ROTHMANS

FOOTBALL

YEARBOOK

2002-2003

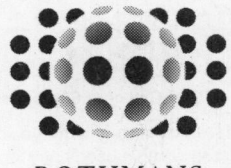

ROTHMANS

EDITORS: GLENDA ROLLIN AND **JACK ROLLIN**

In association with

headline

D1382424

Copyright © 2002 Rothmans Publications Ltd

First published in 2002
by HEADLINE BOOK PUBLISHING

10 9 8 7 6 5 4 3 2 1

All rights reserved. No part of this publication may be reproduced, stored in a retrieval
system, or transmitted, in any form or by any means without the prior written permission
of the publisher, nor be otherwise circulated in any form of binding or cover other than
that in which it is published and without a similar condition being imposed on the
subsequent purchaser.

This publication contains material that is the copyright and database right of
the FA Barclaycard Premiership and the Nationwide Football League Limited.

Front cover photographs: (left and background) Robert Pires (Arsenal) *Actionimages*;
(centre and spine) David Beckham (Manchester United/England) and Trevor Sinclair
(West Ham United/England) *PA Photos*; (right) Robbie Keane (Leeds United/Republic
of Ireland) and Niall Quinn (Sunderland/Republic of Ireland) *Empics*.

Back cover photographs: (top) Neil Lennon (Celtic) and Tore Andre Flo (Rangers)
Actionimages; (bottom) Juan Pablo Angel (Aston Villa) *Actionimages*.

Cataloguing in Publication Data is available from the British Library

ISBN 0 7553 1099 3   (hardback)
ISBN 0 7553 1100 0   (trade paperback)

All calls to ClubCall cost 60p per minute

To subscribe to your ClubCall SMS alerts simply send your club's SMS code to 83131 (e.g.
send LEE to 83131 if you would like to receive Leeds alerts). ClubCall SMS alerts equivalent
to 25p each (inc. VAT) – pre-paid at £1.50 for every 6 alerts. To cancel your alerts at any time
please text <club SMS code> STOP to 81131 (e.g. send LEE STOP to 81131 if you would like
to cancel your Leeds alerts). Unused credits will not be refunded. You may receive further
info/offers, to unsubscribe please text INFO STOP to 81131. Always ask permission of the
bill payer. Users over 16 only. Your network provider will bill you. Customer Helpline
0870 906 3434 (calls charged at national rate). An iTouch UK service, 57–63 Scrutton Street,
London EC2A 4PF. For full Terms and Conditions visit www.clubcall.com

Typeset by Wearset Ltd, Boldon, Tyne and Wear

Printed and bound in Great Britain by
Mackays of Chatham PLC,
Chatham, Kent

HEADLINE BOOK PUBLISHING
A division of Hodder Headline
338 Euston Road
London NW1 3BH

www.headline.co.uk
www.hodderheadline.com

CONTENTS

Introduction and Acknowledgements 5
Editorial 6
Rothmans Football Yearbook Honours 10
Milestones Diary 2001–02 25
Review of the Season 51

THE FA PREMIER LEAGUE AND FOOTBALL LEAGUE: THE CLUBS
Introduction 55
The Clubs 56
English League Clubs Players Directory 426

ENGLISH CLUBS STATISTICS
English League Tables 2001–02 46
Football League Play-Offs 2001–02 48
Leading Goalscorers 2001–02 50
Transfers 2001–02 561
The New Foreign Legion 2001–02 571
The Things They Said 574
Charity Shield 576
English League Honours 1888–89 to 2001–02 577
League Attendances since 1946–47 to 2001–02 586
English League Attendances 2001–02 587

THE LEAGUE CUP AND OTHER FOOTBALL LEAGUE COMPETITIONS
League Cup Finalists 1961–2002 589
Worthington Cup 2001–02 590
Football League Competition Attendances 596
LDV Vans Trophy 2001–02 597

THE FA CUP
FA Cup Attendances 1967–2002 596
FA Cup Finals 1872–2002 601
FA Cup 2001–02 Sponsored by AXA (*preliminary and qualifying rounds*) 603
                                    (*competition proper*) 606

SCOTTISH FOOTBALL
Review of the Scottish Season 616
The Scottish Football League Clubs 618
Scottish League Tables 2001–02 702
Scottish League Honours 1890–91 to 2001–02 703
Scottish League Cup Finals 1946–2002 708
CIS Scottish League Cup 2001–02 709
Bell's League Challenge 2001–02 712
Scottish Cup Finals 1874–2002 714
Tennent's Scottish Cup 2001–02 716

WELSH AND NORTHERN IRISH FOOTBALL
Welsh Football 2001–02 720
Northern Irish Football 2001–02 724

EUROPEAN FOOTBALL
European Cup Finals 728
European Cup 2001–02 729
European Cup 2001–02 (*British & Irish Clubs*) 733
European Cup-Winners' Cup Finals 738
Inter-Cities Fairs Cup Finals 738
UEFA Cup Finals 1972–97 739
UEFA Cup Finals 1998–2002 739
UEFA Cup 2001–02 740
UEFA Cup 2001–02 (*British & Irish Clubs*) 744
European Champions League 2002–03 – Draw 747

Summary of Appearances (*British & Irish Clubs*) 748
Intertoto Cup 2001 749
World Club Championship 750
European Super Cup 750

INTERNATIONAL FOOTBALL
International Directory 751
World Cup 1930–2002 773
FIFA World Cup 2002 Qualifying Competition 774
World Cup Finals Review 802
2002 World Cup Finals 803
EURO 2004 – Fixtures 809
European Football Championship (*formerly European Nations' Cup*) 810
British and Irish International Results 1872–2002 811
Other British and Irish International Matches 2001–02 830
International Appearances 1872–2002 832
British and Irish International Goalscorers since 1872 877
British & Irish International Managers 881
South America 882
Africa 883
UEFA Under-21 Championship 2000–02 884
World Under-17 Championship 885
18th UEFA Under-18 Championship (*Finals in Finland* 885
Under-19 Championship 885
England Under-21 Results 1976–2002 886
England B Results 1949–2002 887
British and Irish Under-21 Teams 2001–02 888
British Under-21 Appearances 1976–2002 890

NON-LEAGUE FOOTBALL
FA Schools and Youth Games 2001–02 902
Women's Football 2001–02 905
Nationwide Conference 2001–02 909
Unibond League 2001–02 913
Dr Martens League 2001–02 917
Ryman Football League 2001–02 922
FA Umbro Trophy 2001–02 929
FA Carlsberg Vase 2001–02 931
The AXA FA Youth Cup 2001–02 (in association with *The Times*) 934
Semi-Professional Internationals 936
FA Umbro Sunday Cup 2001–02 937
FA County Youth Challenge Cup 2001–02 938
FA XI Representative Matches 938
University Football 2001–02 939
Schools Football 2001–02 940
Avon Insurance Combination 2001–02 941
Avon League 2001–02 941
FA Premier Reserve League 2001–02 942
FA Academy Under-17 League 2001–02 943
FA Academy Under-19 League 2001–02 943
Non-League Tables 2001–02 944
Amateur Football Alliance 2001–02 949

INFORMATION AND RECORDS
Rothmans Football Records 11
International Records 24
Football and the Law 45
Refereeing and the Referees 572
National List of Referees for Season 2002–03 572
Football Awards 2002 585
Important Addresses 953
Football Club Chaplaincy 955
Obituaries 956
The FA Barclaycard Premiership and Nationwide Football League Fixtures 2002–03 966
The Scottish Premiership and Scottish Football League Fixtures 2002–03 984
Other Fixtures 2002–03 989
Stop Press 991

INTRODUCTION

In this 33rd edition of Rothmans Football Yearbook, we are delighted to renew the association with both the FA Premier League and Football League, which will certainly help maintain and indeed improve the excellent relationship which we have endured with these two bodies over a number of years. Once again, our new edition features historical and record information for the 92 clubs. The Who's Who style Players Directory which incorporates the total of appearances and goals for each player as in earlier editions, but additionally, features more personal information and a season-by-season account of the individual player's record is again featured. There is also each club's full record in the previous ten seasons and the latest sequences recorded for wins, draws and defeats, etc.

Detailed and varied coverage involves the FA Premier League, Football League, Scottish, Welsh and Irish football, amateur, schools, university, reserve team, extensive non-League information, awards, records and an international directory, Football and the Law, women's football, referees and the work of chaplains.

Transfers fees are given where known. When two clubs have differed as to the amount of a record move, the lower figure has been quoted in both instances. For certain entries, the figure quoted in the list of transfers may be the original one, without extra finance built in for appearances and other reasons, which would appear subsequently as a record fee on the relevant club page. Also, the date when a player is signed often varies from the one given as his registration and the diary occasionally refers to the transfer fee originally discussed, but not ultimately paid.

A frequent question asked is why Football League records have not been changed since the advent of the Premier League. The answer is simple: the Football League still considers its First Division to be a championship which has existed for over 100 years.

The Editors would like to thank Alan Elliott for the Scottish section, Bob Hennessy for the Milestones Diary, Tony Brown for instances of match results in the Records Section and Ian Nannestad for the Obituaries. Thanks are also due to John English, who provided invaluable and conscientious reading of the proofs. The Editors would like to pay tribute to the various organisations who have helped to make this edition complete, especially Mike Foster and Zoe Ward of the FA Premier League, Debbie Birch and Louise Standing from the Football League, as well as David C. Thomson from the Scottish League.

ACKNOWLEDGEMENTS

The editors would like to express appreciation of the following individuals and organisations for their co-operation: Heather Elliott, Dr Malcolm Brodie, Wally Goss (AFA), Rev. Nigel Sands, Edward Grayson, Ken Goldman, Grahame Lloyd, Marshall Gillespie, Ben Jerram, Valery Karpoushkin, Andrew Howe, Mike Kelleher, Ester Kristiansson, Ole Hall, Steven Meeson, Tamar Steinitz and Wendy McCance (Headline Book Publishing).

Special thanks are due to the indefatigable Lorraine Jerram, Headline's Senior Editor for her generosity, expertise, constant support, resilience, patience, sincerity, perspicacity and appreciation, not to mention her unfailing humour, stoicism, quick-wittedness and understated authority.

Finally, sincere thanks to John Anderson, Simon Dunnington, Geoff Turner, Brian Tait and the staff at Wearset for their efforts in the production of this book, which was much appreciated throughout the year.

EDITORIAL

He had flown back from Munich in September with the kind of hope few in England imagined before the trip. It seemed the menace of the Germans had been quelled. No, it was not 1938 and the PM Arthur Neville Chamberlain, but it was another September 63 years later and the man of the hour was England coach Sven Goran Eriksson, albeit from a far less important mission.

Having lifted his team from the pit at the bottom of their World Cup qualifying group, England had crushed Germany 5-1, ironically the most humiliating defeat suffered by them on their own soil since the 6-3 victory in May 1938. More significantly there was expectation of World Cup domination in the 2002 finals.

The narrow squeak of actually qualifying, the Germans failing miserably to top the group and leave us in a play-off situation, was put aside as the nation dressed its expectancy like a suit of armour, believing nothing could prevent ultimate success.

There were the usual sceptics but none behind the St George flags festooning the buildings and vehicles. As a critic wisely reported, the England football team is the only one which unites the country.

By the time of the finals in South Korea and Japan, the working day of the population was centred around England's matches. The media which had fanned the flame of fanaticism to fever pitch ensured blanket coverage to an incredible extent.

The threat of terrorism, the Middle East crisis, stock market slump and the Government's latest gaffe, all were shoved off the front pages of the newspapers, tabloids and broadsheets alike. This was the way to bury bad news. New Labour's heads must have been spinning.

Making Argentina pay the penalty, David Beckham gained his revenge for four years earlier as the infamous Group of Death – without which no self-respecting World Cup seems complete – was safely negotiated. Denmark duly obliged in the defensive error department and then it was Brazil.

We could not match their history; we could do something about their immediate future. Came the day and in our first real attack, Lucio lapsed and there was that little tinker Michael Owen, the fame seeker turned poacher, putting us ahead as Marcos fell to the floor in the wrong direction.

Yet instead of the cavalry pressing home this advantage, we had the pioneer corps preparing to dig in at the back. Brazil drew level before half-time, went ahead with the so-called flukey-floater from Ronaldinho – for which the able Seaman was cruelly castigated in the press for failing to adjust his position – and we were 2-1 down. Even the Brazilian scorer's controversial dismissal leaving them with ten men did nothing to help us. Suddenly it was England with a mountain to climb. Such exertion can be breathtaking and does precious little for the legs.

Brazil cruised along, keeping the ball and we simply finished with tired limbs. England had managed one other shot on target and few could recall it anyway. The chain mail weighed heavier. Down came the flags. Fantasy football was over. And *Past Times* were already selling videos of the Munich match along with Second World War memorabilia.

Now football is a simple game with modest ideals. You want to win. At the same time we know how vulnerable a team is when it scores. Once in the lead they often unconsciously relax, passing the initiative to the opposition, who would be less of a threat nearer their own goal.

The Chinese, who invented the game, have a Confucian saying: *balls in the other half, much less dangerous*. But there is no substitute for technical superiority, even if occasionally the whack and chase has its place.

Once out of the contest we turned our vitriol on the Germans. After all, had we not kicked them severely in the *hosenboden*? Yet here they were heading for the final. While there were no specific references in the press to the Waffen SS or Hitler Youth, you could sense the itch under the surface in the words just falling short of referring to robots in jackboots.

Kaiser Franz Beckenbauer, highly critical of the poor Germans, said this had been a tournament England could have won! Cheers, mate. But in fairness Germany gave Brazil a better game in the final than we did. Ronaldo, erasing the memory of 1998, scored his two goals for the best football team in the competition. Ironically Oliver Kahn, goalkeeper of the tournament, spilled for the first goal; the shot-stopper caught out as they all are in the end.

Referee Pierluigi Collina was the near-perfect man-in-the-middle, booking one from each side early on and then of course no more trouble. The hairless one has few equals. He probably scares seven kinds of muck out of the players.

At home in the aftermath and search for excuses, there were calls for a reduction in the number of league matches and a winter pause to give top players a rest. England went to the finals with two world-class players, Beckham and Owen. We came back with one, Rio Ferdinand. Beckham was not fully fit after playing scarcely any football for weeks and Owen finished it injured.

The real culprit on the fixture front is Europe. In 1966 when England won the World Cup, a team in the European Cup needed only eight games to reach the final. Now it is 16. Clubs are understandably anxious to avoid a reduction in the number of matches for financial reasons. The growing cost of players' wages makes it imperative for income from as many sources as possible. Club versus country continues unresolved.

After a fine World Cup Finals and a summer of speculation, Rio Ferdinand was signed by Manchester United from Leeds United for a British record transfer fee of £30,000,000. (ASP)

Though not affecting the Premier League, the collapse of ITV Digital was a massive blow to the finances of Football League clubs, leaving them with the prospect of vastly reduced funds. Later there was partial replacement with a Sky/BBC resurrection of the system. But one had wondered whether it was being disloyal to watch World Cup games on ITV – or was it just *Coronation Street*, a suggested target of viewer boycotting over the issue. But you knew ITV Digital was in trouble when more people wanted the monkey than the box. The first simian to pay peanuts. When market forces prevail, there is often an early closing day.

That other soap opera, Wembley, dragged on. In the wrong part of London for *EastEnders*, on more neutral ground than *Home and Away*, but certainly at the *Crossroads*. Again money seems to have been poured in its direction, hopefully to filling effect.

Neither did Sky escape criticism. The Professional Footballers Association won an almost 100 per cent vote to strike over money it considered essential for players forced out of the game through injury and illness, before a settlement was reached between the two parties. The union was criticised for looking after the interests of its members because many people outside the game imagine that all footballers are millionaires.

The active life in full-time football lasts on average around eight years. It used to be seven, but improved treatment of injuries has prolonged the timescale. Outside of this the extension into non-league football can take it to 12 again on average.

But a player earning £200,000 a year for eight years will earn as much as the average worker would in a lifetime. Yet the vast majority of full-time players in the lower divisions receive far less than even this figure. The First Division is around £175,000, the Second Division £50,000 and the Third Division £35,000. A brief career which can be shortened further by injury.

These are one set of figures, another represents the saturation point reached in statistics, down to what happens on the pitch and every sod trodden on it. Alas, we still await accurate timing of matches.

Referees have enough with which to contend and it is long overdue that the fourth official should take the watch away from the whistler's bother to end the farce of so-called injury time. Genuine stoppages should be accounted for during 90 minutes play – and not at the end.

The World Cup also revealed that it is essential for that third team on the field, the referee and his two assistants to be just that – a trio, not individuals unused to each other. It could easily be implemented in such tournaments and, if feasible, at others.

One practice which has not been in existence for donkey's years but remains an ass of a law if indeed it exists as such, is the invitation by the referee for a player to strike the ball in the direction of the opposition when the game restarts after injury, in the spirit of fair play. When the ball is dead and a throw-in is taken, there is no problem since a goal cannot be scored direct from a throw. We champion fair play, but what is wrong with a bounce-up?

The way to stop the present system is for the player to take a shot at goal. It will end the idea almost immediately. Also one of the most embarrassing sights in the World Cup was the amount of shirt pulling and wrestling in penalty areas. Who would have the courage to book half a dozen players from both sides? The boy Collina, perhaps.

Talk of conspiracy in the World Cup was laughable. It was even suggested that it was Sepp Blatter's revenge against European countries for voting against him as FIFA President. Incompetent officials, perhaps – dishonest ones, no. But we did back the wrong horse. You can lose your shirt over such bets. Let's hope we don't lose the three lions off ours.

There was criticism of South Korean TV for failing to show the two apparently legitimate goals scored by Spain against their team. English TV did the same when there was film of Geoff Hurst's off-the-bar effort in the 1966 World Cup final, taken from behind the goal and clearly showing the whole of the ball had not crossed the line.

So much for history. In our PC world into which the word discipline has yet to be programmed, conduct on and off the field remains a serious problem. A society yet to embrace zero tolerance and where in some quarters it is the anti-hero who gets the heroin, has pockets which seek a scapegoat by blaming the game for hooliganism, which is still active and better organised. Unfortunately the beautiful game draws unattractive appendages.

David Seaman looks back in despair as a Ronaldinho free kick completely deceives him from 40 yards to give Brazil a winning 2-1 lead over England during the World Cup quarter-final in Shizuoka. (Colorsport)

What of the game's future? We are up to our stocking tops in academies, but one wonders what effect being rejected at the age of seven by a centre of excellence does for an aspiring youngster. There must be a sense of enjoyment in playing, but just where we can find the flair necessary to succeed at the highest level is another matter.

Realising our shortcomings and isolating them to find a solution would be a start. We have to stop telling people how good we are and start proving it. Our Premier League is arguably the finest competition in the world. It attracts many of the world's best players. Over 100 of them were in the World Cup, including the spirited Republic of Ireland contingent.

The clamour for success is relentless. In the search for the elusive, the carnage in managerial casualties reached a new high with more than half the 92 teams in the four divisions changing the man in charge.

Premier League attendances grew to 13,043,118 for an average of 34,324 and Football League crowds jumped to a highly respectable 14,716,162. Such a combined total was last reached in 1971–72. There is blanket coverage of the game on TV, but doubts expressed over the next time Sky's contract comes up for renewal. It will be a poker game for both sides. TV needs football as much as football needs TV.

We are reminded that the pipeline is flooded with outstanding young talent. Our Under-21 squad was favoured to win the European Championship but faltered, losing to two teams already played in the same season; the Under-20s were beaten in a tournament because they could not score enough goals or convert penalties.

Still, the Under-17s did finish top of a competition above Brazil. They will not be ready for 2006 when the finals will be held in Germany, 40 years after England's World Cup triumph. The boys of '66 can rest easy for a while. Bridging the gap between first class and world class is the key. It may need a giant leap for England-man kind. Who's for revenge? It could all change. Even before the wheel was invented, things went in cycles.

ROTHMANS FOOTBALL YEARBOOK HONOURS

For the seventh consecutive year, members of the Football Writers' Association selected their team of the season for Rothmans Football Yearbook. As in previous years, players eligible had to have appeared in FA Barclaycard Premiership matches during the season.

For the 2001–02 Premiership, the majority of members once more chose a 4-4-2 formation. Arsenal's recapture of the title from Manchester United marginally increased their representation in the final team, with both Ashley Cole and Patrick Vieira retaining their positions, while Football Writers' Association Footballer of the Year Robert Pires displaced David Beckham in midfield and Thierry Henry took one of the two striking roles.

While central defenders Rio Ferdinand and Sami Hyypia kept their places, Manchester United provided four players of their own in Gary Neville, Roy Keane, Ryan Giggs and Ruud Van Nistelrooy, the Professional Footballers Association choice as their Player of the Year. The Polish international goalkeeper Jerzy Dudek completed the team.

Arsenal manager Arsène Wenger, who masterminded the club's League and Cup double, was the overwhelming preference in this role.

Rothmans Football Yearbook Team of the Season

Jerzy Dudek
(*Liverpool*)

Gary Neville	Rio Ferdinand	Sami Hyypia	Ashley Cole
(*Manchester U*)	(*Leeds U*)	(*Liverpool*)	(*Arsenal*)

Robert Pires	Patrick Vieira	Roy Keane	Ryan Giggs
(*Arsenal*)	(*Arsenal*)	(*Manchester U*)	(*Manchester U*)

Ruud Van Nistelrooy   Thierry Henry
(*Manchester U*)   (*Arsenal*)

Manager:
Arsène Wenger (*Arsenal*)

Substitutes:
Mikael Silvestre (*Manchester U*)
David Beckham (*Manchester U*)
Michael Owen (*Liverpool*)

In addition this year, the FWA members were asked to select their Team of the Decade 1992–2002, covering the existence of the FA Premier League. Not surprisingly, Manchester United players were well represented during the period in question, since they won seven of the ten championships. Sir Alex Ferguson was an almost unanimous choice as manager.

Rothmans Football Yearbook Team of the Decade – 1992–2002

Peter Schmeichel
(*Manchester U & Aston Villa*)

Lee Dixon	Marcel Desailly	Tony Adams	Denis Irwin
(*Arsenal*)	(*Chelsea*)	(*Arsenal*)	(*Manchester U*)

David Beckham	Patrick Vieira	Roy Keane	Ryan Giggs
(*Manchester U*)	(*Arsenal*)	(*Nottingham F & Manchester U*)	(*Manchester U*)

Eric Cantona   Alan Shearer
(*Leeds U & Manchester U*)   (*Blackburn R & Newcastle U*)

Manager:
Sir Alex Ferguson (*Manchester U*)

Substitutes:
Gary Neville (*Manchester U*)
Dennis Bergkamp (*Arsenal*)
Michael Owen (*Liverpool*)

ROTHMANS FOOTBALL RECORDS

● **TOP TEN**

ALL-TIME PREMIER LEAGUE CHAMPIONSHIP SEASONS IN ORDER OF MERIT

Team	Season	P	W	D	L	F	A	Pts	Pts Av
Man U	1999–2000	38	28	7	3	97	45	91	2.39
Arsenal	2001–02	38	26	9	3	79	36	87	2.26
Man U	1993–94	42	27	11	4	80	38	92	2.19
Man U	1995–96	38	25	7	6	73	35	82	2.15
Blackburn R	1994–95	42	27	8	7	80	39	89	2.11
Man U	2000–01	38	24	8	6	79	31	80	2.09
Man U	1998–99	38	22	13	3	80	37	79	2.07
Arsenal	1997–98	38	23	9	6	68	33	78	2.05
Man U	1992–93	42	24	12	6	67	31	84	2.00
Man U	1996–97	38	21	12	5	76	44	75	1.97

WORLD TRANSFERS

		£	Year
Zinedine Zidane	Juventus to Real Madrid	46.5m	2001
Luis Figo	Barcelona to Real Madrid	37.4m	2000
Hernan Crespo	Parma to Lazio	35.7m	2000
Gianluigi Buffon	Parma to Juventus	34m	2001
Christian Vieri	Lazio to Internationale	31m	1999
Rio Ferdinand	Leeds U to Manchester U	30m	2002
Giazka Mendieta	Valencia to Lazio	29m	2001
Juan Sebastian Veron	Lazio to Manchester United	28.1m	2001
Rui Costa	Fiorentina to AC Milan	28m	2001
Lilian Thuram	Parma to Juventus	25.9m	2001
Filippo Inzaghi	Juventus to AC Milan	25.9m	2001
Pavel Nedved	Lazio to Juventus	25.9m	2001

Source: National Press.

BRITISH TRANSFERS

		£	Year
Rio Ferdinand	Leeds U to Manchester U	30m	2002
Juan Sebastian Veron	Lazio to Manchester U	28.1m	2001
Ruud Van Nistelrooy	PSV Eindhoven to Manchester U	19m	2001
Rio Ferdinand	West Ham U to Leeds U	18m	2000
Alan Shearer	Blackburn R to Newcastle U	15m	1996
Jimmy Floyd Hasselbaink	Atletico Madrid to Chelsea	15m	2000
Nicolas Anelka	Paris St Germain to Manchester C	13m	2002
Dwight Yorke	Aston Villa to Manchester U	12m	1998
Tor Andre Flo	Chelsea to Rangers	12m	2000
Sylvain Wiltord	Bordeaux to Arsenal	11m	2000

Source: National Press.

TOP TEN TRANSFER SPENDERS 2001

Figures in £'s

Manchester United	50.2m
Fulham	43.95m
Arsenal	33.1m
Chelsea	32.2m
Leeds U	29m
Aston Villa	25m
West Ham U	21.7m
Blackburn R	20.95m
Newcastle U	19.29m
Liverpool	18.22m

Source: National Press.

TOP TEN WORLD STARS ANNUAL WAGES

Figures in £'s

Zinedine Zidane	Real Madrid	8.7m
David Beckham	Manchester United	6.5m
Gabriel Batistuta	Roma	6.5m
Hidetoshi Nakata	Parma	6.1m
Ronaldo	Internazionale	5.9m
Christian Vieira	Internazionale	5.7m
Raul	Real Madrid	5.5m
Alvaro Recoba	Internazionale	5.5m
Luis Figo	Real Madrid	5.4m
Sol Campbell	Arsenal	5.4m

TOP TEN PREMIER LEAGUE AVERAGE ATTENDANCES 2001–02

Manchester U	67,586
Newcastle U	51,373
Sunderland	44,108
Liverpool	43,389
Leeds U	39,789
Chelsea	39,033
Arsenal	38,054
Aston Villa	35,012
Tottenham H	34,878
Everton	34,004

TOP TEN FOOTBALL LEAGUE AVERAGE ATTENDANCES 2001–02

Manchester C	33,059
Wolverhampton W	23,796
Birmingham C	21,854
Nottingham F	21,701
Sheffield W	20,864
WBA	20,691
Norwich C	18,738
Sheffield U	18,020
Crystal Palace	17,177
Bradford C	15,489

TOP TEN AVERAGE ATTENDANCES

Manchester United	2001–02	67,586
Manchester United	2000–01	67,544
Manchester United	1999–2000	58,017
Manchester United	1967–68	57,552
Newcastle United	1947–48	56,283
Tottenham Hotspur	1950–51	55,509
Manchester United	1998–99	55,188
Manchester United	1997–98	55,168
Manchester United	1996–97	55,081
Arsenal	1947–48	54,982

TOP TEN ALL-TIME ENGLAND GOALSCORERS

Bobby Charlton	49
Gary Lineker	48
Jimmy Greaves	44
Tom Finney	30
Nat Lofthouse	30
Alan Shearer	30
Vivian Woodward	29
Steve Bloomer	28
David Platt	27
Bryan Robson	26

TOP TEN ALL-TIME ENGLAND CAPS

Peter Shilton	125
Bobby Moore	108
Bobby Charlton	106
Billy Wright	105
Bryan Robson	90
Kenny Sansom	86
Ray Wilkins	84
Gary Lineker	80
John Barnes	79
Stuart Pearce	78

TOP TEN AVERAGE WORLD CUP FINAL CROWDS

In USA	1994	68,604
In Brazil	1950	60,772
In Mexico	1970	52,311
In England	1966	50,458
In Italy	1990	48,368
In Mexico	1986	46,956
In West Germany	1974	46,684
In France	1998	43,366
In Argentina	1978	42,374
In South Korea/Japan	2002	42,274

TOP TEN GOALSCORERS IN WORLD CUP FINAL TOURNAMENTS

Gerd Muller (West Germany)	1970, 74	14
Just Fontaine (France)	1958	13
Pele (Brazil)	1958, 70	12
Ronaldo (Brazil)	1998, 2002	12
Sandor Kocsis (Hungary)	1954	11
Jurgen Klinsmann (Germany)	1990, 98	11
Helmut Rahn (West Germany)	1954, 58	10
Teofilo Cubillas (Peru)	1970, 78	10
Grzegorz Lato (Poland)	1974, 82	10
Gary Lineker (England)	1986, 90	10
Gabriel Batistuta (Argentina)	1994, 2002	10

● HIGHEST WINS

First-Class Match		Arbroath *(Scottish Cup 1st Round)*	36	Bon Accord	0	12 Sept 1885
International Match		England	13	Ireland	0	18 Feb 1882
FA Cup		Preston NE *(1st Round)*	26	Hyde U	0	15 Oct 1887
League Cup		West Ham U *(2nd Round, 2nd Leg)*	10	Bury	0	25 Oct 1983
		Liverpool *(2nd Round, 1st Leg)*	10	Fulham	0	23 Sept 1986
FA PREMIER LEAGUE	*(Home)*	Manchester U	9	Ipswich T	0	4 March 1995
	(Away)	Nottingham F	1	Manchester U	8	6 Feb 1999
FOOTBALL LEAGUE						
Division 1	*(Home)*	WBA	12	Darwen	0	4 April 1892
		Nottingham F	12	Leicester Fosse	0	21 April 1909
	(Away)	Newcastle U	1	Sunderland	9	5 Dec 1908
		Cardiff C	1	Wolverhampton W	9	3 Sept 1955
Division 2	*(Home)*	Newcastle U	13	Newport Co	0	5 Oct 1946
	(Away)	Burslem PV	0	Sheffield U	10	10 Dec 1892
Division 3	*(Home)*	Gillingham	10	Chesterfield	0	5 Sept 1987
	(Away)	Barnet	1	Peterborough U	9	5 Sept 1998
Division 3(S)	*(Home)*	Luton T	12	Bristol R	0	13 April 1936
	(Away)	Northampton T	0	Walsall	8	2 Feb 1947
Division 3(N)	*(Home)*	Stockport Co	13	Halifax T	0	6 Jan 1934
	(Away)	Accrington S	0	Barnsley	9	3 Feb 1934
Division 4	*(Home)*	Oldham Ath	11	Southport	0	26 Dec 1962
	(Away)	Crewe Alex	1	Rotherham U	8	8 Sept 1973
Aggregate Division 3(N)		Tranmere R	13	Oldham Ath	4	26 Dec 1935
SCOTTISH LEAGUE						
Premier	*(Home)*	Aberdeen	8	Motherwell	0	26 March 1979
Division	*(Away)*	Hamilton A	0	Celtic	8	5 Nov 1988
Division 1	*(Home)*	Celtic	11	Dundee	0	26 Oct 1895
	(Away)	Airdrieonians	1	Hibernian	11	24 Oct 1950
Division 2	*(Home)*	Airdrieonians	15	Dundee Wanderers	1	1 Dec 1894
	(Away)	Alloa Ath	0	Dundee	10	8 March 1947
Aggregate Division 2		Airdrieonians	15	Dundee Wanderers	1	1 Dec 1894

● MOST GOALS FOR IN A SEASON

	Season	Team	Goals	Games
FA PREMIER LEAGUE	1999–2000	Manchester U	97	38
FOOTBALL LEAGUE				
Division 1	1930–31	Aston V	128	42
Division 2	1926–27	Middlesbrough	122	42
Division 3(S)	1927–28	Millwall	127	42
Division 3(N)	1928–29	Bradford C	128	42
Division 3	1961–62	QPR	111	46
Division 4	1960–61	Peterborough U	134	46
SCOTTISH PREMIER LEAGUE	2001–02	Celtic	94	38
SCOTTISH LEAGUE				
Premier Division	1991–92	Rangers	101	44
	1982–83	Dundee U	90	36
	1982–83	Celtic	90	36
	1986–87	Celtic	90	44
Division 1	1957–58	Hearts	132	34
Division 2	1937–38	Raith R	142	34
New Division 1	1993–94	Dunfermline Ath	93	44
	1981–82	Motherwell	92	39
New Division 2	1987–88	Ayr U	95	39
New Division 3	1997–98	Alloa	78	36

● FEWEST GOALS FOR IN A SEASON

	Season	Team	Goals	Games
FA PREMIER LEAGUE	1996–97	Leeds U	28	38
FOOTBALL LEAGUE (minimum 42 games)				
Division 1	1984–85	Stoke C	24	42
Division 2	1971–72	Watford	24	42
	1994–95	Leyton Orient	30	46
Division 3(S)	1950–51	Crystal Palace	33	46
Division 3(N)	1923–24	Crewe Alex	32	42
Division 3	1969–70	Stockport Co	27	46
Division 4	1981–82	Crewe Alex	29	46
SCOTTISH PREMIER LEAGUE	2001–02	St Johnstone	24	38
SCOTTISH LEAGUE (minimum 30 games)				
Premier Division	1988–89	Hamilton A	19	36
	1991–92	Dunfermline Ath	22	44
Division 1	1993–94	Brechin C	30	44
	1966–67	Ayr U	20	34
Division 2	1923–24	Lochgelly U	20	38
New Division 1	1980–81	Stirling Alb	18	39
	1995–96	Dumbarton	23	36
New Division 2	1994–95	Brechin C	22	36
New Division 3	1995–96	Alloa	26	36

● MOST GOALS AGAINST IN A SEASON

	Season	Team	Goals	Games
FA PREMIER LEAGUE	1993–94	Swindon T	100	42
FOOTBALL LEAGUE				
Division 1	1930–31	Blackpool	125	42
Division 2	1898–99	Darwen	141	34
Division 3(S)	1929–30	Merthyr T	135	42
Division 3(N)	1927–28	Nelson	136	42
Division 3	1959–60	Accrington S	123	46
Division 4	1959–60	Hartlepools U	109	46
SCOTTISH PREMIER LEAGUE	1999–2000	Aberdeen	83	36
SCOTTISH LEAGUE				
Premier Division	1984–85	Morton	100	36
	1987–88	Morton	100	44
Division 1	1931–32	Leith Ath	137	38
Division 2	1931–32	Edinburgh C	146	38
New Division 1	1988–89	Queen of the S	99	39
	1992–93	Cowdenbeath	109	44
New Division 2	1977–78	Meadowbank T	89	39
New Division 3	1994–95	Albion R	82	36

● FEWEST GOALS AGAINST IN A SEASON

	Season	Team	Goals	Games
FA PREMIER LEAGUE	1998–99	Arsenal	17	38
FOOTBALL LEAGUE (minimum 42 games)				
Division 1	1978–79	Liverpool	16	42
Division 2	1924–25	Manchester U	23	42
	1990–91	West Ham U	34	46
Division 3(S)	1921–22	Southampton	21	42
Division 3(N)	1953–54	Port Vale	21	46
Division 3	1995–96	Gillingham	20	46
Division 4	1980–81	Lincoln C	25	46
SCOTTISH PREMIER LEAGUE	2001–02	Celtic	18	38
SCOTTISH LEAGUE (minimum 30 games)				
Premier Division	1989–90	Rangers	19	36
	1986–87	Rangers	23	44
	1987–88	Celtic	23	44
Division 1	1913–14	Celtic	14	38
Division 3	1966–67	Morton	20	38
New Division 1	1996–97	St Johnstone	23	36
	1980–81	Hibernian	24	39
	1993–94	Falkirk	32	44
New Division 2	1987–88	St Johnstone	24	39
	1990–91	Stirling Alb	24	39
New Division 3	1995–96	Brechin C	21	36

● MOST POINTS IN A SEASON *(under old system of two points for a win)*

	Season	Team	Points	Games
FOOTBALL LEAGUE				
Division 1	1978–79	Liverpool	68	42
Division 2	1919–20	Tottenham H	70	42
Division 3	1971–72	Aston V	70	46
Division 3(S)	1950–51	Nottingham F	70	46
	1954–55	Bristol C	70	46
Division 3(N)	1946–47	Doncaster R	72	42
Division 4	1975–76	Lincoln C	74	46
SCOTTISH LEAGUE				
Premier Division	1984–85	Aberdeen	59	36
	1992–93	Rangers	73	44
Division 1	1920–21	Rangers	76	42
Division 2	1966–67	Morton	69	38
New Division 1	1976–77	St Mirren	62	39
	1993–94	Falkirk	66	44
New Division 2	1983–84	Forfar Ath	63	39

(three points for a win)

	Season	Team	Points	Games
FA PREMIER LEAGUE	1993–94	Manchester U	92	42
FOOTBALL LEAGUE				
Division 1	1998–99	Sunderland	105	46
	1984–85	Everton	90	42
	1987–88	Liverpool	90	40
Division 2	1998–99	Fulham	101	46
Division 3	2001–02	Plymouth Arg	102	46
Division 4	1985–86	Swindon T	102	46
SCOTTISH PREMIER LEAGUE	2001–02	Celtic	103	38
SCOTTISH LEAGUE				
Premier League	1995–96	Rangers	87	36
New Division 1	1998–99	Hibernian	89	36
New Division 2	1995–96	Stirling Alb	81	36
New Division 3	1994–95	Forfar Ath	80	36

● FEWEST POINTS IN A SEASON

	Season	Team	Points	Games
FA PREMIER LEAGUE	1999–2000	Watford	24	38
FOOTBALL LEAGUE (minimum 34 games)				
Division 1	1984–85	Stoke C	17	42
Division 2	1904–05	Doncaster R	8	34
	1899–1900	Loughborough T	8	34
Division 3	1997–98	Doncaster R	20	46
Division 3(S)	1924–25 & 1929–30	Merthyr T	21	42
	1925–26	QPR	21	42
Division 3(N)	1931–32	Rochdale	11	40
Division 4	1976–77	Workington	19	46
SCOTTISH PREMIER LEAGUE	2001–02	St Johnstone	21	38
SCOTTISH LEAGUE (minimum 30 games)				
Premier Division	1975–76	St Johnstone	11	36
	1987–88	Morton	16	44
Division 1	1954–55	Stirling Alb	6	30
Division 2	1936–37	Edinburgh C	7	34
New Division 1	1988–89	Queen of the S	10	39
	1992–93	Cowdenbeath	13	44
New Division 2	1987–88	Berwick R	16	39
	1987–88	Stranraer	16	39
New Division 3	1994–95	Albion R	18	36

● LEAGUE CHAMPIONSHIP HAT-TRICKS

Huddersfield T	1923–24 to 1925–26
Arsenal	1932–33 to 1934–35
Liverpool	1981–82 to 1983–84
Manchester U	1998–99 to 2000–01

● MOST WINS IN A SEASON

	Season	*Team*	*Wins*	*Games*
FA PREMIER LEAGUE	1999–2000	Manchester U	28	38
FOOTBALL LEAGUE				
Division 1	1960–61	Tottenham H	31	42
	2001–02	Manchester C	31	46
Division 2	1919–20	Tottenham H	32	42
Division 3(S)	1927–28	Millwall	30	42
	1929–30	Plymouth Arg	30	42
	1946–47	Cardiff C	30	42
	1950–51	Nottingham F	30	46
	1954–55	Bristol C	30	46
Division 3(N)	1946–47	Doncaster R	33	42
Division 3	1971–72	Aston V	32	46
Division 4	1975–76	Lincoln C	32	46
	1985–86	Swindon T	32	46
SCOTTISH PREMIER LEAGUE	2000–01	Celtic	31	38
SCOTTISH LEAGUE				
Premier Division	1995–96	Rangers	27	36
	1984–85	Aberdeen	27	36
	1991–92	Rangers	33	44
	1992–93	Rangers	33	44
Division 1	1920–21	Rangers	35	42
Division 2	1966–67	Morton	33	38
New Division 1	1998–99	Hibernian	28	36
New Division 2	1983–84	Forfar Ath	27	39
	1987–88	Ayr U	27	39
New Division 3	1994–95	Forfar Ath	25	36

● FEWEST WINS IN A SEASON

	Season	*Team*	*Wins*	*Games*
FA PREMIER LEAGUE	1993–94	Swindon T	5	42
	2001–02	Leicester C	5	38
FOOTBALL LEAGUE				
Division 1	1889–90	Stoke C	3	22
	1912–13	Woolwich Arsenal	3	38
	1984–85	Stoke C	3	42
Division 2	1899–1900	Loughborough T	1	34
	1983–84	Cambridge U	4	42
Division 3(S)	1929–30	Merthyr T	6	42
	1925–26	QPR	6	42
Division 3(N)	1931–32	Rochdale	4	40
Division 3	1973–74	Rochdale	2	46
Division 4	1976–77	Southport	3	46
SCOTTISH PREMIER LEAGUE	1998–99	Dunfermline Ath	4	36
SCOTTISH LEAGUE				
Premier Division	1975–76	St Johnstone	3	36
	1982–83	Kilmarnock	3	36
	1987–88	Morton	3	44
Division 1	1891–92	Vale of Leven	0	22
Division 2	1905–06	East Stirlingshire	1	22
	1974–75	Forfar Ath	1	38
New Division 1	1988–89	Queen of the S	2	39
	1992–93	Cowdenbeath	3	44
New Division 2	1975–76	Forfar Ath	4	26
	1987–88	Stranraer	4	39
New Division 3	1994–95	Albion R	5	36
	2000–01	Elgin C	5	36

● ALL HOME WINS IN A SEASON
Brentford won all 21 games in Division 3(S), 1929–30

● UNDEFEATED AT HOME
Liverpool 85 games (63 League, 9 League Cup, 7 European, 6 FA Cup), Jan 1978–Jan 1981

● RECORD AWAY WINS IN A SEASON
Doncaster R won 18 of 21 games in Division 3(N), 1946–47

● MOST DEFEATS IN A SEASON

	Season	Team	Defeats	Games
FA PREMIER LEAGUE	1994–95	Ipswich T	29	42
FOOTBALL LEAGUE				
Division 1	1984–85	Stoke C	31	42
	2001–02	Stockport Co	32	46
Division 2	1938–39	Tranmere R	31	42
	1992–93	Chester C	33	46
	2000–01	Oxford U	33	46
Division 3	1997–98	Doncaster R	34	46
Division 3(S)	1924–25	Merthyr T	29	42
	1952–53	Walsall	29	46
	1953–54	Walsall	29	46
Division 3(N)	1931–32	Rochdale	33	40
Division 4	1987–88	Newport Co	33	46
SCOTTISH PREMIER LEAGUE	2001–02	St Johnstone	27	38
SCOTTISH LEAGUE				
Premier Division	1984–85	Morton	29	36
Division 1	1920–21	St Mirren	31	42
Division 2	1962–63	Brechin C	30	36
	1923–24	Lochgelly	30	38
New Division 1	1988–89	Queen of the S	29	39
	1995–96	Dumbarton	31	36
	1992–93	Cowdenbeath	34	44
New Division 2	1987–88	Berwick R	29	39
New Division 3	1994–95	Albion R	28	36

● FEWEST DEFEATS IN A SEASON *(Minimum 20 games)*

	Season	Team	Defeats	Games
FA PREMIER LEAGUE	1998–99	Manchester U	3	38
	1998–99	Chelsea	3	38
	1999–2000	Manchester U	3	38
	2001–02	Arsenal	3	38
FOOTBALL LEAGUE				
Division 1	1888–89	Preston NE	0	22
	1990–91	Arsenal	1	38
	1987–88	Liverpool	2	40
	1968–69	Leeds U	2	42
Division 2	1893–94	Liverpool	0	28
	1897–98	Burnley	2	30
	1905–06	Bristol C	2	38
	1963–64	Leeds U	3	42
	1988–89	Chelsea	5	46
Division 3	1966–67	QPR	5	46
	1989–90	Bristol R	5	46
	1997–98	Notts Co	5	46
Division 3(S)	1921–22	Southampton	4	42
	1929–30	Plymouth Arg	4	42
Division 3(N)	1953–54	Port Vale	3	46
	1946–47	Doncaster R	3	42
	1923–24	Wolverhampton W	3	42
Division 4	1975–76	Lincoln C	4	46
	1981–82	Sheffield U	4	46
	1981–82	Bournemouth	4	46
SCOTTISH PREMIER LEAGUE	2001–02	Celtic	1	38
SCOTTISH LEAGUE				
Premier Division	1995–96	Rangers	3	36
	1987–88	Celtic	3	44
Division 1	1898–99	Rangers	0	18
	1920–21	Rangers	1	42
Division 2	1956–57	Clyde	1	36
	1962–63	Morton	1	36
	1967–68	St Mirren	1	36
New Division 1	1975–76	Partick T	2	26
	1976–77	St Mirren	2	39
	1992–93	Raith R	4	44
	1993–94	Falkirk	4	44
New Division 2	1975–76	Raith R	1	26
	1975–76	Clydebank	3	26
	1983–84	Forfar Ath	3	39
	1986–87	Raith R	3	39
	1998–99	Livingston	3	36
New Division 3	2000–01	Hamilton A	4	36

● UNDEFEATED AWAY
Arsenal 19 games FA Premier League 2001–02 (only Preston NE with 11 in 1888–89 had previously remained unbeaten away)

● CONSECUTIVE AWAY WINS
Arsenal 8 games FA Premier League 2001–02

● SCORED IN EVERY PREMIERSHIP GAME
Arsenal 2001–02 38 matches

● HAT-TRICKS
Career 34 Dixie Dean (Tranmere R, Everton, Notts Co, England)
Division 1 (one season post-war) 6 Jimmy Greaves (Chelsea), 1960–61
Three for one team one match
West, Spouncer, Hooper, Nottingham F v Leicester Fosse, Division 1, 21 April 1909
Barnes, Ambler, Davies, Wrexham v Hartlepools U, Division 4, 3 March 1962
Adcock, Stewart, White, Manchester C v Huddersfield T, Division 2, 7 Nov 1987
Loasby, Smith, Wells, Northampton T v Walsall, Division 3S, 5 Nov 1927
Bowater, Hoyland, Readman, Mansfield T v Rotherham U, Division 3N, 27 Dec 1932

● MOST DRAWN GAMES IN A SEASON
	Season	Team	Draws	Games
FA PREMIER LEAGUE	1993–94	Manchester C	18	42
	1993–94	Sheffield U	18	42
	1994–95	Southampton	18	42
FOOTBALL LEAGUE				
Division 1	1978–79	Norwich C	23	42
Division 3	1997–98	Cardiff C	23	46
	1997–98	Hartlepool U	23	46
Division 4	1986–87	Exeter C	23	46
SCOTTISH LEAGUE				
Premier Division	1993–94	Aberdeen	21	44
New Division 1	1986–87	East Fife	21	44

● MOST GOALS IN A GAME
FA PREMIER LEAGUE	19 Sept 1999	Alan Shearer (Newcastle U) 5 goals v Sheffield W
	4 Mar 1995	Andy Cole (Manchester U) 5 goals v Ipswich T
FOOTBALL LEAGUE		
Division 1	14 Dec 1935	Ted Drake (Arsenal) 7 goals v Aston V
Division 2	5 Feb 1955	Tommy Briggs (Blackburn R) 7 goals v Bristol R
	23 Feb 1957	Neville Coleman (Stoke C) 7 goals v Lincoln C
Division 3(S)	13 April 1936	Joe Payne (Luton T) 10 goals v Bristol R
Division 3(N)	26 Dec 1935	Bunny Bell (Tranmere R) 9 goals v Oldham Ath
Division 3	16 Sept 1969	Steve Earle (Fulham) 5 goals v Halifax T
	24 April 1965	Barrie Thomas (Scunthorpe U) 5 goals v Luton T
	20 Nov 1965	Keith East (Swindon T) 5 goals v Mansfield T
	2 Oct 1971	Alf Wood (Shrewsbury T) 5 goals v Blackburn R
	10 Sept 1983	Tony Caldwell (Bolton W) 5 goals v Walsall
	4 May 1987	Andy Jones (Port Vale) 5 goals v Newport Co
	3 April 1990	Steve Wilkinson (Mansfield T) 5 goals v Birmingham C
	5 Sept 1998	Giuliano Grazioli (Peterborough U) 5 goals v Barnet
	6 April 2002	Lee Jones (Wrexham) 5 goals v Cambridge U
Division 4	26 Dec 1962	Bert Lister (Oldham Ath) 6 goals v Southport
FA CUP	20 Nov 1971	Ted MacDougall (Bournemouth) 9 goals v Margate (*1st Round*)
LEAGUE CUP	25 Oct 1989	Frankie Bunn (Oldham Ath) 6 goals v Scarborough
SCOTTISH LEAGUE		
Premier Division	17 Nov 1984	Paul Sturrock (Dundee U) 5 goals v Morton
Division 1	14 Sept 1928	Jimmy McGrory (Celtic) 8 goals v Dunfermline Ath
Division 2	1 Oct 1927	Owen McNally (Arthurlie) 8 goals v Armadale
	2 Jan 1930	Jim Dyet (King's Park) 8 goals v Forfar Ath
	18 April 1936	John Calder (Morton) 8 goals v Raith R
	20 Aug 1937	Norman Hayward (Raith R) 8 goals v Brechin C
SCOTTISH CUP	12 Sept 1885	John Petrie (Arbroath) 13 goals v Bon Accord (*1st Round*)

● MOST CUP GOALS IN A CAREER
FA CUP (post-war)
Ian Rush 43 (Chester, Liverpool)
Pre-Second World war: Henry Cursham 48 (Notts Co)

LEAGUE CUP
Geoff Hurst 49 (West Ham U, Stoke C)
Ian Rush 49 (Chester, Liverpool, Newcastle U)

● MOST LEAGUE GOALS IN A SEASON

	Season	Player	Goals	Games
FA PREMIER	1993–94	Andy Cole (Newcastle U)	34	40
LEAGUE	1994–95	Alan Shearer (Blackburn R)	34	42
Division 1	1927–28	Dixie Dean (Everton)	60	39
Division 2	1926–27	George Camsell (Middlesbrough)	59	37
Division 3(S)	1936–37	Joe Payne (Luton T)	55	39
Division 3(N)	1936–37	Ted Harston (Mansfield T)	55	41
Division 3	1959–60	Derek Reeves (Southampton)	39	46
Division 4	1960–61	Terry Bly (Peterborough U)	52	46
FA CUP	1887–88	Jimmy Ross (Preston NE)	20	8
LEAGUE CUP	1986–87	Clive Allen (Tottenham H)	12	9
SCOTTISH PREMIER				
LEAGUE	2000–01	Henrik Larsson Celtic	35	37
SCOTTISH LEAGUE				
Division 1	1931–32	William McFadyen (Motherwell)	52	34
Division 2	1927–28	Jim Smith (Ayr U)	66	38

● MOST LEAGUE GOALS IN A CAREER

Player	Team	Goals	Games	Season
FOOTBALL LEAGUE				
Arthur Rowley	WBA	4	24	1946–48
	Fulham	27	56	1948–50
	Leicester C	251	303	1950–58
	Shrewsbury T	152	236	1958–65
		———	———	
		434	619	
SCOTTISH LEAGUE				
Jimmy McGrory	Celtic	1	3	1922–23
	Clydebank	13	30	1923–24
	Celtic	396	375	1924–38
		———	———	
		410	408	

● A CENTURY OF LEAGUE AND CUP GOALS IN CONSECUTIVE SEASONS

George Camsell	Middlesbrough	59 Lge	5 Cup	1926–27
(101 goals)		33	4	1927–28
Steve Bull	Wolverhampton W	34 Lge	18 Cup	1987–88
(102 goals)		37	13	1988–89

(Camsell's cup goals were all scored in the FA Cup; Bull had 12 in the Sherpa Van Trophy, 3 Littlewoods Cup, 3 FA Cup in 1987–88; 11 Sherpa Van Trophy, 2 Littlewoods Cup in 1988–89.)

● LONGEST SEQUENCE OF CONSECUTIVE SCORING (Individual)

FA PREMIER LEAGUE

Mark Stein (Chelsea)	9 in 7 games	1993–94
Alan Shearer (Newcastle U)	7 in 7 games	1996–97
Thierry Henry (Arsenal)	9 in 7 games	1999–2000

FOOTBALL LEAGUE RECORD

Tom Phillipson (Wolverhampton W)	23 in 13 games	1926–27

● LONGEST WINNING SEQUENCE

FOOTBALL LEAGUE	Season	Team	Games
FA Premier League	2001–02	Arsenal	13
Division 1	1959–60 (2)	Tottenham H	13
	and 1960–61 (11)		
	1891–92	Preston NE	13
	1891–92	Sunderland	13
Division 2	1904–05	Manchester U	14
	1905–06	Bristol C	14
	1950–51	Preston NE	14
Division 3	1985–86	Reading	13
FROM SEASON'S START			
Division 1	1960–61	Tottenham H	11
	1992–93	Newcastle U	11
	2000–01	Fulham	11
Division 3	1985–86	Reading	13

● LONGEST UNBEATEN SEQUENCE

FOOTBALL LEAGUE	Season	Team	Games
Division 1	Nov 1977–Dec 1978	Nottingham F	42

● LONGEST UNBEATEN CUP SEQUENCE

Liverpool   25 rounds   League/Milk Cup   1980–84

● LONGEST UNBEATEN SEQUENCE IN A SEASON

FOOTBALL LEAGUE	Season	Team	Games
Division 1	1920–21	Burnley	30

● LONGEST UNBEATEN START TO A SEASON

FOOTBALL LEAGUE	Season	Team	Games
Division 1	1973–74	Leeds U	29
	1987–88	Liverpool	29

● LONGEST SEQUENCE WITHOUT A WIN IN A SEASON

FOOTBALL LEAGUE	Season	Team	Games
Division 2	1983–84	Cambridge U	31

● LONGEST SEQUENCE WITHOUT A WIN FROM SEASON'S START

FOOTBALL LEAGUE	Season	Team	Games
Division 1	1990–91	Sheffield U	16

● LONGEST SEQUENCE OF CONSECUTIVE DEFEATS

FOOTBALL LEAGUE	Season	Team	Games
Division 2	1898–99	Darwen	18

● GOALKEEPING RECORDS (without conceding a goal)

BRITISH RECORD (all competitive games)
Chris Woods, Rangers, in 1196 minutes from 26 November 1986 to 31 January 1987.

FOOTBALL LEAGUE
Steve Death, Reading, 1103 minutes from 24 March to 18 August 1979.

● PENALTIES

Most in a Season (individual)	*Goals*		*Season*	
Division 1	Francis Lee (Manchester C)		13	1971–72
Most awarded in one game				
Five	Crystal Palace (4 – 1 scored, 3 missed) v Brighton & HA (1 scored), Div 2			1988–89
Most saved in a Season				
Division 1	Paul Cooper (Ipswich T)		8 (of 10)	1979–80

● MOST FA CUP FINAL GOALS

Ian Rush (Liverpool) 5: 1986(2), 1989(2), 1992(1)

● MOST LEAGUE MEDALS

Phil Neal (Liverpool) 8: 1976, 1977, 1979, 1980, 1982, 1983, 1984, 1986
Alan Hansen (Liverpool) 8: 1979, 1980, 1982, 1983, 1984, 1986, 1988, 1990

● MANAGERS

Most successful	Sir Alex Ferguson CBE	(Manchester U)	14 major trophies in 12 seasons: 7 Premier League, 4 FA Cup, 1 European Cup, 1 Cup-Winners' Cup, 1 League Cup.
		(Aberdeen)	1976–86 – 9 trophies: 3 League, 4 Scottish Cup, 1 League Cup, 1 Cup-Winners' Cup.
	Bob Paisley	(Liverpool)	1974–83 – 13 trophies: 6 League, 3 European Cup, 3 League Cup, 1 UEFA Cup,

● MOST LEAGUE APPEARANCES (750+ matches)

1005   Peter Shilton (286 Leicester City, 110 Stoke City, 202 Nottingham Forest, 188 Southampton, 175 Derby County, 34 Plymouth Argyle, 1 Bolton Wanderers, 9 Leyton Orient) 1966–97

931   Tony Ford (355 Grimsby T, 9 Sunderland (loan), 112 Stoke C, 114 WBA, 68 Grimsby T, 5 Bradford C (loan), 76 Scunthorpe U, 103 Mansfield T, 89 Rochdale) 1975–2002

909   Graeme Armstrong (204 Stirling A, 83 Berwick R, 353 Meadowbank T, 268 Stenhousemuir, 1 Alloa) 1975–2001

863   Tommy Hutchison (165 Blackpool, 314 Coventry City, 46 Manchester City, 92 Burnley, 178 Swansea City, 68 Alloa) 1965–91

824   Terry Paine (713 Southampton, 111 Hereford United) 1957–77

782   Robbie James (484 Swansea C, 48 Stoke C, 87 QPR, 23 Leicester C, 89 Bradford C, 51 Cardiff C) 1973–94

777   Alan Oakes (565 Manchester C, 211 Chester C, 1 Port Vale) 1959–84

771   John Burridge (27 Workington, 134 Blackpool, 65 Aston Villa, 6 Southend U (loan), 88 Crystal Palace, 39 QPR, 74 Wolverhampton W, 6 Derby Co (loan), 109 Sheffield U, 62 Southampton, 67 Newcastle U, 65 Hibernian, 3 Scarborough, 4 Lincoln C, 3 Aberdeen, 3 Dumbarton, 3 Falkirk, 4 Manchester C, 3 Darlington, 6 Queen of the South) 1968–96

770   John Trollope (all for Swindon Town) 1960–80†

764   Jimmy Dickinson (all for Portsmouth) 1946–65

761   Roy Sproson (all for Port Vale) 1950–72

760   Mick Tait (64 Oxford U, 106 Carlisle U, 33 Hull C, 240 Portsmouth, 99 Reading, 79 Darlington, 139 Hartlepool U) 1975–97

758   Ray Clemence (48 Scunthorpe United, 470 Liverpool, 240 Tottenham Hotspur) 1966–87

758   Billy Bonds (95 Charlton Ath, 663 West Ham U) 1964–88

757   Pat Jennings (48 Watford, 472 Tottenham Hotspur, 237 Arsenal) 1963–86

757   Frank Worthington (171 Huddersfield T, 210 Leicester C, 84 Bolton W, 75 Birmingham C, 32 Leeds U, 19 Sunderland, 34 Southampton, 31 Brighton & HA, 59 Tranmere R, 23 Preston NE, 19 Stockport Co) 1966–88

† record for one club

CONSECUTIVE
401   Harold Bell (401 Tranmere R; 459 in all games) 1946–55

FA CUP
88   Ian Callaghan (79 Liverpool, 7 Swansea C, 2 Crewe Alex)

MOST SENIOR MATCHES
1390   Peter Shilton (1005 League, 86 FA Cup, 102 League Cup, 125 Internationals, 13 Under-23, 4 Football League XI, 20 European Cup, 7 Texaco Cup, 5 Simod Cup, 4 European Super Cup, 4 UEFA Cup, 3 Screen Sport Super Cup, 3 Zenith Data Systems Cup, 2 Autoglass Trophy, 2 Charity Shield, 2 Full Members Cup, 1 Anglo-Italian Cup, 1 Football League play-offs, 1 World Club Championship)

● OTHER RECORDS

YOUNGEST PLAYERS
FA Premier League   Gary McSheffrey, 16 years, 198 days, Coventry C v Aston Villa, 27.2.99.
FA Premier League scorer   Michael Owen, 17 years 144 days, Liverpool v Wimbledon, 6.5.97.
Football League   Albert Geldard, 15 years 158 days, Bradford Park Avenue v Millwall, Division 2, 16.9.29; and Ken Roberts, 15 years 158 days, Wrexham v Bradford Park Avenue, Division 3N, 1.9.51
Football League scorer   Ronnie Dix, 15 years 180 days, Bristol Rovers v Norwich City, Division 3S, 3.3.28.
Division 1   Derek Forster, 15 years 185 days, Sunderland v Leicester City, 22.8.64.
Division 1 scorer   Jason Dozzell, 16 years 57 days as substitute Ipswich Town v Coventry City, 4.2.84
Division 1 hat-tricks   Alan Shearer, 17 years 240 days, Southampton v Arsenal, 9.4.88
   Jimmy Greaves, 17 years 10 months, Chelsea v Portsmouth, 25.12.57
FA Cup (any round)   Andy Awford, 15 years 88 days as substitute Worcester City v Boreham Wood, 3rd Qual. rd, 10.10.87
FA Cup proper   Scott Endersby, 15 years 288 days, Kettering v Tilbury, 1st rd, 26.11.77
FA Cup Final   James Prinsep, 17 years 245 days, Clapham Rovers v Old Etonians, 1879
FA Cup Final scorer   Norman Whiteside, 18 years 18 days, Manchester United v Brighton & Hove Albion, 1983
FA Cup Final captain   David Nish, 21 years 212 days, Leicester City v Manchester City, 1969
League Cup Final scorer   Norman Whiteside, 17 years 324 days, Manchester United v Liverpool, 1983
League Cup Final captain   Barry Venison, 20 years 7 months 8 days, Sunderland v Norwich City, 1985

OLDEST PLAYERS
Football League   Neil McBain, 52 years 4 months, New Brighton v Hartlepools United, Div 3N, 15.3.47 (McBain was New Brighton's manager and had to play in an emergency)
Division 1   Stanley Matthews, 50 years 5 days, Stoke City v Fulham, 6.2.65

● SENDINGS-OFF

Season	371 (League alone)	1998–99
Day	15 (all League)	31 Oct 1998
	15 (3 League, 12 FA Cup*)	20 Nov 1982
	worst overall FA Cup total	
	26 (14 English, 12 Scottish)	16 Oct 1999
	(On 17 Oct 1999 a further 1 English made it 27 for the weekend)	
Weekend	15 (League alone)	22/23 Dec 1990
FA Cup Final	Kevin Moran, Manchester U v Everton	1985
Quickest	Walter Boyd, Swansea C v Darlington Div 3 as substitute in zero seconds	23 Nov 1999
Most in one game	Five: Chesterfield (2) v Plymouth Arg (3)	22 Feb 1997
	Five: Wigan Ath (1) v Bristol R (4)	2 Dec 1997
Most in one team	Wigan Ath (1) v Bristol R (4)	2 Dec 1997
	Hereford U (4) v Northampton T (0)	11 Nov 1992

● RECORD ATTENDANCES

FA Premier League	67,683	Manchester U v Middlesbrough, Old Trafford	23.3.2002
Football League	83,260	Manchester U v Arsenal, Maine Road	17.1.1948
Scottish League	118,567	Rangers v Celtic, Ibrox Stadium	2.1.1939
FA Cup Final	126,047*	Bolton W v West Ham U, Wembley	28.4.1923
European Cup	135,826	Celtic v Leeds U, semi-final at Hampden Park	15.4.1970
Scottish Cup	146,433	Celtic v Aberdeen, Hampden Park	24.4.37
World Cup	199,854†	Brazil v Uruguay, Maracana, Rio	16.7.50

* It has been estimated that as many as 70,000 more broke in without paying.
† 173,830 paid.

● GOALS PER GAME

(from 1992–93)

Goals per game	Premier Games	Goals	Division 1 Games	Goals	Division 2 Games	Goals	Division 3 Games	Goals
0	366	0	475	0	461	0	446	0
1	749	749	1024	1024	1035	1035	1020	1020
2	1006	2012	1387	2774	1423	2846	1326	2652
3	815	2445	1141	3423	1204	3612	1138	3414
4	560	2240	794	3176	748	2992	677	2708
5	288	1440	419	2095	385	1925	358	1790
6	162	972	189	1134	155	930	175	1050
7	64	448	66	462	76	532	72	504
8	29	232	20	160	23	184	27	216
9	7	63	3	27	8	72	8	72
10	0	0	2	20	2	20	2	20
11	0	0	0	0	0	0	1	11
	4046	**10601**	**5520**	**14295**	**5520**	**14148**	**5250**	**13457**

(Football League to 1991–92)

Goals per game	Division 1 Games	Goals	Division 2 Games	Goals	Division 3 Games	Goals	Division 4 Games	Goals	Division 3(S) Games	Goals	Division 3(N) Games	Goals
0	2465	0	2665	0	1446	0	1438	0	997	0	803	0
1	5606	5606	5836	5836	3225	3225	3106	3106	2073	2073	1914	1914
2	8275	16550	8609	17218	4569	9138	4441	8882	3314	6628	2939	5878
3	7731	23193	7842	23526	3784	11352	4041	12123	2996	8988	2922	8766
4	6230	24920	5897	23588	2837	11348	2784	11136	2445	9780	2410	9640
5	3751	18755	3634	18170	1566	7830	1506	7530	1554	7770	1599	7995
6	2137	12822	2007	12042	769	4614	786	4716	870	5220	930	5580
7	1092	7644	1001	7007	357	2499	336	2352	451	3157	461	3227
8	542	4336	376	3008	135	1080	143	1144	209	1672	221	1768
9	197	1773	164	1476	64	576	35	315	76	684	102	918
10	83	830	68	680	13	130	8	80	33	330	45	450
11	37	407	19	209	2	22	7	77	15	165	15	165
12	12	144	17	204	1	12	0	0	7	84	8	96
13	4	52	4	52	0	0	0	0	2	26	4	52
14	2	28	1	14	0	0	0	0	0	0	0	0
17	0	0	0	0	0	0	0	0	0	0	1	17
	38164	**117060**	**38140**	**113030**	**18768**	**51826**	**18631**	**51461**	**15042**	**46577**	**14374**	**46466**

New Overall Totals (since 1992)

Games	20336
Goals	52501

Complete Overall Totals (since 1888–89)

Games	163455
Goals	478921

● **COMMON RESULTS** – the season given is the final year of the season.

Season	Games	Score 0-0		Score 1-0		Score 0-1		Score 2-0		Score 1-1		Score 2-1		Other	
		No.	%	No.	%	No.	%	No.	%	No.	%	No.	%	No.	%
1889	132	2	1.52	5	3.79	1	0.76	6	4.55	6	4.55	16	12.12	96	72.73
1890	132	1	0.76	1	0.76	4	3.03	5	3.79	11	8.33	9	6.82	101	76.52
1891	132	4	3.03	9	6.82	5	3.79	7	5.30	7	5.30	8	6.06	92	69.70
1892	182	1	0.55	11	6.04	7	3.85	10	5.49	12	6.59	11	6.04	130	71.43
1893	372	6	1.61	22	5.91	15	4.03	25	6.72	23	6.18	26	6.99	255	68.55
1894	450	10	2.22	21	4.67	18	4.00	24	5.33	31	6.89	37	8.22	309	68.67
1895	480	9	1.88	25	5.21	11	2.29	25	5.21	25	5.21	44	9.17	341	71.04
1896	480	12	2.50	41	8.54	14	2.92	32	6.67	37	7.71	49	10.21	295	61.46
1897	480	22	4.58	30	6.25	22	4.58	36	7.50	39	8.13	31	6.46	300	62.50
1898	480	21	4.38	31	6.46	21	4.38	34	7.08	53	11.04	47	9.79	273	56.88
1899	612	32	5.23	53	8.66	29	4.74	57	9.31	64	10.46	48	7.84	329	53.76
1900	612	44	7.19	63	10.29	27	4.41	63	10.29	48	7.84	44	7.19	323	52.78
1901	612	51	8.33	78	12.75	44	7.19	59	9.64	60	9.80	58	9.48	262	42.81
1902	612	44	7.19	71	11.60	29	4.74	65	10.62	61	9.97	43	7.03	299	48.86
1903	612	32	5.23	58	9.48	43	7.03	57	9.31	48	7.84	57	9.31	317	51.80
1904	612	46	7.52	53	8.66	32	5.23	46	7.52	53	8.66	55	8.99	327	53.43
1905	612	44	7.19	54	8.82	37	6.05	62	10.13	45	7.35	57	9.31	313	51.14
1906	760	41	5.39	69	9.08	46	6.05	68	8.95	63	8.29	58	7.63	415	54.61
1907	760	42	5.53	74	9.74	40	5.26	74	9.74	67	8.82	70	9.21	393	51.71
1908	760	49	6.45	66	8.68	42	5.53	69	9.08	71	9.34	70	9.21	393	51.71
1909	760	44	5.79	76	10.00	44	5.79	73	9.61	85	11.18	62	8.16	376	49.47
1910	760	53	6.97	62	8.16	44	5.79	63	8.29	61	8.03	69	9.08	408	53.68
1911	760	49	6.45	90	11.84	47	6.18	77	10.13	87	11.45	64	8.42	346	45.53
1912	760	59	7.76	93	12.24	45	5.92	65	8.55	71	9.34	63	8.29	364	47.89
1913	760	57	7.50	62	8.16	41	5.39	71	9.34	83	10.92	58	7.63	388	51.05
1914	760	58	7.63	81	10.66	53	6.97	70	9.21	73	9.61	78	10.26	347	45.66
1915	760	52	6.84	81	10.66	37	4.87	57	7.50	73	9.61	64	8.42	396	52.11
1920	924	73	7.90	97	10.50	63	6.82	85	9.20	76	8.23	79	8.55	451	48.81
1921	1386	147	10.61	169	12.19	102	7.36	133	9.60	180	12.99	94	6.78	561	40.48
1922	1766	159	9.00	214	12.12	144	8.15	188	10.65	187	10.59	135	7.64	739	41.85
1923	1766	183	10.36	225	12.74	126	7.13	186	10.53	182	10.31	154	8.72	710	40.20
1924	1848	225	12.18	241	13.04	117	6.33	176	9.52	220	11.90	140	7.58	729	39.45
1925	1848	171	9.25	238	12.88	140	7.58	184	9.96	232	12.55	136	7.36	747	40.42
1926	1848	86	4.65	117	6.33	96	5.19	153	8.28	153	8.28	137	7.41	1106	59.85
1927	1848	77	4.17	137	7.41	77	4.17	127	6.87	158	8.55	144	7.79	1128	61.04
1928	1848	100	5.41	104	5.63	73	3.95	109	5.90	166	8.98	143	7.74	1153	62.39
1929	1848	73	3.95	137	7.41	66	3.57	109	5.90	174	9.42	153	8.28	1136	61.47
1930	1848	71	3.84	126	6.82	63	3.41	127	6.87	181	9.79	146	7.90	1134	61.36
1931	1848	84	4.55	123	6.66	57	3.08	131	7.09	165	8.93	137	7.41	1151	62.28
1932	1806	59	3.27	115	6.37	74	4.10	126	6.98	166	9.19	152	8.42	1114	61.68
1933	1848	80	4.33	131	7.09	69	3.73	141	7.63	188	10.17	155	8.39	1084	58.66
1934	1848	100	5.41	134	7.25	82	4.44	136	7.36	188	10.17	142	7.68	1066	57.68
1935	1848	91	4.92	123	6.66	74	4.00	142	7.68	181	9.79	159	8.60	1078	58.33
1936	1848	120	6.49	142	7.68	79	4.27	141	7.63	183	9.90	154	8.33	1029	55.68
1937	1848	90	4.87	145	7.85	65	3.52	146	7.90	202	10.93	159	8.60	1041	56.33
1938	1848	130	7.03	177	9.58	97	5.25	162	8.77	211	11.42	173	9.36	898	48.59
1939	1848	128	6.93	150	8.12	84	4.55	164	8.87	192	10.39	149	8.06	981	53.08
1947	1848	88	4.76	146	7.90	92	4.98	133	7.20	172	9.31	152	8.23	1065	57.63
1948	1848	136	7.36	176	9.52	116	6.28	132	7.14	222	12.01	155	8.39	911	49.30
1949	1848	155	8.39	179	9.69	106	5.74	157	8.50	222	12.01	174	9.42	855	46.27
1950	1848	143	7.74	201	10.88	113	6.11	159	8.60	227	12.28	162	8.77	843	45.62
1951	2028	114	5.62	203	10.01	103	5.08	158	7.79	227	11.19	187	9.22	1036	51.08

● COMMON RESULTS – *continued*

Season	Games	Score 0-0 No.	%	Score 1-0 No.	%	Score 0-1 No.	%	Score 2-0 No.	%	Score 1-1 No.	%	Score 2-1 No.	%	Other No.	%
1952	2028	99	4.88	186	9.17	96	4.73	159	7.84	221	10.90	181	8.93	1086	53.55
1953	2028	119	5.87	160	7.89	85	4.19	163	8.04	245	12.08	161	7.94	1095	53.99
1954	2028	106	5.23	155	7.64	111	5.47	151	7.45	222	10.95	193	9.52	1090	53.75
1955	2028	100	4.93	178	8.78	110	5.42	147	7.25	210	10.36	173	8.53	1110	54.73
1956	2028	100	4.93	136	6.71	104	5.13	153	7.54	190	9.37	185	9.12	1160	57.20
1957	2028	112	5.52	152	7.50	70	3.45	127	6.26	203	10.01	166	8.19	1198	59.07
1958	2028	102	5.03	143	7.05	73	3.60	125	6.16	208	10.26	181	8.93	1196	58.97
1959	2028	99	4.88	142	7.00	89	4.39	124	6.11	201	9.91	173	8.53	1200	59.17
1960	2028	84	4.14	152	7.50	114	5.62	149	7.35	214	10.55	175	8.63	1140	56.21
1961	2028	84	4.14	140	6.90	96	4.73	145	7.15	190	9.37	178	8.78	1195	58.93
1962	1982	100	5.05	134	6.76	86	4.34	153	7.72	193	9.74	181	9.13	1135	57.27
1963	2028	119	5.87	156	7.69	70	3.45	145	7.15	209	10.31	189	9.32	1140	56.21
1964	2028	113	5.57	173	8.53	97	4.78	155	7.64	221	10.90	150	7.40	1119	55.18
1965	2028	114	5.62	147	7.25	105	5.18	158	7.79	208	10.26	177	8.73	1119	55.18
1966	2028	107	5.28	198	9.76	128	6.31	168	8.28	222	10.95	179	8.83	1026	50.59
1967	2028	137	6.76	202	9.96	116	5.72	144	7.10	241	11.88	204	10.06	984	48.52
1968	2028	139	6.85	186	9.17	127	6.26	181	8.93	272	13.41	179	8.83	944	46.55
1969	2028	202	9.96	239	11.79	143	7.05	178	8.78	275	13.56	180	8.88	811	39.99
1970	2028	174	8.58	214	10.55	140	6.90	178	8.78	287	14.15	179	8.83	856	42.21
1971	2028	173	8.53	252	12.43	148	7.30	182	8.97	283	13.95	181	8.93	809	39.89
1972	2028	206	10.16	220	10.85	138	6.80	194	9.57	232	11.44	201	9.91	837	41.27
1973	2028	181	8.93	247	12.18	140	6.90	208	10.26	281	13.86	201	9.91	770	37.97
1974	2027	205	10.11	256	12.63	146	7.20	164	8.09	290	14.31	190	9.37	776	38.28
1975	2028	184	9.07	254	12.52	129	6.36	207	10.21	267	13.17	194	9.57	793	39.10
1976	2028	179	8.83	251	12.38	144	7.10	171	8.43	265	13.07	177	8.73	841	41.47
1977	2028	169	8.33	248	12.23	133	6.56	179	8.83	255	12.57	192	9.47	852	42.01
1978	2028	207	10.21	221	10.90	104	5.13	188	9.27	272	13.41	202	9.96	834	41.12
1979	2028	185	9.12	243	11.98	144	7.10	185	9.12	288	14.20	179	8.83	804	39.64
1980	2028	187	9.22	227	11.19	125	6.16	190	9.37	261	12.87	189	9.32	849	41.86
1981	2028	207	10.21	246	12.13	153	7.54	199	9.81	225	11.09	189	9.32	809	39.89
1982	2028	183	9.02	222	10.95	147	7.25	162	7.99	253	12.48	196	9.66	865	42.65
1983	2028	159	7.84	206	10.16	118	5.82	177	8.73	246	12.13	196	9.66	926	45.66
1984	2028	153	7.54	214	10.55	149	7.35	160	7.89	244	12.03	203	10.01	905	44.63
1985	2028	161	7.94	221	10.90	141	6.95	169	8.33	223	11.00	196	9.66	917	45.22
1986	2028	123	6.07	209	10.31	137	6.76	167	8.23	259	12.77	177	8.73	956	47.14
1987	2028	158	7.79	246	12.13	140	6.90	184	9.07	274	13.51	178	8.78	848	41.81
1988	2030	178	8.77	188	9.26	163	8.03	150	7.39	251	12.36	202	9.95	898	44.24
1989	2036	153	7.51	221	10.85	153	7.51	159	7.81	263	12.92	194	9.53	893	43.86
1990	2036	160	7.86	218	10.71	173	8.50	167	8.20	263	12.92	191	9.38	864	42.44
1991	2036	168	8.25	222	10.90	143	7.02	171	8.40	254	12.48	207	10.17	871	42.78
1992	2028	157	7.74	249	12.28	152	7.50	170	8.38	265	13.07	185	9.12	1017	50.15
1993	2028	158	7.79	195	9.62	152	7.50	175	8.63	252	12.43	178	8.78	1072	52.86
1994	2028	157	7.74	213	10.50	148	7.30	153	7.54	276	13.61	205	10.11	1054	51.97
1995	2028	189	9.32	215	10.60	157	7.74	173	8.53	246	12.13	180	8.88	1016	50.10
1996	2036	182	8.94	244	11.98	146	7.17	141	6.93	294	14.44	185	9.09	1040	51.08
1997	2036	191	9.38	234	11.49	147	7.22	189	9.28	267	13.11	190	9.33	987	48.48
1998	2036	192	9.43	246	12.08	152	7.47	146	7.17	257	12.62	215	10.56	987	48.48
1999	2036	178	8.74	230	11.30	173	8.50	168	8.25	253	12.43	179	8.79	855	41.99
2000	2036	164	8.06	236	11.59	178	8.74	153	7.51	260	12.77	211	10.36	834	40.96
2001	2036	161	7.91	227	11.15	163	8.01	175	8.60	273	13.41	183	8.99	854	41.94
2002	2036	176	8.64	207	10.17	165	8.10	161	7.91	227	11.15	194	9.53	906	44.50
	163455	11562	7.07	15851	9.70	9737	5.96	13345	8.16	18563	11.36	14491	8.87	81077	49.60

The season is the final year of the season.

INTERNATIONAL RECORDS

● MOST GOALS IN AN INTERNATIONAL

Record/World Cup	Archie Thompson (Australia) 13 goals v American Samoa	11.4.2001
England	Malcolm Macdonald (Newcastle U) 5 goals v Cyprus, at Wembley	16.4.1975
	Willie Hall (Tottenham H) 5 goals v Ireland, at Old Trafford	16.11.1938
	Steve Bloomer (Derby Co) 5 goals v Wales, at Cardiff	16.3.1896
	Howard Vaughton (Aston Villa) 5 goals v Ireland, at Belfast	18.2.1882
Northern Ireland	Joe Bambrick (Linfield) 6 goals v Wales, at Belfast	1.2.1930
Wales	John Price (Wrexham) 4 goals v Ireland, at Wrexham	25.2.1882
	Mel Charles (Cardiff C) 4 goals v Ireland, at Cardiff	11.4.1962
	Ian Edwards (Chester) 4 goals v Malta, at Wrexham	25.10.1978

● MOST GOALS IN AN INTERNATIONAL CAREER

		Goals	Games
England	Bobby Charlton (Manchester U)	49	106
Scotland	Denis Law (Huddersfield T, Manchester C, Torino, Manchester U)	30	55
	Kenny Dalglish (Celtic, Liverpool)	30	102
Northern Ireland	Colin Clarke (Bournemouth, Southampton, QPR, Portsmouth)	13	38
Wales	Ian Rush (Liverpool, Juventus)	28	73
Republic of Ireland	Niall Quinn (Arsenal, Manchester C, Sunderland)	21	91

● HIGHEST SCORES

Record/World Cup Match	Australia	31	American Samoa	0	2001
European Championship	Spain	12	Malta	1	1983
Olympic Games	Denmark	17	France	1	1908
	Germany	16	USSR	0	1912
Other International Match	Libya	21	Oman	0	1966
European Cup	Feyenoord	12	K R Reykjavik	2	1969
European Cup-Winners' Cup	Sporting Lisbon	16	Apoel Nicosia	1	1963
Fairs & UEFA Cups	Ajax	14	Red Boys	0	1984

● GOALSCORING RECORDS

World Cup Final	Geoff Hurst (England) 3 goals v West Germany	1966
World Cup Final tournament	Just Fontaine (France) 13 goals	1958
Career	Artur Friedenreich (Brazil) 1329 goals	1910–30
	Pele (Brazil) 1281 goals	*1956–78
	Franz 'Bimbo' Binder (Austria, Germany) 1006 goals	1930–50
World Cup Finals fastest	Hakan Sukur (Turkey) 10.8 secs v South Korea	2002

Pele subsequently scored two goals in Testimonial matches making his total 1283.

● MOST CAPPED INTERNATIONALS IN BRITISH ISLES

England	Peter Shilton	125 appearances	1970–90
Northern Ireland	Pat Jennings	119 appearances	1964–86
Scotland	Kenny Dalglish	102 appearances	1971–86
Wales	Neville Southall	92 appearances	1982–97
Republic of Ireland	Steve Staunton	102 appearances	1988–2002

MILESTONES DIARY 2001–02

June 2001
Chelsea land Lampard ... CBE for Gentle Giant ... Gunners get Bronckhorst ... Geordies bag Bellamy ... Petit at The Bridge ... Wilkinson steps down ... Saints appoint Gray

14 Chelsea splash £11m for West Ham's Frank Lampard. Everton's Francis Jeffers joins Arsenal for £10m. Dutch captain Frank de Boer is banned for a year after testing positive for the banned steroid Nandrolone.
15 Peter Taylor cuts his coaching ties with England to concentrate on managerial duties at Leicester. In the Queen's Birthday Honours Alan Shearer becomes an OBE, with Welsh legend John Charles celebrating a CBE.
16 Ten days after the 2000–01 campaign close down minnows Carmarthen get the season underway holding Swedish giants AIK Stockholm scoreless in their Intertoto Cup tie at Aberystwyth before 1,624.
17 Roma clinch their 3rd Italian title – and a 1st in 18 years – amid scenes of chaos as fans invade the pitch and tear the kit from the players' backs – 6 min before the whistle. Blackburn tie up £7m deal for striker Corrado Grabbi.
18 Norwegian John Arne Riise agrees a 5-year deal on Merseyside with the £4m transfer to Liverpool set to be completed on July 1. Trevor Brooking who made 622 League and cup appearances for West Ham returns to the club as a non-executive director. Former Latvian national coach Gary Johnson takes charge at Conference club Yeovil Town.
19 Arsenal's second big-fee summer signing in less than a week sees Giovanni Van Bronckhorst join for £8.5m from Rangers. Football League newcomers Rushden & Diamonds draw Burnley in Worthington Cup.
20 Manager Keegan makes Stuart Pearce, 39, his 1st signing at Man City.
21 Less than 2 months after resigning at West Ham, Harry Redknapp becomes Director of Football at Pompey. In new season fixture list Div 1 champions Fulham begin at Man U. Coventry, campaigning outside the top flight for the 1st time in almost 35 years, travel to Stockport Co.
22 Eric Cantona, representing France in the Pro Beach Soccer tournament in Hyde Park, pours cold water on rumours he will coach at Man U.
23 Tiny Welsh side Carmarthen's Intertoto Cup hopes end losing 3-0 at AIK Stockholm.
24 Arsenal play down reports midfielder Vieira has agreed a £150,000-a-week deal with Juventus.
25 Newcastle snap up Coventry striker Craig Bellamy for £6.5m. Tottenham's Ian Walker tells boss Hoddle he wants to leave.
26 Emmanuel Petit finally signs for Chelsea in £7.5m move from Barcelona ending a nightmare 12-month spell at the Nou Camp.
27 Gerry Francis returns for a 2nd spell in charge of relegated Bristol Rovers. Sunderland land French striker Lilian Laslandes from Bordeaux for £3.6m.
28 At Oxford Utd's new stadium, vandals cause thousands of pounds worth of damage shattering glass panels in the semi-circular entrance area; in April arsonists caused a £60,000 fire in the main stands.
29 Howard Wilkinson finally bows to pressure from within the FA and announces he is stepping aside from the U-21 set-up. Southampton install Stuart Gray as Hoddle's successor after chairman Lowe interviews then rejects 6 applicants with greater managerial experience.
30 Greenland beat Tibet 4-1 in an unofficial friendly on Copenhagen neutral ground; the match went ahead amid considerable diplomatic wrangling, with China threatening Greenland's large export of prawns! With just 2 years left in the game David Elleray, a Harrow School housemaster, is given special dispensation to join the elite list of referees without giving up his day job forfeiting the £33,000 annual retainer but being paid a £600 match fee.

July 2001
Anfield mourn Fagan loss ... Campbell becomes a Gunner ... Pallister forced to quit ... Goalie Wright for Highbury ... James heads to Hammers ... Man U entice £28m man Veron ... Great Dane returns ... Platt is U-21 boss ... Sir Alex to remain at club ... Barry fly Welsh flag ... McFarland gets Gulls post ... Everton's ground plans ... Black Cats are bad boys ... Agent Roach charged ... White Feather is a Ram ... Fulham goalie capture

1 Cameroon become the 1st team to qualify for World Cup 2002 finals beating Togo 2-0. Arsenal's Marieanne Spacey, 35, retires from international women's football after collecting 91 England caps.
2 Chelsea will make history on Sunday Aug 19 when they stage the 1st of 40 Premiership pay-per-view matches against Newcastle. Liverpool mourn the loss of Joe Fagan, 80, who led the club to an unprecedented treble in 1984 of the Championship, League Cup and European Cup in his 1st season.
3 Sol Campbell rejects overtures from at least 6 of the continent's leading clubs, shocking Tottenham supporters by joining north London rivals Arsenal on a free transfer and a hefty salary. Anfield suffers its 2nd loss in 3 days after the legendary Billy Liddell dies, aged 79, following a long battle against Alzheimer's Disease.
4 Boro's former Man U defender Gary Pallister, 36, is forced to retire through injury. Charlton splash £4.75m on Wimbledon's Jason Euell.
5 Ipswich goalie Richard Wright agrees his £6m switch to Arsenal. New Boro boss Steve McClaren appoints sports psychologist Bill Beswick and adds Villa pair Steve Harrison and Paul Barron to his coaching staff.
6 Three Man U players commit their long term futures to the club, Scholes signing for 6 years, Butt for 5 with Irwin remaining another year.
7 England's Eriksson tells a Swedish newspaper he already knows his line-up for the crucial World Cup qualifier in Germany in September.

8　Former FA Cup final ref Neil Midgley, 58, dies after a short illness. FIFA congress in Buenos Aires agree new transfer system which effectively gives the green light for players to walk out on clubs after 3 years of their contracts up to the age of 28, and 2 years over 28, with any fee decided by a tribunal if their contract has not expired.

9　Real Madrid raise the stakes to crazy new heights signing French ace Zinedine Zidane from Juventus for £48m and paying £20m in wages over 4 years. Spurs goalie Walker completes £3m move to Leicester. Defender Wes Brown becomes the 10th Man U player to agree a new contract signing a 4-year deal. Southampton break their club record signing Derby's Rory Delap for £4m. Mick Harford is Luton's new coach.

10　Glenn Roeder appoints Ipswich youth team manager Paul Goddard, a former Hammers striker, as his No. 2. A revolutionary new system to help linesmen judge offside will undergo tests by the FA next season, consisting of prismed lights at 1.2m intervals along the touchline which can only be seen when the linesman is directly opposite them.

11　David James completes his £3.5m move to West Ham claiming Villa's lack of ambition drew him back to London. Chelsea's Gustavo Poyet crosses London in £2m move to Spurs.

12　Juan Sebastian Veron's £28.1m arrival at Man U takes Ferguson's summer spending to £42m; the Argentine, 26, leaves Lazio for a 5-year contract. At Villa Park, Great Dane Peter Schmeichel, 37, is unveiled as a surprise but bargain free transfer capture, from Sporting Lisbon. David Platt, 35, leaves his Forest post to take over as England U-21 boss. Swansea City is sold for £1 only to chief executive Mike Lewis who agrees to repay £802,000 owed by the club. Boro's McClaren hails the leadership qualities of £6.5m signing Gareth Southgate, previously skipper at Villa.

13　Man U's Ferguson, who threatened to sever all links in May 2002 when his managerial deal runs out, confirms acceptance of a 5-year contract, believed to be worth around £1m a year, to remain as a consultant.

14　Intertoto Cup action sees Villa lose in Croatia, while Newcastle open up a 4-0 advantage over Lokeren.

15　Former West Ham, Everton and England striker Tony Cottee, 36, announces his retirement after a 19-year career.

16　Christian Ziege seals a £4m move from Liverpool to Spurs, flies home to Germany and will be unveiled later as Hoddle's 4th summer signing.

17　Arsenal's Wenger claims Man U contacted under-contract midfielder Vieira without permission. Palace are trying to forge a link with Walt Disney World to become the company's official club. Forest's new manager Paul Hart begins his reign by clearing out the backroom staff left by David Platt. Former Boro striker Ravanelli moves a step closer to his Premiership return after agreeing, in principle, a 2-year Derby Co deal worth £3.5m.

18　FIFA's world rankings list England equal 14th with Colombia, with Scotland slipping to 37th. Wales lie 105th, N Ireland 106th, and the Republic of Ireland 23rd. Little Barry Town make history becoming the 1st Welsh club to make the 2nd qualifying rd of the Champions League winning 1-0 (agg 3-0) in Azerbaijan against Shamkir. Two of Ireland's best known tycoons, Geneva-based JP McManus and racehorse owner John Magnier, buy a £30m stake in Man U. Swedish defender Olof Mellberg completes £5m move from Racing Santander to Villa.

19　Before 65,000 in Bangkok, Liverpool defeat Thailand's national side 3-1 to lift the Coca-Cola Super Cup. Christian Karembeu claims Boro's sacking of Bryan Robson triggered his £3.5m move to Olympiakos.

20　Former Cambridge and Derby boss Roy McFarland is back in management with Torquay. Sir Geoff Hurst is backing a campaign to keep Wembley as the national stadium claiming its world wide reputation is irreplaceable. Graham Taylor and Robbie Earle sign up as resident experts for ITV Digital's Nationwide League highlights show.

21　Bookies offer 4/5 odds about Southampton's Stuart Gray being the new season's 1st Premiership sacking. Peter Schmeichel, who bowed out with Man U's European Cup final win over Bayern Munich in Barcelona, makes his eagerly awaited return to English football in Villa's Intertoto Cup win over Slaven Belupu.

22　Stephen Froggatt, 28, Coventry's former Villa winger, is forced to retire. Before 80,000 in Kuala Lumpur, Ruud Van Nistelrooy is off the mark in Man U's 6-0 trouncing of a Malaysian side. A record Intertoto Cup crowd of 29,021 witness Newcastle's win over Lokeren.

23　Arsenal's new £3.5m capture, Gamba Osaka's Junichi Inamoto, 21, becomes the 1st Japanese signing into English football. Everton get permission to build a 55,000 capacity stadium on the Merseyside waterfront at Kings Dock and have 6 months to prove the £155m scheme is viable. QPR sign the Nationwide League's 1st Iranian player, Hamid Barr from Fisher Athletic.

24　An appeal by the Nationwide Conference to introduce promotion play-offs is turned down by the FA. Sunderland, with 78 bookings and 5 sending-offs, have the worst disciplinary record in the Premiership. Ipswich show the best record, 32 cautions and just 2 dismissals. Chelsea's Frank Leboeuf returns to France joining Marseille.

25　Ex-Tranmere boss John Aldridge admits being a manager left him mentally and physically drained and on the verge of a breakdown. Minnows Barry Town are swept aside 8-0 at FC Porto. SPL restore the Old Firm battles to traditional Saturday afternoon.

26　Marcel Desailly will succeed Dennis Wise as Chelsea's new captain.

27　Graham Poll says new guidelines given to refs could mean 10 min of stoppage time being added on at some matches, with 30 additional sec allowed per goal, caution and substitutions. The managers of Rangers and Celtic combine to back a move to the English Premiership. Top agent Dennis Roach is charged with 5 breaches of FA regulations after investigations into deals involving Duncan Ferguson and Paulo Wanchope. After negotiating his £600,000 pay-off from Lazio, Ravanelli finally signs a 2-year deal with Derby.

28　Ajax take Liverpool to the cleaners winning 3-1 which means the Merseysiders finish last in the 4-team Amsterdam tournament. Scottish football gets under way with predictable results, Rangers and Celtic chalk-

ing up 3-0 wins. Pompey agree compensation of around £200,000 and a testimonial to Steve Claridge who lasted 22 weeks before being replaced by Graham Rix.

29   Wrexham defeat Burnley to win the Isle of Man's long-standing pre-season tournament.

30   New boss Paul Hart slaps a 'for sale' sign on the entire Forest squad. Leicester snap up Ipswich's Jamie Scowcroft for £3m. Campbell makes his Arsenal debut in Austria figuring in the last 10 min of the win over Mallorca.

31   Fulham pull off a transfer coup securing Dutch international goalie Edwin van der Sar from Juventus for £7m. Minister for Sport Richard Caborn is to ask the Treasury to review the law on the testimonial system describing it as 'a hangover from the past'.

August 2001

Barry shock Porto ... Newcastle splash £10m ... Hartson heads to Celtic ... Zenden zooms in ... The Dons look to New Town ... Evans gets Robins job ... Sky Blues entice Hughes ... Bradford's bonus boost ... Saints in new stadium ... Action under Welsh roof ... Spend, spend, spend on foreigners ... Bees offer free game ... Fowler bust-up ... MOTD gives way to The Premiership ... Sealey sadness ... Anfield fans acknowledged ... Stam bombed out to Lazio ... Marlet enters The Cottage ... Blanc joins Man U ... Two costly keepers for Anfield

1   A near-capacity 67,000 turn up for Ryan Giggs' testimonial but visiting Celtic win a hotly contested clash 4-3. Barry Town pull off a shock 3-1 win over FC Porto but lose 9-3 on agg. Newcastle complete £10m signing of PSG's Laurent Robert. Swindon announce they 'wish to part company' with manager Andy King, at the club just 9 months. Ex Real Madrid and Barcelona star Robert Prosinecki, 32, links with Portsmouth.

2   To beat the registration deadline for European competitions Celtic make 3 signings, Coventry striker John Hartson, Leicester's Steve Guppy and St Johnstone wing back Momo Sylla for a combined £7.5m fee. Chelsea pay £7.5m for Barcelona's Boudewijn Zenden. Poorly supported Wimbledon announce plans to relocate in Milton Keynes. Leeds make Rio Ferdinand, 22, the youngest Premiership captain.

3   Swindon unveil new management duo of Roy Evans and Neil Ruddock. FA announce a prize money boost which increases through the FA Cup rounds – the 32 winners of the 4th qualifying rd ties each getting £20,000 – with the victors earning up to £4m.

4   SPL newcomers Livingston hold Rangers scoreless at Ibrox. The testimonial for Wrexham's management pairing of Brian Flynn and Kevin Reeves attracts 7,614.

5   Pompey goalie Aaron Flahavan, 25, dies following a car crash near Bournemouth. Everton reveal loss of £100,000 each season because thousands of adult supporters have been sneaking into Goodison Park using children's discounted tickets.

6   Terry Venables calls off Greek national post interest because the arrangements were leaked by officials.

7   Bryan Robson is given temporary coaching role at Old Trafford.

8   Owen nets a hat-trick as Liverpool hit 5 at FC Haka. Celtic's Martin O'Neill describes as 'immense' their 3-1 triumph at Ajax. Coventry complete £5m transfer of Albion's Lee Hughes. Spurs pay tribute and give rousing reception to double-winning boss Bill Nicholson, 82, before the friendly against Fiorentina. Former bustling striker Mick Quinn may not apply for his trainer's licence again until 1 Jan 2003 after Jockey Club ban him for 'the poor and unacceptable condition' of 3 of his horses.

9   Rotherham boss Ronnie Moore describes as 'frightening' the spiralling wages gap between Div 2 and Div 1 clubs, revealing that his top player earned £62,000 last year. Confident of returning to the top flight Bradford players opt for a new bonus system paying out for wins and draws – only if they are in the top 10 of Div 1. Villa snatch £6m Croatia striker Bosko Balaban, 22, from under the noses of Fiorentina and Marseille.

10   Former Labour leader Michael Foot joins Plymouth's board as one of 6 directors, each with an equal share. Owen Hargreaves, 20, Calgary-born midfielder playing with Bayern Munich, gets call-up to the England squad to face Holland.

11   Newcomers Rushden & Diamonds open with an away win at York. Mansfield's Les Robinson chalks up his 700th senior appearance. Gills record their biggest Nationwide League success beating Premiership play-off losers Preston 5-0. Over 23,000 flock to Southampton's new £32m St Mary's Stadium officially opened by Ted Bates who has been associated with the club as a player, manager and now president, for over 60 years. David O'Leary threatens to quit over a hate-campaign being waged against chairman Peter Ridsdale. At Oxford U's new £15m Kassam Stadium, Rochdale's Tony Ford, 42, the League's oldest outfield player and a veteran of over 1,000 appearances, performs at his 101st League ground.

12   In the 1st domestic match contested under a roof, Cardiff's Millennium Stadium, Liverpool beat Man U in the Charity Shield before 70,227. PFA's Gordon Taylor insists a row over TV money could end with a shutdown of Premiership football.

13   In his autobiography *Head to Head* being serialised in the *Mirror* newspaper Jaap Stam reveals Man U's Ferguson had arranged a secret meeting – before his £10m move – to entice him from PSV Eindhoven. Derby gain approval to build a £6m Academy on green belt land at Morley.

14   England U-21 boss Platt gets off to a dream start with a 4-0 win over Holland. A fear of violence has resulted in a ban being placed on visiting supporters for the games between Man City and Millwall. English clubs spent more on foreign players than home-grown talent for the 1st time last year.

15   Holland give England a lesson in passing and finishing in 2-0 friendly win at White Hart Lane. Former Pompey manager Tony Pulis issues a High Court writ against the club claiming money owed totalling £350,000. Brentford will allow all fans free admission against Posh on Oct 13. Palace's Clinton Morrison crowns his sub debut for the Republic of Ireland with a goal.

16   Football League unanimously reject Wimbledon's attempt to relocate in Milton Keynes; the League also refuse Brentford's application to ground-share at Woking.

17 Robbie Fowler is steadfastly refusing to apologise after his training-ground bust-up with Liverpool assistant manager Phil Thompson. Ipswich secure a £25m package to boost capacity to 30,000 at Portman Road, and build a new training centre. Sampdoria goalie Matteo Sereni joins Ipswich for £4.5m.

18 Kevin Nolan nets the 1st Premiership goal of the 2001–02 season in Bolton's 5-0 win at Leicester. Sunderland attract the best attendance, 47,370. ITV launch Saturday early evening prime-time *The Premiership*, successor to *MOTD*. Charlton have to turn away 1,800 season-ticket holding supporters because the Valley's north stand is still being rebuilt.

19 Champs Man U commence with win over Fulham, and Newcastle hold Chelsea in London. Coventry's 1st home game outside the top flight for 34 years brings little cause for joy losing to Wolves. Fowler settles his feud with staff at Liverpool. Les Sealey, 43, the former Man U goalie who had a career lasting 22 years and taking in 564 games, suffers a fatal heart attack. Sheff Wed up-and-coming young centre-back Tom Staniforth, 20, collapses and dies while on a night out in York.

20 ITV's *The Premiership* is watched by 4.3 million but is panned by the media for showing only 28 min of action, 13 min of adverts and 27 min of chat. FA is to stage all 4 FA Cup quarter-finals on Sunday Mar 10, Mothering Sunday, with each tie broadcast live on television with staggered times. Spurs hold on for a point at Everton despite finishing with 9 men.

21 Sir Geoff Hurst is to accept a substantial offer from West Ham, thought to be around £150,000, for his 1966 World Cup winners medal. Ref Jeff Winter has his work cut out dispensing 11 yellow cards and dismissing the Leeds pair Mills and Bowyer, against Arsenal. Notts Co goalie Steve Mildenhall scores from a free-kick in his own half in 4-3 win over Mansfield at Field Mill.

22 Ferguson drops Jaap Stam at Blackburn stressing it has nothing to do with the Dutch player's autobiography comments. Denis Irwin, a stalwart for 12 years, announces his intention to quit Man U at the end of the season. In the UEFA Gala awards Liverpool's Gary McAllister is shortlisted for the most valuable player award. Bobby Johnstone, former Hibs, Man City and Scotland star nicknamed 'Bobby Dazzler' dies, aged 71. Celtic squeeze into Champions League group stage but Rangers miss out.

23 Eight days before the nations meet in a World Cup qualifier, Liverpool will meet Borussia Dortmund in the Champions League, with German opposition, in the shape of Schalke 04, awaiting Arsenal. Man U must face Deportivo La Coruna and Celtic, Juventus. The sporting behaviour of Liverpool and Alaves fans is acknowledged by UEFA's Supporters of the Year awards. Convinced of beating England, Germany has arranged 3 friendlies for November – when World Cup play-offs are scheduled.

24 Liverpool lift their 5th trophy in 6 months defeating Bayern Munich to take UEFA's Super Cup in Monaco. The 1st week of the Premiership action throws up 63 cautions and 9 red cards.

25 Brum win at Walsall but end up with 9 men. Arsenal's Vieira and Dennis Wise (Leicester), a volatile pair who between them share a staggering 18 red cards, go head to head and are dismissed at Highbury. After complaints, ITV's *The Premiership* ups the action to 38 min.

26 Newcastle's Shearer ends 5 months of injury coming off the bench in the draw with Sunderland. Shocked Jaap Stam, who signed a new 5-year deal 6 months ago, is distraught at being forced to quit Man U after a £16.5m move to Lazio is hastily concluded.

27 Forest's 9 men hold Coventry scoreless at Highfield Road. Holdsworth's 90th min winner against Liverpool puts Bolton top. Southampton chairman Rupert Lowe makes official complaint over Tottenham's behaviour in their bid to sign Dean Richards. David Elleray admits a mistake in red-carding Tottenham's Gary Doherty and the player will now not even pick up a caution. Fulham take their summer spending to over £30m, buying Olympique Lyon striker Steve Marlet for £11.5m.

28 Skipper Beckham faces 3 days of intense treatment on a groin injury to face Germany, but coach Eriksson says with or without the player England can win.

29 Former jockey Willie Carson is taking the battle for control of Swindon to the High Court.

30 After years of trying, Ferguson finally gets his man, Laurent Blanc, 35, to join Man U on a one year deal reportedly worth £2m. Scotland's Paul Lambert, 32, will bow out of the international scene at the end of the season. Paul Bracewell becomes the season's 1st managerial casualty quitting Halifax. Most managers attending UEFA elite coaches' forum in Geneva call for the abolition of the golden goal rule.

31 Liverpool follow up their completion of £4.85m deal for Feyenoord's Polish goalie Jerzy Dudek by swooping for Coventry's Chris Kirkland (£5m rising with appearances to £8m) leaving No 1 Sander Westerveld sweating on his Anfield future. Arsenal move defender Silvinho out to Celta Vigo for £5m. FA intend developing shortly the 350-acre Staffordshire site following planning permission for the new National Football Centre. A goal in stoppage-time gives England U-21's victory over Germany in Freiburg.

September 2001
England triumph in Germany ... Brian Moore sadness ... Ossie out-then-in ... Albania spread panic ... Hutchison returns to Hammers ... Babbel mystery illness ... Leeds to relocate ... No Scots in Celtic team ... Coventry and Strachan part ... Respect shown for NY disaster ... Addison leads The Swans ... Another red for Keane ... Harris wins battle ... Spurs get Saint Richards ... Chelsea players' shame ... Owen kops long contract ... Cherries new home ... FA cut back on sponsors ... Leicester sack Taylor

1 With an historic Owen treble England devastate Germany with a stunning 5-1 win in Munich, sparking a carnival atmosphere throughout towns and cities at home. The victory was the 1st in a World Cup qualifier on German soil and the 1st success in that country since 1965. Thousands of dejected home fans head for the exits when Heskey nets the 5th in the 74th min, and later coach Eriksson is even greeted with a round of applause in the press room. Down to 10 men Ireland pull off a shock 1-0 win over favourites Holland which effectively leaves the Dutch requiring miracles to make the World Cup finals. Wales, Scotland and N Ireland all draw. Grimsby become undisputed leaders of Div 1 for the 1st time in 20 years. Respected commentator Brian Moore, 69, the voice of ITV football for over 30 years, dies peacefully in Kent.

2   Burnley shade a thriller at Bradford before 17,547, an ideal attendance for crowd shots captured by producers of a new drama series, *Playing The Field*. Audience figures reveal that by the end of the Germany-England clash 14.6 million had tuned in to BBC 1 – its highest Saturday audience for 5 years. Stan Harland, captain of Div 3 Swindon which created a major upset beating Arsenal in the League Cup final at Wembley in 1969, dies after a heart attack at his Somerset home, aged 61.

3   After losing his job with Japan's Yokohama Marinos, Ossie Ardiles joins Saudi Arabia side Al Ittihad. Despite England's success LMA's John Barnwell maintains Eriksson's appointment is an 'insult' to English coaches.

4   Liverpool's Houllier confirms Jerzy Dudek will be 1st choice goalie. Over 23,000 at The Riverside see Jeffers hit 3 in England U-21 win over Albania.

5   England, needing to clinch a victory and clinging to an Owen 44th min goal, is made to sweat against Albania at St James' Park with Fowler's 88th min score finally calming the nerves. Outclassed Scotland see their World Cup hopes in tatters in Belgium. Captain Giggs is dismissed for the 1st time as Wales lose in Norway. George McCartney, 20, scores on his N Ireland debut.

6   Journalists asked by Gillette to pick the greatest individual performance to celebrate the company's 100th anniversary, choose Roger Bannister's historic 4-min mile ahead of World Cup 1966 hat-trick hero Hurst. West Ham unveil Don Hutchison as their record £5m signing from Sunderland. Liverpool's Marcus Babbel is struck down by an illness which weakens his immune system.

7   Feyenoord's De Kuip Stadium is the venue for the UEFA Cup final. Sam Allardyce is the Barclaycard Premiership Manager of the Month, while Fulham's Louis Saha takes the August top player award. Leeds announce their intention to move from Elland Road to a £70m super stadium.

8   Liverpool's Gerrard is dismissed for a shocking lunge on Villa's Boateng with TV pictures making a mockery of Houllier's feeble defence. Boss Strachan runs rowdy gauntlet of jeering home fans requiring an escort as Coventry lose to Grimsby. Sheff U and Bradford draw in the 2,000th game at Bramall Lane. For the 1st time in the club's history Celtic's line-up contained no Scots.

9   The Leeds chairman appeals for fans to stay seated or risk the closing of Elland Road. Red card for The Dons' goalie Paul Heald allows Watford to net 3 goals in the following 10 min.

10   After 5 years at the helm Gordon Strachan leaves Coventry with Roland Nilsson taking temporary charge.

11   The New York World Trade Center attack and the huge loss of life brings a minute's silence before the evening games. Cole's dismissal after conceding a 12th min penalty loses Arsenal the tie at Real Mallorca. Matt Le Tissier is to get a testimonial for 16 years service at Southampton. Liverpool return to Europe's premier club competition after 16 years, against Boavista.

12   John Hollins and assistant Alan Curtis part company with Swansea. Out of respect UEFA take the historic step of postponing all tonight's Champions League games, and tomorrow's UEFA Cup ties.

13   Football League are planning to invite Celtic and Rangers to take part in next season's Worthington Cup. Alex Scott, who won League titles with Rangers and Everton, dies after a short illness, aged 64. Swansea put Colin Addison, 61, in charge with Peter Nicholas his No. 2.

14   Leeds pair Bowyer and Mills are charged with misconduct for bad-mouthing officials at Highbury. Ref Steve Lodge is engaged to work with the Leeds squad in a bid to promote better understanding and communication.

15   With a minute's silence, football across the UK pays its respects to those who perished in the US Trade Center disaster. Fiery Keane receives the 9th red card of his Man U career in defeat at Newcastle. QPR's Andy Thomson nets a hat-trick. According to police the 165th Everton-Liverpool clash was the 1st to end with no arrests.

16   Leicester's Savage, castigated by Ipswich a week earlier, is a target of abuse at Derby where he wins a penalty, 'celebrating' excitedly and sparking pitch trouble and a tunnel fracas. Man U dismiss claims they have lined up Roma coach Fabio Capello to succeed Sir Alex. Spurs, at home, fail for the 26th time since 1990 to defeat Chelsea.

17   Arsenal, Chelsea, Fulham and Man U are on collision course with France regarding the release of players for a Nov 11 friendly in Australia. New Carlisle boss Roddy Collins transfer-lists 8 1st teamers.

18   UEFA agree to compensate each of the 51 travelling clubs, including Man U and Leeds, who had ties postponed whilst respecting the US Trade Center disaster. Beckham saves the blushes with a vital last gasp Man U winner over Lille. Celtic lose to last min penalty at Juventus. Posh put 6 past Bournemouth. Millwall welcome back Neil Harris after winning his battle against testicular cancer.

19   Arsenal have a nail-biting win over Schalke, but Liverpool are held scoreless in Dortmund. England move from 15th to 9th in FIFA's ranking list.

20   Chelsea's Ranieri celebrates a year in charge with 3-0 win over Levski Sofia. Charlton's Alan Curbishley says the concept of the player-exchange agreement with Inter was good but did not materialise when injury-cover was needed. Tickets for England's World Cup qualifier against Greece are sold out within 2 hours. Neil Redfearn and Tony Parks take temporary charge at Halifax.

21   Tottenham complete the £8.1m transfer of Dean Richards with Saints chairman Rupert Lowe claiming it is 'a slap in the face' for his clubs' supporters. Tranmere's Stuart Barlow nets his 2nd hat-trick in 4 days against Wrexham.

22   The Conference fail in their bid for promotion to the Nationwide League to be decided by an end of season play-off programme. Flo claims a hat-trick in Rangers' 6-1 thrashing of Dundee U. Sharpshooter Owen leaves Anfield on crutches and is out of England's against Greece. Early indications show players will, if asked by the PFA, back strike action over the distribution of TV monies. Ipswich receive apology from fierce rivals Norwich after the electronic scoreboard at Carrow Road described them as 'scum'.

23   Four Chelsea players, Lampard, Terry, Morris and Gudjohnsen are branded 'irresponsible' and fined 2 weeks wages for drunken and disorderly behaviour and showing a lack of sensitivity in a hotel where worried

Americans were waiting news of flights home. Div 3 Exeter sack manager Noel Blake after winning just 20 out of 87 games in his 19-month reign.

24 Out of favour Liverpool goalie Sander Westerveld turns down a loan move to Alaves. Former Everton and Norwich boss Mike Walker is sacked by Apoel two games into the new season. Grimsby goalie Danny Coyne gets a Wales recall after 5 years. Ian Rush joins League of Wales side TNS as non-executive director.

25 Late Deportivo double shatters Man U in La Coruna. Celtic register 1st win of their Champions League campaign beating Porto. Brighton remain top of Div 2 after win at Wycombe. Luton clinch top spot in Div 3.

26 Litmanen's quality finish gives Liverpool a win over Kiev. Arsenal fail miserably at Panathinaikos, their 6th defeat in their last 7 away ties in Europe. Northampton sack boss Kevin Wilson. FA charge Blackburn and Oldham with misconduct following ugly scenes in which 3 players were sent off in a Worthington Cup tie. Striker Owen signs to stay at Liverpool until 2005 on a reported £60,000 a week. Chairman Charles Koppel reveals The Dons require a £7m cash injection to survive. Bournemouth's new all-seater Kings Park ground will be called Fitness First Stadium, after securing a 10-year deal with the health and fitness chain.

27 Villa crash to Croatian minnows Varteks. Leeds beat Maritimo. Ipswich mark their return to continental soil winning at Torpedo Moscow. Chelsea progress past Levski Sofia. Ipswich secure the medals of World Cup-winning England manager Sir Alf Ramsey. Hibs go out to AEK Athens, and Viking FC advance at Kilmarnock's expense.

28 FA is accused of lacking courtesy by AXA after the sponsors of the FA Cup claim they were not informed of a changed policy, meaning that from 2002–03 the FA will reduce the number of sponsors from 10 to 5.

29 Spurs, at home to Man U, let slip a 3-0 lead losing 5-3 with United boss Ferguson describing it as his best result achieved away during his entire reign. West Ham go under 5-0 at Everton. Phillips nets his 100th goal in 147 League games for Sunderland. Arsenal's Keown is the 36th dismissal in manager Wenger's Arsenal reign.

30 Leeds go back top at Ipswich. Celtic go 7 pts clear with win at Rangers. With just 5 pts from 8 games Leicester's slump results in the departure of Peter Taylor, the 1st Premiership casualty, after spending £25m.

October 2001

Beckham secures World Cup dream … Brown quits Scotland … Smith gets Wrexham job … Bald Eagle leaves Derby … Webb and Shrimpers part … Trouble-shooter Bassett for Foxes … Houllier's heart surgery … Bates denies revolt … Francis ends Blues link … Nilsson suits Sky Blues … Taylor is back in work … Broadcasters secure World Cup viewing … Schmeichel scores … Strachan is a Saint … Double-winner dies … Managerial departures continue

1 Roy Keane absolves the summer signings from blame for Man U's poor start, claiming several established players should be contributing more. Brum clear the air with manager Francis denying he is on the way out.

2 Dave Jones (Wolves) is Div 1 Manager of the Month, with Mickey Adams (Brighton) and Plymouth's Paul Sturrock also divisional winners. Villa's Dublin becomes 6th Premiership player this season to have a red card rescinded. Joe Royle, unhappy with £200,000 pay-off, is suing Man City. Chelsea will black-out the Dubai-based sponsor Emirates Airlines from their shirts when they play in Israel for fear of inflaming the delicate political situation.

3 Watford's Paolo Vernazza is out for some weeks after being stabbed by an intruder in Islington. A hip injury ends the career of Tottenham's Willen Korsten. Steven Gerrard apologises to coach Eriksson for much-publicised late tackle. Man U's Jesper Blomqvist plays his 1st competitive game for over 2 years.

4 Bradford sack two youth players, Ben Jones and Adam Hardy, for alleged bullying on the training pitch. Chelsea's UEFA tie in Tel Aviv is causing concern and might be switched after an aeroplane from Israel mysteriously explodes and crashes in the Black Sea with the loss of 77 lives.

5 England U-21's show the way against Greece clinching a European Championship play-off place. On eve of their World Cup tie with Greece, Newcastle's Nikos Dabizas claims England is a nation of boozers. Stoke is over £6m in debt and losing £33,000 weekly. Against Greece, skipper Beckham intends sporting boots emblazoned with the St George cross.

6 Trailing 2-1 to Greece in the final seconds, inspirational Beckham sends a trademark 25-yard free kick whistling to the net dramatically securing England's finals spot. With Germany suffering a 0-0 draw at home to Finland – they tackle the play-offs – coach Eriksson's team top Group 9. On his 35th birthday Niall Quinn heads his way into the record books with his 21st goal for the Republic who get the required win over Cyprus and finish joint-top with Portugal. But they must beat the runners-up from the Asian qualifiers in a play-off to make the finals. Craig Brown resigns after hollow victory over Croatia. Hartson's goal give victory over Belarus before 10,200 and prevents Wales going a record 13 games without a win. Sammy McIlroy is sent from the dug-out as N Ireland win in Malta. Carlisle v Bristol Rovers is the only League game which kicks off at the same time as England, watched by 1,849.

7 Ex-Scots boss Brown is to remain as technical director to the association preferring his replacement to be a Scot. For only the 3rd time since 1893, neither Owls nor Blades can manage a goal in the 101st Sheffield league derby, before 29,281. Former Coventry, Chelsea and England goalie Reg Matthews dies, aged 68, after a short illness.

8 As a show of thanks to supporters, FA announce half-price tickets, with children at £5, for friendly against Sweden. Denis Smith replaces Brian Flynn at Wrexham. Derby part company with Jim Smith after 6 years, putting Colin Todd in charge. Gil Prescott relinquishes his managerial post at Macclesfield.

9 With a mere 15,000 seeing the Panathinaikos-Arsenal clash, lower than expected viewing figures on ITV's new digital sport channel, there are increased fears about too much football on television. George Graham rules himself out of the vacant Scots national post. In Worthington Cup, Robbie Keane nets 3 as Leeds put 6 past Leicester. Grimsby provide the big shock knocking out Liverpool – at Anfield. David Webb quits the Southend job. Arsenal's former skipper Frank McLintock is selling his collection of medals.

10 Man U triumph at Olympiakos, the Greek team's 1st defeat in 14 Champions League home ties. Celtic grab a priceless victory over Rosenborg. Troubled Leicester install Dave Bassett as boss with Mickey Adams leaving Brighton to be No. 2. Jocky Scott parts company with Notts Co. Cardiff, Swansea and Wrexham's attempts to play in both English and Welsh competitions, having two chances of getting into Europe, is rejected by UEFA.

11 Bryan Robson, forced out last summer, accuses Boro of stabbing him in the back and appointing Steve McClaren without his knowledge. Premier League insist that the clubs' new offer of £10m a year to the PFA is 'reasonable' as the Players' Union spent 'only £766,000 looking after ex-players last year'. The PFA want £25m a year. Kevin Keen is the caretaker manager at Macclesfield.

12 West Ham's Canadian goalie Craig Forrest reveals he has undergone surgery for suspected testicular cancer but is hopeful of making a full recovery. Villa's John Gregory and Veron (Man U) take the Barclaycard Premier awards for September. Alan Little succeeds Paul Bracewell at Halifax.

13 Gerard Houllier is rushed to hospital for heart surgery after suffering chest pains following his half-time talk during Liverpool's match at Anfield against Leeds. Houllier, 54, is initially treated by the club physio and doctor and only the subs, last out of the dressing-room, are aware of what is happening. The 1,500th competitive game at Maine Road sees Man City draw with Stockport. 'Anoraks' reveal that Arsenal, for the 1st time in 16 years, went into their game at Southampton without a member of the Famous Five defenders, messers Adams, Keown, Dixon, and, of course, no Bould or Winterburn. Forest hand a sub debut to Craig Westcarr, 16. In a bold move to stimulate interest and with entrance free to all, 11,097 see Brentford beat Peterborough, but the home club forfeit around £70,000 in gate receipts.

14 The Hammers' defence wilts alarmingly conceding 7 at Blackburn. Ken Bates denies a dressing-room revolt with anxious players ready to pull out of their UEFA Cup tie in Tel Aviv.

15 Trevor Francis' love-hate relationship with Brum ends with the manager leaving by mutual consent after 5 years. Tommy Taylor resigns after 5 years in charge at Leyton Orient with Paul Brush stepping up. Leeds and Wales legend John 'Gentle Giant' Charles receives his CBE. Just 9 weeks into the season, 15 bosses have been sacked or left their clubs.

16 Shaken by Houllier's health problems Liverpool lift his spirits by winning in Kiev. Arsenal's £6m goalie Richard Wright makes his European debut a winning one against Panathinaikos. Roland Nilsson officially succeeds Gordon Strachan as Coventry boss.

17 Captain Desailly and 5 other senior players are missing when Chelsea check in for their controversial flight to Israel. Barthez makes outstanding saves and 2 costly blunders as a strange-looking Man U formation lose at Deportivo La Coruna. Peter Taylor makes a quick return to take over at Brighton. Peter Shreeves leaves struggling Sheff Wed.

18 Melchiot is off as Chelsea hit a new low in Tel Aviv with late, late 2-0 defeat by Hapoel. Leeds, who parade new £7m signing Seth Johnson, progress past Troyes. Rangers notch win over Dynamo Moscow. BBC and ITV pay £160m to screen the next two World Cups.

19 Northampton's board put the club up for sale. Boss O'Leary stokes up feelings for Sunday's visit of Chelsea wondering if Yorkshire and Leeds is a safe enough place for the Londoners.

20 Bolton pull off the result of the season so far, deserving their smash-and-grab win at Old Trafford. Fowler claims a classy hat-trick in Liverpool's win at Leicester. Goalie Schmeichel abandons duties to pop up and volley a late goal against Everton, but Villa still lose. Oxford U manager Mark Wright and 2 of his players are red-carded against Scunthorpe.

21 Incensed Leeds manager O'Leary is dismissed after Graeme Le Saux's sickening two-footed lunge at Danny Mills; this clash with Chelsea, taking the disciplinary record for their last 11 meetings to 71 yellow and 5 red cards. Second from bottom Southampton sack Stuart Gray. Supporters fighting on the pitch and police in riot gear mar the Potteries derby clash at Vale Park.

22 Boro's Ince sees red in clash with Sunderland. Saints unveil Gordon Strachan as new boss. Concerned LMA's John Barnwell hits out at the high rate of managerial sackings. ITV's flagship programme *The Premiership* is moving from its 7pm slot to 10.30. Bertie Mee, Arsenal's double-winning manager, dies, aged 82. Caretaker Rob Newman gets the post at Southend. Chelsea's Le Saux apologises to Leeds management and staff for his disgraceful challenge on Danny Mills.

23 Nerve-tingling night but Man U eventually defeat Olympiakos, advancing to the Champions League 2nd phase. FA is threatened with legal action for the recovery of £120m of National Lottery money if it does not build a stadium at Wembley. Celtic freeze in Norway losing to Rosenborg with both scores coming from ex-Parkhead striker Brattbakk.

24 Gunners seal their 2nd phase passage late with Henry's 17th goal in 31 European ties, against Real Mallorca. Recovering Houllier gets a tonic tuning into TV highlights of Liverpool's away draw at Boavista. Gary Bennett becomes the 18th casualty tendering his resignation at Darlington. Brum co-owner David Sullivan puts the club up for sale.

25 Charlton's Andy Todd is transfer-listed after 'unsavoury incidents' at the training ground which leaves goalie Dean Kiely with facial injuries. In the present climate, Nigel Spackman is sacked by Barnsley, the 19th departing manager in just over 2 months. Northampton hand the managerial post to Kevan Broadhurst. Tommy Taylor has the post at Darlington until the end of the season.

26 Bristol Rovers become the 3rd Football League club this week to be put up for sale. UEFA charge Boavista over racial taunting directed at Liverpool's Heskey. Former favourite Bernie Slaven is standing as a candidate for Middlesbrough's 1st mayor.

27 Villa's win over Bolton sits them at the pinnacle of English football for the 1st time in 3 years. Roland Nilsson's transformation of the Sky Blues continues as they head the Nationwide League. Brentford's 6th successive win keeps them top of Div 2. In FA Cup draw, last year's semi-finalists Wycombe will meet Hayes.

28 Former Liverpool goalie Bruce Grobbelaar loses his coaching job at S African club Supersport Utd. Despite 4 stewards having to separate the pair, Chelsea's Desailly and Ravanelli (Derby) continue holding up the London-bound departure of the team bus outside Pride Park. Plymouth return to top of Div 3 taking their unbeaten run to 13 games.

29 Fulham confirm they will play at QPR's Loftus Road or West Ham's Upton Park next season if given approval for Craven Cottage's £70m revamp. Manager Andy Kilner is dismissed at Stockport Co. After 5 successive defeats, Leicester gain a point at Blackburn. Ref Dermot Gallagher is demoted from Premiership for an undisclosed period, damned by his own admission, for failing to send off hands-raised Robbie Keane at Old Trafford.

30 On a night when Houllier's name is chanted constantly Liverpool join Arsenal and Man U in the final 16 of the Champions League beating Borussia Dortmund. Ragged Arsenal lose the plot on their travels having Luzhny dismissed early and going under 3-1 at Schalke. John Cornforth is the new boss at Exeter. Burnley's point at Gillingham is overshadowed by the road accident death of Tim, 28, son of Turf Moor assistant boss Sam Ellis.

31 Celtic's brave last stand is not enough to progress despite the stunning 4-3 win over Juventus. Iran, having beaten UAE over 2 legs, will now meet Ireland for a place in the World Cup finals.

November 2001

Europe over for Chelsea ... Attendances on the up ... Eriksson's homeland award ... Palmer gets chance ... Deepdale honours goalie Kelly ... Motty chalks up a century ... McCarthy's men for World Cup ... Stam's drug shock ... Canvey's cup triumph ... Gradi's memorable occasion ... TV agreements avert strike ... Phoenix League talk ... Brave bookie pays out ... Fowler quits Merseyside ... FIFA acknowledge Di Canio ... Francis arrives at Palace

1 Chelsea embarassingly tumble out of the UEFA Cup drawing with Hapoel Tel Aviv. Ipswich win at Helsingborg, while Leeds scramble through at Troyes. Rangers win well at Dynamo Moscow. Nationwide League attendances are up 16 per cent on last season.

2 Palace dig in to prevent under-contract Steve Bruce leaving for Brum refusing to accept his resignation, and handing duties to Steve Kember and Terry Bullivant.

3 Leicester's £5m Akinbiyi at last nets his 1st goal in the League for 203 days. Ravanelli scores on his return to The Riverside, but Derby lose 5-1. David Healy grabs a hat-trick in Preston's 6-0 thrashing of Stockport. Mansfield finish with 9 against Luton. Fan Zhiyi's debut for Dundee ends in shame as the Chinese skipper is red-carded against local rivals Utd. Man City's Goater notches 20 goals by the 1st week in November.

4 A ruthless 3-1 Liverpool performance on Man U puts them top for a half hour, at least. Ticket prices cut to £5 attracts 28,436 to St Andrews, Brum's biggest gate of the season. Charlton net 4 in 18 min to shock Arsenal at Highbury.

5 Bruce Rioch, most recently in charge at Wigan, returns to take temporary charge of Dr Martens League side Gresley Rovers. Coach Eriksson wins Sweden's Personality of the Year award at Stockholm's Football Gala. Sunderland sharpshooter Phillips, 28, is the surprise in England's squad to meet Sweden.

6 Carlton Palmer gets the managerial job of lifting Stockport Co from Div 1 basement. Barnet's Wayne Purser scores one of the fastest hat-tricks in FA Cup history notching his goals in 5 min against Havant & Waterlooville. Celtic sweep aside Stirling 8-0 in CIS Insurance Cup.

7 FA charge Oxford boss Mark Wright for his outburst to ref Joe Ross. Newcastle send home 4 players from their Spanish training camp. Mick Wadsworth becomes Oldham's head coach.

8 Preston's new 6,000-seater, named the Alan Kelly Town End Stand after the goalie who made a club record 512 appearances, is officially opened against Barnsley. West Ham reveal that during Harry Redknapp's tenure, 134 players were bought and sold at a deficit of £16m with one loan recruit costing the club more than £720,000 yet only figuring for 86 min. David Moss is the new manager at struggling Macclesfield.

9 Just 4,937 frozen souls, The Dons' lowest of the season, watches them draw with Sheff U. Blackburn's Dunn impresses on England U-21 duty in Holland. This season's 21st managerial appointment arrives with Steve Parkin replacing Nigel Spackman at Barnsley. A published report predicts English football attendance figures are surging towards the best since the 1960s, with the 4 pro divisions set to exceed 28 million. In their dispute over TV monies, PFA report 99 per cent of pro players will vote in favour of strike action.

10 At Old Trafford Beckham's penalty gives England a draw in friendly with Sweden. Bournemouth's long wait for a new home ends when the Fitness First Stadium opens against Wrexham on the site of what used to be Dean Court. BBC's John Motson commentates on his 100th England international. Ireland gain a 2-goal cushion against Iran in Dublin World Cup play-off.

11 Leeds, Wolves, Brighton and Plymouth lead their respective divisions. In Scotland, Celtic are top with Partick, Clydebank and Brechin other divisional leaders. A flared-up knee injury rules out Ireland skipper Keane from return play-off tie in Iran.

12 Tottenham's Hoddle is Barclaycard Manager of the Month with Rio Ferdinand (Leeds) taking the player award. Walsall appoint former boss Chris Nicholl as 1st team coach. Iain Dowie secures a similar post at Oldham.

13 Carrick's goal against Holland clinches England's U-21's a place at the 8-nation European Championship. Lowly Wigan's 6-goal onslaught stuns high-flying Stoke. New Saints boss Strachan spends £3.2m on Ecuador striker Agustin Delgado.

14 Portugal's friendly in Lisbon is abandoned with 22 min remaining after 4 Angola players are sent-off and another leaves the field injured. Willie Donachie leaves his coaching post at Man City to link with Sheff Wed's new boss Terry Yorath. Germany qualify for their 15th World Cup finals sweeping aside Ukraine in play-offs. Ossie Ardiles is dismissed despite his Al Ittihad club being top.

15   Ireland clinch their World Cup finals place despite conceding a goal 30 sec from the whistle in Iran. Liverpool's Houllier, steadily recuperating from his 6-hour life-saving operation, confesses that he knew 2 months beforehand something was wrong. It is believed just 22 unnamed players voted against PFA strike action. Former West Ham and Arsenal striker Davor Suker signs for Munich 1860.

16   Rochdale put David Hamilton in temporary charge. Jaap Stam, Lazio's £16.5m former Man U defender, insists he is innocent despite testing positive for the banned steroid Nandrolone.

17   Arsenal's Sol Campbell endures a hate-filled afternoon returning to Tottenham. Newcastle fail again to win in London, their defeat at Fulham stretching the sequence to 27 matches. Blackburn's Souness and Thompson (Liverpool) exchange handshakes but their personal feud from Anfield days still lingers. FA Cup giant-killing result belongs to Canvey Island who snatch late 1-0 win at Wigan, while Whitby hold Plymouth.

18   Ipswich's dismal run continues losing at home to Bolton, their 11th League game without success. A near 20,000 witness Wolves–Sheff Wed scoreless draw. In televised FA Cup tie Hereford pick up £150,000 beating Wrexham.

19   West Ham's Kitson, starting for the 1st time in 21 months, claims only the 2nd Premiership's hat-trick of the season, in 4-4 thriller at Charlton. Bradford plan to frisk fans to stop them taking confetti into games because it is blocking drains at Valley Parade.

20   Dario Gradi, 60, appointed 18 years ago, is England's longest-serving boss, and duly celebrates his 1000th game in charge of Crewe, at Norwich. Man U share a 1-1 draw at Bayern Munich. Liverpool suffer their 1st European defeat in 15 games enduring a painful experience as classy Barcelona turn on the style. PFA call strike action for weekend of 1 and 2 Dec.

21   Gunners suffer their 6th consecutive away defeat in Europe losing at Deportivo. UEFA is considering scrapping the 2nd phase of the Champions League hinting at declining interest.

22   Ipswich upstage Inter in UEFA Cup with Armstrong's late home winner. Leeds advance at Grasshoppers. Rangers are held scoreless by PSG. Palace win 1st leg High Court battle with want-away manager Bruce. John Beck resigns after 8 months at struggling Cambridge U. Oxford suspend manager Mark Wright.

23   After 8 hours of discussion, common sense prevails so avoiding a players' strike with a £52.5m over 3 years guarantee to the PFA, thereby ending their dispute over television monies with the Premier League. In front- and back-page exposures the *Daily Mail* reveals advanced secret talks, driven by TV finance, of a revolutionary Phoenix League. The Blueprint would result in an elite new League with 6 clubs breaking away from Nationwide League to form a Premiership Div Two incorporating Celtic and Rangers.

24   Before a club record 31,198, Southampton's 1st victory at their new St Mary's ground lifts them off the bottom. Derby's 12-year St James' Park hoodoo continues. The Gills turn up without their correct shirts, borrowing Millwall's away strip, and then netting winner and full points. Only 3 goals to show in a reduced programme of 6 Premiership fixtures. Scunthorpe put 7 past Darlington who are reduced to 9 men after 33 min. Former Scotland and Celtic winger Jimmy Johnstone, 57, is diagnosed with Motor Neurone Disease.

25   Celtic inflict a 5th successive Old Firm defeat on Rangers. Arsenal feast on Barthez blunders to land Highbury win over Man U. Fiery Smith puts Leeds ahead against Villa, then receives the 5th red card of his fledgling career.

26   PFA confirm the deal to avert a strike will remain for 10 years, not 3 as initially announced. Bookmaker Fred Done agrees to pay out now on Celtic winning the League.

27   Shearer reaches his goal-scoring century for Newcastle. Rangers launch world-wide search for new 1st team coach as Dick Advocaat prepares to move upstairs at Ibrox.

28   ITV tell Football League they intend to fulfill their £315m television contract despite reports the ITV Sport channel is running into payment difficulties. Liverpool's Robbie Fowler agrees £11m shock move to Leeds. In a fixture which has a reputation for foul play – 71 yellows and 4 red cards in the 11 previous clashes – only 2 cautions are added to the tally as spirited Chelsea win comfortably the League Cup clash at Elland Road.

29   After stormy meeting of all 72 Football League chairmen at Meadow Lane, FL's Keith Harris says there was 'a lot more noise than substance' in reporting of a breakaway (Phoenix) League, although Bradford's Geoffrey Richmond makes it clear that Premiership Div Two is on the way. Paolo Di Canio wins FIFA's Fair Play Award for 2001. Fevernova is the £55 new type of Adidas ball for the World Cup finals. An official report lists Rangers, with a turnover of £51.7m, as the richest in Scotland, 15th in the world, with Man U retaining their top spot for the 4th year running.

30   Sepp Blatter stuns the gathering in Busan announcing the 2202 World Cup winners must qualify for the 2006 finals in Germany. The governing body also decide refs can carry advertising on their shirts. Mark Wright resigns from Oxford U. Palace welcome Trevor Francis as new boss, their 12th managerial switch in the past 5 years. As Leeds unveil new recruit Fowler, the former Liverpool favourite claims there was no contract offer on the table for him at Anfield, where he scored 171 goals. Chairman Bates labels some of his under-achieving Chelsea players as 'lemons.'

December 2001

Tough World Cup draw ... Sir Geoff declines BA ... Wenger puts pen to paper ... Chelsea's Hutchinson bows out ... BBC award for Beckham ... Schmeichel MBE ... Rangers name McLeish ... Bruce in charge at Brum ... Leeds players get verdicts ... Ferdinand's milestone score ... Westerveld off to Spain ... O'Leary's book rumpus ... Owen's Europe award ... Bowyer reverses request ... Evans out at Swindon ... France football praises Vieira ... Anelka arrives at Anfield ... Finland honours Hyypia ... Lawrence out at Mariners ... Striker Cole joins Blackburn

1   In World Cup finals draw, England find themselves in a group with favourites Argentina, Sweden and Nigeria. The draw is much kinder to the Republic of Ireland who tackle Germany, Saudi Arabia and Cameroon. Chelsea humiliate Man U at Old Trafford with a resounding 3-0 win.

2   England ask Holland to help with a friendly under the roof at the Amsterdam ArenA in an attempt to replicate indoor conditions in Japan on June 7 when they face Argentina.

3   Shearer's dismissal at Charlton is annulled after ref Andy D'Urso reviews television footage. Phil Thompson's work as stand-in wins him the Manager of the Month award with Anfield's Danny Murphy taking the player prize. Divisional awards go to Burnley's Stan Ternent, Reading's Alan Pardew, and Jan Molby (Kidderminster). Concerned Sir Geoff Hurst says he will not be using British Airways following the Sept 11 New York atrocities. Peter Withe declines an offer to renew his contract as Thailand coach for another year after learning it was £60,000, half his previous salary.

4   Arsenal are fully deserving their fine Highbury win over Juventus. On the eve of Liverpool's tie at Roma, it is learned Markus Babbel is suffering from the neurological condition Guillan-Barre Syndrome.

5   Man U resume normal service beating Boavista. Liverpool dig in for scoreless draw at Roma. Charlton leave Chelsea with a narrow win. Brett Ormerod's move to Southampton provides Blackpool with a £1.75m windfall. The UK Coach of the Year award is shared by England's Eriksson and athletics coach Alex Stanton.

6   Arsenal's Wenger signs, at last, a 4-year contract extension. Vieri's treble wrecks the Ipswich dream at Inter. Rangers win shoot-out at PSG. Leeds advance at the expense of Grasshoppers.

7   FA clear Tottenham of blame for rowdy fan behaviour at the derby clash with Arsenal. Colin Hutchinson is to step down at Chelsea after 15 years at the club. Willie Carson's consortium takes over at Swindon.

8   Defoe clinches West Ham's 1st League victory at Old Trafford since 1986 with Ferguson's selection again under fire. Tranmere hit 6 FA Cup goals past Carlisle. Bobby Zamora's 18th goal against Rushden & Diamonds creates a Brighton club record of scoring for the 9th successive game. A 15-man brawl resulting in 2 dismissals mars Fulham's win over Everton.

9   Neil Gregory, a house-husband, helps Canvey pull off FA Cup shock win over Northampton. Advocaat sparks a mystery revealing he is about to quit the Rangers hot seat. In Cup draw holders Liverpool will host Brum. In hotly contested Lancs clash before 20,370 Burnley win at Preston. Beckham lifts BBC Sports Personality of the Year award.

10   Gerard Houllier breaks down making an emotional address to Liverpool shareholders. Former Blackburn boss Roy Hodgson loses his job at Udinese. Villa's Schmeichel gets an honorary MBE for services to football. Cardiff's request to stage their Leeds cup tie at the 72,500-capacity Millennium Stadium is turned down. Islington council give Arsenal the green light for a new stadium at nearby Ashburton Grove.

11   Hibs boss Alex McLeish, 42, is named Rangers' 11th manager in the club's 130-year history. John Hollins, sacked by Swansea in September, is put in charge at Rochdale. In League Cup Spurs put 6 past Bolton, and Blackburn hammer in 4 against weakened Gunners.

12   Derby are routed as hunger returns to Man U. The 20 Premiership chairmen vote overwhelmingly against a 2nd breakaway (Phoenix) League and direct access to Celtic and Rangers. Steve Bruce starts his 5th job in three and a half years signing a 5-year contract at Brum.

13   Wolves pay £3m for Rangers striker Kenny Miller. Old Trafford is to host the 2003 Champions League final.

14   At Hull Crown court Lee Bowyer is cleared of affray and GBH with Leeds colleague Jonathan Woodgate sentenced to 100 hours community service after being found guilty of affray. Club captain Franck Sauzee replaces McLeish at Hibs.

15   Nine years after Sheff U's Brian Deane starts the ball rolling, Tottenham's Ferdinand fires home the 10,000th Premiership goal, earning a £10,000 charity cheque from Barclaycard. Table-topping Plymouth extend their unbeaten run to 19 matches.

16   Chelsea sweep aside Liverpool 4-0. A £3.6m deal takes out-of-favour Liverpool goalie Sander Westerveld to Real Sociedad, managed by John Toshack. Manager O'Leary defends his decision to take payments for a controversial book, *Leeds United On Trial* in which he makes exclusive comments on the trial of players Bowyer and Woodgate. Supporters representing 89 other clubs, including Barcelona, Ajax and Feyenoord, make their way to south London to show solidarity with Wimbledon fans who use the day to protest at franchising.

17   In Zurich, English football celebrates Michael Owen named European Footballer of the Year, only the 6th British winner, while David Beckham is runner-up to Luis Figo as FIFA World Player of the Year. Ref Gerald Ashby, 52, who took charge of the 1995 FA Cup final, dies after a heart attack. Leeds' disgraced pair Woodgate and Bowyer are to face private legal action by the young Asian student they were cleared of assaulting.

18   Newcastle at last clock up their 1st victory in the capital in 30 attempts, shocking Arsenal with a deserved 3-1 success and going top. A survey reports that since Dario Gradi's June 1983 appointment at Crewe, 864 managers have taken charge of Premiership and FL clubs. Neville Southall, 43, takes the managerial reins at Conference side Dover Ath. Leeds put Bowyer on the list over his reluctance to accept a club 4-week wages fine.

19   Wembley is finally chosen as the site for the new national £715m football stadium. Dagenham & Redbridge demolish Exeter to earn an FA Cup clash with Ipswich.

20   Bowyer backs down over Leeds club fine and comes off the transfer list. As instances of footballers' misbehaviour surface, West Ham fine Hayden Foxe heavily for disgracing himself at the club's Christmas party. Roy Evans becomes the 50th manager departing in 2001, resigning as Director of Football at Swindon. Arsenal's Vieira is France's Footballer of the Year.

21   In surprise swoop Liverpool recruit Nicolas Anelka from Paris St Germain on an extended loan until the end of the season.

22   Newcastle come from 3-1 down at Elland Road to snatch 4-3 success. Van Nistelrooy nets after 30 sec, the fastest of the season, in Man U's 6-1 trouncing of Southampton. Leeds chairman Peter Ridsdale admits to BBC Radio 5 Live he would not sign Lee Bowyer if the midfielder was playing for another club. Four months

after being sacked, Andy King is reinstated at Swindon. Scunthorpe end Argyle's record as the only club unbeaten on their travels in the Nationwide League. Celtic lose their 1st League game at Aberdeen.

23   Gunners have Van Bronckhorst sent-off for diving, the 40th dismissal under manager Wenger – yet pull off a dramatic win at Liverpool to go 2nd.

24   West Ham deny speculation about Di Canio and Man U. Ray Parlour pledges his long-term future to Arsenal. Jim Jefferies quits at Bradford. Gerry Francis resigns from his position as manager and Director of Football at Bristol Rovers because of personal problems.

26   Chelsea's Le Saux sparks a 20-man fracas as Arsenal dig deep winning at Highbury. Leaders Newcastle beat Boro. Three red cards are produced at Swindon versus Bournemouth. Woodgate makes his 1st Premiership start since January but new signing Fowler grabs the limelight with a Leeds hat-trick at Bolton.

27   Liverpool's Sami Hyypia is Finland's sporting personality of the year. Over 80 per cent of supporters back John Fashanu's bid to buy Northampton.

28   An abysmal run of Grimsby results – winning 19 of their 69 games – results in Lennie Lawrence's departure. Bristol Rovers upgrade caretaker Garry Thompson to boss. Leeds dismiss as 'laughable' suggestions boss O'Leary is earmarked for Man U in the summer.

29   Owen comes off the bench to net his 100th goal at West Ham. Blackburn clinch the £8m signing of Andy Cole from Man U. Ryman Premier League side Aldershot Town attract 2,630 against Canvey Island.

30   Days after his Grimsby sacking, Lennie Lawrence is bouncing back as Cardiff's Director of Football. Five wins on the spin sweep Man U to within 3 pts of the leaders. Until they repay £50,000 to PFA, Swindon are banned by FA from the transfer market. Over the weekend matches 14 players are dismissed – 1 red card from the record.

31   The year bows out with Arsenal, Burnley, Bristol City and Plymouth topping their respective divisions. In Scotland, Celtic have 10 pt lead, with other divisions led by Airdrie, Clydebank and Brechin.

January 2002

Honours List awards ... Sky Blues for Bald Eagle ... Cup disgrace at Cardiff ... Whistlers make World Cup ... Internet screen first ... Grip's heart scare ... Bobic at Bolton ... Todd out at Derby ... Bluebirds charged ... Baggies idol dies ... Saddlers sack Graydon ... Spurs reach final ... Premiership crowds rise ... Gregory quits ... Euro 2004 ... Dutch name Advocaat ... Cooper sadness ... Boost for Afghanistan ... Rams return for Gregory

1   Football is recognised in the New Year Honour's List with an OBE for Graham Taylor, England's manager 1990 to 1993, and Gary McAllister, 37, getting an MBE. Freezing weather affects fixtures, just a couple surviving Div 2 and Torquay v Cheltenham the only Div 3 match to go ahead.

2   Sunderland announce a testimonial for Niall Quinn who intends raising £1m to be divided between children's charities locally and in Dublin. Football League impose a transfer embargo on Swansea after the club falls behind on pension payments to staff. Monthly divisional awards go to Barnsley's Steve Parkin, Danny Wilson (Bristol City) and Luton's Joe Kinnear.

3   Former Derby boss Jim Smith returns as assistant manager to Coventry's Roland Nilsson. Sacked Oldham manager Andy Ritchie is Leeds U's new youth academy director.

4   Chelsea's John Terry is charged with affray and assault after arrest in a London nightclub. Under-pressure Walter Smith is given full backing from the Everton board.

5   FA Cup 3rd round glory comes to an end for non-League clubs Canvey Island and Dagenham & Redbridge. Holders Liverpool advance beating Birmingham.

6   Billy Dearden becomes the 1st manager to leave his club in 2002 resigning from Mansfield. Caretaker John Taylor takes the reins at Cambridge U. With legendary John Charles watching at Ninian Park, ugly scenes of taunting fans and baton-wielding police mar Cardiff's 2-1 tempestuous FA Cup defeat of Leeds.

7   FA announce joint inquiry with FAW into crowd disorder and the attack by Cardiff fans on the Leeds trio of Bowyer, Batty and Viduka. Manager O'Leary slams the 'walk round the pitch' behaviour of Bluebirds owner Sam Hammam. Notts Co appoint Billy Dearden as boss, a day after he leaves Mansfield. England's Graham Poll and Hugh Dallas (Scotland) are among 72 officials appointed for World Cup duty.

8   New £8m signing Andy Cole opens his account for Blackburn in the Worthington Cup clash with Sheff Wed, taking the club to the verge of their 1st major domestic Cup final for 42 years. Former Oxford U manager Mark Wright takes charge at Chester City. Cardiff's owner Hammam vows to give up his touchline strolling.

9   Mark McGhee signs new contract to stay at Millwall until 2004. Deputy Stuart Watkiss takes charge at Mansfield. Man U's clash with Liverpool on Jan 22 will be the 1st to be screened on the Internet. In LDV Vans Trophy pairing, Bristol City beat rivals Rovers 3-0 watched by 17,367. England No. 2 Tord Grip leaves hospital after a heart scare and a series of stringent health checks.

10   A review overturns the caution Chelsea's Le Saux received for diving at Southampton. Peter Beardsley slams a PFA move to use convicted drink-driver Tony Adams, former drugs user Paul Merson and wife-beater Paul Gascoigne as role models in an education initiative. Millwall's Mark McGhee and Steve Bruce of Birmingham are sent from the dug out in a stormy New Den clash where the assistant ref is struck a meat pie.

11   Borussia Dortmund striker Fredi Bobic signs on loan for Bolton. Ruud Van Nistelrooy, with 21 goals so far, is Carling's Player of the Month.

12   Danny Mills is dismissed for the 2nd time this season taking the Leeds tally of red cards to 5. Everton's Blomqvist nets his 1st Premiership goal since Oct 1998. Smith's goal for Leeds after 24 seconds is the fastest of the season.

13   Man U hit the top for the 1st time this season winning at Southampton. Man City boss Keegan is forced to wrestle red-carded Danny Tiatto down the tunnel after the volatile Australian flies off the handle. In a major policy change Tony Blair, speaking on BBC TV, backs plans for a national stadium – but not with direct government money.

14 Colin Todd's reign at Derby ends after 98 days following Saturday's defeat at Villa, his 11th reverse in 17 matches. Eriksson is named Coach of the Year at Swedish television's annual sports gala awards. Dick Advocaat turns down the opportunity to coach Holland for a 2nd time.

15 At the end of a troubled week for English football the weekend's Premiership programme is scrutinised closely. Of 306,595 attending the 10 elite matches only 20 are arrested and 58 ejected. Safety officers and police record no incidents of violence with only one fan encroaching the field of play and being arrested.

16 A chance sighting with his agent at Barajas airport earlier in the week snowballs into a £26m transfer speculation story that Arsenal's Vieira is heading to Real Madrid. Two potential buyers emerge for troubled York, £1m in debt and losing £15,000 weekly. Chelsea's Zola dedicates his 'special' back-heel flick goal against Norwich to an 8 year old fan dying of a brain tumour who he comforted in hospital.

17 Former Chelsea, Luton and QPR striker Roy Wegerle, now on the pro golf circuit, tees off in the Alfred Dunhill Championship. Premier League's Richard Scudamore says his clubs will impose bigger fines on troublesome employees exceeding PFA's maximum of 2 weeks wages. Paul Bracewell is among 5 national coach newcomers helping England's youth teams from ages 16–21.

18 FA charge Cardiff with misconduct after an investigation into crowd trouble but Leeds escape with a warning. Pompey Director of Football Harry Redknapp confirms he has been offered but has rejected the chance to replace Graham Rix. Football League admit discussing the prospect of Celtic and Rangers joining next season's Worthington Cup. FA will not consider Chelsea's John Terry for England until the player's legal case, denying affray charges, is complete. Man U pay £7.5m for Independiente striker Diego Forlan.

19 WBA legend and England-capped striker Jeff Astle dies suddenly, aged 59, after collapsing at his daughter's home. Van Nistelrooy nets for a record 8th successive Premiership match. Supporters of Aberdeen and Rangers clash at the 5.35 kick-off sparking shameful scenes of violence with riot police drafted in while players leave the pitch for their own safety and a 20 minute stoppage. Scunthorpe skipper Peter Beagrie chalks up the 600th game of his 18-year career. Wigan notch their 1,500th League goal at Brentford.

20 Chelsea hit 5 against West Ham who have Di Canio sent off for stamping. WBA's Jason Roberts runs off celebrating his winning score, his T-shirt top revealing a picture of Baggies hero, the late Jeff Astle who had netted 174 goals in 361 appearances. Arsenal become the 1st Premiership club reaching 50 cautions, at Leeds.

21 Brum announce increased losses of £2.63m. FA will look at video footage which appears to show Viduka of Leeds elbowing Arsenal's Keown.

22 Blackburn reach the Worthington Cup final. Ray Graydon, who led Walsall to 2 promotions after taking over in May 1998, is sacked, becoming the 33rd manager to depart an English club this season. After Liverpool's win at Old Trafford blows open the title race boss Ferguson claims the Merseysiders had 'just kicked the ball forward hoping to get a break'.

23 At the 27th attempt and spanning a 12-year wait, Spurs gain revenge outplaying Chelsea 5-1 and reaching the Worthington Cup final next month, but following a goal-mouth skirmish ref Halsey dismisses Hasselbaink in error, leaving guilty Melchiot remaining on the pitch. Walsall act quickly installing former Wolves boss Colin Lee as new manager. Figures released show Premiership football boasting the highest attendances of any European League averaging crowds of 34,000. Swindon have a transfer embargo imposed on them for the 2nd time in 3 weeks. Michael Knighton agrees to end his 9-year reign at Carlisle selling to Irish businessman John Courtenay.

24 John Gregory resigns his Villa managerial post just short of his 4th anniversary in the job, and coming after 2 successive Premiership wins lifting the club into 7th place. Gregory who had complained about lack of transfer funding spent £71.5m and recouping £46m. FA find Villa's Ginola guilty of misconduct fining him £22,000 with a 2-match suspension on top. Chairman Peter Ridsdale reveals Leeds have turned down a £25m bid, reportedly from a European club, for Rio Ferdinand. Two days before their FA Cup tie against struggling York, Fulham pledge their club's share of the receipts estimated at £30,000 to the York City Supporters Trust.

25 With overwhelming television evidence, Chelsea's Hasselbaink has his red card against Spurs annulled with colleague Melchiot being hit with a 3-match ban. At the draw in Oporto for Euro 2004 England is grouped with Turkey, Slovakia, Macedonia and Liechtenstein. Scotland must meet Germany, Iceland, Lithuania and Faeroes. Wales journey to Italy, Yugoslavia, Finland and Azerbaijan, while N Ireland tackle Spain, Ukraine, Greece and Armenia. The Republic meet Russia, Switzerland, Georgia and Albania. Dick Advocaat is to coach Holland on a part-time basis combining his duties at Rangers.

26 Boro, struggling for their Premiership lives, survive a shocking 1st half to score 2 late goals, dumping a careless and wasteful Man U from the FA Cup. But just hours after playing in the tie, tragedy strikes for Colin Cooper when his 2 year old son, Finlay, is pronounced dead at Harrogate hospital after choking on a plastic toy at tea-time. Inverness Caledonian Thistle who famously beat Celtic 2 years ago take another scalp defeating Hearts 3-1 in the Scottish Cup.

27 Liverpool's Carragher is struck by a coin at Highbury and reacts by flinging it back into the East Stand leaving the ref no alternative but to send him off. It is the 3rd red card Mike Riley shows after Keown and Bergkamp go in the previous 5 min. Billy O'Rourke, the former Blackpool and Tranmere goalie, dies of a suspected brain haemorrhage, aged 41.

28 Man U's head of security Ned Kelly is suspended pending an investigation into allegations of ticket-touting. Plans for a British Cup replacing the League Cup format in England and Scotland faces opposition from UEFA. Morecambe's Alan Hardiker, 19, becomes the most expensive player to leave the Nationwide Conference for the FL when he joins Stockport for £150,000.

29 Brentford chairman Ron Noades offers £10m to buy QPR's Loftus Road ground. Sheff U and rivals Wednesday serve up a frenzied goalless derby before 29,364.

30 Ipswich skipper Matt Holland reaches a modern-day landmark playing his 200th consecutive game since his £800,000 arrival from Bournemouth in July 1997. Abel Xavier is only the 3rd player in 67 years to move from

Everton to Liverpool. Lawrie McMenemy and Gary Mabbutt will coach the Afghanistan national side and an International Security Force Select in a challenge match in Kabul next month. John Gregory takes the managerial helm at Derby signing a three and a half year deal. Oleg Luzhny is sent off against Blackburn, the 11th this season and 43rd in all, since Arsène Wenger was appointed in September 1996.

31   FA charge Vieira and Hasselbaink, also the Leeds pair Smith and Viduka with misconduct. Bradford hit rebel Benito Carbone with £80,000 fine after he refused to play as a sub.

February 2002
City bad boys ... £5m for 18 year old ... Sir Alex U-turn ... Villa name Taylor ... Community kick-off ... Fashanu's Cobblers bid ... Scots Boss Berti ... Winterbottom sadness ... Cardiff land Lennie ... ITV Digital worries ... Red again for Ray ... Di Matteo quits ... OT statue of 'The King' ... Rovers' Cup success ... Shreeves in – Little and AXA out

1   Villa put non-executive director and former manager Graham Taylor in temporary charge. Exeter apply for an emergency PFA loan to pay players for the next 2 months.

2   Millwall's Mark McGhee and Walsall's Colin Lee, once close friends and together for 8 years at Reading, Leicester and Wolves, ignore each other in the New Den 2-2 clash. A waterlogged pitch ends the Brum v Crewe fixture after 55 min. Luton have their 1st sell-out crowd in years, 9,585, in table-topping clash with Plymouth. Pompey's Robert Prosinecki nets the fastest goal of the day and completes his hat-trick in 4-4 result with Barnsley. Beckham, who never wears the same footwear twice, swops his white boots to experiment with a new all-black prototype heavily disguising the words 'technologies on trial' – and smashes in a trademark free kick. Shortly before kick-off the 1st Norwich side to win promotion to the top division, Ron Saunders' team of 1971–72, parades around Carrow road.

3   Leeds fall to their biggest Elland Road defeat in 22 months losing 4-0 to Liverpool. Once compensation with Kuwaiti's Federation is complete SFA is confident Bert Vogts will be at the helm for the friendly with France next month. Sunderland's Kevin Phillips undergoes a series of precautionary injections on the advice of his club's medical staff after being spat on by Boro's Gianluca Festa. Stuart Pearce's dismissal, the 8th this season for Man City, gives them the worst disciplinary record in the division.

4   Newcastle pay £5m, a record for an English teenager, to take Forest's 18 year old Jermaine Jenas. Teams knocked out in the early stages of the Champions League will not now be able to join the UEFA Cup. Indications are that Sir Alex Ferguson, 60, is having a re-think about his future and is starting negotiations to remain in charge for another 2 or more seasons. While Craven Cottage has a £70m makeover Fulham tie up £1m ground-sharing deal with cash-strapped QPR.

5   Graham Taylor takes over in charge at Villa, agreeing a two and a half year contract and admitting he desperately fancies making a real challenge for the Premiership. Lee Bowyer receives a 6-match Leeds ban. Football League want to combine the Worthington Cup and its Scottish counterpart the CIS Insurance Cup, from the semi-final stages.

6   Boss Ferguson says his wife and family changed his mind about continuing at Man U. Exeter's entire squad hand in a transfer request in protest over non-payment of monthly wages. Advisors inform The Dons there is no chance of planning permission for a return to Plough Lane.

7   Despite being bottom of Div 1, Stockport manager Carlton Palmer gets a 1-year contract extension. A minute's silence is observed before Palace's match against Wolves to remember ex-boss Bert Head who died earlier in the week. Palace's £2.4m signing Ade Akinbiyi sports a No. 55 shirt.

8   The Charity Shield will be renamed the FA Community Shield. Everton spring a surprise by recruiting Villa's flamboyant Frenchman David Ginola. Southampton's Gordon Strachan takes the Barclaycard Manager of the month award.

9   Manager Burley admits Ipswich were fortunate to get away with only a 6-0 hammering by a rampant Liverpool side. The Football Supporters Association is concerned at the increasing number of games being switched from the once sacrosanct 3 pm Saturday slot to cater for television. Hibs go 17 League games without a win.

10   Port Vale win the Potteries derby in front of the largest League crowd at the Britannia Stadium for more than 2 seasons, 23,019. The lead changes hands for the 25th time in the most unpredictable Premiership title race with Man U leap-frogging Liverpool once more.

11   FAI sign up Mick McCarthy on a new 2-year contract. Skipper Beckham models the new reversible away England red strip, price £40, which doubles as a blue leisure top.

12   Hearts ban for life the season ticket-holder who disrupts the 1 minute silence in honour of Princess Margaret. Dick Advocaat raises the stakes for tomorrow's clash in Amsterdam by accusing England of playing boring football.

13   A flying-volley score for Darius Vassell, on his debut, earns England a 1-1 draw in Holland. A 65,000 attendance at the Millennium Stadium see Wales hold Argentina 1-1. John Fashanu submits his bid for cash-strapped Northampton Town. Posh's Andy Clarke tests positive for a banned substance. SFA confirm the appointment of Berti Vogts taking effect from Mar 1.

14   Halifax, 5 points adrift at the bottom of the League, are put up for sale. The Supporters Trust trying to save York receive a £50,000 cheque from Fulham's Mohamed Al Fayed, his team's share of the recent FA Cup gate receipts.

15   Before 30,000 Kabul Select and a British Army XI meet in Afghanistan's Olympic Stadium, frequently the venue for public executions. Official police stats show Cardiff the club with the worst behaved fans with 99 banned from watching in England, Wales or abroad. UEFA, concerned with the finances and near bankrupt state of some leading European clubs, will refuse entry to the Champions League and UEFA Cup of those heavily in debt.

16 Walter Winterbottom who took charge of England from 1946–62, dies aged 89, in Guildford. The country's 1st manager, at one time he had no control over selection with the choice resting on the opinion of FA committee men. The highest attendance in the Conference, 4,458, watch the Yeovil v Dagenham & Redbridge 3-3 draw. Three women officiate at the Farnborough v Telford clash in which not a single player is cautioned – but all three are embarrassingly listed in the programme as Mr!

17 Solano's goal against Man City ruins Keegan's return to Tyneside. The Hasselbaink-Gudjohnsen 42-goal partnership sees Chelsea through against Preston in Cup tie. Boos ring out at Everton, held scoreless by Crewe.

18 Lennie Lawrence, dismissed by Grimsby at Christmas, returns as boss to Cardiff following the resignation of Alan Cork. Villa put in provisional entry for the Intertoto Cup. Aldershot attract over 60 applications following manager George Borg's departure. Amidst threats that ITV Digital will abandon their £312m ITV contract, Nationwide League chairmen fear the £104m due to them next season will not be paid.

19 Parlour is sent off, his 3rd dismissal, as Arsenal concede 90th min equaliser at Bayer Leverkusen. Chelsea's Roberto Di Matteo announces his retirement at the age of 31 because of injury.

20 Man U snatch last-minute draw at Nantes. Chelsea fork out £125.000 on a new pitch surface ready for use in a fortnight. Former England defender Ray Wilson is selling his 1966 World Cup winner's medal.

21 Goalie Martyn stars as Leeds hold Dutch champs PSV in Eindhoven. Chairmen give their support to the Worthington Cup and to maintaining a UEFA Cup place for the winners, while the so-called British Cup, supposedly involving Celtic and Rangers, is not mentioned. Franck Sauzee lasts 2 months as Hibs manager steps down after 1 victory in 15 games. Watford boss Vialli receives a vote of confidence.

22 John Still quits as Barnet manager to concentrate on his boardroom role. Arsenal's Wenger maintains the UEFA Cup spot should go to the club finishing 6th in the Premiership, not the Worthington Cup winners.

23 Anelka nets his 1st for Liverpool in drawn 166th Merseyside derby. Eight Frenchmen take the field, 11 including the subs, in Arsenal's win over Fulham. A statue of Denis 'King' Law, European Footballer of the Year in 1964 and scorer of 236 goals for Man U, is unveiled at Old Trafford.

24 Blackburn upset the odds beating Spurs in the Worthington Cup final, giving Rovers their 1st major cup success for 74 years. Newcastle end a 6-year spell without victories over their local rivals winning 1-0 at Sunderland. Kilmarnock boss Bobby Williamson resigns.

25 FA charge Blackburn manager Graeme Souness and Mauricio Taricco of Spurs with misconduct. Serb millionaire chairman Milan Mandaric gives boss Rix a stern ultimatum about improving results at Pompey. David O'Leary claims his Leeds club has become the most hated in the country. The much-maligned Worthington Cup attracts around 5.6 million TV viewers, 24,000 more than last season's showpiece FA Cup final.

26 Man U sweep away Nantes 5-1. Heskey's saver gives hope to Liverpool in Galatasaray. Premiership League survey indicates as many as 40 per cent of all new supporters are female and account for 15 per cent in the top division. Peter Shreeves is the new head coach at Barnet.

27 Arsenal put in a stunning performance to demolish Bayer Leverkusen 4-1. West Brom reveal record signing Jason Roberts has broken his left foot for the 3rd time in 7 months. Hull part company with Brian Little after less than 2 years. Debt-ridden ITV Digital is on the brink of being sold or closing as owners Carlton and Granada call in advisers.

28 The *Daily Mail* continues to publish revelations about alleged corruption and major money problems at FIFA questioning also the methods used which brought Sepp Blatter to power 4 years ago. FA's 4-year partnership with AXA as sponsors of the FA Cup will conclude at the end of the season. Sir Alex Ferguson signs for another 3 years.

March 2002
Final closes the season ... Keane signs ... Filbert St sold ... Leeds cash loss ... Tosh axed ... Moyes replaces Smith ... Kop fine ... Bramall shame ... Stockport drop down ... Hampden needs new top ... Houllier welcome back ... Upsurge in FL crowds ... Pires shock ... Redknapp back ... Sadly, It's now all over ... Pilgrims promotion ... Pele's shirt ... Le Tissier au revoir

1 The FA Cup final will return to its customary position in next season's calendar, the 17 May 2003, date coming a week after the end of the Premiership campaign. With the PFA deeming his actions unlawful Pompey chairman Mandaric ends his wage-freeze war with under-achieving staff by paying the monthly salaries, a total of £700,000.

2 Roy Keane puts pen to paper on a new 4-year Man U contract reportedly worth £90,000 weekly, the highest paid player in the club's history. Blackburn's Andy Cole is sent off for stamping on Bolton's Mike Whitlow.

3 Derby have a dramatic last minute 'goal' winner controversially chalked off against Man U. Barracking at Brian Kidd prompts Peter Ridsdale to remonstrate with disgruntled Leeds fans following the scoreless draw at Everton, while furious boss O'Leary then offers to quit if taunting continues.

4 Brighton's Peter Taylor says he is refusing to sign a 3-year contract until the club's training facilities are improved. Man City boost their run-in by signing Preston striker Jon Macken for £5m.

5 Pompey's former Spurs defender Justin Edinburgh, 33, is forced to retire. FA fine Fulham £30,000 and Everton £25,000 following a pitch brawl in December. Bottom club Stockport notch their 1st win in 19 games.

6 Leicester sell the Filbert Street ground in £3.75m deal with development company. Pompey appoint Peter Storrie as chief executive. Nine Northampton pubs win licences for breakfast-time opening during the World Cup. FA suspend Posh striker Andy Clarke after testing positive for a banned substance. PFA's Gordon Taylor fears English football will be forced by FIFA to have a transfer window next season.

7 Swansea will not be offering new contracts to manager Colin Addison and assistant Peter Nicholas. Villa and AB Copenhagen announce details of a tie-up to improve youth development, scouting and training methods. The Fraud squad charge former Vale commercial director Neil Hughes with theft and false accounting.

8   Leeds announce a £13.8m loss which may spark players being sold. Bobby Robson is Barclaycard Manager of the Month. Keegan persuades Man City players to pledge £2,500 to the 'Buy-a-seat' appeal by neighbours Bury.

9   Stockport have their 4th player sent-off in 5 games, against Burnley.

10 Chelsea gain 4-0 FA Cup win over Spurs to avenge their Worthington Cup 5-1 mauling, but have Le Saux red-carded. The 3rd Old Firm clash of the season ends 1-1 at Ibrox.

11 John Toshack gets the sack at Sociedad. England have bust-up with Turkey over Euro 2004 dates with nothing resolved after 5-hour meeting in Istanbul. FA sign up an 8-year agreement with shirt sponsors Umbro worth over £120m.

12 Deportivo La Coruna dish out a 2-0 lesson to below-par Arsenal who miss a penalty. Walter Smith's troubled 3 and a half year reign ends with Everton now targeting Peston's David Moyes as the man to help stave off relegation worries.

13 In the latest running feud Chelsea run out 4-0 winners over Spurs with Argentine defender Mauricio Taricco's wild tackle on Le Saux resulting in a dismissal. Slick Liverpool spurn ample chances to win in Barcelona but come away with scoreless draw. Man U earn a place in Champions League quarter-final after 0-0 with Bayern Munich. Tommy Burns is Scotland's No. 2 to coach Berti Vogts. Leicester tell Micky Adams he will be made team manager this summer. Dover sack boss Neville Southall.

14 Fined £20,000 for approaching Christian Ziege, then at Boro but now with Spurs, Liverpool chief executive Rick Parry warns there 'would be dozens of similar cases to investigate. Everton unveil David Moyes, 39, as manager after thrashing out £1m compensation settlement with Preston.

15 Bury is given 6 more weeks to stave off financial ruin. Motor sport entrepreneur John Batchelor pays £4m for York City and earmarks 2 sites for a 15,000-stadium.

16 On a day of shame at Bramall Lane, Sheffield U's clash with WBA is abandoned in the 82nd minute with the Blades down to 6 players. Ref Eddie Wolstenholme has no alternative after 3 United players are dismissed and a further 2 hauled off injured with no subs to send on. Baggies boss Gary Megson then says he will refuse to take part in a re-arranged fixture following a mass brawl on the pitch and a dug-out area bust-up. Gascoigne quits Everton to join Burnley for the remainder of the season netting a reported £200,000 fee. Stockport become the 1st team to be relegated. Bobby Zamora is the 1st Brighton player to bag 30 goals in successive seasons.

17 Rangers end a 22-month trophy drought capturing the CIS Insurance Cup with victory over Ayr. Former Man U defender Jaap Stam makes his Lazio comeback from a 4-month drug ban. FIFA declare that from July 1 revealing messages on T-shirts is banned.

18 Wolves sell almost 13,000 season tickets for next term after giving existing holders the chance to renew at no extra cost. New Scots boss Vogts selects 7 uncapped players in a youthful 1st squad to meet World champions France. The pitch at Hampden Park, venue for the European Cup final, is to be re-laid.

19 With an emotional but calm Gerard Houllier on the Anfield bench after 5 months out Liverpool roar into the Champions League quarter-final with 2-0 win over Lazio. Man U top their group defeating Boavista in Oporto. Doomed Stockport shock champions-elect Man City.

20 Media concern surfaces again that the ITV Sports Channel could close plunging Nationwide League clubs due to be paid £179m, closer to financial ruin. Arsenal's treble hopes end in the hushed surroundings of the Stadio delle Alpi losing to Juventus before just 8,562 spectators. Barnet get planning permission to build a £12m stadium.

21 The 72 Football League clubs warn they will take legal action against Granada and Carlton if the co-owners of ITV Digital refuse to pay up on their £315m 3-year contract. WBA is awarded the 3 pts from their abandoned game against Sheff U.

22 Carlton Palmer breaks the wall of silence confessing he was asked to hand over a £50,000 bribe to an agent before he could land a player; the former England midfielder, now Stockport's manager, refused to pay. Nationwide League crowds are primed to reach the 15 million mark with the Premiership heading for a 13 million audience.

23 The season looks all over for Arsenal's Robert Pires stretchered-off with damaged knee ligaments. Boro blow a gaping hole in Man U's title ambitions snatching a narrow Old Trafford win. No teams in the Premiership win at home while just 12 home successes are registered in the entire League.

24 Smicer's last minute volley sends Liverpool top. Rangers clinch a Tennent's Scottish Cup final spot and will meet Celtic. Coach Eriksson insists it was his choice not to consider Jonathan Woodgate for the World Cup squad.

25 Stuart Pearce, now 39, expects to retire at the end of the season but would like to remain at Man City in a coaching capacity. Graham Rix is sacked at Pompey with Harry Redknapp becoming their 6th manager in 4 years.

26 Doping-control officials refute Italian newspaper claims, and innuendo quotes from Roma's Fabio Capello, hinting the 'powerful physiques' of Liverpool players. FA's Alan Hodson says the Anfield squad had been randomly tested 5 times this season. The death is announced of Kenneth Wolstenholme, 81, the 1st commentator and presenter of BBC *MOTD*, fondly remembered for his spontaneous 'They think it's all over' comment in the dying seconds of the 1966 World Cup final. Plymouth clinch promotion to Div 2.

27 Italy come from behind to defeat England at Elland Road. France defeat Scotland 5-0 giving boss Vogts an international debut to forget. Ireland beat Denmark, Wales hold Czech Republic scoreless. Swindon go into administration. ITV's Digital Channel, losing £3m weekly, is put into administration heralding a financial crisis to lower division clubs. Warren Feeney makes history in 0-0 with Liechtenstein following his father and late grandfather playing for N Ireland. The No. 10 shirt worn by Pele during the 1970 World Cup finals fetches a record £157,750 at Christie's auction.

28   On what is traditionally the busiest trading day of the season, the transfer deadline passes with only 3 cash deals completed, Nathan Ellington's £750,000 Bristol Rovers move to Wigan coming tops. England's Euro 2004 fixture schedule, drawn by UEFA, will mean a final showdown in Turkey in October 2003. Matt Le Tissier retires after 16 years and 209 senior goals for Southampton, his only club. Chelsea's Colin Hutchinson will leave the club to work as a consultant with top agent Paul Stretford.

29   Lively Dyer orchestrates Newcastle's 6-2 defeat of Everton. Jan Molby tenders his resignation at Kidderminster Harriers – days after his wife tells a Danish newspaper he would be taking charge at Hull.

30   In the tightest race for years and after a nail-biting 4-3 win at Leeds, Man U still cling to their ambition of recording a 4th straight Premiership title. But Liverpool maintain their chance beating Charlton. In-form Gunners chalk up win over Sunderland with Tony Adams making his 500th appearance. Luton gain automatic promotion back into Div 2 securing a club record 10 straight wins.

31   Football chiefs decide not to postpone tomorrow's Easter Bank holiday programme following the Queen Mother's death. Liverpool remain top of the Fair Play League, Leicester bottom. Dave Beasant, the Football League's oldest goalie, is offered a new 1-year contract with Pompey which will take him past his 44th birthday.

April 2002

Riot at Millwall ... Halifax drop again ... Time up say Worthington ... Adams takes charge ... Celtic tops ... City's Premiership return ... Notts freeze prices ... FA have a McDonalds ... Great Dane's return ... Sven scraps friendlies ... Ruud acknowledged ... Spur for Redknapp ... Shearer's landmark ... Pires top vote ... Baggies go up ... Neville heartache ... McAllister is boss ... Yorath leads Owls ... Boss Butcher's start ... Boston make it ... Preston name Brown

1   Liverpool's Houllier is given the *Legion d'honneur*, one of France's top civil awards. Former Palace boss Steve Bruce is abused from start to finish on Brum's visit to Selhurst Park. Doomed Halifax return to the Conference 4 years after regaining League status.

2   In arguably their best performance for some years, Man U triumph in one of the most forbidding venues on the continent, at Deportivo La Coruna. Crisis club Bury plead with the League to help avoid a fixture clash with Man U next season.

3   Hyypia's goal edges Liverpool ahead against Bayer Leverkusen but the Anfield club's unexciting display is a poor return for viewers watching in 60 countries. Coors Brewery call time on their Worthington Cup sponsorship after next year's final. Huddersfield reveal a crippling annual loss of over £6m.

4   Leicester announce Micky Adams as their new manager with Dave Bassett becoming Director of Football. Jan Molby takes charge at Hull. Beckenbauer criticises Liverpool's defensive approach against Leverkusen stating that it was hard to tell who had home advantage.

5   FA issue 6 charges against Sheffield U relating to their abandoned match with WBA.

6   Lauren's late penalty gives Arsenal a crucial derby win over Spurs. Celtic clinch their 2nd successive title with Larsson scoring his 11th hat-trick and completing a century of Premier League goals with his third strike. Man City take the Div 1 title crushing Barnsley 5-1. Bobic's hat-trick against Ipswich almost certainly preserves Bolton's status. Carlisle sack manager Roddy Collins following post match comments about owner Michael Knighton. Tom Finney leads out the team at Deepdale to mark his 80th birthday.

7   Reading's draw at Tranmere means Brighton gain their 2nd successive promotion. Keegan breaks his silence about his time in charge of England claiming the FA would not allow him the freedom to do the job his way and, in particular, appoint his mentor Arthur Cox as No. 2 because he was over 60.

8   Halifax release manager Alan Little from his contract. Film star Sean Bean is to become a director of boyhood club Sheffield U. Notts Co thank fans for the biggest crowd of the season at Meadow Lane last Saturday – 9,014 saw the win over Blackpool – by freezing season ticket prices for 5 years.

9   Owen squanders a hat-trick of opportunities as Liverpool crash out at Leverkusen. Garry Thompson is sacked at Bristol Rovers after 4 months in charge.

10   Beckham's World Cup participation is in doubt after breaking a bone in his left ankle following a reckless tackle by Deportivo's Pedro Duscher. Leicester to change the name of their new £35m ground to The Walkers Stadium after original choice, The Walkers Bowl receives widespread criticism. Man City make Arthur Cox assistant manager. Cash-strapped Lincoln persuade Powergen not to pull the plug on their ground over an unpaid £10,000 bill.

11   Holiday company Thomson agree to become Tottenham's shirt sponsor for 2 years. McDonalds is believed to be paying £30m over 4 years becoming the 3rd company joining the FA's new 5-pronged sponsorship strategy following Nationwide and Umbro.

12   Peter Schmeichel, 38, is ditched by Villa with Graham Taylor opting to push younger highly rated Finn, Peter Enckelman. Claudio Ranieri signs a 3-year extension to his Chelsea contract.

13   Div 1 champs Man City move quickly and agree a 1-year deal with Villa's Schmeichel. In a letter sent out to the top flight bosses England's Eriksson says that from next season he will scrap friendlies replacing them with squad get-togethers.

14   Ruud Van Nistelrooy wins the PFA Players' Player of the year pipping Thierry Henry with Newcastle's Craig Bellamy taking the Young Player award. The double is on for the Gunners after booking their FA Cup final place beating Boro. John Terry's goal against Fulham sets up the 1st Cockney Cup final in 20 years and Chelsea's 4th appearance in 8 years.

15   Plymouth clinch the Div 3 title in emphatic style winning 4-1 at Darlington. Defiant FA insist Villa Park was the best venue to stage Sunday's Cup semi-final between Fulham and Chelsea although thousands were held up in road congestion, and 6,000 unsold seats meant a deflated atmosphere. Mike Riley is to ref the FA Cup final. Spurs clinch a £15m kit manufacturing deal with Kappa.

16 FA agree World Cup bonuses rewarding players up to £50,000 for reaching the 2nd rd, rising to about £200,000 for success in the final. Jamie Redknapp ends an 11-year association at Liverpool joining Spurs on a free. After losing their 34-year top flight status Coventry relieve Roland Nilsson and Jim Smith his assistant of their duties. Scottish Premier League clubs outside the Old Firm announce intentions to resign from the League after Rangers and Celtic veto the proposed SPL TV contract.

17 Skipper Owen nets his 15th goal in 34 internationals in England win over Paraguay. Bury coach Billy Ayre, 39, a former Blackpool, Scarborough and Cardiff manager, loses his battle against cancer.

18 Arsène Wenger, who has extensive knowledge of Japan when he coached at Grampus Eight and Nagoya, offers his advice to the FA. Sacked Pompey boss Rix accepts a £200,000 settlement.

19 Arsenal clinch a club record £10m sponsorship deal, over 2 years, with mobile communications company 02.

20 Revelations about the relationship between coach Eriksson and Swedish TV personality Ulrika Jonsson is heavily splashed in the media. Derby's defeat at Liverpool brings relegation. Shearer nets his 200th Premiership goal with his nearest challenger Andy Cole 61 goals behind. Reading clinch promotion in nail-biter at Brentford. Bournemouth crash through the Div 2 trap-door. Plymouth break the 100 point barrier, the only side in England to do so. Mansfield go up. Arsenal's sidelined French winger Robert Pires is the FWA's Footballer of the Year nudging out Van Nistelrooy by just 5 pts.

21 After a 16 year wait – and at the expense of their bitter rivals and near neighbours Wolves – WBA return to the top level. Crewe lose their Div 1 status after 5 years. Hartson, Mjallby and Ricksen are all dismissed in Old Firm draw at Parkhead.

22 Amidst rumours of being enticed back to Lazio after the World Cup England's in-the-spotlight coach Eriksson confirms his future is with the national side – and has Euro 2004 in his sights.

23 Shearer's goal at Blackburn ensures Newcastle a Champions League place. Roy McFarland becomes the 1st managerial casualty of the ITV Digital fiasco leaving Torquay because of staff cost-cutting.

24 Bayer Leverkusen grab the away goals advantage at Man U with Gary Neville breaking a foot bone seriously jeopardising his World Cup chances. Gary McAllister who played 119 games for the club is the new manager at Coventry with ex-Motherwell boss Eric Black set to team up with him.

25 The number of managers sacked over the last year rises to 50 with the departure of Terry Burton from Wimbledon and Alan Buckley at Lincoln. Ray Graydon lands the post at Bristol Rovers while Ian Britton is the new man in charge at Kidderminster. Football League crowds reach an encouraging 14.8 million flocking to games in all divisions.

26 A new biography of Sir Alex Ferguson claims chief executive Peter Kenyon was on the brink of agreeing a deal to install Sven Goran Eriksson – but the FA and the coach himself strongly deny this. Terry Yorath earns a new 2-year contract for keeping £16m in-the-red Sheffield Wed up.

27 Former Sports minister Kate Hoey calls for the Wembley project's £120m lottery grant to be returned; mean-while, the FA still need to raise £485m for the £715m venture. Johnny Haynes, the 1st £100 a week footballer, leads a parade of Fulham's greatest players on to the famous Craven Cottage pitch, soon to be reduced to rubble after 105 years. Crisis-torn Motherwell give new manager Terry Butcher a dream 4-1 winning start. Ayr's game is abandoned after demonstrating Airdrie fans invade the pitch, break a crossbar and later destroy the goalposts.

28 Wolves lose 1st leg play-off at Carrow Road with Dave Jones labelling the ref an 'old tug boat' and accusing Norwich of 'arrogance' after they print Millennium Stadium directions in the match programme. Boston join the ranks of the Football League for the 1st time. Little Livingston clinch UEFA Cup place.

29 Former Scots boss Craig Brown signs a 3-year contract as new manager of Preston. Frustrated Peter Taylor shocks promoted Brighton by resigning. Lively Ljungberg launches Arsenal to victory at Bolton and now need only a draw at Man U next week to claim the title.

30 Man U depart the Champions League semi-final at Leverkusen losing on the away goals rule. The ITV net-work gets the all-clear to pick up transmission of the play-offs. Roberto Di Matteo who was forced to retire is to lead out Chelsea in the FA Cup final. According to *France Football* David Beckham is the 2nd best-paid footballer in the world picking up a staggering £6.6m a year, with Zinedine Zidane topping the survey earning £8.7m

May 2002
Germans buy Wembley ... Gunners and Gers take Cups ... Fergie lets rip ... Bosmans on view ... Arsenal seal it at OT ... Ravanelli bye-bye ... Gills striker jailed ... Irwin severs connection ... Ipswich relegated ... Big time for Brum ... Gerrard agony ... Madrid's Hampden win ... Stoke sack boss ... Liverpool on move ... Baresi for Cottagers ... World Cup exit for Keane ... Cotterill is Stoke's man ... Elton stands down ... Senegal shock

1 Second leg wins put Norwich, Stoke and Brentford into divisional play-off finals. Baggies chairman resigns following an ongoing feud with promotion-winning manager Megson.

2 FA fine Sheff Utd £10,000 and find manager Neil Warnock guilty of improper conduct. Birmingham advance to Div 1 play-off final defeating Millwall 1-0 but afterwards yobs run riot torching 2 parked cars and leaving 47 officers and 26 police horses injured.

3 Gary Neville admits a broken foot bone means his World Cup dream is over. Rebuilding the state-of-the-art 90,000- capacity Wembley is given the green light, financed by a German bank, built by an Australian firm and up and running for the grand opening for the FA 2005 Cup final.

4 Two classy finishes from Parlour and Ljungberg against Chelsea light up a less than enthralling clash to land Arsenal the FA Cup with Tony Adams, 35, lifting the trophy on his 669th club appearance. Rangers snatch a last-gasp 3-2 winner over Celtic in the 117th Scottish Cup final at Hampden. Sir Alex Ferguson's colt Rock of Gibraltar wins the 2000 Guineas, the 1st classic of the season, at Newmarket.

5   Partick Thistle's John Lambie caps a memorable season winning the Tennent's Manager of the Year award and becoming the 1st recipient from outside the top flight to do so. Lincoln name caretaker Keith Alexander as their new manager.

6   Cheltenham Town's play-off final win means that all 11 matches in Wales' Millennium Stadium have gone in favour of the team using the North dressing-room. Former Barnsley caretaker-manager Eric Winstanley gets a new 3-year deal in charge of the West Indies islands St Kitts & Nevis. Agitated Ferguson blows his top at a press conference blistering the air in a foul-mouthed attack on media critics questioning the £28m Veron signing.

7   Celtic win 4-1 at Leeds in Gary Kelly's testimonial attracting a crowd of 26,440 and producing receipts of £600,000 which the player is donating to a cancer charity. Forty-four free-agent players from across the globe put their skills in the shop window in 6 games of 45 minutes at Luton, attracting reps from 47 clubs. Outspoken Roy Keane claims many of his under-achieving colleagues at Man U have not been pulling their weight.

8   Jubilant Arsenal deservedly clinch the Premiership title – and the double – in Man U's backyard, with Wiltord's 57th minute goal moving them 8pts clear. Man U will finish the season empty-handed for only the 3rd time in 13 years. The Gunners protect a record of never having lost away in the League, a feat not achieved in the top flight since Preston NE in the 19th century.

9   Vieira ends speculation on his immediate Arsenal future by declaring he will be at the club for next season. Coach Eriksson names his 23-man squad claiming England can be the 'dark horse' of the World Cup. Ravanelli is surplus to requirements at relegated Derby. Torquay give the managerial post to Leroy Rosenoir.

10 Gills striker Marlon King is jailed for 18 months for handling a stolen BMW convertible worth £32,000. Arsenal's Wenger and Ljungberg are Barclaycard Manager and Player of the Month. Stubborn Ferguson backs off after Eriksson insists recovering Beckham joins the rest and relaxation trip to Dubai.

11 Denis Irwin bows out after 12 years in his 527th appearance for Man U. Stoke beat Brentford in play-off for Div 1 spot ending the so-called south changing-room hoodoo which 11 sides at the Millennium Stadium had used. A brutal tackle by Southampton's El Khalej puts Kieron Dyer's World Cup participation in doubt. Liverpool clinch an automatic Champions League spot banishing Ipswich to relegation. In a carnival-type atmosphere Arsenal wrap up their double campaign beating Everton 4-3.

12 England's World Cup preparations are in disarray as coach Eriksson rules out Kieron Dyer and expects to lose Steven Gerrard. Football League chief executive David Burns dismisses claims Rangers and Celtic will be invited to join Div 1 next season. Birmingham, last in the top flight in 1986, win Div 1 play-off final on penalties.

13 New boss McAllister announces his arrival at Coventry by releasing 11. Rochdale sack John Hollins after he stalls on signing a new deal. Blackburn release Mark Hughes. Tony Adams, 19 years at Arsenal, takes a 2nd testimonial, against Celtic.

14 Scans reveal England's Gerrard requires immediate groin surgery ruling him out of the World Cup. A 35,702 crowd at Sunderland helps raise £750,000 for charity in Niall Quinn's benefit game. Over 31,000 turn up at Southampton for Matt Le Tissier's farewell. Cardiff's Robert Earnshaw caps a dream debut with the goal in Wales' win over Germany. Divisional Manager of the Year awards go to Gary Megson (WBA), Peter Taylor (Brighton) and Paul Sturrock (Plymouth). Football League begin proceedings to sue the owners of ITV Digital for £178m, and will seek a further £500m damages from the stricken channel.

15 Forty-two years after Real Madrid's epic European Cup final success before 137,000 at Hampden Park, Zidane lights up the Scottish venue with a stunning volley to seal the Madrid masters' 2-1 win over Bayer Leverkusen. Brum report the sale of over half their 21,500 season tickets for their Premiership return. Man U claim they are still owed £12m from the £16m transfer of Jaap Stam to Lazio. Millwall's Steven Reid is on his way to Gatwick en route for a Barbados holiday when a message on his mobile has him doing a U-turn and heading to Dublin to join Ireland's World Cup party.

16 Newcastle's Dyer signs a £12.5m 4-year contract before jetting out with England's squad. Ireland have 1st defeat in Dublin for 2 years going under to Nigeria. Stoke sack Gudjon Thordarson 5 days after steering the club into Div 1. FAW fine Cardiff £20,000 following crowd disturbances. Bradford, £13m in the red, go into administration.

17 Relegated Ipswich sack coach Bryan Hamilton. Liverpool announce plans for a new 55,000-seater stadium at Stanley Park 300 yards away from Anfield.

18 Villa beat Everton over 2 legs to take the FA Youth Cup. After their short Dubai holiday with loved ones England arrive at their training base in the South Korean paradise island of Jeju.

19 Bookies make France World Cup favourites shortening their odds to 100/30. The 1st football yob, an England fan, is sent home from the Far East. In a biography of Sven Goran Eriksson, FA's Adam Crozier says Kevin Keegan's walk-out left England 'completely rudderless'.

20 Dyer becomes England's 1st serious casualty. Berti Vogts enters the history books for all the wrong reasons recording his 4th consecutive defeat, the worst for a Scotland manager in 36 years. Liverpool's Houllier will not be making permanent Anelka's £12m move from PSG. Man City pay £3.8m for defender Sylvain Distin.

21 Owen nets his 16th goal in 36 internationals in the England warm-up draw with South Korea. Roy Keane has a training ground bust-up clashing with the goalkeeping coach, then does a U-turn after telling manager McCarthy he wants to go home. Fulham recruit Franco Baresi as their Director of Football. Boro lose their £7m damages claim over Christian Ziege's move to Liverpool.

22 Trevor Sinclair declines stand-by duties and heads back to London – then alarm bells ring over an injury to midfielder Danny Murphy. With just minutes to spare the FAI officially register a revised squad to FIFA reinstating skipper Keane. Leeds transfer-list Lee Bowyer.

23 The major shock of the World Cup so far erupts with controversial captain Keane sent packing by Mick McCarthy for being a 'disruptive influence' after launching an abusive tirade on the Irish boss. Scotland get a win over the Hong Kong League. Bradford dismiss 19 with administrators calculating the action will save £20,000 per day and possibly their future. Man City agree £10m deal to take Nicolas Anelka.

24 Ex-Liverpool defender Steve Nicol is the new head coach at New England Revolution. Roy Paul, the former Man City and Wales captain, dies, aged 80.

25 A report lists 101 English-based players at the World Cup finals, from 20 different nations with 85 represent-ing the Barclaycard Premiership, a notable increase on US '94 (26) and (70) at France '98. After a last minute panic the final batch of 100,000 delayed World Cup tickets arrive from Japan to be hastily delivered to fans' homes by express courier. Pierluigi Collina, arguably the highest-profile ref, is to take charge of the England–Argentina clash. Coach Eriksson admits for the 1st time Beckham will be omitted from the squad if his fitness cannot be guaranteed.

26 Fowler's late equaliser saves England blushes in 2-2 warm-up against Cameroon in Kobe. Ireland players publicly rally behind Mick McCarthy who states he will quit if his authority is questioned by the FAI. Disgraced Diego Maradona is refused entry into Japan.

27 In RTE television interview which grips the Irish nation, Roy Keane talks emotionally about perhaps still fig-uring in the World Cup – but noticeably offers no apology for his foul-mouthed and personal attack on man-ager McCarthy. Steve Cotterill leaves Cheltenham to take the managerial post at promoted Stoke. The Archbishop of Canterbury Dr George Carey, an Arsenal fan, gives dispensation for altered Sunday service times when England kick-off against Sweden at 10.30 am.

28 Sir Elton John resigns as Watford chairman. Phil Babb, voted Portugal's best overseas defender, leaves double-winning Sporting Lisbon to join Sunderland. An Independent Commission allows Wimbledon to relo-cate to Milton Keynes, 50 miles from their adopted Selhurst Park base. Relegated Ipswich are handed a UEFA place courtesy of the Fair Play draw. McCarthy agrees a U-turn, if his squad players want it, but ban-ished Keane announces afresh he will not be returning to Japan.

29 Sir Alex Ferguson is ambassador for the Scotland-Ireland bid to host Euro 2008. Sepp Blatter wins a land-slide victory to keep his FIFA president's job. Andy Dibble, 37, agrees a 1-year deal with Wrexham, his 18th club. Winger Paul Simpson lands the managerial post at Rochdale.

30 Brum complete the £2.3m signing of Leicester's Welsh midfielder Robbie Savage. Cheltenham's coach Graham Allner steps up to take charge. Andy Hunt, ex-WBA and Charlton striker who quit after losing his fight against chronic fatigue syndrome, is keeping chickens and growing organic veg in Belize. Former Sheff Wed player Ian Nolan wins £35,000 settlement after pursuing a claim for a double-fracture tackle by Justin Edinburgh, then at Spurs.

31 The month-long 64-match tournament which brings 32 countries to high-tech stadiums in Japan and South Korea and is the 1st World Cup to be held in Asia, kicks-off in Seoul with an elaborate opening ceremony costing £6m. Outsiders Senegal set the finals alight with an extraordinary victory over champions France. Oldham sack Mick Wadsworth upgrading coach Iain Dowie.

June 2002

Empty World Cup seats . . . Sir Bobby Robson . . . Staunton's ton-up . . . Coppell quits Bees . . . England revenge . . . Conference play-offs . . . Beckham lifted high . . . French short stay . . . Don't cry for me . . . Lions fan ban . . . England bow to Brazil . . . Germany reach final but lose to Brazil . . . Venables replaces O'Leary at Leeds

1 Holland's equaliser earns Ireland an opening draw with Cameroon. Germany demolish and humiliate an inept S Arabia team whose goalie Mohammed Al Deayea, making his 163rd appearance, concedes 8. Concern to FIFA at this early stage is why there were 3,500 empty seats for Senegal-France. El Hadji Diouf, one of the Senegal heroes, confirms a 5-year contract with Liverpool with a fee around £10m.

2 England start with an unconvincing draw against Sweden who enjoy a good 2nd period with their hopes only denied by an alert Seaman. Eriksson contends that games against Argentina and Nigeria are now 'like two finals for us if we want to stay in the World Cup'.

3 Italy come through over a nervous Ecuador while Mexico surprise Croatia. Rivaldo provides the 1st moment of blatant cheating by plummeting to the ground clutching his head – after Hakan Unsal clearly kicks the ball at the Brazilian's legs out by a corner flag. The Turk is one of two red-carded with Brazil winning 2-1.

4 Co-hosts South Korea, inspired by a volcano of noisy support, overwhelm Poland. Meanwhile, Japan with man-of-the-match Inamoto of Arsenal scoring, secure their country's 1st ever World Cup point.

5 Steve Staunton becomes the 1st Ireland performer to earn 100 caps as Robbie Keane snatches a dramatic last-gasp equaliser against Germany. Three down to the US after just 36 minutes hotly-tipped Portugal claw their way back with 2 but never look like rescuing themselves nor depriving the Americans of an historic result.

6 Thanks to Barthez, France just stay alive but have Henry red-carded after 25 minutes yet hang on for score-less result with Uruguay. Danish coach Morten Olsen complains to FIFA having to play 3 times under searing sun while France enjoy relatively cool evening starts. Rivaldo's play-acting against Turkey earns him a 'simulation' fine of £4,500. Released stats show that earlier in the week the official World Cup website scored a massive 79.7 million hits in a single day, thought to be a sports site record. Nicolas Anelka finally signs for Man City. Steve Coppell quits at Brentford. Man U name Portuguese globe-trotter Carlos Queiroz, 49, as No. 2 to Ferguson. PFA release the full list of players available: 562 professionals, 101 'football scholars' in acade-mies, 5 under contract but transfer-listed and 5 exercising their right to go because they are under 23. The total is only marginally over the 636 of a year ago.

7 Amidst delirious scenes throughout UK venues – and in particular the Falklands Globe Tavern in Port Stanley – England skipper Beckham wipes out 4 years of misery with a penalty winner taking sweet revenge

over Argentina who concede the spot-kick by decking Owen. In the same group Larsson's brace for Sweden ends Nigerian interest.

8   Graham Poll is branded a 'village ref' by the complaining Italian camp after twice ruling out scores flagged by an assistant meaning Croatia grab a vital win. Blackburn's Matt Jansen is left in a coma for 2 days after a taxi sent him crashing from his motorbike in Rome. Nationwide Conference will stage play-offs next season.

9   Over 66,000 in the Yokohama Stadium, plus the entire country, goes wild with Japan grabbing their 1st win, beating Russia. In contrast, rioting turns the centre of Moscow into a battlefield, the worst scenes seen since Boris Yeltsin used tanks to put down an armed insurrection in 1993. An unsightly dug-out melee between players and coaching staff from both sides explodes 2 minutes from the end of the Costa Rica–Turkey drawn clash.

10   FIFA are financing the £20,000 operational costs for Afghanistan's war-torn capital Kabul to broadcast World Cup football free on a giant TV screen. Portuguese nerves are calmed against Poland by Pauleta's hat-trick, emulating the watching Eusebio, the last from the country to register the feat 36 years ago against North Korea at Goodison Park. Blackburn and US goalie Friedel saves a penalty and makes a string of stops to help scrape a draw with the lively South Koreans. Culture secretary Tessa Jowell says an export ban will be imposed to prevent Wembley's Royal Box and famous 39 steps being sold abroad.

11   A waxwork model of Beckham suddenly appears across the London skyline after being transferred from Madame Tussaud's to a plinth in Tralfalgar Square, and under the watchful gaze of Admiral Nelson. Ireland progress to the 2nd rd scoring 3 without reply against S Arabia. Passionless France meekly surrender their crown and suffer humiliation of an early return home after losing to Denmark. Sixteen yellow cards – a tournament record – are brandished, and one player each from Germany and Cameroon is shown red, in an explosive scrap. In an unprecedented measure, and with the police laying down the law, Millwall are to ban away fans from 6 high-profile fixtures, against Wolves, Burnley, Forest, Stoke, Pompey and Leicester.

12   In 93 degree midday temperatures and 30 per cent humidity – players wrapping up in revolutionary ice jackets at half-time – England and Nigeria draw 0-0. However, the result is made sweeter by Argentina's exit, dumped out by Sweden. Watford sack assistant Ray Wilkins and 3 other backroom staff. The 72 Football League chairmen will stage a peaceful picket outside the London offices of the television company Carlton & Granada.

13   Brazil crush Costa Rica 5-2 to breeze into the last 16 in search of a record 5th trophy. Croatia, holding all the cards, unexpectedly blow their chance losing to Ecuador handing Italy (1-1 with Mexico) survival on a plate. The Premiership newcomers WBA mark their return to the top flight after 16 years with a daunting trip to Man U on Aug 17. Boston tackle Bournemouth.

14   Portugal have two sent off in losing 1-0 to South Korea. USA beaten 3-1 by Poland, still reach last 16. Minor earthquake in Tokyo, but more movement in Osaka as Japan cruise into the next round 2-0 v Tunisia. Belgium edge out Russia 3-2 and go also through.

15   Germans leave it late against Paraguay in poor game, but England say thank you for Danish defensive errors and comfortably progress 3-0.

16   Harte has a 62nd minute penalty saved against Spain and Kilbane hits the rebound wide, but Keane sends it into extra time at 1-1 with a last minute spot kick. The Irish lose the penalty shoot-out. Holland, Connolly and Kilbane again miss. Senegal's sudden death goal ends Sweden's chances.

17   Two fine goals put Brazil 2-0 in front of Belgium who gave the South Americans a difficult game. Encouraged by a telephone call from President George W. Bush, the USA beat Mexico 2-0.

18   Ahn Jung-Hwan turns from villain to hero after missing a penalty. He scores in extra time to dump sorry Italy 2-1. Turkey end the dream for Japan.

19   Liverpool home in on Senegal's Salif Diao (Sedan). Perugia sack South Korea's goalscoring hero!

20   Chelsea secure £4.3m club record sponsorship with all;sports. Newcastle pay world record fee for Hugo Viana, 19, from Sporting Lisbon.

21   Owen puts England in front against Brazil, but Rivaldo equalises and Ronaldinho makes it 2-1 before harshly being sent off. Germany, on the rack, managed to beat the Americans 1-0.

22   Spanish fury over two disallowed goals and disbelief after losing on penalties to Korea. Ilhan is Turkey's man-of-the-moment in sudden death demise of Senegal.

23   Franz Beckenbauer says: 'America were the better team.' Nobby Stiles recovering from heart attack sustained on 5 June. Intertoto starts up.

24   Manchester United said to be making £30m bid for Ferdinand. Liverpool hope to add El Hadji Diouf (Lens) another Senegalese for £9.5m. Shaka Hislop follows Foxe and Todorov to Portsmouth from West Ham. AFC Wimbledon, newly formed, join Combined Counties League.

25   Michael Ballack scores, is booked for professional foul and is to miss final. German manager Rudi Voller says: 'He sacrificed himself and should be treated with the highest respect.' The other Wimbledon to stay at Selhurst Park for another year.

26   Ronaldo becomes a 49er – his goal timed then sees off Turkey and though 11-2 at the start of finals, Brazil are 5-2 on. Boston hit by 16 FA charges; hearing on 18 July. Jim Smith is Portsmouth's assistant-manager.

27   Leeds shock: O'Leary sacked. They are £77m in the red. Newcastle sign Titus Bramble from Ipswich for £5m. 'Retired' Marieanne Spacey joins Fulham Ladies from Arsenal.

28   Martin O'Neill and Steve McClaren emerge as the favourites to take over Leeds.

29   Hakan Sukur scores the fastest goal in World Cup finals history 10.8 secs and the second Asian dream fades as South Korea lose third place 3-2.

30   Ronaldo's double gives Brazil the trophy after a better-than expected final with much-criticised Germany playing their part. It is Brazil's fifth trophy. Kahn the winner of the Lev Yashin award spills for the first goal. Belgium win the Fair Play accolade. Terry Venables is the latest Leeds name in the Leeds frame followed by McCarthy and Hiddink.

FOOTBALL AND THE LAW

The Golden Jubilee World Cup Competition found the law had dispelled all fears for its enjoyment off the field, both home and away, during the last season 2001–02. Parliament's Football Spectator Act 1989 amended by the Football (Offences and Disorder) Act 2000 was activated before the games began when the courts imposed banning orders on previously convicted offenders. They were thereby prevented from attending certain domestic football matches and from leaving the country when special occasions such as the World Cup took place. The precedents will apply to all future comparable occasions.

Another High Court decision overturned a local Bristol licensing magistrates court to grant special occasion licences for permitting access to drinking during the unusual hours coinciding with the games outside the conventional European hours. This, too, will be used to benefit special events.

More directly linked to the field of play, Bruce Grobbelaar's libel jury's damages award for alleged corrupt practices for fixing matches was reversed in an unprecedented Court of Appeal decision to have been perverse; but at the time of this report, the highest court in the land at the House of Lords is hearing arguments against that Judgment to restore the original decision.

Another High Court decision which is at the same time being considered by the European Court of Justice which could have wide ranging effect, concerned the attempt by Arsenal to prevent a local trader selling merchandise of comparable Arsenal's symbols. The club failed in its claim that there had been a passing off and also a potential infringement of the Trade Marks Act 1994. The Trade Marks decision will be a landmark for future activities to not only clubs, but also players.

The media coverage of the negotiations for Beckham's image rights when arriving at his contract with Manchester United had echoes of this.

Finally, again to reflect the ongoing involvement with the law, Boston United's promotion from the Conference to the Football League is at present in the public eye because of F.A. charges of alleged irregularities which will have been heard by the time these pages appear.

The Laws of the Game will now never be far from the Laws of the Land.

EDWARD GRAYSON
Founder President, British Association for Sport and the Law.

David Beckham and Ronaldo during the World Cup quarter-final. Beckham's image rights were reported to be at the forefront of his contract negotiations with Manchester United. (Colorsport)

ENGLISH LEAGUE TABLES 2001–02

FA BARCLAYCARD PREMIERSHIP

		P	W	D	L	F	A	W	D	L	F	A	GD	Pts
			Home			**Goals**		**Away**			**Goals**			
1	Arsenal	38	12	4	3	42	25	14	5	0	37	11	43	87
2	Liverpool	38	12	5	2	33	14	12	3	4	34	16	37	80
3	Manchester U	38	11	2	6	40	17	13	3	3	47	28	42	77
4	Newcastle U	38	12	3	4	40	23	9	5	5	34	29	22	71
5	Leeds U	38	9	6	4	31	21	9	6	4	22	16	16	66
6	Chelsea	38	11	4	4	43	21	6	9	4	23	17	28	64
7	West Ham U	38	12	4	3	32	14	3	4	12	16	43	–9	53
8	Aston Villa	38	8	7	4	22	17	4	7	8	24	30	–1	50
9	Tottenham H	38	10	4	5	32	24	4	4	11	17	29	–4	50
10	Blackburn R	38	8	6	5	33	20	4	4	11	22	31	4	46
11	Southampton	38	7	5	7	23	22	5	4	10	23	32	–8	45
12	Middlesbrough	38	7	5	7	23	26	5	4	10	12	21	–12	45
13	Fulham	38	7	7	5	21	16	3	7	9	15	28	–8	44
14	Charlton Ath	38	5	6	8	23	30	5	8	6	15	19	–11	44
15	Everton	38	8	4	7	26	23	3	6	10	19	34	–12	43
16	Bolton W	38	5	7	7	20	31	4	6	9	24	31	–18	40
17	Sunderland	38	7	7	5	18	16	3	3	13	11	35	–22	40
18	Ipswich T	38	6	4	9	20	24	3	5	11	21	40	–23	36
19	Derby Co	38	5	4	10	20	26	3	2	14	13	37	–30	30
20	Leicester C	38	3	7	9	15	34	2	6	11	15	30	–34	28

NATIONWIDE FOOTBALL LEAGUE DIVISION 1

		P	W	D	L	F	A	W	D	L	F	A	GD	Pts
			Home			**Goals**		**Away**			**Goals**			
1	Manchester C	46	19	3	1	63	19	12	3	8	45	33	56	99
2	WBA	46	15	4	4	36	11	12	4	7	25	18	32	89
3	Wolverhampton W	46	13	4	6	33	18	12	7	4	43	25	33	86
4	Millwall	46	15	3	5	43	22	7	8	8	26	26	21	77
5	Birmingham C	46	14	4	5	44	20	7	9	7	26	29	21	76
6	Norwich C	46	15	6	2	36	16	7	3	13	24	35	9	75
7	Burnley	46	11	7	5	39	29	10	5	8	31	33	8	75
8	Preston NE	46	13	7	3	45	21	7	5	11	26	38	12	72
9	Wimbledon	46	9	8	6	30	22	9	5	9	33	35	6	67
10	Crystal Palace	46	13	3	7	42	22	7	3	13	28	40	8	66
11	Coventry C	46	12	4	7	33	19	8	2	13	26	34	6	66
12	Gillingham	46	12	5	6	38	26	6	5	12	26	41	–3	64
13	Sheffield U	46	8	8	7	34	30	7	7	9	19	24	–1	60
14	Watford	46	10	5	8	38	30	6	6	11	24	26	6	59
15	Bradford C	46	10	1	12	41	39	5	9	9	28	37	–7	55
16	Nottingham F	46	7	11	5	26	21	5	7	11	24	30	–1	54
17	Portsmouth	46	9	6	8	36	31	4	8	11	24	41	–12	53
18	Walsall	46	10	6	7	29	27	3	6	14	22	44	–20	51
19	Grimsby T	46	9	7	7	34	28	3	7	13	16	44	–22	50
20	Sheffield W	46	6	7	10	28	37	6	7	10	21	34	–22	50
21	Rotherham U	46	7	13	3	32	29	3	6	14	20	37	–14	49
22	Crewe Alex	46	8	8	7	23	32	4	5	14	24	44	–29	49
23	Barnsley	46	9	9	5	37	33	2	6	15	22	53	–27	48
24	Stockport Co	46	5	1	17	19	44	1	7	15	23	58	–60	26

NATIONWIDE FOOTBALL LEAGUE DIVISION 2

		P	W	D	L	F	A	W	D	L	F	A	GD	Pts
			Home			*Goals*		*Away*			*Goals*			
1	Brighton & HA	46	17	5	1	42	16	8	10	5	24	26	24	90
2	Reading	46	12	7	4	36	20	11	8	4	34	23	27	84
3	Brentford	46	17	5	1	48	12	7	6	10	29	31	34	83
4	Cardiff C	46	12	8	3	39	25	11	6	6	36	25	25	83
5	Stoke C	46	16	4	3	43	12	7	7	9	24	28	27	80
6	Huddersfield T	46	13	7	3	35	19	8	8	7	30	28	18	78
7	Bristol C	46	13	6	4	38	21	8	4	11	30	32	15	73
8	QPR	46	11	10	2	35	18	8	4	11	25	31	11	71
9	Oldham Ath	46	14	6	3	47	27	4	10	9	30	38	12	70
10	Wigan Ath	46	9	6	8	36	23	7	10	6	30	28	15	64
11	Wycombe W	46	13	5	5	38	26	4	8	11	20	38	−6	64
12	Tranmere R	46	10	9	4	39	19	6	6	11	24	41	3	63
13	Swindon T	46	10	7	6	26	21	5	7	11	20	35	−10	59
14	Port Vale	46	11	6	6	35	24	5	4	14	16	38	−11	58
15	Colchester U	46	9	6	8	35	33	6	6	11	30	43	−11	57
16	Blackpool	46	8	9	6	39	31	6	5	12	27	38	−3	56
17	Peterborough U	46	11	5	7	46	26	4	5	14	18	33	5	55
18	Chesterfield	46	9	3	11	35	36	4	10	9	18	29	−12	52
19	Notts Co	46	8	7	8	28	29	5	4	14	31	42	−12	50
20	Northampton T	46	9	4	10	30	33	5	3	15	24	46	−25	49
21	Bournemouth	46	9	4	10	36	33	1	10	12	20	38	−15	44
22	Bury	46	6	9	8	26	32	5	2	16	17	43	−32	44
23	Wrexham	46	7	7	9	29	32	4	3	16	27	57	−33	43
24	Cambridge U	46	7	7	9	29	34	0	6	17	18	59	−46	34

NATIONWIDE FOOTBALL LEAGUE DIVISION 3

		P	W	D	L	F	A	W	D	L	F	A	GD	Pts
			Home			*Goals*		*Away*			*Goals*			
1	Plymouth Arg	46	19	2	2	41	11	12	7	4	30	17	43	102
2	Luton T	46	15	5	3	50	18	15	2	6	46	30	48	97
3	Mansfield T	46	17	3	3	49	24	7	4	12	23	36	12	79
4	Cheltenham T	46	11	11	1	40	20	10	4	9	26	29	17	78
5	Rochdale	46	13	8	2	41	22	8	7	8	24	30	13	78
6	Rushden & Diamonds	46	14	5	4	40	20	6	8	9	29	33	16	73
7	Hartlepool U	46	12	6	5	53	23	8	5	10	21	25	26	71
8	Scunthorpe U	46	14	5	4	43	22	5	9	9	31	34	18	71
9	Shrewsbury T	46	13	4	6	36	19	7	6	10	28	34	11	70
10	Kidderminster H	46	13	6	4	35	17	6	3	14	21	30	9	66
11	Hull C	46	12	6	5	38	18	4	7	12	19	33	6	61
12	Southend U	46	12	5	6	36	22	3	8	12	15	32	−3	58
13	Macclesfield T	46	7	7	9	23	25	8	6	9	18	27	−11	58
14	York C	46	11	5	7	36	20	5	4	14	28	47	−13	57
15	Darlington	46	11	6	6	37	25	4	5	14	23	46	−11	56
16	Exeter C	46	7	9	7	25	32	7	4	12	23	41	−25	55
17	Carlisle U	46	11	5	7	31	21	1	11	11	18	35	−7	52
18	Leyton Orient	46	10	7	6	37	25	3	6	14	18	46	−16	52
19	Torquay U	46	8	6	9	27	31	4	9	10	19	32	−17	51
20	Swansea C	46	7	8	8	26	26	6	4	13	27	51	−24	51
21	Oxford U	46	8	7	8	34	28	3	7	13	19	34	−9	47
22	Lincoln C	46	8	4	11	25	27	2	12	9	19	35	−18	46
23	Bristol R	46	8	7	8	28	28	3	5	15	12	32	−20	45
24	Halifax T	46	5	9	9	24	28	3	3	17	15	56	−45	36

FOOTBALL LEAGUE PLAY-OFFS 2001–02

DIV 1 SEMI-FINALS FIRST LEG

28 APR

Birmingham C (0) 1 *(Hughes B 56)*
Millwall (0) 1 *(Dublin 80)*   28,282
Birmingham C: Vaesen; Kenna, Grainger, Hughes B, Purse, Tebily, Johnson D, Carter, Horsfield, John, Mooney (Lazaridis).
Millwall: Warner; Lawrence, Bull, Cahill, Nethercott, Ward, Ifill, Livermore, Harris (Claridge), Dublin, Reid.

Norwich C (0) 3 *(Rivers 56, McVeigh 73, Mackay 90)*
Wolverhampton W (1) 1 *(Sturridge 22)*   20,127
Norwich C: Green; Kenton, Drury, Mackay, Fleming, Holt, Rivers (Roberts I), Mulryne, McVeigh (Notman), Nielsen (Libbra), Easton.
Wolverhampton W: Oakes; Halle, Camara, Lescott, Butler, Cameron, Newton (Miller), Rae, Blake (Proudlock), Sturridge, Cooper.

DIV 2 SEMI-FINALS FIRST LEG

28 APR

Huddersfield T (0) 0
Brentford (0) 0   16,523
Huddersfield T: Margetson; Moses, Evans, Irons, Ifil, Gray, Thorrington, Holland, Booth, Heary (Hay), Facey.
Brentford: Smith P; Dobson, Anderson, Ingimarsson, Powell, Sidwell, Evans, Rowlands, Owusu, Burgess, Hunt.

Stoke C (0) 1 *(Burton 84)*
Cardiff C (1) 2 *(Earnshaw 12, Fortune-West 59)* 21,245
Stoke C: Cutler; Thomas, Clarke, Handyside, Shtanyuk, Dinning, Gudjonsson (Vandeurzen), O'Connor, Cooke, Iwelumo (Dadason), Goodfellow (Burton).
Cardiff C: Alexander; Weston, Croft, Bonner, Young, Prior, Earnshaw (Campbell), Kavanagh, Fortune-West, Thorne (Collins), Boland.

DIV 3 SEMI-FINALS FIRST LEG

27 APR

Hartlepool U (1) 1 *(Williams E 45)*
Cheltenham T (0) 1 *(Grayson 89)*   7135
Hartlepool U: Williams A; Barron, Robinson (Stephenson), Lee, Westwood, Clarke, Boyd, Humphreys, Williams E, Watson (Henderson), Smith.
Cheltenham T: Book; Griffin, Victory, Lee, Walker, Duff, Finnigan, Devaney (Williams), Alsop, Grayson, Yates.

Rushden & D (1) 2 *(Wardley 34, Butterworth 73)*
Rochdale (1) 2 *(McEvilly 8, Simpson 57)*   6015
Rushden & D: Turley; Mustafa, Underwood, Butterworth, Peters, Tillson, Hall, Wardley, Partridge (Angell), Lowe, Burgess.
Rochdale: Edwards; Evans, Doughty, McLoughlin, Jobson, Griffiths, Flitcroft, McEvilly, Platt (Townson), Oliver, Simpson.

DIV 1 SEMI-FINALS SECOND LEG

1 MAY

Wolverhampton W (0) 1 *(Cooper 77)*
Norwich C (0) 0   27,418
Wolverhampton W: Oakes; Halle (Miller), Camara, Lescott, Butler, Cameron, Newton (Kennedy), Rae, Blake, Sturridge, Cooper.
Norwich C: Green; Kenton, Drury, Mackay, Fleming, Holt, Rivers (Sutch), Mulryne, McVeigh (Notman), Nielsen (Roberts I), Easton.
Norwich C won 3-2 on aggregate.

2 MAY

Millwall (0) 0
Birmingham C (0) 1 *(John 90)*   16,391
Millwall: Warner; Lawrence, Bull, Cahill, Nethercott, Ward, Ifill, Livermore, Claridge, Dublin, Reid.
Birmingham C: Vaesen; Kenna, Grainger, Hughes B, Purse, Vickers, Devlin, Tebily, Horsfield (Johnson A), John, Mooney (Lazaridis).
Birmingham C won 2-1 on aggregate.

Stoke City's 2-0 win over Brentford in the Nationwide Division Two play-off final was the first time in 12 attempts that the team allocated the South Stand changing rooms at the Millennium Stadium had been victorious. (Actionimages)

Birmingham City players begin their promotion celebration after a penalty shoot-out win over Norwich City in the Nationwide Division One play-off final. (Actionimages)

DIV 2 SEMI-FINALS SECOND LEG

1 MAY

Brentford (1) 2 *(Powell 14, Owusu 46)*
Huddersfield T (1) 1 *(Booth 2)*　　11,191
Brentford: Smith P; Dobson, Anderson, Ingimarsson, Powell, Sidwell, Evans, Rowlands (O'Connor), Owusu, Burgess (Boxall), Hunt.
Huddersfield T: Margetson; Evans, Jenkins, Irons, Ifil, Gray, Thorrington, Holland, Booth, Heary (Hay), Facey.
Brentford won 2-1 on aggregate.

Cardiff C (0) 0
Stoke C (0) 2 *(O'Connor 90, Oulare 115)*　　19,367
Cardiff C: Alexander; Weston, Croft, Bonner (Maxwell), Young, Prior, Earnshaw (Campbell), Kavanagh, Fortune-West, Thorne (Bowen), Boland.
Stoke C: Cutler; Thomas, Clarke, Handyside, Shtanyuk, Dinning (Van Deurzen), Gudjonsson, O'Connor, Burton, Gunnlaugsson (Cooke), Iwelumo (Oulare).
aet; Stoke C won 3-2 on aggregate.

DIV 3 SEMI-FINALS SECOND LEG

30 APR

Cheltenham T (1) 1 *(Williams 26)*
Hartlepool U (1) 1 *(Arnison 17)*　　7165
Cheltenham T: Book; Griffin, Victory, Williams (Devaney), Walker, Duff, Finnigan, Milton (Lee), Alsop, Naylor (Grayson), Yates.
Hartlepool U: Williams A; Barron, Arnison, Lee, Westwood, Clarke, Humphreys, Stephenson, Williams E (Henderson), Watson, Smith.
aet; Cheltenham T won 5-4 on penalties.

Rochdale (0) 1 *(Peters 65 (og))*
Rushden & D (0) 2 *(Lowe 67, Hall 76)*　　8547
Rochdale: Edwards; Evans, Doughty, McLoughlin, Jobson (Coleman), Griffiths, Flitcroft (McCourt), Townson (Connor), McEvilly, Oliver, Simpson.
Rushden & D: Turley; Mustafa, Underwood (Gray), Butterworth, Peters, Tillson, Hall, Wardley, Partridge, Lowe, Burgess.
Rushden & D won 4-3 on aggregate.

DIV 3 FINAL

(at Millennium Stadium)

6 MAY

Cheltenham T (1) 3 *(Devaney 27, Alsop 49, Finnigan 80)*
Rushden & D (1) 1 *(Hall 28)*　　24,368
Cheltenham T: Book; Griffin, Victory, Williams, Walker, Duff, Finnigan, Devaney (Grayson), Alsop, Naylor, Yates.
Rushden & D: Turley; Mustafa, Underwood, Butterworth, Peters, Tillson, Hall, Wardley, Partridge (Angell), Lowe, Gray (Brady).

DIV 2 FINAL

(at Millennium Stadium)

11 MAY

Brentford (0) 0
Stoke C (2) 2 *(Burton 16, Burgess 45 (og))*　　42,523
Brentford: Smith P; Dobson, Anderson, Ingimarsson, Powell, Sidwell, Evans, Rowlands (O'Connor), Owusu, Burgess (McCammon), Hunt.
Stoke C: Cutler; Thomas, Clarke, Handyside, Shtanyuk, Dinning (Brightwell), Gudjonsson, O'Connor, Burton, Gunnlaugsson (Van Deurzen), Iwelumo (Cooke).

DIV 1 FINAL

(at Millennium Stadium)

12 MAY

Birmingham C (0) 1 *(Horsfield 102)*
Norwich C (0) 1 *(Roberts I 91)*　　71,597
Birmingham C: Vaesen; Kenna, Grainger, Hughes B, Vickers (Carter), Johnson M, Devlin, Tebily, Horsfield (Johnson A), John, Mooney (Lazaridis).
Norwich C: Green; Kenton, Drury, Mackay, Fleming, Holt, Rivers (Notman), Mulryne, McVeigh (Sutch), Nielsen (Roberts I), Easton.
aet; Birmingham C won 4-2 on penalties.

LEADING GOALSCORERS 2001–02

FA BARCLAYCARD PREMIERSHIP	League	FA Cup	Worthington Cup	Other	Total
Thierry Henry (Arsenal)	24	1	0	7	32
Ruud Van Nistelrooy (Manchester U)	23	2	0	11	36
Jimmy Floyd Hasselbaink (Chelsea)	23	3	3	0	29
Alan Shearer (Newcastle U)	23	2	2	0	27
Michael Owen (Liverpool)	19	2	0	6	27
Ole Gunnar Solskjaer (Manchester U)	17	1	0	7	25
Robbie Fowler (Leeds U)	15	0	0	1	16
(including 3 League goals and 1 European Cup goal for Liverpool)					
Eidur Gudjohnsen (Chelsea)	14	3	3	3	23
Marian Pahars (Southampton)	14	1	1	0	16
Frederik Ljungberg (Arsenal)	12	2	0	3	17
Michael Ricketts (Bolton W)	12	1	2	0	15
Juan Angel (Aston Villa)	12	0	0	2	14
James Beattie (Southampton)	12	0	2	0	14
Darius Vassell (Aston Villa)	12	0	0	0	12
Mark Viduka (Leeds U)	11	1	1	3	16
David Beckham (Manchester U)	11	0	0	5	16
Jason Euell (Charlton Ath)	11	1	1	0	13
Kevin Phillips (Sunderland)	11	1	1	0	13
Frederic Kanoute (West Ham U)	11	1	0	0	12

NATIONWIDE DIVISION 1					
Shaun Goater (Manchester C)	28	2	2	0	32
Clint Morrison (Crystal Palace)	22	0	2	0	24
Darren Huckerby (Manchester C)	20	1	5	0	26
Stern John (Birmingham C)	20	0	1	1	22
(Including 13 League goals and 1 Worthington Cup goal for Nottingham F)					
Doug Freedman (Crystal Palace)	20	0	1	0	21
Dean Sturridge (Wolverhampton W)	20	0	0	1	21
Peter Crouch (Portsmouth)	18	0	1	0	19
David Connolly (Wimbledon)	18	0	0	0	18
Marlon King (Gillingham)	17	1	2	0	20
Steve Claridge (Millwall)	17	0	1	0	18
Gareth Taylor (Burnley)	16	0	0	0	16
Mark Robins (Rotherham U)	15	0	1	0	16
Bruce Dyer (Barnsley)	14	1	3	0	18
Richard Sadlier (Millwall)	14	2	1	0	17
Lee Hughes (Coventry C)	14	0	0	0	14
Eoin Jess (Bradford C)	14	0	0	0	14
Richard Cresswell (Preston NE)	13	2	1	0	16
Tommy Mooney (Birmingham C)	13	0	2	0	15
Iwan Roberts (Norwich C)	13	0	0	1	14
Tim Cahill (Millwall)	13	0	0	0	13
Marcelo (Walsall)	13	0	0	0	13
(including 12 League goals for Birmingham C)					

NATIONWIDE DIVISION 2					
Bobby Zamora (Brighton & HA)	28	2	2	0	32
Andy Thomson (QPR)	21	0	0	0	21
Lloyd Owusu (Brentford)	20	0	1	1	22
Danny Allsopp (Notts Co)	19	2	4	3	28
Nicky Forster (Reading)	19	0	0	0	19
Leon McKenzie (Peterborough U)	18	1	0	1	20
Andy Liddell (Wigan Ath)	18	0	0	0	18
Ben Burgess (Brentford)	17	1	0	0	18
Jamie Forrester (Northampton T)	17	0	1	0	18
Tony Thorpe (Bristol C)	16	0	1	1	18
Leon Knight (Huddersfield T (on loan))	16	1	0	0	17
Lee Peacock (Bristol C)	15	0	0	2	17
Jamie Cureton (Reading)	15	1	0	0	16
Scott McGleish (Colchester U)	15	1	0	0	16
Simon Haworth (Tranmere R)	15	0	1	0	16
(including 10 League goals and 1 Worthington Cup goal for Wigan Ath)					
Stuart Barlow (Tranmere R)	14	1	2	0	17
Paul Evans (Brentford)	14	0	0	0	14

NATIONWIDE DIVISION 3					
Steve Howard (Luton T)	24	0	0	0	24
Luke Rodgers (Shrewsbury T)	22	0	0	0	22
Chris Greenacre (Mansfield T)	21	5	2	0	28
Julian Alsop (Cheltenham T)	20	4	0	2	26
Onandi Lowe (Rushden & D)	19	0	0	1	20
Gordon Watson (Hartlepool U)	18	0	0	0	18
Gary Alexander (Hull C)	17	2	1	3	23
Nathan Ellington (Bristol R)	15	4	0	2	21
Ian Clark (Darlington)	15	0	0	0	15
(including 2 League goals for Hartlepool U)					
Dean Crowe (Luton T)	15	0	0	0	15
Richie Foran (Carlisle U)	14	1	0	1	16
Kevin Townson (Rochdale)	14	0	0	1	15
Michael Proctor (York C (on loan))	14	0	0	0	14
Martin Carruthers (Scunthorpe U)	13	3	0	1	17
Steve Torpey (Scunthorpe U)	13	0	0	2	15
Paul Moody (Oxford U)	13	0	0	0	13
Lee Nogan (York C)	13	0	0	0	13
Lee Thorpe (Lincoln C)	13	0	0	0	13

Other matches consist of European games, LDV Vans Trophy, Charity Shield and Football League play-offs. Only goals scored in the respective divisions count in the table. Players listed in order of League goals total.

REVIEW OF THE SEASON

Arsenal's League and Cup double dominated the domestic scene and their race to the championship had the pages of the record books overturning, time and again. Thirteen consecutive wins, unbeaten away and scoring in every Premiership match, their last League defeat was 3-1 at home to Newcastle on 18 December, a fixture they might well have found themselves well behind in during its early stages. They made no mistakes after this one.

With squad systems in operation in the Premier League, it was no surprise that Arsenal used 25 players, none of whom reached ever-present stage. Patrick Vieira with 36 appearances came closest and Thierry Henry with 24 goals was the Gunners' leading scorer. Again with the nucleus of many of the French national team, one of their number Robert Pires was voted Football Writers' Association Footballer of the Year.–

The FA Cup also came to Highbury after an all-London final against Chelsea and the only disappointment for Arsenal was in the quiet exit from the Champions League, which might have proved a blessing in view of their subsequent home achievements.

Liverpool pipped Manchester United for runners-up position and they, too, had a useful run-in at the end, losing only one of their last 17. Though they took only one point off Arsenal, they again did the double over Manchester United.

Third place was unusual in Premiership terms for the Old Trafford club who never recovered from an erratic start in which they sometimes looked unbeatable, on other occasions inept. Much speculation as to the cause, not the least the fact that Sir Alex Ferguson took a while to decide to continue at the helm after the end of the season.

In Ruud Van Nistelrooy, their Dutch striker they unearthed a good one, having waited a year for the player to recover full fitness. He was amply rewarded by being voted Player of the Year by his peers.

On 8 December they were as low as ninth before responding with eight consecutive wins. Half a dozen points below them came Newcastle for whom Bobby Robson earned a knighthood for his longevity in the game. Around Christmas they were even top and stayed on well for their fourth place.

Unbeaten in their opening 11 matches, Leeds' season was marred by off the field events and they had to settle for fifth place.

Chelsea were inconsistent as ever in the League. Their 4-0 win over Liverpool was probably the high spot, but they did manage to reach the FA Cup final where they were badly served by injuries, before and during the encounter with Arsenal.

Seventh place seemed a high ideal for West Ham for most of the season when they were occasionally ill-served by a leaky defence, while a few more wins out of their 14 drawn affairs would have pushed Aston Villa into a more challenging team.

Three wins in a row in October was the best sequence enjoyed by Tottenham who were more than disappointed by losing to Blackburn in the Worthington Cup final.

Silvain Wiltord moves away from Mikael Silvestre. Arsenal moved away from Manchester United to claim their second double in five years. (ASP)

Rushden and Diamonds defender Paul Underwood battles for possession during the Nationwide Division Three play-off final defeat at the hands of Cheltenham Town. (Actionimages)

Rovers for their part found their cup exploits helped towards improved Premier League performances. They did beat West Ham 7-1 in October, but found further wins of any description difficult to obtain until late on.

Southampton in their new home struggled to win there and it was late November before the first arrived. Subsequently they improved enough to stay out of trouble.

Goalscoring was a problem for Middlesbrough from mid-November to Boxing Day with only one goal in six matches, yet but for losing their last four, they could have finished much higher.

Fulham who had spent lavishly for their first season in the top bracket were consolidating nicely until only two points came from a possible 27 from mid-February. Eighth place at the turn of the year was the best for Charlton, but they, too, tailed off at the end with no wins in the last eight.

A change of manager at Everton pulled them to safety after mid-February being two off the bottom. David Moyes from Preston certainly turned things round. Yet Bolton, top in September, gradually slid down the table and at one time had gone 12 games without a win.

Sunderland had to wait until the last day of the season to be sure of survival after just isolated victories had kept them afloat. However, not so fortunate were Ipswich, Derby and Leicester.

Yet Ipswich after just one win in the first 17 seemed to have found the right formula with seven wins out of eight, before they won only one other fixture. Derby were one off the cellar from January and their eight wins were spaced apart. For Leicester, 16 games without a win condemned them to the inevitable early in the New Year.

In the First Division, Manchester City achieved the remarkable feat of equalling their record of goalscoring with 108. They just missed out on a century of points, too. Second half of the campaign clusters of wins kept the momentum going well.

West Bromwich joined them in automatic promotion, thanks to a mean defence which let in only 29 goals. They had 24 clean sheets. Fellow midlanders Birmingham came through the play-offs after finishing fifth. Their fine second half of the season was the prime factor.

Once more Wolves failed to clinch it, despite third place. Only one win in the last four enabled Albion to overtake them for the automatic place and Norwich beat them in the play-offs. Millwall lost to Birmingham at this stage.

Norwich had come with a gallop at the closure, unbeaten in seven while Millwall were not far behind in the finish, not losing in the last five.

Burnley missed out on goal difference after heading the table for much of the middle part of the season. Preston, too, were disappointed Lancastrians, as high as fourth in November.

Wimbledon were ruled out of anything better by losing their last three matches and stable companions Crystal Palace had a poor second half of the season to finish a point behind the Dons.

Coventry took only one point from their last seven matches but Gillingham looked a better balanced outfit after the turn of the year. Sheffield United were middle of the table throughout, their best spell being eight games without defeat.

Expectations rarely materialized at Watford, though the defence at times looked pretty solid. Bradford were off to a flier, but settled down to mid-table and too many drawn games kept Nottingham Forest from leaping ahead.

Eight games without a win for Portsmouth was a sad end to events at Fratton Park, but undefeated in the last five, Walsall escaped the drop in dramatic fashion. Grimsby 23rd even in late February, also hauled themselves up.

In Sheffield Wednesday's case it was a more steady pull out of trouble, but draw champions Rotherham needed goal difference to save them, and they failed to win any of the last ten.

The relegation trio consisted of Crewe, Barnsley and Stockport. Crewe after many years of staying in the First Division had gone eleven games without a win when they played their last game with Rotherham needing a cricket score to survive. They won 2-0.

Twelve unbeaten games mid-season should have been of benefit to Barnsley but they drifted away and Stockport took only two points from a run of 17 matches.

In Division Two the Brighton story continued in successful vein with another title. They also set a club record for the fewest defeats with only six losses and stuttered only briefly from late December.

Reading squeezed into the automatic promotion place at the expense of Brentford, the two meeting on the last day at Griffin Park, with Reading needing just a point which they managed in a 1-1 draw, their ninth such in the last ten matches. Just two wins in a run of 12 matches mid-way through the season had hampered Brentford's challenge.

An unbeaten 13-game run at the season's end shot Cardiff into the play-offs, but having apparently achieved the difficult task of winning at Stoke, they lost at home in extra time. Stoke had been top on 15 December, but suffered in-an-out form later. To add a touch of irony, they beat Brentford in the final at Cardiff!

Huddersfield had slipped up at the end of the campaign with only one win in the last six when first time promotion was still on the agenda, but Bristol City never maintained their useful start.

Queens Park Rangers were fifth half-way through but were unable to sustain anything more substantial, while Oldham were even top of the table at the end of September.

Tenth place in the final reckoning was the best achieved by Wigan all season, in what was merely a gentle improvement, but play-off possibilities dimmed for Wycombe after the turn of the year.

Only three wins out of the last 19 matches confined Tranmere to 12th position and two in 13 did the same for Swindon from an earlier run. The eight games without defeat for Port Vale to late February gave rise to expectations, but only one win followed.

Colchester began with a stunning 6-3 win at Chesterfield, won the second game, then did not manage two in a row afterwards. A mid-season collapse took the edge off Blackpool's efforts, but they did take the LDV Vans Trophy back to Bloomfield Road.

Two consecutive wins in the middle of 20 matches without any other successes said it all for Peterborough and three consecutive wins on two occasions was the high spot of Chesterfield's season.

From late September to the end of February, there were just two victories for Notts County and the heady heights of 19th was the pinnacle of Northampton's campaign.

The relegation quartet proved to be Bournemouth, Bury, Wrexham and Cambridge. Bournemouth had one win from November to March, Bury eight consecutive defeats after the first win and Wrexham were never out of the bottom four from September. Seven wins in total and never off the bottom from mid-January was the tale at Cambridge, who did however reach the LDV Vans Trophy final.

Making his first start of the season in March, Newcastle's Carl Cort is challenged by Liverpool's Sami Hyypia and Danny Murphy. Two goals from Murphy helped Liverpool to a 3-1 victory. (Actionimages)

Record-breaking Plymouth boasted the best defence in the country, conceding only 28 goals. Their total of 102 points equalled the record for the bottom division and set a new one for the Third Division. They had 27 clean sheets.

Luton did well to cling on to the champions tail, were well clear by 18 points of third place and with thirteen wins and a draw from the run-in finished in fine style.

Mansfield had to be on their toes at the end after a couple of heavy defeats threatened to derail their aims. But they duly beat Carlisle 2-0 on the last day. This scuppered Cheltenham's hopes, beaten by the same scoreline at Plymouth. It was the play-offs for them. Sixteen unbeaten matches had put them well in contention in the New Year.

Rochdale also missed out on promotion having finished fifth. They were never able to put together too many sequences without a defeat spoiling it, but Rushden adjusted to the Third Division after a slow start.

Hartlepool edged out Scunthorpe from the final play-off position, by a better goals against record than their rivals. So it was to be Cheltenham ousting Hartlepool and Rushden surprising Rochdale, leaving two of the newest members to fight out the remaining promotion berth. It was Cheltenham 3-1 over Rushden. In fact Hartlepool had had one win in the first nine, Scunthorpe two in the opening ten.

Shrewsbury were never out of the top nine after the early stages, but failed to capitalize on the situation and it was the 15th League game before Kidderminster managed more than the one goal they had scored in any of the previous fixtures.

All-change Hull with a host of new signings were still third in December, but suffered badly thereafter and Southend only once managed two successive wins. A marked second half of the season recovery helped goal-shy Macclesfield.

Goalscoring was a problem for York. They registered five in one run of nine matches and neighbouring Darlington had one run of eight and another of ten games without a win. Exeter recovered from a poor beginning but spoiled it with just one win in the last eleven.

Bottom in November, Carlisle hauled themselves up, but Leyton Orient ruined their chances with a spell of no wins in eleven outings as did Torquay who finished just a point below them.

Swansea had 18 games without a goal and Oxford assembled only one point from the last six matches. Lincoln failed to win any of their last eleven and Bristol Rovers had two disastrous spells, one in which a solitary goal came from eleven games, another with five goals in a similar sequence.

Back to the Conference for a second time went Halifax stuck on the foot of the table from December and nine points worse off than Rovers. Replacing them came Boston United who start with a four-point handicap.

Referee Graham Poll is called into action as Tottenham's Les Ferdinand and Blackburn's Henning Berg wrestle during the Worthington Cup Final at the Millennium Stadium. Poll was to be the English representative in the World Cup finals in Japan and South Korea. (Actionimages)

INTRODUCTION TO THE CLUB SECTION

This year's Rothmans Football Yearbook again features the who's who style players directory which incorporates the total of appearances and goals for each player as in earlier editions but, additionally, features more personal information and a season-by-season account of the individual player's record. It is again featured in A to Z form for easy reference (see pages 426 to 560). There is also each club's full record in the previous ten seasons and the latest sequences recorded for wins, draws and defeats, etc.

The club section again comprises four pages as last year, the first two feature new entries in the 'It's a fact!' and 'Did you know?' series. Record transfer fees are usually left to the discretion of the club concerned.

The third and fourth pages of this section present a complete record of the League season, including date, venue, opponents, results, half-time score, League position, goalscorers, attendances and complete line-ups including substitutes where used, for every League game in the 2001–02 season. Again goal times have been added, though not official they give an indication of when goals were scored. These appear as superior figures [10, 20, 30].

Squad numbers have not been included; those used are the familiar ones, 1–11 while the introduction of a third outfield substitute has been recognised as follows:- the first substitute No. 12, the second No. 13 and the third No. 14. However, if there is a substitute goalkeeper he is represented by No. 15 but *only* if he replaces the first choice goalkeeper. Otherwise he adopts one of the other three substitute numbers, as there have been several instances where a goalkeeper has been used as an outfield player because of injuries during the game. Players replaced are respectively noted with superior figures [1], [2], [3] and [g] for goalkeeper. These third and fourth pages also include consolidated lists of goalscorers for the club in League, Worthington Cup and FA Cup matches plus a summary of results in these two main domestic competitions.

The continued increase in the number of matches played on Sundays has resulted in the League positions shown after every League result being taken on that day. Full holiday programmes are also recorded, but the position after mid-week fixtures will not normally have been updated. Attendance figures quoted for the Nationwide Football League are those which appeared in the Press at the time. But those in the FA Carling Premiership are official. The attendance statistics published on pages 587–588 are those officially issued by the FA Premier League but not the Football League at the end of the season.

In the totals at the top of each column on page 4, substitute appearances are listed separately by the '+', but have been amalgamated in the totals which feature in the players historical section in the directory mentioned above. Thus these appearances include those as substitute. In fact the directory again features those names appearing on the FA Premier League and Football League's Retained list, which is published at the end of May. Each player's height and weight where known, plus birth place, birth date and source together with total League goals and appearances for each club he has represented, can be found as in previous editions. The player's details remain under the club which retained him at the end of the season. An asterisk '*' by a player's name indicates that he was given a free transfer at the end of the 2001–02 season, a dagger '†' against a name means that he is a non-contract player, a double dagger '‡' indicates that the player's registration was cancelled during the season and a section mark '§' shows the player to be a trainee or associated schoolboy who has made League appearances. The symbol # indicates players aged 24 and over who are out of contract but who were offered re-engagement by their clubs. Appearances by players in the play-offs are not included in their career totals. International appearances for foreign players reflect latest information available.

ARSENAL   FA Premiership

FOUNDATION

Formed by workers at the Royal Arsenal, Woolwich in 1886, they began as Dial Square (name of one of the workshops), and included two former Nottingham Forest players, Fred Beardsley and Morris Bates. Beardsley wrote to his old club seeking help and they provided the new club with a full set of red jerseys and a ball. The club became known as the 'Woolwich Reds' although their official title soon after formation was Woolwich Arsenal.

Arsenal Stadium, Highbury, London N5 1BU.

Telephone: (020) 7704 4000. **Fax:** (020) 7704 4001.
Box Office: (020) 7704 4040. **Commercial & Marketing:** (020) 7704 4100. **Recorded Information:** (020) 7704 4242.

Ground Capacity: 38,500 all seated.

Record Attendance: 73,295 v Sunderland, Div 1, 9 March 1935.

At Wembley: 73,455 v Panathinaikos, European Cup Group E, 30 September 1998.

Record Receipts: £902,000 v Everton, FA Barclaycard Premiership, 11 May, 2002.

Pitch Measurements: 110yd x 73yd.

Life President: Sir Robert Bellinger GBE, D.SC.
Chairman: P. D. Hill-Wood. **Vice-chairman:** D. Dein.
Directors: R. G. Gibbs, C. E. B. L. Carr, R. C. L. Carr, D. D. Fiszman, K. J. Friar.

Managing Director: K. Edelman.

Manager: Arsène Wenger.

Assistant Manager: Pat Rice.

First Team Coach: Boro Primorac.

Head Youth Coach: Don Howe.

Head of Youth Development: Liam Brady.

Physio: Gary Lewin.

Reserve Coach: Eddie Niedzwiecki.

Company Secretary: David Miles.

Commercial Manager: John Hazell.

Stadium Manager: John Beattie.

Colours: Red shirts with white sleeves, white shorts, white socks with red trim.

Change Colours: Light blue shirts with navy sleeves and red trim, navy shorts and socks with red trim.

Year Formed: 1886.

Turned Professional: 1891.

Ltd Co: 1893.

HONOURS

FA Premier League: Champions 1997–98, 2001–02. Runners-up 1998–99, 1999–2000, 2000–01.

Football League: Division 1 – Champions 1930–31, 1932–33, 1933–34, 1934–35, 1937–38, 1947–48, 1952–53, 1970–71, 1988–89, 1990–91; Runners-up 1925–26, 1931–32, 1972–73; Division 2 – Runners-up 1903–04.

FA Cup: Winners 1930, 1936, 1950, 1971, 1979, 1993, 1998, 2002; Runners-up 1927, 1932, 1952, 1972, 1978, 1980, 2001.

Double performed: 1970–71, 1997–98, 2001–02.

Football League Cup: Winners 1987, 1993; Runners-up 1968, 1969, 1988.

European Competitions: Fairs Cup: 1963–64, 1969–70 (winners), 1970–71. *European Cup:* 1971–72, 1991–92, 1998–99, 1999–2000, 2000–01, 2001–02. *UEFA Cup:* 1978–79, 1981–82, 1982–83, 1996–97, 1997–98, 1999–2000 (runners-up). *European Cup-Winners' Cup:* 1979–80 (runners-up), 1993–94 (winners), 1994–95 (runners-up).

IT'S A FACT !

On 29 September 2001, Arsène Wenger celebrated his fifth anniversary as Arsenal manager in a 2-0 win at Derby County. Seventeen years earlier to the day, the club had gone top after a 2-1 win at Coventry City.

Previous Names: 1886, Dial Square; 1886, Royal Arsenal; 1891, Woolwich Arsenal; 1914 Arsenal.

Club Nickname: 'Gunners'.

Previous Grounds: 1886, Plumstead Common; 1887, Sportsman Ground; 1888, Manor Ground; 1890, Invicta Ground; 1893, Manor Ground; 1913, Highbury.

First Football League Game: 2 September 1893, Division 2, v Newcastle U (h) D 2–2 – Williams; Powell, Jeffrey; Devine, Buist, Howat; Gemmell, Henderson, Shaw (1), Elliott (1), Booth.

Record League Victory: 12–0 v Loughborough T, Division 2, 12 March 1900 – Orr; McNichol, Jackson; Moir, Dick (2), Anderson (1); Hunt, Cottrell (2), Main (2), Gaudie (3), Tennant (2).

Record Cup Victory: 11–1 v Darwen, FA Cup 3rd rd, 9 January 1932 – Moss; Parker, Hapgood; Jones, Roberts, John; Hulme (2), Jack (3), Lambert (2), James, Bastin (4).

Record Defeat: 0–8 v Loughborough T, Division 2, 12 December 1896.

Most League Points (2 for a win): 66, Division 1, 1930–31.

Most League Points (3 for a win): 87, Premier League 2001–02.

Most League Goals: 127, Division 1, 1930–31.

Highest League Scorer in Season: Ted Drake, 42, 1934–35.

Most League Goals in Total Aggregate: Cliff Bastin, 150, 1930–47.

Most League Goals in One Match: 7, Ted Drake v Aston Villa, Division 1, 14 December 1935.

Most Capped Player: Kenny Sansom, 77 (86), England, 1981–88.

Most League Appearances: David O'Leary, 558, 1975–93.

Youngest League Player: Gerry Ward, 16 years 321 days v Huddersfield T, 22 August 1953 (Jermaine Pennant, 16 years 319 days v Middlesbrough, League Cup, 30 November 1999).

Record Transfer Fee Received: A reported £22,900,000 from Real Madrid for Nicolas Anelka, August 1999.

Record Transfer Fee Paid: A reported £11,000,000 to Bordeaux for Sylvain Wiltord, August 2000.

Football League Record: 1893 Elected to Division 2; 1904–13 Division 1; 1913–19 Division 2; 1919–92 Division 1; 1992– FA Premier League.

LATEST SEQUENCES

Longest Sequence of League Wins: 13, 10.2.02 – 11.5.02 (continuing).

Longest Sequence of League Defeats: 7, 12.2.77 – 12.3.77.

Longest Sequence of League Draws: 6, 4.3.61 – 1.4.61.

Longest Sequence of Unbeaten League Matches: 26, 28.4.90 – 19.1.91.

Longest Sequence Without a League Win: 23, 28.9.12 – 1.3.13.

MANAGERS

Sam Hollis 1894–97
Tom Mitchell 1897–98
George Elcoat 1898–99
Harry Bradshaw 1899–1904
Phil Kelso 1904–08
George Morrell 1908–15
Leslie Knighton 1919–25
Herbert Chapman 1925–34
George Allison 1934–47
Tom Whittaker 1947–56
Jack Crayston 1956–58
George Swindin 1958–62
Billy Wright 1962–66
Bertie Mee 1966–76
Terry Neill 1976–83
Don Howe 1984–86
George Graham 1986–95
Bruce Rioch 1995–96
Arsène Wenger September 1996–

TEN YEAR LEAGUE RECORD

		P	W	D	L	F	A	Pts	Pos
1991-92	Div 1	42	19	15	8	81	46	72	4
1992-93	PR Lge	42	15	11	16	40	38	56	10
1993-94	PR Lge	42	18	17	7	53	28	71	4
1994-95	PR Lge	42	13	12	17	52	49	51	12
1995-96	PR Lge	38	17	12	9	49	32	63	5
1996-97	PR Lge	38	19	11	8	62	32	68	3
1997-98	PR Lge	38	23	9	6	68	33	78	1
1998-99	PR Lge	38	22	12	4	59	17	78	2
1999-2000	PR Lge	38	22	7	9	73	43	73	2
2000-01	PR Lge	38	20	10	8	63	38	70	2

DID YOU KNOW ?

There were Premier League records for Arsenal in 2001–02: they scored in every League game and had 13 consecutive wins. In addition the Gunners were unbeaten away (last achieved 1888–89 by Preston North End).

ARSENAL 2001–02 LEAGUE RECORD

Match No.	Date	Venue	Opponents	Result	H/T Score	Lg. Pos.	Goalscorers	Attendance
1	Aug 18	A	Middlesbrough	W 4-0	1-0	—	Henry [43], Pires (pen) [87], Bergkamp 2 [88, 90]	31,557
2	21	H	Leeds U	L 1-2	1-1	—	Wiltord [32]	38,062
3	25	H	Leicester C	W 4-0	2-0	3	Ljungberg [17], Wiltord [28], Henry [77], Kanu [90]	37,909
4	Sept 8	A	Chelsea	D 1-1	1-1	4	Henry [17]	40,883
5	15	A	Fulham	W 3-1	1-0	2	Ljungberg [17], Henry [82], Bergkamp [90]	20,805
6	22	H	Bolton W	D 1-1	0-0	3	Jeffers [74]	38,014
7	29	A	Derby Co	W 2-0	1-0	2	Henry 2 (1 pen) [21, 63 (p)]	29,200
8	Oct 13	A	Southampton	W 2-0	1-0	2	Pires [5], Henry [74]	29,759
9	20	H	Blackburn R	D 3-3	0-1	2	Pires [48], Bergkamp [53], Henry [78]	38,108
10	27	A	Sunderland	D 1-1	1-0	3	Kanu [40]	45,989
11	Nov 4	H	Charlton Ath	L 2-4	1-2	5	Henry 2 (1 pen) [7, 60 (p)]	38,010
12	17	A	Tottenham H	D 1-1	0-0	5	Pires [81]	36,066
13	25	H	Manchester U	W 3-1	0-1	3	Ljungberg [48], Henry 2 [80, 85]	38,174
14	Dec 1	A	Ipswich T	W 2-0	1-0	2	Ljungberg [5], Henry (pen) [56]	24,631
15	9	H	Aston Villa	W 3-2	0-2	2	Wiltord [46], Henry 2 [72, 90]	38,074
16	15	A	West Ham U	D 1-1	1-1	2	Cole [39]	34,523
17	18	H	Newcastle U	L 1-3	1-0	—	Pires [20]	38,012
18	23	A	Liverpool	W 2-1	1-0	2	Henry (pen) [45], Ljungberg [53]	44,297
19	26	H	Chelsea	W 2-1	0-1	2	Campbell [49], Wiltord [71]	38,079
20	29	H	Middlesbrough	W 2-1	0-1	1	Pires [55], Cole [80]	37,928
21	Jan 13	H	Liverpool	D 1-1	0-0	4	Ljungberg [62]	38,132
22	20	A	Leeds U	D 1-1	1-1	4	Pires [45]	40,143
23	23	A	Leicester C	W 3-1	2-0	—	Van Bronckhorst [33], Henry [43], Wiltord [90]	21,344
24	30	A	Blackburn R	W 3-2	2-2	—	Bergkamp 2 [14, 75], Henry [21]	25,983
25	Feb 2	H	Southampton	D 1-1	1-0	4	Wiltord [40]	38,024
26	10	A	Everton	W 1-0	0-0	4	Wiltord [62]	30,859
27	23	H	Fulham	W 4-1	3-1	3	Lauren [5], Vieira [15], Henry 2 [38, 59]	38,029
28	Mar 2	A	Newcastle U	W 2-0	2-0	2	Bergkamp [11], Campbell [41]	52,087
29	5	H	Derby Co	W 1-0	0-0	—	Pires [69]	37,898
30	17	A	Aston Villa	W 2-1	1-0	2	Edu [15], Pires [60]	41,520
31	30	H	Sunderland	W 3-0	3-0	3	Vieira [2], Bergkamp [4], Wiltord [30]	38,047
32	Apr 1	A	Charlton Ath	W 3-0	3-0	1	Henry 2 [16, 25], Ljungberg [21]	26,336
33	6	H	Tottenham H	W 2-1	1-0	1	Ljungberg [24], Lauren (pen) [86]	38,186
34	21	H	Ipswich T	W 2-0	0-0	1	Ljungberg 2 [68, 78]	38,058
35	24	H	West Ham U	W 2-0	0-0	—	Ljungberg [77], Kanu [80]	38,038
36	29	A	Bolton W	W 2-0	2-0	—	Ljungberg [36], Wiltord [44]	27,351
37	May 8	A	Manchester U	W 1-0	0-0	—	Wiltord [57]	67,580
38	11	H	Everton	W 4-3	2-2	1	Bergkamp [4], Henry 2 [33, 72], Jeffers [83]	38,240

Final League Position: 1

GOALSCORERS

League (79): Henry 24 (4 pens), Ljungberg 12, Wiltord 10, Bergkamp 9, Pires 9 (1 pen), Kanu 3, Campbell 2, Cole 2, Jeffers 2, Lauren 2 (1 pen), Vieira 2, Edu 1, Van Bronckhorst 1.
Worthington Cup (6): Wiltord 4 (1 pen), Edu 1, Kanu 1 (pen).
FA Cup (17): Bergkamp 3, Kanu 2, Ljungberg 2, Parlour 2, Wiltord 2, Adams 1, Campbell 1, Edu 1, Henry 1, Pires 1, own goal 1.

Seaman D 17	Lauren E 27	Cole A 29	Vieira P 35+1	Campbell S 29+2	Adams T 10	Parlour R 25+2	Ljungberg F 24+1	Wiltord S 23+10	Henry T 31+2	Pires R 27+1	Grimandi G 11+15	Van Bronckhorst G 13+8	Bergkamp D 22+11	Jeffers F 2+4	Kanu N 9+14	Keown M 21+1	Luzhny O 15+3	Upson M 10+4	Wright R 12	Taylor S 9+1	Edu 8+6	Dixon L 3+10	Stepanovs 16	Aliadiere J —+1	Match No.
1	2	3	4	5	6	7	8¹	9²	10³	11	12	13	14												1
1	2	3	4	5	6	7¹	8¹	9²	10	11	13	12	14												2
1	2	3	4	5	6		8²	9¹	12	11	13	7	10³		14										3
1	2	3		12	6¹		13	9²	8	11	4	7	10³		14	5									4
1	2	3	4	5		7	8	12	9²	11	13		14		10³										5
1		3	4		6	7¹	8	9	12	5³	11²	10	13			2	14								6
	2	3	4				8²	9¹		11	12	7	10²		13	5	14	6	1						7
	2	3	4	5		12	8¹	9³	10	11	13	7²	14			6	1								8
	2		4			7²	12	9	11¹	6	8	10			13	5	3	1							9
	2		4	5		7	8	9¹	12		11	13	10²			6	3	1							10
	2	3¹		4			8	12	9	11	6	7	10			5		1							11
	2	3	4	5		7		9		11	8	10¹	12			6		1							12
	2	3	4	5		7	8		10	11¹ 12		13	9²			6		1							13
	2	3	4	5		7	8²		10	11¹	12	13	9²			6	1	14							14
	2	3	4	5		7	8¹	12	9	11			10²			6³	1								15
	2	3	4	5			8²	9	11¹	7			10			12	6	1	13						16
	2	3	4	5		7		9²	10	11		12	13		8¹	6	1								17
	2	3		5		8	12	10¹	11²		4			9²	6	14	13	1							18
	2	3		5		7²	8¹	12	10	11		13	14		9³	6		1							19
		3	4	5			8¹	12	10³	11	14	7	13		9²	6	2		1						20
		4	5				8	12	10	11¹	7		13		9²	6	2³	3	1			14			21
		3	4	5		7	8²	12	9	11		13	10¹			6	2³	1			14				22
		3	4	5		7²		12	9	11	13	8³	10¹			6	2	14	1						23
		3	4	5		7		8¹	9	11²	13	12	10			6³	2	14	1						24
	3²	4¹	5			7		8	9	11	13	12	10³			2	6	1	14						25
		4	5		7		9	10		8	11			2	3¹	1			12	6					26
1	7	4	5		8		9	10³	11	12	3²			2				13	6	14					27
1	7	4	5			9²		11	8	10¹	12		3					13	2	6					28
1	2	4	5		7		8	9	11	10		3²						12	13	6					29
1	2	4	5		7¹	9		11	12	10²		13	3					8	14	6³					30
	3	4	5	6		11³	7²	9		12	10²	13	14	2				8							31
	3¹	4	5			11	7	9		8	10²		6	12		13	2								32
1	2	4	5	6	12	11	7³	9		10¹	13	3			8²	14									33
1	2	3	4		6	7	11		9	10¹	13	5			8²										34
1	2	3	4		6	7	11³	9		10¹	13	5			8² 14										35
1	2	3	4	12	6	7	11	9¹		10²	13	5			8³ 14										36
1	2	3	4	5		7	11	10		9¹	6		8	12											37
		3	12			7²		11¹	9	4	10	13			5		1⁶ 15	8	2	6					38

Worthington Cup

Third Round	Manchester U	(h)	4-0
Fourth Round	Grimsby T	(h)	2-0
Fifth Round	Blackburn R	(a)	0-4

FA Cup

Third Round	Watford	(a)	4-2
Fourth Round	Liverpool	(h)	1-0
Fifth Round	Gillingham	(h)	5-2
Sixth Round	Newcastle U	(a)	1-1
		(h)	3-0
Semi-Final	Middlesbrough		1-0
(at Old Trafford)			
Final	Chelsea		2-0
(at Millennium Stadium)			

ASTON VILLA   FA Premiership

FOUNDATION

Cricketing enthusiasts of Villa Cross Wesleyan Chapel, Aston, Birmingham decided to form a football club during the winter of 1874–75. Football clubs were few and far between in the Birmingham area and in their first game against Aston Brook St Mary's Rugby team they played one half rugby and the other soccer. In 1876 they were joined by a Scottish soccer enthusiast George Ramsay who was immediately appointed captain and went on to lead Aston Villa from obscurity to one of the country's top clubs in a period of less than 10 years.

Villa Park, Trinity Rd, Birmingham B6 6HE.
Telephone: (0121) 327 2299. *Fax:* (0121) 322 2107.
Commercial Dept: (0121) 327 5399.
ClubCall: 09068 121 148. *Commercial Fax:* (0121) 328 2099. *Ticket Information:* (0121) 327 5353.
Ticketline: 09068 121 848. *Club Shop:* (0121) 327 2800.
Ground Capacity: 42,584.
Record Attendance: 76,588 v Derby Co, FA Cup 6th rd, 2 March 1946.
Record Receipts: £1,196,712 Portugal v Czech Republic, Euro '96, 23 June 1996.
Pitch Measurements: 115yd × 72yd.
President: J. A. Alderson. *Chairman:* H. D. Ellis.
Deputy Chief Executive and Finance Director: M. J. Ansell. *Operations Director and Secretary:* S. M. Stride.
Non Executive Directors: D. M. Owen, A. J. Hales, G. Taylor, P. D. Ellis.
Manager: Graham Taylor. *Assistant Manager:* John Deehan. *First Team Coach:* Stuart Gray. *Coaches:* Kevin MacDonald, Gordon Cowans.
Physio: Jim Walker. *Reserve Team Manager:* Kevin MacDonald. *Youth Team Manager:* Tony McAndrew. *Youth Team Coach:* Gordon Cowans.
Youth Development Officer: Alan Miller.
Commercial Manager: Abdul Rashid.
Stadium Manager: Tony Diffley.
Football Academy Director: Bryan Jones.
Assistant Academy Director: Steve Burns.
Colours: Claret shirts with blue and yellow trim, white shorts with claret and blue side trim, sky blue and claret stockings with white turnover.
Change Colours: Silver shirts with navy and lime green trim, navy and grey shorts with lime green side trim, navy and lime green stockings with grey turnover.
Year Formed: 1874. *Turned Professional:* 1885. *Ltd Co.:* 1896.
Club Nickname: 'The Villans'.

HONOURS

FA Premier League: Runners-up 1992–93.

Football League: Division 1 – Champions 1893–94, 1895–96, 1896–97, 1898–99, 1899–1900, 1909–10, 1980–81; Runners-up 1888–89, 1902–03, 1907–08, 1910–11, 1912–13, 1913–14, 1930–31, 1932–33, 1989–90; Division 2 – Champions 1937–38, 1959–60; Runners-up 1974–75, 1987–88; Division 3 – Champions 1971–72.

FA Cup: Winners 1887, 1895, 1897, 1905, 1913, 1920, 1957; Runners-up 1892, 1924, 2000.

Double Performed: 1896–97.

Football League Cup: Winners 1961, 1975, 1977, 1994, 1996; Runners-up 1963, 1971.

European Competitions: European Cup: 1981–82 (winners), 1982–83. *UEFA Cup:* 1975–76, 1977–78, 1983–84, 1990–91, 1993–94, 1994–95, 1996–97, 1997–98, 1998–99, 2001–02. *World Club Championship:* 1982. *European Super Cup:* 1982–83 (winners).

IT'S A FACT !

In 1971–72, Aston Villa attracted an average League attendance of 31,952 despite being in Division Three at the time. They were the thirteenth best supported team in the entire Football League.

Previous Grounds: 1874 Wilson Road and Aston Park (also used Aston Lower Grounds for some matches); 1876 Wellington Road, Perry Barr; 1897 Villa Park.

First Football League Game: 8 September 1888, Football League, v Wolverhampton W (a) D 1–1 – Warner; Cox, Coulton; Yates, H. Devey, Dawson; A. Brown, Green (1), Allen, Garvey, Hodgetts.

Record League Victory: 12–2 v Accrington S, Division 1, 12 March 1892 – Warner; Evans, Cox; Harry Devey, Jimmy Cowan, Baird; Athersmith (1), Dickson (2), John Devey (4), L. Campbell (4), Hodgetts (1).

Record Cup Victory: 13–0 v Wednesbury Old Ath, FA Cup 1st rd, 30 October 1886 – Warner; Coulton, Simmonds; Yates, Robertson, Burton (2); R. Davis (1), A. Brown (3), Hunter (3), Loach (2), Hodgetts (2).

Record Defeat: 1–8 v Blackburn R, FA Cup 3rd rd, 16 February 1889.

Most League Points (2 for a win): 70, Division 3, 1971–72.

Most League Points (3 for a win): 78, Division 2, 1987–88.

Most League Goals: 128, Division 1, 1930–31.

Highest League Scorer in Season: 'Pongo' Waring, 49, Division 1, 1930–31.

Most League Goals in Total Aggregate: Harry Hampton, 215, 1904–15.

Most League Goals in One Match: 5, Harry Hampton v Sheffield W, Division 1, 5 October 1912; 5, Harold Halse v Derby Co, Division 1, 19 October 1912; 5, Len Capewell v Burnley, Division 1, 29 August 1925; 5, George Brown v Leicester C, Division 1, 2 January 1932; 5, Gerry Hitchens v Charlton Ath, Division 2, 18 November 1959.

Most Capped Player: Steve Staunton 64 (102), Republic of Ireland.

Most League Appearances: Charlie Aitken, 561, 1961–76.

Youngest League Player: Jimmy Brown, 15 years 349 days v Bolton W, 17 September 1969.

Record Transfer Fee Received: £12,600,000 from Manchester U for Dwight Yorke, August 1998.

Record Transfer Fee Paid: A reported figure of £9,500,000 to River Plate for Juan Pablo Angel, January 2001.

Football League Record: 1888 Founder Member of the League; 1936–38 Division 2; 1938–59 Division 1; 1959–60 Division 2; 1960–67 Division 1; 1967–70 Division 2; 1970–72 Division 3; 1972–75 Division 2; 1975–87 Division 1; 1987–88 Division 2; 1988–92 Division 1; 1992– FA Premier League.

MANAGERS

George Ramsay 1884–1926
(Secretary-Manager)
W. J. Smith 1926–34
(Secretary-Manager)
Jimmy McMullan 1934–35
Jimmy Hogan 1936–44
Alex Massie 1945–50
George Martin 1950–53
Eric Houghton 1953–58
Joe Mercer 1958–64
Dick Taylor 1964–67
Tommy Cummings 1967–68
Tommy Docherty 1968–70
Vic Crowe 1970–74
Ron Saunders 1974–82
Tony Barton 1982–84
Graham Turner 1984–86
Billy McNeill 1986–87
Graham Taylor 1987–90
Dr Jozef Venglos 1990–91
Ron Atkinson 1991–94
Brian Little 1994–98
John Gregory 1998–2002
Graham Taylor February 2002–

LATEST SEQUENCES

Longest Sequence of League Wins: 9, 15.10.10 – 10.12.10.

Longest Sequence of League Defeats: 11, 23.3.63 – 4.5.63.

Longest Sequence of League Draws: 6, 12.9.81 – 10.10.81.

Longest Sequence of Unbeaten League Matches: 15, 12.3.49 – 27.8.49.

Longest Sequence Without a League Win: 12, 27.12.86 – 25.3.87.

TEN YEAR LEAGUE RECORD

		P	W	D	L	F	A	Pts	Pos
1991-92	Div 1	42	17	9	16	48	44	60	7
1992-93	PR Lge	42	21	11	10	57	40	74	2
1993-94	PR Lge	42	15	12	15	46	50	57	10
1994-95	PR Lge	42	11	15	16	51	56	48	18
1995-96	PR Lge	38	18	9	11	52	35	63	4
1996-97	PR Lge	38	17	10	11	47	34	61	5
1997-98	PR Lge	38	17	6	15	49	48	57	7
1998-99	PR Lge	38	15	10	13	51	46	55	6
1999-2000	PR Lge	38	15	13	10	46	35	58	6
2000-01	PR Lge	38	13	15	10	46	43	54	8

DID YOU KNOW ❓

In the 1920s, the Aston Villa half-back line of Jimmy Gibson, Alec Talbot and Joe Tate were respectively nicknamed Wind, Sleet and Rain.

ASTON VILLA 2001–02 LEAGUE RECORD

Match No.	Date	Venue	Opponents	Result	H/T Score	Lg. Pos.	Goalscorers	Atten- dance
1	Aug 18	A	Tottenham H	D	0-0	0-0	—	36,056
2	26	H	Manchester U	D	1-1	1-0	15	Vassell [4]	42,632
3	Sept 8	A	Liverpool	W	3-1	1-0	8	Dublin [31], Hendrie [55], Vassell [86]	44,102
4	16	H	Sunderland	D	0-0	0-0	9		31,668
5	24	A	Southampton	W	3-1	2-1	—	Boateng [9], Angel [15], Hadji [79]	26,794
6	30	H	Blackburn R	W	2-0	0-0	4	Angel [46], Vassell [72]	28,623
7	Oct 14	H	Fulham	W	2-0	0-0	4	Vassell [50], Taylor [61]	28,579
8	20	A	Everton	L	2-3	0-1	5	Hadji [71], Schmeichel [90]	33,352
9	24	H	Charlton Ath	W	1-0	1-0	—	Kachloul [9]	27,701
10	27	H	Bolton W	W	3-2	2-1	1	Angel 2 (1 pen) [13, 47 (p)], Vassell [43]	33,599
11	Nov 3	A	Newcastle U	L	0-3	0-1	3		51,057
12	17	H	Middlesbrough	D	0-0	0-0	3		35,424
13	25	A	Leeds U	D	1-1	1-1	5	Kachloul [35]	40,159
14	Dec 1	H	Leicester C	L	0-2	0-1	6		30,711
15	5	A	West Ham U	D	1-1	1-0	—	Dublin [1]	28,377
16	9	A	Arsenal	L	2-3	2-0	6	Merson [21], Stone [34]	38,074
17	17	H	Ipswich T	W	2-1	1-1	—	Angel 2 [44, 70]	29,320
18	22	A	Derby Co	L	1-3	1-1	8	Angel [45]	28,001
19	26	H	Liverpool	L	1-2	1-1	8	Hendrie [21]	42,602
20	29	H	Tottenham H	D	1-1	0-1	8	Angel (pen) [90]	41,134
21	Jan 1	A	Sunderland	D	1-1	0-0	9	Taylor [59]	41,672
22	12	H	Derby Co	W	2-1	2-1	7	Vassell [12], Angel [26]	28,881
23	21	A	Charlton Ath	W	2-1	2-0	—	Vassell [8], Angel [42]	25,605
24	30	H	Everton	D	0-0	0-0	—		32,460
25	Feb 2	A	Fulham	D	0-0	0-0	7		20,041
26	9	H	Chelsea	D	1-1	1-0	7	Merson [28]	41,137
27	23	A	Manchester U	L	0-1	0-0	7		67,592
28	Mar 2	H	West Ham U	W	2-1	1-1	7	Angel [23], Vassell [90]	37,341
29	5	A	Blackburn R	L	0-3	0-1	—		21,988
30	17	H	Arsenal	L	1-2	0-1	7	Dublin [69]	41,520
31	23	A	Ipswich T	D	0-0	0-0	7		25,428
32	30	A	Bolton W	L	2-3	2-2	7	Warhurst (og) [15], Taylor [17]	24,600
33	Apr 2	H	Newcastle U	D	1-1	1-1	—	Crouch [26]	36,597
34	6	A	Middlesbrough	L	1-2	0-1	10	Angel [80]	26,001
35	13	A	Leeds U	L	0-1	0-1	10		40,039
36	20	A	Leicester C	D	2-2	2-1	10	Vassell [22], Hitzlsperger [27]	18,125
37	27	H	Southampton	W	2-1	2-0	9	Vassell 2 [8, 42]	35,255
38	May 11	A	Chelsea	W	3-1	1-0	8	Crouch [21], Vassell [63], Dublin [88]	40,709

Final League Position: 8

GOALSCORERS

League (46): Angel 12 (2 pens), Vassell 12, Dublin 4, Taylor 3, Crouch 2, Hadji 2, Hendrie 2, Kachloul 2, Merson 2, Boateng 1, Hitzlsperger 1, Schmeichel 1, Stone 1, own goal 1.
Worthington Cup (1): Dublin 1.
FA Cup (2): Taylor 1, own goal 1.

Schmeichel P 29	Delaney M 30	Wright A 23	Mellberg O 32	Alpay O 14	Boateng G 37	Merson P 18+3	Hendrie L 25+4	Angel J 26+3	Vassell D 30+6	Kachloul H 17+5	Ginola D —+5	Hadji M 17+6	Stone S 14+8	Balaban B —+8	Staunton S 30+3	Dublin D 9+12	Samuel J 17+6	Taylor I 7+9	Enckelman P 9	Barry G 16+4	Hitzlsperger T 11+1	Crouch P 7	Match No.
1	2	3	4	5	6	7	8	9^1	10^2	11^3	12	13	14										1
1	2	3	4	5	6	7^1	8	9^2	10	11		12	13										2
1	2	3	4	5	6	7^1	8^2		10	11	12				13	9							3
1	2	3	4	5	6	7^1	8		10	11	12				13	9^2							4
1	2	3	4	5	6		8^1	10^2	11^2	7		12	14	13	9								5
1	2	3		5	6		8	9^1	10	11^2	7				4	12	13						6
1		3		5	6		8	9^1	10	11^2	7	2	12	4		13							7
1	2	3		5^2	6		8^1	9^2	10	12	11	4	13	14	7								8
1	2	3		5	6		8^1		10	11	7		4	9	12								9
1	2	3		5	6	12	8^3	9^1	10^1	11	7		4	13	14								10
1	2	3		5	6		8^2	9^1	10	11	7		4	12	13								11
1	2^1	3	4	5	6		8	9	10	11^1	12	7				13							12
1		3	4	5	6	7	8^2	9^1	10	11		2			12	13							13
1	2	3	4	5^2	6	7	8^1	9	10^2		12	11	14	13									14
	2^2	3	4		6	10^1	8	12				7		5	9	13			1	11			15
		3	4		6	10	8	12				7		5	9	2			1	11^1			16
1		3	4		6	10	8^2	9^1	12			7		5	13	2				11			17
1		3	4		6^3	8	12	10		13		7	14	5	9	2^2				11^1			18
1		3	4		6	7	8^2	9	10	11		12		5		2^1	13						19
1		3^1	4		6^2	7	8	9	10	11		12		5		2	13						20
1		3	4			8		10	11^1			7		5	9	2	6			12			21
1	3		4		6	11^3	8^2	9	10	12	13			5		2	7^1			14			22
1	2		4		6	7	8^1	9	10	11				5	3		12						23
	2		4		6	11	8^1	9	10^2	12		7		5	13	3		1					24
	2		4		6	11	8^2	9^1	10	12		7	13	5		3		1					25
	2		4^3		6	11	8^2	9	10^1			7	13	5	12	3		1	14				26
1	2		4		6			9	10			8^2	7	5	12	3^1			11	13			27
1	2		4		6	12		9	10			7^1		5		3			11	8			28
1	2		4		6	12	13	9^3	10			7^1	14	5		3			11	8^2			29
1	2		4		6	9^1	12		10^2	7^3		14		5	13	3			11	8			30
1	2		4		6			10		7				5	9	3^1	12			11	8		31
1	2^2		4		6			12	10^1	11				5		13	7			3	8	9	32
1	2		4		6^2			10	12	11^1	13	14		5			7			3	8	9^3	33
1	2		4		6			10	12	11^1				5			7			3	8	9	34
	2		4		6^2			10^1	12	11^2	13			5		14	7^1		1	3	8	9	35
	2		4		6				10^2	12		7	13	5		3^1			1	11	8	9	36
	2	3	4		6			12	10		13	7^2		5		14			1	11^1	8	9^1	37
	2	3	4		6			12	13	10^3		7		5	14				1	11	8^1	9^2	38

Worthington Cup
Third Round   Reading   (h)   1-0
Fourth Round   Sheffield W   (h)   0-1

FA Cup
Third Round   Manchester U   (h)   2-3

BARNSLEY

FOUNDATION

Many clubs owe their inception to the church and Barnsley are among them, for they were formed in 1887 by the Rev. T. T. Preedy, curate of Barnsley St Peter's and went under that name until it was dropped in 1897 a year before being admitted to the Second Division of the Football League.

Oakwell Stadium, Barnsley, South Yorkshire S71 1ET

Telephone: (01226) 211 211. *Fax:* (01226) 211 444.
Website: barnsleyfc.co.uk
Email: thereds@barnsleyfc.co.uk
ClubCall: 09068 121 152.

Ground Capacity: 23,186.

Record Attendance: 40,255 v Stoke C, FA Cup 5th rd, 15 February 1936.

Record Receipts: undisclosed.

Pitch Measurements: 110yd × 75yd.

Chairman: J. A. Dennis. *Directors:* C. B. Taylor (Vice-chairman), M. Hanson, C. H. Harrison, M. R. Hayselden, J. N. Kelly, I. D. Potter.

Manager: Steve Parkin. *First Team Coach:* Tony Ford. *Physio:* Jim Webb.

General Manager/Secretary: Michael Spinks.
Sales and Marketing Manager: Graham Barlow.

Colours: Red shirts, white shorts, red stockings.

Change Colours: (To be announced.)

Year Formed: 1887. *Turned Professional:* 1888. *Ltd Co.:* 1899.

Previous Name: 1887, Barnsley St Peter's; 1897, Barnsley.

Club Nickname: 'The Tykes', 'Reds' or 'Colliers'.

First Football League Game: 1 September 1898, Division 2, v Lincoln C (a) L 0–1 – Fawcett; McArtney, Nixon; King, Burleigh, Porteous; Davis, Lees, Murray, McCullough, McGee.

Record League Victory: 9–0 v Loughborough T, Division 2, 28 January 1899 – Greaves; McArtney, Nixon; Porteous, Burleigh, Howard; Davis (4), Hepworth (1), Lees (1), McCullough (1), Jones (2). 9–0 v Accrington S, Division 3 (N), 3 February 1934 – Ellis; Cookson, Shotton; Harper, Henderson, Whitworth; Spence (2), Smith (1), Blight (4), Andrews (1), Ashton (1).

Record Cup Victory: 6–0 v Blackpool, FA Cup 1st rd replay, 20 January 1910 – Mearns; Downs, Ness; Glendinning, Boyle (1), Utley; Bartrop, Gadsby (1), Lillycrop (2), Tufnell (2), Forman. 6–0 v Peterborough U, League Cup 1st rd 2nd leg, 15 September 1981 – Horn; Joyce, Chambers, Glavin (2), Banks, McCarthy, Evans, Parker (2), Aylott (1), McHale, Barrowclough (1).

HONOURS

Football League: Division 1 – Runners-up 1996–97; Division 3 (N) – Champions 1933–34; 1938–39; 1954–55; Runners-up 1953–54; Division 3 – Runners-up 1980–81; Division 4 – Runners-up 1967–68; Promoted 1978–79.

FA Cup: Winners 1912; Runners-up 1910.

Football League Cup: best season: 5th rd, 1982.

IT'S A FACT !

Barnsley had more varied success in 1938–39 than any other Football League team as champions of Division Three (North): most points (67), most home wins (18), and away (12), most goals (94).

Record Defeat: 0–9 v Notts Co, Division 2, 19 November 1927.

Most League Points (2 for a win): 67, Division 3 (N), 1938–39.

Most League Points (3 for a win): 82, Division 1, 1999–2000.

Most League Goals: 118, Division 3 (N), 1933–34.

Highest League Scorer in Season: Cecil McCormack, 33, Division 2, 1950–51.

Most League Goals in Total Aggregate: Ernest Hine, 123, 1921–26 and 1934–38.

Most League Goals in One Match: 5, Frank Eaton v South Shields, Division 3N, 9 April 1927; 5, Peter Cunningham v Darlington, Division 3N, 4 February 1933; 5, Beau Asquith v Darlington, Division 3N, 12 November 1938; 5, Cecil McCormack v Luton T, Division 2, 9 September 1950.

Most Capped Player: Gerry Taggart, 35 (50), Northern Ireland.

Most League Appearances: Barry Murphy, 514, 1962–78.

Youngest League Player: Alan Ogley, 16 years 226 days v Bristol R, 18 September 1962.

Record Transfer Fee Received: £4,250,000 from Blackburn R for Ashley Ward, December 1998.

Record Transfer Fee Paid: £1,500,000 to Partizan Belgrade for Georgi Hristov, June 1997.

Football League Record: 1898 Elected to Division 2; 1932–34 Division 3 (N); 1934–38 Division 2; 1938–39 Division 3 (N); 1946–53 Division 2; 1953–55 Division 3 (N); 1955–59 Division 2; 1959–65 Division 3; 1965–68 Division 4; 1968–72 Division 3; 1972–79 Division 4; 1979–81 Division 3; 1981–92 Division 2; 1992–97 Division 1; 1997–98 FA Premier League; 1998–2002 Division 1; 2002–Division 2.

MANAGERS

Arthur Fairclough 1898–1901
  (Secretary-Manager)
John McCartney 1901–04
  (Secretary-Manager)
Arthur Fairclough 1904–12
John Hastie 1912–14
Percy Lewis 1914–19
Peter Sant 1919–26
John Commins 1926–29
Arthur Fairclough 1929–30
Brough Fletcher 1930–37
Angus Seed 1937–53
Tim Ward 1953–60
Johnny Steele 1960–71
  (continued as General Manager)
John McSeveney 1971–72
Johnny Steele *(General Manager)*
  1972–73
Jim Iley 1973–78
Allan Clarke 1978–80
Norman Hunter 1980–84
Bobby Collins 1984–85
Allan Clarke 1985–89
Mel Machin 1989–93
Viv Anderson 1993–94
Danny Wilson 1994–98
John Hendrie 1998–99
Dave Bassett 1999–2000
Nigel Spackman 2001
Steve Parkin November 2001–

LATEST SEQUENCES

Longest Sequence of League Wins: 10, 5.3.55 – 23.4.55.

Longest Sequence of League Defeats: 9, 14.3.53 – 25.4.53.

Longest Sequence of League Draws: 7, 28.3.11 – 22.4.11.

Longest Sequence of Unbeaten League Matches: 21, 1.1.34 – 5.5.34.

Longest Sequence Without a League Win: 26, 13.12.52 – 26.8.53.

TEN YEAR LEAGUE RECORD

		P	W	D	L	F	A	Pts	Pos
1991-92	Div 2	46	16	11	19	46	57	59	16
1992-93	Div 1	46	17	9	20	56	60	60	13
1993-94	Div 1	46	16	7	23	55	67	55	18
1994-95	Div 1	46	20	12	14	63	52	72	6
1995-96	Div 1	46	14	18	14	60	66	60	10
1996-97	Div 1	46	22	14	10	76	55	80	2
1997-98	PR Lge	38	10	5	23	37	82	35	19
1998-99	Div 1	46	14	17	15	59	56	59	13
1999-2000	Div 1	46	24	10	12	88	67	82	4
2000-01	Div 1	46	15	9	22	49	62	54	16

DID YOU KNOW ?

Barnsley were undefeated at Oakwell from 21 January 1933 to 8 December 1934, a run of home matches totalling 36 games, during the club's move into the Second Division.

BARNSLEY 2001–02 LEAGUE RECORD

Match No.	Date	Venue	Opponents	Result	H/T Score	Lg. Pos.	Goalscorers	Attendance
1	Aug 11	A	Bradford C	L 0-4	0-2	—		16,367
2	18	H	Nottingham F	W 2-1	1-0	16	Gallen [40], Rankin [90]	14,203
3	25	A	Gillingham	L 0-3	0-1	19		8292
4	27	H	Rotherham U	D 1-1	0-1	19	Dyer [79]	15,552
5	Sept 1	A	Grimsby T	L 0-1	0-1	19		6173
6	8	H	Stockport Co	D 2-2	0-0	17	Sheron [48], Briggs (og) [64]	11,192
7	15	H	Crewe Alex	W 2-0	0-0	11	Gorre [50], Neil [78]	10,976
8	18	A	Millwall	L 1-3	1-0	—	Dyer [39]	10,021
9	22	A	Crystal Palace	L 0-1	0-0	20		15,433
10	25	H	Coventry C	D 1-1	0-0	—	Dyer [79]	11,692
11	28	H	Portsmouth	L 1-4	1-2	—	Barnard (pen) [9]	11,660
12	Oct 13	H	Birmingham C	L 1-3	0-1	22	Sand [54]	11,910
13	20	A	Burnley	D 3-3	1-2	22	Lumsdon (pen) [45], Morgan [52], Barnard [88]	14,690
14	24	A	Sheffield W	L 1-3	1-1	—	Gallen [5]	21,008
15	28	H	WBA	W 3-2	2-1	22	Dyer 2 [11, 89], Lumsdon (pen) [45]	12,490
16	31	H	Manchester C	L 0-3	0-3	—		15,159
17	Nov 3	A	Watford	L 0-3	0-0	23		13,964
18	8	A	Preston NE	D 2-2	1-0	—	Barnard [44], Neil [58]	19,042
19	17	H	Wimbledon	D 1-1	0-0	23	Dyer [51]	11,088
20	24	A	Norwich C	L 1-2	0-1	23	Barker [56]	17,333
21	27	H	Wolverhampton W	L 1-4	1-2	—	Barker [44]	19,231
22	Dec 2	H	Sheffield W	W 3-0	2-0	23	Morgan [5], Sheron 2 [41, 85]	16,714
23	8	H	Walsall	W 4-1	2-0	21	Sheron 2 [26, 82], Dyer [40], Donovan [52]	12,509
24	14	A	Sheffield U	D 1-1	0-0	—	Sheron [58]	17,858
25	22	H	Gillingham	W 4-1	2-1	20	Lumsdon [16], Barnard [21], Dyer [48], Jones G [78]	11,965
26	26	A	Stockport Co	W 3-1	1-0	20	Sheron [15], Palmer (og) [49], Morgan [79]	6885
27	29	A	Rotherham U	D 1-1	0-0	19	Morgan [51]	9737
28	Jan 1	H	Grimsby T	D 0-0	0-0	19		13,325
29	12	A	Nottingham F	D 0-0	0-0	19		18,190
30	19	H	Bradford C	D 3-3	2-1	18	Lumsdon (pen) [40], Sheron 2 [43, 60]	13,856
31	29	H	Wolverhampton W	W 1-0	1-0	—	Sheron [40]	13,825
32	Feb 2	A	Portsmouth	D 4-4	1-2	18	Lumsdon 2 (1 pen) [16, 84 (p)], Barker [48], Sheron [90]	12,756
33	9	H	Burnley	D 1-1	1-1	18	Barnard [6]	14,411
34	16	A	Birmingham C	L 0-1	0-0	19		19,208
35	23	A	Coventry C	L 0-4	0-3	19		15,092
36	26	H	Crystal Palace	L 1-4	1-1	—	Dyer [41]	11,207
37	Mar 2	H	Millwall	D 1-1	0-1	20	Lumsdon (pen) [58]	11,816
38	5	A	Crewe Alex	L 0-2	0-1	—		6258
39	9	H	Sheffield U	D 1-1	1-1	21	Dyer [40]	15,430
40	16	A	Walsall	L 1-2	1-0	23	Dyer [22]	7495
41	23	A	Watford	W 2-0	1-0	22	Dyer [33], Barnard (pen) [47]	12,449
42	30	A	WBA	L 1-3	0-1	22	Barnard (pen) [72]	23,167
43	Apr 1	H	Preston NE	W 2-1	1-0	21	Gorre [27], Dyer [60]	14,188
44	6	A	Manchester C	L 1-5	1-2	22	Dyer [43]	33,628
45	13	H	Norwich C	L 0-2	0-1	23		18,803
46	21	A	Wimbledon	W 1-0	1-0	23	Sheron [13]	5379

Final League Position: 23

GOALSCORERS
League (59): Dyer 14, Sheron 12, Barnard 7 (3 pens), Lumsdon 7 (5 pens), Morgan 4, Barker 3, Gallen 2, Gorre 2, Neil 2, Donovan 1, Jones G 1, Rankin 1, Sand 1, own goals 2.
Worthington Cup (5): Dyer 3, Jones G 1, Tinkler 1.
FA Cup (2): Barnard 1, Dyer 1.

Miller K 28	Crooks L 20+6	Barker C 43+1	Morgan C 42	Chettle S 31+1	Ward M 12+3	Donovan K 28+4	Gorre D 14+5	Gallen K 8+1	Dyer B 42+2	Barnard D 34+4	Regan C 6+4	Tinkler E 8+8	Sheron M 23+10	Rankin I 2+7	Neil A 17+8	Fallon R 2+7	O'Callaghan B 1+5	Corbo M —+1	Marriott A 17+1	Jones L 2+11	Parkin J 4	Key A —+1	Sand P 4+2	Lumsdon C 32	Oster J 2	Mulligan D 27+1	Bertos L 2+2	Jones G 25	McSwegan G 1+4	Scothern A —+1	Bedeau A —+3	Betsy K 10	Naylor R 7+1	Flynn M 7	Gibbs P 4	Ghent M 1	Christie J —+1	Match No.
1	2[1]	3	4	5	6	7	8[2]	9[3]	10	11	12	13	14																									1
1	2	3	4	5	6[2]	7	8[3]	9[1]	10	11		12	13	14																								2
1	2[1]	3	4	5		7		9[3]	10	11	12	8	13	14	6[2]																							3
1	2	3[4]	4	5		7		9	11[3]	8	10	12	13		6[1]	14																						4
1	2	3	4	5	12	7[2]	8		10	11[1]			9		6[2]				14	13																		5
1	2	3	4	5	6	7[1]	8		10[2]	12			9		11					13																		6
	5	3	4		6	12	8[2]		10	11	2	13	9[3]		7[1]				1	14																		7
	5[1]	3	4	12	6		8		10	11	2		9[2]		7				1	13																		8
		3	4		6	7	8[3]		9	11	2	13	12		10[2]				1	14			5															9
		3	4		6[2]	12		9	10	11	2	13			7	14			1					8[3]		5[1]												10
		3	4			7	9[1]		10	11	2		8[2]		6				1				5					13										11
	2	3	4		12	7			10			13	9[2]	14					1					8[3]		5[1]		6	11									12
	2	3	4		6[2]	7[1]	12			9		13							1					5[3]		10	11	8										13
	5	3	4			7		9		11[3]	12	13			8[3]				1	14			6[2]	2	10													14
1	2	3	4	5				9[1]	10	11			8		6[2]	12								13		7												15
1		3	4	5				9[2]	10	11		2[3]	8		12	13								6[1]		7		14										16
1		3	4	5			8[1]	12	10	11					6[2]	9	14							13		7		2[3]										17
1		3	4	5			8		9[1]	10	11				6	12								7				2										18
1		3	4	5			8		9[3]	10	11[1]	12			6	13								7				2										19
1	12	3	4	5				13	10	11		8[3]			6[1]									7				2	9[2]									20
1	12	3	4	5			8[3]		9	11[2]		10[1]	13		6									7				2	14									21
1		3	4	5			8		10[1]	11			9										12	7		2		6										22
1		3	4	5[2]			8		10	11			9[1]		12	13								7		2		6[3]										23
1	4	3		5			8		10[2]	11			9		12									7		2[1]		6	13									24
1		3	4	5			8		10[2]	11			9[1]										12	7		2		6	13									25
1		3	4	5			8		10[1]	11			9											7		2		6	12									26
1	2	3	4	5						11			9										12	7				6	10[1]									27
1	2	3	4	5			8		10[1]	11			9		12									7[3]				6	13									28
1	5	3	4				8		10[1]	11			9											7		2		6				12						29
1		3	4	5			8		10	11			9											7		2		6										30
1		3	4	5			8		10	11			9											7		2		6										31
1		3	4	5			8[1]		10[2]	11			9											7		2	12	6				13						32
1		3	4	5	12		8		10	11			9[2]											7[1]		2		6				13						33
1	5	3	4		11		8[2]		10[3]				9		13	12								7		2[1]		6				14						34
1	12	3	4	5	6	13			11[2]	10			9[3]		14									7				8[1]										35
1	12	3	4	5			8[1]		10[2]	11			9		13									7				6										36
13		3	4	5[2]		12			10	11			9[3]		14								1	7		2		6				8[1]						37
	5	3	4		11[3]	13			12				9[1]			14							1	7		2		6[2]				8	10					38
	5	3	4		11[1]				10	12													1	7		2		6				8	9					39
	2	11[2]							10				13		12	14							1			7[3]		6				8	9[1]	4	3			40
			5									10[1]	11		12	7							1			2		6				8	9	4	3			41
13	3		5					14				10	11		12	7							1			2[2]		6[3]				8	9[1]	4				42
		3	4					11[1]				10	12		13								1			7		6				8	9[2]	5	3			43
			4	6				13		9[3]					12	11[1]							1			7		2[2]	10			8	14	5	3			44
	12		4							11			10		13	14							1			7[3]		2				8	9[2]	5	3			45
		3	4									11	10[1]		9	12										2	7[2]	6				8		5		1	13	46

Worthington Cup

First Round	Halifax T	(h)	2-0
Second Round	Colchester U	(a)	3-1
Third Round	Newcastle U	(h)	0-1

FA Cup

Third Round	Blackburn R	(h)	1-1
		(a)	1-3

BIRMINGHAM CITY   FA Premiership

FOUNDATION

In 1875, cricketing enthusiasts who were largely members of Trinity Church, Bordesley, determined to continue their sporting relationships throughout the year by forming a football club which they called Small Heath Alliance. For their earliest games played on waste land in Arthur Street, the team included three Edden brothers and two James brothers.

St Andrews, Birmingham B9 4NH.

Telephone: 0121 772 0101. *Fax:* (0121) 766 7866.
Website: www.bcfc.com *ClubCall:* 09068 121 188.
Club Soccer Shop: 0121 772 0101 (ext. 8).

Ground Capacity: 30,009.

Record Attendance: 66,844 v Everton, FA Cup 5th rd, 11 February 1939.

Record Receipts: £396,113 v Preston NE, (play off semi-final 1st leg), 13 May 2001.

Pitch Measurements: 110yd × 74yd.

Chairman: D. Gold. *Vice-chairman:* J. F. Wiseman.
Directors: D. Sullivan, R. Gold, B. Gold, H. Brandman, A. G. Jones, M. Wiseman.
Managing Director: K. R. Brady.

Manager: Steve Bruce. *Coach:* Mark Bowen.
Reserve Team Coach: Keith Bertschin.
Physio: John Pryce.

General Manager: John Benson. *Sales & Marketing Director:* Jason Holloway. *Safety Officer:* Brian Tew.
Secretary: A. G. Jones BA, MBA.

Colours: Blue shirts, blue shorts, blue and white stockings.

Change Colours: Black shirts, black shorts, black stockings.

Year Formed: 1875.

Turned Professional: 1885.

Ltd Co.: 1888.

Previous Names: 1875, Small Heath Alliance; 1888, dropped 'Alliance'; 1905, Birmingham; 1945, Birmingham City.

Club Nickname: 'Blues'.

Previous Grounds: 1875, waste ground near Arthur St; 1877, Muntz St, Small Heath; 1906, St Andrews.

First Football League game: 3 September 1892, Division 2, v Burslem Port Vale (h) W 5–1 – Charsley; Bayley, Speller; Ollis, Jenkyns, Devey; Hallam (1), Edwards (1), Short (1), Wheldon (2), Hands.

Record League Victory: 12–0 v Walsall T Swifts, Division 2, 17 December 1892 – Charsley; Bayley, Jones; Ollis, Jenkyns, Devey; Hallam (2), Walton (3), Mobley (3), Wheldon (2), Hands (2). 12–0 v Doncaster R, Division 2, 11 April 1903 – Dorrington; Goldie, Wassell; Beer, Dougherty (1), Howard; Athersmith (1), Leonard (3), McRoberts (1), Wilcox (4), Field (1). Aston, (1 og).

HONOURS

Football League: Promoted from Division 1 (play offs) 2001–02; Division 2 – Champions 1892–93, 1920–21, 1947–48, 1954–55, 1994–95; Runners-up 1893–94, 1900–01, 1902–03, 1971–72, 1984–85; Division 3 Runners-up 1991–92.

FA Cup: Runners-up 1931, 1956.

Football League Cup: Winners 1963; Runners-up 2001.

Leyland Daf Cup: Winners 1991.

Auto Windscreens Shield: Winners 1995.

European Competitions: European Fairs Cup: 1955–58, 1958–60 (runners-up), 1960–61 (runners-up), 1961–62.

IT'S A FACT !

On 7 September 1968 Geoff Vowden came on as a substitute for Birmingham City and scored a hat-trick aginast Huddersfield Town in a 5-1 win.

Record Cup Victory: 9–2 v Burton W, FA Cup 1st rd, 31 October 1885 – Hedges; Jones, Evetts (1); F. James, Felton, A. James (1); Davenport (2), Stanley (4), Simms, Figures, Morris (1).

Record Defeat: 1–9 v Sheffield W, Division 1, 13 December 1930. 1–9 v Blackburn R, Division 1, 5 January 1895.

Most League Points (2 for a win): 59, Division 2, 1947–48.

Most League Points (3 for a win): 89, Division 2, 1994–95.

Most League Goals: 103, Division 2, 1893–94 (only 28 games).

Highest League Scorer in Season: Joe Bradford, 29, Division 1, 1927–28.

Most League Goals in Total Aggregate: Joe Bradford, 249, 1920–35.

Most League Goals in One Match: 5, Walter Abbott v Darwen, Division 2, 26 November, 1898; 5, John McMillan v Blackpool, Division 2, 2 March 1901; 5, James Windridge v Glossop, Division 2, 23 January 1915.

Most Capped Player: Malcolm Page, 28, Wales.

Most League Appearances: Frank Womack, 491, 1908–28.

Youngest League Player: Trevor Francis, 16 years 7 months v Cardiff C, 5 September 1970.

Record Transfer Fee Received: £2,500,000 from Coventry C for Gary Breen, January 1997.

Record Transfer Fee Paid: £2,250,000 to Fulham for Geoff Horsfield, July 2000.

MANAGERS

Alfred Jones 1892–1908 (*Secretary-Manager*)
Alec Watson 1908–10
Bob McRoberts 1910–15
Frank Richards 1915–23
Billy Beer 1923–27
Leslie Knighton 1928–33
George Liddell 1933–39
Harry Storer 1945–48
Bob Brocklebank 1949–54
Arthur Turner 1954–58
Pat Beasley 1959–60
Gil Merrick 1960–64
Joe Mallett 1965
Stan Cullis 1965–70
Fred Goodwin 1970–75
Willie Bell 1975–77
Jim Smith 1978–82
Ron Saunders 1982–86
John Bond 1986–87
Garry Pendrey 1987–89
Dave Mackay 1989–91
Lou Macari 1991
Terry Cooper 1991–93
Barry Fry 1993–96
Trevor Francis 1996–2001
Steve Bruce December 2001–

Football League Record: 1892 elected to Division 2; 1894–96 Division 1; 1896–1901 Division 2; 1901–02 Division 1; 1902–03 Division 2; 1903–08 Division 1; 1908–21 Division 2; 1921–39 Division 1; 1946–48 Division 2; 1948–50 Division 1; 1950–55 Division 2; 1955–65 Division 1; 1965–72 Division 2; 1972–79 Division 1; 1979–80 Division 2; 1980–84 Division 1; 1984–85 Division 2; 1985–86 Division 1; 1986–89 Division 2; 1989–92 Division 3; 1992–94 Division 1; 1994–95 Division 2; 1995–2002 Division 1; 2002– FA Premier League.

LATEST SEQUENCES

Longest Sequence of League Wins: 13, 17.12.1892 – 16.9.1893.

Longest Sequence of League Defeats: 8, 28.9.85 – 23.11.85.

Longest Sequence of League Draws: 8, 18.9.90 – 23.10.90.

Longest Sequence of Unbeaten League Matches: 20, 3.9.94 – 2.1.95.

Longest Sequence Without a League Win: 17, 28.9.85 – 18.1.86.

TEN YEAR LEAGUE RECORD

		P	W	D	L	F	A	Pts	Pos
1991-92	Div 3	46	23	12	11	69	52	81	2
1992-93	Div 1	46	13	12	21	50	72	51	19
1993-94	Div 1	46	13	12	21	52	69	51	22
1994-95	Div 2	46	25	14	7	84	37	89	1
1995-96	Div 1	46	15	13	18	61	64	58	15
1996-97	Div 1	46	17	15	14	52	48	66	10
1997-98	Div 1	46	19	17	10	60	35	74	7
1998-99	Div 1	46	23	12	11	66	37	81	4
1999-2000	Div 1	46	22	11	13	65	44	77	5
2000-01	Div 1	46	23	9	14	59	48	78	5

DID YOU KNOW ?

Despite drawing as many as 15 League matches in 1947–48, Birmingham City won the Second Division championship, conceding only 24 goals, 17 better than anyone else.

BIRMINGHAM CITY 2001–02 LEAGUE RECORD

Match No.	Date	Venue	Opponents	Result	H/T Score	Lg. Pos.	Goalscorers	Attendance
1	Aug 11	A	Wimbledon	L	1-3	0-1	—	Hughes B [87]	9142
2	19	H	Millwall	W	4-0	4-0	8	Hughes B 2 [22,27], Horsfield [30], Eaden [45]	19,091
3	25	A	Walsall	W	2-1	2-0	7	Mooney [20], Horsfield [41]	7245
4	27	H	Stockport Co	W	2-1	2-0	3	Grainger [2], Mooney (pen) [21]	18,478
5	Sept 8	H	Sheffield W	W	2-0	1-0	3	Johnson A [43], Hughes B [63]	19,421
6	15	A	Manchester C	L	0-3	0-3	7		31,714
7	18	H	Burnley	L	2-3	2-2	—	Johnson A 2 [19,40]	18,426
8	23	H	Preston NE	L	0-1	0-0	13		23,004
9	26	A	Watford	D	3-3	1-2	—	Hughes B [4], Horsfield [47], Grainger [85]	13,091
10	29	A	Crewe Alex	D	0-0	0-0	14		7314
11	Oct 13	A	Barnsley	W	3-1	1-0	12	Marcelo [36], Horsfield [55], Furlong [83]	11,910
12	17	A	Nottingham F	D	0-0	0-0	—		18,210
13	20	H	Bradford C	W	4-0	3-0	7	Marcelo 3 [37,45,48], Sonner [39]	25,011
14	23	H	Gillingham	W	2-1	1-0	—	Horsfield 2 [36,47]	27,101
15	26	A	Grimsby T	L	1-3	0-2	—	Marcelo [49]	5149
16	30	H	Portsmouth	D	1-1	1-1	—	Marcelo [25]	15,612
17	Nov 4	H	Rotherham U	D	2-2	1-1	10	Branston (og) [45], Horsfield [51]	28,436
18	7	H	WBA	L	0-1	0-1	—		23,554
19	17	A	Sheffield U	L	0-4	0-1	12		15,686
20	25	H	Coventry C	W	2-0	1-0	11	Marcelo 2 [17,61]	18,279
21	30	A	Gillingham	D	1-1	0-1	—	Marcelo [63]	6575
22	Dec 8	H	Norwich C	W	4-0	2-0	10	Mooney 3 (1 pen) [30,45,58(p)], Marcelo [46]	17,310
23	11	A	Crystal Palace	W	1-0	0-0	—	Mooney (pen) [64']	20,119
24	16	A	Wolverhampton W	L	1-2	1-1	10	Marcelo [40]	21,482
25	22	H	Walsall	W	1-0	1-0	8	Purse (pen) [14]	20,127
26	26	A	Sheffield W	W	1-0	0-0	8	Horsfield [77]	24,335
27	29	A	Stockport Co	W	3-0	1-0	6	Vickers [18], Marcelo [49], Mooney [76]	5827
28	Jan 1	H	Nottingham F	D	1-1	1-1	7	Mooney [4]	19,770
29	10	A	Millwall	D	1-1	1-0	—	Mooney [45]	11,856
30	19	A	Wimbledon	L	0-2	0-0	8		17,766
31	29	A	WBA	L	0-1	0-1	—		25,266
32	Feb 16	H	Barnsley	W	1-0	0-0	9	John [51]	19,208
33	23	H	Watford	W	3-2	2-0	9	Purse [21], Mooney 2 (1 pen) [42,53(p)]	18,059
34	26	H	Burnley	W	1-0	1-0	—	Mooney [25]	13,504
35	Mar 2	A	Preston NE	L	0-1	0-1	9		15,543
36	5	H	Manchester C	L	1-2	1-1	—	Johnson M [4]	24,160
37	9	H	Wolverhampton W	D	2-2	2-2	10	John [36], Devlin [45]	22,104
38	12	A	Bradford C	W	3-1	2-1	—	Purse [6], John [31], Horsfield [82]	13,105
39	15	H	Norwich C	W	1-0	1-0	—	John [22]	18,258
40	24	A	Coventry C	D	1-1	0-0	7	Horsfield [81]	17,945
41	30	H	Grimsby T	W	4-0	2-0	6	Hughes B 2 [22,31], John [50], Johnson D [64]	23,249
42	Apr 1	A	Crystal Palace	D	0-0	0-0	6		19,598
43	7	A	Portsmouth	D	1-1	1-0	6	John [2]	25,030
44	10	H	Crewe Alex	W	3-1	2-0	—	John [30], Carter [45], Mooney [49]	28,615
45	13	A	Rotherham U	D	2-2	1-1	5	Grainger [38], Beech (og) [70]	10,536
46	21	H	Sheffield U	W	2-0	0-0	5	Horsfield [61], Grainger [63]	29,178

Final League Position: 5

GOALSCORERS

League (70): Mooney 13 (4 pens), Marcelo 12, Horsfield 11, Hughes B 7, John 7, Grainger 4, Johnson A 3, Purse 3 (1 pen), Carter 1, Devlin 1, Eaden 1, Furlong 1, Johnson D 1, Johnson M 1, Sonner 1, Vickers 1, own goals 2.
Worthington Cup (6): Mooney 2 (1 pen), Hughes B 1, Johnson A 1, Johnson M 1, own goal 1.
FA Cup (0).

Vaesen N 22+1	Gill J 14	Grainger M 39+1	Sonner D 10+5	Purse D 35+1	Johnson M 30+2	Eaden N 24+5	O'Connor M 24	Horsfield G 33+7	Mooney T 29+4	Lazaridis S 22+10	Hughes B 27+4	Holdsworth D 3+1	Furlong P 2+9	Woodhouse C 18+10	Kelly A 6	Johnson A 9+14	Burrows D 9+3	Bragstad B 3	Luntala T 9+6	Marcelo 17+4	Hutchinson J —+3	Ferrari C —+4	Fleming C 6	Vickers S 13+1	Bennett I 18	Hyde G 1+4	Kenna J 21	McCarthy J 3+1	Bak A 2+2	Carter D 12+1	Devlin P 11+2	John S 15	Williams T 4	Johnson D 5+3	Tebily O 7	Hughes M 3	Match No.
1	2^1	3^2	4	5	6	7	8	9^1	10	11	12	13	14																								1
1	2	3	12	5	6	7	8^1	9^3	10^2	11	4				13	14																					2
	2	3	12	5	6	7	8	9^3	10^2	11	4				13		1	14																			3
	2^1	3	12	5	6	7	8	9^3	10^3	11	4				13		1	14																			4
	2				6	7	8	9^2			4		12	11^3	1	10^1	3	5	13	14																	5
	2	3			6		7^3	8	9		12		4		13	11^1	1	10^2	5		14																6
	2	3		7	6		8^1	9		11^2			13	12	1	10	5^3		14																		7
15	2	3	8		6^2	7		9		11^1	4	5		12	16^0	10				13																	8
1	2	3	12		6	7^1		9	13	11^1	4	5		8		10^3			14																		9
1		3	7^2		6	2		9^1	11^1	12	4	5	8		10		13	14																			10
1	2	3		5	6	7	8	9^1		11	4^1		13	12			14	10^3																			11
1	2	3	12	5	6	7^1	8	9^2					13	4			11	10																			12
1	2	3	4	5	6		8^1			11^2		9	12			13		7	10^3	14																	13
1	2	3	4	5	6		8	9		11			12					7	10^2	13																	14
1	2^2	3	4	5	6	7		9		11			12			13		8^1	10																		15
1		3	4	5	6	2		9		11			8					7	10																		16
1		3	4	5	6	2	8	9		11^2			7^1	10^2		12			13																		17
1		3	4	5	6	2	8^1	9	11^2				7	10		12			13																		18
1		3		5			7	8	9	11			12	13		6^1	10^3					2	4														19
	11		5^1		7	8	9						6			3		12	10			2	4	1													20
	11^1		5	14	7	8	9^2	13					6				12	3			10^1		2	4	1												21
			5		7	8		9^1	11					12	3		6	10			2	4	1													22
			5		7	8^1		9	11					3			6	10			2	4	1	12												23
	12		5		7^3	13		9^2	11			8		14	3	2	6^1	10			2	4	1													24
	3			5	7	8	9		11		12		6^1		13	2		10^2				4	1													25
	3			5	8	9	10	11^1	12			6		13							4	1		2	7^2											26
	3		5		8^3	9^2	11					6		12					10^1		4	1	13	2	7	14										27
	3^1			12			8	9	11				13	5					10		4	1	6^3	2	7^3	14										28
			5			7	8	9^1	11	12	7	13		14^3					10^1		4	1	2		6^2											29
	3			5			8^1	9	11	12	7		13						10^3		4^3	1		2	14	6										30
	3		5	6	7			12	11	4		9^1		10					13			1		2^2		8										31
	3		5					9	11^1	12	4			10									6	1	2		8	7	10							32
	3		5	6	12			9	11^1	4												1	13	2		8	7^1	10								33
	3		5	6	12			9	13	4			11^2									1		2		8	7^1	10								34
	3		5	6^3				12	9	13	4		11^2	14								1		2		8	7	10^1								35
	3^1		5	6				9	11	4			12									1	13	2		8	7	10^2								36
	3		5	6				9^1	11	4^2			12											2		8	7	10								37
1	3		5	6	13			12	9^1	14	4													2		8	7	10^2	11^3							38
1	3		5	6	13			12	9^2		4	8												2			7	10^1	11	5						39
1	3^1		6					9	13	4^2														2		8	7^3	10	11	14	5					40
1			6	13				9	11	4														2		14		10^1	3	7^2	5	8^3				41
1			6					9^1	12	13	4	4^3			8									2			14	10	3^2	7	5	11				42
1	3		13	6^2				12	9^1	11	4													2			14	10^3		7	5	8				43
1	3		5					9	11^1	12	4													2		8	7	10^1		13	6					44
1	3		5					9	11		4													2		8		10		7	6					45
1	3		5					9^1	11		4			12									13	2		8	7^3	10^2		14	6					46

Worthington Cup
First Round   Southend U   (h)   3-0
Second Round   Bristol R   (a)   3-0
Third Round   Manchester C   (a)   0-6

FA Cup
Third Round   Liverpool   (a)   0-3

BLACKBURN ROVERS   FA Premiership

FOUNDATION

It was in 1875 that some Public School old boys called a meeting at which the Blackburn Rovers club was formed and the colours blue and white adopted. The leading light was John Lewis, later to become a founder of the Lancashire FA, a famous referee who was in charge of two FA Cup Finals, and a vice-president of both the FA and the Football League.

Ewood Park, Blackburn BB2 4JF.

Telephone: (01254) 698 888. *Fax:* (01254) 671 042.
Website: www.rovers.co.uk *Email:* enquiries@rovers.co.uk
Ticket Hotline: (01254) 671 666. *ClubCall:* 09068 121 179.
Mail Order: 08080 20 20 20. *Club Shop:* (01254) 665 606.

Ground Capacity: 31,367.

Record Attendance: 62,522 v Bolton W, FA Cup 6th rd, 2 March 1929.

Record Receipts: £438,868 (gross) v Newcastle U, FA Cup 5th rd, 31 January 2000.

Pitch Measurements: 115yd × 72yd.

Chairman: R. D. Coar BSC.
Vice-chairman: R. L. Matthewman.
Directors: R. D. Coar BSC, R. L. Matthewman, J. O. Williams BSC (Chief Executive), Tom Finn, K. C. Lee, G. R. Root, I. R. Stanners, D. M. Brown.

Manager: Graeme Souness. *Physio:* Dave Fevre.
Assistant Manager: Tony Parkes. *Coach:* Phil Boersma.

Commercial Manager: Ken Beamish.

Secretary: Tom Finn. *Stadium Manager:* J. Newsham.

Colours: Blue and white halved shirts, white shorts with navy blue strip, white stockings with navy blue trim.

Change Colours: Red shirts with black trim, black shorts with red panel and red stockings with black turnover.

Year Formed: 1875.

Turned Professional: 1880.

Ltd Co.: 1897.

Club Nickname: Rovers.

Previous Grounds: 1875, all matches played away; 1876, Oozehead Ground; 1877, Pleasington Cricket Ground; 1878, Alexandra Meadows; 1881, Leamington Road; 1890, Ewood Park.

First Football League Game: 15 September 1888, Football League, v Accrington (h) D 5–5 – Arthur; Beverley, James Southworth; Douglas, Almond, Forrest; Beresford (1), Walton, John Southworth (1), Fecitt (1), Townley (2).

HONOURS

FA Premier League: Champions 1994–95; Runners-up 1993–94.

Football League: Division 1 – Champions 1911–12, 1913–14; Runners-up 2000–01; Division 2 – Champions 1938–39; Runners-up 1957–58; Division 3 – Champions 1974–75; Runners-up 1979–80.

FA Cup: Winners 1884, 1885, 1886, 1890, 1891, 1928; Runners-up 1882, 1960.

Football League Cup: Winners 2002.

Full Members' Cup: Winners 1987.

European Competitions: European Cup: 1995–96. UEFA Cup: 1994–95, 1998–99.

IT'S A FACT *!*

On 14 October 2001, Blackburn Rovers defeated West Ham United 7-1 to equal their biggest margin of victory over their opponents since the 8-2 win at West Ham on 26 December 1963.

Record League Victory: 9–0 v Middlesbrough, Division 2, 6 November 1954 – Elvy; Suart, Eckersley; Clayton, Kelly, Bell; Mooney (3), Crossan (2), Briggs, Quigley (3), Langton (1).

Record Cup Victory: 11–0 v Rossendale, FA Cup 1st rd, 13 October 1884 – Arthur; Hopwood, McIntyre; Forrest, Blenkhorn, Lofthouse; Sowerbutts (2), J. Brown (1), Fecitt (4), Barton (3), Birtwistle (1).

Record Defeat: 0–8 v Arsenal, Division 1, 25 February 1933.

Most League Points (2 for a win): 60, Division 3, 1974–75.

Most League Points (3 for a win): 91, Division 1, 2000–01.

Most League Goals: 114, Division 2, 1954–55.

Highest League Scorer in Season: Ted Harper, 43, Division 1, 1925–26.

Most League Goals in Total Aggregate: Simon Garner, 168, 1978–92.

Most League Goals in One Match: 7, Tommy Briggs v Bristol R, Division 2, 5 February 1953.

Most Capped Player: Henning Berg, 52 (90), Norway.

Most League Appearances: Derek Fazackerley, 596, 1970–86.

Youngest League Player: Harry Dennison, 16 years 155 days v Bristol C, 8 April 1911.

Record Transfer Fee Received: £15,000,000 from Newcastle U for Alan Shearer, July 1996.

Record Transfer Fee Paid: £7,500,000 to Manchester U for Andy Cole, December 2001.

Football League Record: 1888 Founder Member of the League; 1936–39 Division 2; 1946–48 Division 1; 1948–58 Division 2; 1958–66 Division 1; 1966–71 Division 2; 1971–75 Division 3; 1975–79 Division 2; 1979–80 Division 3; 1980–92 Division 2; 1992–99 FA Premier League; 1999–2001 Division 1; 2001– FA Premier League.

LATEST SEQUENCES

Longest Sequence of League Wins: 8, 1.3.80 – 7.4.80.

Longest Sequence of League Defeats: 7, 12.3.66 – 16.4.66.

Longest Sequence of League Draws: 5, 11.10.75 – 1.11.75.

Longest Sequence of Unbeaten League Matches: 23, 30.9.87 – 27.3.88.

Longest Sequence Without a League Win: 16, 11.11.78 – 24.3.79.

MANAGERS

Thomas Mitchell 1884–96
(Secretary-Manager)
J. Walmsley 1896–1903
(Secretary-Manager)
R. B. Middleton 1903–25
Jack Carr 1922–26
(Team Manager under Middleton to 1925)
Bob Crompton 1926–30
(Hon. Team Manager)
Arthur Barritt 1931–36
(had been Secretary from 1927)
Reg Taylor 1936–38
Bob Crompton 1938–41
Eddie Hapgood 1944–47
Will Scott 1947
Jack Bruton 1947–49
Jackie Bestall 1949–53
Johnny Carey 1953–58
Dally Duncan 1958–60
Jack Marshall 1960–67
Eddie Quigley 1967–70
Johnny Carey 1970–71
Ken Furphy 1971–73
Gordon Lee 1974–75
Jim Smith 1975–78
Jim Iley 1978
John Pickering 1978–79
Howard Kendall 1979–81
Bobby Saxton 1981–86
Don Mackay 1987–91
Kenny Dalglish 1991–95
Ray Harford 1995–97
Roy Hodgson 1997–98
Brian Kidd 1998–99
Tony Parkes 1999–2000
Graeme Souness March 2000–

TEN YEAR LEAGUE RECORD

		P	W	D	L	F	A	Pts	Pos
1991-92	Div 2	46	21	11	14	70	53	74	6
1992-93	PR Lge	42	20	11	11	68	46	71	4
1993-94	PR Lge	42	25	9	8	63	36	84	2
1994-95	PR Lge	42	27	8	7	80	39	89	1
1995-96	PR Lge	38	18	7	13	61	47	61	7
1996-97	PR Lge	38	9	15	14	42	43	42	13
1997-98	PR Lge	38	16	10	12	57	52	58	6
1998-99	PR Lge	38	7	14	17	38	52	35	19
1999-2000	Div 1	46	15	17	14	55	51	62	11
2000-01	Div 1	46	26	13	7	76	39	91	2

DID YOU KNOW ?

Harry Campbell became the first player to achieve Scottish Cup and FA Cup winning medals when he played for Blackburn Rovers in 1890. Two years earlier, he had appeared north of the border with Renton.

BLACKBURN ROVERS 2001–02 LEAGUE RECORD

Match No.	Date	Venue	Opponents	Result	H/T Score	Lg. Pos.	Goalscorers	Attendance
1	Aug 18	A	Derby Co	L	1-2	0-1	—	Blake [73]	28,236
2	22	H	Manchester U	D	2-2	0-1	—	Beckham (og) [49], Gillespie [69]	29,836
3	25	H	Tottenham H	W	2-1	1-0	8	Mahon [7], Duff [71]	24,922
4	Sept 8	A	Sunderland	L	0-1	0-0	15		43,028
5	16	A	Ipswich T	D	1-1	0-1	13	Jansen [54]	22,095
6	19	H	Bolton W	D	1-1	0-0	—	Neill [87]	25,949
7	22	H	Everton	W	1-0	1-0	7	Grabbi [37]	27,732
8	30	A	Aston Villa	L	0-2	0-0	11		28,623
9	Oct 14	H	West Ham U	W	7-1	3-1	11	Flitcroft [18], Dunn [27], Johnson [28], McCann (og) [63], Tugay [80], Jansen [82], Hignett [90]	22,712
10	20	A	Arsenal	D	3-3	1-0	11	Van Bronckhorst (og) [41], Dunn 2 [58, 89]	38,108
11	29	H	Leicester C	D	0-0	0-0	—		21,873
12	Nov 3	H	Southampton	W	2-1	1-1	8	Tugay [45], Hignett [90]	30,523
13	17	H	Liverpool	D	1-1	0-1	9	Jansen [52]	28,859
14	24	A	Chelsea	D	0-0	0-0	10		37,978
15	Dec 1	H	Middlesbrough	L	0-1	0-1	11		23,849
16	9	H	Leeds U	L	1-2	0-0	14	Berg [83]	28,309
17	15	H	Newcastle U	L	1-2	1-0	15	Dunn [34]	50,064
18	22	A	Charlton Ath	W	2-0	0-0	12	Duff [57], Dunn [90]	25,837
19	26	H	Sunderland	L	0-3	0-2	14		29,869
20	29	H	Derby Co	L	0-1	0-1	14		23,529
21	Jan 1	A	Tottenham H	L	0-1	0-1	15		35,131
22	12	H	Charlton Ath	W	4-1	2-0	14	Tugay [5], Cole [45], Hignett [85], Jansen [89]	23,365
23	19	A	Manchester U	L	1-2	0-1	15	Hignett [49]	67,552
24	30	H	Arsenal	L	2-3	2-2	—	Jansen 2 [31, 39]	25,983
25	Feb 2	H	West Ham U	L	0-2	0-1	17		35,307
26	9	A	Fulham	L	0-2	0-1	18		19,580
27	Mar 2	A	Bolton W	D	1-1	0-1	18	Jansen [68]	27,203
28	5	H	Aston Villa	W	3-0	1-0	—	Dunn [7], Duff [85], Cole [89]	21,988
29	13	H	Ipswich T	W	2-1	2-0	—	Duff [20], Cole [43]	23,305
30	17	A	Leeds U	L	1-3	0-2	16	Jansen [49]	39,857
31	30	A	Leicester C	L	1-2	0-1	17	Hughes [46]	16,236
32	Apr 1	A	Southampton	W	2-0	2-0	17	Duff [27], Yordi [29]	28,979
33	10	H	Chelsea	D	0-0	0-0	—		25,441
34	20	A	Middlesbrough	W	3-1	1-0	16	Yordi [33], Cole [74], Dunn (pen) [83]	26,935
35	23	H	Newcastle U	D	2-2	1-0	—	Gillespie [28], Cole [67]	26,712
36	28	A	Everton	W	2-1	1-0	—	Jansen [10], Cole [63]	34,976
37	May 8	A	Liverpool	L	3-4	1-2	—	Duff [28], Cole [49], Jansen [80]	40,663
38	11	H	Fulham	W	3-0	0-0	10	Cole 2 [53, 81], Duff [66]	30,487

Final League Position: 10

GOALSCORERS

League (55): Jansen 10, Cole 9, Duff 7, Dunn 7 (1 pen), Hignett 4, Tugay 3, Gillespie 2, Yordi 2, Berg 1, Blake 1, Flitcroft 1, Grabbi 1, Hughes 1, Johnson 1, Mahon 1, Neill 1, own goals 3.
Worthington Cup (18): Jansen 6, Cole 3, Hignett 3, Duff 1, Dunning 1, Hughes 1, Johansson 1, Johnson 1, Short 1.
FA Cup (5): Cole 1, Dunn 1 (pen), Grabbi 1, Hignett 1, Johansson 1.

Friedel B 36	Curtis J 10	Bjornebye S 23	Short C 21+1	Berg H 34	Dunn D 26+3	Gillespie K 21+11	Flitcroft G 26+3	Grabbi C 10+4	Jansen M 34+1	Duff D 31+1	Blake N —+3	Hignett C 4+16	Bent M 1+8	Mahon A 10+3	Taylor Martin 12+7	Neill L 31	Hughes M 4+17	McKeer J 1+3	Tugay K 32+1	Johnson D 6+1	Ostenstad E 2+2	Johansson N 14+6	Cole A 15	Yordi 5+3	Unsal H 7+1	Kelly A 2	Match No.
1	2	3^1	4	5	6^2	7	8	9^3	10	11	12	13	14														1
1	2	3	4	5		7	8^2	9^1	10^3	11	12	13				6	14										2
1	2		4	5		7^3	8	9^1	10	11	12	13	14			6^2	3										3
1		3		5		7^3	8		10	11				9^1	6^2	4	2	13	12	14							4
1				5		7	8	9^1	10	11		12				6	3	2	4								5
1		3		5			8	9^1	10	11		12		4^2		2	14	13	6	7^3							6
1		3		5			8	9^1	10	11^1		13		12		2	14	4^2	6	7							7
1		3		5	6^2		8		10			13		11	2	9^3	12		4	7^3	14						8
1		3	12	5^1		11	8	9^2	10				14			2		13	6	7^3		4					9
1		3	4	5	11	7^3	8	9^2				14	12			2		13	6	10^3							10
1		3^3		5	11	12	8	9^3	10			14		13		2		4	7^1	6							11
1				5	11	7	8^2		10			13	12		3	2^3	9^1	4	14	6							12
1	2	3	4	5	10	7	8^2	9		11^1		13	12						6								13
1	2	3	4	5^1	10	7		9		11							8^1		12	6	13						14
1			4^3	5	10	7		12	8	11^2		13			3	2			6	9^1		14					15
1	2^1		4^2	5	10	7		12	9	11		8			3				6		13						16
1	2^1		4	5	10	7	8	12	9^2	11		14			3		13^3		6								17
1		3	4	5	12	7	8	9^2		11		10				2		13	6^1								18
1			4	5^2		7		2	8	9^1		13		11	10	14	3^2		12	6							19
1		3	4^2	5	12	7	8^1		10	11		13				14	2		6	9^3							20
1		3^1	4	5	12	7^3	8		10^3	11		13				2			6		14		9				21
1	2	3		5			8		10	11		7				4			6				9				22
1		3^1					8^2	13	12	10^3		11		7		5	2	14	4		6		9				23
1		3^2				12	8		10	11		7^1				5	2	13	4		6		9				24
1		3^1				12	8^2		10	11		7		13		5	2		4		6		9				25
1	2^2		4	5			8	12	10^3			13				3	7^1		6			14	9				26
1		3^3	4	5		12		7	8			13				2	10^1		6				9	14	11^2		27
1				5		7		12	8			10^3		11		13	2		4^1		6		9	14	3^2		28
1				5		7^1		12	8			10		11		13	2	14	4		6		9	10^3	3^2		29
1				5		7		12^2	8			9		11		13	2	14	4^3		6		10		3		30
1		3^1		5		12		7				9				14	2	8^3	4		6			10^2	11		31
1		3	4	5	8^1	7^3		12	9	11		13				2		14	6			10^3					32
1		3	4	5	8	7			10	11						2			6				9				33
1		3	4	5	8	7^1		12		11						2		13	6				9	10^2			34
1			4	5	8	7			10	11						2^1			6				12	9	3		35
1			4	5		7		12	8			10		11		2			6^1				13	9	3^2		36
1	2^1		4	5^2	8			12				10		11		7		13	6^2				3	9		1	37
1				5	8	7						10^1		11		4	2	12	6^2			3^3	9	13	14	1	38

Worthington Cup

Second Round	Oldham Ath	(h)	2-0
Third Round	Middlesbrough	(h)	2-1
Fourth Round	Manchester C	(h)	2-0
Fifth Round	Arsenal	(h)	4-0
Semi-Final	Sheffield W	(a)	2-1
		(h)	4-2
Final	Tottenham H		2-1
(at Millennium Stadium)			

FA Cup

Third Round	Barnsley	(a)	1-1
		(h)	3-1
Fourth Round	Millwall	(a)	1-0
Fifth Round	Middlesbrough	(a)	0-1

BLACKPOOL   Division 2

FOUNDATION

Old boys of St John's School who had formed themselves into a
football club decided to establish a club bearing the name of their
town and Blackpool FC came into being at a meeting at the
Stanley Arms Hotel in the summer of 1887. In their first season
playing at Raikes Hall Gardens, the club won both the Lancashire
Junior Cup and the Fylde Cup.

Bloomfield Rd Ground, Blackpool FY1 6JJ.

Telephone: (01253) 404 331 (Ticket/Credit Bookings),
(01253) 405 331 (Shop/General Enquiries).
Fax: (01253) 405 011. *Website:* www.blackpoolfc.co.uk
Email: info@blackpoolfc.co.uk *ClubCall:* 09068 121 648

Ground Capacity: 11,000.

Record Attendance: 38,098 v Wolverhampton W,
Division 1, 17 September 1955.

Record Receipts: £79,420 v Preston NE, Division 2,
21 November 1998.

Pitch Measurements: 112yd × 74yd.

Chairman: Mr K. Oyston.

Directors: C. Muir OBE, O. J. Oyston, G. Warburton,
P. Smith, P. Whitehead.

Manager: Steve McMahon.

Secretary: Petra Collins.

Commercial Director: Geoff Warburton.

Physio: Phil Horner.

Stadium Manager: John Turner.

Colours: Tangerine shirts, white shorts, tangerine stockings.

Change Colours: White shirts, tangerine shorts, white stockings.

Year Formed: 1887.

Turned Professional: 1887.

Ltd Co.: 1896.

Previous Name: 'South Shore' combined with Blackpool in 1899, twelve years after the latter had been
formed on the breaking up of the old 'Blackpool St John's' club.

Club Nickname: 'The Seasiders'.

Previous Grounds: 1887, Raikes Hall Gardens; 1897, Athletic Grounds; 1899, Raikes Hall Gardens;
1899, Bloomfield Road.

First Football League game: 5 September 1896, Division 2, v Lincoln C (a) L 1–3 – Douglas; Parr,
Bowman; Stuart, Stirzaker, Norris; Clarkin, Donnelly, R. Parkinson, Mount (1), J. Parkinson.

HONOURS

Football League: Division 1 –
Runners-up 1955–56; Division 2 –
Champions 1929–30; Runners-up
1936–37, 1969–70; Promoted from
Division 3 – 2000–01 (play-offs);
Division 4 – Runners-up 1984–85.
FA Cup: Winners 1953; Runners-up
1948, 1951.
Football League Cup: Semi-final 1962.
Anglo-Italian Cup: Winners 1971;
Runners-up 1972.
LDV Vans Trophy: Winners 2002.

IT'S A FACT !

Blackpool centre-half Louis Cardwell had played 70
League games for the club before scoring his first goal in
March 1936. It proved habit-forming, as he scored again
in each of the next three matches.

Record League Victory: 7–0 v Reading, Division 2, 10 November 1928 – Mercer; Gibson, Hamilton, Watson, Wilson, Grant, Ritchie, Oxberry (2), Hampson (5), Tufnell, Neal. 7–0 v Preston NE (away), Division 1, 1 May 1948 – Robinson; Shimwell, Crosland; Buchan, Hayward, Kelly; Hobson, Munro (1), McIntosh (5), McCall, Rickett (1). 7–0 v Sunderland, Division 1, 5 October 1957 – Farm; Armfield, Garrett, Kelly (J), Gratrix, Kelly (H), Matthews, Taylor (2), Charnley (2), Durie (2), Perry (1).

Record Cup Victory: 7–1 v Charlton Ath, League Cup 2nd rd, 25 September 1963 – Harvey; Armfield, Martin; Crawford, Gratrix, Cranston; Lea, Ball (1), Charnley (4), Durie (1), Oates (1).

Record Defeat: 1–10 v Small Heath, Division 2, 2 March 1901 and v Huddersfield T, Division 1, 13 December 1930.

Most League Points (2 for a win): 58, Division 2, 1929–30 and Division 2, 1967–68.

Most League Points (3 for a win): 86, Division 4, 1984–85.

Most League Goals: 98, Division 2, 1929–30.

Highest League Scorer in Season: Jimmy Hampson, 45, Division 2, 1929–30.

Most League Goals in Total Aggregate: Jimmy Hampson, 246, 1927–38.

Most League Goals in One Match: 5, Jimmy Hampson v Reading, Division 2, 10 November 1928; 5, Jimmy McIntosh v Preston NE, Division 1, 1 May 1948.

Most Capped Player: Jimmy Armfield, 43, England.

Most League Appearances: Jimmy Armfield, 568, 1952–71.

Youngest League Player: Trevor Sinclair, 16 years 170 days v Wigan Ath, 19 August 1989.

Record Transfer Fee Received: £1,500,000 from Southampton for Brett Ormerod, December 2001.

Record Transfer Fee Paid: £275,000 to Millwall for Chris Malkin, October 1996.

Football League Record: 1896 Elected to Division 2; 1899 Failed re-election; 1900 Re-elected; 1900–30 Division 2; 1930–33 Division 1; 1933–37 Division 2; 1937–67 Division 1; 1967–70 Division 2; 1970–71 Division 1; 1971–78 Division 2; 1978–81 Division 3; 1981–85 Division 4; 1985–90 Division 3; 1990–92 Division 4; 1992–2000 Division 2; 2000–01 Division 3; 2001– Division 2.

MANAGERS

Tom Barcroft 1903–33
(Secretary-Manager)
John Cox 1909–11
Bill Norman 1919–23
Maj. Frank Buckley 1923–27
Sid Beaumont 1927–28
Harry Evans 1928–33
(Hon. Team Manager)
Alex 'Sandy' Macfarlane 1933–35
Joe Smith 1935–58
Ronnie Suart 1958–67
Stan Mortensen 1967–69
Les Shannon 1969–70
Bob Stokoe 1970–72
Harry Potts 1972–76
Allan Brown 1976–78
Bob Stokoe 1978–79
Stan Ternent 1979–80
Alan Ball 1980–81
Allan Brown 1981–82
Sam Ellis 1982–89
Jimmy Mullen 1989–90
Graham Carr 1990
Bill Ayre 1990–94
Sam Allardyce 1994–96
Gary Megson 1996–97
Nigel Worthington 1997–99
Steve McMahon January 2000–

LATEST SEQUENCES

Longest Sequence of League Wins: 9, 21.11.36 – 1.1.37.

Longest Sequence of League Defeats: 8, 26.11.1898 – 7.1.1899.

Longest Sequence of League Draws: 5, 4.12.76 – 1.1.77.

Longest Sequence of Unbeaten League Matches: 17, 6.4.68 – 21.9.68.

Longest Sequence Without a League Win: 19, 19.12.70 – 24.4.71.

TEN YEAR LEAGUE RECORD

		P	W	D	L	F	A	Pts	Pos
1991-92	Div 4	42	22	10	10	71	45	76	4
1992-93	Div 2	46	12	15	19	63	75	51	18
1993-94	Div 2	46	16	5	25	63	75	53	20
1994-95	Div 2	46	18	10	18	64	70	64	12
1995-96	Div 2	46	23	13	10	67	40	82	3
1996-97	Div 2	46	18	15	13	60	47	69	7
1997-98	Div 2	46	17	11	18	59	67	62	12
1998-99	Div 2	46	14	14	18	44	54	56	14
1999-2000	Div 2	46	8	17	21	49	77	41	22
2000-01	Div 2	46	22	6	18	74	58	72	7

DID YOU KNOW ❓

Stan Mortensen, who scored for Blackpool in every round of the FA Cup in 1947–48, contributed a total of 28 goals in the competition over eight seasons.

BLACKPOOL 2001–02 LEAGUE RECORD

Match No.	Date	Venue	Opponents	Result	H/T Score	Lg. Pos.	Goalscorers	Attendance
1	Aug 11	H	Reading	L	0-2	0-1	—	5613
2	18	A	Bournemouth	W	1-0	1-0	14	Hills [8]	3709
3	25	H	Wycombe W	D	2-2	2-1	14	Ormerod [3], Thompson [14]	5010
4	27	A	Brighton & HA	L	0-4	0-1	16		6696
5	Sept 8	A	Oldham Ath	L	1-2	0-1	18	Ormerod [78]	6650
6	15	A	Huddersfield T	W	4-2	2-1	16	Collins [26], Ormerod 3 [30, 64, 90]	10,691
7	18	H	QPR	D	2-2	0-1	—	O'Kane [52], Fenton [89]	5774
8	22	H	Cambridge U	W	1-1	1-0	17	Ormerod [4]	5096
9	25	A	Northampton T	W	3-1	2-0	—	Ormerod 2 [31, 45], Fenton [79]	5103
10	29	H	Wigan Ath	W	3-1	1-0	14	Murphy J [8], Coid [85], MacKenzie [88]	5279
11	Oct 4	A	Tranmere R	L	0-4	0-3	—		10,354
12	13	H	Colchester U	W	2-1	0-0	13	Ormerod 2 [50, 90]	5546
13	20	A	Peterborough U	L	2-3	2-1	14	O'Kane [7], Murphy J [16]	3500
14	23	A	Wrexham	D	1-1	0-1	—	Ormerod [59]	5640
15	27	H	Chesterfield	W	1-0	0-0	14	Fenton [70]	5395
16	Nov 3	A	Brentford	L	0-2	0-0	15		7605
17	6	H	Stoke C	D	2-2	0-0	—	Ormerod 2 [73, 79]	4921
18	10	H	Swindon T	W	1-0	1-0	12	Coid [3]	5018
19	20	H	Notts Co	D	0-0	0-0	—		4118
20	24	A	Bristol C	L	1-2	0-1	14	Simpson (pen) [84]	9876
21	Dec 1	A	Port Vale	D	1-1	1-0	13	Coid [36]	5390
22	15	H	Cardiff C	D	1-1	0-0	13	Hills [66]	4880
23	22	A	Bury	D	1-1	1-0	13	Payton [40]	4830
24	26	H	Oldham Ath	L	0-2	0-0	13		5772
25	29	H	Brighton & HA	D	2-2	0-2	14	Hughes [55], Collins [90]	5419
26	Jan 1	A	Stoke C	L	0-2	0-1	14		16,615
27	12	A	Bournemouth	W	4-3	2-2	15	Walker [27], Hills (pen) [31], Hayter (og) [69], Fenton [82]	4583
28	19	A	Reading	L	0-3	0-2	17		13,732
29	26	H	Bury	L	0-1	0-1	18		4923
30	Feb 2	A	Wigan Ath	W	1-0	1-0	16	Murphy J [11]	7357
31	9	A	Peterborough U	D	2-2	1-1	17	O'Kane [45], Hills [64]	4604
32	16	A	Colchester U	D	1-1	1-0	17	Walker [41]	3553
33	19	A	Wycombe W	W	4-1	2-0	—	Taylor [20], Walker 2 [23, 48], Murphy J [87]	5803
34	23	H	Huddersfield T	L	1-2	0-0	16	Marshall [47]	8981
35	26	A	Cambridge U	W	3-0	1-0	—	Walker 2 [35, 55], O'Kane [72]	2986
36	Mar 2	A	QPR	L	0-2	0-1	16		10,203
37	5	H	Northampton T	L	1-2	0-1	—	Fenton [59]	4924
38	9	A	Cardiff C	D	2-2	2-1	15	Murphy J 2 [19, 27]	11,629
39	12	H	Tranmere R	D	1-1	1-0	—	Murphy J [12]	6860
40	16	H	Port Vale	W	4-0	0-0	15	Murphy J 2 [51, 84], Walker [70], Bullock [90]	7811
41	19	H	Brentford	L	1-3	0-2	—	Taylor [81]	4865
42	30	A	Swindon T	L	0-1	0-0	16		5085
43	Apr 1	A	Wrexham	W	3-0	1-0	15	Pejic (og) [41], Murphy J [67], Wellens [84]	7066
44	6	A	Notts Co	L	0-1	0-0	15		7783
45	13	H	Bristol C	W	5-1	4-0	15	Walker [9], Murphy J 2 [13, 29], Bullock [34], Hills [49]	9333
46	20	A	Chesterfield	L	1-2	0-1	16	Murphy J [75]	4788

Final League Position: 16

GOALSCORERS

League (66): Murphy J 13, Ormerod 13, Walker 8, Fenton 5, Hills 5 (1 pen), O'Kane 4, Coid 3, Bullock 2, Collins 2, Taylor 2, Hughes 1, MacKenzie 1, Marshall 1, Payton 1, Simpson 1 (pen), Thompson 1, Wellens 1, own goals 2.
Worthington Cup (3): Ormerod 3.
FA Cup (9): Murphy J 2, Ormerod 2, Hills 1, Jaszczun 1, McKenzie 1 (pen), Simpson 1, own goal 1.

Barnes P 30	Parkinson G 13+2	Jaszczun T 36+4	O'Kane J 34+4	Hughes I 13+7	Reid B 26	Wellens R 31+5	Simpson P 25+7	Murphy J 33+4	Ormerod B 21	Hills J 30+7	Collins L 24+8	Bullock M 37+6	MacKenzie N 6+8	Thompson P 10+3	Milligan J 9+8	Murphy N 1	Clarkson P 1+1	Pullen J 16	Coid D 24+3	Fenton G 6+9	Caldwell S 6	Milligan M 1+1	Blinkhorn M —+3	Marshall I 21	Payton A 4	Walker R 16+5	Day R 4+5	Taylor S 13+4	Clarke C 10+1	Dunning D 5	Match No.
1	2	3	4	5	6¹	7²	8³	9	10	11	12	13	14																		1
1	2	12	4	5		7²	8³	9	10	3¹		13	11	6	14																2
1		3	4	5¹	2		8²	9	10	12		7	11	6	13																3
1		3	4		2		9	10¹	11	6	8	12		7²	5		13														4
		4	5		6		2	12	9¹	10	3	7	8	11²				1	13												5
		3	4		6		7	12	9³	10	2	5²	8¹	13				1	11	14											6
		3	4		6		7²	12	9	10	2¹	5	8					1	11	13											7
		3			6		8¹	9	10	2	4	7		5				1	11	12											8
	12	3¹	2		6		8	9³	10	4²	7	13		5				1	11	14											9
		3	2		6		8³	9	10	4²	7¹	12		5	13			1	11	14											10
	12	3¹	2		6		8	9	10	4	7	6³		5	14			1	11	13											11
	2		4		6		8	12	9	11²	13	7						1	3				10¹	5							12
	2		4		6¹		8	9³	10	11	12	13	7					1	3				5²	14							13
	2		4		6		8¹	9	10	5	7							1	3			11	12								14
	2¹	12	4		6		13	8	9	11²		7						1	3				10	5							15
	2	3	4		6		12	8	9	13	10	7¹						1	11²					5							16
	3	4			6²	12	8	9	13	11	7¹							1	2					5		10					17
	3	4			7¹	8	9	11	6	12								1	2					5		10					18
1	3	4	5		7	8²	9¹	10	12	13	6								2					11							19
1	3	4	12	6¹	7	8²	9	10	13		11								2					5							20
1	4		6	7¹	8	9	10	3	12	11									2					5							21
1	2	3	12	5		8	9		13	4	7	11²														6		10¹			22
1	2	3	4	5		8	9		12	7¹	11															6		10²	13		23
1	2¹	3	4	5		12	8²		11³	6	7	13	14													10	9				24
1	3²	4¹	12		2	13		11	7	8	5															6	10	9			25
1	3		5		2¹	12		11	7	8	13	4³														6	10²	9	14		26
1	3			6	7	12	9²		11¹	4	8								2	13						5³	10	14			27
1	3³	12	13	5²	7			11	4	8									2	10¹						6		9	14		28
1		12	5		7		8³	13		3	11¹			6²	14				2				14				9	4	10		29
1	3	4²	12		7		9		11	13	8								2							6		5	10		30
1	3	4¹			7		9		11	12	8²								2						6	13	5	10			31
1	3	4		6	7		9		11	2	12															5	8¹		10		32
1	3	2		5	7		9		11	4	12															6	8¹		10		33
1	3	2		5	7		9		11	4	12															6	8¹		10		34
1	3	2		6³	7		9²		11	4	13								12							5	8¹		10	14	35
1	3²	2			7	12	13		11	4	8²															6³	9	14	10	5	36
1	12		13		7	8¹	9		3	4	11								2³	10		14				6²			5		37
1	3		12		7	8	9			11¹			4						2							6		13	10	5	38
1	3		12		7		9		11	4	8²								2							6¹	13		10	5	39
1	12	13	6		7	11¹	9		3	4	8								2²								14		10	5	40
	2²	3	4	5	6		11	12		13						7		8	1	9¹						10³	14				41
1	2	3		6²		7		9		11		8²							12							14	13	10¹	5	4	42
	2	3			6	7		9³		11		8²			12			1				14				10		13	5	4¹	43
1		3	2		6	7¹		9		11	12	8															10²		13	5	4	44
1		3²	2		6	7¹		9		11	12	8³												13			10		14	5	4	45
1		3	2		6	12		9		11²	7													13			10		8³	5	4	46

Worthington Cup

First Round	Wigan Ath	(h)	3-2
Second Round	Leicester C	(h)	0-1

FA Cup

First Round	Newport Co	(h)	2-2
		(a)	4-1
Second Round	Rochdale	(h)	2-0
Third Round	Charlton Ath	(a)	1-2

BOLTON WANDERERS FA Premiership

FOUNDATION

In 1874 boys of Christ Church Sunday School, Blackburn Street, led by their master Thomas Ogden, established a football club which went under the name of the school and whose president was Vicar of Christ Church. Membership was 6d (two and a half pence). When their president began to lay down too many rules about the use of church premises, the club broke away and formed Bolton Wanderers in 1877, holding their earliest meetings at the Gladstone Hotel.

Reebok Stadium, Burnden Way, Lostock, Bolton BL6 6JW.

Telephone: (01204) 673 673. *Fax:* (01204) 673 773.
Ticket Office: (0871) 871 2932. *ClubCall:* 09068 121 164.

Ground Capacity: 27,879.

Record Attendance: 69,912 v Manchester C, FA Cup 5th rd, 18 February 1933.

Record Receipts: £335,468 v WBA, Division 1, play-off semi-final, 17 May 2001.

Pitch Measurements: 114yd × 74yd.

President: Nat Lofthouse OBE. *Chairman:* P. A. Gartside.
Directors: G. Seymour, G. Warburton, W. B. Warburton, I. Currie, E. Davies OBE, D. Speakman, D. McBain.

Team Manager: Sam Allardyce.

Physio: Mark Taylor.

Chief Executive & Secretary: Simon Marland.

Commercial Director: G. Moores.

Colours: White shirts, navy blue shorts, blue stockings.

Change Colours: Blue shirts with white sash, white shorts, blue stockings.

Year Formed: 1874.

Turned Professional: 1880.

Ltd Co.: 1895.

Previous Name: 1874, Christ Church FC; 1877, Bolton Wanderers.

Club Nickname: 'The Trotters'.

Previous Grounds: Park Recreation Ground and Cockle's Field before moving to Pike's Lane ground 1881; 1895, Burnden Park; 1997, Reebok Stadium.

First Football League Game: 8 September 1888, Football League, v Derby Co (h) L 3–6 – Harrison; Robinson, Mitchell; Roberts, Weir, Bullough, Davenport (2), Milne, Coupar, Barbour, Brogan (1).

Record League Victory: 8–0 v Barnsley, Division 2, 6 October 1934 – Jones; Smith, Finney; Goslin, Atkinson, George Taylor; George T. Taylor (2), Eastham, Milsom (1), Westwood (4), Cook, (1 og).

HONOURS

Football League: Division 1 – Champions 1996–97; Promoted from Division 1 (play-offs) 2000–01. Division 2 – Champions 1908–09, 1977–78; Runners-up 1899–1900, 1904–05, 1910–11, 1934–35, 1992–93; Division 3 – Champions 1972–73.
FA Cup: Winners 1923, 1926, 1929, 1958; Runners-up 1894, 1904, 1953.
Football League Cup: Runners-up 1995.
Freight Rover Trophy: Runners-up 1986.
Sherpa Van Trophy: Winners 1989.

IT'S A FACT !

Right-back Joe Threlfall, a Second World War discovery by Bolton Wanderers from Ashton National, was offered full-time professional forms by the club but decided to remain part-time and on the staff of Ashton Gas Works.

Record Cup Victory: 13–0 v Sheffield U, FA Cup 2nd rd,
1 February 1890 – Parkinson; Robinson (1), Jones;
Bullough, Davenport, Roberts; Rushton, Brogan (3),
Cassidy (5), McNee, Weir (4).

Record Defeat: 1–9 v Preston NE, FA Cup 2nd rd, 10
December 1887.

Most League Points (2 for a win): 61, Division 3, 1972–73.

Most League Points (3 for a win): 98, Division 1, 1996–97.

Most League Goals: 100, Division 1, 1996–97.

Highest League Scorer in Season: Joe Smith, 38, Division 1,
1920–21.

Most League Goals in Total Aggregate: Nat Lofthouse,
255, 1946–61.

Most League Goals in One Match: 5, Tony Caldwell v
Walsall, Division 3, 10 September 1983.

Most Capped Player: Mark Fish, 34 (60), South Africa.

Most League Appearances: Eddie Hopkinson, 519, 1956–70.

Youngest League Player: Ray Parry, 15 years 267 days v
Wolverhampton W, 13 October 1951.

Record Transfer Fee Received: £4,500,000 from Liverpool
for Jason McAteer, September 1995.

Record Transfer Fee Paid: £3,500,000 for Dean Holdsworth
from Wimbledon, October 1997.

Football League Record: 1888 Founder Member of the
League; 1899–1900 Division 2; 1900–03 Division 1; 1903–05
Division 2; 1905–08 Division 1; 1908–09 Division 2; 1909–10
Division 1; 1910–11 Division 2; 1911–33 Division 1; 1933–35
Division 2; 1935–64 Division 1; 1964–71 Division 2; 1971–73
Division 3; 1973–78 Division 2; 1978–80 Division 1; 1980–83
Division 2; 1983–87 Division 3; 1987–88 Division 4; 1988–92
Division 3; 1992–93 Division 2; 1993–95 Division 1; 1995–96
FA Premier League; 1996–97 Division 1; 1997–98 FA
Premier League; 1998–2001 Division 1; 2001– FA Premier
League.

LATEST SEQUENCES

Longest Sequence of League Wins: 11, 5.11.04 – 2.1.05.

Longest Sequence of League Defeats: 11, 7.4.02 – 18.10.02.

Longest Sequence of League Draws: 6, 25.1.13 – 8.3.13.

Longest Sequence of Unbeaten League Matches: 23, 13.10.90 – 9.3.91.

Longest Sequence Without a League Win: 26, 7.4.02 – 10.1.03.

MANAGERS

Tom Rawthorne 1874–85
  (Secretary)
J. J. Bentley 1885–86
  (Secretary)
W. G. Struthers 1886–87
  (Secretary)
Fitzroy Norris 1887
  (Secretary)
J. J. Bentley 1887–95
  (Secretary)
Harry Downs 1895–96
  (Secretary)
Frank Brettell 1896–98
  (Secretary)
John Somerville 1898–1910
Will Settle 1910–15
Tom Mather 1915–19
Charles Foweraker 1919–44
Walter Rowley 1944–50
Bill Ridding 1951–68
Nat Lofthouse 1968–70
Jimmy McIlroy 1970
Jimmy Meadows 1971
Nat Lofthouse 1971
  (then Admin. Manager to 1972)
Jimmy Armfield 1971–74
Ian Greaves 1974–80
Stan Anderson 1980–81
George Mulhall 1981–82
John McGovern 1982–85
Charlie Wright 1985
Phil Neal 1985–92
Bruce Rioch 1992–95
Roy McFarland 1995–96
Colin Todd 1996–99
Sam Allardyce October 1999–

TEN YEAR LEAGUE RECORD

		P	W	D	L	F	A	Pts	Pos
1991-92	Div 3	46	14	17	15	57	56	59	13
1992-93	Div 2	46	27	9	10	80	41	90	2
1993-94	Div 1	46	15	14	17	63	64	59	14
1994-95	Div 1	46	21	14	11	67	45	77	3
1995-96	PR Lge	38	8	5	25	39	71	29	20
1996-97	Div 1	46	28	14	4	100	53	98	1
1997-98	PR Lge	38	9	13	16	41	61	40	18
1998-99	Div 1	46	20	16	10	78	59	76	6
1999-2000	Div 1	46	21	13	12	69	50	76	6
2000-01	Div 1	46	24	15	7	76	45	87	3

DID YOU KNOW ?

In November 1960, Nat
Lofthouse, John Higgins,
Derek Hennin and Dennis
Stevens each received a
£1,000 benefit from Bolton
Wanderers. In the case of
Lofthouse it was his third
such award.

BOLTON WANDERERS 2001–02 LEAGUE RECORD

Match No.	Date	Venue	Opponents	Result		H/T Score	Lg. Pos.	Goalscorers	Attendance
1	Aug 18	A	Leicester C	W	5-0	4-0	—	Nolan 2 [15, 41], Ricketts [33], Frandsen 2 [45, 83]	19,987
2	21	H	Middlesbrough	W	1-0	1-0	—	Ricketts [39]	20,747
3	27	H	Liverpool	W	2-1	1-0	—	Ricketts [27], Holdsworth [90]	27,205
4	Sept 8	A	Leeds U	D	0-0	0-0	1		40,153
5	15	H	Southampton	L	0-1	0-0	3		24,378
6	19	A	Blackburn R	D	1-1	0-0	—	Wallace [69]	25,949
7	22	A	Arsenal	D	1-1	0-0	2	Ricketts [83]	38,014
8	29	H	Sunderland	L	0-2	0-0	5		24,520
9	Oct 13	H	Newcastle U	L	0-4	0-1	8		25,631
10	20	A	Manchester U	W	2-1	1-1	6	Nolan [35], Ricketts [84]	67,559
11	27	A	Aston Villa	L	2-3	1-2	9	Ricketts 2 [2, 75]	33,599
12	Nov 3	H	Everton	D	2-2	1-1	10	Frandsen [10], Ricketts [90]	27,343
13	18	A	Ipswich T	W	2-1	2-1	8	Bergsson [6], Ricketts [25]	22,321
14	24	H	Fulham	D	0-0	0-0	9		23,848
15	Dec 3	A	Tottenham H	L	2-3	1-0	—	Ricketts [8], Wallace [56]	32,971
16	8	A	Derby Co	L	0-1	0-0	12		25,712
17	15	H	Charlton Ath	D	0-0	0-0	12		20,834
18	23	A	Chelsea	L	1-5	1-2	14	Nolan [3]	34,063
19	26	H	Leeds U	L	0-3	0-2	15		27,060
20	29	H	Leicester C	D	2-2	1-2	15	Nolan [34], Ricketts [90]	23,037
21	Jan 1	A	Liverpool	D	1-1	0-0	14	Nolan [78]	43,710
22	12	H	Chelsea	D	2-2	0-0	16	Ricketts [56], Nolan [79]	23,891
23	19	A	Middlesbrough	D	1-1	0-1	16	Hansen [73]	26,104
24	29	H	Manchester U	L	0-4	0-2	—		27,350
25	Feb 2	A	Newcastle U	L	2-3	2-2	18	Gardner [19], Southall [34]	52,094
26	9	H	West Ham U	W	1-0	1-0	17	Gardner [38]	24,342
27	23	A	Southampton	D	0-0	0-0	17		31,380
28	Mar 2	H	Blackburn R	D	1-1	1-0	17	Wallace [45]	27,203
29	5	A	Sunderland	L	0-1	0-1	—		39,730
30	16	H	Derby Co	L	1-3	0-1	18	Gardner [46]	25,893
31	23	A	Charlton Ath	W	2-1	2-0	16	Djorkaeff 2 [15, 39]	26,296
32	30	H	Aston Villa	W	3-2	2-2	15	Delaney (og) [8], Bobic [40], Nolan [76]	24,600
33	Apr 1	A	Everton	L	1-3	0-1	16	N'Gotty [75]	39,784
34	6	H	Ipswich T	W	4-1	4-0	14	Bobic 3 [2, 30, 38], Djorkaeff [35]	25,817
35	20	H	Tottenham H	D	1-1	0-1	15	Holdsworth [71]	25,817
36	23	A	Fulham	L	0-3	0-1	—		18,107
37	29	H	Arsenal	L	0-2	0-2	—		27,351
38	May 11	A	West Ham U	L	1-2	0-1	16	Djorkaeff [67]	35,546

Final League Position: 16

GOALSCORERS

League (44): Ricketts 12, Nolan 8, Bobic 4, Djorkaeff 4, Frandsen 3, Gardner 3, Wallace 3, Holdsworth 2, Bergsson 1, Hansen 1, N'Gotty 1, Southall 1, own goal 1.
Worthington Cup (7): Holdsworth 2 (1 pen), Ricketts 2, Nishizawa 1, Pedersen 1, Wallace 1.
FA Cup (4): Bergsson 1, Norris 1, Pedersen 1, Ricketts 1.

Jaaskelainen J 34	Barness A 19+6	Charlton S 35+1	Warhurst P 25	Bergsson G 30	Whitlow M 28+1	Nolan K 34+1	Frandsen P 25+4	Hansen B 10+7	Ricketts M 26+11	Gardner R 29+2	Southall N 10+8	Marshall I —+2	Pedersen H 5+6	Holdsworth D 9+22	Diawara D 4+5	Farrelly G 11+7	Richardson L —+1	N'Gotty B 24+2	Wallace R 14+5	Johnson J 4+6	Banks S 1	Poole K 3	Hendry C 3	Bobic F 14+2	Tofting S 6	Djorkaeff Y 12	Espartero M —+3	Konstantinidis K 3	Smith J —+1	Match No.
1	2	3	4^1	5^2	6	7	8	9	10	11^3	12	13	14																	1
1	2	3	4^1	5	6	7^2	8	9	10^2	11	12	13			14															2
1	2	3	4	5	6	7^2	8^2	9	10^1	11				12	14	13														3
1	2	3		5	6	7	8	9^2	10^1				4	12		11	13													4
1	2	3	4	5	6	7^2	8^1	9	10^3	13	12			11	14															5
1	2	3	4	5	6	7		9^1	10^2	11				8^3	12			14	13											6
1	2	3	4^2	5	6	7				12	11			8^3	10^1	13		14	9											7
1	2	3	4	5	6	8^2	13	12	14	11				9				7^2	10^1											8
1	2^2	3^3	4	5	6		9	12	11	7^1			10	14		13		8												9
1	12	3	4^2	5	6	7	8	9^1	10	11								2	13											10
12		3		5		8	4	9^3	10	11					13	6	7^2	2^1	14		1									11
	3^3	4^1	5	6	7	8		9	11						13	14	12	2	10^2			1								12
	3	4^1	5	6	7	8		9	11						13		12	2	10^2			1								13
1		3	4	5	6	7	8^2		9	11^1					12		13	2	10											14
1		3		5	6	8	4	12	9^2	11^3					13		7^1	2	10	14										15
1	2	3	4^3	5	6	7	8^2		9	11					12		13		10^1	14										16
1		3	4	5	6	7	8^2		9	11					12			2	10^1											17
1		3	4^1		6	7	8^2	12	9	11					14		13	2	10^3				5							18
1	2^1	3	4^3		6	7	8		11	12		13	9	5	10^2				14											19
1	2^3	3	4		7	8		9		12		13	10	14	11^1	6								5^2						20
1		3	4		7	8		9		11				12	10^1	6	13							5^2						21
1	12	3		5		6	8^2		9	13	11		10^3		4	7		2^1								14				22
1	12	3^2		5		6	8^1	13	10	11	2		14			7		4								9^2				23
1	4	12		5	6	7		8^3	10	3	2^1			13		11			14							9^2				24
1	4	3		5	6	8^2		14	10^3	11	2			13	12		7									9^1				25
1		3	4^2	5	6	7		12	10^3	11	13			14				2								9^1	8			26
1		3^1		5	6	7		12	10	11					13			2	13							9^2	8	4^2	14	27
1	12			5	6	7			13	3	2^1			14				4	10^3							9^2	8	11		28
1	12		7^3	5	6^1				10^2	3	2			13				4	9								8	11	14	29
1		3	4	5^2	6^1		12		10	11	13							2	9						14	8^3	7			30
1	2	3	4		6	8	12	11	13				10^2					5								9^1	7			31
	3	4		12	7	6^1		13	11				10					2				1		9		8^2		5		32
	3	4		6	7	12		13	11				10^1					2	14			1		9^2		8^3		5		33
1	5	3	4^1		6	7	12	13	11^2					14				2	10							9^3	8			34
1		3		5	6	8	4	12		7					13			2	10^1							9^2	11			35
1	2	3		5		8	4	12		7^3					13	6		10^1								9^2	11	14		36
1	2	3		5		8	4	12		7					13		7	6	10^2	13						9^1	11			37
1	2	3		5		12	4		10^2						13		7							9		8^1	11		6^9 14	38

Worthington Cup

Second Round	Walsall	(h)	4-3
Third Round	Nottingham F	(h)	1-0
Fourth Round	Southampton	(h)	2-2
Fifth Round	Tottenham H	(a)	0-6

FA Cup

Third Round	Stockport Co	(a)	4-1
Fourth Round	Tottenham H	(a)	0-4

BOSTON UNITED
Division 3

FOUNDATION

Although it was 1934 before the name Boston United first appeared, football had been played in the town since the late 1800s and indeed, always on the same site as the present York Street stadium. In fact Boston Football Club was established in March 1870 playing their first match against Louth the following month. Before the First World War, there were two clubs, Boston Town, whose headquarters were The Coach and Horses, and Boston Swifts, who used The Indian Queen. In fact, as both public houses were situated on Main Ridge and the pitch was virtually just opposite, it was not surprising that for the first forty years or so, that was what the ground was called. Swifts never reappeared after the First World War and it was left to the club called simply Boston to achieve the first giant-killing in the FA Cup by beating Bradford Park Avenue 1-0 on 12 December 1925. The club was now competing in the Midland League and subsequently reformed under the new title of Boston United.

York Street, Boston, Lincolnshire PE21 6HJ.

Telephone: (01205) 365 525.

Fax: (01205) 354 063.

Ticket office: (01205) 364 403

ClubCall: 09068 121 539

Website: www.bostonunited.co.uk.

Ground Capacity: 8,781

Record Attendance: 10,086 v Corby Town, Friendly, 1955.

Chairman: P. Mackinson.

Chief Executive: K. Mugleston.

Directors: T. Ruck, R. Hackford, R. Carrington, C. Woodcock.

General Manager/Secretary: John Blackwell.

Manager: To be appointed.

Physio: Jim Woods.

HONOURS

Conference: Champions 2001–02.
Dr. Martens: Champions 1999–2000. Runners-up: 1998–99.
Unibond League: Runners-up 1995–96, 1997–98.
Unibond Challenge Cup: Runners-up 1996–97.
FA Trophy: Runners-up 1984–85.
Northern Premier League: Champions 1972–73, 1973–74, 1976–77, 1977–78.
Northern Premier League Cup: Winners 1974, 1976.
Northern Premier League Challenge Shield: Winners 1974, 1975, 1977, 1978.
Lincolnshire Senior Cup: Winners 1935, 1937, 1938, 1946, 1950, 1955, 1956, 1960, 1977, 1979, 1986, 1988, 1989.
Non-League Champions of Champions Cup: Winners 1973, 1977.
East Anglian Cup: Winners 1961.
Central Alliance League: Champions 1961–62.
United Counties League: Champions 1965–66.
West Midlands League: Champions 1966–67, 1967–68.
Eastern Professional Floodlit Cup: Winners 1972.

IT'S A FACT !

On 10 December 1955, Boston United defeated Derby County 6-1, a record score by a non-League club against a Football League team on their own ground, in an FA Cup second round tie. Boston included eight ex-Derby players.

Colours
Amber and black striped shirts, black shorts with amber stripe, black stockings with yellow top.

Change Colours
White shirts with black and amber trim, white shorts, white stockings.

Year formed: 1934.

Club Nickname: 'The Pilgrims'.

Record League Victory: 12-0 v Spilsby T, Grace Swan Cup, 1992–93.

Record Transfer Fee Received: £50,000 from Bolton W for David Norris, 2000.

Record Transfer Fee Paid: £14,000 to Wycombe Wanderers for Micky Nuttell.

MANAGERS
George Kerr/Dave Cusack
Dave Cusack
Peter Morris
Mel Sterland
Greg Fee
Steve Evans, October 1998–

BOSTON UNITED ROLL CALL 2001–02

Player	Date of Birth	Signed from	Position
Paul Bastock	19-05-70	Kettering T	Goalkeeper
Nick Conroy	09-04-76	Yaxley	Goalkeeper
Jim Rodwell	20-11-70	Rushden & D	Defender
Paul Ellender	21-10-74	Scarborough	Defender
Mark Monington	21-10-70	Rochdale	Defender
Andy Lodge	17-05-78	Stamford AFC	Defender
Ross Weatherstone	16-05-81	Oxford U	Defender
Neil Thompson	02-10-63	Scarborough	Defender
Ray Warburton	07-10-67	Rushden & D	Defender
Simon Rusk	17-12-81	Peterborough U	Midfielder
Mark Clifford	11-09-77	Ilkeston T	Midfielder
Peter Costello	31-10-69	Hong Kong	Midfielder
Darren Beesley	16-03-81	Airdrie	Midfielder
James Gould	15-01-82	Northampton T	Midfielder
Mickey Brown	08-02-68	Shrewsbury T	Midfielder
Jamie Cook	02-08-79	Oxford U	Forward
David Town	09-12-76	Rushden & D	Forward
Daryl Clare	01-08-78	Grimsby T	Forward
Simon Weatherstone	26-01-80	Oxford U	Forward
Anthony Elding	16-04-82	Lincoln C	Forward
Neil Tarrant	24-06-79	Ross Co	Forward
Mark Angel	23-08-75	Darlington	Forward

TEN YEAR LEAGUE RECORD

		P	W	D	L	F	A	Pts	Pos
1991–92	Conf.	42	18	9	15	71	66	63	8
1992–93	Conf.	42	9	13	20	50	69	40	22
1993–94	NP pr	42	23	9	10	90	43	78	3
1994–95	NP pr	42	20	11	11	80	43	71	5
1995–96	NP pr	42	23	6	13	86	59	75	2
1996–97	NP pr	44	22	13	9	74	47	79	6
1997–98	NP pr	42	22	12	8	55	40	78	2
1998–99	SL pr	42	17	16	9	69	51	67	2
1999–2000	SL pr	42	27	11	4	102	39	92	1
2000–01	Conf.	42	13	17	12	74	63	56	12

DID YOU KNOW ?

In the 1970s, Boston United completed 51 consecutive home and away League games without defeat and had a similar success with 64 home League matches.

AFC BOURNEMOUTH

Division 3

FOUNDATION

There was a Bournemouth FC as early as 1875, but the present club arose out of the remnants of the Boscombe St John's club (formed 1890). The meeting at which Boscombe FC came into being was held at a house in Gladstone Road in 1899. They began by playing in the Boscombe and District Junior League.

The Fitness First Stadium at Dean Court, Bournemouth, Dorset BH7 7AF.

Telephone: (01202) 726 300. *Fax:* (01202) 726 301.
Website: http://www.afcb.co.uk *Fansline:* tba.
Ticket Office: (01202) 726 303.

Ground Capacity: 9,600 seats, rising to 12,000 all-seater.

Record Attendance: 28,799 v Manchester U, FA Cup 6th rd, 2 March 1957.

Record Receipts: £80,267 v Walsall, Auto Windscreens Shield Southern Area Final, 17 March 1998.

Pitch Measurements: 105m × 78m.

Chairman: A. Swaisland. *Directors:* A. H. Kaye (Vice-chairman), Mel Machin (Director of Football).

Secretary: K. R. J. MacAlister.

HONOURS

Football League: Division 3 – Champions 1986–87; Division 3 (S) – Runners-up 1947–48; Division 4 – Runners-up 1970–71; Promotion from Division 4 1981–82 (4th).

FA Cup: best season: 6th rd, 1957.

Football League Cup: best season: 4th rd, 1962, 1964.

Associate Members' Cup: Winners 1984.

Auto Windscreens Shield: Runners-up 1998.

Manager: Sean O'Driscoll. *Head Coach:* Peter Grant. *Physio:* John Cooper.

Corporate Manager: Mrs D. Rackley. *Groundsman:* D. Edwards.

Colours: Red and black striped shirts, black shorts, black stockings.

Change Colours: White shirts with red and black trim, black or white shorts, black or white stockings.

Year Formed: 1899.

Turned Professional: 1912.

Ltd Co.: 1914.

Previous Names: 1890, Boscombe St Johns; 1899, Boscombe FC; 1923, Bournemouth & Boscombe Ath FC; 1971, AFC Bournemouth.

Club Nickname: 'Cherries'.

Previous Grounds: 1899, Castlemain Road, Pokesdown; 1910, Dean Court.

First Football League Game: 25 August 1923, Division 3 (S), v Swindon T (a), L 1–3 – Heron; Wingham, Lamb; Butt, C. Smith, Voisey; Miller, Lister (1), Davey, Simpson, Robinson.

Record League Victory: 7–0 v Swindon T, Division 3 (S), 22 September 1956 – Godwin; Cunningham, Keetley; Clayton, Crosland, Rushworth; Siddall (1), Norris (2), Arnott (1), Newsham (2), Cutler (1). 10–0 win v Northampton T at start of 1939–40 expunged from the records on outbreak of war.

IT'S A FACT !

Ron Eyre, who made his Bournemouth debut on 3 January 1925 v Luton Town, having been signed from Sheffield Wednesday, went on to score 259 goals in 367 appearances in all matches over eight and a half seasons.

Record Cup Victory: 11–0 v Margate, FA Cup 1st rd, 20 November 1971 – Davies; Machin (1), Kitchener, Benson, Jones, Powell, Cave (1), Boyer, MacDougall (9 incl. 1p), Miller, Scott (De Garis).

Record Defeat: 0–9 v Lincoln C, Division 3, 18 December 1982.

Most League Points (2 for a win): 62, Division 3, 1971–72.

Most League Points (3 for a win): 97, Division 3, 1986–87.

Most League Goals: 88, Division 3 (S), 1956–57.

Highest League Scorer in Season: Ted MacDougall, 42, 1970–71.

Most League Goals in Total Aggregate: Ron Eyre, 202, 1924–33.

Most League Goals in One Match: 4, Jack Russell v Clapton Orient, Division 3S, 7 January 1933; 4, Jack Russell v Bristol C, Division 3S, 28 January 1933; 4, Harry Mardon v Southend U, Division 3S, 1 January 1938; 4, Jack McDonald v Torquay U, Division 3S, 8 November 1947; 4, Ted MacDougall v Colchester U, 18 September 1970; 4, Brian Clark v Rotherham U, 10 October 1972, 4, Luther Blissett v Hull C, 29 November 1988; 4, James Hayter v Bury, Division 2, 21 October 2000.

Most Capped Player: Gerry Peyton, 7 (33), Republic of Ireland.

Most League Appearances: Sean O'Driscoll, 423, 1984–95.

Youngest League Player: Jimmy White, 15 years 321 days v Brentford, 30 April 1958.

Record Transfer Fee Received: £800,000 from Everton for Joe Parkinson, March 1994.

Record Transfer Fee Paid: £210,000 to Gillingham for Gavin Peacock, August 1989.

Football League Record: 1923 Elected to Division 3 (S) and remained a Third Division club for record number of years until 1970; 1970–71 Division 4; 1971–75 Division 3; 1975–82 Division 4; 1982–87 Division 3; 1987–90 Division 2; 1990–92 Division 3; 1992– 2002 Division 2; 2002– Division 3.

MANAGERS

Vincent Kitcher 1914–23
(Secretary-Manager)
Harry Kinghorn 1923–25
Leslie Knighton 1925–28
Frank Richards 1928–30
Billy Birrell 1930–35
Bob Crompton 1935–36
Charlie Bell 1936–39
Harry Kinghorn 1939–47
Harry Lowe 1947–50
Jack Bruton 1950–56
Fred Cox 1956–58
Don Welsh 1958–61
Bill McGarry 1961–63
Reg Flewin 1963–65
Fred Cox 1965–70
John Bond 1970–73
Trevor Hartley 1974–75
John Benson 1975–78
Alec Stock 1979–80
David Webb 1980–82
Don Megson 1983
Harry Redknapp 1983–92
Tony Pulis 1992–94
Mel Machin 1994–2000
Sean O'Driscoll August 2000–

LATEST SEQUENCES

Longest Sequence of League Wins: 7, 22.8.70 – 23.9.70.

Longest Sequence of League Defeats: 7, 13.8.94 – 13.9.94.

Longest Sequence of League Draws: 5, 25.4.00 – 12.8.00.

Longest Sequence of Unbeaten League Matches: 18, 6.3.82 – 28.8.82.

Longest Sequence Without a League Win: 14, 6.3.74 – 27.4.74.

TEN YEAR LEAGUE RECORD

		P	W	D	L	F	A	Pts	Pos
1991-92	Div 3	46	20	11	15	52	48	71	8
1992-93	Div 2	46	12	17	17	45	52	53	17
1993-94	Div 2	46	14	15	17	51	59	57	17
1994-95	Div 2	46	13	11	22	49	69	50	19
1995-96	Div 2	46	16	10	20	51	70	58	14
1996-97	Div 2	46	15	15	16	43	45	60	16
1997-98	Div 2	46	18	12	16	57	52	66	9
1998-99	Div 2	46	21	13	12	63	41	76	7
1999-2000	Div 2	46	16	9	21	59	62	57	16
2000-01	Div 2	46	20	13	13	79	55	73	7

DID YOU KNOW ?

Bournemouth had a marathon semi-final tie with Queens Park Rangers in the Division Three (South) Cup in 1945–46. At Dean Court it finished 1-1 and in the replay sudden death ended it, thanks to Bournemouth's Jack Kirkham after 136 minutes' play.

AFC BOURNEMOUTH 2001–02 LEAGUE RECORD

Match No.	Date	Venue	Opponents	Result	H/T Score	Lg. Pos.	Goalscorers	Attendance
1	Aug 11	A	Huddersfield T	L 0-1	0-0	—		10,137
2	18	H	Blackpool	L 0-1	0-1	23		3709
3	25	A	Cardiff C	D 2-2	0-1	19	Feeney (pen) [62], Tindall [65]	13,383
4	Sept 1	A	Cambridge U	D 2-2	1-1	20	Elliott 2 [20, 85]	2754
5	8	H	Swindon T	D 0-0	0-0	19		3770
6	15	H	Bury	W 3-2	2-2	17	Hayter [9], Feeney (pen) [22], Stock [90]	3004
7	18	A	Peterborough U	L 0-6	0-3	—		3445
8	22	H	Brighton & HA	L 1-2	0-1	21	Howe [76]	6714
9	25	H	Reading	W 1-0	0-0	—	Hayter [71]	3691
10	29	A	Stoke C	L 0-2	0-1	20		14,803
11	Oct 5	H	Oldham Ath	W 3-2	0-1	—	Hayter [57], Holmes [60], Elliott [65]	3312
12	9	H	Wigan Ath	W 2-0	1-0	—	Hayter [14], Elliott [90]	2908
13	13	A	Wycombe W	D 1-1	1-0	15	Holmes [21]	6810
14	20	H	Brentford	L 0-2	0-1	16		3934
15	23	A	Bristol C	L 0-1	0-1	—		9972
16	27	H	Notts Co	W 4-2	3-2	16	Elliott 2 (2 pens) [37, 45], Fletcher C [41], Feeney [71]	3209
17	Nov 3	A	Colchester U	W 2-1	2-1	16	Feeney [13], Howe [20]	4369
18	10	H	Wrexham	W 3-0	2-0	15	Stock [29], Hayter [45], Tindall [64]	5031
19	20	H	Port Vale	D 0-0	0-0	—		4428
20	24	A	Chesterfield	L 1-2	1-1	15	Feeney [27]	4353
21	Dec 1	H	Tranmere R	L 0-2	0-1	16		6035
22	15	A	Northampton T	L 0-1	0-1	17		3909
23	22	H	QPR	L 1-2	0-1	17	Fletcher C [89]	8147
24	26	A	Swindon T	D 0-0	0-0	18		6790
25	29	A	Wigan Ath	D 0-0	0-0	19		5011
26	Jan 12	H	Blackpool	L 3-4	2-2	19	Hayter [8], Fletcher C 2 [45, 89]	4583
27	19	A	Huddersfield T	L 2-3	0-3	19	Holmes [58], Feeney [90]	5307
28	22	A	QPR	D 1-1	0-1	—	Feeney [50]	10,901
29	26	A	Oldham Ath	D 3-3	0-1	19	Howe [53], Feeney (pen) [56], Hughes [66]	4853
30	Feb 2	H	Stoke C	W 3-1	2-0	19	Purches [6], Hughes [43], Feeney [56]	6027
31	5	H	Cardiff C	L 1-3	0-2	—	Holmes [73]	4336
32	9	A	Brentford	L 0-1	0-0	19		6698
33	16	H	Wycombe W	L 1-2	0-0	19	Howe [76]	5807
34	23	A	Bury	L 1-2	1-1	20	Holmes [14]	4218
35	26	H	Brighton & HA	D 1-1	1-1	—	Holmes [36]	6337
36	Mar 2	H	Peterborough U	L 0-2	0-1	21		5163
37	5	A	Reading	D 2-2	0-1	—	Hayter [48], Holmes [71]	13,538
38	9	H	Northampton T	W 5-1	0-0	20	Feeney 2 [33, 74], Tindall [55], Holmes [65], Purches [90]	6322
39	16	A	Tranmere R	D 0-0	0-0	22		7829
40	19	H	Cambridge U	D 2-2	1-1	—	Feeney [24], Elliott (pen) [49]	7082
41	23	H	Bristol C	L 1-3	0-2	22	McAnespie [90]	7033
42	30	A	Notts Co	L 0-2	0-1	22		9014
43	Apr 2	H	Colchester U	L 0-1	0-0	—		5908
44	6	A	Port Vale	D 0-0	0-0	22		3514
45	13	H	Chesterfield	W 3-1	1-0	21	Holmes [33], Feeney [54], Elliott (pen) [57]	6068
46	20	A	Wrexham	L 1-2	1-0	21	Fletcher C [7]	4200

Final League Position: 21

GOALSCORERS

League (56): Feeney 13 (3 pens), Holmes 9, Elliott 8 (4 pens), Hayter 7, Fletcher C 5, Howe 4, Tindall 3, Hughes 2, Purches 2, Stock 2, McAnespie 1.
Worthington Cup (0).
FA Cup (3): Fletcher S 1, Hayter 1, Hughes 1.

Stewart G 45	Broadhurst K 22+1	Elliott W 40+6	Howe E 38	Tindall J 44	Purches S 41	Feeney W 35+2	Hayter J 43+1	Eribenne C 6+18	Fletcher C 35	Hughes R 16+6	Foyewa A 1+7	O'Connor G 12+16	Birmingham D 3+1	Ford J 5+2	Maher S 28+3	Huck W —+7	Stock B 19+7	Holmes D 34+3	Bernard N 4+4	Smith D 1+2	Kandol T 3+9	Fletcher S 1+1	Melligan J 7+1	Thomas D 3+9	McAnespie K 3+4	Young N 10+1	Cooke S 6+1	Menetrier M 1	Match No
1	2^1	3	4	5	6	7	8^2	9	10	11	12	13																	1
1	2^3	3	4		6	7	8^1	9	10			13	12	14	11^2	5													2
1	2	11	4	5	3^2	7	8		10			9^1	12		6	13													3
1	2	11	4	5	6^1		8	9^1	10			7^2		12	3	13	14												4
1	2^2	11	4	5	3	7	8	9^1	10			12			6	13													5
1		11	4	5	3	7^2	8	12	10			2^1			6		13	9											6
1		3	4	5	2	7	9^2	12	10	11^3		13			6		14	8^1											7
1		11	4	5	3^1	7	9	12	10			13			2^1	6		8											8
1	12	11	4	5	3	7^1	9	13	10						2	6		8^2											9
1		11	4	5	3	7^1	9^1	12	10			13			2^1	6	14	8											10
1	2	11	4	5			9	12	10						7^1		13	6^3	8	3^2	14								11
1	2	3	4	5		8	9^1	10				11^2			12	6	7	13											12
1	2	11	4	5		8	9^2	10				12			6	7^1	3	13											13
1	2	3	4			9	12	10				8^3			13	6^2	7	14	5^1	11									14
1	2	11	4	5	6^2	9	12	10				13			8^3	7	3^1	14											15
1	2	11	4^3	5	6	12	9^2	13	10	14					8	7	3^1												16
1	2	3	4	5	6	7	9^2	12	10	13					8^2	11^1	14												17
1	2	3	4	5	6	7^2	9		10	12		14			8^1	11	13^3												18
1	2	3	4	5	6	7	9^1		11	12					8^2	10		13											19
1	2	3	4	5	6	7		12		11					8	10^1		13	9^2										20
1	2	3	4	5	6^1		9	12		11		13			8^2	10^3		14				7							21
1	2^1	12	4	5	3	7	9	13	10^2	11		14			8						6^3								22
1	2^1	3	4	5	6	7	9		10	11					12						8								23
1	2^1	3	4	5	6	7	9		10	11^3			12				13	8											24
1		3	4	5		7	9^1	10				2			6		8	12				11							25
1		3		5	6	7	9	12	10			2^1			4		8					11							26
1	2	3		5	6	7	9		10	12		4^1			8		13					11^2							27
1	2	12	4	5	3	7	9^1		10	11					13		6^2	8											28
1	2	3^1	4	5	6^2	7^3	9		10	11		12			13			8	14										29
1		12	4	5	3	7	9^1		10	11	13	2^1			6		14	8^2											30
1		12	4	5	3^2	7	9^1		10	13		2			6		8^1	11					14						31
1		12	4	5	3^1	7^2	13			11		2			6		8	9^1			10			14					32
1		3^2	4	5	2		9	12	10	11	13	7^3			6							8^1		14					33
1		12	4	5^1	3	7^3	9		10	11^4		2			6		8						13	14					34
1		3		5	6	9						8	12	4		10					13		11^2	7	2^1				35
1		3	4	5^2	2	12	9					8		6		10						11	7^1	13					36
1		11	4	5	3	7^1	9	12				8			6		10					13	2^2						37
1		11	4	5	3	7	9	12							6		10^1					13	14	2^3	8^2				38
1		11	4	5	3	7^1	9					12			6		10				13		2	8^1	1				39
1		11	4	5	3	7	9	12				13			6^2		10^1					14	2^3	8					40
1		11	4	5	3^2	7	9								6	12					13	10^1	2	8					41
1		3		5	6	7			10	11^2	12				4		13^1	9					14	2^3	8^1				42
1		3		5	6	7	8		10	11^2	12				4^3		9						14	2^1	13				43
1		3		5	6	7	8^2		10						4		12	9					13	2	11^1				44
1		11	4	5	3	7^2	8^3		10			12			4		6^1	9			13		14	2					45
1		3^2		5	6	7	8		10			12			4		11^1	9					13	2					46

Worthington Cup
First Round   Torquay U   (h)   0-2

FA Cup
First Round   Worksop T   (h)   3-0
Second Round   Peterborough U   (a)   0-1

BRADFORD CITY   Division 1

FOUNDATION

Bradford was a rugby stronghold around the turn of the century but after Manningham RFC held an archery contest to help them out of financial difficulties in 1903, they were persuaded to give up the handling code and turn to soccer. So they formed Bradford City and continued at Valley Parade. Recognising this as an opportunity of spreading the dribbling code in this part of Yorkshire, the Football League immediately accepted the new club's first application for membership of the Second Division.

Bradford & Bingley Stadium, Valley Parade, Bradford BD8 7DY.

Telephone: (01274) 773 355 (Office). *Fax:* (01274) 773 356.
Ticket Office: (01274) 770 022.
Website: www.bradfordcity.co.uk
Email: bradfordcityfc@compuserve.com
ClubCall: 09068 888 640.

Ground Capacity: 25,000.

Record Attendance: 39,146 v Burnley, FA Cup 4th rd, 11 March 1911.

Record Receipts: £164,567 v Sheffield Wednesday, FA Cup 5th rd, 16 February 1997.

Pitch Measurements: 110yd × 73yd.

HONOURS

Football League: Division 1 – Runners-up 1998–99; Division 2 – Champions 1907–08; Promoted from Division 2 1995–96 (play-offs); Division 3 – Champions 1984–85; Division 3 (N) – Champions 1928–29; Division 4 – Runners-up 1981–82.
FA Cup: Winners 1911.
Football League Cup: best season: 5th rd, 1965, 1989.

Chairman: Geoffrey Richmond. *Directors:* David Richmond, Elizabeth Richmond, Michael Richmond, Julian Rhodes, Prof. David Rhodes.

Managing Director: Shaun Harvey.

Manager: Nicky Law. *Assistant Manager:* Ian Banks. *Youth Coach:* Steve Smith.
Reserve Coach: Mark Prudhoe. *Physio:* Steve Redmond.

Secretary: Jon Pollard.

Stadium Manager: Allan Gilliver.

Colours: Claret and amber shirts, black shorts, amber stockings.

Change Colours: Burgundy and navy shirts, navy shorts and stockings with burgundy trim.

Year Formed: 1903.

Turned Professional: 1903.

Ltd Co.: 1908.

Club Nickname: 'The Bantams'.

First Football League Game: 1 September 1903, Division 2, v Grimsby T (a) L 0–2 – Seymour; Wilson, Halliday; Robinson, Millar, Farnall; Guy, Beckram, Forrest, McMillan, Graham.

Record League Victory: 11–1 v Rotherham U, Division 3 (N), 25 August 1928 – Sherlaw; Russell, Watson; Burkinshaw (1), Summers, Bauld; Harvey (2), Edmunds (3), White (3), Cairns, Scriven (2).

IT'S A FACT *!*

In successive Division 2 matches in December 1931, Bradford City won 5-1 at Tottenham Hotspur and 4-3 at home to Manchester United.

Record Cup Victory: 11–3 v Walker Celtic, FA Cup 1st rd (replay), 1 December 1937 – Parker; Rookes, McDermott; Murphy, Mackie, Moore; Bagley (1), Whittingham (1), Deakin (4 incl. 1p), Cooke (1), Bartholomew (4).

Record Defeat: 1–9 v Colchester U, Division 4, 30 December 1961.

Most League Points (2 for a win): 63, Division 3 (N), 1928–29.

Most League Points (3 for a win): 94, Division 3, 1984–85.

Most League Goals: 128, Division 3 (N), 1928–29.

Highest League Scorer in Season: David Layne, 34, Division 4, 1961–62.

Most League Goals in Total Aggregate: Bobby Campbell, 121, 1981–84, 1984–86.

Most League Goals in One Match: 7, Albert Whitehurst v Tranmere R, Division 3N, 6 March 1929.

Most Capped Player: Jamie Lawrence, 12, Jamaica.

Most League Appearances: Cec Podd, 502, 1970–84.

Youngest League Player: Robert Cullingford, 16 years 141 days v Mansfield T, 22 April 1970.

Record Transfer Fee Received: £2,000,000 from Newcastle U for Des Hamilton, March 1997 and £2,000,000 from Newcastle U for Andrew O'Brien, March 2001.

Record Transfer Fee Paid: £2,500,000 to Leeds U for David Hopkin, July 2000.

Football League Record: 1903 Elected to Division 2; 1908–22 Division 1; 1922–27 Division 2; 1927–29 Division 3 (N); 1929–37 Division 2; 1937–61 Division 3; 1961–69 Division 4; 1969–72 Division 3; 1972–77 Division 4; 1977–78 Division 3; 1978–82 Division 4; 1982–85 Division 3; 1985–90 Division 3; 1990–92 Division 3; 1992–96 Division 2; 1996–99 Division 1; 1999–2001 FA Premier League; 2001– Division 1.

MANAGERS

Robert Campbell 1903–05
Peter O'Rourke 1905–21
David Menzies 1921–26
Colin Veitch 1926–28
Peter O'Rourke 1928–30
Jack Peart 1930–35
Dick Ray 1935–37
Fred Westgarth 1938–43
Bob Sharp 1943–46
Jack Barker 1946–47
John Milburn 1947–48
David Steele 1948–52
Albert Harris 1952
Ivor Powell 1952–55
Peter Jackson 1955–61
Bob Brocklebank 1961–64
Bill Harris 1965–66
Willie Watson 1966–69
Grenville Hair 1967–68
Jimmy Wheeler 1968–71
Bryan Edwards 1971–75
Bobby Kennedy 1975–78
John Napier 1978
George Mulhall 1978–81
Roy McFarland 1981–82
Trevor Cherry 1982–87
Terry Dolan 1987–89
Terry Yorath 1989–90
John Docherty 1990–91
Frank Stapleton 1991–94
Lennie Lawrence 1994–95
Chris Kamara 1995–98
Paul Jewell 1998–2000
Chris Hutchings 2000
Jim Jefferies 2000–01
Nicky Law January 2002–

LATEST SEQUENCES

Longest Sequence of League Wins: 10, 26.11.83 – 3.2.84.

Longest Sequence of League Defeats: 8, 21.1.33 – 11.3.33.

Longest Sequence of League Draws: 6, 30.1.76 – 13.3.76.

Longest Sequence of Unbeaten League Matches: 21, 11.1.69 – 2.5.69.

Longest Sequence Without a League Win: 16, 28.8.48 – 20.11.48.

TEN YEAR LEAGUE RECORD

		P	W	D	L	F	A	Pts	Pos
1991-92	Div 3	46	13	19	14	62	61	58	16
1992-93	Div 2	46	18	14	14	69	67	68	10
1993-94	Div 2	46	19	13	14	61	53	70	7
1994-95	Div 2	46	16	12	18	57	64	60	14
1995-96	Div 2	46	22	7	17	71	69	73	6
1996-97	Div 1	46	12	12	22	47	72	48	21
1997-98	Div 1	46	14	15	17	46	59	57	13
1998-99	Div 1	46	26	9	11	82	47	87	2
1999-2000	PR Lge	38	9	9	20	38	68	36	17
2000-01	PR Lge	38	5	11	22	30	70	26	20

DID YOU KNOW ?

Bradford City were the first Football League club to advertise matches on TV. In January 1974, two peak viewing slots previewed the FA Cup tie with Alvechurch. A season's best crowd of 13,062 turned up to watch the 4-2 win.

BRADFORD CITY 2001–02 LEAGUE RECORD

Match No.	Date	Venue	Opponents	Result	H/T Score	Lg. Pos.	Goalscorers	Attendance
1	Aug 11	H	Barnsley	W 4-0	2-0	—	Ward 2 (2 pens) 16,67, Jess 29, Carbone 75	16,367
2	18	A	Portsmouth	W 1-0	0-0	1	Jess 71	17,239
3	24	H	Coventry C	W 2-1	0-0	—	Myers 50, Locke 55	15,085
4	Sept 2	H	Burnley	L 2-3	0-0	4	Ward 61, McCall 81	17,547
5	8	A	Sheffield U	D 2-2	2-2	6	Jess 2, Tod 39	17,394
6	14	H	Gillingham	W 5-1	1-0	—	Wetherall 12, Tod 57, Jess 60, Blake 81, Carbone 84	14,101
7	17	A	Sheffield W	D 1-1	0-0	—	Carbone 47	18,012
8	20	A	Nottingham F	L 0-1	0-0	—		28,546
9	25	H	Stockport Co	L 2-4	1-1	—	Carbone 41, Myers 61	12,940
10	29	H	Grimsby T	W 3-2	2-0	8	Blake 11, Jess 25, Ward 87	13,778
11	Oct 13	H	Wolverhampton W	L 0-3	0-1	10		16,878
12	16	A	Crystal Palace	L 0-2	0-1	—		15,721
13	20	A	Birmingham C	L 0-4	0-3	15		25,011
14	23	A	Millwall	L 1-3	0-1	—	Locke 69	11,071
15	27	H	Watford	W 4-3	2-0	13	Etherington 6, Jess 3 38,47,66	16,860
16	30	H	Wimbledon	D 3-3	1-3	—	Tod 2 40,80, Jess 77	18,255
17	Nov 2	A	Crewe Alex	D 2-2	1-1	—	Blake 29, McCall 71	6597
18	10	A	Norwich C	W 4-1	2-0	12	Jess 42, Blake 2 (1 pen) 44,64 (p), Bower 90	17,414
19	17	A	Walsall	W 2-0	1-0	11	Jess 35, Juanjo 79	14,251
20	20	A	Preston NE	D 1-1	1-0	—	Blake 26	13,763
21	24	A	WBA	L 0-1	0-1	12		18,910
22	Dec 1	H	Millwall	L 1-2	0-1	15	Blake 89	14,148
23	8	A	Rotherham U	W 3-1	0-0	13	Blake 2 (1 pen) 55 (p), 57, Ward 82	14,529
24	16	A	Manchester C	L 1-3	1-1	15	Dunne (og) 15	30,749
25	23	A	Coventry C	L 0-4	0-2	16		14,977
26	26	H	Sheffield U	L 1-2	0-1	17	Ward 60	18,869
27	29	H	Crystal Palace	L 1-2	1-1	17	Blake 45	14,233
28	Jan 12	H	Portsmouth	W 3-1	1-1	17	Grant 18, Sharpe (pen) 59, Halle 89	14,306
29	19	A	Barnsley	D 3-3	1-2	16	Sharpe 26, Ward 2 82,88	13,856
30	29	H	Preston NE	L 0-1	0-0	—		15,217
31	Feb 2	H	Grimsby T	W 1-0	0-0	17	Carbone 61	5054
32	16	A	Wolverhampton W	L 1-3	1-0	17	Ward 31	21,935
33	23	A	Gillingham	W 4-0	3-0	16	Patterson (og) 8, Ward 38, Lawrence 45, Cadamarteri 68	7789
34	26	H	Nottingham F	W 2-1	1-0	—	Jess 23, Lawrence 88	13,505
35	Mar 2	H	Sheffield W	L 0-2	0-1	16		16,904
36	5	A	Stockport Co	L 0-1	0-1	—		4148
37	8	H	Manchester C	L 0-2	0-1	—		18,168
38	12	H	Birmingham C	L 1-3	1-2	—	Jess 45	13,105
39	16	A	Rotherham U	D 1-1	0-0	17	Jacobs 71	7182
40	20	A	Burnley	D 1-1	0-1	—	Jorgensen 78	19,479
41	23	H	Crewe Alex	W 2-0	1-0	17	Wetherall 12, McCall 89	12,846
42	29	H	Watford	D 0-0	0-0	—		14,001
43	Apr 1	H	Norwich C	L 0-1	0-0	16		14,143
44	6	A	Wimbledon	W 2-1	1-0	15	Jess 31, Bower 69	5595
45	13	A	WBA	L 0-1	0-0	16		20,209
46	21	A	Walsall	D 2-2	0-2	15	Cadamarteri 73, Uhlenbeek (og) 83	8079

Final League Position: 15

GOALSCORERS

League (69): Jess 14, Blake 10 (2 pens), Ward 10 (2 pens), Carbone 5, Tod 4, McCall 3, Bower 2, Cadamarteri 2, Lawrence 2, Locke 2, Myers 2, Sharpe 2 (1 pen), Wetherall 2, Etherington 1, Grant 1, Halle 1, Jacobs 1, Jorgensen 1, Juanjo 1, own goals 3.
Worthington Cup (7): Blake 2 (1 pen), Tod 2, Lawrence 1, McCall 1, Ward 1 (pen).
FA Cup (0).

Walsh G 17 + 1	Halle G 31 + 1	Jacobs W 37 + 1	McCall S 42 + 1	Molenaar R 21	Myers A 28 + 4	Locke G 26 + 5	Whalley G 21 + 2	Ward A 27	Carbone B 10 + 1	Jess E 43 + 2	Wetherall D 17 + 2	Blake R 19 + 7	Sharpe L 11 + 7	Lawrence J 13 + 8	Tod A 25 + 5 -	Makel L 2 + 11	Emanuel L 8 + 1	Grant G 4 + 6	Etherington M 12 + 1	Davison A 9	Atherton P 1	Bower M 9 + 1	Juanjo 5 + 12	Jorgensen C 13 + 5	Caldwell S 9	Muggleton C 4	Combe A 16	Grayson S 7	Cadamarteri D 14	Kearney T 5	Lee A — + 1	Match No.
1	2	3	4	5^1	6	7	8	9	10^2	11^3	12	13	14																			1
1	2	3	4	5	6	7^2	8	9	10^1	11^3		12	14	13																		2
1	2	3	4	5	6	7	8	9	10	11^3				12																		3
1	2^1	3	4	5	6	7	8	9	10	11			12																			4
1	2	3	4	5^1	6	7	8		11	12	9^2	13	10																			5
1	2	3	4^2	5		7	8^1		10	11	6	13	12	9	14																	6
1	2	3	4	5	12	7^2	8		10	11^3	6	14	13	9																		7
1	2^1	3	4	5		7	8^2	9	10	11	6	12	13																			8
1	2	3^1	4		6	7^2	8		10	11	5	9	12	13																		9
1	2		4^1	5		7	8^2	9		11	6	10	12	13	3																	10
1	2	3	4			7	8^1	9	10	11	5	12	6																			11
1	2		4	5	6	7^1	12	9	13	11	3	8^2	10																			12
1	12		4	5^1	6	7	8^2	9	11^3	3	10	2	13	14																		13
1	2		4	5	6	7	8		11^3	3	9	10		12																		14
1	2	3	4	5			8		11^1	6	9	10	12	7																		15
1	2	3	4	5^1	6	12	8^1		11	9	10	13	7																			16
	2	3	4	5	6		8		11	9	10		7	1																		17
	2	3	4		6		8		11	9	10		7	1		5^1	12															18
	2	3	4		6	8		11	9^1	10	7	1	12																			19
		3	4	5^2	6	8		11^1	9	10	12	7	1	13	2																	20
	2	3	4^3	5^2	6	8^1		11	9	10^2	12	7	1	13	14																	21
	2	3	4	5	6	8^1		11	9	$10^{2?}$	12	7	1	13																		22
		4		6			9	11	10	12		5	2	7^1	1	8		3														23
	3		6				9^1	11	8	10	12	4^2	2	7^1	1	13		5														24
15	2^1	3		8		9	11	10	6^2		7	1	13	12		5																25
1		3	4	5	2^1		9	11	10	8	12	6																				26
	3	4	5^1	12		9	11	8	6	7	2	1																				27
3		6	7		11		10	8	2	9	4	5	1																			28
2		12	6	7^1	8	11^2	10	13	14	3	9^2	4	5	1																		29
2	12	4	6	9	11	10	13	8^3	3^1	14	7^2	5	1																			30
2	3	4	6	9	8	12	10^1	7	13	11^2	5	1																				31
3	4	6	7	8^2	9	12	11	5	10^1	13	1	2																				32
3	4	6	12	8^1	9	11	7	5	13	1	2	10^2																				33
3	4	6	12	8^2	9	11^1	13	7	5	14	1	2	10^3																			34
3	4	6		9	11^1	8	7	5	12	1	2	10																				35
3	4	6	7^2	8^1	9	12	11^2	5	13	14	1	2	10																			36
5	3	4	6^1	8	9	11	7^2	12	13	14	1	2	10																			37
5	3	4		8^1	9	11	7	6	12	2	1	10																				38
5	3	4		9	11^2	8	7	12	6	13	1	2	10^1																			39
2	3	4	12	9	11^1	5	8	6	7	1	10																					40
2	3	4		9	11	5	8	6	7	1	10																					41
	3	4		9	11	5	7	12	6	2	1	10^1	8																			42
	3	4		11	5	12^7	7	9^1	6	2	1	10	8																			43
	3	4		11	5	12	7^1	6	9^2	2	1	10	8																			44
	3	4^2	12	13	9	11^3	5	14	6	7	2^1	1	10	8																		45
	3	4	12	13	11^3	5	7	6	9^2	2	1	10	8	14																		46

Worthington Cup

First Round	Macclesfield T	(a)	2-1
Second Round	Rotherham U	(a)	4-0
Third Round	Watford	(a)	1-4

FA Cup

Third Round	Walsall	(a)	0-2

BRENTFORD

Division 2

FOUNDATION

Formed as a small amateur concern in 1889 they were very successful in local circles. They won the championship of the West London Alliance in 1893 and a year later the West Middlesex Junior Cup before carrying off the Senior Cup in 1895. After winning both the London Senior Amateur Cup and the Middlesex Senior Cup in 1898 they were admitted to the Second Division of the Southern League.

Griffin Park, Braemar Rd, Brentford, Middlesex TW8 0NT.
Telephone: (020) 8847 2511. *Fax:* (020) 8568 9940.
Commercial Dept: (020) 8847 2511
Press Office: (020) 8847 2511. *ClubCall:* 09068 121 108.

Ground Capacity: 12,500.

Record Attendance: 38,678 v Leicester C, FA Cup 6th rd, 26 February 1949.

Record Receipts: £162,314 v Tottenham H, Worthington Cup 2nd rd, 15 September 1998.

Pitch Measurements: 111yd × 74yd.

Chairman: Ron Noades. *President:* E. J. Radley-Smith.
Managing Director: G. Hargraves.
Directors: J. Herting, E. Rogers, J. McGlashan.

Manager: Wally Downes.
Coach: Roberto Forzoni.
Director of Youth Football: Geoff Taylor.
Physio: Phil McLoughlin.

Community Officer: Lee Doyle. *Secretary:* Polly Kates.

Safety Officer: Roy King.

Communications Manager: Peter Gilham.

Corporate Sales Manager: Samantha Taylor.

Colours: Red and white vertical striped shirts, black shorts, black stockings.

Change Colours: Black shirts, black shorts, black stockings.

Year Formed: 1889.

Turned Professional: 1899.

Ltd Co.: 1901.

Club Nickname: 'The Bees'.

Previous Grounds: 1889, Clifden Road; 1891, Benns Fields, Little Ealing; 1895, Shotters Field; 1898, Cross Road, S. Ealing; 1900, Boston Park; 1904, Griffin Park.

First Football League Game: 28 August 1920, Division 3, v Exeter C (a) L 0–3 – Young; Hodson, Rosier, Elliott J, Levitt, Amos, Smith, Thompson, Spreadbury, Morley, Henery.

Record League Victory: 9–0 v Wrexham, Division 3, 15 October 1963 – Cakebread; Coote, Jones;

HONOURS

Football League: Division 1 best season: 5th, 1935–36; Division 2 – Champions 1934–35; Division 3 – Champions 1991–92, 1998–99; Division 3 (S) – Champions 1932–33, Runners-up 1929–30, 1957–58; Division 4 – Champions 1962–63.

FA Cup: best season: 6th rd, 1938, 1946, 1949, 1989.

Football League Cup: best season: 4th rd, 1983.

Freight Rover Trophy: Runners-up 1985.

LDV Vans Trophy: Runners-up 2001.

IT'S A FACT !

When Brentford won the Second Division Championship in 1934–35, they called upon the services of only 17 different players and the entire squad cost less than £5,000.

Slater, Scott, Higginson; Summers (1), Brooks (2), McAdams (2), Ward (2), Hales (1), (1 og).

Record Cup Victory: 7–0 v Windsor & Eton (away), FA Cup 1st rd, 20 November 1982 – Roche; Rowe, Harris (Booker), McNichol (1), Whitehead, Hurlock (2), Kamara, Joseph (1), Mahoney (3), Bowles, Roberts. *N.B.* 8-0 v Windsor & Eton, FA Cup, 3rd Qual rd, 31 October 1903.

Record Defeat: 0–7 v Swansea T, Division 3 (S), 8 November 1924 and v Walsall, Division 3 (S), 19 January 1957.

Most League Points (2 for a win): 62, Division 3 (S), 1932–33 and Division 4, 1962–63.

Most League Points (3 for a win): 85, Division 2, 1994–95 and Division 3, 1998–99.

Most League Goals: 98, Division 4, 1962–63.

Highest League Scorer in Season: Jack Holliday, 38, Division 3 (S), 1932–33.

Most League Goals in Total Aggregate: Jim Towers, 153, 1954–61.

Most League Goals in One Match: 5, Jack Holliday v Luton T, Division 3S, 28 January 1933; Billy Scott v Barnsley, Division 2, 15 December 1934; Peter McKennan v Bury, Division 2, 18 February 1949.

Most Capped Player: John Buttigieg, 22 (98), Malta.

Most League Appearances: Ken Coote, 514, 1949–64.

Youngest League Player: Danis Salman, 15 years 243 days v Watford, 15 November 1975.

Record Transfer Fee Received: £2,500,000 from Wimbledon for Hermann Hreidarsson, October 1999.

Record Transfer Fee Paid: £850,000 to Crystal Palace for Hermann Hreidarsson, September 1998.

Football League Record: 1920 Original Member of Division 3; 1921–33 Division 3 (S); 1933–35 Division 2; 1935–47 Division 1; 1947–54 Division 2; 1954–62 Division 3 (S); 1962–63 Division 4; 1963–66 Division 3; 1966–72 Division 4; 1972–73 Division 3; 1973–78 Division 4; 1978–92 Division 3; 1992–93 Division 1; 1993–98 Division 2; 1998 –99 Division 3; 1999– Division 2.

MANAGERS

Will Lewis 1900–03
  (Secretary-Manager)
Dick Molyneux 1902–06
W. G. Brown 1906–08
Fred Halliday 1908–12, 1915–21, 1924–26
  (only Secretary to 1922)
Ephraim Rhodes 1912–15
Archie Mitchell 1921–24
Harry Curtis 1926–49
Jackie Gibbons 1949–52
Jimmy Blain 1952–53
Tommy Lawton 1953
Bill Dodgin Snr 1953–57
Malcolm Macdonald 1957–65
Tommy Cavanagh 1965–66
Billy Gray 1966–67
Jimmy Sirrel 1967–69
Frank Blunstone 1969–73
Mike Everitt 1973–75
John Docherty 1975–76
Bill Dodgin Jnr 1976–80
Fred Callaghan 1980–84
Frank McLintock 1984–87
Steve Perryman 1987–90
Phil Holder 1990–93
David Webb 1993–97
Eddie May 1997
Micky Adams 1997–98
Ron Noades 1998–2000
Ray Lewington 2001
Steve Coppell 2001–02

LATEST SEQUENCES

Longest Sequence of League Wins: 9, 30.4.32 – 24.9.32.
Longest Sequence of League Defeats: 9, 20.10.28 – 25.12.28.
Longest Sequence of League Draws: 5, 16.3.57 – 6.4.57.
Longest Sequence of Unbeaten League Matches: 26, 20.2.99 – 16.10.99.
Longest Sequence Without a League Win: 16, 19.2.94 – 7.5.94.

TEN YEAR LEAGUE RECORD

		P	W	D	L	F	A	Pts	Pos
1991-92	Div 3	46	25	7	14	81	55	82	1
1992-93	Div 1	46	13	10	23	52	71	49	22
1993-94	Div 2	46	13	19	14	57	55	58	16
1994-95	Div 2	46	25	10	11	81	39	85	2
1995-96	Div 2	46	15	13	18	43	49	58	15
1996-97	Div 2	46	20	14	12	56	43	74	4
1997-98	Div 2	46	11	17	18	50	71	50	21
1998-99	Div 3	46	26	7	13	79	56	85	1
1999-2000	Div 2	46	13	13	20	47	61	52	17
2000-01	Div 2	46	14	17	15	56	70	59	14

DID YOU KNOW ❓

Goalkeeper Joe Crozier was the only Brentford player to be ever-present in the 1938–39 season and again after the war, in 1946–47.

BRENTFORD 2001–02 LEAGUE RECORD

Match No.	Date	Venue	Opponents	Result	H/T Score	Lg. Pos.	Goalscorers	Attendance
1	Aug 11	A	Wigan Ath	D	1-1	1-0	—	Ingimarsson [45]	5952
2	18	H	Port Vale	W	2-0	0-0	5	Evans [53], Burgess [84]	4561
3	25	A	Chesterfield	W	1-0	1-0	3	Evans [2]	3571
4	27	H	Cambridge U	W	2-1	1-0	2	Evans 2 (1 pen) [35 (p), 48]	4674
5	Sept 8	H	Tranmere R	W	4-0	1-0	1	Owusu [30], Burgess [58], Evans [76], Williams [89]	5211
6	15	A	Notts Co	D	0-0	0-0	3		5043
7	18	H	Bristol C	D	2-2	2-1	—	Burgess [24], Powell [29]	6342
8	22	H	Oldham Ath	D	2-2	0-1	2	Owusu [47], Evans (pen) [50]	5525
9	25	A	Swindon T	L	0-2	0-1	—		5519
10	29	H	Colchester U	W	4-1	2-1	4	Evans 2 (1 pen) [5 (p), 62], Burgess [34], Owusu [83]	5179
11	Oct 5	A	Brighton & HA	W	2-1	1-0	—	Rowlands [27], Ingimarsson [74]	6823
12	13	H	Peterborough U	W	2-1	2-0	1	Owusu [21], Evans [45]	11,097
13	20	A	Bournemouth	W	2-0	1-0	1	Hunt 2 [4, 66]	3934
14	23	H	Bury	W	5-1	2-0	—	Owusu 2 [1, 51], Gibbs 2 (2 pens) [10, 86], Burgess [75]	5389
15	27	A	Reading	W	2-1	0-0	1	Ingimarsson [69], Price [73]	14,680
16	Nov 3	H	Blackpool	W	2-0	0-0	1	Sidwell [65], Owusu [88]	7605
17	10	A	Stoke C	L	2-3	1-1	2	Burgess [45], Owusu [55]	17,953
18	20	A	Huddersfield T	D	1-1	0-0	—	Burgess [90]	8518
19	24	H	QPR	D	0-0	0-0	3		10,849
20	Dec 1	A	Wycombe W	L	3-5	2-1	3	Owusu [13], Evans (pen) [26], Burgess [59]	8013
21	4	A	Cardiff C	L	1-3	0-2	—	Evans [69]	10,184
22	15	H	Wrexham	W	3-0	1-0	3	Hunt [5], Burgess [50], Ingimarsson [63]	5326
23	21	A	Northampton T	W	3-0	0-0	—	Evans (pen) [76], Burgess [80], Owusu [88]	5142
24	26	A	Cambridge U	L	1-2	1-0	1	Burgess [5]	3989
25	29	A	Tranmere R	L	0-1	0-0	4		9389
26	Jan 12	A	Port Vale	L	1-2	1-1	5	Owusu [31]	4588
27	19	H	Wigan Ath	L	0-1	0-0	6		5549
28	22	A	Northampton T	L	0-1	0-0	—		4184
29	24	H	Brighton & HA	W	4-0	2-0	—	Ingimarsson [22], Burgess 2 [35, 59], Sidwell [62]	7475
30	Feb 2	A	Colchester U	D	1-1	1-0	5	Owusu [25]	3657
31	9	H	Bournemouth	W	1-0	0-0	6	Owusu [84]	6698
32	12	H	Cardiff C	W	2-1	0-1	—	Hunt [54], Burgess [78]	6718
33	16	A	Peterborough U	D	1-1	1-0	5	Owusu [41]	5100
34	23	H	Notts Co	W	2-1	0-0	3	Evans (pen) [77], Burgess [90]	5367
35	26	A	Oldham Ath	L	2-3	1-1	—	Burgess 2 [30, 87]	4935
36	Mar 2	A	Bristol C	W	2-0	0-0	4	Rowlands [54], Owusu [56]	11,421
37	5	H	Swindon T	W	2-0	1-0	—	Owusu 2 [43, 69]	5644
38	9	A	Wrexham	W	3-0	2-0	3	Evans [30], Rowlands 2 [40, 78]	3343
39	12	H	Chesterfield	D	0-0	0-0	—		5372
40	16	H	Wycombe W	W	1-0	1-0	3	Ingimarsson [6]	7165
41	19	A	Blackpool	W	3-1	2-0	—	Rowlands [15], Owusu 2 [22, 47]	4865
42	30	H	Stoke C	W	1-0	0-0	3	Sidwell [67]	8837
43	Apr 1	A	Bury	L	0-2	0-0	3		4332
44	6	H	Huddersfield T	W	3-0	3-0	3	Owusu [28], Sidwell [35], Rowlands [41]	7393
45	13	A	QPR	D	0-0	0-0	3		18,346
46	20	H	Reading	D	1-1	0-0	3	Rowlands [51]	11,303

Final League Position: 3

GOALSCORERS

League (77): Owusu 20, Burgess 17, Evans 14 (6 pens), Rowlands 7, Ingimarsson 6, Hunt 4, Sidwell 4, Gibbs 2 (2 pens), Powell 1, Price 1, Williams 1.
Worthington Cup (2): O'Connor 1, Owusu 1.
FA Cup (3): Burgess 1, Dobson 1, Gibbs 1.

Gottskalksson O 28	Dobson M 38 + 1	Anderson I 33 + 2	Ingimarsson I 46	Powell D 41	Price J 15	Evans P 40	Mahon G 34 + 1	Owusu L 43 + 1	O'Connor K 13 + 12	Gibbs P 23 + 4	Partridge S — + 1	Williams M — + 20	Burgess B 43	Hunt S 34 + 1	Caceres A 5	Rowlands M 13 + 10	Lovett J 2	Bryan D — + 1	Hutchinson E 2 + 7	McCammon M 1 + 13	Sidwell S 29 + 1	Theobald D 5 + 1	Smith P 18	Tabb J — + 3	Boxall D — + 5	Match No.
1	2	3	4	5	6	7	8	9	10¹	11	12															1
1	2	3	4	5	6	7	8¹		10	11²		12	9	13												2
1	2		4	5	3	7	8		10	11			9	6												3
1	2		4	5	3	7	8	9¹	12	11			13	10	6²											4
1	2		4	5	3	7	8	9¹	12	11			13	10¹	6²	14										5
1	2		4	5	6²	7	8	9	12	3			10¹	11	13											6
1			4	5	6	7	8	9¹	12	3			13	10		11³	14	2²								7
1	2	12	4	5	6²	7	8	9¹					13	10		11³	14									8
1	12		4	5	6	7	8	9		3¹			13	10		11³	14	2²								9
1	2	3	4	5	6²	7	8	9¹				12	10						13							10
1		3	4	5	6	7	8	9	10			12		2		11¹										11
1	12		4	5	6	7	8	9¹		3			10	2		11²			13							12
1		3	4	5	6		8	9²				12	10¹	2		11³			14	13	7					13
1		3	4	5	6		8	9²				12	10	2¹		11¹			13	14	7					14
1		3	4	5	6		8	9²				12	10¹	2		11					7					15
1	2	3	4	5			8	9					10	11		7					6					16
1	2	3¹	4	5			8	9				12	10²	11					13	14	7	6¹				17
1	2		4	5		7¹	8	9		3		12	10²	11					13	14		6²				18
1	2		4	5		7	8	9		3²		12	10	11					13		6¹					19
1	2¹		4	5		7	8	9		3		12	10	11							6					20
1	2		4	5		7	8	9²		3		12	10¹	11³					13	14	6					21
1	2	3	4	5		7	8	9²				12	10¹	11³					13	14	6					22
1	2	3	4	5		7	8	9				12	10	11							6¹					23
1	2	3	4			7	8	9				12	10	11²					13		6¹	5				24
1	2	3	4			7	8	9				12	10	11²					13		6¹					25
1	2	3	4	5		7	8	9				12²	10	11	6¹				13							26
1	2	3	4	5		7	8	9					10	11	6											27
1	2	3	4	5	12	13	8	9²					10	11		7¹					6					28
	2	3	4	5		7	8	9					10¹	11							6		1	12		29
	2		4	5		7	8	9		3		12	10¹	11							6		1			30
	2	3	4	5		7	8	9				12	10²	11¹					13		6		1			31
	2	3	4	5		7	8	9					10	11							6		1			32
	2	3	4	5		7	8	9				12	10	11¹							6		1			33
	2	3	4	5		7	8¹	9				12	10	11							6		1			34
	2¹	3	4	5		7	8	9				12	10	11							6		1			35
	2	3	4	5		7		9					10	11		8					6		1			36
	2	3	4	5		7		9				12	10	11¹		8²				13	6		1			37
	2	3	4	5		7		9²				12	10	11¹		8³				13	6		1		14	38
	2	3	4	5¹		7		9²				12	10	11		8				13	6		1			39
	2	3	4	5		7		9					10	11¹		8					6	5	1	12		40
	2	3	4			7		9¹				12	10	11²		8³					6	5	1	13	14	41
	2	3	4			7		9				12	10¹	11³		8²				13	6	5	1		14	42
	2	3	4			7		9				12	10	11		8¹				13	6²	5	1			43
	2	3	4	5²		7		9¹				12	10	11		8³				13	6		1		14	44
	2	3	4	5		7		9				12	10¹	11		8²					6		1	13		45
	2	3	4	5		7		9				12	10	11¹		8					6		1			46

Worthington Cup

First Round	Norwich C	(h)	1-0	
Second Round	Newcastle U	(a)	1-4	

FA Cup

First Round	Morecambe	(h)	1-0	
Second Round	Scunthorpe U	(a)	2-3	

BRIGHTON & HOVE ALBION   Division 1

FOUNDATION

A professional club Brighton United was formed in November 1897 at the Imperial Hotel, Queen's Road, but folded in March 1900 after less than two seasons in the Southern League at the County Ground. An amateur team, Brighton & Hove Rangers was then formed by some prominent United supporters and after one season at Withdean, decided to turn semi-professional and play at the County Ground. Rangers were accepted into the Southern League but then also folded June 1901. John Jackson the former United manager organised a meeting at the Seven Stars public house, Ship Street on 24 June 1901 at which a new third club Brighton & Hove United was formed. They took over Rangers' place in the Southern League and pitch at County Ground. The name was changed to Brighton & Hove Albion before a match was played because of objections by Hove FC.

Offices: Fifth floor, Hanover House, 118 Queens Road, Brighton BN1 3XG.

Ground Address: Withdean Stadium, Tongdean Lane, Brighton BN1 5JD. **Administration Offices:** 118 Queens Road.

Telephone: (01273) 778 855. **Fax:** (01273) 321 095. **ClubCall:** 09068 800 609.

Ground Capacity: 6,960.

Record Attendance: 36,747 v Fulham, Division 2, 27 December 1958.

Record Receipts: £109,615.65 v Crawley T, FA Cup 3rd rd, 4 January 1992.

Pitch Measurements: 110yd × 70yd.

Directors: Dick Knight (Chairman), Ray Bloom, Derek Chapman, Martin Perry, Bob Pinnock FCA, Kevin Griffiths, Chris Kidger.
Non-executive Director: Sir John Smith QPM.

HONOURS

Football League: Division 1 best season: 13th, 1981–82; Division 2 – Champions 2001–02; Runners-up 1978–79; Division 3 (S) – Champions 1957–58; Runners-up 1953–54, 1955–56; Division 3 – Champions 2000–01; Runners-up 1971–72, 1976–77, 1987–88; Division 4 – Champions 1964–65.

FA Cup: Runners-up 1983.

Football League Cup: best season: 5th rd, 1979.

Manager: Martin Hinshelwood. **Assistant Manager:** Bob Booker. **Physio:** Malcolm Stuart.
Youth Team Coach: Dean Wilkins.

Chief Executive: Martin Perry. **Secretary:** Derek Allan.

Colours: Blue and white striped shirts, white shorts, white stockings.

Change Colours: Black shirts, black shorts, black stockings.

Year Formed: 1901.

Turned Professional: 1901. **Ltd Co.:** 1904.

Previous Grounds: 1901, County Ground; 1902, Goldstone Ground. **Club Nickname:** 'The Seagulls'.

First Football League Game: 28 August 1920, Division 3, v Southend U (a) L 0–2 – Hayes; Woodhouse, Little; Hall, Comber, Bentley; Longstaff, Ritchie, Doran, Rodgerson, March.

IT'S A FACT!

Brighton & Hove Albion celebrated their centenary on 22 September 2001 with a 2-1 win over Bournemouth. It was also their 12th successive home League victory.

Record League Victory: 9–1 v Newport Co, Division 3 (S), 18 April 1951 – Ball; Tennant (1p), Mansell (1p); Willard, McCoy, Wilson; Reed, McNichol (4), Garbutt, Bennett (2), Keene (1). 9–1 v Southend U, Division 3, 27 November 1965 – Powney; Magill, Baxter; Leck, Gall, Turner; Gould (1), Collins (1), Livesey (2), Smith (3), Goodchild (2).

Record Cup Victory: 10–1 v Wisbech, FA Cup 1st rd, 13 November 1965 – Powney; Magill, Baxter; Collins (1), Gall, Turner; Gould, Smith (2), Livesey (3), Cassidy (2), Goodchild (1), (1 og).

Record Defeat: 0–9 v Middlesbrough, Division 2, 23 August 1958.

Most League Points (2 for a win): 65, Division 3 (S), 1955–56 and Division 3, 1971–72.

Most League Points (3 for a win): 92, Division 3, 2000–01.

Most League Goals: 112, Division 3 (S), 1955–56.

Highest League Scorer in Season: Peter Ward, 32, Division 3, 1976–77.

Most League Goals in Total Aggregate: Tommy Cook, 114, 1922–29.

Most League Goals in One Match: 5, Jack Doran v Northampton T, Division 3S, 5 November 1921; 5, Adrian Thorne v Watford, Division 3S, 30 April 1958.

Most Capped Player: Steve Penney, 17, Northern Ireland.

Most League Appearances: 'Tug' Wilson, 509, 1922–36.

Youngest League Player: Ian Chapman, 16 years 259 days v Birmingham C, 14 February 1987.

Record Transfer Fee Received: £900,000 from Liverpool for Mark Lawrenson, August 1981.

Record Transfer Fee Paid: £500,000 to Manchester U for Andy Ritchie, October 1980.

Football League Record: 1920 Original Member of Division 3; 1921–58 Division 3 (S); 1958–62 Division 2; 1962–63 Division 3; 1963–65 Division 4; 1965–72 Division 3; 1972–73 Division 2; 1973–77 Division 3; 1977–79 Division 2; 1979–83 Division 1; 1983–87 Division 2; 1987–88 Division 3; 1988–96 Division 2; 1996–2001 Division 3; 2001–02 Division 2; 2002– Division 1.

MANAGERS

John Jackson 1901–05
Frank Scott-Walford 1905–08
John Robson 1908–14
Charles Webb 1919–47
Tommy Cook 1947
Don Welsh 1947–51
Billy Lane 1951–61
George Curtis 1961–63
Archie Macaulay 1963–68
Fred Goodwin 1968–70
Pat Saward 1970–73
Brian Clough 1973–74
Peter Taylor 1974–76
Alan Mullery 1976–81
Mike Bailey 1981–82
Jimmy Melia 1982–83
Chris Cattlin 1983–86
Alan Mullery 1986–87
Barry Lloyd 1987–93
Liam Brady 1993–95
Jimmy Case 1995–96
Steve Gritt 1996–98
Brian Horton 1998–99
Jeff Wood 1999
Micky Adams 1999–2001
Peter Taylor 2001–02
Martin Hinshelwood July 2002–

LATEST SEQUENCES

Longest Sequence of League Wins: 9, 2.10.26 – 20.11.26.

Longest Sequence of League Defeats: 12, 11.11.72 – 27.1.73.

Longest Sequence of League Draws: 6, 16.2.80 – 15.3.80.

Longest Sequence of Unbeaten League Matches: 16, 8.10.30 – 28.1.31.

Longest Sequence Without a League Win: 15, 21.10.72 – 27.1.73.

TEN YEAR LEAGUE RECORD

		P	W	D	L	F	A	Pts	Pos
1991-92	Div 2	46	12	11	23	56	77	47	23
1992-93	Div 2	46	20	9	17	63	59	69	9
1993-94	Div 2	46	15	14	17	60	67	59	14
1994-95	Div 2	46	14	17	15	54	53	59	16
1995-96	Div 2	46	10	10	26	46	69	40	23
1996-97	Div 3	46	13	10	23	53	70	47	23
1997-98	Div 3	46	6	17	23	38	66	35	23
1998-99	Div 3	46	16	7	23	49	66	55	17
1999-2000	Div 3	46	17	16	13	64	46	67	11
2000-01	Div 3	46	28	8	10	73	35	92	1

DID YOU KNOW ?

Bobby Zamora became the first Brighton & Hove Albion player to score as many as 30 goals in successive seasons, a feat he achieved in 2000–01 and again in 2001–02.

BRIGHTON & HOVE ALBION 2001–02 LEAGUE RECORD

Match No.	Date	Venue	Opponents	Result	H/T Score	Lg. Pos.	Goalscorers	Attendance
1	Aug 11	A	Cambridge U	D	0-0	0-0	—	4509
2	18	H	Wigan Ath	W	2-1	1-1	6	Zamora (pen) [39], Steele [79]	6518
3	25	A	Tranmere R	D	0-0	0-0	12		8162
4	27	H	Blackpool	W	4-0	1-0	5	Oatway [38], Carpenter [47], Steele [62], Zamora [72]	6696
5	31	A	Northampton T	L	0-2	0-0	—		5408
6	Sept 8	H	QPR	W	2-1	0-0	6	Zamora [67], Watson [90]	6820
7	14	A	Wrexham	W	2-1	0-0	—	Zamora 2 (1 pen) [68, 77 (p)]	3434
8	18	H	Stoke C	W	1-0	0-0	—	Watson [90]	6627
9	22	H	Bournemouth	W	2-1	1-0	1	Watson [13], Howe (og) [61]	6714
10	25	A	Wycombe W	D	1-1	1-0	—	Jones [11]	7097
11	29	A	Cardiff C	D	1-1	1-0	2	Zamora [36]	12,022
12	Oct 5	H	Brentford	L	1-2	0-1	—	Steele [52]	6823
13	13	A	Huddersfield T	W	2-1	1-0	3	Zamora [35], Hart [64]	10,727
14	20	H	Oldham Ath	W	3-0	3-0	2	Rogers [7], Steele 2 [14, 28]	6793
15	23	A	Notts Co	D	2-2	0-1	—	Hart [63], Zamora [74]	5092
16	27	H	Colchester U	W	1-0	1-0	2	Zamora [16]	6531
17	Nov 3	A	Bristol C	W	1-0	1-0	2	Zamora [37]	13,955
18	10	H	Port Vale	W	1-0	0-0	1	Zamora [49]	6648
19	21	H	Peterborough U	D	1-1	1-1	—	Zamora (pen) [12]	6547
20	24	A	Swindon T	D	1-1	1-0	1	Zamora [14]	8830
21	Dec 1	A	Bury	W	2-0	1-0	1	Brooker [19], Zamora [61]	3782
22	21	H	Chesterfield	D	2-2	1-0	—	Zamora [5], Steele [49]	6371
23	26	A	QPR	D	0-0	0-0	3		16,412
24	29	A	Blackpool	D	2-2	2-0	3	Steele [21], Jones [39]	5419
25	Jan 12	A	Wigan Ath	L	0-3	0-2	4		6203
26	19	H	Cambridge U	W	4-3	1-1	4	Hart [25], Zamora 3 (1 pen) [50 (p), 75, 88]	6575
27	21	A	Chesterfield	W	2-1	0-0	—	Zamora 2 [49, 68]	4689
28	24	A	Brentford	L	0-4	0-2	—		7475
29	31	H	Cardiff C	W	1-0	1-0	—	Zamora (pen) [14]	6117
30	Feb 5	H	Tranmere R	W	1-0	0-0	—	Hart [61]	6279
31	9	A	Oldham Ath	L	0-2	0-1	2		6951
32	11	H	Reading	W	3-1	0-0	—	Zamora [60], Melton [64], Lewis [88]	6756
33	16	H	Huddersfield T	W	1-0	0-0	2	Lewis [54]	6744
34	23	H	Wrexham	D	0-0	0-0	2		6649
35	26	A	Bournemouth	D	1-1	1-1	—	Brooker [37]	6337
36	Mar 1	A	Stoke C	L	1-3	0-1	—	Steele [54]	16,092
37	5	H	Wycombe W	W	4-0	1-0	—	Zamora 2 [40, 76], Brooker [58], Watson [81]	6398
38	9	A	Reading	D	0-0	0-0	2		22,009
39	12	H	Northampton T	W	2-0	1-0	—	Zamora [37], Morgan [59]	6363
40	16	H	Bury	W	2-1	2-0	2	Kenny (og) [21], Zamora (pen) [45]	6609
41	23	H	Notts Co	D	2-2	1-0	2	Zamora [5], Webb [48]	6538
42	30	A	Colchester U	W	4-1	3-0	2	Carpenter 2 [23, 90], Gray [27], Brooker [29]	4881
43	Apr 1	A	Bristol C	W	2-1	1-0	1	Lewis [41], Steele [90]	6759
44	6	A	Peterborough U	W	1-0	0-0	1	Zamora [63]	8321
45	13	H	Swindon T	D	0-0	0-0	1		6870
46	20	A	Port Vale	W	1-0	0-0	1	Watson [72]	8812

Final League Position: 1

GOALSCORERS

League (66): Zamora 28 (6 pens), Steele 9, Watson 5, Brooker 4, Hart 4, Carpenter 3, Lewis 3, Jones 2, Gray 1, Melton 1, Morgan 1, Oatway 1, Rogers 1, Webb 1, own goals 2.
Worthington Cup (2): Zamora 2.
FA Cup (3): Zamora 2, Cullip 1.

Kuipers M 39	Watson P 45	Jones N 29+7	Morgan S 42	Cullip D 44	Carpenter R 45	Hart G 34+5	Rogers P 19+6	Lehmann D 3+4	Zamora B 40+1	Brooker P 30+11	Melton S 5+5	Steele L 20+17	Oatway C 27+5	Mayo K 30+3	Pitcher D 2+8	Crosby A —+2	Pethick R 13+11	Wicks M 2	Virgo A 4+2	Royce S 6	Webb D 7+5	Lewis J 14+1	Lee D —+2	McPhee C 2	Gray W 3+1	Hadland P —+2	Packham W 1	Match No.
1	2	3	4	5	6	7^1	8	9^2	10	11^3	12	13	14															1
1	2	3	4	5	6	7	8	9^1	10	11			12															2
1	2	3^2	4	5	6	7^3		9^1	10	11	8	12			13	14												3
1	2	3	4^3	5	6	7^1	8		10	9^2		12	11		13	14												4
1	2	3^3	4	5	6^2	12	7^1		10	11		9	8		13		14											5
1	2	3	4	5	6	12	7^3	13	10	11^1		9^2	8	14														6
1	2	11^2	4		6	7^3	12		10	13		14	9	3		8^1		5										7
1	2	12	4	5	6	13	7		10	14		9^1	8^1	3	11^3													8
1	2	3	4	5	6	12	7^1		10	11^2		9	8	13														9
1	2	11	4	5	6	7^1	8		10	12			9^2	3	13													10
1	2	11^1	4	5	6	9^2	8		10	12		13	7^2	3	14													11
1	2^3	11	4	5	6	12	7^2	9	10			13	8	3	14													12
1	2	12	4	5	6^2	7	13		10	11^1		9	8	3														13
1	2	12	4	5		7	8	13	10	6^1		9^2	11^3	3	14													14
1	2	12	4	5	6	7	13	14	10	11^1		9^1	8^2	3														15
1	2	11	4^2		6	7			10	12		9	8	3	13			5										16
1	2	11	4	5	6	7			10^1			9	8	3	12													17
1	2	11	4	5	6	7			10			9	8	3														18
1	2	11^2	4	5	6	7	12		10	13	14	9^1	8^3	3														19
1	2	11	4	5	6^1	7			9	12			8	3			10											20
1	2	11	4	5	6	7			10			9	8	3														21
1	3	11^1	4	5	6	12			10			9^2	7^2	8	13		2					14						22
	3	11^2	4	5	6	7			10	13	12	9^1	8				2			1								23
	3	11	4	5	6	7			10	12		9^1	8				2			1								24
	2	11	4^2	5	6	7^1			10	12		9	8	3^2			13			1		14						25
	2	11^3	4	5	6	7	8		10	9^1	12			3^2			13			1		14						26
	2	11	4^2	5	6	9^2	7		10^1	12			8	3			13			1		14						27
	2	11^1		5	6	7^2	9		10	13	14	12	8^3	3					4	1							1	28
1		11		5	6	7			10	12			8	3			2		4			9^1						29
1	3	11^2	4	5	6	9	7		10	12			8^1				2					13						30
1	3		4	5	6	9	7^2		12	11	13		8^3				2					10^1	14					31
1	3			5	6	9			10	11			7				2		4			8						32
1	3		4	5	6	9			10	11			7				2					8						33
1	3		4	5	6	9^2				11	12		7^1				2					8		13	10			34
1		11							10		12		7^1	3			2		4			8		9				35
1	11	12	4	5	6	7^2			10	13		9		3^1			2^3					14	8					36
1	2		4	5	6^1	7	12		10^2	11		9^2	13	3								14	8					37
1	2		4	5	6	7			10	11		9^1		3								12	8					38
1	2		4	5	6	7			10	11				3									8	9				39
1	2		4	5	6	7			10	11		9^1		3								12	8					40
1	2		4	5	6	7^1			10^3	11		12	13	3								14	8		9^2			41
1	2	12	4	5	6	7^2				11			13	3								14	8^2		9	10^1		42
1	2	11	4	5	6	7			10^1				12	3									8		9^2	13		43
1	2	12	4	5	6	7^2			10	11		9^1		3			13						8					44
1	2	11^3	4	5	6				10			12	7^1	3								9^2	8		13	14		45
	2	11	4	5	6^3	12	7		10^2				8	3			13							14	9^1		1	46

Worthington Cup

First Round	Wimbledon	(h)	2-1
Second Round	Southampton	(h)	0-3

FA Cup

First Round	Shrewsbury T	(h)	1-0
Second Round	Rushden & D	(h)	2-1
Third Round	Preston NE	(h)	0-2

BRISTOL CITY   Division 2

FOUNDATION

The name Bristol City came into being in 1897 when the Bristol South End club, formed three years earlier, decided to adopt professionalism and apply for admission to the Southern League after competing in the Western League. The historic meeting was held at The Albert Hall, Bedminster. Bristol City employed Sam Hollis from Woolwich Arsenal as manager and gave him £40 to buy players. In 1901 they merged with Bedminster, another leading Bristol club.

Ashton Gate, Bristol BS3 2EJ.

Telephone: (0117) 963 0630 (5 lines).
Fax: (0117) 963 0700. **Website:** www.bcfc.co.uk
Commercial: (0117) 963 0600. **Shop:** (0117) 963 0637.
ClubCall: 09068 121 176. **Supporters Club:** (0117) 966 5554. **Community Dept:** (0117) 963 0636.

Ground Capacity: 21,479.

Record Attendance: 43,335 v Preston NE, FA Cup 5th rd, 16 February 1935.

Record Receipts: £251,612 v Everton, FA Cup 4th rd, 23 January 1999.

Pitch Measurements: 115yd × 75yd.

Chairman: J. Laycock.

Directors: S. Lansdown, K. Dawe, A. Gooch.

Chief Executive: Colin Sexstone.

Football Secretary: Michelle McDonald.

Manager: Danny Wilson. **Physio:** Gill O'Shea.

Stadium Manager: Dave Lewis.

Commercial Manager: Richard Gould.

Safety Officer: Keith Draisey.

Colours: Red shirts, red shorts, white stockings.

Change Colours: (To be announced.)

Year Formed: 1894.

Turned Professional: 1897.

Ltd Co.: 1897. Bristol City Football Club Ltd.

Previous Name: 1894, Bristol South End; 1897, Bristol City.

Club Nickname: 'Robins'.

Previous Grounds: 1894, St John's Lane; 1904, Ashton Gate.

First Football League Game: 7 September 1901, Division 2, v Blackpool (a) W 2–0 – Moles; Tuft, Davies; Jones, McLean, Chambers; Bradbury, Connor, Boucher, O'Brien (2), Flynn.

HONOURS

Football League: Division 1 – Runners-up 1906–07; Division 2 – Champions 1905–06; Runners-up 1975–76, 1997–98; Division 3 (S) – Champions 1922–23, 1926–27, 1954–55; Runners-up 1937–38; Division 3 – Runners-up 1964–65, 1989–90.
FA Cup: Runners-up 1909.
Football League Cup: Semi-final 1971, 1989.
Welsh Cup: Winners 1934.
Anglo-Scottish Cup: Winners 1978.
Freight Rover Trophy: Winners 1986; Runners-up 1987.
Auto Windscreens Shield: Runners-up 2000.

IT'S A FACT !

Bob Etheridge became a Bristol City player in September 1956 and within an hour of signing for the Ashton Gate club, also became a professional with Gloucestershire County Cricket Club.

Record League Victory: 9–0 v Aldershot, Division 3 (S), 28 December 1946 – Eddols; Morgan, Fox; Peacock, Roberts, Jones (1); Chilcott, Thomas, Clark (4 incl. 1p), Cyril Williams (1), Hargreaves (3).

Record Cup Victory: 11–0 v Chichester C, FA Cup 1st rd, 5 November 1960 – Cook; Collinson, Thresher; Connor, Alan Williams, Etheridge; Tait (1), Bobby Williams (1), Atyeo (5), Adrian Williams (3), Derrick, (1 og).

Record Defeat: 0–9 v Coventry C, Division 3 (S), 28 April 1934.

Most League Points (2 for a win): 70, Division 3 (S), 1954–55.

Most League Points (3 for a win): 91, Division 3, 1989–90.

Most League Goals: 104, Division 3 (S), 1926–27.

Highest League Scorer in Season: Don Clark, 36, Division 3 (S), 1946–47.

Most League Goals in Total Aggregate: John Atyeo, 314, 1951–66.

Most League Goals in One Match: 6, Tommy 'Tot' Walsh v Gillingham, Division 3S, 15 January 1927.

Most Capped Player: Billy Wedlock, 26, England.

Most League Appearances: John Atyeo, 597, 1951–66.

Youngest League Player: Nyrere Kelly, 16 years 213 days v Hartlepool U, 16 October 1982.

Record Transfer Fee Received: £3,000,000 from Wolverhampton W for Ade Akinbiyi, September 1999.

Record Transfer Fee Paid: £1,200,000 to Gillingham for Ade Akinbiyi, May 1998.

Football League Record: 1901 Elected to Division 2; 1906–11 Division 1; 1911–22 Division 2; 1922–23 Division 3 (S); 1923–24 Division 2; 1924–27 Division 3 (S); 1927–32 Division 2; 1932–55 Division 3 (S); 1955–60 Division 2; 1960–65 Division 3; 1965–76 Division 2; 1976–80 Division 1; 1980–81 Division 2; 1981–82 Division 3; 1982–84 Division 4; 1984–90 Division 3; 1990–92 Division 2; 1992–95 Division 1; 1995–98 Division 2; 1998–99 Division 1; 1999– Division 2.

MANAGERS

Sam Hollis 1897–99
Bob Campbell 1899–1901
Sam Hollis 1901–05
Harry Thickett 1905–10
Sam Hollis 1911–13
George Hedley 1913–15
Jack Hamilton 1915–19
Joe Palmer 1919–21
Alex Raisbeck 1921–29
Joe Bradshaw 1929–32
Bob Hewison 1932–49
   (under suspension 1938–39)
Bob Wright 1949–50
Pat Beasley 1950–58
Peter Doherty 1958–60
Fred Ford 1960–67
Alan Dicks 1967–80
Bobby Houghton 1980–82
Roy Hodgson 1982
Terry Cooper 1982–88
   (Director from 1983)
Joe Jordan 1988–90
Jimmy Lumsden 1990–92
Denis Smith 1992–93
Russell Osman 1993–94
Joe Jordan 1994–97
John Ward 1997–98
Benny Lennartsson 1998–99
Tony Pulis 1999
Tony Fawthrop 2000
Danny Wilson June 2000–

LATEST SEQUENCES

Longest Sequence of League Wins: 14, 9.9.05 – 2.12.05.

Longest Sequence of League Defeats: 7, 3.10.70 – 7.11.70.

Longest Sequence of League Draws: 4, 6.11.99 – 27.11.99.

Longest Sequence of Unbeaten League Matches: 24, 9.9.05 – 10.2.06.

Longest Sequence Without a League Win: 15, 29.4.33 – 4.11.33.

TEN YEAR LEAGUE RECORD

		P	W	D	L	F	A	Pts	Pos
1991-92	Div 2	46	13	15	18	55	71	54	17
1992-93	Div 1	46	14	14	18	49	67	56	15
1993-94	Div 1	46	16	16	14	47	50	64	13
1994-95	Div 1	46	11	12	23	42	63	45	23
1995-96	Div 2	46	15	15	16	55	60	60	13
1996-97	Div 2	46	21	10	15	69	51	73	5
1997-98	Div 2	46	25	10	11	69	39	85	2
1998-99	Div 1	46	9	15	22	57	80	42	24
1999-2000	Div 2	46	15	19	12	59	57	64	9
2000-01	Div 2	46	18	14	14	70	56	68	9

DID YOU KNOW ?

On 6 December 1947, Bristol City beat Dartford 9-2 in an FA Cup first round replay following a goalless draw. There were hat-tricks each for Don Clark, Len Townsend and Cyril Williams.

BRISTOL CITY 2001–02 LEAGUE RECORD

Match No.	Date	Venue	Opponents	Result	H/T Score	Lg. Pos.	Goalscorers	Attendance
1	Aug 11	A	Northampton T	W 3-0	3-0	—	Thorpe 3 (1 pen) [6, 22 (p), 28]	5528
2	18	H	Swindon T	W 3-1	1-0	1	Tinnion [34], Matthews [61], Jones S [74]	13,818
3	25	A	Wigan Ath	W 2-1	0-0	1	Murray [47], Thorpe [52]	6231
4	30	A	QPR	D 0-0	0-0	—		11,655
5	Sept 8	H	Port Vale	D 1-1	0-1	5	Thorpe [49]	12,560
6	15	H	Colchester U	W 3-1	1-1	2	Murray [40], Jones S [47], Clist [89]	9992
7	18	A	Brentford	D 2-2	1-2	—	Tinnion [18], Bell (pen) [76]	6342
8	22	A	Peterborough U	L 1-4	0-3	7	Murray [61]	5550
9	25	H	Tranmere R	W 2-0	2-0	—	Jones S [21], Thorpe [45]	9634
10	29	A	Huddersfield T	L 0-1	0-0	6		10,652
11	Oct 5	H	Chesterfield	W 3-0	2-0	—	Thorpe [31], Jones S 2 [38, 49]	10,718
12	9	H	Cardiff C	D 1-1	0-1	—	Bell [56]	13,804
13	13	H	Oldham Ath	W 1-0	1-0	2	Murray [39]	6565
14	20	H	Wycombe W	L 0-1	0-0	3		11,452
15	23	H	Bournemouth	W 1-0	1-0	—	Tinnion [38]	9972
16	27	A	Stoke C	L 0-1	0-0	4		16,828
17	Nov 3	H	Brighton & HA	L 0-1	0-1	4		13,955
18	10	A	Reading	L 2-3	1-2	7	Amankwaah [34], Thorpe [59]	14,060
19	20	A	Bury	D 2-2	1-1	—	Peacock 2 (1 pen) [20, 89 (p)]	2608
20	24	A	Blackpool	W 2-1	1-0	5	Thorpe [45], Murray [90]	9876
21	Dec 1	H	Notts Co	W 3-2	1-0	5	Ireland (og) [12], Peacock 2 (1 pen) [67 (p), 74]	9411
22	8	A	Wrexham	W 2-0	0-0	—	Roberts (og) [55], Thorpe [62]	3091
23	15	A	Cambridge U	W 3-0	2-0	4	Peacock 2 [12, 43], Duncan (og) [88]	3561
24	22	H	Wrexham	W 1-0	0-0	3	Carey (og) [80]	12,137
25	26	A	Port Vale	L 0-1	0-0	4		5682
26	29	H	Cardiff C	W 3-1	0-0	1	Murray 2 [56, 58], Matthews [60]	16,149
27	Jan 5	H	Wigan Ath	D 2-2	2-0	3	Peacock 2 [14, 23]	9991
28	13	A	Swindon T	W 2-1	1-0	2	Hill [21], Peacock [51]	7273
29	19	H	Northampton T	L 1-3	0-2	2	Thorpe [62]	11,733
30	Feb 2	H	Huddersfield T	D 1-1	0-0	4	Peacock [68]	10,643
31	5	H	QPR	W 2-0	2-0	—	Murray [9], Thorpe [45]	11,654
32	9	A	Wycombe W	L 1-2	0-0	4	Peacock [63]	7972
33	16	H	Oldham Ath	W 3-0	0-0	3	Peacock [47], Thorpe (pen) [70], Lever [72]	10,849
34	23	A	Colchester U	D 0-0	0-0	4		3558
35	26	A	Peterborough U	W 1-0	1-0	—	Thorpe [15]	8299
36	Mar 2	H	Brentford	L 0-2	0-0	5		11,421
37	5	A	Tranmere R	L 0-1	0-1	—		7735
38	9	H	Cambridge U	W 2-0	2-0	5	Bell 2 [9, 17]	9817
39	16	H	Notts Co	L 0-2	0-1	6		7521
40	19	A	Chesterfield	L 1-2	0-1	—	Matthews [90]	3630
41	23	A	Bournemouth	W 3-1	2-0	6	Bell (pen) [34], Peacock [43], Thorpe [90]	7033
42	30	H	Reading	D 3-3	2-3	6	Peacock [6], Bell (pen) [13], Robinson [59]	15,609
43	Apr 1	A	Brighton & HA	L 1-2	0-1	7	Doherty [52]	6759
44	6	H	Bury	W 2-0	0-0	7	Bell [85], Peacock [90]	9449
45	13	A	Blackpool	L 1-5	0-4	7	Thorpe [61]	9333
46	20	A	Stoke C	D 1-1	0-1	7	Brown A [68]	11,277

Final League Position: 7

GOALSCORERS

League (68): Thorpe 16 (2 pens), Peacock 15 (2 pens), Murray 8, Bell 7 (3 pens), Jones S 5, Matthews 3, Tinnion 3, Amankwaah 1, Brown A 1, Clist 1, Doherty 1, Hill 1, Lever 1, Robinson 1, own goals 4.
Worthington Cup (4): Amankwaah 1, Clist 1, Jones S 1, Thorpe 1.
FA Cup (0).

Stowell M 25	Amankwaah K 18 + 6	Bell M 41 + 1	Hill M 40	Lever M 26 + 3	Carey L 34 + 1	Doherty T 27 + 7	Brown A 34 + 2	Jones S 17 + 6	Thorpe T 36 + 6	Tinnion B 35 + 3	Murray S 34 + 3	Clist S 9 + 11	Matthews L 6 + 16	Goodridge G — + 2	Burnell J 26 + 4	Phillips S 21 + 1	Summerbell M 5	Coles D 20 + 3	Peacock L 28 + 3	Brown M 1 + 9	Woodman C 5 + 1	Hulbert R 4 + 7	Fortune C — + 1	Rodrigues D — + 4	Singh H 3	Robinson S 6	Roberts C 4	Jones D 1 + 1	Rosenior L — + 1	Match No.
1	2^1	3	4	5	6	7^2	8	9	10^3	11	12	13	14																	1
1	2^1	3	4	5	6	7	8^2	9	10^3	11	12	13	14																	2
1	12	3	4	5	6	7^2	8	9	10	11	2^1	13																		3
1		3	4	5	6		8	9	10	11	2	7^1	12																	4
1	12	3	4	5	6		8	9	10	11	2	7^1																		5
1		3	4	5	6	7^1	8	9	10^2	11	2	12	13																	6
1	2	3	4	5		7^1	8	9	10^2	11	6	12			13															7
1	2^1	3	4	5		7^2	8	9	10	11	12	13	14		6															8
1	2	3^1	4	5		12	8	9	10	11	7	6																		9
1^9	2	3	4	5			8	9	10	11	7	6^1	12		15															10
	2	3	4	5		12	8^2	9^2	10	11^1	7	13	14			1	6													11
	2	3	4	5		12	8^2	9^2	10	11	7	13	14			1	6^1													12
	2^1	3	4	5			9	10	11	7	8^1				12	1	6													13
		3	4^3	5		12		9	10	11	7	8^2			2	1		6^1	14	13										14
		3	4	5		8^1		10	11	7	12	13			2	1		6	9^2											15
1		3	4	5	6^1	12	8	9^2	10	11	7				2				13											16
1	12	3	4	5	6^1	7	8^2	9^1	10	11	2							13	14											17
1	2^2	3	4	5^3	6	7	8		10	11^1		12	13					14	9											18
1		3	4		6	7	8		10^2	11^1	2				12			5	9	13										19
1		3	4		6	7	8		10	11^1	2				12			5	9											20
1		3	4		6	7	8		10	11^2	2				12			5	9	3^1	13									21
1		3	4		6	7	8		10^1		2				12			5	9	12	11									22
1		3	4		6	7^2	8		10^1		2							5	9	12	11^3	13	14							23
1	2^2	12			6	7	8^3		10	13								3	5	9	14	11^1								24
1		3	4		6	7^1	8		10	12	2							11^2	5	9	13									25
1	12	3	4	13	6		8		10	11^2	7		9^1		2			5												26
1	6^1	3	4			7	8^3		10	12	2		13		9^1			5	9^2	14										27
		4	3	6	12		8^1		10^3	11^2	2				7	1		5	9		13	14								28
		4^1	3	6		12	8		10	11^2	2				7	1		5	9	13										29
		3	4	12	6		8		10	11^1	2				7	1		5	9											30
		4	3	5		6^1	7^1		13	10	11	2			8	1			9^2		12									31
		3	4		6		8^1	13		11	2	12			10	1		5	9	7^2										32
		3		5	2		8^2		10	11	7^3				4^1	1		6	9	14	13	12								33
	2	3	4	5	6		8		10	11					1				9		7									34
	2	3	4	5	6		8^1	13	10^2	11		12			1				9		7									35
	2^1	3	4	5^3	6	12		14	10	11^2		13			7^1	1			9	8										36
12	3		4		6	7^2	13	14	10^3	11					2^1	1		5	9	8										37
12	3		4		6	7^2			8				10^1		2^1	1		5	9	13		11								38
	3	4		2	7^2	12			8				10^1		6^1	1		5	9	14	13	11^3								39
	3	4		6	12			9^2	13	8			10		2	1		5						14	11^1	7^3				40
	3	4^2	5	6	7			12	11	2			10^1		13	1			9							8				41
	3		5	6	7			12	11	2			10^1		4^1	1			9			13				8^2				42
1	3		5	6	7^1	12		13	11	2		14			4				9^3							8	10^2			43
1	3		6	7	8			12		2		13			4			5	9							11^2	10^1			44
1	3		6	7	8			12		2		13			4			5^1	9							11^3	10^2	14		45
		5	6	7	8^1			2					11^2	1				9	12	3						10	4	13		46

Worthington Cup
First Round	Cheltenham T	(h)	2-1	
Second Round	Watford	(h)	2-3	

FA Cup
First Round	Leyton Orient	(h)	0-1

BRISTOL ROVERS   Division 3

FOUNDATION

Bristol Rovers were formed at a meeting in Stapleton Road, Eastville, in 1883. However, they first went under the name of the Black Arabs (wearing black shirts). Changing their name to Eastville Rovers in their second season, they won the Gloucestershire Senior Cup in 1888–89. Original members of the Bristol & District League in 1892, this eventually became the Western League and Eastville Rovers adopted professionalism in 1897.

Registered Offices: The Memorial Stadium, Filton Avenue, Horfield, Bristol BS7 0BF. (0117) 909 6648.

Ground: The Memorial Stadium.

Training Ground: (0117) 942 1912.

Matchday Ticket Office: (0117) 9421912.
ClubCall: 09068 121 131. *Fax:* (0117) 908 5530.
Community Office: (0117) 907 6555.
Ticket Office: (0117) 924 7474.

Ground Capacity: 11,976.

Record Attendance: 11,433 v Sunderland, Worthington Cup 3rd rd, 31 October 2000 (Memorial Stadium). 9464 v Liverpool, FA Cup 4th rd, 8 February 1992 (Twerton Park). 38,472 v Preston NE, FA Cup 4th rd, 30 January 1960 (Eastville).

HONOURS

Football League: Division 2 best season: 4th, 1994–95; Division 3 (S) – Champions 1952–53; Division 3 – Champions 1989–90; Runners-up 1973–74.

FA Cup: best season: 6th rd, 1951, 1958.

Football League Cup: best season: 5th rd, 1971, 1972.

Record Receipts: £115,000 v Sunderland, Worthington Cup 3rd rd, 31 October 2000.

Pitch Measurements: 101m × 68m.

Vice-presidents: Dr W. T. Cussen, A. I. Seager, R. Redmond. *Chairman:* G. M. H. Dunford.
Vice-chairman: R. Craig. *Directors:* D. H. A. Dunford, B. Andrews, V. Stokes, B. Bradshaw, C. Williams. *Associate Director:* S. Burns.

Director of Football and Team Manager: Ray Graydon. *Assistant Manager:* John Still.

Physio: Phil Kite. *Director of Youth:* Phil Bater.

Community Scheme Organiser: Peter Aitken.

Club Secretary: Roger Brinsford. *Office Manager:* Mrs Angela Mann.

Sales Manager: Graham Bowen.

Colours: Blue and white quartered shirts, white shorts, blue stockings.

Change Colours: Orange shirts, black shorts and stockings.

Year Formed: 1883. *Turned Professional:* 1897. *Ltd Co.:* 1896.

Previous Names: 1883, Black Arabs; 1884, Eastville Rovers; 1897, Bristol Eastville Rovers; 1898, Bristol Rovers. *Club Nickname:* 'Pirates'.

Previous Grounds: 1883, Purdown; Three Acres, Ashley Hill; Rudgeway, Fishponds; 1897, Eastville; 1986, Twerton Park; 1996, The Memorial Stadium.

First Football League Game: 28 August 1920, Division 3, v Millwall (a) L 0–2 – Stansfield; Bethune, Panes; Boxley, Kenny, Steele; Chance, Bird, Sims, Bell, Palmer.

IT'S A FACT !

In 1949, of the 34 professionals with Bristol Rovers, 25 were products of Bristol & District Football and just six had been signed from other professional clubs.

Record League Victory: 7–0 v Brighton & HA, Division 3 (S), 29 November 1952 – Hoyle; Bamford, Fox; Pitt, Warren, Sampson; McIlvenny, Roost (2), Lambden (1), Bradford (1), Petherbridge (2), (1 og). 7–0 v Swansea T, Division 2, 2 October 1954 – Radford; Bamford, Watkins; Pitt, Muir, Anderson; Petherbridge, Bradford (2), Meyer, Roost (1), Hooper (2), (2 og). 7–0 v Shrewsbury T, Division 3, 21 March 1964 – Hall; Hillard, Gwyn Jones; Oldfield, Stone (1), Mabbutt; Jarman (2), Brown (1), Biggs (1p), Hamilton, Bobby Jones (2).

Record Cup Victory: 6–0 v Merthyr Tydfil, FA Cup 1st rd, 14 November 1987 – Martyn; Alexander (Dryden), Tanner, Hibbitt, Twentyman, Jones, Holloway, Meacham (1), White (2), Penrice (3) (Reece), Purnell.

Record Defeat: 0–12 v Luton T, Division 3 (S), 13 April 1936.

Most League Points (2 for a win): 64, Division 3 (S), 1952–53.

Most League Points (3 for a win): 93, Division 3, 1989–90.

Most League Goals: 92, Division 3 (S), 1952–53.

Highest League Scorer in Season: Geoff Bradford, 33, Division 3 (S), 1952–53.

Most League Goals in Total Aggregate: Geoff Bradford, 242, 1949–64.

Most League Goals in One Match: 4, Sidney Leigh v Exeter C, Division 3S, 2 May 1921; 4, Jonah Wilcox v Bournemouth, Division 3S, 12 December 1925; 4, Bill Culley v QPR, Division 3S, 5 March 1927; Frank Curran v Swindon T, Division 3S, 25 March 1939; Vic Lambden v Aldershot, Division 3S, 29 March 1947; George Petherbridge v Torquay U, Division 3S, 1 December 1951; Vic Lambden v Colchester U, Division 3S, 14 May 1952; Geoff Bradford v Rotherham U, Division 2, 14 March 1959; Robin Stubbs v Gillingham, Division 2, 10 October 1970; Alan Warboys v Brighton & HA, Division 3, 1 December 1973; Jamie Cureton v Reading, Division 2, 16 January 1999.

Most Capped Player: Vitalijs Astafjevs, 21 (83), Latvia.

Most League Appearances: Stuart Taylor, 546, 1966–80.

Youngest League Player: Ronnie Dix, 15 years 180 days v Norwich C, 3 March 1928.

Record Transfer Fee Received: £2,000,000 from Fulham for Barry Hayles, November 1998 and £2,000,000 from WBA for Jason Roberts, July 2000.

Record Transfer Fee Paid: £370,000 to QPR for Andy Tillson, November 1992.

Football League Record: 1920 Original Member of Division 3; 1921–53 Division 3 (S); 1953–62 Division 2; 1962–74 Division 3; 1974–81 Division 2; 1981–90 Division 3; 1990–92 Division 2. 1992–93 Division 1; 1993–2001 Division 2; 2001– Division 3.

MANAGERS

Alfred Homer 1899–1920
(*continued as Secretary to 1928*)
Ben Hall 1920–21
Andy Wilson 1921–26
Joe Palmer 1926–29
Dave McLean 1929–30
Albert Prince-Cox 1930–36
Percy Smith 1936–37
Brough Fletcher 1938–49
Bert Tann 1950–68 (*continued as General Manager to 1972*)
Fred Ford 1968–69
Bill Dodgin Snr 1969–72
Don Megson 1972–77
Bobby Campbell 1978–79
Harold Jarman 1979–80
Terry Cooper 1980–81
Bobby Gould 1981–83
David Williams 1983–85
Bobby Gould 1985–87
Gerry Francis 1987–91
Martin Dobson 1991
Dennis Rofe 1992
Malcolm Allison 1992–93
John Ward 1993–96
Ian Holloway 1996–2001
Garry Thompson 2001
Gerry Francis 2001
Garry Thompson 2001–02
Ray Graydon April 2002–

LATEST SEQUENCES

Longest Sequence of League Wins: 12, 18.10.52 – 17.1.53.
Longest Sequence of League Defeats: 8, 29.4.61 – 9.9.61.
Longest Sequence of League Draws: 5, 1.11.75 – 22.11.75.
Longest Sequence of Unbeaten League Matches: 32, 7.4.73 – 27.1.74.
Longest Sequence Without a League Win: 20, 5.4.80 – 1.11.80.

TEN YEAR LEAGUE RECORD

		P	W	D	L	F	A	Pts	Pos
1991-92	Div 2	46	16	14	16	60	63	62	13
1992-93	Div 1	46	10	11	25	55	87	41	24
1993-94	Div 2	46	20	10	16	60	59	70	8
1994-95	Div 2	46	22	16	8	70	40	82	4
1995-96	Div 2	46	20	10	16	57	60	70	10
1996-97	Div 2	46	15	11	20	47	50	56	17
1997-98	Div 2	46	20	10	16	70	64	70	5
1998-99	Div 2	46	13	17	16	65	56	56	13
1999-2000	Div 2	46	23	11	12	69	45	80	7
2000-01	Div 2	46	12	15	19	53	57	51	21

DID YOU KNOW ❓

Meeting Aldershot in the FA Cup in 1950–51, Bristol Rovers produced the fastest goal in the competition by Vic Lambden after eight seconds and helped them reach the sixth round. In 2001–02, a replay victory over Aldershot Town ushered them to the second round.

BRISTOL ROVERS 2001–02 LEAGUE RECORD

Match No.	Date		Venue	Opponents		Result	H/T Score	Lg. Pos.	Goalscorers	Attendance
1	Aug	11	H	Torquay U	W	1-0	0-0	—	Foster [79]	10,127
2		18	A	Scunthorpe U	W	2-1	2-1	2	Ellington [28], Weare [45]	3593
3		25	H	Luton T	W	3-2	1-1	1	Ellington [30], Hillier [64], Gall [75]	9057
4		27	A	Darlington	L	0-1	0-0	4		4487
5	Sept	1	H	Shrewsbury T	D	0-0	0-0	4		6942
6		8	A	Leyton Orient	L	1-3	0-0	9	Gall [89]	5433
7		15	A	Lincoln C	W	1-0	1-0	6	Gall [37]	3204
8		18	H	Southend U	W	2-1	1-1	—	Foran [40], Thomson [90]	5743
9		22	H	York C	D	2-2	0-0	7	Cameron [68], Potter (og) [94]	6933
10		29	H	Oxford U	D	1-1	1-1	8	Cameron [45]	7678
11	Oct	6	A	Carlisle U	L	0-1	0-1	8		1849
12		13	H	Macclesfield T	L	0-2	0-0	8		6554
13		20	A	Halifax T	D	0-0	0-0	9		1898
14		23	A	Exeter C	L	0-1	0-1	—		3879
15		28	H	Plymouth Arg	L	1-2	0-1	15	Cameron [85]	6889
16	Nov	3	A	Kidderminster H	L	0-2	0-1	19		3588
17		6	A	Cheltenham T	D	0-0	0-0	—		4913
18		10	H	Rochdale	L	0-2	0-0	19		5675
19		20	H	Mansfield T	L	0-1	0-0	—		5043
20		24	A	Hull C	D	0-0	0-0	20		9680
21	Dec	1	A	Rushden & D	L	1-3	0-2	21	Cameron (pen) [54]	4570
22		21	A	Swansea C	L	1-2	1-2	—	Ellington [3]	2734
23		26	H	Leyton Orient	W	5-3	2-0	20	Ellington 3 [25, 28, 73], Astafjevs [47], Ommel [89]	7458
24		29	H	Darlington	W	1-0	0-0	19	Ellington [85]	7567
25	Jan	12	H	Scunthorpe U	D	1-1	1-0	19	Ellington [17]	6691
26		15	A	Shrewsbury T	W	1-0	0-0	—	Ommel [90]	3475
27		19	A	Torquay U	L	1-2	0-1	16	Ellington [55]	3493
28		22	H	Swansea C	W	4-1	2-0	—	Ellington 3 (1 pen) [42 (p), 53, 86], Ommel [45]	5725
29	Feb	2	A	Oxford U	D	0-0	0-0	16		7457
30		9	H	Halifax T	W	2-0	1-0	15	Ommel [39], Ellington [72]	6921
31		12	H	Hartlepool U	L	0-1	0-1	—		6482
32		16	A	Macclesfield T	L	1-2	1-0	17	Ommel [8]	2149
33		19	A	Luton T	L	0-3	0-0	—		5651
34		23	H	Lincoln C	L	1-2	1-1	19	Ommel [26]	5741
35		26	A	Southend U	L	1-2	1-1	—	Ellington [36]	2477
36	Mar	5	H	Cheltenham T	L	1-2	1-1	—	Ommel [42]	5909
37		9	A	Hartlepool U	D	1-1	0-1	20	Ellington [64]	3699
38		12	H	Carlisle U	D	0-0	0-0	—		4457
39		16	H	Rushden & D	L	0-3	0-1	23		5240
40		23	H	Exeter C	D	0-0	0-0	22		6105
41		30	A	Plymouth Arg	L	0-1	0-1	23		15,732
42	Apr	1	H	Kidderminster H	W	2-1	1-1	22	Quinn (pen) [5], Ommel [88]	5711
43		6	A	Mansfield T	L	0-2	0-0	22		3996
44		13	H	Hull C	D	1-1	0-1	22	Foran [67]	6340
45		16	A	York C	L	0-3	0-2	—		2983
46		20	A	Rochdale	L	1-2	1-0	23	Thomas [29]	5292

Final League Position: 23

GOALSCORERS
League (40): Ellington 15 (1 pen), Ommel 8, Cameron 4 (1 pen), Gall 3, Foran 2, Astafjevs 1, Foster 1, Hillier 1, Quinn 1 (pen), Thomas 1, Thomson 1, Weare 1, own goal 1.
Worthington Cup (1): Hillier 1.
FA Cup (8): Ellington 4, Astafjevs 1, Hogg 1, Ommel 1, Walters 1.

Howie S 46	Wilson C 38	Challis T 28+1	Foster S 33	Thomson A 29+2	Trought M 17+3	Mauge R 14+1	Gall K 25+6	Ellington N 27	Weare R 9+1	Bryant S 8	Pritchard D 1+4	Cameron M 10+15	Jones S 14+5	Hillier D 27	Gilroy D 2+2	Lopez R 5+2	Bubb A 3+10	Hammond E 3+4	Foran M 30+1	Hogg L 22+1	Smith M 17+2	Walters M 7+19	Plummer D 12+3	Ross N 2+3	Astafjevs V 14+5	Ommel S 18+15	McKeever M 6+2	Lopez C 6	Shore D 9	Thomas J 7	Quinn J 6	Carlisle W 5	Toner C 6	Richards J —+1	Clarke R —+1	Arndale N —+1	Match No.
1	2	3	4	5	6	7¹	8	9	10	11	12²	13																									1
1	2	3¹	4	5	6	7	8	9	10¹			12	13	11																							2
1	2		4	5	6	7	8	9				10¹		3		11	12																				3
1	2		4	5	6	7	8					10		3¹		11	9²	12	13																		4
1	2		4	5	6	7	8		10¹			12		3²		11		13	9																		5
1	2		4	5	6	7	8	9				12		3¹		11			10																		6
1	2		4	5	12	7	8	9¹				10²		13		11		3¹		14	6																7
1	2		4	5		7	8		10¹			13	12			11²		3		9	6																8
1	2		4	5	12	7	8	9³				13	10			11²		3¹		14	6																9
1	2		4	5²			8	9			11	12	10	13				3¹	6	7																	10
1	2		4		6		8²	9				11		10⁵				3²		14	12	7	5	13													11
1	2		4	5	6		8	9¹	10	11									13	12	7²		5	13													12
1	2	3	4	5			8							11	9				6			7	10														13
1	2	3	4	5			8							11²	9¹				12	6		7	10	13													14
1	2	3¹	4	5			8							13	12	9²			14	6		7³	11	10													15
1	2	12	4	5		7²	13							11³	9	3¹			14			6	8	10													16
1	2	3	4	5			9	8						11					10¹	6		7²	12	13													17
1	2	3⁴	4	5			9	8				12		11					10¹	6			13	7													18
1	2	3⁴	4	5	6			10				9		11					12				13		8¹	7											19
1		3	4	5	6	7	8					10²		11¹							2	12	9			13											20
1		3	4²	5	6³	7	12	9				10		11					13		2¹				8	14											21
1	2	3		5¹	6		12	9											4	8	11	7	10														22
1	2				6¹		4²	9				12		11					5	8	3	13			7	10											23
1		3					12	9				6²		11			13		5	8¹	2	4	14		7³	10											24
1		3					4²	9				12		6		11			5	8	2	13	7			10¹											25
1		3					4²	9				12		6		11			5	8	2	13	7			10¹											26
1		3¹					12	4³	9					13		6		11	5	8	2	14	7			10⁴											27
1		3	4									9		12		11			5	9²	2	13	6		7	10¹											28
1			4					7				9		12		6	11²	3	5		2		13		8	10¹											29
1		3	4									9		6		11			5	8	2¹		12		7	10											30
1		3²	4			7	9¹					12		6					5	8			13		11	10		2									31
1		3	4									12		6			9		5	8	14	11²	13		7	10		2³									32
1	2		4	5				9						3					6¹	8²	7	12	11			10	13										33
1	2	3	4	5				9						11				12		8²			13		6	10	7¹										34
1	6	3	4	5				9²						11				12		8			13			10	7¹	2									35
1	5	3				6¹	12	9						13	11²					8		4	14		7³	10		2									36
1	6	3	4					9	12					11					5	8	2					10¹			7								37
1	6	3	4				12	9	10³					11¹					5	8	2¹	13				14			7								38
1	6	3	4				12	9	13					11					5	8	2³	14				10²			7¹								39
1	2	3⁴	4					9		6²									5	8	13					12				7	10	11					40
1	2	3	4					9											5							12		11¹	7	10	9	6	8				41
1	4	3																	5		13				12	14	11²	2²	7	10	9³	6	8				42
1	2	3	4																5	12			13				11²	10³	7¹	9	6	8	14				43
1	2	3	4¹		12		6												5	6³			13		14				7²	10	9		11				44
1	2	3	4				8²												5						12	13			7	10	9¹	6	11				45
1⁹		3	4	5								12										7			8	2²		10¹	9	6	11				15	13	46

Worthington Cup

First Round	Wycombe W	(a)	1-0
Second Round	Birmingham C	(h)	0-3

FA Cup

First Round	Aldershot T	(a)	0-0
		(h)	1-0
Second Round	Plymouth Arg	(a)	1-1
		(h)	3-2
Third Round	Derby Co	(a)	3-1
Fourth Round	Gillingham	(a)	0-1

BURNLEY

Division 1

FOUNDATION

The majority of those responsible for the formation of the Burnley club in 1881 were from the defunct rugby club Burnley Rovers. Indeed, they continued to play rugby for a year before changing to soccer and dropping 'Rovers' from their name. The changes were decided at a meeting held in May 1882 at the Bull Hotel.

Turf Moor, Burnley BB10 4BX.

Telephone: (01282) 700 000. *Fax:* (01282) 700 014.
ClubCall: 09068 121 153. *Ticket Office:* (01282) 700 010.
Community Programme: (01282) 700 081.
Commercial Department: (01282) 700 007.

Ground Capacity: 22,619.

Record Attendance: 54,775 v Huddersfield T, FA Cup 3rd rd, 23 February 1924.

Record Receipts: £183,000 v Preston NE, Division 2, 4 March 2000.

Pitch Measurements: 112yd × 70yd.

Chairman: B. Kilby. *Vice-chairman:* R. Ingleby.
President: Dr R. D. Iven MRCS (Eng), LRCP (Lond), MRCGP.
Directors: C. Holt, R. Blakeborough, J. Turkington, M. Hobbs, C. Duckworth.

Manager: Stan Ternent. *Chief Executive:* A. Watson.
Assistant Manager: Sam Ellis. *Chief Scout:* Cliff Roberts.

Company Secretary: Cathy Pickup.

Coaches: Ronnie Jepson, Michael Docherty, James Robson, Terry Pashley.

Sales Manager: Anthony Fairclough.

Colours: Claret body with blue sleeves, white shorts, white stockings.

Change Colours: Navy shirts with sky blue sleeves, sky blue shorts, navy stockings.

Year Formed: 1882.

Turned Professional: 1883. *Ltd Co.:* 1897.

Previous Name: 1881, Burnley Rovers; 1882, Burnley.

Club Nickname: 'The Clarets'.

Previous Grounds: 1881, Calder Vale; 1882, Turf Moor.

First Football League Game: 8 September 1888, Football League, v Preston NE (a) L 2–5 – Smith; Lang, Bury, Abrams, Friel, Keenan, Brady, Tait, Poland (1), Gallocher (1), Yates.

Record League Victory: 9–0 v Darwen, Division 1, 9 January 1892 – Hillman; Walker, McFettridge, Lang, Matthews, Keenan, Nicol (3), Bowes, Espie (1), McLardie (3), Hill (2).

HONOURS

Football League: Division 1 – Champions 1920–21, 1959–60; Runners-up 1919–20, 1961–62; Division 2 – Champions 1897–98, 1972–73; Runners-up 1912–13, 1946–47, 1999–2000; Promoted from Division 2, 1993–94 (play-offs); Division 3 – Champions 1981–82; Division 4 – Champions 1991–92. Record 30 consecutive Division 1 games without defeat 1920–21.

FA Cup: Winners 1914; Runners-up 1947, 1962.

Football League Cup: Semi-final 1961, 1969, 1983.

Anglo–Scottish Cup: Winners 1979.

Sherpa Van Trophy: Runners-up 1988.

European Competitions: European Cup: 1960–61. European Fairs Cup: 1966–67.

IT'S A FACT !

Tom Nicol made a sensational debut for Burnley scoring a hat-trick against Preston North End at Turf Moor on 7 March 1891 in a 6-2 win. However, many contemporary reports awarded him four goals.

Record Cup Victory: 9–0 v Crystal Palace, FA Cup 2nd rd (replay), 10 February 1909 – Dawson; Barron, McLean; Cretney (2), Leake, Moffat; Morley, Ogden, Smith (3), Abbott (2), Smethams (1). 9–0 v New Brighton, FA Cup 4th rd, 26 January 1957 – Blacklaw; Angus, Winton; Seith, Adamson, Miller; Newlands (1), McIlroy (3), Lawson (3), Cheesebrough (1), Pilkington (1). 9–0 v Penrith, FA Cup 1st rd, 17 November 1984 – Hansbury; Miller, Hampton, Phelan, Overson (Kennedy), Hird (3 incl. 1p), Grewcock (1), Powell (2), Taylor (3), Biggins, Hutchison.

Record Defeat: 0–10 v Aston Villa, Division 1, 29 August 1925 and v Sheffield U, Division 1, 19 January 1929.

Most League Points (2 for a win): 62, Division 2, 1972–73.

Most League Points (3 for a win): 88, Division 2, 1999–2000.

Most League Goals: 102, Division 1, 1960–61.

Highest League Scorer in Season: George Beel, 35, Division 1, 1927–28.

Most League Goals in Total Aggregate: George Beel, 178, 1923–32.

Most League Goals in One Match: 6, Louis Page v Birmingham C, Division 1, 10 April 1926.

Most Capped Player: Jimmy McIlroy, 51 (55), Northern Ireland.

Most League Appearances: Jerry Dawson, 522, 1907–28.

Youngest League Player: Tommy Lawton, 16 years 174 days v Doncaster R, 28 March 1936.

Record Transfer Fee Received: £750,000 from Luton T for Steve Davis, August 1995.

Record Transfer Fee Paid: £1,000,000 to Stockport C for Ian Moore, October 2000. £1,000,000 to Bradford C for Robbie Blake, January 2002.

Football League Record: 1888 Original Member of the Football League; 1897–98 Division 2; 1898–1900 Division 1; 1900–13 Division 2; 1913–30 Division 1; 1930–47 Division 2; 1947–71 Division 1; 1971–73 Division 2; 1973–76 Division 1; 1976–80 Division 2; 1980–82 Division 3; 1982–83 Division 2; 1983–85 Division 3; 1985–92 Division 4; 1992–94 Division 2; 1994–95 Division 1; 1995–2000 Division 2; 2000– Division 1.

MANAGERS

Arthur F. Sutcliffe 1893–96
(Secretary-Manager)
Harry Bradshaw 1896–99
(Secretary-Manager)
Ernest Magnall 1899–1903
(Secretary-Manager)
Spen Whittaker 1903–10
R. H. Wadge 1910–11
(Secretary-Manager)
John Haworth 1911–25
Albert Pickles 1925–32
Tom Bromilow 1932–35
Alf Boland 1935–39
(Secretary-Manager)
Cliff Britton 1945–48
Frank Hill 1948–54
Alan Brown 1954–57
Billy Dougall 1957–58
Harry Potts 1958–70
(General Manager to 1972)
Jimmy Adamson 1970–76
Joe Brown 1976–77
Harry Potts 1977–79
Brian Miller 1979–83
John Bond 1983–84
John Benson 1984–85
Martin Buchan 1985
Tommy Cavanagh 1985–86
Brian Miller 1986–89
Frank Casper 1989–91
Jimmy Mullen 1991–96
Adrian Heath 1996–97
Chris Waddle 1997–98
Stan Ternent June 1998–

LATEST SEQUENCES

Longest Sequence of League Wins: 10, 16.11.12 – 18.1.13.
Longest Sequence of League Defeats: 8, 2.1.95 – 25.2.95.
Longest Sequence of League Draws: 6, 21.2.31 – 28.3.31.
Longest Sequence of Unbeaten League Matches: 30, 6.9.20 – 25.3.21.
Longest Sequence Without a League Win: 24, 16.4.79 – 17.11.79.

TEN YEAR LEAGUE RECORD

		P	W	D	L	F	A	Pts	Pos
1991-92	Div 4	42	25	8	9	79	43	83	1
1992-93	Div 2	46	15	16	15	57	59	61	13
1993-94	Div 2	46	21	10	15	79	58	73	6
1994-95	Div 1	46	11	13	22	49	74	46	22
1995-96	Div 2	46	14	13	19	56	68	55	17
1996-97	Div 2	46	19	11	16	71	55	68	9
1997-98	Div 2	46	13	13	20	55	65	52	20
1998-99	Div 2	46	13	16	17	54	73	55	15
1999-2000	Div 2	46	25	13	8	69	47	88	2
2000-01	Div 2	46	21	9	16	50	54	72	7

DID YOU KNOW

On 27 January 1973, the Football League launched its Leagueline train taking 500 Burnley supporters to Queens Park Rangers. The coaches included one fitted with four television screens and another kitted out as a disco.

BURNLEY 2001–02 LEAGUE RECORD

Match No.	Date	Venue	Opponents	Result	H/T Score	Lg. Pos.	Goalscorers	Atten-dance
1	Aug 12	A	Sheffield W	W 2-0	0-0	—	Taylor [57], Cook (pen) [79]	21,766
2	18	H	Wimbledon	W 3-2	3-1	3	Moore A [12], Cook (pen) [31], Armstrong [40]	14,473
3	25	A	Millwall	W 2-0	0-0	2	Moore I [63], Moore A [68]	11,903
4	27	H	Manchester C	L 2-4	1-1	4	Davis [25], Briscoe [52]	19,602
5	Sept 2	A	Bradford C	W 3-2	0-0	1	Little 2 [46, 79], Ellis [85]	17,547
6	8	H	Rotherham U	W 3-0	0-0	1	Moore I [48], Weller [49], Payton (pen) [90]	14,820
7	15	H	Walsall	W 5-2	2-0	1	Taylor [31], Moore I [45], Briscoe 2 [69, 72], Cook [80]	14,019
8	18	A	Birmingham C	W 3-2	2-2	—	Little 2 [10, 72], Moore I [34]	18,426
9	22	A	Norwich C	L 1-2	0-1	1	Armstrong [58]	19,849
10	25	H	Crewe Alex	D 3-3	0-2	—	Taylor [62], Payton 2 (1 pen) [83 (p), 90]	13,964
11	29	H	WBA	L 0-1	0-0	2		21,442
12	Oct 13	A	Nottingham F	L 0-1	0-0	2		24,016
13	20	H	Barnsley	D 3-3	2-1	5	Morgan (og) [23], Briscoe [36], Payton (pen) [86]	14,690
14	23	H	Crystal Palace	W 1-0	1-0	—	Cook [17]	14,713
15	28	A	Wolverhampton W	L 0-3	0-3	4		24,893
16	30	A	Gillingham	D 2-2	1-2	—	Taylor [32], Little (pen) [52]	8067
17	Nov 4	H	Sheffield U	W 2-0	2-0	9	Taylor [30], Cook [33]	13,166
18	10	H	Portsmouth	D 1-1	0-0	5	Taylor [69]	14,123
19	13	H	Watford	W 1-0	1-0	—	Little [2]	13,162
20	17	A	Coventry C	W 2-0	2-0	1	Taylor [11], Little [33]	16,849
21	23	H	Grimsby T	W 1-0	1-0	—	Taylor [3]	18,535
22	Dec 1	A	Crystal Palace	W 2-1	1-1	1	Moore I 2 [23, 63]	18,457
23	9	A	Preston NE	W 3-2	2-2	1	Gnohere 2 [17, 61], Little [25]	20,370
24	15	H	Stockport Co	W 3-2	1-1	1	Little (pen) [9], Taylor [66], Moore I [70]	15,526
25	22	H	Millwall	D 0-0	0-0	1		16,131
26	29	A	Manchester C	L 1-5	0-4	1	Moore I [61]	34,250
27	Jan 12	A	Wimbledon	D 0-0	0-0	3		7675
28	19	H	Sheffield W	L 1-2	0-1	5	Taylor (pen) [77]	16,081
29	Feb 3	H	WBA	L 0-2	0-2	7		15,846
30	6	A	Watford	W 2-1	0-1	—	Cox [72], Weller [90]	12,160
31	9	A	Barnsley	D 1-1	1-1	5	Taylor [38]	14,411
32	12	A	Rotherham U	D 1-1	1-1	—	Taylor (pen) [9]	9021
33	16	H	Nottingham F	D 1-1	0-0	5	Gnohere [88]	15,085
34	23	A	Crewe Alex	W 2-1	1-0	5	Taylor [20], Moore A [58]	6458
35	26	H	Birmingham C	L 0-1	0-1	—		13,504
36	Mar 2	H	Norwich C	D 1-1	1-0	5	Taylor [6]	14,679
37	5	A	Walsall	L 0-1	0-0	—		5611
38	9	A	Stockport Co	W 2-0	0-0	6	Taylor [51], Cox [83]	6410
39	17	H	Preston NE	W 2-1	2-0	4	Moore I [5], Johnson [25]	18,388
40	20	H	Bradford C	D 1-1	1-0	—	Johnson [20]	19,479
41	23	A	Sheffield U	L 0-3	0-1	4		19,003
42	30	H	Wolverhampton W	L 2-3	0-3	4	Moore I [47], Johnson [85]	21,823
43	Apr 1	A	Portsmouth	D 1-1	1-0	4	Johnson [20]	18,020
44	6	H	Gillingham	W 2-0	0-0	4	Moore I [55], Johnson [62]	16,236
45	13	A	Grimsby T	L 1-3	0-3	6	Briscoe [90]	9275
46	21	H	Coventry C	W 1-0	0-0	7	Taylor [68]	18,751

Final League Position: 7

GOALSCORERS

League (70): Taylor 16 (2 pens), Moore I 11, Little 9 (2 pens), Briscoe 5, Cook 5 (2 pens), Johnson 5, Payton 4 (3 pens), Gnohere 3, Moore A 3, Armstrong 2, Cox 2, Weller 2, Davis 1, Ellis 1, own goal 1.
Worthington Cup (2): McGregor 1, Moore A 1.
FA Cup (5): Moore I 3, Little 1, Moore A 1.

Michopoulos N 33	West D 43+1	Armstrong G 11+7	Cox I 32+2	Davis S 22+1	Briscoe L 43+1	Little G 31+6	Cook P 25+3	Moore I 41+5	Taylor G 35+5	Weller P 29+9	Payton A —+15	Ellis T —+11	Moore A 23+6	Mullin J —+4	Ball K 37+5	Gnohere A 31+3	Thomas M 10+2	Grant T 26+2	Papadopoulos D —+6	Maylett B —+10	Johnrose L —+6	Branch G 8+2	Beresford M 13	Blake R 1+9	McGregor M 1	Johnson D 8	Gascoigne P 3+3	Match No.
1	2	3	4	5	6	7	8	9^1	10^2	11^3	12	13	14															1
1	2	3	4	5	6	7	8	9^1	10				12		11^2	13												2
1	2	3^1	4	5	6	7^3	8	9^1	10			13	12		11	14												3
1	2^3	3	4	5	6^2	7	8^1	9	10	12	13		11	14														4
1	2	3		5	6	10	8	9^1		4		12	11		7													5
1	2	3		5		10	8	9^1	12	4^2	13		11		7	6												6
1	2			5	12	7	8	9^1	10^2		13	11^3	14	4	6	3												7
1	2	3		5	6	7	8^2	9^1	10		13	11^2		4	12	14												8
1	2	3		5	6	7^2	8	9^3	10	12	14	13	11^1		4													9
1	2^2	3^3		5	4		8^1	9	10	7	13		12	11	6	14												10
1	2		4^3	5	3		8	9^1	10	7	14	13		12	11^2	6												11
1	2		4	5	3		8^1	9^3	10	11	12			7	6^3	13	14											12
1	2^2	12	4	5	3		8^3	9^1	10	11	13			7	6		14											13
1		12	4	5	3	13	8^1	9^3	10^2	11	14			7	6	2												14
1	12	13	4^3	5	3	14	8^1	9	10	11				7	6	2^2												15
1	2		4	5	3	7	8^1	9^2	10	11	13			12	6^3		14											16
1	2		4		3	7^1	8^2	9^3	10	11				6	5	14	12	13										17
1	2		4		3	7	8^2	9^1	10	11	12			6	5		13											18
1	2		4		3	7	8^2	9	10	11^1				12	6	5	13											19
1	2		4		3^1	7	8^2	9	10	11		13		12	6	5												20
1	2		4			7	8^2	9	10^3	11^1	14	13		12	6	5		3										21
1	2		4		3	8^2		9		7^1	13	11^3		12	6	5	14	10										22
1	2		4		3	10^1		9	13	12		11^3		7	6	5	14	8^2										23
1	2	12	4		3	10		9^3	8	13		11^2		7	6		14		5^1									24
1	2		4		3	10		9^1	8	12		11		7	6	5												25
1	2^2		4		3	7		9^1	10		12	11		8	6	5	13											26
1	2		4		3			8^1	9		13	11		7	6	5	12^2		10									27
1	2		4		3			9^1	8			11		7	6	5	12	13	10^2									28
	2		4		3	12	8^1	9^1	10	13		11^2		7	6	5				1	14							29
	2	12			3	7	9	8^1	11			4		6	5	14	10^2	1	13^3									30
	2		4		3	7^2		9^3	10	11		12		8	6	5^1	13		1	14								31
	2		4		3	7^1		9^3	10^2	8		11		5	6		12	13	1	14								32
	2	14	4^1		3	7		12	9	10		11		8	6	5^2			1	13^3								33
	2	3^3	4		6	9^1	8	12	10	7		11		5			13	1										34
	2	4	12		6	7	8^2	13	9	10		11^3		5		3^1		1	14									35
	2	14		5	3	7^1		12	10	8		11^2		4	6		13	1	9^1									36
	2^1	8^2	12	5	3		13	9	10	7^3		11		4	6		14	1										37
		4		5^3	7		12	9	10	11				6	3	8^1	13	1	14	2^2								38
	2	5		3	12	13	9^3		7^1			11		8	6	4			1	14				10^2				39
	2	5		3	7^1		9			12		11		6	4	13			1	14				10^2	8^1			40
	2	5^2		3			9^1	10	12	14	13		11		6	5			14	1					7	8^3		41
	1	2			3	12		13	10^2	7^3			11		4	6	5	14							9	8^1		42
	1	2	12			3	13		9^2		7^3		11		8	6	5	4^1									10	14	43
	1	2			5	3	7		9	12	13				8	6	4	11^2									10^1		44
	1	2^1			5	11	7^4		9	13	12				8^3	6	3	4									10	14	45
	1	2^2			5	11	8		9^1	12	7	13			4	6	3^1										10	14	46

Worthington Cup
First Round   Rushden & D   (h)   2-3

FA Cup
Third Round   Canvey Island   (h)   4-1
Fourth Round   Cheltenham T   (a)   1-2

BURY   Division 3

FOUNDATION

A meeting at the Waggon & Horses Hotel, attended largely by members of Bury Wesleyans and Bury Unitarians football clubs, decided to form a new Bury club. This was officially formed at a subsequent gathering at the Old White Horse Hotel, Fleet Street, Bury on 24 April 1885.

Gigg Lane, Bury BL9 9HR.

Telephone: (0161) 764 4881. *Fax:* (0161) 764 5521.
Commercial Dept: (0161) 705 2144. *Fax:* (0161) 763 3103.
Community Programme: (0161) 797 5423.
Info line: 0900 809 0003.

Social Club: (0161) 764 6771.

Ground Capacity: 11,669.

Record Attendance: 35,000 v Bolton W, FA Cup 3rd rd, 9 January 1960.

Record Receipts: £86,000 v Manchester C, Division 1, 12 September 1997.

Pitch Measurements: 112yd × 70yd.

Joint Chairmen: J. Smith, F. Mason.

Manager: Andy Preece. *Assistant Manager:* Graham Barrow.
Physios: Alan Raw, Lee Nobes. *Youth Development:* Andy Feeley.

Safety Officer: Richard Ambler.

Secretary: Jill Neville.

Commercial Manager: Peter Young.

Colours: White shirts, royal blue shorts, royal blue stockings.

Change Colours: Silver and blue.

Year Formed: 1885.

Turned professional: 1885.

Ltd Co.: 1897.

Club Nickname: 'Shakers'.

Club Sponsors: Bury Metro.

HONOURS

Football League: Division 1 best season: 4th, 1925–26; Division 2 – Champions 1894–95, 1996–97; Runners-up 1923–24; Division 3 – Champions 1960–61; Runners-up 1967–68; Promoted from Division 3 (3rd) 1995–96.
FA Cup: Winners 1900, 1903.
Football League Cup: Semi-final 1963.

First Football League Game: 1 September 1894, Division 2, v Manchester C (h) W 4–2 – Lowe; Gillespie, Davies; White, Clegg, Ross; Wylie, Barbour (2), Millar (1), Ostler (1), Plant.

Record League Victory: 8–0 v Tranmere R, Division 3, 10 January 1970 – Forrest; Tinney, Saile; Anderson, Turner, McDermott; Hince (1), Arrowsmith (1), Jones (4), Kerr (1), Grundy, (1 og).

Record Cup Victory: 12–1 v Stockton, FA Cup 1st rd (replay), 2 February 1897 – Montgomery; Darroch, Barbour; Hendry (1), Clegg, Ross (1); Wylie (3), Pangbourn, Millar (4), Henderson (2), Plant, (1 og).

IT'S A FACT !

Bury's first season in the Second Division in 1894–95 brought instant success with the championship and a 100 per cent home record. Their winning margin of nine points stayed as a division record until 1974.

Record Defeat: 0–10 v West Ham U, Milk Cup 2nd rd 2nd leg, 25 October 1983.

Most League Points (2 for a win): 68, Division 3, 1960–61.

Most League Points (3 for a win): 84, Division 4, 1984–85 and Division 2, 1996–97.

Most League Goals: 108, Division 3, 1960–61.

Highest League Scorer in Season: Craig Madden, 35, Division 4, 1981–82.

Most League Goals in Total Aggregate: Craig Madden, 129, 1978–86.

Most League Goals in One Match: 5, Eddie Quigley v Millwall, Division 2, 15 February 1947; 5, Ray Pointer v Rotherham U, Division 2, 2 October 1965.

Most Capped Player: Bill Gorman, 11 (13), Republic of Ireland and (4), Northern Ireland.

Most League Appearances: Norman Bullock, 506, 1920–35.

Youngest League Player: Brian Williams, 16 years 133 days v Stockport Co, 18 March 1972.

Record Transfer Fee Received: £1,100,000 from Ipswich T for David Johnson, November 1997.

Record Transfer Fee Paid: £200,000 to Ipswich T for Chris Swailes, November 1997 and to Swindon T for Darren Bullock, February 1999.

Football League Record: 1894 Elected to Division 2; 1895–1912 Division 1; 1912–24 Division 2; 1924–29 Division 1; 1929–57 Division 2; 1957–61 Division 3; 1961–67 Division 2; 1967–68 Division 3; 1968–69 Division 2; 1969–71 Division 3; 1971–74 Division 4; 1974–80 Division 3; 1980–85 Division 4; 1985–96 Division 3; 1996–97 Division 2; 1997–99 Division 1; 1999–2002 Division 2; 2002– Division 3.

MANAGERS

T. Hargreaves 1887
 (Secretary-Manager)
H. S. Hamer 1887–1907
 (Secretary-Manager)
Archie Montgomery 1907–15
William Cameron 1919–23
James Hunter Thompson 1923–27
Percy Smith 1927–30
Arthur Paine 1930–34
Norman Bullock 1934–38
Jim Porter 1944–45
Norman Bullock 1945–49
John McNeil 1950–53
Dave Russell 1953–61
Bob Stokoe 1961–65
Bert Head 1965–66
Les Shannon 1966–69
Jack Marshall 1969
Les Hart 1970
Tommy McAnearney 1970–72
Alan Brown 1972–73
Bobby Smith 1973–77
Bob Stokoe 1977–78
David Hatton 1978–79
Dave Connor 1979–80
Jim Iley 1980–84
Martin Dobson 1984–89
Sam Ellis 1989–90
Mike Walsh 1990–95
Stan Ternent 1995–98
Neil Warnock 1998–99
Andy Preece May 2000–

LATEST SEQUENCES

Longest Sequence of League Wins: 9, 26.9.60 – 19.11.60.

Longest Sequence of League Defeats: 8, 18.8.01 – 25.9.01.

Longest Sequence of League Draws: 6, 6.3.99 – 3.4.99.

Longest Sequence of Unbeaten League Matches: 18, 4.2.61 – 29.4.61.

Longest Sequence Without a League Win: 19, 1.4.11 – 2.12.11.

TEN YEAR LEAGUE RECORD

		P	W	D	L	F	A	Pts	Pos
1991-92	Div 3	46	13	12	21	55	74	51	21
1992-93	Div 3	42	18	9	15	63	55	63	7
1993-94	Div 3	42	14	11	17	55	56	53	13
1994-95	Div 3	42	23	11	8	73	36	80	4
1995-96	Div 3	46	22	13	11	66	48	79	3
1996-97	Div 2	46	24	12	10	62	38	84	1
1997-98	Div 1	46	11	19	16	42	58	52	17
1998-99	Div 1	46	10	17	19	35	60	47	22
1999-2000	Div 2	46	13	18	15	61	64	57	15
2000-01	Div 2	46	16	10	20	45	59	58	16

DID YOU KNOW ?

Billy Hibbert of Bury scored six goals for the FA touring team against Kuip River District at Ladysmith on 20 June 1910 and five against Western Province at Cape Town on 28 May.

BURY 2001–02 LEAGUE RECORD

Match No.	Date	Venue	Opponents	Result		H/T Score	Lg. Pos.	Goalscorers	Attendance
1	Aug 11	A	Tranmere R	W	2-1	1-0	—	Newby [4], Reid [84]	9114
2	18	H	QPR	L	1-2	1-1	11	Nelson [4]	4167
3	25	A	Huddersfield T	L	0-2	0-0	15		8684
4	27	H	Swindon T	L	0-3	0-0	17		3202
5	Sept 8	H	Wigan Ath	L	0-2	0-1	22		4175
6	11	A	Wrexham	L	0-1	0-0	—		2470
7	15	A	Bournemouth	L	2-3	2-2	23	Jarrett [6], Reid [44]	3004
8	22	H	Stoke C	L	0-1	0-1	24		4727
9	25	A	Oldham Ath	L	0-4	0-2	—		5605
10	29	A	Reading	D	1-1	0-1	24	Lawson [90]	10,035
11	Oct 2	H	Wycombe W	D	1-1	1-1	—	Reid (pen) [19]	2459
12	13	A	Cambridge U	L	1-3	1-1	24	Singh [26]	3252
13	20	H	Chesterfield	W	2-1	0-1	24	Seddon 2 [65, 68]	2898
14	23	A	Brentford	L	1-5	0-2	—	Siros [63]	5389
15	27	H	Peterborough U	W	2-0	1-0	24	Unsworth [31], Clegg [87]	2784
16	Nov 3	H	Port Vale	L	0-1	0-0	24		4688
17	7	H	Cardiff C	W	3-0	1-0	—	Jarrett [10], Seddon [52], Borley [79]	2549
18	11	H	Northampton T	W	2-1	0-1	20	Lawson [77], Swailes [82]	3539
19	20	H	Bristol C	D	2-2	1-1	—	Newby (pen) [42], Singh [49]	2608
20	24	A	Colchester U	W	1-0	0-0	20	Newby [82]	3534
21	Dec 1	H	Brighton & HA	L	0-2	0-1	20		3782
22	15	A	Notts Co	W	2-1	2-0	20	Borley (pen) [36], Seddon [43]	4395
23	22	H	Blackpool	D	1-1	0-1	19	Stuart [53]	4830
24	26	A	Wigan Ath	D	1-1	0-0	19	Redmond [77]	6751
25	29	A	Swindon T	L	1-3	1-2	20	Newby [25]	7624
26	Jan 12	A	QPR	L	0-3	0-1	21		10,003
27	15	H	Huddersfield T	D	0-0	0-0	—		3462
28	19	A	Tranmere R	L	0-1	0-1	20		4245
29	26	A	Blackpool	W	1-0	1-0	20	Seddon [8]	4923
30	29	H	Wrexham	D	2-2	1-2	—	Clegg [28], Lawson [86]	2735
31	Feb 2	H	Reading	D	1-1	1-0	20	Newby [22]	3667
32	9	A	Chesterfield	L	0-2	0-0	20		5132
33	16	H	Cambridge U	D	2-2	1-1	20	Borley [15], Clegg [65]	3547
34	19	A	Cardiff C	L	0-1	0-1	—		8273
35	23	A	Bournemouth	W	2-1	1-1	19	Clegg [45], Lawson [64]	4218
36	26	A	Stoke C	L	0-4	0-1	—		9635
37	Mar 2	A	Wycombe W	W	2-0	0-0	19	Rogers (og) [54], Nelson [63]	6409
38	5	H	Oldham Ath	D	1-1	1-0	—	Forrest [14]	7953
39	9	H	Notts Co	L	0-4	0-3	—		5435
40	16	A	Brighton & HA	L	1-2	0-2	21	Preece [68]	6609
41	23	H	Port Vale	D	1-1	0-0	21	Newby [70]	3700
42	29	A	Northampton T	L	0-1	0-0	—		6522
43	Apr 1	H	Brentford	W	2-0	0-0	21	Billy 2 [47, 74]	4332
44	6	A	Bristol C	L	0-2	0-0	21		9449
45	13	H	Colchester U	L	1-3	0-1	22	Billy [74]	5014
46	20	A	Peterborough U	L	1-2	0-1	22	Seddon [77]	5754

Final League Position: 22

GOALSCORERS

League (43): Newby 6 (1 pen), Seddon 6, Clegg 4, Lawson 4, Billy 3, Borley 3 (1 pen), Reid 3 (1 pen), Jarrett 2, Nelson 2, Singh 2, Forrest 1, Preece 1, Redmond 1, Siros 1, Stuart 1, Swailes 1, Unsworth 1, own goal 1.
Worthington Cup (1): Reid 1 (pen).
FA Cup (2): Seddon 1, Singh 1.

Kenny P 41	Barrass M 6+1	Armstrong C 11	Nelson M 28+3	Collins S 26+3	Redmond S 26	Billy C 19+2	Forrest M 31+3	Bhutia B 3	Newby J 46	Reid P 23+5	Jarrett J 32+5	Seddon G 23+12	Murphy M 5+4	Unsworth L 34+1	Bullock D 2+2	Preece A 4+9	Swailes D 26+2	Clegg G 25+6	Singh H 11+1	Siros G 9	Lawson I 12+12	Stuart J 24	O'Shaughnessy P —+2	Borley D 16+5	Garner G 5+2	Connell L 9+4	Hill N 3+2	Nugent D 1+4	Clarkson P 4	Evans G 1	Gunby S —+1	Match No.
1	2	3	4	5	6	7	8¹	9²	10	11	12	13																				1
1	2³	3	4	5	6	7	8¹	9²	10	11	12	13	14																			2
1		3	4	5	6¹	7	8³		9	11	12	10²		2	14	13																3
1	2		4	5	6¹	7			9	10	11²	13	12	3	14	8³																4
1		3	4¹	12		7			9	11³	8	13	6	2	14		5	10²														5
1	2³	3		12	6¹	7	8		9²	11		10	13				5	14	4													6
1		3		6		7	8		9			10¹		2			5	11	4		12											7
1		3		6		7¹	8		9			12		2			5	11	4		10											8
1		3		6		7	8		9²		12	13	14	2¹			5	11	4		10³											9
1		3	4	6		7	8		9	10				2¹			5	11			12											10
1		3		6²		7	8¹		9	10	12	13		2			5	11	4													11
1		3		6		7	8		9		12	13		2²			5	11	4¹		10											12
1				6		7	8		9		12	10²		2			5				11¹	4		3		13						13
1				5¹	6	7²	8		9	11	12	10		2					4		13			3								14
1			4		6	7	8		9	11				2			5	12				10¹		3								15
1			4		6	7	8²		9	11³	12	13	14	2			5					10¹		3								16
1			4		6	7	8		9	11				2			5	12				10¹		3								17
1			4		6²	7	8¹		9		12	13		2			5	11				10		3⁹	15							18
1			4		6	7	8		9		12			2			5	11¹				10		3								19
1				5	6	7¹	8		9			13		2				11	4²		12	10		3								20
1			4		6³	7¹	8		9			13	14	2			5	11			12	10²		3								21
1			4	5	6	7	8¹		9					2							12	10		3		11						22
1			4	5	6	7	8		9					2								10		3		11						23
1			4	5	6	7			9	11				2				8¹			12	10		3²		13						24
1			4		6	7			9	11				2²		12	5	8				10¹		3		13						25
1			4		6				9					2		12	5	8				10		3		11	7¹					26
1			4		6	7²			9					2			5	8			12	10		3		11¹	13					27
1		4³			6				9	11²	12	13		2	14		5	8				10		3			7¹					28
1			4		6				9	7				2		12	5	8				10¹		3		11						29
1			4		6				9	7⁵	12			2			5	8			13	10		3		11¹						30
1			4		6				9	7				2			5	8				10		3		11						31
1	12		4		3				9	7	11²			2			5¹	8								13	6					32
1		4	5	6	3				9	7								8			12					11⁹	15					33
1		4	5	6²			2		9	11				12			8					10		3		13	7¹					34
1		4	5	6¹	7				9	11				2			8					10		3		12						35
1		4	5	6³	7				9	12	10¹	14		2²		13	8							3		11						36
1		4	5	6					9	7				10			8							3		11	1	2				37
1		4	5	6					9	7	12			10			8							3		11¹	1	2				38
1	4¹	5		6					9	7	11²	10	14			12	8³				13			3			2					39
		4		6²					9	7²	11	12		2			10¹	5				8		13		3	14					40
		4		6					9	7²	11			2			10³	5				8		12		3	13					41
1	12	4		13	6				9	11³				2			10	5				8¹	14	3²			7					42
1			4		7	6			9²					5		12		3				10¹		11		2	13	8				43
1	12		4²		7	6			9					5				3				10³		11		2¹	13	14	8			44
1		3¹		5		7	8		9		12			6				11			10					2²	13	4				45
	6²					2³	7¹		9	12				10			4	5			8	1		13		11			3		14	46

Worthington Cup
First Round   Sheffield W   (h) 1-3

FA Cup
First Round   Lincoln C   (a) 1-1
                                          (h) 1-1

CAMBRIDGE UNITED   Division 3

FOUNDATION

The football revival in Cambridge began soon after World War II when the Abbey United club (formed 1912) decided to turn professional in 1949. In 1951 they changed their name to Cambridge United. They were competing in the United Counties League before graduating to the Eastern Counties League in 1951 and the Southern League in 1958.

Abbey Stadium, Newmarket Rd, Cambridge, CB5 8LN.

Telephone: (01223) 566 500. *Fax:* (01223) 566 502.
ClubCall: 09068 555 885.
Website: cambridge-united.co.uk

Ground Capacity: 9,247.

Record Attendance: 14,000 v Chelsea, Friendly,
1 May 1970.

Record Receipts: £86,308 v Manchester U,
Rumbelows Cup 2nd rd 2nd leg, 9 October 1991.

Pitch Measurements: 110yd × 74yd.

Life President: R. H. Smart. *Chairman:* G. G. Harwood.
Vice-chairman: R. F. Hunt.

Directors: J. Howard, R. Hunt, G. Lowe, R. Summerfield,
P. S. Barry, R. L. Sargent.

HONOURS

Football League: Division 2 best season: 5th, 1991–92; Division 3 – Champions 1990–91; Runners-up 1977–78, 1998–99; Division 4 – Champions 1976–77; Promoted from Division 4 1989–90 (play-offs).
FA Cup: best season: 6th rd, 1990 (shared record for Fourth Division club), 1991.
Football League Cup: best season: 5th rd, 1993.
LDV Vans Trophy: Runners-up 2002.

Manager: John Taylor. *Assistant Manager:* Dale Brooks.

Physio: Stuart Ayres.

Secretary: Andrew Pincher.

Stadium Manager: Ian Darler.

Colours: Amber shirts with black trim, black shorts, amber stockings.

Change Colours: All navy with Cambridge blue trim.

Year Formed: 1912.

Turned Professional: 1949.

Ltd Co.: 1948.

Previous Name: 1919, Abbey United; 1951, Cambridge United.

Club Nickname: The 'U's'.

First Football League Game: 15 August 1970, Division 4, v Lincoln C (h) D 1–1 – Roberts;
Thompson, Meldrum (1), Slack, Eades, Hardy, Leggett, Cassidy, Lindsey, McKinven, Harris.

IT'S A FACT !

In 1976–77 when Cambridge United won the Fourth Division title, the club's youth team also covered itself with honours, winning five domestic competitions and a tournament in Holland (without conceding a goal).

Record League Victory: 6–0 v Darlington, Division 4,
18 September 1971 – Roberts; Thompson, Akers, Guild,
Eades, Foote, Collins (1p), Horrey, Hollett, Greenhalgh (4),
Phillips, (1 og). 6–0 v Hartlepool U, Division 4, 11 February
1989 – Vaughan; Beck, Kimble, Turner, Chapple (1), Daish,
Clayton, Holmes, Taylor (3 incl. 1p), Bull (1), Leadbitter (1).

Record Cup Victory: 5–1 v Bristol C, FA Cup 5th rd second
replay, 27 February 1990 – Vaughan; Fensome, Kimble,
Bailie (O'Shea), Chapple, Daish, Cheetham (Robinson),
Leadbitter (1), Dublin (2), Taylor (1), Philpott (1).

Record Defeat: 0–6 v Aldershot, Division 3, 13 April 1974;
v Darlington, Division 4, 28 September 1974. 0–6 v Chelsea,
Division 2, 15 January 1983 and v Brentford, Division 2,
28 January 1995.

Most League Points (2 for a win): 65, Division 4, 1976–77.

Most League Points (3 for a win): 86, Division 3, 1990–91.

Most League Goals: 87, Division 4, 1976–77.

Highest League Scorer in Season: David Crown, 24,
Division 4, 1985–86.

Most League Goals in Total Aggregate: John Taylor, 86,
1988–92; 1996–2001.

Most League Goals in One Match: 5, Steve Butler v Exeter C, Division 2, 4 April 1994.

Most Capped Player: Tom Finney, 7 (15), Northern Ireland.

Most League Appearances: Steve Spriggs, 416, 1975–87.

Youngest League Player: Andy Sinton, 16 years 228 days v Wolverhampton W, 2 November 1982.

Record Transfer Fee Received: £1,000,000 from Manchester U for Dion Dublin, August 1992.

Record Transfer Fee Paid: £190,000 to Luton T for Steve Claridge, November 1992.

Football League Record: 1970 Elected to Division 4; 1973–74 Division 3; 1974–77 Division 4;
1977–78 Division 3; 1978–84 Division 2; 1984–85 Division 3; 1985–90 Division 4; 1990–91 Division 3;
1991–92 Division 2; 1992–93 Division 1; 1993–95 Division 2; 1995–99 Division 3; 1999–2002 Division 2;
2002– Division 3.

MANAGERS

Bill Whittaker 1949–55
Gerald Williams 1955
Bert Johnson 1955–59
Bill Craig 1959–60
Alan Moore 1960–63
Roy Kirk 1964–66
Bill Leivers 1967–74
Ron Atkinson 1974–78
John Docherty 1978–83
John Ryan 1984–85
Ken Shellito 1985
Chris Turner 1985–90
John Beck 1990–92
Ian Atkins 1992–93
Gary Johnson 1993–95
Tommy Taylor 1995–96
Roy McFarland 1996–2001
John Beck 2001
John Taylor January 2002–

LATEST SEQUENCES

Longest Sequence of League Wins: 7, 19.2.77 – 1.4.77.

Longest Sequence of League Defeats: 7, 8.4.85 – 30.4.85.

Longest Sequence of League Draws: 6, 6.9.86 – 30.9.86.

Longest Sequence of Unbeaten League Matches: 14, 9.9.72 – 10.11.72.

Longest Sequence Without a League Win: 31, 8.10.83 – 23.4.84.

TEN YEAR LEAGUE RECORD

		P	W	D	L	F	A	Pts	Pos
1991-92	Div 2	46	19	17	10	65	47	74	5
1992-93	Div 1	46	11	16	19	48	69	49	23
1993-94	Div 2	46	19	9	18	79	73	66	10
1994-95	Div 2	46	11	15	20	52	69	48	20
1995-96	Div 3	46	14	12	20	61	71	54	16
1996-97	Div 3	46	18	11	17	53	59	65	10
1997-98	Div 3	46	14	18	14	63	57	60	16
1998-99	Div 3	46	23	12	11	78	48	81	2
1999-2000	Div 2	46	12	12	22	64	65	48	19
2000-01	Div 2	46	14	11	21	61	77	53	19

DID YOU KNOW ?

While still known as Abbey
United, Cambridge United
enjoyed a highly successful
1928–29 season, winning
Section A of the Cambridge
League Division One, the
Cambridge Challenge Cup
and four other district cup
competitions.

CAMBRIDGE UNITED 2001–02 LEAGUE RECORD

Match No.	Date	Venue	Opponents	Result		H/T Score	Lg. Pos.	Goalscorers	Attendance
1	Aug 11	H	Brighton & HA	D	0-0	0-0	—		4509
2	18	A	Notts Co	L	1-2	0-1	18	Kitson [86]	5744
3	25	H	Stoke C	L	0-2	0-0	21		3336
4	27	A	Brentford	L	1-2	0-1	23	Wanless [80]	4674
5	Sept 1	H	Bournemouth	D	2-2	1-1	22	Revell [4], Kitson [70]	2754
6	8	A	Peterborough U	L	0-1	0-0	24		8656
7	15	H	Cardiff C	W	2-1	1-0	21	Kitson [15], Wanless [71]	3454
8	18	A	Reading	L	0-1	0-0	—		8348
9	22	A	Blackpool	D	1-1	0-1	20	Kitson [83]	5096
10	25	H	Wigan Ath	D	2-2	1-1	—	Prokas [31], Youngs [52]	2969
11	29	H	QPR	W	2-1	1-0	18	Kitson [3], Youngs [56]	4508
12	Oct 5	A	Port Vale	L	0-5	0-1	—		4119
13	13	H	Bury	W	3-1	1-1	20	One [17], Youngs [50], Revell [71]	3252
14	20	A	Colchester U	L	1-3	1-2	20	One [14]	4684
15	24	A	Swindon T	L	0-2	0-0	—		4882
16	27	H	Northampton T	D	3-3	3-1	20	Kitson [18], One 2 [29, 42]	3682
17	Nov 3	A	Chesterfield	L	0-2	0-0	21		3729
18	10	H	Oldham Ath	D	1-1	0-1	22	Kitson [58]	3378
19	20	H	Wrexham	L	0-2	0-0	—		2648
20	24	A	Tranmere R	L	1-6	0-2	23	Youngs (pen) [83]	8004
21	Dec 1	A	Huddersfield T	L	1-2	1-0	23	Tudor [32]	9513
22	15	H	Bristol C	L	0-3	0-2	24		3561
23	22	A	Wycombe W	L	0-2	0-2	24		6560
24	26	H	Brentford	W	2-1	0-1	23	Wanless [76], Chillingworth [85]	3989
25	29	H	Peterborough U	D	0-0	0-0	23		5665
26	Jan 12	H	Notts Co	L	0-2	0-0	23		3747
27	19	A	Brighton & HA	L	3-4	1-1	24	Tudor [27], Guttridge [54], Wanless (pen) [81]	6575
28	22	H	Wycombe W	W	2-0	1-0	—	Chillingworth [8], Wanless [46]	2623
29	Feb 2	A	QPR	D	0-0	0-0	24		18,071
30	6	A	Stoke C	L	0-5	0-2	—		9570
31	9	H	Colchester U	L	1-2	1-0	24	Youngs [1]	3954
32	13	H	Port Vale	L	0-1	0-1	—		2379
33	16	A	Bury	D	2-2	1-1	24	Wanless [44], Youngs [66]	3547
34	23	A	Cardiff C	L	0-2	0-1	24		10,182
35	26	H	Blackpool	L	0-3	0-1	—		2986
36	Mar 2	H	Reading	D	2-2	2-0	24	Kitson [14], Youngs [32]	3841
37	5	A	Wigan Ath	L	1-4	0-1	—	Ashbee (pen) [65]	3535
38	9	A	Bristol C	L	0-2	0-2	24		9817
39	16	H	Huddersfield T	L	0-1	0-0	24		3728
40	19	A	Bournemouth	D	2-2	1-1	—	Cowan [18], Jackman [58]	7082
41	30	A	Oldham Ath	D	2-2	1-1	24	Ashbee [37], Guttridge (pen) [57]	4957
42	Apr 2	H	Chesterfield	W	4-1	3-0	—	Kitson [5], Tudor [30], Youngs [35], Scully [64]	2669
43	6	A	Wrexham	L	0-5	0-1	24		2581
44	9	A	Swindon T	L	1-2	1-1	—	Scully [32]	2406
45	13	H	Tranmere R	W	2-1	0-1	24	Bridges [50], Youngs [71]	4627
46	20	A	Northampton T	D	2-2	1-1	24	Youngs 2 [4, 71]	6723

Final League Position: 24

GOALSCORERS

League (47): Youngs 11 (1 pen), Kitson 9, Wanless 6 (1 pen), One 4, Tudor 3, Ashbee 2 (1 pen), Chillingworth 2, Guttridge 2 (1 pen), Revell 2, Scully 2, Bridges 1, Cowan 1, Jackman 1, Prokas 1.
Worthington Cup (1): Alcide 1.
FA Cup (1): Tudor 1.

Perez L 42	Cowan T 3+2	Warner P 11+1	Walling D 20	Angus S 41	Ashbee I 38	Wanless P 28+1	Fleming T 28+6	Kitson D 30+3	Alcide C 7+1	Traore D 2+5	Richardson M 4+2	Duncan A 20+4	Byrne D 3+1	Youngs T 36+6	Kelly L 1+1	Revell A 7+17	Guttridge L 27+2	Kandol T 2+2	Clements M —+1	One A 18+14	Prokas R 8+1	McAnespie S —+1	Goodhind W 11+3	Chillingworth D 10+2	Tudor S 31+1	Scully T 19+6	Marshall S 4+3	Tann A 24+1	Taylor S —+3	Murray F 21	Mustoe N —+5	Austin K 4+2	Jackman D 5+2	Bridges D 1+6	Match No.
1	2^1	3	4	5	6	7	8	9	10	11	12																								1
1		3^2	4	5^1	6	7	2	9	10	11		8^3	13	12	14																				2
1	12		4	5	6	7	2	9	10^1	13		8^2	14	3		11^3																			3
1			4	5	6	7	2	9			12	8^2	11	3	13	10^1																			4
1			4	5	6	7	2	9			12			3		11	8^2	13		10^1															5
1	12		4	5	6	7	2	9^2						11		8^1	3			10^3	13	14													6
1			4	5	6	7^2	2	9			8		11			12	10^1	3	13																7
1	3^1		4	5	6		2	9			8		11	12		13	10^2	7																	8
1			4	5	6		2	9			8		11	12			10^1	7	3																9
1		3	4	5	6		8	9					11	12			10^1	7	2																10
1		3	4	5	6	7		9					11	12^2	13		10^1	8	2																11
1		3	4	5^2	6	7	12	9		13			11				10^3	8	2^1	14															12
1	3^2	4		6	7	2	9^1			5			11	12			10^1	8	13	14															13
1		3	4	5	6	7	2	9					11				10	8	3																14
1		3	4	5	6	7	2	12	9^1				11	13			10^2			8															15
1		3	4	5		7	2	9	8^1				11				10	12		6															16
1		3	4	5	6	7^1	12	13	9				11^2		2		10			8^3	14														17
1		4	5^1	6	7	2	9	8			12	11					10^2			3	13														18
1		4	5	6		2	9^1	12	7				11				10			8	3														19
1	3^6	4^2	5	6		9	7						11	12	2					8	10^1	15	13												20
1	3		5	6	7	12		9^2	4			11^1	13		2^3						8	10														21
			6	7				9^1	4							12	3^2			10					8	11	1	2	13	5					22
1			6	7					4							12	10^1	3		9			8		11		2		5						23
1			6	7					4							12	9^2	3		13			10^1		8	11^3		2	14	5					24
1			5		7				4							9^1	3		12				10		8	11		2	13	6					25
1			5	6					4							12	9^2	3		13				10	8	11^1		2	7						26
1			5	6	7				4							9^1	3		14				12	13	10^3	8	11^2	2							27
1			5^2	6	7				4		12					9	3								10^3	8	11^6	15	2	13					28
1			5	6			2	9^1				13				7^1				10					8	11^3		4	3	12	14				29
			5	6^1	12		2	9^2				13				11				10^3			8	14				4	3	7					30
			5		2											11^3	9^1	6		13			12	10^2	8	14		4	3	7					31
1			2		7	12						5^1		11			6^1		10					9^2	8	13		4	3	14					32
1			2		7	6			13					9					12						8	11^1		4	3		5	10^2			33
1			2		7	6	12		5					11			13								8	4^1		4	3		9				34
1			5	2	7^1	12								11			13	6							8	11		4	3		9				35
1			5	6		2	9							10			12	7		13					8^1	11^2		4	3						36
1			5	6				9^1						10			7			12					8^2	11	2	4	3		13				37
1			5	6	7									4		11	9^1	8		10^2						12	2		3		13				38
1				6	7									4		10	12	11							2	8^2	13	5	3^3		9^1	14			39
1	3^2		5		6			9^1						11^3		12	7								2	8		4	13	10	14				40
1			5	6		2	9					4^1				7		13							8^3	11	4	3	12		14				41
1			5	6^2		2	9^3							10^1		12	7								8	11	4	3	13		14				42
1			5	6		2^2	9							10		12	7								8	11^1	4	3	13						43
1			5	6		2^1	9							10			7		13				12		8^1	11	4	3							44
1^0			5^2	6			9							10		7	12		14				2^1		8^1	11	15	4	3			13			45
	12		5^2		9			10	13					7		14	2^1						8		11^3	1	4	3	6						46

Worthington Cup
First Round   WBA   (h)   1-1

FA Cup
First Round   Notts Co   (h)   1-1
                                        (a)   0-2

CARDIFF CITY   Division 2

FOUNDATION

Credit for the establishment of a first class professional football club in such a rugby stronghold as Cardiff, is due to members of the Riverside club formed in 1899 out of a cricket club of that name. Cardiff became a city in 1905 and in 1908 the South Wales and Monmouthshire FA granted Riverside permission to call themselves Cardiff City.

Ninian Park, Cardiff CF11 8SX.

Telephone: (029) 2022 1001. *Fax:* (029) 2034 1148.
Ticket Office: 0845 345 1400.
ClubCall: 09068 121 171. *Website:* www.cardiffcityfc.co.uk
Email: reception@cardiffcityfc.co.uk

Ground Capacity: 20,000.

Record Attendance: 62,634, Wales v England, 17 October 1959.

Club Record Attendance: 57,893 v Arsenal, Division 1, 22 April 1953.

Record Receipts: £141,756 v Manchester C, FA Cup 4th rd, 29 January 1994.

Pitch Measurements: 120yd × 72yd.

Owner: Sam Hammam. *Vice-chairman:* Steve Borley.
Chief Executive: David Temme.

Directors: Sam Hammam, Steve Borley, Paul Guy, Kim Walker, Samesh Kumar, Michael Isaac, Jonathan Crystal QC. *Advisor:* Tony Clemo.

Manager: Lennie Lawrence.
Assistant Manager: Ian Butterworth.
Physios: Clive Goodyear, Jimmy Goodfellow.

Club Secretary: Jason Turner.
Commercial Manager: Neil Hughes. *Sales Manager:* Kathryn Scruby.

Colours: Blue shirts, blue shorts, blue stockings.

Change Colours: Yellow shirts, yellow shorts, yellow stockings.

Year Formed: 1899. *Turned Professional:* 1910. *Ltd Co.:* 1910.

Previous Names: 1899, Riverside; 1902, Riverside Albion; 1908, Cardiff City.

Club Nickname: 'Bluebirds'.

Previous Grounds: Riverside, Sophia Gardens, Old Park and Fir Gardens. Moved to Ninian Park, 1910.

First Football League Game: 28 August 1920, Division 2, v Stockport Co (a) W 5–2 – Kneeshaw; Brittan, Leyton; Keenor (1), Smith, Hardy; Grimshaw (1), Gill (2), Cashmore, West, Evans (1).

Record League Victory: 9–2 v Thames, Division 3 (S), 6 February 1932 – Farquharson; E. L. Morris, Roberts; Galbraith, Harris, Ronan; Emmerson (1), Keating (1), Jones (1), McCambridge (1), Robbins (5).

HONOURS

Football League: Division 1 – Runners-up 1923–24; Division 2 – Runners-up 1920–21, 1951–52, 1959–60; Division 3 (S) – Champions 1946–47; Division 3 – Champions 1992–93. Runners-up 1975–76, 1982–83, 2000–01; Division 4 – Runners-up 1987–88.

FA Cup: Winners 1927 (only occasion the Cup has been won by a club outside England); Runners-up 1925.

Football League Cup: Semi-final 1966.

Welsh Cup: Winners 21 times.

Charity Shield: Winners 1927.

European Competitions: *European Cup-Winners' Cup:* 1964–65, 1965–66, 1967–68 (semi-finalists), 1968–69, 1969–70, 1970–71, 1971–72, 1973–74, 1974–75, 1976–77, 1977–78, 1988–89, 1991–92, 1992–93, 1993–94.

IT'S A FACT !

An administrative error prevented Leslie Lea making his debut for Cardiff City at Plymouth Argyle on 16 December 1967, after transfer from Blackpool. For the only time in the club's history, they were unable to have a substitute on the bench.

Record Cup Victory: 8–0 v Enfield, FA Cup 1st rd, 28
November 1931 – Farquharson; Smith, Roberts; Harris (1),
Galbraith, Ronan; Emmerson (2), Keating (3); O'Neill (2),
Robbins, McCambridge.

Record Defeat: 2–11 v Sheffield U, Division 1, 1 January 1926.

Most League Points (2 for a win): 66, Division 3 (S), 1946–47.

Most League Points (3 for a win): 86, Division 3, 1982–83.

Most League Goals: 95, Division 3, 2000–01.

Highest League Scorer in Season: Stan Richards, 30,
Division 3 (S), 1946–47.

Most League Goals in Total Aggregate: Len Davies, 128,
1920–31.

Most League Goals in One Match: 5, Hugh Ferguson v
Burnley, Division 1, 1 September 1928; 5, Walter Robbins v
Thames, Division 3S, 6 February 1932; 5, William
Henderson v Northampton T, Division 3S, 22 April 1933.

Most Capped Player: Alf Sherwood, 39 (41), Wales.

Most League Appearances: Phil Dwyer, 471, 1972–85.

Youngest League Player: John Toshack, 16 years 236 days v
Leyton Orient, 13 November 1965.

Record Transfer Fee Received: £500,000 from Coventry C
for Simon Haworth, June 1997.

Record Transfer Fee Paid: £1,700,000 to Stoke C for Peter
Thorne, September 2001.

Football League Record: 1920 Elected to Division 2;
1921–29 Division 1; 1929–31 Division 2; 1931–47
Division 3 (S); 1947–52 Division 2; 1952–57 Division 1;
1957–60 Division 2; 1960–62 Division 1; 1962–75 Division 2;
1975–76 Division 3; 1976–82 Division 2; 1982–83 Division 3;
1983–85 Division 2; 1985–86 Division 3; 1986–88 Division 4;
1988–90 Division 3; 1990–92 Division 4; 1992–93 Division 3;
1993–95 Division 3; 1995–99 Division 3; 1999–2000
Division 2; 2000–01 Division 3; 2001– Division 2.

MANAGERS

Davy McDougall 1910–11
Fred Stewart 1911–33
Bartley Wilson 1933–34
B. Watts-Jones 1934–37
Bill Jennings 1937–39
Cyril Spiers 1939–46
Billy McCandless 1946–48
Cyril Spiers 1948–54
Trevor Morris 1954–58
Bill Jones 1958–62
George Swindin 1962–64
Jimmy Scoular 1964–73
Frank O'Farrell 1973–74
Jimmy Andrews 1974–78
Richie Morgan 1978–82
Len Ashurst 1982–84
Jimmy Goodfellow 1984
Alan Durban 1984–86
Frank Burrows 1986–89
Len Ashurst 1989–91
Eddie May 1991–94
Terry Yorath 1994–95
Eddie May 1995
Kenny Hibbitt *(Chief Coach)*
1995
Phil Neal 1996
Russell Osman 1996–97
Kenny Hibbitt 1996–98
Frank Burrows 1998–99
Billy Ayre 1999–2000
Bobby Gould 2000
Alan Cork 2000–02
Lennie Lawrence February 2002–

LATEST SEQUENCES

Longest Sequence of League Wins: 9, 26.10.46 – 28.12.46.

Longest Sequence of League Defeats: 7, 4.11.33 – 25.12.33.

Longest Sequence of League Draws: 6, 29.11.80 – 17.1.81.

Longest Sequence of Unbeaten League Matches: 21, 21.9.46 – 1.3.47.

Longest Sequence Without a League Win: 15, 21.11.36 – 6.3.37.

TEN YEAR LEAGUE RECORD

		P	W	D	L	F	A	Pts	Pos
1991-92	Div 4	42	17	15	10	66	53	66	9
1992-93	Div 3	42	25	8	9	77	47	83	1
1993-94	Div 2	46	13	15	18	66	79	54	19
1994-95	Div 2	46	9	11	26	46	74	38	22
1995-96	Div 3	46	11	12	23	41	64	45	22
1996-97	Div 3	46	20	9	17	56	54	69	7
1997-98	Div 3	46	9	23	14	48	52	50	21
1998-99	Div 3	46	22	14	10	60	39	80	3
1999-2000	Div 2	46	9	17	20	45	67	44	21
2000-01	Div 3	46	23	13	10	95	58	82	2

DID YOU KNOW

On 26 August 1986 in the
League Cup, Cardiff City
were losing 4-1 at home to
Plymouth Argyle at half-
time, but eventually
recovered to win 5-4.

CARDIFF CITY 2001–02 LEAGUE RECORD

Match No.	Date	Venue	Opponents	Result	H/T Score	Lg. Pos.	Goalscorers	Attendance
1	Aug 11	H	Wycombe W	W 1-0	1-0	—	Gabbidon [17]	17,403
2	18	A	Peterborough U	D 1-1	1-1	7	Kavanagh [18]	6437
3	25	H	Bournemouth	D 2-2	1-0	11	Fortune-West [39], Earnshaw [49]	13,383
4	Sept 8	A	Reading	W 2-1	2-1	9	Fortune-West 2 [13,36]	13,017
5	15	A	Cambridge U	L 1-2	0-1	13	Legg [90]	3454
6	18	H	Northampton T	W 2-0	1-0	—	Kavanagh [28], Brayson (pen) [72]	11,232
7	22	H	Huddersfield T	L 1-2	1-1	15	Thorne [8]	12,280
8	25	A	QPR	L 1-2	1-0	—	Kavanagh (pen) [38]	11,667
9	29	H	Brighton & HA	D 1-1	0-1	17	Brayson [79]	12,022
10	Oct 9	A	Bristol C	D 1-1	1-0	—	Earnshaw (pen) [45]	13,804
11	12	H	Wigan Ath	D 2-2	0-1	—	Thorne [53], Brayson [84]	11,072
12	21	A	Swindon T	W 3-0	1-0	15	Earnshaw [36], Bowen [46], Kavanagh [81]	8373
13	24	A	Port Vale	W 2-0	2-0	—	Prior [19], Earnshaw [34]	4552
14	27	H	Tranmere R	D 1-1	1-0	15	Bowen [39]	13,070
15	Nov 4	A	Wrexham	W 3-1	2-1	11	Gordon G [33], Kavanagh [45], Fortune-West [55]	5832
16	7	A	Bury	L 0-3	0-1	—		2549
17	10	H	Chesterfield	W 2-1	2-1	8	Earnshaw (pen) [4], Fortune-West [24]	9516
18	20	H	Colchester U	D 1-1	1-0	—	Collins [33]	8013
19	24	A	Notts Co	D 0-0	0-0	10		6313
20	Dec 1	H	Oldham Ath	W 3-1	1-0	9	Earnshaw [37], Kavanagh 2 [74,90]	10,004
21	4	H	Brentford	W 3-1	2-0	—	Thorne [15], Earnshaw [36], Gabbidon [75]	10,184
22	15	A	Blackpool	D 1-1	0-0	6	Gordon D [68]	4880
23	19	A	Stoke C	D 1-1	0-0	—	Gordon D [83]	14,331
24	26	H	Reading	D 2-2	1-0	6	Earnshaw 2 [29,67]	16,708
25	29	H	Bristol C	L 1-3	0-0	10	Kavanagh [47]	16,149
26	Jan 12	A	Peterborough U	L 0-2	0-1	12		11,301
27	19	A	Wycombe W	W 1-0	0-0	10	Kavanagh [67]	7165
28	22	H	Stoke C	W 2-0	1-0	—	Gudjonsson (og) [19], Legg [71]	11,771
29	31	A	Brighton & HA	L 0-1	0-1	—		6117
30	Feb 5	A	Bournemouth	W 3-1	2-0	—	Kavanagh [15], Earnshaw [21], Boland [52]	4336
31	9	H	Swindon T	W 3-0	1-0	8	Earnshaw [19], Bowen 2 [71,81]	12,045
32	12	A	Brentford	L 1-2	1-0	—	Bowen [18]	6718
33	16	A	Wigan Ath	L 0-4	0-2	11		5487
34	19	H	Bury	W 1-0	1-0	—	Kavanagh (pen) [43]	8273
35	23	H	Cambridge U	W 2-0	1-0	7	Kavanagh 2 (1 pen) [36, 62 (p)]	10,182
36	Mar 2	A	Northampton T	W 2-1	2-1	8	Maxwell [32], Campbell [37]	5495
37	5	H	QPR	D 1-1	0-1	—	Young [59]	13,425
38	9	H	Blackpool	D 2-2	1-2	8	Campbell 2 [30,66]	11,629
39	16	A	Oldham Ath	W 7-1	5-0	7	Young [6], Fortune-West 2 [22,45], Thorne [23], Campbell 3 [30,64,73]	6786
40	22	H	Wrexham	W 3-2	2-1	—	Young [14], Thorne [17], Gabbidon [47]	15,702
41	30	A	Chesterfield	W 2-0	2-0	6	Fortune-West [6], Campbell [30]	5442
42	Apr 1	H	Port Vale	W 1-0	0-0	6	Thorne [74]	15,556
43	6	A	Colchester U	W 1-0	1-0	5	Prior [20]	3970
44	9	A	Huddersfield T	D 2-2	1-0	—	Thorne 2 [39, 62]	11,660
45	13	A	Notts Co	W 2-1	0-1	4	Fortune-West [52], Young [78]	17,105
46	20	A	Tranmere R	W 1-0	0-0	4	Croft [72]	8375

Final League Position: 4

GOALSCORERS

League (75): Kavanagh 13 (3 pens), Earnshaw 11 (2 pens), Fortune-West 9, Thorne 8, Campbell 7, Bowen 5, Young 4, Brayson 3 (1 pen), Gabbidon 3, Gordon D 2, Legg 2, Prior 2, Boland 1, Collins 1, Croft 1, Gordon G 1, Maxwell 1, own goal 1.
Worthington Cup (1): Earnshaw 1.
FA Cup (9): Earnshaw 2, Kavanagh 2 (1 pen), Brayson 1, Fortune-West 1, Gordon G 1, Hamilton 1, Young 1.

Alexander N 46	Simpkins M 13+4	Low J 11+11	Weston R 35+2	Young S 30+3	Gabbidon D 44	Hamilton D 14+5	Kavanagh G 43	Gordon G 12+3	Legg A 27+8	Earnshaw R 28+2	Brayson P 16+19	Hughes D 1+1	Fortune-West L 18+18	Boland W 40+4	Prior S 33+4	Bonner M 25+4	Maxwell L 5+12	Jeanne L —+2	Thorne P 23+3	Bowen J 21+4	Collins J 2+5	Nugent K 1	Gordon D 7	Campbell A 8	Jones G —+1	Croft G 3+3	Match No.
1	2	3^1	4	5^2	6	7	8	9^3	10	11	12	13	14														1
1	2	3^1	4		6	7^2	8	9^2	10	11	12	5	13	14													2
1	2^1	12	4		6	7^2	8		10	3	13		9	11	5												3
1	2	12	4		3	7^2	8		10^2	13	11^1		9	5	6	14											4
1	2		4		6	7^2	8	12		3			9^3	5	11	10^1	13	14									5
1	2		4		6	7^1	8			3	9		12	13	5	11^2	10										6
1	2		4		6		8			3	11^1		9	7	5		10	12									7
1	2	12	4		6	7^2	8			3^2	13		9	11	5		10										8
1	2^1	3^1	4		6	7	8^3			12	9		11	5		13	10	14									9
1	2	4^1		6	12	8		9		3			11	5	13		10	7^2									10
1	2^2		4	12	6		8			9	13		3	11	5^1		10	7									11
1	2^1	13	4		6		8	14	11	12	9^2			7	5		10^3	3									12
1	12	2	13		6		8	10^3	11^1	3^2	9		14	4	5		7										13
1	12	2			6	13	8	10^1	11	3	9^1			4	5		7^2										14
1		2^1	12		6	13	8	10^1	11	3	9		14	4	5		7^2										15
1	12	2			6	7	8		11^2	3	9		10^3	4^1	5			13			14						16
1	12		2		6	7^2	8^3		11	3	9^1		10	4	5	13	14										17
1			4	2	7		8^1		11	3			10^2	6	5	12	13			9							18
1		6	2					11	12				13	4	5	8^4	14		7^1	10	9^2	3					19
1		6	2				8	11					12	7	5	4	13		10^1	9^2		3					20
1		6	2				8	9^2					12	11	5	4	13		10^1	7		3					21
1		6	2				8	9^1	10		12		13	11	5	4			7^1			3					22
1	12	6^1	2				8	9	10		13		14	11	5	4^3			7^2			3					23
1		6	2				8^2	9^3	10	13	12		14	11	5	4			7^1			3					24
1		6	2				8	9	10	12	13		14	11	5	4^3			7^2			3^1					25
1	12	13	6	2			8	9^4	10	3	7		14	11^1	5^2	4											26
1	7	6	5	2			8	9	10^3	3	12			11	4^3	14			13								27
1	12	4	5	6	2^1		8	9^1	10^2	3	13		14	11					7								28
1	12	6	5	2	13		8		3				10	11	4^1	9^2			7								29
1	12	6^1	5	2	7		8	13	9^3	3	14			11	4				10^2								30
1		6	5	2	7^1	8	13	9^2	3					11	12	4			14	10							31
1	3^1	2^4	5	6		8				12			10^3	11		7	13		14	9							32
1		2^1	4	5	6^2		8			3	12			11	13	7			10^3	9	14						33
1		2	4	5	6		8			3	12			13^1	11	7			10^2	9^1							34
1		2	4	5	6		8			3				11		7^1	12		10	9							35
1	12	2	4	5	6^1					3	9^2		14^1	11	13		7		10					8^3			36
1		2	4^1	5	6					3	8^2		13	11	12		7		10					9			37
1		2^1		5	6	14	8			3	12		13^1	11^2	4		7		10^1					9			38
1	12		4	5	2^1		8^2			3			9	11	6		10		13					7^3	14		39
1	12	2^3	5	6		8				3	13		9	11	4		10^2	14						7^1			40
1		2	5^1	6		8				3^2	12		9	11	4	13		10						7^1	14		41
1		2	5^3	3		8		12		13			9	11	6	4^3		10^2						7^1	14		42
1		2	6			8		12					9	11	5	4		10						7^1		3	43
1		2	5	3^2		8				7^1			9	11	6	4	12	10								13	44
1		2	5			8				7^1	12		9	11	6	4		10								3	45
1		2	5^3			8				7^2			9	11	6	4^1	12	10	13	14						3	46

Worthington Cup
First Round   Millwall   (a)   1-2

FA Cup
First Round (at Cardiff)   Tiverton T   (a)   3-1
Second Round   Port Vale   (h)   3-0
Third Round   Leeds U   (h)   2-1
Fourth Round   Tranmere R   (a)   1-3

CARLISLE UNITED
Division 3

FOUNDATION

Carlisle United came into being in 1903 through the amalgamation of Shaddongate United and Carlisle Red Rose. The new club was admitted to the Second Division of the Lancashire Combination in 1905–06, winning promotion the following season. Devonshire Park was officially opened on 2 September 1905, when St Helens Town were the visitors. Despite defeat in a disappointing 3-2 start, a respectable mid-table position was achieved.

Brunton Park, Carlisle CA1 1LL.

Telephone: (01228) 526 237. *Fax:* (01228) 530 138.
Website: www.carlisleunited.co.uk

Ground Capacity: 16,651.

Record Attendance: 27,500 v Birmingham C, FA Cup 3rd rd, 5 January 1957 and v Middlesbrough, FA Cup 5th rd, 7 February 1970.

Record Receipts: £146,000 v Tottenham H, Coca-Cola Cup 2nd rd, 30 September 1997.

Pitch Measurements: 117yd × 72yd.

Directors: Mark Knighton, Andrea Whittaker.

Manager: To be appointed.

Physio: Neil Dalton.

Secretary: Sarah McKnight.

Colours: Blue shirts, blue shorts, blue stockings.

Change Colours: All white with green and red trim.

Year Formed: 1903.

Ltd Co.: 1921.

Previous Name: 1903, Shaddongate United; 1904, Carlisle United.

Club Nicknames: 'Cumbrians' or 'The Blues'.

Previous Grounds: 1903, Milholme Bank; 1905, Devonshire Park; 1909, Brunton Park.

First Football League Game: 25 August 1928, Division 3 (N), v Accrington S (a) W 3–2 – Prout; Coulthard, Cook; Harrison, Ross, Pigg; Agar (1), Hutchison, McConnell (1), Ward (1), Watson.

Record League Victory: 8–0 v Hartlepool U, Division 3 (N), 1 September 1928 – Prout; Smiles, Cook; Robinson (1) Ross, Pigg; Agar (1), Hutchison (1), McConnell (4), Ward (1), Watson. 8–0 v Scunthorpe U, Division 3 (N), 25 December 1952 – MacLaren; Hill, Scott; Stokoe, Twentyman, Waters; Harrison (1), Whitehouse (5), Ashman (2), Duffett, Bond.

HONOURS

Football League: Division 1 best season: 22nd, 1974–75; Promoted from Division 2 (3rd) 1973–74; Division 3 – Champions 1964–65, 1994–95; Runners-up 1981–82; Promoted from Division 3 1996–97; Division 4 – Runners-up 1963–64.

FA Cup: best season: 6th rd 1975.

Football League Cup: Semi-final 1970.

Auto Windscreens Shield: Winners 1997; Runners-up 1995.

IT'S A FACT !

Victories over Chelsea, Middlesbrough and Tottenham Hotspur put Carlisle United at the top of the First Division at the start of the 1974–75 season.

Record Cup Victory: 6–0 v Shepshed Dynamo, FA Cup 1st rd, 16 November 1996 – Caig; Hopper, Archdeacon (pen), Walling, Robinson, Pounewatchy, Peacock (1), Conway (1) (Jansen), Smart (McAlindon (1)), Hayward, Aspinall (Thorpe), (2 og).

Record Defeat: 1–11 v Hull C, Division 3 (N), 14 January 1939.

Most League Points (2 for a win): 62, Division 3 (N), 1950–51.

Most League Points (3 for a win): 91, Division 3, 1994–95.

Most League Goals: 113, Division 4, 1963–64.

Highest League Scorer in Season: Jimmy McConnell, 42, Division 3 (N), 1928–29.

Most League Goals in Total Aggregate: Jimmy McConnell, 126, 1928–32.

Most League Goals in One Match: 5, Hugh Mills v Halifax T, Division 3N, 11 September 1937; 5, Jim Whitehouse v Scunthorpe U, Division 3N, 25 December 1952.

Most Capped Player: Eric Welsh, 4, Northern Ireland.

Most League Appearances: Allan Ross, 466, 1963–79.

Youngest League Player: John Slaven, 16 years 162 days v Scunthorpe U, 16 March 2002.

Record Transfer Fee Received: £1,500,000 from Crystal Palace for Matt Jansen, February 1998.

Record Transfer Fee Paid: £121,000 to Notts Co for David Reeves, December 1993.

Football League Record: 1928 Elected to Division 3 (N); 1958–62 Division 4; 1962–63 Division 3; 1963–64 Division 4; 1964–65 Division 3; 1965–74 Division 2; 1974–75 Division 1; 1975–77 Division 2; 1977–82 Division 3; 1982–86 Division 2; 1986–87 Division 3; 1987–92 Division 4; 1992–95 Division 3; 1995–96 Division 2; 1996–97 Division 3; 1997–98 Division 2; 1998– Division 3.

LATEST SEQUENCES

Longest Sequence of League Wins: 6, 27.8.94 – 17.9.94.

Longest Sequence of League Defeats: 8, 8.11.86 – 3.1.87.

Longest Sequence of League Draws: 6, 11.2.78 – 11.3.78.

Longest Sequence of Unbeaten League Matches: 19, 1.10.94 – 11.2.95.

Longest Sequence Without a League Win: 14, 19.1.35 – 19.4.35.

MANAGERS

Harry Kirkbride 1904–05
    (Secretary-Manager)
McCumiskey 1905–06
    (Secretary-Manager)
Jack Houston 1906–08
    (Secretary-Manager)
Bert Stansfield 1908–10
Jack Houston 1910–12
Davie Graham 1912–13
George Bristow 1913–30
Billy Hampson 1930–33
Bill Clarke 1933–35
Robert Kelly 1935–36
Fred Westgarth 1936–38
David Taylor 1938–40
Howard Harkness 1940–45
Bill Clark 1945–46 *(Secretary-Manager)*
Ivor Broadis 1946–49
Bill Shankly 1949–51
Fred Emery 1951–58
Andy Beattie 1958–60
Ivor Powell 1960–63
Alan Ashman 1963–67
Tim Ward 1967–68
Bob Stokoe 1968–70
Ian MacFarlane 1970–72
Alan Ashman 1972–75
Dick Young 1975–76
Bobby Moncur 1976–80
Martin Harvey 1980
Bob Stokoe 1980–85
Bryan 'Pop' Robson 1985
Bob Stokoe 1985–86
Harry Gregg 1986–87
Cliff Middlemass 1987–91
Aidan McCaffery 1991–92
David McCreery 1992–93
Mick Wadsworth *(Director of Coaching)* 1993–96
Mervyn Day 1996–97
David Wilkes and John Halpin *(Directors of Coaching)*, and Michael Knighton 1997–99
Martin Wilkinson 1999–2000
Ian Atkins 2000–01
Roddy Collins 2001–02

TEN YEAR LEAGUE RECORD

		P	W	D	L	F	A	Pts	Pos
1991-92	Div 4	42	7	13	22	41	67	34	22
1992-93	Div 3	42	11	11	20	51	65	44	18
1993-94	Div 3	42	18	10	14	57	42	64	7
1994-95	Div 3	42	27	10	5	67	31	91	1
1995-96	Div 2	46	12	13	21	57	72	49	21
1996-97	Div 3	46	24	12	10	67	44	84	3
1997-98	Div 2	46	12	8	26	57	73	44	23
1998-99	Div 3	46	11	16	19	43	53	49	23
1999-2000	Div 3	46	9	12	25	42	75	39	23
2000-01	Div 3	46	11	15	20	42	65	48	22

DID YOU KNOW

In 1907–08, Carlisle reached the last 32 in the FA Cup after a marathon run, beating Carlisle City (!), Lancaster Town, Windermere, Workington, Darlington, Southend United and Brentford after a replay.

CARLISLE UNITED 2001–02 LEAGUE RECORD

Match No.	Date	Venue	Opponents	Result	H/T Score	Lg. Pos.	Goalscorers	Attendance
1	Aug 11	H	Luton T	L 0-2	0-0	—		4432
2	18	A	Leyton Orient	D 0-0	0-0	22		4693
3	25	H	Hull C	D 0-0	0-0	19		3695
4	27	A	Torquay U	L 1-2	1-1	22	Stevens [42]	2274
5	Sept 1	H	Rochdale	L 1-2	0-2	23	Allan [80]	3373
6	8	A	Darlington	D 2-2	2-1	23	Halliday [19], Foran (pen) [37]	4677
7	15	A	Cheltenham T	L 0-2	0-1	24		3081
8	18	H	York C	W 2-1	1-0	—	Foran [34], Hews [48]	2705
9	22	H	Lincoln C	D 2-2	1-1	22	Halliday [29], Foran [90]	3105
10	25	A	Southend U	L 2-3	1-1	—	Foran [24], Hopper [83]	2967
11	29	A	Hartlepool U	L 1-3	1-1	23	Hews [4]	3854
12	Oct 6	H	Bristol R	W 1-0	1-0	22	Halliday [11]	1849
13	13	A	Exeter C	L 0-1	0-0	24		3151
14	20	H	Kidderminster H	W 1-0	0-0	22	Foran [49]	2556
15	23	A	Oxford U	D 1-1	0-0	—	Rogers [54]	7405
16	27	H	Halifax T	D 0-0	0-0	22		3157
17	Nov 3	A	Macclesfield T	D 1-1	1-0	21	Foran [43]	2432
18	10	H	Mansfield T	L 0-1	0-1	22		2546
19	20	A	Shrewsbury T	L 0-1	0-0	—		2003
20	24	A	Plymouth Arg	L 0-3	0-2	24		5870
21	Dec 1	H	Scunthorpe U	W 3-0	2-0	23	Soley [13], Stevens [20], Hadland [53]	2702
22	15	A	Swansea C	D 0-0	0-0	23		2906
23	22	A	Rushden & D	L 1-3	1-1	23	Green [26]	4142
24	Jan 12	H	Leyton Orient	W 6-1	5-0	23	Stevens 3 [2, 15, 32], Soley [7], Foran (pen) [18], McGill [82]	2955
25	15	A	Hull C	W 1-0	1-0	—	Foran [9]	8526
26	19	H	Luton T	D 1-1	0-0	22	Soley [52]	6647
27	22	A	Rushden & D	W 3-0	2-0	—	Green [24], Foran [29], Halliday [65]	2864
28	29	A	Rochdale	D 1-1	1-0	—	Halliday [18]	3008
29	Feb 5	H	Darlington	L 1-3	1-1	—	Foran (pen) [45]	5226
30	9	A	Kidderminster H	D 2-2	1-1	20	Halliday 2 [26, 57]	3295
31	16	H	Exeter C	W 1-0	0-0	19	Soley [71]	4929
32	19	H	Torquay U	W 2-0	0-0	—	Winstanley [82], Green [88]	3823
33	Mar 2	A	Lincoln C	L 1-3	0-2	19	McGill [46]	2751
34	5	H	Southend U	D 0-0	0-0	—		3045
35	9	H	Swansea C	W 3-1	3-0	18	Stevens [5], Whitehead [19], Allan [29]	3349
36	12	A	Bristol R	D 0-0	0-0	—		4457
37	16	A	Scunthorpe U	L 1-2	0-2	17	McDonagh [77]	4109
38	19	A	Hartlepool U	L 0-2	0-1	—		3147
39	23	H	Oxford U	W 2-1	1-1	16	Stevens [17], Foran [90]	3349
40	29	A	Halifax T	D 2-2	1-1	—	Stevens [34], Foran [90]	2728
41	Apr 1	H	Macclesfield T	W 3-2	0-2	15	Foran 2 (2 pens) [50, 90], McAughtrie [89]	3625
42	6	A	Shrewsbury T	L 0-1	0-1	15		3969
43	9	A	York C	D 0-0	0-0	—		2809
44	13	H	Plymouth Arg	L 0-2	0-1	17		3080
45	16	H	Cheltenham T	D 0-0	0-0	—		2184
46	20	A	Mansfield T	L 0-2	0-2	17		8638

Final League Position: 17

GOALSCORERS

League (49): Foran 14 (5 pens), Stevens 8, Halliday 7, Soley 4, Green 3, Allan 2, Hews 2, McGill 2, Hadland 1, Hopper 1, McAughtrie 1, McDonagh 1, Rogers 1, Whitehead 1, Winstanley 1.
Worthington Cup (0).
FA Cup (2): Foran 1, Soley 1.

Weaver L 10	Andrews L 37 + 2	Maddison L 5 + 2	Whitehead S 29 + 3	Winstanley M 36	Morley D 14 + 4	Soley S 19 + 2	Hopper T 20 + 9	Allan J 10 + 19	Thurston M 1	Halliday S 28 + 15	Murphy P 39 + 1	Stevens I 23 + 3	Willis S — + 1	Birch M 42	Elliott S 6	McAughtrie C 2 + 3	Harkin M 2 + 2	Berkley A 2 + 3	Haddow A 4	Foran R 37	McGill B 27 + 1	Hews C 4 + 1	Hore J — + 3	Rogers D 26 + 1	Jack M 16 + 16	Keen P 36	Dickinson M — + 1	Skinner S 1 + 5	Friars S — + 1	Hadland P 4	Green S 16	McDonagh W 7 + 5	Slaven J — + 2	Bell S 3 + 2	Thwaites A — + 1	Rooke S — + 1	Match No.
1	2	3	4^1	5	6	7	8	9^2	10^3	11	12	13	14																								1
1	2^1	3	4		6		8	12		11	5	9^2		7	10	13																					2
1			4	5			8			11	3	9^1		2	10	12	7^2	13	6																		3
1	12		4	5	13		8			11	6^2	9^3		2	10	14	7	3^1																		4
1			4	5	12		8	13		11^2	6			2	3^3		7	14	10^1	9																5
1	12		4	5^1			8^3			11	6			2	10		13	14	3^2	9	7															6
1	5	3^1	4		6					11	8			2^2	10^3			7			9	12	13	14												7
1	5		4		6					11	10			2						9	7	8^1		3	12											8
1	5		4^1		6			12		11	10			2						9	7	8^2	13	3												9
1	10		4	5	6			13		11^3				2^1						9	7	8^2	12	3	14											10
	10		4	5	6			12		11^3				2^1						9	7	8^2		3	13	1	14									11
	10		4^1	5	6	12				11^3	8			2						9	7^2			3	13	1		14								12
			4	5	6		8^1			11	10			2^1	12					9^1	7			3	13	1		14								13
			4	5	6		8	13		11^3	10^1			2						9	7^2			3	12	1		14								14
13			4	5	6^1		8	14		12	10			2						9	7			3^2		1		11^3								15
3			4	5	6^2	8	2	12		11^1	10			2						9	7					1		13								16
			4	5	12	8^1	6			11^3	10^2			2						9	7			3	13	1		14								17
12			4	5^1	6		8^1	9^2		11	10			2							7			3	13	1			14							18
5				6	12		8^1			10^2	4			2						9	7			3	13	1				11						19
3			4	5	12	8		10^3	13		9	6^2		2^1							7			14	1				11							20
5					8							6	10	2						9	7			3	4	1			11							21
2		5					12					6	10	2						9	7			3	8	1			11^1	4						22
2	4	5			7		8			12	3	10^1		2						9					11	1			6							23
4	12	5			8			11^3		3	10			2						9	7^1				1				6	13						24
4	12	5			8			11^1		13	3	10		2						9	7^2				1				6							25
6	4	5			8	13				12	11	10^1		2^2						9				3		1			7							26
6	4	5			7			13		12	3	10^1		2						9				11^2	1			8							27
6	4	5			7		12			11	3			2						9				10^1	1			8							28
6	4	5			13	10				12	3	8^1		2						9				11^2	1			7							29
6	4	5			8	12				10	3^2			2						9				13	11^1	1			7							30
6	4	5			8	12				10	3			2						9	7^1			13	1			11^2								31
6	4^1	5			8^2	13				10	3			2						9	7			12^2	1			11	14							32
6		5			8	4^2	13			10^1	3	12		2^3						9	7			14	1			11								33
6	4					8^2				10^1	5	9		2							7			3	12	1			11	13						34
6	4^3	5			8^1		13			10^3	3	9		2							7^2			12	1			11	14							35
8		5					13			12	6	10^1		2						9				3^2	7	1			11	4						36
8		5					13			10^1	6	12		2						9^3				3	7	1			11^2	4	14					37
4		5			10	13				12	6	8^1		2						9				3	11^2	1			7							38
4	12	5^2			10^3	14				13	6	8^1		2						9				3	11^1	1			7							39
5					10	7^1				12	6	8		2						9				3	11	1			4							40
5					10	13				12		8^1		2	6					9				3	11	1			4^2	14	7^3					41
5					14	13				12	4	8^1		2	6					9	7			3	11^2	1			10^3							42
4		5			10	12				9	6^2	8		2						7^1				3	11	1						13				43
4		5			10^2	6^3				12		8^1		2						9	7			3	11	1					13	14				44
4	3	5			10	14				12		8		2						9^2	7^1			6	13	1							11^3			45
4	3	5			10	7^3				12		8^1		2						9				6		1						11^2	13	14		46

Worthington Cup
First Round Stockport Co (a) 0-3

FA Cup
First Round Barnet (a) 0-0
(h) 1-0
Second Round Tranmere R (a) 1-6

CHARLTON ATHLETIC   FA Premiership

FOUNDATION

The club was formed on 9 June 1905, by a group of 14- and 15-year-old youths living in streets by the Thames in the area which now borders the Thames Barrier. The club's progress through local leagues was so rapid that after the First World War they joined the Kent League where they spent a season before turning professional and joining the Southern League in 1920. A year later they were elected to the Football League's Division 3 (South).

The Valley, Floyd Road, Charlton, London SE7 8BL.

Telephone: (020) 8333 4000. *Fax:* (020) 8333 4001.
Website: www.cafc.co.uk *Email:* info@cafc.co.uk
Box Office: (020) 8333 4010. *ClubCall:* 09068 121 146.

Ground Capacity: 20,043, rising to 26,500 December 2001.

Record Attendance: 75,031 v Aston Villa, FA Cup 5th rd, 12 February 1938 (at The Valley).

Record Receipts: £201,711 v QPR, FA Cup 5th rd, 8 January 2000.

Pitch Measurements: 111yd × 73yd.

Chairman: M. A. Simons.
Deputy Chairman: R. A. Murray.
Group Chief Executive: P. D. Varney.
Directors: R. N. Alwen, G. P. Bone, N. E. Capelin, R. D. Collins, D. J. Hughes, M. C. Stevens, D. C. Sumners, D. G. Ufton, R. C. Whitehand, G. B. C. Franklin, D. White.

HONOURS

Football League: Division 1 – Champions 1999–2000; Runners-up 1936–37; Promoted from Division 1, 1997–98 (play-offs); Division 2 – Runners-up 1935–36, 1985–86; Division 3 (S) – Champions 1928–29, 1934–35; Promoted from Division 3 (3rd) 1974–75, 1980–81.

FA Cup: Winners 1947; Runners-up 1946.

Football League Cup: best season: 4th rd, 1963, 1966, 1979.

Full Members' Cup: Runners-up 1987.

Manager: Alan Curbishley. *Assistant Manager:* Keith Peacock. *First Team Coach:* Mervyn Day. *Academy Director:* Mick Browne. *Physio:* Andy Jones.

Football Secretary: Chris Parkes.

Safety Officer: John Little.

Media and PR: Rick Everitt.

Colours: Red shirts, white shorts, red stockings.

Change Colours: White shirts, red shorts, white stockings.

Year Formed: 1905.

Turned Professional: 1920. *Ltd Co.:* 1919.

Club Nickname: 'Addicks'.

Previous Grounds: 1906, Siemen's Meadow; 1907, Woolwich Common; 1909, Pound Park; 1913, Horn Lane; 1920, The Valley; 1923, Catford (The Mount); 1924, The Valley; 1985, Selhurst Park; 1991, Upton Park; 1992, The Valley.

First Football League Game: 27 August 1921, Division 3 (S), v Exeter C (h) W 1–0 – Hughes; Mitchell, Goodman; Dowling (1), Hampson, Dunn; Castle, Bailey, Halse, Green, Wilson.

IT'S A FACT !

Between 8 December and 25 December 1934, Charlton Athletic enjoyed a remarkable sequence in scoring 21 goals in 16 days, with wins of 6-0, 6-3, 3-1 and 6-0.

Record League Victory: 8–1 v Middlesbrough, Division 1, 12 September 1953 – Bartram; Campbell, Ellis; Fenton, Ufton, Hammond; Hurst (2), O'Linn (2), Leary (1), Firmani (3), Kiernan.

Record Cup Victory: 7–0 v Burton A, FA Cup 3rd rd, 7 January 1956 – Bartram; Campbell, Townsend; Hewie, Ufton, Hammond; Hurst (1), Gauld (1), Leary (3), White, Kiernan (2).

Record Defeat: 1–11 v Aston Villa, Division 2, 14 November 1959.

Most League Points (2 for a win): 61, Division 3 (S), 1934–35.

Most League Points (3 for a win): 91, Division 1, 1999–2000.

Most League Goals: 107, Division 2, 1957–58.

Highest League Scorer in Season: Ralph Allen, 32, Division 3 (S), 1934–35.

Most League Goals in Total Aggregate: Stuart Leary, 153, 1953–62.

MANAGERS
Bill Rayner 1920–25
Alex McFarlane 1925–27
Albert Lindon 1928
Alex McFarlane 1928–32
Jimmy Seed 1933–56
Jimmy Trotter 1956–61
Frank Hill 1961–65
Bob Stokoe 1965–67
Eddie Firmani 1967–70
Theo Foley 1970–74
Andy Nelson 1974–79
Mike Bailey 1979–81
Alan Mullery 1981–82
Ken Craggs 1982
Lennie Lawrence 1982–91
Steve Gritt/Alan Curbishley 1991–95
Alan Curbishley June 1995–

Most League Goals in One Match: 5, Wilson Lennox v Exeter C, Division 3S, 2 February 1929; 5, Eddie Firmani v Aston Villa, Division 1, 5 February 1955; 5, John Summers v Huddersfield T, Division 2, 21 December 1957; 5, John Summers v Portsmouth, Division 2, 1 October 1960.

Most Capped Player: John Robinson, 30, Wales.

Most League Appearances: Sam Bartram, 583, 1934–56.

Youngest League Player: Paul Konchesky, 16 years 93 days v Oxford U, 16 August 1997.

Record Transfer Fee Received: £4,370,000 from Leeds U for Danny Mills, June 1999.

Record Transfer Fee Paid: £4,750,000 to Wimbledon for Jason Euell, July 2001.

Football League Record: 1921 Elected to Division 3 (S); 1929–33 Division 2; 1933–35 Division 3 (S); 1935–36 Division 2; 1936–57 Division 1; 1957–72 Division 2; 1972–75 Division 3; 1975–80 Division 2; 1980–81 Division 3; 1981–86 Division 2; 1986–90 Division 1; 1990–92 Division 2; 1992–98 Division 1; 1998–99 FA Premier League; 1999–2000 Division 1; 2000– FA Premier League.

LATEST SEQUENCES

Longest Sequence of League Wins: 12, 26.12.99 – 7.3.00.

Longest Sequence of League Defeats: 10, 11.4.90 – 15.9.90.

Longest Sequence of League Draws: 6, 13.12.92 – 16.1.93.

Longest Sequence of Unbeaten League Matches: 15, 4.10.80 – 20.12.80.

Longest Sequence Without a League Win: 16, 26.2.55 – 22.8.55.

TEN YEAR LEAGUE RECORD

		P	W	D	L	F	A	Pts	Pos
1991-92	Div 2	46	20	11	15	54	48	71	7
1992-93	Div 1	46	16	13	17	49	46	61	12
1993-94	Div 1	46	19	8	19	61	58	65	11
1994-95	Div 1	46	16	11	19	58	66	59	15
1995-96	Div 1	46	17	20	9	57	45	71	6
1996-97	Div 1	46	16	11	19	52	66	59	15
1997-98	Div 1	46	26	10	10	80	49	88	4
1998-99	PR Lge	38	8	12	18	41	56	36	18
1999-2000	Div 1	46	27	10	9	79	45	91	1
2000-01	PR Lge	38	14	10	14	50	57	52	9

DID YOU KNOW ?

On 4 November 2001, Charlton Athletic won 4-2 at Arsenal, their first success at Highbury since 29 October 1955 when they had been successful by the same scoreline.

CHARLTON ATHLETIC 2001–02 LEAGUE RECORD

Match No.	Date	Venue	Opponents	Result	H/T Score	Lg. Pos.	Goalscorers	Attendance
1	Aug 18	H	Everton	L 1-2	0-0	—	Johansson [58]	20,451
2	25	A	Ipswich T	W 1-0	0-0	13	Lisbie [85]	22,518
3	Sept 9	H	Fulham	D 1-1	1-1	14	Melville (og) [34]	20,451
4	16	H	Leeds U	L 0-2	0-1	16		20,451
5	22	A	Sunderland	D 2-2	1-0	16	Quinn (og) [11], Brown [61]	44,478
6	29	H	Leicester C	W 2-0	1-0	12	Johansson [45], Bartlett [56]	20,451
7	Oct 13	H	Middlesbrough	D 0-0	0-0	12		20,451
8	20	A	Derby Co	D 1-1	0-1	13	Euell [73]	30,221
9	24	A	Aston Villa	L 0-1	0-1	—		27,701
10	27	H	Liverpool	L 0-2	0-2	16		22,658
11	Nov 4	A	Arsenal	W 4-2	2-1	15	Brown [35], Wright (og) [43], Jensen [49], Euell [53]	38,010
12	19	H	West Ham U	D 4-4	2-2	—	Euell 2 [21, 28], Johansson 2 [51, 90]	23,198
13	24	A	Southampton	L 0-1	0-0	16		31,198
14	Dec 1	H	Newcastle U	D 1-1	0-0	15	MacDonald [83]	24,179
15	5	A	Chelsea	W 1-0	0-0	—	Lisbie [89]	33,504
16	8	H	Tottenham H	W 3-1	2-0	10	Stuart [4], Lisbie 2 [19, 78]	25,103
17	15	A	Bolton W	D 0-0	0-0	11		20,834
18	22	H	Blackburn R	L 0-2	0-0	13		25,837
19	26	A	Fulham	D 0-0	0-0	12		17,900
20	29	A	Everton	W 3-0	1-0	9	Stuart [29], Euell [68], Konchesky [80]	31,131
21	Jan 1	H	Ipswich T	W 3-2	2-2	8	Robinson [16], Parker [32], Euell [61]	25,858
22	12	A	Blackburn R	L 1-4	0-2	10	Euell [53]	23,365
23	21	A	Aston Villa	L 1-2	0-2	—	Stuart [88]	25,605
24	29	H	Derby Co	W 1-0	0-0	—	Bart-Williams [79]	25,300
25	Feb 3	A	Middlesbrough	D 0-0	0-0	8		24,041
26	10	H	Manchester U	L 0-2	0-1	10		26,459
27	24	A	Leeds U	D 0-0	0-0	10		39,374
28	Mar 2	H	Chelsea	W 2-1	0-0	9	Euell 2 [72, 89]	26,333
29	9	A	Leicester C	D 1-1	1-1	9	Euell [42]	18,562
30	18	A	Tottenham H	W 1-0	0-0	—	Powell [70]	29,596
31	23	H	Bolton W	L 1-2	0-2	8	Johansson [52]	26,286
32	30	A	Liverpool	L 0-2	0-2	9		44,094
33	Apr 1	H	Arsenal	L 0-3	0-3	11		26,336
34	6	A	West Ham U	L 0-2	0-2	12		32,389
35	13	H	Southampton	D 1-1	1-0	12	Rufus [17]	26,551
36	20	A	Newcastle U	L 0-3	0-1	13		51,360
37	27	H	Sunderland	D 2-2	1-2	13	Euell [2], Lisbie [82]	26,606
38	May 11	A	Manchester U	D 0-0	0-0	14		67,579

Final League Position: 14

GOALSCORERS

League (38): Euell 11, Johansson 5, Lisbie 5, Stuart 3, Brown 2, Bart-Williams 1, Bartlett 1, Jensen 1, Konchesky 1, MacDonald 1, Parker 1, Powell 1, Robinson 1, Rufus 1, own goals 3.
Worthington Cup (5): Brown 1, Euell 1 (pen), Fortune 1, Konchesky 1, Robinson 1.
FA Cup (3): Stuart 2 (1 pen), Euell 1.

Kiely D 38	Young L 34	Powell C 35 + 1	Stuart G 31	Brown S 11 + 3	Fish M 25	Parker S 36 + 2	Euell J 31 + 5	Bartlett S 10 + 4	Johansson J 21 + 9	Salako J 2 + 1	Peacock G 1 + 4	Lisbie K 10 + 12	Fortune J 14 + 5	Rufus R 10	Konchesky P 22 + 12	Todd A 3 + 2	Robinson J 16 + 12	Kinsella M 14 + 3	Jensen C 16 + 2	MacDonald C — + 2	Costa J 22 + 2	Bart-Williams C 10 + 6	Svensson M 6 + 6	Kishishev R — + 3	Match No.
1	2	3	4	5	6	7^1	8	9^2	10	11^3	12	13	14												1
1	2	3	4	12	6	7	8		10^3	11^2	9	13			5^1	14									2
1	2	3	4	5	6	7^2	8	9^1			12	11^3			13	10	14								3
1	2^1	3	7	5	6	10	8^2	9			12				4	11	13								4
1	2	3	7^3	5	6	11^2	12	9	10^1						4	13	14	8							5
1	2	3^1	7	5	6	11	13	9^2	10						4	12	14	8^3							6
1	2	3			6	8	12	9^1	10						4	5	11^2	7	13						7
1	2^2	3			6	11	12	9^1	10				14		4	5	13	7	8^3						8
1	2	3^3		5	6	11	12	9^1	10				14		4		13	7	8^2						9
1	2	3		5	6	12	9		10			13			4^2	11		7	8^1						10
1	2	3		5	6	11^3	9		10^2		12		14		4	13		7	8^1						11
1	2^2	3		5	6	11^1	9		10		12				4	13		7	8						12
1	2	3	11^3	5	6		12	9	10						4^2	13		7^1	8					14	13
1	2	3	4^3	5^2	6	7		9^1	10		12	13			11			8						14	14
1	2	3	4		6^3	7		9	10^1		12				5	13	11^2		8					14	15
1	2	3	7^3		6	11		9^1	10		12				5	13			8^2		4			14	16
1	2	3^2	7		6	11^1		9	10		12				5	13			8		4				17
1	2	3^2	7		6	11^3	8	9			12				5^1	13			10		4			14	18
1	2	3	4		6^2	7^3	8	9							5^1	11^1			10	13				14	19
1	2	3	4^1		6	7	8	9			12				5		11		10^2	13					20
1	2	3			6	7^3	8	9^1			12	13			5		11		10^2					14	21
1		3	2^3		6	7	8	9^1			12				5^2		11		10	13	4			14	22
1	2^2	3	4		6	7^3		9	10		12		14		5	13	11	8^1							23
1		3	2		6	7^2	10^1	9^3			12				5		11				4	8	13	14	24
1		3	2		6^2	7	10^1	9^3			12		13		5		11				4	8		14	25
1	2	3	4^3		6	7	8^1	9^2			12		13		5		11		10		4			14	26
1	2	3	4		6	11^1	8				12				5			7	10	13		9^2			27
1	2	3	4		6	11		9^1			12				5			7^2	8	13		10			28
1	2	3	4		6	11		9			12				5			7^1	8			10			29
1	2	3^2	7		6	11^1		9			12	13			5				8		4	10			30
1	2^2	3^1	7		6	11		9			12	13	14		5				8^1		4	10			31
1	2	3	7		6^3	11^2		9			12	13	14		5				8		4	10^1			32
1	2	3	4		6	7		9	10		12				5		11^1		8						33
1	2		4		6	11		9	10						3	5		7	8						34
1		3	2		6	7^1		9	10		12	13			5		11		8^2		4				35
1	2		4		6	7^1		9^2	10		12	13			3		11		8		5				36
1	2	12	4		6	7		9	10			13			5		11^3		8^2		3^1			14	37
1	2	3	7^1		6	11		9	10^3		12	13			5				8^2		4			14	38

Worthington Cup

Second Round	Port Vale	(h)	2-0
Third Round	WBA	(a)	1-0
Fourth Round	Watford	(a)	2-3

FA Cup

Third Round	Blackpool	(h)	2-1
Fourth Round	Walsall	(h)	1-2

CHELSEA   FA Premiership

FOUNDATION

Chelsea may never have existed but for the fact that Fulham rejected an offer to rent the Stamford Bridge ground from Mr H. A. Mears who had owned it since 1904. Fortunately he was determined to develop it as a football stadium rather than sell it to the Great Western Railway and got together with Frederick Parker, who persuaded Mears of the financial advantages of developing a major sporting venue. Chelsea FC was formed in 1905, and when admission to the Southern League was denied, they immediately gained admission to the Second Division of the Football League.

Stamford Bridge, London SW6 1HS.

Telephone: (020) 7385 5545. *Fax:* (020) 7381 4831.
ClubCall: 09068 121 159. *Ticket News and Promotions:* 09068 121 011. *Ticket Credit Card Service:* (020) 7386 7799.

Ground Capacity: 42,449.

Record Attendance: 82,905 v Arsenal, Division 1, 12 October 1935.

Record Receipts: £1,064,561 v Tottenham H, FA Premier League, 28 October 2000.

Pitch Measurements: 113yd × 74yd.

Chairman: K. W. Bates.
Directors: T. Birch (Managing), Ms Y. S. Todd. M. Russell ACMA.

Head Coach: Claudio Ranieri. *Assistant Manager:* Gwyn Williams. *First Team Coach:* Angelo Antenucci. *Physio:* Michael Banks. *Reserve Team Manager:* Mick McGiven.

Company Secretary: Alan Shaw.

Assistant Secretary: Claire Lait.

Corporate Sales Manager: Carole Phair.

Safety Officer: Jill Dawson.

HONOURS

Football League: Division 1 – Champions 1954–55; Division 2 – Champions 1983–84, 1988–89; Runners-up 1906–07, 1911–12, 1929–30, 1962–63, 1976–77.

FA Cup: Winners 1970, 1997, 2000; Runners-up 1915, 1967, 1994, 2002.

Football League Cup: Winners 1965, 1998; Runners-up 1972.

Full Members' Cup: Winners 1986.

Zenith Data Systems Cup: Winners 1990.

European Competitions: European Cup: 1999–2000. European Fairs Cup: 1958–60, 1965–66, 1968–69. European Cup-Winners' Cup: 1970–71 (winners), 1971–72, 1994–95, 1997–98 (winners), 1998–99 (semi-finals). UEFA Cup: 2000–01, 2001–02. Super Cup: 1998–99 (winners).

Colours: Royal blue shirts and shorts with white trim, white stockings with royal blue trim.

Change Colours: Midnight/deep royal shirts, midnight/deep royal shorts, midnight/deep royal stockings.

Year Formed: 1905. *Turned Professional:* 1905. *Ltd Co.:* 1905. *Club Nickname:* 'The Blues'.

First Football League Game: 2 September 1905, Division 2, v Stockport Co (a) L 0–1 – Foulke; Mackie, McEwan; Key, Harris, Miller; Moran, J. T. Robertson, Copeland, Windridge, Kirwan.

IT'S A FACT !

In 1954–55 when Chelsea were First Division champions, their reserve team won the Football Combination title while the A team took the Metropolitan League, its Challenge Cup and Professional Cup.

Record League Victory: 9–2 v Glossop N E, Division 2,
1 September 1906 – Byrne; Walton, Miller; Key (1),
McRoberts, Henderson; Moran, McDermott (1),
Hilsdon (5), Copeland (1), Kirwan (1).

Record Cup Victory: 13–0 v Jeunesse Hautcharage, ECWC,
1st rd 2nd leg, 29 September 1971 – Bonetti; Boyle,
Harris (1), Hollins (1p), Webb (1), Hinton, Cooke,
Baldwin (3), Osgood (5), Hudson (1), Houseman (1).

Record Defeat: 1–8 v Wolverhampton W, Division 1,
26 September 1953.

Most League Points (2 for a win): 57, Division 2, 1906–07.

Most League Points (3 for a win): 99, Division 2, 1988–89.

Most League Goals: 98, Division 1, 1960–61.

Highest League Scorer in Season: Jimmy Greaves, 41,
1960–61.

Most League Goals in Total Aggregate: Bobby Tambling,
164, 1958–70.

Most League Goals in One Match: 5, George Hilsdon v
Glossop, Division 2, 1 September 1906; 5, Jimmy Greaves v
Wolverhampton W, Division 1, 30 August 1958; 5, Jimmy
Greaves v Preston NE, Division 1, 19 December 1959;
5, Jimmy Greaves v WBA, Division 1, 3 December 1960;
5, Bobby Tambling v Aston Villa, Division 1, 17 September
1966; 5, Gordon Durie v Walsall, Division 2, 4 February 1989.

Most Capped Player: Marcel Desailly, 48 (97), France.

Most League Appearances: Ron Harris, 655, 1962–80.

Youngest League Player: Ian Hamilton, 16 years 138 days v Tottenham H, 18 March 1967.

Record Transfer Fee Received: £12,000,000 from Rangers for Tor Andre Flo, November 2000.

Record Transfer Fee Paid: £15,000,000 to Atletico Madrid for Jimmy Floyd Hasselbaink, June 2000.

Football League Record: 1905 Elected to Division 2; 1907–10 Division 1; 1910–12 Division 2;
1912–24 Division 1; 1924–30 Division 2; 1930–62 Division 1; 1962–63 Division 2; 1963–75 Division 1;
1975–77 Division 2; 1977–79 Division 1; 1979–84 Division 2; 1984–88 Division 1; 1988–89 Division 2;
1989–92 Division 1; 1992– FA Premier League.

MANAGERS

John Tait Robertson 1905–07
David Calderhead 1907–33
Leslie Knighton 1933–39
Billy Birrell 1939–52
Ted Drake 1952–61
Tommy Docherty 1962–67
Dave Sexton 1967–74
Ron Suart 1974–75
Eddie McCreadie 1975–77
Ken Shellito 1977–78
Danny Blanchflower 1978–79
Geoff Hurst 1979–81
John Neal 1981–85 *(Director to
1986)*
John Hollins 1985–88
Bobby Campbell 1988–91
Ian Porterfield 1991–93
David Webb 1993
Glenn Hoddle 1993–96
Ruud Gullit 1996–98
Gianluca Vialli 1998–2000
Claudio Ranieri September 2000–

LATEST SEQUENCES

Longest Sequence of League Wins: 8, 15.3.89 – 8.4.89.

Longest Sequence of League Defeats: 7, 1.11.52 – 20.12.52.

Longest Sequence of League Draws: 6, 20.8.69 – 13.9.69.

Longest Sequence of Unbeaten League Matches: 27, 29.10.88 – 8.4.89.

Longest Sequence Without a League Win: 21, 3.11.87 – 2.4.88.

TEN YEAR LEAGUE RECORD

		P	W	D	L	F	A	Pts	Pos
1991-92	Div 1	42	13	14	15	50	60	53	14
1992-93	PR Lge	42	14	14	14	51	54	56	11
1993-94	PR Lge	42	13	12	17	49	53	51	14
1994-95	PR Lge	42	13	15	14	50	55	54	11
1995-96	PR Lge	38	12	14	12	46	44	50	11
1996-97	PR Lge	38	16	11	11	58	55	59	6
1997-98	PR Lge	38	20	3	15	71	43	63	4
1998-99	PR Lge	38	20	15	3	57	30	75	3
1999-2000	PR Lge	38	18	11	9	53	34	65	5
2000-01	PR Lge	38	17	10	11	68	45	61	6

DID YOU KNOW ?

In 1930, Chelsea paid almost
£25,000 for three Scottish
internationals: £10,000 for
Hughie Gallacher; £6,000 for
winger Alec Cheyne and
shortly afterwards £8,500 for
Huddersfield Town's Alec
Jackson.

CHELSEA 2001–02 LEAGUE RECORD

Match No.	Date	Venue	Opponents	Result	H/T Score	Lg. Pos.	Goalscorers	Attendance
1	Aug 19	H	Newcastle U	D 1-1	1-0	—	Zenden [8]	40,153
2	25	A	Southampton	W 2-0	1-0	6	Hasselbaink [33], Stanic [90]	31,107
3	Sept 8	H	Arsenal	D 1-1	1-1	9	Hasselbaink (pen) [31]	40,883
4	16	A	Tottenham H	W 3-2	1-0	6	Hasselbaink 2 (1 pen) [45, 81 (p)], Desailly [90]	33,485
5	23	H	Middlesbrough	D 2-2	2-0	5	Hasselbaink 2 [3, 37]	36,767
6	30	A	Fulham	D 1-1	1-0	9	Hasselbaink [32]	21,159
7	Oct 13	H	Leicester C	W 2-0	2-0	6	Hasselbaink (pen) [20], Gudjohnsen [45]	40,371
8	21	A	Leeds U	D 0-0	0-0	7		40,171
9	24	A	West Ham U	L 1-2	1-2	—	Hasselbaink [22]	26,520
10	28	A	Derby Co	D 1-1	0-1	8	Hasselbaink [48]	28,910
11	Nov 4	H	Ipswich T	W 2-1	1-0	7	Zola [36], Dalla Bona [90]	40,456
12	18	A	Everton	D 0-0	0-0	7		30,555
13	24	H	Blackburn R	D 0-0	0-0	8		37,978
14	Dec 1	A	Manchester U	W 3-0	1-0	5	Melchiot [6], Hasselbaink [64], Gudjohnsen [86]	67,544
15	5	H	Charlton Ath	L 0-1	0-0	—		33,504
16	9	A	Sunderland	D 0-0	0-0	5		44,907
17	16	H	Liverpool	W 4-0	2-0	5	Le Saux [3], Hasselbaink [28], Dalla Bona [71], Gudjohnsen [90]	41,175
18	23	H	Bolton W	W 5-1	2-1	6	Gudjohnsen [41], Hasselbaink [45], Zenden [56], Hendry (og) [76], Lampard [87]	34,063
19	26	A	Arsenal	L 1-2	1-0	6	Lampard [31]	38,079
20	29	A	Newcastle U	W 2-1	2-1	6	Gudjohnsen 2 [35, 45]	52,123
21	Jan 1	H	Southampton	L 2-4	2-1	6	Gudjohnsen [20], Hasselbaink [45]	35,164
22	12	A	Bolton W	D 2-2	0-0	6	Gudjohnsen [53], Forssell [65]	23,891
23	20	H	West Ham U	W 5-1	1-0	6	Hasselbaink 2 [45, 60], Gudjohnsen 2 [51, 87], Forssell [90]	40,054
24	30	H	Leeds U	W 2-0	2-0	—	Gudjohnsen [2], Dalla Bona [31]	40,615
25	Feb 2	A	Leicester C	W 3-2	0-1	5	Hasselbaink 2 [62, 90], Zola [79]	19,950
26	9	A	Aston Villa	D 1-1	0-1	5	Lampard [65]	41,137
27	Mar 2	A	Charlton Ath	L 1-2	0-0	6	Lampard [83]	26,333
28	6	H	Fulham	W 3-2	2-1	—	Melchiot [18], Gudjohnsen [29], Forssell [82]	39,744
29	13	H	Tottenham H	W 4-0	1-0	—	Hasselbaink 3 [24, 89, 81], Lampard [90]	39,652
30	16	H	Sunderland	W 4-0	1-0	5	Gallas [24], Gudjohnsen [73], Forssell [84], Dalla Bona [90]	40,223
31	24	A	Liverpool	L 0-1	0-0	6		44,203
32	30	H	Derby Co	W 2-1	0-0	5	Terry [50], Petit [86]	37,849
33	Apr 1	A	Ipswich T	D 0-0	0-0	5		27,929
34	6	H	Everton	W 3-0	2-0	4	Hasselbaink 2 [26, 44], Zola [90]	40,545
35	10	A	Blackburn R	D 0-0	0-0	—		25,441
36	20	H	Manchester U	L 0-3	0-2	5		41,725
37	27	A	Middlesbrough	W 2-0	2-0	5	Cole [38], Zenden [43]	28,686
38	May 11	H	Aston Villa	L 1-3	0-1	6	Gudjohnsen (pen) [70]	40,709

Final League Position: 6

GOALSCORERS

League (66): Hasselbaink 23 (3 pens), Gudjohnsen 14 (1 pen), Lampard 5, Dalla Bona 4, Forssell 4, Zenden 3, Zola 3, Melchiot 2, Cole 1, Desailly 1, Gallas 1, Le Saux 1, Petit 1, Stanic 1, Terry 1, own goal 1.
Worthington Cup (8): Gudjohnsen 3, Hasselbaink 3, Forssell 2.
FA Cup (16): Forssell 3, Gudjohnsen 3, Hasselbaink 3, Terry 2, Gallas 1, Lampard 1, Le Saux 1, Stanic 1, Zola 1.

De Goey E 6	Melchiot M 35 + 2	Le Saux G 26 + 1	Petit E 26 + 1	Terry J 32 + 1	Desailly M 24	Gronkjaer J 11 + 2	Lampard F 34 + 3	Hasselbaink J 35	Zola G 19 + 16	Zenden B 13 + 9	Gallas W 27 + 3	Jokanovic S 12 + 8	Morris J 2 + 3	Stanic M 18 + 9	Gudjohnsen E 26 + 6	Babayaro C 18	Ferrer A 2 + 2	Dalla Bona S 16 + 8	Cudicini C 27 + 1	Forssell M 2 + 20	Bosnich M 5	Keenan J —+ 1	Cole C 2 + 1	Huth R —+ 1	Match No.
1	2	3	4	5¹	6	7	8	9	10	11²	12	13													1
1	2	3	4²	5	6	7¹	8	9	12	11³				10	13	14									2
1	12	3	4	5	6	7²	8	9	10	11¹	2				13										3
1	2	3	4	5¹	6	7	8	9	10³	11²	12	13			14										4
1	2	12		5	6		8³	9	13	11²	4	7	14	10	3¹										5
1	2²		8	5	6		9	10¹	11³	4	7		12	3	13	14									6
12		4	5	6	13	9²	10	11¹	2	7		8³	3		1	14									7
	2	11	4	5		7	9	12	6			10²	3¹	8	13	1									8
	2	3	4³	5		8²	9	10	12	6	7	11¹	14	13	1										9
	2²	3	8	5	6	12	9	10³	11	4	7¹		13	14	1										10
	2²			5	6	8	9	10	12	7¹	14	13	3	4	11³	1									11
	2			5	6	8	9	10	12	6	7¹	13	3	11²	15	16									12
	2	3	4	5		8	9	10¹	11²	6	7	12	13	1											13
	2	11²		5		4	9³	12	6	7	13	10¹	3	8	1	14									14
	2			5		4	9	12	11¹	6	7	10²	3	8	1	13									15
	2			5		4	9		6	11	7	10¹	3	8	1	12									16
	2	11²		5		7	9¹	12	13	6	14	4³	10	3	8	1									17
	2	3³	12	5		4	9	13	11¹	6		7	10²	14	8	1									18
	2	11¹	4	5		8	9	12	6		7²	10³	3	13	1	14									19
	2	11		5		4	9¹	12	6	13	7²	10³	3	8	1	14									20
	2	11		5		4	9	12	6	13	7²	10	3¹	8³	1	14									21
	2	3		5	6	4	10²		12	11¹	7	9	8	1	13										22
	2	4²	5	6		8	9¹	11¹	12	3	13	7	10	1	14										23
	2	3	4	5	6	8	9		7	10¹	11	1	12												24
	2	3	4	5	6	8	9	12	7	10¹	11	1	13												25
		3	4	5³	6	8	9	12	7	10²	2¹	11	1	13	14										26
	2	11	4		12	8	9	13	5	6²	7	10	3¹	1	14										27
	2	11	4¹		6	13	8	9	7²	5	10³	3	12	1	14										28
	2	11	4		6	7³	8	9	12	5	13	10¹	3	1	14										29
	2	11¹		6	7²	4	9	12	5	13	10³	3	8	1	14										30
	2	4	6	11	8	9	12	5	7	10¹	3	1													31
	2	3	4	12	6	11	8	9	13	5¹	7²	10³	1	14											32
	2	3		5	6	12	9	11	13		4	7²	14	8¹	1	10³									33
	2	3	4²	5¹	6	8	9¹	11	12	13	7	10	1	14											34
	2	4	5	6	8	9	11	12	7	10¹	3	1													35
	2	4²	5	6	7	8	9	11	12	3	10¹	13	1												36
	2	4¹	5	6	7²	8		10	11	3	12	14	13	1	9³										37
	2	3³	4	5	7¹	8		10	11²	6	13	12	1	9	14										38

Worthington Cup

Third Round	Coventry C	(a)	2-0
Fourth Round	Leeds U	(a)	2-0
Fifth Round	Newcastle U	(h)	1-0
Semi-Final	Tottenham H	(h)	2-1
		(a)	1-5

FA Cup

Third Round	Norwich C	(a)	0-0
		(h)	4-0
Fourth Round	West Ham U	(h)	1-1
		(a)	3-2
Fifth Round	Preston NE	(h)	3-1
Sixth Round	Tottenham H	(a)	4-0
Semi-Final (at Villa Park)	Fulham		1-0
Final (at Millennium Stadium)	Arsenal		0-2

CHELTENHAM TOWN   Division 2

FOUNDATION

Although a scratch team representing Cheltenham played a match against Gloucester in 1884, the earliest recorded match for Cheltenham Town FC was a friendly against Dean Close School on 12 March 1892. The School won 4–3 and the match was played at Prestbury (half a mile from Whaddon Road). Cheltenham Town played Wednesday afternoon friendlies at a local cricket ground until entering the Mid Gloucester League. In those days the club played in deep red coloured shirts and were nicknamed 'the Rubies'. The club moved to Whaddon Lane for season 1901–02 and changed to red and white colours two years later.

Whaddon Road, Cheltenham, Gloucester GL52 5NA.

Telephone: (01242) 573 558.

Fax: (01242) 224 675 (due to change).

ClubCall: 09066 555 833.

Website: www.cheltenhamtownfc.com

Ground Capacity: 7,407.

Record Attendance: at Whaddon Road: 8,326 v Reading, FA Cup 1st rd, 17 November 1956; at Cheltenham Athletic Ground: 10,389 v Blackpool, FA Cup 3rd rd, 13 January 1934.

Record Receipts: £78,895 v Burnley, FA Cup 4th rd, 27 January 2002.

Pitch Measurements: 111yd × 72yd.

Chairman: Paul Baker.

Directors: Rod Burge, Colin Farmer, Arthur Hayward, Brian Sandland, John Wood, Barrie Wood, David Reynolds.

Manager: Graham Allner.

Assistant Manager: Mike Davis.

First Team Coach: Graham Allner.

Youth Team Manager: Bob Bloomer.

Secretary: Paul Godfrey.

Physio: John Atkinson. *Head of Youth:* Brian Forsbrook.

Colours: Red and white striped shirts, white shorts, white stockings.

Change Colours: All orange.

HONOURS

Football League: Promoted from Division 3 (play-offs) 2001–02. *Football Conference:* Champions 1998–99, runners-up 1997–98. *FA Trophy:* Winners 1997–98. *Southern League:* Champions 1984–85; *Southern League Cup:* Winners 1957–58, runners-up 1968–69, 1984–85; *Southern League Merit Cup:* Winners 1984–85; *Southern League Championship Shield:* Winners 1985.

Gloucestershire Senior Cup: Winners 1998–99; *Gloucestershire Northern Senior Professional Cup:* Winners 30 times; *Midland Floodlit Cup:* Winners 1985–86, 1986–87, 1987–88; *Mid Gloucester League:* Champions 1896–97; *Gloucester and District League:* Champions 1902–03, 1905–06; *Cheltenham League:* Champions 1910–11, 1913–14; *North Gloucestershire League:* Champions 1913–14; *Gloucestershire Northern Senior League:* Champions 1928–29, 1932–33; *Gloucestershire Northern Senior Amateur Cup:* Winners 1929–30, 1930–31, 1932–33, 1933–34, 1934–35; *Leamington Hospital Cup:* Winners 1934–35.

IT'S A FACT !

Billy James scored five goals out of seven in an FA Cup preliminary round tie for Cheltenham Town against Abergavenny Thursday on 7 September 1963.

Year Formed: 1892.

Turned Professional: 1932.

Ltd Co.: 1937.

Club Nickname: 'The Robins'.

Previous Grounds: Grafton Cricket Ground, Whaddon Lane, Carter's Field (pre 1932).

Record League Victory: 11–0 v Bourneville Ath, Birmingham Combination, 29 April 1933 – Davis; Jones, Williams; Lang (1), Blackburn, Draper; Evans, Hazard (4), Haycox (4), Goodger (1), Hill (1).

Record Cup Victory: 12–0 v Chippenham R, FA Cup 3rd qual. rd, 2 November 1935 – Bowles; Whitehouse, Williams; Lang, Devonport (1), Partridge (2); Perkins, Hackett, Jones (4), Black (4), Griffiths (1).

Record Defeat: 1–10 v Merthyr T, Southern League, 8 March 1952.

Most League Points (2 for a win): 60, Southern League Division 1, 1963–64.

Most League Points (3 for a win): 86, Southern League Premier Division, 1994–95.

Most League Goals: 115, Southern League, 1957–58.

Highest League Scorer in Season: Dave Lewis, 33 (53 in all competitions), Southern League Division 1, 1974–75.

Most League Goals in Total Aggregate: Dave Lewis, 205 (290 in all competitions), 1970–83.

Most Capped Player: Michael Duff, 1, Northern Ireland.

Most League Appearances: Roger Thorndale, 523 (702 in all competitions), 1958–76.

Record Transfer Fee Received: £60,000 from Southampton for Christer Warren, 1995.

Record Transfer Fee Paid: £25,000 to Kidderminster H for Kim Casey, 1991.

MANAGERS

George Blackburn 1932–34
George Carr 1934–37
Jimmy Brain 1937–48
Cyril Dean 1948–50
George Summerbee 1950–52
William Raeside 1952–53
Arch Anderson 1953–58
Ron Lewin 1958–60
Peter Donnelly 1960–61
Tommy Cavanagh 1961
Arch Anderson 1961–65
Harold Fletcher 1965–66
Bob Etheridge 1966–73
Willie Penman 1973–74
Dennis Allen 1974–79
Terry Paine 1979
Alan Grundy 1979–82
Alan Wood 1982–83
John Murphy 1983–88
Jim Barron 1988–90
John Murphy 1990
Dave Lewis 1990–91
Ally Robertson 1991–92
Lindsay Parsons 1992–95
Chris Robinson 1995–97
Steve Cotterill 1997–2002
Graham Allner July 2002–

LATEST SEQUENCES

Longest Sequence of League Wins: not more than 3.

Longest Sequence of League Defeats: 5, 13.1.01 – 13.2.01.

Longest Sequence of League Draws: not more than 2.

Longest Sequence of Unbeaten League Matches: 16, 1.12.01 – 12.3.02.

Longest Sequence Without a League Win: 6, 11.8.01 – 8.9.01.

TEN YEAR LEAGUE RECORD

		P	W	D	L	F	A	Pts	Pos
1991–92	Conf	42	10	13	19	56	82	43	21
1992–93	Sth L	40	21	10	9	76	40	73	2
1993–94	Sth L	42	21	12	9	67	38	75	2
1994–95	Sth L	42	25	11	6	87	39	86	2
1995–96	Sth L	42	21	11	10	76	57	74	3
1996–97	Sth L	42	21	11	10	76	44	74	2
1997–98	Conf	42	23	9	10	63	43	78	2
1998-99	Conf	42	22	14	6	71	36	80	1
1999-2000	Div 3	46	20	10	16	50	42	70	8
2000-01	Div 3	46	18	14	14	59	52	68	9

DID YOU KNOW ?

The first player to score an FA Cup hat-trick for Cheltenham Town from the first round proper onwards was centre-forward Peter Goring in a 5-0 win over Street on 29 November 1947.

CHELTENHAM TOWN 2001–02 LEAGUE RECORD

Match No.	Date	Venue	Opponents	Result	H/T Score	Lg. Pos.	Goalscorers	Attendance
1	Aug 11	H	Leyton Orient	D	1-1	0-0	—	White [64]	4115
2	18	A	Luton T	L	1-2	0-2	16	Howarth [71]	6177
3	25	H	Mansfield T	L	2-3	0-1	20	Alsop 2 [62, 66]	3105
4	27	A	Swansea C	D	2-2	0-2	21	Duff [70], Yates [90]	3343
5	Sept 1	H	Torquay U	D	2-2	1-2	22	Milton [36], Yates [90]	3167
6	8	A	Shrewsbury T	L	1-2	0-2	22	Yates [57]	3395
7	15	H	Carlisle U	W	2-0	1-0	20	Victory [16], Grayson (pen) [66]	3081
8	18	A	Hartlepool U	W	1-0	0-0	—	Devaney [78]	2599
9	22	A	Rushden & D	L	0-1	0-0	16		4116
10	28	A	Southend U	W	1-0	1-0	—	Alsop [26]	3709
11	Oct 5	H	Lincoln C	W	2-1	1-0	—	Milton [11], Naylor [47]	3315
12	13	A	Kidderminster H	D	0-0	0-0	10		3554
13	20	H	Exeter C	W	3-1	2-0	8	Alsop 2 [30, 40], Naylor [81]	3393
14	23	A	Rochdale	D	2-2	1-0	—	Victory 2 [6, 84]	3279
15	27	H	Scunthorpe U	D	3-3	2-2	10	Victory [36], Howells [45], Alsop [61]	3295
16	Nov 3	A	Hull C	L	1-5	0-3	10	Alsop [69]	9435
17	6	H	Bristol R	D	0-0	0-0	—		4913
18	9	H	Plymouth Arg	D	0-0	0-0	—		5035
19	20	H	Macclesfield T	W	4-1	1-0	—	Alsop [30], Duff [64], Priest (og) [86], Williams [90]	2402
20	24	A	Oxford U	L	0-3	0-2	11		6740
21	Dec 1	H	Halifax T	W	2-1	1-1	10	Victory [17], Alsop [66]	3304
22	15	A	York C	W	3-1	2-1	8	Naylor 2 [29, 42], Alsop [60]	2082
23	26	H	Shrewsbury T	W	1-0	1-0	8	Naylor [26]	4561
24	29	H	Swansea C	D	2-2	0-2	8	Alsop [60], Naylor [61]	4130
25	Jan 1	A	Torquay U	W	1-0	0-0	7	Williams [58]	2952
26	12	H	Luton T	D	1-1	1-0	8	Naylor [22]	5026
27	19	A	Leyton Orient	W	2-0	1-0	7	Victory [39], Alsop [68]	4868
28	23	H	Darlington	D	0-0	0-0	—		2808
29	Feb 9	A	Exeter C	W	2-0	0-0	9	Yates [64], Naylor [90]	3837
30	12	A	Darlington	W	2-0	2-0	—	Yates (pen) [6], Alsop [41]	3338
31	19	H	Southend U	D	1-1	0-0	—	Howells [51]	4015
32	26	H	Hartlepool U	W	3-0	2-0	—	Naylor 2 [41, 74], Alsop [43]	3257
33	Mar 2	H	Rushden & D	D	1-1	1-1	6	Alsop [25]	4584
34	5	A	Bristol R	W	2-1	1-1	—	Walker [45], Alsop [70]	5909
35	9	H	York C	W	4-0	1-0	6	Alsop 2 [22, 63], Yates [80], Finnigan [87]	3958
36	12	H	Lincoln C	W	1-0	0-0	6	Alsop [62]	2026
37	16	A	Halifax T	L	1-4	1-1	5	Victory [14]	1870
38	23	H	Rochdale	D	1-1	1-0	5	Williams [3]	4643
39	26	H	Kidderminster H	W	2-1	1-1	—	Naylor [40], Tyson [76]	5016
40	30	A	Scunthorpe U	W	2-1	1-0	3	Alsop [38], Naylor [77]	5086
41	Apr 1	H	Hull C	W	1-0	0-0	3	Brough [71]	5546
42	6	A	Macclesfield T	L	0-1	0-0	3		2270
43	9	A	Mansfield T	L	1-2	1-1	—	Yates [25]	8633
44	13	H	Oxford U	W	2-0	2-0	3	Finnigan [16], Duff [45]	7013
45	16	A	Carlisle U	D	0-0	0-0	—		2184
46	20	A	Plymouth Arg	L	0-2	0-2	4		18,517

Final League Position: 4

GOALSCORERS
League (66): Alsop 20, Naylor 12, Victory 7, Yates 7 (1 pen), Duff 3, Williams 3, Finnigan 2, Howells 2, Milton 2, Brough 1, Devaney 1, Grayson 1 (pen), Howarth 1, Tyson 1, Walker 1, White 1, own goal 1.
Worthington Cup (1): Grayson 1.
FA Cup (12): Naylor 5, Alsop 4, Devaney 1, Howells 1, Milton 1.

Muggleton C 7	Jones S 2+3	Victory J 45+1	Banks C 38	Walker R 11+1	Duff M 45	Milton R 37+2	Devaney M 8+17	Alsop J 38+3	McAuley H 3+4	Yates M 45	White J —+4	Hopkins G —+3	Howarth N 18+8	Naylor T 43+1	Grayson N 13+21	Howells L 31	Hill K 2+3	Brough J 9+12	Book S 39	Williams L 36+2	Jackson M —+1	Griffin A 21+3	Finnigan J 12	Higgs S —+1	Tyson N 1+7	Lee M 2+3	Match No.
1	2^1	3	4	5	6^2	7	8^3	9	10	11	12	13	14														1
1	2^1	3	4	5	6	7	8	9^2	10^3	11			12	13	14												2
1		3	4	5	2	6	8^1	12		11^1		13	14	10	9^2	7											3
1		3^1	4	5	2	8^2	12	9^2		11			6	10	13	7	14										4
1	12	4	5^2	2	8	13				11	14		6^1	10	9	7	3^3										5
1		3	4		2	6^1	8^3			11		13	12	10	9^2	7	5	14									6
		3	4	5	2	6	8^3	12		11				10^2	9^1	7	14	13	1								7
		3	4	5	2	6	8^3	12		11			13	10	9^1	7		14	1								8
		3	4	5^1	2	6^3	8^2	9		11			10			7	12	13	1	14							9
		3	4		2	6^1	13	9		11^2			5	10^1		7		13	1	8							10
		3	4		2	6^1	13	9		11			5	10^1		7		14	1	8^1							11
		3	4		2	6	12	9		11^2			5	10^2		7		13	1	8^1	14						12
		3	4		2	6^2	12	9	13	11			5	10^1		7			1	8^1		14					13
		3	4		2	6	12	9		11			5	10^2	13	7			1	8^1							14
		3	4		2	6		9		11			5	10^1	12	7		13	1	8^2							15
		3	4		2	6	12	9	13	11^2			5	10^1	14	7			1	8^1							16
		3	4		2	6		9		11			5	10^1	12	7			1	8							17
		3	4		2	6	12	9	8^1	11			5	10^1		7			1	13							18
		3	4		2	6	12	9	13	11^2			5	10^1	14	7			1	8							19
		3	4		2	6	8	9^1	12				5^3	10^2	13	7			1	11	14						20
	12	3	5		6		13	9		11				10^2		7		8	1	4		2^1			14		21
		3	5		6		12	9^2		11		13		10^1		7		8	1	4		2					22
		3	5		6			9^1		11				10		7	12	8	1	4		2					23
		3	5		6	12	13	9		11				10^1		7		8^2	1	4		2					24
		3	5		6			9		11				10		7		8	1	4		2					25
		3	5		6	8				11				10	9	7			1	4		2					26
		3	5		6	7		9		11				10				8	1	4		2					27
		3	5		6	8	12			11				10^1	13	7			1	4^2		2					28
		3	5		6	8		9		11				10		7			1	4		2					29
	12	3	5			8		9		11				10^2	13	7	6		1	4^1		2					30
		3	5			8		9		11				10		7			1	4		2					31
		3	5^3		6	8	12	9^2		11				10^1	13	7	14		1	4		2					32
		3			6	8^1		9		11				10	12	7	5		1	4		2					33
		3	5	12	6	8^2	14	9		11				10	13	7^1			1	4^3		2					34
		3	5	4	6			9^1		11			13	10^2		12	14		1	7^2		2	8				35
		3	5	4	6			9		11				10				8	1			2	7				36
		3	5	4^1	6			9		11	12			10^2	13			8	1			2	7	15			37
		3	5		6	8		9		11				10					1	4		2	7				38
		3	5^2		6	8^3		9		11	12			10	13				1	4^1		2	7		14		39
1	12	3			6			9		11			5	10^2					1	4^1		2	7		13	8	40
		3			6	12		9		11			5	10^2	13				1	4^3		2	7		14	8^1	41
		3			6	8^3		9		11			5^1	10	12	7			1	4^2		2			13	14	42
		3			6	8^1	13			11			5	10	12	7			1	4^3		2			9^2	14	43
		3			6	8				11			5	10^2	9	7			1	4^1		2	12		13		44
		3			6	8^2		9		11			5	10^1	12	7			1	4^3		2			14	13	45
		3			6	8		9^1	12	11			5^1	10	13	7			1	4^2		2			14		46

Worthington Cup

First Round	Bristol C	(a)	1-2

FA Cup

First Round	Kettering T	(a)	6-1
Second Round	Hinckley U	(a)	2-0
Third Round	Oldham Ath	(h)	2-1
Fourth Round	Burnley	(h)	2-1
Fifth Round	WBA	(a)	0-1

CHESTERFIELD   Division 2

FOUNDATION

Chesterfield are fourth only to Stoke, Notts County and Nottingham Forest in age for they can trace their existence as far back as 1866, although it is fair to say that they were somewhat casual in the first few years of their history playing only a few friendlies a year. However, their rules of 1871 are still in existence showing an annual membership of 2s (10p), but it was not until 1891 that they won a trophy (the Barnes Cup) and followed this a year later by winning the Sheffield Cup, Barnes Cup and the Derbyshire Junior Cup.

Recreation Ground, Chesterfield S40 4SX.

Telephone: (01246) 209 765. *Fax:* (01246) 556 799.
Commercial Dept: (01246) 231 535.
ClubCall: 09068 555 818.

Ground Capacity: 6,879.

Record Attendance: 30,968 v Newcastle U, Division 2, 7 April 1939.

Record Receipts: £45,000 v Mansfield T, Division 3 play-off semi-final, 17 May 1995.

Pitch Measurements: 113yd × 71yd.

President: His Grace the Duke of Devonshire MC, DL, JP.

Chief Executive: Alan Walters.

Manager: Dave Rushbury. *Assistant Manager:* Lee Richardson.
Physio: Jamie Hewitt.

Secretary: Alan Walters. *Commercial Manager:* Jim Brown. *Stadium Manager:* W. W. Kenworthy.

Colours: All blue.

Change Colours: Red shirts, red shorts, red stockings.

Year Formed: 1866.

Turned Professional: 1891.

Ltd Co: 1871.

Previous Name: Chesterfield Town.

Club Nicknames: 'Blues' or 'Spireites'.

First Football League Game: 2 September 1899, Division 2, v Sheffield W (a) L 1–5 – Hancock; Pilgrim, Fletcher; Ballantyne, Bell, Downie; Morley, Thacker, Gooing, Munday (1), Geary.

Record League Victory: 10–0 v Glossop NE, Division 2, 17 January 1903 – Clutterbuck; Thorpe, Lerper; Haig, Banner, Thacker; Tomlinson (2), Newton (1), Milward (3), Munday (2), Steel (2).

Record Cup Victory: 5–0 v Wath Ath (a), FA Cup 1st rd, 28 November 1925 – Birch; Saxby, Dennis; Wass, Abbott, Thompson; Fisher (1), Roseboom (1), Cookson (2), Whitfield (1), Hopkinson.

HONOURS

Football League: Division 2 best season: 4th, 1946–47; Division 3 (N) – Champions 1930–31, 1935–36; Runners-up 1933–34; Promoted to Division 2 (3rd) – 2000–01; Division 4 – Champions 1969–70, 1984–85.
FA Cup: Semi-final 1997.
Football League Cup: best season: 4th rd, 1965.
Anglo-Scottish Cup: Winners 1981.

IT'S A FACT !

Chesterfield hold the record for the highest score in the Third Division (North) Cup. In 1934–35 they had an 8-1 victory over Mansfield Town.

Record Defeat: 0–10 v Gillingham, Division 3, 5 September 1987.

Most League Points (2 for a win): 64, Division 4, 1969–70.

Most League Points (3 for a win): 91, Division 4, 1984–85.

Most League Goals: 102, Division 3 (N), 1930–31.

Highest League Scorer in Season: Jimmy Cookson, 44, Division 3 (N), 1925–26.

Most League Goals in Total Aggregate: Ernie Moss, 161, 1969–76, 1979–81 and 1984–86.

Most League Goals in One Match: 4, Jimmy Cookson v Accrington S, Division 3N, 16 January 1926; 4, Jimmy Cookson v Ashington, Division 3N, 1 May 1926; 4, Jimmy Cookson v Wigan Borough, Division 3N, 4 September 1926; 4, Tommy Lyon v Southampton, Division 2, 3 December 1938.

Most Capped Player: Walter McMillen, 4 (7), Northern Ireland; Mark Williams, 4 (17), Northern Ireland.

Most League Appearances: Dave Blakey, 613, 1948–67.

Youngest League Player: Dennis Thompson, 16 years 160 days v Notts Co, 26 December 1950.

Record Transfer Fee Received: £750,000 from Southampton for Kevin Davies, May 1997.

Record Transfer Fee Paid: £250,000 to Watford for Jason Lee, August 1998.

Football League Record: 1899 Elected to Division 2; 1909 failed re-election; 1921–31 Division 3 (N); 1931–33 Division 2; 1933–36 Division 3 (N); 1936–51 Division 2; 1951–58 Division 3 (N); 1958–61 Division 3; 1961–70 Division 4; 1970–83 Division 3; 1983–85 Division 4; 1985–89 Division 3; 1989–92 Division 4; 1992–95 Division 3; 1995–2000 Division 2; 2000–01 Division 3; 2001– Division 2.

MANAGERS

E. Russell Timmeus 1891–95
  (Secretary-Manager)
Gilbert Gillies 1895–1901
E. F. Hind 1901–02
Jack Hoskin 1902–06
W. Furness 1906–07
George Swift 1907–10
G. H. Jones 1911–13
R. L. Weston 1913–17
T. Callaghan 1919
J. J. Caffrey 1920–22
Harry Hadley 1922
Harry Parkes 1922–27
Alec Campbell 1927
Ted Davison 1927–32
Bill Harvey 1932–38
Norman Bullock 1938–45
Bob Brocklebank 1945–48
Bobby Marshall 1948–52
Ted Davison 1952–58
Duggie Livingstone 1958–62
Tony McShane 1962–67
Jimmy McGuigan 1967–73
Joe Shaw 1973–76
Arthur Cox 1976–80
Frank Barlow 1980–83
John Duncan 1983–87
Kevin Randall 1987–88
Paul Hart 1988–91
Chris McMenemy 1991–93
John Duncan 1993–2000
Nicky Law 2000–02
Dave Rushbury January 2002–

LATEST SEQUENCES

Longest Sequence of League Wins: 10, 6.9.33 – 4.11.33.

Longest Sequence of League Defeats: 9, 22.10.60 – 27.12.60.

Longest Sequence of League Draws: 5, 19.9.90 – 6.10.90.

Longest Sequence of Unbeaten League Matches: 21, 26.12.94 – 29.4.95.

Longest Sequence Without a League Win: 18, 11.9.99 – 3.1.00.

TEN YEAR LEAGUE RECORD

		P	W	D	L	F	A	Pts	Pos
1991-92	Div 4	42	14	11	17	49	61	53	13
1992-93	Div 3	42	15	11	16	59	63	56	12
1993-94	Div 3	42	16	14	12	55	48	62	8
1994-95	Div 3	42	23	12	7	62	37	81	3
1995-96	Div 2	46	20	12	14	56	51	72	7
1996-97	Div 2	46	18	14	14	42	39	68	10
1997-98	Div 2	46	16	17	13	46	44	65	10
1998-99	Div 2	46	17	13	16	46	44	64	9
1999-2000	Div 2	46	7	15	24	34	63	36	24
2000-01	Div 3	46	25	14	7	79	42	80*	3

*9 pts deducted.

DID YOU KNOW ?

Alan Birch's penalty goal against Exeter City in the final match of 1979–80 was Chesterfield's 4,000th goal in the Football League in their 2,646th match.

CHESTERFIELD 2001–02 LEAGUE RECORD

Match No.	Date	Venue	Opponents	Result	H/T Score	Lg. Pos.	Goalscorers	Attendance
1	Aug 11	H	Colchester U	L	3-6	1-3	—	Willis [10], Beckett [47], Payne [55]	3939
2	18	A	Oldham Ath	D	1-1	0-1	21	Willis [70]	5534
3	25	H	Brentford	L	0-1	0-1	22		3571
4	27	A	Notts Co	D	1-1	0-0	19	Booty [90]	6236
5	Sept 1	H	Peterborough U	L	0-1	0-1	23		3555
6	8	A	Wycombe W	D	0-0	0-0	21		5644
7	15	A	Northampton T	W	2-0	1-0	19	Beckett [15], Breckin [79]	4535
8	18	H	Wrexham	W	3-2	1-0	—	Ebdon [7], Beckett [68], Edwards [90]	3538
9	22	H	Swindon T	W	4-0	0-0	12	Reeves [46], Richardson [53], Hyde [66], Howard [75]	4275
10	25	A	Huddersfield T	D	0-0	0-0	—		9399
11	29	H	Tranmere R	L	0-2	0-1	16		4790
12	Oct 5	A	Bristol C	L	0-3	0-2	—		10,718
13	13	H	Port Vale	D	1-1	0-0	19	Willis [54]	4348
14	20	A	Bury	L	1-2	1-0	19	Beckett [4]	2898
15	23	A	Stoke C	L	1-2	0-0	—	Reeves (pen) [64]	5141
16	27	H	Blackpool	L	0-1	0-0	19		5395
17	Nov 3	H	Cambridge U	W	2-0	0-0	18	Beckett 2 [59, 85]	3729
18	10	A	Cardiff C	L	1-2	1-2	18	D'Auria [45]	9516
19	20	A	Wigan Ath	D	1-1	0-0	—	Howard [71]	4071
20	24	H	Bournemouth	W	2-1	1-1	19	Reeves [35], Howard [89]	4353
21	Dec 1	A	Reading	W	1-0	1-0	19	Howard [10]	11,209
22	15	H	QPR	L	2-3	0-0	18	Reeves (pen) [61], Howard [79]	4611
23	21	D	Brighton & HA	D	2-2	0-1	—	Parrish [60], Innes [80]	6371
24	29	H	Notts Co	W	2-1	1-0	18	Innes [43], Allott [84]	5139
25	Jan 12	H	Oldham Ath	W	4-2	0-1	17	Allott [53], Hurst 2 [54, 90], Burt [66]	4716
26	19	A	Colchester U	W	2-1	1-0	16	Burt [17], Hurst [75]	4060
27	21	A	Brighton & HA	L	1-2	0-0	—	Willis [86]	4689
28	Feb 2	A	Tranmere R	D	0-0	0-0	18		8477
29	5	A	Peterborough U	D	1-1	1-0	—	Burt [45]	4401
30	9	H	Bury	W	2-0	0-0	15	Burt 2 [58, 90]	5132
31	12	H	Wycombe W	L	0-1	0-0	—		3654
32	16	A	Port Vale	L	1-4	0-1	16	Hurst [68]	5529
33	23	H	Northampton T	D	2-2	1-2	17	Ebdon [13], Burt [53]	4186
34	26	A	Swindon T	L	1-2	1-1	—	Hurst [39]	4580
35	Mar 2	A	Wrexham	W	1-0	1-0	17	Hurst [44]	3328
36	5	H	Huddersfield T	D	1-1	1-0	—	Booty [42]	4740
37	9	A	QPR	D	0-0	0-0	18		10,434
38	12	A	Brentford	D	0-0	0-0	—		5372
39	16	A	Reading	L	0-2	0-2	17		5145
40	19	H	Bristol C	W	2-1	1-0	—	Allott [21], Hurst [54]	3630
41	23	A	Stoke C	L	0-1	0-1	17		14,841
42	30	H	Cardiff C	L	0-2	0-2	18		5442
43	Apr 2	A	Cambridge U	L	1-4	0-3	—	Hurst [76]	2669
44	6	H	Wigan Ath	L	1-2	1-2	18	Allott (pen) [19]	3896
45	13	A	Bournemouth	L	1-3	0-1	18	Howson [87]	6068
46	20	H	Blackpool	W	2-1	1-0	18	Hurst [13], Burt [88]	4788

Final League Position: 18

GOALSCORERS

League (53): Hurst 9, Burt 7, Beckett 6, Howard 5, Allott 4 (1 pen), Reeves 4 (2 pens), Willis 4, Booty 2, Ebdon 2, Innes 2, Breckin 1, D'Auria 1, Edwards 1, Howson 1, Hyde 1, Parrish 1, Payne 1, Richardson 1.
Worthington Cup (1): Rowland 1.
FA Cup (4): Beckett 2, D'Auria 1, own goal 1.

Abbey N 46	Booty M 40	Edwards R 30+1	Breckin I 42	Blatherwick S 4+1	Payne S 44	Williams D 19+5	Ebdon M 29+2	Willis R 11+13	Beckett L 20+1	Rowland K 6+3	Reeves D 20+2	Ingledow J 12+5	Rushbury A —+3	Pearce G 5+2	Hyde G 8+1	Howard J 12+8	Richardson L 13+1	Jones M 1+5	D'Auria D 10+4	Moore S 1+1	Parrish S 11+9	Hitzlsperger T 5	Hurst G 22+1	Burt J 18+6	Allott M 19+2	Innes M 22+1	Hewitt J 1	Walsh D —+1	O'Hare A 19	Howson S 13	Buchanan W 3	Match No.
1	2	3	4	5[1]	6	7	8[2]	9[3]	10	11	12	13	14																			1
1	2	4[1]	5		6	7		8	10	3[3]	9	11		12	13																	2
1	2	3[1]	5		6	7	11	12	10[1]		9	4[2]	14	8	13																	3
1	2		5		6	7		11[1]	10		4	9		12	3	8																4
1	2		5		6	7[2]	12	11[1]	10		4	9		13	3	8																5
1	2		5		6	7	8		10		9				4	11	3															6
1	2	12	5		6	7[1]	8		10		9	13			4	11[2]	3															7
1	2	3	5		6	13	7		10		9	12[2]		4	9[1]	11																8
1	2	3	5		6	12	8		10[3]		9	13		4[2]	7	11[1]	14															9
1	2	3	5		6		7		10		9	4			8	11																10
1	2	3	5		6[1]	12	7	13	10		9	14		4	8[3]	11[2]																11
1	2	3	5		6	7		8	10		9[1]	4			11	12																12
1	2	3	5		6	7	8	9[1]	10		12	4			11																	13
1	2	3	5		6		8	7[1]	10		9	4[2]			11	12	13															14
1	2	3	5		6		7	12	10		9				11	4[1]	8															15
1	2	3	5		6		7		10		9				11[1]	12	8	4[2]	13													16
1	2	3	5		6		7	12	10		9[1]				11	8			4													17
1	2	3	5		6		8	12	10[1]		9	7		13	11[3]	14	4[2]															18
1	2	3	5		6		8		10		9	7[1]		12	11[2]	13	4															19
1	2	3	5		6		7		10		9[1]			8	11	12	4															20
1	2	3	5		6			12	10[1]		9			7		8	11	4														21
1	2	3	5		6				9					10	11	8[1]		4		7	12											22
1		3			6	7		12					5	10				4		11	8[1]	9	2									23
1		3			6	8		12					5					4		7	10	9	11	2[1]								24
1	2	3	5		6	8								12				4		7	10[1]	9	11									25
1	2[3]	3	5		6	8		12						14	13			4		7	10[2]	9[1]	11									26
1		3	5		6			12			4		2[2]					8		7	10	9[1]	11	13								27
1		3	5		6	8	12				4[1]									7	10	9	11		2							28
1		3	5		6	8	7[1]				4							12			10	9	11		2							29
1		3	5		6	8[1]	7	13			4[3]			12				14			10	9[2]	11		2							30
1	2[1]	3	5		6		7							8						12	10	9[1]	11		4							31
1	2	3	5		6									12				8		7	10	9[1]	11		4							32
1	2	3[1]	5		6	8	7											12		9	10		11		4							33
1	2		5		6		8	9										12		7	10[2]	13	11[1]		3	4						34
1	2		5		6		8	10[2]										12		7	13	9	11[1]		3	4						35
1	2		5		6	10[1]	8											12		7	12	9	11		3	4						36
1	2		4	5	6		8	9[1]										12		7		11			10	3						37
1	2		4	5[1]	6	12	8	13												7	9[2]		11		10	3						38
1	2		5		6	4[1]	8					13								7	9	12	11		10[2]	3						39
1	2		5		6			8[2]				13						12		7	10	9	11[1]		3	4						40
1	2		5		6		8													7	10	9			3	4	11					41
1	5		12	6												8[1]	13			7	10	9	11		3[2]	4	2					42
1	4		5[1]			13										12		14		8	7	10[2]	9[1]	11		3	6	2				43
1	2		5		12		13									10			8[3]	4	7	14	9[2]	11		3[1]	6					44
1	2		5		6[2]		8				13					12				10	7		9	11[1]		3	4					45
1	2	11[3]	5		6		8		10[1]											12	7	13	9	14		3[2]	4					46

Worthington Cup
First Round · Port Vale · (a) · 1-2

FA Cup
First Round · Stalybridge C · (a) · 3-0
Second Round · Southend U · (h) · 1-1
· · (a) · 0-2

COLCHESTER UNITED
Division 2

FOUNDATION

Colchester United was formed in 1937 when a number of enthusiasts of the much older Colchester Town club decided to establish a professional concern as a limited liability company. The new club continued at Layer Road which had been the amateur club's home since 1909.

Layer Rd Ground, Colchester, Essex CO2 7JJ.

Telephone: (01206) 508 800. *Fax:* (01206) 508 827
Club Shop: (01206) 508 809.
Soccer Centre: (01206) 572 378. *Lottery:* (01206) 508 820.

Ground Capacity: 7,341.

Record Attendance: 19,072 v Reading, FA Cup 1st rd, 27 November 1948.

Record Receipts: £35,431 v Burnley, Div 2, 26 February 2000.

Pitch Measurements: 110yd × 71yd.

Patron: The Mayor of Colchester.

Chairman: Peter Heard.

Directors: John Worsp, Peter Powell.

Chief Executive: Marie Partner.

Manager: Steve Whitton.

Assistant Manager/Coach: Geraint Williams.

Director of Youth: Micky Cook.

Physios: Frank Reepe, Graham Jones.

Consultant Physio: Ray Cole.

Secretary: Miss Sonya Constantine.

Corporate and Promotions Consultant: John Schultz.

Commercial and Marketing Manager: Jerry Carter.

Stadium Manager: David Blacknall.

Colours: Blue and white striped shirts, navy shorts, white stockings.

Change Colours: White shirts, navy shorts, navy stockings.

Year Formed: 1937.

Turned Professional: 1937.

Ltd Co.: 1937.

Club Nickname: 'The U's'.

First Football League Game: 19 August 1950, Division 3 (S), v Gillingham (a) D 0–0 – Wright; Kettle, Allen; Bearryman, Stewart, Elder; Jones, Curry, Turner, McKim, Church.

HONOURS

Football League: Promoted from Division 3 – 1997–98 (play-offs); Division 4 – Runners-up 1961–62.

FA Cup: best season: 6th rd, 1971.

Football League Cup: best season: 5th rd, 1975.

Auto Windscreens Shield: Runners-up 1997.

GM Vauxhall Conference: Winners 1991–92.

FA Trophy: Winners 1992.

IT'S A FACT !

In 1938–39, Colchester United won the Southern League and the Eastern Counties League and were runners-up in the Southern League Midweek Section and the Eastern Counties Cup.

Record League Victory: 9–1 v Bradford C, Division 4, 30 December 1961 – Ames; Millar, Fowler; Harris, Abrey, Ron Hunt; Foster, Bobby Hunt (4), King (4), Hill (1), Wright.

Record Cup Victory: 7–1 v Yeovil T (away), FA Cup 2nd rd (replay), 11 December 1958 – Ames; Fisher, Fowler; Parker, Milligan, Hammond; Williams (1), McLeod (2), Langman (4), Evans, Wright. 7–1 v Yeading, FA Cup 1st rd (replay), 22 November 1994 – Cheesewright; Betts, English, Cawley, Caesar, Locke (Dennis), Fry, Brown (2), Whitton (2) (Thompson), Kinsella (1), Abrahams (2).

Record Defeat: 0–8 v Leyton Orient, Division 4, 15 October 1989.

Most League Points (2 for a win): 60, Division 4, 1973–74.

Most League Points (3 for a win): 81, Division 4, 1982–83.

Most League Goals: 104, Division 4, 1961–62.

Highest League Scorer in Season: Bobby Hunt, 38, Division 4, 1961–62.

Most League Goals in Total Aggregate: Martyn King, 130, 1956–64.

Most League Goals in One Match: 4, Bobby Hunt v Bradford C, Division 4, 30 December 1961; 4, Martyn King v Bradford C, Division 4, 30 December 1961; 4, Bobby Hunt v Doncaster R, Division 4, 30 April 1962.

Most Capped Player: None.

Most League Appearances: Micky Cook, 613, 1969–84.

Youngest League Player: Lindsay Smith, 16 years 218 days v Grimsby T, 24 April 1971.

Record Transfer Fee Received: £2,250,000 from Newcastle U for Lomano Lua-Lua, September 2000.

Record Transfer Fee Paid: £50,000 to Norwich C for Adrian Coote, December 2001.

Football League Record: 1950 Elected to Division 3 (S); 1958–61 Division 3; 1961–62 Division 4; 1962–65 Division 3; 1965–66 Division 4; 1966–68 Division 3; 1968–74 Division 4; 1974–76 Division 3, 1976–77 Division 4; 1977–81 Division 3; 1981–90 Division 4; 1990–92 GM Vauxhall Conference; 1992–98 Division 3; 1998– Division 2.

MANAGERS

Ted Fenton 1946–48
Jimmy Allen 1948–53
Jack Butler 1953–55
Benny Fenton 1955–63
Neil Franklin 1963–68
Dick Graham 1968–72
Jim Smith 1972–75
Bobby Roberts 1975–82
Allan Hunter 1982–83
Cyril Lea 1983–86
Mike Walker 1986–87
Roger Brown 1987–88
Jock Wallace 1989
Mick Mills 1990
Ian Atkins 1990–91
Roy McDonough 1991–94
George Burley 1994
Steve Wignall 1995–99
Mick Wadsworth 1999
Steve Whitton August 1999–

LATEST SEQUENCES

Longest Sequence of League Wins: 7, 29.11.68 – 1.2.69.

Longest Sequence of League Defeats: 8, 9.10.54 – 4.12.54.

Longest Sequence of League Draws: 6, 21.3.77 – 11.4.77.

Longest Sequence of Unbeaten League Matches: 20, 22.12.56 – 19.4.57.

Longest Sequence Without a League Win: 20, 2.3.68 – 31.8.68.

TEN YEAR LEAGUE RECORD

		P	W	D	L	F	A	Pts	Pos
1991-92	Conf	42	28	10	4	98	40	94	1
1992-93	Div 3	42	18	5	19	67	76	59	10
1993-94	Div 3	42	13	10	19	56	71	49	17
1994-95	Div 3	42	16	10	16	56	64	58	10
1995-96	Div 3	46	18	18	10	61	51	72	7
1996-97	Div 3	46	17	17	12	62	51	68	8
1997-98	Div 3	46	21	11	14	72	60	74	4
1998-99	Div 2	46	12	16	18	52	70	52	18
1999-2000	Div 2	46	14	10	22	59	82	52	18
2000-01	Div 2	46	15	12	19	55	59	57	17

DID YOU KNOW ?

Vic Keeble was the first Colchester United player to score a hat-trick in the Football League, a feat he achieved in a spell of only 12 minutes against Plymouth Argyle on 17 March 1951.

COLCHESTER UNITED 2001–02 LEAGUE RECORD

Match No.	Date	Venue	Opponents	Result	H/T Score	Lg. Pos.	Goalscorers	Attendance
1	Aug 11	A	Chesterfield	W 6-3	3-1	—	Dunne [9], Booty (og) [26], Stockwell [37], Rapley [48], McGleish 2 [62, 78]	3939
2	18	H	Tranmere R	W 2-1	0-0	2	Rapley [84], McGleish [89]	3618
3	25	A	Wrexham	D 1-1	1-0	2	Stockwell [20]	2952
4	27	H	Port Vale	W 2-0	1-0	1	Keith [21], McGleish [46]	3611
5	Sept 1	A	Swindon T	L 0-1	0-0	3		4889
6	8	H	Northampton T	W 3-1	3-0	2	Rapley [7], McGleish (pen) [8], Hope (og) [42]	3705
7	15	A	Bristol C	L 1-3	1-1	5	Rapley [45]	9992
8	18	H	Oldham Ath	W 2-1	2-0	—	Izzet [10], McGleish [27]	2991
9	22	H	Notts Co	L 0-1	0-0	4		3796
10	26	A	Stoke C	L 0-3	0-1	—		9515
11	29	A	Brentford	L 1-4	1-2	11	McGleish [17]	5179
12	Oct 5	H	Reading	W 2-0	2-0	—	Rapley [8], McGleish [26]	3691
13	13	A	Blackpool	L 1-2	0-0	11	Izzet [86]	5546
14	20	H	Cambridge U	W 3-1	2-1	8	McGleish 2 [37, 87], Johnson G [42]	4684
15	23	H	Wycombe W	D 2-2	2-2	—	Stockwell [13], Rapley [28]	5186
16	27	A	Brighton & HA	L 0-1	0-1	9		6531
17	Nov 3	H	Bournemouth	L 1-2	1-2	13	Duguid [25]	4369
18	9	A	Wigan Ath	W 3-2	0-2	—	Stockwell 2 [13, 19], Johnson R [77]	5735
19	20	A	Cardiff C	D 1-1	0-1	—	Dunne [87]	8013
20	24	H	Bury	L 0-1	0-0	13		3534
21	Dec 1	A	QPR	D 2-2	2-1	12	Stockwell [29], Keith [39]	11,158
22	15	H	Peterborough U	W 2-1	1-1	11	McGleish [8], White [70]	3480
23	22	A	Huddersfield T	D 3-3	2-1	12	Duguid [9], Stockwell [23], McGleish [74]	3543
24	26	A	Northampton T	W 3-2	1-1	12	Sampson (og) [45], Barrett 2 [50, 66]	4740
25	29	A	Port Vale	L 1-3	0-2	12	Duguid [90]	4444
26	Jan 5	H	Wrexham	W 2-1	1-1	12	Stockwell [12], Bowry [78]	2835
27	12	A	Tranmere R	D 0-0	0-0	10		8387
28	19	H	Chesterfield	L 1-2	0-1	12	Barrett [49]	4060
29	22	A	Huddersfield T	L 1-2	0-2	—	White [83]	7179
30	26	A	Reading	L 0-3	0-1	12		12,743
31	30	H	Swindon T	L 1-3	1-0	—	Keith (pen) [41]	3132
32	Feb 2	H	Brentford	D 1-1	0-1	14	Coote [66]	3657
33	9	A	Cambridge U	W 2-1	0-1	13	Coote [68], Rapley [85]	3954
34	16	A	Blackpool	D 1-1	0-1	13	Keith (pen) [72]	3553
35	23	H	Bristol C	D 0-0	0-0	14		3558
36	26	A	Notts Co	D 1-1	1-0	—	White [36]	3140
37	Mar 2	A	Oldham Ath	L 1-4	1-2	15	Izzet [12]	5457
38	5	H	Stoke C	L 1-3	0-2	—	Duguid [54]	3866
39	9	A	Peterborough U	L 1-3	0-2	16	Barrett [87]	4625
40	16	H	QPR	W 3-1	1-0	16	Rapley 2 [12, 85], McGleish [53]	4903
41	23	H	Wycombe W	D 0-0	0-0	16		6737
42	30	H	Brighton & HA	L 1-4	0-3	17	Stockwell [88]	4881
43	Apr 2	A	Bournemouth	W 1-0	0-0	—	Maher (og) [62]	5908
44	6	H	Cardiff C	L 0-1	0-1	16		3970
45	13	H	Bury	W 3-1	1-0	16	McGleish [45], Coote 2 [72, 87]	5014
46	20	H	Wigan Ath	D 2-2	2-0	15	McGleish [42], MacDonald [45]	3672

Final League Position: 15

GOALSCORERS

League (65): McGleish 15 (1 pen), Rapley 9, Stockwell 9, Barrett 4, Coote 4, Duguid 4, Keith 4 (2 pens), Izzet 3, White 3, Dunne 2, Bowry 1, Johnson G 1, Johnson R 1, MacDonald 1, own goals 4.
Worthington Cup (3): Izzet 1, Keith 1, Stockwell 1.
FA Cup (2): Duguid 1, McGleish 1.

Woodman A 26	Dunne J 6 + 2	Johnson G 19 + 1	Pinault T 37 + 5	Fitzgerald S 36 + 1	Clark S 19 + 2	Izzet K 36 + 4	Gregory D 15 + 1	Bapley K 26 + 9	Stockwell M 45 + 1	McGleish S 44 + 2	Keith J 33 + 8	Bowry B 27 + 9	Duguid K 36 + 5	Morgan D 1 + 29	White A 28 + 5	Johnson R 13 + 3	Opara L — + 1	Barrett G 19 + 1	Coote A 5 + 14	Brown S 19	Halls J 6	Blatsis C 7	MacDonald C 2 + 2	Canham M — + 1	Chambers T — + 1	Knight R 1	Match No.
1	2	3[1]	4[2]	5	6	7	8	9	10[3]	11	12	13	14														1
1	2		4[1]	5	6	7	8	9[2]	10	11	3	12		13													2
1	2		4	5	6[2]	8[1]	7	9	10[1]	11	3	12		13	14												3
1	2[1]		4	5		7	8	9	10[2]	11[3]	3	13	12	14	6												4
1			4	5		7[1]	8	9[2]	10	11	3	12	2	13	6												5
1	12		4	5	6	7	8	9[2]	10[1]	11[3]	3	13	2	14													6
1	7		4	5	6[3]	12	8[1]	9	10	11[2]	3		2	13	14												7
1	8		4	5		7		9	10	11	3		2		6												8
1	12	8	4[2]	5[1]	13	7		9	10[3]	11	3		2	14	6												9
1	3		4[1]		6	7	8	9	10[2]	11		12	2	13	5												10
1	3		4		6	7	8	9[1]	10	11			2	12	5												11
1	3[2]	4			6	7[1]	8	9	12	11	13	10	2		5												12
1	3				6	7	8[1]	9	10[3]	11[2]	4		2	13	12	5	14										13
1	3		4		6	7		9[2]	10[1]	11	12	8	2	13		5											14
1	3		4		6	7		9[2]	10[1]	11	12	8	2	13		5											15
1	3		4[1]		6	7		9[2]	10	11	12	8	2	13		5											16
1	3[2]	12	5	6	7		8[1]	9	10	11	13	4	2	14													17
1	2	12	5			7		13	10[3]	9	3	8[1]	11	14	4	6											18
1	2	7	4	5				12	10[2]	9	3[1]	8	11	13		6											19
1	2[2]	7	4	5				9[1]	10	11	12	8	3	13		6											20
1			4	5	12			9[2]	10	11	3	8	7	13	2	6[1]											21
1			7	5	6			9[2]	10[1]	11	3	8	2	12	4	13											22
1			7	5[2]	6			10	11	3[1]	8	2	12	4	13		9[3]	14									23
1			7[1]		6	12		13	10[2]	11[3]	3	8	2		4	5	9	14									24
1			4		6	7		12	10[2]	11[1]	3	8	2		5	13	9	14									25
1			4[2]	12	6	7			10[1]	11		8	2		5	3	9	13									26
		12	5	6	7				10	11	3[2]	8[1]	2	13	4		9									1	27
			7	5		8			10[1]	11[2]	3		2	12	4		9	13	1	6							28
			8	5		7			10[1]	11[2]	3		2	12	4		9	13	1	6							29
		12	13	5		7			10	11	3[1]	8[2]	2		4		9		1	6							30
		6		5		7			10[2]	12	3	8	2	13	4		9	11[1]	1								31
		2		5	12				13	10[1]	11	3	8		4		9	7[2]	1	6							32
		4		5	12				10	11[1]	3	8[2]	2	13			9	7	1	6							33
		8[1]	12	5					14	10	11	3	2		4		9	7[3]	1	6[2]							34
			4	5		7			8[2]	10[1]	11	3	12	2			6		9	13	1						35
			4	5		7			8[2]	10[1]	11	3	12	2			6		9	13	1						36
			4	5		7	2	12	10	11[2]	3	8[1]					6		9	13	1						37
			4	5		7	12		10[1]	11		8[2]	2	13	6		3		9		1						38
			4	5		7		12	10	11[1]	13	8[3]	2	14	6[2]		3		9		1						39
			4	5		7	2	8	10[1]	11	3		12						9			6					40
			4	5		7	2	8	10[2]	11[3]	3		12						9[1]	14		6					41
			8	5		7			9[1]	10	11[2]	3		2	12	4[3]			13			6	14				42
			4	5		7			9	10[1]	11[2]	3	8	2		12			13			6					43
									10[2]	12	3	8[2]	2						11[1]	1		6	9	14	13		44
			4	5		7			10	9[3]	3	8[1]	11[3]	2	12				13			6	14		1		45
			4	5		7			10[1]	11[3]	3	8	12	13	2				14			6	9[2]				46

Worthington Cup
First Round   Portsmouth   (a)   2-1
Second Round   Barnsley   (h)   1-3

FA Cup
First Round   York C   (h)   0-0
　　　　　　　　　　　　　(a)   2-2

COVENTRY CITY   Division 1

FOUNDATION

Workers at Singers' cycle factory formed a club in 1883. The first
success of Singers' FC was to win the Birmingham Junior Cup in
1891 and this led in 1894 to their election to the Birmingham and
District League. Four years later they changed their name to
Coventry City and joined the Southern League in 1908 at which
time they were playing in blue and white quarters.

*Highfield Road Stadium, King Richard Street, Coventry
CV2 4FW.*

Telephone: (024) 7623 4000. *Fax:* (024) 7623 4099.
Ticket Office: (024) 7623 4020. *Ticket Office Fax:* (024)
7623 4023. *Sales & Marketing:* (024) 7623 4010.
ClubCall: 09068 121 166. *Website:* http://www.ccfc.co.uk
Email: info@ccfc.co.uk

Ground Capacity: 23,633.

Record Attendance: 51,455 v Wolverhampton W,
Division 2, 29 April 1967.

Record Receipts: £405,369 v Charlton Ath, FA Cup
5th rd, 29 January 2000.

Pitch Measurements: 110yd × 75yd.

President: G. Robinson MP.

HONOURS

Football League: Division 1 best
season: 6th, 1969–70; Division 2 –
Champions 1966–67; Division 3 –
Champions 1963–64; Division 3 (S) –
Champions 1935–36; Runners-up
1933–34; Division 4 – Runners-up
1958–59.

FA Cup: Winners 1987.

Football League Cup: Semi-final 1981,
1990.

European Competitions: European
Fairs Cup: 1970–71.

Chairman: M. C. McGinnity.
Deputy Chairman: J. F. W. Reason.
Directors: A. M. Jepson, J. F. W. Reason, D. A. Higgs, Miss B. Price, G. P. Hover.
Chief Executive: Graham Hover.

Manager: Gary McAllister. *Assistant Manager:* Eric Black. *Physio:* Stuart Collie.

Commercial: Ric Allison.

Stadium Manager: Don Blair.

Club Statistician: Jim Brown.

Colours: Sky blue shirts with navy mesh panels and navy collar, navy shorts with sky blue stitching, sky
blue stockings with navy piping.

Change Colours: Navy blue shirts with sky blue chest panel and white piping, navy shorts with white
piping, navy stockings with sky blue panel.

Year Formed: 1883.

Turned Professional: 1893.

Ltd Co.: 1907.

Previous Names: 1883, Singers FC; 1898, Coventry City FC.

Club Nickname: 'Sky Blues'.

Previous Grounds: 1883, Binley Road; 1887, Stoke Road; 1899, Highfield Road.

First Football League Game: 30 August 1919, Division 2, v Tottenham H (h) L 0–5 – Lindon;
Roberts, Chaplin, Allan, Hawley, Clarke, Sheldon, Mercer, Sambrooke, Lowes, Gibson.

IT'S A FACT !

On 9 February 2002, Coventry City won 6-1 at Crewe
Alexandra. It was their biggest away win in the Football
League since St Valentine's Day 1959, when they won
6-1 at Carlisle United.

Record League Victory: 9–0 v Bristol C, Division 3 (S), 28 April 1934 – Pearson; Brown, Bisby; Perry, Davidson, Frith; White (2), Lauderdale, Bourton (5), Jones (2), Lake.

Record Cup Victory: 7–0 v Scunthorpe U, FA Cup 1st rd, 24 November 1934 – Pearson; Brown, Bisby; Mason, Davidson, Boileau; Birtley (2), Lauderdale (2), Bourton (1), Jones (1), Liddle (1).

Record Defeat: 2–10 v Norwich C, Division 3 (S), 15 March 1930.

Most League Points (2 for a win): 60, Division 4, 1958–59 and Division 3, 1963–64.

Most League Points (3 for a win): 66, Division 1, 2001–02.

Most League Goals: 108, Division 3 (S), 1931–32.

Highest League Scorer in Season: Clarrie Bourton, 49, Division 3 (S), 1931–32.

Most League Goals in Total Aggregate: Clarrie Bourton, 171, 1931–37.

Most League Goals in One Match: 5, Clarrie Bourton v Bournemouth, Division 3S, 17 October 1931; 5, Arthur Bacon v Gillingham, Division 3S, 30 December 1933.

Most Capped Player: Magnus Hedman 44 (49), Sweden.

Most League Appearances: Steve Ogrizovic, 507, 1984–2000.

Youngest League Player: Gary McSheffrey, 16 years 198 days v Aston Villa, 27 February 1999.

Record Transfer Fee Received: £12,500,000 from Internazionale for Robbie Keane, July 2000.

Record Transfer Fee Paid: £6,000,000 to Wolverhampton W for Robbie Keane, August 1999.

Football League Record: 1919 Elected to Division 2; 1925–26 Division 3 (N); 1926–36 Division 3 (S); 1936–52 Division 2; 1952–58 Division 3 (S); 1958–59 Division 4; 1959–64 Division 3; 1964–67 Division 2; 1967–92 Division 1; 1992–2001 FA Premier League; 2001– Division 1.

LATEST SEQUENCES

Longest Sequence of League Wins: 6, 25.4.64 – 5.9.64.
Longest Sequence of League Defeats: 9, 30.8.19 – 11.10.19.
Longest Sequence of League Draws: 6, 28.9.96 – 16.11.96.
Longest Sequence of Unbeaten League Matches: 25, 26.11.66 – 13.5.67.
Longest Sequence Without a League Win: 19, 30.8.19 – 20.12.19.

MANAGERS

H. R. Buckle 1909–10
Robert Wallace 1910–13
  (Secretary-Manager)
Frank Scott-Walford 1913–15
William Clayton 1917–19
H. Pollitt 1919–20
Albert Evans 1920–24
Jimmy Kerr 1924–28
James McIntyre 1928–31
Harry Storer 1931–45
Dick Bayliss 1945–47
Billy Frith 1947–48
Harry Storer 1948–53
Jack Fairbrother 1953–54
Charlie Elliott 1954–55
Jesse Carver 1955–56
Harry Warren 1956–57
Billy Frith 1957–61
Jimmy Hill 1961–67
Noel Cantwell 1967–72
Bob Dennison 1972
Joe Mercer 1972–75
Gordon Milne 1972–81
Dave Sexton 1981–83
Bobby Gould 1983–84
Don Mackay 1985–86
George Curtis 1986–87
  (became Managing Director)
John Sillett 1987–90
Terry Butcher 1990–92
Don Howe 1992
Bobby Gould 1992–93
Phil Neal 1993–95
Ron Atkinson 1995–96
  (became Director of Football)
Gordon Strachan 1996–2001
Roland Nilsson 2001–02
Gary McAllister April 2002–

TEN YEAR LEAGUE RECORD

		P	W	D	L	F	A	Pts	Pos
1991-92	Div 1	42	11	11	20	35	44	44	19
1992-93	PR Lge	42	13	13	16	52	57	52	15
1993-94	PR Lge	42	14	14	14	43	45	56	11
1994-95	PR Lge	42	12	14	16	44	62	50	16
1995-96	PR Lge	38	8	14	16	42	60	38	16
1996-97	PR Lge	38	9	14	15	38	54	41	17
1997-98	PR Lge	38	12	16	10	46	44	52	11
1998-99	PR Lge	38	11	9	18	39	51	42	15
1999-2000	PR Lge	38	12	8	18	47	54	44	14
2000-01	PR Lge	38	8	10	20	36	63	34	19

DID YOU KNOW ?

Arguably Coventry City's finest First Division performance was the 4-0 win over Liverpool on 10 December 1983. It was the Merseyside club's biggest defeat for seven years and Terry Gibson scored a hat-trick.

COVENTRY CITY 2001–02 LEAGUE RECORD

Match No.	Date	Venue	Opponents	Result	H/T Score	Lg. Pos.	Goalscorers	Attendance
1	Aug 11	A	Stockport Co	W 2-0	1-0	—	Hughes [29], Carsley [75]	9329
2	19	H	Wolverhampton W	L 0-1	0-1	11		22,092
3	24	A	Bradford C	L 1-2	0-0	—	Bothroyd [78]	15,085
4	27	H	Nottingham F	D 0-0	0-0	15		18,467
5	Sept 8	H	Grimsby T	L 0-1	0-0	18		14,980
6	15	A	Sheffield U	W 1-0	0-0	13	Delorge [72]	16,168
7	19	H	Manchester C	W 4-3	2-1	—	Pearce (og) [16], Konjic [45], Hughes [66], Thompson [89]	18,804
8	22	H	Portsmouth	W 2-0	1-0	9	Bothroyd [17], Carsley [71]	18,303
9	25	A	Barnsley	D 1-1	0-0	—	Martinez [54]	11,692
10	29	A	Gillingham	W 2-1	2-0	9	Martinez [14], Chippo [45]	9435
11	Oct 14	A	Walsall	W 1-0	1-0	5	Thompson [14]	7515
12	17	H	Rotherham U	D 0-0	0-0	—		6582
13	21	H	Crewe Alex	W 1-0	1-0	4	Hughes (pen) [30]	15,788
14	24	A	Wimbledon	W 1-0	0-0	—	Thompson [75]	5883
15	27	H	Sheffield W	W 2-0	1-0	3	Safri [39], Hughes (pen) [64]	17,381
16	31	H	Preston NE	D 2-2	1-1	—	Thompson 2 [5, 78]	15,755
17	Nov 3	A	Millwall	L 2-3	0-0	4	Martinez [60], Bothroyd [68]	15,748
18	17	H	Burnley	L 0-2	0-2	8		16,849
19	25	A	Birmingham C	L 0-2	0-1	9		18,279
20	28	A	Crystal Palace	W 2-0	0-0	—	Delorge [62], Mills [80]	13,695
21	Dec 1	H	Wimbledon	W 3-1	2-1	5	Hughes [20], Mills [43], Thompson [79]	17,303
22	9	H	Watford	L 0-2	0-0	7		13,251
23	12	A	WBA	L 0-1	0-0	—		22,543
24	15	A	Norwich C	L 0-2	0-1	8		17,889
25	23	H	Bradford C	W 4-0	2-0	6	Hughes 2 (1 pen) [41, 49 (p)], Thompson [43], Joachim [81]	14,977
26	26	A	Grimsby T	W 1-0	1-0	6	Hughes [40]	7568
27	29	A	Nottingham F	L 1-2	1-0	8	Chippo [31]	22,706
28	Jan 13	A	Wolverhampton W	L 1-3	0-0	10	Bothroyd [90]	21,009
29	19	H	Stockport Co	D 0-0	0-0	9		12,448
30	29	A	Crystal Palace	W 3-1	2-0	—	Bothroyd [12], Hall M [36], McSheffery [75]	16,197
31	Feb 2	H	Gillingham	L 1-2	0-1	10	Bothroyd [86]	14,337
32	6	H	Rotherham U	W 2-0	0-0	—	Konjic [79], Hughes [90]	12,893
33	9	A	Crewe Alex	W 6-1	2-1	6	Delorge 2 [37, 57], Hughes 3 [45, 48, 70], Thompson [67]	7835
34	19	H	Walsall	W 2-1	1-1	—	Thompson [21], Chippo [82]	13,736
35	23	H	Barnsley	W 4-0	3-0	6	Chippo [1], Thompson 2 [19, 44], Mills [60]	15,092
36	26	A	Portsmouth	L 0-1	0-0	—		12,336
37	Mar 3	A	Manchester C	L 2-4	1-3	6	Mills 2 [19, 88]	33,335
38	6	H	Sheffield U	W 1-0	1-0	—	Thompson [45]	12,963
39	9	H	Norwich C	W 2-1	0-1	4	Hughes 2 (1 pen) [51 (p), 90]	16,744
40	16	A	Watford	L 0-3	0-2	5		15,833
41	24	H	Birmingham C	D 1-1	0-0	5	Healy [61]	17,945
42	29	A	Sheffield W	L 1-2	1-1	—	Healy [21]	21,470
43	Apr 1	H	WBA	L 0-1	0-1	8		21,513
44	6	A	Preston NE	L 0-4	0-2	10		15,665
45	12	H	Millwall	L 0-1	0-1	—		15,335
46	21	A	Burnley	L 0-1	0-0	11		18,751

Final League Position: 11

GOALSCORERS

League (59): Hughes 14 (4 pens), Thompson 12, Bothroyd 6, Mills 5, Chippo 4, Delorge 4, Martinez 3, Carsley 2, Healy 2, Konjic 2, Hall M 1, Joachim 1, McSheffrey 1, Safri 1, own goal 1.
Worthington Cup (2): Carsley 1, Thompson 1.
FA Cup (0).

Kirkland C 1	Nilsson R 9	Hall M 27 + 2	Williams P 4 + 1	Konjic M 38	Carsley L 25 + 1	Thompson D 35 + 2	Chippo Y 29 + 5	Hughes L 35 + 3	O'Neill K 7 + 4	Bothroyd J 24 + 7	Shaw R 29 + 3	Hedman M 34	Strachan G — + 1	Zuniga Y 1 + 6	Quinn B 18 + 4	Edworthy M 18 + 2	Breen G 30	Eustace J 5 + 1	Safri V 32 + 1	Joachim J 4 + 12	Guerrero I 3 + 1	Delorge L 21 + 7	Martinez J 5 + 6	Goram A 6 + 1	Normann R — + 2	Antonelius T 3 + 2	Davenport C 1 + 2	McSheffrey G 1 + 7	Fowler L 5 + 8	Mills L 19 + 1	Betts R 4 + 5	Healy C 17	Flowers T 5	Carbonari H 5	Trollope P 5 + 1	Pead C 1	Match No.
1	2	3	4	5[1]	6	7	8	9	10	11	12																										1
	2	3	4		6	7	8[1]	9	10[2]	11	5	1	12	13																							2
	2	3	4		6	7[1]	12	9	10	11	5	1			13	8[1]																					3
	2	3	4[1]	5	6	7[1]	8	9	10	11		1	12	13																						4
	2	3		5	6	12	8[2]		10	11[1]		1		13					4	7[3]		14	9														5
	2[2]	3		5	6	7		9	12	13		1							4	11	10[3]	8[1]	14														6
		3		5	6	7	8[1]	9	10[2]	12	2	1							4	11		13															7
				5	6	7[2]	8	9	10[3]	12	3	1		2					4	11[1]		13	14														8
	2				6	7[2]	8[1]	9	10[3]	12	5	1		3					4	11		13	14														9
	2[1]	13		5[1]	7		8		12	6				14	3	4[2]			11			9	10	1													10
		3		5	6	7	8	9	12		2	1							4	11[2]	10[1]																11
		3		5	6	7	8[1]	9	10		2	1							4	11	12																12
		3		5	6	7	8	9	10[1]		2	1							4	11	12	1															13
		12		5	6	7		9	10[2]		3								2	4	11	8[1]	13	1													14
				5	6	7		9	10[2]		3				12	2	4		11[1]		8[3]	13	1	14													15
				5	6	7		9	10[1]		3					2	4		11		8[2]	12	1	13													16
				5	6	7		9	12		3	1				2	4		11		8	10															17
	11				6		9[1]		3	1				8[2]	2	4			7	10					5	12	13										18
		3		5	6		8	9	10[1]		1				2	4		11	12	7[2]						13											19
		3[2]		5	6	7	4[3]	9		1				2		11	12		8						13	14	10[1]										20
		3		5	6	7	4	9		1				2		11	12		8						13	10[1]											21
		3[2]		5	6[1]		4	9	12	1[0]				2		11	13		8	15						10											22
		3		5		7[2]		9	4[1]	6				2		13	12		8	1						11	10										23
				5		7	6	9[1]	4	3	1				2		11	12		8[2]						13	10										24
		3[3]		5	12	7	6[1]	9	4	1				14	2		11	13		8							10[2]										25
				5		7	6	9	4	1				3		11				12	2					8[1]	10										26
				5		7	6	9	4	1				3[2]	2		11	12			13		4			8[1]	10										27
					6	7			12	5	1				2	4			9	8[2]			3			11	10	13									28
		3		5	8	7			6	1				13	4			12	2	9[1]						10	11[2]										29
		3			6			10	5	1				2	4			9[3]	7[2]						13	14	11	12	8[1]								30
		3[2]			6		9	12	5	1				2	4			7							14	13	10[1]	11[1]	8								31
		3		5	11		12	9[1]		1				2	4[2]	8		7							13		14	12	10[1]	13	6[2]						32
		3		5	11		9			1				2	4	8		7[1]									14	12	10[1]	13	6[2]						33
		3		5	11	12	9[1]			1				2	4	8		7[2]									13		10	6	1						34
		3[1]		5	7[2]	9				1				2	4	8	12	11[3]									13	10	14	6	1						35
		3		5	9	7				1				2	4	8	12	11[1]										10	6	1							36
		3		5		7	9	12		1				2[1]	4	8												10	11	6	1						37
				5		7[3]	13	9[1]	11[2]		3				2	4	8	12										10	14	6	1						38
				5		11	7	9	10		3	1			2	4	8													6							39
				5		11	7	9	10[1]		3	1			2	4	8												12	6							40
				5		11	12	9[2]	10[1]		3	1			13	2			8											6			4	7		41
				5		11[1]	12	9	10[2]		3	1			13	2[1]		4	14	8										6			5	7		42
		12		5		7	9[2]	13			1			11		4[1]	3[1]	8										14		10	6	2		4[1]	11	43
	2	3		5		12	7[2]	13	9		1					10	8													6	1			4		44
				5		7	9	10[2]			3	1			2		11[1]		12									13		6			4	8		45
				5		7	12				4	1			3	8[2]												10	9	2	6			13	11[1]	46

Worthington Cup
Second Round   Peterborough U   (a)   2-2
Third Round   Chelsea   (h)   0-2

FA Cup
Third Round   Tottenham H   (h)   0-2

CREWE ALEXANDRA   Division 2

FOUNDATION

The first match played at Crewe was on 1 December 1877 against Basford, the leading North Staffordshire team of that time. During the club's history they have also played in a number of other leagues including the Football Alliance, Football Combination, Lancashire League, Manchester League, Central League and Lancashire Combination. Two former players, Aaron Scragg in 1899 and Jackie Pearson in 1911, had the distinction of refereeing FA Cup finals. Pearson was also capped for England against Ireland in 1892.

Football Ground, Gresty Road, Crewe CW2 6EB.

Telephone: (01270) 213 014. **ClubCall:** 09068 121 647.

Ground Capacity: 10,046.

Record Attendance: 20,000 v Tottenham H, FA Cup 4th rd, 30 January 1960.

Record Receipts: £102,877 v Everton, FA Cup 5th rd replay, 26 February 2002.

Pitch Measurements: 112yd × 74yd.

President: N. Rowlinson.

Chairman: J. Bowler.

Vice-chairman: N. Hassall.

Directors: D. Rowlinson, R. Clayton, J. McMillan, D. Gradi.

Manager: Dario Gradi MBE.

Secretary: Mrs Gill Palin.

Marketing Manager: Alison Bowler.

Colours: Red shirts, white shorts, red stockings.

Change Colours: Blue shirts, navy shorts, white stockings.

Year Formed: 1877.

Turned Professional: 1893.

Ltd Co.: 1892.

Club Nickname: 'Railwaymen'.

First Football League Game: 3 September 1892, Division 2, v Burton Swifts (a) L 1–7 – Hickton; Moore, Cope; Linnell, Johnson, Osborne; Bennett, Pearson (1), Bailey, Barnett, Roberts.

Record League Victory: 8–0 v Rotherham U, Division 3 (N), 1 October 1932 – Foster; Pringle, Dawson; Ward, Keenor (1), Turner (1); Gillespie, Swindells (1), McConnell (2), Deacon (2), Weale (1).

HONOURS

Football League: Promoted from Division 2 1996–97 (play-offs).

FA Cup: Semi-final 1888.

Football League Cup: best season: 3rd rd, 1975, 1976, 1979, 1993, 1999, 2000, 2002.

Welsh Cup: Winners 1936, 1937.

IT'S A FACT !

On 20 November 2001, Dario Gradi celebrated his 1,000th match in charge of Crewe Alexandra in a 2-2 draw at Norwich City. Before the match, City manager Nigel Worthington presented him with a cut-glass decanter.

Record Cup Victory: 8–0 v Hartlepool U, Auto Windscreens Shield 1st rd, 17 October 1995 – Gayle; Collins (1), Booty, Westwood (Unsworth), Macauley (1), Whalley (1), Garvey (1), Murphy (1), Savage (1) (Rivers (1p)), Lennon, Edwards, (1 og).

Record Defeat: 2–13 v Tottenham H, FA Cup 4th rd replay, 3 February 1960.

Most League Points (2 for a win): 59, Division 4, 1962–63.

Most League Points (3 for a win): 83, Division 2, 1994–95.

Most League Goals: 95, Division 3 (N), 1931–32.

Highest League Scorer in Season: Terry Harkin, 35, Division 4, 1964–65.

Most League Goals in Total Aggregate: Bert Swindells, 126, 1928–37.

Most League Goals in One Match: 5, Tony Naylor v Colchester U, Division 3, 24 April 1993.

Most Capped Player: Clayton Ince (29), Trinidad & Tobago.

Most League Appearances: Tommy Lowry, 436, 1966–78.

Youngest League Player: Steve Walters, 16 years 119 days v Peterborough U, 6 May 1988.

Record Transfer Fee Received: £3,000,000 Derby Co for Seth Johnson, May 1999.

Record Transfer Fee Paid: £650,000 to Torquay U for Rodney Jack, June 1998.

Football League Record: 1892 Original Member of Division 2; 1896 Failed re-election; 1921 Re-entered Division 3 (N); 1958–63 Division 3; 1963–64 Division 3; 1964–68 Division 4; 1968–69 Division 3; 1969–89 Division 4; 1989–91 Division 3; 1991–92 Division 4; 1992–94 Division 3; 1994–97 Division 2; 1997–2002 Division 1; 2002– Division 2.

MANAGERS

W. C. McNeill 1892–94
  (Secretary-Manager)
J. G. Hall 1895–96
  (Secretary-Manager)
R. Roberts *(1st team Secretary-Manager)* 1897
J. B. Blomerley 1898–1911
  (Secretary-Manager, continued as Hon. Secretary to 1925)
Tom Bailey *(Secretary only)* 1925–38
George Lillycrop *(Trainer)* 1938–44
Frank Hill 1944–48
Arthur Turner 1948–51
Harry Catterick 1951–53
Ralph Ward 1953–55
Maurice Lindley 1956–57
Willie Cook 1957–58
Harry Ware 1958–60
Jimmy McGuigan 1960–64
Ernie Tagg 1964–71
  (continued as Secretary to 1972)
Dennis Viollet 1971
Jimmy Melia 1972–74
Ernie Tagg 1974
Harry Gregg 1975–78
Warwick Rimmer 1978–79
Tony Waddington 1979–81
Arfon Griffiths 1981–82
Peter Morris 1982–83
Dario Gradi June 1983–

LATEST SEQUENCES

Longest Sequence of League Wins: 7, 30.4.94 – 3.9.94.

Longest Sequence of League Defeats: 10, 16.4.79 – 22.8.79.

Longest Sequence of League Draws: 5, 31.8.87 – 18.9.87.

Longest Sequence of Unbeaten League Matches: 17, 25.3.95 – 16.9.95.

Longest Sequence Without a League Win: 30, 22.9.56 – 6.4.57.

TEN YEAR LEAGUE RECORD

		P	W	D	L	F	A	Pts	Pos
1991-92	Div 4	42	20	10	12	66	51	70	6
1992-93	Div 3	42	21	7	14	75	56	70	6
1993-94	Div 3	42	21	10	11	80	61	73	3
1994-95	Div 2	46	25	8	13	80	68	83	3
1995-96	Div 2	46	22	7	17	77	60	73	5
1996-97	Div 2	46	22	7	17	56	47	73	6
1997-98	Div 1	46	18	5	23	58	65	59	11
1998-99	Div 1	46	12	12	22	54	78	48	18
1999-2000	Div 1	46	14	9	23	46	67	51	19
2000-01	Div 1	46	15	10	21	47	62	55	14

DID YOU KNOW ?

In 1967–68, Crewe Alexandra's promotion season included an unbeaten home record for the first time in the club's history. It comprised 13 wins and ten draws.

CREWE ALEXANDRA 2001–02 LEAGUE RECORD

Match No.	Date	Venue	Opponents	Result	H/T Score	Lg. Pos.	Goalscorers	Attendance
1	Aug 11	A	Grimsby T	L	0-1	0-0	—	5368
2	18	H	Sheffield W	L	0-2	0-1	23	7933
3	25	A	Manchester C	L	2-5	2-2	23	Hulse [44], Little [45]	32,844
4	28	H	Millwall	W	1-0	0-0	—	Hulse [85]	5913
5	Sept 8	H	Walsall	W	2-1	1-0	14	Jack [38], Lunt [51]	6809
6	15	A	Barnsley	L	0-2	0-0	19		10,976
7	18	H	Wimbledon	L	0-4	0-1	—		5563
8	22	H	Watford	W	1-0	1-0	18	Hulse [37]	6507
9	25	A	Burnley	D	3-3	2-0	—	Lunt [17], Foster [28], Hulse [89]	13,964
10	29	H	Birmingham C	D	0-0	0-0	19		7314
11	Oct 13	H	Preston NE	W	2-1	1-0	17	Ashton [32], Foster [90]	7746
12	16	A	Wolverhampton W	W	1-0	0-0	—	Hulse [53]	22,569
13	21	A	Coventry C	L	0-1	0-1	16		15,788
14	24	H	Stockport Co	D	0-0	0-0	—		6679
15	27	A	Sheffield U	L	0-1	0-1	16		15,185
16	30	A	Rotherham U	D	2-2	2-1	—	Brammer [9], Lunt [12]	5971
17	Nov 2	H	Bradford C	D	2-2	1-1	—	Ashton [35], Foster [87]	6597
18	10	H	Gillingham	D	0-0	0-0	16		5419
19	17	A	Crystal Palace	L	1-4	1-4	18	Ashton [41]	21,802
20	20	A	Norwich C	D	2-2	1-1	—	Walton [6], Brammer [86]	15,710
21	24	H	Nottingham F	L	0-3	0-1	20		8402
22	Dec 1	A	Stockport Co	W	1-0	0-0	19	Foster [67]	5308
23	8	A	Portsmouth	W	4-2	2-1	18	Hulse [9], Sodje [29], Charnock [65], Lunt [68]	14,430
24	15	H	WBA	D	1-1	1-1	18	Thomas [31]	8154
25	26	A	Walsall	L	1-2	0-2	19	Jack [60]	7325
26	29	A	Millwall	L	0-2	0-1	20		11,630
27	Jan 12	A	Sheffield W	L	0-1	0-1	20		16,737
28	19	H	Grimsby T	W	2-0	2-0	19	Thomas [9], Smith S (pen) [25]	5974
29	29	H	Norwich C	W	1-0	0-0	—	Ashton [74]	6285
30	Feb 9	H	Coventry C	L	1-6	1-2	20	Hulse [45]	7835
31	20	H	Wolverhampton W	L	1-4	0-0	—	Jack [88]	8371
32	23	H	Burnley	L	1-2	0-1	21	Hulse [63]	6458
33	Mar 2	A	Watford	W	1-0	0-0	21	Ashton [73]	15,199
34	5	H	Barnsley	W	2-0	1-0	—	Ashton [43], Street [90]	6258
35	12	H	Manchester C	L	1-3	0-2	—	Jack [55]	10,092
36	16	A	Portsmouth	D	1-1	1-1	20	Hulse [37]	7170
37	20	A	Preston NE	D	2-2	1-2	—	Lunt [17], Hulse [77]	13,396
38	23	A	Bradford C	L	0-2	0-1	21		12,846
39	26	A	WBA	L	1-4	1-2	—	Ashton [39]	21,303
40	30	H	Sheffield U	D	2-2	2-1	21	Hulse [43], Foster [45]	7855
41	Apr 1	A	Gillingham	L	0-1	0-1	23		7748
42	4	A	Wimbledon	L	0-2	0-0	—		5007
43	7	H	Crystal Palace	D	0-0	0-0	23		6724
44	10	A	Birmingham C	L	1-3	0-2	—	Jack [85]	28,615
45	13	A	Nottingham F	D	2-2	0-0	22	Jack [77], Hulse [81]	22,870
46	21	H	Rotherham U	W	2-0	2-0	22	Jack [26], Sodje [33]	7904

Final League Position: 22

GOALSCORERS

League (47): Hulse 12, Ashton 7, Jack 7, Foster 5, Lunt 5, Brammer 2, Sodje 2, Thomas 2, Charnock 1, Little 1, Smith S 1 (pen), Street 1, Walton 1.
Worthington Cup (6): Brammer 1, Hulse 1, Little 1, Richards 1, Smith S 1 (pen), Watson 1.
FA Cup (7): Ashton 3, Foster 1, Rix 1, Thomas 1, Vaughan 1.

Bankole A 28	Navarro A 7	Smith S 41 + 1	Foster S 29 + 5	Walton D 29 + 2	Charnock P 21 + 2	Grant J 1	Lunt K 45	Jack R 24 + 9	Tait P 3 + 9	Sorvel N 31 + 7	Little C 8 + 9	Richards M 1 + 3	Brammer D 29 + 1	Sodje E 34 + 2	Collins W 13 + 7	Hulse R 40 + 1	Macauley S 9	Jones S 1 + 5	Barrett G 2 + 1	Thomas G 8 + 6	Street K 2 + 7	Wright D 29 + 1	Ashton D 29 + 2	Rix B 6 + 15	Ince C 18 + 1	Vaughan D 11 + 2	McCready C — + 1	Walker R — + 1	Whalley G 7	Match No.
1	2	3	4	5	6¹	7	8	9	10²	11³	12	13	14																	1
1	2	3		5	6³		8	9	10²		12	13	11¹	4	14	7														2
1	2¹	3					8	9³			12		10²	13	4	6	11	7	5	14										3
1	2	3					8	9			12		13	10²	4¹	6	11	7	5											4
1	2	3	12				8	9			13		10²	4	6¹	11	7	5												5
1	2	3	6				8			12			10	4	13	11	7	5²		9¹										6
1	2	3	6				8²			12			10¹	4		11	7	5		9	13									7
1		3	2	5	6²			9³		11		10¹	4	8	12	7				13	14									8
1		3	4	5	6		8	9¹		11			2	10		7				13	12									9
1		3	12	5	6		8	9¹		11			4²	10	13	7			14		2¹									10
1		3	2	5	6¹		8	9		11			4	10		7					12									11
1		3	2	5			8	9¹		11			4	6	12	7²				13		10								12
1		3	2	5			8	9¹		11			4	6		7						10	12							13
1		3	2	5			8	9		11			4¹	6		7				12		10								14
		3³	2	5	12		8			11¹	13		4	6		7		9²				14	10		1					15
		3	4	5	6		8			11				7¹								2	10		1					16
1		3	4	5	6		8			11¹			10	7								2	9	12						17
1		3	4	5	6¹		8	9		11	12		10	7								2								18
1		3	4	5	6¹		8	12		11²			10³	7						13		2	9	14						19
1		3	4	5	6		8						10	7						11¹		2	9	12						20
1		3	4	5	6		8			12	10²		7				13			11¹		2	9							21
		3	4		6¹		8	12					10	5		7				11		2	9		1					22
		3	4		6		8	12					10	5		7				11		2	9¹		1					23
		3	4		6		8	12	13				10	5		7²				11		2	9¹		1					24
		3			6²		8	9					4	5	7¹					11		2	10	12	1	13				25
		3	4				8	9¹		11				5¹	6²		12					2	10	13	1	7	14			26
		3	4				8	12	13	11				5		7				10³		2	9²	14	1	6¹				27
1		3	4				8	9²	13	12			6	5						11¹		2	10	14		7²				28
1			4	3			8	9¹		11¹			6	5	13	12						2	10	14		7²				29
1⁰		3	4¹	12			8²			11			6	5		7						2	9	13	15	10				30
		3	4				8³	12	13	11			6	5	14	9¹						2	10²	7	1					31
		3³	12	4			8	13					6	5	7¹	9						2	10²	14	1	11				32
		3	4				8			11	12			5	6	9						2	10	7¹	1					33
		3	4				8			11	12			5	6¹	9			13			2	10	7²	1					34
		4	3³				8	12		11		7¹		5		9			13			2	10²	14	1	6				35
	12	4	3				8	13	10⁵	11	7²			5		9					2	4	2¹		1	6				36
		3	4	12			8	10		11				5	2	9			13				7²	1		6¹				37
		3	4	6²			8	10		11				5		9			12			2	13	7¹	1					38
		3	4				8²	10		11	12			6	7¹	5						2⁸	9	13	1			14		39
		3	4				8	10²		11			12	2	9	5¹		6					13	1				7		40
1		3	2				8			12				5	9	6	13		4²				11¹	10				7		41
1		12	2	5	6¹		8			11	13			9³	4²	14				3		10						7		42
1		3	12	6			4	8		11				5¹		9						2	10	13				7²		43
1		3		4			8	12	13	11				5		9²						2	10²	14		6		7³		44
1		3		6			4	8		11				5		9						2	10					7		45
1		3	12	6¹			4	8	13	11³				5	14	9²						2	10					7		46

Worthington Cup

First Round	York C	(a)	2-2	
Second Round	Rushden & D	(h)	2-0	
Third Round	Ipswich T	(h)	2-3	

FA Cup

Third Round	Sheffield W	(h)	2-1	
Fourth Round	Rotherham U	(a)	4-2	
Fifth Round	Everton	(a)	0-0	
		(h)	1-2	

CRYSTAL PALACE   Division 1

FOUNDATION

There was a Crystal Palace club as early as 1861 but the present organisation was born in 1905 after the formation of a club by the company that controlled the Crystal Palace (building), had been rejected by the FA who did not like the idea of the Cup Final hosts running their own club. A separate company had to be formed and they had their home on the old Cup Final ground until 1915.

Selhurst Park, London SE25 6PU.

Telephone: (020) 8768 6000. *Fax:* (020) 8771 5311.
Lottery Office: (020) 8768 6094.
Club Shop: (020) 8768 6100.
Dial-A-Seat Ticketline: (020) 8771 8841.
PR and Communications: (020) 8768 6020.
Fax: (020) 8768 6114. *ClubCall:* 09068 400 333.

Ground Capacity: 26,400.

Record Attendance: 51,482 v Burnley, Division 2, 11 May 1979.

Record Receipts: £327,124 v Manchester U, FA Premier League, 21 April 1993 (League); £336,583 v Chelsea, Coca-Cola Cup 5th rd, 6 January 1993.

Pitch Measurements: 110yd × 74yd.

Chairman: Simon Jordan.

Manager: Trevor Francis.

Physio: George Cooper.

Stadium Manager: Vic Worrall.

Club Secretary: Mike Hurst.

PR and Communications Manager: Terry Byfield.

Colours: Red and blue vertical striped shirts, red shorts, red stockings with blue tops.

Change Colours: All white with red and blue sash on shirt.

Year Formed: 1905. *Turned Professional:* 1905. *Ltd Co.:* 1905.

Club Nickname: 'The Eagles'.

Previous Grounds: 1905, Crystal Palace; 1915, Herne Hill; 1918, The Nest; 1924, Selhurst Park.

First Football League Game: 28 August 1920, Division 3, v Merthyr T (a) L 1–2 – Alderson; Little, Rhodes; McCracken, Jones, Feebury; Bateman, Conner, Smith, Milligan (1), Whibley.

Record League Victory: 9–0 v Barrow, Division 4, 10 October 1959 – Rouse; Long, Noakes; Truett, Evans, McNichol; Gavin (1), Summersby (4 incl. 1p), Sexton, Byrne (2), Colfar (2).

HONOURS

Football League: Division 1 – Champions 1993–94; Promoted from Division 1, 1996–97 (play-offs); Division 2 – Champions 1978–79; Runners-up 1968–69; Division 3 – Runners-up 1963–64; Division 3 (S) – Champions 1920–21; Runners-up 1928–29, 1930–31, 1938–39; Division 4 – Runners-up 1960–61.
FA Cup: Runners-up 1990.
Football League Cup: Semi-final 1993, 1995, 2001.
Zenith Data Systems Cup: Winners 1991.

IT'S A FACT !

Frank Morris turned professional with Crystal Palace in 1956. Once a right-back, he switched to left-wing and as an ABA amateur boxer, had represented Great Britain as a lightweight against Germany.

Record Cup Victory: 8–0 v Southend U, Rumbelows League Cup 2nd rd (1st leg), 25 September 1989 – Martyn; Humphrey (Thompson (1)), Shaw, Pardew, Young, Thorn, McGoldrick, Thomas, Bright (3), Wright (3), Barber (Hodges (1)).

Record Defeat: 0–9 v Burnley, FA Cup 2nd rd replay, 10 February 1909. 0–9 v Liverpool, Division 1, 12 September 1990.

Most League Points (2 for a win): 64, Division 4, 1960–61.

Most League Points (3 for a win): 90, Division 1, 1993–94.

Most League Goals: 110, Division 4, 1960–61.

Highest League Scorer in Season: Peter Simpson, 46, Division 3 (S), 1930–31.

Most League Goals in Total Aggregate: Peter Simpson, 153, 1930–36.

Most League Goals in One Match: 6, Peter Simpson v Exeter C, Division 3S, 4 October 1930.

Most Capped Player: Eric Young, 19 (21), Wales.

Most League Appearances: Jim Cannon, 571, 1973–88.

Youngest League Player: Phil Hoadley, 16 years 112 days v Bolton W, 27 April 1968.

Record Transfer Fee Received: £4,500,000 from Tottenham H for Chris Armstrong, June 1995.

Record Transfer Fee Paid: £2,750,000 to RC Strasbourg for Valerien Ismael, January 1998.

Football League Record: 1920 Original Members of Division 3; 1921–25 Division 2; 1925–58 Division 3 (S); 1958–61 Division 4; 1961–64 Division 3; 1964–69 Division 2; 1969–73 Division 1; 1973–74 Division 2; 1974–77 Division 3; 1977–79 Division 2; 1979–81 Division 1; 1981–89 Division 2; 1989–92 Division 1; 1992–93 FA Premier League; 1993–94 Division 1; 1994–95 FA Premier League; 1995–97 Division 1; 1997–98 FA Premier League; 1998– Division 1.

LATEST SEQUENCES

Longest Sequence of League Wins: 8, 9.2.21 – 26.3.21.

Longest Sequence of League Defeats: 8, 10.1.98 – 14.3.98.

Longest Sequence of League Draws: 5, 30.12.78 – 24.2.79.

Longest Sequence of Unbeaten League Matches: 18, 22.2.69 – 13.8.69.

Longest Sequence Without a League Win: 20, 3.3.62 – 8.9.62.

MANAGERS

John T. Robson 1905–07
Edmund Goodman 1907–25
  (had been Secretary since 1905 and afterwards continued in this position to 1933)
Alec Maley 1925–27
Fred Mavin 1927–30
Jack Tresadern 1930–35
Tom Bromilow 1935–36
R. S. Moyes 1936
Tom Bromilow 1936–39
George Irwin 1939–47
Jack Butler 1947–49
Ronnie Rooke 1949–50
Charlie Slade and Fred Dawes
  (Joint Managers) 1950–51
Laurie Scott 1951–54
Cyril Spiers 1954–58
George Smith 1958–60
Arthur Rowe 1960–62
Dick Graham 1962–66
Bert Head 1966–72 *(continued as General Manager to 1973)*
Malcolm Allison 1973–76
Terry Venables 1976–80
Ernie Walley 1980
Malcolm Allison 1980–81
Dario Gradi 1981
Steve Kember 1981–82
Alan Mullery 1982–84
Steve Coppell 1984–93
Alan Smith 1993–95
Steve Coppell *(Technical Director)* 1995–96
Dave Bassett 1996–97
Steve Coppell 1997–98
Attilio Lombardo 1998
Terry Venables *(Head Coach)* 1998–99
Steve Coppell 1999–2000
Alan Smith 2000–01
Steve Bruce 2001
Trevor Francis November 2001–

TEN YEAR LEAGUE RECORD

		P	W	D	L	F	A	Pts	Pos
1991-92	Div 1	42	14	15	13	53	61	57	10
1992-93	PR Lge	42	11	16	15	48	61	49	20
1993-94	Div 1	46	27	9	10	73	46	90	1
1994-95	PR Lge	42	11	12	19	34	49	45	19
1995-96	Div 1	46	20	15	11	67	48	75	3
1996-97	Div 1	46	19	14	13	78	48	71	6
1997-98	PR Lge	38	8	9	21	37	71	33	20
1998-99	Div 1	46	14	16	16	58	71	58	14
1999-2000	Div 1	46	13	15	18	57	67	54	15
2000-01	Div 1	46	12	13	21	57	70	49	21

DID YOU KNOW ?

Crystal Palace won a marathon FA Cup second round tie against Notts County in 1923–24, succeeding after three goalless draws with a 2-1 win at Villa Park.

CRYSTAL PALACE 2001–02 LEAGUE RECORD

Match No.	Date	Venue	Opponents	Result	H/T Score	Lg. Pos.	Goalscorers	Attendance
1	Aug 11	A	Rotherham U	W 3-2	1-2	—	Freedman (pen) [39], Riihilahti [57], Smith [77]	6994
2	18	H	Stockport Co	W 4-1	0-0	2	Riihilahti [52], Morrison 2 [68, 90], Freedman [85]	15,760
3	25	A	Nottingham F	L 2-4	1-2	8	Freedman 2 [28, 50]	18,239
4	Sept 8	H	Millwall	L 1-3	1-1	12	Morrison [45]	21,641
5	15	A	Portsmouth	L 2-4	1-2	15	Rodger [11], Freedman [70]	18,149
6	18	H	Grimsby T	W 5-0	2-0	—	Kirovski [32], Popovic 2 [39, 51], Freedman [65], Morrison [90]	13,970
7	22	H	Barnsley	W 1-0	0-0	10	Riihilahti [90]	15,433
8	25	A	Sheffield U	W 3-1	1-0	—	Smith [12], Freedman (pen) [78], Hopkin [90]	14,180
9	29	H	Sheffield W	W 4-1	3-1	5	Freedman 2 [6, 14], Morrison 2 [26, 52]	17,066
10	Oct 13	H	Wimbledon	W 4-0	2-0	4	Morrison [33], Kirovski [42], Riihilahti [79], Brown (og) [85]	20,009
11	16	H	Bradford C	W 2-0	1-0	—	Morrison 2 [18, 90]	15,721
12	20	A	Wolverhampton W	W 1-0	1-0	1	Kirovski [45]	26,471
13	23	A	Burnley	L 0-1	0-1	—		14,713
14	28	H	Norwich C	W 3-2	1-0	2	Morrison 2 [41, 53], Freedman [65]	19,553
15	31	H	WBA	L 0-1	0-0	—		17,273
16	Nov 3	A	Walsall	D 2-2	1-2	3	Hopkin [30], Freedman [78]	6795
17	17	H	Crewe Alex	W 4-1	4-1	3	Walton (og) [25], Morrison [31], Kirovski [34], Freedman [45]	21,802
18	21	A	Gillingham	L 0-3	0-3	—		9396
19	24	A	Preston NE	L 1-2	1-0	6	Freedman [16]	15,264
20	28	A	Coventry C	L 0-2	0-0	—		13,695
21	Dec 1	H	Burnley	L 1-2	1-1	8	Morrison [38]	18,457
22	8	H	Manchester C	W 2-1	2-0	6	Freedman [31], Kirovski [45]	22,080
23	11	A	Birmingham C	L 0-1	0-0	—		20,119
24	15	A	Watford	L 0-1	0-1	7		16,499
25	20	H	Nottingham F	D 1-1	1-1	—	Morrison [37]	15,645
26	26	A	Millwall	L 0-3	0-0	10		16,630
27	29	A	Bradford C	W 2-1	1-1	9	Berhalter [34], Benjamin [46]	14,233
28	Jan 13	A	Stockport Co	W 1-0	0-0	8	Freedman [67]	5541
29	16	H	Gillingham	W 3-1	1-1	—	Morrison 2 [3, 65], Freedman [87]	17,646
30	19	H	Rotherham U	W 2-0	0-0	6	Morrison [55], Smith [79]	17,311
31	29	H	Coventry C	L 1-3	0-2	—	Freedman [57]	16,197
32	Feb 2	A	Sheffield W	W 3-1	3-1	5	Morrison [31], Freedman [35], Smith [37]	20,099
33	7	A	Wolverhampton W	L 0-2	0-1	—		18,475
34	16	A	Wimbledon	D 1-1	0-1	6	Morrison [80]	13,564
35	23	H	Sheffield U	L 0-1	0-0	8		18,009
36	26	A	Barnsley	W 4-1	1-1	—	Freedman [29], Riihilahti [56], Akinbiyi [83], Gray [85]	11,207
37	Mar 2	A	Grimsby T	L 2-5	0-3	7	Gray [84], Morrison [80]	5924
38	5	H	Portsmouth	D 0-0	0-0	—		15,915
39	9	H	Watford	L 0-2	0-1	8		16,817
40	16	A	Manchester C	L 0-1	0-1	10		33,637
41	23	H	Walsall	W 2-0	0-0	10	Morrison [77], Freedman (pen) [80]	21,038
42	30	H	Norwich C	L 1-2	0-2	10	Morrison [50]	21,251
43	Apr 1	H	Birmingham C	D 0-0	0-0	11		19,598
44	7	A	Crewe Alex	D 0-0	0-0	11		6724
45	13	H	Preston NE	W 2-0	0-0	10	Hopkin [55], Akinbiyi [64]	21,361
46	21	A	WBA	L 0-2	0-1	10		26,712

Final League Position: 10

GOALSCORERS

League (70): Morrison 22, Freedman 20 (3 pens), Kirovski 5, Riihilahti 5, Smith 4, Hopkin 3, Akinbiyi 2, Gray 2, Popovic 2, Benjamin 1, Berhalter 1, Rodger 1, own goals 2.
Worthington Cup (7): Black 2, Morrison 2, Freedman 1 (pen), Riihilahti 1, Rodger 1.
FA Cup (0).

Kolinko A 18+1	Smith J 28+4	Gray J 35+8	Austin D 27+8	Zhiyi F 2	Riihilahti A 45	Mullins H 43	Kirovski J 25+11	Morrison C 45	Freedman D 39+1	Hopkin D 13+7	Berhalter G 6+8	Rodger S 29+7	Black T 5+20	Rubins A —+7	Thomson S 10+13	Popovic T 20	Clarke M 28	Harrison C 4+2	Kabba S 1+3	Vickers S 6	Routledge W —+2	Edwards C 9	Symons K 9	Benjamin T 5+1	Gooding S —+1	Fleming C 17	Granville D 16	Murphy S 11	Akinbiyi A 9+5	Carasso C —+1	Frampton A 1+1	Match No.
1	2	3	4	5	6	7	8[1]	9	10	11[2]	12	13																				1
1	2	3	4[1]	5	6	7		9	10[3]	12	8	13	14		11																	2
1	2	3			6	7	12	9	10	4	13	8[2]	14		11[3]	5[1]																3
	2	11	4		6[2]	7	12	9	10			8	13			5	1	3[1]														4
	2		4		6	7	11	9	10		12	8[1]	13			5	1	3[1]	14													5
	2	3	4		6	7	11[3]	9	10[1]		12	8[2]	14		13	5	1															6
	2	3			6	7	11[2]	9	10		12	8[1]	14		13	5	1	4														7
	2	3	12		6	7	11[1]	9	10[2]			13	8			5	1	4														8
	2[1]	3	12		6[2]	7	11[3]	9	10		14	8	13			5	1	4														9
	2	3	12		6	7	11	9	10[2]			13	8[3]		14	5	1	4[1]														10
	2	3	4		6	7	11[1]	9	10[2]		12	13	8			5	1															11
	2	3	12		6	7	11[2]	9	10[1]			13	8			5	1	4														12
	2[1]	3			6	7	10	9		11		8[2]	12		13	5	1	4														13
	2	3	4		6	7	11	9	10		12	8[1]				5	1															14
	2[1]	3	4		6	7	11[3]	9	10			13	8		12	5[2]	1				14											15
		3	2		6	5	11	9	10	7		4	8				1															16
15		3	2		6[1]	5	11	9	10	7			8		12		1[0]				4											17
		3	4		6	2	11[2]	9	10	7	13		8[1]		12		1				5											18
		3	4		6	2	11	9	10				8		7		1				5											19
		3	4		6	2	11	9[2]	10	7[1]			8		12		1				13	5										20
		3	4		6	2	11	9	10				5		8		1				7											21
1	2[1]	3	12		6	7	11[2]	9[1]	10				8		13						14	4	5									22
1	2[1]	3	12		6	7	11		10				8[3]		14	13					9[2]	4	5									23
1	2				6	7[1]	12	9	10	11[3]			8[2]		14	13					3	4	5									24
1	2		12		6		13	9	10[2]	7	14				11			3[1]				4	5	8								25
1	2[3]	3			6	11[1]		9		7			8		12			13				4	5[2]	10	14							26
1		3[1]			6	2	11	9		7		4			8	5		12						10								27
1	13	14			6	7	12[2]	9	10[3]				11[1]			5							4	8		2	3					28
1	12	11[2]			6	7		9	10				13			5							4	8		2	3					29
1	12	13			6	7	11[1]	9	10				8[2]			5							4	14		2	3					30
1	2[3]	8	12		6	7		9	10				13	14		5[1]							4[2]			3	11					31
1	2[1]	7[2]	4		6		12	9	10		13		8													3	11	5				32
1		12			6	4		9	10	7[1]			8													2	3	5	11			33
	2	12	4		6	7		9	10			14	8[1]		13		1										3[3]	5	11[2]			34
	2[1]	12	5		4	11[2]	9		7	6			8[3]	13			14		1								3		10			35
	2	11	4		6	7	12	9	10[3]		13		8[2]				1										3	5	14			36
	8[2]	11	12		6	7		9	10		13					4	1									2[3]	3	5	14			37
	12	11[2]	4		6	8		9	10				7				1									2[1]	3	5	13			38
	2	11	4		6	8	12	9	10				7[3]	13			1										3[2]	5	14			39
	2[2]	11	4		6	7	12	9	10[3]		13		8				1										3	5	14			40
		11	4		6	7	8[2]	9	12		14		13				1									2[3]	3[1]	5	10			41
		12	4		6	7	13	9	10		14		8				1									2	3[1]	5[3]	11[2]			42
		12	4		6	7		9	10[2]		13		8			1[0]										2	3	5	11	15		43
1		7	4		6	5	9[2]	10		12	13[3]		8[1]													2	3	11			14	44
1		11[3]	4		6	7		9	12		13[3]					5					14					2	3	10	8[1]			45
1		4			6[1]	7	12	9		11			8[3]	13	14	5										2	3	10[2]				46

Worthington Cup
First Round   Leyton Orient   (a)   4-2
Second Round   Everton   (a)   1-1
Third Round   Sheffield W   (a)   2-2

FA Cup
Third Round   Newcastle U   (a)   0-2

DARLINGTON   Division 3

FOUNDATION

A football club was formed in Darlington as early as 1861 but the present club began in 1883 and reached the final of the Durham Senior Cup in their first season, losing to Sunderland in a replay after complaining that they had suffered from intimidation in the first. On 5 April 1884, Sunderland had defeated Darlington 4-3. Darlington's objection was upheld by the referee and the replay took place on 3 May. The new referee for the match was Major Marindin, appointed by the Football Association to ensure fair play. Sunderland won 2-0. The following season Darlington won this trophy and for many years were one of the leading amateur clubs in their area.

Feethams Ground, Darlington DL1 5JB.

Telephone: (01325) 240 240.

Fax: (01325) 240 500.

Ground Capacity: 8,500.

Record Attendance: 21,023 v Bolton W, League Cup 3rd rd, 14 November 1960.

Record Receipts: £32,300 v Rochdale, Division 4, 11 May 1991.

Pitch Measurements: 110yd × 74yd.

President: A. Noble.

Chairman: George Reynolds.

Vice-chairman: G. Hodgson.
Manager: Tommy Taylor.

Assistant Manager: Mick Tait.

Football Secretary: Lisa Charlton.

Colours: White and black with red piping.

Change Colours: Red, black and white.

Year Formed: 1883.

Turned Professional: 1908.

Ltd Co.: 1891.

Club Nickname: 'The Quakers'.

First Football League Game: 27 August 1921, Division 3 (N), v Halifax T (h) W 2–0 – Ward; Greaves, Barbour; Dickson (1), Sutcliffe, Malcolm; Dolphin, Hooper (1), Edmunds, Wolstenholme, Winship.

Record League Victory: 9–2 v Lincoln C, Division 3 (N), 7 January 1928 – Archibald; Brooks, Mellen; Kelly, Waugh, McKinnell; Cochrane (1), Gregg (1), Ruddy (3), Lees (3), McGiffen (1).

HONOURS

Football League: Division 2 best season: 15th, 1925–26; Division 3 (N) – Champions 1924–25; Runners-up 1921–22; Division 4 – Champions 1990–91; Runners-up 1965–66.

FA Cup: best season: 5th rd, 1958.

Football League Cup: best season: 5th rd, 1968.

GM Vauxhall Conference: Champions 1989–90.

IT'S A FACT !

Despite failing to score in their opening three games of 1965–66, Darlington finished second in Division 4 on goal average behind Doncaster Rovers and won promotion.

Record Cup Victory: 7–2 v Evenwood T, FA Cup 1st rd, 17 November 1956 – Ward; Devlin, Henderson; Bell (1p), Greener, Furphy; Forster (1), Morton (3), Tulip (2), Davis, Moran.

Record Defeat: 0–10 v Doncaster R, Division 4, 25 January 1964.

Most League Points (2 for a win): 59, Division 4, 1965–66.

Most League Points (3 for a win): 85, Division 4, 1984–85.

Most League Goals: 108, Division 3 (N), 1929–30.

Highest League Scorer in Season: David Brown, 39, Division 3 (N), 1924–25.

Most League Goals in Total Aggregate: Alan Walsh, 90, 1978–84.

Most League Goals in One Match: 5, Tom Ruddy v South Shields, Division 2, 23 April 1927; 5, Maurice Wellock v Rotherham U, Division 3N, 15 February 1930.

Most Capped Player: Jason Devos, 3, Canada.

Most League Appearances: Ron Greener, 442, 1955–68.

Youngest League Player: Dale Anderson, 16 years 254 days v Chesterfield, 4 May 1987.

Record Transfer Fee Received: £400,000 from Dundee U for Jason Devos, October 1998.

Record Transfer Fee Paid: £95,000 to Motherwell for Nick Cusack, January 1992.

Football League Record: 1921 Original Member Division 3 (N); 1925–27 Division 2; 1927–58 Division 3 (N); 1958–66 Division 4; 1966–67 Division 3; 1967–85 Division 4; 1985–87 Division 3; 1987–89 Division 4; 1989–90 GM Vauxhall Conference; 1990–91 Division 4; 1991– Division 3.

LATEST SEQUENCES

Longest Sequence of League Wins: 6, 6.2.00 – 7.3.00.

Longest Sequence of League Defeats: 8, 31.8.85 – 19.10.85.

Longest Sequence of League Draws: 5, 31.12.88 – 28.1.89.

Longest Sequence of Unbeaten League Matches: 17, 27.4.68 – 19.10.68.

Longest Sequence Without a League Win: 19, 27.4.88 – 8.11.88.

MANAGERS

Tom McIntosh 1902–11
W. L. Lane 1911–12
  (Secretary-Manager)
Dick Jackson 1912–19
Jack English 1919–28
Jack Fairless 1928–33
George Collins 1933–36
George Brown 1936–38
Jackie Carr 1938–42
Jack Surtees 1942
Jack English 1945–46
Bill Forrest 1946–50
George Irwin 1950–52
Bob Gurney 1952–57
Dick Duckworth 1957–60
Eddie Carr 1960–64
Lol Morgan 1964–66
Jimmy Greenhalgh 1966–68
Ray Yeoman 1968–70
Len Richley 1970–71
Frank Brennan 1971
Ken Hale 1971–72
Allan Jones 1972
Ralph Brand 1972–73
Dick Conner 1973–74
Billy Horner 1974–76
Peter Madden 1976–78
Len Walker 1978–79
Billy Elliott 1979–83
Cyril Knowles 1983–87
Dave Booth 1987–89
Brian Little 1989–91
Frank Gray 1991–92
Ray Hankin 1992
Billy McEwan 1992–93
Alan Murray 1993–95
Paul Futcher 1995
David Hodgson/Jim Platt
  (Director of Coaching) 1995
Jim Platt 1995–96
David Hodgson 1996–2000
Gary Bennett 2000–01
Tommy Taylor October 2001–

TEN YEAR LEAGUE RECORD

		P	W	D	L	F	A	Pts	Pos
1991-92	Div 3	46	10	7	29	56	90	37	24
1992-93	Div 3	42	12	14	16	48	53	50	15
1993-94	Div 3	42	10	11	21	42	64	41	21
1994-95	Div 3	42	11	8	23	43	57	41	20
1995-96	Div 3	46	20	18	8	60	42	78	5
1996-97	Div 3	46	14	10	22	64	78	52	18
1997-98	Div 3	46	14	12	20	56	72	54	19
1998-99	Div 3	46	18	11	17	69	58	65	11
1999-2000	Div 3	46	21	16	9	66	36	79	4
2000-01	Div 3	46	12	13	21	44	56	49	20

DID YOU KNOW

On 26 January 2002, Mark Sheeran began as a striker and finished as a sweeper, coming on as a 73rd minute substitute against Luton Town. He scored two goals, but finished the day as usual cleaning out the dressing rooms.

DARLINGTON 2001–02 LEAGUE RECORD

Match No.	Date	Venue	Opponents	Result	H/T Score	Lg. Pos.	Goalscorers	Attendance
1	Aug 11	A	Southend U	L	0-1	0-0	—		4725
2	18	H	Kidderminster H	W	2-0	0-0	11	Ford (pen) [69], Mellanby [72]	3677
3	25	A	Hartlepool U	W	2-1	2-1	6	Atkinson [35], Mellanby [42]	4842
4	27	H	Bristol R	W	1-0	0-0	3	Conlon [67]	4487
5	Sept 1	A	Lincoln C	D	1-1	1-0	3	Ford (pen) [20]	3021
6	8	H	Carlisle U	D	2-2	1-2	7	Wainwright [45], Conlon [90]	4677
7	15	A	Torquay U	L	1-2	0-0	8	Ford [52]	2065
8	18	H	Leyton Orient	W	3-0	1-0	—	Conlon [45], Heckingbottom [66], Harper [86]	3357
9	22	H	Exeter C	W	4-0	1-0	4	Hodgson [5], Convery [62], Mellanby [67], Ford [82]	4039
10	25	A	Macclesfield T	D	1-1	0-1	—	Conlon [77]	1556
11	29	H	Rushden & D	D	0-0	0-0	6		4365
12	Oct 5	A	Luton T	L	2-5	1-1	—	Mellanby [25], Wainwright [50]	7219
13	13	H	Mansfield T	L	0-1	0-0	7		4021
14	23	A	Swansea C	L	0-2	0-0	—		2926
15	27	H	Hull C	L	0-1	0-1	14		5163
16	Nov 3	A	Halifax T	D	2-2	1-1	13	Campbell [16], Wainwright [71]	2192
17	6	A	Shrewsbury T	L	0-3	0-0	—		3084
18	10	H	Oxford U	W	1-0	0-0	9	Healy [74]	3358
19	20	H	Rochdale	W	1-0	0-0	—	Clark (pen) [78]	3362
20	24	A	Scunthorpe U	L	1-7	0-4	13	Chillingworth [73]	3662
21	Dec 1	H	York C	W	3-1	2-0	11	Clark [23], Conlon 2 [27, 75]	4014
22	15	A	Plymouth Arg	L	0-1	0-0	12		5041
23	29	A	Bristol R	L	0-1	0-0	17		7567
24	Jan 12	A	Kidderminster H	L	0-1	0-0	17		2756
25	19	H	Southend U	D	2-2	1-0	17	Heckingbottom [37], Ford (pen) [58]	3365
26	23	A	Cheltenham T	D	0-0	0-0	—		2808
27	26	H	Luton T	W	3-2	1-1	15	Pearson [29], Sheeran 2 [81, 88]	3560
28	29	H	Lincoln C	W	2-1	0-0	15	Heckingbottom [66], Sheeran [90]	2984
29	Feb 2	A	Rushden & D	L	1-2	0-1	14	Liddle [55]	4383
30	5	A	Carlisle U	W	3-1	1-1	—	Ford [1], Clark [52], Liddle [82]	5226
31	9	H	Shrewsbury T	D	3-3	1-1	12	Conlon [45], Clark [47], Hodgson [77]	3444
32	12	H	Cheltenham T	L	0-2	0-2	—		3338
33	16	A	Mansfield T	L	2-4	1-3	12	Clark (pen) [23], Sheeran [74]	5107
34	19	H	Hartlepool U	D	1-1	1-0	—	Clark [37]	6339
35	23	H	Torquay U	L	1-3	0-1	14	Clark [69]	3119
36	26	A	Leyton Orient	D	0-0	0-0	—		3284
37	Mar 2	A	Exeter C	L	2-4	1-1	16	Maddison [33], Wainwright [62]	3117
38	5	H	Macclesfield T	L	0-1	0-0	—		2729
39	16	H	York C	L	0-2	0-0	18		3903
40	23	H	Swansea C	D	0-0	0-0	19		2915
41	30	A	Hull C	W	2-1	1-0	17	Conlon [17], Clark [78]	8642
42	Apr 1	H	Halifax T	W	5-0	2-0	16	Clark 2 (1 pen) [9, 16 (p)], Conlon [60], Ford [64], Sheeran [89]	3401
43	6	A	Rochdale	L	1-3	1-3	16	Conlon [4]	3055
44	13	H	Scunthorpe U	W	2-1	1-0	16	Clark 2 (1 pen) [34 (p), 73]	4218
45	15	H	Plymouth Arg	L	1-4	1-3	—	Clark (pen) [34]	4089
46	20	A	Oxford U	W	2-1	0-0	15	Naylor [72], Sheeran [77]	6167

Final League Position: 15

GOALSCORERS

League (60): Clark 13 (5 pens), Conlon 10, Ford 7 (3 pens), Sheeran 6, Mellanby 4, Wainwright 4, Heckingbottom 3, Hodgson 2, Liddle 2, Atkinson 1, Campbell 1, Chillingworth 1, Convery 1, Harper 1, Healy 1, Maddison 1, Naylor 1, Pearson 1.
Worthington Cup (0).
FA Cup (5): Wainwright 2, Campbell 1, Chillingworth 1, Conlon 1.

	Collett A 28	Harper S 15+8	Betts S 29	Liddle C 31	Brightwell D 22	Ford M 34+1	Hodgson R 24+12	Convery M 6+11	Conlon B 35	Maddison N 24+6	Atkinson B 35	Mellanby D 22+2	Jackson K 1+10	Wainwright N 32+3	Heckingbottom P 40+2	Jeannin A 11	Brunwell P 16+6	Marcelle C —+3	Marsh A 1	Campbell P 8+8	Reed A 7	Healy B 1+1	Caldwell G 4	Chillingworth D 2+2	Clark I 28	McGurk D 10+2	Pearson G 9	Sheeran M 1+21	Finch K 11+1	Rundle A 5+7	Kilty M 1	Porter C 7	Naylor G 6	Keltie C —+1	Match No.
	1	2	3	4	5	6¹	7	8	9²	10	11	12	13																						1
	1	2	3	4	5	6	12	13	9	10	11²	8³	14	7¹																					2
	1	2	3	4	5	6	12		9²	10¹	11	8		7	13																				3
	1	2	3	4	5	6		8	12	9	11¹	10		7																					4
	1	2	3	4	5	6¹		8	12	9	11			10	13	7²																			5
	1	2³	3	4	5	6		8²	12	9	11			10	13	7¹	14																		6
	1		3	4		6	7		9	8	11	10¹	12		2	5																			7
	1	12	3	4		6	7¹	13	9	8²	11	10			2	5																			8
	1	12	3	4		6	7²	8¹	9		11	10			2	5	13																		9
	1	12	3	4		6	7	8¹	9		11	10			2	5																			10
	1	12	3	4		6	7¹	8²	9¹		11	10	14	13	2	5																			11
	1		3	4				8¹	9		11	10	12	7	2	5	6																		12
	1	2¹	3	4				12	9	13	11	10³		7	8	5	6³	14																	13
	1	12	3	4				8	9	6	11	10²		7¹	2	5	13																		14
	1	12	3¹	4				13	9	8	11	10³			2	5	6	14		7²															15
	1	2	3	4					9	10		12		7	6	5	11			8¹															16
	1	2¹	3	4				12	13	9	8		14	7²	6	5	11			10³															17
	1		3		5			8	12	9	11	10¹		7	4	6²	2	13																	18
	1		3		5	12		8	13		14	7²		4	6		10	2							9³	11¹									19
	1		3		5	7	8¹	12	9					4	6		10¹	2							13	11									20
	1		3		5	6		8	9		11			7¹	4										2	12	10								21
	1		3		5				12	11	10			7	4	6	13								2	9²	8								22
	1		3		4			8		10	7	5		12	11											2	9								23
	1		3		4	7	8¹	10²	9	12	5	6	13		11³											2		14							24
	1		3	4	5	6			9	8	10			7	2												11								25
	1		3		4				9	8	11	10¹		7	2										6		5	12							26
	1	12		4		8	13	9²		10²	11			7¹	2										3		5	14							27
	1³	2		4		6	8¹		9	11²	7				3					10						5		12	15	13					28
		2		4		6			9	12	11			7	3		13			14						8¹		5²	10²	1					29
		2		4		6²			9	12	11³			7	3		13			10						5		14	1	8³			2¹		30
				4		6			12	9	11			7	3		13			10						5²		14	1	8²			2¹		31
		12		4		6²			9	13	11	10³		7	2			3¹								5		14	1	8					32
		12							9	6	11	10²		7	3		4	2								5		13	1	8¹					33
		2		5		12			9	6	11			7	4		10²	3								13			1	8¹					34
		2²		4		6			12	9	7			11³	10¹		3			8						5		13	1	14					35
		2		5		6			9¹	13	11			7	4					8						10	3	12²	1						36
		2		5		6	13		12²	9³	11			7	4					8¹						10	3	14	1						37
		2		4	5	6	12	8¹	9²		11			7	3											10³			1	13			14		38
				4	5¹	6			9	11³	7			2	3²		12			8						13	10	14	1						39
				4		6	8		11²	12	7			5	13		2			10¹							3	14			1		9²		40
				4		6	7		9²	11¹	3			12	5		8			2						13		14	1		1		10³		41
				4		6	7¹	12	9		8			3	5					11						2		14	1		1		10¹		42
				4		6	7¹		9	8	12			3	13		5²			11						2		14	1		1		10¹		43
				4		6¹	7³		8		11		12	3	2		5			10						13		14	1		1		9²		44
				4		6	7²	9³	8		11			5	2¹		12			10						3		13	14	1	1				45
			3	4		6	7		10					5	2¹		8²			11						12		14	1		1		9³	13	46

Worthington Cup
First Round   Sheffield U   (h)   0-1

FA Cup
First Round   Kidderminster H   (a)   1-0
Second Round   Altrincham   (a)   2-1
Third Round   Peterborough U   (h)   2-2
                                       (a)   0-2

DERBY COUNTY   Division 1

FOUNDATION

Derby County was formed by members of the Derbyshire County Cricket Club in 1884, when football was booming in the area and the cricketers thought that a football club would help boost finances for the summer game. To begin with, they sported the cricket club's colours of amber, chocolate and pale blue, and went into the game at the top immediately entering the FA Cup.

Pride Park Stadium, Derby DE24 8XL.

Telephone: (01332) 202 202. *Fax:* (01332) 667 519.
ClubCall: 09068 121 187.

Ground Capacity: 33,597.

Record Attendance: 41,826 v Tottenham H, Division 1, 20 September 1969.

Record Receipts: £425,804 v Huddersfield T, FA Cup 5th rd replay, 24 February 1999.

Pitch Measurements: 110yd × 72yd.

Chairman: L. V. Pickering.

Director: F. Vinton.

Manager: John Gregory.

First Team Coach: Billy McEwan.

Medical Manager: Peter Melville.

Chief Executive: Keith Loring.

Secretary: Keith Pearson ACIS.

General Sales Manager: Andy Dawson.

Colours: White shirts with black piping, black shorts, white stockings.

Change Colours: Navy blue shirts, navy blue shorts with white trim, navy blue stockings.

Year Formed: 1884.

Turned Professional: 1884.

Ltd Co.: 1896.

Club Nickname: 'The Rams'.

Previous Grounds: 1884, Racecourse Ground; 1895, Baseball Ground; 1997, Pride Park.

First Football League Game: 8 September 1888, Football League, v Bolton W (a) W 6–3 – Marshall; Latham, Ferguson, Williamson; Monks, W. Roulstone; Bakewell (2), Cooper (2), Higgins, H. Plackett, L. Plackett (2).

HONOURS

Football League: Division 1 – Champions 1971–72, 1974–75; Runners-up 1895–96, 1929–30, 1935–36, 1995–96; Division 2 – Champions 1911–12, 1914–15, 1968–69, 1986–87; Runners-up 1925–26; Division 3 (N) Champions 1956–57; Runners-up 1955–56.

FA Cup: Winners 1946; Runners-up 1898, 1899, 1903.

Football League Cup: Semi-final 1968.

Texaco Cup: Winners 1972.

European Competitions: *European Cup:* 1972–73, 1975–76. *UEFA Cup:* 1974–75, 1976–77. *Anglo-Italian Cup:* Runners-up 1993.

IT'S A FACT *!*

On 22 November 1987, Derby County appeared live on television for the first time. It was also goalkeeper Peter Shilton's 1,000th competitive club match and John Gregory scored the second goal in a 2-0 win over Chelsea.

Record League Victory: 9–0 v Wolverhampton W, Division 1, 10 January 1891 – Bunyan; Archie Goodall, Roberts; Walker, Chalmers, Roulston (1); Bakewell, McLachlan, Johnny Goodall (1), Holmes (2), McMillan (5). 9–0 v Sheffield W, Division 1, 21 January 1899 – Fryer; Methven, Staley; Cox, Archie Goodall, May; Oakden (1), Bloomer (6), Boag, McDonald (1), Allen, (1 og).

Record Cup Victory: 12–0 v Finn Harps, UEFA Cup 1st rd 1st leg, 15 September 1976 – Moseley; Thomas, Nish, Rioch (1), McFarland, Todd (King), Macken, Gemmill, Hector (5), George (3), James (3).

Record Defeat: 2–11 v Everton, FA Cup 1st rd, 1889–90.

Most League Points (2 for a win): 63, Division 2, 1968–69 and Division 3 (N), 1955–56 and 1956–57.

Most League Points (3 for a win): 84, Division 3, 1985–86 and Division 3, 1986–87.

Most League Goals: 111, Division 3 (N), 1956–57.

Highest League Scorer in Season: Jack Bowers, 37, Division 1, 1930–31; Ray Straw, 37 Division 3 (N), 1956–57.

Most League Goals in Total Aggregate: Steve Bloomer, 292, 1892–1906 and 1910–14.

Most League Goals in One Match: 6, Steve Bloomer v Sheffield W, Division 1, 2 January 1899.

Most Capped Player: Deon Burton, 40, Jamaica.

Most League Appearances: Kevin Hector, 486, 1966–78 and 1980–82.

Youngest League Player: Steve Powell, 16 years 33 days v Arsenal, 23 October 1971.

Record Transfer Fee Received: £7 million rising to £9 million for Seth Johnson from Leeds U, October 2001.

Record Transfer Fee Paid: £3,000,000 rising to £4,000,000 for Lee Morris from Sheffield U, October 1999.

Football League Record: 1888 Founder Member of the Football League; 1907–12 Division 2; 1912–14 Division 1; 1914–15 Division 2; 1915–21 Division 1; 1921–26 Division 2; 1926–53 Division 1; 1953–55 Division 2; 1955–57 Division 3 (N); 1957–69 Division 2; 1969–80 Division 1; 1980–84 Division 2; 1984–86 Division 3; 1986–87 Division 2; 1987–91 Division 1; 1991–92 Division 2; 1992–96 Division 1; 1996–2002 FA Premier League; 2002– Division 1.

MANAGERS

Harry Newbould 1896–1906
Jimmy Methven 1906–22
Cecil Potter 1922–25
George Jobey 1925–41
Ted Magner 1944–46
Stuart McMillan 1946–53
Jack Barker 1953–55
Harry Storer 1955–62
Tim Ward 1962–67
Brian Clough 1967–73
Dave Mackay 1973–76
Colin Murphy 1977
Tommy Docherty 1977–79
Colin Addison 1979–82
Johnny Newman 1982
Peter Taylor 1982–84
Roy McFarland 1984
Arthur Cox 1984–93
Roy McFarland 1993–95
Jim Smith 1995–2001
Colin Todd 2001–02
John Gregory January 2002–

LATEST SEQUENCES

Longest Sequence of League Wins: 9, 15.3.69 – 19.4.69.

Longest Sequence of League Defeats: 8, 12.12.87 – 10.2.88.

Longest Sequence of League Draws: 6, 26.3.27 – 18.4.27.

Longest Sequence of Unbeaten League Matches: 22, 8.3.69 – 20.9.69.

Longest Sequence Without a League Win: 20, 15.12.90 – 23.4.91.

TEN YEAR LEAGUE RECORD

		P	W	D	L	F	A	Pts	Pos
1991-92	Div 2	46	23	9	14	69	51	78	3
1992-93	Div 1	46	19	9	18	68	57	66	8
1993-94	Div 1	46	20	11	15	73	68	71	6
1994-95	Div 1	46	18	12	16	66	51	66	9
1995-96	Div 1	46	21	16	9	71	51	79	2
1996-97	PR Lge	38	11	13	14	45	58	46	12
1997-98	PR Lge	38	16	7	15	52	49	55	9
1998-99	PR Lge	38	13	13	12	40	45	52	8
1999-2000	PR Lge	38	9	11	18	44	57	38	16
2000-01	PR Lge	38	10	12	16	37	59	42	17

DID YOU KNOW ?

Although the Baseball Ground had been officially opened on 14 September 1895 with Sunderland as visitors, Derby County had also met them in 1892 when the races had prevented the match taking place at the then County Ground.

DERBY COUNTY 2001–02 LEAGUE RECORD

Match No.	Date	Venue	Opponents	Result		H/T Score	Lg. Pos.	Goalscorers	Attendance
1	Aug 18	H	Blackburn R	W	2-1	1-0	—	Ravanelli [45], Christie [65]	28,236
2	21	A	Ipswich T	L	1-3	0-1	—	Ravanelli [84]	21,133
3	25	A	Fulham	D	0-0	0-0	9		18,607
4	Sept 8	H	West Ham U	D	0-0	0-0	12		27,802
5	15	H	Leicester C	L	2-3	1-1	15	Burton [4], Ravanelli (pen) [86]	26,863
6	23	A	Leeds U	L	0-3	0-1	18		39,155
7	29	H	Arsenal	L	0-2	0-1	19		29,200
8	Oct 15	A	Tottenham H	L	1-3	1-2	—	Ravanelli [15]	30,150
9	20	H	Charlton Ath	D	1-1	1-0	18	Ravanelli [15]	30,221
10	28	H	Chelsea	D	1-1	1-0	18	Ravanelli [7]	28,910
11	Nov 3	A	Middlesbrough	L	1-5	0-0	20	Ravanelli [89]	28,099
12	17	H	Southampton	W	1-0	1-0	17	Mawene [25]	32,063
13	24	A	Newcastle U	L	0-1	0-1	18		50,070
14	Dec 1	H	Liverpool	L	0-1	0-1	19		33,289
15	8	H	Bolton W	W	1-0	0-0	18	Christie [66]	25,712
16	12	A	Manchester U	L	0-5	0-2	—		67,577
17	15	A	Everton	L	0-1	0-0	19		38,615
18	22	H	Aston Villa	W	3-1	1-1	18	Ravanelli [45], Carbone [67], Christie [87]	28,001
19	26	A	West Ham U	L	0-4	0-1	18		31,397
20	29	A	Blackburn R	W	1-0	1-0	18	Christie [40]	23,529
21	Jan 2	A	Fulham	L	0-1	0-0	—		28,165
22	12	A	Aston Villa	L	1-2	1-2	19	Powell [23]	28,881
23	19	H	Ipswich T	L	1-3	0-0	19	Christie [79]	29,658
24	29	A	Charlton Ath	L	0-1	0-0	—		25,300
25	Feb 2	H	Tottenham H	W	1-0	1-0	19	Morris [43]	27,721
26	9	H	Sunderland	L	0-1	0-0	19		31,771
27	23	A	Leicester C	W	3-0	0-0	19	Kinkladze [53], Strupar [64], Morris [89]	21,620
28	Mar 3	H	Manchester U	D	2-2	1-1	19	Christie 2 [8, 77]	33,041
29	5	A	Arsenal	L	0-1	0-0	—		37,898
30	16	A	Bolton W	W	3-1	1-0	19	Christie [22], Ravanelli [53], Higginbotham (pen) [87]	25,893
31	23	H	Everton	L	3-4	0-1	19	Strupar 2 [57, 81], Morris [76]	33,297
32	30	A	Chelsea	L	1-2	0-0	19	Strupar [60]	37,849
33	Apr 1	H	Middlesbrough	L	0-1	0-1	19		30,822
34	6	A	Southampton	L	0-2	0-1	19		29,263
35	13	H	Newcastle U	L	2-3	0-0	19	Christie [46], Morris [53]	31,031
36	20	A	Liverpool	L	0-2	0-1	19		43,510
37	27	H	Leeds U	L	0-1	0-1	19		30,735
38	May 11	A	Sunderland	D	1-1	0-1	19	Robinson [66]	47,989

Final League Position: 19

GOALSCORERS

League (33): Christie 9, Ravanelli 9 (1 pen), Morris 4, Strupar 4, Burton 1, Carbone 1, Higginbotham 1 (pen), Kinkladze 1, Mawene 1, Powell 1, Robinson 1.
Worthington Cup (5): Burton 2, Burley 1, Kinkladze 1, Ravanelli 1.
FA Cup (1): Ravanelli 1.

Poom M 15	Daino D 2	Boertien P 23 + 9	Riggott C 37	Higginbotham D 37	O'Neil B 8 + 2	Burley C 11	Morris L 9 + 6	Christie M 27 + 8	Ravanelli F 30 + 1	Powell D 23	Kinkladze G 13 + 11	Murray A 3 + 3	Johnson S 7	Burton D 8 + 9	Oakes A 20	Mawene Y 17	Jackson R 6 + 1	Feuer I 2	Valakari S 6 + 3	Zavagno L 26	Ducrocq P 19	Carbone B 13	Grenet F 12 + 3	Bolder A 2 + 9	Elliott S 2 + 4	Carbonari H 3	Barton W 14	Lee R 13	Foletti P 1 + 1	Strupar B 8 + 4	Evatt I 1 + 2	Robinson M — + 2	Twigg G — + 1	Match No.
1	2	3	4	5	6	7	8^1	9	10	11	12																							1
1	2^1	3	4	5	6	7		9	10	11^2	12		8	13																				2
		3	4	5	6	7		9^1	10	11	12	13	10	8	1		2^2																	3
		3	4	5		7		9^1	10	11	12				1	6	2		8															4
		3	4	5	6	7	8	9	10	11	12				1		2^1																	5
		3	4	5	6	7^3	8	9	10^1	11	12	13			1		2																	6
		3	4	5	6	7^3	8	9	10	11	12	13			1		2^1																	7
			4	5		7	8^3	9^1	10	11	12	13			1	6	2			3														8
			4	5		7		9^1	10	11	12	13			1		2		8	3	6^2													9
1			4	5		7		9^1	10	11	12						2		8	3	6													10
1			4	5		7		9	10	11	12						2		8	3	6^1													11
1		12	4	5		7		9	10	11		13				6	2^2		8	3^1														12
1		12	4	5		7		9	10	11^2		13				6	2		8	3^1														13
1			4	5				9	10	11						6	2		8	3	7													14
1			4	5				9^1	10	11		13				6	2		8^3	3	7		12											15
		13	4	5				9^2	10	11					1	6^1	2		8	3	7^3		12				14							16
		12	4	5				9	10	11^3		13			1	6^2	2^1		8	3	7						14							17
		3	4	5				9^1	10	11		13				6	2^3		8^2		7		12				14							18
1		3	4^2	5				9	10	11		13				6	2		8		7^1		12											19
1		12	4	5				9	10	11		13				6	2^1		8^2	3	7													20
1		12	4	5				9	10	11		13				6^1	2		8^2	3	7^3						14							21
1		3	4	5				9	10	11^2		13				6^1	2		8		7		12											22
		12	4	5				9	10	11		13			1	6^1	2		8	3^4	7													23
		3	4	5				9	10	11					1	6	2		8		7^1		12											24
		12	4	5				9	10	11		13			1	6^1	2		8^2	3	7													25
		12	4	5				9	10	11^1		13			1	6	2		8^2	3	7													26
		11	4	5				9				13			1	6	2		8^1	3	7	10^2	12									15		27
		11	4	5				9	10^3			13			1	6^1	2		8^2	3	7^3		12				14							28
		11	4	5				9	10^3			13			1	6	2		8^2	3	7^3		12				14							29
		11	4	5				9^1	10^3			13			1	6	2		8^2	3	7		12				14							30
		11	4	5				9^1	10			13			1	6	2		8	3^3	7		12											31
		11	4	5				9^1	10			13			1	6	2		8	3^3	7		12											32
		11	4	5				9^2	10^1			13			1	6	2		8	3^3	7		12				14							33
		11	4	5				9	10^3			13			1	6	2		8^1	3^2	7		12				14							34
		3	4	5				9^1	10	11^2		13			1	6	2		8	3	7^3		12				14							35
		11	4	5				9	10						1	6	2		8	3	7													36
1		11	4	5				9	10^3			13				6^2	2		8^1	3	7		12				14							37
1		11^3	4	5				9	10^2			13				6	2		8	3^1	7		12				14							38

Worthington Cup
Second Round	Hull C	(h)	3-0
Third Round	Fulham	(a)	2-5

FA Cup
| Third Round | Bristol R | (h) | 1-3 |

EVERTON   FA Premiership

FOUNDATION

St Domingo Church Sunday School formed a football club in 1878 which played at Stanley Park. Enthusiasm was so great that in November 1879 they decided to expand membership and changed the name to Everton playing in black shirts with a scarlet sash and nicknamed the 'Black Watch'. After wearing several other colours, royal blue was adopted in 1901.

Goodison Park, Liverpool L4 4EL.

Telephone: (0151) 330 2200. *Fax:* (0151) 286 9112.
Ticket Infoline: 09068 121 599. *ClubCall:* 09068 121 199.

Ground Capacity: 40,170.

Record Attendance: 78,299 v Liverpool, Division 1,
18 September 1948.

Record Receipts: £730,000 v Manchester U, FA Premier League, 16 September 2000.

Pitch Measurements: 110yd × 70yd.

Chairman: Sir Philip Carter CBE.

Deputy-chairman: Bill Kenwright CBE.

Directors: Keith Tamlin, Arthur Abercromby, Paul Gregg, Jon Woods.

Manager: David Moyes.

Assistant Manager: Alan Irvine.

Chief Executive: Michael J. Dunford.

Club Secretary: David Harrison.

Stadium Manager: Alan Bowen.

Head of Marketing: Andy Oldknow.

Head of Corporate Affairs & PR: Ian Ross.

Head of Physiotherapy: Rob Ryles, Grad. Dip. Phys., MCSP, SRP.

Colours: Royal blue shirts with white panels, white shorts with blue trim, blue stockings with white trim.

Change Colours: Silver shirts, black shorts, silver and black stockings.

Year Formed: 1878.

Turned Professional: 1885.

Ltd Co.: 1892.

Previous Name: 1878, St Domingo FC; 1879, Everton.

Club Nickname: 'The Toffees'.

Previous Grounds: 1878, Stanley Park; 1882, Priory Road; 1884, Anfield Road; 1892, Goodison Park.

HONOURS

Football League: Division 1 – Champions 1890–91, 1914–15, 1927–28, 1931–32, 1938–39, 1962–63, 1969–70, 1984–85, 1986–87; Runners-up 1889–90, 1894–95, 1901–02, 1904–05, 1908–09, 1911–12, 1985–86; Division 2 – Champions 1930–31; Runners-up 1953–54.

FA Cup: Winners 1906, 1933, 1966, 1984, 1995; Runners-up 1893, 1897, 1907, 1968, 1985, 1986, 1989.

Football League Cup: Runners-up 1977, 1984.

League Super Cup: Runners-up 1986.

Simod Cup: Runners-up 1989.

Zenith Data Systems Cup: Runners-up 1991.

European Competitions: European Cup: 1963–64, 1970–71. European Cup-Winners' Cup: 1966–67, 1984–85 (winners), 1995–96. European Fairs Cup: 1962–63, 1964–65, 1965–66. UEFA Cup: 1975–76, 1978–79, 1979–80.

IT'S A FACT !

Bertie Freeman, who scored 36 goals in 37 matches for Everton in 1908–09, had a run of ten successive games in which he scored at least once for a total of 17.

First Football League Game: 8 September 1888, Football League, v Accrington (h) W 2–1 – Smalley; Dick, Ross; Holt, Jones, Dobson; Fleming (2), Waugh, Lewis, E. Chadwick, Farmer.

Record League Victory: 9–1 v Manchester C, Division 1, 3 September 1906 – Scott; Balmer, Crelley; Booth, Taylor (1), Abbott (1); Sharp, Bolton (1), Young (4), Settle (2), George Wilson. 9–1 v Plymouth Arg, Division 2, 27 December 1930 – Coggins; Williams, Cresswell; McPherson, Griffiths, Thomson; Critchley, Dunn, Dean (4), Johnson (1), Stein (4).

Record Cup Victory: 11–2 v Derby Co, FA Cup 1st rd, 18 January 1890 – Smalley; Hannah, Doyle (1); Kirkwood, Holt (1), Parry; Latta, Brady (3), Geary (3), Chadwick, Millward (3).

Record Defeat: 4–10 v Tottenham H, Division 1, 11 October 1958.

Most League Points (2 for a win): 66, Division 1, 1969–70.

Most League Points (3 for a win): 90, Division 1, 1984–85.

Most League Goals: 121, Division 2, 1930–31.

Highest League Scorer in Season: William Ralph 'Dixie' Dean, 60, Division 1, 1927–28 (All-time League record).

Most League Goals in Total Aggregate: William Ralph 'Dixie' Dean, 349, 1925–37.

Most League Goals in One Match: 6, Jack Southworth v WBA, Division 1, 30 December 1893.

Most Capped Player: Neville Southall, 92, Wales.

Most League Appearances: Neville Southall, 578, 1981–98.

Youngest League Player: Joe Royle, 16 years 282 days v Blackpool, 15 January 1966.

Record Transfer Fee Received: £10,000,000 from Arsenal for Francis Jeffers, June 2001.

Record Transfer Fee Paid: £5,750,000 to Middlesbrough for Nick Barmby, October 1996.

Football League Record: 1888 Founder Member of the Football League; 1930–31 Division 2; 1931–51 Division 1; 1951–54 Division 2; 1954–92 Division 1; 1992– FA Premier League.

LATEST SEQUENCES

Longest Sequence of League Wins: 12, 24.3.1894 – 13.10.1894.

Longest Sequence of League Defeats: 6, 26.12.96 – 29.1.97.

Longest Sequence of League Draws: 5, 4.5.77 – 16.5.77.

Longest Sequence of Unbeaten League Matches: 20, 29.4.78 – 16.12.78.

Longest Sequence Without a League Win: 14, 6.3.37 – 4.9.37.

MANAGERS

W. E. Barclay 1888–89
(Secretary-Manager)
Dick Molyneux 1889–1901
(Secretary-Manager)
William C. Cuff 1901–18
(Secretary-Manager)
W. J. Sawyer 1918–19
(Secretary-Manager)
Thomas H. McIntosh 1919–35
(Secretary-Manager)
Theo Kelly 1936–48
Cliff Britton 1948–56
Ian Buchan 1956–58
Johnny Carey 1958–61
Harry Catterick 1961–73
Billy Bingham 1973–77
Gordon Lee 1977–81
Howard Kendall 1981–87
Colin Harvey 1987–90
Howard Kendall 1990–93
Mike Walker 1994
Joe Royle 1994–97
Howard Kendall 1997–98
Walter Smith 1998–2002
David Moyes March 2002–

TEN YEAR LEAGUE RECORD

		P	W	D	L	F	A	Pts	Pos
1991-92	Div 1	42	13	14	15	52	51	53	12
1992-93	PR Lge	42	15	8	19	53	55	53	13
1993-94	PR Lge	42	12	8	22	42	63	44	17
1994-95	PR Lge	42	11	17	14	44	51	50	15
1995-96	PR Lge	38	17	10	11	64	44	61	6
1996-97	PR Lge	38	10	12	16	44	57	42	15
1997-98	PR Lge	38	9	13	16	41	56	40	17
1998-99	PR Lge	38	11	10	17	42	47	43	14
1999-2000	PR Lge	38	12	14	12	59	49	50	13
2000-01	PR Lge	38	11	9	18	45	59	42	16

DID YOU KNOW ?

Jesper Blomqvist returned to Premier League action with Everton and scored against Sunderland at Goodison Park on 12 January 2002. It was his first goal since one for Manchester United in October 1998 on the same ground.

EVERTON 2001–02 LEAGUE RECORD

Match No.	Date	Venue	Opponents	Result	H/T Score	Lg. Pos.	Goalscorers	Attendance
1	Aug 18	A	Charlton Ath	W	2-1	0-0	—	Ferguson (pen) [64], Weir [77]	20,451
2	20	H	Tottenham H	D	1-1	0-1	—	Ferguson (pen) [65]	29,503
3	25	H	Middlesbrough	W	2-0	1-0	1	Campbell [17], Gemmill [52]	32,829
4	Sept 8	A	Manchester U	L	1-4	0-2	5	Campbell [68]	67,534
5	15	H	Liverpool	L	1-3	1-2	8	Campbell [5]	39,554
6	22	A	Blackburn R	L	0-1	0-1	11		27,732
7	29	H	West Ham U	W	5-0	1-0	10	Campbell [45], Hutchison (og) [52], Gravesen [56], Watson [75], Radzinski [79]	32,049
8	Oct 13	A	Ipswich T	D	0-0	0-0	10		22,820
9	20	H	Aston Villa	W	3-2	1-0	9	Watson [31], Radzinski [59], Gravesen [62]	33,352
10	27	H	Newcastle U	L	1-3	0-1	10	Weir [51]	37,524
11	Nov 3	A	Bolton W	D	2-2	1-1	11	Stubbs [43], Gascoigne [57]	27,343
12	18	H	Chelsea	D	0-0	0-0	12		30,555
13	24	A	Leicester C	D	0-0	0-0	12		21,539
14	Dec 2	H	Southampton	W	2-0	0-0	9	Radzinski [50], Pembridge [87]	28,138
15	8	A	Fulham	L	0-2	0-1	11		19,338
16	15	H	Derby Co	W	1-0	0-0	9	Moore [76]	38,615
17	19	A	Leeds U	L	2-3	0-2	—	Moore [84], Weir [90]	40,201
18	22	A	Sunderland	L	0-1	0-0	9		42,486
19	26	H	Manchester U	L	0-2	0-0	13		39,948
20	29	H	Charlton Ath	L	0-3	0-1	13		31,131
21	Jan 1	A	Middlesbrough	L	0-1	0-0	13		27,463
22	12	H	Sunderland	W	1-0	1-0	13	Blomqvist [27]	30,736
23	19	A	Tottenham H	D	1-1	1-1	13	Weir [8]	36,075
24	30	A	Aston Villa	D	0-0	0-0	—		32,460
25	Feb 2	H	Ipswich T	L	1-2	1-2	14	Unsworth (pen) [28]	33,069
26	10	H	Arsenal	L	0-1	0-0	15		30,859
27	23	A	Liverpool	D	1-1	0-0	16	Radzinski [52]	44,371
28	Mar 3	H	Leeds U	D	0-0	0-0	15		33,226
29	6	A	West Ham U	L	0-1	0-0	—		29,883
30	16	H	Fulham	W	2-1	2-0	15	Unsworth [1], Ferguson [13]	34,639
31	23	A	Derby Co	W	4-3	1-0	13	Unsworth [38], Stubbs [52], Alexandersson [54], Ferguson [71]	33,297
32	29	A	Newcastle U	L	2-6	2-2	—	Ferguson [6], Alexandersson [34]	51,921
33	Apr 1	H	Bolton W	W	3-1	1-0	12	Pistone [41], Radzinski [57], Chadwick [86]	39,784
34	6	A	Chelsea	L	0-3	0-2	13		40,545
35	13	H	Leicester C	D	2-2	0-2	13	Chadwick [64], Ferguson [86]	35,580
36	20	H	Southampton	W	1-0	1-0	11	Watson [41]	31,785
37	28	H	Blackburn R	L	1-2	0-1	12	Chadwick [51]	34,976
38	May 11	A	Arsenal	L	3-4	2-2	15	Carsley [20], Radzinski [31], Watson [89]	38,240

Final League Position: 15

GOALSCORERS

League (45): Ferguson 6 (2 pens), Radzinski 6, Campbell 4, Watson 4, Weir 4, Chadwick 3, Unsworth 3 (1 pen), Alexandersson 2, Gravesen 2, Moore 2, Stubbs 2, Blomqvist 1, Carsley 1, Gascoigne 1, Gemmill 1, Pembridge 1, Pistone 1, own goal 1.
Worthington Cup (1): Ferguson 1 (pen).
FA Cup (7): Campbell 3, Ferguson 1, Radzinski 1, Stubbs 1, own goal 1.

Gerrard P 13	Watson S 24 + 1	Pistone A 25	Stubbs A 29 + 2	Weir D 36	Gravesen T 22 + 3	Alexandersson N 28 + 3	Gemmill S 31 + 1	Campbell K 21 + 2	Ferguson D 17 + 5	Pembridge M 10 + 4	Unsworth D 28 + 5	Moore J 3 + 13	Tal 11 + 6	Naysmith G 23 + 1	Xavier A 11 + 1	Gascoigne P 8 + 10	Hibbert T 7 + 3	Radzinski T 23 + 4	Simonsen S 25	Cleland A — + 3	Cadamarteri D 2 + 1	Chadwick N 2 + 7	Blomqvist J 10 + 5	Clarke P 5 + 2	Linderoth T 4 + 4	Carsley L 8	Ginola D 2 + 3	Match No.
1	2	3	4	5	6	7¹	8	9	10	11	12																	1
1	2²	3	4	5	6¹	7³	8	9	10	11	12	13	14															2
1	2	3	4	5		7¹	8	9	10	11¹	6			12	13													3
1	2	6	4²	5³		7¹	8	9	10	11	3	12	13		14													4
1	2		4	5	8	7³		9	10		6¹			3	11²	12	14	13										5
1			4	5	6¹	7		9	10		12	13		2	3	8	11²											6
1	2	6		5	11	7		9	12²				14	3	4	8¹	13	10³										7
1	2¹		4	5	12	7		9	10³	11²		13	14	3	6	8												8
1	2	6		5	8³	7	12	9	13	11¹				3	4	14		10²										9
1	2	12		5	8	7	11	9²	13	6²				3	4¹	14		10										10
	2		4	5	10	7	11				6			3		8¹		9²	1	12	13							11
10	2		4	5	6	7¹	8		12					3		11		9	1									12
10	2		4	5	6²	7	8		12					3		11¹	13	9	1									13
9	2		4	5	8	7²	11	12			6¹			3		13		10	1									14
	2	6	4	5	10²	12	7	11				13		3		8¹		9	1									15
9	2²		4¹	5	6³	7	8	11	12			13		3		14		10	1									16
9	2²			5	7³	8	11¹				6	13	14	3	4	12		10	1									17
	2				6¹	12	11			4		9	7³	3	5	8		10²	1			13	14					18
	2			5	9²	7³	8	12		6		13		3	4	14		10	1				11¹					19
	2			5	7³	8	12		6	9		13		3	4	14		10¹	1				11²					20
2²			4	5	7³	8	10	11	12					3	6	13			1			9¹	14					21
			4	5	7¹	10	9				6			3	8	2			1	12		13	11²					22
			4	5	7²	11	9	10		6	12			3	8¹	2			1		13							23
			4		11	9	10	6	7		3			2²		1	13	8¹	12			5						24
			4	5	11	9	10	2¹	12	3	8			1		7	6²	13										25
			4	5	9	12	3²	14	11	13				1		7¹	2³	8	6	10								26
	3	4	5	12	8	9	11	13		1				2	7¹	6	10²											27
	2	4	5	12	8	9	3	10	1	11²				7¹	6	13												28
	2	4	5	12	7¹	8	9²	3	10	1	11	14	6³	13														29
	2	4	5	8	11	10	3²	12	7	9¹	13	6																30
4⁵	5	7	12	8	13	10	3	2	9²	1	11	14	6¹															31
12	3³	4	5	6	7	8	10	11	2¹	9²	1	13	14															32
2	3	4	5	7	8	10	6	9¹	1	12	11¹	13																33
2	3	5	6	7¹	8	10	9	1	12	11²	4	13																34
2¹	3	4	5	6	7	8	12	10	11	9²	13																	35
1	2	3	4	5	10	8	9	11	12	7¹	6																	36
1	2	3	4	5	6	7¹	8	9	11²	12	10	13																37
2	4	5	7¹	9	11	3	10	1	8	6	12																	38

Worthington Cup

Second Round	Crystal Palace	(h)	1-1

FA Cup

Third Round	Stoke C	(a)	1-0
Fourth Round	Leyton Orient	(h)	4-1
Fifth Round	Crewe Alex	(h)	0-0
		(a)	2-1
Sixth Round	Middlesbrough	(a)	0-3

EXETER CITY
Division 3

FOUNDATION

Exeter City was formed in 1904 by the amalgamation of St Sidwell's United and Exeter United. The club first played in the East Devon League and then the Plymouth & District League. After an exhibition match between West Bromwich Albion and Woolwich Arsenal was held to test interest as Exeter was then a rugby stronghold, Exeter City decided at a meeting at the Red Lion Hotel to turn professional in 1908.

St James Park, Exeter EX4 6PX.

Telephone: (01392) 411 243.

Fax: (01392) 413 959.

ClubCall: 09068 121 634.

Website: www.exetercityfc.co.uk

Training Ground: (01395) 232784.

Ground Capacity: 9,036.

Record Attendance: 20,984 v Sunderland, FA Cup 6th rd (replay), 4 March 1931.

Record Receipts: £59,862.98 v Aston Villa, FA Cup 3rd rd, 8 January 1994.

Pitch Measurements: 114yd × 73yd.

Chairman: A. I. Doble.

Directors: P. Carter, I. M. Couch, S. W. Dawe, M. Vandale, J. Gadston.

Associate Directors: M. Shelbourne, P. Dobson, J. Tagg, S. Perryman, D. Newbery.

Manager: John Cornforth.

Physio: Damien Davey.

Chief Executive: Bernard Frowd OBE.

Secretary: Stuart Brailey.

Company Secretary: P. Carter.

Colours: Red and white shirts, white shorts, white stockings.

Change Colours: Purple and white.

Year Formed: 1904.

Turned Professional: 1908.

Ltd Co.: 1908.

Club Nickname: 'The Grecians'.

First Football League Game: 28 August 1920, Division 3, v Brentford (h) W 3–0 – Pym; Coleburne, Feebury (1p); Crawshaw, Carrick, Mitton; Appleton, Makin, Wright (1), Vowles (1), Dockray.

HONOURS

Football League: Division 3 best season: 8th, 1979–80; Division 3 (S) – Runners-up 1932–33; Division 4 – Champions 1989–90; Runners-up 1976–77.

FA Cup: best season: 6th rd replay, 1931, 6th rd 1981.

Football League Cup: never beyond 4th rd.

Division 3 (S) Cup: Winners 1934.

IT'S A FACT !

In 1930–31, Exeter City defeated Northfleet United, Coventry City after a replay, Derby County, Bury and Leeds United in the FA Cup and forced Sunderland to a sixth round replay.

Record League Victory: 8–1 v Coventry C, Division 3 (S), 4 December 1926 – Bailey; Pollard, Charlton; Pullen, Pool, Garrett; Purcell (2), McDevitt, Blackmore (2), Dent (2), Compton (2). 8–1 v Aldershot, Division 3 (S), 4 May 1935 – Chesters; Gray, Miller; Risdon, Webb, Angus; Jack Scott (1), Wrightson (1), Poulter (3), McArthur (1), Dryden (1), (1 og).

Record Cup Victory: 14–0 v Weymouth, FA Cup 1st qual rd, 3 October 1908 – Fletcher; Craig, Bulcock; Ambler, Chadwick, Wake; Parnell (1), Watson (1), McGuigan (4), Bell (6), Copestake (2).

Record Defeat: 0–9 v Notts Co, Division 3 (S), 16 October 1948. 0–9 v Northampton T, Division 3 (S), 12 April 1958.

Most League Points (2 for a win): 62, Division 4, 1976–77.

Most League Points (3 for a win): 89, Division 4, 1989–90.

Most League Goals: 88, Division 3 (S), 1932–33.

Highest League Scorer in Season: Fred Whitlow, 33, Division 3 (S), 1932–33.

Most League Goals in Total Aggregate: Tony Kellow, 129, 1976–78, 1980–83, 1985–88.

Most League Goals in One Match: 4, Harold 'Jazzo' Kirk v Portsmouth, Division 3S, 3 March 1923; 4, Fred Dent v Bristol R, Division 3S, 5 November 1927; 4, Fred Whitlow v Watford, Division 3S, 29 October 1932.

Most Capped Player: Dermot Curtis, 1 (17), Eire.

Most League Appearances: Arnold Mitchell, 495, 1952–66.

Youngest League Player: Cliff Bastin, 16 years 31 days v Coventry C, 14 April 1928.

MANAGERS

Arthur Chadwick 1910–22
Fred Mavin 1923–27
Dave Wilson 1928–29
Billy McDevitt 1929–35
Jack English 1935–39
George Roughton 1945–52
Norman Kirkman 1952–53
Norman Dodgin 1953–57
Bill Thompson 1957–58
Frank Broome 1958–60
Glen Wilson 1960–62
Cyril Spiers 1962–63
Jack Edwards 1963–65
Ellis Stuttard 1965–66
Jock Basford 1966–67
Frank Broome 1967–69
Johnny Newman 1969–76
Bobby Saxton 1977–79
Brian Godfrey 1979–83
Gerry Francis 1983–84
Jim Iley 1984–85
Colin Appleton 1985–87
Terry Cooper 1988–91
Alan Ball 1991–94
Terry Cooper 1994–95
Peter Fox 1995–2000
Noel Blake 2000–01
John Cornforth October 2001–

Record Transfer Fee Received: £500,000 from Manchester C for Martin Phillips, November 1995.

Record Transfer Fee Paid: £65,000 to Blackpool for Tony Kellow, March 1980.

Football League Record: 1920 Elected Division 3; 1921–58 Division 3 (S); 1958–64 Division 4; 1964–66 Division 3; 1966–77 Division 4; 1977–84 Division 3; 1984–90 Division 4; 1990–92 Division 3; 1992–94 Division 2; 1994– Division 3.

LATEST SEQUENCES

Longest Sequence of League Wins: 7, 23.4.77 – 20.8.77.

Longest Sequence of League Defeats: 7, 14.1.84 – 25.2.84.

Longest Sequence of League Draws: 6, 13.9.86 – 4.10.86.

Longest Sequence of Unbeaten League Matches: 13, 23.8.86 – 25.10.86.

Longest Sequence Without a League Win: 18, 21.2.95 – 19.8.95.

TEN YEAR LEAGUE RECORD

		P	W	D	L	F	A	Pts	Pos
1991-92	Div 3	46	14	11	21	57	80	53	20
1992-93	Div 2	46	11	17	18	54	69	50	19
1993-94	Div 2	46	11	12	23	52	83	45	22
1994-95	Div 3	42	8	10	24	36	70	34	22
1995-96	Div 3	46	13	18	15	46	53	57	14
1996-97	Div 3	46	12	12	22	48	73	48	22
1997-98	Div 3	46	15	15	16	68	63	60	15
1998-99	Div 3	46	17	12	17	47	50	63	12
1999-2000	Div 3	46	11	11	24	46	72	44	21
2000-01	Div 3	46	12	14	20	40	58	50	19

DID YOU KNOW ?

Rod Williams scored two goals in each of the three successive FA Cup ties for Exeter City during 1936–37, his only season with the club.

EXETER CITY 2001–02 LEAGUE RECORD

Match No.	Date	Venue	Opponents	Result	H/T Score	Lg. Pos.	Goalscorers	Attendance
1	Aug 11	H	Hull C	L	1-3	1-1	—	Campbell [22]	4677
2	18	A	Halifax T	D	1-1	1-1	20	Kerr [2]	1937
3	25	H	Scunthorpe U	L	0-4	0-2	23		2798
4	27	A	Rochdale	L	0-2	0-2	24		3003
5	Sept 1	H	Luton T	D	2-2	1-1	24	Flack [29], Mansell (og) [68]	3088
6	8	A	Swansea C	L	2-4	1-3	24	Roberts [13], McConnell [85]	3889
7	15	H	Oxford U	W	3-2	3-1	23	McCarthy [2], Flack [15], Breslan [45]	3268
8	18	A	Plymouth Arg	L	2-3	2-1	—	Curran [7], Roberts [18]	5756
9	22	A	Darlington	L	0-4	0-1	24		4039
10	25	H	Rushden & D	D	1-1	0-0	—	McCarthy [56]	2622
11	29	H	Macclesfield T	D	0-0	0-0	24		2833
12	Oct 6	A	York C	W	3-2	2-0	23	McCarthy [31], Roberts 2 [34, 70]	2054
13	13	H	Carlisle U	W	1-0	0-0	22	Tomlinson [65]	3151
14	20	A	Cheltenham T	L	1-3	0-2	23	Roberts [90]	3393
15	23	H	Bristol R	W	1-0	1-0	—	Breslan [34]	3879
16	27	A	Lincoln C	D	0-0	0-0	19		2719
17	Nov 3	H	Southend U	W	2-1	2-1	16	Cort (og) [37], Roberts [45]	3269
18	10	A	Hartlepool U	L	0-2	0-1	20		3222
19	20	A	Torquay U	W	2-0	0-0	—	McCarthy 2 [46, 61]	3764
20	24	H	Leyton Orient	D	0-0	0-0	14		3364
21	Dec 1	A	Shrewsbury T	W	1-0	1-0	14	Power [20]	3565
22	15	H	Kidderminster H	W	2-1	0-1	10	Tomlinson [69], Flack [74]	2707
23	21	H	Mansfield T	W	1-0	0-0	—	McConnell (pen) [53]	3958
24	26	H	Swansea C	L	0-3	0-0	10		4123
25	29	H	Rochdale	D	1-1	0-1	10	Watson [62]	2994
26	Jan 12	H	Halifax T	D	0-0	0-0	11		2763
27	15	A	Scunthorpe U	W	4-3	1-1	—	Flack [35], Roberts 2 [50, 74], Roscoe [90]	2877
28	19	A	Hull C	L	0-2	0-1	11		8459
29	22	A	Mansfield T	L	0-1	0-1	—		3106
30	Feb 2	A	Macclesfield T	W	2-1	0-0	11	Tomlinson [54], Flack [67]	1719
31	9	H	Cheltenham T	L	0-2	0-0	13		3837
32	16	A	Carlisle U	L	0-1	0-0	13		4929
33	23	A	Oxford U	W	2-1	1-1	12	Roscoe 2 [20, 50]	6051
34	26	H	Plymouth Arg	L	0-3	0-2	—		16,369
35	Mar 2	H	Darlington	W	4-2	1-1	12	Roscoe 2 [42, 57], Roberts 2 [50, 74]	3117
36	5	A	Rushden & D	L	1-2	0-2	—	McCarthy [65]	3343
37	9	A	Kidderminster H	L	1-3	0-2	14	McConnell (pen) [49]	2615
38	12	H	Luton T	L	0-3	0-1	—		6327
39	16	H	Shrewsbury T	D	2-2	0-1	14	Tomlinson [58], Roscoe [65]	3020
40	19	H	York C	W	2-1	0-0	—	Roberts [64], Buckle (pen) [88]	2038
41	23	A	Bristol R	D	0-0	0-0	13		6105
42	30	H	Lincoln C	D	1-1	1-0	14	Roscoe [28]	2609
43	Apr 1	A	Southend U	L	1-3	1-2	14	Tomlinson [21]	3588
44	7	H	Torquay U	D	0-0	0-0	14		3580
45	13	A	Leyton Orient	D	1-1	1-1	14	Flack [20]	5332
46	20	H	Hartlepool U	L	0-2	0-1	16		3595

Final League Position: 16

GOALSCORERS

League (48): Roberts 11, Roscoe 7, Flack 6, McCarthy 5, Tomlinson 5, McConnell 3 (2 pens), Breslan 2, Buckle 1 (pen), Campbell 1, Curran 1, Kerr 1, Power 1, Watson 1, own goals 2.
Worthington Cup (0).
FA Cup (3): Curran 1, Roscoe 1, Tomlinson 1.

Van Heusden A 33	Buckle P 19+6	Campbell J 14+2	Kerr D 5	Watson A 42+1	Burrows M 6+3	Flack S 27+9	Ampadu K 33+3	McCarthy S 18+8	Birch G 5+10	Barlow M 26+4	Roberts C 34+3	Richardson J 5+13	Tomlinson G 25+7	Power G 36+1	Curran C 35+2	Whitworth N 12+3	Moor R —+2	Gross M 1	McConnell B 30+2	Cronin G 24+6	Roscoe A 35+3	Breslan G 21+12	Zabek L 2	Walker A 1	Gregg M 2	Diallo C —+2	Read P 3+12	Fraser S 10+2	Elliott S —+1	Goff S 2	Afful L —+2	Match No.
1	2	3	4	5	6	7^1	8^2	9	10^3	11	12	13	14																			1
1		2		4	5		12	13		9^1	10^3	11	14	8		3^2	6	7														2
1	7^1	3^3	4	5		9	8			12	10	11				13	6	2^2	14													3
1			4^3	5		12		10	8	11		9^1	3	6					2^4	13	14	7										4
1	2		5			9		12	10	11^3		3			14				6	4^2	13	7^1	8									5
	4		5^3	6	9			10	11			3	12						2	14	13	7^1	8^2	1								6
	4		5	10	12	9^1		11	8		3	6	2^2						13	14	7^3			1								7
	2		5	12	8	9^2		10	11^1		3	6			4					7			1	13								8
1		4	5	2^2	8^1		9	12	10		3	6								7				13								9
1	5		12		8^2	4^1	9	13	10	11	3	6			2					7												10
1	12	5			4	9^1	13	10^3	8	14	3	6			2					7^1	11											11
1	12	5			4	9^2	13	10	8		3	6			2					7^1	11											12
1	12	5	6		4	9^2	8	10			13^3	3			2					7	11^1			14								13
1	4^1	5	6		8	12	9	10^2	11		3				2	13				7^3				14								14
1	4	12	6		8^1	9	13	11^2	14		3	5			2	10^3				7												15
1	2		6		4	9	12	8	13		3	5			10	7^2	11															16
1	2		6		4^1	9	13	12	8^3		3	5			10	7	11^2							14								17
1	4^1		6			9^2	12	10	11	14	3	5			2	8	7^2	13														18
1	4		6		12	8^2	9^2		11	13	10^1	3	5		2	7	13															19
1	4		6		12	8^3	9^2		11	13	10^1	3	5		2	14	7															20
1	4	12	6^1		8				10^1	11	9	3	5		2	7^2	13															21
1			6		10	4		8		13	9	9	3	5		2	7^1	11^2						12								22
1	5		6		12	8		13	11	14	9^2		4		2	3	7^2						10^1									23
1^0	5		6		12	8			11	13	9^1		4		2	3	7^2						10	15								24
			6	12	8	4			11		9^2	3		5^1	2	10	7						13	1								25
1^0			6		8		12		10^1	11^2	9		5	4	2	3	7^1						13	15								26
			6		8^2			10^1	11	12	9^1	3	5	13	2	4	7							1								27
			6		8^1	12		10^1	11	13	9	3	5		2	4	7^2						14	1								28
			6	13	8^1	4^1		12	11		9		5	3^2	2	10	7	14						1								29
			6		8	4		10^1	11		9^1	3	5		2	7							1	12								30
			6		8	4		10^2	11		9^1	3	5		2	13	7						12	1								31
			6		8	4	12		11		9^2	3	5		2	10	7^1	13						1								32
			6^1		8	4	12		11		9^2	3	5		2	10	7^1	13						1								33
13			6		8^1	4	12		11		9^3	3	5		2	10^2	7	14						1								34
1	12			4	9^1			8^2	13	3	5	6			2	10	7^1	11^1						14								35
1	14		6	12	4^3	9^2	8	13		3	5				2	10	7	11^1														36
1	4		6	8^2		11		9^1		3	5				2	10	7	12	13													37
1	4		6	12			10	11	8		3	5			2	7^2	13						9^1									38
1	2		6	8^1	4^2		10	11	12	9^0	3	5				7	13						14									39
1	2		6	12	4		10^1	8	13	9^1	3	5				14	7	11^2														40
1	2		6	8	4					12	9	3	5			10	7^1	11														41
1	2		6	8	4	12				9^3	3^1	5	14			10	7^1	11	13													42
1	2		6	10^1	8	12				14	9	5^2	13			4	7^3	11										3				43
1	2		6	3	10^1	8	12	13		4	9		5			11^2	7^3	14														44
1	2		6	3	10	8				4^2	9^3	12			5^1	11	7	13												14		45
			6	5	10^2	8^2	9^1			13	12				2	4	7	11						1					3	14		46

Worthington Cup
First Round   Walsall   (h) 0-1

FA Cup
First Round   Cambridge C   (h) 3-0
Second Round   Dagenham & R   (h) 0-0
                                        (a) 0-3

FULHAM   FA Premiership

FOUNDATION

Churchgoers were responsible for the foundation of Fulham, which first saw the light of day as Fulham St Andrew's Church Sunday School FC in 1879. They won the West London Amateur Cup in 1887 and the championship of the West London League in its initial season of 1892–93. The name Fulham had been adopted in 1888.

South Africa Road, London W12 7PA. (QPR)

Telephone: (020) 7893 8383. *Fax:* (020) 7384 4715.
Website: http://www.fulhamfc.co.uk
ClubCall: 09068 440 044.

Ground Capacity: 19,148.

Record Attendance: 49,335 v Millwall, Division 2, 8 October 1938.

Record Receipts: £139,235 v Watford, Division 2, 2 May 1998.

Pitch Measurements: 110yd × 75yd.

Chairman: M. Al Fayed.

Directors: W. F. Muddyman (Vice-chairman), Stuart Benson, Andy Muddyman, Tim Delaney, Lee Hoos, Andy Ambler, Juliet Slot, Jean Tigana, Mark Collins, Moody Fayed.

HONOURS

Football League: Division 1 – Champions 2000–01; Division 2 – Champions 1948–49, 1998–99; Runners-up 1958–59; Division 3 (S) – Champions 1931–32; Division 3 – Runners-up 1970–71, 1996–97.

FA Cup: Runners-up 1975.

Football League Cup: best season: 5th rd, 1968, 1971, 2000.

Acting Managing Director: Mark Collins. *Manager:* Jean Tigana.
Director of Football: Franco Baresi. *Chief Scout:* John Marshall. *Academy Director:* Steve Kean.

Community Department Manager: Gary Mulcahey (020) 7384 4759. *Stadium Manager:* Francis Broughton. *Club Secretary & Deputy Managing Director:* Lee Hoos. *Sales and Marketing Director:* Juliet Slot. *PR Manager:* Sarah Brookes.

Colours: White shirts, black trim, black shorts, white stockings red and black trim.

Change Colours: Red and black striped shirts, red shorts and stockings.

Year Formed: 1879.

Turned Professional: 1898.

Ltd Co.: 1903.

Reformed: 1987.

Previous Name: 1879, Fulham St Andrew's; 1888, Fulham.

Club Nickname: 'Cottagers'.

Previous Grounds: 1879, Star Road, Fulham; c.1883, Eel Brook Common, 1884, Lillie Road; 1885, Putney Lower Common; 1886, Ranelagh House, Fulham; 1888, Barn Elms, Castelnau; 1889, Purser's Cross (Roskell's Field), Parsons Green Lane; 1891, Eel Brook Common; 1891, Half Moon, Putney; 1895, Captain James Field, West Brompton; 1896, Craven Cottage.

First Football League Game: 3 September 1907, Division 2, v Hull C (h) L 0–1 – Skene; Ross, Lindsay; Collins, Morrison, Goldie; Dalrymple, Freeman, Bevan, Hubbard, Threlfall.

Record League Victory: 10–1 v Ipswich T, Division 1, 26 December 1963 – Macedo; Cohen, Langley; Mullery (1), Keetch, Robson (1); Key, Cook (1), Leggat (4), Haynes, Howfield (3).

IT'S A FACT !

On 23 April 1966, Fulham were away to Northampton Town. The winners would avoid relegation at the expense of the losers. Despite twice going behind, Fulham won 4-2 with a Steve Earle hat-trick and a goal from Bobby Robson.

Record Cup Victory: 7–0 v Swansea C, FA Cup 1st rd, 11 November 1995 – Lange; Jupp (1), Herrera, Barkus (Brooker (1)), Moore, Angus, Thomas (1), Morgan, Brazil (Hamill), Conroy (3) (Bolt), Cusack (1).

Record Defeat: 0–10 v Liverpool, League Cup 2nd rd 1st leg, 23 September 1986.

Most League Points (2 for a win): 60, Division 2, 1958–59 and Division 3, 1970–71.

Most League Points (3 for a win): 101, Division 2, 1998–99.

Most League Goals: 111, Division 3 (S), 1931–32.

Highest League Scorer in Season: Frank Newton, 43, Division 3 (S), 1931–32.

Most League Goals in Total Aggregate: Gordon Davies, 159, 1978–84, 1986–91.

Most League Goals in One Match: 5, Fred Harrison v Stockport Co, Division 2, 5 September 1908; 5, Bedford Jezzard v Hull C, Division 2, 8 October 1955; 5, Jimmy Hill v Doncaster R, Division 2, 15 March 1958; 5, Steve Earle v Halifax T, Division 3, 16 September 1969.

Most Capped Player: Johnny Haynes, 56, England.

Most League Appearances: Johnny Haynes, 594, 1952–70.

Youngest League Player: Tony Mahoney, 17 years 38 days v Cardiff C, 6 November 1976.

Record Transfer Fee Received: £800,000 from Bristol C for Tony Thorpe, February 1998.

Record Transfer Fee Paid: £11,500,000 to Lyon for Steve Marlet, August 2001.

Football League Record: 1907 Elected to Division 2; 1928–32 Division 3 (S); 1932–49 Division 2; 1949–52 Division 1; 1952–59 Division 2; 1959–68 Division 1; 1968–69 Division 2; 1969–71 Division 3; 1971–80 Division 2; 1980–82 Division 3; 1982–86 Division 2; 1986–92 Division 3; 1992–94 Division 2; 1994–97 Division 3; 1997–99 Division 2; 1999–2001 Division 1; 2001– FA Premier League.

LATEST SEQUENCES

Longest Sequence of League Wins: 11, 12.8.00 – 18.10.00.

Longest Sequence of League Defeats: 11, 2.12.61 – 24.2.62.

Longest Sequence of League Draws: 6, 14.10.95 – 18.11.95.

Longest Sequence of Unbeaten League Matches: 15, 26.1.99 – 13.4.99.

Longest Sequence Without a League Win: 15, 25.2.50 – 23.8.50.

MANAGERS

Harry Bradshaw 1904–09
Phil Kelso 1909–24
Andy Ducat 1924–26
Joe Bradshaw 1926–29
Ned Liddell 1929–31
Jim MacIntyre 1931–34
Jimmy Hogan 1934–35
Jack Peart 1935–48
Frank Osborne 1948–64
    (was Secretary-Manager or General Manager for most of this period)
Bill Dodgin Snr 1949–53
Duggie Livingstone 1956–58
Bedford Jezzard 1958–64
    (General Manager for last two months)
Vic Buckingham 1965–68
Bobby Robson 1968
Bill Dodgin Jnr 1969–72
Alec Stock 1972–76
Bobby Campbell 1976–80
Malcolm Macdonald 1980–84
Ray Harford 1984–96
Ray Lewington 1986–90
Alan Dicks 1990–91
Don Mackay 1991–94
Ian Branfoot 1994–96
    (continued as General Manager)
Micky Adams 1996–97
Ray Wilkins 1997–98
Kevin Keegan 1998–99
    (Chief Operating Officer)
Paul Bracewell 1999–2000
Jean Tigana July 2000–

TEN YEAR LEAGUE RECORD

		P	W	D	L	F	A	Pts	Pos
1991-92	Div 3	46	19	13	14	57	53	70	9
1992-93	Div 2	46	16	17	13	57	55	65	12
1993-94	Div 2	46	14	10	22	50	63	52	21
1994-95	Div 3	42	16	14	12	60	54	62	8
1995-96	Div 3	46	12	17	17	57	63	53	17
1996-97	Div 3	46	25	12	9	72	38	87	2
1997-98	Div 2	46	20	10	16	60	43	70	6
1998-99	Div 2	46	31	8	7	79	32	101	1
1999-2000	Div 1	46	17	16	13	49	41	67	9
2000-01	Div 1	46	30	11	5	90	32	101	1

DID YOU KNOW

On 30 March 2001, Fulham's 4-1 win at Tranmere Rovers was their 12th away from home and equalled a club record. They went on to record 14 by the season's end.

FULHAM 2001–02 LEAGUE RECORD

Match No.	Date	Venue	Opponents	Result	H/T Score	Lg. Pos.	Goalscorers	Attendance
1	Aug 19	A	Manchester U	L	2-3	1-1	—	Saha 2 [4, 48]	67,534
2	22	H	Sunderland	W	2-0	0-0	—	Hayles [70], Saha [85]	20,197
3	25	H	Derby Co	D	0-0	0-0	7		18,607
4	Sept 9	A	Charlton Ath	D	1-1	1-1	10	Boa Morte [38]	20,451
5	15	H	Arsenal	L	1-3	0-1	14	Malbranque [48]	20,805
6	22	A	Leicester C	D	0-0	0-0	14		18,918
7	30	H	Chelsea	D	1-1	0-1	14	Hayles [56]	21,159
8	Oct 14	A	Aston Villa	L	0-2	0-0	15		28,579
9	21	H	Ipswich T	D	1-1	1-0	14	Hayles [23]	17,221
10	27	H	Southampton	W	2-1	2-1	14	Malbranque 2 [25, 33]	18,771
11	Nov 3	A	West Ham U	W	2-0	1-0	12	Legwinski [44], Malbranque [65]	26,217
12	17	H	Newcastle U	W	3-1	2-0	11	Saha [20], Legwinski [28], Hayles [70]	21,159
13	24	A	Bolton W	D	0-0	0-0	11		23,848
14	Dec 2	H	Leeds U	D	0-0	0-0	12		20,918
15	8	H	Everton	W	2-0	1-0	8	Hayles 2 [36, 50]	19,338
16	12	A	Liverpool	D	0-0	0-0	—		37,163
17	15	A	Tottenham H	L	0-4	0-2	10		36,054
18	26	H	Charlton Ath	D	0-0	0-0	10		17,900
19	30	H	Manchester U	L	2-3	1-2	12	Legwinski [45], Marlet [89]	21,159
20	Jan 2	A	Derby Co	W	1-0	0-0	—	Carbonari (og) [72]	28,165
21	12	H	Middlesbrough	W	2-1	2-1	9	Saha [40], Marlet [45]	18,975
22	19	A	Sunderland	D	1-1	1-0	9	Malbranque [15]	41,305
23	30	A	Ipswich T	L	0-1	0-1	—		25,149
24	Feb 2	H	Aston Villa	D	0-0	0-0	10		20,041
25	9	H	Blackburn R	W	2-0	1-0	9	Hayles [31], Malbranque [63]	19,580
26	19	A	Middlesbrough	L	1-2	0-1	—	Marlet [56]	26,277
27	23	A	Arsenal	L	1-4	1-3	9	Marlet [10]	38,029
28	Mar 2	A	Liverpool	L	0-2	0-1	10		21,103
29	6	A	Chelsea	L	2-3	1-2	—	Saha 2 (1 pen) [20 (p), 73]	39,744
30	16	A	Everton	L	1-2	0-2	12	Malbranque [52]	34,639
31	24	H	Tottenham H	L	0-2	0-2	14		15,885
32	30	A	Southampton	D	1-1	1-1	13	Marlet [7]	31,616
33	Apr 1	H	West Ham U	L	0-1	0-1	15		19,416
34	8	A	Newcastle U	D	1-1	0-1	—	Saha [77]	50,017
35	20	A	Leeds U	W	1-0	0-0	14	Malbranque [52]	39,811
36	23	H	Bolton W	W	3-0	1-0	—	Goldbaek [42], Marlet [72], Hayles [76]	18,107
37	27	H	Leicester C	D	0-0	0-0	11		21,016
38	May 11	A	Blackburn R	L	0-3	0-0	13		30,487

Final League Position: 13

GOALSCORERS

League (36): Hayles 8, Malbranque 8, Saha 8 (1 pen), Marlet 6, Legwinski 3, Boa Morte 1, Goldbaek 1, own goal 1.
Worthington Cup (8): Hayles 2, Boa Morte 1, Brevett 1, Collins 1, Legwinski 1, Malbranque 1 (pen), Saha 1.
FA Cup (8): Marlet 3, Hayles 2, Legwinski 1, Malbranque 1, own goal 1.

Van der Sar E 37	Finnan S 38	Harley J 5 + 5	Melville A 35	Goma A 32 + 1	Davis S 25 + 5	Goldbaek B 8 + 5	Collins J 29 + 5	Saha L 28 + 8	Hayles B 27 + 8	Malbranque S 33 + 4	Stolcers A — + 5	Betsy K — + 1	Ouaddou A 4 + 4	Brevett R 34 + 1	Symons K 2 + 2	Legwinski S 30 + 3	Clark L 5 + 4	Boa Morte L 15 + 8	Marlet S 21 + 5	Knight Z 8 + 2	Willock C — + 2	Taylor M 1	Lewis E 1	Match No.
1	2	3	4	5	6	7^1	8	9	10^2	11^3	12	13	14											1
1	2	12	4	5	6	7	8	9	10	11				3^1										2
1	2	12	4	5^2	6	7^1	8^3	9	10	11				3		13	14							3
1	2		4		6		8	9^1	12	13				3	5	7		11^2	10					4
1	2		4		6		8	9	12	11				3	5	7^2			10^1	13				5
1	2		4		6		8	9		14				3	12	13^1	11	10^2	7	5^1				6
1	2		4		6	7^1	8^3	9	10	13				3		11^2	12	14	5					7
1	2		4	12	6^2		8	9	13	11				3		7	14	10^2	5^1					8
1	2		4	5	12		8	13	10^2	14				3		7	6^1	9^3						9
1	2		4	5			8	12	10	6				3		7		11	9^1					10
1	2		4	5	12	13	8^2	9^1	10	6^3	14			3		7		11						11
1	2		4	5	6	12	8^2	9	10	11^1				3		7	13							12
1	2		4	5	6		8	9	10^1	11^2				3		7	13	12						13
1	2		4	5	12		8	9	10	6				3		7^1		11						14
1	2		4	5	12		8	9^1	10	6				3		7		11						15
1	2		4	5	6^1		8	9	10	11				3	12		7							16
1	2		4	5			8^1	9	10	6				3		7	12	11						17
1	2		4	5	6		12	9	10	11				3		7^1	8^2	13						18
1	2		4	5	12		8	9	10^2	6				3		7^1		11	13					19
1	2		4	5	6		8	12	10^1	11				3				9	7					20
1	2		4	5	6		8	12	10^2	11				3		7^1		9	13					21
1	2		4	5			8		10^1	6	13			3		7		12^2	9	11				22
1	2		4	5		8^1	13	9	12	6			14	3		7^3			10	11^2				23
1	2	3	4	5		12		9	10	6						7			8	11^1				24
1	2		4	5	6		8		10	11				3		7			9^1		12			25
1	2		4	5	6		8^1	12	10	11				3		7			9					26
1	2	12	4	5			8	13	10^2	11				3		7		14	9	6^1				27
1	2		5		6^2		8	14	9	12	11		4	3		7	13^3	10^1	8					28
1	2	11	5				8	9	12	6			4	3		7^1		10						29
1	2		4	5^2	12		8	9	13	6			14	3		7^1		11^2	10					30
1	2	3^1	5		6			9	10	11			4		12	7		8						31
1	2	12	4	5	6^2		8^1	13	10^2	11				3		7		14	9					32
1	2	12	4	5	6^1		8^3	9^1	10	11				3		7		13	14					33
1	2		4	5	6		8	9		11				3		7		10						34
1	2		4	5	6^3	12		9^1	13	8			14	3		7		11^1	10					35
1	2		4	5	6^1	7	12	9^1	10	11^1	13			3		8		14						36
1	2		4	5	6	7^2	12	13	10	11^1				3		8^1		9						37
	2	3	4		6	7		9			12				5^2		8^1		10^3	13	14	1	11	38

Worthington Cup

Second Round	Rochdale	(a)	2-2
Third Round	Derby Co	(h)	5-2
Fourth Round	Tottenham H	(h)	1-2

FA Cup

Third Round	Wycombe W	(a)	2-2
		(h)	1-0
Fourth Round	York C	(a)	2-0
Fifth Round	Walsall	(a)	2-1
Sixth Round	WBA	(a)	1-0
Semi-Final (at Villa Park)	Chelsea		0-1

GILLINGHAM
Division 1

FOUNDATION

The success of the pioneering Royal Engineers of Chatham excited the interest of the residents of the Medway Towns and led to the formation of many clubs including Excelsior. After winning the Kent Junior Cup and the Chatham District League in 1893, Excelsior decided to go for bigger things and it was at a meeting in the Napier Arms, Brompton, in 1893 that New Brompton FC came into being, buying and developing the ground which is now Priestfield Stadium.

Priestfield Stadium, Gillingham, ME7 4DD.

Telephone: (01634) 851 854 or 300 000.
Fax: (01634) 850 986. *ClubCall:* 09068 332 211.

Ground Capacity: 10,600.

Record Attendance: 23,002 v QPR, FA Cup 3rd rd, 10 January 1948.

Record Receipts: £80,184 v Sheffield W, FA Cup 3rd rd, 7 January 1995.

Pitch Measurements: 114yd × 75yd.

Chairman/Chief Executive: P. D. P. Scally.

Directors: P. A. Spokes, M. J. Quarlington (non-executive).
Associate Director: Yvonne Paulley.

Player Manager: Andy Hessenthaler.

Assistant Manager: Richard Hill.

First Team Coach: Wayne Jones.

Physio: Ken Steggles.

Secretary: Mrs G. E. Poynter.

Colours: Blue.

Change Colours: Red or white.

Year Formed: 1893.

Turned Professional: 1894.

Ltd Co.: 1893.

Previous Name: 1893, New Brompton; 1913, Gillingham.

Club Nickname: 'The Gills'.

First Football League Game: 28 August 1920, Division 3, v Southampton (h) D 1–1 – Branfield; Robertson, Sissons; Battiste, Baxter, Wigmore; Holt, Hall, Gilbey (1), Roe, Gore.

Record League Victory: 10–0 v Chesterfield, Division 3, 5 September 1987 – Kite; Haylock, Pearce, Shipley (2) (Lillis), West, Greenall (1), Pritchard (2), Shearer (2), Lovell, Elsey (2), David Smith (1).

HONOURS

Football League: Promoted from Division 2 1999–2000 (play-offs); Division 3 – Runners-up 1995-96; Division 4 – Champions 1963–64; Runners-up 1973–74.
FA Cup: best season: 6th rd, 2000.
Football League Cup: best season: 4th rd, 1964, 1997.

IT'S A FACT !

In 1945–46, Gillingham set a Kent County record, in winning the Kent League, League Cup, Senior Cup, Senior Shield and becoming joint holders with Millwall of the Kent Championship Cup, succeeding in every competition for which they entered.

Record Cup Victory: 10–1 v Gorleston, FA Cup 1st rd, 16 November 1957 – Brodie; Parry, Hannaway; Riggs, Boswell, Laing; Payne, Fletcher (2), Saunders (5), Morgan (1), Clark (2).

Record Defeat: 2–9 v Nottingham F, Division 3 (S), 18 November 1950.

Most League Points (2 for a win): 62, Division 4, 1973–74.

Most League Points (3 for a win): 85, Division 2, 1999–2000.

Most League Goals: 90, Division 4, 1973–74.

Highest League Scorer in Season: Ernie Morgan, 31, Division 3 (S), 1954–55; Brian Yeo, 31, Division 4, 1973–74.

Most League Goals in Total Aggregate: Brian Yeo, 135, 1963–75.

Most League Goals in One Match: 6, Fred Cheesmur v Merthyr T, Division 3S, 26 April 1930.

Most Capped Player: Tony Cascarino, 3 (88), Republic of Ireland.

Most League Appearances: John Simpson, 571, 1957–72.

Youngest League Player: Billy Hughes, 15 years 275 days v Southend U, 13 April 1976.

Record Transfer Fee Received: £1,500,000 from Manchester C for Robert Taylor, November 1999.

Record Transfer Fee Paid: £600,000 to Reading for Carl Asaba, August 1998.

Football League Record: 1920 Original Member of Division 3; 1921 Division 3 (S); 1938 Failed re-election; Southern League 1938–44; Kent League 1944–46; Southern League 1946–50; 1950 Re-elected to Division 3 (S); 1958–64 Division 4; 1964–71 Division 3; 1971–74 Division 4; 1974–89 Division 3; 1989–92 Division 4; 1992–96; Division 3; 1996–2000 Division 2; 2000– Division 1.

MANAGERS

W. Ironside Groombridge
1896–1906 *(Secretary-Manager)*
(previously Financial Secretary)
Steve Smith 1906–08
W. I. Groombridge 1908–19
(Secretary-Manager)
George Collins 1919–20
John McMillan 1920–23
Harry Curtis 1923–26
Albert Hoskins 1926–29
Dick Hendrie 1929–31
Fred Mavin 1932–37
Alan Ure 1937–38
Bill Harvey 1938–39
Archie Clark 1939–58
Harry Barratt 1958–62
Freddie Cox 1962–65
Basil Hayward 1966–71
Andy Nelson 1971–74
Len Ashurst 1974–75
Gerry Summers 1975–81
Keith Peacock 1981–87
Paul Taylor 1988
Keith Burkinshaw 1988–89
Damien Richardson 1989–93
Mike Flanagan 1993–95
Neil Smillie 1995
Tony Pulis 1995–99
Peter Taylor 1999–2000
Andy Hessenthaler June 2000–

LATEST SEQUENCES

Longest Sequence of League Wins: 7, 18.12.54 – 29.1.55.

Longest Sequence of League Defeats: 10, 20.9.88 – 5.11.88.

Longest Sequence of League Draws: 5, 28.8.93 – 18.9.93.

Longest Sequence of Unbeaten League Matches: 20, 13.10.73 – 10.2.74.

Longest Sequence Without a League Win: 15, 1.4.72 – 2.9.72.

TEN YEAR LEAGUE RECORD

		P	W	D	L	F	A	Pts	Pos
1991-92	Div 4	42	15	12	15	63	53	57	11
1992-93	Div 3	42	9	13	20	48	64	40	21
1993-94	Div 3	42	12	15	15	44	51	51	16
1994-95	Div 3	42	10	11	21	46	64	41	19
1995-96	Div 3	46	22	17	7	49	20	83	2
1996-97	Div 2	46	19	10	17	60	59	67	11
1997-98	Div 2	46	19	13	14	52	47	70	8
1998-99	Div 2	46	22	14	10	75	44	80	4
1999-2000	Div 2	46	25	10	11	79	48	85	3
2000-01	Div 1	46	13	16	17	61	66	55	13

DID YOU KNOW ?

Harry Loasby's hat-trick in an FA Cup first round tie against Guildford City on 29 November 1930 in a 7-2 win were all the goals he scored in the competition for the club.

GILLINGHAM 2001–02 LEAGUE RECORD

Match No.	Date	Venue	Opponents	Result	H/T Score	Lg. Pos.	Goalscorers	Attendance
1	Aug 11	H	Preston NE	W 5-0	2-0	—	Browning 2 [14, 67], Ashby [17], Onuora [71], Gooden [74]	9412
2	18	A	Sheffield U	D 0-0	0-0	5		16,998
3	25	H	Barnsley	W 3-0	1-0	3	Onuora [39], King 2 [72, 84]	8292
4	27	A	WBA	L 0-1	0-1	7		18,180
5	Sept 8	A	Portsmouth	L 1-2	1-0	10	Onuora [34]	17,224
6	14	A	Bradford C	L 1-5	0-1	—	King [90]	14,101
7	18	H	Wolverhampton W	L 2-3	0-2	—	Ipoua [84], King (pen) [90]	8966
8	22	H	Rotherham U	W 2-1	1-0	15	King [27], Hope [54]	7688
9	25	A	Grimsby T	W 2-1	1-0	—	Hope [17], King [54]	4859
10	29	H	Coventry C	L 1-2	0-2	15	Shaw [90]	9435
11	Oct 13	H	Norwich C	L 0-2	0-0	18		9166
12	20	A	Wimbledon	L 1-3	0-1	20	Butters [82]	8042
13	23	A	Birmingham C	L 1-2	0-1	—	Ipoua [53]	27,101
14	27	H	Walsall	W 2-0	1-0	20	Perpetuini [24], Ipoua [67]	7548
15	30	H	Burnley	D 2-2	2-1	—	Osborn [6], Ipoua [15]	8067
16	Nov 3	A	Manchester C	L 1-4	0-3	20	King [70]	33,067
17	10	A	Crewe Alex	D 0-0	0-0	21		5419
18	18	H	Watford	D 0-0	0-0	20		8733
19	21	H	Crystal Palace	W 3-0	3-0	—	Ipoua 2 [9, 33], Onuora [20]	9396
20	24	A	Millwall	W 2-1	0-0	17	Ipoua [83], King [88]	15,214
21	27	A	Stockport Co	W 2-0	1-0	—	Onuora [32], King [88]	4854
22	30	H	Birmingham C	D 1-1	1-0	—	Purse (og) [16]	6575
23	Dec 8	A	Nottingham F	D 2-2	1-1	15	Shaw 2 [5, 70]	18,303
24	15	H	Sheffield W	W 2-1	2-1	12	Shaw [20], Osborn [26]	8586
25	22	A	Barnsley	L 1-4	1-2	13	Morgan (og) [45]	11,965
26	26	H	Portsmouth	W 2-0	2-0	12	King [22], Shaw [29]	10,477
27	29	H	WBA	W 2-1	1-0	12	Hope [45], Smith [90]	9912
28	Jan 12	H	Sheffield U	L 0-1	0-0	13		8814
29	16	A	Crystal Palace	L 1-3	1-1	—	Onuora [29]	17,646
30	19	A	Preston NE	W 2-0	1-0	11	Osborn [29], Smith [87]	13,289
31	29	H	Stockport Co	D 3-3	3-2	—	Woodthorpe (og) [12], Osborn [38], King (pen) [45]	7217
32	Feb 2	A	Coventry C	W 2-1	1-0	11	Onuora [19], King [77]	14,337
33	9	H	Wimbledon	D 0-0	0-0	11		8494
34	23	H	Bradford C	L 0-4	0-3	12		7789
35	26	A	Rotherham U	L 2-3	0-1	—	Onuora [76], King [85]	6005
36	Mar 2	A	Wolverhampton W	L 0-2	0-2	15		25,908
37	5	H	Grimsby T	W 2-1	1-1	—	Shaw [45], Ipoua [55]	7025
38	9	A	Sheffield W	D 0-0	0-0	13		20,361
39	16	H	Nottingham F	W 3-1	0-1	13	King 2 [49, 81], Browning [83]	8928
40	19	A	Norwich C	L 1-2	1-0	—	Onuora [17]	16,479
41	24	A	Millwall	W 1-0	0-0	12	King [69]	8082
42	30	A	Walsall	D 1-1	0-1	12	Saunders [87]	6190
43	Apr 1	H	Crewe Alex	W 1-0	1-0	12	King (pen) [45]	7748
44	6	A	Burnley	L 0-2	0-0	12		16,236
45	13	H	Manchester C	L 1-3	1-2	12	Onuora [34]	9494
46	21	A	Watford	W 3-2	1-1	12	Hope [42], Shaw [69], Onuora [85]	15,674

Final League Position: 12

GOALSCORERS

League (64): King 17 (3 pens), Onuora 11, Ipoua 8, Shaw 7, Hope 4, Osborn 4, Browning 3, Smith 2, Ashby 1, Butters 1, Gooden 1, Perpetuini 1, Saunders 1, own goals 3.
Worthington Cup (4): King 2 (1 pen), Onuora 1, own goal 1.
FA Cup (4): Gooden 1, King 1, Shaw 1, own goal 1.

Bartram V 36	Patterson M 17 + 3	Edge R 14	Hope C 46	Ashby B 28	Pennock A 9 + 1	Smith P 46	Browning M 38 + 4	Onuora I 31 + 2	Ipoua G 20 + 20	Gooden T 20 + 5	Perpetuini D 25 + 9	Saunders M 6 + 13	Shaw P 27 + 10	King M 38 + 4	Hessenthaler A 10 + 7	Spiller D — + 1	James K — + 10	Butters G 21 + 2	Nosworthy N 29	Osborn S 23 + 5	Taylor R 3 + 8	Samuel J 7 + 1	Brown J 10	Rose R 2 + 1	Match No.
1	2	3^1	4	5	6	7	8	9	10^3	11	12	13	14												1
1	2	3	4	5	6	7	8	9	10^1	11				12											2
1	2	3	4	5	6	7	8^2	9^1		11^3		13		12	10	14									3
1	2	3	4	5	6	7	8^2	9^1	12	11				10	13										4
1	2	3	4	5	6	7	8^2	9		11				12	10^1	13									5
1	2^1		4	5	6	7	11^2		12		3^3	13	10	9	8	14									6
1			4	5		7	2		12	11^2	3	6^3	10^1	9	8	14	13								7
1	2	3	4	5		7	6	9^1		11^2		13		12	10	8									8
1	2	3	4	5		7	6	9		11^1	12	13		10	8^2										9
1		3	4	5		7	6^1	9	12	11^2		13	14	10	8				2^3						10
1	2	3	4		6	7	8^2	9^1		11				10				5	13	12					11
1	2	3	4		6	7	8	9^2		11^3	12			10^1				5	14	13					12
1	2		4		6^3	7		9	12	11			10^2				14	5^1	3	8	13				13
1	2		4			7		9^1	12	11			10^2					5	3	8	13	6			14
1	2^1		4			7		9^2	12	11		13		10				5	3	8		6			15
1			4			7		9^2	12		3	13		10^3	8^1			5	2	11	14	6			16
1			4	5		7		9^2	12	11	3			10^1					2	8	13	6			17
1			4	5		7		9^2	12	11	3			10^1					2	8		6			18
1			4	5		7	6^2	9^1	12	11	3	13	10						2	8					19
1			4	5^2		7	6	9^1	12	11	3^3	13	10				14		2	8					20
1			4			7		9^2	12	11	3			10^1				5	2	8		6			21
1			4			7		9^2	12	11	3	13		10^1				5	2	8		6			22
1			4			7	6	9^1		11	3		10^2				13	5	2	8	12				23
1			4			7	6	9		11	3		10^1					5	2	8	12				24
1			4			7	6			11^1	3		10				12	5	2	8	9				25
1			4	5		7	6	9^1	12	11^2	3	13							2	8	10				26
1			4	5		7	6	9^2	12	11	3^1	13							2	8	10				27
1			4	5		7	6	9	12	11^1	3		10						2	8					28
1			4	5		7	6^3	9^2	12	11	3^1	13	10				14		2	8					29
1	2		4	5		7	6	9^1	12	11^3		13	10^2				14		2	8					30
1			4	5		7	6^3	9	12	11	3	13	10^2				14		2^1	8					31
1	2		4	5		7	6	9	12	11	3		10^1				12			8					32
1	2		4	5		7	6^3	9^1	12	11^2	3	13	10				14			8					33
1	2		4	5		7	6^3	9	12	11	3	13	10^1				14			8^2					34
1			4	5		7	6	9	12	11	3		10						2	8					35
1	3		4	5		7	6^1	9	12	11^2		13	10				14		2	8^3					36
		3	4			7^2	6^1	9	12	11		13	10^3				14	5	2	8			1		37
		3	4			7	6	9^1	12	11			10				14	5	2	8			1		38
		3^2	4			7	6	9^1	12	11^3		13	10				14	5	2	8			1		39
			4			7	6^3	9^1	12	11^{12}	3	13	10				14	5	2	8			1		40
			4			7	6	9	12	11	3	13	10^2					5	2	8^1			1		41
			4			7	6^3	9	12	11^2	3	13	10^1				14	5	2	8			1		42
			4			7	6	9	12	11^3	3	13	10^2				14	5	2^1	8			1		43
	2		4			7	6	9	12	11	3^3	13	10^1					5		8^2			1	14	44
	2		4			7	6	9^1	12	11^2		13	10				14	5		8^3			1	3	45
	2	13	4			7	6	9	12	11^2			10^1				14	5		8^3			1	3	46

Worthington Cup

First Round	Oxford U	(a)	2-1
Second Round	Millwall	(h)	2-1
Third Round	Southampton	(h)	0-2

FA Cup

Third Round	Wolverhampton W	(a)	1-0
Fourth Round	Bristol R	(h)	1-0
Fifth Round	Arsenal	(a)	2-5

GRIMSBY TOWN

FOUNDATION

Grimsby Pelham FC, as they were first known, came into being at a meeting held at the Wellington Arms in September 1878. Pelham is the family name of big landowners in the area, the Earls of Yarborough. The receipts for their first game amounted to 6s. 9d. (approx. 39p). After a year, the club name was changed to Grimsby Town.

Blundell Park, Cleethorpes, North East Lincolnshire DN35 7PY.

Telephone: (01472) 605 050. **Fax:** (01472) 693 665. **ClubCall:** 09068 555 855.

Ground Capacity: 10,033.

Record Attendance: 31,657 v Wolverhampton W, FA Cup 5th rd, 20 February 1937.

Record Receipts: £119,799 v Aston Villa, FA Cup 4th rd, 29 January 1994.

Pitch Measurements: 111yd × 75yd.

Life President: T. J. Lindley.

Chairman: P. W. Furneaux.

Directors: J. Arnell, C. Graves, J. Fenty, M. Rouse, A. King, D. Ramsden.

Manager: Paul Groves.
Assistant Manager: Graham Rodger.

Chief Executive/Company Secretary: Ian Fleming.
Physio: Paul Mitchell.

Commercial Manager: Tony Richardson.

Press Officer: Tim Harvey.

Colours: Black and white striped shirts, black shorts, black stockings with red turnover.

Change Colours: Sky blue shirts with navy trim, sky blue shorts with navy trim, sky blue stockings with navy trim.

Year Formed. 1878.

Turned Professional: 1890.

Ltd Co.: 1890.

Previous Name: 1878, Grimsby Pelham; 1879, Grimsby Town.

Club Nickname: 'The Mariners'.

Previous Grounds: 1880, Clee Park; 1889, Abbey Park; 1899, Blundell Park.

First Football League Game: 3 September 1892, Division 2, v Northwich Victoria (h) W 2–1 – Whitehouse; Lundie, T. Frith; C. Frith, Walker, Murrell; Higgins, Henderson, Brayshaw, Riddoch (2), Ackroyd.

HONOURS

Football League: Division 1 best season: 5th, 1934–35; Division 2 – Champions 1900–01, 1933–34; Runners-up 1928–29; Promoted from Division 2 1997–98 (play-offs); Division 3 (N) – Champions 1925–26, 1955–56; Runners-up 1951–52; Division 3 – Champions 1979–80; Runners-up 1961–62; Division 4 – Champions 1971–72; Runners-up 1978–79; 1989–90.

FA Cup: Semi-finals, 1936, 1939.

Football League Cup: best season: 5th rd, 1980, 1985.

League Group Cup: Winners 1982.

Auto Windscreen Shield: Winners 1998.

IT'S A FACT !

When Grimsby Town won 1-0 at Crewe Alexandra on 2 August 2001, it was the first time in 17 years that they had succeeded in winning the opening Football League game of the season.

Record League Victory: 9–2 v Darwen, Division 2, 15 April 1899 – Bagshaw; Lockie, Nidd; Griffiths, Bell (1), Nelmes; Jenkinson (3), Richards (1), Cockshutt (3), Robinson, Chadburn (1).

Record Cup Victory: 8–0 v Darlington, FA Cup 2nd rd, 21 November 1885 – G. Atkinson; J. H. Taylor, H. Taylor; Hall, Kimpson, Hopewell; H. Atkinson (1), Garnham, Seal (3), Sharman, Monument (4).

Record Defeat: 1–9 v Arsenal, Division 1, 28 January 1931.

Most League Points (2 for a win): 68, Division 3 (N), 1955–56.

Most League Points (3 for a win): 83, Division 3, 1990–91.

Most League Goals: 103, Division 2, 1933–34.

Highest League Scorer in Season: Pat Glover, 42, Division 2, 1933–34.

Most League Goals in Total Aggregate: Pat Glover, 180, 1930–39.

Most League Goals in One Match: 6, Tommy McCairns v Leicester Fosse, Division 2, 11 April 1896.

Most Capped Player: Pat Glover, 7, Wales.

Most League Appearances: John McDermott, 497, 1987– .

Youngest League Player: Tony Ford, 16 years 143 days v Walsall, 4 October 1975.

Record Transfer Fee Received: £1,500,000 from Everton for John Oster, July 1997.

Record Transfer Fee Paid: £500,000 to Preston NE for Lee Ashcroft, August 1998.

Football League Record: 1892 Original Member Division 2; 1901–03 Division 1; 1903 Division 2; 1910 Failed re-election; 1911 re-elected Division 2; 1920–21 Division 3; 1921–26 Division 3 (N); 1926–29 Division 3; 1929–32 Division 1; 1932–34 Division 2; 1934–48 Division 1; 1948–51 Division 2; 1951–56 Division 3 (N); 1956–59 Division 2; 1959–62 Division 3; 1962–64 Division 2; 1964–68 Division 3; 1968–72 Division 4; 1972–77 Division 3; 1977–79 Division 4; 1979–80 Division 3; 1980–87 Division 2; 1987–88 Division 3; 1988–90 Division 4; 1990–91 Division 3; 1991–92 Division 2; 1992–97 Division 1; 1997–98 Division 2; 1998– Division 1.

MANAGERS

H. N. Hickson 1902–20
  (Secretary-Manager)
Haydn Price 1920
George Fraser 1921–24
Wilf Gillow 1924–32
Frank Womack 1932–36
Charles Spencer 1937–51
Bill Shankly 1951–53
Billy Walsh 1954–55
Allenby Chilton 1955–59
Tim Ward 1960–62
Tom Johnston 1962–64
Jimmy McGuigan 1964–67
Don McEvoy 1967–68
Bill Harvey 1968–69
Bobby Kennedy 1969–71
Lawrie McMenemy 1971–73
Ron Ashman 1973–75
Tom Casey 1975–76
Johnny Newman 1976–79
George Kerr 1979–82
David Booth 1982–85
Mike Lyons 1985–87
Bobby Roberts 1987–88
Alan Buckley 1988–94
Brian Laws 1994–96
Kenny Swain 1997
Alan Buckley 1997–2000
Lennie Lawrence 2000–01
Paul Groves December 2001–

LATEST SEQUENCES

Longest Sequence of League Wins: 11, 19.1.52 – 29.3.52.

Longest Sequence of League Defeats: 9, 30.11.07 – 18.1.08.

Longest Sequence of League Draws: 5, 6.2.65 – 6.3.65.

Longest Sequence of Unbeaten League Matches: 19, 16.2.80 – 30.8.80.

Longest Sequence Without a League Win: 18, 10.10.81 – 16.3.82.

TEN YEAR LEAGUE RECORD

		P	W	D	L	F	A	Pts	Pos
1991-92	Div 2	46	14	11	21	47	62	53	19
1992-93	Div 1	46	19	7	20	58	57	64	9
1993-94	Div 1	46	13	20	13	52	47	59	16
1994-95	Div 1	46	17	14	15	62	56	65	10
1995-96	Div 1	46	14	14	18	55	69	56	17
1996-97	Div 1	46	11	13	22	60	81	46	22
1997-98	Div 2	46	19	15	12	55	37	72	3
1998-99	Div 1	46	17	10	19	40	52	61	11
1999-2000	Div 1	46	13	12	21	41	67	51	20
2000-01	Div 1	46	14	10	22	43	62	52	18

DID YOU KNOW ?

Fred Smith scored four goals in seven minutes for Grimsby Town in a Division Three (North) match against Hartlepools United on 15 November 1952, the goals registering in 14, 17, 19 and 21 minutes of a 7-0 win.

GRIMSBY TOWN 2001–02 LEAGUE RECORD

Match No.	Date	Venue	Opponents	Result	H/T Score	Lg. Pos.	Goalscorers	Atten-dance
1	Aug 11	H	Crewe Alex	W 1-0	0-0	—	Burnett [50]	5368
2	18	A	WBA	W 1-0	0-0	4	Pouton (pen) [77]	17,971
3	25	H	Preston NE	D 2-2	1-1	4	Rowan [27], Pouton (pen) [54]	5789
4	27	A	Portsmouth	L 2-4	0-1	9	Butterfield [50], Jeffrey [73]	13,614
5	Sept 1	H	Barnsley	W 1-0	1-0	2	Jevons [22]	6173
6	8	A	Coventry C	W 1-0	0-0	2	Jevons [59]	14,980
7	15	H	Nottingham F	D 0-0	0-0	3		8746
8	18	A	Crystal Palace	L 0-5	0-2	—		13,970
9	22	A	Stockport Co	D 3-3	1-2	6	Rowan [22], Burnett [64], Campbell [75]	7834
10	25	H	Gillingham	L 1-2	0-1	—	Allen [76]	4859
11	29	A	Bradford C	L 2-3	0-2	12	Rowan [58], Boulding [80]	13,778
12	Oct 5	H	Rotherham U	L 0-2	0-1	—		6662
13	13	A	Sheffield U	L 1-3	0-2	15	Willems [87]	15,442
14	20	H	Watford	L 0-3	0-2	18		5506
15	23	A	Manchester C	L 0-4	0-3	—		30,797
16	26	H	Birmingham C	W 3-1	2-0	—	Boulding 2 [28, 52], Jevons [35]	5149
17	30	H	Norwich C	L 0-2	0-1	—		5489
18	Nov 3	A	Wimbledon	L 1-2	0-1	19	Campbell [49]	6189
19	10	A	Sheffield W	D 0-0	0-0	20		17,507
20	17	H	Millwall	D 2-2	0-0	19	Rowan [49], Boulding [88]	5037
21	23	A	Burnley	L 0-1	0-1	—		18,535
22	Dec 1	H	Manchester C	L 0-2	0-0	22		7960
23	7	H	Wolverhampton W	D 1-1	1-1	—	Jevons [2]	5143
24	15	A	Walsall	L 0-4	0-1	23		5080
25	22	A	Preston NE	D 0-0	0-0	23		14,667
26	26	H	Coventry C	L 0-1	0-1	23		7568
27	29	H	Portsmouth	W 3-1	2-1	22	Jevons 2 (1 pen) [40, 80 (p)], Ford [44]	5217
28	Jan 1	A	Barnsley	D 0-0	0-0	22		13,325
29	12	H	WBA	D 0-0	0-0	23		6011
30	19	A	Crewe Alex	L 0-2	0-2	23		5974
31	29	A	Rotherham U	D 1-1	1-0	—	Taylor [36]	6098
32	Feb 2	H	Bradford C	L 0-1	0-0	23		5054
33	10	A	Watford	L 0-2	0-1	23		12,163
34	16	H	Sheffield U	W 1-0	0-0	23	Campbell [77]	7141
35	23	H	Nottingham F	D 0-0	0-0	23		21,081
36	26	H	Stockport Co	W 3-1	3-1	—	Todd [7], Groves [32], Allen [45]	6836
37	Mar 2	H	Crystal Palace	W 5-2	3-0	22	Todd [31], Boulding [44], Allen [45], Fleming (og) [58], Smith D [88]	5924
38	5	A	Gillingham	L 1-2	1-1	—	Boulding [19]	7025
39	9	H	Walsall	D 2-2	1-0	22	Groves [11], Roper (og) [52]	7016
40	16	A	Wolverhampton W	W 1-0	0-0	21	Todd [79]	25,967
41	23	H	Wimbledon	W 6-2	2-2	19	Boulding 3 [31, 85, 87], Pouton 3 (2 pens) [45, 72 (p), 85 (p)]	6473
42	30	A	Birmingham C	L 0-4	0-2	20		23,249
43	Apr 1	H	Sheffield W	D 0-0	0-0	20		9236
44	6	A	Norwich C	D 1-1	0-1	21	Cooke [84]	20,075
45	13	H	Burnley	W 3-1	3-0	18	Boulding 2 [5, 43], Allen [12]	9275
46	21	A	Millwall	L 1-3	1-3	19	Butterfield [11]	17,004

Final League Position: 19

GOALSCORERS

League (50): Boulding 11, Jevons 6 (1 pen), Pouton 5 (4 pens), Allen 4, Rowan 4, Campbell 3, Todd 3, Burnett 2, Butterfield 2, Groves 2, Cooke 1, Ford 1, Jeffrey 1, Smith D 1, Taylor 1, Willems 1, own goals 2.
Worthington Cup (7): Broomes 2, Jevons 2, Allen 1, Jeffrey 1, Rowan 1.
FA Cup (0).

Coyne D 45	McDermott J 24	Gallimore T 38	Beharall D 13+1	Groves P 43	Butterfield D 43+3	Pouton A 35	Willems M 27+3	Rowan J 19+5	Jevons P 25+6	Campbell S 32+1	Burnett W 18+14	Jeffrey M 4+14	Busscher R —+1	Allen B 19+9	Smith D 4	Broomes M 13+2	Boulding M 24+11	Chapman B 12+5	Croudson S 1	Coldicott S 19+7	Neilson A 8+2	Thompson C 4+4	Raven P 4+5	Ford S 8+5	Taylor R 4	Todd A 12	Pringle M 2	Robinson P 1+4	Falconer W 1+1	Livingstone S —+3	Cooke T 3	Ward 11	Match No.
1	2	3^1	4	5	6	7	8	9^2	10	11	12	13																					1
1	2	3	4	5	6	7	8^2	9^1	10	11		12	13																				2
1	2	3^1	4	5	6	7	8	9^2	10	11	12	13																					3
1	2	3	4	5	6	7^2	8	9	10	11	13	12																					4
1	2	3	4	5	6	7	8^2	9^1	10	11	13	12																					5
1	2	3	4	5	6	7	8	9^1	10^2	11	13	12																					6
1	2	3	4	5	6	7	8	9^1	10^1	11^2	13	12		14																			7
1	2			5	6	7^1	8	9^2		11	12	10		13		3	4																8
1	2	3	4	5	6^1		8	9		11	7	10^1		12		13	14																9
1	2	3		5	12	7	8^1	9	10^2	11^3	6	13		14		4																	10
1		3	4	5	2	7		9^1	10^2	11	6	12		8^2		13	14																11
1		3	4^1	5	2	7		9	10^2	11	6			8		12	13		1														12
1		3	4	5	2^3	7	12	9	10	11^2				13		6	8^1			14													13
1		3		5	4	7^1	8	9	10^3	11^2				14		6	12	13			2												14
1		3		5		7	8^2	9^1	10	12				13		4	11			6	2												15
1		3	4		8	7				12		10^1		9		5	11	13		6	2^2												16
1		3	4		8	7				12	13	10		9^2		5	11	2^1		6^1		14											17
1		3	12	5	2^3	7	8	9^2		11		10				4	13	14		6^1													18
1		3		5	2	6	8	12	10^1	11				9^2		4	7						13										19
1		5	2		8^1	9^1				11	12			10^2		4	7	3			13	14											20
1		5	6	7	8^2	9^3	12			13		10^1				4	11	3			2	14											21
1		3		5	2	7	8	9^1	10				12			4	11			6^1	13												22
1		3		5	2	7^1	8		10					9		4	11			6	12												23
1		3		5		7		8		10		12		9^2			11			6^1	2	13	4										24
1	6			5		7		8				10^1		11^3		12		13		3		14	2	9^2	4								25
1	6			5		7		8^2				10^3		11		12		9		3		13	2	14	4^1								26
1	6			5		7				12		10^2		11		13		14		3		8	2^1	9^3	4								27
1	6			5		2				8		10^1		7		12		13		3		11		9^2	4								28
1	6			5		2				8				10	11^1	7		12		3				9	4								29
1	6	5^2			2		8							10	11	7^3		12		3^1		14			13	4	9						30
1		3		5	2		8								11	7		9		6					12	4^1	10						31
1	2^2	3				13	7^1	8		12		11						9		6					5	4	10						32
1	2	3		5	12	7^3	8			13	11^1	4		14				9						6		10^2							33
1	2	3		5		7				11		8		10				9		6					4^1	12							34
1	2	3		5		7	8			11		4		12				9										6	10^1				35
1	2	3		5		7	8			11		4		9			3	12									13	6^1	10^1				36
1	2			5		7	8		12	11		4		10^2		3		9^1		13						14		6^1					37
1	2			5		7	8			11		4		10^1		3^2		9	13	12						6							38
1	2	3		5		7	8			11		4		10^1				9		12						6							39
1	2	3		5		7	8			12	11	13		10^1				9		4^2						6							40
1	2	3		5		7	8			12	13	11	14	10^1				9^2		4^3						6							41
1	2	3		5		7	8			11		12		10^2				9^3		4^1						6		14	13				42
1	2	3		5		7	8			11^1				10				9		4						6		12					43
1	2^2	3		5		7	8			12						4		9		13						6		10^1	9^3	14	11		44
1	2^1			5		7^2	8							10^3				9	3	4						12		6	13	14	11		45
1	2^1			5		7	8			12				10^3				9	3	4						6		13	14	11^2		2^1	46

Worthington Cup

First Round	Lincoln C	(h)	2-1
Second Round	Sheffield U	(h)	3-3
Third Round	Liverpool	(a)	2-1
Fourth Round	Arsenal	(a)	0-2

FA Cup

Third Round	York C	(h)	0-0
		(a)	0-1

HALIFAX TOWN   Conference

FOUNDATION

The real pioneer behind the setting up of the club was Mr A. E. Jones, who, using the *nom de plume* 'Old Sport', wrote to the *Halifax Evening Courier*. His letter suggesting a club be set up and inviting public opinion was published on 20 April 1911. A public meeting was held at the Saddle Hotel on 23 May 1911, whereafter Dr A. H. Muir became the club's first president and Joe McClelland its first secretary. Mr Jones proposed the following: 'That this meeting of townsmen of Halifax heartily approves of the establishment of a town's Association football club on the basis of scheme 1 (the formation of a limited company) and pledges itself to adopt every legitimate means to that end.' Mr Charles Deantry seconded the motion and the resolution was carried unanimously. The chairman asked for a show of hands of those willing to become guarantors of £1. There was an immediate response from 46 of the assembly.

The Shay Stadium, Shaw Hill, Halifax HX1 2YS.

Telephone: (01422) 345 543. *Fax:* (01422) 349 487.
Souvenir Shop: (01422) 353 423.

Ground Capacity: 9,900.

Record Attendance: 36,885 v Tottenham H, FA Cup 5th rd, 15 February 1953.

Record Receipts: £36,267 v Bradford C, Worthington Cup, 2nd rd, 1st leg, 15 September 1998.

Pitch Measurements: 110yd × 70yd.

President: Robert Holmes.

Vice-presidents: Jack Haymer and Bill King.

Chairman: R. F. Walker. *Directors:* R. Crabtree, D. Tait, D. Cairns, A. Hall.
General Manager: Tony Kniveton.

Manager: Chris Wilder. *Assistant Manager:* Graham Mitchell.

Youth Team Coach: Steve Thornber.

Acting Secretary: Jenna Helliwell.

Colours: Blue shirts, blue shorts, blue stockings with white band.

Change Colours: White shirts with blue trim, white shorts and stockings.

Year Formed: 1911.

Turned Professional: 1911. *Ltd Co.:* 1911.

Club Nickname: 'The Shaymen'.

Previous Grounds: 1911, Sandhall; 1919, Exley; 1921, The Shay.

Club Sponsors: Nationwide.

First Football League Game: 27 August 1921, Division 3 (N), v Darlington (a) L 0-2 – Haldane; Hawley, Mackrill; Hall, Wellock, Challinor; Pinkey, Hetherington, Woods, Dent, Phipps.

HONOURS

Football League: Division 3 best season: 3rd, 1970–71; Division 3 (N) – Runners-up 1934–35; Division 4: Runners-up 1968–69.

FA Cup: best season: 5th rd, 1933, 1953.

Football League Cup: best season: 4th rd, 1964.

Vauxhall Conference: Champions 1997–98.

IT'S A FACT !

On 14 November 1959, Halifax Town full-back Phil Roscoe scored in an FA Cup first round tie at Gateshead with a shot from inside his own half of the pitch, in a 4-3 win.

Record League Victory: 6–0 v Bradford PA, Division 3 (N), 3 December 1955 – Johnson; Griffiths, Ferguson; Watson, Harris, Bell; Hampson (2), Baker (3), Watkinson (1), Capel, Lonsdale. 6–0 v Doncaster R, Division 4, 2 November 1976 – Gennoe; Trainer, Loska (Bradley), McGill, Dunleavy (1), Phelan, Hoy (2), Carroll (1), Bullock (1), Lawson (1), Johnston.

Record Cup Victory: 7–0 v Bishop Auckland, FA Cup 2nd rd (replay), 10 January 1967 – White; Russell, Bodell; Smith, Holt, Jeff Lee; Taylor (2), Hutchison (2), Parks (2), Atkins (1), McCarthy.

Record Defeat: 0–13 v Stockport Co, Division 3 (N), 6 January 1934.

Most League Points (2 for a win): 57, Division 4, 1968–69.

Most League Points (3 for a win): 66, Division 3, 1998–99.

Most League Goals: 83, Division 3 (N), 1957–58.

Highest League Scorer in Season: Albert Valentine, 34, Division 3 (N), 1934–35.

Most League Goals in Total Aggregate: Ernest Dixon, 129, 1922–30.

Most League Goals in One Match: 6, William Chambers v Hartlepools U, Division 3N, 7 April 1934.

Most Capped Player: None.

Most League Appearances: John Pickering, 367, 1965–74.

Youngest League Player: Robert Herbert, 16 years 13 days v Brighton & HA, 11 September 1999.

Record Transfer Fee Received: £350,000 from Fulham for Geoff Horsfield, October 1998.

Record Transfer Fee Paid: £150,000 to Scarborough for Chris Tate, July 1999.

Football League Record: 1921 Original Member of Division 3 (N); 1958–63 Division 3; 1963–69 Division 4; 1969–76 Division 3; 1976–92 Division 4; 1992–93 Division 3; 1993–98 Vauxhall Conference; 1998–2002 Division 3; 2002– Conference.

MANAGERS

A. M. Ricketts 1911–12
(Secretary-Manager)
Joe McClelland 1912–30
Alec Raisbeck 1930–36
Jimmy Thomson 1936–47
Jack Breedon 1947–50
William Wootton 1951–52
Gerald Henry 1952–54
Willie Watson 1954–56
Billy Burnikell 1956
Harry Hooper 1957–62
Willie Watson 1964–66
Vic Metcalfe 1966–67
Alan Ball Snr 1967–70
George Kirby 1970–71
Ray Henderson 1971–72
George Mulhall 1972–74
Johnny Quinn 1974–76
Alan Ball Snr 1976–77
Jimmy Lawson 1977–78
George Kirby 1978–81
Mick Bullock 1981–84
Mick Jones 1984–86
Bill Ayre 1986–90
Jim McCalliog 1990–91
John McGrath 1991–92
Peter Wragg 1992–93
John Bird 1993–95
John Carroll 1996
George Mulhall 1996–98
Kieran O'Regan 1998–99
Mark Lillis 1999–2000
Paul Bracewell 2000–01
Alan Little 2001–02
Neil Redfearn 2002
Chris Wilder July 2002–

LATEST SEQUENCES

Longest Sequence of League Wins: 7, 22.2.64 – 21.3.64.

Longest Sequence of League Defeats: 8, 7.12.46 – 13.1.47.

Longest Sequence of League Draws: 7, 22.1.82 – 20.2.82.

Longest Sequence of Unbeaten League Matches: 17, 14.1.69 – 21.4.69.

Longest Sequence Without a League Win: 22, 26.8.78 – 10.2.79.

TEN YEAR LEAGUE RECORD

		P	W	D	L	F	A	Pts	Pos
1991-92	Div 4	42	10	8	24	34	75	38	20
1992-93	Div 3	42	9	9	24	45	68	36	22
1993-94	Conf	42	13	16	13	55	49	55	13
1994-95	Conf	42	17	12	13	68	54	63	8
1995-96	Conf	42	13	13	16	49	63	52	15
1996-97	Conf	42	12	12	18	55	74	48	19
1997-98	Conf	42	25	12	5	74	43	87	1
1998-99	Div 3	46	17	15	14	58	56	66	10
1999-2000	Div 3	46	15	9	22	44	58	54	18
2000-01	Div 3	46	12	11	23	54	68	47	23

DID YOU KNOW ?

Left-winger Sammy Watters, a pre-war player with Third Lanark, was recruited by Halifax Town in July 1946 and finished as top scorer with 11 League and Cup goals from a total of only 46 in all competitions.

HALIFAX TOWN 2001–02 LEAGUE RECORD

Match No.	Date	Venue	Opponents	Result	H/T Score	Lg. Pos.	Goalscorers	Attendance
1	Aug 11	A	Lincoln C	W	2-1	2-1	—	Midgley [38], Harsley [39]	3753
2	18	H	Exeter C	D	1-1	1-1	6	Swales [22]	1937
3	25	A	Southend U	L	1-4	0-1	15	Redfearn (pen) [66]	3525
4	27	H	Oxford U	L	0-2	0-2	19		2271
5	Sept 1	A	York C	L	0-1	0-0	21		2646
6	8	H	Macclesfield T	D	0-0	0-0	19		1714
7	15	A	Swansea C	W	2-0	1-0	15	Harsley 2 [25, 46]	3794
8	18	H	Mansfield T	W	1-0	1-0	—	Jones [29]	1880
9	22	H	Leyton Orient	D	0-0	0-0	10		2021
10	25	A	Rochdale	L	0-2	0-0	—		3410
11	29	A	Hull C	L	0-3	0-1	18		9572
12	Oct 5	H	Scunthorpe U	D	0-0	0-0	—		2603
13	13	A	Plymouth Arg	L	0-3	0-3	21		5065
14	20	H	Bristol R	D	0-0	0-0	20		1898
15	23	H	Luton T	L	2-4	1-2	—	Harsley [6], Fitzpatrick [78]	2140
16	27	A	Carlisle U	D	0-0	0-0	24		3157
17	Nov 3	H	Darlington	D	2-2	1-1	23	Redfearn [22], Fitzpatrick [90]	2192
18	10	A	Rushden & D	L	1-2	0-1	24	Redfearn [89]	3883
19	20	A	Hartlepool U	L	0-3	0-1	—		2963
20	24	H	Torquay U	W	2-0	1-0	23	Middleton [45], Fitzpatrick [57]	1681
21	Dec 1	A	Cheltenham T	L	1-2	1-1	24	Harsley [14]	3304
22	15	H	Shrewsbury T	L	1-2	0-0	24	Harsley [88]	1703
23	26	A	Macclesfield T	D	1-1	1-0	24	Bushell [33]	2421
24	29	A	Oxford U	L	1-6	0-2	24	Harsley [48]	6046
25	Jan 12	A	Exeter C	D	0-0	0-0	24		2763
26	19	H	Lincoln C	W	3-0	1-0	24	Jones 2 [30, 66], Fitzpatrick [85]	2007
27	22	A	Kidderminster H	L	0-2	0-1	—		2295
28	26	A	Scunthorpe U	L	0-4	0-2	24		3465
29	29	H	Southend U	D	1-1	1-0	—	Jones [16]	1251
30	Feb 2	H	Hull C	L	0-1	0-1	24		3400
31	9	A	Bristol R	L	0-2	0-1	24		6921
32	12	H	York C	D	1-1	1-0	—	Fitzpatrick [13]	2818
33	16	H	Plymouth Arg	L	0-2	0-2	24		2330
34	23	A	Swansea C	L	0-1	0-1	24		1601
35	26	A	Mansfield T	L	1-2	1-0	—	Fitzpatrick [31]	4513
36	Mar 2	A	Leyton Orient	L	1-3	0-1	24	Redfearn [51]	4748
37	5	H	Rochdale	L	1-2	1-0	—	Redfearn [32]	2825
38	9	A	Shrewsbury T	L	0-3	0-1	24		3729
39	12	H	Kidderminster H	W	1-0	1-0	—	Midgley [9]	1227
40	16	H	Cheltenham T	W	4-1	1-1	24	Midgley [25], Fitzpatrick [53], Harsley 2 (1 pen) [81 (p), 85]	1870
41	23	H	Luton T	L	0-5	0-2	24		6830
42	29	H	Carlisle U	D	2-2	1-1	—	Woodward [22], Redfearn [56]	2728
43	Apr 1	A	Darlington	L	0-5	0-2	24		3401
44	6	H	Hartlepool U	L	0-2	0-1	24		1838
45	13	A	Torquay U	W	4-2	1-1	24	Stoneman [45], Harsley [63], Middleton [78], Clarke M [82]	2692
46	20	H	Rushden & D	L	2-4	1-0	24	Harsley (pen) [23], Fitzpatrick [85]	2699

Final League Position: 24

GOALSCORERS

League (39): Harsley 11 (2 pens), Fitzpatrick 8, Redfearn 6 (1 pen), Jones 4, Midgley 3, Middleton 2, Bushell 1, Clarke M 1, Stoneman 1, Swales 1, Woodward 1.
Worthington Cup (0).
FA Cup (3): Harsley 1, Middleton 1, Wood 1.

Butler L 21+1	Harsley P 45	Jules M 34+1	Woodward A 29+1	Clarke C 24	Stoneman P 32	Swales S 20+4	Redfearn N 27+3	Kerrigan S 23+7	Wood J 10+6	Midgley C 12+12	Mitchell G 41+2	Jones G 20+15	Wright P 3+11	Middleton C 21+8	Reilly A —+2	Clarke M 22+9	Smith G 11	Fitzpatrick J 26+3	Bushell S 25	Ludden D 2	Crookes P 1	Herbert R 11+1	Richardson B 24	Winder N —+1	Houghton S 7	Richards M 5	Farrell A 7+2	Oleksewycz S —+2	Heinemann N 3	Smith C —+2	Match No.
1	2	3	4^1	5	6	7	8	9^2	10	11^3	12	13	14																		1
1	2	3	4	5	6	7	8	9	10^1	11^2	12	13																			2
1	2	3	4	5	6	7^3	8	9	10^1	11^2	12	13	14																		3
1	2	3	4		6^3	12	8	9	10^2	5	11	13	7^5	14																	4
1	2	3	4	5	6	7	8	9^2	12	11	10^1						13														5
1	2	3	4	5	6	7^1	8				11	9	12			13	10^2														6
1	2	3	4	5	6	7	8				11	9				12	10^1														7
1	2	3	4	5	6	7	8				11	9				12	10^1														8
1	2	3	4^1	5	6	7			14		11	9		8^3	12^2	13	10														9
1	2	3		5	6	7	8	12		4		9^2		11		13	10^1														10
1	2	3		5^1	6	7	8	11		4		9				12	10														11
1	2	3		5^1	6	7	8	11^3	14	12	4	9^2			13		10														12
1	2	3^1			6	7	8^2	11^3	14	12	4	9			13	5	10														13
1	2	3			6	7		11	12	4		9^1		8^2		5	10	13													14
1	2	3			6	7^2		9^1	13		4	12		11		5	10	8													15
1	2	3			6			12	8	9	4			11^1		5	10	7													16
1	2	3			6^1			12	8^2	9	14	10^3	4	13		11	5	7													17
1	2	3			6	7		8	9		12			4	13	11^3	5	10^2													18
1	2	12	13		6	7	8	14			9			3^2	4^1	11	5	10^2													19
1	2		4		6			12	9^2	13				3		11	5	10^1	8			7									20
1	2		4		6			12	13	9^3	14			3		11^1	5	10^2	8			7									21
15	2		4		6			9^1	12					3	13	11	5	10	7		1	8^2									22
	2		4		6			12	9^2	13				3		11	5	10^1	7			8	1								23
	2		4		6			12	9^1			10		3	13	11^2	5		7			8	1								24
	2	3			6			9^1	12					4	10	11	5	7				8	1								25
	2	3			6			9						4		11	5	10	7			8	1								26
	2	3			6	4		9^2		11				13	12		5	10	7^1			8	1		14						27
	2	3	4	5	6			9^1				7			13	11		10^2				8	1								28
	2	3^1	4		6	7		9				12				11	5	10				8	1								29
	2		4		6			9						3	12	11	5	13	7			8^1	1		10^2						30
	2		4	5	6			9^1						3	13	11		12	7			8^3	1		10						31
	2		4	5	6			9^1	12					3				10	7				1		11	8					32
	2		4		6			9				13^3		3	14		5^2	10^1	7				1		11	8	12				33
		3	4^1	5	6	7		9				12		2				10	8				1		11						34
	2	3		5	6	7^1			12	4					13			10	8				1		11		9^2				35
	2	3	4	5	6	7^1			12					14	13			10	8				1		11^3		9^2				36
	2	3	4	5	6	7		9^1				12				11		10				8	1								37
	2	3	4	5	6	7		9^1				12				11		10^2				8	1			13					38
	2	3	4	5	6	7		9				10						12				8	1		11^1						39
	2	3	4	5	6	7		9										10				8	1		11						40
	2	3	4		6	7		9^1	12					14	13		5^1	10				8	1		11^3						41
	2	3	4	5	6	7		9				12						10^2				8	1		11^1	13					42
	2	3	4	11	6	7		9^1									5	10^2				8	1		12	13					43
	2		4	5^2	6	7		9^3				12			13			10				8	1		11^1				3	14	44
	2				6	7		9	12	4							5	10^1				8	1		11				3		45
	2^3	3			6	7		9^2	12	4		10						8	13				1		11		5^1		3	14	46

Worthington Cup
First Round   Barnsley   (a)   0-2

FA Cup
First Round   Farnborough T   (h)   2-1
Second Round   Stoke C   (h)   1-1
    (a)   0-3

HARTLEPOOL UNITED   Division 3

FOUNDATION

The inspiration for the launching of Hartlepool United was the West Hartlepool club which won the FA Amateur Cup in 1904–05. They had been in existence since 1881 and their Cup success led in 1908 to the formation of the new professional concern which first joined the North-Eastern League. In those days they were Hartlepools United and won the Durham Senior Cup in their first two seasons.

Victoria Park, Clarence Road, Hartlepool TS24 8BZ.

Telephone: (01429) 272 584. *Fax:* (01429) 863 007.
Commercial Dept: (01429) 272 584.
Website: www.hartlepoolunited.co.uk
Email: info@hartlepoolunited.co.uk
Football in the Community: (01429) 862 595.

Ground Capacity: 7,629.

Record Attendance: 17,426 v Manchester U, FA Cup 3rd rd, 5 January 1957.

Record Receipts: £59,800 (inc. VAT) v Cheltenham T, Play-off semi-final, 27 April 2002.

Pitch Measurements: 100 × 66 metres.

Chairman: K. Hodcroft.

Directors: H. Hornsey, I. Prescott.

Manager: Chris Turner.

Assistant Manager: Colin West.

Youth Coach: Martin Scott.

Physios: John Murray, Ian Gallagher.

Commercial Manager: John Breward.

Secretary: Maureen Smith.

Football in the Community Officers: Keith Nobbs, Peter Smith.

Safety Officer: Maurice Russell.

Colours: Royal blue and white striped shirts.

Change Colours: (To be announced.)

Year Formed: 1908.

Turned Professional: 1908.

Ltd Co.: 1908.

Previous Names: 1908, Hartlepools United; 1968, Hartlepool; 1977, Hartlepool United.

Club Nickname: 'The Pool'.

First Football League Game: 27 August 1921, Division 3 (N), v Wrexham (a) W 2–0 – Gill; Thomas, Crilly; Dougherty, Hopkins, Short; Kessler, Mulholland (1), Lister (1), Robertson, Donald.

HONOURS

Football League: Division 3 (N) – Runners-up 1956–57.

FA Cup: best season: 4th rd, 1955, 1978, 1989, 1993.

Football League Cup, best season: 4th rd, 1975.

IT'S A FACT !

On 10 February 1990, Hartlepool United beat Stockport County 5-0. The previous occasion in which Hartlepool had scored five times in a League game had been on 3 April 1985 when they beat Stockport 5-1.

Record League Victory: 10–1 v Barrow, Division 4, 4 April 1959 – Oakley; Cameron, Waugh; Johnson, Moore, Anderson; Scott (1), Langland (1), Smith (3), Clark (2), Luke (2), (1 og).

Record Cup Victory: 6–0 v North Shields, FA Cup 1st rd, 30 November 1946 – Heywood; Brown, Gregory; Spelman, Lambert, Jones; Price, Scott (2), Sloan (4), Moses, McMahon.

Record Defeat: 1–10 v Wrexham, Division 4, 3 March 1962.

Most League Points (2 for a win): 60, Division 4, 1967–68.

Most League Points (3 for a win): 82, Division 4, 1990–91.

Most League Goals: 90, Division 3 (N), 1956–57.

Highest League Scorer in Season: William Robinson, 28, Division 3 (N), 1927–28; Joe Allon, 28, Division 4, 1990–91.

Most League Goals in Total Aggregate: Ken Johnson, 98, 1949–64.

Most League Goals in One Match: 5, Harry Simmons v Wigan Borough, Division 3N, 1 January 1931; 5, Bobby Folland v Oldham Ath, Division 3N, 15 April 1961.

Most Capped Player: Ambrose Fogarty, 1 (11), Republic of Ireland.

Most League Appearances: Wattie Moore, 447, 1948–64.

Youngest League Player: John McGovern, 16 years 205 days v Bradford C, 21 May 1966.

Record Transfer Fee Received: £750,000 from Ipswich T for Tommy Miller, July 2001.

Record Transfer Fee Paid: £75,000 to Notts Co for Gary Jones, March 1999; £75,000 to Mansfield T for Darrell Clarke, July 2001.

Football League Record: 1921 Original Member of Division 3 (N); 1958–68 Division 4; 1968–69 Division 3; 1969–91 Division 4; 1991–92 Division 3; 1992–94 Division 2; 1994– Division 3.

LATEST SEQUENCES

Longest Sequence of League Wins: 7, 1.4.68 – 26.4.68.

Longest Sequence of League Defeats: 8, 27.1.93 – 27.2.93.

Longest Sequence of League Draws: 5, 24.2.01 – 17.3.01.

Longest Sequence of Unbeaten League Matches: 21, 2.12.00 – 31.3.01.

Longest Sequence Without a League Win: 18, 9.1.93 – 3.4.93.

MANAGERS

Alfred Priest 1908–12
Percy Humphreys 1912–13
Jack Manners 1913–20
Cecil Potter 1920–22
David Gordon 1922–24
Jack Manners 1924–27
Bill Norman 1927–31
Jack Carr 1932–35
   (had been Player-Coach since 1931)
Jimmy Hamilton 1935–43
Fred Westgarth 1943–57
Ray Middleton 1957–59
Bill Robinson 1959–62
Allenby Chilton 1962–63
Bob Gurney 1963–64
Alvan Williams 1964–65
Geoff Twentyman 1965
Brian Clough 1965–67
Angus McLean 1967–70
John Simpson 1970–71
Len Ashurst 1971–74
Ken Hale 1974–76
Billy Horner 1976–83
Johnny Duncan 1983
Mike Docherty 1983
Billy Horner 1984–86
John Bird 1986–88
Bobby Moncur 1988–89
Cyril Knowles 1989–91
Alan Murray 1991–93
Viv Busby 1993
John MacPhail 1993–94
David McCreery 1994–95
Keith Houchen 1995–96
Mick Tait 1996–99
Chris Turner March 1999–

TEN YEAR LEAGUE RECORD

		P	W	D	L	F	A	Pts	Pos
1991-92	Div 3	46	18	11	17	57	57	65	11
1992-93	Div 2	46	14	12	20	42	60	54	16
1993-94	Div 2	46	9	9	28	41	87	36	23
1994-95	Div 3	42	11	10	21	43	69	43	18
1995-96	Div 3	46	12	13	21	47	67	49	20
1996-97	Div 3	46	14	9	23	53	66	51	20
1997-98	Div 3	46	12	23	11	61	53	59	17
1998-99	Div 3	46	13	12	21	52	65	51	22
1999-2000	Div 3	46	21	9	16	60	49	72	7
2000-01	Div 3	46	21	14	11	71	54	77	4

DID YOU KNOW ?

On Good Friday 1951, Hartlepools United beat neighbours Darlington 6-1, with right-back Joe Willetts converting three penalty kicks during the match.

HARTLEPOOL UNITED 2001–02 LEAGUE RECORD

Match No.	Date	Venue	Opponents	Result	H/T Score	Lg. Pos.	Goalscorers	Attendance
1	Aug 11	H	Mansfield T	D 1-1	0-1	—	Clark [78]	3534
2	18	A	Shrewsbury T	W 3-1	0-1	3	Clark (pen) [61], Henderson [66], Tinkler [76]	2783
3	25	H	Darlington	L 1-2	1-2	13	Tinkler [15]	4842
4	27	A	Leyton Orient	L 0-2	0-1	17		3719
5	Sept 8	A	Scunthorpe U	L 0-1	0-1	20		3206
6	15	A	Southend U	D 0-0	0-0	21		3933
7	18	H	Cheltenham T	L 0-1	0-0	—		2599
8	22	H	Kidderminster H	D 1-1	0-0	23	Watson [54]	3130
9	25	A	Lincoln C	L 0-2	0-1	—		2306
10	29	H	Carlisle U	W 3-1	1-1	22	Tinkler [34], Watson [66], Boyd [88]	3854
11	Oct 5	A	Rushden & D	L 1-2	1-1	—	Watson [45]	3929
12	13	H	York C	W 3-0	1-0	23	Tinkler [39], Boyd 2 [47, 64]	3603
13	20	A	Torquay U	L 0-1	0-0	24		2148
14	23	A	Macclesfield T	W 1-0	0-0	—	Boyd [77]	1356
15	27	H	Oxford U	L 0-1	0-0	21		3595
16	Nov 3	A	Plymouth Arg	L 0-1	0-1	24		5723
17	6	H	Hull C	W 4-0	2-0	—	Watson 3 [33, 40, 90], Barron [84]	3183
18	10	H	Exeter C	W 2-0	1-0	15	Watson [37], Lormor [90]	3222
19	20	A	Halifax T	W 3-0	1-0	—	Watson [35], Tinkler [60], Widdrington [65]	2963
20	23	A	Swansea C	W 1-0	1-0	—	Smith [20]	4161
21	30	H	Rochdale	D 1-1	0-0	—	Bass [74]	4162
22	Dec 8	H	Luton T	L 1-2	0-2	—	Humphreys [64]	3585
23	22	A	Luton T	D 2-2	1-1	12	Clarke 2 [45, 59]	6739
24	29	H	Leyton Orient	W 3-1	2-0	12	Watson [4], Smith [37], Tinkler [86]	3832
25	Jan 12	H	Shrewsbury T	D 2-2	1-0	13	Watson [26], Lee [89]	3447
26	19	A	Mansfield T	L 0-3	0-1	13		4349
27	26	H	Rushden & D	W 5-1	1-0	13	Watson 2 [29, 64], Humphreys [62], Widdrington [69], Coppinger [78]	3513
28	29	H	Scunthorpe U	W 3-2	1-1	—	Tinkler [12], Watson [77], Smith [82]	3294
29	Feb 5	A	Hull C	D 1-1	0-1	—	Boyd [90]	8419
30	9	H	Torquay U	W 4-1	3-0	11	Boyd 2 [13, 14], Lee [20], Easter [65]	3658
31	12	A	Bristol R	W 1-0	1-0	—	Boyd [19]	6482
32	16	A	York C	L 0-1	0-0	10		4823
33	19	A	Darlington	D 1-1	0-1	—	Tinkler [59]	6339
34	23	H	Southend U	W 5-1	2-0	10	Humphreys 2 [9, 66], Coppinger [35], Smith [69], Easter [71]	3609
35	26	A	Cheltenham T	L 0-3	0-2	—		3257
36	Mar 2	A	Kidderminster H	L 2-3	1-0	11	Humphreys [4], Tinkler [73]	2894
37	5	H	Lincoln C	D 1-1	0-0	—	Clarke [77]	3126
38	9	H	Bristol R	D 1-1	1-0	11	Watson [29]	3699
39	16	A	Rochdale	D 0-0	0-0	11		3219
40	19	A	Carlisle U	W 2-0	1-0	—	Lee [22], Watson [68]	3147
41	22	H	Macclesfield T	L 1-2	0-1	—	Westwood [90]	3819
42	30	A	Oxford U	W 2-1	2-1	10	Williams E 2 [12, 23]	5767
43	Apr 1	H	Plymouth Arg	W 1-0	0-0	9	Clarke [86]	3725
44	6	A	Halifax T	W 2-0	1-0	9	Watson [9], Lee [63]	1838
45	13	H	Swansea C	W 7-1	2-1	8	Clarke 3 [20, 45, 65], Williams E [47], Boyd [69], Watson (pen) [75], Henderson [77]	4033
46	20	A	Exeter C	W 2-0	1-0	7	Watson [9], Williams E [56]	3595

Final League Position: 7

GOALSCORERS

League (74): Watson 18 (1 pen), Boyd 9, Tinkler 9, Clarke 7, Humphreys 5, Lee 4, Smith 4, Williams E 4, Clark 2 (1 pen), Coppinger 2, Easter 2, Henderson 2, Widdrington 2, Barron 1, Bass 1, Lormor 1, Westwood 1.
Worthington Cup (0).
FA Cup (1): Clarke 1.

Holland M 3	Bass J 19+1	Clark 15+2	Barron M 39	Lee G 38+1	Westwood C 35	Tinkler M 39+1	Humphreys R 42+4	Henderson K 13+10	Widdrington T 24	Stephenson P 23+6	Sharp J 13+2	Lormor T 4+13	Clarke D 24+9	Easter J —+12	Williams A 43	Arnison P 11+8	Robinson M 33+4	Simms G 6+4	Watson G 31+1	Omerod A 2	Boyd A 10+19	Sweeney A —+2	Smith P 30+1	Parkin J —+1	Coppinger J 14	Williams E 5+3	Match No
1	2	3	4	5	6¹	7	8	9²	10	11	12	13															1
1	2	3³	4	5¹	6	7	8²	9	10	11	12	13	14														2
1	2¹	3	4	5	6	7	9³	10	8	11²		12	13	14													3
	2³	3	4¹	5		7	8²	10	11	6		9	12	13	1	14											4
	2		5			7	9¹	10	8	11		6	12	4	1		3										5
	2		5			7	9¹	10	8	11		6	12	4	1		3²	13									6
	2	12	5³			7	9	10⁴	8¹	11		6		4	13	1	3	14									7
	2	12				7	13			11		6	9	4²	1		3	5	10	8¹							8
	2	4				8	12			11		6	9		1		3	5	10	7¹							9
	2	4	12			7³	13	9	8	11¹		6			1		3	5¹	10	14							10
	2³	4	5			7	12	9¹	8	11		6²	13		1		3		10	14							11
		4	5			7¹	8	11		6					1	2	3		10		9	12					12
		4	5			7	8	11		6¹	12				1	2	3		10		9²	13					13
		4	5			7	8³	9²	11	12	6				1	2	3	13	10¹	14							14
		4³	5¹			7	8	13	11	14	6	12			1	2	3²		10	9							15
	2	4	5	8	9¹		11³				6²	12	7		3	13	10			14							16
	2	4²	5	9	12	8				7			1	3	6	10¹	13	11									17
	2	4	5	12	9²	8		13	7				1	3¹	6	10³	14	11									18
	2	4	5	6	8	9³	11	12	7				1	13	10¹	14	3²										19
	2	4	5	6	8	9	11	12	7				1		10¹	3											20
	2	4	5	6	8	9	11		7				1		10¹	12	3										21
	2¹	4	5	8	10	11	9²	7			1	12	14	6³	13	3											22
	2	4	5	8	9	6			7		1	3	10¹	12	11												23
12	2¹	4	5	8	9	6			7		1	3	10²	13	11												24
	2	4	5	8	9²	6¹	12		7		1	3³	10	13	11	14											25
2¹		4	5	6	8	9			7		1	12	3²	10	13	11											26
	2	4	5	8³	9	6¹	12			1	13	3	10	14	11	7²											27
	2	4	5	8	9	6²		14		1	12	3	10	13³	11	7¹											28
	2	4	5	6	9	12				1		3	10¹	8	11	7											29
		4	5	6¹	9	10³	12	13	14	1	2	3	8²	11	7												30
	2	4	5	6	9	10²	7¹	12	13	1	3	8		11													31
	2	4	5	6	9	10¹		12		1	3	8		11	7												32
	2	4	5	6¹	9	12	8²	13	14	1	3		10³	11	7												33
	2	4	5	6	9		8²	12	14	1	13	3	10³	11	7¹												34
	2	4	5	6	9		8	12	13	1	3		10²	11	7¹												35
	2	4	5	6	9	10³	8²	12	13	1	3	14		11	7¹												36
	2	4	5	6	9²	8	12	13		1	3	10		11	7¹												37
	2¹	4	5	6	9	8	7	1	12	3	10²	11		13													38
	2	4	5	6	9	8	7	1	3	10	11																39
		4	5	6	8	9¹	12	11	7	1	2	10²	3	13													40
		4	5	6	8²	9	11	7	1	2¹	12	10³	13	3	14												41
		4	5	6	8	12	11²	7	1	2	13	10¹	3	9													42
	2	4	5	8	12	6	1	3	10	13	11	7²	9														43
	2	4	5	8	12	6	1	3	10	13	11	7²	9¹														44
	2²	4	5	8	12	6	1	13	3²	10	14	11	7	9¹													45
		4	5	8	12	13	6	1	2	3	10¹	14	11	7³	9²												46

Worthington Cup
First Round   Nottingham F   (h)   0-2

FA Cup
First Round   Swindon T   (a)   1-3

HUDDERSFIELD TOWN   Division 2

FOUNDATION

A meeting, attended largely by members of the Huddersfield & District FA, was held at the Imperial Hotel in 1906 to discuss the feasibility of establishing a football club in this rugby stronghold. However, it was not until a man with both the enthusiasm and the money to back the scheme came on the scene, that real progress was made. This benefactor was Mr Hilton Crowther and it was at a meeting at the Albert Hotel in 1908, that the club formally came into existence with a capital of £2,000 and joined the North-Eastern League.

The Alfred McAlpine Stadium, Leeds Rd, Huddersfield HD1 6PX.

Telephone: (01484) 484 100. *Fax:* (01484) 484 101.
ClubCall: 09068 121 635. *Ticket Office:* (01484) 484 123.
Club Shop: (01484) 484 144.

Ground Capacity: 24,500.

Record Attendance: 67,037 v Arsenal, FA Cup 6th rd, 27 February 1932 (at Leeds Road);
23,678 v Liverpool, FA Cup 3rd rd, 12 December 1999 (at Alfred McAlpine Stadium).

Record Receipts: £243,081 v Liverpool, FA Cup 3rd rd, 12 December 1999.

Pitch Measurements: 115yd × 76yd.

President: Lawrence Batley OBE.

Chairman: David Taylor.

Directors: P. Haigh, G. Headey, P. Bane.

Manager: Mick Wadsworth. *First Team Coach:* David Wilkes.

Secretary: Ann Hough.

Physio: Alex Moreno.

Stadium Manager: Phil Armitage.

Colours: Blue and white striped shirts, white shorts, white stockings with blue trim.

Change Colours: Black shirts and shorts with royal blue trim, black stockings with royal blue turnover.

Year Formed: 1908.

Turned Professional: 1908.

Ltd Co.: 1908.

Club Nickname: 'The Terriers'.

Previous Ground: 1908, Leeds Road; 1994, The Alfred McAlpine Stadium.

First Football League Game: 3 September 1910, Division 2, v Bradford PA (a) W 1–0 – Mutch; Taylor, Morris; Beaton, Hall, Bartlett; Blackburn, Wood, Hamilton (1), McCubbin, Jee.

HONOURS

Football League: Division 1 – Champions 1923–24, 1924–25, 1925–26; Runners-up 1926–27, 1927–28, 1933–34; Division 2 – Champions 1969–70; Runners-up 1919–20, 1952–53; Promoted from Division 2 1994–95 (play-offs); Division 4 – Champions 1979–80.
FA Cup: Winners 1922; Runners-up 1920, 1928, 1930, 1938.
Football League Cup: Semi-final 1968.
Autoglass Trophy: Runners-up 1994.

IT'S A FACT !

On Christmas Eve 1956, Denis Law aged 16 years 303 days, made his Huddersfield Town debut at inside-right against Notts County. His wing partner was Kevin McHale at 17 years 84 days. Huddersfield won 2-0.

Record League Victory: 10–1 v Blackpool, Division 1,
13 December 1930 – Turner; Goodall, Spencer; Redfern,
Wilson, Campbell; Bob Kelly (1), McLean (4), Robson (3),
Davies (1), Smailes (1).

Record Cup Victory: 7–0 v Lincoln U, FA Cup 1st rd,
16 November 1991 – Clarke; Trevitt, Charlton,
Donovan (2), Mitchell, Doherty, O'Regan (1), Stapleton (1)
(Wright), Roberts (2), Onuora (1), Barnett (Ireland).
N.B. 11-0 v Heckmondwike (a), FA Cup 1st pr rd
18 September 1909.

Record Defeat: 1–10 v Manchester C, Division 2,
7 November 1987.

Most League Points (2 for a win): 66, Division 4, 1979–80.

Most League Points (3 for a win): 82, Division 3, 1982–83.

Most League Goals: 101, Division 4, 1979–80.

Highest League Scorer in Season: Sam Taylor, 35,
Division 2, 1919–20; George Brown, 35, Division 1, 1925–26.

Most League Goals in Total Aggregate: George Brown,
142, 1921–29; Jimmy Glazzard, 142, 1946–56.

Most League Goals in One Match: 5, Dave Mangnall v
Derby Co, Division 1, 21 November 1931; 5, Alf Lythgoe v
Blackburn R, Division 1, 13 April 1935.

Most Capped Player: Jimmy Nicholson, 31 (41),
Northern Ireland.

Most League Appearances: Billy Smith, 520, 1914–34.

Youngest League Player: Denis Law, 16 years 303 days v
Notts Co, 24 December 1956.

Record Transfer Fee Received: £2,700,000 from Sheffield W
for Andy Booth, July 1996.

Record Transfer Fee Paid: £1,200,000 to Bristol R for
Marcus Stewart, July 1996.

MANAGERS

Fred Walker 1908–10
Richard Pudan 1910–12
Arthur Fairclough 1912–19
Ambrose Langley 1919–21
Herbert Chapman 1921–25
Cecil Potter 1925–26
Jack Chaplin 1926–29
Clem Stephenson 1929–42
David Steele 1943–47
George Stephenson 1947–52
Andy Beattie 1952–56
Bill Shankly 1956–59
Eddie Boot 1960–64
Tom Johnston 1964–68
Ian Greaves 1968–74
Bobby Collins 1974
Tom Johnston 1975–78
   *(had been General Manager
   since 1975)*
Mike Buxton 1978–86
Steve Smith 1986–87
Malcolm Macdonald 1987–88
Eoin Hand 1988–92
Ian Ross 1992–93
Neil Warnock 1993–95
Brian Horton 1995–97
Peter Jackson 1997–99
Steve Bruce 1999–2000
Lou Macari 2000–02
Mick Wadsworth July 2002–

Football League Record: 1910 Elected to Division 2; 1920–52 Division 1; 1952–53 Division 2;
1953–56 Division 1; 1956–70 Division 2; 1970–72 Division 1; 1972–73 Division 2; 1973–75 Division 3;
1975–80 Division 4; 1980–83 Division 3; 1983–88 Division 2; 1988–92 Division 3; 1992–95 Division 2;
1995–2001 Division 1; 2001– Division 2.

LATEST SEQUENCES

Longest Sequence of League Wins: 11, 5.4.20 – 4.9.20.
Longest Sequence of League Defeats: 7, 8.10.55 – 19.11.55.
Longest Sequence of League Draws: 6, 3.3.87 – 3.4.87.
Longest Sequence of Unbeaten League Matches: 27, 24.1.25 – 17.10.25.
Longest Sequence Without a League Win: 22, 4.12.71 – 29.4.72.

TEN YEAR LEAGUE RECORD

		P	W	D	L	F	A	Pts	Pos
1991-92	Div 3	46	22	12	12	59	38	78	3
1992-93	Div 2	46	17	9	20	54	61	60	15
1993-94	Div 2	46	17	14	15	58	61	65	11
1994-95	Div 2	46	22	15	9	79	49	81	5
1995-96	Div 1	46	17	12	17	61	58	63	8
1996-97	Div 1	46	13	15	18	48	61	54	20
1997-98	Div 1	46	14	11	21	50	72	53	16
1998-99	Div 1	46	15	16	15	62	71	61	10
1999-2000	Div 1	46	21	11	14	62	49	74	8
2000-01	Div 1	46	11	15	20	48	57	48	22

DID YOU KNOW ?

Unusually for a
championship-winning team,
Huddersfield Town achieved
more points away from home
than on their own ground. In
1924–25, they achieved 30 on
their travels compared with
28 at Leeds Road.

HUDDERSFIELD TOWN 2001–02 LEAGUE RECORD

Match No.	Date	Venue	Opponents	Result	H/T Score	Lg. Pos.	Goalscorers	Attendance
1	Aug 11	H	Bournemouth	W 1-0	0-0	—	Irons [50]	10,137
2	18	A	Reading	L 0-1	0-1	12		11,915
3	25	H	Bury	W 2-0	0-0	8	Schofield 2 [82, 88]	8684
4	27	A	Peterborough U	W 2-1	0-0	4	Booth [52], Beech [71]	5253
5	Sept 2	H	Wycombe W	W 2-1	1-1	1	Thorrington [38], Brown (og) [70]	9750
6	8	A	Stoke C	D 1-1	1-0	3	Schofield [32]	13,319
7	15	H	Blackpool	L 2-4	1-2	6	Clarke [18], Thorrington [87]	10,691
8	18	A	Wigan Ath	L 0-1	0-0	—		5717
9	22	A	Cardiff C	W 2-1	1-1	6	Mattis [20], Schofield [56]	12,280
10	25	H	Chesterfield	D 0-0	0-0	—		9399
11	29	H	Bristol C	W 1-0	0-0	3	Thorrington [71]	10,652
12	Oct 7	A	QPR	L 2-3	1-1	7	Hay [33], Ben Askar (og) [90]	10,668
13	13	H	Brighton & HA	L 1-2	0-1	9	Irons [74]	10,727
14	20	A	Tranmere R	L 0-1	0-0	12		8632
15	23	A	Northampton T	W 3-0	2-0	—	Booth 3 [30, 45, 70]	5926
16	27	H	Wrexham	W 5-1	1-1	6	Thorrington (pen) [29], Holland [48], Knight 2 [64, 66], Booth [87]	9888
17	Nov 3	A	Oldham Ath	D 1-1	1-0	5	Schofield [23]	8859
18	9	H	Notts Co	D 2-2	1-0	—	Jenkins [37], Knight [83]	10,168
19	20	H	Brentford	D 1-1	0-0	—	Knight [56]	8518
20	24	A	Port Vale	D 1-1	0-0	7	Knight [67]	5026
21	Dec 1	H	Cambridge U	W 2-1	0-1	7	Hay [76], Booth [88]	9513
22	22	A	Colchester U	D 3-3	1-2	10	Booth 2 [40, 61], Schofield [59]	3543
23	26	H	Peterborough U	W 3-1	1-0	8	Thorrington 2 [34, 52], Irons [66]	11,446
24	29	H	Stoke C	D 0-0	0-0	9		16,041
25	Jan 12	A	Reading	L 0-1	0-0	11		10,775
26	15	A	Bury	D 0-0	0-0	—		3462
27	19	A	Bournemouth	W 3-2	3-0	9	Booth [3], Hay [24], Knight [37]	5307
28	22	H	Colchester U	W 2-1	2-0	—	Schofield 2 [5, 25]	7179
29	26	H	QPR	W 1-0	1-0	6	Booth [37]	9433
30	Feb 2	A	Bristol C	D 1-1	0-0	7	Knight [90]	10,643
31	5	A	Swindon T	W 1-0	0-0	—	Hay [54]	5094
32	9	H	Tranmere R	W 2-1	0-1	5	Armstrong [78], Wijnhard [81]	15,784
33	16	A	Brighton & HA	L 0-1	0-0	6		6744
34	23	A	Blackpool	W 2-1	0-0	6	Knight 2 [70, 90]	8981
35	Mar 2	H	Wigan Ath	D 0-0	0-0	7		12,844
36	5	A	Chesterfield	D 1-1	0-1	—	Knight [83]	4740
37	9	H	Swindon T	W 2-0	1-0	6	Irons [21], Knight [52]	9569
38	12	A	Wycombe W	W 4-2	2-0	—	Knight 2 [28, 89], Gray [36], Irons [90]	5546
39	16	A	Cambridge U	W 1-0	0-0	5	Knight [64]	3728
40	23	H	Northampton T	W 2-0	2-0	5	Knight 2 [27, 33]	10,783
41	30	A	Wrexham	D 1-1	0-0	5	Facey [53]	4448
42	Apr 1	H	Oldham Ath	D 0-0	0-0	5		14,343
43	6	A	Brentford	L 0-3	0-3	6		7393
44	9	H	Cardiff C	D 2-2	0-1	—	Irons (pen) [79], Hay [82]	11,660
45	13	H	Port Vale	W 2-1	1-1	6	Facey [42], Booth [65]	12,270
46	20	A	Notts Co	L 1-2	0-1	6	Irons (pen) [83]	15,618

Final League Position: 6

GOALSCORERS

League (65): Knight 16, Booth 11, Schofield 8, Irons 7 (2 pens), Thorrington 6 (1 pen), Hay 5, Facey 2, Armstrong 1, Beech 1, Clarke 1, Gray 1, Holland 1, Jenkins 1, Mattis 1, Wijnhard 1, own goals 2.
Worthington Cup (0).
FA Cup (2): Knight 1, Moses 1.

Margetson M 46	Jenkins S 40	Evans G 35	Irons K 34+7	Lucketti C 2	Gray K 44	Beech C 6+3	Holland C 35+2	Booth A 30+6	Hay C 19+12	Armstrong C 7+4	Thorrington J 29+2	Schofield D 39+1	Mattis D 21+8	Macari P —+6	Heary T 21+11	Moses A 13+4	Baldry S 3+1	Clarke N 36	Knight L 31	Wijnhard C 2+11	Facey D 11+2	Ifil J 1+1	Delaney D 1+1	Match No.
1	2	3	4	5	6	7¹	8	9	10²	11	12	13												1
1	2	3	4²	5	6	7	8	9	10³	11¹	12	13	14											2
1	2	3			6	12	8	9	10¹	11²	4	7	13					5						3
1	2	3	12		6	7²	13	9	10¹	11²	4	8	14					5						4
1		3			6	11²	8	9	12		4	10	13			2		5	7¹					5
		3	12		6	7¹	8	9²		11	4	10	13			2		5						6
1	2	3	12		6	11¹	8	9²		4	10	13	14		7³			5						7
1	2	3²	4		6		8¹	9	12		7	10	11	13				5						8
1	2	3	4		6		8	9			7	10	11					5						9
1	2	3	4		6		8	9			7	10	11					5						10
1	2	3	4		6		8	9			7	10	11					5						11
1	2	3¹	4		6		8	9	10²		7	11³	12	14				13	5					12
1	2	3¹	4		6		8	9			7	10	11	12				5						13
1	2				6		8	9	12		7	10	11	3	4¹			5						14
1	2				6	12	8	9²	13		4¹	10	11	14	3			5	7³					15
1	2²		12		6		8	9			4	10	11	3	13			5	7¹					16
1	2		4		6		8	9¹	12			10	11	3				5	7					17
1	2		4		6			8			7	10	11	3				5	9					18
1	2		4		6		8	9				10	11	3				5	7					19
1	2		4¹		6		8	9	12			10	11	3				5	7					20
1	2		4		6		8	9	12			10	11	3¹				5	7					21
1	2	3	4		6			9				10	11			5	7¹		8	12				22
1	2	3	4¹		6			9²	13		7³	10	11	12		5			8	14				23
1	2	3	4		6			9	13³		7²	10	11	12		5			8	14				24
1		3	4¹		6	8²	9	11	12		10			2	5				7	13				25
1		3	4		6	8	9	11			10¹			2				5	7	12				26
1	2	3	4²		6	8	9	11	13		10			12				5	7¹					27
1	2	3	4		6	8	9¹	11²	12		10							5	7	13				28
1	2	3	4		6	8	9	11¹	12		10			13				5	7²					29
1		3	4¹			9	11¹	8			10			2	6			5	7	12				30
1	2	3	4			12	9	8²	11	4	10¹			13	6			5	7					31
1	2	3			6		8	9¹	10	4	7							5	11	12				32
1	2	3	12		6	8		9			10			4				5	7	11¹				33
1	2		12		6	8²			7¹	10	13			3	4			5	11	9²	14			34
1	2²		12		6	8		9¹			7	10	13	4³	3			5	11		14			35
1	2	3²	4¹		6	8			7	10				12				5	9	13	11			36
1	2	3	4		6¹	8			7²	10			13	12				5	9¹	14	11			37
1	2	3¹	4		6	8			7	10			12					5	9		11			38
1	2	3²	4		6	8		12	7	10¹			13					5	9	14	11³			39
1	2	3	4		6		8	12	13		7¹	10²		14				5	9		11²			40
1	2		4¹		6		12		7	10³	8			3²				5	9		11	13	14	41
1	2	3	4		6		12		7	10	8							5	9		11¹			42
1	2	3	4		6		12		7	10¹	8²			13				5	9		11			43
1	2	3	4		6		12	10	7¹					8				5	9		11			44
1	2	3	4		6		12	10¹	7					8				5	9		11			45
1		3	4¹		6	12	8	9	13		7²	14			5				11			2	10³	46

Worthington Cup
First Round   Rochdale   (h)   0-1

FA Cup
First Round   Gravesend & N   (h)   2-1
Second Round   Mansfield T   (a)   0-4

HULL CITY

Division 3

FOUNDATION

The enthusiasts who formed Hull City in 1904 were brave men indeed. More than that they were audacious for they immediately put the club on the map in this Rugby League fortress by obtaining a three-year agreement with the Hull Rugby League club to rent their ground! They had obtained quite a number of conversions to the dribbling code, before the Rugby League forbade the use of any of their club grounds by Association Football clubs. By that time, Hull City were well away having entered the FA Cup in their initial season and the Football League, Second Division after only a year.

Boothferry Park, Hull HU4 6EU.

Telephone: (01482) 575 263. **Fax:** (01482) 565 752.
Club Shop: Ground: (01482) 575 263. Princes Quay: (01482) 227 654. **ClubCall:** 09068 888 688.

Ground Capacity: 15,756.

Record Attendance: 55,019 v Manchester U, FA Cup 6th rd, 26 February 1949.

Record Receipts: £79,604 v Liverpool, FA Cup 5th rd, 18 February 1989.

Pitch Measurements: 115yd × 75yd.

Chairman/Chief Executive: Adam Pearson.

Manager: Jan Molby.

Physios: Keith Warner, Mick Mathews.

Sales Director: John Holm.

HONOURS

Football League: Division 2 best season: 3rd, 1909–10; Division 3 (N) – Champions 1932–33, 1948–49; Division 3 – Champions 1965–66; Runners-up 1958–59; Division 4 – Runners-up 1982–83.

FA Cup: Semi-final 1930.

Football League Cup: best season: 4th, 1974, 1976, 1978.

Associate Members' Cup: Runners-up 1984.

Football in the Community Office: John Davies (01482) 568 088. **Marketing Manager:** Rob Smith.
Ticket Office Manager: Carol Taylor. **Club Secretary:** Phil Hough.

Hon. Medical Officers: Mr F. R. Howell MA, FRCS, Dr T. Jackson.

Colours: Black, amber and white shirts, black shorts, black stockings.

Change Colours: All white.

Year Formed: 1904.

Turned Professional: 1905.

Ltd Co.: 1905.

Club Nickname: 'The Tigers'.

Previous Grounds: 1904, Boulevard Ground (Hull RFC); 1905, Anlaby Road (Hull CC); 1944, Boulevard Ground; 1946, Boothferry Park.

First Football League Game: 2 September 1905, Division 2, v Barnsley (h) W 4–1 – Spendiff; Langley, Jones; Martin, Robinson, Gordon (2); Rushton, Spence (1), Wilson (1), Howe, Raisbeck.

Record League Victory: 11–1 v Carlisle U, Division 3 (N), 14 January 1939 – Ellis; Woodhead, Dowen;

IT'S A FACT !

In 2001–02, Gary Alexander became the first Hull City player for 35 years to have reached double figures in League goals by the start of November. In 1966–67, Ken Wagstaff had managed 14 goals in 14 games.

Robinson (1), Blyth, Hardy; Hubbard (2), Richardson (2), Dickinson (2), Davies (2), Cunliffe (2).

Record Cup Victory: 8–2 v Stalybridge Celtic (a), FA Cup 1st rd, 26 November 1932 – Maddison; Goldsmith, Woodhead; Gardner, Hill (1), Denby; Forward (1), Duncan, McNaughton (1), Wainscoat (4), Sargeant (1).

Record Defeat: 0–8 v Wolverhampton W, Division 2, 4 November 1911.

Most League Points (2 for a win): 69, Division 3, 1965–66.

Most League Points (3 for a win): 90, Division 4, 1982–83.

Most League Goals: 109, Division 3, 1965–66.

Highest League Scorer in Season: Bill McNaughton, 39, Division 3 (N), 1932–33.

Most League Goals in Total Aggregate: Chris Chilton, 195, 1960–71.

Most League Goals in One Match: 5, Ken McDonald v Bristol C, Division 2, 17 November 1928; 5, Simon 'Slim' Raleigh v Halifax T, Division 3N, 26 December 1930.

Most Capped Player: Theo Whitmore, Jamaica.

Most League Appearances: Andy Davidson, 520, 1952–67.

Youngest League Player: Matthew Edeson, 16 years 63 days v Fulham, 10 October 1992.

Record Transfer Fee Received: £750,000 from Middlesbrough for Andy Payton, November 1991.

Record Transfer Fee Paid: £210,000 to Leicester C for Lawrie Dudfield, July 2001.

Football League Record: 1905 Elected to Division 2; 1930–33 Division 3 (N); 1933–36 Division 2; 1936–49 Division 3 (N); 1949–56 Division 2; 1956–58 Division 3 (N); 1958–59 Division 3; 1959–60 Division 2; 1960–66 Division 3; 1966–78 Division 2; 1978–81 Division 3; 1981–83 Division 4; 1983–85 Division 3; 1985–91 Division 2; 1991–92 Division 3; 1992–96 Division 2; 1996– Division 3.

MANAGERS

James Ramster 1904–05
(Secretary-Manager)
Ambrose Langley 1905–13
Harry Chapman 1913–14
Fred Stringer 1914–16
David Menzies 1916–21
Percy Lewis 1921–23
Bill McCracken 1923–31
Haydn Green 1931–34
John Hill 1934–36
David Menzies 1936
Ernest Blackburn 1936–46
Major Frank Buckley 1946–48
Raich Carter 1948–51
Bob Jackson 1952–55
Bob Brocklebank 1955–61
Cliff Britton 1961–70
(continued as General Manager to 1971)
Terry Neill 1970–74
John Kaye 1974–77
Bobby Collins 1977–78
Ken Houghton 1978–79
Mike Smith 1979–82
Bobby Brown 1982
Colin Appleton 1982–84
Brian Horton 1984–88
Eddie Gray 1988–89
Colin Appleton 1989
Stan Ternent 1989–91
Terry Dolan 1991–97
Mark Hateley 1997–98
Warren Joyce 1998–2000
Brian Little 2000–02
Jan Molby April 2002–

LATEST SEQUENCES

Longest Sequence of League Wins: 10, 23.2.66 – 20.4.66.

Longest Sequence of League Defeats: 8, 7.4.34 – 8.9.34.

Longest Sequence of League Draws: 5, 30.3.29 – 15.4.29.

Longest Sequence of Unbeaten League Matches: 19, 13.3.01 – 22.9.01.

Longest Sequence Without a League Win: 27, 27.3.89 – 4.11.89.

TEN YEAR LEAGUE RECORD

		P	W	D	L	F	A	Pts	Pos
1991-92	Div 3	46	16	11	19	54	54	59	14
1992-93	Div 2	46	13	11	22	46	69	50	20
1993-94	Div 2	46	18	14	14	62	54	68	9
1994-95	Div 2	46	21	11	14	70	57	74	8
1995-96	Div 2	46	5	16	25	36	78	31	24
1996-97	Div 3	46	13	18	15	44	50	57	17
1997-98	Div 3	46	11	8	27	56	83	41	22
1998-99	Div 3	46	14	11	21	44	62	53	21
1999-2000	Div 3	46	15	14	17	43	43	59	14
2000-01	Div 3	46	19	17	10	47	39	74	6

DID YOU KNOW

On 11 January 1930, Stan Alexander scored three times for Hull City in a 4-3 win at Plymouth Argyle in a third round FA Cup tie. It was the first treble by a Hull player in the competition proper.

HULL CITY 2001–02 LEAGUE RECORD

Match No.	Date	Venue	Opponents	Result	H/T Score	Lg. Pos.	Goalscorers	Attendance
1	Aug 11	A	Exeter C	W 3-1	1-1	—	Whitmore [33], Greaves [57], Dudfield [85]	4677
2	18	H	Plymouth Arg	D 0-0	0-0	4		10,755
3	25	A	Carlisle U	D 0-0	0-0	9		3695
4	27	H	Kidderminster H	W 2-1	0-0	6	Alexander 2 [52, 90]	8835
5	Sept 8	H	York C	W 4-0	1-0	4	Mohan [23], Dudfield (pen) [61], Alexander [73], Lee [90]	9737
6	15	A	Macclesfield T	D 0-0	0-0	7		2740
7	18	H	Rochdale	W 3-1	1-1	—	Alexander 2 [28, 51], Dudfield [63]	10,213
8	22	H	Swansea C	W 2-1	1-0	2	Dudfield [34], Johnsson [47]	10,440
9	25	A	Mansfield T	L 2-4	0-3	2	Alexander [56], Reddy [85]	5702
10	29	H	Halifax T	W 3-0	1-0	2	Dudfield [23], Reddy 2 [73, 85]	9572
11	Oct 5	A	Shrewsbury T	D 1-1	0-1	—	Alexander [90]	5010
12	13	H	Torquay U	W 1-0	0-0	3	Reddy [75]	9102
13	20	A	Rushden & D	D 3-3	1-3	4	Alexander [5], Hunter (og) [47], Rowe [54]	4676
14	23	H	Leyton Orient	D 1-1	0-0	—	Alexander [77]	9843
15	27	A	Darlington	W 1-0	1-0	4	Alexander (pen) [44]	5163
16	Nov 3	H	Cheltenham T	W 5-1	3-0	3	Banks (og) [4], Dudfield [22], Alexander [26], Whitmore [78], Beresford [81]	9435
17	6	A	Hartlepool U	L 0-4	0-2	—		3183
18	10	A	Lincoln C	L 1-2	0-1	5	Alexander [90]	4950
19	20	A	Luton T	W 1-0	0-0	—	Matthews [51]	7214
20	24	H	Bristol R	D 0-0	0-0	4		9680
21	Dec 1	H	Oxford U	W 3-0	3-0	3	Matthews [13], Dudfield [19], Alexander [38]	9552
22	15	A	Scunthorpe U	L 1-2	0-1	4	Dudfield [65]	6479
23	21	H	Southend U	D 0-0	0-0	—		8678
24	29	A	Kidderminster H	L 0-3	0-1	4		3962
25	Jan 12	A	Plymouth Arg	L 0-1	0-1	6		9134
26	15	H	Carlisle U	L 0-1	0-1	—		8526
27	19	H	Exeter C	W 2-0	1-0	5	Johnsson [26], Alexander [67]	8459
28	22	A	Southend U	L 0-2	0-1	—		3341
29	26	H	Shrewsbury T	W 3-0	3-0	5	Williams R (pen) [19], Dudfield [29], Edwards [32]	8534
30	29	A	York C	L 1-2	0-2	—	Rowe (pen) [72]	6495
31	Feb 2	A	Halifax T	W 1-0	1-0	4	Johnsson [38]	3400
32	5	H	Hartlepool U	D 1-1	1-0	—	Williams R [6]	8419
33	9	H	Rushden & D	W 2-1	1-0	5	Alexander [12], Van Blerk [70]	8825
34	16	A	Torquay U	D 1-1	1-0	5	Alexander [30]	2403
35	22	H	Macclesfield T	L 0-1	0-0	—		8431
36	Mar 1	A	Swansea C	L 0-1	0-0	—		5006
37	5	H	Mansfield T	W 4-1	2-0	—	Philpott [14], Bradshaw [22], Norris [49], Johnsson [78]	9158
38	9	H	Scunthorpe U	L 0-1	0-0	8		12,529
39	16	A	Oxford U	L 0-1	0-0	9		5952
40	23	A	Leyton Orient	D 0-0	0-0	9		4265
41	30	H	Darlington	L 1-2	0-1	11	Alexander [68]	8642
42	Apr 1	A	Cheltenham T	L 0-1	0-0	11		5546
43	6	H	Luton T	L 0-4	0-2	11		9379
44	9	A	Rochdale	L 2-3	2-1	—	Dudfield 2 [26, 45]	3433
45	13	A	Bristol R	D 1-1	1-0	11	Matthews [36]	6340
46	20	H	Lincoln C	D 1-1	1-1	11	Dudfield [45]	11,890

Final League Position: 11

GOALSCORERS

League (57): Alexander 17 (1 pen), Dudfield 12 (1 pen), Johnsson 4, Reddy 4, Matthews 3, Rowe 2 (1 pen), Whitmore 2, Williams R 2 (1 pen), Beresford 1, Bradshaw 1, Edwards 1, Greaves 1, Lee 1, Mohan 1, Norris 1, Philpott 1, Van Blerk 1, own goals 2.
Worthington Cup (3): Alexander 1, Greaves 1, Whitmore 1.
FA Cup (7): Alexander 2, Dudfield 2, Johnsson 1, Matthews 1, own goal 1.

Glennon M 26	Edwards M 38+1	Goodison I 14+2	Whittle J 35+1	Greaves M 25+1	Mohan N 26+1	Williams R 26+3	Johnsson J 38+2	Alexander G 43	Dudfield L 32+6	Beresford D 33+8	Whitmore T 23+11	Price M —+1	Philpott L 9+2	Matthews R 9+6	Rowe R 5+9	Lee D 2+9	Petty B 22+5	Holt A 24+6	Reddy M 1+4	Bloomer M —+3	Tait P —+2	Sneekes R 17+5	Folan C —+1	Musselwhite P 20	Wicks M 14	Morley B 1+2	Roberts N 3+3	Van Blerk J 10	Bradshaw G 3	Norris D 3+3	Lightbourne K 3+1	Caceres A 1+3	Match No.
1	2	3	4	5	6	7¹	8	9	10²	11³	12	13	14																				1
1	2	3	4	5	6		8	9	10²	11	7¹				12	13																	2
1	2	3	4	5	6		8	9¹	10²	11	7				12	13																	3
1	2	3	4	5²	6		8	9	10¹	11	7³				12	13	14																4
1	2		4		6	8²	9³	7	11	12					5		10¹	14	13	3													5
1	2		4		6		8	9	10¹	11	7				5		12			3													6
1	2			5	6		8	9	10	11	7						4			3													7
1	2			5	6		8	9²	10	11	7		12				4		3	13													8
1	2			5	6³		8	9	10	11	7²		12				4		3	13	14												9
1	2			5	6		8	9¹	10	11	7						12	4²	3	13													10
1	2			5	4²12		8	9	10	11							6		3	7¹13													11
1	2	4		5			7¹	8	9	10	11						6		3	12													12
1	2			5	6	7	8³	9	10²	11¹					12	13	14	4	3														13
1	2			5	6	7	8	9		11	4				10¹	12			3														14
1	2			5	6	7³	8	9²	12	11	4				10¹	14	13		3														15
1	2	12		5		7¹	8	9	10	11	4²					13	6		3	14													16
1	2	4		5	7	8		9	11	10							6¹		3			12											17
1	2	4	5	6	7		9	10²	8						12		11	3¹			13												18
1	2	3	5		7	8	9	10	4						11		6																19
1	2	3	5		7¹	8	9	10²	12	4					11	13	6																20
1	2	3	5			8²	9	10³	11	4					7¹		6	12				13	14										21
1	2	3	5			8	9	10	11¹	4					7²		6	12				13											22
1	2	3	5		12	8	9	10²	11¹	4					7	13	6																23
		4	5¹	6		8	9	12	11	7²					13		2	3				10	1										24
		4	5	11³	12	8¹	9	10	13	7							2	3²				14	1	6									25
3		5	12		13	9	14	11	8¹	7	10³						2					4²	1	6									26
2		5¹	6	12	7	8	9	10	11								3						1	4									27
2²		6	4	7	8	9	10	11¹	12								3					13	1	5									28
2³		6	4	7			10²	11	12						13		3					8	1	5	14	9¹							29
		2³	4	7³	12		9	11¹	8						13		3					6	1	5	14	10							30
2		4		7	8	9		11							10¹		3					6	1	5	12								31
2		4		7	8	9		11	12								3					6	1	5	10¹	3							32
2	12	4		7³	8	9	10	11³					13				14					6¹	1	5	3								33
2		5	4	7¹	8²	9	10	11²12					11				3					13	1	6	14	3						34
2		5	4	7¹		9	10	11²12									3					8	1	6	13	3¹						35
2		5	3	7¹	8	9		12	13	11							10	1	6						4²								36
2		5	6	7	8	9	12	13		11²							4³	1	3						10¹	14							37
2	12	5	6		8	9	10²	7		11³	13						4	1	3¹						14								38
		5	6		8	9	12	13	7¹	11²			2	3			4	1							10								39
		5	6¹		7	8	9			11			2	12			4	1						3			10²13						40
		5	6		7²		9		12	13	11¹		2				4	1						3		8	14	10³					41
2		5		6	7	8³	9		12	13			14				4²	1						3		11²	14	10³					42
2			4	6	7¹	9				12			5	13			8	1						3		11²	14	10³					43
1	12		5	4	6		9	10²	11					2	7		8¹									3					13		44
1			5	4	6		8	9	10²	12				7¹			2	11								3					13		45
1	2			4	5	7¹	8	9	12	11				6²10³			14	13								3							46

Worthington Cup
First Round Wrexham (a) 3-2
Second Round Derby Co (a) 0-3

FA Cup
First Round Northwich Vic (a) 5-2
Second Round Oldham Ath (h) 2-3

IPSWICH TOWN   Division 1

FOUNDATION

Considering that Ipswich Town only reached the Football League in 1938, many people outside of East Anglia may be surprised to learn that this club was formed at a meeting held in the Town Hall as far back as 1878 when Mr T. C. Cobbold, MP, was voted president. Originally it was the Ipswich Association FC to distinguish it from the older Ipswich Football Club which played rugby. These two amalgamated in 1888 and the handling game was dropped in 1893.

Portman Road, Ipswich, Suffolk IP1 2DA.

Telephone: (01473) 400 500 (4 lines).
Fax: (01473) 400 040. *Ticket Office:* (01473) 400 555.
Website: www.itfc.co.uk *Email:* enquiries@itfc.co.uk
Sales Dept: (01473) 400 523.

Ground Capacity: 30,250.

Record Attendance: 38,010 v Leeds U, FA Cup 6th rd, 8 March 1975.

Record Receipts: £105,950 v AZ 67 Alkmaar, UEFA Cup Final 1st leg, 6 May 1981.

Pitch Measurements: 101m × 65m.

Chairman and Chief Executive: David Sheepshanks.

Vice-presidents: Kenneth H. Brightwell, Harold R. Smith.

Directors: P. Hope-Cobbold, R. Moore, John Kerr MBE, R. J. Finbow, Lord Ryder OBE.

Manager: George Burley. *Reserve Team Manager:* Dale Roberts. *First Team Coach:* Tony Mowbray. *Chief Scout:* Colin Suggett. *Academy Director:* Bryan Klug. *Physio:* Dave Williams.

Secretary: David C. Rose.

Director of Communications & Marketing: Alesha Gooderham. *Publications Manager:* Mike Noye.

Director of Commercial Affairs: Paul Clouting. *Director of Finance:* Mike Cooper.

Colours: Blue shirts, white shorts, blue stockings.

Change Colours: Wine red shirts with navy sleeves and white trim, navy shorts, white stockings.

Year Formed: 1878.

Turned Professional: 1936.

Ltd Co.: 1936.

Club Nicknames: 'Blues' or 'Town'.

HONOURS

Football League: Division 1 – Champions 1961–62; Runners-up 1980–81, 1981–82; Promoted from Division 1 1999–2000 (play-offs); Division 2 – Champions 1960–61, 1967–68, 1991–92; Division 3 (S) – Champions 1953–54, 1956–57.
FA Cup: Winners 1978.
Football League Cup: Semi-final 1982, 1985.
Texaco Cup: Winners 1973.
European Competitions: *European Cup:* 1962–63. *European Cup-Winners' Cup:* 1978–79. *UEFA Cup:* 1973–74, 1974–75, 1975–76, 1977–78, 1979–80, 1980–81 (winners), 1981–82, 1982–83, 2001–02.

IT'S A FACT !

John Gammage, one-time treasurer of Ipswich Town's Supporters Club, was the originator of the club's badge, based as it is on the Suffolk Punch horse. Punch also became the club's official leisurewear brand.

First Football League Game: 27 August 1938, Division 3 (S), v Southend U (h) W 4–2 – Burns; Dale, Parry; Perrett, Fillingham, McLuckie; Williams, Davies (1), Jones (2), Alsop (1), Little.

Record League Victory: 7–0 v Portsmouth, Division 2, 7 November 1964 – Thorburn; Smith, McNeil; Baxter, Bolton, Thompson; Broadfoot (1), Hegan (2), Baker (1), Leadbetter, Brogan (3). 7–0 v Southampton, Division 1, 2 February 1974 – Sivell; Burley, Mills (1), Morris, Hunter, Beattie (1), Hamilton (2), Viljoen, Johnson, Whymark (2), Lambert (1) (Woods). 7–0 v WBA, Division 1, 6 November 1976 – Sivell; Burley, Mills, Talbot, Hunter, Beattie (1), Osborne, Wark (1), Mariner (1) (Bertschin), Whymark (4), Woods.

Record Cup Victory: 10–0 v Floriana, European Cup prel. rd, 25 September 1962 – Bailey; Malcolm, Compton; Baxter, Laurel, Elsworthy (1); Stephenson, Moran (2), Crawford (5), Phillips (2), Blackwood.

Record Defeat: 1–10 v Fulham, Division 1, 26 December 1963.

Most League Points (2 for a win): 64, Division 3 (S), 1953–54 and 1955–56.

Most League Points (3 for a win): 87, Division 1, 1999–2000.

Most League Goals: 106, Division 3 (S), 1955–56.

Highest League Scorer in Season: Ted Phillips, 41, Division 3 (S), 1956–57.

Most League Goals in Total Aggregate: Ray Crawford, 203, 1958–63 and 1966–69.

Most League Goals in One Match: 5, Alan Brazil v Southampton, Division 1, 16 February 1981.

Most Capped Player: Allan Hunter, 47 (53), Northern Ireland.

Most League Appearances: Mick Mills, 591, 1966–82.

Youngest League Player: Jason Dozzell, 16 years 56 days v Coventry C, 4 February 1984.

Record Transfer Fee Received: £6,000,000 from Newcastle U for Kieron Dyer, July 1999; £6,000,000 from Arsenal for Richard Wright, July 2001.

Record Transfer Fee Paid: £4,750,000 to Sampdoria for Matteo Sereni.

Football League Record: 1938 Elected to Division 3 (S); 1954–55 Division 2; 1955–57 Division 3 (S); 1957–61 Division 2; 1961–64 Division 1; 1964–68 Division 2; 1968–86 Division 1; 1986–92 Division 2; 1992–95 FA Premier League; 1995–2000 Division 1; 2000–02 FA Premier League; 2002– Division 1.

MANAGERS

Mick O'Brien 1936–37
Scott Duncan 1937–55
    (continued as Secretary)
Alf Ramsey 1955–63
Jackie Milburn 1963–64
Bill McGarry 1964–68
Bobby Robson 1969–82
Bobby Ferguson 1982–87
Johnny Duncan 1987–90
John Lyall 1990–94
George Burley December 1994–

LATEST SEQUENCES

Longest Sequence of League Wins: 8, 23.9.53 – 31.10.53.

Longest Sequence of League Defeats: 10, 4.9.54 – 16.10.54.

Longest Sequence of League Draws: 7, 10.11.90 – 21.12.90.

Longest Sequence of Unbeaten League Matches: 23, 8.12.79 – 26.4.80.

Longest Sequence Without a League Win: 21, 28.8.63 – 14.12.63.

TEN YEAR LEAGUE RECORD

		P	W	D	L	F	A	Pts	Pos
1991-92	Div 2	46	24	12	10	70	50	84	1
1992-93	PR Lge	42	12	16	14	50	55	52	16
1993-94	PR Lge	42	9	16	17	35	58	43	19
1994-95	PR Lge	42	7	6	29	36	93	27	22
1995-96	Div 1	46	19	12	15	79	69	69	7
1996-97	Div 1	46	20	14	12	68	50	74	4
1997-98	Div 1	46	23	14	9	77	43	83	5
1998-99	Div 1	46	26	8	12	69	32	86	3
1999-2000	Div 1	46	25	12	9	71	42	87	3
2000-01	PR Lge	38	20	6	12	57	42	66	5

DID YOU KNOW ?

Tommy Parker signed from the Navy, played his first game for Ipswich Town on 3 November 1945 at Watford and his last on 25 August 1956, making 493 appearances in all first class games in which he scored 100 goals.

IPSWICH TOWN 2001–02 LEAGUE RECORD

Match No.	Date	Venue	Opponents	Result	H/T Score	Lg. Pos.	Goalscorers	Attendance
1	Aug 18	A	Sunderland	L	0-1	0-1	—	45,173
2	21	H	Derby Co	W	3-1	1-0	—	George 2 [14, 76], Naylor [48]	21,133
3	25	A	Charlton Ath	L	0-1	0-0	12		22,518
4	Sept 8	A	Leicester C	D	1-1	1-0	13	Stewart [13]	18,774
5	16	H	Blackburn R	D	1-1	1-0	12	Armstrong [15]	22,095
6	22	A	Manchester U	L	0-4	0-2	17		67,551
7	30	H	Leeds U	L	1-2	1-0	17	Stewart [22]	22,628
8	Oct 13	H	Everton	D	0-0	0-0	16		22,820
9	21	A	Fulham	D	1-1	0-1	17	Wright [55]	17,221
10	24	A	Southampton	D	3-3	1-2	—	Stewart 2 [38, 73], Venus [64]	29,614
11	28	H	West Ham U	L	2-3	0-1	17	Hreidarsson [63], Holland [90]	22,826
12	Nov 4	A	Chelsea	L	1-2	0-1	18	Stewart (pen) [83]	40,456
13	18	H	Bolton W	L	1-2	1-2	19	Holland [45]	22,321
14	25	A	Middlesbrough	D	0-0	0-0	20		32,586
15	Dec 1	H	Arsenal	L	0-2	0-1	20		24,631
16	9	H	Newcastle U	L	0-1	0-1	20		24,749
17	17	A	Aston Villa	L	1-2	1-1	—	George [18]	29,320
18	22	A	Tottenham H	W	2-1	1-1	20	George [40], Armstrong [88]	36,044
19	26	H	Leicester C	W	2-0	0-0	19	Bent M [48], Peralta [55]	24,394
20	29	H	Sunderland	W	5-0	4-0	19	Armstrong 2 [15, 27], Gaardsoe [26], George [31], Clapham [86]	24,546
21	Jan 1	A	Charlton Ath	L	2-3	2-2	19	Bent M 2 [1, 5]	25,858
22	12	H	Tottenham H	W	2-1	1-0	22	Bent M [12], McGreal [81]	25,057
23	19	A	Derby Co	W	3-1	0-0	17	Bent M [47], Peralta [67], Reuser [87]	29,658
24	30	H	Fulham	W	1-0	1-0	—	Bent M [10]	25,149
25	Feb 2	A	Everton	W	2-1	2-1	12	Peralta [11], Holland [44]	33,069
26	9	H	Liverpool	L	0-6	0-2	13		25,607
27	Mar 2	H	Southampton	L	1-3	0-0	16	George [82]	25,430
28	6	A	Leeds U	L	0-2	0-0	—		39,414
29	13	A	Blackburn R	L	1-2	0-2	—	Stewart [55]	23,305
30	16	H	Newcastle U	D	2-2	0-0	17	Bent M 2 [50, 63]	51,115
31	23	H	Aston Villa	D	0-0	0-0	18		25,428
32	30	A	West Ham U	L	1-3	0-1	18	Bent M [71]	33,871
33	Apr 1	D	Chelsea	D	0-0	0-0	18		27,929
34	6	A	Bolton W	L	1-4	0-4	18	Clapham [90]	25,817
35	21	A	Arsenal	L	0-2	0-0	18		38,058
36	24	H	Middlesbrough	W	1-0	0-0	17	Bent D [58]	25,979
37	27	H	Manchester U	L	0-1	0-1	18		28,286
38	May 11	A	Liverpool	L	0-5	0-2	18		44,088

Final League Position: 18

GOALSCORERS

League (41): Bent M 9, George 6, Stewart 6 (1 pen), Armstrong 4, Holland 3, Peralta 3, Clapham 2, Bent D 1, Gaardsoe 1, Hreidarsson 1, McGreal 1, Naylor 1, Reuser 1, Venus 1, Wright 1.
Worthington Cup (4): Reuser 2, Armstrong 1, Bent M 1.
FA Cup (5): Peralta 2, Bent M 1, Muggleton 1, Stewart 1.

Sereni M 25	Makin C 30	Hreidarsson H 38	Bramble T 16 + 2	McGreal J 27	Reuser M 18 + 6	Magilton J 16 + 8	Holland M 38	Stewart M 20 + 8	George F 21 + 4	Wright J 24 + 5	Clapham J 22 + 10	Counago P 1 + 12	Wilnis F 6 + 8	Naylor R 5 + 9	Armstrong A 21 + 11	Branagan K — +1	Venus M 29	Peralta S 16 + 6	Gaardsoe T 3 + 1	Le Pen U — +1	Bent M 22 + 3	Miller T 5 + 3	Marshall A 13	Bent D 2 + 3	Ambrose D — +1	Match No.
1	2	3	4	5¹	6	7⁴	8	9	10	11	12	13														1
1	2	5	4	6		8	9¹	10	7	3³	12	14	11²	13												2
1	2	5	4	6	13	8	9²	10	7	3³	12		11¹	14												3
1	2	3	4	5	6	7	8	9¹	10⁵	11			12	15												4
1	2	3	4	5	6²	7	8	9	11¹			13	12	14	10³											5
1	2³	3	4	5	12	7	8	9	11¹	13	14		6²		10											6
1	2³	3		5		7	8	9	11¹	6²	12	13	14		10		4									7
1	2²	3		5	6	7	8	9	12	11¹		13			10		4									8
1	7	6		5	12	13	8	14	10²	11	3		2¹		9		4²									9
1	2¹	6		5			8	9	11	3		12	13	10²			4	7								10
1	2	6			7	12	8	9	11¹	3³	13				10²		4	14	5							11
1	2	6	5		12	7	8	9	11	3¹	13		10²				4									12
1	2³	3		5	6	7¹	8		12			10	13		4	11		14					9²			13
1	2	6	5			8			7	3	12	13	10¹		4	11³					9²	14				14
1	2¹	6	5			8		12	7	3	13		10²		4	11³	14				9					15
1	2	3		5		8		11³	7²	6	12		13		10¹	4	14				9					16
1	2	3		5		7	8		11¹	7²	6	12			10	9²	4				13					17
1	2	3	12	5¹	6	7²	8		10	11				14	13		4				9³					18
1	2	3		5		6	12	8		11²	13			14	10³		4	7¹			9					19
1	2	3			6³	7	8		11	12	13			14	10²		4		5		9¹					20
1	2	3			12	7²	8		11			6¹			10		4	13	5		9					21
	2	3		5	6²	7³	8	12		11	13				10¹		4	14			9		1			22
	2	3		5	6¹		8	9³		11	12			14	13		4	7			10²		1			23
	2	3		5	13		8	12		11²	6				10¹		4	7			9		1			24
	2	3		5			12	8	13	11¹	6				10²		4	7			9		1			25
	2	3		5			12	8	13	11²	6				10¹		4	7			9		1			26
	2²	3	5		6¹	7	8	9³	11	13	12	14					4				10		1			27
		6		5		7	8	9³	11²		3	12	2		10¹		4				14	13	1			28
1	2	6		5		7	8	9	12	11	3¹				10³		4	13			14					29
1	2	6		5		12	8	9		11	3				13		4	7¹			10²					30
1	2¹	6		5	13	12	8	9³	11²	7	3				14		4				10					31
1		6		5			8	9	12	11²	3		2				4	7¹			10	13				32
	3		5				8	12	11²		13		2		10¹		4	7³			9	6	1		14	33
	3	12	5				8	13	11¹	14			2		10		4²	7³			9	6	1			34
	6	2	5	4³			8	9	11²	3					12			13			10¹	7	1		14	35
	6	2	5	11			8	9²		3	12				13		4¹	7			10³		1		14	36
	6	2	5	4³			8		11¹	3	12				13			7			9²	10	1		14	37
	3	2	5²	11			8	12				6			13		14	4			9³	7	1	10¹		38

Worthington Cup

| Third Round | Crewe Alex | (a) | 3-2 |
| Fourth Round | Newcastle U | (a) | 1-4 |

FA Cup

| Third Round | Dagenham & R | (a) | 4-1 |
| Fourth Round | Manchester C | (h) | 1-4 |

KIDDERMINSTER HARRIERS   Division 3

FOUNDATION

Kidderminster Harriers were originally formed as a rugby team and played their first game as a soccer club on 18 September 1886 away to Wilden. Harriers won 2-1 with goals from Arthur Millward and William Colsey. Millward was vice-captain and later Kidderminster's first representative on the executive of the Birmingham County FA in 1897. Colsey was to die in tragic circumstances following an accidental injury sustained in a match only two months later.

Aggborough Stadium, Hoo Road, Kidderminster DY10 1NB.

Telephone: (01562) 823 931.

Fax: (01562) 827 329.

Website: www.harriers.co.uk

E-mail: info@harriers.co.uk

ClubCall: 09066 555 815.

Ground Capacity: 6,229 (1,100 seated).

Record Attendance: 9,155 v Hereford U, 27 November 1948.

Chairman: C. C. Youngjohns.

Vice-chairman: B. Norgrove.

Director: R. Painter.

Chief Executive: N. Morris.

Manager: Ian Britton.

Youth Team Manager: John Deakin.

Medical Officers: Dr. K. O'Connor, Dr. V. P. Schreiber.

Physio: Jim Conway.

General Manager: Geoff Butler.

Football Secretary: Roger Barlow.

Safety Officer: Peter Picken.

IT'S A FACT !

Wing-half Wally Birch, signed by Kidderminster Harriers from Sheffield Wednesday in 1933, was promised a benefit in 1939, but the war interrupted. However, he was presented with a cheque for £40 seven years later.

Stadium Manager: Roger Barlow.

Media Manager: Steve Thomas.

Year Formed: 1886.

Club Nickname: 'Harriers'.

Record Cup Victory: 4–0 v Halesowen T, FA Cup 1st rd replay, 16 November 1987.

Record Defeat: 0–13 v Darwen, FA Cup 1st rd replay, 24 January 1891.

Most League Points (3 for a win): 66, Division 3, 2001–02.

Most League Goals: 56, Division 3, 2001–02.

Record Transfer Fee Received: £380,000 from WBA for Lee Hughes, 1997.

Record Transfer Fee Paid: £100,000 to Nuneaton Borough for Andy Ducros, July 2000.

Colours: Red shirts with white flash, red shorts and stockings with white trim.

Change Colours: Silver shirts, silver shorts, black stockings.

HONOURS

Conference: – Champions 1993–94, 1999–2000; Runners-up 1996–97.
FA Trophy: 1986–87 (winners); 1990–91, 1994–95 (runners-up).
League Cup: 1996–97 (winners).
Welsh FA Cup: 1985–86 (runners-up), 1988–89 (runners-up).
Southern League Cup: 1979–80 (winners).
Worcester Senior Cup: (22)
Birmingham Senior Cup: (7)
Staffordshire Senior Cup: (4)
West Midland League: Champions (6) Runners-up (3)
Southern Premier: Runners-up (1)
West Midland League Cup: Winners (7)
Keys Cup: Winners (7)
Border Counties Floodlit League: Champions: (3)
Camkin Floodlit Cup: Winners (3)
Bass County Vase: Winners (1)
Conference Fair Play Trophy: (5)

First Football League Game: 12 August 2000, Division 3, v Torquay U W 2–0 – Clarke; Clarkson, Stamps, Webb, Hinton, Smith, Bennett, Horne (1), Foster, Hadley (1), Ducros (Bird).

Record League Victory: 4–1 v York C, Division 3, 23 October 2001 – Brock; Clarkson, Stamps, Blake, Hinton, Sall (1), Bennett, Foster (1) (Hadley), Broughton (2), Larkin (Lewis), Williams (Shilton). 4–1 v Rochdale, Division 3, 26 December 2001 – Brock; Clarkson, Stamps, Blake (1), Hinton, Sall, Bennett (1), Appleby, Henriksen (2) (Broughton), Larkin, Williams. 4–1 v Torquay U (a), 5 January 2002 – Brock; Clarkson (Ayres), Stamps, Blake, Hinton, Williams, Bennett, Appleby (1), Henriksen (1), Larkin (Foster (2)), Shilton (Broughton).

LATEST SEQUENCES

Longest Sequence of League Wins: 4, 3.11.01 – 24.11.01.
Longest Sequence Without a League Win: 8, 25.2.01 – 24.3.01

TEN YEAR LEAGUE RECORD

		P	W	D	L	F	A	Pts	Pos
1991-92	Conf	42	12	9	21	56	77	45	19
1992-93	Conf	42	14	16	12	60	60	58	9
1993-94	Conf	42	22	9	11	63	35	75	1
1994-95	Conf	42	16	9	17	63	61	57	11
1995-96	Conf	42	18	10	14	78	66	64	7
1996-97	Conf	42	26	7	9	84	42	85	2
1997-98	Conf	42	11	14	17	56	63	47	17
1998-99	Conf	42	14	9	19	56	52	51	15
1999-2000	Conf	42	26	7	9	75	40	85	1
2000-01	Div 3	46	13	14	19	47	61	53	16

DID YOU KNOW ❓

The longest result among current Football League clubs was recorded in 1988–89 in the third round of the Welsh Cup: Kidderminster Harriers 3, Llanfairpwllgwyngyllgo-cerychwyrndrobwllilanty-siliogogogoch 0.

KIDDERMINSTER HARRIERS 2001–02 LEAGUE RECORD

Match No.	Date	Venue	Opponents	Result		H/T Score	Lg. Pos.	Goalscorers	Attendance
1	Aug 11	H	Scunthorpe U	W	1-0	0-0	—	Ducros [62]	3173
2	18	A	Darlington	L	0-2	0-0	13		3677
3	25	H	Torquay U	W	1-0	0-0	8	Bird (pen) [90]	2440
4	27	A	Hull C	L	1-2	0-0	10	Bird (pen) [81]	8835
5	Sept 1	H	Mansfield T	D	1-1	0-1	12	Blake [53]	2387
6	8	A	Rochdale	L	0-2	0-1	15		2885
7	15	H	Plymouth Arg	D	0-0	0-0	16		2801
8	18	A	Shrewsbury T	L	0-4	0-2	—		3530
9	22	A	Hartlepool U	D	1-1	0-0	19	Blake [57]	3130
10	25	H	Oxford U	D	0-0	0-0	—		2663
11	29	H	Swansea C	L	0-2	0-2	21		2796
12	Oct 7	A	Macclesfield T	W	1-0	1-0	19	Larkin [23]	1859
13	13	H	Cheltenham T	D	0-0	0-0	19		3554
14	20	A	Carlisle U	L	0-1	0-0	19		2556
15	23	H	York C	W	4-1	1-1	—	Broughton 2 [13, 63], Sall [49], Foster [50]	2002
16	27	A	Southend U	L	0-1	0-1	18		3990
17	Nov 3	H	Bristol R	W	2-0	1-0	15	Bennett [33], Broughton [61]	3588
18	10	A	Leyton Orient	W	3-1	1-0	12	Bennett [20], Appleby [80], Henriksen [83]	4321
19	20	A	Lincoln C	W	1-0	0-0	—	Bennett [85]	2249
20	24	H	Rushden & D	W	3-0	1-0	8	Bennett [28], Blake [84], Larkin [85]	3014
21	Dec 15	A	Exeter C	L	1-2	1-0	11	Bennett [31]	2707
22	26	H	Rochdale	W	4-1	2-1	11	Henriksen 2 [4, 44], Blake [51], Bennett [84]	3856
23	29	H	Hull C	W	3-0	1-0	9	Henriksen [25], Larkin [48], Bennett [68]	3962
24	Jan 5	A	Torquay U	W	4-1	2-1	9	Henriksen [7], Appleby [45], Foster 2 [72, 90]	2129
25	8	H	Luton T	L	1-4	0-0	—	Williams [50]	4147
26	12	A	Darlington	W	1-0	0-0	7	Ducros [53]	2756
27	19	A	Scunthorpe U	L	0-1	0-1	9		3360
28	22	H	Halifax T	W	2-0	1-0	—	Foster 2 (1 pen) [15, 89 (p)]	2295
29	29	A	Mansfield T	D	1-1	1-0	—	Smith [19]	4321
30	Feb 9	H	Carlisle U	D	2-2	1-1	10	Smith [9], Appleby [84]	3295
31	12	A	Swansea C	L	1-2	1-1	—	Henriksen [19]	3508
32	19	H	Macclesfield T	L	0-1	0-0	—		2256
33	23	A	Plymouth Arg	L	1-2	1-0	11	Broughton [33]	8758
34	26	A	Shrewsbury T	W	1-0	1-0	—	Heathcote (og) [13]	3625
35	Mar 2	H	Hartlepool U	W	3-2	0-1	10	Sall [58], Larkin [64], Bennett [87]	2894
36	5	A	Oxford U	D	1-1	0-0	—	Broughton [63]	5027
37	9	H	Exeter C	W	3-1	2-0	10	Foster 2 [10, 89], Broughton [31]	2615
38	12	A	Halifax T	L	0-1	0-1	—		1227
39	16	A	Luton T	L	0-1	0-1	10		6488
40	23	A	York C	W	1-0	0-0	10	Larkin [81]	2787
41	26	A	Cheltenham T	L	1-2	1-1	—	Larkin [19]	5016
42	30	H	Southend U	W	2-0	1-0	8	Henriksen [37], Foster [77]	2804
43	Apr 1	A	Bristol R	L	1-2	1-1	10	Broughton [36]	5711
44	6	H	Lincoln C	D	1-1	0-0	10	Broughton [48]	2578
45	13	A	Rushden & D	W	2-0	0-0	10	Appleby [52], Henriksen [76]	5478
46	20	H	Leyton Orient	L	0-1	0-1	10		3138

Final League Position: 10

GOALSCORERS
League (56): Bennett 8, Broughton 8, Foster 8 (1 pen), Henriksen 8, Larkin 6, Appleby 4, Blake 4, Bird 2 (2 pens), Ducros 2, Sall 2, Smith 2, Williams 1, own goal 1.
Worthington Cup (2): Bird 2.
FA Cup (0).

Brock S 42	Medou-Otye P 2	Stamps S 36+1	Blake M 23+1	Hinton C 41	Smith A 33+3	Bird T 14+12	Davies B 9	Hadley S 5+5	Ducros A 7+7	Shilton S 12+12	Foster I 21+12	Bennett D 39+3	Ayres L 5+1	Broughton D 23+15	Williams D 37+1	Clarkson J 36+3	Joy I 13+3	Shail M 4	Larkin C 31+2	Nixon E 2	Sall A 27	Lewis M —+2	Appleby R 18+1	Henriksen B 24+1	Corbett A —+2	Doyle D —+1	Danby J —+2	Montgomery G 2	Match No.
1	2	3	4	5	6	7	8	9	10^1	11^2	12	13																	1
1	2	3	4	5	6	7	8	9	10^1	11	12																		2
1		3	4	5	2	7		8^2	9^1	12	11	10^1	13	6	14														3
1		3	4	5	2	7				12	11	13	8	6^2	9^1	10													4
1		3^2	4^1	5	6	7		9		11	12	13	10^2	8	2		14												5
1				5	6	7	8	9^1			11	10	12	4	2	3													6
1	12		4		6	7^1				13	11^1	9		14	8	2	3	5	10^3										7
1		3	4		6	12		8		13	11^1	14	10^2		9	7^3	2	5											8
1		10	4	5	7	8					11	9			2	3	6												9
1		11	4	5	7	8						9			2	3	6		10										10
1		11^1	4	5	7^2	8^3					12	9		13	14	2	3	6	10										11
1		3	4	5	6						11	7		9	8	2			10										12
		3		5	6	7		12			11	8		9^1	4	2			10	1									13
		3	4	5	6	7^1				12		8		9	11	2			10	1									14
1		3	4	5						12	13	7		8^1	2	9	11^2		10^2		6	14							15
1		3	4	5						12	13	7		8^2	2	9	11^3		10^1		6								16
1		3	4^1	5						12	13	7		8^2	2	9	11		10^1		6								17
1		3	4	5						12		7		8^2	2^1	9	11		10^3		6	13	14						18
1		3	4	5						12	13	7	14		11	2			10^3		6		8^2	9^1					19
1		3	4	5						12	13	7			11	2			10^2		6	14	8^1	9^3					20
1		3	4	5							12	7			11	2			10		6		8	9^1					21
1		3	4	5							12	7			11	2			10		6		8	9^1					22
1		3	4	5						12		7	14	13	11	2			10^1		6^3		8	9^2					23
1		3	4	5						11^2	12	7	14	13	6	2^3			10^1				8	9					24
1		3^4	4	5						12		7	6	10	11	2	13						8^1	9					25
1			5	12						8	11	10^2	7	6	13	4	2^1	3						9					26
1		3	4	5						12		7		8^2	2	13	11		10		6			9^1					27
1		3	4^3	5						12	13	7	14		2	11			10^1		6		8	9^2					28
1		3	4	5						12	13	7		10	2	11					6		8^1	9^1					29
1		3	12^2	5							13	7^3	14		2^1	11			10		6		8	9					30
1	2		5	6						11	12	7		4^2	13	3			10				8	9^1					31
1		3		5	6					11	12	7	4^1	9	2				10^3			14	8^2		13				32
1		3	4	5	7		8^1			10	11	9			2	12					6								33
1		3	4	5						11		7		9	2				10		6		8						34
1		3^2	4	5	12					11^1		7	13	8	2				10		6			9					35
1		3	4	5	3	12				11		7		9	4	2			10^1		6		8						36
1			4	5	12					11^3	8	7		9	2				10^1		6				13				37
1		3	4	5	12					13	8	7		9	2^1	11			10^2		6								38
1		3	4	5	7							8^1		9	2^6	11	12				6		10				15		39
1		3	4	5	12					13	14	7^2		9	2^1	11^3			10		6		8						40
1		3	5	2	12					13	14	7		9^4					10^3		6		11^1	8					41
1		3	5	2	12					13	10	7		9	4						6		11^2	8^1				1	42
1		3	5	2	12						10	7		9^1	4	13					6		11^6	8^2			15	1	43
1		3^1	5	2								7		9	4	12			10		6		11	8					44
1			5	2				8				7		4	3				10		6		11	9					45
1			5	6	12			11^1				7		4	2	3			10				8	9					46

Worthington Cup
First Round   Preston NE   (h)   2-3

FA Cup
First Round   Darlington   (h)   0-1

LEEDS UNITED

FA Premiership

FOUNDATION

Immediately the Leeds City club (founded in 1904) was wound up by the FA in October 1919, following allegations of illegal payments to players, a meeting was called by a Leeds solicitor, Mr Alf Masser, at which Leeds United was formed. They joined the Midland League playing their first game in that competition in November 1919. It was in this same month that the new club had discussions with the directors of a virtually bankrupt Huddersfield Town who wanted to move to Leeds in an amalgamation. But Huddersfield survived even that crisis.

Elland Road, Leeds LS11 0ES.

Telephone: (0113) 226 6000. *Fax:* (0113) 226 6050.

Website: www.leedsunited.com

Ticket Information: 09068 121 680.

ClubCall: 09068 121 180.

Ground Capacity: 40,296.

Record Attendance: 57,892 v Sunderland, FA Cup 5th rd (replay), 15 March 1967.

Record Receipts: £781,445 v Liverpool, FA Cup 4th rd, 27 January 2001.

Pitch Measurements: 105m × 68m.

President: The Right Hon. The Earl of Harewood KBE, LLD.

Chairman: Peter Ridsdale.

Directors: S. Harrison, A. Hudson, I. Silvester, D. Spencer, D. Walker.

Manager: Terry Venables.

Assistant Manager: Eddie Gray MBE.

Club Secretary: Ian Silvester.

Physio: Dave Hancock.

Commercial Manager: Phil Brining.

Stadium Manager: Harry Stokey.

Colours: All white with royal blue trim.

Change Colours: All blue with yellow trim.

Year Formed: 1919, as Leeds United after disbandment (by FA order) of Leeds City (formed in 1904).

Turned Professional: 1920.

Ltd Co.: 1920.

Club Nickname: 'United'.

HONOURS

Football League: Division 1 – Champions 1968–69, 1973–74, 1991–92; Runners-up 1964–65, 1965–66, 1969–70, 1970–71, 1971–72; Division 2 – Champions 1923–24, 1963–64, 1989–90; Runners-up 1927–28, 1931–32, 1955–56.

FA Cup: Winners 1972; Runners-up 1965, 1970, 1973.

Football League Cup: Winners 1968; Runners-up 1996.

European Competitions: *European Cup:* 1969–70, 1974–75 (runners-up), 1992–93, 2000–01 (semi-finalists). *European Cup-Winners' Cup:* 1972–73 (runners-up). *European Fairs Cup:* 1965–66, 1966–67 (runners-up), 1967–68 (winners), 1968–69, 1970–71 (winners). *UEFA Cup:* 1971–72, 1973–74, 1979–80, 1995–96, 1998–99, 1999–2000 (semi-finalists), 2001–02.

IT'S A FACT *!*

In 1953, John Charles scored three hat-tricks for Leeds United against Rotherham United: 17 January in a 4-0 home win, 22 August in a 4-2 away victory and 19 December in a 4-2 success at Elland Road.

First Football League Game: 28 August 1920, Division 2,
v Port Vale (a) L 0–2 – Down; Duffield, Tillotson;
Musgrove, Baker, Walton; Mason, Goldthorpe, Thompson,
Lyon, Best.

Record League Victory: 8–0 v Leicester C, Division 1,
7 April 1934 – Moore; George Milburn, Jack Milburn;
Edwards, Hart, Copping; Mahon (2), Firth (2), Duggan (2),
Furness (2), Cochrane.

Record Cup Victory: 10–0 v Lyn (Oslo), European Cup
1st rd 1st leg, 17 September 1969 – Sprake; Reaney, Cooper,
Bremner (2), Charlton, Hunter, Madeley, Clarke (2),
Jones (3), Giles (2) (Bates), O'Grady (1).

Record Defeat: 1–8 v Stoke C, Division 1, 27 August 1934.

Most League Points (2 for a win): 67, Division 1, 1968–69.

Most League Points (3 for a win): 85, Division 2, 1989–90.

Most League Goals: 98, Division 2, 1927–28.

Highest League Scorer in Season: John Charles, 42,
Division 2, 1953–54.

Most League Goals in Total Aggregate: Peter Lorimer,
168, 1965–79 and 1983–86.

Most League Goals in One Match: 5, Gordon Hodgson v
Leicester C, Division 1, 1 October 1938.

Most Capped Player: Billy Bremner, 54, Scotland.

Most League Appearances: Jack Charlton, 629, 1953–73.

Youngest League Player: Peter Lorimer, 15 years 289 days v Southampton, 29 September 1962.

Record Transfer Fee Received: £30,000,000 from Manchester U for Rio Ferdinand, July 2002.

Record Transfer Fee Paid: £18,000,000 to West Ham United for Rio Ferdinand, November 2000.

Football League Record: 1920 Elected to Division 2; 1924–27 Division 1; 1927–28 Division 2;
1928–31 Division 1; 1931–32 Division 2; 1932–47 Division 1; 1947–56 Division 2; 1956–60 Division 1;
1960–64 Division 2; 1964–82 Division 1; 1982–90 Division 2; 1990–92 Division 1; 1992– FA Premier
League.

MANAGERS

Dick Ray 1919–20
Arthur Fairclough 1920–27
Dick Ray 1927–35
Bill Hampson 1935–47
Willis Edwards 1947–48
Major Frank Buckley 1948–53
Raich Carter 1953–58
Bill Lambton 1958–59
Jack Taylor 1959–61
Don Revie OBE 1961–74
Brian Clough 1974
Jimmy Armfield 1974–78
Jock Stein CBE 1978
Jimmy Adamson 1978–80
Allan Clarke 1980–82
Eddie Gray MBE 1982–85
Billy Bremner 1985–88
Howard Wilkinson 1988–96
George Graham 1996–98
David O'Leary 1998–2002
Terry Venables July 2002–

LATEST SEQUENCES

Longest Sequence of League Wins: 9, 26.9.31 – 21.11.31.

Longest Sequence of League Defeats: 6, 6.4.96 – 2.5.96.

Longest Sequence of League Draws: 5, 19.4.97 – 9.8.97.

Longest Sequence of Unbeaten League Matches: 34, 26.10.68 – 26.8.69.

Longest Sequence Without a League Win: 17, 1.2.47 – 26.5.47.

TEN YEAR LEAGUE RECORD

		P	W	D	L	F	A	Pts	Pos
1991-92	Div 1	42	22	16	4	74	37	82	1
1992-93	PR Lge	42	12	15	15	57	62	51	17
1993-94	PR Lge	42	18	16	8	65	39	70	5
1994-95	PR Lge	42	20	13	9	59	38	73	5
1995-96	PR Lge	38	12	7	19	40	57	43	13
1996-97	PR Lge	38	11	13	14	28	38	46	11
1997-98	PR Lge	38	17	8	13	57	46	59	5
1998-99	PR Lge	38	18	13	7	62	34	67	4
1999-2000	PR Lge	38	21	6	11	58	43	69	3
2000-01	PR Lge	38	20	8	10	64	43	68	4

DID YOU KNOW ?

In the 1921–22 season, Leeds
United scored in just 11 of
their first 17 matches. Tommy
Howarth was on target in
each one for a total of 12
goals.

LEEDS UNITED 2001–02 LEAGUE RECORD

Match No.	Date	Venue	Opponents	Result	H/T Score	Lg. Pos.	Goalscorers	Attendance
1	Aug 18	H	Southampton	W 2-0	0-0	—	Bowyer [67], Smith [81]	39,715
2	21	A	Arsenal	W 2-1	1-1	—	Harte [29], Viduka [53]	38,062
3	25	A	West Ham U	D 0-0	0-0	2		24,517
4	Sept 8	H	Bolton W	D 0-0	0-0	3		40,153
5	16	A	Charlton Ath	W 2-0	1-0	1	Keane [21], Mills [62]	20,451
6	23	H	Derby Co	W 3-0	1-0	1	Bakke [9], Kewell 2 [74, 78]	39,155
7	30	A	Ipswich T	W 2-1	0-1	1	Keane [70], Venus (og) [86]	22,628
8	Oct 13	A	Liverpool	D 1-1	1-0	1	Kewell [27]	44,352
9	21	H	Chelsea	D 0-0	0-0	1		40,171
10	27	A	Manchester U	D 1-1	0-0	2	Viduka [77]	67,555
11	Nov 4	H	Tottenham H	W 2-1	0-0	1	Harte [61], Kewell [82]	40,203
12	18	A	Sunderland	L 0-2	0-0	2		46,017
13	25	A	Aston Villa	D 1-1	1-1	2	Smith [18]	40,159
14	Dec 2	A	Fulham	D 0-0	0-0	3		20,918
15	9	A	Blackburn R	W 2-1	0-0	3	Kewell 2 [55, 62]	28,309
16	16	H	Leicester C	D 2-2	1-0	4	Kewell [7], Viduka [59]	38,337
17	19	H	Everton	W 3-2	2-0	—	Viduka [19], Fowler 2 [26, 71]	40,201
18	22	H	Newcastle U	L 3-4	1-1	4	Bowyer [38], Viduka [50], Harte [56]	40,287
19	26	A	Bolton W	W 3-0	2-0	4	Fowler 3 [2, 16, 89]	27,060
20	29	A	Southampton	W 1-0	0-0	3	Bowyer [89]	31,622
21	Jan 1	H	West Ham U	W 3-0	2-0	1	Viduka 2 [4, 7], Fowler [50]	39,322
22	12	A	Newcastle U	L 1-3	1-1	3	Smith [1]	52,130
23	20	H	Arsenal	D 1-1	1-1	3	Fowler [6]	40,143
24	30	A	Chelsea	L 0-2	0-2	—		40,615
25	Feb 3	H	Liverpool	L 0-4	0-1	6		40,216
26	9	A	Middlesbrough	D 2-2	1-0	6	Bakke [19], Fowler [54]	30,221
27	24	H	Charlton Ath	D 0-0	0-0	6		39,374
28	Mar 3	A	Everton	D 0-0	0-0	5		33,226
29	6	H	Ipswich T	W 2-0	0-0	—	Fowler [46], Harte (pen) [78]	39,414
30	17	H	Blackburn R	W 3-1	2-0	6	Fowler 2 [5, 8], Kewell [71]	39,857
31	23	A	Leicester C	W 2-0	2-0	5	Viduka [18], Fowler [31]	18,976
32	30	H	Manchester U	L 3-4	1-3	6	Viduka [20], Harte [62], Bowyer [80]	40,058
33	Apr 1	A	Tottenham H	L 1-2	0-2	6	Viduka [52]	35,167
34	7	H	Sunderland	W 2-0	1-0	6	Craddock (og) [9], Keane [83]	39,195
35	13	A	Aston Villa	W 1-0	1-0	6	Viduka [29]	40,039
36	20	H	Fulham	L 0-1	0-0	6		39,811
37	27	A	Derby Co	W 1-0	1-0	6	Bowyer [16]	30,735
38	May 11	H	Middlesbrough	W 1-0	0-0	5	Smith [63]	40,218

Final League Position: 5

GOALSCORERS
League (53): Fowler 12, Viduka 11, Kewell 8, Bowyer 5, Harte 5 (1 pen), Smith 4, Keane 3, Bakke 2, Mills 1, own goals 2.
Worthington Cup (6): Keane 3, Bakke 1, Kewell 1, Viduka 1.
FA Cup (1): Viduka 1.

Martyn N 38	Mills D 28	Harte I 34 + 2	Batty D 30 + 6	Ferdinand R 31	Matteo D 32	Dacourt O 16 + 1	Keane R 16 + 9	Viduka M 33	Kewell H 26 + 1	Bowyer L 24 + 1	Bakke E 20 + 7	Smith A 19 + 4	Kelly G 19 + 1	Woodgate J 11 + 2	Maybury A — + 1	Wilcox J 4 + 9	McPhail S — + 1	Johnson S 12 + 2	Fowler R 22	Duberry M 3	Match No.
1	2	3	4¹	5	6	7	8²	9	10	11	12	13									1
1	2	3	12	5	6	7		10	11³	8		4²	9³	13	14						2
1	2	3¹	4	5	6	7²	8	9	10	11			12	13							3
1		3	4	5	6	7	8	9	10		12		2				11¹				4
1	2	3	4	5	6	7¹	8	9	10	11								12			5
1	2	3	4	5	6		8	9	10	11	7										6
1	2	3	4	5	6		8	9	10	11	7										7
1	2	3	12	5	6	7	8¹	9	10	11	4										8
1	2	3		5	6	7	8¹	9	10	11	4	12									9
1	2	3	12	5	6	7	8¹	9	10²	11	4	13									10
1	2	3	12	5	6	7¹	8²	9	10	11³	4	13		14							11
1	2	3	4	5	6	7	8			11	9							10			12
1	2	3	4	5	6		8			7	9				11			10			13
1	6	3	4	5		12		9	7¹		8	2						11	10		14
1	2	3	4	5		11¹		9	10			7		12				8		6	15
1	2	3	4	5	6			9	10			12	7					11¹	8		16
1	2	3	4²	5	6			9¹	10		12	13	7					11	8		17
1	6	3	4	5				9	10¹	7	12	2						11	8		18
1	12	4	5	3¹		8		9	7²	11		6	2					13	10		19
1	2	3	4	5				9		11		8	7	6				12	10¹		20
1	2	3	4	5				9		11¹		8	7	6				12	10		21
1	2		4		3			9		11		8	7	6				12	10¹	5	22
1	2		4	5	3			9		7			6					11	10	8	23
1	12	4	5	3		14		9	13	7		2	6¹					11	10³	8²	24
1		3	4	5	6	7²	12	9	10¹	11		2						13	8		25
1		3	4	5	6	7¹		9	10	11		2						12	8		26
1		3	12	5	6	7¹	8	9	11		4		2						10		27
1		3	4		6			9	11			7	8	2					10	5	28
1		3	4	5	6			12	9	11¹		7	8	2					10		29
1	2	3	4	5		7²	12	9	11³			13	8¹		6			14	10		30
1	2	3	4		6	7¹		9	11				8		5			12	10		31
1	2	3	4³		6		12	9	11²	13	14		8		5			7¹	10		32
1	2	3	4		6		12	9	11	7¹	8				5				10		33
1	2	3	4		6		12	9	11	7	8				5				10¹		34
1	5	3	4		6		10	9	11	7	8	2									35
1	2	3	4	5	6		9		11	7	8								10		36
1		3	12	5	6	13		11¹		7	4	8	2					10	9²		37
1		3		5	6	9		11¹		7	4	8	2					12	10		38

Worthington Cup
Third Round   Leicester C   (a)   6-0
Fourth Round   Chelsea   (h)   0-2

FA Cup
Third Round   Cardiff C   (a)   1-2

LEICESTER CITY   Division 1

FOUNDATION

In 1884 a number of young footballers who were mostly old boys of Wyggeston School, held a meeting at a house on the Roman Fosse Way and formed Leicester Fosse FC. They collected 9d (less than 4p) towards the cost of a ball, plus the same amount for membership. Their first professional, Harry Webb from Stafford Rangers, was signed in 1888 for 2s 6d (12p) per week, plus travelling expenses.

The Walkers Stadium, Filbert Way, Leicester LE2 7FL.

Telephone: (0116) 291 5000. *Fax:* (0116) 247 0585.
Ticket Office: (0116) 291 5232. *ClubCall:* 09068 121 185.
24hr Ticket Information: 09068 121 028.
Website: www.lcfc.co.uk

Ground Capacity: 32,500.

Record Attendance: 47,298 v Tottenham H, FA Cup 5th rd, 18 February 1928.

Record Receipts: £377,467 v Aston Villa, League Cup semi-final, 2nd leg, 2 February 2000.

Pitch Measurements: 110yd × 76yd.

President: T. W. Shipman. *Chairman:* Sir Rodney Walker. *Chief Executive:* Steve Kind FCCA. *Directors:* G. Clarke, J. M. Elsom FCA, M. George. M. Fenoughty (Finance Director).

Manager: Micky Adams.
Director of Football: Dave Bassett.
Physios: David Rennie and Mick Yeoman.

Director of Media and Communications: Paul Mace. *Director of Football Administration and Club Secretary:* Andrew Neville. *Stadium Manager:* John Petherick.

Colours: Royal blue shirts, royal blue shorts, blue stockings.

Change Colours: Amber shirts, navy shorts, navy stockings.

Year Formed: 1884.

Turned Professional: 1888. *Ltd Co:* 1897.

Previous Name: 1884, Leicester Fosse; 1919, Leicester City.

Club Nickname: 'Foxes'.

Previous Grounds: 1884, Victoria Park; 1887, Belgrave Road; 1888, Victoria Park; 1891, Filbert Street.

First Football League Game: 1 September 1894, Division 2, v Grimsby T (a) L 3–4 – Thraves; Smith, Bailey; Seymour, Brown, Henrys; Hill, Hughes, McArthur (1), Skea (2), Priestman.

Record League Victory: 10–0 v Portsmouth, Division 1, 20 October 1928 – McLaren; Black, Brown; Findlay, Carr, Watson; Adcock, Hine (3), Chandler (6), Lochhead, Barry (1).

Record Cup Victory: 8–1 v Coventry C (a), League Cup 5th rd, 1 December 1964 – Banks; Sjoberg,

HONOURS

Football League: Division 1 – Runners-up 1928–29; Promoted from Division 1 1993–94 (play-offs) and 1995–96 (play-offs); Division 2 – Champions 1924–25, 1936–37, 1953–54, 1956–57, 1970–71, 1979–80; Runners-up 1907–08.

FA Cup: Runners-up 1949, 1961, 1963, 1969.

Football League Cup: Winners 1964, 1997, 2000; Runners-up 1965, 1999.

European Competitions: *European Cup-Winners' Cup:* 1961–62. *UEFA Cup:* 1997–98, 2000–01.

IT'S A FACT !

Inside-right Johnny Duncan scored six goals in succession for Leicester City, the last half dozen in a 7-0 Christmas Day 1924 victory over Port Vale.

Norman (2); Roberts, King, McDerment; Hodgson (2), Cross, Goodfellow, Gibson (1), Stringfellow (2), (1 og).

Record Defeat: 0–12 (as Leicester Fosse) v Nottingham F, Division 1, 21 April 1909.

Most League Points (2 for a win): 61, Division 2, 1956–57.

Most League Points (3 for a win): 77, Division 2, 1991–92.

Most League Goals: 109, Division 2, 1956–57.

Highest League Scorer in Season: Arthur Rowley, 44, Division 2, 1956–57.

Most League Goals in Total Aggregate: Arthur Chandler, 259, 1923–35.

Most League Goals in One Match: 6, John Duncan v Port Vale, Division 2, 25 December 1924; 6, Arthur Chandler v Portsmouth, Division 1, 20 October 1928.

Most Capped Player: John O'Neill, 39, Northern Ireland.

Most League Appearances: Adam Black, 528, 1920–35.

Youngest League Player: Dave Buchanan, 16 years 192 days v Oldham Ath, 1 January 1979.

Record Transfer Fee Received: £11,000,000 from Liverpool for Emile Heskey, March 2000.

Record Transfer Fee Paid: £5,000,000 to Wolverhampton W for Ade Akinbiyi, July 2000.

Football League Record: 1894 Elected to Division 2; 1908–09 Division 1; 1909–25 Division 2; 1925–35 Division 1; 1935–37 Division 2; 1937–39 Division 1; 1946–54 Division 2; 1954–55 Division 1; 1955–57 Division 2; 1957–69 Division 1; 1969–71 Division 2; 1971–78 Division 1; 1978–80 Division 2; 1980–81 Division 1; 1981–83 Division 2; 1983–87 Division 1; 1987–92 Division 2; 1992–94 Division 1; 1994–95 FA Premier League; 1995–96 Division 1; 1996–2002 FA Premier League; 2002– Division 1.

MANAGERS

Frank Gardner 1884–92
Ernest Marson 1892–94
J. Lee 1894–95
Henry Jackson 1895–97
William Clark 1897–98
George Johnson 1898–1912
Jack Bartlett 1912–14
Louis Ford 1914–15
Harry Linney 1915–19
Peter Hodge 1919–26
Willie Orr 1926–32
Peter Hodge 1932–34
Arthur Lochhead 1934–36
Frank Womack 1936–39
Tom Bromilow 1939–45
Tom Mather 1945–46
John Duncan 1946–49
Norman Bullock 1949–55
David Halliday 1955–58
Matt Gillies 1958–68
Frank O'Farrell 1968–71
Jimmy Bloomfield 1971–77
Frank McLintock 1977–78
Jock Wallace 1978–82
Gordon Milne 1982–86
Bryan Hamilton 1986–87
David Pleat 1987–91
Gordon Lee 1991
Brian Little 1991–94
Mark McGhee 1994–95
Martin O'Neill 1995–2000
Peter Taylor 2000–01
Dave Bassett 2001–02
Micky Adams April 2002–

LATEST SEQUENCES

Longest Sequence of League Wins: 7, 28.2.93 – 27.3.93.

Longest Sequence of League Defeats: 8, 17.3.01 – 28.4.01.

Longest Sequence of League Draws: 6, 21.8.76 – 18.9.76.

Longest Sequence of Unbeaten League Matches: 19, 6.2.71 – 18.8.71.

Longest Sequence Without a League Win: 18, 12.4.75 – 1.11.75.

TEN YEAR LEAGUE RECORD

		P	W	D	L	F	A	Pts	Pos
1991-92	Div 2	46	23	8	15	62	55	77	4
1992-93	Div 1	46	22	10	14	71	64	76	6
1993-94	Div 1	46	19	16	11	72	59	73	4
1994-95	PR Lge	42	6	11	25	45	80	29	21
1995-96	Div 1	46	19	14	13	66	60	71	5
1996-97	PR Lge	38	12	11	15	46	54	47	9
1997-98	PR Lge	38	13	14	11	51	41	53	10
1998-99	PR Lge	38	12	13	13	40	46	49	10
1999-2000	PR Lge	38	16	7	15	55	55	55	8
2000-01	PR Lge	38	14	6	18	39	51	48	13

DID YOU KNOW ?

Leicester City made a master stroke signing in Jack Bowers from Derby County in November 1936. He scored 33 goals in only 27 League matches to help City win the Second Division title, having earlier scored 12 in 15 games for Derby.

LEICESTER CITY 2001–02 LEAGUE RECORD

Match No.	Date	Venue	Opponents	Result	H/T Score	Lg. Pos.	Goalscorers	Attendance
1	Aug 18	H	Bolton W	L	0-5	0-4	—	19,987
2	25	A	Arsenal	L	0-4	0-2	20	37,909
3	Sept 8	H	Ipswich T	D	1-1	0-1	18	Sturridge [90]	18,774
4	15	A	Derby Co	W	3-2	1-1	17	Sturridge 2 [30, 64], Izzet (pen) [90]	26,863
5	17	H	Middlesbrough	L	1-2	1-0	—	Jones [10]	15,412
6	22	H	Fulham	D	0-0	0-0	19		18,918
7	26	A	Newcastle U	L	0-1	0-1	—		49,185
8	29	A	Charlton Ath	L	0-2	0-1	20		20,451
9	Oct 13	A	Chelsea	L	0-2	0-2	20		40,371
10	20	H	Liverpool	L	1-4	0-3	20	Wise [58]	21,886
11	29	A	Blackburn R	D	0-0	0-0	—		21,873
12	Nov 3	H	Sunderland	W	1-0	0-0	17	Akinbiyi [61]	20,573
13	17	A	Manchester U	L	0-2	0-1	18		67,651
14	24	H	Everton	D	0-0	0-0	19		21,539
15	Dec 1	A	Aston Villa	W	2-0	1-0	17	Akinbiyi [12], Scowcroft [51]	30,711
16	8	H	Southampton	L	0-4	0-1	19		20,321
17	16	A	Leeds U	D	2-2	0-1	18	Deane [78], Scowcroft [89]	38,337
18	22	H	West Ham U	D	1-1	1-0	19	Izzet [43]	20,131
19	26	A	Ipswich T	L	0-2	0-0	20		24,394
20	29	A	Bolton W	D	2-2	2-1	20	Ricketts (og) [22], Deane [27]	23,037
21	Jan 12	A	West Ham U	L	0-1	0-1	20		34,698
22	19	H	Newcastle U	D	0-0	0-0	20		21,354
23	23	H	Arsenal	L	1-3	0-2	—	Izzet [68]	21,344
24	30	A	Liverpool	L	0-1	0-0	—		42,305
25	Feb 2	H	Chelsea	L	2-3	1-0	20	Scowcroft 2 [24, 68]	19,950
26	9	A	Tottenham H	L	1-2	0-1	20	Oakes [79]	35,973
27	23	H	Derby Co	L	0-3	0-0	20		21,620
28	Mar 2	A	Middlesbrough	L	0-1	0-1	20		25,734
29	9	H	Charlton Ath	D	1-1	1-1	20	Scowcroft [20]	18,562
30	16	A	Southampton	D	2-2	2-1	20	Deane 2 [21, 25]	30,012
31	23	H	Leeds U	L	0-2	0-2	20		18,976
32	30	H	Blackburn R	W	2-1	1-0	20	Dickov 2 [9, 77]	16,236
33	Apr 1	A	Sunderland	L	1-2	1-2	20	Dickov [9]	40,862
34	6	H	Manchester U	L	0-1	0-0	20		21,447
35	13	A	Everton	D	2-2	2-0	20	Deane 2 [18, 27]	35,580
36	20	H	Aston Villa	D	2-2	1-2	20	Izzet (pen) [25], Stevenson [67]	18,125
37	27	A	Fulham	D	0-0	0-0	20		21,016
38	May 11	H	Tottenham H	W	2-1	0-0	20	Dickov [60], Piper [71]	21,716

Final League Position: 20

GOALSCORERS

League (30): Deane 6, Scowcroft 5, Dickov 4, Izzet 4 (2 pens), Sturridge 3, Akinbiyi 2, Jones 1, Oakes 1, Piper 1, Stevenson 1, Wise 1, own goal 1.
Worthington Cup (1): Akinbiyi 1.
FA Cup (2): Scowcroft 2.

Flowers T 3 + 1	Impey A 20 + 7	Davidson C 29 + 1	Elliott M 31	Rowett G 9 + 2	Sinclair F 33 + 2	Savage R 35	Izzet M 29 + 2	Akinbiyi A 16 + 5	Sturridge D 8 + 1	Wise D 15 + 2	Lewis J 4 + 2	Marshall L 29 + 6	Gunnlaugsson A — + 2	Stewart J 9 + 3	Delaney D 2 + 1	Scowcroft J 21 + 3	Jones M 6 + 4	Walker I 35	Benjamin T 4 + 7	Oakes S 16 + 5	Heath M 3 + 2	Piper M 14 + 2	Rogers A 9 + 4	Deane B 13 + 2	Laursen J 10	Stevenson J — + 6	Dickov P 11 + 1	Reeves M 1 + 4	Ashton J 3 + 4	Wright T — + 1	Williamson T — + 1	Taggart G — + 1	Match No.
1	2	3¹	4	5	6	7	8	9²	10³	11	12	13	14																				1
1	2			5¹	6	7	8²	9		11	4	12		3	13	10³	14																2
	2	3	4	5²	6		8	9¹		12	11			7		13	10	1															3
			4	5	6	7	8	9	10¹	11				2	3	12		1															4
	12		4	5¹	6	7		9	10²	11				2	3	8³		1	13	14													5
	12		4	5²	6	7	8	9		11	13			2	3	10		1															6
		3	4	5	6	7	8	9¹		11¹	12			2		10	14	1															7
		3	4	5¹	6	7	8	9		12			14	2		10²	11	1			13³	4											8
	12		4	5	6	7	8	9	10³	11		13	14	2¹		3²		1															9
	12		4	5	6	7		9	10¹	11				2		3²		1				8	13										10
		3	4	5	6	7	8	9		11				2		12		1				10¹											11
		3	4	5	6	7	8	9		11				2		12		1				10¹											12
		3²	4		6	7	8	9		11				2	5	12		1				10¹	13										13
		3	4	5	6	7²	8	9¹		11				2		10		1				12	13										14
			4	5	6	7	8	9¹		11			13	2		10		1				12	3²										15
			4	5	6	7	8	9³			12			2¹		10		1			3	13		11²	14								16
		3	4	5	6	7¹	8				12			2		10		1				11		9									17
			4	5	6	7³	8				12		13	2	3	10		1				11²	14	9¹									18
	12	13	4	5	6		8						14	2¹	3²	10		1				7	11³	9									19
	12	3	4	5	6²				13	10³				7			2	1	8	14		11¹	9										20
	2			5	6	7		8²		11		12				10		1				3¹	9	4	13								21
15	2	3		5	6	8	9				12			10		1⁶			7¹			11	4										22
	1	7	3²		2	6	9	12								10¹	14		13	8³		11	5										23
	2	3	4		8					12				6²		10	7¹	1	13	11²		9	14					5					24
	2¹	3	4		6	7	8							12		10		1		11		9						5					25
	2	3	4		6	7										10		1		11		9						5					26
	2¹	3	4		6	7	8				12					10		1		11²		9¹	13	5	14								27
		3	4		5	6	8					2				10		1		12		7	11				9¹						28
			4		6	8						2		3		10¹		1		12		7	9	5	11								29
		4			6	8						2		3				1		11	12	7	10¹	5		9²	13						30
		4		12	6	8						2¹						1		11²		7	10	5		9			3	13			31
		4	12	5	6	8						2						1		11		7²	10			9	13	3¹					32
		4	5	3	6	8³						2						1		11¹	12		10	13		9	7²	14					33
	6¹	4	5	3		7						2						1		11²	8		10			9	13	12					34
	3		2	5	6	7												1		11	4	8²	10¹	14		9³	13	12					35
	3¹	4	2	5	6	8						7²						1		11³	12	10		14		9	13						36
	3¹	4	2	5	6	8						7						1		12		10	11	13	9²								37
	2	6	4	5		8²						7						1		10	11		12	9³		3¹		13	14				38

Worthington Cup
Second Round	Blackpool	(a)	1-0
Third Round	Leeds U	(h)	0-6

FA Cup
Third Round	Mansfield T	(h)	2-1
Fourth Round	WBA	(a)	0-1

LEYTON ORIENT   Division 3

FOUNDATION

There is some doubt about the foundation of Leyton Orient, and, indeed, some confusion with clubs like Leyton and Clapton over their early history. As regards the foundation, the most favoured version is that Leyton Orient was formed originally by members of Homerton Theological College who established Glyn Cricket Club in 1881 and then carried on through the following winter playing football. Eventually many employees of the Orient Shipping Line became involved and so the name Orient was chosen in 1888.

Leyton Stadium, Brisbane Road, Leyton, London E10 5NE.

Telephone: (020) 8926 1111. *Fax:* (020) 8926 1110.
ClubCall: 09068 121 150.

Ground Capacity: 11,127.

Record Attendance: 34,345 v West Ham U, FA Cup 4th rd, 25 January 1964.

Record Receipts: £87,867.92 v West Ham U, FA Cup 3rd rd, 10 January 1987.

Pitch Measurements: 110yd × 80yd.

Chairman: Barry Hearn.

Chief Executive: Steve Dawson.

HONOURS

Football League: Division 1 best season: 22nd, 1962–63; Division 2 – Runners-up 1961–62; Division 3 – Champions 1969–70; Division 3 (S) – Champions 1955–56; Runners-up 1954–55; Promoted from Division 4 1988–89 (play-offs).

FA Cup: Semi-final 1978.

Football League Cup: best season: 5th rd, 1963.

Directors: Tony Wood OBE, John Goldsmith FRIBA, David Dodd, Steve Davis, Nick Levene.

Manager: Paul Brush. *First Team Coach:* Martin Ling. *Physio:* Tony Flynn.

Secretary: Kirstine Nicholson. *General Manager, Commercial and Stadium:* John Hines.

Colours: Red shirts with white chest panel, red shorts, white stockings.

Change Colours: Blue and yellow.

Year Formed: 1881. *Turned Professional:* 1903. *Ltd Co.:* 1906.

Previous Names: 1881, Glyn Cricket and Football Club; 1886, Eagle Football Club; 1888, Orient Football Club; 1898, Clapton Orient; 1946, Leyton Orient; 1966, Orient; 1987, Leyton Orient.

Club Nickname: 'The O's'.

Previous Grounds: 1884, Glyn Road; 1896, Whittles Athletic Ground; 1900, Millfields Road; 1930, Lea Bridge Road; 1937, Brisbane Road.

First Football League Game: 2 September 1905, Division 2, v Leicester Fosse (a) L 1–2 – Butler; Holmes, Codling; Lamberton, Boden, Boyle; Kingaby (1), Wootten, Leigh, Evenson, Bourne.

Record League Victory: 8–0 v Crystal Palace, Division 3 (S), 12 November 1955 – Welton; Lee, Earl; Blizzard, Aldous, McKnight; White (1), Facey (3), Burgess (2), Heckman, Hartburn (2). 8–0 v Rochdale, Division 4, 20 October 1987 – Wells; Howard, Dickenson (1), Smalley (1), Day, Hull, Hales (2), Castle (Sussex), Shinners (2), Godfrey (Harvey), Comfort (2). 8–0 v Colchester U, Division 4, 15 October 1988 – Wells; Howard, Dickenson, Hales (1p), Day (1), Sitton (1), Baker (1), Ward, Hull (3), Juryeff, Comfort (1). 8–0 v Doncaster R, Division 3, 28 December 1997 – Hyde; Channing, Naylor, Smith (1p), Hicks, Clark, Ling, Joseph R, Griffiths (3) (Harris), Richards (2) (Baker (1)), Inglethorpe (1) (Simpson).

IT'S A FACT !

In their 1955–56 promotion season, Leyton Orient conceded the fewest goals (49) in the division, achieved most away wins (11) and scored the most goals at home (76).

Record Cup Victory: 9–2 v Chester, League Cup 3rd rd, 15 October 1962 – Robertson; Charlton, Taylor; Gibbs, Bishop, Lea; Deeley (1), Waites (3), Dunmore (2), Graham (3), Wedge.

Record Defeat: 0–8 v Aston Villa, FA Cup 4th rd, 30 January 1929.

Most League Points (2 for a win): 66, Division 3 (S), 1955–56.

Most League Points (3 for a win): 75, Division 4, 1988–89.

Most League Goals: 106, Division 3 (S), 1955–56.

Highest League Scorer in Season: Tom Johnston, 35, Division 2, 1957–58.

Most League Goals in Total Aggregate: Tom Johnston, 121, 1956–58, 1959–61.

Most League Goals in One Match: 4, Wally Leigh v Bradford C, Division 2, 13 April 1906; 4, Albert Pape v Oldham Ath, Division 2, 1 September 1924; 4, Peter Kitchen v Millwall, Division 3, 21 April 1984.

Most Capped Players: Tunji Banjo, 7 (7), Nigeria; John Chiedozie, 7 (9), Nigeria; Tony Grealish, 7 (45), Eire.

Most League Appearances: Peter Allen, 432, 1965–78.

Youngest League Player: Paul Went, 15 years 327 days v Preston NE, 4 September 1965.

Record Transfer Fee Received: £600,000 from Notts Co, for John Chiedozie, August 1981.

Record Transfer Fee Paid: £175,000 to Wigan Ath for Paul Beesley, October 1989.

Football League Record: 1905 Elected to Division 2; 1929–56 Division 3 (S); 1956–62 Division 2; 1962–63 Division 1; 1963–66 Division 2; 1966–70 Division 3; 1970–82 Division 2; 1982–85 Division 3; 1985–89 Division 4; 1989–92 Division 3; 1992–95 Division 2; 1995– Division 3.

LATEST SEQUENCES

Longest Sequence of League Wins: 10, 21.1.56 – 30.3.56.

Longest Sequence of League Defeats: 9, 1.4.95 – 6.5.95.

Longest Sequence of League Draws: 6, 30.11.74 – 28.12.74.

Longest Sequence of Unbeaten League Matches: 13, 30.10.54 – 19.2.55.

Longest Sequence Without a League Win: 23, 6.10.62 – 13.4.63.

MANAGERS

Sam Omerod 1905–06
Ike Ivenson 1906
Billy Holmes 1907–22
Peter Proudfoot 1922–29
Arthur Grimsdell 1929–30
Peter Proudfoot 1930–31
Jimmy Seed 1931–33
David Pratt 1933–34
Peter Proudfoot 1935–39
Tom Halsey 1939
Bill Wright 1939–45
Willie Hall 1945
Bill Wright 1945–46
Charlie Hewitt 1946–48
Neil McBain 1948–49
Alec Stock 1949–59
Les Gore 1959–61
Johnny Carey 1961–63
Benny Fenton 1963–64
Dave Sexton 1965
Dick Graham 1966–68
Jimmy Bloomfield 1968–71
George Petchey 1971–77
Jimmy Bloomfield 1977–81
Paul Went 1981
Ken Knighton 1981
Frank Clark 1982–91 *(Managing Director)*
Peter Eustace 1991–94
Chris Turner/John Sitton 1994–95
Pat Holland 1995–96
Tommy Taylor 1996–2001
Paul Brush October 2001–

TEN YEAR LEAGUE RECORD

		P	W	D	L	F	A	Pts	Pos
1991-92	Div 3	46	18	11	17	62	52	65	10
1992-93	Div 2	46	21	9	16	69	53	72	7
1993-94	Div 2	46	14	14	18	57	71	56	18
1994-95	Div 2	46	6	8	32	30	75	26	24
1995-96	Div 3	46	12	11	23	44	63	47	21
1996-97	Div 3	46	15	12	19	50	58	57	16
1997-98	Div 3	46	19	12	15	62	47	66	11
1998-99	Div 3	46	19	15	12	68	59	72	6
1999-2000	Div 3	46	13	13	20	47	52	52	19
2000-01	Div 3	46	20	15	11	59	51	75	5

DID YOU KNOW ?

Ron Heckman scored five goals for Leyton Orient in an FA Cup first round tie against Lovells Athletic on 19 November 1955 in a 7-1 win.

LEYTON ORIENT 2001–02 LEAGUE RECORD

Match No.	Date	Venue	Opponents	Result	H/T Score	Lg. Pos.	Goalscorers	Atten- dance
1	Aug 11	A	Cheltenham T	D 1-1	0-0	—	Lockwood 55	4115
2	18	H	Carlisle U	D 0-0	0-0	14		4693
3	25	A	York C	L 1-2	0-1	17	McLean 75	2661
4	27	H	Hartlepool U	W 2-0	1-0	12	Ibehre 45, Houghton 90	3719
5	Sept 1	A	Southend U	W 2-1	1-0	9	Constantine 2, Smith 79	5853
6	8	H	Bristol R	W 3-1	0-0	6	Constantine 56, Minton 60, Gough 90	5433
7	15	H	Rushden & D	W 2-1	2-0	4	Ibehre 17, Houghton (pen) 37	5287
8	18	A	Darlington	L 0-3	0-1	—		3357
9	22	A	Halifax T	D 0-0	0-0	9		2021
10	25	H	Luton T	L 1-3	0-1	—	Houghton (pen) 85	6540
11	29	H	Torquay U	L 1-2	1-1	9	Constantine 25	4414
12	Oct 5	A	Mansfield T	L 2-3	1-3	—	Houghton 21, Watts 70	5168
13	13	H	Shrewsbury T	L 2-4	1-2	13	Watts 2 4, 90	4436
14	20	A	Swansea C	W 1-0	0-0	11	Minton 90	3645
15	23	A	Hull C	D 1-1	0-0	—	Whittle (og) 90	9843
16	27	H	Rochdale	W 4-2	2-0	9	Ibehre 34, Minton 39, Watts 51, Joseph 59	4631
17	Nov 3	A	Scunthorpe U	L 1-4	0-2	9	Minton 70	3356
18	10	H	Kidderminster H	L 1-3	0-1	14	Minton 59	4321
19	20	H	Oxford U	W 3-0	2-0	—	Watts 16, Martin 23, Ibehre 59	3753
20	24	A	Exeter C	D 0-0	0-0	12		3364
21	Dec 1	H	Plymouth Arg	D 0-0	0-0	13		6342
22	15	A	Macclesfield T	L 1-2	1-2	15	Watts 9	2618
23	22	H	Lincoln C	W 5-0	1-0	11	Gray 8, Watts 2 49, 62, Canham 76, Houghton 84	3874
24	26	A	Bristol R	L 3-5	0-2	13	Watts 56, Gray 2 75, 90	7458
25	29	H	Hartlepool U	L 1-3	0-2	15	Harris 75	3832
26	Jan 12	A	Carlisle U	L 1-6	0-5	16	Gray 72	2955
27	19	H	Cheltenham T	L 0-2	0-1	19		4868
28	22	A	Lincoln C	L 0-2	0-1	—		1935
29	Feb 2	A	Torquay U	D 1-1	1-0	21	Canham 29	1993
30	9	H	Swansea C	D 2-2	0-1	21	McGhee 62, Gray 66	4590
31	16	A	Shrewsbury T	L 0-1	0-0	22		3299
32	19	A	York C	L 1-2	0-1	—	Hadland 77	3663
33	23	H	Rushden & D	L 0-1	0-0	23		4507
34	26	H	Darlington	D 0-0	0-0	—		3284
35	Mar 2	H	Halifax T	W 3-1	1-0	22	Canham 2 31, 48, Christie 63	4748
36	5	A	Luton T	L 0-3	0-1	—		6683
37	9	H	Macclesfield T	W 2-0	2-0	21	Christie 27, Lockwood (pen) 45	3839
38	12	H	Southend U	W 2-1	2-0	—	Nugent 12, Christie 31	4840
39	16	A	Plymouth Arg	L 0-3	0-1	20		9438
40	19	H	Mansfield T	W 2-0	0-0	—	Hutchings 77, Martin 81	3316
41	23	H	Hull C	D 0-0	0-0	18		4265
42	30	A	Rochdale	L 0-3	0-2	19		3021
43	Apr 1	H	Scunthorpe U	D 0-0	0-0	19		4221
44	6	A	Oxford U	D 1-1	0-0	20	McGhee 58	5740
45	13	H	Exeter C	D 1-1	1-1	20	Newton 23	5332
46	20	A	Kidderminster H	W 1-0	1-0	18	Smith 7	3138

Final League Position: 18

GOALSCORERS

League (55): Watts 9, Gray 5, Houghton 5 (2 pens), Minton 5, Canham 4, Ibehre 4, Christie 3, Constantine 3, Lockwood 2 (1 pen), Martin 2, McGhee 2, Smith 2, Gough 1, Hadland 1, Harris 1, Hutchings 1, Joseph 1, McLean 1, Newton 1, Nugent 1, own goal 1.
Worthington Cup (2): Houghton 1, Minton 1.
FA Cup (8): Watts 3, Canham 1, Christie 1, Gray 1, Ibehre 1, Smith 1.

Bayes A 12+1	Joseph M 29+1	Lockwood M 20+4	Smith D 45	McGhee D 39+1	Downer S 11+1	Harris A 45	Ibehre J 21+7	Tate C 1+6	Oakes S 11	Minton J 32+1	McLean A 4+23	Castle S —+1	Houghton S 10+11	Watts S 22+8	Fletcher G 3+6	Hadland P —+5	Gough N 1+10	Martin J 29+2	Constantine L 9+1	Beall B 7+4	Barnard D 6+4	Barrett S 32	Jones B 16	Canham S 23+1	Herrera R 2	McElholm B —+2	Dorrian C 2+1	Hatcher D 2+6	Leigertwood M 8	Gray W 13+2	Christie J 19+6	Partridge D 6+1	Brazier M 8	Nugent K 7+2	Hutchings C 9+1	Newton A 10	Morris G 2	Match No.
1	2	3	4	5	6	7	8	9¹	10²	11³	12	13	14																									1
1	2	3	4	5	6	7	12	10¹	11				8	9²	13																							2
1	2	3¹	4		5	6	8²	10	13	11	9³	12	14	7																								3
1	2		3	4	5	6	8²	12	10³	11	13	7					9¹	14																				4
1	2		3	4	5	6	8¹	10²	11				7				12	9	13																			5
1	2		3	4	5	6	8¹	10	11				7				12	9																				6
	2		4	5	6	8¹	10	11					7				12	9	3	1																		7
	2		4	5	6³	8¹	10²	11					7			13	12	9	14	3	1																	8
1	2		4		5	6	8	10¹	11				7	9	12			3																				9
1	2	3	4	5	6	8	10²	11			12		14	13	7¹	9³																						10
	2		4	5	12	6	11	13			7	10²	9	8	1	3¹																						11
	2	4¹	12	5	6	8²	10³	11	13		7	14	9	1	3																							12
	2³		4	5	6	11	12	9	10²	7¹	13		1	3	14	8																						13
	2		5	4	6	12	13	11	8¹	9²	7		10	1	3³	14																						14
	2		5	4	6	8²	14	11	13	12	9	7¹	10¹	1	3																							15
	2³		5	4	6	8²	11	13	12	9	7	10¹	1	3	14																							16
	2		4	5	6¹	8²	14	11	13	12	9²	7	10	1	3																							17
	2		4	5	6	12	11	8¹	13	9	14	7³	10²	1	3																							18
	2		4	5	6	8²	11	12	9¹	1	3³											14	13	10														19
	12		4	5	6	8³	11		13	9	7²	1	3¹									2	14	10														20
2	12		4	5	6	8	11²	9³	7¹	1	3¹											13	10	14														21
2	12		4	5	6	8³	11	13	9	7¹	1	3²											10	14														22
	2		4	5	6	12	13	14	9²	7	1	3	11³										10	8¹														23
2	12	4²	5	6	13	14	9	7	1	3¹	11²											10	8															24
	3		5	6	12	13	9¹	7³	10	1	11²										2	14	4	8														25
	4		5	8³	11	7²	13	2¹	3	10	1	12	6	9	14																							26
2	3		4	5	6	11	9	7¹	10²	1	12	8	13																									27
2	3	4²	5	7¹	11	10	14	12²	1	8	9	13	6																									28
2		4	5	7	11	12	7	1	8¹	13	6	3	10¹	9²																								29
2		4	5	7	11	13	12	1	8¹	9	6	3	10²																									30
2³		4	5	7	11¹	13	12	7	1	8	9	6	3	10²	14																							31
	4		6	13	9³	12	7	2¹	8²	1	10	5	3	14	11																							32
3	4	5	6	13	14	9³	12	2¹	1	8²	10	11	7																									33
2	4	5	6	11	12	13	1	8	10¹	9	3²	7																										34
2	4	5	6	11	12	14	1	8³	10²	9¹	3	13	7																									35
2	4	5	6	13	12	14	7³	1	8	9²	3	10¹	11																									36
15	2	4	5	6	13	12	7	1²	8	9²	10¹	11	3																									37
1	2	4	5	6	12	7	13	8²	10	9	11	3²																										38
1	2	4	6	12	10¹	7	13	8²	9	5	11	3																										39
2	4	5	6	12	13	10²	7	1	8	9¹	11	3																										40
1	2	4	5	6	12	11	13	10¹	7	1	8	9²	3																									41
1	2	4	5	6	13	11	14	10²	12	7¹	8	9²	3																									42
	2	4	5	6	9	11	10²	13	7	1	8	12	3¹																									43
	2	4³	5	6	9²	11	13	10¹	7	1	8	12	14	3																							44
12	2	4	5	6	9³	14	13	7²	11¹	8	10	3	1																									45
2	3	4²	5	6	12	7	13	8	10¹	9	11	1																										46

Worthington Cup

First Round   Crystal Palace   (h)   2-4

FA Cup

First Round	Bristol C	(a)	1-0
Second Round	Lincoln C	(h)	2-1
Third Round	Portsmouth	(a)	4-1
Fourth Round	Everton	(a)	1-4

LINCOLN CITY   Division 3

FOUNDATION

The original Lincoln Football Club was established in the early 1860's and was one of the first provisional clubs to affiliate to the Football Association. In their early years, they regularly played matches against the famous Sheffield Club and later became known as Lincoln Lindum. The present organisation was formed at a public meeting held in the Monson Arms Hotel in June 1884 and won the Lincolnshire Cup in only their third season. They were founder members of the Midland League in 1889 and that competition's first champions.

Sincil Bank, Lincoln LN5 8LD.

Telephone: (01522) 880 011. **Fax:** (01522) 880 020.
Website: www.redimps.com **ClubCall:** 09066 555 900.

Ground Capacity: 10,147.

Record Attendance: 23,196 v Derby Co, League Cup 4th rd, 15 November 1967.

Record Receipts: £44,184.46 v Everton, Coca-Cola Cup 2nd rd 1st leg, 21 September 1993.

Pitch Measurements: 110yd × 71yd.

President: J. Jennison. **Chairman:** R. Bradley.
Vice-chairman: J. Hicks. **Directors:** K. Roe, S. Wright, K. Cooke.
Hon. Consultant Surgeon: Mr Brian Smith.
Hon. Club Doctor: Chris Batty.
Company Secretary: J. Hicks.

Manager: Keith Alexander.

Physio: Keith Oakes.

HONOURS

Football League: Division 2 best season: 5th, 1901–02; Promotion from Division 3, 1997–98; Division 3 (N) – Champions 1931–32, 1947–48, 1951–52; Runners-up 1927–28, 1930–31, 1936–37; Division 4 – Champions 1975–76; Runners-up 1980–81.

FA Cup: best season: 1st rd of Second Series (5th rd equivalent), 1887, 2nd rd (5th rd equivalent), 1890, 1902.

Football League Cup: best season: 4th rd, 1968.

GM Vauxhall Conference: Champions 1987–88.

Commercial Manager: W. Bavin. **Secretary:** F. J. Martin. **Stadium Manager:** Nigel Dennis.

Colours: Red and white striped shirts, red shorts and stockings.

Change Colours: Gold and black.

Year Formed: 1884. **Turned Professional:** 1892.

Ltd Co.: 1895.

Club Nickname: 'The Red Imps'.

Previous Grounds: 1883, John O'Gaunt's; 1894, Sincil Bank.

First Football League Game: 3 September 1892, Division 2, v Sheffield U (a) L 2–4 – W. Gresham; Coulton, Neill; Shaw, Mettam, Moore; Smallman, Irving (1), Cameron (1), Kelly, J. Gresham.

Record League Victory: 11–1 v Crewe Alex, Division 3 (N), 29 September 1951 – Jones; Green (1p), Varney; Wright, Emery, Grummett (1); Troops (1), Garvey, Graver (6), Whittle (1), Johnson (1).

IT'S A FACT !

On 26 March 2002, Grant Brown completed his 403rd Football League game for Lincoln City at York City to break Tony Emery's appearance record at the club.

Record Cup Victory: 8–1 v Bromley, FA Cup 2nd rd, 10 December 1938 – McPhail; Hartshorne, Corbett; Bean, Leach, Whyte (1); Hancock, Wilson (1), Ponting (3), Deacon (1), Clare (2).

Record Defeat: 3–11 v Manchester C, Division 2, 23 March 1895.

Most League Points (2 for a win): 74, Division 4, 1975–76.

Most League Points (3 for a win): 77, Division 3, 1981–82.

Most League Goals: 121, Division 3 (N), 1951–52.

Highest League Scorer in Season: Allan Hall, 42, Division 3 (N), 1931–32.

Most League Goals in Total Aggregate: Andy Graver, 143, 1950–55 and 1958–61.

Most League Goals in One Match: 6, Frank Keetley v Halifax T, Division 3N, 16 January 1932; 6, Andy Graver v Crewe Alex, Division 3N, 29 September 1951.

Most Capped Player: David Pugh, 3 (7), Wales; George Moulson, 3, Republic of Ireland.

Most League Appearances: Grant Brown, 407, 1989–2002.

Youngest League Player: Shane Nicholson, 16 years 172 days v Burnley, 22 November 1986.

Record Transfer Fee Received: £500,000 from Port Vale for Gareth Ainsworth, September 1997.

Record Transfer Fee Paid: £75,000 to Carlisle U for Dean Walling, September 1997; £75,000 to Bury for Tony Battersby, August 1998.

Football League Record: 1892 Founder member of Division 2. Remained in Division 2 until 1920 when they failed re-election but also missed seasons 1908–09 and 1911–12 when not re-elected. 1921–32 Division 3 (N); 1932–34 Division 2; 1934–48 Division 3 (N); 1948–49 Division 2; 1949–52 Division 3 (N); 1952–61 Division 2; 1961–62 Division 3; 1962–76 Division 4; 1976–79 Division 3; 1979–81 Division 4; 1981–86 Division 3; 1986–87 Division 4; 1987–88 GM Vauxhall Conference; 1988–92 Division 4; 1992–98 Division 3; 1998–99 Division 2; 1999– Division 3.

MANAGERS

David Calderhead 1900–07
John Henry Strawson 1907–14
(had been Secretary)
George Fraser 1919–21
David Calderhead Jnr. 1921–24
Horace Henshall 1924–27
Harry Parkes 1927–36
Joe McClelland 1936–46
Bill Anderson 1946–65
(General Manager to 1966)
Roy Chapman 1965–66
Ron Gray 1966–70
Bert Loxley 1970–71
David Herd 1971–72
Graham Taylor 1972–77
George Kerr 1977–78
Willie Bell 1977–78
Colin Murphy 1978–85
John Pickering 1985
George Kerr 1985–87
Peter Daniel 1987
Colin Murphy 1987–90
Allan Clarke 1990
Steve Thompson 1990–93
Keith Alexander 1993–94
Sam Ellis 1994–95
Steve Wicks *(Head Coach)* 1995
John Beck 1995–98
Shane Westley 1998
John Reames 1998–99
Phil Stant 2000–01
Alan Buckley 2001–02
Keith Alexander May 2002–

LATEST SEQUENCES

Longest Sequence of League Wins: 10, 1.9.30 – 18.10.30.

Longest Sequence of League Defeats: 12, 21.9.1896 – 9.1.1897.

Longest Sequence of League Draws: 5, 21.2.81 – 7.3.81.

Longest Sequence of Unbeaten League Matches: 18, 11.3.80 – 13.9.80.

Longest Sequence Without a League Win: 19, 22.8.78 – 23.12.78.

TEN YEAR LEAGUE RECORD

		P	W	D	L	F	A	Pts	Pos
1991-92	Div 4	42	17	11	14	50	44	62	10
1992-93	Div 3	42	18	9	15	57	53	63	8
1993-94	Div 3	42	12	11	19	52	63	47	18
1994-95	Div 3	42	15	11	16	54	55	56	12
1995-96	Div 3	46	13	14	19	57	73	53	18
1996-97	Div 3	46	18	12	16	70	69	66	9
1997-98	Div 3	46	20	15	11	60	51	72	3
1998-99	Div 2	46	13	7	26	42	74	46	23
1999-2000	Div 3	46	15	14	17	67	69	59	15
2000-01	Div 3	46	12	15	19	58	66	51	18

DID YOU KNOW ?

In their penultimate League game in 1947–48, Lincoln City beat nearest championship challengers Rotherham United 2-0 away on 24 April, with goals from Willie Windle and Jimmy McCormick, both of whom hailed from the Rotherham area.

LINCOLN CITY 2001–02 LEAGUE RECORD

Match No.	Date	Venue	Opponents	Result	H/T Score	Lg. Pos.	Goalscorers	Attendance
1	Aug 11	H	Halifax T	L	1-2	1-2	—	Thorpe [44]	3753
2	16	A	Rushden & D	D	0-0	0-0	—		5018
3	25	H	Swansea C	W	3-0	0-0	12	Thorpe 2 [49, 66], Holmes (pen) [63]	2593
4	27	A	Scunthorpe U	D	1-1	1-1	11	Sedgemore [22]	4349
5	Sept 1	H	Darlington	D	1-1	0-1	13	Cameron [79]	3021
6	8	A	Mansfield T	L	1-2	0-1	16	Cameron [56]	3878
7	15	H	Bristol R	L	0-1	0-1	19		3204
8	18	A	Luton T	D	1-1	0-1	—	Coyne (og) [86]	5066
9	22	A	Carlisle U	D	2-2	1-1	20	Black 2 [15, 50]	3105
10	25	H	Hartlepool U	W	2-0	1-0	—	Thorpe [37], Holmes (pen) [66]	2306
11	29	H	York C	L	1-3	0-2	19	Cameron [83]	2994
12	Oct 5	A	Cheltenham T	L	1-2	0-1	—	Black [63]	3315
13	13	H	Oxford U	W	1-0	0-0	16	Thorpe [90]	3124
14	20	A	Macclesfield T	W	1-0	0-0	13	Barnett J [90]	1845
15	23	A	Plymouth Arg	L	0-2	0-1	—		6572
16	27	H	Exeter C	D	0-0	0-0	16		2719
17	Nov 3	A	Shrewsbury T	D	1-1	1-1	17	Holmes (pen) [27]	3437
18	10	H	Hull C	W	2-1	1-0	13	Cameron [30], Battersby [64]	4950
19	20	H	Kidderminster H	L	0-1	0-0	—		2249
20	24	A	Rochdale	D	2-2	0-1	15	Battersby [89], Holmes [90]	3139
21	Dec 1	A	Southend U	D	1-1	1-1	15	Thorpe [27]	3979
22	15	H	Torquay U	D	0-0	0-0	16		2747
23	22	A	Leyton Orient	L	0-5	0-1	19		3874
24	29	H	Scunthorpe U	W	3-2	2-1	18	Cameron [18], Gain [45], Thorpe [76]	5235
25	Jan 5	A	Swansea C	D	0-0	0-0	18		3409
26	12	H	Rushden & D	L	2-4	2-2	18	Black [32], Battersby [38]	3170
27	19	A	Halifax T	L	0-3	0-1	20		2007
28	22	H	Leyton Orient	W	2-0	1-0	—	Sedgemore [25], Thorpe [86]	1935
29	29	A	Darlington	L	1-2	0-0	—	Morgan [49]	2984
30	Feb 9	H	Macclesfield T	W	1-0	1-0	17	Battersby (pen) [36]	3374
31	12	H	Mansfield T	L	1-4	0-3	—	Thorpe [47]	4072
32	16	A	Oxford U	L	1-2	0-2	20	Thorpe [66]	6596
33	23	A	Bristol R	W	2-1	1-1	20	Gain [18], Walker [90]	5741
34	26	H	Luton T	L	0-1	0-1	—		2921
35	Mar 2	H	Carlisle U	W	3-1	2-0	18	Thorpe [29], Battersby [45], Walker [82]	2751
36	5	A	Hartlepool U	D	1-1	0-0	—	Walker [54]	3126
37	9	A	Torquay U	L	0-2	0-0	19		2255
38	12	H	Cheltenham T	L	0-1	0-0	—		2026
39	16	H	Southend U	L	0-1	0-1	19		2328
40	23	H	Plymouth Arg	L	0-1	0-0	21		4019
41	26	A	York C	L	0-2	0-2	—		2755
42	30	A	Exeter C	D	1-1	0-1	22	Black [86]	2609
43	Apr 1	H	Shrewsbury T	L	1-2	0-1	23	Thorpe [26]	2778
44	6	A	Kidderminster H	D	1-1	0-0	23	Cameron [90]	2578
45	13	H	Rochdale	D	1-1	1-0	23	Thorpe [30]	5849
46	20	A	Hull C	D	1-1	1-1	22	Barnett J [12]	11,890

Final League Position: 22

GOALSCORERS

League (44): Thorpe 13, Cameron 6, Battersby 5 (1 pen), Black 5, Holmes 4 (3 pens), Walker 3, Barnett J 2, Gain 2, Sedgemore 2, Morgan 1, own goal 1.
Worthington Cup (1): Battersby 1.
FA Cup (3): Cameron 1, Hamilton 1, Holmes 1.

Marriott A 43	Barnett J 23+3	Bimson S 34+1	Morgan P 32+2	Holmes S 18+2	Finnigan J 21+2	Black K 30+1	Sedgemore B 33+10	Battersby T 28+11	Thorpe L 37	Gain P 35+7	Cameron D 23+21	Buckley A 19+12	Pettinger P 3	Walker J 24+7	Mayo P 11+3	Brown G 32+4	Bailey M 18	Betts R 1+2	Camm M 5+11	Hamilton I 26	Logan R —+2	Smith P 6+2	Horrigan D —+1	Blooner M 4+1	Match No.
1	2	3	4	5	6	7[1]	8	9	10	11	12														1
1	2	3	4	5	6	7	8	9	10	11															2
1	2	3	4	5	6	7	8	9[1]	10[2]	11	12	13													3
1	2	3	4	5	6	7	8	9		11	10														4
	2	3[2]	4	5	6	7	8[3]	9	10[1]	11	12	13	1	14											5
	2[2]		4	5	6	7	8	9[1]	10	11	12	13	1	14	3[2]										6
	2		4	5	6	7	8[1]	9	10	3	12	11	1												7
1	2[2]		4	5	6	7	8[2]	9	10	3	12	11		13		14									8
1	2		4	5	6	7[1]	12	9	10[2]	3	13	11[3]		8		14									9
1	2	3	4	5	6	7	8	9	10	11[2]	12	13													10
1	2[1]	3	4	5	6[3]	7	8	9	10	11	12			13		14									11
1	2	3	4	5		7	8	9	10	11	12				6[2]	13									12
1	12	3		5		7	8		10	11	13			9		6		2[1]	4[2]						13
1	12	3	13	5		7	8	9[1]		11[3]	10	14		4		6		2[1]							14
1	4[1]	3		5		7	8[3]	12		11[2]	9	13		10		6		2		14					15
1	12	3	4	13		7	8	9[1]		14	10	11[3]		5		6		2[2]							16
1	5[2]	3	4[1]	12		7	8	13		10	9	11				6		2							17
1	4	3		5		7	8[3]	9		10[2]	11[1]			12		6		2	13	14					18
1	3			5		7[1]	8[3]	9		12	10	11[1]		13		6		2	14	4					19
1	3[1]			5			8[3]	12	10	11	9	13		7		6		2[1]	14	4					20
1							8[1]		10	3	9	11		7	5	6		2	12	4					21
1	12		13				8	14	10	3	9	11[1]		7[1]	5	6		2	4[3]						22
1	3	4		6		7[1]	12	9	10[2]	11[1]	13	14				5		2	8						23
1	3	4		6	12	8		10	11	9				4		5		2	7[1]						24
1	3[1]		4		8			10	11	9	12			6		5		2	7						25
1		4	7	8	9			3	10	11				6		5	2[1]	12							26
1	13	2	7	8[2]	9[1]	10	3	12	11[1]	14	6	5				4									27
1	2	3	4	6	11	8	10	9						5				7							28
1	2	3	4	6		8	12	10	11[2]	9	13			5				7[1]							29
1	3	4	6	11[2]	8	9	10	13	12					5	2			7							30
1	3	4	6	11[1]	8[2]	9	10	12		13				5	2			7							31
1	3	4	6	12	13	10	11	9		8		5[2]	2[2]					7[1]	14						32
1	3	4		8	10	11	9			6		5	2			7[1]		12							33
1	3	4	12	13	10	11[1]	9	14		6	5	2						8[3]	7[2]						34
1	3	4	12	9[1]	10	11[1]	13	14		6	5	2						8[1]	7						35
1	3	4	12	9	10	11	13			6	5	2						8[1]	7						36
1	3	4	12	9[1]	10	11[1]	13			6	5		2[3]	8	14	7									37
1	3	4	12	9	10	11[3]	13			6	14	5	2[1]			8[2]		7							38
1[3]	3[1]	4	7	12	10	13	9	11		6		5				8[1]			2	15					39
1	2	3[1]	4	7[2]	12	10	13	9	11	6		5				8[1]		14							40
1	2[1]	3[1]	4	7[2]	12	10		9	11	6		5		13	8					14					41
1	2[1]	4	7	13	12	9	10		11	6		5		14	8[2]					3[3]					42
1	2		7[2]	8	9[1]	10	3[2]	12	11	6	13	5		14						4					43
1	3[3]		8	9[1]	10	12	13	11[1]		6	4	5		14	7					2					44
1	2	4	8	12	10[1]	13	9	11		6	5[2]			14	7[1]					3					45
1	2	4	12	9	3	10	11[2]	8		6	5			13	7[1]										46

Worthington Cup
First Round — Grimsby T — (a) — 1-2

FA Cup
First Round — Bury — (h) — 1-1
— (a) — 1-1
Second Round — Leyton Orient — (a) — 1-2

LIVERPOOL   FA Premiership

FOUNDATION

But for a dispute between Everton FC and their landlord at Anfield in 1892, there may never have been a Liverpool club. This dispute persuaded the majority of Evertonians to quit Anfield for Goodison Park, leaving the landlord, Mr John Houlding, to form a new club. He originally tried to retain the name 'Everton' but when this failed, he founded Liverpool Association FC on 15 March 1892.

Anfield Road, Liverpool L4 0TH.

Telephone: (0151) 263 2361. *Fax:* (0151) 260 8813.
Website: www.liverpoolfc.tv *ClubCall:* 09068 121 184.
Ticket and Match Information: 0870 444 4949
(24-hour service) or 0870 220 2345 (office hours).
Credit Card Bookings: 0870 220 2151.
International Supporters Club: (0151) 261 1444.
Museum and Stadium Tours: (0151) 260 6677.
LFC Direct Mail Order: (0990) 532 532.

Ground Capacity: 45,362.

Record Attendance: 61,905 v Wolverhampton W, FA Cup 4th rd, 2 February 1952.

Record Receipts: £604,048 v Celtic, UEFA Cup, 30 September 1997.

Pitch Measurements: 111yd × 74yd.

Chairman: D. R. Moores.

Chief Executive: Rick Parry BSC, FCA.

Director of Finance: Les Wheatley BSC, FCA.

Directors: N. White FSCA, T. D. Smith, J. Burns, K. E. B. Clayton FCA.

Vice-presidents: H. E. Roberts, J. T. Cross, P. B. Robinson.

Manager: Gerard Houllier.

Assistant Manager: Phil Thompson.

Physio: Dave Galley.

Secretary: Bryce Morrison.

Press Officer: Ian Cotton.

Stadium Manager: Ged Poynton.

Academy Director: Steve Heighway.

Colours: All red.

Change Colours: (To be announced.)

Year Formed: 1892. *Turned Professional:* 1892.
Ltd Co.: 1892.

HONOURS

Football League: Division 1 – Champions 1900–01, 1905–06, 1921–22, 1922–23, 1946–47, 1963–64, 1965–66, 1972–73, 1975–76, 1976–77, 1978–79, 1979–80, 1981–82, 1982–83, 1983–84, 1985–86, 1987–88, 1989–90 (Liverpool have a record number of 18 League Championship wins); Runners-up 1898–99, 1909–10, 1968–69, 1973–74, 1974–75, 1977–78, 1984–85, 1986–87, 1988–89, 1990–91, 2001–02; Division 2 – Champions 1893–94, 1895–96, 1904–05, 1961–62.
FA Cup: Winners 1965, 1974, 1986, 1989, 1992, 2001; Runners-up 1914, 1950, 1971, 1977, 1988, 1996;
Football League Cup: Winners 1981, 1982, 1983, 1984, 1995, 2001; Runners-up 1978, 1987.
League Super Cup: Winners 1986.
European Competitions: European Cup: 1964–65, 1966–67, 1973–74, 1976–77 (winners), 1977–78 (winners), 1978–79, 1979–80, 1980–81 (winners), 1981–82, 1982–83, 1983–84 (winners), 1984–85 (runners-up), 2001–02. *European Cup-Winners' Cup:* 1965–66 (runners-up), 1971–72, 1974–75, 1992–93, 1996–97 (s-f.). *European Fairs Cup:* 1967–68, 1968–69, 1969–70, 1970–71. *UEFA Cup:* 1972–73 (winners), 1975–76 (winners), 1991–92, 1995–96, 1997–98, 1998–99, 2000–01 (winners). *Super Cup:* 1977 (winners), 1978, 1984, 2001 (winners). *World Club Championship:* 1981 (runners-up), 1984 (runners-up).

IT'S A FACT !

Liverpool supplied both goalkeepers for the Scotland v Northern Ireland International on 13 March 1920: Elisha Scott (Northern Ireland) and Kenny Campbell (Scotland). Scotland won 3-0.

Club Nicknames: 'Reds' or 'Pool'.

First Football League Game: 2 September 1893, Division 2, v Middlesbrough Ironopolis (a) W 2–0 – McOwen; Hannah, McLean; Henderson, McQue (1), McBride; Gordon, McVean (1), M. McQueen, Stott, H. McQueen.

Record League Victory: 10–1 v Rotherham T, Division 2, 18 February 1896 – Storer; Goldie, Wilkie; McCartney, McQue, Holmes; McVean (3), Ross (2), Allan (4), Becton (1), Bradshaw.

Record Cup Victory: 11–0 v Stromsgodset Drammen, ECWC 1st rd 1st leg, 17 September 1974 – Clemence; Smith (1), Lindsay (1p), Thompson (2), Cormack (1), Hughes (1), Boersma (2), Hall, Heighway (1), Kennedy (1), Callaghan (1).

Record Defeat: 1–9 v Birmingham C, Division 2, 11 December 1954.

Most League Points (2 for a win): 68, Division 1, 1978–79.

Most League Points (3 for a win): 90, Division 1, 1987–88.

Most League Goals: 106, Division 2, 1895–96.

Highest League Scorer in Season: Roger Hunt, 41, Division 2, 1961–62.

Most League Goals in Total Aggregate: Roger Hunt, 245, 1959–69.

Most League Goals in One Match: 5, Andy McGuigan v Stoke C, Division 1, 4 January 1902; 5, John Evans v Bristol R, Division 2, 15 September 1954; 5, Ian Rush v Luton T, Division 1, 29 October 1983.

Most Capped Player: Ian Rush, 67 (73), Wales.

Most League Appearances: Ian Callaghan, 640, 1960–78.

Youngest League Player: Max Thompson, 17 years 128 days v Tottenham H, 8 May 1974.

Record Transfer Fee Received: £12,500,000 from Leeds U for Robbie Fowler, November 2001.

Record Transfer Fee Paid: £11,000,000 to Leicester C for Emile Heskey, March 2000.

Football League Record: 1893 Elected to Division 2; 1894–95 Division 1; 1895–96 Division 2; 1896–1904 Division 1; 1904–05 Division 2; 1905–54 Division 1; 1954–62 Division 2; 1962–92 Division 1; 1992– FA Premier League.

MANAGERS

W. E. Barclay 1892–96
Tom Watson 1896–1915
David Ashworth 1920–23
Matt McQueen 1923–28
George Patterson 1928–36
(continued as Secretary)
George Kay 1936–51
Don Welsh 1951–56
Phil Taylor 1956–59
Bill Shankly 1959–74
Bob Paisley 1974–83
Joe Fagan 1983–85
Kenny Dalglish 1985–91
Graeme Souness 1991–94
Roy Evans January 1994–98
(then Joint Manager)
Gerard Houllier July 1998–

LATEST SEQUENCES

Longest Sequence of League Wins: 12, 21.4.90 – 6.10.90.

Longest Sequence of League Defeats: 9, 29.4.1899 – 14.10.1899.

Longest Sequence of League Draws: 6, 19.2.75 – 19.3.75.

Longest Sequence of Unbeaten League Matches: 31, 4.5.87 – 16.3.88.

Longest Sequence Without a League Win: 14, 12.12.53 – 20.3.54.

TEN YEAR LEAGUE RECORD

		P	W	D	L	F	A	Pts	Pos
1991-92	Div 1	42	16	16	10	47	40	64	6
1992-93	PR Lge	42	16	11	15	62	55	59	6
1993-94	PR Lge	42	17	9	16	59	55	60	8
1994-95	PR Lge	42	21	11	10	65	37	74	4
1995-96	PR Lge	38	20	11	7	70	34	71	3
1996-97	PR Lge	38	19	11	8	62	37	68	4
1997-98	PR Lge	38	18	11	9	68	42	65	3
1998-99	PR Lge	38	15	9	14	68	49	54	7
1999-2000	PR Lge	38	19	10	9	51	30	67	4
2000-01	PR Lge	38	20	9	9	71	39	69	3

DID YOU KNOW ?

The fastest scoring Liverpool player to reach a century of goals in all matches was Roger Hunt in 144 games. Michael Owen achieved his 100th after 184 appearances.

LIVERPOOL 2001–02 LEAGUE RECORD

Match No.	Date	Venue	Opponents	Result	H/T Score	Lg. Pos.	Goalscorers	Attendance
1	Aug 18	H	West Ham U	W 2-1	1-1	—	Owen 2 [18, 77]	43,935
2	27	A	Bolton W	L 1-2	0-1	—	Heskey [66]	27,205
3	Sept 8	H	Aston Villa	L 1-3	0-1	16	Gerrard [46]	44,102
4	15	A	Everton	W 3-1	2-1	10	Gerrard [12], Owen (pen) [31], Riise [52]	39,554
5	22	H	Tottenham H	W 1-0	0-0	6	Litmanen [57]	44,116
6	30	H	Newcastle U	W 2-0	1-0	6	Riise [3], Murphy [86]	52,095
7	Oct 13	H	Leeds U	D 1-1	0-1	7	Murphy [69]	44,352
8	20	A	Leicester C	W 4-1	3-0	4	Fowler 3 [5, 43, 90], Hyypia [10]	21,886
9	27	A	Charlton Ath	W 2-0	2-0	4	Redknapp [14], Owen [43]	22,658
10	Nov 4	H	Manchester U	W 3-1	2-0	2	Owen 2 [32, 51], Riise [39]	44,361
11	17	A	Blackburn R	D 1-1	1-0	1	Owen [30]	28,859
12	25	H	Sunderland	W 1-0	1-0	1	Heskey [22]	43,537
13	Dec 1	A	Derby Co	W 1-0	1-0	1	Owen [6]	33,289
14	8	H	Middlesbrough	W 2-0	2-0	1	Owen [27], Berger [45]	43,674
15	12	H	Fulham	D 0-0	0-0	—		37,163
16	16	A	Chelsea	L 0-4	0-2	1		41,175
17	23	H	Arsenal	L 1-2	0-1	3	Litmanen [55]	44,297
18	26	A	Aston Villa	W 2-1	1-1	3	Litmanen [9], Smicer [73]	42,602
19	29	A	West Ham U	D 1-1	0-1	4	Owen [88]	35,103
20	Jan 1	H	Bolton W	D 1-1	0-0	4	Gerrard [50]	43,710
21	9	A	Southampton	L 0-2	0-0	—		31,527
22	13	A	Arsenal	D 1-1	0-0	5	Riise [68]	38,132
23	19	H	Southampton	D 1-1	1-0	5	Owen [8]	43,710
24	22	A	Manchester U	W 1-0	0-0	—	Murphy [85]	67,599
25	30	H	Leicester C	W 1-0	0-0	—	Heskey [57]	42,305
26	Feb 3	A	Leeds U	W 4-0	1-0	3	Ferdinand (og) [16], Heskey 2 [61, 63], Owen [90]	40,216
27	9	A	Ipswich T	W 6-0	2-0	2	Xavier [16], Heskey 2 [43, 90], Hyypia [52], Owen 2 [62, 71]	25,607
28	23	H	Everton	D 1-1	0-0	4	Anelka [72]	44,371
29	Mar 2	A	Fulham	W 2-0	1-0	3	Anelka [13], Litmanen [90]	21,103
30	6	H	Newcastle U	W 3-0	1-0	—	Murphy 2 [32, 53], Hamann [75]	44,204
31	16	A	Middlesbrough	W 2-1	1-0	3	Heskey [33], Riise [84]	31,253
32	24	H	Chelsea	W 1-0	0-0	1	Smicer [90]	44,203
33	30	H	Charlton Ath	W 2-0	2-0	1	Smicer [23], Owen [36]	44,094
34	Apr 13	A	Sunderland	W 1-0	0-0	2	Owen [55]	46,062
35	20	H	Derby Co	W 2-0	1-0	2	Owen 2 [16, 90]	43,510
36	27	H	Tottenham H	L 0-1	0-1	3		36,017
37	May 8	H	Blackburn R	W 4-3	2-1	—	Murphy [23], Anelka [39], Hyypia [52], Heskey [86]	40,663
38	11	H	Ipswich T	W 5-0	2-0	2	Riise 2 [13, 35], Owen [46], Smicer [57], Anelka [88]	44,088

Final League Position: 2

GOALSCORERS

League (67): Owen 19 (1 pen), Heskey 9, Riise 7, Murphy 6, Anelka 4, Litmanen 4, Smicer 4, Fowler 3, Gerrard 3, Hyypia 3, Berger 1, Hamann 1, Redknapp 1, Xavier 1, own goal 1.
Worthington Cup (1): McAllister 1 (pen).
FA Cup (3): Owen 2, Anelka 1.

Arphexad P 1+1	Babbel M 2	Carragher J 33	Hamann D 31	Henchoz S 37	Hyypia S 37	Murphy D 31+5	Litmanen J 8+13	Owen M 25+4	McAllister G 14+11	Biscan I 4+1	Riise J 34+4	Redknapp J 2+2	Barmby N 2+4	Westerveld S 1	Gerrard S 26+2	Fowler R 8+2	Heskey E 26+9	Dudek J 35	Vignal G 3+1	Smicer V 13+9	Wright S 10+2	Berger P 12+9	Anelka N 13+7	Xavier A 9+1	Kirkland C 1	Match No.
1	2¹	3	4	5	6	7²	8	9	10	11³	12	13	14													1
	2¹	3	4	5	6	11		10	8		12			1	7	9²	13									2
	2		4	5²	6	13		12	8		3³		11¹		7	10	9	1	14							3
	2		4	5	6	11¹		10	12		3				7²		9	1	8	13						4
	2		4	5	6	10¹	12²	13	11		3				8	9³	14	1	7							5
	2			5	6	7		8	11		3					10	9	1	4							6
	2			5	6	7	13		11³		3	14	12		4	10	9²	1	8							7
		5			6	11		12	8		3	4²			7³	10	9¹	1	13	2	14					8
		6	4	5		11		9¹	10¹		3		8³		7	13	12	1	2	14						9
	2		4	5	6	11		10¹			3				7	12	9	1		8²		13				10
	2		4	5	6	12		10²	8		3				7	13	9	1				11¹				11
	2		4	5	6	11³		12			3				7	10¹	9	1		8²	13	14				12
	2		4	5	6	8		12	10¹	13	3				7		9	1				11²				13
	2		4	5	6	7		9	10¹	8	3						12	1				11				14
	2			5	6	8¹	12	10		4	3	13			7		9	1				11¹				15
	2			5	6	11		10	8	4¹	3				7		9	1		12						16
	2			5	6	7		12	10	8¹	3				4		9²	1		13		11				17
	2		4	5	6	12		9³	10	13	3				7¹			1		8²		11	14			18
	2			5	6	7¹		12	13	4³	3				14		9	1		8¹		11	10			19
			4	5	6	12		10			3				7		9	1		8²	2	11¹	13			20
		3	4	5	6	11³		9	12						7	13		1		8²	2¹	14	10			21
	2		4	5	6	8²		10	12		3				7	13		1				11	9¹			22
	2		4	5	6	8¹		10	12		3				7²		9	1		13³		11	14			23
		3	4	5	6	8¹		10²					11		7		9	1			2	12	13			24
		3	4	5	6	12		8¹					13				9	1		7	2	11²	10			25
		3	4	5	6	8		10	12				11		7¹		9	1			2					26
15			4	5	6	8		10	12				11²		7¹		9	1⁹			2		13	3		27
			4	5	6	7		10	8²				11		12					13	3¹	9	2		1	28
			4	5	6	7		12					11			13	9	1		8²	3	10¹	2			29
			4	5	6	7		12	10¹		3		11			13		1		8²		9	2			30
		3	4	5	6	7							11		12		9	1		8¹		10	2			31
		3	4	5	6	8		12	13				11		7³		9	1		14		10¹	2⁴			32
	2		4	5	6	7		12	10¹	13	3						9³	1		14		11²	8			33
		3	4	5	6	12		9¹	10²				11		7			1				13	8	2		34
	2		4	5	6	11¹		12	10		3				7	13		1		8¹		14	9²			35
		3	4	5	6	7¹		12	10				11				9³	1		8		13	14	2²		36
	2		4²	5	6	11		10¹			3				7		9	1		12		8	13			37
		3	4	5	6	8¹		10	12				11		7²		9	1		13		14	2³			38

Worthington Cup
Third Round   Grimsby T   (h)   1-2

FA Cup
Third Round   Birmingham C   (h)   3-0
Fourth Round   Arsenal   (a)   0-1

LUTON TOWN   Division 2

FOUNDATION

Formed by an amalgamation of two leading local clubs, Wanderers and Excelsior a works team, at a meeting in Luton Town Hall in April 1885. The Wanderers had three months earlier changed their name to Luton Town Wanderers and did not take too kindly to the formation of another Town club but were talked around at this meeting. Wanderers had already appeared in the FA Cup and the new club entered in its inaugural season.

Kenilworth Road Stadium, 1 Maple Rd, Luton, Beds LU4 8AW.

Telephone: (01582) 411 622. **Ticket Office:** (01582) 416 976. **Credit Hotline:** (01582) 307 48 (24 hrs). **ClubCall:** 09068 121 123.

Ground Capacity: 9,975.

Record Attendance: 30,069 v Blackpool, FA Cup 6th rd replay, 4 March 1959.

Record Receipts: £115,541.20 v West Ham U, FA Cup 6th rd, 23 March 1994.

Pitch Measurements: 110yd × 72yd.

Chairman: M. Watson-Challis.

Directors: E. Hood, J. Mitchell, C. Bassett, R. Stringer, Y. Fletcher, R. H. E. Kelly.

Manager: Joe Kinnear

Coach: Mick Harford. **Physio:** Bruce Sewell.

Secretary: Cherry Newbery.

Commercial Manager: Linda Layton.

Safety Officer: Geoff Lovell.

Colours: White shirts with orange and black trim, black shorts with orange and white trim, black stockings with two white hoops.

Change Colours: Orange shirts with white and royal trim, royal shorts with orange and white trim, royal stockings with two white hoops.

Year Formed: 1885.

Turned Professional: 1890.

Ltd Co.: 1897.

Club Nickname: 'The Hatters'.

Previous Grounds: 1885, Excelsior, Dallow Lane; 1897, Dunstable Road; 1905, Kenilworth Road.

First Football League Game: 4 September 1897, Division 2, v Leicester Fosse (a) D 1–1 – Williams; McCartney, McEwen; Davies, Stewart, Docherty; Gallacher, Coupar, Birch, McInnes, Ekins (1).

HONOURS

Football League: Division 1 best season: 7th, 1986–87; Division 2 – Champions 1981–82; Runners-up 1954–55, 1973–74; Division 3 – Runners-up 1969–70, 2001–02; Division 4 – Champions 1967–68; Division 3 (S) – Champions 1936–37; Runners-up 1935–36.

FA Cup: Runners-up 1959.

Football League Cup: Winners 1988; Runners-up 1989.

Simod Cup: Runners-up 1988.

IT'S A FACT !

Highest scorers among Football League clubs in 1937–38 were Luton Town with 89 goals, despite finishing 12th in Division Two, their haul included two 6s, a five and eight 4s.

Record League Victory: 12–0 v Bristol R, Division 3 (S), 13 April 1936 – Dolman; Mackey, Smith; Finlayson, Nelson, Godfrey; Rich, Martin (1), Payne (10), Roberts (1), Stephenson.

Record Cup Victory: 9–0 v Clapton, FA Cup 1st rd (replay after abandoned game), 30 November 1927 – Abbott; Kingham, Graham; Black, Rennie, Fraser; Pointon, Yardley (4), Reid (2), Woods (1), Dennis (2).

Record Defeat: 0–9 v Small Heath, Division 2, 12 November 1898.

Most League Points (2 for a win): 66, Division 4, 1967–68.

Most League Points (3 for a win): 97, Division 3, 2001–02.

Most League Goals: 103, Division 3 (S), 1936–37.

Highest League Scorer in Season: Joe Payne, 55, Division 3 (S), 1936–37.

Most League Goals in Total Aggregate: Gordon Turner, 243, 1949–64.

Most League Goals in One Match: 10, Joe Payne v Bristol R, Division 3S, 13 April 1936.

Most Capped Player: Mal Donaghy, 58 (91), Northern Ireland.

Most League Appearances: Bob Morton, 495, 1948–64.

Youngest League Player: Mike O'Hara, 16 years 32 days v Stoke C, 1 October 1960.

Record Transfer Fee Received: £2,500,000 from Arsenal for John Hartson, January 1995.

Record Transfer Fee Paid: £850,000 to Odense for Lars Elstrup, August 1989.

Football League Record: 1897 Elected to Division 2; 1900 Failed re-election; 1920 Division 3; 1921–37 Division 3 (S); 1937–55 Division 2; 1955–60 Division 1; 1960–63 Division 2; 1963–65 Division 3; 1965–68 Division 4; 1968–70 Division 3; 1970–74 Division 2; 1974–75 Division 1; 1975–82 Division 2; 1982–96 Division 1; 1996–2001 Division 2; 2001–02 Division 3; 2002– Division 2.

MANAGERS

Charlie Green 1901–28
  (Secretary-Manager)
George Thomson 1925
John McCartney 1927–29
George Kay 1929–31
Harold Wightman 1931–35
Ted Liddell 1936–38
Neil McBain 1938–39
George Martin 1939–47
Dally Duncan 1947–58
Syd Owen 1959–60
Sam Bartram 1960–62
Bill Harvey 1962–64
George Martin 1965–66
Allan Brown 1966–68
Alec Stock 1968–72
Harry Haslam 1972–78
David Pleat 1978–86
John Moore 1986–87
Ray Harford 1987–89
Jim Ryan 1900–91
David Pleat 1991–95
Terry Westley 1995
Lennie Lawrence 1995–2000
Ricky Hill 2000
Lil Fuccillo 2000
Joe Kinnear January 2001–

LATEST SEQUENCES

Longest Sequence of League Wins: 12, 19.2.02 – 6.4.02.

Longest Sequence of League Defeats: 8, 11.11.1899 – 6.1.1900.

Longest Sequence of League Draws: 5, 28.8.71 – 18.9.71.

Longest Sequence of Unbeaten League Matches: 19, 8.4.69 – 7.10.69.

Longest Sequence Without a League Win: 16, 9.9.64 – 6.11.64.

TEN YEAR LEAGUE RECORD

		P	W	D	L	F	A	Pts	Pos
1991-92	Div 1	42	10	12	20	38	71	42	20
1992-93	Div 1	46	10	21	15	48	62	51	20
1993-94	Div 1	46	14	11	21	56	60	53	20
1994-95	Div 1	46	15	13	18	61	64	58	16
1995-96	Div 1	46	11	12	23	40	64	45	24
1996-97	Div 2	46	21	15	10	71	45	78	3
1997-98	Div 2	46	14	15	17	60	64	57	17
1998-99	Div 2	46	16	10	20	51	60	58	12
1999-2000	Div 2	46	17	10	19	61	65	61	13
2000-01	Div 2	46	9	13	24	52	80	40	22

DID YOU KNOW ?

Marvin Johnson has played in four different divisions of the Football League for Luton Town, if you count the Football League First Division before the FA Premier League as a separate competition.

LUTON TOWN 2001–02 LEAGUE RECORD

Match No.	Date	Venue	Opponents	Result	H/T Score	Lg. Pos.	Goalscorers	Attendance
1	Aug 11	A	Carlisle U	W 2-0	0-0	—	Nicholls [46], Griffiths [57]	4432
2	18	H	Cheltenham T	W 2-1	2-0	1	Hughes [30], Griffiths [37]	6177
3	25	A	Bristol R	L 2-3	1-1	5	Taylor [42], Mansell [81]	9057
4	27	H	Southend U	W 2-0	0-0	2	Griffiths [80], Fotiadis [83]	6496
5	Sept 1	A	Exeter C	D 2-2	1-1	2	Taylor 2 [35, 53]	3088
6	8	H	Oxford U	D 1-1	1-1	5	Nicholls [9]	6736
7	15	A	York C	W 2-1	1-1	3	Griffiths [42], Hillier [74]	3247
8	18	A	Lincoln C	D 1-1	1-0	—	Skelton [9]	5066
9	22	H	Torquay U	W 5-1	3-1	3	Howard [18], Griffiths 3 [31, 45, 79], Valois [61]	6392
10	25	A	Leyton Orient	W 3-1	1-0	—	Taylor [30], Valois [52], Howard [66]	6540
11	29	A	Plymouth Arg	L 1-2	1-2	3	Crowe [15]	5782
12	Oct 5	H	Darlington	W 5-2	1-1	2	Spring [35], Howard [48], Crowe [67], Nicholls (pen) [73], Valois [83]	7219
13	13	A	Scunthorpe U	W 2-0	0-0	1	Forbes [65], Perrett [72]	3939
14	20	H	Rochdale	L 0-1	0-1	3		7696
15	23	A	Halifax T	W 4-2	2-1	—	Crowe 2 [31, 45], Nicholls [86], Forbes [88]	2140
16	27	A	Swansea C	W 3-0	1-0	2	Crowe [23], Perrett [55], Forbes [61]	6705
17	Nov 3	A	Mansfield T	L 1-4	0-1	4	Crowe [86]	5973
18	9	H	Shrewsbury T	W 1-0	0-0	—	Spring [72]	6809
19	20	H	Hull C	L 0-1	0-0	—		7214
20	24	A	Macclesfield T	L 1-4	1-1	5	Howard [33]	2250
21	Dec 8	A	Hartlepool U	W 2-1	2-0	—	Crowe [30], Taylor [45]	3585
22	15	H	Rushden & D	W 1-0	1-0	2	Crowe [34]	7495
23	22	H	Hartlepool U	D 2-2	1-1	2	Howard [35], Johnson [84]	6739
24	26	A	Oxford U	W 2-1	1-1	2	Crowe [39], Spring [46]	11,121
25	29	A	Southend U	W 2-1	0-0	2	Crowe [68], Taylor [83]	5973
26	Jan 8	A	Kidderminster H	W 4-1	0-0	—	Taylor [53], Spring 2 [55, 70], Howard [58]	4147
27	12	H	Cheltenham T	D 1-1	1-0	2	Howard [73]	5026
28	19	H	Carlisle U	D 1-1	0-0	2	Perrett [68]	6647
29	26	A	Darlington	L 2-3	1-1	2	Howard [13], Valois [60]	3560
30	Feb 2	H	Plymouth Arg	W 2-0	0-0	2	Nicholls (pen) [80], Howard [87]	9585
31	9	H	Rochdale	L 0-1	0-1	2		4306
32	16	H	Scunthorpe U	L 2-3	1-2	3	Howard [36], Taylor [78]	6371
33	19	H	Bristol R	W 3-0	0-0	—	Howard [47], Coyne [65], Nicholls (pen) [77]	5651
34	23	H	York C	W 2-1	1-1	2	Howard 2 [19, 50]	6188
35	26	A	Lincoln C	W 1-0	1-0	—	Taylor [42]	2921
36	Mar 2	H	Torquay U	W 1-0	1-0	2	Brkovic [20]	3280
37	5	H	Leyton Orient	W 3-0	1-0	—	Coyne [36], Crowe [49], Forbes [66]	6683
38	9	A	Rushden & D	W 2-1	0-0	2	Crowe [58], Howard [82]	5876
39	12	A	Exeter C	W 3-0	1-0	—	Howard 2 [27, 65], Taylor [79]	6327
40	16	H	Kidderminster H	W 1-0	1-0	2	Hughes [16]	6488
41	23	H	Halifax T	W 5-0	2-0	2	Spring [21], Coyne [32], Howard [49], Crowe [75], Valois [87]	6830
42	30	A	Swansea C	W 3-1	1-0	2	Taylor [31], Holmes [58], Howard [78]	5436
43	Apr 1	H	Mansfield T	W 5-3	4-2	2	Valois [11], Crowe [22], Nicholls (pen) [30], Howard 2 [35, 50]	8231
44	6	A	Hull C	W 4-0	2-0	1	Howard 3 [23, 79, 89], Crowe [38]	9379
45	13	H	Macclesfield T	D 0-0	0-0	2		7873
46	20	A	Shrewsbury T	W 2-0	1-0	2	Rioch (og) [36], Howard [90]	7858

Final League Position: 2

GOALSCORERS

League (96): Howard 24, Crowe 15, Taylor 11, Griffiths 7, Nicholls 7 (4 pens), Spring 6, Valois 6, Forbes 4, Coyne 3, Perrett 3, Hughes 2, Brkovic 1, Fotiadis 1, Hillier 1, Holmes 1, Johnson 1, Mansell 1, Skelton 1, own goal 1.
Worthington Cup (0).
FA Cup (2): Brkovic 1, Forbes 1.

Emberson C 33	Skelton A 9	Taylor M 43	Boyce E 30 + 7	Perrett R 39 + 1	Johnson M 11 + 7	Nicholls K 42	Mansell L 6 + 5	Howard S 42	Griffiths C 10	Hughes P 12 + 10	Locke A 1 + 2	Douglas S 2 + 7	Foiadis A — + 8	Hillier I 11 + 12	Forbes A 15 + 25	George L 2 + 2	Stirling J 1	Dryden R 2 + 1	Spring M 42	Holmes P 4 + 3	Coyne C 29 + 2	Ovendale M 13	Valois J 32 + 2	Crowe D 32 + 2	Brkovic A 17 + 4	Street K 1 + 1	Bayliss D 15 + 3	McSwegan G 2 + 1	Neilson A 8	Kabba S — + 3	Match No.
1	2	3	4	5	6^1	7	8^2	9	10^3	11	12	13	14																		1
1		3	4	5		7	8	9^1	10^2	11	12	13		2	6^3	14															2
1		3	4	5	6	7	8	9	10^2	11^2	12	13	14	2^3																	3
1		3		5	6	7	8	9^1	10	11^2	12	13		2					4												4
1		3	2	5	6	7	8	9^1	10^3	11	12^2	13	14						4												5
1	2	3	4	5	6	7	8^2	9	10^1	11	12	13																			6
1	2	3^1	4	5	6	7	8	9	10^2	11	12	13	14																		7
1	2^3	3	4	5		7	8^2	9	10^1	11	12	13	14																		8
		3	2	5		7	8^1	9	10		12^2	13	14		6				4			1	11^3								9
		3	2	5		7	8^1	9			12	13			6				4			1	11	10^2							10
		3	2	5		7	8^2	9	10		12	13	14		6				4^1			1	11^2								11
1		3	2	5		7^1	8^2	9			12	13			6				4				11	10							12
1		3	2^2	5		7	8^3	9			12	13	14		6				4				11^1	10							13
1		3		5^1		7	8^3	9			12^2	13	14	2	6				4				11^1	10							14
1		3		5		7	8	9			12			2	6				4				11^1	10							15
1	2	3		5		7	8	9^1			12	13			6				4				11	10^2							16
1	2	3		5		7	8^1	9			12	13			6				4				11^2	10							17
1	2^1	3		5		7	8	9			12				6				4				11	10							18
1		3		5^1		7	8^2	9			12	13	14	2	6				4				11	10^1							19
1	2^2	3		5		7	8	9			12	13	14		6				4				11^3	10^1							20
		3	4			7	8	9			12			2	6						1		11	10^1			5				21
		3	2			7		9			12	13	14		6^1				4^3		1		11^2	10	8		5				22
		3	2	5		7		9			12	13	14						4		1		11^3	10^2	8^1		6				23
		3	2	5		7		9			12	13							4		1		11^1	10	8^2		6				24
		3	2	5		7		9			12	13							4		1		11^1	10	8^2		6				25
		3	2	5		7		9^1			12	13	14						4		1		11^3	10	8^1		6				26
		3	4	5		7		9			12	13	14	2^3							1		11	10^1	8^2		6				27
		3	2	5		7		9			12	13							4		1		11	10^1	8^2		6				28
		3		5^1	6	7		9			12	13	14	2					4		1		11^3	10^2	8						29
1		3	2	5		7		9			12								4				11	10^1	8		6				30
1		3	2	5		7		9			12								4	13			11^2	10^1	8		6				31
1		3		5		7		9			12	13		2					4				11	10^1	8^2		6				32
1		3	2	5		7		9			12								4	13			11^2	10^1	8		6				33
1	2^1	3		5				9			12	13			6				4				11^2	10	8				7		34
1		3	4	5		7		9		11				2	6									10	8						35
1		3	4^1	5		7					12	13	14	2	6								11	10	8^2			9^2			36
1		3		5		7^2		9^1			12	13	14	2	6				4				11^1	10	8						37
1		3	4^2	5		7		9			12	13		2	6								11	10	8^1						38
1		3		5		7		9			12	13		2	6				4				11^2	10	8^1						39
		3		5		7		9		11	12	13		2^1	6				4			1		10^2	8						40
1		3		5		7	8	9		11	12			2	6				4					10^1							41
1		3^1	4	5		7		9			12	13	14	2^2	6								11^3	10	8						42
1		3	2	5		7		9			12				6				4				11^1	10^2	8					13	43
1		3	2	5		7		9			12	13	14		6				4				11^1	10^3	8^2						44
1		3	2	5		7		9			12	13			6				4				11^2	10^3	8^1					14	45
1		3		5		7		9			12	13	14		6				4				11^2	10^3	8^1			2		14	46

Worthington Cup
First Round   Reading   (a) 0-4

FA Cup
First Round   Southend U   (a) 2-3

MACCLESFIELD TOWN   Division 3

FOUNDATION

From the mid-19th Century until 1874, Macclesfield Town FC played under rugby rules. In 1891 they moved to the Moss Rose and finished champions of the Manchester & District League in 1906 and 1908. By 1911, they had carried off the Cheshire Senior Cup five times. Macclesfield were founder members of the Cheshire County League in 1919.

The Moss Rose Ground, London Road, Macclesfield, Cheshire SK11 7SP.

Telephone: (01625) 264 686. *Fax:* (01625) 264 692.

Website: www.mtfc.co.uk

Email: office@mtfc.co.uk

Commercial Office: (01625) 264 693.

Social Club: (01625) 424 324.

Press Box: (01625) 264 690/1.

ClubCall: 09066 555 835.

Ground Capacity: 6,235 (seated 2,537, standing 3,698).

Record Attendance: 9,008 v Winsford U, Cheshire Senior Cup 2nd rd, 4 February 1948.

Pitch Measurements: 100m × 66m.

Chief Executive: Colin Garlick.

Directors: E. Furlong, C. Garlick, M. Rance, A. Cash, R. Bickerton.

Director of Football: Gil Prescott.

Manager: David Moss.

Reserve Team Manager: John Askey.

Secretary: Colin Garlick.

Administration Manager: Dianne Hehir.

Commercial Manager: Matthew Lenton.

Club Doctors: Dr Mike Whiteside, Mike Hughes.

Physio: Andrew Balderston.

Colours: Royal blue shirts, white shorts, blue stockings.

Change Colours: All tangerine.

Year formed: 1874.

HONOURS

Football League: Division 3 – Runners-up 1997–98.

FA Cup: best season: 3rd rd, 1968, 1988, 2002.

Vauxhall Conference: Champions 1994–95, 1996–97.

FA Trophy: Winners 1969–70, 1995–96; Runners-up 1988–89.

Bob Lord Trophy: Winners 1993–94; Runners-up 1995–96, 1996–97.

Vauxhall Conference Championship Shield: Winners 1996, 1997, 1998.

Northern Premier League: Winners 1968–69, 1969–70, 1986–87; Runners-up 1984–85.

Northern Premier League Challenge Cup: Winners 1986–87; Runners-up 1969–70, 1970–71, 1982–83.

Northern Premier League Presidents Cup: Winners 1986–87; Runners-up 1984–85.

Cheshire Senior Cup: Winners 20 times; Runners-up 11.

IT'S A FACT !

In 1983, Macclesfield Town were granted a £10,000 loan by the Football Association to install new floodlights at their Moss Rose ground. They became one of the best systems outside the Football League.

Club Nickname: 'The Silkmen'.

Previous Ground: 1874, Rostron Field; 1891, Moss Rose.

First Football League Game: 9 August 1997, Division 3, v Torquay U (h) W 2–1 – Price; Tinson, Rose, Payne (Edey), Howarth, Sodje (1), Askey, Wood, Landon (1) (Power), Mason, Sorvel.

Record League Victory: 5–2 v Mansfield T, Division 3, 2 November 1999 – Martin; Ingram, Rioch, Collins, Tinson, Sedgemore (1), Askey (1), Priest (1), Barker (2), Davies (Wood), Durkan.

Record Win: 15–0 v Chester St Marys, Cheshire Senior Cup, 2nd rd, 16 February 1886.

Record Defeat: 1–13 v Tranmere R reserves, 3 May 1929.

Most League Points (3 for a win): 82, Division 3, 1997–98.

Most League Goals: 66, Division 3, 1999–2000.

Highest League Scorer in Season: Richard Barker, 16, Division 3, 1999–2000.

Most League Goals in Total Aggregate: John Askey, 29, 1997–2002.

Most League Appearances: Darren Tinson, 218, 1997–2002.

Youngest League Player: Peter Griffiths, 18 years 44 days v Reading, 26 September 1998.

Record Transfer Fee Received: £100,600 from Rotherham U for Richard Barker, January 2001.

Record Transfer Fee Paid: £30,000 to Stevenage Borough for Efetobore Sodje, August 1997; £30,000 to Altrincham for Danny Adams, September 2000.

Football League Record: Promoted to Division 3 1997; 1998–99 Division 2; 1999– Division 3.

MANAGERS

Since 1967
Keith Goalen 1967–68
Frank Beaumont 1968–72
Billy Haydock 1972–74
Eddie Brown 1974
John Collins 1974
Willie Stevenson 1974
John Collins 1975–76
Tony Coleman 1976
John Barnes 1976
Brian Taylor 1976
Dave Connor 1976–78
Derek Partridge 1978
Phil Staley 1978–80
Jimmy Williams 1980–81
Brian Booth 1981–85
Neil Griffiths 1985–86
Roy Campbell 1986
Peter Wragg 1986–93
Sammy McIlroy 1993–2000
Peter Davenport 2000
Gil Prescott 2001
David Moss November 2001–

LATEST SEQUENCES

Longest Sequence of League Wins: 5, 16.10.99 – 6.11.99.

Longest Sequence of League Defeats: 6, 26.12.98 –6.2.99.

Longest Sequence of League Draws: 3, 27.9.97 – 11.10.97.

Longest Sequence of Unbeaten League Matches: 8, 16.10.99 – 27.11.99.

Longest Sequence Without a League Win: 10, 21.11.98 – 6.2.99.

TEN YEAR LEAGUE RECORD

		P	W	D	L	F	A	Pts	Pos
1991-92	Conf	42	13	13	16	50	50	52	13
1992-93	Conf	42	12	13	17	40	50	49	18
1993-94	Conf	42	16	11	15	48	49	59	7
1994-95	Conf	42	24	8	10	70	40	80	1
1995-96	Conf	42	22	9	11	66	49	75	4
1996-97	Conf	42	27	9	6	80	30	90	1
1997-98	Div 3	46	23	13	10	63	44	82	2
1998-99	Div 2	46	11	10	25	43	63	43	24
1999-2000	Div 3	46	18	11	17	66	61	65	13
2000-01	Div 3	46	14	14	18	51	62	56	14

DID YOU KNOW ?

Four goals in eight minutes by Macclesfield Town against Swansea City in a second round FA Cup tie on 8 December 2001, represented the fastest sequence of such goalscoring in the club's history.

MACCLESFIELD TOWN 2001–02 LEAGUE RECORD

Match No.	Date	Venue	Opponents	Result	H/T Score	Lg. Pos.	Goalscorers	Attendance
1	Aug 11	H	Swansea C	L 1-3	1-2	—	Glover (pen) [34]	2309
2	18	A	Rochdale	D 1-1	1-1	21	Glover (pen) [18]	3346
3	25	H	Rushden & D	D 0-0	0-0	18		1950
4	27	A	Mansfield T	L 0-4	0-2	23		2681
5	Sept 1	H	Scunthorpe U	W 4-3	2-2	16	Tracey 2 [14, 86], Glover 2 (1 pen) [45 (p), 68]	1740
6	8	A	Halifax T	D 0-0	0-0	17		1714
7	15	H	Hull C	D 0-0	0-0	18		2740
8	18	A	Oxford U	W 2-0	1-0	—	Glover [45], Lightbourne [48]	4964
9	22	A	Plymouth Arg	L 0-2	0-1	15		4227
10	25	H	Darlington	D 1-1	1-0	—	Glover [13]	1556
11	29	A	Exeter C	D 0-0	0-0	16		2833
12	Oct 7	H	Kidderminster H	L 0-1	0-1	20		1859
13	13	A	Bristol R	W 2-0	0-0	14	Lightbourne [50], Glover [71]	6554
14	20	H	Lincoln C	L 0-1	0-0	17		1845
15	23	H	Hartlepool U	L 0-1	0-0	—		1356
16	27	A	York C	L 0-1	0-0	23		2253
17	Nov 3	H	Carlisle U	D 1-1	0-1	22	Lightbourne [77]	2432
18	9	A	Southend U	L 0-3	0-1	—		2889
19	20	A	Cheltenham T	L 1-4	0-1	—	Byrne [73]	2402
20	24	H	Luton T	W 4-1	1-1	22	Lambert 3 [10, 63, 90], Byrne [53]	2250
21	Dec 1	A	Torquay U	W 2-1	1-1	19	Lambert 2 [28, 73]	1702
22	15	H	Leyton Orient	W 2-1	2-1	18	Smith J [43], Byrne [44]	2618
23	21	A	Shrewsbury T	D 1-1	1-0	—	Glover [25]	3511
24	26	H	Halifax T	D 1-1	0-1	17	Smith J [89]	2421
25	29	H	Mansfield T	L 0-1	0-0	20		2550
26	Jan 12	H	Rochdale	L 0-1	0-0	20		3002
27	19	A	Swansea C	W 1-0	0-0	18	Byrne [51]	3753
28	22	H	Shrewsbury T	W 2-1	2-1	—	Lightbourne [25], Tretton (og) [38]	1688
29	29	A	Rushden & D	L 0-2	0-0	—		2771
30	Feb 2	H	Exeter C	L 1-2	0-0	17	Whittaker [82]	1719
31	9	A	Lincoln C	L 0-1	0-1	19		3374
32	12	A	Scunthorpe U	D 1-1	1-0	—	Hitchen [36]	2870
33	16	H	Bristol R	W 2-1	0-1	18	Lambert [70], Byrne [82]	2149
34	19	A	Kidderminster H	W 1-0	0-0	—	Byrne [60]	2256
35	22	H	Hull C	W 1-0	0-0	—	Lambert [50]	8431
36	26	H	Oxford U	L 0-1	0-1	—		1401
37	Mar 2	H	Plymouth Arg	D 1-1	0-0	15	Priest [90]	2557
38	5	A	Darlington	W 1-0	0-0	—	Askey [76]	2729
39	9	A	Leyton Orient	L 0-2	0-2	13		3839
40	16	H	Torquay U	L 0-2	0-1	15		2085
41	22	A	Hartlepool U	W 2-1	1-0	—	Tipton [33], Lambert [62]	3819
42	30	H	York C	W 2-1	1-1	13	Tipton [18], Glover (pen) [59]	1928
43	Apr 1	A	Carlisle U	L 2-3	2-0	13	Tinson [19], Whittaker [39]	3625
44	6	H	Cheltenham T	W 1-0	0-0	13	Tipton [84]	2270
45	13	A	Luton T	D 0-0	0-0	13		7873
46	20	H	Southend U	D 0-0	0-0	13		2415

Final League Position: 13

GOALSCORERS

League (41): Glover 9 (4 pens), Lambert 8, Byrne 6, Lightbourne 4, Tipton 3, Smith J 2, Tracey 2, Whittaker 2, Askey 1, Hitchen 1, Priest 1, Tinson 1, own goal 1.
Worthington Cup (1): Glover 1.
FA Cup (7): Byrne 2, Glover 2, Lambert 2, Keen 1.

Martin L 8 + 1	Hitchen S 28 + 2	Adams D 38 + 1	Keen K 29 + 1	Tinson D 46	Ridler D 37 + 2	McAvoy A 4 + 6	Byrne C 26 + 6	Lightbourne K 22 + 7	Glover L 38 + 5	Eyre R 12 + 2	Tracey R 10 + 10	Askey J 1 + 17	O'Neill P 7 + 4	Priest C 32 + 1	Munroe K 19 + 11	Wilson S 38	Lambert R 32 + 3	Abbey G 15 + 2	Woolley M — + 3	Shuttleworth B — + 3	Bullock M 2 + 1	Whitehead D 1 + 1	Smith J 7 + 1	Macauley S 12	Came S 1	Whitaker D 15 + 1	Tipton M 12 + 1	Welch M 6	Smith D 8	Match No.
1	2	3	4	5	6	7^1	8	9	10^2	11	12	13																		1
1	2	3	4	5^2	6	7^1	8	9	10	11	12		13																	2
1	2	3	4	5	6			9^2	10	11			7	13	8^1	12														3
1	2	3	4	5	6	12		9	10^3	11^1			7	14	8^2	13														4
	2	3	4	5	6			9^2	10	11^1			7	13	8	1	12													5
	2	3	4^1	5	6			9^2	10	12			7	13	8	1	11													6
	2	3	4	5	6			9^2	10^1				7	13	8	1	11	12												7
	2	3^2	4	5	6			9	10^1			13	7	12	8	1	11													8
	2^1		4	5	6	14		9^2	10			12	7	13	8	1	11^3	3												9
	2		4^1	5	6	12		9^2	10	11			7	13	8	1		3												10
	2		4^2	5	6			9	10^3	11^1		13	7	12	8	1	14	3												11
	2		4	5	6			9^2	10	11^1			7	12	8	1	13	3												12
	2		4	5	6			9^2	10				7		8	1	11^1	3			12	13								13
	2		4	5	6			9^1	10				7	12	8	1	11^2	3				13								14
	2	12	4^2	5	6			10					7		9^1	8	13	1				3		11						15
	2^1	3	4	5	6			10					9		8	1	11	7						12						16
		3	7	5	6			4	9	10				8		1	2							11^1		12				17
		3	4	5	6			12	10	11^1				8		1	7	2						9						18
	2	3	7^2	5^1	6			13	11	10				4	8	12	1	9												19
	2	3	7	5	6	10^1	4					12		8		1	9							11						20
	2	3	7	5	6		4	10^1				12		8^2	13	1	9							11						21
	2	3	7	5	12		4	13	10					8^3	14	1	9^2							11^1					6	22
	2	3	7	5			4	12^2	10			13		8^3	14	1	9^1	11											6	23
	2^2	3	7	5	13		4		10			12		8^1		1	9							11					6	24
	2	3	7	5^1	12		4		10			13		8^2		1	9							11					6	25
15	2^2	3		5			4	9	10			12		8		1^6	7	13						11^1	6					26
1		3	7	5	6		4	9^2	10					8	12		11	2^1						13						27
1		3	7	5	6	12	4	9	10^1					8			11	2												28
1		3^4		5	6	10^2	4	9				12	13	8	7^1		11	2	14											29
1		3^2		5	6	12	4	9				7^1		8^3			10	2	13							14		11		30
	2	3		5	6			13	9^1	10		12		8^2			1	7								4		11		31
	2^2	3		5	6		8	12	10				7			1	9^1	13								4		11		32
		3		5	6	12	13	14	10^3					2^2		1	7							4			8	9^1	11	33
		3		5	6	8^3	12	13				14		2^2		1	10							4		7	9^1		11	34
		3^4		5	6			12						2		1	10^1							4		7	9		11	35
		3		5		8	12	13					6^2	2^1		1	10							4		7	9		11	36
	12	3		5		4^1	9^2	10				13		8		1	7							6		2			11	37
	2	3	12	5		4^1	10					13		8		1	11							6		7	9^2			38
	2	3	4	5		12	13	10^3				14		8^1		1	11							6		7	9^2			39
	2	7	5	3		4^1	10^3					12		9^2		1	9	13						6		11	14			40
	2	3	4	5	6	8		12								1	10							7			9^1	11		41
		3		5	6		8	10				2	7			1	11										9		4	42
		3^1		5	6		8	12				4	2			1	10							7			9	11		43
	12	3		5	6		4	10						2^1		1	11							7			9	8		44
	2	3		5	6			10				12				1	11^1							8			9	4		45
		3		5	6			10^1				12			7	1	11	2						8			9	4		46

Worthington Cup

First Round	Bradford C	(h)	1-2

FA Cup

First Round	Forest Green R	(h)	2-2
		(a)	1-1
Second Round	Swansea C	(h)	4-1
Third Round	West Ham U	(h)	0-3

MANCHESTER CITY   FA Premiership

FOUNDATION

Manchester City was formed as a Limited Company in 1894 after their predecessors Ardwick had been forced into bankruptcy. However, many historians like to trace the club's lineage as far back as 1880 when St Mark's Church, West Gorton added a football section to their cricket club. They amalgamated with Gorton Athletic in 1884 as Gorton FC. Because of a change of ground they became Ardwick in 1887.

Maine Road, Moss Side, Manchester M14 7WN.

Telephone: (0161) 232 3000. *Fax:* (0161) 232 8999.
Ticket Office: (0161) 226 2224. *ClubCall:* 09068 121 191.
Dial-A-Seat: (0161) 828 1200. *Development Office:* (0161) 226 3143.

Ground Capacity: 34,026.

Record Attendance: 84,569 v Stoke C, FA Cup 6th rd, 3 March 1934 (British record for any game outside London or Glasgow).

Record Receipts: £512,235 Manchester U v Oldham Ath, FA Cup semi-final replay, 13 April 1994.

Pitch Measurements: 116.5yd × 75yd.

Chairman: D. A. Bernstein. *Directors:* J. Wardle, D. Tueart, A. Lewis, A. Thomas, B. Bodek, C. Bird, A. Mackintosh. *General Secretary:* J. B. Halford.

Manager: Kevin Keegan. *Assistant Manager:* Arthur Cox. *Reserve Team Coach:* Asa Hartford. *Physio:* Rob Harris. *Youth Team Coach:* Alex Gibson. *Youth Academy Director:* Jim Cassell.

Colours: Lazer blue shirts, white shorts, lazer blue and navy stockings.

HONOURS

Football League: Division 1 – Champions 1936–37, 1967–68, 2001–02; Runners-up 1903–04, 1920–21, 1976–77, 1999–2000; Division 2 – Champions 1898–99, 1902–03, 1909–10, 1927–28, 1946–47, 1965–66; Runners-up 1895–96, 1950–51, 1987–88; Promoted from Division 2 (play-offs) 1998–99.

FA Cup: Winners 1904, 1934, 1956, 1969; Runners-up 1926, 1933, 1955, 1981.

Football League Cup: Winners 1970, 1976; Runners-up 1974.

European Competitions: European Cup: 1968–69. European Cup-Winners' Cup: 1969–70 (winners), 1970–71. UEFA Cup: 1972–73, 1976–77, 1977–78, 1978–79.

Change Colours: Silver with yellow and navy striped shirts, navy shorts with yellow trim, yellow stockings.

Year Formed: 1887 as Ardwick FC; 1894 as Manchester City.

Turned Professional: 1887 as Ardwick FC.

Ltd Co.: 1894.

Previous Names: 1887, Ardwick FC (formed through the amalgamation of West Gorton and Gorton Athletic, the latter having been formed in 1880); 1894, Manchester City.

Club Nicknames: 'Blues' or 'The Citizens'.

Previous Grounds: 1880, Clowes Street; 1881, Kirkmanshulme Cricket Ground; 1882, Queens Road; 1884, Pink Bank Lane; 1887, Hyde Road (1894–1923 as City); 1923, Maine Road.

First Football League Game: 3 September 1892, Division 2, v Bootle (h) W 7–0 – Douglas; McVickers, Robson; Middleton, Russell, Hopkins; Davies (3), Morris (2), Angus (1), Weir (1), Milarvie.

IT'S A FACT !

In 1887, Jack Hodgetts was said to be the first professional player employed by Manchester City at the princely wage of five shillings (25p). The rest of the team were unpaid amateurs.

Record League Victory: 10–1 v Huddersfield T, Division 2, 7 November 1987 – Nixon; Gidman, Hinchcliffe, Clements, Lake, Redmond, White (3), Stewart (3), Adcock (3), McNab (1), Simpson.

Record Cup Victory: 10–1 v Swindon T, FA Cup 4th rd, 29 January 1930 – Barber; Felton, McCloy; Barrass, Cowan, Heinemann; Toseland, Marshall (5), Tait (3), Johnson (1), Brook (1).

Record Defeat: 1–9 v Everton, Division 1, 3 September 1906.

Most League Points (2 for a win): 62, Division 2, 1946–47.

Most League Points (3 for a win): 99, Division 1, 2001–02.

Most League Goals: 108, Division 2, 1926–27, 108, Division 1, 2001–02.

Highest League Scorer in Season: Tommy Johnson, 38, Division 1, 1928–29.

Most League Goals in Total Aggregate: Tommy Johnson, 158, 1919–30.

Most League Goals in One Match: 5, Fred Williams v Darwen, Division 2, 18 February 1899; 5, Tom Browell v Burnley, Division 2, 24 October 1925; 5, Tom Johnson v Everton, Division 1, 15 September 1928; 5, George Smith v Newport Co, Division 2, 14 June 1947.

Most Capped Player: Colin Bell, 48, England.

Most League Appearances: Alan Oakes, 565, 1959–76.

Youngest League Player: Glyn Pardoe, 15 years 314 days v Birmingham C, 11 April 1961.

Record Transfer Fee Received: £4,925,000 from Ajax for Georgi Kinkladze, May 1998.

Record Transfer Fee Paid: £3,000,000 to Portsmouth for Lee Bradbury, July 1997.

Football League Record: 1892 Ardwick elected founder member of Division 2; 1894 Newly-formed Manchester C elected to Division 2; Division 1 1899–1902, 1903–09, 1910–26, 1928–38, 1947–50, 1951–63, 1966–83, 1985–87, 1989–92; Division 2 1902–03, 1909–10, 1926–28, 1938–47, 1950–51, 1963–66, 1983–85, 1987–89; 1992–96 FA Premier League; 1996–98 Division 1; 1998–99 Division 2; 1999–2000 Division 1; 2000–01 FA Premier League; 2001–02 Division 1; 2002– FA Premier League.

MANAGERS

Joshua Parlby 1893–95
  (Secretary-Manager)
Sam Omerod 1895–1902
Tom Maley 1902–06
Harry Newbould 1906–12
Ernest Magnall 1912–24
David Ashworth 1924–25
Peter Hodge 1926–32
Wilf Wild 1932–46
  (continued as Secretary to 1950)
Sam Cowan 1946–47
John 'Jock' Thomson 1947–50
Leslie McDowall 1950–63
George Poyser 1963–65
Joe Mercer 1965–71
  (continued as General Manager to 1972)
Malcolm Allison 1972–73
Johnny Hart 1973
Ron Saunders 1973–74
Tony Book 1974–79
Malcolm Allison 1979–80
John Bond 1980–83
John Benson 1983
Billy McNeill 1983–86
Jimmy Frizzell 1986–87
  (continued as General Manager)
Mel Machin 1987–89
Howard Kendall 1990
Peter Reid 1990–93
Brian Horton 1993–95
Alan Ball 1995–96
Steve Coppell 1996
Frank Clark 1996–98
Joe Royle 1998–2001
Kevin Keegan May 2001–

LATEST SEQUENCES

Longest Sequence of League Wins: 9, 8.4.12 – 28.9.12.

Longest Sequence of League Defeats: 8, 23.8.95 – 14.10.95.

Longest Sequence of League Draws: 6, 5.4.13 – 6.9.13.

Longest Sequence of Unbeaten League Matches: 22, 16.11.46 – 19.4.47.

Longest Sequence Without a League Win: 17, 26.12.79 – 7.4.80.

TEN YEAR LEAGUE RECORD

		P	W	D	L	F	A	Pts	Pos
1991-92	Div 1	42	20	10	12	61	48	70	5
1992-93	PR Lge	42	15	12	15	56	51	57	9
1993-94	PR Lge	42	9	18	15	38	49	45	16
1994-95	PR Lge	42	12	13	17	53	64	49	17
1995-96	PR Lge	38	9	11	18	33	58	38	18
1996-97	Div 1	46	17	10	19	59	60	61	14
1997-98	Div 1	46	12	12	22	56	57	48	22
1998-99	Div 2	46	22	16	8	69	33	82	3
1999-2000	Div 1	46	26	11	9	78	40	89	2
2000-01	PR Lge	38	8	10	20	41	65	34	18

DID YOU KNOW ?

Shaun Goater became the first Manchester City player for 30 years to score more than 30 goals in a season in 2001–02 with 32 in League and Cup matches. Francis Lee had scored 35 in 1971–72.

MANCHESTER CITY 2001–02 LEAGUE RECORD

Match No.	Date	Venue	Opponents	Result	H/T Score	Lg. Pos.	Goalscorers	Attendance
1	Aug 11	H	Watford	W	3-0	0-0	—	Goater [59], Berkovic [64], Pearce [87]	33,939
2	18	A	Norwich C	L	0-2	0-0	10		18,745
3	25	H	Crewe Alex	W	5-2	2-2	6	Wanchope 2 [33, 90], Pearce (pen) [42], Goater 2 [80, 88]	32,844
4	27	A	Burnley	W	4-2	1-1	1	Goater 3 [17, 62, 86], Wanchope [50]	19,602
5	Sept 8	A	WBA	L	0-4	0-1	8		23,524
6	15	H	Birmingham C	W	3-0	3-0	6	Goater 2 [23, 42], Dunne [24]	31,714
7	19	A	Coventry C	L	3-4	1-2	—	Benarbia [30], Horlock [57], Hall (og) [74]	18,804
8	22	A	Sheffield W	W	6-2	2-1	4	Benarbia [32], Goater 2 [35, 70], Granville [59], Wanchope 2 (1 pen) [68, 80 (p)]	25,731
9	25	H	Walsall	W	3-0	2-0	—	Benarbia [24], Goater [41], Wanchope (pen) [60]	31,525
10	29	H	Wimbledon	L	0-4	0-2	6		32,989
11	Oct 13	H	Stockport Co	D	2-2	0-0	6	Benarbia [51], Goater [84]	34,214
12	16	H	Sheffield U	D	0-0	0-0	—		32,454
13	21	A	Preston NE	L	1-2	1-1	9	Huckerby [38]	21,014
14	23	H	Grimsby T	W	4-0	3-0	—	Goater [2], Howey [21], Huckerby 2 [24, 64]	30,797
15	28	A	Nottingham F	D	1-1	1-1	7	Goater [8]	28,226
16	31	A	Barnsley	W	3-0	3-0	—	Goater [14], Pearce [36], Huckerby [45]	15,159
17	Nov 3	H	Gillingham	W	4-1	3-0	5	Goater 3 [18, 20, 53], Huckerby [35]	33,067
18	17	A	Portsmouth	L	1-2	1-0	9	Huckerby [28]	19,103
19	24	H	Rotherham U	W	2-1	1-1	7	Negouai [43], Benarbia [88]	34,223
20	Dec 1	A	Grimsby T	W	2-0	0-0	6	Huckerby (pen) [74], Goater [90]	7960
21	4	A	Millwall	W	3-2	1-1	—	Goater [23], Huckerby [68], Wright-Phillips [83]	13,026
22	8	A	Crystal Palace	L	1-2	0-2	3	Goater [68]	22,080
23	11	H	Wolverhampton W	W	1-0	1-0	—	Horlock [21]	33,639
24	16	A	Bradford C	W	3-1	1-1	2	Mettomo [35], Horlock [58], Wright-Phillips [64]	30,749
25	26	H	WBA	D	0-0	0-0	2		34,407
26	29	H	Burnley	W	5-1	4-0	2	Wanchope 3 [2, 28, 45], Berkovic [38], Huckerby [90]	34,250
27	Jan 1	A	Sheffield U	W	3-1	0-0	1	Goater [55], Berkovic [68], Wright-Phillips [90]	26,291
28	13	A	Norwich C	W	3-1	1-0	1	Berkovic 2 [43, 66], Wanchope (pen) [62]	31,794
29	20	A	Watford	W	2-1	1-1	1	Wanchope [30], Helguson (og) [80]	17,074
30	30	H	Millwall	W	2-0	0-0	1	Goater 2 [78, 87]	30,238
31	Feb 3	H	Wimbledon	L	1-2	0-1	1	Benarbia [54]	10,664
32	10	A	Preston NE	W	3-2	0-0	1	Wright-Phillips [49], Howey [56], Wanchope [74]	34,220
33	23	A	Walsall	D	0-0	0-0	2		7618
34	27	H	Sheffield W	W	4-0	2-0	—	Horlock [9], Huckerby [32], Berkovic [76], Goater [88]	33,682
35	Mar 3	H	Coventry C	W	4-2	3-1	2	Huckerby [15], Tiatto [35], Wright-Phillips 2 [42, 71]	33,335
36	5	A	Birmingham C	W	2-1	1-1	—	Jensen [45], Horlock [67]	24,160
37	8	A	Bradford C	W	2-0	1-0	—	Huckerby [44], Macken [90]	18,168
38	12	A	Crewe Alex	W	3-1	2-0	—	Benarbia [29], Huckerby [45], Goater [75]	10,092
39	16	H	Crystal Palace	W	1-0	1-0	1	Horlock [10]	33,637
40	19	A	Stockport Co	L	1-2	1-0	1	Macken [19]	9532
41	23	A	Rotherham U	D	1-1	0-1	1	Benarbia [60]	11,426
42	30	H	Nottingham F	W	3-0	2-0	1	Huckerby 3 (1 pen) [40, 45, 84 (p)]	34,345
43	Apr 1	A	Wolverhampton W	W	2-0	1-0	1	Wright-Phillips 2 [36, 80]	28,015
44	6	A	Barnsley	W	5-1	2-1	1	Huckerby 3 [12, 36, 63], Macken 2 [53, 70]	33,628
45	13	A	Gillingham	W	3-1	2-1	1	Horlock [20], Goater [39], Huckerby [85]	9494
46	21	H	Portsmouth	W	3-1	2-0	1	Howey [9], Goater [27], Macken [86]	34,657

Final League Position: 1

GOALSCORERS

League (108): Goater 28, Huckerby 20 (2 pens), Wanchope 12 (3 pens), Benarbia 8, Wright-Phillips 8, Horlock 7, Berkovic 6, Macken 5, Howey 3, Pearce 3 (1 pen), Dunne 1, Granville 1, Jensen 1, Mettomo 1, Negouai 1, Tiatto 1, own goals 2.
Worthington Cup (10): Huckerby 5, Goater 2, Dickov 1, Shuker 1, own goal 1.
FA Cup (6): Goater 2, Berkovic 1, Horlock 1, Huckerby 1, Wanchope 1.

Nash C 22+1	Charvet L 3	Granville D 12+4	Dunne R 41+2	Howey S 34	Pearce S 38	Wiekens G 24+5	Berkovic E 20+5	Wanchope P 14+1	Goater S 42	Tiatto D 36+1	Whitley J —+2	Huckerby D 30+10	Dickov P —+7	Weaver N 24+1	Horlock K 33+9	Grant T 2+1	Wright-Phillips S 31+4	Edghill R 9+2	Colosimo S —+6	Benarbia A 38	Etuhu D 11+1	Shuker C —+2	Toure A —+1	Mettomo L 17+6	Negouai C 2+3	Mike L 1+1	Killen C —+3	Ritchie P —+8	Haaland A —+3	Jensen N 16+2	Jihai S 2+5	Macken J 4+4	Mears T —+1	Match No.
1	2	3	4	5	6	7	8¹	9	10³	11	12	13	14																					1
1⁸	2	3	4	5	6	7	8¹	9	10	11	12²			15	13																			2
	2¹	3	4	5	6	8²		9	10	11					12	1	14	13	7³															3
		3	4	5	6			9	10	11						1			7	8	2													4
		3²	4	5	6	12			10	11		9		13		1			7¹	8	2³	14												5
		3	4	5	6			9¹	10²	11		12		13		1	14			2				7³	8									6
		3		5	6	4		9	10	11¹						1				12	2		13	7	8²									7
		3	12	5	6	4		9	10²	11					13	1	14			2¹				7³	8									8
		3¹	2	5	6	4		9	10¹	11					12	1	13							7²	8	14								9
		3	2³	5	6	4²			10	11		9				1				12			13	7	8¹	14								10
		3¹	2²	5	6	4³	12		10	11		9				1				13				7	8		14							11
	2		5¹	6		12		9		3						1	10	11²		13				7	8	4								12
	3	2		6¹		4	13		10	11		9³	12			1				14	7²	8		5										13
		2³	5	6			13		10¹	3		9	12		1	11		14			7⁴	8		4										14
		12	2	5	3	4¹			10			9			1	11					7	8		6										15
		12	2	5	6¹		8³		10²	3		9	13		1					11			14	7		4								16
		2³	5²	6			8¹		10	3		9			1	12		11	14	7	13			4										17
		2	5	3					10¹						1	8	11			7				6		4	12							18
		2	5¹	6	12					3²		9			1	13	11			7				4		8	10³	14						19
1			2			4	8		10	3		9			6		11			7				5										20
1	12		2			4	8		10	3¹		9			6		11			7				5										21
1			2			4¹	8		10	3		9			6		11			7²				5	12									22
1	12		2			4	8³		10	3¹		9			6		11			7²				5	13		14							23
1			2			4		12	10¹	3		9			6		11²	3	8³	7				5				13	14					24
1		5¹		4	8²	9	10²	3							11		12	2		7				6				13	14					25
1	12	5		4¹	8	9	10²	3							11		14	2³		7				6				13	14					26
1		4	5			8³	9	10¹	3³						12		11	7	2					6				13	14					27
1		4	5¹	6		8²	9	10¹	3			12			11		2											13	14					28
1		5	6	4	8	9	10¹	3			12			11		2			7²									13						29
		5	6	4	8		10¹					9	12	1	11		2			7								3						30
		5	6	4²	8¹		10					9		1	11		2	12		7			13					3						31
		4	5	6	12	8²	9		13	10		1	11		2¹			7³					14					3						32
1		4	5	6		8		10	11		9¹		1		7	2				12							3							33
1		4	5	6		8²	10	11	9				1	7	2¹	12							13				3							34
		5	6³		8²	10	3	9					1	11	2		7	4¹			12		13	14										35
15		4	5¹	6		10	11		9	1⁹	8	2	7		12									3										36
1		5	6	4		10¹	11		9		8	2	7											3				12						37
1		5	6	4		10	11		9		8	2	7											3										38
1		5	6	4		10¹	11²		9		8	2	7										13	12				3						39
1		4	5	6	8	10	11					2¹	7		12									3				9						40
1		4	5	6	8¹	10		9				11	2		7									3				12						41
1		4¹	5	6³		10²		9		8		11	7		12									3				2	13	14				42
1		4	5	6				9		8		11	2		7									3				2	10					43
1		4	5¹	6²	12			11³		9		8	2		7								13	3				14	10					44
1		4²	5	6			10	11³		12		8	2		7								13	3				14	9¹					45
1		4	5¹	6	12	13		10³	11²	9		8	2		7								3					14						46

Worthington Cup
Second Round	Notts Co	(a)	4-2
Third Round	Birmingham C	(h)	6-0
Fourth Round	Blackburn R	(a)	0-2

FA Cup
Third Round	Swindon T	(h)	2-0
Fourth Round	Ipswich T	(a)	4-1
Fifth Round	Newcastle U	(a)	0-1

MANCHESTER UNITED   FA Premiership

FOUNDATION

Manchester United was formed as comparatively recently as 1902 after their predecessors, Newton Heath, went bankrupt. However, it is usual to give the date of the club's foundation as 1878 when the dining room committee of the carriage and waggon works of the Lancashire and Yorkshire Railway Company formed Newton Heath L and YR Cricket and Football Club. They won the Manchester Cup in 1886 and as Newton Heath FC were admitted to the Second Division in 1892.

Sir Matt Busby Way, Old Trafford, Manchester M16 0RA.

Telephone: (0161) 868 8000. *Fax:* (0161) 868 8804.
Textphone for Deaf/Impaired Hearing: (0161) 868 8668.
Ticket and Match Information: (0870) 757 1968.
Membership and Supporters Club Enquiries:
(0870) 442 1994.

Ground Capacity: 68,210.

Record Attendance: 76,962 Wolverhampton W v
Grimsby T, FA Cup semi-final, 25 March 1939.

Club record: 70,504 v Aston Villa, Division 1,
27 December 1920.

Record Receipts: £1,124,195.24 (net of VAT),
£1,320,929.99 (including VAT) v Olympiakos, European
Champions League Group G, 23 October 2001.

Pitch Measurements: 116yd × 76yd.

Chairman/Chief Executive: C. M. Edwards.
Directors: J. M. Edelson, Sir Bobby Charlton CBE,
E. M. Watkins LL.M., R. L. Olive, P. F. Kenyon, D. A. Gill.

Manager: Sir Alex Ferguson CBE. *First Team Coach:*
Carlos Queiroz. *Secretary:* Kenneth Merrett. *Stadium
Manager:* Alan Bird.

Colours: Red shirts, white shorts, black stockings.

Change Colours: White shirts, black shorts, black and
white stockings.

Year Formed: 1878 as Newton Heath LYR; 1902,
Manchester United.

Turned Professional: 1885. *Ltd Co.:* 1907.

Previous Name: 1880, Newton Heath; 1902, Manchester
United. *Club Nickname:* 'Red Devils'.

Previous Grounds: 1880, North Road, Monsall Road;
1893, Bank Street; 1910, Old Trafford (played at Maine
Road 1941–49).

HONOURS

FA Premier League – Champions
1992–93, 1993–94, 1995–96, 1996–97,
1998–99, 1999–2000, 2000–01;
Runners-up 1994–95, 1997–98.

Football League: Division 1 –
Champions 1907–08, 1910–11,
1951–52, 1955–56, 1956–57, 1964–65,
1966–67; Runners-up 1946–47,
1947–48, 1948–49, 1950–51, 1958–59,
1963–64, 1967–68, 1979–80, 1987–88,
1991–92. Division 2 – Champions
1935–36, 1974–75; Runners-up
1896–97, 1905–06, 1924–25, 1937–38.

FA Cup: Winners 1909, 1948, 1963,
1977, 1983, 1985, 1990, 1994, 1996,
1999; Runners-up 1957, 1958, 1976,
1979, 1995.

Football League Cup: Winners 1992;
Runners-up 1983, 1991, 1994.

European Competitions: *European
Cup:* 1956–57 (s-f), 1957–58 (s-f),
1965–66 (s-f), 1967–68 (winners),
1968–69 (s-f), 1993–94, 1994–95,
1996–97 (s-f), 1997–98, 1998–99
(winners), 1999–2000, 2000–01,
2001–02 (s-f). *European Cup-Winners'
Cup:* 1963–64, 1977–78, 1983–84,
1990–91 (winners). 1991–92. *European
Fairs Cup:* 1964–65. *UEFA Cup:*
1976–77, 1980–81, 1982–83, 1984–85,
1992–93, 1995–96. *Super Cup:* 1991
(winners), 1999 (runners-up). *Inter-
Continental Cup:* 1999 (winners), 1968
(runners-up)

IT'S A FACT !

Jack Rowley scored four goals for Manchester United
against Swansea Town on 4 December 1937 at the
tender age of 17 years 58 days.

First Football League Game: 3 September 1892, Division 1, v Blackburn R (a) L 3–4 – Warner; Clements, Brown; Perrins, Stewart, Erentz; Farman (1), Coupar (1), Donaldson (1), Carson, Mathieson.

Record League Victory (as Newton Heath): 10–1 v Wolverhampton W, Division 1, 15 October 1892 – Warner; Mitchell, Clements; Perrins, Stewart (3), Erentz; Farman (1), Hood (1), Donaldson (3), Carson (1), Hendry (1).

Record League Victory (as Manchester U): 9–0 v Ipswich T, FA Premier League, 4 March 1995 – Schmeichel; Keane (1) (Sharpe), Irwin, Bruce (Butt), Kanchelskis, Pallister, Cole (5), Ince (1), McClair, Hughes (2), Giggs.

Record Cup Victory: 10–0 v RSC Anderlecht, European Cup prel. rd 2nd leg, 26 September 1956 – Wood; Foulkes, Byrne; Colman, Jones, Edwards; Berry (1), Whelan (2), Taylor (3), Viollet (4), Pegg.

Record Defeat: 0–7 v Blackburn R, Division 1, 10 April 1926. 0–7 v Aston Villa, Division 1, 27 December 1930. 0–7 v Wolverhampton W, Division 2, 26 December 1931.

Most League Points (2 for a win): 64, Division 1, 1956–57.

Most League Points (3 for a win): 92, FA Premier League, 1993–94.

Most League Goals: 103, Division 1, 1956–57 and 1958–59.

Highest League Scorer in Season: Dennis Viollet, 32, 1959–60.

Most League Goals in Total Aggregate: Bobby Charlton, 199, 1956–73.

Most Capped Player: Bobby Charlton, 106, England.

Most League Appearances: Bobby Charlton, 606, 1956–73.

Youngest League Player: Jeff Whitefoot, 16 years 105 days v Portsmouth, 15 April 1950.

Record Transfer Fee Received: £15,250,000 from Lazio for Jaap Stam, August 2001.

Record Transfer Fee Paid: £30,000,000 to Leeds U for Rio Ferdinand, July 2002.

Football League Record: 1892 Newton Heath elected to Division 1; 1894–1906 Division 2; 1906–22 Division 1; 1922–25 Division 2; 1925–31 Division 1; 1931–36 Division 2; 1936–37 Division 1; 1937–38 Division 2; 1938–74 Division 1; 1974–75 Division 2; 1975–92 Division 1; 1992– FA Premier League.

MANAGERS

J. Ernest Mangnall 1903–12
John Bentley 1912–14
John Robson 1914–21
    (Secretary-Manager from 1916)
John Chapman 1921–26
Clarence Hilditch 1926–27
Herbert Bamlett 1927–31
Walter Crickmer 1931–32
Scott Duncan 1932–37
Walter Crickmer 1937–45
    (Secretary-Manager)
Matt Busby 1945–69
    (continued as General Manager then Director)
Wilf McGuinness 1969–70
Sir Matt Busby 1970–71
Frank O'Farrell 1971–72
Tommy Docherty 1972–77
Dave Sexton 1977–81
Ron Atkinson 1981–86
Alex Ferguson November 1986–

LATEST SEQUENCES

Longest Sequence of League Wins: 14, 15.10.04 – 3.1.05.
Longest Sequence of League Defeats: 14, 26.4.30 – 25.10.30.
Longest Sequence of League Draws: 6, 30.10.88 – 27.11.88.
Longest Sequence of Unbeaten League Matches: 29, 26.12.98 – 25.9.99.
Longest Sequence Without a League Win: 16, 19.4.30 – 25.10.30.

TEN YEAR LEAGUE RECORD

		P	W	D	L	F	A	Pts	Pos
1991-92	Div 1	42	21	15	6	63	33	78	2
1992-93	PR Lge	42	24	12	6	67	31	84	1
1993-94	PR Lge	42	27	11	4	80	38	92	1
1994-95	PR Lge	42	26	10	6	77	28	88	2
1995-96	PR Lge	38	25	7	6	73	35	82	1
1996-97	PR Lge	38	21	12	5	76	44	75	1
1997-98	PR Lge	38	23	8	7	73	26	77	2
1998-99	PR Lge	38	22	13	3	80	37	79	1
1999-2000	PR Lge	38	28	7	3	97	45	91	1
2000-01	PR Lge	38	24	8	6	79	31	80	1

DID YOU KNOW ?

On 29 September 2001, Manchester United were three goals down at Tottenham Hotspur by half-time. They scored five times in the second half to win 5-3. On 5 September 1936, 4-1 down to Derby County after 51 minutes, United had won 5-4.

MANCHESTER UNITED 2001–02 LEAGUE RECORD

Match No.	Date	Venue	Opponents	Result	H/T Score	Lg. Pos.	Goalscorers	Attendance
1	Aug 19	H	Fulham	W 3-2	1-1	—	Beckham [35], Van Nistelrooy 2 [51, 53]	67,534
2	22	A	Blackburn R	D 2-2	1-0	—	Giggs [20], Beckham [78]	29,836
3	26	A	Aston Villa	D 1-1	0-1	5	Alpay (og) [90]	42,632
4	Sept 8	H	Everton	W 4-1	2-0	2	Veron [22], Cole [40], Fortune [46], Beckham [90]	67,534
5	15	A	Newcastle U	L 3-4	1-2	5	Van Nistelrooy [29], Giggs [62], Veron [64]	52,056
6	22	H	Ipswich T	W 4-0	2-0	4	Johnsen [13], Solskjaer 2 [20, 90], Cole [89]	67,551
7	29	A	Tottenham H	W 5-3	0-3	3	Cole [46], Blanc [58], Van Nistelrooy [72], Veron [76], Beckham [87]	36,049
8	Oct 13	A	Sunderland	W 3-1	1-0	3	Varga (og) [35], Giggs [59], Cole [66]	47,433
9	20	H	Bolton W	L 1-2	1-1	3	Veron [25]	67,559
10	27	H	Leeds U	D 1-1	0-0	5	Solskjaer [89]	67,555
11	Nov 4	A	Liverpool	L 1-3	0-2	6	Beckham [50]	44,361
12	17	A	Leicester C	W 2-0	1-0	4	Van Nistelrooy [21], Yorke [50]	67,651
13	25	A	Arsenal	L 1-3	1-0	6	Scholes [14]	38,174
14	Dec 1	H	Chelsea	L 0-3	0-1	7		67,544
15	8	H	West Ham U	L 0-1	0-0	9		67,582
16	12	A	Derby Co	W 5-0	2-0	—	Solskjaer 2 [6, 58], Keane [10], Van Nistelrooy [63], Scholes [89]	67,577
17	15	A	Middlesbrough	W 1-0	0-0	6	Van Nistelrooy [75]	34,358
18	22	H	Southampton	W 6-1	3-0	5	Van Nistelrooy 3 [1, 34, 54], Solskjaer [41], Keane [72], Neville P [78]	67,638
19	26	A	Everton	W 2-0	0-0	5	Giggs [78], Van Nistelrooy [85]	39,948
20	30	A	Fulham	W 3-2	2-1	5	Giggs 2 [5, 47], Van Nistelrooy [45]	21,159
21	Jan 2	H	Newcastle U	W 3-1	1-0	—	Van Nistelrooy [24], Scholes 2 [50, 62]	67,646
22	13	A	Southampton	W 3-1	2-1	1	Van Nistelrooy [9], Beckham [45], Solskjaer [63]	31,858
23	19	H	Blackburn R	W 2-1	1-0	1	Van Nistelrooy (pen) [45], Keane [81]	67,552
24	22	H	Liverpool	L 0-1	0-0	—		67,599
25	29	A	Bolton W	W 4-0	2-0	—	Solskjaer 3 [15, 39, 64], Van Nistelrooy [84]	27,350
26	Feb 2	H	Sunderland	W 4-1	4-1	1	Neville P. [6], Beckham [25], Van Nistelrooy 2 (1 pen) [28, 44 (p)]	67,587
27	10	A	Charlton Ath	W 2-0	1-0	1	Solskjaer 2 [33, 74]	26,459
28	23	H	Aston Villa	W 1-0	0-0	1	Van Nistelrooy [50]	67,592
29	Mar 3	A	Derby Co	D 2-2	1-1	1	Scholes [41], Veron [60]	33,041
30	6	H	Tottenham H	W 4-0	2-0	—	Beckham 2 [15, 64], Van Nistelrooy 2 (1 pen) [43 (p), 76]	67,599
31	16	A	West Ham U	W 5-3	2-2	1	Beckham 2 (1 pen) [17, 89 (p)], Butt [22], Scholes [55], Solskjaer [64]	35,281
32	23	H	Middlesbrough	L 0-1	0-1	2		67,683
33	30	A	Leeds U	W 4-3	3-1	2	Scholes [9], Solskjaer 2 [37, 39], Giggs [55]	40,058
34	Apr 6	A	Leicester C	W 1-0	0-0	2	Solskjaer [61]	21,447
35	20	A	Chelsea	W 3-0	2-0	3	Scholes [15], Van Nistelrooy [41], Solskjaer [86]	41,725
36	27	A	Ipswich T	W 1-0	1-0	2	Van Nistelrooy (pen) [45]	28,286
37	May 8	H	Arsenal	L 0-1	0-0	—		67,580
38	11	H	Charlton Ath	D 0-0	0-0	3		67,579

Final League Position: 3

GOALSCORERS

League (87): Van Nistelrooy 23 (4 pens), Solskjaer 17, Beckham 11 (1 pen), Scholes 8, Giggs 7, Veron 5, Cole 4, Keane 3, Neville P 2, Blanc 1, Butt 1, Fortune 1, Johnsen 1, Yorke 1, own goals 2.
Worthington Cup (0).
FA Cup (3): Van Nistelrooy 2, Solskjaer 1.

Barthez F 32	Irwin D 10 + 2	Silvestre M 31 + 4	Neville G 31 + 3	Neville P 21 + 7	Stam J 1	Beckham D 23 + 5	Scholes P 30 + 5	Van Nistelrooy R 29 + 3	Veron J 24 + 2	Giggs R 18 + 7	Cole A 7 + 4	Chadwick L 5 + 3	Brown W 15 + 2	Keane R 28	Johnsen R 9 + 1	Yorke D 4 + 6	Carroll R 6 + 1	Solskjaer O 23 + 7	Blanc L 29	Fortune Q 8 + 6	May D 2	Butt N 20 + 5	Stewart M 2 + 1	O'Shea J 4 + 5	Wallwork R — + 1	Forlan D 6 + 7	Van der Gouw R — + 1	Match No.
1	2	3	4	5^1	6	7	8	9^3	10^3	11	12	13	14															1
1	2^1	3	12			7	8^3	9^4	10	11	13			4	5	6	14											2
	3^1	2	12			7^2	8^3	9	10	11	13			4	5	6	1		14									3
1	12	2^1	3			13		14	10		9	7^2	4	5			8^3		6	11								4
1		2	3			7	12	9	8	11	10^1			4	5			6										5
1	3		2			12		13		9	7^1			5^2	6			10		11		4	8					6
1	3^1	12	2			7	5	9	11		10			4				13	6			8^2						7
	3	2	12			5^3		11^2	9	7	4			13	1	10	6^1					8	14					8
1	3	12	2			5^2		11	13	9	14	4			10^3	7				6^1	8							9
1	3	2				7	5	9	10	11			4					12	6			8^1						10
1	3^1	6	2			7^1	12	9	10				4			13		8^2		11		5	14					11
1	3^1	12	2			7	8	9	11^2				4	5				10		6	13							12
1	3^1	2	12			7	8	9^2	10^3				4	5		14	13	6	11									13
1		12	3			7^2	2	9	8	10^3	14	4	5			13	6	11^1										14
1	6	2	3			12	11			13	7^1			5		10^3	9		14	8^2		4						15
1^8	3	2				11	9^1	7					5		12	15	10	6		8		4						16
1	3	2	12			11	9	7	13				5		1	10	6	8^2		4^1								17
1	3	4	2			12	11	9	7^1	13			5^3			10^2	6	8					14					18
1	3	4	2			12		9	7	11			5			10	6	8^1										19
1	3	4	2			7	10	9		11			5			10^1	6	8										20
1	3	4	2			12	11	9^2	7				5		13	10^1	6	8										21
1	12	3	4	2^1		7	11	9^2	8	13			5			10	6											22
1	12	3^1	4	2		7	11	9	8^3	13			5			10^2	6			14								23
1		3	4	2		7^1	10	9	8	11			5			12	6											24
1		3	4	2		7	8	9		11			5^1			10^3	6^2			12		13		14				25
1		3	4	2		7	8	9		11^3			5^1			10	6^2			12		13		14				26
		3	4	2		7	8	9^1	12	11^4			5			1	10^3	6		13				14				27
1	2^1	3	4				9	11					5	12		10	6											28
1	2^1	3	4			7	5	9	8	11^1			6			10							12		13			29
1		3	2^1	12		7	11^3	9	8^2				5	4			6	13	14					10				30
1		3	2			7	11	9^1					5	4			10^2	6	12		8				13			31
1		3	2	12		7	12	9	8^1	11			5	4			6	13		5				10^2				32
1		3	2	12		7	10		11^2				5	4		9	6		8					13				33
	2^3	3	4	5		11	12		13				14			1	9	6	7^1	8				10^2				34
1		3	2	12		8	9		11^2				4			10	6	7^1		5				13				35
	3	12		2		13	9^2			7^1	4	5				1	14			8	11^2	6		10				36
1		3	2			8	12	7^1	11				4	5			9	6	13						10^8			37
1^8	2^2		3			8		12					4	5			9	6	11				7^1	13		10	15	38

Worthington Cup
Third Round   Arsenal   (a)   0-4

FA Cup
Third Round   Aston Villa   (a)   3-2
Fourth Round   Middlesbrough   (a)   0-2

MANSFIELD TOWN   Division 2

FOUNDATION

The club was formed as Mansfield Wesleyans in 1897, and changed their name to Mansfield Wesley in 1906 and Mansfield Town in 1910. This was after the Mansfield Wesleyan Chapel trustees had requested that the club change its name as 'it has no longer had any connection with either the chapel or school'. The new club participated in the Notts and Derby District League, but in the following season 1911–12 joined the Central Alliance.

Field Mill Ground, Quarry Lane, Mansfield NG18 5DA.

Telephone: 0870 756 3160. *Fax:* (01623) 482 495.
Marketing: 0870 756 3160. *ClubCall:* 09068 121 311.
Football in the Community: (07977) 428 147.

Ground Capacity: 9,990.

Record Attendance: 24,467 v Nottingham F, FA Cup 3rd rd, 10 January 1953.

Record Receipts: £46,915 v Sheffield W, FA Cup 3rd rd, 5 January 1991.

Pitch Measurements: 114yd × 70yd.

Chairman/Chief Executive: Keith Haslam.

Associate Directors: K. Woodcock, S. Whetton, M. Murphy.

Manager: Stuart Watkiss.

Physio: Barry Statham.

Community Scheme Organiser: John Gannon.

Secretary: Christine Reynolds.

Commercial Manager: Bob Gorrill.

Colours: Amber shirts with royal blue trim, royal blue shorts with amber trim, amber stockings with blue trim.

Change Colours: All navy.

Year Formed: 1897.

Turned Professional: 1906.

Ltd Co.: 1922.

Previous Name: 1897, Mansfield Wesleyans; 1906, Mansfield Wesley; 1910, Mansfield Town.

Previous Grounds: 1897–99, Westfield Lane; 1899–1901, Ratcliffe Gate; 1901–12, Newgate Lane; 1912–16, Ratcliffe Gate.

Club Nickname: 'The Stags'.

First Football League Game: 29 August 1931, Division 3 (S), v Swindon T (h) W 3–2 – Wilson; Clifford, England; Wake, Davis, Blackburn; Gilhespy, Readman (1), Johnson, Broom (2), Baxter.

HONOURS

Football League: Division 2 best season: 21st, 1977–78; Division 3 – Champions 1976–77; Promoted to Division 2 (3rd) 2001–02; Division 4 – Champions 1974–75; Division 3 (N) – Runners-up 1950–51.

FA Cup: best season: 6th rd, 1969.

Football League Cup: best season: 5th rd, 1976.

Freight Rover Trophy: Winners 1987.

IT'S A FACT !

In 1950–51, Mansfield Town finished runners-up in Division Three (North) and also reached the fifth round of the FA Cup. They were the only unbeaten team at home in the Football League, conceding just 19 goals.

Record League Victory: 9–2 v Rotherham U,
Division 3 (N), 27 December 1932 – Wilson; Anthony,
England; Davies, S. Robinson, Slack; Prior, Broom,
Readman (3), Hoyland (3), Bowater (3).

Record Cup Victory: 8–0 v Scarborough (a), FA Cup 1st rd,
22 November 1952 – Bramley; Chessell, Bradley; Field,
Plummer, Lewis; Scott, Fox (3), Marron (2), Sid Watson (1),
Adam (2).

Record Defeat: 1–8 v Walsall, Division 3 (N),
19 January 1933.

Most League Points (2 for a win): 68, Division 4, 1974–75.

Most League Points (3 for a win): 81, Division 4, 1985–86.

Most League Goals: 108, Division 4, 1962–63.

Highest League Scorer in Season: Ted Harston, 55,
Division 3 (N), 1936–37.

Most League Goals in Total Aggregate: Harry Johnson,
104, 1931–36.

Most League Goals in One Match: 7, Ted Harston v
Hartlepools U, Division 3N, 23 January 1937.

Most Capped Player: John McClelland, 6 (53), Northern
Ireland.

Most League Appearances: Rod Arnold, 440, 1970–83.

Youngest League Player: Cyril Poole, 15 years 351 days v
New Brighton, 27 February 1937.

Record Transfer Fee Received: £655,000 from Tottenham H
for Colin Calderwood, July 1993.

Record Transfer Fee Paid: £150,000 to Carlisle U for
Lee Peacock, October 1997.

Football League Record: 1931 Elected to Division 3 (S);
1932–37 Division 3 (N); 1937–47 Division 3 (S); 1947–58
Division 3 (N); 1958–60 Division 3; 1960–63 Division 4; 1963–72 Division 3; 1972–75 Division 4;
1975–77 Division 3; 1977–78 Division 2; 1978–80 Division 3; 1980–86 Division 4; 1986–91 Division 3;
1991–92 Division 4; 1992–93 Division 2; 1993–2002 Division 3; 2002– Division 2.

MANAGERS

John Baynes 1922–25
Ted Davison 1926–28
Jack Hickling 1928–33
Henry Martin 1933–35
Charlie Bell 1935
Harold Wightman 1936
Harold Parkes 1936–38
Jack Poole 1938–44
Lloyd Barke 1944–45
Roy Goodall 1945–49
Freddie Steele 1949–51
George Jobey 1952–53
Stan Mercer 1953–55
Charlie Mitten 1956–58
Sam Weaver 1958–60
Raich Carter 1960–63
Tommy Cummings 1963–67
Tommy Eggleston 1967–70
Jock Basford 1970–71
Danny Williams 1971–74
Dave Smith 1974–76
Peter Morris 1976–78
Billy Bingham 1978–79
Mick Jones 1979–81
Stuart Boam 1981–83
Ian Greaves 1983–89
George Foster 1989–93
Andy King 1993–96
Steve Parkin 1996–99
Bill Dearden 1999–2002
Stuart Watkiss January 2002–

LATEST SEQUENCES

Longest Sequence of League Wins: 7, 13.9.91 – 26.10.91.

Longest Sequence of League Defeats: 7, 18.1.47 – 15.3.47.

Longest Sequence of League Draws: 5, 18.10.86 – 22.11.86.

Longest Sequence of Unbeaten League Matches: 20, 14.2.76 – 21.8.76.

Longest Sequence Without a League Win: 14, 25.3.00 – 2.9.00.

TEN YEAR LEAGUE RECORD

		P	W	D	L	F	A	Pts	Pos
1991-92	Div 4	42	23	8	11	75	53	77	3
1992-93	Div 2	46	11	11	24	52	80	44	22
1993-94	Div 3	42	15	10	17	53	62	55	12
1994-95	Div 3	42	18	11	13	84	59	65	6
1995-96	Div 3	46	11	20	15	54	64	53	19
1996-97	Div 3	46	16	16	14	47	45	64	11
1997-98	Div 3	46	16	17	13	64	55	65	12
1998-99	Div 3	46	19	10	17	60	58	67	8
1999-2000	Div 3	46	16	8	22	50	65	56	17
2000-01	Div 3	46	15	13	18	64	72	68	13

DID YOU KNOW ?

In 2000–01, Halifax-born
Chris Greenacre dealt
severely with his home town
club, scoring three times for
Mansfield Town against
Halifax Town on 9
September and twice on 10
February in the return match.

MANSFIELD TOWN 2001–02 LEAGUE RECORD

Match No.	Date	Venue	Opponents	Result	H/T Score	Lg. Pos.	Goalscorers	Attendance
1	Aug 11	A	Hartlepool U	D	1-1	1-0		Greenacre [8]	3534
2	18	H	Southend U	D	0-0	0-0	15		2774
3	25	A	Cheltenham T	W	3-2	1-0	10	Disley 2 [30, 47], Corden [90]	3105
4	27	H	Macclesfield T	W	4-0	2-0	5	Greenacre [15], Disley 2 [20, 67], White A [46]	2681
5	Sept 1	A	Kidderminster H	D	1-1	1-0	6	Greenacre [28]	2387
6	8	H	Lincoln C	W	2-1	1-0	3	Greenacre [28], Corden [86]	3878
7	14	H	Shrewsbury T	W	2-1	0-1	—	Bacon [69], Greenacre [90]	4759
8	18	A	Halifax T	L	0-1	0-1	—		1880
9	22	A	Scunthorpe U	D	0-0	0-0	8		3857
10	25	H	Hull C	W	4-2	3-0		Disley [34], Hassell [35], Reddington [40], Greenacre [58]	5702
11	29	A	Rochdale	L	1-3	0-1	7	Greenacre [90]	3963
12	Oct 5	H	Leyton Orient	W	3-2	3-1	—	Williamson [15], Disley [33], Greenacre [39]	5168
13	13	A	Darlington	W	1-0	0-0	5	Tankard [79]	4021
14	20	H	Plymouth Arg	L	0-3	0-0	5		4621
15	23	H	Torquay U	W	2-0	0-0		Greenacre [75], Corden [87]	4059
16	27	A	Rushden & D	L	1-3	1-2	5	Bradley [5]	4937
17	Nov 3	H	Luton T	W	4-1	1-0	5	Greenacre 2 [21, 56], Pemberton [63], Bradley [80]	5973
18	10	A	Carlisle U	W	1-0	1-0	4	Greenacre [28]	2546
19	20	A	Bristol R	W	1-0	0-0	—	Lawrence [56]	5043
20	23	H	York C	D	1-1	0-0	—	Disley [90]	4877
21	Dec 1	H	Swansea C	W	3-0	2-0	2	Greenacre 2 [15, 45], Piper [77]	3240
22	15	A	Oxford U	L	2-3	1-0	3	Corden (pen) [23], Hatswell (og) [69]	5437
23	21	H	Exeter C	L	0-1	0-0	—		3958
24	29	A	Macclesfield T	W	1-0	0-0	3	Tankard [90]	2550
25	Jan 12	A	Southend U	L	0-1	0-1	3		3300
26	19	H	Hartlepool U	W	3-0	1-0	3	Lee (og) [3], Corden [78], Greenacre [90]	4349
27	22	A	Exeter C	W	1-0	1-0	—	Lawrence [9]	3106
28	29	H	Kidderminster H	D	1-1	0-1	—	Pemberton [87]	4321
29	Feb 2	H	Rochdale	W	3-1	2-0	3	Greenacre 2 [37, 86], Pemberton [38]	4876
30	9	A	Plymouth Arg	L	0-1	0-0	4		14,716
31	12	A	Lincoln C	W	4-1	3-0	—	Corden [15], Williamson 2 [42, 45], Pemberton [48]	4072
32	16	H	Darlington	W	4-2	3-1	2	Kelly 2 [2, 77], Corden (pen) [21], Greenacre [32]	5107
33	23	H	Shrewsbury T	L	0-3	0-2	3		4120
34	26	H	Halifax T	W	2-1	0-1		Kelly [53], Greenacre [66]	4513
35	Mar 2	H	Scunthorpe U	W	2-1	0-1	3	Murray 2 [51, 70]	6292
36	5	A	Hull C	L	1-4	0-2		Bradley [82]	9158
37	9	H	Oxford U	W	2-1	2-0	3	Kelly [29], Murray [45]	4916
38	16	A	Swansea C	L	0-2	0-1	3		3527
39	19	A	Leyton Orient	L	0-2	0-0	—		3316
40	23	H	Torquay U	D	0-0	0-0	3		2679
41	30	H	Rushden & D	L	1-4	0-1	4	Murray [49]	5807
42	Apr 1	A	Luton T	L	3-5	2-4	4	Murray [12], Sellars [42], Greenacre [90]	8231
43	6	H	Bristol R	W	2-0	0-0	4	Murray [57], White A [79]	3996
44	9	A	Cheltenham T	W	2-1	1-0	—	Greenacre [4], White A [77]	8633
45	13	A	York C	L	1-3	1-1	4	Murray [40]	5460
46	20	H	Carlisle U	W	2-0	2-0	3	Corden [5], White A [30]	8638

Final League Position: 3

GOALSCORERS

League (72): Greenacre 21, Corden 8 (2 pens), Disley 7, Murray 7, Kelly 4, Pemberton 4, White A 4, Bradley 3, Williamson 3, Lawrence 2, Tankard 2, Bacon 1, Hassell 1, Piper 1, Reddington 1, Sellars 1, own goals 2.
Worthington Cup (3): Greenacre 2, White A 1.
FA Cup (6): Greenacre 5, Corden 1.

Pilkington K 45	Hassell B 43	Tankard A 22 + 8	Robinson L 36	Reddington S 34 + 4	Williamson L 44 + 2	Lawrence L 32	Disley C 31 + 5	White A 16 + 6	Greenacre C 43 + 1	Corden W 46	Pemberton M 33 + 5	Bacon D 1 + 7	Asher A 1 + 9	Williams L — + 2	White J 6 + 1	Harris R — + 6	Bradley S 7 + 9	Barrett A 26 + 3	Piper M 8	Jervis D — + 3	Kelly D 11 + 6	Murray A 13	Wheatcroft P 1 + 1	Bingham M 1 + 1	Sellers S 5 + 1	Clarke J 1	Match No.
1	2	3	4	5	6	7	8	9	10	11																	1
1	2	3^1	4	5	6	7	8	9	10	11	12																2
1	2	3	4	5	6	7^1	8	9^2	10	11	12	13															3
1	2^2	3	4	5	6	7^1	8	9^1	10	11	12	13	14														4
1	2	3^1	4	5	6	7	8	9^2	10	11	12	13															5
1	2		4	5	6	7	8	9	10	11	3																6
1	2		4	5	6	7	8^2	9^2	10	11	3	12	13														7
1	2	12	4	5	6	7	8^1	9^2	10	11^3	3	14	13														8
1	2		4	5	6	7	8		10	11	3				9												9
1	2	12	4	5	6	7	8	13	10	11^1	3				9^2												10
1	2		4	5	6	7	8		10	11	3	12			9^2	13											11
1	2	12	4	5	6	7	8		10	11	3				9^2	13											12
1	2	12	4	5	6	7	8		10^3	11	3		13		9^2	14											13
1	2^1		4	5	6	7	8		10	11	3				9^2	12	13										14
1	2		4^2	5	6	7	8		10^1	11	3			12	9	13											15
1	2	12		5	6	7	8			11^2	3	9	13	10	4												16
1	2		4	12	6	7	8		10^2	11	3		13		9			5									17
1	2	12	4		6	7	8^1		10	11	3		9					5									18
1	2	3	4		6	7	8		10	11								5	9								19
1		3	4	12	6	7	8		10	11^2			2				13	5^1	9								20
1	2	3	4	5^1	6	7	8		10	11							12		9								21
1	2	3	4		6	7^1	8		10	11							12	5	9								22
1	2	3^1	4		6	7	8		10	11^2			12				13	5	9								23
1	2	3	4		6	7	8		10	11								5	9								24
1	2	3	4	12	6	7			10	11			8					5	9								25
1	2^1	3^2		5	6	7			10	11			8				12	4	9		13						26
1	2	3^4	4		6	7			10	11			8				12	5	9		13						27
1	2	3	4		6^2	7			10	11^1			8	12			13	5	9								28
1	2	3	4		6	7^2			10^1	11			8	12			13	5	9^3				14				29
1	2	3	4		6	7			10	11			8					5	9								30
1	2	3	4		6	7				11			8^1				12	5	9						10		31
1		3^1	4	5	6	7			10	11			8	12					9	2							32
1	2	3^2	4		6		8		10	11			7	13			12	5	9^1								33
1	2		4		6				10	11	3						12	5	9		7		8^1				34
1	2	3	4		6		12		10^1	11							13	5	9^2		7		8				35
1	2	3^1	4		6		13		10^2	11							12	5	9		7		8				36
1	2	5	4		6		12	8^1	10	11	3^2						13		9		7						37
1	2		4	5	6		8										12		9^6		7^2	13		15			38
1	2		4	5	6		8	12	10	11	3								9^1		7						39
1	2		4		6		8	12	10^1	11	3							5	9^2		7	13					40
	2		4		6^3		8	12	10	11^2	3						13	5	9^1		7		1		14		41
1	2	4^1	12		6		8			11^2	3						13	5	9		7				10		42
1	2	12	4	13	6		8	9	10^3	11	3^1							5			7^2	14					43
1	2	12	4	13	6		8^1	9	10^3	11	3^2							5			7	14					44
1	2	3	4		6^1		12	9	10	11								5^2				13			8	7	45
1	2^3	3	4		6		12	9	10^2	11								5		14		13			8	7^1	46

Worthington Cup

First Round	Notts Co	(h)	3-4

FA Cup

First Round	Oxford U	(h)	1-0
Second Round	Huddersfield T	(h)	4-0
Third Round	Leicester C	(a)	1-2

MIDDLESBROUGH   FA Premiership

FOUNDATION

A previous belief that Middlesbrough Football Club was founded at a tripe supper at the Corporation Hotel has proved to be erroneous. In fact, members of Middlesbrough Cricket Club were responsible for forming it at a meeting in the gymnasium of the Albert Park Hotel in 1875.

Riverside Stadium, Middlesbrough, TS3 6RS.

Telephone: (01642) 877 700. *Fax:* (01642) 877 840.
Website: www.mfc.co.uk *ClubCall:* 09068 121 181.
Ticket Office: (01642) 877 745.
Ticket Information Line: (01642) 877 809.
Club Tours: (01642) 877 730.
Stadium Store: (01642) 877 720.
Town Centre Store: (01642) 877 849.
Mail Order: (01642) 866 642.
Lottery Office: (01642) 877 790.

Ground Capacity: 35,049.

Record Attendance: Ayresome Park: 53,536 v Newcastle U, Division 1, 27 December 1949. BT Cellnet Riverside Stadium: 34,800 v Leeds U, FA Premier League, 26 February 2000.

Record Receipts: £486,229 v Newcastle U, FA Premier League, 6 December 1998.

Pitch measurements: 105m × 68m.

HONOURS

Football League: Division 1 – Champions 1994–95; Runners-up 1997–98; Division 2 – Champions 1926–27, 1928–29, 1973–74; Runners-up 1901–02, 1991–92; Division 3 – Runners-up 1966–67, 1986–87.

FA Cup: Runners-up 1997.

Football League Cup: Runners-up 1997, 1998.

Amateur Cup: Winners 1895, 1898.

Anglo-Scottish Cup: Winners 1976.

Zenith Data Systems Cup: Runners-up 1990.

Chairman: Steve Gibson. *Chief Executive:* Keith Lamb.
Secretary: Karen Nelson.

Manager: Steve McClaren. *Assistant Manager:* Bill Beswick. *First Team Coach:* Steve Harrison.
Reserve Team Coach: Steve Round. *Physio:* Bob Ward.
Youth Academy Director: David Parnaby *Chief Scout:* Ray Train.

Commercial Manager: Graham Fordy. *Media & Communications Manager:* Dave Allan.
Stadium Manager: Terry Tasker. *Head of Finance & Administration:* Alan Baige.

Colours: Red and white.

Change Colours: All white.

Year Formed: 1876; re-formed 1986.

Turned Professional: 1889; became amateur 1892, and professional again, 1899.

Ltd Co: 1892. *Club Nickname:* 'Boro'.

Previous Grounds: 1877, Old Archery Ground, Albert Park; 1879, Breckon Hill; 1882, Linthorpe Road Ground; 1903, Ayresome Park; 1995, Cellnet Riverside Stadium.

First Football League Game: 2 September 1899, Division 2, v Lincoln C (a) L 0–3 – Smith; Shaw, Ramsey; Allport, McNally, McCracken; Wanless, Longstaffe, Gettins, Page, Pugh.

Record League Victory: 9–0 v Brighton & HA, Division 2, 23 August 1958 – Taylor; Bilcliff, Robinson; Harris (2p), Phillips, Walley; Day, McLean, Clough (5), Peacock (2), Holliday.

IT'S A FACT !

An important milestone date in the history of the Middlesbrough club is 16 May. On that day in 1918, Wilf Mannion was born and in 1967 John O'Rourke scored a hat-trick to achieve promotion.

Record Cup Victory: 7–0 v Hereford U, Coca-Cola Cup 2nd rd, 1st leg, 18 September 1996 – Miller; Fleming (1), Branco (1), Whyte, Vickers, Whelan, Emerson (1), Mustoe, Stamp, Juninho, Ravanelli (4).

Record Defeat: 0–9 v Blackburn R, Division 2, 6 November 1954.

Most League Points (2 for a win): 65, Division 2, 1973–74.

Most League Points (3 for a win): 94, Division 3, 1986–87.

Most League Goals: 122, Division 2, 1926–27.

Highest League Scorer in Season: George Camsell, 59, Division 2, 1926–27 (Second Division record).

Most League Goals in Total Aggregate: George Camsell, 325, 1925–39.

Most League Goals in One Match: 5, Andy Wilson v Nottingham F, Division 1, 6 October 1923; 5, George Camsell v Manchester C, Division 2, 25 December 1926; 5, George Camsell v Aston Villa, Division 1, 9 September 1935; 5, Brian Clough v Brighton & HA, Division 2, 22 August 1958.

Most Capped Player: Wilf Mannion, 26, England.

Most League Appearances: Tim Williamson, 563, 1902–23.

Youngest League Player: Stephen Bell, 16 years 323 days v Southampton, 30 January 1982; Sam Lawrie, 16 years 323 days v Arsenal, 3 November 1951.

Record Transfer Fee Received: £12,000,000 from Atletico Madrid for Juninho, July 1997.

Record Transfer Fee Paid: £8,000,000 to Aston Villa for Ugo Ehiogu, October 2000.

Football League Record: 1899 Elected to Division 2; 1902–24 Division 1; 1924–27 Division 2; 1927–28 Division 1; 1928–29 Division 2; 1929–54 Division 1; 1954–66 Division 2; 1966–67 Division 3; 1967–74 Division 2; 1974–82 Division 1; 1982–86 Division 2; 1986–87 Division 3; 1987–88 Division 2; 1988–89 Division 1; 1989–92 Division 2; 1992–93 FA Premier League; 1993–95 Division 1; 1995–97 FA Premier League; 1997–98 Division 1; 1998– FA Premier League.

MANAGERS

John Robson 1899–1905
Alex Mackie 1905–06
Andy Aitken 1906–09
J. Gunter 1908–10
  (Secretary-Manager)
Andy Walker 1910–11
Tom McIntosh 1911–19
Jimmy Howie 1920–23
Herbert Bamlett 1923–26
Peter McWilliam 1927–34
Wilf Gillow 1934–44
David Jack 1944–52
Walter Rowley 1952–54
Bob Dennison 1954–63
Raich Carter 1963–66
Stan Anderson 1966–73
Jack Charlton 1973–77
John Neal 1977–81
Bobby Murdoch 1981–82
Malcolm Allison 1982–84
Willie Maddren 1984–86
Bruce Rioch 1986–90
Colin Todd 1990–91
Lennie Lawrence 1991–94
Bryan Robson 1994–2001
Steve McClaren July 2001–

LATEST SEQUENCES

Longest Sequence of League Wins: 9, 16.2.74 – 6.4.74.

Longest Sequence of League Defeats: 8, 26.12.95 – 17.2.96.

Longest Sequence of League Draws: 8, 3.4.71 – 1.5.71.

Longest Sequence of Unbeaten League Matches: 24, 8.9.73 – 19.1.74.

Longest Sequence Without a League Win: 19, 3.10.81 – 6.3.82.

TEN YEAR LEAGUE RECORD

		P	W	D	L	F	A	Pts	Pos
1991-92	Div 2	46	23	11	12	58	41	80	2
1992-93	PR Lge	42	11	11	20	54	75	44	21
1993-94	Div 1	46	18	13	15	66	54	67	9
1994-95	Div 1	46	23	13	10	67	40	82	1
1995-96	PR Lge	38	11	10	17	35	50	43	12
1996-97	PR Lge	38	10	12	16	51	60	39	19
1997-98	Div 1	46	27	10	9	77	41	91	2
1998-99	PR Lge	38	12	15	11	48	54	51	9
1999-2000	PR Lge	38	14	10	14	46	52	52	12
2000-01	PR Lge	38	9	15	14	44	44	42	14

DID YOU KNOW ?

On 16 February 2002, Robbie Mustoe played in his 87th different cup match for Middlesbrough to establish a club record.

MIDDLESBROUGH 2001–02 LEAGUE RECORD

Match No.	Date	Venue	Opponents	Result		H/T Score	Lg. Pos.	Goalscorers	Attendance
1	Aug 18	H	Arsenal	L	0-4	0-1	—		31,557
2	21	A	Bolton W	L	0-1	0-1	—		20,747
3	25	A	Everton	L	0-2	0-1	19		32,829
4	Sept 8	H	Newcastle U	L	1-4	1-1	20	Cooper [4]	30,004
5	15	H	West Ham U	W	2-0	2-0	19	Deane [31], Johnston [41]	25,406
6	17	A	Leicester C	W	2-1	0-1	—	Ince [85], Greening [88]	15,412
7	23	A	Chelsea	D	2-2	0-2	12	Stockdale [61], Boksic (pen) [90]	36,767
8	29	H	Southampton	L	1-3	0-0	15	Boksic (pen) [75]	26,142
9	Oct 13	A	Charlton Ath	D	0-0	0-0	14		20,451
10	22	H	Sunderland	W	2-0	2-0	—	Queudrue [2], Boksic [21]	28,422
11	27	A	Tottenham H	L	1-2	1-0	15	Boksic [9]	36,046
12	Nov 3	H	Derby Co	W	5-1	0-0	13	Nemeth [49], Marinelli 2 [57, 82], Boksic [61], Mustoe [73]	28,099
13	17	A	Aston Villa	D	0-0	0-0	14		35,424
14	25	A	Ipswich T	D	0-0	0-0	14		32,586
15	Dec 1	H	Blackburn R	W	1-0	1-0	14	Boksic [45]	23,849
16	8	A	Liverpool	L	0-2	0-2	15		43,674
17	15	H	Manchester U	L	0-1	0-0	16		34,358
18	26	A	Newcastle U	L	0-3	0-1	16		52,127
19	29	A	Arsenal	L	1-2	1-0	16	Whelan [22]	37,928
20	Jan 1	H	Everton	W	1-0	0-0	16	Festa [50]	27,463
21	12	A	Fulham	L	1-2	1-2	17	Cooper [8]	18,975
22	19	H	Bolton W	D	1-1	1-0	18	Whelan [38]	26,104
23	29	A	Sunderland	W	1-0	1-0	—	Whelan [14]	41,955
24	Feb 3	H	Charlton Ath	D	0-0	0-0	16		24,041
25	9	H	Leeds U	D	2-2	0-1	16	Ince [51], Windass [88]	30,221
26	19	H	Fulham	W	2-1	1-0	—	Boksic [27], Nemeth [77]	26,277
27	23	A	West Ham U	L	0-1	0-0	12		35,420
28	Mar 2	H	Leicester C	W	1-0	1-0	12	Sinclair (og) [4]	25,734
29	6	A	Southampton	D	1-1	0-1	—	Whelan [57]	28,931
30	16	H	Liverpool	L	1-2	0-1	13	Southgate [89]	31,253
31	23	A	Manchester U	W	1-0	1-0	10	Boksic [9]	67,683
32	30	H	Tottenham H	D	1-1	0-1	11	Queudrue [69]	31,258
33	Apr 1	A	Derby Co	W	1-0	1-0	10	Mustoe [12]	30,822
34	6	H	Aston Villa	W	2-1	1-0	9	Carbone [39], Ehiogu [65]	26,001
35	20	H	Blackburn R	L	1-3	0-1	9	Nemeth [90]	26,935
36	24	A	Ipswich T	L	0-1	0-0	—		25,979
37	27	H	Chelsea	L	0-2	0-2	10		28,686
38	May 11	A	Leeds U	L	0-1	0-0	12		40,218

Final League Position: 12

GOALSCORERS

League (35): Boksic 8 (2 pens), Whelan 4, Nemeth 3, Cooper 2, Ince 2, Marinelli 2, Mustoe 2, Queudrue 2, Carbone 1, Deane 1, Ehiogu 1, Festa 1, Greening 1, Johnston 1, Southgate 1, Stockdale 1, Windass 1, own goal 1.
Worthington Cup (4): Nemeth 2, Murphy 1, Wilson 1.
FA Cup (8): Whelan 3, Campbell 1, Ehiogu 1, Ince 1, Nemeth 1, own goal 1.

Schwarzer M 21	Fleming C 8	Cooper C 14 + 4	Southgate G 37	Ehiogu U 29	Mustoe R 31 + 5	Greening J 36	Windass D 8 + 19	Boksic A 20 + 2	Job J 3 + 1	Ince P 31	Wilson M 2 + 8	Ricard H 6 + 3	Okon P 1 + 3	Deane B 6 + 1	Vickers S 2	Nemeth S 11 + 10	Crossley M 17 + 1	Johnston A 13 + 4	Gavin J 5 + 4	Marinelli C 12 + 8	Stockdale R 26 + 2	Queudrue F 28	Stamp P 3 + 3	Hudson M — + 2	Beresford M — + 1	Whelan N 18 + 1	Campbell A — + 4	Festa G 8	Gordon D — + 1	Carbone B 13	Murphy D — + 5	Wilkshire L 6 + 1	Debeve M 1 + 3	Downing S 2 + 1	Match No.
1	2	3	4	5	6¹	7	8²	9	10	11	12	13																							1
1	2	3	4	5	6²	7	12	8		11		9¹	13	10																					2
1	2	3	4	5	12	7	13		10	11		9²	8¹			6²	14																		3
1	2	3	4		6	7	8⁶			11	12	9				5	15	10¹																	4
1	2	3²	4	5	6	7	8			11	12	9					10¹	13																	5
1	2	3	4	5	6²	7	8³			11	12	9				13	10¹	14																	6
	2²	3	4		6¹	7		9	10	11	12						1	8³	5	13	14														7
1	2	3	4	5	6¹	7		9		11	12					10³	14	8²		13															8
			4	5	12	7	13	9²		11						10³	1	6¹	14	8	2	3													9
1			4	5	6	7	12	9		11						13		10¹	14	8²	2	3													10
1		12	4	5	6³	7	13	9		11								10¹	14	8	2²	3													11
1			4	5	6	7¹	12	9²		11						13		10¹	14	8	2	3													12
	12		4	5	6	7	13	9	10²	11							1	8²	14		2	3²													13
			4	5	6	7	12	9	10¹	11¹						13	1		14	8²	2	3													14
	2		4	5	6	7	12	9¹	10	11						13	1		14	8²		3²													15
	2		4	5	6	7	12	9		11						13	1⁶	10¹		8²		3	15												16
			4	5	6	7		9		11						10¹	1			8	2	3	12												17
			4	5	6	7	12	9¹		11						13	1		14	8²	2	3				10³									18
	12		4	5¹	6	7		9		11						13	1		14	8²	2	3				10³									19
			4	5	6	7²	12	9		11						13	1		14	8¹	2	3³				10									20
		3	4	5		7	8	9²		11	12		14				1			13	2					10		8²							21
	12		4	5	6	7		9³		11²			14			13	1				2	3¹				10		8							22
			4	5	6	7	8³	9²		11	12						1		14	13	2	3				10¹									23
			4	5	6	7	8¹	9		11	12						1			13	2²	3				10									24
			4	5	6¹	7¹	12	9		11			14			13	1				2	3				10³		8							25
1			4	5	6¹	7	12	9		11						13					2	3				10¹		8²				14			26
1			4	5	6¹	7²	12	9		11						13					2	3				10²		8				14			27
1			4	5	6	7	12	9²		11						13					2	3				10³		8				14			28
1			4	5	6	7		9¹		11											2	3	12			10		8							29
1			4		6²	7		9		11	12					13			14		2³	3				10		5	8	10¹					30
1			4	5	6	7¹	12	9¹		11											2	3				10¹		8		13					31
			4	5	6	7	12	9									1				2	3				10¹		8		13	11²				32
			4	5	6	7		9		11							1				2	3				10		8							33
1			4	5	6	7	12	9¹		11											2	3				10		8							34
1			4		6¹	7³	12	9		11						10²					2	3						8		13		5		14	35
1		4		5	6	7¹	12	9													2²	3				10		8		13			11		36
1			4		6¹	7	12	9		11						10³					2	3						8²		13		14	11¹		37
1		3²	4	5	6	7³	12	9													2					10		8		13		14	11¹		38

Worthington Cup

Second Round	Northampton T	(h)	3-1
Third Round	Blackburn R	(a)	1-2

FA Cup

Third Round	Wimbledon	(a)	0-0
		(h)	2-0
Fourth Round	Manchester U	(h)	2-0
Fifth Round	Blackburn R	(h)	1-0
Sixth Round	Everton	(h)	3-0
Semi-Final	Arsenal		0-1
(at Old Trafford)			

MILLWALL
Division 1

FOUNDATION

Formed in 1885 as Millwall Rovers by employees of Morton & Co,
a jam and marmalade factory in West Ferry Road. The founders
were predominantly Scotsmen. Their first headquarters was The
Islanders pub in Tooke Street, Millwall. Their first trophy was the
East End Cup in 1887.

Millwall Football & Athletic Company (1985) plc,
The Den, Zampa Road, Bermondsey SE16 3LN.

Telephone: (020) 7232 1222. *Fax:* (020) 7231 3663.
Ticket Office: (020) 7231 9999. *ClubCall:* 09068 400 300.
Club Shop: (020) 7231 9845.

Ground Capacity: 20,146 (all-seater).

Record Attendance: 20,093 v Arsenal, FA Cup 3rd rd,
10 January 1994.

Record Receipts: undisclosed.

Pitch Measurements: 100m × 68m.

Chairman: Theo Paphitis. *Life President:* Reg Burr.
Directors: Peter Mead, Doug Woodward, David Sullivan.
Secretary: Yvonne Haines.

Manager: Mark McGhee. *Assistant Manager:* Steve Gritt.
Physio: Gerry Docherty.

Youth Development Officer & Senior Scout: Bob Pearson.
Assistant Youth Development Officer: Dave Mehmet.
Hon. Medical Officer: Dr. Des Thompson.

Stadium Manager: Colin Sayer.
Sales and Promotions Manager: Mark Cole.

Colours: Blue shirts, white shorts.

Change Colours: Silver shirts, black shorts.

Year Formed: 1885. *Turned Professional:* 1893. *Ltd Co.:* 1894.

Previous Names: 1885, Millwall Rovers; 1889, Millwall Athletic; 1985, Millwall Football & Athletic
Company.

Club Nickname: 'The Lions'.

Previous Grounds: 1885, Glengall Road, Millwall; 1886, Back of 'Lord Nelson'; 1890, East Ferry Road;
1901, North Greenwich; 1910, The Den, Cold Blow Lane; 1993, The Den, Bermondsey.

First Football League Game: 28 August 1920, Division 3, v Bristol R (h) W 2–0 – Lansdale; Fort,
Hodge; Voisey (1), Riddell, McAlpine; Waterall, Travers, Broad (1), Sutherland, Dempsey.

Record League Victory: 9–1 v Torquay U, Division 3 (S), 29 August 1927 – Lansdale, Tilling, Hill,
Amos, Bryant (3), Graham, Chance, Hawkins (3), Landells (1), Phillips (2), Black. 9–1 v Coventry C,
Division 3 (S), 19 November 1927 – Lansdale, Fort, Hill, Amos, Collins (1), Graham, Chance,
Landells (4), Cock (2), Phillips (2), Black.

HONOURS

Football League: Division 1 best
season: 3rd, 1993–94; Division 2 –
Champions 1987–88, 2000–01;
Division 3 (S) – Champions 1927–28,
1937–38; Runners-up 1952–53;
Division 3 – Runners–up 1965–66,
1984–85; Division 4 – Champions
1961–62; Runners-up 1964–65.

FA Cup: Semi-final 1900, 1903, 1937
(first Division 3 side to reach
semi-final).

Football League Cup: best season:
5th rd, 1974, 1977, 1995.

Football League Trophy: Winners
1983.

Auto Windscreens Shield: Runners-up
1999.

IT'S A FACT !

On 5 March 1900, Southern League Millwall won a
marathon third round FA Cup tie against Aston Villa,
the then Football League champions, winning 2-1 at
Reading after two drawn games.

Record Cup Victory: 7–0 v Gateshead, FA Cup 2nd rd,
12 December 1936 – Yuill; Ted Smith, Inns; Brolly,
Hancock, Forsyth; Thomas (1), Mangnall (1),
Ken Burditt (2), McCartney (2), Thorogood (1).

Record Defeat: 1–9 v Aston Villa, FA Cup 4th rd,
28 January 1946.

Most League Points (2 for a win): 65, Division 3 (S),
1927–28 and Division 3, 1965–66.

Most League Points (3 for a win): 93, Division 2, 2000–01.

Most League Goals: 127, Division 3 (S), 1927–28.

Highest League Scorer in Season: Richard Parker, 37,
Division 3 (S), 1926–27.

Most League Goals in Total Aggregate: Teddy
Sheringham, 93, 1984–91.

Most League Goals in One Match: 5, Richard Parker v
Norwich C, Division 3S, 28 August 1926.

Most Capped Player: Eamonn Dunphy, 22 (23), Republic
of Ireland.

Most League Appearances: Barry Kitchener, 523, 1967–82.

Youngest League Player: David Mehmet, 16 years 163 days
v Burnley, 14 May 1977.

Record Transfer Fee Received: £2,300,000 from Liverpool
for Mark Kennedy, March 1995.

Record Transfer Fee Paid: £800,000 to Derby Co for Paul
Goddard, December 1989.

Football League Record: 1920 Original Members of
Division 3; 1921 Division 3 (S); 1928–34 Division 2; 1934–38
Division 3 (S); 1938–48 Division 2; 1948–58 Division 3 (S);
1958–62 Division 4; 1962–64 Division 3; 1964–65 Division 4;
1965–66 Division 3; 1966–75 Division 2; 1975–76 Division 3;
1976–79 Division 2; 1979–85 Division 3; 1985–88 Division 2;
1988–90 Division 1; 1990–92 Division 2; 1992–96 Division 1;
1996–2001 Division 2; 2001– Division 1.

MANAGERS

F. B. Kidd 1894–99
  (Hon. Treasurer/Manager)
E. R. Stopher 1899–1900
  (Hon. Treasurer/Manager)
George Saunders 1900–11
  (Hon. Treasurer/Manager)
Herbert Lipsham 1911–19
Robert Hunter 1919–33
Bill McCracken 1933–36
Charlie Hewitt 1936–40
Bill Voisey 1940–44
Jack Cock 1944–48
Charlie Hewitt 1948–56
Ron Gray 1956–57
Jimmy Seed 1958–59
Reg Smith 1959–61
Ron Gray 1961–63
Billy Gray 1963–66
Benny Fenton 1966–74
Gordon Jago 1974–77
George Petchey 1978–80
Peter Anderson 1980–82
George Graham 1982–86
John Docherty 1986–90
Bob Pearson 1990
Bruce Rioch 1990–92
Mick McCarthy 1992–96
Jimmy Nicholl 1996–97
John Docherty 1997
Billy Bonds 1997–98
Keith Stevens May 1998–2000
  (then Joint Manager)
(plus Alan McLeary 1999–2000)
Mark McGhee September 2000–

LATEST SEQUENCES

Longest Sequence of League Wins: 10, 10.3.28 – 25.4.28.

Longest Sequence of League Defeats: 11, 10.4.29 – 16.9.29.

Longest Sequence of League Draws: 5, 22.12.73 – 12.1.74.

Longest Sequence of Unbeaten League Matches: 19, 22.8.59 – 31.10.59.

Longest Sequence Without a League Win: 20, 26.12.89 – 5.5.90.

TEN YEAR LEAGUE RECORD

		P	W	D	L	F	A	Pts	Pos
1991-92	Div 2	46	17	10	19	64	71	61	15
1992-93	Div 1	46	18	16	12	65	53	70	7
1993-94	Div 1	46	19	17	10	58	49	74	3
1994-95	Div 1	46	16	14	16	60	60	62	12
1995-96	Div 1	46	13	13	20	43	63	52	22
1996-97	Div 2	46	16	13	17	50	55	61	14
1997-98	Div 2	46	14	13	19	43	54	55	18
1998-99	Div 2	46	17	11	18	52	59	62	10
1999-2000	Div 2	46	23	13	10	76	50	82	5
2000-01	Div 2	46	28	9	9	89	38	93	1

DID YOU KNOW ?

Billy Keen scored all four
goals for Millwall in a 4-0 win
over Swansea Town in a third
round FA Cup tie on 18
February 1922.

MILLWALL 2001–02 LEAGUE RECORD

Match No.	Date	Venue	Opponents	Result	H/T Score	Lg. Pos.	Goalscorers	Attendance
1	Aug 11	H	Norwich C	W 4-0	2-0	—	Claridge [12], Reid [43], Cahill [66], Neill [90]	14,501
2	19	A	Birmingham C	L 0-4	0-4	12		19,091
3	25	H	Burnley	L 0-2	0-0	17		11,903
4	28	A	Crewe Alex	L 0-1	0-0	—		5913
5	Sept 8	A	Crystal Palace	W 3-1	1-1	13	Sadlier [45], Claridge 2 [50, 90]	21,641
6	15	A	Preston NE	L 0-1	0-1	16		11,371
7	18	H	Barnsley	W 3-1	0-1	—	Claridge 2 [59, 70], Cahill [80]	10,021
8	22	H	Sheffield U	W 2-0	1-0	14	Nethercott [16], Kinet [82]	12,276
9	25	A	Wimbledon	D 2-2	2-1	—	Cahill [43], Reid [45]	7020
10	29	A	Walsall	D 0-0	0-0	13		6289
11	Oct 11	A	WBA	W 2-0	2-0	—	Sadlier 2 [19, 27]	17,335
12	20	H	Nottingham F	D 3-3	1-0	13	Cahill [14], Ifill [86], Sadlier [90]	14,154
13	23	H	Bradford C	W 3-1	1-0	—	Sadlier [33], Cahill 2 [61, 86]	11,071
14	27	A	Stockport Co	W 4-0	3-0	8	Cahill [13], Reid [29], Claridge 2 (1 pen) [39, 47 (p)]	5371
15	31	A	Wolverhampton W	L 0-1	0-0	—		23,018
16	Nov 3	H	Coventry C	W 3-2	0-0	8	Claridge [55], Kinet [81], Sadlier [90]	15,748
17	9	H	Rotherham U	W 1-0	1-0	—	Cahill [23]	12,173
18	17	A	Grimsby T	D 2-2	0-0	6	Sadlier [76], Claridge [90]	5037
19	24	H	Gillingham	L 1-2	0-0	8	Cahill [69]	15,214
20	Dec 1	A	Bradford C	W 2-1	1-0	9	Claridge [41], Dyche [90]	14,148
21	4	H	Manchester C	L 2-3	1-1	—	Sadlier [45], Claridge (pen) [77]	13,026
22	8	A	Sheffield W	D 1-1	0-0	9	Sadlier [89]	21,304
23	13	H	Portsmouth	W 1-0	0-0	—	Sadlier [79]	11,527
24	22	A	Burnley	D 0-0	0-0	7		16,131
25	26	H	Crystal Palace	W 3-0	0-0	7	Claridge [51], Sadlier 2 [53, 56]	16,630
26	29	H	Crewe Alex	W 2-0	1-0	5	Cahill [28], Reid [78]	11,630
27	Jan 1	A	Watford	W 4-1	1-0	5	Cahill [32], Sadlier [59], Reid [69], Harris [90]	15,300
28	10	H	Birmingham C	D 1-1	0-1	—	Dyche [70]	11,856
29	15	H	Watford	W 1-0	1-0	—	Claridge (pen) [33]	12,531
30	20	A	Norwich C	D 0-0	0-0	3		18,969
31	30	A	Manchester C	L 0-2	0-0	—		30,238
32	Feb 2	H	Walsall	D 2-2	0-0	4	Sadlier [67], Harris (pen) [83]	11,285
33	9	A	Nottingham F	W 2-1	2-0	4	Ifill [7], Cahill [42]	18,511
34	19	H	WBA	W 1-0	1-0	—	Cahill [10]	13,716
35	23	H	Wimbledon	L 0-1	0-1	4		13,788
36	Mar 2	A	Barnsley	D 1-1	1-0	4	Kinet [37]	11,816
37	5	H	Preston NE	W 2-1	1-0	—	Claridge 2 [29, 65]	11,071
38	9	A	Portsmouth	L 0-3	0-2	5		15,221
39	16	H	Sheffield W	L 1-2	0-0	6	Dyche [82]	13,074
40	19	A	Sheffield U	L 2-3	1-0	—	Ifill [29], Nethercott [73]	16,037
41	24	A	Gillingham	L 0-1	0-0	6		8082
42	30	H	Stockport Co	W 3-0	1-0	5	Dublin [12], Nethercott [81], Ifill [87]	13,570
43	Apr 1	A	Rotherham U	D 0-0	0-0	5		6888
44	5	H	Wolverhampton W	W 1-0	0-0	—	Claridge (pen) [73]	17,058
45	12	A	Coventry C	W 1-0	1-0	—	Claridge [24]	15,335
46	21	H	Grimsby T	W 3-1	3-1	4	Dublin [6], Harris 2 [23, 31]	17,004

Final League Position: 4

GOALSCORERS

League (69): Claridge 17 (4 pens), Sadlier 14, Cahill 13, Reid 5, Harris 4 (1 pen), Ifill 4, Dyche 3, Kinet 3, Nethercott 3, Dublin 2, Neill 1.
Worthington Cup (3): Claridge 1 (pen), Moody 1, Sadlier 1.
FA Cup (2): Sadlier 2.

Warner T 46	Neill L 2+2	Ryan R 32+5	Cahill T 43	Nethercott S 46	Dyche S 35	Ifill P 27+13	Livermore D 43	Claridge S 39+2	Sadlier R 36+2	Reid S 33+2	Bircham M 22+2	Bull R 20+6	Lawrence M 24+2	Savarese G —+1	Stamp P —+1	Phillips M 1	Kinet C 11+6	Tuttle D 5	Moody P —+1	Harris N 9+12	Hearn C —+2	Ward D 10+4	Green R 12+1	Gueret W —+1	Odunsi L —+2	Naylor R 2+1	Braniff K —+1	McPhail S 3	Dunne A —+1	Dublin D 5	Sweeney P —+1	Match No.
1	2	3	4	5	6	7	8	9	10	11																						1
1	2	3	4[2]	5	6	7[1]	8	9	10	11[3]	13	14	12																			2
1	12	3[2]	4	5	6	7[1]	8	9	10	11	2	13																				3
1	12	3	4	5	6	11	8	9	10	7[1]	2																					4
1		3[1]	4	5	6	7	8	9	10	11[1]	2	12																				5
1		3[1]	4	5		7	8	9[1]	10	11	12		2[1]				13	6		14												6
1		3	4	5		7[1]	8	9	10[2]	11	12		2					6		13												7
1		3	4	5		7	8	9	10	11			2					6														8
1		3	4	5	12	7	8	9[2]	10	11[1]			2					6		13												9
1		3	4	5		7	8	9	10	11[1]	12		2					6														10
1			4	5	6	12	8	9	10	11	7[1]	3	2																			11
1			4	5	6	12	8	9	10	11	7[1]	3	2																			12
1			4	5	6	12	8	9	10	11	7	3	2																			13
1	12		4[3]	5	6	13	8	9	10	11[1]	7[2]	3	2	14																		14
1		3	4	5	6	7	8	9	10	11[1]	12		2																			15
1	13		4	5	6	7	8	9	10	11	12[2]	3[1]	2																			16
1[4]		3	4	5	6[2]	11	8	9	10	7[1]	12	13	2	15																		17
1		3	4	5	6	7	8	9	10	11			2																			18
1		3	4	5	6	7	8	9	10	11			2																			19
1		3	4	5	6		8	9	10	11	7		2																			20
1		3[1]	4	5	6	12	8	9	10	11	7		2																			21
1		3	4	5	6	12	8	9[1]	10	11	7[1]	13	2																			22
1		3	4	5	6	7[1]	8	9	10	11	12		2																			23
1		3	4	5	6	12	8	9	10	11[1]	7		2																			24
1		3	4	5	6	12	8	9[2]	10	13	7		2				11[1]															25
1		3	4	5	6		8	9	10	12	7		2				11															26
1		3	4	5	6		8	9	10	11	7		2				12															27
1		3		5	6		8	9		11	7[2]	4[1]	2	12						10	13											28
1				5	6			9[1]	10	11	4	3	2	12			7[3]			13	14											29
1		3[1]		5	6	12	8	9		11	7	4[1]	2							10	13											30
1	12		4	5	6	7[1]	8		10[3]	11		3	2[2]							13		14	9									31
1		3	4	5	6	12	8		10	11[2]	7		2							13			9[1]									32
1		3	4	5	6	7	8		10		12		2				11[1]			9												33
1		3	4	5	6	12	8		10	11		13	2				7[2]			9[1]												34
1		3	4	5	6	7	8[1]		10				2				11			9		12										35
1		3	4	5		7	8	9	10				2				11	6														36
1		3	4	5	12		8	9	10[2]		7[1]		2				11	6		13												37
1		3	4	5	6	7	8	9			12		2				11[1]			10[2]		13										38
1		3[1]	4	5	6	7[2]	8[3]	9		11	12		2							13		14	10									39
1			4	5	6	7	8	9			2	3					11			10[1]		12										40
1	12		4	5	6	7	8	9			2	3[1]					11			13			10[2]									41
1			4	5	6[2]	7	8	9[1]			12	3	2				11[3]			13		14								10		42
1			4	5		7	8	12	10[1]	11		3	2					6		9												43
1			4	5		7	8	9		11		3	2					6												10		44
1			4	5		7	8	9[1]		11	12	3	2					6												10		45
1	13		4	5		7	8	12[2]		11		3	2	14				6		9[2]										10[1]		46

Worthington Cup

First Round	Cardiff C	(h)	2-1
Second Round	Gillingham	(a)	1-2

FA Cup

Third Round	Scunthorpe U	(h)	2-1
Fourth Round	Blackburn R	(h)	0-1

NEWCASTLE UNITED FA Premiership

FOUNDATION

It stemmed from a newly formed club called Stanley in 1881.
In October 1882 they changed their name to Newcastle East End to
avoid confusion with two other local clubs, Stanley Nops and
Stanley Albion. Shortly afterwards another club Rosewood merged
with them. Newcastle West End had been formed in August 1882
and they played on a pitch which was part of the Town Moor.
Moved to Brandling Park 1885 and St James' Park 1886 (home of
Newcastle Rangers). West End went out of existence after a bad
run and the remaining committee men invited East End to move to
St James' Park. They accepted and, at a meeting in Bath Lane Hall
in 1892, changed their name to Newcastle United.

St James' Park, Newcastle-upon-Tyne NE1 4ST.

Telephone: (0191) 201 8400. *Fax:* (0191) 201 8600.
ClubCall: 09068 121 190. *Box Office:* (0191) 261 1571.
Mail Order: 0870 442 1892. *Club Shop:* (0191) 201 8426.
Football in the Community: (0191) 222 0134.
Travel Club: (0191) 201 8550.
Magpies Club: (0191) 201 8472.
Corporate Hospitality: (0191) 201 8704.
Conference and Banqueting: (0191) 201 8525.
Club United: (0191) 201 8581.
Press Office: (0191) 201 8420.
Commercial Department: (0191) 201 8421.
Lottery Office: (0191) 201 8502.
Photographic Dept: (0191) 201 8579.

Ground Capacity: 52,193.

Record Attendance: 68,386 v Chelsea, Division 1,
3 September 1930.

Record Receipts: £830,271 v Everton, FA Cup 6th rd,
7 March 1999.

Pitch Measurements: 105m × 68m.

HONOURS

FA Premier League: Runners-up
1995–96, 1996–97; *Football League:*
Division 1 – Champions 1904–05,
1906–07, 1908–09, 1926–27, 1992–93;
Division 2 – Champions 1964–65;
Runners-up 1897–98, 1947–48.
FA Cup: Winners 1910, 1924, 1932,
1951, 1952, 1955; Runners-up 1905,
1906, 1908, 1911, 1974, 1998, 1999.
Football League Cup: Runners-up 1976.
Texaco Cup: Winners 1974, 1975.
European Competitions: *European Cup:*
1997–98. *European Fairs Cup:* 1968–69
(winners), 1969–70, 1970–71. *UEFA Cup:*
1977–78, 1994–95, 1996–97, 1999–2000.
European Cup Winners' Cup: 1998–99.
Anglo-Italian Cup: Winners 1972–73.

President: Sir John Hall. *Patron:* T. Bennett. *Honorary
President:* B. Young.

Chairman: W. F. Shepherd. *Deputy Chairman:* D. S. Hall.
Directors: W. F. Shepherd, D. S. Hall, R. Jones, R. Cushing, K. Slater (Finance Director).

Manager: Sir Bobby Robson cbe. *Director of Football:* Gordon Milne. *Chief Scout:* Charlie Woods.
Coaches: John Carver, Tommy Craig, Simon Smith. *Academy Director:* Kenny Wharton.
Senior Physio: Derek Wright. *Physio:* Paul Ferris. *Fitness Coach:* Paul Winsper.

Chief Operating Officer: Russell Cushing. *Director of Commercial Affairs:* Trevor Garwood.
Safety Officer: Dave Pattison. *Team Administrator:* Tony Toward. *Assistant Secretary:* Lee Charnley.

Colours: Black and white striped shirts, black shorts, black stockings.

Change Colours: Dark marine and opal shirts, dark marine shorts, dark marine stockings.

Year Formed: 1881. *Turned Professional:* 1889. *Ltd Co.:* 1890.

Previous Names: 1881, Stanley; 1882, Newcastle East End; 1892, Newcastle United.

IT'S A FACT *!*

On 18 December 2001, Newcastle United's 3-1 win at
Arsenal lifted them to top place in the FA Premier
League and ended their four-year hoodoo of no wins in
the capital.

Club Nickname: 'The Magpies'.

Previous Grounds: 1881, South Byker; 1886, Chillingham Road, Heaton, 1892, St James' Park.

First Football League Game: 2 September 1893, Division 2, v Royal Arsenal (a) D 2–2 – Ramsay; Jeffery, Miller; Criely, Graham, McKane; Bowman, Crate (1), Thompson, Sorley (1), Wallace. Graham and not Crate scored according to some reports.

Record League Victory: 13–0 v Newport Co, Division 2, 5 October 1946 – Garbutt; Cowell, Graham; Harvey, Brennan, Wright; Milburn (2), Bentley (1), Wayman (4), Shackleton (6), Pearson.

Record Cup Victory: 9–0 v Southport (at Hillsborough), FA Cup 4th rd, 1 February 1932 – McInroy; Nelson, Fairhurst; McKenzie, Davidson, Weaver (1); Boyd (1), Jimmy Richardson (3), Cape (2), McMenemy (1), Lang (1).

Record Defeat: 0–9 v Burton Wanderers, Division 2, 15 April 1895.

Most League Points (2 for a win): 57, Division 2, 1964–65.

Most League Points (3 for a win): 96, Division 1, 1992–93.

Most League Goals: 98, Division 1, 1951–52.

Highest League Scorer in Season: Hughie Gallacher, 36, Division 1, 1926–27.

Most League Goals in Total Aggregate: Jackie Milburn, 177, 1946–57.

Most League Goals in One Match: 6, Len Shackleton v Newport Co, Division 2, 5 October 1946.

Most Capped Player: Alf McMichael, 40, Northern Ireland.

Most League Appearances: Jim Lawrence, 432, 1904–22.

Youngest League Player: Steve Watson, 16 years 223 days v Wolverhampton W, 10 November 1990.

Record Transfer Fee Received: £8,000,000 from Liverpool for Dieter Hamann, July 1999.

Record Transfer Fee Paid: £15,000,000 to Blackburn R for Alan Shearer, July 1996.

Football League Record: 1893 Elected to Division 2; 1898–1934 Division 1; 1934–48 Division 2; 1948–61 Division 1; 1961–65 Division 2; 1965–78 Division 1; 1978–84 Division 2; 1984–89 Division 1; 1989–92 Division 2; 1992–93 Division 1; 1993– FA Premier League.

MANAGERS

Frank Watt 1895–32
  (Secretary-Manager)
Andy Cunningham 1930–35
Tom Mather 1935–39
Stan Seymour 1939–47
  (Hon. Manager)
George Martin 1947–50
Stan Seymour 1950–54
  (Hon. Manager)
Duggie Livingstone 1954–56
Stan Seymour 1956–58
  (Hon. Manager)
Charlie Mitten 1958–61
Norman Smith 1961–62
Joe Harvey 1962–75
Gordon Lee 1975–77
Richard Dinnis 1977
Bill McGarry 1977–80
Arthur Cox 1980–84
Jack Charlton 1984
Willie McFaul 1985–88
Jim Smith 1988–91
Ossie Ardiles 1991–92
Kevin Keegan 1992–97
Kenny Dalglish 1997–98
Ruud Gullit 1998–99
Bobby Robson September 1999–

LATEST SEQUENCES

Longest Sequence of League Wins: 13, 25.4.92 – 18.10.92.
Longest Sequence of League Defeats: 10, 23.8.77 – 15.10.77.
Longest Sequence of League Draws: 4, 20.1.90 – 24.2.90.
Longest Sequence of Unbeaten League Matches: 14, 22.4.50 – 30.9.50.
Longest Sequence Without a League Win: 21, 14.1.78 – 23.8.78.

TEN YEAR LEAGUE RECORD

		P	W	D	L	F	A	Pts	Pos
1991-92	Div 2	46	13	13	20	66	84	52	20
1992-93	Div 1	46	29	9	8	92	38	96	1
1993-94	PR Lge	42	23	8	11	82	41	77	3
1994-95	PR Lge	42	20	12	10	67	47	72	6
1995-96	PR Lge	38	24	6	8	66	37	78	2
1996-97	PR Lge	38	19	11	8	73	40	68	2
1997-98	PR Lge	38	11	11	16	35	44	44	13
1998-99	PR Lge	38	11	13	14	48	54	46	13
1999-2000	PR Lge	38	14	10	14	63	54	52	11
2000-01	PR Lge	38	14	9	15	44	50	51	11

DID YOU KNOW ?

On 20 April 2002, Alan Shearer's goal for Newcastle United in the 3-0 win over Charlton Athletic was his 200th since the formation of the FA Premier League in 1992.

NEWCASTLE UNITED 2001–02 LEAGUE RECORD

Match No.	Date	Venue	Opponents	Result	H/T Score	Lg. Pos.	Goalscorers	Attendance
1	Aug 19	A	Chelsea	D	1-1	0-1	—	Acuna [77]	40,153
2	26	H	Sunderland	D	1-1	1-1	14	Bellamy [43]	52,021
3	Sept 8	A	Middlesbrough	W	4-1	1-1	7	Shearer 2 (1 pen) [34 (p), 76], Dabizas [59], Robert [62]	30,004
4	15	H	Manchester U	W	4-3	2-1	4	Robert [5], Lee [34], Dabizas [52], Brown (og) [82]	52,056
5	23	A	West Ham U	L	0-3	0-1	9		24,840
6	26	H	Leicester C	W	1-0	1-0	—	Solano [33]	49,185
7	30	H	Liverpool	L	0-2	0-1	8		52,095
8	Oct 13	A	Bolton W	W	4-0	1-0	5	Solano [41], Robert [62], Shearer [72], Bellamy [84]	25,631
9	21	H	Tottenham H	L	0-2	0-2	8		50,593
10	27	A	Everton	W	3-1	1-0	6	Bellamy [19], Solano [49], Acuna [86]	37,524
11	Nov 3	H	Aston Villa	W	3-0	1-0	4	Bellamy 2 [37, 82], Shearer [50]	51,057
12	17	A	Fulham	L	1-3	0-2	6	Speed [65]	21,159
13	24	H	Derby Co	W	1-0	1-0	4	Shearer (pen) [30]	50,070
14	Dec 1	A	Charlton Ath	D	1-1	0-0	4	Speed [73]	24,179
15	9	A	Ipswich T	W	1-0	1-0	4	Solano [20]	24,749
16	15	H	Blackburn R	W	2-1	0-1	3	Bernard [65], Speed [70]	50,064
17	18	A	Arsenal	W	3-1	0-1	—	O'Brien [60], Shearer (pen) [86], Robert [90]	38,012
18	22	A	Leeds U	W	4-3	1-1	1	Bellamy [38], Elliott [59], Shearer (pen) [71], Solano [90]	40,287
19	26	H	Middlesbrough	W	3-0	1-0	1	Shearer [29], Speed [58], Bernard [83]	52,127
20	29	H	Chelsea	L	1-2	1-2	2	Shearer [37]	52,123
21	Jan 2	A	Manchester U	L	1-3	0-1	—	Shearer [69]	67,646
22	12	H	Leeds U	W	3-1	1-1	2	Duberry (og) [44], Dyer [60], Bellamy [87]	52,130
23	19	A	Leicester C	D	0-0	0-0	2		21,354
24	30	H	Tottenham H	W	3-1	0-1	—	Acuna [67], Shearer [69], Bellamy [78]	36,005
25	Feb 2	H	Bolton W	W	3-2	2-2	2	Shearer 2 [23, 43], Bellamy [79]	52,094
26	9	H	Southampton	W	3-1	3-1	3	Robert [24], Shearer 2 (1 pen) [29, 45 (p)]	51,857
27	24	A	Sunderland	W	1-0	0-0	2	Dabizas [64]	47,204
28	Mar 2	H	Arsenal	L	0-2	0-2	4		52,087
29	6	A	Liverpool	L	0-3	0-1	—		44,204
30	16	H	Ipswich T	D	2-2	0-0	4	Robert [60], Shearer [88]	51,115
31	29	H	Everton	W	6-2	2-2	—	Shearer [13], Cort [15], O'Brien [59], Solano 2 [71, 73], Bernard [88]	51,921
32	Apr 2	A	Aston Villa	D	1-1	1-1	—	Shearer [3]	36,597
33	8	H	Fulham	D	1-1	1-0	—	Dyer [21]	50,017
34	13	A	Derby Co	W	3-2	0-0	4	Robert [73], Dyer [76], Lua-Lua [90]	31,031
35	20	H	Charlton Ath	W	3-0	1-0	4	Speed [22], Lua-Lua [46], Shearer [89]	51,360
36	23	A	Blackburn R	D	2-2	0-1	4	Shearer 2 [63, 71]	26,712
37	27	H	West Ham U	W	3-1	1-1	4	Shearer [41], Lua-Lua [53], Robert [66]	52,127
38	May 11	A	Southampton	L	1-3	0-2	4	Shearer [55]	31,973

Final League Position: 4

GOALSCORERS

League (74): Shearer 23 (5 pens), Bellamy 9, Robert 8, Solano 7, Speed 5, Acuna 3, Bernard 3, Dabizas 3, Dyer 3, Lua-Lua 3, O'Brien 2, Cort 1, Elliott 1, Lee 1, own goals 2.
Worthington Cup (9): Bellamy 4, Ameobi 2, Shearer 2, Robert 1.
FA Cup (8): Shearer 2 (1 pen), Acuna 1, Hughes 1, McClen 1, O'Brien 1, Robert 1, Solano 1.

Given S 38	Barton W 4+1	Elliott R 26+1	Dabizas N 33+2	Hughes A 34	Acuna C 10+6	Lee R 15+1	Bassedas C 1+1	Ameobi F 4+11	Bellamy C 26+1	Robert L 34+2	O'Brien A 31+3	Griffin A 3+1	Lua-Lua L 4+16	Solano N 37	Speed G 28+1	Shearer A 36+1	Distin S 20+8	Bernard O 4+12	Dyer K 15+3	McClen J 3	Jenas J 6+6	Cort C 6+2	Match No.
1	2	3	4	5	6¹	7	8²	9³	10	11	12	13	14										1
1	2	3¹	4	5	12	7		9¹	10	11	13			6	8¹	14							2
1	2³	3	4	5	8	7			12	10²	11	14		13	6	9¹							3
1	12	3	4		8	7¹			10²	11	5	2			6	9	13						4
1	2²	3	4		8	7			12	10	11	5			6¹	9	13						5
1		3	4		8	7			12	10	11	5	2		6	9¹							6
1		3	4		8²	7			12	10	11	5	2	6¹	13	9							7
1		3	4³	5		7		12	10²	11	13	2	14	6	8¹	9							8
1			4			7²	13	12	10	11	5	2¹	14	6¹	8	9	3						9
1		3	4			7			10	11	5	2	12	6¹	8	9							10
1		3	4			7			10	11	5	2		6	8	9	12						11
1		3	4³			7¹		12	10	11	5	2	13	6²	8	9		14					12
1		3	4			7			10	11¹	5	2	12	6	8	9							13
1		3	4			7		12	10¹	11²	5	2	13	6	8	9							14
1		3	4			7			10	11¹	5	2		6²	8	9	12	13					15
1		3				7²		12	10¹		5	2		6	8	9	4	11	13				16
1		3¹	4					12	10	11	5	2		6²	8	9	13	14	7³				17
1		3	4²						10¹	11³	5	2	12	6	8	9	13	14	7				18
1		3						12	10	11³	5	2	13	6¹	8	9	4	14	7²				19
1		3²						12	10	11	5	2		6¹	8	9	4	13	7				20
1		3	4			7		12	10¹	11		2		6²	8	9	5	13					21
1		3	4						10	11	5¹	2		6	8	9	12		7				22
1		3	4						10	11		2		6	8	9	5		7				23
1		3¹	4		8			12	10		5	2				9	6	11	7				24
1			4					12	10	11	5	2		6	8	9	3		7¹				25
1	12		4						10	11	5	2		6	8	9	3¹		7²		13		26
1			4					12	10	11¹	5	2		6	8	9	3		7				27
1			4					12	10¹	11	5	2⁵		6	8	9	3		7		13		28
1			4					12		11	5	2		6	8¹	9	3	13	7			10²	29
1			4		8			12		11	5	2	13	6²		9	3	14	7³			10¹	30
1			4					12		11¹	5	2	13	6	8	9	3	14	7¹			10²	31
1			4					12		11²	5	2		6	8	9	3	13	7			10¹	32
1		3						12		11	5¹	2		6	8	9	4		7		13	10²	33
1			4					12		11	5²	2		6	8	9³	3	13	7		14	10¹	34
1		3						12	10	11¹	5¹	2		6³	8	9	4	13	7			14	35
1		3²	4					12	10¹	11	5	2		6	8	9		13	7				36
1			4						10³	11	5¹	2		6	8	9	12	3	7²		13	14	37
1			4						10	11	5	2		6	8	9	3		7¹		12		38

Worthington Cup

Second Round	Brentford	(h)	4-1
Third Round	Barnsley	(a)	1-0
Fourth Round	Ipswich T	(h)	4-1
Fifth Round	Chelsea	(a)	0-1

FA Cup

Third Round	Crystal Palace	(h)	2-0
Fourth Round	Peterborough U	(a)	4-2
Fifth Round	Manchester C	(h)	1-0
Sixth Round	Arsenal	(h)	1-1
		(a)	0-3

NORTHAMPTON TOWN   Division 2

FOUNDATION

Formed in 1897 by school teachers connected with the
Northampton and District Elementary Schools' Association, they
survived a financial crisis at the end of their first year when they
were £675 in the red and became members of the Midland League
– a fast move indeed for a new club. They achieved Southern
League membership in 1901.

Sixfields Stadium, Upton Way, Northampton NN5 5QA.

Telephone: (01604) 757 773. *Fax:* (01604) 751 613.
Website: www.ntfc.co.uk
Email: via website.
Ticket Office: (01604) 588 338.

Ground Capacity: 7,653 (all seated).

Record Attendance: (at County Ground): 24,523 v
Fulham, Division 1, 23 April 1966; (at Sixfields Stadium):
7,557 v Manchester C, Division 2, 26 September 1998.

Record Receipts (at Sixfields): £102,979 v Tottenham H,
Worthington Cup 3rd rd, 27 October 1998.

Pitch Measurements: 116yd × 72yd.

Chairman: B. J. Stonhill. *Directors:* B. Hancock,
C. Smith, T. Clarke MP, P. Randall.

HONOURS

Football League: Division 1 best
season: 21st, 1965–66; Division 2 –
Runners-up 1964–65; Division 3 –
Champions 1962–63; Promoted from
Division 3 1996–97 (play-offs);
Division 3 (S) – Runners-up 1927–28,
1949–50; Division 4 – Champions
1986–87; Runners-up 1975–76.
FA Cup: best season: 5th rd, 1934,
1950, 1970.
Football League Cup: best season:
5th rd, 1965, 1967.

Secretary: Norman Howells. *Company Secretary:* B. J. Stonhill.

Manager: Kevan Broadhurst. *Assistant Manager:* Martin Wilkinson.

Coach: Mark Kearney.

Physio: Denis Casey.

Sales Manager: Paul Martin.

Stadium Manager: Tom Holland.

Colours: Claret shirts with thin white piping, white shorts, claret stockings.

Change Colours: All white.

Year Formed: 1897.

Turned Professional: 1901.

Ltd Co.: 1901.

Previous Ground: 1897, County Ground; 1994, Sixfields Stadium.

Club Nickname: 'The Cobblers'.

First Football League Game: 28 August 1920, Division 3, v Grimsby T (a) L 0–2 – Thorpe; Sproston,
Hewison; Jobey, Tomkins, Pease; Whitworth, Lockett, Thomas, Freeman, MacKechnie.

Record League Victory: 10–0 v Walsall, Division 3 (S), 5 November 1927 – Hammond; Watson, Jeffs;
Allen, Brett, Odell; Daley, Smith (3), Loasby (3), Hoten (1), Wells (3).

IT'S A FACT !

Eric Tomkins captained the first England schoolboy
team against Scotland. Later in 1911–12 he was at left-
half, promoted to the Northampton Town first team
from the reserves and played 79 consecutive matches.

Record Cup Victory: 10–0 v Sutton T, FA Cup prel rd, 7 December 1907 – Cooch; Drennan, Lloyd Davies, Tirrell (1), McCartney, Hickleton, Badenock (3), Platt (3), Lowe (1), Chapman (2), McDiarmid.

Record Defeat: 0–11 v Southampton, Southern League, 28 December 1901.

Most League Points (2 for a win): 68, Division 4, 1975–76.

Most League Points (3 for a win): 99, Division 4, 1986–87.

Most League Goals: 109, Division 3, 1962–63 and Division 3 (S), 1952–53.

Highest League Scorer in Season: Cliff Holton, 36, Division 3, 1961–62.

Most League Goals in Total Aggregate: Jack English, 135, 1947–60.

Most League Goals in One Match: 5, Ralph Hoten v Crystal Palace, Division 3S, 27 October 1928.

Most Capped Player: E. Lloyd Davies, 12 (16), Wales.

Most League Appearances: Tommy Fowler, 521, 1946–61.

Youngest League Player: Adrian Mann, 16 years 297 days v Bury, 5 May 1984.

Record Transfer Fee Received: £265,000 from Watford for Richard Hill, July 1987.

Record Transfer Fee Paid: £150,000 to FC Utrecht for Jamie Forrester, July 2000.

Football League Record: 1920 Original Member of Division 3; 1921 Division 3 (S); 1958–61 Division 4; 1961–63 Division 3; 1963–65 Division 2; 1965–66 Division 1; 1966–67 Division 2; 1967–69 Division 3; 1969–76 Division 4; 1976–77 Division 3; 1977–87 Division 4; 1987–90 Division 3; 1990–92 Division 4; 1992–97 Division 3; 1997–99 Division 2; 1999–2000 Division 3; 2000– Division 2.

LATEST SEQUENCES

Longest Sequence of League Wins: 8, 27.8.60 – 19.9.60.

Longest Sequence of League Defeats: 8, 26.10.35 – 21.12.35.

Longest Sequence of League Draws: 6, 18.9.83 – 15.10.83.

Longest Sequence of Unbeaten League Matches: 21, 27.9.86 – 6.2.87.

Longest Sequence Without a League Win: 18, 26.3.69 – 20.9.69.

MANAGERS

Arthur Jones 1897–1907
  (Secretary-Manager)
Herbert Chapman 1907–12
Walter Bull 1912–13
Fred Lessons 1913–19
Bob Hewison 1920–25
Jack Tresadern 1925–30
Jack English 1931–35
Syd Puddefoot 1935–37
Warney Cresswell 1937–39
Tom Smith 1939–49
Bob Dennison 1949–54
Dave Smith 1954–59
David Bowen 1959–67
Tony Marchi 1967–68
Ron Flowers 1968–69
Dave Bowen 1969–72
  (continued as General Manager
  and Secretary to 1985 when
  joined the board)
Billy Baxter 1972–73
Bill Dodgin Jnr 1973–76
Pat Crerand 1976–77
Bill Dodgin Jnr 1977
John Petts 1977–78
Mike Keen 1978–79
Clive Walker 1979–80
Bill Dodgin Jnr 1980–82
Clive Walker 1982–84
Tony Barton 1984–85
Graham Carr 1985–90
Theo Foley 1990–92
Phil Chard 1992–93
John Barnwell 1993–95
Ian Atkins 1995–99
Kevin Wilson 1999–2001
Kevan Broadhurst October 2001–

TEN YEAR LEAGUE RECORD

		P	W	D	L	F	A	Pts	Pos
1991-92	Div 4	42	11	13	18	46	57	46	16
1992-93	Div 3	42	11	8	23	48	74	41	20
1993-94	Div 3	42	9	11	22	44	66	38	22
1994-95	Div 3	42	10	14	18	45	67	44	17
1995-96	Div 3	46	18	13	15	51	44	67	11
1996-97	Div 3	46	20	12	14	67	44	72	4
1997-98	Div 2	46	18	17	11	52	37	71	4
1998-99	Div 2	46	10	18	18	43	57	48	22
1999-2000	Div 3	46	25	7	14	63	45	82	3
2000-01	Div 2	46	15	12	19	46	59	57	18

DID YOU KNOW ❓

Jack Jennings, who arrived at Northampton Town during the war, later became trainer, player-coach and caretaker manager with the club, as well as coach to the British Olympic team, England Amateurs and masseur to the Indian Cricket touring team in 1946.

NORTHAMPTON TOWN 2001–02 LEAGUE RECORD

Match No.	Date	Venue	Opponents	Result	H/T Score	Lg. Pos.	Goalscorers	Attendance
1	Aug 11	H	Bristol C	L 0-3	0-3	—		5528
2	18	A	Stoke C	L 0-2	0-0	24		12,845
3	25	H	Notts Co	L 0-2	0-1	24		4648
4	28	A	Oldham Ath	L 2-4	0-2	—	Hope 2 [53, 90]	4941
5	31	H	Brighton & HA	W 2-0	0-0	—	Gabbiadini [74], Asamoah [90]	5408
6	Sept 8	A	Colchester U	L 1-3	0-3	23	Hargreaves [78]	3705
7	15	H	Chesterfield	L 0-2	0-1	24		4535
8	18	A	Cardiff C	L 0-2	0-1	—		11,232
9	22	A	Port Vale	W 1-0	0-0	23	Hunter [73]	4419
10	25	H	Blackpool	L 1-3	0-2	—	Burgess [83]	5103
11	29	H	Swindon T	D 1-1	0-0	22	Hunter [66]	5104
12	Oct 7	A	Peterborough U	L 0-2	0-1	22		8101
13	13	H	Tranmere R	W 4-1	2-1	21	Forrester 2 [9, 72], Hope [45], McGregor [48]	4636
14	20	A	QPR	W 1-0	1-0	21	Hunt [11]	10,444
15	23	H	Huddersfield T	L 0-3	0-2	—		5926
16	27	A	Cambridge U	D 3-3	1-3	21	Gabbiadini [38], Forrester 2 (2 pens) [71, 87]	3682
17	Nov 3	H	Reading	L 0-2	0-0	22		5162
18	11	A	Bury	L 1-2	1-0	23	Hope [11]	3539
19	20	A	Wycombe W	L 1-2	1-1	—	Gabbiadini [39]	5817
20	24	H	Wigan Ath	L 0-2	0-1	24		4267
21	Dec 1	A	Wrexham	L 2-3	1-1	24	Forrester [14], McGregor [51]	2708
22	15	H	Bournemouth	W 1-0	0-0	23	Forrester [81]	3909
23	21	A	Brentford	L 0-3	0-0	—		5142
24	26	H	Colchester U	L 2-3	1-1	24	Hope [36], Forrester [80]	4740
25	29	A	Oldham Ath	L 0-1	0-0	24		4760
26	Jan 13	H	Stoke C	D 1-1	0-1	24	Parkin [82]	5636
27	19	A	Bristol C	W 3-1	2-0	23	Forrester 2 (1 pen) [36 (p), 37], Hunt [69]	11,733
28	22	H	Brentford	W 1-0	0-0	—	Asamoah [86]	4184
29	29	A	Notts Co	W 3-0	1-0	—	Gabbiadini [12], Forrester 2 (2 pens) [64, 69]	4182
30	Feb 2	H	Swindon T	L 1-2	0-1	22	Forrester [81]	6585
31	9	H	QPR	D 2-2	0-2	22	Asamoah [78], Parkin [88]	6424
32	12	A	Tranmere R	L 0-2	0-0	—		7739
33	19	A	Peterborough U	W 2-1	2-1	—	Parkin [17], Forrester [38]	6064
34	23	A	Chesterfield	D 2-2	2-1	21	Hope [3], Forrester [22]	4186
35	26	H	Port Vale	W 1-0	1-0	—	Forrester [19]	5155
36	Mar 2	H	Cardiff C	L 1-2	1-2	20	Gabbiadini [35]	5495
37	5	A	Blackpool	W 2-1	1-0	—	Gabbiadini 2 [8, 54]	4924
38	9	A	Bournemouth	L 1-5	1-1	21	McGregor [46]	6322
39	12	A	Brighton & HA	L 0-2	0-1	—		6363
40	16	H	Wrexham	W 4-1	1-1	19	Hunt [42], Hunter 2 (2 pens) [77, 90], Parkin [82]	5029
41	23	A	Huddersfield T	L 0-2	0-2	20		10,783
42	29	H	Bury	W 1-0	0-0	—	Hunt [58]	6522
43	Apr 1	A	Reading	D 0-0	0-0	19		16,495
44	6	A	Wycombe W	W 4-1	0-1	19	Hargreaves 2 [52, 65], Forrester [77], Carruthers [84]	5851
45	13	A	Wigan Ath	L 0-3	0-2	19		5938
46	20	H	Cambridge U	D 2-2	1-1	20	Forrester (pen) [23], Hodge [90]	6723

Final League Position: 20

GOALSCORERS

League (54): Forrester 17 (6 pens), Gabbiadini 7, Hope 6, Hunt 4, Hunter 4 (2 pens), Parkin 4, Asamoah 3, Hargreaves 3, McGregor 3, Burgess 1, Carruthers 1, Hodge 1.
Worthington Cup (3): Forrester 1, McGregor 1, Parkin 1.
FA Cup (2): Gabbiadini 2.

Welch K 38	Lavin G 2	Spedding D 22 + 1	Frain J 25 + 2	Burgess D 36	Hope R 35 + 8	Hunt J 38	Parkin S 31 + 9	Forrester J 40 + 3	Gabbiadini M 30 + 5	Hargreaves C 38 + 1	Evatt I 10 + 1	Asamoah D 3 + 37	McGregor P 37 + 2	Wolleaston R 2 + 5	Sollitt A 8 + 2	Dempsey P 13 + 7	Hodge J 4 + 15	Hunter R 38 + 2	Cavill A — + 1	Marsh C 26	Carruthers C 6 + 7	Sampson I 24 + 3	Morison S — + 1	Match No.
1	2	3¹	4	5	6	7	8²	9	10	11	12	13												1
1	2	3	4		6	7	8¹	9	10²	11³	5	12	13	14										2
		3	4		6		8²	9	10³	11	5	9	7¹	12	1	2		13	14					3
		3	4		6			9	10	11	5	8		1	2			7¹	12					4
		4	3	6		12		9¹	10¹	11	5	14	8²	13	1	2		7						5
		4³		6	7¹			9	10²	11	5	13	8	12	1			3		2	14			6
	6		4	7	9	12	10		5³	13	8¹	11²	1	14		3		2						7
1	6		4	7	10	9			12	8	11¹		5			3		2³	13					8
1	3		6	4	7	10¹	9²	12	11³	5	13		2			8			14					9
1	3		6	4	7³		9	10²		5	12	11¹		2	13	8			14					10
1	3		6	4	7	12	9		5²	11¹	13		2	14	8			10³						11
1	11	10¹	4	6	7	14	9		12	5³		8²	2	13	3									12
1	6	12	2	5	7¹	10	9²		11	13	8		14	3				4³						13
1		4	5	6	7	8		10¹	11	12	9		13			2	3²							14
1		4	5	6	7	8¹	12	10²	11		13	9		3³		2	14							15
1		4	5	6	7	12	9	10¹	11		8		2			3								16
1	3	4	5	6	7		9	12	11		10²			13	2¹		8							17
1	3	2	5	6	7	12		10¹	11		13	9²		8			4							18
1	3	2	5	6	7	12	9¹	10²	11		13			8			4							19
1	3	2	5	6	7³	12	9	10	11		13	8²		14	4									20
1⁸	3	4	5	6	7	12	9¹	10			13	11²	15		8	2								21
1		2	5	6		8¹	9²	12		13	11		14	7³	3			10	4					22
1		6	2		4		8	9	10	11	12		5	7¹	3									23
		3²	2	5	6³		8	9		11	12	10¹	1	14	13	7						4		24
1		3	5			8¹	9	10	11		12	7²	15	2⁹	13	6						4		25
			5		6	8	9	10	11		12	7¹	1	2¹	13	3						4		26
			5		6	8	9	10	11		7		1		3			2	4					27
1	2		5	13	6	8	9²	10	11		12	7¹			3				4					28
1		5	12	6	8	9	10	11¹		13	7³	14		3	2			4						29
1		5	6	8	9	10²		12	7	2¹	13	11	3			4								30
1		5	6	8	9	11		12	10¹	14	7²	3	2	13³		4								31
1		5	6	7	8	9²		11	12	10¹		13	3	2		4								32
1		5	12	6	8	9²	10³	11	13	7¹	14	3	2			4								33
1		5	6	3	8	9¹	10	11	12	7		2	4											34
1	12	5	4	6	8	9²	10¹	11	13	7³	14	3	2											35
1	3	5	4	6	9	10³	11	12	7¹	13	8	2²	14											36
1	3	12	5	4	6	9¹	10²	11	13	7¹	8	2	14											37
1	3	5	4	6	12	9	10³	11	13	7¹	8	2	14											38
1	6	5	12	10	8²	9³	13	11	14	7	3	2¹	4											39
1	6³	5	12	10	8	9²	11	13	7¹	14	3	2	4											40
1	6	5	12	10	8	9²	13	11	14	7³	3	2¹	4											41
1	6	5	12	7	8	9	11	13	10¹	3	2	4												42
1	7	5	6	8	10²	12	11	13	9¹	3	2	4												43
1	6³	5	12	7	8	9	10¹	11	13	3	2	14	4⁸											44
1	6	7	8¹	9	10	11	12	5	2	3	4													45
1	6	7	8²	9⁵	11	10	12	5	2	3	4	13												46

Worthington Cup
First Round   QPR   (h) 2-1
Second Round Middlesbrough (a) 1-3

FA Cup
First Round   Torquay U   (a) 2-1
Second Round Canvey Island (a) 0-1

NORWICH CITY   Division 1

FOUNDATION

Formed in 1902, largely through the initiative of two local schoolmasters who called a meeting at the Criterion Cafe, they were shocked by an FA Commission which in 1904 declared the club professional and ejected them from the FA Amateur Cup. However, this only served to strengthen their determination. New officials were appointed and a professional club established at a meeting in the Agricultural Hall in March 1905.

Carrow Road, Norwich NR1 1JE.

Telephone: (01603) 760 760. *Fax:* (01603) 613 886.
Box Office: 0870 444 1902. *ClubCall:* 09068 121 144.

Ground Capacity: 21,468.

Record Attendance: 43,984 v Leicester C, FA Cup 6th rd, 30 March 1963.

Record Receipts: £339,005 v Chelsea, FA Cup 3rd rd, 5 January 2002.

Pitch Measurements: 114yd × 74yd.

President: G. C. Watling. *Chairman:* Bob Cooper.
Deputy Chairman: B. J. Skipper.
Company Secretary: N. A. Doncaster.
Directors: M. M. Foulger, M. Wynn Jones, D. Smith, R. J. Munby, R. Stuart.

HONOURS

FA Premier League: best season: 3rd 1992–93.

Football League: Division 2 – Champions 1971–72, 1985–86; Division 3 (S) – Champions 1933–34; Division 3 – Runners-up 1959–60.

FA Cup: Semi-finals 1959, 1989, 1992.

Football League Cup: Winners 1962, 1985; Runners-up 1973, 1975.

European Competitions: UEFA Cup: 1993–94.

First Team Manager: Nigel Worthington. *Assistant Manager:* Doug Livermore.

First Team Coach: Steve Foley. *Director of Academy:* Sammy Morgan.

Coach: Keith Webb.

Physio: Neil Reynolds, MCSP, SRP.

Club Secretary: Kevan Platt.

Colours: Yellow shirts, green shorts, yellow stockings.

Change Colours: All red.

Year Formed: 1902.

Turned Professional: 1905.

Ltd Co.: 1905.

Club Nickname: 'The Canaries'.

Previous Grounds: 1902, Newmarket Road; 1908, The Nest, Rosary Road; 1935, Carrow Road.

First Football League Game: 28 August 1920, Division 3, v Plymouth Arg (a) D 1–1 – Skermer; Gray, Gadsden; Wilkinson, Addy, Martin; Laxton, Kidger, Parker, Whitham (1), Dobson.

Record League Victory: 10–2 v Coventry C, Division 3 (S), 15 March 1930 – Jarvie; Hannah, Graham; Brown, O'Brien, Lochhead (1); Porter (1), Anderson, Hunt (5), Scott (2), Slicer (1).

IT'S A FACT !

The first League match staged at Carrow Road on 31 August 1935 saw Norwich City defeat West Ham United 4-3, with Doug Lochhead scoring the Canaries' first goal.

Record Cup Victory: 8–0 v Sutton U, FA Cup 4th rd, 28 January 1989 – Gunn; Culverhouse, Bowen, Butterworth, Linighan, Townsend (Crook), Gordon, Fleck (3), Allen (4), Phelan, Putney (1).

Record Defeat: 2–10 v Swindon T, Southern League, 5 September 1908.

Most League Points (2 for a win): 64, Division 3 (S), 1950–51.

Most League Points (3 for a win): 84, Division 2, 1985–86.

Most League Goals: 99, Division 3 (S), 1952–53.

Highest League Scorer in Season: Ralph Hunt, 31, Division 3 (S), 1955–56.

Most League Goals in Total Aggregate: Johnny Gavin, 122, 1945–54, 1955–58.

Most League Goals in One Match: 5, Tommy Hunt v Coventry C, Division 3S, 15 March 1930; 5, Roy Hollis v Walsall, Division 3S, 29 December 1951.

Most Capped Player: Mark Bowen, 35 (41), Wales.

Most League Appearances: Ron Ashman, 592, 1947–64.

Youngest League Player: Ian Davies, 17 years 29 days v Birmingham C, 27 April 1974.

Record Transfer Fee Received: £5,000,000 from Blackburn R for Chris Sutton, July 1994.

Record Transfer Fee Paid: £1,000,000 to Leeds U for Jon Newsome, June 1994.

Football League Record: 1920 Original Member of Division 3; 1921 Division 3 (S): 1934–39 Division 2; 1946–58 Division 3 (S); 1958–60 Division 3; 1960–72 Division 2; 1972–74 Division 1; 1974–75 Division 2; 1975–81 Division 1; 1981–82 Division 2; 1982–85 Division 1; 1985–86 Division 2; 1986–92 Division 1; 1992–95 FA Premier League; 1995– Division 1.

MANAGERS

John Bowman 1905–07
James McEwen 1907–08
Arthur Turner 1909–10
Bert Stansfield 1910–15
Major Frank Buckley 1919–20
Charles O'Hagan 1920–21
Albert Gosnell 1921–26
Bert Stansfield 1926
Cecil Potter 1926–29
James Kerr 1929–33
Tom Parker 1933–37
Bob Young 1937–39
Jimmy Jewell 1939
Bob Young 1939–45
Cyril Spiers 1946–47
Duggie Lochhead 1947–50
Norman Low 1950–55
Tom Parker 1955–57
Archie Macaulay 1957–61
Willie Reid 1961–62
George Swindin 1962
Ron Ashman 1962–66
Lol Morgan 1966–69
Ron Saunders 1969–73
John Bond 1973–80
Ken Brown 1980–87
Dave Stringer 1987–92
Mike Walker 1992–94
John Deehan 1994–95
Martin O'Neill 1995
Gary Megson 1995–96
Mike Walker 1996–98
Bruce Rioch 1998–2000
Bryan Hamilton 2000
Nigel Worthington January 2001–

LATEST SEQUENCES

Longest Sequence of League Wins: 10, 23.11.85 – 25.1.86.

Longest Sequence of League Defeats: 7, 1.4.95 – 6.5.95.

Longest Sequence of League Draws: 7, 15.1.94 – 26.2.94.

Longest Sequence of Unbeaten League Matches: 20, 31.8.50 – 30.12.50.

Longest Sequence Without a League Win: 25, 22.9.56 – 23.2.57.

TEN YEAR LEAGUE RECORD

		P	W	D	L	F	A	Pts	Pos
1991-92	Div 1	42	11	12	19	47	63	45	18
1992-93	PR Lge	42	21	9	12	61	65	72	3
1993-94	PR Lge	42	12	17	13	65	61	53	12
1994-95	PR Lge	42	10	13	19	37	54	43	20
1995-96	Div 1	46	14	15	17	59	55	57	16
1996-97	Div 1	46	17	12	17	63	68	63	13
1997-98	Div 1	46	14	13	19	52	69	55	15
1998-99	Div 1	46	15	17	14	62	61	62	9
1999-2000	Div 1	46	14	15	17	45	50	57	12
2000-01	Div 1	46	14	12	20	46	58	54	15

DID YOU KNOW ?

Marc Libbra (squad number 19) took 19 seconds to score on his debut as substitute for Norwich City against Manchester City on 18 August 2001 and had a t-shirt suitably inscribed.

NORWICH CITY 2001–02 LEAGUE RECORD

Match No.	Date	Venue	Opponents	Result	H/T Score	Lg. Pos.	Goalscorers	Attendance
1	Aug 11	A	Millwall	L	0-4	0-2	—		14,501
2	18	H	Manchester C	W	2-0	0-0	15	Libbra [75], McVeigh [90]	18,745
3	25	A	Wimbledon	W	1-0	0-0	9	Libbra [89]	6084
4	27	H	Sheffield W	W	2-0	1-0	5	Roberts I [37], McVeigh [74]	16,820
5	Sept 8	H	Nottingham F	W	1-0	1-0	4	Abbey [14]	18,061
6	15	A	Rotherham U	D	1-1	0-0	5	Scott (og) [51]	6099
7	18	H	Watford	W	3-1	2-1	—	Roberts I [20], Nedergaard [25], MacKay [68]	17,885
8	22	H	Burnley	W	2-1	1-0	2	Holt [4], Roberts I [55]	19,849
9	26	A	Preston NE	L	0-4	0-4	—		12,014
10	29	A	Sheffield U	L	1-2	0-2	4	Nedergaard [83]	15,523
11	Oct 9	A	Walsall	L	0-2	0-1	—		5713
12	13	A	Gillingham	W	2-0	0-0	3	Roberts I 2 [81, 90]	9166
13	19	H	WBA	W	2-0	2-0	—	Roberts I [13], Rivers [16]	20,465
14	23	H	Portsmouth	D	0-0	0-0	—		19,962
15	28	A	Crystal Palace	L	2-3	0-1	5	Libbra [70], Roberts I (pen) [86]	19,553
16	30	A	Grimsby T	W	2-0	1-0	—	Mulryne 2 [19, 58]	5489
17	Nov 3	H	Wolverhampton W	W	2-0	2-0	2	Roberts I [7], McVeigh [33]	20,335
18	10	H	Bradford C	L	1-4	0-2	3	McVeigh [67]	17,414
19	15	A	Stockport Co	L	1-2	0-1	—	Mulryne [85]	6551
20	20	H	Crewe Alex	D	2-2	1-1	—	Libbra 2 [14, 50]	15,710
21	24	H	Barnsley	W	2-1	1-0	3	Roberts I [30], Mulryne [82]	17,333
22	Dec 2	A	Portsmouth	W	2-1	1-1	3	Roberts I [17], Tiler (og) [85]	13,286
23	8	A	Birmingham C	L	0-4	0-2	4		17,310
24	15	H	Coventry C	W	2-0	1-0	5	Rivers [12], Nielsen [88]	17,889
25	22	H	Wimbledon	W	2-1	1-0	4	Nielsen [17], Roberts I (pen) [59]	17,286
26	26	A	Nottingham F	L	0-2	0-2	4		23,003
27	29	A	Sheffield W	W	5-0	4-0	4	Kenton [5], Nielsen 2 [17, 27], McVeigh [38], Holt [76]	19,205
28	Jan 1	H	Walsall	D	1-1	1-0	4	Nielsen [13]	19,434
29	13	A	Manchester C	L	1-3	0-1	5	Nielsen [47]	31,794
30	20	H	Millwall	D	0-0	0-0	7		18,969
31	29	A	Crewe Alex	L	0-1	0-0	—		6285
32	Feb 3	H	Sheffield U	W	2-1	0-0	6	Kenton 2 [72, 74]	17,348
33	10	A	WBA	L	0-1	0-1	8		19,115
34	22	H	Preston NE	W	3-0	3-0	—	Roberts I [62], Alexander (og) [81], Mulryne [88]	19,506
35	26	A	Watford	L	1-2	0-2	—	Roberts I [66]	12,622
36	Mar 2	A	Burnley	D	1-1	0-1	8	Libbra [55]	14,679
37	5	H	Rotherham U	D	0-0	0-0	—		18,485
38	9	A	Coventry C	L	1-2	1-0	9	Libbra [45]	16,744
39	15	H	Birmingham C	L	0-1	0-1	—		18,258
40	19	H	Gillingham	W	2-1	0-1	—	Easton [55], Kenton [65]	16,479
41	23	A	Wolverhampton W	D	0-0	0-0	9		26,280
42	30	H	Crystal Palace	W	2-1	2-0	9	Nielsen [42], McVeigh [45]	21,251
43	Apr 1	A	Bradford C	W	1-0	0-0	7	McVeigh [86]	14,143
44	6	H	Grimsby T	D	1-1	1-0	8	MacKay [4]	20,075
45	13	A	Barnsley	W	2-0	1-0	7	Nielsen [41], McVeigh [51]	18,803
46	21	H	Stockport Co	W	2-0	1-0	6	Mulryne [45], MacKay [75]	20,897

Final League Position: 6

GOALSCORERS

League (60): Roberts I 13 (2 pens), McVeigh 8, Nielsen 8, Libbra 7, Mulryne 6, Kenton 4, MacKay 3, Holt 2, Nedergaard 2, Rivers 2, Abbey 1, Easton 1, own goals 3.
Worthington Cup (0).
FA Cup (0).

Green R 41	Kenton D 30+3	Drury A 35	Mackay M 44	Fleming C 46	Holt G 46	Mulryne P 29+1	Emblen M 1+1	Roberts I 29+1	Abbey Z 6	Llewellyn C 5+8	McGovern B 5+4	Russell D 13+10	Easton C 10+4	Nedergaard S 37+3	Libbra M 17+17	McVeigh P 37+5	Notman A 6+24	Rivers M 19+13	Sutch D 6+13	Nielsen D 22+1	Crichton P 5+1	Roberts A 4+1	Benjamin T 3+3	Match No
1	2¹	3	4	5	6	7	8²	9	10	11³	12	13	14											1
1	2	3	4	5	6	7		9³	10	11²		8³		14	12	13								2
1	2	3	4	5	6	7		9	10¹		13	8³		14	12	11²								3
1	2	3	4	5	6	8		9³	10²			12		7¹	13	11	14							4
1	2	3	4	5	6	8		9³	10			12		7	13	11¹								5
1		3	4	5	6	8		9	10²	2		12		7	13	11¹								6
1		3	4	5	6	8¹		9		2	12			7³	10²	11	13	14						7
1	2²	3	4	5	6		12	9			13	8		7	10¹	11³	14							8
1	2	3		5	6			9³				4	8³	13	7	10¹	11	12	14					9
1	3		4	5	6	8		9						11²	7	12		10¹	13	2				10
1	2¹	3	4	5	6	8		9			12			7³	13	11		10						11
1		3	4	5	6	7				12		8		2	11²			10¹	13					12
1	12	3¹	4	5	6	7		9		13		14		2	8²	11		10³						13
1	3		4	5	6	7		9		12				2	10¹	11	13	8²						14
1		3	4	5	6	7		9		12			8²	2³	13	11		10¹	14					15
1		3	4	5	6	7		9		11²		12		8³	10¹	13	14	2						16
1		3	4	5	6	7		9						2	8	11	12	10¹						17
1	3		4	5	6	7		9						2	8	11	12	10¹						18
1	3¹		4	5	6	7		9		11³				12	10²	7	13	14	2					19
1	12	3	4	5	6	7		9						2	8¹	11	13	10¹						20
1		3	4	5	6	7		9						2	8	11	12	10¹						21
1		3	4	5	6	7		9					8	2		11	12	10¹						22
1	12	3	4	5	6	7		9²					8¹	2	13	11	14	10³						23
1		3	4	5	6	7						12		2	8²	11	9	10¹		13				24
1		3	4	5	6	7		9				12		2	13	11¹	14	10³		8²				25
1		3	4	5	6	7		9		11¹			8³	2	13	12	14			10²				26
1	3		4	5	6	7		9³				8	12		11	14	13		2¹	10²				27
1	2¹	3	4	5	6	7						8²			12	11	13	9¹	14	10				28
1	2	3	4	5	6							8¹	13	7³	12	11	9¹	14		10				29
	2	3	4	5	6							12	8	7	13	11³	9¹	14		10²	1			30
	2	3²	4³	5	6								8	7	12	11	9¹	13		10	1	14		31
1	3		4	5	6	12								2	9³	11	13	7¹		10		8		32
1	3		4	5	6	7¹								2³	11²	12	13	14		10		8	9	33
1			4	5	6	7		9						2	11	12	8¹	3		10²		13		34
1⁵	4			5	6			9				8	12	2	11²	7¹	3	10	15			13		35
	3³		4	5	6	7		9¹						2	12		13	14		10²	1	8	11	36
	3		4	5	6	7								2	9	12	13			10²	1	8¹	11	37
	2¹	3	4	5	6	8									11	7	9	12		10²	1	13		38
1		3	4	5	6	7						12		2	11¹	9	13	8²		10				39
1	2	3	4	5	6							12		11	7	9³	13			10¹				40
1	2²	3	4	5	6	8						12		11¹	7	9	13	14		10³				41
1	2	3	4	5	6	8								11²	7	9¹	13	12	14	10³				42
1	2	3	4	5	6	8								11¹	7	9²	12	13		10				43
1	2¹	3	4	5	6	8						12		11¹	7	9²	13	14		10				44
1	2	3	4	5	6	8								11²	12	9¹	13	7³	14	10				45
1	2	3	4	5	6	8								11		9	12	7¹		10				46

Worthington Cup
First Round   Brentford   (a)   0-1

FA Cup
Third Round   Chelsea   (h)   0-0
(a)   0-4

NOTTINGHAM FOREST   Division 1

FOUNDATION

One of the oldest football clubs in the world, Nottingham Forest was formed at a meeting in the Clinton Arms in 1865. Known originally as the Forest Football Club, the game which first drew the founders together was 'shinney', a form of hockey. When they determined to change to football in 1865, one of their first moves was to buy a set of red caps to wear on the field.

City Ground, Nottingham NG2 5FJ.

Telephone: (0115) 982 4444. *Fax:* (0115) 982 4455.
Information Desk: (0115) 982 4449.
Commercial Office: (0115) 982 4450. *Fax:* (0115) 982 4410. *Ticket Office:* (0115) 982 4445. *Souvenir Shop:* (0115) 982 4447. *Junior Reds:* (0115) 982 4400.
ClubCall: 09068 121 174.
Website: www.nottinghamforest.co.uk

Ground Capacity: 30,602.

Record Attendance: 49,946 v Manchester U, Division 1, 28 October 1967.

Record Receipts: £499,099 v Bayern Munich, UEFA Cup quarter-final 2nd leg, 19 March 1996.

Pitch Measurements: 112yd × 74yd.

Chairman: N. E. Doughty.
Chief Executive: M. A. Arthur.
Finance Director: J. D. Pelling.
Board of Directors: N. E. Doughty, M. A. Arthur, J. D. Pelling, N. G. Candeland.

Manager: Paul Hart. *First Team Coaches:* Ian Bowyer, Liam O'Kane. *Reserve Team Coach:* Ian McParland.
Goalkeeping Coach: Andy Beesley.
Physios: John Haselden, Gary Fleming.

Secretary: Paul White. *Press Officer:* Fraser Nicholson.

Colours: Red shirts, white shorts, red stockings.

Change Colours: Blue shirts, blue shorts, blue stockings.

Year Formed: 1865. *Turned Professional:* 1889. *Ltd Co.:* 1982. *Club Nickname:* 'Reds'.

Previous Grounds: 1865, Forest Racecourse; 1879, The Meadows; 1880, Trent Bridge Cricket Ground; 1882, Parkside, Lenton; 1885, Gregory, Lenton; 1890, Town Ground; 1898, City Ground.

First Football League Game: 3 September 1892, Division 1, v Everton (a) D 2–2 – Brown; Earp, Scott; Hamilton, A. Smith, McCracken; McCallum, W. Smith, Higgins (2), Pike, McInnes.

Record League Victory: 12–0 v Leicester Fosse, Division 1, 12 April 1909 – Iremonger; Dudley, Maltby; Hughes (1), Needham, Armstrong; Hooper (3), Marrison, West (3), Morris (2), Spouncer (3 incl. 1p).

HONOURS

Football League: Division 1 – Champions 1977–78, 1997–98; Runners-up 1966–67, 1978–79; Division 2 – Champions 1906–07, 1921–22; Runners-up 1956–57; Division 3 (S) – Champions 1950–51.

FA Cup: Winners 1898, 1959; Runners-up 1991.

Football League Cup: Winners 1978, 1979, 1989, 1990; Runners-up 1980, 1992.

Anglo-Scottish Cup: Winners 1977;

Simod Cup: Winners 1989.

Zenith Data Systems Cup: Winners 1992.

European Competitions: European Fairs Cup: 1961–62, 1967–68. European Cup: 1978–79 (winners), 1979–80 (winners), 1980–81. Super Cup: 1979–80 (winners), 1980–81 (runners-up). World Club Championship: 1980. UEFA Cup: 1983–84, 1984–85, 1995–96.

IT'S A FACT !

Oddly enough, Nottingham Forest twice ended lengthy unbeaten runs by Burnley. One was of 20 matches in 1913 with a 5-3 win, the other a run of 16 ended on Boxing Day 1946 with a 1-0 win.

Record Cup Victory: 14–0 v Clapton (away), FA Cup 1st rd, 17 January 1891 – Brown; Earp, Scott; A. Smith, Russell, Jeacock; McCallum (2), 'Tich' Smith (1), Higgins (5), Lindley (4), Shaw (2).

Record Defeat: 1–9 v Blackburn R, Division 2, 10 April 1937.

Most League Points (2 for a win): 70, Division 3 (S), 1950–51.

Most League Points (3 for a win): 94, Division 1, 1997–98.

Most League Goals: 110, Division 3 (S), 1950–51.

Highest League Scorer in Season: Wally Ardron, 36, Division 3 (S), 1950–51.

Most League Goals in Total Aggregate: Grenville Morris, 199, 1898–1913.

Most League Goals in One Match: 4, Enoch West v Sunderland, Division 1, 9 November 1907; 4, Tommy Gibson v Burnley, Division 2, 25 January 1913; 4, Tom Peacock v Port Vale, Division 2, 23 December 1933; 4, Tom Peacock v Barnsley, Division 2, 9 November 1935; 4, Tom Peacock v Port Vale, Division 2, 23 November 1935; 4, Tom Peacock v Doncaster R, Division 2, 26 December 1935; 4, Tommy Capel v Gillingham, Division 3S, 18 November 1950; 4, Wally Ardron v Hull C, Division 2, 26 December 1952; 4, Tommy Wilson v Barnsley, Division 2, 9 February 1957; 4, Peter Withe v Ipswich T, Division 1, 4 October 1977.

Most Capped Player: Stuart Pearce, 76 (78), England.

Most League Appearances: Bob McKinlay, 614, 1951–70.

Youngest League Player: Craig Westcarr, 16 years 257 days v Burnley, 13 October 2001.

Record Transfer Fee Received: £8,500,000 from Liverpool for Stan Collymore, June 1995.

Record Transfer Fee Paid: £3,500,000 to Celtic for Pierre van Hooijdonk, March 1997.

Football League Record: 1892 Elected to Division 1; 1906–07 Division 2; 1907–11 Division 1; 1911–22 Division 2; 1922–25 Division 1; 1925–49 Division 2; 1949–51 Division 3 (S); 1951–57 Division 2; 1957–72 Division 1; 1972–77 Division 2; 1977–92 Division 1; 1992–93 FA Premier League; 1993–94 Division 1; 1994–97 FA Premier League; 1997–98 Division 1; 1998–99 FA Premier League; 1999– Division 1.

MANAGERS

Harry Radford 1889–97 *(Secretary-Manager)*
Harry Haslam 1897–1909 *(Secretary-Manager)*
Fred Earp 1909–12
Bob Masters 1912–25
John Baynes 1925–29
Stan Hardy 1930–31
Noel Watson 1931–36
Harold Wightman 1936–39
Billy Walker 1939–60
Andy Beattie 1960–63
Johnny Carey 1963–68
Matt Gillies 1969–72
Dave Mackay 1972
Allan Brown 1973–75
Brian Clough 1975–93
Frank Clark 1993–96
Stuart Pearce 1996–97
Dave Bassett 1997–98 *(previously General Manager from February)*
Ron Atkinson 1998–99
David Platt 1999–2001
Paul Hart July 2001–

LATEST SEQUENCES

Longest Sequence of League Wins: 7, 9.5.79 – 1.9.79.

Longest Sequence of League Defeats: 14, 21.3.13 – 27.9.13.

Longest Sequence of League Draws: 7, 29.4.78 – 2.9.78.

Longest Sequence of Unbeaten League Matches: 42, 26.11.77 – 25.11.78.

Longest Sequence Without a League Win: 19, 8.9.98 – 16.1.99.

TEN YEAR LEAGUE RECORD

		P	W	D	L	F	A	Pts	Pos
1991-92	Div 1	42	16	11	15	60	58	59	8
1992-93	PR Lge	42	10	10	22	41	62	40	22
1993-94	Div 1	46	23	14	9	74	49	83	2
1994-95	PR Lge	42	22	11	9	72	43	77	3
1995-96	PR Lge	38	15	13	10	50	54	58	9
1996-97	PR Lge	38	6	16	16	31	59	34	20
1997-98	Div 1	46	28	10	8	82	42	94	1
1998-99	PR Lge	38	7	9	22	35	69	30	20
1999-2000	Div 1	46	14	14	18	53	55	56	14
2000-01	Div 1	46	20	8	18	55	53	68	11

DID YOU KNOW

When centre-half Ernie Jardine first played for Nottingham Forest in 1878, he paid an entrance fee of five shillings (25p) for the privilege as did his contemporaries. Later he became Sir Ernest Jardine and president of the club.

NOTTINGHAM FOREST 2001–02 LEAGUE RECORD

Match No.	Date	Venue	Opponents	Result	H/T Score	Lg. Pos.	Goalscorers	Attendance
1	Aug 11	H	Sheffield U	D	1-1	1-0	—	Harewood [20]	25,513
2	18	A	Barnsley	L	1-2	0-1	18	Jenas [87]	14,203
3	25	H	Crystal Palace	W	4-2	2-1	10	Prutton [18], John 2 [23, 83], Harewood [72]	18,239
4	27	A	Coventry C	D	0-0	0-0	12		18,467
5	Sept 8	A	Norwich C	L	0-1	0-1	15		18,061
6	15	A	Grimsby T	D	0-0	0-0	14		8746
7	17	H	Rotherham U	W	2-0	2-0	—	Bart-Williams (pen) [30], Doig [38]	15,632
8	20	A	Bradford C	W	1-0	0-0	—	Jenas [73]	28,546
9	25	A	Wolverhampton W	L	0-1	0-0	—		24,350
10	29	H	Stockport Co	W	2-1	2-0	11	Lester 2 [11, 19]	17,584
11	Oct 13	H	Burnley	W	1-0	0-0	9	Bart-Williams [79]	24,016
12	17	A	Birmingham C	D	0-0	0-0	—		18,210
13	20	A	Millwall	D	3-3	0-1	10	John 3 [59, 63, 88]	14,154
14	23	A	Watford	W	2-1	0-0	—	Johnson D [61], John [82]	16,355
15	28	H	Manchester C	D	1-1	0-0	10	Bart-Williams [7]	28,226
16	31	H	Sheffield W	L	0-1	0-0	—		20,206
17	Nov 4	A	WBA	L	0-1	0-1	12		18,281
18	11	A	Walsall	L	0-2	0-2	15		6754
19	17	H	Preston NE	D	1-1	1-1	15	Jenas [8]	21,020
20	24	A	Crewe Alex	W	3-0	1-0	14	Johnson D 2 [12, 55], John [82]	8402
21	28	A	Portsmouth	L	2-3	2-1	—	Summerbee [12], Jenas (pen) [33]	14,837
22	Dec 1	H	Watford	D	0-0	0-0	13		24,015
23	8	A	Gillingham	D	2-2	1-1	14	John 2 [21, 64]	18,303
24	16	A	Wimbledon	L	0-1	0-0	17		5920
25	20	A	Crystal Palace	D	1-1	1-1	—	John [3]	15,645
26	26	H	Norwich C	W	2-0	2-0	15	Prutton [24], John [34]	23,003
27	29	H	Coventry C	W	2-1	0-1	13	John (pen) [59], Summerbee [66]	22,706
28	Jan 1	A	Birmingham C	D	1-1	1-1	13	John [26]	19,770
29	12	H	Barnsley	D	0-0	0-0	12		18,190
30	19	A	Sheffield U	D	0-0	0-0	13		18,352
31	30	A	Portsmouth	L	0-1	0-0	—		26,476
32	Feb 2	A	Stockport Co	W	3-1	0-0	12	Jones [58], Harewood [65], Roget (og) [90]	6513
33	9	H	Millwall	L	1-2	0-2	14	Harewood (pen) [87]	18,511
34	16	A	Burnley	D	1-1	0-0	14	Harewood (pen) [69]	15,085
35	23	H	Grimsby T	D	0-0	0-0	15		21,081
36	26	A	Bradford C	L	1-2	0-1	—	Harewood [46]	13,505
37	Mar 2	A	Rotherham U	W	2-1	0-0	14	Lester [49], Harewood [58]	8455
38	6	H	Wolverhampton W	D	2-2	0-1	—	Gray [54], Harewood [67]	21,010
39	9	H	Wimbledon	D	0-0	0-0	14		24,292
40	16	A	Gillingham	L	1-3	1-0	14	Lester [10]	8928
41	22	H	WBA	L	0-1	0-0	—		24,788
42	30	A	Manchester C	L	0-3	0-2	17		34,345
43	Apr 1	H	Walsall	L	2-3	1-2	17	Harewood 2 (1 pen) [20, 89 (p)]	16,659
44	6	A	Sheffield W	W	2-0	1-0	16	Lester [42], Prutton [48]	21,782
45	13	H	Crewe Alex	D	2-2	0-0	15	Bopp [51], Louis-Jean [66]	22,870
46	21	A	Preston NE	L	1-2	1-0	16	Harewood [30]	17,390

Final League Position: 16

GOALSCORERS

League (50): John 13 (1 pen), Harewood 11 (3 pens), Lester 5, Jenas 4 (1 pen), Bart-Williams 3 (1 pen), Johnson D 3, Prutton 3, Summerbee 2, Bopp 1, Doig 1, Gray 1, Jones 1, Louis-Jean 1, own goal 1.
Worthington Cup (3): Bart-Williams 1, John 1, Lester 1.
FA Cup (0).

Ward D 46	Louis-Jean M 37 + 1	Foy K 2	Bart-Williams C 17	Hjelde J 42	Doig C 8	Prutton D 43	Jenas J 28	Harewood M 20 + 8	Lester J 23 + 9	Williams G 44	John S 20 + 6	Scimeca R 35 + 2	Johnson D 17 + 5	Edwards C 2 + 4	Brennan J 41	Johnson A — + 1	Reid A 19 + 10	Gray A 8 + 8	Bopp E 12 + 7	Westcar C — + 8	Rogers A 3	Vaughan T 5 + 3	Summerbee N 17	Edds G — + 1	Thompson J 8	Jones G 2 + 3	Cash B — + 5	Dawson K 3	Proudlock A 3	Dawson M 1	Match No.
1	2	3	4	5	6	7	8	9	10¹	11	12																				1
1	2	3	4	5	6	7¹	8	9¹	10	11		12	13³	14																	2
1	2		4²	5	6	7	8	9¹	12	11	10³				3	13	14														3
1	2		4	5	6	7	8	12²	10	9				13	3		11														4
1	2		4	5		7³	8	10¹	11	12	9²	6			3	13	14														5
1				5	6	7³	8	12	10¹	4	9	2			3	11²	13	14													6
1	12		4	5	6		8³	13	10	11¹	9	2			3	7²	14														7
1			4	5	6	7	8	12	10¹	11	9	2			3																8
1			4	5	6²	7	8	12	10¹	11	9	2		13	3																9
1	2²		4	5		7	8	10	11¹	9²		6	13	14	3		12														10
1	2		4	5		7	8	9³	10¹	11	12	6			3	13	14														11
1	2		4	5		7	8	9³	10¹		12	6			3	13	14	11²													12
1	2		4	5		7	8	9¹	10	11	12	6			3																13
1	2		4	5		7	8	9	10	11		6			3																14
1	2		4	5		7	8	9	10²	11		6			3	12	13														15
1	2		4	5		7	8³	9²	10¹	11	12	6			3	13	14														16
1	2		4²	5		7	8	9¹	10²	11	12	6			3	13	14														17
1	2²		4	5			8	9	10		12	6			3		7¹	11	13												18
1	2			5		7	8	9	10¹			6	4		3		12				11										19
1	2			5		7	8	9¹			12	6	4		3		10²	13			11										20
1	2			5		7	8	9¹			12	6	4		3		10				11										21
1	2			5		7	8	9¹			12	6	4		3		10²	13			11										22
1	2			5		7	8	9¹			12	6	4		3		10				11										23
1	2			5		7	8	9¹			12	6	4		3		10	13			11²										24
1	2			5		7	8¹	9			12	6	4		3		10				11										25
1	2			5		7	8	9				6	4		3		10				11										26
1	2²			5		7	8	9			12	6	4		3		10¹	13			11										27
1				5		7	8	9	10			6	4		3						11				2						28
1	2³			5		7	8	9¹			12	6	4		3		10	13			11²		14								29
1				5			8	9¹	10		12	6	4		3		7²		13		11				2						30
1				5		7	8	9¹	10¹		12	6	4		3		13				11				2						31
1				5		7		9²			12	6	4		3		10³				11				2		8¹	14			32
1				5		7		9			12	6	4		3		10				11²				2		8¹	13			33
1	2			5		7		9	10			6	4		3		8						11			6					34
1	2			5¹		7		9²	10		12	6	4		3		8	13					11³			6	14				35
1	2					7		9	10		12	6	4		3		8						11¹			5					36
1	2					7		9	10¹			6			3		8	11	4							5	12				37
1	2					7		9	10			6	4		3		8	11								6		5			38
1	2			5		7		9	10			6	4		3		8²	11¹								13	6				39
1	2			5		7			10		4	6			3		9¹	11	12								6				40
1	2			5		7		9	10		4	6			3		11											8			41
1	2			5		7		9²			4	6			3		10³	11	8¹	13			12	14							42
1	2			5		7		9	12		4	6			3		8¹	11²	13									10	6		43
1	2			5		7		9	10		4¹	6			3		8	11	12												44
1	2			5		7		9	10		6				3		11	4	12									8¹			45
1	2			5		7		9	10		4	6			3		8	12	11¹												46

Worthington Cup

First Round	Hartlepool U	(a)	2-0
Second Round	Stockport Co	(h)	1-1
Third Round	Bolton W	(a)	0-1

FA Cup

Third Round	Sheffield U	(a)	0-1

NOTTS COUNTY   Division 2

FOUNDATION

According to the official history of Notts County 'the true date of Notts' foundation has to be the meeting at the George Hotel on 7 December 1864'. However, in the same opening chapter is the following: *The Nottingham Guardian* on 28 November 1862 carried the following report: 'The opening of the Nottingham Football Club commenced on Tuesday last at Cremorne Gardens. A side was chosen by W. Arkwright and Chas Deakin. A very spirited game resulted in the latter scoring two goals and two rouges against one and one'.

The Aaron Scargill Stadium, Meadow Lane, Nottingham NG2 3HJ.

Telephone: (0115) 952 9000. *Fax:* (0115) 955 3994.
Ticket Office: (0115) 955 7210. *ClubCall:* 09068 888 684.
Football in the Community: (0115) 955 7215.
Supporters Club: (0115) 955 7255.

Ground Capacity: 20,300.

Record Attendance: 47,310 v York C, FA Cup 6th rd, 12 March 1955.

Record Receipts: £124,539.10 v Manchester C, FA Cup 6th rd, 16 February 1991.

Pitch Measurements: 113yd × 72yd.

Chairman: A. Scardino. *Directors:* B. Barrowcliffe, D. Rhodes, P. Joyce, J. Scardino, D. Ward.

Manager: Billy Dearden. *Assistant Manager:* Gary Brazil. *Youth Coach:* John Gaunt. *Secretary:* Tony Cuthbert. *Physio:* Roger Cleary.

Commercial Manager: Shuna Thompson. *Conference & Banqueting Manager:* Matthew Foote. *Stadium Manager:* Bob Davy.

Colours: Black with white striped shirts, black shorts, black stockings.

Change Colours: All amber.

Year Formed: 1862* (*see Foundation*).

Turned Professional: 1885. *Ltd Co.:* 1888. *Club Nickname:* 'Magpies'.

Previous Grounds: 1862, The Park; 1864, The Meadows; 1877, Beeston Cricket Ground; 1880, Castle Ground; 1883, Trent Bridge; 1910, Meadow Lane.

First Football League Game: 15 September 1888, Football League, v Everton (a) L 1–2 – Holland; Guttridge, McLean; Brown, Warburton, Shelton; Hodder, Harker, Jardine, Moore (1), Wardle.

Record League Victory: 11–1 v Newport Co, Division 3 (S), 15 January 1949 – Smith; Southwell, Purvis; Gannon, Baxter, Adamson; Houghton (1), Sewell (4), Lawton (4), Pimbley, Johnston (2).

Record Cup Victory: 15–0 v Rotherham T (at Trent Bridge), FA Cup 1st rd, 24 October 1885 – Sherwin; Snook, H. T. Moore; Dobson (1), Emmett (1), Chapman; Gunn (1), Albert Moore (2), Jackson (3), Daft (2), Cursham (4), (1 og).

HONOURS

Football League: Division 1 best season: 3rd, 1890–91, 1900–01; Division 2 – Champions 1896–97, 1913–14, 1922–23; Runners-up 1894–95, 1980–81; Promoted from Division 2 1990–91 (play-offs); Division 3 (S) – Champions 1930–31, 1949–50; Runners-up 1936–37; Division 3 – Champions 1997–98; Runners-up 1972–73; Promoted from Division 3 1989–90 (play-offs); Division 4 – Champions 1970–71; Runners-up 1959–60.

FA Cup: Winners 1894; Runners-up 1891.

Football League Cup: best season: 5th rd, 1964, 1973, 1976.

Anglo-Italian Cup: Winners 1995; Runners-up 1994.

IT'S A FACT !

In 1922–23, Notts County, as champions of Division Two, scored only 46 goals in 42 matches, failing to find the target in 11 of them. They did, however, record 23 clean sheets.

Record Defeat: 1–9 v Blackburn R, Division 1, 16 November 1889. 1–9 v Aston Villa, Division 1, 29 September 1888. 1–9 v Portsmouth, Division 2, 9 April 1927.

Most League Points (2 for a win): 69, Division 4, 1970–71.

Most League Points (3 for a win): 99, Division 3, 1997–98.

Most League Goals: 107, Division 4, 1959–60.

Highest League Scorer in Season: Tom Keetley, 39, Division 3 (S), 1930–31.

Most League Goals in Total Aggregate: Les Bradd, 124, 1967–78.

Most League Goals in One Match: 5, Robert Jardine v Burnley, Division 1, 27 October 1888; 5, Daniel Bruce v Port Vale, Division 2, 26 February 1895; 5, Bertie Mills v Barnsley, Division 2, 19 November 1927.

Most Capped Player: Kevin Wilson, 15 (42), Northern Ireland.

Most League Appearances: Albert Iremonger, 564, 1904–26.

Youngest League Player: Tony Bircumshaw, 16 years 54 days v Brentford, 3 April 1961.

Record Transfer Fee Received: £2,500,000 from Derby Co for Craig Short, September 1992.

Record Transfer Fee Paid: £685,000 to Sheffield U for Tony Agana, November 1991.

Football League Record: 1888 Founder Member of the Football League; 1893–97 Division 2; 1897–1913 Division 1; 1913–14 Division 2; 1914–20 Division 1; 1920–23 Division 2; 1923–26 Division 1; 1926–30 Division 2; 1930–31 Division 3 (S); 1931–35 Division 2; 1935–50 Division 3 (S); 1950–58 Division 2; 1958–59 Division 3; 1959–60 Division 4; 1960–64 Division 3; 1964–71 Division 4; 1971–73 Division 3; 1973–81 Division 2; 1981–84 Division 1; 1984–85 Division 2; 1985–90 Division 3; 1990–91 Division 2; 1991–95 Division 1; 1995–97 Division 2; 1997–98 Division 3; 1998– Division 2.

LATEST SEQUENCES

Longest Sequence of League Wins: 10, 3.12.97 – 31.1.98.

Longest Sequence of League Defeats: 7, 3.9.83 – 16.10.83.

Longest Sequence of League Draws: 5, 2.12.78 – 26.12.78.

Longest Sequence of Unbeaten League Matches: 19, 26.4.30 – 6.12.30.

Longest Sequence Without a League Win: 20, 3.12.96 – 31.3.97.

MANAGERS

Edwin Browne 1883–93 *(Secretary-Manager)*
Tom Featherstone 1893 *(Secretary-Manager)*
Tom Harris 1893–1913 *(Secretary-Manager)*
Albert Fisher 1913–27
Horace Henshall 1927–34
Charlie Jones 1934–35
David Pratt 1935
Percy Smith 1935–36
Jimmy McMullan 1936–37
Harry Parkes 1938–39
Tony Towers 1939–42
Frank Womack 1942–43
Major Frank Buckley 1944–46
Arthur Stollery 1946–49
Eric Houghton 1949–53
George Poyser 1953–57
Tommy Lawton 1957–58
Frank Hill 1958–61
Tim Coleman 1961–63
Eddie Lowe 1963–65
Tim Coleman 1965–66
Jack Burkitt 1966–67
Andy Beattie *(General Manager)* 1967
Billy Gray 1967–68
Jimmy Sirrel 1969–75
Ron Fenton 1975–77
Jimmy Sirrel 1978–82 *(continued as General Manager to 1984)*
Howard Wilkinson 1982–83
Larry Lloyd 1983–84
Richie Barker 1984–85
Jimmy Sirrel 1985–87
John Barnwell 1987–88
Neil Warnock 1989–93
Mick Walker 1993–94
Russell Slade 1994–95
Howard Kendall 1995
Colin Murphy June 1995 *(continued as General Manager to 1996)*
Steve Thompson 1996
Sam Allardyce 1997–99
Gary Brazil 1999–2000
Jocky Scott 2000–01
Gary Brazil 2001
Billy Dearden January 2002–

TEN YEAR LEAGUE RECORD

		P	W	D	L	F	A	Pts	Pos
1991-92	Div 1	42	10	10	22	40	62	40	21
1992-93	Div 1	46	12	16	18	55	70	52	17
1993-94	Div 1	46	20	8	18	65	69	68	7
1994-95	Div 1	46	9	13	24	45	66	40	24
1995-96	Div 2	46	21	15	10	63	39	78	4
1996-97	Div 2	46	7	14	25	33	59	35	24
1997-98	Div 3	46	29	12	5	82	43	99	1
1998-99	Div 2	46	14	12	20	52	61	54	16
1999-2000	Div 2	46	18	11	17	61	55	65	8
2000-01	Div 2	46	19	12	15	62	66	69	8

DID YOU KNOW

Notts County's first promotion season in 1896–97 saw them score in all 30 League games and fail to score in only one of the four Test matches. Tom Boucher and John Murphy shared the goalscoring honours with 22 goals each.

NOTTS COUNTY 2001–02 LEAGUE RECORD

Match No.	Date	Venue	Opponents	Result		H/T Score	Lg. Pos.	Goalscorers	Attendance
1	Aug 11	A	Port Vale	L	2-4	1-1	—	Cas [28], Allsopp [53]	6076
2	18	H	Cambridge U	W	2-1	1-0	13	Ireland [4], Stallard [67]	5744
3	25	A	Northampton T	W	2-0	1-0	9	Baraclough [3], Stallard [90]	4648
4	27	H	Chesterfield	D	1-1	0-0	8	Owers [60]	6236
5	Sept 8	H	Wrexham	D	2-2	2-1	10	Allsopp 2 (1 pen) [7 (p), 45]	4776
6	15	H	Brentford	D	0-0	0-0	11		5043
7	18	A	Tranmere R	L	2-4	2-1	—	Caskey [26], Cas [30]	7343
8	22	A	Colchester U	W	1-0	0-0	13	Allsopp [62]	3796
9	25	A	Peterborough U	W	1-0	0-0	—	Stallard [90]	5633
10	29	A	Oldham Ath	L	1-4	0-2	15	Stallard [62]	6864
11	Oct 6	H	Wycombe W	L	0-1	0-0	14		4483
12	13	A	Stoke C	L	0-1	0-0	16		13,220
13	20	H	Reading	L	3-4	1-4	18	Allsopp 2 (1 pen) [7, 68 (p)], Grayson [84]	5604
14	23	H	Brighton & HA	D	2-2	1-0	—	Fenton [41], Richardson I [53]	5092
15	27	A	Bournemouth	L	2-4	2-3	18	Hackworth [3], Allsopp [24]	3209
16	Nov 3	H	QPR	L	0-2	0-0	19		6231
17	9	A	Huddersfield T	D	2-2	0-1	—	Baraclough [73], Caskey [89]	10,168
18	20	A	Blackpool	D	0-0	0-0	—		4118
19	24	H	Cardiff C	D	0-0	0-0	21		6313
20	Dec 1	A	Bristol C	L	2-3	0-1	21	Quinn [65], Chilvers [76]	9411
21	11	A	Wigan Ath	D	1-1	0-1	—	Heffernan [76]	3827
22	15	H	Bury	L	1-2	0-2	21	Quinn [62]	4395
23	21	H	Swindon T	W	3-1	2-1	—	Quinn [42], Caskey [45], Cas [78]	4197
24	26	A	Wrexham	L	1-2	1-1	21	Allsopp [2]	3707
25	29	A	Chesterfield	L	1-2	0-1	21	Fenton [47]	5139
26	Jan 12	A	Cambridge U	W	2-0	0-0	20	Caskey [75], Heffernan [77]	3747
27	19	H	Port Vale	L	1-3	0-2	21	Fenton [86]	6006
28	22	H	Swindon T	L	0-1	0-0	—		3821
29	26	A	Wycombe W	L	0-3	0-1	21		5574
30	29	H	Northampton T	L	0-3	0-1	—		4182
31	Feb 2	H	Oldham Ath	L	0-2	0-0	23		4555
32	9	A	Reading	L	1-2	1-1	23	Liburd [18]	13,564
33	16	H	Stoke C	D	0-0	0-0	23		7501
34	19	H	Wigan Ath	L	1-3	0-1	—	Richardson I [63]	3358
35	23	A	Brentford	L	1-2	0-0	23	Caskey [59]	5367
36	26	H	Colchester U	D	1-1	0-1	—	Allsopp [51]	3140
37	Mar 2	H	Tranmere R	W	3-0	3-0	23	Allsopp 3 [14, 32, 39]	4562
38	5	A	Peterborough U	W	1-0	1-0	—	Heffernan [6]	4415
39	9	A	Bury	W	4-0	3-0	22	Allsopp 2 [6, 26], Heffernan [19], Cas [49]	5435
40	16	H	Bristol C	W	2-0	1-0	20	Cas [17], Heffernan [73]	7521
41	23	A	Brighton & HA	D	2-2	0-1	19	Allsopp [70], Cas [85]	6538
42	30	H	Bournemouth	W	2-0	1-0	19	Allsopp 2 [27, 87]	9014
43	Apr 1	A	QPR	L	2-3	2-1	20	Heffernan [5], Baraclough [34]	10,966
44	6	H	Blackpool	W	1-0	0-0	20	Allsopp (pen) [47]	7783
45	13	A	Cardiff C	L	1-2	1-0	20	Liburd [12]	17,105
46	20	H	Huddersfield T	W	2-1	1-0	19	Allsopp [14], Nicholson [61]	15,618

Final League Position: 19

GOALSCORERS
League (59): Allsopp 19 (3 pens), Cas 6, Heffernan 6, Caskey 5, Stallard 4, Baraclough 3, Fenton 3, Quinn 3, Liburd 2, Richardson I 2, Chilvers 1, Grayson 1, Hackworth 1, Ireland 1, Nicholson 1, Owers 1.
Worthington Cup (6): Allsopp 4 (1 pen), Mildenhall 1, Stallard 1.
FA Cup (3): Allsopp 2, Owers 1.

Mildenhall S 25+1	Fenton N 41+1	Baraclough I 30+3	Caskey D 39+3	Wilkie L 2	Ireland C 26+1	Owers G 26+4	Cas M 39+1	Stallard M 21+5	Allsopp D 43	Nicholson K 15+9	Warren M 12+5	Liburd R 22+3	Heffernan P 18+5	Hackworth T 9+24	Grayson S 10	Richardson I 21+3	Hamilton 16+3	Jorgensen H —+2	Brough M 14+7	Chilvers 9	Bolland P 16+3	Stone D 5+1	Richardson L 20+1	Quinn J 6	Riley P 3+3	Garden S 21	Holmes R 1	McNamara N —+4	Whitley J 6	Match No.
1	2	3	4	5	6¹	7	8	9	10	11³	12	13																		1
1	2	3	4	5¹	6	7	8	9	10		12	11																		2
1	2	3	4		6	7	8	9	10¹		5	11	12																	3
1	2	3	4		6	7	8	9	10	12	5	11¹																		4
1	2	3	4²		6¹	7	8	9	10	12	11			13	5															5
1	2	3	4¹			7	8	9	10	11²	5			13		12	6													6
1	2	3	4²			7	8	9	10	11¹	5			13		12	6													7
1	2	3	4²			7	8	9¹	10					12		6	5	11	13											8
1	2	3	4			7	8	9	10¹					12		6	5	11												9
1	2	3	4			7¹	8	9	10					12		6	5	11												10
1	2³	3	4			7²	8	9	10¹	13		14		12		6	5	11												11
1		3	4			7	8	9	10¹	13	5					12	6	2	11²											12
1		3	4¹				8	9	10²	12	5	11		13		6	2	14	7³											13
1	2	3	4			7	8	9	10¹	12				13		6	5		11²											14
1	2	3²	4¹			7	8	9	10	12		13				6	5	14	11³											15
1	2	3	4²			7	8	9	10¹	12				13	5³	6	14		11											16
1	2	3	4				8	9	10¹		5			13		12	6	14				7³	11²							17
1	2	3	4				8	9¹	10					12		5					6	7	11							18
1	2	3	4				8	9	10							5			12		6	7¹	11							19
1		3	4	5		7¹	8	9	10					12		6²					13	2	11							20
1	2	3						9	10	12		11²				5			13		7	6	4¹		8					21
	2	3	4					9	10	12		11¹				5		14	13			6²	7³		8	1				22
1	2	3	4¹		6	7	8	9						13		12	5	14				10²	11³			1				23
1	2	3³			6	7		9	10¹	12				13			5	14			11		8		4²	1				24
15	2				6⁶	7	8		10							5			11		9		3			1				25
1	2		4	5		7	8	9¹	10					13					12		11	6			3²					26
1	2				6²	7	8	9	10	12						5					11	3	4¹		13					27
1	2		4				8²	9	10					13		12	5				7¹	6	11		3					28
1	2		4				8	9	10	12				13			5				7²	6	11		3¹					29
	2		4			7	8³	9	10	12				13	5			14				6	11²		3¹	1				30
	2	3	4				8		10						5	7	9		12		6¹		11			1				31
	2¹	3	4		6		8	9¹	10	12					5	7			13				11			1				32
		3	4¹		6		8	9²	10	12				13	5	7						2	11			1				33
12		3	4³		6		8	9¹	10						5	7		14	13			2	11¹			1				34
	2	3	4		6		8		10¹							7	9		11		5					1		12		35
	2	3	4		6		8	9	10							7¹			12		11		5			1				36
5		3	4		6		8³		10¹							7	9		12		13	2²	11			1				37
	2	3	4		6		8¹		10							7	9		12		11		5			1				38
5¹		3	4		6		8		10							7³	9²	14	12		13	2	11			1				39
5		3	4		6		8		10							7	9		12			2	11			1				40
5		3	4		6		8		10²		12						9				13	2	11¹			1		7		41
5		3	4³		6		8		10²		12						9	14	11¹		13	2				1		7		42
5		3	4		6			9¹	10					13		7²			11		12	2				1		8		43
5		3			6		8		10		12					7	9		11¹		13	2				1		4		44
5		3	4²		6			9	10¹					13		7			11		12	2				1		8		45
5		3	4		6		8²		10¹	12							9		11		13	2				1		7		46

Worthington Cup

First Round	Mansfield T	(a)	4-3	
Second Round	Manchester C	(h)	2-4	

FA Cup

First Round	Cambridge U	(a)	1-1	
		(h)	2-0	
Second Round	Wycombe W	(a)	0-3	

OLDHAM ATHLETIC

Division 2

FOUNDATION

It was in 1895 that John Garland, the landlord of the Featherstall and Junction Hotel, decided to form a football club. As Pine Villa they played in the Oldham Junior League. In 1899 the local professional club, Oldham County, went out of existence and one of the liquidators persuaded Pine Villa to take over their ground at Sheepfoot Lane and change their name to Oldham Athletic.

Boundary Park, Oldham OL1 2PA.

Telephone: 0870 753 2000, *07000 Latics:* 0161 624 4972. *Fax:* (0161) 627 5915. *Website:* www.oldhamathletic.co.uk *ClubCall:* 09068 121 142. *Commercial Office:* (0161) 627 1802. *Fax:* (0161) 652 6501.

Ground Capacity: (all seated) 13,559.

Record Attendance: 46,471 v Sheffield W, FA Cup 4th rd, 25 January 1930.

Record Receipts: £138,680 v Manchester U, FA Premier League, 29 December 1993.

Pitch Measurements: 110yd × 74yd.

Chairman: C. E. Moore.
Directors: Alan Hardy, Martin J. Hogarty, Nigel D. Horn.
Associate Directors: Paul Thompson, Jean Howard.

Manager: Iain Dowie.

Chief Executive/Secretary: Alan Hardy.

Marketing and Public Relations Manager: Sean Jarvis.

Stadium Manager: George Furniss.

Safety Officer: Peter Davis.

Club Accountant: Neil Joy.

Physio: Paul Caton.

Senior Youth Coach: David Cross. *Assistant Youth Coach:* Tony Philliskirk.
Director of Youth Development: Andy Beaglehole.

Colours: Blue shirts, blue shorts, blue stockings.

Change Colours: Burgundy shirts, burgundy shorts, navy stockings.

Year Formed: 1895.

Turned Professional: 1899. *Ltd Co.:* 1906.

Previous Name: 1895, Pine Villa; 1899, Oldham Athletic.

Club Nickname: 'The Latics'.

Previous Grounds: 1895, Sheepfoot Lane; 1900, Hudson Field; 1906, Sheepfoot Lane; 1907, Boundary Park.

HONOURS

Football League: Division 1 – Runners-up 1914–15; Division 2 – Champions 1990–91; Runners-up 1909–10; Division 3 (N) – Champions 1952–53; Division 3 – Champions 1973–74; Division 4 – Runners-up 1962–63.

FA Cup: Semi-final 1913, 1990, 1994.

Football League Cup: Runners-up 1990.

IT'S A FACT !

In 1913, Oldham Athletic signed England centre-half Charlie Roberts from Manchester United for a fee of £1,750 and he subsequently became the club's manager.

First Football League Game: 9 September 1907, Division 2,
v Stoke (a) W 3–1 – Hewitson; Hodson, Hamilton; Fay,
Walders, Wilson; Ward, W. Dodds (1), Newton (1),
Hancock, Swarbrick (1).

Record League Victory: 11–0 v Southport, Division 4,
26 December 1962 – Bollands; Branagan, Marshall; McCall,
Williams, Scott; Ledger (1), Johnstone, Lister (6),
Colquhoun (1), Whitaker (3).

Record Cup Victory: 10–1 v Lytham, FA Cup 1st rd,
28 November 1925 – Gray; Wynne, Grundy; Adlam,
Heaton, Naylor (1), Douglas, Pynegar (2), Ormston (2),
Barnes (3), Watson (2).

Record Defeat: 4–13 v Tranmere R, Division 3 (N),
26 December 1935.

Most League Points (2 for a win): 62, Division 3, 1973–74.

Most League Points (3 for a win): 88, Division 2, 1990–91.

Most League Goals: 95, Division 4, 1962–63.

Highest League Scorer in Season: Tom Davis, 33,
Division 3 (N), 1936–37.

Most League Goals in Total Aggregate: Roger Palmer, 141,
1980–94.

Most League Goals in One Match: 7, Eric Gemmell v
Chester, Division 3N, 19 January 1952.

Most Capped Player: Gunnar Halle, 24 (64), Norway.

Most League Appearances: Ian Wood, 525, 1966–80.

MANAGERS

David Ashworth 1906–14
Herbert Bamlett 1914–21
Charlie Roberts 1921–22
David Ashworth 1923–24
Bob Mellor 1924–27
Andy Wilson 1927–32
Jimmy McMullan 1933–34
Bob Mellor 1934–45
  (continued as Secretary to 1953)
Frank Womack 1945–47
Billy Wootton 1947–50
George Hardwick 1950–56
Ted Goodier 1956–58
Norman Dodgin 1958–60
Jack Rowley 1960–63
Les McDowall 1963–65
Gordon Hurst 1965–66
Jimmy McIlroy 1966–68
Jack Rowley 1968–69
Jimmy Frizzell 1970–82
Joe Royle 1982–94
Graeme Sharp 1994–97
Neil Warnock 1997–98
Andy Ritchie 1998–2001
Mick Wadsworth 2001–02
Iain Dowie May 2002–

Youngest League Player: Wayne Harrison, 15 years 11 months v Notts Co, 27 October 1984.

Record Transfer Fee Received: £1,700,000 from Aston Villa for Earl Barrett, February 1992.

Record Transfer Fee Paid: £750,000 to Aston Villa for Ian Olney, June 1992.

Football League Record: 1907 Elected to Division 2; 1910–23 Division 1; 1923–35 Division 2;
1935–53 Division 3 (N); 1953–54 Division 2; 1954–58 Division 3 (N); 1958–63 Division 4;
1963–69 Division 3; 1969–71 Division 4; 1971–74 Division 3; 1974–91 Division 2; 1991–92 Division 1;
1992–94 FA Premier League; 1994–97 Division 1; 1997– Division 2.

LATEST SEQUENCES

Longest Sequence of League Wins: 10, 12.1.74 – 12.3.74.

Longest Sequence of League Defeats: 8, 15.12.34 – 2.2.35.

Longest Sequence of League Draws: 5, 26.12.82 – 15.1.83.

Longest Sequence of Unbeaten League Matches: 20, 1.5.90 – 10.11.90.

Longest Sequence Without a League Win: 17, 4.9.20 – 18.12.20.

TEN YEAR LEAGUE RECORD

		P	W	D	L	F	A	Pts	Pos
1991-92	Div 1	42	14	9	19	63	67	51	17
1992-93	PR Lge	42	13	10	19	63	74	49	19
1993-94	PR Lge	42	9	13	20	42	68	40	21
1994-95	Div 1	46	16	13	17	60	60	61	14
1995-96	Div 1	46	14	14	18	54	50	56	18
1996-97	Div 1	46	10	13	23	51	66	43	23
1997-98	Div 2	46	15	16	15	62	54	61	13
1998-99	Div 2	46	14	9	23	48	66	51	20
1999-2000	Div 2	46	16	12	18	50	55	60	14
2000-01	Div 2	46	15	13	18	53	65	58	15

DID YOU KNOW

Discarded by Atherton, full-
back Teddy Ivill made 244
consecutive League and Cup
appearances for Oldham
Athletic before being
transferred to
Wolverhampton Wanderers
in 1932.

OLDHAM ATHLETIC 2001–02 LEAGUE RECORD

Match No.	Date	Venue	Opponents	Result	H/T Score	Lg. Pos.	Goalscorers	Attendance
1	Aug 11	A	Wrexham	D 3-3	1-0	—	Allott [38], Eyres [73], Corazzin [90]	4881
2	18	H	Chesterfield	D 1-1	1-0	15	Allott [33]	5534
3	25	A	Swindon T	W 2-0	2-0	10	Sheridan J [17], Balmer [39]	5219
4	28	H	Northampton T	W 4-2	2-0	—	Balmer [6], Rickers [35], Duxbury [63], Tipton [78]	4941
5	Sept 1	A	Tranmere R	D 2-2	2-1	6	Sheridan D [12], Eyre [33]	8716
6	8	H	Blackpool	W 2-1	1-0	4	Sheridan D [30], Duxbury [88]	6650
7	15	H	Peterborough U	W 2-0	0-0	1	Corazzin [86], Tipton (pen) [90]	4855
8	18	A	Colchester U	L 1-2	0-2	—	Eyres [81]	2991
9	22	A	Brentford	D 2-2	1-0	3	Rickers [34], Corazzin [74]	5525
10	25	H	Bury	W 4-0	2-0	—	Duxbury [8], Tipton [45], Corazzin [63], Allott [90]	5605
11	29	H	Notts Co	W 4-1	2-0	1	Fenton (og) [20], Dudley [22], Eyre [84], Corazzin (pen) [90]	6864
12	Oct 5	A	Bournemouth	L 2-3	1-0	—	Tipton [1], Tindall (og) [66]	3312
13	13	H	Bristol C	L 0-1	0-1	4		6565
14	20	A	Brighton & HA	L 0-3	0-3	7		6793
15	23	H	Reading	L 0-1	0-1	—		4901
16	27	A	QPR	D 1-1	0-1	8	Balmer [65]	10,556
17	Nov 3	H	Huddersfield T	D 1-1	1-1	10	Balmer [76]	8859
18	10	A	Cambridge U	D 1-1	1-0	13	Allott [18]	3378
19	21	A	Stoke C	D 0-0	0-0	—		11,031
20	24	H	Wycombe W	W 2-0	2-0	8	Tipton [31], Rammell (og) [39]	4731
21	Dec 1	A	Cardiff C	L 1-3	0-1	11	Eyre [75]	10,004
22	15	H	Wigan Ath	D 1-1	0-0	12	Beharall [89]	6407
23	21	H	Port Vale	W 2-0	1-0	—	Eyres [30], Reeves [57]	4317
24	26	A	Blackpool	W 2-0	0-0	10	Reeves 2 (1 pen) [56 (p), 66]	5772
25	29	A	Northampton T	W 1-0	0-0	7	Eyres [80]	4760
26	Jan 12	A	Chesterfield	L 2-4	1-0	8	Murray [11], Eyres [47]	4716
27	16	H	Swindon T	W 2-0	1-0	—	Eyre 2 [45, 81]	3970
28	19	H	Wrexham	W 3-1	1-1	7	Murray [34], Sheridan J (pen) [56], Corazzin [90]	5451
29	22	A	Port Vale	L 2-3	0-2	—	Appleby [48], Corazzin [70]	4408
30	26	H	Bournemouth	D 3-3	1-0	8	Balmer [18], Broadhurst (og) [56], Eyres [63]	4853
31	Feb 2	A	Notts Co	W 2-0	0-0	6	Murray [49], Corazzin [54]	4555
32	9	H	Brighton & HA	W 2-0	1-0	7	Appleby [30], Eyres [81]	6951
33	16	A	Bristol C	L 0-3	0-0	7		10,849
34	19	H	Tranmere R	D 1-1	0-1	—	Colusso [60]	5998
35	23	A	Peterborough U	D 2-2	2-1	8	Murray [11], Smart [15]	4308
36	26	H	Brentford	W 3-2	1-1	—	Eyres (pen) [45], Smart 2 [62, 69]	4935
37	Mar 2	H	Colchester U	W 4-1	2-1	6	Smart [24], Murray [44], Eyres [77], Corazzin [90]	5457
38	5	A	Bury	D 1-1	0-1	—	Colusso [90]	7953
39	9	A	Wigan Ath	L 0-1	0-0	7		7389
40	16	H	Cardiff C	L 1-7	0-5	8	Balmer [74]	6786
41	23	A	Reading	D 2-2	1-2	8	Duxbury [31], Smart [75]	15,191
42	30	H	Cambridge U	D 2-2	1-1	9	Holden 2 [45, 90]	4957
43	Apr 1	A	Huddersfield T	D 0-0	0-0	9		14,343
44	6	H	Stoke C	W 2-1	1-0	9	Carss [25], Hall [88]	6548
45	13	A	Wycombe W	L 1-2	0-2	9	Smart (pen) [82]	6728
46	20	H	QPR	W 1-0	1-0	9	Baudet [10]	7262

Final League Position: 9

GOALSCORERS

League (77): Corazzin 9 (1 pen), Eyres 9 (1 pen), Balmer 6, Smart 6 (1 pen), Eyre 5, Murray 5, Tipton 5 (1 pen), Allott 4, Duxbury 4, Reeves 3 (1 pen), Appleby 2, Colusso 2, Holden 2, Rickers 2, Sheridan D 2, Sheridan J 2 (1 pen), Baudet 1, Beharall 1, Carss 1, Dudley 1, Hall 1, own goals 4.
Worthington Cup (0).
FA Cup (6): Eyres 3, Duxbury 2, Sheridan J 1.

Kelly G 22+1	McNiven S 32+3	Sheridan D 25+3	Garnett S 4+4	Balmer S 35+1	Duxbury L 34+6	Rickers P 13+11	Sheridan J 24+3	Tipton M 11+11	Allott M 9+6	Boshell D 2+2	Eyres D 40+5	Corazzin C 24+9	Carss T 7+7	Prenderville B 10+2	Eyre J 11+9	Dudley C 6+3	Innes M —+5	Holden D 20+3	Gill W 3	Richards M 3+2	Armstrong C 31+1	Miskelly D 4	Rachubka P 16	Beharall D 18	Bauder J 13+7	Smart A 14+7	Murray P 23+1	Hardy L —+1	Reeves D 11+2	Haining W 1+3	Appleby M 16+1	Colusso C 6+7	Clegg M 5+1	Goram A 4	Adebola D 5	Hall F 4	Griffin A —+1	Match No.
1	2	3	4	5	6	7¹	8	9	10²	11³	12	13	14																									1
1	2	3	4³	5	6	12	8¹	9²	10		11				7	14	13																					2
1	2	3	12	5¹	6	7	8³	13	9		14				11		4	10²																				3
1	2	3	12	5¹	6	7	8³	13	9		14				11		4	10²																				4
1	2	3	12	5	6	7	8²	9			13				11		4¹	10																				5
1	2	3	12	5	6	7¹	8	13	9²		14				11		4	10³																				6
1	2	3	4	5	6	7	8³	12	9¹		11	13						10²	14																			7
1	2	3	4²	5	6	7³	8		9¹		11	12	13						10	14																		8
1	2	3		5	6	7		9			12				11	10¹	4	8																				9
1	2	3¹		5	6³	7	12	9			13				11	10²	4	8	14																			10
1	2			5	6³	7	8	9²	13		3	10			4	12	11¹	14																				11
1	2			5	6	7		9¹			8³	3	10		4	12	11																					12
1				5	6	7²		12			3	10	4		9²	11	13	2		8¹	14																	13
1	2			5	6	12	8	9³			11	10²			4¹	13	3			7	14																	14
1	4	3		5	6	12		9²	13		11					10	2³	7¹	8	14																		15
1	4	10		5	6	7¹	8	12	13		11³						14	2		9²	3																	16
1	4	8		5	6	12		13	14		11	10³			9¹		2	7²			3																	17
1	4	7		5	6	12	8¹	13			11	10³			14		2				3																	18
15	4²	9		5	6		8	12			11	10¹			13		2				3	1⁰			7													19
	12	7		5	6	13	8²	9¹			11	10³			14		2				3	1		4														20
		7		5	6		8	9³			11²	12	13				2				3	1		4	14	10¹												21
		7²		5	6		8	9¹	12		11	10³				13	2				3¹	1		4		14												22
		7		5	6¹		8²	12			11³					2					3	1		4	13	10	14	9										23
	12	7			13		8²		11		2²										3	1	4	5	10¹	6³	9	14										24
	7			12	13		8³		11		2²										3	1	4	5¹	10	6	9	14										25
	7³			5	6²		12				11					13					2¹	3	1	4	14	10	8	9										26
		2		5	6²		8³				11					12					3	1	4		13	10¹	7	9	14									27
		2		5	6	12	8	13			11²	14				9³					3	1	4		7			10¹										28
		2		5	6	12					11	10				9¹					3	1	4²	13	7			8									29
		2		5	6¹	12	8				9	10									3	1	4	13	7			11²									30
		2			12		8¹				11	10²				13					3	1	4	5	6			9	7									31
		2			12		8¹				11	10									3	1	4	5	13	6	9²	7	14									32
		2			6¹						11³	10²	12								3	1	4	5	13	7	9	8	14									33
		2	4		12						11	13									3	1		5	10²	6	9	8	7¹									34
		2	4								11	10¹									3	1		5	7³	6	9	8	12	13								35
1	12	13	4								11	10									3			5¹	9³	6	14	8	7²	2								36
1	13	5		12							11	10									3		4	9³	6	14	8¹	7²	2									37
1	7	5²										10									3		4	12	11	6	9¹	8	13	2								38
1	7³	5		12							11	10				13					3		4	6	9	8¹	14	2²										39
	12	5		13							11¹	10	14								3		4	9²	6	8	7³	2	1									40
	4			6²							11	12	13				2				3		5	14	8	10	7³	1	9¹									41
	4	8		6							11	12	13				2				3²		5¹	9³	7	14		1	10									42
	4			6¹	12						11	10	13				2				3²		14	7	8		1	9³	5									43
	4			6³	12						11	10	8				2		3			1	13	7¹	14			9²	5									44
	4			6¹							11³	10	8				2		3			1	12	13	7	14			9²	5								45
											11³	12	13				2		3			1	4	9¹	7	6			8²	10		5			14		46

Worthington Cup
First Round   Stoke C   (a)   0-0
Second Round   Blackburn R   (a)   0-2

FA Cup
First Round   Barrow   (h)   1-1
                               (a)   1-0
Second Round   Hull C   (a)   3-2
Third Round   Cheltenham T   (a)   1-2

OXFORD UNITED   Division 3

FOUNDATION

There had been an Oxford United club around the time of World War I but only in the Oxfordshire Thursday League and there is no connection with the modern club which began as Headington in 1893, adding 'United' a year later. Playing first on Quarry Fields and subsequently Wootten's Fields, they owe much to a Dr Hitchings for their early development.

The Kassam Stadium, Grenoble Road, Oxford OX4 4XP.

Telephone: (01865) 337 500. *ClubCall:* 09068 440 055.
Fax: 01865 337 555. *Ticketline:* 01865 337 533.
Website: www.oufc.co.uk
Email: admin@oufc.co.uk

Ground Capacity: 12,450.

Record Attendance: 22,730 v Preston NE, FA Cup 6th rd, 29 February 1964.

Record Receipts: £136,423 v Chelsea, FA Cup 4th rd, 25 January 1999.

Pitch Measurements: 115yd × 74yd.

HONOURS

Football League: Division 1 best season: 12th, 1997–98; Division 2 – Champions 1984–85; Runners-up 1995–96; Division 3 – Champions 1967–68, 1983–84; Division 4 – Promoted 1964–65 (4th).

FA Cup: best season: 6th rd, 1964 (shared record for 4th Division club).

Football League Cup: Winners 1986.

President: The Duke of Marlborough.
Chairman: Firoz Kassam. *Directors:* F. Higgins, A. Tawakley. *Associate Directors:* B. Cross, Lord Faulkner, M. Matthews, B. Smith.

Manager: Ian Atkins.

Reserve Team Coach: Mike Ford.

Physio: Neal Reynolds.

Secretary: Mick Brown.

Stadium Manager: Tony Ashley.

Colours: Yellow shirts with navy trim, navy shorts, navy stockings.

Change Colours: Navy shirts with white trim, white shorts, white stockings.

Year Formed: 1893.

Turned Professional: 1949.

Ltd Co.: 1949.

Club Nickname: 'The U's'.

Previous Names: 1893, Headington; 1894, Headington United; 1960, Oxford United.

Previous Grounds: 1893, Headington Quarry; 1894, Wootten's Field; 1898, Sandy Lane Ground; 1902, Britannia Field; 1909, Sandy Lane; 1910, Quarry Recreation Ground; 1914, Sandy Lane; 1922, The Paddock Manor Road; 1925, Manor Ground.

First Football League Game: 18 August 1962, Division 4, v Barrow (a) L 2–3 – Medlock; Beavon, Quartermain; R. Atkinson, Kyle, Jones; Knight, G. Atkinson (1), Houghton (1), Cornwell, Colfar.

IT'S A FACT !

Oxford United's Division Three championship winning season of 1983–84 also saw them reach the fifth round in both League Cup and FA Cup for a total of 64 competitive matches of which only nine resulted in defeat.

Record League Victory: 7–0 v Barrow, Division 4,
19 December 1964 – Fearnley; Beavon, Quartermain;
R. Atkinson (1), Kyle, Jones; Morris, Booth (3), Willey (1),
G. Atkinson (1), Harrington (1).

Record Cup Victory: 9–1 v Dorchester T, FA Cup 1st rd,
11 November 1995 – Whitehead; Wood (2), Ford M (1),
Smith, Elliott, Gilchrist, Rush (1), Massey (Murphy),
Moody (3), Ford R (1), Angel (Beauchamp (1)).

Record Defeat: 0–7 v Sunderland, Division 1, 19 September
1998.

Most League Points (2 for a win): 61, Division 4, 1964–65.

Most League Points (3 for a win): 95, Division 3, 1983–84.

Most League Goals: 91, Division 3, 1983–84.

Highest League Scorer in Season: John Aldridge, 30,
Division 2, 1984–85.

Most League Goals in Total Aggregate: Graham Atkinson,
77, 1962–73.

Most League Goals in One Match: 4, Tony Jones v
Newport Co, Division 4, 22 September 1962; 4, Arthur
Longbottom v Darlington, Division 4, 26 October 1963; 4,
Richard Hill v Walsall, Division 2, 26 December 1988; 4,
John Durnin v Luton T, 14 November 1992.

Most Capped Player: Jim Magilton, 18 (52\), Northern Ireland.

Most League Appearances: John Shuker, 478, 1962–77.

Youngest League Player: Jason Seacole, 16 years 149 days v Mansfield T, 7 September 1976.

Record Transfer Fee Received: £1,600,000 from Leicester C for Matt Elliott, January 1997.

Record Transfer Fee Paid: £475,000 to Aberdeen for Dean Windass, August 1998.

Football League Record: 1962 Elected to Division 4; 1965–68 Division 3; 1968–76 Division 2;
1976–84 Division 3; 1984–85 Division 2; 1985–88 Division 1; 1988–92 Division 2; 1992–94 Division 1;
1994–96 Division 2; 1996–99 Division 1; 1999–2001 Division 2; 2001– Division 3.

MANAGERS

Harry Thompson 1949–58
　(Player-Manager) 1949-51
Arthur Turner 1959–69
　*(continued as General Manager
　to 1972)*
Ron Saunders 1969
Gerry Summers 1969–75
Mick Brown 1975–79
Bill Asprey 1979–80
Ian Greaves 1980–82
Jim Smith 1982–85
Maurice Evans 1985–88
Mark Lawrenson 1988
Brian Horton 1988–93
Denis Smith 1993–97
Malcolm Crosby 1997
Malcolm Shotton 1998–99
Denis Smith 2000
David Kemp 2000–01
Mark Wright 2001
Ian Atkins November 2001–

LATEST SEQUENCES

Longest Sequence of League Wins: 6, 6.4.85 – 24.4.85.

Longest Sequence of League Defeats: 7, 4.5.91 – 7.9.91.

Longest Sequence of League Draws: 5, 7.10.78 – 28.10.78.

Longest Sequence of Unbeaten League Matches: 20, 17.3.84 – 29.9.84.

Longest Sequence Without a League Win: 27, 14.11.87 – 27.8.88.

TEN YEAR LEAGUE RECORD

		P	W	D	L	F	A	Pts	Pos
1991-92	Div 2	46	13	11	22	66	73	50	21
1992-93	Div 1	46	14	14	18	53	56	56	14
1993-94	Div 1	46	13	10	23	54	75	49	23
1994-95	Div 2	46	21	12	13	66	52	75	7
1995-96	Div 2	46	24	11	11	76	39	83	2
1996-97	Div 1	46	16	9	21	64	68	57	17
1997-98	Div 1	46	16	10	20	60	64	58	12
1998-99	Div 1	46	10	14	22	48	71	44	23
1999-2000	Div 2	46	12	9	25	43	73	45	20
2000-01	Div 2	46	7	6	33	53	100	27	24

DID YOU KNOW ?

On 21 April 2001, goalkeeper
Phil Wilson saved a penalty
with his first touch of the ball
as a Football League player,
having come on against
Bristol Rovers as a
replacement for the dismissed
Richard Knight.

OXFORD UNITED 2001–02 LEAGUE RECORD

Match No.	Date	Venue	Opponents	Result	H/T Score	Lg. Pos.	Goalscorers	Attendance
1	Aug 11	H	Rochdale	L	1-2	0-1	—	Brooks [52]	7842
2	18	A	Swansea C	D	0-0	0-0	18		5501
3	25	H	Shrewsbury T	L	0-1	0-0	21		5667
4	27	A	Halifax T	W	2-0	2-0	16	Scott [6], Gray [12]	2271
5	Sept 1	H	Rushden & D	W	3-2	0-0	10	Whitehead [51], Thomas [53], Bolland [69]	6289
6	8	A	Luton T	D	1-1	1-1	12	Scott [5]	6736
7	15	A	Exeter C	L	2-3	1-3	13	Brooks [11], Thomas (pen) [69]	3268
8	18	H	Macclesfield T	L	0-2	0-1	—		4964
9	22	H	Southend U	W	2-0	1-0	11	Moody [29], Ricketts [46]	5724
10	25	A	Kidderminster H	D	0-0	0-0	—		2663
11	29	A	Bristol R	D	1-1	1-1	13	Omoyinmi [1]	7678
12	Oct 6	H	Plymouth Arg	D	1-1	0-0	13	Moody (pen) [74]	6017
13	13	A	Lincoln C	L	0-1	0-0	17		3124
14	20	H	Scunthorpe U	L	0-1	0-0	18		5006
15	23	H	Carlisle U	D	1-1	0-0	—	Brooks [66]	7405
16	27	A	Hartlepool U	W	1-0	0-0	17	Moody [48]	3595
17	Nov 3	H	York C	D	2-2	0-1	18	Brooks 2 [48, 83]	5487
18	10	A	Darlington	L	0-1	0-0	21		3358
19	20	A	Leyton Orient	L	0-3	0-2	—		3753
20	24	H	Cheltenham T	W	3-0	2-0	18	Moody [7], Brooks [38], Powell [56]	6740
21	Dec 1	A	Hull C	L	0-3	0-3	18		9552
22	15	H	Mansfield T	W	3-2	0-1	17	Morley [59], Gray 2 [77, 87]	5437
23	22	A	Torquay U	D	3-3	0-2	17	Omoyinmi [45], Crosby [57], Moody [79]	2463
24	26	H	Luton T	L	1-2	1-1	18	Scott [20]	11,121
25	29	H	Halifax T	W	6-1	2-0	16	Moody 3 (1 pen) [25, 33, 83 (p)], Scott [69], Savage [79], Omoyinmi [84]	6046
26	Jan 8	A	Shrewsbury T	L	0-1	0-1	—		2576
27	12	H	Swansea C	W	2-1	2-1	14	Moody [16], Scott [31]	5934
28	19	A	Rochdale	D	1-1	0-1	14	Moody [83]	3355
29	22	H	Torquay U	D	1-1	0-0	—	Moody (pen) [83]	5480
30	26	A	Plymouth Arg	L	2-4	2-3	14	Morley [34], Powell [41]	8239
31	Feb 2	H	Bristol R	D	0-0	0-0	15		7457
32	5	A	Rushden & D	L	1-2	0-1	—	Morley [74]	4484
33	9	A	Scunthorpe U	L	0-1	0-0	16		3504
34	16	H	Lincoln C	W	2-1	2-0	16	Gray [19], Scott (pen) [21]	6596
35	23	A	Exeter C	L	1-2	1-1	18	Beauchamp [33]	6051
36	26	A	Macclesfield T	W	1-0	1-0	—	Powell [24]	1401
37	Mar 2	A	Southend U	D	2-2	1-2	17	Scott [45], Powell (pen) [71]	3701
38	5	H	Kidderminster H	D	1-1	0-0	—	Brooks [80]	5027
39	9	H	Mansfield T	L	1-2	0-2	16	Moody (pen) [50]	4916
40	16	H	Hull C	W	1-0	0-0	16	Brooks [82]	5952
41	23	A	Carlisle U	L	1-2	1-1	17	Brooks [35]	3349
42	30	H	Hartlepool U	L	1-2	1-2	18	Moody [33]	5767
43	Apr 1	A	York C	L	0-1	0-0	21		3290
44	6	A	Leyton Orient	D	1-1	0-0	21	Scott [84]	5740
45	13	A	Cheltenham T	L	0-2	0-2	21		7013
46	20	H	Darlington	L	1-2	0-0	21	Brooks [57]	6167

Final League Position: 21

GOALSCORERS
League (53): Moody 13 (4 pens), Brooks 10, Scott 8 (1 pen), Gray 4, Powell 4 (1 pen), Morley 3, Omoyinmi 3, Thomas 2 (1 pen), Beauchamp 1, Bolland 1, Crosby 1, Ricketts 1, Savage 1, Whitehead 1.
Worthington Cup (1): Scott 1.
FA Cup (0).

Knight R 3	Stockley S 39+2	Powell P 33+3	Guyett S 20+2	Hatswell W 21	Bolland P 20	Savage D 42	Tait P 13+1	Scott A 25+5	Brooks J 18+7	Thomas M 13+1	Ricketts S 19+10	Onuoyinmi E 11+12	McCaldon I 28	Beauchamp J 2+1	Folland R —+10	Gray P 14+7	Whitehead D 30+10	Quinn R 11+5	Richardson J 16+2	Moody P 29+6	Hackett C 5+10	Douglas S 1+3	Crosby A 22+1	Morley D 16+2	Bound M 22	Woodman A 15	Maddison L 11	Patterson D 2	Waterman D 4+1	King S 1+1	Louis J —+1	Match No.
1	2	3¹	4	5	6	7	8	9	10	11²	12	13																				1
	2		4	5	6	7		9	10	8		3	1			11																2
	2		4	5	6	8		9	10¹	11		3²	1	12	13	7³	14															3
	2		4	5	6	8²		9	12	11³		3	1			10¹	7	13														4
	2²			5	6	7		9	12	11¹		3	1		14	10¹	8	13	4													5
	2		4	5	6	7		9		11		3	1			10	8															6
	2		4	5	6²	7¹		9		11		3	12			10	8	13														7
	2	3¹	4	5	6	7		9		11²	12	8	1		14	10³	13															8
	2		4	5	6	7		9¹		11		3	1			12	8		10													9
	2		4	5	6	7				11		3	1			10	8			9												10
	2		4	5	6	7				11		3	1			10	8			9												11
	2		4	5	6	7	8¹				12	3	1			10	11			9												12
	2	12	4	5		7²			13	11		3³	1		14	10¹	8		6	9												13
	2¹	3	4	5	6	7			10²		12	11¹	1		13	8				9	14											14
12		3¹	4		6	7			10			2³	13		14	8		5	9	11²												15
	2	3¹	4		6	7			10²		12		1		13	8	11	5	9³	14												16
	2²	3			6	7			10			4	8²	1		13	12	11¹	5	9	14											17
	2²	3	4		6	7			10¹				11	1		13	8		5	9	12											18
	2²	3	4	5	6¹	7			10	11			1		13	8		12	9²	14												19
	2	3	4	5	6	7			10	12			1			8		11	9	13												20
	2	3	4	5	6	7¹	10²			12	13		1		14	8		11	9⁴													21
	2¹	3		5		7	10²			12			1		13			8	6	9			4	11								22
	2²	3	5¹			7	10			12			1		13	14		8	11	9¹			4	6								23
	2	3	5²			7	9			12			1		10¹	14	8²	11	13				4	6								24
	2	3				7	10³	12		5²	13		1		14	8		11	9¹				4	6								25
	2	3¹				7	10²	13		5	12		1			8		11	9⁴				4	6								26
	2²	11	12				13	10		3		1		14	8	7	5¹	9⁴				4	6									27
	2¹	3				7	8⁵	9			12			10²	11	14		13				4	6	5	1							28
	2²	3				7		10		13	12				8	11¹		9				4	6	5	1							29
		3				7		9		2	12			10²	8¹	11		13				4	6	5	1							30
	2²	3	8			7¹				11				13	10		9	12				4	6	5	1							31
1	2¹	11				7			8					13	10²		9	12				4	6	5			3					32
		11³				7		13		14	9¹			10²	8		2		12			4	6	5	1		3					33
		11				7		10		12				9²	8	13			3			4¹	6	5	1	2						34
		11				4		9		2		7²		10¹	14	8³		12	13				6	5	1	3						35
	2	11	4			7		10		12				8			9¹						6	5	1	3						36
	2	11				7¹		10						8	12		9					4	6	5	1	3						37
	2	11					8¹	10	12					7		6²	9					4	13	5	1	3						38
	2	11				7	8¹	10	12					13			9					4	6²	5	1	3						39
	2	11³				7	8	10						12	6²		9¹	13				4	14	5	1	3						40
1	2¹	11				7	8¹		10²					9³	12		13	14				4	6	5			3					41
	2	12				7	8¹	13	10			1					9	11				4		5		3²		6				42
	2	12				7	8¹	13	10			1		9²				11		14		4		5		3³	6	4				43
12		3³				7	8²	13	10					6¹			9	11		4			5	1					2	14		44
		11²	12			7	8³	9	10	3							13	14		4		6		5	1				2¹			45
	2	11²				7³		12	10					8			9	3¹		4			5	1				13	6	14	46

PETERBOROUGH UNITED   Division 2

FOUNDATION

The old Peterborough & Fletton club, founded in 1923, was suspended by the FA during season 1932–33 and disbanded. Local enthusiasts determined to carry on and in 1934 a new professional club, Peterborough United, was formed and entered the Midland League the following year. Peterborough's first success came in 1939–40, but from 1955–56 to 1959–60 they won five successive titles. During the 1958–59 season they were undefeated in the Midland League. They reached the third round of the FA Cup, won the Northamptonshire Senior Cup, the Maunsell Cup and were runners-up in the East Anglian Cup.

London Road Ground, Peterborough PE2 8AL.

Telephone: 08700 550 442. **Fax:** (01733) 344 140.
ClubCall: 09068 121 654. **Website:** www.theposh.com
Email: info@pufc-theposhisp.com

Ground Capacity: 15,314.

Record Attendance: 30,096 v Swansea T, FA Cup 5th rd, 20 February 1965.

Record Receipts: £51,315 v Brighton & HA, FA Cup 5th rd, 15 February 1986.

Pitch Measurements: 112yd × 71yd.

Chairman: Peter Boizot MBE, DL.
Vice-chairman: Roger Terrell. **Directors:** A. Hand, P. Sagar.

Chief Executive: Geoff Davey.

Company Secretary: Timothy Warren.

Club Secretary: Julie Etherington.

First Team Manager: Barry Fry.

Head Coach: Phil Chapple.

Youth Academy Director: Dan Ashworth.

Physio: Paul Showler.

Colours: Royal blue shirts, white shorts, blue stockings with white tops.

Change Colours: (To be announced.)

Year Formed: 1934.

Turned Professional: 1934.

Ltd Co.: 1934.

Club Nickname: 'The Posh'.

First Football League Game: 20 August 1960, Division 4, v Wrexham (h) W 3–0 – Walls; Stafford, Walker; Rayner, Rigby, Norris; Hails, Emery (1), Bly (1), Smith, McNamee (1).

HONOURS

Football League: Division 1 best season: 10th, 1992–93. Promoted from Division 3 1999–2000 (play-offs); Division 4 – Champions 1960–61, 1973–74.

FA Cup: best season: 6th rd, 1965.

Football League Cup: Semi-final 1966.

IT'S A FACT !

From 29 September 1956 until gaining election to the Football League in 1960, Peterborough United did not lose a home Midland League game for nearly four years.

Record League Victory: 9–1 v Barnet (a) Division 3, 5 September 1998 – Griemink; Hooper (1), Drury (Farell), Gill, Bodley, Edwards, Davies, Payne, Grazioli (5), Quinn (2) (Rowe), Houghton (Etherington) (1).

Record Cup Victory: 7–0 v Harlow T, FA Cup 1st rd, 16 November 1991 – Barber; Luke, Johnson, Halsall (1), Robinson D, Welsh, Sterling (1) (Butterworth), Cooper G (2 incl. 1p), Riley (1) (Culpin (1)), Charlery (1), Kimble.

Record Defeat: 1–8 v Northampton T, FA Cup 2nd rd (2nd replay), 18 December 1946.

Most League Points (2 for a win): 66, Division 4, 1960–61.

Most League Points (3 for a win): 82, Division 4, 1981–82.

Most League Goals: 134, Division 4, 1960–61.

Highest League Scorer in Season: Terry Bly, 52, Division 4, 1960–61.

Most League Goals in Total Aggregate: Jim Hall, 122, 1967–75.

Most League Goals in One Match: 5, Guiliano Grazioli v Barnet, Division 3, 5 September 1998.

Most Capped Player: Tony Millington, 8 (21), Wales.

Most League Appearances: Tommy Robson, 482, 1968–81.

Youngest League Player: Matthew Etherington, 15 years 262 days v Brentford, 3 May 1997.

Record Transfer Fee Received: £700,000 from Tottenham H for Simon Davies, December 1999.

Record Transfer Fee Paid: £350,000 to Walsall for Martin O'Connor, July 1996.

Football League Record: 1960 Elected to Division 4; 1961–68 Division 3, when they were demoted for financial irregularities; 1968–74 Division 4; 1974–79 Division 3; 1979–91 Division 4; 1991–92 Division 3; 1992–94 Division 1; 1994–97 Division 2; 1997–2000 Division 3; 2000– Division 2.

MANAGERS

Jock Porter 1934–36
Fred Taylor 1936–37
Vic Poulter 1937–38
Sam Madden 1938–48
Jack Blood 1948–50
Bob Gurney 1950–52
Jack Fairbrother 1952–54
George Swindin 1954–58
Jimmy Hagan 1958–62
Jack Fairbrother 1962–64
Gordon Clark 1964–67
Norman Rigby 1967–69
Jim Iley 1969–72
Noel Cantwell 1972–77
John Barnwell 1977–78
Billy Hails 1978–79
Peter Morris 1979–82
Martin Wilkinson 1982–83
John Wile 1983–86
Noel Cantwell 1986–88
   (continued as
   General Manager)
Mick Jones 1988–89
Mark Lawrenson 1989–90
Chris Turner 1991–92
Lil Fuccillo 1992–93
John Still 1994–95
Mick Halsall 1995–96
Barry Fry May 1996–

LATEST SEQUENCES

Longest Sequence of League Wins: 9, 1.2.92 – 14.3.92.

Longest Sequence of League Defeats: 5, 8.10.96 – 26.10.96.

Longest Sequence of League Draws: 8, 18.12.71 – 12.2.72.

Longest Sequence of Unbeaten League Matches: 17, 17.12.60 – 8.4.61.

Longest Sequence Without a League Win: 17, 23.9.78 – 30.12.78.

TEN YEAR LEAGUE RECORD

		P	W	D	L	F	A	Pts	Pos
1991-92	Div 3	46	20	14	12	65	58	74	6
1992-93	Div 1	46	16	14	16	55	63	62	10
1993-94	Div 1	46	8	13	25	48	76	37	24
1994-95	Div 2	46	14	18	14	54	69	60	15
1995-96	Div 2	46	13	13	20	59	66	52	19
1996-97	Div 2	46	11	14	21	55	73	47	21
1997-98	Div 3	46	18	13	15	63	51	67	10
1998-99	Div 3	46	18	12	16	72	56	66	9
1999-2000	Div 3	46	22	12	12	63	54	78	5
2000-01	Div 2	46	15	14	17	61	66	59	12

DID YOU KNOW ❓

On 31 December 1938, Peterborough United achieved their highest score in a Midland League match by beating Boston United 12-0. Charlie MacCartney scored six times.

PETERBOROUGH UNITED 2001–02 LEAGUE RECORD

Match No.	Date	Venue	Opponents	Result	H/T Score	Lg. Pos.	Goalscorers	Attendance
1	Aug 11	A	Swindon T	D	0-0	0-0	—	7934
2	18	H	Cardiff C	D	1-1	1-1	16	Farrell [44]	6437
3	25	A	Port Vale	L	1-4	0-1	17	Cullen [67]	4925
4	27	H	Huddersfield T	L	1-2	0-0	20	Farrell [46]	5253
5	Sept 1	A	Chesterfield	W	1-0	1-0	16	McKenzie [18]	3555
6	8	H	Cambridge U	W	1-0	0-0	13	MacDonald [68]	8656
7	15	A	Oldham Ath	L	0-2	0-0	14		4855
8	18	H	Bournemouth	W	6-0	3-0	—	Joseph [2], Bullard [10], McKenzie [43], Fenn 2 [50, 55], French [67]	3445
9	22	A	Bristol C	W	4-1	3-0	9	Clarke A 2 [14, 42], Joseph [39], Bullard [75]	5550
10	25	A	Notts Co	L	0-1	0-0	—		5633
11	29	A	Wrexham	W	2-1	0-0	8	Bullard [48], McKenzie [78]	2640
12	Oct 7	H	Northampton T	W	2-0	1-0	6	Bullard (pen) [45], Clarke A [54]	8101
13	13	A	Brentford	L	1-2	0-2	7	Rea [79]	11,097
14	20	H	Blackpool	W	3-2	1-2	5	McKenzie 2 [36, 90], Williams T [53]	3500
15	23	H	QPR	W	4-1	2-1	—	Farrell [39], Fenn 2 [45, 84], McKenzie [49]	7427
16	27	A	Bury	L	0-2	0-1	5		2784
17	Nov 3	H	Wigan Ath	L	0-2	0-1	6		5405
18	10	A	Wycombe W	L	0-3	0-1	10		6025
19	21	A	Brighton & HA	D	1-1	1-1	—	McKenzie [21]	6547
20	24	H	Reading	L	1-2	1-0	12	Clarke A [6]	5695
21	Dec 15	A	Colchester U	L	1-2	1-1	15	Edwards [7]	3480
22	26	A	Huddersfield T	L	1-3	0-1	16	Clarke A [86]	11,446
23	29	A	Cambridge U	D	0-0	0-0	17		5665
24	Jan 8	H	Port Vale	W	3-0	1-0	—	Williams T [20], Bullard [47], Oldfield [65]	3747
25	12	A	Cardiff C	W	2-0	1-0	14	McKenzie [45], Fenn [54]	11,301
26	19	H	Swindon T	D	1-1	0-1	15	Bullard [59]	6598
27	22	H	Tranmere R	L	0-1	0-1	—		7342
28	29	H	Stoke C	L	1-2	1-1	—	Farrell [2]	5173
29	Feb 2	H	Wrexham	L	2-3	1-1	17	Cowan [16], Green [69]	4675
30	5	H	Chesterfield	D	1-1	0-1	—	Forinton [48]	4401
31	9	A	Blackpool	D	2-2	1-1	18	Bullard (pen) [33], Edwards [78]	4604
32	16	A	Brentford	D	1-1	0-1	18	McKenzie [84]	5100
33	19	A	Northampton T	L	1-2	1-2	—	Bullard [2]	6064
34	23	H	Oldham Ath	D	2-2	1-2	18	Forinton [9], Fenn [65]	4308
35	26	A	Bristol C	L	0-1	0-1	—		8299
36	Mar 2	H	Bournemouth	W	2-0	1-0	18	Gill [7], McKenzie [47]	5163
37	5	H	Notts Co	L	0-1	0-1	—		4415
38	9	H	Colchester U	W	3-1	2-0	17	Farrell [26], Green [39], McKenzie [77]	4625
39	16	A	Stoke C	L	0-1	0-1	18		12,983
40	19	H	Tranmere R	W	5-0	3-0	—	McKenzie 3 [18, 52, 74], Danielsson 2 [22, 28]	3995
41	23	A	QPR	L	0-1	0-1	18		10,324
42	30	H	Wycombe W	W	2-1	1-0	15	McKenzie [14], Green [60]	4926
43	Apr 1	A	Wigan Ath	L	1-2	0-2	16	Farrell [49]	4497
44	6	A	Brighton & HA	L	0-1	0-0	17		8321
45	13	A	Reading	D	2-2	1-0	17	Gill [29], McKenzie [83]	22,151
46	20	H	Bury	W	2-1	1-0	17	McKenzie 2 (1 pen) [27 (p), 79]	5754

Final League Position: 17

GOALSCORERS
League (64): McKenzie 18 (1 pen), Bullard 8 (2 pens), Farrell 6, Fenn 6, Clarke A 5, Green 3, Danielsson 2, Edwards 2, Forinton 2, Gill 2, Joseph 2, Williams T 2, Cowan 1, Cullen 1, French 1, MacDonald 1, Oldfield 1, Rea 1.
Worthington Cup (4): Clarke A 1, Fenn 1, Forsyth 1, own goal 1.
FA Cup (9): Clarke A 2, Farrell 2, Bullard 1 (pen), Danielsson 1, Fenn 1, McKenzie 1, own goal 1.

Tyler M 44	Joseph M 44	Williams T 31+3	Cullen J 10+3	Rea S 27+3	Edwards A 44	Bullard J 36+4	Oldfield D 27+3	Clarke A 19+9	Green F 12+11	Furlong H 13+4	Forsyth R 30+2	Farrell D 35+3	Fenn N 25+11	Connor D —+1	Danielsson H 20+11	MacDonald G 7+1	Hooper D 7+6	Hanlon R —+1	McKenzie L 28+2	Jelleyman G 6+4	Shields T 6+9	French D 1+9	Pearce D 8+1	Clarke L —+1	Toner C 6	Cowan T 4+1	Gill M 11+1	Kimble A 3	Steele L 2	Match No.
1	2	3	4[1]	5	6	7	8	9	10[2]	11[3]	12	13	14																	1
1[9]	2	3	10	5[2]	6		8	9	12	11[1]	4	7			15	13														2
1	2	3	6[1]		5	12	8	9	10[2]		4	13	11			7[3]	14													3
1	5	3	10[1]		6	12	8[3]	9	13		4	7	11[2]			2	14													4
1	2		10	5	6		8	12			4	7	11			3			9[1]											5
1	2		10[1]	5	6	12	8	13			4	7	11			3			9[2]											6
1	4	3[2]	8	5	6	7					11	10[3]	9[1]		12	2				13	14									7
1	2	3	12	5	6	7					4[2]		10		8				9[1]	11[3]	13	14								8
1	2	3		5	6	7		9[1]	12		4[2]	11	10		8						13									9
1	2[2]	3		5	6	7		9	12		4	11	10[3]		8[1]	13					14									10
1	2	3		5	6	7			12		4	11	10[1]		8[2]				9[3]	14	13									11
1	5	3			6	7		9	12		4	11	10[1]		8[2]	2			13											12
1	5	3[2]	12		6	7		9			4	11	13		8[1]	2			10											13
1	2	3		5	6	7		9[2]			4	11	10		8[1]				12	13										14
1	2	3		5	6	7[3]	12				4[2]	11	10		14				9[1]	8	13									15
1	2	3[2]		5	6	7	8		10[2]		12				9	11	4[1]	13	14											16
1	2	3[2]	4[1]	5		7[2]	6				12		10		8				9	11	13									17
1	2	12		5[2]	6			9			7	13			8	14			10	11[2]	4	3[1]								18
1	2	3		5	6				11	12	4	7	10		8				9[1]											19
1	5	3			6	12	11	9			4	7	10[1]		8[2]	13	2													20
1	2	12	4[2]	5	6	7	8[3]	9	10[1]		11									3	13				14					21
1	2	12	13	5	6	7[3]	8	9	10		11	14								3[1]					4[2]					22
1	2	3		5	6	7	8	12			11	10[1]							9						4					23
1	2	3		5	6	7	8	12	13		11	10[2]		14					9[1]						4[3]					24
1	2	3	12	5[1]	6	7	8	13			11	10			14				9[2]						4					25
1	5			6	7	8[1]	9				12	11	10		2				13						4[2]	3				26
1		7	12	6[1]					10			9[3]	11		8	5	2			13	14				4[2]	3				27
1	2	8			6	7		9			4	11	10			5[1]	12									3				28
1	2	8		5	6	7		9	13	14	4[1]	11	10[3]		12											3[2]				29
1	2	3		5	6	7		9[1]	12	10	4	11			8															30
1	2	3		5	6	7	8		10		4	11			9															31
1	2	3		5	6	7	8[2]		10[1]		4	11	12		9								13							32
1	2[3]	3		5	6	7	8[2]		10		4	11	12		9[1]								13			14				33
1	2	3			6	7			12	10	4[2]	11	9		13								8[1]			5				34
1	2	3	12		6	7		8[3]	10	11	9[1]				13								4[2]	14		5				35
1	2	3		5	6		8		12	10[1]	11				13				9				7[2]			4				36
1	2	3			6	7	8		12	10[1]	11	13			14				9				4[2]			5[3]				37
1	2	3			6	7	8		10		11				12				9				4[1]			5				38
1				5	6	7			10	12		11			4				9[1]							2	3			39
1	5				6	7	8		10[2]	12	4[3]	13			11				9[1]				14	3		2				40
1	5				6	7	8[2]		10		4		12		11				9[1]				13	3		2				41
1	5				6	7	8[1]		10		4				11				9				12	3		2				42
1	5				6	7		9	8		4	11			2				10				3							43
1	5				6	7		9[3]	8		4	11[1]	12		2				10				3			13				44
	5				6	7	12	13			4	14	10[2]		11				9				8			2[1]	3[3]	1		45
	5					7	12	13	8[1]		4[3]	14	11	6					9				2[2]			10	3	1		46

Worthington Cup

First Round	Swansea C	(a)	2-0
Second Round	Coventry C	(h)	2-2

FA Cup

First Round	Bedford T	(a)	0-0
		(h)	2-1
Second Round	Bournemouth	(h)	1-0
Third Round	Darlington	(a)	2-2
		(h)	2-0
Fourth Round	Newcastle U	(h)	2-4

PLYMOUTH ARGYLE   Division 2

FOUNDATION

The club was formed in September 1886 as the Argyle Football Club by former public and private school pupils who wanted to continue playing the game. The meeting was held in a room above the Borough Arms (a Coffee House), Bedford Street, Plymouth. It was common then to choose a local street/terrace as a club name and Argyle or Argyll was a fashionable name throughout the land due to Queen Victoria's great interest in Scotland.

Home Park, Plymouth, Devon PL2 3DQ.

Telephone: (01752) 562 561. **Fax:** (01752) 606 167.
Pilgrim Shop: (01752) 558 292.

Ground Capacity: 20,134.

Record Attendance: 43,596 v Aston Villa, Division 2, 10 October 1936.

Record Receipts: £128,000 v Burnley, Division 2 play-off, 18 May 1994.

Pitch Measurements: 110yd × 72yd.

President: S. J. Rendell.

Chairman: Paul Stapleton. **Vice-chairman:** Peter Jones.

Directors: Phil Gill, Nick Warren, Rt Hon Michael Foot.
Assistant Directors: Ken Jones, John McNulty.

Manager: Paul Sturrock.
Assistant Manager: Kevin Summerfield.
Physio: Paul Maxwell.

Chief Executive: David Tall. **Secretary:** Carole Rowntree.

Colours: Green shirts, green shorts, green stockings.

Change Colours: Tangerine shirts, green shorts, tangerine stockings.

Year Formed: 1886.

Turned Professional: 1903.

Ltd Co.: 1903.

Previous Name: 1886, Argyle Athletic Club; 1903, Plymouth Argyle.

Club Nickname: 'The Pilgrims'.

First Football League game: 28 August 1920, Division 3, v Norwich C (h) D 1–1 – Craig; Russell, Atterbury; Logan, Dickinson, Forbes; Kirkpatrick, Jack, Bowler, Heeps (1), Dixon.

Record League Victory: 8–1 v Millwall, Division 2, 16 January 1932 – Harper; Roberts, Titmuss; Mackay, Pullan, Reed; Grozier, Bowden (2), Vidler (3), Leslie (1), Black (1), (1 og). 8–1 v Hartlepool U (a), Division 2, 7 May 1994 – Nicholls; Patterson (Naylor), Hill, Burrows, Comyn, McCall (1), Barlow, Castle (1), Landon (3), Marshall (1), Dalton (2).

HONOURS

Football League: Division 2 best season: 4th, 1931–32, 1952–53; Division 3 (S) – Champions 1929–30, 1951–52; Runners-up 1921–22, 1922–23, 1923–24, 1924–25, 1925–26, 1926–27 (record of six consecutive years); Division 3 – Champions 1958–59, 2001–02; Runners-up 1974–75, 1985–86, Promoted 1995–96 (play-offs).
FA Cup: Semi-final 1984.
Football League Cup: Semi-final 1965, 1974.

IT'S A FACT !

Ray Bowden, a one-time auctioneer's clark, was snapped up by Plymouth Argyle after scoring 10 goals for Looe v Tavistock in 1926. Later with Arsenal, he was capped by England.

Record Cup Victory: 6–0 v Corby T, FA Cup 3rd rd, 22 January 1966 – Leiper; Book, Baird; Williams, Nelson, Newman; Jones (1), Jackson (1), Bickle (3), Piper (1), Jennings.

Record Defeat: 0–9 v Stoke C, Division 2, 17 December 1960.

Most League Points (2 for a win): 68, Division 3 (S), 1929–30.

Most League Points (3 for a win): 102, Division 3, 2001–02.

Most League Goals: 107, Division 3 (S), 1925–26 and 1951–52.

Highest League Scorer in Season: Jack Cock, 32, Division 3 (S), 1925–26.

Most League Goals in Total Aggregate: Sammy Black, 180, 1924–38.

Most League Goals in One Match: 5, Wilf Carter v Charlton Ath, Division 2, 27 December 1960.

Most Capped Player: Moses Russell, 20 (23), Wales.

Most League Appearances: Kevin Hodges, 530, 1978–92.

Youngest League Player: Lee Phillips, 16 years 43 days v Gillingham, 29 October 1996.

Record Transfer Fee Received: £750,000 from Southampton for Mickey Evans, March 1997.

Record Transfer Fee Paid: £250,000 to Hartlepool U for Paul Dalton, June 1992.

Football League Record: 1920 Original Member of Division 3; 1921–30 Division 3 (S); 1930–50 Division 2; 1950–52 Division 3 (S); 1952–56 Division 2; 1956–58 Division 3 (S); 1958–59 Division 3; 1959–68 Division 2; 1968–75 Division 3; 1975–77 Division 2; 1977–86 Division 3; 1986–95 Division 2; 1995–96 Division 3; 1996–98 Division 2; 1998–2002 Division 3; 2002– Division 2.

MANAGERS

Frank Brettell 1903–05
Bob Jack 1905–06
Bill Fullerton 1906–07
Bob Jack 1910–38
Jack Tresadern 1938–47
Jimmy Rae 1948–55
Jack Rowley 1955–60
Neil Dougall 1961
Ellis Stuttard 1961–63
Andy Beattie 1963–64
Malcolm Allison 1964–65
Derek Ufton 1965–68
Billy Bingham 1968–70
Ellis Stuttard 1970–72
Tony Waiters 1972–77
Mike Kelly 1977–78
Malcolm Allison 1978–79
Bobby Saxton 1979–81
Bobby Moncur 1981–83
Johnny Hore 1983–84
Dave Smith 1984–88
Ken Brown 1988–90
David Kemp 1990–92
Peter Shilton 1992–95
Steve McCall 1995
Neil Warnock 1995–97
Mick Jones 1997–98
Kevin Hodges 1998–2000
Paul Sturrock October 2000–

LATEST SEQUENCES

Longest Sequence of League Wins: 9, 8.3.86 – 12.4.86.

Longest Sequence of League Defeats: 9, 12.10.63 – 7.12.63.

Longest Sequence of League Draws: 5, 26.2.00 – 14.3.00.

Longest Sequence of Unbeaten League Matches: 22, 20.4.29 – 21.12.29.

Longest Sequence Without a League Win: 13, 27.4.63 – 2.10.63.

TEN YEAR LEAGUE RECORD

		P	W	D	L	F	A	Pts	Pos
1991-92	Div 2	46	13	9	24	42	64	48	22
1992-93	Div 2	46	16	12	18	59	64	60	14
1993-94	Div 2	46	25	10	11	88	56	85	3
1994-95	Div 2	46	12	10	24	45	83	46	21
1995-96	Div 3	46	22	12	12	68	49	79	4
1996-97	Div 2	46	12	18	16	47	58	54	19
1997-98	Div 2	46	12	13	21	55	70	49	22
1998-99	Div 3	46	17	10	19	58	54	61	13
1999-2000	Div 3	46	16	18	12	55	51	66	12
2000-01	Div 3	46	15	13	18	54	61	58	12

DID YOU KNOW ?

On 24 November 2001, Plymouth Argyle completed a post-war club record of 17 unbeaten League matches with a 3-0 win over Carlisle United. It was also their seventh consecutive home win.

PLYMOUTH ARGYLE 2001–02 LEAGUE RECORD

Match No.	Date	Venue	Opponents	Result		H/T Score	Lg. Pos.	Goalscorers	Attendance
1	Aug 11	H	Shrewsbury T	L	0-1	0-0	—		5087
2	18	A	Hull C	D	0-0	0-0	19		10,755
3	25	H	Rochdale	L	1-2	1-1	22	Coleman (og) [16]	4198
4	27	A	Rushden & D	W	3-2	1-2	18	Evans [45], Coughlan [51], McGlinchey [71]	4414
5	Sept 8	A	Torquay U	W	1-0	0-0	14	Friio [58]	4217
6	11	H	Swansea C	W	3-1	2-0	—	Wotton (pen) [24], Banger [45], Phillips M [61]	3850
7	15	A	Kidderminster H	D	0-0	0-0	9		2801
8	18	A	Exeter C	W	3-2	1-2	—	Phillips M [6], Evans [65], Stonebridge [90]	5756
9	22	H	Macclesfield T	W	2-0	1-0	5	Hodges L [45], Friio [65]	4227
10	25	A	York C	D	0-0	0-0	—		2282
11	29	H	Luton T	W	2-1	2-1	4	Phillips M [22], Friio [45]	5782
12	Oct 6	A	Oxford U	D	1-1	0-0	5	Banger [80]	6017
13	13	H	Halifax T	W	3-0	3-0	4	Coughlan [16], Phillips M [23], Hodges L [26]	5065
14	20	A	Mansfield T	W	3-0	0-0	2	Evans [54], Friio [89], Stonebridge [90]	4621
15	23	H	Lincoln C	W	2-0	1-0	—	Friio [28], Coughlan [75]	6572
16	28	A	Bristol R	W	2-1	1-0	1	Phillips M [2], Hodges L [58]	6889
17	Nov 3	H	Hartlepool U	W	1-0	1-0	1	Friio [41]	5723
18	9	A	Cheltenham T	D	0-0	0-0	—		5035
19	20	A	Southend U	W	1-0	1-0	—	Adams [43]	3716
20	24	H	Carlisle U	W	3-0	2-0	1	Evans [17], Bent [45], Phillips M [88]	5870
21	Dec 1	A	Leyton Orient	D	0-0	0-0	1		6342
22	15	H	Darlington	W	1-0	0-0	1	Friio [81]	5041
23	22	A	Scunthorpe U	L	1-2	0-2	1	Coughlan [51]	3602
24	26	H	Torquay U	D	2-2	0-0	1	Coughlan [50], Stonebridge [52]	13,677
25	29	H	Rushden & D	W	1-0	0-0	1	Keith [81]	9503
26	Jan 12	H	Hull C	W	1-0	1-0	1	Stonebridge [20]	9134
27	19	A	Shrewsbury T	L	1-3	1-1	1	Evans [5]	4796
28	22	H	Scunthorpe U	W	2-1	1-1	—	Wotton (pen) [44], Keith [54]	5804
29	26	H	Oxford U	W	4-2	3-2	1	Coughlan [21], Hodges L [24], Stonebridge 2 [45, 46]	8239
30	Feb 2	A	Luton T	L	0-2	0-0	1		9585
31	5	A	Swansea C	W	1-0	1-0	—	Sturrock [39]	4060
32	9	H	Mansfield T	W	1-0	0-0	1	Friio [85]	14,716
33	16	A	Halifax T	W	2-0	2-0	1	Hodges L [41], Wotton (pen) [43]	2330
34	23	H	Kidderminster H	W	2-1	0-1	1	Coughlan [67], Wotton (pen) [81]	8758
35	26	H	Exeter C	W	3-0	2-0	—	Adams [5], Keith 2 [29, 74]	16,369
36	Mar 2	A	Macclesfield T	D	1-1	0-0	1	Coughlan [71]	2557
37	5	H	York C	W	1-0	1-0	—	Potter (og) [45]	10,801
38	16	H	Leyton Orient	W	3-0	1-0	1	Stonebridge [6], Coughlan [78], Evans [81]	9438
39	23	A	Lincoln C	W	1-0	0-0	1	Stonebridge [71]	4019
40	26	A	Rochdale	W	3-1	0-0	—	Keith [66], Coughlan [81], Hodges L [83]	4457
41	30	H	Bristol R	W	1-0	1-0	1	Keith [1]	15,732
42	Apr 1	A	Hartlepool U	L	0-1	0-0	1		3725
43	6	A	Southend U	D	0-0	0-0	2		10,021
44	13	A	Carlisle U	W	2-0	1-0	1	Keith [20], Wotton [53]	3080
45	15	A	Darlington	W	4-1	3-1	—	Evans [10], Keith 2 [17, 28], Bent [59]	4089
46	20	H	Cheltenham T	W	2-0	2-0	1	Bent [4], Coughlan [24]	18,517

Final League Position: 1

GOALSCORERS
League (71): Coughlan 11, Keith 9, Friio 8, Stonebridge 8, Evans 7, Hodges L 6, Phillips M 6, Wotton 5 (4 pens), Bent 3, Adams 2, Banger 2, McGlinchey 1, Sturrock 1, own goals 2.
Worthington Cup (0).
FA Cup (7): Friio 2, Phillips M 2, Bent 1, Stonebridge 1, Wotton 1.

Larrieu R 45	Adams S 40+6	Beswetherick J 27+5	Friio D 41	Wotton P 46	Coughlan G 46	Phillips M 37+2	Wills K 13+5	Stonebridge I 29+13	Evans M 30+8	McGlinchey B 26+3	Evers S 3+4	Crowe D —+1	Gritton M —+2	Hodges L 42+3	Broad J 1+6	Worrell D 42	Banger N 3+7	Bent J 16+5	Keith M 13+10	Sturrock B 4+15	Heaney N 1+7	Adamson C 1	Taylor C —+1	Match No.
1	2	3^1	4	5	6	7	8	9^2	10^3	11	12	13	14											1
1	2	3	4	5	6	7	12	9^1	11	10^2				8	13									2
1	2	12		5	6	7		9^3	10	11	4^1			8	13	3^2	14							3
1	2	3		5	6	7	8	9^1	11		12			10	4									4
1	2	3	4	5	6	7		9	10^2	12				8		11	13							5
1	2	3	4	5	6	7		9	11					12		8	10^1							6
1	2	3	4	5	6	7	11^3	12	9^1	13				9^2		10	14							7
1	2	3^2	4	5	6	7		12	9	11				13		10	8^1							8
1	3		4	5	6	7		9	10^1	11				8		2	12							9
1	6		4	3	5	7	8^1	12	9	11				10		2								10
1	6		4	3	5	7^2	12	9	10	11				13		2	8^1							11
1	6		4	3	5	7^2	13	12	9^1	11				8		2	14	10^3						12
1	12		4	3	5	7^1		9	13	11				8		2	10^2	6						13
1	11	12	4	5	6	7^1	8^3	13	9^2	3				10	14	2								14
1	12		4	5	6	7^1		9^2	10	3				8		2	13	11						15
1	11	12	4	5	6	7^3	8^1	13	9^2	3				10		2	14							16
1	12		4	5	6	7^2		9^1	10	3				8		2	13	11						17
1	10^1		4	5	6	7^3	13	12	9	3				8		2	14	11^2						18
1	7		4	5	6		8		9	3				10		2	11							19
1	12	13	4^1		5	6		9^3	10	3				8^2		2	11	14						20
1	4	3		5	6	7^1	8		9	11	12			10		2								21
1	12	3^2	4	5	6	7^3		9^1		11				8		2	10	13	14					22
1	11		4	5	6	7	10^1	9^2		3				8		2	12	13						23
1	11		4	5	6	7^3	12	9^2		3				8		2	10^1	13	14					24
1	11		4	5	6	7^1		9^2		3	12			8		2	10	13						25
1	11		4	5	6	7^2		9	12	3				8		2	13	10^1						26
1	11		4	5	6	7^1		12	9^1	3	10^2			8		2	13	14						27
	11	12	4	5	6	7		9	13	3^1				8		2	10^2		1					28
1	11	3	4	5	6	7		9	12					8		2	10^1							29
1	11	3	4	5	6	7^2		9^1	12		13			8		2	10^1	14						30
1	11	3	4	5	6			12	10					8	13	2			9^1	7^2				31
1	11	3	4	5	6	7^2		9^1	10^1					8		2	12	13	14					32
1	11	3	4	5	6	12	7^2	9						8	13	2			10^1					33
1	11	3	4	5	6	7^1		9^1	10					8^2		2	12	13	14					34
1	11	3	4	5	6	7^3	12	9^1						8^1		2	10	13	14					35
1	11	3	4	5	6		10^1	9^1						8	12	2	13	7						36
1	11	3	4	5	6	7^1		9						8		2	10^2	12			13			37
1	11	4^3	5	6		7^2		9	12					8		2	13	10^1	14					38
1	11	3	4	5	6	7^2	10^1	12	9					8		2		13						39
1	11^3	3	4	5	6			12	9^1					8		2	10	13	7^2	14				40
1	11	3	4	5	6	7^2		9^1	12					8		2	13	10^1	14					41
1	11^2	3	4	5	6		7^3	12	9^1					8		2	10	13	14					42
1	12	3	4	5	6	7		9^2	10					8^1		2	11^3	13	14					43
1	11	3		5	6			9	10					8		2	4	7						44
1	11	3		5	6	12		9^1	10^2	13				8^3		2	4	7	14					45
1	11	3	4	5	6			9^2	12					8		2	7	10^1	13					46

Worthington Cup
First Round   Watford   (a)   0-1

FA Cup
First Round   Whitby T   (a) 1-1 (h) 3-2
Second Round   Bristol R   (h) 1-1 (a) 2-3

PORTSMOUTH
Division 1

FOUNDATION

At a meeting held in his High Street, Portsmouth offices in 1898, solicitor Alderman J. E. Pink and five other business and professional men agreed to buy some ground close to Goldsmith Avenue for £4,950 which they developed into Fratton Park in record breaking time. A team of professionals was signed up by manager Frank Brettell and entry to the Southern League obtained for the new club's September 1899 kick-off.

Fratton Park, Frogmore Rd, Portsmouth PO4 8RA.

Telephone: (023) 9273 1204. **Fax:** (023) 9273 4129

Ticket Office: (023) 9261 8777.

ClubCall: 09068 121 182.

Ground Capacity: 19,179.

Record Attendance: 51,385 v Derby Co, FA Cup 6th rd, 26 February 1949.

Record Receipts: £233,000 v Chelsea, FA Cup 6th rd, 9 March 1997.

Pitch Measurements: 110yd × 72yd.

Chairman: Milan Mandaric.
Directors: F. Dinenage, T. Brady.
Chief Executive: Peter Storrie.

Manager: Harry Redknapp. **Assistant Manager:** Jim Smith.

Goalkeeper Coach: Alan Knight.

Secretary: Paul Weld.

Youth Team Manager: Mark O'Connor.

Physio: Gary Sadler.

Colours: Blue shirts, white shorts, red stockings.

Change Colours: Gold and navy shirts, gold and navy shorts, navy stockings.

Year Formed: 1898.

Turned Professional: 1898.

Ltd Co.: 1898.

Club Nickname: 'Pompey'.

First Football League Game: 28 August 1920, Division 3, v Swansea T (h) W 3–0 – Robson; Probert, Potts; Abbott, Harwood, Turner; Thompson, Stringfellow (1), Reid (1), James (1), Beedie.

Record League Victory: 9–1 v Notts Co, Division 2, 9 April 1927 – McPhail; Clifford, Ted Smith; Reg Davies (1), Foxall, Moffat; Forward (1), Mackie (2), Haines (3), Watson, Cook (2).

HONOURS

Football League: Division 1 – Champions 1948–49, 1949–50; Division 2 – Runners-up 1926–27, 1986–87; Division 3 (S) – Champions 1923–24; Division 3 – Champions 1961–62, 1982–83.

FA Cup: Winners 1939; Runners-up 1929, 1934.

Football League Cup: best season: 5th rd, 1961, 1986.

IT'S A FACT !

Former miner John Gilfillan, developed with Hearts as a goalkeeper and loaned to East Fife, played in the 1937 Scottish Cup Final. Transferred to Portsmouth, he added appearances in the FA Cup in 1929 and 1933.

Record Cup Victory: 7–0 v Stockport Co, FA Cup 3rd rd, 8 January 1949 – Butler; Rookes, Ferrier; Scoular, Flewin, Dickinson; Harris (3), Barlow, Clarke (2), Phillips (2), Froggatt.

Record Defeat: 0–10 v Leicester C, Division 1, 20 October 1928.

Most League Points (2 for a win): 65, Division 3, 1961–62.

Most League Points (3 for a win): 91, Division 3, 1982–83.

Most League Goals: 91, Division 4, 1979–80.

Highest League Scorer in Season: Guy Whittingham, 42, Division 1, 1992–93.

Most League Goals in Total Aggregate: Peter Harris, 194, 1946–60.

Most League Goals in One Match: 5, Alf Strange v Gillingham, Division 3, 27 January 1923; 5, Peter Harris v Aston Villa, Division 1, 3 September 1958.

Most Capped Player: Jimmy Dickinson, 48, England.

Most League Appearances: Jimmy Dickinson, 764, 1946–65.

Youngest League Player: Clive Green, 16 years 259 days v Wrexham, 21 August 1976.

Record Transfer Fee Received: £4,500,000 from Aston Villa for Peter Crouch, March 2002.

Record Transfer Fee Paid: £1,400,000 to Yokohama Marinos for Yoshikatsu Kawaguchi, October 2001.

Football League Record: 1920 Original Member of Division 3; 1921 Division 3 (S); 1924–27 Division 2; 1927–59 Division 1; 1959–61 Division 2; 1961–62 Division 3; 1962–76 Division 2; 1976–78 Division 3; 1978–80 Division 4; 1980–83 Division 3; 1983–87 Division 2; 1987–88 Division 1; 1988–92 Division 2; 1992– Division 1.

MANAGERS

Frank Brettell 1898–1901
Bob Blyth 1901–04
Richard Bonney 1905–08
Bob Brown 1911–20
John McCartney 1920–27
Jack Tinn 1927–47
Bob Jackson 1947–52
Eddie Lever 1952–58
Freddie Cox 1958–61
George Smith 1961–70
Ron Tindall 1970–73
(General Manager to 1974)
John Mortimore 1973–74
Ian St John 1974–77
Jimmy Dickinson 1977–79
Frank Burrows 1979–82
Bobby Campbell 1982–84
Alan Ball 1984–89
John Gregory 1989–90
Frank Burrows 1990–91
Jim Smith 1991–95
Terry Fenwick 1995–98
Alan Ball 1998–99
Tony Pulis 2000
Steve Claridge 2000–01
Graham Rix 2001–02
Harry Redknapp March 2002–

LATEST SEQUENCES

Longest Sequence of League Wins: 7, 22.1.83 – 26.2.83.

Longest Sequence of League Defeats: 9, 21.10.75 – 6.12.75.

Longest Sequence of League Draws: 5, 6.12.00 – 13.1.01.

Longest Sequence of Unbeaten League Matches: 15, 18.4.24 – 18.10.24.

Longest Sequence Without a League Win: 25, 29.11.58 – 22.8.59.

TEN YEAR LEAGUE RECORD

		P	W	D	L	F	A	Pts	Pos
1991-92	Div 2	46	19	12	15	65	51	69	9
1992-93	Div 1	46	26	10	10	80	46	88	3
1993-94	Div 1	46	15	13	18	52	58	58	17
1994-95	Div 1	46	15	13	18	53	63	58	18
1995-96	Div 1	46	13	13	20	61	69	52	21
1996-97	Div 1	46	20	8	18	59	53	68	7
1997-98	Div 1	46	13	10	23	51	63	49	20
1998-99	Div 1	46	11	14	21	57	73	47	19
1999-2000	Div 1	46	13	12	21	55	66	51	18
2000-01	Div 1	46	10	19	17	47	59	49	20

DID YOU KNOW ?

Robert Blyth was unique in his time with Portsmouth, serving the club as player, captain, manager, director, vice-chairman and finally chairman from 1925–34, though he stayed on the board until 1938.

PORTSMOUTH 2001–02 LEAGUE RECORD

Match No.	Date	Venue	Opponents	Result	H/T Score	Lg. Pos.	Goalscorers	Attendance
1	Aug 11	A	Wolverhampton W	D	2-2	2-1	—	Crouch [8], Crowe [20]	23,012
2	18	H	Bradford C	L	0-1	0-0	19		17,239
3	25	A	Stockport Co	W	1-0	0-0	12	Prosinecki (pen) [61]	5090
4	27	H	Grimsby T	W	4-2	1-0	8	Burchill 2 [28, 78], Crouch 2 [63, 79]	13,614
5	Sept 8	H	Gillingham	W	2-1	0-1	7	Barrett [58], Zamperini [90]	17,224
6	12	A	Wimbledon	D	3-3	0-1	—	Burchill [67], Crouch [76], Bradbury (pen) [90]	7138
7	15	H	Crystal Palace	W	4-2	2-1	2	Zamperini [5], Prosinecki [38], Burchill (pen) [63], Crouch [76]	18,149
8	18	A	Walsall	D	0-0	0-0	—		6153
9	22	A	Coventry C	L	0-2	0-1	5	—	18,303
10	25	H	WBA	L	1-2	1-1	—	Prosinecki (pen) [6]	17,287
11	28	A	Barnsley	W	4-1	2-1	—	Vincent [23], Crouch [45], Bradbury 2 (1 pen) [51 (p), 59]	11,660
12	Oct 12	A	Rotherham U	L	1-2	0-1	—	Crouch [58]	6427
13	20	H	Sheffield U	W	1-0	1-0	8	Edinburgh [40]	15,538
14	23	A	Norwich C	D	0-0	0-0	—		19,962
15	27	H	Preston NE	L	0-1	0-1	12		15,402
16	30	A	Birmingham C	D	1-1	1-1	—	Bradbury [40]	15,612
17	Nov 3	A	Sheffield W	W	3-2	2-1	11	Crouch 2 [6, 39], Barrett [59]	18,212
18	10	A	Burnley	D	1-1	0-0	10	Crouch [72]	14,123
19	17	H	Manchester C	W	2-1	0-1	10	Bradbury [54], Crouch [77]	19,103
20	25	A	Watford	L	0-3	0-2	10		15,631
21	28	H	Nottingham F	W	3-2	1-2	—	Hjelde (og) [10], Bradbury 2 (1 pen) [50, 83 (p)]	14,837
22	Dec 2	H	Norwich C	L	1-2	1-1	10	Harper [23]	13,286
23	8	H	Crewe Alex	L	2-4	1-2	11	Lovell [44], Crouch [81]	14,430
24	13	A	Millwall	L	0-1	0-0	—		11,527
25	22	H	Stockport Co	W	2-0	0-0	12	Crouch [71], Lovell [82]	13,887
26	26	A	Gillingham	L	0-2	0-2	13		10,477
27	29	A	Grimsby T	L	1-3	1-2	14	Crouch [32]	5217
28	Jan 12	A	Bradford C	L	1-3	1-1	16	Primus [2]	14,306
29	17	H	Wolverhampton W	L	2-3	1-1	—	Quashie [11], Prosinecki [79]	13,105
30	30	A	Nottingham F	W	1-0	0-0	—	Prosinecki [83]	26,476
31	Feb 2	H	Barnsley	D	4-4	2-1	16	Prosinecki 3 (1 pen) [5 (p), 61, 69], Primus [41]	12,756
32	9	A	Sheffield U	L	3-4	2-3	16	Crouch [6], Prosinecki [45], Quashie [60]	17,553
33	16	H	Rotherham U	D	0-0	0-0	16		13,313
34	23	A	WBA	L	0-5	0-4	17		21,028
35	26	H	Coventry C	W	1-0	0-0	—	Crouch [54]	12,336
36	Mar 2	H	Walsall	D	1-1	0-0	17	Crouch [66]	13,203
37	5	A	Crystal Palace	D	0-0	0-0	—		15,915
38	9	H	Millwall	W	3-0	2-0	16	Biagini [5], O'Neil [10], Pitt [52]	15,221
39	12	H	Wimbledon	L	1-2	1-0	—	Biagini [4]	13,118
40	16	A	Crewe Alex	D	1-1	1-1	16	Crouch [24]	7170
41	23	H	Sheffield W	D	0-0	0-0	15		14,819
42	30	H	Preston NE	L	0-2	0-0	16		16,832
43	Apr 1	A	Burnley	D	1-1	0-1	15	Todorov [75]	18,020
44	7	A	Birmingham C	D	1-1	0-1	17	Pitt [84]	25,030
45	13	H	Watford	L	0-1	0-0	17		16,302
46	21	A	Manchester C	L	1-3	0-2	17	Pitt [59]	34,657

Final League Position: 17

GOALSCORERS

League (60): Crouch 18, Prosinecki 9 (3 pens), Bradbury 7 (3 pens), Burchill 4 (1 pen), Pitt 3, Barrett 2, Biagini 2, Lovell 2, Primus 2, Quashie 2, Zamperini 2, Crowe 1, Edinburgh 1, Harper 1, O'Neil 1, Todorov 1, Vincent 1, own goal 1.
Worthington Cup (1): Crouch 1.
FA Cup (1): own goal 1.

Beasant D 27	Crowe J 18+4	Vincent J 29+5	Hiley S 28+5	Moore D 2	Zamperini A 16	O'Neil G 27+6	Miglioranzi S 1+2	Crouch P 37	Bradbury L 17+5	Quashie N 33+2	Harper K 37+2	Panopoulos M 1+1	Pitt C 29+10	Derry S 12	Prosinecki R 30+3	Buxton L 27+2	Barrett N 23+3	Howe E 1	Burchill M 5+1	Summerbell M 5	Tardif C 1	Ilic S 7	Vine R 3+8	Brady G 1+5	Edinburgh J 7	Primus L 21+1	Lovell S 8+12	Mills L 2	Kawaguchi Y 11	Waterman D 8+1	Tiler C 7+1	Thogersen T 2+3	Curtis T 3+6	Rudonja M 2+1	Biagini L 6+2	Pettefer C 1+1	Cooper S 3+4	Todorov S 3	Wilson S 5	Match No.
1	2¹	3	4	5	6	7	8²	9	10³	11	12	13	14																											1
1		3	4	5	6	7		9	10	11			2¹	12	8²	13																								2
1	12	3	4		6	11²		9	10³	13			2¹		8	5	7		14																					3
	12		4		6¹	13		9	14	11	2		3		8	5	7²		10³			1																		4
			4		6			9		11	2		3		8	5	7		10			1																		5
	12		4		6	13		9	14	11	2		3¹		8²	5³	7		10			1																		6
2			5		6³	12		9	13	11¹	4		3		8²	14	7		10			1																		7
2	12		4		6³			9²	13	11	7		3¹		14	5	8		10			1																		8
2		3	5		6	7¹		9	10³	11²	4		12		8							1	14	13																9
2		3²			6	13		9	12	11	4¹		7		8	5	10					1																		10
4	2		5		6			9	10	11			12		8¹	7					1		3																	11
1			4					9	10	11³			3		2	8	7						12	6		5														12
1	2		4					9	10¹	11			6		8	7									3	5	12													13
1	2		4		6				10	11			8¹	12	7									13	3	5	9²													14
1	2¹		4		6				10	11					7									13	3	5	9													15
1	2		4		6			9	10¹				7		11	8									3	5	9													16
1	2		4		6			9	10¹				7		2	8	11								3	5	12			1										17
	12		4		6			9		11			3		8²		7									5	13	10	1	2										18
5	4		6		11			9					10		3	2	8									7			1	·1										19
	4	3	5		6³	8³		9	10	11			12		2											7¹	13		1				14							20
	4	12	5		6	8¹		9		11			10¹		2		3²									7	13		1					14						21
2²	3¹	4			6			9	10	11	7		12		8											13			1			5								22
2	3¹	4			6			9	10	11	7		12													8²			1			5	13							23
	12							9	10²				2		3¹	8	6									5	13		1			4								24
	12							9					2		3¹	8	6									5	10		1			4								25
2²	3³				12			9		11			13		8	6	7¹		14							5	10		1			4								26
	3¹	12						9		7			2		11	8			13							5	10²		1			4	6³	14						27
1	12							9		11			10		2	3¹	4	8	13	7²						5						6								28
1	2	3	4²					9		11	10¹				7	8	6									5	13													29
1	3	12						7			2²		11	4	8	6										5	10³							14	13	9¹				30
1	2		12		6	7		9			10		3¹	11	8	4										5														31
1	2	3						9			7		10	11¹	4	8	6									5	12													32
1	3	12			6	8¹		9		11	2		7²	4		5											13								10					33
1	3	4			6			9		11					8	5													12		7¹		10	2						34
1	3¹	4				10		9		11	2²		7		8	5													6			12	13							35
1	3	4²				10		9		7			2³		8	5										12			6			13	11³	14						36
1	3							9		11			2¹	8		6	13								12	5			4		7					10²				37
1	3	12				7²		9		11			2³	8		6										5¹	14		4		13	10								38
1	3¹	4						9		11¹				7		5	13						12				8²		6		2	10	14							39
1	3							9		11	12		7²			5	7³									8²			6		4	10¹	14	2						40
1	3							9		11	7²		2¹	4³	12	5	14												6		13			8	10					41
1	3					10				11	2				5		4	7	12	8¹									6				13	9	6²					42
1	3	4²				10³	13			11	2		12		8	5		7													14			9	6¹					43
1	3					10	12			11			2¹		8	6		7	13		5											9²		4						44
1	3					10				11			2²	8¹		6		7	9	12	5													13				4		45
1	3									11	10²		2¹		8	6		7	9	12	5													13				4		46

Worthington Cup
First Round   Colchester U   (h)   1-2

FA Cup
Third Round   Leyton Orient   (h)   1-4

PORT VALE   Division 2

FOUNDATION

Formed in 1876 as Port Vale, adopting the prefix 'Burslem' in 1884 upon moving to that part of the city. It was dropped in 1909.

Vale Park, Hamil Road, Burslem, Stoke-on-Trent ST6 1AW.

Telephone: (01782) 655 800. *Fax:* (01782) 834 981.
ClubCall: 09068 121 636. *Club Shop:* (01782) 833 545.
Community: (01782) 575 594. *Marketing Dept:* (01782) 835 524. *Marketing Fax:* (01782) 836 875.

Ground Capacity: 17,677.

Record Attendance: 49,768 v Aston Villa, FA Cup 5th rd, 20 February 1960.

Record Receipts: £170,349 v Everton, FA Cup 4th rd, 14 February 1996.

Pitch Measurements: 114yd × 75yd.

Chairman: W. T. Bell LAE, TECH. ENG, MIMI.

Directors: Andrew Belfield, Jim Lloyd, Alan Jones.

Manager: Brian Horton. *Physio:* Matthew Radcliffe.

Medical Officer: Dr D. Phillips.

Secretary: F. W. Lodey.

Safety Officer: W. Stevenson.

Groundsman: S. Speed.

Community Scheme Officer: Jim Cooper (01782 575594).

Colours: White shirts, black shorts, black and white stockings.

Change Colours: All yellow.

Year Formed: 1876.

Turned Professional: 1885.

Ltd Co.: 1911.

Previous Name: 1876, Port Vale; 1884, Burslem Port Vale; 1909, Port Vale.

Club Nickname: 'Valiants'.

Previous Grounds: 1876, Limekin Lane, Longport; 1881, Westport; 1884, Moorland Road, Burslem; 1886, Athletic Ground, Cobridge; 1913, Recreation Ground, Hanley; 1950, Vale Park.

First Football League Game: 3 September 1892, Division 2, v Small Heath (a) L 1–5 – Frail; Clutton, Elson; Farrington, McCrindle, Delves; Walker, Scarratt, Bliss (1), Jones. (Only 10 men).

Record League Victory: 9–1 v Chesterfield, Division 2, 24 September 1932 – Leckie; Shenton, Poyser; Sherlock, Round, Jones; McGrath, Mills, Littlewood (6), Kirkham (2), Morton (1).

HONOURS

Football League: Division 2 – Runners-up 1993–94; Division 3 (N) – Champions 1929–30, 1953–54; Runners-up 1952–53; Division 4 – Champions 1958–59; Promoted 1969–70 (4th).

FA Cup: Semi-final 1954, when in Division 3.

Football League Cup: best season: 3rd rd 1992, 1997.

Autoglass Trophy: Winners 1993.

Anglo-Italian Cup: Runners-up 1996.

LDV Vans Trophy: Winners 2001.

IT'S A FACT !

Port Vale's first venture in the LDV Vans Trophy competition on 9 January 2001, ended a nightmare extending over 18 cup matches without a win in either the FA Cup or League Cup. Port Vale defeated Notts County 3-0.

Record Cup Victory: 7–1 v Irthlingborough, FA Cup 1st rd, 12 January 1907 – Matthews; Dunn, Hamilton; Eardley, Baddeley, Holyhead; Carter, Dodds (2), Beats, Mountford (2), Coxon (3).

Record Defeat: 0–10 v Sheffield U, Division 2, 10 December 1892. 0–10 v Notts Co, Division 2, 26 February 1895.

Most League Points (2 for a win): 69, Division 3 (N), 1953–54.

Most League Points (3 for a win): 89, Division 2, 1992–93.

Most League Goals: 110, Division 4, 1958–59.

Highest League Scorer in Season: Wilf Kirkham 38, Division 2, 1926–27.

Most League Goals in Total Aggregate: Wilf Kirkham, 154, 1923–29, 1931–33.

Most League Goals in One Match: 6, Stewart Littlewood v Chesterfield, Division 2, 24 September 1922.

Most Capped Player: Tony Rougier, Trinidad & Tobago.

Most League Appearances: Roy Sproson, 761, 1950–72.

Youngest League Player: Malcolm McKenzie, 15 years 347 days v Newport Co, 12 April 1966.

Record Transfer Fee Received: £2,000,000 from Wimbledon for Gareth Ainsworth, October 1998.

Record Transfer Fee Paid: £500,000 to Lincoln C for Gareth Ainsworth, September 1997.

Football League Record: 1892 Original Member of Division 2. Failed re-election in 1896; Re-elected 1898; Resigned 1907; Returned in Oct, 1919, when they took over the fixtures of Leeds City; 1929–30 Division 3 (N); 1930–36 Division 2; 1936–38 Division 3 (N); 1938–52 Division 3 (S); 1952–54 Division 3 (N); 1954–57 Division 2; 1957–58 Division 3 (S); 1958–59 Division 4; 1959–65 Division 3; 1965–70 Division 4; 1970–78 Division 3; 1978–83 Division 4; 1983–84 Division 3; 1984–86 Division 4; 1986–89 Division 3; 1989–94 Division 2; 1994–2000 Division 1; 2000– Division 2.

MANAGERS

Sam Gleaves 1896–1905
  (Secretary-Manager)
Tom Clare 1905–11
A. S. Walker 1911–12
H. Myatt 1912–14
Tom Holford 1919–24
  (continued as Trainer)
Joe Schofield 1924–30
Tom Morgan 1930–32
Tom Holford 1932–35
Warney Cresswell 1936–37
Tom Morgan 1937–38
Billy Frith 1945–46
Gordon Hodgson 1946–51
Ivor Powell 1951
Freddie Steele 1951–57
Norman Low 1957–62
Freddie Steele 1962–65
Jackie Mudie 1965–67
Sir Stanley Matthews
  (General Manager) 1965–68
Gordon Lee 1968–74
Roy Sproson 1974–77
Colin Harper 1977
Bobby Smith 1977–78
Dennis Butler 1978–79
Alan Bloor 1979
John McGrath 1980–83
John Rudge 1984–99
Brian Horton February 1999–

LATEST SEQUENCES

Longest Sequence of League Wins: 8, 8.4.1893 – 30.9.1893.

Longest Sequence of League Defeats: 9, 9.3.57 – 20.4.57.

Longest Sequence of League Draws: 6, 26.4.81 – 12.9.81.

Longest Sequence of Unbeaten League Matches: 19, 5.5.69 – 8.11.69.

Longest Sequence Without a League Win: 17, 7.12.91 – 21.3.92.

TEN YEAR LEAGUE RECORD

		P	W	D	L	F	A	Pts	Pos
1991-92	Div 2	46	10	15	21	42	59	45	24
1992-93	Div 2	46	26	11	9	79	44	89	3
1993-94	Div 2	46	26	10	9	79	46	88	2
1994-95	Div 1	46	15	13	18	58	64	58	17
1995-96	Div 1	46	15	15	16	59	66	60	12
1996-97	Div 1	46	17	16	13	58	55	67	8
1997-98	Div 1	46	13	10	23	56	66	49	19
1998-99	Div 1	46	13	8	25	45	75	47	21
1999-2000	Div 1	46	7	15	24	48	69	36	23
2000-01	Div 2	46	16	14	16	55	49	62	11

DID YOU KNOW

Bycars Park, Port Vale's training area, was renamed Sproson Park in March 2002 in recognition of this family. Roy Sproson, brother Jess and Jess's son Phil between them appeared in more than 1,300 games for the club.

PORT VALE 2001–02 LEAGUE RECORD

Match No.	Date	Venue	Opponents	Result		H/T Score	Lg. Pos.	Goalscorers	Attendance
1	Aug 11	H	Notts Co	W	4-2	1-1	—	McPhee [21], O'Callaghan 2 [47, 62], Dodd [70]	6076
2	18	A	Brentford	L	0-2	0-0	10		4561
3	25	H	Peterborough U	W	4-1	1-0	6	Hardy [32], Cummins [50], Brooker [78], McPhee [90]	4925
4	27	A	Colchester U	L	0-2	0-1	11		3611
5	Sept 1	H	Reading	L	0-2	0-1	13		5196
6	8	A	Bristol C	D	1-1	1-0	15	O'Callaghan [10]	12,560
7	15	A	QPR	L	1-4	0-0	15	Brooker [55]	9295
8	18	H	Swindon T	L	0-2	0-1	—		3737
9	22	H	Northampton T	L	0-1	0-0	19		4419
10	25	A	Wrexham	W	3-1	1-0	—	McPhee 2 [42, 82], Killen [46]	3091
11	29	A	Wycombe W	L	1-3	0-3	19	Killen [53]	5714
12	Oct 5	H	Cambridge U	W	5-0	1-0	—	Cummins [39], Armstrong [46], Killen 2 [55, 59], Brooker [57]	4119
13	13	A	Chesterfield	D	1-1	0-0	18	Brooker [64]	4348
14	21	H	Stoke C	D	1-1	0-0	17	McPhee [63]	10,344
15	24	H	Cardiff C	L	0-2	0-2	—		4552
16	27	A	Wigan Ath	W	1-0	1-0	17	Killen [21]	5634
17	Nov 3	H	Bury	W	1-0	0-0	17	Killen [63]	4688
18	10	A	Brighton & HA	L	0-1	0-0	17		6648
19	20	A	Bournemouth	D	0-0	0-0	—		4428
20	24	H	Huddersfield T	D	1-1	0-0	17	Cummins [81]	5026
21	Dec 1	H	Blackpool	D	1-1	0-1	18	Cummins [78]	5390
22	15	A	Tranmere R	L	1-3	1-2	19	Cummins [30]	7859
23	21	A	Oldham Ath	L	0-2	0-1	—		4317
24	26	H	Bristol C	W	1-0	0-0	17	McPhee [63]	5682
25	29	H	Colchester U	W	3-1	2-0	16	Armstrong [35], Rowland [39], Brooker [69]	4444
26	Jan 1	A	Reading	L	0-2	0-0	16		10,743
27	8	A	Peterborough U	L	0-3	0-1	—		3747
28	12	H	Brentford	W	2-1	1-1	16	McPhee (pen) [45], Armstrong [70]	4588
29	19	A	Notts Co	W	3-1	2-0	14	Brooker 2 [16, 76], McPhee (pen) [38]	6006
30	22	H	Oldham Ath	W	3-2	2-0	—	McClare [22], Brooker [45], McPhee [80]	4408
31	Feb 2	H	Wycombe W	D	1-1	1-0	13	Durnin [23]	4737
32	10	A	Stoke C	W	1-0	1-0	12	Cummins [36]	23,019
33	13	A	Cambridge U	W	1-0	1-0	—	McPhee [37]	2379
34	16	H	Chesterfield	W	4-1	1-0	12	Cummins 2 [41, 72], Bridge-Wilkinson 2 [89, 90]	5529
35	23	H	QPR	W	1-0	1-0	12	Bridge-Wilkinson [18]	6228
36	26	A	Northampton T	L	0-1	0-1	—		5155
37	Mar 2	A	Swindon T	L	0-3	0-2	12		5867
38	5	H	Wrexham	L	1-3	0-1	—	McPhee [59]	4436
39	9	H	Tranmere R	D	1-1	1-1	13	Bridge-Wilkinson [23]	4630
40	16	A	Blackpool	L	0-4	0-0	13		7811
41	23	A	Bury	D	1-1	0-0	13	Bridge-Wilkinson [79]	3700
42	30	H	Wigan Ath	W	1-0	1-0	12	Brooker [45]	4359
43	Apr 1	A	Cardiff C	L	0-1	0-0	13		15,556
44	6	H	Bournemouth	D	0-0	0-0	13		3514
45	13	A	Huddersfield T	L	1-2	1-1	13	Bridge-Wilkinson [7]	12,270
46	20	H	Brighton & HA	L	0-1	0-0	14		8812

Final League Position: 14

GOALSCORERS

League (51): McPhee 11 (2 pens), Brooker 9, Cummins 8, Bridge-Wilkinson 6, Killen 6, Armstrong 3, O'Callaghan 3, Dodd 1, Durnin 1, Hardy 1, McClare 1, Rowland 1.
Worthington Cup (2): McPhee 2.
FA Cup (3): Brooker 1, Burgess 1, Cummins 1.

Goodlad M 43	Cummins M 46	Ingram R 22 + 2	Carragher M 41	Walsh M 27 + 1	Burton S 33 + 4	O'Callaghan G 8 + 3	Brisco N 34 + 3	Brooker S 41	McPhee S 44	Armstrong J 20 + 11	Dodd A 5 + 4	Paynter B 2 + 5	Hardy P 8	Bridge-Wilkinson M 15 + 4	Torpey S — + 1	Burns L 30 + 3	Osborn S 7	Delany D 3 + 1	Burgess R 1 + 1	Killen C 8 + 1	Maye D — + 2	Gibson A 1	Donnelly P 1 + 5	McClare S 19 + 4	Rowland S 25	Webber D 2 + 2	Durnin J 18 + 1	Byrne P 1 + 1	Atangana M 1 + 1	Birchall C — + 1	Match No.
1	2	3	4	5	6	7	8	9	10	11¹	12																				1
1	2¹	3	4	5	6	7	8	9	10		11	12																			2
1	2¹	3	4	5	6	7	8²	9	10		12			11		13															3
1	2	3	4	5	6	7²	8	9	10	13	12			11¹																	4
1	2	3	4		5	7¹	6	9	10	8				11	12																5
1	2	3	4			7	6	9	10					11		5	8														6
1	2	3	4			7¹	6	9	10	12				11		5	8			15											7
1	2¹	3	4		6	7²	12	9	10					11		5	8	13													8
1	2	3	4¹		6	11		9	10	12						5	8			7											9
1	2	3			4			9	10					11		5	8						7								10
	2¹	3		12	6	13	4	9	10	14				11³		5	8²	1		7											11
1	2	3		5	6			10	9	11¹						4	8						7	12							12
1	2	3			6	12	8	9	10	11¹						5							7	4²	13						13
1	2	3	4		6		8	9	10	11	7¹					5								12							14
1	2	3¹	4		6		8	9	10	11	7²					5			12					13							15
1	2		4		6		8	9	10					11		5¹			7					12	3						16
1	2		4		6		5	9	10	11									7					8	3						17
1	2		4		6			9	10	12				11¹					7					8	3						18
1	2	3	4		6		8	9		11¹						12					10			7	5						19
1	2	3	4		6		8	9	10							5								7¹	11	12					20
1	2	3	4		6		8	9	10															7	5	11					21
1	2	3	4		6			9	10	11														7	5	8	12				22
1	2	3²	4	5	6			10	11				13			12								7	8	9					23
1	2		4	5	6	12		9	10	11¹														7	3		8				24
1	2		4	5	6			9	10	11¹														7	3	12	8				25
1	2		4	5	6			9	10	11														7	3		8				26
1	2		4	5	6	12		9	10	13						3¹								7			8		11²		27
1	2		4	5	6			9	10	11¹														7	3		8				28
1	2			5			6¹	9	10	11					12	4								7	3		8				29
	2¹			4	5	12		8	9	10	11					13	6							7²	3				14		30
1	2	12		4	5				10	11						13	6¹							7	3		8		9²		31
1	2		4	5				11	9	10						7	6								3		8				32
1	2		4	5				11	9	10						7	6								3		8				33
1	2		4	5				11	9	10¹	12					7	6								3		8				34
1	2		4	5	12			11	9	10						7	6								3		8¹				35
1	2		4	5	13			11²	9¹	10	12					7	6								3		8				36
1	2		4	5¹	12			10³		9	11			14		7	6							13	3		8²				37
1	2		4	5	6			11	10	12				9		7	3										8¹				38
	2		4	5¹			8		10					9		11	6	1					12	7	3						39
	2		4¹	5			8	9	10	12						11	6	1						7	3						40
1	2		4	6				11	9	10						7	5								3		8¹				41
1	2	12²	4	5	6				9	10	11					7	13								3¹		8				42
1	2¹		4	5	6				9	10	11			13		7	3²							12			8				43
1	2		4	5¹	6			8	9	10	11					7²	3			13				12							44
1	2	3	4		6			8¹	9	10	12					11	5²							13	7						45
1	2	3	4	5	6			8²	9	10						11									7¹			12		13	46

Worthington Cup
First Round — Chesterfield — (h) — 2-1
Second Round — Charlton Ath — (a) — 0-2

FA Cup
First Round — Aylesbury U — (h) — 3-0
Second Round — Cardiff C — (a) — 0-3

PRESTON NORTH END   Division 1

FOUNDATION

North End Cricket and Rugby Club which was formed in 1863, indulged in most sports before taking up soccer in about 1879. In 1881 they decided to stick to football to the exclusion of other sports and even a 16–0 drubbing by Blackburn Rovers in an invitation game at Deepdale, a few weeks after taking this decision, did not deter them for they immediately became affiliated to the Lancashire FA.

Deepdale, Preston PR1 6RU.
Telephone: (01772) 902 020. **Fax:** (01772) 653 266.
Website: www.pnefc.net
Email: enquiries@pnefc.net
Ticket Enquiries: 0870 442 1966.
Ticket Office Credit Card Bookings: 0870 442 1966.
Corporate Hospitality: (01772) 902 030.
Media/Press: (01772) 902 002.
Community: (01772) 902 061.
Kit 1 Shop at Deepdale: (01772) 902 040.

Ground Capacity: 22,226.

Record Attendance: 42,684 v Arsenal, Division 1, 23 April 1938.

Record Receipts: £108,920 v Stockport Co, FA Cup 3rd rd, 6 January 2001.

Pitch Measurements: 110yd × 77yd.

President: Sir Tom Finney OBE, JP.

Acting Chairman: Derek Shaw.

Directors: T. Scholes (Chief Executive), Simon Beard.
Non-Executive: D. Taylor, H. Nash, K. W. Leeming, M. J. Woodhouse (snr).

Manager: Craig Brown.

Coach: Jimmy Lumsden. **Secretary:** G. E. Harrison.

Colours: White shirts, navy shorts, white stockings.

Change Colours: Navy shirts, white shorts, navy stockings.

Year Formed: 1881.

Turned Professional: 1885.

Ltd Co.: 1893.

Club Nicknames: 'The Lilywhites' or 'North End'.

First Football League Game: 8 September 1888, Football League, v Burnley (h) W 5–2 – Trainer; Howarth, Holmes; Robertson, W. Graham, J. Graham; Gordon (1), Ross (2), Goodall, Dewhurst (2), Drummond.

HONOURS

Football League: Division 1 – Champions 1888–89 (first champions) 1889–90; Runners-up 1890–91, 1891–92, 1892–93, 1905–06, 1952–53, 1957–58; Division 2 – Champions 1903–04, 1912–13, 1950–51, 1999–2000; Runners-up 1914–15, 1933–34; Division 3 – Champions 1970–71, 1995–96; Division 4 – Runners-up 1986–87.
FA Cup: Winners 1889, 1938; Runners-up 1888, 1922, 1937, 1954, 1964.
Double Performed: 1888–89.
Football League Cup: best season: 4th rd, 1963, 1966, 1972, 1981.

IT'S A FACT !

When Preston North End signed the legendary Alex James in 1925, his registration form was not received by the Football League until three days after his debut against Middlesbrough on 23 September. The club was fined 10 Guineas (£10.50) but no points deducted.

Record League Victory: 10–0 v Stoke, Division 1,
14 September 1889 – Trainer; Howarth, Holmes; Kelso,
Russell (1), Graham; Gordon, Jimmy Ross (2),
Nick Ross (3), Thomson (2), Drummond (2).

Record Cup Victory: 26–0 v Hyde, FA Cup 1st rd,
15 October 1887 – Addison; Howarth, Nick Ross;
Russell (1), Thomson (5), Graham (1); Gordon (5), Jimmy
Ross (8), John Goodall (1), Dewhurst (3), Drummond (2).

Record Defeat: 0–7 v Blackpool, Division 1, 1 May 1948.

Most League Points (2 for a win): 61, Division 3, 1970–71.

Most League Points (3 for a win): 95, Division 2, 1999–2000.

Most League Goals: 100, Division 2, 1927–28 and
Division 1, 1957–58.

Highest League Scorer in Season: Ted Harper, 37,
Division 2, 1932–33.

Most League Goals in Total Aggregate: Tom Finney, 187,
1946–60.

Most League Goals in One Match: 7, Jimmy Ross v Stoke,
Division 1, 6 October 1888.

Most Capped Player: Tom Finney, 76, England.

Most League Appearances: Alan Kelly, 447, 1961–75.

Youngest League Player: Steve Doyle, 16 years 166 days v
Tranmere R, 15 November 1974.

Record Transfer Fee Received: £1,250,000 from WBA for
Kevin Kilbane, June 1997.

Record Transfer Fee Paid: £1,500,000 to Manchester U for
David Healy, December 2000.

Football League Record: 1888 Founder Member of League;
1901–04 Division 2; 1904–12 Division 1; 1912–13 Division 2;
1913–14 Division 1; 1914–15 Division 2; 1919–25 Division 1; 1925–34 Division 2; 1934–49 Division 1;
1949–51 Division 2; 1951–61 Division 1; 1961–70 Division 2; 1970–71 Division 3; 1971–74 Division 2;
1974–78 Division 3; 1978–81 Division 2; 1981–85 Division 3; 1985–87 Division 4; 1987–92 Division 3;
1992–93 Division 2; 1993–96 Division 3; 1996–2000 Division 2; 2000– Division 1.

MANAGERS
Charlie Parker 1906–15
Vincent Hayes 1919–23
Jim Lawrence 1923–25
Frank Richards 1925–27
Alex Gibson 1927–31
Lincoln Hayes 1931–32
Run by committee 1932–36
Tommy Muirhead 1936–37
Run by committee 1937–49
Will Scott 1949–53
Scot Symon 1953–54
Frank Hill 1954–56
Cliff Britton 1956–61
Jimmy Milne 1961–68
Bobby Seith 1968–70
Alan Ball Sr 1970–73
Bobby Charlton 1973–75
Harry Catterick 1975–77
Nobby Stiles 1977–81
Tommy Docherty 1981
Gordon Lee 1981–83
Alan Kelly 1983–85
Tommy Booth 1985–86
Brian Kidd 1986
John McGrath 1986–90
Les Chapman 1990–92
John Beck 1992–94
Gary Peters 1994–98
David Moyes 1998–2002
Craig Brown April 2002–

LATEST SEQUENCES

Longest Sequence of League Wins: 14, 25.12.50 – 27.3.51.

Longest Sequence of League Defeats: 8, 22.9.84 – 27.10.84.

Longest Sequence of League Draws: 6, 24.2.79 – 20.3.79.

Longest Sequence of Unbeaten League Matches: 23, 8.9.1888 – 14.9.1889.

Longest Sequence Without a League Win: 15, 14.4.23 – 20.10.23.

TEN YEAR LEAGUE RECORD									
		P	W	D	L	F	A	Pts	Pos
1991-92	Div 3	46	15	12	19	61	72	57	17
1992-93	Div 2	46	13	8	25	65	94	47	21
1993-94	Div 3	42	18	13	11	79	60	67	5
1994-95	Div 3	42	19	10	13	58	41	67	5
1995-96	Div 3	46	23	17	6	78	38	86	1
1996-97	Div 2	46	18	7	21	49	55	61	15
1997-98	Div 2	46	15	14	17	56	56	59	15
1998-99	Div 2	46	22	13	11	78	50	79	5
1999-2000	Div 2	46	28	11	7	74	37	95	1
2000-01	Div 1	46	23	9	14	64	52	78	4

DID YOU KNOW

George Mutch, scorer of
Preston North End's goal in
the 1938 FA Cup Final, was
presented with the ball used
in the pre-match kick-in,
suitably autographed – but
not until 1966.

PRESTON NORTH END 2001–02 LEAGUE RECORD

Match No.	Date	Venue	Opponents	Result		H/T Score	Lg. Pos.	Goalscorers	Attendance
1	Aug 11	A	Gillingham	L	0-5	0-2	—		9412
2	18	H	Walsall	D	1-1	0-1	20	Murdock [54]	11,402
3	25	A	Grimsby T	D	2-2	1-1	20	Murdock [31], Healy [47]	5789
4	27	H	Wimbledon	D	1-1	0-1	21	Keane [64]	13,349
5	Sept 8	H	Wolverhampton W	L	1-2	1-0	22	Lucketti [34]	14,381
6	15	H	Millwall	W	1-0	1-0	18	Anderson [3]	11,371
7	18	A	WBA	L	0-2	0-1	—		18,209
8	23	A	Birmingham C	W	1-0	0-0	17	Edwards [58]	23,004
9	26	H	Norwich C	W	4-0	4-0	—	Alexander (pen) [2], Macken 2 [14, 45], Edwards [33]	12,014
10	30	A	Watford	D	1-1	1-0	16	Macken [22]	18,911
11	Oct 13	A	Crewe Alex	L	1-2	0-1	19	Rankine [60]	7746
12	16	H	Sheffield W	W	2-1	0-1	—	Rankine [46], Macken [80]	15,592
13	21	H	Manchester C	W	2-1	0-1	12	Healy [51], Macken [67]	21,014
14	23	H	Sheffield U	W	3-0	2-0	—	Macken [8], Healy [30], Gallacher [88]	14,027
15	27	A	Portsmouth	W	1-0	1-0	6	Cartwright [45]	15,402
16	31	A	Coventry C	D	2-2	1-1	—	Cresswell 2 [41, 78]	15,755
17	Nov 3	H	Stockport Co	W	6-0	3-0	6	Healy 3 [11, 29, 38], Lucketti [54], Cresswell [61], McKenna [83]	13,776
18	8	H	Barnsley	D	2-2	0-1	—	Rankine [54], Cresswell [88]	19,042
19	17	A	Nottingham F	D	1-1	1-1	7	Cresswell [40]	21,020
20	20	A	Bradford C	D	1-1	0-1	—	Alexander (pen) [53]	13,763
21	24	H	Crystal Palace	W	2-1	0-1	4	Cresswell [52], Alexander (pen) [80]	15,264
22	Dec 1	A	Sheffield U	D	2-2	2-0	7	Healy [13], Cresswell [45]	16,270
23	9	A	Burnley	L	2-3	2-2	8	McKenna [29], Alexander (pen) [41]	20,370
24	15	A	Rotherham U	L	0-1	0-1	9		6558
25	22	H	Grimsby T	D	0-0	0-0	10		14,667
26	26	A	Wolverhampton W	W	3-2	0-1	9	Healy [47], Anderson [56], Gregan [73]	24,024
27	29	A	Wimbledon	L	0-2	0-0	10		6501
28	Jan 12	A	Walsall	W	2-1	0-0	9	Anderson [75], Basham [85]	6314
29	19	H	Gillingham	L	0-2	0-1	10		13,289
30	29	H	Bradford C	W	1-0	0-0	—	Keane [47]	15,217
31	31	H	Watford	D	1-1	1-0	—	Alexander [32]	12,749
32	Feb 5	H	Sheffield W	W	4-2	2-1	—	Etuhu [16], Macken [24], Reid [67], Healy [74]	14,038
33	10	A	Manchester C	L	2-3	0-0	9	Macken [47], Anderson [90]	34,220
34	22	A	Norwich C	L	0-3	0-3	—		19,506
35	26	H	WBA	W	1-0	0-0	—	Etuhu [57]	14,487
36	Mar 2	H	Birmingham C	W	1-0	1-0	10	Purse (og) [35]	15,543
37	5	A	Millwall	L	1-2	0-1	—	Healy [84]	11,071
38	9	H	Rotherham U	W	2-1	1-0	7	Cresswell 2 [45, 70]	14,579
39	17	A	Burnley	L	1-2	0-2	8	Anderson [84]	18,388
40	20	H	Crewe Alex	D	2-2	2-1	—	McKenna [1], Cresswell [19]	13,396
41	23	A	Stockport Co	W	2-0	1-0	8	McKenna [45], Cresswell [51]	6139
42	30	H	Portsmouth	W	2-0	0-0	8	Wijnhard [64], Alexander (pen) [70]	16,832
43	Apr 1	A	Barnsley	L	1-2	0-1	9	Wijnhard [69]	14,188
44	6	H	Coventry C	W	4-0	2-0	7	Wijnhard [5], Etuhu [27], Ainsworth [87], Cresswell [89]	15,665
45	13	A	Crystal Palace	L	0-2	0-0	8		21,361
46	21	H	Nottingham F	W	2-1	0-1	8	Rankine [75], Cresswell [87]	17,390

Final League Position: 8

GOALSCORERS

League (71): Cresswell 13, Healy 10, Macken 8, Alexander 6 (5 pens), Anderson 5, McKenna 4, Rankine 4, Etuhu 3, Wijnhard 3, Edwards 2, Keane 2, Lucketti 2, Murdock 2, Ainsworth 1, Basham 1, Cartwright 1, Gallacher 1, Gregan 1, Reid 1, own goal 1.
Worthington Cup (4): Cresswell 1, Gallacher 1, Jackson 1, Macken 1.
FA Cup (5): Cresswell 2, Alexander 1 (pen), Macken 1, Skora 1.

Lucas D 23+1	Alexander G 45	Edwards R 36	Murdock C 22+1	Jackson M 12+1	Gregan S 40+1	Cartwright L 34+2	Rankine M 24+2	Macken J 28+3	Healy D 35+9	Cresswell R 27+13	McKenna P 37+1	Anderson I 16+15	Gallacher K 1+4	Barry-Murphy B 2+2	Lucketti C 40	Keane M 17+3	Moilanen T 23+1	Robinson S —+2	Basham S —+16	Kidd R 5+1	Eaton A 6+6	Skora E 2+2	Etuhu D 16	Reid P —+1	Gudjonsson T 4+3	Hendry C 2	Wijnhard C 6	Ainsworth G 3+2	Match No.
1	2	3	4	5	6	7	8	9	10	11																			1
1	2	3	4	5	6	11	8	9³	10¹	12	7²	13	14																2
1	2		4		6	11	12	9	10	13			14	7³	3	5	8¹												3
1⁹	2		4		6	11	8¹	9²	10						3	5	7	15	12	13									4
1	2		4		6	12		9	10³		7	11¹			5	8²	13	14	3										5
	2	3	4		6		8	12	10¹		7	11²	13³		5		1								14				6
	2	3	4		6¹	11	8	9	10	12	7				5		1												7
	2	3	4		6	11	8	9	10		7				5		1												8
	2	3	4		6		8	9	10¹	12	7	11²	13		5		1												9
	2	3	4		6	11	8	9	10¹	12	7				5		1												10
	2	3	4		6	11	8	9¹	10	12	7	13			5		1												11
	2	3	4		6	7	8	9	10¹	12		13		11²	5		1												12
	2	3	4		6	11	8	9	10¹	12	7				5		1												13
	2	3¹	4	12	6	11	8	9	10³		7	13	14		5		1												14
	2	3⁴	4		6	11	8	9	10¹	12	7				5	13	1												15
	2		4		6	11	8	9	10¹	12	7				5		1	3											16
15	2		4		6	11	8	9²	10¹	12	7	13			5	1⁰		3											17
1	2		4		6	11²	8	9	10¹	12	7	13			5			3³	14										18
1	2		4		6	11	8	9¹	10		7				5				12	3									19
1	2	3	4		6¹	11	8	9	10		7	12			5														20
1	2	3	4		6	11	8	9	10¹		7				5				12										21
1	2	3	4		6	11	8	12	10¹	9	7				5														22
1	2	3	4		6	11¹	8	9²	10	12	7				5				13										23
1	2	3	4¹		6	11³	8²	9	10	12	7		14		5				13										24
1	2	3	4		6	11¹	8	9	10	12	7				5														25
1	2	3		4	6	11¹	8	9¹	10	12	7				5	13													26
1	2	3	4		6²	11³	8	9	10	12	7		14		5	13													27
1	2	3	4		6¹	11	8	9	10	12	7				5						8								28
	2	3	4¹	12	6	11	8²	9	10	13	7				5		1				6								29
	2	3	4	12	6	7		9¹	10			11			5		1				3		8						30
	2		4	12	6	7²		9¹	10³	11		12	14		5	13	1	3			3		8						31
	2		4	5	6²	7		9	10	12		11¹					1	3			3	13	8						32
	2	3	4		6	7²		9	10	11¹		12			5		1						8		13				33
	2	3	4³		6	7¹		9	10	12		11²	14		5		1						8		13				34
1	2		4		6	7		9	10¹	12		11²			5	13		3			8		8						35
1	2	3	4		6	7		9²	10¹	12		11²	14		5	13					8		8					4	36
1	2	3	4²		6³	7		9	10	12		11²	14		5	13					8		8					6³	37
1	2	3	4¹	12	6	7		9	10			11²			5	13					6		8¹						38
1	2	3	4³		6	7²	8	9	10²	12		11	14		5	13													39
1	2	3	4		6	7	8	9	10¹	12		11			5						4								40
1	2	3	4		6	7	8	9		12		11			5						4							10¹	41
	2	3²	4	12	6	7²	8	9				11			5	1	1				13		4					10¹14	42
	2		4	12	6	7²	8²	9		13		11			5¹	4	1	3										10 14	43
	2	3	4	5	6	7¹		9		11		12			4	1							8					10	44
	2	3	4	5	6	7¹		9		11		13			4²	1							8					10	45
	2	3	4	5	6	7		9		11		14			4¹	13	1						8³					10²	46

Worthington Cup
First Round   Kidderminster H   (a)   3-2
Second Round   Tranmere R   (a)   1-4

FA Cup
Third Round   Brighton & HA   (a)   2-0
Fourth Round   Sheffield U   (h)   2-1
Fifth Round   Chelsea   (a)   1-3

QUEENS PARK RANGERS — Division 2

FOUNDATION

There is an element of doubt about the date of the foundation of this club, but it is believed that in either 1885 or 1886 it was formed through the amalgamation of Christchurch Rangers and St Jude's Institute FC. The leading light was George Wodehouse, whose family maintained a connection with the club until comparatively recent times. Most of the players came from the Queen's Park district so this name was adopted after a year as St Jude's Institute.

South Africa Road, London W12 7PA.

Telephone: (020) 8743 0262. **Fax:** (020) 8749 0994.
Club Shop: (020) 8749 2509. **Box Office:** (020) 8740 2575.
Supporters Club: (020) 8740 2534.
Commercial: (020) 8740 2588.
ClubCall: 09068 121 162.

Ground Capacity: 19,148.

Record Attendance: 35,353 v Leeds U, Division 1, 27 April 1974.

Record Receipts: £218,475 v Manchester U, FA Premier League, 5 February 1994.

Pitch Measurements: 112yd × 72yd.

Directors: Nick Blackburn, David Davies, Ross Jones.

Manager: Ian Holloway. **Secretary:** Sheila Marson.
Physio: Prav Mathema.

Commercial and Marketing Director: Mark Devlin.

Year Formed: 1885* (see Foundation). **Turned Professional:** 1898. **Ltd Co.:** 1899.

Previous Name: 1885, St Jude's; 1887, Queens Park Rangers. **Club Nicknames:** 'Rangers' or 'Rs'.

Colours: Blue and white hooped shirts, white shorts and stockings.

Change Colours: Red and black half shirts, black shorts, black stockings.

Previous Grounds: 1885* (see Foundation), Welford's Fields; 1888–99; London Scottish Ground, Brondesbury, Home Farm, Kensal Rise Green, Gun Club Wormwood Scrubs, Kilburn Cricket Ground; 1899, Kensal Rise Athletic Ground; 1901, Latimer Road, Notting Hill; 1904, Agricultural Society, Park Royal; 1907, Park Royal Ground; 1917, Loftus Road; 1931, White City; 1933, Loftus Road; 1962, White City; 1963, Loftus Road.

First Football League Game: 28 August 1920, Division 3, v Watford (h) L 1–2 – Price; Blackman, Wingrove; McGovern, Grant, O'Brien; Faulkner, Birch (1), Smith, Gregory, Middlemiss.

Record League Victory: 9–2 v Tranmere R, Division 3, 3 December 1960 – Drinkwater; Woods, Ingham; Keen, Rutter, Angell; Lazarus (2), Bedford (2), Evans (2), Andrews (1), Clark (2).

HONOURS

Football League: Division 1 – Runners-up 1975–76; Division 2 – Champions 1982–83; Runners-up 1967–68, 1972–73; Division 3 (S) – Champions 1947–48; Runners-up 1946–47; Division 3 – Champions 1966–67.

FA Cup: Runners-up 1982.

Football League Cup: Winners 1967; Runners-up 1986. (In 1966–67 won Division 3 and Football League Cup.)

European Competitions: UEFA Cup: 1976–77, 1984–85.

IT'S A FACT !

In 1936–37, Queens Park Rangers were the only team in Division Three (South) to achieve a home and away double over the divisional winners, Luton Town.

Record Cup Victory: 8–1 v Bristol R (away), FA Cup 1st rd, 27 November 1937 – Gilfillan; Smith, Jefferson; Lowe, James, March; Cape, Mallett, Cheetham (3), Fitzgerald (3) Bott (2). 8–1 v Crewe Alex, Milk Cup 1st rd, 3 October 1983 – Hucker; Neill, Dawes, Waddock (1), McDonald (1), Fenwick, Micklewhite (1), Stewart (1), Allen (1), Stainrod (3), Gregory.

Record Defeat: 1–8 v Mansfield T, Division 3, 15 March 1965. 1–8 v Manchester U, Division 1, 19 March 1969.

Most League Points (2 for a win): 67, Division 3, 1966–67.

Most League Points (3 for a win): 85, Division 2, 1982–83.

Most League Goals: 111, Division 3, 1961–62.

Highest League Scorer in Season: George Goddard, 37, Division 3 (S), 1929–30.

Most League Goals in Total Aggregate: George Goddard, 172, 1926–34.

Most League Goals in One Match: 4, George Goddard v Merthyr T, Division 3S, 9 March 1929; 4, George Goddard v Swindon T, Division 3S, 12 April 1930; 4, George Goddard v Exeter C, Division 3S, 20 December 1930; 4, George Goddard v Watford, Division 3S, 19 September 1931; 4, Tom Cheetham v Aldershot, Division 3S, 14 September 1935; 4, Tom Cheetham v Aldershot, Division 3S, 12 November 1938.

Most Capped Player: Alan McDonald, 52, Northern Ireland.

Most League Appearances: Tony Ingham, 519, 1950–63.

Youngest League Player: Frank Sibley, 16 years 97 days v Bristol C, 10 March 1964.

Record Transfer Fee Received: £6,000,000 from Newcastle U for Les Ferdinand, June 1995.

Record Transfer Fee Paid: £2,750,000 to Stoke C for Mike Sheron, July 1997.

Football League Record: 1920 Original Members of Division 3; 1921–48 Division 3 (S); 1948–52 Division 3 (S); 1952–58 Division 3 (S); 1958–67 Division 3; 1967–68 Division 2; 1968–69 Division 1; 1969–73 Division 2; 1973–79 Division 1; 1979–83 Division 2; 1983–92 Division 1; 1992–96 FA Premier League; 1996–2001 Division 1; 2001– Division 2.

LATEST SEQUENCES

Longest Sequence of League Wins: 8, 7.11.31 – 28.12.31.

Longest Sequence of League Defeats: 9, 25.2.69 – 5.4.69.

Longest Sequence of League Draws: 6, 29.1.00 – 5.3.00.

Longest Sequence of Unbeaten League Matches: 20, 11.3.72 – 23.9.72.

Longest Sequence Without a League Win: 20, 7.12.68 – 7.4.69.

MANAGERS

James Cowan 1906–13
Jimmy Howie 1913–20
Ted Liddell 1920–24
Will Wood 1924–25
　(had been Secretary since 1903)
Bob Hewison 1925–30
John Bowman 1930–31
Archie Mitchell 1931–33
Mick O'Brien 1933–35
Billy Birrell 1935–39
Ted Vizard 1939–44
Dave Mangnall 1944–52
Jack Taylor 1952–59
Alec Stock 1959–65
　(General Manager to 1968)
Bill Dodgin Jnr 1968
Tommy Docherty 1968
Les Allen 1968–71
Gordon Jago 1971–74
Dave Sexton 1974–77
Frank Sibley 1977–78
Steve Burtenshaw 1978–79
Tommy Docherty 1979–80
Terry Venables 1980–84
Gordon Jago 1984
Alan Mullery 1984
Frank Sibley 1984–85
Jim Smith 1985–88
Trevor Francis 1988–90
Don Howe 1990–91
Gerry Francis 1991–94
Ray Wilkins 1994–96
Stewart Houston 1996–97
Ray Harford 1997–98
Gerry Francis 1998–2001
Ian Holloway February 2001–

TEN YEAR LEAGUE RECORD

		P	W	D	L	F	A	Pts	Pos
1991-92	Div 1	42	12	18	12	48	47	54	11
1992-93	PR Lge	42	17	12	13	63	55	63	5
1993-94	PR Lge	42	16	12	14	62	61	60	9
1994-95	PR Lge	42	17	9	16	61	59	60	8
1995-96	PR Lge	38	9	6	23	38	57	33	19
1996-97	Div 1	46	18	12	16	64	60	66	9
1997-98	Div 1	46	10	19	17	51	63	49	21
1998-99	Div 1	46	12	11	23	52	61	47	20
1999-2000	Div 1	46	16	18	12	62	53	66	10
2000-01	Div 1	46	7	19	20	45	75	40	23

DID YOU KNOW ?

Queens Park Rangers' tour of Ireland in 1947 produced wins of 9-0, 6-1, 5-0 and 6-1. In the first match, an Irish player was injured, and with no replacement available, Rangers withdrew Albert Parkinson to level the teams.

QUEENS PARK RANGERS 2001–02 LEAGUE RECORD

Match No.	Date	Venue	Opponents	Result	H/T Score	Lg. Pos.	Goalscorers	Attendance
1	Aug 11	H	Stoke C	W 1-0	1-0	—	Thomson [23]	14,357
2	18	A	Bury	W 2-1	1-1	4	Thomson (pen) [30], Bruce [67]	4167
3	25	A	Reading	D 0-0	0-0	5		13,829
4	27	A	Wycombe W	L 0-1	0-0	9		9217
5	30	H	Bristol C	D 0-0	0-0	—		11,655
6	Sept 8	A	Brighton & HA	L 1-2	0-0	12	Thomson [79]	6820
7	15	H	Port Vale	W 4-1	0-0	8	Palmer [84], Thomson 3 (1 pen) [72, 76 (p), 90]	9295
8	18	A	Blackpool	D 2-2	1-0	—	Griffiths 2 [32, 46]	5774
9	22	A	Wigan Ath	W 2-1	1-1	8	Thomson [45], Brannan (og) [90]	6686
10	25	H	Cardiff C	W 2-1	0-1	—	Thomson 2 (1 pen) [54 (p), 61]	11,667
11	29	A	Cambridge U	L 1-2	0-1	7	Connolly [75]	4508
12	Oct 7	H	Huddersfield T	W 3-2	1-1	5	Thomson [13], Rose [56], Palmer [61]	10,668
13	13	A	Wrexham	L 0-1	0-1	6		4474
14	20	H	Northampton T	L 0-1	0-1	10		10,444
15	23	A	Peterborough U	L 1-4	1-2	—	Palmer [4]	7427
16	27	H	Oldham Ath	D 1-1	1-0	13	Dodou [26]	10,556
17	Nov 3	H	Notts Co	W 2-0	0-0	9	Thomson 2 [72, 73]	6231
18	10	A	Tranmere R	L 1-2	0-0	14	Thomson [89]	9024
19	21	H	Swindon T	W 4-0	3-0	—	Dodou [3], Burgess [8], Gallen [37], Thomson [90]	8847
20	24	A	Brentford	D 0-0	0-0	11		10,849
21	Dec 1	H	Colchester U	D 2-2	1-2	10	Gallen 2 [22, 54]	11,158
22	15	A	Chesterfield	W 3-2	0-0	10	Thomson (pen) [65], Shittu [69], Rose [71]	4611
23	22	A	Bournemouth	W 2-1	1-0	8	Thomson 2 (1 pen) [5, 69 (p)]	8147
24	26	H	Brighton & HA	D 0-0	0-0	9		16,412
25	29	H	Wycombe W	W 4-3	1-1	6	Thomson [26], Gallen [54], Connolly [61], Peacock [76]	14,834
26	Jan 5	A	Reading	L 0-1	0-0	6		19,329
27	12	H	Bury	W 3-0	1-0	6	Griffiths [19], Pacquette [56], Bonnot [90]	10,003
28	19	A	Stoke C	W 1-0	0-0	5	Peacock [81]	16,725
29	22	H	Bournemouth	D 1-1	1-0	—	Palmer [39]	10,901
30	26	A	Huddersfield T	L 0-1	0-1	7		9433
31	Feb 2	H	Cambridge U	D 0-0	0-0	8		18,071
32	5	A	Bristol C	L 0-2	0-2	—		11,654
33	9	A	Northampton T	D 2-2	2-0	9	Connolly 2 (1 pen) [12 (p), 21]	6424
34	16	H	Wrexham	W 2-1	0-1	8	Langley [59], Gallen [89]	9706
35	23	A	Port Vale	L 0-1	0-1	11		6228
36	26	H	Wigan Ath	D 1-1	0-0	—	Gallen [90]	8519
37	Mar 2	H	Blackpool	W 2-0	1-0	9	Gallen [43], Langley [60]	10,203
38	5	A	Cardiff C	D 1-1	1-0	—	Pacquette [12]	13,425
39	9	H	Chesterfield	D 0-0	0-0	9		10,434
40	16	A	Colchester U	L 1-3	0-1	10	Dodou [90]	4903
41	23	H	Peterborough U	W 1-0	1-0	10	Thomson (pen) [34]	10,324
42	30	A	Tranmere R	W 3-2	1-0	8	Thomson 2 [14, 90], Langley [77]	8619
43	Apr 1	H	Notts Co	W 3-2	1-2	8	Shittu [45], Rose [62], Foley [84]	10,966
44	6	A	Swindon T	W 1-0	0-0	8	Thomas [76]	6774
45	13	H	Brentford	D 0-0	0-0	8		18,346
46	20	A	Oldham Ath	L 0-1	0-1	8		7262

Final League Position: 8

GOALSCORERS

League (60): Thomson 21 (6 pens), Gallen 7, Connolly 4 (1 pen), Palmer 4, Dodou 3, Griffiths 3, Langley 3, Rose 3, Pacquette 2, Peacock 2, Shittu 2, Bonnot 1, Bruce 1, Burgess 1, Foley 1, Thomas 1, own goal 1.
Worthington Cup (1): own goal 1.
FA Cup (0).

Day C 16	Forbes T 43	Bruce P 13	Palmer S 46	Ben Askar A 18	Perry M 13 + 3	Bignot M 41 + 4	Bonnot A 17 + 5	Thomson A 29 + 9	Wardley S 5 + 5	Connolly K 24 + 9	Griffiths L 23 + 7	Koejoe S — + 2	Warren C 8 + 6	Rose M 37 + 2	Dodou E 20 + 16	Pacquette R 8 + 8	McEwen D 2 + 3	Taylor R 3 + 1	Burgess 4	Shittu D 27	De Ornelas F 1 + 1	Foley D 3 + 2	Digby F 19	Plummer C 1	Gallen K 25	Murphy D 10 + 2	Peacock G 19 + 1	Langley R 15 + 3	Leaburn C — + 1	Fitzgerald B — + 1	Evans R 11	Oli D — + 2	Daly W 1	Thomas J 4	Agogo M — + 2	Match No.
1	2	3	4	5	6	7	8	9	10¹	11³	12²	13	14																							1
1	2	3	4	5	6	7	8³	9	10²	11¹		13	12	14																						2
1	2		4	5	6¹	7	8	9²	10³	11				3	12	13	14																			3
1	2		4	5	3	7	8	9		11²	13		6		12	10¹																				4
1	2	3	4	5	6	7	12	9²		11¹	14		8		13	10³																				5
1	2	3	4	5	6	7	12			11²	10	13	14	8³	9¹																					6
1	2	3	4		7	6	9	11	8				5	12		10¹																				7
1	2	3	4		7		9²	10	11¹	8	12	5	6		13																					8
1	2		4	5	6	7	9¹	11	10	3		8	12																							9
1	2		4	5	6	7	9	12		11²	10	3¹	8	13																						10
1	2		4	5	6	12	8¹	9		13	10²	3	7	11³	14																					11
1	2		4	5	12	7	8	9	13	11²	10¹	3	6																							12
1	2	3	4	5	12	7¹	8	9	13	11²	10³		6	14																						13
1		3	4	6²	7	8	9	12	10³	11¹			5	13	14	2																				14
1		3	4		7	8	12	11	13				5	9¹	10²	6	2																			15
1	2	3	4		7	8	13	11					5	9	12²	6³	14	10¹																		16
	2	3	4		6	7	9	12	11	13			5	10²		8¹		1																		17
	2	3	4		6¹	7	9	10	11	12			8					1	5																	18
	2		4			12	8	13	11		3		5	10²		7¹		6	1			9														19
	2		4			7	8	12	11		3		5	10¹				6	1			9														20
	2		4			7	8	10	11		3¹		5	12				6	1			9														21
	2		4	5	12	14	9	11²		7	13³		6					1		9	10	3¹	8													22
	2		4			7	12	10¹	13	5	11²		6					1		9	3	8														23
	2		4			7¹	10	12		5	11		6					1		9	3	8														24
	2		4	5	12	10	11¹		6	7								1		9	3	8														25
	2	3²	4	5	7	12	10	11¹		6¹								1		9	8	13	14													26
	2		4	12	7	8	10		9	6²			5					1		3¹	11	13														27
	2		4	7		13	12	10		5	9¹	11²	6					1		3	8															28
	2		4	7		9	12	10		5	11²		6					1		3¹	8	13														29
	2		4	7		10¹	12	11¹		5	13	14	6					1		9	3²	8														30
2³			4		3	10¹	12	11		5	7	13						6		1	9²	8	14													31
	2		4			12	13	11	14	5	7²	10¹						6		1	9	3³	8													32
	2		4		3		11	10¹		5	12		6					1		9	8	7														33
2³			4		3	12	11¹	10²		5	13	14	6					1		9	8	7														34
			4	2²	3	8	10¹			5	11	12	6					1		9	13	7														35
	2		4	5	3	8		10²	12		11¹		6							9		7		1	13											36
	2		4	5	3	10	8		12		11¹		6							9		7		1												37
	2		4	5	3		12	8		11			6							9¹		7		1												38
2³			4	5	3	12	10²	8	13		11¹		6							9	14	7		1												39
	2		4		6	10		12	13	5				9	3³	8	7			1	11¹																40
	2		4		3	10²	12			5	11¹		6							9	8	7		1	13											41
	2		4		3	10	12			5			6							9	8	7		1	11¹											42
	2		4		3	10¹				5	6	12								9	8	7		1	11											43
	2		4		3					5	6	10¹								9	8	7		1	11	12										44
	2		4		3	12				5	6	10¹								9	8	7		1	11											45
	2		4	3¹		10	11³			5	6	13		9²	12	8	7			1						14										46

Worthington Cup
First Round   Northampton T   (a)   1-2

FA Cup
First Round   Swansea C   (a)   0-4

READING
Division 1

FOUNDATION

Reading was formed as far back as 1871 at a public meeting held at the Bridge Street Rooms. They first entered the FA Cup as early as 1877 when they amalgamated with the Reading Hornets. The club was further strengthened in 1889 when Earley FC joined them. They were the first winners of the Berks and Bucks Cup in 1878–79.

Madejski Stadium, Junction 11, M4, Reading, Berks RG2 0FL.

Telephone: (0118) 968 1100. *Fax:* (0118) 968 1101.

ClubCall: 09068 121 000. *Website:* www.readingfc.co.uk
Email: comments@readingfc.co.uk
Ticket Office: (0118) 968 1000.
Ticket Office Fax: (0118) 968 1001.

Ground Capacity: 24,200.

Record Attendance: 33,042 v Brentford, FA Cup 5th rd, 19 February 1927.

Record Receipts: £171,203 v Manchester C, Division 2, 27 March 1999.

Pitch Measurements: 112yd × 77yd.

President: F. Orton.

Chairman: John Madejski OBE, DL.

Director: I. Wood-Smith.

Manager: Alan Pardew.

Chief Executive: Nigel Howe.

Physio: Jon Fearn.

Commercial Manager: Kevin Girdler.

Secretary: Ms Sue Hewett.

Colours: Blue and white hooped shirts, white shorts, white stockings with blue bands.

Change Colours: Burgundy shirts with navy and gold trim, navy shorts with gold trim, navy stockings with gold bands.

Year Formed: 1871.

Turned Professional: 1895.

Ltd Co.: 1895.

Club Nickname: 'The Royals'.

Previous Grounds: 1871, Reading Recreation; Reading Cricket Ground; 1882, Coley Park; 1889, Caversham Cricket Ground; 1896, Elm Park; 1998, Madejski Stadium.

First Football League Game: 28 August 1920, Division 3, v Newport Co (a) W 1–0 – Crawford; Smith, Horler; Christie, Mavin, Getgood; Spence, Weston, Yarnell, Bailey (1), Andrews.

HONOURS

Football League: Division 1 – Runners-up 1994–95; Division 2 – Champions 1993–94; Runners-up 2001–02; Division 3 – Champions 1985–86; Division 3 (S) – Champions 1925–26; Runners-up 1931–32, 1934–35, 1948–49, 1951–52; Division 4 – Champions 1978–79.

FA Cup: Semi-final 1927.

Football League Cup: best season: 5th rd, 1996.

Simod Cup: Winners 1988.

IT'S A FACT !

Fred Gregory played as an emergency goalkeeper, at full-back, half-back and centre-forward for Reading from 1933 and once cost Manchester City £2,500 at the age of 17 from Doncaster Rovers.

Record League Victory: 10–2 v Crystal Palace, Division 3 (S),
4 September 1946 – Groves; Glidden, Gulliver; McKenna,
Ratcliffe, Young; Chitty, Maurice Edelston (3), McPhee (4),
Barney (1), Deverell (2).

Record Cup Victory: 6–0 v Leyton, FA Cup 2nd rd,
12 December 1925 – Duckworth; Eggo, McConnell; Wilson,
Messer, Evans; Smith (2), Braithwaite (1), Davey (1),
Tinsley, Robson (2).

Record Defeat: 0–18 v Preston NE, FA Cup 1st rd, 1893–94.

Most League Points (2 for a win): 65, Division 4, 1978–79.

Most League Points (3 for a win): 94, Division 3, 1985–86.

Most League Goals: 112, Division 3 (S), 1951–52.

Highest League Scorer in Season: Ronnie Blackman, 39,
Division 3 (S), 1951–52.

Most League Goals in Total Aggregate: Ronnie Blackman,
158, 1947–54.

Most League Goals in One Match: 6, Arthur Bacon v
Stoke C, Division 2, 3 April 1931.

Most Capped Player: Jimmy Quinn, 17 (46), Northern
Ireland.

Most League Appearances: Martin Hicks, 500, 1978–91.

Youngest League Player: Steve Hetzke, 16 years 184 days v
Darlington, 4 December 1971.

Record Transfer Fee Received: £1,575,000 from
Newcastle U for Shaka Hislop, August 1995.

Record Transfer Fee Paid: £800,000 to Brentford for Carl
Asaba, August 1997.

Football League Record: 1920 Original Member of
Division 3; 1921–26 Division 3 (S); 1926–31 Division 2; 1931–58 Division 3 (S); 1958–71 Division 3;
1971–76 Division 4; 1976–77 Division 3; 1977–79 Division 4; 1979–83 Division 3; 1983–84 Division 4;
1984–86 Division 3; 1986–88 Division 2; 1988–92 Division 3; 1992–94 Division 2; 1994–98 Division 1;
1998–2002 Division 2; 2002– Division 1.

MANAGERS

Thomas Sefton 1897–1901
(Secretary-Manager)
James Sharp 1901–02
Harry Matthews 1902–20
Harry Marshall 1920–22
Arthur Chadwick 1923–25
H. S. Bray 1925–26
(Secretary only since 1922 and 1926–35)
Andrew Wylie 1926–31
Joe Smith 1931–35
Billy Butler 1935–39
John Cochrane 1939
Joe Edelston 1939–47
Ted Drake 1947–52
Jack Smith 1952–55
Harry Johnston 1955–63
Roy Bentley 1963–69
Jack Mansell 1969–71
Charlie Hurley 1972–77
Maurice Evans 1977–84
Ian Branfoot 1984–89
Ian Porterfield 1989–91
Mark McGhee 1991–94
Jimmy Quinn/Mick Gooding 1994–97
Terry Bullivant 1997–98
Tommy Burns 1998–99
Alan Pardew October 1999–

LATEST SEQUENCES

Longest Sequence of League Wins: 13, 17.8.85 – 19.10.85.

Longest Sequence of League Defeats: 7, 10.4.98 – 15.8.98.

Longest Sequence of League Draws: 6, 23.3.02 – 20.4.02 (continuing).

Longest Sequence of Unbeaten League Matches: 19, 21.4.73 – 27.10.73.

Longest Sequence Without a League Win: 14, 30.4.27 – 29.10.27.

TEN YEAR LEAGUE RECORD

		P	W	D	L	F	A	Pts	Pos
1991-92	Div 3	46	16	13	17	59	62	61	12
1992-93	Div 2	46	18	15	13	66	51	69	8
1993-94	Div 2	46	26	11	9	81	44	89	1
1994-95	Div 1	46	23	10	13	58	44	79	2
1995-96	Div 1	46	13	17	16	54	63	56	19
1996-97	Div 1	46	15	12	19	58	67	57	18
1997-98	Div 1	46	11	9	26	39	78	42	24
1998-99	Div 2	46	16	13	17	54	63	61	11
1999-2000	Div 2	46	16	14	16	57	63	62	10
2000-01	Div 2	46	25	11	10	86	52	86	3

DID YOU KNOW ?

Dennis Watkin scored only
four FA Cup goals for
Reading – but all in one tie
on 12 December 1936 against
Newport County in a second
round game, won 7-2.

READING 2001–02 LEAGUE RECORD

Match No.	Date	Venue	Opponents	Result		H/T Score	Lg. Pos.	Goalscorers	Attendance
1	Aug 11	A	Blackpool	W	2-0	1-0	—	Parkinson [33], Forster [75]	5613
2	18	H	Huddersfield T	W	1-0	1-0	3	Forster [8]	11,915
3	25	A	QPR	D	0-0	0-0	4		13,829
4	Sept 1	A	Port Vale	W	2-0	1-0	4	Cureton 2 [45, 62]	5196
5	8	H	Cardiff C	L	1-2	1-2	7	Smith A [32]	13,017
6	15	A	Stoke C	L	0-2	0-2	10		11,752
7	18	H	Cambridge U	W	1-0	0-0	—	Harper [63]	8348
8	22	H	Wycombe W	W	2-0	2-0	5	Williams [16], Henderson [18]	13,565
9	25	A	Bournemouth	L	0-1	0-0	—		3691
10	29	H	Bury	D	1-1	1-0	9	Igoe [45]	10,035
11	Oct 5	A	Colchester U	L	0-2	0-2	—		3691
12	13	H	Swindon T	L	1-3	0-1	14	Henderson [80]	14,389
13	20	A	Notts Co	W	4-3	4-1	11	Hughes [4], Cureton 2 [13, 43], Smith A [45]	5604
14	23	A	Oldham Ath	W	1-0	1-0	—	Cureton [19]	4901
15	27	H	Brentford	L	1-2	0-0	11	Butler (pen) [53]	14,680
16	Nov 3	A	Northampton T	W	2-0	0-0	8	Cureton [52], Butler [90]	5162
17	6	H	Wrexham	W	2-0	0-0	—	Forster [69], Henderson [84]	8081
18	10	H	Bristol C	W	3-2	2-1	4	Mackie [12], Lever (og) [44], Salako [51]	14,060
19	20	H	Tranmere R	W	4-1	2-0	—	Smith N [25], Forster 2 [38, 61], Henderson [90]	9007
20	24	A	Peterborough U	W	2-1	0-1	4	Henderson 2 [83, 90]	5695
21	Dec 1	H	Chesterfield	L	0-1	0-1	4		11,209
22	22	H	Wigan Ath	D	1-1	1-0	5	Salako [6]	15,808
23	26	A	Cardiff C	D	2-2	0-1	5	Forster [56], Salako [78]	16,708
24	29	A	Wrexham	W	2-0	1-0	5	Forster [33], Salako [67]	3885
25	Jan 1	H	Port Vale	W	2-0	0-0	4	Cureton 2 (1 pen) [83 (p), 89]	10,743
26	5	H	QPR	W	1-0	0-0	2	Hughes [57]	19,329
27	12	A	Huddersfield T	W	1-0	0-0	1	Forster [56]	10,775
28	19	H	Blackpool	W	3-0	2-0	1	Forster 3 [20, 22, 51]	13,732
29	22	A	Wigan Ath	W	2-0	2-0	—	Hughes [25], Forster [42]	5546
30	26	H	Colchester U	W	3-0	1-0	1	Forster 2 (1 pen) [38 (p), 69], Hughes [48]	12,743
31	Feb 2	A	Bury	D	1-1	0-1	1	Salako [79]	3667
32	9	H	Notts Co	W	2-1	1-1	1	Garden (og) [25], Cureton [90]	13,564
33	11	A	Brighton & HA	L	1-3	0-0	—	Cureton [90]	6756
34	14	A	Swindon T	D	0-0	0-0	—		10,200
35	23	H	Stoke C	W	1-0	0-0	1	Cureton [52]	21,032
36	26	A	Wycombe W	W	2-0	0-0	—	Cureton [68], Henderson [90]	9250
37	Mar 2	A	Cambridge U	D	2-2	0-2	1	Viveash [57], Forster [74]	3841
38	5	H	Bournemouth	D	2-2	1-0	—	Cureton [5], Hughes [80]	13,538
39	9	H	Brighton & HA	D	0-0	0-0	1		22,009
40	16	A	Chesterfield	W	2-0	2-0	1	Forster [30], Cureton [45]	5145
41	23	A	Oldham Ath	D	2-2	2-1	1	Mackie [8], Parkinson [45]	15,191
42	30	A	Bristol C	D	3-3	3-2	1	Hughes [2], Forster (pen) [5], Watson [14]	15,609
43	Apr 1	H	Northampton T	D	0-0	0-0	2		16,495
44	7	A	Tranmere R	D	2-2	0-1	2	Rougier [50], Salako [72]	9282
45	13	A	Peterborough U	D	2-2	0-1	2	Forster 2 [73, 79]	22,151
46	20	A	Brentford	D	1-1	0-0	2	Cureton [77]	11,303

Final League Position: 2

GOALSCORERS

League (70): Forster 19 (2 pens), Cureton 15 (1 pen), Henderson 7, Hughes 6, Salako 6, Butler 2 (1 pen), Mackie 2, Parkinson 2, Smith A 2, Harper 1, Igoe 1, Rougier 1, Smith N 1, Viveash 1, Watson 1, Williams 1, own goals 2.
Worthington Cup (4): Henderson 2, Parkinson 1, Smith A 1.
FA Cup (1): Cureton 1.

Whitehead P 33	Murty G 43	Robinson M 14	Whitbread A 14	Williams A 33+2	Parkinson P 32+1	Hughes A 34+5	Harper J 19+7	Butler M 14+3	Forster N 36+6	Smith A 12+1	Gamble J 2+4	Henderson D 2+36	Igoe S 27+8	Rougier T 20+13	Cureton J 24+14	Jones K 10+6	Smith N 3+11	Sharey N 32	Viveash A 18	Watson K 12	Salako J 31	Mackie J 27	Ashdown J 1	Hahnemann M 6	Roberts B 6	Roget L 1	Tyson N —+1	Branch M —+2	Savage B —+1	Match No.
1	2	3	4	5	6	7^1	8	9^2	10^3	11	12	13	14																	1
1	2	3	4	5	6	7^1	8		9	10		13	12	11^2																2
1	2	3	4	5	6	12	8	9^3	10			13	7^1	11^2	14															3
1	2	3	4	5	6	12	8	13	10^3				14	7	11^2	9^1														4
1	2	3	4	5	6		8	12		10^1		13	7	11^3	9															5
1	2	3	4	5	6		8		10	12	11^2	13	7^1		9^3				14											6
1	2	3	4	5	6		8	9^1	10^2	11^1	12	13	7						14											7
1	2	3	4	5			8	9^2	10	12			11^1	7	6^3				14											8
1	2	3	4	5			8		9	10		11^2	7^3	12	13	6^1			14											9
1	2	3	4	5			8	9^2	10^3	11^1		13	7	12		14			6											10
1	2	3^2	4	5	6		8^1		10	12	11	13	14		9	7^3														11
1		2		5	6	12	8		10^2	11^1			14	7^3	13		9	3	4											12
1	2	3		5	6	7^1	8^2		10	12	11		14		9^1				4											13
1	2	3		5^2	6	7^3	8		10	12	11				9^1				4											14
1	2	3		5	6	7^1	8		10	12	11^2	13			9				4											15
1	2			5		7	8		10	12					9^1	13		3	4	6^2	11									16
1	2			5		7	8		10^2	12		13			9^2	14		3	4	6^3	11									17
1	2					7^1			10^3			13	12		9^2	14		3	4	6	11	8			5					18
1	2					7^1		12	10^2			13	14		9			3	4	6	11	8^1			5					19
1	2	12				7^2			10			13	14		9			3	4	6	11	8^3			5^1					20
	2			5		7^1		12	10			13	14		9^3			3	4	6	11	8^1		1						21
	2			5	12	7^3			10			14	13		9^2			3	4	6^1	11	8		1						22
	2			5	6	12			10				7		9^1			3	4		11	8		1						23
	2			5	6	12			10			13	7		9^2			3	4		11	8^1		1						24
	2^2			5		7			10			14	12		9^1	13		3	4	6	11	8^2		1						25
	2			5	6	7			10^1			13	12		9^2	14		3	4		11	8^3		1						26
		2		5	6	7^2			10			13	12		9			3	4		11	8		1						27
	2			5	6^3	7			10^2			14	12		9^1	13		3	4		11	8		1						28
	2			5	6	7			10^1			13	12		9^2			3	4		11	8		1						29
	2			5	6^2	7			10^1			14	12		9	13		3	4		11	8		1						30
	2			5	6	7			10^1			13	12		9			3	4		11	8		1						31
	2			5	6^3	7			10			14	12		9^1	13		3	4		11	8		1						32
	2			5	6	7^2			10			13	12		9	14		3	4		11	8		1						33
1	2				6	7			10^1			13	12		9^3	14		3	4		11^2	8			5					34
1	2				6	7			10^2			13	12		9^1			3	4		11	8			5					35
1	2				6	7			10^1				12		9^2	13		3	4		11	8			5					36
1	2				6	7^3			10^3			13	12		9	14		3	4		11	8^1			5					37
1	2				6^1	7			10^2			13	12		9	14		3	4^3		11	8			5					38
1	2			5	6	7			10^1				12		9			3	4		11^2	8							13	39
1		2		5	6	7^2			10			13	12		9^3	14		3	4		11	8^1								40
1	2			5	6	7			10			13	12		9^1			3	4		11^2	9^3						14		41
1	2			5	6	7^1		12	10				14		9^2			3	4		11	8						13^3		42
1	2				6	7^1		12	10^2			13	14		9			3	4		11^3	8			5					43
1	2				6	7			10						9			3	4		11	8			5					44
1	2	12^2			6	7			10			13	14		9^3			3	4		11	8			5^1					45
1	2			5	6	8			10						9^2	7^1		3	4		11	12			13					46

Worthington Cup

First Round	Luton T	(h)	4-0	
Second Round	West Ham U	(h)	0-0	
Third Round	Aston Villa	(a)	0-1	

FA Cup

First Round	Welling U	(h)	1-0	
Second Round	York C	(a)	0-2	

ROCHDALE   Division 3

FOUNDATION

Considering the love of rugby in their area, it is not surprising that Rochdale had difficulty in establishing an Association Football club. The earlier Rochdale Town club formed in 1900 went out of existence in 1907 when the present club was immediately established and joined the Manchester League, before graduating to the Lancashire Combination in 1908.

Spotland, Sandy Lane, Rochdale OL11 5DS.

Telephone: (01706) 644 648.

Fax: (01706) 648 466.

Commercial: (01706) 647 521.

Ground Capacity: 10,208.

Record Attendance: 24,231 v Notts Co, FA Cup 2nd rd, 10 December 1949.

Record Receipts: £46,000 v Burnley, Division 4, 5 May 1992.

Pitch Measurements: 114yd × 76yd.

President: Mrs L. Stoney.

Chairman: D. F. Kilpatrick.

Directors: G. R. Brierley, C. Dunphy, J. Marsh, G. Morris, R. Bott, I. H. Stott.

Manager: Paul Simpson.

Secretary: Hilary Molyneux Dearden.

Lottery and Merchandising Manager: P. Woodhouse.

Advertising and Sponsorship Manager: L. Duckworth.

Stadium Manager: Ronnie Cowgill.

Physio: Andy Thorpe.

Colours: Blue shirts with white trim, blue shorts, blue stockings with white hoop on turnover.

Change Colours: Jade green and black shirts, white shorts, black socks.

Year Formed: 1907.

Turned Professional: 1907.

Ltd Co.: 1910.

Club Nickname: 'The Dale'.

First Football League Game: 27 August 1921, Division 3 (N), v Accrington Stanley (h) W 6–3 – Crabtree; Nuttall, Sheehan; Hill, Farrer, Yarwood; Hoad, Sandiford, Dennison (2), Owens (3), Carney (1).

HONOURS

Football League: Division 3 best season: 9th, 1969–70; Division 3 (N) – Runners-up 1923–24, 1926–27.

FA Cup: best season: 5th rd, 1990.

Football League Cup: Runners-up 1962 (record for 4th Division club).

IT'S A FACT !

Terry Owen, signed by Rochdale from Chester in 1977, was the club's top goalscorer in his first season and voted Player of the Year. His son is Michael Owen.

Record League Victory: 8–1 v Chesterfield, Division 3 (N),
18 December 1926 – Hill; Brown, Ward; Hillhouse, Parkes,
Braidwood; Hughes, Bertram, Whitehurst (5), Schofield (2),
Martin (1).

Record Cup Victory: 8–2 v Crook T, FA Cup 1st rd,
26 November 1927 – Moody; Hopkins, Ward; Braidwood,
Parkes, Barker; Tompkinson, Clennell (3) Whitehurst (4),
Hall, Martin (1).

Record Defeat: 1–9 v Tranmere R, Division 3 (N),
25 December 1931.

Most League Points (2 for a win): 62, Division 3 (N),
1923–24.

Most League Points (3 for a win): 78, Division 3, 2001–02.

Most League Goals: 105, Division 3 (N), 1926–27.

Highest League Scorer in Season: Albert Whitehurst, 44,
Division 3 (N), 1926–27.

Most League Goals in Total Aggregate: Reg Jenkins, 119,
1964–73.

Most League Goals in One Match: 6, Tommy Tippett v
Hartlepools U, Division 3N, 21 April 1930.

Most Capped Players: Patrick McCourt, 1, Northern
Ireland and Lee McEvilly, 1, Northern Ireland.

Most League Appearances: Graham Smith, 317, 1966–74.

Youngest League Player: Zac Hughes, 16 years 105 days v
Exeter C, 19 September 1987.

Record Transfer Fee Received: £400,000 from West Ham U
for Stephen Bywater, August 1998.

Record Transfer Fee Paid: £150,000 to Stoke C for Paul
Connor, March 2001.

Football League Record: 1921 Elected to Division 3 (N);
1958–59 Division 3; 1959–69 Division 4; 1969–74 Division 3;
1974–92 Division 4; 1992– Division 3.

MANAGERS

Billy Bradshaw 1920
Run by committee 1920–22
Tom Wilson 1922–23
Jack Peart 1923–30
Will Cameron 1930–31
Herbert Hopkinson 1932–34
Billy Smith 1934–35
Ernest Nixon 1935–37
Sam Jennings 1937–38
Ted Goodier 1938–52
Jack Warner 1952–53
Harry Catterick 1953–58
Jack Marshall 1958–60
Tony Collins 1960–68
Bob Stokoe 1967–68
Len Richley 1968–70
Dick Conner 1970–73
Walter Joyce 1973–76
Brian Green 1976–77
Mike Ferguson 1977–78
Doug Collins 1979
Bob Stokoe 1979–80
Peter Madden 1980–83
Jimmy Greenhoff 1983–84
Vic Halom 1984–86
Eddie Gray 1986–88
Danny Bergara 1988–89
Terry Dolan 1989–91
Dave Sutton 1991–94
Mick Docherty 1995–96
Graham Barrow 1996–99
Steve Parkin 1999–2001
John Hollins 2001–02
Paul Simpson May 2002–

LATEST SEQUENCES

Longest Sequence of League Wins: 8, 29.9.69 – 3.11.69.
Longest Sequence of League Defeats: 17, 14.11.31 – 12.3.32.
Longest Sequence of League Draws: 6, 17.8.68 – 14.9.68.
Longest Sequence of Unbeaten League Matches: 20, 15.9.23 – 19.1.24.
Longest Sequence Without a League Win: 28, 14.11.31 – 29.8.32.

TEN YEAR LEAGUE RECORD

		P	W	D	L	F	A	Pts	Pos
1991-92	Div 4	42	18	13	11	57	53	67	8
1992-93	Div 3	42	16	10	16	70	70	58	11
1993-94	Div 3	42	16	12	14	63	51	60	9
1994-95	Div 3	42	12	14	16	44	67	50	15
1995-96	Div 3	46	14	13	19	57	61	55	15
1996-97	Div 3	46	14	16	16	58	58	58	14
1997-98	Div 3	46	17	7	22	56	55	58	18
1998-99	Div 3	46	13	15	18	42	55	54	19
1999-2000	Div 3	46	18	14	14	57	54	68	10
2000-01	Div 3	46	18	17	11	59	48	71	8

DID YOU KNOW ?

Despite having not had a
player capped as a full
international prior to the
2001–02 season, Rochdale
had both Pat McCourt and
Lee McEvilly chosen for the
full Northern Ireland
international team.

ROCHDALE 2001–02 LEAGUE RECORD

Match No.	Date	Venue	Opponents	Result	H/T Score	Lg. Pos.	Goalscorers	Attendance
1	Aug 11	A	Oxford U	W 2-1	1-0	—	Doughty 30, Coleman 66	7842
2	18	H	Macclesfield T	D 1-1	1-1	7	Ford 26	3346
3	25	A	Plymouth Arg	W 2-1	1-1	3	Jones G 17, Connor 77	4198
4	27	H	Exeter C	W 2-0	2-0	1	Jones G (pen) 29, Townson 30	3003
5	Sept 1	A	Carlisle U	W 2-1	2-0	1	Oliver 11, Platt 12	3373
6	8	H	Kidderminster H	W 2-0	1-0	1	Griffiths 2 2, 76	2885
7	15	H	Scunthorpe U	D 2-2	0-1	1	Oliver 59, Jones G (pen) 81	3468
8	18	A	Hull C	L 1-3	1-1	—	Townson 30	10,213
9	22	A	Shrewsbury T	L 0-1	0-0	6		4612
10	25	A	Halifax T	W 2-0	0-0	—	Platt 2 62, 77	3410
11	29	H	Mansfield T	W 3-1	1-0	1	Platt 32, Jones G 64, Wheatcroft 81	3963
12	Oct 9	A	Swansea C	W 1-0	1-0	—	Ford 31	3533
13	13	H	Rushden & D	D 0-0	0-0	2		4345
14	20	A	Luton T	W 1-0	1-0	1	Wheatcroft 39	7696
15	23	H	Cheltenham T	D 2-2	0-1	—	Wheatcroft 52, Townson 72	3279
16	27	A	Leyton Orient	L 2-4	0-2	3	Townson 2 77, 90	4631
17	Nov 3	A	Torquay U	W 2-0	0-0	2	Townson 2 49, 90	3078
18	10	A	Bristol R	W 2-0	0-0	2	Platt 50, Jones G 70	5675
19	20	A	Darlington	L 0-1	0-0	—		3362
20	24	H	Lincoln C	D 2-2	1-0	2	Jobson 43, Durkan 70	3139
21	30	H	Hartlepool U	D 1-1	0-0	—	Oliver 59	4162
22	Dec 15	H	Southend U	L 0-1	0-1	5		2849
23	26	A	Kidderminster H	L 1-4	1-2	5	Oliver 38	3856
24	29	A	Exeter C	D 1-1	1-0	5	Townson 2	2994
25	Jan 12	A	Macclesfield T	W 1-0	0-0	5	Townson 51	3002
26	19	H	Oxford U	D 1-1	1-0	6	McCourt 7	3355
27	22	A	York C	D 0-0	0-0	—		2317
28	26	H	Swansea C	W 2-0	2-0	4	Oliver 40, Sharp (og) 45	2819
29	29	H	Carlisle U	D 1-1	0-1	—	Griffiths 62	3008
30	Feb 2	A	Mansfield T	L 1-3	0-2	5	Oliver 89	4876
31	5	H	York C	W 5-4	2-2	—	Townson 2 (1 pen) 16 (p), 45, McEvilly 49, Jobson 2 54, 77	2823
32	9	H	Luton T	W 1-0	1-0	3	McCourt 12	4306
33	16	A	Rushden & D	D 1-1	0-0	4	Townson 90	4672
34	23	A	Scunthorpe U	L 1-2	1-2	5	Jones S 10	4521
35	Mar 2	H	Shrewsbury T	W 1-0	0-0	4	Griffiths 80	3353
36	5	A	Halifax T	W 2-1	0-1	—	McEvilly 81, McCourt 90	2825
37	9	A	Southend U	D 0-0	0-0	5		3429
38	16	H	Hartlepool U	D 0-0	0-0	6		3219
39	23	A	Cheltenham T	D 1-1	0-1	6	Platt 53	4643
40	26	H	Plymouth Arg	L 1-3	0-0	—	Simpson 54	4457
41	30	H	Leyton Orient	W 3-0	2-0	5	McEvilly 6, Simpson 30, Townson 82	3021
42	Apr 1	A	Torquay U	L 0-3	0-1	6		3136
43	6	H	Darlington	W 3-1	3-1	5	Platt 7, McEvilly 27, Simpson 35	3055
44	9	H	Hull C	W 3-2	1-2	—	Oliver 32, McCourt 57, Townson 64	3433
45	13	A	Lincoln C	D 1-1	0-1	5	Simpson 81	5849
46	20	H	Bristol R	W 2-1	0-1	5	Simpson 63, McLoughlin (pen) 86	5292

Final League Position: 5

GOALSCORERS

League (65): Townson 14 (1 pen), Oliver 7, Platt 7, Jones G 5 (2 pens), Simpson 5, Griffiths 4, McCourt 4, McEvilly 4, Jobson 3, Wheatcroft 3, Ford 2, Coleman 1, Connor 1, Doughty 1, Durkan 1, Jones S 1, McLoughlin 1 (pen), own goal 1.
Worthington Cup (1): Ford 1.
FA Cup (2): Doughty 1, Oliver 1.

Gilks M 19	Evans W 43	Todd L 8+2	Jones G 20	Coleman S 6+3	Griffiths G 41	Ford T 17	Connor P 11+6	Platt C 41+2	Oliver M 45	Doughty M 32+4	Townson K 17+24	Durkan K 16+14	Flitcroft D 21+14	Edwards N 7	McAuley S 23	Bayliss D 9	Ware P 4+4	Duffy L 1+5	Atkinson G 8+3	Jobson R 34+1	Wheatcroft P 6	Hahnemann M 5	McCourt P 10+13	Dunning D 4+1	Banks S 15	McLoughlin A 15+3	McEvilly L 13+5	Jones S 6+3	Simpson P 7	Match No.
1	2	3	4	5	6	7	8^1	9	10	11^2	12	13																		1
1	2	3	4	5	6	7	8^1	9	10^1	11^2	12	13	14																	2
	2		4	5		7^1	12	9^1	10	13	11^3	8		1	3	6	14													3
1	2		4	5		7^1	8^1	9	10	12	11	13			3	6														4
1	2		4	5		7		9	10	12		11^1	8		3	6														5
1	2		4		5	7	13	9	10	14	8^2	11^1	12		3	6														6
1	2^1	12	4		5	7	8^2	9	10		13	11			3	6														7
1	2		4		5	7	8^2	9	10	3^1	13	11	12			6		14												8
1	2		4		5	7^1		9	10	3	12	11^2	8			6		13												9
1	2	3	4		5	7^1		9	10	13	8		12			6^3		14		11^2										10
1	2		4		6	7		9	10	3	12	13							11^1	5	8									11
1	2		4		6	7		9	10	3	12	11	13						11^2	5	8^1									12
	2		4		6	7		9	10^2	3	12	11	13							5	8^1	1								13
	2		4		6	7^2		9	10	11	12		13		3					5	8^1	1								14
	2		4		6	7^2		9	10	11^1	12		13		3					5	8	1								15
1	2		4		6	7^2		9	10	11^1	12	14	13		3					5	8^1									16
	2		4		6	7.		9^2	10	12	8	11^1			3					5		1	13							17
	2		4		6	7.		9	10	11	8^2		12		3					5		1	13							18
1	2		4			7		9	10	11	8		12		3	6				5										19
	2		4		6	7	8^1	9	10^2	11	12	13		1	3					5										20
	2				6	7	8^1	9	10	11^2	12	13			3					5					1	4				21
	2				6	7^2	8	9^2	10	11^1	12				3					5			13		1	4				22
	2				6		8	9^2	11	12					3					5			10		1	4		7^1	13	23
	2				6		8	9	11	12		13			3					5			10^2		1	4^1		7		24
	2			5	6		8	9	10	11	12				3					5			7^1		1	4				25
	2			5^3	6		8^1	9	10	11	12	13			3								7^2		1	4	14			26
1	2				6		8^{12}	9	10	3	13									11^1						4^3				27
	2				6	7	8^1	9	10	11^2	12				3		4			5			13		1		14			28
	2				6	7	8^1	9	10	11	12^2				3		4			5					1		13			29
	2				6	7	8^2	9	10	11^3					3		4^1	12		5			13		1		14			30
	2				6	7	8	10^1	11	3^2							4^3			5			13		1	12	14	9		31
	2				6	7.	8	11	3											5			4		1	13	10^1	9^3		32
	2	12			6	7	8	11	3											5			10^1		1	4		9		33
	2	3	12	6^1		7	8	9	11											5			13		1	4	10^2			34
	2	3			6	7	8	9	10	11	12	4								5			13		1	4	8^1	7^2		35
	2	3^3			6	7	8	9	10^2	11	12									5			4		1	13	8	14		36
	2				6		8	12	11	3							13	14		5			10^3		1	4	9^1	7^2		37
1	2				6	7	8^1	12	10	3										11^2			13			4	9^3	14		38
1	2^1		12		6	7		9	11	3	13	14								5			8^3			4	10^2			39
1					6	7^1	8^2	9	10	3	12				2								4				13	11	11	40
1	2				6	7^3		9^2	10	3	12	13								5			14			4	8^1		11	41
1	2				6	7^3	4^2	9	10	3	12									5			14			4	8^2		11	42
	2				6	7^3		9	10	3	12	13	1							5			14			4	8^2		11	43
	2				6	7^2		9	10	3	12		1							5			13			4	8		11	44
	2				6	7^2		9	10	3	12	13	1							5						4	8^1		11	45
	2^1		12		6	7^2		9	10	3		14	1							5			13^3			4	8		11	46

Worthington Cup
First Round   Huddersfield T   (a)   1-0

FA Cup
First Round   Tamworth   (a)   1-1
                            (h)   1-0
Second Round   Blackpool   (a)   0-2

ROTHERHAM UNITED   Division 1

FOUNDATION

Rotherham were formed in 1870 before becoming Town in the late 1880s. Thornhill United were founded in 1877 and changed their name to Rotherham County in 1905. The Town amalgamated with Rotherham County to form Rotherham United in 1925.

Millmoor Ground, Rotherham S60 1HR.

Telephone: (01709) 512 434. *Fax:* (01709) 512 762.
Ticket Office: (01709) 309 440.
Commercial Dept: (01709) 512 760.
Fax: (01709) 512 763. *ClubCall:* 09068 121 637.

Football in the Community: (01709) 512 761.

Ground Capacity: 11,486.

Record Attendance: 25,170 v Sheffield U, Division 2, 13 December 1952.

Record Receipts: £106,182 v Southampton, FA Cup 3rd rd, 16 January 2002.

Pitch Measurements. 115yd × 70yd.

Chairman: K. F. Booth. *Directors:* C. A. Luckock, T. Smallwood OBE.

Chief Executive: Phil Henson.

Manager: Ronnie Moore. *Assistant Manager:* John Breckin.

Youth Development Coach: John Bilton. *Physios:* Denis Circuit, Ian Bailey.

Stadium Manager: Peter Chapman. *Safety Officer:* David Sumner.

Commercial Manager: D. Nicholls.

Year Formed: 1870. *Turned Professional:* 1905. *Ltd Co.:* 1920. *Club Nickname:* 'The Merry Millers'.

Colours: Red and white.

Change Colours: Black and blue striped shirts, black shorts, black stockings.

Previous Names: 1877, Thornhill United; 1905, Rotherham County; 1925, amalgamated with Rotherham Town under Rotherham United.

Previous Ground: 1870, Red House Ground; 1907, Millmoor.

First Football League Game: 2 September 1893, Division 2, Rotherham T v Lincoln C (a) D 1–1 – McKay; Thickett, Watson; Barr, Brown, Broadhead; Longden, Cutts, Leatherbarrow, McCormick, Pickering, (1 og). 30 August 1919, Division 2, Rotherham Co v Nottingham F (h) W 2–0 – Branston; Alton, Baines; Bailey, Coe, Stanton; Lee (1), Cawley (1), Glennon, Lees, Lamb.

Record League Victory: 8–0 v Oldham Ath, Division 3 (N), 26 May 1947 – Warnes; Selkirk, Ibbotson; Edwards, Horace Williams, Danny Williams; Wilson (2), Shaw (1), Ardron (3), Guest (1), Hainsworth (1).

Record Cup Victory: 6–0 v Spennymoor U, FA Cup 2nd rd, 17 December 1977 – McAlister; Forrest, Breckin, Womble, Stancliffe, Green, Finney, Phillips (3), Gwyther (2) (Smith), Goodfellow, Crawford (1). 6–0 v Wolverhampton W, FA Cup 1st rd, 16 November 1985 – O'Hanlon; Forrest, Dungworth, Gooding

HONOURS

Football League: Division 2 – runners-up 2000–01; Division 3 – Champions 1980–81; Runners-up 1999–2000; Division 3 (N) – Champions 1950–51; Runners-up 1946–47, 1947–48, 1948–49; Division 4 – Champions 1988–89; Runners-up 1991–92.

FA Cup: best season: 5th rd, 1953, 1968.

Football League Cup: Runners-up 1961.

Auto Windscreens Shield: Winners 1996.

IT'S A FACT !

In 1946–47, the five Rotherham United forwards counted for all but ten of the 114 League goals scored by the club: Wally Ardron (38), Stewart McLean (19), Albert Wilson (19), Gladstone Guest (15) and Jack Shaw (13).

(1), Smith (1), Pickering, Birch (2), Emerson, Tynan (1), Simmons (1), Pugh. 6–0 v Kings Lynn, FA Cup 2nd rd, 6 December 1997 – Mimms; Clark, Hurst (Goodwin), Garner (1) (Hudson) (1), Warner (Bass), Richardson (1), Berry (1), Thompson, Druce (1), Glover (1), Roscoe.

Record Defeat: 1–11 v Bradford C, Division 3 (N), 25 August 1928.

Most League Points (2 for a win): 71, Division 3 (N), 1950–51.

Most League Points (3 for a win): 91, Division 2, 2000–01.

Most League Goals: 114, Division 3 (N), 1946–47.

Highest League Scorer in Season: Wally Ardron, 38, Division 3 (N), 1946–47.

Most League Goals in Total Aggregate: Gladstone Guest, 130, 1946–56.

Most League Goals in One Match: 4, Roland Bastow v York C, Division 3N, 9 November 1935; 4, Roland Bastow v Rochdale, Division 3N, 7 March 1936; 4, Wally Ardron v Crewe Alex, Division 3N, 5 October 1946; 4, Wally Ardron v Carlisle U, Division 3N, 13 September 1947; 4, Wally Ardron v Hartlepools U, Division 3N, 13 October 1948; 4, Ian Wilson v Liverpool, Division 2, 2 May 1955; 4, Carl Gilbert v Swansea C, Division 3, 28 September 1971; 4, Carl Airey v Chester, Division 3, 31 August 1987; 4, Shaun Goater v Hartlepool U, Division 3, 9 April 1994; 4, Lee Glover v Hull C, Division 3, 28 December 1997.

Most Capped Player: Shaun Goater 14 (19), Bermuda.

Most League Appearances: Danny Williams, 459, 1946–62.

Youngest League Player: Kevin Eley, 16 years 72 days v Scunthorpe U, 15 May 1984.

Record Transfer Fee Received: £325,000 from Sheffield W for Matt Clarke, July 1996.

Record Transfer Fee Paid: £150,000 to Millwall for Tony Towner, August 1980; £150,000 to Port Vale for Lee Glover, August 1996; £150,000 to Burnley for Alan Lee, September 2000.

Football League Record: 1893 Rotherham Town elected to Division 2; 1896 Failed re-election; 1919 Rotherham County elected to Division 2; 1923–51 Division 3 (N); 1951–68 Division 2; 1968–73 Division 3; 1973–75 Division 4; 1975–81 Division 3; 1981–83 Division 2; 1983–88 Division 3; 1988–89 Division 4; 1989–91 Division 3; 1991–92 Division 4; 1992–97 Division 2; 1997–2000 Division 3; 2000–01 Division 2; 2001– Division 1.

MANAGERS

Billy Heald 1925–29 *(Secretary only for long spell)*
Stanley Davies 1929–30
Billy Heald 1930–33
Reg Freeman 1934–52
Andy Smailes 1952–58
Tom Johnston 1958–62
Danny Williams 1962–65
Jack Mansell 1965–67
Tommy Docherty 1967–68
Jimmy McAnearney 1968–73
Jimmy McGuigan 1973–79
Ian Porterfield 1979–81
Emlyn Hughes 1981–83
George Kerr 1983–85
Norman Hunter 1985–87
Dave Cusack 1987–88
Billy McEwan 1988–91
Phil Henson 1991–94
Archie Gemmill/John McGovern 1994–96
Danny Bergara 1996–97
Ronnie Moore May 1997–

LATEST SEQUENCES

Longest Sequence of League Wins: 9, 2.2.82 – 6.3.82.

Longest Sequence of League Defeats: 8, 7.4.56 – 18.8.56.

Longest Sequence of League Draws: 6, 13.10.69 – 22.11.69.

Longest Sequence of Unbeaten League Matches: 18, 13.10.69 – 7.2.70.

Longest Sequence Without a League Win: 14, 8.10.77 – 2.1.78.

TEN YEAR LEAGUE RECORD

		P	W	D	L	F	A	Pts	Pos
1991-92	Div 4	42	22	11	9	70	37	77	2
1992-93	Div 2	46	17	14	15	60	60	65	11
1993-94	Div 2	46	15	13	18	63	60	58	15
1994-95	Div 2	46	14	14	18	57	61	56	17
1995-96	Div 2	46	14	14	18	54	62	56	16
1996-97	Div 2	46	7	14	25	39	70	35	23
1997-98	Div 3	46	16	19	11	67	61	67	9
1998-99	Div 3	46	20	13	13	79	61	73	5
1999-2000	Div 3	46	24	12	10	72	36	84	2
2000-01	Div 2	46	27	10	9	79	55	91	2

DID YOU KNOW ?

On 19 January 1929, Rotherham United celebrated the opening of the new Millmoor Lane covered stand by beating Hartlepools United 3-2 before a crowd of 4,339.

ROTHERHAM UNITED 2001–02 LEAGUE RECORD

Match No.	Date	Venue	Opponents	Result	H/T Score	Lg. Pos.	Goalscorers	Attendance
1	Aug 11	H	Crystal Palace	L	2-3	2-1	—	Branston [30], Robins [33]	6994
2	18	A	Watford	L	2-3	1-2	21	Robins 2 [20, 66]	13,839
3	23	H	Sheffield U	D	1-1	1-0	—	Scott R [23]	7515
4	27	A	Barnsley	D	1-1	1-0	22	Robins [16]	15,552
5	Sept 8	A	Burnley	L	0-3	0-0	23		14,820
6	15	H	Norwich C	D	1-1	0-0	23	Robins (pen) [70]	6099
7	17	A	Nottingham F	L	0-2	0-2	—		15,632
8	22	A	Gillingham	L	1-2	0-1	24	Robins [90]	7688
9	25	H	Sheffield W	D	1-1	0-0	—	McIntosh [58]	8474
10	29	H	Wolverhampton W	L	0-3	0-2	24		8298
11	Oct 5	A	Grimsby T	W	2-0	1-0	—	Robins 2 [26, 66]	6662
12	12	H	Portsmouth	W	2-1	1-0	—	Monkhouse [4], Beech [85]	6427
13	17	H	Coventry C	D	0-0	0-0	—		6582
14	20	A	Stockport Co	W	1-0	1-0	19	Talbot [43]	6616
15	23	H	Walsall	L	2-3	0-3	—	Scott R [89], Monkhouse [90]	6162
16	27	H	Wimbledon	W	3-2	2-2	19	Swailes [18], Robins (pen) [40], McIntosh [76]	5586
17	30	H	Crewe Alex	D	2-2	1-2	—	Robins [10], Swailes [48]	5971
18	Nov 4	A	Birmingham C	D	2-2	1-1	17	Lee [16], Swailes [54]	28,436
19	9	A	Millwall	L	0-1	0-1	—		12,173
20	17	H	WBA	W	2-1	1-0	17	Swailes [23], Lee [70]	8509
21	24	A	Manchester C	L	1-2	1-1	18	Swailes [24]	34,223
22	Dec 1	H	Walsall	W	2-0	1-0	18	Mullin [34], Lee [76]	6273
23	8	A	Bradford C	L	1-3	0-0	18	Scott R [74]	14,529
24	15	H	Preston NE	W	1-0	1-0	19	McIntosh [3]	6558
25	22	A	Sheffield U	D	2-2	0-0	18	Watson [66], Swailes [78]	22,749
26	29	H	Barnsley	D	1-1	0-0	18	Barker [58]	9737
27	Jan 12	H	Watford	D	1-1	0-1	18	Barker [59]	6409
28	19	A	Crystal Palace	L	0-2	0-0	20		17,311
29	29	H	Grimsby T	D	1-1	0-1	—	Lee [61]	6098
30	Feb 2	A	Wolverhampton W	L	1-2	1-0	20	Lee [43]	22,591
31	6	A	Coventry C	L	0-2	0-0	—		12,893
32	9	H	Stockport Co	W	3-2	1-0	19	Sedgwick [33], Robins 2 (1 pen) [83 (p), 90]	6413
33	12	H	Burnley	D	1-1	1-1	—	Robins (pen) [12]	9021
34	16	A	Portsmouth	D	0-0	0-0	18		13,313
35	23	A	Sheffield W	W	2-1	0-0	18	Lee [50], Barker [90]	28,179
36	26	H	Gillingham	W	3-2	1-0	—	Robins [34], Mullin [48], Daws [52]	6005
37	Mar 2	H	Nottingham F	L	1-2	0-0	18	Robins (pen) [67]	8455
38	5	A	Norwich C	D	0-0	0-0	—		18,485
39	9	A	Preston NE	L	1-2	0-1	18	Lee [66]	14,579
40	16	H	Bradford C	D	1-1	0-0	18	Lee (pen) [89]	7182
41	23	H	Manchester C	D	1-1	1-0	18	Lee [45]	11,426
42	30	A	Wimbledon	L	0-1	0-1	19		4751
43	Apr 1	H	Millwall	D	0-0	0-0	19		6888
44	7	A	WBA	D	1-1	0-1	19	Byfield [50]	22,376
45	13	H	Birmingham C	D	2-2	1-1	20	Byfield [36], McIntosh [59]	10,536
46	21	A	Crewe Alex	L	0-2	0-2	21		7904

Final League Position: 21

GOALSCORERS

League (52): Robins 15 (5 pens), Lee 9 (1 pen), Swailes 6, McIntosh 4, Barker 3, Scott R 3, Byfield 2, Monkhouse 2, Mullin 2, Beech 1, Branston 1, Daws 1, Sedgwick 1, Talbot 1, Watson 1.
Worthington Cup (2): Lee 1, Robins 1.
FA Cup (4): Mullin 2, Barker 1, Warne 1.

Pollitt M 46	Bryan M 19	Hurst P 45	Sedgwick C 39 + 5	Swailes C 44	Branston G 10	Talbot S 36 + 2	Watson K 19	Barker R 11 + 24	Robins M 34 + 7	Warne P 14 + 11	Monkhouse A 21 + 17	Daws N 21 + 14	Scott R 35 + 3	Beech C 2 + 6	McIntosh M 39	Lee A 37 + 1	Miranda J 2	Mullin J 27 + 7	Gray I — + 1	Lowndes N 2	Byfield D 3	Match No.
1	2	3	4¹	5	6	7	8²	9	10	11	12	13										1
1	2	3¹	4	5	6	7¹	8	9	10	11³	12	13	14									2
1	2	3	12	5		7¹	8	13	10	11³	14				4	6		9²				3
1	2	3	7²	5			8	12	10	13	11				4	6		9¹				4
1	2	3	7²	5		11	8³	12	10¹		13	14			4	6		9				5
1	2	3	12	5		7	8²		10	11¹	13				4	6		9				6
1	2	3	12	5		7²	8		10	11¹	13				4	6		9				7
1	2	3²	12	5¹		7	8	13	10	11³	14				4	6		9				8
1	2	3	4	5		7¹	8		10	11²	12	13				6		9				9
1	2³	3	4	5		7	8²	12	10	11	14	13				6		9¹				10
1		3	4	5		7	8	12	10	11					2	6		9¹				11
1		3	4	5		7	8²	12	10	11³	13		14		2	6		9¹				12
1		3	4	5		7¹	8		10	11	12				2	6		9				13
1		3	4	5		7²	8	12	10¹	11		13			2	6		9				14
1		3	4	5		7	8	12	10²	11		13			2	6		9¹				15
1		3	4	5		7	8	12	10¹	11					2	6		9				16
1		3	4	5		7	8	12	10¹	11					2	6		9				17
1		3	4	5	6	7	8	12	10¹	11					2			9				18
1		3	4	5²	6³	7	8	12	10¹	11		13	14		2			9				19
1		3	4	5		7	8	12	10¹	11					2	6		9				20
1		3	4	5		7	8³	12	10¹	11		13	14		2	6		9¹				21
1		3	4	5		7	8	12	10²	11		13			2	6		9¹				22
1		3	4	5		7	8³	12	10²	11		13	14		2	6		9¹				23
1		3	4¹	5		7	8²	12	10	11		13			2	6		9				24
1		3	4	5		7	8¹	12	10²	11		13			2	6		9				25
1		3	4	5		7	8¹	12	10	11		13			2²	6		9				26
1		3	4¹	5	6	7	8	12	10	11					2			9				27
1		3	4	5		7	8¹	12	10	11					2	6		9				28
1		3	4	5		7	8	12	10²	11		13			2	6		9¹				29
1		3	4¹	5		7²	8	12	10	11		13			2	6		9				30
1		3	4	5		7²	8³	12	10¹	11		13	14		2	6		9				31
1	2	3	4	5		7¹	8²	12	10	11		13				6		9				32
1	2	3	4	5		7³	8²	12	10	11		13	14			6		9¹				33
1	2	3	4	5		7	8	12	10²	11¹		13				6		9				34
1	2	3	4²	5		7	8	12	10¹	11		13				6		9				35
1	2	3	4²	5		7³	8	12	10¹	11		13	14			6		9				36
1	2	3	4³	5		7²	8	12	10	11		13	14			6		9¹				37
1	2	3		5	6	7¹	8		10	11	12				4			9				38
1³	2	3	4²	5	6	7	8	12	10	11		13						9¹		15		39
1	2	3	12	5		7³	8		10²	11	14	13			4¹	6		9				40
1		3	4	5		7	8	12	10¹	11					2	6		9				41
1		3	4	5		7	8	12	10	11⁴		13	14		2³	6		9¹				42
1		3	4	5		7	8	12	10²	11³		13	14		2	6		9¹				43
1		3	4	5		7	8			11					2	6		9			10	44
1		3	4	5		7	8	12		11²		13			2	6		9¹			10	45
1	11	3	4	5		7³	8	12				13	14		2	6		9¹			10²	46

Worthington Cup

First Round	Scunthorpe U	(a)	2-0
Second Round	Bradford C	(h)	0-4

FA Cup

Third Round	Southampton	(h)	2-1
Fourth Round	Crewe Alex	(h)	2-4

RUSHDEN & DIAMONDS   Division 3

FOUNDATION

Rushden & Diamonds were formed in 1992 from an amalgamation of Rushden Town and Irthlingborough Diamonds. At the end of 1990–91, Rushden Town had been relegated to the Southern League Midland Division as their ground was unfit for Premier Division football. Irthlingborough Diamonds were competing in the United Counties League at the time. The idea for this merger came from Max Griggs (owner of Dr Martens) a local multi-millionaire businessman. He invested several million pounds and they have been able to achieve Football League status in nine years.

Nene Park, Diamond Way, Irthlingborough, Northants NN9 5QF.

MANAGERS

Roger Ashby 1992–97
Brian Talbot 1997–

Telephone: (01933) 652 000.

Fax: (01933) 650 418.

Website: www.thediamondsfc.com

R&DFC ClubCall: 09068 440033.

Radio Diamonds: (01933) 653 535.

Ground Capacity: 6,441.

Record Attendance: 6,431 v Leeds U, FA Cup 3rd rd, 2 January 1999.

Record Receipts: £46,592 v Rochdale, Division 3 Play-off semi-final first leg, 27 April 2002.

Pitch Measurements: 111yd x 75yd.

Directors: W.M. Griggs CBE, MA (Chairman), M.G. Darnell (Managing), S.W. Griggs, H.M. Johnstone, A.C. Jones, R.W. Langley, C.M. Smith.

President: D. Attley.

Manager: Brian Talbot.

First Team Coach: Steve Spooner.

Youth Team Coach: Brian Sparrow.

Physio: Simon Parsell.

Secretary: David Joyce.

Colours: White shirts with blue trim and red piping, blue shorts, white stockings.

Change Colours: Yellow shirts with black sleeves, black shorts, yellow stockings.

IT'S A FACT !

The newly formed Rushden & Diamonds played its first game as such at the start of the 1992–93 season with a 2-2 draw against Bilston Town, watched by a crowd of 315.

Year formed: 1992.

Turned Professional: 1992.

Ltd Co.: 1992.

Club Nickname: 'The Diamonds'.

Record League Victory: 7–0 v Redditch U, Southern League, Midland Division, 7 May 1994:– Fox; Wooding (1), Johnson, Flower (1), Beech, Page, Coe, Mann (2), Nuttell (1), Watkins (1), Keast (1).

Record Cup Victory: 8–0 v Desborough T, Northants F.A. Hillier Senior Cup, 1st rd, 27 September 1994:– Fox; Wooding, Johnson, Flower, Keast, Page, Collins, Butterworth, Nuttell (2), Watkins (2), Mann (2). Subs:– Capone (2), Mason.

HONOURS
Conference – Champions 2000–01.
Conference Championship Shield – Winners 2001.
Southern League Midland Division – Champions 1993–94.
Premier Division – Champions 1995–96.
FA Trophy – Semi-finalists 1994.
Northants FA Hillier Senior Cup – Winners 1993–94, 1998–99.
Maunsell Premier Cup –Winners 1994–95, 1998–99; Finalists 2001–02

Record Defeat: 1–7 v Cardiff C, LDV Vans Trophy 1st rd, 16 October 2001.

Most League Points (3 for a win): 98, Southern League Midland Division, 1993–94.

Most League Goals: 109, Southern League Midland Division, 1993–94.

Highest League Scorer in Season: Darren Collins, 30 (40 in all competitions), Southern League Premier Division, 1995–96.

Most League Goals in Total Aggregate: Darren Collins, 112 (153 in all competitions), 1994–2000.

Most Capped Player: Onandi Lowe 1, Jamaica.

Most League Appearances: Garry Butterworth, 286 (371 in all competitions), 1994–2002.

Record Transfer Fee Received: £25,000 from Kettering T for Darren Collins, November 2000.

Record Transfer Fee Paid: Undisclosed to Kansas City Wizards for Onandi Lowe, February 2002.

LATEST SEQUENCES

Longest Sequence of League Wins: 4, 16.3.02 – 1.4.02.

Longest Sequence of League Defeats: 4, 27.8.01 – 15.9.01.

Longest Sequence of League Draws: not more than 2.

Longest Sequence of Unbeaten League Matches: 12, 18.9.01 – 20.11.01.

Longest Sequence Without a League Win: 7, 16.8.01 – 18.9.01

TEN YEAR LEAGUE RECORD

		P	W	D	L	F	A	Pts	Pos
1991-92	Rushden T in SL mid; Diamonds in UCL								
1992-93	SL mid	42	25	10	7	85	41	85	3
1993-94	SL mid	42	29	11	2	109	37	98	1
1994-95	SL pr	42	19	11	12	99	65	68	5
1995-96	SL pr	42	29	7	6	99	41	94	1
1996-97	Conf.	42	14	11	17	61	63	53	12
1997-98	Conf.	42	23	5	14	79	57	74	4
1998-99	Conf.	42	20	12	10	71	42	72	4
1999-2000	Conf.	42	21	13	8	71	42	76	2
2000-01	Conf.	42	25	11	6	78	36	86	1

DID YOU KNOW ?

In 2001–02, Rushden & Diamonds had a David Bell and a David Bell Jr on their professional staff. The younger was a cousin of his namesake.

RUSHDEN & DIAMONDS 2001–02 LEAGUE RECORD

Match No.	Date	Venue	Opponents	Result	H/T Score	Lg. Pos.	Goalscorers	Attendance
1	Aug 11	A	York C	W 1-0	1-0	—	Patmore [27]	4307
2	16	H	Lincoln C	D 0-0	0-0	—		5018
3	25	A	Macclesfield T	D 0-0	0-0	11		1950
4	27	H	Plymouth Arg	L 2-3	2-1	13	Darby 2 [30, 42]	4414
5	Sept 1	A	Oxford U	L 2-3	0-0	14	Darby 2 [85, 88]	6289
6	8	H	Southend U	L 0-1	0-0	18		4583
7	15	A	Leyton Orient	L 1-2	0-2	22	Hanlon (pen) [76]	5287
8	18	H	Torquay U	D 0-0	0-0	—		3258
9	22	H	Cheltenham T	W 1-0	0-0	17	Sigere [47]	4116
10	25	A	Exeter C	D 1-1	0-0	—	Hanlon [90]	2622
11	29	A	Darlington	D 0-0	0-0	20		4365
12	Oct 5	H	Hartlepool U	W 2-1	1-1	—	Barron (og) [30], Hunter [67]	3929
13	13	A	Rochdale	D 0-0	0-0	12		4345
14	20	H	Hull C	D 3-3	3-1	16	Edwards (og) [9], Burgess 2 [19, 26]	4676
15	23	A	Shrewsbury T	W 2-0	1-0	—	Setchell [20], Darby [69]	4016
16	27	H	Mansfield T	W 3-1	2-1	8	Hassell (og) [31], Burgess [35], Partridge [77]	4937
17	Nov 3	A	Swansea C	D 0-0	0-0	8		3970
18	10	H	Halifax T	W 2-1	1-0	8	Partridge [32], Thomson [72]	3883
19	20	H	Scunthorpe U	D 0-0	0-0	—		3533
20	24	A	Kidderminster H	L 0-3	0-1	10		3014
21	Dec 1	A	Bristol R	W 3-1	2-0	8	Partridge 2 [2, 46], Lowe [13]	4570
22	15	A	Luton T	L 0-1	0-1	9		7495
23	22	H	Carlisle U	W 3-1	1-1	8	Lowe [28], Hall [50], Whitehead (og) [84]	4142
24	26	A	Southend U	L 2-4	2-0	9	Butterworth [5], Partridge [35]	5878
25	29	A	Plymouth Arg	L 0-1	0-0	11		9503
26	Jan 12	A	Lincoln C	W 4-2	2-2	10	Lowe [5], Hall 2 [16, 74], Darby [80]	3170
27	19	H	York C	W 3-0	2-0	10	Darby [4], McElhatton [45], Lowe [87]	4605
28	22	H	Carlisle U	L 0-3	0-2	—		2864
29	26	A	Hartlepool U	L 1-5	0-1	11	Duffy [90]	3513
30	29	H	Macclesfield T	W 2-0	0-0	—	Lowe [52], Wardley [90]	2771
31	Feb 2	H	Darlington	W 2-1	1-0	9	Hall [45], Lowe [78]	4383
32	5	H	Oxford U	W 2-1	1-0	—	Lowe [36], Brady [80]	4484
33	9	A	Hull C	L 1-2	0-1	8	Hanlon (pen) [77]	8825
34	16	H	Rochdale	D 1-1	0-0	9	Hall [88]	4672
35	23	H	Leyton Orient	W 1-0	0-0	8	Wardley [63]	4507
36	26	H	Torquay U	D 1-1	1-0	—	Wardley [38]	1709
37	Mar 2	A	Cheltenham T	D 1-1	1-1	9	Lowe [40]	4584
38	5	H	Exeter C	W 2-1	2-0	—	Burgess [31], Hanlon (pen) [34]	3343
39	9	H	Luton T	L 1-2	0-0	9	Hall [49]	5876
40	16	A	Bristol R	W 3-0	1-0	8	Lowe 2 [43, 68], Hanlon [67]	5240
41	23	H	Shrewsbury T	W 3-0	3-0	7	Lowe [33], Hanlon [39], Mustafa [45]	5432
42	30	A	Mansfield T	W 4-1	1-0	8	Lowe 3 [39, 53, 64], Angell [79]	5807
43	Apr 1	H	Swansea C	W 4-0	2-0	5	Hall [2], Lowe 2 [17, 56], Angell [54]	4671
44	6	A	Scunthorpe U	D 1-1	0-1	6	Lowe [79]	4794
45	13	H	Kidderminster H	L 0-2	0-0	6		5478
46	20	A	Halifax T	W 4-2	0-1	6	Lowe 2 [46, 49], Wardley [62], Hall [76]	2699

Final League Position: 6

GOALSCORERS

League (69): Lowe 19, Hall 8, Darby 7, Hanlon 6 (3 pens), Partridge 5, Burgess 4, Wardley 4, Angell 2, Brady 1, Butterworth 1, Duffy 1, Hunter 1, McElhatton 1, Mustafa 1, Patmore 1, Setchell 1, Sigere 1, Thomson 1, own goals 4.
Worthington Cup (3): Darby 1, Mustafa 1, Peters 1.
FA Cup (2): Hanlon 2 (1 pen).

Turley B 43	Mustafa T 21+2	Underwood P 40	Talbot D 2+1	Peters M 40	Rodwell J 8+1	Butterworth G 28+1	Brady J 9+13	Patmore W 4	Jackson J 5	Mills G 3+6	Setchell G 13+9	Darby D 17+13	Carey S 7+1	Angell B 3+2	Gray S 12	Sigere J 4+3	Solkhon B —+1	Burgess A 28+4	Wormull S 4+1	Sambrook A 25+1	Hunter B 23	Hanlon R 33+2	Pennock T 3+2	Partridge S 26+11	Duffy R 1+7	Lee C 1	Folan C 1+5	Hall P 34	Thomson P 1+1	Lowe O 25	McElhatton M 4+3	Bell Jnr D —+1	Warburton R 1	Dempster J —+2	Douglas S 4+5	Carr D 1	Wardley S 18	Tillson A 14	Match No.
1	2	3	4¹	5	6	7	8	9²	10	11³	12	13	14																										1
1	2	3		5	6	7	8	9¹	10		12		4	11																									2
1	2	3		5	6	7	8	9¹	10		12		4	11																									3
1	2	3		5	6	7	8		10²		12		9	4	11¹	13																							4
1	2	3		5	6	7²	8		10³		13		11¹	9	4			14	12																				5
1	2	3		5	6		8²	9¹		11		10	4		12	7	13																						6
1	2²	3		5			8¹			12			4		9⁶		10		13	6	7	15	11																7
1				5		7							4		9¹		10	3	2	6	8		11	12														8
1	3¹			5	12	7	13								9³		10	6²	2	4	8		11	14														9
				5		7	12					3			9²		10	6¹	2	4	8	1	11	13														10
				5		7	12					3			13		10	6¹	2	4	8	1	11	9²														11
	3			5		7	8								10			2	6	4	1	11		9¹	12													12
1	3			5		4					12				10			2	6	8		11¹		9	7													13
1	3			5		4						12	9²		10¹			2	6	8		11		13	7													14
	3			5		4							10	9¹				2	6	8		11		12	7													15
1	3⁴			5		4	12					13	9		10¹			2	6	8		11³		14	7													16
1	10¹			5		4	12					3	9					2	6	8		11²		13	7													17
1	3			5		4	12						9²		10¹			2	6	8		11			7	13												18
1	3			5		4							9		10			2	6	8		11			7													19
1	3	12	5		4	13						10²						2	6	8		11	14		7¹	9³												20
1	3		5	4	8					6								2	10¹		11	12		7	9													21
1	3			5		4					9¹							11	2	6	8²	12		7	10	13												22
1	3			5		4²					12							10	2	6¹	8	11		7	9	13												23
1	3			5		4³					13	12						10	2		8	11²		7	9	14												24
1	12	3		5		4					10	13		6²				2¹				11		7	9	8³	14											25
1		3				4					10	12		6²				13	2	5		11¹		7	9	8												26
1		3				4¹					11	9³		6²				13	2	5	12	14		7	10	8												27
1											3	9	11¹		12²	2	6	4						7	10	8	5¹	14	13									28
1	12										3		11			2¹	6	4		10²	13			7				14	9	5³	8							29
1	2	5					12					3¹	9²		11			6	4	13				7		10³				14		8							30
1	2	3		5			12						9²		11			6	4¹	13				7		10³				14		8							31
1	2¹	3		5								12			11			6	4	9³				7		10²				14		8							32
1	2	3		5			12²						14		11¹			4		9³				7		10				13		8	6						33
1	2	3		5								12						11		4				7		10¹				9		8	6						34
1	2	3		5								12						10		4	12			7		11				9¹		8	6						35
1		2		5		11						12						4	3			13		7		10¹				9²		8	6						36
	2			5		11²						12						4	3	13		9¹		7		10						8	6						37
1	2	3		5								12						11		4		9¹		7		10						8	6						38
1	2	3		5								12						11		4		9¹		7		10						8	6						39
1	3²			5			12					14	9					11		2¹		4		7		13				10		8	6						40
1	2	3		5							12	9						11		4¹		13		7		10²						8	6						41
1	2	3		5			12					9²	14					11		4		13		7¹		10³						8	6						42
1	2	3²	5¹				12	13				9						11		4		14		7		10³						8	6						43
1	2	3		5								12		9²				11		4¹		13		7		10						8	6						44
1	2	3		5			12					4		9²				11¹		13				7		10						8	6						45
1⁶	2	3		5			4					12		13				11		15		9¹		7		10²						8	6						46

Worthington Cup

First Round	Burnley	(a)	3-2
Second Round	Crewe Alex	(a)	0-2

FA Cup

First Round	Worcester C	(a)	1-0
Second Round	Brighton & HA	(a)	1-2

SCUNTHORPE UNITED   Division 3

FOUNDATION

The year of foundation for Scunthorpe United has often been quoted as 1910, but the club can trace its history back to 1899 when Brumby Hall FC, who played on the Old Showground, consolidated their position by amalgamating with some other clubs and changing their name to Scunthorpe United. The year 1910 was when that club amalgamated with North Lindsey United as Scunthorpe and Lindsey United. The link is Mr W. T. Lockwood whose chairmanship covers both years.

Glanford Park, Scunthorpe, North Lincolnshire DN15 8TD.

Telephone: (01724) 848 077. *Fax:* (01724) 857 986.
ClubCall: 09068 121 652.

Ground Capacity: 9,183.

Record Attendance: Old Showground: 23,935 v Portsmouth, FA Cup 4th rd, 30 January 1954. Glanford Park: 8,775 v Rotherham U, Division 4, 1 May 1989.

Record Receipts: £47,252 v Burnley, Division 2, 6 May 2000.

Pitch Measurements: 110yd × 71yd.

HONOURS

Football League: Division 2 best season: 4th, 1961–62; Division 3 (N) – Champions 1957–58. Promoted from Division 3 1998–99 (play-offs).

FA Cup: best season: 5th rd, 1958, 1970.

Football League Cup: never past 3rd rd.

Vice-presidents: I. T. Botham, G. Johnson, A. Harvey, R. Ashman, K. Waters, J. Brownsword, B. Heywood, Dr J. Zacarias. *Chairman:* K. Wagstaff. *Vice-chairman:* R. Garton.

Directors: J. B. Borrill, B. Collen, J. A. C. Godfrey CBE, J. S. Wharton, C. Holland.

Team Manager: Brian Laws.

Chief Executive/Secretary: A. D. Rowing.

Commercial Manager: A. D. Rowing.

Colours: White shirt with claret and blue trim, white shorts with claret and blue trim, white stockings with claret and blue top.

Change Colours: Lime green shirt with navy trim, navy shorts with lime trim, navy stockings with lime top.

Year Formed: 1899. *Turned Professional:* 1912.

Ltd Co.: 1912.

Club Nickname: 'The Iron'.

Previous Names: Amalgamated first with Brumby Hall then North Lindsey United to become Scunthorpe & Lindsey United, 1910; dropped '& Lindsey' in 1958.

Previous Ground: 1899, Old Showground; 1988, Glanford Park.

First Football League Game: 19 August 1950, Division 3 (N), v Shrewsbury T (h) D 0–0 – Thompson; Barker, Brownsword; Allen, Taylor, McCormick; Mosby, Payne, Gorin, Rees, Boyes.

IT'S A FACT !

In 1935–36, Scunthorpe United met Coventry City in the FA Cup, earned a replay in a 1-1 draw and though two goals down at one stage, won this match 4-2 against the Division Three (South) champions that season.

Record League Victory: 8–1 v Luton T, Division 3,
24 April 1965 – Sidebottom; Horstead, Hemstead; Smith,
Neale, Lindsey; Bramley (1), Scott, Thomas (5), Mahy (1),
Wilson (1). 8–1 v Torquay U (a), Division 3, 28 October
1995 – Samways; Housham, Wilson, Ford (1), Knill (1),
Hope (Nicholson), Thornber, Bullimore (Walsh),
McFarlane (4) (Young), Eyre (2), Paterson.

Record Cup Victory: 9–0 v Boston U, FA Cup 1st rd,
21 November 1953 – Malan; Hubbard, Brownsword;
Sharpe, White, Bushby; Mosby (1), Haigh (3), Whitfield (2),
Gregory (1), Mervyn Jones (2).

Record Defeat: 0–8 v Carlisle U, Division 3 (N),
25 December 1952.

Most League Points (2 for a win): 66, Division 3 (N),
1956–57, 1957–58.

Most League Points (3 for a win): 83, Division 4, 1982–83.

Most League Goals: 88, Division 3 (N), 1957–58.

Highest League Scorer in Season: Barrie Thomas, 31,
Division 2, 1961–62.

Most League Goals in Total Aggregate: Steve Cammack,
110, 1979–81, 1981–86.

Most League Goals in One Match: 5, Barrie Thomas v
Luton T, Division 3, 24 April 1965.

Most Capped Player: None.

Most League Appearances: Jack Brownsword, 595, 1950–65.

Youngest League Player: Mike Farrell, 16 years 240 days v
Workington, 8 November 1975.

Record Transfer Fee Received: £350,000 from Aston Villa for Neil Cox, February 1991.

Record Transfer Fee Paid: £200,000 to Bristol C for Steve Torpey, February 2000.

Football League Record: 1950 Elected to Division 3 (N); 1958–64 Division 2; 1964–68 Division 3;
1968–72 Division 4; 1972–73 Division 3; 1973–83 Division 4; 1983–84 Division 3; 1984–92 Division 4;
1992–99 Division 3; 1999–2000 Division 2; 2000– Division 3.

MANAGERS

Harry Allcock 1915–53
(Secretary-Manager)
Tom Crilly 1936–37
Bernard Harper 1946–48
Leslie Jones 1950–51
Bill Corkhill 1952–56
Ron Suart 1956–58
Tony McShane 1959
Bill Lambton 1959
Frank Soo 1959–60
Dick Duckworth 1960–64
Fred Goodwin 1964–66
Ron Ashman 1967–73
Ron Bradley 1973–74
Dick Rooks 1974–76
Ron Ashman 1976–81
John Duncan 1981–83
Allan Clarke 1983–84
Frank Barlow 1984–87
Mick Buxton 1987–91
Bill Green 1991–93
Richard Money 1993–94
David Moore 1994–96
Mick Buxton 1996–97
Brian Laws February 1997–

LATEST SEQUENCES

Longest Sequence of League Wins: 6, 18.10.69 – 25.11.69.

Longest Sequence of League Defeats: 8, 29.11.97 – 20.1.98.

Longest Sequence of League Draws: 6, 2.1.84 – 25.2.84.

Longest Sequence of Unbeaten League Matches: 15, 13.11.71 – 26.2.72.

Longest Sequence Without a League Win: 14, 22.3.75 – 6.9.75.

TEN YEAR LEAGUE RECORD

			P	W	D	L	F	A	Pts	Pos
1991-92	Div 4		42	21	9	12	64	59	72	5
1992-93	Div 3		42	14	12	16	57	54	54	14
1993-94	Div 3		42	15	14	13	64	56	59	11
1994-95	Div 3		42	18	8	16	68	63	62	7
1995-96	Div 3		46	15	15	16	67	61	60	12
1996-97	Div 3		46	18	9	19	59	62	63	13
1997-98	Div 3		46	19	12	15	56	52	69	8
1998-99	Div 3		46	22	8	16	69	58	74	4
1999-2000	Div 2		46	9	12	25	40	74	39	23
2000-01	Div 3		46	18	11	17	62	52	65	10

DID YOU KNOW ?

On 24 November 2001,
Scunthorpe United's 7-1 win
over Darlington was the
highest score achieved by the
club at Glanford Park and a
goal short of equalling their
record League victory.

SCUNTHORPE UNITED 2001–02 LEAGUE RECORD

Match No.	Date	Venue	Opponents	Result	H/T Score	Lg. Pos.	Goalscorers	Attendance
1	Aug 11	A	Kidderminster H	L	0-1	0-0	—	3173
2	18	H	Bristol R	L	1-2	1-2	23	Quailey [45]	3593
3	25	A	Exeter C	W	4-0	2-0	16	Carruthers 2 [14, 67], Grant [45], Bradshaw [61]	2798
4	27	A	Lincoln C	D	1-1	1-1	15	Beagrie [1]	4349
5	Sept 1	A	Macclesfield T	L	3-4	2-2	17	Jackson [6], Carruthers [32], Sheldon [51]	1740
6	8	H	Hartlepool U	W	1-0	1-0	13	Torpey [29]	3206
7	15	A	Rochdale	D	2-2	1-0	12	Brough [13], Beagrie (pen) [83]	3468
8	18	H	Swansea C	D	2-2	2-2	—	Carruthers [31], Torpey [39]	2574
9	22	H	Mansfield T	D	0-0	0-0	13		3857
10	25	A	Torquay U	D	0-0	0-0		—	1982
11	29	H	Shrewsbury T	W	3-1	2-0	10	Thom [22], Carruthers [28], Quailey [66]	3047
12	Oct 5	A	Halifax T	D	0-0	0-0		—	2603
13	13	H	Luton T	L	0-2	0-0	11		3939
14	20	A	Oxford U	W	1-0	0-0	10	Torpey [72]	5006
15	23	H	Southend U	W	2-0	0-0	—	Carruthers [61], Beagrie [88]	2956
16	27	A	Cheltenham T	D	3-3	2-2	7	Carruthers [14], Beagrie [33], Quailey [90]	3295
17	Nov 3	H	Leyton Orient	W	4-1	2-0	6	Torpey 2 [11, 20], Hodges [47], Beagrie [90]	3356
18	9	A	York C	W	2-0	0-0		Carruthers [50], Calvo-Garcia [83]	3192
19	20	A	Rushden & D	D	0-0	0-0		—	3533
20	24	H	Darlington	W	7-1	4-0	7	Carruthers 2 [7, 45], Torpey 2 [21, 69], Beagrie (pen) [32], Sheldon [66], Kell [78]	3662
21	Dec 1	A	Carlisle U	L	0-3	0-2	7		2702
22	15	H	Hull C	W	2-1	1-0	7	Hodges [2], Torpey [53]	6479
23	22	H	Plymouth Arg	W	2-1	2-0	6	Hodges 2 [6, 25]	3602
24	29	A	Lincoln C	L	2-3	1-2	7	Calvo-Garcia [32], Beagrie (pen) [58]	5235
25	Jan 12	A	Bristol R	D	1-1	0-1	9	Calvo-Garcia [49]	6691
26	15	H	Exeter C	L	3-4	1-1	—	Torpey [22], Beagrie (pen) [79], Quailey [89]	2877
27	19	H	Kidderminster H	W	1-0	1-0	8	Torpey [44]	3360
28	22	H	Plymouth Arg	L	1-2	1-1	—	Carruthers [13]	5804
29	26	H	Halifax T	W	4-0	2-0	7	Thom [19], Torpey 2 [23, 90], Calvo-Garcia [84]	3465
30	29	A	Hartlepool U	L	2-3	1-1		Beagrie 2 (1 pen) [28, 66 (p)]	3294
31	Feb 2	A	Shrewsbury T	D	2-2	2-2	7	Jackson [20], Quailey [43]	3345
32	9	H	Oxford U	W	1-0	0-0	6	Hodges [90]	3504
33	12	H	Macclesfield T	D	1-1	0-1	—	Torpey [55]	2870
34	16	A	Luton T	W	3-2	2-1	6	Beagrie [9], Graves [45], Sparrow [90]	6371
35	23	A	Rochdale	W	2-1	2-1	4	Graves 2 [27, 38]	4521
36	26	A	Swansea C	D	2-2	1-1	—	Calvo-Garcia [30], Quailey [89]	3085
37	Mar 2	A	Mansfield T	L	1-2	1-0	5	Quailey [27]	6292
38	5	H	Torquay U	W	1-0	0-0	—	Quailey [53]	2838
39	9	A	Hull C	W	1-0	0-0	4	Jackson [90]	12,529
40	16	H	Carlisle U	W	2-1	2-0	4	Jeffrey [18], Hodges [37]	4109
41	23	A	Southend U	L	0-2	0-2	4		3818
42	30	H	Cheltenham T	L	1-2	0-1	6	Calvo-Garcia [90]	5086
43	Apr 1	A	Leyton Orient	D	0-0	0-0	7		4221
44	6	H	Rushden & D	D	1-1	1-0	7	Underwood (og) [44]	4794
45	13	A	Darlington	L	1-2	0-1	9	Carruthers [89]	4218
46	20	H	York C	W	1-0	0-0	8	Carruthers [90]	5159

Final League Position: 8

GOALSCORERS

League (74): Carruthers 13, Torpey 13, Beagrie 11 (5 pens), Quailey 8, Calvo-Garcia 6, Hodges 6, Graves 3, Jackson 3, Sheldon 2, Thom 2, Bradshaw 1, Brough 1, Grant 1, Jeffrey 1, Kell 1, Sparrow 1, own goal 1.
Worthington Cup (0).
FA Cup (7): Carruthers 3, Calvo-Garcia 2, Hodges 1, McCombe 1.

Evans T 42	Stanton N 39+3	Dawson A 44	Bradshaw C 18+3	Jackson M 45	Thom S 17+3	Sheldon G 6+8	Graves W 16+1	Carruthers M 30+3	Grant K 3+1	Beagrie P 39+1	Quailey B 15+15	Croudson S 4	Wilcox R 6+3	Brough S 5+14	Barwick T 7+3	Ridley L 2+2	Torpey S 37+2	Hodges L 26+9	Kell R 16	Cotterill J 8+2	Calvo-Garcia A 33+1	McCombe J 11+6	Sparrow M 20+4	Dudley C 1+3	Anderson M —+1	McGibbon P 6	Parton A 1	Pepper N —+1	Jeffrey M 4+2	Vaughan T 5	Match No.
1	2	3	4	5	6	7	8	9	10^1	11	12																				1
		3	4	5	6	7	8	9		11	10^1	1	2	12																	2
2	3^4	4	5	6	12		8	9	10^3	11^1		1	13		7	14															3
2	3	4	5	6	12		8	9	10^2	11		1			7^1	13															4
2	3	4	5	6	7^1		8	9		11		1		12			10														5
1		3	4	5	6		8^1	9		11			2	12	7		10														6
1	2	3	4	5	6^1					11	12			8	7^2		9	13	10												7
1	2	3	4	5				9^1		11	12		6		7^2	14	10	13	8^3												8
1	2	3	4	5	6			9^1		11	12				7^2		10	13	8												9
1	2	3	4	5	6			9		11	12			13			10^2	7^1	8												10
1	2^3	3	4^2	5	6			9		11	10			12	13			7^1	8	14											11
1	12	3	4	5	6			9^2		11	10			14			13	7	8^3	2^1											12
1	2	3	4	5	12			9		11	10^2			13			7^1	8^3	6	14											13
1	12	3		5	6	13		14		11					7^3	4^2		8	2^1	9											14
1	12	3	2^1	5	6			9^2		11	13			14			10	4^3	8	7											15
1	2	3		5	6^2			9^1		11	12		13	14			10	4^3	8	7											16
1	2	3		5				9^1		11^2	12			13			10	6	8^3		7	4	14								17
1	2	3		5				9^1		11^2	12			13			10	6^2	8		7	4	14								18
1	2	3		5				9^1		11	12						10	6	8		7	4									19
1	2^1	3	12	5		13		9^2		11							10	6^3	8		7	4									20
1	2^1	3	12	5				9		11	13						10	6^2	8		7	4									21
1	2	3	12	5				9^1		11				13	14		10	6^2	8^3		7	4									22
1	2	3	4^1	5				9		11							10	8			7	6	12								23
1	2	3	4	5				11		9							10	8			7	6									24
1	2	3	5^1	12			8	9		11							10				7	4	6								25
1	2	3	5	12			8^3	9^2		11	13						10	6^1			7	4	14								26
1	2	3	5	6				11		9					4		10	8			7										27
1	2	3	5	6			8^3	9^2		11	13						10	12			7^1	14	4								28
1	2	3	5	6^3				9^1		11^2	12			13			10	8			7	14	4								29
1	2	3	5	12			8^2	9^1		11	13						10				7	6	4								30
1	2	3	5^1				8			11	9^2						10			6	7	12	4	13							31
1		3	5							11	9	6						8		2	7		4	10^1	12						32
1	6	3	5							11	9^1						10	8		2	7		4	12							33
1	2	3	5				8^1			11	9						10	12			7		4			6					34
1	2	3	5				8^1			11^2	9						10	12			7		4	13		6					35
1		3	4	5				9		11^1		2					10	12		13	7		8	6^2		6^3					36
1	2	3	5				12			9							10	8		6	7		11		4^1						37
1	2	3	5				11			9							10	8^1			7		4		6			12			38
1	2	3	5				11			9^1							10	8			7		4		6						39
1	2	3					11^1			10							8		5	7	12		4		6			9			40
1	3		4	5			12			13			6^2				2^3	10	8	7	14	11						9^1			41
1	2		5				12	13		11		3					10	8^1		7	4							9^2	6		42
1	2	3	5				8^2	9^1		11	12						10	13			7	4							6		43
1	2	3	5				12	8^1	9^2	11							10				7	4						13	6		44
1	2	3	5				12^3	8^1	9	11							10	14			7^2	4						13	6		45
1	2	3	5							9				11	12		8^2				7	13	4						10^1	6	46

Worthington Cup

First Round	Rotherham U	(h)	0-2

FA Cup

First Round	Doncaster R	(a)	3-2
Second Round	Brentford	(h)	3-2
Third Round	Millwall	(a)	1-2

SHEFFIELD UNITED — Division 1

FOUNDATION

In March 1889, Yorkshire County Cricket Club formed Sheffield United six days after an FA Cup semi-final between Preston North End and West Bromwich Albion had finally convinced Charles Stokes, a member of the cricket club, that the formation of a professional football club would prove successful at Bramall Lane. The United's first secretary, Mr J. B. Wostinholm was also secretary of the cricket club.

Bramall Lane Ground, Sheffield S2 4SU.

Telephone: (0114) 221 5757. *Fax:* (0114) 272 3030.
ISDN: (0114) 221 3148. *Website:* http://www.sufc.co.uk
Email: info@sufc.co.uk *Box Office:* (0114) 221 1889.
Box Office Promotions: (0114) 221 3131.
ClubCall: 09068 888 650. *Club Shop:* (0114) 221 3132.
Executive Suite: (0114) 221 3195.
Football in the Community: (0114) 276 9314.

Ground Capacity: 30,945.

Record Attendance: 68,287 v Leeds U, FA Cup 5th rd, 15 February 1936.

Record Receipts: £298,364 v Coventry C, FA Cup 6th rd replay, 17 March 1998.

Pitch Measurements: 112yd × 72yd.

Chairman: D. Dooley (football club), K. McCabe (plc).

Directors: K. McCabe, A. Laver, M. Dudley, A. Bamford, S. Slinn, C. Steer, S. Bean.

Football Executive: Terry Robinson.

Manager: Neil Warnock. *Assistant Manager:* Kevin Blackwell. *Player-Coach:* Keith Curle.

Physios: Dennis Pettitt, Nigel Cox.

Estates Manager: Steve Hicks.

General Manager, Commercial: Andy Daykin.

Secretary: J. Howarth.

Community Programme Organiser: Tony Currie, Tel: (0114) 2769314.

Colours: Red and white striped shirts with white trim, white shorts, white stockings.

Change Colours: All navy with red trim.

Year Formed: 1889.

Turned Professional: 1889.

Ltd Co.: 1899.

Club Nickname: 'The Blades'.

First Football League Game: 3 September 1892, Division 2, v Lincoln C (h) W 4–2 – Lilley; Witham, Cain; Howell, Hendry, Needham (1); Wallace, Dobson, Hammond (3), Davies, Drummond.

HONOURS

Football League: Division 1 – Champions 1897–98; Runners-up 1896–97, 1899–1900; Division 2 – Champions 1952–53; Runners-up 1892–93, 1938–39, 1960–61, 1970–71, 1989–90; Division 4 – Champions 1981–82.

FA Cup: Winners 1899, 1902, 1915, 1925; Runners-up 1901, 1936.

Football League Cup: best season: 5th rd, 1962, 1967, 1972.

IT'S A FACT !

Sheffield United left-winger Bob Evans had played ten times for Wales before it was discovered in 1910 that he had been born just inside the English border. England subsequently capped him four times.

Record League Victory: 10–0 v Burslem Port Vale (a), Division 2, 10 December 1892 – Howlett; Witham, Lilley; Howell, Hendry, Needham; Drummond (1), Wallace (1), Hammond (4), Davies (2), Watson (2).

Record Cup Victory: 6–1 v Lincoln C, League Cup, 22 August 2000 – Tracey; Uhlenbeek, Weber, Woodhouse (Ford), Murphy, Sandford, Devlin (pen), Ribeiro (Santos), Bent (3), Kelly (1) (Thompson), Jagielka, og (1). 6–1 v Loughborough, FA Cup 4th qualifying rd, 6 December 1890; 6–1 v Scarborough (a), FA Cup 1st qualifying rd, 5 October 1889.

Record Defeat: 0–13 v Bolton W, FA Cup 2nd rd, 1 February 1890.

Most League Points (2 for a win): 60, Division 2, 1952–53.

Most League Points (3 for a win): 96, Division 4, 1981–82.

Most League Goals: 102, Division 1, 1925–26.

Highest League Scorer in Season: Jimmy Dunne, 41, Division 1, 1930–31.

Most League Goals in Total Aggregate: Harry Johnson, 205, 1919–30.

Most League Goals in One Match: 5, Harry Hammond v Bootle, Division 2, 26 November 1892; 5, Harry Johnson v West Ham U, Division 1, 26 December 1927.

Most Capped Player: Billy Gillespie, 25, Northern Ireland.

Most League Appearances: Joe Shaw, 629, 1948–66.

Youngest League Player: Graham French, 16 years 177 days v Reading, 30 September 1961.

Record Transfer Fee Received: £2,700,000 from Leeds U for Brian Deane, July 1993.

Record Transfer Fee Paid: £1,200,000 to West Ham U for Don Hutchison, January 1996.

Football League Record: 1892 Elected to Division 2; 1893–1934 Division 1; 1934–39 Division 2; 1946–49 Division 1; 1949–53 Division 2; 1953–56 Division 1; 1956–61 Division 2; 1961–68 Division 1; 1968–71 Division 2; 1971–76 Division 1; 1976–79 Division 2; 1979–81 Division 3; 1981–82 Division 4; 1982–84 Division 3; 1984–88 Division 2; 1988–89 Division 3; 1989–90 Division 2; 1990–92 Division 1; 1992–94 FA Premier League; 1994– Division 1.

MANAGERS

J. B. Wostinholm 1889–99
    (Secretary-Manager)
John Nicholson 1899–1932
Ted Davison 1932–52
Reg Freeman 1952–55
Joe Mercer 1955–58
Johnny Harris 1959–68
    (continued as General Manager to 1970)
Arthur Rowley 1968–69
Johnny Harris *(General Manager resumed Team Manager duties)* 1969–73
Ken Furphy 1973–75
Jimmy Sirrel 1975–77
Harry Haslam 1978–81
Martin Peters 1981
Ian Porterfield 1981–86
Billy McEwan 1986–88
Dave Bassett 1988–95
Howard Kendall 1995–97
Nigel Spackman 1997–98
Steve Bruce 1998–99
Adrian Heath 1999
Neil Warnock December 1999–

LATEST SEQUENCES

Longest Sequence of League Wins: 8, 14.9.60 – 22.10.60.

Longest Sequence of League Defeats: 7, 19.8.75 – 20.9.75.

Longest Sequence of League Draws: 6, 6.5.01 – 8.9.01.

Longest Sequence of Unbeaten League Matches: 22, 2.9.1899 – 13.1.1900.

Longest Sequence Without a League Win: 19, 27.9.75 – 7.2.76.

TEN YEAR LEAGUE RECORD

		P	W	D	L	F	A	Pts	Pos
1991-92	Div 1	42	16	9	17	65	63	57	9
1992-93	PR Lge	42	14	10	18	54	53	52	14
1993-94	PR Lge	42	8	18	16	42	60	42	20
1994-95	Div 1	46	17	17	12	74	55	68	8
1995-96	Div 1	46	16	14	16	57	54	62	9
1996-97	Div 1	46	20	13	13	75	52	73	5
1997-98	Div 1	46	19	17	10	69	54	74	6
1998-99	Div 1	46	18	13	15	71	66	67	8
1999-2000	Div 1	46	13	15	18	59	71	54	16
2000-01	Div 1	46	19	11	16	52	49	68	10

DID YOU KNOW ?

On 11 September 1897, Sheffield United found themselves two goals down in five minutes to visiting Stoke at Bramall Lane, but recovered to win 4-3.

SHEFFIELD UNITED 2001–02 LEAGUE RECORD

Match No.	Date	Venue	Opponents	Result	H/T Score	Lg. Pos.	Goalscorers	Attendance
1	Aug 11	A	Nottingham F	D	1-1	0-1	—	Devlin [88]	25,513
2	18	H	Gillingham	D	0-0	0-0	17		16,998
3	23	A	Rotherham U	D	1-1	0-1	—	D'Jaffo (pen) [67]	7515
4	27	H	Wolverhampton W	D	2-2	0-1	14	D'Jaffo (pen) [49], Asaba [83]	16,497
5	Sept 8	H	Bradford C	D	2-2	2-2	16	Curle [16], Asaba [36]	17,394
6	15	H	Coventry C	L	0-1	0-0	20		16,168
7	18	A	Stockport Co	W	2-1	2-0	—	Nicholson (pen) [30], Ndlovu [33]	5137
8	22	A	Millwall	L	0-2	0-1	19		12,276
9	25	H	Crystal Palace	L	1-3	0-1	—	Nicholson [74]	14,180
10	29	H	Norwich C	W	2-1	2-0	18	Asaba [40], Suffo [45]	15,523
11	Oct 7	A	Sheffield W	D	0-0	0-0	17		29,281
12	13	H	Grimsby T	W	3-1	2-0	14	Suffo 2 [14, 27], Brown [62]	15,442
13	16	A	Manchester C	D	0-0	0-0	—		32,454
14	20	A	Portsmouth	L	0-1	0-1	17		15,538
15	23	A	Preston NE	L	0-3	0-2	—		14,027
16	27	H	Crewe Alex	W	1-0	1-0	15	Tonge [28]	15,185
17	30	H	Watford	L	0-2	0-0	—		14,338
18	Nov 4	A	Burnley	L	0-2	0-2	18		13,166
19	9	A	Wimbledon	D	1-1	0-0	—	Santos [57]	4937
20	17	H	Birmingham C	W	4-0	1-0	16	Montgomery [16], Brown [65], Peschisolido 2 [79, 82]	15,686
21	24	A	Walsall	W	2-1	2-1	16	Peschisolido [43], Nicholson (pen) [45]	6415
22	Dec 1	H	Preston NE	D	2-2	0-2	16	Peschisolido [47], Santos [80]	16,270
23	8	A	WBA	W	1-0	0-0	16	Asaba [90]	19,462
24	14	A	Barnsley	D	1-1	0-0	—	Peschisolido [81]	17,858
25	22	H	Rotherham U	D	2-2	0-0	15	Suffo [48], Devlin [61]	22,749
26	26	A	Bradford C	W	2-1	1-0	14	Asaba 2 [12, 54]	18,869
27	29	A	Wolverhampton W	L	0-1	0-1	16		24,138
28	Jan 1	H	Manchester C	L	1-3	0-0	16	Brown [89]	26,291
29	12	A	Gillingham	W	1-0	0-0	14	Tonge [63]	8814
30	19	H	Nottingham F	D	0-0	0-0	15		18,352
31	29	H	Sheffield W	D	0-0	0-0	—		29,364
32	Feb 3	A	Norwich C	L	1-2	0-0	15	Brown [77]	17,348
33	9	H	Portsmouth	W	4-3	3-2	15	Montgomery [18], Furlong 2 (1 pen) [25, 90 (p)], Asaba [40]	17,553
34	16	A	Grimsby T	L	0-1	0-0	15		7141
35	23	A	Crystal Palace	W	1-0	0-0	13	Brown [60]	18,009
36	Mar 2	H	Stockport Co	W	3-0	0-0	11	Woodthorpe (og) [51], Peschisolido [55], Ndlovu [61]	15,642
37	6	A	Coventry C	L	0-1	0-1	—		12,963
38	9	A	Barnsley	D	1-1	1-1	15	D'Jaffo [29]	15,430
39	16	H	WBA	L	0-3	0-1	15		17,692
40	19	H	Millwall	W	3-2	0-1	—	Tonge [68], Ndlovu 2 [88, 90]	16,037
41	23	H	Burnley	W	3-0	1-0	13	Jagielka 2 [19, 88], D'Jaffo [47]	19,003
42	30	A	Crewe Alex	D	2-2	1-2	13	D'Jaffo [40], Doane [72]	7855
43	Apr 1	H	Wimbledon	L	0-1	0-1	13		19,712
44	6	A	Watford	W	3-0	2-0	13	Javary [13], Jagielka [41], Lovell [63]	13,377
45	13	H	Walsall	L	0-1	0-1	13		20,520
46	21	A	Birmingham C	L	0-2	0-0	13		29,178

Final League Position: 13

GOALSCORERS

League (53): Asaba 7, Peschisolido 6, Brown 5, D'Jaffo 5 (2 pens), Ndlovu 4, Suffo 4, Jagielka 3, Nicholson 3 (2 pens), Tonge 3, Devlin 2, Furlong 2 (1 pen), Montgomery 2, Santos 2, Curle 1, Doane 1, Javary 1, Lovell 1, own goal 1.
Worthington Cup (4): Devlin 1, D'Jaffo 1, Ndlovu 1, Suffo 1.
FA Cup (1): Brown 1.

Tracey S 41	Kozluk R 6+2	Phelan T 8	Ford B 20+6	Murphy S 27	Page R 43	Devlin P 14+5	Jagielka P 14+9	Asaba C 26+3	Peschisolido P 19+10	Ndlovu P 41+4	Montgomery N 14+17	Curle K 30+2	Santos G 14+16	D'Jaffo L 23+9	Brown M 36	Uhlenbeek G 19+1	Nicholson S 21+4	Suffo P 10+10	Sandford L 5+1	De Vogt W 5+1	Tonge M 27+3	Mallon R —+1	Doane B 14	Ward M —+1	Littlejohn A 1+2	Ullathorne R 14	Furlong P 4	Smith G 1+6	Javary J 6+1	Lovell S 3+2	Killeen L —+1	Cryan C —+1	Match No.
1	2¹	3	4	5	6	7	8²	9	10	11	12	13																					1
1		3	8	5	2	7	12	9	10³	11³	13	6	4²	14																			2
1	12	3¹	11	5	2	7		9²	13	14		6	4³	10	8																		3
1	2	3	4¹	5		7		13	10²	11		6	12	9	8																		4
1		3	4	5		7		9	12	11¹		6	13	10²	8	2																	5
1			4	5	2	7		9	12	11²		6	13	10¹	8³		3	14															6
1		7	5	2				9³		11¹	13	12	4	10	8²		3	14	6														7
1		7²	5	2				9	12	11¹	13		4	10³	8		3	14	6														8
1	12		4	5	2¹	7	11	9²	13	14					8		3	10³	6														9
1	2		12	5	4			9	13	11		6	14		8		3¹	10²		1	7³												10
1	2			5	4	12		9	13	11¹		6	14		8		3³	10²			7												11
1	2			5	4	12				11³		6	13	9	8		3²	10¹			7	14											12
1	2²			5	3	12		9³		11	4	6	13	14	8			10¹			7												13
1				5	3	12				11	4²	6³	13	9	8	2	14	10¹			7												14
1		3		5	6	7				11	12		13	9²	8	10¹					4		2										15
1		3		5	6	7	12			10³	11				8	13					4¹		2	14	9²								16
1		3		5	6	7²	12			10¹	11	13			9³	8					4		2		14								17
1		4¹	5	3						11	12	6		9²	8			10			7		2	13									18
1				5		12	9			11	4	6		10	8		3				7¹		2										19
1				5		12	9	10²		11	4	6	7¹		8		3	13					2										20
1				5		12	9¹	10²		11	4		7		8	3	13	6					2										21
1				5		12	9	10¹		11²	4	6	7		8	3	13						2										22
1	12			5				13	9	10³	11¹	4		7	8	14	3		6		2³												23
1	12			5	6			9	10³	11²	4¹			7	8	2	3	13			14												24
1			5	3	12			10		11	4¹	6	7	13	8	2		9²															25
1			5	6	7		9			12		11		8	2	3	10¹				4												26
1		11	5	6	7		9²			12	14		8	13		2	3	10¹			4³												27
1			5	6	7		9			12	4		10²			2	3¹	13			11												28
1		7	5			9			11	6	12	10¹	8	2							4					3							29
1		4	5			9			11	12	6	13	10¹	8	2					1	7²					3							30
1		4	5			9			11	6		10	8	2				7								3							31
1		4	5	10		9²	12	11¹	13	6		14	8	2				7²								3							32
1			4	5			12	9¹	13	11	7²	6			8			14			2					3		9³	10				33
1		7		5			12	9¹	13	11	4³	6			14	8	2									3			10				34
1		4		5		7			10³	11¹	6	12	13	8	2		14									3		9²					35
1		4³		5		7			10¹	11	6	12	13	8	2						14					3		9²					36
1			5			7²	12	10	11	14	6	13	9	8	2						4³					3							37
1			5			7	12	10	11³		6	13	9¹	8	2	14					4²					3							38
1			5			7		10	11⁵		6	12	9	8²	2	13		15			4¹					3							39
1			5	7		10¹	11	13		6	12			2	3			4³											14	8	9²		40
1	12		5	7		10¹	11	13		6				9	2	3			4²										14	8³			41
1	12		5	7		10¹	11	4²	6					9¹	3						1	8³	2						14	8			42
1	10		5	7		11	4¹	6					9²	3						1	8³	2						13	14	12		43
1		6	5	7		11	13					9³	12							1	4²	2			3		14	8	10¹			44
1		6	5	7		11¹	12					9									4	2			3		13	8¹	10³	14		45
1		5	6³	7		11	12					9									4	2			3		10¹	8²	13		14	46

Worthington Cup
First Round — Darlington — (a) — 1-0
Second Round — Grimsby T — (a) — 3-3

FA Cup
Third Round — Nottingham F — (h) — 1-0

SHEFFIELD WEDNESDAY   Division 1

FOUNDATION

Sheffield being one of the principal centres of early Association Football, this club was formed as long ago as 1867 by the Sheffield Wednesday Cricket Club (formed 1825) and their colours from the start were blue and white. The inaugural meeting was held at the Adelphi Hotel and the original committee included Charles Stokes who was subsequently a founder member of Sheffield United.

Hillsborough, Sheffield S6 1SW.

Telephone: (0114) 221 2121. *Fax:* (0114) 221 2122.
ClubCall: 09068 121 186. *Website:* www.swfc.co.uk
Email: enquiries@swfc.co.uk
Ticket Office: (0114) 221 2400.

Ground Capacity: 39,859.

Record Attendance: 72,841 v Manchester C, FA Cup 5th rd, 17 February 1934.

Record Receipts: £533,918 Sunderland v Norwich C, FA Cup semi-final, 5 April 1992.

Pitch Measurements: 115yd × 74yd.

President: K. T. Addy.

Chairman: G. K. Hulley. *Vice-chairman:* K. T. Addy.

Directors: G. K. Hulley, R. M. Grierson FCA, K. T. Addy, G. A. Thorpe, D. E. D. Allen, M. G. Wright.

Manager: Terry Yorath.

First Team Coach: Willie Donachie. *Physio:* John Dickens.

Chief Executive: Alan D. Sykes.

Commercial Director: Kaven Walker.

Stadium Manager: Trevor Grayson.

Colours: Blue and white striped shirts, black shorts, blue stockings.

Change Colours: All navy with white trim.

Year Formed: 1867 (fifth oldest League club).

Turned Professional: 1887.

Ltd Co.: 1899.

Former Names: The Wednesday until 1929.

Club Nickname: 'The Owls'.

Previous Grounds: 1867, Highfield; 1869, Myrtle Road; 1877, Sheaf House; 1887, Olive Grove; 1899, Owlerton (since 1912 known as Hillsborough). Some games were played at Endcliffe in the 1880s. Until 1895 Bramall Lane was used for some games.

First Football League Game: 3 September 1892, Division 1, v Notts Co (a) W 1–0 – Allan; Tom Brandon (1), Mumford; Hall, Betts, Harry Brandon; Spiksley, Brady, Davis, R. N. Brown, Dunlop.

HONOURS

Football League: Division 1 – Champions 1902–03, 1903–04, 1928–29, 1929–30; Runners-up 1960–61; Division 2 – Champions 1899–1900, 1925–26, 1951–52, 1955–56, 1958–59; Runners-up 1949–50, 1983–84.

FA Cup: Winners 1896, 1907, 1935; Runners-up 1890, 1966, 1993.

Football League Cup: Winners 1991; Runners-up 1993.

European Competitions: European Fairs Cup: 1961–62, 1963–64. UEFA Cup: 1992–93.

IT'S A FACT !

In 1876–77, the Sheffield Association instituted a Challenge Cup. Sheffield Wednesday met Heeley in the final but found themselves 3-0 down at half-time. They levelled by the end of full-time and won 4-3 during the extra period.

Record League Victory: 9–1 v Birmingham, Division 1, 13 December 1930 – Brown; Walker, Blenkinsop; Strange, Leach, Wilson; Hooper (3), Seed (2), Ball (2), Burgess (1), Rimmer (1).

Record Cup Victory: 12–0 v Halliwell, FA Cup 1st rd, 17 January 1891 – Smith; Thompson, Brayshaw; Harry Brandon (1), Betts, Cawley (2); Winterbottom, Mumford (2), Bob Brandon (1), Woolhouse (5), Ingram (1).

Record Defeat: 0–10 v Aston Villa, Division 1, 5 October 1912.

Most League Points (2 for a win): 62, Division 2, 1958–59.

Most League Points (3 for a win): 88, Division 2, 1983–84.

Most League Goals: 106, Division 2, 1958–59.

Highest League Scorer in Season: Derek Dooley, 46, Division 2, 1951–52.

Most League Goals in Total Aggregate: Andy Wilson, 199, 1900–20.

Most League Goals in One Match: 6, Doug Hunt v Norwich C, Division 2, 19 November 1938.

Most Capped Player: Nigel Worthington, 50 (66), Northern Ireland.

Most League Appearances: Andrew Wilson, 501, 1900–20.

Youngest League Player: Peter Fox, 15 years 269 days v Orient, 31 March 1973.

Record Transfer Fee Received: £2,750,000 from Blackburn R for Paul Warhurst, September 1993.

Record Transfer Fee Paid: £4,500,000 to Celtic for Paolo Di Canio, August 1997.

Football League Record: 1892 Elected to Division 1; 1899–1900 Division 2; 1900–20 Division 1; 1920–26 Division 2; 1926–37 Division 1; 1937–50 Division 2; 1950–51 Division 1; 1951–52 Division 2; 1952–55 Division 1; 1955–56 Division 2; 1956–58 Division 2; 1958–59 Division 2; 1959–70 Division 1; 1970–75 Division 2; 1975–80 Division 3; 1980–84 Division 2; 1984–90 Division 1; 1990–91 Division 2; 1991–92 Division 1; 1992–2000 FA Premier League; 2000– Division 1.

MANAGERS

Arthur Dickinson 1891–1920
  (Secretary-Manager)
Robert Brown 1920–33
Billy Walker 1933–37
Jimmy McMullan 1937–42
Eric Taylor 1942–58
  (continued as General Manager to 1974)
Harry Catterick 1958–61
Vic Buckingham 1961–64
Alan Brown 1964–68
Jack Marshall 1968–69
Danny Williams 1969–71
Derek Dooley 1971–73
Steve Burtenshaw 1974–75
Len Ashurst 1975–77
Jackie Charlton 1977–83
Howard Wilkinson 1983–88
Peter Eustace 1988–89
Ron Atkinson 1989–91
Trevor Francis 1991–95
David Pleat 1995–97
Ron Atkinson 1997–98
Danny Wilson 1998–2000
Peter Shreeves (Acting) 2000
Paul Jewell 2000–01
Peter Shreeves 2001
Terry Yorath November 2001–

LATEST SEQUENCES

Longest Sequence of League Wins: 9, 23.4.04 – 15.10.04.

Longest Sequence of League Defeats: 8, 9.9.2000 – 17.10.2000.

Longest Sequence of League Draws: 5, 24.10.92 – 28.11.92.

Longest Sequence of Unbeaten League Matches: 19, 10.12.60 – 8.4.61.

Longest Sequence Without a League Win: 20, 11.1.75 – 30.8.75.

TEN YEAR LEAGUE RECORD

		P	W	D	L	F	A	Pts	Pos
1991-92	Div 1	42	21	12	9	62	49	75	3
1992-93	PR Lge	42	15	14	13	55	51	59	7
1993-94	PR Lge	42	16	16	10	76	54	64	7
1994-95	PR Lge	42	13	12	17	49	57	51	13
1995-96	PR Lge	38	10	10	18	48	61	40	15
1996-97	PR Lge	38	14	15	9	50	51	57	7
1997-98	PR Lge	38	12	8	18	52	67	44	16
1998-99	PR Lge	38	13	7	18	41	42	46	12
1999-2000	PR Lge	38	8	7	23	38	70	31	19
2000-01	Div 1	46	15	8	23	52	71	53	17

DID YOU KNOW ?

On 22 May 1967, Sheffield Wednesday were involved in a unique transfer deal. Goalkeeper Ron Springett, aged 31, returned to his former club Queens Park Rangers, who signed him in exchange for brother Peter, aged 21.

SHEFFIELD WEDNESDAY 2001–02 LEAGUE RECORD

Match No.	Date	Venue	Opponents	Result		H/T Score	Lg. Pos.	Goalscorers	Attendance
1	Aug 12	H	Burnley	L	0-2	0-0	—		21,766
2	18	A	Crewe Alex	W	2-0	1-0	13	Sibon [4], McLaren [70]	7933
3	25	H	WBA	D	1-1	1-1	13	Sibon [5]	18,844
4	27	A	Norwich C	L	0-2	0-1	18		16,820
5	Sept 8	A	Birmingham C	L	0-2	0-1	21		19,421
6	15	A	Wimbledon	D	1-1	1-0	21	Johnson T [40]	7348
7	17	H	Bradford C	D	1-1	0-0	—	Di Piedi [60]	18,012
8	22	H	Manchester C	L	2-6	1-2	21	Bonvin [3], Bromby [47]	25,731
9	25	A	Rotherham U	D	1-1	0-0	—	Westwood [68]	8474
10	29	A	Crystal Palace	L	1-4	1-3	21	Johnson T [42]	17,066
11	Oct 7	H	Sheffield U	D	0-0	0-0	21		29,281
12	13	A	Watford	L	1-3	1-2	23	Johnson T [18]	14,456
13	16	H	Preston NE	L	1-2	1-0	—	Sibon [27]	15,592
14	20	H	Walsall	W	2-1	0-1	21	Sibon [71], Bonvin [90]	16,275
15	24	H	Barnsley	W	3-1	1-1	—	Sibon [24], Bonvin 2 [57, 81]	21,008
16	27	A	Coventry C	L	0-2	0-1	21		17,381
17	31	A	Nottingham F	W	1-0	0-0	—	Morrison [79]	20,206
18	Nov 3	H	Portsmouth	L	2-3	1-2	21	Donnelly [1], Sibon (pen) [67]	18,212
19	10	H	Grimsby T	D	0-0	0-0	22		17,507
20	18	A	Wolverhampton W	D	0-0	0-0	22		19,947
21	24	H	Stockport Co	W	5-0	1-0	19	Maddix [37], Sibon (pen) [70], Morrison [83], Soltvedt [85], Ekoku [86]	17,365
22	Dec 2	A	Barnsley	L	0-3	0-2	20		16,714
23	8	H	Millwall	D	1-1	0-0	20	Ekoku [49]	21,304
24	15	A	Gillingham	L	1-2	1-2	21	Sibon (pen) [23]	8586
25	22	A	WBA	D	1-1	0-0	21	Ekoku [55]	20,340
26	26	H	Birmingham C	L	0-1	0-0	22		24,335
27	29	H	Norwich C	L	0-5	0-4	23		19,205
28	Jan 12	A	Crewe Alex	W	1-0	1-0	22	Sibon [44]	16,737
29	19	A	Burnley	W	2-1	1-0	21	McLaren [33], Kuqi [90]	16,081
30	29	A	Sheffield U	D	0-0	0-0	—		29,364
31	Feb 2	H	Crystal Palace	L	1-3	1-3	22	Ekoku [43]	20,099
32	5	A	Preston NE	L	2-4	1-2	—	Quinn [37], Ekoku (pen) [86]	14,038
33	9	A	Walsall	W	3-0	1-0	21	Ekoku [32], Kuqi [79], Sibon [90]	8290
34	16	H	Watford	W	2-1	0-1	20	Ekoku (pen) [58], Kuqi [78]	18,244
35	23	H	Rotherham U	L	1-2	0-0	20	Kuqi [70]	28,179
36	27	A	Manchester C	L	0-4	0-2	—		33,682
37	Mar 2	A	Bradford C	W	2-0	1-0	19	Johnson D [27], Kuqi [57]	16,904
38	6	H	Wimbledon	L	1-2	1-1	—	Johnson D [12]	18,930
39	9	H	Gillingham	D	0-0	0-0	20		20,361
40	16	H	Millwall	W	2-1	0-0	19	Donnelly 2 [74, 75]	13,074
41	23	A	Portsmouth	D	0-0	0-0	20		14,819
42	29	H	Coventry C	W	2-1	1-1	—	Sibon 2 [40, 58]	21,470
43	Apr 1	A	Grimsby T	D	0-0	0-0	18		9236
44	6	H	Nottingham F	L	0-2	0-1	18		21,782
45	13	A	Stockport Co	L	1-3	1-1	21	Quinn [9]	8706
46	21	H	Wolverhampton W	D	2-2	1-1	20	Donnelly [43], Kuqi [53]	29,772

Final League Position: 20

GOALSCORERS
League (49): Sibon 12 (3 pens), Ekoku 7 (2 pens), Kuqi 6, Bonvin 4, Donnelly 4, Johnson T 3, Johnson D 2, McLaren 2, Morrison 2, Quinn 2, Bromby 1, Di Piedi 1, Maddix 1, Soltvedt 1, Westwood 1.
Worthington Cup (17): Ekoku 5 (1 pen), Soltvedt 2, Bonvin 1, Crane 1, Di Piedi 1, Hamshaw 1, McLaren 1, Maddix 1, Morrison 1 (pen), O'Donnell 1, Sibon 1, Westwood 1.
FA Cup (1): Hamshaw 1.

Stringer C 1	Hendon I 9	Geary D 29+3	Solvedt T 38	Bromby L 26	Maddix D 33+3	Haslam S 39+2	Sibon G 31+4	McLaren P 29+6	Quinn A 35+3	Lescott A 2+5	Morrison O 11+13	Di Piedi M 2+10	Pressman K 40	Bonvin P 7+16	Westwood A 25+1	Palmer C 10	Johnson T 8	Donnelly S 14+9	Hamshaw M 13+8	Crane T 4+11	O'Donnell P 6+2	Djordjic B 4+1	Windass D 2	Broomes M 18+1	Hinchcliffe A 1	Kuqi S 17	Roberts S —+1	Heald P 5	Armstrong C 7+1	Johnson D 7	Burrows D 8	McCarthy J 4	Gallacher K —+4	Match No.
1	2^1	3	4	5	6	7	8	9	10^2	11^3	12	13	14																					1
	2	3	4	5	6	7	8	9	10^2	11^1	12	13	1																					2
	2	3	4	5	6	7	8	9	10^2	11^1	12		1				13																	3
	2^2	3	4	5	6	7	8^3	9	10	11^1	12		1			13	14																	4
		3	4	5	6	2	8^1	9		11	12	13	1		14		7^2	10^3																5
		3	4		6	2^1	8	9		11	12	13	1			5	7	10^2																6
		3	4		6	2^1	8	9^2		11	12	13	1	14		5	7	10^3																7
		3	4		6		8^1	9	2	11^1	12	13	1	14		5	7	10^2																8
		3	4	2	6	12	8^1	9^3		11	13		1	14		5	7	10^2																9
		3	4	2	6	12	8^1	9^3		11	13		1	14		5^2	7	10																10
		3	4	2	6			9^1		11	12	13	1		5	8	10	13	7^2															11
		3^2	4	2	6	7	12	8		11³	13	14	1			5	10	9																12
	2	3		6	7	8^1		11^2			9	12	1		5	10^3		13	14															13
	2^2		4	3^1	6	7	8			11	12		1	13	5	10		9^1	14															14
	2	3	4		6	7	8^2	12	10^3	11^1	13		1	9	5			14																15
	2	3	4		6	7	8			11^2	12	1	1	9^1	5	10		13																16
	2		4	3	6		8			11	7	9	1		5	10																		17
		3	4	2	6^1		8			11	7^2	9	1	13	5	10		12																18
		3	4	2	6^3		8	12	7	11^1	13		1	9^1	5	10^2	14																	19
		3	4	2		7	8^2	12	11^1	9		1	1	5^8	10	14	13	6																20
		3	4	5	6	2	8	12	11^1	9^9		1	13	10	7																			21
		3	4	5	6	2	8	9	12	11^1		1	13	10^2	7																			22
		3^2	4	5^1	12	2	8^3	9	13			1	14	6			7	11	10															23
		3^1	4		6	7	8	9			12^1	25	1	13	11^2	10	2																	24
		3	4		6	7	8	9	10		1			12	5^{11}	11^1	2																	25
		3	4		6	7	8	9^3	12	13^1	5		10^1		14	11^2	2																	26
		3^1	4		6	7	8	9	10	1			11	12	5^2	13	2																	27
	2		6		4	8	9		11	1		5	7			12	3^1	10																28
	12	4	6		2	11	9	8	13	1^8	5		7^2			3^1	10	15																29
		4	6		2	8	9	10	11^3	12	5		7^1			3		1																30
	13	4	6		2	8^1	9	10	11^3	12	5^2		14			3	7	1																31
	3	4	6^1	12	2		9	8	11	13	5^3		7^2	14			1	10																32
		3	4		6	2	12	9^1	11		13		7^2	5		8	1	10																33
		4		6^2	2	12	9	8			5^1		13	14	11^3		7	1	3	10														34
		4			2	8^1	9	6	11		1		12			7		3	10															35
		4			2	12	8	11		1		5	7^1		6	9		3	10															36
		6	4	12	2		8	11		1^{13}		14	7^3		5	9		3^1	10^2															37
		6	4		2	12	13	8^3	11	1		14	7^1		5	9		3^1	10^2															38
		6	4^3		2	7^1		11	12	1	10^2	14	13		5	9		8	3															39
			6	2			8	11	12	1		10^2	7^3	13	5	9		4	3															40
			6	2	8	12	4	11		1		10^1	7^3	13	5	9			3															41
			6	2	8^1		4	11	12	1		10^2			5	9			3	7	13													42
		14	6	2	8^2	12	4	11		1		10^3	13		5	9^1			3	7														43
			6	2	8^1	12	4	11		1		10^2			5	9		13	3	7^3	14													44
	2		6	4^2	8		10^3	11	12	1		13			5	9			3	7^1	14													45
		5		2	8^1		4^2	11	12	1		10	7		6	9			3		13													46

Worthington Cup

First Round	Bury	(a)	3-1
Second Round	Sunderland	(h)	4-2
Third Round	Crystal Palace	(h)	2-2
Fourth Round	Aston Villa	(a)	1-0
Fifth Round	Watford	(h)	4-0
Semi-Final	Blackburn R	(h)	1-2
		(a)	2-4

FA Cup

Third Round	Crewe Alex	(a)	1-2

SHREWSBURY TOWN

Division 3

FOUNDATION

Shrewsbury School having provided a number of the early England and Wales international players it is not surprising that there was a Town club as early as 1876 which won the Birmingham Senior Cup in 1879. However, the present Shrewsbury Town club was formed in 1886 and won the Welsh FA Cup as early as 1891.

Gay Meadow, Shrewsbury SY2 6AB.

Telephone: (01743) 360 111. *Fax:* (01743) 236 384.
Commercial Dept: (01743) 356 316.
ClubCall: 09068 121 194.
Community Officer: Brian Williams (01743) 356 623.

Ground Capacity: 8,000.

Record Attendance: 18,917 v Walsall, Division 3, 26 April 1961.

Record Receipts: £80,610 v Arsenal, FA Cup 5th rd, 27 February 1991.

Pitch Measurements: 114yd × 74yd.

Life Vice-presidents: Dr J. Millard Bryson, G. W. Nelson, W.H. Richards.

Chairman: R. Wycherley.

Directors: A. Hopkins, M. J. Starkey, K. R. Woodhouse, T. J. Allen, K. J. Sayfritz. *Associate Directors:* M. R. Ashton, H. J. Wilson, A. T. Jones.

Manager: Kevin Ratcliffe. *Physio:* Simon Shakeshaft. *Coach:* Dave Fogg.

Commercial Manager: M. Thomas. *Secretary:* Mrs J. Shone. *Operations Manager:* M. R. Ashton.

Chaplain: Rev. Tim Welch.

Colours: Amber and blue shirts, blue shorts, blue stockings with amber trim.

Change Colours: All white.

Year Formed: 1886.

Turned Professional: 1896.

Ltd Co.: 1936.

Club Nickname: 'Town', 'Blues' or 'Salop'. The name 'Salop' is a colloquialism for the county of Shropshire. Since Shrewsbury is the only club in Shropshire, cries of 'Come on Salop' are frequently used!

Previous Ground: Old Shrewsbury Racecourse.

First Football League Game: 19 August 1950, Division 3 (N), v Scunthorpe U (a) D 0–0 – Egglestone; Fisher, Lewis; Wheatley, Depear, Robinson; Griffin, Hope, Jackson, Brown, Barker.

HONOURS

Football League: Division 2 best season: 8th, 1983–84, 1984–85; Division 3 – Champions 1978–79, 1993–94; Division 4 – Runners-up 1974–75.

FA Cup: best season: 6th rd, 1979, 1982.

Football League Cup: Semi-final 1961.

Welsh Cup: Winners 1891, 1938, 1977, 1979, 1984, 1985; Runners-up 1931, 1948, 1980.

Auto Windscreens Shield: Runners-up 1996

IT'S A FACT !

Five of the bottom six clubs in 1950–51, Shrewsbury Town's first season in the Third Division (North), subsequently lost their Football League status: Barrow, Southport, Halifax Town, Accrington Stanley and New Brighton. Shrewsbury finished 20th.

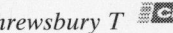

Record League Victory: 7–0 v Swindon T, Division 3 (S), 6 May 1955 – McBride; Bannister, Skeech; Wallace, Maloney, Candlin; Price, O'Donnell (1), Weigh (4), Russell, McCue (2).

Record Cup Victory: 11–2 v Marine, FA Cup 1st rd, 11 November 1995 – Edwards, Seabury (Dempsey (1)), Withe (1), Evans (1), Whiston (2), Scott (1), Woods, Stevens (1), Spink (3) (Anthrobus), Walton, Berkley, (1 og).

Record Defeat: 1–8 v Norwich C, Division 3 (S), 13 September 1952. 1–8 v Coventry C, Division 3, 22 October 1963.

Most League Points (2 for a win): 62, Division 4, 1974–75.

Most League Points (3 for a win): 79, Division 3, 1993–94.

Most League Goals: 101, Division 4, 1958–59.

Highest League Scorer in Season: Arthur Rowley, 38, Division 4, 1958–59.

Most League Goals in Total Aggregate: Arthur Rowley, 152, 1958–65 (thus completing his League record of 434 goals).

Most League Goals in One Match: 5, Alf Wood v Blackburn R, Division 3, 2 October 1971.

Most Capped Player: Jimmy McLaughlin, 5 (12), Northern Ireland; Bernard McNally, 5, Northern Ireland.

Most League Appearances: Mickey Brown, 418, 1986–91; 1992–94; 1996–2001.

Youngest League Player: Graham French, 16 years 177 days v Reading, 30 September 1961.

Record Transfer Fee Received: £500,000 from Crewe Alex for Dave Walton, October 1997.

Record Transfer Fee Paid: £100,000 to Aldershot for John Dungworth, November 1979 and £100,000 to Southampton for Mark Blake, August 1990.

Football League Record: 1950 Elected to Division 3 (N); 1951–58 Division 3 (S); 1958–59 Division 4; 1959–74 Division 3; 1974–75 Division 4; 1975–79 Division 3; 1979–89 Division 2; 1989–94 Division 3; 1994– Division 2.

MANAGERS

W. Adams 1905–12
(Secretary-Manager)
A. Weston 1912–34
(Secretary-Manager)
Jack Roscamp 1934–35
Sam Ramsey 1935–36
Ted Bousted 1936–40
Leslie Knighton 1945–49
Harry Chapman 1949–50
Sammy Crooks 1950–54
Walter Rowley 1955–57
Harry Potts 1957–58
Johnny Spuhler 1958
Arthur Rowley 1958–68
Harry Gregg 1968–72
Maurice Evans 1972–73
Alan Durban 1974–78
Richie Barker 1978
Graham Turner 1978–84
Chic Bates 1984–87
Ian McNeill 1987–90
Asa Hartford 1990–91
John Bond 1991–93
Fred Davies 1994–97
(previously Caretaker-Manager 1993–94)
Jake King 1997–99
Kevin Ratcliffe November 1999–

LATEST SEQUENCES

Longest Sequence of League Wins: 7, 28.10.95 – 16.12.95.

Longest Sequence of League Defeats: 7, 17.10.87 – 14.11.87.

Longest Sequence of League Draws: 6, 30.10.63 – 14.12.63.

Longest Sequence of Unbeaten League Matches: 16, 30.10.93 – 26.2.94.

Longest Sequence Without a League Win: 17, 25.1.92 – 11.4.92.

TEN YEAR LEAGUE RECORD

		P	W	D	L	F	A	Pts	Pos
1991-92	Div 3	46	12	11	23	53	68	47	22
1992-93	Div 3	42	17	11	14	57	52	62	9
1993-94	Div 3	42	22	13	7	63	39	79	1
1994-95	Div 2	46	13	14	19	54	62	53	18
1995-96	Div 2	46	13	14	19	58	70	53	18
1996-97	Div 2	46	11	13	22	49	74	46	22
1997-98	Div 3	46	16	13	17	61	62	61	13
1998-99	Div 3	46	14	14	18	52	63	56	15
1999-2000	Div 3	46	9	13	24	40	67	40	22
2000-01	Div 3	46	15	10	21	49	65	55	15

DID YOU KNOW?

William Hewitson signed from Oldham Athletic, scored 72 goals for Shrewsbury Town in the Birmingham League, FA Cup and Welsh Cup for Shrewsbury Town in 1935–36, before transferring to York City.

SHREWSBURY TOWN 2001–02 LEAGUE RECORD

Match No.	Date	Venue	Opponents	Result		H/T Score	Lg. Pos.	Goalscorers	Attendance
1	Aug 11	A	Plymouth Arg	W	1-0	0-0	—	Jemson [73]	5087
2	18	H	Hartlepool U	L	1-3	1-0	12	Rodgers [40]	2783
3	25	A	Oxford U	W	1-0	0-0	7	Jemson [67]	5667
4	28	H	York C	W	3-2	1-0	—	Rodgers [9], Jagielka [66], Jemson [89]	3002
5	Sept 1	A	Bristol R	D	0-0	0-0	5		6942
6	8	H	Cheltenham T	W	2-1	2-0	2	Jemson [20], Rodgers [39]	3395
7	14	A	Mansfield T	L	1-2	1-0	—	Rodgers [8]	4759
8	18	H	Kidderminster H	W	4-0	2-0	—	Jagielka [5], Rodgers 3 [45, 49, 80]	3530
9	22	H	Rochdale	W	1-0	0-0	1	Rodgers [90]	4612
10	25	A	Swansea C	D	3-3	1-2	—	Jemson 2 (1 pen) [1, 83 (p)], Murray [73]	3131
11	29	A	Scunthorpe U	L	1-3	0-2	5	Rodgers [80]	3047
12	Oct 5	H	Hull C	D	1-1	0-0	—	Rodgers [16]	5010
13	13	A	Leyton Orient	W	4-2	2-1	6	Redmile [31], Rodgers 2 [33, 63], Jagielka [67]	4436
14	23	H	Rushden & D	L	0-2	0-1	—		4016
15	27	A	Torquay U	L	1-2	0-1	6	Rioch [90]	2356
16	Nov 3	H	Lincoln C	D	1-1	1-1	7	Heathcote [9]	3437
17	6	H	Darlington	W	3-0	0-0	—	Moss [71], Jemson (pen) [74], Rodgers [79]	3084
18	9	A	Luton T	L	0-1	0-0	—		6809
19	20	A	Carlisle U	W	1-0	0-0	—	Jemson [86]	2003
20	24	H	Southend U	W	2-0	1-0	6	Jemson [40], Rioch [58]	3452
21	Dec 1	H	Exeter C	L	0-1	0-1	6		3565
22	15	A	Halifax T	W	2-1	0-0	6	Atkins 2 (1 pen) [69, 82 (p)]	1703
23	21	H	Macclesfield T	D	1-1	0-1	—	Rodgers [71]	3511
24	26	A	Cheltenham T	L	0-1	0-1	7		4561
25	29	A	York C	D	1-1	1-0	6	Lowe [20]	2413
26	Jan 8	H	Oxford U	W	1-0	1-0	—	Moss [29]	2576
27	12	A	Hartlepool U	D	2-2	0-1	4	Murray [57], Rodgers [78]	3447
28	15	H	Bristol R	L	0-1	0-0	—		3475
29	19	H	Plymouth Arg	W	3-1	1-1	4	Rodgers [44], Aiston [50], Lowe [84]	4796
30	22	A	Macclesfield T	L	1-2	1-2	—	Rodgers [41]	1688
31	26	A	Hull C	L	0-3	0-3	6		8534
32	Feb 2	H	Scunthorpe U	D	2-2	2-2	6	Jemson [10], Rodgers [13]	3345
33	9	A	Darlington	D	3-3	1-1	7	Woan [13], Rodgers [50], Jagielka [61]	3444
34	16	H	Leyton Orient	W	1-0	0-0	7	Jagielka [51]	3299
35	23	H	Mansfield T	W	3-0	2-0	7	Lowe [34], Lormor [42], Woan [84]	4120
36	26	A	Kidderminster H	L	0-1	0-1	—		3625
37	Mar 2	A	Rochdale	L	0-1	0-0	8		3353
38	5	H	Swansea C	W	3-0	1-0	—	Lormor [40], Lowe 2 [87, 90]	3168
39	9	H	Halifax T	W	3-0	1-0	7	Heathcote [1], Rodgers [55], Aiston [70]	3729
40	16	A	Exeter C	D	2-2	1-0	7	Rodgers [17], Redmile [62]	3020
41	23	A	Rushden & D	L	0-3	0-3	8		5432
42	30	H	Torquay U	L	0-1	0-1	9		4510
43	Apr 1	A	Lincoln C	W	2-1	1-1	8	Rodgers [5], Tolley [90]	2778
44	6	H	Carlisle U	W	1-0	1-0	8	Lowe [38]	3969
45	13	A	Southend U	W	2-0	1-0	7	Woan [22], Lowe [67]	5023
46	20	H	Luton T	L	0-2	0-1	9		7858

Final League Position: 9

GOALSCORERS

League (64): Rodgers 22, Jemson 10 (2 pens), Lowe 7, Jagielka 5, Woan 3, Aiston 2, Atkins 2 (1 pen), Heathcote 2, Lormor 2, Moss 2, Murray 2, Redmile 2, Rioch 2, Tolley 1.
Worthington Cup (1): Jemson 1.
FA Cup (0).

Cartwright M 14	Jenkins I 3 + 2	Rioch G 38	Redmile M 44	Heathcote M 33 + 1	Wilding P 12 + 10	Murray K 25 + 9	Atkins M 42	Rodgers L 38	Jemson N 28	Jagielka S 25 + 6	Tretton A 15 + 4	Walker J — + 3	Freestone C 3 + 4	Moss D 23 + 8	Drysdale L 22 + 4	Aiston S 22 + 13	Lowe R 22 + 16	Dunbavin I 32 + 2	Murphy C — + 4	Tolley J 19 + 4	Fallon R 8 + 3	Thompson A 13 + 1	Woan I 14	Lormor T 7	Guinan S 4 + 1	Match No.
1	2	3	4	5	6¹	7	8	9²	10³	11	12	13	14													1
1	2³	3	4	5	6	7	8	9²	10¹	11	13	12	14													2
1		3	4	5	6		8	7	10	11				9¹		2	12									3
1		3	4	5	6		8	7	10	11				9¹		2	12									4
1		3		5	6	7		8²	10	11	4			9¹		2	12	13								5
1		3	4	5	6	12	8	9	10	11¹					2	7²	13									6
1		3	4	5	6		8	9¹	10	11					2	7	12									7
1		3	4	5		6	8	9	10	11			12		2	7¹										8
1		3	4	5		6	8	9	10	11					2	7										9
1		3	4	5	12	6	8	9	10	11			13		2²	7¹										10
1		3	4	5		6	8	9	10	11			12		2¹	7²	13									11
1	12	3¹	4	5		6	8	9	10	11					2	7²	13									12
1⁵		3	4	5	6¹	7	8	9²	10	11				2		12	15	13								13
13		3	4	5		6	8	9	10	11²		12	2		7¹	1										14
		3	4	5	6⁸		8	9	10	11		12	2²	13		7¹	1		14							15
1		3	4	5		6	8	9¹	10	11			7⁸	2		12	15									16
		3	4	5		6	8³	9²	10¹	11		13	7	7	2		12	1	14							17
		3	4		6	8	9	10	11	5			7¹	2		12	1									18
		3		5	12	6¹		9	10	13	4		7³	2	8²	14	1		11							19
		3	4	5	12		8	9	10²	11³	13		14	2	7		1		6							20
2²	3	4	5¹			8	9	10		12			7		11	13	1		6							21
		3	4	6¹	13	8	9³			5			12	2	11²	14	1		7	10						22
		3	4	12	6	8	9	10		5			7¹	2²	13	1		11³								23
		3	4	6²	8		9¹	10		5			7³	2	12	11	1		13	14						24
		3	4	12	6			10		5¹			7²	2	13	8	1	14	11	9³						25
		3	4			8		10		5			2	12	11	7¹	1		6	9						26
		3	4	12	13	8	9		14	5			2		11¹	7²	1		6	10³						27
		3	4		12	8	9		13	5			2		11	7	1		6¹	10²						28
		3	4	12		8	9²		13	5			2		11	7	1		6	10³	14					29
3¹		4		13	8	9	10		5			7		12	11²	1		6		2						30
		3	4			8	10	12	5			2		11	7	1		6	9¹	3						31
		3	4		8	9	10²	12	5			2		7	7	1		6	13	3	11¹					32
		4	12	13	8	9		11³	5¹			2			10	1		6²	14	3	7					33
		4	5	12	6	8		11²				2	13		10¹	1	14		3	7	9²					34
		4	5	12	6	8		11¹				2		13	10	1			3	7	9²					35
		4	5		6¹	8		7				2	12	11	10	1			3		9					36
		4	5	2	6	8		11						12	10¹	1			3	7	9					37
		4	5		6	8		10⁵						2	11	12	1		3	7	9					38
		3	4	5	12	6	8¹	9					2	11	13	1			7	10⁵						39
		3	4	5	2	6²	8	9					11	12	1		13	7	10¹							40
		3	4¹	5		8	9		12				2	11	10	1		6		7						41
		3	4	5	12	8	9					2¹	11³	10	1	13	6		7²	14						42
		3	4	5	12	8¹	9						13	10	1		6		2	7	11²					43
3²		4	5		8	9⁵					13	12	10	1		6		2	7	11						44
		3	4	5		8	9						12	10	1		6		2	7	11¹					45
3¹		4	5	13	8²	9					12	14	10	1		6		2	7	11³						46

Worthington Cup
First Round   Tranmere R   (a)   1-3

FA Cup
First Round   Brighton & HA   (a)   0-1

SOUTHAMPTON FA Premiership

FOUNDATION

Formed largely by players from the Deanery FC, which had been established by school teachers in 1880. Most of the founders were connected with the young men's association of St Mary's Church. At the inaugural meeting held in November 1885 the club was named Southampton St Mary's and the church's curate was elected president.

The Friends Provident St Mary's Stadium, Britannia Road, Southampton SO14 5FP.

Telephone: (0870) 2200 000. *Fax:* (023) 8072 7727.
ClubCall: 09068 121 178. *Website:* www.saintsfc.co.uk
Email: sfc@saintsfc.co.uk
Recorded Ticket Information: 0870 220 0150.

Ground Capacity: 32,551.

Record Attendance: 31,973 v Newcastle U, FA Premier League, 11 May 2002.

Record Receipts: £686,160 v Manchester U, FA Premier League, 13 January 2002.

Pitch Measurements: 112yd × 74yd.

President: E. T. Bates. *Chairman:* R. J. G. Lowe.
Vice-chairman: B. H. D. Hunt.
Directors: I. L. Gordon, K. St. J. Wiseman,
M. R. Richards FCA, A. Cowen, R. M. Withers.

Manager: Gordon Strachan.

Assistant Manager: Gary Pendrey.

Academy Director: Huw Jennings.

Physios: Jim Joyce, Phil Wilson.

Secretary: Brian Truscott.

HONOURS

Football League: Division 1 –
Runners-up 1983–84; Division 2 –
Runners-up 1965–66, 1977–78;
Division 3 (S) – Champions 1921–22;
Runners-up 1920–21; Division 3 –
Champions 1959–60.
FA Cup: Winners 1976; Runners-up 1900, 1902.
Football League Cup: Runners-up 1979.
Zenith Data Systems Cup: Runners-up 1992.
European Competitions: European Fairs Cup: 1969–70. UEFA Cup: 1971–72, 1981–82, 1982–83, 1984–85. European Cup-Winners' Cup: 1976–77.

Colours: Red and white striped shirts, black shorts, white stockings with black and red trim.

Change Colours: White with red shoulder markings, red shorts with white trim, red stockings.

Year Formed: 1885.

Turned Professional: 1894.

Ltd Co.: 1897.

Previous Name: 1885, Southampton St Mary's; 1897, Southampton.

Club Nickname: 'The Saints'.

Previous Grounds: 1885, Antelope Ground; 1897, County Cricket Ground; 1898, The Dell; 2001, St Mary's.

First Football League Game: 28 August 1920, Division 3, v Gillingham (a) D 1–1 – Allen; Parker, Titmuss; Shelley, Campbell, Turner; Barratt, Dominy (1), Rawlings, Moore, Foxall.

IT'S A FACT !

On 23 November 2001, Pagan Priestess Cerradwen 'Dragonoak' Connelly performed an exorcism at Southampton's St Mary's Stadium, site of the Anglo-Saxon settlement of Hamwick, to banish the curse of no home wins. The next day saw a 1-0 victory over Charlton.

Record League Victory: 9–3 v Wolverhampton W,
Division 2, 18 September 1965 – Godfrey; Jones, Williams;
Walker, Knapp, Huxford; Paine (2), O'Brien (1), Melia,
Chivers (4), Sydenham (2).

Record Cup Victory: 7–1 v Ipswich T, FA Cup 3rd rd,
7 January 1961 – Reynolds; Davies, Traynor; Conner, Page,
Huxford; Paine (1), O'Brien (3 incl. 1p), Reeves,
Mulgrew (2), Penk (1).

Record Defeat: 0–8 v Tottenham H, Division 2,
28 March 1936. 0–8 v Everton, Division 1, 20 November 1971.

Most League Points (2 for a win): 61, Division 3 (S),
1921–22 and Division 3, 1959–60.

Most League Points (3 for a win): 77, Division 1, 1983–84.

Most League Goals: 112, Division 3 (S), 1957–58.

Highest League Scorer in Season: Derek Reeves, 39,
Division 3, 1959–60.

Most League Goals in Total Aggregate: Mike Channon,
185, 1966–77, 1979–82.

Most League Goals in One Match: 5, Charlie Wayman v
Leicester C, Division 2, 23 October 1948.

Most Capped Player: Peter Shilton, 49 (125), England.

Most League Appearances: Terry Paine, 713, 1956–74.

Youngest League Player: Danny Wallace, 16 years 313 days
v Manchester U, 29 November 1980.

Record Transfer Fee Received: £8,000,000 from
Tottenham H for Dean Richards, October 2001.

Record Transfer Fee Paid: £4,000,000 to Derby Co for
Rory Delap, July 2001.

Football League Record: 1920 Original Member of
Division 3; 1921–22 Division 3 (S); 1922–53 Division 2;
1953–58 Division 3 (S); 1958–60 Division 3; 1960–66
Division 2; 1966–74 Division 1; 1974–78 Division 2; 1978–92
Division 1; 1992– FA Premier League.

LATEST SEQUENCES

Longest Sequence of League Wins: 6, 3.3.92 – 4.4.92.

Longest Sequence of League Defeats: 5, 16.8.98 – 12.9.98.

Longest Sequence of League Draws: 7, 28.12.94 – 11.2.95.

Longest Sequence of Unbeaten League Matches: 19, 5.9.21 – 31.12.21.

Longest Sequence Without a League Win: 20, 30.8.69 – 27.12.69.

MANAGERS

Cecil Knight 1894–95
(Secretary-Manager)
Charles Robson 1895–97
E. Arnfield 1897–1911
(Secretary-Manager)
(continued as Secretary)
George Swift 1911–12
Ernest Arnfield 1912–19
Jimmy McIntyre 1919–24
Arthur Chadwick 1925–31
George Kay 1931–36
George Gross 1936–37
Tom Parker 1937–43
*J. R. Sarjantson stepped down
from the board to act as
Secretary-Manager 1943–47
with the next two listed being
team Managers during this
period*
Arthur Dominy 1943–46
Bill Dodgin Snr 1946–49
Sid Cann 1949–51
George Roughton 1952–55
Ted Bates 1955–73
Lawrie McMenemy 1973–85
Chris Nicholl 1985–91
Ian Branfoot 1991–94
Alan Ball 1994–95
Dave Merrington 1995–96
Graeme Souness 1996–97
Dave Jones 1997–2000
Glenn Hoddle 2000–01
Stuart Gray 2001
Gordon Strachan October 2001–

TEN YEAR LEAGUE RECORD

		P	W	D	L	F	A	Pts	Pos
1991-92	Div 1	42	14	10	18	39	55	52	16
1992-93	PR Lge	42	13	11	18	54	61	50	18
1993-94	PR Lge	42	12	7	23	49	66	43	18
1994-95	PR Lge	42	12	18	12	61	63	54	10
1995-96	PR Lge	38	9	11	18	34	52	38	17
1996-97	PR Lge	38	10	11	17	50	56	41	16
1997-98	PR Lge	38	14	6	18	50	55	48	12
1998-99	PR Lge	38	11	8	19	37	64	41	17
1999-2000	PR Lge	38	12	8	18	45	62	44	15
2000-01	PR Lge	38	14	10	14	40	48	52	10

DID YOU KNOW ?

Having pioneered the advent
of Latvian internationals in
the Premier League with
Marian Pahars, Southampton
introduced Ecuador
international centre-forward
Agustin Delgado during the
2001–02 season.

SOUTHAMPTON 2001–02 LEAGUE RECORD

Match No.	Date	Venue	Opponents	Result	H/T Score	Lg. Pos.	Goalscorers	Attendance
1	Aug 18	A	Leeds U	L	0-2	0-0	—		39,715
2	25	H	Chelsea	L	0-2	0-1	18		31,107
3	Sept 9	A	Tottenham H	L	0-2	0-0	19		33,658
4	15	A	Bolton W	W	1-0	0-0	18	Pahars [77]	24,378
5	24	H	Aston Villa	L	1-3	1-2	—	Pahars [45]	26,794
6	29	A	Middlesbrough	W	3-1	0-0	16	Beattie 2 [66, 86], Pahars (pen) [73]	26,142
7	Oct 13	H	Arsenal	L	0-2	0-1	17		29,759
8	20	A	West Ham U	L	0-2	0-0	19		25,842
9	24	H	Ipswich T	D	3-3	2-1	—	Beattie [14], Pahars [23], Marsden [52]	29,614
10	27	A	Fulham	L	1-2	1-2	19	Beattie [32]	18,771
11	Nov 3	H	Blackburn R	L	1-2	1-1	19	Pahars [36]	30,523
12	17	A	Derby Co	L	0-1	0-1	20		32,063
13	24	H	Charlton Ath	W	1-0	0-0	17	Pahars [59]	31,198
14	Dec 2	A	Everton	L	0-2	0-0	18		28,138
15	8	A	Leicester C	W	4-0	1-0	17	Svensson 2 [12, 75], Beattie [64], Pahars [90]	20,321
16	15	H	Sunderland	W	2-0	1-0	17	Craddock (og) [43], Pahars [67]	29,459
17	22	A	Manchester U	L	1-6	0-3	17	Pahars [55]	67,638
18	26	H	Tottenham H	W	1-0	0-0	17	Beattie [56]	31,719
19	29	H	Leeds U	L	0-1	0-0	17		31,622
20	Jan 1	A	Chelsea	W	4-2	1-2	17	Beattie 2 [7, 73], Pahars [55], Marsden [64]	35,164
21	9	H	Liverpool	W	2-0	0-0	—	Beattie (pen) [63], Riise (og) [71]	31,527
22	13	A	Manchester U	L	1-3	1-2	15	Beattie [3]	31,858
23	19	A	Liverpool	D	1-1	0-1	14	Davies [46]	43,710
24	30	H	West Ham U	W	2-0	1-0	—	Davies [43], Fernandes [66]	31,879
25	Feb 2	A	Arsenal	D	1-1	0-1	13	Tessem [80]	38,024
26	9	A	Newcastle U	L	1-3	1-3	14	Pahars [39]	51,857
27	23	H	Bolton W	D	0-0	0-0	13		31,380
28	Mar 2	A	Ipswich T	W	3-1	0-0	11	Delap [52], Ormerod [61], Marsden [88]	25,430
29	6	H	Middlesbrough	D	1-1	1-0	—	Svensson [38]	28,931
30	16	H	Leicester C	D	2-2	1-2	11	Pahars 2 (1 pen) [29, 87 (p)]	30,012
31	23	A	Sunderland	D	1-1	0-0	11	Tessem [88]	42,799
32	30	H	Fulham	D	1-1	1-1	12	Delap [22]	31,616
33	Apr 1	A	Blackburn R	L	0-2	0-2	13		28,979
34	6	H	Derby Co	W	2-0	1-0	11	Oakley [29], Pahars [55]	29,263
35	13	A	Charlton Ath	D	1-1	0-1	11	El Khalej [85]	26,551
36	20	H	Everton	L	0-1	0-1	12		31,785
37	27	A	Aston Villa	L	1-2	0-2	14	Beattie [52]	35,255
38	May 11	H	Newcastle U	W	3-1	2-0	11	Svensson [17], Beattie (pen) [24], Telfer [90]	31,973

Final League Position: 11

GOALSCORERS

League (46): Pahars 14 (2 pens), Beattie 12 (2 pens), Svensson 4, Marsden 3, Davies 2, Delap 2, Tessem 2, El Khalej 1, Fernandes 1, Oakley 1, Ormerod 1, Telfer 1, own goals 2.
Worthington Cup (7): Beattie 2 (1 pen), Svensson 2, Davies 1, El-Khalej 1, Pahars 1.
FA Cup (1): Pahars 1 (pen).

Jones P 36	Delap R 24+4	Bridge W 38	Marsden C 27+1	Lundekvam C 34	Richards D 4	Svensson A 33+1	Oakley M 26+1	Roster U 3+1	Pahars M 33+3	Davies K 18+5	Tessem J 7+15	Benali F —+3	Beattie J 24+4	Ripley S 1+4	El Khalej T 12+2	Murray P —+1	Draper M 1+1	McDonald S —+2	Le Tissier M —+4	Monk G 1+1	Dodd J 26+3	Petrescu D —+2	Williams P 27+1	Telfer P 27+1	Ormerod B 8+10	Fernandes F 6+5	Delgado A —+1	Bleidelis I —+1	Moss N 2	Match No.
1	2	3	4¹	5	6	7	8	9²	10³	11	12	13	14																	1
1	2	3	4²	5	6	7	8	9²	10¹	11	14				12	13														2
1	2	3			6	7²	4	9	10¹	8	11³				12			5	14	13										3
1	2	3	12	5	6	7	8	13	10	11¹	9		4²																	4
1	2	3		5		7	4		10³	8²	11¹	12	9		6			13	14											5
1	2³	3	4	5		7¹	8		10³	11	12		9	13							6		14							6
1		3	4	5³		7²	8¹		10	11	12		9		13						2	14	6							7
1	7	3	4	5			12		10²	11¹			9		13						2		8							8
1	2³	3	4	5		8		12	10	11¹			9		7²			13	14		6									9
1	2	3		5³		7	8		10	11²	12		9¹		4			13	14		6									10
1	11	3	4			8			10				9		5						2		6	7						11
1	12	3	4			8			10	11¹			9²					13			2		6	7						12
1		3	4	5		8			10¹	11	12		9								2		6	7						13
1		3	4¹	5		8			10	11	12		9								2		6	7						14
1	12	3	4			8¹			10	11			9								2		6	7						15
1		3	4	5		8			10¹	11			9								2		6	7	12					16
1	12	3	4			8²			10	11¹			9								2		6	7	13					17
1	8	3	4	5					10¹	11			9								2		6	7	12					18
1	8	3	4	5					10	11			9								2		6	7¹		12				19
1	8	3	4	5					10¹	11			9								2		6	7	12					20
1	8¹	3	4	5					10²	11	12		9								2		6	7	13					21
1		3	4	5					10	11			9²								2		6	7	12	8¹	13			22
1		3	4	5					10²	11	12		9					13			2		6	7	8¹					23
1		3		5			4¹		10	11	12		9²					13			2		6	7	8³	14				24
1		3	4	5		8²			10	11			9¹					12			2		6	7	13					25
1	12	3	4	5		8²			10	11			9					13			2		6	7¹						26
1	7	3	4	5					10²	11			9								2	12	6		13	8¹				27
1	7	3	4	5		8			10	11			9¹								2		6							28
1	7	3	4	5		8	12		10	11¹			9								2		6							29
1		3	4	5¹		7	8		10	11³	13	12	9								2		6		14					30
1		3	4²	5		7	8		10	11¹	12		9			13					2		6							31
1	8	3		5			4		10²	11	12	13	9								2		6	7						32
1	4	3		5		8			10¹	11²	12	13	9								2		6	7						33
1	11	3	4¹			8			10²	12			9		5						2		6	7	13					34
1	4	3				8¹			10²	11	12		9		5						2		6	7	13					35
1	4	3							10	11		8¹	9								2²		6	7	13	12				36
	4	3		5					11		12	13	9		14						2	6³	7		10¹	8²	1			37
	4	3		5					11²	10²		12	9		6			13			2		7		8¹	14	1			38

Worthington Cup
Second Round	Brighton & HA	(a)	3-0
Third Round	Gillingham	(a)	2-0
Fourth Round	Bolton W	(a)	2-2

FA Cup
Third Round	Rotherham U	(a)	1-2

SOUTHEND UNITED   Division 3

FOUNDATION

The leading club in Southend around the turn of the century was Southend Athletic, but they were an amateur concern. Southend United was a more ambitious professional club when they were founded in 1906, employing Bob Jack as secretary-manager and immediately joining the Second Division of the Southern League.

Roots Hall Football Ground, Victoria Avenue, Southend-on-Sea SS2 6NQ.

Telephone: (01702) 304 050. *Fax:* (01702) 304 124.
Commercial: (01702) 304 147. *ClubCall:* 09068 121 105.
Ticket Office: (01702) 304 090.

Ground Capacity: 12,392.

Record Attendance: 31,090 v Liverpool, FA Cup 3rd rd, 10 January 1979.

Record Receipts: £83,999 v West Ham U, Division 1, 7 April 1993.

Pitch Measurements: 110yd × 74yd.

Deputy-chairman: G. King.
Directors: D. M. Markscheffel, R. J. Osborne, P. Robinson, D. A. J. Wilshire, F. Van Wezel, R. Martin.

Secretary: Miss Helen Giles.

Manager: Rob Newman. *Joint Assistant Managers:* David Crown, Steve Tilson.

Physio: John Gowens.

Commercial Manager: Brian Wheeler.

Safety Officer: David Jobson.

Club Nickname: 'The Blues' or 'The Shrimpers'.

Colours: Navy blue.

Change Colours: All white.

Year Formed: 1906.

Turned Professional: 1906.

Ltd Co.: 1919.

Previous Grounds: 1906, Roots Hall, Prittlewell; 1920, Kursaal; 1934, Southend Stadium; 1955, Roots Hall Football Ground.

First Football League Game: 28 August 1920, Division 3, v Brighton & HA (a) W 2–0 – Capper; Reid, Newton; Wileman, Henderson, Martin; Nicholls, Nuttall, Fairclough (2), Myers, Dorsett.

Record League Victory: 9–2 v Newport Co, Division 3 (S), 5 September 1936 – McKenzie; Nelson, Everest (1); Deacon, Turner, Carr; Bolan, Lane (1), Goddard (4), Dickinson (2), Oswald (1).

HONOURS

Football League: Division 1 best season: 13th, 1994–95. Division 3 – Runners-up 1990–91; Division 4 – Champions 1980–81; Runners-up 1971–72, 1977–78.
FA Cup: best season: old 3rd rd, 1921; 5th rd, 1926, 1952, 1976, 1993.
Football League Cup: never past 3rd rd.

IT'S A FACT !

The first Southend United player to score as many as four goals in one match was Billy Goodwin against Millwall on 24 February 1923 in a 4-0 win.

Record Cup Victory: 10–1 v Golders Green, FA Cup 1st rd, 24 November 1934 – Moore; Morfitt, Kelly; Mackay, Joe Wilson, Carr (1); Lane (1), Johnson (5), Cheesmuir (2), Deacon (1), Oswald. 10–1 v Brentwood, FA Cup 2nd rd, 7 December 1968 – Roberts; Bentley, Birks; McMillan (1) Beesley, Kurila; Clayton, Chisnall, Moore (4), Best (5), Hamilton. 10–1 v Aldershot, Leyland Daf Cup Prel rd, 6 November 1990 – Sansome; Austin, Powell, Cornwell, Prior (1), Tilson (3), Cawley, Butler, Ansah (1), Benjamin (1), Angell (4).

Record Defeat: 1–9 v Brighton & HA, Division 3, 27 November 1965.

Most League Points (2 for a win): 67, Division 4, 1980–81.

Most League Points (3 for a win): 85, Division 3, 1990–91.

Most League Goals: 92, Division 3 (S), 1950–51.

Highest League Scorer in Season: Jim Shankly, 31, 1928–29; Sammy McCrory, 1957–58, both in Division 3 (S).

Most League Goals in Total Aggregate: Roy Hollis, 122, 1953–60.

Most League Goals in One Match: 5, Jim Shankly v Merthyr T, Division 3S, 1 March 1930.

Most Capped Player: George Mackenzie, 9, Eire.

Most League Appearances: Sandy Anderson, 452, 1950–63.

Youngest League Player: Phil O'Connor, 16 years 76 days v Lincoln C, 26 December 1969.

Record Transfer Fee Received: £3,570,000 from Nottingham F for Stan Collymore, June 1993.

Record Transfer Fee Paid: £750,000 to Crystal Palace for Stan Collymore, November 1992.

Football League Record: 1920 Original Member of Division 3; 1921–58 Division 3 (S); 1958–66 Division 3; 1966–72 Division 4; 1972–76 Division 3; 1976–78 Division 4; 1978–80 Division 3; 1980–81 Division 4; 1981–84 Division 3; 1984–87 Division 4; 1987–89 Division 3; 1989–90 Division 4; 1990–91 Division 3; 1991–92 Division 2; 1992–97 Division 1; 1997–98 Division 2; 1998– Division 3.

MANAGERS

Bob Jack 1906–10
George Molyneux 1910–11
O. M. Howard 1911–12
Joe Bradshaw 1912–19
Ned Liddell 1919–20
Tom Mather 1920–21
Ted Birnie 1921–34
David Jack 1934–40
Harry Warren 1946–56
Eddie Perry 1956–60
Frank Broome 1960
Ted Fenton 1961–65
Alvan Williams 1965–67
Ernie Shepherd 1967–69
Geoff Hudson 1969–70
Arthur Rowley 1970–76
Dave Smith 1976–83
Peter Morris 1983–84
Bobby Moore 1984–86
Dave Webb 1986–87
Dick Bate 1987
Paul Clark 1987–88
Dave Webb *(General Manager)* 1988–92
Colin Murphy 1992–93
Barry Fry 1993
Peter Taylor 1993–95
Steve Thompson 1995
Ronnie Whelan 1995–97
Alvin Martin 1997–99
Alan Little 1999–2000
David Webb 2000–01
Rob Newman October 2001–

LATEST SEQUENCES

Longest Sequence of League Wins: 7, 27.4.90 – 18.9.90.

Longest Sequence of League Defeats: 6, 29.8.87 – 19.9.87.

Longest Sequence of League Draws: 6, 30.1.82 – 19.2.82.

Longest Sequence of Unbeaten League Matches: 16, 20.2.32 – 29.8.32.

Longest Sequence Without a League Win: 17, 31.12.83 – 14.4.84.

TEN YEAR LEAGUE RECORD

		P	W	D	L	F	A	Pts	Pos
1991-92	Div 2	46	17	11	18	63	63	62	12
1992-93	Div 1	46	13	13	20	54	64	52	18
1993-94	Div 1	46	17	8	21	63	67	59	15
1994-95	Div 1	46	18	8	20	54	73	62	13
1995-96	Div 1	46	15	14	17	52	61	59	14
1996-97	Div 1	46	8	15	23	42	86	39	24
1997-98	Div 2	46	11	10	25	47	79	43	24
1998-99	Div 3	46	14	12	20	52	58	54	18
1999-2000	Div 3	46	15	11	20	53	61	56	16
2000-01	Div 3	46	15	18	13	55	53	63	11

DID YOU KNOW ❓

Derek Woodley, the Southend United winger, scored the fastest goal ever seen at Wembley playing for England Boys against Wales in 1957. It came after 13 seconds following a three man move from the kick-off. England won 2-0.

SOUTHEND UNITED 2001–02 LEAGUE RECORD

Match No.	Date	Venue	Opponents	Result		H/T Score	Lg. Pos.	Goalscorers	Attendance
1	Aug 11	H	Darlington	W	1-0	0-0	—	Rawle [80]	4725
2	18	A	Mansfield T	D	0-0	0-0	9		2774
3	25	H	Halifax T	W	4-1	1-0	2	Richards 2 [45, 90], Johnson [56], Webb [80]	3525
4	27	A	Luton T	L	0-2	0-0	7		6496
5	Sept 1	H	Leyton Orient	L	1-2	0-1	11	Whelan [48]	5853
6	8	A	Rushden & D	W	1-0	0-0	8	Searle [75]	4583
7	15	H	Hartlepool U	D	0-0	0-0	10		3933
8	18	A	Bristol R	L	1-2	1-1	—	Johnson [29]	5743
9	22	A	Oxford U	L	0-2	0-1	12		5724
10	25	H	Carlisle U	W	3-2	1-1	—	Whelan [44], Webb [54], Maher [88]	2967
11	28	H	Cheltenham T	L	0-1	0-1	—		3709
12	Oct 5	A	Torquay U	L	1-2	0-0	—	Hutchings [55]	2329
13	13	H	Swansea C	W	4-2	0-1	9	Bramble [57], Belgrave [63], Maher 2 (2 pens) [81, 90]	3622
14	20	A	York C	L	1-2	1-1	14	Rawle [14]	2270
15	23	A	Scunthorpe U	L	0-2	0-0	—		2956
16	27	H	Kidderminster H	W	1-0	1-0	12	Hutchings [2]	3990
17	Nov 3	A	Exeter C	L	1-2	1-2	14	Bramble [3]	3269
18	9	H	Macclesfield T	W	3-0	1-0	—	Rawle 2 [2, 72], Bramble [78]	2889
19	20	H	Plymouth Arg	L	0-1	0-1	—		3716
20	24	A	Shrewsbury T	L	0-2	0-1	16		3452
21	Dec 1	H	Lincoln C	D	1-1	1-1	16	Bramble [29]	3979
22	15	A	Rochdale	W	1-0	1-0	14	Broad [7]	2849
23	21	A	Hull C	D	0-0	0-0	—		8678
24	26	H	Rushden & D	W	4-2	0-2	12	Cort [50], Belgrave 2 [59, 75], Bramble [67]	5878
25	29	H	Luton T	L	1-2	0-0	13	Hutchings [53]	5973
26	Jan 12	H	Mansfield T	W	1-0	1-0	12	Bramble [23]	3300
27	19	A	Darlington	D	2-2	0-1	12	Maher [78], Belgrave [89]	3365
28	22	H	Hull C	W	2-0	1-0	—	Rawle [36], Hutchings (pen) [71]	3341
29	26	A	Torquay U	D	1-1	0-0	10	Whelan [49]	4184
30	29	A	Halifax T	D	1-1	0-1	—	Woodward (og) [82]	1251
31	Feb 9	H	York C	L	0-1	0-0	14		3967
32	15	A	Swansea C	L	2-3	1-2	—	Cort [6], Whelan [86]	3600
33	19	A	Cheltenham T	D	1-1	0-0	—	Newman [83]	4015
34	23	A	Hartlepool U	L	1-5	0-2	16	Belgrave [90]	3609
35	26	H	Bristol R	W	2-1	1-1	—	Bramble 2 (1 pen) [45 (p), 57]	2477
36	Mar 2	H	Oxford U	D	2-2	2-1	14	Bramble (pen) [29], Cort [43]	3701
37	5	A	Carlisle U	D	0-0	0-0	—		3045
38	9	H	Rochdale	D	0-0	0-0	12		3429
39	12	A	Leyton Orient	L	1-2	0-2	—	Barry-Murphy [63]	4840
40	16	A	Lincoln C	W	1-0	1-0	12	Clark S [7]	2328
41	23	H	Scunthorpe U	W	2-0	2-0	12	Cort [17], Newman [26]	3818
42	30	A	Kidderminster H	L	0-2	0-1	12		2804
43	Apr 1	H	Exeter C	W	3-1	2-1	12	Maher [39], Whelan [41], Broad [75]	3588
44	6	A	Plymouth Arg	D	0-0	0-0	12		10,021
45	13	H	Shrewsbury T	L	0-2	0-1	12		5023
46	20	A	Macclesfield T	D	0-0	0-0	12		2415

Final League Position: 12

GOALSCORERS

League (51): Bramble 9 (2 pens), Belgrave 5, Maher 5 (2 pens), Rawle 5, Whelan 5, Cort 4, Hutchings 4 (1 pen), Broad 2, Johnson 2, Newman 2, Richards 2, Webb 2, Barry-Murphy 1, Clark S 1, Searle 1, own goal 1.
Worthington Cup (0).
FA Cup (7): Bramble 3, Belgrave 2, Rawle 1, Whelan 1.

Flahavan D 41	Broad S 30 + 2	Searle D 41 + 2	Johnson L 24 + 4	Cort L 43 + 2	Whelan P 43 + 1	Holness D 1 + 1	Maher K 36	Webb D 10 + 6	Richards T 9 + 8	Thurgood S 34 + 5	Rawle M 25 + 5	Risbridger G — + 1	Hutchings C 28 + 1	Smith B — + 1	Bramble T 32 + 3	McSweeney D 13 + 8	Forbes S 3 + 10	Belgrave B 32 + 2	Kerrigan D 6 + 5	Harris J 2 + 3	Beard M 5 + 9	Dsane R 1 + 1	Clark S 9 + 3	Newman R 10 + 1	Gay D 5 + 1	Selley I 14	Barry-Murphy B 8	Szmid M 1 + 1	Clark A — + 2	Lunan D — + 1	Wallace A — + 2	Alderton R — + 2	Match No.
1	2	3	4	5	6	7[1]	8	9[1]	10	11	12[2]	13	14																				1
1	2	3	4	5	6		8	9		11	10		7																				2
1		3		5	6	4	8		10	7	9[2]		2	13	11[1]	12																	3
1		3		5	6	12	4	8[1]	10	7	9		2		11[2]	13																	4
1		3		5	6	4	8		10	7	9[1]		2		11				12														5
1	5	11	3	6		4	9[1]		10	7			2		12	13		8[2]															6
1	5	6	3	12		4	8		10	7			2		11[1]			9															7
1	5[1]	3	4	12	6		8		10	7			2		11[1]			9															8
1		3	4	5	6		8		12	10[2]	7		2		11[1]			9	13														9
1	12	4		5	6		8		9		7		2		10	11	3[1]																10
1	12	4		5	6		7		9[1]		2[3]	13	14		10	11	3[2]																11
1		3	4[2]	5	6		8		9	10[1]	7		12		2	11	13																12
1		3	4	5	6		8		9		7				11[1]	2[2]	10	12	13														13
1		3[1]	4	5	6		8[2]		12	9	7				11	2[2]	10	13	14														14
1		3	4	5	6		8[1]		9		7				11	2[2]	10	12	13														15
1		3	4[1]	5	6				13	12	9		7		11[2]	2	10[2]	8	14														16
1		3	4	5	6				9	12	7				11	2[1]	13	10[2]	8[2]	14													17
1		3	4[3]	5	6		8		12	9	7				11		13	10[2]	14		2												18
1		3	4[2]	5	6[1]		8		12		7	9				10					2		13	11									19
1	2	3	4[1]	5	6		8		12		7	9[2]				10			14			13		11[3]									20
1	2	3		5	6		8		12		7	9[1]			4	10		11															21
1	2	3		5	6		8			11	9[6]		7			10									4	15							22
1	2	3		5	6		8			11	9[1]		7			10			12						4								23
1	2	3	12	5	6		8			11	13		7[1]			10[2]		9						14	4[3]								24
	2[1]	3		5	6		8			7[3]	13				4	10		12[2]		14			9	11	1								25
1	2	3		5	6		8			12	7[2]				4	10		13					9	11[1]									26
1	2	3		5	6		8			12	13	14	7[2]			9							11[1]		4[3]								27
1	2	3	13	5	6					12	7[2]		9[3]		4	10		11[1]	8[2]	14													28
1	2	3		5	6		8			12	7[2]		9[3]		4			11[1]	13	10	14												29
1	2	3	13	5	6		8[1]			12	9[2]		4[3]		11			7	14														30
1	2	3	14	5	6					12	11	9[3]	7[2]		10[1]	13	8	4															31
1	2	3		5	6					11	12				10	9[1]							4			7	8						32
1	2	3[1]		5	6					11					9	10		12					4			7	8						33
1	2	3		5	6					11					9	10		12	13				4[2]			7	8[2]	14					34
1	2	3		5	6										4	9[1]	10	12			11					7	8						35
1	2	3		5	6					12					4[1]	9[2]	10				13	11				7	8						36
1	2	3		5	6		8								4	10[1]	9				12					7	11						37
1	2	3		5	6		8	9[1]							4	10					12					7	11						38
1	2	3		5	6		8				4[1]					10		12	13							7	11	9[2]					39
	2	3	4	5			8				12				6	10[1]					11		9		1	7							40
	2	3	4	5			8								6	10					11		9		1	7							41
	2	3	4[2]	5	12		8			10					6		13				11[3]	9[1]	1			7		14					42
1	12	3		5	9		8			13					6[2]	10[4]	4		2[1]	11			7								14		43
1	2	3		5	9		8			11					6	10[1]	4		7												12		44
	12	3	4[2]	5	9		8			11					6	10			2[1]				1			7[3]					13	14	45
1	2	3		5	6		8				4	11[2]			9[1]	12	10[3]									7				13		14	46

Worthington Cup

First Round	Birmingham C	(a)	0-3

FA Cup

First Round	Luton T	(h)	3-2
Second Round	Chesterfield	(a)	1-1
		(h)	2-0
Third Round	Tranmere R	(h)	1-3

STOCKPORT COUNTY — Division 2

FOUNDATION

Formed at a meeting held at Wellington Road South by members of Wycliffe Congregational Chapel in 1883, they called themselves Heaton Norris Rovers until changing to Stockport County in 1890, a year before joining the Football Combination.

Edgeley Park, Hardcastle Road, Stockport, Cheshire SK3 9DD.

Telephone: (0161) 286 8888. **Fax:** (0161) 286 8900.
Club Shop: (0161) 286 8899. **ClubCall:** 09068 121 638.
Website: www.stockportcounty.com

Ground Capacity: 10,817.

Record Attendance: 27,833 v Liverpool, FA Cup 5th rd, 11 February 1950.

Record Receipts: £181,449 v Middlesbrough, Coca-Cola Cup Semi-final 1st leg, 26 February 1997.

Pitch Measurements: 111yd × 72yd.

Hon. Vice-presidents: Freddie Pye, Andrew Barlow, Graham White.

Chairman: Brendan Elwood.

Directors: Mike Baker, Michael Rains, Brian Taylor.

Secretary: Gary Glendenning BA (HONS), FCCA.

Manager: Carlton Palmer. **Assistant Manager:** Kevin Richardson. **Physio:** Rodger Wylde.

Assistant Secretary: Andrea Dawson. **Commercial Manager:** John Rutter.
Marketing Manager: Steve Bellis. **Programme Editor:** Chris Jolley.

Year Formed: 1883.

Turned Professional: 1891. **Ltd Co.:** 1908.

Previous Names: 1883, Heaton Norris Rovers; 1888, Heaton Norris; 1890, Stockport County.

Club Nicknames: 'County' or 'Hatters'.

Colours: Royal blue shirts with white trim, royal blue shorts with white trim, white stockings with blue trim.

Change Colours: White shirts with black trim, black shorts with white trim, white stockings with black trim.

Previous Grounds: 1883 Heaton Norris Recreation Ground; 1884 Heaton Norris Wanderers Cricket Ground; 1885 Chorlton's Farm, Chorlton's Lane; 1886 Heaton Norris Cricket Ground; 1887 Wilkes' Field, Belmont Street; 1889 Nursery Inn, Green Lane; 1902 Edgeley Park.

First Football League Game: 1 September 1900, Division 2, v Leicester Fosse (a) D 2–2 – Moores; Earp, Wainwright; Pickford, Limond, Harvey; Stansfield, Smith (1), Patterson, Foster, Betteley (1).

Record League Victory: 13–0 v Halifax T, Division 3 (N), 6 January 1934 – McGann; Vincent (1p); Jenkinson; Robinson, Stevens, Len Jones; Foulkes (1), Hill (3), Lythgoe (2), Stevenson (2), Downes (4).

HONOURS

Football League: Division 1 best season: 8th, 1997–98; Division 2 – Runners-up 1996–97; Division 3 (N) – Champions 1921–22, 1936–37; Runners-up 1928–29, 1929-30, 1996–97; Division 4 – Champions 1966–67; Runners-up 1990–91.
FA Cup: best season: 5th rd, 1935, 1950, 2001.
Football League Cup: Semi-final 1997.
Autoglass Trophy: Runners-up 1992, 1993.

IT'S A FACT !

Chelsea's first Football League game was played at Stockport County on 2 September 1905 in Division Two. Stockport won 1-0 with a goal from Bob Manson.

Record Cup Victory: 5–0 v Lincoln C, FA Cup 1st rd, 11 November 1995 – Edwards; Connelly, Todd, Bennett, Flynn, Gannon (Dinning), Beaumont, Oliver, Ware, Eckhardt (3), Armstrong (1) (Mike), Chalk, (1 og).

Record Defeat: 1–8 v Chesterfield, Division 2, 19 April 1902.

Most League Points (2 for a win): 64, Division 4, 1966–67.

Most League Points (3 for a win): 85, Division 2, 1993–94.

Most League Goals: 115, Division 3 (N), 1933–34.

Highest League Scorer in Season: Alf Lythgoe, 46, Division 3 (N), 1933–34.

Most League Goals in Total Aggregate: Jack Connor, 132, 1951–56.

Most League Goals in One Match: 5, Joe Smith v Southport, Division 3N, 7 January 1928; 5, Joe Smith v Lincoln C, Division 3N, 15 September 1928; 5, Frank Newton v Nelson, Division 3N, 21 September 1929; 5, Alf Lythgoe v Southport, Division 3N, 25 August 1934; 5, Billy McNaughton v Mansfield T, Division 3N, 14 December 1935; 5, Jack Connor v Workington, Division 3N, 8 November 1952; 5, Jack Connor v Carlisle U, Division 3N, 7 April 1956.

Most Capped Player: Jarkko Wiss, 9 (36), Finland.

Most League Appearances: Andy Thorpe, 489, 1978–86, 1988–92.

Youngest League Player: Jimmy Collier, 16 years 227 days v Bristol R, 8 April 1969.

Record Transfer Fee Received: £1,600,000 from Middlesbrough for Alun Armstrong, February 1998.

Record Transfer Fee Paid: £800,000 to Nottingham F for Ian Moore, July 1998.

Football League Record: 1900 Elected to Division 2; 1904 Failed re-election; 1905–21 Division 2; 1921–22 Division 3 (N); 1922–26 Division 2; 1926–37 Division 3 (N); 1937–38 Division 2; 1938–58 Division 3 (N); 1958–59 Division 3; 1959–67 Division 4; 1967–70 Division 3; 1970–91 Division 4; 1991–92 Division 3; 1992–97 Division 2; 1997–2002 Division 1; 2002– Division 2.

LATEST SEQUENCES

Longest Sequence of League Wins: 8, 26.12.27 – 28.1.28.

Longest Sequence of League Defeats: 10, 24.11.01 – 13.01.02.

Longest Sequence of League Draws: 7, 17.3.89 – 14.4.89.

Longest Sequence of Unbeaten League Matches: 18, 28.1.33 – 28.8.33.

Longest Sequence Without a League Win: 19, 28.12.99 – 22.4.00.

MANAGERS

Fred Stewart 1894–1911
Harry Lewis 1911–14
David Ashworth 1914–19
Albert Williams 1919–24
Fred Scotchbrook 1924–26
Lincoln Hyde 1926–31
Andrew Wilson 1932–33
Fred Westgarth 1934–36
Bob Kelly 1936–38
George Hunt 1938–39
Bob Marshall 1939–49
Andy Beattie 1949–52
Dick Duckworth 1952–56
Billy Moir 1956–60
Reg Flewin 1960–63
Trevor Porteous 1963–65
Bert Trautmann
   (*General Manager*) 1965–66
Eddie Quigley (*Team Manager*) 1965–66
Jimmy Meadows 1966–69
Wally Galbraith 1969–70
Matt Woods 1970–71
Brian Doyle 1972–74
Jimmy Meadows 1974–75
Roy Chapman 1975–76
Eddie Quigley 1976–77
Alan Thompson 1977–78
Mike Summerbee 1978–79
Jimmy McGuigan 1979–82
Eric Webster 1982–85
Colin Murphy 1985
Les Chapman 1985–86
Jimmy Melia 1986
Colin Murphy 1986–87
Asa Hartford 1987–89
Danny Bergara 1989–95
Dave Jones 1995–97
Gary Megson 1997–99
Andy Kilner 1999–2001
Carlton Palmer November 2001–

TEN YEAR LEAGUE RECORD

		P	W	D	L	F	A	Pts	Pos
1991-92	Div 3	46	22	10	14	75	51	76	5
1992-93	Div 2	46	19	15	12	81	57	72	6
1993-94	Div 2	46	24	13	9	74	44	85	4
1994-95	Div 2	46	19	8	19	63	60	65	11
1995-96	Div 2	46	19	13	14	61	47	70	9
1996-97	Div 2	46	23	13	10	59	41	82	2
1997-98	Div 1	46	19	8	19	71	69	65	8
1998-99	Div 1	46	12	17	17	49	60	53	16
1999-2000	Div 1	46	13	15	18	55	67	54	17
2000-01	Div 1	46	11	18	17	58	65	51	19

DID YOU KNOW ?

When Shefki Kuqi came on as a 63rd minute substitute for Finland against England on 24 March 2001, it was the first time Stockport County had had two full internationals in one match. Jarkko Wiss was already on the pitch.

STOCKPORT COUNTY 2001–02 LEAGUE RECORD

Match No.	Date	Venue	Opponents	Result	H/T Score	Lg. Pos.	Goalscorers	Attendance
1	Aug 11	H	Coventry C	L	0-2	0-1	—		9329
2	18	A	Crystal Palace	L	1-4	0-0	24	Fradin [62]	15,760
3	25	H	Portsmouth	L	0-1	0-0	24		5090
4	27	A	Birmingham C	L	1-2	0-2	24	Kuqi (pen) [86]	18,478
5	Sept 8	A	Barnsley	D	2-2	0-0	24	Flynn [62], Taylor [90]	11,192
6	15	A	Wolverhampton W	D	2-2	1-0	24	Kuqi [24], Taylor [71]	20,742
7	18	H	Sheffield U	L	1-2	0-2	—	Roget (pen) [80]	5137
8	22	H	Grimsby T	D	3-3	2-1	23	Hardy 2 [3, 45], Wilbraham [69]	7834
9	25	A	Bradford C	W	4-2	1-1	—	Hurst 2 [12, 54], Taylor 2 [52, 84]	12,940
10	29	A	Nottingham F	L	1-2	0-2	22	Flynn [47]	17,584
11	Oct 13	H	Manchester C	D	2-2	0-0	24	Hurst [50], Kuqi (pen) [68]	34,214
12	16	H	WBA	L	1-2	0-1	—	Fradin [88]	6052
13	20	H	Rotherham U	L	0-1	0-1	24		6616
14	24	A	Crewe Alex	D	0-0	0-0	—		6679
15	27	H	Millwall	L	0-4	0-3	24		5371
16	30	H	Walsall	L	0-2	0-1	—		4553
17	Nov 3	A	Preston NE	L	0-6	0-3	24		13,776
18	10	A	Watford	D	1-1	0-0	24	Robinson (og) [80]	12,576
19	15	H	Norwich C	W	2-1	1-0	—	Hurst [28], Palmer [60]	6551
20	24	A	Sheffield W	L	0-5	0-1	24		17,365
21	27	H	Gillingham	L	0-2	0-1	—		4854
22	Dec 1	A	Crewe Alex	L	0-1	0-0	24		5308
23	8	H	Wimbledon	L	1-2	1-2	24	Wilbraham [42]	4673
24	15	A	Burnley	L	2-3	1-1	24	McSheffrey [11], Kuqi (pen) [90]	15,526
25	22	A	Portsmouth	L	0-2	0-0	24		13,887
26	26	H	Barnsley	L	1-3	0-1	24	Kuqi [83]	6885
27	29	A	Birmingham C	L	0-3	0-1	24		5827
28	Jan 1	A	WBA	L	0-4	0-2	24		20,541
29	13	H	Crystal Palace	L	0-1	0-0	24		5541
30	19	A	Coventry C	D	0-0	0-0	24		12,448
31	29	H	Gillingham	D	3-3	2-3	—	Beckett 2 [27, 39], Ross [47]	7217
32	Feb 2	H	Nottingham F	L	1-3	0-0	24	Palmer [87]	6513
33	9	A	Rotherham U	L	2-3	0-1	24	Hardiker [77], Delaney [86]	6413
34	23	H	Wolverhampton W	L	1-4	1-3	24	Beckett [33]	8481
35	26	A	Grimsby T	L	1-3	1-3	—	Palmer [42]	6836
36	Mar 2	A	Sheffield U	L	0-3	0-0	24		15,642
37	5	H	Bradford C	W	1-0	1-0	—	Beckett [11]	4148
38	9	H	Burnley	L	0-2	0-0	24		6410
39	16	A	Wimbledon	L	1-3	0-1	24	Daly [78]	5224
40	19	H	Manchester C	W	2-1	0-1	—	Hardiker 2 [85, 90]	9532
41	23	H	Preston NE	L	0-2	0-1	24		6139
42	30	A	Millwall	L	0-3	0-1	24		13,570
43	Apr 1	H	Watford	W	2-1	1-0	24	McLachlan [11], Beckett [59]	4086
44	6	A	Walsall	L	0-1	0-0	24		6322
45	13	H	Sheffield W	W	3-1	1-1	24	Wilbraham [10], Beckett 2 [51, 90]	8706
46	21	A	Norwich C	L	0-2	0-1	24		20,897

Final League Position: 24

GOALSCORERS

League (42): Beckett 7, Kuqi 5 (3 pens), Hurst 4, Taylor 4, Hardiker 3, Palmer 3, Wilbraham 3, Flynn 2, Fradin 2, Hardy 2, Daly 1, Delaney 1, McLachlan 1, McSheffrey 1, Roget 1 (pen), Ross 1, own goal 1.
Worthington Cup (4): Taylor 3, Kuqi 1.
FA Cup (1): Daly 1 (pen).

Jones L 21 + 3	Gibb A 40 + 1	Clark P 12 + 2	Roget L 20 + 2	Clare R 21 + 2	Hancock G — + 1	Woodthorpe C 22 + 12	Helin P 10 + 3	Kuqi S 15 + 3	Wilbraham A 19 + 2	Taylor S 19 + 9	Fradin K 18 + 2	Hurst G 12 + 3	Van Blerk J 13	Carratt P — + 2	Flynn M 26	Briggs K 30 + 2	Wiss J 7 + 4	Hardy N 4 + 6	Smith D 9 + 2	Wild P 1	Ross N 2 + 1	Arphexad P 3	Sandford L 7	McLachlan F 11	Turner S 4 + 2	Bryngelsson F 3	Flowers T 4	Byrne M 1 + 4	Welsh A 9 + 6	Daly J 11 + 2	Williams C 1 + 4	Palmer C 20 + 1	Lescott A 17	Spence J 1 + 1	Delaney D 10 + 2	Ellison K 6 + 5	Holt D — + 1	McSheffrey G 3 + 2	Beckett L 17 + 2	Dibble A 13	Challinor D 18	Hardiker J 11 + 1	Thomas A 7 + 3	Match No.
1	2	3	4	5	6		7	8	9	10¹	11	12																																1
1	2	12	4	5	6	7²	8	9	13	11			3¹	10																														2
1	7	12	4			8	9¹	10			3	5	2	6	13	11																												3
1	7		4	6	12	8	13	9³			3	5	2	10¹	14	11²																												4
1	7		4		12	8		9	10	13	3¹	5	2¹	14	11		6³																											5
1			4	2¹	3	6	8		9³	11	7		5		13		12	10²	14																									6
1	2		4	6¹	3	12	8³	9	10	11		5		13	14		7²																											7
1	2		4	12	3	6¹		9	13	10	7	5				11²	8																											8
1	2¹		4		12			9	13	10	7	3	5			8²	11	6																										9
	2		4		12		13	9	10	8	7	3¹	5		14		11³	6²		1																								10
	2			12	7	8³	9¹	14	10	11	3	5					13	4³		1	6																							11
15	2			12	7	13	9¹	10	8	11	3	5						4¹		1³	6																							12
1	2			12		8	13	9	10	11²	3¹	5	4			7					6																							13
	4			12	7	8	9	10	11		3	5									6	1	2¹																					14
	4			12	7³	8	9²	10	11¹		3	5			13						6		2	1	14																			15
	7					9	10¹				3	5	2³		12	11	13				6		4²	1	8	14																		16
	7	2	4			9¹	10		8	3	5				11						6		1	12																				17
	7	3	4		12		9²	10		11		5	2	8¹		6						15	1⁶		13																			18
1	7	3	4				9	10	11			2	8¹																	5	6	12												19
1	13		4		3		9	10	12	11		5	2	6³																14	8²	7¹												20
1	7		4		3		9²	10		12		5	2	8¹																13	11	6												21
1			4		3	12	13	10³		11		5	2¹																	8²	7	6	9	14										22
1	2		4		3	7	10	9¹	12			5																		11²	6	13	8											23
1	7		4		3	2	10					5	12																	6¹	9	8	11²	13									24
1	2	3	4			9		12			5	7¹																		6	11	8	13	10²									25
	2	3				9	8¹				5	7	6											1					11	4	12	10											26
	2	3¹	6		12			13			5	7												1				8	10	14	4²	11		9³									27
	2	3	4¹	12				13			5	7												1				8	10		6	11		9²									28
			4	3				13				7												9¹					5	10	11	8²		12	1	6						29
	2		4	3								7												9					12	5	8	11		10¹	1	6						30
15	7		12	5	3							4												9²					8	2	11		10¹	1	6						31
15	7		12	5¹	3							4												9²					8	2	11	13	10	1⁶	6						32
1	2²			6	14			12				7															3¹		9	8	11		10		5	13	4³				33
1			5				3	12	7		11															9	8		10	6	2	4¹			34
1			5	3			11			7														12	8	9	4¹		10	6²	2	13			35
1⁸	7		4	3			11²	13						8	15			9	5			10	6	2¹	12			36
	2		4¹	3			7	11		8					9	5		10	1	6	12			37
	7		3			11	12		8				9	5		10	1	6	4	2¹		38
	2		5	11			7	10¹		8	13	12	9			1	6	4	3¹		39
	2		4			7		8	13	12	9²	5		10	1	6	3	11¹		40
	2		4	12			7		8²	9	13	5		10	1	6	3	11¹		41
	2		4	3			7		8	11	9		10	1	5	6		42
	3	6¹	4	12			7		8	14	11²	9³	1	13	10	1	5	2		43
	3	6	4			7		8	11²	9¹	12	13	10	1	5	2		44
	7²	3	6		9	4		12		8	11	13	10	1	5	2¹		45
	2	6		4		7		8	12²	11	9	13	15	10¹	1	5	3⁶	46

Worthington Cup
First Round   Carlisle U   (h)   3-0
Second Round   Nottingham F   (a)   1-1

FA Cup
Third Round   Bolton W   (h)   1-4

STOKE CITY   Division 1

FOUNDATION

The date of the formation of this club has long been in doubt. The year 1863 was claimed, but more recent research by Wade Martin has uncovered nothing earlier than 1868, when a couple of Old Carthusians, who were apprentices at the local works of the old North Staffordshire Railway Company, met with some others from that works, to form Stoke Ramblers. It should also be noted that the old Stoke club went bankrupt in 1908 when a new club was formed.

Britannia Stadium, Stoke-on-Trent ST4 4EG.

Telephone: (01782) 592 222. *Fax:* (01782) 592 221.
Commercial Dept: (01782) 592 211.
Football in the Community: (01782) 592 255.
ClubCall: 09068 121 040.

Ground Capacity: 28,218.

Record Attendance: 51,380 v Arsenal, Division 1, 29 March 1937.

Record Receipts: £379,000 v Everton, FA Cup 3rd rd, 5 January 2002.

Pitch Measurements: 116yd × 72yd.

Vice-president: Stefan Geir Thorisson.

Chairman: Gunnar Thor Gislason.

Directors: Asgeir Sigurvinsson, Peter Coates, Keith Humphreys.

Chief Executive: Jonathan Fuller.

Manager: Steve Cotterill. *Physio:* Stefan Stefansson.

Stadium Manager/Safety Officer: J. Alcock.

HONOURS

Football League: Division 1 best season: 4th, 1935–36, 1946–47; Division 2 – Champions 1932–33, 1962–63, 1992–93; Runners-up 1921–22; Promoted 1978–79 (3rd), Promoted from Division 2 (play-offs) 2001–02; Division 3 (N) – Champions 1926–27.

FA Cup: Semi-finals 1899, 1971, 1972.

Football League Cup: Winners 1972.

Autoglass Trophy: Winners: 1992.

Auto Windscreens Shield: Winners: 2000.

European Competitions: UEFA Cup: 1972–73, 1974–75.

Colours: Red and white striped shirts, white shorts, red and white hooped stockings.

Change Colours: Blue shirts and shorts with red and white stripe on left hand side, white stockings with blue turnover.

Year Formed: 1863 *(see Foundation). Turned Professional:* 1885. *Ltd Co.:* 1908.

Previous Names: 1868, Stoke Ramblers; 1870, Stoke; 1925, Stoke City.

Club Nickname: 'The Potters'.

Previous Grounds: 1875, Sweeting's Field; 1878, Victoria Ground (previously known as the Athletic Club Ground); 1997, Britannia Stadium.

First Football League Game: 8 September 1888, Football League, v WBA (h) L 0–2 – Rowley; Clare, Underwood; Ramsey, Shutt, Smith; Sayer, McSkimming, Staton, Edge, Tunnicliffe.

Record League Victory: 10–3 v WBA, Division 1, 4 February 1937 – Doug Westland; Brigham, Harbot; Tutin, Turner (1p), Kirton; Matthews, Antonio (2), Freddie Steele (5), Jimmy Westland, Johnson (2).

IT'S A FACT !

Stoke City introduced a full matchday programme in the 1903–04 season. Although the price of one old penny was doubled shortly afterwards, it stayed at that price until after the Second World War.

Record Cup Victory: 7–1 v Burnley, FA Cup 2nd rd (replay), 20 February 1896 – Clawley; Clare, Eccles; Turner, Grewe, Robertson; Willie Maxwell, Dickson, A. Maxwell (3), Hyslop (4), Schofield.

Record Defeat: 0–10 v Preston NE, Division 1, 14 September 1889.

Most League Points (2 for a win): 63, Division 3 (N), 1926–27.

Most League Points (3 for a win): 93, Division 2, 1992–93.

Most League Goals: 92, Division 3 (N), 1926–27.

Highest League Scorer in Season: Freddie Steele, 33, Division 1, 1936–37.

Most League Goals in Total Aggregate: Freddie Steele, 142, 1934–49.

Most League Goals in One Match: 7, Neville Coleman v Lincoln C, Division 2, 23 February 1957.

Most Capped Player: Gordon Banks, 36 (73), England.

Most League Appearances: Eric Skeels, 506, 1958–76.

Youngest League Player: Peter Bullock, 16 years 163 days v Swansea C, 19 April 1958.

Record Transfer Fee Received: £2,750,000 from QPR for Mike Sheron, July 1997.

Record Transfer Fee Paid: £600,000 to Orgryte for Brynjar Gunnarsson, December 1999.

Football League Record: 1888 Founder Member of Football League; 1890 Not re-elected; 1891 Re-elected; relegated in 1907, and after one year in Division 2, resigned for financial reasons; 1919 re-elected to Division 2; 1922–23 Division 1; 1923–26 Division 2; 1926–27 Division 3 (N); 1927–33 Division 2; 1933–53 Division 1; 1953–63 Division 2; 1963–77 Division 1; 1977–79 Division 2; 1979–85 Division 1; 1985–90 Division 2; 1990–92 Division 3; 1992–93 Division 2; 1993–98 Division 1; 1998–2002 Division 2; 2002– Division 1.

MANAGERS

Tom Slaney 1874–83
  (Secretary-Manager)
Walter Cox 1883–84
  (Secretary-Manager)
Harry Lockett 1884–90
Joseph Bradshaw 1890–92
Arthur Reeves 1892–95
William Rowley 1895–97
H. D. Austerberry 1897–1908
A. J. Barker 1908–14
Peter Hodge 1914–15
Joe Schofield 1915–19
Arthur Shallcross 1919–23
John 'Jock' Rutherford 1923
Tom Mather 1923–35
Bob McGrory 1935–52
Frank Taylor 1952–60
Tony Waddington 1960–77
George Eastham 1977–78
Alan A'Court 1978
Alan Durban 1978–81
Richie Barker 1981–83
Bill Asprey 1984–85
Mick Mills 1985–89
Alan Ball 1989–91
Lou Macari 1991–93
Joe Jordan 1993–94
Lou Macari 1994–97
Chic Bates 1997–98
Chris Kamara 1998
Brian Little 1998–99
Gary Megson 1999
Gudjon Thordarson 1999–2002
Steve Cotterill May 2002–

LATEST SEQUENCES

Longest Sequence of League Wins: 8, 30.3.1895 – 21.9.1895.

Longest Sequence of League Defeats: 11, 6.4.85 – 17.8.85.

Longest Sequence of League Draws: 5, 21.3.87 – 11.4.87.

Longest Sequence of Unbeaten League Matches: 25, 5.9.92 – 20.2.93.

Longest Sequence Without a League Win: 17, 22.4.89 – 14.10.89.

TEN YEAR LEAGUE RECORD

		P	W	D	L	F	A	Pts	Pos
1991-92	Div 3	46	21	14	11	69	49	77	4
1992-93	Div 2	46	27	12	7	73	34	93	1
1993-94	Div 1	46	18	13	15	57	59	67	10
1994-95	Div 1	46	16	15	15	50	53	63	11
1995-96	Div 1	46	20	13	13	60	49	73	4
1996-97	Div 1	46	18	10	18	51	57	64	12
1997-98	Div 1	46	11	13	22	44	74	46	23
1998-99	Div 2	46	21	6	19	59	63	69	8
1999-2000	Div 2	46	23	13	10	68	42	82	6
2000-01	Div 2	46	21	14	11	74	49	77	5

DID YOU KNOW ?

For their successful League Cup Final appearance in 1972, Stoke City had a song *We'll be with you*, written by Jackie Trent and Tony Hatch, and recorded by The Potters.

STOKE CITY 2001–02 LEAGUE RECORD

Match No.	Date	Venue	Opponents	Result	H/T Score	Lg. Pos.	Goalscorers	Attendance
1	Aug 11	A	QPR	L	0-1	0-1	—	14,357
2	18	H	Northampton T	W	2-0	0-0	9	Cooke [52], Thorne [54]	12,845
3	25	A	Cambridge U	W	2-0	0-0	7	Thorne [48], Cooke [51]	3336
4	27	H	Tranmere R	L	1-2	0-1	10	Thorne (pen) [90]	12,031
5	Sept 8	H	Huddersfield T	D	1-1	0-1	14	Thorne [90]	13,319
6	15	H	Reading	W	2-0	2-0	9	Gudjonsson [25], Cooke [30]	11,752
7	18	A	Brighton & HA	L	0-1	0-0	—		6627
8	22	A	Bury	W	1-0	1-0	10	Van Doerzen [32]	4727
9	26	H	Colchester U	W	3-0	1-0	—	Van Doerzen [45], Thordarson 2 [57, 90]	9515
10	29	H	Bournemouth	W	2-0	1-0	5	Maher (og) [11], Thomas [47]	14,803
11	Oct 13	H	Notts Co	W	1-0	0-0	5	Hoekstra (pen) [47]	13,220
12	21	A	Port Vale	D	1-1	0-0	4	Iwelumo [78]	10,344
13	23	A	Chesterfield	W	2-1	0-0	—	Hoekstra 2 (1 pen) [67, 90 (p)]	5141
14	27	H	Bristol C	W	1-0	0-0	3	Gunnarsson [88]	16,828
15	Nov 3	A	Swindon T	W	3-0	1-0	3	Gunnarsson [28], Iwelumo [65], O'Connor [86]	7981
16	6	A	Blackpool	D	2-2	0-0	—	Iwelumo 2 [63, 64]	4921
17	10	H	Brentford	W	3-2	1-1	3	Gunnarsson [32], Iwelumo [49], Shtanyuk [80]	17,953
18	13	A	Wigan Ath	L	1-6	1-3	—	Van Doerzen [6]	7047
19	21	H	Oldham Ath	D	0-0	0-0	—	—	11,031
20	24	A	Wrexham	W	1-0	0-0	2	Cooke [67]	5477
21	Dec 15	H	Wycombe W	W	5-1	3-1	1	Gunnarsson 2 [19, 44], Iwelumo [30], Cooke [58], Goodfellow [85]	12,911
22	19	H	Cardiff C	D	1-1	0-0	—	Gabbidon (og) [77]	14,331
23	26	A	Tranmere R	D	2-2	1-1	2	Cooke [19], Dadason (pen) [90]	12,201
24	29	A	Huddersfield T	D	0-0	0-0	2		16,041
25	Jan 1	H	Blackpool	W	2-0	1-0	1	Shtanyuk [13], O'Connor [82]	16,615
26	13	A	Northampton T	D	1-1	1-0	3	Goodfellow [36]	5636
27	19	H	QPR	L	0-1	0-0	3		16,725
28	22	A	Cardiff C	L	0-2	0-1	—		11,771
29	26	H	Wigan Ath	D	2-2	1-2	4	Goodfellow [37], Dadason (pen) [67]	13,361
30	29	A	Peterborough U	W	2-1	1-1	—	Dadason [21], Goodfellow [90]	5173
31	Feb 2	A	Bournemouth	L	1-3	0-2	3	Dadason (pen) [63]	6027
32	6	H	Cambridge U	W	5-0	2-0	—	Cooke [22], Gudjonsson [27], Thordarson [61], Tann (og) [71], Goodfellow [89]	9570
33	10	H	Port Vale	L	0-1	0-1	3		23,019
34	16	A	Notts Co	D	0-0	0-0	4		7501
35	23	A	Reading	L	0-1	0-0	5		21,032
36	26	H	Bury	W	4-0	1-0	—	Iwelumo 2 [45, 56], Van Doerzen [73], Thordarson [84]	9635
37	Mar 1	H	Brighton & HA	W	3-1	1-0	—	Iwelumo [29], Gunnlaugsson (pen) [58], Clarke [86]	16,092
38	5	A	Colchester U	W	3-1	2-0	—	Gudjonsson [42], Burton 2 [45, 80]	3866
39	9	A	Wycombe W	L	0-1	0-0	4		7344
40	16	A	Peterborough U	W	1-0	1-0	4	Gunnlaugsson [10]	12,983
41	23	H	Chesterfield	W	1-0	1-0	4	Gunnlaugsson [23]	14,841
42	30	A	Brentford	L	0-1	0-0	4		8837
43	Apr 1	H	Swindon T	W	2-0	0-0	4	Thomas [60], Iwelumo [68]	13,530
44	6	A	Oldham Ath	L	1-2	0-1	4	Holden (og) [63]	6548
45	13	H	Wrexham	W	1-0	1-0	5	Cooke [30]	14,298
46	20	A	Bristol C	D	1-1	1-0	5	Cooke [16]	11,277

Final League Position: 5

GOALSCORERS

League (67): Iwelumo 10, Cooke 9, Goodfellow 5, Gunnarsson 5, Dadason 4 (3 pens), Thordarson 4, Thorne 4 (1 pen), Van Deurzen 4, Gudjonsson 3, Gunnlaugsson 3 (1 pen), Hoekstra 3 (2 pens), Burton 2, O'Connor 2, Shtanyuk 2, Thomas 2, Clarke 1, own goals 4.
Worthington Cup (0).
FA Cup (6): Gunnarsson 2, Cooke 1, Gudjohnson 1, Handyside 1, Iwelumo 1.

Ward G 10	Thomas W 40	Clarke C 42 + 1	Handyside P 34	Shtanyuk S 40	Van Deurzen J 37 + 3	Gudjonsson B 46	O'Connor J 43	Cooke A 26 + 9	Thorne P 5	Hoekstra P 20 + 4	Rowson D 8 + 5	Iwelumo C 22 + 16	Goodfellow M 11 + 12	Thordarson S 3 + 18	Henry K 9 + 15	Gunnarsson B 21 + 2	Cutler N 36	Neal L 6 + 5	Smart A — + 2	Dadason R 6 + 5	Flynn M 11 + 2	Oulare S — + 1	Wilson B — + 1	Marteinsson P 2 + 1	Burton D 11 + 1	Gunnlaugsson A 9	Brightwell I 3 + 1	Dinning T 5	Miles J — + 1	Match No.
1	2	3^1	4	5	6	7	8	9^2	10	11	12	13																		1
1	2		4	5	3	6	7	9^1	10	11^3	8		12	13																2
1	2	12	4	5	3	6	8	9^3	10^1	11^1	7		14	13																3
1	2	3	4	5	6	7	8	9^3	10	11^1		12		13																4
1	2	3			6	7	8	9	10	11^2		12		13	4^1	5														5
1	2	3	4	5	10	7	8	9^1		11		12				6														6
1	2	3	4	5	10	7	8	9		11		12				6														7
	2	3	4	5	10	7	8	9		11^1		12^2		13	14	6^3	1													8
	2	3	4	5	10	7	8	9			11	12				6^1	1													9
	2	3	4	5	10	7	8	9^1		12		11	13			6^2	1													10
1	2	3	4	5	10	7	8	9^1		11		12				6														11
	2	3	4	5	10^2	7	8	9		11^1		12				6	1	13												12
	2^2	3	4	5	10^1	7	8	12		11		9		13		6	1													13
	2^2	3^1	4	5	10	7	8	12		11		9^1		13		6	1	14												14
	2^2	3	4	5		7	8	12		11^1		9		13		6	1	10												15
		3	4	5	10	7	8	9			12	11		2^1		6	1													16
	2	3	4	5	10	7		12		11	13	9^2				6	1	8^1												17
	2	3	4	5	10	7		11	6^1	9						6	1		12											18
1	2^2	3	4	5	10^1	7	8	12		11^3		6						13	14											19
1	2	3	4	5	10^1	7	8	9		11	12					6														20
	2	3^1	4	5	11	7	8	9				10^2	12			6	1				13									21
	2	3	4	5	11^1	7	8	9				10^2	12			6	1				13									22
5	3	4				7	8	9				10^2	12		2	6	1	11^1			13									23
	2	3	4	5	11^1	7	8	9^2				10	12		13	6^2		14												24
4	3		5	6	7	8	9^1					12	10^2	11	2		1	14												25
	5	3			7	8		9^1				12	10	9	6^1		1	12			11^1	4	13							26
		3			5	6^1	7	8	9			2	12	10			1				11	4								27
	2	3			5	11^1	7^2	8	9			8	10	12		13	1				4		13							28
	2	3			5	10^2	7			11^3	6^1	12	9	14			1			6^2	10^1	4	11^3							29
	2	3			5	7	8	12				13^3	9	14			1			6^2	10^1	4	11^3							30
	2^2	3			5	13	7	8	12			9	14				1			6^1	10	4	11^3							31
	2	3			5	6^3	7^1	8	9			10^3	11	13	12		1			4	14									32
	2	3			5	6^2	7	8	9			12	11	14	13		1							10^3	4^1					33
	3	4	5	6^1	7	8	9					12	10^2	13	2		1					11								34
	2	3	4	5		7	8	12				13		14		11	1							6^2	9^1	10^3				35
	2	3	4^3	5	6	7	8					11^2	13				1				14				9^1	10^1				36
	2	3	4	5	6	7	8					11^3	14		13	1	1								9^2	10^1				37
	2^3	3	4	5	6	7	8					11^3	14		12	1	1					13			9^1	10^1				38
	2	3				6	7	8	12^2			11^3	13	14		5	1					4			9^1	10^1				39
	2	3				6	7	8				4^2	11	12	14	13	5	1							9^1	10^3				40
	2	3	4		12	7^3	8					13	14		11	6^1	5^1	1							9^1	10^2				41
5	3	4			7	8				11^1		13	12				1								9	10	2^2	6		42
	2	3	4	5		7	8			11^1		12	13	14			1								9^1	10^2		6		43
	2	3^1	4	5	10^3	7^2	8					11	13	12			1								9		14	6		44
	3^1	4	5	12	7	8	9					13	11		14		1								10^2		2	6^3		45
		4	5	3	7^3	8	9^2					10	11		12		1								13		2^1	6	14	46

Worthington Cup

First Round	Oldham Ath	(h)	0-0

FA Cup

First Round (at Stoke)	Lewes	(a)	2-0
Second Round	Halifax T	(a)	1-1
		(h)	3-0
Third Round	Everton	(h)	0-1

SUNDERLAND   FA Premiership

FOUNDATION

A Scottish schoolmaster named James Allan, working at Hendon Board School, took the initiative in the foundation of Sunderland in 1879 when they were formed as The Sunderland and District Teachers' Association FC at a meeting in the Adults School, Norfolk Street. Due to financial difficulties, they quickly allowed members from outside the teaching profession and so became Sunderland AFC in October 1880.

Sunderland Stadium of Light, Sunderland, Tyne and Wear SR5 1SU.
Telephone: (0191) 551 5000. *Fax:* (0191) 551 5123.
Website: www.safc.com
ClubCall: 09068 121 140. *Ticket Office:* (0191) 551 5151.
Club Shop: (0191) 551 5050.
Tour Hotline: (0191) 551 5055.
Ground Capacity: 48,353
Record Attendance: Stadium of Light: 48,353 v Liverpool, FA Premier League, 13 April 2002. FA Premier League figure (46,062). Roker Park: 75,118 v Derby Co, FA Cup 6th rd replay, 8 March 1933.
Record Receipts: £862,840 v Manchester U, FA Premier League, 13 October 2001.
Pitch Measurements: 105m × 68m.
Chairman: R. S. Murray. *Vice-chairman:* John Fickling.
Directors: Jim Slater, Lesley Callaghan, Mark Blackbourne, Peter Walker.
Associate Directors: G. S. Wood, J. G. Wood.
Manager: Peter Reid. *Assistant Manager:* Adrian Heath.
Player-First Team Coach: Niall Quinn. *Reserve Team Manager:* Ricky Sbragia.
Physio: Mark Leather.
Community Programme Officer: Bob Oates.
Secretary: Jane Purdon.
Marketing Director: Jim Slater.
Safety Officer: John Davidson.
Colours: Red and white striped shirts, black shorts, black stockings.
Change Colours: Baltic blue shirt with white trim, white shorts with baltic blue piping, baltic blue stockings with white trim.
Year Formed: 1879.
Turned Professional: 1886. *Ltd Co.:* 1906.
Previous Name: 1879, Sunderland and District Teacher's AFC; 1880, Sunderland.
Previous Grounds: 1879, Blue House Field, Hendon; 1882, Groves Field, Ashbrooke; 1883, Horatio Street; 1884, Abbs Field, Fulwell; 1886, Newcastle Road; 1898, Roker Park; 1997, Stadium of Light.

HONOURS

Football League: Division 1 – Champions 1891–92, 1892–93, 1894–95, 1901–02, 1912–13, 1935–36, 1995–96, 1998–99; Runners-up 1893–94, 1897–98, 1900–01, 1922–23, 1934–35; Division 2 – Champions 1975–76; Runners-up 1963–64, 1979–80; Division 3 – Champions 1987–88.

FA Cup: Winners 1937, 1973; Runners-up 1913, 1992.

Football League Cup: Runners-up 1985.

European Competitions: European Cup-Winners' Cup: 1973–74.

IT'S A FACT !

On 27 January 1951, Sunderland had to borrow a set of Newcastle United's black and white striped shirts for their fourth round FA Cup tie with Southampton. They won 2-0 with a brace of goals from Dickie Davis.

First Football League Game: 13 September 1890, Football League, v Burnley (h) L 2–3 – Kirtley; Porteous, Oliver; Wilson, Auld, Gibson; Spence (1), Miller, Campbell (1), Scott, D. Hannah.

Record League Victory: 9–1 v Newcastle U (a), Division 1, 5 December 1908 – Roose; Forster, Melton; Daykin, Thomson, Low; Mordue (1), Hogg (3), Brown, Holley (3), Bridgett (2).

Record Cup Victory: 11–1 v Fairfield, FA Cup 1st rd, 2 February 1895 – Doig; McNeill, Johnston; Dunlop, McCreadie (1), Wilson; Gillespie (1), Millar (5), Campbell, Hannah (3), Scott (1).

Record Defeat: 0–8 v Sheff Wed, Division 1, 26 December 1911. 0–8 v West Ham U, Division 1, 19 October 1968. 0–8 v Watford, Division 1, 25 September 1982.

Most League Points (2 for a win): 61, Division 2, 1963–64.

Most League Points (3 for a win): 105, Division 1, 1998–99 (Football League Record).

Most League Goals: 109, Division 1, 1935–36.

Highest League Scorer in Season: Dave Halliday, 43, Division 1, 1928–29.

Most League Goals in Total Aggregate: Charlie Buchan, 209, 1911–25.

Most League Goals in One Match: 5, Charlie Buchan v Liverpool, Division 1, 7 December 1919; 5, Bobby Gurney v Bolton W, Division 1, 7 December 1935; 5, Dominic Sharkey v Norwich C, Division 2, 20 February 1962.

Most Capped Player: Charlie Hurley, 38 (40), Republic of Ireland.

Most League Appearances: Jim Montgomery, 537, 1962–77.

Youngest League Player: Derek Forster, 15 years 184 days v Leicester C, 22 August 1964.

Record Transfer Fee Received: £5,600,000 from Leeds U for Michael Bridges, July 1999.

Record Transfer Fee Paid: £4,500,000 to Chelsea for Emerson Thome, September 2000 and £4,500,000 to Rangers for Claudio Reyna, December 2001.

Football League Record: 1890 Elected to Division 1; 1958–64 Division 2; 1964–70 Division 1; 1970–76 Division 2; 1976–77 Division 1; 1977–80 Division 2; 1980–85 Division 1; 1985–87 Division 2; 1987–88 Division 3; 1988–90 Division 2; 1990–91 Division 1; 1991–92 Division 2; 1992–96 Division 1; 1996–97 FA Premier League; 1997–99 Division 1; 1999– FA Premier League.

MANAGERS

Tom Watson 1888–96
Bob Campbell 1896–99
Alex Mackie 1899–1905
Bob Kyle 1905–28
Johnny Cochrane 1928–39
Bill Murray 1939–57
Alan Brown 1957–64
George Hardwick 1964–65
Ian McColl 1965–68
Alan Brown 1968–72
Bob Stokoe 1972–76
Jimmy Adamson 1976–78
Ken Knighton 1979–81
Alan Durban 1981–84
Len Ashurst 1984–85
Lawrie McMenemy 1985–87
Denis Smith 1987–91
Malcolm Crosby 1992–93
Terry Butcher 1993
Mick Buxton 1993–95
Peter Reid March 1995–

LATEST SEQUENCES

Longest Sequence of League Wins: 13, 14.11.1891 – 2.4.1892.

Longest Sequence of League Defeats: 9, 23.11.76 – 15.1.77.

Longest Sequence of League Draws: 6, 26.3.49 – 19.4.49.

Longest Sequence of Unbeaten League Matches: 19, 3.5.98 – 14.11.98.

Longest Sequence Without a League Win: 14, 16.4.85 – 14.9.85.

TEN YEAR LEAGUE RECORD

		P	W	D	L	F	A	Pts	Pos
1991-92	Div 2	46	14	11	21	61	65	53	18
1992-93	Div 1	46	13	11	22	50	64	50	21
1993-94	Div 1	46	19	8	19	54	57	65	12
1994-95	Div 1	46	12	18	16	41	45	54	20
1995-96	Div 1	46	22	17	7	59	33	83	1
1996-97	PR Lge	38	10	10	18	35	53	40	18
1997-98	Div 1	46	26	12	8	86	50	90	3
1998-99	Div 1	46	31	12	3	91	28	105	1
1999-2000	PR Lge	38	16	10	12	57	56	58	7
2000-01	PR Lge	38	15	12	11	46	41	57	7

DID YOU KNOW ?

Despite taking only two points from their opening seven League matches in 1912–13, Sunderland went on to win the First Division Championship and also to reach the FA Cup Final.

SUNDERLAND 2001–02 LEAGUE RECORD

Match No.	Date	Venue	Opponents	Result		H/T Score	Lg. Pos.	Goalscorers	Attendance
1	Aug 18	H	Ipswich T	W	1-0	1-0	—	Phillips (pen) [38]	45,173
2	22	A	Fulham	L	0-2	0-0	—		20,197
3	26	A	Newcastle U	D	1-1	1-1	10	Phillips [34]	52,021
4	Sept 8	H	Blackburn R	W	1-0	0-0	6	Quinn [81]	43,028
5	16	A	Aston Villa	D	0-0	0-0	7		31,668
6	19	H	Tottenham H	L	1-2	0-1	—	Phillips [79]	43,599
7	22	H	Charlton Ath	D	2-2	0-1	8	Quinn 2 [74, 77]	44,478
8	29	A	Bolton W	W	2-0	0-0	7	Phillips [77], Craddock [83]	24,520
9	Oct 13	H	Manchester U	L	1-3	0-1	9	Phillips [83]	47,433
10	22	A	Middlesbrough	L	0-2	0-2	—		28,422
11	27	H	Arsenal	D	1-1	0-1	13	Schwarz [54]	45,989
12	Nov 3	A	Leicester C	L	0-1	0-0	16		20,573
13	18	H	Leeds U	W	2-0	0-0	13	Arca [48], Phillips [55]	46,017
14	25	A	Liverpool	L	0-1	0-1	13		43,537
15	Dec 1	H	West Ham U	W	1-0	0-0	13	Phillips [85]	45,367
16	9	H	Chelsea	D	0-0	0-0	13		44,907
17	15	A	Southampton	L	0-2	0-1	13		29,459
18	22	H	Everton	W	1-0	0-0	11	Reyna [77]	42,486
19	26	A	Blackburn R	W	3-0	2-0	9	Quinn 2 [17, 32], Kilbane [90]	29,869
20	29	A	Ipswich T	L	0-5	0-4	10		24,546
21	Jan 1	H	Aston Villa	D	1-1	0-0	10	Emerson [86]	41,672
22	12	A	Everton	L	0-1	0-1	12		30,736
23	19	H	Fulham	D	1-1	0-1	11	Phillips [67]	41,305
24	29	H	Middlesbrough	L	0-1	0-1	—		41,955
25	Feb 2	A	Manchester U	L	1-4	1-4	15	Phillips [12]	67,587
26	9	A	Derby Co	W	1-0	0-0	11	Quinn [80]	31,771
27	24	H	Newcastle U	L	0-1	0-0	14		47,204
28	Mar 2	A	Tottenham H	L	1-2	1-1	14	Mboma [45]	36,062
29	5	H	Bolton W	W	1-0	1-0	—	McAteer [42]	39,730
30	16	A	Chelsea	L	0-4	0-1	14		40,223
31	23	H	Southampton	D	1-1	0-0	15	McAteer [62]	42,799
32	30	A	Arsenal	L	0-3	0-3	16		38,047
33	Apr 1	H	Leicester C	W	2-1	2-1	14	Reyna 2 [3, 18]	40,862
34	7	A	Leeds U	L	0-2	0-1	15		39,195
35	13	H	Liverpool	L	0-1	0-0	15		46,062
36	20	A	West Ham U	L	0-3	0-1	17		33,319
37	27	A	Charlton Ath	D	2-2	2-1	17	Kilbane [2], Phillips [11]	26,606
38	May 11	H	Derby Co	D	1-1	1-0	17	Phillips [17]	47,989

Final League Position: 17

GOALSCORERS

League (29): Phillips 11 (1 pen), Quinn 6, Reyna 3, Kilbane 2, McAteer 2, Arca 1, Craddock 1, Emerson 1, Mboma 1, Schwarz 1.
Worthington Cup (2): Laslandes 1, Phillips 1.
FA Cup (1): Phillips 1.

Sorensen T 34	Haas B 27	Gray M 35	McCann G 29	Craddock J 30	Emerson 12	Schwarz S 18 + 2	Arca J 20 + 2	Laslandes L 5 + 7	Phillips K 37	Kilbane K 24 + 4	Rae A 1 + 2	Quinn N 24 + 14	McCartney G 12 + 6	Bellion D — + 9	Hutchison D 2	Macho J 4	Williams D 23 + 5	Varga S 9	Thirlwell P 11 + 3	McAteer J 26	Butler T 2 + 5	Reyna C 17	Kyle K — + 6	Bjorklund J 11 + 1	Mboma P 5 + 4	Match No.
1	2	3	4	5	6	7	8^1	9^1	10	11	12	13														1
1	2	3	4	5		7^2		9^1	10	11		12	6	13	8											2
1	2	3	4	5	6	7^1			10	11	12	9		13	8^2											3
1	2	3	4	5		7	8	9^1	10	12	11^1	13	6													4
	2	3	4	5		7	8	12	10	11		9^1	6				1									5
	2	3	4	5		7	8	12	10	11^1		9	6^2				1	13								6
	2	3	4	5		7	8	11	10			9					1	6								7
1		3	4	5		7	8		10	11		9					2	6								8
1		3		5		7	8		10	11^1		9		12			2	6	4							9
1	2	3	4	5		11^2	8	12	10			9^1		13			6		7							10
1	2^1	3	10^2	5	6	11	8		9			12					13	4	7							11
1	2	3	10	5^2	6	11	8		9			12	13				4^1		7							12
1	2	3	4		6		8	12	10			9^1	13				5		11	7^2						13
1	2	3	4		6		8^3	12	10			9	13				5^2		11^1	7	14					14
1	2	3	4		6		8	12	10			9^1					5		11	7^2	13					15
1		2	4		6		8	9^1	10	11		12	3				5		7							16
1	2	3	4	5				12	9	11^1		13					6		8^1	7	10					17
1	2	3	4		6		8		10			9^1					5		7	11	12					18
1	2	3	4		6		8^1		10	12		9^2					5		7	11	13					19
1	2	3^2	4		6		8		10	12		9^2	13				5		7^1	11	14					20
1	2	3	4		6		8		10			9					5		12	7	11^1					21
1	2	3	4	5			8^2		9	11		12		13					6	10	7^1					22
1	2	3	4^1	5			8		10	11		9					12	6		7						23
1	2^2	3		5		4	12		10	11		9	13						6	7^1	8					24
	2^3	3		5			13		9	11		12	14			1	10	6^2		7	8		4			25
1	2	3		5		4	8^1		10			9^3	12				13		7	11	14	6^2				26
1	2	3		5		4^1			10	11		9^2							7	12	8	6^1		13		27
1	2	3		5		12			10	11		13	4				14		7		8^3	6^1			9^2	28
1	2	3		5		8			10	11		12	6				4		7						9^1	29
1	2	3	4	5		6^2				11		12	10	13			6		7^1						9	30
1		3	4	5					10	11^2		12	6^3				2		13	7		8		14	9^1	31
1		3	4	5					10^1			12	13				2		11	7^3	14	8		6	9^2	32
1		3	4	5					10	11		9					2		12	7	8^1	6				33
1			4	5					10^2	11		9	3	12			2^1			7	8	6			13	34
1			4	5					10	11		9	3				2				8		12	6		35
1			4	5		12			10^1	11		9^2	3				2		7^3	14	8			13	6	36
1		3^1		5					10^2	11		9		12			2			8	7	4		6	13	37
1		3		5					10	11		9^1					2			7	4	8		6	12	38

Worthington Cup
Second Round   Sheffield W   (a)   2-4

FA Cup
Third Round   WBA   (h)   1-2

SWANSEA CITY

Division 3

FOUNDATION

The earliest Association Football in Wales was played in the Northern part of the country and no international took place in the South until 1894, when a local paper still thought it necessary to publish an outline of the rules and an illustration of the pitch markings. There had been an earlier Swansea club, but this has no connection with Swansea Town (now City) formed at a public meeting in June 1912.

Vetch Field, Swansea SA1 3SU.
Telephone: (01792) 633 400. *Fax:* (01792) 646 120.
ClubCall: 09068 121 639. *Website:* www.swanseacity.net
Email: swans.prom@btinternet.com
Club Shop: (01792) 633 425.
Commercial Department: (01792) 633 422.
Youth Development: (01792) 633 410.

Ground Capacity: 10,402.

Record Attendance: 32,796 v Arsenal, FA Cup 4th rd,
17 February 1968.

Record Receipts: £36,477.42 v Liverpool, Division 1,
18 September 1982.

Pitch Measurements: 112yd × 74yd.

Directors: David Morgan, Leigh Dineen, Brian Katzen,
Hugh Jenkins, Don Keefe, Steve Penny.

Player-Coach: Nick Cusack.

Assistant Coach: Alan Curtis.

Physio: Richard Evans.

Youth Development Officer: Wayne Powell.

Football Development Officer: Lyndon Jones.

Club Secretary: Jackie Rockey.

Commercial Manager: Dianne Griffiths.

Safety Officer: John Morgan.

Programme Editor: Colin Jones (01792) 633 419.

Colours: All white with black trim.

Change Colours: All yellow with black trim.

Year Formed: 1912. *Turned Professional:* 1912. *Ltd Co.:* 1912.

Previous Name: Swansea Town until February 1970. *Club Nicknames:* 'The Swans', 'The Jacks'.

First Football League Game: 28 August 1920, Division 3, v Portsmouth (a) L 0–3 – Crumley; Robson, Evans; Smith, Holdsworth, Williams; Hole, I. Jones, Edmundson, Rigsby, Spottiswood.

Record League Victory: 8–0 v Hartlepool U, Division 4, 1 April 1978 – Barber; Evans, Bartley, Lally (1) (Morris), May, Bruton, Kevin Moore, Robbie James (3 incl. 1p), Curtis (3), Toshack (1), Chappell.

HONOURS

Football League: Division 1 best season: 6th, 1981–82; Division 2 – Promoted 1980–81 (3rd); Division 3 (S) – Champions 1924–25, 1948–49; Division 3 – Champions 1999–2000; Promoted 1978–79 (3rd); Division 4 – Promoted 1969–70 (3rd), 1977–78 (3rd), 1987–88 (play-offs).

FA Cup: Semi-finals 1926, 1964.

Football League Cup: best season: 4th rd. 1965, 1977.

Welsh Cup: Winners 9 times; Runners-up 8 times.

Autoglass Trophy: Winners 1994.

European Competitions: European Cup-Winners' Cup: 1961–62, 1966–67, 1981–82, 1982–83, 1983–84, 1989–90, 1991–92.

IT'S A FACT !

On 9 January 1915, the then Swansea Town, a Southern League team at the time, beat League champions Blackburn Rovers 1-0 in a first round FA Cup tie.

Record Cup Victory: 12–0 v Sliema W (Malta), ECWC
1st rd 1st leg, 15 September 1982 – Davies; Marustik,
Hadziabdic (1), Irwin (1), Kennedy, Rajkovic (1),
Loveridge (2) (Leighton James), Robbie James, Charles (2),
Stevenson (1), Latchford (1) (Walsh (3)).

Record Defeat: 0–8 v Liverpool, FA Cup 3rd rd, 9 January
1990. 0–8 v Monaco, ECWC, 1st rd 2nd leg, 1 October 1991.

Most League Points (2 for a win): 62, Division 3 (S),
1948–49.

Most League Points (3 for a win): 85, Division 3,
1999–2000.

Most League Goals: 90, Division 2, 1956–57.

Highest League Scorer in Season: Cyril Pearce, 35,
Division 2, 1931–32.

Most League Goals in Total Aggregate: Ivor Allchurch,
166, 1949–58, 1965–68.

Most League Goals in One Match: 5, Jack Fowler v
Charlton Ath, Division 3S, 27 December 1924.

Most Capped Player: Ivor Allchurch, 42 (68), Wales.

Most League Appearances: Wilfred Milne, 585, 1919–37.

Youngest League Player: Nigel Dalling, 15 years 289 days v
Southport, 6 December 1974.

Record Transfer Fee Received: £400,000 from Bristol C for
Steve Torpey, August 1997.

Record Transfer Fee Paid: £340,000 to Liverpool for
Colin Irwin, August 1981.

Football League Record: 1920 Original Member of
Division 3; 1921–25 Division 3 (S); 1925–47 Division 2;
1947–49 Division 3 (S); 1949–65 Division 2; 1965–67
Division 3; 1967–70 Division 4; 1970–73 Division 3; 1973–78
Division 4; 1978–79 Division 3; 1979–81 Division 2; 1981–83
Division 1; 1983–84 Division 2; 1984–86 Division 3; 1986–88 Division 4; 1988–92 Division 3; 1992–96
Division 2; 1996–2000 Division 3; 2000–01 Division 2; 2001– Division 3.

MANAGERS

Walter Whittaker 1912–14
William Bartlett 1914–15
Joe Bradshaw 1919–26
Jimmy Thomson 1927–31
Neil Harris 1934–39
Haydn Green 1939–47
Bill McCandless 1947–55
Ron Burgess 1955–58
Trevor Morris 1958–65
Glyn Davies 1965–66
Billy Lucas 1967–69
Roy Bentley 1969–72
Harry Gregg 1972–75
Harry Griffiths 1975–77
John Toshack 1978–83
   *(resigned October re-appointed
   in December) 1983–84*
Colin Appleton 1984
John Bond 1984–85
Tommy Hutchison 1985–86
Terry Yorath 1986–89
Ian Evans 1989–90
Terry Yorath 1990–91
Frank Burrows 1991–95
Kevin Cullis 1996
Jan Molby 1996–97
Micky Adams 1997
Alan Cork 1997–98
John Hollins 1998–2001
Colin Addison 2001–02
Nick Cusack March 2002–

LATEST SEQUENCES

Longest Sequence of League Wins: 9, 27.11.99 – 22.100.
Longest Sequence of League Defeats: 9, 26.1.91 – 19.3.91.
Longest Sequence of League Draws: 5, 5.1.93 – 5.2.93.
Longest Sequence of Unbeaten League Matches: 19, 19.10.70 – 9.3.71.
Longest Sequence Without a League Win: 15, 25.3.89 – 2.9.89.

TEN YEAR LEAGUE RECORD

		P	W	D	L	F	A	Pts	Pos
1991-92	Div 3	46	14	14	18	55	65	56	19
1992-93	Div 2	46	20	13	13	65	47	73	5
1993-94	Div 2	46	16	12	18	56	58	60	13
1994-95	Div 2	46	19	14	13	57	45	71	10
1995-96	Div 2	46	11	14	21	43	79	47	22
1996-97	Div 3	46	21	8	17	62	58	71	5
1997-98	Div 3	46	13	11	22	49	62	50	20
1998-99	Div 3	46	19	14	13	56	48	71	7
1999-2000	Div 3	46	24	13	9	51	30	85	1
2000-01	Div 2	46	8	13	25	47	73	37	23

DID YOU KNOW ?

Jack Fowler scored in five
successive FA Cup ties for
Swansea Town in 1925–26
including four goals against
Stoke City and the winning
effort against Arsenal.

SWANSEA CITY 2001–02 LEAGUE RECORD

Match No.	Date	Venue	Opponents	Result	H/T Score	Lg. Pos.	Goalscorers	Attendance
1	Aug 11	A	Macclesfield T	W 3-1	2-1	—	Phillips [5], Sidibe [22], Watkin (pen) [87]	2309
2	18	H	Oxford U	D 0-0	0-0	5		5501
3	25	A	Lincoln C	L 0-3	0-0	14		2593
4	27	H	Cheltenham T	D 2-2	2-0	14	Roberts [14], Bound (pen) [40]	3343
5	Sept 8	H	Exeter C	W 4-2	3-1	11	O'Leary [26], Roberts [36], Bound (pen) [37], Williams [90]	3889
6	11	A	Plymouth Arg	L 1-3	0-2	—	Sidibe [79]	3850
7	15	H	Halifax T	L 0-2	0-1	14		3794
8	18	A	Scunthorpe U	D 2-2	2-2	—	Coates [8], Williams [25]	2574
9	22	A	Hull C	L 1-2	0-1	18	Roberts [72]	10,440
10	25	H	Shrewsbury T	D 3-3	2-1	20	Roberts [24], Coates 2 [26, 77]	3131
11	29	A	Kidderminster H	W 2-0	2-0	14	Jenkins [7], Williams [20]	2796
12	Oct 9	H	Rochdale	L 0-1	0-1	—		3533
13	13	A	Southend U	L 2-4	1-0	20	Howard [38], Roberts [86]	3622
14	20	A	Leyton Orient	L 0-1	0-0	21		3645
15	23	H	Darlington	W 2-0	0-0	—	Cusack [51], Tyson [54]	2926
16	27	A	Luton T	L 0-3	0-1	20		6705
17	Nov 3	H	Rushden & D	D 0-0	0-0	20		3970
18	10	A	Torquay U	W 2-1	0-1	18	Sidibe 2 [65, 82]	2276
19	20	A	York C	W 2-0	1-0	—	Lacey [27], Sidibe [74]	1840
20	23	H	Hartlepool U	L 0-1	0-1	—		4161
21	Dec 1	A	Mansfield T	L 0-3	0-2	17		3240
22	15	H	Carlisle U	D 0-0	0-0	19		2906
23	21	H	Bristol R	W 2-1	2-1	—	Sidibe [15], Watkin [17]	2734
24	26	A	Exeter C	W 3-0	0-0	14	Watkin 2 (1 pen) [57 (p), 69], Coates [86]	4123
25	29	A	Cheltenham T	D 2-2	2-0	14	Williams [5], Brodie [12]	4130
26	Jan 5	H	Lincoln C	D 0-0	0-0	13		3409
27	12	A	Oxford U	L 1-2	1-2	15	Coates [11]	5934
28	19	H	Macclesfield T	L 0-1	0-0	15		3753
29	22	H	Bristol R	L 1-4	0-2	—	Watkin [61]	5725
30	26	A	Rochdale	L 0-2	0-2	19		2819
31	Feb 5	H	Plymouth Arg	L 0-1	0-1	—		4060
32	9	A	Leyton Orient	D 2-2	1-0	18	Cusack [20], Mumford [81]	4590
33	12	H	Kidderminster H	W 2-1	1-1	—	Todd [36], Sharp [59]	3508
34	15	H	Southend U	W 3-2	2-1	—	Todd 2 [1, 32], Sidibe [75]	3600
35	23	A	Halifax T	W 1-0	1-0	15	Watkin [10]	1601
36	26	H	Scunthorpe U	D 2-2	1-1	—	Phillips [41], Mumford [90]	3085
37	Mar 1	H	Hull C	W 1-0	0-0	—	Watkin [86]	5006
38	5	A	Shrewsbury T	L 0-3	0-1	—		3168
39	9	A	Carlisle U	L 1-3	0-3	15	Brodie [80]	3349
40	16	H	Mansfield T	W 2-0	1-0	13	Watkin (pen) [30], Romo [81]	3527
41	23	A	Darlington	D 0-0	0-0	14		2915
42	30	H	Luton T	L 1-3	0-1	15	Mumford [90]	5436
43	Apr 1	A	Rushden & D	L 0-4	0-2	17		4671
44	6	A	York C	L 0-1	0-0	19		2677
45	13	A	Hartlepool U	L 1-7	1-2	19	Mumford [26]	4033
46	20	H	Torquay U	D 2-2	2-1	20	Mumford [1], O'Leary [17]	3265

Final League Position: 20

GOALSCORERS

League (53): Watkin 8 (3 pens), Sidibe 7, Coates 5, Mumford 5, Roberts 5, Williams 4, Todd 3, Bound 2 (2 pens), Brodie 2, Cusack 2, O'Leary 2, Phillips 2, Howard 1, Jenkins 1, Lacey 1, Romo 1, Sharp 1, Tyson 1.
Worthington Cup (0).
FA Cup (5): Cusack 2, Sidibe 1, Watkin 1, Williams 1.

Freestone R 43	Jenkins L 14+1	Howard M 42	Cusack N 33+2	O'Leary K 30+1	Todd C 28+4	Roberts S 13	Phillips G 29+6	Sidibe M 26+5	Watkin S 25+6	Coates J 44+1	Romo D 3+7	De-Vulgt L 7+3	Williams J 26+15	Appleby R 3+7	Mazzina N 3	Keegan M —+2	Bound M 18	Tyson N 7+4	Mumford A 28+4	Draper C —+2	Casey R 6+10	Sharp N 22+3	Smith J 7+1	Lacey D 5+11	Evans T 16	Evans S 4	Brodie S 21+5	Jones J 3	Match No.
1	2	3	4¹	5	6	7²	8	9³	10	11	12	13	14																1
1	2	3	4		5	7¹	8	9	10²	11	6		13	12															2
1	2	3	4	5	6²	7		9	10¹	11		13	12		8³	14													3
1	2	3	4	5	6	7	8¹	9		11	12						10												4
1	2	3		5			7¹	8	9	11			12	13	6		4	10¹											5
1	2	3	12	5	13	7	8	9		11			14		6²		4	10³											6
1	2	3		5	6¹	7	8²	9²		11		13	10	12		4		14											7
1	2	3		5	6	7	8			11			10¹	12		4		9											8
1	2	3		5	6	7	8			11	12		10²	13		4		9¹											9
1	2	3	4	5	6	7¹	8			11			9²	12		10	13												10
1	2	3	4	5	6	7	8						9²	11¹		10	13	12											11
1	2	3	4		6¹	7		12		11			10	8²		5	13		9³	14									12
1		3	4	5	6	7		12		11	13	2	10¹	8²			14		9²									13
1		3	4¹	5	6		8			11		2³	9	12	13	7	10³	14										14
1		3	4	5	6		8		12	11			9			7	10²	13	2¹										15
1		3	4		6		8		12	11³			9			5	10		7¹	2²	13	14							16
1		3¹	4				8		12	11¹			9			5	10		13	6	7		2						17
1		4					8²	9		11			12			5	10		7	6¹	13	2	3						18
1		4	13				12	9		11			10²			5			8²	6	7	2	3	14					19
1			5				12	9	13	11			10			6			14	4¹	7²	2	3	8³					20
1		4	5					9	12	11			10¹			8			13	6³	7²	2	3	14					21
1	3	4				7	12	10²	11			9¹			5	6	13					2	8						22
1	3	4				7	9	10	11							6		5				2	8						23
1	3	4	5			12	9¹	10	11			13				6		7				2	8¹						24
1	3	4	5				10	11¹				9				7		6	12	2									25
1	3	4	5			12	10²	11³				9				7	13	6	14	2	8¹								26
1	3	4	5				10	11				9				7	12	6	8¹	2									27
1	3¹	4	5			12	10	11¹				9³				7	13	6	14	2	8								28
1	3	4	5			12	10	11¹				9²				7		6	13	2	8								29
1	3	4	5¹	12			10	11				9				7²		6	13	2	8								30
1	13	4	4³	5			9	10¹	11²			12				7		6	14	2	8								31
1	8	3	4	12	5		9	10³	11			7						6¹	13	2²	14								32
1	2	3	8	5		7²	9	12	11¹							4		6	13	10									33
1	2	4	5			7	9²	10¹	11		12					3		6	13	8									34
1	3		5	6		7	9	10	11		12							2	4¹	8									35
1	2	4	5			7	9	10	11		12					3		6		8¹									36
1	2	4	5			7	9	10	11²		12					3	13	6		8¹									37
1	2¹	4	5			7	9	10	11¹		12					3	13	6		8									38
1	2		5	6		7	9²	10	11		8¹					3	12	4		13									39
1	2¹		5	6		7		10	11	12	9					3	4			8									40
1	2		5	6			12	10	11	13	4	9¹				3	7²			8									41
1	2		5	6			12	10	11	13	4	9¹				3	7²			8									42
	3	4		6		7	9¹	10	11		2					8²	13	5				12	1						43
1	3	12	5	13		7	9		11¹	8	2	10¹				6	14	4²											44
	3		5	6³		7	9		12	8²	2	13				4	11¹14				10	1							45
	3	4²	5			2	9¹	10	11			12				7	13	6				8	1						46

Worthington Cup
First Round   Peterborough U   (h)   0-2

FA Cup
First Round   QPR   (h)   4-0
Second Round   Macclesfield T   (a)   1-4

SWINDON TOWN   Division 2

FOUNDATION

It is generally accepted that Swindon Town came into being in 1881, although there is no firm evidence that the club's founder, Rev. William Pitt, captain of the Spartans (an offshoot of a cricket club) changed his club's name to Swindon Town before 1883, when the Spartans amalgamated with St Mark's Young Men's Friendly Society.

County Ground, Swindon, Wiltshire SN1 2ED.

Telephone: (01793) 333 700. *Fax:* (01793) 333 703.

Marketing: (01793) 333 718. *Fax:* (01793) 333 719.

Superstore: (01793) 333 778. *Fax:* (01793) 333 780.

Community Office: (01793) 421 303.

ClubCall: 09068 121 640.

Ground Capacity: 15,728.

Record Attendance: 32,000 v Arsenal, FA Cup 3rd rd, 15 January 1972.

Record Receipts: £149,371 v Bolton W, Coca-Cola Cup semi-final, 1st leg, 12 February 1995.

Pitch Measurements: 110yd × 70yd.

Chief Executive: Peter Rowe.

Chairman: Willie Carson.

Directors: R. Holt, N. Prescott, Mrs W. Godwin.

Manager: Andy King.

Assistant Manager: Malcolm Crosby.

Player-Coach: Neil Ruddock.

Physio: Dick Mackey.

Company Secretary: Mike Squires.

Colours: Red shirts, white shorts, red stockings.

Change Colours: Light blue/dark blue panelled shirts and shorts, light blue stockings.

Year Formed: 1881* (*see Foundation*).

Turned Professional: 1894.

Ltd Co.: 1894.

Club Nickname: 'Robins'.

Previous Ground: 1881, The Croft; 1896, County Ground.

First Football League Game: 28 August 1920, Division 3, v Luton T (h) W 9–1 – Nash; Kay, Macconachie; Langford, Hawley, Wareing; Jefferson (1), Fleming (4), Rogers, Batty (2), Davies (1), (1 og).

HONOURS

FA Premier League: best season: 22nd 1993–94.

Football League: Division 2 – Champions 1995–96; Division 3 – Runners-up 1962–63, 1968–69; Division 4 – Champions 1985–86 (with record 102 points).

FA Cup: Semi-finals 1910, 1912.

Football League Cup: Winners 1969.

Anglo-Italian Cup: Winners 1970.

IT'S A FACT !

The youngest full-back partnership in Football League history was established when Terry Wollen and Norman Trollope paired each other in defence for Swindon Town in 1960–61. Wollen was 17 in August 1960, Trollope in the July.

Record League Victory: 9–1 v Luton T, Division 3 (S), 28 August 1920 – Nash; Kay, Macconachie; Langford, Hawley, Wareing; Jefferson (1), Fleming (4), Rogers, Batty (2), Davies (1), (1 og).

Record Cup Victory: 10–1 v Farnham U Breweries (away), FA Cup 1st rd (replay), 28 November 1925 – Nash; Dickenson, Weston, Archer, Bew, Adey; Denyer (2), Wall (1), Richardson (4), Johnson (3), Davies.

Record Defeat: 1–10 v Manchester C, FA Cup 4th rd (replay), 25 January 1930.

Most League Points (2 for a win): 64, Division 3, 1968–69.

Most League Points (3 for a win): 102, Division 4, 1985–86.

Most League Goals: 100, Division 3 (S), 1926–27.

Highest League Scorer in Season: Harry Morris, 47, Division 3 (S), 1926–27.

Most League Goals in Total Aggregate: Harry Morris, 216, 1926–33.

Most League Goals in One Match: 5, Harry Morris v QPR, Division 3S, 18 December 1926; 5, Harry Morris v Norwich C, Division 3S, 26 April 1930; 5, Keith East v Mansfield T, Division 3, 20 November 1965.

Most Capped Player: Rod Thomas, 30 (50), Wales.

Most League Appearances: John Trollope, 770, 1960–80.

Youngest League Player: Paul Rideout, 16 years 107 days v Hull C, 29 November 1980.

Record Transfer Fee Received: £1,500,000 from Manchester C for Kevin Horlock, January 1997.

Record Transfer Fee Paid: £800,000 to West Ham U for Joey Beauchamp, August 1994.

Football League Record: 1920 Original Member of Division 3; 1921–58 Division 3 (S); 1958–63 Division 3; 1963–65 Division 2; 1965–69 Division 3; 1969–74 Division 2; 1974–82 Division 3; 1982–86 Division 4; 1986–87 Division 3; 1987–92 Division 2; 1992–93 Division 1; 1993–94 FA Premier League; 1994–95 Division 1; 1995–96 Division 2; 1996–2000 Division 1; 2000– Division 2.

MANAGERS

Sam Allen 1902–33
Ted Vizard 1933–39
Neil Harris 1939–41
Louis Page 1945–53
Maurice Lindley 1953–55
Bert Head 1956–65
Danny Williams 1965–69
Fred Ford 1969–71
Dave Mackay 1971–72
Les Allen 1972–74
Danny Williams 1974–78
Bobby Smith 1978–80
John Trollope 1980–83
Ken Beamish 1983–84
Lou Macari 1984–89
Ossie Ardiles 1989–91
Glenn Hoddle 1991–93
John Gorman 1993–94
Steve McMahon 1994–99
Jimmy Quinn 1999–2000
Colin Todd 2000
Andy King 2000–01
Roy Evans 2001
Andy King January 2002–

LATEST SEQUENCES

Longest Sequence of League Wins: 8, 12.1.86 – 15.3.86.

Longest Sequence of League Defeats: 6, 2.5.93 – 25.8.93.

Longest Sequence of League Draws: 6, 22.11.91 – 28.12.91.

Longest Sequence of Unbeaten League Matches: 22, 12.1.86 – 23.8.86.

Longest Sequence Without a League Win: 19, 30.10.99 – 4.3.00.

TEN YEAR LEAGUE RECORD

		P	W	D	L	F	A	Pts	Pos
1991-92	Div 2	46	18	15	13	69	55	69	8
1992-93	Div 1	46	21	13	12	74	59	76	5
1993-94	PR Lge	42	5	15	22	47	100	30	22
1994-95	Div 1	46	12	12	22	54	73	48	21
1995-96	Div 2	46	25	17	4	71	34	92	1
1996-97	Div 1	46	15	9	22	52	71	54	19
1997-98	Div 1	46	14	10	22	42	73	52	18
1998-99	Div 1	46	13	11	22	59	81	50	17
1999-2000	Div 1	46	8	12	26	38	77	36	24
2000-01	Div 2	46	13	13	20	47	65	52	20

DID YOU KNOW ?

Manager of the Month Award for Swindon Town's Lou Macari in the 1986–87 promotion season, brought him five gallons of Bell's whisky – but this teetotaller did not take one drop of it.

SWINDON TOWN 2001–02 LEAGUE RECORD

Match No.	Date	Venue	Opponents		Result	H/T Score	Lg. Pos.	Goalscorers	Attendance
1	Aug 11	H	Peterborough U	D	0-0	0-0	—		7934
2	18	A	Bristol C	L	1-3	0-1	19	O'Halloran (pen) [77]	13,818
3	25	H	Oldham Ath	L	0-2	0-2	23		5219
4	27	A	Bury	W	3-0	0-0	14	Osei-Kuffour [48], O'Halloran (pen) [72], Duke [89]	3202
5	Sept 1	H	Colchester U	W	1-0	0-0	11	Ruddock [53]	4889
6	8	A	Bournemouth	D	0-0	0-0	11		3770
7	15	H	Tranmere R	D	2-2	1-1	12	Grazioli [7], Gurney [88]	5922
8	18	A	Port Vale	W	2-0	1-0	—	Invincible [32], Hewlett [60]	3737
9	22	A	Chesterfield	L	0-4	0-0	14		4275
10	25	H	Brentford	W	2-0	1-0	—	Invincible [39], Grazioli [63]	5519
11	29	A	Northampton T	D	1-1	0-0	10	Grazioli [48]	5104
12	Oct 13	A	Reading	W	3-1	1-0	10	Grazioli [38], Invincible [52], Osei-Kuffour [87]	14,389
13	21	H	Cardiff C	L	0-3	0-1	13		8373
14	24	H	Cambridge U	W	2-0	0-0	—	Grazioli 2 [83, 90]	4882
15	27	A	Wycombe W	D	1-1	1-1	10	Carlisle [23]	7127
16	Nov 3	H	Stoke C	L	0-3	0-1	14		7981
17	10	A	Blackpool	L	0-1	0-1	16		5018
18	21	H	QPR	L	0-4	0-3	—		8847
19	24	H	Brighton & HA	D	1-1	0-1	16	Sabin [58]	8830
20	27	A	Wrexham	W	3-1	2-0	—	Sabin [5], Invincible [28], Heywood [60]	4127
21	Dec 1	A	Wigan Ath	L	0-1	0-0	15		5635
22	21	H	Notts Co	L	1-3	1-2	—	Duke [26]	4197
23	26	H	Bournemouth	D	0-0	0-0	15		6790
24	29	H	Bury	W	3-1	2-1	13	Gurney [6], Howe [8], Carlisle [51]	7624
25	Jan 13	H	Bristol C	L	1-2	0-1	18	Foley [56]	7273
26	16	A	Oldham Ath	L	0-2	0-1	—		3970
27	19	A	Peterborough U	D	1-1	1-0	18	Sabin [20]	6598
28	22	H	Notts Co	W	1-0	0-0	—	Invincible [71]	3821
29	26	A	Wrexham	D	2-2	0-1	15	Grazioli [74], Reeves [90]	2879
30	30	A	Colchester U	W	3-1	0-1	—	Gurney 2 (1 pen) [62 (p), 74], Sabin [63]	3132
31	Feb 2	H	Northampton T	W	2-1	1-0	12	Gabbiadini (og) [5], Invincible [64]	6585
32	5	H	Huddersfield T	L	0-1	0-0	—		5094
33	9	A	Cardiff C	L	0-3	0-1	14		12,045
34	14	H	Reading	D	0-0	0-0	—		10,200
35	22	A	Tranmere R	D	0-0	0-0	—		8106
36	26	H	Chesterfield	W	2-1	1-1	—	Grazioli [25], Reeves [64]	4580
37	Mar 2	H	Port Vale	W	3-0	2-0	13	Gurney [43], Heywood [45], Willis [83]	5867
38	5	A	Brentford	L	0-2	0-1	—		5644
39	9	A	Huddersfield T	L	0-2	0-1	14		9569
40	16	H	Wigan Ath	D	1-1	0-0	14	Sabin [64]	6226
41	30	H	Blackpool	W	1-0	0-0	14	Young [47]	5085
42	Apr 1	A	Stoke C	L	0-2	0-0	14		13,530
43	6	H	QPR	L	0-1	0-0	14		6774
44	9	A	Cambridge U	W	2-1	1-1	—	Gurney [44], Angus (og) [83]	2406
45	13	A	Brighton & HA	D	0-0	0-0	14		6870
46	20	H	Wycombe W	D	1-1	0-1	13	Heywood [56]	7492

Final League Position: 13

GOALSCORERS

League (46): Grazioli 8, Gurney 6 (1 pen), Invincible 6, Sabin 5, Heywood 3, Carlisle 2, Duke 2, O'Halloran 2 (2 pens), Osei-Kuffour 2, Reeves 2, Foley 1, Hewlett 1, Howe 1, Ruddock 1, Willis 1, Young 1, own goals 2.
Worthington Cup (2): Howe 1, O'Halloran 1 (pen).
FA Cup (6): Invincible 2, Edwards P 1, Haywood 1, Howe 1, Ruddock 1 (pen).

Griemink B 45	Invincible D 40 + 4	Duke D 36 + 6	Heywood M 42 + 2	Reeves A 24 + 1	Gurney A 43	O'Halloran K 6	Howe B 33 + 6	Sabin E 33 + 1	Grazioli G 24 + 7	Hewlett M 38 + 1	Brayley B — + 7	Robinson S 37 + 3	Davis S 15 + 6	Osei-Kuffour J 4 + 7	Ruddock N 14 + 1	Davies G — + 2	Edwards P 14 + 6	McAreavey P 8 + 11	Edwards N 2 + 5	Carlise W 10 + 1	Willis A 19 + 3	Robinson M 6 + 2	Williams J — + 1	Young A 7 + 7	Foley D 5 + 2	McKinney R 1	Cobian J — + 1	Herring I — + 1	Match No.
1	2¹	3	4		5	6	7	8²	9³	10	11	12	13	14															1
1	2¹	3	4		5	6	7	13	9	10²	11	14	8³	12															2
1	2	11²	4		5	6	7	8¹	9		10	12		3	13														3
1	12	2	4		5	6	7	8	9		11	13		3¹	10²														4
1	12	2²	4		6	7	8	9²		11		13	3	10¹	5	14													5
1	12	2¹	4		6	7²	8		13	11		9	3	10	5														6
1	2	3	4		6		8		10¹	11	12	7		9²	5		13												7
1	2	3	12	5	6		8		10	11		7		4¹		9²	13												8
1	2	3³	4	5	6²		8		10¹	11	12	7		14	13	9													9
1	2	3	4	5	6		8		10	11		7				9													10
1	2	3	4	5	6		8		10¹	11²		7		12	13	9													11
1	2	3	12	5	6		8		10²	11		7³		13		9¹	14												12
1	2	3		5	6		8		10¹	11		7		4		9		12											13
1	2	3¹		5	6		8		10	11		7		4		9			12										14
1	2	3	4						10¹	11		7		12	6	9²	13		8	5									15
1	2	3²	4				8	12	10¹	11				13	5	9		7											16
1	2		4		6		8	9¹	10²	11	12				5		13		7	3¹	14								17
1	10	3	4		6			9¹	12	11		8		13	5				7		2²								18
1	10	3	4		6			9		11		8			5				7		2								19
1	10	3	4		6			9		11		8			5				7		2								20
1	10²	3	4		6		12	9¹		11		8	13			14			7	5	2³								21
1	10	3	4				8³	9	13			2	12²	6		11¹	14		7	5									22
1	2	3	4	5	6		8	9	10			7	12						11²		13								23
1	2	3	4	5	6		8	9	10¹			7				12			11										24
1	10	3	4	5				9²				7	2			8¹		6			12	13	11						25
1	2	3	4	5	6		8¹	9				7				10						12	11						26
1	10	3²	4	5	6		12	9	13			7	2¹					14	8			11²							27
1	10	3	4		6		9	12				7	2					13	8²			11¹							28
1	10	3¹	4	5	6		12	9	13	14		7³	2					8				11²							29
1	7	12	4		6		8²	9	10³	11¹		2	3			13		5				14							30
1	7	12	4		6		8	9	10¹	11		2	3					5											31
1	2	12	4		6		7²	9	10¹	11		3³				8	14	5				13							32
1	10	3²	4		6		12	9¹	13	11		7	2			8¹		5				14							33
1	8		4	5	6		7¹	9	10²	11		2	3			12		13											34
1	7		4	5	6		8²	9	10	11		2	3			13						12							35
1	7		4	5	6		9¹	10	11			2	12			13	3¹												36
1	9	12	4	2			8		10²	11		7	3			13		5				6¹							37
1	9	3	4		6		8²		10¹	11		7	2			12		5				13							38
1	8²	3	4	2			7¹	9	10	11		6				12		5				13							39
1	8²	12	4	2			7	9³		11		6	3¹			14	13	5				10							40
1	10	3	4	2			7	9		11		6						5				8							41
	10	12	4	5³	6		7	9²		11		8¹	3					2				13				1	14		42
1	10	3	4	12			7²	9		11		6				13		5				8¹							43
1	12	3	4	2			13	9		11		6²				7¹	8¹	14				5					10		44
1		3	4	5	2		8	9		11		12				7	13					6¹					10²		45
1		3	4	5	2			9		11		6				8¹	7					10						12	46

Worthington Cup
First Round — Wolverhampton W — (a) — 2-1
Second Round — WBA — (a) — 0-2

FA Cup
First Round — Hartlepool U — (h) — 3-1
Second Round — Hereford U — (h) — 3-2
Third Round — Manchester C — (a) — 0-2

TORQUAY UNITED   Division 3

FOUNDATION

The idea of establishing a Torquay club was agreed by old boys of
Torquay College and Torbay College, while sitting in Princess
Gardens listening to the band. A proper meeting was subsequently
held at Tor Abbey Hotel at which officers were elected. This was
on 1 May 1899 and the club's first competition was the Eastern
League (later known as the East Devon League). As an amateur
club it played at Teignmouth Road, Torquay Recreation Ground
and Cricket Field Road before settling down for four years at
Torquay Cricket Ground where the rugby club now plays. They
became Torquay United in 1921 after merging with Babbacombe
FC.

Plainmoor Ground, Torquay, Devon TQ1 3PS.

Telephone: (01803) 328 666. **Fax:** (01803) 323 976.

Ground Capacity: 6,283.

Record Attendance: 21,908 v Huddersfield T, FA Cup
4th rd, 29 January 1955.

Record Receipts: £30,824 v Plymouth Arg, Division 3,
25 March 2000.

Pitch Measurements: 110yd × 74yd.

Chairman/Managing Director: M. Bateson.

Financial Director: Mrs H. Kindeleit-Badcock.

Directors: Mrs S. Bateson, M. Benney, I. Hayman,
B. Palk.

First Team Coach: Leroy Rosenoir.

Physio: Norman Medhurst.

Company Secretary: Mrs H. Kindeleit-Badcock.

Colours: Yellow shirts with navy and white inserts under arm and white V. neck, yellow shorts,
yellow stockings.

Change Colours: Black and white striped shirts with yellow trim, black shorts with yellow stripes to
sides, black stockings with yellow and white stripes top and bottom.

Year Formed: 1899.

Turned Professional: 1921.

Ltd Co.: 1921.

Previous Name: 1910, Torquay Town; 1921, Torquay United.

Club Nickname: 'The Gulls'.

Previous Grounds: 1899, Teignmouth Road; 1900, Torquay Recreation Ground; 1904, Cricket Field
Road; 1906, Torquay Cricket Ground; 1910, Plainmoor Ground.

HONOURS

Football League: Division 3 best
season: 4th, 1967–68; Division 3 (S) –
Runners-up 1956–57; Division 4 –
Promoted 1959–60 (3rd), 1965–66
(3rd), 1990–91 (play-offs).

FA Cup: best season: 4th rd, 1949,
1955, 1971, 1983, 1990.

Football League Cup: never past
3rd rd.

Sherpa Van Trophy: Runners-up
1989.

IT'S A FACT !

Despite an unbeaten home record in 1956–57, Torquay
United were pipped to promotion in Division Three
(South) on goal average by Ipswich Town. Surprisingly,
having beaten Millwall 7-2 at home, they lost by the
same scoreline at The Den.

First Football League Game: 27 August 1927, Division 3 (S), v Exeter C (h) D 1–1 – Millsom; Cook, Smith; Wellock, Wragg, Connor, Mackey, Turner (1), Jones, McGovern, Thomson.

Record League Victory: 9–0 v Swindon T, Division 3 (S), 8 March 1952 – George Webber; Topping, Ralph Calland; Brown, Eric Webber, Towers; Shaw (1), Marchant (1), Northcott (2), Collins (3), Edds (2).

Record Cup Victory: 7–1 v Northampton T, FA Cup 1st rd, 14 November 1959 – Gill; Penford, Downs; Bettany, George Northcott, Rawson; Baxter, Cox, Tommy Northcott (1), Bond (3), Pym (3).

Record Defeat: 2–10 v Fulham, Division 3 (S), 7 September 1931. 2–10 v Luton T, Division 3 (S), 2 September 1933.

Most League Points (2 for a win): 60, Division 4, 1959–60.

Most League Points (3 for a win): 77, Division 4, 1987–88.

Most League Goals: 89, Division 3 (S), 1956–57.

Highest League Scorer in Season: Sammy Collins, 40, Division 3 (S), 1955–56.

Most League Goals in Total Aggregate: Sammy Collins, 204, 1948–58.

Most League Goals in One Match: 5, Robin Stubbs v Newport Co, Division 4, 19 October 1963.

Most Capped Player: Rodney Jack, St Vincent.

Most League Appearances: Dennis Lewis, 443, 1947–59.

Youngest League Player: David Byng, 16 years 36 days v Walsall, 14 August 1993.

Record Transfer Fee Received: £500,000 from Crewe Alex for Rodney Jack, July 1998.

Record Transfer Fee Paid: £70,000 to Barry T for Eifion Williams, March 1999.

Football League Record: 1927 Elected to Division 3 (S); 1958–60 Division 4; 1960–62 Division 3; 1962–66 Division 4; 1966–72 Division 3; 1972–91 Division 4; 1991– Division 3.

MANAGERS

Percy Mackrill 1927–29
A. H. Hoskins 1929
  (Secretary-Manager)
Frank Womack 1929–32
Frank Brown 1932–38
Alf Steward 1938–40
Billy Butler 1945–46
Jack Butler 1946–47
John McNeil 1947–50
Bob John 1950
Alex Massie 1950–51
Eric Webber 1951–65
Frank O'Farrell 1965–68
Alan Brown 1969–71
Jack Edwards 1971–73
Malcolm Musgrove 1973–76
Mike Green 1977–81
Frank O'Farrell 1981–82
  _(continued as General Manager
  to 1983)_
Bruce Rioch 1982–84
Dave Webb 1984–85
John Sims 1985
Stuart Morgan 1985–87
Cyril Knowles 1987–89
Dave Smith 1989–91
John Impey 1991–92
Ivan Golac 1992
Paul Compton 1992–93
Don O'Riordan 1993–95
Eddie May 1995–96
Kevin Hodges _(Head Coach)_
  1996–98
Wes Saunders 1998–2001
Roy McFarland 2001–02
Leroy Rosenoir June 2002–

LATEST SEQUENCES

Longest Sequence of League Wins: 8, 24.1.98 – 3.3.98.

Longest Sequence of League Defeats: 8, 30.9.95 – 18.11.95.

Longest Sequence of League Draws: 8, 25.10.69 – 13.12.69.

Longest Sequence of Unbeaten League Matches: 15, 5.5.90 – 3.11.90.

Longest Sequence Without a League Win: 17, 5.3.38 – 10.9.38.

TEN YEAR LEAGUE RECORD

		P	W	D	L	F	A	Pts	Pos
1991-92	Div 3	46	13	8	25	42	68	47	23
1992-93	Div 3	42	12	7	23	45	67	43	19
1993-94	Div 3	42	17	16	9	64	56	67	6
1994-95	Div 3	42	14	13	15	54	57	55	13
1995-96	Div 3	46	5	14	27	30	84	29	24
1996-97	Div 3	46	13	11	22	46	62	50	21
1997-98	Div 3	46	21	11	14	68	59	74	5
1998-99	Div 3	46	12	17	17	47	58	53	20
1999-2000	Div 3	46	19	12	15	62	52	69	9
2000-01	Div 3	46	12	13	21	52	77	49	21

DID YOU KNOW

Ralph Birkett became the first Torquay United produced player to later win full England international honours. He made his debut for United on 8 May 1930, creating all seven goals in the win over Bournemouth.

TORQUAY UNITED 2001–02 LEAGUE RECORD

Match No.	Date	Venue	Opponents	Result		H/T Score	Lg. Pos.	Goalscorers	Attendance
1	Aug 11	A	Bristol R	L	0-1	0-0	—		10,127
2	18	H	York C	L	0-3	0-2	24		2659
3	25	A	Kidderminster H	L	0-1	0-0	24		2440
4	27	H	Carlisle U	W	2-1	1-1	20	Hill [7], Russell A [74]	2274
5	Sept 1	A	Cheltenham T	D	2-2	2-1	20	Russell A [5], Graham [22]	3167
6	8	H	Plymouth Arg	L	0-1	0-0	21		4217
7	15	H	Darlington	W	2-1	0-0	17	Russell A (pen) [76], Nicholls [90]	2065
8	18	H	Rushden & D	D	0-0	0-0	—		3258
9	22	A	Luton T	L	1-5	1-3	21	Nicholls (og) [41]	6392
10	25	H	Scunthorpe U	D	0-0	0-0	—		1982
11	29	A	Leyton Orient	W	2-1	1-1	17	Bedeau 2 [42, 81]	4414
12	Oct 5	H	Southend U	W	2-1	0-0	—	Richardson [51], Graham [62]	2329
13	13	A	Hull C	L	0-1	0-0	15		9102
14	20	H	Hartlepool U	W	1-0	0-0	12	Graham [79]	2148
15	23	H	Mansfield T	L	0-2	0-0	—		4059
16	27	H	Shrewsbury T	W	2-1	1-0	11	Graham [24], Roach [46]	2356
17	Nov 3	A	Rochdale	L	0-2	0-0	12		3078
18	10	H	Swansea C	L	1-2	1-0	17	Richardson [10]	2276
19	20	H	Exeter C	L	0-2	0-0	—		3764
20	24	A	Halifax T	L	0-2	0-1	21		1681
21	Dec 1	H	Macclesfield T	L	1-2	1-1	22	Hill [38]	1702
22	15	A	Lincoln C	D	0-0	0-0	21		2747
23	22	A	Oxford U	D	3-3	2-0	20	Graham [19], Goodridge [23], Logan [72]	2463
24	26	A	Plymouth Arg	D	2-2	0-0	21	McGlinchey (og) [67], Logan (pen) [90]	13,677
25	Jan 1	H	Cheltenham T	L	0-1	0-0	21		2952
26	5	H	Kidderminster H	L	1-4	1-2	21	Fowler [10]	2129
27	12	A	York C	D	1-1	0-1	21	Richardson [81]	3445
28	19	A	Bristol R	W	2-1	1-0	21	Brandon [41], Logan [79]	3493
29	22	A	Oxford U	D	1-1	0-0	—	Woods [84]	5480
30	26	A	Southend U	D	1-1	0-0	22	Williams [81]	4184
31	Feb 2	H	Leyton Orient	D	1-1	0-1	22	Logan [83]	1993
32	9	A	Hartlepool U	L	1-4	0-3	23	Brandon [73]	3658
33	16	H	Hull C	D	1-1	0-1	23	Woods [61]	2403
34	19	A	Carlisle U	L	0-2	0-0	—		3823
35	23	A	Darlington	W	3-1	1-0	22	Russell A 3 (1 pen) [24, 60, 90 (p)]	3119
36	26	A	Rushden & D	D	1-1	0-1	—	Sambrook (og) [71]	1709
37	Mar 2	H	Luton T	L	0-1	0-1	23		3280
38	5	A	Scunthorpe U	L	0-1	0-0	—		2838
39	9	H	Lincoln C	W	2-0	0-0	22	Brandon [70], Russell A [76]	2255
40	16	A	Macclesfield T	W	2-0	1-0	21	Graham 2 [38, 90]	2085
41	23	H	Mansfield T	D	0-0	0-0	20		2679
42	30	A	Shrewsbury T	W	1-0	1-0	20	Richardson [3]	4510
43	Apr 1	H	Rochdale	W	3-0	1-0	18	Bedeau [40], Canoville [46], Graham [65]	3136
44	7	A	Exeter C	D	0-0	0-0	17		3580
45	13	H	Halifax T	L	2-4	1-1	18	Ashford [39], Richardson [71]	2692
46	20	A	Swansea C	D	2-2	1-2	19	Richardson [27], Bedeau [78]	3265

Final League Position: 19

GOALSCORERS

League (46): Graham 8, Russell A 7 (2 pens), Richardson 6, Bedeau 4, Logan 4 (1 pen), Brandon 3, Hill 2, Woods 2, Ashford 1, Canoville 1, Fowler 1, Goodridge 1, Nicholls 1, Roach 1, Williams 1, own goals 3.
Worthington Cup (2): Brandon 1, Graham 1.
FA Cup (1): Hill 1.

Dearden K 46	Herrera R 2+1	McNeil M 16	MacDonald C 5	Aggrey J 2	Tully S 17+1	Russell A 33	Brandon C 22+5	Healy B 2	Bedeau A 9+12	Williams E 8+17	Graham D 31+5	O'Brien M —+1	Banger N 1	Roach N 5+7	Rees J 26+7	Hill K 40+4	Woods S 38	Woozley D 15+1	Douglin T 5+1	Martin A 5	Russell L 7+4	Parker K —+2	Greyling A —+2	Nicholls M 4+5	Ashford R 1+1	Law G —+5	Canoville L 10+2	Richardson M 18+12	Holmes P 17+1	Hockley M 12	Williamson M 3	Brahin G 6	Hankin S 27	Benefield J 3+5	Brown D 2	Hanson C 6	Goodridge G 9+8	Fowler J 14	Preece D 4+2	Logan R 16	Hazell R 19	Match No.
1	2	3	4	5	6	7	8	9¹	10²	11	12		13																													1
1	2	3	4	5	6	7	8³	9¹	10¹	11	12	13		14																												2
1		2			11	7				10³	12				9¹	8	3	4	5		6²			13		14																3
1	6	2			11	7			10²		12				9¹	8	3	4	5					13																		4
1	6	2			11	7³			10²						9¹	8	3	4						13		12	14															5
1	12	2			11	7			10				13		9²	8	3¹	4¹	5					14																		6
1	6	2			11				10³		12²				9¹	8	3	4	5		7			13		14																7
1	6	2			11						12				8	3		4	5		7			13			9¹	10²														8
1	6	2¹									12		13		10	8	3	4	5		7²			11			9	14														9
1	6	2				7¹					12				10	8²	3	4	5					13			9	11		4												10
1	6	2²				7									10	8	3¹	4	5	12				13			9	11		4												11
1	6					7²					12				10	8	3	4	5					13		14	9¹	11³	2													12
1	6					7³					12				10	8¹	3	4	5²	13				14			9	11	2													13
1	6			12		7¹					13				10		3	4	5					8			9²	11	2													14
1	6								10¹		12				8	3	4		7²	13				8	9³	11	5	2	14													15
1	6	12									13				10	11²	8¹	3	4		14			7	9²	2	5															16
1	6								13		12				10	11¹	8	3	4		14			7²	9³	2	5															17
1				13					12		10¹			14	8	3	4		6					7²	9	2	5							11³								18
1	2			12					10						8	3	4	5					7²	9¹			11	6	13													19
1		9¹		10							12				3	4		5		13			14	2	11¹	7	8²	6														20
1	12			13					9¹		10				8²	3	4						2		5	14	6	7	11³													21
1		2	3						10		12				4			5		6						7	11	8¹	9													22
1		2	3	13					10		12				4			5		6						7	11	8¹	9²													23
1		2	3	12					10¹		11²				4			5		6						7	8	13	9													24
1		2³	3	13					10²		14				12	4		5		6						7	11	8¹	9													25
1	6			13					10³		12				11	4	3	2		5						7¹	8									14	9²					26
1	6			7					11		4						5		12						3		5	10									8¹	9	2			27
1	3			7			8		11		4						12								2		5	10										9¹	6			28
1	6			7¹			8		11		4						12								3		5	10										9	2			29
1	6			7²			12		8		11				4		13								3³		5	14									10		9¹	2		30
1	10			7¹			12		8		3				4		6								14		2²	13									11³	9	5			31
1	6			10			12		14		8				3		4								5		13										7²	11³	9¹	2		32
1	10			6			7		8		11				4		2								5												9¹		3			33
1	2			6			7³		10²		11				4		12								3		5	13									8	9				34
1	10¹			6			7		12		8				11		4								13		3	5									9²	2				35
1	10²			6			7		12		8				11		4								3		5	13									9¹	2				36
1				6			10		12		8³				11		4								13		3	5								14	7¹	9²	2			37
1				6			9		12		10¹				8		11								14		3²	5									7³	13	2			38
1	10¹			6			7		12		13				11		4								9		3	5									8²	2				39
1	10¹			6			7		13		8				12		11								4		9²	3									5	2				40
1				6			7²		12		8				10¹		11								4		9	3									5	13	2			41
1		11		7			12		8		3			10¹	4										10²		9¹	2									5	13		6		42
1		11		9			8		3		4							12		10²					14		7³	2¹								5	13		6		43
1		11		14			8		13		3¹	4						10³		7							9²						6				12			2		44
1		3		13			8		12		4	5								10²		9	11¹	14										6				7³		2		45
1		11	12				13		8		3	4				5				10²							9¹										6	7		2		46

Worthington Cup
First Round   Bournemouth   (a)   2-0
Second Round   Tottenham H   (a)   0-2

FA Cup
First Round   Northampton T   (h)   1-2

TOTTENHAM HOTSPUR   FA Premiership

FOUNDATION

The Hotspur Football Club was formed from an older cricket club in 1882. Most of the founders were old boys of St John's Presbyterian School and Tottenham Grammar School. The Casey brothers were well to the fore as the family provided the club's first goalposts (painted blue and white) and their first ball. They soon adopted the local YMCA as their meeting place, but after a couple of moves settled at the Red House, which is still their headquarters, although now known simply as 748 High Road.

Bill Nicholson Way, 748 High Rd, Tottenham, London N17 0AP.

Telephone: (020) 8365 5000. *Fax:* (020) 8365 5175.
Spurs ticket line: 08700 112 222.
Spurs Line: 09068 100 500. *Members Office:* (020) 8365 5150. *Commercial Dept:* (020) 8365 5010.

Ground Capacity: 36,236.

Record Attendance: 75,038 v Sunderland, FA Cup 6th rd, 5 March 1938.

Record Receipts: £336,702 v Manchester U, Division 1, 28 September 1991.

Pitch Measurements: 110yd × 73yd.

Chairman: Daniel Levy.

Football Director: D. J. Pleat. *Finance Director:* P. L. Viner. *Property Director:* P. Z. Kemsley.

Non-Executive Directors: D. Buchler (Vice-chairman), M. S. Peters MBE.

President: W. E. Nicholson OBE.

Vice-presidents: N. Solomon, D. A. Alexiou, A. G. Berry.

Manager: Glenn Hoddle. *Assistant Manager:* John Gorman.
First Team Coach: Chris Hughton. *Reserve Team Manager:* Colin Calderwood.
Chief Physio: Alasdair Beattie.

Club Secretary: John Alexander. *Sales Manager:* Scot Gardiner.

Public Relations Officer: John Fennelly.

Colours: White shirts, navy blue shorts, white stockings.

Change Colours: Navy and black shirts, navy and black shorts, navy and black stockings.

Year Formed: 1882. *Turned Professional:* 1895. *Ltd Co.:* 1898.

Previous Name: 1882–84, Hotspur Football Club.

Club Nickname: 'Spurs'.

Previous Grounds: 1882, Tottenham Marshes; 1888, Northumberland Park; 1899, White Hart Lane.

HONOURS

Football League: Division 1 – Champions 1950–51, 1960–61; Runners-up 1921–22, 1951–52, 1956–57, 1962–63; Division 2 – Champions 1919–20, 1949–50; Runners-up 1908–09, 1932–33; Promoted 1977–78 (3rd).

FA Cup: Winners 1901 (as non-League club), 1921, 1961, 1962, 1967, 1981, 1982, 1991; Runners-up 1987.

Football League Cup: Winners 1971, 1973, 1999; Runners-up 1982, 2002.

European Competitions: European Cup: 1961–62. *European Cup-Winners' Cup:* 1962–63 (winners), 1963–64, 1967–68, 1981–82, 1982–83, 1991–92. *UEFA Cup:* 1971–72 (winners), 1972–73, 1973–74 (runners-up), 1983–84 (winners), 1984–85, 1999–2000.

IT'S A FACT !

Tottenham Hotspur, the last non-League club to win the FA Cup, had in 1901 a team composed of five Scots, three Englishmen, two Welshmen and an Irishman, the first finalists to be represented by all four home countries.

First Football League Game: 1 September 1908, Division 2, v Wolverhampton W (h) W 3–0 – Hewitson; Coquet, Burton; Morris (1), D. Steel, Darnell; Walton, Woodward (2), Macfarlane, R. Steel, Middlemiss.

Record League Victory: 9–0 v Bristol R, Division 2, 22 October 1977 – Daines; Naylor, Holmes, Hoddle (1), McAllister, Perryman, Pratt, McNab, Moores (3), Lee (4), Taylor (1).

Record Cup Victory: 13–2 v Crewe Alex, FA Cup 4th rd (replay), 3 February 1960 – Brown; Hills, Henry; Blanchflower, Norman, Mackay; White, Harmer (1), Smith (4), Allen (5), Jones (3 incl. 1p).

Record Defeat: 0–8 v Cologne, UEFA Inter Toto Cup, 22 July 1995.

Most League Points (2 for a win): 70, Division 2, 1919–20.

Most League Points (3 for a win): 77, Division 1, 1984–85.

Most League Goals: 115, Division 1, 1960–61.

Highest League Scorer in Season: Jimmy Greaves, 37, Division 1, 1962–63.

Most League Goals in Total Aggregate: Jimmy Greaves, 220, 1961–70.

Most League Goals in One Match: 5, Ted Harper v Reading, Division 2, 30 August 1930; 5, Alf Stokes v Birmingham C, Division 1, 18 September 1957; 5, Bobby Smith v Aston Villa, Division 1, 29 March 1958.

Most Capped Player: Pat Jennings, 74 (119), Northern Ireland.

Most League Appearances: Steve Perryman, 655, 1969–86.

Youngest League Player: Ally Dick, 16 years 301 days v Manchester C, 20 February 1982.

Record Transfer Fee Received: £5,500,000 from Lazio for Paul Gascoigne, May 1992.

Record Transfer Fee Paid: £11,000,000 to Dynamo Kiev for Sergei Rebrov, May 2000.

Football League Record: 1908 Elected to Division 2; 1909–15 Division 1; 1919–20 Division 2; 1920–28 Division 1; 1928–33 Division 2; 1933–35 Division 1; 1935–50 Division 2; 1950–77 Division 1; 1977–78 Division 2; 1978–92 Division 1; 1992– FA Premier League.

MANAGERS

Frank Brettell 1898–99
John Cameron 1899–1906
Fred Kirkham 1907–08
Peter McWilliam 1912–27
Billy Minter 1927–29
Percy Smith 1930–35
Jack Tresadern 1935–38
Peter McWilliam 1938–42
Arthur Turner 1942–46
Joe Hulme 1946–49
Arthur Rowe 1949–55
Jimmy Anderson 1955–58
Bill Nicholson 1958–74
Terry Neill 1974–76
Keith Burkinshaw 1976–84
Peter Shreeves 1984–86
David Pleat 1986–87
Terry Venables 1987–91
Peter Shreeves 1991–92
Ossie Ardiles 1993–94
Gerry Francis 1994–97
Christian Gross *(Head Coach)* 1997–98
George Graham 1998–2001
Glenn Hoddle April 2001–

LATEST SEQUENCES

Longest Sequence of League Wins: 13, 23.4.60 – 1.10.60.
Longest Sequence of League Defeats: 7, 1.1.94 – 27.2.94.
Longest Sequence of League Draws: 6, 9.1.99 – 27.2.99.
Longest Sequence of Unbeaten League Matches: 22, 31.8.49 – 31.12.49.
Longest Sequence Without a League Win: 16, 29.12.34 – 13.4.35.

TEN YEAR LEAGUE RECORD

		P	W	D	L	F	A	Pts	Pos
1991-92	Div 1	42	15	7	20	58	63	52	15
1992-93	PR Lge	42	16	11	15	60	66	59	8
1993-94	PR Lge	42	11	12	19	54	59	45	15
1994-95	PR Lge	42	16	14	12	66	58	62	7
1995-96	PR Lge	38	16	13	9	50	38	61	8
1996-97	PR Lge	38	13	7	18	44	51	46	10
1997-98	PR Lge	38	11	11	16	44	56	44	14
1998-99	PR Lge	38	11	14	13	47	50	47	11
1999-2000	PR Lge	38	15	8	15	57	49	53	10
2000-01	PR Lge	38	13	10	15	47	54	49	12

DID YOU KNOW ❓

On 15 December 2001, Les Ferdinand's 20th minute goal for Tottenham Hotspur against Fulham was the 10,000th since the Premier League was launched.

TOTTENHAM HOTSPUR 2001–02 LEAGUE RECORD

Match No.	Date	Venue	Opponents	Result		H/T Score	Lg. Pos.	Goalscorers	Atten- dance
1	Aug 18	H	Aston Villa	D	0-0	0-0	—		36,056
2	20	A	Everton	D	1-1	1-0	—	Anderton [45]	29,503
3	25	A	Blackburn R	L	1-2	0-1	16	Ziege [90]	24,922
4	Sept 9	H	Southampton	W	2-0	0-0	11	Ziege [76], Davies [87]	33,658
5	16	H	Chelsea	L	2-3	0-1	11	Sheringham 2 [66,89]	33,485
6	19	A	Sunderland	W	2-1	1-0	—	Ziege [26], Sheringham [51]	43,599
7	22	A	Liverpool	L	0-1	0-0	10		44,116
8	29	H	Manchester U	L	3-5	3-0	13	Richards [15], Ferdinand [25], Ziege [45]	36,049
9	Oct 15	H	Derby Co	W	3-1	2-1	—	Ferdinand [10], Ziege [41], Poyet [90]	30,150
10	21	A	Newcastle U	W	2-0	2-0	10	Speed (og) [8], Poyet [20]	50,593
11	27	H	Middlesbrough	W	2-1	0-1	7	Sheringham (pen) [58], Ferdinand [61]	36,046
12	Nov 4	A	Leeds U	L	1-2	0-0	9	Poyet [52]	40,203
13	17	H	Arsenal	D	1-1	0-0	10	Poyet [90]	36,066
14	24	A	West Ham U	W	1-0	0-0	7	Ferdinand [50]	32,780
15	Dec 3	H	Bolton W	W	3-2	0-1	—	Poyet [47], Ferdinand [48], Sheringham [86]	32,971
16	8	A	Charlton Ath	L	1-3	0-2	7	Poyet [85]	25,103
17	15	H	Fulham	W	4-0	2-0	7	Ferdinand [20], Anderton [40], Davies [71], Rebrov [77]	36,054
18	22	H	Ipswich T	L	1-2	1-1	7	Davies [12]	36,044
19	26	A	Southampton	L	0-1	0-0	7		31,719
20	29	A	Aston Villa	D	1-1	1-0	7	Ferdinand [38]	41,134
21	Jan 1	H	Blackburn R	W	1-0	1-0	7	Richards [45]	35,131
22	12	A	Ipswich T	L	1-2	0-1	8	Poyet [58]	25,057
23	19	H	Everton	D	1-1	1-1	7	Ferdinand [5]	36,075
24	30	H	Newcastle U	L	1-3	1-0	—	Iversen [17]	36,005
25	Feb 2	A	Derby Co	L	0-1	0-1	9		27,721
26	9	H	Leicester C	W	2-1	1-0	8	Anderton [37], Davies [61]	35,973
27	Mar 2	A	Sunderland	W	2-1	1-1	8	Poyet [31], Ferdinand [63]	36,062
28	6	A	Manchester U	L	0-4	0-2	—		67,599
29	13	A	Chelsea	L	0-4	0-1	—		39,652
30	18	H	Charlton Ath	L	0-1	0-0	—		29,596
31	24	H	Fulham	W	2-0	2-0	9	Sheringham [28], Poyet [32]	15,885
32	30	A	Middlesbrough	D	1-1	1-0	8	Iversen [32]	31,258
33	Apr 1	H	Leeds U	W	2-1	2-0	7	Iversen [10], Sheringham [29]	35,167
34	6	A	Arsenal	L	1-2	0-1	8	Sheringham (pen) [61]	38,186
35	13	A	West Ham U	D	1-1	0-0	8	Sheringham [53]	36,083
36	20	A	Bolton W	D	1-1	1-0	8	Iversen [8]	25,817
37	27	H	Liverpool	W	1-0	1-0	7	Poyet [41]	36,017
38	May 11	A	Leicester C	L	1-2	0-0	9	Sheringham (pen) [54]	21,716

Final League Position: 9

GOALSCORERS

League (49): Poyet 10, Sheringham 10 (3 pens), Ferdinand 9, Ziege 5, Davies 4, Iversen 4, Anderton 3, Richards 2, Rebrov 1, own goal 1.
Worthington Cup (21): Ferdinand 5, Davies 3, Rebrov 3, Iversen 2, Sheringham 2 (1 pen), Anderton 1, King 1, Poyet 1, Sherwood 1, Ziege 1, own goal 1.
FA Cup (10): Poyet 3, Anderton 1 (pen), Etherington 1, Ferdinand 1, Iversen 1, Sheringham 1, Ziege 1, own goal 1.

Sullivan N 29	Taricco M 30	Ziege C 27	Freund S 19+1	Doherty G 4+3	Bunjevcevic G 5+1	Poyet G 32+2	Clemence S 4+2	Rebrov S 9+21	Ferdinand L 22+3	King L 32	Perry C 30+3	Anderton D 33+2	Iversen S 12+6	Sheringham T 33+1	Davies S 22+9	Leonhardsen O 2+5	Thelwell A —+2	Richards D 24	Sherwood T 15+4	Thatcher B 11+1	Gardner A 11+4	Keller K 9	Etherington M 3+8	Match No.
1	2^1	3	4^2	5	6	7	8	9	10^3	11	12	13	14											1
1	2	3	4^1	5	6	8	12			11		7	9	10										2
1	2^2	3	12	5		8	11^1	13		4	6	7^3	9	10	14									3
1	2	3	4	5	6	9	11					7^1		10	8	12								4
1	2	3	4^1	6^2		12	9	11		5		7		10	8	13								5
1	2	3	4			11	12	9^1	6	5		7^2		10	8			13						6
1	2	3	4			11	12	9	6	5		7		10	8^1									7
1	2	3	8			11	12	9	4	5		7^1		10				6						8
1	2	3	8			11	12	9^1	4	5		7		10				6						9
1	2^2	3	8			11	12	9^1	4	5		7^3		10	13			6	14					10
1	2^1	3	8			11		9	4	5		7		10				6	12					11
1	2	3	8^1			11^2		9	4	5		7		10	13			6						12
1	2	3	8^2			11	12	9^1	4	5		7		10	13			6						13
1		3	7			11^1		9	4	5	2			10	8	12		6						14
1		3	7^2	12		11		9^2	13	4	5^1	2		10	8	14		6						15
1		3	4^1			7	9	11		5	2		12	10	8^2			6	13					16
1		3	7			11	12	9^1	4	5	2			10	8			6						17
1	2	3	4			12	9^2	13	11	5^3		7		10	8^1			6			14			18
1	2	3	8^3			11^1	12	9	4			7		10	13			6	14	5^2				19
	2	3^2	8			11	12	9^1	4	5		7		10				6			13	1		20
	2	3	8			11^1		9	4	5		7		10				6	12			1		21
1	2^3	3^2			8			9	10^1	11	5	7	12					6	13		4		14	22
1	3^1					12		9^2		5	2	13	10	11	7^3			6	8		4		14	23
1	3		11^2			12			4	5	2		9	10^1	8^3	13		6	7				14	24
1	3^2		11			12			4	5		13	9	10	2^2		8	6	7				14	25
1	3					12		10^1		5		7	9		8		13	6	4	2^2			11	26
1	2^2	3				7	12	9^1		5		10	11					6	8	4	13			27
1	2	3^1				7^1		9^2	13	5	12	10	11					6	8	4			14	28
1	2	3				11	12	9^1		5	13	10	7					6^2	8	4^3	14			29
1		3	11					9^2	10^1	5	6	7	12		2				8	4	13			30
1		3	11					9	10	5	6	7^1	12						8	2	4			31
			8			9^1				5	6	7^2		10	12	13		4		2	3	1	11	32
			12	13	14			2^1	9	10^3	8				6	7		3	4			1	11^2	33
	11^3		8			12			2^4	5	7	9^1	10	13	6			4	3			1	14	34
		3^1	12			11		8		6	7	13	10	2		8		5	4			1		35
3		13	11			12^2				6	7	9^1	10	8				4	5	2		1		36
	2					11	4				5	7	9	10	8			3		6		1		37
	3		12			11	8^1			6	7	9	10	2^2				5	4			1	13	38

Worthington Cup

Second Round	Torquay U	(h)	2-0
Third Round	Tranmere R	(a)	4-0
Fourth Round	Fulham	(a)	2-1
Fifth Round	Bolton W	(h)	6-0
Semi-Final	Chelsea	(a)	1-2
		(h)	5-1
Final	Blackburn R		1-2
(at Millennium Stadium)			

FA Cup

Third Round	Coventry C	(a)	2-0
Fourth Round	Bolton W	(h)	4-0
Fifth Round	Tranmere R	(h)	4-0
Sixth Round	Chelsea	(h)	0-4

TRANMERE ROVERS

Division 2

FOUNDATION

Formed in 1884 as Belmont they adopted their present title the following year and eventually joined their first league, the West Lancashire League in 1889–90, the same year as their first success in the Wirral Challenge Cup. The club almost folded in 1899–1900 when all the players left en bloc to join a rival club, but they survived the crisis and went from strength to strength winning the 'Combination' title in 1907–08 and the Lancashire Combination in 1913–14. They joined the Football League in 1921 from the Central League.

Prenton Park, Prenton Road West, Prenton, Wirral CH42 9PY.

Telephone: (0151) 609 3333. *Fax:* (0151) 608 4385.
Shop: (0151) 609 3311. *Ticket Office:* (0151) 609 3322.
ClubCall: 09068 121 646

Ground Capacity: 16,587 (all seated).

Record Attendance: 24,424 v Stoke C, FA Cup 4th rd, 5 February 1972.

Record Receipts: £268,946 v Liverpool, FA Cup 6th rd, 11 March 2001.

Pitch Measurements: 110yd × 70yd.

Chairperson: Lorraine Rogers.

Directors: Lorraine Rogers, Mick Horton, Richard Hughes.

Secretary: Mick Horton.

Manager: Dave Watson

Assistant Manager: (To be appointed.)

Youth Development Officer: Warwick Rimmer.

Coach and Chief Scout: Dave Philpotts.

Reserve Team Coach: (To be appointed.)

Physio: Les Parry.

Colours: White shirts and shorts with blue trim.

Change Colours: Navy and royal blue shirt and shorts.

Year Formed: 1884.

Turned Professional: 1912.

Ltd Co.: 1920.

Previous Name: 1884, Belmont AFC; 1885, Tranmere Rovers.

Club Nickname: 'The Rovers'.

HONOURS

Football League Division 1 best season: 4th, 1992–93; Promoted from Division 3 1990–91 (play-offs); Division 3 (N) – Champions 1937–38; Promotion to 3rd Division: 1966–67, 1975–76; Division 4 – Runners-up 1988–89.

FA Cup: best season: 6th rd, 2000, 2001.

Football League Cup: Runners-up, 2000.

Welsh Cup: Winners 1935; Runners-up 1934.

Leyland Daf Cup: Winners 1990; Runners-up 1991.

IT'S A FACT !

Legendary Tranmere Rovers marksman Bunny Bell was busy on three pre-war fronts: goalscoring centre-forward, shipping office worker and Birkenhead grocery shop owner.

Previous Grounds: 1884, Steeles Field; 1887, Ravenshaws Field/Old Prenton Park; 1912, Prenton Park.

First Football League Game: 27 August 1921, Division 3 (N), v Crewe Alex (h) W 4–1 – Bradshaw; Grainger, Stuart (1); Campbell, Milnes (1), Heslop; Moreton, Groves (1), Hyam, Ford (1), Hughes.

Record League Victory: 13–4 v Oldham Ath, Division 3 (N), 26 December 1935 – Gray; Platt, Fairhurst; McLaren, Newton, Spencer; Eden, MacDonald (1), Bell (9), Woodward (2), Urmson (1).

Record Cup Victory: 13–0 v Oswestry U, FA Cup 2nd prel rd, 10 October 1914 – Ashcroft; Stevenson, Bullough, Hancock, Taylor, Holden (1), Moreton (1), Cunningham (2), Smith (5), Leck (3), Gould (1).

Record Defeat: 1–9 v Tottenham H, FA Cup 3rd rd (replay), 14 January 1953.

Most League Points (2 for a win): 60, Division 4, 1964–65.

Most League Points (3 for a win): 80, Division 4, 1988–89 and Division 3, 1989–90.

Most League Goals: 111, Division 3 (N), 1930–31.

Highest League Scorer in Season: Bunny Bell, 35, Division 3 (N), 1933–34.

Most League Goals in Total Aggregate: Ian Muir, 142, 1985–95.

Most League Goals in One Match: 9, Bunny Bell v Oldham Ath, Division 3N, 26 December 1935.

Most Capped Player: John Aldridge, 30 (69), Republic of Ireland.

Most League Appearances: Harold Bell, 595, 1946–64 (incl. League record 401 consecutive appearances).

Youngest League Player: Iain Hume, 16 years 167 days v Swindon T, 15 April 2000.

Record Transfer Fee Received: £3,300,000 from Everton for Steve Simonsen, September 1998.

Record Transfer Fee Paid: £450,000 to Aston Villa for Shaun Teale, August 1995.

Football League Record: 1921 Original Member of Division 3 (N): 1938–39 Division 2; 1946–58 Division 3 (N); 1958–61 Division 3; 1961–67 Division 4; 1967–75 Division 3; 1975–76 Division 4; 1976–79 Division 3; 1979–89 Division 4; 1989–91 Division 3; 1991–92 Division 2; 1992–2001 Division 1; 2001– Division 2.

MANAGERS

Bert Cooke 1912–35
Jackie Carr 1935–36
Jim Knowles 1936–39
Bill Ridding 1939–45
Ernie Blackburn 1946–55
Noel Kelly 1955–57
Peter Farrell 1957–60
Walter Galbraith 1961
Dave Russell 1961–69
Jackie Wright 1969–72
Ron Yeats 1972–75
John King 1975–80
Bryan Hamilton 1980–85
Frank Worthington 1985–87
Ronnie Moore 1987
John King 1987–96
John Aldridge 1996–2001
Dave Watson April 2001–

LATEST SEQUENCES

Longest Sequence of League Wins: 9, 9.2.90 – 19.3.90.

Longest Sequence of League Defeats: 8, 29.10.38 – 17.12.38.

Longest Sequence of League Draws: 5, 26.12.97 – 31.1.98.

Longest Sequence of Unbeaten League Matches: 18, 16.3.70 – 4.9.70.

Longest Sequence Without a League Win: 16, 8.11.69 – 14.3.70.

TEN YEAR LEAGUE RECORD

		P	W	D	L	F	A	Pts	Pos
1991-92	Div 2	46	14	19	13	56	56	61	14
1992-93	Div 1	46	23	10	13	72	56	79	4
1993-94	Div 1	46	21	9	16	69	53	72	5
1994-95	Div 1	46	22	10	14	67	58	76	5
1995-96	Div 1	46	14	17	15	64	60	59	13
1996-97	Div 1	46	17	14	15	63	56	65	11
1997-98	Div 1	46	14	14	18	54	57	56	14
1998-99	Div 1	46	12	20	14	63	61	56	15
1999-2000	Div 1	46	15	12	19	57	68	57	13
2000-01	Div 1	46	9	11	26	46	77	38	24

DID YOU KNOW ?

Bob Randles was the scorer of the first goal at Prenton Park on 9 March 1912 and went on to hit three in the 8-0 success over Lancaster Town.

TRANMERE ROVERS 2001–02 LEAGUE RECORD

Match No.	Date	Venue	Opponents	Result	H/T Score	Lg. Pos.	Goalscorers	Attendance
1	Aug 11	H	Bury	L	1-2	0-1	—	Parkinson [74]	9114
2	18	A	Colchester U	L	1-2	0-0	22	Barlow (pen) [90]	3618
3	25	H	Brighton & HA	D	0-0	0-0	20		8162
4	27	A	Stoke C	W	2-1	1-0	15	Hill [13], Flynn [89]	12,031
5	Sept 1	A	Oldham Ath	D	2-2	1-2	15	Barlow [36], Mellon [88]	8716
6	8	A	Brentford	L	0-4	0-1	16		5211
7	15	A	Swindon T	D	2-2	1-1	20	Allen [45], Koumas [74]	5922
8	18	H	Notts Co	W	4-2	1-2	—	Barlow 3 (1 pen) [21, 55 ipl, 59], Koumas [56]	7343
9	21	H	Wrexham	W	5-0	1-0	—	Koumas [45], Barlow 3 [54, 55, 78], Yates [64]	10,285
10	25	A	Bristol C	L	0-2	0-2	—		9634
11	29	H	Chesterfield	W	2-0	1-0	13	Barlow [39], N'Diaye [61]	4790
12	Oct 4	H	Blackpool	W	4-0	3-0	—	Yates [2], Flynn 2 [21, 69], Parkinson [35]	10,354
13	13	A	Northampton T	L	1-4	1-2	12	Flynn [45]	4636
14	20	H	Huddersfield T	W	1-0	0-0	9	Henry [50]	8632
15	23	H	Wigan Ath	L	1-2	0-0	—	N'Diaye [81]	9030
16	27	A	Cardiff C	D	1-1	0-1	12	Rideout [90]	13,070
17	Nov 3	H	Wycombe W	D	1-1	1-1	12	Flynn [12]	8096
18	10	A	QPR	W	2-1	0-0	9	Koumas [72], Barlow [90]	9024
19	20	A	Reading	L	1-4	0-2	—	Price [77]	9007
20	24	H	Cambridge U	W	6-1	2-0	9	Hill [13], Price 2 [39, 88], Koumas [61], Allison [89], Navarro [90]	8004
21	Dec 1	A	Bournemouth	W	2-0	1-0	8	Price [42], Roberts [66]	6035
22	15	H	Port Vale	W	3-1	2-1	7	Allison 2 [34, 83], Yates [38]	7859
23	26	H	Stoke C	D	2-2	1-1	11	Price 2 [42, 72]	12,201
24	29	H	Brentford	W	1-0	0-0	8	Koumas [61]	9389
25	Jan 12	H	Colchester U	D	0-0	0-0	7		8387
26	19	A	Bury	W	1-0	1-0	8	Koumas [28]	4245
27	22	H	Peterborough U	W	1-0	0-0	—	Rideout [14]	7342
28	Feb 2	H	Chesterfield	D	0-0	0-0	9		8477
29	5	A	Brighton & HA	L	0-1	0-0	—		6279
30	9	A	Huddersfield T	L	1-2	1-0	10	Rideout [23]	15,784
31	12	H	Northampton T	W	2-0	0-0	—	Price [65], Allison [87]	7739
32	19	A	Oldham Ath	D	1-1	1-0	—	Rideout [12]	5998
33	22	H	Swindon T	D	0-0	0-0	—		8106
34	26	A	Wrexham	D	1-1	0-0	—	Barlow [82]	5702
35	Mar 2	A	Notts Co	L	0-3	0-3	10		4562
36	5	H	Bristol C	W	1-0	1-0	—	Haworth [14]	7735
37	9	A	Port Vale	D	1-1	1-1	10	Haworth [10]	4630
38	12	A	Blackpool	D	1-1	0-1	—	Haworth [57]	6860
39	16	H	Bournemouth	D	0-0	0-0	9		7829
40	19	A	Peterborough U	L	0-5	0-3	—		3995
41	23	A	Wigan Ath	W	2-1	1-1	9	Thornton [24], Barlow [85]	7783
42	30	H	QPR	L	2-3	0-1	10	Koumas [60], Barlow [70]	8619
43	Apr 1	A	Wycombe W	L	1-2	0-1	10	Haworth [61]	6297
44	7	H	Reading	D	2-2	1-0	10	Barlow [41], Haworth [48]	9282
45	13	A	Cambridge U	L	1-2	1-0	11	Roberts [30]	4627
46	20	H	Cardiff C	L	0-1	0-0	12		8375

Final League Position: 12

GOALSCORERS

League (63): Barlow 14 (2 pens), Koumas 8, Price 7, Flynn 5, Haworth 5, Allison 4, Rideout 4, Yates 3, Hill 2, N'Diaye 2, Parkinson 2, Roberts 2, Allen 1, Henry 1, Mellon 1, Navarro 1, Thornton 1.
Worthington Cup (7): Barlow 2, Flynn 2, Henry 1, Koumas 1, Mellon 1.
FA Cup (16): Koumas 4, Price 4, Flynn 3, Allison 1, Barlow 1 (pen), Navarro 1, Rideout 1, Yates 1.

Murphy J 21+1	Hazell R 6	Roberts G 45	Henry N 39	Challinor D 6	Hill C 30	Flynn S 30+1	Parkinson A 14+17	N'Diaye S 6+5	Barlow S 31+7	Mellon M 23+4	Yates S 36+1	Allison W 13+14	Hume 11+13	Koumas J 38	Thornton S 9+2	Jobson R 1	Hay A 2+1	Allen G 30+1	Sharps I 25+4	Rideout P 14+1	Harrison D 1	Hinds R 6+4	Price J 20+4	Achterberg J 25	Navarro A 21	Haworth S 12	Morgan A 1+1	Nixon E —+1	Match No.
1	2	3	4[1]	5[2]	6	7	8	9	10	11[3]	12	13	14																1
1	2	3	4[1]	5	6	7	8	13	9	11		10[2]	12																2
		3	4	5	6	12	8		9	7[1]	2	10		11															3
		3		5	6	4	8		9[1]	7	2	10	12	11															4
1	6	3	4[2]	5		7	8		9[1]	11	2	10	12		13														5
1	2	3				7	8[1]		9	11	4	12		10			6[2]	13	5										6
1	2	3	4			7	12		9	11	6	10					8[1]	5											7
1	2[2]	3	4			7	8		9	11[1]	6	12		10				5	13										8
1		3	4[2]			7	8	12	9[1]	13	6	10[3]		11				5	2	14									9
1		3	4[1]			7	8[2]	9[3]	10	12	6	13	14	11				5	2										10
1		3	4	5		7	12	13	9	8	6	10[2]		11[1]					2										11
1		3	4			7	8		9	10	11	6						5	2										12
1		3				4	8[1]	9	10	7	6	12	13	11				5	2										13
1		3	4			7	12[2]		10	8	6	14	13	11[1]				5	2	9[1]									14
1		3	4			7	12		10	8			13	11				5	2	9[1]	8[2]								15
1		3	4			7	12		9[2]	13	11	6	8[1]					5[2]	2	10		14							16
1		3	4			7	12		10[3]	8[1]	6	13	14	11				5	2[2]	9									17
1		3	4		6	7						10		11				5		9			8						18
1		3	4[2]		6	7	12		9	13	2	10[1]		11				5					8						19
		3	4		6	7[1]	12				2		13	11				5	9[2]				8	1		10			20
		3	4		6[1]	7					2	10		11				5	12				8	1		9			21
		3	4		6	7	8					10		11				5	2[1]			12	9	1					22
		3	4		6	7	12		8[1]			10		11				5					9	1					23
		3	4		6	7			8			10		11				5					9	1					24
			4		6	7	12		8[2]			3	10[1]	11				5	13			2	9	1					25
		3	4		6	7	12		8			2		11				5	9			10[1]		1					26
		3	4		6	7			12			8	2	11				5	9			10[1]		1					27
		3	4[2]	5		7	12				13	2	14	11					8	9[1]		10[1]			6				28
		3	4		6	7	12					2	13	11				5	9[2]			10[1]	8						29
		3	4		6	7[2]	10				12	2	13	11					9[1]			14	8[2]						30
		3	4	5[2]		7	12		9[2]			2	10	11				13	6			14	8[1]						31
		3	4		6		12					8	2	11				5	9			10[1]		1	7				32
		3	4		6		8[1]					2	13	11				5	9[2]			10[1]		1	7				33
		3	4		6		13		8[1]			2		11				5	9			10[2]		1	7				34
		3[2]	4[1]		6		8					2		11	12			5	13			10		1	7	9			35
		3	4		6		10							11	8			5	2					1	7	9			36
		3			6		10							11	7			5	2			12		1	7	9	4		37
		3			6		10							11	7			5	2			4		1	8	9			38
		3	4				12		10[2]			2	13	11	7			5	6						8[1]	9			39
		3	4				8		10[1]			2	12	11				5[2]	6			13		1	7[3]	9	14		40
		3	4[3]		6		12						14	11	7	10[1]		5[2]	2			13		1	8	9			41
		3	4[1]	5			12		10					11	7				6			2	13	1	8	9[2]			42
		3		5			8				10		12		7				6			2	11[1]	1	4	9			43
15		3	4	5			8[1]		10	12		6		11									10[1]		7	9			44
1[8]		3	4[1]	5			12		10	13	7	6	2	11[2]									8			9		15	45
1		3					12		10	8	2			11	7				6				5		4[1]	9			46

Worthington Cup

First Round	Shrewsbury T	(h)	3-1
Second Round	Preston NE	(h)	4-1
Third Round	Tottenham H	(h)	0-4

FA Cup

First Round	Brigg T	(h)	4-1
Second Round	Carlisle U	(h)	6-1
Third Round	Southend U	(a)	3-1
Fourth Round	Cardiff C	(h)	3-1
Fifth Round	Tottenham H	(a)	0-4

WALSALL   Division 1

FOUNDATION

Two of the leading clubs around Walsall in the 1880s were Walsall Swifts (formed 1877) and Walsall Town (formed 1879). The Swifts were winners of the Birmingham Senior Cup in 1881, while the Town reached the 4th round (5th round modern equivalent) of the FA Cup in 1883. These clubs amalgamated as Walsall Town Swifts in 1888, becoming simply Walsall in 1895.

Bescot Stadium, Bescot Crescent, Walsall WS1 4SA.

Telephone: (01922) 622 791. **Fax:** (01922) 613 202.
ClubCall: 09068 555 800. **Website:** www.saddlers.co.uk
Email: info@walsallfc.co.uk (General Information), commercial@walsallfc.co.uk (Commercial), tickets @walsallfc.co.uk (Ticket Office), a.poole@walsallfc.co.uk (Matchday Programme/ Official Website)

Commercial Dept: (01922) 651 412.

Ground Capacity: 6,700 until December 2002, then 10,700.

Record Attendance: 10,628 B International, England v Switzerland, 20 May 1991.

Record Receipts: £98,828 v Leeds U, FA Cup 3rd rd, 7 January 1995.

Pitch Measurements: 110yd × 73yd.

Chairman: M. N. Lloyd.

Directors: J. W. Bonser, R. E. Tisdale, C. Welch, K. R. Whalley. **Chief Executive:** K. R. Whalley.
Director of Finance: K. Avery. **Director of Conference and Banqueting Services:** C. Deakin.

Manager: Colin Lee. **Assistant Manager:** Dave Merrington. **Physio:** Duncan Russell.
Chief Scout: Bob Rickwood. **Youth/Reserve Team Manager:** Mick Halsall.
Youth Liaison & Recruitment Officer: Bill Jones. **Centre of Excellence Director:** John Kerr.

Secretary/Commercial Director: Roy Whalley.

Year Formed: 1888. **Turned Professional:** 1888. **Ltd Co.:** 1921.

Previous Names: Walsall Swifts (founded 1877) and Walsall Town (founded 1879) amalgamated in 1888 and were known as Walsall Town Swifts until 1895. **Club Nickname:** 'The Saddlers'.

Colours: Red shirts, red shorts, red stockings with black and white trim.

Change Colours: Navy blue shirts, navy blue shorts, navy blue stockings with white trim.

Previous Grounds: 1888, Fellows Park; 1990, Bescot Stadium.

First Football League Game: 3 September 1892, Division 2, v Darwen (h) L 12 – Hawkins; Withington, Pinches; Robinson, Whitrick, Forsyth; Marshall, Holmes, Turner, Gray (1), Pangbourn.

Record League Victory: 10–0 v Darwen, Division 2, 4 March 1899 – Tennent; E. Peers (1), Davies; Hickinbotham, Jenkyns, Taggart; Dean (3), Vail (2), Aston (4), Martin, Griffin.

Record Cup Victory: 7–0 v Macclesfield T (a), FA Cup 2nd rd, 6 December 1997 – Walker; Evans, Marsh, Viveash (1), Ryder, Peron, Boli (2 incl. 1p) (Ricketts), Porter (2), Keates, Watson (Platt), Hodge (2 incl. 1p).

HONOURS

Football League: Division 2: Runners-up, 1998–99, Promoted to Division 1 – 2000–01 (play-offs); Division 3 – Runners-up 1960–61, 1994–95; Division 4 – Champions 1959–60; Runners-up 1979–80.

FA Cup: best season: 5th rd, 1939, 1975, 1978, 1987, 2001 and last 16 1889.

Football League Cup: Semi-final 1984.

IT'S A FACT !

In their 1959–60 championship season, Walsall's five forwards reached double figures in goalscoring: John Davies (12), Roy Faulkner (21), Tony Richards (24), Ken Hodgkisson (12) and Colin Taylor (21).

Record Defeat: 0–12 v Small Heath, 17 December 1892.
0–12 v Darwen, 26 December 1896, both Division 2.

Most League Points (2 for a win): 65, Division 4, 1959–60.

Most League Points (3 for a win): 87, Division 2, 1998–99.

Most League Goals: 102, Division 4, 1959–60.

Highest League Scorer in Season: Gilbert Alsop, 40,
Division 3 (N), 1933–34 and 1934–35.

Most League Goals in Total Aggregate: Tony Richards, 184,
1954–63; Colin Taylor, 184, 1958–63, 1964–68, 1969–73.

Most League Goals in One Match: 5, Gilbert Alsop v
Carlisle U, Division 3N, 2 February 1935; 5, Bill Evans v
Mansfield T, Division 3N, 5 October 1935; 5, Johnny Devlin v
Torquay U, Division 3S, 1 September 1949.

Most Capped Player: Mick Kearns, 15 (18), Republic of Ireland.

Most League Appearances: Colin Harrison, 467, 1964–82.

Youngest League Player: Geoff Morris, 16 years 218 days v
Scunthorpe U, 14 September 1965.

Record Transfer Fee Received: £600,000 from West Ham U
for David Kelly, July 1988.

Record Transfer Fee Paid: £175,000 to Birmingham C for
Alan Buckley, June 1979.

Football League Record: 1892 Elected to Division 2; 1895
Failed re-election; 1896–1901 Division 2; 1901 Failed
re-election; 1921 Original Member of Division 3 (N); 1927–31
Division 3 (S); 1931–36 Division 3 (N); 1936–58 Division 3 (S);
1958–60 Division 4; 1960–61 Division 3; 1961–63 Division 4;
1963–79 Division 3; 1979–80 Division 4; 1980–88 Division 3;
1988–89 Division 2; 1989–90 Division 3; 1990–92 Division 4;
1992–95 Division 3; 1995–99 Division 2; 1999–2000 Division 1;
2000–01 Division 2; 2001– Division 1.

LATEST SEQUENCES

Longest Sequence of League Wins: 7, 10.10.59 – 21.11.59.

Longest Sequence of League Defeats: 15, 29.10.88 – 4.2.89.

Longest Sequence of League Draws: 5, 7.5.88 – 17.9.88.

Longest Sequence of Unbeaten League Matches: 21, 6.11.79 –
22.3.80.

Longest Sequence Without a League Win: 18, 15.10.88 –
4.2.89.

MANAGERS

H. Smallwood 1888–91
(Secretary-Manager)
A. G. Burton 1891–93
J. H. Robinson 1893–95
C. H. Ailso 1895–96
(Secretary-Manager)
A. E. Parsloe 1896–97
(Secretary-Manager)
L. Ford 1897–98
(Secretary-Manager)
G. Hughes 1898–99
(Secretary-Manager)
L. Ford 1899–1901
(Secretary-Manager)
J. E. Shutt 1908–13
(Secretary-Manager)
Haydn Price 1914–20
Joe Burchell 1920–26
David Ashworth 1926–27
Jack Torrance 1927–28
James Kerr 1928–29
Sid Scholey 1929–30
Peter O'Rourke 1930–32
Bill Slade 1932–34
Andy Wilson 1934–37
Tommy Lowes 1937–44
Harry Hibbs 1944–51
Tony McPhee 1951
Brough Fletcher 1952–53
Major Frank Buckley 1953–55
John Love 1955–57
Billy Moore 1957–64
Alf Wood 1964
Reg Shaw 1964–68
Dick Graham 1968
Ron Lewin 1968–69
Billy Moore 1969–72
John Smith 1972–73
Doug Fraser 1973–77
Dave Mackay 1977–78
Alan Ashman 1978
Frank Sibley 1979
Alan Buckley 1979–86
Neil Martin *(Joint Manager with*
Buckley) 1981–82
Tommy Coakley 1986–88
John Barnwell 1989–90
Kenny Hibbitt 1990–94
Chris Nicholl 1994–97
Jan Sorensen 1997–98
Ray Graydon 1998–2002
Colin Lee January 2002–

TEN YEAR LEAGUE RECORD

		P	W	D	L	F	A	Pts	Pos
1991-92	Div 4	42	12	13	17	48	58	49	15
1992-93	Div 3	42	22	7	13	76	61	73	5
1993-94	Div 3	42	17	9	16	48	53	60	10
1994-95	Div 3	42	24	11	7	75	40	83	2
1995-96	Div 2	46	19	12	15	60	45	69	11
1996-97	Div 2	46	19	10	17	54	53	67	12
1997-98	Div 2	46	14	12	20	43	52	54	19
1998-99	Div 2	46	26	9	11	63	47	87	2
1999-2000	Div 1	46	11	13	22	52	77	46	22
2000-01	Div 2	46	23	12	11	79	50	81	4

DID YOU KNOW ?

Alan Buckley is the most
prolific scorer in Walsall's
history, with 205 goals in all
competitions. He was also the
most expensive signing at one
time, costing £175,000 when
returning from Birmingham
City in June 1979.

WALSALL 2001–02 LEAGUE RECORD

Match No.	Date	Venue	Opponents	Result	H/T Score	Lg. Pos.	Goalscorers	Attendance
1	Aug 11	H	WBA	W 2-1	1-0	—	Leitao 37, Barras 62	9181
2	18	A	Preston NE	D 1-1	1-0	6	Herivelto 36	11,402
3	25	H	Birmingham C	L 1-2	0-2	11	Herivelto 90	7245
4	27	A	Watford	L 1-2	0-0	16	Leitao 48	14,652
5	Sept 8	A	Crewe Alex	L 1-2	0-1	19	Simpson 76	6809
6	15	A	Burnley	L 2-5	0-2	22	Wrack 51, Davis (og) 64	14,019
7	18	H	Portsmouth	D 0-0	0-0	—		6153
8	21	H	Wolverhampton W	L 0-3	0-3	—		8327
9	25	A	Manchester C	L 0-3	0-2	—		31,525
10	29	H	Millwall	D 0-0	0-0	23		6289
11	Oct 9	A	Norwich C	W 2-0	1-0	—	Barras 45, Byfield 53	5713
12	14	H	Coventry C	L 0-1	0-1	21		7515
13	20	A	Sheffield W	L 1-2	1-0	23	Byfield 19	16,275
14	23	H	Rotherham U	W 3-2	3-0	—	Matias 2 5, 30, Wrack 36	6162
15	27	H	Gillingham	L 0-2	0-1	23		7548
16	30	A	Stockport Co	W 2-0	1-0	—	Angell 19, Thogersen 73	4553
17	Nov 3	H	Crystal Palace	D 2-2	2-1	22	Barras 2 25, 44	6795
18	11	H	Nottingham F	W 2-0	2-0	20	Matias 27, Angell 33	6754
19	17	A	Bradford C	L 0-2	0-1	21		14,251
20	20	A	Wimbledon	D 2-2	1-1	—	Thogersen 42, Leitao 88	4249
21	24	H	Sheffield U	L 1-2	1-2	21	Wrack 21	6415
22	Dec 1	A	Rotherham U	L 0-2	0-1	21		6273
23	8	A	Barnsley	L 1-4	0-2	23	Aranalde 63	12,509
24	15	H	Grimsby T	W 4-0	1-0	20	Biancalani 33, Angell 68, Leitao 89, Herivelto 90	5080
25	22	A	Birmingham C	L 0-1	0-1	22		20,127
26	26	H	Crewe Alex	W 2-1	2-0	21	Aranalde 17, Biancalani 51	7325
27	29	H	Watford	L 0-3	0-2	21		6882
28	Jan 1	A	Norwich C	D 1-1	0-1	21	Tillson 56	19,434
29	12	H	Preston NE	L 1-2	0-0	21	Wrack 57	6314
30	20	A	WBA	L 0-1	0-1	22		20,290
31	29	H	Wimbledon	W 2-1	1-1	—	Leitao 42, Carbon 85	5388
32	Feb 2	A	Millwall	D 2-2	0-0	21	Matias 76, Keates (pen) 80	11,285
33	9	H	Sheffield W	L 0-3	0-1	22		8290
34	19	A	Coventry C	L 1-2	1-1	—	Holdsworth 25	13,736
35	23	H	Manchester C	D 0-0	0-0	22		7618
36	26	A	Wolverhampton W	L 0-3	0-0	—		27,043
37	Mar 2	A	Portsmouth	D 1-1	0-0	23	O'Connor 59	13,203
38	5	H	Burnley	W 1-0	0-0	—	Marcelo 52	5611
39	9	A	Grimsby T	D 2-2	0-1	23	Leitao 80, Byfield 90	7016
40	16	H	Barnsley	W 2-1	0-1	22	Byfield 68, Goodman 83	7495
41	23	A	Crystal Palace	L 0-2	0-0	23		21,038
42	30	H	Gillingham	D 1-1	1-0	23	Herivelto 32	6190
43	Apr 1	A	Nottingham F	W 3-2	2-1	22	Simpson 5, Matias 45, Corica 86	16,659
44	6	H	Stockport Co	W 1-0	0-0	20	Leitao 50	6322
45	13	H	Sheffield U	W 1-0	1-0	19	Leitao 43	20,520
46	21	H	Bradford C	D 2-2	2-0	18	Corica 2 14, 22	8079

Final League Position: 18

GOALSCORERS

League (51): Leitao 8, Matias 5, Barras 4, Byfield 4, Herivelto 4, Wrack 4, Angell 3, Corica 3, Aranalde 2, Biancalani 2, Simpson 2, Thogersen 2, Carbon 1, Goodman 1, Holdsworth 1, Keates 1 (pen), Marcelo 1, O'Connor 1, Tillson 1, own goal 1.
Worthington Cup (4): Barras 1, Byfield 1, Herivelto 1, Wrack 1.
FA Cup (5): Leitao 2, Angell 1, Bennett 1, Byfield 1.

Walker J 43	Gadsby M 17+5	Aranalde Z 43+2	Tillson A 8+1	Barras T 25+1	Keates D 6+7	Herivelto H 11+13	Bennett T 34+6	Leitao J 24+14	Byfield D 24+13	Matias P 25+5	Brightwell I 25+2	Simpson F 21+7	Wrack D 40+3	Goodman D 7+10	Biancalani F 13+5	Garrocho C 2+2	Roper I 24+3	Harper L 3	Curtis T 3+1	Chettle S 6	Angell B 13+7	Scott D —+1	Thogersen T 7	Carbon M 22	Ofodile A —+1	Birch G —+1	Andre C 5	Holdsworth D 9	O'Connor M 12+1	Marcelo 9	Shields G 7	Corica S 13	Uhlenbeek G 5	Hawley K —+1	Match No.
1	2	3	4	5	6	7¹	8²	9	10³	11	12	13	14																						1
1	2	3	4¹	5	6	7³	8	9²	10		12	11	13	14																					2
1		3	4¹	5	6	7	8	9²	10³	11	2	12	13	14																					3
1	2	3		5	6	7¹	8	12	11²	4	9	10	13																						4
1		3	4	5	6¹	7	8³	9	13	2	12	10²	14		11																				5
1	2¹	3		5			9²	13	11¹	4	8	12	10			14	6																		6
	2¹	3	4	5			12	8	9²	13	6	7	10	11				1																	7
		3	4	5		7	12	13	14	11²	6	8	9³	10			1		2¹																8
	2	3¹	12	6¹			8²	13	9	14	4	10	11					1	7	5															9
1	2	3		6			12	8¹	9²	13	4	10			11				7	5															10
1	2	3		6		7³	8	9	10	12	4				13		11				13		5	14											11
1	2¹	3		6		7³	8	9	10	12	4		13		11								5	14											12
1	2²	3		6			7	9	10	12		8			11		4				5		13												13
1	12	3		6			9	4	10³	11	2¹	8		7			13				5²		14												14
1	2¹	3		6	13	12	8³	14	9	4	10				11		5						7²												15
1		3		5						4		10	11	2	12		7						9¹	8	6										16
1		3		5						4		10¹	11	2			7						9	8	6	12									17
1	2	3								4	12	10¹	11		13		7				14		9²	8	6³										18
1	12	3		5						4	13	10²	11	2¹			7						9	8	6³										19
1	2	3		5	12					4	13	10					7				11	14	9²	8¹	6³										20
1	2	3		5						12	4	13	10	11¹			7				6		9²	8³											21
1	2	12		5					13	4	9²	10³	11¹	8			7		3		6									14					22
1	2²	12		5	6	13	8	9	10²			11	3¹						7				14	4											23
1		3					12	8	13	10²	11	4					7¹		2		5		9	6											24
1		3					12	4	10⁴	13	11	2					7¹		8	5			9	6											25
1	12	3			13			4	10	14	11		2				7		8²		5		9¹	6											26
1	12	3						4	10	14	11²		2				5¹		7		9			6											27
1		3	4	5				8	12	13			2				7		10		9¹		6				11²								28
1		3	4		12					6			10	13	2				7		8		9²				11¹								29
1	2	3						12	7	13								11	8		5		9¹	6			10²	4							30
1		3				12	13	4	9	10²	11³	2									14		6				8¹	5							31
1		3				12		4	9	10²	11	2					7				13		6				8¹	5							32
1		3			13	12²	4	9	14	11²	2¹		7										6				5	8	10						33
1		3					9¹	12	11²						8	13		5						6				4¹	10		2	7			34
1			5				12	9²	13						3		11	8		6								4¹	10		2	7			35
1		3			12			13	9¹	14				8³			11				5			12				6	4²	10	2	7²			36
1		3							9¹					8			11	13			5			12				6	4	10	2	7²			37
1		3							4					11	12	7	8				5							6	2	9					38
1		3					8	12	10					11⁵	13	7	14				5							6	4		2³	9²			39
1		3						4						10³			8²	12	11	13				6				14	9¹		2	7			40
1		3				12		13	10						2¹		14	11	8²					6				4	9³		7				41
1	12	3				7¹								11⁴			10	13						6				4	9³		8	2	14		42
1		3					12							11			8	10¹	7					6				4			9¹	2			43
1		3						12						11			8	10¹	7					6				4			9	2			44
1		3					12	9²						11			8¹	13	7					5				4			10	2			45
1		3					12	9³						11			8¹	13	7					5				4¹			10	2			46

Worthington Cup

First Round	Exeter C	(a)	1-0
Second Round	Bolton W	(a)	3-4

FA Cup

Third Round	Bradford C	(h)	2-0
Fourth Round	Charlton Ath	(a)	2-1
Fifth Round	Fulham	(h)	1-2

WATFORD   Division 1

FOUNDATION

The club was formed as Watford Rovers in 1881. The name was changed to West Herts in 1893 and then the name Watford was adopted after rival club Watford St Mary's was absorbed in 1898.

Vicarage Road Stadium, Watford WD18 0ER.

Telephone: (01923) 496 000. *Fax:* (01923) 496 001.
Ticketline: 09068 400 401. *Ticket Office:* (01923) 496 010.
Ticket Office Fax: (01923) 351 145.
ClubCall: 09068 104 104. *Club Shop:* (01923) 229 859.
Club Shop Fax: (01923) 496 238. *Catering:* (01923) 252 323.
Football in the Community: (01923) 440 449.
Junior Hornets Club: (01923) 496 256.
Marketing: (01923) 496 006. *Press Office:* (01923) 496 234.

Ground Capacity: 20,800.

Record Attendance: 34,099 v Manchester U, FA Cup
4th rd (replay), 3 February 1969.

Record Receipts: £440,349 v Chelsea, FA Premier
League, 18 September 1999.

Pitch Measurements: 113yd × 73yd.

Life Presidents: Sir Elton John CBE, Geoff Smith,
Graham Taylor OBE.

HONOURS

Football League: Division 1 –
Runners-up 1982–83, promoted from
Division 1 1998–99 (play-offs);
Division 2 – Champions 1997–98;
Runners-up 1981–82; Division 3 –
Champions 1968–69; Runners-up
1978–79; Division 4 – Champions
1977–78; Promoted 1959–60 (4th).

FA Cup: Runners-up 1984.

Football League Cup: Semi- final
1979.

European Competitions: UEFA Cup:
1983–84.

Chairman: Sir Elton John CBE. *Vice-chairman:* Haig Oundjian. *Directors:* B. Anderson, D. Meller,
T. Shaw, D. Lester, C. Lissack, C. Norton, G. Simpson, M. Sherwood, N. Wray.
Chief Executive: Tim Shaw. *Football Secretary:* Catherine Alexander.

Football Manager: Ray Lewington. *Assistant Manager:* Terry Byrne.
Academy Director: Peter Trevivian. *Academy Assistant Directors:* Chris Cummins, David Hockaday.

Communications Manager: Andrew French. *Director of Marketing:* Ed Coan.
Safety Officer: Paul Dumpleton. *Stadium Manager:* Paddy Flavin.

Colours: Yellow shirts, red shorts, red stockings with black and yellow turnover.

Change Colours: Black shirts with red and yellow trim around cuffs and collar, black shorts, black
stockings with thick red and thin yellow bands on turnover.

Year Formed: 1881.

Turned Professional: 1897.

Ltd Co.: 1909.

Club Nickname: 'The Hornets'.

Previous Names: 1881, Watford Rovers; 1893, West Herts; 1898, Watford.

Previous Grounds: 1883, Vicarage Meadow, Rose and Crown Meadow; 1889, Colney Butts; 1890,
Cassio Road; 1922, Vicarage Road.

First Football League Game: 28 August 1920, Division 3, v QPR (a) W 2–1 – Williams; Horseman, F.
Gregory; Bacon, Toone, Wilkinson; Bassett, Ronald (1), Hoddinott, White (1), Waterall.

IT'S A FACT !

George Toone completed four years for Watford
without missing a first team game, appearing in 176
consecutive matches between 1919 and 1924.

Record League Victory: 8–0 v Sunderland, Division 1, 25 September 1982 – Sherwood; Rice, Rostron, Taylor, Terry, Bolton, Callaghan (2), Blissett (4), Jenkins (2), Jackett, Barnes.

Record Cup Victory: 10–1 v Lowestoft T, FA Cup 1st rd, 27 November 1926 – Yates; Prior, Fletcher (1); F. Smith, 'Bert' Smith, Strain; Stephenson, Warner (3), Edmonds (3), Swan (1), Daniels (1), (1 og).

Record Defeat: 0–10 v Wolverhampton W, FA Cup 1st rd (replay), 24 January 1912.

Most League Points (2 for a win): 71, Division 4, 1977–78.

Most League Points (3 for a win): 88, Division 2, 1997–98.

Most League Goals: 92, Division 4, 1959–60.

Highest League Scorer in Season: Cliff Holton, 42, Division 4, 1959–60.

Most League Goals in Total Aggregate: Luther Blissett, 148, 1976–83, 1984–88, 1991–92.

Most League Goals in One Match: 5, Eddie Mummery v Newport Co, Division 3S, 5 January 1924.

Most Capped Player: John Barnes, 31 (79), England and Kenny Jackett, 31, Wales.

Most League Appearances: Luther Blissett, 415, 1976–83, 1984–88, 1991–92.

Youngest League Player: Keith Mercer, 16 years 125 days v Tranmere R, 16 February 1973.

Record Transfer Fee Received: £2,300,000 from Chelsea for Paul Furlong, May 1994.

Record Transfer Fee Paid: £2,250,000 to Tottenham H for Allan Nielsen, August 2000.

MANAGERS

John Goodall 1903–10
Harry Kent 1910–26
Fred Pagnam 1926–29
Neil McBain 1929–37
Bill Findlay 1938–47
Jack Bray 1947–48
Eddie Hapgood 1948–50
Ron Gray 1950–51
Haydn Green 1951–52
Len Goulden 1952–55
  (General Manager to 1956)
Johnny Paton 1955–56
Neil McBain 1956–59
Ron Burgess 1959–63
Bill McGarry 1963–64
Ken Furphy 1964–71
George Kirby 1971–73
Mike Keen 1973–77
Graham Taylor 1977–87
Dave Bassett 1987–88
Steve Harrison 1988–90
Colin Lee 1990
Steve Perryman 1990–93
Glenn Roeder 1993–96
Kenny Jackett 1996–97
Graham Taylor 1997–2001
Gianluca Vialli 2001–02
Ray Lewington July 2002–

Football League Record: 1920 Original Member of Division 3; 1921–58 Division 3 (S); 1958–60 Division 4; 1960–69 Division 3; 1969–72 Division 2; 1972–75 Division 3; 1975–78 Division 4; 1978–79 Division 3; 1979–82 Division 2; 1982–88 Division 1; 1988–92 Division 2; 1992–96 Division 1; 1996–98 Division 2; 1998–99 Division 1; 1999–2000 FA Premier League; 2000– Division 1.

LATEST SEQUENCES

Longest Sequence of League Wins: 7, 28.8.00 – 14.10.00.

Longest Sequence of League Defeats: 9, 26.12.72 – 27.2.73.

Longest Sequence of League Draws: 7, 30.11.96 – 27.1.97.

Longest Sequence of Unbeaten League Matches: 22, 1.10.96 – 1.3.97.

Longest Sequence Without a League Win: 19, 27.11.71 – 8.4.72.

TEN YEAR LEAGUE RECORD

		P	W	D	L	F	A	Pts	Pos
1991-92	Div 2	46	18	11	17	51	48	65	10
1992-93	Div 1	46	14	13	19	57	71	55	16
1993-94	Div 1	46	15	9	22	66	80	54	19
1994-95	Div 1	46	19	13	14	52	46	70	7
1995-96	Div 1	46	10	18	18	62	70	48	23
1996-97	Div 2	46	16	19	11	45	38	67	13
1997-98	Div 2	46	24	16	6	67	41	88	1
1998-99	Div 1	46	21	14	11	65	56	77	5
1999-2000	PR Lge	38	6	6	26	35	77	24	20
2000-01	Div 1	46	20	9	17	76	67	69	9

DID YOU KNOW ?

In 1922–23 Fred Pagnam, an ever-present in the team, scored 30 of Watford's 57 League goals including four hat-tricks as the club finished 10th.

WATFORD 2001–02 LEAGUE RECORD

Match No.	Date	Venue	Opponents	Result	H/T Score	Lg. Pos.	Goalscorers	Attendance
1	Aug 11	A	Manchester C	L	0-3	0-0	—		33,939
2	18	H	Rotherham U	W	3-2	2-1	14	Smith 2 [3, 60], Nielsen [44]	13,839
3	25	A	Wolverhampton W	L	0-1	0-1	18		20,257
4	27	H	Walsall	W	2-1	0-0	11	Galli [69], Nielsen [80]	14,652
5	Sept 9	H	Wimbledon	W	3-0	1-0	9	Wooter [45], Gayle [48], Robinson [53]	15,466
6	15	H	WBA	L	1-2	0-1	10	Gayle [60]	15,726
7	18	A	Norwich C	L	1-3	1-2	—	Vega [42]	17,885
8	22	A	Crewe Alex	L	0-1	0-1	16		6507
9	26	H	Birmingham C	D	3-3	2-1	—	Smith [13], Cox [30], Glass [76]	13,091
10	30	H	Preston NE	D	1-1	0-1	17	Jackson (og) [52]	18,911
11	Oct 13	H	Sheffield W	W	3-1	2-1	16	Hyde [3], Noel-Williams [29], Helguson [64]	14,456
12	20	A	Grimsby T	W	3-0	2-0	14	Hyde 2 [19, 58], Noble [44]	5506
13	23	H	Nottingham F	L	1-2	0-0	—	Noel-Williams [54]	16,355
14	27	A	Bradford C	L	3-4	0-2	18	Helguson [63], Smith 2 (1 pen) [76, 79 (p)]	16,860
15	30	A	Sheffield U	W	2-0	0-0	—	Helguson [51], Smith [72]	14,338
16	Nov 3	H	Barnsley	W	3-0	0-0	13	Smith [50], Helguson 2 [61, 90]	13,964
17	10	H	Stockport Co	D	1-1	0-0	13	Smith [90]	12,576
18	13	A	Burnley	L	0-1	0-1	—		13,162
19	18	A	Gillingham	D	0-0	0-0	13		8733
20	25	H	Portsmouth	W	3-0	2-0	13	Robinson [22], Cox [44], Issa [86]	15,631
21	Dec 1	A	Nottingham F	D	0-0	0-0	11		24,015
22	9	A	Coventry C	W	2-0	0-0	12	Glass 2 (1 pen) [74 (p), 87]	13,251
23	15	H	Crystal Palace	W	1-0	1-0	11	Noel-Williams [41]	16,499
24	22	H	Wolverhampton W	D	1-1	1-1	11	Smith [26]	17,389
25	29	A	Walsall	W	3-0	2-0	11	Fisken [21], Nielsen [39], Smith [83]	6882
26	Jan 1	H	Millwall	L	1-4	0-1	11	Helguson [82]	15,300
27	12	A	Rotherham U	D	1-1	1-0	11	Swailes (og) [17]	6409
28	15	A	Millwall	L	0-1	0-1	—		12,531
29	20	H	Manchester C	L	1-2	1-1	12	Smith [26]	17,074
30	31	A	Preston NE	D	1-1	0-1	—	Noel-Williams [65]	12,749
31	Feb 6	H	Burnley	L	1-2	1-0	—	Pennant [23]	12,160
32	10	H	Grimsby T	W	2-0	1-0	12	Robinson [36], Noel-Williams [46]	12,163
33	16	A	Sheffield W	L	1-2	1-0	12	Noel-Williams [43]	18,244
34	19	A	Wimbledon	D	0-0	0-0	—		5551
35	23	H	Birmingham C	L	2-3	0-2	14	Pennant [59], Johnson M (og) [90]	18,059
36	26	H	Norwich C	W	2-1	2-0	—	Hyde [8], Nielsen [41]	12,622
37	Mar 2	H	Crewe Alex	L	0-1	0-0	12		15,199
38	5	A	WBA	D	1-1	0-0	—	Brown [52]	19,580
39	9	A	Crystal Palace	W	2-0	1-0	11	Nielsen [45], Gayle [47]	16,817
40	16	H	Coventry C	W	3-0	2-0	12	Brown 2 [4, 45], Gayle [74]	15,833
41	23	A	Barnsley	L	0-2	0-1	14		12,449
42	29	D	Bradford C	D	0-0	0-0	—		14,001
43	Apr 1	A	Stockport Co	L	1-2	0-1	14	Webber [68]	4086
44	6	H	Sheffield U	L	0-3	0-2	14		13,377
45	13	A	Portsmouth	W	1-0	0-0	14	Webber [50]	16,302
46	21	H	Gillingham	L	2-3	1-1	14	McNamee [12], Nielsen [55]	15,674

Final League Position: 14

GOALSCORERS

League (62): Smith 11 (1 pen), Helguson 6, Nielsen 6, Noel-Williams 6, Gayle 4, Hyde 4, Brown 3, Glass 3 (1 pen), Robinson 3, Cox 2, Pennant 2, Webber 2, Fisken 1, Galli 1, Issa 1, McNamee 1, Noble 1, Vega 1, Wooter 1, own goals 3.
Worthington Cup (11): Gayle 2 (1 pen), Hyde 2, Noel-Williams 2, Vega 2, Helguson 1, Robinson 1, Vernazza 1.
FA Cup (2): Gayle 1, Noel-Williams 1.

Baardsen E 14	Blondeau P 24 + 1	Robinson P 38	Vernazza P 21	Galli F 22 + 1	Vega R 23 + 4	Nielsen A 19 + 3	Hyde M 37 + 2	Gayle M 28 + 8	Smith T 35 + 5	Hughes S 11 + 4	Ward D — + 1	Fisken G 12 + 5	Helguson H 11 + 23	Foley D 1	Noel-Williams G 15 + 14	Cox N 39 + 1	Panayi J — + 2	Wooter N 7 + 10	Glass S 29 + 2	Noble D 5 + 10	Issa P 12 + 3	Doyley L 11 + 9	Chamberlain A 32	Norville J — + 2	Okon P 14 + 1	Pennant J 9	Hand J 4 + 6	Brown W 10 + 1	Cook L 6 + 4	Mahon G 6	McNamee A 2 + 5	Webber D 4 + 1	Gibbs N — + 1	Match No.
1	2	3	4	5	6	7	8[1]	9	10[2]	11[3]	12	13	14																					1
1	2	3	4	5	6	7	8[1]	9	10[2]	12					11	13																		2
1			4	5	6	7	8[1]	9	10	11[2]					12	2	13	3																3
1	2[1]	3	4	5	12	7	8[2]	9	10[3]	13			14			6		11																4
1		3		5	6	7	8	9[1]	10			4[3]	13		12	2		11	7[2]	14														5
1		3[1]		5	6[1]		8	9	10[2]				14		13	12	2		11	7		4												6
1		3[1]	4		6		8[3]	9	12				10[5]		13	2		11	7	14	5													7
1		3	4		6		8	9	10	12[2]			11[1]		13	14		2		7[3]	5													8
1		3	4		6		8[3]	9	10				11		13	2		12[1]	7	5[1]	14													9
1		3	4	5					12	10	13		8[2]	9[3]	14	2		11[1]	7			6												10
1	2[1]	3		5	12		8		10[2]	11			14		9	4		13	7	6[3]														11
1	2	3		5			8[1]		10[2]	11			13		9[1]	4		12	7	6[1]	14													12
1	2	3		5			8[3]		10[2]	11			13		9	4		12	7	6[1]	14													13
1	2	3		5[2]	12				10	11			8[3]		9	4		13	7[1]	6							14							14
	2[2]	3	4[1]		6								10[3]	11	9			5	7	12	8	13	1	14										15
	2[3]	4	5	12			8		10[2]	11			9		3	13		7	14	6			1											16
		3	4		6		8	12	10	11[3]			9[1]			2		13	7		5[2]	1												17
		3	4[1]		6		8	12	10	11[2]			9			2		13		14	5[1]	7	1											18
	2[2]	3	4		6		8	9[1]		11[3]			12		10	5		13	7	14			1											19
	2[3]	3	11		6		8	9[1]	10				12[4]			7		13	5	14		1												20
		3[1]	4		6		8	12	10	11			13			9[1]		5	7		2	1												21
	2	3	4		6		12	9	10[3]	11[1]			8			13		5	7	14		1												22
	2[3]	3	4		6		8	12	10	13			11[2]			9		5	7[1]	14		1												23
		3	4[2]		6		12	8	9	10			11			13		7[1]	2		5	1												24
		3	4		6	7		9	10[2]	11			12			13		2[3]	8[1]		5	14	1											25
	2	3[1]	4		6	7		9	10[1]	11			8		14	13		12			5[3]	1												26
	2		4[2]		6	7	13	9[1]					10			5					3	1			8	11								27
	2			5	8[2]	6	12	10[3]					13		9[1]			7			3	1			11	14								28
			5[3]	6	7	8		10					12		13	2[1]		11[2]	14		3	1			4	9								29
3			5	6	7[2]		12						9			8[1]		2[3]			1			11	10	4	14	13						30
2			5	6	8[2]								10[3]			12	13				1			4	11	14	3	7[1]					31
2[1]			5	12	8	9	13						10[2]			14					1			4	11		6	7[2]					32
3			5[2]	7	8	12	10[1]						9			2[3]					1			4	11	13	6	14					33
3[1]			12	7	8[2]	10							9	5							1			4	11	13	6	14					34
2			5	12	8[1]	9	13						10[2]			6					1			4	11	3							35
3			5	7	8[2]	9[1]	10						12			2			11		1			4	13	6							36
3			5	7	8	9[1]	10[1]						12			2			11[2]		1			4[3]	14	6	13						37
3			5	7	8	9[1]	10	13					12			2			11		1			4[2]	6								38
3			5	7[3]	8	9[1]	10	13					12			2			11[2]	14	1			6	4								39
12	3		5	7	8	9[2]	10[1]						13			2					1			6	4[3]	11	14						40
2	3		5[2]	7	8	9							12			10[3]	4				13			1	6[1]	11	14						41
2	3		5		8[1]	9	10									4		7[2]			13		1	12	6[3]	11	13	14						42
2	3		5[2]			10		12								4		7[3]	8[1]		13	1		6		11	14	9						43
2	3			8		10		7[1]	12							5					13	1		4		6[3]	11[2]	14	9					44
	3			8	10	12			13							5	14		11[3]		2	1		4		6			7[2]	9[1]				45
	3			7[2]	8	10			12							5					2	1		4		6[1]			11	9	13		46

Worthington Cup

First Round	Plymouth Arg	(h)	1-0
Second Round	Bristol C	(a)	3-2
Third Round	Bradford C	(h)	4-1
Fourth Round	Charlton Ath	(h)	3-2
Fifth Round	Sheffield W	(a)	0-4

FA Cup

Third Round	Arsenal	(h)	2-4

WEST BROMWICH ALBION FA Premiership

FOUNDATION

There is a well known story that when employees of Salter's Spring Works in West Bromwich decided to form a football club, they had to send someone to the nearby Association Football stronghold of Wednesbury to purchase a football. A weekly subscription of 2d (less than 1p) was imposed and the name of the new club was West Bromwich Strollers.

The Hawthorns, West Bromwich B71 4LF.

Telephone: (0121) 525 8888 (all Depts).
Fax: (0121) 524 3461.

Registered Office: The Hawthorns, West Bromwich, West Midlands B71 4LF.

Ground Capacity: 28,000 (all seated).

Record Attendance: 64,815 v Arsenal, FA Cup 6th rd, 6 March 1937.

Record Receipts: £375,272 v Cheltenham T, FA Cup 5th rd, 16 February 2002.

Pitch Measurements: 115yd × 74yd.

President: Sir F. A. Millichip.
Vice-president: John G. Silk LL.B (Lond).
Chairman: P. Thompson.
Directors: J. W. Brandrick, B. Hurst, C. Stapleton, J. D. Wile (Chief Executive), J. Peace.

Manager: Gary Megson.
Assistant Manager: Frank Burrows.

Reserve Coach: Gary Shelton.
Youth Coach: Alan Crawford. **Physio:** Nick Worth.

Secretary: Dr John J. Evans BA, PHD. (Wales).

Club Statistician: Tony Matthews.

Colours: Navy blue and white striped shirts, white shorts, blue and white stockings.

Change Colours: Yellow and green striped shirts, green shorts, yellow stockings.

Year Formed: 1878. **Turned Professional:** 1885.

Ltd Co.: 1892. **Plc:** 1996.

Previous Name: 1878, West Bromwich Strollers; 1871, West Bromwich Albion.

Club Nicknames: 'Throstles', 'Baggies', 'Albion'.

Previous Grounds: 1878, Coopers Hill; 1879, Dartmouth Park; 1881, Bunns Field, Walsall Street; 1882, Four Acres (Dartmouth Cricket Club); 1885, Stoney Lane; 1900, The Hawthorns.

First Football League Game: 8 September 1888, Football League, v Stoke (a) W 2–0 – Roberts; J. Horton, Green; E. Horton, Perry, Bayliss; Bassett, Woodhall (1), Hendry, Pearson, Wilson (1).

HONOURS

Football League: Division 1 – Champions 1919–20; Runners-up 1924–25, 1953–54, 2001–02; Division 2 – Champions 1901–02, 1910–11; Runners-up 1930–31, 1948–49; Promoted to Division 1 1975–76 (3rd).
FA Cup: Winners 1888, 1892, 1931, 1954, 1968; Runners-up 1886, 1887, 1895, 1912, 1935.
Football League Cup: Winners 1966; Runners-up 1967, 1970.
European Competitions: European Cup-Winners' Cup: 1968–69.
European Fairs Cup: 1966–67. *UEFA Cup:* 1978–79, 1979–80, 1981–82.

IT'S A FACT !

The 1887 FA Cup semi-final brought West Bromwich Albion a 3-1 victory over Preston North End but not before a pre-match problem. Goalkeeper Bob Roberts missed his train connection and only arrived as the players were kicking-in!

Record League Victory: 12–0 v Darwen, Division 1, 4 April 1892 – Reader; J. Horton, McCulloch; Reynolds (2), Perry, Groves; Bassett (3), McLeod, Nicholls (1), Pearson (4), Geddes (1), (1 og).

Record Cup Victory: 10–1 v Chatham (away), FA Cup 3rd rd, 2 March 1889 – Roberts; J. Horton, Green; Timmins (1), Charles Perry, E. Horton; Bassett (2), Perry (1), Bayliss (2), Pearson, Wilson (3), (1 og).

Record Defeat: 3–10 v Stoke C, Division 1, 4 February 1937.

Most League Points (2 for a win): 60, Division 1, 1919–20.

Most League Points (3 for a win): 89, Division 1, 2001–02.

Most League Goals: 105, Division 2, 1929–30.

Highest League Scorer in Season: William 'Ginger' Richardson, 39, Division 1, 1935–36.

Most League Goals in Total Aggregate: Tony Brown, 218, 1963–79.

Most League Goals in One Match: 6, Jimmy Cookson v Blackpool, Division 2, 17 September 1927.

Most Capped Player: Stuart Williams, 33 (43), Wales.

Most League Appearances: Tony Brown, 574, 1963–80.

Youngest League Player: Charlie Wilson, 16 years 73 days v Oldham Ath, 1 October 1921.

Record Transfer Fee Received: £5,000,001 from Coventry C for Lee Hughes, July 2001.

Record Transfer Fee Paid: £2,100,000 to Bristol R for Jason Roberts, June 2000.

Football League Record: 1888 Founder Member of Football League; 1901–02 Division 2; 1902–04 Division 1; 1904–11 Division 2; 1911–27 Division 1; 1927–31 Division 2; 1931–38 Division 1; 1938–49 Division 2; 1949–73 Division 1; 1973–76 Division 2; 1976–86 Division 1; 1986–91 Division 2; 1991–92 Division 3; 1992–93 Division 2; 1993–2002 Division 1; 2002– FA Premier League.

MANAGERS

Louis Ford 1890–92
(Secretary-Manager)
Henry Jackson 1892–94
(Secretary-Manager)
Edward Stephenson 1894–95
(Secretary-Manager)
Clement Keys 1895–96
(Secretary-Manager)
Frank Heaven 1896–1902
(Secretary-Manager)
Fred Everiss 1902–48
Jack Smith 1948–52
Jesse Carver 1952
Vic Buckingham 1953–59
Gordon Clark 1959–61
Archie Macaulay 1961–63
Jimmy Hagan 1963–67
Alan Ashman 1967–71
Don Howe 1971–75
Johnny Giles 1975–77
Ronnie Allen 1977
Ron Atkinson 1978–81
Ronnie Allen 1981–82
Ron Wylie 1982–84
Johnny Giles 1984–85
Ron Saunders 1986–87
Ron Atkinson 1987–88
Brian Talbot 1988–91
Bobby Gould 1991–92
Ossie Ardiles 1992–93
Keith Burkinshaw 1993–94
Alan Buckley 1994–97
Ray Harford 1997
Denis Smith 1997–2000
Brian Little 2000
Gary Megson March 2000–

LATEST SEQUENCES

Longest Sequence of League Wins: 11, 5.4.30 – 8.9.30.

Longest Sequence of League Defeats: 11, 28.10.95 – 26.12.95.

Longest Sequence of League Draws: 5, 30.8.99 – 3.10.99.

Longest Sequence of Unbeaten League Matches: 17, 7.9.57 – 7.12.57.

Longest Sequence Without a League Win: 14, 28.10.95 – 3.2.96.

TEN YEAR LEAGUE RECORD

		P	W	D	L	F	A	Pts	Pos
1991-92	Div 3	46	19	14	13	64	49	71	7
1992-93	Div 2	46	25	10	11	88	54	85	4
1993-94	Div 1	46	13	12	21	60	69	51	21
1994-95	Div 1	46	16	10	20	51	57	58	19
1995-96	Div 1	46	16	12	18	60	68	60	11
1996-97	Div 1	46	14	15	17	68	72	57	16
1997-98	Div 1	46	16	12	17	50	56	61	10
1998-99	Div 1	46	16	11	19	69	76	59	12
1999-2000	Div 1	46	10	19	17	43	60	49	21
2000-01	Div 1	46	21	11	14	60	52	74	6

DID YOU KNOW

In January 2002, West Bromwich Albion completed 718 minutes of League and Cup football without conceding a goal, until losing 1-0 at Millwall on 19 February.

WEST BROMWICH ALBION 2001–02 LEAGUE RECORD

Match No.	Date	Venue	Opponents	Result	H/T Score	Lg. Pos.	Goalscorers	Attendance
1	Aug 11	A	Walsall	L	1-2	0-1	—	Clement [55]	9181
2	18	H	Grimsby T	L	0-1	0-0	22		17,971
3	25	A	Sheffield W	D	1-1	1-1	22	Dichio [25]	18,844
4	27	H	Gillingham	W	1-0	1-0	17	Dichio [34]	18,180
5	Sept 8	H	Manchester C	W	4-0	1-0	11	McInnes [10], Clement 2 (1 pen) [67 (p), 79], Dobie [83]	23,524
6	15	A	Watford	W	2-1	1-0	9	Dobie 2 [30, 52]	15,726
7	18	H	Preston NE	W	2-0	1-0	—	Dobie 2 [27, 71]	18,209
8	22	H	Wimbledon	L	0-1	0-0	8		19,222
9	25	A	Portsmouth	W	2-1	1-1	—	Clement [27], Dobie [70]	17,287
10	29	H	Burnley	W	1-0	0-0	3	Dobie [67]	21,442
11	Oct 11	H	Millwall	L	0-2	0-2	—		17,335
12	16	A	Stockport Co	W	2-1	1-0	—	Taylor 2 [10, 61]	6052
13	19	A	Norwich C	L	0-2	0-2	—		20,465
14	25	H	Wolverhampton W	D	1-1	0-1	—	Clement [69]	26,143
15	28	A	Barnsley	L	2-3	1-2	11	Johnson [10], Clement [90]	12,490
16	31	A	Crystal Palace	W	1-0	0-0	—	Taylor [63]	17,273
17	Nov 4	H	Nottingham F	W	1-0	1-0	7	Rosler [34]	18,281
18	7	A	Birmingham C	W	1-0	1-0	—	Johnson [37]	23,554
19	17	A	Rotherham U	L	1-2	0-1	4	Moore [90]	8509
20	24	H	Bradford C	W	1-0	1-0	5	McInnes [40]	18,910
21	Dec 2	A	Wolverhampton W	W	1-0	0-0	4	Jordao [59]	27,515
22	8	H	Sheffield U	L	0-1	0-0	5		19,462
23	12	H	Coventry C	W	1-0	0-0	—	Konjic (og) [73]	22,543
24	15	A	Crewe Alex	D	1-1	1-1	4	Jordao [28]	8154
25	22	H	Sheffield W	D	1-1	0-0	5	Fox [64]	20,340
26	26	A	Manchester C	D	0-0	0-0	5		34,407
27	29	A	Gillingham	L	1-2	0-1	7	Johnson [72]	9912
28	Jan 1	H	Stockport Co	W	4-0	2-0	6	Roberts [17], Johnson [28], Dichio 2 [73, 78]	20,541
29	12	A	Grimsby T	D	0-0	0-0	6		6011
30	20	H	Walsall	W	1-0	1-0	4	Roberts [41]	20,290
31	29	H	Birmingham C	W	1-0	1-0	—	Roberts [43]	25,266
32	Feb 3	A	Burnley	W	2-0	2-0	3	Roberts 2 [36, 41]	15,846
33	10	H	Norwich C	W	1-0	1-0	3	Dichio [41]	19,115
34	19	A	Millwall	L	0-1	0-1	—		13,716
35	23	H	Portsmouth	W	5-0	4-0	3	Roberts 2 [8, 80], Sigurdsson [24], Dobie [38], Balis [45]	21,028
36	26	A	Preston NE	L	0-1	0-0	—		14,487
37	Mar 2	A	Wimbledon	W	1-0	0-0	3	Dichio [52]	8363
38	5	H	Watford	D	1-1	0-0	—	Dichio [77]	19,580
39	16	A	Sheffield U	W	3-0	1-0	3	Dobie 2 [18, 77], McInnes [62]	17,692
40	22	A	Nottingham F	W	1-0	0-0	—	Taylor [83]	24,788
41	26	H	Crewe Alex	W	4-1	2-1	—	Jordao 2 [37, 45], Dichio [49], Wright (og) [55]	21,303
42	30	H	Barnsley	W	3-1	1-0	3	Jordao [32], Dichio [59], Benjamin [65]	23,167
43	Apr 1	A	Coventry C	W	1-0	1-0	3	Taylor [16]	21,513
44	7	H	Rotherham U	D	1-1	1-0	2	Taylor [33]	22,376
45	13	A	Bradford C	W	1-0	0-0	2	Balis (pen) [90]	20,209
46	21	H	Crystal Palace	W	2-0	1-0	2	Moore [17], Taylor [54]	26,712

Final League Position: 2

GOALSCORERS

League (61): Dobie 10, Dichio 9, Roberts 7, Taylor 7, Clement 6 (1 pen), Jordao 5, Johnson 4, McInnes 3, Balis 2 (1 pen), Moore 2, Benjamin 1, Fox 1, Rosler 1, Sigurdsson 1, own goals 2.
Worthington Cup (3): Dobie 2, Jordao 1.
FA Cup (4): Clement 2 (2 pens), Dichio 1, Johnson 1.

Hoult R 45	Balis I 32+2	Clement N 45	Sigurdsson L 42+1	Butler T 14+5	Gilchrist P 43	Appleton M 18	McInnes D 45	Dobie S 32+11	Taylor B 18+16	Jordao 19+6	Cummings W 6+8	Quinn J 1+6	Fox R 2+18	Lyttle D 13+10	Chambers A 24+8	Dichio D 26+1	Chambers J 1+4	Roberts J 12+4	Moore D 31+1	Johnson A 28+4	Jensen B 1	Rosler U 5	Varga S 3+1	Benjamin T —+3	Match No.
1	2	3	4	5	6	7	8	9	10²	11³	12	13	14												1
1	2	3	4		5	7	8	9	10²	12	6¹	13	11												2
1		3	4	12	6	11	8³	9²	13	7	5¹					2		14	10						3
1	2³	3	4	5	6	11	7	9¹	10²	12						13	8	14							4
1		3	4	5	6	11	8	12	13							2		7³	10¹	9¹					5
1			4	5	6	11	7	9¹	10³	3	12					2²	8	13	14						6
1		3	4	5	6	11	7	9	10²	12		13				2	8¹								7
1		3	4¹	5	6³	11	7	9	10			12	13			2²	8		14						8
1		6	4	5		11	7	9	10¹	3						2	12	8							9
1		3	4		6	11	7	9	10¹		12					2			5	8					10
		3	4		6	11⁴	7	9	12	13					8	2³	14		5¹	10	1				11
1		3	4		6	11	7	9	10							2			5	8					12
1		3¹	4		6	11²	7	9	10		12				14	13	2		5	8²					13
1		3	4		6	11	7	9¹	10			12			13	2			5	8²					14
1	12	3	4³	13	6	11	7		10						9	14	2¹		5	8²					15
1		3	4		6	11	7		10		12					2			5	8		9¹			16
1	2	3	4		6	11	7	8	10¹										5	12		9			17
1	2²	3	4	5	6	11	7	10	12						13					8		9¹			18
1	2	3¹	4²	12	6		7	10		11³				14	13				5	8		9			19
1	2¹	3	4		6		7	10		11	13			12	8	9			5						20
1	2	3	4		6		7	10		11					8	9			5						21
1	2	3	4		6²		7	10	12	11³	13			14	8	9			5						22
1	2	3	4		6		7	10¹	12	11²					8	9			5	13					23
1	2	3	4		6		7		10¹	11					8²	9		12	5	13					24
1	2	3	4		6¹		7	10		11²		13				9		12	5	8					25
1	2	3	4	12			7	13		11³	6			14		9²			10	5¹	8				26
1	2¹	3		4			7	12		11³	6			13	14	9			10²	5	8				27
1	2	3	4		6		7	11	12						13	9¹			10²	5	8				28
1	2²	3	4		6		7	12							13	11¹	9		10	5	8				29
1	2	3	4		6		7	12	13	11³					14	9¹			10²	5	8				30
1	2³	3	4		6		7	12						13	14	11¹²	9¹		10	5	8				31
1	2²	3	4		6		7	12							13	11	9		10¹	5	8				32
1	2²	3	4		6		7	12							13	11	9¹		10	5	8				33
1	12	3	4	5	6		7		9²	11³				14	2¹		13		10		8				34
1	2	3³	4	5	6		7	9¹	12	13	14				11				10		8²				35
1	2	3	4	5¹	6		7	9	13					14	12	11³			10²		8				36
1	2	3	4	5	6			10	12	11					7	9¹					8				37
1	2	3	4	5²	6		7³	10	14	12		13			11¹	9					8				38
1	2	3	4¹	12	6		7	10	14						13	11³	9		5		8²				39
1	2	3	4		6		7	10	12	11					8	9¹			5						40
1	2²	3	4³		6		7	10¹	12	11		13			8	9			5				14		41
1	2	3		6¹			7	10²		11		13	12		8³	9			5				4	14	42
1	2	3		6			7	12	10¹	11		13			8²	9¹			5				4	14	43
1	2	3	12		6¹		7	13	10³	11		14			9				5	8²			4		44
1	2	3	4		6		7	10	12						11¹²	9¹			5	8				13	45
1	2	3	4		6		7	12	10¹	13				14	11	9³			5	8²					46

Worthington Cup

First Round	Cambridge U	(a)	1-1
Second Round	Swindon T	(h)	2-0
Third Round	Charlton Ath	(h)	0-1

FA Cup

Third Round	Sunderland	(a)	2-1
Fourth Round	Leicester C	(h)	1-0
Fifth Round	Cheltenham T	(h)	1-0
Sixth Round	Fulham	(h)	0-1

WEST HAM UNITED   FA Premiership

FOUNDATION

Thames Iron Works FC was formed by employees of this famous shipbuilding company in 1895 and entered the FA Cup in their initial season at Chatham and the London League in their second. The committee wanted to introduce professional players, so Thames Iron Works was wound up in June 1900 and relaunched a month later as West Ham United.

Boleyn Ground, Green Street, Upton Park, London E13 9AZ.

Telephone General Office: (020) 8548 2748.
Fax: (020) 8548 2758. *Ticket Office:* (020) 8548 2700.
Sportswear Stadium Store: (020) 8548 2794.
Membership Office: (020) 8548 2727.
Commercial: (020) 8548 2777.
Conference & Banqueting: (020) 8548 2775.

Football in the Community: (020) 8548 2707.

ClubCall: 09068 121 110.

Hammers Line: 09065 861 966.

Website: www.whufc.co.uk

Ground Capacity: 35,595.

Record Attendance: 42,322 v Tottenham H, Division 1, 17 October 1970.

Record Receipts: £910,500 v Chelsea, FA Cup 4th rd replay, 6 February 2002.

Pitch Measurements: 112yd × 72yd.

HONOURS

Football League: Division 1 best season: 3rd, 1985–86; Division 2 – Champions 1957–58, 1980–81; Runners-up 1922–23, 1990–91.

FA Cup: Winners 1964, 1975, 1980; Runners-up 1923.

Football League Cup: Runners-up 1966, 1981.

European Competitions: European Cup-Winners' Cup: 1964–65 (winners), 1965–66, 1975–76 (runners-up), 1980–81. *UEFA Cup:* 1999–2000. *Intertoto Cup* (winners) 1999.

Chairman: T. W. Brown FCIS, AII, FCCA. *Vice-chairman:* M. W. Cearns ACIB. *Directors:* C. J. Warner, N. Igoe, C. Manhire, T. Brooking CBE (Non-executive), P. Aldridge (Managing).

Manager: Glenn Roeder. *Assistant Manager:* Paul Goddard. *Reserve Team Coach:* Roger Cross.

Physio: John Green BSC (HONS), MCSP, SRP.

Football Secretary: Peter Barnes.

Stadium Manager: John Ball.

Press Officer: Peter Stewart.

Colours: Claret shirts with sky blue sleeves, white shorts and stockings.

Change Colours: Sky blue shirts with two claret rings, sky blue shorts and stockings.

Year Formed: 1895.

Turned Professional: 1900.

Ltd Co.: 1900.

Previous Name: Thames Iron Works FC, 1895–1900.

Club Nicknames: 'The Hammers', 'The Irons'.

IT'S A FACT !

Dick Walker, the West Ham United defender, served as a paratrooper in the Second World War and during the Arnhem landings, carried a football with him. Both survived, and the ball is now in the club's museum.

Previous Grounds: 1895, Memorial Recreation Ground, Canning Town; 1904, Boleyn Ground.

First Football League Game: 30 August 1919, Division 2, v Lincoln C (h) D 1–1 – Hufton; Cope, Lee; Lane, Fenwick, McCrae; D. Smith, Moyes (1), Puddefoot, Morris, Bradshaw.

Record League Victory: 8–0 v Rotherham U, Division 2, 8 March 1958 – Gregory; Bond, Wright; Malcolm, Brown, Lansdowne; Grice, Smith (2), Keeble (2), Dick (4), Musgrove. 8–0 v Sunderland, Division 1, 19 October 1968 – Ferguson; Bonds, Charles; Peters, Stephenson, Moore (1); Redknapp, Boyce, Brooking (1), Hurst (6), Sissons.

Record Cup Victory: 10–0 v Bury, League Cup 2nd rd (2nd leg), 25 October 1983 – Parkes; Stewart (1), Walford, Bonds (Orr), Martin (1), Devonshire (2), Allen, Cottee (4), Swindlehurst, Brooking (2), Pike.

Record Defeat: 2–8 v Blackburn R, Division 1, 26 December 1963.

Most League Points (2 for a win): 66, Division 2, 1980–81.

Most League Points (3 for a win): 88, Division 1, 1992–93.

Most League Goals: 101, Division 2, 1957–58.

Highest League Scorer in Season: Vic Watson, 42, Division 1, 1929–30.

Most League Goals in Total Aggregate: Vic Watson, 298, 1920–35.

Most League Goals in One Match: 6, Vic Watson v Leeds U, Division 1, 9 February 1929; 6, Geoff Hurst v Sunderland, Division 1, 19 October 1968.

Most Capped Player: Bobby Moore, 108, England.

Most League Appearances: Billy Bonds, 663, 1967–88.

Youngest League Player: Neil Finn, 17 years 3 days v Manchester C, 1 January 1996.

Record Transfer Fee Received: £18,000,000 from Leeds U for Rio Ferdinand, November 2000.

Record Transfer Fee Paid: £5,000,000 to Sunderland for Don Hutchison, August 2001 and £5,000,000 to Sparta Prague for Tomas Repka, September 2001.

Football League Record: 1919 Elected to Division 2; 1923–32 Division 1; 1932–58 Division 2; 1958–78 Division 1; 1978–81 Division 2; 1981–89 Division 1; 1989–91 Division 2; 1991–93 Division 1; 1993– FA Premier League.

MANAGERS

Syd King 1902–32
Charlie Paynter 1932–50
Ted Fenton 1950–61
Ron Greenwood 1961–74
  (continued as General Manager to 1977)
John Lyall 1974–89
Lou Macari 1989–90
Billy Bonds 1990–94
Harry Redknapp 1994–2001
Glenn Roeder June 2001–

LATEST SEQUENCES

Longest Sequence of League Wins: 9, 19.10.85 – 14.12.85.

Longest Sequence of League Defeats: 9, 28.3.32 – 29.8.32.

Longest Sequence of League Draws: 5, 7.9.68 – 5.10.68.

Longest Sequence of Unbeaten League Matches: 27, 27.12.80 – 10.10.81.

Longest Sequence Without a League Win: 17, 31.1.76 – 21.8.76.

TEN YEAR LEAGUE RECORD

		P	W	D	L	F	A	Pts	Pos
1991-92	Div 1	42	9	11	22	37	59	38	22
1992-93	Div 1	46	26	10	10	81	41	88	2
1993-94	PR Lge	42	13	13	16	47	58	52	13
1994-95	PR Lge	42	13	11	18	44	48	50	14
1995-96	PR Lge	38	14	9	15	43	52	51	10
1996-97	PR Lge	38	10	12	16	39	48	42	14
1997-98	PR Lge	38	16	8	14	56	57	56	8
1998-99	PR Lge	38	16	9	13	46	53	57	5
1999-2000	PR Lge	38	15	10	13	52	53	55	9
2000-01	PR Lge	38	10	12	16	45	50	42	15

DID YOU KNOW ?

On 25 November 1936, West Ham United beat visiting Yugoslav team Gradjanski 1-0 at Upton Park. The Hammers donated the entire gate of £117 to the visitors to offset their financial losses on the tour.

WEST HAM UNITED 2001–02 LEAGUE RECORD

Match No.	Date	Venue	Opponents	Result		H/T Score	Lg. Pos.	Goalscorers	Attendance
1	Aug 18	A	Liverpool	L	1-2	1-1	—	Di Canio (pen) [30]	43,935
2	25	H	Leeds U	D	0-0	0-0	17		24,517
3	Sept 8	A	Derby Co	D	0-0	0-0	17		27,802
4	15	A	Middlesbrough	L	0-2	0-2	20		25,406
5	23	H	Newcastle U	W	3-0	1-0	15	Hutchison [18], Di Canio [53], Kanoute [82]	24,840
6	29	A	Everton	L	0-5	0-1	18		32,049
7	Oct 14	A	Blackburn R	L	1-7	1-3	19	Carrick [39]	22,712
8	20	H	Southampton	W	2-0	0-0	16	Kanoute 2 [53, 81]	25,842
9	24	H	Chelsea	W	2-1	2-1	—	Carrick [5], Kanoute [13]	26,520
10	28	A	Ipswich T	W	3-2	1-0	11	Di Canio [22], Kanoute [72], Defoe [90]	22,826
11	Nov 3	H	Fulham	L	0-2	0-1	14		26,217
12	19	A	Charlton Ath	D	4-4	2-2	—	Kitson 3 [3, 30, 64], Defoe [84]	23,198
13	24	H	Tottenham H	L	0-1	0-0	15		32,780
14	Dec 1	A	Sunderland	L	0-1	0-0	16		45,367
15	5	H	Aston Villa	D	1-1	0-1	—	Defoe [90]	28,377
16	8	A	Manchester U	W	1-0	0-0	16	Defoe [64]	67,582
17	15	H	Arsenal	D	1-1	1-1	14	Kanoute [36]	34,523
18	22	A	Leicester C	D	1-1	0-1	15	Di Canio (pen) [74]	20,131
19	26	H	Derby Co	W	4-0	1-0	11	Schemmel [5], Di Canio [73], Sinclair [86], Defoe [90]	31,397
20	29	A	Liverpool	D	1-1	1-0	11	Sinclair [39]	35,103
21	Jan 1	A	Leeds U	L	0-3	0-2	11		39,322
22	12	A	Leicester C	W	1-0	1-0	11	Di Canio [36]	34,698
23	20	A	Chelsea	L	1-5	0-1	12	Defoe [88]	40,054
24	30	A	Southampton	L	0-2	0-1	—		31,879
25	Feb 2	H	Blackburn R	W	2-0	1-0	11	Sinclair [17], Kanoute [56]	35,307
26	9	A	Bolton W	L	0-1	0-1	12		24,342
27	23	H	Middlesbrough	W	1-0	0-0	11	Kanoute [76]	35,420
28	Mar 2	A	Aston Villa	L	1-2	1-1	13	Di Canio (pen) [13]	37,341
29	6	H	Everton	W	1-0	0-0	—	Sinclair [59]	29,883
30	16	H	Manchester U	L	3-5	2-2	10	Lomas [8], Kanoute [20], Defoe [78]	35,281
31	30	H	Ipswich T	W	3-1	1-0	10	Lomas [36], Di Canio [74], Defoe [86]	33,871
32	Apr 1	A	Fulham	W	1-0	1-0	8	Kanoute [45]	19,416
33	6	H	Charlton Ath	W	2-0	2-0	7	Di Canio (pen) [23], Kanoute [34]	32,389
34	13	A	Tottenham H	D	1-1	0-0	7	Pearce [89]	36,083
35	20	H	Sunderland	W	3-0	1-0	7	Sinclair [28], Lomas [52], Defoe [77]	33,319
36	24	A	Arsenal	L	0-2	0-0	—		38,038
37	27	A	Newcastle U	L	1-3	1-1	8	Defoe [20]	52,127
38	May 11	H	Bolton W	W	2-1	1-0	7	Lomas [45], Pearce [89]	35,546

Final League Position: 7

GOALSCORERS

League (48): Kanoute 11, Defoe 10, Di Canio 9 (4 pens), Sinclair 5, Lomas 4, Kitson 3, Carrick 2, Pearce 2, Hutchison 1, Schemmel 1.
Worthington Cup (0).
FA Cup (6): Defoe 4, Cole 1, Kanoute 1.

Hislop S 12	Schemmel S 35	Winterburn N 29+2	Moncur J 7+12	Song R 5	Dailly C 38	Sinclair T 34	Cole J 29+1	Todorov S 2+4	Di Canio P 26	Carrick M 30	McCann G —+3	Courtois L 5+2	Defoe J 14+21	Hutchison D 24	Kanoute F 27	Repka T 31	Soma R 1+2	Byrne S —+1	Kitson P 3+4	Foxe H 4+2	Minto S 5	Lomas S 14+1	James D 26	Camara T —+1	Garcia R 2+6	Labant V 7+5	Pearce I 8+1	Match No.
1	2	3	4[1]	5	6	7	8[2]	9[1]	10	11	12	13	14															1
1	2	3	4[2]	5	6	7	8	9[1]	10	11	13		12															2
1	2	3	12	5	6	7	8[1]	13	10[3]	11			14	4	9[2]													3
1	2	3[3]	7[1]	4[2]	6	9	8	12	11				13	10		5	14											4
1	2	3			6	7			10	11			8[1]	13	9[2]	4	5											5
1	2	3[1]		5	6	7			10	11			8[2]	4	9[3]	12	13	14										6
1	2		4[1]		6[2]	7			10	11	12		8	9	5	3			13									7
1	2	3	12		6	7			10	11		4[1]		8	9	5												8
1	2	3			6	7			10	11		4[1]	12	8	9[2]	5	13											9
1	2	3			6	7			10[1]	11			12	8	9		5	4										10
1	2	3			6	7			10[1]	11		4[1]	12	8	9	5												11
1	2				6	7	12		10	11			13	8[1]	5	9[2]	4	3[3]	14									12
	2		12		6	7	10						11		8	5	9		3			4[1]	1					13
	2		12		6	7	8[1]	13	10				11		9	4	5		3[2]				1					14
	2	3			6	7	8		10	11			9		4	5						1						15
	2	3			6	7	8		10	11			9[1]		4	5						1	12					16
	2	3			6	7	8		10	11	12	4	9[1]	5								1						17
	2	3			6	7	8		10	11		9[1]	4	5		12						1						18
	2	3	12		6	7	8		10[1]	11			13		4	9[2]	5					1						19
	2	3			6	7	8			11		10	4	9	5							1						20
	2	3	11		6	7	8	12	10[1]					4	9[2]	5						1			13			21
	2	3	11[2]		6	7	8		10			12		4	9[1]	5	13					1						22
	2	3			6	7[1]	8		10	11	12	13	4	9[2]	5							1						23
	2	12			6		8		10	11[1]			13	7[2]	9	5						4	1			3		24
	2	3	12		6	11[1]	8		10				13	7[3]	9[2]	5						4	1			14		25
	2				6		8						10	9							12	5	1	3	4	7[1]	11	26
		3	4		6		8			10			7[1]	9	5							11[1]	1		13	12	2	27
	2	3			6	7	8		10				9		5							1			11[1]	12	4	28
	2[2]	3			6	7	8		10				12	9[1]	5							1			13	11	4	29
	2	3[1]			6	7	8		10	7			12	9	5							1				11		30
	2	3	12		6	7	8		10[1]	11			13	9[2]	5						4	1						31
	2		12		6	7	8		10[1]	11			13	9[2]	5						4	1			3[3]	14		32
	2	3	12		6	7	8[1]		10[2]	11			13	9	5						4	1						33
	2	12			6	7				11			10	9	5						8	1				3[1]	4	34
	2[1]	3			6	7	8			11			9[2]		5						10	1			13	12	4	35
	2[2]	3			6	7	8			11			12	9[1]	5						10	1			13		4	36
		12			6	7[1]	8			11			10	9	5						4	1		13	3[2]		2	37
		3	12		6	7	8			11[1]			10	9[2]	5						4	1		13			2	38

Worthington Cup
Second Round   Reading   (a)   0-0

FA Cup
Third Round   Macclesfield T   (a)   3-0
Fourth Round   Chelsea   (a)   1-1
                                 (h)   2-3

WIGAN ATHLETIC   Division 2

FOUNDATION

Following the demise of Wigan Borough and their resignation
from the Football League in 1931, a public meeting was called in
Wigan at the Queen's Hall in May 1932 at which a new club,
Wigan Athletic, was founded in the hope of carrying on in the
Football League. With this in mind, they bought Springfield Park
for £2,250, but failed to gain admission to the Football League
until 46 years later.

*JJB Stadium, Robin Park Complex, Newtown, Wigan
WN5 0UZ.*

Website: www.wiganathletic.tv

Ticket Office: (01942) 770 410.

Telephone: (01942) 774 000.

Fax: (01942) 770 477.

Commercial Dept: (01942) 774 000.

Latics ClubCall: 09068 121 655.

Football in the Community: (01942) 824 599.

Ground Capacity: 25,000.

Record Attendance: 27,526 v Hereford U, 12 December
1953.

Record Receipts: £140,000 v Preston NE, Division 2, 4 April 2000.

Pitch Measurements: 115yd × 75yd.

President: S. Jackson.

Chairman: David Whelan.

Directors: D. Whelan, J. Winstanley, D. Sharpe, P. Williams, B. Ashcroft, B. Spencer.

Chief Executive/Secretary: Mrs Brenda Spencer.

Assistant Secretary: Stuart Hayton.

Manager: Paul Jewell.

Physio: Alex Cribley.

Safety Officer: Raymond Johnston.

Groundsman: Ian Forshaw.

Colours: Blue shirts, blue shorts, blue stockings.

Change Colours: (To be announced.)

Year Formed: 1932.

Club Nickname: 'The Latics'.

First Football League Game: 19 August 1978, Division 4, v Hereford U (a) D 0–0 – Brown; Hinnigan,
Gore, Gillibrand, Ward, Davids, Corrigan, Purdie, Houghton, Wilkie, Wright.

HONOURS

Football League: Division 3
Champions, 1996–97; Division 4 –
Promoted (3rd) 1981–82.
FA Cup: best season: 6th rd, 1987.
Football League Cup: best season:
4th rd, 1982.
Freight Rover Trophy: Winners 1985.
Auto Windscreens Shield: Winners
1999.

IT'S A FACT !

When Wigan Athletic beat Hereford United 4-1 in an
FA Cup second round tie on 12 December 1953, the
attendance at Springfield Park of 27,500 was the highest
for the meeting of two non-League clubs outside a
Wembley final.

Record League Victory: 7–1 v Scarborough, Division 3, 11 March 1997 – Butler L, Butler J, Sharp (Morgan), Greenall, McGibbon (Biggins (1)), Martinez (1), Diaz (2), Jones (Lancashire (1)), Lowe (2), Rogers, Kilford.

Record Cup Victory: 6–0 v Carlisle U (away), FA Cup 1st rd, 24 November 1934 – Caunce; Robinson, Talbot; Paterson, Watson, Tufnell; Armes (2), Robson (1), Roberts (2), Felton, Scott (1).

Record Defeat: 1–6 v Bristol R, Division 3, 3 March 1990.

Most League Points (2 for a win): 55, Division 4, 1978–79 and 1979–80.

Most League Points (3 for a win): 91, Division 4, 1981–82.

Most League Goals: 84, Division 3, 1996–97.

Highest League Scorer in Season: Graeme Jones, 31, Division 3, 1996–97.

Most League Goals in Total Aggregate: David Lowe, 66, 1982–87 and 1995–99.

Most League Goals in One Match: Not more than three goals by one player.

Most Capped Player: Roy Carroll, 9 (11), Northern Ireland.

Most League Appearances: Kevin Langley, 317, 1981–86, 1990–94.

Youngest League Player: Steve Nugent, 16 years 132 days v Leyton Orient, 16 September 1989.

Record Transfer Fee Received: £2,500,000 from Manchester U for Roy Carroll, July 2001

Record Transfer Fee Paid: £750,000 to Wolverhampton W for Tony Dinning, September 2001 and £750,000 to Bristol R for Nathan Ellington, March 2002.

Football League Record: 1978 Elected to Division 4; 1982–92 Division 3; 1992–93 Division 2; 1993–97 Division 3; 1997– Division 2.

LATEST SEQUENCES

Longest Sequence of League Wins: 6, 26.12.87 – 23.1.88.

Longest Sequence of League Defeats: 7, 6.4.93 – 4.5.93.

Longest Sequence of League Draws: 6, 11.12.01 – 5.1.02.

Longest Sequence of Unbeaten League Matches: 25, 8.5.99 – 3.1.00.

Longest Sequence Without a League Win: 14, 9.5.89 – 17.10.89.

MANAGERS

Charlie Spencer 1932–37
Jimmy Milne 1946–47
Bob Pryde 1949–52
Ted Goodier 1952–54
Walter Crook 1954–55
Ron Suart 1955–56
Billy Cooke 1956
Sam Barkas 1957
Trevor Hitchen 1957–58
Malcolm Barrass 1958–59
Jimmy Shirley 1959
Pat Murphy 1959–60
Allenby Chilton 1960
Johnny Ball 1961–63
Allan Brown 1963–66
Alf Craig 1966–67
Harry Leyland 1967–68
Alan Saunders 1968
Ian McNeill 1968–70
Gordon Milne 1970–72
Les Rigby 1972–74
Brian Tiler 1974–76
Ian McNeill 1976–81
Larry Lloyd 1981–83
Harry McNally 1983–85
Bryan Hamilton 1985–86
Ray Mathias 1986–89
Bryan Hamilton 1989–93
Dave Philpotts 1993
Kenny Swain 1993–94
Graham Barrow 1994–95
John Deehan 1995–98
Ray Mathias 1998–99
John Benson 1999–2000
Bruce Rioch 2000–01
Steve Bruce 2001
Paul Jewell June 2001–

TEN YEAR LEAGUE RECORD

		P	W	D	L	F	A	Pts	Pos
1991-92	Div 3	46	15	14	17	58	64	59	15
1992-93	Div 2	46	10	11	25	43	72	41	23
1993-94	Div 3	42	11	12	19	51	70	45	19
1994-95	Div 3	42	14	10	18	53	60	52	14
1995-96	Div 3	46	20	10	16	62	56	70	10
1996-97	Div 3	46	26	9	11	84	51	87	1
1997-98	Div 2	46	17	11	18	64	66	62	11
1998-99	Div 2	46	22	10	14	75	48	76	6
1999-2000	Div 2	46	22	17	7	72	38	83	4
2000-01	Div 2	46	19	18	9	53	42	75	6

DID YOU KNOW ?

In 1934–35, Wigan Athletic were Cheshire League champions and in their FA Cup run from the first qualifying round to the third round proper, scored 27 goals from seven ties.

WIGAN ATHLETIC 2001–02 LEAGUE RECORD

Match No.	Date	Venue	Opponents	Result	H/T Score	Lg. Pos.	Goalscorers	Attendance
1	Aug 11	H	Brentford	D	1-1	0-1	—	McCulloch [66]	5952
2	18	A	Brighton & HA	L	1-2	1-1	17	McCulloch [17]	6518
3	25	H	Bristol C	L	1-2	0-0	18	Ashcroft [73]	6231
4	Sept 8	A	Bury	W	2-0	1-0	17	Billy (og) [26], Haworth [49]	4175
5	15	A	Wycombe W	L	0-1	0-1	22		5400
6	18	H	Huddersfield T	W	1-0	0-0	—	Haworth [49]	5717
7	22	H	QPR	L	1-2	1-1	18	Dinning [42]	6686
8	25	A	Cambridge U	D	2-2	1-1	—	Roberts 2 [17, 72]	2969
9	29	A	Blackpool	L	1-3	0-1	21	Ashcroft (pen) [70]	5279
10	Oct 9	A	Bournemouth	L	0-2	0-1	—		2908
11	12	A	Cardiff C	D	2-2	1-0	—	McGibbon [17], Haworth [52]	11,072
12	20	H	Wrexham	L	2-3	1-1	23	Dinning (pen) [33], Haworth [67]	5979
13	23	A	Tranmere R	W	2-1	0-0	—	Haworth 2 [67, 74]	9030
14	27	H	Port Vale	L	0-1	0-1	23		5634
15	Nov 3	A	Peterborough U	W	2-0	1-0	20	Haworth 2 [11, 83]	5405
16	9	H	Colchester U	L	2-3	0-2	—	Fitzgerald (og) [52], Liddell [56]	5735
17	13	H	Stoke C	W	6-1	3-1	—	Dinning [4], Liddell [14], De Zeeuw [35], Dalglish [49], Ashcroft (pen) [61], Kenna [88]	7047
18	20	H	Chesterfield	D	1-1	0-0	—	Edwards (og) [66]	4071
19	24	A	Northampton T	W	2-0	1-0	18	Dinning [28], Haworth [57]	4267
20	Dec 1	H	Swindon T	W	1-0	0-0	17	Liddell [70]	5635
21	11	H	Notts Co	D	1-1	1-0	—	Liddell [15]	3827
22	15	A	Oldham Ath	D	1-1	0-0	14	Liddell [62]	6407
23	22	A	Reading	D	1-1	0-1	14	Haworth [57]	15,808
24	26	H	Bury	D	1-1	0-0	14	Liddell [51]	6751
25	29	H	Bournemouth	D	0-0	0-0	15		5011
26	Jan 5	A	Bristol C	D	2-2	0-2	13	McCulloch [59], De Vos [78]	9991
27	12	H	Brighton & HA	W	3-0	2-0	13	Liddell 3 (1 pen) [9, 20 (p), 81]	6203
28	19	A	Brentford	W	1-0	0-0	13	Liddell [79]	5549
29	22	H	Reading	L	0-2	0-2	—		5546
30	26	H	Stoke C	D	2-2	2-1	14	Green [20], Dinning [45]	13,361
31	Feb 2	H	Blackpool	L	0-1	0-1	15		7357
32	9	A	Wrexham	L	0-2	0-1	16		4153
33	16	H	Cardiff C	W	4-0	2-0	15	McCulloch [2], De Vos 2 [16, 52], De Zeeuw [67]	5487
34	19	A	Notts Co	W	3-1	1-0	—	McCulloch [15], Teale [81], Dalglish [90]	3358
35	23	H	Wycombe W	D	0-0	0-0	13		4743
36	26	A	QPR	D	1-1	0-0	—	De Vos [70]	8519
37	Mar 2	A	Huddersfield T	D	0-0	0-0	14		12,844
38	5	H	Cambridge U	W	4-1	1-0	—	Liddell 3 (1 pen) [17 (p), 46, 90], McCulloch [71]	3535
39	9	H	Oldham Ath	W	1-0	0-0	12	Liddell [61]	7389
40	16	A	Swindon T	D	1-1	0-0	12	Green [60]	6226
41	23	H	Tranmere R	L	1-2	1-1	12	Liddell (pen) [20]	7783
42	30	A	Port Vale	L	0-1	0-1	13		4359
43	Apr 1	H	Peterborough U	W	2-1	2-0	12	Liddell 2 [5, 12]	4497
44	6	A	Chesterfield	W	2-1	2-1	11	Liddell [6], Ellington [23]	3896
45	13	H	Northampton T	W	3-0	2-0	10	De Vos [7], Ellington [45], Green [69]	5938
46	20	A	Colchester U	D	2-2	0-2	10	Roberts 2 [60, 86]	3672

Final League Position: 10

GOALSCORERS

League (66): Liddell 18 (3 pens), Haworth 10, McCulloch 6, De Vos 5, Dinning 5 (1 pen), Roberts 4, Ashcroft 3 (2 pens), Green 3, Dalglish 2, De Zeeuw 2, Ellington 2, Kenna 1, McGibbon 1, Teale 1, own goals 3.
Worthington Cup (2): Brannan 1, Haworth 1.
FA Cup (0).

Stillie D 13	Mitchell P 16 + 7	Nolan 15 + 3	Bukran G 1	De Vos J 19 + 1	De Zeeuw A 42	Branman G 31 + 2	Adamczuk D 3	Ashcroft L 14 + 2	Liddell A 33 + 1	Kennedy P 29 + 2	McCulloch L 24 + 10	Roberts N 5 + 12	McGibbon P 18	McLoughlin A 1 + 2	Traynor G —+1	Kerr S 8	Sharp K 1 + 1	Dalglish P 17 + 12	Haworth S 19 + 8	Green S 35 + 4	McMillan S 29	Dinning T 32 + 1	Kilford 17 + 13	Santus P —+1	Jackson M 26	Pendlebury 14	Kenna J 6	Cook P 6	Filan J 25	Teale G 22 + 1	Croft G 7	Jarrett J 5	Ellington N 3	Match No.
1	2	3	4	5	6	7	8	9¹	10	11	12																							1
1	2¹	3		5	6	7	8		10³	11³	9	12	4	13	14																			2
	2				6	7	8¹	9		11		12	5			1	3	4	10															3
					6	7		9		11	12		5			1		8	10	2	3¹	4												4
					6	7		9¹	3	11	12		5			1		8	10	2		4												5
					6	7		9	3	11²	13		5			1	12	8¹	10	2		4												6
	12				6	7		9	13	3	10²		5¹			1		8²	11	2		4	14											7
	2				6	7		9		3	10					1		12	11¹	5²	4	8	13											8
	2³				6	7		9		11	13	10¹	5			1		8²	12	14	3	4												9
					6	7		9¹		11	10²	13	5	8³		1		14	12	2	3	4												10
1	12				6	7				11	10³		5					13	14	9	2³	3¹	4	8										11
1	12				6¹			14	10	11	13		5					9	7²	4	8	2	3³											12
1				12				9	8²	11	13		5					10	7	4	6	2	3¹											13
1					6	12		9¹	11	3	13		5					14	10	7²	4	8³	2											14
1	12				6	7		9²	11	13								4¹	10	2	8	5	3											15
1					6	7		10	11¹	12								8	9	2	4	5	3											16
1	13				6	7		9	10	11¹	12							8²		2	4	5	3											17
1					6	7		9¹	10	12	11²							8	13	2		4			5	3								18
1					6	7			10	11								8	9	2		4			5	3								19
1					6	7			10	11	12							4	9¹	2					5	3	8							20
1	13					7			10	11	12		5					4	9¹	2²		3					6	8						21
					6	7			10	11¹									9	2	3	12			5		8		1	4				22
					6				10	11									9	2	3	7			5		8		1	4				23
						7			10	11	6	12						9		2	3	13			5		8²		1	4¹				24
					6	7¹			10		9	12						13		2	3	11			5		8		1	4²				25
	12				6	7			10	11	9²		14					13		2¹	3	8			5				1	4³				26
	2				6	7			10	11	9¹	12						13		3		8			5²				1	4				27
					6	8			10		9		5					2		11		4							1	7	3			28
					6	8			10		9		5					13	12	2¹	11	4							1	7²	3¹			29
					6	8			10		9		5					13		2	11	4	12						1	7²	3¹			30
	14				6	8²			10	12			5³					13	9	2	11	4							1	7	3¹			31
				5	6	8¹			10²	11	9							13	12	3		4							1	7	2			32
				5	6	8¹				11	9		10²	13	14			3³		4	12								1	7	2			33
				5	6	8¹				11	9			13				3		4	12								1	7	2			34
	3			5	6	8²			12	11	9		10¹					4	13	2									1	7				35
8	12			5	6				11	9²			10²	13	14			3	4	2¹									1	7				36
8				5	6				10	9¹	12			7				3	4	13	2								1	11²				37
8	12			5	6				10	9			13	7				3	4	2¹									1	11²				38
8	2			5	6				10	11¹	9			7				3	4	12									1	11¹				39
8	2			5	6				10	9				7				3	4	12									1	11¹				40
8				5	6				10	9	12			7				11	4	2	3¹								1	11				41
4¹				5	6				10	9	8²			7				3	12	2						1	13	11						42
4				5	6				10	9¹	12			7				3		2						1	11	8						43
4	12			5	6				10					7				3	13	2						1	11¹	8²	9					44
4				5	6				10					7				3	12	2						1	11	8²	9					45
4				5	6				10			13		11				12		2	3²					1	7¹	8	9					46

Worthington Cup
First Round   Blackpool   (a)   2-3

FA Cup
First Round   Canvey Island   (h)   0-1

WIMBLEDON   Division 1

FOUNDATION

Old boys from Central School formed this club as Wimbledon Old Centrals in 1889. Their earliest successes were in the Clapham League before switching to the Southern Suburban League in 1902.

Selhurst Park, South Norwood, London SE25 6PY.
Telephone: (020) 8771 2233.
Fax: (020) 8768 0641.
Website: www.wimbledon-fc.co.uk
Box Office: (020) 8771 8841.
ClubCall: 09068 121 175.
Ground Capacity: 26,297.
Record Attendance: 30,115 v Manchester U, FA Premier League, 9 May 1993.
Record Receipts: £531,976 v Tottenham H, Worthington Cup semi-final, 2nd leg, 16 February 1999.
Pitch Measurements: 110yd × 74yd.
Chairman: Charles Koppel.
Deputy Chairman: Peter Lloyd-Cooper.
Directors: K. I. Røkke, B Gjelsten, J. H. Lelliott, P. E. Cork, P. J. B. Miller, M. Hauger, C. Stromberg.
Manager: Stuart Murdoch.
Club Secretary: Steve Rooke.
Director of Media and Communications: Graham Thorley.
Press Manager: Reg Davis.
Chief Scout: Terry Murphy.
Team Physio: Steve Allen. *Club Physio:* John Clinkard.
Stadium Manager: Kevin Corner.
Colours: All navy blue with yellow trim.
Change Colours: All red with black trim.
Year Formed: 1889.
Turned Professional: 1964.
Ltd Co.: 1964.
Previous Name: Wimbledon Old Centrals, 1899–1905.
Previous Ground: 1899, Plough Lane; 1991, Selhurst Park.
Club Nicknames: 'The Dons', 'The Crazy Gang'.

HONOURS

FA Premier League: best season: 6th, 1993–94.
Football League: Division 3 – Runners-up 1983–84; Division 4 – Champions 1982–83.
FA Cup: Winners 1988.
Football League Cup: Semi-final 1996–97, 1998–99.
League Group Cup: Runners-up 1982.
Amateur Cup: Winners 1963; Runners-up 1935, 1947.

IT'S A FACT !

England amateur international Eddie Reynolds was Wimbledon's leading scorer with 43 goals in 1964–65, their first season as a professional club in the Southern League.

First Football League Game: 20 August 1977, Division 4, v Halifax T (h) D 3–3 – Guy; Bryant (1), Galvin, Donaldson, Aitken, Davies, Galliers, Smith, Connell (1), Holmes, Leslie (1).

Record League Victory: 6–0 v Newport Co, Division 3, 3 September 1983 – Beasant; Peters, Winterburn, Galliers, Morris, Hatter, Evans (2), Ketteridge (1), Cork (3 incl. 1p), Downes, Hodges (Driver).

Record Cup Victory: 7–2 v Windsor & Eton, FA Cup 1st rd, 22 November 1980 – Beasant; Jones, Armstrong, Galliers, Mick Smith (2), Cunningham (1), Ketteridge, Hodges, Leslie, Cork (1), Hubbick (3).

Record Defeat: 0–8 v Everton, League Cup 2nd rd, 29 August 1978.

Most League Points (2 for a win): 61, Division 4, 1978–79.

Most League Points (3 for a win): 98, Division 4, 1982–83.

Most League Goals: 97, Division 3, 1983–84.

Highest League Scorer in Season: Alan Cork, 29, 1983–84.

Most League Goals in Total Aggregate: Alan Cork, 145, 1977–92.

Most League Goals in One Match: 4, Alan Cork v Torquay U, Division 4, 28 February 1979.

Most Capped Player: Kenny Cunningham, 40, Republic of Ireland.

Most League Appearances: Alan Cork, 430, 1977–92.

Youngest League Player: Kevin Gage, 17 years 15 days v Bury, 2 May 1981.

Record Transfer Fee Received: £7,000,000 from Newcastle U for Carl Cort, July 2000.

Record Transfer Fee Paid: £7,500,000 to West Ham U for John Hartson, January 1999.

Football League Record: 1977 Elected to Division 4; 1979–80 Division 3; 1980–81 Division 4; 1981–82 Division 3; 1982–83 Division 4; 1983–84 Division 3; 1984–86 Division 2; 1986–92 Division 1; 1992–2000 FA Premier League; 2000– Division 1.

MANAGERS

Les Henley 1955–71
Mike Everitt 1971–73
Dick Graham 1973–74
Allen Batsford 1974–78
Dario Gradi 1978–81
Dave Bassett 1981–87
Bobby Gould 1987–90
Ray Harford 1990–91
Peter Withe 1991
Joe Kinnear 1992–99
Egil Olsen 1999–2000
Terry Burton 2000–02
Stuart Murdoch June 2002–

LATEST SEQUENCES

Longest Sequence of League Wins: 7, 4.9.96 – 19.10.96.

Longest Sequence of League Defeats: 8, 19.3.00 – 30.4.00.

Longest Sequence of League Draws: 4, 26.10.96 – 23.11.96 and 4, 24.4.01 – 6.5.01

Longest Sequence of Unbeaten League Matches: 22, 15.1.83 – 14.5.83.

Longest Sequence Without a League Win: 14, 19.3.00 – 28.8.00.

TEN YEAR LEAGUE RECORD

		P	W	D	L	F	A	Pts	Pos
1991-92	Div 1	42	13	14	15	53	53	53	13
1992-93	PR Lge	42	14	12	16	56	55	54	12
1993-94	PR Lge	42	18	11	13	56	53	65	6
1994-95	PR Lge	42	15	11	16	48	65	56	9
1995-96	PR Lge	38	10	11	17	55	70	41	14
1996-97	PR Lge	38	15	11	12	49	46	56	8
1997-98	PR Lge	38	10	14	14	34	46	44	15
1998-99	PR Lge	38	10	12	16	40	63	42	16
1999-2000	PR Lge	38	7	12	19	46	74	33	18
2000-01	PR Lge	38	17	18	11	71	50	69	8

DID YOU KNOW ?

Alan Cork was the first Wimbledon player to score a hat-trick for the club in the Football League. On 26 August 1978, he hit three in the 4-1 win over Northampton Town.

WIMBLEDON 2001–02 LEAGUE RECORD

Match No.	Date	Venue	Opponents	Result	H/T Score	Lg. Pos.	Goalscorers	Attendance
1	Aug 11	H	Birmingham C	W 3-1	1-0	—	Shipperley [45], Connolly [50], Purse (og) [76]	9142
2	18	A	Burnley	L 2-3	1-3	9	Nielsen [10], Shipperley [65]	14,473
3	25	H	Norwich C	L 0-1	0-0	14		6084
4	27	A	Preston NE	D 1-1	1-0	13	Shipperley [45]	13,349
5	Sept 9	A	Watford	L 0-3	0-1	20		15,466
6	12	H	Portsmouth	D 3-3	1-0	—	Cooper [37], Hughes [48], Connolly [53]	7138
7	15	H	Sheffield W	D 1-1	0-1	17	Hughes [58]	7348
8	18	A	Crewe Alex	W 4-0	1-0	—	Brown [2], Connolly [64], Cooper [75], Nielsen [81]	5563
9	22	A	WBA	W 1-0	0-0	12	Shipperley [90]	19,222
10	25	H	Millwall	D 2-2	1-2	—	Connolly [20], Agyemang [47]	7020
11	29	A	Manchester C	W 4-0	2-0	10	Connolly 2 (1 pen) [23 (p), 35], Shipperley 2 [83, 90]	32,989
12	Oct 13	A	Crystal Palace	L 0-4	0-2	13		20,009
13	20	H	Gillingham	W 3-1	1-0	11	Cooper 2 [43, 53], Hughes [61]	8042
14	24	H	Coventry C	L 0-1	0-0	—		5883
15	27	A	Rotherham U	L 2-3	2-2	14	Connolly [8], McAnuff [9]	5586
16	30	A	Bradford C	D 3-3	3-1	—	Connolly 2 [15, 43], Cooper [17]	18,255
17	Nov 3	H	Grimsby T	W 2-1	1-0	14	Roberts [37], McAnuff [83]	6189
18	9	H	Sheffield U	D 1-1	0-0	14	Cooper [88]	4937
19	17	A	Barnsley	D 1-1	0-0	14	Cooper [87]	11,088
20	20	H	Walsall	D 2-2	1-1	—	Connolly 2 [29, 73]	4249
21	24	H	Wolverhampton W	L 0-1	0-0	15		9873
22	Dec 1	A	Coventry C	L 1-3	1-2	17	McAnuff [45]	17,303
23	8	A	Stockport Co	W 2-1	2-1	17	Cooper [1], Connolly [32]	4673
24	16	H	Nottingham F	W 1-0	0-0	14	Willmott [66]	5920
25	22	A	Norwich C	L 1-2	0-1	14	Connolly (pen) [63]	17,286
26	29	H	Preston NE	W 2-0	0-0	15	Shipperley [87], Agyemang [90]	6501
27	Jan 12	H	Burnley	D 0-0	0-0	15		7675
28	19	A	Birmingham C	W 2-0	0-0	14	Hughes [80], Agyemang [90]	17,766
29	29	A	Walsall	L 1-2	1-1	—	Shipperley [12]	5388
30	Feb 3	H	Manchester C	W 2-1	1-0	13	Shipperley 2 [34, 69]	10,664
31	9	A	Gillingham	D 0-0	0-0	13		8494
32	16	H	Crystal Palace	D 1-1	1-0	13	Francis [7]	13,564
33	19	H	Watford	D 0-0	0-0	—		5551
34	23	A	Millwall	W 1-0	1-0	11	Cooper [15]	13,788
35	Mar 2	H	WBA	L 0-1	0-0	13		8363
36	6	A	Sheffield W	W 2-1	1-1	—	Connolly [45], Ardley [60]	18,930
37	9	A	Nottingham F	D 0-0	0-0	12		24,292
38	12	A	Portsmouth	W 2-1	0-1	—	Cooper [77], Connolly [84]	13,118
39	16	H	Stockport Co	W 3-1	1-0	9	Connolly 2 [25, 65], Ardley [70]	5224
40	23	A	Grimsby T	L 2-6	2-2	11	Shipperley [24], Agyemang [42]	6473
41	30	H	Rotherham U	W 1-0	1-0	11	Morgan [17]	4751
42	Apr 1	A	Sheffield U	W 1-0	1-0	10	Ardley [39]	19,712
43	4	H	Crewe Alex	W 2-0	0-0	—	Shipperley [56], McAnuff [68]	5007
44	6	H	Bradford C	L 1-2	0-1	9	Connolly (pen) [90]	5595
45	14	A	Wolverhampton W	L 0-1	0-1	9		26,920
46	21	H	Barnsley	L 0-1	0-1	9		5379

Final League Position: 9

GOALSCORERS

League (63): Connolly 18 (3 pens), Shipperley 12, Cooper 10, Agyemang 4, Hughes 4, McAnuff 4, Ardley 3, Nielsen 2, Brown 1, Francis 1, Morgan 1, Roberts 1, Willmott 1, own goal 1.
Worthington Cup (1): Williams 1.
FA Cup (0).

Davis K 40	Darlington J 25+4	Kimble A 7+2	Andersen T 27+3	Williams M 4+1	Willmott C 25+2	Ardley N 27+2	Roberts A 18	Shipperley N 36+5	Connolly D 35	Cooper K 39+1	Nielsen D 6+6	Agyemang P 17+16	Jupp D 1+1	Heald P 4	Gier R 3	McAnuff J 22+16	Holloway D 32	Feuer I 2+2	Hughes M 24+2	Brown W 17	Leigertwood M 1	Cunningham K 34	Karlsson P 1+6	Robinson P —+1	Hawkins P 25+4	Mild H 8+1	Francis D 21+2	Ainsworth G —+2	Morgan L 4+7	Nowland A 1+6	Gore S —+1	Byrne D —+1	Reo-Coker N —+1	Match No.
1	2	3	4^1	5	6	7	8	9^2	10	11^3	12	13	14																					1
1	2	3		5	6	7	4	9	10	11		8^1	12																					2
	2	3			6	7	4	9^1	10	11		8^2	12																					3
12	3				6	7	4	9	10	11^1				1		5	13																	4
12	3^1				6	7	8	9	10	11				1		5	4^9	2	15															5
	2	13	4		6	7^1	8	9	10	11				1		5^2	3		12															6
1	2		4		6		8	9	10^1	11	12						3		7			5												7
1	12	3	4^1		6		8	9^2	10	11^3		13				14	2		7			5												8
1	7	3			6		4	9	10^1	11	12						2		8			5												9
1	2				6		8	9^2	10^1	11	12	13				4	3		7			5												10
1	2						8	9^1	10^2	11	12	13				4	3		7	6		5												11
1	2						8	9	10^2	11						4^1	3		7	6		5	12		13									12
1	2						8	9	10^2	11	12					4^1	3^9		7	6		5			13		14							13
1	2						8	9	10	11	12					4	3^1		7	6		5												14
1	2^3						8	9^1	10	11	12					4^2	3		7	6		5			13		14							15
1					6		8	9^1	10	11	12					4^2			7	2		5	13		3									16
1					6		4	9^1	10	11		8^2	12			13			7	2		5			3									17
1	2				6		8^1	9	10^2	11	12	13				4			7			5			3									18
1	2		4					9	10^1	11	12								7	6		5			3		8							19
1	2		4					9	10	11^1						12			7	6		5			3		8							20
1			4					9^1	10	11	12	13				7^2	2		14	6		5			3		8^3							21
1	2					7		9^1	10	11		12				4^2	3		8	6		5			13									22
1	2					7		9	10	11^1						12	3		8	6		5	4^2		13									23
1	2			5		7		9	10	11	12						3		8	6					4^1									24
1	2		4			7		9	10	11^2						12	3^9		15	8		5	13		6^1									25
1	2		4			7		9	10^1	11^2	12					13	3		8			5			6									26
			4					9	10^1	11	12					8^2	2	1	7			5			3	13	6							27
1	3^2		4			7		9	10^1	11	12						2		8			5	13		6									28
1	12		4		13	7		9	10^3	11		2^1				8						5			3		6^2	14						29
1			4			7		9	10^1	11	12						2		8			5			3		6							30
1			4			7		9	10^2	11^1	12						2		8			5			3		6		13					31
1	12		4			7		9^1	10	11		13^3					2		8^2			5			3		6		14					32
1			4			7		9	10^1	11^2	12						2					5			3		8	6	13					33
1	2				12		6	9	10^1	11									7			5	4		3	13	8^4							34
1	2		4			7		9	10	11	12											5			3		8^1	6^2	13					35
1			4		6	7		9^1	10^2	11	12						2					5			3		8		13					36
1			4		6	7		9^1	10	11							2					5			3		8		12					37
1			4^1		6	7	13	9^2	10		12						2					5			3		8		11^2	14				38
1			4^1			7		9^2	10	11^3	12	13					2					5			3		8		14					39
			4		6	7		9	10	11^6	12			1			2^1					5			3		8			15				40
1	2		4		6	7		9	10^2		12											5			3		8		13	11^1				41
1	2		4^1		6^2	7	13	9	10^3		12											5			3		8		14	11				42
1			4		6	7	8	9	10^2	11^1	12						2					5	13		3									43
1			4		6	7		9	10	11^1	13						2					5	12^2		3		8							44
1			4		6	7^1		9	10	11^3	12						2					5	13		3		8^2		14					45
1			4^2	5	6	7		9	10	11^1		10									2				3		8^3		12		13	14		46

Worthington Cup
First Round   Brighton & HA   (a)   1-2

FA Cup
Third Round   Middlesbrough   (h) 0-0
                                                  (a) 0-2

WOLVERHAMPTON WANDERERS Division 1

FOUNDATION

Enthusiasts of the game at St Luke's School, Blakenhall formed a club in 1877. In the same neighbourhood a cricket club called Blakenhall Wanderers had a football section. Several St Luke's footballers played cricket for them and shortly before the start of the 1879–80 season the two amalgamated and Wolverhampton Wanderers FC was brought into being.

Molineux Stadium, Wolverhampton WV1 4QR.

Telephone: (01902) 655 000. *Fax:* (01902) 687 006. *ClubCall:* 09068 121 103.

Ground Capacity: 28,525.

Record Attendance: 61,315 v Liverpool, FA Cup 5th rd, 11 February 1939.

Record Receipts: £369,232 v Norwich C, Division 1 play-off semi-final, 1 May 2002.

Pitch Measurements: 110yd × 75yd.

President and Chairman: Sir Jack Hayward.

Deputy Chairman: Derek Harrington.

Chief Executive: Jez Moxey.

Directors: Jack Harris, John Harris, Rick Hayward, Rachael Heyhoe Flint, Michael Lister, Paul Manduca, Jez Moxey.

Manager: David Jones. *Assistant Manager:* John Ward. *Coach:* Terry Connor. *Physio:* Barry Holmes.

Secretary: Richard Skirrow.

Stadium Manager: Steve Sutton.

Safety Officer: Bob Morrison.

Colours: Gold shirts, black shorts, black stockings.

Change Colours: All white.

HONOURS

Football League: Division 1 – Champions 1953–54, 1957–58, 1958–59; Runners-up 1937–38, 1938–39; 1949–50, 1954–55, 1959–60; Division 2 – Champions 1931–32, 1976–77; Runners-up 1966–67, 1982–83; Division 3 (N) – Champions 1923–24; Division 3 – Champions 1988–89; Division 4 – Champions 1987–88.

FA Cup: Winners 1893, 1908, 1949, 1960; Runners-up 1889, 1896, 1921, 1939.

Football League Cup: Winners 1974, 1980.

Texaco Cup: Winners 1971.

Sherpa Van Trophy: Winners 1988.

European Competitions: European Cup: 1958–59, 1959–60. *European Cup-Winners' Cup:* 1960–61. *UEFA Cup:* 1971–72 (runners-up), 1973–74, 1974–75, 1980–81.

Year Formed: 1877* (*see Foundation*). *Turned Professional:* 1888. *Ltd Co.:* 1923 (but current club is WWFC (1986) Ltd).

Previous Names: 1879, St Luke's combined with Wanderers Cricket Club to become Wolverhampton Wanderers (1923) Ltd. New limited companies followed in 1982 and 1986 (current).

Club Nickname: 'Wolves'.

Previous Grounds: 1877, Windmill Field; 1879, John Harper's Field; 1881, Dudley Road; 1889, Molineux.

First Football League Game: 8 September 1888, Football League, v Aston Villa (h) D 1–1 – Baynton; Baugh, Mason; Fletcher, Allen, Lowder; Hunter, Cooper, Anderson, White, Cannon, (1 og).

Record League Victory: 10–1 v Leicester C, Division 1, 15 April 1938 – Sidlow; Morris, Dowen; Galley, Cullis, Gardiner; Maguire (1), Horace Wright, Westcott (4), Jones (1), Dorsett (4).

IT'S A FACT !

In 1959–60, Wolverhampton Wanderers became the first Football League club to score a century of goals in three successive seasons. The following term, they made it four in a row, consecutively scoring 103, 110, 106 and 103 goals.

Record Cup Victory: 14–0 v Crosswell's Brewery, FA Cup 2nd rd, 13 November 1886 – I. Griffiths; Baugh, Mason; Pearson, Allen (1), Lowder; Hunter (4), Knight (2), Brodie (4), B. Griffiths (2), Wood. Plus one goal 'scrambled through'.

Record Defeat: 1–10 v Newton Heath, Division 1, 15 October 1892.

Most League Points (2 for a win): 64, Division 1, 1957–58.

Most League Points (3 for a win): 92, Division 3, 1988–89.

Most League Goals: 115, Division 2, 1931–32.

Highest League Scorer in Season: Dennis Westcott, 38, Division 1, 1946–47.

Most League Goals in Total Aggregate: Steve Bull, 250, 1986–99.

Most League Goals in One Match: 5, Joe Butcher v Accrington, Division 1, 19 November 1892; 5, Tom Phillipson v Barnsley, Division 2, 26 April 1926; 5, Tom Phillipson v Bradford C, Division 2, 25 December 1926; 5, Billy Hartill v Notts Co, Division 2, 12 October 1929; 5, Billy Hartill v Aston Villa, Division 1, 3 September 1934.

Most Capped Player: Billy Wright, 105, England (70 consecutive).

Most League Appearances: Derek Parkin, 501, 1967–82.

Youngest League Player: Jimmy Mullen, 16 years 43 days v Leeds U, 18 February 1939.

Record Transfer Fee Received: £5,000,000 from Leicester C for Ade Akinbiyi, July 2000.

Record Transfer Fee Paid: £3,000,000 to Bristol C for Ade Akinbiyi, September 1999 and £3,000,000 to Rangers for Kenny Miller, December 2001.

Football League Record: 1888 Founder Member of Football League: 1906–23 Division 2; 1923–24 Division 3 (N); 1924–32 Division 2; 1932–65 Division 1; 1965–67 Division 2; 1967–76 Division 1; 1976–77 Division 2; 1977–82 Division 1; 1982–83 Division 2; 1983–84 Division 1; 1984–85 Division 2; 1985–86 Division 3; 1986–88 Division 4; 1988–89 Division 3; 1989–92 Division 2; 1992– Division 1.

MANAGERS

George Worrall 1877–85 (Secretary-Manager)
John Addenbrooke 1885–1922
George Jobey 1922–24
Albert Hoskins 1924–26 (had been Secretary since 1922)
Fred Scotchbrook 1926–27
Major Frank Buckley 1927–44
Ted Vizard 1944–48
Stan Cullis 1948–64
Andy Beattie 1964–65
Ronnie Allen 1966–68
Bill McGarry 1968–76
Sammy Chung 1976–78
John Barnwell 1978–81
Ian Greaves 1982
Graham Hawkins 1982–84
Tommy Docherty 1984–85
Bill McGarry 1985
Sammy Chapman 1985–86
Brian Little 1986
Graham Turner 1986–94
Graham Taylor 1994–95
Mark McGhee 1995–98
Colin Lee 1998–2000
David Jones January 2001–

LATEST SEQUENCES

Longest Sequence of League Wins: 8, 15.10.88 – 26.11.88.
Longest Sequence of League Defeats: 8, 5.12.81 – 13.2.82.
Longest Sequence of League Draws: 6, 22.4.95 – 20.8.95.
Longest Sequence of Unbeaten League Matches: 20, 24.11.23 – 5.4.24.
Longest Sequence Without a League Win: 19, 1.12.84 – 6.4.85.

TEN YEAR LEAGUE RECORD

		P	W	D	L	F	A	Pts	Pos
1991-92	Div 2	46	18	10	18	61	54	64	11
1992-93	Div 1	46	16	13	17	57	56	61	11
1993-94	Div 1	46	17	17	12	60	47	68	8
1994-95	Div 1	46	21	13	12	77	61	76	4
1995-96	Div 1	46	13	16	17	56	62	55	20
1996-97	Div 1	46	22	10	14	68	51	76	3
1997-98	Div 1	46	18	11	17	57	53	65	9
1998-99	Div 1	46	19	16	11	64	43	73	7
1999-2000	Div 1	46	21	11	14	64	48	74	7
2000-01	Div 1	46	14	13	19	45	48	55	12

DID YOU KNOW ?

In 1951, Wolverhampton Wanderers toured South Africa from 19 May to 30 June, playing 12 matches which produced 12 wins and 60 goals scored for only five against.

WOLVERHAMPTON WANDERERS 2001–02 LEAGUE RECORD

Match No.	Date	Venue	Opponents	Result	H/T Score	Lg. Pos.	Goalscorers	Attendance
1	Aug 11	H	Portsmouth	D	2-2	1-2	—	Newton [45], Roussel [57]	23,012
2	19	A	Coventry C	W	1-0	1-0	7	Robinson [7]	22,092
3	25	H	Watford	W	1-0	1-0.	5	Vega (og) [9]	20,257
4	27	A	Sheffield U	D	2-2	1-0	6	Roussel [29], Lescott [85]	16,497
5	Sept 8	A	Preston NE	W	2-1	0-1	5	Sinton [48], Lescott [61]	14,381
6	15	H	Stockport Co	D	2-2	0-1	8	Robinson [69], Blake [78]	20,742
7	18	A	Gillingham	W	3-2	2-0	—	Blake [37], Miller [40], Newton [90]	8966
8	21	A	Walsall	W	3-0	3-0	—	Kennedy [20], Miller [22], Newton [26]	8327
9	25	H	Nottingham F	W	1-0	0-0	—	Newton [90]	24,350
10	29	A	Rotherham U	W	3-0	2-0	1	Cameron [18], Kennedy [23], Rae [87]	8298
11	Oct 13	A	Bradford C	W	3-0	1-0	1	Proudlock 3 [45, 76, 79]	16,878
12	16	H	Crewe Alex	L	0-1	0-0	—		22,569
13	20	H	Crystal Palace	L	0-1	0-1	2		26,471
14	25	A	WBA	D	1-1	1-0	—	Blake [22]	26,143
15	28	H	Burnley	W	3-0	3-0	1	Taylor (og) [10], Rae [20], Cook (og) [39]	24,893
16	31	H	Millwall	W	1-0	0-0	—	Rae [90]	23,018
17	Nov 3	A	Norwich C	L	0-2	0-2	1		20,335
18	18	H	Sheffield W	D	0-0	0-0	2		19,947
19	24	A	Wimbledon	W	1-0	0-0	2	Sturridge [82]	9873
20	27	H	Barnsley	W	4-1	2-1	—	Sturridge 3 [9, 33, 76], Newton [68]	19,231
21	Dec 2	H	WBA	L	0-1	0-0	2		27,515
22	7	A	Grimsby T	D	1-1	1-1	—	Groves (og) [7]	5143
23	11	A	Manchester C	L	0-1	0-1	—		33,639
24	16	H	Birmingham C	W	2-1	1-1	3	Blake [38], Rae [66]	21,482
25	22	A	Watford	D	1-1	1-1	2	Newton [8]	17,389
26	26	H	Preston NE	L	2-3	1-0	3	Sturridge [19], Blake [65]	24,024
27	29	H	Sheffield U	W	1-0	1-0	3	Sturridge [45]	24,138
28	Jan 13	H	Coventry C	W	3-1	0-0	2	Sturridge 2 [50, 53], Cameron [56]	21,009
29	17	A	Portsmouth	W	3-2	1-1	—	Rae [15], Blake [61], Sturridge [85]	13,105
30	29	A	Barnsley	L	0-1	0-1	—		13,825
31	Feb 2	H	Rotherham U	W	2-1	0-1	2	Sturridge [69], Ndah [77]	22,591
32	7	A	Crystal Palace	W	2-0	1-0	—	Sturridge [13], Newton [85]	18,475
33	16	H	Bradford C	W	3-1	0-1	2	Sturridge 2 (1 pen) [76, 90 (pl)], Newton [83]	21,935
34	20	A	Crewe Alex	W	4-1	0-0	—	Blake 2 [53, 60], Rae [57], Kennedy [67]	8371
35	23	A	Stockport Co	W	4-1	3-1	1	Sturridge 2 (1 pen) [16 (pl), 44], Kennedy 2 [28, 72]	8481
36	26	H	Walsall	W	3-0	0-0	—	Sturridge 2 [54, 76], Blake [77]	27,043
37	Mar 2	H	Gillingham	W	2-0	2-0	1	Rae [26], Blake [45]	25,908
38	6	A	Nottingham F	D	2-2	1-0	—	Sturridge [11], Lescott [60]	21,010
39	9	A	Birmingham C	D	2-2	2-2	1	Butler [20], Lescott [29]	22,104
40	16	H	Grimsby T	L	0-1	0-0	2		25,967
41	23	H	Norwich C	D	0-0	0-0	2		26,280
42	30	A	Burnley	W	3-2	3-0	—	Sturridge 2 [9, 26], Cameron [45]	21,823
43	Apr 1	H	Manchester C	L	0-2	0-1	2		28,015
44	5	A	Millwall	L	0-1	0-0	—		17,058
45	14	H	Wimbledon	W	1-0	1-0	3	Blake [23]	26,920
46	21	A	Sheffield W	D	2-2	1-1	3	Cameron [1], Lescott [56]	29,772

Final League Position: 3

GOALSCORERS

League (76): Sturridge 20 (2 pens), Blake 11, Newton 8, Rae 7, Kennedy 5, Lescott 5, Cameron 4, Proudlock 3, Miller 2, Robinson 2, Roussel 2, Butler 1, Ndah 1, Sinton 1, own goals 4.
Worthington Cup (1): Dinning 1.
FA Cup (0).

Oakes M 46	Muscat K 37	Naylor L 26+1	Lescott J 44	Butler P 43	Dinning T 4	Newton S 45	Robinson C 15+8	Roussel C 6+11	Proudlock A 12+7	Kennedy M 35	Connelly S 5+3	Ketsbaia T —+2	Cameron C 38+3	Sinton A 3+4	Ndah G 1+14	Miller K 5+15	Blake N 38+1	Rae A 31+5	Branch M 5+2	Sturridge D 27	Camara M 23+4	Pollet L 5+3	Andrews K 4+7	Halle G 4+1	Cooper K 4+1	Match No.
1	2	3^1	4	5	6	7	8	9	10	11	12															1
1	2	3	4	5	6	7	8	9^1	10	11		12														2
1	2	3	4	5	6	7	8^2	9	10^1	11^3		12	13	14												3
1	2	3	4	5	6	7		9	10^1			8	11	12												4
1	2	3	4	5		7	8	9	10^2	11^1			6		12	13										5
1	2	3	4	5		7	8		10^1	11			6			12	9									6
1	2	3	4	5		7	8	12	13	11			6			10^2	9^1									7
1	2	3	4	5		7	8	12	13	11^3			6			10^2	9^1	14								8
1	2	3	4	5		7	8		12	11			6			10^3	9									9
1	2	3	4	5		7	8^2	12	10^1	11			6				9	13								10
1	2	3	4	5		7	8^1		10	11			6				9	12								11
1	2	3	4	5		7	8^2	12	10^1	11			6				9	13								12
1	2	3	4	5		7	8^1		10^2	11			6				9	12	13							13
1	2	3	4	5		7		12	13	11			6				9^1	8		10^2						14
1	2	3	4	5		7		12	13	11^2			6^1				9	8		10						15
1	2	3	4	5		7		12	13	11^2			6^1				9	8		10						16
1	2	3	4	5		7		12	13	11^1			6				9	8		10^2						17
1		3	4	5		7^1	12	9		11^2			6	2	13			8	14	10^3						18
1		3	4	5		7	12			11^2			6^1	2	13		9	8		10						19
1		3	4	5^3		7	12	13					6	2^1			9^2	8		10	11	14				20
1		3	4	5		7	12			11			6	2			9^1	8		10						21
1	2	3	4	5		7	12	13		11^3			6^1				9^2	8		10		14				22
1	2	3	4	5		7^1	12	13		11			6^1				9	8		10^3		14				23
1	2	3	4	5		7				11^2			6		12		9^1	8	13	10						24
1	2	3^1	4	5		7				11			6^2		12	13	9	8	14	10^1						25
1	2	3^2	4	5		7^1				11			6		12		9	8	13	10						26
1	2			5		7			12	11			6				9^1	8		10	3	4				27
1	2		4	5		7				11			6		12	13	9^1	8		10^2	3					28
1	2		4	5		7				11^1			6		12		9	8		10	3					29
1	2		4	5						11			6^2		12		9	8	13	10	3	7^1				30
1	2		4	5		7^1				11			6		12	13	9^2	8		10	3					31
1	2		4	5		7^1				11			6^3		12	13	9^1	8		10	3		14			32
1	2		4	5		7				11			6		12		9^1	8		10	3					33
1	2^1		4	5		7				11			6^2		12		9	8		10	3	13				34
1	2		4	5		7				11			6^3		12	13	9^1	8		10^2	3		14			35
1	2		4	5		7^1				11			6		12		9	8^2		10	3	13				36
1	2		4	5		7^2				11^1			6		12	13	9	8		10	3					37
1	2		4	5		7				11			6		12		9^1	8		10	3					38
1	2		4	5		7				11			6^1				9	8		10	3	12				39
1	2		4	5		7				11^2			6^1		13	12	9	8	14	10	3					40
1	2		4			7				11			6		12		9	8		10	3			5^1		41
1			4	5		7							6		12	13	9^1	8		10^2	3		2^3	14	11	42
1			4	5		7							6		12	13	9^2	8		10	3		2		11^1	43
1			4	5		7							6		12	13	9^1	8^3		10	3		2	14	11^2	44
1			4	5^1		7							6			13	9^2	8		10	3	12	2		11	45
1	12		4			7				11^3			6			13	9^2	8		10	3^1		2	5	14	46

Worthington Cup
First Round   Swindon T   (h) 1-2

FA Cup
Third Round   Gillingham   (h) 0-1

WREXHAM

Division 3

FOUNDATION

The club was formed on 28 September 1872 by members of Wrexham Cricket Club, so they could continue playing a sport during the winter months. This meeting was held at the Turf Hotel, which although rebuilt since, still stands at one corner of the present ground. Their first game was a few weeks later and matches often included 17 players on either side! By 1875 team formations were reduced to 11 men and a year later the club was among the founder members of the Cambrian Football Association, which quickly changed its title to the Football Association of Wales.

Racecourse Ground, Mold Road, Wrexham LL11 2AH.

Telephone: (01978) 262 129. **Fax:** (01978) 357 821.
Commercial Dept: (01978) 352 536.
Community Office: (01978) 358 545.
ClubCall: 09068 121 642.

Ground Capacity: 15,500.

Record Attendance: 34,445 v Manchester U, FA Cup 4th rd, 26 January 1957.

Record Receipts: £126,012 v West Ham U, FA Cup 4th rd, 4 February 1992.

Pitch Measurements: 111yd × 71yd.

Chairman: M. Guterman.

Managing Director: D. L. Rhodes (Vice-chairman).

Directors: D. Griffiths, S. Mackarth, G. Jones, D. Bennett.

Manager: Denis Smith.
Assistant Manager: Kevin Russell.
Player-Coach: Joey Jones.
Physio: Mel Pejic.

Secretary: D. L. Rhodes.

Commercial Director: W. Wingrove.

Colours: Red shirts, white shorts, red stockings.

Change Colours: Black and white hoops.

Year Formed: 1872 (oldest club in Wales). **Turned Professional:** 1912. **Ltd Co.:** 1912.

Club Nickname: 'Red Dragons'.

Previous Grounds: 1872, Racecourse Ground; 1883, Rhosddu Recreation Ground; 1887, Racecourse Ground.

First Football League Game: 27 August 1921, Division 3 (N), v Hartlepools U (h) L 0–2 – Godding; Ellis, Simpson; Matthias, Foster, Griffiths; Burton, Goode, Cotton, Edwards, Lloyd.

HONOURS

Football League: Division 2 best season: 7th, 1997–98; Division 3 – Champions 1977–78; Runners-up 1992–93; Division 3 (N) – Runners-up 1932–33; Division 4 – Runners-up 1969–70.

FA Cup: best season: 6th rd, 1974, 1978, 1997.

Football League Cup: best season: 5th rd, 1961, 1978.

Welsh Cup: Winners 23 times (record); Runners-up 22 times (record).

FAW Premier Cup: Winners 1998, 2000.

European Competition: European Cup-Winners' Cup: 1972–73, 1975–76, 1978–79, 1979–80, 1984–85, 1986–87, 1990–91, 1995–96.

IT'S A FACT *!*

The demise of Aldershot as a Football League club in March 1992 left Wrexham with an unbeaten home record against the Hampshire club. It comprised 13 wins and four drawn games at the Racecourse Ground.

Record League Victory: 10–1 v Hartlepool U, Division 4, 3 March 1962 – Keelan; Peter Jones, McGavan; Tecwyn Jones, Fox, Ken Barnes; Ron Barnes (3), Bennion (1), Davies (3), Ambler (3), Ron Roberts.

Record Cup Victory: 11–1 v New Brighton, Football League Northern Section Cup 1st rd, 3 January 1934 – Foster; Alfred Jones, Hamilton, Bulling, McMahon, Lawrence, Bryant (3), Findlay (1), Bamford (5), Snow, Waller (1), (o.g. 1).

Record Defeat: 0–9 v Brentford, Division 3, 15 October 1963.

Most League Points (2 for a win): 61, Division 4, 1969–70 and Division 3, 1977–78.

Most League Points (3 for a win): 80, Division 3, 1992–93.

Most League Goals: 106, Division 3 (N), 1932–33.

Highest League Scorer in Season: Tom Bamford, 44, Division 3 (N), 1933–34.

Most League Goals in Total Aggregate: Tom Bamford, 175, 1928–34.

Most League Goals in One Match: 5, Tom Bamford v Carlisle U, Division 3N, 17 March 1934; 5, Lee Jones v Cambridge U, Division 2, 6 April 2002.

Most Capped Player: Joey Jones, 29 (72), Wales.

Most League Appearances: Arfon Griffiths, 592, 1959–61, 1962–79.

Youngest League Player: Ken Roberts, 15 years 158 days v Bradford PA, 1 September 1951.

Record Transfer Fee Received: £800,000 from Birmingham C for Bryan Hughes, March 1997.

Record Transfer Fee Paid: £210,000 to Liverpool for Joey Jones, October 1978.

Football League Record: 1921 Original Member of Division 3 (N); 1958–60 Division 3; 1960–62 Division 4; 1962–64 Division 3; 1964–70 Division 4; 1970–78 Division 3; 1978–82 Division 2; 1982–83 Division 3; 1983–92 Division 4; 1992–93 Division 3; 1993–2002 Division 2; 2002– Division 3.

MANAGERS

Selection Committee 1872–1924
Charlie Hewitt 1924–25
Selection Committee 1925–29
Jack Baynes 1929–31
Ernest Blackburn 1932–37
James Logan 1937–38
Arthur Cowell 1938
Tom Morgan 1938–42
Tom Williams 1942–49
Les McDowell 1949–50
Peter Jackson 1950–55
Cliff Lloyd 1955–57
John Love 1957–59
Cliff Lloyd 1959–60
Billy Morris 1960–61
Ken Barnes 1961–65
Billy Morris 1965
Jack Rowley 1966–67
Alvan Williams 1967–68
John Neal 1968–77
Arfon Griffiths 1977–81
Mel Sutton 1981–82
Bobby Roberts 1982–85
Dixie McNeil 1985–89
Brian Flynn 1989–2001
Denis Smith October 2001–

LATEST SEQUENCES

Longest Sequence of League Wins: 7, 4.3.78 – 27.3.78.

Longest Sequence of League Defeats: 9, 2.10.63 – 30.10.63.

Longest Sequence of League Draws: 6, 12.11.99 – 26.12.99.

Longest Sequence of Unbeaten League Matches: 16, 3.9.66 – 19.11.66.

Longest Sequence Without a League Win: 16, 25.9.99 – 3.1.00.

TEN YEAR LEAGUE RECORD

		P	W	D	L	F	A	Pts	Pos
1991-92	Div 4	42	14	9	19	52	73	51	14
1992-93	Div 3	42	23	11	8	75	52	80	2
1993-94	Div 2	46	17	11	18	66	77	62	12
1994-95	Div 2	46	16	15	15	65	64	63	13
1995-96	Div 2	46	18	16	12	76	55	70	8
1996-97	Div 2	46	17	18	11	54	50	69	8
1997-98	Div 2	46	18	16	12	55	51	70	7
1998-99	Div 2	46	13	14	19	43	62	53	17
1999-2000	Div 2	46	17	11	18	52	61	62	11
2000-01	Div 2	46	17	12	17	65	71	63	10

DID YOU KNOW ?

Eddie Tunney, whose 15-year Wrexham career spanned the Second World War, was an ever-present in 1938–39 and again in 1947–48 from a total of 222 League appearances.

WREXHAM 2001–02 LEAGUE RECORD

Match No.	Date	Venue	Opponents	Result	H/T Score	Lg. Pos.	Goalscorers	Attendance
1	Aug 11	H	Oldham Ath	D	3-3	0-1	—	Lawrence [51], Edwards [59], Faulconbridge [63]	4881
2	18	A	Wycombe W	L	2-5	0-4	20	Faulconbridge [64], Chalk [90]	5425
3	25	H	Colchester U	D	1-1	0-1	16	Edwards [73]	2952
4	Sept 8	A	Notts Co	D	2-2	1-2	20	Trundle [12], Faulconbridge [50]	4776
5	11	H	Bury	W	1-0	0-0	—	Trundle [84]	2470
6	14	H	Brighton & HA	L	1-2	0-0	—	Thomas [66]	3434
7	18	A	Chesterfield	L	2-3	0-1	—	Roberts [81], Ferguson [87]	3538
8	21	A	Tranmere R	L	0-5	0-1	—		10,285
9	25	H	Port Vale	L	1-3	0-1	—	Faulconbridge [56]	3091
10	29	H	Peterborough U	L	1-2	0-0	23	Faulconbridge [74]	2640
11	Oct 13	H	QPR	W	1-0	1-0	23	Blackwood [43]	4474
12	20	A	Wigan Ath	W	3-2	1-1	22	Hill [44], Sam [70], Faulconbridge [79]	5979
13	23	H	Blackpool	D	1-1	1-0	—	Trundle [33]	5640
14	27	A	Huddersfield T	L	1-5	1-1	22	Chalk [25]	9888
15	Nov 4	H	Cardiff C	L	1-3	1-2	23	Edwards [5]	5832
16	6	A	Reading	L	0-2	0-0	—		8081
17	10	A	Bournemouth	L	0-3	0-2	24		5031
18	20	A	Cambridge U	W	2-0	0-0	—	Ferguson (pen) [47], Faulconbridge [84]	2648
19	24	H	Stoke C	L	0-1	0-0	22		5477
20	27	A	Swindon T	L	1-3	0-2	—	Faulconbridge [56]	4127
21	Dec 1	H	Northampton T	W	3-2	1-1	22	Carey [43], Chalk (pen) [56], Ferguson [86]	2708
22	8	H	Bristol C	L	0-2	0-0	—		3091
23	15	H	Brentford	L	0-3	0-1	22		5326
24	22	A	Bristol C	L	0-1	0-0	22		12,137
25	26	H	Notts Co	W	2-1	1-1	22	Phillips [12], Trundle [87]	3707
26	29	H	Reading	L	0-2	0-1	22		3885
27	Jan 5	A	Colchester U	L	1-2	1-1	22	Thomas [29]	2835
28	12	H	Wycombe W	D	0-0	0-0	22		2752
29	19	A	Oldham Ath	L	1-3	1-1	22	Morrell [11]	5451
30	26	H	Swindon T	D	2-2	1-0	23	Faulconbridge [30], Carey [73]	2879
31	29	A	Bury	D	2-2	2-1	—	Sam 2 (1 pen) [2, 22 (p)]	2735
32	Feb 2	A	Peterborough U	W	3-2	1-1	21	Faulconbridge [15], Blackwood [46], Sam (pen) [90]	4675
33	9	H	Wigan Ath	W	2-0	1-0	21	Faulconbridge [19], Lawrence [67]	4153
34	16	A	QPR	L	1-2	1-0	21	Thomas [2]	9706
35	23	A	Brighton & HA	D	0-0	0-0	22		6649
36	26	H	Tranmere R	D	1-1	0-0	—	Trundle [75]	5702
37	Mar 2	H	Chesterfield	L	0-1	0-1	22		3328
38	5	A	Port Vale	W	3-1	1-0	—	Edwards [36], Trundle 2 (1 pen) [85 (p), 87]	4436
39	9	H	Brentford	L	0-3	0-2	23		3343
40	16	A	Northampton T	L	1-4	1-1	23	Trundle [21]	5029
41	22	A	Cardiff C	L	2-3	1-2	—	Faulconbridge [34], Sam [88]	15,702
42	30	H	Huddersfield T	D	1-1	0-0	23	Faulconbridge [55]	4448
43	Apr 1	A	Blackpool	L	0-3	0-1	23		7066
44	6	H	Cambridge U	W	5-0	1-0	23	Jones 5 [16, 49, 51, 61, 74]	2581
45	13	A	Stoke C	L	0-1	0-1	23		14,298
46	20	H	Bournemouth	W	2-1	0-1	23	Morrell [72], Edwards [89]	4200

Final League Position: 23

GOALSCORERS

League (56): Faulconbridge 13, Trundle 8 (1 pen), Edwards 5, Jones 5, Sam 5 (2 pens), Chalk 3 (1 pen), Ferguson 3 (1 pen), Thomas 3, Blackwood 2, Carey 2, Lawrence 2, Morrell 2, Hill 1, Phillips 1, Roberts 1.
Worthington Cup (2): Faulconbridge 1, Russell 1.
FA Cup (0).

Rogers K 27	Holmes S 39 + 1	Edwards C 10 + 16	Phillips W 27	Carey B 16 + 2	Lawrence D 29 + 3	Warren D 5	Ferguson D 37 + 1	Morrell A 13 + 12	Faulconbridge C 36 + 1	Thomas S 30 + 8	Russell K 8 + 2	Blackwood M 21 + 10	Chalk M 17 + 7	Sam H 15 + 14	Barrett P 10 + 5	Gibson R 11 + 7	Roberts S 24	Trundle L 30 + 6	Miller W 5	Evans M — + 4	Hill K 12	Whitley J 34	Walsh D 7 + 2	Sharp K 12 + 3	Rovde M 12	Moody A — + 1	Pejic S 11 + 1	Bennett D 5 + 1	Jones L 3 + 1	Morgan C — + 2	Match No.
1	2	3	4	5	6	7	8^1	9^2	10	11	12	13																			1
1	2	3^1	4^2	5	6	7	8	9^3	10	11		12	13	14																	2
1	2	3		5	6		8		10	11^1	9	4^2	7		12	13															3
1	2	3			6	7	8	9	11	4							5	10													4
1	2	3^2		5	6	7	8	9^1	11	4		12		13				10													5
1	2	12		5	6	7^2	8	9^1	11	4		13					3	10													6
1		12	4		6		8	9^1	11^2	2^3		13	7	14			5	10	3												7
1	2	12			6		8	9	11	4			7^1				5	10	3												8
1	2	12	4^2		6		8	9	11	13			7^1			5^3		10	3	14											9
1	2		6^3				8^1	9	11	4		13	7	12		5		10	3^2	14											10
1	2						8	9	11	4			7	6	10	5	3														11
1	3				12		8	9	13	4		11^1	14			7^3	5	10^2	6	2											12
1	3				12	11	8	9^2	13	4			7	8^1		5	10		6	2											13
1^6	5						8	12	9	11		7^2	13			6	10^1	4	3	2	15										14
	3^2	12					8	14	9^2	4		11		13		6^1	10		5	2	1	7									15
	3	4^2	6				9		7	12	8	13		10		5	2	1	11^1												16
	3^1	6					13	9	14	12	7	8^2	4^3		10	5	2	1	11												17
1	3				12		8	9		11			7	5	10	6^1	2	4													18
1	3						8	9	12	13		11^1	14	7^3	5	10	6	2	4^2												19
1	3						8	9^2	12	13		11^1	14	7^3	5	10	6	2	4												20
	3			5			4	12	9^1	13		8^3	11	7^2	10	6	2	1	14												21
	3^3						8	9^2	4	12		7^1	14	13	5	10	6	2	1	11											22
1	3			8	5		9		4^1	12		11^2	7		6	10	2	13													23
1				8	5		9^2	4	12	11^1	7	13	6	10		2	3														24
1	12			8		6	9^3	4	11	13		7^2	5	10	14	2	3^1														25
1	3	12	8^1		6		13	9^3	10	4	11	14	7^2	5	2																26
1	3		7		6		8	9	4^1	11	10		5	12	2																27
1	3	12	7^2				8	9	4^3	11^1	14	10	13	6	2																28
1	3		7^1	5	13		8	9	12	4^3	14	11^2	6	10	2																29
1	3	12	7	5			8	9	4	13	11^1	6	10	2^2																	30
	3	12	2	5	6		8	9	4	11^1	7^2	10	13												1						31
	3	2			6		8	12	9	4^3	11^1	7^2	10	13											1	14	5				32
	3	12	7		6		8	9	4	11^2		10^1		5	13	2									1						33
	3		7	12	6		13	9	4	11	14	8^2		5^1	10^3	2									1						34
	3	12	5^2	6			8	9	4^2	11		10^1		13	2										1		14				35
	3	12	7	6			8	9	4^3	11^2	14	10^1		13	2										1		5				36
	3^2	7	6				8	9	4	11^1		10		12	2	15	13	1^6	5												37
	3^2	7	6				8	12	9	4^1		13		10	2	1	11		5												38
	3^1	7	6				8	12	9			13	11^{12}	10	2	1	4		5												39
		6	7	4			8	9		11^1		10			2	3	1		5	12											40
	3	12	7^1	6			8		13	11		10			2		1		5	4^2											41
	3	12	4^2	6			8	9	13	11	7^1	10^3			2		1	5		14											42
	3	4^1	6				8	9	12	14	11^2	7^3	13		2		1	5	10												43
	3	12	7	6			8^1	9		13	11			2		1	5^2	4	10^2	14											44
1	3	12	7^2	6^3			8^1	9	13	10	11			2		5	4	14													45
1	3^1	12	7^2	6			8	9	13	11	14			2		5	4	10^3													46

Worthington Cup
First Round   Hull C   (h)   2-3

FA Cup
First Round   Hereford U   (a)   0-1

WYCOMBE WANDERERS   Division 2

FOUNDATION

In 1887 a group of young furniture trade workers called a meeting at the Steam Engine public house with the aim of forming a football club and entering junior football. It is thought that they were named after the famous FA Cup winners, The Wanderers who had visited the town in 1877 for a tie with the original High Wycombe club. It is also possible that they played informally before their formation, although there is no proof of this.

Adams Park, Hillbottom Road, Sands, High Wycombe HP12 4HJ.

Telephone: (01494) 472 100. **Fax:** (01494) 527 633.
Credit Card Hotline: (01494) 441 118.
Information Line: 09003 446 855.

Ground Capacity: 10,000; new stand now seats 7,350.

Record Attendance: 9,650 v Wimbledon, FA Cup 5th rd, 17 February 2001.

Pitch Measurements: 115yd × 75yd.

President: M. E. Seymour.

Chairman: I. L. Beeks JP.

Directors: G. Peart (Financial), M. Greatwood, R. Tomlin, A. Parry, A. Thibault, B. Kane, D. Vere.

Associate Directors: G. Cox, B. R. Lee, J. Goldsworthy. **Secretary:** Keith J. Allen.

Manager: Lawrie Sanchez. **Assistant Manager:** Terry Gibson.

Physio: David Jones.

Youth Team Manager: Micky Forsyth.

Youth Development Officer: Adrian Cole.

Youth Physio: Terry Evans.

Marketing Manager: Mark Austin.

Promotions Manager: Mike Phillips.

Press Officer: Alan Hutchinson.

Colours: Light and dark blue quartered shirts, navy shorts, light blue stockings.

Change Colours: All yellow.

Year Formed: 1887.

Turned Professional: 1974.

Club Nicknames: 'Chairboys' (after High Wycombe's tradition of furniture making), 'The Blues'.

Previous Grounds: 1887, The Rye; 1893, Spring Meadow; 1895, Loakes Park; 1899, Daws Hill Park; 1901, Loakes Park; 1990, Adams Park.

HONOURS

Football League: Division 2 best season: 6th, 1994–95.

FA Amateur Cup: Winners 1931.

FA Trophy: Winners 1991, 1993.

GM Vauxhall Conference: Winners 1992–93.

FA Cup: semi-final 2001.

Football League Cup: never beyond 2nd rd.

IT'S A FACT !

Wycombe Wanderers' most prolific marksman was Tony Horseman, who in 14 seasons from 1961–62, scored 416 goals in 749 appearances in all matches after a scoring debut on 23 October against Oxford City.

First Football League Game: 14 August 1993, Division 3 v Carlisle U (a) D 2–2: Hyde; Cousins, Horton (Langford), Kerr, Crossley, Ryan, Carroll, Stapleton, Thompson, Scott, Guppy (1) (Hutchinson), (1 og).

Record League Victory: 5–0 v Burnley, Division 2, 15 April 1997 – Parkin; Cousins, Bell, Kavanagh, McCarthy, Forsyth, Carroll (2p) (Simpson), Scott (Farrell), Stallard (1), McGavin (1) (Read (1)), Brown.

Record Cup Victory: 5–0 v Hitchin T (a), FA Cup 2nd rd, 3 December 1994 – Hyde; Cousins, Brown, Crossley, Evans, Ryan (1), Carroll, Bell (1), Thompson, Garner (3) (Hemmings), Stapleton (Langford).

Record Defeat: 0–5 v Walsall, Auto Windscreens Shield 1st rd, 7 November 1995.

Most League Points (3 for a win): 78, Division 2, 1994–95.

Most League Goals: 67, Division 3, 1993–94.

Highest League Goalscorer in Season: Sean Devine, 23, 1999–2000.

Most League Goals in Total Aggregate: Dave Carroll, 41, 1993–2002.

Most League Goals in One Match: 3, Miguel Desouza v Bradford C, Division 2, 26 March 1996; 3, Mark Stallard v Walsall, Division 2, 21 October 1997; 3, Sean Devine v Reading, Division 2, 2 October 1999; 3, Sean Divine v Bury, Division 2, 26 February 2000.

Most Capped Player: Mark Rogers, 5, Canada.

Most League Appearances: Steve Brown, 309, 1994–2002.

Youngest League Player: Roger Johnson, 17 years 8 days v Cambridge U, 6 May 2000.

Record Transfer Fee Received: £375,000 from Swindon T for Keith Scott, November 1993.

Record Transfer Fee Paid: £220,000 to Barnet for Sean Devine, 15 April 1999.

Football League Record: Promoted to Division 3 from GMVC in 1993; 1993–94 Division 3; 1994– Division 2.

MANAGERS

First coach appointed 1951. *Prior to Brian Lee's appointment in 1969 the team was selected by a Match Committee which met every Monday evening.*

James McCormack 1951–52
Sid Cann 1952–61
Graham Adams 1961–62
Don Welsh 1962–64
Barry Darvill 1964–68
Brian Lee 1969–76
Ted Powell 1976–77
John Reardon 1977–78
Andy Williams 1978–80
Mike Keen 1980–84
Paul Bence 1984–86
Alan Gane 1986–87
Peter Suddaby 1987–88
Jim Kelman 1988–90
Martin O'Neill 1990–95
Alan Smith 1995–96
John Gregory 1996–98
Neil Smillie 1998–99
Lawrie Sanchez February 1999–

LATEST SEQUENCES

Longest Sequence of League Wins: 4, 26.2.94 – 19.3.94.

Longest Sequence of League Defeats: 4, 2.1.99 – 30.1.99.

Longest Sequence of League Draws: 4, 16.9.95 – 7.10.95.

Longest Sequence of Unbeaten League Matches: 14, 29.8.95 – 18.11.95.

Longest Sequence Without a League Win: 12, 8.8.98 – 10.10.98.

TEN YEAR LEAGUE RECORD

		P	W	D	L	F	A	Pts	Pos
1991-92	Conf	42	30	4	8	84	35	94	2
1992-93	Conf	42	24	11	7	84	37	83	1
1993-94	Div 3	42	19	13	10	67	53	70	4
1994-95	Div 2	46	21	15	10	60	46	78	6
1995-96	Div 2	46	15	15	16	63	59	60	12
1996-97	Div 2	46	15	10	21	51	56	55	18
1997-98	Div 2	46	14	18	14	51	53	60	14
1998-99	Div 2	46	13	12	21	52	58	51	19
1999-2000	Div 2	46	16	13	17	56	53	61	12
2000-01	Div 2	46	15	14	17	46	53	59	13

DID YOU KNOW ?

Wycombe Wanderers' first victory in the FA Cup against a Football League club occurred on 24 November 1973, when they beat Newport County 3-1 in a first round tie.

WYCOMBE WANDERERS 2001–02 LEAGUE RECORD

Match No.	Date	Venue	Opponents	Result	H/T Score	Lg. Pos.	Goalscorers	Attendance
1	Aug 11	A	Cardiff C	L	0-1	0-1	—	17,403
2	18	H	Wrexham	W	5-2	4-0	8	Bulman [15], Simpson [17], Emblen [24], McCarthy [30], Brown [61]	5425
3	25	A	Blackpool	D	2-2	1-2	13	Brown (pen) [41], Currie [82]	5010
4	27	H	QPR	W	1-0	0-0	6	McCarthy [90]	9217
5	Sept 2	A	Huddersfield T	L	1-2	1-1	9	Holligan [14]	9750
6	8	H	Chesterfield	D	0-0	0-0	8		5644
7	15	H	Wigan Ath	W	1-0	1-0	7	Rammell [34]	5400
8	22	A	Reading	L	0-2	0-2	16		13,565
9	25	H	Brighton & HA	D	1-1	0-1	—	Rammell [62]	7097
10	29	H	Port Vale	W	3-1	3-0	12	Walker 2 [8, 14], Rammell [12]	5714
11	Oct 2	A	Bury	D	1-1	1-1	—	Brown [6]	2459
12	6	A	Notts Co	W	1-0	0-0	9	Rammell [64]	4483
13	13	H	Bournemouth	D	1-1	0-1	8	Rammell [73]	6810
14	20	A	Bristol C	W	1-0	0-0	6	McSporran [53]	11,452
15	23	A	Colchester U	D	2-2	2-2	—	Brown [14], Currie [45]	5186
16	27	H	Swindon T	D	1-1	1-1	7	Walker [45]	7127
17	Nov 3	A	Tranmere R	D	1-1	1-1	7	Currie [16]	8096
18	10	H	Peterborough U	W	3-0	1-0	5	Holligan 2 [34, 75], McCarthy [64]	6025
19	20	A	Northampton T	W	2-1	1-1	—	Rammell 2 [20, 85]	5817
20	24	A	Oldham Ath	L	0-2	0-2	6		4731
21	Dec 1	H	Brentford	W	5-3	1-2	6	Owusu (og) [42], Vinnicombe [52], Rammell 2 [64, 69], Bulman [90]	8013
22	15	A	Stoke C	L	1-5	1-3	8	McSporran [24]	12,911
23	22	H	Cambridge U	W	2-0	2-0	6	Ryan [37], McSporran [44]	6560
24	29	H	QPR	L	3-4	1-1	11	Brown (pen) [31], Bulman [64], Rammell (pen) [80]	14,834
25	Jan 12	A	Wrexham	D	0-0	0-0	9		2752
26	19	H	Cardiff C	L	0-1	0-0	11		7165
27	22	A	Cambridge U	L	0-2	0-1	—		2623
28	26	H	Notts Co	W	3-0	1-0	11	Johnson [22], McSporran [72], Bulman [90]	5574
29	Feb 2	A	Port Vale	D	1-1	0-1	11	Bulman [73]	4737
30	9	H	Bristol C	W	2-1	0-0	11	Devine [70], Rogers [73]	7972
31	12	A	Chesterfield	W	1-0	0-0	—	Devine [52]	3654
32	16	A	Bournemouth	W	2-1	0-0	9	Devine [67], McSporran [90]	5807
33	19	H	Blackpool	L	1-4	0-2	—	McSporran [82]	5803
34	23	A	Wigan Ath	D	0-0	0-0	9		4743
35	26	H	Reading	L	0-2	0-0	—		9250
36	Mar 2	H	Bury	L	0-2	0-0	11		6409
37	5	A	Brighton & HA	L	0-4	0-1	—		6398
38	9	H	Stoke C	W	1-0	0-0	11	McSporran [83]	7344
39	12	H	Huddersfield T	L	2-4	0-2	—	Brown [51], Rogers [86]	5546
40	16	A	Brentford	L	0-1	0-1	11		7165
41	23	H	Colchester U	D	0-0	0-0	11		6737
42	30	A	Peterborough U	L	1-2	0-1	11	Tyler (og) [77]	4926
43	Apr 1	H	Tranmere R	W	2-1	1-0	11	Rammell [29], Brown (pen) [51]	6297
44	6	A	Northampton T	L	1-4	0-0	12	Holligan [17]	5851
45	13	H	Oldham Ath	W	2-1	2-0	12	Devine [3], Brown (pen) [15]	6728
46	20	A	Swindon T	D	1-1	1-0	11	Devine [45]	7492

Final League Position: 11

GOALSCORERS

League (58): Rammell 11 (1 pen), Brown 8 (4 pens), McSporran 7, Bulman 5, Devine 5, Holligan 4, Currie 3, McCarthy 3, Walker 3, Rogers 2, Emblen 1, Johnson 1, Ryan 1, Simpson 1, Vinnicombe 1, own goals 2.
Worthington Cup (0).
FA Cup (9): Currie 3, Rammell 2, Brown 1 (pen), Bulman 1, McSporran 1, Walker 1.

Taylor M 46	Rogers M 39 + 2	Vinnicombe C 42	Bulman D 37 + 9	Cousins J 13 + 6	McCarthy P 28	Currie D 44 + 2	Simpson M 43	McSporran J 19 + 13	Rammell A 27	Brown S 31 + 8	Senda D 38 + 5	Holligan G 11 + 9	Ryan K 12 + 23	Marsh C — + 1	Emblen P 5 + 7	Phelan L — + 1	Walker R 10 + 2	Carroll D 1 + 11	Roberts S 18 + 8	Lee M 2 + 5	Devine S 19 + 1	Johnson R 7	Lopez C 1	Baird A 1 + 5	Tuttle D 4	Leach M 1	Townsend B 2	Harris R 2 + 1	Thomson A 3	Match No.
1	2	3	4	5¹	6	7	8	9³	10³	11	12	13	14																	1
1	2	3	4	5	6³	9	8	12	10²	11		13	14		7¹															2
1	2	3	4	5	6	7	8	9¹	11²	12	10³						13	14												3
1	2	3	4	5	6	9	8	12	10³	11²	13		14		7¹															4
1	2	3	4	5	6	7²	8	12	10³	11	13		9¹	14																5
1	2	3	4²	5	6	9¹	8	12		11	13	10	14		7³															6
1	2	3	4	5		9²	8	10	11¹	6	7³	12		14	13															7
1	2	3	4	5		9¹	8	12	10³	13	11	7	6²		14															8
1	5	3	12		6	7	8	9	10²	4¹	2						13	11												9
1	5	3	12		6	7	8	9¹	10²	4³	2						13	11	14											10
1	5	3	12	13	6	11²	8	9	10¹	4	2						7³	14												11
1	5	3	12		6	11³	8	9²	10¹	4	2						7	14												12
1	5	3	12		6	11²	8	9	10	4³	2	14	13				7													13
1	5	3	4		6	11³	8	9	10²	7¹		2	12				14	13												14
1	5	3	4		6	9¹	8	10	11	2	13	12					7²	14												15
1	5	3	12		6	11	8	10²	4¹	2	14	13					9	7³												16
1	5	3	4	12	6	9			10²	11	2¹		13				8	14	7³											17
1	5	3	12	14	6	9	8		10²	4¹	2	11		13				7³												18
1	5	3	4		6	9¹	8		10	2	11¹	13	12				14	7³												19
1	5	3	4		6	9	8²	10		2	12				11	13	7¹													20
1	5	3	4	12	6¹	9²	8	10		2					11	13	7													21
1	5	3	4³	14	6	9¹	8	10		12	2	13		11				7²												22
1	5	3	12	13	6²	10¹	8	9		11	2	4		14				7³												23
1	5	3	4¹	6		12	8	9	10²	11³	2		7				13	14												24
1	5		4	6		10	8	9¹	3	12	2¹						11	7²	13	14										25
1		3	4	5		11	8	12		9¹	6								7		10	2								26
1		4³	5			9	8	12		2¹		11²		13					7	14	10	6	3							27
1		3	4	5²		11	8	9		12	2	14	13						7¹		10³	6								28
1		3	4			11¹	8	9²		2			6						7	12	10	5		13						29
1	5	3	4¹			11²	8	9¹		12	2		13						7		10	6		14						30
1	5	3	4			9¹	8			11²	2		12						7³	13	10	6		14						31
1	5	3	4			9	8	12		13	2		14						7¹	11¹	10	6³								32
1	5	3	4			9⁴	8	12		13	2	11¹	6						7		10									33
1	5	3	4			7²	8	9		11	2		12								10¹				13	6				34
1	5	3	4			7¹	8	9³		11²	2		12						13		10				14	6				35
1	5	3	4			9¹				12	2	13	14						7	8	10³				11²	6				36
1		3	4			9		12		11	2	6		7¹					13		10				5	8²				37
1	5	3	4			7	8	9		11	2		6						12		10¹									38
1	5	3	4			7	8	9		11¹	2		6						12		10									39
1	5	3	4		6	7	8	12	9	11¹	2										10									40
1	5	3	4		6	7	8	12	9	11¹	2										10									41
1	5		4		6	7	8	9¹	11²	2	12								13		10¹						3	14		42
1	5		4		6	7²	8		9	12	2	10³	13						14								3	11¹		43
1	5	3	4³		6	12	8	13	9	11¹	2	10²	14																7	44
1	12	3	13		6	7	8		9	4¹	2	11²									10								5	45
1	12	3	4		6	7	8		9¹		2	13									10							11²	5	46

Worthington Cup
First Round   Bristol R   (h)   0-1

FA Cup
First Round   Hayes   (a)   4-3
Second Round   Notts Co   (h)   3-0
Third Round   Fulham   (h)   2-2
                                            (a)   0-1

YORK CITY

Division 3

FOUNDATION

Although there was a York City club formed in 1903 by a soccer enthusiast from Darlington, this has no connection with the modern club because it went out of existence during World War I. Unlike many others of that period who restarted in 1919, York City did not re-form until 1922 and the tendency now is to ignore the modern club's pre-1922 existence.

Bootham Crescent, York YO30 7AQ.

Telephone: (01904) 624 447.

Fax: (01904) 631 457.

ClubCall: 09068 121 643

Ground Capacity: 9,496.

Record Attendance: 28,123 v Huddersfield T, FA Cup 6th rd, 5 March 1938.

Record Receipts: £63,680 v Manchester U, Coca-Cola Cup 2nd rd, 2nd leg, 3 October 1995.

Pitch Measurements: 115yd × 74yd.

Chairman: J. Batchelor.

Directors: C. Webb, E. B. Swallow, J. Easby, I. McAndrew, D. M. Craig, N. Townend.

Manager: Terry Dolan.

First Team Coach: Adie Shaw.

Chief Executive: Keith Usher.

Commercial Manager: Peter Salter.

Communications Director: James Richardson.

Physio: Jeff Miller.

Hon. Orthopaedic Surgeon: Mr Peter De Boer MA, FRCS.

Medical Officer: Dr R. Porter.

Colours: Red shirts, red shorts, red stockings.

Change Colours: All yellow.

Year Formed: 1922.

Turned Professional: 1922.

Ltd Co.: 1922.

Club Nickname: 'Minstermen'.

Previous Grounds: 1922, Fulfordgate; 1932, Bootham Crescent.

First Football League Game: 31 August 1929, Division 3 (N), v Wigan Borough (a) W 2–0 – Farmery; Archibald, Johnson; Beck, Davis, Thompson; Evans, Gardner, Cowie (1), Smailes, Stockhill (1).

HONOURS

Football League: Division 3 – Promoted 1973–74 (3rd); Division 4 – Champions 1983–84.

FA Cup: Semi-finals 1955, when in Division 3.

Football League Cup: best season: 5th rd, 1962.

IT'S A FACT !

The survival qualities of York City were well illustrated in the 1930s. In 1932–33, they avoided re-election on goal average and escaped in 1938–39 by a point.

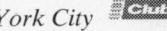
Record League Victory: 9–1 v Southport, Division 3 (N),
2 February 1957 – Forgan; Phillips, Howe; Brown (1),
Cairney, Mollatt; Hill, Bottom (4 incl. 1p), Wilkinson (2),
Wragg (1), Fenton (1).

Record Cup Victory: 6–0 v South Shields (away), FA Cup
1st rd, 16 November 1968 – Widdowson; Baker (1p),
Richardson; Carr, Jackson, Burrows; Taylor, Ross (3),
MacDougall (2), Hodgson, Boyer.

Record Defeat: 0–12 v Chester, Division 3 (N), 1 February
1936.

Most League Points (2 for a win): 62, Division 4, 1964–65.

Most League Points (3 for a win): 101, Division 4, 1983–84.

Most League Goals: 96, Division 4, 1983–84.

Highest League Scorer in Season: Bill Fenton, 31,
Division 3 (N), 1951–52; Arthur Bottom, 31, Division 3 (N),
1954–55 and 1955–56.

Most League Goals in Total Aggregate: Norman
Wilkinson, 125, 1954–66.

Most League Goals in One Match: 5, Alf Patrick v
Rotherham U, Division 3N, 20 November 1948.

Most Capped Player: Peter Scott, 7 (10), Northern Ireland.

Most League Appearances: Barry Jackson, 481, 1958–70.

Youngest League Player: Reg Stockill, 15 years 281 days v
Wigan Borough, 31 August 1929.

Record Transfer Fee Received: £1,000,000 from Manchester U for Jonathan Greening, March 1998.

Record Transfer Fee Paid: £140,000 to Burnley for Adrian Randall, December 1995.

Football League Record: 1929 Elected to Division 3 (N); 1958–59 Division 4; 1959–60 Division 3;
1960–65 Division 4; 1965–66 Division 3; 1966–71 Division 4; 1971–74 Division 3; 1974–76 Division 2;
1976–77 Division 3; 1977–84 Division 4; 1984–88 Division 3; 1988–92 Division 4; 1992–93 Division 3;
1993–99 Division 2; 1999– Division 3.

MANAGERS

Bill Sherrington 1924–60
*(was Secretary for most of this
time but virtually Secretary-
Manager for a long pre-war
spell)*
John Collier 1929–36
Tom Mitchell 1936–50
Dick Duckworth 1950–52
Charlie Spencer 1952–53
Jimmy McCormick 1953–54
Sam Bartram 1956–60
Tom Lockie 1960–67
Joe Shaw 1967–68
Tom Johnston 1968–75
Wilf McGuinness 1975–77
Charlie Wright 1977–80
Barry Lyons 1980–81
Denis Smith 1982–87
Bobby Saxton 1987–88
John Bird 1988–91
John Ward 1991–93
Alan Little 1993–99
Neil Thompson 1999–2000
Terry Dolan February 2000–

LATEST SEQUENCES

Longest Sequence of League Wins: 7, 31.10.64 – 26.12.64.

Longest Sequence of League Defeats: 8, 14.11.66 – 31.12.66.

Longest Sequence of League Draws: 6, 26.12.92 – 22.1.93.

Longest Sequence of Unbeaten League Matches: 21, 10.9.73 – 12.1.74.

Longest Sequence Without a League Win: 17, 4.5.87 – 24.10.87.

TEN YEAR LEAGUE RECORD

		P	W	D	L	F	A	Pts	Pos
1991-92	Div 4	42	8	16	18	42	58	40	19
1992-93	Div 3	42	21	12	9	72	45	75	4
1993-94	Div 2	46	21	12	13	64	40	75	5
1994-95	Div 2	46	21	9	16	67	51	72	9
1995-96	Div 2	46	13	13	20	58	73	52	20
1996-97	Div 2	46	13	13	20	47	68	52	20
1997-98	Div 2	46	14	17	15	52	58	59	16
1998-99	Div 2	46	13	11	22	56	80	50	21
1999-2000	Div 3	46	12	16	18	39	53	52	20
2000-01	Div 3	46	13	13	20	42	63	52	17

DID YOU KNOW ?

In York City's first season in
the Third Division (North) in
1929–30, their average
attendance was 5,247. Almost
20 years later, the club had
virtually doubled this to
10,412 in 1948–49.

YORK CITY 2001–02 LEAGUE RECORD

Match No.	Date	Venue	Opponents	Result		H/T Score	Lg. Pos.	Goalscorers	Attendance
1	Aug 11	H	Rushden & D	L	0-1	0-1	—		4307
2	18	A	Torquay U	W	3-0	2-0	10	Bullock [32], Basham [45], Nogan [49]	2659
3	25	H	Leyton Orient	W	2-1	1-0	4	Nogan [41], Proctor [60]	2661
4	28	A	Shrewsbury T	L	2-3	0-1	—	Bullock [87], Fielding [90]	3002
5	Sept 1	H	Halifax T	W	1-0	0-0	7	Proctor [90]	2646
6	8	A	Hull C	L	0-4	0-1	10		9737
7	15	H	Luton T	L	1-2	1-1	11	Nogan [32]	3247
8	18	A	Carlisle U	L	1-2	0-1	—	Salvati [62]	2705
9	22	A	Bristol R	D	2-2	0-0	14	Potter [74], Cooper [90]	6933
10	25	H	Plymouth Arg	D	0-0	0-0	—		2282
11	Oct 6	A	Lincoln C	W	3-1	2-0	11	Proctor 2 [2, 89], Brass [16]	2994
12	6	H	Exeter C	L	2-3	0-2	15	Bullock [56], Mathie [90]	2054
13	13	A	Hartlepool U	L	0-3	0-1	18		3603
14	20	H	Southend U	W	2-1	1-1	15	Nogan [15], Proctor [65]	2270
15	23	A	Kidderminster H	L	1-4	1-1	—	Nogan [45]	2002
16	27	H	Macclesfield T	W	1-0	0-0	13	Proctor [90]	2253
17	Nov 3	A	Oxford U	D	2-2	1-0	11	Nogan [16], Proctor [51]	5487
18	9	H	Scunthorpe U	L	0-2	0-0	—		3192
19	20	H	Swansea C	L	0-2	0-1	—		1840
20	23	A	Mansfield T	D	1-1	0-0	—	Nogan [74]	4877
21	Dec 1	A	Darlington	L	1-3	0-2	20	Proctor [84]	4014
22	15	H	Cheltenham T	L	1-3	1-2	20	Bullock [32]	2082
23	29	A	Shrewsbury T	D	1-1	0-1	22	Nogan [59]	2413
24	Jan 12	H	Torquay U	D	1-1	1-0	22	Bullock [22]	3445
25	19	A	Rushden & D	L	0-3	0-2	23		4605
26	22	H	Rochdale	D	0-0	0-0	—		2317
27	29	H	Hull C	W	2-1	0-0	—	Proctor [14], Duffield [16]	6495
28	Feb 5	A	Rochdale	L	4-5	2-2	—	Brass [13], Duffield [21], Bullock [51], Proctor [83]	2823
29	9	A	Southend U	W	1-0	0-0	22	Parkin [84]	3967
30	12	A	Halifax T	D	1-1	0-1	—	Mitchell (og) [48]	2818
31	16	H	Hartlepool U	W	1-0	0-0	21	Nogan [68]	4823
32	19	A	Leyton Orient	W	2-1	1-0	—	Duffield [40], Mathie [84]	3663
33	23	A	Luton T	L	1-2	1-1	21	Proctor [17]	6188
34	Mar 5	A	Plymouth Arg	L	0-1	0-1	—		10,801
35	9	A	Cheltenham T	L	0-4	0-1	23		3958
36	16	H	Darlington	W	2-0	0-0	22	Basham [55], Proctor [67]	3903
37	19	A	Exeter C	L	1-2	0-0	—	Nogan [53]	2038
38	23	H	Kidderminster H	L	0-1	0-0	23		2787
39	26	H	Lincoln C	W	2-0	2-0	—	Bullock [2], Nogan [36]	2755
40	30	A	Macclesfield T	L	1-2	1-1	21	Bullock [17]	1928
41	Apr 1	H	Oxford U	W	1-0	0-0	20	Potter [73]	3290
42	6	A	Swansea C	W	1-0	0-0	18	Jones S [78]	2677
43	9	H	Carlisle U	D	0-0	0-0	—		2809
44	13	H	Mansfield T	W	3-1	1-1	15	Nogan [44], Parkin [54], Proctor [68]	5460
45	16	H	Bristol R	W	3-0	2-0	—	Wilson (og) [6], Nogan [32], Proctor [90]	2983
46	20	A	Scunthorpe U	L	0-1	0-0	14		5159

Final League Position: 14

GOALSCORERS

League (54): Proctor 14, Nogan 13, Bullock 8, Duffield 3, Basham 2, Brass 2, Mathie 2, Parkin 2, Potter 2, Cooper 1, Fielding 1, Jones S 1, Salvati 1, own goals 2.
Worthington Cup (2): Brass 1, Bullock 1.
FA Cup (5): Potter 2, Brass 1, Richardson 1, own goal 1.

Fettis A 45	Edmondson D 34+2	Potter G 37	Hocking M 29+4	Basham M 26+3	Hobson G 14+2	Brass C 41	Bullock L 39+1	Nogan L 40+2	Proctor M 40+1	Richardson N 17+5	Duffield P 7+4	Fielding J 9	Cooper R 23+2	Wood L 12+2	Emmerson S —+6	O'Kane A 11+1	Evans M 1+1	Stamp N 5+2	Fox C 5+7	Salvati M 1+7	Mathie A 11+12	Maley M 11+2	Smith C 12+3	Darlow K 1+1	Rhodes B —+1	Parkin J 18	Wise S 3+3	Brackstone S 6+3	Jones S 7+1	Howarth R 1+1	Grant L —+1	Match No.
1	2	3	4	5	6	7	8	9	10	11[1]	12																					1
1	2	3		5		7	8[1]	9[1]	10				4	6	12	13	11															2
1	2	3	12	5[1]		7	8	9	10				4	6			11															3
1	2	3		5		7	8	9	10				4	6		12	11[1]															4
1	2	3	12	5[1]		7	8	9	10	13			4	6			11[2]															5
1	2	3		5		7	8	9	10	11[1]			4	6[2]				13	12													6
1	2	3		5		7	8	9	10	11[2]			4						6[1]		13	12										7
1	2	3[3]	12	5[1]		7	8	9	10	11[2]			4			13					14	6										8
1	2	3		5		7	8	9	10				4[2]	6		11[1]	12	13														9
1	2	3	4	5		7	8	9	10					6		11[1]	12															10
1	2	3	4	5		7	8	9	10					6[1]		12	11															11
1	2	3	4[3]	5[1]		7	8	9	10					6[2]		12	13	11	14													12
1						7	8	9	10	11[2]			4[1]	3					6		13	12	5	2								13
1	2		12			7	8	9[2]	10				6[1]					3	11		13		5	4								14
1	2[2]		12	13		7	8	9	10	14			6					3	11				5[1]	4[1]								15
1	2	3	4	5		7	8[1]	9	10	12			11										6									16
1	2	3	4	5		7	8	9	10				11										6									17
1	2		4		6	7	8	9	10				11[2]		13						12		5			3[1]						18
1	12	3	4	5[2]		7	8	9	10	11[1]			6								13	2[3]	14									19
1	2	3	4			7		9	10	11			6							8		12	5									20
1	2	3	4[1]	12		7	8		10	11			6[2]									5	9					13				21
1	2	3	12	5[1]		7	8	9	10[2]	14			11				13					6[3]	4									22
1	2	3	4	5	6	7	8	9	10	11																						23
1	2	3	4	5[1]	6		8	9	10	11			7									12										24
1	2	3		5	6		8	9[1]	10	11[2]	12		7								13	4										25
1	2	3	4	5	6	7		9	10		12		11								8[1]											26
1		3	4	5	6[3]	7		9[1]	10	2		8[2]	11								13	12	14									27
1	2	3	4	5[1]		7		9	10	11			6[3]									12	13									28
1		3	4	5		7	8[1]		10	12		9[2]									13	2	6			11						29
1		3	4	5		7	8[2]	12	10	13		9										2	6[1]			11						30
1	2	3	4	5		7	12	9[1]	10	11		8[2]									13					6						31
1	2	3	4	5			8	9	10	11[1]			7								12					6						32
1	2	3		5[2]	6	7	8	9	10	11[1]											12							4	13			33
1		3	4	5	6[1]	7	8	9		11											10							2	12			34
1		3	4		6	7	8[1]	9	10	2	12										11							5				35
1		3	4	12	6[1]	7	8	9[1]	10[2]	2	13										11							5	14			36
1		3	4	5		7	8	12	10	13			11[2]								9[1]							6	2			37
1	12	3		5		7	8	9					4		13	11[1]					10[2]							6	2			38
1	2	3	4			7	8	9	10[2]				6								11[1]							5	12	13		39
1	2	3	4			7	8	9					6								11[1]					10			12	5		40
1	2	3	4[2]			7	8	9					6		12											10		13	11[1]	5		41
1	2					7	8	9			12		6				4				11[1]					10	3			5		42
1	2					7	8	9	10[1]				6				4				12					11	3			5		43
1	2					7		9	10				6		8				12							11	3[1]	4		5		44
1[6]	2							9	10				4		7[1]		12				8[2]		3			6		11	5	15	13	45
	2							9	10[2]				12		4		7[1]		13		8		3			6		11	5	1		46

Worthington Cup
First Round   Crewe Alex   (h)   2-2

FA Cup
First Round   Colchester U   (a)   0-0
                                                  (h)   2-2
Second Round   Reading   (h)   2-0
Third Round   Grimsby T   (a)   0-0
                                                  (h)   1-0
Fourth Round   Fulham   (h)   0-2

ENGLISH LEAGUE PLAYERS DIRECTORY

*Free transfer, †Non-contract, ‡Registration cancelled, §Trainee/Scholar/Schoolboy
#Players over age 24, out of contract but who have been made an offer of re-engagement.
Players listed refer to the retain and transfer list May 2002.

ARSENAL

ADAMS, Tony (D)   504 32
H: 6 3   W: 13 02   b.Romford 10-10-66
Source: Apprentice. *Honours:* England Youth, Under-21, B, 66 full caps, 5 goals.

1983–84	Arsenal	3	0		
1984–85	Arsenal	16	0		
1985–86	Arsenal	10	0		
1986–87	Arsenal	42	6		
1987–88	Arsenal	39	2		
1988–89	Arsenal	36	4		
1989–90	Arsenal	38	5		
1990–91	Arsenal	30	1		
1991–92	Arsenal	35	2		
1992–93	Arsenal	35	0		
1993–94	Arsenal	35	0		
1994–95	Arsenal	27	3		
1995–96	Arsenal	21	1		
1996–97	Arsenal	28	3		
1997–98	Arsenal	26	3		
1998–99	Arsenal	26	1		
1999–2000	Arsenal	21	0		
2000–01	Arsenal	26	1		
2001–02	Arsenal	10	0	504	32

ALIADIERE, Jeremie (F)   1 0
H: 6 0   W: 11 00   b.Rambouillet 30-3-83
Source: Scholar.

1999–2000	Arsenal	0	0		
2000–01	Arsenal	0	0		
2001–02	Arsenal	1	0	1	0

BAILEY, Alex (D)   0 0
H: 5 9   W: 10 07   b.Newham 21-9-83
Source: Scholar. *Honours:* England Youth.

2001–02	Arsenal	0	0		

BARRETT, Graham (F)   26 4
H: 5 10   W: 11 07   b.Dublin 6-10-81
Source: Trainee. *Honours:* Eire Schools, Youth, Under-21.

1998–99	Arsenal	0	0		
1999–2000	Arsenal	2	0		
2000–01	Arsenal	0	0		
2000–01	*Bristol R*	1	0	1	0
2001–02	Arsenal	0	0	2	0
2001–02	*Crewe Alex*	3	0	3	0
2001–02	*Colchester U*	20	4	20	4

BENTLEY, David (F)   0 0
H: 5 10   W: 10 07   b.Peterborough 27-8-84
Source: Scholar. *Honours:* England Youth.

2001–02	Arsenal	0	0		

BERGKAMP, Dennis (F)   442 183
H: 6 0   W: 12 05   b.Amsterdam 18-5-69
Honours: Holland 79 full caps, 36 goals.

1986–87	Ajax	14	2		
1987–88	Ajax	25	5		
1988–89	Ajax	30	13		
1989–90	Ajax	25	8		
1990–91	Ajax	33	25		
1991–92	Ajax	30	24		
1992–93	Ajax	28	26	185	103
1993–94	Internazionale	31	8		
1994–95	Internazionale	21	3	52	11
1995–96	Arsenal	33	11		
1996–97	Arsenal	29	12		
1997–98	Arsenal	28	16		
1998–99	Arsenal	29	12		
1999–2000	Arsenal	28	6		
2000–01	Arsenal	25	3		
2001–02	Arsenal	33	9	205	69

BRADLEY, Stephen (M)   0 0
H: 5 8   W: 9 07   b.Dublin 19-11-84
Source: Scholar.

2001–02	Arsenal	0	0		

BROWN, Jermaine (F)   0 0
H: 5 11   W: 11 00   b.Lambeth 12-1-83
Source: Scholar.

2001–02	Arsenal	0	0		

CAMPBELL, Sol (D)   286 12
H: 6 2   W: 14 02   b.Newham 18-9-74
Source: Trainee. *Honours:* England Youth, Under-21, 51 full caps, 1 goal.

1992–93	Tottenham H	1	1		
1993–94	Tottenham H	34	0		
1994–95	Tottenham H	30	0		
1995–96	Tottenham H	31	1		
1996–97	Tottenham H	38	0		
1997–98	Tottenham H	34	0		
1998–99	Tottenham H	37	6		
1999–2000	Tottenham H	29	0		
2000–01	Tottenham H	21	2	255	10
2001–02	Arsenal	31	2	31	2

CHILVERS, Liam (D)   16 1
H: 6 0   W: 12 04   b.Chelmsford 6-10-81
Source: Scholar.

2000–01	Arsenal	0	0		
2000–01	*Northampton T*	7	0	7	0
2001–02	Arsenal	0	0		
2001–02	*Notts Co*	9	1	9	1

CHORLEY, Ben (D)   0 0
H: 6 3   W: 13 02   b.Sidcup 30-9-82
Source: Scholar.

2001–02	Arsenal	0	0		

COLE, Ashley (D)   61 6
H: 5 8   W: 10 10   b.Stepney 20-12-80
Source: Trainee. *Honours:* England Youth, Under-21, 13 full caps.

1998–99	Arsenal	0	0		
1999–2000	Arsenal	1	0		
1999–2000	*Crystal Palace*	14	1	14	1
2000–01	Arsenal	17	3		
2001–02	Arsenal	29	2	47	5

DIXON, Lee* (D)   635 36
H: 5 9   W: 10 12   b.Manchester 17-3-64
Source: Local. *Honours:* England B, 22 full caps, 1 goal.

1982–83	Burnley	3	0		
1983–84	Burnley	1	0	4	0
1983–84	Chester C	16	1		
1984–85	Chester C	41	0	57	1
1985–86	Bury	45	5	45	5
1986–87	Stoke C	42	3		
1987–88	Stoke C	29	2	71	5
1987–88	Arsenal	6	0		
1988–89	Arsenal	33	1		
1989–90	Arsenal	38	5		
1990–91	Arsenal	38	5		
1991–92	Arsenal	38	4		
1992–93	Arsenal	29	0		
1993–94	Arsenal	33	0		
1994–95	Arsenal	39	1		
1995–96	Arsenal	38	2		
1996–97	Arsenal	32	2		
1997–98	Arsenal	28	0		
1998–99	Arsenal	36	0		
1999–2000	Arsenal	28	4		
2000–01	Arsenal	29	1		
2001–02	Arsenal	13	0	458	25

EDU (M)   47 1
H: 6 1   W: 12 04   b.Sao Paulo 15-5-78

1998	Corinthians	1	0		
1999	Corinthians	19	0		
2000	Corinthians	8	0	28	0
2000–01	Arsenal	5	0		
2001–02	Arsenal	14	1	19	1

GARRY, Ryan (D)   0 0
H: 6 2   W: 13 00   b.Hornchurch 29-9-83
Source: Scholar. *Honours:* England Youth.

2001–02	Arsenal	0	0		

GRIMANDI, Gilles* (D)   204 7
H: 5 10   W: 11 08   b.Gap 11-11-70
Source: FC Gap.

1991–92	Monaco	5	0		
1992–93	Monaco	8	0		
1993–94	Monaco	19	1		
1994–95	Monaco	19	1		
1995–96	Monaco	25	1		
1996–97	Monaco	24	1	90	3
1997–98	Arsenal	22	1		
1998–99	Arsenal	8	0		
1999–2000	Arsenal	28	2		
2000–01	Arsenal	30	1		
2001–02	Arsenal	26	0	114	4

GRONDIN, David (D)   1 0
H: 5 9   W: 11 11   b.Paris 8-5-80
Source: St Etienne, France Youth.

1998–99	Arsenal	1	0		
1999–2000	Arsenal	0	0		
2000–01	Arsenal	0	0		
2001–02	Arsenal	0	0	1	0

HALLS, John (D)   6 0
H: 6 0   W: 11 00   b.Islington 14-2-82
Source: Scholar. *Honours:* England Youth, Under-20.

2000–01	Arsenal	0	0		
2001–02	Arsenal	0	0		
2001–02	*Colchester U*	6	0	6	0

HENRY, Thierry (F)   220 81
H: 6 2   W: 13 01   b.Paris 17-8-77
Honours: France 38 full caps, 12 goals.

1994–95	Monaco	8	3		
1995–96	Monaco	18	3		
1996–97	Monaco	36	9		
1997–98	Monaco	30	4		
1998–99	Monaco	13	1	105	20
1998–99	Juventus	16	3	16	3
1999–2000	Arsenal	31	17		
2000–01	Arsenal	35	17		
2001–02	Arsenal	33	24	99	58

INAMOTO, Junichi* (M)   118 16
H: 5 9   W: 12 00   b.Osaka 18-9-79
Honours: Japan 33 full caps, 3 goals.

1997	Gamba Osaka	27	3		
1998	Gamba Osaka	23	6		
1999	Gamba Osaka	22	1		
2000	Gamba Osaka	28	4		
2001	Gamba Osaka	13	2	118	16
2001–02	Arsenal	0	0		

ITONGA, Carlin* (F)   0 0
H: 5 9   W: 11 09   b.Congo DR 11-12-82
Source: Scholar.

2001–02	Arsenal	0	0		

JEFFERS, Francis (F)   55 20
H: 5 10   W: 10 07   b.Liverpool 25-1-81
Source: Trainee. *Honours:* England Schools, Youth, Under-21.

1997–98	Everton	1	0		
1998–99	Everton	15	6		
1999–2000	Everton	21	6		
2000–01	Everton	12	6	49	18
2001–02	Arsenal	6	2	6	2

JUAN (D)   0 0
H: 5 6   W: 9 07   b.Sao Paulo 6-2-82
Source: Sao Paulo.

2001–02	Arsenal	0	0		

KANU, Nwankwo (F)   219 65
H: 6 5   W: 12 01   b.Owerri 1-8-76
Honours: Nigeria 37 full caps, 6 goals.

1991–92	Federation Works	30	9	30	9
1992–93	Iwanyanwu	30	6	30	6
1993–94	Ajax	6	2		
1994–95	Ajax	18	10		
1995–96	Ajax	30	13	54	25
1996–97	Internazionale	0	0		
1997–98	Internazionale	11	1		
1998–99	Internazionale	1	0	12	1
1998–99	Arsenal	12	6		
1999–2000	Arsenal	31	12		
2000–01	Arsenal	27	3		
2001–02	Arsenal	23	3	93	24

KEOWN, Martin (D)   529 8
H: 6 1   W: 12 04   b.Oxford 24-7-66
Source: Apprentice. *Honours:* England Youth, Under-21, B, 43 full caps, 2 goals.

1983–84	Arsenal	0	0		
1984–85	Arsenal	0	0		
1984–85	*Brighton & HA*	16	0		
1985–86	Arsenal	22	0		
1985–86	*Brighton & HA*	7	1	23	1
1986–87	Aston Villa	36	0		
1987–88	Aston Villa	43	3		
1988–89	Aston Villa	34	0	112	3
1989–90	Everton	20	0		
1990–91	Everton	24	0		
1991–92	Everton	39	0		
1992–93	Everton	13	0	96	0
1992–93	Arsenal	16	0		
1993–94	Arsenal	33	0		
1994–95	Arsenal	31	1		
1995–96	Arsenal	34	0		
1996–97	Arsenal	33	1		
1997–98	Arsenal	18	0		
1998–99	Arsenal	34	1		
1999–2000	Arsenal	27	1		
2000–01	Arsenal	28	0		
2001–02	Arsenal	22	0	298	4

LAUREN, Etame-Mayer (M) 188 22
H: 5 11 W: 11 03 b.Londi Keisi 19-1-77
Honours: Cameroon 25 full caps, 1 goal.

1995–96	Utrera	30	5	30	5
1996–97	Sevilla B	17	3	17	3
1997–98	Levante	34	6	34	6
1998–99	Mallorca	32	1		
1999–2000	Mallorca	30	3	62	4
2000–01	Arsenal	18	2		
2001–02	Arsenal	27	2	45	4

LJUNGBERG, Frederik (M) 176 35
H: 5 9 W: 10 13 b.Halmstad 16-4-77
Honours: Sweden 34 full caps, 2 goals.

1994	Halmstad	1	0		
1995	Halmstad	16	1		
1996	Halmstad	20	2		
1997	Halmstad	24	5		
1998	Halmstad	18	2	79	10
1998–99	Arsenal	16	1		
1999–2000	Arsenal	26	6		
2000–01	Arsenal	30	6		
2001–02	Arsenal	25	12	97	25

LUZHNY, Oleg (D) 298 11
H: 5 10 W: 12 01 b.Ukraine 5-8-68
Honours: USSR 8 full caps, Ukraine 44 full caps.

1989	Dynamo Kiev	27	0		
1990	Dynamo Kiev	12	0		
1991	Dynamo Kiev	28	0		
1992–93	Dynamo Kiev	26	3		
1993–94	Dynamo Kiev	34	1		
1994–95	Dynamo Kiev	24	4		
1995–96	Dynamo Kiev	24	1		
1996–97	Dynamo Kiev	28	2		
1997–98	Dynamo Kiev	16	0		
1998–99	Dynamo Kiev	21	0	240	11
1999–2000	Arsenal	21	0		
2000–01	Arsenal	19	0		
2001–02	Arsenal	18	0	58	0

MANNINGER, Alex (G) 68 0
H: 6 2 W: 13 03 b.Salzburg 4-6-77
Honours: Austria Under-21, 10 full caps.

1995–96	Vorwaerts Steyr	5	0	5	0
1995–96	Salzburg	1	0	1	0
1996–97	Graz	23	0	23	0
1997–98	Arsenal	7	0		
1998–99	Arsenal	6	0		
1999–2000	Arsenal	15	0		
2000–01	Arsenal	11	0		
2001–02	Arsenal	0	0	39	0

MENDEZ, Alberto (M) 4 0
H: 5 11 W: 11 09 b.Nuremberg 24-10-74
Source: FC Feucht.

1997–98	Arsenal	3	0		
1998–99	Arsenal	1	0		
1999–2000	Arsenal	0	0		
2000–01	Arsenal	0	0		
2001–02	Arsenal	0	0	4	0

NOBLE, David (M) 15 1
H: 6 0 W: 12 04 b.Hitchin 2-2-82
Source: Scholar. *Honours:* England Youth, Under-20.

2000–01	Arsenal	0	0		
2001–02	Arsenal	0	0		
2001–02	*Watford*	15	1	15	1

OATES, Greg* (D) 0 0
H: 6 0 W: 12 04 b.Maldon 3-10-81
Source: Scholar.

2000–01	Arsenal	0	0		
2001–02	Arsenal	0	0		

OSEI-KUFFOUR, Jo* (F) 11 2
H: 5 7 W: 10 03 b.Edmonton 17-11-81
Source: Scholar.

2000–01	Arsenal	0	0		
2001–02	Arsenal	0	0		
2001–02	*Swindon T*	11	2	11	2

PARLOUR, Ray (M) 295 22
H: 5 10 W: 11 12 b.Romford 7-3-73
Source: Trainee. *Honours:* England Under-21, B, 10 full caps.

1990–91	Arsenal	0	0		
1991–92	Arsenal	6	1		
1992–93	Arsenal	21	1		
1993–94	Arsenal	27	2		
1994–95	Arsenal	30	0		
1995–96	Arsenal	22	0		
1996–97	Arsenal	30	2		
1997–98	Arsenal	34	5		
1998–99	Arsenal	35	6		
1999–2000	Arsenal	30	1		
2000–01	Arsenal	33	4		
2001–02	Arsenal	27	0	295	22

PAULINHO (M) 0 0
H: 5 7 W: 10 04 b.Sao Paulo 2-3-83
Source: Sao Paulo.

2001–02	Arsenal	0	0		

PENNANT, Jermaine (M) 9 2
H: 5 8 W: 10 01 b.Nottingham 15-1-83
Honours: England Schools, Youth, England Under-21.

1998–99	Notts Co	0	0		
1998–99	Arsenal	0	0		
1999–2000	Arsenal	0	0		
2000–01	Arsenal	0	0		
2001–02	*Watford*	9	2	9	2

PIRES, Robert (M) 289 64
H: 6 1 W: 11 09 b.Reims 29-10-73
Honours: France 54 full caps, 10 goals.

1992–93	Metz	2	0		
1993–94	Metz	24	1		
1994–95	Metz	35	9		
1995–96	Metz	38	11		
1996–97	Metz	32	11		
1997–98	Metz	31	11	162	43
1998–99	Marseille	34	6		
1999–2000	Marseille	32	2	66	8
2000–01	Arsenal	33	4		
2001–02	Arsenal	28	9	61	13

RICKETTS, Rohan (M) 0 0
H: 5 9 W: 11 00 b.Clapham 22-12-82
Source: Scholar. *Honours:* England Youth, Under-20.

2001–02	Arsenal	0	0		

SANTRY, Stephen* (M) 0 0
H: 5 7 W: 10 06 b.Westminster 9-9-82
Source: Scholar.

2001–02	Arsenal	0	0		

SEAMAN, David (G) 684 0
H: 6 4 W: 13 00 b.Rotherham 19-9-63
Source: Apprentice. *Honours:* England Under-21, B, 73 full caps.

1981–82	Leeds U	0	0		
1982–83	Peterborough U	38	0		
1983–84	Peterborough U	45	0		
1984–85	Peterborough U	8	0	91	0
1984–85	Birmingham C	33	0		
1985–86	Birmingham C	42	0	75	0
1986–87	QPR	41	0		
1987–88	QPR	32	0		
1988–89	QPR	35	0		
1989–90	QPR	33	0	141	0
1990–91	Arsenal	38	0		
1991–92	Arsenal	42	0		
1992–93	Arsenal	39	0		
1993–94	Arsenal	39	0		
1994–95	Arsenal	31	0		
1995–96	Arsenal	38	0		
1996–97	Arsenal	22	0		
1997–98	Arsenal	31	0		
1998–99	Arsenal	32	0		
1999–2000	Arsenal	24	0		
2000–01	Arsenal	24	0		
2001–02	Arsenal	17	0	377	0

SIDWELL, Steven (M) 30 4
H: 5 10 W: 11 02 b.Wandsworth 14-12-82
Source: Scholar. *Honours:* England Under-20.

2001–02	Arsenal	0	0		
2001–02	*Brentford*	30	4	30	4

SKULASON, Olafur-Ingi (M) 0 0
H: 6 0 W: 11 10 b.Reykjavik 1-4-83
Source: Fylkir.

2001–02	Arsenal	0	0		

SPICER, John (M) 0 0
H: 5 11 W: 11 07 b.Romford 13-9-83
Source: Scholar. *Honours:* England Youth.

2001–02	Arsenal	0	0		

STACK, Graham (G) 0 0
H: 6 2 W: 12 06 b.Hampstead 26-9-81

2000–01	Arsenal	0	0		
2001–02	Arsenal	0	0		

STEPANOVS, Igor (D) 164 13
H: 6 4 W: 13 05 b.Ogre 21-1-76
Honours: Latvia 49 full caps, 2 goals.

1994	Interskonto	20	2	20	2
1995	Skonto Riga	23	1		
1996	Skonto Riga	22	3		
1997	Skonto Riga	22	2		
1998	Skonto Riga	24	0		
1999	Skonto Riga	20	4		
2000	Skonto Riga	18	2	129	11
2001–02	Arsenal	6	0	15	0

SVARD, Sebastian (D) 0 0
H: 6 1 W: 12 02 b.Hvidovre 15-1-83

2000–01	Arsenal	0	0		
2001–02	Arsenal	0	0		

TAVLARIDIS, Efstathios (D) 64 1
H: 6 2 W: 12 11 b.Serres 25-1-80

1996–97	Iraklis	0	0		
1997–98	Iraklis	2	0		
1998–99	Iraklis	12	1		
1999–2000	Iraklis	23	0		
2000–01	Iraklis	27	0	64	1
2001–02	Arsenal	0	0		

TAYLOR, Stuart (G) 30 0
H: 6 5 W: 13 06 b.Romford 28-11-80
Source: Trainee. *Honours:* FA Schools, England Youth, Under-21.

1998–99	Arsenal	0	0		
1999–2000	Arsenal	0	0		
1999–2000	*Bristol R*	4	0	4	0
2000–01	Arsenal	0	0		
2000–01	*Crystal Palace*	10	0	10	0
2000–01	*Peterborough U*	6	0	6	0
2001–02	Arsenal	10	0	10	0

THOMAS, Jerome (M) 4 1
H: 5 10 W: 11 10 b.Brent 23-3-83
Source: Scholar. *Honours:* England Youth.

2001–02	Arsenal	0	0		
2001–02	*QPR*	4	1	4	1

TOURE, Kolo (M) 0 0
H: 5 10 W: 11 09 b.Ivory Coast 19-3-81
Source: ASEC Mimosas.

2001–02	Arsenal	0	0		

UPSON, Matthew (D) 43 0
H: 6 1 W: 11 04 b.Hartismere 18-4-79
Source: Trainee. *Honours:* England Youth, Under-21.

1995–96	Luton T	0	0		
1996–97	Luton T	1	0	1	0
1996–97	Arsenal	0	0		
1997–98	Arsenal	5	0		
1998–99	Arsenal	5	0		
1999–2000	Arsenal	8	0		
2000–01	Arsenal	2	0		
2000–01	*Nottingham F*	1	0	1	0
2000–01	*Crystal Palace*	7	0	7	0
2001–02	Arsenal	14	0	34	0

VAN BRONCKHORST, Giovanni (M) 209 38
H: 5 9 W: 11 03 b.Rotterdam 5-2-75
Source: LMO, SC Feyenoord. *Honours:* Holland 26 full caps, 2 goals.

1993–94	Feyenoord	0	0		
1993–94	RKC	12	2	12	2
1994–95	Feyenoord	10	1		
1995–96	Feyenoord	27	9		
1996–97	Feyenoord	34	4		
1997–98	Feyenoord	32	8	103	22
1998–99	Rangers	35	7		
1999–2000	Rangers	27	4		
2000–01	Rangers	11	2		
2000–01	Rangers	0	0	73	13
2001–02	Arsenal	21	1	21	1

VIEIRA, Patrick (M) 245 18
H: 6 4 W: 13 00 b.Dakar 23-6-76
Honours: France Under-21, 56 full caps, 3 goals.

1993–94	Cannes	5	0		
1994–95	Cannes	31	2		
1995–96	Cannes	13	0	49	2
1995–96	AC Milan	2	0	2	0
1996–97	Arsenal	31	2		
1997–98	Arsenal	33	2		
1998–99	Arsenal	34	3		
1999–2000	Arsenal	30	2		
2000–01	Arsenal	30	5		
2001–02	Arsenal	36	2	194	16

VOLZ, Moritz (D) 0 0
H: 5 10 W: 12 06 b.Siegen 21-1-83

1999–2000	Arsenal	0	0		
2000–01	Arsenal	0	0		
2001–02	Arsenal	0	0		

WILTORD, Sylvain (F) 284 76
H: 5 9 W: 12 04 b.Neuilly-sur-Marne 10-5-74
Honours: France 42 full caps, 12 goals.

1991–92	Rennes	0	0		
1992–93	Rennes	2	0		
1993–94	Rennes	26	8		
1994–95	La Coruna	4	0		
1994–95	Rennes	25	5		
1995–96	Rennes	37	15		
1996–97	Rennes	35	5	125	33
1997–98	Bordeaux	34	10		
1998–99	Bordeaux	33	2		

1999–2000	Bordeaux	32	13	**99**	**25**
2000–01	Arsenal	27	8		
2001–02	Arsenal	33	10	**60**	**18**

WRIGHT, Richard (G) 252 0
H: 6 2   W: 14 04   b.Ipswich 5-11-77
Source: Trainee. *Honours:* England Schools, Youth, Under-21, 2 full caps.

1994–95	Ipswich T	3	0
1995–96	Ipswich T	23	0
1996–97	Ipswich T	40	0
1997–98	Ipswich T	46	0
1998–99	Ipswich T	46	0
1999–2000	Ipswich T	46	0
2000–01	Ipswich T	36	0	**240**	**0**
2001–02	Arsenal	12	0	**12**	**0**

Trainees
Birchall, Adam S; Fowler, Jordan M; Freeman, Brett W; Gordon, Michael A; Holloway, Craig D; Hoyte, Justin R; Kamara, Alfred; Kanu, Samuel; Larsson, Sebastian; Nicolau, Nicky G; O'Sullivan, Wayne; Probets, Ashley; Shiels, Dean A; Simek, Franklin M

ASTON VILLA

ALPAY, Ozalan (D) 247 13
H: 6 2   W: 14 00   b.Izmir 29-5-73
Source: Soma Linyit. *Honours:* Turkey 66 full caps, 4 goals.

1992–93	Altay	23	1	**23**	**1**
1993–94	Besiktas	10	0		
1994–95	Besiktas	29	3		
1995–96	Besiktas	31	2		
1996–97	Besiktas	25	3		
1997–98	Besiktas	26	1		
1998–99	Besiktas	27	0	**148**	**9**
1999–2000	Fenerbahce	29	3	**29**	**3**
2000–01	Aston Villa	33	0		
2001–02	Aston Villa	14	0	**47**	**0**

AMOO, Ryan (M) 0 0
H: 5 10   W: 9 12   b.Leicester 11-10-83
Source: Scholar.

2001–02	Aston Villa	0	0

ANGEL, Juan Pablo (F) 129 58
H: 6 0   W: 12 10   b.Medellin 24-10-75
Source: Nacional. *Honours:* Colombia 21 caps, 5 goals.

1997–98	River Plate	12	2		
1998–99	River Plate	27	11		
1999–2000	River Plate	34	19		
2000–01	River Plate	18	13	**91**	**45**
2000–01	Aston Villa	9	1		
2001–02	Aston Villa	29	12	**38**	**13**

BALABAN, Bosko (F) 130 35
H: 5 10   W: 11 10   b.Rijeka 15-10-78
Honours: Croatia 13 full caps, 6 goals.

1995–96	Rijeka	2	0		
1996–97	Rijeka	17	1		
1997–98	Rijeka	26	1		
1998–99	Rijeka	23	4		
1999–2000	Rijeka	29	15	**97**	**21**
2000–01	Dynamo Zagreb	25	14	**25**	**14**
2001–02	Aston Villa	8	0	**8**	**0**

BARRY, Gareth (D) 114 3
H: 5 11   W: 12 2   b.Hastings 23-2-81
Source: Trainee. *Honours:* England Youth, Under-21, 6 full caps.

1997–98	Aston Villa	2	0		
1998–99	Aston Villa	32	2		
1999–2000	Aston Villa	30	1		
2000–01	Aston Villa	30	0		
2001–02	Aston Villa	20	0	**114**	**3**

BERKS, David‡ (M) 0 0
H: 5 8   W: 10 07   b.Stoke 23-12-81
Source: Scholar.

2000–01	Aston Villa	0	0
2001–02	Aston Villa	0	0

BEWERS, Jonathan (D) 1 0
H: 5 8   W: 9 13   b.Kettering 10-9-82
Source: Trainee. *Honours:* England Youth, Under-20.

1999–2000	Aston Villa	1	0		
2000–01	Aston Villa	0	0		
2001–02	Aston Villa	0	0	**1**	**0**

BOATENG, George (M) 227 10
H: 5 9   W: 10 12   b.Nkawkaw 5-9-75
Honours: Holland 2 full caps.

1994–95	Excelsior	9	0	**9**	**0**
1995–96	Feyenoord	24	1		
1996–97	Feyenoord	21	0		
1997–98	Feyenoord	18	0	**68**	**1**
1997–98	Coventry C	14	1		
1998–99	Coventry C	33	4	**47**	**5**

1999–2000	Aston Villa	33	2		
2000–01	Aston Villa	33	1		
2001–02	Aston Villa	37	1	**103**	**4**

COOKE, Stephen (M) 7 0
H: 5 7   W: 9 00   b.Walsall 15-2-83
Honours: England Youth.

1999–2000	Aston Villa	0	0		
2000–01	Aston Villa	0	0		
2001–02	Aston Villa	0	0		
2001–02	*Bournemouth*	7	0	**7**	**0**

CROUCH, Peter (F) 86 30
H: 6 7   W: 11 12   b.Macclesfield 30-1-81
Source: Trainee. *Honours:* England Youth, Under-20, Under-21.

1998–99	Tottenham H	0	0		
1999–2000	Tottenham H	0	0		
2000–01	QPR	42	10	**42**	**10**
2001–02	Portsmouth	37	18	**37**	**18**
2001–02	Aston Villa	7	2	**7**	**2**

DAVIS, Steven (M) 0 0
H: 5 7   W: 9 07   b.Ballymena 1-1-85
Source: Scholar.

2001–02	Aston Villa	0	0

DELANEY, Mark (D) 107 1
H: 6 1   W: 11 07   b.Haverfordwest 13-5-76
Source: Carmarthen T. *Honours:* Wales 15 full caps.

1998–99	Cardiff C	28	0	**28**	**0**
1998–99	Aston Villa	2	0		
1999–2000	Aston Villa	28	1		
2000–01	Aston Villa	19	0		
2001–02	Aston Villa	30	0	**79**	**1**

DILLON, Sean* (D) 0 0
H: 6 0   W: 12 06   b.Dublin 30-7-83
Source: Scholar.

2000–01	Aston Villa	0	0
2001–02	Aston Villa	0	0

DUBLIN, Dion (F) 422 152
H: 6 2   W: 12 04   b.Leicester 22-4-69
Source: Oakham U. *Honours:* England 4 full caps.

1987–88	Norwich C	0	0		
1988–89	Cambridge U	21	6		
1989–90	Cambridge U	46	15		
1990–91	Cambridge U	46	16		
1991–92	Cambridge U	43	15	**156**	**52**
1992–93	Manchester U	7	1		
1993–94	Manchester U	5	1	**12**	**2**
1994–95	Coventry C	31	13		
1995–96	Coventry C	34	14		
1996–97	Coventry C	34	13		
1997–98	Coventry C	36	18		
1998–99	Coventry C	10	3	**145**	**61**
1998–99	Aston Villa	24	11		
1999–2000	Aston Villa	26	12		
2000–01	Aston Villa	33	8		
2001–02	Aston Villa	21	4	**104**	**35**
2001–02	*Millwall*	5	2	**5**	**2**

EDWARDS, Rob (D) 0 0
H: 6 1   W: 11 10   b.Telford 25-12-82
Source: Trainee.

1999–2000	Aston Villa	0	0
2000–01	Aston Villa	0	0
2001–02	Aston Villa	0	0

ENCKELMAN, Peter (G) 98 0
H: 6 2   W: 12 05   b.Turku 10-3-77
Source: TPS Turku. *Honours:* Finland 3 full caps.

1995	TPS Turku	6	0		
1996	TPS Turku	24	0		
1997	TPS Turku	25	0		
1998	TPS Turku	24	0	**79**	**0**
1998–99	Aston Villa	0	0		
1999–2000	Aston Villa	10	0		
2000–01	Aston Villa	0	0		
2001–02	Aston Villa	9	0	**19**	**0**

ENNIS, Pierre (D) 0 0
H: 5 10   W: 12 03   b.Dublin 25-2-84
Source: Scholar.

2000–01	Aston Villa	0	0
2001–02	Aston Villa	0	0

FAHEY, Keith (M) 0 0
H: 5 10   W: 12 07   b.Dublin 15-1-83
Source: Scholar.

1999–2000	Aston Villa	0	0
2000–01	Aston Villa	0	0
2001–02	Aston Villa	0	0

FOLDS, Liam* (M) 0 0
H: 5 11   W: 12 01   b.Bedford 21-1-82
Source: Scholar.

2000–01	Aston Villa	0	0
2001–02	Aston Villa	0	0

GHRAYIB, Najwan‡ (D) 132 27
H: 5 8   W: 11 04   b.Nazareth 30-1-74
Honours: Israel 18 full caps, 4 goals.

1994–95	Maccabi Haifa	23	4	**23**	**4**
1995–96	Maccabi P-T	27	10		
1996–97	Maccabi P-T	22	4	**49**	**14**
1997–98	Hapoel Haifa	26	2		
1998–99	Hapoel Haifa	29	7	**55**	**9**
1999–2000	Aston Villa	5	0		
2000–01	Aston Villa	0	0		
2001–02	Aston Villa	0	0	**5**	**0**

HADJI, Mustapha (M) 291 50
H: 5 11   W: 11 12   b.Ifrane 16-11-71
Honours: Morocco 60 full caps.

1992–93	Nancy	32	6		
1993–94	Nancy	37	11		
1994–95	Nancy	28	3		
1995–96	Nancy	42	11	**139**	**31**
1996–97	Sporting	27	3		
1997–98	Sporting	9	0	**36**	**3**
1997–98	La Coruna	10	0		
1998–99	La Coruna	21	2	**31**	**2**
1999–2000	Coventry C	33	6		
2000–01	Coventry C	29	6	**62**	**12**
2001–02	Aston Villa	23	2	**23**	**2**

HAYNES, Danny* (D) 0 0
H: 6 2   W: 12 02   b.Nuneaton 24-8-82
Source: Scholar.

2000–01	Aston Villa	0	0
2001–02	Aston Villa	0	0

HENDERSON, Wayne (G) 0 0
H: 5 11   W: 12 02   b.Dublin 16-9-83
Source: Scholar.

2000–01	Aston Villa	0	0
2001–02	Aston Villa	0	0

HENDRIE, Lee (M) 146 15
H: 5 10   W: 11 00   b.Birmingham 18-5-77
Source: Trainee. *Honours:* England Youth, Under-21, B, 1 full cap.

1993–94	Aston Villa	0	0		
1994–95	Aston Villa	0	0		
1995–96	Aston Villa	3	0		
1996–97	Aston Villa	4	0		
1997–98	Aston Villa	17	3		
1998–99	Aston Villa	32	3		
1999–2000	Aston Villa	29	1		
2000–01	Aston Villa	32	6		
2001–02	Aston Villa	29	2	**146**	**15**

HITZLSPERGER, Thomas (D) 18 1
H: 6 0   W: 11 12   b.Germany 5-4-82
Source: Bayern Munich.

2000–01	Aston Villa	1	0		
2001–02	*Chesterfield*	5	0	**5**	**0**
2001–02	Aston Villa	12	1	**13**	**1**

HUSBANDS, Michael (F) 0 0
H: 5 9   W: 9 13   b.Birmingham 13-11-83
Source: Scholar.

2001–02	Aston Villa	0	0

HYLTON, Leon (D) 0 0
H: 5 9   W: 11 00   b.Birmingham 27-1-83
Honours: England Youth.

1999–2000	Aston Villa	0	0
2000–01	Aston Villa	0	0
2001–02	Aston Villa	0	0

HYNES, Peter (F) 0 0
H: 5 9   W: 11 12   b.Dublin 28-11-83
Source: Scholar.

2000–01	Aston Villa	0	0
2001–02	Aston Villa	0	0

JACKMAN, Daniel (D) 7 1
H: 5 4   W: 9 08   b.Worcester 3-1-83
Source: Scholar.

2000–01	Aston Villa	0	0		
2001–02	Aston Villa	0	0		
2001–02	*Cambridge U*	7	1	**7**	**1**

KACHLOUL, Hassan (M) 245 48
H: 6 1   W: 12 01   b.Agadir 19-2-73
Honours: Morocco 12 full caps.

1992–93	Nimes	17	1		
1993–94	Nimes	37	17		
1994–95	Nimes	32	8	**86**	**26**
1995–96	Dunkerque	28	6	**28**	**6**
1996–97	Metz	7	0	**7**	**0**
1997–98	St Etienne	16	0	**16**	**0**
1998–99	Southampton	22	5		
1999–2000	Southampton	32	5		
2000–01	Southampton	32	4	**86**	**14**
2001–02	Aston Villa	22	2	**22**	**2**

MARFELL, Andrew‡ (F) 0 0
H: 6 1   W: 12 07   b.Gloucester 20-2-82
Source: Scholar.

2000–01	Aston Villa	0	0
2001–02	Aston Villa	0	0

McGRATH, John (F) 3 0
H: 5 10 W: 10 04 b.Limerick 27-3-80
Source: Belvedere. *Honours:* Eire Under-21.

1999–2000	Aston Villa	0	0		
2000–01	Aston Villa	3	0		
2001–02	Aston Villa	0	0	3	0

MELAUGH, Gavin (M) 0 0
H: 5 7 W: 9 07 b.Derry 9-7-81
Source: Trainee. *Honours:* Northern Ireland Under-21.

1998–99	Aston Villa	0	0
1999–2000	Aston Villa	0	0
2000–01	Aston Villa	0	0
2001–02	Aston Villa	0	0

MELLBERG, Olof (D) 194 0
H: 6 1 W: 12 10 b.Amncharad 3-9-77
Honours: Sweden 26 full caps.

1996	Degerfors	22	0		
1997	Degerfors	25	0	47	0
1998	AIK Stockholm	17	0	17	0
1998–99	Santander	25	0		
1999–2000	Santander	37	0		
2000–01	Santander	36	0	98	0
2001–02	Aston Villa	32	0	32	0

MERSON, Paul (F) 499 107
H: 6 0 W: 13 02 b.Northolt 20-3-68
Source: Apprentice. *Honours:* England Youth, Under-21, B, 21 full caps, 3 goals.

1985–86	Arsenal	0	0		
1986–87	Arsenal	7	3		
1986–87	Brentford	7	0	7	0
1987–88	Arsenal	15	5		
1988–89	Arsenal	37	10		
1989–90	Arsenal	29	7		
1990–91	Arsenal	37	13		
1991–92	Arsenal	42	12		
1992–93	Arsenal	33	6		
1993–94	Arsenal	33	7		
1994–95	Arsenal	24	4		
1995–96	Arsenal	38	5		
1996–97	Arsenal	32	6	327	78
1997–98	Middlesbrough	45	11		
1998–99	Middlesbrough	3	0	48	11
1998–99	Aston Villa	26	5		
1999–2000	Aston Villa	32	5		
2000–01	Aston Villa	38	6		
2001–02	Aston Villa	21	2	117	18

MOORE, Stefan (F) 2 0
H: 5 10 W: 10 12 b.Birmingham 28-9-83
Source: Scholar. *Honours:* England Youth.

2000–01	Aston Villa	0	0		
2001–02	Aston Villa	0	0		
2001–02	Chesterfield	2	0	2	0

MYHILL, Boaz (G) 0 0
H: 6 3 W: 14 06 b.California 9-11-82
Source: Scholar. *Honours:* England Youth, Under-20.

2000–01	Aston Villa	0	0
2001–02	Aston Villa	0	0
2001–02	Stoke C	0	0

RIDGEWELL, Liam (M) 0 0
H: 5 10 W: 10 03 b.London 21-7-84
Source: Scholar.

2001–02	Aston Villa	0	0

SAMUEL, J Lloyd (D) 43 0
H: 5 11 W: 11 04 b.Trinidad 29-3-81
Source: Charlton Ath Trainee. *Honours:* England Youth, Under-20, Under-21.

1998–99	Aston Villa	0	0		
1999–2000	Aston Villa	9	0		
2000–01	Aston Villa	3	0		
2001–02	Gillingham	8	0	8	0
2001–02	Aston Villa	23	0	35	0

SCHMEICHEL, Peter* (G) 578 9
H: 6 4 W: 16 00 b.Gladsaxe 18-11-63
Honours: Denmark 129 full caps, 1 goal.

1984	Hvidovre	30	0		
1985	Hvidovre	28	6		
1986	Hvidovre	30	0	88	6
1987	Brondby	23	2		
1988	Brondby	26	0		
1989	Brondby	26	0		
1990	Brondby	26	0		
1991	Brondby	18	0	119	2
1991–92	Manchester U	40	0		
1992–93	Manchester U	42	0		
1993–94	Manchester U	40	0		
1994–95	Manchester U	32	0		
1995–96	Manchester U	36	0		
1996–97	Manchester U	36	0		
1997–98	Manchester U	32	0		
1998–99	Manchester U	34	0	292	0
1999–2000	Sporting Lisbon	28	0		
2000–01	Sporting Lisbon	22	0	50	0
2001–02	Aston Villa	29	1	29	1

SCULLION, David (F) 8 2
H: 5 8 W: 10 03 b.Craigavon 27-4-84

2000–01	Portadown	8	2	8	2
2001–02	Aston Villa	0	0		

SMITH, Jay (M) 0 0
H: 5 7 W: 10 00 b.London 24-9-81
Source: Scholar.

2000–01	Aston Villa	0	0
2001–02	Aston Villa	0	0

STAUNTON, Steve (D) 378 17
H: 6 0 W: 12 12 b.Drogheda 19-1-69
Source: Dundalk. *Honours:* Eire Under-21, 102 full caps, 7 goals.

1986–87	Liverpool	0	0		
1987–88	Liverpool	0	0		
1987–88	Bradford C	8	0	8	0
1988–89	Liverpool	21	0		
1989–90	Liverpool	20	0		
1990–91	Liverpool	24	0		
1991–92	Aston Villa	37	4		
1992–93	Aston Villa	42	2		
1993–94	Aston Villa	24	2		
1994–95	Aston Villa	35	5		
1995–96	Aston Villa	13	0		
1996–97	Aston Villa	30	2		
1997–98	Aston Villa	27	1		
1998–99	Liverpool	31	0		
1999–2000	Liverpool	12	0		
2000–01	Liverpool	1	0	109	0
2000–01	Crystal Palace	6	1	6	1
2000–01	Aston Villa	14	0		
2001–02	Aston Villa	33	0	255	16

STONE, Steve (M) 283 27
H: 5 8 W: 12 07 b.Gateshead 20-8-71
Source: Trainee. *Honours:* England 9 full caps, 2 goals.

1989–90	Nottingham F	0	0		
1990–91	Nottingham F	0	0		
1991–92	Nottingham F	1	0		
1992–93	Nottingham F	12	1		
1993–94	Nottingham F	45	5		
1994–95	Nottingham F	41	5		
1995–96	Nottingham F	34	7		
1996–97	Nottingham F	5	0		
1997–98	Nottingham F	29	2		
1998–99	Nottingham F	26	3	193	23
1998–99	Aston Villa	10	0		
1999–2000	Aston Villa	24	1		
2000–01	Aston Villa	34	2		
2001–02	Aston Villa	22	1	90	4

STUART, Cameron (D) 0 0
H: 5 6 W: 10 08 b.York 9-1-84
Source: Scholar.

2001–02	Aston Villa	0	0

TAYLOR, Ian (M) 317 57
H: 6 1 W: 12 00 b.Birmingham 4-6-68
Source: Moor Green.

1992–93	Port Vale	41	15		
1993–94	Port Vale	42	13	83	28
1994–95	Sheffield W	14	1	14	1
1994–95	Aston Villa	22	1		
1995–96	Aston Villa	25	3		
1996–97	Aston Villa	34	2		
1997–98	Aston Villa	32	6		
1998–99	Aston Villa	33	4		
1999–2000	Aston Villa	29	5		
2000–01	Aston Villa	29	4		
2001–02	Aston Villa	16	3	220	28

VASSELL, Darius (F) 76 16
H: 5 7 W: 12 00 b.Birmingham 13-6-80
Source: Trainee. *Honours:* England Youth, Under-21, 8 full caps, 3 goals.

1998–99	Aston Villa	6	0		
1999–2000	Aston Villa	11	0		
2000–01	Aston Villa	23	4		
2001–02	Aston Villa	36	12	76	16

WILLETTS, Ben (D) 0 0
H: 5 9 W: 11 05 b.West Bromwich 10-2-83
Source: Scholar. *Honours:* England Youth.

1999–2000	Aston Villa	0	0
2000–01	Aston Villa	0	0
2001–02	Aston Villa	0	0

WRIGHT, Alan (D) 422 6
H: 5 4 W: 9 09 b.Ashton-under-Lyme 28-9-71
Source: Trainee. *Honours:* England Schools, Youth, Under-21.

1987–88	Blackpool	1	0		
1988–89	Blackpool	16	0		
1989–90	Blackpool	24	0		
1990–91	Blackpool	45	0		
1991–92	Blackpool	12	0	98	0
1991–92	Blackburn R	33	1		
1992–93	Blackburn R	24	0		
1993–94	Blackburn R	12	0		
1994–95	Blackburn R	5	0	74	1
1994–95	Aston Villa	8	0		
1995–96	Aston Villa	38	2		
1996–97	Aston Villa	38	1		
1997–98	Aston Villa	37	0		
1998–99	Aston Villa	38	0		
1999–2000	Aston Villa	32	1		
2000–01	Aston Villa	36	1		
2001–02	Aston Villa	23	0	250	5

Trainees
Atkinson, Jonathan M; Baptist, Adam R; Brazil, Alan; Cormell, Scott; Gahan, Stephen; Marshall, Colin; Nolan, David S; O'Connor, James F; Pecora, Antoni; Whittingham, Pete; Williams, Oliver

BARNSLEY

AUSTIN, Neil (F) 0 0
H: 5 10 W: 11 09 b.Barnsley 26-4-83
Source: Trainee. *Honours:* England Youth.

1999–2000	Barnsley	0	0
2000–01	Barnsley	0	0
2001–02	Barnsley	0	0

BARKER, Christopher (D) 113 3
H: 6 0 W: 11 11 b.Sheffield 2-3-80
Source: Alfreton.

1998–99	Barnsley	0	0		
1999–2000	Barnsley	29	0		
2000–01	Barnsley	40	0		
2001–02	Barnsley	44	3	113	3

BARNARD, Darren‡ (D) 281 45
H: 5 9 W: 12 04 b.Rinteln 30-11-71
Source: Wokingham T. *Honours:* England Schools, Wales 16 full caps.

1990–91	Chelsea	0	0		
1991–92	Chelsea	4	0		
1992–93	Chelsea	13	1		
1993–94	Chelsea	12	1		
1994–95	Chelsea	0	0		
1994–95	Reading	4	0	4	0
1995–96	Chelsea	0	0	29	2
1995–96	Bristol C	34	4		
1996–97	Bristol C	44	11	78	15
1997–98	Barnsley	35	2		
1998–99	Barnsley	26	4		
1999–2000	Barnsley	41	13		
2000–01	Barnsley	30	2		
2001–02	Barnsley	38	7	170	28

BARROWCLOUGH, Carl (F) 7 0
H: 5 7 W: 9 08 b.Doncaster 25-9-81
Source: Scholar.

2000–01	Barnsley	7	0		
2001–02	Barnsley	0	0	7	0

BERNARD, Paul‡ (M) 211 24
H: 6 0 W: 13 01 b.Edinburgh 30-12-72
Source: Trainee. *Honours:* Scotland Under-21, 2 full caps.

1990–91	Oldham Ath	2	1		
1991–92	Oldham Ath	21	5		
1992–93	Oldham Ath	33	4		
1993–94	Oldham Ath	32	5		
1994–95	Oldham Ath	17	2		
1995–96	Oldham Ath	7	1	112	18
1995–96	Aberdeen	31	1		
1996–97	Aberdeen	14	0		
1997–98	Aberdeen	17	0		
1998–99	Aberdeen	9	1		
1999–2000	Aberdeen	25	4		
2000–01	Aberdeen	3	0	99	6
2001–02	Barnsley	0	0		

BERTOS, Leo (M) 6 0
H: 5 8 W: 12 08 b.Wellington 20-12-81

2000–01	Barnsley	2	0		
2001–02	Barnsley	4	0	6	0

BETSY, Kevin (M) 32 1
H: 6 1 W: 12 03 b.Seychelles 20-3-78
Source: Woking.

1998–99	Fulham	7	1		
1999–2000	Fulham	2	0		
1999–2000	Bournemouth	5	0	5	0
1999–2000	Hull C	2	0	2	0
2000–01	Fulham	5	0		
2001–02	Fulham	1	0	15	1
2001–02	Barnsley	10	0	10	0

BROWN, Keith‡ (D) 14 0
H: 5 11 W: 11 01 b.Edinburgh 24-12-79
Source: Trainee. *Honours:* Scotland Youth.

1996–97	Blackburn R	0	0
1997–98	Blackburn R	0	0
1998–99	Blackburn R	0	0
1999–2000	Blackburn R	0	0
1999–2000	Barnsley	10	0
2000–01	Barnsley	1	0

2000–01	Oxford U	3	0	3	0
2001–02	Barnsley	0	0	11	0

CHETTLE, Steve‡ (D)   513 13
H: 6 1   W: 13 06   b.Nottingham 27-9-68
Source: Apprentice. Honours: England Under-21.

1986–87	Nottingham F	0	0		
1987–88	Nottingham F	30	0		
1988–89	Nottingham F	28	2		
1989–90	Nottingham F	22	1		
1990–91	Nottingham F	37	2		
1991–92	Nottingham F	22	1		
1992–93	Nottingham F	30	0		
1993–94	Nottingham F	46	1		
1994–95	Nottingham F	41	0		
1995–96	Nottingham F	37	0		
1996–97	Nottingham F	32	0		
1997–98	Nottingham F	45	1		
1998–99	Nottingham F	30	0		
1999–2000	Nottingham F	11	1	415	11
1999–2000	Barnsley	25	2		
2000–01	Barnsley	35	0		
2001–02	Barnsley	32	0	92	2
2001–02	Walsall	6	0	6	0

CHRISTIE, Jeremy§ (M)   1 0
H: 5 10   W: 10 12   b.Whangarei 22-5-83
Source: Scholar.

2001–02	Barnsley	1	0	1	0

CORBO, Mateo‡ (M)   92 2
H: 5 9   W: 12 12   b.Montevideo 21-4-76

1996	River Plate (Uru)	2	0		
1997	River Plate (Uru)	25	1		
1998	River Plate (Uru)	16	0		
1999	River Plate (Uru)	11	1	68	2
1999–2000	Oviedo	6	0	6	0
2000–01	Barnsley	17	0		
2001–02	Barnsley	1	0	18	0

COULSON, David* (M)   0 0
H: 6 1   W: 12 08   b.Durham 21-3-84

2001–02	Barnsley	0	0	0	0

CROOKS, Lee (D)   105 2
H: 6 2   W: 13 12   b.Wakefield 14-1-78
Source: Trainee. Honours: England Youth.

1994–95	Manchester C	0	0		
1995–96	Manchester C	0	0		
1996–97	Manchester C	15	0		
1997–98	Manchester C	5	0		
1998–99	Manchester C	34	1		
1999–2000	Manchester C	20	1		
2000–01	Manchester C	2	0	76	2
2000–01	Northampton T	3	0	3	0
2000–01	Barnsley	0	0		
2001–02	Barnsley	26	0	26	0

DIXON, Kevin (M)   3 0
H: 5 8   W: 12 08   b.Easington 27-6-80
Source: Trainee. Honours: England Youth.

1997–98	Leeds U	0	0		
1998–99	Leeds U	0	0		
1999–2000	Leeds U	0	0		
1999–2000	York C	3	0	3	0
2000–01	Leeds U	0	0		
2001–02	Barnsley	0	0		

DONOVAN, Kevin (M)   382 45
H: 5 10   W: 11 12   b.Halifax 17-12-71
Source: Trainee.

1989–90	Huddersfield T	1	0		
1990–91	Huddersfield T	6	1		
1991–92	Huddersfield T	10	0		
1991–92	Halifax T	6	0	6	0
1992–93	Huddersfield T	3	0	20	1
1992–93	WBA	32	6		
1993–94	WBA	37	8		
1994–95	WBA	33	5		
1995–96	WBA	34	0		
1996–97	WBA	32	0	168	19
1997–98	Grimsby T	46	16		
1998–99	Grimsby T	28	0		
1999–2000	Grimsby T	41	3		
2000–01	Grimsby T	41	5	156	24
2001–02	Barnsley	32	1	32	1

DUDGEON, James (D)   22 3
H: 6 2   W: 12 04   b.Newcastle 19-3-81
Source: Trainee. Honours: Scotland Youth.

1999–2000	Barnsley	0	0		
2000–01	Barnsley	0	0		
2000–01	Lincoln C	22	3	22	3
2001–02	Barnsley	0	0		

DYER, Bruce (F)   308 85
H: 5 11   W: 12 08   b.Ilford 13-4-75
Source: Trainee. Honours: England Under-21.

1992–93	Watford	2	0		
1993–94	Watford	29	6	31	6
1993–94	Crystal Palace	11	0		
1994–95	Crystal Palace	16	1		
1995–96	Crystal Palace	35	13		
1996–97	Crystal Palace	43	17		
1997–98	Crystal Palace	24	4		
1998–99	Crystal Palace	6	2	135	37
1998–99	Barnsley	28	7		
1999–2000	Barnsley	32	6		
2000–01	Barnsley	38	15		
2001–02	Barnsley	44	14	142	42

FALLON, Rory (F)   21 0
H: 6 2   W: 12 02   b.Gisbourne 20-3-82
Source: North Shore U. Honours: England Youth.

1998–99	Barnsley	0	0		
1999–2000	Barnsley	0	0		
2000–01	Barnsley	1	0		
2001–02	Barnsley	9	0	10	0
2001–02	Shrewsbury T	11	0	11	0

FLYNN, Mike (D)   583 24
H: 6 1   W: 13 05   b.Oldham 23-2-69
Source: Trainee.

1986–87	Oldham Ath	0	0		
1987–88	Oldham Ath	31	1		
1988–89	Oldham Ath	9	0	40	1
1988–89	Norwich C	0	0		
1989–90	Norwich C	0	0		
1989–90	Preston NE	23	1		
1990–91	Preston NE	35	1		
1991–92	Preston NE	43	3		
1992–93	Preston NE	35	2	136	7
1992–93	Stockport Co	10	0		
1993–94	Stockport Co	46	1		
1994–95	Stockport Co	43	2		
1995–96	Stockport Co	46	6		
1996–97	Stockport Co	46	2		
1997–98	Stockport Co	34	1		
1998–99	Stockport Co	46	1		
1999–2000	Stockport Co	46	1		
2000–01	Stockport Co	44	0		
2001–02	Stockport Co	26	2	387	16
2001–02	Stoke C	13	0	13	0
2001–02	Barnsley	7	0	7	0

GARTLAND, Graham‡ (M)   0 0
H: 6 0   W: 11 01   b.Dublin 13-7-83

2000–01	Barnsley	0	0		
2001–02	Barnsley	0	0		

GHENT, Matthew (G)   2 0
H: 6 3   W: 14 09   b.Burton 5-10-80
Source: Trainee. Honours: England Schools, Youth.

1997–98	Aston Villa	0	0		
1998–99	Aston Villa	0	0		
1999–2000	Aston Villa	0	0		
2000–01	Aston Villa	0	0		
2000–01	Lincoln C	1	0	1	0
2001–02	Barnsley	1	0	1	0

GIBBS, Paul (D)   186 16
H: 5 11   W: 11 07   b.Great Yarmouth 26-10-72
Source: Diss T.

1994–95	Colchester U	9	0		
1995–96	Colchester U	24	3		
1996–97	Colchester U	20	0	53	3
1997–98	Torquay U	41	7	41	7
1998–99	Plymouth Arg	27	3		
1999–2000	Plymouth Arg	7	0	34	3
2000–01	Brentford	27	1		
2001–02	Brentford	27	2	54	3
2001–02	Barnsley	4	0	4	0

GORRE, Dean (M)   270 44
H: 5 7   W: 11 09   b.Surinam 10-9-70

1991–92	SVV/Dordrecht	32	8	32	8
1992–93	Feyenoord	25	2		
1993–94	Feyenoord	12	3		
1994–95	Feyenoord	5	1	42	6
1994–95	Groningen	12	3		
1995–96	Groningen	34	4		
1996–97	Groningen	34	11	80	18
1997–98	Ajax	21	3		
1998–99	Ajax	14	1	35	4
1999–2000	Huddersfield T	28	4		
2000–01	Huddersfield T	32	2	62	6
2001–02	Barnsley	19	2	19	2

HAYWARD, Steve (M)   241 22
H: 5 11   W: 12 13   b.Walsall 8-9-71
Source: Trainee. Honours: England Youth.

1988–89	Derby Co	0	0		
1989–90	Derby Co	3	0		
1990–91	Derby Co	1	0		
1991–92	Derby Co	7	0		
1992–93	Derby Co	7	1		
1993–94	Derby Co	5	0		
1994–95	Derby Co	3	0	26	1
1994–95	Carlisle U	9	2		
1995–96	Carlisle U	38	4		
1996–97	Carlisle U	43	7	90	13
1997–98	Fulham	35	4		
1998–99	Fulham	42	3		
1999–2000	Fulham	37	0		
2000–01	Fulham	1	0	115	7
2000–01	Barnsley	10	1		
2001–02	Barnsley	0	0	10	1

JACKSON, Paul‡ (F)   0 0
H: 5 8   W: 11 04   b.Rochdale 14-5-81
Source: Trainee.

1999–2000	Barnsley	0	0		
2000–01	Barnsley	0	0		
2001–02	Barnsley	0	0		

JONES, Gary (M)   173 23
H: 5 11   W: 12 06   b.Birkenhead 3-6-77

1997–98	Swansea C	8	0	8	0
1997–98	Rochdale	17	2		
1998–99	Rochdale	20	0		
1999–2000	Rochdale	39	7		
2000–01	Rochdale	44	8		
2001–02	Rochdale	20	5	140	22
2001–02	Barnsley	25	1	25	1

KAY, Antony (F)   8 0
H: 5 11   W: 11 07   b.Barnsley 21-10-82
Source: Trainee. Honours: England Youth.

1999–2000	Barnsley	0	0		
2000–01	Barnsley	7	0		
2001–02	Barnsley	1	0	8	0

LUMSDON, Chris (M)   56 8
H: 5 11   W: 10 02   b.Newcastle 15-12-79
Source: Trainee.

1997–98	Sunderland	1	0		
1998–99	Sunderland	0	0		
1999–2000	Sunderland	1	0		
1999–2000	Blackpool	6	1	6	1
2000–01	Sunderland	0	0		
2000–01	Crewe Alex	16	0	16	0
2001–02	Sunderland	0	0	2	0
2001–02	Barnsley	32	7	32	7

MARRIOTT, Andy (G)   274 0
H: 6 0   W: 12 05   b.Sutton-in-Ashfield 11-10-70
Source: Trainee. Honours: England Schools, FA Schools, Youth, Under-21, Wales 5 full caps.

1988–89	Arsenal	0	0		
1989–90	Nottingham F	0	0		
1989–90	WBA	3	0	3	0
1989–90	Blackburn R	2	0	2	0
1989–90	Colchester U	10	0	10	0
1990–91	Nottingham F	0	0		
1991–92	Nottingham F	6	0		
1991–92	Burnley	15	0	15	0
1992–93	Nottingham F	5	0		
1993–94	Nottingham F	0	0	11	0
1993–94	Wrexham	36	0		
1994–95	Wrexham	46	0		
1995–96	Wrexham	46	0		
1996–97	Wrexham	43	0		
1997–98	Wrexham	42	0		
1998–99	Wrexham	0	0	213	0
1998–99	Sunderland	1	0		
1999–2000	Sunderland	1	0		
2000–01	Sunderland	0	0	2	0
2000–01	Wigan Ath	0	0		
2000–01	Barnsley	0	0		
2001–02	Barnsley	18	0	18	0

MEECHAN, Gary* (M)   0 0
H: 5 6   W: 10 13   b.Glasgow 18-11-84

2001–02	Barnsley	0	0		

MILLER, Christopher (D)   0 0
H: 5 8   W: 11 09   b.Paisley 19-11-82
Source: Scholar.

2000–01	Barnsley	0	0		
2001–02	Barnsley	0	0		

MILLER, Kevin‡ (G)   496 0
H: 6 1   W: 16 00   b.Falmouth 15-3-69
Source: Newquay.

1988–89	Exeter C	3	0		
1989–90	Exeter C	28	0		
1990–91	Exeter C	46	0		
1991–92	Exeter C	42	0		
1992–93	Exeter C	44	0	163	0
1993–94	Birmingham C	24	0	24	0
1994–95	Watford	44	0		
1995–96	Watford	42	0		
1996–97	Watford	42	0	128	0
1997–98	Crystal Palace	38	0		
1998–99	Crystal Palace	28	0		
1999–2000	Crystal Palace	0	0	66	0
1999–2000	Barnsley	41	0		
2000–01	Barnsley	46	0		
2001–02	Barnsley	28	0	115	0

MORGAN, Chris (D)   149 5
H: 6 1   W: 12 13   b.Barnsley 9-11-77
Source: Trainee.

1996–97	Barnsley	0	0		

1997–98	Barnsley	11	0		
1998–99	Barnsley	19	0		
1999–2000	Barnsley	37	0		
2000–01	Barnsley	40	1		
2001–02	Barnsley	42	4	149	5

MULLIGAN, David (M) 28 0
H: 5 5 W: 9 12 b.Fazakerley 24-3-82
Source: Scholar.

2000–01	Barnsley	0	0		
2001–02	Barnsley	28	0	28	0

NEIL, Alex (M) 73 7
H: 5 9 W: 11 02 b.Bellshill 9-6-81
Source: Dunfermline Ath.

1999–2000	Airdrieonians	16	5	16	5
2000–01	Barnsley	32	0		
2001–02	Barnsley	25	2	57	2

O'CALLAGHAN, Brian (D) 32 0
H: 6 1 W: 12 03 b.Limerick 24-2-81
Source: Pike Rovers.

1998–99	Barnsley	0	0		
1999–2000	Barnsley	0	0		
2000–01	Barnsley	26	0		
2001–02	Barnsley	6	0	32	0

OLDHAM, Adam (M) 0 0
b.Sheffield 26-1-85
Honours: England Youth.

2001–02	Barnsley	0	0		

PARRY, Craig (G) 0 0
H: 5 11 W: 12 04 b.Barnsley 15-3-84
Source: Scholar.

2000–01	Barnsley	0	0		
2001–02	Barnsley	0	0		

RANKIN, Isiah (F) 96 17
H: 5 10 W: 11 00 b.London 22-5-78
Source: Trainee.

1995–96	Arsenal	0	0		
1996–97	Arsenal	0	0		
1997–98	Arsenal	1	0	1	0
1997–98	Colchester U	11	5	11	5
1998–99	Bradford C	27	4		
1999–2000	Bradford C	9	0		
1999–2000	Birmingham C	13	0	13	4
2000–01	Bradford C	1	0	37	4
2000–01	Bolton W	16	2	16	2
2000–01	Barnsley	9	1		
2001–02	Barnsley	9	1	18	2

RAVENHILL, Ricky‡ (F) 0 0
H: 5 10 W: 11 01 b.Doncaster 16-1-81
Source: Trainee.

1999–2000	Barnsley	0	0		
2000–01	Barnsley	0	0		
2001–02	Barnsley	0	0		

REGAN, Carl (D) 37 0
H: 6 0 W: 11 03 b.Liverpool 14-1-80
Source: Trainee. *Honours:* England Youth.

1997–98	Everton	0	0		
1998–99	Everton	0	0		
1999–2000	Everton	0	0		
2000–01	Barnsley	27	0		
2001–02	Barnsley	10	0	37	0

SALLI, Janne (D) 7 0
H: 6 2 W: 12 08 b.Seinajoki 14-12-77
Honours: Finland 8 full caps, 1 goal.

2000–01	Barnsley	7	0		
2001–02	Barnsley	0	0	7	0

SAND, Peter‡ (M) 43 4
H: 6 0 W: 12 02 b.Aalborg 17-7-72

2000–01	Midtjylland	27	3		
2001–02	Midtjylland	10	0	37	3
2001–02	Barnsley	6	1	6	1

(Transferred to Stabaek, February 2002).

SAVIC, Sinisa‡ (M) 0 0
H: 5 8 W: 12 08 b.Starnberg 8-11-80

2000–01	Barnsley	0	0		
2001–02	Barnsley	0	0		

SCOTHERN, Ashley§ (F) 1 0
b.Pontefract 11-9-84
Source: Scholar. *Honours:* England Youth.

2001–02	Barnsley	1	0	1	0

SHERON, Mike (F) 383 104
H: 5 10 W: 12 08 b.Liverpool 11-1-72
Source: Trainee. *Honours:* England Under-21.

1990–91	Manchester C	0	0		
1990–91	Bury	5	1	5	1
1991–92	Manchester C	29	7		
1992–93	Manchester C	38	11		
1993–94	Manchester C	33	6	100	24
1994–95	Norwich C	21	1		
1995–96	Norwich C	7	1	28	2
1995–96	Stoke C	28	15		
1996–97	Stoke C	41	19	69	34
1997–98	QPR	40	11		

1998–99	QPR	23	8	63	19
1998–99	Barnsley	15	2		
1999–2000	Barnsley	36	9		
2000–01	Barnsley	34	1		
2001–02	Barnsley	33	12	118	24

TINKLER, Eric‡ (M) 176 10
H: 6 0 W: 13 12 b.Roodepoort 30-7-70
Honours: South Africa 46 full caps, 1 goal.

1993–94	Vitoria Setubal	21	0		
1994–95	Vitoria Setubal	17	1		
1995–96	Vitoria Setubal	19	0	57	1
1996–97	Cagliari	20	0	20	0
1997–98	Barnsley	25	2		
1998–99	Barnsley	25	3		
1999–2000	Barnsley	33	4		
2000–01	Barnsley	0	0		
2001–02	Barnsley	16	0	99	9

WARD, Mitch (M) 233 12
H: 5 8 W: 11 08 b.Sheffield 19-6-71
Source: Trainee.

1989–90	Sheffield U	0	0		
1990–91	Sheffield U	4	0		
1990–91	Crewe Alex	4	1	4	1
1991–92	Sheffield U	6	2		
1992–93	Sheffield U	26	0		
1993–94	Sheffield U	22	1		
1994–95	Sheffield U	14	2		
1995–96	Sheffield U	42	1		
1996–97	Sheffield U	34	4		
1997–98	Sheffield U	6	1	154	11
1997–98	Everton	8	0		
1998–99	Everton	6	0		
1999–2000	Everton	10	0	24	0
2000–01	Barnsley	36	0		
2001–02	Barnsley	15	0	51	0

Scholars
Baker, Thomas; Black, Grant; Carrington, Richard J; Christie, Jeremy J; Cox, Christopher D; Greaves, Sean; Jones, Griffith T; Pearce, Allan D; Reece, Gary L; Scothern, Ashley; Sedgwick, Craig D; Selby, Callum S; Shackelton, Marc; Tonge, Dale; Williams, Robert; Wordsworth, Dean
Non-Contract
Rhodes, Andrew C

BIRMINGHAM C

ADEBOLA, Dele* (F) 258 70
H: 6 3 W: 15 00 b.Lagos 23-6-75
Source: Trainee.

1992–93	Crewe Alex	6	0		
1993–94	Crewe Alex	0	0		
1994–95	Crewe Alex	30	8		
1995–96	Crewe Alex	29	8		
1996–97	Crewe Alex	32	16		
1997–98	Crewe Alex	27	7	124	39
1997–98	Birmingham C	17	7		
1998–99	Birmingham C	39	13		
1999–2000	Birmingham C	42	5		
2000–01	Birmingham C	31	6		
2001–02	Birmingham C	0	0	129	31
2001–02	Oldham Ath	5	0	5	0

BAK, Arkadiusz‡ (M) 203 55
H: 5 9 W: 11 13 b.Poland 6-1-74
Honours: Poland 14 full caps.

1994–95	Olimpia	32	5		
1995–96	Olimpia	14	2	46	7
1995–96	Amica	16	4	16	4
1996–97	Polonia	14	2		
1997–98	Polonia	30	14		
1998–99	Polonia	28	7		
1999–2000	Polonia	22	4		
2000–01	Polonia	22	7		
2001–02	Polonia	13	6	129	40
2001–02	Widzew	8	4	8	4
2001–02	Birmingham C	4	0	4	0

BARROWMAN, Andrew (F) 0 0
H: 5 11 W: 11 06 b.Wishaw 27-11-84
Source: Scholar.

2001–02	Birmingham C	0	0		

BENNETT, Ian (G) 343 0
H: 6 0 W: 13 10 b.Worksop 10-10-71
Source: Newcastle U Trainee.

1991–92	Peterborough U	7	0		
1992–93	Peterborough U	46	0		
1993–94	Peterborough U	19	0	72	0
1993–94	Birmingham C	22	0		
1994–95	Birmingham C	46	0		
1995–96	Birmingham C	24	0		
1996–97	Birmingham C	40	0		
1997–98	Birmingham C	45	0		
1998–99	Birmingham C	10	0		
1999–2000	Birmingham C	21	0		

2000–01	Birmingham C	45	0		
2001–02	Birmingham C	18	0	271	0

CAPALDI, Tony (D) 0 0
H: 6 0 W: 11 06 b.Porsgrunn 12-8-81
Source: Trainee. *Honours:* Northern Ireland Under-21.

1999–2000	Birmingham C	0	0		
2000–01	Birmingham C	0	0		
2001–02	Birmingham C	0	0		

CARTER, Darren (M) 13 1
H: 6 2 W: 12 11 b.Solihull 18-12-83
Source: Scholar. *Honours:* England Youth.

2001–02	Birmingham C	13	1	13	1

DEVLIN, Paul (F) 382 78
H: 5 8 W: 11 08 b.Birmingham 14-4-72
Source: Stafford R.

1991–92	Notts Co	2	0		
1992–93	Notts Co	32	3		
1993–94	Notts Co	41	7		
1994–95	Notts Co	40	9		
1995–96	Notts Co	26	6		
1995–96	Birmingham C	16	7		
1996–97	Birmingham C	38	16		
1997–98	Birmingham C	22	5		
1997–98	Sheffield U	10	1		
1998–99	Sheffield U	33	5		
1998–99	Notts Co	5	0	146	25
1999–2000	Sheffield U	44	11		
2000–01	Sheffield U	41	5		
2001–02	Sheffield U	19	2	147	24
2001–02	Birmingham C	13	1	89	29

DIAMOND, Ross‡ (M) 0 0
b.Middlesbrough 3-12-81
Source: Scholar.

2001–02	Birmingham C	0	0		

EADEN, Nicky (D) 367 13
H: 5 9 W: 12 04 b.Sheffield 12-12-72
Source: Trainee.

1991–92	Barnsley	0	0		
1992–93	Barnsley	2	0		
1993–94	Barnsley	37	2		
1994–95	Barnsley	45	1		
1995–96	Barnsley	46	2		
1996–97	Barnsley	46	3		
1997–98	Barnsley	35	0		
1998–99	Barnsley	40	1		
1999–2000	Barnsley	42	1	293	10
2000–01	Birmingham C	45	2		
2001–02	Birmingham C	29	1	74	3

FAGAN, Craig (F) 0 0
H: 5 11 W: 11 09 b.Birmingham 11-12-82
Source: Scholar.

2001–02	Birmingham C	0	0		

FERRARI, Carlos‡ (M) 4 0
H: 6 0 W: 12 02 b.Londrina 19-2-79

2001–02	Birmingham C	4	0	4	0

FURLONG, Paul (F) 318 107
H: 6 0 W: 13 11 b.London 1-10-68
Source: Enfield.

1991–92	Coventry C	37	4	37	4
1992–93	Watford	41	19		
1993–94	Watford	38	18	79	37
1994–95	Chelsea	36	10		
1995–96	Chelsea	28	3	64	13
1996–97	Birmingham C	43	10		
1997–98	Birmingham C	25	15		
1998–99	Birmingham C	29	11		
1999–2000	Birmingham C	4	0		
2000–01	QPR	3	1	3	1
2001–02	Birmingham C	11	1	131	50
2001–02	Sheffield U	4	2	4	2

GILBERT, Peter§ (D) 0 0
H: 5 11 W: 12 13 b.Newcastle 31-7-83
Source: Scholar.

2001–02	Birmingham C	0	0		

GILL, Jeremy (D) 60 0
H: 5 11 W: 11 12 b.Clevedon 8-9-70
Source: Yeovil T.

1997–98	Birmingham C	3	0		
1998–99	Birmingham C	3	0		
1999–2000	Birmingham C	11	0		
2000–01	Birmingham C	29	0		
2001–02	Birmingham C	14	0	60	0

GRAINGER, Martin (D) 360 43
H: 5 10 W: 12 11 b.Enfield 23-8-72
Source: Trainee.

1989–90	Colchester U	7	2		
1990–91	Colchester U	0	0		
1991–92	Colchester U	0	0		
1992–93	Colchester U	31	3		
1993–94	Colchester U	8	2	46	7
1993–94	Brentford	31	2		
1994–95	Brentford	37	7		

1995–96	Brentford	33	3	101	12
1995–96	Birmingham C	8	0		
1996–97	Birmingham C	23	3		
1997–98	Birmingham C	33	2		
1998–99	Birmingham C	40	4		
1999–2000	Birmingham C	34	5		
2000–01	Birmingham C	35	6		
2001–02	Birmingham C	40	4	213	24

GRONDIN, Christophe (M)   0 0
b.Toulouse 2-9-83
Source: Toulouse.

2000–01	Birmingham C	0	0
2001–02	Birmingham C	0	0

HOLDSWORTH, David (D)   445 72
H: 6 1 W: 13 02 b.Walthamstow 8-11-68
Source: Trainee. Honours: England Youth, Under-21.

1986–87	Watford	0	0		
1987–88	Watford	0	0		
1988–89	Watford	33	1		
1989–90	Watford	44	3		
1990–91	Watford	15	2		
1991–92	Watford	33	2		
1992–93	Watford	39	0		
1993–94	Watford	28	0		
1994–95	Watford	39	1		
1995–96	Watford	27	1		
1996–97	Watford	0	0	258	10
1996–97	Sheffield U	37	1		
1997–98	Sheffield U	40	2		
1998–99	Sheffield U	16	1	93	4
1998–99	Birmingham C	8	1		
1999–2000	Birmingham C	44	5		
2000–01	Birmingham C	29	1		
2001–02	Birmingham C	4	0	85	7
2001–02	Walsall	9	1	9	1

HORSFIELD, Geoff (F)   155 48
H: 6 0 W: 11 07 b.Barnsley 1-11-73

1992–93	Scarborough	6	1		
1993–94	Scarborough	6	0	12	1

From Witton Alb

1998–99	Halifax T	10	7	10	7
1998–99	Fulham	28	15		
1999–2000	Fulham	31	7	59	22
2000–01	Birmingham C	34	7		
2001–02	Birmingham C	40	11	74	18

HUGHES, Bryan (M)   294 41
H: 5 11 W: 11 03 b.Liverpool 19-6-76
Source: Trainee.

1993–94	Wrexham	11	0		
1994–95	Wrexham	38	9		
1995–96	Wrexham	22	0		
1996–97	Wrexham	23	3	94	12
1996–97	Birmingham C	11	0		
1997–98	Birmingham C	40	5		
1998–99	Birmingham C	28	3		
1999–2000	Birmingham C	45	10		
2000–01	Birmingham C	45	4		
2001–02	Birmingham C	31	7	200	29

HUTCHINSON, Jonathan (D)   3 0
H: 5 11 W: 11 11 b.Middlesbrough 2-4-82
Source: Scholar.

2000–01	Birmingham C	0	0		
2001–02	Birmingham C	3	0	3	0

HYDE, Graham (M)   233 13
H: 5 7 W: 11 09 b.Doncaster 10-11-70
Source: Trainee.

1988–89	Sheffield W	0	0		
1989–90	Sheffield W	0	0		
1990–91	Sheffield W	0	0		
1991–92	Sheffield W	13	0		
1992–93	Sheffield W	20	1		
1993–94	Sheffield W	36	1		
1994–95	Sheffield W	35	5		
1995–96	Sheffield W	26	1		
1996–97	Sheffield W	19	2		
1997–98	Sheffield W	22	1		
1998–99	Sheffield W	1	0	172	11
1998–99	Birmingham C	13	0		
1999–2000	Birmingham C	31	1		
2000–01	Birmingham C	3	0		
2001–02	Birmingham C	5	0	52	1
2001–02	Chesterfield	9	1	9	1

JOHN, Stern (F)   142 69
H: 6 0 W: 12 11 b.Trinidad 30-10-76
Honours: Trinidad & Tobago 16 full caps, 8 goals.

1998	Columbus Crew	27	26		
1999	Columbus Crew	28	18	55	44
1999–2000	Nottingham F	17	3		
2000–01	Nottingham F	29	2		
2001–02	Nottingham F	26	13	72	18
2001–02	Birmingham C	15	7	15	7

JOHNSON, Andrew (F)   83 8
H: 5 7 W: 10 09 b.Bedford 10-2-81
Source: Trainee. Honours: England Youth, Under-20.

1997–98	Birmingham C	0	0		
1998–99	Birmingham C	4	0		
1999–2000	Birmingham C	22	1		
2000–01	Birmingham C	34	4		
2001–02	Birmingham C	23	3	83	8

JOHNSON, Damien (M)   74 4
H: 5 9 W: 11 09 b.Lisburn 18-11-78
Source: Trainee. Honours: Northern Ireland Youth, Under-21, 16 full caps.

1995–96	Blackburn R	0	0		
1996–97	Blackburn R	0	0		
1997–98	Blackburn R	0	0		
1997–98	Nottingham F	6	0	6	0
1998–99	Blackburn R	21	1		
1999–2000	Blackburn R	16	1		
2000–01	Blackburn R	16	0		
2001–02	Blackburn R	7	1	60	3
2001–02	Birmingham C	8	1	8	1

JOHNSON, Michael (D)   363 13
H: 5 11 W: 12 08 b.Nottingham 4-7-73
Source: Trainee. Honours: Jamaica 7 full caps.

1991–92	Notts Co	5	0		
1992–93	Notts Co	37	0		
1993–94	Notts Co	34	0		
1994–95	Notts Co	31	0		
1995–96	Notts Co	0	0	107	0
1995–96	Birmingham C	33	0		
1996–97	Birmingham C	35	0		
1997–98	Birmingham C	38	3		
1998–99	Birmingham C	45	5		
1999–2000	Birmingham C	34	2		
2000–01	Birmingham C	39	2		
2001–02	Birmingham C	32	1	256	13

KENNA, Jeff (D)   307 6
H: 5 11 W: 12 04 b.Dublin 27-8-70
Source: Trainee. Honours: Eire Youth, Under-21, B, 27 full caps.

1988–89	Southampton	0	0		
1989–90	Southampton	0	0		
1990–91	Southampton	2	0		
1991–92	Southampton	14	0		
1992–93	Southampton	29	2		
1993–94	Southampton	41	2		
1994–95	Southampton	28	0	114	4
1994–95	Blackburn R	9	1		
1995–96	Blackburn R	32	0		
1996–97	Blackburn R	37	0		
1997–98	Blackburn R	37	0		
1998–99	Blackburn R	23	0		
1999–2000	Blackburn R	11	0		
2000–01	Blackburn R	6	0		
2000–01	Tranmere R	11	0	11	0
2001–02	Blackburn R	0	0	155	1
2001–02	Wigan Ath	6	1	6	1
2001–02	Birmingham C	21	0	21	0

LAZARIDIS, Stan (M)   236 12
H: 5 9 W: 11 12 b.Perth 16-8-72
Honours: Australia 44 full caps.

1992–93	Adelaide Sharks	28	2		
1993–94	Adelaide Sharks	23	3		
1994–95	Adelaide Sharks	22	0	73	5
1995–96	West Ham U	4	0		
1996–97	West Ham U	22	1		
1997–98	West Ham U	28	2		
1998–99	West Ham U	15	0	69	3
1999–2000	Birmingham C	31	2		
2000–01	Birmingham C	31	2		
2001–02	Birmingham C	32	0	94	4

LUNTALA, Tresor (M)   15 0
H: 5 9 W: 10 11 b.Dreux 31-5-82

1999–2000	Birmingham C	0	0		
2000–01	Birmingham C	0	0		
2001–02	Birmingham C	15	0	15	0

McCARTHY, Jon* (M)   422 50
H: 5 9 W: 11 02 b.Middlesbrough 18-8-70
Honours: Northern Ireland B, 18 full caps.

1987–88	Hartlepool U	1	0	1	0

From Shepshed

1990–91	York C	27	2		
1991–92	York C	42	6		
1992–93	York C	42	7		
1993–94	York C	44	7		
1994–95	York C	44	9	199	31
1995–96	Port Vale	45	7		
1996–97	Port Vale	45	4		
1997–98	Port Vale	4	0	94	11
1997–98	Birmingham C	41	4		
1998–99	Birmingham C	43	0		
1999–2000	Birmingham C	21	4		
2000–01	Birmingham C	15	0		
2001–02	Birmingham C	0	0	124	8
2001–02	Sheffield W	4	0	4	0

MOONEY, Tommy (F)   404 108
H: 5 11 W: 13 08 b.Teeside North 11-8-71
Source: Trainee.

1989–90	Aston Villa	0	0		
1990–91	Scarborough	27	13		
1991–92	Scarborough	40	8		
1992–93	Scarborough	40	9	107	30
1993–94	Southend U	14	5	14	5
1993–94	Watford	10	2		
1994–95	Watford	29	3		
1995–96	Watford	42	6		
1996–97	Watford	37	13		
1997–98	Watford	45	6		
1998–99	Watford	36	9		
1999–2000	Watford	12	2		
2000–01	Watford	39	19	250	60
2001–02	Birmingham C	33	13	33	13

PARKER, Sonny (M)   0 0
b.Middlesbrough 28-2-83
Source: Trainee. Honours: England Youth.

1999–2000	Birmingham C	0	0
2000–01	Birmingham C	0	0
2001–02	Birmingham C	0	0

PURSE, Darren (D)   253 16
H: 6 2 W: 13 01 b.Stepney 14-2-76
Source: Trainee. Honours: England Under-21.

1993–94	Leyton Orient	5	0		
1994–95	Leyton Orient	38	3		
1995–96	Leyton Orient	12	0	55	3
1996–97	Oxford U	31	1		
1997–98	Oxford U	28	4	59	5
1997–98	Birmingham C	8	0		
1998–99	Birmingham C	38	2		
1999–2000	Birmingham C	38	2		
2000–01	Birmingham C	36	3	139	8

RANDRIANANTOANINA, Marco‡ (M)   0 0
b.Bourg La Reine 24-8-83

2000–01	Birmingham C	0	0
2001–02	Birmingham C	0	0

SABATHIER, Mickael‡ (M)   0 0
b.Auch 14-4-82
Source: Toulouse.

2000–01	Birmingham C	0	0
2001–02	Birmingham C	0	0

SADLER, Matthew (D)   0 0
H: 5 11 W: 11 05 b.Birmingham 26-2-85
Source: Scholar. Honours: England Youth.

2001–02	Birmingham C	0	0

SONNER, Danny* (M)   161 11
H: 6 0 W: 12 08 b.Wigan 9-1-72
Source: Wigan Ath. Honours: Northern Ireland B, 7 full caps.

1990–91	Burnley	2	0		
1991–92	Burnley	3	0		
1992–93	Burnley	1	0	6	0
1992–93	Bury	5	3	5	3

From Erzgebirge Aue

1996–97	Ipswich T	29	2		
1997–98	Ipswich T	23	1		
1998–99	Ipswich T	4	0	56	3
1998–99	Sheffield W	26	3		
1999–2000	Sheffield W	27	0	53	3
2000–01	Birmingham C	26	1		
2001–02	Birmingham C	15	1	41	2

TEBILY, Oliver (D)   64 1
H: 6 0 W: 13 05 b.Abidjan 19-12-75
Source: Chateauroux. Honours: Ivory Coast full caps.

1997–98	Chateauroux	11	1	11	1
1998–99	Sheffield U	8	0	8	0
1999–2000	Celtic	23	0		
2000–01	Celtic	4	0		
2001–02	Celtic	11	0	38	0
2001–02	Birmingham C	7	0	7	0

VAESEN, Nico (G)   207 0
H: 6 3 W: 12 13 b.Hasselt 28-9-69
Source: Tongeren.

1993–94	CS Brugge	13	0		
1994–95	CS Brugge	3	0	16	0
1995–96	Aalst	20	0		
1996–97	Aalst	14	0	34	0
1997–98	Aalst	14	0		
1998–99	Huddersfield T	43	0		
1999–2000	Huddersfield T	46	0		
2000–01	Huddersfield T	45	0	134	0
2001–02	Birmingham C	23	0	23	0

VICKERS, Steve (D)   590 20
H: 6 2 W: 12 10 b.Bishop Auckland 13-10-67
Source: Spennymoor U.

1985–86	Tranmere R	3	0
1986–87	Tranmere R	36	2

Season	Club				
1987–88	Tranmere R	46	1		
1988–89	Tranmere R	46	3		
1989–90	Tranmere R	42	3		
1990–91	Tranmere R	42	1		
1991–92	Tranmere R	43	1		
1992–93	Tranmere R	42	0		
1993–94	Tranmere R	11	0	**311**	**11**
1993–94	Middlesbrough	26	3		
1994–95	Middlesbrough	44	3		
1995–96	Middlesbrough	32	1		
1996–97	Middlesbrough	29	0		
1997–98	Middlesbrough	33	0		
1998–99	Middlesbrough	31	1		
1999–2000	Middlesbrough	32	0		
2000–01	Middlesbrough	30	0		
2001–02	Middlesbrough	2	0	**259**	**8**
2001–02	Crystal Palace	6	0	**6**	**0**
2001–02	Birmingham C	14	1	**14**	**1**

WARD, Chris (F) 0 0
H: 6 1 W: 11 00 b.Preston 28-4-81
Source: Lancaster C.

2000–01	Birmingham C	0	0
2001–02	Birmingham C	0	0

WILLIAMS, Jacques‡ (M) 3 0
H: 5 9 W: 11 00 b.Wallasey 25-4-81

1999–2000	Birmingham C	0	0		
2000–01	Birmingham C	3	0		
2001–02	Birmingham C	0	0	**3**	**0**

WILLIAMS, Tom (M) 40 2
H: 6 0 W: 11 13 b.Carshalton 8-7-80
Source: Walton & Hersham. *Honours:*

1999–2000	West Ham U	0	0		
2000–01	West Ham U	0	0		
2000–01	Peterborough U	2	0		
2001–02	Peterborough U	34	2	**36**	**2**
2001–02	Birmingham C	4	0	**4**	**0**

WOODHOUSE, Curtis (M) 149 8
H: 5 7 W: 12 02 b.Driffield 17-4-80
Source: Trainee. *Honours:* England Youth, Under-21.

1997–98	Sheffield U	9	0		
1998–99	Sheffield U	33	3		
1999–2000	Sheffield U	37	3		
2000–01	Sheffield U	25	0	**104**	**6**
2000–01	Birmingham C	17	2		
2001–02	Birmingham C	28	0	**45**	**2**

Scholars
Allen, Mark A; Alsop, Sam; Barnes, Neil; Beauchamp, James FV; Cartledge, Jon; Chisholm, Kelvin S; Cottrill, Christopher; Courtney, Duane; Davies, Clint; Doyle, Colin; Evans, Richard G; Gilbert, Peter; Hipkiss, Robert J; Longthorn, Paul D; Martin, James L; Motteram, Carl; Robertson, Daniel; Tearney, Trevor L

BLACKBURN R

BELL, Andrew (F) 0 0
b.Blackburn 12-2-84
Source: Scholar. *Honours:* England Youth.

2000–01	Blackburn R	0	0
2001–02	Blackburn R	0	0

BERG, Henning* (D) 342 9
H: 6 0 W: 12 07 b.Eidsvoll 1-9-69
Source: Lillestrom. *Honours:* Norway Under-21, 90 full caps, 9 goals.

1990	Viking	22	0		
1991	Viking	0	0	**22**	**0**
1992	Lillestrom	20	1	**20**	**1**
1992–93	Blackburn R	4	0		
1993–94	Blackburn R	41	1		
1994–95	Blackburn R	40	1		
1995–96	Blackburn R	38	0		
1996–97	Blackburn R	36	2		
1997–98	Manchester U	27	1		
1998–99	Manchester U	16	0		
1999–2000	Manchester U	22	1		
2000–01	Manchester U	1	0	**66**	**2**
2000–01	Blackburn R	41	1		
2001–02	Blackburn R	34	1	**234**	**6**

BJORNEBYE, Stig Inge (D) 310 11
H: 5 10 W: 11 09 b.Elverum 11-12-69
Honours: Norway 75 full caps, 1 goal.

1988	Strammen	19	0	**19**	**0**
1989	Kongsvinger	21	2		
1990	Kongsvinger	20	0		
1991	Kongsvinger	21	1	**62**	**3**
1992	Rosenborg	21	3	**21**	**3**
1992–93	Liverpool	11	0		
1993–94	Liverpool	9	0		
1994–95	Liverpool	31	0		
1995–96	Liverpool	2	0		
1996–97	Liverpool	38	2		
1997–98	Liverpool	25	0		
1998–99	Liverpool	23	0	**139**	**2**
1999–2000	Brondby	13	2	**13**	**2**
2000–01	Blackburn R	33	1		
2001–02	Blackburn R	23	0	**56**	**1**

BLAKEMAN, Liam* (M) 0 0
b.Southport 6-9-82
Source: Scholar.

1999–2000	Blackburn R	0	0
2000–01	Blackburn R	0	0
2001–02	Blackburn R	0	0

BURGESS, Ben (F) 45 17
H: 6 4 W: 14 05 b.Buxton 9-11-81
Source: Trainee.

1998–99	Blackburn R	0	0		
1999–2000	Blackburn R	2	0		
2000–01	Blackburn R	0	0		
2001–02	Blackburn R	0	0	**2**	**0**
2001–02	Brentford	43	17	**43**	**17**

COLE, Andy (F) 335 180
H: 5 11 W: 12 04 b.Nottingham 15-10-71
Source: Trainee. *Honours:* England Schools, Youth, Under-21, B, 15 full caps, 1 goal. Football League:

1989–90	Arsenal	0	0		
1990–91	Arsenal	1	0		
1991–92	Arsenal	0	0	**1**	**0**
1991–92	Fulham	13	3	**13**	**3**
1991–92	Bristol C	12	8		
1992–93	Bristol C	29	12	**41**	**20**
1992–93	Newcastle U	12	12		
1993–94	Newcastle U	40	34		
1994–95	Newcastle U	18	9	**70**	**55**
1994–95	Manchester U	18	12		
1995–96	Manchester U	34	11		
1996–97	Manchester U	20	6		
1997–98	Manchester U	33	15		
1998–99	Manchester U	32	17		
1999–2000	Manchester U	28	19		
2000–01	Manchester U	19	9		
2001–02	Manchester U	11	4	**195**	**93**
2001–02	Blackburn R	15	9	**15**	**9**

CORBETT, Jimmy (F) 16 2
H: 5 10 W: 12 00 b.Hackney 6-7-80
Source: Trainee.

1997–98	Gillingham	16	2	**16**	**2**
1998–99	Blackburn R	0	0		
1999–2000	Blackburn R	0	0		
2000–01	Blackburn R	0	0		
2001–02	Blackburn R	0	0		

CREASY, Neil* (M) 0 0
b.Barrow 18-11-82
Source: Scholar.

2001–02	Blackburn R	0	0

CUMMING, Stuart (M) 0 0
b.Aberdeen 30-1-85

2001–02	Blackburn R	0	0

CURTIS, John (D) 97 2
H: 5 10 W: 11 07 b.Nuneaton 3-9-78
Source: Trainee. *Honours:* England Schools, Youth, Under-21, B.

1995–96	Manchester U	0	0		
1996–97	Manchester U	0	0		
1997–98	Manchester U	8	0		
1998–99	Manchester U	4	0		
1999–2000	Manchester U	1	0	**13**	**0**
1999–2000	Barnsley	28	2	**28**	**2**
2000–01	Blackburn R	46	0		
2001–02	Blackburn R	10	0	**56**	**0**

DANNS, Neil (F) 0 0
b.Liverpool 23-11-82
Source: Scholar.

2000–01	Blackburn R	0	0
2001–02	Blackburn R	0	0

DONNELLY, Ciaran (M) 0 0
b.Blackpool 2-4-84
Source: Scholar. *Honours:* England Youth.

2001–02	Blackburn R	0	0

DOUGLAS, Jonathan (M) 0 0
H: 6 0 W: 12 07 b.Monaghan 22-11-81
Source: Trainee.

1999–2000	Blackburn R	0	0
2000–01	Blackburn R	0	0
2001–02	Blackburn R	0	0

DUFF, Damien (F) 158 18
H: 5 10 W: 12 00 b.Ballyboden 3-3-79
Source: Lourdes Celtic. *Honours:* Eire Youth, 30 full caps, 2 goals.

1995–96	Blackburn R	0	0
1996–97	Blackburn R	1	0
1997–98	Blackburn R	26	4
1998–99	Blackburn R	28	1
1999–2000	Blackburn R	39	5
2000–01	Blackburn R	32	1
2001–02	Blackburn R	32	7	**158**	**18**

DUNN, David (M) 108 22
H: 5 10 W: 12 05 b.Blackburn 27-12-79
Source: Trainee. *Honours:* England Youth, Under-21.

1997–98	Blackburn R	0	0		
1998–99	Blackburn R	15	1		
1999–2000	Blackburn R	22	2		
2000–01	Blackburn R	42	12		
2001–02	Blackburn R	29	7	**108**	**22**

DUNNING, Darren (M) 20 0
H: 5 7 W: 11 08 b.Scarborough 8-1-81
Source: Trainee.

1998–99	Blackburn R	0	0		
1999–2000	Blackburn R	0	0		
2000–01	Blackburn R	1	0		
2001–02	Bristol C	9	0	**9**	**0**
2001–02	Blackburn R	0	0	**1**	**0**
2001–02	Rochdale	5	0	**5**	**0**
2001–02	Blackpool	5	0	**5**	**0**

FITZGERALD, John (M) 0 0
b.Dublin 10-2-84
Source: Scholar.

2000–01	Blackburn R	0	0
2001–02	Blackburn R	0	0

FLITCROFT, Garry (M) 288 22
H: 6 1 W: 12 11 b.Bolton 6-11-72
Source: Trainee. *Honours:* England Schools, Under-21.

1991–92	Manchester C	0	0		
1991–92	Bury	12	0	**12**	**0**
1992–93	Manchester C	32	5		
1993–94	Manchester C	21	3		
1994–95	Manchester C	37	5		
1995–96	Blackburn R	25	0	**115**	**13**
1995–96	Blackburn R	3	0		
1996–97	Blackburn R	28	3		
1997–98	Blackburn R	33	0		
1998–99	Blackburn R	8	2		
1999–2000	Blackburn R	19	0		
2000–01	Blackburn R	41	3		
2001–02	Blackburn R	29	1	**161**	**9**

FRIEDEL, Brad (G) 126 0
H: 6 3 W: 14 00 b.Lakewood 18-5-71
Honours: USA 82 full caps.

1996	Columbus Crew	9	0		
1997	Columbus Crew	29	0	**38**	**0**
1997–98	Liverpool	11	0		
1998–99	Liverpool	12	0		
1999–2000	Liverpool	2	0		
2000–01	Liverpool	0	0	**25**	**0**
2000–01	Blackburn R	27	0		
2001–02	Blackburn R	36	0	**63**	**0**

GILLESPIE, Keith (F) 223 21
H: 5 10 W: 11 12 b.Larne 18-2-75
Source: Trainee. *Honours:* Northern Ireland Schools, Youth, Under-21, 41 full caps, 1 goal.

1992–93	Manchester U	0	0		
1993–94	Manchester U	0	0		
1993–94	Wigan Ath	8	4		
1994–95	Wigan Ath	9	1	**9**	**1**
1994–95	Newcastle U	17	2		
1995–96	Newcastle U	28	4		
1996–97	Newcastle U	32	1		
1997–98	Newcastle U	29	4		
1998–99	Newcastle U	7	0	**113**	**11**
1998–99	Blackburn R	16	1		
1999–2000	Blackburn R	22	2		
2000–01	Blackburn R	18	0		
2000–01	Wigan Ath	5	0	**13**	**4**
2001–02	Blackburn R	32	2	**88**	**5**

GRABBI, Corrado (F) 208 77
H: 5 11 W: 12 13 b.Turin 29-7-75

1993–94	Spartta Novara	31	8	**31**	**8**
1994–95	Juventus	2	1	**2**	**1**
1995–96	Lucchese	8	1	**8**	**1**
1995–96	Chievo	18	2	**18**	**2**
1996–97	Modena	31	15		
1997–98	Modena	27	14	**58**	**29**
1998–99	Ternana	14	2		
1999–2000	Ravenna	29	13	**29**	**13**
2000–01	Ternana	34	20	**48**	**22**
2001–02	Blackburn R	14	1	**14**	**1**

(On loan to Messina, January 2002).

GRAYSON, Simon* (M) 307 5
H: 6 0 W: 13 03 b.Ripon 16-12-69
Source: Trainee.

1987–88	Leeds U	2	0		
1988–89	Leeds U	0	0		
1989–90	Leeds U	0	0		
1990–91	Leeds U	0	0		
1991–92	Leeds U	0	0	**2**	**0**
1991–92	Leicester C	13	0		
1992–93	Leicester C	24	1		

1993–94	Leicester C	40	1		
1994–95	Leicester C	34	0		
1995–96	Leicester C	41	2		
1996–97	Leicester C	36	0	188	4
1997–98	Aston Villa	33	0		
1998–99	Aston Villa	15	0	48	0
1999–2000	Blackburn R	34	0		
2000–01	Blackburn R	0	0		
2000–01	*Sheffield W*	5	0	5	0
2000–01	*Stockport Co*	13	0	13	0
2001–02	Blackburn R	0	0	34	0
2001–02	*Notts Co*	10	1	10	1
2001–02	*Bradford C*	7	0	7	0

GREER, Gordon (D)   30   0
H: 6 2   W: 12 05   b.Glasgow 14-12-80
Source: Port Glasgow.

2000–01	Clyde	30	0	30	0
2000–01	Blackburn R	0	0		
2001–02	Blackburn R	0	0		

HEVICON, Ryan* (M)   0   0
b.Manchester 3-12-82
Source: Scholar.

2001–02	Blackburn R	0	0

HIGNETT, Craig (M)   406   112
H: 5 9   W: 11 10   b.Whiston 12-1-70
Source: Liverpool Trainee.

1987–88	Crewe Alex	0	0		
1988–89	Crewe Alex	0	0		
1989–90	Crewe Alex	35	8		
1990–91	Crewe Alex	38	13		
1991–92	Crewe Alex	33	13		
1992–93	Crewe Alex	14	8	121	42
1992–93	Middlesbrough	21	4		
1993–94	Middlesbrough	29	5		
1994–95	Middlesbrough	26	8		
1995–96	Middlesbrough	22	5		
1996–97	Middlesbrough	22	4		
1997–98	Middlesbrough	36	7	156	33
1998–99	Aberdeen	13	2	13	2
1998–99	Barnsley	24	9		
1999–2000	Barnsley	42	19	66	28
2000–01	Blackburn R	30	3		
2001–02	Blackburn R	20	4	50	7

HUGHES, Mark* (F)   606   163
H: 5 10   W: 13 04   b.Wrexham 1-11-63
Source: Apprentice. *Honours:* Wales Schools, Youth, Under-21, 72 full caps, 16 goals.

1980–81	Manchester U	0	0		
1981–82	Manchester U	0	0		
1982–83	Manchester U	0	0		
1983–84	Manchester U	11	4		
1984–85	Manchester U	38	16		
1985–86	Manchester U	40	17		
1986–87	Barcelona	28	4	28	4
1987–88	*Bayern Munich*	18	6	18	6
1988–89	Manchester U	38	14		
1989–90	Manchester U	37	13		
1990–91	Manchester U	31	10		
1991–92	Manchester U	39	11		
1992–93	Manchester U	41	15		
1993–94	Manchester U	36	11		
1994–95	Manchester U	34	8	345	119
1995–96	Chelsea	31	8		
1996–97	Chelsea	35	8		
1997–98	Chelsea	29	9	95	25
1998–99	Southampton	32	1		
1999–2000	Southampton	20	1	52	2
1999–2000	Everton	9	1		
2000–01	Everton	9	0	18	1
2001–02	Blackburn R	29	5		
2001–02	Blackburn R	21	1	50	6

JANSEN, Matt (F)   184   59
H: 5 11   W: 12 04   b.Carlisle 20-10-77
Source: Trainee. *Honours:* England Under-21.

1995–96	Carlisle U	0	0		
1996–97	Carlisle U	19	1		
1997–98	Carlisle U	23	9	42	10
1997–98	Crystal Palace	8	3		
1998–99	Crystal Palace	18	7	26	10
1998–99	Blackburn R	11	2		
1999–2000	Blackburn R	30	4		
2000–01	Blackburn R	40	23		
2001–02	Blackburn R	35	10	116	39

JOHANSSON, Nils-Eric (D)   30   0
H: 6 2   W: 13 03   b.Stockholm 13-1-80
Source: Viksjo, Brommapojkana.

1998	AIK Stockholm	0	0		
1998–99	Bayern Munich	2	0		
1999–2000	Bayern Munich	0	0		
2000–01	Bayern Munich	0	0	2	0
2001–02	Nuremberg	8	0	8	0
2001–02	Blackburn R	20	0	20	0

JOHNSON, Jemal (M)   0   0
b.New Jersey 3-5-84
Source: Scholar.

2001–02	Blackburn R	0	0

KELLY, Alan (G)   405   0
H: 6 2   W: 14 05   b.Preston 1-8-68
Source: Trainee. *Honours:* Eire Youth, Under-21, Under-23, 34 full caps.

1985–86	Preston NE	13	0		
1986–87	Preston NE	22	0		
1987–88	Preston NE	19	0		
1988–89	Preston NE	0	0		
1989–90	Preston NE	42	0		
1990–91	Preston NE	23	0		
1991–92	Preston NE	23	0	142	0
1992–93	Sheffield U	33	0		
1993–94	Sheffield U	30	0		
1994–95	Sheffield U	38	0		
1995–96	Sheffield U	35	0		
1996–97	Sheffield U	39	0		
1997–98	Sheffield U	19	0		
1998–99	Sheffield U	22	0	216	0
1999–2000	Blackburn R	30	0		
2000–01	Blackburn R	7	0		
2000–01	*Stockport Co*	2	0	2	0
2001–02	Blackburn R	2	0	39	0
2001–02	*Birmingham C*	6	0	6	0

MAHON, Alan (M)   152   14
H: 5 8   W: 11 10   b.Dublin 4-4-78
Source: Crumplin U. *Honours:* Eire Under-21, 2 full caps.

1994–95	Tranmere R	0	0		
1995–96	Tranmere R	2	0		
1996–97	Tranmere R	25	2		
1997–98	Tranmere R	18	1		
1998–99	Tranmere R	39	6		
1999–2000	Tranmere R	36	4	120	13
2000–01	Sporting Lisbon	1	0	1	0
2000–01	Blackburn R	18	0		
2001–02	Blackburn R	13	1	31	1

MARTIN, Anthony (M)   0   0
b.Dublin 20-9-83
Source: Scholar.

2000–01	Blackburn R	0	0
2001–02	Blackburn R	0	0

McLEAN, Matthew‡ (M)   0   0
b.Brighton 3-12-83
Source: School.

2000–01	Blackburn R	0	0
2001–02	Blackburn R	0	0

McNAMEE, David (D)   31   0
H: 5 11   W: 11 02   b.Glasgow 10-10-80
Source: St Mirren BC.

1998–99	St Mirren	31	0	31	0
1998–99	Blackburn R	0	0		
1999–2000	Blackburn R	0	0		
2000–01	Blackburn R	0	0		
2001–02	Blackburn R	0	0		

MILLER, Alan (G)   203   0
H: 6 4   W: 14 12   b.Epping 29-3-70
Source: Trainee. *Honours:* England Schools, FA Schools, Under-21.

1987–88	Arsenal	0	0		
1988–89	Arsenal	0	0		
1988–89	*Plymouth Arg*	13	0	13	0
1989–90	Arsenal	0	0		
1990–91	Arsenal	0	0		
1991–92	Arsenal	0	0		
1991–92	*WBA*	3	0		
1991–92	*Birmingham C*	15	0	15	0
1992–93	Arsenal	4	0		
1993–94	Arsenal	4	0	8	0
1994–95	Middlesbrough	41	0		
1995–96	Middlesbrough	6	0		
1996–97	Middlesbrough	10	0	57	0
1996–97	*Huddersfield T*	0	0		
1996–97	*Grimsby T*	3	0	3	0
1996–97	WBA	12	0		
1997–98	WBA	41	0		
1998–99	WBA	20	0		
1999–2000	WBA	25	0	101	0
1999–2000	*Blackburn R*	1	0		
2000–01	*Blackburn R*	0	0		
2000–01	*Bristol C*	4	0	4	0
2000–01	*Coventry C*	1	0	1	0
2001–02	Blackburn R	0	0	1	0

MORGAN, Alan (M)   0   0
b.Edinburgh 27-11-83
Source: Scholar.

2000–01	Blackburn R	0	0
2001–02	Blackburn R	0	0

NEILL, Lucas (M)   183   14
H: 6 1   W: 12 07   b.Sydney 9-3-78
Source: NSW Soccer Academy. *Honours:* Australia Youth, 2 full caps.

1995–96	Millwall	13	0
1996–97	Millwall	39	3
1997–98	Millwall	6	0
1998–99	Millwall	35	6
1999–2000	Millwall	31	1
2000–01	Millwall	24	2
2001–02	Millwall	4	1		
2001–02	Blackburn R	31	1	31	1

(Millwall total: 152   13)

O'BRIEN, Burton (F)   22   1
H: 5 10   W: 10 12   b.South Africa 10-6-81
Source: S Form. *Honours:* Scotland Youth, Under-21.

1998–99	St Mirren	22	1	22	1
1998–99	Blackburn R	0	0		
1999–2000	Blackburn R	0	0		
2000–01	Blackburn R	0	0		
2001–02	Blackburn R	0	0		

OSTENSTAD, Egil (F)   273   93
H: 6 0   W: 12 11   b.Haugesund 2-1-72
Honours: Norway 17 full caps, 6 goals.

1990	Viking	10	1		
1991	Viking	10	1		
1992	Viking	20	1		
1993	Viking	22	10		
1994	Viking	21	6		
1995	Viking	21	12		
1996	Viking	24	23	128	54
1996–97	Southampton	30	9		
1997–98	Southampton	29	11		
1998–99	Southampton	34	7		
1999–2000	Southampton	3	1	96	28
1999–2000	Blackburn R	28	8		
2000–01	Blackburn R	13	3		
2000–01	*Manchester C*	4	0	4	0
2001–02	Blackburn R	4	0	45	11

RENTON, Keiron (G)   0   0
b.Edinburgh 13-2-84
Source: Scholar.

2001–02	Blackburn R	0	0

RICHARDS, Marc (F)   14   0
H: 5 11   W: 12 12   b.Wolverhampton 8-7-82
Source: Trainee. *Honours:* England Youth, Under-20.

1999–2000	Blackburn R	0	0		
2000–01	Blackburn R	0	0		
2001–02	Blackburn R	0	0		
2001–02	*Crewe Alex*	4	0	4	0
2001–02	*Oldham Ath*	5	0	5	0
2001–02	*Halifax T*	5	0	5	0

ROBINSON, Ryan (G)   0   0
H: 6 2   W: 13 02   b.Cumbria 13-10-82
Source: Scholar.

2001–02	Blackburn R	0	0

SHORT, Craig (D)   482   27
H: 6 3   W: 13 12   b.Bridlington 25-6-68
Source: Pickering T. *Honours:* England Schools.

1987–88	Scarborough	21	2		
1988–89	Scarborough	42	5	63	7
1989–90	Notts Co	44	2		
1990–91	Notts Co	0	0		
1990–91	Notts Co	43	0		
1991–92	Notts Co	38	3		
1992–93	Notts Co	3	1	128	6
1992–93	Derby Co	38	3		
1993–94	Derby Co	43	3		
1994–95	Derby Co	37	3	118	9
1995–96	Everton	23	2		
1996–97	Everton	23	2		
1997–98	Everton	31	0		
1998–99	Everton	22	0	99	4
1999–2000	Blackburn R	17	0		
2000–01	Blackburn R	35	1		
2001–02	Blackburn R	22	0	74	1

TAYLOR, Martin (D)   55   3
H: 6 4   W: 15 00   b.Ashington 9-11-79
Source: Trainee. *Honours:* England Youth, Under-21.

1997–98	Blackburn R	0	0		
1998–99	Blackburn R	3	0		
1999–2000	Blackburn R	6	0		
1999–2000	*Darlington*	4	0	4	0
1999–2000	*Stockport Co*	7	0	7	0
2000–01	Blackburn R	16	3		
2001–02	Blackburn R	19	0	44	3

TAYLOR, Michael (M)   0   0
b.Liverpool 21-11-82
Source: Scholar.

1999–2000	Blackburn R	0	0
2000–01	Blackburn R	0	0
2001–02	Blackburn R	0	0

THOMAS, James* (F)   33   5
H: 6 1   W: 13 05   b.Swansea 16-1-79
Source: Trainee. *Honours:* Wales Under-21.

1996–97	Blackburn R	0	0		
1997–98	Blackburn R	0	0		
1997–98	*WBA*	3	0	3	0
1998–99	Blackburn R	0	0		
1999–2000	Blackburn R	0	0		

1999–2000	*Blackpool*	9	2	**9**	**2**
2000–01	Blackburn R	4	1		
2000–01	*Sheffield U*	10	1	**10**	**1**
2001–02	Blackburn R	0	0	**4**	**1**
2001–02	*Bristol R*	7	1	**7**	**1**

TUGAY, Kerimoglu (M) 350 41
H: 5 9 W: 11 00 b.Istanbul 24-8-70
Honours: Turkey 74 full caps, 2 goals.

1988–89	Galatasaray	16	0		
1989–90	Galatasaray	23	0		
1990–91	Galatasaray	12	0		
1991–92	Galatasaray	26	3		
1992–93	Galatasaray	25	6		
1993–94	Galatasaray	25	12		
1994–95	Galatasaray	23	1		
1995–96	Galatasaray	30	3		
1996–97	Galatasaray	33	4		
1997–98	Galatasaray	30	2		
1998–99	Galatasaray	22	2		
1999–2000	Galatasaray	10	1	**275**	**34**
1999–2000	Rangers	16	1		
2000–01	Rangers	26	3	**42**	**4**
2001–02	Blackburn R	33	3	**33**	**3**

UNSAL, Hakan (M) 163 11
H: 5 10 W: 13 01 b.Sinop 14-5-73
Honours: Turkey 29 full caps.

1995–96	Galatasaray	28	1		
1996–97	Galatasaray	29	2		
1997–98	Galatasaray	27	3		
1998–99	Galatasaray	31	3		
1999–2000	Galatasaray	16	1		
2000–01	Galatasaray	16	1		
2001–02	Galatasaray	8	0	**155**	**11**
2001–02	Blackburn R	8	0	**8**	**0**

WATT, Jerome (M) 0 0
b.Preston 20-10-84
Source: Scholar. *Honours:* England Youth.

2001–02	Blackburn R	0	0		

YORDI‡ (F) 236 82
H: 6 1 W: 13 07 b.San Fernando 14-9-74
Source: San Fernando.

1993–94	Sevilla B	14	8		
1994–95	Sevilla B	26	7		
1995–96	Sevilla B	29	16	**69**	**31**
1996–97	Sevilla	6	1	**6**	**1**
1996–97	Atletico Madrid B	34	19	**34**	**19**
1996–97	Atletico Madrid	1	0	**1**	**0**
1997–98	Zaragoza	30	5		
1998–99	Zaragoza	16	5		
1999–2000	Zaragoza	23	9		
2000–01	Zaragoza	31	4		
2001–02	Zaragoza	18	6	**118**	**29**
2001–02	Blackburn R	8	2	**8**	**2**

Trainees
Black, Ian; Bruce, Alex; Cole, Michael J; Cumming, Stuart; Francis, Carl; Gallagher, Paul; Harkins, Gary; Hockenhull, Darren; Howard, Philip; Kebe, Yahia; Marsden, Mark; McEveley, James; McKay, Ross; Nelson, Adam; Stevenson, David WN; Whelan, Daniel

BLACKPOOL

BARNES, Phil (G) 80 0
H: 6 1 W: 11 01 b.Sheffield 2-3-79
Source: Trainee.

1996–97	Rotherham U	2	0	**2**	**0**
1997–98	Blackpool	1	0		
1998–99	Blackpool	1	0		
1999–2000	Blackpool	12	0		
2000–01	Blackpool	34	0		
2001–02	Blackpool	30	0	**78**	**0**

BLINKHORN, Matthew§ (F) 3 0
H: 6 0 W: 10 10 b.Blackpool 2-3-85
Source: Scholar.

2001–02	Blackpool	3	0	**3**	**0**

BULLOCK, Martin (M) 234 7
H: 5 5 W: 10 07 b.Derby 5-3-75
Source: Eastwood T. *Honours:* England Under-21.

1993–94	Barnsley	0	0		
1994–95	Barnsley	29	0		
1995–96	Barnsley	41	1		
1996–97	Barnsley	28	0		
1997–98	Barnsley	33	0		
1998–99	Barnsley	32	2		
1999–2000	Barnsley	4	0		
1999–2000	*Port Vale*	6	1	**6**	**1**
2000–01	Barnsley	18	1		
2001–02	Barnsley	0	0	**185**	**4**
2001–02	Blackpool	43	2	**43**	**2**

CLARKE, Chris (D) 62 1
H: 6 3 W: 12 02 b.Leeds 18-12-80
Source: Wolverhampton W Trainee.

1999–2000	Halifax T	1	0		
2000–01	Halifax T	26	1		
2001–02	Halifax T	24	0	**51**	**1**
2001–02	Blackpool	11	0	**11**	**0**

COID, Danny (M) 95 5
H: 5 11 W: 11 07 b.Liverpool 3-10-81
Source: Trainee.

1998–99	Blackpool	1	0		
1999–2000	Blackpool	21	1		
2000–01	Blackpool	46	1		
2001–02	Blackpool	27	3	**95**	**5**

COLLINS, Lee (M) 168 5
H: 5 8 W: 11 06 b.Bellshill 3-2-74
Source: Possil U.

1993–94	Albion R	20	0		
1994–95	Albion R	17	0		
1995–96	Albion R	8	1	**45**	**1**
1995–96	Swindon T	5	0		
1996–97	Swindon T	4	0		
1997–98	Swindon T	26	1		
1998–99	Swindon T	4	0		
1999–2000	Swindon T	24	1	**63**	**2**
2000–01	Blackpool	28	0		
2001–02	Blackpool	32	2	**60**	**2**

FENTON, Graham (F) 155 25
H: 5 10 W: 12 10 b.Wallsend 22-5-74
Source: Trainee. *Honours:* England Under-21.

1991–92	Aston Villa	0	0		
1992–93	Aston Villa	0	0		
1993–94	Aston Villa	12	1		
1993–94	*WBA*	7	3	**7**	**3**
1994–95	Aston Villa	17	2		
1995–96	Aston Villa	3	0	**32**	**3**
1995–96	Blackburn R	14	6		
1996–97	Blackburn R	13	1	**27**	**7**
1997–98	Leicester C	23	3		
1998–99	Leicester C	9	0		
1999–2000	Leicester C	2	0	**34**	**3**
1999–2000	Walsall	9	1	**9**	**1**
2000–01	Stoke C	5	1	**5**	**1**
2000–01	St Mirren	26	2	**26**	**2**
2001–02	Blackpool	15	5	**15**	**5**

HILLS, John (M) 156 12
H: 5 9 W: 11 02 b.St Annes-on-Sea 22-4-78
Source: Trainee.

1995–96	Blackpool	0	0		
1995–96	Everton	0	0		
1996–97	Everton	3	0		
1996–97	*Swansea C*	11	0		
1997–98	Everton	0	0	**3**	**0**
1997–98	*Swansea C*	7	1	**18**	**1**
1997–98	Blackpool	19	1		
1998–99	Blackpool	28	1		
1999–2000	Blackpool	33	2		
2000–01	Blackpool	18	2		
2001–02	Blackpool	37	5	**135**	**11**

HUGHES, Ian (D) 317 4
H: 5 10 W: 12 08 b.Bangor 2-8-74
Source: Trainee. *Honours:* Wales Youth, Under-21.

1991–92	Bury	17	0		
1992–93	Bury	15	0		
1992–93	Bury	15	0		
1993–94	Bury	38	0		
1994–95	Bury	23	1		
1995–96	Bury	32	0		
1996–97	Bury	22	0		
1997–98	Bury	13	0	**175**	**1**
1997–98	Blackpool	21	0		
1998–99	Blackpool	33	1		
1999–2000	Blackpool	34	0		
2000–01	Blackpool	34	1		
2001–02	Blackpool	20	1	**142**	**3**

JASZCZUN, Tommy (D) 94 0
H: 5 10 W: 10 10 b.Kettering 16-9-77
Source: Trainee.

1996–97	Aston Villa	0	0		
1997–98	Aston Villa	0	0		
1998–99	Aston Villa	0	0		
1999–2000	Aston Villa	0	0		
1999–2000	Blackpool	19	0		
2000–01	Blackpool	35	0		
2001–02	Blackpool	40	0	**94**	**0**

JONES, Eifion* (D) 8 0
H: 6 3 W: 13 00 b.Caernarfon 28-9-80
Source: Trainee. *Honours:* Wales Youth, Under-21.

1997–98	Liverpool	0	0		
1998–99	Liverpool	0	0		
1999–2000	Liverpool	0	0		
1999–2000	Blackpool	1	0		
2000–01	Blackpool	7	0		
2001–02	Blackpool	0	0	**8**	**0**

MACKENZIE, Neil (M) 111 6
H: 6 2 W: 12 12 b.Birmingham 15-4-76
Source: WBA schoolboy.

1996–97	Stoke C	22	1		
1997–98	Stoke C	12	0		
1998–99	Stoke C	6	0		
1998–99	*Cambridge U*	4	1		
1999–2000	Stoke C	2	0	**42**	**1**
1999–2000	Cambridge U	22	0		
2000–01	Cambridge U	6	0	**32**	**1**
2000–01	Kidderminster H	23	3	**23**	**3**
2001–02	Blackpool	14	1	**14**	**1**

MARSHALL, Ian* (D) 411 94
H: 6 2 W: 14 09 b.Liverpool 20-3-66
Source: Apprentice.

1983–84	Everton	0	0		
1984–85	Everton	0	0		
1985–86	Everton	9	0		
1986–87	Everton	2	1		
1987–88	Everton	4	0	**15**	**1**
1987–88	Oldham Ath	10	0		
1988–89	Oldham Ath	41	4		
1989–90	Oldham Ath	25	3		
1990–91	Oldham Ath	26	17		
1991–92	Oldham Ath	41	10		
1992–93	Oldham Ath	27	2	**170**	**36**
1993–94	Ipswich T	29	10		
1994–95	Ipswich T	18	3		
1995–96	Ipswich T	35	19		
1996–97	Ipswich T	2	0	**84**	**32**
1996–97	Leicester C	28	8		
1997–98	Leicester C	24	7		
1998–99	Leicester C	10	3		
1999–2000	Leicester C	21	0	**83**	**18**
2000–01	Bolton W	36	6		
2001–02	Bolton W	2	0	**38**	**6**
2001–02	Blackpool	21	1	**21**	**1**

MILLIGAN, Jamie (M) 27 0
H: 5 6 W: 9 12 b.Blackpool 3-1-80
Source: Trainee. *Honours:* England Youth.

1997–98	Everton	0	0		
1998–99	Everton	3	0		
1999–2000	Everton	1	0		
2000–01	Everton	0	0	**4**	**0**
2000–01	Blackpool	6	0		
2001–02	Blackpool	17	0	**23**	**0**

MILLIGAN, Mike* (M) 448 30
H: 5 8 W: 11 00 b.Manchester 20-2-67
Source: Trainee. *Honours:* Eire Under-21, B, 1 full cap.

1984–85	Oldham Ath	0	0		
1985–86	Oldham Ath	5	1		
1986–87	Oldham Ath	38	2		
1987–88	Oldham Ath	39	1		
1988–89	Oldham Ath	39	6		
1989–90	Oldham Ath	41	7		
1990–91	Everton	17	1	**17**	**1**
1991–92	Oldham Ath	36	3		
1992–93	Oldham Ath	42	3		
1993–94	Oldham Ath	39	0	**279**	**23**
1994–95	Norwich C	26	2		
1995–96	Norwich C	28	2		
1996–97	Norwich C	37	1		
1997–98	Norwich C	20	0		
1998–99	Norwich C	2	0		
1999–2000	Norwich C	11	0	**124**	**5**
2000–01	Blackpool	26	1		
2001–02	Blackpool	2	0	**28**	**1**

MURPHY, John (F) 225 61
H: 6 2 W: 14 00 b.Whiston 18-10-76
Source: Trainee.

1994–95	Chester C	5	0		
1995–96	Chester C	18	3		
1996–97	Chester C	11	1		
1997–98	Chester C	27	4		
1998–99	Chester C	42	12	**103**	**20**
1999–2000	Blackpool	39	10		
2000–01	Blackpool	46	18		
2001–02	Blackpool	37	13	**122**	**41**

MURPHY, Neil* (D) 7 0
H: 5 9 W: 11 00 b.Liverpool 19-5-80
Source: Trainee. *Honours:* England Youth.

1997–98	Liverpool	0	0		
1998–99	Liverpool	0	0		
1999–2000	Liverpool	0	0		
2000–01	Blackpool	6	0		
2001–02	Blackpool	1	0	**7**	**0**

O'CONNOR, Jon* (D) 20 0
H: 5 11 W: 11 12 b.Darlington 29-10-76
Source: Trainee. *Honours:* England Youth, Under-21.

1993–94	Everton	0	0		
1994–95	Everton	0	0		
1995–96	Everton	4	0		

1996–97	Everton	0	0		
1997–98	Everton	1	0	5	0
1997–98	Sheffield U	2	0		
1998–99	Sheffield U	2	0		
1999–2000	Sheffield U	0	0		
2000–01	Sheffield U	0	0	4	0
2000–01	Blackpool	11	0		
2001–02	Blackpool	0	0	11	0

O'KANE, John (D)   120 9
H: 5 10 W: 12 02 b.Nottingham 15-11-74
Source: Trainee.

1992–93	Manchester U	0	0		
1993–94	Manchester U	0	0		
1994–95	Manchester U	0	0		
1994–95	Wimbledon	0	0		
1995–96	Manchester U	1	0		
1996–97	Manchester U	1	0		
1996–97	*Bury*	13	3	13	3
1997–98	Manchester U	0	0	2	0
1997–98	*Bradford C*	7	0	7	0
1997–98	Everton	12	0		
1998–99	Everton	2	0		
1998–99	*Burnley*	8	0	8	0
1999–2000	Everton	0	0	14	0
1999–2000	Bolton W	11	1		
2000–01	Bolton W	27	1	38	2
2001–02	Blackpool	38	4	38	4

PARKINSON, Gary* (D)   454 15
H: 5 11 W: 11 10 b.Middlesbrough 10-1-68
Source: Everton Amateur.

1985–86	Middlesbrough	0	0		
1986–87	Middlesbrough	46	0		
1987–88	Middlesbrough	38	0		
1988–89	Middlesbrough	36	2		
1989–90	Middlesbrough	41	2		
1990–91	Middlesbrough	10	1		
1991–92	Middlesbrough	27	0		
1992–93	Middlesbrough	4	0	202	5
1992–93	*Southend U*	6	0	6	0
1992–93	Bolton W	2	0		
1993–94	Bolton W	1	0	3	0
1993–94	Burnley	20	1		
1994–95	Burnley	43	2		
1995–96	Burnley	29	0		
1996–97	Burnley	43	1	135	4
1997–98	Preston NE	45	5		
1998–99	Preston NE	27	1		
1999–2000	Preston NE	1	0		
2000–01	Preston NE	11	0	84	6
2000–01	Blackpool	9	0		
2001–02	Blackpool	15	0	24	0

REID, Brian (D)   111 8
H: 6 2 W: 11 12 b.Paisley 15-6-70

1998–99	Burnley	31	3	31	3
1999–2000	Dunfermline Ath	23	3		
2000–01	Dunfermline Ath	2	0	25	3
2000–01	Blackpool	29	2		
2001–02	Blackpool	26	0	55	2

TAYLOR, Scott (F)   208 28
H: 5 10 W: 11 06 b.Chertsey 5-5-76
Source: Staines T.

1994–95	Millwall	6	0		
1995–96	Millwall	22	0	28	0
1995–96	Bolton W	1	0		
1996–97	Bolton W	11	1		
1997–98	Bolton W	0	0		
1997–98	*Rotherham U*	10	3	10	3
1997–98	*Blackpool*	5	1		
1998–99	Bolton W	0	0	12	1
1998–99	Tranmere R	36	9		
1999–2000	Tranmere R	35	3		
2000–01	Tranmere R	37	5	108	17
2001–02	Stockport Co	28	4	28	4
2001–02	Blackpool	17	2	22	3

THOMPSON, Phil* (D)   47 3
H: 5 11 W: 12 00 b.Blackpool 1-4-81
Source: Trainee.

1997–98	Blackpool	1	0		
1998–99	Blackpool	22	2		
1999–2000	Blackpool	3	0		
2000–01	Blackpool	8	0		
2001–02	Blackpool	13	1	47	3

WALKER, Richard (F)   78 19
H: 6 0 W: 12 00 b.Sutton Coldfield 8-11-77
Source: Trainee.

1995–96	Aston Villa	0	0		
1996–97	Aston Villa	0	0		
1997–98	Aston Villa	1	0		
1998–99	Aston Villa	0	0		
1998–99	*Cambridge U*	21	3	21	3
1999–2000	Aston Villa	5	2		
2000–01	Aston Villa	0	0		
2000–01	*Blackpool*	18	3		
2001–02	Aston Villa	0	0	6	2
2001–02	*Wycombe W*	12	3	12	3
2001–02	Blackpool	21	8	39	11

WELLENS, Richard (M)   80 9
H: 5 9 W: 11 06 b.Manchester 26-3-80
Source: Trainee. Honours: England Youth.

1996–97	Manchester U	0	0		
1997–98	Manchester U	0	0		
1998–99	Manchester U	0	0		
1999–2000	Manchester U	0	0		
1999–2000	Blackpool	8	0		
2001–02	Blackpool	36	8		
2001–02	Blackpool	36	1	80	9

Scholars
Blinkhorn, Matthew D; Burns, Jamie D;
Carroll, John D; Connors, John J ; Fenech,
Jonathan; Gordon, William D; Heffernan,
Guy; Maden, Wayne T; McInally, Garry;
McMahon, Stephen J; Robinson, Craig;
Robinson, Daniel M; Russell, Mark P; Swan,
Mark L; Wiles, Simon

BOLTON W

BALDACCHINO, Ryan (M)   0 0
H: 5 9 W: 12 03 b.Leicester 13-1-81
Source: Trainee.

1999–2000	Blackburn R	0	0		
1999–2000	Blackburn R	0	0		
2000–01	Blackburn R	0	0		
2001–02	Bolton W	0	0		

BANKS, Steve (G)   253 0
H: 6 0 W: 13 12 b.Hillingdon 9-2-72
Source: Trainee.

1991–92	West Ham U	0	0		
1991–92	West Ham U	0	0		
1993–94	Gillingham	29	0		
1994–95	Gillingham	38	0	67	0
1995–96	Blackpool	24	0		
1996–97	Blackpool	46	0		
1997–98	Blackpool	45	0		
1998–99	Blackpool	35	0	150	0
1998–99	Bolton W	9	0		
1999–2000	Bolton W	2	0		
2000–01	Bolton W	9	0		
2001–02	Bolton W	1	0	21	0
2001–02	*Rochdale*	15	0	15	0

BARNESS, Anthony (D)   187 4
H: 5 11 W: 11 10 b.Lewisham 25-3-73
Source: Trainee.

1990–91	Charlton Ath	0	0		
1991–92	Charlton Ath	22	1		
1992–93	Charlton Ath	5	0		
1992–93	Chelsea	2	0		
1993–94	Chelsea	0	0		
1993–94	*Middlesbrough*	0	0		
1994–95	Chelsea	12	0		
1995–96	Chelsea	0	0	14	0
1995–96	*Southend U*	5	0	5	0
1996–97	Charlton Ath	45	2		
1997–98	Charlton Ath	29	1		
1998–99	Charlton Ath	3	0		
1999–2000	Charlton Ath	19	0	123	4
2000–01	Bolton W	20	0		
2001–02	Bolton W	25	0	45	0

BERGSSON, Gudni* (D)   310 24
H: 6 1 W: 12 11 b.Reykjavik 21-7-65
Source: Valur. Honours: Iceland Youth,
Under-21, 77 full caps, 1 goal.

1988–89	Tottenham H	8	0		
1989–90	Tottenham H	18	0		
1990–91	Tottenham H	12	1		
1991–92	Tottenham H	28	1		
1992–93	Tottenham H	5	0		
1993–94	Tottenham H	0	0	71	2
1994–95	Bolton W	8	0		
1995–96	Bolton W	34	4		
1996–97	Bolton W	33	3		
1997–98	Bolton W	35	2		
1998–99	Bolton W	17	0		
1999–2000	Bolton W	38	4		
2000–01	Bolton W	44	8		
2001–02	Bolton W	30	1	239	22

BOBIC, Fredi‡ (F)   282 116
H: 6 2 W: 12 03 b.Maribor 30-10-71
Honours: Germany 19 full caps, 2 goals.

1992–93	Stuttgart Kickers	30	10		
1993–94	Stuttgart Kickers	32	16	66	26
1994–95	Stuttgart	32	12		
1995–96	Stuttgart	26	17		
1996–97	Stuttgart	33	19		
1997–98	Stuttgart	29	13		
1998–99	Stuttgart	28	8	148	69
1999–2000	Borussia Dortmund	29	7		
2000–01	Borussia Dortmund	24	10		
2001–02	Borussia Dortmund	3	0	56	17
2001–02	Bolton W	16	4	16	4

BON, Jeremy (G)   0 0
b.Begles 21-10-84
Source: Bordeaux.

| 2001–02 | Bolton W | 0 | 0 | | |

BUCHANAN, Wayne (D)   3 0
H: 6 1 W: 13 02 b.Bambridge 12-1-82
Source: Scholar. Honours: Northern Ireland
Under-21.

| 2001–02 | Bolton W | 0 | 0 | | |
| 2001–02 | *Chesterfield* | 3 | 0 | 3 | 0 |

CASSAR, Jeff* (G)   0 0
b.Michigan 2-2-74

| 2001–02 | Bolton W | 0 | 0 | | |

CHARLTON, Simon (D)   368 3
H: 5 8 W: 11 00 b.Huddersfield 25-10-71
Source: Trainee. Honours: FA Schools.

1989–90	Huddersfield T	3	0		
1990–91	Huddersfield T	30	0		
1991–92	Huddersfield T	45	0		
1992–93	Huddersfield T	46	1	124	1
1993–94	Southampton	33	1		
1994–95	Southampton	25	1		
1995–96	Southampton	26	0		
1996–97	Southampton	27	0		
1997–98	Southampton	3	0	114	2
1998–99	Birmingham C	28	0		
1997–98	Birmingham C	24	0		
1999–2000	Birmingham C	20	0	72	0
2000–01	Bolton W	22	0		
2001–02	Bolton W	36	0	58	0

DIAWARA, Djibril‡ (D)   112 1
H: 6 1 W: 12 03 b.Dakar 3-1-75

1994–95	Le Havre	11	1		
1995–96	Le Havre	24	0		
1996–97	Le Havre	23	0	58	1
1997–98	Monaco	11	0		
1998–99	Monaco	13	0	24	0
1999–2000	Torino	14	0		
2000–01	Torino	7	0	21	0
2001–02	Bolton W	9	0	9	0

DJORKAEFF, Youri* (M)   460 169
H: 5 10 W: 11 05 b.Lyon 9-3-68
Honours: France 82 full caps, 28 goals.

1984–85	Grenoble	0	0		
1985–86	Grenoble	6	0		
1986–87	Grenoble	26	4		
1987–88	Grenoble	19	8		
1988–89	Grenoble	25	11		
1989–90	Grenoble	3	0	81	23
1989–90	Strasbourg	28	21		
1990–91	Strasbourg	7	4	35	25
1990–91	Monaco	20	5		
1991–92	Monaco	35	9		
1992–93	Monaco	32	12		
1993–94	Monaco	35	20		
1994–95	Monaco	33	14	155	60
1995–96	Paris St Germain	35	13	35	13
1996–97	Internazionale	33	14		
1997–98	Internazionale	29	8		
1998–99	Internazionale	25	8	87	30
1999–2000	Kaiserslautern	25	11		
2000–01	Kaiserslautern	26	3		
2001–02	Kaiserslautern	4	0	55	14
2001–02	Bolton W	12	4	12	4

DOWNEY, Chris (F)   1 0
H: 5 10 W: 9 11 b.Warrington 19-4-83
Source: Scholar.

| 2000–01 | Bolton W | 1 | 0 | | |
| 2001–02 | Bolton W | 0 | 0 | 1 | 0 |

ESPARTERO, Mario‡ (M)   77 8
H: 5 8 W: 11 01 b.Frejus 17-1-78

1997–98	Louhans	21	2		
1998–99	Louhans	5	2		
1999–2000	Louhans	26	2	52	6
2000–01	Metz	10	2		
2001–02	Metz	12	0	22	2
2001–02	Bolton W	3	0	3	0

FARRELLY, Gareth (M)   115 7
H: 6 1 W: 13 07 b.Dublin 28-8-75
Source: Home Farm. Honours: Eire Under-21, 6 full caps.

1992–93	Aston Villa	0	0		
1993–94	Aston Villa	0	0		
1994–95	Aston Villa	0	0		
1994–95	*Rotherham U*	10	2	10	2
1995–96	Aston Villa	5	0		
1996–97	Aston Villa	3	0	8	0
1997–98	Everton	26	1		
1998–99	Everton	1	0		
1999–2000	Everton	0	0	27	1
1999–2000	Bolton W	11	1		
2000–01	Bolton W	41	3		
2001–02	Bolton W	18	0	70	4

FORSCHELET, Gerald (D)   0   0
b.Papeete 19-9-81
Source: Cannes.
2001–02   Bolton W   0   0

FRANDSEN, Per (M)   418   85
H: 5 11   W: 12 10   b.Copenhagen 6-2-70
Honours: Denmark 20 full caps.
1990   B 1903   25   15   25   15
1990–91   Lille   19   4
1991–92   Lille   27   8
1992–93   Lille   32   3
1993–94   Lille   31   4   109   19
1994–95   FC Copenhagen   29   12
1995–96   FC Copenhagen   26   7   55   19
1996–97   Bolton W   41   5
1997–98   Bolton W   38   2
1998–99   Bolton W   44   8
1999–2000   Bolton W   7   2
1999–2000   Blackburn R   31   5   31   5
2000–01   Bolton W   39   7
2001–02   Bolton W   29   3   198   27

GARDNER, Ricardo (M)   122   13
H: 5 9   W: 11 01   b.St Andrews 25-9-78
Source: Harbour View. *Honours:* Jamaica 37 full caps.
1998–99   Bolton W   30   2
1999–2000   Bolton W   29   5
2000–01   Bolton W   32   3
2001–02   Bolton W   31   3   122   13

HANSEN, Bo (M)   198   58
H: 6 1   W: 12 02   b.Jutland 16-6-72
Honours: Denmark 1 full cap.
1994–95   Brondby   31   11
1995–96   Brondby   14   4
1996–97   Brondby   20   2
1997–98   Brondby   21   14
1998–99   Brondby   16   12   102   43
1998–99   Bolton W   8   0
1999–2000   Bolton W   30   9
2000–01   Bolton W   41   5
2001–02   Bolton W   17   1   96   15

HENDRY, Colin (D)   497   44
H: 6 1   W: 12 07   b.Keith 7-12-65
Source: Islavale. *Honours:* Scotland B, 51 full caps, 3 goals.
1983–84   Dundee   4   0
1984–85   Dundee   4   0
1985–86   Dundee   20   0
1986–87   Dundee   13   2   41   2
1986–87   Blackburn R   13   3
1987–88   Blackburn R   44   12
1988–89   Blackburn R   38   7
1989–90   Blackburn R   7   0
1989–90   Manchester C   25   3
1990–91   Manchester C   32   1
1991–92   Manchester C   6   1   63   5
1991–92   Blackburn R   30   4
1992–93   Blackburn R   41   1
1993–94   Blackburn R   23   0
1994–95   Blackburn R   38   4
1995–96   Blackburn R   33   1
1996–97   Blackburn R   35   1
1997–98   Blackburn R   34   1   336   34
1998–99   Rangers   19   0   19   0
1999–2000   Coventry C   9   0
2000–01   Coventry C   2   0   11   0
2000–01   Bolton W   22   3
2001–02   Bolton W   3   0   25   3
2001–02   Preston NE   2   0   2   0

HOLDEN, Dean (D)   36   3
H: 6 0   W: 12 03   b.Salford 15-9-79
Source: Trainee. *Honours:* England Youth.
1997–98   Bolton W   0   0
1998–99   Bolton W   0   0
1999–2000   Bolton W   12   0
2000–01   Bolton W   1   1
2001–02   Bolton W   0   0   13   1
2001–02   *Oldham Ath*   23   2   23   2

HOLDSWORTH, Dean (F)   466   158
H: 5 11   W: 13 06   b.Walthamstow 8-11-68
Source: Trainee.
1986–87   Watford   2   0
1987–88   *Carlisle U*   4   1   4   1
1987–88   *Port Vale*   6   2   6   2
1988–89   Watford   10   2
1988–89   *Swansea C*   5   1   5   1
1988–89   *Brentford*   7   1
1989–90   Watford   4   1   16   3
1989–90   Brentford   39   24
1990–91   Brentford   30   5
1991–92   Brentford   41   24   117   54
1992–93   Wimbledon   36   19
1993–94   Wimbledon   42   17
1994–95   Wimbledon   28   7
1995–96   Wimbledon   33   10
1996–97   Wimbledon   25   5

1997–98   Wimbledon   5   0   169   58
1997–98   Bolton W   20   3
1998–99   Bolton W   32   12
1999–2000   Bolton W   35   11
2000–01   Bolton W   31   11
2001–02   Bolton W   31   2   149   39

HUNT, Nicky (D)   1   0
H: 6 1   W: 10 06   b.Westhoughton 3-9-83
Source: Scholar.
2000–01   Bolton W   1   0
2001–02   Bolton W   0   0   1   0

JAASKELAINEN, Jussi (G)   247   0
H: 6 3   W: 13 05   b.Mikkeli 19-4-75
Honours: Finland 9 full caps.
1992   MP   6   0
1993   MP   6   0
1994   MP   26   0
1995   MP   26   0   64   0
1996   VPS   27   0
1997   VPS   27   0   54   0
1997–98   Bolton W   0   0
1998–99   Bolton W   34   0
1999–2000   Bolton W   34   0
2000–01   Bolton W   27   0
2001–02   Bolton W   34   0   129   0

JOHNSON, Jermaine (M)   10   0
H: 5 9   W: 11 05   b.Jamaica 25-6-80
Source: Tivoli Gardens.
2001–02   Bolton W   10   0   10   0

KONSTANTINIDIS, Kostas‡ (D)   259   20
H: 6 2   W: 12 13   b.Greece 31-8-72
Honours: Greece 32 full caps, 1 goal.
1991–92   Perikos   30   1
1992–93   Perikos   27   2
1993–94   Perikos   27   2   84   5
1994–95   Ofi Crete   26   1
1995–96   Ofi Crete   26   2
1996–97   Ofi Crete   13   3   65   6
1996–97   Panathinaikos   9   0
1997–98   Panathinaikos   25   3
1998–99   Panathinaikos   26   4   60   7
1999–2000   Hertha Berlin   20   1
2000–01   Hertha Berlin   21   1
2001–02   Hertha Berlin   6   0   47   2
2001–02   Bolton W   3   0   3   0

MORINI, Emmanuelle (F)   2   0
H: 5 8   W: 10 07   b.Rome 31-1-82
Source: Roma.
2000–01   Bolton W   2   0
2001–02   Bolton W   0   0   2   0

N'GOTTY, Bruno (D)   393   21
H: 6 1   W: 13 08   b.Lyon 10-6-71
Honours: France 6 full caps.
1989–90   Lyon   27   0
1990–91   Lyon   37   2
1991–92   Lyon   36   1
1992–93   Lyon   36   3
1993–94   Lyon   36   3
1994–95   Lyon   35   3   207   12
1995–96   Paris St Germain   24   1
1996–97   Paris St Germain   30   4
1997–98   Paris St Germain   26   2   80   7
1998–99   AC Milan   25   1
1999–2000   AC Milan   9   0   34   1
1999–2000   Venezia   16   0   16   0
2000–01   Marseille   30   0   30   0
2001–02   Bolton W   26   1   26   1

NISHIZAWA, Akinori‡ (F)   101   28
H: 5 11   W: 11 00   b.Shizuoka 18-6-76
Honours: Japan 28 full caps, 10 goals.
1996   Cerezo Osaka   14   3
1997   Cerezo Osaka   19   7
1998   Cerezo Osaka   32   7
1999   Cerezo Osaka   30   11   95   28
2000–01   Espanyol   6   0   6   0
2001–02   Bolton W   0   0
(Transferred to Cerezo Osaka, January 2002).

NIVEN, Derek (M)   1   0
H: 6 1   W: 11 02   b.Falkirk 12-12-83
Source: Stenhousemuir.
2000–01   Raith R   1   0   1   0
2001–02   Bolton W   0   0

NOLAN, Kevin (M)   70   9
H: 6 0   W: 14 00   b.Liverpool 24-6-82
Source: Scholar. *Honours:* England Youth, Under-20.
1999–2000   Bolton W   4   0
2000–01   Bolton W   31   1
2001–02   Bolton W   35   8   70   9

NORRIS, David (M)   6   1
H: 5 7   W: 11 06   b.Peterborough 22-2-81
Source: Boston U.
1999–2000   Bolton W   0   0
2000–01   Bolton W   0   0

2001–02   Bolton W   0   0
2001–02   *Hull C*   6   1   6   1

O'HARE, Alan (D)   19   0
H: 6 2   W: 12 02   b.Dundalk 31-7-82
Source: Scholar.
2001–02   Bolton W   0   0
2001–02   *Chesterfield*   19   0   19   0

PEDERSEN, Henrik (F)   133   62
H: 6 1   W: 13 08   b.Denmark 10-6-75
Honours: Denmark 1 full cap.
1995–96   Silkeborg   12   4
1996–97   Silkeborg   2   0
1997–98   Silkeborg   15   9
1998–99   Silkeborg   33   16
1999–2000   Silkeborg   28   13
2000–01   Silkeborg   32   20   122   62
2001–02   Bolton W   11   0   11   0

POOLE, Kevin (G)   299   0
H: 5 10   W: 11 11   b.Bromsgrove 21-7-63
Source: Apprentice.
1981–82   Aston Villa   0   0
1982–83   Aston Villa   0   0
1983–84   Aston Villa   0   0
1984–85   Aston Villa   7   0
1984–85   *Northampton T*   3   0   3   0
1985–86   Aston Villa   11   0
1986–87   Aston Villa   10   0   28   0
1987–88   Middlesbrough   1   0
1988–89   Middlesbrough   12   0
1989–90   Middlesbrough   21   0
1990–91   Middlesbrough   0   0   34   0
1990–91   *Hartlepool U*   12   0   12   0
1991–92   Leicester C   42   0
1992–93   Leicester C   19   0
1993–94   Leicester C   14   0
1994–95   Leicester C   36   0
1995–96   Leicester C   45   0
1996–97   Leicester C   7   0   163   0
1997–98   Birmingham C   1   0
1998–99   Birmingham C   36   0
1999–2000   Birmingham C   18   0
2000–01   Birmingham C   1   0
2001–02   Birmingham C   0   0   56   0
2001–02   Bolton W   3   0   3   0

RICHARDSON, Leam (D)   34   0
H: 5 8   W: 11 04   b.Leeds 19-11-79
Source: Trainee.
1997–98   Blackburn R   0   0
1998–99   Blackburn R   0   0
1999–2000   Blackburn R   0   0
2000–01   Bolton W   12   0
2001–02   Bolton W   1   0   13   0
2001–02   *Notts Co*   21   0   21   0

RICKETTS, Michael (F)   152   45
H: 6 2   W: 11 12   b.Birmingham 4-12-78
Source: Trainee. *Honours:* England 1 full cap.
1995–96   Walsall   1   1
1996–97   Walsall   11   1
1997–98   Walsall   24   1
1998–99   Walsall   8   0
1999–2000   Bolton W   32   11   76   14
2000–01   Bolton W   39   19
2001–02   Bolton W   37   12   76   31

RYAN, Ciaran (D)   0   0
b.Dublin 27-2-83
Source: Scholar.
2001–02   Bolton W   0   0

SMITH, Jeff (M)   13   2
H: 5 10   W: 11 01   b.Middlesbrough 28-6-80
Source: Trainee.
1998–99   Hartlepool U   3   0
1999–2000   Hartlepool U   0   0   3   0
From Bishop Auckland
2000–01   Bolton W   1   0
2001–02   *Macclesfield T*   8   2   8   2
2001–02   Bolton W   1   0   2   0

SNORRASON, Olaf‡ (F)   0   0
H: 5 10   W: 11 00   b.Reykjavik 22-4-82
1998–99   Bolton W   0   0
1999–2000   Bolton W   0   0
2000–01   Bolton W   0   0
2001–02   Bolton W   0   0

SOUTHALL, Nicky (M)   382   47
H: 5 10   W: 12 12   b.Stockton 28-1-72
Source: Trainee.
1990–91   Hartlepool U   0   0
1991–92   Hartlepool U   22   3
1992–93   Hartlepool U   39   6
1993–94   Hartlepool U   40   9
1994–95   Hartlepool U   37   6   138   24
1995–96   Grimsby T   33   2
1996–97   Grimsby T   34   3
1997–98   Grimsby T   5   0   72   5
1997–98   Gillingham   23   2
1998–99   Gillingham   42   4

1999–2000	Gillingham	45	9		
2000–01	Gillingham	44	2	154	17
2001–02	Bolton W	18	1	18	1

TAYLOR, Cleveland (F) 0 0
b.Leicester 9-9-83
Source: Scholar.

| 2001–02 | Bolton W | 0 | 0 | | |

TOFTING, Stig (M) 307 37
H: 5 9 W: 12 08 b.Aarhus 14-8-69
Honours: Denmark 41 full caps, 2 goals.

1990	Aarhus	22	2		
1990–91	Aarhus	18	0		
1991–92	Aarhus	24	2		
1992–93	Aarhus	30	7		
1993–94	Odense	12	3	12	3
1993–94	Hamburg	5	0		
1994–95	Hamburg	3	0		
1994–95	Hamburg	14	2		
1995–96	Hamburg	24	3		
1996–97	Aarhus	32	12	164	28
1997–98	Duisburg	12	0		
1998–99	Duisburg	28	2		
1999–2000	Duisburg	29	2	69	4
2000–01	Hamburg	28	2		
2001–02	Hamburg	20	0	56	2
2001–02	Bolton W	6	0	6	0

WALLACE, Rod* (F) 393 119
H: 5 7 W: 11 03 b.Lewisham 2-10-69
Source: Trainee. *Honours:* England Under-21, B.

1987–88	Southampton	15	1		
1988–89	Southampton	38	12		
1989–90	Southampton	38	18		
1990–91	Southampton	37	14	128	45
1991–92	Leeds U	34	11		
1992–93	Leeds U	32	7		
1993–94	Leeds U	37	17		
1994–95	Leeds U	32	4		
1995–96	Leeds U	24	1		
1996–97	Leeds U	22	3		
1997–98	Leeds U	31	10		
1998–99	Rangers	34	18	34	18
1999–2000	Leeds U	0	0		
2000–01	Leeds U	0	0	212	53
2001–02	Bolton W	19	3	19	3

WALTERS, Jonathan (F) 0 0
b.Birkenhead 20-9-83
Source: Blackburn R Scholar.

| 2001–02 | Bolton W | 0 | 0 | | |

WARHURST, Paul* (D) 301 16
H: 6 0 W: 13 07 b.Stockport 26-9-69
Source: Trainee. *Honours:* England Under-21.

1987–88	Manchester C	0	0		
1988–89	Oldham Ath	4	0		
1989–90	Oldham Ath	30	1		
1990–91	Oldham Ath	33	1	67	2
1991–92	Sheffield W	33	0		
1992–93	Sheffield W	29	6		
1993–94	Sheffield W	4	0	66	6
1993–94	Blackburn R	9	0		
1994–95	Blackburn R	27	2		
1995–96	Blackburn R	10	0		
1996–97	Blackburn R	11	2	57	4
1997–98	Crystal Palace	22	3		
1998–99	Crystal Palace	5	1	27	4
1998–99	Bolton W	20	0		
1999–2000	Bolton W	19	0		
2000–01	Bolton W	20	0		
2001–02	Bolton W	25	0	84	0

WHEATCROFT, Paul* (F) 8 3
H: 5 9 W: 9 11 b.Manchester 22-11-80
Source: Trainee. *Honours:* England Schools, Youth.

1998–99	Manchester U	0	0		
1999–2000	Manchester U	0	0		
2000–01	Bolton W	0	0		
2001–02	Bolton W	0	0		
2001–02	Rochdale	6	3	6	3
2001–02	Mansfield T	2	0	2	0

WHITLOW, Mike (D) 339 14
H: 6 1 W: 13 03 b.Northwich 13-1-68
Source: Witton Alb.

1988–89	Leeds U	20	1		
1989–90	Leeds U	29	1		
1990–91	Leeds U	18	1		
1991–92	Leeds U	10	1	77	4
1991–92	Leicester C	5	0		
1992–93	Leicester C	24	1		
1993–94	Leicester C	31	2		
1994–95	Leicester C	28	2		
1995–96	Leicester C	42	3		
1996–97	Leicester C	17	0		
1997–98	Leicester C	0	0	147	8
1997–98	Bolton W	13	0		
1998–99	Bolton W	28	0		
1999–2000	Bolton W	37	1		
2000–01	Bolton W	8	1		
2001–02	Bolton W	29	0	115	2

Trainees
Bird, Michael; Brabbs, Andrew; Byrne, Michael T; Dootson, Shaun; Eckersley, Michael; Errington, Anthony; Hamlin, Lewis; Livesey, Daniel; Moran, Martin R; Price, Andrew; Rowe, Philip A; Shakes, Ricky U; Taylor, Cleveland; Tubbs, Matthew

AFC BOURNEMOUTH

BERNARD, Narada (M) 22 0
H: 5 7 W: 10 07 b.Bristol 30-1-81
Source: Trainee.

1999–2000	Arsenal	0	0		
2000–01	Bournemouth	14	0		
2001–02	Bournemouth	8	0	22	0

BIRMINGHAM, David‡ (D) 6 0
H: 5 8 W: 11 01 b.Portsmouth 16-4-81
Source: Bournemouth Trainee.

1999–2000	Portsmouth	2	0		
2000–01	Portsmouth	0	0	2	0
2000–01	Bournemouth	0	0		
2001–02	Bournemouth	4	0	4	0

BROADHURST, Karl (D) 69 0
H: 6 1 W: 11 07 b.Portsmouth 18-3-80
Source: Trainee.

1998–99	Bournemouth	0	0		
1999–2000	Bournemouth	16	0		
2000–01	Bournemouth	30	0		
2001–02	Bournemouth	23	0	69	0

ELLIOTT, Wade (M) 94 20
H: 5 10 W: 11 01 b.Southampton 14-12-78

1999–2000	Bournemouth	12	3		
2000–01	Bournemouth	36	9		
2001–02	Bournemouth	46	8	94	20

ERIBENNE, Chukkie (F) 41 1
H: 5 10 W: 11 12 b.London 2-11-80
Source: Trainee.

1997–98	Coventry C	0	0		
1998–99	Coventry C	0	0		
1999–2000	Coventry C	0	0		
2000–01	Bournemouth	17	1		
2001–02	Bournemouth	24	0	41	1

FEENEY, Warren (F) 47 17
H: 5 10 W: 11 05 b.Belfast 17-1-81
Source: Trainee. *Honours:* Northern Ireland Schools, Youth, Under-21, 2 full caps.

1997–98	Leeds U	0	0		
1998–99	Leeds U	0	0		
1999–2000	Leeds U	0	0		
2000–01	Leeds U	0	0		
2000–01	*Bournemouth*	10	4		
2001–02	Bournemouth	37	13	47	17

FLETCHER, Carl (M) 105 14
H: 5 10 W: 11 07 b.Camberley 7-4-80
Source: Trainee.

1997–98	Bournemouth	1	0		
1998–99	Bournemouth	1	0		
1999–2000	Bournemouth	25	3		
2000–01	Bournemouth	43	6		
2001–02	Bournemouth	35	5	105	14

FLETCHER, Steve (F) 345 64
H: 6 2 W: 14 09 b.Hartlepool 26-7-72
Source: Trainee.

1990–91	Hartlepool U	14	2		
1991–92	Hartlepool U	18	2	32	4
1992–93	Bournemouth	31	4		
1993–94	Bournemouth	36	6		
1994–95	Bournemouth	40	6		
1995–96	Bournemouth	7	1		
1996–97	Bournemouth	35	7		
1997–98	Bournemouth	42	12		
1998–99	Bournemouth	39	8		
1999–2000	Bournemouth	36	7		
2000–01	Bournemouth	45	9		
2001–02	Bournemouth	2	0	313	60

FORD, James* (M) 12 0
H: 5 8 W: 11 00 b.Portsmouth 23-10-81
Source: Trainee.

1999–2000	Bournemouth	2	0		
2000–01	Bournemouth	3	0		
2001–02	Bournemouth	7	0	12	0

FOYEWA, Amos (F) 8 0
H: 5 8 W: 12 00 b.Nigeria 26-12-81

| 2001–02 | Bournemouth | 8 | 0 | 8 | 0 |

GRANT, Peter (M) 475 19
H: 5 8 W: 11 00 b.Bellshill 30-8-65
Source: Celtic BC. *Honours:* Scotland Schools, Youth, Under-21, B, 2 full caps.

1982–83	Celtic	0	0		
1983–84	Celtic	3	0		
1984–85	Celtic	20	4		
1985–86	Celtic	30	1		
1986–87	Celtic	37	1		
1987–88	Celtic	37	2		
1988–89	Celtic	21	0		
1989–90	Celtic	26	0		
1990–91	Celtic	27	0		
1991–92	Celtic	22	0		
1992–93	Celtic	31	2		
1993–94	Celtic	28	0		
1994–95	Celtic	28	2		
1995–96	Celtic	30	3		
1996–97	Celtic	23	0	363	15
1997–98	Norwich C	35	3		
1998–99	Norwich C	33	0		
1999–2000	Norwich C	0	0	68	3
1999–2000	Reading	29	1	29	1
2000–01	Bournemouth	15	0		
2001–02	Bournemouth	0	0	15	0

HAYTER, James (F) 142 22
H: 5 9 W: 10 13 b.Newport (IW) 9-4-79
Source: Trainee.

1996–97	Bournemouth	2	0		
1997–98	Bournemouth	5	0		
1998–99	Bournemouth	20	2		
1999–2000	Bournemouth	31	2		
2000–01	Bournemouth	40	11		
2001–02	Bournemouth	44	7	142	22

HOLMES, Derek (F) 83 23
H: 6 2 W: 13 07 b.Lanark 18-10-78
Source: Royal Albert.

1995–96	Hearts	0	0		
1996–97	Hearts	1	0		
1997–98	Hearts	1	1		
1997–98	Cowdenbeath	13	5	13	5
1998–99	Hearts	6	0	8	1
1999–2000	Ross Co	25	8		
2000–01	Ross Co	0	0	25	8
2001–02	Bournemouth	37	9	37	9

HUCK, Willie* (M) 40 0
H: 5 10 W: 11 09 b.Paris 17-3-79
Source: Monaco.

1998–99	Arsenal	0	0		
1998–99	Bournemouth	8	0		
1999–2000	Bournemouth	17	0		
2000–01	Bournemouth	8	0		
2001–02	Bournemouth	7	0	40	0

HUGHES, Richard (M) 131 14
H: 6 2 W: 12 00 b.Glasgow 25-6-79
Source: Atalanta. *Honours:* Scotland Youth, Under-21.

1997–98	Arsenal	0	0		
1998–99	Bournemouth	44	2		
1999–2000	Bournemouth	21	2		
2000–01	Bournemouth	44	8		
2001–02	Bournemouth	22	2	131	14

KANDOL, Tresor (F) 33 3
H: 6 0 W: 13 07 b.Banga 30-8-81
Source: Trainee.

1998–99	Luton T	4	0		
1999–2000	Luton T	4	0		
2000–01	Luton T	13	3	21	3
2001–02	Bournemouth	12	0	12	0

MAHER, Shaun (D) 97 2
H: 6 1 W: 13 02 b.Dublin 20-6-78
Source: Bohemians.

1996–97	Bohemians	2	0		
1997–98	Fulham	0	0		
1997–98	Bohemians	11	0		
1998–99	Bohemians	25	1		
1999–2000	Bohemians	28	1		
2000–01	Bohemians	0	0	66	2
2001–02	Bournemouth	31	0	31	0

MATHIE, Graeme‡ (D) 0 0
H: 6 1 W: 12 00 b.Lanark 17-10-82
Source: Trainee.

1999–2000	Coventry C	0	0		
2000–01	Coventry C	0	0		
2001–02	Bournemouth	0	0		

MENETRIER, Michael (G) 13 0
H: 6 0 W: 13 02 b.Reims 23-9-78
Source: Metz.

| 2000–01 | Bournemouth | 12 | 0 | | |
| 2001–02 | Bournemouth | 1 | 0 | 13 | 0 |

O'CONNOR, Gareth (F) 80 5
H: 5 10 W: 11 00 b.Dublin 10-11-78
Source: Bohemians.

1998–99	Shamrock R	8	0	8	0
1999–2000	Bohemians	22	4	22	4
2000–01	Bournemouth	22	1		
2001–02	Bournemouth	28	0	50	1

PURCHES, Stephen (M)   75   2
H: 5 11　W: 11 09　b.Ilford 14-1-80
Source: Trainee.

Season	Club				
1998–99	West Ham U	0	0		
1999–2000	West Ham U	0	0		
2000–01	Bournemouth	34	0		
2001–02	Bournemouth	41	2	75	2

SMITH, Danny* (D)   18   0
H: 5 11　W: 11 04　b.Southampton 17-8-82
Source: Trainee.

1999–2000	Bournemouth	1	0		
2000–01	Bournemouth	14	0		
2001–02	Bournemouth	3	0	18	0

STEWART, Gareth (G)   83   0
H: 6 0　W: 12 08　b.Preston 3-2-80
Source: Trainee. Honours: England Schools, Youth.

1996–97	Blackburn R	0	0		
1997–98	Blackburn R	0	0		
1998–99	Blackburn R	0	0		
1999–2000	Bournemouth	3	0		
2000–01	Bournemouth	35	0		
2001–02	Bournemouth	45	0	83	0

STOCK, Brian (M)   32   2
H: 5 11　W: 11 02　b.Winchester 24-12-81
Source: Trainee.

1999–2000	Bournemouth	5	0		
2000–01	Bournemouth	1	0		
2001–02	Bournemouth	26	2	32	2

TETU, Pascal‡ (M)   0   0
H: 5 11　W: 12 00　b.Bordeaux 22-4-80
Source: Bordeaux.

2001–02	Bournemouth	0	0

THOMAS, Danny (M)   15   0
H: 5 7　W: 10 10　b.Leamington Spa 1-5-81
Source: Trainee.

1997–98	Nottingham F	0	0		
1997–98	Leicester C	0	0		
1998–99	Leicester C	0	0		
1999–2000	Leicester C	3	0		
2000–01	Leicester C	0	0		
2001–02	Leicester C	0	0	3	0
2001–02	Bournemouth	12	0	12	0

TINDALL, Jason (M)   114   5
H: 6 1　W: 12 01　b.Stepney 15-11-77
Source: Trainee.

1996–97	Charlton Ath	0	0		
1997–98	Charlton Ath	0	0		
1998–99	Bournemouth	17	1		
1999–2000	Bournemouth	8	0		
2000–01	Bournemouth	45	1		
2001–02	Bournemouth	44	3	114	5

YOUNG, Neil# (D)   260   3
H: 5 9　W: 12 00　b.Harlow 31-8-73
Source: Trainee.

1991–92	Tottenham H	0	0		
1992–93	Tottenham H	0	0		
1993–94	Tottenham H	0	0		
1994–95	Bournemouth	32	0		
1995–96	Bournemouth	41	0		
1996–97	Bournemouth	44	0		
1997–98	Bournemouth	44	2		
1998–99	Bournemouth	44	1		
1999–2000	Bournemouth	37	0		
2000–01	Bournemouth	7	0		
2001–02	Bournemouth	11	0	260	3

BRADFORD C

ATHERTON, Peter (D)   513   10
H: 5 11　W: 13 12　b.Wigan 6-4-70
Source: Trainee. Honours: England Schools, Under-21.

1987–88	Wigan Ath	16	0		
1988–89	Wigan Ath	40	1		
1989–90	Wigan Ath	46	0		
1990–91	Wigan Ath	46	0		
1991–92	Wigan Ath	1	0	149	1
1991–92	Coventry C	35	0		
1992–93	Coventry C	39	0		
1993–94	Coventry C	40	0	114	0
1994–95	Sheffield W	41	1		
1995–96	Sheffield W	36	0		
1996–97	Sheffield W	37	2		
1997–98	Sheffield W	27	3		
1998–99	Sheffield W	38	2		
1999–2000	Sheffield W	35	1	214	9
2000–01	Bradford C	25	0		
2000–01	*Birmingham C*	10	0	10	0
2001–02	Bradford C	1	0	26	0

BOWER, Mark (D)   49   4
H: 5 10　W: 11 00　b.Bradford 23-1-80
Source: Trainee.

1997–98	Bradford C	3	0		
1998–99	Bradford C	0	0		
1999–2000	Bradford C	0	0		
1999–2000	York C	15	1		
2000–01	Bradford C	0	0		
2000–01	*York C*	21	1	36	2
2001–02	Bradford C	10	2	13	2

CADAMARTERI, Danny (F)   112   16
H: 5 9　W: 12 10　b.Bradford 12-10-79
Source: Trainee. Honours: England Youth, Under-21.

1996–97	Everton	1	0		
1997–98	Everton	26	4		
1998–99	Everton	30	4		
1999–2000	Everton	17	1		
1999–2000	*Fulham*	5	1	5	1
2000–01	Everton	16	4		
2001–02	Everton	3	0	93	13
2001–02	Bradford C	14	2	14	2

CARBONE, Benito (F)   375   65
H: 5 7　W: 10 10　b.Begnara 14-8-71

1988–89	Torino	3	0		
1989–90	Torino	5	0		
1990–91	Reggina	31	5	31	5
1991–92	Casert	31	4	31	4
1992–93	Ascoli	28	6	28	6
1993–94	Torino	28	3	36	3
1994–95	Napoli	29	5	29	5
1995–96	Internazionale	31	2		
1996–97	Internazionale	1	0	32	2
1996–97	Sheffield W	25	6		
1997–98	Sheffield W	33	9		
1998–99	Sheffield W	31	8		
1999–2000	Sheffield W	7	2	96	25
1999–2000	*Aston Villa*	24	3	24	3
2000–01	Bradford C	31	5		
2001–02	Bradford C	11	5	42	10
2001–02	*Derby Co*	13	1	13	1
2001–02	*Middlesbrough*	13	1	13	1

COMBE, Alan (G)   226   0
H: 6 1　W: 12 02　b.Edinburgh 3-4-74
Source: Kelty Hearts.

1992–93	Cowdenbeath	18	0	18	0
1993–94	St Mirren	16	0		
1994–95	St Mirren	21	0		
1995–96	St Mirren	21	0		
1996–97	St Mirren	36	0		
1997–98	St Mirren	30	0	124	0
1998–99	Dundee U	10	0		
1999–2000	Dundee U	35	0		
2000–01	Dundee U	23	0		
2001–02	Dundee U	0	0	68	0
2001–02	Bradford C	16	0	16	0

DAVISON, Aidan (G)   187   0
H: 6 1　W: 13 12　b.Sedgefield 11-5-68
Source: Billingham Synthonia. Honours: Northern Ireland B, 3 full caps.

1987–88	Notts Co	0	0		
1988–89	Notts Co	1	0		
1989–90	Notts Co	0	0	1	0
1989–90	*Leyton Orient*	0	0		
1989–90	*Bury*	0	0		
1989–90	*Chester C*	0	0		
1990–91	Bury	0	0		
1990–91	*Blackpool*	0	0		
1991–92	Millwall	33	0		
1992–93	Millwall	1	0	34	0
1993–94	Bolton W	31	0		
1994–95	Bolton W	4	0		
1995–96	Bolton W	2	0		
1996–97	Bolton W	0	0	37	0
1996–97	*Ipswich T*	0	0		
1996–97	*Hull C*	9	0	9	0
1996–97	Bradford C	10	0		
1997–98	Grimsby T	42	0		
1998–99	Grimsby T	35	0		
1999–2000	Grimsby T	0	0	77	0
1999–2000	*Sheffield U*	2	0	2	0
1999–2000	Bradford C	6	0		
2000–01	Bradford C	0	0		
2001–02	Bradford C	9	0	27	0

EMANUEL, Lewis (D)   9   0
H: 5 8　W: 12 01　b.Bradford 14-10-83
Source: Scholar. Honours: England Youth.

2001–02	Bradford C	9	0	9	0

GRANT, Gareth‡ (F)   30   1
H: 5 9　W: 10 03　b.Leeds 6-9-80
Source: Trainee.

1997–98	Bradford C	3	0		
1998–99	Bradford C	5	0		
1998–99	*Halifax T*	3	0	3	0
1999–2000	*Bolton W*	0	0		
2000–01	Bradford C	5	0		
2000–01	*Lincoln C*	3	0	3	0
2001–02	Bradford C	10	1	24	1

HALLE, Gunnar* (D)   346   22
H: 5 11　W: 11 02　b.Oslo 11-8-65
Source: Lillestrom. Honours: Norway 64 full caps, 5 goals.

1990–91	Oldham Ath	17	0		
1991–92	Oldham Ath	10	0		
1992–93	Oldham Ath	41	5		
1993–94	Oldham Ath	23	1		
1994–95	Oldham Ath	40	5		
1995–96	Oldham Ath	37	3		
1996–97	Oldham Ath	20	3	188	17
1996–97	Leeds U	20	0		
1997–98	Leeds U	33	2		
1998–99	Leeds U	17	2	70	4
1999–2000	Bradford C	38	0		
2000–01	Bradford C	13	0		
2001–02	Bradford C	32	1	83	1
2001–02	*Wolverhampton W*	5	0	5	0

JACOBS, Wayne (D)   445   18
H: 5 9　W: 11 02　b.Sheffield 3-2-69
Source: Apprentice.

1986–87	Sheffield W	0	0		
1987–88	Sheffield W	6	0	6	0
1987–88	Hull C	6	0		
1988–89	Hull C	33	0		
1989–90	Hull C	46	3		
1990–91	Hull C	19	1		
1991–92	Hull C	25	0		
1992–93	Hull C	0	0	129	4
1993–94	Rotherham U	42	2	42	2
1994–95	Bradford C	38	1		
1995–96	Bradford C	28	0		
1996–97	Bradford C	39	3		
1997–98	Bradford C	36	2		
1998–99	Bradford C	44	3		
1999–2000	Bradford C	24	0		
2000–01	Bradford C	21	2		
2001–02	Bradford C	38	1	268	12

JESS, Eoin (F)   398   96
H: 5 10　W: 11 09　b.Aberdeen 13-12-70
Source: Rangers 'S' Form. Honours: Scotland Under-21, B, 18 full caps, 2 goals.

1987–88	Aberdeen	0	0		
1988–89	Aberdeen	2	0		
1989–90	Aberdeen	11	3		
1990–91	Aberdeen	27	13		
1991–92	Aberdeen	39	12		
1992–93	Aberdeen	31	12		
1993–94	Aberdeen	41	6		
1994–95	Aberdeen	25	1		
1995–96	Aberdeen	25	3		
1995–96	Coventry C	12	1		
1996–97	Coventry C	27	0	39	1
1997–98	Aberdeen	34	9		
1998–99	Aberdeen	36	14		
1999–2000	Aberdeen	26	5		
2000–01	Aberdeen	0	0	297	78
2000–01	Bradford C	17	3		
2001–02	Bradford C	45	14	62	17

JONES, Kingsley‡ (M)   0   0
b.Bradford 2-10-82
Source: Scholar.

2001–02	Bradford C	0	0

JORGENSEN, Claus (M)   105   15
H: 5 11　W: 11 00　b.Holstebro 27-4-76
Source: Resen-Humlum, Struer BK, Holstebro, Aarhus, AC Horsens.

1999–2000	Bournemouth	44	6		
2000–01	Bournemouth	43	8	87	14
2001–02	Bradford C	18	1	18	1

JUANJO (F)   125   14
H: 5 9　W: 10 08　b.Barcelona 4-5-77

1997–98	Barcelona B	36	4	36	4
1998–99	Hearts	11	0		
1999–2000	Hearts	15	3		
2000–01	Hearts	37	4		
2001–02	Hearts	9	2	72	9
2001–02	Bradford C	17	1	17	1

KEARNEY, Tom (M)   5   0
H: 5 11　W: 10 08　b.Liverpool 7-10-81
Source: Trainee.

1999–2000	Everton	0	0		
2000–01	Everton	0	0		
2001–02	Everton	0	0		
2001–02	Bradford C	5	0	5	0

LAWRENCE, Jamie (M)   215   15
H: 5 9　W: 12 10　b.Balham 8-3-70
Source: Cowes. Honours: Jamaica 12 full caps.

1993–94	Sunderland	4	0	4	0
1993–94	Doncaster R	9	1		
1994–95	Doncaster R	16	2	25	3
1994–95	Leicester C	17	1		
1995–96	Leicester C	15	0		
1996–97	Leicester C	15	0	47	1
1997–98	Bradford C	43	3		

1998–99 Bradford C 35 2
1999–2000 Bradford C 23 3
2000–01 Bradford C 17 1
2001–02 Bradford C 21 2 **139 11**

LEE, Andrew (F) **1 0**
H: 5 7 W: 9 07 b.Bradford 18-8-82
Source: Scholar.
2001–02 Bradford C 1 0 **1 0**

LOCKE, Gary (M) **179 7**
H: 6 0 W: 11 13 b.Edinburgh 16-6-75
Source: Whitehill Welfare. Honours: Scotland Under-21.
1992–93 Hearts 1 0
1993–94 Hearts 33 0
1994–95 Hearts 9 0
1995–96 Hearts 29 4
1996–97 Hearts 11 0
1997–98 Hearts 21 0
1998–99 Hearts 25 1
1999–2000 Hearts 12 0
2000–01 Hearts 0 0 **141 5**
2000–01 Bradford C 7 0
2001–02 Bradford C 31 2 **38 2**

MAKEL, Lee‡ (M) **115 7**
H: 5 10 W: 11 04 b.Sunderland 11-1-73
Source: Trainee.
1990–91 Newcastle U 3 0
1991–92 Newcastle U 9 1 **12 1**
1992–93 Blackburn R 1 0
1993–94 Blackburn R 2 0
1994–95 Blackburn R 0 0
1995–96 Blackburn R 3 0 **6 0**
1995–96 Huddersfield T 33 2
1996–97 Huddersfield T 19 3
1997–98 Huddersfield T 13 0 **65 5**
1997–98 Hearts 5 0
1998–99 Hearts 14 1
1999–2000 Hearts
2000–01 Hearts 0 0 **19 1**
2001–02 Bradford C 13 0 **13 0**
(Transferred to Livingston, December 2001).

McCALL, Stuart* (M) **692 65**
H: 5 8 W: 11 13 b.Leeds 10-6-64
Source: Apprentice. Honours: Scotland Under-21, 40 full caps, 1 goal.
1982–83 Bradford C 28 4
1983–84 Bradford C 46 5
1984–85 Bradford C 46 8
1985–86 Bradford C 38 4
1986–87 Bradford C 36 7
1987–88 Bradford C 44 9
1988–89 Everton 33 0
1989–90 Everton 37 3
1990–91 Everton 33 3 **103 6**
1991–92 Rangers 36 1
1992–93 Rangers 36 5
1993–94 Rangers 34 3
1994–95 Rangers 30 2
1995–96 Rangers 21 3
1996–97 Rangers 7 0
1997–98 Rangers 30 0 **194 14**
1998–99 Bradford C 43 3
1999–2000 Bradford C 34 1
2000–01 Bradford C 37 1
2001–02 Bradford C 43 3 **395 45**

MOLENAAR, Robert (D) **217 9**
H: 6 2 W: 14 04 b.Zaandam 27-2-69
1992–93 Volendam 28 2
1993–94 Volendam 27 1
1994–95 Volendam 31 0
1995–96 Volendam 21 0
1996–97 Volendam 17 0 **124 3**
1996–97 Leeds U 12 1
1997–98 Leeds U 22 2
1998–99 Leeds U 17 2
1999–2000 Leeds U 0 0
2000–01 Leeds U 0 0 **51 5**
2000–01 Bradford C 21 1
2001–02 Bradford C 21 0 **42 1**

MYERS, Andy (D) **157 5**
H: 5 10 W: 13 12 b.Hounslow 3-11-73
Source: Trainee. Honours: England Schools, Youth, Under-21.
1990–91 Chelsea 3 0
1991–92 Chelsea 11 1
1992–93 Chelsea 3 0
1993–94 Chelsea 6 0
1994–95 Chelsea 10 0
1995–96 Chelsea 20 0
1996–97 Chelsea 18 1
1997–98 Chelsea 12 0 **84 2**
1998–99 Chelsea 1 0
1999–2000 Bradford C 13 0
1999–2000 Portsmouth 8 0 **8 0**
2000–01 Bradford C 20 1
2001–02 Bradford C 32 2 **65 3**

SHARPE, Lee‡ (M) **313 33**
H: 6 0 W: 12 13 b.Halesowen 27-5-71
Source: Trainee. Honours: England Under-21, B, 8 full caps.
1987–88 Torquay U 14 3 **14 3**
1988–89 Manchester U 22 0
1989–90 Manchester U 18 1
1990–91 Manchester U 23 2
1991–92 Manchester U 14 1
1992–93 Manchester U 27 1
1993–94 Manchester U 30 9
1994–95 Manchester U 28 3
1995–96 Manchester U 31 4 **193 21**
1996–97 Leeds U 26 5
1997–98 Leeds U 4 0
1998–99 Leeds U 20 4 **30 5**
1998–99 *Bradford C* 9 2
1998–99 *Sampdoria* 3 0 **3 0**
1999–2000 Bradford C 18 0
2000–01 Bradford C 11 0
2000–01 *Portsmouth* 17 0 **17 0**
2001–02 Bradford C 2 0 **56 4**

STANDING, Michael (M) **0 0**
H: 5 10 W: 10 05 b.Shoreham 20-3-81
Source: Trainee. Honours: England Schools.
1997–98 Aston Villa 0 0
1998–99 Aston Villa 0 0
1999–2000 Aston Villa 0 0
2000–01 Aston Villa 0 0
2001–02 Aston Villa 0 0
2001–02 Bradford C 0 0

TOD, Andrew (D) **267 41**
H: 5 10 W: 11 13 b.Dunfermline 4-11-71
Source: Kelty Hearts.
1993–94 Dunfermline Ath 22 11
1994–95 Dunfermline Ath 35 6
1995–96 Dunfermline Ath 35 5
1996–97 Dunfermline Ath 35 4
1997–98 Dunfermline Ath 35 6
1998–99 Dunfermline Ath 25 1
1999–2000 Dunfermline Ath 30 1
2000–01 Dunfermline Ath 0 0
2000–01 *Stockport Co* 11 3 **11 3**
2001–02 Dunfermline Ath 0 0 **226 34**
2001–02 Bradford C 30 4 **30 4**

WALSH, Gary (G) **235 0**
H: 6 3 W: 14 13 b.Wigan 21-3-68
Source: Apprentice. Honours: England Under-21.
1984–85 Manchester U 0 0
1985–86 Manchester U 0 0
1986–87 Manchester U 14 0
1987–88 Manchester U 16 0
1988–89 Manchester U 0 0
1988–89 *Airdrieonians* 3 0 **3 0**
1989–90 Manchester U 0 0
1990–91 Manchester U 5 0
1991–92 Manchester U 2 0
1992–93 Manchester U 0 0
1993–94 Manchester U 3 0
1993–94 *Oldham Ath* 6 0 **6 0**
1994–95 Manchester U 10 0 **50 0**
1995–96 Middlesbrough 32 0
1996–97 Middlesbrough 12 0
1997–98 Middlesbrough 0 0
1997–98 Bradford C 35 0
1998–99 Bradford C 46 0
1999–2000 Bradford C 11 0
2000–01 Bradford C 19 0
2000–01 *Middlesbrough* 3 0 **47 0**
2001–02 Bradford C 18 0 **129 0**

WARD, Ashley (F) **331 102**
H: 6 0 W: 11 00 b.Manchester 24-11-70
Source: Trainee.
1989–90 Manchester C 1 0
1990–91 Manchester C 0 0 **1 0**
1991–92 *Wrexham* 4 2 **4 2**
1991–92 Leicester C 10 0
1992–93 Leicester C 0 0 **10 0**
1992–93 *Blackpool* 2 1 **2 1**
1992–93 Crewe Alex 20 4
1993–94 Crewe Alex 25 13
1994–95 Crewe Alex 16 8 **61 25**
1994–95 Norwich C 25 8
1995–96 Norwich C 28 10 **53 18**
1995–96 Derby Co 7 1
1996–97 Derby Co 30 8
1997–98 Derby Co 3 0 **40 9**
1997–98 Barnsley 29 8
1998–99 Barnsley 17 12 **46 20**
1998–99 Blackburn R 17 5
1999–2000 Blackburn R 37 8 **54 13**
2000–01 Bradford C 33 4
2001–02 Bradford C 27 10 **60 14**

WETHERALL, David (D) **277 17**
H: 6 3 W: 13 12 b.Sheffield 14-3-71
Source: School. Honours: England Schools.
1989–90 Sheffield W 0 0
1990–91 Sheffield W 0 0
1991–92 Leeds U 1 0
1992–93 Leeds U 13 1
1993–94 Leeds U 32 1
1994–95 Leeds U 38 3
1995–96 Leeds U 34 4
1996–97 Leeds U 29 0
1997–98 Leeds U 34 3
1998–99 Leeds U 21 0 **202 12**
1999–2000 Bradford C 38 2
2000–01 Bradford C 18 1
2001–02 Bradford C 19 2 **75 5**

WHALLEY, Gareth* (M) **290 12**
H: 5 10 W: 11 11 b.Manchester 19-12-73
Source: Trainee.
1992–93 Crewe Alex 25 1
1993–94 Crewe Alex 15 1
1994–95 Crewe Alex 40 1
1995–96 Crewe Alex 44 2
1996–97 Crewe Alex 38 3
1997–98 Crewe Alex 45 2
1998–99 Bradford C 16 1
2000–01 Bradford C 19 0
2001–02 Bradford C 23 0 **103 3**
2001–02 *Crewe Alex* 7 0 **187 9**

Scholars
Beach, Nicholas; Bentham, Craig; Brodie, Keith J; Fishlock, Craig C; Flynn, Liam D; Forrest, Daniel PH; Hatton, Philip D; McGahey, Phillip M; Morgan, Robert D; Penford, Thomas J; Sanasy, Kevin R; Swift, John M; Worsnop, Jon A
Players who do not hold a current contract but their registration has been retained by the club
Hutton, Peter; Tomlinson, Paul; Holmes, Richard

BRENTFORD

ANDERSON, Ijah (D) **193 4**
H: 5 9 W: 11 09 b.Hackney 30-12-75
Source: Tottenham H Trainee.
1994–95 Southend U 1 0
1995–96 Brentford 25 2
1996–97 Brentford 46 1
1997–98 Brentford 17 0
1998–99 Brentford 38 1
1999–2000 Brentford 31 0
2000–01 Brentford 1 0
2001–02 Brentford 35 0 **193 4**

BOXALL, Danny* (D) **94 1**
H: 5 11 W: 12 08 b.Croydon 24-8-77
Source: Trainee. Honours: Eire Under-21.
1994–95 Crystal Palace 1 0
1995–96 Crystal Palace 1 0
1996–97 Crystal Palace 6 0
1997–98 Crystal Palace 1 0 **8 0**
1997–98 *Oldham Ath* 18 0 **18 0**
1998–99 Brentford 38 1
1999–2000 Brentford 25 0
2000–01 Brentford 0 0
2001–02 Brentford 5 0 **68 1**

BRYAN, Derek‡ (F) **50 7**
H: 5 11 W: 12 13 b.Hammersmith 11-11-74
Source: Hampton.
1997–98 Brentford 11 2
1998–99 Brentford 20 4
1999–2000 Brentford 18 1
2000–01 Brentford 0 0
2001–02 Brentford 1 0 **50 7**

CHARLES, Julian* (F) **12 0**
H: 5 9 W: 12 04 b.Plaistow 5-2-77
Source: Hampton & Richmond B. Honours: St. Vincent & the Grenadines 2 full caps.
1999–2000 Brentford 2 0
2000–01 Brentford 10 0
2001–02 Brentford 0 0 **12 0**

DOBSON, Michael (D) **65 0**
H: 6 0 W: 13 05 b.Isleworth 9-4-81
Source: Trainee.
1999–2000 Brentford 0 0
2000–01 Brentford 26 0
2001–02 Brentford 39 0 **65 0**

EVANS, Paul* (M) **328 57**
H: 5 8 W: 12 06 b.Oswestry 1-9-74
Source: Trainee. Honours: Wales Youth, Under-21, 1 full cap.
1991–92 Shrewsbury T 2 0

1992–93	Shrewsbury T	4	0		
1993–94	Shrewsbury T	13	0		
1994–95	Shrewsbury T	32	5		
1995–96	Shrewsbury T	34	3		
1996–97	Shrewsbury T	42	6		
1997–98	Shrewsbury T	39	6		
1998–99	Shrewsbury T	32	6	198	26
1998–99	Brentford	14	3		
1999–2000	Brentford	33	7		
2000–01	Brentford	43	7		
2001–02	Brentford	40	14	130	31

EVANS, Stephen (M)   10 0
H: 5 11 W: 11 02 b.Caerphilly 25-9-80
Source: Wales Youth, Under-21.

1998–99	Crystal Palace	4	0		
1999–2000	Crystal Palace	1	0		
2000–01	Crystal Palace	1	0		
2001–02	Crystal Palace	0	0	6	0
2001–02	Swansea C	4	0	4	0
2001–02	Brentford	0	0		

FIELDWICK, Lee (D)   0 0
H: 5 11 W: 11 09 b.Croydon 6-9-82
Source: Trainee.

2001–02	Brentford	0	0		

FOLAN, Tony‡ (F)   60 7
H: 5 11 W: 11 08 b.Lewisham 18-9-81
Source: Trainee. *Honours:* Eire Under-21.

1995–96	Crystal Palace	0	0		
1996–97	Crystal Palace	0	0		
1997–98	Crystal Palace	1	0		
1998–99	Crystal Palace	0	0	1	0
1998–99	Brentford	29	4		
1999–2000	Brentford	9	1		
2000–01	Brentford	21	2		
2001–02	Brentford	0	0	59	7

(Transferred to Bohemians, November 2001).

GOTTSKALKSSON, Olafur (G)   304 0
H: 6 3 W: 13 12 b.Keflavik 12-3-68
Honours: Iceland 9 full caps.

1988	IA Akranes	18	0		
1989	IA Akranes	15	0	33	0
1990	KR	18	0		
1991	KR	18	0		
1992	KR	18	0		
1993	KR	17	0	71	0
1994	Keflavik	18	0		
1995	Keflavik	17	0		
1996	Keflavik	18	0		
1997	Keflavik	10	0	63	0
1997–98	Hibernian	16	0		
1998–99	Hibernian	36	0		
1999–2000	Hibernian	0	0		
2000–01	Hibernian	12	0	64	0
2000–01	Brentford	45	0		
2001–02	Brentford	28	0	73	0

HUNT, Steve (F)   38 4
H: 5 8 W: 10 12 b.Waterford 1-8-80
Source: Trainee.

1999–2000	Crystal Palace	3	0		
2000–01	Crystal Palace	0	0	3	0
2001–02	Brentford	35	4	35	4

HUTCHINSON, Eddie (M)   16 0
H: 6 2 W: 13 01 b.Kingston 23-2-82
Source: Sutton U.

2000–01	Brentford	7	0		
2001–02	Brentford	9	0	16	0

INGIMARSSON, Ivar* (D)   198 21
H: 6 0 W: 13 05 b.Reykjavik 20-8-77
Honours: Iceland 3 full caps.

1995	Valur	12	0		
1996	Valur	17	2		
1997	Valur	16	3	45	5
1998	IBV	18	1		
1999	IBV	18	4	36	5
1999–2000	Torquay U	4	1	4	1
1999–2000	Brentford	25	1		
2000–01	Brentford	42	3		
2001–02	Brentford	46	6	113	10

JULIAN, Alan (G)   0 0
H: 6 2 W: 13 05 b.Ashford 11-3-83
Source: Trainee.

2001–02	Brentford	0	0		

LOVETT, Jay (D)   27 0
H: 6 2 W: 12 04 b.Brighton 22-1-78
Source: Crawley T.

2000–01	Brentford	25	0		
2001–02	Brentford	2	0	27	0

MARSHALL, Scott (D)   106 4
H: 6 1 W: 12 13 b.Edinburgh 1-5-73
Source: Trainee. *Honours:* Scotland Youth, Under-21.

1992–93	Arsenal	2	0		
1993–94	Arsenal	0	0		
1993–94	*Rotherham U*	10	1	10	1
1993–94	*Oxford U*	0	0		
1994–95	Arsenal	0	0		
1994–95	*Sheffield U*	17	0	17	0
1995–96	Arsenal	11	1		
1996–97	Arsenal	8	0		
1997–98	Arsenal	3	0	24	1
1998–99	Southampton	2	0		
1998–99	Celtic	2	0	2	0
1999–2000	Southampton	0	0	2	0
1999–2000	Brentford	22	2		
2000–01	Brentford	29	0		
2001–02	Brentford	0	0	51	2

McCAMMON, Mark (F)   50 3
H: 6 3 W: 15 00 b.Barnet 7-8-78
Source: Cambridge C.

1997–98	Cambridge U	2	0		
1998–99	Cambridge U	2	0	4	0
1998–99	Charlton Ath	0	0		
1999–2000	Charlton Ath	4	0	4	0
1999–2000	*Swindon T*	4	0	4	0
2000–01	Brentford	24	3		
2001–02	Brentford	14	0	38	3

O'CONNOR, Kevin (F)   42 1
H: 5 11 W: 12 02 b.Blackburn 24-2-82
Source: Trainee.

1999–2000	Brentford	6	0		
2000–01	Brentford	11	1		
2001–02	Brentford	25	0	42	1

OWUSU, Lloyd* (F)   164 64
H: 6 2 W: 13 05 b.Slough 12-12-76
Source: Slough T.

1998–99	Brentford	46	22		
1999–2000	Brentford	41	12		
2000–01	Brentford	33	10		
2001–02	Brentford	44	20	164	64

PETERS, Mark (F)   0 0
H: 5 8 W: 10 08 b.Frimley 4-10-83
Source: Scholar.

2000–01	Southampton	0	0		
2001–02	Southampton	0	0		
2001–02	Brentford	0	0		

POWELL, Darren (D)   128 6
H: 6 4 W: 13 03 b.Hammersmith 10-3-76
Source: Hampton.

1998–99	Brentford	33	2		
1999–2000	Brentford	36	2		
2000–01	Brentford	18	1		
2001–02	Brentford	41	1	128	6

ROWLANDS, Martin (F)   131 19
H: 5 8 W: 11 07 b.Hammersmith 8-2-79
Source: Farnborough T. *Honours:* Eire Under-21.

1998–99	Brentford	36	4		
1999–2000	Brentford	40	6		
2000–01	Brentford	32	2		
2001–02	Brentford	23	7	131	19

SMITH, Jay (D)   3 0
H: 5 11 W: 11 11 b.Lambeth 29-12-81
Source: Trainee.

2000–01	Brentford	3	0		
2001–02	Brentford	0	0	3	0

SMITH, Paul (G)   20 0
H: 6 4 W: 14 00 b.Epsom 17-12-79
Source: Trainee.

1998–99	Charlton Ath	0	0		
1998–99	*Brentford*	0	0		
1999–2000	Charlton Ath	0	0		

From Carshalton Ath.

2000–01	Brentford	2	0		
2001–02	Brentford	18	0	20	0

SOMNER, Matt (D)   3 0
H: 6 0 W: 13 01 b.Isleworth 8-12-82
Source: Trainee.

2000–01	Brentford	3	0		
2001–02	Brentford	0	0	3	0

TABB, Jay (M)   5 0
H: 5 7 W: 11 03 b.Tooting 21-2-84
Source: Trainee.

2000–01	Brentford	2	0		
2001–02	Brentford	3	0	5	0

THEOBALD, David* (D)   31 0
H: 6 3 W: 12 08 b.Cambridge 15-12-78
Source: Trainee.

1997–98	Ipswich T	0	0		
1998–99	Ipswich T	0	0		
1999–2000	Brentford	10	0		
2000–01	Brentford	15	0		
2001–02	Brentford	6	0	31	0

WILLIAMS, Mark (F)   50 3
H: 5 9 W: 11 03 b.Chatham 19-10-81
Source: Scholar.

2000–01	Brentford	30	2		
2001–02	Brentford	20	1	50	3

Trainees
Allen-Page, Danny L; Blackman, Lloyd J; Hollands, Michael R; Hughes, Stephen T; Johnson, Paul; Rehman, Rizwan; Thomas, Daniel K; Traynor, Robert T

Scholars
Gauci, Dominique V; Marchena, Barry J; McNamara, Steven; Paterson, Matthew J; Scotchford, Mark N; Wells, Dean T

BRIGHTON & HA

BROOKER, Paul (F)   153 13
H: 5 8 W: 10 04 b.Hammersmith 25-11-76
Source: Fulham.

1995–96	Fulham	20	2		
1996–97	Fulham	26	2		
1997–98	Fulham	9	0		
1998–99	Fulham	1	0		
1999–2000	Fulham	0	0	56	4
1999–2000	*Brighton & HA*	15	2		
2000–01	Brighton & HA	41	3		
2001–02	Brighton & HA	41	4	97	9

CARPENTER, Richard (M)   342 22
H: 6 0 W: 13 00 b.Sheppey 30-9-72
Source: Trainee.

1990–91	Gillingham	9	1		
1991–92	Gillingham	3	0		
1992–93	Gillingham	28	0		
1993–94	Gillingham	40	3		
1994–95	Gillingham	29	0		
1995–96	Gillingham	12	0		
1996–97	Gillingham	1	0	122	4
1996–97	Fulham	34	5		
1997–98	Fulham	24	2	58	7
1998–99	Cardiff C	42	1		
1999–2000	Cardiff C	33	1	75	2
2000–01	Brighton & HA	42	6		
2001–02	Brighton & HA	45	3	87	9

CULLIP, Danny (D)   180 6
H: 6 0 W: 13 04 b.Ascot 17-9-76
Source: Trainee.

1995–96	Oxford U	0	0		
1996–97	Fulham	29	1		
1997–98	Fulham	21	1	50	2
1997–98	Brentford	13	0		
1998–99	Brentford	2	0		
1999–2000	Brentford	0	0	15	0
1999–2000	Brighton & HA	33	2		
2000–01	Brighton & HA	38	2		
2001–02	Brighton & HA	44	0	115	4

FREEMAN, Darren‡ (F)   134 27
H: 5 11 W: 13 00 b.Brighton 22-8-73
Source: Horsham T.

1994–95	Gillingham	2	0		
1995–96	Gillingham	10	0	12	0
1996–97	Fulham	39	9		
1997–98	Fulham	7	0	46	9
1998–99	Brentford	22	6	22	6
1999–2000	Brighton & HA	38	12		
2000–01	Brighton & HA	16	0		
2001–02	Brighton & HA	0	0	54	12

HADLAND, Phil* (M)   43 4
H: 5 9 W: 11 05 b.Warrington 20-10-80
Source: Trainee.

2001–02	*Carlisle U*	4	1	4	1
1999–2000	Reading	0	0		
2000–01	Rochdale	32	2	32	2
2001–02	Leyton Orient	5	1	5	1
2001–02	Brighton & HA	2	0	2	0

HART, Gary (F)   171 32
H: 5 9 W: 12 07 b.Harlow 21-9-76
Source: Stansted.

1998–99	Brighton & HA	44	12		
1999–2000	Brighton & HA	43	9		
2000–01	Brighton & HA	45	7		
2001–02	Brighton & HA	39	4	171	32

JONES, Chris* (G)   30 0
H: 6 0 W: 13 08 b.Melbourne 10-7-75

1997–98	South Melbourne	1	0		
1998–99	South Melbourne	0	0		
1999–2000	South Melbourne	25	0		
2000–01	South Melbourne	2	0		
2001–02	South Melbourne	2	0	30	0
2001–02	Brighton & HA	0	0		

JONES, Nathan (M)   184 8
H: 5 6 W: 11 07 b.Rhondda 28-5-73
Source: Cardiff C Trainee, Maesteg Park, Ton Pentre, Merthyr T.

1995–96	Luton T	0	0		

Badajoz, Numancia

1997–98	Southend U	39	0		
1998–99	Southend U	17	0		
1998–99	*Scarborough*	9	0	9	0

1999–2000	Southend U	43	2	99 2
2000–01	Brighton & HA	40	4	
2001–02	Brighton & HA	36	2	76 6

KUIPERS, Michels (G)   **74 0**
H: 6 2 W: 14 09 b.Amsterdam 26-6-74

1998–99	Bristol R	1	0	
1999–2000	Bristol R	0	0	1 0
2000–01	Brighton & HA	34	0	
2001–02	Brighton & HA	39	0	73 0

LEE, David (M)   **55 9**
H: 5 10 W: 12 07 b.Basildon 28-3-80
Source: Trainee.

1998–99	Tottenham H	0	0	
1999–2000	Tottenham H	0	0	
2000–01	Southend U	42	8	42 8
2001–02	Hull C	11	1	11 1
2001–02	Brighton & HA	2	0	2 0

LEHMANN, Dirk‡ (F)   **93 11**
H: 6 1 W: 12 01 b.Aachen 16-8-71
Source: Energie Cottbus.

1998–99	Fulham	26	2	26 2
1999–2000	Hibernian	30	7	
2000–01	Hibernian	30	2	60 9
2001–02	Brighton & HA	7	0	7 0

(On loan to Motherwell, January 2002).

MARNEY, Daniel (F)   **0 0**
H: 5 9 W: 10 12 b.Sidcup 2-10-81
Source: Scholar.

2001–02	Brighton & HA	0	0	

MAYO, Kerry (D)   **202 9**
H: 5 9 W: 13 05 b.Cuckfield 21-9-77
Source: Trainee.

1996–97	Brighton & HA	24	0	
1997–98	Brighton & HA	44	6	
1998–99	Brighton & HA	25	1	
1999–2000	Brighton & HA	31	1	
2000–01	Brighton & HA	45	1	
2001–02	Brighton & HA	33	0	202 9

McARTHUR, Duncan (M)   **3 0**
H: 5 9 W: 12 06 b.Brighton 6-5-81
Source: Trainee.

1998–99	Brighton & HA	3	0	
1999–2000	Brighton & HA	0	0	
2000–01	Brighton & HA	0	0	
2001–02	Brighton & HA	0	0	3 0

McPHEE, Christopher§ (M)   **6 0**
H: 5 11 W: 11 09 b.Eastbourne 20-3-83
Source: Scholar.

1999–2000	Brighton & HA	4	0	
2000–01	Brighton & HA	0	0	
2001–02	Brighton & HA	2	0	6 0

MELTON, Steve (M)   **46 2**
H: 5 11 W: 12 03 b.Lincoln 3-10-78
Source: Trainee.

1995–96	Nottingham F	0	0	
1996–97	Nottingham F	0	0	
1997–98	Nottingham F	0	0	
1998–99	Nottingham F	1	0	
1999–2000	Nottingham F	2	0	3 0
1999–2000	Stoke C	5	0	5 0
2000–01	Brighton & HA	28	1	
2001–02	Brighton & HA	10	1	38 2

MORGAN, Simon* (D)   **555 52**
H: 5 11 W: 12 00 b.Birmingham 5-9-66
Source: Trainee. *Honours:* England Under-21.

1984–85	Leicester C	0	0	
1985–86	Leicester C	30	0	
1986–87	Leicester C	41	1	
1987–88	Leicester C	40	0	
1988–89	Leicester C	32	0	
1989–90	Leicester C	17	2	
1990–91	Leicester C	0	0	160 3
1990–91	Fulham	32	0	
1991–92	Fulham	36	3	
1992–93	Fulham	39	8	
1993–94	Fulham	37	6	
1994–95	Fulham	42	11	
1995–96	Fulham	41	6	
1996–97	Fulham	44	8	
1997–98	Fulham	19	1	
1998–99	Fulham	34	5	
1999–2000	Fulham	28	0	
2000–01	Fulham	1	0	353 48
2001–02	Brighton & HA	42	1	42 1

OATWAY, Charlie (M)   **271 6**
H: 5 7 W: 11 11 b.Hammersmith 28-11-73
Source: Yeading.

1994–95	Cardiff C	30	0	
1995–96	Cardiff C	2	0	32 0
1995–96	Torquay U	24	0	
1996–97	Torquay U	41	1	
1997–98	Torquay U	2	0	67 1
1997–98	Brentford	33	0	

1998–99	Brentford	24	0	57 0
1998–99	Lincoln C	3	0	3 0
1999–2000	Brighton & HA	42	4	
2000–01	Brighton & HA	38	0	
2001–02	Brighton & HA	32	1	112 5

PACKHAM, Will (G)   **2 0**
H: 6 2 W: 13 02 b.Brighton 13-1-81
Source: Trainee.

1999–2000	Brighton & HA	0	0	
2000–01	Brighton & HA	1	0	
2001–02	Brighton & HA	1	0	2 0

PETHICK, Robbie (D)   **276 5**
H: 5 10 W: 12 02 b.Tavistock 8-9-70
Source: Weymouth.

1993–94	Portsmouth	18	0	
1994–95	Portsmouth	44	1	
1995–96	Portsmouth	38	0	
1996–97	Portsmouth	35	0	
1997–98	Portsmouth	44	2	
1998–99	Portsmouth	10	0	189 3
1998–99	Bristol R	9	0	
1999–2000	Bristol R	41	2	
2000–01	Bristol R	13	0	63 2
2001–02	Brighton & HA	24	0	24 0

PITCHER, Geoff (M)   **24 2**
H: 5 7 W: 11 11 b.Sutton 15-8-75
Source: Millwall Trainee. *Honours:*

1994–95	Watford	4	1	
1995–96	Watford	9	1	13 2

From Kingstonian.

1996–97	Colchester U	1	0	1 0

From Kingstonian.

2001–02	Brighton & HA	10	0	10 0

RAMSAY, Scott‡ (M)   **35 2**
H: 6 0 W: 13 00 b.Hastings 16-10-80
Source: Trainee.

1999–2000	Brighton & HA	24	2	
2000–01	Brighton & HA	11	0	
2001–02	Brighton & HA	0	0	35 2

ROGERS, Paul (M)   **362 32**
H: 6 0 W: 12 12 b.Portsmouth 21-3-65
Source: Sutton U.

1991–92	Sheffield U	13	0	
1992–93	Sheffield U	27	3	
1993–94	Sheffield U	25	3	
1994–95	Sheffield U	44	4	
1995–96	Sheffield U	16	0	125 10
1995–96	Notts Co	21	2	
1996–97	Notts Co	1	0	22 2
1996–97	Wigan Ath	20	3	
1997–98	Wigan Ath	38	0	
1998–99	Wigan Ath	42	2	100 5
1999–2000	Brighton & HA	45	8	
2000–01	Brighton & HA	45	6	
2001–02	Brighton & HA	25	1	115 15

STEELE, Lee* (F)   **173 48**
H: 5 7 W: 12 06 b.Liverpool 2-12-73
Source: Bootle, Northwich V.

1997–98	Shrewsbury T	38	13	
1998–99	Shrewsbury T	38	13	
1999–2000	Shrewsbury T	37	11	113 37
2000–01	Brighton & HA	37	9	
2001–02	Brighton & HA	37	9	60 11

VIRGO, Adam (D)   **12 0**
H: 6 2 W: 13 12 b.Brighton 25-1-83

2000–01	Brighton & HA	6	0	
2001–02	Brighton & HA	6	0	12 0

WATSON, Paul (D)   **282 20**
H: 5 8 W: 11 05 b.Hastings 4-1-75
Source: Trainee.

1992–93	Gillingham	1	0	
1993–94	Gillingham	14	0	
1994–95	Gillingham	39	2	
1995–96	Gillingham	8	0	62 2
1996–97	Fulham	44	3	
1997–98	Fulham	6	1	50 4
1997–98	Brentford	25	0	
1998–99	Brentford	12	0	37 0
1999–2000	Brighton & HA	46	5	
2000–01	Brighton & HA	46	5	
2001–02	Brighton & HA	45	5	133 14

WILKINSON, Shaun (M)   **3 0**
H: 5 6 W: 10 08 b.Portsmouth 12-9-81
Source: Scholar.

1999–2000	Brighton & HA	2	0	
2000–01	Brighton & HA	1	0	
2001–02	Brighton & HA	0	0	3 0

ZAMORA, Bobby (F)   **94 62**
H: 6 1 W: 11 11 b.Barking 16-1-81
Source: Trainee. *Honours:* England Under-21.

1999–2000	Bristol R	4	0	4 0
1999–2000	*Brighton & HA*	6	6	

2000–01	Brighton & HA	43	28	
2001–02	Brighton & HA	41	28	90 62

Scholars
Bartholomew, Philip O; Beck, Daniel G;
Bridle, Nicholas P; Bryant, Alexander E;
Budd, Darren L; El Abd, Adam; Greatwich,
Christopher R; Hammond, Dean J; Harding,
Daniel A; Hemsley, Kevin C; Hinshelwood,
Adam; Jackson, Mark A; McPhee,
Christopher SI; Sansom, Rupert; Windsor,
Mark L; Wojciechowski, Stefan
Non-Contract
Keeley, John H
**Players who do not hold a current contract
but their registration has been retained by the
club**
McArthur, Duncan E; Geard, Matthew J

BRISTOL C

AMANKWAAH, Kevin (D)   **43 1**
H: 6 1 W: 12 10 b.London 19-5-82
Source: Scholar. *Honours:* England Youth.

1999–2000	Bristol C	5	0	
2000–01	Bristol C	14	0	
2001–02	Bristol C	24	1	43 1

ANYINSAH, Joseph (M)   **0 0**
b.Bristol 8-10-84
Source: Scholar.

2001–02	Bristol C	0	0	

ATTWELL, Jamie* (G)   **0 0**
H: 6 1 W: 15 00 b.Bristol 8-6-82
Source: Tottenham H scholar.

2001–02	Bristol C	0	0	

BEADLE, Peter (F)   **319 76**
H: 6 2 W: 15 00 b.Lambeth 13-5-72
Source: Trainee.

1988–89	Gillingham	0	0	
1989–90	Gillingham	10	2	
1990–91	Gillingham	22	7	
1991–92	Gillingham	33	5	67 14
1992–93	Tottenham H	0	0	
1992–93	Bournemouth	9	2	9 2
1993–94	Tottenham H	0	0	
1993–94	Southend U	8	1	8 1
1994–95	Tottenham H	0	0	
1994–95	Watford	20	1	
1995–96	Watford	3	0	23 1
1995–96	Bristol R	27	12	
1996–97	Bristol R	42	12	
1997–98	Bristol R	40	15	109 39
1998–99	Port Vale	26	3	26 6
1998–99	Notts Co	14	3	
1999–2000	Notts Co	8	0	22 3
1999–2000	Bristol C	35	4	
2000–01	Bristol C	33	4	
2001–02	Bristol C	0	0	58 10

BELL, Mickey (D)   **467 47**
H: 5 8 W: 12 09 b.Newcastle 15-11-71
Source: Trainee.

1989–90	Northampton T	6	0	
1990–91	Northampton T	2	0	
1991–92	Northampton T	30	4	
1992–93	Northampton T	39	5	
1993–94	Northampton T	38	0	
1994–95	Northampton T	12	1	153 10
1994–95	Wycombe W	31	3	
1995–96	Wycombe W	44	1	
1996–97	Wycombe W	46	2	118 6
1997–98	Bristol C	44	10	
1998–99	Bristol C	33	5	
1999–2000	Bristol C	36	5	
2000–01	Bristol C	41	0	
2001–02	Bristol C	42	7	196 31

BROWN, Aaron (M)   **103 6**
H: 5 10 W: 13 01 b.Bristol 14-3-80
Source: Trainee. *Honours:* England Schools.

1997–98	Bristol C	0	0	
1998–99	Bristol C	14	0	
1999–2000	Bristol C	13	2	
1999–2000	*Exeter C*	5	1	5 1
2000–01	Bristol C	35	2	
2001–02	Bristol C	36	1	98 5

BROWN, Marvin (F)   **17 0**
H: 5 8 W: 11 12 b.Bristol 6-7-83
Honours: England Youth.

1999–2000	Bristol C	2	0	
2000–01	Bristol C	5	0	
2001–02	Bristol C	10	0	17 0

BURKE, Andrew (M)   **0 0**
b.Camden 9-1-83

2000–01	Bristol C	0	0	
2001–02	Bristol C	0	0	

BURNELL, Joe (D)   70 0
H: 5 9 W: 11 13 b.Bristol 10-10-80
Source: Trainee.

1999-2000	Bristol C	17	0		
2000-01	Bristol C	23	0		
2001-02	Bristol C	30	0	70	0

BURNS, John (M)   14 0
H: 5 10 W: 11 04 b.Dublin 4-12-77
Source: Belvedere, Trainee.

1994-95	Nottingham F	0	0		
1995-96	Nottingham F	0	0		
1996-97	Nottingham F	0	0		
1997-98	Nottingham F	0	0		
1998-99	Nottingham F	0	0		
1999-2000	Nottingham F	3	0	3	0
1999-2000	Bristol C	11	0		
2000-01	Bristol C	0	0		
2001-02	Bristol C	0	0	11	0

CAREY, Louis (D)   247 3
H: 5 10 W: 12 06 b.Bristol 20-1-77
Source: Trainee. Honours: Scotland Under-21.

1995-96	Bristol C	23	0		
1996-97	Bristol C	42	0		
1997-98	Bristol C	38	0		
1998-99	Bristol C	41	0		
1999-2000	Bristol C	22	0		
2000-01	Bristol C	46	3		
2001-02	Bristol C	35	0	247	3

CLEVERLEY, Benjamin (M)   0 0
H: 5 9 W: 10 00 b.Bristol 12-9-81
Source: Scholar.

| 2001-02 | Bristol C | 0 | 0 | | |

CLIST, Simon (M)   67 5
H: 5 9 W: 11 05 b.Bournemouth 13-6-81
Source: Tottenham H Trainee.

1999-2000	Bristol C	9	0		
2000-01	Bristol C	38	4		
2001-02	Bristol C	20	1	67	5

COLES, Daniel (D)   26 0
H: 6 0 W: 12 08 b.Bristol 31-10-81
Source: Scholar.

1999-2000	Bristol C	1	0		
2000-01	Bristol C	2	0		
2001-02	Bristol C	23	0	26	0

CORREIA, Albano (F)   0 0
H: 6 2 W: 12 13 b.Guinea Bissau 18-10-81

| 2000-01 | Bristol C | 0 | 0 | | |
| 2001-02 | Bristol C | 0 | 0 | | |

DEW, Simon* (M)   0 0
b.Bristol 21-7-83
Source: Scholar.

| 2000-01 | Bristol C | 0 | 0 | | |
| 2001-02 | Bristol C | 0 | 0 | | |

DOHERTY, Tom (M)   88 4
H: 5 8 W: 11 07 b.Bristol 17-3-79
Source: Trainee.

1997-98	Bristol C	30	2		
1998-99	Bristol C	23	1		
1999-2000	Bristol C	1	0		
2000-01	Bristol C	0	0		
2001-02	Bristol C	34	1	88	4

EDWARDS, Jamie‡ (D)   0 0
H: 5 5 W: 10 05 b.Hereford 18-2-83
Source: Scholar.

1999-2000	Bristol C	0	0		
2000-01	Bristol C	0	0		
2001-02	Bristol C	0	0		

FORTUNE, Clayton (D)   1 0
H: 6 3 W: 13 10 b.Forest Gate 10-11-82
Source: Tottenham H Scholar.

| 2000-01 | Bristol C | 0 | 0 | | |
| 2001-02 | Bristol C | 1 | 0 | 1 | 0 |

HARRHY, Nicholas* (M)   0 0
b.Abergavenny 14-9-82

| 2000-01 | Bristol C | 0 | 0 | | |
| 2001-02 | Bristol C | 0 | 0 | | |

HILL, Matt (D)   91 1
H: 5 8 W: 11 10 b.Bristol 26-3-81
Source: Trainee.

1998-99	Bristol C	3	0		
1999-2000	Bristol C	14	0		
2000-01	Bristol C	34	0		
2001-02	Bristol C	40	1	91	1

HOLLAND, Paul‡ (M)   313 38
H: 5 11 W: 13 05 b.Lincoln 8-7-73
Source: School. Honours: England Schools, Under-21.

1990-91	Mansfield T	1	0		
1991-92	Mansfield T	38	6		
1992-93	Mansfield T	39	3		
1993-94	Mansfield T	38	7		
1994-95	Mansfield T	33	9	149	25
1995-96	Sheffield U	18	1	18	1
1995-96	Chesterfield	17	2		
1996-97	Chesterfield	25	3		
1997-98	Chesterfield	35	3		
1998-99	Chesterfield	33	3		
1999-2000	Chesterfield	4	0	114	11
1999-2000	Bristol C	27	0		
2000-01	Bristol C	5	1		
2001-02	Bristol C	0	0	32	1

HULBERT, Robin (M)   61 0
H: 5 10 W: 11 10 b.Plymouth 14-3-80
Source: Trainee. Honours: England Youth.

1997-98	Swindon T	1	0		
1997-98	Newcastle U	0	0		
1998-99	Swindon T	16	0		
1999-2000	Swindon T	12	0	29	0
1999-2000	Bristol C	2	0		
2000-01	Bristol C	19	0		
2001-02	Bristol C	11	0	32	0

JONES, Darren (D)   2 0
H: 6 1 W: 14 00 b.Newport 28-8-83
Source: Scholar. Honours: Wales Schools, Youth.

| 2000-01 | Bristol C | 0 | 0 | | |
| 2001-02 | Bristol C | 2 | 0 | 2 | 0 |

JONES, Steve (F)   214 51
H: 6 1 W: 13 04 b.Cambridge 17-3-70
Source: Billericay T.

1992-93	West Ham U	6	2		
1993-94	West Ham U	8	2		
1994-95	West Ham U	3	0		
1994-95	Bournemouth	30	9		
1995-96	Bournemouth	44	17		
1995-96	West Ham U	0	0		
1996-97	West Ham U	8	0	24	4
1996-97	Charlton Ath	2	0		
1997-98	Charlton Ath	23	7		
1997-98	Bournemouth	5	4	79	30
1998-99	Charlton Ath	25	1		
1999-2000	Charlton Ath	2	0	52	8
1999-2000	Bristol C	14	2		
1999-2000	Brentford	8	0	8	0
1999-2000	Southend U	9	2	9	2
2000-01	Bristol C	0	0		
2000-01	Wycombe W	5	0	5	0
2001-02	Bristol C	23	5	37	7

JORDAN, Thomas* (D)   0 0
H: 6 4 W: 13 01 b.Manchester 24-5-81
Source: School.

| 2000-01 | Bristol C | 0 | 0 | | |
| 2001-02 | Bristol C | 0 | 0 | | |

LEVER, Mark (D)   392 9
H: 6 1 W: 13 12 b.Beverley 29-3-70
Source: Trainee.

1987-88	Grimsby T	1	0		
1988-89	Grimsby T	37	2		
1989-90	Grimsby T	38	2		
1990-91	Grimsby T	40	2		
1991-92	Grimsby T	36	0		
1992-93	Grimsby T	14	1		
1993-94	Grimsby T	22	0		
1994-95	Grimsby T	31	0		
1995-96	Grimsby T	24	1		
1996-97	Grimsby T	21	0		
1997-98	Grimsby T	38	0		
1998-99	Grimsby T	24	0		
1999-2000	Grimsby T	35	0	361	8
2000-01	Bristol C	2	0		
2001-02	Bristol C	29	1	31	1

LOURENCO‡ (F)   3 1
b.Luanda 5-6-83
Source: Sporting Lisbon.

| 2000-01 | Bristol C | 3 | 1 | | |
| 2001-02 | Bristol C | 0 | 0 | 3 | 1 |

LOXTON, Craig (M)   0 0
b.Bath 14-9-84
Source: Scholar.

| 2001-02 | Bristol C | 0 | 0 | | |

MATTHEWS, Lee (F)   41 6
H: 5 9 W: 13 04 b.Middlesbrough 16-1-79
Source: Trainee. Honours: England Youth.

1995-96	Leeds U	0	0		
1996-97	Leeds U	0	0		
1997-98	Leeds U	3	0		
1998-99	Leeds U	0	0		
1998-99	Notts Co	5	0	5	0
1999-2000	Leeds U	0	0		
1999-2000	Gillingham	5	0	5	0
2000-01	Leeds U	0	0	3	0
2000-01	Bristol C	6	3		
2001-02	Bristol C	22	3	28	6

MERCER, Billy (G)   282 0
H: 6 1 W: 13 02 b.Liverpool 22-5-69
Source: Trainee.

1987-88	Liverpool	0	0		
1988-89	Liverpool	0	0		
1988-89	Rotherham U	0	0		
1989-90	Rotherham U	2	0		
1990-91	Rotherham U	13	0		
1991-92	Rotherham U	35	0		
1992-93	Rotherham U	36	0		
1993-94	Rotherham U	17	0		
1994-95	Rotherham U	1	0	104	0
1994-95	Sheffield U	3	0		
1994-95	Nottingham F	0	0		
1995-96	Sheffield U	1	0	4	0
1995-96	Chesterfield	34	0		
1996-97	Chesterfield	35	0		
1997-98	Chesterfield	36	0		
1998-99	Chesterfield	44	0		
1999-2000	Chesterfield	0	0	149	0
1999-2000	Bristol C	25	0		
2000-01	Bristol C	0	0		
2001-02	Bristol C	0	0	25	0

MILLEN, Keith* (D)   527 26
H: 6 2 W: 13 03 b.Croydon 26-9-66
Source: Juniors.

1984-85	Brentford	17	0		
1985-86	Brentford	32	2		
1986-87	Brentford	39	2		
1987-88	Brentford	40	3		
1988-89	Brentford	36	3		
1989-90	Brentford	32	0		
1990-91	Brentford	32	2		
1991-92	Brentford	34	1		
1992-93	Brentford	43	4		
1993-94	Brentford	0	0	305	17
1993-94	Watford	10	0		
1994-95	Watford	31	1		
1995-96	Watford	33	0		
1996-97	Watford	42	2		
1997-98	Watford	38	1		
1998-99	Watford	11	1		
1999-2000	Watford	0	0	165	5
1999-2000	Bristol C	28	2		
2000-01	Bristol C	29	2		
2001-02	Bristol C	0	0	57	4

MURRAY, Scott (M)   183 27
H: 5 8 W: 11 02 b.Aberdeen 26-5-74
Source: Fraserburgh.

1993-94	Aston Villa	0	0		
1994-95	Aston Villa	0	0		
1995-96	Aston Villa	3	0		
1996-97	Aston Villa	1	0		
1997-98	Aston Villa	0	0	4	0
1997-98	Bristol C	23	0		
1998-99	Bristol C	32	3		
1999-2000	Bristol C	41	6		
2000-01	Bristol C	46	10		
2001-02	Bristol C	37	8	179	27

ODEJAYI, Kayode* (F)   6 0
H: 6 1 W: 12 08 b.Ibadon 21-2-82
Source: Scholar.

1999-2000	Bristol C	3	0		
2000-01	Bristol C	3	0		
2001-02	Bristol C	0	0	6	0

PEACOCK, Lee (F)   239 68
H: 5 9 W: 14 05 b.Paisley 9-10-76
Source: Trainee. Honours: Scotland Youth, Under-21.

1993-94	Carlisle U	1	0		
1994-95	Carlisle U	7	0		
1995-96	Carlisle U	22	2		
1996-97	Carlisle U	44	9		
1997-98	Carlisle U	2	0	76	11
1997-98	Mansfield T	32	5		
1998-99	Mansfield T	45	17		
1999-2000	Mansfield T	12	7	89	29
1999-2000	Manchester C	8	0	8	0
2000-01	Bristol C	35	13		
2001-02	Bristol C	31	15	66	28

PHILLIPS, Steve (G)   100 0
H: 6 1 W: 13 02 b.Bath 6-5-78
Source: Paulton R.

1996-97	Bristol C	0	0		
1997-98	Bristol C	0	0		
1998-99	Bristol C	15	0		
1999-2000	Bristol C	21	0		
2000-01	Bristol C	42	0		
2001-02	Bristol C	22	0	100	0

PIKE, James* (F)   0 0
H: 5 10 W: 11 09 b.Bristol 15-11-82
Source: Scholar.

1999-2000	Bristol C	0	0		
2000-01	Bristol C	0	0		
2001-02	Bristol C	0	0		

ROBERTS, Chris (F)   106 22
H: 5 11 W: 11 06 b.Cardiff 22-10-79
Source: Trainee. Honours: Wales Youth, Under-21.

| 1997-98 | Cardiff C | 11 | 3 | | |

Season	Club				
1998–99	Cardiff C	4	0		
1999–2000	Cardiff C	8	0	23	3
2000–01	Exeter C	42	8		
2001–02	Exeter C	37	11	79	19
2001–02	Bristol C	4	0	4	0

ROSENIOR, Liam (F)   1   0
b.London 9-7-84
Source: Scholar.

2001–02	Bristol C	1	0	1	0

SHANAHAN, Aaron (M)   0   0
b.Coventry 10-9-82
Source: Coventry C Scholar.

2000–01	Bristol C	0	0
2001–02	Bristol C	0	0

SHEPPARD, Kyle (D)   0   0
b.Cardiff 4-12-82
Source: Chelsea Scholar.

2000–01	Bristol C	0	0
2001–02	Bristol C	0	0

SPENCER, Damien* (F)   19   1
H: 6 0   W: 14 05   b.Ascot 19-9-81
Source: Scholar.

1999–2000	Bristol C	9	1		
2000–01	Bristol C	4	0		
2000–01	Exeter C	6	0	6	0
2001–02	Bristol C	0	0	13	1

STOWELL, Mike (G)   453   0
H: 6 2   W: 14 01   b.Preston 19-4-65
Source: Leyland Motors.

1984–85	Preston NE	0	0		
1985–86	Preston NE	0	0		
1985–86	Everton	0	0		
1986–87	Everton	0	0		
1987–88	*Chester C*	14	0	14	0
1987–88	*York C*	6	0	6	0
1987–88	*Manchester C*	14	0	14	0
1988–89	Everton	0	0		
1988–89	*Port Vale*	7	0	7	0
1988–89	*Wolverhampton W*	7	0		
1989–90	Everton	0	0		
1989–90	*Preston NE*	2	0	2	0
1990–91	Wolverhampton W	39	0		
1991–92	Wolverhampton W	46	0		
1992–93	Wolverhampton W	26	0		
1993–94	Wolverhampton W	46	0		
1994–95	Wolverhampton W	37	0		
1995–96	Wolverhampton W	38	0		
1996–97	Wolverhampton W	46	0		
1997–98	Wolverhampton W	35	0		
1998–99	Wolverhampton W	46	0		
1999–2000	Wolverhampton W	18	0		
2000–01	Wolverhampton W	1	0	385	0
2001–02	Bristol C	25	0	25	0

TESTIMITANU, Ivan* (M)   114   26
H: 5 10   W: 11 02   b.Moldova 27-4-74
Honours: Moldova 38 full caps, 6 goals.

1995–96	Zimbru Chisinau	28	11		
1996–97	Zimbru Chisinau	25	4		
1997–98	Zimbru Chisinau	26	9	79	24
1998–99	Bristol C	8	0		
1999–2000	Bristol C	16	2		
2000–01	Bristol C	11	0		
2001–02	Bristol C	0	0	35	2

THORPE, Tony* (F)   279   109
H: 5 9   W: 12 01   b.Leicester 10-4-74
Source: Leicester C.

1992–93	Luton T	0	0		
1993–94	Luton T	14	1		
1994–95	Luton T	4	0		
1995–96	Luton T	33	7		
1996–97	Luton T	41	28		
1997–98	Luton T	28	14		
1997–98	Fulham	13	3	13	3
1998–99	Bristol C	16	2		
1998–99	*Reading*	6	1	6	1
1998–99	*Luton T*	8	4		
1999–2000	Bristol C	31	13		
1999–2000	*Luton T*	4	1	132	55
2000–01	Bristol C	39	19		
2001–02	Bristol C	42	16	128	50

TINNION, Brian (M)   528   48
H: 6 2   W: 13 01   b.Stanley 23-3-68
Source: Apprentice.

1985–86	Newcastle U	0	0		
1986–87	Newcastle U	3	0		
1987–88	Newcastle U	16	1		
1988–89	Newcastle U	13	1	32	2
1988–89	Bradford C	14	1		
1989–90	Bradford C	37	5		
1990–91	Bradford C	41	5		
1991–92	Bradford C	26	8		
1992–93	Bradford C	27	3	145	22
1992–93	Bristol C	11	2		
1993–94	Bristol C	41	5		
1994–95	Bristol C	35	2		
1995–96	Bristol C	30	3		
1996–97	Bristol C	32	1		
1997–98	Bristol C	44	3		
1998–99	Bristol C	35	1		
1999–2000	Bristol C	43	3		
2000–01	Bristol C	42	1		
2001–02	Bristol C	38	3	351	24

WOODMAN, Craig (D)   8   0
H: 5 9   W: 10 11   b.Tiverton 22-12-82
Source: Trainee.

1999–2000	Bristol C	0	0		
2000–01	Bristol C	2	0		
2001–02	Bristol C	6	0	8	0

Scholars
Aubrey, Matthew D; Blake, David J; Clayton, Jonathan J; Elmore, Barry M; Folkes, Peter; Gibbs, Stuart J; Harley, Ryan; Hawkins, Darren; Horseman, David J; Jacobs, Thomas; Lindsay, Dean L; Lita, Leroy H; Moundi, Didier; Palmer, Marc K; Platt, Daniel G; Simpson, Sekani; Trace, Benjamin; Turnor, James M

BRISTOL R

ANDREASSON, Marcus (D)   27   1
H: 6 4   W: 13 04   b.Liberia 13-7-78

1997	Osters	21	0		
1998	Osters	4	0	12	0
1998–99	Bristol R	5	0		
1999–2000	Bristol R	6	0		
2000–01	Bristol R	4	1		
2001–02	Bristol R	0	0	15	1

ARNDALE, Neil§ (M)   1   0
b.Bristol 26-4-84
Source: Scholar. *Honours:* England Youth.

2001–02	Bristol R	1	0	1	0

ASTAFJEVS, Vitalijs (M)   256   69
H: 5 11   W: 12 04   b.Riga 3-4-71
Honours: Latvia 83 full caps, 10 goals.

1992	Skonto Riga	21	0		
1993	Skonto Riga	11	5		
1994	Skonto Riga	21	7		
1995	Skonto Riga	28	19		
1996	Skonto Riga	18	12		
1996–97	*FK Austria*	26	1	26	1
1997	Skonto Riga	14	1		
1998	Skonto Riga	23	7		
1999	Skonto Riga	18	9	154	60
1999–2000	Bristol R	16	2		
2000–01	Bristol R	41	5		
2001–02	Bristol R	19	1	76	8

BRYANT, Simon (M)   53   1
H: 5 11   W: 12 11   b.Bristol 22-11-82
Source: Scholar. *Honours:* England Youth.

1999–2000	Bristol R	15	0		
2000–01	Bristol R	30	1		
2001–02	Bristol R	8	0	53	1

BUBB, Alvin* (F)   14   0
H: 5 4   W: 10 03   b.Paddington 11-10-80
Source: Trainee.

1998–99	QPR	0	0		
1999–2000	QPR	0	0		
2000–01	QPR	1	0	1	0
2001–02	Bristol R	0	0	13	0

CAMERON, Martin (F)   39   6
H: 6 2   W: 14 01   b.Dunfermline 16-6-78

2000–01	Bristol R	14	2		
2001–02	Bristol R	25	4	39	6

CARLISLE, Wayne‡ (F)   62   5
H: 5 7   W: 10 00   b.Lisburn 9-9-79
Source: Trainee. *Honours:* Northern Ireland Schools, Youth, Under-21.

1996–97	Crystal Palace	0	0		
1997–98	Crystal Palace	0	0		
1998–99	Crystal Palace	6	0		
1999–2000	Crystal Palace	26	3		
2000–01	Crystal Palace	14	0		
2001–02	Crystal Palace	0	0	46	3
2001–02	*Swindon T*	11	2	11	2
2001–02	Bristol R	5	0	5	0

CHALLIS, Trevor (D)   142   1
H: 5 8   W: 11 13   b.Paddington 23-10-75
Source: Trainee. *Honours:* England Youth, Under-21.

1994–95	QPR	0	0		
1995–96	QPR	11	0		
1996–97	QPR	2	0		
1997–98	QPR	0	0	13	0
1998–99	Bristol R	38	0		
1999–2000	Bristol R	40	1		
2000–01	Bristol R	22	0		
2001–02	Bristol R	29	0	129	1

CLARKE, Ryan (G)   1   0
H: 6 3   W: 12 13   b.Bristol 30-4-82
Source: Scholar.

2001–02	Bristol R	1	0	1	0

ELLIS, Clinton‡ (F)   15   1
H: 5 6   W: 12 06   b.Ealing 7-7-77

1999–2000	Bristol R	0	0		
2000–01	Bristol R	15	1		
2001–02	Bristol R	0	0	15	1

FORAN, Mark* (D)   121   5
H: 6 5   W: 14 04   b.Aldershot 30-10-73
Source: Trainee.

1991–92	Millwall	0	0		
1992–93	Millwall	0	0		
1993–94	Millwall	0	0		
1993–94	Sheffield U	0	0		
1994–95	Sheffield U	4	1		
1994–95	*Rotherham U*	3	0	3	0
1995–96	Sheffield U	7	0	11	1
1995–96	*Wycombe W*	5	0	5	0
1995–96	Peterborough U	17	1		
1996–97	Peterborough U	4	0		
1996–97	*Lincoln C*	2	0	2	0
1996–97	*Oldham Ath*	1	0	1	0
1997–98	Peterborough U	4	0	25	1
1997–98	Crewe Alex	12	1		
1998–99	Crewe Alex	6	0		
1999–2000	Crewe Alex	13	0	31	1
2000–01	Bristol R	12	0		
2001–02	Bristol R	31	2	43	2

FOSTER, Stephen* (D)   202   7
H: 6 2   W: 12 08   b.Mansfield 3-12-74
Source: Trainee.

1993–94	Mansfield T	5	0	5	0

From Woking

1997–98	Bristol R	34	0		
1998–99	Bristol R	43	1		
1999–2000	Bristol R	43	1		
2000–01	Bristol R	44	4		
2001–02	Bristol R	33	1	197	7

GALL, Kevin (M)   41   5
H: 5 9   W: 10 08   b.Merthyr 4-2-82
Source: Trainee. *Honours:* Wales Schools, Youth, Under-21.

1998–99	Newcastle U	0	0		
1999–2000	Newcastle U	0	0		
2000–01	Newcastle U	0	0		
2000–01	Bristol R	10	2		
2001–02	Bristol R	31	3	41	5

GILROY, David§ (F)   4   0
H: 5 11   W: 11 00   b.Yeovil 23-12-82
Source: Scholar.

2001–02	Bristol R	4	0	4	0

HILLIER, David* (M)   254   7
H: 5 10   W: 12 00   b.Blackheath 19-12-69
Source: Trainee. *Honours:* England Under-21.

1987–88	Arsenal	0	0		
1988–89	Arsenal	0	0		
1989–90	Arsenal	0	0		
1990–91	Arsenal	16	0		
1991–92	Arsenal	27	1		
1992–93	Arsenal	30	1		
1993–94	Arsenal	15	0		
1994–95	Arsenal	9	0		
1995–96	Arsenal	5	0		
1996–97	Arsenal	2	0	104	2
1996–97	Portsmouth	21	2		
1997–98	Portsmouth	30	2		
1998–99	Portsmouth	16	0	67	4
1998–99	Bristol R	13	0		
1999–2000	Bristol R	39	0		
2000–01	Bristol R	4	0		
2001–02	Bristol R	27	1	83	1

HOGG, Lewis (M)   57   3
H: 5 9   W: 11 04   b.Bristol 13-9-82
Source: Trainee.

1999–2000	Bristol R	0	0		
2000–01	Bristol R	34	3		
2001–02	Bristol R	23	0	57	3

HOWIE, Scott (G)   257   0
H: 6 4   W: 14 04   b.Motherwell 4-1-72
Source: Ferguslie U. *Honours:* Scotland Under-21.

1991–92	Clyde	15	0		
1992–93	Clyde	39	0		
1993–94	Clyde	1	0	55	0
1993–94	Norwich C	2	0	2	0
1994–95	Motherwell	3	0		

Season	Club	Apps	Gls	Tot Apps	Tot Gls
1995–96	Motherwell	36	0		
1996–97	Motherwell	30	0		
1997–98	Motherwell	0	0	69	0
1997–98	Reading	7	0		
1998–99	Reading	42	0		
1999–2000	Reading	36	0		
2000–01	Reading	0	0	85	0
2001–02	Bristol R	46	0	46	0

JONES, Scott (D) 155 8
H: 5 10 W: 12 01 b.Sheffield 1-5-75
Source: Trainee.

Season	Club	Apps	Gls	Tot Apps	Tot Gls
1993–94	Barnsley	0	0		
1994–95	Barnsley	0	0		
1995–96	Barnsley	4	0		
1996–97	Barnsley	18	0		
1997–98	Barnsley	12	1		
1997–98	*Mansfield T*	6	0	6	0
1997–98	*Notts Co*	0	0		
1998–99	Barnsley	29	3		
1999–2000	Barnsley	20	0		
2000–01	Barnsley	0	0	83	4
2000–01	Bristol R	39	3		
2001–02	Bristol R	19	0	58	3
2001–02	York C	8	1	8	1

LOPEZ, Carlos (D) 6 0
H: 5 11 W: 12 07 b.Madrid 22-7-79

Season	Club	Apps	Gls	Tot Apps	Tot Gls
2001–02	Bristol R	6	0	6	0

LOPEZ, Rik‡ (D) 7 0
H: 5 10 W: 11 04 b.Northwick Park 25-12-79
Source: Arsenal Trainee.

Season	Club	Apps	Gls	Tot Apps	Tot Gls
1996–97	QPR	0	0		
1997–98	QPR	0	0		
1998–99	QPR	0	0		
1999–2000	QPR	0	0		
2001–02	Bristol R	7	0	7	0

MAUGE, Ronnie* (M) 346 26
H: 5 10 W: 11 11 b.Islington 10-3-69
Source: Trainee. *Honours:* Trinidad & Tobago 8 full caps, 1 goal.

Season	Club	Apps	Gls	Tot Apps	Tot Gls
1987–88	Charlton Ath	0	0		
1988–89	Fulham	13	0		
1989–90	Fulham	37	2	50	2
1990–91	Bury	29	6		
1991–92	Bury	22	0		
1991–92	*Manchester C*	0	0		
1992–93	Bury	13	1		
1993–94	Bury	26	3		
1994–95	Bury	18	0	108	10
1995–96	Plymouth Arg	37	7		
1996–97	Plymouth Arg	35	3		
1997–98	Plymouth Arg	31	1		
1998–99	Plymouth Arg	32	3	135	14
1999–2000	Bristol R	22	0		
2000–01	Bristol R	16	0		
2001–02	Bristol R	15	0	53	0

McKEEVER, Mark (M) 42 2
H: 5 11 W: 12 00 b.Derry 16-11-78
Source: Trainee. *Honours:* Northern Ireland Youth. Eire Under-21.

Season	Club	Apps	Gls	Tot Apps	Tot Gls
1996–97	Peterborough U	3	0	3	0
1996–97	Sheffield W	0	0		
1997–98	Sheffield W	0	0		
1998–99	Sheffield W	3	0		
1998–99	*Bristol R*	7	0		
1998–99	*Reading*	7	2	7	2
1999–2000	Sheffield W	2	0		
2000–01	Sheffield W	0	0	5	0
2000–01	Bristol R	12	0		
2001–02	Bristol R	8	0	27	0

OMMEL, Sergio (F) 56 14
H: 6 2 W: 12 06 b.The Hague 2-9-77

Season	Club	Apps	Gls	Tot Apps	Tot Gls
1996–97	Groningen	5	0		
1997–98	Groningen	5	1		
1998–99	Groningen	20	5	33	6
2001–02	Bristol R	23	8	23	8

PIERRE, Nigel‡ (F) 3 0
H: 5 11 W: 11 11 b.Port of Spain 2-6-79
Source: Joe Public.

Season	Club	Apps	Gls	Tot Apps	Tot Gls
1999–2000	Bristol R	3	0		
2000–01	Bristol R	0	0		
2001–02	Bristol R	0	0	3	0

PLUMMER, Dwayne (M) 49 1
H: 5 9 W: 11 00 b.Bristol 12-5-78
Source: Trainee.

Season	Club	Apps	Gls	Tot Apps	Tot Gls
1995–96	Bristol C	11	0		
1996–97	Bristol C	2	0		
1997–98	Bristol C	1	0		
1998–99	Bristol C	0	0		
1999–2000	Bristol C	0	0	14	0

From St'age, Cheshm

Season	Club	Apps	Gls	Tot Apps	Tot Gls
2000–01	Bristol R	20	1		
2001–02	Bristol R	15	0	35	1

PRITCHARD, David‡ (D) 168 1
H: 5 8 W: 11 10 b.Wolverhampton 27-5-72
Source: Telford U. *Honours:* Wales B.

Season	Club	Apps	Gls	Tot Apps	Tot Gls
1990–91	WBA	0	0		
1991–92	WBA	5	0	5	0
1993–94	Bristol R	11	0		
1994–95	Bristol R	43	0		
1995–96	Bristol R	12	0		
1996–97	Bristol R	26	0		
1997–98	Bristol R	33	0		
1998–99	Bristol R	12	0		
1999–2000	Bristol R	21	1		
2000–01	Bristol R	0	0		
2001–02	Bristol R	5	0	163	1

RICHARDS, Justin (F) 9 0
H: 6 0 W: 13 11 b.Sandwell 16-10-80
Source: Trainee.

Season	Club	Apps	Gls	Tot Apps	Tot Gls
1998–99	WBA	1	0		
1999–2000	WBA	0	0		
2000–01	WBA	0	0	1	0
2000–01	Bristol R	7	0		
2001–02	Bristol R	1	0	8	0

SHORE, Drew† (M) 9 0
H: 5 11 W: 11 12 b.Poole 8-4-82
Source: Trainee.

Season	Club	Apps	Gls	Tot Apps	Tot Gls
2001–02	Bristol R	9	0	9	0

SHORE, Jamie (M) 24 2
H: 5 9 W: 12 05 b.Bristol 1-9-77
Source: Trainee. *Honours:* England Youth.

Season	Club	Apps	Gls	Tot Apps	Tot Gls
1994–95	Norwich C	0	0		
1995–96	Norwich C	0	0		
1996–97	Norwich C	0	0		
1997–98	Norwich C	0	0		
1998–99	Bristol R	24	2		
1999–2000	Bristol R	0	0		
2001–02	Bristol R	0	0	24	2

SMITH, Mark* (D) 33 0
H: 5 11 W: 13 02 b.Bristol 13-9-77
Source: Trainee.

Season	Club	Apps	Gls	Tot Apps	Tot Gls
1998–99	Bristol R	14	0		
1999–2000	Bristol R	0	0		
2000–01	Bristol R	0	0		
2001–02	Bristol R	19	0	33	0

TROUGHT, Michael* (D) 33 0
H: 6 2 W: 13 03 b.Bristol 19-10-80
Source: Trainee.

Season	Club	Apps	Gls	Tot Apps	Tot Gls
1998–99	Bristol R	9	0		
1999–2000	Bristol R	4	0		
2000–01	Bristol R	0	0		
2001–02	Bristol R	20	0	33	0

WALTERS, Mark* (M) 600 128
H: 5 10 W: 12 10 b.Birmingham 2-6-64
Source: Apprentice. *Honours:* England Schools, Youth, Under-21, B, 1 full cap.

Season	Club	Apps	Gls	Tot Apps	Tot Gls
1981–82	Aston Villa	0	0		
1982–83	Aston Villa	22	1		
1983–84	Aston Villa	37	8		
1984–85	Aston Villa	36	10		
1985–86	Aston Villa	40	10		
1986–87	Aston Villa	21	3		
1987–88	Aston Villa	24	7	181	39
1987–88	Rangers	18	7		
1988–89	Rangers	31	8		
1989–90	Rangers	27	5		
1990–91	Rangers	30	12	106	32
1991–92	Liverpool	25	3		
1992–93	Liverpool	34	11		
1993–94	Liverpool	17	0		
1993–94	Stoke C	9	2	9	2
1994–95	Liverpool	18	0		
1994–95	Wolverhampton W	11	3	11	3
1995–96	Liverpool	0	0	94	14
1995–96	Southampton	5	0	5	0
1996–97	Swindon T	27	7		
1997–98	Swindon T	34	6		
1998–99	Swindon T	38	10		
1999–2000	Swindon T	13	2	112	25
1999–2000	Bristol R	30	9		
2000–01	Bristol R	26	4		
2001–02	Bristol R	26	0	82	13

WEARE, Ross* (F) 14 1
H: 6 2 W: 13 09 b.Perivale 19-3-77
Source: East Ham U.

Season	Club	Apps	Gls	Tot Apps	Tot Gls
1998–99	QPR	0	0		
1999–2000	QPR	4	0		
2000–01	QPR	0	0	4	0
2001–02	Bristol R	10	1	10	1

WILSON, Che‡ (D) 97 0
H: 5 10 W: 11 12 b.Ely 17-1-79
Source: Trainee.

Season	Club	Apps	Gls	Tot Apps	Tot Gls
1997–98	Norwich C	1	0		
1998–99	Norwich C	17	0		
1999–2000	Norwich C	5	0	22	0
2000–01	Bristol R	37	0		
2001–02	Bristol R	38	0	75	0

Scholars
Arndale, Neil D; Chambers, Andrew J; Davis, Anthony S; Gilroy, David M; Greaves, Daniel G; Guibarra, Daniel G; Hobbs, Shane M; Kershaw, Keven JJ; Scott, Robert T; Spencer, Lance JM; Webb, Victor; Weisberg, Ryan P; Wilson, Dene
Non-Contract
Shore, Andrew J

BURNLEY

ARMSTRONG, Gordon# (D) 529 60
H: 6 0 W: 13 04 b.Newcastle 15-7-67
Source: Apprentice.

Season	Club	Apps	Gls	Tot Apps	Tot Gls
1984–85	Sunderland	4	0		
1985–86	Sunderland	14	2		
1986–87	Sunderland	41	5		
1987–88	Sunderland	37	5		
1988–89	Sunderland	45	8		
1989–90	Sunderland	46	8		
1990–91	Sunderland	35	6		
1991–92	Sunderland	40	10		
1992–93	Sunderland	45	3		
1993–94	Sunderland	26	2		
1994–95	Sunderland	15	1		
1995–96	Sunderland	1	0	349	50
1995–96	*Bristol C*	6	0	6	0
1995–96	*Northampton T*	4	1	4	1
1996–97	Bury	32	2		
1997–98	Bury	37	2		
1998–99	Bury	2	0	71	4
1998–99	Burnley	40	2		
1999–2000	Burnley	22	1		
2000–01	Burnley	19	0		
2001–02	Burnley	18	2	99	5

BALL, Kevin* (M) 544 27
H: 5 10 W: 12 04 b.Hastings 12-11-64
Source: Apprentice.

Season	Club	Apps	Gls	Tot Apps	Tot Gls
1983–84	Portsmouth	1	0		
1984–85	Portsmouth	9	0		
1985–86	Portsmouth	9	0		
1986–87	Portsmouth	16	0		
1987–88	Portsmouth	29	1		
1988–89	Portsmouth	14	1		
1989–90	Portsmouth	36	2	105	4
1990–91	Sunderland	33	3		
1991–92	Sunderland	33	1		
1992–93	Sunderland	43	3		
1993–94	Sunderland	36	0		
1994–95	Sunderland	42	2		
1995–96	Sunderland	36	4		
1996–97	Sunderland	32	3		
1997–98	Sunderland	31	3		
1998–99	Sunderland	42	2		
1999–2000	Sunderland	11	0	339	21
1999–2000	Fulham	18	0	18	0
2000–01	Burnley	40	2		
2001–02	Burnley	42	0	82	2

BLAKE, Robbie (F) 242 62
H: 5 9 W: 12 06 b.Middlesbrough 4-3-76
Source: Trainee.

Season	Club	Apps	Gls	Tot Apps	Tot Gls
1994–95	Darlington	9	0		
1995–96	Darlington	29	11		
1996–97	Darlington	30	10	68	21
1996–97	Bradford C	5	0		
1997–98	Bradford C	34	8		
1998–99	Bradford C	39	16		
1999–2000	Bradford C	28	2		
2000–01	Bradford C	11	0		
2000–01	*Nottingham F*	11	1	11	1
2001–02	Bradford C	26	10	153	40
2001–02	Burnley	10	0	10	0

BRANCH, Graham (F) 232 23
H: 6 2 W: 12 02 b.Liverpool 12-2-72
Source: Heswall.

Season	Club	Apps	Gls	Tot Apps	Tot Gls
1991–92	Tranmere R	4	0		
1992–93	Tranmere R	3	0		
1992–93	*Bury*	4	1	4	1
1993–94	Tranmere R	13	0		
1994–95	Tranmere R	1	0		
1995–96	Tranmere R	21	2		
1996–97	Tranmere R	35	5		
1997–98	Tranmere R	25	3	102	10
1997–98	*Wigan Ath*	3	0	3	0
1998–99	Stockport Co	14	3	14	3
1998–99	Burnley	20	1		
1999–2000	Burnley	44	3		

| 2000–01 | Burnley | 35 | 5 | | |
| 2001–02 | Burnley | 10 | 0 | 109 | 9 |

BRISCOE, Lee (D) 156 7
H: 5 11 W: 11 12 b.Pontefract 30-9-75
Source: Trainee. Honours: England Under-21.

1993–94	Sheffield W	1	0		
1994–95	Sheffield W	6	0		
1995–96	Sheffield W	26	0		
1996–97	Sheffield W	6	0		
1997–98	Sheffield W	7	0		
1997–98	*Manchester C*	5	1	5	1
1998–99	Sheffield W	16	1		
1999–2000	Sheffield W	16	0	78	1
2000–01	Burnley	29	0		
2001–02	Burnley	44	5	73	5

CENNAMO, Luigi* (G) 0 0
H: 6 0 W: 12 12 b.Munich 7-2-80
Source: Olympiakos.

| 2001–02 | Burnley | 0 | 0 | | |

COOK, Paul (M) 558 55
H: 5 11 W: 11 00 b.Liverpool 22-6-67
Source: Marine.

1984–85	Wigan Ath	2	0		
1985–86	Wigan Ath	13	2		
1986–87	Wigan Ath	27	4		
1987–88	Wigan Ath	41	8		
1988–89	Norwich C	4	0		
1989–90	Norwich C	2	0	6	0
1989–90	Wolverhampton W	28	2		
1990–91	Wolverhampton W	42	6		
1991–92	Wolverhampton W	43	8		
1992–93	Wolverhampton W	44	1		
1993–94	Wolverhampton W	36	2	193	19
1994–95	Coventry C	34	3		
1995–96	Coventry C	3	0	37	3
1995–96	Tranmere R	15	1		
1996–97	Tranmere R	36	3		
1997–98	Tranmere R	9	0	60	4
1997–98	Stockport Co	25	3		
1998–99	Stockport Co	24	0	49	3
1998–99	Burnley	12	1		
1999–2000	Burnley	44	3		
2000–01	Burnley	40	3		
2001–02	Burnley	28	5	124	12
2001–02	*Wigan Ath*	6	0	89	14

COX, Ian (D) 276 20
H: 6 0 W: 12 00 b.Croydon 25-3-71
Source: Carshalton Ath. Honours: Trinidad & Tobago 5 full caps.

1993–94	Crystal Palace	0	0		
1994–95	Crystal Palace	11	0		
1995–96	Crystal Palace	4	0	15	0
1995–96	Bournemouth	8	0		
1996–97	Bournemouth	44	8		
1997–98	Bournemouth	46	3		
1998–99	Bournemouth	46	5		
1999–2000	Bournemouth	28	0	172	16
1999–2000	Burnley	17	1		
2000–01	Burnley	38	1		
2001–02	Burnley	34	2	89	4

DAVIS, Steve (D) 446 59
H: 6 2 W: 14 07 b.Hexham 30-10-68
Source: Trainee.

1987–88	Southampton	0	0		
1988–89	Southampton	0	0		
1989–90	Southampton	4	0		
1989–90	*Burnley*	9	0		
1990–91	Southampton	3	0	7	0
1990–91	*Notts Co*	2	0	2	0
1991–92	Burnley	40	6		
1992–93	Burnley	37	2		
1993–94	Burnley	42	7		
1994–95	Burnley	43	7		
1995–96	Luton T	36	2		
1996–97	Luton T	44	8		
1997–98	Luton T	38	5		
1998–99	Luton T	20	6	138	21
1998–99	Burnley	19	3		
1999–2000	Burnley	42	7		
2000–01	Burnley	44	5		
2001–02	Burnley	23	1	299	38

ELLIS, Tony* (F) 517 179
H: 5 11 W: 11 00 b.Salford 20-10-64
Source: Horwich RMI, Northwich Vic.

1986–87	Oldham Ath	5	0		
1987–88	Oldham Ath	3	0	8	0
1987–88	Preston NE	24	4		
1988–89	Preston NE	45	19		
1989–90	Preston NE	17	3		
1989–90	Stoke C	24	6		
1990–91	Stoke C	38	9		
1991–92	Stoke C	15	4	77	19
1992–93	Preston NE	35	22		
1993–94	Preston NE	37	26	158	74
1994–95	Blackpool	40	17		
1995–96	Blackpool	43	14		
1996–97	Blackpool	45	15		
1997–98	Blackpool	18	8	146	54
1997–98	Bury	22	6		
1998–99	Bury	16	2	38	8
1998–99	Stockport Co	16	6		
1999–2000	Stockport Co	4	0	20	6
1999–2000	Rochdale	31	11		
2000–01	Rochdale	28	6	59	17
2001–02	Burnley	11	1	11	1

GASCOIGNE, Paul* (M) 378 81
H: 5 10 W: 11 11 b.Gateshead 27-5-67
Source: Apprentice. Honours: England, Under-21 B, 57 full caps, 10 goals.

1984–85	Newcastle U	2	0		
1985–86	Newcastle U	31	9		
1986–87	Newcastle U	24	5		
1987–88	Newcastle U	35	7	92	21
1988–89	Tottenham H	32	6		
1989–90	Tottenham H	34	6		
1990–91	Tottenham H	26	7		
1991–92	Tottenham H	0	0	92	19
1992–93	Lazio	22	4		
1993–94	Lazio	17	2		
1994–95	Lazio	2	0	41	6
1995–96	Rangers	28	14		
1996–97	Rangers	26	13		
1997–98	Rangers	20	3	74	30
1997–98	Middlesbrough	7	0		
1998–99	Middlesbrough	26	3		
1999–2000	Middlesbrough	8	1	41	4
2000–01	Everton	14	0		
2001–02	Everton	18	1	32	1
2001–02	Burnley	6	0	6	0

GNOHERE, Arthur (D) 62 5
H: 6 0 W: 13 00 b.Yamoussoukro 20-11-78

| 2000–01 | Caen | 28 | 2 | 28 | 2 |
| 2001–02 | Burnley | 34 | 3 | 34 | 3 |

GRANT, Tony (M) 127 3
H: 5 11 W: 10 10 b.Liverpool 14-11-74
Source: Trainee. Honours: England Under-21.

1993–94	Everton	0	0		
1994–95	Everton	5	0		
1995–96	Everton	13	1		
1995–96	Swindon T	3	1	3	1
1996–97	Everton	18	0		
1997–98	Everton	7	1		
1998–99	Everton	16	0		
1999–2000	Everton	2	0	61	2
1999–2000	*Tranmere R*	9	0	9	0
1999–2000	Manchester C	8	0		
2000–01	Manchester C	10	0		
2000–01	WBA	5	0	5	0
2001–02	Manchester C	3	0	21	0
2001–02	Burnley	28	0	28	0

JOHNROSE, Lenny* (M) 371 46
H: 5 11 W: 12 06 b.Preston 27-11-69
Source: Trainee.

1987–88	Blackburn R	1	0		
1988–89	Blackburn R	0	0		
1989–90	Blackburn R	8	3		
1990–91	Blackburn R	26	7		
1991–92	Blackburn R	7	1	42	11
1991–92	*Preston NE*	3	1	3	1
1991–92	Hartlepool U	15	2		
1992–93	Hartlepool U	38	6		
1993–94	Hartlepool U	13	3	66	11
1993–94	Bury	14	0		
1994–95	Bury	26	4		
1995–96	Bury	34	6		
1996–97	Bury	43	4		
1997–98	Bury	44	3		
1998–99	Bury	27	2	188	19
1998–99	Burnley	12	1		
1999–2000	Burnley	35	2		
2000–01	Burnley	19	1		
2001–02	Burnley	6	0	72	4

LITTLE, Glen (M) 185 26
H: 6 3 W: 13 00 b.Wimbledon 15-10-75
Source: Trainee.

1994–95	Crystal Palace	0	0		
1995–96	Crystal Palace	0	0		
1996–97	Glentoran	6	2	6	2
1996–97	Burnley	9	0		
1997–98	Burnley	24	4		
1998–99	Burnley	34	5		
1999–2000	Burnley	41	3		
2000–01	Burnley	34	3		
2001–02	Burnley	37	9	179	24

MAYLETT, Brad (M) 39 0
H: 5 8 W: 10 07 b.Manchester 24-12-80
Source: Trainee.

1998–99	Burnley	17	0		
1999–2000	Burnley	10	0		
2000–01	Burnley	12	0		
2001–02	Burnley	10	0	39	0

McGREGOR, Mark (D) 245 11
H: 5 9 W: 12 08 b.Chester 16-2-77
Source: Trainee.

1994–95	Wrexham	1	0		
1995–96	Wrexham	32	1		
1996–97	Wrexham	38	1		
1997–98	Wrexham	42	2		
1998–99	Wrexham	43	1		
1999–2000	Wrexham	45	1		
2000–01	Wrexham	43	5		
2001–02	Wrexham	0	0	244	11
2001–02	Burnley	1	0	1	0

MICHOPOULOS, Nick (G) 174 0
H: 6 3 W: 14 00 b.Karditsa 20-2-70
Honours: Greece 13 full caps.

1996–97	PAOK Salonika	34	0		
1997–98	PAOK Salonika	32	0		
1998–99	PAOK Salonika	19	0		
1999–2000	PAOK Salonika	17	0	102	0
2000–01	Burnley	39	0		
2001–02	Burnley	33	0	72	0

MOORE, Alan (M) 152 17
H: 5 10 W: 11 11 b.Dublin 25-11-74
Source: Rivermount. Honours: Eire Under-21, 8 full caps.

1991–92	Middlesbrough	0	0		
1992–93	Middlesbrough	2	0		
1993–94	Middlesbrough	42	10		
1994–95	Middlesbrough	37	4		
1995–96	Middlesbrough	12	0		
1996–97	Middlesbrough	17	0		
1997–98	Middlesbrough	4	0		
1998–99	Middlesbrough	4	0		
1998–99	*Barnsley*	5	0	5	0
1999–2000	Middlesbrough	0	0		
2000–01	Middlesbrough	0	0	118	14
2001–02	Burnley	29	3	29	3

MOORE, Ian (F) 246 49
H: 5 11 W: 12 02 b.Birkenhead 26-8-76
Source: Trainee. Honours: England Youth, Under-21.

1994–95	Tranmere R	1	0		
1995–96	Tranmere R	36	9		
1996–97	Tranmere R	21	3	58	12
1996–97	*Bradford C*	6	0	6	0
1996–97	Nottingham F	5	0		
1997–98	Nottingham F	10	1	15	1
1997–98	*West Ham U*	1	0	1	0
1998–99	Stockport Co	38	3		
1999–2000	Stockport Co	38	10		
2000–01	Stockport Co	17	7	93	20
2000–01	Burnley	27	5		
2001–02	Burnley	46	11	73	16

PAPADOPOULOS, Dimitri (F) 6 0
H: 5 8 W: 11 04 b.Kazakhstan 20-9-81
Source: Akratitos.

| 2001–02 | Burnley | 6 | 0 | 6 | 0 |

PAYTON, Andy (F) 508 200
H: 5 9 W: 11 13 b.Whalley 23-10-67
Source: Apprentice.

1985–86	Hull C	0	0		
1986–87	Hull C	21	2		
1987–88	Hull C	28	4		
1988–89	Hull C	39	17		
1989–90	Hull C	43	25		
1990–91	Hull C	10	7	143	55
1991–92	Middlesbrough	19	3	19	3
1992–93	Celtic	29	13		
1993–94	Celtic	7	2	36	15
1993–94	Barnsley	25	12		
1994–95	Barnsley	43	12		
1995–96	Barnsley	40	17	108	41
1996–97	Huddersfield T	38	17		
1997–98	Huddersfield T	5	0	43	17
1997–98	Burnley	19	9		
1998–99	Burnley	40	9		
1999–2000	Burnley	41	27		
2000–01	Burnley	40	9		
2001–02	Burnley	15	4	155	68
2001–02	*Blackpool*	4	1	4	1

RASMUSSEN, Mark (M) 0 0
H: 5 6 W: 10 10 b.Newcastle 28-11-83

SHANDRAN, Anthony (F) 1 0
H: 5 9 W: 12 10 b.North Shields 17-9-81
Source: Scholar.

| 2000–01 | Burnley | 1 | 0 | | |
| 2001–02 | Burnley | 0 | 0 | 1 | 0 |

TAYLOR, Gareth (F) 259 72

H: 6 2 W: 13 07 b.Weston-Super-Mare 25-2-73
Source: Southampton Trainee. *Honours:* Wales Under-21, 9 full caps.

Season	Club				
1991–92	Bristol R	1	0		
1992–93	Bristol R	0	0		
1993–94	Bristol R	0	0		
1994–95	Bristol R	39	12		
1995–96	Bristol R	7	4	47	16
1995–96	Crystal Palace	20	1	20	1
1995–96	Sheffield U	10	2		
1996–97	Sheffield U	34	12		
1997–98	Sheffield U	28	10		
1998–99	Sheffield U	12	1	84	25
1998–99	Manchester C	26	4		
1999–2000	Manchester C	17	5		
1999–2000	Port Vale	4	0	4	0
1999–2000	QPR	6	1	6	1
2000–01	Manchester C	0	0	43	9
2000–01	*Burnley*	15	4		
2001–02	Burnley	40	16	55	20

THOMAS, Mitchell* (D) 586 15

H: 6 2 W: 14 00 b.Luton 2-10-64
Source: Apprentice. *Honours:* England Youth, Under-21, B.

Season	Club				
1982–83	Luton T	4	0		
1983–84	Luton T	26	0		
1984–85	Luton T	36	0		
1985–86	Luton T	41	1		
1986–87	Tottenham H	39	4		
1987–88	Tottenham H	36	0		
1988–89	Tottenham H	25	1		
1989–90	Tottenham H	26	1		
1990–91	Tottenham H	31	0	157	6
1991–92	West Ham U	35	3		
1992–93	West Ham U	3	0		
1993–94	West Ham U	0	0	38	3
1993–94	Luton T	20	1		
1994–95	Luton T	36	0		
1995–96	Luton T	27	0		
1996–97	Luton T	42	3		
1997–98	Luton T	28	1		
1998–99	Luton T	32	0	292	6
1999–2000	Burnley	44	0		
2000–01	Burnley	43	0		
2001–02	Burnley	12	0	99	0

WELLER, Paul (M) 185 11

H: 5 8 W: 11 02 b.Brighton 6-3-75
Source: Trainee.

Season	Club				
1993–94	Burnley	3	0		
1994–95	Burnley	0	0		
1995–96	Burnley	25	1		
1996–97	Burnley	31	2		
1997–98	Burnley	39	2		
1998–99	Burnley	1	0		
1999–2000	Burnley	7	1		
2000–01	Burnley	44	3		
2001–02	Burnley	38	2	185	11

WEST, Dean# (D) 314 28

H: 5 10 W: 11 07 b.Leeds 5-12-72
Source: Leeds U Schoolboy.

Season	Club				
1990–91	Lincoln C	1	1		
1991–92	Lincoln C	32	3		
1992–93	Lincoln C	19	3		
1993–94	Lincoln C	18	6		
1994–95	Lincoln C	41	6		
1995–96	Lincoln C	8	1	119	20
1995–96	Bury	37	1		
1996–97	Bury	46	4		
1997–98	Bury	4	0		
1998–99	Bury	23	3	110	8
1999–2000	Burnley	34	0		
2000–01	Burnley	7	0		
2001–02	Burnley	44	0	85	0

WILLIAMSON, John* (D) 1 0

H: 6 1 W: 11 06 b.Derby 3-3-81
Source: Trainee.

Season	Club				
1998–99	Burnley	1	0		
1999–2000	Burnley	0	0		
2000–01	Burnley	0	0		
2001–02	Burnley	0	0	1	0

Scholars

Barrett, Paul J; Blakey, Sean; Carpenter, Rhys E; Chaplow, Richard D; Davis, Earl A; Eves, Liam J; Fogarty, Brian W; Grimes, Robert J; Hindle, Damien; Leeson, Andrew; O'Neill, Matthew P; Pilkington, Joel T; Richardson, Steven; Salisbury, James A; Scott, Paul D; Waine, Andrew P

BURY

BARRASS, Matt (D) 37 1

H: 5 10 W: 12 05 b.Bury 28-2-81
Source: Trainee.

Season	Club				
1999–2000	Bury	25	1		
2000–01	Bury	5	0		
2001–02	Bury	7	0	37	1

BHUTIA, Baichung* (F) 37 3

H: 5 8 W: 10 00 b.Sikkim 15-6-76
Source: East Bengal. *Honours:* India full caps.

Season	Club				
1999–2000	Bury	14	2		
2000–01	Bury	20	1		
2001–02	Bury	3	0	37	3

BILLY, Chris (M) 358 20

H: 6 0 W: 12 13 b.Huddersfield 2-1-73
Source: Trainee.

Season	Club				
1991–92	Huddersfield T	10	2		
1992–93	Huddersfield T	13	0		
1993–94	Huddersfield T	34	0		
1994–95	Huddersfield T	37	2	94	4
1995–96	Plymouth Arg	32	4		
1996–97	Plymouth Arg	45	3		
1997–98	Plymouth Arg	41	2	118	9
1998–99	Notts Co	6	0	6	0
1998–99	Bury	37	0		
1999–2000	Bury	36	4		
2000–01	Bury	46	0		
2001–02	Bury	21	3	140	7

BORLEY, David (M) 21 3

H: 5 9 W: 12 08 b.Newcastle 17-4-83
Source: Scholar. *Honours:* England Schools.

Season	Club				
2001–02	Bury	21	3	21	3

BULLOCK, Darren (M) 253 23

H: 5 9 W: 12 10 b.Worcester 12-2-69
Source: Nuneaton Bor.

Season	Club				
1993–94	Huddersfield T	20	3		
1994–95	Huddersfield T	39	6		
1995–96	Huddersfield T	42	6		
1996–97	Huddersfield T	27	1	128	16
1996–97	Swindon T	13	1		
1997–98	Swindon T	31	0		
1998–99	Swindon T	22	1	66	2
1998–99	Bury	12	1		
1999–2000	Bury	27	2		
2000–01	Bury	10	2		
2000–01	*Sheffield U*	6	0	6	0
2001–02	Bury	4	0	53	5

CLARKSON, Phil‡ (M) 325 81

H: 5 10 W: 12 05 b.Garstang 13-11-68
Source: Fleetwood T.

Season	Club				
1991–92	Crewe Alex	28	6		
1992–93	Crewe Alex	35	13		
1993–94	Crewe Alex	7	2		
1994–95	Crewe Alex	23	6		
1995–96	Crewe Alex	5	0	98	27
1995–96	Scunthorpe U	24	6		
1996–97	Scunthorpe U	28	13	52	19
1997–98	Blackpool	17	5		
1997–98	Blackpool	45	13		
1998–99	Blackpool	44	9		
1999–2000	Blackpool	35	3		
2000–01	Blackpool	28	5		
2001–02	Blackpool	2	0	171	35
2001–02	Bury	4	0	4	0

CLEGG, George (M) 41 4

H: 5 10 W: 12 00 b.Manchester 16-11-80
Source: Trainee.

Season	Club				
1999–2000	Manchester U	0	0		
2000–01	Manchester U	0	0		
2000–01	*Wycombe W*	10	0	10	0
2001–02	Bury	31	4	31	4

COLLINS, Sam* (D) 119 2

H: 6 3 W: 14 02 b.Pontefract 5-6-77
Source: Trainee.

Season	Club				
1994–95	Huddersfield T	0	0		
1995–96	Huddersfield T	0	0		
1996–97	Huddersfield T	4	0		
1997–98	Huddersfield T	10	0		
1998–99	Huddersfield T	23	0	37	0
1999–2000	Bury	19	0		
2000–01	Bury	34	2		
2001–02	Bury	29	0	82	2

CONNELL, Lee (D) 16 1

H: 6 1 W: 13 01 b.Bury 24-6-81
Source: Trainee.

Season	Club				
1999–2000	Bury	2	0		
2000–01	Bury	1	1		
2001–02	Bury	13	0	16	1

EVANS, Gary (D) 1 0

H: 5 9 W: 12 03 b.Doncaster 13-9-82
Source: Scholar.

Season	Club				
2001–02	Bury	1	0	1	0

FORREST, Martyn (M) 77 1

H: 5 9 W: 11 07 b.Bury 2-1-79

Season	Club				
1997–98	Bury	0	0		
1998–99	Bury	1	0		
1999–2000	Bury	15	0		
2000–01	Bury	27	0		
2001–02	Bury	34	1	77	1

GARNER, Glyn (G) 7 0

H: 6 2 W: 13 04 b.Pontypool 9-12-76
Source: Llanelli.

Season	Club				
2000–01	Bury	0	0		
2001–02	Bury	7	0	7	0

GUNBY, Stephen§ (M) 1 0

H: 5 11 W: 13 03 b.Lincoln 14-4-84
Source: Scholar.

Season	Club				
2001–02	Bury	1	0	1	0

HALFORD, Stephen‡ (D) 5 0

H: 5 10 W: 12 10 b.Bury 21-9-80
Source: Trainee.

Season	Club				
1999–2000	Bury	2	0		
2000–01	Bury	3	0		
2001–02	Bury	0	0	5	0

HILL, Nicky (D) 20 0

H: 6 0 W: 13 07 b.Accrington 26-2-81
Source: Trainee.

Season	Club				
1999–2000	Bury	5	0		
2000–01	Bury	10	0		
2001–02	Bury	5	0	20	0

KENNY, Paddy (G) 133 0

H: 6 1 W: 15 00 b.Halifax 15-5-78
Source: Bradford PA.

Season	Club				
1998–99	Bury	0	0		
1999–2000	Bury	46	0		
2000–01	Bury	46	0		
2001–02	Bury	41	0	133	0

LAWSON, Ian (F) 125 27

H: 5 11 W: 12 08 b.Huddersfield 4-11-77
Source: Trainee.

Season	Club				
1994–95	Huddersfield T	0	0		
1995–96	Huddersfield T	0	0		
1996–97	Huddersfield T	18	3		
1997–98	Huddersfield T	18	0		
1998–99	Huddersfield T	6	1	42	5
1998–99	*Blackpool*	9	3	9	3
1999–2000	Bury	25	11		
1999–2000	Stockport Co	15	4		
2000–01	Stockport Co	10	0		
2001–02	*Stockport Co*	0	0	25	4
2001–02	Bury	24	4	49	15

MARTIN, Adam* (F) 0 0

H: 6 2 W: 12 07 b.Manchester 12-10-81
Source: Scholar.

Season	Club				
2001–02	Bury	0	0		

MURPHY, Matt* (M) 258 38

H: 6 1 W: 12 12 b.Northampton 20-8-71
Source: Corby T.

Season	Club				
1992–93	Oxford U	2	0		
1993–94	Oxford U	0	0		
1994–95	Oxford U	22	7		
1995–96	Oxford U	34	5		
1996–97	Oxford U	30	3		
1997–98	Oxford U	29	2		
1997–98	*Scunthorpe U*	3	0	3	0
1998–99	Oxford U	43	4		
1999–2000	Oxford U	46	11		
2000–01	Oxford U	40	6	246	38
2001–02	Bury	9	0	9	0

NELSON, Michael (D) 33 3

H: 6 2 W: 13 03 b.Gateshead 15-3-82

Season	Club				
2000–01	Bury	2	1		
2001–02	Bury	31	2	33	3

NEWBY, Jon (F) 83 11

H: 5 11 W: 11 00 b.Warrington 28-11-78
Source: Trainee.

Season	Club				
1998–99	Liverpool	0	0		
1999–2000	Liverpool	1	0		
1999–2000	*Crewe Alex*	6	0	6	0
2000–01	Liverpool	0	0	1	0
2000–01	*Sheffield U*	13	0	13	0
2000–01	Bury	17	5		
2001–02	Bury	46	6	63	11

NUGENT, Dave (F) 5 0

H: 5 11 W: 12 00 b.Liverpool 2-5-85
Source: Scholar.

Season	Club				
2001–02	Bury	5	0	5	0

O'SHAUGHNESSY, Paul (M) 2 0

H: 5 10 W: 11 10 b.Bury 3-10-81
Source: Scholar.

Season	Club				
2001–02	Bury	2	0	2	0

PEYTON, Warren‡ (M) — 2 0
H: 5 9 W: 11 03 b.Manchester 13-12-79

Season	Club				
1999–2000	Rochdale	1	0	1	0
2000–01	Bury	1	0		
2001–02	Bury	0	0	1	0

PREECE, Andy (F) — 420 106
H: 6 2 W: 13 01 b.Evesham 27-3-67
Source: Evesham U.

Season	Club				
1988–89	Northampton T	1	0	1	0
From Worcester C					
1989–90	Wrexham	7	1		
1990–91	Wrexham	34	4		
1991–92	Wrexham	10	2	51	7
1991–92	Stockport Co	25	13		
1992–93	Stockport Co	29	8		
1993–94	Stockport Co	43	21	97	42
1994–95	Crystal Palace	20	4	20	4
1995–96	Blackpool	41	14		
1996–97	Blackpool	41	10		
1997–98	Blackpool	44	11	126	35
1998–99	Bury	39	3		
1999–2000	Bury	43	12		
2000–01	Bury	30	2		
2001–02	Bury	13	1	125	18

REDMOND, Steve (D) — 564 15
H: 5 11 W: 13 02 b.Liverpool 2-11-67
Source: Apprentice. Honours: England Youth, Under-21.

Season	Club				
1984–85	Manchester C	0	0		
1985–86	Manchester C	9	0		
1986–87	Manchester C	30	2		
1987–88	Manchester C	44	0		
1988–89	Manchester C	46	1		
1989–90	Manchester C	38	0		
1990–91	Manchester C	37	3		
1991–92	Manchester C	31	1	235	7
1992–93	Oldham Ath	31	0		
1993–94	Oldham Ath	33	1		
1994–95	Oldham Ath	43	0		
1995–96	Oldham Ath	40	1		
1996–97	Oldham Ath	24	2		
1997–98	Oldham Ath	34	0	205	4
1998–99	Bury	26	0		
1999–2000	Bury	33	1		
2000–01	Bury	39	2		
2001–02	Bury	26	1	124	4

REID, Paul* (M) — 531 57
H: 5 8 W: 12 03 b.Oldbury 19-1-68
Source: Apprentice.

Season	Club				
1985–86	Leicester C	0	0		
1986–87	Leicester C	6	0		
1987–88	Leicester C	26	5		
1988–89	Leicester C	45	6		
1989–90	Leicester C	40	8		
1990–91	Leicester C	33	2		
1991–92	Leicester C	12	0	162	21
1991–92	Bradford C	7	0		
1992–93	Bradford C	44	6		
1993–94	Bradford C	38	9	89	15
1994–95	Huddersfield T	42	6		
1995–96	Huddersfield T	13	0		
1996–97	Huddersfield T	22	0	77	6
1996–97	Oldham Ath	9	1		
1997–98	Oldham Ath	44	4		
1998–99	Oldham Ath	40	1	93	6
1999–2000	Bury	39	2		
2000–01	Bury	43	4		
2001–02	Bury	28	3	110	9

SEDDON, Gareth (F) — 35 6
H: 5 9 W: 12 04 b.Burnley 23-5-80
Source: Atherstone U.

Season	Club				
2001–02	Bury	35	6	35	6

STUART, Jamie (D) — 119 4
H: 5 10 W: 11 02 b.Southwark 5-10-76
Source: Trainee. Honours: England Youth, Under-21.

Season	Club				
1994–95	Charlton Ath	12	0		
1995–96	Charlton Ath	27	2		
1996–97	Charlton Ath	10	1		
1997–98	Charlton Ath	1	0	50	3
1998–99	Millwall	35	0		
1999–2000	Millwall	9	0		
2000–01	Millwall	1	0		
2001–02	Millwall	0	0	45	0
2001–02	Bury	24	1	24	1

SWAILES, Danny (D) — 63 4
H: 6 3 W: 13 03 b.Bolton 1-4-79
Source: Trainee.

Season	Club				
1997–98	Bury	0	0		
1998–99	Bury	0	0		
1999–2000	Bury	24	3		
2000–01	Bury	11	0		
2001–02	Bury	28	1	63	4

SYROS, George‡ (D) — 9 1
H: 6 2 W: 13 07 b.Athens 8-2-76
Source: Akratitos.

Season	Club				
2001–02	Bury	9	1	9	1

(Transferred to Akratitos, December 2001).

TARSUSLUGIL, Edward (D) — 0 0
H: 5 9 W: 11 07 b.Leeds 3-11-82
Source: Doncaster R.

Season	Club				
2001–02	Bury	0	0		

THOMPSON, Nick* (D) — 0 0
H: 6 0 W: 11 00 b.Manchester 7-9-81
Source: Scholar.

Season	Club				
2001–02	Bury	0	0		

UNSWORTH, Lee (D) — 176 1
H: 5 11 W: 11 09 b.Eccles 25-2-73
Source: Ashton U.

Season	Club				
1994–95	Crewe Alex	0	0		
1995–96	Crewe Alex	29	0		
1996–97	Crewe Alex	29	0		
1997–98	Crewe Alex	36	0		
1998–99	Crewe Alex	24	0		
1999–2000	Crewe Alex	8	0	126	0
2000–01	Bury	15	0		
2001–02	Bury	35	1	50	1

WHITEMAN, Marc* (M) — 0 0
H: 5 9 W: 12 02 b.St Hellier 1-10-82
Source: Scholar.

Season	Club				
2000–01	Manchester U	0	0		
2001–02	Bury	0	0		

Scholars
Abbiss, Graham, P; Blackley, John A; Buckley, Craig; Gunby, Stephen R; Joseph, Daniel; Kennedy, Thomas G; Lobban, Alexander; Maden, Steven A; Morris, James P; Morris, Matthew; Nugent, David J; Rowe, Sebastian; Thompson, James; Whaley, Simon; Winstanley, Richard A
Player who does not hold a current contract but his registration has been retained by the club
Bullock, Darren.

CAMBRIDGE U

ALCIDE, Colin (F) — 211 37
H: 6 2 W: 13 11 b.Huddersfield 14-4-72
Source: Emley.

Season	Club				
1995–96	Lincoln C	27	6		
1996–97	Lincoln C	42	7		
1997–98	Lincoln C	29	12		
1998–99	Lincoln C	23	1	121	26
1998–99	Hull C	17	3		
1999–2000	Hull C	12	1	29	4
1999–2000	York C	15	2		
2000–01	York C	38	5	53	7
2001–02	Cambridge U	8	0	8	0

ANGUS, Stevland (D) — 50 0
H: 6 0 W: 12 00 b.Essex 16-9-80
Source: Trainee.

Season	Club				
1999–2000	West Ham U	0	0		
2000–01	West Ham U	0	0		
2000–01	Bournemouth	9	0	9	0
2001–02	Cambridge U	41	0	41	0

ASHBEE, Ian* (M) — 204 11
H: 6 1 W: 14 04 b.Birmingham 6-9-76
Source: Trainee. Honours: England Youth.

Season	Club				
1994–95	Derby Co	1	0		
1995–96	Derby Co	0	0		
1996–97	Derby Co	0	0	1	0
1996–97	Cambridge U	18	0		
1997–98	Cambridge U	27	1		
1998–99	Cambridge U	31	4		
1999–2000	Cambridge U	45	1		
2000–01	Cambridge U	44	3		
2001–02	Cambridge U	38	2	203	11

AUSTIN, Kevin‡ (D) — 250 5
H: 6 1 W: 15 00 b.Hackney 12-2-73
Source: Saffron Walden. Honours: Trinidad & Tobago 1 full cap.

Season	Club				
1993–94	Leyton Orient	30	0		
1994–95	Leyton Orient	39	2		
1995–96	Leyton Orient	40	1	109	3
1996–97	Lincoln C	44	1		
1997–98	Lincoln C	46	0		
1998–99	Lincoln C	39	1	129	2
1999–2000	Barnsley	3	0		
2000–01	Barnsley	0	0	3	0
2000–01	Brentford	3	0	3	0
2001–02	Cambridge U	6	0	6	0

BOURGEOIS, Daryl (D) — 0 0
b.Newham 22-9-82
Source: Southend U Scholar.

Season	Club				
2001–02	Cambridge U	0	0		

BRIDGES, David (M) — 7 1
H: 6 0 W: 12 00 b.Huntingdon 22-9-82
Source: Scholar.

Season	Club				
2001–02	Cambridge U	7	1	7	1

BUTTERWORTH, Adam‡ (D) — 1 0
H: 6 1 W: 12 00 b.Paignton 9-8-82

Season	Club				
2000–01	Cambridge U	1	0		
2001–02	Cambridge U	0	0	1	0

CHILLINGWORTH, Daniel (F) — 20 3
H: 6 0 W: 12 06 b.Cambridge 13-9-81
Source: Scholar.

Season	Club				
1999–2000	Cambridge U	3	0		
2000–01	Cambridge U	1	0		
2001–02	*Darlington*	4	1	4	1
2001–02	Cambridge U	12	2	16	2

CLARK, George§ (G) — 0 0
H: 6 4 W: 13 10 b.Cambridge 9-9-84
Source: Scholar.

Season	Club				
2001–02	Cambridge U	0	0		

CLEMENTS, Matt‡ (M) — 1 0
b.Birmingham 17-9-77
Source: Mildenhall.

Season	Club				
2001–02	Cambridge U	1	0	1	0

COCKRILL, Dale‡ (D) — 0 0
H: 6 0 W: 12 00 b.Great Yarmouth 23-11-82

Season	Club				
2001–02	Cambridge U	0	0		
2001–02	Cambridge U	0	0		

COWAN, Tom* (D) — 299 15
H: 5 9 W: 11 10 b.Bellshill 28-8-69
Source: Netherdale BC.

Season	Club				
1988–89	Clyde	16	2	16	2
1988–89	Rangers	4	0		
1989–90	Rangers	3	0		
1990–91	Rangers	5	0	12	0
1991–92	Sheffield U	20	0		
1992–93	Sheffield U	21	0		
1993–94	Sheffield U	4	0	45	0
1993–94	Stoke C	14	0	14	0
1993–94	Huddersfield T	10	0		
1994–95	Huddersfield T	37	2		
1995–96	Huddersfield T	43	2		
1996–97	Huddersfield T	42	4		
1997–98	Huddersfield T	0	0		
1998–99	Huddersfield T	5	0	137	8
1998–99	Burnley	12	1		
1999–2000	Burnley	8	0	20	1
1999–2000	*Cambridge U*	4	0		
2000–01	Cambridge U	41	2		
2001–02	Cambridge U	5	1	50	3
2001–02	Peterborough U	5	1	5	1

DUNCAN, Andy* (D) — 140 3
H: 5 11 W: 14 03 b.Hexham 20-10-77
Source: Trainee. Honours: England Schools.

Season	Club				
1996–97	Manchester U	0	0		
1997–98	Manchester U	0	0		
1997–98	Cambridge U	19	0		
1998–99	Cambridge U	45	1		
1999–2000	Cambridge U	13	1		
2000–01	Cambridge U	39	1		
2001–02	Cambridge U	24	0	140	3

FLEMING, Terry (M) — 320 12
H: 5 9 W: 10 01 b.Marston Green 1-5-73
Source: Trainee.

Season	Club				
1990–91	Coventry C	2	0		
1991–92	Coventry C	0	0		
1992–93	Coventry C	11	0	13	0
1993–94	Northampton T	31	1	31	1
1994–95	Preston NE	27	2		
1995–96	Preston NE	5	0	32	2
1995–96	Lincoln C	22	0		
1996–97	Lincoln C	37	0		
1997–98	Lincoln C	40	3		
1998–99	Lincoln C	43	0		
1999–2000	Lincoln C	41	5	183	8
2000–01	Plymouth Arg	17	0	17	0
2000–01	Cambridge U	10	1		
2001–02	Cambridge U	34	0	44	1

GOODHIND, Warren (D) — 107 3
H: 5 11 W: 11 02 b.Johannesburg 16-8-77
Source: Trainee.

Season	Club				
1996–97	Barnet	3	0		
1997–98	Barnet	35	1		
1998–99	Barnet	15	1		
1999–2000	Barnet	9	0		
2000–01	Barnet	31	1		
2001–02	Barnet	0	0	93	3
2001–02	Cambridge U	14	0	14	0

GUTTRIDGE, Luke (M) — 31 3
H: 5 5 W: 8 06 b.Barnstaple 27-3-82
Source: Trainee.

Season	Club				
1999–2000	Torquay U	5	0		
2000–01	Torquay U	0	0	1	0

2000–01	Cambridge U	1	1		
2001–02	Cambridge U	29	2	30	3

KELLY, Leon* (M) 2 0
H: 6 1 W: 12 04 b.Coventry 26-6-78
Source: Atherstone U.

2001–02	Cambridge U	2	0	2	0

KITSON, Dave (F) 41 10
H: 6 3 W: 13 00 b.Hitchin 21-1-80
Source: Arlesey.

2000–01	Cambridge U	8	1		
2001–02	Cambridge U	33	9	41	10

MARSHALL, Shaun (G) 64 0
H: 6 1 W: 13 03 b.Fakenham 3-10-78
Source: Trainee.

1996–97	Cambridge U	1	0		
1997–98	Cambridge U	2	0		
1998–99	Cambridge U	19	0		
1999–2000	Cambridge U	24	0		
2000–01	Cambridge U	11	0		
2001–02	Cambridge U	7	0	64	0

McANESPIE, Steve‡ (D) 102 0
H: 5 9 W: 10 09 b.Kilmarnock 1-2-72
Source: Aberdeen, Vasterhauringe. *Honours:* Scotland Youth.

1993–94	Raith R	3	0		
1994–95	Raith R	34	0		
1995–96	Raith R	3	0	40	0
1995–96	Bolton W	9	0		
1996–97	Bolton W	13	0		
1997–98	Bolton W	2	0	24	0
1997–98	Fulham	4	0		
1997–98	*Bradford C*	7	0	7	0
1998–99	Fulham	3	0		
1999–2000	Fulham	0	0	7	0
2000–01	Cambridge U	23	0		
2001–02	Cambridge U	1	0	24	0

(Transferred to Partick T, March 2002).

MURRAY, Fred (D) 21 0
H: 5 10 W: 11 12 b.Tipperary 22-5-82
Source: Trainee.

1998–99	Blackburn R	0	0		
1999–2000	Blackburn R	0	0		
2000–01	Blackburn R	0	0		
2001–02	Blackburn R	0	0		
2001–02	Cambridge U	21	0	21	0

MUSTOE, Neil* (M) 99 4
H: 5 9 W: 12 02 b.Gloucester 5-11-76
Source: Trainee.

1995–96	Manchester U	0	0		
1996–97	Manchester U	0	0		
1997–98	Manchester U	0	0		
1998–99	Cambridge U	34	3		
1999–2000	Cambridge U	33	0		
2000–01	Cambridge U	27	1		
2001–02	Cambridge U	5	0	99	4

NACCA, Franco (D) 0 0
H: 5 6 W: 10 00 b.Venezuela 9-11-82
Source: Scholar.

2000–01	Cambridge U	0	0		
2001–02	Cambridge U	0	0		

ONE, Armand (F) 32 4
H: 6 4 W: 14 00 b.Paris 15-3-83
Source: Nantes.

2001–02	Cambridge U	32	4	32	4

PAYNTER, Owen (M) 0 0
b.Newmarket 22-10-82
Source: Scholar.

2001–02	Cambridge U	0	0		

PEREZ, Lionel* (G) 345 0
H: 5 11 W: 13 04 b.Bagnols Coze 24-4-67

1989–90	Nimes	3	0		
1990–91	Nimes	34	0		
1991–92	Nimes	38	0		
1992–93	Nimes	36	0	111	0
1993–94	Bordeaux	9	0		
1994–95	Bordeaux	7	0	16	0
1995–96	Laval	42	0	42	0
1996–97	Sunderland	29	0		
1997–98	Sunderland	46	0	75	0
1998–99	Newcastle U	0	0		
1999–2000	Newcastle U	0	0		
1999–2000	*Scunthorpe U*	13	0	13	0
1999–2000	*Cambridge U*	9	0		
2000–01	Cambridge U	37	0		
2001–02	Cambridge U	42	0	88	0

PROKAS, Richard (M) 216 4
H: 5 9 W: 11 05 b.Penrith 22-1-76
Source: Trainee.

1994–95	Carlisle U	39	1		
1995–96	Carlisle U	20	0		
1996–97	Carlisle U	13	1		
1997–98	Carlisle U	34	0		
1998–99	Carlisle U	34	0		
1999–2000	Carlisle U	35	1		
2000–01	Carlisle U	29	0	204	3
2000–01	Cambridge U	3	0		
2001–02	Cambridge U	9	1	12	1

REVELL, Alex (F) 28 2
H: 6 3 W: 13 00 b.Cambridge 7-7-83
Source: Scholar.

2000–01	Cambridge U	4	0		
2001–02	Cambridge U	24	2	28	2

RUSH, Graham† (D) 0 0
H: 5 11 W: 12 00 b.Cambridge 8-9-82
Source: Scholar.

2001–02	Cambridge U	0	0		

SCULLY, Tony (M) 108 4
H: 5 7 W: 11 06 b.Dublin 12-6-76
Source: Trainee. *Honours:* Eire Under-21.

1993–94	Crystal Palace	0	0		
1994–95	Crystal Palace	0	0		
1994–95	*Bournemouth*	10	0	10	0
1995–96	Crystal Palace	2	0		
1995–96	*Cardiff C*	14	0	14	0
1996–97	Crystal Palace	1	0		
1997–98	Crystal Palace	0	0	3	0
1997–98	*Manchester C*	9	0	9	0
1997–98	*Stoke C*	7	0	7	0
1997–98	QPR	7	0		
1998–99	QPR	23	2		
1999–2000	QPR	8	0		
2000–01	QPR	2	0	40	2
2001–02	Cambridge U	25	2	25	2

TANN, Adam (D) 26 0
H: 6 0 W: 11 05 b.Fakenham 12-5-82
Source: Scholar. *Honours:* England Youth.

1999–2000	Cambridge U	0	0		
2000–01	Cambridge U	1	0		
2001–02	Cambridge U	25	0	26	0

TAYLOR, John (F) 506 151
H: 6 2 W: 15 00 b.Norwich 24-10-64
Source: Local.

1982–83	Colchester U	0	0		
1983–84	Colchester U	0	0		
1984–85	Colchester U	0	0		
From Sudbury T					
1988–89	Cambridge U	40	12		
1989–90	Cambridge U	45	15		
1990–91	Cambridge U	40	14		
1991–92	Cambridge U	35	5		
1991–92	Bristol R	8	7		
1992–93	Bristol R	42	14		
1993–94	Bristol R	45	23	95	44
1994–95	Bradford C	36	11	36	11
1994–95	Luton T	9	3		
1995–96	Luton T	28	0		
1996–97	Luton T	0	0	37	3
1996–97	*Lincoln C*	5	2	5	2
1996–97	*Colchester U*	8	5	8	5
1996–97	Cambridge U	21	4		
1997–98	Cambridge U	34	10		
1998–99	Cambridge U	40	17		
1999–2000	Cambridge U	40	6		
2000–01	Cambridge U	30	3		
2001–02	Cambridge U	0	0	325	86

TAYLOR, Scott‡ (M) 306 33
H: 5 9 W: 11 05 b.Portsmouth 23-11-70
Source: Trainee.

1988–89	Reading	3	0		
1989–90	Reading	29	2		
1990–91	Reading	32	1		
1991–92	Reading	29	2		
1992–93	Reading	32	5		
1993–94	Reading	38	6		
1994–95	Reading	44	8	207	24
1995–96	Leicester C	39	6		
1996–97	Leicester C	25	0		
1997–98	Leicester C	0	0		
1998–99	Leicester C	0	0		
1999–2000	Leicester C	0	0	64	6
1999–2000	*Wolverhampton W*	28	3		
2000–01	Wolverhampton W	4	0	32	3
2001–02	Cambridge U	3	0	3	0

THORNTON, Rob§ (G) 0 0
H: 5 11 W: 12 06 b.Bedford 21-11-83
Source: Scholar.

2001–02	Cambridge U	0	0		

TRAORE, Demba* (F) 8 0
H: 6 2 W: 12 00 b.Stockholm 22-4-82

2000–01	Cambridge U	1	0		
2001–02	Cambridge U	7	0	8	0

TUDOR, Shane (M) 33 3
H: 5 8 W: 11 00 b.Wolverhampton 10-2-82
Source: Trainee.

1999–2000	Wolverhampton W	0	0		
2000–01	Wolverhampton W	1	0		
2001–02	Wolverhampton W	0	0	1	0
2001–02	Cambridge U	32	3	32	3

WALLING, Dean* (D) 359 35
H: 6 0 W: 10 08 b.Leeds 17-4-69
Source: Apprentice.

1986–87	Leeds U	0	0		
1987–88	Rochdale	12	2		
1988–89	Rochdale	34	3		
1989–90	Rochdale	19	3	65	8
From Guiseley					
1991–92	Carlisle U	37	5		
1992–93	Carlisle U	23	0		
1993–94	Carlisle U	40	5		
1994–95	Carlisle U	41	7		
1995–96	Carlisle U	43	2		
1996–97	Carlisle U	46	3		
1997–98	Carlisle U	6	0	236	22
1997–98	Lincoln C	35	5		
1998–99	Lincoln C	3	0		
1999–2000	Lincoln C	0	0		
2000–01	Lincoln C	0	0	38	5
2001–02	Cambridge U	20	0	20	0

WANLESS, Paul (M) 285 39
H: 6 1 W: 14 08 b.Banbury 14-12-73
Source: Trainee.

1991–92	Oxford U	6	0		
1992–93	Oxford U	7	0		
1993–94	Oxford U	9	0		
1994–95	Oxford U	10	0	32	0
1995–96	Lincoln C	8	0	8	0
1995–96	*Cambridge U*	14	1		
1996–97	Cambridge U	30	3		
1997–98	Cambridge U	42	8		
1998–99	Cambridge U	45	8		
1999–2000	Cambridge U	42	3		
2000–01	Cambridge U	43	10		
2001–02	Cambridge U	29	6	245	39

WARNER, Phil (D) 32 0
H: 5 10 W: 11 12 b.Southampton 2-2-79
Source: Trainee.

1997–98	Southampton	1	0		
1998–99	Southampton	5	0		
1999–2000	Southampton	0	0		
1999–2000	*Brentford*	14	0	14	0
2000–01	Southampton	0	0	6	0
2001–02	Cambridge U	12	0	12	0

YOUNGS, Tom (F) 115 33
H: 5 9 W: 11 01 b.Bury St Edmunds 31-8-79
Source: Trainee.

1997–98	Cambridge U	4	0		
1998–99	Cambridge U	10	0		
1999–2000	Cambridge U	21	8		
2000–01	Cambridge U	38	14		
2001–02	Cambridge U	42	11	115	33

Scholars
Bennett, Lee; Clark, George; George, Rikki; Gleeson, Daniel; Hammond, Daniel J; Heathcote, Jonathan; Huggins, Daniel J; Meddows, Leigh J; Shinn, Michael J; Stephenson-Lowe, Jermaine J; Thornton, Robert I; Winkworth, Kevin P
Non-Contract
Rush, Graham
Player who does not hold a current contract but his registration has been retained by the club
Millership, Jamie C

CARDIFF C

ALEXANDER, Neil (G) 154 0
H: 6 0 W: 11 11 b.Edinburgh 10-3-78
Source: Edina Hibs. *Honours:* Scotland Under-21.

1996–97	Stenhousemuir	12	0		
1997–98	Stenhousemuir	36	0	48	0
1998–99	Livingston	21	0		
1999–2000	Livingston	13	0		
2000–01	Livingston	26	0	60	0
2001–02	Livingston	46	0	46	0

BOLAND, Willie (M) 158 3
H: 5 9 W: 12 02 b.Ennis 6-8-74
Source: Trainee. *Honours:* Eire Youth, Under-21.

1992–93	Coventry C	1	0		
1993–94	Coventry C	27	0		
1994–95	Coventry C	12	0		
1995–96	Coventry C	3	0		
1996–97	Coventry C	1	0		
1997–98	Coventry C	19	0		
1998–99	Coventry C	0	0	63	0
1999–2000	Cardiff C	28	1		
2000–01	Cardiff C	25	1		
2001–02	Cardiff C	42	1	95	3

BONNER, Mark (M) 288 17
H: 5 10 W: 11 00 b.Ormskirk 7-7-74
Source: Trainee.

Season	Club	Apps	Gls	Tot A	Tot G
1991–92	Blackpool	3	0		
1992–93	Blackpool	15	0		
1993–94	Blackpool	40	7		
1994–95	Blackpool	17	0		
1995–96	Blackpool	42	3		
1996–97	Blackpool	29	1		
1997–98	Blackpool	32	3	178	14
1998–99	Cardiff C	25	1		
1998–99	*Hull C*	1	1	1	1
1999–2000	Cardiff C	31	0		
2000–01	Cardiff C	24	1		
2001–02	Cardiff C	29	0	109	2

BOWEN, Jason (F) 311 65
H: 5 7 W: 11 02 b.Merthyr 24-8-72
Source: Trainee. *Honours:* Wales Schools, Youth, Under-21, 2 full caps.

Season	Club	Apps	Gls	Tot A	Tot G
1990–91	Swansea C	3	0		
1991–92	Swansea C	11	0		
1992–93	Swansea C	38	10		
1993–94	Swansea C	41	11		
1994–95	Swansea C	31	5	124	26
1995–96	Birmingham C	23	4		
1996–97	Birmingham C	25	3		
1997–98	Birmingham C	0	0	48	7
1997–98	*Southampton*	3	0	3	0
1997–98	Reading	14	1		
1998–99	Reading	1	0	15	1
1998–99	Cardiff C	17	2		
1999–2000	Cardiff C	39	12		
2000–01	Cardiff C	40	12		
2001–02	Cardiff C	25	5	121	31

BRAYSON, Paul* (F) 136 25
H: 5 4 W: 11 04 b.Newcastle 16-9-77
Source: Trainee. *Honours:* England Youth.

Season	Club	Apps	Gls	Tot A	Tot G
1995–96	Newcastle U	1	0		
1996–97	Newcastle U	0	0		
1996–97	*Swansea C*	11	5	11	5
1997–98	Newcastle U	0	0		
1997–98	Reading	6	1		
1998–99	Reading	28	0		
1999–2000	Reading	7	0	41	1
1999–2000	*Cardiff C*	9	1		
2000–01	Cardiff C	40	15		
2001–02	Cardiff C	35	3	84	19

CAMPBELL, Andy (F) 81 14
H: 5 11 W: 11 07 b.Middlesbrough 18-4-79
Source: Trainee. *Honours:* England Youth, Under-21.

Season	Club	Apps	Gls	Tot A	Tot G
1995–96	Middlesbrough	2	0		
1996–97	Middlesbrough	3	0		
1997–98	Middlesbrough	7	0		
1998–99	Middlesbrough	8	0		
1998–99	*Sheffield U*	11	3	11	3
1999–2000	Middlesbrough	25	4		
2000–01	Middlesbrough	7	0		
2000–01	*Bolton W*	6	0	6	0
2001–02	Middlesbrough	4	0	56	4
2001–02	Cardiff C	8	7	8	7

COLLINS, James (F) 10 1
H: 6 2 W: 13 01 b.Newport 23-4-83
Source: Scholar. *Honours:* Wales Youth.

Season	Club	Apps	Gls	Tot A	Tot G
2000–01	Cardiff C	3	0		
2001–02	Cardiff C	7	1	10	1•

DIMOND, Kristian (M) 0 0
b.Cardiff 1-2-83
Source: Trainee.

Season	Club	Apps	Gls
1999–2000	Crystal Palace	0	0
2000–01	Crystal Palace	0	0
2001–02	Crystal Palace	0	0
2001–02	Cardiff C	0	0

EARNSHAW, Robert (F) 85 34
H: 5 8 W: 10 07 b.Zambia 6-4-81
Source: Trainee. *Honours:* Wales Youth, Under-21, 1 full cap, 1 goal.

Season	Club	Apps	Gls	Tot A	Tot G
1997–98	Cardiff C	5	0		
1998–99	Cardiff C	5	1		
1998–99	*Middlesbrough*	0	0		
1999–2000	Cardiff C	6	1		
1999–2000	*Morton*	3	2	3	2
2000–01	Cardiff C	36	19		
2001–02	Cardiff C	30	11	82	32

EVANS, Kevin (M) 32 3
H: 6 2 W: 12 01 b.Carmarthen 16-12-80
Source: Trainee. *Honours:* Wales Youth, Under-21.

Season	Club	Apps	Gls	Tot A	Tot G
1997–98	Leeds U	0	0		
1998–99	Leeds U	0	0		
1999–2000	Leeds U	0	0		
1999–2000	*Swansea C*	2	0	2	0
2000–01	Cardiff C	30	3		
2001–02	Cardiff C	0	0	30	3

FISH, Nicholas (M) 0 0
b.Cardiff 15-9-84
Source: Scholar.

Season	Club	Apps	Gls
2001–02	Cardiff C	0	0

FORTUNE-WEST, Leo (F) 229 70
H: 6 3 W: 14 01 b.Stratford 9-4-71
Source: Tiptree, Dagenham, Dartford, Bishops Stortford, Stevenage Bor.

Season	Club	Apps	Gls	Tot A	Tot G
1995–96	Gillingham	40	12		
1996–97	Gillingham	7	2		
1996–97	*Leyton Orient*	5	0	5	0
1997–98	Gillingham	20	4	67	18
1998–99	Lincoln C	9	1	9	1
1998–99	Brentford	11	0	11	0
1998–99	Rotherham U	20	12		
1999–2000	Rotherham U	39	17		
2000–01	Rotherham U	5	1	64	30
2000–01	Cardiff C	37	12		
2001–02	Cardiff C	36	9	73	21

GABBIDON, Daniel (D) 107 6
H: 5 10 W: 12 01 b.Cwmbran 8-8-79
Source: Trainee. *Honours:* Wales Youth, Under-21, 1 full cap.

Season	Club	Apps	Gls	Tot A	Tot G
1998–99	WBA	2	0		
1999–2000	WBA	18	0		
2000–01	WBA	0	0	20	0
2000–01	Cardiff C	43	3		
2001–02	Cardiff C	44	3	87	6

GILES, Martyn (D) 5 0
H: 6 0 W: 11 04 b.Cardiff 10-4-83
Source: Scholar. *Honours:* Wales Youth.

Season	Club	Apps	Gls	Tot A	Tot G
2000–01	Cardiff C	5	0		
2001–02	Cardiff C	0	0	5	0

GORDON, Gavin (F) 162 39
H: 6 1 W: 12 00 b.Manchester 24-6-79
Source: Trainee.

Season	Club	Apps	Gls	Tot A	Tot G
1995–96	Hull C	13	3		
1996–97	Hull C	20	4		
1997–98	Hull C	5	2	38	9
1997–98	Lincoln C	13	3		
1998–99	Lincoln C	27	5		
1999–2000	Lincoln C	41	11		
2000–01	Lincoln C	18	9	99	28
2000–01	Cardiff C	10	1		
2001–02	Cardiff C	15	1	25	2

HAMILTON, Des (M) 148 6
H: 5 11 W: 14 04 b.Bradford 15-8-76
Source: Trainee. *Honours:* England Under-21.

Season	Club	Apps	Gls	Tot A	Tot G
1993–94	Bradford C	2	1		
1994–95	Bradford C	30	1		
1995–96	Bradford C	24	3		
1996–97	Bradford C	32	0	88	5
1996–97	Newcastle U	0	0		
1997–98	Newcastle U	12	0		
1998–99	Newcastle U	0	0		
1998–99	*Sheffield U*	6	0	6	0
1998–99	*Huddersfield T*	10	1	10	1
1999–2000	Newcastle U	0	0		
1999–2000	*Norwich C*	7	0	7	0
2000–01	Newcastle U	0	0	12	0
2000–01	*Tranmere R*	6	0	6	0
2001–02	Cardiff C	19	0	19	0

HEAL, Simon (M) 0 0
b.Barnstaple 10-11-82
Source: Scholar.

Season	Club	Apps	Gls
2001–02	Cardiff C	0	0

HUGHES, Ceri* (M) 240 20
H: 5 10 W: 12 07 b.Pontypridd 26-2-71
Source: Trainee. *Honours:* Wales Youth, B, 8 full caps.

Season	Club	Apps	Gls	Tot A	Tot G
1989–90	Luton T	1	0		
1990–91	Luton T	17	1		
1991–92	Luton T	18	0		
1992–93	Luton T	29	2		
1993–94	Luton T	42	7		
1994–95	Luton T	9	2		
1995–96	Luton T	23	1		
1996–97	Luton T	36	4	175	17
1997–98	Wimbledon	17	1		
1998–99	Wimbledon	14	0		
1999–2000	Wimbledon	0	0	31	1
1999–2000	Portsmouth	15	2		
2000–01	Portsmouth	19	0		
2001–02	Portsmouth	0	0	34	2
2001–02	Cardiff C	0	0		

HUGHES, David (D) 68 3
H: 6 4 W: 14 01 b.Wrexham 1-2-79
Source: Trainee. *Honours:* Wales Youth, Under-21, B.

Season	Club	Apps	Gls	Tot A	Tot G
1996–97	Aston Villa	7	0		
1997–98	Aston Villa	0	0		
1997–98	*Carlisle U*	1	0	1	0
1998–99	Aston Villa	0	0		
1999–2000	Aston Villa	0	0	7	0
1999–2000	Shrewsbury T	22	1		
2000–01	Shrewsbury T	24	2	46	3
2000–01	Cardiff C	12	0		
2001–02	Cardiff C	2	0	14	0

INGRAM, Richard (M) 0 0
b.Merthyr 15-2-85
Source: Scholar.

Season	Club	Apps	Gls
2001–02	Cardiff C	0	0

JEANNE, Leon (M) 14 0
H: 5 10 W: 11 01 b.Cardiff 17-1-80
Source: Trainee. *Honours:* Wales Under-21.

Season	Club	Apps	Gls	Tot A	Tot G
1997–98	QPR	0	0		
1998–99	QPR	10	0		
1999–2000	QPR	2	0		
2000–01	QPR	0	0	12	0
2001–02	Cardiff C	2	0	2	0

JONES, Gethin (D) 3 0
H: 5 11 W: 12 00 b.Carmarthen 8-8-81
Source: Carmarthen T.

Season	Club	Apps	Gls	Tot A	Tot G
2000–01	Cardiff C	2	0		
2001–02	Cardiff C	1	0	3	0

JORDAN, Andrew (D) 16 0
H: 6 1 W: 13 01 b.Manchester 14-12-79
Source: Trainee. *Honours:* Scotland Under-21.

Season	Club	Apps	Gls	Tot A	Tot G
1997–98	Bristol C	0	0		
1998–99	Bristol C	1	0		
1999–2000	Bristol C	8	0		
2000–01	Bristol C	2	0	11	0
2000–01	Cardiff C	5	0		
2001–02	Cardiff C	0	0	5	0

KAVANAGH, Graham (M) 289 51
H: 5 10 W: 12 01 b.Dublin 2-12-73
Source: Home Farm. *Honours:* Eire Under-21, 3 full caps, 1 goal.

Season	Club	Apps	Gls	Tot A	Tot G
1991–92	Middlesbrough	0	0		
1992–93	Middlesbrough	10	0		
1993–94	Middlesbrough	11	2		
1993–94	*Darlington*	5	0	5	0
1994–95	Middlesbrough	7	0		
1995–96	Middlesbrough	7	1		
1996–97	Middlesbrough	0	0	35	3
1996–97	Stoke C	38	4		
1997–98	Stoke C	44	5		
1998–99	Stoke C	36	11		
1999–2000	Stoke C	45	7		
2000–01	Stoke C	43	8	206	35
2001–02	Cardiff C	43	13	43	13

KENDALL, Lee (G) 0 0
H: 5 11 W: 14 04 b.Newport 8-1-81
Source: Trainee. *Honours:* Wales Under-21.

Season	Club	Apps	Gls
1997–98	Crystal Palace	0	0
1998–99	Crystal Palace	0	0
1999–2000	Crystal Palace	0	0
2000–01	Crystal Palace	0	0
2001–02	Cardiff C	0	0

LEGG, Andy (M) 460 53
H: 5 8 W: 10 01 b.Neath 28-7-66
Source: Briton Ferry. *Honours:* Wales 6 full caps.

Season	Club	Apps	Gls	Tot A	Tot G
1988–89	Swansea C	6	0		
1989–90	Swansea C	26	3		
1990–91	Swansea C	39	5		
1991–92	Swansea C	46	9		
1992–93	Swansea C	46	12	163	29
1993–94	Notts Co	30	2		
1994–95	Notts Co	34	3		
1995–96	Notts Co	25	4	89	9
1995–96	Birmingham C	12	1		
1996–97	Birmingham C	33	4		
1997–98	Birmingham C	0	0	45	5
1997–98	*Ipswich T*	6	1	6	1
1997–98	Reading	10	0		
1998–99	Reading	2	0	12	0
1998–99	*Peterborough U*	5	0	5	0
1998–99	Cardiff C	24	2		
1999–2000	Cardiff C	42	2		
2000–01	Cardiff C	39	3		
2001–02	Cardiff C	35	2	140	9

LOW, Josh (M) 102 7
H: 6 1 W: 14 03 b.Bristol 15-2-79
Source: Trainee. *Honours:* Wales Youth, Under-21.

Season	Club	Apps	Gls	Tot A	Tot G
1995–96	Bristol R	1	0		
1996–97	Bristol R	3	0		
1997–98	Bristol R	10	0		
1998–99	Bristol R	8	0	22	0
1999–2000	*Leyton Orient*	5	1	5	1
1999–2000	Cardiff C	17	2		
2000–01	Cardiff C	36	4		
2001–02	Cardiff C	22	0	75	6

MAXWELL, Leyton (M) 37 3
H: 5 8 W: 12 01 b.Rhyl 3-10-79
Source: Trainee. *Honours:* Wales Youth, Under-21.

1997-98	Liverpool	0	0	
1998-99	Liverpool	0	0	
1999-2000	Liverpool	0	0	
2000-01	Liverpool	0	0	
2000-01	*Stockport Co*	20	2	20 2
2001-02	Cardiff C	17	1	17 1

McCULLOCH, Scott‡ (D) 130 6
H: 6 0 W: 13 04 b.Cumnock 29-11-75
Source: Rangers BC. *Honours:* Scotland Schools.

1992-93	Rangers	0	0	
1993-94	Rangers	0	0	
1994-95	Hamilton A	8	1	
1995-96	Hamilton A	10	1	
1996-97	Hamilton A	24	1	
1997-98	Hamilton A	15	1	57 4
1997-98	Dunfermline Ath	18	0	
1998-99	Dunfermline Ath	19	1	37 1
1999-2000	Dundee U	15	0	15 0
2000-01	Cardiff C	21	1	
2001-02	Cardiff C	0	0	21 1

NOGAN, Kurt* (F) 333 113
H: 6 1 W: 12 05 b.Cardiff 9-9-70
Source: Trainee. *Honours:* Wales Under-21, B.

1989-90	Luton T	10	2	
1990-91	Luton T	9	0	
1991-92	Luton T	14	1	33 3
1992-93	Peterborough U	0	0	
1992-93	Brighton & HA	30	20	
1993-94	Brighton & HA	41	22	
1994-95	Brighton & HA	26	7	97 49
1994-95	Burnley	15	3	
1995-96	Burnley	46	20	
1996-97	Burnley	31	10	92 33
1996-97	Preston NE	7	0	
1997-98	Preston NE	22	5	
1998-99	Preston NE	42	18	
1999-2000	Preston NE	22	4	93 27
1999-2000	Cardiff C	6	0	
2000-01	Cardiff C	12	1	
2001-02	Cardiff C	0	0	18 1

PARKINS, Michael (M) 0 0
b.Cardiff 12-1-85
Source: Scholar.

2001-02	Cardiff C	0	0

PRIOR, Spencer (D) 394 11
H: 6 3 W: 13 01 b.Rochford 22-4-71
Source: Trainee.

1988-89	Southend U	14	1	
1989-90	Southend U	15	1	
1990-91	Southend U	19	0	
1991-92	Southend U	42	1	
1992-93	Southend U	45	0	135 3
1993-94	Norwich C	13	0	
1994-95	Norwich C	12	0	
1995-96	Norwich C	44	1	74 1
1996-97	Leicester C	34	0	
1997-98	Leicester C	30	0	64 0
1998-99	Derby Co	34	1	
1999-2000	Derby Co	20	0	54 1
1999-2000	Manchester C	9	3	
2000-01	Manchester C	21	1	30 4
2001-02	Cardiff C	37	2	37 2

SIMPKINS, Mike (D) 43 0
H: 6 1 W: 12 00 b.Sheffield 28-11-78
Source: Trainee.

1997-98	Sheffield W	0	0	
1997-98	Chesterfield	0	0	
1998-99	Chesterfield	1	0	
1999-2000	Chesterfield	9	0	
2000-01	Chesterfield	16	0	26 0
2001-02	Cardiff C	17	0	17 0

THORNE, Peter (F) 272 100
H: 6 0 W: 12 09 b.Manchester 21-6-73
Source: Trainee.

1991-92	Blackburn R	0	0	
1992-93	Blackburn R	0	0	
1993-94	Blackburn R	0	0	
1993-94	*Wigan Ath*	11	0	11 0
1994-95	Blackburn R	0	0	
1994-95	Swindon T	20	5	
1995-96	Swindon T	26	10	
1996-97	Swindon T	31	8	77 27
1997-98	Stoke C	36	12	
1998-99	Stoke C	34	9	
1999-2000	Stoke C	45	24	
2000-01	Stoke C	38	16	
2001-02	Stoke C	5	4	158 65
2001-02	Cardiff C	26	8	26 8

WALLIS, Tony (M) 0 0
b.Portsmouth 9-10-82
Source: Scholar.

2001-02	Cardiff C	0	0

WALTON, Mark (G) 210 0
H: 6 4 W: 16 03 b.Merthyr 1-6-69
Source: Swansea C. *Honours:* Wales Under-21.

1986-87	Luton T	0	0	
1987-88	Luton T	0	0	
1987-88	Colchester U	17	0	
1988-89	Colchester U	23	0	40 0
1989-90	Norwich C	1	0	
1990-91	Norwich C	4	0	
1991-92	Norwich C	17	0	
1992-93	Norwich C	0	0	
1993-94	Norwich C	0	0	
1993-94	*Wrexham*	6	0	6 0
1993-94	Dundee	0	0	
1993-94	Bolton W	3	0	3 0
From Fakenham T.				
1996-97	Fulham	28	0	
1997-98	Fulham	12	0	40 0
1997-98	*Gillingham*	1	0	1 0
1997-98	*Norwich C*	0	0	22 0
1998-99	Brighton & HA	19	0	
1999-2000	Brighton & HA	39	0	58 0
2000-01	Cardiff C	40	0	
2001-02	Cardiff C	0	0	40 0

WESTON, Rhys (D) 66 0
H: 6 0 W: 12 09 b.Kingston 27-10-80
Source: Trainee. *Honours:* Wales Schools, Youth, Under-21, 1 full cap.

1999-2000	Arsenal	1	0	
2000-01	Arsenal	0	0	1 0
2000-01	Cardiff C	28	0	
2001-02	Cardiff C	37	0	65 0

YOUNG, Scott (D) 265 21
H: 6 2 W: 13 01 b.Pontypridd 14-1-76
Source: Trainee. *Honours:* Wales Under-21, B.

1993-94	Cardiff C	6	0	
1994-95	Cardiff C	22	0	
1995-96	Cardiff C	41	0	
1996-97	Cardiff C	32	1	
1997-98	Cardiff C	31	3	
1998-99	Cardiff C	33	1	
1999-2000	Cardiff C	22	2	
2000-01	Cardiff C	45	10	
2001-02	Cardiff C	33	4	265 21

Scholars
Anthony, Byron; Bailey, John; Brimble, Daniel; Busby, Dean C; Evans, Gari; Fleetwood, Stuart; Hayward, Michael; Huggins, Kirk; Khalil, Tareq; Lippiett, Darren; Parslow, Daniel; Porter, Marc A; Taylor, Anthony P; Thomas, Daniel; Williams, Steven P

CARLISLE U

ALLAN, Jonny* (F) 29 2
H: 6 0 W: 11 03 b.Penrith 24-5-83
Source: Trainee.

2000-01	Carlisle U	0	0	
2001-02	Carlisle U	29	2	29 2

ANDREWS, Lee (D) 39 0
H: 6 0 W: 10 11 b.Carlisle 23-4-83
Source: Scholar.

2001-02	Carlisle U	39	0	39 0

ANTONY, Paul‡ (M) 0 0
H: 5 10 W: 11 00 b.Barnet 4-3-82
Source: Trainee.

2000-01	Carlisle U	0	0
2001-02	Carlisle U	0	0

BELL, Stuart§ (M) 5 0
H: 5 9 W: 11 04 b.Carlisle 15-3-84
Source: Trainee.

2001-02	Carlisle U	5	0	5 0

BERKLEY, Austin‡ (M) 181 12
H: 5 9 W: 10 10 b.Gravesend 28-1-77
Source: Trainee.

1990-91	Gillingham	0	0	
1991-92	Gillingham	3	0	3 0
1992-93	Swindon T	0	0	
1993-94	Swindon T	0	0	
1994-95	Swindon T	1	0	1 0
1995-96	Shrewsbury T	38	1	
1996-97	Shrewsbury T	24	0	
1997-98	Shrewsbury T	36	3	
1998-99	Shrewsbury T	41	8	
1999-2000	Shrewsbury T	33	0	172 12
2000-01	Barnet	0	0	
2001-02	Carlisle U	5	0	5 0

BIRCH, Mark (D) 86 0
H: 5 10 W: 11 08 b.Stoke 5-1-77
Source: Trainee.

1997-98	Stoke C	0	0	
From Northwich V.				
2000-01	Carlisle U	44	0	
2001-02	Carlisle U	42	0	86 0

DICKINSON, Mike§ (F) 1 0
H: 5 11 W: 10 08 b.Newcastle 4-5-84
Source: Trainee.

2001-02	Carlisle U	1	0	1 0

FORAN, Richie (F) 65 25
H: 6 1 W: 12 10 b.Dublin 16-6-80

2000-01	Shelbourne	28	11	28 11
2001-02	Carlisle U	37	14	37 14

FRIARS, Sean‡ (F) 2 0
H: 5 8 W: 10 07 b.Derry 15-5-79
Source: Trainee. *Honours:* Northern Ireland Under-21.

1995-96	Liverpool	0	0	
1996-97	Liverpool	0	0	
1997-98	Liverpool	0	0	
1998-99	Ipswich T	0	0	
1999-2000	Ipswich T	1	0	
2000-01	Ipswich T	0	0	1 0
2001-02	Carlisle U	1	0	1 0

GALLOWAY, Mick (M) 147 7
H: 5 11 W: 11 05 b.Nottingham 13-10-74
Source: Trainee.

1993-94	Notts Co	0	0	
1994-95	Notts Co	7	0	
1995-96	Notts Co	9	0	
1996-97	Notts Co	5	0	21 0
1996-97	*Gillingham*	9	1	
1997-98	Gillingham	39	1	
1998-99	Gillingham	25	3	
1999-2000	Gillingham	2	0	75 5
1999-2000	*Lincoln C*	5	0	5 0
1999-2000	Chesterfield	15	1	
2000-01	Chesterfield	5	0	20 1
2000-01	Carlisle U	26	1	
2001-02	Carlisle U	0	0	26 1

HADDOW, Alex* (M) 7 0
H: 5 8 W: 11 00 b.Fleet 18-1-82
Source: Trainee.

1999-2000	Reading	2	0	
2000-01	Reading	1	0	3 0
2001-02	Carlisle U	4	0	4 0

HALLIDAY, Steve‡ (F) 227 40
H: 5 10 W: 12 10 b.Sunderland 3-5-76
Source: Charlton Ath.

1993-94	Hartlepool U	11	0	
1994-95	Hartlepool U	28	5	
1995-96	Hartlepool U	39	7	
1996-97	Hartlepool U	31	8	
1997-98	Hartlepool U	31	5	140 25
1998-99	Motherwell	4	0	4 0
1999-2000	Carlisle U	16	7	
2000-01	Carlisle U	24	1	
2001-02	Carlisle U	43	7	83 15

HARKIN, Maurice‡ (F) 77 2
H: 5 8 W: 11 05 b.Derry 16-8-79
Source: Trainee. *Honours:* Northern Ireland Youth, Under-21.

1996-97	Wycombe W	4	0	
1997-98	Wycombe W	35	2	
1998-99	Wycombe W	2	0	
1999-2000	Wycombe W	17	0	
2000-01	Wycombe W	15	0	
2001-02	Wycombe W	0	0	73 2
2001-02	Carlisle U	4	0	4 0

HEWS, Chay‡ (F) 126 8
b.Norrkoping 30-9-76

1994-95	Brisbane Strikers	4	0	
1995-96	Brisbane Strikers	15	0	
1996-97	Brisbane Strikers	18	0	
1997-98	Brisbane Strikers	23	0	
1998-99	Brisbane Strikers	19	1	
1999-2000	Brisbane Strikers	16	2	
From Hiratsuka.				
2000-01	Brisbane Strikers	17	0	112 3
2002	Sylvia	9	3	9 3
2001-02	Carlisle U	5	2	5 2

HOOLICKIN, Lee‡ (M) 0 0
b.Carlisle 30-10-82
Source: Trainee.

2001-02	Carlisle U	0	0

HOPPER, Tony* (M) 138 2
H: 5 11 W: 12 08 b.Carlisle 31-5-76
Source: Trainee.

1992-93	Carlisle U	1	0
1993-94	Carlisle U	5	0
1994-95	Carlisle U	5	0
1995-96	Carlisle U	5	0

1996–97	Carlisle U	20	1
1997–98	Carlisle U	19	0
1998–99	Carlisle U	23	0
1999–2000	Carlisle U	27	0
2000–01	Carlisle U	9	0
2001–02	Carlisle U	29	1	**138**	**2**

HORE, John* (M)   **5 0**
H: 5 11   W: 10 12   b.Liverpool 18-8-82
Source: Trainee.
1999–2000	Carlisle U	1	0
2000–01	Carlisle U	1	0
2001–02	Carlisle U	3	0	**5**	**0**

JACK, Michael‡ (M)   **32 0**
H: 5 8   W: 10 02   b.Carlisle 2-10-82
Source: Trainee.
| 2001–02 | Carlisle U | 32 | 0 | **32** | **0** |

KEEN, Peter‡ (G)   **52 1**
H: 6 0   W: 11 09   b.Middlesbrough 16-11-76
Source: Trainee.
1995–96	Newcastle U	0	0
1996–97	Newcastle U	0	0
1997–98	Newcastle U	0	0
1998–99	Newcastle U	0	0
1999–2000	Carlisle U	6	0
2000–01	Carlisle U	3	1
2000–01	*Darlington*	7	0	**7**	**0**
2001–02	Carlisle U	36	0	**45**	**1**

LEWIS, Craig‡ (M)   **0 0**
b.Whitehaven 6-10-82
Source: Trainee.
| 2001–02 | Carlisle U | 0 | 0 |

MADDISON, Lee (D)   **245 0**
H: 5 11   W: 11 00   b.Bristol 5-10-72
Source: Trainee.
1991–92	Bristol R	10	0
1992–93	Bristol R	12	0
1993–94	Bristol R	37	0
1994–95	Bristol R	14	0
1995–96	Bristol R	0	0	**73**	**0**
1995–96	Northampton T	21	0
1996–97	Northampton T	34	0	**55**	**0**
1997–98	Dundee	24	1
1998–99	Dundee	21	0
1999–2000	Dundee	20	0
2000–01	Dundee	0	0	**65**	**1**
2000–01	Carlisle U	34	0
2001–02	Carlisle U	7	0	**41**	**0**
2001–02	*Oxford U*	11	0	**11**	**0**

MAY, Kyle* (M)   **0 0**
b.Doncaster 7-9-82
Source: Trainee.
| 2001–02 | Carlisle U | 0 | 0 |

McAUGHTRIE, Craig* (D)   **10 1**
H: 6 4   W: 13 10   b.Burton-on-Trent 3-3-81
Source: Trainee.
1999–2000	Sheffield U	0	0
2000–01	Carlisle U	5	0
2001–02	Carlisle U	5	1	**10**	**1**

McDONAGH, Will (D)   **12 1**
H: 6 1   W: 12 01   b.Dublin 14-3-83
Source: Bohemians.
| 2001–02 | Carlisle U | 12 | 1 | **12** | **1** |

MURPHY, Peter (D)   **61 1**
H: 5 11   W: 12 07   b.Dublin 27-10-80
Source: Trainee. *Honours:* Eire Under-21.
1998–99	Blackburn R	0	0
1999–2000	Blackburn R	0	0
2000–01	Blackburn R	0	0
2000–01	*Halifax T*	21	1	**21**	**1**
2001–02	Blackburn R	0	0
2001–02	Carlisle U	40	0	**40**	**0**

NICHOLSON, Richard§ (G)   **0 0**
H: 6 1   W: 11 10   b.Newcastle 24-9-83
Source: Trainee.
| 2001–02 | Carlisle U | 0 | 0 |

NIXON, Marc§ (F)   **0 0**
H: 5 10   W: 11 10   b.Hexham 29-1-84
Source: Trainee.
| 2001–02 | Carlisle U | 0 | 0 |

ROGERS, Dave‡ (D)   **112 4**
H: 6 0   W: 12 00   b.Liverpool 25-8-75
Source: Trainee.
1994–95	Tranmere R	0	0
1995–96	Chester C	20	1
1996–97	Chester C	5	0	**25**	**1**
From Southport.			
1997–98	Dundee	32	1
1998–99	Dundee	11	0	**43**	**1**
1999–2000	Ayr U	16	1	**16**	**1**
2000–01	Scunthorpe U	1	0	**1**	**0**
2001–02	Carlisle U	27	1	**27**	**1**

ROOKE, Steven* (D)   **1 0**
b.Carlisle 21-9-82
Source: Trainee.
| 2001–02 | Carlisle U | 1 | 0 | **1** | **0** |

SKINNER, Stephen‡ (F)   **8 0**
H: 6 0   W: 12 03   b.Whitehaven 25-11-81
Source: Trainee.
1999–2000	Carlisle U	2	0
2000–01	Carlisle U	0	0
2001–02	Carlisle U	6	0	**8**	**0**

SLAVEN, John§ (F)   **2 0**
H: 5 11   W: 10 02   b.Edinburgh 8-10-85
| 2001–02 | Carlisle U | 2 | 0 | **2** | **0** |

SOLEY, Steve* (M)   **101 16**
H: 5 11   W: 12 08   b.Widnes 22-4-71
Source: Warrington, Leek T.
1998–99	Portsmouth	8	0
1998–99	*Macclesfield T*	10	0	**10**	**0**
1999–2000	Portsmouth	0	0	**8**	**0**
1999–2000	Carlisle U	37	8
2000–01	Carlisle U	25	4
2001–02	Carlisle U	21	4	**83**	**16**

STEVENS, Ian* (F)   **443 134**
H: 5 10   W: 12 07   b.Malta 21-10-69
Source: Trainee.
1984–85	Preston NE	4	1
1985–86	Preston NE	7	1	**11**	**2**
1986–87	Stockport Co	2	0	**2**	**0**
From Lancaster C			
1986–87	Bolton W	8	2
1987–88	Bolton W	9	0
1988–89	Bolton W	21	5
1989–90	Bolton W	4	0
1990–91	Bolton W	5	0	**47**	**7**
1991–92	Bury	45	17
1992–93	Bury	32	14
1993–94	Bury	33	7	**110**	**38**
1994–95	Shrewsbury T	38	8
1995–96	Shrewsbury T	32	12
1996–97	Shrewsbury T	41	17	**111**	**37**
1996–97	Carlisle U	0	0
1997–98	Carlisle U	37	17
1998–99	Carlisle U	41	9
1999–2000	Wrexham	16	4	**16**	**4**
1999–2000	*Cheltenham T*	1	0	**1**	**0**
2000–01	Carlisle U	41	12
2001–02	Carlisle U	26	8	**145**	**46**

THURSTON, Mark (D)   **6 0**
H: 6 2   W: 11 08   b.Carlisle 10-2-80
Source: Trainee.
1998–99	Carlisle U	0	0
1999–2000	Carlisle U	0	0
2000–01	Carlisle U	5	0
2001–02	Carlisle U	1	0	**6**	**0**

THWAITES, Adam (D)   **1 0**
H: 5 10   W: 11 10   b.Carlisle 18-12-81
Source: Trainee.
| 2000–01 | Carlisle U | 0 | 0 |
| 2001–02 | Carlisle U | 1 | 0 | **1** | **0** |

VARTY, Will‡ (D)   **129 1**
H: 6 0   W: 12 00   b.Workington 1-10-76
Source: Trainee.
1995–96	Carlisle U	0	0
1996–97	Carlisle U	32	0
1997–98	Carlisle U	44	1
1998–99	Carlisle U	6	0
1998–99	*Rotherham U*	14	0
1999–2000	Rotherham U	27	0
2000–01	Rotherham U	6	0	**47**	**0**
2001–02	Carlisle U	0	0	**82**	**1**

WAKE, Brian (M)   **0 0**
b.Stockton 13-8-82
| 2001–02 | Carlisle U | 0 | 0 |

WEAVER, Luke (G)   **68 0**
H: 6 1   W: 13 02   b.Woolwich 26-6-79
Source: Trainee. *Honours:* England Schools, Youth.
1996–97	Leyton Orient	9	0
1996–97	*West Ham U*	0	0
1997–98	Leyton Orient	0	0	**9**	**0**
1997–98	Sunderland	0	0
1998–99	Sunderland	0	0
1998–99	*Scarborough*	6	0	**6**	**0**
1999–2000	Sunderland	0	0
1999–2000	Carlisle U	29	0
2000–01	Carlisle U	14	0
2001–02	Carlisle U	10	0	**53**	**0**

WHITEHEAD, Stuart (D)   **143 2**
H: 6 0   W: 12 02   b.Bromsgrove 17-7-77
Source: Bromsgrove R.
1995–96	Bolton W	0	0
1996–97	Bolton W	0	0
1997–98	Bolton W	0	0
1998–99	Carlisle U	37	0

1999–2000	Carlisle U	29	0
2000–01	Carlisle U	45	1
2001–02	Carlisle U	32	1	**143**	**2**

WILLIS, Scott‡ (M)   **1 0**
H: 5 9   W: 11 07   b.Liverpool 20-2-82
Source: Wigan Ath Trainee.
1999–2000	Mansfield T	0	0
2000–01	Mansfield T	0	0
2001–02	Carlisle U	1	0	**1**	**0**

WINSTANLEY, Mark‡ (D)   **485 10**
H: 6 1   W: 12 07   b.St Helens 22-1-68
Source: Trainee.
1984–85	Bolton W	0	0
1985–86	Bolton W	3	0
1986–87	Bolton W	13	0
1987–88	Bolton W	8	1
1988–89	Bolton W	44	0
1989–90	Bolton W	43	1
1990–91	Bolton W	32	0
1991–92	Bolton W	27	0
1992–93	Bolton W	29	1
1993–94	Bolton W	21	0	**220**	**3**
1994–95	Burnley	44	2
1995–96	Burnley	45	3
1996–97	Burnley	35	0
1997–98	Burnley	27	0
1998–99	Burnley	1	0	**152**	**5**
1998–99	*Shrewsbury T*	8	0
1998–99	*Scunthorpe U*	1	0
1998–99	*Preston NE*	0	0
1999–2000	Shrewsbury T	33	1	**41**	**1**
2000–01	Carlisle U	36	0
2001–02	Carlisle U	36	1	**72**	**1**

Trainees
Bell, Stuart; Blades, Neil; Brown, Gary; Bruce, Paul R; Dickinson, Michael J; Gardiner, Mark; Hewitt, Steven E; Lynn, Charles D; McKie, Michael J; McNeil, Steven; Mitchell, Andrew R; Nicholson, Richard A; Nixon, Marc S; Reed, Michael T; Robinson, Nicholas A; Taylor, Tyran D
Non-Contract
Dalton, Neil J

CHARLTON ATH

BAGHERI, Karim‡ (M)   **52 6**
H: 6 1   W: 12 04   b.Tabriz 20-2-74
Source: Teraktor Sazi, Keshavarz, Pirouzi.
Honours: Iran 48 full caps.
1997–98	Arminia Bielefeld	18	3
1998–99	Arminia Bielefeld	22	2
1999–2000	Arminia Bielefeld	11	1	**51**	**6**
From Pirouzi			
2000–01	Charlton Ath	0	0
2001–02	Charlton Ath	0	0	**1**	**0**

BART-WILLIAMS, Chris (M)   **383 49**
H: 5 11   W: 12 07   b.Freetown 16-6-74
Source: Trainee. *Honours:* England Youth, Under-21.
1990–91	Leyton Orient	21	2
1991–92	Leyton Orient	15	0	**36**	**2**
1991–92	Sheffield W	15	0
1992–93	Sheffield W	34	6
1993–94	Sheffield W	37	8
1994–95	Sheffield W	38	2	**124**	**16**
1995–96	Nottingham F	33	0
1996–97	Nottingham F	16	1
1997–98	Nottingham F	33	4
1998–99	Nottingham F	24	3
1999–2000	Nottingham F	38	5
2000–01	Nottingham F	46	14
2001–02	Nottingham F	17	3	**207**	**30**
2001–02	Charlton Ath	16	1	**16**	**1**

BARTLETT, Shaun (F)   **166 50**
H: 6 0   W: 12 06   b.Cape Town 31-10-72
Honours: Cape Town Spurs. South Africa 60 full caps, 24 goals.
1996	Colorado Rapids	26	8
1996–97	Amazulu	0	0
1997	New York/	13	2	**13**	**2**
	New Jersey M		
1997	Colorado Rapids	10	1	**36**	**9**
1998	Cape Town Spurs	18	8	**18**	**8**
1998–99	Zurich	27	13
1999–2000	Zurich	20	2
2000–01	Zurich	20	8	**67**	**23**
2000–01	Charlton Ath	18	7
2001–02	Charlton Ath	14	1	**32**	**8**

BRENNAN, Martin* (G)   **0 0**
H: 6 1   W: 12 00   b.Whipps Cross 14-9-82
| 2000–01 | Charlton Ath | 0 | 0 |
| 2001–02 | Charlton Ath | 0 | 0 |

BROWN, Steve (D) 239 9
H: 6 1 W: 14 10 b.Brighton 13-5-72
Source: Trainee.

1990–91	Charlton Ath	0	0		
1991–92	Charlton Ath	1	0		
1992–93	Charlton Ath	0	0		
1993–94	Charlton Ath	19	0		
1994–95	Charlton Ath	42	3		
1995–96	Charlton Ath	19	0		
1996–97	Charlton Ath	27	0		
1997–98	Charlton Ath	34	2		
1998–99	Charlton Ath	18	0		
1999–2000	Charlton Ath	40	2		
2000–01	Charlton Ath	25	0		
2001–02	Charlton Ath	14	2	**239**	**9**

COLLIS, Dave‡ (D) 2 0
H: 5 10 W: 10 12 b.London 8-11-81

2000–01	Charlton Ath	0	0		
2000–01	*Barnet*	2	0	**2**	**0**
2001–02	Charlton Ath	0	0		

COSTA, Jorge* (D) 259 16
H: 6 2 W: 14 00 b.Oporto 14-10-71
Honours: Portugal 51 full caps, 2 goals.

1990–91	Penafiel	19	3	**19**	**3**
1991–92	Maritimo	31	1	**31**	**1**
1992–93	Porto	9	1		
1993–94	Porto	13	0		
1994–95	Porto	13	1		
1995–96	Porto	21	1		
1996–97	Porto	26	4		
1997–98	Porto	13	0		
1998–99	Porto	33	2		
1999–2000	Porto	31	1		
2000–01	Porto	20	1		
2001–02	Porto	6	1	**185**	**12**
2001–02	Charlton Ath	24	0	**24**	**0**

DE BOLLA, Mark (F) 0 0
H: 5 7 W: 11 09 b.London 1-1-83
Source: Trainee.

1999–2000	Aston Villa	0	0		
2000–01	Charlton Ath	0	0		
2001–02	Charlton Ath	0	0		

DEANE, Adrian (M) 0 0
H: 5 10 W: 10 00 b.London 24-2-83

2001–02	Charlton Ath	0	0		

DINCER, Fatih (D) 0 0
H: 5 8 W: 11 00 b.Stockholm 13-7-83

2000–01	Charlton Ath	0	0		
2001–02	Charlton Ath	0	0		

EUELL, Jason (F) 177 52
H: 5 11 W: 11 13 b.Lambeth 6-2-77
Source: Trainee. *Honours:* England Youth, Under-21.

1995–96	Wimbledon	9	2		
1996–97	Wimbledon	7	2		
1997–98	Wimbledon	19	4		
1998–99	Wimbledon	33	10		
1999–2000	Wimbledon	37	4		
2000–01	Wimbledon	36	19	**141**	**41**
2001–02	Charlton Ath	36	11	**36**	**11**

FISH, Mark (D) 297 13
H: 6 4 W: 12 11 b.Cape Town 14-3-74
Source: Arcadia Shepherds. *Honours:* South Africa 60 full caps, 2 goals.

1992	Jomo Cosmos	14	1		
1993	Jomo Cosmos	41	1	**55**	**2**
1994	Orlando Pirates	37	5		
1995	Orlando Pirates	38	1	**75**	**6**
1996–97	Lazio	15	1	**15**	**1**
1997–98	Bolton W	22	2		
1998–99	Bolton W	36	1		
1999–2000	Bolton W	31	0		
2000–01	Bolton W	14	0	**103**	**3**
2000–01	Charlton Ath	24	1		
2001–02	Charlton Ath	25	0	**49**	**1**

FORTUNE, Jon (D) 37 0
H: 6 2 W: 12 12 b.Islington 23-8-80
Source: Trainee.

1998–99	Charlton Ath	0	0		
1999–2000	Charlton Ath	0	0		
1999–2000	*Mansfield T*	4	0		
2000–01	Charlton Ath	0	0		
2000–01	*Mansfield T*	14	0	**18**	**0**
2001–02	Charlton Ath	19	0	**19**	**0**

GEORGE, Kevin* (M) 0 0
H: 5 11 W: 12 04 b.London 21-11-82
Source: Scholar.

2000–01	Charlton Ath	0	0		
2001–02	Charlton Ath	0	0		

HUNT, Andy‡ (F) 341 122
H: 6 1 W: 12 08 b.Thurrock 9-6-70
Source: Kettering T.

1990–91	Newcastle U	16	2		
1991–92	Newcastle U	27	9		
1992–93	Newcastle U	0	0	**43**	**11**
1992–93	*WBA*	10	9		
1993–94	WBA	35	12		
1994–95	WBA	39	13		
1995–96	WBA	45	14		
1996–97	WBA	45	15		
1997–98	WBA	38	13	**212**	**76**
1998–99	Charlton Ath	34	7		
1999–2000	Charlton Ath	44	24		
2000–01	Charlton Ath	8	4		
2001–02	Charlton Ath	0	0	**86**	**35**

ILIC, Sasa* (G) 59 0
H: 6 4 W: 14 12 b.Melbourne 18-7-72
Source: Partizan Belgrade, Radnicki, Ringwood, Daewoo Royals, St Leonards Stamcroft. *Honours:* Yugoslavia 1 full cap.

1997–98	Charlton Ath	14	0		
1998–99	Charlton Ath	23	0		
1999–2000	Charlton Ath	1	0		
1999–2000	*West Ham U*	1	0	**1**	**0**
2000–01	Charlton Ath	13	0		
2001–02	Charlton Ath	0	0	**51**	**0**
2001–02	*Portsmouth*	7	0	**7**	**0**

JENSEN, Claus (M) 208 28
H: 6 1 W: 13 04 b.Nykobing 29-4-77
Source: Stubbekobing, Nykobing. *Honours:* Denmark Under-21, 15 full caps, 1 goal.

1995–96	Naestved	4	0	**4**	**0**
1996–97	Lyngby	31	3		
1997–98	Lyngby	31	11	**62**	**14**
1998–99	Bolton W	44	2		
1999–2000	Bolton W	42	6	**86**	**8**
2000–01	Charlton Ath	38	5		
2001–02	Charlton Ath	18	1	**56**	**6**

JOHANSSON, Jonatan (F) 149 45
H: 6 1 W: 12 08 b.Stockholm 16-8-75
Source: Flora Tallinn. *Honours:* Finland 42 full caps, 9 goals.

1995	TPS Turku	9	0		
1996	TPS Turku	23	6	**32**	**6**
1996–97	Flora Tallinn	9	9	**9**	**9**
1997–98	Rangers	6	0		
1998–99	Rangers	25	8		
1999–2000	Rangers	16	6	**47**	**14**
2000–01	Charlton Ath	31	11		
2001–02	Charlton Ath	30	5	**61**	**16**

KIELY, Dean (G) 455 0
H: 6 0 W: 12 13 b.Salford 10-10-70
Source: WBA School. *Honours:* England Schools, FA Schools, Youth, Eire 6 full caps.

1987–88	Coventry C	0	0		
1988–89	Coventry C	0	0		
1989–90	Coventry C	0	0		
1989–90	*Ipswich T*	0	0		
1989–90	*York C*	0	0		
1990–91	York C	17	0		
1991–92	York C	21	0		
1992–93	York C	40	0		
1993–94	York C	46	0		
1994–95	York C	46	0		
1995–96	York C	40	0	**210**	**0**
1996–97	Bury	46	0		
1997–98	Bury	46	0		
1998–99	Bury	45	0	**137**	**0**
1999–2000	Charlton Ath	45	0		
2000–01	Charlton Ath	25	0		
2001–02	Charlton Ath	38	0	**108**	**0**

KINSELLA, Mark (M) 388 46
H: 5 8 W: 12 01 b.Dublin 12-8-72
Source: Home Farm. *Honours:* Eire 32 full caps, 3 goals.

1989–90	Colchester U	6	0		
1990–91	Colchester U	0	0		
1991–92	Colchester U	0	0		
1992–93	Colchester U	38	6		
1993–94	Colchester U	42	8		
1994–95	Colchester U	42	6		
1995–96	Colchester U	45	5		
1996–97	Colchester U	7	2	**180**	**27**
1996–97	Charlton Ath	37	6		
1997–98	Charlton Ath	46	6		
1998–99	Charlton Ath	38	2		
1999–2000	Charlton Ath	38	3		
2000–01	Charlton Ath	32	2		
2001–02	Charlton Ath	17	0	**208**	**19**

KISHISHEV, Radostin (D) 223 17
H: 5 10 W: 12 08 b.Bourgas 30-7-74
Honours: Bulgaria 41 full caps.

1991–92	Chernomorets	6	1		
1992–93	Chernomorets	23	2		
1993–94	Chernomorets	23	1	**52**	**4**
1994–95	Neftochimik	14	0		
1995–96	Neftochimik	30	0		
1996–97	Neftochimik	30	6		
1997–98	Neftochimik	1	0	**75**	**6**
1997–98	Bursaspor	20	3	**20**	**3**
1997–98	Litets Lovch	5	0	**5**	**0**
1998–99	Litets Lovech	26	2		
1999–2000	Litets Lovech	15	2	**41**	**4**
2000–01	Charlton Ath	27	0		
2001–02	Charlton Ath	3	0	**30**	**0**

KONCHESKY, Paul (D) 70 1
H: 5 8 W: 11 07 b.Barking 15-5-81
Source: Trainee. *Honours:* England Youth, Under-20, Under-21.

1997–98	Charlton Ath	3	0		
1998–99	Charlton Ath	2	0		
1999–2000	Charlton Ath	8	0		
2000–01	Charlton Ath	23	0		
2001–02	Charlton Ath	34	1	**70**	**1**

LISBIE, Kevin (F) 94 11
H: 5 10 W: 11 01 b.Hackney 17-10-78
Source: Trainee. *Honours:* England Youth. Jamaica 2 full caps.

1996–97	Charlton Ath	25	1		
1997–98	Charlton Ath	17	1		
1998–99	Charlton Ath	1	0		
1998–99	*Gillingham*	7	4	**7**	**4**
1999–2000	Charlton Ath	0	0		
1999–2000	*Reading*	2	0	**2**	**0**
2000–01	Charlton Ath	18	0		
2000–01	*QPR*	2	0	**2**	**0**
2001–02	Charlton Ath	22	5	**83**	**7**

LONG, Stacy (F) 0 0
H: 5 8 W: 10 00 b.Bromley 11-1-85
Source: Scholar. *Honours:* England Youth.

2001–02	Charlton Ath	0	0		

MACDONALD, Charlie* (F) 25 4
H: 5 8 W: 12 10 b.Southwark 13-2-81
Source: Trainee.

1998–99	Charlton Ath	0	0		
1999–2000	Charlton Ath	3	0		
2000–01	Charlton Ath	3	0		
2000–01	*Cheltenham T*	8	2	**8**	**2**
2001–02	Charlton Ath	2	1	**8**	**1**
2001–02	*Torquay U*	5	0	**5**	**0**
2001–02	*Colchester U*	4	1	**4**	**1**

MARTIN, Alex* (M) 0 0
H: 5 8 W: 11 04 b.Harlow 2-5-83
Source: Scholar. *Honours:* England Youth.

2000–01	Charlton Ath	0	0		
2001–02	Charlton Ath	0	0		

McCAFFERTY, Neil (M) 0 0
H: 5 7 W: 10 00 b.Derry 19-7-84
Source: Scholar.

2001–02	Charlton Ath	0	0		

MENDONCA, Clive‡ (F) 359 131
H: 5 10 W: 12 10 b.Islington 9-9-68
Source: Apprentice.

1986–87	Sheffield U	2	0		
1987–88	Sheffield U	11	4		
1987–88	*Doncaster R*	2	0	**2**	**0**
1987–88	Rotherham U	8	2		
1988–89	Rotherham U	10	1		
1989–90	Rotherham U	32	14		
1990–91	Rotherham U	34	10	**84**	**27**
1991–92	Sheffield U	10	1	**23**	**5**
1991–92	*Grimsby T*	10	3		
1992–93	Grimsby T	42	10		
1993–94	Grimsby T	39	14		
1994–95	Grimsby T	22	11		
1995–96	Grimsby T	8	4		
1996–97	Grimsby T	45	17	**166**	**59**
1997–98	Charlton Ath	40	23		
1998–99	Charlton Ath	25	8		
1999–2000	Charlton Ath	19	9		
2000–01	Charlton Ath	0	0		
2001–02	Charlton Ath	0	0	**84**	**40**

PARKER, Scott (M) 86 4
H: 5 8 W: 11 02 b.Lambeth 13-10-80
Source: Trainee. *Honours:* England Schools, Youth, Under-21.

1997–98	Charlton Ath	3	0		
1998–99	Charlton Ath	4	0		
1999–2000	Charlton Ath	15	1		
2000–01	Charlton Ath	20	1		
2000–01	*Norwich C*	6	1	**6**	**1**
2001–02	Charlton Ath	38	1	**80**	**3**

POWELL, Chris (D) 500 5
H: 5 10 W: 11 13 b.Lambeth 8-9-69
Source: Trainee. *Honours:* England 5 full caps.

1987–88	Crystal Palace	0	0		
1988–89	Crystal Palace	3	0		
1989–90	Crystal Palace	0	0	**3**	**0**
1989–90	*Aldershot*	11	0	**11**	**0**
1990–91	Southend U	45	1		
1991–92	Southend U	44	0		
1992–93	Southend U	42	2		
1993–94	Southend U	46	0		
1994–95	Southend U	44	0		

1995–96	Southend U	27	0	248	3
1995–96	Derby Co	19	0		
1996–97	Derby Co	35	0		
1997–98	Derby Co	37	1	91	1
1998–99	Charlton Ath	38	0		
1999–2000	Charlton Ath	40	0		
2000–01	Charlton Ath	33	0		
2001–02	Charlton Ath	36	1	147	1

PRINGLE, Martin (F) 165 29
H: 6 2 W: 12 03 b.Gothenburg 18-11-70
Source: Stenungsund. *Honours:* Sweden 2 full caps, 1 goal.

1994	Helsingborg	21	3		
1995	Helsingborg	22	7		
1996	Helsingborg	21	5	64	15
1996–97	Benfica	15	3		
1997–98	Benfica	14	2		
1998–99	Benfica	12	1	41	6
1998–99	Charlton Ath	18	3		
1999–2000	Charlton Ath	32	4		
2000–01	Charlton Ath	8	1		
2001–02	Charlton Ath	0	0	58	8
2001–02	*Grimsby T*	2	0	2	0

RACHUBKA, Paul (G) 17 0
H: 6 1 W: 13 01 b.San Luis Opispo 21-5-81
Source: Trainee. *Honours:* England Youth.

1999–2000	Manchester U	0	0		
2000–01	Manchester U	1	0		
2001–02	Manchester U	0	0	1	0
2001–02	*Oldham Ath*	16	0	16	0
2001–02	Charlton Ath	0	0		

ROBERTS, Ben (G) 68 0
H: 6 2 W: 13 00 b.Bishop Auckland 22-6-75
Source: Trainee. *Honours:* England Under-21.

1992–93	Middlesbrough	0	0		
1993–94	Middlesbrough	0	0		
1994–95	Middlesbrough	0	0		
1995–96	Middlesbrough	0	0		
1995–96	*Hartlepool U*	4	0	4	0
1995–96	*Wycombe W*	15	0	15	0
1996–97	Middlesbrough	10	0		
1996–97	*Bradford C*	2	0	2	0
1997–98	Middlesbrough	6	0		
1998–99	Middlesbrough	0	0		
1998–99	*Millwall*	11	0	11	0
1999–2000	Middlesbrough	0	0	16	0
1999–2000	*Luton T*	14	0	14	0
2000–01	Charlton Ath	0	0		
2001–02	Charlton Ath	0	0		
2001–02	*Reading*	6	0	6	0

ROBINSON, John (M) 381 46
H: 5 10 W: 12 01 b.Bulawayo 29-8-71
Source: Apprentice. *Honours:* Wales Under-21, 30 full caps, 3 goals.

1989–90	Brighton & HA	5	0		
1990–91	Brighton & HA	15	0		
1991–92	Brighton & HA	36	6		
1992–93	Brighton & HA	6	0	62	6
1992–93	Charlton Ath	15	2		
1993–94	Charlton Ath	27	1		
1994–95	Charlton Ath	21	3		
1995–96	Charlton Ath	44	6		
1996–97	Charlton Ath	42	3		
1997–98	Charlton Ath	38	8		
1998–99	Charlton Ath	30	2		
1999–2000	Charlton Ath	45	7		
2000–01	Charlton Ath	29	2		
2001–02	Charlton Ath	28	1	319	35

ROBSON, Paul (D) 0 0
H: 5 9 W: 11 05 b.Hull 4-8-83
Source: Doncaster R.

2001–02	Charlton Ath	0	0

ROWETT, Gary (D) 325 19
H: 6 0 W: 12 10 b.Bromsgrove 6-3-74
Source: Trainee.

1991–92	Cambridge U	13	2		
1992–93	Cambridge U	21	2		
1993–94	Cambridge U	29	5	63	9
1993–94	Everton	2	0		
1994–95	Everton	2	0	4	0
1994–95	*Blackpool*	17	0	17	0
1995–96	Derby Co	35	0		
1996–97	Derby Co	35	1		
1997–98	Derby Co	35	1		
1998–99	Derby Co	0	0	105	2
1998–99	Birmingham C	42	5		
1999–2000	Birmingham C	45	1	87	6
2000–01	Leicester C	38	2		
2001–02	Leicester C	11	0	49	2
2001–02	Charlton Ath				

RUFUS, Richard (D) 258 10
H: 6 1 W: 12 12 b.Lewisham 12-1-75
Source: Trainee. *Honours:* England Under-21.

1993–94	Charlton Ath	0	0		
1994–95	Charlton Ath	28	0		
1995–96	Charlton Ath	41	0		
1996–97	Charlton Ath	34	0		
1997–98	Charlton Ath	42	0		
1998–99	Charlton Ath	27	1		
1999–2000	Charlton Ath	44	6		
2000–01	Charlton Ath	32	2		
2001–02	Charlton Ath	10	1	258	10

SHIELDS, Greg (D) 111 2
H: 5 10 W: 11 04 b.Falkirk 21-8-76
Source: Rangers BC. *Honours:* Scotland Schools, Youth, Under-21.

1994–95	Rangers	0	0		
1995–96	Rangers	1	0		
1996–97	Rangers	6	0	7	0
1997–98	Dunfermline Ath	36	0		
1998–99	Dunfermline Ath	36	0	72	0
1999–2000	Charlton Ath	21	2		
2000–01	Charlton Ath	4	0		
2001–02	Charlton Ath	0	0	25	2
2001–02	*Walsall*	7	0	7	0

SNODIN, Lee* (M) 0 0
H: 5 10 W: 11 10 b.Doncaster 19-6-83
Source: Doncaster R.

2001–02	Charlton Ath	0	0

STUART, Graham (M) 388 66
H: 5 8 W: 12 00 b.Tooting 24-10-70
Source: Trainee. *Honours:* FA Schools, England Under-21.

1989–90	Chelsea	2	1		
1990–91	Chelsea	19	4		
1991–92	Chelsea	27	0		
1992–93	Chelsea	39	9	87	14
1993–94	Everton	30	3		
1994–95	Everton	28	3		
1995–96	Everton	29	9		
1996–97	Everton	35	5		
1997–98	Everton	14	2	136	22
1997–98	Sheffield U	28	5		
1998–99	Sheffield U	25	6	53	11
1998–99	Charlton Ath	9	4		
1999–2000	Charlton Ath	37	7		
2000–01	Charlton Ath	35	5		
2001–02	Charlton Ath	31	3	112	19

SVENSSON, Mathias (F) 157 43
H: 6 1 W: 12 08 b.Boras 24-9-74
Honours: Sweden 3 full caps.

1996	Elfsborg	22	15	22	15
1996–97	Portsmouth	19	6		
1997–98	Portsmouth	26	4	45	10
1998–99	Innsbruck	6	1	6	1
1998–99	Crystal Palace	8	1		
1999–2000	Crystal Palace	24	9	32	10
1999–2000	Charlton Ath	18	2		
2000–01	Charlton Ath	22	5		
2001–02	Charlton Ath	12	0	52	7

TODD, Andy (D) 157 6
H: 5 11 W: 13 04 b.Derby 21-9-74
Source: Trainee.

1991–92	Middlesbrough	0	0		
1992–93	Middlesbrough	0	0		
1993–94	Middlesbrough	3	0		
1994–95	Middlesbrough	5	0	8	0
1994–95	*Swindon T*	13	0	13	0
1995–96	Bolton W	12	2		
1996–97	Bolton W	15	0		
1997–98	Bolton W	25	0		
1998–99	Bolton W	20	0		
1999–2000	Bolton W	12	0	84	2
1999–2000	Charlton Ath	12	0		
2000–01	Charlton Ath	23	1		
2001–02	Charlton Ath	5	0	40	1
2001–02	*Grimsby T*	12	3	12	3

TURNER, Michael (D) 0 0
H: 6 4 W: 12 06 b.Lewisham 9-11-83
Source: Scholar.

2001–02	Charlton Ath	0	0

YOUDS, Eddie* (D) 217 13
H: 6 2 W: 14 10 b.Liverpool 3-5-70
Source: Trainee.

1988–89	Everton	0	0		
1989–90	Everton	0	0		
1989–90	*Cardiff C*	1	0	1	0
1989–90	*Wrexham*	20	2	20	2
1990–91	Everton	8	0		
1991–92	Everton	0	0	8	0
1991–92	Ipswich T	1	0		
1992–93	Ipswich T	16	0		
1993–94	Ipswich T	23	1		
1994–95	Ipswich T	10	0	50	1
1994–95	Bradford C	17	3		
1995–96	Bradford C	30	4		
1996–97	Bradford C	0	0		
1997–98	Bradford C	38	1	85	8
1997–98	Charlton Ath	8	0		
1998–99	Charlton Ath	22	2		
1999–2000	Charlton Ath	23	0		
2000–01	Charlton Ath	0	0		
2001–02	Charlton Ath	0	0	53	2

YOUNG, Luke (D) 92 0
H: 5 11 W: 12 06 b.Harlow 19-7-79
Source: Trainee. *Honours:* England Youth, Under-21.

1997–98	Tottenham H	0	0		
1998–99	Tottenham H	15	0		
1999–2000	Tottenham H	20	0		
2000–01	Tottenham H	23	0	58	0
2001–02	Charlton Ath	34	0	34	0

Trainees
Beckford, Karl L; Campbell-Ryce, Jamal; Cerroni, Christopher; Delo, Jack N; Frempong, Ralph; Fuller, Barry M; Funna, Charles; Jackson, Simon P; Martin, Jamie N; Nunn, Christopher R; Penfold, Darren; Ricketts, Mark J; Sankofa, Osei OK; Savage, Anthony J; Varney, Alexander

CHELSEA

ALEKSIDZE, Rati (F) 79 33
H: 6 0 W: 12 02 b.Georgia 3-8-78
Honours: Georgia 10 full caps, 1 goal.

1996–97	Dynamo Tbilisi	5	2		
1997–98	Dynamo Tbilisi	29	6		
1998–99	Dynamo Tbilisi	29	13		
1999–2000	Dynamo Tbilisi	14	12	77	33
2000–01	Chelsea	2	0		
2001–02	Chelsea	0	0	2	0

AMBROSETTI, Gabriele (M) 230 44
H: 5 11 W: 11 05 b.Varese 7-8-73

1990–91	Varese	8	0		
1991–92	Varese	16	2		
1992–93	Varese	26	9	50	11
1993–94	Brescia	25	8		
1994–95	Venezia	18	3	18	3
1995–96	Brescia	9	2	43	12
1995–96	Vicenza	24	3		
1996–97	Vicenza	25	6		
1997–98	Vicenza	30	5		
1998–99	Vicenza	24	4	103	18
1999–2000	Chelsea	16	0		
2001–02	Chelsea	0	0	16	0

BABAYARO, Celestine (D) 178 11
H: 5 9 W: 11 09 b.Kaduna 29-8-78
Source: Plateau U. *Honours:* Nigeria 26 full caps.

1994–95	Anderlecht	22	0		
1995–96	Anderlecht	28	5		
1996–97	Anderlecht	25	3	75	8
1997–98	Chelsea	8	0		
1998–99	Chelsea	28	3		
1999–2000	Chelsea	25	0		
2000–01	Chelsea	24	0		
2001–02	Chelsea	18	0	103	3

BOGARDE, Winston (D) 201 26
H: 6 3 W: 14 02 b.Rotterdam 22-10-70
Honours: Holland 20 full caps.

1988–89	SVV	9	1		
1989–90	SVV	2	0		
1989–90	Excelsior	10	1	10	1
1990–91	SVV	0	0	11	1
1991–92	Sparta	0	0		
1992–93	Sparta	32	3		
1993–94	Sparta	33	11	65	14
1994–95	Ajax	13	0		
1995–96	Ajax	33	2		
1996–97	Ajax	16	4	62	6
1997–98	AC Milan	3	0	3	0
1997–98	Barcelona	19	2		
1998–99	Barcelona	1	0		
1999–2000	Barcelona	21	2	41	4
2000–01	Chelsea	9	0		
2001–02	Chelsea	0	0	9	0

BOSNICH, Mark (G) 215 0
H: 6 2 W: 14 10 b.Fairfield 13-1-72
Honours: Australia Youth, Under-20, Under-23, 17 full caps, 1 goal.

1989–90	Manchester U	1	0		
1990–91	Manchester U	2	0		
1991–92	Sydney U	3	0	5	0
1991–92	Aston Villa	1	0		
1992–93	Aston Villa	17	0		

1993–94	Aston Villa	28	0		
1994–95	Aston Villa	30	0		
1995–96	Aston Villa	38	1		
1996–97	Aston Villa	20	0		
1997–98	Aston Villa	30	0		
1998–99	Aston Villa	15	0	**179**	**0**
1999–2000	Manchester U	23	0		
2000–01	Manchester U	0	0	**26**	**0**
2000–01	Chelsea	0	0		
2001–02	Chelsea	5	0	**5**	**0**

COLE, Carlton (F) **3** **1**
H: 6 3 W: 12 13 b.Surrey 12-11-83
Source: Scholar. *Honours:* England Youth.

2000–01	Chelsea	0	0		
2001–02	Chelsea	3	1	**3**	**1**

CUDICINI, Carlo (G) **136** **0**
H: 6 1 W: 12 02 b.Milan 6-9-73

1991–92	AC Milan	0	0		
1992–93	AC Milan	0	0		
1993–94	Como	6	0	**6**	**0**
1994–95	AC Milan	0	0		
1995–96	AC Milan	0	0		
1995–96	Prato	30	0	**30**	**0**
1996–97	Lazio	1	0	**1**	**0**
1997–98	Castel di Sangro	14	0		
1998–99	Castel di Sangro	32	0	**46**	**0**
1999–2000	Chelsea	1	0		
2000–01	Chelsea	24	0		
2001–02	Chelsea	28	0	**53**	**0**

CUMMINGS, Warren (D) **27** **1**
H: 5 9 W: 11 05 b.Aberdeen 15-10-80
Source: Trainee. *Honours:* Scotland Under-21, 1 full cap.

1999–2000	Chelsea	0	0		
2000–01	Chelsea	0	0		
2000–01	*Bournemouth*	10	1	**10**	**1**
2000–01	*WBA*	3	0		
2001–02	Chelsea	0	0		
2001–02	*WBA*	14	0	**17**	**0**

DALLA BONA, Samuele (F) **55** **6**
H: 6 0 W: 13 03 b.San Dona di Piave 6-2-81

1997–98	Atalanta	0	0		
1998–99	Chelsea	0	0		
1999–2000	Chelsea	2	0		
2000–01	Chelsea	29	2		
2001–02	Chelsea	24	4	**55**	**6**

DE GOEY, Ed (G) **467** **0**
H: 6 6 W: 14 05 b.Gouda 20-12-66
Honours: Holland 31 full caps.

1985–86	Sparta	12	0		
1986–87	Sparta	34	0		
1987–88	Sparta	34	0		
1988–89	Sparta	31	0		
1989–90	Sparta	34	0	**145**	**0**
1990–91	Feyenoord	34	0		
1991–92	Feyenoord	34	0		
1992–93	Feyenoord	33	0		
1993–94	Feyenoord	34	0		
1994–95	Feyenoord	32	0		
1995–96	Feyenoord	34	0	**201**	**0**
1997–98	Chelsea	28	0		
1998–99	Chelsea	35	0		
1999–2000	Chelsea	37	0		
2000–01	Chelsea	15	0		
2001–02	Chelsea	6	0	**121**	**0**

DE OLIVEIRA, Filipe (F) **0** **0**
H: 5 10 W: 10 12 b.Braga 27-5-84

2001–02	Chelsea	0	0		

DESAILLY, Marcel (D) **459** **15**
H: 6 0 W: 13 05 b.Accra 7-9-68
Honours: France 97 full caps, 3 goals.

1986–87	Nantes	15	0		
1987–88	Nantes	11	0		
1988–89	Nantes	36	1		
1989–90	Nantes	36	1		
1990–91	Nantes	34	1		
1991–92	Nantes	32	2	**164**	**5**
1992–93	Marseille	31	1		
1993–94	Marseille	15	0	**46**	**1**
1993–94	AC Milan	22	1		
1994–95	AC Milan	22	1		
1995–96	AC Milan	32	2		
1996–97	AC Milan	29	1		
1997–98	AC Milan	33	0	**137**	**5**
1998–99	Chelsea	31	0		
1999–2000	Chelsea	23	1		
2000–01	Chelsea	34	2		
2001–02	Chelsea	24	1	**112**	**4**

DI CESARE, Valerio (D) **0** **0**
H: 6 2 W: 11 13 b.Rome 23-5-83

2000–01	Chelsea	0	0		
2001–02	Chelsea	0	0		

DI MATTEO, Roberto* (M) **323** **31**
H: 5 10 W: 12 04 b.Schaffhausen 29-5-70
Honours: Italy 34 full caps, 2 goals.

1988–89	Schaffhausen	18	0		
1989–90	Schaffhausen	31	2		
1990–91	Schaffhausen	1	0	**50**	**2**
1991–92	Zurich	34	6	**34**	**6**
1992–93	Aarau	32	1	**32**	**1**
1993–94	Lazio	29	4		
1994–95	Lazio	28	1		
1995–96	Lazio	31	2	**88**	**7**
1996–97	Chelsea	34	7		
1997–98	Chelsea	30	4		
1998–99	Chelsea	30	2		
1999–2000	Chelsea	18	2		
2000–01	Chelsea	7	0		
2001–02	Chelsea	0	0	**119**	**15**

EVANS, Rhys (G) **15** **0**
H: 6 1 W: 11 12 b.Swindon 27-1-82
Source: Trainee. *Honours:* England Schools, Youth, Under-20.

1998–99	Chelsea	0	0		
1999–2000	Chelsea	0	0		
1999–2000	*Bristol R*	4	0	**4**	**0**
2000–01	Chelsea	0	0		
2001–02	Chelsea	0	0		
2001–02	*QPR*	11	0	**11**	**0**

FERRER, Albert (D) **295** **1**
H: 5 6 W: 12 02 b.Barcelona 6-6-70
Honours: Spain 36 full caps.

1989–90	Tenerife	17	0	**17**	**0**
1990–91	Barcelona	26	0		
1991–92	Barcelona	12	1		
1992–93	Barcelona	32	0		
1993–94	Barcelona	34	0		
1994–95	Barcelona	31	0		
1995–96	Barcelona	28	0		
1996–97	Barcelona	18	0		
1997–98	Barcelona	24	0	**205**	**1**
1998–99	Chelsea	30	0		
1999–2000	Chelsea	25	0		
2000–01	Chelsea	14	0		
2001–02	Chelsea	4	0	**73**	**0**

FORSSELL, Mikael (F) **101** **22**
H: 6 0 W: 12 08 b.Steinfurt 15-3-81
Honours: Finland 19 full caps, 7 goals.

1997	HJK Helsinki	1	0		
1998	HJK Helsinki	16	1	**17**	**1**
1998–99	Chelsea	10	1		
1999–2000	Chelsea	0	0		
1999–2000	*Crystal Palace*	13	3		
2000–01	Chelsea	0	0		
2000–01	*Crystal Palace*	39	13	**52**	**16**
2001–02	Chelsea	22	4	**32**	**5**

GALLAS, William (D) **133** **3**
H: 6 0 W: 11 13 b.Asnieres 17-8-77

1996–97	Caen	18	0	**18**	**0**
1997–98	Marseille	3	0		
1998–99	Marseille	30	0		
1999–2000	Marseille	22	0		
2000–01	Marseille	30	2	**85**	**2**
2001–02	Chelsea	30	1	**30**	**1**

GRONKJAER, Jesper (M) **169** **22**
H: 6 2 W: 13 03 b.Nuuk 12-8-77
Honours: Denmark 30 full caps, 2 goals.

1995–96	Aalborg	29	3		
1996–97	Aalborg	28	1		
1997–98	Aalborg	29	6	**86**	**10**
1998–99	Ajax	25	8		
1999–2000	Ajax	25	3		
2000–01	Ajax	6	0	**56**	**11**
2000–01	Chelsea	14	1		
2001–02	Chelsea	13	0	**27**	**1**

GUDJOHNSEN, Eidur (F) **153** **52**
H: 6 1 W: 14 01 b.Reykjavik 15-9-78
Honours: Iceland Youth, 16 full caps, 3 goals.

1994–95	Valur	17	7	**17**	**7**
1995–96	PSV Eindhoven	13	3		
1996–97	PSV Eindhoven	0	0	**13**	**3**
1998	KR	6	0	**6**	**0**
1998–99	Bolton W	14	5		
1999–2000	Bolton W	41	13	**55**	**18**
2000–01	Chelsea	30	10		
2001–02	Chelsea	32	14	**62**	**24**

HASSELBAINK, Jimmy Floyd (F) **233** **136**
H: 5 10 W: 13 10 b.Paramaribo 27-3-72
Honours: Holland 19 full caps, 7 goals.

1995–96	Campomaiorense	31	12	**31**	**12**
1996–97	Boavista	29	20	**29**	**20**
1997–98	Leeds U	33	16		
1998–99	Leeds U	36	18	**69**	**34**
1999–2000	Atletico Madrid	34	24	**34**	**24**
2000–01	Chelsea	35	23		
2001–02	Chelsea	35	23	**70**	**46**

HUTH, Robert (D) **1** **0**
H: 6 2 W: 12 12 b.Berlin 18-8-84

2001–02	Chelsea	1	0	**1**	**0**

JEFFREYS, Danny (M) **0** **0**
H: 5 7 W: 9 04 b.Hammersmith 21-1-85
Source: Scholar. *Honours:* England Youth.

2001–02	Chelsea	0	0		

JOKANOVIC, Slavisa* (M) **315** **52**
H: 6 3 W: 13 03 b.Novi Sad 16-8-68
Honours: Yugoslavia 58 full caps, 9 goals.

1990–91	Partizan Belgrade	20	4		
1991–92	Partizan Belgrade	16	4		
1992–93	Partizan Belgrade	32	13	**68**	**21**
1993–94	Oviedo	32	7		
1994–95	Oviedo	30	5	**62**	**12**
1995–96	Tenerife	34	2		
1996–97	Tenerife	30	10		
1997–98	Tenerife	30	3		
1998–99	Tenerife	29	2	**123**	**17**
1999–2000	La Coruna	23	2	**23**	**2**
2000–01	Chelsea	19	0		
2001–02	Chelsea	20	0	**39**	**0**

KEENAN, Joe (M) **1** **0**
H: 5 8 W: 9 12 b.Southampton 14-10-82
Source: Trainee. *Honours:* England Youth, Under-20.

1999–2000	Chelsea	0	0		
2000–01	Chelsea	0	0		
2001–02	Chelsea	1	0	**1**	**0**

KITAMIRIKE, Joel (D) **0** **0**
H: 5 11 W: 12 08 b.Uganda 5-4-84
Source: Scholar. *Honours:* England Youth.

2000–01	Chelsea	0	0		
2001–02	Chelsea	0	0		

KNEISSL, Sebastian (F) **0** **0**
H: 5 11 W: 11 05 b.Germany 13-1-83

2000–01	Chelsea	0	0		
2001–02	Chelsea	0	0		

KNIGHT, Leon (F) **42** **16**
H: 5 4 W: 9 04 b.Hackney 16-9-82
Source: Trainee. *Honours:* England Youth, Under-20.

1999–2000	Chelsea	0	0		
2000–01	Chelsea	0	0		
2000–01	*QPR*	11	0	**11**	**0**
2001–02	Chelsea	0	0		
2001–02	*Huddersfield T*	31	16	**31**	**16**

LAMPARD, Frank (M) **194** **29**
H: 6 0 W: 14 00 b.Romford 21-6-78
Source: Trainee. *Honours:* England Youth, Under-21, B, 7 full caps.

1994–95	West Ham U	0	0		
1995–96	West Ham U	2	0		
1995–96	*Swansea C*	9	1	**9**	**1**
1996–97	West Ham U	13	0		
1997–98	West Ham U	31	4		
1998–99	West Ham U	38	5		
1999–2000	West Ham U	34	7		
2000–01	West Ham U	30	7	**148**	**23**
2001–02	Chelsea	37	5	**37**	**5**

LE SAUX, Graeme (D) **331** **17**
H: 5 10 W: 11 09 b.Jersey 17-10-68
Source: St Pauls. *Honours:* England Under-21, B, 36 full caps, 1 goal.

1987–88	Chelsea	0	0		
1988–89	Chelsea	1	0		
1989–90	Chelsea	7	1		
1990–91	Chelsea	28	4		
1991–92	Chelsea	40	3		
1992–93	Chelsea	14	0		
1992–93	Blackburn R	9	0		
1993–94	Blackburn R	41	2		
1994–95	Blackburn R	39	3		
1995–96	Blackburn R	14	1		
1996–97	Blackburn R	26	1	**129**	**7**
1997–98	Chelsea	26	1		
1998–99	Chelsea	31	0		
1999–2000	Chelsea	8	0		
2000–01	Chelsea	20	0		
2001–02	Chelsea	27	1	**202**	**10**

MARTELLA, Antonio* (M) **0** **0**
H: 5 6 W: 10 06 b.Isernia 17-3-84
Source: San Leucio Soccer School.

2001–02	Chelsea	0	0		

MELCHIOT, Mario (D) **146** **3**
H: 6 2 W: 11 11 b.Amsterdam 4-11-76
Honours: Holland 9 full caps.

1996–97	Ajax	23	0		
1997–98	Ajax	26	0		
1998–99	Ajax	24	1	**73**	**1**
1999–2000	Chelsea	5	0		
2000–01	Chelsea	31	0		
2001–02	Chelsea	37	2	**73**	**2**

MORRIS, Jody (M) 99 5
H: 5 5 W: 10 04 b.Hammersmith 22-12-78
Source: Trainee. *Honours:* England Schools, Youth, Under-21.

1995–96	Chelsea	1	0	
1996–97	Chelsea	12	0	
1997–98	Chelsea	12	1	
1998–99	Chelsea	18	1	
1999–2000	Chelsea	30	3	
2000–01	Chelsea	21	0	
2001–02	Chelsea	5	0	99 5

NICOLAS, Alexis (M) 0 0
H: 5 10 W: 9 12 b.London 13-2-83
Source: Scholar.

2000–01	Aston Villa	0	0
2001–02	Aston Villa	0	0
2001–02	Chelsea	0	0

PARKIN, Sam (F) 62 12
H: 6 2 W: 13 03 b.Roehampton 14-3-81
Honours: England Schools.

1998–99	Chelsea	0	0	
1999–2000	Chelsea	0	0	
2000–01	Chelsea	0	0	
2000–01	Millwall	7	4	7 4
2000–01	Wycombe W	8	1	8 1
2000–01	Oldham Ath	7	3	7 3
2001–02	Chelsea	0	0	
2001–02	*Northampton T*	40	4	40 4

PETIT, Emmanuel (M) 357 15
H: 6 1 W: 13 03 b.Dieppe 22-9-70
Source: ES Arques. *Honours:* France 60 full caps, 6 goal.

1988–89	Monaco	9	0	
1989–90	Monaco	28	0	
1990–91	Monaco	27	1	
1991–92	Monaco	28	0	
1992–93	Monaco	25	1	
1993–94	Monaco	28	0	
1994–95	Monaco	25	1	
1995–96	Monaco	23	1	
1996–97	Monaco	29	0	222 4
1997–98	Arsenal	32	2	
1998–99	Arsenal	27	4	
1999–2000	Arsenal	26	3	85 9
2000–01	Barcelona	23	1	23 1
2001–02	Chelsea	27	1	27 1

SLATTER, Danny* (D) 0 0
H: 5 8 W: 10 01 b.Cardiff 15-11-80
Source: Trainee. *Honours:* Wales Under-21.

1998–99	Chelsea	0	0
1999–2000	Chelsea	0	0
2000–01	Chelsea	0	0
2001–02	Chelsea	0	0

STANIC, Mario (M) 304 84
H: 6 2 W: 13 07 b.Zagreb 10-4-72
Honours: Croatia 45 full caps, 7 goals.

1988–89	Zeljeznicar	14	0	
1989–90	Zeljeznicar	14	0	
1990–91	Zeljeznicar	28	1	
1991–92	Zeljeznicar	21	11	77 12
1992–93	Croatia Zagreb	26	11	26 11
1993–94	Gijon	34	7	34 7
1994–95	Benfica	14	5	14 5
1995–96	FC Brugge	30	20	
1996–97	FC Brugge	7	7	37 27
1996–97	Parma	13	3	
1997–98	Parma	23	4	
1998–99	Parma	18	7	
1999–2000	Parma	23	5	77 19
2000–01	Chelsea	12	2	
2001–02	Chelsea	27	1	39 3

TERRY, John (D) 67 2
H: 6 1 W: 12 13 b.Barking 7-12-80
Source: Trainee. *Honours:* England Under-21.

1997–98	Chelsea	0	0	
1998–99	Chelsea	2	0	
1999–2000	Chelsea	4	0	
1999–2000	*Nottingham F*	6	0	6 0
2000–01	Chelsea	22	1	
2001–02	Chelsea	33	1	61 2

THORNTON, Paul (D) 0 0
H: 5 8 W: 11 00 b.Surrey 7-1-83
Source: Trainee.

1999–2000	Chelsea	0	0
2000–01	Chelsea	0	0
2001–02	Chelsea	0	0

WOLLEASTON, Robert (M) 18 0
H: 5 11 W: 11 07 b.Perivale 21-12-79
Source: Trainee.

1998–99	Chelsea	0	0	
1999–2000	Chelsea	1	0	
1999–2000	*Bristol R*	4	0	4 0
2000–01	*Portsmouth*	6	0	6 0

2001–02	Chelsea	0	0	1 0
2001–02	*Northampton T*	7	0	7 0

ZENDEN, Boudewijn (F) 197 29
H: 5 8 W: 11 09 b.Maastricht 15-8-76
Honours: Holland 36 full caps, 6 goals.

1994–95	PSV Eindhoven	27	5	
1995–96	PSV Eindhoven	25	7	
1996–97	PSV Eindhoven	34	8	
1997–98	PSV Eindhoven	25	3	111 23
1998–99	Barcelona	25	0	
1999–2000	Barcelona	29	2	
2000–01	Barcelona	10	1	64 3
2001–02	Chelsea	22	3	22 3

ZOLA, Gianfranco (F) 517 157
H: 5 6 W: 10 08 b.Oliena 5-7-66
Honours: Italy 35 full caps, 8 goals.

1984–85	Nuorese	4	0	
1985–86	Nuorese	27	10	31 10
1986–87	Torres	30	8	
1987–88	Torres	24	2	
1988–89	Torres	34	11	88 21
1989–90	Napoli	18	2	
1990–91	Napoli	20	6	
1991–92	Napoli	34	12	
1992–93	Napoli	33	12	105 32
1993–94	Parma	33	18	
1994–95	Parma	32	19	
1995–96	Parma	29	10	
1996–97	Parma	8	2	102 49
1996–97	Chelsea	23	8	
1997–98	Chelsea	27	8	
1998–99	Chelsea	37	13	
1999–2000	Chelsea	33	4	
2000–01	Chelsea	36	9	
2001–02	Chelsea	35	3	191 45

Trainees
Cousins, Scott R; Pidgeley, Leonard J; Ross, Andrew C; Sentance, Billy; Tillen, Samuel L; Watt, Steven M; Wizik, Glenn PP; Woodards, Daniel M

CHELTENHAM T

ALSOP, Julian (F) 203 45
H: 6 5 W: 14 04 b.Nuneaton 28-5-73
Source: Nuneaton, VS Rugby, RC Warwick, Tamworth, Halesowen T.

1996–97	Bristol R	16	3	
1997–98	Bristol R	17	1	33 4
1997–98	Swansea C	12	3	
1998–99	Swansea C	41	10	
1999–2000	Swansea C	37	3	90 16
2000–01	Cheltenham T	39	5	
2001–02	Cheltenham T	41	20	80 25

BANKS, Chris# (D) 230 3
H: 5 11 W: 12 05 b.Stone 12-11-65
Source: local.

1982–83	Port Vale	0	0	
1983–84	Port Vale	0	0	
1984–85	Port Vale	7	0	
1985–86	Port Vale	19	1	
1986–87	Port Vale	25	0	
1987–88	Port Vale	14	0	65 1
1988–89	Exeter C	45	1	45 1

From Bath C.

1999–2000	Cheltenham T	42	0	
2000–01	Cheltenham T	40	1	
2001–02	Cheltenham T	38	0	120 1

BENBOW, Steve‡ (G) 0 0
H: 5 10 W: 10 10 b.Cheltenham 5-4-82

1999–2000	Cheltenham T	0	0
2000–01	Cheltenham T	0	0
2001–02	Cheltenham T	0	0

BIRD, David (M) 0 0
H: 5 8 W: 12 00 b.Gloucester 26-12-84
Source: Cinderford T.

2001–02	Cheltenham T	0	0

BOOK, Steve (G) 131 0
H: 5 11 W: 11 08 b.Bournemouth 7-7-69

1997–98	Brighton & HA	0	0	
1998–99	Lincoln C	0	0	

From Forest Green R.

1999–2000	Cheltenham T	46	0	
2000–01	Cheltenham T	46	0	
2001–02	Cheltenham T	39	0	131 0

BROUGH, John# (D) 163 7
H: 6 0 W: 13 00 b.Ilkeston 8-1-73

1991–92	Notts Co	0	0	
1992–93	Shrewsbury T	14	1	
1993–94	Shrewsbury T	2	0	16 1

From Telford U.

1994–95	Hereford U	18	1	
1995–96	Hereford U	22	1	
1996–97	Hereford U	39	1	79 3

1999–2000	Cheltenham T	37	2	
2000–01	Cheltenham T	10	0	
2001–02	Cheltenham T	21	1	68 3

DEVANEY, Martin (F) 85 17
H: 5 11 W: 12 05 b.Cheltenham 1-6-80
Source: Trainee.

1997–98	Coventry C	0	0	
1998–99	Coventry C	0	0	
1999–2000	Cheltenham T	26	6	
2000–01	Cheltenham T	34	10	
2001–02	Cheltenham T	25	1	85 17

DUFF, Michael (D) 115 10
H: 6 1 W: 12 05 b.Belfast 11-1-78
Source: Trainee. *Honours:* Northern Ireland 1 full cap.

1999–2000	Cheltenham T	31	2	
2000–01	Cheltenham T	39	5	
2001–02	Cheltenham T	45	3	115 10

DUFF, Shane (D) 0 0
H: 6 1 W: 12 10 b.Wroughton 2-4-82

2000–01	Cheltenham T	0	0
2001–02	Cheltenham T	0	0

FINNIGAN, John# (M) 155 5
H: 5 8 W: 10-10 b.Wakefield 29-3-76
Source: Trainee.

1992–93	Nottingham F	0	0	
1993–94	Nottingham F	0	0	
1994–95	Nottingham F	0	0	
1995–96	Nottingham F	0	0	
1996–97	Nottingham F	0	0	
1997–98	Nottingham F	0	0	
1997–98	*Lincoln C*	6	0	
1998–99	Lincoln C	37	1	
1999–2000	Lincoln C	37	2	
2000–01	Lincoln C	40	0	
2001–02	Lincoln C	23	0	143 3
2001–02	Cheltenham T	12	2	12 2

GRAYSON, Neil* (F) 273 61
H: 5 10 W: 13 04 b.York 1-11-64
Source: Rowntree Mackintosh.

1989–90	Doncaster R	6	1	
1990–91	Doncaster R	23	5	29 6
1990–91	York C	1	0	
1991–92	Chesterfield	15	0	15 0

From Gateshead, Boston U

1994–95	Northampton			
1995–96	Northampton T	42	1	
1996–97	Northampton T	40	12	120 31

From Hereford U.

1999–2000	Cheltenham T	43	10	
2000–01	Cheltenham T	31	13	
2001–02	Cheltenham T	34	1	108 24

GRIFFIN, Anthony (D) 76 1
H: 5 11 W: 11 07 b.Bournemouth 22-3-79
Source: Trainee.

1997–98	Bournemouth	0	0	
1998–99	Bournemouth	6	0	6 0
1999–2000	Cheltenham T	24	0	
2000–01	Cheltenham T	22	1	
2001–02	Cheltenham T	24	0	70 1

HIGGS, Shane# (G) 12 0
H: 6 3 W: 14 12 b.Oxford 13-5-77
Source: Trainee.

1994–95	Bristol R	0	0	
1995–96	Bristol R	0	0	
1996–97	Bristol R	2	0	
1997–98	Bristol R	8	0	10 0

From Worcester C.

1999–2000	Cheltenham T	0	0	
2000–01	Cheltenham T	1	0	
2001–02	Cheltenham T	1	0	2 0

HILL, Keith (D) 412 12
H: 6 0 W: 12 12 b.Bolton 17-5-69
Source: Apprentice.

1986–87	Blackburn R	0	0	
1987–88	Blackburn R	1	0	
1988–89	Blackburn R	15	1	
1989–90	Blackburn R	25	0	
1990–91	Blackburn R	22	2	
1991–92	Blackburn R	32	0	
1992–93	Blackburn R	1	0	96 3
1992–93	Plymouth Arg	36	0	
1993–94	Plymouth Arg	29	1	
1994–95	Plymouth Arg	34	1	
1995–96	Plymouth Arg	24	0	123 2
1996–97	Rochdale	43	3	
1997–98	Rochdale	37	2	
1998–99	Rochdale	33	1	
1999–2000	Rochdale	38	0	
2000–01	Rochdale	25	0	176 6
2001–02	Cheltenham T	5	0	5 0
2001–02	*Wrexham*	12	1	12 1

HOPKINS, Gareth* (F) 8 0
H: 6 2 W: 13 07 b.Cheltenham 14-6-80
Source: Trainee.
1999–2000 Cheltenham T 1 0
2000–01 Cheltenham T 4 0
2001–02 Cheltenham T 3 0 8 0

HOWARTH, Neil# (D) 154 9
H: 6 2 W: 13 00 b.Bolton 15-11-71
Source: Trainee.
1989–90 Burnley 1 0 1 0
From Macclesfield T.
1997–98 Macclesfield T 41 3
1998–99 Macclesfield T 19 0 60 3
1999–2000 Cheltenham T 44 2
2000–01 Cheltenham T 23 3
2001–02 Cheltenham T 26 1 93 6

HOWELLS, Lee (M) 112 6
H: 5 11 W: 11 12 b.Fremantle 14-10-68
Source: Apprentice.
1986–87 Bristol R 0 0
From Brisbane Lions.
1999–2000 Cheltenham T 45 3
2000–01 Cheltenham T 36 1
2001–02 Cheltenham T 31 2 112 6

JACKSON, Michael D* (M) 9 0
H: 5 7 W: 11 00 b.Cheltenham 26-6-80
Source: Trainee.
1999–2000 Cheltenham T 2 0
2000–01 Cheltenham T 6 0
2001–02 Cheltenham T 1 0 9 0

JONES, Steve (D) 151 4
H: 5 10 W: 12 00 b.Bristol 25-12-70
Source: Cheltenham T.
1995–96 Swansea C 7 0
1996–97 Swansea C 46 1
1997–98 Swansea C 0 0
1998–99 Swansea C 32 2
1999–2000 Swansea C 38 0
2000–01 Swansea C 13 1 146 4
2001–02 Cheltenham T 5 0 5 0

KEAR, Richard (F) 0 0
H: 5 9 W: 11 00 b.Gloucester 5-11-83
Source: Trainee.
2001–02 Cheltenham T 0 0

McAULEY, Hugh* (M) 81 7
H: 5 10 W: 11 08 b.Plymouth 13-5-77
Source: Leek T.
1999–2000 Cheltenham T 39 4
2000–01 Cheltenham T 35 3
2001–02 Cheltenham T 7 0 81 7

MILTON, Russell# (M) 96 12
H: 5 8 W: 11 08 b.Folkestone 12-1-69
Source: Apprentice.
1986–87 Arsenal 0 0
1987–88 Arsenal 0 0
From Dover Ath.
1999–2000 Cheltenham T 38 9
2000–01 Cheltenham T 19 1
2001–02 Cheltenham T 39 2 96 12

MUGGLETON, Carl‡ (G) 282 0
H: 6 2 W: 14 00 b.Leicester 13-9-68
Source: Apprentice. *Honours:* England Under-21.
1986–87 Leicester C 0 0
1987–88 Leicester C 0 0
1987–88 *Chesterfield* 17 0
1987–88 *Blackpool* 2 0 2 0
1988–89 Leicester C 3 0
1988–89 *Hartlepool U* 8 0 8 0
1989–90 Leicester C 0 0
1989–90 *Stockport Co* 4 0 4 0
1990–91 Leicester C 22 0
1990–91 *Liverpool* 0 0
1991–92 Leicester C 4 0
1992–93 Leicester C 17 0
1993–94 Leicester C 0 0 46 0
1993–94 *Stoke C* 6 0
1993–94 *Sheffield U* 0 0
1993–94 *Celtic* 12 0 12 0
1994–95 Stoke C 24 0
1995–96 Stoke C 6 0
1995–96 *Rotherham U* 6 0 6 0
1995–96 *Sheffield U* 1 0 1 0
1996–97 Stoke C 33 0
1997–98 Stoke C 34 0
1998–99 Stoke C 40 0
1999–2000 Stoke C 0 0
1999–2000 *Mansfield T* 9 0 9 0
1999–2000 *Chesterfield* 5 0 22 0
2000–01 Stoke C 12 0 155 0
2000–01 *Cardiff C* 6 0 6 0
2001–02 *Cheltenham T* 7 0 7 0
2001–02 *Bradford C* 4 0 4 0

NAYLOR, Tony (F) 419 128
H: 5 4 W: 10 13 b.Manchester 29-3-67
Source: Droylsden.
1989–90 Crewe Alex 2 0
1990–91 Crewe Alex 14 1
1991–92 Crewe Alex 34 15
1992–93 Crewe Alex 35 16
1993–94 Crewe Alex 37 13 122 45
1994–95 Port Vale 33 9
1995–96 Port Vale 39 11
1996–97 Port Vale 43 17
1997–98 Port Vale 38 10
1998–99 Port Vale 22 4
1999–2000 Port Vale 36 6
2000–01 Port Vale 42 14 253 71
2001–02 Cheltenham T 44 12 44 12

VICTORY, Jamie (D) 111 13
H: 5 11 W: 12 13 b.London 14-11-75
Source: Trainee.
1994–95 West Ham U 0 0
1995–96 Bournemouth 16 1
1996–97 Bournemouth 0 0 16 1
1999–2000 Cheltenham T 46 4
2000–01 Cheltenham T 3 1
2001–02 Cheltenham T 46 7 95 12

WALKER, Richard (D) 126 5
H: 5 10 W: 13 00 b.Derby 9-11-71
Source: Trainee.
1991–92 Notts Co 0 0
1992–93 Notts Co 12 3
1993–94 Notts Co 21 1
1994–95 Notts Co 7 0
1994–95 *Mansfield T* 4 0 4 0
1995–96 Notts Co 11 0
1996–97 Notts Co 16 0 67 4
From Hereford U.
1999–2000 Cheltenham T 7 0
2000–01 Cheltenham T 36 0
2001–02 Cheltenham T 12 1 55 1

WHITE, Jason* (F) 319 77
H: 6 1 W: 13 00 b.Meriden 19-10-71
Source: Derby Co Trainee. *Honours:*
1991–92 Scunthorpe U 22 11
1992–93 Scunthorpe U 37 5
1993–94 Scunthorpe U 9 0 68 16
1993–94 *Darlington* 4 1 4 1
1993–94 Scarborough 24 9
1994–95 Scarborough 39 11 63 20
1995–96 Northampton T 45 16
1996–97 Northampton T 32 2
1997–98 Northampton T 0 0 77 18
1997–98 Rotherham U 27 13
1998–99 Rotherham U 26 5
1999–2000 Rotherham U 20 4 73 22
2000–01 Cheltenham T 27 0 27 0
2001–02 *Mansfield T* 7 0 7 0

WILLIAMS, Lee# (M) 309 13
H: 5 7 W: 11 10 b.Edgbaston 3-2-73
Source: Trainee.
1991–92 Aston Villa 0 0
1992–93 Aston Villa 0 0
1992–93 *Shrewsbury T* 3 0 3 0
1993–94 Aston Villa 0 0
1993–94 Peterborough U 18 0
1994–95 Peterborough U 40 1
1995–96 Peterborough U 33 0 91 1
1996–97 Tranmere R 0 0
1996–97 Mansfield T 6 0
1997–98 Mansfield T 38 3
1998–99 Mansfield T 44 2
1999–2000 Mansfield T 46 0
2000–01 Mansfield T 41 4
2001–02 Mansfield T 2 0 177 9
2001–02 Cheltenham T 38 3 38 3

YATES, Mark (M) 256 26
H: 5 11 W: 13 01 b.Birmingham 24-1-70
1987–88 Birmingham C 3 0
1988–89 Birmingham C 20 3
1989–90 Birmingham C 20 2
1990–91 Birmingham C 9 1
1991–92 Birmingham C 2 0 54 6
1991–92 Burnley 17 1
1992–93 Burnley 1 0 18 1
1992–93 *Lincoln C* 14 0 14 0
1993–94 *Doncaster R* 34 4 34 4
From Kidderminster H
1999–2000 Cheltenham T 46 2
2000–01 Cheltenham T 45 6
2001–02 Cheltenham T 45 7 136 15

CHESTERFIELD

ABBEY, Nathan* (G) 101 0
H: 6 1 W: 11 13 b.Islington 11-7-78
Source: Trainee.
1995–96 Luton T 0 0
1996–97 Luton T 0 0
1997–98 Luton T 0 0
1998–99 Luton T 2 0
1999–2000 Luton T 33 0
2000–01 Luton T 20 0 55 0
2001–02 Chesterfield 46 0 46 0

ALLOTT, Mark (F) 175 35
H: 5 11 W: 10 12 b.Middleton 16-3-78
Source: Trainee.
1995–96 Oldham Ath 0 0
1996–97 Oldham Ath 5 1
1997–98 Oldham Ath 22 2
1998–99 Oldham Ath 41 7
1999–2000 Oldham Ath 32 10
2000–01 Oldham Ath 39 7
2001–02 Oldham Ath 15 4 154 31
2001–02 Chesterfield 21 4 21 4

ARMSTRONG, Joel* (G) 4 0
H: 5 11 W: 12 07 b.Chesterfield 25-9-81
Source: Scholar.
1999–2000 Chesterfield 3 0
2000–01 Chesterfield 1 0
2001–02 Chesterfield 0 0 4 0

BARRETT, Danny* (M) 3 0
H: 6 0 W: 11 12 b.Bradford 25-9-80
Source: Trainee.
1999–2000 Chesterfield 2 0
2000–01 Chesterfield 1 0
2001–02 Chesterfield 0 0 3 0

BLATHERWICK, Steve (D) 146 3
H: 6 1 W: 15 00 b.Nottingham 20-9-73
Source: Notts Co.
1992–93 Nottingham F 0 0
1993–94 Nottingham F 3 0
1993–94 *Wycombe W* 2 0 2 0
1994–95 Nottingham F 0 0
1995–96 Nottingham F 0 0
1995–96 *Hereford U* 10 1 10 1
1996–97 Nottingham F 7 0 10 0
1996–97 *Reading* 7 0 7 0
1997–98 Burnley 21 0
1998–99 Burnley 3 0 24 0
1998–99 Chesterfield 14 1
1999–2000 Chesterfield 36 0
2000–01 Chesterfield 38 1
2001–02 Chesterfield 5 0 93 2

BOOTY, Martyn (D) 285 8
H: 5 8 W: 12 03 b.Kirby Muxloe 30-5-71
Source: Trainee.
1991–92 Coventry C 3 0
1992–93 Coventry C 0 0
1993–94 Coventry C 2 0 5 0
1993–94 Crewe Alex 31 1
1994–95 Crewe Alex 44 2
1995–96 Crewe Alex 21 2 96 5
1995–96 Reading 17 1
1996–97 Reading 14 0
1997–98 Reading 25 0
1998–99 Reading 8 0 64 1
1998–99 Southend U 20 0
1999–2000 Southend U 28 0
2000–01 Southend U 32 0 80 0
2001–02 Chesterfield 40 2 40 2

BRECKIN, Ian (D) 344 14
H: 5 11 W: 11 07 b.Rotherham 24-2-75
Source: Trainee.
1993–94 Rotherham U 10 0
1994–95 Rotherham U 41 2
1995–96 Rotherham U 39 1
1996–97 Rotherham U 42 3 132 6
1997–98 Chesterfield 43 1
1998–99 Chesterfield 44 2
1999–2000 Chesterfield 38 1
2000–01 Chesterfield 45 3
2001–02 Chesterfield 42 1 212 8

BURT, Jamie (F) 24 7
H: 5 10 W: 12 00 b.Ashington 29-9-79
Source: Whitby T.
2001–02 Chesterfield 24 7 24 7

D'AURIA, David (M) 283 37
H: 5 9 W: 11 11 b.Swansea 26-3-70
Source: Trainee. *Honours:* Wales Youth.
1987–88 Swansea C 4 0
1988–89 Swansea C 14 2
1989–90 Swansea C 7 0
1990–91 Swansea C 20 4 45 6
From Barry T
1994–95 Scarborough 34 7

1995–96	Scarborough	18	1	52 8
1995–96	Scunthorpe U	27	5	
1996–97	Scunthorpe U	39	3	
1997–98	Scunthorpe U	41	10	107 18
1998–99	Hull C	42	4	
1999–2000	Hull C	12	0	54 4
1999–2000	Chesterfield	5	0	
2000–01	Chesterfield	6	0	
2001–02	Chesterfield	14	1	25 1

DAVIES, Gareth (D) 172 5
H: 6 1 W: 11 12 b.Hereford 11-12-73
Source: Trainee. Honours: Wales Under-21.

1991–92	Hereford U	4	0	
1992–93	Hereford U	32	1	
1993–94	Hereford U	31	0	
1994–95	Hereford U	28	0	95 1
1995–96	Crystal Palace	20	2	
1996–97	Crystal Palace	6	0	
1996–97	Cardiff C	6	2	6 2
1997–98	Crystal Palace	1	0	27 2
1997–98	Reading	18	0	
1998–99	Reading	1	0	19 0
1998–99	Swindon T	6	0	
1999–2000	Swindon T	17	0	
2000–01	Swindon T	0	0	
2001–02	Swindon T	2	0	25 0
2001–02	Chesterfield	0	0	

EBDON, Marcus (M) 315 24
H: 5 10 W: 11 02 b.Pontypool 17-10-70
Source: Trainee. Honours: Wales Youth, Under-21.

1988–89	Everton	0	0	
1989–90	Everton	0	0	
1990–91	Everton	0	0	
1991–92	Peterborough U	15	2	
1992–93	Peterborough U	28	4	
1993–94	Peterborough U	10	0	
1994–95	Peterborough U	35	6	
1995–96	Peterborough U	39	2	
1996–97	Peterborough U	20	1	147 15
1996–97	Chesterfield	12	1	
1997–98	Chesterfield	33	2	
1998–99	Chesterfield	40	1	
1999–2000	Chesterfield	11	0	
2000–01	Chesterfield	41	3	
2001–02	Chesterfield	31	2	168 9

EDWARDS, Rob (M) 358 63
H: 5 9 W: 12 04 b.Manchester 23-2-70
Source: Trainee.

1987–88	Crewe Alex	6	1	
1988–89	Crewe Alex	4	0	
1989–90	Crewe Alex	4	0	
1990–91	Crewe Alex	29	11	
1991–92	Crewe Alex	28	6	
1992–93	Crewe Alex	23	7	
1993–94	Crewe Alex	12	2	
1994–95	Crewe Alex	17	2	
1995–96	Crewe Alex	32	15	155 44
1995–96	Huddersfield T	13	7	
1996–97	Huddersfield T	33	3	
1997–98	Huddersfield T	38	1	
1998–99	Huddersfield T	45	2	
1999–2000	Huddersfield T	9	1	
2000–01	Huddersfield T	0	0	138 14
2000–01	Chesterfield	34	4	
2001–02	Chesterfield	31	1	65 5

HEWITT, Jamie* (M) 539 26
H: 5 10 W: 10 08 b.Chesterfield 17-5-68
Source: School.

1984–85	Chesterfield	0	0	
1985–86	Chesterfield	17	0	
1986–87	Chesterfield	42	2	
1987–88	Chesterfield	28	2	
1988–89	Chesterfield	40	1	
1989–90	Chesterfield	42	6	
1990–91	Chesterfield	43	0	
1991–92	Chesterfield	37	3	
1992–93	Doncaster R	27	0	
1993–94	Doncaster R	6	0	33 0
1993–94	Chesterfield	29	3	
1994–95	Chesterfield	38	3	
1995–96	Chesterfield	28	2	
1996–97	Chesterfield	37	1	
1997–98	Chesterfield	44	1	
1998–99	Chesterfield	40	2	
1999–2000	Chesterfield	40	0	
2000–01	Chesterfield	1	0	
2001–02	Chesterfield	1	0	506 26

HOWARD, Jonathan# (F) 263 44
H: 5 11 W: 11 07 b.Sheffield 7-10-71
Source: Trainee.

1990–91	Rotherham U	1	0	
1991–92	Rotherham U	10	3	
1992–93	Rotherham U	17	2	
1993–94	Rotherham U	8	0	
1994–95	Rotherham U	0	0	36 5
1994–95	Chesterfield	12	1	
1995–96	Chesterfield	30	2	
1996–97	Chesterfield	35	9	
1997–98	Chesterfield	35	6	
1998–99	Chesterfield	37	9	
1999–2000	Chesterfield	27	2	
2000–01	Chesterfield	31	5	
2001–02	Chesterfield	20	5	227 39

HOWSON, Stuart (M) 13 1
H: 6 1 W: 12 13 b.Chorley 30-9-81
Source: Trainee.

1999–2000	Blackburn R	0	0	
2000–01	Blackburn R	0	0	
2001–02	Blackburn R	0	0	
2001–02	Chesterfield	13	1	13 1

HURST, Glynn (F) 124 46
H: 5 10 W: 11 06 b.Barnsley 17-1-76
Source: Tottenham H Trainee.

1994–95	Barnsley	2	0	
1995–96	Barnsley	5	0	
1995–96	Swansea C	2	1	2 1
1996–97	Barnsley	1	0	8 0
1996–97	Mansfield T	6	0	6 0
1998–99	Ayr U	34	18	
1999–2000	Ayr U	25	14	59 32
2000–01	Stockport Co	11	0	
2001–02	Stockport Co	15	4	26 4
2001–02	Chesterfield	23	9	23 9

INGLEDOW, Jamie* (M) 66 5
H: 5 7 W: 11 01 b.Barnsley 23-8-80
Source: Trainee.

1998–99	Rotherham U	21	2	
1999–2000	Rotherham U	4	0	25 2
2000–01	Chesterfield	24	3	
2001–02	Chesterfield	17	0	41 3

INNES, Mark (D) 96 3
H: 5 10 W: 12 04 b.Bellshill 27-9-78
Source: Trainee.

1995–96	Oldham Ath	0	0	
1996–97	Oldham Ath	0	0	
1997–98	Oldham Ath	4	0	
1998–99	Oldham Ath	13	1	
1999–2000	Oldham Ath	21	0	
2000–01	Oldham Ath	30	0	
2001–02	Oldham Ath	5	0	73 1
2001–02	Chesterfield	23	2	23 2

JONES, Mark (F) 15 0
H: 5 10 W: 12 07 b.Walsall 7-9-79
Source: Trainee. Honours: England Schools.

1996–97	Wolverhampton W	0	0	
1997–98	Wolverhampton W	0	0	
1998–99	Wolverhampton W	2	0	
1999–2000	Wolverhampton W	1	0	3 0
1999–2000	Cheltenham T	3	0	3 0
2000–01	Chesterfield	3	0	
2001–02	Chesterfield	6	0	9 0

(Transferred to Raith R, November 2001).

PARRISH, Sean# (M) 233 32
H: 5 10 W: 11 05 b.Wrexham 14-3-72
Source: Trainee.

1989–90	Shrewsbury T	2	0	
1990–91	Shrewsbury T	1	0	3 0
From Telford U				
1994–95	Doncaster R	25	3	
1995–96	Doncaster R	41	5	66 8
1996–97	Northampton T	39	8	
1997–98	Northampton T	12	1	
1998–99	Northampton T	33	1	
1999–2000	Northampton T	25	3	109 13
2000–01	Chesterfield	35	10	
2001–02	Chesterfield	20	1	55 11

PAYNE, Steve# (D) 174 7
H: 5 11 W: 12 05 b.Castleford 1-8-75
Source: Trainee.

1993–94	Huddersfield T	0	0	
1994–95	Huddersfield T	0	0	
1995–96	Huddersfield T	0	0	
1996–97	Huddersfield T	0	0	
1997–98	Macclesfield T	39	0	
1998–99	Macclesfield T	38	2	77 2
1999–2000	Chesterfield	18	3	
2000–01	Chesterfield	35	1	
2001–02	Chesterfield	44	1	97 5

PEARCE, Greg* (M) 19 0
H: 6 0 W: 11 00 b.Bolton 26-5-80
Source: Trainee.

1997–98	Chesterfield	0	0	
1998–99	Chesterfield	1	0	
1999–2000	Chesterfield	10	0	
2000–01	Chesterfield	1	0	
2001–02	Chesterfield	7	0	19 0

RICHARDSON, Lee J# (M) 402 38
H: 5 11 W: 10 06 b.Halifax 12-3-69
Source: Trainee.

1986–87	Halifax T	1	0	
1987–88	Halifax T	35	5	
1988–89	Halifax T	25	1	56 2
1988–89	Watford	9	0	
1989–90	Watford	32	1	41 1
1990–91	Blackburn R	38	2	
1991–92	Blackburn R	24	1	
1992–93	Blackburn R	0	0	62 3
1992–93	Aberdeen	29	2	
1993–94	Aberdeen	35	4	64 6
1994–95	Oldham Ath	30	6	
1995–96	Oldham Ath	27	11	
1996–97	Oldham Ath	31	4	
1997–98	Oldham Ath	0	0	88 21
1997–98	Stockport Co	6	0	6 0
1997–98	Huddersfield T	21	3	
1998–99	Huddersfield T	15	0	
1999–2000	Huddersfield T	0	0	36 3
1999–2000	Bury	5	1	5 1
1999–2000	Livingston	0	0	
2000–01	Chesterfield	30	0	
2001–02	Chesterfield	14	1	44 1

ROWLAND, Keith (M) 231 8
H: 5 10 W: 10 07 b.Portadown 1-9-71
Source: Trainee. Honours: Northern Ireland Youth, B, 19 full caps, 1 goal.

1990–91	Bournemouth	0	0	
1991–92	Bournemouth	37	0	
1992–93	Bournemouth	35	2	72 2
1992–93	Coventry C	2	0	2 0
1993–94	West Ham U	23	0	
1994–95	West Ham U	12	0	
1995–96	West Ham U	23	0	
1996–97	West Ham U	15	1	
1997–98	West Ham U	7	0	80 1
1997–98	QPR	7	0	
1998–99	QPR	30	3	
1999–2000	QPR	15	0	
2000–01	QPR	4	0	56 3
2000–01	Luton T	12	2	12 2
2001–02	Chesterfield	9	0	9 0

RUSHBURY, Andy§ (M) 5 0
H: 5 10 W: 11 07 b.Carlisle 7-3-83
Source: Scholar.

2000–01	Chesterfield	2	0	
2001–02	Chesterfield	3	0	5 0

TUTILL, Steve (D) 390 7
H: 5 10 W: 12 06 b.Derwent 1-10-69
Source: Trainee. Honours: England Schools.

1987–88	York C	21	0	
1988–89	York C	22	1	
1989–90	York C	42	0	
1990–91	York C	42	0	
1991–92	York C	39	1	
1992–93	York C	3	0	
1993–94	York C	46	4	
1994–95	York C	39	0	
1995–96	York C	25	0	
1996–97	York C	15	0	
1997–98	York C	2	0	301 6
1997–98	Darlington	7	0	
1998–99	Darlington	36	0	
1999–2000	Darlington	27	0	70 0
2000–01	Chesterfield	19	1	
2001–02	Chesterfield	0	0	19 1

WALSH, Danny‡ (M) 3 0
H: 5 11 W: 12 03 b.Manchester 16-9-78
Source: Trainee.

1998–99	Oldham Ath	1	0	
1999–2000	Oldham Ath	0	0	
2000–01	Oldham Ath	0	0	
2001–02	Oldham Ath	1	0	2 0
2001–02	Chesterfield	1	0	1 0

WILDING, Craig* (M)
H: 5 10 W: 11 11 b.Birmingham 30-10-81
Source: Scholar.

2001–02	Chesterfield	0	0

WILLIAMS, Danny* (M) 31 0
H: 5 9 W: 9 13 b.Sheffield 2-3-81
Source: Trainee.

1999–2000	Chesterfield	5	0	
2000–01	Chesterfield	2	0	
2001–02	Chesterfield	24	0	31 0

WILLIS, Roger* (M) 314 54
H: 6 0 W: 12 00 b.Islington 17-6-67
Source: Dunkirk.

1989–90	Grimsby T	9	0	9 0
From Barnet				
1991–92	Barnet	38	12	
1992–93	Barnet	6	1	44 13
1992–93	Watford	32	2	
1993–94	Watford	4	0	36 2
1993–94	Birmingham C	16	5	
1994–95	Birmingham C	3	0	19 5
1994–95	Southend U	21	4	
1995–96	Southend U	10	3	31 7
1996–97	Peterborough U	40	6	40 6
1997–98	Chesterfield	34	8	

1998–99	Chesterfield	17	0		
1999-2000	Chesterfield	28	4		
2000–01	Chesterfield	32	5		
2001–02	Chesterfield	24	4	135	21

Scholars
Atkinson, Joe; Cooke, Nicholas J; Cressey, Ben; Hall, Jordan; Hogg, Timothy G; Mitchell, Adam T; Richmond, Andrew J; Rushbrary, Andrew J; Shaw, Craig P; Smith, Mark; Smith, Nathan A; Stone, Joseph; Tuckwood, Stephen A; Warne, Stephen J; Wharton, Lee; Worthington, Matthew A; Young, Matthew P

COLCHESTER U

ALLMAN, Anthon* (M)   0 0
H: 5 10 W: 11 08 b.Sidcup 14-12-80
Source: Trainee. *Honours:* England Schools.

1997–98	Charlton Ath	0	0
1998–99	Charlton Ath	0	0
1999-2000	Charlton Ath	0	0
2000–01	Charlton Ath	0	0
2001–02	Colchester U	0	0

BLACKWELL, Oliver‡ (D)   0 0
H: 6 2 W: 12 04 b.Colchester 15-10-82

2001–02	Colchester U	0	0

BLATSIS, Con‡ (D)   111 5
H: 6 3 W: 13 10 b.Australia 6-7-77
Honours: Australia Under-20, Under-23, 2 full caps.

1995–96	South Melbourne	19	1		
1996–97	South Melbourne	23	2		
1997–98	South Melbourne	23	1		
1998–99	South Melbourne	7	0		
1999-2000	South Melbourne	24	1	96	5
2000–01	Derby Co	2	0		
2000–01	Sheffield W	6	0	6	0
2001–02	Derby Co	0	0	2	0
2001–02	Colchester U	7	0	7	0

BOWRY, Bobby# (M)   226 7
H: 5 10 W: 11 00 b.Hampstead 19-5-71
Honours: St. Kitts & Nevis full caps.

1990–91	QPR	0	0		
From Carshalton Ath					
1991–92	Crystal Palace	0	0		
1992–93	Crystal Palace	11	1		
1993–94	Crystal Palace	21	0		
1994–95	Crystal Palace	18	0	50	1
1995–96	Millwall	38	2		
1996–97	Millwall	28	1		
1997–98	Millwall	43	2		
1998–99	Millwall	25	0		
1999-2000	Millwall	5	0		
2000–01	Millwall	1	0	140	5
2001–02	Colchester U	36	1	36	1

BROWN, Simon (G)   76 0
H: 6 2 W: 13 00 b.Chelmsford 3-12-76
Source: Trainee.

1995–96	Tottenham H	0	0		
1996–97	Tottenham H	0	0		
1997–98	Tottenham H	0	0		
1997–98	Lincoln C	1	0	1	0
1998–99	Tottenham H	0	0		
1998–99	Fulham	0	0		
1999-2000	Colchester U	38	0		
2000–01	Colchester U	18	0		
2001–02	Colchester U	19	0	75	0

CANHAM, Marc§ (M)   1 0
b.Wefburg 11-9-82
Source: Scholar.

2001–02	Colchester U	1	0	1	0

CHAMBERS, Triston§ (F)   1 0
b.Enfield 25-12-82
Source: Scholar.

2001–02	Colchester U	1	0	1	0

CLARK, Simon‡ (D)   260 13
H: 6 1 W: 13 04 b.Boston 12-3-67
Source: Boston U, Holbeach, Kings Lynn, Hendon, Stevenage Borough.

1993–94	Peterborough U	1	0		
1994–95	Peterborough U	32	0		
1995–96	Peterborough U	40	1		
1996–97	Peterborough U	34	3	107	4
1997–98	Leyton Orient	39	4		
1998–99	Leyton Orient	40	4		
1999-2000	Leyton Orient	19	1	98	9
2000–01	Colchester U	34	0		
2001–02	Colchester U	21	0	55	0

COOTE, Adrian (F)   73 7
H: 6 2 W: 12 10 b.Gt Yarmouth 30-9-78
Source: Trainee. *Honours:* Northern Ireland Under-21, B, 6 full caps.

1997–98	Norwich C	23	2
1998–99	Norwich C	6	0
1999-2000	Norwich C	11	1
2000–01	Norwich C	14	0
2001–02	Norwich C	0	0	54	3
2001–02	Colchester U	19	4	19	4

DOZZELL, Jason‡ (M)   535 79
H: 6 2 W: 13 07 b.Ipswich 9-12-67
Source: School. *Honours:* England Youth, Under-21.

1983–84	Ipswich T	5	1		
1984–85	Ipswich T	14	2		
1985–86	Ipswich T	41	3		
1986–87	Ipswich T	42	2		
1987–88	Ipswich T	39	1		
1988–89	Ipswich T	29	11		
1989–90	Ipswich T	46	8		
1990–91	Ipswich T	30	6		
1991–92	Ipswich T	45	11		
1992–93	Ipswich T	41	7		
1993–94	Tottenham H	32	8		
1994–95	Tottenham H	7	0		
1995–96	Tottenham H	28	3		
1996–97	Tottenham H	17	2	84	13
1997–98	Ipswich T	8	1	340	53
1997–98	Northampton T	21	4	21	4
1998–99	Colchester U	29	4		
1999-2000	Colchester U	39	5		
2000–01	Colchester U	22	0		
2001–02	Colchester U	0	0	90	9

DUGUID, Karl (F)   213 32
H: 5 11 W: 11 07 b.Hitchin 21-3-78
Source: Trainee.

1995–96	Colchester U	16	1		
1996–97	Colchester U	20	3		
1997–98	Colchester U	21	3		
1998–99	Colchester U	33	4		
1999-2000	Colchester U	41	12		
2000–01	Colchester U	41	5		
2001–02	Colchester U	41	4	213	32

DUNNE, Joe# (D)   278 7
H: 5 9 W: 11 10 b.Dublin 25-5-73
Source: Trainee. *Honours:* Eire Youth, Under-21.

1990–91	Gillingham	26	0		
1991–92	Gillingham	11	0		
1992–93	Gillingham	4	0		
1993–94	Gillingham	37	0		
1994–95	Gillingham	35	1		
1995–96	Gillingham	2	0	115	1
1995–96	Colchester U	5	1		
1996–97	Colchester U	35	0		
1997–98	Colchester U	25	2		
1998–99	Colchester U	36	0		
From Dover Ath.					
1999-2000	Colchester U	20	0		
2000–01	Colchester U	34	1		
2001–02	Colchester U	8	2	163	6

FITZGERALD, Scott (D)   268 2
H: 6 1 W: 13 00 b.Westminster 13-8-69
Source: Trainee. *Honours:* Eire Under-21, B.

1988–89	Wimbledon	0	0		
1989–90	Wimbledon	1	0		
1990–91	Wimbledon	0	0		
1991–92	Wimbledon	36	1		
1992–93	Wimbledon	20	0		
1993–94	Wimbledon	28	0		
1994–95	Wimbledon	17	0		
1995–96	Wimbledon	4	0		
1995–96	Sheffield U	6	0	6	0
1996–97	Wimbledon	0	0	106	1
1996–97	Millwall	7	0		
1997–98	Millwall	18	0		
1998–99	Millwall	32	1		
1999-2000	Millwall	31	0		
2000–01	Millwall	1	0	89	1
2000–01	Colchester U	30	0		
2001–02	Colchester U	37	0	67	0

GREGORY, David# (M)   262 22
H: 5 10 W: 12 00 b.Polstead 23-1-70
Source: Trainee.

1987–88	Ipswich T	0	0		
1988–89	Ipswich T	2	0		
1989–90	Ipswich T	4	0		
1990–91	Ipswich T	21	1		
1991–92	Ipswich T	1	0		
1992–93	Ipswich T	3	1		
1993–94	Ipswich T	0	0		
1994–95	Ipswich T	1	0	32	2
1994–95	Hereford U	2	0	2	0
1995–96	Peterborough U	3	0	3	0
1995–96	Colchester U	10	0		
1996–97	Colchester U	38	1		
1997–98	Colchester U	44	5		
1998–99	Colchester U	44	11		
1999-2000	Colchester U	45	0		
2000–01	Colchester U	28	3		
2001–02	Colchester U	16	0	225	20

IZZET, Kem (M)   46 4
H: 5 7 W: 11 00 b.Whitechapel 29-9-80
Source: Trainee.

1998–99	Charlton Ath	0	0		
1999-2000	Charlton Ath	0	0		
2000–01	Charlton Ath	0	0		
2001–02	Colchester U	40	3	46	4

JOHNSON, Gavin# (D)   323 22
H: 5 11 W: 12 13 b.Eye 10-10-70
Source: Trainee.

1988–89	Ipswich T	4	0		
1989–90	Ipswich T	6	0		
1990–91	Ipswich T	7	0		
1991–92	Ipswich T	42	5		
1992–93	Ipswich T	40	5		
1993–94	Ipswich T	16	1		
1994–95	Ipswich T	17	0	132	11
1995–96	Luton T	5	0	5	0
1995–96	Wigan Ath	27	3		
1996–97	Wigan Ath	37	3		
1997–98	Wigan Ath	20	2	84	8
1998–99	Dunfermline Ath	6	0	18	0
1999-2000	Colchester U	27	0		
2000–01	Colchester U	37	2		
2001–02	Colchester U	20	1	84	5

JOHNSON, Ross* (D)   184 3
H: 6 0 W: 13 00 b.Brighton 2-1-76
Source: Trainee.

1993–94	Brighton & HA	2	0		
1994–95	Brighton & HA	20	0		
1995–96	Brighton & HA	20	0		
1996–97	Brighton & HA	29	0		
1997–98	Brighton & HA	38	0		
1998–99	Brighton & HA	34	2		
1999-2000	Brighton & HA	9	0	132	2
1999-2000	Colchester U	18	0		
2000–01	Colchester U	18	0		
2001–02	Colchester U	16	1	52	1

KEEBLE, Chris (M)   22 2
H: 5 10 W: 10 12 b.Colchester 17-9-78
Source: Trainee.

1997–98	Ipswich T	1	0		
1998–99	Ipswich T	0	0		
1999-2000	Ipswich T	0	0	1	0
1999-2000	Colchester U	5	1		
2000–01	Colchester U	16	1		
2001–02	Colchester U	0	0	21	2

KEITH, Joe (D)   113 8
H: 5 7 W: 11 00 b.London 1-10-78
Source: Trainee.

1997–98	West Ham U	0	0		
1998–99	West Ham U	0	0		
1999-2000	Colchester U	45	1		
2000–01	Colchester U	27	3		
2001–02	Colchester U	41	4	113	8

McGLEISH, Scott (F)   287 77
H: 5 9 W: 11 12 b.Camden Town 10-2-74
Source: Edgware T.

1994–95	Charlton Ath	6	0	6	0
1994–95	*Leyton Orient*	6	1		
1995–96	Peterborough U	12	0		
1995–96	*Colchester U*	15	6		
1996–97	Peterborough U	1	0	13	0
1996–97	*Cambridge U*	10	7	10	7
1996–97	Leyton Orient	28	7		
1997–98	Leyton Orient	8	0	42	8
1997–98	Barnet	37	13		
1998–99	Barnet	36	8		
1999-2000	Barnet	42	10		
2000–01	Barnet	19	5	134	36
2000–01	Colchester U	21	5		
2001–02	Colchester U	46	15	82	26

MORGAN, Dean (F)   34 0
H: 6 0 W: 12 01 b.Enfield 3-10-83
Source: Scholar.

2000–01	Colchester U	4	0		
2001–02	Colchester U	30	0	34	0

MORROW, Steve‡ (D)   186 3
H: 6 0 W: 12 06 b.Bangor 2-7-70
Source: Trainee. *Honours:* Northern Ireland Schools, Youth, Under-23, B, 39 full caps, 1 goal.

1987–88	Arsenal	0	0		
1988–89	Arsenal	0	0		
1989–90	*Reading*	10	0		
1990–91	Arsenal	2	0		
1991–92	*Watford*	8	0	8	0
1991–92	*Reading*	3	0	13	0
1991–92	*Barnet*	1	0	1	0
1992–93	Arsenal	16	0		
1993–94	Arsenal	11	0		
1994–95	Arsenal	15	1		
1995–96	Arsenal	4	0		

Season	Club				
1996–97	Arsenal	14	0	62	1
1996–97	QPR	5	1		
1997–98	QPR	31	1		
1998–99	QPR	24	0		
1999–2000	QPR	7	0		
2000–01	QPR	24	0	91	2
2000–01	Peterborough U	11	0	11	0
2001–02	Colchester U	0	0		

OPARA, Lloyd§ (F) 1 0
b.Edmonton 6-1-84
Source: Scholar.

2001–02	Colchester U	1	0	1	0

PINAULT, Thomas (M) 51 1
H: 5 9 W: 11 10 b.Grasse 4-12-81
Source: Cannes.

1999–2000	Colchester U	4	0		
2000–01	Colchester U	5	1		
2001–02	Colchester U	42	0	51	1

RAPLEY, Kevin (F) 159 29
H: 5 10 W: 12 02 b.Reading 21-9-77
Source: Trainee.

1996–97	Brentford	2	0		
1997–98	Brentford	37	9		
1998–99	Brentford	12	3	51	12
1998–99	Southend U	9	4	9	4
1998–99	Notts Co	16	2		
1999–2000	Notts Co	29	2		
2000–01	Notts Co	7	0	52	4
2000–01	Exeter C	7	0	7	0
2000–01	Scunthorpe U	5	0	5	0
2001–02	Colchester U	35	9	35	9

STOCKWELL, Mick# (M) 598 55
H: 5 6 W: 12 00 b.Maldon 14-2-65
Source: Apprentice.

1982–83	Ipswich T	2	0		
1983–84	Ipswich T	0	0		
1984–85	Ipswich T	0	0		
1985–86	Ipswich T	8	0		
1986–87	Ipswich T	21	1		
1987–88	Ipswich T	43	1		
1988–89	Ipswich T	23	2		
1989–90	Ipswich T	34	3		
1990–91	Ipswich T	44	6		
1991–92	Ipswich T	46	2		
1992–93	Ipswich T	39	4		
1993–94	Ipswich T	42	1		
1994–95	Ipswich T	15	0		
1995–96	Ipswich T	37	1		
1996–97	Ipswich T	43	7		
1997–98	Ipswich T	46	3		
1998–99	Ipswich T	30	2		
1999–2000	Ipswich T	35	2	506	35
2000–01	Colchester U	46	11		
2001–02	Colchester U	46	9	92	20

WHITE, Alan# (D) 149 6
H: 6 2 W: 13 07 b.Darlington 22-3-76
Source: Derby Co Schoolboy.

1994–95	Middlesbrough	0	0		
1995–96	Middlesbrough	0	0		
1996–97	Middlesbrough	0	0		
1997–98	Middlesbrough	0	0		
1997–98	Luton T	28	1		
1998–99	Luton T	13	1		
1999–2000	Luton T	19	1	80	3
1999–2000	Colchester U	4	0		
2000–01	Colchester U	32	0		
2001–02	Colchester U	33	3	69	3

WIGNALL, Jack‡ (D) 1 0
H: 6 1 W: 11 01 b.Liverpool 26-9-81
Source: Trainee.

1999–2000	Colchester U	1	0		
2000–01	Colchester U	0	0		
2001–02	Colchester U	0	0	1	0

Scholars
Canham, Marc D; Chambers, Tristan; Cranfield, Ben MD; Crouch, Ross A; Driver, Sherdan; Edwards, Dwayne W; Gerken, Dean J; Hadrava, David L; Halford, Gregory; Hanna, Aaron J; Hearn, Matthew J; Opara, Lloyd; Redmond, Gary St C; Williamson, Glenn A

COVENTRY C

ANTONELIUS, Tomas‡ (D) 5 0
H: 5 10 W: 12 00 b.Stockholm 7-5-73
Source: AIK Stockholm. Honours: Sweden 6 full caps.

2001–02	Coventry C	5	0	5	0

(Transferred to AB Copenhagen, February 2002).

BETTS, Robert (D) 22 0
H: 5 10 W: 11 00 b.Doncaster 21-12-81
Source: School.

1997–98	Doncaster R	3	0	3	0
1998–99	Coventry C	0	0		
1999–2000	Coventry C	2	0		
2000–01	Coventry C	1	0		
2000–01	Plymouth Arg	4	0	4	0
2001–02	Lincoln C	3	0	3	0
2001–02	Coventry C	9	0	12	0

BOTHROYD, Jay (F) 39 6
H: 6 3 W: 13 00 b.Islington 7-5-82
Source: Trainee. Honours: England Youth, Under-20, Under-21.

1999–2000	Arsenal	0	0		
2000–01	Coventry C	8	0		
2001–02	Coventry C	31	6	39	6

BRANCATI, Marco (M) 0 0
H: 5 10 W: 11 05 b.Rome 16-4-83

2000–01	Coventry C	0	0		
2001–02	Coventry C	0	0		

BREEN, Gary* (D) 325 5
H: 6 1 W: 11 12 b.London 12-12-73
Source: Charlton Ath. Honours: Eire Under-21, 47 full caps, 6 goals.

1991–92	Maidstone U	19	0	19	0
1992–93	Gillingham	29	0		
1993–94	Gillingham	22	0	51	0
1994–95	Peterborough U	44	1		
1995–96	Peterborough U	25	0	69	1
1995–96	Birmingham C	18	1		
1996–97	Birmingham C	22	1	40	2
1996–97	Coventry C	9	0		
1997–98	Coventry C	30	1		
1998–99	Coventry C	25	0		
1999–2000	Coventry C	21	0		
2000–01	Coventry C	31	1		
2001–02	Coventry C	30	0	146	2

CHIPPO, Youssef (M) 129 8
H: 5 11 W: 12 00 b.Rabat 10-5-73
Source: Al Arabi. Honours: Morocco 43 full caps.

1997–98	Porto	18	2		
1998–99	Porto	12	0	30	2
1999–2000	Coventry C	33	2		
2000–01	Coventry C	32	0		
2001–02	Coventry C	34	4	99	6

CUDWORTH, Thomas* (D) 0 0
H: 5 10 W: 11 00 b.Coventry 3-8-82
Source: Trainee.

1999–2000	Coventry C	0	0		
2000–01	Coventry C	0	0		
2001–02	Coventry C	0	0		

DAHL, Andreas (M) 0 0
H: 5 11 W: 12 10 b.Sweden 6-6-84
Source: IFK Hassleholm.

2001–02	Coventry C	0	0		

DAVENPORT, Calum (D) 4 0
H: 6 4 W: 14 00 b.Bedford 1-1-83
Source: Trainee. Honours: England Youth.

1999–2000	Coventry C	0	0		
2000–01	Coventry C	1	0		
2001–02	Coventry C	3	0	4	0

DELORGE, Laurent (M) 38 9
H: 5 10 W: 11 12 b.Leuven 21-7-79
Honours: .

1998–99	Gent	10	5	10	5
1998–99	Coventry C	0	0		
1999–2000	Coventry C	0	0		
2000–01	Coventry C	0	0		
2001–02	Coventry C	28	4	28	4

EDWORTHY, Marc* (D) 271 2
H: 5 11 W: 10 03 b.Barnstaple 24-12-72
Source: Trainee.

1990–91	Plymouth Arg	0	0		
1991–92	Plymouth Arg	15	0		
1992–93	Plymouth Arg	15	0		
1993–94	Plymouth Arg	12	0		
1994–95	Plymouth Arg	27	1	69	1
1995–96	Crystal Palace	44	0		
1996–97	Crystal Palace	45	0		
1997–98	Crystal Palace	34	0		
1998–99	Crystal Palace	3	0	126	0
1998–99	Coventry C	22	0		
1999–2000	Coventry C	10	0		
2000–01	Coventry C	24	1		
2001–02	Coventry C	20	0	76	1

EUSTACE, John (M) 65 4
H: 5 11 W: 11 12 b.Solihull 3-11-79
Source: Trainee.

1996–97	Coventry C	0	0		
1997–98	Coventry C	0	0		
1998–99	Coventry C	0	0		
1998–99	Dundee U	11	1	11	1
1999–2000	Coventry C	16	1		
2000–01	Coventry C	32	2		
2001–02	Coventry C	6	0	54	3

FAHLMAN, Per (G) 0 0
H: 6 0 W: 12 07 b.Sweden 26-4-84

2000–01	Coventry C	0	0		
2001–02	Coventry C	0	0		

FERGUSON, Barry‡ (D) 13 0
H: 6 3 W: 13 00 b.Dublin 7-9-79
Source: Home Farm. Honours: Eire Under-21.

1998–99	Coventry C	0	0		
1999–2000	Coventry C	0	0		
1999–2000	Colchester U	6	0	6	0
2000–01	Coventry C	0	0		
2000–01	Hartlepool U	4	0	4	0
2000–01	Northampton T	3	0	3	0
2001–02	Coventry C	0	0		

FORD, Brian (D) 0 0
H: 5 11 W: 12 00 b.Edinburgh 23-9-82
Source: Trainee.

1999–2000	Coventry C	0	0		
2000–01	Coventry C	0	0		
2001–02	Coventry C	0	0		

FOWLER, Lee (M) 13 0
H: 5 7 W: 10 00 b.Cardiff 10-6-83
Source: Scholar.

2000–01	Coventry C	0	0		
2001–02	Coventry C	13	0	13	0

FROGGATT, Steve‡ (F) 190 11
H: 5 11 W: 11 00 b.Lincoln 9-3-73
Source: Trainee. Honours: England Under-21.

1990–91	Aston Villa	0	0		
1991–92	Aston Villa	9	0		
1992–93	Aston Villa	17	1		
1993–94	Aston Villa	9	1	35	2
1994–95	Wolverhampton W	20	2		
1995–96	Wolverhampton W	18	1		
1996–97	Wolverhampton W	27	2		
1997–98	Wolverhampton W	33	2		
1998–99	Wolverhampton W	8	0	106	7
1998–99	Coventry C	23	1		
1999–2000	Coventry C	26	1		
2000–01	Coventry C	0	0		
2001–02	Coventry C	0	0	49	2

GALLIERI, Antonio (F) 0 0
H: 5 8 W: 11 00 b.Rome 5-7-83

2000–01	Coventry C	0	0		
2001–02	Coventry C	0	0		

GORAM, Andy* (G) 595 1
H: 5 11 W: 11 06 b.Bury 13-4-64
Source: West Bromwich Apprentice, Scotland Under-21, 43 full caps.

1981–82	Oldham Ath	3	0		
1982–83	Oldham Ath	38	0		
1983–84	Oldham Ath	22	0		
1984–85	Oldham Ath	41	0		
1985–86	Oldham Ath	41	0		
1986–87	Oldham Ath	41	0		
1987–88	Oldham Ath	9	0		
1987–88	Hibernian	33	1		
1988–89	Hibernian	36	0		
1989–90	Hibernian	34	0		
1990–91	Hibernian	35	0	138	1
1991–92	Rangers	44	0		
1992–93	Rangers	34	0		
1993–94	Rangers	8	0		
1994–95	Rangers	19	0		
1995–96	Rangers	30	0		
1996–97	Rangers	25	0		
1997–98	Rangers	24	0	184	0
1998–99	Notts Co	1	0	1	0
1998–99	Sheffield U	7	0	7	0
1998–99	Motherwell	13	0		
1999–2000	Motherwell	22	0		
2000–01	Motherwell	22	0	57	0
2000–01	Manchester U	2	0	2	0
2001–02	Oldham Ath	4	0	199	0
2001–02	Coventry C	7	0	7	0

GRANT, Stephen (D) 0 0
H: 5 7 W: 10 12 b.Kirkcaldy 28-7-84
Source: Scholar.

2001–02	Coventry C	0	0		

GUERRERO, Ivan (D) 7 0
H: 5 7 W: 10 00 b.Comayagua 30-11-77
Source: Motagua. Honours: Honduras full caps.

2000–01	Coventry C	3	0		
2001–02	Coventry C	4	0	7	0

HALL, Marcus* (D)   132 2
H: 6 1 W: 12 02 b.Coventry 24-3-76
Source: Trainee. *Honours:* England Under-21, B.

1994–95	Coventry C	5	0		
1995–96	Coventry C	25	0		
1996–97	Coventry C	13	0		
1997–98	Coventry C	25	1		
1998–99	Coventry C	5	0		
1999–2000	Coventry C	9	0		
2000–01	Coventry C	21	0		
2001–02	Coventry C	29	1	132	2

HEDMAN, Magnus (G)   261 0
H: 6 3 W: 14 00 b.Stockholm 19-3-73
Honours: Sweden 49 full caps.

1990	AIK Stockholm	2	0		
1991	AIK Stockholm	2	0		
1992	AIK Stockholm	7	0		
1993	AIK Stockholm	26	0		
1994	AIK Stockholm	26	0		
1995	AIK Stockholm	25	0		
1996	AIK Stockholm	26	0		
1997	AIK Stockholm	13	0	127	0
1997–98	Coventry C	14	0		
1998–99	Coventry C	36	0		
1999–2000	Coventry C	35	0		
2000–01	Coventry C	35	0		
2001–02	Coventry C	34	0	134	0

HIGGINS, Ruaidhri (M)   0 0
H: 5 10 W: 12 00 b.Derry 23-10-84
Source: Scholar.

2001–02	Coventry C	0	0

HOPE, Shaun* (D)   0 0
H: 5 11 W: 12 00 b.Hartlepool 15-12-82
Source: Scholar.

2000–01	Coventry C	0	0
2001–02	Coventry C	0	0

HUGHES, Lee (F)   194 92
H: 6 0 W: 11 06 b.Birmingham 22-5-76
Source: Kidderminster H.

1997–98	WBA	37	14		
1998–99	WBA	42	31		
1999–2000	WBA	36	12		
2000–01	WBA	41	21	156	78
2001–02	Coventry C	38	14	38	14

HYLDGAARD, Morten (G)   5 0
H: 6 6 W: 14 00 b.Herning 26-1-78
Source: Ikast.

1999–2000	Coventry C	0	0		
1999–2000	*Scunthorpe U*	5	0	5	0
2000–01	Coventry C	0	0		
2001–02	*Grimsby T*	0	0		

JOACHIM, Julian (F)   256 65
H: 5 6 W: 12 00 b.Boston 20-9-74
Source: Trainee. *Honours:* England Youth, Under-21.

1992–93	Leicester C	26	10		
1993–94	Leicester C	36	11		
1994–95	Leicester C	15	3		
1995–96	Leicester C	22	1	99	25
1995–96	Aston Villa	11	1		
1996–97	Aston Villa	15	3		
1997–98	Aston Villa	26	8		
1998–99	Aston Villa	36	14		
1999–2000	Aston Villa	33	6		
2000–01	Aston Villa	20	7	141	39
2001–02	Coventry C	16	1	16	1

KENNA, Conor (D)   0 0
H: 5 10 W: 12 00 b.Dublin 21-11-84
Source: Scholar.

2001–02	Coventry C	0	0

KONJIC, Muhamed (D)   216 14
H: 6 3 W: 13 00 b.Bosnia 14-5-70
Honours: Bosnia 23 full caps, 3 goals.

1990–91	Tuzla	3	0		
1991–92	Tuzla	5	0	8	0
1992–93	Belisce	18	0	18	0
1993–94	Zagreb	29	3		
1994–95	Zagreb	19	1		
1995–96	Zagreb	15	1	63	5
1996–97	Zurich	29	2		
1997–98	Zurich	7	3	36	5
1997–98	Monaco	19	0		
1998–99	Monaco	18	2	37	2
1998–99	Coventry C	4	0		
1999–2000	Coventry C	4	0		
2000–01	Coventry C	8	0		
2001–02	Coventry C	38	2	54	2

MAGENNIS, Mark* (M)   0 0
H: 5 7 W: 10 02 b.Newtonards 15-3-83
Source: Scholar.

2000–01	Coventry C	0	0
2001–02	Coventry C	0	0

MARTINEZ, Jairo (F)   11 3
H: 5 9 W: 11 08 b.Honduras 14-5-78
Honours: Honduras full caps.

2000–01	Coventry C	0	0		
2001–02	Coventry C	11	3	11	3

McSHEFFREY, Gary (F)   17 2
H: 5 8 W: 10 06 b.Coventry 13-8-82
Source: Trainee. *Honours:* England Youth, Under-20.

1998–99	Coventry C	1	0		
1999–2000	Coventry C	3	0		
2000–01	Coventry C	0	0		
2001–02	*Stockport Co*	5	1	5	1
2001–02	Coventry C	8	1	12	1

MILLER, Kirk (D)   0 0
H: 5 10 W: 11 10 b.Coventry 15-9-83
Source: Scholar.

2000–01	Coventry C	0	0
2001–02	Coventry C	0	0

MILLS, Lee (F)   264 81
H: 6 4 W: 12 09 b.Mexborough 10-7-70
Source: Stocksbridge PS.

1992–93	Wolverhampton W	0	0		
1993–94	Wolverhampton W	14	1		
1994–95	Wolverhampton W	11	1	25	2
1994–95	Derby Co	16	7	16	7
1995–96	Port Vale	32	8		
1996–97	Port Vale	35	13		
1997–98	Port Vale	42	14	109	35
1998–99	Bradford C	44	23		
1999–2000	Bradford C	21	5	65	28
1999–2000	*Manchester C*	3	0	3	0
2000–01	Portsmouth	24	4		
2001–02	Portsmouth	2	0	26	4
2001–02	Coventry C	20	5	20	5

MONTGOMERY, Gary (G)   2 0
H: 6 1 W: 13 07 b.Leamington Spa 8-10-82
Source: Scholar.

2000–01	Coventry C	0	0		
2001–02	Coventry C	0	0		
2001–02	*Crewe Alex*	0	0		
2001–02	*Kidderminster H*	2	0	2	0

NILSSON, Roland‡ (D)   486 22
H: 5 10 W: 11 10 b.Helsingborg 27-11-63
Honours: Sweden 116 full caps, 2 goals.

1981	Helsingborg	16	1		
1982	Helsingborg	22	2		
1983	IFK Gothenburg	13	1		
1984	IFK Gothenburg	22	1		
1985	IFK Gothenburg	22	1		
1986	IFK Gothenburg	23	3		
1987	IFK Gothenburg	23	2		
1988	IFK Gothenburg	22	0		
1989	IFK Gothenburg	21	0	124	7
1989–90	Sheffield W	20	0		
1990–91	Sheffield W	22	0		
1991–92	Sheffield W	39	1		
1992–93	Sheffield W	32	1		
1993–94	Sheffield W	38	0	151	2
1994	Helsingborg	17	0		
1995	Helsingborg	16	1		
1996	Helsingborg	25	4		
1997	Helsingborg	6	1		
1997–98	Coventry C	32	0		
1998–99	Coventry C	28	0		
1999	Helsingborg	19	2		
2000	Helsingborg	21	2	142	13
2001–02	Coventry C	9	0	9	0

NOON, Mark (M)   0 0
H: 5 10 W: 12 00 b.Leamington Spa 23-9-83
Source: Scholar.

2001–02	Coventry C	0	0

NORMANN, Runar (M)   51 6
H: 5 11 W: 12 00 b.Harstad 1-3-78
Source: Harstad.

1997	Lillestrom	1	1		
1998	Lillestrom	23	2		
1999	Lillestrom	17	3	41	6
1999–2000	Coventry C	8	0		
2000–01	Coventry C	0	0		
2001–02	Coventry C	2	0	10	0

O'NEILL, Keith (M)   121 9
H: 6 1 W: 13 03 b.Dublin 16-12-76
Source: Trainee. *Honours:* Eire 13 full caps, 4 goals.

1994–95	Norwich C	1	0		
1995–96	Norwich C	19	1		
1996–97	Norwich C	26	6		
1997–98	Norwich C	9	0		
1998–99	Norwich C	18	1	73	9
1998–99	Middlesbrough	6	0		
1999–2000	Middlesbrough	16	0		
2000–01	Middlesbrough	15	0	37	0
2001–02	Coventry C	11	0	11	0

PEAD, Craig (M)   1 0
H: 5 9 W: 11 06 b.Bromsgrove 15-9-81
Source: Trainee. *Honours:* England Youth, Under-20.

1998–99	Coventry C	0	0		
1999–2000	Coventry C	0	0		
2000–01	Coventry C	0	0		
2001–02	Coventry C	1	0	1	0

PIPE, David (M)   0 0
H: 5 9 W: 12 01 b.Caerphilly 5-11-83
Source: Scholar.

2000–01	Coventry C	0	0
2001–02	Coventry C	0	0

QUIGLEY, Stephen (D)   0 0
b.Dublin 13-1-85
Source: Scholar.

2001–02	Coventry C	0	0

QUINN, Barry (M)   65 0
H: 6 0 W: 12 02 b.Dublin 9-5-79
Source: Trainee. *Honours:* Eire Under-21, 4 full caps.

1996–97	Coventry C	0	0		
1997–98	Coventry C	7	0		
1998–99	Coventry C	11	0		
2000–01	Coventry C	25	0		
2001–02	Coventry C	22	0	65	0

REGAN, Martin (D)   0 0
b.Tralee 29-1-85
Source: Scholar.

2001–02	Coventry C	0	0

RICE, Stephen (M)   0 0
H: 5 9 W: 10 10 b.Dublin 6-10-84
Source: Scholar.

2001–02	Coventry C	0	0

SAFRI, Youseff (M)   33 1
H: 5 8 W: 10 12 b.Casablanca 13-1-77
Source: Raja. *Honours:* Morocco full caps.

2001–02	Coventry C	33	1	33	1

SHAW, Richard (D)   422 3
H: 5 9 W: 12 08 b.Brentford 11-9-68
Source: Apprentice.

1986–87	Crystal Palace	0	0		
1987–88	Crystal Palace	3	0		
1988–89	Crystal Palace	14	0		
1989–90	Crystal Palace	21	0		
1989–90	*Hull C*	4	0	4	0
1990–91	Crystal Palace	36	1		
1991–92	Crystal Palace	10	0		
1992–93	Crystal Palace	33	0		
1993–94	Crystal Palace	34	2		
1994–95	Crystal Palace	41	0		
1995–96	Crystal Palace	15	0	207	3
1995–96	Coventry C	21	0		
1996–97	Coventry C	35	0		
1997–98	Coventry C	33	0		
1998–99	Coventry C	37	0		
1999–2000	Coventry C	29	0		
2000–01	Coventry C	24	0		
2001–02	Coventry C	32	0	211	0

SPONG, Richard (D)   0 0
H: 5 11 W: 11 09 b.Falun 23-9-83
Source: Scholar.

2000–01	Coventry C	0	0
2001–02	Coventry C	0	0

STRACHAN, Craig* (M)   0 0
H: 5 8 W: 10 06 b.Aberdeen 19-5-82
Source: Scholar.

1999–2000	Coventry C	0	0
2000–01	Coventry C	0	0
2001–02	Coventry C	0	0

STRACHAN, Gavin (M)   21 0
H: 5 10 W: 11 07 b.Aberdeen 23-12-78
Source: Trainee. *Honours:* Scotland Youth, Under-21.

1996–97	Coventry C	0	0		
1997–98	Coventry C	9	0		
1998–99	Coventry C	0	0		
1998–99	*Dundee*	6	0	6	0
1999–2000	Coventry C	3	0		
2000–01	Coventry C	2	0		
2001–02	Coventry C	1	0	15	0

THOMPSON, David (M)   120 20
H: 5 7 W: 10 00 b.Birkenhead 12-9-77
Source: Trainee. *Honours:* England Youth, Under-21.

1994–95	Liverpool	0	0		
1995–96	Liverpool	0	0		
1996–97	Liverpool	2	0		
1997–98	Liverpool	5	1		
1997–98	*Swindon T*	10	0	10	0
1998–99	Liverpool	14	1		
1999–2000	Liverpool	27	3	48	5

2000–01	Coventry C	25	3		
2001–02	Coventry C	37	12	62	15

THORNTON, Barry (F) 0 0
b.Dublin 21-1-85
Source: Scholar.

2001–02	Coventry C	0	0		

TROLLOPE, Paul* (M) 269 27
H: 6 0 W: 11 05 b.Swindon 3-6-72
Source: Trainee. *Honours:* Wales B, 6 full caps.

1989–90	Swindon T	0	0		
1990–91	Swindon T	0	0		
1991–92	Swindon T	0	0		
1991–92	Torquay U	10	0		
1992–93	Torquay U	36	2		
1993–94	Torquay U	42	10		
1994–95	Torquay U	18	4	106	16
1994–95	Derby Co	24	4		
1995–96	Derby Co	17	0		
1996–97	Derby Co	14	1		
1996–97	Grimsby T	7	1	7	1
1996–97	Crystal Palace	9	0	9	0
1997–98	Derby Co	10	0	65	5
1997–98	Fulham	24	3		
1998–99	Fulham	20	2		
1999–2000	Fulham	22	0		
2000–01	Fulham	10	0		
2001–02	Fulham	0	0	76	5
2001–02	Coventry C	6	0	6	0

YAZDANI, Hussain (M) 0 0
b.Dublin 6-1-85
Source: Scholar.

2001–02	Coventry C	0	0		

ZUNIGA, Ysrael (F) 53 22
H: 5 9 W: 11 00 b.Lima 27-8-76
Honours: Peru 17 full caps, 2 goals.

1999	Melgar	25	19	25	19
1999–2000	Coventry C	6	2		
2000–01	Coventry C	15	1		
2001–02	Coventry C	7	0	28	3

Scholars
Ashby, Jason C; Brush, Richard J; Cook, Matthew; Cooney, Sean P; Jephcott, Avun Cyd; May, Rory J; Nelson, Daniel M; O'Donovan, Roy S; Stanford, Edward J; Whing, Andrew J

CREWE ALEX

ASHTON, Dean (F) 52 15
H: 6 2 W: 12 08 b.Swindon 24-11-83
Source: Schoolboy. *Honours:* England Youth.

2000–01	Crewe Alex	21	8		
2001–02	Crewe Alex	31	7	52	15

BANKOLE, Ademola (G) 56 0
H: 6 3 W: 14 08 b.Lagos 9-9-69
Source: Leyton Orient.

1996–97	Crewe Alex	3	0		
1997–98	Crewe Alex	3	0		
1998–99	QPR	0	0		
1998–99	Grimsby T	0	0		
1999–2000	QPR	1	0	1	0
1999–2000	Bradford C	0	0		
2000–01	Crewe Alex	21	0		
2001–02	Crewe Alex	28	0	55	0

BELL, Lee (M) 0 0
H: 5 11 W: 11 05 b.Crewe 26-1-83
Source: Scholar.

2000–01	Crewe Alex	0	0	
2001–02	Crewe Alex	0	0	

BETTS, Tom (D) 0 0
H: 6 0 W: 12 00 b.Stone 3-12-82
Source: Scholar.

2000–01	Crewe Alex	0	0	
2001–02	Crewe Alex	0	0	

BRAMMER, Dave (M) 240 17
H: 5 11 W: 12 00 b.Bromborough 28-2-75
Source: Trainee.

1992–93	Wrexham	2	0		
1993–94	Wrexham	22	2		
1994–95	Wrexham	14	1		
1995–96	Wrexham	11	2		
1996–97	Wrexham	21	1		
1997–98	Wrexham	33	4		
1998–99	Wrexham	34	2	137	12
1998–99	Port Vale	9	0		
1999–2000	Port Vale	29	0		
2000–01	Port Vale	35	3	73	3
2001–02	Crewe Alex	30	2	30	2

CHARLES, Anthony‡ (D) 0 0
H: 6 0 W: 12 00 b.Isleworth 11-3-81
Source: Brook House.

1999–2000	Crewe Alex	0	0	

2000–01	Crewe Alex	0	0		
2001–02	Crewe Alex	0	0		

CHARNOCK, Phil* (M) 161 8
H: 5 10 W: 11 05 b.Southport 14-2-75
Source: Trainee.

1992–93	Liverpool	0	0		
1993–94	Liverpool	0	0		
1994–95	Liverpool	0	0		
1995–96	Liverpool	0	0		
1995–96	Blackpool	4	0	4	0
1996–97	Liverpool	0	0		
1996–97	Crewe Alex	32	1		
1997–98	Crewe Alex	33	3		
1998–99	Crewe Alex	44	2		
1999–2000	Crewe Alex	16	1		
2000–01	Crewe Alex	9	0		
2001–02	Crewe Alex	23	1	157	8

COLLINS, James‡ (M) 24 1
H: 5 8 W: 10 00 b.Liverpool 28-5-78
Source: Trainee.

1996–97	Crewe Alex	0	0		
1997–98	Crewe Alex	1	0		
1998–99	Crewe Alex	6	1		
1999–2000	Crewe Alex	13	0		
2000–01	Crewe Alex	4	0		
2001–02	Crewe Alex	0	0	24	1

COLLINS, Wayne (M) 226 24
H: 5 10 W: 12 02 b.Manchester 4-3-69
Source: Winsford U.

1993–94	Crewe Alex	35	2		
1994–95	Crewe Alex	40	11		
1995–96	Crewe Alex	42	1		
1996–97	Sheffield W	12	1		
1997–98	Sheffield W	19	5	31	6
1997–98	Fulham	13	1		
1998–99	Fulham	21	2		
1999–2000	Fulham	19	1		
2000–01	Fulham	5	0	58	4
2001–02	Crewe Alex	20	0	137	14

EDWARDS, Paul (F) 0 0
H: 6 0 W: 10 09 b.Derby 10-11-82
Source: Scholar.

2000–01	Crewe Alex	0	0	
2001–02	Crewe Alex	0	0	

FOSTER, Stephen (D) 65 5
H: 5 11 W: 11 00 b.Warrington 10-9-80
Source: Trainee. *Honours:* England Schools.

1998–99	Crewe Alex	0	0		
1999–2000	Crewe Alex	0	0		
2000–01	Crewe Alex	30	0		
2001–02	Crewe Alex	34	5	65	5

FROST, Carl (M) 0 0
H: 5 9 W: 10 07 b.Chester 19-7-83
Source: Scholar.

2000–01	Crewe Alex	0	0	
2001–02	Crewe Alex	0	0	

GRANT, John* (F) 7 0
H: 5 11 W: 10 08 b.Manchester 9-8-81
Source: Trainee.

1999–2000	Crewe Alex	4	0		
2000–01	Crewe Alex	2	0		
2001–02	Crewe Alex	1	0	7	0
2001–02	Rushden & D	0	0		

HIGDON, Michael (F) 0 0
H: 6 1 W: 11 03 b.Liverpool 2-9-83
Source: School.

2000–01	Crewe Alex	0	0	
2001–02	Crewe Alex	0	0	

HOWELL, Dean‡ (D) 5 0
H: 6 1 W: 12 05 b.Burton-on-Trent 29-11-80
Source: Trainee.

1999–2000	Notts Co	1	0	1	0
2000–01	Crewe Alex	1	0		
2000–01	Rochdale	3	0	3	0
2001–02	Crewe Alex	0	0	1	0

HULSE, Rob (F) 78 24
H: 6 1 W: 12 08 b.Crewe 25-10-79
Source: Trainee.

1998–99	Crewe Alex	0	0		
1999–2000	Crewe Alex	4	1		
2000–01	Crewe Alex	33	11		
2001–02	Crewe Alex	41	12	78	24

INCE, Clayton (G) 21 0
H: 6 3 W: 13 00 b.Trinidad 13-7-72
Source: Defence Force. *Honours:* Trinidad & Tobago 29 full caps.

1999–2000	Crewe Alex	1	0		
2000–01	Crewe Alex	1	0		
2001–02	Crewe Alex	19	0	21	0

JACK, Rodney (F) 212 48
H: 5 7 W: 10 07 b.Kingston, Jamaica 28-9-72
Source: Lambada. *Honours:* St Vincent full caps.

1995–96	Torquay U	14	2		
1996–97	Torquay U	33	10		
1997–98	Torquay U	40	12	87	24
1998–99	Crewe Alex	39	9		
1999–2000	Crewe Alex	23	4		
2000–01	Crewe Alex	30	4		
2001–02	Crewe Alex	33	7	125	24

JEFFS, Ian (M) 0 0
H: 5 7 W: 10 02 b.Chester 12-10-82
Source: Scholar.

2000–01	Crewe Alex	0	0	
2001–02	Crewe Alex	0	0	

JONES, Steve (F) 15 1
H: 5 10 W: 10 05 b.Derry 25-10-76
Source: Leigh RMI.

2001–02	Rochdale	9	1	9	1
2001–02	Crewe Alex	6	0	6	0

LIDDLE, Gareth (D) 0 0
H: 6 0 W: 12 05 b.Manchester 10-8-82
Source: Scholar.

2000–01	Crewe Alex	0	0	
2001–02	Crewe Alex	0	0	

LITTLE, Colin (F) 187 33
H: 5 10 W: 11 00 b.Wythenshaw 4-11-72
Source: Hyde U.

1995–96	Crewe Alex	12	1		
1996–97	Crewe Alex	17	0		
1997–98	Crewe Alex	40	13		
1998–99	Crewe Alex	37	10		
1999–2000	Crewe Alex	37	4		
2000–01	Crewe Alex	27	4		
2001–02	Crewe Alex	17	1	187	33

LUNT, Kenny (M) 193 12
H: 5 10 W: 10 02 b.Runcorn 20-11-79
Source: Trainee. *Honours:* England Schools, Youth.

1997–98	Crewe Alex	41	2		
1998–99	Crewe Alex	18	1		
1999–2000	Crewe Alex	43	3		
2000–01	Crewe Alex	46	1		
2001–02	Crewe Alex	45	5	193	12

MACAULEY, Steve* (D) 273 26
H: 6 1 W: 12 05 b.Lytham 4-3-69
Source: Fleetwood T.

1991–92	Crewe Alex	9	1		
1992–93	Crewe Alex	25	3		
1993–94	Crewe Alex	17	3		
1994–95	Crewe Alex	43	4		
1995–96	Crewe Alex	29	7		
1996–97	Crewe Alex	42	2		
1997–98	Crewe Alex	20	1		
1998–99	Crewe Alex	20	1		
1999–2000	Crewe Alex	37	4		
2000–01	Crewe Alex	30	1		
2001–02	Crewe Alex	9	0	261	26
2001–02	Macclesfield T	12	0	12	0

McCREADY, Chris (D) 1 0
H: 6 1 W: 12 05 b.Chester 5-9-81
Source: Scholar.

2000–01	Crewe Alex	0	0		
2001–02	Crewe Alex	1	0	1	0

MORRIS, Alexander (M) 0 0
b.Stoke 5-10-82
Source: Scholar.

2000–01	Crewe Alex	0	0	
2001–02	Crewe Alex	0	0	

RIX, Ben (F) 21 0
H: 5 9 W: 11 05 b.Wolverhampton 11-12-82
Source: Scholar.

2000–01	Crewe Alex	0	0		
2001–02	Crewe Alex	21	0	21	0

ROBINSON, James (M) 0 0
H: 5 10 W: 11 03 b.Whiston 18-9-82
Source: Scholar.

2001–02	Crewe Alex	0	0	

SMITH, Shaun* (D) 409 41
H: 5 10 W: 11 02 b.Leeds 9-4-71
Source: Trainee.

1988–89	Halifax T	1	0		
1989–90	Halifax T	6	0		
1990–91	Halifax T	0	0	7	0
1991–92	Crewe Alex	10	0		
1992–93	Crewe Alex	36	4		
1993–94	Crewe Alex	37	7		
1994–95	Crewe Alex	45	8		
1995–96	Crewe Alex	29	1		
1996–97	Crewe Alex	38	4		
1997–98	Crewe Alex	43	6		

1998–99	Crewe Alex	46	4		
1999–2000	Crewe Alex	31	2		
2000–01	Crewe Alex	45	4		
2001–02	Crewe Alex	42	1	402	41

SODJE, Efetobar (D) 163 8
H: 6 1 W: 12 00 b.Greenwich 5-10-72
Source: Delta Steel Pioneer, Stevenage Bor.
Honours: Nigeria 8 full caps, 1 goal.

1997–98	Macclesfield T	41	3		
1998–99	Macclesfield T	42	3	83	6
1999–2000	Luton T	9	0	9	0
1999–2000	Colchester U	3	0	3	0
2000–01	Crewe Alex	32	0		
2001–02	Crewe Alex	36	2	68	2

SORVEL, Neil (M) 225 14
H: 6 0 W: 12 05 b.Widnes 2-3-73
Source: Trainee.

1991–92	Crewe Alex	9	0		
1992–93	Crewe Alex	9	0		
1997–98	Macclesfield T	45	3		
1998–99	Macclesfield T	41	4	86	7
1999–2000	Crewe Alex	46	6		
2000–01	Crewe Alex	46	1		
2001–02	Crewe Alex	38	0	139	7

STREET, Kevin* (M) 117 9
H: 5 10 W: 11 02 b.Crewe 25-11-77
Source: Trainee.

1996–97	Crewe Alex	0	0		
1997–98	Crewe Alex	32	4		
1998–99	Crewe Alex	23	2		
1999–2000	Crewe Alex	28	1		
2000–01	Crewe Alex	23	1		
2001–02	Luton T	2	0	2	0
2001–02	Crewe Alex	9	1	115	9

TAIT, Paul* (F) 70 6
H: 6 1 W: 11 00 b.Newcastle 24-10-74
Source: Trainee.

1993–94	Everton	0	0		
1994–95	Wigan Ath	5	0		
1995–96	Wigan Ath	0	0	5	0

From Northwich Vic.

1999–2000	Crewe Alex	33	6		
2000–01	Crewe Alex	18	0		
2001–02	Hull C	2	0	2	0
2001–02	Crewe Alex	12	0	63	6

THOMAS, Geoff* (M) 462 66
H: 5 10 W: 13 05 b.Manchester 5-8-64
Source: Local. *Honours:* England B, 9 full caps.

1981–82	Rochdale	0	0		
1982–83	Rochdale	1	0		
1983–84	Rochdale	10	1	11	1
1983–84	Crewe Alex	8	1		
1984–85	Crewe Alex	40	4		
1985–86	Crewe Alex	37	6		
1986–87	Crewe Alex	40	9		
1987–88	Crystal Palace	41	6		
1988–89	Crystal Palace	22	5		
1989–90	Crystal Palace	35	1		
1990–91	Crystal Palace	38	6		
1991–92	Crystal Palace	30	6		
1992–93	Crystal Palace	29	2	195	26
1993–94	Wolverhampton W	8	4		
1994–95	Wolverhampton W	14	1		
1995–96	Wolverhampton W	2	0		
1996–97	Wolverhampton W	22	3	46	8
1997–98	Nottingham F	20	3		
1998–99	Nottingham F	5	1	25	4
1999–2000	Barnsley	27	4		
2000–01	Barnsley	11	0	38	4
2000–01	Notts Co	8	1	8	1
2001–02	Crewe Alex	14	2	139	22

TRAINER, Phil* (M) 0 0
H: 6 0 W: 12 00 b.Wolverhampton 3-7-81

2000–01	Crewe Alex	0	0	
2001–02	Crewe Alex	0	0	

VAUGHAN, David (M) 14 0
H: 5 7 W: 11 00 b.St Asaph 18-2-83
Source: Scholar.

2000–01	Crewe Alex	1	0		
2001–02	Crewe Alex	13	0	14	0

WALKER, Richard (D) 4 0
H: 6 2 W: 12 07 b.Stafford 17-9-80
Source: Brook House.

1999–2000	Crewe Alex	0	0		
2000–01	Crewe Alex	3	0		
2001–02	Crewe Alex	1	0	4	0

WALTON, David (D) 255 12
H: 6 2 W: 13 09 b.Bellingham 10-4-73
Source: Trainee.

1991–92	Sheffield U	0	0	
1992–93	Sheffield U	0	0	
1993–94	Sheffield U	0	0	
1993–94	Shrewsbury T	27	5	
1994–95	Shrewsbury T	36	3	
1995–96	Shrewsbury T	35	0	
1996–97	Shrewsbury T	24	1	
1997–98	Shrewsbury T	6	1	128 10
1997–98	Crewe Alex	27	0	
1998–99	Crewe Alex	38	1	
1999–2000	Crewe Alex	11	0	
2000–01	Crewe Alex	20	0	
2001–02	Crewe Alex	31	1	127 2

WRIGHT, David (D) 140 1
H: 5 11 W: 10 09 b.Warrington 1-5-80
Source: Trainee. *Honours:* England Youth.

1997–98	Crewe Alex	3	0		
1998–99	Crewe Alex	20	1		
1999–2000	Crewe Alex	45	0		
2000–01	Crewe Alex	42	0		
2001–02	Crewe Alex	30	0	140	1

YATES, Adam (D) 0 0
H: 5 10 W: 10 07 b.Stoke 28-5-83
Source: Scholar.

2000–01	Crewe Alex	0	0	
2001–02	Crewe Alex	0	0	

Scholars
Anderson, Joshua; Austin, Ryan; Ball, Craig; Booth, Martin T; Brown, Alexander JA; Clare, Craig G; Clark, James; Coverley, Neil; Garner, Matt NP; Hawthorne, Robert; Jenkins, Byron K; Lee, Jamie A; Malbon, Craig D; McGowan, Lloyd E; Platt, Matthew; Roberts, Mark A; Tomlinson, Stuart; Westwood, Lee K; Wilcock, James W; Wilson, Nicholas D

CRYSTAL PALACE

AKINBIYI, Ade (F) 279 87
H: 6 1 W: 12 08 b.Hackney 10-10-74
Source: Trainee. *Honours:* Nigeria full caps.

1992–93	Norwich C	0	0		
1993–94	Norwich C	2	0		
1993–94	*Hereford U*	4	2	4	2
1994–95	Norwich C	13	0		
1994–95	*Brighton & HA*	7	4	7	4
1995–96	Norwich C	22	3		
1996–97	Norwich C	12	0	49	3
1996–97	Gillingham	19	7		
1997–98	Gillingham	44	21	63	28
1998–99	Bristol C	44	19		
1999–2000	Bristol C	3	2	47	21
1999–2000	Wolverhampton W	37	16	37	16
2000–01	Leicester C	37	9		
2001–02	Leicester C	21	2	58	11
2001–02	Crystal Palace	14	2	14	2

AUSTIN, Dean‡ (D) 359 8
H: 5 11 W: 11 11 b.Hemel Hempstead 26-4-70
Source: St. *Honours:* Albans C.

1989–90	Southend U	7	0		
1990–91	Southend U	44	0		
1991–92	Southend U	45	2	96	2
1992–93	Tottenham H	34	0		
1993–94	Tottenham H	23	0		
1994–95	Tottenham H	24	0		
1995–96	Tottenham H	28	0		
1996–97	Tottenham H	15	0		
1997–98	Tottenham H	0	0	124	0
1998–99	Crystal Palace	20	1		
1999–2000	Crystal Palace	45	2		
2000–01	Crystal Palace	39	3		
2001–02	Crystal Palace	35	0	139	6

BERHALTER, Gregg (D) 122 5
H: 6 1 W: 12 05 b.Englewood 1-8-73
Honours: USA 29 full caps.

1994–95	Zwolle	23	1		
1995–96	Zwolle	14	1	37	2
1996–97	Sparta	8	0		
1997–98	Sparta	2	0	10	0
1998–99	Cambuur	28	2		
1999–2000	*Cambuur*	28	0	56	2
2000–01	Crystal Palace	5	0		
2001–02	Crystal Palace	14	1	19	1

BLACK, Tommy (M) 75 5
H: 5 7 W: 11 10 b.Chigwell 26-11-79
Source: Trainee.

1998–99	Arsenal	0	0		
1999–2000	Arsenal	1	0	1	0
1999–2000	*Carlisle U*	5	1	5	1
1999–2000	*Bristol C*	4	0	4	0
2000–01	Crystal Palace	40	4		
2001–02	Crystal Palace	25	0	65	4

BOARDMAN, Jonathan‡ (D) 0 0
H: 6 2 W: 13 11 b.Reading 27-1-81
Source: Trainee.

1999–2000	Crystal Palace	0	0	
2000–01	Crystal Palace	0	0	
2001–02	Crystal Palace	0	0	

CARASSO, Cedric (G) 1 0
H: 6 3 W: 13 12 b.Avignon 30-12-81
Source: Avignon.

2001–02	Marseille	0	0		
2001–02	Crystal Palace	1	0	1	0

CLARKE, Matt (G) 202 0
H: 6 4 W: 13 08 b.Sheffield 3-11-73
Source: Trainee.

1992–93	Rotherham U	9	0		
1993–94	Rotherham U	30	0		
1994–95	Rotherham U	45	0		
1995–96	Rotherham U	40	0	124	0
1996–97	Sheffield W	1	0		
1997–98	Sheffield W	3	0		
1998–99	Sheffield W	0	0	4	0
1999–2000	Bradford C	21	0		
2000–01	Bradford C	17	0		
2000–01	*Bolton W*	8	0	8	0
2001–02	Bradford C	0	0	38	0
2001–02	*Fulham*	0	0		
2001–02	Crystal Palace	28	0	28	0

FLEMING, Curtis (D) 289 3
H: 5 10 W: 12 09 b.Manchester 8-10-68
Source: St Patrick's Ath. *Honours:* Eire Youth, Under-21, B, 10 full caps.

1991–92	Middlesbrough	28	0		
1992–93	Middlesbrough	24	0		
1993–94	Middlesbrough	40	0		
1994–95	Middlesbrough	21	0		
1995–96	Middlesbrough	13	1		
1996–97	Middlesbrough	30	0		
1997–98	Middlesbrough	31	1		
1998–99	Middlesbrough	14	1		
1999–2000	Middlesbrough	27	0		
2000–01	Middlesbrough	30	0		
2001–02	Middlesbrough	8	0	266	3
2001–02	*Birmingham C*	6	0	6	0
2001–02	Crystal Palace	17	0	17	0

FRAMPTON, Andrew (D) 27 0
H: 5 11 W: 10 10 b.Wimbledon 3-9-79
Source: Trainee.

1998–99	Crystal Palace	6	0		
1999–2000	Crystal Palace	9	0		
2000–01	Crystal Palace	10	0		
2001–02	Crystal Palace	2	0	27	0

FREEDMAN, Dougie (F) 302 117
H: 5 9 W: 12 05 b.Glasgow 21-1-74
Source: Trainee. *Honours:* Scotland Schools, Under-21, B, 2 full caps, 1 goal.

1991–92	QPR	0	0		
1992–93	QPR	0	0		
1993–94	QPR	0	0		
1994–95	Barnet	42	24		
1995–96	Barnet	5	3	47	27
1995–96	Crystal Palace	39	20		
1996–97	Crystal Palace	44	11		
1997–98	Crystal Palace	7	0		
1997–98	Wolverhampton W	29	10	29	10
1998–99	Nottingham F	31	9		
1999–2000	Nottingham F	34	9		
2000–01	Nottingham F	5	0	70	18
2000–01	Crystal Palace	26	11		
2001–02	Crystal Palace	40	20	156	62

FULLER, Ricardo‡ (F) 8 0
b.Kingston, Jamaica 31-10-79
Source: Tivoli Gardens. *Honours:* Jamaica full caps.

2000–01	Crystal Palace	8	0		
2001–02	Crystal Palace	0	0	8	0

GOODING, Scott‡ (M) 1 0
H: 5 10 W: 11 07 b.Croydon 2-1-82
Source: Scholar.

2001–02	Crystal Palace	1	0	1	0

GRANVILLE, Danny (D) 218 10
H: 6 0 W: 12 00 b.Islington 19-1-75
Source: Trainee. *Honours:* England Under-21.

1993–94	Cambridge U	11	5		
1994–95	Cambridge U	16	2		
1995–96	Cambridge U	35	0		
1996–97	Cambridge U	37	0	99	7
1996–97	Chelsea	5	0		
1997–98	Chelsea	13	0	18	0
1998–99	Leeds U	9	0		
1999–2000	Leeds U	0	0	9	0
1999–2000	Manchester C	35	2		
2000–01	Manchester C	19	0		
2000–01	*Norwich C*	6	0	6	0
2001–02	Manchester C	16	1	70	3
2001–02	Crystal Palace	16	0	16	0

GRAY, Julian (M) 67 3
H: 6 1 W: 11 08 b.Lewisham 21-9-79
Source: Trainee.

1998–99	Arsenal	0	0		
1999–2000	Arsenal	1	0	1	0
2000–01	Crystal Palace	23	1		
2001–02	Crystal Palace	43	2	66	3

GREGG, Matt‡ (G) 46 0
H: 5 11 W: 12 00 b.Cheltenham 30-11-78
Source: Trainee.

1995–96	Torquay U	1	0		
1996–97	Torquay U	1	0		
1997–98	Torquay U	19	0		
1998–99	Torquay U	11	0	32	0
1998–99	Crystal Palace	0	0		
1998–99	*Swansea C*	5	0	5	0
1999–2000	Crystal Palace	6	0		
2000–01	Crystal Palace	1	0		
2001–02	Crystal Palace	0	0	7	0
2001–02	*Exeter C*	2	0	2	0

GWILLIM, Gareth‡ (M) 0 0
b.Farnborough 9-2-83

| 2000–01 | Crystal Palace | 0 | 0 |
| 2001–02 | Crystal Palace | 0 | 0 |

HARRISON, Craig (D) 68 0
H: 6 0 W: 11 08 b.Middlesbrough 10-11-77
Source: Trainee.

1996–97	Middlesbrough	0	0		
1997–98	Middlesbrough	20	0		
1998–99	Middlesbrough	4	0		
1998–99	*Preston NE*	6	0	6	0
1999–2000	Middlesbrough	0	0		
2000–01	Middlesbrough	0	0	24	0
2000–01	Crystal Palace	32	0		
2001–02	Crystal Palace	6	0	38	0

HEEROO, Gavin (M) 0 0
b.London 2-9-84

| 2001–02 | Crystal Palace | 0 | 0 |

HOPKIN, David (M) 254 32
H: 6 1 W: 13 13 b.Greenock 21-8-70
Source: Pt Glasgow R BC. Honours: Scotland B, 7 full caps, 2 goals.

1989–90	Morton	8	0		
1990–91	Morton	10	0		
1991–92	Morton	0	0	18	0
1992–93	Chelsea	4	0		
1993–94	Chelsea	21	0		
1994–95	Chelsea	15	1	40	1
1995–96	Crystal Palace	42	8		
1996–97	Crystal Palace	41	13		
1997–98	Leeds U	25	1		
1998–99	Leeds U	34	4		
1999–2000	Leeds U	14	1	73	6
2000–01	Bradford C	11	0	11	0
2001–02	Crystal Palace	20	3	112	25

HOWELL, Richard‡ (M) 0 0
b.Hitchin 29-8-82

1999–2000	Crystal Palace	0	0
2000–01	Crystal Palace	0	0
2001–02	Crystal Palace	0	0

KABBA, Steven (F) 9 0
H: 5 10 W: 11 07 b.Lambeth 7-3-81
Source: Trainee.

1999–2000	Crystal Palace	1	0		
2000–01	Crystal Palace	1	0		
2001–02	Crystal Palace	4	0	6	0
2001–02	*Luton T*	3	0	3	0

KEMBER, Robert* (M) 0 0
b.Wimbledon 21-8-81

| 2000–01 | Crystal Palace | 0 | 0 |
| 2001–02 | Crystal Palace | 0 | 0 |

KIROVSKI, Jovan* (M) 81 8
H: 6 1 W: 12 01 b.Escondido 18-3-76
Source: San Diego Nomads. Honours: USA 54 full caps, 7 goals.

1994–95	Manchester U	0	0		
1995–96	Borussia Dortmund	0	0		
1996–97	Borussia Dortmund	7	1		
1997–98	Borussia Dortmund	13	0		
1998–99	Fortuna Cologne	20	2	20	2
1999–2000	Borussia Dortmund	0	0	20	1
2000–01	Sporting Lisbon	5	0	5	0
2001–02	Crystal Palace	36	5	36	5

KOLINKO, Aleksandrs (G) 162 0
H: 6 2 W: 14 02 b.Latvia 18-6-75
Honours: Latvia 29 full caps.

1994	Interskonto	22	0	22	0
1995	Skonto Metals	25	0	25	0
1996	Skonto Riga	9	0		
1997	Skonto Riga	12	0		
1998	Skonto Riga	5	0		
1999	Skonto Riga	18	0		
2000	Skonto Riga	17	0	61	0
2000–01	Crystal Palace	35	0		
2001–02	Crystal Palace	19	0	54	0

MORRISON, Clinton (F) 157 62
H: 6 1 W: 11 02 b.Tooting 14-5-79
Source: Trainee. Honours: Eire 7 full caps, 2 goals.

1996–97	Crystal Palace	0	0		
1997–98	Crystal Palace	1	1		
1998–99	Crystal Palace	37	12		
1999–2000	Crystal Palace	29	13		
2000–01	Crystal Palace	45	14		
2001–02	Crystal Palace	45	22	157	62

MULLINS, Hayden (D) 169 16
H: 6 0 W: 11 12 b.Reading 27-3-79
Source: Trainee. Honours: England Under-21.

1996–97	Crystal Palace	0	0		
1997–98	Crystal Palace	0	0		
1998–99	Crystal Palace	40	5		
1999–2000	Crystal Palace	45	10		
2000–01	Crystal Palace	41	1		
2001–02	Crystal Palace	43	0	169	16

POLLOCK, Jamie (M) 295 31
H: 6 0 W: 13 03 b.Stockton 16-2-74
Source: Trainee. Honours: England Youth, Under-21.

1990–91	Middlesbrough	0	0		
1991–92	Middlesbrough	26	1		
1992–93	Middlesbrough	22	1		
1993–94	Middlesbrough	34	9		
1994–95	Middlesbrough	41	5		
1995–96	Middlesbrough	31	1	155	17
1996–97	Osasuna	0	0		
1996–97	Bolton W	20	4		
1997–98	Bolton W	26	1	46	5
1997–98	Manchester C	8	1		
1998–99	Manchester C	26	1		
1999–2000	Manchester C	24	3	58	5
2000–01	Crystal Palace	31	4		
2000–01	*Birmingham C*	5	0	5	0
2001–02	Crystal Palace	0	0	31	4

POPOVIC, Tony (D) 269 29
H: 6 5 W: 13 01 b.Australia 7-4-73
Honours: Australia 39 full caps, 6 goals.

1989–90	Sydney U	13	0		
1990–91	Sydney U	17	1		
1991–92	Sydney U	20	1		
1992–93	Sydney U	24	2		
1993–94	Sydney U	27	2		
1994–95	Sydney U	25	3		
1995–96	Sydney U	29	4		
1995–96	Wolverhampton W	0	0		
1996–97	Wolverhampton W	0	0		
1996–97	Sydney U	7	2	162	15
1997	Sanfrecce	11	0		
1998	Sanfrecce	25	4		
1999	Sanfrecce	23	6		
2000	Sanfrecce	21	2		
2001	Sanfrecce	7	0	87	12
2001–02	Crystal Palace	20	2	20	2

RIIHILAHTI, Aki (M) 79 11
H: 5 11 W: 12 06 b.Helsinki 9-9-76
Honours: Finland 36 full caps, 7 goals.

1999	Valerenga	25	5	25	5
2000–01	Crystal Palace	9	1		
2001–02	Crystal Palace	45	5	54	6

RODGER, Simon* (M) 289 12
H: 5 9 W: 11 09 b.Shoreham 3-10-71
Source: Trainee.

1989–90	Crystal Palace	0	0		
1990–91	Crystal Palace	0	0		
1991–92	Crystal Palace	22	0		
1992–93	Crystal Palace	23	2		
1993–94	Crystal Palace	42	3		
1994–95	Crystal Palace	24	0		
1995–96	Crystal Palace	11	0		
1996–97	*Manchester C*	8	1	8	1
1996–97	*Stoke C*	5	0	5	0
1997–98	Crystal Palace	29	2		
1998–99	Crystal Palace	18	1		
1999–2000	Crystal Palace	34	2		
2000–01	Crystal Palace	33	0		
2001–02	Crystal Palace	36	1	276	11

ROUTLEDGE, Wayne§ (F) 2 0
H: 5 6 W: 10 07 b.Eltham 7-1-85
Source: Scholar. Honours: England Youth.

| 2001–02 | Crystal Palace | 2 | 0 | 2 | 0 |

RUBINS, Andrejs (M) 96 14
H: 5 8 W: 10 13 b.Latvia 26-11-78
Honours: Latvia 31 full caps, 3 goals.

1998	Skonto Riga	19	1		
1999	Skonto Riga	25	6		
2000	Skonto Riga	23	7	67	14
2000–01	Crystal Palace	22	0		
2001–02	Crystal Palace‡	7	0	29	0

SHARPLING, Christopher‡ (F) 6 0
H: 5 11 W: 11 10 b.Bromley 21-4-81
Source: Trainee.

1998–99	Crystal Palace	0	0		
1999–2000	Crystal Palace	6	0		
2000–01	Crystal Palace	0	0		
2001–02	Crystal Palace‡	0	0	6	0

SMITH, Jamie (D) 228 5
H: 5 8 W: 11 02 b.Birmingham 17-9-74
Source: Trainee.

1992–93	Wolverhampton W	0	0		
1994–95	Wolverhampton W	25	0		
1995–96	Wolverhampton W	13	0		
1996–97	Wolverhampton W	38	0		
1997–98	Wolverhampton W	11	0	87	0
1997–98	Crystal Palace	18	0		
1998–99	Crystal Palace	26	0		
1998–99	*Fulham*	9	1	9	1
1999–2000	Crystal Palace	27	0		
2000–01	Crystal Palace	29	0		
2001–02	Crystal Palace	32	4	132	4

SYMONS, Kit (D) 396 27
H: 6 1 W: 13 00 b.Basingstoke 8-3-71
Source: Trainee. Honours: Wales Youth, Under-21, B, 36 full caps, 2 goals.

1988–89	Portsmouth	2	0		
1989–90	Portsmouth	1	0		
1990–91	Portsmouth	46	1		
1991–92	Portsmouth	41	2		
1992–93	Portsmouth	29	3		
1993–94	Portsmouth	40	4		
1995–96	Portsmouth	1	0	161	10
1995–96	Manchester C	38	2		
1996–97	Manchester C	44	0		
1997–98	Manchester C	42	2	124	4
1998–99	Fulham	45	11		
1999–2000	Fulham	29	2		
2000–01	Fulham	24	0		
2001–02	Fulham	4	0	102	13
2001–02	Crystal Palace	9	0	9	0

THOMSON, Steve (M) 78 0
H: 5 8 W: 10 04 b.Glasgow 23-1-78
Source: Trainee. Honours: Scotland Youth.

1995–96	Crystal Palace	0	0		
1996–97	Crystal Palace	0	0		
1997–98	Crystal Palace	16	0		
1998–99	Crystal Palace	21	0		
2000–01	Crystal Palace	18	0		
2001–02	Crystal Palace	23	0	78	0

WILLIAMS, Ryan* (M) 0 0
b.Reading 16-4-82
Source: Scholar.

| 2001–02 | Crystal Palace | 0 | 0 |

WINDEGAARD, Stephen‡ (M) 0 0
b.Chertsey 6-8-82
Honours: England Schools.

| 2000–01 | Crystal Palace | 0 | 0 |
| 2001–02 | Crystal Palace | 0 | 0 |

ZHIYI, Fan (M) 88 4
H: 6 0 W: 12 01 b.Shanghai 22-1-70
Source: Shanghai Shenhua. Honours: China 106 full caps, 16 goals.

1998–99	Crystal Palace	29	2		
1999–2000	Crystal Palace	29	1		
2000–01	Crystal Palace	28	1		
2001–02	Crystal Palace	2	0	88	4

(Transferred to Dundee, October 2001).

Scholars
Amoako, Adolf; Antwi, William; Bashkal, Kerem; Borrowdale, Gary I; Dobson, Craig G; Elsegood, Christopher J; Gibson, James D; Hay, Adam; Hunt, David; Julius, Andrew; Nabil, Tariq; Routledge, Wayne; Smith, Robert J; Surey, Ben D; Togwell, Samuel; Watson, Ben; Williams, Gareth A

DARLINGTON

ATKINSON, Brian (M) 336 15
H: 5 10 W: 12 05 b.Darlington 19-1-71
Source: Trainee. Honours: England Under-21.

1988–89	Sunderland	3	0		
1989–90	Sunderland	13	0		
1990–91	Sunderland	6	0		
1991–92	Sunderland	30	2		
1992–93	Sunderland	36	2		
1993–94	Sunderland	29	0		
1994–95	Sunderland	17	0		
1995–96	Sunderland	7	0	141	4

1995–96	Carlisle U	2	0	2	0
1996–97	Darlington	30	3		
1997–98	Darlington	32	1		
1998–99	Darlington	43	2		
1999–2000	Darlington	30	0		
2000–01	Darlington	23	4		
2001–02	Darlington	35	1	193	11

BETTS, Simon (M)   220 11
H: 5 8 W: 11 00 b.Middlesbrough 3-3-73
Source: Trainee.

1991–92	Ipswich T	0	0		
1992–93	Scarborough	0	0		
1992–93	Colchester U	23	0		
1993–94	Colchester U	33	1		
1994–95	Colchester U	35	2		
1995–96	Colchester U	45	5		
1996–97	Colchester U	10	1		
1997–98	Colchester U	17	0		
1998–99	Colchester U	28	2		
1999–2000	Colchester U	0	0		
2000–01	Colchester U	0	0	191	11

From Yeovil T.

| 2001–02 | Darlington | 29 | 0 | 29 | 0 |

BRIGHTWELL, David (D)   257 8
H: 6 2 W: 12 09 b.Lutterworth 7-1-71
Source: Trainee.

1987–88	Manchester C	0	0		
1988–89	Manchester C	0	0		
1989–90	Manchester C	0	0		
1990–91	Manchester C	0	0		
1990–91	*Chester C*	6	0	6	0
1991–92	Manchester C	4	0		
1992–93	Manchester C	8	0		
1993–94	Manchester C	22	1		
1994–95	Manchester C	9	0		
1995–96	Manchester C	0	0	43	1
1995–96	*Lincoln C*	5	0	5	0
1995–96	*Stoke C*	1	0	1	0
1995–96	Bradford C	22	0		
1996–97	Bradford C	2	0	24	0
1996–97	*Blackpool*	2	0	2	0
1997–98	Northampton T	35	1	35	1
1998–99	Carlisle U	41	4		
1999–2000	Carlisle U	37	0	78	4
2000–01	Hull C	27	2	27	2
2000–01	Darlington	14	0		
2001–02	Darlington	22	0	36	0

BRUMWELL, Phil (M)   203 1
H: 5 8 W: 11 00 b.Darlington 8-8-75
Source: Trainee.

1994–95	Sunderland	0	0		
1995–96	Darlington	28	0		
1996–97	Darlington	38	1		
1997–98	Darlington	35	0		
1998–99	Darlington	37	0		
1999–2000	Darlington	18	0		
2000–01	Hull C	4	0	4	0
2000–01	Darlington	21	0		
2001–02	Darlington	22	0	199	1

CAMPBELL, Paul (M)   56 6
H: 6 0 W: 11 05 b.Middlesbrough 29-1-80
Source: Trainee.

1997–98	Darlington	6	1		
1998–99	Darlington	9	1		
1999–2000	Darlington	9	2		
2000–01	Darlington	16	1		
2001–02	Darlington	16	1	56	6

CAU, Jean-Michel‡ (F)   1 0
b.Corsica 27-10-80
Source: Gazelec.

| 2000–01 | Darlington | 1 | 0 | | |
| 2001–02 | Darlington | 0 | 0 | 1 | 0 |

CLARK, Ian (M)   211 33
H: 5 11 W: 11 07 b.Stockton 23-10-74
Source: Stockton.

1995–96	Doncaster R	23	1		
1996–97	Doncaster R	20	2		
1997–98	Doncaster R	2	0	45	3
1997–98	Hartlepool U	24	7		
1998–99	Hartlepool U	39	4		
1999–2000	Hartlepool U	44	6		
2000–01	Hartlepool U	24	0		
2001–02	Hartlepool U	7	2	138	17
2001–02	Darlington	28	13	28	13

COLLETT, Andy (G)   187 0
H: 6 0 W: 12 01 b.Middlesbrough 28-10-73
Source: Trainee.

1991–92	Middlesbrough	0	0		
1992–93	Middlesbrough	2	0		
1993–94	Middlesbrough	0	0		
1994–95	Middlesbrough	0	0	2	0
1994–95	Bristol R	4	0		
1995–96	Bristol R	26	0		
1996–97	Bristol R	44	0		
1997–98	Bristol R	30	0		
1998–99	Bristol R	3	0	107	0

1999–2000	Darlington	13	0		
2000–01	Darlington	37	0		
2001–02	Darlington	28	0	78	0

CONLON, Barry (F)   163 38
H: 6 3 W: 13 07 b.Drogheda 1-10-78
Source: QPR Trainee. *Honours:* Eire Under-21.

1997–98	Manchester C	7	0		
1997–98	*Plymouth Arg*	13	2	13	2
1998–99	Manchester C	0	0	7	0
1998–99	Southend U	34	7	34	7
1999–2000	York C	40	11		
2000–01	York C	8	0	48	11
2000–01	*Colchester U*	26	8	26	8
2001–02	Darlington	35	10	35	10

CONVERY, Mark (M)   28 1
H: 5 6 W: 10 05 b.Newcastle 29-5-81
Source: Trainee.

1998–99	Sunderland	0	0		
1999–2000	Sunderland	0	0		
2000–01	Sunderland	0	0		
2000–01	Darlington	11	0		
2001–02	Darlington	17	1	28	1

FINCH, Keith‡ (G)   12 0
H: 6 0 W: 12 02 b.Easington 6-5-82
Source: Scholar.

| 2001–02 | Darlington | 12 | 0 | 12 | 0 |

FORD, Mark (M)   166 14
H: 5 8 W: 10 01 b.Pontefract 10-10-75
Source: Trainee. *Honours:* England Youth, Under-21.

1992–93	Leeds U	1	0		
1993–94	Leeds U	1	0		
1994–95	Leeds U	0	0		
1995–96	Leeds U	12	0		
1996–97	Leeds U	16	1	29	1
1997–98	Burnley	36	1		
1998–99	Burnley	12	0	48	1
1999–2000	Lommel	15	0	15	0
2000–01	Torquay U	28	3	28	3
2000–01	Darlington	11	2		
2001–02	Darlington	35	4	46	9

GRAINGER, Andrew* (M)   0 0
b.Ashington 21-9-82

| 2001–02 | Darlington | 0 | 0 | | |

GRAY, Martin‡ (M)   262 5
H: 5 9 W: 11 05 b.Stockton 17-8-71
Source: Trainee.

1989–90	Sunderland	0	0		
1990–91	Sunderland	0	0		
1990–91	*Aldershot*	5	0	5	0
1991–92	Sunderland	1	0		
1992–93	Sunderland	12	1		
1993–94	Sunderland	22	0		
1994–95	Sunderland	22	0		
1995–96	Sunderland	7	0	64	1
1995–96	*Fulham*	6	0	6	0
1995–96	Oxford U	7	0		
1996–97	Oxford U	43	2		
1997–98	Oxford U	31	2		
1998–99	Oxford U	40	0	121	4
1999–2000	Darlington	41	0		
2000–01	Darlington	25	0		
2001–02	Darlington	0	0	66	0

HARPER, Steve* (M)   504 54
H: 5 10 W: 11 12 b.Newcastle-under-Lyme 3-2-69
Source: Trainee.

1987–88	Port Vale	21	2		
1988–89	Port Vale	7	0	28	2
1988–89	Preston NE	5	0		
1989–90	Preston NE	36	10		
1990–91	Preston NE	36	0	77	10
1991–92	Burnley	35	3		
1992–93	Burnley	34	5		
1993–94	Burnley	0	0	69	8
1993–94	Doncaster R	31	2		
1994–95	Doncaster R	33	9		
1995–96	Doncaster R	1	0	65	11
1995–96	Mansfield T	29	5		
1996–97	Mansfield T	40	2		
1997–98	Mansfield T	46	5		
1998–99	Mansfield T	45	6	160	18
1999–2000	Hull C	38	4		
2000–01	Hull C	27	0	65	4
2000–01	Darlington	17	0		
2001–02	Darlington	23	1	40	1

HEALY, Brian‡ (M)   61 12
H: 6 1 W: 13 08 b.Glasgow 27-12-68
Source: West Auckland, Billingham T, Bishop Auckland, Gateshead, Spennymoor U, Morecambe.

1998–99	Torquay U	19	2		
1999–2000	Torquay U	38	9		
2000–01	Torquay U	0	0		

| 2001–02 | Torquay U | 2 | 0 | 59 | 11 |
| 2001–02 | Darlington | 2 | 1 | 2 | 1 |

HECKINGBOTTOM, Paul* (D)   149 6
H: 6 0 W: 12 03 b.Barnsley 17-7-77
Source: Manchester U Trainee.

1995–96	Sunderland	0	0		
1996–97	Sunderland	0	0		
1997–98	Sunderland	0	0		
1997–98	*Scarborough*	29	0	29	0
1998–99	Sunderland	0	0		
1998–99	*Hartlepool U*	5	1	5	1
1998–99	*Darlington*	10	0		
1999–2000	Darlington	45	1		
2000–01	Darlington	18	1		
2001–02	Darlington	42	3	115	5

HIMSWORTH, Gary‡ (M)   391 26
H: 5 8 W: 11 00 b.York 19-12-69
Source: Trainee.

1987–88	York C	31	2		
1988–89	York C	32	2		
1989–90	York C	23	4		
1990–91	York C	2	0		
1990–91	Scarborough	23	1		
1991–92	Scarborough	36	4		
1992–93	Scarborough	33	1	92	6
1993–94	Darlington	28	3		
1994–95	Darlington	38	2		
1995–96	Darlington	28	3		
1995–96	York C	8	1		
1996–97	York C	33	2		
1997–98	York C	15	0		
1998–99	York C	13	0	157	11
1998–99	Darlington	14	1		
1999–2000	Darlington	19	0		
2000–01	Darlington	15	0		
2001–02	Darlington	0	0	142	9

HODGSON, Richard (M)   72 4
H: 5 10 W: 11 08 b.Sunderland 1-10-79
Source: Trainee.

1996–97	Nottingham F	0	0		
1997–98	Nottingham F	0	0		
1998–99	Nottingham F	0	0		
1999–2000	Nottingham F	0	0		
1999–2000	Scunthorpe U	1	0	1	0
2000–01	Darlington	35	2		
2001–02	Darlington	36	2	71	4

JACKSON, Kirk‡ (F)   21 1
H: 5 10 W: 11 07 b.Barnsley 16-10-76
Source: Trainee.
From Worksop T.

| 2000–01 | Darlington | 10 | 1 | | |
| 2001–02 | Darlington | 11 | 0 | 21 | 1 |

JEANNIN, Alex‡ (D)   22 0
H: 6 0 W: 11 06 b.Troyes 30-12-77
Source: Troyes.

| 2000–01 | Darlington | 11 | 0 | | |
| 2001–02 | Darlington | 11 | 0 | 22 | 0 |

KELTIE, Clark (M)   1 0
H: 5 11 W: 11 05 b.Gateshead 31-8-83
Source: Shildon.

| 2001–02 | Darlington | 1 | 0 | 1 | 0 |

KILTY, Mark (D)   23 1
H: 5 11 W: 12 05 b.Sunderland 24-6-81
Source: Trainee.

1998–99	Darlington	2	0		
1999–2000	Darlington	2	0		
2000–01	Darlington	18	1		
2001–02	Darlington	1	0	23	1

LIDDLE, Craig (D)   205 8
H: 5 11 W: 12 07 b.Newcastle 21-10-71
Source: Blyth Spartans.

1994–95	Middlesbrough	1	0		
1995–96	Middlesbrough	13	0		
1996–97	Middlesbrough	5	0		
1997–98	Middlesbrough	6	0	25	0
1997–98	*Darlington*	15	0		
1998–99	Darlington	44	3		
1999–2000	Darlington	45	1		
2000–01	Darlington	45	2		
2001–02	Darlington	31	2	180	8

LIDDLE, Graham‡ (M)   0 0
b.Durham 19-9-81

| 2001–02 | Darlington | 0 | 0 | | |

MADDISON, Neil (M)   265 25
H: 5 10 W: 12 00 b.Darlington 2-10-69
Source: Trainee.

1987–88	Southampton	0	0		
1988–89	Southampton	5	2		
1989–90	Southampton	2	0		
1990–91	Southampton	4	0		
1991–92	Southampton	6	0		
1992–93	Southampton	37	4		
1993–94	Southampton	41	7		
1994–95	Southampton	35	3		

1995–96	Southampton	15	1	
1996–97	Southampton	18	1	
1997–98	Southampton	6	1	169 19
1997–98	Middlesbrough	22	4	
1998–99	Middlesbrough	21	0	
1999–2000	Middlesbrough	13	0	
2000–01	Middlesbrough	0	0	56 4
2000–01	*Barnsley*	3	0	3 0
2000–01	*Bristol C*	7	1	7 1
2001–02	Darlington	30	1	30 1

MARCELLE, Clint* (M) 168 13
H: 5 5 W: 10 00 b.Port of Spain 9-11-68
Source: Vitoria Setubal, Rio Ave. *Honours:*
Trinidad & Tobago full caps.

1994–95	Falgueiras	30	3	
1995–96	Falgueiras	21	0	51 3
1996–97	Barnsley	40	8	
1997–98	Barnsley	20	0	
1998–99	Barnsley	9	0	
1999–2000	Barnsley	0	0	
1999–2000	*Scunthorpe U*	10·	0	10 0
2000–01	Barnsley	0	0	69 8
2000–01	*Hull C*	23	2	23 2
2000–01	Darlington	12	0	
2001–02	Darlington	3	0	15 0

MARSH, Adam* (F) 8 0
H: 5 11 W: 11 08 b.Derby 20-2-82
Source: Worksop T.

2000–01	Darlington	7	0	
2001–02	Darlington	1	0	8 0

McGURK, David§ (D) 12 0
H: 6 0 W: 11 10 b.Middlesbrough 30-9-82
Source: Scholar.

2001–02	Darlington	12	0	12 0

MELLANBY, Danny (F) 24 4
H: 5 10 W: 11 09 b.Bishop Auckland 17-7-79
Source: Bishop Auckland.

2001–02	Darlington	24	4	24 4

NAYLOR, Glenn (F) 311 74
H: 6 0 W: 11 08 b.Goole 11-8-72
Source: Trainee.

1989–90	York C	1	0	
1990–91	York C	20	5	
1991–92	York C	21	8	
1992–93	York C	4	0	
1993–94	York C	10	1	
1994–95	York C	29	9	
1995–96	York C	25	7	
1995–96	*Darlington*	4	1	
1996–97	York C	1	0	111 30
1996–97	Darlington	37	11	
1997–98	Darlington	42	8	
1998–99	Darlington	42	9	
1999–2000	Darlington	25	3	
2000–01	Darlington	44	11	
2001–02	Darlington	6	1	200 44

PEARSON, Gary (D) 9 1
H: 6 0 W: 12 04 b.Easington 7-12-76
Source: Trainee.

1995–96	Sheffield U	0	0	
1996–97	Sheffield U	0	0	
1997–98	Sheffield U	0	0	
1998–99	Sheffield U	0	0	
From Durham C.				
2001–02	Darlington	9	1	9 1

PORTER, Chris† (G) 7 0
H: 6 2 W: 12 03 b.Middlesbrough 17-7-79
Source: Trainee.

1998–99	Sunderland	0	0	
1999–2000	Sunderland	0	0	
2000–01	Hartlepool U	0	0	
2000–01	Southend U	0	0	
2001–02	Darlington	7	0	7 0

REED, Adam (D) 169 3
H: 6 0 W: 12 00 b.Bishop Auckland 18-2-75
Source: Trainee.

1991–92	Darlington	1	0	
1992–93	Darlington	0	0	
1993–94	Darlington	13	0	
1994–95	Darlington	38	1	
1995–96	Blackburn R	0	0	
1996–97	Blackburn R	0	0	
1996–97	*Darlington*	14	0	
1997–98	Blackburn R	0	0	
1997–98	*Rochdale*	10	0	10 0
1998–99	Darlington	29	2	
1999–2000	Darlington	23	0	
2000–01	Darlington	34	0	
2001–02	Darlington	7	0	159 3

RUNDLE, Adam§ (F) 12 0
H: 5 10 W: 11 02 b.Durham 8-7-84
Source: Scholar.

2001–02	Darlington	12	0	12 0

SHEERAN, Mark§ (F) 22 6
H: 6 0 W: 11 10 b.Newcastle 9-9-82
Source: Scholar.

2001–02	Darlington	22	6	22 6

VAN DER GEEST, Frank‡ (G) 61 0
H: 6 2 W: 11 06 b.Beverwijk 30-4-73

1993–94	AZ	1	0	
1994–95	AZ	2	0	3 0
From ADO 20				
1995–96	Sparta	0	0	
1996–97	Sparta	2	0	2 0
1997–98	Heracles	22	0	
1998–99	Heracles	32	0	54 0
2000–01	Darlington	2	0	
2001–02	Darlington	0	0	2 0

WAINWRIGHT, Neil (M) 78 11
H: 6 1 W: 12 00 b.Warrington 4-11-77
Source: Trainee.

1996–97	Wrexham	0	0	
1997–98	Wrexham	11	3	11 3
1998–99	Sunderland	2	0	
1999–2000	Sunderland	0	0	
1999–2000	*Darlington*	17	4	
2000–01	Sunderland	0	0	
2000–01	*Halifax T*	13	0	13 0
2001–02	Sunderland	0	0	2 0
2001–02	Darlington	35	4	52 8

WALLER, Russell (M) 0 0
b.Adelaide 6-2-84

2001–02	Darlington	0	0	

Scholars
Bond, Michael; Coghlan, Michael J; Collins,
Paul; Ellenden, John; Hughes, Christopher;
Jarvis, Marc; Lawton, Mark; McGurk, David;
Morley, Steven; Paxton, Richard J; Rundle,
Adam; Sheeran, Mark J; Smith, Martin M;
Thompson, David J; Trainer, Lee GE
Non-Contract
Porter, Christopher I

DERBY CO

BANNISTER, Patrick (M) 0 0
b.Walsall 3-12-83
Source: Scholar.

2000–01	Derby Co	0	0	
2001–02	Derby Co	0	0	

BARTON, Warren (D) 400 14
H: 6 3 W: 11 13 b.Islington 19-3-69
Source: Leytonstone/Ilford. *Honours:*
England B, 3 full caps.

1989–90	Maidstone U	42	0	42 0
1990–91	Wimbledon	37	3	
1991–92	Wimbledon	42	1	
1992–93	Wimbledon	23	2	
1993–94	Wimbledon	39	2	
1994–95	Wimbledon	39	2	180 10
1995–96	Newcastle U	31	0	
1996–97	Newcastle U	18	1	
1997–98	Newcastle U	23	3	
1998–99	Newcastle U	24	0	
1999–2000	Newcastle U	34	0	
2000–01	Newcastle U	29	0	
2001–02	Newcastle U	5	0	164 4
2001–02	Derby Co	14	0	14 0

BOERTIEN, Paul (D) 62 2
H: 5 11 W: 11 11 b.Carlisle 21-1-79
Source: Trainee.

1996–97	Carlisle U	0	0	
1997–98	Carlisle U	9	0	
1998–99	Carlisle U	8	1	17 1
1998–99	Derby Co	1	0	
1999–2000	Derby Co	2	0	
1999–2000	*Crewe Alex*	2	0	2 0
2000–01	Derby Co	8	1	
2001–02	Derby Co	32	0	43 1

BOLDER, Adam (M) 33 0
H: 5 8 W: 11 13 b.Hull 25-10-80
Source: Trainee.

1998–99	Hull C	1	0	
1999–2000	Hull C	19	0	20 0
1999–2000	Derby Co	0	0	
2000–01	Derby Co	2	0	
2001–02	Derby Co	11	0	13 0

BRAGSTAD, Bjorn (D) 209 26
H: 6 3 W: 14 06 b.Trondheim 5-1-71
Honours: Norway 15 full caps.

1989	Rosenborg	2	0	
1990	Rosenborg	9	0	

1991	Rosenborg	6	1	
1992	Rosenborg	16	4	
1993	Rosenborg	20	4	
1994	Rosenborg	21	3	
1995	Rosenborg	25	6	
1996	Rosenborg	8	2	
1997	Rosenborg	22	0	
1998	Rosenborg	25	4	
1999	Rosenborg	25	1	
2000	Rosenborg	16	1	194 26
2000–01	Derby Co	12	0	
2001–02	Derby Co	0	0	12 0
2001–02	*Birmingham C*	3	0	3 0

BURLEY, Craig (M) 222 33
H: 6 1 W: 13 03 b.Ayr 24-9-71
Source: Trainee. *Honours:* Scotland Schools,
Youth, Under-21, 45 full caps, 3 goals.

1989–90	Chelsea	1	0	
1990–91	Chelsea	11	0	
1991–92	Chelsea	8	0	
1992–93	Chelsea	3	0	
1993–94	Chelsea	23	3	
1994–95	Chelsea	25	2	
1995–96	Chelsea	22	0	
1996–97	Chelsea	31	2	113 7
1997–98	Celtic	35	10	
1998–99	Celtic	21	9	
1999–2000	Celtic	0	0	56 19
1999–2000	Derby Co	18	5	
2000–01	Derby Co	24	2	
2001–02	Derby Co	11	0	53 7

BURTON, Deon (F) 200 36
H: 5 9 W: 12 08 b.Reading 25-10-77
Source: Trainee. *Honours:* Jamaica 40 full
caps, 4 goals.

1993–94	Portsmouth	2	0	
1994–95	Portsmouth	7	2	
1995–96	Portsmouth	32	7	
1996–97	Portsmouth	21	1	62 10
1996–97	*Cardiff C*	5	2	5 2
1997–98	Derby Co	29	3	
1998–99	Derby Co	21	9	
1998–99	*Barnsley*	3	0	3 0
1999–2000	Derby Co	19	4	
2000–01	Derby Co	32	5	
2001–02	Derby Co	17	1	118 22
2001–02	*Stoke C*	12	2	12 2

CARBONARI, Horace Angel (D) 228 34
H: 6 3 W: 14 08 b.Rosario 2-5-71

1993–94	Rosario Central	23	2	
1994–95	Rosario Central	15	3	
1995–96	Rosario Central	32	7	
1996–97	Rosario Central	31	5	
1997–98	Rosario Central	34	9	135 26
1998–99	Derby Co	29	5	
1999–2000	Derby Co	29	2	
2000–01	Derby Co	27	1	
2001–02	Derby Co	3	0	88 8
2001–02	*Coventry C*	5	0	5 0

CHRISTIE, Malcolm (F) 92 22
H: 6 0 W: 12 06 b.Peterborough 11-4-79
Source: Nuneaton B. *Honours:* England
Under-21.

1998–99	Derby Co	2	0	
1999–2000	Derby Co	21	5	
2000–01	Derby Co	34	8	
2001–02	Derby Co	35	9	92 22

CLEARY, Sean‡ (M) 0 0
b.Belfast 26-2-83
Source: Scholar.

2001–02	Derby Co	0	0	

DAINO, Daniele‡ (D) 65 0
H: 5 11 W: 11 11 b.Alessandria 8-9-79

1996–97	AC Milan	5	0	
1997–98	AC Milan	14	0	
1998–99	Napoli	35	0	35 0
1999–2000	Perugia	8	0	8 0
2000–01	AC Milan	1	0	20 0
2001–02	Derby Co	2	0	2 0
(Transferred to AC Milan, November 2001).				

DUCROCQ, Pierre‡ (M) 158 3
H: 5 11 W: 12 00 b.Pontoise 18-12-76

1994–95	Paris St Germain	2	0	
1995–96	Paris St Germain	1	0	
1996–97	Laval	35	1	35 1
1997–98	Paris St Germain	28	0	
1998–99	Paris St Germain	33	1	
2000–01	Paris St Germain	27	0	
2001–02	Paris St Germain	1	0	104 2
2001–02	Derby Co	19	0	19 0

ELLIOTT, Steve (D) 46 0
H: 6 2 W: 14 08 b.Derby 29-10-78
Source: Trainee.

1996–97	Derby Co	0	0	

1997–98 Derby Co 3 0
1998–99 Derby Co 11 0
1999–2000 Derby Co 20 0
2000–01 Derby Co 6 0
2001–02 Derby Co 6 0 46 0

ERANIO, Stefano‡ (M) 406 26
H: 5 11 W: 12 08 b.Genoa 29-12-66
Honours: Italy 20 full caps, 3 goals.
1984–85 Genoa 9 0
1985–86 Genoa 13 0
1986–87 Genoa 36 3
1987–88 Genoa 34 0
1988–89 Genoa 35 4
1989–90 Genoa 25 0
1990–91 Genoa 32 4
1991–92 Genoa 29 2 213 13
1992–93 AC Milan 21 2
1993–94 AC Milan 21 1
1994–95 AC Milan 11 0
1995–96 AC Milan 24 1
1996–97 AC Milan 21 2 98 6
1997–98 Derby Co 23 5
1998–99 Derby Co 25 0
1999–2000 Derby Co 19 0
2000–01 Derby Co 28 2
2001–02 Derby Co 0 0 95 7

EVATT, Ian (D) 15 0
H: 6 3 W: 14 04 b.Coventry 23-11-81
Source: Trainee.
1998–99 Derby Co 0 0
1999–2000 Derby Co 0 0
2000–01 Derby Co 1 0
2001–02 *Northampton T* 11 0 11 0
2001–02 Derby Co 3 0 4 0

FLANAGAN, Martin (M) 0 0
b.Omagh 13-1-84
Source: Scholar.
2000–01 Derby Co 0 0
2001–02 Derby Co 0 0

FOLETTI, Patrick‡ (G) 89 0
H: 6 3 W: 13 00 b.Sorengo 27-5-74
1994–95 Grasshoppers 1 0
1995–96 Grasshoppers 10 0
1996–97 Grasshoppers 0 0
1997–98 Grasshoppers 0 0 11 0
From Schaffhausen
1999–2000 Lucerne 32 0
2000–01 Lucerne 22 0
2001–02 Lucerne 22 0 76 0
2001–02 Derby Co 2 0 2 0

GRANT, Lee (G) 0 0
H: 6 2 W: 13 00 b.Watford 27-1-83
Source: Scholar. *Honours:* England Youth.
2000–01 Derby Co 0 0
2001–02 Derby Co 0 0

GRENET, Francois (D) 192 4
H: 5 11 W: 11 06 b.Bordeaux 8-3-75
1992–93 Bordeaux 1 0
1993–94 Bordeaux 3 0
1994–95 Bordeaux 5 1
1995–96 Bordeaux 26 0
1996–97 Bordeaux 27 1
1997–98 Bordeaux 24 2
1998–99 Bordeaux 23 0
1999–2000 Bordeaux 31 0
2000–01 Bordeaux 29 0
2001–02 Bordeaux 8 0 177 4
2001–02 Derby Co 15 0 15 0

HIGGINBOTHAM, Danny (D) 67 1
H: 6 1 W: 13 03 b.Manchester 29-12-78
Source: Trainee.
1997–98 Manchester U 1 0
1998–99 Manchester U 0 0
1999–2000 Manchester U 3 0 4 0
2000–01 Derby Co 26 0
2001–02 Derby Co 37 1 63 1

HOLMES, Gareth* (M) 0 0
b.Mansfield 1-10-82
Source: Scholar.
2001–02 Derby Co 0 0

HUNT, Lewis (D) 0 0
H: 5 11 W: 12 08 b.Birmingham 25-8-82
Source: Scholar.
2000–01 Derby Co 0 0
2001–02 Derby Co 0 0

JACKSON, Richard (D) 33 0
H: 5 7 W: 11 02 b.Whitby 18-4-80
Source: Trainee.
1997–98 Scarborough 2 0
1998–99 Scarborough 20 0 22 0
1998–99 Derby Co 0 0
1999–2000 Derby Co 2 0
2000–01 Derby Co 2 0
2001–02 Derby Co 7 0 11 0

KINKLADZE, Georgiou (M) 339 82
H: 5 6 W: 11 05 b.Tbilisi 6-7-73
Source: Dynamo Tbilisi. *Honours:* Georgia 44 full caps, 8 goals.
1990 Mretebi 34 8
1991 Mretebi 16 1
1991–92 Mretebi 30 9 80 18
1992–93 Dynamo Tbilisi 30 14
1993–94 Dynamo Tbilisi 14 13
1993–94 Saarbrucken 11 0 11 0
1994–95 Dynamo Tbilisi 21 14 65 41
1995–96 Manchester C 37 4
1996–97 Manchester C 39 12
1997–98 Manchester C 30 4 106 20
1998–99 Ajax 12 0 12 0
1999–2000 Derby Co 17 1
2000–01 Derby Co 24 1
2001–02 Derby Co 24 1 65 3

LEE, Robert (M) 614 103
H: 5 10 W: 11 10 b.Plaistow 1-2-66
Source: Hornchurch. *Honours:* England Under-21, 21 full caps, 2 goals.
1983–84 Charlton Ath 11 4
1984–85 Charlton Ath 39 10
1985–86 Charlton Ath 35 8
1986–87 Charlton Ath 33 3
1987–88 Charlton Ath 23 2
1988–89 Charlton Ath 31 5
1989–90 Charlton Ath 37 1
1990–91 Charlton Ath 43 13
1991–92 Charlton Ath 39 12
1992–93 Charlton Ath 7 1 298 59
1992–93 Newcastle U 36 10
1993–94 Newcastle U 41 7
1994–95 Newcastle U 35 9
1995–96 Newcastle U 36 8
1996–97 Newcastle U 33 5
1997–98 Newcastle U 28 4
1998–99 Newcastle U 26 0
1999–2000 Newcastle U 30 0
2000–01 Newcastle U 22 0
2001–02 Newcastle U 16 1 303 44
2001–02 Derby Co 13 0 13 0

MAWENE, Youl (D) 31 1
H: 6 1 W: 13 05 b.Caen 16-7-79
1999–2000 Lens 6 0 6 0
2000–01 Derby Co 8 0
2001–02 Derby Co 17 1 25 1

McARDLE, Fiachra (M) 0 0
b.Newry 18-8-83
Source: Scholar.
2000–01 Derby Co 0 0
2001–02 Derby Co 0 0

McKEOWN, Gareth‡ (D) 0 0
b.Belfast 14-7-83
Source: Scholar.
2001–02 Derby Co 0 0

MORRIS, Lee (F) 69 11
H: 5 9 W: 11 02 b.Driffield 30-4-80
Source: Trainee. *Honours:* England Youth.
1997–98 Sheffield U 5 0
1998–99 Sheffield U 20 6
1999–2000 Sheffield U 1 0 26 6
1999–2000 Derby Co 3 0
2000–01 Derby Co 20 0
2000–01 *Huddersfield T* 5 1 5 1
2001–02 Derby Co 15 4 38 4

MOUKOKO, Tonton (M) 0 0
b.Congo 22-12-83
Source: Scholar.
2000–01 Derby Co 0 0
2001–02 Derby Co 0 0

MURRAY, Adam (M) 45 7
H: 5 9 W: 11 11 b.Birmingham 30-9-81
Source: Trainee. *Honours:* England Youth, Under-20.
1998–99 Derby Co 4 0
1999–2000 Derby Co 8 0
2000–01 Derby Co 14 0
2001–02 Derby Co 6 0 32 0
2001–02 *Mansfield T* 13 7 13 7

O'NEIL, Brian (M) 218 12
H: 6 0 W: 13 10 b.Paisley 6-9-72
Source: X Form. *Honours:* Scotland Schools, Youth, Under-21, 6 full caps.
1991–92 Celtic 28 1
1992–93 Celtic 17 3
1993–94 Celtic 28 2
1994–95 Celtic 26 0
1995–96 Celtic 5 0
1996–97 Celtic ·16 2 120 8
1996–97 *Nottingham F* 5 0 5 0
1997–98 Aberdeen 29 1 29 1
1998–99 Wolfsburg 26 2
1999–2000 Wolfsburg 16 1

2000–01 Wolfsburg 8 0 50 3
2000–01 Derby Co 4 0
2001–02 Derby Co 10 0 14 0

OAKES, Andy (G) 45 0
H: 6 1 W: 12 04 b.Crewe 11-1-77
1995–96 Bury 0 0
1996–97 Bury 0 0
1997–98 Bury 0 0
From Winsford U.
1998–99 Hull C 19 0 19 0
1999–2000 Derby Co 0 0
1999–2000 *Port Vale* 0 0
2000–01 Derby Co 6 0
2001–02 Derby Co 20 0 26 0

POOM, Mart (G) 178 0
H: 6 4 W: 14 03 b.Tallinn 3-2-72
Honours: Estonia 79 full caps.
1992–93 Flora Tallinn 11 0
1993–94 Flora Tallinn 11 0
1994–95 Portsmouth 0 0
1995–96 Portsmouth 4 0
1995–96 Flora Tallinn 7 0
1996–97 Portsmouth 0 0 4 0
1996–97 Flora Tallinn 12 0 41 0
1996–97 Derby Co 4 0
1997–98 Derby Co 36 0
1998–99 Derby Co 17 0
1999–2000 Derby Co 28 0
2000–01 Derby Co 33 0
2001–02 Derby Co 15 0 133 0

POWELL, Darryl (M) 339 26
H: 6 1 W: 13 03 b.Lambeth 15-11-71
Source: Trainee. *Honours:* Jamaica full caps.
1988–89 Portsmouth 3 0
1989–90 Portsmouth 0 0
1990–91 Portsmouth 8 0
1991–92 Portsmouth 36 6
1992–93 Portsmouth 23 0
1993–94 Portsmouth 28 5
1994–95 Portsmouth 34 5 132 16
1995–96 Derby Co 37 5
1996–97 Derby Co 33 1
1997–98 Derby Co 33 0
1998–99 Derby Co 33 0
1999–2000 Derby Co 31 2
2000–01 Derby Co 27 1
2001–02 Derby Co 23 1 207 10

RAVANELLI, Fabrizio (F) 458 176
H: 6 2 W: 13 04 b.Perugia 11-12-68
Honours: Italy 21 full caps, 9 goals.
1986–87 Perugia 26 5
1987–88 Perugia 32 23
1988–89 Perugia 32 13 90 41
1989–90 Avellino 7 0
1989–90 Casertana 27 12 27 12
1990–91 Avellino 0 0 7 0
1990–91 Reggiana 34 16
1991–92 Reggiana 32 8 66 24
1992–93 Juventus 22 5
1993–94 Juventus 30 9
1994–95 Juventus 33 15
1995–96 Juventus 26 12 111 41
1996–97 Middlesbrough 33 16
1997–98 Middlesbrough 2 1 35 17
1997–98 Marseille 21 9
1998–99 Marseille 29 13
1999–2000 Marseille 14 6 64 28
2000–01 Lazio 16 2
2001–02 Lazio 11 2 27 4
2001–02 Derby Co 31 9 31 9

RIGGOTT, Chris (D) 69 3
H: 6 2 W: 13 09 b.Derby 1-9-80
Source: Trainee. *Honours:* England Youth, Under-21.
1998–99 Derby Co 0 0
1999–2000 Derby Co 1 0
2000–01 Derby Co 31 3
2001–02 Derby Co 37 0 69 3

ROBINSON, Marvin (F) 14 2
H: 6 0 W: 13 05 b.Crewe 11-4-80
Source: Trainee.
1998–99 Derby Co 1 0
1999–2000 Derby Co 8 0
2000–01 Derby Co 0 0
2000–01 *Stoke C* 3 1 3 1
2001–02 Derby Co 2 1 11 1

STRUPAR, Branko (F) 146 76
H: 6 3 W: 14 06 b.Zagreb 9-2-70
Source: Spansko. *Honours:* Belgium 17 full caps, 5 goals.
1996–97 Genk 31 12
1997–98 Genk 31 22
1998–99 Genk 33 18
1999–2000 Genk 15 9 110 61
1999–2000 Derby Co 15 5

2000–01	Derby Co	9	6	
2001–02	Derby Co	12	4	**36 15**

TWIGG, Gary (F) — **1 0**
H: 6 0 W: 11 02 b.Glasgow 19-3-84
Source: Scholar.

2000–01	Derby Co	0	0
2001–02	Derby Co	1	0

VALAKARI, Simo (M) — **172 6**
H: 5 11 W: 12 08 b.Helsinki 24-4-73
Honours: Finland 22 full caps.

1995	Finn PA	22	3	
1996	Finn PA	26	2	**48 5**
1996–97	Motherwell	11	0	
1997–98	Motherwell	28	0	
1998–99	Motherwell	35	0	
1999–2000	Motherwell	30	0	**104 0**
2000–01	Derby Co	11	1	
2001–02	Derby Co	9	0	**20 1**

WECKSTROM, Kristoffer (F) — **0 0**
b.Helsinki 26-5-83
Source: IFK Mariehamn.

2000–01	Derby Co	0	0
2001–02	Derby Co	0	0

ZAVAGNO, Luciano (D) — **87 1**
H: 5 11 W: 11 07 b.Rosario 6-8-77

1997–98	Strasbourg	5	0	
1998–99	Strasbourg	9	1	**14 1**
1999–2000	Troyes	26	0	
2000–01	Troyes	13	0	
2001–02	Troyes	8	0	**47 0**
2001–02	Derby Co	26	0	**26 0**

Trainees
Camp, Lee MJ; Donnelly, Sean; Francis, Carl; Freeman, Jim; Hamilton, Lewis E; Harmainen, Higginbott; Keenan, Colin P; Kuduzovic, Fahrudin; Lambert, Jordan K; McLeod, Izale M; Mills, Pablo; Molloy, Barry; O'Halloran, Matthew V; Palmer, Christopher L; Porter, Justin L; Tosh, Bryan R; Tudgay, Marcus; Turner, James J

EVERTON

ALEXANDERSSON, Niclas (M) — **323 50**
H: 5 9 W: 11 08 b.Halmstad 29-12-71
Honours: Sweden 63 full caps, 7 goals.

1989	Halmstad	4	0	
1990	Halmstad	22	2	
1991	Halmstad	16	3	
1992	Halmstad	27	7	
1993	Halmstad	25	4	
1994	Halmstad	25	4	
1995	Halmstad	26	5	**145 25**
1996	IFK Gothenburg	26	7	
1997	IFK Gothenburg	26	6	**52 13**
1997–98	Sheffield W	6	0	
1998–99	Sheffield W	32	3	
1999–2000	Sheffield W	37	5	**75 8**
2000–01	Everton	20	2	
2001–02	Everton	31	2	**51 4**

BECK, Steven (M) — **0 0**
b.Liverpool 4-6-84
Source: Scholar. *Honours:* England Youth.

2001–02	Everton	0	0

BLOMQVIST, Jesper* (M) — **197 31**
H: 5 10 W: 11 06 b.Tavelsjo 5-2-74
Honours: Sweden 30 full caps.

1992	Umea	27	6	
1993	Umea	11	2	**38 8**
1993	IFK Gothenburg	6	1	
1994	IFK Gothenburg	24	8	
1995	IFK Gothenburg	18	3	
1996	IFK Gothenburg	23	7	**71 19**
1996–97	AC Milan	19	1	
1997–98	AC Milan	1	0	**20 1**
1997–98	Parma	28	1	**28 1**
1998–99	Manchester U	25	1	
1999–2000	Manchester U	0	0	
2000–01	Manchester U	0	0	
2001–02	Manchester U	0	0	**25 1**
2001–02	Everton	15	1	**15 1**

BROWN, Scott (M) — **0 0**
b.Chester 8-5-85
Source: Scholar. *Honours:* England Youth.

2001–02	Everton	0	0

CAMPBELL, Kevin (F) — **376 131**
H: 6 0 W: 13 13 b.Lambeth 4-2-70
Source: Trainee. *Honours:* England Under-21, B.

1987–88	Arsenal	1	0	
1988–89	Arsenal	0	0	
1988–89	Leyton Orient	16	9	**16 9**
1989–90	Arsenal	15	2	
1989–90	Leicester C	11	5	**11 5**
1990–91	Arsenal	22	9	
1991–92	Arsenal	31	13	
1992–93	Arsenal	37	4	
1993–94	Arsenal	37	14	
1994–95	Arsenal	23	4	**166 46**
1995–96	Nottingham F	21	3	
1996–97	Nottingham F	17	6	
1997–98	Nottingham F	42	23	**80 32**
1998–99	Trabzonspor	17	5	**17 5**
1998–99	Everton	8	9	
1999–2000	Everton	26	12	
2000–01	Everton	29	9	
2001–02	Everton	23	4	**86 34**

CARNEY, David (M) — **0 0**
b.Sydney 30-11-83
Source: Scholar.

2000–01	Everton	0	0
2001–02	Everton	0	0

CARSLEY, Lee (M) — **239 20**
H: 5 10 W: 12 04 b.Birmingham 28-2-74
Source: Trainee. *Honours:* Eire 20 full caps.

1992–93	Derby Co	0	0	
1993–94	Derby Co	0	0	
1994–95	Derby Co	23	2	
1995–96	Derby Co	35	1	
1996–97	Derby Co	24	0	
1997–98	Derby Co	34	1	
1998–99	Derby Co	22	1	**138 5**
1998–99	Blackburn R	8	0	
1999–2000	Blackburn R	30	10	
2000–01	Blackburn R	8	0	**46 10**
2000–01	Coventry C	21	2	
2001–02	Coventry C	26	2	**47 4**
2001–02	Everton	8	1	**8 1**

CHADWICK, Nick (F) — **9 3**
H: 5 11 W: 10 09 b.Stoke 26-10-82

1999–2000	Everton	0	0	
2000–01	Everton	0	0	
2001–02	Everton	9	3	**9 3**

CLARKE, Peter (D) — **8 0**
H: 6 0 W: 12 00 b.Southport 3-1-82
Source: Trainee. *Honours:* England Youth, Under-20.

1998–99	Everton	0	0	
1999–2000	Everton	0	0	
2000–01	Everton	1	0	
2001–02	Everton	7	0	**8 0**

CLELAND, Alec* (D) — **282 12**
H: 5 10 W: 11 07 b.Glasgow 10-12-70
Source: 'S' Form. *Honours:* Scotland Schools, Under-21, B.

1987–88	Dundee U	0	0	
1988–89	Dundee U	9	0	
1989–90	Dundee U	15	0	
1990–91	Dundee U	20	2	
1991–92	Dundee U	31	4	
1992–93	Dundee U	24	0	
1993–94	Dundee U	33	1	
1994–95	Dundee U	18	1	**151 8**
1994–95	Rangers	10	0	
1995–96	Rangers	25	1	
1996–97	Rangers	32	0	
1997–98	Rangers	29	3	**96 4**
1998–99	Everton	18	0	
1999–2000	Everton	9	0	
2000–01	Everton	5	0	
2001–02	Everton	3	0	**35 0**

CROWDER, Martin (D) — **0 0**
b.Liverpool 11-4-84
Source: Scholar.

2001–02	Everton	0	0

CURRAN, Damien* (M) — **0 0**
H: 5 9 W: 12 01 b.Antrim 17-10-81
Source: Trainee.

1999–2000	Everton	0	0
2000–01	Everton	0	0
2001–02	Everton	0	0

EATON, David* (F) — **0 0**
b.Liverpool 30-9-81
Source: Scholar.

2001–02	Everton	0	0

FERGUSON, Duncan (F) — **271 87**
H: 6 4 W: 13 07 b.Stirling 27-12-71
Source: Carse T. *Honours:* Scotland Schools, Youth, Under-21, B, 7 full caps.

1990–91	Dundee U	9	1	
1991–92	Dundee U	38	15	
1992–93	Dundee U	30	12	**77 28**
1993–94	Rangers	10	1	
1994–95	Rangers	4	1	**14 2**
1994–95	Everton	23	7	
1995–96	Everton	18	0	
1996–97	Everton	33	10	
1997–98	Everton	29	11	
1998–99	Everton	13	4	
1998–99	Newcastle U	7	2	
1999–2000	Newcastle U	23	6	**30 8**
2000–01	Everton	12	6	
2001–02	Everton	22	6	**150 49**

GARSIDE, Craig (D) — **0 0**
H: 5 11 W: 13 00 b.Chester 11-1-85
Source: Scholar.

2001–02	Everton	0	0

GEMMILL, Scot (M) — **326 26**
H: 5 10 W: 11 08 b.Paisley 2-1-71
Source: School. *Honours:* Scotland Under-21, B, 23 full caps, 1 goal.

1989–90	Nottingham F	0	0	
1990–91	Nottingham F	4	0	
1991–92	Nottingham F	39	8	
1992–93	Nottingham F	33	1	
1993–94	Nottingham F	31	8	
1994–95	Nottingham F	19	1	
1995–96	Nottingham F	31	1	
1996–97	Nottingham F	24	0	
1997–98	Nottingham F	44	2	
1998–99	Nottingham F	20	0	**245 21**
1998–99	Everton	17	1	
1999–2000	Everton	14	1	
2000–01	Everton	28	2	
2001–02	Everton	32	1	**81 5**

GERRARD, Paul (G) — **223 1**
H: 6 2 W: 13 11 b.Heywood 22-1-73
Source: Trainee. *Honours:* England Under-21.

1991–92	Oldham Ath	0	0	
1992–93	Oldham Ath	25	0	
1993–94	Oldham Ath	16	0	
1994–95	Oldham Ath	42	0	
1995–96	Oldham Ath	36	1	**119 1**
1996–97	Everton	5	0	
1997–98	Everton	4	0	
1998–99	Everton	0	0	
1998–99	Oxford U	16	0	**16 0**
1999–2000	Everton	34	0	
2000–01	Everton	32	0	
2001–02	Everton	13	0	**88 0**

GINOLA, David* (M) — **502 75**
H: 5 10 W: 12 07 b.Gassin 25-1-67
Honours: France 17 full caps, 3 goals.

1985–86	Toulon	14	0	
1986–87	Toulon	34	0	
1987–88	Toulon	33	4	**81 4**
1988–89	Racing Paris	29	7	
1989–90	Racing Paris	32	1	**61 8**
1990–91	Brest	33	1	
1991–92	Brest	17	9	**50 10**
1991–92	Paris St Germain	15	2	
1992–93	Paris St Germain	34	6	
1993–94	Paris St Germain	38	13	
1994–95	Paris St Germain	28	11	**115 32**
1995–96	Newcastle U	34	5	
1996–97	Newcastle U	24	1	**58 6**
1997–98	Tottenham H	34	6	
1998–99	Tottenham H	30	3	
1999–2000	Tottenham H	36	3	**100 12**
2000–01	Aston Villa	27	3	
2001–02	Aston Villa	5	0	**32 3**
2001–02	Everton	5	0	**5 0**

GRAVESEN, Thomas (M) — **189 20**
H: 5 9 W: 13 06 b.Vejle 11-3-76
Honours: Denmark 27 full caps, 2 goals.

1995–96	Vejle	28	2	
1996–97	Vejle	30	8	**58 10**
1997–98	Hamburg	26	2	
1998–99	Hamburg	22	3	
1999–2000	Hamburg	26	1	**74 6**
2000–01	Everton	32	2	
2001–02	Everton	25	2	**57 4**

HIBBERT, Tony (D) — **13 0**
H: 5 9 W: 13 06 b.Liverpool 20-2-81
Source: Trainee.

1998–99	Everton	0	0	
1999–2000	Everton	0	0	
2000–01	Everton	3	0	
2001–02	Everton	10	0	**13 0**

LINDEROTH, Tobias (M) — **133 13**
H: 5 10 W: 11 08 b.Marseille 21-4-79
Honours: Sweden 25 full caps, 1 goal.

1996	Elfsborg	10	0	
1997	Elfsborg	25	1	
1998	Elfsborg	22	3	**57 4**
1999	Stabaek	23	3	
2000	Stabaek	24	4	
2001	Stabaek	21	2	**68 9**
2001–02	Everton	8	0	**8 0**

McKAY, Matt* (M) — **5 0**
H: 6 0 W: 11 05 b.Warrington 21-1-81
Source: Trainee.

1997–98	Chester C	5	0	**5 0**

1997–98	Everton	0	0		
1998–99	Everton	0	0		
1999–2000	Everton	0	0		
2000–01	Everton	0	0		
2001–02	Everton	0	0		

McLEOD, Kevin (M)   **5 0**
H: 5 11   W: 12 00   b.Liverpool 12-9-80
Source: Trainee.

1998–99	Everton	0	0
1999–2000	Everton	0	0
2000–01	Everton	5	0
2001–02	Everton	0	0 **5 0**

MOOGAN, Alan (M)   **0 0**
b.Liverpool 22-2-84
Source: Scholar. *Honours:* England Youth.

2000–01	Everton	0	0
2001–02	Everton	0	0

MOOGAN, Brian (D)   **0 0**
b.Liverpool 22-2-84
Source: Scholar.

2001–02	Everton	0	0

MOORE, Joe-Max (F)   **129 45**
H: 5 8   W: 11 06   b.USA 23-2-71
Honours: USA 100 full caps, 24 goals.

1996	New England Rev	14	11
1997	New England Rev	13	4
1998	New England Rev	21	7
1999	New England Rev	29	15 **77 37**
1999–2000	Everton	15	6
2000–01	Everton	21	0
2001–02	Everton	16	2 **52 8**

MYHRE, Thomas‡ (G)   **174 0**
H: 6 3   W: 13 13   b.Sarpsborg 16-10-73
Honours: Norway 28 full caps.

1993	Viking	22	0
1994	Viking	22	0
1995	Viking	24	0
1996	Viking	0	0
1997	Viking	26	0 **94 0**
1997–98	Everton	22	0
1998–99	Everton	38	0
1999–2000	Everton	4	0
1999–2000	Birmingham C	7	0 **7 0**
2000–01	Everton	6	0
2000–01	*Tranmere R*	3	0 **3 0**
2001–02	Everton	0	0 **70 0**

(Transferred to Besiktas, November 2001).

NAYSMITH, Gary (D)   **141 5**
H: 5 9   W: 12 01   b.Edinburgh 16-11-78
Source: Whitehill Welfare Colts. *Honours:*
Scotland Schools, Under-21, 6 full caps.

1995–96	Hearts	1	0
1996–97	Hearts	10	0
1997–98	Hearts	16	2
1998–99	Hearts	26	0
1999–2000	Hearts	35	1
2000–01	Hearts	9	0 **97 3**
2000–01	Everton	20	2
2001–02	Everton	24	0 **44 2**

NYARKO, Alex (M)   **144 14**
H: 6 0   W: 13 00   b.Accra 15-10-73
Source: Asanti Kotoko, Deawe Youngsters.
Honours: Ghana full caps.

1994–95	Sportul	0	0
1995–96	Basle	26	3
1996–97	Basle	29	5 **55 8**
1997–98	Karlsruhe	22	1 **22 1**
1998–99	Lens	24	3
1999–2000	Lens	21	1 **45 4**
2000–01	Everton	22	1
2001–02	Everton	0	0 **22 1**

O'HANLON, Sean (D)   **0 0**
H: 6 1   W: 12 05   b.Southport 2-1-83
Honours: England Youth.

1999–2000	Everton	0	0
2000–01	Everton	0	0
2001–02	Everton	0	0

OSMAN, Leon (F)   **0 0**
H: 5 8   W: 10 09   b.Billinge 17-5-81
Source: Trainee. *Honours:* England Schools,
Youth.

1998–99	Everton	0	0
1999–2000	Everton	0	0
2000–01	Everton	0	0
2001–02	Everton	0	0

PEMBRIDGE, Mark (M)   **348 49**
H: 5 7   W: 11 09   b.Merthyr 29-11-70
Source: Trainee. *Honours:* Wales Schools,
Under-21, B, 42 full caps, 6 goals.

1989–90	Luton T	0	0
1990–91	Luton T	18	1
1991–92	Luton T	42	5 **60 6**
1992–93	Derby Co	42	8
1993–94	Derby Co	41	11

1994–95	Derby Co	27	9	**110 28**	
1995–96	Sheffield W	25	1		
1996–97	Sheffield W	34	6		
1997–98	Sheffield W	34	4	**93 11**	
1998–99	Benfica	19	1	**19 1**	
1999–2000	Everton	31	2		
2000–01	Everton	21	0		
2001–02	Everton	14	1	**66 3**	

PENMAN, Craig‡ (D)   **0 0**
H: 5 11   W: 11 06   b.Falkirk 9-9-82
Source: Trainee.

1999–2000	Everton	0	0
2000–01	Everton	0	0
2001–02	Everton	0	0

PETTINGER, Andrew (G)   **0 0**
b.Scunthorpe 21-4-84
Source: Scunthorpe U.

2000–01	Everton	0	0
2001–02	Everton	0	0

PILKINGTON, George (D)   **0 0**
H: 5 11   W: 11 00   b.Rugeley 7-11-81
Source: Trainee. *Honours:* England Youth.

1998–99	Everton	0	0
1999–2000	Everton	0	0
2000–01	Everton	0	0
2001–02	Everton	0	0

PISTONE, Alessandro (D)   **178 8**
H: 5 11   W: 11 08   b.Milan 27-7-75

1992–93	Vicenza	0	0
1993–94	Solbiatese	20	1 **20 1**
1994–95	Crevalcore	29	4 **29 4**
1995–96	Vicenza	6	0 **6 0**
1995–96	Internazionale	19	1
1996–97	Internazionale	26	0 **45 1**
1997–98	Newcastle U	28	0
1998–99	Newcastle U	3	0
1999–2000	Newcastle U	15	1 **46 1**
2000–01	Everton	7	0
2001–02	Everton	25	1 **32 1**

RADZINSKI, Tomasz (F)   **209 100**
H: 5 7   W: 11 10   b.Poznan 14-12-73
Source: Toronto Rockets, St Catherines
Roma. *Honours:* Canada 15 full caps, 3 goals.

1994–95	Ekeren	22	9
1995–96	Ekeren	22	9
1996–97	Ekeren	23	8
1997–98	Ekeren	31	19 **104 42**
1998–99	Anderlecht	22	15
1999–2000	Anderlecht	25	14
2000–01	Anderlecht	31	23 **78 52**
2001–02	Everton	27	6 **27 6**

SCHUMACHER, Steven (M)   **0 0**
b.Liverpool 30-4-84
Source: Scholar. *Honours:* England Youth.

2000–01	Everton	0	0
2001–02	Everton	0	0

SIMONSEN, Steve (G)   **62 0**
H: 6 2   W: 14 00   b.South Shields 3-4-79
Source: Trainee. *Honours:* England Youth,
Under-21.

1996–97	Tranmere R	0	0
1997–98	Tranmere R	30	0
1998–99	Tranmere R	5	0 **35 0**
1998–99	Everton	0	0
1999–2000	Everton	1	0
2000–01	Everton	1	0
2001–02	Everton	25	0 **27 0**

SOUTHERN, Keith (M)   **0 0**
H: 5 10   W: 12 04   b.Gateshead 24-4-81
Source: Trainee.

1998–99	Everton	0	0
1999–2000	Everton	0	0
2000–01	Everton	0	0
2001–02	Everton	0	0

SOUTHERN, Robert (M)   **0 0**
b.Gateshead 24-9-83
Source: Scholar.

2000–01	Everton	0	0
2001–02	Everton	0	0

STUBBS, Alan (D)   **339 14**
H: 6 2   W: 13 12   b.Kirkby 6-10-71
Source: Trainee.

1990–91	Bolton W	23	0
1991–92	Bolton W	32	1
1992–93	Bolton W	42	2
1993–94	Bolton W	41	1
1994–95	Bolton W	39	1
1995–96	Bolton W	25	4 **202 9**
1996–97	Celtic	20	0
1997–98	Celtic	29	1
1998–99	Celtic	23	1
1999–2000	Celtic	23	0
2000–01	Celtic	11	1 **106 3**
2001–02	Everton	31	2 **31 2**

SYMES, Michael (F)   **0 0**
H: 6 2   W: 12 00   b.Gt Yarmouth 31-10-83
Source: Scholar.

2001–02	Everton	0	0

TAL, Idan (M)   **157 20**
H: 5 10   W: 10 13   b.Petah Tikva 13-9-75
Honours: Israel 29 full caps, 2 goals.

1996–97	Maccabi Petah Tikva	27	1
1997–98	Maccabi Petah Tikva	29	6
1998–99	Maccabi Petah Tikva	15	3
1998–99	Hapoel Tel Aviv	14	2 **14 2**
1999–2000	Merida	36	5 **36 5**
2000–01	Maccabi Petah Tikva	7	1 **78 11**
2000–01	Everton	22	2
2001–02	Everton	7	0 **29 2**

UNSWORTH, Dave (D)   **277 28**
H: 6 1   W: 15 02   b.Chorley 16-10-73
Source: Trainee. *Honours:* England Youth,
Under-21, 1 full cap.

1991–92	Everton	2	1
1992–93	Everton	3	0
1993–94	Everton	8	0
1994–95	Everton	38	3
1995–96	Everton	31	2
1996–97	Everton	34	5
1997–98	West Ham U	32	2 **32 2**
1998–99	Aston Villa	0	0
1998–99	Everton	34	1
1999–2000	Everton	33	6
2000–01	Everton	29	5
2001–02	Everton	33	3 **245 26**

VALENTINE, Ryan* (D)   **0 0**
H: 5 10   W: 11 07   b.Wrexham 19-8-82
Source: Trainee. *Honours:* Wales Under-21.

1999–2000	Everton	0	0
2000–01	Everton	0	0
2001–02	Everton	0	0

WATSON, Steve (D)   **308 16**
H: 6 0   W: 12 07   b.North Shields 1-4-74
Source: Trainee. *Honours:* England Youth,
Under-21, B.

1990–91	Newcastle U	24	0
1991–92	Newcastle U	28	1
1992–93	Newcastle U	2	0
1993–94	Newcastle U	32	2
1994–95	Newcastle U	27	4
1995–96	Newcastle U	23	3
1996–97	Newcastle U	36	1
1997–98	Newcastle U	29	1
1998–99	Newcastle U	7	0 **208 12**
1998–99	Aston Villa	27	0
1999–2000	Aston Villa	14	0 **41 0**
2000–01	Everton	34	0
2001–02	Everton	25	4 **59 4**

WEIR, David (D)   **347 23**
H: 6 5   W: 14 03   b.Falkirk 10-5-70
Source: Celtic BC. *Honours:* Scotland 35 full
caps, 1 goal.

1992–93	Falkirk	30	1
1993–94	Falkirk	37	3
1994–95	Falkirk	32	1
1995–96	Falkirk	34	3 **133 8**
1996–97	Hearts	34	6
1997–98	Hearts	35	1
1998–99	Hearts	23	1 **92 8**
1998–99	Everton	14	0
1999–2000	Everton	35	2
2000–01	Everton	37	1
2001–02	Everton	36	4 **122 7**

Trainees
Colbeck, Franklyn A; Cole, Alex

EXETER C

AFFUL, Leslie§ (M)   **2 0**
H: 5 6   W: 10 00   b.Liverpool 4-2-84
Source: Scholar.

2001–02	Exeter C	2	0 **2 0**

AMPADU, Kwame (M)   **348 18**
H: 5 10   W: 11 10   b.Bradford 20-12-70
Source: Belvedere, Trainee. *Honours:* Eire
Youth, Under-21.

1988–89	Arsenal	0	0
1989–90	Arsenal	0	0
1990–91	Arsenal	0	0 **2 0**
1990–91	*Plymouth Arg*	6	1 **6 1**
1990–91	WBA	7	1
1991–92	WBA	21	3
1992–93	WBA	10	0
1993–94	WBA	11	0 **49 4**

1993–94 Swansea C 13 0
1994–95 Swansea C 44 6
1995–96 Swansea C 43 2
1996–97 Swansea C 29 4
1997–98 Swansea C 18 0 147 12
1998–99 Leyton Orient 29 1
1999–2000 Leyton Orient 43 0 72 1
2000–01 Exeter C 36 0
2001–02 Exeter C 36 0 72 0

BARLOW, Martin* (M) 359 24
H: 5 7 W: 10 03 b.Barnstable 25-6-71
Source: Trainee.
1988–89 Plymouth Arg 1 0
1989–90 Plymouth Arg 1 0
1990–91 Plymouth Arg 30 1
1991–92 Plymouth Arg 28 3
1992–93 Plymouth Arg 24 1
1993–94 Plymouth Arg 26 2
1994–95 Plymouth Arg 42 2
1995–96 Plymouth Arg 28 5
1996–97 Plymouth Arg 40 1
1997–98 Plymouth Arg 42 4
1998–99 Plymouth Arg 45 5
1999–2000 Plymouth Arg 2 0
2000–01 Plymouth Arg 20 0 329 24
2001–02 Exeter C 30 0 30 0

BLAKE, Noel‡ (D) 602 37
H: 6 2 W: 14 05 b.Kingston, Jamaica 12-1-62
Source: Walsall Amateur, Sutton Coldfield T.
1979–80 Aston Villa 3 0
1980–81 Aston Villa 0 0
1981–82 Aston Villa 1 0
1981–82 *Shrewsbury T* 6 0 6 0
1982–83 Aston Villa 0 0 4 0
1982–83 Birmingham C 37 3
1983–84 Birmingham C 39 2 76 5
1984–85 Portsmouth 42 3
1985–86 Portsmouth 42 4
1986–87 Portsmouth 41 3
1987–88 Portsmouth 19 0 144 10
1988–89 Leeds U 44 4
1989–90 Leeds U 7 0 51 4
1989–90 Stoke C 18 0
1990–91 Stoke C 44 3
1991–92 Stoke C 13 0 75 3
1991–92 *Bradford C* 6 0
1992–93 Bradford C 32 3
1993–94 Bradford C 7 0 45 3
1993–94 Dundee 23 2
1994–95 Dundee 31 0 54 2
1995–96 Exeter C 44 2
1996–97 Exeter C 46 6
1997–98 Exeter C 38 1
1998–99 Exeter C 7 0
1999–2000 Exeter C 7 1
2000–01 Exeter C 5 0
2001–02 Exeter C 0 0 147 10

BRESLAN, Geoff (M) 99 6
H: 5 9 W: 10 05 b.Torbay 4-6-80
Source: Trainee.
1997–98 Exeter C 1 0
1998–99 Exeter C 34 4
1999–2000 Exeter C 29 0
2000–01 Exeter C 2 0
2001–02 Exeter C 33 2 99 6

BUCKLE, Paul (M) 336 24
H: 5 8 W: 11 08 b.Welwyn 16-12-70
Source: Trainee.
1987–88 Brentford 1 0
1988–89 Brentford 0 0
1989–90 Brentford 10 0
1990–91 Brentford 26 0
1991–92 Brentford 15 1
1992–93 Brentford 5 0
1993–94 Brentford 0 0 57 1
1993–94 Torquay U 16 2
1994–95 Torquay U 32 3
1995–96 Torquay U 11 4 59 9
1995–96 Exeter C 22 2
1996–97 *Northampton T* 0 0
1996–97 *Wycombe W* 0 0
1996–97 Colchester U 24 0
1997–98 Colchester U 38 5
1998–99 Colchester U 43 2 105 7
1999–2000 Exeter C 27 1
2000–01 Exeter C 41 3
2001–02 Exeter C 25 1 115 7

BURROWS, Mark (D) 38 0
H: 6 3 W: 12 08 b.Kettering 14-8-80
Source: Trainee.
1997–98 Coventry C 0 0
1998–99 Coventry C 0 0
1999–2000 Coventry C 0 0
2000–01 Exeter C 29 0
2001–02 Exeter C 9 0 38 0

CAMPBELL, Jamie‡ (D) 290 17
H: 6 1 W: 12 07 b.Birmingham 21-10-72
Source: Trainee.
1991–92 Luton T 11 0
1992–93 Luton T 9 1
1993–94 Luton T 16 0
1994–95 Luton T 0 0 36 1
1994–95 *Mansfield T* 3 1 3 1
1994–95 Cambridge U 12 0
1995–96 Barnet 24 1
1996–97 Barnet 43 4 67 5
1997–98 Cambridge U 46 2
1998–99 Cambridge U 45 4 103 6
1999–2000 Brighton & HA 23 1 23 1
2000–01 Exeter C 42 2
2001–02 Exeter C 16 1 58 3

CRONIN, Glenn (M) 30 0
H: 5 8 W: 10 11 b.Dublin 14-9-81
Source: Trainee.
2000–01 Exeter C 0 0
2001–02 Exeter C 30 0 30 0

CURRAN, Chris* (D) 326 10
H: 5 11 W: 12 12 b.Birmingham 17-9-71
Source: Trainee.
1989–90 Torquay U 1 0
1990–91 Torquay U 13 0
1991–92 Torquay U 17 0
1992–93 Torquay U 34 0
1993–94 Torquay U 41 1
1994–95 Torquay U 27 2
1995–96 Torquay U 19 1 152 4
1995–96 Plymouth Arg 8 0
1996–97 Plymouth Arg 22 0 30 0
1997–98 Exeter C 9 0
1998–99 Exeter C 34 4
1999–2000 Exeter C 38 1
2000–01 Exeter C 26 0
2001–02 Exeter C 37 1 144 6

DIALLO, Cherif‡ (D) 2 0
H: 5 8 W: 10 11 b.Dakar 23-12-76
Source: Scarborough.
From Scarborough.
2001–02 Exeter C 2 0 2 0

ELLIOTT, Stuart‡ (D) 80 0
H: 5 8 W: 11 05 b.London 27-8-77
Source: Trainee.
1995–96 Newcastle U 0 0
1996–97 Newcastle U 0 0
1996–97 *Hull C* 3 0 3 0
1997–98 Newcastle U 0 0
1997–98 *Swindon T* 2 0 2 0
1998–99 Newcastle U 0 0
1998–99 *Gillingham* 5 0 5 0
1998–99 *Hartlepool U* 5 0 5 0
1998–99 *Wrexham* 9 0 9 0
1999–2000 Newcastle U 0 0
1999–2000 *Bournemouth* 8 0 8 0
1999–2000 *Stockport Co* 5 0 5 0
2000–01 Darlington 24 0 24 0
2000–01 Plymouth Arg 12 0 12 0
2001–02 Carlisle U 6 0 6 0
2001–02 Exeter C 1 0 1 0

FRASER, Stuart (G) 19 0
H: 6 0 W: 12 00 b.Cheltenham 1-8-78
Source: Cheltenham T.
1996–97 Stoke C 0 0
1997–98 Stoke C 0 0
1998–99 Stoke C 1 0
1999–2000 Stoke C 0 0 1 0
2000–01 Exeter C 6 0
2001–02 Exeter C 12 0 18 0

GOFF, Shaun§ (D) 2 0
H: 5 10 W: 11 10 b.Tiverton 13-4-84
Source: Trainee.
2001–02 Exeter C 2 0 2 0

GROSS, Marcus‡ (D) 1 0
H: 6 0 W: 12 00 b.Barnstaple 15-12-82
Source: Scholar.
2001–02 Exeter C 1 0 1 0

KERR, Dylan‡ (D) 202 11
H: 5 9 W: 11 04 b.Valletta 14-1-67
Source: Arcadia Shepherds.
1988–89 Leeds U 3 0
1989–90 Leeds U 5 0

1990–91 Leeds U 0 0
1991–92 Leeds U 0 0
1991–92 Doncaster R 7 1 7 1
1991–92 *Blackpool* 12 1 12 1
1992–93 Leeds U 5 0 13 0
1993–94 Reading 45 2
1994–95 Reading 36 1
1995–96 Reading 8 2
1996–97 Reading 0 0 89 5
1996–97 Carlisle U 1 0 1 0
1996–97 Kilmarnock 27 0
1997–98 Kilmarnock 14 0
1998–99 Kilmarnock 16 0
1999–2000 Kilmarnock 0 0 57 0
2000–01 Kidderminster H 1 0 1 0
2000–01 Hamilton A 17 3 17 3
2001–02 Exeter C 5 1 5 1

McCARTHY, Sean (F) 547 172
H: 6 1 W: 12 05 b.Bridgend 12-9-67
Source: Bridgend. *Honours:* Wales B.
1985–86 Swansea C 22 3
1986–87 Swansea C 44 14
1987–88 Swansea C 25 8 91 25
1988–89 Plymouth Arg 38 8
1989–90 Plymouth Arg 32 11
1990–91 Bradford C 42 13
1991–92 Bradford C 29 16
1992–93 Bradford C 42 17
1993–94 Bradford C 18 14 131 60
1993–94 Oldham Ath 20 4
1994–95 Oldham Ath 39 18
1995–96 Oldham Ath 35 10
1996–97 Oldham Ath 21 3
1997–98 Oldham Ath 25 7 140 42
1997–98 *Bristol C* 1 1 1 1
1998–99 Plymouth Arg 16 3
1999–2000 Plymouth Arg 29 6
2000–01 Plymouth Arg 37 10 152 38
2001–02 Exeter C 26 6 26 6

McCONNELL, Barry (D) 141 15
H: 5 11 W: 10 10 b.Exeter 1-1-77
Source: Trainee.
1995–96 Exeter C 8 0
1996–97 Exeter C 34 0
1997–98 Exeter C 16 6
1998–99 Exeter C 22 5
1999–2000 Exeter C 25 1
2000–01 Exeter C 4 0
2001–02 Exeter C 32 3 141 15

MOOR, Reinier§ (F) 2 0
H: 5 10 W: 12 00 b.Holland 12-6-83
Source: Scholar.
2001–02 Exeter C 2 0 2 0

MUDGE, James (F) 3 0
H: 5 11 W: 11 09 b.Exeter 25-3-83
Source: Scholar.
2000–01 Exeter C 3 0
2001–02 Exeter C 0 0 3 0

POWER, Graeme (D) 167 2
H: 5 11 W: 11 07 b.Northwick Park 7-8-77
Source: Trainee. *Honours:* England Schools, Youth.
1994–95 QPR 0 0
1995–96 QPR 0 0
1996–97 Bristol R 16 0
1997–98 Bristol R 10 0 26 0
1998–99 Exeter C 40 0
1999–2000 Exeter C 29 0
2000–01 Exeter C 35 1
2001–02 Exeter C 37 1 141 2

READ, Paul* (F) 98 11
H: 5 8 W: 12 06 b.Harlow 25-9-73
Source: Trainee. *Honours:* England Schools.
1991–92 Arsenal 0 0
1992–93 Arsenal 0 0
1993–94 Arsenal 0 0
1994–95 Arsenal 0 0
1994–95 *Leyton Orient* 11 0 11 0
1995–96 Arsenal 0 0
1995–96 *Southend U* 4 1 4 1
1996–97 Arsenal 0 0
1996–97 Wycombe W 13 4
1997–98 Wycombe W 28 4
1998–99 Wycombe W 16 1
1999–2000 Wycombe W 0 0 57 9
From OFK Ostersund
2000–01 Exeter C 11 1
2001–02 Exeter C 15 0 26 1

RICHARDSON, Jay (M) 18 0
H: 5 9 W: 11 09 b.Kenton 14-11-79
Source: Trainee.
1997–98 Chelsea 0 0
1998–99 Chelsea 0 0
1999–2000 Chelsea 0 0
2000–01 Chelsea 0 0
2001–02 Exeter C 18 0 18 0

ROSCOE, Andy (M) 325 28
H: 5 9 W: 12 00 b.Liverpool 4-6-73
Source: Trainee.

1991–92	Liverpool	0	0	
1992–93	Bolton W	0	0	
1993–94	Bolton W	3	0	
1994–95	Bolton W	0	0	3 0
1994–95	Rotherham U	31	4	
1995–96	Rotherham U	45	2	
1996–97	Rotherham U	43	0	
1997–98	Rotherham U	45	7	
1998–99	Rotherham U	38	5	202 18
1999–2000	Mansfield T	39	2	39 2
2000–01	Exeter C	43	1	
2001–02	Exeter C	38	7	81 8

TOMLINSON, Graeme* (F) 136 20
H: 5 10 W: 12 00 b.Watford 10-12-75
Source: Trainee.

1993–94	Bradford C	17	6	17 6
1994–95	Manchester U	0	0	
1995–96	Manchester U	0	0	
1995–96	*Luton T*	7	0	7 0
1996–97	Manchester U	0	0	
1997–98	Manchester U	0	0	
1997–98	*Bournemouth*	7	1	7 1
1997–98	*Millwall*	3	1	3 1
1998–99	Macclesfield T	28	4	
1999–2000	Macclesfield T	18	2	46 6
2000–01	Exeter C	24	1	
2001–02	Exeter C	32	5	56 6

VAN HEUSDEN, Arjan* (G) 154 0
H: 6 4 W: 14 05 b.Alphen 11-12-72
Source: Noordwijk.

1994–95	Port Vale	2	0	
1995–96	Port Vale	7	0	
1996–97	Port Vale	13	0	
1997–98	Port Vale	5	0	27 0
1997–98	*Oxford U*	11	0	11 0
1998–99	Cambridge U	27	0	
1999–2000	Cambridge U	15	0	42 0
2000–01	Exeter C	41	0	
2001–02	Exeter C	33	0	74 0

WALKER, Andy‡ (G) 4 0
H: 6 0 W: 12 03 b.Bexley 30-9-81

1998–99	Colchester U	1	0	
1999–2000	Colchester U	2	0	
2000–01	Colchester U	0	0	3 0
2001–02	Exeter C	1	0	1 0

WATSON, Alex (D) 415 15
H: 6 1 W: 12 00 b.Liverpool 5-4-68
Source: Apprentice. *Honours:* England Youth.

1984–85	Liverpool	0	0	
1985–86	Liverpool	0	0	
1986–87	Liverpool	0	0	
1987–88	Liverpool	2	0	
1988–89	Liverpool	2	0	
1989–90	Liverpool	0	0	
1990–91	Liverpool	0	0	4 0
1990–91	*Derby Co*	0	0	5 0
1990–91	Bournemouth	23	3	
1991–92	Bournemouth	15	0	
1992–93	Bournemouth	46	1	
1993–94	Bournemouth	45	1	
1994–95	Bournemouth	22	0	
1995–96	Bournemouth	0	0	151 5
1995–96	*Gillingham*	10	1	10 1
1995–96	Torquay U	29	2	
1996–97	Torquay U	46	1	
1997–98	Torquay U	46	1	
1998–99	Torquay U	8	0	
1999–2000	Torquay U	43	4	
2000–01	Torquay U	30	0	202 8
2001–02	Exeter C	43	1	43 1

WHITWORTH, Neil (D) 179 7
H: 6 0 W: 12 13 b.Ince 12-4-72
Source: Trainee. *Honours:* England Youth.

1989–90	Wigan Ath	2	0	
1990–91	Manchester U	0	0	
1991–92	Manchester U	0	0	
1991–92	*Preston NE*	6	0	6 0
1991–92	*Barnsley*	11	0	11 0
1992–93	Manchester U	0	0	
1992–93	*Rotherham U*	8	1	8 1
1993–94	*Blackpool*	3	0	3 0
1994–95	Kilmarnock	30	3	
1995–96	Kilmarnock	28	0	
1996–97	Kilmarnock	7	0	
1997–98	Kilmarnock	11	0	76 3
1997–98	Wigan Ath	4	0	4 0
1998–99	Hull C	18	2	
1999–2000	Hull C	1	0	19 2
2000–01	Exeter C	34	1	
2001–02	Exeter C	15	0	49 1

ZABEK, Lee* (M) 62 1
H: 6 0 W: 10 10 b.Bristol 13-10-78
Source: Trainee.

1996–97	Bristol R	1	0	
1997–98	Bristol R	13	1	
1998–99	Bristol R	11	0	
1999–2000	Bristol R	4	0	29 1
2000–01	Exeter C	31	0	
2001–02	Exeter C	2	0	33 0

Scholars
Afful, Leslie S; Arscott, Michael J; Bowker, Scott; Bradford, Jamie; Bull, James J; Canham, Sean; Drake, David; Gillingham, Michael J; Goff, Shaun J; Harris, Ben; Johns, Steven S; Lock, Matthew J; McShane, Kevin JP; Moor, Reinier S; Murphy, Nathan J; Parker, Lee; Reed, Lewis C; Tippett, Rhys J
Players who do not hold a current contract but their registration has been retained by the club
Breslan, Gavin; Mudge, James

FULHAM

BOA MORTE, Luis (F) 101 20
H: 5 10 W: 11 10 b.Lisbon 4-8-77
Source: Sporting Lisbon, Lourihanense (loan). *Honours:* Portugal Under-21, 2 full caps.

1997–98	Arsenal	15	0	
1998–99	Arsenal	8	0	
1999–2000	Arsenal	2	0	25 0
1999–2000	Southampton	14	1	
2000–01	Southampton	0	0	14 1
2000–01	*Fulham*	39	18	
2001–02	Fulham	23	1	62 19

BREVETT, Rufus (D) 414 5
H: 5 8 W: 11 13 b.Derby 24-9-69
Source: Trainee.

1987–88	Doncaster R	17	0	
1988–89	Doncaster R	23	0	
1989–90	Doncaster R	42	0	
1990–91	Doncaster R	27	3	109 3
1990–91	QPR	10	0	
1991–92	QPR	7	0	
1992–93	QPR	15	0	
1993–94	QPR	7	0	
1994–95	QPR	19	0	
1995–96	QPR	27	1	
1996–97	QPR	44	0	
1997–98	QPR	23	0	152 1
1997–98	Fulham	11	0	
1998–99	Fulham	45	1	
1999–2000	Fulham	23	0	
2000–01	Fulham	39	0	
2001–02	Fulham	35	0	153 1

CLARK, Lee (M) 364 54
H: 5 8 W: 11 10 b.Wallsend 27-10-72
Source: Trainee. *Honours:* England Schools, Youth, Under-21.

1989–90	Newcastle U	0	0	
1990–91	Newcastle U	19	2	
1991–92	Newcastle U	29	5	
1992–93	Newcastle U	46	9	
1993–94	Newcastle U	29	2	
1994–95	Newcastle U	19	1	
1995–96	Newcastle U	28	2	
1996–97	Newcastle U	25	2	195 23
1997–98	Sunderland	46	13	
1998–99	Sunderland	27	3	73 16
1999–2000	Fulham	42	8	
2000–01	Fulham	45	7	
2001–02	Fulham	9	0	96 15

COLEMAN, Chris (D) 478 23
H: 6 2 W: 14 07 b.Swansea 10-6-70
Source: Apprentice. *Honours:* Wales Schools, Youth, Under-21, 32 full caps, 4 goals.

1987–88	Swansea C	30	0	
1988–89	Swansea C	43	0	
1989–90	Swansea C	46	2	
1990–91	Swansea C	41	0	160 2
1991–92	Crystal Palace	18	4	
1992–93	Crystal Palace	38	5	
1993–94	Crystal Palace	46	3	
1994–95	Crystal Palace	35	1	
1995–96	Crystal Palace	17	0	154 13
1995–96	Blackburn R	20	0	
1996–97	Blackburn R	8	0	
1997–98	Blackburn R	0	0	28 0
1997–98	Fulham	26	1	
1998–99	Fulham	45	4	
1999–2000	Fulham	40	3	
2000–01	Fulham	25	0	
2001–02	Fulham	0	0	136 8

COLLINS, John (M) 549 76
H: 5 8 W: 10 10 b.Galashiels 31-1-68
Source: Hutchison Vale BC. *Honours:* Scotland Youth, Under-21, 58 full caps, 12 goals.

1984–85	Hibernian	0	0	
1985–86	Hibernian	19	1	
1986–87	Hibernian	30	1	
1987–88	Hibernian	44	6	
1988–89	Hibernian	35	2	
1989–90	Hibernian	35	6	163 16
1990–91	Celtic	35	1	
1991–92	Celtic	38	11	
1992–93	Celtic	43	8	
1993–94	Celtic	38	8	
1994–95	Celtic	34	8	
1995–96	Celtic	29	11	217 47
1996–97	Monaco	28	6	
1997–98	Monaco	25	1	53 7
1998–99	Everton	20	1	
1999–2000	Everton	35	2	55 3
2000–01	Fulham	27	3	
2001–02	Fulham	34	0	61 3

CORNWALL, Luke (F) 14 5
H: 5 10 W: 10 02 b.Lambeth 23-7-80
Source: Trainee.

1998–99	Fulham	4	1	
1999–2000	Fulham	0	0	
2000–01	Fulham	0	0	
2000–01	*Grimsby T*	10	4	10 4
2001–02	Fulham	0	0	4 1

DAVIS, Sean (M) 103 6
H: 5 9 W: 12 09 b.Lambeth 20-9-79
Source: Trainee. *Honours:* England Under-21.

1996–97	Fulham	1	0	
1997–98	Fulham	0	0	
1998–99	Fulham	6	0	
1999–2000	Fulham	26	0	
2000–01	Fulham	40	6	
2001–02	Fulham	30	0	103 6

DOHERTY, Sean (M) 0 0
H: 5 8 W: 10 00 b.Basingstoke 10-5-85
Source: Scholar. *Honours:* England Youth.

2001–02	Fulham	0	0	

FINNAN, Steve (D) 252 14
H: 5 10 W: 12 04 b.Limerick 20-4-76
Source: Welling U. *Honours:* Eire 19 full caps, 1 goal.

1995–96	Birmingham C	12	1	
1995–96	*Notts Co*	17	2	
1996–97	Birmingham C	3	0	15 1
1996–97	Notts Co	23	0	
1997–98	Notts Co	44	5	
1998–99	Notts Co	13	0	97 7
1998–99	Fulham	22	2	
1999–2000	Fulham	35	2	
2000–01	Fulham	45	2	
2001–02	Fulham	38	0	140 6

GOLDBAEK, Bjarne (M) 287 41
H: 5 10 W: 12 04 b.Denmark 6-10-68
Honours: Denmark 28 full caps.

1991–92	Kaiserslautern	24	2	
1992–93	Kaiserslautern	28	5	
1993–94	Kaiserslautern	3	0	55 7
1993–94	Tennis Borussia	24	5	24 5
1994–95	Cologne	14	0	
1995–96	Cologne	16	2	30 2
1996–97	FC Copenhagen	32	7	
1997–98	FC Copenhagen	30	6	
1998–99	FC Copenhagen	12	3	74 16
1998–99	Chelsea	23	5	
1999–2000	Chelsea	6	0	29 5
1999–2000	Fulham	18	3	
2000–01	Fulham	44	2	
2001–02	Fulham	13	1	75 6

GOMA, Alain (D) 265 5
H: 6 0 W: 13 05 b.Sault 15-10-72
Honours: France 2 full caps.

1990–91	Auxerre	1	0	
1991–92	Auxerre	1	0	
1992–93	Auxerre	15	1	
1993–94	Auxerre	33	0	
1994–95	Auxerre	28	0	
1995–96	Auxerre	33	0	
1996–97	Auxerre	34	2	
1997–98	Auxerre	22	1	166 4
1998–99	Paris St Germain	30	0	30 0
1999–2000	Newcastle U	14	0	
2000–01	Newcastle U	19	1	33 1
2000–01	Fulham	3	0	
2001–02	Fulham	33	0	36 0

HAHNEMANN, Marcus* (G) 79 0
H: 6 3 W: 16 02 b.Seattle 15-6-72
Honours: USA 4 full caps.
1997   Colorado Rapids 25 0
1998   Colorado Rapids 28 0
1999   Colorado Rapids 13 0 66 0
1999–2000 Fulham   0 0
2000–01   Fulham   2 0
2001–02   Fulham   0 0 2 0
2001–02   *Rochdale*   5 0 5 0
2001–02   *Reading*   6 0 6 0

HAMMOND, Elvis (F) 7 0
H: 5 10 W: 11 06 b.Accra 6-10-80
Source: Trainee.
1999–2000 Fulham   0 0
2000–01   Fulham   0 0
2001–02   Fulham   0 0
2001–02   *Bristol R*   7 0 7 0

HARLEY, Jon (D) 46 4
H: 5 9 W: 11 05 b.Maidstone 26-9-79
Source: Trainee. *Honours:* England Under-21.
1996–97   Chelsea   0 0
1997–98   Chelsea   3 0
1998–99   Chelsea   0 0
1999–2000 Chelsea   17 2
2000–01   Chelsea   10 0 30 2
2000–01   *Wimbledon*   6 2 6 2
2001–02   Fulham   10 0 10 0

HAYLES, Barry (F) 197 71
H: 5 10 W: 12 11 b.Lambeth 17-5-72
Source: Stevenage Bor. *Honours:* Jamaica 6 full caps.
1997–98   Bristol R   45 23
1998–99   Bristol R   17 9 62 32
1998–99   Fulham   30 8
1999–2000 Fulham   35 5
2000–01   Fulham   35 18
2001–02   Fulham   35 8 135 39

HUDSON, Mark (D) 0 0
H: 6 3 W: 12 06 b.Guildford 30-3-82
Source: Trainee.
1998–99   Fulham   0 0
1999–2000 Fulham   0 0
2000–01   Fulham   0 0
2001–02   Fulham   0 0

HUTCHINSON, Tom (D) 0 0
H: 6 1 W: 12 06 b.Kingston 23-2-82
1998–99   Fulham   0 0
1999–2000 Fulham   0 0
2000–01   Fulham   0 0
2001–02   Fulham   0 0

KNIGHT, Zat (D) 18 0
H: 6 6 W: 14 06 b.Solihull 2-5-80
Honours: England Under-21.
1998–99   Fulham   0 0
1999–2000 Fulham   0 0
1999–2000 *Peterborough U* 8 0 8 0
2000–01   Fulham   0 0
2001–02   Fulham   10 0 10 0

LEGWINSKI, Sylvain (M) 203 18
H: 6 1 W: 11 10 b.Clermont-Ferrand 6-10-73
1992–93   Monaco   2 0
1993–94   Monaco   0 0
1994–95   Monaco   21 1
1995–96   Monaco   29 2
1996–97   Monaco   37 9
1997–98   Monaco   22 0
1998–99   Monaco   14 1 125 13
1999–2000 Bordeaux   13 1
2000–01   Bordeaux   32 1 45 2
2001–02   Fulham   33 3 33 3

LEWIS, Eddie (M) 131 9
H: 5 10 W: 10 13 b.California 17-5-74
Honours: USA 43 full caps, 3 goals.
1996   San Jose Clash 25 0
1997   San Jose Clash 29 2
1998   San Jose Clash 32 3
1999   San Jose Clash 29 4 115 9
1999–2000 Fulham   8 0
2000–01   Fulham   7 0
2001–02   Fulham   1 0 16 0

MALBRANQUE, Steed (M) 114 13
H: 5 8 W: 11 10 b.Mouscron 6-1-80
1997–98   Lyon   2 0
1998–99   Lyon   21 0
1999–2000 Lyon   28 3
2000–01   Lyon   26 2 77 5
2001–02   Lyon   37 8 37 8

MARLET, Steve (F) 164 43
H: 5 11 W: 11 10 b.Pithiviers 1-10-74
Honours: France 8 full caps, 2 goals.
1996–97   Auxerre   24 3
1997–98   Auxerre   18 6
1998–99   Auxerre   32 7
1999–2000 Auxerre   33 9 107 25
2000–01   Lyon   31 12 31 12
2001–02   Fulham   26 6 26 6

McANESPIE, Kieran (D) 57 6
H: 5 8 W: 11 06 b.Gosport 11-9-79
Source: St Johnstone BC. *Honours:* Scotland Under-17, Under-21.
1995–96   St Johnstone   0 0
1996–97   St Johnstone   9 2
1997–98   St Johnstone   3 0
1998–99   St Johnstone   18 2
1999–2000 St Johnstone   20 1 50 5
2000–01   Fulham   0 0
2001–02   Fulham   2 0
2001–02   *Bournemouth*   7 1 7 1

McFREDERICK, William‡ (M) 0 0
b.Enniskillen 24-2-85
2001–02   Fulham   0 0

MELVILLE, Andy (D) 638 54
H: 6 1 W: 12 13 b.Swansea 29-11-68
Source: School. *Honours:* Wales Under-21, B, 51 full caps, 3 goals.
1985–86   Swansea C   1 0
1986–87   Swansea C   42 3
1987–88   Swansea C   37 4
1988–89   Swansea C   45 10
1989–90   Swansea C   46 5 175 22
1990–91   Oxford U   42 3
1991–92   Oxford U   45 4
1992–93   Oxford U   44 6 135 13
1993–94   Sunderland   44 2
1994–95   Sunderland   36 3
1995–96   Sunderland   40 4
1996–97   Sunderland   30 2
1997–98   Sunderland   10 1
1997–98   *Bradford C*   6 1 6 1
1998–99   Sunderland   44 2 204 14
1999–2000 Fulham   40 3
2000–01   Fulham   43 1
2001–02   Fulham   35 0 118 4

OUADDOU, Abdes (D) 55 0
H: 6 4 W: 12 03 b.Ksar-Askour 1-11-78
Honours: Morocco full caps.
1999–2000 Nancy   16 0
2000–01   Nancy   31 0 47 0
2001–02   Fulham   8 0 8 0

PRATLEY, Darren (F) 0 0
H: 6 0 W: 10 13 b.Barking 22-4-85
Source: Scholar.
2001–02   Fulham   0 0

REHMAN, Zesh (M) 0 0
H: 6 2 W: 12 09 b.Birmingham 14-10-83
Source: Scholar. *Honours:* England Youth.
2001–02   Fulham   0 0

SAHA, Louis (F) 137 41
H: 6 1 W: 12 06 b.Paris 8-8-78
1997–98   Metz   21 1
1998–99   Metz   3 0
1998–99   Newcastle U   11 1 11 1
1999–2000 Metz   23 4 47 5
2000–01   Fulham   43 27
2001–02   Fulham   36 8 79 35

SHEVEL, David (M) 0 0
H: 5 8 W: 9 10 b.Croydon 14-9-83
Source: Scholar.
2000–01   Fulham   0 0
2001–02   Fulham   0 0

STOLCERS, Andrejs (M) 130 36
H: 5 11 W: 11 00 b.Latvia 8-7-74
Honours: Latvia 57 full caps, 7 goals.
1996   Skonto Riga   26 6
1997   Skonto Riga   23 9 49 15
1997–98   Shakhtar Donetsk 13 4
1998–99   Shakhtar Donetsk 21 6
1999–2000 Shakhtar Donetsk 15 4 49 14
2000   Spartak Moscow 12 5 12 5
2000–01   Fulham   15 2
2001–02   Fulham   5 0 20 2

TAYLOR, Maik (G) 253 0
H: 6 3 W: 14 02 b.Hildesheim 4-9-71
Source: Farnborough T. *Honours:* Northern Ireland Under-21, B, 21 full caps.
1995–96   Barnet   45 0
1996–97   Barnet   25 0 70 0
1996–97   Southampton   18 0
1997–98   Southampton   0 0 18 0
1997–98   Fulham   28 0
1998–99   Fulham   46 0
1999–2000 Fulham   46 0
2000–01   Fulham   44 0
2001–02   Fulham   1 0 165 0

THOMPSON, Glyn (G) 17 0
H: 6 2 W: 13 01 b.Telford 24-2-81
Source: Trainee.
1998–99   Shrewsbury T   1 0
1999–2000 Shrewsbury T   0 0
1999–2000 Fulham   0 0
1999–2000 *Mansfield T*   16 0 16 0
2000–01   Fulham   0 0
2001–02   *Shrewsbury T* 0 0 1 0
2001–02   Fulham   0 0

VAN DER SAR, Edwin (G) 329 1
H: 6 5 W: 14 08 b.Voorhout 29-10-70
Honours: Holland 66 full caps.
1990–91   Ajax   9 0
1991–92   Ajax   0 0
1992–93   Ajax   19 0
1993–94   Ajax   32 0
1994–95   Ajax   33 0
1995–96   Ajax   33 0
1996–97   Ajax   33 0
1997–98   Ajax   33 1 192 1
1998–99   Juventus   34 0
1999–2000 Juventus   32 0
2000–01   Juventus   34 0 100 0
2001–02   Fulham   37 0 37 0

WILLOCK, Calum (F) 3 0
H: 6 0 W: 12 09 b.London 29-10-81
Source: Scholar. *Honours:* England Schools.
2000–01   Fulham   1 0
2001–02   Fulham   2 0 3 0

Trainees
Buari, Malik; Davis, Thomas; Flitney, Ross; Green, Adam; Leacock, Dean; Lock, Christopher; McClements, Eddie; McFrederick, William S; Noble, Stuart W; Timlin, Michael

GILLINGHAM

ASHBY, Barry (D) 425 13
H: 6 1 W: 14 04 b.London 2-11-70
Source: Trainee.
1988–89   Watford   0 0
1989–90   Watford   18 1
1990–91   Watford   23 0
1991–92   Watford   21 0
1992–93   Watford   35 0
1993–94   Watford   17 2 114 3
1993–94   Brentford   8 1
1994–95   Brentford   40 1
1995–96   Brentford   33 1
1996–97   Brentford   40 1 121 4
1997–98   Gillingham   43 0
1998–99   Gillingham   38 1
1999–2000 Gillingham   41 3
2000–01   Gillingham   40 1
2001–02   Gillingham   28 1 190 6

BARTRAM, Vince (G) 347 0
H: 6 2 W: 15 04 b.Birmingham 7-8-68
Source: Local.
1985–86   Wolverhampton W 0 0
1986–87   Wolverhampton W 1 0
1987–88   Wolverhampton W 0 0
1988–89   Wolverhampton W 0 0
1989–90   Wolverhampton W 0 0
1989–90   *Blackpool*   9 0 9 0
1990–91   Wolverhampton W 4 0
1990–91   WBA   0 0
1991–92   Bournemouth   46 0
1992–93   Bournemouth   45 0
1993–94   Bournemouth   41 0 132 0
1994–95   Arsenal   11 0
1995–96   Arsenal   9 0
1996–97   Arsenal   0 0
1996–97   *Wolverhampton W* 0 0 5 0
1997–98   Arsenal   0 0 11 0
1997–98   *Huddersfield T* 12 0 12 0
1997–98   Gillingham   9 0
1998–99   Gillingham   44 0
1999–2000 Gillingham   43 0
2000–01   Gillingham   46 0
2001–02   Gillingham   36 0 178 0

BROWN, Jason (G) 10 0
H: 6 0 W: 15 05 b.Southwark 18-5-82
Source: Charlton Ath Scholar.
2000–01   Gillingham   0 0
2001–02   Gillingham   10 0 10 0

BROWNING, Marcus* (M) 292 21
H: 6 0 W: 13 02 b.Bristol 22-4-71
Source: Trainee. *Honours:* Wales 5 full caps.
1989–90   Bristol R   1 0
1990–91   Bristol R   0 0
1991–92   Bristol R   11 0
1992–93   Bristol R   19 1
1992–93   *Hereford U*   7 5 7 5

1993–94	Bristol R	31	4		
1994–95	Bristol R	41	2		
1995–96	Bristol R	45	4		
1996–97	Bristol R	26	2	174	13
1996–97	Huddersfield T	13	0		
1997–98	Huddersfield T	14	0		
1998–99	Huddersfield T	6	0	33	0
1998–99	Gillingham	4	0		
1999–2000	Gillingham	1	0		
2000–01	Gillingham	31	0		
2001–02	Gillingham	42	3	78	3

BUTTERS, Guy (D)   367   27
H: 6 2   W: 16 04   b.Hillingdon 30-10-69
Source: Trainee. *Honours:* England Under-21.

1988–89	Tottenham H	28	1		
1989–90	Tottenham H	7	0	35	1
1989–90	Southend U	16	3	16	3
1990–91	Portsmouth	23	0		
1991–92	Portsmouth	33	2		
1992–93	Portsmouth	15	1		
1993–94	Portsmouth	15	1		
1994–95	Portsmouth	24	0		
1994–95	Oxford U	3	1	3	1
1995–96	Portsmouth	37	2		
1996–97	Portsmouth	7	0	154	6
1996–97	Gillingham	30	0		
1997–98	Gillingham	31	7		
1998–99	Gillingham	23	3		
1999–2000	Gillingham	40	2		
2000–01	Gillingham	12	3		
2001–02	Gillingham	23	1	159	16

CROFTS, Andrew§ (D)   1   0
H: 5 9   W: 10 02   b.Chatham 29-5-84
Source: Trainee.

2000–01	Gillingham	1	0		
2001–02	Gillingham	0	0	1	0

EDGE, Roland (D)   68   1
H: 5 9   W: 12 09   b.Gillingham 25-11-78
Source: Trainee.

1997–98	Gillingham	0	0		
1998–99	Gillingham	8	0		
1999–2000	Gillingham	26	1		
2000–01	Gillingham	20	0		
2001–02	Gillingham	14	0	68	1

GOODEN, Ty (M)   205   14
H: 5 8   W: 12 08   b.Canvey Island 23-10-72
Source: Arsenal, Wycombe W.

1993–94	Swindon T	4	0		
1994–95	Swindon T	16	2		
1995–96	Swindon T	26	3		
1996–97	Swindon T	13	1		
1997–98	Swindon T	39	2		
1998–99	Swindon T	38	1		
1999–2000	Swindon T	10	0	146	9
1999–2000	Gillingham	16	4		
2000–01	Gillingham	18	0		
2001–02	Gillingham	25	1	59	5

HESSENTHALER, Andy (M)   396   27
H: 5 7   W: 11 10   b.Gravesend 17-6-65
Source: Dartford, Redbridge Forest.

1991–92	Watford	35	1		
1992–93	Watford	45	3		
1993–94	Watford	42	5		
1994–95	Watford	43	2		
1995–96	Watford	30	0	195	11
1996–97	Gillingham	38	2		
1997–98	Gillingham	42	0		
1998–99	Gillingham	39	7		
1999–2000	Gillingham	42	5		
2000–01	Gillingham	23	2		
2001–02	Gillingham	17	0	201	16

HOPE, Chris (D)   379   25
H: 6 1   W: 12 11   b.Sheffield 14-11-72
Source: Darlington.

1991–92	Nottingham F	0	0		
1992–93	Nottingham F	0	0		
1993–94	Scunthorpe U	41	0		
1994–95	Scunthorpe U	24	0		
1995–96	Scunthorpe U	40	3		
1996–97	Scunthorpe U	46	3		
1997–98	Scunthorpe U	46	5		
1998–99	Scunthorpe U	46	5		
1999–2000	Scunthorpe U	44	3	287	19
2000–01	Gillingham	46	2		
2001–02	Gillingham	46	4	92	6

IPOUA, Guy (F)   138   34
H: 6 0   W: 13 13   b.Douala 14-1-76
Source: Atletico Madrid, Novelda.

1998–99	Bristol R	24	3	24	3
1999–2000	Scunthorpe U	40	9		
2000–01	Scunthorpe U	25	14	65	23
2000–01	Gillingham	9	0		
2001–02	Gillingham	40	8	49	8

JAMES, Kevin (F)   17   0
H: 5 7   W: 11 12   b.Southwark 3-1-80
Source: Trainee.

1998–99	Charlton Ath	0	0		
1999–2000	Charlton Ath	0	0		
2000–01	Gillingham	7	0		
2001–02	Gillingham	10	0	17	0

KING, Marlon (F)   133   46
H: 6 0   W: 12 10   b.Dulwich 26-4-80
Source: Trainee.

1998–99	Barnet	22	6		
1999–2000	Barnet	31	8	53	14
2000–01	Gillingham	38	15		
2001–02	Gillingham	42	17	80	32

LOVELL, Mark* (F)   1   0
H: 5 11   W: 12 07   b.Beckenham 16-7-83
Source: Trainee.

2000–01	Gillingham	1	0		
2001–02	Gillingham	0	0	1	0

NOSWORTHY, Nayron (D)   71   1
H: 6 1   W: 12 10   b.London 11-10-80
Source: Trainee.

1998–99	Gillingham	3	0		
1999–2000	Gillingham	29	1		
2000–01	Gillingham	10	0		
2001–02	Gillingham	29	0	71	1

ONUORA, Iffy* (F)   414   112
H: 6 2   W: 14 08   b.Glasgow 28-7-67
Source: British Univ.

1989–90	Huddersfield T	20	3		
1990–91	Huddersfield T	43	7		
1991–92	Huddersfield T	41	8		
1992–93	Huddersfield T	39	6		
1993–94	Huddersfield T	22	6	165	30
1994–95	Mansfield T	14	7		
1995–96	Mansfield T	14	1	28	8
1996–97	Gillingham	40	21		
1997–98	Gillingham	22	2		
1997–98	Swindon T	6	1		
1998–99	Swindon T	43	20		
1999–2000	Swindon T	24	4	73	25
1999–2000	Gillingham	22	6		
2000–01	Gillingham	31	9		
2001–02	Gillingham	33	11	148	49

OSBORN, Simon (M)   302   27
H: 5 8   W: 11 08   b.New Addington 19-1-72
Source: Apprentice.

1989–90	Crystal Palace	0	0		
1990–91	Crystal Palace	4	0		
1991–92	Crystal Palace	14	2		
1992–93	Crystal Palace	31	2		
1993–94	Crystal Palace	6	1	55	5
1994–95	Reading	32	5	32	5
1995–96	QPR	9	1	9	1
1995–96	Wolverhampton W	21	2		
1996–97	Wolverhampton W	35	5		
1997–98	Wolverhampton W	24	2		
1998–99	Wolverhampton W	37	2		
1999–2000	Wolverhampton W	25	0		
2000–01	Wolverhampton W	20	0	162	11
2000–01	Tranmere R	9	1	9	1
2001–02	Port Vale	7	0	7	0
2001–02	Gillingham	28	4	28	4

PATTERSON, Mark (D)   329   8
H: 5 8   W: 12 08   b.Leeds 13-9-68
Source: Trainee.

1986–87	Carlisle U	6	0		
1987–88	Carlisle U	16	0	22	0
1987–88	Derby Co	0	0		
1988–89	Derby Co	1	0		
1989–90	Derby Co	9	0		
1990–91	Derby Co	11	1		
1991–92	Derby Co	12	2		
1992–93	Derby Co	18	0	51	3
1993–94	Plymouth Arg	41	0		
1994–95	Plymouth Arg	38	3		
1995–96	Plymouth Arg	43	0		
1996–97	Plymouth Arg	12	0		
1997–98	Plymouth Arg	0	0	134	3
1997–98	Gillingham	23	0		
1998–99	Gillingham	42	2		
1999–2000	Gillingham	9	0		
2000–01	Gillingham	28	0		
2001–02	Gillingham	20	0	122	2

PENNOCK, Adrian (D)   297   11
H: 6 1   W: 14 03   b.Ipswich 27-3-71

1989–90	Norwich C	1	0		
1990–91	Norwich C	0	0		
1991–92	Norwich C	0	0	1	0
1992–93	Bournemouth	43	1		
1993–94	Bournemouth	40	3		
1994–95	Bournemouth	31	5		
1995–96	Bournemouth	17	0		
1996–97	Bournemouth	0	0	131	9

1996–97	Gillingham	26	2		
1997–98	Gillingham	20	0		
1998–99	Gillingham	40	0		
1999–2000	Gillingham	34	0		
2000–01	Gillingham	35	0		
2001–02	Gillingham	10	0	165	2

PERPETUINI, David (M)   53   2
H: 5 10   W: 12 01   b.Hitchin 26-9-79
Source: Trainee.

1997–98	Watford	0	0		
1998–99	Watford	1	0		
1999–2000	Watford	13	1		
2000–01	Watford	5	0	19	1
2001–02	Gillingham	34	1	34	1

PHILLIPS, Michael (M)   1   0
H: 5 10   W: 10 00   b.Camberwell 22-1-83
Source: Trainee.

2000–01	Gillingham	1	0		
2001–02	Gillingham	0	0	1	0

ROSE, Richard (D)   7   0
H: 6 0   W: 11 07   b.Pembury 8-9-82

2000–01	Gillingham	4	0		
2001–02	Gillingham	3	0	7	0

SAUNDERS, Mark* (M)   186   22
H: 6 0   W: 12 07   b.Reading 23-7-71
Source: Tiverton.

1995–96	Plymouth Arg	10	1		
1996–97	Plymouth Arg	25	3		
1997–98	Plymouth Arg	37	7	72	11
1998–99	Gillingham	34	4		
1999–2000	Gillingham	26	1		
2000–01	Gillingham	35	5		
2001–02	Gillingham	19	1	114	11

SHAW, Paul (F)   218   45
H: 5 11   W: 13 03   b.Burnham 4-9-73
Source: Trainee.

1991–92	Arsenal	0	0		
1992–93	Arsenal	0	0		
1993–94	Arsenal	1	0		
1994–95	Arsenal	9	4	9	4
1995–96	Burnley	9	4		
1995–96	Arsenal	3	0		
1995–96	Cardiff C	6	0	6	0
1995–96	Peterborough U	12	5	12	5
1996–97	Arsenal	8	2		
1997–98	Arsenal	0	0	12	2
1997–98	Millwall	40	11		
1998–99	Millwall	34	10		
1999–2000	Millwall	35	5	109	26
2000–01	Gillingham	33	1		
2001–02	Gillingham	37	7	70	8

SMITH, Paul (M)   402   27
H: 6 0   W: 14 00   b.East Ham 18-9-71
Source: Trainee.

1989–90	Southend U	10	1		
1990–91	Southend U	2	0		
1991–92	Southend U	0	0		
1992–93	Southend U	8	0	20	1
1993–94	Brentford	32	3		
1994–95	Brentford	35	3		
1995–96	Brentford	46	4		
1996–97	Brentford	46	1	159	11
1997–98	Gillingham	46	3		
1998–99	Gillingham	45	6		
1999–2000	Gillingham	44	1		
2000–01	Gillingham	42	3		
2001–02	Gillingham	46	2	223	15

SPILLER, Daniel (M)   1   0
H: 5 7   W: 11 01   b.Maidstone 10-10-81
Source: Trainee.

2000–01	Gillingham	0	0		
2001–02	Gillingham	1	0	1	0

WHITE, Ben (D)   0   0
H: 6 0   W: 14 01   b.Hastings 2-6-82
Source: Trainee.

2000–01	Gillingham	0	0		
2001–02	Gillingham	0	0		

Scholars

Awuah, Jones; Beckwith, Dean S; Benjamin, Ronayne; Crofts, Andrew L; Flaherty, Darren S; Green, Mark; Millar, James SBM; Peters, Ryan J; Vella, Daniel MT

GRIMSBY T

ALLEN, Bradley* (F)   205   52
H: 5 8   W: 11 00   b.Harold Wood 13-9-71
Source: School. *Honours:* England Youth, Under-21.

1988–89	QPR	1	0		
1989–90	QPR	0	0		
1990–91	QPR	10	2		
1991–92	QPR	11	5		

1992–93	QPR	25	10	
1993–94	QPR	21	7	
1994–95	QPR	5	2	
1995–96	QPR	8	1	81 27
1995–96	Charlton Ath	10	3	
1996–97	Charlton Ath	18	4	
1997–98	Charlton Ath	12	2	
1998–99	Charlton Ath	0	0	40 9
1998–99	Colchester U	4	1	4 1
1999–2000	Grimsby T	31	8	
2000–01	Grimsby T	21	3	
2001–02	Grimsby T	28	4	80 15

BOLDER, Chris (M) 0 0
H: 5 11 W: 12 00 b.Hull 19-8-82
Source: Hull C scholar.
2001–02 Grimsby T 0 0

BOULDING, Mick* (F) 101 23
H: 5 10 W: 11 03 b.Sheffield 8-2-76
1999–2000 Mansfield T 33 6
2000–01 Mansfield T 33 6
2001–02 Mansfield T 0 0 66 12
2001–02 Grimsby T 35 11 35 11

BURNETT, Wayne* (M) 268 9
H: 5 11 W: 12 07 b.Lambeth 4-9-71
Source: Trainee.
1989–90 Leyton Orient 3 0
1990–91 Leyton Orient 1 0
1991–92 Leyton Orient 36 0 40 0
1992–93 Blackburn R 0 0
1993–94 Plymouth Arg 32 2
1994–95 Plymouth Arg 32 1
1995–96 Plymouth Arg 6 0 70 3
1995–96 Bolton W 1 0
1996–97 Bolton W 1 0 2 0
1996–97 Huddersfield T 35 0
1997–98 Huddersfield T 15 0 50 0
1997–98 Grimsby T 21 1
1998–99 Grimsby T 20 2
1999–2000 Grimsby T 10 0
2000–01 Grimsby T 23 1
2001–02 Grimsby T 32 2 106 6

BUSSCHER, Robbie‡ (M) 1 0
H: 5 8 W: 11 05 b.Leischenden 23-11-82
Source: Feyenoord.
2001–02 Grimsby T 1 0 1 0

BUTTERFIELD, Danny* (D) 124 3
H: 5 10 W: 11 06 b.Boston 21-11-79
Source: Trainee. Honours: England Youth.
1997–98 Grimsby T 7 0
1998–99 Grimsby T 12 0
1999–2000 Grimsby T 29 0
2000–01 Grimsby T 30 1
2001–02 Grimsby T 46 2 124 3

CAMPBELL, Stuart (M) 110 5
H: 5 10 W: 10 13 b.Corby 9-12-77
Source: Trainee. Honours: Scotland Under-21.
1996–97 Leicester C 10 0
1997–98 Leicester C 11 0
1998–99 Leicester C 12 0
1999–2000 Leicester C 4 0
1999–2000 Birmingham C 2 0 2 0
2000–01 Leicester C 0 0 37 0
2000–01 Grimsby T 38 2
2001–02 Grimsby T 33 3 71 5

CHAPMAN, Ben* (M) 21 0
H: 5 6 W: 11 05 b.Scunthorpe 2-3-79
Source: Trainee.
1997–98 Grimsby T 0 0
1998–99 Grimsby T 1 0
1999–2000 Grimsby T 1 0
2000–01 Grimsby T 2 0
2001–02 Grimsby T 17 0 21 0

COLDICOTT, Stacy (M) 254 6
H: 5 8 W: 12 08 b.Worcester 29-4-74
Source: Trainee.
1991–92 WBA 0 0
1992–93 WBA 14 0
1993–94 WBA 5 0
1994–95 WBA 11 0
1995–96 WBA 33 0
1996–97 WBA 19 3
1996–97 Cardiff C 6 0 6 0
1997–98 WBA 22 0 104 3
1998–99 Grimsby T 37 0
1999–2000 Grimsby T 44 2
2000–01 Grimsby T 37 1
2001–02 Grimsby T 26 0 144 3

COOKE, Terry (M) 88 10
H: 5 7 W: 10 08 b.Marston Green 5-8-76
Source: Trainee. Honours: England Youth, Under-21.
1994–95 Manchester U 0 0
1995–96 Manchester U 4 0
1995–96 Sunderland 6 0 6 0

1996–97 Manchester U 0 0
1996–97 Birmingham C 4 0 4 0
1997–98 Manchester U 0 0
1998–99 Manchester U 0 0 4 0
1998–99 Wrexham 10 0 10 0
1998–99 Manchester C 21 7
1999–2000 Manchester C 13 0
1999–2000 Wigan Ath 10 1 10 1
2000–01 Manchester C 0 0
2000–01 Sheffield W 17 1 17 1
2001–02 Manchester C 0 0 34 7
2001–02 Grimsby T 3 1 3 1

COYNE, Danny (G) 246 0
H: 6 0 W: 13 04 b.Prestatyn 27-8-73
Source: Trainee. Honours: Wales Schools, Youth, Under-21, B, 2 full caps.
1991–92 Tranmere R 0 0
1992–93 Tranmere R 1 0
1993–94 Tranmere R 5 0
1994–95 Tranmere R 5 0
1995–96 Tranmere R 46 0
1996–97 Tranmere R 21 0
1997–98 Tranmere R 16 0
1998–99 Tranmere R 17 0 111 0
1999–2000 Grimsby T 44 0
2000–01 Grimsby T 46 0
2001–02 Grimsby T 45 0 135 0

CRANLEY, Morgan‡ (M) 0 0
H: 5 10 W: 10 08 b.Dublin 12-1-84
2000–01 Grimsby T 0 0
2001–02 Grimsby T 0 0

CROUDSON, Steve (G) 10 0
H: 6 0 W: 11 12 b.Grimsby 14-9-79
Source: Trainee.
1998–99 Grimsby T 2 0
1999–2000 Grimsby T 3 0
2000–01 Grimsby T 0 0
2001–02 Scunthorpe U 4 0 4 0
2001–02 Grimsby T 1 0 6 0

ERMES, Ronald‡ (G) 0 0
H: 6 4 W: 13 00 b.Amsterdam 14-4-81
Source: Feyenoord.
2001–02 Grimsby T 0 0

FALCONER, Willie‡ (M) 456 74
H: 6 1 W: 11 09 b.Aberdeen 5-4-66
Source: Lewis United. Honours: Scotland Schools, Youth.
1982–83 Aberdeen 1 0
1983–84 Aberdeen 8 1
1984–85 Aberdeen 16 4
1985–86 Aberdeen 8 0
1986–87 Aberdeen 8 0
1987–88 Aberdeen 36 8 77 13
1988–89 Watford 33 5
1989–90 Watford 30 3
1990–91 Watford 35 4 98 12
1991–92 Middlesbrough 25 5
1992–93 Middlesbrough 28 5 53 10
1993–94 Sheffield U 23 3 23 3
1993–94 Celtic 14 1
1994–95 Celtic 26 4
1995–96 Celtic 2 0 42 5
1995–96 Motherwell 15 5
1996–97 Motherwell 21 2
1997–98 Motherwell 22 3 58 10
1998–99 Dundee 33 4
1999–2000 Dundee 31 13
2000–01 Dundee 14 1 78 18
2001–02 St Johnstone 25 3 25 3
2001–02 Grimsby T 2 0

FORD, Simon (D) 13 1
H: 6 1 W: 12 04 b.Lincoln 17-11-81
Source: Charlton Ath scholar.
2001–02 Grimsby T 13 1 13 1

GALLIMORE, Tony (D) 386 13
H: 5 11 W: 13 04 b.Crewe 21-2-72
Source: Trainee.
1989–90 Stoke C 1 0
1990–91 Stoke C 7 0
1991–92 Stoke C 3 0
1991–92 Carlisle U 16 0
1992–93 Stoke C 0 0 11 0
1992–93 Carlisle U 8 1
1993–94 Carlisle U 40 5
1994–95 Carlisle U 40 5
1995–96 Carlisle U 36 2 140 0
1995–96 Grimsby T 10 1
1996–97 Grimsby T 42 1
1997–98 Grimsby T 35 2
1998–99 Grimsby T 43 0
1999–2000 Grimsby T 39 0
2000–01 Grimsby T 28 0
2001–02 Grimsby T 38 0 235 4

GROVES, Paul (M) 567 95
H: 5 11 W: 13 04 b.Derby 28-2-66
Source: Burton Alb.
1987–88 Leicester C 1 1
1988–89 Leicester C 15 0
1989–90 Leicester C 0 0 16 1
1989–90 Lincoln C 8 1 8 1
1989–90 Blackpool 19 1
1990–91 Blackpool 46 11
1991–92 Blackpool 42 9 107 21
1992–93 Grimsby T 46 12
1993–94 Grimsby T 46 11
1994–95 Grimsby T 46 5
1995–96 Grimsby T 46 10
1996–97 WBA 29 4 29 4
1997–98 Grimsby T 46 7
1998–99 Grimsby T 46 14
1999–2000 Grimsby T 43 3
2000–01 Grimsby T 45 4
2001–02 Grimsby T 43 2 407 68

HOCKLESS, Graham* (M) 0 0
H: 5 7 W: 10 02 b.Hull 20-10-82
2001–02 Grimsby T 0 0

JEFFREY, Mike* (F) 262 54
H: 6 1 W: 11 09 b.Liverpool 11-8-71
Source: Trainee.
1988–89 Bolton W 9 0
1989–90 Bolton W 4 0
1990–91 Bolton W 0 0
1991–92 Bolton W 2 0 15 0
1991–92 Doncaster R 11 6
1992–93 Doncaster R 30 12
1993–94 Doncaster R 8 1 49 19
1993–94 Newcastle U 2 0
1994–95 Newcastle U 0 0 2 0
1995–96 Rotherham U 22 5 22 5
1995–96 Fortuna Sittard 19 4
1996–97 Fortuna Sittard 25 8
1997–98 Fortuna Sittard 31 8
1998–99 Fortuna Sittard 28 5 103 25
1999–2000 Kilmarnock 18 2 18 2
2000–01 Grimsby T 29 1
2001–02 Grimsby T 18 1 47 2
2001–02 Scunthorpe U 6 1 6 1

JEVONS, Phil (F) 39 6
H: 5 11 W: 12 00 b.Liverpool 1-8-79
Source: Trainee.
1996–97 Everton 0 0
1997–98 Everton 0 0
1998–99 Everton 1 0
1999–2000 Everton 3 0
2000–01 Everton 4 0 8 0
2001–02 Grimsby T 31 6 31 6

LIVINGSTONE, Steve (F) 326 55
H: 6 1 W: 15 03 b.Middlesbrough 8-9-68
Source: Trainee.
1986–87 Coventry C 3 0
1987–88 Coventry C 4 0
1988–89 Coventry C 1 0
1989–90 Coventry C 13 3
1990–91 Coventry C 10 2 31 5
1990–91 Blackburn R 18 9
1991–92 Blackburn R 10 1
1992–93 Blackburn R 2 0 30 10
1992–93 Chelsea 1 0
1993–94 Chelsea 0 0 1 0
1993–94 Port Vale 5 0 5 0
1993–94 Grimsby T 27 3
1994–95 Grimsby T 34 8
1995–96 Grimsby T 38 11
1996–97 Grimsby T 32 6
1997–98 Grimsby T 41 5
1998–99 Grimsby T 23 0
1999–2000 Grimsby T 29 0
2000–01 Grimsby T 32 7
2001–02 Grimsby T 3 0 259 40

McDERMOTT, John (D) 497 7
H: 5 7 W: 10 13 b.Middlesbrough 3-2-69
Source: Trainee.
1986–87 Grimsby T 13 0
1987–88 Grimsby T 28 0
1988–89 Grimsby T 38 1
1989–90 Grimsby T 39 0
1990–91 Grimsby T 43 0
1991–92 Grimsby T 39 1
1992–93 Grimsby T 38 2
1993–94 Grimsby T 26 0
1994–95 Grimsby T 12 0
1995–96 Grimsby T 28 1
1996–97 Grimsby T 29 1
1997–98 Grimsby T 41 1
1998–99 Grimsby T 37 0
1999–2000 Grimsby T 26 0
2000–01 Grimsby T 36 0
2001–02 Grimsby T 24 0 497 7

MORGAN, David‡ (D)   0 0
H: 5 10   W: 11 00   b.Middlesbrough 9-12-81
Source: Sunderland scholar.
2001–02   Grimsby T   0 0

MURRAY, Neil (M)   68 1
H: 5 9   W: 10 10   b.Bellshill 21-2-73
Source: Rangers Amateur. *Honours:* Scotland Schools, Under-21.
1989–90   Rangers   0 0
1990–91   Rangers   0 0
1991–92   Rangers   16 0
1992–93   Rangers   22 0
1993–94   Rangers   20 1
1995–96   Rangers   5 0   63 1
From Lorient.
1998–99   Dundee U   3 0
1999–2000   Dundee U   0 0   3 0
2000–01   Grimsby T   2 0
2001–02   Grimsby T   0 0   2 0

POUTON, Alan (M)   181 14
H: 6 0   W: 12 10   b.Newcastle 1-2-77
Source: Newcastle U Trainee.
1995–96   Oxford U   0 0
1995–96   York C   0 0
1996–97   York C   22 1
1997–98   York C   41 5
1998–99   York C   27 1
1999–2000   York C   0 0   90 7
1999–2000   Grimsby T   35 1
2000–01   Grimsby T   21 1
2001–02   Grimsby T   35 5   91 7

RAVEN, Paul (D)   353 21
H: 6 1   W: 12 11   b.Salisbury 28-7-70
Source: School. *Honours:* England Schools, Youth.
1987–88   Doncaster R   17 3
1988–89   Doncaster R   35 1
1988–89   WBA   3 0
1989–90   WBA   7 0
1990–91   WBA   13 0
1991–92   WBA   7 1
1991–92   *Doncaster R*   7 0   59 4
1992–93   WBA   44 7
1993–94   WBA   34 1
1994–95   WBA   31 0
1995–96   WBA   40 4
1996–97   WBA   33 1
1997–98   WBA   8 0
1998–99   WBA   7 0
1998–99   *Rotherham U*   11 2   11 2
1999–2000   WBA   32 1   259 15
2000–01   Grimsby T   15 0
2001–02   Grimsby T   9 0   24 0

ROWAN, Jonathan (F)   29 4
H: 5 10   W: 11 00   b.Grimsby 29-11-81
2000–01   Grimsby T   5 0
2001–02   Grimsby T   24 4   29 4

SMITH, David‡ (M)   407 33
H: 5 7   W: 11 11   b.Gloucester 29-5-68
Source: Apprentice. *Honours:* England Under-21.
1986–87   Coventry C   0 0
1987–88   Coventry C   16 4
1988–89   Coventry C   35 3
1989–90   Coventry C   37 6
1990–91   Coventry C   36 1
1991–92   Coventry C   24 4
1992–93   Coventry C   6 1   154 19
1992–93   *Bournemouth*   1 0   1 0
1992–93   Birmingham C   13 1
1993–94   Birmingham C   25 2   38 3
1993–94   WBA   18 0
1994–95   WBA   22 0
1995–96   WBA   16 0
1996–97   WBA   24 2
1997–98   WBA   22 0   102 2
1997–98   Grimsby T   17 1
1998–99   Grimsby T   31 5
1999–2000   Grimsby T   36 1
2000–01   Grimsby T   24 1
2001–02   Grimsby T   4 1   112 9

TAYLOR, Robert† (F)   351 114
H: 6 1   W: 13 08   b.Norwich 30-4-71
Source: Trainee.
1989–90   Norwich C   0 0
1990–91   Norwich C   0 0
1990–91   *Leyton Orient*   3 1
1991–92   Birmingham C   0 0
1991–92   Leyton Orient   11 1
1992–93   Leyton Orient   39 18
1993–94   Leyton Orient   23 1   76 21
1993–94   Brentford   5 2
1994–95   Brentford   43 23
1995–96   Brentford   42 11
1996–97   Brentford   43 7

1997–98   Brentford   40 13   173 56
1998–99   Gillingham   43 16
1999–2000   Gillingham   15 15
1999–2000   Manchester C   16 5   16 5
2000–01   Wolverhampton W   0 0
2001–02   Wolverhampton W   9 0   9 0
2001–02   QPR   4 0   4 0
2001–02   *Gillingham*   11 0   69 31
2001–02   Grimsby T   4 1   4 1

THOMPSON, Chris (F)   8 0
H: 5 10   W: 11 12   b.Warrington 7-2-82
Source: Liverpool scholar.
2001–02   Grimsby T   8 0   8 0

THOMPSON, Ross‡ (M)   0 0
H: 5 9   W: 11 08   b.Torquay 25-5-84
2001–02   Grimsby T   0 0

WARD, Iain (D)   1 0
H: 6 0   W: 10 10   b.Cleethorpes 13-5-83
2000–01   Grimsby T   0 0
2001–02   Grimsby T   1 0   1 0

WILLEMS, Menno (M)   92 3
H: 6 0   W: 11 13   b.Amsterdam 10-3-77
1996–97   Ajax   2 0   2 0
1997–98   Vitesse   11 1
1998–99   Vitesse   1 0
1999–2000   Den Bosch   24 0   24 0
2000–01   Vitesse   0 0   12 1
2000–01   Grimsby T   24 1
2001–02   Grimsby T   30 1   54 2

Scholars
Beesley, Lee G; Butterwood, Michael S; Carchedi, Giovanni R; Cass, Frederick A; Gibson, Thomas W; Haseley, Ashley; Hildred, Ashley; Kirwin, Jonathan G; Mansaram, Darren; Moran, Gary; Morfitt, Adrian J; Newton, Mark; Nimmo, Liam; Parker, Wesley; Soames, David M; Thorne, Sam; Wall, Christopher A; White, Russell
Non-Contract
Taylor, Robert A

HALIFAX T

BRACEWELL, Paul‡ (M)   587 22
H: 5 9   W: 12 03   b.Heswall 19-7-62
Source: Apprentice. *Honours:* England Under-21, 3 full caps.
1979–80   Stoke C   6 0
1980–81   Stoke C   40 2
1981–82   Stoke C   42 1
1982–83   Stoke C   41 2   129 5
1983–84   Sunderland   38 4
1984–85   Everton   37 2
1985–86   Everton   38 3
1986–87   Everton   0 0
1987–88   Everton   20 2
1988–89   Everton   0 0
1989–90   Everton   0 0   95 7
1989–90   Sunderland   37 2
1990–91   Sunderland   37 0
1991–92   Sunderland   39 0
1992–93   Newcastle U   25 2
1993–94   Newcastle U   32 1
1994–95   Newcastle U   16 0   73 3
1995–96   Sunderland   38 0
1996–97   Sunderland   38 0
1997–98   Sunderland   1 0   228 6
1997–98   Fulham   36 0
1998–99   Fulham   26 1
1999–2000   Fulham   0 0   62 1
2000–01   Halifax T   0 0
2001–02   Halifax T   0 0

BUSHELL, Steve‡ (M)   278 17
H: 5 8   W: 11 01   b.Manchester 28-12-72
Source: Trainee.
1990–91   York C   15 0
1991–92   York C   16 0
1992–93   York C   8 0
1993–94   York C   31 4
1994–95   York C   10 1
1995–96   York C   23 0
1996–97   York C   31 3
1997–98   York C   40 2   174 10
1998–99   Blackpool   31 3
1999–2000   Blackpool   24 2
2000–01   Blackpool   24 1   79 6
From Stalybridge C.
2001–02   Halifax T   25 1   25 1

BUTLER, Lee‡ (G)   355 0
H: 6 1   W: 13 08   b.Sheffield 30-5-66
Source: Haworth Colliery. *Honours:*
1986–87   Lincoln C   30 0   30 0
1987–88   Aston Villa   0 0
1988–89   Aston Villa   4 0

1989–90   Aston Villa   0 0
1990–91   Aston Villa   4 0   8 0
1990–91   *Hull C*   4 0   4 0
1991–92   Barnsley   43 0
1992–93   Barnsley   28 0
1993–94   Barnsley   37 0
1994–95   Barnsley   9 0
1995–96   Barnsley   3 0   120 0
1995–96   *Scunthorpe U*   2 0   2 0
1996–97   Wigan Ath   46 0
1997–98   Wigan Ath   17 0   63 0
1998–99   Dunfermline Ath   35 0   35 0
1999–2000   Halifax T   38 0
2000–01   Halifax T   33 0
2001–02   Halifax T   22 0   93 0

CLARKE, Matthew (F)   69 2
H: 6 3   W: 13 00   b.Leeds 18-12-80
Source: Wolverhampton W Trainee.
1999–2000   Halifax T   19 0
2000–01   Halifax T   19 1
2001–02   Halifax T   31 1   69 2

CROOKES, Peter* (G)   1 0
H: 6 0   W: 14 02   b.Liverpool 7-6-82
Source: Liverpool Scholar. *Honours:* England Schools.
2000–01   Halifax T   0 0
2001–02   Halifax T   1 0   1 0

FARRELL, Andy§ (F)   9 0
H: 5 11   W: 11 00   b.Easington 21-12-83
Source: Scholar.
2001–02   Halifax T   9 0   9 0

FITZPATRICK, Ian* (F)   49 10
H: 5 9   W: 11 00   b.Manchester 22-9-80
Source: Trainee. *Honours:* England Schools.
1998–99   Manchester U   0 0
1999–2000   Manchester U   0 0
1999–2000   Halifax T   8 0
2000–01   Halifax T   12 2
2001–02   Halifax T   29 8   49 10

HARSLEY, Paul (M)   173 16
H: 5 10   W: 11 11   b.Scunthorpe 29-5-78
Source: Trainee.
1996–97   Grimsby T   0 0
1997–98   Scunthorpe U   15 1
1998–99   Scunthorpe U   34 0
1999–2000   Scunthorpe U   46 3
2000–01   Scunthorpe U   33 1   128 5
2001–02   Halifax T   45 11   45 11

HEINEMANN, Nicky§ (F)   3 0
H: 6 0   W: 12 00   b.Bradford 4-1-85
Source: Scholar.
2001–02   Halifax T   3 0   3 0

HERBERT, Robert (M)   25 1
H: 5 10   W: 12 04   b.Durham 29-8-83
Source: Scholar.
1999–2000   Halifax T   4 0
2000–01   Halifax T   9 1
2001–02   Halifax T   12 0   25 1

JONES, Gary* (F)   343 80
H: 6 1   W: 12 00   b.Huddersfield 6-4-69
Source: Rossington Main.
1988–89   Doncaster R   17 2
1989–90   Doncaster R   3 0   20 2
From Boston U.
1993–94   Southend U   22 3
1993–94   *Lincoln C*   4 2   4 2
1994–95   Southend U   25 11
1995–96   Southend U   23 2   70 16
1995–96   Notts Co   18 5
1996–97   Notts Co   27 3
1996–97   *Scunthorpe U*   11 5   11 5
1997–98   Notts Co   44 28
1998–99   Notts Co   28 2   117 38
1998–99   Hartlepool U   12 1
1999–2000   Hartlepool U   33 6   45 7
1999–2000   *Halifax T*   8 1
2000–01   Halifax T   33 5
2001–02   Halifax T   35 4   76 10

JULES, Mark* (D)   360 21
H: 5 7   W: 12 01   b.Bradford 5-9-71
Source: Trainee.
1990–91   Bradford C   0 0
1991–92   Scarborough   41 8
1992–93   Scarborough   36 8   77 16
1993–94   Chesterfield   33 1
1994–95   Chesterfield   23 0
1995–96   Chesterfield   32 2
1996–97   Chesterfield   42 0
1997–98   Chesterfield   33 1
1998–99   Chesterfield   23 0   186 4
1999–2000   Halifax T   42 0
2000–01   Halifax T   20 1
2001–02   Halifax T   35 0   97 1

KERRIGAN, Steve (F) 291 73
H: 6 1 W: 12 01 b.Bailleston 9-10-72
Source: Newmains J.

1992-93	Albion R	29	8		
1993-94	Albion R	24	6	53	14
1993-94	Clydebank	15	0		
1994-95	Clydebank	14	0		
1995-96	Clydebank	1	0	30	0
1995-96	Stranraer	21	5	21	5
1996-97	Ayr U	27	14		
1997-98	Ayr U	6	3	33	17
1997-98	Shrewsbury T	14	2		
1998-99	Shrewsbury T	37	10		
1999-2000	Shrewsbury T	25	3	76	15
1999-2000	Halifax T	7	3		
2000-01	Halifax T	41	19		
2001-02	Halifax T	30	0	78	22

LUDDEN, Dominic (D) 130 1
H: 5 7 W: 10 09 b.Basildon 30-3-74
Source: Trainee. Honours: England Schools.

1992-93	Leyton Orient	24	1		
1993-94	Leyton Orient	34	0	58	1
1994-95	Watford	1	0		
1995-96	Watford	12	0		
1996-97	Watford	20	0		
1997-98	Watford	0	0	33	0
1998-99	Preston NE	32	0		
1999-2000	Preston NE	3	0		
2000-01	Preston NE	2	0		
2001-02	Preston NE	0	0	37	0
2001-02	Halifax T	2	0	2	0

MIDDLETON, Craig* (M) 263 28
H: 5 11 W: 12 03 b.Nuneaton 10-9-70
Source: Trainee.

1989-90	Coventry C	1	0		
1990-91	Coventry C	0	0		
1991-92	Coventry C	1	0		
1992-93	Coventry C	1	0	3	0
1993-94	Cambridge U	19	2		
1994-95	Cambridge U	0	0		
1995-96	Cambridge U	40	8	59	10
1996-97	Cardiff C	41	4		
1997-98	Cardiff C	33	0		
1998-99	Cardiff C	35	4		
1999-2000	Cardiff C	10	0	119	8
1999-2000	Plymouth Arg	6	2	6	2
1999-2000	Halifax T	10	1		
2000-01	Halifax T	37	5		
2001-02	Halifax T	29	2	76	8

MIDGLEY, Craig (F) 154 25
H: 5 7 W: 11 06 b.Hartlepool 24-5-76
Source: Trainee.

1994-95	Bradford C	3	0		
1995-96	Bradford C	5	1		
1995-96	Scarborough	16	1		
1996-97	Bradford C	1	0		
1996-97	Scarborough	6	2	22	3
1997-98	Bradford C	2	0	11	1
1997-98	Darlington	1	0	1	0
1997-98	Hartlepool U	9	3		
1998-99	Hartlepool U	29	7		
1999-2000	Hartlepool U	17	0		
2000-01	Hartlepool U	41	8	96	18
2001-02	Halifax T	24	3	24	3

MITCHELL, Graham* (D) 512 6
H: 6 1 W: 13 11 b.Shipley 16-2-68
Source: Apprentice.

1986-87	Huddersfield T	17	0		
1987-88	Huddersfield T	29	1		
1988-89	Huddersfield T	34	0		
1989-90	Huddersfield T	37	1		
1990-91	Huddersfield T	46	0		
1991-92	Huddersfield T	43	0		
1992-93	Huddersfield T	4	0		
1993-94	Huddersfield T	22	0		
1993-94	Bournemouth	4	0	4	0
1994-95	Huddersfield T	12	0	244	2
1994-95	Bradford C	26	0		
1995-96	Bradford C	33	1		
1996-97	Bradford C	6	0	65	1
1996-97	Raith R	20	0		
1997-98	Raith R	3	0	23	0
1998-99	Cardiff C	46	0	46	0
1999-2000	Halifax T	45	2		
2000-01	Halifax T	42	1		
2001-02	Halifax T	43	0	130	3

MYERS, Peter§ (M) 1 0
H: 5 11 W: 11 03 b.Dronfield 15-9-82
Source: Scholar.

| 2000-01 | Halifax T | 1 | 0 | | |
| 2001-02 | Halifax T | 0 | 0 | 1 | 0 |

OLEKSEWYCZ, Stephen (F) 5 0
H: 5 8 W: 11 00 b.Halifax 24-2-83

| 2000-01 | Halifax T | 3 | 0 | | |
| 2001-02 | Halifax T | 2 | 0 | 5 | 0 |

PARKS, Tony* (G) 264 0
H: 5 10 W: 11 05 b.Hackney 28-1-63
Source: Apprentice.

1980-81	Tottenham H	0	0		
1981-82	Tottenham H	0	0		
1982-83	Tottenham H	1	0		
1983-84	Tottenham H	16	0		
1984-85	Tottenham H	0	0		
1985-86	Tottenham H	0	0		
1986-87	Tottenham H	2	0		
1986-87	Oxford U	5	0	5	0
1987-88	Tottenham H	16	0	37	0
1987-88	Gillingham	2	0	2	0
1988-89	Brentford	33	0		
1989-90	Brentford	37	0		
1990-91	Brentford	1	0	71	0
1990-91	QPR	0	0		
1990-91	Fulham	2	0	2	0
1991-92	West Ham U	6	0	6	0
1992-93	Stoke C	2	0	2	0
1992-93	Falkirk	15	0		
1993-94	Falkirk	41	0		
1994-95	Falkirk	28	0		
1995-96	Falkirk	28	0	112	0
1996-97	Blackpool	0	0		
1997-98	Burnley	0	0		
1997-98	Doncaster R	6	0	6	0
1998-99	Burnley	0	0		
From Barrow					
1998-99	Scarborough	15	0	15	0
1999-2000	Halifax T	1	0		
2000-01	Halifax T	5	0		
2001-02	Halifax T	0	0	6	0

POTTER, Lee* (F) 22 2
H: 5 11 W: 12 10 b.Salford 3-9-78
Source: Trainee.

1997-98	Bolton W	0	0		
1998-99	Bolton W	0	0		
1999-2000	Bolton W	0	0		
1999-2000	Halifax T	19	2		
2000-01	Halifax T	3	0		
2001-02	Halifax T	0	0	22	2

REDFEARN, Neil (M) 727 145
H: 5 11 W: 13 01 b.Dewsbury 20-6-65
Source: Nottingham F Apprentice.

1982-83	Bolton W	10	0		
1983-84	Bolton W	25	1	35	1
1983-84	Lincoln C	10	1		
1984-85	Lincoln C	45	4		
1985-86	Lincoln C	45	8	100	13
1986-87	Doncaster R	46	14	46	14
1987-88	Crystal Palace	42	8		
1988-89	Crystal Palace	15	2	57	10
1988-89	Watford	12	2		
1989-90	Watford	12	1	24	3
1989-90	Oldham Ath	17	2		
1990-91	Oldham Ath	45	14	62	16
1991-92	Barnsley	36	4		
1992-93	Barnsley	46	3		
1993-94	Barnsley	46	12		
1994-95	Barnsley	39	11		
1995-96	Barnsley	45	14		
1996-97	Barnsley	43	17		
1997-98	Barnsley	37	10	292	71
1998-99	Charlton Ath	30	3	30	3
1999-2000	Bradford C	17	1	17	1
1999-2000	Wigan Ath	12	6		
2000-01	Wigan Ath	10	1	22	7
2000-01	Halifax T	12	0		
2001-02	Halifax T	30	6	42	6

REILLY, Alan* (M) 45 2
H: 5 11 W: 14 02 b.Dublin 22-8-80
Source: Trainee.

1998-99	Manchester C	0	0		
1999-2000	Manchester C	0	0		
1999-2000	Halifax T	20	0		
2000-01	Halifax T	23	2		
2001-02	Halifax T	2	0	45	2

REZAI, Carl (D) 11 0
H: 5 9 W: 11 00 b.Manchester 16-10-82

| 2000-01 | Halifax T | 11 | 0 | | |
| 2001-02 | Halifax T | 0 | 0 | 11 | 0 |

RICHARDSON, Barry* (G) 307 0
H: 6 1 W: 13 00 b.Willington Quay 5-8-69
Source: Trainee.

1987-88	Sunderland	0	0		
1988-89	Scunthorpe U	0	0		
1989-90	Scarborough	24	0		
1990-91	Scarborough	6	0	30	0
1991-92	Northampton T	27	0		
1992-93	Northampton T	42	0		
1993-94	Northampton T	27	0	96	0
1994-95	Preston NE	17	0		
1995-96	Preston NE	3	0	20	0
1995-96	Lincoln C	34	0		
1996-97	Lincoln C	45	0		
1997-98	Lincoln C	26	0		
1998-99	Lincoln C	13	0		
1999-2000	Lincoln C	22	0		
1999-2000	Mansfield T	6	0	6	0
1999-2000	Sheffield W	0	0		
2000-01	Lincoln C	0	0	131	0
From Doncaster R.					
2001-02	Halifax T	24	0	24	0

SMITH, Craig (M) 2 0
H: 5 8 W: 10 10 b.Bradford 8-6-84
Source: Scholar.

| 2001-02 | Halifax T | 2 | 0 | 2 | 0 |

STONEMAN, Paul* (D) 185 13
H: 6 0 W: 13 09 b.Whitley Bay 26-2-73
Source: Trainee.

1991-92	Blackpool	19	0		
1992-93	Blackpool	10	0		
1993-94	Blackpool	10	0		
1994-95	Blackpool	4	0	43	0
1994-95	Colchester U	3	1	3	1
1998-99	Halifax T	40	5		
1999-2000	Halifax T	37	4		
2000-01	Halifax T	30	2		
2001-02	Halifax T	32	1	139	12

SWALES, Steve* (M) 189 3
H: 5 10 W: 11 06 b.Whitby 26-12-73
Source: Trainee.

1991-92	Scarborough	4	0		
1992-93	Scarborough	3	0		
1993-94	Scarborough	26	0		
1994-95	Scarborough	21	1	54	1
1995-96	Reading	9	0		
1996-97	Reading	3	0		
1997-98	Reading	31	1		
1998-99	Reading	0	0	43	1
1998-99	Hull C	22	0		
1999-2000	Hull C	20	0		
2000-01	Hull C	26	0	68	0
2001-02	Halifax T	24	1	24	1

WINDER, Nathan§ (D) 1 0
H: 6 1 W: 12 05 b.Barnsley 17-2-83
Source: Scholar.

| 2001-02 | Halifax T | 1 | 0 | 1 | 0 |

WOOD, Jamie* (F) 63 6
H: 5 11 W: 12 11 b.Salford 21-9-78
Source: Trainee. Honours: Cayman Islands 2 full caps.

1997-98	Manchester U	0	0		
1998-99	Manchester U	0	0		
1999-2000	Hull C	32	6		
2000-01	Hull C	15	0	47	6
2001-02	Halifax T	16	0	16	0

WOODWARD, Andy (D) 180 2
H: 6 0 W: 13 08 b.Stockport 23-9-73
Source: Trainee.

1992-93	Crewe Alex	6	0		
1993-94	Crewe Alex	12	0		
1994-95	Crewe Alex	2	0	20	0
1994-95	Bury	8	0		
1995-96	Bury	1	0		
1996-97	Bury	23	0		
1997-98	Bury	32	0		
1998-99	Bury	37	1		
1999-2000	Bury	14	0	115	1
1999-2000	Sheffield U	3	0		
2000-01	Sheffield U	0	0	3	0
2000-01	Scunthorpe U	12	0	12	0
2001-02	Halifax T	30	1	30	1

WRIGHT, Peter* (F) 14 0
H: 5 8 W: 10 10 b.Preston 15-8-82
Source: Newcastle U Scholar.

| 2001-02 | Halifax T | 14 | 0 | 14 | 0 |

Scholars
Birchall, Gary N; Boulton, Matthew J; Clamp, Jimmy; Dunnan, Ryan P; Farrell, Andrew; Harris, Chad; Heinemann, Nicky; Lewins, Gareth O; Mierzwinski, Mark F; Myers, Peter W; Poole, Ryan; Smith, Craig M; Vincent, Alexander C; Winder, Nathan J; Wood, Simon; Woodcock, Gary R

HARTLEPOOL U

ARNISON, Paul# (D) 54 2
H: 5 10 W: 10 12 b.Hartlepool 18-9-77
Source: Trainee.

1995-96	Newcastle U	0	0		
1996-97	Newcastle U	0	0		
1997-98	Newcastle U	0	0		
1998-99	Newcastle U	0	0		
1999-2000	Newcastle U	0	0		
1999-2000	Hartlepool U	8	1		
2000-01	Hartlepool U	27	1		
2001-02	Hartlepool U	19	0	54	2

BARRON, Micky (D) 197 2
H: 5 11 W: 11 10 b.Lumley 22-12-74
Source: Trainee.

1992–93	Middlesbrough	0	0		
1993–94	Middlesbrough	2	0		
1994–95	Middlesbrough	0	0		
1995–96	Middlesbrough	1	0		
1996–97	Middlesbrough	0	0	**3**	**0**
1996–97	*Hartlepool U*	16	0		
1997–98	Hartlepool U	33	0		
1998–99	Hartlepool U	38	1		
1999–2000	Hartlepool U	40	0		
2000–01	Hartlepool U	28	0		
2001–02	Hartlepool U	39	1	**194**	**2**

BASS, Jonathan (D) 98 1
H: 6 0 W: 12 02 b.Weston-Super-Mare 1-1-76
Source: Trainee. *Honours:* England Schools.

1994–95	Birmingham C	0	0		
1995–96	Birmingham C	5	0		
1996–97	Birmingham C	13	0		
1996–97	*Carlisle U*	3	0	**3**	**0**
1997–98	Birmingham C	30	0		
1998–99	Birmingham C	11	0		
1999–2000	Birmingham C	8	0		
1999–2000	*Gillingham*	7	0	**7**	**0**
2000–01	Birmingham C	1	0	**68**	**0**
2001–02	Hartlepool U	20	1	**20**	**1**

BOYD, Adam (F) 38 10
H: 5 9 W: 10 12 b.Hartlepool 25-5-82
Source: Scholar.

1999–2000	Hartlepool U	4	1		
2000–01	Hartlepool U	5	0		
2001–02	Hartlepool U	29	9	**38**	**10**

CLARKE, Darrell (M) 194 31
H: 5 10 W: 11 06 b.Mansfield 16-12-77
Source: Trainee.

1995–96	Mansfield T	3	0		
1996–97	Mansfield T	19	2		
1997–98	Mansfield T	35	4		
1998–99	Mansfield T	33	5		
1999–2000	Mansfield T	39	7		
2000–01	Mansfield T	32	6	**161**	**24**
2001–02	Hartlepool U	33	7	**33**	**7**

EASTER, Jermaine (F) 16 2
H: 5 10 W: 12 03 b.Cardiff 15-1-82
Source: Trainee. *Honours:* Wales Youth.

2000–01	Wolverhampton W	0	0		
2000–01	Hartlepool U	4	0		
2001–02	Hartlepool U	12	2	**16**	**2**

HENDERSON, Kevin (F) 112 28
H: 5 11 W: 13 12 b.Ashington 8-6-74
Source: Morpeth Town.

1997–98	Burnley	7	0		
1998–99	Burnley	7	1	**14**	**1**
1999–2000	Hartlepool U	35	8		
2000–01	Hartlepool U	40	17		
2001–02	Hartlepool U	23	2	**98**	**27**

HOLLUND, Martin* (G) 141 0
H: 6 2 W: 12 09 b.Stord 11-8-74

1994	Brann	3	0		
1995	Brann	15	0		
1996	Brann	0	0		
1997	Brann	6	0	**24**	**0**
1997–98	Hartlepool U	28	0		
1998–99	Hartlepool U	41	0		
1999–2000	Hartlepool U	40	0		
2000–01	Hartlepool U	5	0		
2001–02	Hartlepool U	3	0	**117**	**0**

HUMPHREYS, Richie (M) 135 16
H: 5 11 W: 12 07 b.Sheffield 30-11-77
Source: Trainee. *Honours:* England Youth, Under-21.

1995–96	Sheffield W	5	0		
1996–97	Sheffield W	29	3		
1997–98	Sheffield W	7	0		
1998–99	Sheffield W	19	1		
1999–2000	Sheffield W	0	0		
1999–2000	*Scunthorpe U*	6	2	**6**	**2**
1999–2000	*Cardiff C*	9	2	**9**	**2**
2000–01	Sheffield W	7	0	**67**	**4**
2000–01	Cambridge U	7	3	**7**	**3**
2001–02	Hartlepool U	46	5	**46**	**5**

LEE, Graeme (D) 174 17
H: 6 2 W: 13 08 b.Middlesbrough 31-5-78
Source: Trainee.

1995–96	Hartlepool U	6	0		
1996–97	Hartlepool U	24	0		
1997–98	Hartlepool U	37	3		
1998–99	Hartlepool U	24	3		
1999–2000	Hartlepool U	38	7		
2000–01	Hartlepool U	6	0		
2001–02	Hartlepool U	39	4	**174**	**17**

LORMOR, Tony* (F) 374 102
H: 6 2 W: 13 13 b.Ashington 29-10-70
Source: Trainee.

1987–88	Newcastle U	5	2		
1988–89	Newcastle U	3	1		
1988–89	*Norwich C*	0	0		
1989–90	Newcastle U	0	0	**8**	**3**
1989–90	Lincoln C	21	8		
1990–91	Lincoln C	34	12		
1991–92	Lincoln C	35	9		
1992–93	Lincoln C	0	0		
1993–94	Lincoln C	10	1	**100**	**30**
1994–95	Peterborough U	5	0	**5**	**0**
1994–95	Chesterfield	23	10		
1995–96	Chesterfield	41	13		
1996–97	Chesterfield	36	8		
1997–98	Chesterfield	13	4	**113**	**35**
1997–98	Preston NE	12	3	**12**	**3**
1997–98	*Notts Co*	7	0	**7**	**0**
1998–99	Mansfield T	41	11		
1999–2000	Mansfield T	33	9	**74**	**20**
2000–01	Hartlepool U	31	8		
2001–02	Hartlepool U	17	1	**48**	**9**
2001–02	*Shrewsbury T*	7	2	**7**	**2**

PROVETT, Jim (G) 0 0
H: 5 11 W: 11 12 b.Stockton 22-12-82
Source: Trainee.

1999–2000	Hartlepool U	0	0
2000–01	Hartlepool U	0	0
2001–02	Hartlepool U	0	0

ROBINSON, Mark (D) 43 0
H: 5 9 W: 11 00 b.Guisborough 24-7-81
Source: Trainee.

1999–2000	Hartlepool U	0	0		
2000–01	Hartlepool U	6	0		
2001–02	Hartlepool U	37	0	**43**	**0**

ROSS, Brian (M) 0 0
H: 5 6 W: 10 02 b.Hartlepool 21-8-83

2001–02	Hartlepool U	0	0

SHARP, James (D) 49 2
H: 6 2 W: 14 06 b.Reading 2-1-76
Source: Reading, Florida Tech, Aldershot T, Wokingham, Andover T.

2000–01	Hartlepool U	34	2		
2001–02	Hartlepool U	15	0	**49**	**2**

SIMMS, Gordon (D) 10 0
H: 6 3 W: 12 03 b.Larne 23-3-81
Source: Trainee. *Honours:* Northern Ireland Under-21.

1997–98	Wolverhampton W	0	0		
1998–99	Wolverhampton W	0	0		
1999–2000	Wolverhampton W	0	0		
2000–01	Wolverhampton W	0	0		
2000–01	Hartlepool U	0	0		
2001–02	Hartlepool U	10	0	**10**	**0**

SMITH, Paul (M) 147 9
H: 6 0 W: 13 03 b.Easington 22-1-76
Source: Trainee.

1993–94	Burnley	1	0		
1994–95	Burnley	0	0		
1995–96	Burnley	10	0		
1996–97	Burnley	37	4		
1997–98	Burnley	14	0		
1998–99	Burnley	12	0		
1999–2000	Burnley	24	0		
2000–01	Burnley	14	1	**112**	**5**
2000–01	*Oldham Ath*	4	0	**4**	**0**
2001–02	Torquay U	0	0		
2001–02	Hartlepool U	31	4	**31**	**4**

STEPHENSON, Paul (M) 483 28
H: 5 10 W: 12 12 b.Wallsend 2-1-68
Source: Apprentice. *Honours:* England Youth.

1985–86	Newcastle U	22	1		
1986–87	Newcastle U	24	0		
1987–88	Newcastle U	7	0		
1988–89	Newcastle U	8	0	**61**	**1**
1989–90	Millwall	12	1		
1989–90	Millwall	23	2		
1990–91	Millwall	30	1		
1991–92	Millwall	28	2		
1992–93	Millwall	5	0	**98**	**6**
1992–93	*Gillingham*	12	2	**12**	**2**
1992–93	Brentford	11	0		
1993–94	Brentford	25	0		
1994–95	Brentford	34	2	**70**	**2**
1995–96	York C	27	2		
1996–97	York C	35	1		
1997–98	York C	35	5	**97**	**8**
1997–98	Hartlepool U	3	0		
1998–99	Hartlepool U	27	2		
1999–2000	Hartlepool U	46	5		
2000–01	Hartlepool U	40	2		
2001–02	Hartlepool U	29	0	**145**	**9**

SWEENEY, Anthony (M) 2 0
H: 6 0 W: 11 07 b.Stockton 5-9-83
Source: Scholar.

2001–02	Hartlepool U	2	0	**2**	**0**

TENNEBO, Thomas‡ (M) 13 0
H: 6 2 W: 12 00 b.Bergen 19-3-75
Source: Fana.

1999–2000	Hartlepool U	11	0		
2000–01	Hartlepool U	2	0		
2001–02	Hartlepool U	0	0	**13**	**0**

TINKLER, Mark (M) 239 21
H: 6 2 W: 13 00 b.Bishop Auckland 24-10-74
Source: Trainee. *Honours:* England Schools, Youth.

1991–92	Leeds U	0	0		
1992–93	Leeds U	7	0		
1993–94	Leeds U	3	0		
1994–95	Leeds U	3	0		
1995–96	Leeds U	9	0		
1996–97	Leeds U	3	0	**25**	**0**
1996–97	York C	9	1		
1997–98	York C	44	5		
1998–99	York C	37	2		
1999–2000	York C	0	0	**90**	**8**
1999–2000	Southend U	41	0		
2000–01	Southend U	15	1	**56**	**1**
2000–01	Hartlepool U	28	3		
2001–02	Hartlepool U	40	9	**68**	**12**

WATSON, Gordon# (F) 208 53
H: 5 10 W: 12 08 b.Sidcup 20-3-71
Source: Trainee. *Honours:* England Under-21.

1988–89	Charlton Ath	0	0		
1989–90	Charlton Ath	9	0		
1990–91	Charlton Ath	22	7	**31**	**7**
1990–91	Sheffield W	5	0		
1991–92	Sheffield W	4	0		
1992–93	Sheffield W	11	1		
1993–94	Sheffield W	23	12		
1994–95	Sheffield W	23	2	**66**	**15**
1994–95	Southampton	12	3		
1995–96	Southampton	25	3		
1996–97	Southampton	15	2	**52**	**8**
1996–97	Bradford C	3	1		
1997–98	Bradford C	0	0		
1998–99	Bradford C	18	4	**21**	**5**
1999–2000	Bournemouth	6	0		
2000–01	Bournemouth	0	0	**6**	**0**
2001–02	Hartlepool U	32	18	**32**	**18**

WESTWOOD, Chris# (D) 126 3
H: 5 11 W: 12 10 b.Dudley 13-2-77
Source: Trainee.

1995–96	Wolverhampton W	0	0		
1996–97	Wolverhampton W	0	0		
1997–98	Wolverhampton W	4	1		
1998–99	Wolverhampton W	0	0	**4**	**1**
1998–99	Hartlepool U	4	0		
1999–2000	Hartlepool U	37	0		
2000–01	Hartlepool U	46	1		
2001–02	Hartlepool U	35	1	**122**	**2**

WIDDRINGTON, Tommy (M) 276 21
H: 5 9 W: 11 12 b.Newcastle 1-10-71
Source: Trainee.

1989–90	Southampton	0	0		
1990–91	Southampton	0	0		
1991–92	Southampton	3	0		
1991–92	*Wigan Ath*	6	0	**6**	**0**
1992–93	Southampton	12	0		
1993–94	Southampton	11	1		
1994–95	Southampton	28	0		
1995–96	Southampton	21	2	**75**	**3**
1996–97	Grimsby T	42	4		
1997–98	Grimsby T	21	3		
1998–99	Grimsby T	26	1	**89**	**8**
1998–99	*Port Vale*	9	1		
1999–2000	Port Vale	38	5		
2000–01	Port Vale	35	2	**82**	**8**
2001–02	Hartlepool U	24	2	**24**	**2**

WILLIAMS, Anthony (G) 110 0
H: 6 2 W: 13 08 b.Ogwr 20-9-77
Source: Trainee. *Honours:* Wales Youth, Under-21.

1996–97	Blackburn R	0	0		
1997–98	Blackburn R	0	0		
1997–98	*QPR*	0	0		
1998–99	Blackburn R	0	0		
1998–99	*Macclesfield T*	4	0		
1998–99	*Huddersfield T*	0	0		
1998–99	*Bristol R*	9	0	**9**	**0**
1999–2000	Blackburn R	0	0		
1999–2000	*Gillingham*	2	0	**2**	**0**
1999–2000	*Macclesfield T*	11	0	**15**	**0**
2000–01	Hartlepool U	41	0		
2001–02	Hartlepool U	43	0	**84**	**0**

WILLIAMS, Eifion (F) 119 28
H: 5 11 W: 11 02 b.Bangor 15-11-75
Source: Barry T. *Honours:* Wales B.
1998–99 Torquay U 7 5
1999–2000 Torquay U 42 9
2000–01 Torquay U 37 9
2001–02 Torquay U 25 1 111 24
2001–02 Hartlepool U 8 4 8 4

Scholars
Batey, Marc; Brackstone, John; Craddock, Darren; Duncan, Kevin M; Flett, Martyn J; Flockett, Stephen; Hill, Andrew S; Manson, Stephen; McKenzie, Colin JF; Peachey, Lee G; Piggott, David J; Robson, Matthew J; Watts, Andrew; Wear, Joseph M

HUDDERSFIELD T

BALDRY, Simon (M) 129 6
H: 5 10 W: 12 11 b.Huddersfield 12-2-76
Source: Trainee.
1993–94 Huddersfield T 10 2
1994–95 Huddersfield T 11 0
1995–96 Huddersfield T 14 0
1996–97 Huddersfield T 7 0
1997–98 Huddersfield T 11 1
1998–99 Huddersfield T 13 0
1998–99 Bury 5 0 5 0
1999–2000 Huddersfield T 19 1
2000–01 Huddersfield T 35 2
2001–02 Huddersfield T 4 0 124 6

BEECH, Chris* (M) 247 38
H: 5 10 W: 12 04 b.Blackpool 16-9-74
Source: Trainee.
1992–93 Blackpool 1 0
1993–94 Blackpool 35 2
1994–95 Blackpool 28 2
1995–96 Blackpool 18 0 82 4
1996–97 Hartlepool U 42 7
1997–98 Hartlepool U 36 6
1998–99 Hartlepool U 16 9 94 22
1998–99 Huddersfield T 17 2
1999–2000 Huddersfield T 35 9
2000–01 Huddersfield T 10 0
2001–02 Huddersfield T 9 1 71 12

BOOTH, Andy (F) 304 96
H: 6 0 W: 12 04 b.Huddersfield 6-12-73
Source: Trainee. *Honours:* England Under-21.
1991–92 Huddersfield T 3 0
1992–93 Huddersfield T 5 2
1993–94 Huddersfield T 26 10
1994–95 Huddersfield T 46 26
1995–96 Huddersfield T 43 16
1996–97 Sheffield W 35 10
1997–98 Sheffield W 23 7
1998–99 Sheffield W 34 6
1999–2000 Sheffield W 23 2
2000–01 Sheffield W 18 3 133 28
2000–01 Tottenham H 4 0 4 0
2001–02 Huddersfield T 8 3
2001–02 Huddersfield T 36 11 167 68

BROWN, Nathaniel (F) 0 0
H: 6 2 W: 12 05 b.Sheffield 15-6-81
Source: Trainee.
1999–2000 Huddersfield T 0 0
2000–01 Huddersfield T 0 0
2001–02 Huddersfield T 0 0

CLARKE, Doni (M) 0 0
H: 5 8 W: 10 11 b.Burnley 18-9-81
Source: Scholar.
2001–02 Huddersfield T 0 0

CLARKE, Nathan (D) 36 1
H: 6 2 W: 11 11 b.Halifax 30-7-83
Source: Scholar.
2001–02 Huddersfield T 36 1 36 1

DYSON, Jon* (D) 213 9
H: 5 10 W: 12 07 b.Mirfield 18-12-71
Source: School.
1991–92 Huddersfield T 0 0
1992–93 Huddersfield T 15 0
1993–94 Huddersfield T 22 0
1994–95 Huddersfield T 28 2
1995–96 Huddersfield T 17 0
1996–97 Huddersfield T 23 0
1997–98 Huddersfield T 36 1
1998–99 Huddersfield T 14 1
1999–2000 Huddersfield T 28 2
2000–01 Huddersfield T 30 3
2001–02 Huddersfield T 0 0 213 9

EVANS, Gareth (M) 36 0
H: 5 10 W: 12 01 b.Leeds 10-4-81
Source: Trainee. *Honours:* England Youth.
1997–98 Leeds U 0 0
1998–99 Leeds U 0 0
1999–2000 Leeds U 0 0
2000–01 Leeds U 1 0 1 0
2001–02 Huddersfield T 35 0 35 0

EVANS, Paul‡ (G) 0 0
H: 6 4 W: 14 04 b.South Africa 28-12-73
Source: Witts Univ.
1995–96 Leeds U 0 0
1995–96 *Crystal Palace* 0 0
1996–97 Leeds U 0 0
1996–97 *Bradford C* 0 0
From Jomo Cosmos.
2001–02 Huddersfield T 0 0

FACEY, Delroy (F) 75 15
H: 6 0 W: 14 12 b.Huddersfield 22-4-80
Source: Trainee.
1996–97 Huddersfield T 3 0
1997–98 Huddersfield T 3 0
1998–99 Huddersfield T 20 3
1999–2000 Huddersfield T 2 0
2000–01 Huddersfield T 34 10
2001–02 Huddersfield T 13 2 75 15

FOWLER, Adam (M) 0 0
H: 5 9 W: 10 10 b.Huddersfield 11-9-81
Source: Scholar.
2001–02 Huddersfield T 0 0

GRAY, Kevin# (D) 372 9
H: 6 0 W: 14 06 b.Sheffield 7-1-72
Source: Trainee.
1988–89 Mansfield T 1 0
1989–90 Mansfield T 16 0
1990–91 Mansfield T 31 1
1991–92 Mansfield T 18 0
1992–93 Mansfield T 33 0
1993–94 Mansfield T 42 2 141 3
1994–95 Huddersfield T 5 0
1995–96 Huddersfield T 38 0
1996–97 Huddersfield T 39 1
1997–98 Huddersfield T 35 1
1998–99 Huddersfield T 34 1
1999–2000 Huddersfield T 18 2
2000–01 *Stockport Co* 1 0 1 0
2000–01 Huddersfield T 17 0
2001–02 Huddersfield T 44 1 230 6

HAY, Chris* (F) 161 39
H: 6 1 W: 12 08 b.Glasgow 28-8-74
Source: Giffnock N.
1993–94 Celtic 2 0
1994–95 Celtic 5 0
1995–96 Celtic 4 0
1996–97 Celtic 14 4 25 4
1997–98 Swindon T 36 14
1998–99 Swindon T 27 6
1999–2000 Swindon T 31 10 94 30
1999–2000 Huddersfield T 7 0
2000–01 Huddersfield T 4 0
2001–02 Huddersfield T 31 5 42 5

HAY, Nathan (D) 0 0
H: 5 7 W: 10 07 b.Leeds 5-10-81
Source: Scholar.
2001–02 Huddersfield T 0 0

HEARY, Thomas (D) 72 0
H: 5 10 W: 12 06 b.Dublin 14-2-79
Source: Trainee. *Honours:* Eire Under-21.
1995–96 Huddersfield T 0 0
1996–97 Huddersfield T 5 0
1997–98 Huddersfield T 3 0
1998–99 Huddersfield T 3 0
1999–2000 Huddersfield T 1 0
2000–01 Huddersfield T 28 0
2001–02 Huddersfield T 32 0 72 0

HOLLAND, Chris (M) 157 2
H: 6 1 W: 12 10 b.Clitheroe 11-9-75
Source: Trainee. *Honours:* England Youth, Under-21.
1993–94 Preston NE 1 0 1 0
1993–94 Newcastle U 3 0
1994–95 Newcastle U 0 0
1995–96 Newcastle U 0 0
1996–97 Newcastle U 0 0 3 0
1996–97 Birmingham C 32 0
1997–98 Birmingham C 10 0
1998–99 Birmingham C 14 0
1999–2000 Birmingham C 14 0 70 0
1999–2000 Huddersfield T 17 1
2000–01 Huddersfield T 29 0
2001–02 Huddersfield T 37 1 83 2

IRONS, Kenny (M) 465 64
H: 5 10 W: 12 06 b.Liverpool 4-11-70
Source: Trainee.
1989–90 Tranmere R 3 0
1990–91 Tranmere R 32 6
1991–92 Tranmere R 43 7
1992–93 Tranmere R 42 7
1993–94 Tranmere R 34 3
1994–95 Tranmere R 38 4
1995–96 Tranmere R 32 3
1996–97 Tranmere R 41 5
1997–98 Tranmere R 43 4
1998–99 Tranmere R 43 15 351 54
1999–2000 Huddersfield T 40 3
2000–01 Huddersfield T 33 0
2001–02 Huddersfield T 41 7 114 10

JENKINS, Steve (D) 400 5
H: 5 11 W: 12 12 b.Merthyr 16-7-72
Source: Trainee. *Honours:* Wales Youth, Under-21, 16 full caps.
1990–91 Swansea C 1 0
1991–92 Swansea C 34 0
1992–93 Swansea C 33 0
1993–94 Swansea C 40 1
1994–95 Swansea C 42 0
1995–96 Swansea C 15 0 165 1
1995–96 Huddersfield T 31 1
1996–97 Huddersfield T 33 0
1997–98 Huddersfield T 29 1
1998–99 Huddersfield T 36 1
1999–2000 Huddersfield T 33 0
2000–01 Huddersfield T 30 0
2000–01 *Birmingham C* 3 0 3 0
2001–02 Huddersfield T 40 1 232 4

MACARI, Paul (F) 9 0
H: 5 6 W: 12 02 b.Manchester 23-8-76
Source: Trainee.
1993–94 Stoke C 0 0
1994–95 Stoke C 0 0
1995–96 Stoke C 0 0
1996–97 Stoke C 0 0
1997–98 Stoke C 3 0 3 0
1998–99 *Sheffield U* 0 0
1999–2000 Sheffield U 0 0
2000–01 Huddersfield T 0 0
2001–02 Huddersfield T 6 0 6 0

MARGETSON, Martyn# (G) 134 0
H: 6 0 W: 13 08 b.West Neath 8-9-71
Source: Trainee. *Honours:* Wales Schools, Youth, Under-21, B.
1990–91 Manchester C 2 0
1991–92 Manchester C 3 0
1992–93 Manchester C 1 0
1993–94 Manchester C 0 0
1993–94 *Bristol R* 3 0 3 0
1993–94 *Bolton W* 0 0
1994–95 Manchester C 0 0
1994–95 *Luton T* 5 0
1995–96 Manchester C 0 0
1996–97 Manchester C 17 0
1997–98 Manchester C 28 0 51 0
1998–99 Southend U 32 0 32 0
1999–2000 Huddersfield T 0 0
2000–01 Huddersfield T 2 0
2001–02 Huddersfield T 46 0 48 0

MATTIS, Dwayne (M) 31 1
H: 6 0 W: 12 03 b.Huddersfield 31-7-81
Source: Trainee.
1998–99 Huddersfield T 2 0
1999–2000 Huddersfield T 0 0
2000–01 Huddersfield T 0 0
2001–02 Huddersfield T 29 1 31 1

MOSES, Adi (D) 180 3
H: 5 10 W: 12 12 b.Doncaster 4-5-75
Source: School. *Honours:* England Under-21.
1993–94 Barnsley 0 0
1994–95 Barnsley 4 0
1995–96 Barnsley 24 1
1996–97 Barnsley 28 2
1997–98 Barnsley 35 0
1998–99 Barnsley 34 0
1999–2000 Barnsley 12 0
2000–01 Barnsley 14 0 151 3
2000–01 Huddersfield T 12 0
2001–02 Huddersfield T 17 0 29 0

SCHOFIELD, Danny (F) 44 8
H: 5 10 W: 11 09 b.Doncaster 10-4-80
Source: Brodsworth.
1998–99 Huddersfield T 1 0
1999–2000 Huddersfield T 2 0
2000–01 Huddersfield T 1 0
2001–02 Huddersfield T 40 8 44 8

SCOTT, Paul (M) 0 0
H: 5 11 W: 12 08 b.Wakefield 5-11-79
Source: Trainee.
1998–99 Huddersfield T 0 0
1999–2000 Huddersfield T 0 0
2000–01 Huddersfield T 0 0
2001–02 Huddersfield T 0 0

SENIOR, Chris (F) 0 0
H: 5 6 W: 9 01 b.Huddersfield 18-11-81
Source: Scholar.
2001–02 Huddersfield T 0 0

SENIOR, Michael (M) 4 0
H: 5 9 W: 10 07 b.Huddersfield 3-3-81
Source: Trainee.

1999-2000	Huddersfield T	0	0		
2000-01	Huddersfield T	4	0		
2001-02	Huddersfield T	0	0	4	0

SENIOR, Philip (G) 0 0
H: 5 11 W: 10 12 b.Huddersfield 30-10-82
Source: Trainee.

1999-2000	Huddersfield T	0	0
2000-01	Huddersfield T	0	0
2001-02	Huddersfield T	0	0

SIMPSON, Neil (M) 0 0
H: 5 7 W: 10 00 b.Bradford 2-12-81
Source: Scholar.

| 2001-02 | Huddersfield T | 0 | 0 |

SMITH, Martin (F) 187 47
H: 5 11 W: 11 13 b.Sunderland 13-11-74
Source: Trainee. *Honours:* England Schools, Under-21.

1992-93	Sunderland	0	0		
1993-94	Sunderland	29	8		
1994-95	Sunderland	35	10		
1995-96	Sunderland	20	2		
1996-97	Sunderland	11	0		
1997-98	Sunderland	16	2		
1998-99	Sunderland	8	3	119	25
1999-2000	Sheffield U	26	10	26	10
1999-2000	Huddersfield T	12	4		
2000-01	Huddersfield T	30	8		
2001-02	Huddersfield T	0	0	42	12

STEAD, Jonathan (M) 0 0
b.Huddersfield 7-4-83
Source: Scholar.

| 2001-02 | Huddersfield T | 0 | 0 |

THORRINGTON, John (M) 31 6
H: 5 8 W: 10 06 b.Johannesburg 10-7-79
Source: US College. *Honours:* USA 1 full cap.

1997-98	Manchester U	0	0		
1998-99	Manchester U	0	0		
1999-2000	Manchester U	0	0		
2000-01	Huddersfield T	0	0		
2001-02	Huddersfield T	31	6	31	6

WORTHINGTON, Jonathan (M) 0 0
b.Dewsbury 16-4-83
Source: Scholar.

| 2001-02 | Huddersfield T | 0 | 0 |

Scholars
Ahmed, Aadnan; Austin, Ben; Brown, Christopher T; Clapham, Daniel D; Greaves, Robert A; Holdsworth, Andrew; Kelly, Gregory; Kenworthy, Steven P; Lloyd, Anthony F; McAliskey, John J; McCombe, John P; Mirfin, David M; Padgett, Lee J; Tunnacliffe, Michael; Walsh, Joseph J; Washington, Joe

HULL C

ALEXANDER, Gary (F) 117 40
H: 5 11 W: 13 00 b.Lambeth 15-8-79
Source: Trainee.

1998-99	West Ham U	0	0		
1999-2000	West Ham U	0	0		
1999-2000	Exeter C	37	16	37	16
2000-01	Swindon T	37	7	37	7
2001-02	Hull C	43	17	43	17

BERESFORD, David (M) 154 6
H: 5 5 W: 11 04 b.Middleton 11-11-76
Source: Trainee. *Honours:* England Schools, Youth.

1993-94	Oldham Ath	1	0		
1994-95	Oldham Ath	2	0		
1995-96	Oldham Ath	28	2		
1995-96	Swansea C	6	0	6	0
1996-97	Oldham Ath	33	0	64	2
1996-97	Huddersfield T	6	1		
1997-98	Huddersfield T	8	0		
1998-99	Huddersfield T	19	2		
1999-2000	Huddersfield T	0	0		
1999-2000	Preston NE	4	0	4	0
2000-01	Huddersfield T	2	0	35	3
2000-01	Port Vale	4	0		
2001-02	Hull C	41	1	41	1

BLOOMER, Matt (D) 20 0
H: 6 1 W: 13 00 b.Cleethorpes 3-11-78
Source: Trainee.

1997-98	Grimsby T	0	0		
1998-99	Grimsby T	4	0		
1999-2000	Grimsby T	2	0		
2001-02	Grimsby T	6	0		
2001-02	Grimsby T	0	0	12	0

| 2001-02 | Hull C | 3 | 0 | 3 | 0 |
| 2001-02 | Lincoln C | 5 | 0 | 5 | 0 |

BRADSHAW, Gary (F) 17 1
H: 5 6 W: 10 06 b.Hull 30-12-82
Source: Scholar.

1999-2000	Hull C	12	0		
2000-01	Hull C	2	0		
2001-02	Hull C	3	1	17	1

CACERES, Adrian‡ (F) 9 0
H: 5 10 W: 12 05 b.Buenos Aires 10-1-82
Source: Perth SC.

2000-01	Southampton	0	0		
2001-02	Southampton	0	0		
2001-02	Brentford	5	0	5	0
2001-02	Hull C	4	0	4	0

DUDFIELD, Lawrie (F) 57 15
H: 6 1 W: 13 09 b.Southwark 7-5-80
Source: Kettering T.

1997-98	Leicester C	0	0		
1998-99	Leicester C	0	0		
1999-2000	Leicester C	2	0		
2000-01	Leicester C	0	0	2	0
2000-01	Lincoln C	3	0	3	0
2000-01	Chesterfield	14	3	14	3
2001-02	Hull C	38	12	38	12

EDWARDS, Mike (D) 172 6
H: 6 0 W: 12 10 b.North Ferriby 25-4-80
Source: Trainee.

1997-98	Hull C	21	0		
1998-99	Hull C	30	0		
1999-2000	Hull C	40	1		
2000-01	Hull C	42	4		
2001-02	Hull C	39	1	172	6

FENTON, Anthony‡ (D) 1 0
H: 5 10 W: 11 12 b.Preston 23-11-79
Source: Trainee.

1996-97	Manchester C	0	0		
1997-98	Manchester C	0	0		
1998-99	Manchester C	0	0		
1998-99	Portsmouth	0	0		
1999-2000	Portsmouth	1	0		
2000-01	Portsmouth	0	0	1	0
2001-02	Hull C	0	0		

GLENNON, Matt (G) 56 0
H: 6 2 W: 14 09 b.Stockport 8-10-78
Source: Trainee.

1997-98	Bolton W	0	0		
1998-99	Bolton W	0	0		
1999-2000	Bolton W	0	0		
1999-2000	Port Vale	0	0		
2000-01	Bolton W	0	0		
2000-01	Bristol R	1	0	1	0
2000-01	Carlisle U	29	0	29	0
2001-02	Hull C	26	0	26	0

GOODISON, Ian‡ (D) 70 1
H: 6 1 W: 12 06 b.St James, Jamaica 21-11-72
Source: Olympic Gardens. *Honours:* Jamaica full caps.

1999-2000	Hull C	18	0		
2000-01	Hull C	36	1		
2001-02	Hull C	16	0	70	1

GREAVES, Mark (D) 174 10
H: 6 1 W: 13 00 b.Hull 22-1-75
Source: Brigg Town.

1996-97	Hull C	30	2		
1997-98	Hull C	25	2		
1998-99	Hull C	25	0		
1999-2000	Hull C	38	3		
2000-01	Hull C	30	2		
2001-02	Hull C	26	1	174	10

HOLT, Andy (M) 164 12
H: 6 1 W: 12 07 b.Stockport 21-5-78
Source: Trainee.

1996-97	Oldham Ath	1	0		
1997-98	Oldham Ath	14	1		
1998-99	Oldham Ath	43	5		
1999-2000	Oldham Ath	46	3		
2000-01	Oldham Ath	20	1	124	10
2000-01	Hull C	10	2		
2001-02	Hull C	30	0	40	2

JOHNSSON, Julian (M) 44 4
H: 6 1 W: 12 08 b.Denmark 24-2-75
Honours: Faroes 40 full caps, 1 goal.

| 2001 | Sogndal | 4 | 0 | 4 | 0 |
| 2001-02 | Hull C | 40 | 4 | 40 | 4 |

JOYCE, Warren* (M) 608 78
H: 5 9 W: 12 00 b.Oldham 20-1-65
Source: School.

1982-83	Bolton W	8	0		
1983-84	Bolton W	45	3		
1984-85	Bolton W	45	5		
1985-86	Bolton W	44	5		
1986-87	Bolton W	44	5		
1987-88	Bolton W	11	0	184	17
1987-88	Preston NE	22	0		
1988-89	Preston NE	40	9		
1989-90	Preston NE	44	11		
1990-91	Preston NE	42	9		
1991-92	Preston NE	29	5	177	34
1992-93	Plymouth Arg	30	3	30	3
1993-94	Burnley	22	4		
1994-95	Burnley	5	0		
1994-95	Hull C	9	3		
1995-96	Burnley	43	5	70	9
1996-97	Hull C	45	5		
1997-98	Hull C	45	4		
1998-99	Hull C	29	2		
1999-2000	Hull C	19	1		
2000-01	Hull C	0	0		
2001-02	Hull C	0	0	147	15

KERR, Scott (M) 1 0
H: 5 9 W: 10 08 b.Leeds 11-12-81
Source: Scholar.

| 2000-01 | Bradford C | 1 | 0 | 1 | 0 |
| 2001-02 | Hull C | 0 | 0 | | |

MANN, Neil (M) 175 9
H: 5 10 W: 12 01 b.Nottingham 19-11-72
Source: Notts Co, Spalding U, Grantham T.

1993-94	Hull C	5	0		
1994-95	Hull C	31	2		
1995-96	Hull C	38	1		
1996-97	Hull C	32	2		
1997-98	Hull C	34	3		
1998-99	Hull C	20	1		
1999-2000	Hull C	2	0		
2000-01	Hull C	13	0		
2001-02	Hull C	0	0	175	9

MATTHEWS, Rob (M) 220 34
H: 6 0 W: 13 00 b.Slough 14-10-70
Source: Loughborough Univ. *Honours:* England Schools.

1991-92	Notts Co	5	3		
1992-93	Notts Co	8	2		
1993-94	Notts Co	12	3		
1994-95	Notts Co	18	3	43	11
1994-95	Luton T	11	0		
1995-96	Luton T	0	0	11	0
1995-96	York C	17	1	17	1
1995-96	Bury	16	4		
1996-97	Bury	27	5		
1997-98	Bury	15	0		
1998-99	Bury	16	2	74	11
1998-99	Stockport Co	23	2		
1999-2000	Stockport Co	4	1		
1999-2000	Blackpool	6	2	6	2
2000-01	Stockport Co	11	1	38	4
2000-01	Halifax T	8	2	8	2
2000-01	Hull C	8	0		
2001-02	Hull C	15	3	23	3

MOHAN, Nicky (D) 387 18
H: 6 1 W: 14 00 b.Middlesbrough 6-10-70
Source: Trainee.

1987-88	Middlesbrough	0	0		
1988-89	Middlesbrough	6	0		
1989-90	Middlesbrough	22	0		
1990-91	Middlesbrough	0	0		
1991-92	Middlesbrough	27	2		
1992-93	Middlesbrough	18	2		
1992-93	Hull C	5	1		
1993-94	Middlesbrough	26	0	99	4
1994-95	Leicester C	23	0	23	0
1995-96	Bradford C	39	4		
1996-97	Bradford C	44	0		
1997-98	Bradford C	0	0	83	4
1997-98	Wycombe W	33	0		
1998-99	Wycombe W	25	2	58	2
1998-99	Stoke C	15	0		
1999-2000	Stoke C	40	5		
2000-01	Stoke C	37	1	92	6
2001-02	Hull C	27	1	32	2

MORLEY, Ben* (D) 26 0
H: 5 9 W: 10 11 b.Hull 22-12-80
Source: Trainee.

1997-98	Hull C	8	0		
1998-99	Hull C	12	0		
1999-2000	Hull C	1	0		
2000-01	Hull C	2	0		
2001-02	Hull C	3	0	26	0

MUSSELWHITE, Paul (G) 501 0
H: 6 2 W: 14 02 b.Portsmouth 22-12-68
Source: Apprentice.

1987-88	Portsmouth	0	0		
1988-89	Scunthorpe U	41	0		
1989-90	Scunthorpe U	29	0		
1990-91	Scunthorpe U	38	0		
1991-92	Scunthorpe U	24	0	132	0
1992-93	Port Vale	41	0		
1993-94	Port Vale	46	0		

1994–95	Port Vale	44	0	
1995–96	Port Vale	39	0	
1996–97	Port Vale	33	0	
1997–98	Port Vale	41	0	
1998–99	Port Vale	38	0	
1999–2000	Port Vale	30	0	312 0
2000–01	Sheffield W	0	0	
2000–01	Hull C	37	0	
2001–02	Hull C	20	0	57 0

PETTY, Ben (D)   73 0
H: 6 0 W: 12 05 b.Solihull 22-3-77
Source: Trainee.

1994–95	Aston Villa	0	0
1995–96	Aston Villa	0	0
1996–97	Aston Villa	0	0
1997–98	Aston Villa	0	0
1998–99	Aston Villa	0	0
1998–99	Stoke C	11	0
1999–2000	Stoke C	13	0
2000–01	Stoke C	22	0	46 0
2001–02	Hull C	27	0	27 0

PHILPOTT, Lee (M)   384 30
H: 5 10 W: 11 08 b.Barnet 21-2-70
Source: Trainee.

1987–88	Peterborough U	1	0		
1988–89	Peterborough U	3	0	4 0
1989–90	Cambridge U	42	5		
1990–91	Cambridge U	45	5		
1991–92	Cambridge U	31	5		
1992–93	Cambridge U	16	2	134 17
1992–93	Leicester C	27	3		
1993–94	Leicester C	19	0		
1994–95	Leicester C	23	0		
1995–96	Leicester C	6	0	75 3
1995–96	Blackpool	10	0		
1996–97	Blackpool	26	3		
1997–98	Blackpool	35	2	71 5
1998–99	Lincoln C	24	0		
1999–2000	Lincoln C	23	3	47 3
2000–01	Hull C	42	1		
2001–02	Hull C	11	1	53 2

PRICE, Mike (D)   1 0
H: 5 9 W: 11 01 b.Wrexham 29-4-82
Source: Trainee. *Honours:* Wales Under-21.

1999–2000	Everton	0	0
2000–01	Everton	0	0
2001–02	Hull C	1	0	1 0

ROWE, Rodney* (F)   214 37
H: 5 8 W: 12 08 b.Huddersfield 30-7-75
Source: Trainee.

1993–94	Huddersfield T	13	1		
1994–95	Huddersfield T	0	0		
1994–95	*Scarborough*	14	1	14 1
1994–95	*Bury*	3	0	3 0
1995–96	Huddersfield T	14	1		
1996–97	Huddersfield T	7	0	34 2
1996–97	York C	10	3		
1997–98	York C	41	10		
1998–99	York C	39	7		
1999–2000	York C	7	0	97 20
1999–2000	*Halifax T*	9	2	9 2
1999–2000	Gillingham	22	4		
2000–01	Gillingham	0	0	22 4
2000–01	Hull C	21	6		
2001–02	Hull C	14	2	35 8

SNEEKES, Richard‡ (M)   473 65
H: 5 11 W: 12 03 b.Amsterdam 30-10-68
Honours: Holland Under-21.

1985–86	Ajax	1	0		
1986–87	Ajax	1	0		
1987–88	Ajax	1	0	3 0
1988–89	Volendam	31	7	31 7
1989–90	Fortuna Sittard	32	2		
1990–91	Fortuna Sittard	32	7		
1991–92	Fortuna Sittard	33	5		
1992–93	Fortuna Sittard	29	6	126 20

From Locarno, Fortuna Sittard.

1994–95	Bolton				
1995–96	Bolton W	17	1	55 7
1995–96	WBA	13	10		
1996–97	WBA	45	8		
1997–98	WBA	42	3		
1998–99	WBA	40	4		
1999–2000	WBA	42	3		
2000–01	WBA	45	3	227 31
2001–02	Stockport Co	9	0	9 0
2001–02	Hull C	22	0	22 0

VAN BLERK, Jason* (D)   358 21
H: 6 1 W: 13 00 b.Sydney 16-3-68
Honours: Australia 27 full caps, 1 goal.

1989	Blackdown City	24	3	24 3
1989–90	Leichhardt	25	1		
1990–91	St Truiden	23	2	23 2
1991–92	Leichhardt	14	4	39 5
1992–93	Go Ahead	18	1		
1993–94	Go Ahead	30	4	48 5

1994–95	Millwall	27	1		
1995–96	Millwall	42	1		
1996–97	Millwall	4	0	73 2
1997–98	Manchester C	19	0	19 0
1997–98	WBA	8	0		
1998–99	WBA	30	0		
1999–2000	WBA	35	1		
2000–01	WBA	36	2	109 3
2001–02	Stockport Co	13	0	13 0
2001–02	Hull C	1	0	10 1

WHITMORE, Theo‡ (M)   77 9
H: 6 2 W: 12 10 b.Montego Bay 5-8-72
Source: Seba U. *Honours:* Jamaica full caps.

1999–2000	Hull C	17	2	
2000–01	Hull C	26	5	
2001–02	Hull C	34	2	77 9

WHITNEY, Jon‡ (D)   188 11
H: 5 10 W: 13 08 b.Nantwich 23-12-70
Source: Winsford U.

1993–94	Huddersfield T	14	0		
1994–95	Huddersfield T	0	0		
1994–95	*Wigan Ath*	12	0	12 0
1995–96	Huddersfield T	4	0	18 0
1995–96	Lincoln C	26	2		
1996–97	Lincoln C	18	3		
1997–98	Lincoln C	44	1		
1998–99	Lincoln C	13	2	101 8
1998–99	Hull C	21	1		
1999–2000	Hull C	21	1		
2000–01	Hull C	15	1		
2001–02	Hull C	0	0	57 3

WHITTLE, Justin (D)   215 2
H: 6 1 W: 13 00 b.Derby 18-3-71
Source: Celtic.

1994–95	Stoke C	0	0		
1995–96	Stoke C	8	0		
1996–97	Stoke C	37	0		
1997–98	Stoke C	20	0		
1998–99	Stoke C	14	1	79 1
1998–99	Hull C	24	1		
1999–2000	Hull C	38	0		
2000–01	Hull C	38	0		
2001–02	Hull C	36	0	136 1

WICKS, Matt (D)   77 3
H: 6 2 W: 13 05 b.Reading 8-9-78
Source: Manchester U Trainee. *Honours:* England Youth.

1995–96	Arsenal	0	0		
1996–97	Arsenal	0	0		
1997–98	Arsenal	0	0		
1998–99	Crewe Alex	6	0	6 0
1998–99	Peterborough U	11	0		
1999–2000	Peterborough U	20	0		
2000–01	Peterborough U	0	0	31 0
2000–01	Brighton & HA	24	3		
2001–02	Brighton & HA	2	0	26 3
2001–02	Hull C	14	0	14 0

WILLIAMS, Ryan (F)   135 18
H: 5 4 W: 11 04 b.Sutton-in-Ashfield 31-8-78
Source: Trainee. *Honours:* England Youth.

1995–96	Mansfield T	10	3		
1996–97	Mansfield T	16	0	26 3
1997–98	Tranmere R	7	0		
1998–99	Tranmere R	5	0		
1999–2000	Tranmere R	0	0	5 0
1999–2000	Chesterfield	30	5		
2000–01	Chesterfield	45	8	75 13
2001–02	Hull C	29	2	29 2

Scholars
Bowsley, Anthony J; Burton, Steven PG; Chapman, Liam J; Crutwell, Ian G; Donaldson, Clayton A; Heard, Jamie; Hudson, Christopher; Kaveney, Gene; Mulchinock, Daniel T; Peat, Nathan NM; Russell, Simon C; Tomlinson, James; Turnbull, Peter E; Van der Ville, Lenuel N

IPSWICH T

ABIDALLAH, Nabil (M)   2 0
H: 5 7 W: 9 00 b.Amsterdam 5-8-82

2000–01	Ipswich T	2	0	
2001–02	Ipswich T	0	0	2 0

AMBROSE, Darren (M)   1 0
H: 6 0 W: 11 07 b.Harlow 29-2-84
Source: Scholar. *Honours:* England Youth.

2001–02	Ipswich T	1	0	1 0

ARMSTRONG, Alun (F)   247 68
H: 6 0 W: 13 08 b.Gateshead 22-2-75
Source: School.

1993–94	Newcastle U	0	0
1994–95	Stockport Co	45	14
1995–96	Stockport Co	46	13

1996–97	Stockport Co	39	9		
1997–98	Stockport Co	29	12	159 48
1997–98	Middlesbrough	11	7		
1998–99	Middlesbrough	6	1		
1999–2000	Middlesbrough	12	1		
1999–2000	*Huddersfield T*	6	0	6 0
2000–01	Middlesbrough	0	0	29 9
2000–01	Ipswich T	21	7		
2001–02	Ipswich T	32	4	53 11

ARTUN, Erdem (D)   0 0
b.London 11-11-82
Source: Trainee.

1999–2000	Ipswich T	0	0
2000–01	Ipswich T	0	0
2001–02	Ipswich T	0	0

BEEVERS, Lee (D)   0 0
H: 6 1 W: 12 07 b.Doncaster 4-12-83
Source: Scholar.

2000–01	Ipswich T	0	0
2001–02	Ipswich T	0	0

BENT, Darren (F)   5 1
H: 5 11 W: 11 07 b.Tooting 6-2-84
Source: Scholar. *Honours:* England Youth.

2001–02	Ipswich T	5	1	5 1

BENT, Marcus (F)   231 51
H: 6 2 W: 12 04 b.Hammersmith 19-5-78
Source: Trainee. *Honours:* England Under-21.

1995–96	Brentford	12	1		
1996–97	Brentford	34	3		
1997–98	Brentford	24	4	70 8
1997–98	Crystal Palace	16	5		
1998–99	Crystal Palace	12	0	28 5
1998–99	Port Vale	15	0		
1999–2000	Port Vale	8	1	23 1
1999–2000	Sheffield U	32	15		
2000–01	Sheffield U	16	5	48 20
2000–01	Blackburn R	28	8		
2001–02	Blackburn R	9	0	37 8
2001–02	Ipswich T	25	9	25 9

BLOOMFIELD, Matt (M)   0 0
H: 5 8 W: 11 00 b.Ipswich 8-2-84
Source: Scholar. *Honours:* England Youth.

2001–02	Ipswich T	0	0

BONWICK, Guy* (D)   0 0
b.Herts 16-9-83
Source: Scholar.

2001–02	Ipswich T	0	0

BRAMBLE, Titus (D)   50 1
H: 6 2 W: 14 10 b.Ipswich 31-7-81
Source: Trainee. *Honours:* England Under-21.

1998–99	Ipswich T	4	0		
1999–2000	Ipswich T	0	0		
1999–2000	*Colchester U*	2	0	2 0
2000–01	Ipswich T	26	1		
2001–02	Ipswich T	18	0	48 1

BRANAGAN, Keith (G)   376 0
H: 6 0 W: 14 00 b.Fulham 10-7-66
Honours: Eire B. 1 full cap.

1983–84	Cambridge U	1	0		
1984–85	Cambridge U	19	0		
1985–86	Cambridge U	9	0		
1986–87	Cambridge U	46	0		
1987–88	Cambridge U	35	0	110 0
1987–88	Millwall	1	0		
1988–89	Millwall	0	0		
1989–90	Millwall	16	0		
1989–90	*Brentford*	2	0	2 0
1990–91	Millwall	18	0		
1991–92	Millwall	12	0	46 0
1991–92	*Gillingham*	1	0	1 0
1991–92	*Fulham*	7	0		
1992–93	Bolton W	46	0		
1993–94	Bolton W	10	0		
1994–95	Bolton W	43	0		
1995–96	Bolton W	31	0		
1996–97	Bolton W	36	0		
1997–98	Bolton W	34	0		
1998–99	Bolton W	3	0		
1999–2000	Bolton W	11	0	214 0
1999–2000	Ipswich T	0	0		
2000–01	Ipswich T	2	0		
2001–02	Ipswich T	1	0	3 0

BROWN, Wayne (D)   63 4
H: 6 0 W: 12 06 b.Barking 20-8-77
Source: Trainee.

1995–96	Ipswich T	0	0		
1996–97	Ipswich T	0	0		
1997–98	Ipswich T	3	0		
1997–98	*Colchester U*	2	0	2 0
1998–99	Ipswich T	1	0		
1999–2000	Ipswich T	25	0		
2000–01	Ipswich T	4	0		
2000–01	*QPR*	2	0	2 0

2001–02	Ipswich T	0 0	**31 0**
2001–02	Wimbledon	17 1	**17 1**
2001–02	Watford	11 3	**11 3**

CLAPHAM, Jamie (M) **193 9**
H: 5 9 W: 11 05 b.Lincoln 7-12-75
Source: Trainee.

1994–95	Tottenham H	0 0	
1995–96	Tottenham H	0 0	
1996–97	Tottenham H	1 0	
1996–97	Leyton Orient	6 0	**6 0**
1996–97	Bristol R	5 0	**5 0**
1997–98	Tottenham H	0 0	**1 0**
1997–98	Ipswich T	22 0	
1998–99	Ipswich T	46 3	
1999–2000	Ipswich T	46 2	
2000–01	Ipswich T	35 2	
2001–02	Ipswich T	32 2	**181 9**

COUNAGO, Pablo (F) **61 5**
H: 5 11 W: 11 06 b.Pontevedra 9-8-79

1998–99	Numancia	13 1	**13 1**
1998–99	Celta Vigo	1 0	
1999–2000	Huelva	26 4	**26 4**
2000–01	Celta Vigo	8 0	**9 0**
2001–02	Ipswich T	13 0	**13 0**

CROFT, Gary (D) **231 6**
H: 5 8 W: 11 08 b.Stafford 17-2-74
Source: Trainee. *Honours:* England Under-21.

1990–91	Grimsby T	1 0	
1991–92	Grimsby T	0 0	
1992–93	Grimsby T	32 0	
1993–94	Grimsby T	36 1	
1994–95	Grimsby T	44 1	
1995–96	Grimsby T	36 1	**149 3**
1995–96	Blackburn R	0 0	
1996–97	Blackburn R	5 0	
1997–98	Blackburn R	23 1	
1998–99	Blackburn R	12 0	
1999–2000	Blackburn R	0 0	**40 1**
1999–2000	Ipswich T	21 1	
2000–01	Ipswich T	8 0	
2001–02	Ipswich T	0 0	**29 1**
2001–02	Wigan Ath	7 0	**7 0**
2001–02	Cardiff C	6 1	**6 1**

DICKINSON, Robert (M) **0 0**
H: 5 9 W: 10 00 b.Leeds 27-11-83
Source: Scholar.

2000–01	Ipswich T	0 0	
2001–02	Ipswich T	0 0	

GAARDSOE, Thomas (M) **66 6**
H: 6 2 W: 12 06 b.Denmark 23-11-79

1996–97	Aalborg	0 0	
1997–98	Aalborg	6 1	
1998–99	Aalborg	17 2	
1999–2000	Aalborg	18 2	
2000–01	Aalborg	20 0	**62 5**
2001–02	Ipswich T	4 1	**4 1**

GEORGE, Finidi (F) **272 67**
H: 6 0 W: 12 04 b.Port Harcourt 15-4-71
Honours: Nigeria full caps.

1993–94	Ajax	27 4	
1994–95	Ajax	30 8	
1995–96	Ajax	29 6	**86 18**
1996–97	Betis	36 10	
1997–98	Betis	34 9	
1998–99	Betis	36 11	
1999–2000	Betis	24 8	**130 38**
2000–01	Mallorca	31 5	**31 5**
2001–02	Ipswich T	25 6	**25 6**

GRAAVEN, Guillermo‡ (M) **0 0**
H: 6 0 W: 11 06 b.Amsterdam 17-1-82

2000–01	Ipswich T	0 0	
2001–02	Ipswich T	0 0	

HOLLAND, Matt (M) **318 49**
H: 5 9 W: 12 07 b.Bury 11-4-74
Source: Trainee. *Honours:* Eire 23 full caps, 4 goals.

1992–93	West Ham U	0 0	
1993–94	West Ham U	0 0	
1994–95	West Ham U	0 0	
1994–95	Bournemouth	16 1	
1995–96	Bournemouth	43 10	
1996–97	Bournemouth	45 7	**104 18**
1997–98	Ipswich T	46 10	
1998–99	Ipswich T	46 5	
1999–2000	Ipswich T	46 10	
2000–01	Ipswich T	38 3	
2001–02	Ipswich T	38 3	**214 31**

HREIDARSSON, Hermann (D) **242 16**
H: 6 3 W: 13 01 b.Iceland 11-7-74
Honours: Iceland 41 full caps, 2 goals.

1993	IBV	2 0	
1994	IBV	18 2	
1995	IBV	18 1	
1996	IBV	17 2	
1997	IBV	11 0	**66 5**
1997–98	Crystal Palace	30 2	
1998–99	Crystal Palace	7 0	**37 2**
1998–99	Brentford	33 4	
1999–2000	Brentford	8 2	**41 6**
1999–2000	Wimbledon	24 1	**24 1**
2000–01	Ipswich T	36 1	
2001–02	Ipswich T	38 1	**74 2**

KARIC, Amir (D) **186 28**
H: 5 11 W: 12 08 b.Oramovica Ponja 31-12-73
Honours: Slovenia 46 full caps, 1 goal.

1991–92	Rudar	7 0	
1992–93	Rudar	27 10	**34 10**
1993–94	Maribor	20 0	
1994–95	Maribor	28 2	
1995–96	Maribor	21 4	
1996–97	Maribor	25 6	
1997	Gamba Osaka	5 0	
1998	Gamba Osaka	7 0	**12 0**
1998–99	Maribor	15 3	
1999–2000	Maribor	25 3	
2000–01	Maribor	3 0	**137 18**
2000–01	Ipswich T	0 0	
2000–01	*Crystal Palace*	3 0	**3 0**
2001–02	Ipswich T	0 0	

(On loan to Maribor, January 2002).

KELLY, Darren (G) **0 0**
b.Dublin 30-5-84
Source: Scholar.

2001–02	Ipswich T	0 0	

LE PEN, Ulrich (M) **81 9**
H: 5 7 W: 9 09 b.Auray 21-1-74

1994–95	Rennes	20 1	
1995–96	Rennes	31 0	
1996–97	Rennes	17 0	**68 1**

From Laval

2001–02	Lorient	12 0	**12 0**
2001–02	Ipswich T	1 0	**1 0**

LOGAN, Richard (F) **24 5**
H: 6 0 W: 12 05 b.Bury St Edmunds 4-1-82
Source: Trainee. *Honours:* England Youth.

1998–99	Ipswich T	2 0	
1999–2000	Ipswich T	1 0	
2000–01	Ipswich T	0 0	
2000–01	*Cambridge U*	5 1	**5 1**
2001–02	Ipswich T	0 0	**3 0**
2001–02	*Torquay U*	16 4	**16 4**

MAGILTON, Jim (M) **421 56**
H: 6 0 W: 13 10 b.Belfast 6-5-69
Source: Apprentice. *Honours:* Northern Ireland Schools, Youth, Under-21, Under-23, 52 full caps, 5 goals. Football League.

1986–87	Liverpool	0 0	
1987–88	Liverpool	0 0	
1988–89	Liverpool	0 0	
1989–90	Liverpool	0 0	
1990–91	Liverpool	0 0	
1990–91	Oxford U	37 6	
1991–92	Oxford U	44 12	
1992–93	Oxford U	40 11	
1993–94	Oxford U	29 5	**150 34**
1993–94	Southampton	15 0	
1994–95	Southampton	42 6	
1995–96	Southampton	31 3	
1996–97	Southampton	37 4	
1997–98	Southampton	5 0	**130 13**
1997–98	Sheffield W	21 1	
1998–99	Sheffield W	6 0	**27 1**
1998–99	Ipswich T	19 3	
1999–2000	Ipswich T	38 4	
2000–01	Ipswich T	33 1	
2001–02	Ipswich T	24 0	**114 8**

MAKIN, Chris (D) **298 7**
H: 5 10 W: 11 02 b.Manchester 8-5-73
Source: Trainee. *Honours:* England Schools, Under-21.

1991–92	Oldham Ath	0 0	
1992–93	Oldham Ath	0 0	
1992–93	Wigan Ath	15 2	**15 2**
1993–94	Oldham Ath	27 1	
1994–95	Oldham Ath	28 1	
1995–96	Oldham Ath	39 2	**94 4**
1996–97	Marseille	29 0	**29 0**
1997–98	Sunderland	25 0	
1998–99	Sunderland	38 0	
1999–2000	Sunderland	23 0	**120 1**
2000–01	Ipswich T	10 0	
2001–02	Ipswich T	30 0	**40 0**

MARSHALL, Andy (G) **224 0**
H: 6 2 W: 13 07 b.Bury 14-4-75
Source: Trainee. *Honours:* England Under-21.

1993–94	Norwich C	0 0	
1994–95	Norwich C	21 0	
1995–96	Norwich C	3 0	
1996–97	Norwich C	7 0	
1996–97	Bournemouth	11 0	**11 0**
1996–97	Gillingham	5 0	**5 0**
1997–98	Norwich C	42 0	
1998–99	Norwich C	37 0	
1999–2000	Norwich C	44 0	
2000–01	Norwich C	41 0	**195 0**
2001–02	Ipswich T	13 0	**13 0**

McGREAL, John (D) **284 3**
H: 5 11 W: 13 00 b.Birkenhead 2-6-72
Source: Trainee.

1990–91	Tranmere R	3 0	
1991–92	Tranmere R	0 0	
1992–93	Tranmere R	0 0	
1993–94	Tranmere R	15 1	
1994–95	Tranmere R	43 0	
1995–96	Tranmere R	32 0	
1996–97	Tranmere R	24 0	
1997–98	Tranmere R	42 0	
1998–99	Tranmere R	36 0	**195 1**
1999–2000	Ipswich T	34 0	
2000–01	Ipswich T	28 1	
2001–02	Ipswich T	27 1	**89 2**

MILLER, Justin (D) **0 0**
H: 6 0 W: 11 07 b.Johannesburg 16-12-80
Source: Academy.

1999–2000	Ipswich T	0 0	
2000–01	Ipswich T	0 0	
2001–02	Ipswich T	0 0	

MILLER, Tommy (M) **145 35**
H: 6 1 W: 11 12 b.Easington 8-1-79
Source: Trainee.

1997–98	Hartlepool U	13 1	
1998–99	Hartlepool U	34 4	
1999–2000	Hartlepool U	44 14	
2000–01	Hartlepool U	46 16	
2001–02	Hartlepool U	0 0	**137 35**
2001–02	Ipswich T	8 0	**8 0**

NAYLOR, Richard (F) **136 21**
H: 6 1 W: 13 07 b.Leeds 28-2-77
Source: Trainee.

1995–96	Ipswich T	0 0	
1996–97	Ipswich T	27 4	
1997–98	Ipswich T	5 2	
1998–99	Ipswich T	30 5	
1999–2000	Ipswich T	36 8	
2000–01	Ipswich T	13 1	
2001–02	Ipswich T	14 1	**125 21**
2001–02	*Millwall*	3 0	**3 0**
2001–02	*Barnsley*	8 0	**8 0**

NICHOLLS, Ashley* (M) **0 0**
H: 5 11 W: 11 11 b.Suffolk 30-10-81
Source: Ipswich W. *Honours:* England Schools.

2000–01	Ipswich T	0 0	
2001–02	Ipswich T	0 0	

PERALTA, Sixto‡ (M) **133 22**
H: 6 1 W: 12 02 b.Comodoro Rivadavia 16-4-79

1996–97	Huracan	27 2	
1997–98	Huracan	25 1	
1998–99	Huracan	29 9	**81 12**
1999–2000	Racing	26 6	**26 6**
2000–01	Internazionale	0 0	
2000–01	Torino	4 1	**4 1**
2001–02	Ipswich T	22 3	**22 3**

PULLEN, James (G) **16 0**
H: 6 2 W: 14 00 b.Chelmsford 18-3-82
Source: Heybridge S.

1999–2000	Ipswich T	0 0	
2000–01	Ipswich T	0 0	
2001–02	Ipswich T	0 0	
2001–02	*Blackpool*	16 0	**16 0**

REUSER, Martijn (M) **156 29**
H: 5 7 W: 12 10 b.Amsterdam 1-2-75
Honours: Holland 1 full cap.

1993–94	Ajax	2 0	
1994–95	Ajax	18 2	
1995–96	Ajax	18 3	
1996–97	Ajax	19 3	
1997–98	Ajax	1 0	**42 6**
1997–98	Vitesse	24 6	
1998–99	Vitesse	32 8	**56 14**
1999–2000	Ipswich T	22 0	
2000–01	Ipswich T	26 6	
2001–02	Ipswich T	24 1	**58 9**

RICHARDS, Matthew (D) **0 0**
b.Harlow 26-12-84
Source: Scholar.

2001–02	Ipswich T	0 0	

SALMON, Mike* (G) 410 0
H: 6 2 W: 14 00 b.Leyland 14-7-64
Source: Local.

1981–82	Blackburn R	1	0	
1982–83	Blackburn R	0	0	1 0
1982–83	*Chester C*	16	0	16 0
1983–84	Stockport Co	46	0	
1984–85	Stockport Co	46	0	
1985–86	Stockport Co	26	0	118 0
1986–87	Bolton W	26	0	26 0
1986–87	*Wrexham*	17	0	
1987–88	*Wrexham*	40	0	
1988–89	*Wrexham*	43	0	100 0
1989–90	Charlton Ath	0	0	
1990–91	Charlton Ath	7	0	
1991–92	Charlton Ath	0	0	
1992–93	Charlton Ath	19	0	
1993–94	Charlton Ath	41	0	
1994–95	Charlton Ath	20	0	
1995–96	Charlton Ath	27	0	
1996–97	Charlton Ath	25	0	
1997–98	Charlton Ath	9	0	
1998–99	Charlton Ath	0	0	148 0
1998–99	*Oxford U*	1	0	1 0
1999–2000	Ipswich T	0	0	
2000–01	Ipswich T	0	0	
2001–02	Ipswich T	0	0	

SERENI, Matteo (G) 174 0
H: 6 1 W: 12 07 b.Parma 11-2-75

1993–94	Sampdoria	0	0	
1994–95	Crevalcore	0	0	
1995–96	Sampdoria	4	0	
1996–97	Sampdoria	6	0	
1997–98	Piacenza	34	0	34 0
1998–99	Empoli	30	0	30 0
1999–2000	Sampdoria	37	0	
2000–01	Sampdoria	38	0	85 0
2001–02	Ipswich T	25	0	25 0

STEWART, Marcus (F) 376 142
H: 5 10 W: 11 08 b.Bristol 7-11-72
Source: Trainee. *Honours:* England Schools, Football League.

1991–92	Bristol R	33	5	
1992–93	Bristol R	38	11	
1993–94	Bristol R	29	5	
1994–95	Bristol R	27	15	
1995–96	Bristol R	44	21	171 57
1996–97	Huddersfield T	20	7	
1997–98	Huddersfield T	41	15	
1998–99	Huddersfield T	43	22	
1999–2000	Huddersfield T	29	14	133 58
1999–2000	Ipswich T	10	2	
2000–01	Ipswich T	34	19	
2001–02	Ipswich T	28	6	72 27

VENUS, Mark (D) 492 24
H: 6 0 W: 13 02 b.Hartlepool 6-4-67

1984–85	Hartlepool U	4	0	4 0
1985–86	Leicester C	1	0	
1986–87	Leicester C	39	0	
1987–88	Leicester C	21	1	61 1
1987–88	Wolverhampton W	4	0	
1988–89	Wolverhampton W	35	0	
1989–90	Wolverhampton W	44	2	
1990–91	Wolverhampton W	6	0	
1991–92	Wolverhampton W	46	1	
1992–93	Wolverhampton W	12	0	
1993–94	Wolverhampton W	39	1	
1994–95	Wolverhampton W	39	3	
1995–96	Wolverhampton W	22	0	
1996–97	Wolverhampton W	40	0	287 7
1997–98	Ipswich T	14	1	
1998–99	Ipswich T	44	9	
1999–2000	Ipswich T	28	2	
2000–01	Ipswich T	25	3	
2001–02	Ipswich T	29	1	140 16

WILNIS, Fabian (D) 337 7
H: 5 8 W: 12 06 b.Paramaribo 23-8-70
Source: Het Noorden, NOC, De Zwervers, Sparta.

1990–91	NAC	7	3	
1991–92	NAC	30	0	
1992–93	NAC	32	0	
1993–94	NAC	34	0	
1994–95	NAC	31	0	134 3
1995–96	De Graafschap	32	0	
1996–97	De Graafschap	24	0	
1997–98	De Graafschap	33	1	
1998–99	De Graafschap	19	0	107 1
1998–99	Ipswich T	18	1	
1999–2000	Ipswich T	35	0	
2000–01	Ipswich T	29	2	
2001–02	Ipswich T	14	0	96 3

WRIGHT, Jermaine (M) 182 9
H: 5 10 W: 12 07 b.Greenwich 21-10-75
Source: Trainee. *Honours:* England Youth.

1992–93	Millwall	0	0	
1993–94	Millwall	0	0	
1994–95	Millwall	0	0	
1994–95	Wolverhampton W	6	0	
1995–96	Wolverhampton W	7	0	
1995–96	*Doncaster R*	13	0	13 0
1996–97	Wolverhampton W	3	0	
1997–98	Wolverhampton W	4	0	20 0
1997–98	Crewe Alex	5	0	
1998–99	Crewe Alex	44	5	49 5
1999–2000	Ipswich T	34	1	
2000–01	Ipswich T	37	2	
2001–02	Ipswich T	29	1	100 4

Trainees
Boardley, Stuart; Burton, Steven P; Chaffey, Lee; Hill, Victor; Hogg, Christopher; Mayes, Mark; Morrow, Samuel; Murray, Antonio; O'Connor, Gerard; Okay, Erkan; Peat, Scott; Robinson, Matthew A; Smith, Marc; Westlake, Ian J

KIDDERMINSTER H

APPLEBY, Ritchie# (M) 142 15
H: 5 9 W: 11 04 b.Stockton 18-9-75
Source: Trainee. *Honours:* England Youth.

1993–94	Newcastle U	0	0	
1994–95	Newcastle U	0	0	
1994–95	*Darlington*	0	0	
1995–96	Ipswich T	3	0	3 0
1996–97	Swansea C	11	1	
1997–98	Swansea C	35	3	
1998–99	Swansea C	39	3	
1999–2000	Swansea C	20	4	
2000–01	Swansea C	5	0	
2001–02	Swansea C	10	0	120 11
2001–02	Kidderminster H	19	4	19 4

AYRES, Lee (D) 6 0
H: 6 1 W: 11 00 b.Birmingham 28-8-82

2001–02	Kidderminster H	6	0	6 0

BARNETT, Gary‡ (M) 397 59
H: 5 6 W: 9 13 b.Stratford upon Avon 11-3-63
Source: Apprentice.

1980–81	Coventry C	0	0	
1981–82	Coventry C	0	0	
1982–83	Oxford U	22	2	
1982–83	*Wimbledon*	5	1	5 1
1983–84	Oxford U	19	7	
1984–85	Oxford U	2	0	
1984–85	*Fulham*	2	1	
1985–86	Oxford U	2	0	45 9
1985–86	Fulham	36	6	
1986–87	Fulham	42	9	
1987–88	Fulham	42	9	
1988–89	Fulham	28	5	
1989–90	Fulham	32	1	182 31
1990–91	Huddersfield T	22	1	
1991–92	Huddersfield T	31	3	
1992–93	Huddersfield T	46	7	
1993–94	Huddersfield T	1	0	100 11
1993–94	Leyton Orient	36	7	
1994–95	Leyton Orient	27	0	63 7

From Barry T.

2000–01	Kidderminster H	2	0	
2001–02	Kidderminster H	0	0	2 0

BENNETT, Dean (M) 85 12
H: 5 10 W: 11 00 b.Wolverhampton 13-12-77

1996–97	WBA	1	0	
1997–98	WBA	0	0	1 0

From Bromsgrove R

2000–01	Kidderminster H	42	4	
2001–02	Kidderminster H	42	8	84 12

BIRD, Tony* (F) 212 34
H: 5 11 W: 12 10 b.Cardiff 1-9-74
Source: Trainee. *Honours:* Wales Youth, Under-21.

1991–92	Cardiff C	0	0	
1992–93	Cardiff C	9	1	
1993–94	Cardiff C	35	5	
1994–95	Cardiff C	19	4	
1995–96	Cardiff C	12	3	75 13

From Barry T

1997–98	Swansea C	41	14	
1998–99	Swansea C	29	3	
1999–2000	Swansea C	16	1	86 18
2000–01	Kidderminster H	25	1	
2001–02	Kidderminster H	26	2	51 3

BLAKE, Mark (M) 266 24
H: 5 11 W: 13 05 b.Nottingham 16-12-70
Source: Trainee. *Honours:* England Schools, Youth, Under-21.

1989–90	Aston Villa	9	0	
1990–91	Aston Villa	7	0	
1990–91	*Wolverhampton W*	2	0	2 0
1991–92	Aston Villa	14	2	
1992–93	Aston Villa	1	0	31 2
1993–94	Portsmouth	15	0	15 0
1993–94	Leicester C	11	1	
1994–95	Leicester C	30	3	
1995–96	Leicester C	8	0	49 4
1996–97	Walsall	38	4	
1997–98	Walsall	23	1	61 5
1999–2000	Mansfield T	43	1	
2000–01	Mansfield T	41	8	84 9
2001–02	Kidderminster H	24	4	24 4

BROCK, Stuart (G) 63 0
H: 6 1 W: 13 03 b.Sandwell 26-9-76
Source: Trainee.

1994–95	Aston Villa	0	0	
1995–96	Aston Villa	0	0	
1996–97	Aston Villa	0	0	
1996–97	Northampton T	0	0	
1997–98	Northampton T	0	0	
1998–99	Northampton T	0	0	
1999–2000	Northampton T	0	0	
2000–01	Kidderminster H	21	0	
2001–02	Kidderminster H	42	0	63 0

BROUGHTON, Drewe (F) 106 24
H: 6 3 W: 12 04 b.Hitchin 25-10-78
Source: Trainee.

1996–97	Norwich C	8	1	
1997–98	Norwich C	1	0	
1997–98	*Wigan Ath*	4	0	4 0
1998–99	Norwich C	0	0	9 1
1998–99	*Brentford*	1	0	1 0
1998–99	Peterborough U	25	7	
1999–2000	Peterborough U	10	1	
2000–01	Peterborough U	0	0	35 8
2000–01	Kidderminster H	19	7	
2001–02	Kidderminster H	38	8	57 15

CLARKSON, Ian* (D) 382 1
H: 5 10 W: 12 00 b.Solihull 4-12-70
Source: Trainee.

1988–89	Birmingham C	9	0	
1989–90	Birmingham C	20	0	
1990–91	Birmingham C	37	0	
1991–92	Birmingham C	42	0	
1992–93	Birmingham C	28	0	
1993–94	Birmingham C	0	0	136 0
1993–94	Stoke C	14	0	
1994–95	Stoke C	18	0	
1995–96	Stoke C	43	0	75 0
1996–97	Northampton T	45	0	
1997–98	Northampton T	42	1	
1998–99	Northampton T	5	0	
1999–2000	Northampton T	2	0	94 1
2000–01	Kidderminster H	38	0	
2001–02	Kidderminster H	39	0	77 0

CORBETT, Andy (F) 8 0
H: 6 0 W: 11 04 b.Worcester 20-2-82

2000–01	Kidderminster H	6	0	
2001–02	Kidderminster H	2	0	8 0

DANBY, John (G) 2 0
b.Stoke 20-9-83

2001–02	Kidderminster H	2	0	2 0

DAVIES, Ben‡ (M) 12 0
H: 5 6 W: 10 07 b.Birmingham 27-5-81
Source: Walsall trainee.

2000–01	Kidderminster H	3	0	
2001–02	Kidderminster H	9	0	12 0

DOYLE, Daire (M) 16 0
H: 5 10 W: 11 06 b.Dublin 18-10-80
Source: Cherry Orchard.

1998–99	Coventry C	0	0	
1999–2000	Coventry C	0	0	
2000–01	Coventry C	0	0	
2000–01	Kidderminster H	15	0	
2001–02	Kidderminster H	1	0	16 0

DUCROS, Andy (F) 56 4
H: 5 6 W: 9 08 b.Evesham 16-9-77
Source: Trainee. *Honours:* England Schools, Youth.

1994–95	Coventry C	0	0	
1995–96	Coventry C	0	0	
1996–97	Coventry C	5	0	
1997–98	Coventry C	3	0	
1998–99	Coventry C	0	0	8 0

From Nuneaton B

2000–01	Kidderminster H	34	2	
2001–02	Kidderminster H	14	2	48 4

FAULDS, Peter* (M) 0 0
H: 5 7 W: 10 00 b.Birmingham 26-8-82

2001–02	Kidderminster H	0	0	

FOSTER, Ian (F) 62 10
H: 5 7 W: 10 07 b.Merseyside 11-11-76
Source: Liverpool Schoolboy. *Honours:* England Schools.

1996–97	Hereford U	19	0	19 0

From Barrow
2000–01 Kidderminster H 10 2
2001–02 Kidderminster H 33 8 43 10

HADLEY, Stewart (F)   167 37
H: 5 11 W: 13 05 b.Stourbridge 30-12-73
Source: Halesowen T.
1992–93 Derby Co 0 0
1993–94 Derby Co 0 0
1993–94 Mansfield T 14 5
1994–95 Mansfield T 39 14
1995–96 Mansfield T 33 8
1996–97 Mansfield T 36 4
1997–98 Mansfield T 2 0 124 31
2000–01 Kidderminster H 33 6
2001–02 Kidderminster H 10 0 43 6

HENRIKSEN, Bo (F)   141 42
H: 5 11 W: 11 11 b.Roskilde 7-2-75
1995–96 Odense 10 3
1996–97 Odense 23 8 33 11
1997–98 Aarhus 0 0
1997–98 Herfolge 15 6
1998–99 Herfolge 23 6
1999–2000 Herfolge 10 1
2000–01 Herfolge 21 1
2000–01 *Frem* 4 3 4 3
2001–02 Herfolge 10 6 79 20
2001–02 Kidderminster H 25 8 25 8

HINTON, Craig (D)   87 2
H: 5 11 W: 11 00 b.Wolverhampton 26-11-77
Source: Trainee.
1996–97 Birmingham C 0 0
1997–98 Birmingham C 0 0
2000–01 Kidderminster H 46 2
2001–02 Kidderminster H 41 0 87 2

JOY, Ian (D)   41 2
H: 5 10 W: 11 00 b.San Diego 14-7-81
Source: Trainee.
1998–99 Tranmere R 0 0
1999–2000 Tranmere R 0 0
2000–01 Montrose 25 2 25 2
2001–02 Kidderminster H 16 0 16 0

LEWIS, Matt (F)   2 0
b.Coventry 20-3-84
Source: Marconi.
2001–02 Kidderminster H 2 0 2 0

MEDOU-OTYE, Parfait‡ (D)   29 0
H: 5 10 W: 12 00 b.Ekoundendi 29-11-76
1998–99 Le Havre 0 0
From Le Mans UC 72
2000–01 Morton 10 0 10 0
2000–01 Kidderminster H 17 0
2001–02 Kidderminster H 2 0 19 0

MURPHY, Brendan‡ (G)   0 0
H: 5 11 W: 11 12 b.Wexford 19-8-75
Source: Bradford C Trainee. *Honours:* Eire Youth, Under-21, B.
1994–95 Wimbledon 0 0
1995–96 Wimbledon 0 0
1996–97 Wimbledon 0 0
1997–98 Wimbledon 0 0
1998–99 Wimbledon 0 0
From Dundalk
2000–01 Kidderminster H 0 0
2001–02 Kidderminster H 0 0

SALL, Abdou (D)   27 2
H: 6 3 W: 12 13 b.Senegal 1-11-80
Source: Toulouse.
2001–02 Kidderminster H 27 2 27 2

SHAIL, Mark‡ (D)   168 5
H: 6 1 W: 12 06 b.Sweden 15-10-66
Source: Yeovil T.
1992–93 Bristol C 4 0
1993–94 Bristol C 36 2
1994–95 Bristol C 38 2
1995–96 Bristol C 12 0
1996–97 Bristol C 11 0
1997–98 Bristol C 2 0
1998–99 Bristol C 24 0
1999–2000 Bristol C 1 0 128 4
2000–01 Kidderminster H 36 1
2001–02 Kidderminster H 4 0 40 1

SHILTON, Sam (M)   88 7
H: 5 11 W: 11 06 b.Nottingham 21-7-78
Source: School.
1994–95 Plymouth Arg 2 0
1995–96 Plymouth Arg 1 0 3 0
1995–96 Coventry C 0 0
1996–97 Coventry C 0 0
1997–98 Coventry C 2 0
1998–99 Coventry C 5 0
1999–2000 Coventry C 0 0 7 0
1999–2000 Hartlepool U 21 3
2000–01 Hartlepool U 33 4 54 7
2001–02 Kidderminster H 24 0 24 0

SMITH, Adie (D)   70 7
H: 5 10 W: 12 00 b.Birmingham 11-8-73
Source: Bromsgrove R.
2000–01 Kidderminster H 34 5
2001–02 Kidderminster H 36 2 70 7

STAMPS, Scott (D)   213 6
H: 5 11 W: 11 09 b.Edgbaston 20-3-75
Source: Trainee.
1992–93 Torquay U 2 0
1993–94 Torquay U 6 0
1994–95 Torquay U 25 1
1995–96 Torquay U 23 1
1996–97 Torquay U 30 3 86 5
1996–97 Colchester U 8 0
1997–98 Colchester U 27 1
1998–99 Colchester U 21 0 56 1
2000–01 Kidderminster H 34 0
2001–02 Kidderminster H 37 0 71 0

WEBB, Paul‡ (M)   32 1
H: 5 9 W: 13 07 b.Wolverhampton 30-11-67
Source: Bromsgrove R.
2000–01 Kidderminster H 32 1
2001–02 Kidderminster H 0 0 32 1

WILLIAMS, Danny (M)   77 4
H: 6 2 W: 13 01 b.Wrexham 12-7-79
Source: Trainee. *Honours:* Wales Under-21.
1996–97 Liverpool 0 0
1997–98 Liverpool 0 0
1998–99 Liverpool 0 0
1998–99 Wrexham 0 0
1999–2000 Wrexham 24 1
2000–01 Wrexham 15 2 39 3
2001–02 Kidderminster H 38 1 38 1

LEEDS U

ALLAWAY, Shaun (G)   0 0
H: 6 2 W: 12 00 b.Reading 16-2-83
Source: Trainee. *Honours:* England Youth.
1999–2000 Reading 0 0
1999–2000 Leeds U 0 0
2000–01 Leeds U 0 0
2001–02 Leeds U 0 0

ARMSTRONG, Chris (F)   0 0
H: 6 1 W: 13 02 b.Durham 8-11-84
Source: Scholar.
2001–02 Leeds U 0 0

BAKKE, Eirik (M)   161 23
H: 5 11 W: 12 05 b.Sogndal 13-9-77
Honours: Norway 17 full caps.
1994 Sogndal 5 0
1995 Sogndal
1996 Sogndal 19 8
1997 Sogndal 25 4
1998 Sogndal 19 2
1999 Sogndal 8 3 76 17
1999–2000 Leeds U 29 2
2000–01 Leeds U 29 2
2001–02 Leeds U 27 2 85 6

BATTY, David (M)   426 8
H: 5 8 W: 12 00 b.Leeds 2-12-68
Source: Trainee. *Honours:* England Under-21, B, 42 full caps.
1987–88 Leeds U 23 1
1988–89 Leeds U 30 0
1989–90 Leeds U 42 0
1990–91 Leeds U 37 0
1991–92 Leeds U 40 2
1992–93 Leeds U 30 1
1993–94 Leeds U 9 0
1993–94 Blackburn R 26 0
1994–95 Blackburn R 5 0
1995–96 Blackburn R 23 1 54 1
1995–96 Newcastle U 11 1
1996–97 Newcastle U 32 1
1997–98 Newcastle U 32 1
1998–99 Newcastle U 8 0 83 3
1998–99 Leeds U 10 0
1999–2000 Leeds U 16 0
2000–01 Leeds U 16 0
2001–02 Leeds U 36 0 289 4

BOWYER, Lee (M)   234 43
H: 5 9 W: 10 04 b.London 3-1-77
Source: Trainee. *Honours:* England Youth, Under-21.
1993–94 Charlton Ath 1 0
1994–95 Charlton Ath 5 0
1995–96 Charlton Ath 41 8 46 8
1996–97 Leeds U 32 4
1997–98 Leeds U 25 3
1998–99 Leeds U 35 9
1999–2000 Leeds U 33 5
2000–01 Leeds U 38 9
2001–02 Leeds U 25 5 188 35

BOYLE, West‡ (F)   1 0
H: 5 10 W: 11 11 b.Portadown 30-3-79
Source: Trainee. *Honours:* Northern Ireland Under-21.
1995–96 Leeds U 0 0
1996–97 Leeds U 1 0
1997–98 Leeds U 0 0
1998–99 Leeds U 0 0
1999–2000 Leeds U 0 0
2000–01 Leeds U 0 0
2001–02 Leeds U 0 0 1 0

BREEN, Gerard (M)   0 0
H: 5 11 W: 13 01 b.County Louth 29-3-84
Source: Scholar.
2000–01 Leeds U 0 0
2001–02 Leeds U 0 0

BRIDGES, Michael (F)   120 35
H: 6 1 W: 12 05 b.North Shields 5-8-78
Source: Trainee. *Honours:* England Schools, Youth, Under-21.
1995–96 Sunderland 15 4
1996–97 Sunderland 25 3
1997–98 Sunderland 9 1
1998–99 Sunderland 30 8 79 16
1999–2000 Leeds U 34 19
2000–01 Leeds U 7 0
2001–02 Leeds U 0 0 41 19

BURNS, Jacob (M)   86 8
H: 5 10 W: 11 11 b.Sydney 21-4-78
Honours: Australia 2 full caps.
1996–97 Sydney U 5 0
1997–98 Sydney U 25 2
1998–99 Sydney U 27 3 57 5
1999–2000 Parramatta Power 25 3 25 3
2000–01 Leeds U 4 0
2001–02 Leeds U 0 0 4 0

CANDSELL-SHERIFF, Shane (D)   0 0
H: 6 0 W: 11 12 b.Sydney 10-11-82
Source: NSW Academy.
1999–2000 Leeds U 0 0
2000–01 Leeds U 0 0
2001–02 Leeds U 0 0

CORR, Barry (F)   0 0
H: 6 2 W: 11 06 b.Co Wicklow 2-4-85
Source: Scholar.
2001–02 Leeds U 0 0

COUSINS, Andrew (M)   0 0
H: 5 6 W: 10 08 b.Dublin 30-1-85
Source: Scholar.
2001–02 Leeds U 0 0

COYLES, William (G)   0 0
H: 6 0 W: 11 09 b.Co Antrim 20-12-84
Source: Scholar.
2001–02 Leeds U 0 0

CRAMER, Martin‡ (M)   0 0
H: 5 4 W: 10 02 b.Dublin 15-11-82
Source: Maryland Boys.
1999–2000 Leeds U 0 0
2000–01 Leeds U 0 0
2001–02 Leeds U 0 0

CRONIN, Kevin (M)   0 0
b.Dublin 18-5-85
Source: Scholar.
2001–02 Leeds U 0 0

DACOURT, Olivier (M)   233 11
H: 5 9 W: 11 07 b.Montreuil 25-9-74
Honours: France 3 full caps.
1992–93 Strasbourg 6 0
1993–94 Strasbourg 8 0
1994–95 Strasbourg 18 0
1995–96 Strasbourg 34 0
1996–97 Strasbourg 31 1
1997–98 Strasbourg 30 3 127 4
1998–99 Everton 30 2 30 2
1999–2000 Lens 26 2 26 2
2000–01 Leeds U 33 3
2001–02 Leeds U 17 0 50 3

DUBERRY, Michael (D)   114 2
H: 6 0 W: 14 00 b.Enfield 14-10-75
Source: Trainee. *Honours:* England Under-21.
1993–94 Chelsea 1 0
1994–95 Chelsea 0 0
1995–96 Chelsea 22 0
1995–96 Bournemouth 7 0 7 0
1996–97 Chelsea 15 1
1997–98 Chelsea 23 0
1998–99 Chelsea 25 0 86 1
1999–2000 Leeds U 13 1
2000–01 Leeds U 5 0

2001–02	Leeds U	3	0	21	1

EDWARDS, Stewart (D) 0 0
H: 5 9 W: 11 00 b.Swansea 1-10-84
Source: Scholar.

2001–02	Leeds U	0	0

FARRELL, Craig (F) 0 0
H: 6 0 W: 12 11 b.Middlesbrough 5-12-82
Source: Trainee.

1999–2000	Leeds U	0	0
2000–01	Leeds U	0	0
2001–02	Leeds U	0	0

FARREN, Larry (D) 0 0
H: 6 0 W: 11 11 b.Donegal 29-7-83
Source: Scholar.

2000–01	Leeds U	0	0
2001–02	Leeds U	0	0

FERDINAND, Rio (D) 191 4
H: 6 2 W: 13 12 b.Peckham 7-11-78
Source: Trainee. *Honours:* England Youth, Under-21, 27 full caps, 1 goal.

1995–96	West Ham U	1	0		
1996–97	West Ham U	15	2		
1996–97	*Bournemouth*	10	0	10	0
1997–98	West Ham U	35	0		
1998–99	West Ham U	31	0		
1999–2000	West Ham U	33	0		
2000–01	West Ham U	12	0	127	2
2000–01	Leeds U	23	2		
2001–02	Leeds U	31	0	54	2

FERGUSON, Steven (M) 0 0
H: 5 7 W: 9 13 b.Newry 25-2-83
Source: St Andrew's.

1999–2000	Leeds U	0	0
2000–01	Leeds U	0	0
2001–02	Leeds U	0	0

FOLAN, Caleb (F) 7 0
H: 6 2 W: 13 00 b.Leeds 26-10-82
Source: Trainee.

1999–2000	Leeds U	0	0		
2000–01	Leeds U	0	0		
2001–02	Leeds U	0	0		
2001–02	*Rushden & D*	6	0	6	0
2001–02	*Hull C*	1	0	1	0

FOWLER, Robbie (F) 258 132
H: 5 8 W: 11 06 b.Liverpool 9-4-75
Source: Trainee. *Honours:* England Youth, B, Under-21, 26 full caps, 7 goals.

1991–92	Liverpool	0	0		
1992–93	Liverpool	0	0		
1993–94	Liverpool	28	12		
1994–95	Liverpool	42	25		
1995–96	Liverpool	38	28		
1996–97	Liverpool	32	18		
1997–98	Liverpool	20	9		
1998–99	Liverpool	25	14		
1999–2000	Liverpool	14	3		
2000–01	Liverpool	27	8		
2001–02	Liverpool	10	3	236	120
2001–02	Leeds U	22	12	22	12

HARTE, Ian (D) 163 24
H: 5 9 W: 12 06 b.Drogheda 31-8-77
Source: Trainee. *Honours:* Eire 44 full caps, 8 goals.

1995–96	Leeds U	4	0		
1996–97	Leeds U	14	2		
1997–98	Leeds U	12	0		
1998–99	Leeds U	35	4		
1999–2000	Leeds U	33	6		
2000–01	Leeds U	29	7		
2001–02	Leeds U	36	5	163	24

HAY, Danny* (D) 52 2
H: 6 4 W: 14 07 b.Auckland 15-5-75
Source: Waitakere, Central Utd. *Honours:* New Zealand 11 full caps.

1997–98	Perth Glory	24	1		
1998–99	Perth Glory	24	1	48	2
1999–2000	Leeds U	0	0		
2000–01	Leeds U	4	0		
2001–02	Leeds U	0	0	4	0

JOHNSON, Seth (M) 180 8
H: 5 8 W: 12 04 b.Birmingham 12-3-79
Source: Trainee. *Honours:* England Youth, Under-21, 1 full cap.

1996–97	Crewe Alex	11	1		
1997–98	Crewe Alex	40	1		
1998–99	Crewe Alex	42	4	93	6
1999–2000	Derby Co	36	1		
2000–01	Derby Co	30	1		
2001–02	Derby Co	7	0	73	2
2001–02	Leeds U	14	0	14	0

JOHNSON, Simon (F) 0 0
H: 5 9 W: 11 12 b.West Bromwich 9-3-83
Source: Scholar. *Honours:* England Youth.

2000–01	Leeds U	0	0
2001–02	Leeds U	0	0

KAMARA, Christopher‡ (D) 0 0
H: 5 9 W: 12 06 b.York 27-2-84
Source: Scholar.

2000–01	Leeds U	0	0
2001–02	Leeds U	0	0

KEANE, Robbie (F) 153 48
H: 5 9 W: 12 06 b.Dublin 8-7-80
Source: Trainee. *Honours:* Eire 37 full caps, 13 goals.

1997–98	Wolverhampton W	38	11		
1998–99	Wolverhampton W	33	11		
1999–2000	Wolverhampton W	2	2	73	24
1999–2000	Coventry C	31	12	31	12
2000–01	Internazionale	6	0	6	0
2000–01	Leeds U	18	9		
2001–02	Leeds U	25	3	43	12

KEEGAN, Paul (M) 0 0
H: 5 11 W: 11 11 b.Dublin 5-7-84
Source: Scholar.

2000–01	Leeds U	0	0
2001–02	Leeds U	0	0

KELLY, Gary (D) 265 2
H: 5 8 W: 11 00 b.Drogheda 9-7-74
Source: Home Farm. *Honours:* Eire Youth, 50 full caps, 2 goals.

1991–92	Leeds U	2	0		
1992–93	Leeds U	0	0		
1993–94	Leeds U	42	0		
1994–95	Leeds U	42	0		
1995–96	Leeds U	34	0		
1996–97	Leeds U	36	2		
1997–98	Leeds U	34	0		
1998–99	Leeds U	0	0		
1999–2000	Leeds U	31	0		
2000–01	Leeds U	24	0		
2001–02	Leeds U	20	0	265	2

KEWELL, Harry (F) 150 31
H: 5 11 W: 13 04 b.Sydney 22-9-78
Source: NSW Soccer Academy. *Honours:* Australia 12 full caps, 3 goals.

1995–96	Leeds U	2	0		
1996–97	Leeds U	1	0		
1997–98	Leeds U	29	5		
1998–99	Leeds U	38	6		
1999–2000	Leeds U	36	10		
2000–01	Leeds U	17	2		
2001–02	Leeds U	27	8	150	31

KEYES, Edward (D) 0 0
H: 5 7 W: 9 05 b.Dublin 2-5-85
Source: Scholar.

2001–02	Leeds U	0	0

KILGALLON, Matthew (D) 0 0
H: 6 1 W: 12 04 b.York 8-1-84
Source: Scholar. *Honours:* England Youth.

2000–01	Leeds U	0	0
2001–02	Leeds U	0	0

KINSELLA, Alan (F) 0 0
H: 5 8 W: 11 00 b.Dublin 2-2-84
Source: Scholar.

2000–01	Leeds U	0	0
2001–02	Leeds U	0	0

KRIEF, Dominique (M) 0 0
H: 5 9 W: 10 02 b.Leeds 15-9-83
Source: Scholar.

2000–01	Leeds U	0	0
2001–02	Leeds U	0	0

LAVERY, Sean (M) 0 0
H: 5 7 W: 11 12 b.Lurgan 16-11-83
Source: Scholar.

2000–01	Leeds U	0	0
2001–02	Leeds U	0	0

LENNON, Anthony‡ (F) 0 0
H: 5 10 W: 10 09 b.Leeds 16-5-82
Source: Trainee.

1998–99	Leeds U	0	0
1999–2000	Leeds U	0	0
2000–01	Leeds U	0	0
2001–02	Leeds U	0	0

MARTIN, Alan‡ (D) 0 0
H: 5 10 W: 11 05 b.Dublin 21-11-81
Source: Trainee.

1998–99	Leeds U	0	0
1999–2000	Leeds U	0	0
2000–01	Leeds U	0	0
2001–02	Leeds U	0	0

MARTYN, Nigel (G) 580 0
H: 6 1 W: 14 00 b.St Austell 11-8-66
Source: St Blazey. *Honours:* England Under-21, B, 23 full caps.

1987–88	Bristol R	39	0		
1988–89	Bristol R	46	0		
1989–90	Bristol R	16	0	101	0
1989–90	Crystal Palace	25	0		
1990–91	Crystal Palace	38	0		
1991–92	Crystal Palace	38	0		
1992–93	Crystal Palace	42	0		
1993–94	Crystal Palace	46	0		
1994–95	Crystal Palace	37	0		
1995–96	Crystal Palace	46	0	272	0
1996–97	Leeds U	37	0		
1997–98	Leeds U	37	0		
1998–99	Leeds U	34	0		
1999–2000	Leeds U	38	0		
2000–01	Leeds U	23	0		
2001–02	Leeds U	38	0	207	0

MATTEO, Dominic (D) 190 1
H: 6 1 W: 12 08 b.Dumfries 28-4-74
Source: Trainee. *Honours:* England Youth, Under-21, B, Scotland 6 full caps.

1992–93	Liverpool	0	0		
1993–94	Liverpool	11	0		
1994–95	Liverpool	7	0		
1994–95	*Sunderland*	1	0	1	0
1995–96	Liverpool	5	0		
1996–97	Liverpool	26	0		
1997–98	Liverpool	26	0		
1998–99	Liverpool	20	1		
1999–2000	Liverpool	32	0		
2000–01	Liverpool	0	0	127	1
2000–01	Leeds U	30	0		
2001–02	Leeds U	32	0	62	0

MAYBURY, Alan‡ (D) 28 0
H: 5 8 W: 11 08 b.Dublin 8-8-78
Source: Trainee. *Honours:* Eire Under-21, 2 full caps.

1995–96	Leeds U	1	0		
1996–97	Leeds U	0	0		
1997–98	Leeds U	12	0		
1998–99	Leeds U	0	0		
1998–99	*Reading*	8	0	8	0
1999–2000	Leeds U	0	0		
2000–01	Leeds U	0	0		
2000–01	*Crewe Alex*	6	0	6	0
2001–02	Leeds U	1	0	14	0

(Transferred to Hearts, October 2001.)

McCARGO, Gerard‡ (F) 0 0
H: 5 4 W: 9 06 b.Belfast 3-11-82
Source: Celtic (Belfast) Boys.

1999–2000	Leeds U	0	0
2000–01	Leeds U	0	0
2001–02	Leeds U	0	0

McMASTER, Jamie (M) 0 0
H: 5 10 W: 11 11 b.Sydney 29-11-82
Source: NSW Academy. *Honours:* England Youth, Under-20.

1999–2000	Leeds U	0	0
2000–01	Leeds U	0	0
2001–02	Leeds U	0	0

McPHAIL, Stephen (M) 56 2
H: 5 8 W: 12 05 b.London 9-12-79
Source: Trainee. *Honours:* Eire Under-21, 5 full caps, 1 goal.

1996–97	Leeds U	0	0		
1997–98	Leeds U	4	0		
1998–99	Leeds U	17	0		
1999–2000	Leeds U	24	2		
2000–01	Leeds U	7	0		
2001–02	Leeds U	1	0	53	2
2001–02	*Millwall*	3	0	3	0

McSTAY, Henry (D) 0 0
H: 5 9 W: 11 03 b.Co Armagh 6-3-85
Source: Scholar.

2001–02	Leeds U	0	0

MILLS, Danny (D) 179 5
H: 5 10 W: 12 05 b.Norwich 18-5-77
Source: Trainee. *Honours:* England Youth, Under-21, 1 full caps.

1994–95	Norwich C	0	0		
1995–96	Norwich C	14	0		
1996–97	Norwich C	32	0		
1997–98	Norwich C	20	0	66	0
1997–98	Charlton Ath	9	1		
1998–99	Charlton Ath	36	2	45	3
1999–2000	Leeds U	17	1		
2000–01	Leeds U	23	0		
2001–02	Leeds U	28	1	68	2

MILOSEVIC, Danny (G) 31 0
H: 6 3 W: 14 12 b.Carlton 26-6-78

1995–96	Canberra Cosmos	3	0		
1996–97	Canberra Cosmos	11	0	14	0

1997–98	Arminia Bielefeld	0	0		
1997–98	Prussen Munster	0	0		
1998–99	Perth Glory	17	0	17	0
1999–2000	Leeds U	0	0		
2000–01	Leeds U	0	0		
2001–02	Leeds U	0	0		
2001–02	*Wolverhampton W*	0	0		

MITCHELL, Peter (D) 0 0
H:5 8 W:11 00 b.Londonderry 10-4-84
Source: Scholar.

| 2000–01 | Leeds U | 0 | 0 |
| 2001–02 | Leeds U | 0 | 0 |

NEWEY, Tom (D) 0 0
H:5 10 W:10 02 b.Sheffield 31-10-82
Source: Scholar.

| 2000–01 | Leeds U | 0 | 0 |
| 2001–02 | Leeds U | 0 | 0 |

RADEBE, Lucas (D) 164 0
H:6 1 W:12 04 b.Johannesburg 12-4-69
Source: Kaizer Chiefs. Honours: South Africa 70 full caps, 1 goal.

1994–95	Leeds U	12	0		
1995–96	Leeds U	13	0		
1996–97	Leeds U	32	0		
1997–98	Leeds U	27	0		
1998–99	Leeds U	29	0		
1999–2000	Leeds U	31	0		
2000–01	Leeds U	20	0		
2001–02	Leeds U	0	0	164	0

RICHARDSON, Frazer (D) 0 0
H:5 11 W:11 11 b.Rotherham 29-10-82
Source: Trainee. Honours: England Youth, Under-20.

1999–2000	Leeds U	0	0
2000–01	Leeds U	0	0
2001–02	Leeds U	0	0

ROBINSON, Paul (G) 21 0
H:6 4 W:15 09 b.Beverley 15-10-79
Source: Trainee. Honours: England Under-21.

1996–97	Leeds U	0	0		
1997–98	Leeds U	0	0		
1998–99	Leeds U	5	0		
1999–2000	Leeds U	0	0		
2000–01	Leeds U	16	0		
2001–02	Leeds U	0	0	21	0

SHIELDS, Robbie (M) 0 0
H:5 6 W:9 03 b.Dublin 1-5-84
Source: Scholar.

| 2000–01 | Leeds U | 0 | 0 |
| 2001–02 | Leeds U | 0 | 0 |

SINGH, Harpal (F) 15 2
H:5 7 W:10 09 b.Bradford 15-9-81
Source: Trainee.

1998–99	Leeds U	0	0		
1999–2000	Leeds U	0	0		
2000–01	Leeds U	0	0		
2001–02	Leeds U	0	0		
2001–02	*Bury*	12	2	12	2
2001–02	*Bristol C*	3	0	3	0

SMITH, Alan (F) 104 26
H:5 10 W:11 11 b.Leeds 28-10-80
Source: Trainee. Honours: England Youth, Under-21, 3 full caps.

1997–98	Leeds U	0	0		
1998–99	Leeds U	22	7		
1999–2000	Leeds U	26	4		
2000–01	Leeds U	33	11		
2001–02	Leeds U	23	4	104	26

STIENS, Craig (F) 0 0
H:5 8 W:12 04 b.Swansea 31-7-84
Source: Scholar.

| 2000–01 | Leeds U | 0 | 0 |
| 2001–02 | Leeds U | 0 | 0 |

TYRRELL, Derek (D) 0 0
H:6 0 W:11 02 b.Dublin 14-4-85
Source: Scholar.

| 2001–02 | Leeds U | 0 | 0 |

VIDUKA, Mark (F) 236 138
H:6 2 W:14 11 b.Melbourne 9-10-75
Honours: Australia 19 full caps, 2 goals.

1992–93	Melbourne Knights	4	2		
1993–94	Melbourne Knights				
1994–95	Melbourne Knights	24	21	48	40
1995–96	Croatia Zagreb	27	12		
1996–97	Croatia Zagreb	25	18		
1997–98	Croatia Zagreb	25	8		
1998–99	Croatia Zagreb	7	2	84	40
1998–99	Celtic	9	5		
1999–2000	Celtic	28	25	37	30
2000–01	Leeds U	34	17		
2001–02	Leeds U	33	11	67	28

WARD, Michael (F) 0 0
H:5 8 W:11 00 b.Omagh 17-4-84
Source: Scholar.

| 2000–01 | Leeds U | 0 | 0 |
| 2001–02 | Leeds U | 0 | 0 |

WILCOX, Jason (M) 319 34
H:6 0 W:11 11 b.Bolton 15-7-71
Source: Trainee. Honours: England B, 3 full caps.

1989–90	Blackburn R	1	0		
1990–91	Blackburn R	18	0		
1991–92	Blackburn R	38	4		
1992–93	Blackburn R	33	4		
1993–94	Blackburn R	33	6		
1994–95	Blackburn R	27	5		
1995–96	Blackburn R	10	3		
1996–97	Blackburn R	28	2		
1997–98	Blackburn R	31	4		
1998–99	Blackburn R	30	3		
1999–2000	Blackburn R	20	0	269	31
1999–2000	Leeds U	20	3		
2000–01	Leeds U	17	0		
2001–02	Leeds U	13	0	50	3

WOODGATE, Jonathan (D) 86 4
H:6 2 W:13 00 b.Middlesbrough 22-1-80
Source: Trainee. Honours: England Youth, Under-21, 1 full cap.

1996–97	Leeds U	0	0		
1997–98	Leeds U	0	0		
1998–99	Leeds U	25	2		
1999–2000	Leeds U	34	1		
2000–01	Leeds U	14	1		
2001–02	Leeds U	13	0	86	4

Trainees
Winter, Jamie

LEICESTER C

ASHTON, Jon (D) 7 0
H:6 2 W:13 05 b.Nuneaton 4-10-82
Source: Scholar.

| 2000–01 | Leicester C | 0 | 0 | | |
| 2001–02 | Leicester C | 7 | 0 | 7 | 0 |

BENJAMIN, Trevor (F) 170 38
H:6 2 W:14 02 b.Kettering 8-2-79
Source: Trainee. Honours: England Under-21.

1995–96	Cambridge U	5	0		
1996–97	Cambridge U	7	1		
1997–98	Cambridge U	25	4		
1998–99	Cambridge U	42	10		
1999–2000	Cambridge U	44	20	123	35
2000–01	Leicester C	21	1		
2001–02	Leicester C	11	0	32	1
2001–02	*Crystal Palace*	6	1	6	1
2001–02	*Norwich C*	6	0	6	0
2001–02	*WBA*	3	1	3	1

DARBY, Brett (F) 0 0
H:5 8 W:11 09 b.Leicester 10-11-83
Source: Scholar.

| 2000–01 | Leicester C | 0 | 0 |
| 2001–02 | Leicester C | 0 | 0 |

DAVIDSON, Callum (D) 167 6
H:5 10 W:12 10 b.Stirling 25-6-76
Source: 'S' Form. Honours: Scotland Under-21, 15 full caps.

1994–95	St Johnstone	7	1		
1995–96	St Johnstone	2	0		
1996–97	St Johnstone	20	2		
1997–98	St Johnstone	15	1	44	4
1997–98	Blackburn R	1	0		
1998–99	Blackburn R	34	1		
1999–2000	Blackburn R	30	0	65	1
2000–01	Leicester C	28	1		
2001–02	Leicester C	30	0	58	1

DEANE, Brian (F) 527 161
H:6 3 W:14 03 b.Leeds 7-2-68
Source: Apprentice. Honours: England B, 3 full caps.

1985–86	Doncaster R	3	0		
1986–87	Doncaster R	20	2		
1987–88	Doncaster R	43	10	66	12
1988–89	Sheffield U	43	22		
1989–90	Sheffield U	45	21		
1990–91	Sheffield U	38	13		
1991–92	Sheffield U	30	12		
1992–93	Sheffield U	41	14		
1993–94	Leeds U	41	11		
1994–95	Leeds U	35	9		
1995–96	Leeds U	34	7		
1996–97	Leeds U	28	5	138	32
1997–98	Sheffield U	24	11	221	93

From Benfica.

1998–99	Middlesbrough	26	6		
1999–2000	Middlesbrough	29	9		
2000–01	Middlesbrough	25	2		
2001–02	Middlesbrough	7	1	87	18
2001–02	Leicester C	15	6	15	6

DELANEY, Damien (D) 22 1
H:6 3 W:13 10 b.Cork 20-7-81
Source: Cork C.

2000–01	Leicester C	5	0		
2001–02	Leicester C	3	0	8	0
2001–02	*Stockport Co*	12	1	12	1
2001–02	*Huddersfield T*	2	0	2	0

DICKOV, Paul (F) 212 46
H:5 8 W:10 13 b.Glasgow 1-11-72
Source: Trainee. Honours: Scotland Schools, Youth, Under-21, 3 full caps.

1992–93	Arsenal	3	2		
1993–94	Arsenal	1	0		
1993–94	*Luton T*	15	1	15	1
1993–94	*Brighton & HA*	8	5	8	5
1994–95	Arsenal	9	0		
1995–96	Arsenal	7	1		
1996–97	Arsenal	1	0	21	3
1996–97	Manchester C	29	5		
1997–98	Manchester C	30	9		
1998–99	Manchester C	35	10		
1999–2000	Manchester C	34	5		
2000–01	Manchester C	21	4		
2001–02	Manchester C	7	0	156	33
2001–02	Leicester C	12	4	12	4

EADIE, Darren (F) 208 37
H:5 7 W:10 09 b.Chippenham 10-6-75
Source: Trainee. Honours: England Youth, Under-21.

1992–93	Norwich C	0	0		
1993–94	Norwich C	15	3		
1994–95	Norwich C	26	2		
1995–96	Norwich C	31	6		
1996–97	Norwich C	42	17		
1997–98	Norwich C	19	3		
1998–99	Norwich C	22	3		
1999–2000	Norwich C	13	1	168	35
1999–2000	Leicester C	16	0		
2000–01	Leicester C	24	2		
2001–02	Leicester C	0	0	40	2

ELLIOTT, Matt (D) 525 65
H:6 3 W:15 01 b.Roehampton 1-11-68
Source: Epsom & Ewell. Honours: Scotland 18 full caps, 1 goal.

1988–89	Charlton Ath	0	0		
1988–89	Torquay U	13	2		
1989–90	Torquay U	33	2		
1990–91	Torquay U	45	6		
1991–92	Torquay U	33	5	124	15
1991–92	*Scunthorpe U*	8	1		
1992–93	Scunthorpe U	39	6		
1993–94	Scunthorpe U	14	1	61	8
1993–94	Oxford U	32	5		
1994–95	Oxford U	45	4		
1995–96	Oxford U	45	8		
1996–97	Oxford U	26	4	148	21
1996–97	Leicester C	16	4		
1997–98	Leicester C	37	7		
1998–99	Leicester C	37	4		
1999–2000	Leicester C	37	6		
2000–01	Leicester C	34	2		
2001–02	Leicester C	31	0	192	21

FLOWERS, Tim (G) 503 0
H:6 2 W:15 01 b.Kenilworth 3-2-67
Source: Apprentice. Honours: England Youth, Under-21, 11 full caps.

1984–85	Wolverhampton W	38	0		
1985–86	Wolverhampton W	25	0	63	0
1985–86	*Southampton*	0	0		
1986–87	Southampton	9	0		
1986–87	*Swindon T*	2	0		
1987–88	Southampton	9	0		
1987–88	*Swindon T*	5	0	7	0
1988–89	Southampton	7	0		
1989–90	Southampton	35	0		
1990–91	Southampton	37	0		
1991–92	Southampton	41	0		
1992–93	Southampton	42	0		
1993–94	Southampton	12	0	192	0
1993–94	Blackburn R	29	0		
1994–95	Blackburn R	39	0		
1995–96	Blackburn R	37	0		
1996–97	Blackburn R	36	0		
1997–98	Blackburn R	25	0		
1998–99	Blackburn R	11	0	177	0
1999–2000	Leicester C	29	0		
2000–01	Leicester C	22	0		
2001–02	Leicester C	4	0	55	0
2001–02	*Stockport Co*	4	0	4	0
2001–02	*Coventry C*	5	0	5	0

HEATH, Matthew (D)   5 0
H: 6 4   W: 14 03   b.Leicester 1-11-81
Source: Scholar.
2000–01	Leicester C	0	0	
2001–02	Leicester C	5	0	5 0

IMPEY, Andrew (M)   321 14
H: 5 8   W: 11 08   b.Hammersmith 30-9-71
Source: Yeading. Honours: England Under-21.
1990–91	QPR	0	0	
1991–92	QPR	13	0	
1992–93	QPR	40	2	
1993–94	QPR	33	3	
1994–95	QPR	40	3	
1995–96	QPR	29	3	
1996–97	QPR	32	2	187 13
1997–98	West Ham U	19	0	
1998–99	West Ham U	8	0	27 0
1998–99	Leicester C	18	0	
1999–2000	Leicester C	29	1	
2000–01	Leicester C	33	0	
2001–02	Leicester C	27	0	107 1

IZZET, Muzzy (M)   201 32
H: 5 10   W: 10 11   b.Hackney 31-10-74
Source: Trainee. Honours: Turkey 8 full caps.
1993–94	Chelsea	0	0	
1994–95	Chelsea	0	0	
1995–96	Chelsea	0	0	
1995–96	Leicester C	9	1	
1996–97	Leicester C	35	3	
1997–98	Leicester C	36	4	
1998–99	Leicester C	31	5	
1999–2000	Leicester C	32	8	
2000–01	Leicester C	27	7	
2001–02	Leicester C	31	4	201 32

JONES, Matthew (M)   44 1
H: 5 11   W: 12 09   b.Llanelli 1-9-80
Source: Trainee. Honours: Wales Youth, Under-21, B, 11 full caps.
1997–98	Leeds U	0	0	
1998–99	Leeds U	8	0	
1999–2000	Leeds U	11	0	
2000–01	Leeds U	4	0	23 0
2000–01	Leicester C	11	0	
2001–02	Leicester C	10	1	21 1

LAURSEN, Jacob (D)   372 15
H: 6 0   W: 12 13   b.Vejle 6-10-71
Honours: Denmark 22 full caps.
1990	Vejle	0	0	
1990–91	Vejle	18	0	
1991–92	Vejle	17	1	55 1
1992–93	Silkeborg	32	0	
1993–94	Silkeborg	30	1	
1994–95	Silkeborg	31	3	
1995–96	Silkeborg	32	4	125 8
1996–97	Derby Co	36	1	
1997–98	Derby Co	28	1	
1998–99	Derby Co	37	0	
1999–2000	Derby Co	36	1	137 3
2000–01	FC Copenhagen	28	3	
2001–02	FC Copenhagen	17	0	45 3
2001–02	Leicester C	10	0	10 0
2001–02	Wolverhampton W	0	0	

LEWIS, Junior (F)   101 11
H: 6 2   W: 11 08   b.Wembley 9-10-73
Source: Trainee.
1992–93	Fulham	6	0	6 0
From Dover, Hendon				
1999–2000	Gillingham	42	6	
2000–01	Gillingham	17	2	59 8
2000–01	Leicester C	15	0	
2001–02	Leicester C	6	0	21 0
2001–02	Brighton & HA	15	3	15 3

LYTH, Ashley (D)   0 0
H: 5 10   W: 11 00   b.Whitby 14-6-83
2000–01	Leicester C	0	0	
2001–02	Leicester C	0	0	

MARSHALL, Lee (D)   161 11
H: 6 2   W: 12 12   b.Islington 21-1-79
Source: Enfield. Honours: England Under-21.
1996–97	Norwich C	0	0	
1997–98	Norwich C	4	0	
1998–99	Norwich C	44	3	
1999–2000	Norwich C	33	5	
2000–01	Norwich C	36	3	117 11
2000–01	Leicester C	9	0	
2001–02	Leicester C	35	0	44 0

McSWEENEY, Leon (F)   0 0
H: 5 10   W: 10 05   b.Cork 19-2-83
Source: Cork C.
2001–02	Leicester C	0	0	

MORTIMER, Alex (M)   0 0
H: 5 10   W: 10 06   b.Manchester 28-11-82
Source: Trainee.
1999–2000	Leicester C	0	0	

2000–01	Leicester C	0	0	
2001–02	Leicester C	0	0	

NOBLE, Karl (M)   0 0
H: 5 10   W: 11 12   b.Leicester 5-9-82
Source: Scholar.
2001–02	Leicester C	0	0	

OAKES, Stefan (M)   59 2
H: 5 11   W: 12 12   b.Leicester 6-9-78
Source: Trainee.
1997–98	Leicester C	0	0	
1998–99	Leicester C	3	0	
1999–2000	Leicester C	22	1	
2000–01	Leicester C	13	0	
2001–02	Leicester C	21	1	59 2

PIPER, Matt (F)   24 2
H: 6 1   W: 12 09   b.Leicester 29-9-81
Source: Trainee.
1999–2000	Leicester C	0	0	
2000–01	Leicester C	0	0	
2001–02	Mansfield T	8	1	8 1
2001–02	Leicester C	16	1	16 1

PRICE, Michael (G)   0 0
H: 6 3   W: 13 11   b.Ashington 3-4-83
Source: Scholar.
2000–01	Leicester C	0	0	
2001–02	Leicester C	0	0	

REEVES, Martin (M)   5 0
H: 6 1   W: 11 09   b.Birmingham 7-9-81
Source: Scholar.
2000–01	Leicester C	0	0	
2001–02	Leicester C	5	0	5 0

ROGERS, Alan (M)   207 18
H: 5 10   W: 12 08   b.Liverpool 3-1-77
Source: Trainee.
1995–96	Tranmere R	26	2	
1996–97	Tranmere R	31	0	57 2
1997–98	Nottingham F	46	1	
1998–99	Nottingham F	34	3	
1999–2000	Nottingham F	37	9	
2000–01	Nottingham F	17	3	
2001–02	Nottingham F	3	0	137 16
2001–02	Leicester C	13	0	13 0

ROYCE, Simon (G)   182 0
H: 6 2   W: 12 10   b.Newham 9-9-71
Source: Heybridge Swifts. Honours:
1991–92	Southend U	1	0	
1992–93	Southend U	3	0	
1993–94	Southend U	6	0	
1994–95	Southend U	13	0	
1995–96	Southend U	46	0	
1996–97	Southend U	43	0	
1997–98	Southend U	37	0	149 0
1998–99	Charlton Ath	8	0	
1999–2000	Charlton Ath	0	0	8 0
2000–01	Leicester C	19	0	
2001–02	Leicester C	0	0	19 0
2001–02	Brighton & HA	6	0	6 0
2001–02	Manchester C	0	0	

SAVAGE, Robbie (M)   249 18
H: 5 11   W: 11 01   b.Wrexham 18-10-74
Source: Trainee. Honours: Wales Schools, Youth, Under-21, 25 full caps, 2 goals.
1993–94	Manchester U	0	0	
1994–95	Crewe Alex	6	2	
1995–96	Crewe Alex	30	7	
1996–97	Crewe Alex	41	1	77 10
1997–98	Leicester C	35	2	
1998–99	Leicester C	34	1	
1999–2000	Leicester C	35	1	
2000–01	Leicester C	33	4	
2001–02	Leicester C	35	0	172 8

SCOWCROFT, James (F)   226 52
H: 6 1   W: 14 08   b.Bury St Edmunds 15-11-75
Source: Trainee. Honours: England Under-21.
1994–95	Ipswich T	0	0	
1995–96	Ipswich T	23	2	
1996–97	Ipswich T	41	9	
1997–98	Ipswich T	31	6	
1998–99	Ipswich T	32	13	
1999–2000	Ipswich T	41	13	
2000–01	Ipswich T	34	4	202 47
2001–02	Leicester C	24	5	24 5

SHERMAN, David (D)   0 0
H: 5 9   W: 12 07   b.Wegberg 19-5-83
Source: Scholar. Honours: England Youth.
2000–01	Leeds U	0	0	
2000–01	Leicester C	0	0	
2001–02	Leicester C	0	0	

SINCLAIR, Frank (D)   292 9
H: 5 10   W: 12 03   b.Lambeth 3-12-71
Source: Trainee. Honours: Jamaica 19 full caps.
1989–90	Chelsea	0	0	
1990–91	Chelsea	4	0	
1991–92	Chelsea	8	1	
1991–92	WBA	6	1	6 1
1992–93	Chelsea	32	0	
1993–94	Chelsea	35	0	
1994–95	Chelsea	35	3	
1995–96	Chelsea	13	1	
1996–97	Chelsea	20	1	
1997–98	Chelsea	22	1	169 7
1998–99	Leicester C	31	1	
1999–2000	Leicester C	34	0	
2000–01	Leicester C	17	0	
2001–02	Leicester C	35	0	117 1

SMITH, Matthew‡ (D)   0 0
H: 5 11   W: 11 08   b.Liverpool 1-9-82
Source: Derby Co trainee. Honours:
2000–01	Leicester C	0	0	
2001–02	Leicester C	0	0	

STEVENSON, Jon (F)   6 1
H: 5 6   W: 11 06   b.Leicester 13-10-82
Source: Scholar.
2000–01	Leicester C	0	0	
2001–02	Leicester C	6	1	6 1

STEWART, Jordan (D)   17 0
H: 6 0   W: 11 09   b.Birmingham 3-3-82
Source: Trainee. Honours: England Youth.
1999–2000	Leicester C	1	0	
1999–2000	Bristol R	4	0	4 0
2000–01	Leicester C	0	0	
2001–02	Leicester C	12	0	13 0

TAGGART, Gerry (D)   364 29
H: 6 2   W: 14 03   b.Belfast 18-10-70
Source: Trainee. Honours: Northern Ireland Schools, Youth, Under-23, 50 full caps, 7 goals.
1988–89	Manchester C	11	1	
1989–90	Manchester C	1	0	12 1
1989–90	Barnsley	21	2	
1990–91	Barnsley	30	2	
1991–92	Barnsley	38	3	
1992–93	Barnsley	44	4	
1993–94	Barnsley	38	2	
1994–95	Barnsley	41	3	212 16
1995–96	Bolton W	11	1	
1996–97	Bolton W	43	3	
1997–98	Bolton W	15	0	69 4
1998–99	Leicester C	15	0	
1999–2000	Leicester C	31	6	
2000–01	Leicester C	24	2	
2001–02	Leicester C	1	0	71 8

WALKER, Ian (G)   296 0
H: 6 2   W: 13 04   b.Watford 31-10-71
Source: Trainee. Honours: England Youth, Under-21, B, 3 full caps.
1989–90	Tottenham H	1	0	
1990–91	Tottenham H	1	0	
1990–91	Oxford U	2	0	2 0
1990–91	Ipswich T	0	0	
1991–92	Tottenham H	18	0	
1992–93	Tottenham H	17	0	
1993–94	Tottenham H	11	0	
1994–95	Tottenham H	41	0	
1995–96	Tottenham H	38	0	
1996–97	Tottenham H	37	0	
1997–98	Tottenham H	29	0	
1998–99	Tottenham H	25	0	
1999–2000	Tottenham H	38	0	
2000–01	Tottenham H	4	0	259 0
2001–02	Leicester C	35	0	35 0

WEBB, Mark‡ (M)   0 0
H: 5 10   W: 12 00   b.Wolverhampton 21-9-82
Source: Scholar.
2000–01	Leicester C	0	0	
2001–02	Leicester C	0	0	

WILLIAMSON, Tom (M)   1 0
H: 5 9   W: 10 02   b.Leicester 24-12-84
Source: Scholar.
2001–02	Leicester C	1	0	1 0

WISE, Dennis (M)   484 81
H: 5 6   W: 10 07   b.Kensington 15-12-66
Source: Southampton Apprentice. Honours: England Under-21, B, 21 full caps, 1 goal.
1984–85	Wimbledon	0	0	
1985–86	Wimbledon	4	0	
1986–87	Wimbledon	28	4	
1987–88	Wimbledon	30	10	
1988–89	Wimbledon	37	5	
1989–90	Wimbledon	35	8	135 27
1990–91	Chelsea	33	10	

1991–92	Chelsea	38	10		
1992–93	Chelsea	27	3		
1993–94	Chelsea	35	4		
1994–95	Chelsea	19	6		
1995–96	Chelsea	35	7		
1996–97	Chelsea	31	3		
1997–98	Chelsea	26	3		
1998–99	Chelsea	22	0		
1999–2000	Chelsea	30	4		
2000–01	Chelsea	36	3	332	53
2001–02	Leicester C	17	1	17	1

WRIGHT, Thomas (M)   1   0
H: 6 0 W: 11 12 b.Leicester 28-9-84
Source: Trainee.

2001–02	Leicester C	1	0	1	0

ZAYED, Eamon (F)   0   0
H: 6 0 W: 12 07 b.Dublin 4-10-83
Source: St Josephs.

2001–02	Leicester C	0	0

Trainees
Campbell, Gareth; Deen, Ahmead; Doyle, Jamie; Howard, Chris; Larvin, Kevin; Mortimer, Benjamin; Pearmain, Dominic; Tozer, Lewis; Williamson, Tom; Woollard, Thomas; Wright, Thomas
Non-Contract
Andrews, Ian E

LEYTON ORIENT

BARNARD, Donny§ (D)   10   0
H: 6 0 W: 11 00 b.Forest Gate 1-7-84

2001–02	Leyton Orient	10	0	10	0

BARNES, Nicholas‡ (M)   0   0
H: 5 10 W: 10 10 b.Chatham 20-10-82
Source: Scholar.

2001–02	Leyton Orient	0	0

BARRETT, Scott (G)   362   0
H: 5 11 W: 14 06 b.Ilkeston 2-4-63
Source: Ilkeston T.

1984–85	Wolverhampton W	4	0		
1985–86	Wolverhampton W	21	0		
1986–87	Wolverhampton W	5	0	30	0
1987–88	Stoke C	27	0		
1988–89	Stoke C	17	0		
1989–90	Stoke C	7	0	51	0
1989–90	Colchester U	13	0		
1989–90	Stockport Co	10	0	10	0
1990–91	Colchester U	1	0		
1991–92	Colchester U	0	0	13	0
1992–93	Gillingham	34	0		
1993–94	Gillingham	13	0		
1994–95	Gillingham	4	0	51	0
1995–96	Cambridge U	31	0		
1996–97	Cambridge U	45	0		
1997–98	Cambridge U	43	0		
1998–99	Cambridge U	0	0	119	0
1998–99	Leyton Orient	20	0		
1999–2000	Leyton Orient	29	0		
2000–01	Leyton Orient	7	0		
2001–02	Leyton Orient	32	0	88	0

BAYES, Ashley* (G)   297   0
H: 6 1 W: 14 00 b.Lincoln 19-4-72
Source: Trainee.

1989–90	Brentford	1	0		
1990–91	Brentford	1	0		
1991–92	Brentford	1	0		
1992–93	Brentford	2	0	4	0
1993–94	Torquay U	32	0		
1994–95	Torquay U	37	0		
1995–96	Torquay U	28	0	97	0
1996–97	Exeter C	41	0		
1997–98	Exeter C	45	0		
1998–99	Exeter C	41	0	127	0
1999–2000	Leyton Orient	17	0		
2000–01	Leyton Orient	39	0		
2001–02	Leyton Orient	13	0	69	0

BEALL, Billy‡ (M)   165   10
H: 5 5 W: 11 00 b.Enfield 4-12-77
Source: Trainee.

1995–96	Cambridge U	15	4		
1996–97	Cambridge U	36	2		
1997–98	Cambridge U	30	1		
1998–99	Cambridge U	0	0	81	7
1998–99	Leyton Orient	23	2		
1999–2000	Leyton Orient	33	1		
2000–01	Leyton Orient	17	0		
2001–02	Leyton Orient	11	0	84	3

BRAZIER, Matt (M)   133   8
H: 5 10 W: 10 10 b.Whipps Cross 2-7-76
Source: Trainee.

1994–95	QPR	0	0
1995–96	QPR	11	0
1996–97	QPR	27	2

1997–98	QPR	11	0	49	2
1997–98	Fulham	7	1		
1998–99	Fulham	2	0	9	1
1998–99	Cardiff C	11	2		
1999–2000	Cardiff C	30	1		
2000–01	Cardiff C	26	2		
2001–02	Cardiff C	0	0	67	5
2001–02	Leyton Orient	8	0	8	0

BROWN, Craig* (M)   0   0
H: 5 9 W: 10 09 b.Kingston 13-1-83
Source: Reading scholar.

2001–02	Leyton Orient	0	0

CANHAM, Scott# (M)   85   5
H: 5 8 W: 11 06 b.Newham 5-11-74
Source: Trainee.

1993–94	West Ham U	0	0		
1994–95	West Ham U	0	0		
1995–96	West Ham U	0	0		
1995–96	Torquay U	3	0	3	0
1995–96	Brentford	14	0		
1996–97	Brentford	13	1		
1997–98	Brentford	22	0	49	1
1998–99	Leyton Orient	8	0		
1999–2000	Leyton Orient	1	0		
2000–01	Leyton Orient	0	0		
2001–02	Leyton Orient	24	4	33	4

CASTLE, Steve* (M)   489   110
H: 5 11 W: 13 04 b.Barkingside 17-5-66
Source: Apprentice.

1984–85	Orient	21	1		
1985–86	Orient	23	4		
1986–87	Orient	24	5		
1987–88	Orient	42	10		
1988–89	Orient	24	6		
1989–90	Orient	27	7		
1990–91	Orient	45	12		
1991–92	Orient	37	10	243	55
1992–93	Plymouth Arg	31	11		
1993–94	Plymouth Arg	44	21		
1994–95	Plymouth Arg	26	3	101	35
1995–96	Birmingham C	15	1		
1995–96	Gillingham	6	1	6	1
1996–97	Birmingham C	8	0	23	1
1996–97	Leyton Orient	4	1		
1996–97	Peterborough U	4	0		
1997–98	Peterborough U	37	3		
1998–99	Peterborough U	26	4		
1999–2000	Peterborough U	39	10	102	17
2000–01	Leyton Orient	9	0		
2001–02	Leyton Orient	1	0	14	1

CHRISTIE, Iyseden* (F)   152   30
H: 6 0 W: 14 05 b.Coventry 14-11-76
Source: Trainee.

1994–95	Coventry C	0	0		
1995–96	Coventry C	1	0		
1995–96	Coventry C	0	0	1	0
1996–97	Bournemouth	4	0		
1996–97	Mansfield T	8	0	4	0
1997–98	Mansfield T	39	10		
1998–99	Mansfield T	42	8	89	18
1999–2000	Leyton Orient	36	7		
2000–01	Leyton Orient	7	2		
2001–02	Leyton Orient	15	3	58	12

DORRIAN, Chris‡ (D)   5   0
H: 5 11 W: 11 05 b.Harlow 3-4-82
Source: Trainee.

2000–01	Leyton Orient	2	0		
2001–02	Leyton Orient	3	0	5	0

DOWNER, Simon (D)   68   0
H: 6 1 W: 13 02 b.Romford 19-10-81
Source: Trainee.

1998–99	Leyton Orient	1	0		
1999–2000	Leyton Orient	24	0		
2000–01	Leyton Orient	31	0		
2001–02	Leyton Orient	12	0	68	0

FLETCHER, Gary (F)   14   0
H: 5 11 W: 12 06 b.Liverpool 4-6-81
Source: Northwich Vic. *Honours:* England Schools.

2000–01	Hull C	5	0	5	0
2001–02	Leyton Orient	9	0	9	0

GOUGH, Neil‡ (F)   15   1
H: 6 0 W: 11 12 b.Harlow 1-9-81
Source: Trainee.

1999–2000	Leyton Orient	4	0		
2000–01	Leyton Orient	0	0		
2001–02	Leyton Orient	11	1	15	1

GOULD, Ronnie‡ (F)   2   0
H: 5 11 W: 11 11 b.London 27-9-82
Source: Trainee.

1999–2000	Leyton Orient	2	0		
2000–01	Leyton Orient	0	0		
2001–02	Leyton Orient	0	0	2	0

GRIMSDELL, Danny‡ (M)   0   0
H: 6 0 W: 11 00 b.Islington 23-1-83
Source: Trainee.

2001–02	Leyton Orient	0	0

HARRIS, Andy (D)   176   1
H: 5 11 W: 12 05 b.Springs 26-2-77
Source: Trainee.

1993–94	Liverpool	0	0		
1994–95	Liverpool	0	0		
1995–96	Liverpool	0	0		
1996–97	Southend U	44	0		
1997–98	Southend U	27	0		
1998–99	Southend U	1	0	72	0
1999–2000	Leyton Orient	15	0		
2000–01	Leyton Orient	44	0		
2001–02	Leyton Orient	45	1	104	1

HATCHER, Daniel§ (F)   10   0
H: 5 10 W: 11 00 b.Newport (IW) 24-12-83
Source: Scholar.

2000–01	Leyton Orient	2	0		
2001–02	Leyton Orient	8	0	10	0

HERRERA, Robbie‡ (D)   276   2
H: 5 7 W: 10 06 b.Torbay 12-6-70
Source: Trainee.

1987–88	QPR	0	0		
1988–89	QPR	2	0		
1989–90	QPR	1	0		
1990–91	QPR	3	0		
1991–92	QPR	0	0		
1991–92	Torquay U	11	0		
1992–93	QPR	0	0		
1992–93	Torquay U	5	0		
1993–94	QPR	0	0	6	0
1993–94	Fulham	23	1		
1994–95	Fulham	27	0		
1995–96	Fulham	43	0		
1996–97	Fulham	26	0		
1997–98	Fulham	26	0	145	1
1998–99	Torquay U	40	0		
1999–2000	Torquay U	35	0		
2000–01	Torquay U	29	1		
2001–02	Torquay U	3	0	123	1
2001–02	Leyton Orient	2	0	2	0

HOUGHTON, Scott* (M)   319   46
H: 5 5 W: 12 02 b.Hitchin 22-10-71
Source: Trainee. *Honours:* England Schools, Youth.

1990–91	Tottenham H	0	0		
1990–91	Ipswich T	8	1	8	1
1991–92	Tottenham H	10	2		
1992–93	Tottenham H	0	0	10	2
1992–93	Cambridge U	0	0		
1992–93	Gillingham	3	0	3	0
1992–93	Charlton Ath	6	0	6	0
1993–94	Luton T	15	1		
1994–95	Luton T	1	0	16	1
1994–95	Walsall	38	8		
1995–96	Walsall	40	6	78	14
1996–97	Peterborough U	32	8		
1997–98	Peterborough U	30	4		
1998–99	Peterborough U	8	1	70	13
1998–99	Southend U	3	0		
1999–2000	Southend U	43	4		
2000–01	Southend U	9	2	79	9
2000–01	Leyton Orient	21	1		
2001–02	Leyton Orient	21	5	42	6
2001–02	Halifax T	7	0	7	0

HUTCHINGS, Carl (M)   267   15
H: 6 0 W: 11 06 b.Hammersmith 24-9-74
Source: Trainee.

1993–94	Brentford	29	0		
1994–95	Brentford	39	0		
1995–96	Brentford	23	0		
1996–97	Brentford	28	2		
1997–98	Brentford	43	5		
1998–99	Bristol C	21	2		
1999–2000	Bristol C	21	1		
1999–2000	Brentford	8	0	170	7
2000–01	Bristol C	0	0	42	3
2000–01	Exeter C	2	0	2	0
2000–01	Southend U	14	0		
2001–02	Southend U	29	4	43	4
2001–02	Leyton Orient	10	1	10	1

IBEHRE, Jabo (F)   36   6
H: 6 2 W: 13 00 b.Islington 28-1-83
Source: Trainee.

1999–2000	Leyton Orient	3	0		
2000–01	Leyton Orient	5	2		
2001–02	Leyton Orient	28	4	36	6

JONES, Billy (D)   17   0
H: 6 1 W: 11 04 b.Chatham 26-6-83
Source: Trainee.

2000–01	Leyton Orient	1	0		
2001–02	Leyton Orient	16	0	17	0

JOSEPH, Matt (D) 322 8
H: 5 5 W: 10 07 b.Bethnal Green 30-9-72
Source: Trainee. *Honours:* Barbados 2 full caps.

1991–92	Arsenal	0	0	
1992–93	Gillingham	0	0	
1993–94	Cambridge U	27	2	
1994–95	Cambridge U	39	2	
1995–96	Cambridge U	42	0	
1996–97	Cambridge U	44	0	
1997–98	Cambridge U	7	0	159 6
1997–98	Leyton Orient	14	1	
1998–99	Leyton Orient	34	0	
1999–2000	Leyton Orient	41	0	
2000–01	Leyton Orient	44	0	
2001–02	Leyton Orient	30	1	163 2

LING, Martin† (M) 565 64
H: 5 7 W: 10 08 b.West Ham 15-7-66
Source: Apprentice.

1983–84	Exeter C	29	0	
1984–85	Exeter C	42	6	
1985–86	Exeter C	45	8	116 14
1986–87	Swindon T	2	0	
1986–87	Southend U	24	8	
1987–88	Southend U	42	7	
1988–89	Southend U	44	6	
1989–90	Southend U	25	10	
1990–91	Southend U	3	0	138 31
1990–91	Mansfield T	3	0	3 0
1990–91	Swindon T	1	0	
1991–92	Swindon T	21	3	
1992–93	Swindon T	43	3	
1993–94	Swindon T	33	1	
1994–95	Swindon T	36	3	
1995–96	Swindon T	16	0	152 10
1996–97	Leyton Orient	44	1	
1997–98	Leyton Orient	46	2	
1998–99	Leyton Orient	44	4	
1999–2000	Leyton Orient	14	1	
1999–2000	Brighton & HA	8	1	8 1
2000–01	Leyton Orient	0	0	
2001–02	Leyton Orient	0	0	148 8

LOCKWOOD, Matt (D) 197 19
H: 5 10 W: 11 07 b.Rochford 17-10-76
Source: Trainee.

1994–95	QPR	0	0	
1995–96	QPR	0	0	
1996–97	Bristol R	39	1	
1997–98	Bristol R	24	0	63 1
1998–99	Leyton Orient	37	3	
1999–2000	Leyton Orient	41	6	
2000–01	Leyton Orient	32	7	
2001–02	Leyton Orient	24	2	134 18

MARTIN, John (M) 60 2
H: 5 8 W: 10 03 b.Bethnal Green 15-7-81
Source: Trainee.

1997–98	Leyton Orient	1	0	
1998–99	Leyton Orient	1	0	
1999–2000	Leyton Orient	8	0	
2000–01	Leyton Orient	19	0	
2001–02	Leyton Orient	31	2	60 2

McELHOLM, Brendan‡ (M) 17 0
H: 5 11 W: 11 07 b.Omagh 7-7-82
Source: Trainee. *Honours:* Northern Ireland Youth.

1999–2000	Leyton Orient	3	0	
2000–01	Leyton Orient	12	0	
2001–02	Leyton Orient	2	0	17 0

McGHEE, Dave (D) 219 14
H: 6 0 W: 13 07 b.Worthing 19-6-76
Source: Trainee.

1994–95	Brentford	7	1	
1995–96	Brentford	36	5	
1996–97	Brentford	45	1	
1997–98	Brentford	29	1	
1998–99	Brentford	0	0	117 8
From Stevenage Bor.				
1999–2000	Leyton Orient	23	1	
2000–01	Leyton Orient	39	3	
2001–02	Leyton Orient	40	2	102 6

McLEAN, Aaron (F) 32 2
H: 5 9 W: 10 10 b.Hammersmith 25-5-83
Source: Trainee.

1999–2000	Leyton Orient	3	0	
2000–01	Leyton Orient	2	1	
2001–02	Leyton Orient	27	1	32 2

MINTON, Jeff* (M) 254 43
H: 5 07 W: 11 04 b.Hackney 28-12-73
Source: Trainee.

1991–92	Tottenham H	2	1	
1992–93	Tottenham H	0	0	
1993–94	Tottenham H	0	0	2 1
1994–95	Brighton & HA	39	5	
1995–96	Brighton & HA	39	8	
1996–97	Brighton & HA	25	3	
1997–98	Brighton & HA	36	6	
1998–99	Brighton & HA	35	9	174 31
1999–2000	Port Vale	23	3	
2000–01	Port Vale	13	1	36 4
2000–01	Rotherham U	9	2	9 2
2001–02	Leyton Orient	33	5	33 5

MORGAN, Thomas‡ (M) 0 0
H: 5 7 W: 10 07 b.Enfield 8-4-83
Source: Trainee.

2001–02	Leyton Orient	0	0

MORRIS, Glenn§ (G) 2 0
H: 6 0 W: 11 00 b.Woolwich 20-12-83
Source: Scholar.

2001–02	Leyton Orient	2	0	2 0

MURRAY, Jade‡ (F) 2 0
H: 5 10 W: 11 06 b.Islington 23-9-81
Source: Trainee.

1999–2000	Leyton Orient	2	0	
2000–01	Leyton Orient	0	0	
2001–02	Leyton Orient	0	0	2 0

NUGENT, Kevin (F) 403 96
H: 6 1 W: 13 07 b.Edmonton 10-4-69
Source: Trainee. *Honours:* Eire Youth.

1987–88	Leyton Orient	11	3	
1988–89	Leyton Orient	3	0	
1989–90	Leyton Orient	11	0	
1990–91	Leyton Orient	33	5	
1991–92	Leyton Orient	36	12	
1991–92	Plymouth Arg	4	0	
1992–93	Plymouth Arg	45	11	
1993–94	Plymouth Arg	39	14	
1994–95	Plymouth Arg	37	7	
1995–96	Plymouth Arg	6	0	131 32
1995–96	Bristol C	34	8	
1996–97	Bristol C	36	6	70 14
1997–98	Cardiff C	4	0	
1998–99	Cardiff C	41	15	
1999–2000	Cardiff C	39	10	
2000–01	Cardiff C	14	4	
2001–02	Cardiff C	1	0	99 29
2001–02	Leyton Orient	9	1	103 21

OAKES, Scott‡ (F) 229 28
H: 5 10 W: 11 09 b.Leicester 5-8-72
Source: Trainee.

1989–90	Leicester C	2	0	
1990–91	Leicester C	0	0	
1991–92	Leicester C	1	0	3 0
1991–92	Luton T	21	2	
1992–93	Luton T	44	5	
1993–94	Luton T	36	8	
1994–95	Luton T	43	9	
1995–96	Luton T	29	3	173 27
1996–97	Sheffield W	19	1	
1997–98	Sheffield W	4	0	
1998–99	Sheffield W	1	0	
1999–2000	Sheffield W	0	0	24 1
2000–01	Cambridge U	18	0	18 0
2001–02	Leyton Orient	11	0	11 0

OPARA, Kelechi‡ (F) 25 0
H: 6 1 W: 13 07 b.Oweri Imo State 21-12-81
Source: Trainee.

1998–99	Colchester U	1	0	
1999–2000	Colchester U	16	0	
2000–01	Colchester U	2	0	19 0
2000–01	Leyton Orient	6	0	
2001–02	Leyton Orient	0	0	6 0

PARSONS, David‡ (M) 1 0
H: 6 0 W: 13 09 b.Greenwich 26-2-82
Source: Trainee.

1999–2000	Leyton Orient	1	0	
2000–01	Leyton Orient	0	0	
2001–02	Leyton Orient	0	0	1 0

PARTRIDGE, David (D) 70 0
H: 6 1 W: 13 08 b.Westminster 26-11-78
Source: Trainee.

1997–98	West Ham U	0	0	
1998–99	Dundee U	1	0	
1998–99	Dundee U	1	0	
1999–2000	Dundee U	29	0	
2000–01	Dundee U	19	0	
2001–02	Dundee U	13	0	63 0
2001–02	*Leyton Orient*	7	0	7 0

SMITH, Dean (D) 471 50
H: 6 0 W: 13 03 b.West Bromwich 19-3-71
Source: Trainee.

1988–89	Walsall	15	0	
1989–90	Walsall	7	0	
1990–91	Walsall	33	0	
1991–92	Walsall	9	0	
1992–93	Walsall	42	1	
1993–94	Walsall	36	1	142 2
1994–95	Hereford U	35	3	
1995–96	Hereford U	40	8	
1996–97	Hereford U	42	8	117 19
1997–98	Leyton Orient	43	9	
1998–99	Leyton Orient	37	9	
1999–2000	Leyton Orient	44	4	
2000–01	Leyton Orient	43	5	
2001–02	Leyton Orient	45	2	212 29

TATE, Chris (F) 96 20
H: 6 0 W: 12 08 b.York 27-12-77
Source: York C Trainee.

1996–97	Sunderland	0	0	
1997–98	Scarborough	24	1	
1998–99	Scarborough	25	12	49 13
1999–2000	Halifax T	18	4	18 4
From Scarborough.				
2000–01	Leyton Orient	22	3	
2001–02	Leyton Orient	7	0	29 3

THORPE, Lee (F) 204 58
H: 6 0 W: 11 13 b.Wolverhampton 14-12-75
Source: Trainee.

1993–94	Blackpool	1	0	
1994–95	Blackpool	1	0	
1995–96	Blackpool	1	0	
1996–97	Blackpool	9	0	12 0
1997–98	Lincoln C	44	14	
1998–99	Lincoln C	38	8	
1999–2000	Lincoln C	42	16	
2000–01	Lincoln C	31	7	
2001–02	Lincoln C	37	13	192 58
2001–02	Leyton Orient	0	0	

TONER, Ciaran (M) 12 0
H: 6 1 W: 12 02 b.Craigavon 30-6-81
Source: Trainee. *Honours:* Northern Ireland Under-21.

1999–2000	Tottenham H	0	0	
2000–01	Tottenham H	0	0	
2001–02	Tottenham H	0	0	
2001–02	*Peterborough U*	6	0	6 0
2001–02	*Bristol R*	6	0	6 0
2001–02	Leyton Orient	0	0	

UKA, Niam‡ (M) 0 0
H: 5 6 W: 11 00 b.Kosovo 26-10-81
Source: Partizani.

1999–2000	Leyton Orient	0	0
2000–01	Leyton Orient	0	0
2001–02	Leyton Orient	0	0

WATTS, Steve (F) 126 29
H: 6 0 W: 14 02 b.Lambeth 11-7-76
Source: Fisher Ath.

1998–99	Leyton Orient	28	6	
1999–2000	Leyton Orient	32	6	
2000–01	Leyton Orient	36	8	
2001–02	Leyton Orient	30	9	126 29

Scholars
Barnard, Donny G; Berry, Jimmie; Bray, Thomas J; Butler, Graeme; Forbes, Boniek MG; Game, Matthew; Hatcher, Daniel I; Holder, Philip; Levy, Adam H; McGee, Paul; Morris, Glenn J; Rodden, James C; Stephens, Kevin; Wareham, Ross; Wild, Christopher; Williams, Andre
Non-Contract
Ling, Martin

LINCOLN C

BAILEY, Mark (D) 85 1
H: 5 8 W: 11 07 b.Stoke 12-8-76
Source: Trainee.

1994–95	Stoke C	0	0	
1995–96	Stoke C	0	0	
1996–97	Stoke C	0	0	
1996–97	Rochdale	15	0	
1997–98	Rochdale	33	0	
1998–99	Rochdale	19	1	
1999–2000	Rochdale	0	0	
2000–01	Rochdale	0	0	67 1
From Northwich Vic.				
2001–02	Lincoln C	18	0	18 0

BARNETT, Jason* (D) 207 6
H: 5 9 W: 13 06 b.Shrewsbury 21-4-76
Source: Trainee.

1994–95	Wolverhampton W	0	0	
1995–96	Wolverhampton W	0	0	
1995–96	Lincoln C	32	2	
1996–97	Lincoln C	36	0	
1997–98	Lincoln C	33	0	
1998–99	Lincoln C	29	1	
1999–2000	Lincoln C	18	0	
2000–01	Lincoln C	33	1	
2001–02	Lincoln C	26	2	207 6

BATTERSBY, Tony (F) 237 40
H: 6 0 W: 13 07 b.Doncaster 30-8-75
Source: Trainee.

1993–94	Sheffield U	0	0

1994–95	Sheffield U	0	0		
1994–95	Southend U	8	1	8	1
1995–96	Sheffield U	10	1	10	1
1995–96	Notts Co	21	7		
1996–97	Notts Co	18	1	39	8
1996–97	*Bury*	11	2		
1997–98	Bury	37	6		
1998–99	Bury	0	0	48	8
1998–99	Lincoln C	39	7		
1999–2000	Lincoln C	16	3		
1999–2000	*Northampton T*	3	1	3	1
2000–01	Lincoln C	35	6		
2001–02	Lincoln C	39	5	129	21

BIMSON, Stuart (D)   169 3
H: 5 11 W: 11 06 b.Liverpool 29-9-69
Source: Macclesfield T.

1994–95	Bury	19	0		
1995–96	Bury	16	0		
1996–97	Bury	1	0	36	0
1997–98	Lincoln C	15	1		
1997–98	Lincoln C	12	0		
1998–99	Lincoln C	31	2		
1999–2000	Lincoln C	20	0		
2000–01	Lincoln C	20	0		
2001–02	Lincoln C	35	0	133	3

BLACK, Kingsley (M)   416 56
H: 5 10 W: 12 00 b.Luton 22-6-68
Source: School. *Honours:* England Schools,
Northern Ireland Under-21, 30 full caps, 1
goal.

1986–87	Luton T	0	0		
1987–88	Luton T	13	0		
1988–89	Luton T	37	8		
1989–90	Luton T	36	11		
1990–91	Luton T	37	7		
1991–92	Luton T	4	0	127	26
1991–92	Nottingham F	25	4		
1992–93	Nottingham F	24	5		
1993–94	Nottingham F	37	3		
1994–95	Nottingham F	10	2		
1994–95	*Sheffield U*	11	2	11	2
1995–96	Nottingham F	2	0	98	14
1995–96	Millwall	3	1	3	1
1996–97	Grimsby T	24	0		
1997–98	Grimsby T	39	2		
1998–99	Grimsby T	42	4		
1999–2000	Grimsby T	31	2		
2000–01	Grimsby T	5	0	141	8
2000–01	*Lincoln C*	5	0		
2001–02	Lincoln C	31	5	36	5

BROWN, Grant* (D)   421 15
H: 6 0 W: 12 08 b.Sunderland 19-11-69
Source: Trainee.

1987–88	Leicester C	2	0		
1988–89	Leicester C	12	0	14	0
1989–90	Lincoln C	34	2		
1990–91	Lincoln C	32	1		
1991–92	Lincoln C	37	1		
1992–93	Lincoln C	40	1		
1993–94	Lincoln C	38	3		
1994–95	Lincoln C	39	3		
1995–96	Lincoln C	34	0		
1996–97	Lincoln C	34	1		
1997–98	Lincoln C	15	0		
1998–99	Lincoln C	22	1		
1999–2000	Lincoln C	26	0		
2000–01	Lincoln C	20	2		
2001–02	Lincoln C	36	0	407	15

BUCKLEY, Adam (M)   46 0
H: 5 9 W: 11 07 b.Nottingham 2-8-79
Source: WBA schoolboy.

1997–98	Grimsby T	0	0		
1998–99	Grimsby T	2	0		
1999–2000	Grimsby T	13	0		
2000–01	Grimsby T	0	0	15	0
2001–02	Lincoln C	31	0	31	0

CAMERON, Dave* (F)   88 10
H: 6 1 W: 12 13 b.Bangor 24-8-75

1998–99	St Mirren	2	1	11	2
1999–2000	Brighton & HA	17	0	17	0

From Worthing.

2000–01	Lincoln C	16	2		
2001–02	Lincoln C	44	6	60	8

CAMM, Mark (D)   19 0
H: 5 8 W: 11 05 b.Mansfield 1-10-80
Source: Trainee.

1999–2000	Sheffield U	0	0		
2000–01	Lincoln C	3	0		
2001–02	Lincoln C	16	0	19	0

GAIN, Peter (M)   102 9
H: 5 9 W: 11 07 b.Hammersmith 2-11-76
Source: Trainee.

1995–96	Tottenham H	0	0		
1996–97	Tottenham H	0	0		
1997–98	Tottenham H	0	0		
1998–99	Tottenham H	0	0		
1998–99	Lincoln C	4	0		
1999–2000	Lincoln C	32	2		
2000–01	Lincoln C	24	5		
2001–02	Lincoln C	42	2	102	9

HAMILTON, Ian (M)   520 46
H: 5 10 W: 12 07 b.Stevenage 14-12-67
Source: Apprentice.

1985–86	Southampton	0	0		
1986–87	Southampton	0	0		
1987–88	Southampton	0	0		
1987–88	Cambridge U	9	1		
1988–89	Cambridge U	15	0	24	1
1988–89	Scunthorpe U	27	1		
1989–90	Scunthorpe U	43	6		
1990–91	Scunthorpe U	34	2		
1991–92	Scunthorpe U	41	9	145	18
1992–93	WBA	46	7		
1993–94	WBA	42	3		
1994–95	WBA	35	4		
1995–96	WBA	41	3		
1996–97	WBA	39	5		
1997–98	WBA	37	1	240	23
1997–98	Sheffield U	8	1		
1998–99	Sheffield U	30	2		
1999–2000	Sheffield U	7	0		
1999–2000	*Grimsby T*	6	1	6	1
2000–01	Sheffield U	0	0	45	3
2000–01	Notts Co	25	0		
2001–02	Notts Co	9	0	34	0
2001–02	Lincoln C	26	0	26	0

HOLMES, Steve* (D)   219 36
H: 6 2 W: 13 08 b.Middlesbrough 13-1-71
Source: Guisborough T.

1993–94	Preston NE	0	0		
1994–95	Preston NE	5	1		
1994–95	*Hartlepool U*	5	2	5	2

From Guisborough T

1995–96	Preston NE	8	0	13	1
1995–96	Lincoln C	23	2		
1996–97	Lincoln C	28	4		
1997–98	Lincoln C	46	4		
1998–99	Lincoln C	37	6		
1999–2000	Lincoln C	9	2		
2000–01	Lincoln C	38	11		
2001–02	Lincoln C	20	4	201	33

HORRIGAN, Darren§ (G)   1 0
b.Middlesbrough 2-6-83
Source: Scholar.

2001–02	Lincoln C	1	0	1	0

LOGAN, Richard (D)   218 20
H: 6 0 W: 13 03 b.Barnsley 24-5-69
Source: Guisborough T.

1993–94	Huddersfield T	16	0		
1994–95	Huddersfield T	27	1		
1995–96	Huddersfield T	2	0	45	1
1995–96	Plymouth Arg	31	4		
1996–97	Plymouth Arg	28	4		
1997–98	Plymouth Arg	27	4	86	12
1997–98	Scunthorpe U	41	6		
1999–2000	Scunthorpe U	39	1	80	7
2000–01	Lincoln C	5	0		
2001–02	Lincoln C	2	0	7	0

MARRIOTT, Alan (G)   91 0
H: 5 11 W: 12 01 b.Bedford 3-9-78
Source: Trainee.

1997–98	Tottenham H	0	0		
1998–99	Tottenham H	0	0		
1999–2000	Lincoln C	18	0		
2000–01	Lincoln C	30	0		
2001–02	Lincoln C	43	0	91	0

MAYO, Paul (D)   60 0
H: 5 11 W: 11 08 b.Lincoln 13-10-81
Source: Scholar.

1999–2000	Lincoln C	19	0		
2000–01	Lincoln C	27	0		
2001–02	Lincoln C	14	0	60	0

MORGAN, Paul (D)   34 1
H: 6 0 W: 11 05 b.Belfast 23-10-78
Source: Trainee. *Honours:* Northern Ireland
Under-21.

1997–98	Preston NE	0	0		
1998–99	Preston NE	0	0		
1999–2000	Preston NE	0	0		
2000–01	Preston NE	0	0		
2001–02	Lincoln C	34	1	34	1

PETTINGER, Paul (G)   23 0
H: 6 0 W: 13 00 b.Sheffield 1-10-75
Source: Barnsley. *Honours:* England Schools,
Youth.

1992–93	Leeds U	0	0		
1993–94	Leeds U	0	0		
1994–95	Leeds U	0	0		
1994–95	*Torquay U*	3	0	3	0
1995–96	Leeds U	0	0		
1995–96	*Rotherham U*	1	0		
1995–96	Gillingham	0	0		
1996–97	Carlisle U	0	0		
1997–98	Rotherham U	3	0		
1998–99	Rotherham U	0	0		
1999–2000	Rotherham U	0	0		
2000–01	Rotherham U	13	0	17	0
2001–02	Lincoln C	3	0	3	0

PINKNEY, Grant§ (M)   0 0
H: 5 7 W: 11 07 b.Evesham 31-1-83

1999–2000	Birmingham C	0	0		
2000–01	Lincoln C	0	0		
2001–02	Lincoln C	0	0		

SCHOFIELD, Jon† (D)   471 23
H: 5 10 W: 11 08 b.Barnsley 16-5-65
Source: Gainsborough T.

1988–89	Lincoln C	29	2		
1989–90	Lincoln C	29	2		
1990–91	Lincoln C	42	3		
1991–92	Lincoln C	39	1		
1992–93	Lincoln C	40	0		
1993–94	Lincoln C	40	2		
1994–95	Lincoln C	12	1		
1994–95	Doncaster R	27	1		
1995–96	Doncaster R	41	4		
1996–97	Doncaster R	42	7	110	12
1997–98	Mansfield T	44	0		
1998–99	Mansfield T	42	0	86	0
1999–2000	Hull C	25	0	25	0
2000–01	Lincoln C	19	0		
2001–02	Lincoln C	0	0	250	11

SEDGEMORE, Ben (M)   249 15
H: 5 10 W: 12 13 b.Wolverhampton 5-8-75
Source: Trainee. *Honours:* England Schools.

1993–94	Birmingham C	0	0		
1994–95	Birmingham C	0	0		
1994–95	*Northampton T*	1	0	1	0
1995–96	Birmingham C	0	0		
1995–96	*Mansfield T*	9	0		
1995–96	Peterborough U	17	0		
1996–97	Peterborough U	0	0	17	0
1996–97	Mansfield T	39	4		
1997–98	Mansfield T	28	2	76	6
1997–98	Macclesfield T	5	0		
1998–99	Macclesfield T	35	2		
1999–2000	Macclesfield T	35	1		
2000–01	Macclesfield T	27	3	102	6
2000–01	Lincoln C	10	1		
2001–02	Lincoln C	43	2	53	3

SMITH, Andy‡ (M)   0 0
b.Blackpool 13-1-80

2000–01	Grimsby T	0	0		
2001–02	Lincoln C	0	0		

SMITH, Paul (M)   120 17
H: 5 11 W: 11 10 b.Hastings 25-1-76
Source: Hastings T.

1994–95	Nottingham F	0	0		
1995–96	Nottingham F	0	0		
1996–97	Nottingham F	0	0		
1997–98	*Nottingham F*	0	0		
1997–98	*Lincoln C*	17	3		
1998–99	Lincoln C	28	2		
1999–2000	Lincoln C	27	5		
2000–01	Lincoln C	40	7		
2001–02	Lincoln C	8	0	120	17

WALKER, Justin* (M)   208 6
H: 5 11 W: 12 04 b.Nottingham 6-9-75
Source: Trainee. *Honours:* England Schools,
Youth.

1992–93	Nottingham F	0	0		
1993–94	Nottingham F	0	0		
1994–95	Nottingham F	0	0		
1995–96	Nottingham F	0	0		
1996–97	Nottingham F	0	0		
1996–97	Scunthorpe U	9	0		
1997–98	Scunthorpe U	40	1		
1998–99	Scunthorpe U	41	1		
1999–2000	Scunthorpe U	42	0	132	2
2000–01	Lincoln C	45	1		
2001–02	Lincoln C	31	3	76	4

Scholars
Basker, Carl; Bent, Daniel; Bone, Liam K;
Byrne, Richard A; Cochrane, Gary J; Davies,
Christopher M; Fisher, Daniel; Garfoot,
Stephen R; Holtham, Adam D; Horrigan,
Darren; Kerley, Adam L; Kinsella, Sean I;
McConville, Christopher; Pinkney, Grant E;
Stant, Craig PA; Trout, Charlie JS
Non-Contract
Schofield, John D

LIVERPOOL

ANELKA, Nicolas (F) 153 40
H: 6 1 W: 12 04 b.Versailles 14-3-79
Honours: France Youth, Under-21, 28 full caps, 6 goals.

1995–96	Paris St Germain	2	0	
1996–97	Paris St Germain	8	1	
1996–97	Arsenal	4	0	
1997–98	Arsenal	26	6	
1998–99	Arsenal	35	17	65 23
1999–2000	Real Madrid	19	2	19 2
2000–01	Paris St Germain	27	8	
2001–02	Paris St Germain	12	2	49 11
2001–02	Liverpool	20	4	20 4

ARPHEXAD, Pegguy (G) 29 0
H: 6 2 W: 13 07 b.Abymes 18-5-73
Source: Brest.

1994–95	Lens	0	0	
1995–96	Lens	3	0	
1996–97	Lens	0	0	3 0
1997–98	Leicester C	6	0	
1998–99	Leicester C	4	0	
1999–2000	Leicester C	11	0	21 0
2000–01	Liverpool	0	0	
2001–02	Stockport Co	3	0	3 0
2001–02	Liverpool	2	0	2 0

BABBEL, Markus (D) 282 13
H: 6 0 W: 13 05 b.Munich 8-9-72
Honours: Germany 51 full caps, 1 goal.

1991–92	Bayern Munich	12	0	
1992–93	Hamburg	27	1	
1993–94	Hamburg	33	0	60 1
1994–95	Bayern Munich	26	2	
1995–96	Bayern Munich	30	2	
1996–97	Bayern Munich	31	2	
1997–98	Bayern Munich	30	1	
1998–99	Bayern Munich	27	1	
1999–2000	Bayern Munich	26	1	182 9
2000–01	Liverpool	38	3	
2001–02	Liverpool	2	0	40 3

BARMBY, Nick (M) 277 48
H: 5 6 W: 11 04 b.Hull 11-2-74
Source: Trainee. *Honours:* England Schools, Youth, Under-21, B, 23 full caps, 4 goals.

1991–92	Tottenham H	0	0	
1992–93	Tottenham H	22	6	
1993–94	Tottenham H	27	5	
1994–95	Tottenham H	38	9	87 20
1995–96	Middlesbrough	32	7	
1996–97	Middlesbrough	10	1	42 8
1996–97	Everton	21	4	
1997–98	Everton	30	2	
1998–99	Everton	24	3	
1999–2000	Everton	37	9	116 18
2000–01	Liverpool	26	2	
2001–02	Liverpool	6	0	32 2

BAROS, Milan (F) 61 11
H: 6 0 W: 13 02 b.Valassake Mezirici 28-10-81
Honours: Czech Republic 10 full caps, 4 goals.

1998–99	Banik Ostrava	6	0	
1999–2000	Banik Ostrava	29	6	
2000–01	Banik Ostrava	26	5	61 11
2001–02	Liverpool	0	0	

BERGER, Patrik (M) 260 56
H: 6 1 W: 13 00 b.Prague 10-11-73
Honours: Czechoslovakia 2 full caps.Czech Republic 44 full caps, 18 goals.

1991–92	Slavia Prague	20	3	
1992–93	Slavia Prague	29	10	
1993–94	Slavia Prague	12	4	
1994–95	Slavia Prague	28	7	89 24
1995–96	Borussia Dortmund	25	4	25 4
1996–97	Liverpool	23	6	
1997–98	Liverpool	22	3	
1998–99	Liverpool	32	7	
1999–2000	Liverpool	34	9	
2000–01	Liverpool	14	2	
2001–02	Liverpool	21	1	146 28

BISCAN, Igor (M) 97 12
H: 6 3 W: 12 08 b.Zagreb 4-5-78
Honours: Croatia 15 full caps, 1 goal.

1997–98	Samobor	12	1	12 1
1997–98	Dynamo Zagreb	5	0	
1998–99	Dynamo Zagreb	19	2	
1998–99	Dynamo Zagreb	15	0	
1999–2000	Dynamo Zagreb	29	6	
2000–01	Dynamo Zagreb	14	3	67 11
2000–01	Liverpool	13	0	
2001–02	Liverpool	5	0	18 0

CARRAGHER, Jamie (M) 159 2
H: 6 1 W: 12 05 b.Liverpool 28-1-78
Source: Trainee. *Honours:* England Youth, Under-21, 8 full caps.

1995–96	Liverpool	0	0	
1996–97	Liverpool	2	1	
1997–98	Liverpool	20	0	
1998–99	Liverpool	34	1	
1999–2000	Liverpool	36	0	
2000–01	Liverpool	34	0	
2001–02	Liverpool	33	0	159 2

CULSHAW, Paul* (M) 0 0
b.Liverpool 17-9-81
Source: Scholar.

2001–02	Liverpool	0	0

DIOMEDE, Bernard (M) 178 30
H: 5 9 W: 12 04 b.Bourges 23-1-74
Honours: France 8 full caps.

1992–93	Auxerre	7	0	
1993–94	Auxerre	2	0	
1994–95	Auxerre	26	3	
1995–96	Auxerre	33	9	
1996–97	Auxerre	31	6	
1997–98	Auxerre	31	4	
1998–99	Auxerre	27	5	
1999–2000	Auxerre	19	3	176 30
2000–01	Liverpool	2	0	
2001–02	Liverpool	0	0	2 0

DUDEK, Jerzy (G) 186 0
H: 6 2 W: 12 08 b.Ribnek 23-3-73
Source: GKS Tychy. *Honours:* Poland 23 full caps.

1995–96	Sokol Tychy	15	0	15 0
1996–97	Feyenoord	0	0	
1997–98	Feyenoord	34	0	
1998–99	Feyenoord	34	0	
1999–2000	Feyenoord	34	0	
2000–01	Feyenoord	34	0	136 0
2001–02	Liverpool	35	0	35 0

FOLEY-SHERIDAN, Michael (M) 0 0
b.Dublin 9-3-83

1999–2000	Liverpool	0	0
2000–01	Liverpool	0	0
2001–02	Liverpool	0	0

GERRARD, Steven (M) 102 11
H: 6 1 W: 12 03 b.Whiston 30-5-80
Source: Trainee. *Honours:* England Youth, Under-21, 10 full caps, 1 goal.

1997–98	Liverpool	0	0	
1998–99	Liverpool	12	0	
1999–2000	Liverpool	29	1	
2000–01	Liverpool	33	7	
2001–02	Liverpool	28	3	102 11

HAMANN, Dietmar (M) 217 14
H: 6 2 W: 12 01 b.Waldasson 27-8-73
Source: Wacker Munich. *Honours:* Germany 46 full caps, 4 goals.

1993–94	Bayern Munich	5	1	
1994–95	Bayern Munich	30	0	
1995–96	Bayern Munich	20	2	
1996–97	Bayern Munich	22	1	
1997–98	Bayern Munich	28	2	105 6
1998–99	Newcastle U	23	4	23 4
1999–2000	Liverpool	28	1	
2000–01	Liverpool	30	2	
2001–02	Liverpool	31	1	89 4

HEGGEM, Vegard (D) 111 8
H: 5 11 W: 12 04 b.Trondheim 13-7-75
Honours: Norway 21 full caps, 3 goals.

1995	Rosenborg	15	1	
1996	Rosenborg	14	1	
1997	Rosenborg	23	3	
1998	Rosenborg	5	0	57 5
1998–99	Liverpool	29	2	
1999–2000	Liverpool	22	1	
2000–01	Liverpool	3	0	
2001–02	Liverpool	0	0	54 3

HENCHOZ, Stephane (D) 308 3
H: 6 1 W: 12 13 b.Billens 7-9-74
Source: Bulle. *Honours:* Switzerland 53 full caps.

1992–93	Neuchatel Xamax	35	0	
1993–94	Neuchatel Xamax	21	1	
1994–95	Neuchatel Xamax	35	0	91 1
1995–96	Hamburg	31	2	
1996–97	Hamburg	18	0	49 2
1997–98	Blackburn R	36	0	
1998–99	Blackburn R	34	0	70 0
1999–2000	Liverpool	29	0	
2000–01	Liverpool	32	0	
2001–02	Liverpool	37	0	98 0

HESKEY, Emile (F) 237 66
H: 6 1 W: 14 04 b.Leicester 11-1-78
Source: Trainee. *Honours:* England Youth, Under-21, B, 29 full caps, 4 goals.

1994–95	Leicester C	1	0	
1995–96	Leicester C	30	7	
1996–97	Leicester C	35	10	
1997–98	Leicester C	35	10	
1998–99	Leicester C	30	6	
1999–2000	Leicester C	23	7	154 40
1999–2000	Liverpool	12	3	
2000–01	Liverpool	36	14	
2001–02	Liverpool	35	9	83 26

HYYPIA, Sami (D) 273 14
H: 6 4 W: 13 11 b.Porvoo 7-10-73
Source: KuMu. *Honours:* Finland 45 full caps, 1 goal.

1993	MyPa 47	12	0	
1994	MyPa 47	25	0	
1995	MyPa 47	26	3	63 3
1996–97	Willem II	14	0	
1997–98	Willem II	30	1	
1997–98	Willem II	30	0	
1998–99	Willem II	26	2	100 3
1999–2000	Liverpool	38	2	
2000–01	Liverpool	35	3	
2001–02	Liverpool	37	3	110 8

KIPPE, Frode (D) 68 3
H: 6 4 W: 14 02 b.Oslo 17-1-78

1997	Lillestrom	9	0	
1998	Lillestrom	25	2	34 2
1998–99	Liverpool	0	0	
1999–2000	Liverpool	0	0	
1999–2000	Stoke C	15	1	
2000–01	Liverpool	0	0	
2000–01	Stoke C	19	0	34 1
2001–02	Liverpool	0	0	

(Transferred to Lillestrom, January 2001).

KIRKLAND, Christopher (G) 25 0
H: 6 6 W: 14 12 b.Leicester 2-5-81
Source: Trainee. *Honours:* England Youth, Under-21.

1997–98	Coventry C	0	0	
1998–99	Coventry C	0	0	
1999–2000	Coventry C	0	0	
2000–01	Coventry C	23	0	
2001–02	Coventry C	1	0	24 0
2001–02	Liverpool	1	0	1 0

LITMANEN, Jari (F) 337 149
H: 6 0 W: 12 10 b.Lahti 20-2-71
Honours: Finland 76 full caps, 21 goals.

1987	Reipas Lahti	9	0	
1988	Reipas Lahti	26	8	
1989	Reipas Lahti	25	6	
1990	Reipas Lahti	26	14	86 28
1990	HJK Helsinki	27	16	27 16
1991	MyPa	18	7	18 7
1992–93	Ajax	12	1	
1993–94	Ajax	30	26	
1994–95	Ajax	27	17	
1995–96	Ajax	26	13	
1996–97	Ajax	16	6	
1997–98	Ajax	25	16	
1998–99	Ajax	23	11	159 90
1999–2000	Barcelona	21	3	
2000–01	Barcelona	0	0	21 3
2000–01	Liverpool	5	1	
2001–02	Liverpool	21	4	26 5

MASSIE, Jason (M) 0 0
b.Whiston 13-9-84
Honours: England Youth.

2001–02	Liverpool	0	0

McALLISTER, Gary (M) 665 109
H: 6 1 W: 11 11 b.Motherwell 25-12-64
Source: Fir Park BC. *Honours:* Scotland Under-21, B, 57 full caps, 5 goals.

1981–82	Motherwell	1	0	
1982–83	Motherwell	1	0	
1983–84	Motherwell	21	0	
1984–85	Motherwell	35	6	
1985–86	Motherwell	1	0	59 6
1985–86	Leicester C	31	7	
1986–87	Leicester C	39	10	
1987–88	Leicester C	42	9	
1988–89	Leicester C	46	11	
1989–90	Leicester C	43	10	201 47
1990–91	Leeds U	38	2	
1991–92	Leeds U	42	5	
1992–93	Leeds U	42	6	
1993–94	Leeds U	42	8	
1994–95	Leeds U	41	6	
1995–96	Leeds U	36	5	231 31
1996–97	Coventry C	38	6	
1997–98	Coventry C	14	0	
1998–99	Coventry C	29	3	
1999–2000	Coventry C	38	11	119 20

2000–01 Liverpool 30 5
2001–02 Liverpool 25 0 55 5

McNULTY, Stephen (D) 0 0
b.Liverpool 26-9-83
Source: Scholar.
2001–02 Liverpool 0 0

MELLOR, Neil (F) 0 0
b.Sheffield 4-11-82
Source: Scholar.
2001–02 Liverpool 0 0

MURPHY, Danny (M) 253 41
H: 5 9 W: 12 08 b.Chester 18-3-77
Source: Trainee. *Honours:* England Schools, Youth, Under-21, 4 full caps, 1 goal.
1993–94 Crewe Alex 12 2
1994–95 Crewe Alex 35 5
1995–96 Crewe Alex 42 10
1996–97 Crewe Alex 45 10
1997–98 Liverpool 16 0
1998–99 Liverpool 1 0
1998–99 *Crewe Alex* 16 1 150 28
1999–2000 Liverpool 23 3
2000–01 Liverpool 27 4
2001–02 Liverpool 36 6 103 13

NIELSEN, Jorgen* (G) 2 0
H: 6 0 W: 12 11 b.Nykobing 6-5-71
1993–94 Naestved 2 0
1994–95 Naestved 2 0
1995–96 Hvidovre 0 0
1996–97 Liverpool 0 0
1997–98 Liverpool 0 0
1998–99 Liverpool 0 0
1998–99 *Wolverhampton W* 0 0
1999–2000 Liverpool 0 0
2000–01 Liverpool 0 0
2001–02 Liverpool 0 0

O'BRIEN, Chris (M) 0 0
b.Liverpool 13-1-82
Source: Trainee. *Honours:* England Schools.
1998–99 Liverpool 0 0
1999–2000 Liverpool 0 0
2000–01 Liverpool 0 0
2001–02 Liverpool 0 0

OTSEMOBOR, John (D) 0 0
b.Liverpool 23-3-83
Source: Trainee. *Honours:* England Youth.
1999–2000 Liverpool 0 0
2000–01 Liverpool 0 0
2001–02 Liverpool 0 0

OWEN, Michael (F) 152 83
H: 5 8 W: 10 13 b.Chester 14-12-79
Source: Trainee. *Honours:* England Schools, Youth, Under-21, 41 full caps, 18 goals.
1996–97 Liverpool 2 1
1997–98 Liverpool 36 18
1998–99 Liverpool 30 18
1999–2000 Liverpool 27 11
2000–01 Liverpool 28 16
2001–02 Liverpool 29 19 152 83

PARTRIDGE, Richie (M) 6 1
H: 5 8 W: 10 07 b.Dublin 12-9-80
Source: Trainee. *Honours:* Eire Under-21.
1998–99 Liverpool 0 0
1999–2000 Liverpool 0 0
2000–01 Liverpool 0 0
2000–01 *Bristol R* 6 1 6 1
2001–02 Liverpool 0 0

PEERS, Mark (F) 0 0
b.St Helens 14-5-84
Honours: England Youth.
2001–02 Liverpool 0 0

POTTER, Darren (F) 0 0
b.Liverpool 21-12-84
Source: Scholar.
2001–02 Liverpool 0 0

RAVEN, David (D) 0 0
b.Wirral 10-3-85
Source: Scholar. *Honours:* England Youth.
2001–02 Liverpool 0 0

RIISE, John Arne (M) 82 11
H: 6 1 W: 12 08 b.Molde 24-9-80
Honours: Norway 15 full caps, 1 goal.
1998–99 Monaco 0 0
1999–2000 Monaco 21 1
2000–01 Monaco 16 3 44 4
2001–02 Liverpool 38 7 38 7

SJOLUND, Danny (F) 0 0
H: 5 11 W: 12 00 b.Mariehamn 22-4-83
1999–2000 West Ham U 0 0
2000–01 West Ham U 0 0
2000–01 Liverpool 0 0
2001–02 Liverpool 0 0

SMICER, Vladimir (M) 242 49
H: 5 10 W: 12 02 b.Degin 24-5-73
Honours: Czechoslovakia 1 full cap, Czech Republic 56 full caps, 20 goals.
1992–93 Slavia Prague 21 8
1993–94 Slavia Prague 17 6
1994–95 Slavia Prague 15 3
1995–96 Slavia Prague 28 9 81 26
1996–97 Lens 33 5
1997–98 Lens 28 7
1998–99 Lens 30 4 91 16
1999–2000 Liverpool 21 1
2000–01 Liverpool 27 2
2001–02 Liverpool 22 4 70 7

SMYTH, Mark (M) 0 0
b.Liverpool 9-1-85
Source: Scholar. *Honours:* England Youth.
2001–02 Liverpool 0 0

TRAORE, Djimi (D) 8 0
H: 6 1 W: 12 06 b.Saint-Ouen 1-3-80
Source: Laval.
1998–99 Liverpool 0 0
1999–2000 Liverpool 0 0
2000–01 Liverpool 8 0
2001–02 Liverpool 0 0 8 0

VAUGHAN, Stephen (D) 0 0
b.Liverpool 22-1-85
Source: Scholar.
2001–02 Liverpool 0 0

VIGNAL, Gregory (D) 10 0
H: 5 11 W: 12 03 b.Montpellier 19-7-81
2000–01 Liverpool 6 0
2001–02 Liverpool 4 0 10 0

WARNOCK, Stephen (M) 0 0
b.Ormskirk 12-12-81
Source: Trainee. *Honours:* England Schools, Youth.
1998–99 Liverpool 0 0
1999–2000 Liverpool 0 0
2000–01 Liverpool 0 0
2001–02 Liverpool 0 0

WELSH, John (D) 0 0
b.Liverpool 10-1-84
Source: Scholar. *Honours:* England Youth.
2000–01 Liverpool 0 0
2001–02 Liverpool 0 0

WESTERVELD, Sander (G) 189 0
H: 6 4 W: 13 08 b.Enschede 23-10-74
Source: Tubanters. *Honours:* Holland 6 full caps.
1994–95 Twente 3 0
1995–96 Twente 11 0 14 0
1996–97 Vitesse 34 0
1997–98 Vitesse 34 0
1998–99 Vitesse 32 0 100 0
1999–2000 Liverpool 38 0
2000–01 Liverpool 38 0
2001–02 Liverpool 1 0 75 0
(Transferred to Real Sociedad, December 2001).

WRIGHT, Andrew (M) 0 0
b.Southport 15-1-85
Source: Scholar.
2001–02 Liverpool 0 0

WRIGHT, Stephen (D) 37 0
H: 6 0 W: 11 11 b.Liverpool 8-2-80
Source: Trainee. *Honours:* England Youth, Under-21.
1997–98 Liverpool 0 0
1998–99 Liverpool 0 0
1999–2000 Liverpool 0 0
1999–2000 *Crewe Alex* 23 0 23 0
2000–01 Liverpool 2 0
2001–02 Liverpool 12 0 14 0

XAVIER, Abel (D) 227 7
H: 6 3 W: 12 07 b.Mozambique 30-11-72
Honours: Portugal 19 full caps, 2 goals.
1990–91 Amadora 6 0
1991–92 Amadora 21 0
1992–93 Amadora 0 0 43 0
1993–94 Benfica 24 1
1994–95 Benfica 22 3 46 4
1995–96 Bari 8 0 8 0
1996–97 Oviedo 27 0
1997–98 Oviedo 31 0 58 0
1998–99 PSV Eindhoven 19 2 19 2
1999–2000 Everton 20 0
2000–01 Everton 11 0
2001–02 Everton 12 0 43 0
2001–02 Liverpool 10 1 10 1

Trainees
Butler, Christopher W; Clampitt, Carl E; Dawes, Ian; Dittmer, Timothy S; Flynn, Adam J; Gillespie, Steven; Harrison, Paul A; Massie, Jason D; McGrath, Christopher E; Murray, Matthew J; Nicholas, Andrew P; Whitbread, Zak B; Wright, Andrew D

LUTON T

BAYLISS, Dave (D) 204 9
H: 6 0 W: 12 08 b.Liverpool 8-6-76
Source: Trainee.
1994–95 Rochdale 1 0
1995–96 Rochdale 28 0
1996–97 Rochdale 24 0
1997–98 Rochdale 29 2
1998–99 Rochdale 25 1
1999–2000 Rochdale 29 3
2000–01 Rochdale 41 3
2001–02 Rochdale 9 0 186 9
2001–02 Luton T 18 0 18 0

BOYCE, Emmerson (D) 110 4
H: 6 0 W: 12 03 b.Aylesbury 24-9-79
Source: Trainee.
1997–98 Luton T 0 0
1998–99 Luton T 0 0
1999–2000 Luton T 30 1
2000–01 Luton T 42 3
2001–02 Luton T 37 0 110 4

BRENNAN, Dean‡ (M) 9 0
H: 5 9 W: 11 08 b.Dublin 17-6-80
1997–98 Sheffield W 0 0
1998–99 Sheffield W 0 0
1999–2000 Sheffield W 0 0
2000–01 Luton T 9 0
2001–02 Luton T 0 0 9 0

BRKOVIC, Ahmet* (M) 90 9
H: 5 8 W: 11 10 b.Dubrovnik 23-9-74
Source: Dubrovnik.
1999–2000 Leyton Orient 29 5
2000–01 Leyton Orient 40 3
2001–02 Leyton Orient 0 0 69 8
2001–02 Luton T 21 1 21 1

BRUCE, Joseph* (D) 0 0
H: 6 0 W: 12 00 b.London 5-7-83
2000–01 Luton T 0 0
2001–02 Luton T 0 0

COYNE, Chris (D) 60 3
H: 6 1 W: 13 08 b.Brisbane 20-12-78
Source: Perth SC.
1995–96 West Ham U 0 0
1996–97 West Ham U 0 0
1997–98 West Ham U 0 0
1998–99 West Ham U 1 0 1 0
1998–99 *Brentford* 7 0 7 0
1998–99 *Southend U* 1 0 1 0
1999–2000 Dundee 2 0
2000–01 Dundee 18 0 20 0
2001–02 Luton T 31 3 31 3

CROWE, Dean (F) 111 29
H: 5 6 W: 11 07 b.Stockport 6-6-79
Source: Trainee.
1996–97 Stoke C 0 0
1997–98 Stoke C 16 4
1998–99 Stoke C 38 8
1999–2000 Stoke C 6 0
1999–2000 *Northampton T* 5 0 5 0
1999–2000 *Bury* 4 1
2000–01 Stoke C 0 0
2000–01 *Bury* 7 1 11 2
2001–02 Stoke C 0 0 60 12
2001–02 *Plymouth Arg* 1 0 1 0
2001–02 Luton T 34 15 34 15

DOUGLAS, Stuart* (F) 159 18
H: 5 9 W: 12 05 b.London 9-4-78
Source: Trainee.
1995–96 Luton T 8 1
1996–97 Luton T 9 0
1997–98 Luton T 17 1
1998–99 Luton T 42 9
1999–2000 Luton T 40 3
2000–01 Luton T 21 4
2001–02 Luton T 9 0 146 18
2001–02 *Oxford U* 4 0 4 0
2001–02 *Rushden & D* 9 0 9 0

DRYDEN, Richard* (D) 285 11
H: 6 0 W: 14 03 b.Stroud 14-6-69
Source: Trainee.
1986–87 Bristol R 6 0
1987–88 Bristol R 6 0
1988–89 Bristol R 1 0 13 0
1988–89 Exeter C 21 0
1989–90 Exeter C 30 7 51 7
1990–91 *Manchester C* 0 0
1991–92 Notts Co 29 1
1992–93 Notts Co 2 0 31 1
1992–93 *Plymouth Arg* 5 0 5 0
1992–93 Birmingham C 11 0

Season	Club				
1993–94	Birmingham C	34	0		
1994–95	Birmingham C	3	0	48	0
1994–95	Bristol C	19	1		
1995–96	Bristol C	18	1	37	2
1996–97	Southampton	29	1		
1997–98	Southampton	13	0		
1998–99	Southampton	4	0		
1999–2000	Southampton	1	0		
1999–2000	Stoke C	13	0	13	0
2000–01	Southampton	0	0	47	1
2000–01	Northampton T	10	0	10	0
2000–01	Swindon T	7	0	7	0
2000–01	Luton T	20	0		
2001–02	Luton T	3	0	23	0

EMBERSON, Carl (G) 233 0
H: 6 2 W: 15 00 b.Epsom 13-7-73
Source: Trainee.

Season	Club				
1991–92	Millwall	0	0		
1992–93	Millwall	0	0		
1992–93	Colchester U	13	0		
1993–94	Millwall	0	0		
1994–95	Colchester U	20	0		
1995–96	Colchester U	41	0		
1996–97	Colchester U	35	0		
1997–98	Colchester U	46	0		
1998–99	Colchester U	37	0	192	0
1999–2000	Walsall	5	0		
2000–01	Walsall	3	0	8	0
2001–02	Luton T	33	0	33	0

EVERITT, Adam‡ (M) 0 0
b.Hemel Hempstead 28-6-82

Season	Club				
2001–02	Luton T	0	0		

FORBES, Adrian (M) 152 12
H: 5 7 W: 11 12 b.Greenford 23-1-79
Source: Trainee. Honours: England Youth.

Season	Club				
1996–97	Norwich C	1	0		
1997–98	Norwich C	33	4		
1998–99	Norwich C	15	0		
1999–2000	Norwich C	25	1		
2000–01	Norwich C	29	3	112	8
2001–02	Luton T	40	4	40	4

FOTIADIS, Andrew (F) 106 12
H: 6 0 W: 12 13 b.Hitchin 6-9-77
Source: School. Honours: England Schools.

Season	Club				
1996–97	Luton T	17	3		
1997–98	Luton T	15	1		
1998–99	Luton T	21	2		
1999–2000	Luton T	23	2		
2000–01	Luton T	22	3		
2001–02	Luton T	8	1	106	12

FRASER, Stuart‡ (D) 44 1
H: 5 10 W: 11 12 b.Edinburgh 9-1-80
Source: Trainee. Honours: Scotland Under-21.

Season	Club				
1997–98	Luton T	1	0		
1998–99	Luton T	8	0		
1999–2000	Luton T	20	1		
2000–01	Luton T	15	0		
2001–02	Luton T	0	0	44	1

GEORGE, Liam‡ (F) 102 20
H: 5 9 W: 11 04 b.Luton 2-2-79
Source: Trainee. Honours: Eire Under-21.

Season	Club				
1996–97	Luton T	1	0		
1997–98	Luton T	1	0		
1998–99	Luton T	12	0		
1999–2000	Luton T	42	13		
2000–01	Luton T	43	7		
2001–02	Luton T	4	0	102	20

GRIFFITHS, Carl (F) 331 123
H: 5 11 W: 12 04 b.Oswestry 15-7-71
Source: Trainee. Honours: Wales Youth, Under-21, B.

Season	Club				
1988–89	Shrewsbury T	28	6		
1989–90	Shrewsbury T	18	4		
1990–91	Shrewsbury T	19	4		
1991–92	Shrewsbury T	27	8		
1992–93	Shrewsbury T	42	27		
1993–94	Shrewsbury T	9	5	143	54
1993–94	Manchester C	16	4		
1994–95	Manchester C	2	0		
1995–96	Manchester C	0	0	18	4
1995–96	Portsmouth	14	2	14	2
1995–96	Peterborough U	4	1		
1996–97	Peterborough U	12	1	16	2
1996–97	Leyton Orient	13	6		
1997–98	Leyton Orient	33	18		
1998–99	Leyton Orient	24	8		
1998–99	Wrexham	4	3	4	3
1998–99	Port Vale	3	1		
1999–2000	Port Vale	5	0	8	1
1999–2000	Leyton Orient	11	4		
2000–01	Leyton Orient	37	14	118	50
2001–02	Leyton Orient	10	7	10	7

HILLIER, Ian (D) 23 1
H: 6 1 W: 11 12 b.Neath 26-12-79
Source: Trainee. Honours: Wales Schools, Youth, Under-21.

Season	Club				
1998–99	Tottenham H	0	0		
1999–2000	Tottenham H	0	0		
2000–01	Tottenham H	0	0		
2001–02	Tottenham H	0	0		
2001–02	Luton T	23	1	23	1

HOLMES, Peter (M) 25 2
H: 5 11 W: 11 05 b.Bishop Auckland 18-11-80
Source: Trainee. Honours: England Schools.

Season	Club				
1997–98	Sheffield W	0	0		
1998–99	Sheffield W	0	0		
1999–2000	Sheffield W	0	0		
2000–01	Luton T	18	1		
2001–02	Luton T	7	1	25	2

HOWARD, Steve (F) 282 72
H: 6 3 W: 15 00 b.Durham 10-5-76
Source: Tow Law T.

Season	Club				
1995–96	Hartlepool U	39	7		
1996–97	Hartlepool U	32	8		
1997–98	Hartlepool U	43	7		
1998–99	Hartlepool U	28	5	142	27
1998–99	Northampton T	12	0		
1999–2000	Northampton T	41	10		
2000–01	Northampton T	33	8	86	18
2000–01	Luton T	12	3		
2001–02	Luton T	42	24	54	27

HUGHES, Paul* (M) 54 5
H: 6 0 W: 12 08 b.Hammersmith 17-4-76
Source: Trainee. Honours: England Schools.

Season	Club				
1994–95	Chelsea	0	0		
1995–96	Chelsea	0	0		
1996–97	Chelsea	12	2		
1997–98	Chelsea	9	0		
1998–99	Chelsea	0	0		
1998–99	Stockport Co	7	0	7	0
1998–99	Norwich C	4	1	4	1
1999–2000	Chelsea	0	0	21	2
1999–2000	Crewe Alex	0	0		
2000–01	Southampton	0	0		
2001–02	Southampton	0	0		
2001–02	Luton T	22	2	22	2

JOHNSON, Marvin* (D) 373 7
H: 6 0 W: 13 02 b.Wembley 29-10-68
Source: Apprentice.

Season	Club				
1986–87	Luton T	0	0		
1987–88	Luton T	9	0		
1988–89	Luton T	16	0		
1989–90	Luton T	12	0		
1990–91	Luton T	26	0		
1991–92	Luton T	0	0		
1992–93	Luton T	40	3		
1993–94	Luton T	17	0		
1994–95	Luton T	46	1		
1995–96	Luton T	36	0		
1996–97	Luton T	44	0		
1997–98	Luton T	14	2		
1998–99	Luton T	42	0		
1999–2000	Luton T	44	0		
2000–01	Luton T	9	0		
2001–02	Luton T	18	1	373	7

KARLSEN, Kent‡ (D) 68 1
H: 6 2 W: 13 00 b.Norway 17-2-73

Season	Club				
1996	Valerengen	24	0		
1997	Valerengen	6	0		
1998	Valerengen	6	0		
1999	Valerengen	8	0		
2000	Valerengen	3	0	41	0
2000	Haugesund	21	1	21	1
2000–01	Luton T	6	0		
2001–02	Luton T	0	0	6	0

LEARY, Michael (M) 0 0
H: 5 11 W: 12 03 b.Ealing 17-4-83
Source: Scholar.

Season	Club				
2001–02	Luton T	0	0		

LOCKE, Adam* (M) 283 21
H: 5 11 W: 13 02 b.Croydon 20-8-70
Source: Trainee.

Season	Club				
1988–89	Crystal Palace	0	0		
1989–90	Crystal Palace	0	0		
1990–91	Southend U	28	4		
1991–92	Southend U	10	0		
1992–93	Southend U	27	0		
1993–94	Southend U	8	0	73	4
1993–94	Colchester U	4	0		
1994–95	Colchester U	22	1		
1995–96	Colchester U	25	3		
1996–97	Colchester U	32	4	83	8
1997–98	Bristol C	37	1		
1998–99	Bristol C	28	3	65	4
1999–2000	Luton T	34	3		

Season	Club				
2000–01	Luton T	25	2		
2001–02	Luton T	3	0	62	5

MANSELL, Lee (M) 29 6
H: 5 9 W: 10 12 b.Gloucester 28-10-82
Source: Scholar.

Season	Club				
2000–01	Luton T	18	5		
2001–02	Luton T	11	1	29	6

McSWEGAN, Gary (F) 262 82
H: 5 8 W: 10 09 b.Glasgow 24-9-70
Source: Rangers Amateur BC.

Season	Club				
1986–87	Rangers	1	0		
1987–88	Rangers	1	0		
1988–89	Rangers	1	0		
1989–90	Rangers	3	0		
1990–91	Rangers	3	0		
1991–92	Rangers	4	0		
1992–93	Rangers	9	4	18	4
1993–94	Notts Co	37	15		
1994–95	Notts Co	22	6		
1995–96	Notts Co	3	0	62	21
1995–96	Dundee U	25	17		
1996–97	Dundee U	31	7		
1997–98	Dundee U	31	5		
1998–99	Dundee U	5	3	92	32
1998–99	Hearts	21	7		
1999–2000	Hearts	30	13		
2000–01	Hearts	26	5		
2001–02	Hearts	5	0	82	25
2001–02	Barnsley	5	0	5	0
2001–02	Luton T	3	0	3	0

MURPHY, Daryl‡ (F) 0 0
H: 6 0 W: 12 13 b.Waterford 15-3-83

Season	Club				
2000–01	Luton T	0	0		
2001–02	Luton T	0	0		

NEILSON, Alan (D) 144 3
H: 5 11 W: 12 08 b.Wegburg 26-9-72
Source: Trainee. Honours: Wales Under-21, B, 5 full caps.

Season	Club				
1990–91	Newcastle U	3	0		
1991–92	Newcastle U	16	1		
1992–93	Newcastle U	3	0		
1993–94	Newcastle U	14	0		
1994–95	Newcastle U	6	0	42	1
1995–96	Southampton	18	0		
1996–97	Southampton	29	0		
1997–98	Southampton	8	0	55	0
1997–98	Fulham	17	0		
1998–99	Fulham	4	1		
1999–2000	Fulham	5	1		
2000–01	Fulham	3	0		
2001–02	Fulham	0	0	29	2
2001–02	Grimsby T	10	0	10	0
2001–02	Luton T	8	0	8	0

NICHOLLS, Kevin (M) 86 9
H: 5 10 W: 12 02 b.Newham 2-1-79
Source: Trainee. Honours: England Youth.

Season	Club				
1995–96	Charlton Ath	0	0		
1996–97	Charlton Ath	6	1		
1997–98	Charlton Ath	6	0		
1998–99	Charlton Ath	0	0	12	1
1998–99	Brighton & HA	4	1	4	1
1999–2000	Wigan Ath	8	0		
2000–01	Wigan Ath	20	0	28	0
2001–02	Luton T	42	7	42	7

OVENDALE, Mark (G) 134 0
H: 6 2 W: 14 00 b.Leicester 22-11-73
Source: Wisbech T.

Season	Club				
1994–95	Northampton T	6	0	6	0

From Barry T.

Season	Club				
1997–98	Bournemouth	0	0		
1998–99	Bournemouth	46	0		
1999–2000	Bournemouth	43	0	89	0
2000–01	Luton T	26	0		
2001–02	Luton T	13	0	39	0

PERRETT, Russell (D) 141 6
H: 6 1 W: 12 09 b.Barton-on-Sea 18-6-73
Source: AFC Lymington.

Season	Club				
1995–96	Portsmouth	9	0		
1996–97	Portsmouth	32	1		
1997–98	Portsmouth	16	1		
1998–99	Portsmouth	15	0	72	2
1999–2000	Cardiff C	27	1		
2000–01	Cardiff C	2	0	29	1
2001–02	Luton T	40	3	40	3

SKELTON, Aaron (M) 142 18
H: 5 11 W: 12 09 b.Welwyn 22-11-74
Source: Trainee.

Season	Club				
1992–93	Luton T	0	0		
1993–94	Luton T	0	0		
1994–95	Luton T	5	0		
1995–96	Luton T	0	0		
1996–97	Luton T	3	0		
1997–98	Colchester U	39	7		
1998–99	Colchester U	9	0		
1999–2000	Colchester U	33	4		

```
2000–01   Colchester U      44   6   125  17
2001–02   Luton T            9   1    17   1
```

SPRING, Matthew (M)   185 19
H:6 0   W: 12 08   b.Harlow 17-11-79
Source: Trainee.
```
1997–98   Luton T           12   0
1998–99   Luton T           45   3
1999–2000 Luton T           45   6
2000–01   Luton T           41   4
2001–02   Luton T           42   6   185  19
```

STIRLING, Jude‡ (D)   10 0
H:6 2   W: 12 13   b.Enfield 29-6-82
Source: Trainee.
```
1999–2000 Luton T            0   0
2000–01   Luton T            9   0
2001–02   Luton T            1   0    10   0
```

TAYLOR, Matthew (D)   129 16
H:5 11 W: 11 08 b.Oxford 27-11-81
Source: Trainee.
```
1998–99   Luton T            0   0
1999–2000 Luton T           41   4
2000–01   Luton T           45   1
2001–02   Luton T           43  11   129  16
```

THOMSON, Peter‡ (F)   18 3
H:6 3   W: 13 04   b.Crumpsall 30-6-77
Source: Stand Ath.
```
1995–96   Bury               0   0
1996–97   Bury               0   0
From Lancaster C
1998–99   NAC Breda          3   0
1999–2000 NAC Breda          2   0     5   0
2000–01   Luton T           11   2
2001–02   Luton T            0   0    11   2
2001–02   Rushden & D        2   1     2   1
```

VALOIS, Jean-Louis* (M)   43 7
H:5 11   W: 11 11   b.Saint-Priest 15-10-73
```
2000–01   Lille              9   1     9   1
2001–02   Luton T           34   6    34   6
```

WARD, Scott* (G)   1 0
H:6 2   W: 14 09   b.Brent 5-10-81
Source: Trainee.
```
1998–99   Luton T            0   0
1999–2000 Luton T            0   0
2000–01   Luton T            0   0
2001–02   Luton T            0   0     1   0
```

Scholars
Beckwith, Robert; Carroll, John M; Chatfield, Jonathan D; Clarke, Duane L; Davies, Curtis; Deeney, Joseph E; Dillon, Christopher H; Dogbe, Steven YS; Foley, Kevin P; Gillman, Robert; James-Barriteau, Rene WJ; Jeffrey, Marcus P; Judge, Matthew P; Mortara, Dean P; O'Leary, Stephen; Okai, Parys; Osborn, James

MACCLESFIELD T

ABBEY, George (D)   53 0
H:5 8   W: 10 08   b.Port Harcourt 20-10-78
Source: Sharks.
```
1999–2000 Macclesfield T    18   0
2000–01   Macclesfield T    18   0
2001–02   Macclesfield T    17   0    53   0
```

ADAMS, Daniel (D)   76 0
H:5 8   W: 13 08   b.Manchester 3-1-76
Source: Altrincham.
```
2000–01   Macclesfield T    37   0
2001–02   Macclesfield T    39   0    76   0
```

ALDRIDGE, Paul† (F)   6 0
H:5 11   W: 11 07   b.Liverpool 2-12-81
Source: Scholar.
```
1999–2000 Tranmere R         4   0
2000–01   Tranmere R         2   0
2001–02   Tranmere R         0   0     6   0
2001–02   Macclesfield T     0   0
```

ASKEY, John† (F)   172 29
H:6 0   W: 12 02   b.Stoke 4-11-64
Source: Port Vale.
```
1997–98   Macclesfield T    39   6
1998–99   Macclesfield T    38   4
1999–2000 Macclesfield T    40  15
2000–01   Macclesfield T    37   3
2001–02   Macclesfield T    18   1   172  29
```

BAMBER, Michael‡ (D)   6 0
H:5 7   W: 10 02   b.Preston 1-10-80
Source: Blackpool Trainee.
```
1999–2000 Macclesfield T     1   0
2000–01   Macclesfield T     5   0
2001–02   Macclesfield T     0   0     6   0
```

BYRNE, Chris (M)   101 17
H:5 9   W: 10 00   b.Hulme 9-2-75
Source: Crewe Alex, Macclesfield T.
```
1997–98   Sunderland         8   0     8   0
1997–98   Stockport Co      26   7
1998–99   Stockport Co      11   2
1999–2000 Stockport Co      18   2
1999–2000 Macclesfield T     5   0
2000–01   Stockport Co       1   0    56  11
2001–02   Macclesfield T    32   6    37   6
```

CAME, Shaun (D)   8 0
H:6 3   W: 13 00   b.Crewe 15-6-83
Source: Trainee.
```
2000–01   Macclesfield T     7   0
2001–02   Macclesfield T     1   0     8   0
```

EYRE, Richard‡ (M)   62 1
H:5 9   W: 10 10   b.Stockport 15-9-76
Source: Trainee.
```
1995–96   Port Vale          0   0
1996–97   Port Vale          0   0
1997–98   Port Vale          1   0
1998–99   Port Vale         11   0
1999–2000 Port Vale         30   1
2000–01   Port Vale          6   0    48   1
2001–02   Macclesfield T    14   0    14   0
```

GLOVER, Lee# (F)   318 63
H:5 11   W: 11 09   b.Kettering 24-4-70
Source: Trainee. *Honours:* Scotland Youth, Under-21.
```
1986–87   Nottingham F       0   0
1987–88   Nottingham F      20   3
1988–89   Nottingham F       0   0
1989–90   Nottingham F       0   0
1989–90   Leicester C        5   1     5   1
1989–90   Barnsley           8   0     8   0
1990–91   Nottingham F       8   1
1991–92   Nottingham F      16   0
1991–92   Luton T            1   0     1   0
1992–93   Nottingham F      14   0
1993–94   Nottingham F      18   5    76   9
1994–95   Port Vale         28   4
1995–96   Port Vale         24   3    52   7
1996–97   Rotherham U       22   1
1996–97   Huddersfield T    11   0    11   0
1997–98   Rotherham U       37  17
1998–99   Rotherham U       19  10
1999–2000 Rotherham U        7   1    85  29
2000–01   Macclesfield T    38   5
2001–02   Macclesfield T    43   9    80  17
```

HARRIES, Paul‡ (F)   32 3
H:6 1   W: 13 00   b.Sydney 19-11-77
```
1997–98   Portsmouth         1   0     1   0
1998–99   Crystal Palace     0   0
1998–99   Torquay U          5   0     5   0
1999–2000 Carlisle U        20   2
2000–01   Wollongong Wolves  6   1     6   1
2000–01   Carlisle U         0   0    20   2
2001–02   Macclesfield T     0   0
```

HITCHEN, Steve (D)   109 1
H:5 8   W: 11 07   b.Salford 28-11-76
Source: Trainee.
```
1995–96   Blackburn R        0   0
1996–97   Blackburn R        0   0
1997–98   Macclesfield T     2   0
1998–99   Macclesfield T    35   0
1999–2000 Macclesfield T     5   0
2000–01   Macclesfield T    37   0
2001–02   Macclesfield T    30   1   109   1
```

HODGSON, Steven‡ (G)   0 0
H:5 11   W: 11 00   b.Macclesfield 23-12-81
Source: Scholar. *Honours:* England Youth.
```
1998–99   Manchester C       0   0
1999–2000 Manchester C       0   0
2000–01   Manchester C       0   0
2001–02   Macclesfield T     0   0
```

KEEN, Kevin* (M)   500 40
H:5 6   W: 10 10   b.Amersham 25-2-67
Source: Wycombe W and Apprentice.
Honours: England Schools, Youth.
```
1983–84   West Ham U         0   0
1984–85   West Ham U         0   0
1985–86   West Ham U         0   0
1986–87   West Ham U        13   0
1987–88   West Ham U        23   1
1988–89   West Ham U        24   3
1989–90   West Ham U        44  10
1990–91   West Ham U        40   0
1991–92   West Ham U        29   0
1992–93   West Ham U        46   7   219  21
1993–94   Wolverhampton W   41   7
1994–95   Wolverhampton W    1   0    42   7
1994–95   Stoke C           21   2
1995–96   Stoke C           33   3
1996–97   Stoke C           16   1
```

LIGHTBOURNE, Kyle (F)   344 95
H:6 2   W: 12 02   b.Bermuda 29-9-68
Source: Trainee. *Honours:* Bermuda 22 full caps.
```
1992–93   Scarborough       19   3
1993–94   Scarborough       10   0    19   3
1993–94   Walsall           35   7
1994–95   Walsall           42  23
1995–96   Walsall           43  15
1996–97   Walsall           45  20   165  65
1997–98   Coventry C         7   0     7   0
1997–98   Fulham             4   2     4   2
1997–98   Stoke C           13   2
1998–99   Stoke C           36   7
1999–2000 Stoke C           40   7
2000–01   Stoke C           22   5   111  21
2000–01   Swindon T          2   0     2   0
2000–01   Cardiff C          3   0     3   0
2001–02   Macclesfield T    29   4    29   4
2001–02   Hull C             4   0     4   0
```

MARTIN, Lee (G)   240 0
H:6 0   W: 13 07   b.Huddersfield 9-9-68
Source: Trainee. *Honours:* England Schools.
```
1987–88   Huddersfield T    18   0
1988–89   Huddersfield T     0   0
1989–90   Huddersfield T    25   0
1990–91   Huddersfield T     4   0
1991–92   Huddersfield T     7   0    54   0
1992–93   Blackpool         24   0
1993–94   Blackpool         43   0
1994–95   Blackpool         31   0
1995–96   Blackpool          0   0
1995–96   Bradford C         0   0
1996–97   Blackpool          0   0    98   0
1997–98   Rochdale           0   0
1998–99   Halifax T         37   0    37   0
1999–2000 Macclesfield T    21   0
2000–01   Macclesfield T    21   0
2001–02   Macclesfield T     9   0    51   0
```

McAVOY, Andy‡ (M)   31 0
H:6 0   W: 12 00   b.Middlesbrough 28-8-79
Source: Trainee.
```
1997–98   Blackburn R        0   0
1998–99   Blackburn R        0   0
1999–2000 Blackburn R        0   0
1999–2000 Hartlepool U      16   0
2000–01   Hartlepool U       5   0    21   0
2001–02   Hartlepool U      10   0    10   0
```

MORRIS, Adam* (M)   0 0
b.Crewe 13-1-83
Source: Trainee.
```
2001–02   Macclesfield T     0   0
```

MUNROE, Karl* (D)   59 1
H:6 0   W: 10 08   b.Manchester 23-9-79
Source: Trainee.
```
1997–98   Swansea C          1   0
1998–99   Swansea C          0   0
1999–2000 Swansea C          0   0     1   0
1999–2000 Macclesfield T     5   0
2000–01   Macclesfield T    23   1
2001–02   Macclesfield T    30   0    58   1
```

O'NEILL, Paul (D)   24 0
H:5 11   W: 11 02   b.Bolton 17-6-82
Source: Trainee.
```
1999–2000 Macclesfield T     1   0
2000–01   Macclesfield T    12   0
2001–02   Macclesfield T    11   0    24   0
```

PRIEST, Chris (M)   251 35
H:5 10   W: 12 00   b.Leigh 18-10-73
Source: Trainee.
```
1992–93   Everton            0   0
1993–94   Everton            0   0
1994–95   Everton            0   0
1994–95   Chester C         24   1
1995–96   Chester C         39  13
1996–97   Chester C         32   2
1997–98   Chester C         37   6
1998–99   Chester C         35   4   167  26
1999–2000 Macclesfield T    36   4
2000–01   Macclesfield T    15   4
2001–02   Macclesfield T    33   1    84   9
```

RIDLER, Dave (D)   155 1
H:6 0   W: 11 00   b.Liverpool 12-3-76
Source: Prescot T.
```
1996–97   Wrexham           11   0
1997–98   Wrexham           20   0
1998–99   Wrexham           36   1
1999–2000 Wrexham           25   0
2000–01   Wrexham           24   0   116   1
2001–02   Macclesfield T    39   0    39   0
```

SHUTTLEWORTH, Barry‡ (D) 22 1
H: 5 8 W: 11 00 b.Accrington 9-7-77
Source: Trainee.

Season	Club	App	Gls	Tot App	Tot Gls
1995-96	Bury	0	0		
1996-97	Bury	0	0		
1997-98	Rotherham U	0	0		
1998-99	Blackpool	14	1		
1999-2000	Blackpool	5	0		
2000-01	Blackpool	0	0	19	1

From Scarborough.

2001-02	Macclesfield T	3	0	3	0

TINSON, Darren (D) 218 5
H: 6 0 W: 13 07 b.Birmingham 15-11-69
Source: Northwich V.

Season	Club	App	Gls	Tot App	Tot Gls
1997-98	Macclesfield T	44	0		
1998-99	Macclesfield T	37	0		
1999-2000	Macclesfield T	46	1		
2000-01	Macclesfield T	45	3		
2001-02	Macclesfield T	46	1	218	5

TIPTON, Matthew (F) 125 18
H: 5 10 W: 11 02 b.Bridgend 29-6-80
Source: Trainee. Honours: Wales Youth, Under-21.

Season	Club	App	Gls	Tot App	Tot Gls
1997-98	Oldham Ath	30	0		
1998-99	Oldham Ath	28	2		
1999-2000	Oldham Ath	29	3		
2000-01	Oldham Ath	30	5		
2001-02	Oldham Ath	22	5	112	15
2001-02	Macclesfield T	13	3	13	3

TRACEY, Richard‡ (F) 89 16
H: 5 11 W: 12 04 b.Muirfield 9-7-79
Source: Trainee.

Season	Club	App	Gls	Tot App	Tot Gls
1997-98	Sheffield U	0	0		
1997-98	Rotherham U	0	0		
1998-99	Rotherham U	3	0	3	0
1998-99	Carlisle U	11	3		
1999-2000	Carlisle U	36	7		
2000-01	Carlisle U	6	1	53	11
2000-01	Macclesfield T	13	3		
2001-02	Macclesfield T	20	2	33	5

WELCH, Michael (D) 6 0
H: 6 3 W: 11 12 b.Crewe 11-1-82
Source: Barnsley Scholar. Honours:

2001-02	Macclesfield T	6	0	6	0

WHITEHEAD, Damien* (F) 58 14
H: 5 10 W: 12 00 b.Whiston 24-4-79
Source: Warrington T.

Season	Club	App	Gls	Tot App	Tot Gls
1999-2000	Macclesfield T	23	6		
2000-01	Macclesfield T	33	8		
2001-02	Macclesfield T	2	0	58	14

WHITTAKER, Dan (M) 16 2
H: 5 10 W: 11 00 b.Manchester 14-11-80

Season	Club	App	Gls	Tot App	Tot Gls
2000-01	Macclesfield T	0	0		
2001-02	Macclesfield T	16	2	16	2

WILSON, Steve* (G) 220 0
H: 5 10 W: 10 07 b.Hull 24-4-74
Source: Trainee.

Season	Club	App	Gls	Tot App	Tot Gls
1990-91	Hull C	2	0		
1991-92	Hull C	3	0		
1992-93	Hull C	26	0		
1993-94	Hull C	9	0		
1994-95	Hull C	20	0		
1995-96	Hull C	19	0		
1996-97	Hull C	15	0		
1997-98	Hull C	37	0		
1998-99	Hull C	23	0		
1999-2000	Hull C	27	0		
2000-01	Hull C	0	0	181	0
2000-01	Macclesfield T	1	0		
2001-02	Macclesfield T	38	0	39	0

WOOLLEY, Matt* (M) 5 0
H: 5 10 W: 11 02 b.Manchester 22-2-82

Season	Club	App	Gls	Tot App	Tot Gls
2000-01	Macclesfield T	2	0		
2001-02	Macclesfield T	3	0	5	0

Scholars
Bayliss, Richard L; Brackenridge, Stephen J; Campbell, John R; Carr, Michael A; Dolphin, Wesley D; Drummond, Philip A; Goodeve, Jordan; Higgins, Matthew R; Naylor, Adam R

Non-Contract
Aldridge, Paul J; Askey, John C

MANCHESTER C

ALMOND, James (F) 0 0
b.Northallerton 5-10-83
Source: Scholar. Honours: England Youth.

2000-01	Manchester C	0	0		
2001-02	Manchester C	0	0		

BARTON, Joey (M) 0 0
H: 5 9 W: 11 00 b.Huyton 2-9-82
Source: Scholar.

2001-02	Manchester C	0	0		

BENARBIA, Ali (M) 396 42
H: 5 8 W: 10 08 b.Oran 8-10-68

Season	Club	App	Gls	Tot App	Tot Gls
1988-89	Martigues	30	2		
1989-90	Martigues	28	3		
1990-91	Martigues	29	5		
1991-92	Martigues	24	2		
1992-93	Martigues	25	2		
1993-94	Martigues	34	2		
1994-95	Martigues	31	7	201	23
1995-96	Monaco	25	4		
1996-97	Monaco	35	3		
1997-98	Monaco	30	1	90	8
1998-99	Bordeaux	25	3	25	3
1999-2000	Paris St Germain	27	0		
2000-01	Paris St Germain	14	0		
2001-02	Paris St Germain	1	0	42	0
2001-02	Manchester C	38	8	38	8

BERKOVIC, Eyal (M) 289 57
H: 5 7 W: 10 12 b.Haifa 2-4-72
Honours: Israel 73 full caps, 9 goals.

Season	Club	App	Gls	Tot App	Tot Gls
1992-93	Maccabi Haifa	32	7		
1993-94	Maccabi Haifa	38	10		
1994-95	Maccabi Haifa	29	3		
1995-96	Maccabi Haifa	29	3	128	25
1996-97	Southampton	28	4	28	4
1997-98	West Ham U	35	7		
1998-99	West Ham U	30	3	65	10
1999-2000	Celtic	28	9		
2000-01	Celtic	4	1	32	10
2000-01	Blackburn R	11	2	11	2
2001-02	Manchester C	25	6	25	6

BROWNE, Gary (F) 0 0
H: 5 10 W: 10 10 b.Dundonald 17-1-83
Source: Scholar.

2000-01	Manchester C	0	0		
2001-02	Manchester C	0	0		

CHARVET, Laurent (D) 173 22
H: 5 11 W: 13 07 b.Beziers 8-5-73

Season	Club	App	Gls	Tot App	Tot Gls
1994-95	Cannes	19	4		
1995-96	Cannes	31	8		
1996-97	Cannes	38	6		
1997-98	Cannes	11	1	99	19
1997-98	Chelsea	11	2	11	2
1998-99	Newcastle U	31	1		
1999-2000	Newcastle U	2	0		
2000-01	Newcastle U	7	0	40	1
2000-01	Manchester C	20	0		
2001-02	Manchester C	3	0	23	0

COLOSIMO, Simon‡ (D) 74 12
H: 5 11 W: 12 01 b.Melbourne 8-1-79
Honours: Australia 13 full caps, 2 goals.

Season	Club	App	Gls	Tot App	Tot Gls
1997-98	Carlton	21	1		
1998-99	Carlton	13	5		
1999-2000	Carlton	11	2		
2000-01	Carlton	5	2	50	10
2000-01	South Melbourne	18	2	18	2
2001-02	Manchester C	6	0	6	0

DAY, Rhys (D) 9 0
H: 6 2 W: 12 10 b.Bridgend 31-8-82
Source: Scholar. Honours: Wales Under-21.

Season	Club	App	Gls	Tot App	Tot Gls
1999-2000	Manchester C	0	0		
2000-01	Manchester C	0	0		
2001-02	Manchester C	0	0		
2001-02	Blackpool	9	0	9	0

DUNFIELD, Terry (M) 1 0
H: 5 10 W: 11 02 b.Canada 20-2-82
Source: Trainee.

Season	Club	App	Gls	Tot App	Tot Gls
1998-99	Manchester C	0	0		
1999-2000	Manchester C	0	0		
2000-01	Manchester C	1	0		
2001-02	Manchester C	0	0	1	0

DUNNE, Richard (D) 128 1
H: 6 1 W: 16 05 b.Dublin 21-9-79
Source: Trainee. Honours: Eire Under-21, 14 full caps, 3 goals.

Season	Club	App	Gls	Tot App	Tot Gls
1996-97	Everton	7	0		
1997-98	Everton	3	0		
1998-99	Everton	16	0		
1999-2000	Everton	31	0		
2000-01	Everton	3	0	60	0
2000-01	Manchester C	25	0		
2001-02	Manchester C	43	1	68	1

EDGHILL, Richard* (D) 184 1
H: 5 9 W: 12 01 b.Oldham 23-9-74
Source: Trainee. Honours: England Under-21.

Season	Club	App	Gls	Tot App	Tot Gls
1992-93	Manchester C	0	0		
1993-94	Manchester C	22	0		
1994-95	Manchester C	14	0		
1995-96	Manchester C	13	0		
1996-97	Manchester C	0	0		
1997-98	Manchester C	36	0		
1998-99	Manchester C	38	0		
1999-2000	Manchester C	41	1		
2000-01	Manchester C	6	0		
2000-01	Birmingham C	3	0	3	0
2001-02	Manchester C	11	0	181	1

ELLEGAARD, Kevin Stuhr (G) 0 0
H: 6 5 W: 14 00 b.Denmark 23-5-83
Source: Farum.

2001-02	Manchester C	0	0		

ELLIOTT, Stephen (F) 0 0
b.Dublin 6-1-84
Source: School.

2000-01	Manchester C	0	0		
2001-02	Manchester C	0	0		

FLOOD, William (M) 0 0
b.Dublin 10-4-85

2001-02	Manchester C	0	0		

GOATER, Shaun (F) 443 187
H: 6 0 W: 12 06 b.Bermuda 25-2-70
Honours: Bermuda 19 full caps.

Season	Club	App	Gls	Tot App	Tot Gls
1988-89	Manchester U	0	0		
1989-90	Manchester U	0	0		
1989-90	Rotherham U	12	2		
1990-91	Rotherham U	22	2		
1991-92	Rotherham U	24	9		
1992-93	Rotherham U	23	7		
1993-94	Rotherham U	39	13		
1993-94	Notts Co	0	1	1	0
1994-95	Rotherham U	45	19		
1995-96	Rotherham U	44	18	209	70
1996-97	Bristol C	42	23		
1997-98	Bristol C	33	17	75	40
1997-98	Manchester C	7	3		
1998-99	Manchester C	43	17		
1999-2000	Manchester C	40	23		
2000-01	Manchester C	26	6		
2001-02	Manchester C	42	28	158	77

HAALAND, Alf-Inge (D) 187 18
H: 6 1 W: 12 02 b.Bryne 23-11-72
Source: Bryne. Honours: Norway 34 full caps.

Season	Club	App	Gls	Tot App	Tot Gls
1993-94	Nottingham F	3	0		
1994-95	Nottingham F	20	1		
1995-96	Nottingham F	17	0		
1996-97	Nottingham F	35	6	75	7
1997-98	Leeds U	32	7		
1998-99	Leeds U	29	1		
1999-2000	Leeds U	13	0	74	8
2000-01	Manchester C	35	3		
2001-02	Manchester C	3	0	38	3

HARRIS, Richard* (M) 0 0
b.Shrewsbury 14-9-84

2001-02	Manchester C	0	0		

HODGSON, David (M) 0 0
b.Billinge 2-9-83

2001-02	Manchester C	0	0		

HOGAN, Barry* (D) 0 0
H: 5 8 W: 9 12 b.St Helens 15-2-83
Source: Scholar.

2000-01	Manchester C	0	0		
2001-02	Manchester C	0	0		

HORLOCK, Kevin (M) 337 59
H: 5 11 W: 12 12 b.Erith 1-11-72
Source: Trainee. Honours: Northern Ireland B, 29 full caps.

Season	Club	App	Gls	Tot App	Tot Gls
1991-92	West Ham U	0	0		
1992-93	West Ham U	0	0		
1992-93	Swindon T	14	1		
1993-94	Swindon T	38	0		
1994-95	Swindon T	38	1		
1995-96	Swindon T	45	12		
1996-97	Swindon T	28	8	163	22
1997-98	Manchester C	18	4		
1998-99	Manchester C	25	5		
1999-2000	Manchester C	37	9		
1999-2000	Manchester C	38	10		
2000-01	Manchester C	14	2		
2001-02	Manchester C	42	7	174	37

HOWEY, Steve (D) 261 15
H: 6 1 W: 13 05 b.Sunderland 26-10-71
Source: Trainee. Honours: England 4 full caps.

Season	Club	App	Gls	Tot App	Tot Gls
1988-89	Newcastle U	1	0		
1989-90	Newcastle U	0	0		
1990-91	Newcastle U	11	0		
1991-92	Newcastle U	21	1		
1992-93	Newcastle U	41	2		
1993-94	Newcastle U	14	0		
1994-95	Newcastle U	30	1		
1995-96	Newcastle U	28	1		
1996-97	Newcastle U	8	1		
1997-98	Newcastle U	14	0		
1998-99	Newcastle U	14	0		
1999-2000	Newcastle U	9	0	191	6

2000–01 Manchester C 36 6
2001–02 Manchester C 34 3 **70 9**

HUCKERBY, Darren (F) **222 59**
H: 5 10 W: 12 05 b.Nottingham 23-4-76
Source: Trainee. *Honours:* England Under-21, B.
1993–94 Lincoln C 6 1
1994–95 Lincoln C 6 2
1995–96 Lincoln C 16 2 **28 5**
1995–96 Newcastle U 1 0
1996–97 Newcastle U 0 0 **1 0**
1996–97 Millwall 6 3 **6 3**
1996–97 Coventry C 25 5
1997–98 Coventry C 34 14
1998–99 Coventry C 34 9
1999–2000 Coventry C 1 0 **94 28**
1999–2000 Leeds U 33 2
2000–01 Leeds U 7 0 **40 2**
2000–01 Manchester C 13 1
2001–02 Manchester C 40 20 **53 21**

JAMES, William (M) **0 0**
b.Swansea 11-1-84
Source: Scholar.
2001–02 Manchester C 0 0

JENSEN, Niclas (D) **236 15**
H: 6 0 W: 12 00 b.Copenhagen 17-8-74
Honours: Denmark 11 full caps.
1992–93 Lyngby 12 2
1993–94 Lyngby 21 0
1994–95 Lyngby 20 1
1995–96 Lyngby 32 3
1996–97 Lyngby 7 1 **92 7**
1996–97 PSV Eindhoven 2 0
1997–98 PSV Eindhoven 2 0 **4 0**
1997–98 FC Copenhagen 10 0
1998–99 FC Copenhagen 33 4
1999–2000 FC Copenhagen 29 1
2000–01 FC Copenhagen 32 1
2001–02 FC Copenhagen 18 1 **122 7**
2001–02 Manchester C 18 1 **18 1**

JIHAI, Sun (D) **30 0**
H: 5 10 W: 10 07 b.Dalian 30-9-77
Source: Dalian Wanda. *Honours:* China 61 full caps.
1998–99 Crystal Palace 23 0 **23 0**
From Dalian Wanda.
2001–02 Manchester C 7 0 **7 0**

JORDAN, Stephen (D) **0 0**
H: 6 0 W: 11 13 b.Warrington 6-3-82
Source: Scholar.
1998–99 Manchester C 0 0
1999–2000 Manchester C 0 0
2000–01 Manchester C 0 0
2001–02 Manchester C 0 0

JOYCE, Damien (M) **0 0**
H: 5 8 W: 12 03 b.Dublin 8-3-83
Source: Scholar.
1999–2000 Manchester C 0 0
2000–01 Manchester C 0 0
2001–02 Manchester C 0 0

KILHEENEY, Ciaran (F) **0 0**
b.Stockport 9-1-84
2001–02 Manchester C 0 0

KILLEN, Chris (F) **24 9**
H: 6 0 W: 12 11 b.Wellington 8-10-81
Source: Miramar R. *Honours:* New Zealand 4 full caps.
1998–99 Manchester C 0 0
1999–2000 Manchester C 0 0
2000–01 Manchester C 0 0
2000–01 Wrexham 12 3 **12 3**
2001–02 Port Vale 9 6 **9 6**
2001–02 Manchester C 3 0 **3 0**

MACKEN, Jonathan (F) **192 68**
H: 5 10 W: 12 00 b.Manchester 7-9-77
Source: Trainee. *Honours:* England Youth.
1996–97 Manchester U 0 0
1997–98 Preston NE 29 6
1998–99 Preston NE 42 8
1999–2000 Preston NE 44 22
2000–01 Preston NE 38 19
2001–02 Preston NE 31 8 **184 63**
2001–02 Manchester C 8 5 **8 5**

McCARTHY, Patrick (D) **0 0**
H: 6 1 W: 12 08 b.Dublin 31-5-83
Source: Scholar.
2000–01 Manchester C 0 0
2001–02 Manchester C 0 0

McDOWALL, Ryan (M) **0 0**
b.Knowsley 30-3-84
Source: School.
2000–01 Manchester C 0 0
2001–02 Manchester C 0 0

McTAGGART, Daniel (M) **0 0**
b.St Asaph 1-12-83
Source: Scholar.
2001–02 Manchester C 0 0

MEARS, Tyrone (D) **1 0**
H: 5 11 W: 11 11 b.Stockport 18-2-83
2000–01 Manchester C 0 0
2001–02 Manchester C 1 0 **1 0**

METTOMO, Lucien (D) **99 10**
H: 6 0 W: 12 00 b.Douala 19-4-77
Source: Ocean Kribi. *Honours:* Cameroon 16 full caps, 1 goal.
1998–99 St Etienne 33 7
1999–2000 St Etienne 26 1
2000–01 St Etienne 17 1 **76 9**
2001–02 Manchester C 23 1 **23 1**

MIKE, Leon (F) **12 0**
H: 5 10 W: 13 04 b.Manchester 4-9-81
Source: Scholar. *Honours:* England Schools, Youth.
1998–99 Manchester C 0 0
1999–2000 Manchester C 0 0
2000–01 Manchester C 0 0
2000–01 Oxford U 3 0 **3 0**
2000–01 Halifax T 7 0 **7 0**
2001–02 Manchester C 2 0 **2 0**
(Transferred to Aberdeen, October 2001).

MORRISON, Andy‡ (D) **262 16**
H: 5 11 W: 15 07 b.Inverness 30-7-70
Source: Trainee.
1987–88 Plymouth Arg 1 0
1988–89 Plymouth Arg 2 0
1989–90 Plymouth Arg 19 1
1990–91 Plymouth Arg 32 2
1991–92 Plymouth Arg 30 3
1992–93 Plymouth Arg 29 0 **113 6**
1993–94 Blackburn R 5 0
1994–95 Blackburn R 0 0 **5 0**
1994–95 Blackpool 18 0
1995–96 Blackpool 29 3
1996–97 Huddersfield T 10 1
1997–98 Huddersfield T 23 1
1998–99 Huddersfield T 12 0 **45 2**
1998–99 Manchester C 22 4
1999–2000 Manchester C 12 0
2000–01 Manchester C 3 0
2000–01 Blackpool 6 1 **53 4**
2000–01 Crystal Palace 5 0 **5 0**
2000–01 Sheffield U 4 0 **4 0**
2001–02 Manchester C 0 0 **37 4**

MURPHY, Brian (G) **0 0**
H: 6 0 W: 13 01 b.Waterford 7-5-83
2000–01 Manchester C 0 0
2001–02 Manchester C 0 0

NASH, Carlo (G) **139 0**
H: 6 4 W: 14 05 b.Bolton 13-9-73
Source: Clitheroe.
1996–97 Crystal Palace 21 0
1997–98 Crystal Palace 0 0 **21 0**
1998–99 Stockport Co 43 0
1999–2000 Stockport Co 38 0
2000–01 Stockport Co 8 0 **89 0**
2000–01 Manchester C 6 0
2001–02 Manchester C 23 0 **29 0**

NEGOUAI, Christian (M) **40 5**
H: 6 4 W: 13 00 b.Martinique 20-1-75
1999–2000 Charleroi 9 0
2000–01 Charleroi 26 4
2001–02 Charleroi 0 0 **35 4**
2001–02 Manchester C 5 1 **5 1**

PAISLEY, Stephen (D) **0 0**
H: 6 1 W: 12 08 b.Dublin 28-7-83
Source: Scholar.
2000–01 Manchester C 0 0
2001–02 Manchester C 0 0

PEARCE, Stuart* (D) **569 72**
H: 5 10 W: 12 12 b.Hammersmith 24-4-62
Source: Wealdstone. *Honours:* England Under-21, 78 full caps, 5 goals.
1983–84 Coventry C 23 0
1984–85 Coventry C 28 4 **51 4**
1985–86 Nottingham F 30 1
1986–87 Nottingham F 39 6
1987–88 Nottingham F 34 5
1988–89 Nottingham F 36 6
1989–90 Nottingham F 34 5
1990–91 Nottingham F 33 11
1991–92 Nottingham F 30 5
1992–93 Nottingham F 23 2
1993–94 Nottingham F 42 6
1994–95 Nottingham F 36 8
1995–96 Nottingham F 31 3
1996–97 Nottingham F 33 5 **401 63**
1997–98 Newcastle U 25 0
1998–99 Newcastle U 12 0 **37 0**

1999–2000 West Ham U 8 0
2000–01 West Ham U 34 2 **42 2**
2001–02 Manchester C 38 3 **38 3**

RITCHIE, Paul (D) **167 4**
H: 5 11 W: 12 10 b.Kirkcaldy 21-8-75
Source: Links U. *Honours:* Scotland Schools, Under-21, B, 6 full caps, 1 goal.
1992–93 Hearts 0 0
1993–94 Hearts 0 0
1994–95 Hearts 0 0
1995–96 Hearts 28 1
1996–97 Hearts 28 1
1997–98 Hearts 34 0
1998–99 Hearts 29 1
1999–2000 Hearts 14 1 **133 4**
1999–2000 Bolton W 14 0 **14 0**
2000–01 Manchester C 12 0
2001–02 Manchester C 8 0 **20 0**

SHUKER, Chris (F) **11 1**
H: 5 4 W: 9 06 b.Liverpool 9-5-82
Source: Scholar.
1999–2000 Manchester C 0 0
2000–01 Manchester C 0 0
2000–01 *Macclesfield T* 9 1 **9 1**
2001–02 Manchester C 2 0 **2 0**

TIATTO, Danny (D) **191 8**
H: 5 7 W: 11 06 b.Melbourne 22-5-73
Honours: Australia 19 full caps, 1 goal.
1994–95 Melbourne Knights 25 3
1995–96 Melbourne Knights 18 0 **43 3**
1996–97 Salernitana 11 1 **11 1**
1997–98 Stoke C 15 1 **15 1**
1998–99 Manchester C 17 0
1999–2000 Manchester C 35 0
2000–01 Manchester C 33 2
2001–02 Manchester C 37 1 **122 3**

TICKLE, David (M) **0 0**
b.Billinge 3-9-83
2001–02 Manchester C 0 0

TOURE, Alioune (F) **50 3**
H: 5 8 W: 11 05 b.Saint-Denis 9-9-78
1996–97 Nantes 2 0
1997–98 Nantes 9 0
1998–99 Nantes 17 2
1999–2000 Nantes 6 1
2000–01 Nantes 15 0 **49 3**
2001–02 Manchester C 1 0 **1 0**

TUNNICLIFFE, Andrew* (F) **0 0**
H: 5 6 W: 9 08 b.Manchester 24-5-83
Source: Scholar.
2000–01 Manchester C 0 0
2001–02 Manchester C 0 0

WANCHOPE, Paulo (F) **149 56**
H: 6 3 W: 13 08 b.Heredia 31-7-76
Source: Herediano. *Honours:* Costa Rica 53 full caps, 37 goals.
1996–97 Derby Co 5 1
1997–98 Derby Co 32 13
1998–99 Derby Co 35 9 **72 23**
1999–2000 West Ham U 35 12 **35 12**
2000–01 Manchester C 27 9
2001–02 Manchester C 15 12 **42 21**

WEAVER, Nick (G) **147 0**
H: 6 4 W: 14 05 b.Sheffield 2-3-79
Source: Trainee. *Honours:* England Under-21.
1995–96 Mansfield T 1 0
1996–97 Mansfield T 0 0 **1 0**
1996–97 Manchester C 0 0
1997–98 Manchester C 0 0
1998–99 Manchester C 45 0
1999–2000 Manchester C 45 0
2000–01 Manchester C 31 0
2001–02 Manchester C 25 0 **146 0**

WESTWOOD, Keiren (G) **0 0**
b.Manchester 23-10-84
2001–02 Manchester C 0 0

WHELAN, Glenn (M) **0 0**
H: 5 10 W: 11 13 b.Dublin 13-1-84
Source: Scholar.
2000–01 Manchester C 0 0
2001–02 Manchester C 0 0

WHITLEY, Jeff (M) **138 10**
H: 5 8 W: 11 00 b.Zambia 28-1-79
Source: Trainee. *Honours:* Northern Ireland Under-21, B, 7 full caps, 1 goal.
1995–96 Manchester C 0 0
1996–97 Manchester C 23 1
1997–98 Manchester C 17 1
1998–99 Manchester C 8 1
1998–99 *Wrexham* 9 2 **9 2**
1999–2000 Manchester C 42 4

2000–01	Manchester C	31	1		
2001–02	Manchester C	2	0	**123**	**8**
2001–02	*Notts Co*	6	0	**6**	**0**

WIEKENS, Gerard (D) 209 11
H: 6 0 W: 13 06 b.Tolhuiswyk 25-2-73

1996–97	Veendam	33	1	**33**	**1**
1997–98	Manchester C	37	5		
1998–99	Manchester C	42	2		
1999–2000	Manchester C	34	1		
2000–01	Manchester C	34	2		
2001–02	Manchester C	29	0	**176**	**10**

WRIGHT-PHILLIPS, Shaun (F) 54 8
H: 5 4 W: 9 10 b.London 25-10-81
Honours: England Under-21.

1998–99	Manchester C	0	0		
1999–2000	Manchester C	4	0		
2000–01	Manchester C	15	0		
2001–02	Manchester C	35	8	**54**	**8**

Scholars
Almond, Michael J; Croft, Lee D; Douglas-Pringle, Daniel F; Egerton, Mark C; Furnival, Gary R; Gilder, Phillip G; Matthews, James L; Murphy, Paul J; Orr, Adrian; Pearson, Sean C; Proffitt, Dorryl; Slack, Leyton L; Smith, Craig C; Tandy, Jamie R; Wright-Phillips, Bradley E

MANCHESTER U

BARTHEZ, Fabien (G) 337 0
H: 5 11 W: 12 08 b.Lavelanet 28-6-71
Honours: France 51 full caps.

1991–92	Toulouse	26	0	**26**	**0**
1992–93	Marseille	30	0		
1993–94	Marseille	37	0		
1994–95	Marseille	39	0	**106**	**0**
1995–96	Monaco	21	0		
1996–97	Monaco	36	0		
1997–98	Monaco	30	0		
1998–99	Monaco	32	0		
1999–2000	Monaco	24	0	**143**	**0**
2000–01	Manchester U	30	0		
2001–02	Manchester U	32	0	**62**	**0**

BAXTER, Nick* (G) 0 0
H: 6 3 W: 13 10 b.Bridlington 25-3-83
Source: Scholar.

2000–01	Manchester U	0	0		
2001–02	Manchester U	0	0		

BECKHAM, David (M) 239 57
H: 6 0 W: 11 13 b.Leytonstone 2-5-75
Source: Trainee. *Honours:* England Youth, Under-21, 54 full caps, 7 goals.

1992–93	Manchester U	0	0		
1993–94	Manchester U	0	0		
1994–95	Manchester U	4	0		
1994–95	*Preston NE*	5	2	**5**	**2**
1995–96	Manchester U	33	7		
1996–97	Manchester U	36	7		
1997–98	Manchester U	37	9		
1998–99	Manchester U	34	6		
1999–2000	Manchester U	31	6		
2000–01	Manchester U	31	9		
2001–02	Manchester U	28	11	**234**	**55**

BLANC, Laurent* (D) 583 124
H: 6 3 W: 13 10 b.Ales 19-11-65
Honours: France 97 full caps, 16 goals.

1983–84	Montpellier	15	0		
1984–85	Montpellier	32	5		
1985–86	Montpellier	29	6		
1986–87	Montpellier	34	18		
1987–88	Montpellier	24	6		
1988–89	Montpellier	35	15		
1989–90	Montpellier	36	12		
1990–91	Montpellier	38	14	**243**	**76**
1991–92	Napoli	31	6	**31**	**6**
1992–93	Nimes	29	1	**29**	**1**
1993–94	St Etienne	33	5		
1994–95	St Etienne	37	13	**70**	**18**
1995–96	Auxerre	23	2	**23**	**2**
1996–97	Barcelona	28	1	**28**	**1**
1997–98	Marseille	31	11		
1998–99	Marseille	32	2	**63**	**13**
1999–2000	Internazionale	34	3		
2000–01	Internazionale	33	3	**67**	**6**
2001–02	Manchester U	29	1	**29**	**1**

BROWN, Wes (D) 61 0
H: 6 1 W: 13 11 b.Manchester 13-10-79
Source: Trainee. *Honours:* England Schools, Youth, Under-21, 6 full caps.

1996–97	Manchester U	0	0		
1997–98	Manchester U	2	0		
1998–99	Manchester U	14	0		
1999–2000	Manchester U	0	0		
2000–01	Manchester U	28	0		
2001–02	Manchester U	17	0	**61**	**0**

BUTT, Nicky (M) 231 20
H: 5 10 W: 11 11 b.Manchester 21-1-75
Source: Trainee. *Honours:* England Schools, Youth, Under-21, 22 full caps.

1992–93	Manchester U	1	0		
1993–94	Manchester U	1	0		
1994–95	Manchester U	22	1		
1995–96	Manchester U	32	2		
1996–97	Manchester U	26	5		
1997–98	Manchester U	33	3		
1998–99	Manchester U	31	2		
1999–2000	Manchester U	32	3		
2000–01	Manchester U	28	3		
2001–02	Manchester U	25	1	**231**	**20**

CARROLL, Roy (G) 188 0
H: 6 2 W: 13 12 b.Enniskillen 30-9-77
Source: Trainee. *Honours:* Northern Ireland Youth, Under-21, 11 full caps.

1995–96	Hull C	23	0		
1996–97	Hull C	23	0	**46**	**0**
1996–97	Wigan Ath	0	0		
1997–98	Wigan Ath	29	0		
1998–99	Wigan Ath	43	0		
1999–2000	Wigan Ath	34	0		
2000–01	Wigan Ath	29	0	**135**	**0**
2001–02	Manchester U	7	0	**7**	**0**

CHADWICK, Luke (F) 24 2
H: 5 11 W: 11 08 b.Cambridge 18-11-80
Source: Trainee. *Honours:* England Youth, Under-21.

1998–99	Manchester U	0	0		
1999–2000	Manchester U	0	0		
2000–01	Manchester U	16	2		
2001–02	Manchester U	8	0	**24**	**2**

CLEGG, Steven* (D) 0 0
H: 5 9 W: 12 08 b.Ashton-under-Lyne 16-4-82
Source: Scholar.

2000–01	Manchester U	0	0		
2001–02	Manchester U	0	0		

COGGER, John (D) 0 0
H: 5 10 W: 13 05 b.Waltham Forest 12-9-83
Source: Scholar.

2001–02	Manchester U	0	0		

CULKIN, Nick (G) 50 0
H: 6 2 W: 13 09 b.York 6-7-78
Source: York C.

1995–96	Manchester U	0	0		
1996–97	Manchester U	0	0		
1997–98	Manchester U	0	0		
1998–99	Manchester U	0	0		
1999–2000	Manchester U	1	0		
1999–2000	*Hull C*	4	0	**4**	**0**
2000–01	Manchester U	0	0		
2000–01	*Bristol R*	45	0	**45**	**0**
2001–02	Manchester U	0	0	**1**	**0**

DAVIS, Jimmy (F) 0 0
H: 5 8 W: 11 05 b.Bromsgrove 6-2-82
Source: Trainee. *Honours:* England Youth, Under-20.

1999–2000	Manchester U	0	0		
2000–01	Manchester U	0	0		
2001–02	Manchester U	0	0		

DJORDJIC, Bojan (F) 6 0
H: 5 10 W: 11 01 b.Belgrade 6-2-82
Source: On loan to Brommapojkarna.

1998–99	Manchester U	0	0		
1999–2000	Manchester U	0	0		
2000–01	Manchester U	1	0		
2001–02	Manchester U	0	0	**1**	**0**
2001–02	*Sheffield W*	5	0	**5**	**0**

FLETCHER, Darren (M) 0 0
H: 6 0 W: 13 01 b.Edinburgh 1-2-84
Source: Scholar.

2000–01	Manchester U	0	0		
2001–02	Manchester U	0	0		

FORLAN, Diego (F) 90 36
H: 5 8 W: 11 11 b.Montevideo 19-5-79
Honours: Uruguay 5 full caps, 2 goals.

1998–99	Independiente	2	0		
1999–2000	Independiente	24	7		
2000–01	Independiente	36	18		
2001–02	Independiente	15	11	**77**	**36**
2001–02	Manchester U	13	0	**13**	**0**

FORTUNE, Quinton (F) 123 13
H: 5 9 W: 11 09 b.Cape Town 21-5-77
Source: Kaizer Chiefs, Tottenham H schoolboy. *Honours:* South Africa 43 full caps.

1995–96	Mallorca	8	1	**8**	**1**
1995–96	Atletico Madrid	3	0		
1996–97	Atletico Madrid B	30	2		
1996–97	Atletico Madrid	2	0		
1997–98	Atletico Madrid B	31	1		
1997–98	Atletico Madrid	0	0		
1998–99	Atletico Madrid	2	0		
1998–99	Atletico Madrid B	20	4	**7**	**0**
1999–2000	Manchester U	6	2		
2000–01	Manchester U	7	2		
2001–02	Manchester U	14	1	**27**	**5**

FOX, David (M) 0 0
H: 5 9 W: 12 02 b.Stoke 13-12-83
Source: Scholar. *Honours:* England Youth.

2000–01	Manchester U	0	0		
2001–02	Manchester U	0	0		

GIGGS, Ryan (F) 346 71
H: 5 11 W: 11 00 b.Cardiff 29-11-73
Source: School. *Honours:* England Schools, Wales Youth, Under-21, 36 full caps, 7 goals.

1990–91	Manchester U	2	1		
1991–92	Manchester U	38	4		
1992–93	Manchester U	41	9		
1993–94	Manchester U	38	13		
1994–95	Manchester U	29	1		
1995–96	Manchester U	33	11		
1996–97	Manchester U	26	3		
1997–98	Manchester U	29	8		
1998–99	Manchester U	24	3		
1999–2000	Manchester U	30	6		
2000–01	Manchester U	31	5		
2001–02	Manchester U	25	7	**346**	**71**

HEATH, Colin (F) 0 0
H: 6 0 W: 13 01 b.Chesterfield 31-12-83
Source: Scholar.

2000–01	Manchester U	0	0		
2001–02	Manchester U	0	0		

HILTON, Kirk (D) 0 0
H: 5 7 W: 10 01 b.Flixton 2-4-81
Source: Trainee.

1999–2000	Manchester U	0	0		
2000–01	Manchester U	0	0		
2001–02	Manchester U	0	0		

HUMPHREYS, Chris (F) 0 0
H: 5 9 W: 13 05 b.Manchester 22-9-83
Source: Scholar.

2001–02	Manchester U	0	0		

IRWIN, Denis* (D) 607 27
H: 5 8 W: 10 11 b.Cork 31-10-65
Source: Apprentice. *Honours:* Eire Schools, Youth, Under-21, B, 56 full caps, 4 goals.

1983–84	Leeds U	12	0		
1984–85	Leeds U	41	1		
1985–86	Leeds U	19	0	**72**	**1**
1986–87	Oldham Ath	41	1		
1987–88	Oldham Ath	43	0		
1988–89	Oldham Ath	41	2		
1989–90	Oldham Ath	42	1	**167**	**4**
1990–91	Manchester U	34	0		
1991–92	Manchester U	38	4		
1992–93	Manchester U	40	5		
1993–94	Manchester U	42	2		
1994–95	Manchester U	40	2		
1995–96	Manchester U	31	1		
1996–97	Manchester U	31	1		
1997–98	Manchester U	25	2		
1998–99	Manchester U	29	2		
1999–2000	Manchester U	25	3		
2000–01	Manchester U	21	0		
2001–02	Manchester U	12	0	**368**	**22**

JOHNSEN, Ronny* (D) 175 19
H: 6 3 W: 13 06 b.Sandefjord 10-6-69
Honours: Norway 48 full caps, 3 goals.

1992	Lyn	12	1		
1993	Lyn	19	6	**31**	**7**
1994	Lillestrom	10	3		
1995	Lillestrom	13	1	**23**	**4**
1995–96	Besiktas	22	1	**22**	**1**
1996–97	Manchester U	31	0		
1997–98	Manchester U	22	2		
1998–99	Manchester U	22	3		
1999–2000	Manchester U	3	0		
2000–01	Manchester U	11	1		
2001–02	Manchester U	10	1	**99**	**7**

JOHNSON, Eddie (F) 0 0
H: 5 10 W: 13 05 b.Chester 20-9-84
Source: Scholar. *Honours:* England Youth.

2001–02	Manchester U	0	0		

JOWSEY, James (G) 0 0
H: 6 0 W: 12 04 b.Scarborough 24-11-83
Source: Scholar.

2000–01	Manchester U	0	0		
2001–02	Manchester U	0	0		

KEANE, Roy (M) 355 51
H: 5 11 W: 11 10 b.Cork 10-8-71
Source: Cobh Ramb. *Honours:* Eire Youth, Under-21, 58 full caps, 9 goals.

1990–91	Nottingham F	35	8		

1991–92	Nottingham F	39	8		
1992–93	Nottingham F	40	6	114	22
1993–94	Manchester U	37	5		
1994–95	Manchester U	25	2		
1995–96	Manchester U	29	6		
1996–97	Manchester U	21	2		
1997–98	Manchester U	9	2		
1998–99	Manchester U	35	2		
1999–2000	Manchester U	29	5		
2000–01	Manchester U	28	2		
2001–02	Manchester U	28	3	241	29

LYNCH, Mark (D) 0 0
H: 5 11 W: 11 03 b.Manchester 2-9-81
Source: Trainee.

1999–2000	Manchester U	0	0
2000–01	Manchester U	0	0
2001–02	Manchester U	0	0

MAY, David (D) 208 9
H: 6 0 W: 13 05 b.Oldham 24-6-70
Source: Trainee.

1988–89	Blackburn R	1	0		
1989–90	Blackburn R	17	0		
1990–91	Blackburn R	19	1		
1991–92	Blackburn R	12	0		
1992–93	Blackburn R	34	1		
1993–94	Blackburn R	40	1	123	3
1994–95	Manchester U	19	2		
1995–96	Manchester U	16	1		
1996–97	Manchester U	29	3		
1997–98	Manchester U	9	0		
1998–99	Manchester U	6	0		
1999–2000	Manchester U	1	0		
1999–2000	*Huddersfield T*	1	0	1	0
2000–01	Manchester U	2	0		
2001–02	Manchester U	2	0	84	6

McDERMOTT, Alan* (D) 0 0
H: 6 1 W: 11 07 b.Dublin 22-1-82
Source: Trainee.

1998–99	Manchester U	0	0
1999–2000	Manchester U	0	0
2000–01	Manchester U	0	0
2001–02	Manchester U	0	0

MOONIARUCK, Kalam (F) 0 0
H: 5 8 W: 11 09 b.Yeovil 22-11-83
Source: Scholar. Honours: England Youth.

2000–01	Manchester U	0	0
2001–02	Manchester U	0	0

MORAN, David* (G) 0 0
H: 6 0 W: 14 05 b.Ballinasloe 16-4-82
Source: Scholar.

2000–01	Manchester U	0	0
2001–02	Manchester U	0	0

MUIRHEAD, Ben (F) 0 0
H: 5 9 W: 10 05 b.Doncaster 5-1-83
Source: Trainee. Honours: England Youth.

1999–2000	Manchester U	0	0
2000–01	Manchester U	0	0
2001–02	Manchester U	0	0

NARDIELLO, Daniel (F) 0 0
H: 5 11 W: 11 04 b.Coventry 22-10-82
Source: Trainee.

1999–2000	Manchester U	0	0
2000–01	Manchester U	0	0
2001–02	Manchester U	0	0

NEVILLE, Gary (D) 237 3
H: 5 11 W: 12 04 b.Bury 18-2-75
Source: Trainee. Honours: England Youth, 52 full caps.

1992–93	Manchester U	0	0		
1993–94	Manchester U	1	0		
1994–95	Manchester U	18	0		
1995–96	Manchester U	31	0		
1996–97	Manchester U	31	1		
1997–98	Manchester U	34	0		
1998–99	Manchester U	34	1		
1999–2000	Manchester U	22	0		
2000–01	Manchester U	32	1		
2001–02	Manchester U	34	0	237	3

NEVILLE, Phil (D) 188 6
H: 5 11 W: 12 00 b.Bury 21-1-77
Source: Trainee. Honours: England Schools, Youth, Under-21, 37 full caps.

1994–95	Manchester U	2	0		
1995–96	Manchester U	24	0		
1996–97	Manchester U	18	0		
1997–98	Manchester U	30	1		
1998–99	Manchester U	28	0		
1999–2000	Manchester U	29	0		
2000–01	Manchester U	29	1		
2001–02	Manchester U	28	2	188	4

O'SHEA, John (D) 19 1
H: 6 3 W: 12 10 b.Waterford 30-4-81
Source: Waterford. Honours: Eire Under-21, 1 full cap.

1998–99	Manchester U	0	0		
1999–2000	Manchester U	0	0		
1999–2000	*Bournemouth*	10	1	10	1
2000–01	Manchester U	0	0		
2001–02	Manchester U	9	0	9	0

PUGH, Danny (M) 0 0
H: 6 0 W: 12 10 b.Manchester 19-10-82
Source: Scholar.

2000–01	Manchester U	0	0
2001–02	Manchester U	0	0

RANKIN, John (M) 0 0
H: 5 8 W: 12 08 b.Bellshill 27-6-83
Source: Scholar.

2000–01	Manchester U	0	0
2001–02	Manchester U	0	0

ROCHE, Lee (D) 41 0
H: 5 10 W: 10 10 b.Bolton 28-10-80
Source: Trainee. Honours: England Youth, Under-21.

1998–99	Manchester U	0	0		
1999–2000	Manchester U	0	0		
2000–01	Manchester U	0	0		
2000–01	*Wrexham*	41	0	41	0
2001–02	Manchester U	0	0		

SAMPSON, Gary* (M) 0 0
H: 5 9 W: 11 02 b.Manchester 13-9-82
Source: Scholar.

2000–01	Manchester U	0	0
2001–02	Manchester U	0	0

SCHOLES, Paul (M) 227 55
H: 5 7 W: 11 00 b.Salford 16-11-74
Source: Trainee. Honours: England Youth, 49 full caps, 13 goals.

1992–93	Manchester U	0	0		
1993–94	Manchester U	0	0		
1994–95	Manchester U	17	5		
1995–96	Manchester U	26	10		
1996–97	Manchester U	24	3		
1997–98	Manchester U	31	8		
1998–99	Manchester U	31	6		
1999–2000	Manchester U	31	9		
2000–01	Manchester U	32	6		
2001–02	Manchester U	35	8	227	55

SILVESTRE, Mikael (D) 163 2
H: 6 0 W: 13 01 b.Chambray les Tours 9-8-77
Honours: France 11 full caps, 1 goal.

1995–96	Rennes	1	0		
1996–97	Rennes	16	0		
1997–98	Rennes	32	0	49	0
1998–99	Internazionale	18	1	18	1
1999–2000	Manchester U	31	0		
2000–01	Manchester U	30	1		
2001–02	Manchester U	35	0	96	1

SOLSKJAER, Ole Gunnar (F) 205 105
H: 5 10 W: 11 11 b.Kristiansund 26-2-73
Honours: Norway Under-21, 48 full caps, 19 goals.

1995	Molde	26	20		
1996	Molde	16	11	42	31
1996–97	Manchester U	33	17		
1997–98	Manchester U	22	6		
1998–99	Manchester U	19	12		
1999–2000	Manchester U	28	12		
2000–01	Manchester U	31	10		
2001–02	Manchester U	30	17	163	74

STAM, Jaap (D) 272 18
H: 6 3 W: 15 00 b.Kampen 17-7-72
Honours: Holland 45 full caps, 3 goals.

1992–93	Zwolle	32	1	32	1
1993–94	Cambuur	33	1		
1994–95	Cambuur	33	2	66	3
1995–96	Willem II	19	1	19	1
1995–96	PSV Eindhoven	14	1		
1996–97	PSV Eindhoven	33	7		
1997–98	PSV Eindhoven	29	4	76	12
1998–99	Manchester U	30	1		
1999–2000	Manchester U	33	0		
2000–01	Manchester U	15	0		
2001–02	Manchester U	0	0	79	1

STEELE, Luke (G) 2 0
H: 6 2 W: 12 00 b.Peterborough 24-9-84
Source: Scholar. Honours: England Youth.

2001–02	Peterborough U	2	0	2	0
2001–02	Manchester U	0	0		

STEWART, Michael (M) 6 0
H: 5 11 W: 11 11 b.Edinburgh 26-2-81
Source: Trainee. Honours: Scotland Schools, Under-21, 3 full caps.

1997–98	Manchester U	0	0		
1998–99	Manchester U	0	0		
1999–2000	Manchester U	0	0		
2000–01	Manchester U	3	0		
2001–02	Manchester U	3	0	6	0

TATE, Alan (D) 0 0
H: 6 1 W: 13 05 b.Easington 2-9-82
Source: Scholar.

2000–01	Manchester U	0	0
2001–02	Manchester U	0	0

(On loan to Antwerp, December 2001).

TAYLOR, Andrew* (M) 0 0
H: 5 9 W: 12 10 b.Exeter 17-9-82
Source: Scholar.

2000–01	Manchester U	0	0
2001–02	Manchester U	0	0

TAYLOR, Kris (M) 0 0
H: 5 9 W: 13 05 b.Stafford 12-1-84
Source: Scholar. Honours: England Youth.

2000–01	Manchester U	0	0
2001–02	Manchester U	0	0

TIERNEY, Paul (M) 0 0
H: 5 10 W: 12 10 b.Salford 15-9-82
Source: Scholar.

2000–01	Manchester U	0	0
2001–02	Manchester U	0	0

TIMM, Mads (F) 0 0
H: 5 9 W: 12 10 b.Odense 31-10-84
Source: Scholar.

2001–02	Manchester U	0	0

VAN NISTELROOY, Ruud (F) 199 115
H: 6 2 W: 12 13 b.Oss 1-7-76
Source: Nooit Gedacht, Margriet. *Honours:* Holland 18 full caps, 8 goals.

1993–94	Den Bosch	2	0		
1994–95	Den Bosch	15	3		
1995–96	Den Bosch	21	2		
1996–97	Den Bosch	31	12	69	17
1997–98	Heerenveen	31	13	31	13
1998–99	PSV Eindhoven	34	31		
1999–2000	PSV Eindhoven	23	29		
2000–01	PSV Eindhoven	10	2	67	62
2001–02	Manchester U	32	23	32	23

VAN DER GOUW, Raimond* (G) 392 0
H: 6 3 W: 13 09 b.Oldenzaal 24-3-63

1985–86	Go Ahead	28	0		
1986–87	Go Ahead	34	0		
1987–88	Go Ahead	35	0	97	0
1988–89	Vitesse	36	0		
1989–90	Vitesse	34	0		
1990–91	Vitesse	31	0		
1991–92	Vitesse	34	0		
1992–93	Vitesse	34	0		
1993–94	Vitesse	34	0		
1994–95	Vitesse	34	0		
1995–96	Vitesse	21	0	258	0
1996–97	Manchester U	2	0		
1997–98	Manchester U	5	0		
1998–99	Manchester U	5	0		
1999–2000	Manchester U	14	0		
2000–01	Manchester U	10	0		
2001–02	Manchester U	1	0	37	0

VERON, Juan Sebastian (F) 243 35
H: 6 1 W: 12 08 b.Buenos Aires 9-3-75
Honours: Argentina 50 full caps, 8 goals.

1993–94	Estudiantes	7	0		
1994–95	Estudiantes	38	5		
1995–96	Estudiantes	15	2	60	7
1995–96	Boca Juniors	17	4	17	4
1996–97	Sampdoria	32	5		
1997–98	Sampdoria	29	2	61	7
1998–99	Parma	26	1	26	1
1999–2000	Lazio	31	8		
2000–01	Lazio	22	3	53	11
2001–02	Manchester U	26	5	26	5

WALLWORK, Ronnie (D) 36 1
H: 5 10 W: 13 01 b.Manchester 10-9-77
Source: Trainee. Honours: England Youth.

1994–95	Manchester U	0	0		
1995–96	Manchester U	0	0		
1996–97	Manchester U	0	0		
1997–98	Manchester U	1	0		
1997–98	*Carlisle*	10	1	10	1
1997–98	*Stockport Co*	7	0	7	0
1998–99	Manchester U	0	0		
1999–2000	Manchester U	5	0		
2000–01	Manchester U	12	0		
2001–02	Manchester U	1	0	19	0

WEBBER, Danny (F) 9 2
H: 5 9 W: 10 08 b.Manchester 28-12-81
Source: Trainee. Honours: England Youth, Under-20.

1998–99	Manchester U	0	0
1999–2000	Manchester U	0	0
2000–01	Manchester U	0	0

2001–02	Manchester U	0	0		
2001–02	*Port Vale*	4	0	**4**	**0**
2001–02	*Watford*	5	2	**5**	**2**

WILLIAMS, Ben (G) **0 0**
H: 6 0 W: 13 01 b.Manchester 27-8-82
Source: Scholar. *Honours:* England Schools.

2001–02	Manchester U	0	0		

WILLIAMS, Matthew (F) **0 0**
H: 5 8 W: 9 11 b.St Asaph 5-11-82
Honours: Wales Under-21.

1999–2000	Manchester U	0	0		
2000–01	Manchester U	0	0		
2001–02	Manchester U	0	0		

WOOD, Neil (F) **0 0**
H: 5 10 W: 13 02 b.Manchester 4-1-83
Source: Trainee. *Honours:* England Youth.

1999–2000	Manchester U	0	0		
2000–01	Manchester U	0	0		
2001–02	Manchester U	0	0		

(On loan to Antwerp, December 2001).

YORKE, Dwight (F) **327 121**
H: 5 10 W: 12 03 b.Canaan 3-11-71
Source: St Clair's, Tobago. *Honours:* Trinidad & Tobago full caps.

1989–90	Aston Villa	2	0		
1990–91	Aston Villa	18	2		
1991–92	Aston Villa	32	11		
1992–93	Aston Villa	27	6		
1993–94	Aston Villa	12	2		
1994–95	Aston Villa	37	6		
1995–96	Aston Villa	35	17		
1996–97	Aston Villa	37	17		
1997–98	Aston Villa	30	12		
1998–99	Aston Villa	1	0	**231**	**73**
1998–99	Manchester U	32	18		
1999–2000	Manchester U	32	20		
2000–01	Manchester U	22	9		
2001–02	Manchester U	10	1	**96**	**48**

Trainees
Bardsley, Phillip A; Byrne, Daniel T; Collett, Benjamin; Jones, David FL; Lawrence, Lee A; Poole, David A; Richardson, Kieran E; Sims, Lee M

MANSFIELD T

ANDREWS, John‡ (D) **38 1**
H: 6 1 W: 12 08 b.Cork 27-9-78
From Grantham T.

1996–97	Coventry C	0	0		
1997–98	Coventry C	0	0		

From Shepshd, Grantam

1999–2000	Mansfield T	30	1		
2000–01	Mansfield T	8	0		
2001–02	Mansfield T	0	0	**38**	**1**

ASHER, Alistair* (D) **73 0**
H: 6 0 W: 11 06 b.Leicester 14-10-80
Source: Trainee.

1999–2000	Mansfield T	35	0		
2000–01	Mansfield T	28	0		
2001–02	Mansfield T	10	0	**73**	**0**

BACON, Danny (F) **38 4**
H: 5 10 W: 10 12 b.Mansfield 20-9-80
Source: Trainee.

1999–2000	Mansfield T	8	2		
2000–01	Mansfield T	22	1		
2001–02	Mansfield T	8	1	**38**	**4**

BARRETT, Adam* (D) **89 4**
H: 5 10 W: 12 00 b.Dagenham 29-11-79
Source: Leyton Orient Trainee.

1998–99	Plymouth Arg	1	0		
1999–2000	Plymouth Arg	42	3		
2000–01	Plymouth Arg	9	0	**52**	**3**
2000–01	Mansfield T	8	1		
2001–02	Mansfield T	29	0	**37**	**1**

BINGHAM, Michael (G) **2 0**
H: 6 0 W: 12 07 b.Preston 21-5-81
Source: Trainee. *Honours:* England Schools.

1998–99	Blackburn R	0	0		
1999–2000	Blackburn R	0	0		
2000–01	Blackburn R	0	0		
2001–02	Mansfield T	2	0	**2**	**0**

BRADLEY, Shayne (F) **61 11**
H: 5 11 W: 13 02 b.Gloucester 8-12-79
Source: Trainee. *Honours:* England Schools.

1997–98	Southampton	0	0		
1998–99	Southampton	3	0		
1998–99	*Swindon T*	7	0	**7**	**0**
1999–2000	Southampton	1	0		
1999–2000	*Exeter C*	8	1	**8**	**1**
2000–01	Southampton	0	0	**4**	**0**
2000–01	Mansfield T	26	7		
2001–02	Mansfield T	16	3	**42**	**10**

CLARKE, Jamie§ (M) **1 0**
b.Sunderland 18-9-82
Source: Scholar.

2001–02	Mansfield T	1	0	**1**	**0**

CORDEN, Wayne# (F) **146 12**
H: 5 9 W: 11 03 b.Leek 1-11-75
Source: Trainee.

1994–95	Port Vale	1	0		
1995–96	Port Vale	2	0		
1996–97	Port Vale	12	0		
1997–98	Port Vale	33	1		
1998–99	Port Vale	16	0		
1999–2000	Port Vale	2	0	**66**	**1**
2000–01	Mansfield T	34	3		
2001–02	Mansfield T	46	8	**80**	**11**

DISLEY, Craig (M) **65 7**
H: 5 10 W: 11 00 b.Worksop 24-8-81
Source: Trainee.

1999–2000	Mansfield T	5	0		
2000–01	Mansfield T	24	0		
2001–02	Mansfield T	36	7	**65**	**7**

GREENACRE, Chris* (F) **156 54**
H: 5 11 W: 12 08 b.Halifax 23-12-77
Source: Trainee.

1995–96	Manchester C	0	0		
1996–97	Manchester C	4	0		
1997–98	Manchester C	3	1		
1997–98	*Cardiff C*	11	2	**11**	**2**
1997–98	*Blackpool*	4	0	**4**	**0**
1998–99	Manchester C	1	0		
1998–99	*Scarborough*	12	2	**12**	**2**
1999–2000	Manchester C	0	0	**8**	**1**
1999–2000	Mansfield T	31	9		
2000–01	Mansfield T	46	19		
2001–02	Mansfield T	44	21	**121**	**49**

HASSELL, Bobby (D) **106 3**
H: 5 9 W: 12 06 b.Derby 4-6-80
Source: Trainee.

1997–98	Mansfield T	9	0		
1998–99	Mansfield T	3	0		
1999–2000	Mansfield T	11	1		
2000–01	Mansfield T	40	1		
2001–02	Mansfield T	43	1	**106**	**3**

HICKS, Stuart‡ (D) **402 5**
H: 6 1 W: 13 00 b.Peterborough 30-5-67
Source: Peterborough U Apprentice, Wisbech T.

1987–88	Colchester U	7	0		
1988–89	Colchester U	37	0		
1989–90	Colchester U	20	0	**64**	**0**
1990–91	Scunthorpe U	46	1		
1991–92	Scunthorpe U	21	0	**67**	**1**
1992–93	Doncaster R	36	0		
1993–94	Doncaster R	0	0	**36**	**0**
1993–94	Huddersfield T	22	1	**22**	**1**
1993–94	Preston NE	4	0		
1994–95	Preston NE	8	0	**12**	**0**
1994–95	Scarborough	6	0		
1995–96	Scarborough	41	1		
1996–97	Scarborough	38	1	**85**	**2**
1997–98	Leyton Orient	35	1		
1998–99	Leyton Orient	29	0		
1999–2000	Leyton Orient	14	0	**78**	**1**
1999–2000	Chester C	13	0	**13**	**0**
2000–01	Mansfield T	25	0		
2001–02	Mansfield T	0	0	**25**	**0**

JERVIS, David (D) **25 0**
H: 5 10 W: 11 00 b.Worksop 18-1-82
Source: Trainee.

2000–01	Mansfield T	22	0		
2001–02	Mansfield T	3	0	**25**	**0**

KELLY, David‡ (F) **581 186**
H: 5 11 W: 12 01 b.Birmingham 25-11-65
Source: Alvechurch. *Honours:* Eire Under-21, Under-23, B, 26 full caps, 9 goals.

1983–84	Walsall	6	3		
1984–85	Walsall	32	7		
1985–86	Walsall	28	10		
1986–87	Walsall	42	23		
1987–88	Walsall	39	20	**147**	**63**
1988–89	West Ham U	25	6		
1989–90	West Ham U	16	1	**41**	**7**
1989–90	Leicester C	10	7		
1990–91	Leicester C	44	14		
1991–92	Leicester C	12	1	**66**	**22**
1991–92	Newcastle U	25	11		
1992–93	Newcastle U	45	24	**70**	**35**
1993–94	Wolverhampton W	36	11		
1994–95	Wolverhampton W	42	15		
1995–96	Wolverhampton W	5	0	**83**	**26**
1995–96	Sunderland	10	2		
1996–97	Sunderland	24	0	**34**	**2**
1997–98	Tranmere R	29	11		
1998–99	Tranmere R	27	4		
1999–2000	Tranmere R	32	6	**88**	**21**
2000–01	Sheffield U	35	6	**35**	**6**
2001–02	Mansfield T	17	4	**17**	**4**

LAWRENCE, Liam (M) **52 6**
H: 5 10 W: 11 03 b.Retford 14-12-81
Source: Trainee.

1999–2000	Mansfield T	2	0		
2000–01	Mansfield T	18	4		
2001–02	Mansfield T	32	2	**52**	**6**

PILKINGTON, Kevin (G) **99 0**
H: 6 1 W: 13 00 b.Hitchin 8-3-74
Source: Trainee. *Honours:* England Schools.

1992–93	Manchester U	0	0		
1993–94	Manchester U	0	0		
1994–95	Manchester U	1	0		
1995–96	Manchester U	3	0		
1995–96	*Rochdale*	6	0	**6**	**0**
1996–97	Manchester U	0	0		
1996–97	*Rotherham U*	17	0	**17**	**0**
1997–98	Manchester U	2	0		
1998–99	Manchester U	0	0	**6**	**0**
1998–99	Port Vale	8	0		
1999–2000	Port Vale	15	0	**23**	**0**
2000–01	Macclesfield T	0	0		
2000–01	Wigan Ath	0	0		
2000–01	Mansfield T	2	0		
2001–02	Mansfield T	45	0	**47**	**0**

REDDINGTON, Stuart (D) **47 1**
H: 6 4 W: 13 07 b.Lincoln 21-2-78
Source: Lincoln U.

1999–2000	Chelsea	0	0		
2000–01	Chelsea	0	0		
2000–01	*Mansfield T*	9	0		
2001–02	Mansfield T	38	1	**47**	**1**

ROBINSON, Les (D) **628 18**
H: 5 9 W: 12 04 b.Shirebrook 1-3-67
Source: Local.

1984–85	Mansfield T	6	0		
1985–86	Mansfield T	7	0		
1986–87	Mansfield T	2	0		
1986–87	Stockport Co	30	1		
1987–88	Stockport Co	37	2	**67**	**3**
1987–88	Doncaster R	7	1		
1988–89	Doncaster R	43	3		
1989–90	Doncaster R	32	8	**82**	**12**
1989–90	Oxford U	1	0		
1990–91	Oxford U	43	0		
1991–92	Oxford U	27	0		
1992–93	Oxford U	16	0		
1993–94	Oxford U	36	2		
1994–95	Oxford U	46	0		
1995–96	Oxford U	41	0		
1996–97	Oxford U	38	0		
1997–98	Oxford U	46	1		
1998–99	Oxford U	44	0		
1999–2000	Oxford U	46	0	**384**	**3**
2000–01	Mansfield T	44	0		
2001–02	Mansfield T	36	0	**95**	**0**

SELLARS, Scott‡ (M) **531 70**
H: 5 8 W: 10 00 b.Sheffield 27-11-65
Source: Apprentice. *Honours:* England Under-21.

1982–83	Leeds U	1	0		
1983–84	Leeds U	19	3		
1984–85	Leeds U	39	7		
1985–86	Leeds U	17	2		
1986–87	Blackburn R	32	4		
1987–88	Blackburn R	42	7		
1988–89	Blackburn R	46	2		
1989–90	Blackburn R	43	14		
1990–91	Blackburn R	9	1		
1991–92	Blackburn R	30	7	**202**	**35**
1992–93	Leeds U	7	0	**83**	**12**
1992–93	Newcastle U	13	2		
1993–94	Newcastle U	30	3		
1994–95	Newcastle U	12	0		
1995–96	Newcastle U	6	0	**61**	**5**
1995–96	Bolton W	22	3		
1996–97	Bolton W	42	8		
1997–98	Bolton W	22	2		
1998–99	Bolton W	25	2	**111**	**15**
1999–2000	Huddersfield T	34	1		
2000–01	Huddersfield T	14	0	**48**	**1**
2000–01	Aarhus	9	1		
2001–02	Aarhus	11	0	**20**	**1**
2001–02	Port Vale	0	0		
2001–02	Mansfield T	6	1	**6**	**1**

SISSON, Michael (M) **31 2**
H: 5 9 W: 10 10 b.Sutton-in-Ashfield 24-11-78
Source: Trainee.

1997–98	Mansfield T	1	0		
1998–99	Mansfield T	1	0		
1999–2000	Mansfield T	25	2		
2000–01	Mansfield T	4	0		
2001–02	Mansfield T	0	0	**31**	**2**

TANKARD, Allen# (D) 519 17
H: 5 10 W: 11 10 b.Fleet 21-5-69
Source: Trainee. Honours: England Youth.

1985-86	Southampton	3	0		
1986-87	Southampton	2	0		
1987-88	Southampton	0	0	5	0
1988-89	Wigan Ath	33	1		
1989-90	Wigan Ath	45	1		
1990-91	Wigan Ath	46	1		
1991-92	Wigan Ath	44	0		
1992-93	Wigan Ath	41	1	209	4
1993-94	Port Vale	26	0		
1994-95	Port Vale	39	1		
1995-96	Port Vale	29	0		
1996-97	Port Vale	37	1		
1997-98	Port Vale	39	0		
1998-99	Port Vale	37	4		
1999-2000	Port Vale	35	1		
2000-01	Port Vale	33	4	275	11
2001-02	Mansfield T	30	2	30	2

WHITE, Andy (F) 26 4
H: 6 4 W: 14 03 b.Derby 6-11-81
Source: Hucknall T.

2000-01	Mansfield T	4	0		
2001-02	Mansfield T	22	4	26	4

WILLIAMSON, Lee (M) 65 3
H: 5 10 W: 10 04 b.Derby 7-6-82
Source: Trainee.

1999-2000	Mansfield T	4	0		
2000-01	Mansfield T	15	0		
2001-02	Mansfield T	46	3	65	3

Scholars
Beardsley, Christopher K; Carter, Mark; Clarke, James W; Davies, Andrew P; Elliott, Dominic S; Ghaichem, James JF; Gibson, Christopher J; Holyoak, Daniel; Hurst, Mark; Lazarus, Neil P; Mitchell, Craig R; Murcott, Scott A; Rew, David J; Robinson, Mark; Shaw, James R; Swinscoe, Craig A

MIDDLESBROUGH

BAKER, Steve‡ (D) 25 0
H: 6 0 W: 12 04 b.Pontefract 8-9-78
Source: Trainee. Honours: Eire Under-21.

1997-98	Middlesbrough	6	0		
1998-99	Middlesbrough	2	0		
1999-2000	Middlesbrough	0	0		
1999-2000	Huddersfield T	3	0	3	0
1999-2000	Darlington	5	0	5	0
2000-01	Middlesbrough	0	0		
2000-01	Hartlepool U	9	0	9	0
2001-02	Middlesbrough	0	0	8	0

BERESFORD, Marlon* (G) 299 0
H: 6 1 W: 13 00 b.Lincoln 2-9-69
Source: Trainee.

1987-88	Sheffield W	0	0		
1988-89	Sheffield W	0	0		
1989-90	Sheffield W	0	0		
1989-90	Bury	1	0	1	0
1989-90	Ipswich T	0	0		
1990-91	Sheffield W	0	0		
1990-91	Northampton T	13	0		
1990-91	Crewe Alex	3	0	3	0
1991-92	Sheffield W	0	0		
1991-92	Northampton T	15	0	28	0
1992-93	Burnley	44	0		
1993-94	Burnley	46	0		
1994-95	Burnley	40	0		
1995-96	Burnley	36	0		
1996-97	Burnley	40	0		
1997-98	Burnley	34	0		
1997-98	Middlesbrough	3	0		
1998-99	Middlesbrough	4	0		
1999-2000	Middlesbrough	1	0		
2000-01	Middlesbrough	1	0		
2000-01	Sheffield W	4	0	4	0
2001-02	Middlesbrough	1	0	10	0
2001-02	Wolverhampton W	0	0		
2001-02	Burnley	13	0	253	0

BERNHARDT, Arthur (F) 0 0
H: 6 1 W: 12 00 b.Santa Catarina 27-8-82
Source: Hamburg.

1999-2000	Middlesbrough	0	0		
2000-01	Middlesbrough	0	0		
2001-02	Middlesbrough	0	0		

BOKSIC, Alen (F) 332 107
H: 6 1 W: 14 01 b.Niakarska 21-1-70
Honours: Croatia 39 full caps, 10 goals.

1987-88	Hajduk Split	3	2		
1988-89	Hajduk Split	26	7		
1989-90	Hajduk Split	30	7		
1990-91	Hajduk Split	29	6	95	27
1991-92	Cannes	1	0	1	0
1992-93	Marseille	37	23		
1993-94	Marseille	12	3	49	26
1993-94	Lazio	21	4		
1994-95	Lazio	23	9		
1995-96	Lazio	23	4		
1996-97	Juventus	22	3	22	3
1997-98	Lazio	26	10		
1998-99	Lazio	3	0		
1999-2000	Lazio	19	4	115	31
2000-01	Middlesbrough	28	12		
2001-02	Middlesbrough	22	8	50	20

CADE, Jamie (F) 0 0
H: 5 8 W: 10 10 b.Durham 15-1-84
Source: Scholar. Honours: England Youth.

2001-02	Middlesbrough	0	0		

CLOSE, Brian (D) 0 0
H: 5 10 W: 12 03 b.Belfast 27-1-82
Honours: Northern Ireland Under-21.

1999-2000	Middlesbrough	0	0		
2000-01	Middlesbrough	0	0		
2001-02	Middlesbrough	0	0		

COOPER, Colin (D) 548 37
H: 5 11 W: 11 11 b.Sedgefield 28-2-67
Honours: England Under-21, 2 full caps.

1984-85	Middlesbrough	0	0		
1985-86	Middlesbrough	11	0		
1986-87	Middlesbrough	46	0		
1987-88	Middlesbrough	43	2		
1988-89	Middlesbrough	35	2		
1989-90	Middlesbrough	21	2		
1990-91	Middlesbrough	32	0		
1991-92	Millwall	36	2		
1992-93	Millwall	41	4	77	6
1993-94	Nottingham F	37	7		
1994-95	Nottingham F	35	1		
1995-96	Nottingham F	36	2		
1996-97	Nottingham F	36	2		
1997-98	Nottingham F	35	5		
1998-99	Nottingham F	0	0	180	20
1998-99	Middlesbrough	32	1		
1999-2000	Middlesbrough	26	0		
2000-01	Middlesbrough	27	2		
2001-02	Middlesbrough	18	2	291	11

CROSSLEY, Mark (G) 339 0
H: 6 0 W: 15 09 b.Barnsley 16-6-69
Source: Trainee. Honours: England Under-21, Wales B, 5 full caps.

1987-88	Nottingham F	1	0		
1988-89	Nottingham F	2	0		
1989-90	Nottingham F	8	0		
1989-90	Manchester U	0	0		
1990-91	Nottingham F	36	0		
1991-92	Nottingham F	36	5		
1992-93	Nottingham F	37	0		
1993-94	Nottingham F	37	0		
1994-95	Nottingham F	42	0		
1995-96	Nottingham F	38	0		
1996-97	Nottingham F	33	0		
1997-98	Nottingham F	0	0		
1997-98	Millwall	13	0	13	0
1998-99	Nottingham F	12	0		
1999-2000	Nottingham F	20	0	303	0
2000-01	Middlesbrough	5	0		
2001-02	Middlesbrough	18	0	23	0

DEBEVE, Mickael* (M) 362 30
H: 6 0 W: 12 08 b.Abbeville 1-12-70

1986-87	Toulouse	2	0		
1987-88	Toulouse	2	0		
1988-89	Toulouse	1	0		
1989-90	Toulouse	18	2		
1990-91	Toulouse	31	4		
1991-92	Toulouse	34	3		
1992-93	Toulouse	29	3		
1993-94	Toulouse	23	2	139	14
1994-95	Lens	38	4		
1995-96	Lens	36	2		
1996-97	Lens	35	2		
1997-98	Lens	29	2		
1998-99	Lens	29	3		
1999-2000	Le Havre	27	2	27	2
2000-01	Lens	25	1	192	14
2001-02	Middlesbrough	4	0	4	0

DOVE, Craig (M) 0 0
H: 5 8 W: 11 00 b.Hartlepool 6-8-83
Source: Scholar. Honours: England Youth.

2000-01	Middlesbrough	0	0		
2001-02	Middlesbrough	0	0		

DOWNING, Stewart (M) 3 0
H: 6 0 W: 11 00 b.Middlesbrough 22-7-84
Source: Scholar. Honours: England Youth.

2001-02	Middlesbrough	3	0	3	0

EHIOGU, Ugo (D) 289 16
H: 6 2 W: 14 10 b.Hackney 3-11-72
Source: Trainee. Honours: England Under-21, B, 4 full caps, 1 goal.

1990-91	WBA	2	0	2	0
1991-92	Aston Villa	8	0		
1992-93	Aston Villa	4	0		
1993-94	Aston Villa	17	0		
1994-95	Aston Villa	39	3		
1995-96	Aston Villa	36	1		
1996-97	Aston Villa	38	3		
1997-98	Aston Villa	37	2		
1998-99	Aston Villa	25	2		
1999-2000	Aston Villa	31	1		
2000-01	Aston Villa	2	0	237	12
2000-01	Middlesbrough	21	3		
2001-02	Middlesbrough	29	1	50	4

FESTA, Gianluca (D) 407 16
H: 5 11 W: 13 00 b.Cagliari 15-3-69

1986-87	Cagliari	3	0		
1987-88	Fersuicis	26	2	26	2
1988-89	Cagliari	27	0		
1989-90	Cagliari	36	0		
1990-91	Cagliari	28	0		
1991-92	Cagliari	31	0		
1992-93	Cagliari	31	0	156	0
1993-94	Internazionale	4	0		
1993-94	Roma	21	1	21	1
1994-95	Internazionale	26	2		
1995-96	Internazionale	31	1		
1996-97	Internazionale	5	0	66	3
1996-97	Middlesbrough	13	1		
1997-98	Middlesbrough	38	2		
1998-99	Middlesbrough	25	2		
1999-2000	Middlesbrough	29	2		
2000-01	Middlesbrough	25	2		
2001-02	Middlesbrough	8	1	138	10

GAVIN, Jason (D) 31 0
H: 6 0 W: 11 12 b.Dublin 14-3-80
Source: Trainee. Honours: Eire Under-21.

1996-97	Middlesbrough	0	0		
1997-98	Middlesbrough	0	0		
1998-99	Middlesbrough	2	0		
1999-2000	Middlesbrough	6	0		
2000-01	Middlesbrough	14	0		
2001-02	Middlesbrough	9	0	31	0

GILROY, Keith (M) 0 0
H: 5 10 W: 10 13 b.Sligo 8-7-83

2000-01	Middlesbrough	0	0		
2001-02	Middlesbrough	0	0		

GORDON, Dean* (D) 271 26
H: 6 0 W: 13 08 b.Thornton Heath 10-2-73
Source: Trainee. Honours: England Under-21.

1991-92	Crystal Palace	4	0		
1992-93	Crystal Palace	10	0		
1993-94	Crystal Palace	45	5		
1994-95	Crystal Palace	41	2		
1995-96	Crystal Palace	34	8		
1996-97	Crystal Palace	30	3		
1997-98	Crystal Palace	37	2	201	20
1998-99	Middlesbrough	38	3		
1999-2000	Middlesbrough	4	0		
2000-01	Middlesbrough	20	1		
2001-02	Middlesbrough	1	0	63	4
2001-02	Cardiff C	7	2	7	2

GREENING, Jonathan (M) 75 3
H: 6 0 W: 11 13 b.Scarborough 2-1-79
Source: Trainee. Honours: England Youth, Under-21.

1996-97	York C	5	0		
1997-98	York C	20	2	25	2
1997-98	Manchester U	0	0		
1998-99	Manchester U	3	0		
1999-2000	Manchester U	4	0		
2000-01	Manchester U	7	0	14	0
2001-02	Middlesbrough	36	1	36	1

GULLIVER, Philip (D) 0 0
H: 6 2 W: 13 05 b.Bishop Auckland 12-9-82
Source: Scholar.

2000-01	Middlesbrough	0	0		
2001-02	Middlesbrough	0	0		

HANSON, Christian* (D) 14 0
H: 6 1 W: 12 11 b.Middlesbrough 3-8-81
Source: Trainee. Honours: England Schools, Youth.

1998-99	Middlesbrough	0	0		
1999-2000	Middlesbrough	0	0		
2000-01	Middlesbrough	0	0		
2000-01	Cambridge U	8	0	8	0
2001-02	Middlesbrough	0	0		
2001-02	Torquay U	6	0	6	0

HUDSON, Mark (M) 5 0
H: 5 10 W: 11 03 b.Bishop Auckland 24-10-80
Source: Trainee.

1999-2000	Middlesbrough	0	0		
2000-01	Middlesbrough	3	0		
2001-02	Middlesbrough	2	0	5	0

INCE, Paul* (M) 490 61
H: 5 10 W: 12 04 b.Ilford 21-10-67
Source: Trainee. *Honours:* England Youth, Under-21, B, 53 full caps, 2 goals.

1985–86	West Ham U	8	0	
1986–87	West Ham U	10	1	
1987–88	West Ham U	28	3	
1988–89	West Ham U	33	3	
1989–90	West Ham U	1	0	72 7
1989–90	Manchester U	26	0	
1990–91	Manchester U	31	3	
1991–92	Manchester U	33	3	
1992–93	Manchester U	41	5	
1993–94	Manchester U	39	8	
1994–95	Manchester U	36	5	206 24
1995–96	Internazionale	30	3	
1996–97	Internazionale	24	6	54 9
1997–98	Liverpool	31	8	
1998–99	Liverpool	34	6	65 14
1999–2000	Middlesbrough	32	3	
2000–01	Middlesbrough	30	2	
2001–02	Middlesbrough	31	2	93 7

JOB, Joseph-Desire (F) 81 18
H: 5 11 W: 11 00 b.Venissieux 1-12-77
Honours: Cameroon 35 full caps, 5 goals.

1997–98	Lyon	22	5	
1998–99	Lyon	19	6	41 11
1999–2000	Lens	24	4	24 4
2000–01	Middlesbrough	12	3	
2001–02	Middlesbrough	4	0	16 3

(On loan to Metz, December 2001).

JOHNSTON, Allan (M) 252 37
H: 5 10 W: 11 12 b.Glasgow 14-12-73
Source: Tynecastle BC. *Honours:* Scotland Under-21, B, 16 full caps, 2 goals.

1991–92	Hearts	0	0	
1992–93	Hearts	2	1	
1993–94	Hearts	28	1	
1994–95	Hearts	21	1	
1995–96	Hearts	33	9	84 12
1996–97	Rennes	23	2	23 2
1996–97	Sunderland	6	1	
1997–98	Sunderland	40	11	
1998–99	Sunderland	40	7	86 19
1999–2000	Rangers	0	0	
1999–2000	Birmingham C	9	0	9 0
1999–2000	Bolton W	19	3	19 3
2000–01	Rangers	13	0	
2001–02	Rangers	1	0	14 0
2001–02	Middlesbrough	17	1	17 1

JONES, Brad (G) 0 0
H: 6 3 W: 12 01 b.Armadale 19-3-82
Source: Trainee.

1998–99	Middlesbrough	0	0
1999–2000	Middlesbrough	0	0
2000–01	Middlesbrough	0	0
2001–02	Middlesbrough	0	0

KILGANNON, Sean‡ (M) 1 0
H: 5 11 W: 12 04 b.Stirling 8-3-81
Source: Trainee.

1999–2000	Middlesbrough	1	0
2000–01	Middlesbrough	0	0
2001–02	Middlesbrough	0	0

(Transferred to Dunfermline Ath, March 2002).

MARINELLI, Carlos (M) 35 2
H: 5 8 W: 11 06 b.Buenos Aires 4-3-82
Source: Boca Juniors.

1999–2000	Middlesbrough	2	0	
2000–01	Middlesbrough	13	0	
2001–02	Middlesbrough	20	2	35 2

MURPHY, David (D) 5 0
H: 6 1 W: 12 03 b.Hartlepool 1-3-84
Source: Scholar. *Honours:* England Youth.

2001–02	Middlesbrough	5	0	5 0

MUSTOE, Robbie* (M) 456 35
H: 6 0 W: 12 03 b.Oxford 28-8-68

1986–87	Oxford U	3	0	
1987–88	Oxford U	17	0	
1988–89	Oxford U	33	3	
1989–90	Oxford U	38	7	91 10
1990–91	Middlesbrough	41	4	
1991–92	Middlesbrough	30	2	
1992–93	Middlesbrough	23	1	
1993–94	Middlesbrough	38	2	
1994–95	Middlesbrough	27	3	
1995–96	Middlesbrough	21	1	
1996–97	Middlesbrough	31	3	
1997–98	Middlesbrough	32	3	
1998–99	Middlesbrough	33	4	
1999–2000	Middlesbrough	28	0	
2000–01	Middlesbrough	25	0	
2001–02	Middlesbrough	36	2	365 25

NELSON, Craig‡ (F) 0 0
H: 5 9 W: 9 12 b.South Shields 14-10-81
Source: Scholar.

2000–01	Middlesbrough	0	0
2001–02	Middlesbrough	0	0

NEMETH, Szilard (F) 177 87
H: 5 11 W: 11 04 b.Komarno 8-8-77
Honours: Slovakia 31 full caps, 10 goals.

1994–95	Slovan Bratislava	3	0	
1995–96	Slovan Bratislava	28	12	
1996–97	Slovan Bratislava	30	13	61 25
1997–98	Kosice	18	12	
1998–99	Kosice	19	8	37 20
1999–2000	Inter Bratislava	26	16	26 16
2000–01	Inter Bratislava	32	23	32 23
2001–02	Middlesbrough	21	3	21 3

ORMEROD, Anthony* (M) 38 3
H: 5 10 W: 11 13 b.Middlesbrough 31-3-79
Source: Trainee. *Honours:* England Youth.

1995–96	Middlesbrough	0	0	
1996–97	Middlesbrough	0	0	
1997–98	Middlesbrough	18	3	
1998–99	Middlesbrough	0	0	
1998–99	Carlisle U	5	0	5 0
1999–2000	Middlesbrough	1	0	
1999–2000	York C	12	0	12 0
2000–01	Middlesbrough	0	0	
2001–02	Middlesbrough	0	0	19 3
2001–02	Hartlepool U	2	0	2 0

PARNABY, Stuart (M) 6 0
H: 5 11 W: 11 00 b.Durham City 19-7-82
Source: Trainee. *Honours:* England Youth, Under-20.

1999–2000	Middlesbrough	0	0	
2000–01	Middlesbrough	0	0	
2000–01	Halifax T	6	0	6 0
2001–02	Middlesbrough	0	0	

QUEUDRUE, Franck (D) 70 4
H: 6 1 W: 12 07 b.Paris 27-8-78
Source: Meaux.

1999–2000	Lens	16	1	
2000–01	Lens	24	1	
2001–02	Lens	2	0	42 2
2001–02	Middlesbrough	28	2	28 2

RICARD, Hamilton‡ (F) 115 33
H: 6 1 W: 14 05 b.Choco 12-1-74
Source: Deportivo Cali. *Honours:* Colombia 21 full caps, 4 goals.

1997–98	Middlesbrough	9	2	
1998–99	Middlesbrough	36	15	
1999–2000	Middlesbrough	34	12	
2000–01	Middlesbrough	27	4	
2001–02	Middlesbrough	9	0	115 33

(Transferred to CSKA Sofia, March 2002).

RUSSELL, Sam (G) 0 0
H: 6 0 W: 10 13 b.Middlesbrough 4-10-82
Source: Scholar.

2000–01	Middlesbrough	0	0
2001–02	Middlesbrough	0	0

SCHWARZER, Mark (G) 242 0
H: 6 5 W: 15 01 b.Sydney 6-10-72
Honours: Australia 19 full caps.

1990–91	Marconi Stallions	1	0	
1991–92	Marconi Stallions	9	0	
1992–93	Marconi Stallions	23	0	
1993–94	Marconi Stallions	25	0	58 0
1994–95	Dynamo Dresden	2	0	2 0
1995–96	Kaiserslautern	4	0	
1996–97	Kaiserslautern	0	0	4 0
1996–97	Bradford C	13	0	13 0
1996–97	Middlesbrough	7	0	
1997–98	Middlesbrough	35	0	
1998–99	Middlesbrough	34	0	
1999–2000	Middlesbrough	37	0	
2000–01	Middlesbrough	31	0	
2001–02	Middlesbrough	21	0	165 0

SOUTHGATE, Gareth (D) 380 23
H: 6 0 W: 12 03 b.Watford 3-9-70
Source: Trainee. *Honours:* England 49 full caps, 1 goal.

1988–89	Crystal Palace	0	0	
1989–90	Crystal Palace	0	0	
1990–91	Crystal Palace	1	0	
1991–92	Crystal Palace	30	0	
1992–93	Crystal Palace	33	3	
1993–94	Crystal Palace	46	9	
1994–95	Crystal Palace	42	3	152 15
1995–96	Aston Villa	31	1	
1996–97	Aston Villa	28	1	
1997–98	Aston Villa	32	0	
1998–99	Aston Villa	38	1	
1999–2000	Aston Villa	31	2	
2000–01	Middlesbrough	31	2	191 7
2001–02	Middlesbrough	37	1	37 1

STAMP, Phil (M) 117 6
H: 5 11 W: 14 09 b.Middlesbrough 12-12-75
Source: Trainee. *Honours:* England Youth.

1992–93	Middlesbrough	0	0	
1993–94	Middlesbrough	10	0	
1994–95	Middlesbrough	3	0	
1995–96	Middlesbrough	12	2	
1996–97	Middlesbrough	24	1	
1997–98	Middlesbrough	10	0	
1998–99	Middlesbrough	16	2	
1999–2000	Middlesbrough	16	0	
2000–01	Middlesbrough	19	1	
2001–02	Middlesbrough	6	0	116 6
2001–02	Millwall	1	0	1 0

STEPHENSON, Paul‡ (D) 0 0
H: 6 2 W: 11 12 b.Hartlepool 3-1-82
Source: Scholar.

2000–01	Middlesbrough	0	0
2001–02	Middlesbrough	0	0

STOCKDALE, Robbie (D) 65 2
H: 6 0 W: 12 03 b.Redcar 30-11-79
Source: Trainee. *Honours:* England Under-21, Scotland 4 full caps.

1997–98	Middlesbrough	1	0	
1998–99	Middlesbrough	19	0	
1999–2000	Middlesbrough	11	1	
2000–01	Middlesbrough	0	0	
2000–01	Sheffield W	6	0	6 0
2001–02	Middlesbrough	28	1	59 2

SUMMERBELL, Mark (M) 61 1
H: 5 9 W: 11 01 b.Durham 30-10-76
Source: Trainee.

1995–96	Middlesbrough	1	0	
1996–97	Middlesbrough	2	0	
1997–98	Middlesbrough	11	0	
1998–99	Middlesbrough	11	0	
1999–2000	Middlesbrough	19	0	
2000–01	Middlesbrough	7	1	
2001–02	Middlesbrough	0	0	51 1
2001–02	Bristol C	5	0	5 0
2001–02	Portsmouth	5	0	5 0

WHELAN, Noel (F) 228 43
H: 6 2 W: 12 03 b.Leeds 30-12-74
Source: Trainee. *Honours:* England Under-21.

1992–93	Leeds U	1	0	
1993–94	Leeds U	16	0	
1994–95	Leeds U	23	7	
1995–96	Leeds U	8	0	48 7
1995–96	Coventry C	21	8	
1996–97	Coventry C	35	6	
1997–98	Coventry C	21	6	
1998–99	Coventry C	31	10	
1999–2000	Coventry C	26	1	134 31
2000–01	Middlesbrough	27	1	
2001–02	Middlesbrough	19	4	46 5

WILFORD, Aaron‡ (D) 0 0
H: 6 3 W: 14 07 b.Scarborough 14-1-82
Source: Harrogate College.

1999–2000	Middlesbrough	0	0
2000–01	Middlesbrough	0	0
2001–02	Middlesbrough	0	0

WILKSHIRE, Luke (M) 7 0
H: 5 8 W: 11 00 b.Wollongong 2-10-81

1998–99	Middlesbrough	0	0	
1999–2000	Middlesbrough	0	0	
2000–01	Middlesbrough	0	0	
2001–02	Middlesbrough	7	0	7 0

WILSON, Mark (M) 26 4
H: 5 10 W: 12 07 b.Scunthorpe 9-2-79
Source: Trainee. *Honours:* England Schools, Under-21.

1995–96	Manchester U	0	0	
1996–97	Manchester U	0	0	
1997–98	Manchester U	0	0	
1997–98	Wrexham	13	4	13 4
1998–99	Manchester U	0	0	
1999–2000	Manchester U	3	0	
2000–01	Manchester U	0	0	3 0
2001–02	Middlesbrough	10	0	10 0

WINDASS, Dean (F) 393 112
H: 5 10 W: 12 06 b.North Ferriby 1-4-69
Source: N Ferriby U.

1991–92	Hull C	32	6	
1992–93	Hull C	41	7	
1993–94	Hull C	43	23	
1994–95	Hull C	44	17	
1995–96	Hull C	16	4	176 57
1995–96	Aberdeen	20	6	
1996–97	Aberdeen	29	10	
1997–98	Aberdeen	24	5	73 21
1998–99	Oxford U	33	15	33 15
1998–99	Bradford C	12	3	
1999–2000	Bradford C	38	10	

2000–01	Bradford C	24	3	**74**	**16**
2000–01	Middlesbrough	8	2		
2001–02	Middlesbrough	27	1	**35**	**3**
2001–02	*Sheffield W*	2	0	**2**	**0**

Trainees
Agbatar, Jonathan T; Brunt, Christopher; Davies, Andrew; Emms, Christopher J; Garbutt, Christopher J; Harrison, Alan G; Kelly, Andrew J; Nordgren, Niklas; O'Shea, Andrew C; Smith, Gary S; Storey, Anthony; Turnball, Ross

MILLWALL

BIRCHAM, Marc# (M)   **104**   **3**
H: 5 11   W: 12 06   b.Brent 11-5-78
Source: Trainee. *Honours:* Canada 13 full caps, 1 goal.

1996–97	Millwall	6	0
1997–98	Millwall	4	0
1998–99	Millwall	28	0
1999–2000	Millwall	22	1
2000–01	Millwall	20	2
2001–02	Millwall	24	0 **104** **3**

BOOTH, Stuart (M)   **0**   **0**
H: 5 11   W: 11 11   b.Roehampton 7-12-83
Source: School.

2000–01	Millwall	0	0
2001–02	Millwall	0	0

BRANIFF, Kevin (F)   **6**   **0**
H: 5 11   W: 10 03   b.Belfast 4-3-83
Source: Scholar. *Honours:* Northern Ireland Schools, Youth, Under-21.

1999–2000	Millwall	0	0
2000–01	Millwall	5	0
2001–02	Millwall	1	0 **6** **0**

BULL, Ronnie (D)   **38**   **0**
H: 5 7   W: 10 10   b.Hackney 26-12-80
Source: Trainee.

1998–99	Millwall	1	0
1999–2000	Millwall	9	0
2000–01	Millwall	2	0
2001–02	Millwall	26	0 **38** **0**

CAHILL, Tim (M)   **166**   **40**
H: 5 10   W: 10 10   b.Sydney 6-12-79
Source: Sydney U.

1997–98	Millwall	1	0
1998–99	Millwall	36	6
1999–2000	Millwall	45	12
2000–01	Millwall	41	9
2001–02	Millwall	43	13 **166** **40**

CLARIDGE, Steve (F)   **534**   **175**
H: 6 0   W: 12 07   b.Portsmouth 10-4-66
Source: Portsmouth, Fareham T.

1984–85	Bournemouth	6	1		
1985–86	Bournemouth	1	0	**7**	**1**
From Weymouth					
1988–89	Crystal Palace	0	0		
1988–89	Aldershot	37	9		
1989–90	Aldershot	25	10	**62**	**19**
1989–90	Cambridge U	20	4		
1990–91	Cambridge U	30	12		
1991–92	Cambridge U	29	12		
1992–93	Luton T	16	2	**16**	**2**
1992–93	Cambridge U	29	7		
1993–94	Cambridge U	24	11	**132**	**46**
1993–94	Birmingham C	18	7		
1994–95	Birmingham C	42	20		
1995–96	Birmingham C	28	8	**88**	**35**
1995–96	Leicester C	14	5		
1996–97	Leicester C	32	11		
1997–98	Leicester C	17	0	**63**	**16**
1997–98	*Portsmouth*	10	2		
1997–98	Wolverhampton W	5	0	**5**	**0**
1998–99	Portsmouth	39	9		
1999–2000	Portsmouth	34	14		
2000–01	Portsmouth	31	11	**114**	**36**
2000–01	*Millwall*	6	3		
2001–02	Millwall	41	17	**47**	**20**

COGAN, Barry (M)   **0**   **0**
H: 5 9   W: 9 0   b.Sligo 4-11-84
Source: Scholar.

2001–02	Millwall	0	0

CONSTANTINE, Leon* (F)   **11**   **3**
H: 6 3   W: 11 10   b.Hackney 24-2-78
Source: Edgware T.

2000–01	Millwall	1	0		
2001–02	Millwall	0	0	**1**	**0**
2001–02	*Leyton Orient*	10	3	**10**	**3**

(On loan to Partick T, January 2002).

DOLAN, Joe (D)   **46**   **3**
H: 6 3   W: 13 02   b.Harrow 27-5-80
Source: Chelsea Trainee. *Honours:* Northern Ireland Youth, Under-21.

1998–99	Millwall	9	1		
1999–2000	Millwall	17	1		
2000–01	Millwall	20	1		
2001–02	Millwall	0	0	**46**	**3**

DUNNE, Alan (D)   **1**   **0**
H: 5 10   W: 10 13   b.Dublin 23-8-82
Source: Trainee.

1999–2000	Millwall	0	0		
2000–01	Millwall	0	0		
2001–02	Millwall	1	0	**1**	**0**

DYCHE, Sean# (D)   **331**   **12**
H: 6 1   W: 13 09   b.Kettering 28-6-71
Source: Trainee.

1988–89	Nottingham F	0	0		
1989–90	Nottingham F	0	0		
1989–90	Chesterfield	22	2		
1990–91	Chesterfield	28	2		
1991–92	Chesterfield	42	3		
1992–93	Chesterfield	20	1		
1993–94	Chesterfield	20	0		
1994–95	Chesterfield	22	0		
1995–96	Chesterfield	41	0		
1996–97	Chesterfield	36	0	**231**	**8**
1997–98	Bristol C	11	0		
1998–99	Bristol C	6	0	**17**	**0**
1998–99	*Luton T*	14	1	**14**	**1**
1999–2000	Millwall	1	0		
2000–01	Millwall	33	0		
2001–02	Millwall	35	3	**69**	**3**

ELLIOTT, Marvin (M)   **0**   **0**
b.Wandsworth 15-9-84
Source: Scholar.

2001–02	Millwall	0	0

GREEN, Ryan* (M)   **31**   **0**
H: 5 7   W: 10 10   b.Cardiff 20-10-80
Source: Danes Court. *Honours:* Wales Youth, Under-21, 2 full caps.

1997–98	Wolverhampton W	0	0		
1998–99	Wolverhampton W	1	0		
1999–2000	Wolverhampton W	0	0		
2000–01	Wolverhampton W	7	0		
2000–01	*Torquay U*	10	0	**10**	**0**
2001–02	Wolverhampton W	0	0	**8**	**0**
2001–02	*Millwall*	13	0	**13**	**0**

GUERET, Willy (G)   **12**   **0**
H: 6 1   W: 13 05   b.Saint Claude 3-8-73

2000–01	Millwall	11	0		
2001–02	Millwall	1	0	**12**	**0**

HARPUR, Chad (G)   **0**   **0**
H: 5 10   W: 12 11   b.Johannesburg 3-9-82

2000–01	Leeds U	0	0
2001–02	Millwall	0	0

HARRIS, Neil (F)   **143**   **71**
H: 5 11   W: 12 00   b.Orsett 12-7-77
Source: Cambridge C.

1997–98	Millwall	3	0		
1998–99	Millwall	39	15		
1999–2000	Millwall	38	25		
2000–01	Millwall	42	27		
2001–02	Millwall	21	4	**143**	**71**

HEARN, Charley (M)   **2**   **0**
H: 5 10   W: 12 00   b.Ashford 5-11-83
Source: School.

2000–01	Millwall	0	0		
2001–02	Millwall	2	0	**2**	**0**

HICKS, Mark* (M)   **1**   **0**
H: 5 8   W: 9 12   b.Belfast 24-7-81

1998–99	Millwall	1	0		
1999–2000	Millwall	0	0		
2000–01	Millwall	0	0		
2001–02	Millwall	0	0	**1**	**0**

IFILL, Paul (M)   **134**   **22**
H: 6 0   W: 12 01   b.Brighton 20-10-79
Source: Trainee.

1998–99	Millwall	15	1		
1999–2000	Millwall	44	11		
2000–01	Millwall	35	6		
2001–02	Millwall	40	4	**134**	**22**

KINET, Christophe (M)   **112**   **11**
H: 5 8   W: 10 12   b.Huy 31-12-74

1995–96	Ekeren	15	1		
1996–97	Ekeren	23	3	**38**	**4**
1997–98	Strasbourg	17	2		
1998–99	Strasbourg	10	0	**27**	**2**
1999–2000	Millwall	3	0		
2000–01	Millwall	27	2		
2001–02	Millwall	17	3	**47**	**5**

LAMBU, Goma (M)   **0**   **0**
H: 5 3   W: 9 0   b.London 10-11-84
Source: Scholar. *Honours:* England Youth.

2001–02	Millwall	0	0

LAWRENCE, Matthew (D)   **218**   **5**
H: 6 1   W: 12 08   b.Northampton 19-6-74
Source: Grays Ath. *Honours:* England Schools.

1995–96	Wycombe W	3	0		
1996–97	Wycombe W	13	1		
1996–97	Fulham	15	0		
1997–98	Fulham	43	0		
1998–99	Fulham	1	0	**59**	**0**
1998–99	Wycombe W	34	2		
1999–2000	Wycombe W	29	2	**79**	**5**
1999–2000	Millwall	9	0		
2000–01	Millwall	45	0		
2001–02	Millwall	26	0	**80**	**0**

LIVERMORE, David (M)   **114**   **5**
H: 5 11   W: 12 03   b.Edmonton 20-5-80
Source: Trainee.

1998–99	Arsenal	0	0		
1999–2000	Millwall	32	2		
2000–01	Millwall	39	3		
2001–02	Millwall	43	0	**114**	**5**

LOMBARDO, Daniel* (M)   **0**   **0**
b.London 18-9-82

2001–02	Millwall	0	0

MAY, Ben (F)   **0**   **0**
H: 6 1   W: 12 06   b.Gravesend 10-3-84

2000–01	Millwall	0	0
2001–02	Millwall	0	0

NETHERCOTT, Stuart (D)   **235**   **8**
H: 6 1   W: 13 08   b.Ilford 21-3-73
Source: Trainee. *Honours:* England Under-21.

1991–92	Tottenham H	0	0		
1991–92	*Maidstone U*	13	1	**13**	**1**
1991–92	*Barnet*	3	0	**3**	**0**
1992–93	Tottenham H	5	0		
1993–94	Tottenham H	10	0		
1994–95	Tottenham H	17	0		
1995–96	Tottenham H	13	0		
1996–97	Tottenham H	9	0		
1997–98	Tottenham H	0	0	**54**	**0**
1997–98	Millwall	10	0		
1998–99	Millwall	37	2		
1999–2000	Millwall	37	0		
2000–01	Millwall	35	2		
2001–02	Millwall	46	3	**165**	**7**

ODUNSI, Leke (M)   **17**   **0**
H: 5 9   W: 11 07   b.Walworth 5-12-80
Source: Trainee.

1998–99	Millwall	3	0		
1999–2000	Millwall	4	0		
2000–01	Millwall	8	0		
2001–02	Millwall	2	0	**17**	**0**

PHILLIPS, Mark (D)   **1**   **0**
H: 6 1   W: 11 00   b.Lambeth 27-1-82
Source: Scholar.

1999–2000	Millwall	0	0		
2000–01	Millwall	0	0		
2001–02	Millwall	1	0	**1**	**0**

REES, Matthew (M)   **0**   **0**
H: 6 2   W: 12 00   b.Swansea 2-9-82
Source: Trainee.

1999–2000	Millwall*	0	0
2000–01	Millwall	0	0
2001–02	Millwall	0	0

REID, Steven (M)   **119**   **12**
H: 6 0   W: 12 02   b.Kingston 10-3-81
Source: Trainee. *Honours:* England Youth. Eire 7 full caps, 2 goals.

1997–98	Millwall	1	0		
1998–99	Millwall	25	0		
1999–2000	Millwall	21	0		
2000–01	Millwall	37	7		
2001–02	Millwall	35	5	**119**	**12**

ROBINSON, Paul (D)   **0**   **0**
H: 6 1   W: 11 09   b.Barnet 7-1-82
Source: Scholar.

2000–01	Millwall	0	0
2001–02	Millwall	0	0

RYAN, Robbie (D)   **170**   **0**
H: 5 10   W: 12 01   b.Dublin 16-5-77
Source: Belvedere. *Honours:* Eire Youth, Under-21.

1994–95	Huddersfield T	0	0		
1995–96	Huddersfield T	0	0		
1996–97	Huddersfield T	5	0		
1997–98	Huddersfield T	10	0	**15**	**0**
1997–98	Millwall	16	0		
1998–99	Millwall	26	0		
1999–2000	Millwall	34	0		

2000–01 Millwall 42 0
2001–02 Millwall 37 0 **155 0**

SADLIER, Richard (F) **138 33**
H: 6 2 W: 13 02 b.Dublin 14-1-79
Source: Belvedere. Honours: Eire Youth, Under-21, 1 full cap.
1996–97 Millwall 10 0
1997–98 Millwall 4 3
1998–99 Millwall 31 5
1999–2000 Millwall 27 5
2000–01 Millwall 29 6
2001–02 Millwall 37 14 **138 33**

SAMBA, Cherno (M) **0 0**
H: 5 10 W: 10 01 b.Gambia 10-1-85
Source: Scholar. Honours: England Youth.
2001–02 Millwall 0 0

SAVARESE, Giovanni‡ (F) **148 64**
H: 6 0 W: 11 03 b.Caracas 14-7-71
Honours: Venezuela 22 full caps, 4 goals.
1996 New York/ 26 13
New Jersey M
1997 New York/ 29 14
New Jersey M
1998 New York/ 30 15 **85 42**
New Jersey M
1999 New England 27 10 **27 10**
Rev
2000 San Jose Earth 4 0 **4 0**
2000–01 Swansea C 31 12 **31 12**
2001–02 Millwall 1 0 **1 0**

STEELE, Daniel* (M) **0 0**
b.London 11-10-82
2001–02 Millwall 0 0

SWEENEY, Peter (F) **1 0**
H: 6 0 W: 12 01 b.Glasgow 25-9-84
Source: Scholar.
2001–02 Millwall 1 0 **1 0**

TUTTLE, David (D) **202 6**
H: 6 2 W: 15 00 b.Reading 6-2-72
Source: Trainee. Honours: England Youth.
1989–90 Tottenham H 0 0
1990–91 Tottenham H 6 0
1991–92 Tottenham H 2 0
1992–93 Tottenham H 5 0 **13 0**
1992–93 Peterborough U 7 0 **7 0**
1993–94 Sheffield U 31 0
1994–95 Sheffield U 6 0
1995–96 Sheffield U 26 1 **63 1**
1995–96 Crystal Palace 10 1
1996–97 Crystal Palace 39 2
1997–98 Crystal Palace 9 0
1998–99 Crystal Palace 22 2
1998–99 Charlton Ath 0 0
1999–2000 Crystal Palace 1 0 **81 5**
1999–2000 Barnsley 12 0 **12 0**
1999–2000 Millwall 8 0
2000–01 Millwall 9 0
2001–02 Millwall 5 0 **22 0**
2001–02 Wycombe W 4 0 **4 0**

WARD, Darren (D) **87 2**
H: 6 4 W: 11 04 b.Kenton 13-9-78
Source: Trainee.
1995–96 Watford 1 0
1996–97 Watford 7 0
1997–98 Watford 0 0
1998–99 Watford 1 0
1999–2000 Watford 9 1
1999–2000 QPR 14 0 **14 0**
2000–01 Watford 40 1
2001–02 Watford 1 0 **59 2**
2001–02 Watford 14 0 **14 0**

WARNER, Tony (G) **137 0**
H: 6 4 W: 15 07 b.Liverpool 11-5-74
Source: School.
1993–94 Liverpool 0 0
1994–95 Liverpool 0 0
1995–96 Liverpool 0 0
1996–97 Liverpool 0 0
1997–98 Liverpool 0 0
1997–98 Swindon T 2 0 **2 0**
1998–99 Liverpool 0 0
1998–99 Celtic 3 0 **3 0**
1998–99 Aberdeen 6 0 **6 0**
1999–2000 Millwall 45 0
2000–01 Millwall 35 0
2001–02 Millwall 46 0 **126 0**

Scholars
Cant, Steven; Craig, Tony A; Donovan, James; Hart, Edward M; Kevin, Joseph S; McCartney, David J; Robinson, Trevor; Rose, Jason; Simpson, James W; Taylor, William B; Tiesse, Alex; Worsfold, Dean C

NEWCASTLE U

ACUNA, Clarence (M) **213 25**
H: 5 10 W: 12 00 b.Rancagua 8-2-75
Honours: Chile 56 full caps, 3 goals.
1994 O'Higgins 28 2
1995 O'Higgins 26 3
1996 O'Higgins 27 3 **81 8**
1997 Univ de Chile 27 3
1998 Univ de Chile 27 3
1999 Univ de Chile 36 5 **90 11**
2000–01 Newcastle U 26 3
2001–02 Newcastle U 16 3 **42 6**

AMEOBI, Foluwashola (F) **35 2**
H: 6 3 W: 12 03 b.Zaria 12-10-81
Source: Trainee. Honours: England Under-21.
1998–99 Newcastle U 0 0
1999–2000 Newcastle U 0 0
2000–01 Newcastle U 20 2
2001–02 Newcastle U 15 0 **35 2**

BASSEDAS, Christian (M) **292 22**
H: 5 8 W: 11 09 b.Buenos Aires 16-2-73
Honours: Argentina 22 full caps.
1990–91 Velez Sarsfield 12 1
1991–92 Velez Sarsfield 36 4
1992–93 Velez Sarsfield 32 1
1993–94 Velez Sarsfield 26 1
1994–95 Velez Sarsfield 21 2
1995–96 Velez Sarsfield 32 2
1996–97 Velez Sarsfield 23 4
1997–98 Velez Sarsfield 31 2
1998–99 Velez Sarsfield 28 2
1999–2000 Velez Sarsfield 27 2 **268 21**
2000–01 Newcastle U 22 1
2001–02 Newcastle U 2 0 **24 1**
(On loan to Tenerife, January 2002).

BEAUMONT, James (M) **0 0**
H: 5 7 W: 10 10 b.Stockton 11-12-84
Source: Scholar.
2001–02 Newcastle U 0 0

BELLAMY, Craig (F) **145 47**
H: 5 10 W: 11 00 b.Cardiff 13-7-79
Source: Trainee. Honours: Wales Schools, Youth, Under-21, 16 full caps, 4 goals.
1996–97 Norwich C 3 0
1997–98 Norwich C 36 13
1998–99 Norwich C 40 17
1999–2000 Norwich C 4 2
2000–01 Norwich C 1 0 **84 32**
2000–01 Coventry C 34 6 **34 6**
2001–02 Newcastle U 27 9 **27 9**

BERNARD, Olivier (D) **26 5**
H: 5 7 W: 10 11 b.Lyon 14-10-79
2000–01 Newcastle U 0 0
2000–01 Darlington 10 2 **10 2**
2001–02 Newcastle U 16 3 **16 3**

BOYD, Mark* (M) **0 0**
H: 5 10 W: 12 04 b.Carlisle 22-10-81
Source: Trainee.
1998–99 Newcastle U 0 0
1999–2000 Newcastle U 0 0
2000–01 Newcastle U 0 0
2001–02 Newcastle U 0 0

BRADY, Gary‡ (M) **0 0**
b.Newcastle 18-12-83
2001–02 Newcastle U 0 0

BRENNAN, Stephen (D) **0 0**
H: 5 8 W: 11 10 b.Dublin 26-3-83
1999–2000 Newcastle U 0 0
2000–01 Newcastle U 0 0
2001–02 Newcastle U 0 0

CALDWELL, Gary (D) **4 0**
H: 5 11 W: 11 10 b.Stirling 12-4-82
Source: Trainee. Honours: Scotland Under-21, 4 full caps.
1998–99 Newcastle U 0 0
1999–2000 Newcastle U 0 0
2000–01 Newcastle U 0 0
2001–02 Darlington 4 0 **4 0**

CALDWELL, Steven (D) **24 0**
H: 6 0 W: 11 05 b.Stirling 12-9-80
Source: Trainee. Honours: Scotland Youth, Under-21, 1 full cap.
1997–98 Newcastle U 0 0
1998–99 Newcastle U 0 0
1999–2000 Newcastle U 0 0
2000–01 Newcastle U 9 0
2001–02 Blackpool 6 0 **6 0**
2001–02 Bradford C 9 0 **9 0**

CHOPRA, Michael (F) **0 0**
H: 5 8 W: 9 06 b.Newcastle 23-12-83
Source: Scholar. Honours: England Youth.
2000–01 Newcastle U 0 0
2001–02 Newcastle U 0 0

COLLEY, Karl (D) **0 0**
H: 6 1 W: 12 06 b.Sheffield 13-10-83
Source: Scholar.
2000–01 Sheffield W 0 0
2001–02 Sheffield W 0 0
2001–02 Newcastle U 0 0

COPPINGER, James (F) **25 5**
H: 5 7 W: 10 03 b.Middlesbrough 18-1-81
Source: Scholar. Darlington Trainee. Honours: England Youth.
1997–98 Newcastle U 0 0
1998–99 Newcastle U 0 0
1999–2000 Newcastle U 0 0
1999–2000 Hartlepool U 10 3
2000–01 Newcastle U 1 0
2001–02 Newcastle U 0 0 **1 0**
2001–02 Hartlepool U 14 2 **24 5**

CORT, Carl (F) **100 24**
H: 6 4 W: 12 07 b.Southwark 1-11-77
Source: Trainee. Honours: England Under-21.
1996–97 Wimbledon 1 0
1996–97 Lincoln C 6 1 **6 1**
1997–98 Wimbledon 22 4
1998–99 Wimbledon 16 3
1999–2000 Wimbledon 34 9 **73 16**
2000–01 Newcastle U 13 6
2001–02 Newcastle U 8 1 **21 7**

COWAN, David* (D) **0 0**
H: 5 11 W: 11 02 b.Whitehaven 5-3-82
Source: Trainee.
1999–2000 Newcastle U 0 0
2000–01 Newcastle U 0 0
2001–02 Newcastle U 0 0

DABIZAS, Nikos (D) **218 18**
H: 6 1 W: 12 07 b.Amindeo 3-8-73
Honours: Greece 50 full caps.
1994–95 Olympiakos 26 2
1995–96 Olympiakos 27 1
1996–97 Olympiakos 31 0
1997–98 Olympiakos 20 5 **104 8**
1997–98 Newcastle U 11 1
1998–99 Newcastle U 30 3
1999–2000 Newcastle U 29 3
2000–01 Newcastle U 9 0
2001–02 Newcastle U 35 3 **114 10**

DIMAS, Pedro* (M) **0 0**
H: 6 0 W: 11 00 b.Dexira 22-4-82
Source: Porto.
2000–01 Newcastle U 0 0
2001–02 Newcastle U 0 0

DISTIN, Sylvain (D) **115 4**
H: 6 3 W: 13 12 b.Bagnolet 16-12-77
1998–99 Tours 26 3 **26 3**
1999–2000 Gueugnon 33 1 **33 1**
2000–01 Paris St Germain 28 0 **28 0**
2001–02 Newcastle U 28 0 **28 0**

DIXON, Kevin* (M) **0 0**
H: 5 9 W: 10 11 b.Preston 17-3-83
Source: Scholar.
2000–01 Newcastle U 0 0
2001–02 Newcastle U 0 0

DYER, Kieron (M) **165 20**
H: 5 7 W: 9 07 b.Ipswich 29-12-78
Source: Trainee. Honours: England Youth, Under-21, B, 12 full caps.
1996–97 Ipswich T 13 0
1997–98 Ipswich T 41 4
1998–99 Ipswich T 37 5 **91 9**
1999–2000 Newcastle U 30 3
2000–01 Newcastle U 26 5
2001–02 Newcastle U 18 3 **74 11**

ELLIOTT, Robbie (D) **192 15**
H: 5 8 W: 12 03 b.Gosforth 25-12-73
Source: Trainee. Honours: England Under-21.
1990–91 Newcastle U 6 0
1991–92 Newcastle U 9 0
1992–93 Newcastle U 8 0
1993–94 Newcastle U 15 0
1994–95 Newcastle U 14 2
1995–96 Newcastle U 6 0
1996–97 Newcastle U 29 7
1997–98 Bolton W 4 0
1998–99 Bolton W 22 0
1999–2000 Bolton W 27 3
2000–01 Bolton W 33 2 **86 5**
2001–02 Newcastle U 27 1 **106 10**

GARDNER, Ross (M)   **0 0**
H: 5 8   W: 10 06   b.South Shields 15-12-85
Source: Scholar. *Honours:* England Youth.
2001–02   Newcastle U   0   0

GAVILAN, Diego (M)   **7 1**
H: 5 8   W: 10 07   b.Asuncion 1-3-80
Source: Cerro Porteno. *Honours:* Paraguay 23
full caps.
1999–2000   Newcastle U   6   1
2000–01   Newcastle U   1   0
2001–02   Newcastle U   0   0   **7 1**

GIVEN, Shay (G)   **165 0**
H: 6 1   W: 13 04   b.Lifford 20-4-76
Source: Celtic. *Honours:* Eire Under-21, 43
full caps.
1994–95   Blackburn R   0   0
1994–95   *Swindon T*   0   0
1995–96   Blackburn R   0   0
1995–96   *Swindon T*   5   0   **5 0**
1995–96   *Sunderland*   17   0   **17 0**
1996–97   Blackburn R   2   0   **2 0**
1997–98   Newcastle U   24   0
1998–99   Newcastle U   31   0
1999–2000   Newcastle U   14   0
2000–01   Newcastle U   34   0
2001–02   Newcastle U   38   0   **141 0**

GREEN, Stuart (M)   **16 3**
H: 5 10   W: 11 00   b.Carlisle 15-6-81
Source: Trainee.
1999–2000   Newcastle U   0   0
2000–01   Newcastle U   0   0
2001–02   Newcastle U   0   0
2001–02   *Carlisle U*   16   3   **16 3**

GRIFFIN, Andy (D)   **101 3**
H: 5 9   W: 10 10   b.Billinge 7-3-79
Source: Trainee. *Honours:* England Youth,
Under-21.
1996–97   Stoke C   34   1
1997–98   Stoke C   23   1   **57 2**
1997–98   Newcastle U   4   0
1998–99   Newcastle U   14   0
1999–2000   Newcastle U   3   1
2000–01   Newcastle U   19   0
2001–02   Newcastle U   4   0   **44 1**

HARPER, Steve (G)   **71 0**
H: 6 2   W: 13 00   b.Easington 14-3-75
Source: Seaham Red Star.
1993–94   Newcastle U   0   0
1994–95   Newcastle U   0   0
1995–96   Newcastle U   0   0
1995–96   *Bradford C*   1   0   **1 0**
1996–97   Newcastle U   0   0
1996–97   *Stockport Co*   0   0
1997–98   Newcastle U   0   0
1997–98   *Hartlepool U*   15   0   **15 0**
1997–98   *Huddersfield T*   24   0   **24 0**
1998–99   Newcastle U   8   0
1999–2000   Newcastle U   18   0
2000–01   Newcastle U   5   0
2001–02   Newcastle U   0   0   **31 0**

HEINIGER, Carl* (M)   **0 0**
b.Durham 27-10-82
Source: Scholar.
2001–02   Newcastle U   0   0

HOGG, Ryan (D)   **0 0**
H: 6 2   W: 13 00   b.Ashington 20-11-82
Source: Scholar.
2001–02   Newcastle U   0   0

HUGHES, Aaron (D)   **114 2**
H: 6 1   W: 11 02   b.Cookstown 8-11-79
Source: Trainee. *Honours:* Northern Ireland
Youth, B, 24 full caps.
1996–97   Newcastle U   0   0
1997–98   Newcastle U   14   0
1998–99   Newcastle U   40   0
1999–2000   Newcastle U   27   2
2000–01   Newcastle U   35   0
2001–02   Newcastle U   34   0   **114 2**

JENAS, Jermaine (M)   **41 4**
H: 5 10   W: 12 00   b.Nottingham 18-2-83
Source: Scholar. *Honours:* England Youth,
Under-21.
1999–2000   Nottingham F   0   0
2000–01   Nottingham F   0   0
2001–02   Nottingham F   28   4   **29 4**
2001–02   Newcastle U   12   0   **12 0**

KARELSE, John (G)   **385**
H: 6 3   W: 13 07   b.Kapelle 17-5-70
1986–87   NAC Breda   8   0
1987–88   NAC Breda   13   0
1988–89   NAC Breda   36   0
1989–90   NAC Breda   34   0
1990–91   NAC Breda   38   0
1991–92   NAC Breda   37   0

1992–93   NAC Breda   33   0
1993–94   NAC Breda   34   0
1994–95   NAC Breda   32   0
1995–96   NAC Breda   29   0
1996–97   NAC Breda   27   0
1997–98   NAC Breda   33   0
1998–99   NAC Breda   28   0   **382 0**
1999–2000   Newcastle U   3   0
2000–01   Newcastle U   0   0
2001–02   Newcastle U   0   0   **3 0**

KENDRICK, Joseph (D)   **0 0**
H: 6 0   W: 11 05   b.Dublin 26-6-83
Source: Scholar.
2000–01   Newcastle U   0   0
2001–02   Newcastle U   0   0

KERR, Brian (M)   **1 0**
H: 5 10   W: 10 11   b.Motherwell 12-10-81
Source: Trainee. *Honours:* Scotland Schools,
Youth.
1998–99   Newcastle U   0   0
1999–2000   Newcastle U   0   0
2000–01   Newcastle U   1   0
2001–02   Newcastle U   0   0   **1 0**

LUA-LUA, Lomano (F)   **102 18**
H: 5 8   W: 12 00   b.Kinshasa 28-12-80
Honours: DR Congo 4 full caps.
1998–99   Colchester U   3   1
1999–2000   Colchester U   41   12
2000–01   Colchester U   7   2   **61 15**
2000–01   Newcastle U   21   0
2001–02   Newcastle U   20   3   **41 3**

MAKONGO, Calvin (F)   **0 0**
H: 6 1   W: 12 00   b.Kinshasha 31-12-84
Source: Scholar.
2001–02   Newcastle U   0   0

MANN, Jonathan* (F)   **0 0**
H: 5 9   W: 10 00   b.Blyth 21-11-82
Source: Scholar.
2000–01   Newcastle U   0   0
2001–02   Newcastle U   0   0

MARCELINO, Elena (D)   **134 9**
H: 6 2   W: 13 00   b.Gijon 26-9-71
Honours: Spain 5 full caps.
1993–94   Gijon   2   0
1994–95   Gijon   8   0
1995–96   Gijon   4   0   **14 0**
1996–97   Mallorca   33   4
1997–98   Mallorca   36   2
1998–99   Mallorca   34   3   **103 9**
1999–2000   Newcastle U   11   0
2000–01   Newcastle U   6   0
2001–02   Newcastle U   0   0   **17 0**

McCLEN, Jamie (M)   **13 0**
H: 5 8   W: 10 07   b.Newcastle 13-5-79
Source: Trainee.
1997–98   Newcastle U   0   0
1998–99   Newcastle U   1   0
1999–2000   Newcastle U   9   0
2000–01   Newcastle U   0   0
2001–02   Newcastle U   3   0   **13 0**

McDERMOTT, Neale (M)   **0 0**
H: 5 9   W: 10 11   b.Newcastle 8-3-85
Source: Scholar. *Honours:* England Youth.

McGUFFIE, Ryan* (D)   **0 0**
H: 6 0   W: 11 01   b.Dumfries 22-7-80
Source: Trainee.
2000–01   Newcastle U   0   0
2001–02   Newcastle U   0   0

McMAHON, David‡ (F)   **8 1**
H: 6 1   W: 11 05   b.Dublin 17-1-81
Source: Trainee.
1997–98   Newcastle U   0   0
1998–99   Newcastle U   0   0
1999–2000   Newcastle U   0   0
2000–01   Newcastle U   0   0
2000–01   *Darlington*   8   1   **8 1**
2001–02   Newcastle U   0   0

McMENAMIN, Colin* (F)   **0 0**
H: 5 9   W: 10 12   b.Glasgow 12-2-81
2000–01   Newcastle U   0   0
2001–02   Newcastle U   0   0

O'BRIEN, Alan (M)   **0 0**
H: 5 9   W: 11 00   b.Dublin 20-2-85
Source: Scholar.
2001–02   Newcastle U   0   0

O'BRIEN, Andy (D)   **176 6**
H: 6 3   W: 11 05   b.Harrogate 29-6-79
Source: Trainee. *Honours:* England Youth,
Under-21, Eire Under-21, 5 full caps.
1996–97   Bradford C   22   2
1997–98   Bradford C   26   0
1998–99   Bradford C   31   0
1999–2000   Bradford C   36   1

2000–01   Bradford C   18   0   **133 3**
2000–01   Newcastle U   9   1
2001–02   Newcastle U   34   2   **43 3**

OFFIONG, Richard (F)   **0 0**
H: 5 11   W: 12 00   b.South Shields 17-12-83
Source: Scholar. *Honours:* England Youth.
2001–02   Newcastle U   0   0

ORR, Bradley (M)   **0 0**
H: 6 0   W: 11 11   b.Liverpool 1-11-82
Source: Scholar.
2001–02   Newcastle U   0   0

PRINGLE, Philip* (G)   **0 0**
H: 6 1   W: 14 09   b.Newcastle 1-1-83
Source: Scholar.
2000–01   Newcastle U   0   0
2001–02   Newcastle U   0   0

QUINN, Wayne (D)   **154 6**
H: 5 10   W: 11 12   b.Truro 19-11-76
Source: Trainee. *Honours:* England Under-
21, B.
1994–95   Sheffield U   0   0
1995–96   Sheffield U   0   0
1996–97   Sheffield U   0   0
1997–98   Sheffield U   28   2
1998–99   Sheffield U   44   1
1999–2000   Sheffield U   43   1
2000–01   Sheffield U   24   2   **139 6**
2000–01   Newcastle U   15   0
2001–02   Newcastle U   0   0   **15 0**

ROBERT, Laurent (F)   **221 50**
H: 5 8   W: 10 13   b.Saint-Benoit 21-5-75
Honours: France 9 full caps, 1 goal.
1994–95   Montpellier   7   0
1995–96   Montpellier   21   5
1996–97   Nancy   38   1   **38 1**
1997–98   Montpellier   26   2
1998–99   Montpellier   32   11   **86 18**
1999–2000   Paris St Germain   28   9
2000–01   Paris St Germain   32   14
2001–02   Paris St Germain   1   0   **61 23**
2001–02   Newcastle U   36   8   **36 8**

ROBSON, Craig‡ (M)   **0 0**
b.Congo 31-12-84
2001–02   Newcastle U   0   0

ROBSON, Damon (M)   **0 0**
H: 5 7   W: 13 06   b.Co Durham 19-9-83
Source: Scholar. *Honours:* England Youth.
2000–01   Newcastle U   0   0
2001–02   Newcastle U   0   0

SHEARER, Alan (F)   **427 227**
H: 6 0   W: 12 06   b.Newcastle 13-8-70
Source: Trainee. *Honours:* England Youth,
Under-21, B, 63 full caps, 30 goals.
1987–88   Southampton   5   3
1988–89   Southampton   10   0
1989–90   Southampton   26   3
1990–91   Southampton   36   4
1991–92   Southampton   41   13   **118 23**
1992–93   Blackburn R   21   16
1993–94   Blackburn R   40   31
1994–95   Blackburn R   42   34
1995–96   Blackburn R   35   31   **138 112**
1996–97   Newcastle U   31   25
1997–98   Newcastle U   17   2
1998–99   Newcastle U   30   14
1999–2000   Newcastle U   37   23
2000–01   Newcastle U   19   5
2001–02   Newcastle U   37   23   **171 92**

SOLANO, Nolberto (M)   **236 59**
H: 5 9   W: 11 02   b.Callao 12-12-74
Honours: Peru 57 full caps, 11 goals.
1994–95   Sporting Cristal   38   12
1995–96   Sporting Cristal   26   13
1996–97   Sporting Cristal   11   7   **75 32**
1997–98   Boca Juniors   32   5   **32 5**
1998–99   Newcastle U   29   6
1999–2000   Newcastle U   30   3
2000–01   Newcastle U   33   6
2001–02   Newcastle U   37   7   **129 22**

SPEED, Gary (M)   **457 79**
H: 5 10   W: 10 12   b.Deeside 8-9-69
Source: Trainee. *Honours:* Wales Youth,
Under-21, 68 full caps, 4 goals.
1988–89   Leeds U   1   0
1989–90   Leeds U   25   3
1990–91   Leeds U   38   7
1991–92   Leeds U   41   7
1992–93   Leeds U   39   7
1993–94   Leeds U   36   10
1994–95   Leeds U   39   3
1995–96   Leeds U   29   2   **248 39**
1996–97   Everton   37   9
1997–98   Everton   21   7   **58 16**
1997–98   Newcastle U   13   1

1998–99	Newcastle U	38	4		
1999–2000	Newcastle U	36	9		
2000–01	Newcastle U	35	5		
2001–02	Newcastle U	29	5	151	24

Trainees
Bell, Carl W; Brittain, Martin; Carr, Christopher; Collin, Adam J; Dunn, Paul J; English, Thomas M; Ferrell, Andrew E; Gate, Kristopher; Guy, Lewis B; Labonte, Aaron M; Moore, James C; Norton, Lee F; Ramage, Peter I

NORTHAMPTON T

ASAMOAH, Derek (F) 40 3
H: 5 6 W: 10 04 b.Ghana 1-5-81
Source: Slough T.

| 2001–02 | Northampton T | 40 | 3 | 40 | 3 |

BURGESS, Daryl (D) 368 11
H: 5 11 W: 11 04 b.Birmingham 24-1-71
Source: Trainee.

1989–90	WBA	34	0		
1990–91	WBA	25	0		
1991–92	WBA	36	2		
1992–93	WBA	18	1		
1993–94	WBA	43	2		
1994–95	WBA	22	0		
1995–96	WBA	45	2		
1996–97	WBA	33	1		
1997–98	WBA	27	1		
1998–99	WBA	20	0		
1999–2000	WBA	26	1		
2000–01	WBA	3	0	332	10
2001–02	Northampton T	36	1	36	1

CARRUTHERS, Chris (M) 16 1
H: 6 1 W: 12 03 b.Kettering 19-8-83
Source: Scholar.

| 2000–01 | Northampton T | 3 | 0 | | |
| 2001–02 | Northampton T | 13 | 1 | 16 | 1 |

CAVILL, Aaran§ (M) 1 0
b.Bedford 5-3-84
Source: Scholar.

| 2001–02 | Northampton T | 1 | 0 | 1 | 0 |

DEMPSEY, Paul‡ (D) 26 0
H: 5 11 W: 12 00 b.Birkenhead 3-12-81
Source: Scholar.

2000–01	Sheffield U	0	0		
2000–01	Northampton T	6	0		
2001–02	Northampton T	20	0	26	0

FORRESTER, Jamie (F) 267 84
H: 5 6 W: 11 00 b.Bradford 1-11-74
Source: Auxerre. *Honours:* England Schools, Youth.

1992–93	Leeds U	6	0		
1993–94	Leeds U	3	0		
1994–95	Leeds U	0	0		
1994–95	Southend U	5	0	5	0
1994–95	Grimsby T	9	1		
1995–96	Leeds U	0	0	9	0
1995–96	Grimsby T	28	5		
1996–97	Grimsby T	13	1	50	7
1997–98	Scunthorpe U	10	6		
1997–98	Scunthorpe U	45	11		
1998–99	Scunthorpe U	46	20	101	37
1999–2000	Utrecht	1	0	1	0
1999–2000	Walsall	5	0	5	0
1999–2000	Northampton T	10	6		
2000–01	Northampton T	43	17		
2001–02	Northampton T	43	17	96	40

FRAIN, John (D) 467 27
H: 5 10 W: 12 04 b.Birmingham 8-10-68
Source: Apprentice.

1985–86	Birmingham C	3	0		
1986–87	Birmingham C	3	1		
1987–88	Birmingham C	14	2		
1988–89	Birmingham C	28	3		
1989–90	Birmingham C	38	1		
1990–91	Birmingham C	42	3		
1991–92	Birmingham C	44	5		
1992–93	Birmingham C	45	6		
1993–94	Birmingham C	26	2		
1994–95	Birmingham C	7	0		
1995–96	Birmingham C	23	0		
1996–97	Birmingham C	1	0	274	23
1996–97	Northampton T	13	0		
1997–98	Northampton T	45	1		
1998–99	Northampton T	41	0		
1999–2000	Northampton T	40	2		
2000–01	Northampton T	27	1		
2001–02	Northampton T	27	0	193	4

GABBIADINI, Marco (F) 603 205
H: 5 10 W: 13 04 b.Nottingham 20-1-68
Source: Apprentice. *Honours:* England Under-21, B.

1984–85	York C	1	0		
1985–86	York C	22	4		
1986–87	York C	29	9		
1987–88	York C	8	1		
1987–88	Sunderland	35	21		
1988–89	Sunderland	36	18		
1989–90	Sunderland	46	21		
1990–91	Sunderland	31	9		
1991–92	Sunderland	9	5	157	74
1991–92	Crystal Palace	15	5	15	5
1991–92	Derby Co	20	6		
1992–93	Derby Co	44	9		
1993–94	Derby Co	39	13		
1994–95	Derby Co	32	11		
1995–96	Derby Co	39	11		
1996–97	Derby Co	14	0	188	50
1996–97	Birmingham C	2	0	2	0
1996–97	Oxford U	5	1	5	1
1997–98	Stoke C	8	0	8	0
1997–98	York C	7	1	67	15
1998–99	Darlington	40	23		
1999–2000	Darlington	42	24	82	47
2000–01	Northampton T	44	6		
2001–02	Northampton T	35	7	79	13

HARGREAVES, Chris# (M) 311 19
H: 5 11 W: 12 02 b.Cleethorpes 12-5-72
Source: Trainee.

1989–90	Grimsby T	19	2		
1990–91	Grimsby T	18	3		
1991–92	Grimsby T	10	0		
1992–93	Grimsby T	4	0		
1992–93	Scarborough	3	0	3	0
1993–94	Grimsby T	0	0	51	5
1993–94	Hull C	28	0		
1994–95	Hull C	21	0	49	0
1995–96	WBA	1	0	1	0
1995–96	Hereford U	17	2		
1996–97	Hereford U	44	4		
1997–98	Hereford U	0	0	61	6

From Hereford U.

1998–99	Plymouth Arg	32	2		
1999–2000	Plymouth Arg	44	3	76	5
2000–01	Northampton T	31	0		
2001–02	Northampton T	39	3	70	3

HODGE, John* (M) 362 35
H: 5 7 W: 11 12 b.Skelmersdale 4-1-69
Source: Exmouth.

1991–92	Exeter C	23	1		
1992–93	Exeter C	42	9	65	10
1993–94	Swansea C	27	2		
1994–95	Swansea C	44	7		
1995–96	Swansea C	41	1		
1996–97	Swansea C	0	0	112	10
1996–97	Walsall	37	4		
1997–98	Walsall	39	8	76	12
1998–99	Gillingham	34	1		
1999–2000	Gillingham	15	0	49	1
1999–2000	Northampton T	8	0		
2000–01	Northampton T	33	1		
2001–02	Northampton T	19	1	60	2

HOPE, Richard (D) 175 7
H: 6 3 W: 13 05 b.Middlesbrough 22-6-78
Source: Trainee.

1995–96	Blackburn R	0	0		
1996–97	Blackburn R	0	0		
1996–97	Darlington	20	0		
1997–98	Darlington	35	1		
1998–99	Darlington	8	0	63	1
1998–99	Northampton T	19	0		
1999–2000	Northampton T	17	0		
2000–01	Northampton T	33	0		
2001–02	Northampton T	43	6	112	6

HUNT, James# (M) 191 9
H: 5 11 W: 12 07 b.Derby 17-12-76
Source: Trainee.

1994–95	Notts Co	5	0		
1995–96	Notts Co	10	1		
1996–97	Notts Co	9	0	19	1
1997–98	Northampton T	21	0		
1998–99	Northampton T	35	2		
1999–2000	Northampton T	37	1		
2000–01	Northampton T	32	2		
2001–02	Northampton T	38	4	172	8

HUNTER, Roy# (M) 186 18
H: 5 10 W: 12 08 b.Saltburn 29-10-73
Source: Trainee.

1991–92	WBA	6	1		
1992–93	WBA	1	0		
1993–94	WBA	2	0		
1994–95	WBA	0	0	9	1
1995–96	Northampton T	34	0		
1996–97	Northampton T	36	6		
1997–98	Northampton T	28	3		
1998–99	Northampton T	18	1		
1999–2000	Northampton T	17	3		
2000–01	Northampton T	4	0		
2001–02	Northampton T	40	4	177	17

LAVIN, Gerard (D) 226 3
H: 5 10 W: 11 10 b.Corby 5-2-74
Source: Trainee. *Honours:* Scotland Under-21.

1991–92	Watford	1	0		
1992–93	Watford	28	0		
1993–94	Watford	46	3		
1994–95	Watford	35	0		
1995–96	Watford	16	0	126	3
1995–96	Millwall	20	0		
1996–97	Millwall	9	0		
1997–98	Millwall	7	0		
1998–99	Millwall	38	0	74	0
1999–2000	Bristol C	19	0		
2000–01	Bristol C	3	0	22	0
2000–01	Wycombe W	2	0	2	0
2001–02	Northampton T	2	0	2	0

LOPES, Richard* (F) 6 0
H: 5 7 W: 10 05 b.Waterford 10-8-81
Source: Scholar.

2000–01	Sheffield U	0	0		
2000–01	Northampton T	6	0		
2001–02	Northampton T	0	0	6	0

LOWE, Daniel§ (F) 4 0
H: 5 7 W: 10 05 b.Barnsley 12-1-84
Source: Scholar.

| 2000–01 | Northampton T | 4 | 0 | | |
| 2001–02 | Northampton T | 0 | 0 | 4 | 0 |

MARSH, Chris (D) 430 23
H: 5 11 W: 13 02 b.Sedgley 14-1-70
Source: Trainee.

1987–88	Walsall	3	0		
1988–89	Walsall	13	0		
1989–90	Walsall	9	0		
1990–91	Walsall	23	2		
1991–92	Walsall	37	1		
1992–93	Walsall	33	3		
1993–94	Walsall	39	4		
1994–95	Walsall	38	9		
1995–96	Walsall	41	2		
1996–97	Walsall	30	0		
1997–98	Walsall	36	0		
1998–99	Walsall	43	2		
1999–2000	Walsall	40	0		
2000–01	Walsall	7	0	392	23
2000–01	Wycombe W	11	0		
2001–02	Wycombe W	1	0	12	0
2001–02	Northampton T	26	0	26	0

McGREGOR, Paul (M) 160 28
H: 5 10 W: 11 06 b.Liverpool 17-12-74
Source: Trainee.

1991–92	Nottingham F	0	0		
1992–93	Nottingham F	0	0		
1993–94	Nottingham F	0	0		
1994–95	Nottingham F	11	1		
1995–96	Nottingham F	14	2		
1996–97	Nottingham F	5	0		
1997–98	Nottingham F	0	0		
1998–99	Nottingham F	0	0	30	3
1998–99	Carlisle U	10	3	10	3
1998–99	Preston NE	4	0	4	0
1999–2000	Plymouth Arg	44	13		
2000–01	Plymouth Arg	33	6	77	19
2001–02	Northampton T	39	3	39	3

MORISON, Steven§ (F) 1 0
b.London 29-8-83
Source: Scholar.

| 2001–02 | Northampton T | 1 | 0 | 1 | 0 |

SAMPSON, Ian# (D) 337 24
H: 6 2 W: 13 05 b.Wakefield 14-11-68
Source: Goole T.

1990–91	Sunderland	0	0		
1991–92	Sunderland	8	0		
1992–93	Sunderland	5	1		
1993–94	Sunderland	4	0	17	1
1993–94	Northampton T	8	0		
1994–95	Northampton T	42	2		
1995–96	Northampton T	33	4		
1996–97	Northampton T	43	5		
1997–98	Northampton T	39	3		
1998–99	Northampton T	42	1		
1999–2000	Northampton T	45	6		
2000–01	Northampton T	41	2		
2001–02	Northampton T	27	0	320	23

SOLLITT, Adam* (G) 16 0
H: 6 0 W: 11 04 b.Sheffield 22-6-77
Source: Gainsborough Tr, Kettering T. *Honours:* England semi-pro.

| 1995–96 | Barnsley | 0 | 0 | | |
| 1996–97 | Barnsley | 0 | 0 | | |

2000–01	Northampton T	6	0		
2001–02	Northampton T	10	0	**16**	**0**

SPEDDING, Duncan (D) **119** **2**
H: 6 2 W: 11 01 b.Frimley 7-9-77
Source: Trainee.

1996–97	Southampton	0	0		
1997–98	Southampton	7	0	**7**	**0**
1998–99	Northampton T	24	1		
1999–2000	Northampton T	44	1		
2000–01	Northampton T	21	0		
2001–02	Northampton T	23	0	**112**	**2**

THOMPSON, Chris§ (M) **0** **0**
b.Swindon 15-8-82
Source: Scholar.

2001–02	Northampton T	0	0		

WELCH, Keith# (G) **593** **0**
H: 6 2 W: 13 07 b.Bolton 3-10-68
Source: Trainee.

1986–87	Bolton W	0	0		
1986–87	Rochdale	24	0		
1987–88	Rochdale	46	0		
1988–89	Rochdale	46	0		
1989–90	Rochdale	46	0		
1990–91	Rochdale	43	0	**205**	**0**
1991–92	Bristol C	26	0		
1992–93	Bristol C	45	0		
1993–94	Bristol C	45	0		
1994–95	Bristol C	44	0		
1995–96	Bristol C	35	0		
1996–97	Bristol C	11	0		
1997–98	Bristol C	44	0		
1998–99	Bristol C	21	0	**271**	**0**
1999–2000	Northampton T	39	0		
2000–01	Northampton T	40	0		
2001–02	Northampton T	38	0	**117**	**0**

Scholars
Bunn, Mark; Cavill, Aaran; Champelovier, Neil M; Cracknell, Dean P; Daly, Ben AJ; Georcelin, Justin S; Howard, Matthew A; Laws, Michael J; Lowe, Daniel J; Meade, Nathan S; Morison, Steven; Nash, Ryan M; Spooner, Mark S; Stirling, James S; Thompson, Christopher D; White, Robert

NORWICH C

ABBEY, Zema (F) **48** **7**
H: 6 1 W: 12 09 b.Luton 17-4-77
Source: Arlesey, Baldock T, Hitchin T.

1999–2000	Cambridge U	8	0		
2000–01	Cambridge U	14	5	**22**	**5**
2000–01	Norwich C	20	1		
2001–02	Norwich C	6	1	**26**	**2**

BLOIS, Lewis* (M) **0** **0**
H: 5 9 W: 11 04 b.Aylsham 14-12-81
Source: Scholar.

2001–02	Norwich C	0	0		

BLOOMFIELD, Danny* (F) **0** **0**
H: 5 8 W: 11 07 b.Ipswich 28-7-82
Source: Felixstowe & Walton U.

2000–01	Norwich C	0	0		
2001–02	Norwich C	0	0		

CRICHTON, Paul (G) **418** **0**
H: 6 1 W: 13 05 b.Pontefract 3-10-68
Source: Apprentice.

1986–87	Nottingham F	0	0		
1986–87	*Notts Co*	5	0	**5**	**0**
1986–87	*Darlington*	5	0		
1986–87	*Peterborough U*	4	0		
1987–88	Nottingham F	0	0		
1987–88	*Darlington*	3	0	**8**	**0**
1987–88	*Swindon T*	4	0	**4**	**0**
1987–88	*Rotherham U*	6	0	**6**	**0**
1988–89	Nottingham F	0	0		
1988–89	*Torquay U*	13	0	**13**	**0**
1988–89	Peterborough U	31	0		
1989–90	Peterborough U	16	0	**51**	**0**
1990–91	Doncaster R	20	0		
1991–92	Doncaster R	16	0		
1992–93	Doncaster R	41	0	**77**	**0**
1993–94	Grimsby T	46	0		
1994–95	Grimsby T	43	0		
1995–96	Grimsby T	44	0		
1996–97	Grimsby T	0	0	**133**	**0**
1996–97	WBA	30	0		
1997–98	WBA	2	0		
1997–98	*Aston Villa*	0	0		
1998–99	WBA	0	0	**32**	**0**
1998–99	Burnley	29	0		
1999–2000	Burnley	46	0		
2000–01	Burnley	8	0	**83**	**0**
2001–02	Norwich C	6	0	**6**	**0**

DRURY, Adam (D) **189** **2**
H: 5 10 W: 11 06 b.Cottenham 29-8-78
Source: Trainee.

1995–96	Peterborough U	1	0		
1996–97	Peterborough U	5	1		
1997–98	Peterborough U	31	0		
1998–99	Peterborough U	40	0		
1999–2000	Peterborough U	42	1		
2000–01	Peterborough U	29	0	**148**	**2**
2000–01	Norwich C	6	0		
2001–02	Norwich C	35	0	**41**	**0**

EASTON, Clint (M) **78** **2**
H: 5 11 W: 10 09 b.Barking 1-11-77
Source: Trainee. *Honours:* England Youth.

1996–97	Watford	17	1		
1997–98	Watford	12	0		
1998–99	Watford	7	0		
1999–2000	Watford	17	0		
2000–01	Watford	11	0	**64**	**1**
2001–02	Norwich C	14	1	**14**	**1**

EMBLEN, Neil (M) **229** **16**
H: 6 1 W: 13 08 b.Bromley 19-6-71
Source: Tonbridge, Sittingbourne.

1993–94	Millwall	12	0	**12**	**0**
1994–95	Wolverhampton W	27	7		
1995–96	Wolverhampton W	33	2		
1996–97	Wolverhampton W	28	0		
1997–98	Wolverhampton W	7	0		
1997–98	Crystal Palace	13	0	**13**	**0**
1998–99	Wolverhampton W	33	2		
1999–2000	Wolverhampton W	46	5		
2000–01	Wolverhampton W	28	0	**202**	**16**
2001–02	Norwich C	2	0	**2**	**0**

FLEMING, Craig (D) **404** **8**
H: 5 11 W: 12 09 b.Halifax 6-10-71
Source: Trainee.

1988–89	Halifax T	1	0		
1989–90	Halifax T	10	0		
1990–91	Halifax T	46	0	**57**	**0**
1991–92	Oldham Ath	32	1		
1992–93	Oldham Ath	24	0		
1993–94	Oldham Ath	37	0		
1994–95	Oldham Ath	5	0		
1995–96	Oldham Ath	22	0		
1996–97	Oldham Ath	44	0	**164**	**1**
1997–98	Norwich C	22	1		
1998–99	Norwich C	37	3		
1999–2000	Norwich C	39	3		
2000–01	Norwich C	39	0		
2001–02	Norwich C	46	0	**183**	**7**

GIALLANZA, Gaetano* (F) **82** **31**
H: 5 11 W: 11 05 b.Basle 6-6-74

1996–97	Basle	32	19	**32**	**19**
1997–98	Nantes	12	2	**12**	**2**
1997–98	Bolton W	3	0	**3**	**0**
1998–99	Lugano	21	8	**21**	**8**
1999–2000	Norwich C	3	0		
2000–01	Norwich C	11	2		
2001–02	Norwich C	0	0	**14**	**2**

GREEN, Robert (G) **51** **0**
H: 6 3 W: 13 00 b.Chertsey 18-1-80
Source: Trainee. *Honours:* England Youth.

1997–98	Norwich C	0	0		
1998–99	Norwich C	2	0		
1999–2000	Norwich C	3	0		
2000–01	Norwich C	5	0		
2001–02	Norwich C	41	0	**51**	**0**

HOLT, Gary (M) **202** **11**
H: 6 1 W: 11 13 b.Irvine 9-3-73
Source: Celtic. *Honours:* Scotland 3 full caps.

1994–95	Stoke C	0	0		
1995–96	Kilmarnock	26	0		
1996–97	Kilmarnock	12	1		
1997–98	Kilmarnock	27	2		
1998–99	Kilmarnock	33	3		
1999–2000	Kilmarnock	35	0		
2000–01	Kilmarnock	19	3	**152**	**9**
2000–01	Norwich C	4	0		
2001–02	Norwich C	46	2	**50**	**2**

KENTON, Darren (D) **121** **8**
H: 5 11 W: 12 00 b.Wandsworth 13-9-78
Source: Trainee.

1997–98	Norwich C	11	0		
1998–99	Norwich C	22	1		
1999–2000	Norwich C	26	1		
2000–01	Norwich C	29	2		
2001–02	Norwich C	33	4	**121**	**8**

LIBBRA, Marc (F) **276** **63**
H: 6 2 W: 12 06 b.Toulon 5-8-72

1991–92	Marseille	1	0		
1992–93	Istres	10	1	**10**	**1**
1993–94	Marseille	13	1		
1994–95	Marseille	37	7		
1995–96	Marseille	38	14		
1996–97	Marseille	35	7		
1997–98	Marseille	6	0	**130**	**29**
1997–98	Guingamp	13	1	**13**	**1**
1998–99	Cannes	29	8	**29**	**8**
1999–2000	Toulouse	34	11		
2000–01	Toulouse	15	1	**49**	**12**
2000–01	Hibernian	11	5	**11**	**5**
2001–02	Norwich C	34	7	**34**	**7**

LLEWELLYN, Chris (M) **137** **17**
H: 6 0 W: 11 10 b.Merthyr 29-8-79
Source: Trainee. *Honours:* Wales Youth, Under-21, B, 2 full caps.

1996–97	Norwich C	0	0		
1997–98	Norwich C	15	4		
1998–99	Norwich C	31	2		
1999–2000	Norwich C	36	3		
2000–01	Norwich C	42	8		
2001–02	Norwich C	13	0	**137**	**17**

MACKAY, Malky (D) **237** **15**
H: 6 3 W: 13 01 b.Bellshill 19-2-72
Source: Queen's Park Youth.

1990–91	Queen's Park	10	0		
1991–92	Queen's Park	27	3		
1992–93	Queen's Park	33	3	**70**	**6**
1993–94	Celtic	0	0		
1994–95	Celtic	1	0		
1995–96	Celtic	11	1		
1996–97	Celtic	20	1		
1997–98	Celtic	4	1		
1998–99	Celtic	1	1	**37**	**4**
1998–99	Norwich C	27	1		
1999–2000	Norwich C	21	0		
2000–01	Norwich C	38	1		
2001–02	Norwich C	44	3	**130**	**5**

McGOVERN, Brian (D) **27** **1**
H: 6 3 W: 12 07 b.Dublin 28-4-80
Source: Cherry Orchard. *Honours:* Eire Youth, Under-21.

1997–98	Arsenal	0	0		
1998–99	Arsenal	0	0		
1999–2000	Arsenal	1	0		
1999–2000	*QPR*	5	0	**5**	**0**
2000–01	Arsenal	0	0	**1**	**0**
2000–01	Norwich C	12	1		
2001–02	Norwich C	9	0	**21**	**1**

McVEIGH, Paul (M) **57** **10**
H: 5 6 W: 10 07 b.Belfast 6-12-77
Source: Trainee. *Honours:* Northern Ireland Schools, Youth, Under-21, 3 full caps.

1995–96	Tottenham H	0	0		
1996–97	Tottenham H	3	1		
1997–98	Tottenham H	0	0		
1998–99	Tottenham H	0	0		
1999–2000	Tottenham H	0	0	**3**	**1**
1999–2000	Norwich C	1	0		
2000–01	Norwich C	11	1		
2001–02	Norwich C	42	8	**54**	**9**

MULRYNE, Phil# (M) **85** **9**
H: 5 9 W: 11 04 b.Belfast 1-1-78
Source: Trainee. *Honours:* Northern Ireland Youth, Under-21, B, 16 full caps, 3 goals.

1994–95	Manchester U	0	0		
1995–96	Manchester U	0	0		
1996–97	Manchester U	0	0		
1997–98	Manchester U	1	0		
1998–99	Manchester U	0	0	**1**	**0**
1998–99	Norwich C	7	2		
1999–2000	Norwich C	9	0		
2000–01	Norwich C	28	1		
2001–02	Norwich C	40	6	**84**	**9**

NEDERGAARD, Steen (M) **255** **23**
H: 6 1 W: 11 11 b.Odense 25-2-70

1991–92	Odense	17	0		
1992–93	Odense	30	9		
1993–94	Odense	25	1		
1994–95	Odense	27	1		
1995–96	Odense	30	1		
1996–97	Odense	24	4		
1997–98	Odense	21	2		
1998–99	Odense	0	0		
1999–2000	Odense	26	2	**200**	**20**
2000–01	Norwich C	15	1		
2001–02	Norwich C	40	2	**55**	**3**

NIELSEN, David (F) **171** **53**
H: 6 0 W: 12 00 b.Sonderborg 1-12-76

1996–97	FC Copenhagen	14	1		
1997–98	FC Copenhagen	31	11		
1998–99	FC Copenhagen	30	15		
1999–2000	FC Copenhagen	26	8		
2000–01	FC Copenhagen	7	1	**108**	**36**
2000–01	Grimsby T	17	5	**17**	**5**
2000–01	Wimbledon	11	2		
2001–02	Wimbledon	12	2	**23**	**4**
2001–02	Norwich C	23	8	**23**	**8**

NOTMAN, Alex (F) 57 4
H: 5 7 W: 10 13 b.Edinburgh 10-12-79
Source: Trainee. *Honours:* Scotland Schools, Youth, Under-21.

1996–97	Manchester U	0	0		
1997–98	Manchester U	0	0		
1998–99	Manchester U	0	0		
1998–99	*Aberdeen*	2	0	**2**	**0**
1999–2000	Manchester U	0	0		
1999–2000	*Sheffield U*	10	3	**10**	**3**
2000–01	Manchester U	0	0		
2000–01	Norwich C	15	1		
2001–02	Norwich C	30	0	**45**	**1**

RIVERS, Mark (F) 235 45
H: 5 10 W: 11 00 b.Crewe 26-11-75
Source: Trainee.

1993–94	Crewe Alex	0	0		
1994–95	Crewe Alex	0	0		
1995–96	Crewe Alex	33	10		
1996–97	Crewe Alex	27	6		
1997–98	Crewe Alex	35	6		
1998–99	Crewe Alex	43	7		
1999–2000	Crewe Alex	32	7		
2000–01	Crewe Alex	33	7	**203**	**43**
2001–02	Norwich C	32	2	**32**	**2**

ROBERTS, Iwan (F) 532 181
H: 6 3 W: 13 01 b.Bangor 26-6-68
Source: Trainee. *Honours:* Wales Schools, Youth, B, 15 full caps.

1985–86	Watford	4	0		
1986–87	Watford	3	1		
1987–88	Watford	25	2		
1988–89	Watford	22	6		
1989–90	Watford	9	0	**63**	**9**
1990–91	Huddersfield T	44	13		
1991–92	Huddersfield T	46	24		
1992–93	Huddersfield T	37	9		
1993–94	Huddersfield T	15	4	**142**	**50**
1993–94	Leicester C	26	13		
1994–95	Leicester C	37	9		
1995–96	Leicester C	37	19	**100**	**41**
1996–97	Wolverhampton W	33	12	**33**	**12**
1997–98	Norwich C	31	5		
1998–99	Norwich C	45	19		
1999–2000	Norwich C	44	17		
2000–01	Norwich C	44	15		
2001–02	Norwich C	30	13	**194**	**69**

RUSSELL, Darel (M) 111 7
H: 6 0 W: 12 04 b.Mile End 22-10-80
Source: Trainee. *Honours:* England Youth.

1997–98	Norwich C	1	0		
1998–99	Norwich C	13	1		
1999–2000	Norwich C	33	4		
2000–01	Norwich C	41	2		
2001–02	Norwich C	23	0	**111**	**7**

SUTCH, Daryl (D) 305 9
H: 5 11 W: 12 05 b.Lowestoft 11-9-71
Source: Trainee. *Honours:* England Youth, Under-21.

1989–90	Norwich C	0	0		
1990–91	Norwich C	4	0		
1991–92	Norwich C	9	0		
1992–93	Norwich C	22	2		
1993–94	Norwich C	3	0		
1994–95	Norwich C	30	1		
1995–96	Norwich C	13	0		
1996–97	Norwich C	44	3		
1997–98	Norwich C	40	1		
1998–99	Norwich C	36	0		
1999–2000	Norwich C	45	2		
2000–01	Norwich C	40	0		
2001–02	Norwich C	19	0	**305**	**9**

Scholars
Batt, Damian AN; Chick, David R; Crane, Gregory W; Davey, Thomas; Dodsworth, Paul; Goodchild, Richard I; Hayes, Paul E; Henderson, Ian; Lee-Barrett, Arran; Merrick, Michael T; Osborne, Aaron A; Oxby, Andrew D; Self, Daniel G; Shackell, Jason; Sinclair, Dean M; Thompson, Ben; Woodrow, Richard

NOTTINGHAM F

ANTOINE-CURIER, Mickael (F) 0 0
H: 6 0 W: 12 00 b.Orsay 5-3-83

2000–01	Preston NE	0	0		
2001–02	Nottingham F	0	0		

BIRCH, Jay (F) 0 0
b.Barnsley 23-11-83
Source: Scholar.

2001–02	Nottingham F	0	0		

BOPP, Eugene (M) 19 1
H: 5 11 W: 12 03 b.Kiev 5-9-83
Source: Bayern Munich.

2000–01	Nottingham F	0	0		
2001–02	Nottingham F	19	1	**19**	**1**

BRENNAN, Jim (D) 135 3
H: 5 11 W: 13 01 b.Toronto 8-5-77
Source: Sora Lazio. *Honours:* Canada 31 full caps, 2 goals.

1994–95	Bristol C	0	0		
1995–96	Bristol C	0	0		
1996–97	Bristol C	8	0		
1997–98	Bristol C	6	0		
1998–99	Bristol C	29	1		
1999–2000	Bristol C	12	2	**55**	**3**
1999–2000	Nottingham F	25	0		
2000–01	Nottingham F	12	0		
2000–01	*Huddersfield T*	2	0	**2**	**0**
2001–02	Nottingham F	41	0	**78**	**0**

CASH, Brian (M) 5 0
H: 5 9 W: 11 01 b.Dublin 24-11-82
Source: Trainee.

1999–2000	Nottingham F	0	0		
2000–01	Nottingham F	0	0		
2001–02	Nottingham F	5	0	**5**	**0**

DAWSON, Kevin* (D) 16 0
H: 6 0 W: 12 06 b.Northallerton 18-6-81
Source: Trainee.

1998–99	Nottingham F	0	0		
1999–2000	Nottingham F	7	0		
2000–01	Nottingham F	1	0		
2000–01	*Barnet*	5	0	**5**	**0**
2001–02	Nottingham F	3	0	**11**	**0**

DAWSON, Michael (D) 1 0
H: 6 2 W: 12 02 b.Northallerton 18-11-83
Source: School. *Honours:* England Youth.

2000–01	Nottingham F	0	0		
2001–02	Nottingham F	1	0	**1**	**0**

DOIG, Chris (D) 36 1
H: 6 2 W: 13 07 b.Dumfries 13-2-81
Source: Trainee. *Honours:* Scotland Schools, Youth, Under-21.

1997–98	Nottingham F	0	0		
1998–99	Nottingham F	2	0		
1999–2000	Nottingham F	11	0		
2000–01	Nottingham F	15	0		
2001–02	Nottingham F	8	1	**36**	**1**

EDDS, Gareth* (M) 16 1
H: 6 0 W: 12 00 b.Sydney 3-2-81
Source: Trainee.

1997–98	Nottingham F	0	0		
1998–99	Nottingham F	0	0		
1999–2000	Nottingham F	2	0		
2000–01	Nottingham F	13	1		
2001–02	Nottingham F	1	0	**16**	**1**

EDWARDS, Christian (D) 186 8
H: 6 2 W: 12 03 b.Caerphilly 23-11-75
Source: Trainee. *Honours:* Wales Under-21, B, 1 full cap.

1994–95	Swansea C	9	0		
1995–96	Swansea C	38	2		
1996–97	Swansea C	36	0		
1997–98	Swansea C	32	2	**115**	**4**
1997–98	Nottingham F	0	0		
1998–99	Nottingham F	12	0		
1998–99	*Bristol C*	3	0	**3**	**0**
1999–2000	Nottingham F	0	0		
1999–2000	*Oxford U*	5	1	**5**	**1**
2000–01	Nottingham F	36	3		
2001–02	Nottingham F	6	0	**54**	**3**
2001–02	*Crystal Palace*	9	0	**9**	**0**

FENTON, Paul‡ (F) 0 0
H: 5 7 W: 10 10 b.Cork 8-3-83
Source: Scholar.

1999–2000	Nottingham F	0	0		
2000–01	Nottingham F	0	0		
2001–02	Nottingham F	0	0		

FORMANN, Pascal (G) 0 0
H: 6 1 W: 11 07 b.Werne 16-11-82

2000–01	Nottingham F	0	0		
2001–02	Nottingham F	0	0		

FOY, Keith (D) 22 1
H: 5 10 W: 13 01 b.Crumlin 30-12-81
Source: Trainee.

1998–99	Nottingham F	0	0		
1999–2000	Nottingham F	0	0		
2000–01	Nottingham F	20	1		
2001–02	Nottingham F	2	0	**22**	**1**

FREEMAN, David* (F) 11 0
H: 5 10 W: 11 09 b.Dublin 25-11-79
Source: Cherry Orchard. *Honours:* Eire Under-21.

1996–97	Nottingham F	0	0		
1997–98	Nottingham F	0	0		
1998–99	Nottingham F	0	0		
1999–2000	Nottingham F	3	0		
2000–01	Nottingham F	5	0		
2000–01	*Port Vale*	3	0	**3**	**0**
2001–02	Nottingham F	0	0	**8**	**0**

GRAY, Andy* (M) 101 2
H: 6 1 W: 13 04 b.Harrogate 15-11-77
Source: Trainee. *Honours:* Scotland Youth.

1995–96	Leeds U	15	0		
1996–97	Leeds U	7	0		
1997–98	Leeds U	0	0		
1997–98	*Bury*	6	1	**6**	**1**
1998–99	Leeds U	0	0	**22**	**0**
1998–99	Nottingham F	8	0		
1998–99	*Preston NE*	5	0	**5**	**0**
1998–99	*Oldham Ath*	4	0	**4**	**0**
1999–2000	Nottingham F	22	0		
2000–01	Nottingham F	18	0		
2001–02	Nottingham F	16	1	**64**	**1**

HAIGH, Phil* (D) 0 0
b.Boston 27-9-82

2000–01	Nottingham F	0	0		
2001–02	Nottingham F	0	0		

HAREWOOD, Marlon (F) 125 20
H: 6 1 W: 13 07 b.Hampstead 25-8-79
Source: Trainee.

1996–97	Nottingham F	0	0		
1997–98	Nottingham F	1	0		
1998–99	Nottingham F	23	1		
1998–99	*Ipswich T*	6	1	**6**	**1**
1999–2000	Nottingham F	34	4		
2000–01	Nottingham F	33	3		
2001–02	Nottingham F	28	11	**119**	**19**

HASKINS, Andy (M) 0 0
b.York 30-4-84
Source: School. *Honours:* England Youth.

2000–01	Nottingham F	0	0		
2001–02	Nottingham F	0	0		

HJELDE, Jon Olav (D) 158 5
H: 6 3 W: 13 07 b.Levanger 30-7-72

1994	Rosenborg	1	0		
1995	Rosenborg	7	0		
1996	Rosenborg	16	1		
1997	Rosenborg	3	0	**27**	**1**
1997–98	Nottingham F	28	1		
1998–99	Nottingham F	17	1		
1999–2000	Nottingham F	33	0		
2000–01	Nottingham F	11	2		
2001–02	Nottingham F	42	0	**131**	**4**

HUDSON, Niall* (D) 0 0
H: 5 8 W: 11 04 b.Dublin 17-1-82
Source: Trainee.

1998–99	Nottingham F	0	0		
1999–2000	Nottingham F	0	0		
2000–01	Nottingham F	0	0		
2001–02	Nottingham F	0	0		

JEFFREY, Richard (F) 0 0
H: 5 9 W: 11 00 b.Derby 4-11-83
Source: Scholar.

2000–01	Nottingham F	0	0		
2001–02	Nottingham F	0	0		

JOHNSON, David (F) 284 85
H: 5 6 W: 12 00 b.Kingston, Jamaica 15-8-76
Source: Trainee. *Honours:* England Schools, B. Jamaica 4 full caps.

1994–95	Manchester U	0	0		
1995–96	Bury	36	5		
1996–97	Bury	44	8		
1997–98	Bury	17	5	**97**	**18**
1997–98	Ipswich T	31	20		
1998–99	Ipswich T	42	13		
1999–2000	Ipswich T	44	22		
2000–01	Ipswich T	14	0	**131**	**55**
2000–01	Nottingham F	19	2		
2001–02	Nottingham F	22	3	**41**	**5**
2001–02	*Sheffield W*	7	2	**7**	**2**
2001–02	*Burnley*	8	5	**8**	**5**

JONES, Gary (F) 214 30
H: 6 3 W: 14 07 b.Chester 10-5-75
Source: Trainee.

1993–94	Tranmere R	6	2		
1994–95	Tranmere R	19	3		
1995–96	Tranmere R	23	1		
1996–97	Tranmere R	30	6		
1997–98	Tranmere R	43	8		
1998–99	Tranmere R	26	5		
1999–2000	Tranmere R	31	3	**178**	**28**
2000–01	Nottingham F	31	1		
2001–02	Nottingham F	5	1	**36**	**2**

KEARNEY, Liam (M) 0 0
H: 5 7 W: 10 12 b.Dublin 10-1-83
Source: Scholar.

1999–2000	Nottingham F	0	0		

Season	Club				
2000–01	Nottingham F	0	0		
2001–02	Nottingham F	0	0		

LESTER, Jack (F) 210 32
H: 5 11 W: 11 06 b.Sheffield 8-10-75
Source: Trainee. *Honours:* England Schools.

Season	Club				
1994–95	Grimsby T	7	0		
1995–96	Grimsby T	5	0		
1996–97	Grimsby T	22	5		
1996–97	Doncaster R	11	1	11	1
1997–98	Grimsby T	40	4		
1998–99	Grimsby T	33	4		
1999–2000	Grimsby T	26	4	133	17
1999–2000	Nottingham F	15	2		
2000–01	Nottingham F	19	7		
2001–02	Nottingham F	32	5	66	14

LOUIS-JEAN, Mathieu (D) 172 1
H: 5 9 W: 11 03 b.Mont-St-Aignan 22-2-76

Season	Club				
1993–94	Le Havre	7	0		
1994–95	Le Havre	9	0		
1995–96	Le Havre	15	0		
1996–97	Le Havre	31	0		
1997–98	Le Havre	16	0	78	0
1998–99	Nottingham F	16	0		
1999–2000	Nottingham F	27	0		
2000–01	Nottingham F	13	0		
2001–02	Nottingham F	38	1	94	1

LOVE, Gordon* (F) 0 0
H: 5 7 W: 10 00 b.Bellshill 17-3-83

Season	Club				
1999–2000	Nottingham F	0	0		
2000–01	Nottingham F	0	0		
2001–02	Nottingham F	0	0		

LYNCH, Damien‡ (D) 0 0
H: 5 10 W: 11 04 b.Dublin 31-7-79

Season	Club				
1996–97	Leeds U	0	0		
1997–98	Leeds U	0	0		
1998–99	Leeds U	0	0		
1999–2000	Leeds U	0	0		
2000–01	Leeds U	0	0		
2001–02	Nottingham F	0	0		

PEYTON, Emmet (G) 0 0
b.Castlebar 26-10-83

Season	Club				
2000–01	Nottingham F	0	0		
2001–02	Nottingham F	0	0		

PRUTTON, David (M) 119 6
H: 6 0 W: 12 00 b.Hull 12-9-81
Source: Trainee. *Honours:* England Youth, Under-21.

Season	Club				
1998–99	Nottingham F	0	0		
1999–2000	Nottingham F	34	2		
2000–01	Nottingham F	42	1		
2001–02	Nottingham F	43	3	119	6

REID, Andrew (G) 0 0
b.Aberdeen 3-6-85
Source: Scholar.

Season	Club				
2001–02	Nottingham F	0	0		

REID, Andy (F) 43 2
H: 5 8 W: 11 02 b.Dublin 29-7-82
Source: Trainee.

Season	Club				
1999–2000	Nottingham F	0	0		
2000–01	Nottingham F	14	2		
2001–02	Nottingham F	29	0	43	2

ROBERTSON, Gregor (D) 0 0
b.Edinburgh 19-1-84

Season	Club				
2000–01	Nottingham F	0	0		
2001–02	Nottingham F	0	0		

ROCHE, Barry (G) 2 0
H: 6 5 W: 14 00 b.Dublin 6-4-82
Source: Trainee.

Season	Club				
1999–2000	Nottingham F	0	0		
2000–01	Nottingham F	2	0		
2001–02	Nottingham F	0	0	2	0

SAMUEL, Jake* (M) 0 0
b.Nottingham 5-11-84
Source: Academy.

Season	Club				
2001–02	Nottingham F	0	0		

SCIMECA, Riccardo (D) 184 6
H: 6 1 W: 13 05 b.Leamington Spa 13-6-75
Source: Trainee. *Honours:* England Under-21, B.

Season	Club				
1993–94	Aston Villa	0	0		
1994–95	Aston Villa	0	0		
1995–96	Aston Villa	17	0		
1996–97	Aston Villa	17	0		
1997–98	Aston Villa	21	0		
1998–99	Aston Villa	18	2	73	2
1999–2000	Nottingham F	38	0		
2000–01	Nottingham F	36	4		
2001–02	Nottingham F	37	0	111	4

SUMMERBEE, Nicky‡ (M) 365 22
H: 5 11 W: 12 03 b.Altrincham 26-8-71
Source: Trainee. *Honours:* England Under-21.

Season	Club				
1989–90	Swindon T	1	0		
1990–91	Swindon T	7	0		
1991–92	Swindon T	27	0		
1992–93	Swindon T	39	3		
1993–94	Swindon T	38	3	112	6
1994–95	Manchester C	41	1		
1995–96	Manchester C	37	1		
1996–97	Manchester C	44	4		
1997–98	Manchester C	9	0		
1997–98	Sunderland	25	3		
1998–99	Sunderland	36	3		
1999–2000	Sunderland	32	1		
2000–01	Sunderland	0	0	93	7
2000–01	Bolton W	12	1	12	1
2001–02	Manchester C	0	0	131	6
2001–02	Nottingham F	17	2	17	2

THOMPSON, John (D) 8 0
H: 6 0 W: 12 01 b.Dublin 12-10-81

Season	Club				
1999–2000	Nottingham F	0	0		
2000–01	Nottingham F	0	0		
2001–02	Nottingham F	8	0	8	0

TYNAN, Scott (M) 0 0
b.Knowsley 27-11-83
Source: Wigan Ath Scholar.

Season	Club				
2001–02	Nottingham F	0	0		

VAUGHAN, Tony (D) 187 6
H: 6 1 W: 13 04 b.Manchester 11-10-75
Source: Trainee. *Honours:* England Schools.

Season	Club				
1994–95	Ipswich T	10	0		
1995–96	Ipswich T	25	1		
1996–97	Ipswich T	32	2	67	3
1997–98	Manchester C	19	1		
1998–99	Manchester C	38	1		
1999–2000	Manchester C	1	0	58	2
1999–2000	Cardiff C	14	0	14	0
1999–2000	Nottingham F	10	0		
2000–01	Nottingham F	25	1		
2001–02	Nottingham F	8	0	43	1
2001–02	Scunthorpe U	5	0	5	0

WARD, Darren (G) 378 0
H: 6 0 W: 13 02 b.Worksop 11-5-74
Source: Trainee. *Honours:* Wales Under-21, B, 2 full caps.

Season	Club				
1992–93	Mansfield T	13	0		
1993–94	Mansfield T	33	0		
1994–95	Mansfield T	35	0	81	0
1995–96	Notts C	46	0		
1996–97	Notts C	38	0		
1997–98	Notts C	44	0		
1998–99	Notts C	43	0		
1999–2000	Notts C	45	0		
2000–01	Notts C	35	0	251	0
2000–01	Nottingham F	0	0		
2001–02	Nottingham F	46	0	46	0

WEBB, Steven (M) 0 0
b.Macclesfield 13-9-84
Source: Academy.

Season	Club				
2001–02	Nottingham F	0	0		

WESTCARR, Craig (F) 8 0
H: 5 11 W: 11 04 b.Nottingham 29-1-85
Source: Scholar. *Honours:* England Youth.

Season	Club				
2001–02	Nottingham F	8	0	8	0

WILLIAMS, Gareth (M) 63 0
H: 6 1 W: 12 03 b.Glasgow 16-12-81
Source: Trainee. *Honours:* Scotland Youth, Under-21, 4 full caps.

Season	Club				
1998–99	Nottingham F	0	0		
1999–2000	Nottingham F	2	0		
2000–01	Nottingham F	17	0		
2001–02	Nottingham F	44	0	63	0

Scholars
Biggins, James W; Bodkin, Matthew J; Ervin, Robert J; Freyne, David P; Groves, Thomas A; Hawkins, Nicholas C; Jenkins, Ryan M; Lorrimer, Wayne RG; McClean, Craig; Morgan, Neil; Myhill, Craig J; Plummer, Michael J

NOTTS CO

ALLSOPP, Danny (F) 149 46
H: 6 1 W: 14 00 b.Melbourne 10-8-78
Honours: Australia Youth, Under-23.

Season	Club				
1995–96	South Melbourne	14	1		
1996–97	South Melbourne	4	1	20	2
1997–98	Carlton	16	3	16	3
1998–99	Manchester C	24	4		
1999–2000	Manchester C	4	0		
1999–2000	Notts C	3	1		
1999–2000	Wrexham	3	4	3	4
2000–01	Manchester C	1	0	29	4
2000–01	Bristol R	6	0	6	0
2000–01	Notts C	29	13		
2001–02	Notts C	43	19	75	33

BARACLOUGH, Ian (D) 403 31
H: 6 1 W: 12 11 b.Leicester 4-12-70
Source: Trainee.

Season	Club				
1988–89	Leicester C	0	0		
1989–90	Leicester C	0	0		
1989–90	Wigan Ath	9	2	9	2
1990–91	Leicester C	0	0		
1990–91	Grimsby T	4	0		
1991–92	Grimsby T	0	0		
1992–93	Grimsby T	1	0	5	0
1992–93	Lincoln C	36	5		
1993–94	Lincoln C	37	5	73	10
1994–95	Mansfield T	36	3		
1995–96	Mansfield T	11	2	47	5
1995–96	Notts C	35	2		
1996–97	Notts C	38	2		
1997–98	Notts C	38	6		
1997–98	QPR	8	0		
1998–99	QPR	43	1		
1999–2000	QPR	45	0		
2000–01	QPR	29	0	125	1
2001–02	Notts C	33	3	144	13

BOLLAND, Paul (M) 76 1
H: 5 11 W: 12 10 b.Bradford 23-12-79
Source: Trainee.

Season	Club				
1997–98	Bradford C	10	0		
1998–99	Bradford C	2	0	12	0
1998–99	Notts C	13	0		
1999–2000	Notts C	25	1		
2000–01	Notts C	7	0		
2001–02	Notts C	19	0	64	1

BROUGH, Michael (M) 48 1
H: 6 0 W: 12 05 b.Nottingham 1-8-81
Source: Trainee.

Season	Club				
1999–2000	Notts C	11	0		
2000–01	Notts C	16	1		
2001–02	Notts C	21	0	48	1

CAS, Marcel (M) 106 12
H: 6 1 W: 12 10 b.Breda 30-4-72

Season	Club				
1997–98	RBC	27	3		
1998–99	RBC	9	1		
1999–2000	RBC	30	2	66	6
2001–02	Notts C	40	6	40	6

CASKEY, Darren (M) 282 45
H: 5 8 W: 12 04 b.Basildon 21-8-74
Source: Trainee. *Honours:* England Schools, Youth.

Season	Club				
1991–92	Tottenham H	0	0		
1992–93	Tottenham H	0	0		
1993–94	Tottenham H	25	4		
1994–95	Tottenham H	4	0		
1995–96	Tottenham H	3	0	32	4
1995–96	Watford	6	1	6	1
1995–96	Reading	15	2		
1996–97	Reading	35	0		
1997–98	Reading	23	0		
1998–99	Reading	42	7		
1999–2000	Reading	44	17		
2000–01	Reading	43	9	202	35
2001–02	Notts C	42	5	42	5

CROSS, David§ (M) 1 0
H: 5 10 W: 10 07 b.Bromley 7-9-82
Source: Scholar.

Season	Club				
1999–2000	Notts C	1	0		
2000–01	Notts C	0	0		
2001–02	Notts C	0	0	1	0

DEENEY, Saul (G) 0 0
H: 6 1 W: 12 07 b.Londonderry 12-3-83
Source: Scholar.

Season	Club				
2000–01	Notts C	0	0		
2001–02	Notts C	0	0		

FENTON, Nick (D) 113 6
H: 6 0 W: 12 04 b.Preston 23-11-79
Source: Trainee. *Honours:* England Youth.

Season	Club				
1996–97	Manchester C	0	0		
1997–98	Manchester C	0	0		
1998–99	Manchester C	15	0		
1999–2000	Manchester C	0	0		
1999–2000	Notts C	13	1		
1999–2000	Bournemouth	8	0		
2000–01	Manchester C	0	0	15	0
2000–01	Bournemouth	5	0	13	0
2000–01	Notts C	30	2		
2001–02	Notts C	42	3	85	6

FORD, Ryan‡ (M) 1 0
H: 5 9 W: 10 13 b.Worksop 3-9-78
Source: Trainee.

Season	Club				
1997–98	Manchester U	0	0		
1998–99	Manchester U	0	0		
1999–2000	Manchester U	0	0		
1999–2000	Notts C	1	0		
2000–01	Notts C	0	0		
2001–02	Notts C	0	0	1	0

GARDEN, Stuart (G)   21 0
H: 6 0   W: 12 06   b.Dundee 10-2-72

Season	Club				
2001–02	Notts Co	21	0	21	0

HACKWORTH, Tony (F)   33 1
H: 6 1   W: 13 07   b.Durham 19-5-80
Source: Trainee. *Honours:* England Youth.

1997–98	Leeds U	0	0		
1998–99	Leeds U	0	0		
1999–2000	Leeds U	0	0		
2000–01	Leeds U	0	0		
2001–02	Notts Co	33	1	33	1

HEFFERNAN, Paul (F)   26 6
H: 5 10   W: 11 05   b.Dublin 29-12-81
Source: Newton.

1999–2000	Notts Co	2	0		
2000–01	Notts Co	1	0		
2001–02	Notts Co	23	6	26	6

HOLMES, Richard (D)   55 0
H: 5 11   W: 11 08   b.Grantham 7-11-80
Source: Trainee.

1998–99	Notts Co	8	0		
1999–2000	Notts Co	41	0		
2000–01	Notts Co	5	0		
2001–02	Notts Co	1	0	55	0

IRELAND, Craig (D)   126 6
H: 6 3   W: 13 09   b.Dundee 29-11-75
Source: Aberdeen Lads.

1994–95	Aberdeen	0	0		
1995–96	Aberdeen	0	0		
1995–96	Dunfermline Ath	10	0		
1996–97	Dunfermline Ath	9	1		
1997–98	Dunfermline Ath	12	1		
1998–99	Dunfermline Ath	23	0		
1999–2000	Dunfermline Ath	3	0	57	2
1999–2000	Dundee	14	1	14	1
2000–01	Airdrieonians	12	2	12	2
2000–01	Notts Co	16	0		
2001–02	Notts Co	27	1	43	1

JORGENSEN, Henrik‡ (D)   7 0
H: 6 2   W: 14 00   b.Bogense 12-1-79

2000–01	Notts Co	5	0		
2001–02	Notts Co	2	0	7	0

LIBURD, Richard (D)   250 11
H: 5 9   W: 11 08   b.Nottingham 26-9-73
Source: Forest Ath.

1992–93	Middlesbrough	0	0		
1993–94	Middlesbrough	41	1	41	1
1994–95	Bradford C	9	1		
1995–96	Bradford C	33	1		
1996–97	Bradford C	36	1		
1997–98	Bradford C	0	0	78	3
1997–98	Carlisle U	9	0	9	0
1998–99	Notts Co	35	1		
1999–2000	Notts Co	31	1		
2000–01	Notts Co	31	3		
2001–02	Notts Co	25	2	122	7

McCAIG, John* (D)   0 0
H: 6 1   W: 12 04   b.Ayr 19-11-82

2000–01	Notts Co	0	0		
2001–02	Notts Co	0	0		

McNAMARA, Niall* (F)   4 0
H: 6 1   W: 12 07   b.Limerick 26-1-82
Source: Trainee.

1998–99	Nottingham F	0	0		
1999–2000	Nottingham F	0	0		
2000–01	Nottingham F	0	0		
2001–02	Notts Co	4	0	4	0

MILDENHALL, Steve (G)   59 0
H: 6 4   W: 15 01   b.Swindon 13-5-78
Source: Trainee.

1996–97	Swindon T	1	0		
1997–98	Swindon T	4	0		
1998–99	Swindon T	0	0		
1999–2000	Swindon T	5	0		
2000–01	Swindon T	23	0	33	0
2001–02	Notts Co	26	0	26	0

NICHOLSON, Kevin (M)   43 3
H: 5 8   W: 12 01   b.Derby 2-10-80
Source: Trainee. *Honours:* England Schools.

1997–98	Sheffield W	0	0		
1998–99	Sheffield W	0	0		
1999–2000	Sheffield W	0	0		
2000–01	Sheffield W	1	0	1	0

From Forest Green R

2000–01	Northampton T	7	0	7	0
2000–01	Notts Co	11	2		
2001–02	Notts Co	24	1	35	3

OWERS, Gary* (M)   548 46
H: 5 11   W: 12 07   b.Newcastle 3-10-68
Source: Apprentice.

1986–87	Sunderland	0	0		
1987–88	Sunderland	37	4		
1988–89	Sunderland	38	3		
1989–90	Sunderland	43	9		
1990–91	Sunderland	38	1		
1991–92	Sunderland	30	4		
1992–93	Sunderland	33	1		
1993–94	Sunderland	30	2		
1994–95	Sunderland	19	1	268	25
1994–95	Bristol C	21	2		
1995–96	Bristol C	37	2		
1996–97	Bristol C	46	4		
1997–98	Bristol C	22	1	126	9
1998–99	Notts Co	39	3		
1999–2000	Notts Co	45	4		
2000–01	Notts Co	40	4		
2001–02	Notts Co	30	1	154	12

RICHARDSON, Ian* (D)   176 17
H: 6 0   W: 12 04   b.Barking 22-10-70
Source: Dagenham & Redbridge.

1995–96	Birmingham C	7	0	7	0
1995–96	Notts Co	15	0		
1996–97	Notts Co	19	1		
1997–98	Notts Co	30	2		
1998–99	Notts Co	23	7		
1999–2000	Notts Co	33	4		
2000–01	Notts Co	25	1		
2001–02	Notts Co	24	2	169	17

RILEY, Paul (D)   6 0
H: 5 9   W: 10 07   b.Nottingham 29-9-82
Source: Scholar.

2001–02	Notts Co	6	0	6	0

STALLARD, Mark (F)   266 78
H: 6 0   W: 13 09   b.Derby 24-10-74
Source: Trainee.

1991–92	Derby Co	3	0		
1992–93	Derby Co	5	0		
1993–94	Derby Co	0	0		
1994–95	Derby Co	16	2		
1994–95	Fulham	4	3	4	3
1995–96	Derby Co	3	0	27	2
1995–96	Bradford C	21	9		
1996–97	Bradford C	22	1	43	10
1996–97	Preston NE	4	1	4	1
1996–97	Wycombe W	12	4		
1997–98	Wycombe W	43	17		
1998–99	Wycombe W	15	2	70	23
1998–99	Notts Co	14	4		
1999–2000	Notts Co	36	14		
2000–01	Notts Co	42	17		
2001–02	Notts Co	26	4	118	39

STONE, Danny (D)   6 0
H: 6 0   W: 12 03   b.Liverpool 14-9-82
Honours: Blackburn R Scholar.

2001–02	Notts Co	6	0	6	0

WARREN, Mark* (D)   240 6
H: 6 0   W: 12 10   b.Clapton 12-11-74
Source: Trainee.

1991–92	Leyton Orient	1	0		
1992–93	Leyton Orient	14	0		
1993–94	Leyton Orient	6	0		
1993–94	West Ham U	0	0		
1994–95	Leyton Orient	31	3		
1995–96	Leyton Orient	22	1		
1996–97	Leyton Orient	27	1		
1997–98	Leyton Orient	41	0		
1998–99	Leyton Orient	10	0	152	5
1998–99	Oxford U	4	0	4	0
1998–99	Notts Co	18	0		
1999–2000	Notts Co	33	1		
2000–01	Notts Co	16	0		
2001–02	Notts Co	17	0	84	1

WILKIE, Lee (D)   37 0
H: 6 4   W: 13 00   b.Dundee 20-4-80
Source: Downfield J. *Honours:* Scotland Under-21, 2 full caps.

1999–2000	Dundee	24	0		
2000–01	Dundee	9	0		
2000–01	Plymouth Arg	2	0	2	0
2001–02	Dundee	0	0	33	0
2001–02	Notts Co	2	0	2	0

Scholars
Appleby, Craig; Berry, Dean; Bostock, Daniel; Clarke, Ryan A; Commons, Spencer J; Cross, David B; Dunn, Mark A; Francis, Willis D; Harrad, Shaun; McCaul, Matthew J; Osborne, Calum G; Poznanski, Lee J; Richardson, Ben; Screaton, Iain P; Smith, Gregory M

OLDHAM ATH

ANDREWS, Wayne (F)   40 9
H: 5 10   W: 11 09   b.Paddington 25-11-77
Source: Trainee.

1995–96	Watford	1	0		
1996–97	Watford	25	4		
1997–98	Watford	2	0		
1998–99	Watford	0	0	28	4
1998–99	*Cambridge U*	2	0	2	0
1998–99	*Peterborough U*	10	5	10	5

From Chesham U

2001–02	Oldham Ath	0	0		

APPLEBY, Matty (M)   265 17
H: 5 10   W: 11 10   b.Middlesbrough 16-4-72
Source: Trainee.

1989–90	Newcastle U	0	0		
1990–91	Newcastle U	1	0		
1991–92	Newcastle U	18	0		
1992–93	Newcastle U	0	0		
1993–94	Newcastle U	1	0	20	0
1993–94	*Darlington*	10	1		
1994–95	Darlington	36	1		
1995–96	Darlington	43	6	89	8
1996–97	Barnsley	35	0		
1997–98	Barnsley	15	0		
1998–99	Barnsley	34	0		
1999–2000	Barnsley	36	5		
2000–01	Barnsley	19	2		
2001–02	Barnsley	0	0	139	7
2001–02	Oldham Ath	17	2	17	2

ARMSTRONG, Chris (D)   65 1
H: 5 9   W: 11 00   b.Newcastle 5-8-82
Source: Scholar. *Honours:* England Under-20.

2000–01	Bury	22	1		
2001–02	Bury	11	0	33	1
2001–02	Oldham Ath	32	0	32	0

BALMER, Stuart (D)   364 18
H: 6 0   W: 13 02   b.Falkirk 20-9-69
Source: Celtic BC. *Honours:* Scotland Schools, Youth.

1987–88	Celtic	0	0		
1988–89	Celtic	0	0		
1989–90	Celtic	0	0		
1990–91	Charlton Ath	24	0		
1991–92	Charlton Ath	18	0		
1992–93	Charlton Ath	45	2		
1993–94	Charlton Ath	31	1		
1994–95	Charlton Ath	29	2		
1995–96	Charlton Ath	32	1		
1996–97	Charlton Ath	32	2		
1997–98	Charlton Ath	16	0		
1998–99	Charlton Ath	0	0	227	8
1998–99	Wigan Ath	36	1		
1999–2000	Wigan Ath	41	2		
2000–01	Wigan Ath	24	1	101	4
2001–02	Oldham Ath	36	6	36	6

BAUDET, Julien (D)   20 1
H: 6 3   W: 12 08   b.St Martin D'heres 13-1-79
Source: Toulouse.

2001–02	Oldham Ath	20	1	20	1

BEHARALL, David (D)   38 1
H: 6 2   W: 11 12   b.Newcastle 8-3-79
Source: Trainee.

1997–98	Newcastle U	0	0		
1998–99	Newcastle U	4	0		
1999–2000	Newcastle U	2	0		
2000–01	Newcastle U	0	0	6	0
2001–02	Grimsby T	14	0	14	0
2001–02	Oldham Ath	18	1	18	1

BOSHELL, Daniel (M)   30 1
H: 5 11   W: 11 11   b.Bradford 30-5-81
Source: Trainee.

1998–99	Oldham Ath	0	0		
1999–2000	Oldham Ath	8	0		
2000–01	Oldham Ath	18	1		
2001–02	Oldham Ath	4	0	30	1

CARSS, Tony (M)   190 7
H: 5 10   W: 11 09   b.Alnwick 31-3-76
Source: Bradford C Trainee.

1994–95	Blackburn R	0	0		
1995–96	Darlington	28	2		
1996–97	Darlington	29	0	57	2
1997–98	Cardiff C	42	1	42	1
1998–99	Chesterfield	4	0		
1999–2000	Chesterfield	31	1	35	1
2000–01	Carlisle U	7	0	7	0
2000–01	Oldham Ath	35	2		
2001–02	Oldham Ath	14	1	49	3

CLEGG, Michael (D)   24 0
H: 5 8   W: 11 01   b.Ashton-under-Lyne 3-7-77
Source: Trainee. *Honours:* England Under-21.

1995–96	Manchester U	0	0		
1996–97	Manchester U	4	0		
1997–98	Manchester U	3	0		
1998–99	Manchester U	0	0		
1999–2000	Manchester U	2	0		
1999–2000	Ipswich T	3	0	3	0
1999–2000	Wigan Ath	6	0	6	0
2000–01	Manchester U	0	0		

Season	Club				
2001–02	Manchester U	0	0	9	0
2001–02	Oldham Ath	6	0	6	0

COLUSSO, Cristian‡ (M)   13 2
H: 5 9 W: 11 06 b.Buenos Aires 7-2-77

Season	Club				
2001–02	Oldham Ath	13	2	13	2

CORAZZIN, Carlo (F)   328 107
H: 5 10 W: 12 07 b.Canada 25-12-71
Source: Vancouver 86ers. *Honours:* Canada 54 full caps, 10 goals.

Season	Club				
1993–94	Cambridge U	28	10		
1994–95	Cambridge U	46	19		
1995–96	Cambridge U	31	10	105	39
1995–96	Plymouth Arg	6	1		
1996–97	Plymouth Arg	30	5		
1997–98	Plymouth Arg	38	16	74	22
1998–99	Northampton T	39	16		
1999–2000	Northampton T	39	14	78	30
2000–01	Oldham Ath	38	7		
2001–02	Oldham Ath	33	9	71	16

DUDLEY, Craig (F)   108 15
H: 5 11 W: 10 02 b.Ollerton 12-9-79
Source: Trainee. *Honours:* England Youth.

Season	Club				
1996–97	Notts Co	10	2		
1997–98	Notts Co	17	1		
1997–98	*Shrewsbury T*	4	0	4	0
1998–99	Notts Co	4	0	31	3
1998–99	*Hull C*	7	2	7	2
1998–99	Oldham Ath	0	0		
1999–2000	Oldham Ath	25	5		
1999–2000	*Chesterfield*	2	0	2	0
2000–01	Oldham Ath	26	4		
2001–02	Oldham Ath	9	1	60	10
2001–02	*Scunthorpe U*	4	0	4	0

DUXBURY, Lee (M)   525 62
H: 5 10 W: 10 07 b.Keighley 7-10-69
Source: Trainee.

Season	Club				
1988–89	Bradford C	1	0		
1989–90	Bradford C	12	1		
1989–90	*Rochdale*	10	0	10	0
1990–91	Bradford C	45	5		
1991–92	Bradford C	46	5		
1992–93	Bradford C	42	5		
1993–94	Bradford C	43	9		
1994–95	Bradford C	20	0		
1994–95	Huddersfield T	26	2		
1995–96	Huddersfield T	3	0	29	2
1995–96	Bradford C	30	4		
1996–97	Bradford C	33	3	272	32
1997–98	Oldham Ath	12	1		
1997–98	Oldham Ath	38	5		
1998–99	Oldham Ath	41	6		
1999–2000	Oldham Ath	43	4		
2000–01	Oldham Ath	40	8		
2001–02	Oldham Ath	40	4	214	8

EYRE, John (F)   255 70
H: 6 0 W: 12 06 b.Hull 9-10-74
Source: Trainee.

Season	Club				
1993–94	Oldham Ath	2	0		
1994–95	Oldham Ath	8	1		
1994–95	*Scunthorpe U*	9	8		
1995–96	Scunthorpe U	39	10		
1996–97	Scunthorpe U	42	8		
1997–98	Scunthorpe U	42	10		
1998–99	Scunthorpe U	41	15	173	51
1999–2000	Hull C	24	8		
2000–01	Hull C	28	5	52	13
2001–02	Oldham Ath	20	5	30	6

EYRES, David (M)   516 106
H: 5 11 W: 11 06 b.Liverpool 26-2-64
Source: Rhyl.

Season	Club				
1989–90	Blackpool	35	7		
1990–91	Blackpool	36	6		
1991–92	Blackpool	41	9		
1992–93	Blackpool	46	16	158	38
1993–94	Burnley	45	19		
1994–95	Burnley	39	8		
1995–96	Burnley	42	6		
1996–97	Burnley	36	3		
1997–98	Burnley	13	1	175	37
1997–98	Preston NE	28	4		
1998–99	Preston NE	34	8		
1999–2000	Preston NE	41	7		
2000–01	Preston NE	5	0	108	19
2000–01	Oldham Ath	30	3		
2001–02	Oldham Ath	45	9	75	12

FUTCHER, Ben‡ (D)   10 0
Source: Trainee.

Season	Club				
1999–2000	Oldham Ath	5	0		
2000–01	Oldham Ath	5	0		
2001–02	Oldham Ath	0	0	10	0

GARNETT, Shaun (D)   332 17
H: 6 2 W: 13 01 b.Wallasey 22-11-69
Source: Trainee.

Season	Club				
1987–88	Tranmere R	1	0		
1988–89	Tranmere R	0	0		
1989–90	Tranmere R	4	0		
1990–91	Tranmere R	16	1		
1991–92	Tranmere R	8	0		
1992–93	Tranmere R	5	1		
1992–93	*Chester C*	9	0	9	0
1992–93	*Preston NE*	10	2	10	2
1992–93	*Wigan Ath*	13	1	13	1
1993–94	Tranmere R	26	2		
1994–95	Tranmere R	34	1		
1995–96	Tranmere R	18	0	112	5
1995–96	Swansea C	9	0		
1996–97	Swansea C	6	0	15	0
1996–97	Oldham Ath	23	1		
1997–98	Oldham Ath	34	3		
1998–99	Oldham Ath	37	2		
1999–2000	Oldham Ath	32	2		
2000–01	Oldham Ath	39	1		
2001–02	Oldham Ath	8	0	173	9

GILL, Wayne (M)   33 9
H: 5 9 W: 11 00 b.Chorley 28-11-75
Source: Trainee.

Season	Club				
1994–95	Blackburn R	0	0		
1995–96	Blackburn R	0	0		
1996–97	Blackburn R	0	0		
1997–98	Blackburn R	0	0		
1997–98	*Dundee U*	2	0	2	0
1998–99	Blackburn R	0	0		
1999–2000	Blackburn R	0	0		
1999–2000	*Blackpool*	12	7	12	7
2000–01	Tranmere R	16	2		
2001–02	Tranmere R	0	0	16	2
2001–02	Oldham Ath	3	0	3	0

GRIFFIN, Adam§ (M)   1 0
H: 5 10 W: 11 02 b.Manchester 28-8-84
Source: Scholar.

Season	Club				
2001–02	Oldham Ath	1	0	1	0

HAINING, Will§ (D)   4 0
H: 6 0 W: 12 04 b.Glasgow 2-10-82
Source: Scholar.

Season	Club				
2001–02	Oldham Ath	4	0	4	0

HALL, Fitz (D)   4 1
H: 6 4 W: 12 01 b.Walthamstow 20-12-80
Source: Barnet Trainee, Chesham U.

Season	Club				
2001–02	Oldham Ath	4	1	4	1

HARDY, Lee* (M)   1 0
H: 5 11 W: 11 04 b.Blackpool 26-11-81
Source: Scholar.

Season	Club				
2000–01	Blackburn R	0	0		
2001–02	Oldham Ath	1	0	1	0

HOTTE, Mark‡ (M)   65 0
H: 5 11 W: 11 00 b.Bradford 27-9-78
Source: Trainee.

Season	Club				
1997–98	Oldham Ath	1	0		
1998–99	Oldham Ath	1	0		
1999–2000	Oldham Ath	35	0		
2000–01	Oldham Ath	28	0		
2001–02	Oldham Ath	0	0	65	0

JONES, Paul* (D)   28 3
H: 6 1 W: 11 09 b.Liverpool 3-6-78
Source: Trainee.

Season	Club				
1995–96	Tranmere R	0	0		
1996–97	Tranmere R	0	0		
1996–97	*Blackpool*	0	0		
From Barrow, Leigh RMI					
1999–2000	Oldham Ath	16	1		
2000–01	Oldham Ath	12	2		
2001–02	Oldham Ath	0	0	28	3

KELLY, Gary (G)   519 0
H: 5 11 W: 12 08 b.Fulwood 3-8-66
Source: Apprentice. *Honours:* Eire Under-21, B.

Season	Club				
1984–85	Newcastle U	0	0		
1985–86	Newcastle U	0	0		
1986–87	Newcastle U	3	0		
1987–88	Newcastle U	37	0		
1988–89	Newcastle U	9	0		
1988–89	*Blackpool*	5	0	5	0
1989–90	Newcastle U	4	0	53	0
1989–90	Bury	38	0		
1990–91	Bury	46	0		
1991–92	Bury	46	0		
1992–93	Bury	42	0		
1993–94	Bury	1	0		
1993–94	*West Ham U*	0	0		
1994–95	Bury	38	0		
1995–96	Bury	25	0	236	0
1996–97	Oldham Ath	42	0		
1997–98	Oldham Ath	26	0		
1998–99	Oldham Ath	45	0		
1999–2000	Oldham Ath	44	0		
2000–01	Oldham Ath	45	0		
2001–02	Oldham Ath	23	0	225	0

McNIVEN, Scott* (D)   222 3
H: 5 10 W: 10 08 b.Leeds 27-5-78
Source: Trainee. *Honours:* Scotland Youth, Under-21.

Season	Club				
1994–95	Oldham Ath	1	0		
1995–96	Oldham Ath	15	0		
1996–97	Oldham Ath	12	0		
1997–98	Oldham Ath	32	1		
1998–99	Oldham Ath	37	1		
1999–2000	Oldham Ath	45	1		
2000–01	Oldham Ath	45	0		
2001–02	Oldham Ath	35	0	222	3

MISKELLY, David (G)   9 0
H: 6 0 W: 12 02 b.Ards 3-9-79
Source: Trainee. *Honours:* Northern Ireland Youth, Under-21.

Season	Club				
1997–98	Oldham Ath	0	0		
1998–99	Oldham Ath	1	0		
1999–2000	Oldham Ath	2	0		
2000–01	Oldham Ath	2	0		
2001–02	Oldham Ath	4	0	9	0

MURRAY, Paul (M)   206 13
H: 5 8 W: 10 05 b.Carlisle 31-8-76
Source: Trainee. *Honours:* England Youth, Under-21, B.

Season	Club				
1993–94	Carlisle U	8	0		
1994–95	Carlisle U	5	0		
1995–96	Carlisle U	28	1	41	1
1995–96	QPR	1	0		
1996–97	QPR	32	5		
1997–98	QPR	32	1		
1998–99	QPR	39	1		
1999–2000	QPR	30	0		
2000–01	QPR	6	0	140	7
2001–02	Southampton	1	0	1	0
2001–02	Oldham Ath	24	5	24	5

PRENDERVILLE, Barry‡ (D)   49 2
H: 6 0 W: 12 08 b.Dublin 16-10-76
Source: Trainee.

Season	Club				
1994–95	Coventry C	0	0		
1995–96	Coventry C	0	0		
1996–97	Coventry C	0	0		
1997–98	Coventry C	0	0		
1998–99	Coventry C	0	0		
1998–99	*Hibernian*	13	2	13	2
1999–2000	*St Patrick's Ath*	15	0	15	0
2000–01	Oldham Ath	9	0		
2001–02	Oldham Ath	12	0	21	0

REEVES, David (F)   545 156
H: 6 0 W: 12 06 b.Birkenhead 19-11-67
Source: Heswall.

Season	Club				
1986–87	Sheffield W	0	0		
1986–87	Scunthorpe U	4	2		
1987–88	Sheffield W	0	0		
1987–88	Scunthorpe U	6	4	10	6
1987–88	*Burnley*	16	8	16	8
1988–89	Sheffield W	17	2	17	2
1989–90	Bolton W	41	10		
1990–91	Bolton W	44	10		
1991–92	Bolton W	35	8		
1992–93	Bolton W	14	1	134	29
1992–93	Notts Co	9	2		
1993–94	Notts Co	4	0	13	2
1993–94	Carlisle U	34	11		
1994–95	Carlisle U	42	21		
1995–96	Carlisle U	43	13		
1996–97	Carlisle U	8	3	127	48
1996–97	Preston NE	34	11		
1997–98	Preston NE	13	1	47	12
1997–98	Chesterfield	26	5		
1998–99	Chesterfield	40	10		
1999–2000	Chesterfield	43	14		
2000–01	Chesterfield	37	13		
2001–02	Chesterfield	22	4	168	46
2001–02	Oldham Ath	13	3	13	3

RICKERS, Paul* (M)   261 20
H: 5 10 W: 11 04 b.Dewsbury 9-5-75
Source: Trainee.

Season	Club				
1993–94	Oldham Ath	0	0		
1994–95	Oldham Ath	4	1		
1995–96	Oldham Ath	23	0		
1996–97	Oldham Ath	46	4		
1997–98	Oldham Ath	40	4		
1998–99	Oldham Ath	44	4		
1999–2000	Oldham Ath	41	3		
2000–01	Oldham Ath	38	2		
2001–02	Oldham Ath	24	2	261	20

SALT, Philip‡ (D)   22 0
H: 5 10 W: 11 02 b.Huddersfield 2-3-79
Source: Trainee.

Season	Club				
1997–98	Oldham Ath	2	0		
1998–99	Oldham Ath	9	0		
1999–2000	Oldham Ath	5	0		
2000–01	Oldham Ath	6	0		
2001–02	Oldham Ath	0	0	22	0

SHEPHERD, Paul‡ (D) 16 1
H: 5 11 W: 12 00 b.Leeds 17-11-77
Source: Trainee. Honours: England Youth.
1995–96 Leeds U 0 0
1996–97 Leeds U 1 0
1997–98 Leeds U 0 0
1997–98 *Ayr U* 6 1 6 1
1998–99 Leeds U 0 0
1998–99 *Tranmere R* 1 0 1 0
1999–2000 Leeds U 0 0 1 0
2000–01 Scunthorpe U 1 0 1 0
2000–01 Luton T 7 0 7 0
2001–02 Oldham Ath 0 0

SHERIDAN, Darren (M) 257 10
H: 5 6 W: 11 04 b.Manchester 8-12-67
Source: Winsford U.
1993–94 Barnsley 3 0
1994–95 Barnsley 35 2
1995–96 Barnsley 41 0
1996–97 Barnsley 41 2
1997–98 Barnsley 26 0
1998–99 Barnsley 25 1 171 5
1999–2000 Wigan Ath 31 3
2000–01 Wigan Ath 27 0 58 3
2001–02 Oldham Ath 28 2 28 2

SHERIDAN, John (M) 579 83
H: 5 10 W: 11 12 b.Stretford 1-10-64
Source: Local. Honours: Eire Youth, Under-21, Under-23, B, 34 full caps, 5 goals.
1981–82 Leeds U 0 0
1982–83 Leeds U 27 2
1983–84 Leeds U 11 1
1984–85 Leeds U 42 6
1985–86 Leeds U 32 4
1986–87 Leeds U 40 15
1987–88 Leeds U 38 12
1988–89 Leeds U 40 7 230 47
1989–90 Nottingham F 0 0
1989–90 Sheffield W 27 2
1990–91 Sheffield W 46 10
1991–92 Sheffield W 24 6
1992–93 Sheffield W 25 3
1993–94 Sheffield W 20 3
1994–95 Sheffield W 36 1
1995–96 Sheffield W 17 0
1995–96 *Birmingham C* 2 0 2 0
1996–97 Sheffield W 2 0 197 25
1996–97 Bolton W 20 2
1997–98 Bolton W 12 0 32 2
From Doncaster R
1998–99 Oldham Ath 30 2
1999–2000 Oldham Ath 36 1
2000–01 Oldham Ath 25 4
2001–02 Oldham Ath 27 2 118 9

SMART, Allan (F) 154 40
H: 6 2 W: 12 04 b.Perth 8-7-74
1994–95 Caledonian Th 4 0 4 0
1994–95 Preston NE 19 6
1995–96 Preston NE 2 0
1995–96 *Carlisle U* 4 0
1996–97 Preston NE 0 0 21 6
1996–97 *Northampton T* 1 0 1 0
1996–97 Carlisle U 28 10
1997–98 Carlisle U 16 6 48 16
1998–99 Watford 35 7
1999–2000 Watford 14 5
2000–01 Watford 8 0
2001–02 Watford 0 0 57 12
2001–02 *Stoke C* 2 0 2 0
2001–02 Oldham Ath 21 6 21 6

SMITH, Ben* (F) 0 0
H: 5 4 W: 10 07 b.Oldham 25-8-82
Source: Scholar.
2001–02 Oldham Ath 0 0

SUGDEN, Ryan‡ (F) 21 1
H: 6 0 W: 12 07 b.Bradford 26-12-80
1998–99 Oldham Ath 2 0
1999–2000 Oldham Ath 17 1
2000–01 Oldham Ath 2 0
2001–02 Oldham Ath 0 0 21 1

Scholars
Davenport, Michael J; Donnelly, Anthony M; Doran, Joseph R; Duncan, Kevin; Fleming, Craig M; Grange, Christopher D; Griffin, Adam; Haining, William W; Hall, Daniel A; Lavery, Karl A; O'Grady, Paul JO; Roca, Carlos J; Sutcliffe, Arren; Vernon, Scott M; Whittle, Thomas J; Yates, Daniel T

OXFORD U

ALEXIS, Michael (M) 0 0
b.Oxford 2-1-85
2001–02 Oxford U 0 0

BEAUCHAMP, Joey* (M) 412 68
H: 5 10 W: 12 12 b.Oxford 13-3-71
Source: Trainee.
1988–89 Oxford U 1 0
1989–90 Oxford U 3 0
1990–91 Oxford U 4 0
1991–92 Oxford U 27 7
1991–92 *Swansea C* 5 2 5 2
1992–93 Oxford U 44 7
1993–94 Oxford U 45 6
1994–95 West Ham U 0 0
1994–95 Swindon T 42 3
1995–96 Swindon T 3 0 45 3
1995–96 Oxford U 32 7
1996–97 Oxford U 45 7
1997–98 Oxford U 44 13
1998–99 Oxford U 37 4
1999–2000 Oxford U 34 4
2000–01 Oxford U 43 7
2001–02 Oxford U 3 1 362 63

BOLLAND, Phil‡ (D) 20 1
H: 6 4 W: 13 12 b.Liverpool 26-8-76
2001–02 Oxford U 20 1 20 1

BOUND, Matt (D) 256 15
H: 6 2 W: 14 06 b.Bradford-on-Avon 9-11-72
Source: Trainee.
1990–91 Southampton 1 0
1991–92 Southampton 0 0
1992–93 Southampton 3 0
1993–94 Southampton 1 0
1993–94 *Hull C* 7 1 7 1
1994–95 Southampton 0 0 5 0
1994–95 Stockport Co 14 0
1995–96 Stockport Co 26 5
1995–96 *Lincoln C* 4 0 4 0
1996–97 Stockport Co 4 0
1997–98 Stockport Co 0 0 44 5
1997–98 Swansea C 28 0
1998–99 Swansea C 45 2
1999–2000 Swansea C 43 2
2000–01 Swansea C 40 3
2001–02 Swansea C 18 2 174 9
2001–02 Oxford U 22 0 22 0

BROOKS, Jamie (F) 29 11
H: 5 9 W: 10 08 b.Oxford 12-8-83
Source: Scholar.
2000–01 Oxford U 4 1
2001–02 Oxford U 25 10 29 11

CROSBY, Andy (D) 368 13
H: 6 2 W: 13 13 b.Rotherham 3-3-73
Source: Leeds U Trainee.
1991–92 Doncaster R 22 0
1992–93 Doncaster R 29 0
1993–94 Doncaster R 0 0 51 0
1993–94 Darlington 25 0
1994–95 Darlington 35 0
1995–96 Darlington 45 1
1996–97 Darlington 42 1
1997–98 Darlington 34 1 181 3
1998–99 Chester C 41 4 41 4
1999–2000 Brighton & HA 36 3
2000–01 Brighton & HA 34 2
2001–02 Brighton & HA 0 2 72 5
2001–02 Oxford U 23 1 23 1

FOLLAND, Rob‡ (D) 40 2
H: 5 9 W: 10 07 b.Swansea 16-9-79
Source: Trainee. Honours: Wales Youth, Under-21.
1997–98 Oxford U 2 0
1998–99 Oxford U 0 0
1999–2000 Oxford U 23 1
2000–01 Oxford U 5 1
2001–02 Oxford U 10 0 40 2

GIBBENS, Kevin‡ (M) 11 0
H: 5 10 W: 13 06 b.Southampton 4-11-79
Source: Trainee.
1997–98 Southampton 2 0
1998–99 Southampton 4 0
1999–2000 Southampton 0 0
1999–2000 *Stockport Co* 2 0 2 0
2000–01 Southampton 3 0
2001–02 Southampton 0 0 9 0
2001–02 Oxford U 2 0

GRAY, Phil‡ (F) 347 94
H: 5 9 W: 12 07 b.Belfast 2-10-68
Source: Apprentice. Honours: Northern Ireland Schools, Youth, Under-23, 26 full caps, 6 goals.
1986–87 Tottenham H 0 0
1987–88 Tottenham H 1 0
1988–89 Tottenham H 1 0
1989–90 Tottenham H 6 0
1989–90 *Barnsley* 3 0 3 0
1990–91 Tottenham H 0 0 9 0

1990–91 Fulham 3 0 3 0
1991–92 Luton T 14 3
1992–93 Luton T 45 19
1993–94 Sunderland 41 14
1994–95 Sunderland 42 12
1995–96 Sunderland 32 8 115 34
1996–97 Nancy 16 4 16 4
1996–97 Fortuna Sittard 12 1 12 1
1997–98 Luton T 17 2
1998–99 Luton T 35 8
1999–2000 Luton T 29 11 140 43
2000–01 Burnley 5 1 5 1
2000–01 Oxford U 23 7
2001–02 Oxford U 21 4 44 11

GUYETT, Scott (D) 22 0
H: 6 2 W: 12 09 b.Ascot 20-1-76
2001–02 Oxford U 22 0 22 0

HACKETT, Chris (M) 33 2
H: 6 0 W: 11 09 b.Oxford 1-3-83
Source: Scholar.
1999–2000 Oxford U 2 0
2000–01 Oxford U 16 2
2001–02 Oxford U 15 0 33 2

HATSWELL, Wayne‡ (D) 48 0
H: 6 0 W: 13 10 b.Swindon 8-2-75
Source: Forest Green R.
2000–01 Oxford U 27 0
2001–02 Oxford U 21 0 48 0

HOLDER, Jorden‡ (M) 2 0
b.Oxford 22-10-82
Source: Scholar.
2000–01 Oxford U 2 0
2001–02 Oxford U 0 0 2 0

KING, Simon (D) 4 0
H: 6 0 W: 12 08 b.Oxford 11-4-83
Source: Scholar.
2000–01 Oxford U 2 0
2001–02 Oxford U 2 0 4 0

KNIGHT, Richard‡ (G) 60 0
H: 6 1 W: 13 11 b.Burton 3-8-79
Source: Burton Alb. Honours: England Youth.
1997–98 Derby Co 0 0
1998–99 Derby Co 0 0
1998–99 *Carlisle U* 6 0 6 0
1999–2000 *Birmingham C* 0 0
1999–2000 *Hull C* 1 0 1 0
1999–2000 *Macclesfield T* 3 0 3 0
1999–2000 *Oxford U* 13 0
2000–01 Oxford U 33 0
2001–02 Oxford U 3 0 49 0
2001–02 *Colchester U* 1 0 1 0

LOUIS, Jefferson (F) 1 0
H: 6 2 W: 14 12 b.Harrow 22-2-79
Source: Thame U.
2001–02 Oxford U 1 0 1 0

McCALDON, Ian (G) 108 0
H: 6 5 W: 16 00 b.Liverpool 14-9-74
Source: Glenafton Ath.
1996–97 Livingston 0 0
1997–98 Livingston 36 0
1998–99 Livingston 15 0
1999–2000 Livingston 23 0
2000–01 Livingston 6 0 80 0
2001–02 Oxford U 28 0 28 0

MOODY, Paul (F) 288 106
H: 6 3 W: 16 00 b.Portsmouth 13-6-67
Source: Waterlooville.
1991–92 Southampton 4 0
1992–93 Southampton 3 0
1992–93 *Reading* 5 1 5 1
1993–94 Southampton 5 0 12 0
1993–94 Oxford U 15 8
1994–95 Oxford U 41 20
1995–96 Oxford U 42 17
1996–97 Oxford U 38 4
1997–98 Fulham 33 15
1998–99 Fulham 7 4 40 19
1999–2000 Millwall 32 11
2000–01 Millwall 27 13
2001–02 Millwall 1 0 60 24
2001–02 Oxford U 35 13 171 62

MORLEY, Dave* (D) 142 5
H: 6 3 W: 13 11 b.St Helens 25-9-77
Source: Trainee.
1995–96 Manchester C 0 0
1996–97 Manchester C 0 0
1997–98 Manchester C 3 1
1997–98 *Ayr U* 4 0 4 0
1998–99 Manchester C 0 0 3 1
1998–99 Southend U 27 0
1999–2000 Southend U 32 0
2000–01 Southend U 17 0 76 0

Season	Club	A	G	Tot A	Tot G
2000–01	Carlisle U	23	1		
2001–02	Carlisle U	18	0	41	1
2001–02	Oxford U	18	3	18	3

OMOYINMI, Emmanuel (M)　　92　13
H: 5 7　W: 10 11　b.Nigeria 28-12-77
Source: Trainee. *Honours:* England Schools.

Season	Club	A	G	Tot A	Tot G
1994–95	West Ham U	0	0		
1995–96	West Ham U	0	0		
1996–97	West Ham U	1	0		
1996–97	*Bournemouth*	7	0	7	0
1997–98	West Ham U	5	2		
1997–98	*Dundee U*	4	0	4	0
1998–99	West Ham U	3	0		
1998–99	*Leyton Orient*	4	1	4	1
1999–2000	West Ham U	0	0	9	2
1999–2000	*Gillingham*	9	3	9	3
1999–2000	*Scunthorpe U*	6	1	6	1
1999–2000	*Barnet*	6	0	6	0
2000–01	Oxford U	24	3		
2001–02	Oxford U	23	3	47	6

PATTERSON, Darren‡ (D)　　222　8
H: 6 1　W: 12 10　b.Belfast 15-10-69
Source: Trainee. *Honours:* Northern Ireland Youth, Under-21, B, 17 full caps, 1 goal.

Season	Club	A	G	Tot A	Tot G
1988–89	WBA	0	0		
1989–90	Wigan Ath	29	1		
1990–91	Wigan Ath	28	4		
1991–92	Wigan Ath	40	1	97	6
1992–93	Crystal Palace	0	0		
1993–94	Crystal Palace	0	0		
1994–95	Crystal Palace	22	1	22	1
1995–96	Luton T	23	0		
1996–97	Luton T	10	0		
1996–97	*Preston NE*	2	0	2	0
1997–98	Luton T	23	0	56	0
1998–99	Dundee U	19	0		
1999–2000	Dundee U	0	0		
2000–01	Dundee U	0	0	19	0
2000–01	York C	6	0	6	0
2000–01	Oxford U	18	1		
2001–02	Oxford U	2	0	20	1

POWELL, Paul (M)　　164　15
H: 5 8　W: 12 02　b.Wallingford 30-6-78
Source: Trainee.

Season	Club	A	G	Tot A	Tot G
1995–96	Oxford U	3	0		
1996–97	Oxford U	0	0		
1997–98	Oxford U	21	1		
1998–99	Oxford U	44	3		
1999–2000	Oxford U	40	6		
2000–01	Oxford U	20	1		
2001–02	Oxford U	36	4	164	15

QUINN, Robert‡ (M)　　161　5
H: 6 0　W: 12 08　b.Sidcup 8-11-76
Source: Trainee.

Season	Club	A	G	Tot A	Tot G
1994–95	Crystal Palace	0	0		
1995–96	Crystal Palace	0	0		
1996–97	Crystal Palace	21	1		
1997–98	Crystal Palace	0	0	23	1
1998–99	Brentford	43	2		
1999–2000	Brentford	44	0		
2000–01	Brentford	22	0	109	2
2000–01	Oxford U	13	2		
2001–02	Oxford U	16	0	29	2

RICHARDSON, Jon‡ (D)　　306　10
H: 6 1　W: 12 02　b.Nottingham 29-8-75
Source: Trainee.

Season	Club	A	G	Tot A	Tot G
1993–94	Exeter C	7	0		
1994–95	Exeter C	38	1		
1995–96	Exeter C	43	1		
1996–97	Exeter C	43	1		
1997–98	Exeter C	41	2		
1998–99	Exeter C	40	2		
1999–2000	Exeter C	35	1	247	8
2000–01	Oxford U	41	2		
2001–02	Oxford U	18	0	59	2

RICKETTS, Sam (D)　　43　1
H: 6 1　W: 11 09　b.Wendover 11-10-81
Source: Trainee.

Season	Club	A	G	Tot A	Tot G
1999–2000	Oxford U	0	0		
2000–01	Oxford U	14	0		
2001–02	Oxford U	29	1	43	1

SAVAGE, David (M)　　287　25
H: 6 2　W: 13 06　b.Dublin 30-7-73
Source: Longford T. *Honours:* Eire Under-21, 5 full caps.

Season	Club	A	G	Tot A	Tot G
1994–95	Millwall	37	2		
1995–96	Millwall	27	0		
1996–97	Millwall	35	3		
1997–98	Millwall	31	1		
1998–99	Millwall	2	0	132	6
1998–99	Northampton T	27	5		
1999–2000	Northampton T	43	5		
2000–01	Northampton T	43	8	113	18
2001–02	Oxford U	42	1	42	1

SCOTT, Andy (F)　　257　50
H: 6 1　W: 12 03　b.Epsom 2-8-72
Source: Sutton U.

Season	Club	A	G	Tot A	Tot G
1992–93	Sheffield U	2	1		
1993–94	Sheffield U	15	0		
1994–95	Sheffield U	37	4		
1995–96	Sheffield U	7	0		
1996–97	Sheffield U	8	1		
1996–97	*Chesterfield*	5	3	5	3
1996–97	*Bury*	8	0	8	0
1997–98	Sheffield U	6	0	75	6
1997–98	Brentford	26	5		
1998–99	Brentford	34	7		
1999–2000	Brentford	36	3		
2000–01	Brentford	22	13	118	28
2000–01	Oxford U	21	5		
2001–02	Oxford U	30	8	51	13

SHEPHEARD, Jon‡ (D)　　7　0
H: 6 2　W: 12 04　b.Oxford 31-3-81
Source: Trainee.

Season	Club	A	G	Tot A	Tot G
1999–2000	Oxford U	2	0		
2000–01	Oxford U	5	0		
2001–02	Oxford U	0	0	7	0

STOCKLEY, Sam (D)　　223　2
H: 6 0　W: 12 08　b.Tiverton 5-9-77
Source: Trainee.

Season	Club	A	G	Tot A	Tot G
1996–97	Southampton	0	0		
1996–97	Barnet	21	0		
1997–98	Barnet	41	0		
1998–99	Barnet	41	0		
1999–2000	Barnet	34	1		
2000–01	Barnet	45	1	182	2
2001–02	Oxford U	41	0	41	0

SYLLA, Norman (M)　　0　0
b.Bondy 27-9-82

Season	Club	A	G	Tot A	Tot G
2001–02	Oxford U	0	0	0	0

TAIT, Paul‡ (M)　　264　17
H: 5 11　W: 11 10　b.Sutton Coldfield 31-7-71
Source: Trainee.

Season	Club	A	G	Tot A	Tot G
1987–88	Birmingham C	1	0		
1988–89	Birmingham C	10	0		
1989–90	Birmingham C	14	2		
1990–91	Birmingham C	17	3		
1991–92	Birmingham C	12	0		
1992–93	Birmingham C	28	2		
1993–94	Birmingham C	10	0		
1993–94	*Millwall*	0	0		
1994–95	Birmingham C	25	4		
1995–96	Birmingham C	27	3		
1996–97	Birmingham C	26	0		
1997–98	Birmingham C	0	0		
1997–98	*Northampton T*	3	0	3	0
1998–99	Birmingham C	0	0	170	14
1998–99	Oxford U	17	0		
1999–2000	Oxford U	34	0		
2000–01	Oxford U	26	3		
2001–02	Oxford U	14	0	91	3

THOMAS, Martin‡ (M)　　208　20
H: 5 8　W: 11 07　b.Lyndhurst 12-9-73
Source: Trainee.

Season	Club	A	G	Tot A	Tot G
1992–93	Southampton	0	0		
1993–94	Southampton	0	0		
1993–94	*Leyton Orient*	5	2	5	2
1994–95	Fulham	23	3		
1995–96	Fulham	37	5		
1996–97	Fulham	26	0		
1997–98	Fulham	4	0	90	8
1998–99	Swansea C	30	3		
1999–2000	Swansea C	40	4		
2000–01	Swansea C	21	1	91	8
2000–01	Brighton & HA	8	0	8	0
2001–02	Oxford U	14	2	14	2

WATERMAN, David (M)　　85　0
H: 5 11　W: 11 13　b.Guernsey 16-5-77
Source: Trainee. *Honours:* Northern Ireland Under-21.

Season	Club	A	G	Tot A	Tot G
1995–96	Portsmouth	0	0		
1996–97	Portsmouth	4	0		
1997–98	Portsmouth	15	0		
1998–99	Portsmouth	10	0		
1999–2000	Portsmouth	20	0		
2000–01	Portsmouth	22	0		
2001–02	Portsmouth	9	0	80	0
2001–02	Oxford U	5	0	5	0

WHITEHEAD, Dean (M)　　60　1
H: 6 0　W: 12 04　b.Oxford 12-1-82
Source: Trainee.

Season	Club	A	G	Tot A	Tot G
1999–2000	Oxford U	0	0		
2000–01	Oxford U	20	0		
2001–02	Oxford U	40	1	60	1

WILSON, Philip§ (G)　　2　0
H: 6 4　W: 14 04　b.Oxford 17-10-82
Source: Scholar.

Season	Club	A	G	Tot A	Tot G
2000–01	Oxford U	2	0		
2001–02	Oxford U	0	0	2	0

WOODMAN, Andy (G)　　316　0
H: 6 2　W: 14 08　b.Camberwell 11-8-71
Source: Apprentice.

Season	Club	A	G	Tot A	Tot G
1989–90	Crystal Palace	0	0		
1990–91	Crystal Palace	0	0		
1991–92	Crystal Palace	0	0		
1992–93	Crystal Palace	0	0		
1993–94	Crystal Palace	0	0		
1994–95	Exeter C	6	0	6	0
1994–95	Northampton T	10	0		
1995–96	Northampton T	44	0		
1996–97	Northampton T	45	0		
1997–98	Northampton T	46	0		
1998–99	Northampton T	18	0	163	0
1998–99	Brentford	22	0		
1999–2000	Brentford	39	0		
1999–2000	Peterborough U	0	0		
2000–01	Brentford	0	0	61	0
2000–01	*Southend U*	17	0	17	0
2000–01	Colchester U	28	0		
2001–02	Colchester U	26	0	54	0
2001–02	Oxford U	15	0	15	0

Scholars
Brandish, Matthew; Carbon, Josias; Ciampoli, Dwight M; Cruse, Robert P; Davis, Scott J; Garner, Adam R; Lovegrove, Robert T; McIntosh, Kelvin R; Spence, Brynley J; Wilson, Philip J

PETERBOROUGH U

BULLARD, Jimmy (M)　　40　8
H: 5 9　W: 10 00　b.Newham 23-10-78
Source: Corinthian, Dartford, Gravesend & N.

Season	Club	A	G	Tot A	Tot G
1998–99	West Ham U	0	0		
1999–2000	West Ham U	0	0		
2000–01	West Ham U	0	0		
2001–02	Peterborough U	40	8	40	8

CHAPPLE, Phil‡ (D)　　346　35
H: 6 2　W: 13 01　b.Norwich 21-11-66
Source: Apprentice.

Season	Club	A	G	Tot A	Tot G
1984–85	Norwich C	0	0		
1985–86	Norwich C	0	0		
1986–87	Norwich C	0	0		
1987–88	Norwich C	0	0		
1987–88	Cambridge U	6	1		
1988–89	Cambridge U	46	3		
1989–90	Cambridge U	45	5		
1990–91	Cambridge U	45	5		
1991–92	Cambridge U	45	5	187	19
1992–93	Charlton Ath	44	5		
1993–94	Charlton Ath	21	2		
1994–95	Charlton Ath	16	2		
1995–96	Charlton Ath	26	2		
1996–97	Charlton Ath	35	4	142	15
1997–98	Peterborough U	1	0		
1998–99	Peterborough U	16	1		
1999–2000	Peterborough U	0	0		
2000–01	Peterborough U	0	0	17	1

CLARKE, Andy# (F)　　287　46
H: 5 10　W: 11 07　b.Islington 22-7-67
Source: Barnet.

Season	Club	A	G	Tot A	Tot G
1990–91	Wimbledon	12	3		
1991–92	Wimbledon	34	3		
1992–93	Wimbledon	33	5		
1993–94	Wimbledon	23	2		
1994–95	Wimbledon	25	1		
1995–96	Wimbledon	18	2		
1996–97	Wimbledon	11	1		
1997–98	Wimbledon	14	0		
1998–99	Wimbledon	0	0	170	17
1998–99	*Port Vale*	6	0	6	0
1998–99	*Northampton T*	4	0	4	0
1998–99	Peterborough U	0	0		
1999–2000	Peterborough U	37	15		
2000–01	Peterborough U	42	9		
2001–02	Peterborough U	28	5	107	29

CLARKE, Lee (F)　　1　0
H: 5 11　W: 10 08　b.Peterborough 28-7-83
Source: Yaxley.

Season	Club	A	G	Tot A	Tot G
2001–02	Peterborough U	1	0	1	0

CONNOR, Dan (G)　　4　0
H: 6 2　W: 13 04　b.Dublin 31-1-81
Source: Trainee.

Season	Club	A	G	Tot A	Tot G
1997–98	Peterborough U	0	0		
1998–99	Peterborough U	2	0		
1999–2000	Peterborough U	1	0		

2000–01 Peterborough U 0 0
2001–02 Peterborough U 1 0 **4 0**

CULLEN, Jon (M) 123 23
H: 6 0 W: 13 00 b.Durham 10-1-73
Source: Trainee.
1990–91 Doncaster R 1 0
1991–92 Doncaster R 8 0
1992–93 Doncaster R 0 0
1993–94 Doncaster R 0 0 **9 0**
From Morpeth T
1996–97 Hartlepool U 6 0
1997–98 Hartlepool U 28 12 **34 12**
1997–98 Sheffield U 2 0
1998–99 Sheffield U 2 0
1999–2000 Sheffield U 0 0 **4 0**
1999–2000 *Shrewsbury T* 10 1 **10 1**
1999–2000 *Halifax T* 11 5 **11 5**
1999–2000 Peterborough U 13 3
2000–01 Peterborough U 18 1
2000–01 *Carlisle U* 11 0 **11 0**
2001–02 Peterborough U 13 1 **44 5**

DANIELSSON, Helgi (M) 37 2
H: 6 0 W: 12 00 b.Reykjavik 13-7-81
Source: Fylkir. *Honours:* Iceland 1 full cap.
1998–99 Peterborough U 0 0
1999–2000 Peterborough U 0 0
2000–01 Peterborough U 6 0
2001–02 Peterborough U 31 2 **37 2**

EDWARDS, Andy (D) 430 15
H: 6 2 W: 12 13 b.Epping 17-9-71
Source: Trainee.
1988–89 Southend U 1 0
1989–90 Southend U 8 0
1990–91 Southend U 2 1
1991–92 Southend U 9 0
1992–93 Southend U 41 0
1993–94 Southend U 42 1
1994–95 Southend U 44 3 **147 5**
1995–96 Birmingham C 37 1
1996–97 Birmingham C 3 0 **40 1**
1996–97 Peterborough U 25 0
1997–98 Peterborough U 46 2
1998–99 Peterborough U 41 2
1999–2000 Peterborough U 44 2
2000–01 Peterborough U 43 1
2001–02 Peterborough U 44 2 **243 9**

FARRELL, Dave (M) 267 35
H: 5 11 W: 11 08 b.Birmingham 11-11-71
Source: Redditch U.
1992–93 Aston Villa 2 0
1992–93 *Scunthorpe U* 5 1 **5 1**
1993–94 Aston Villa 4 0
1994–95 Aston Villa 0 0
1995–96 Aston Villa 0 0 **6 0**
1995–96 Wycombe W 33 7
1996–97 Wycombe W 27 1 **60 8**
1997–98 Peterborough U 42 6
1998–99 Peterborough U 37 4
1999–2000 Peterborough U 35 3
2000–01 Peterborough U 44 7
2001–02 Peterborough U 38 6 **196 26**

FENN, Neale (F) 62 7
H: 5 9 W: 10 12 b.Edmonton 18-1-77
Source: Trainee. *Honours:* Eire Youth, Under-21.
1995–96 Tottenham H 0 0
1996–97 Tottenham H 4 0
1997–98 Tottenham H 4 0
1997–98 *Leyton Orient* 3 0 **3 0**
1997–98 *Norwich C* 7 1 **7 1**
1998–99 Tottenham H 0 0
1998–99 *Swindon T* 4 0 **4 0**
1998–99 *Lincoln C* 4 0 **4 0**
1999–2000 Tottenham H 0 0
2000–01 Tottenham H 0 0 **8 0**
2001–02 Peterborough U 36 6 **36 6**

FORINTON, Howard (F) 64 14
H: 5 11 W: 12 04 b.Boston 18-9-75
Source: Yeovil T.
1997–98 Birmingham C 1 0
1998–99 Birmingham C 3 1
1998–99 *Plymouth Arg* 9 3 **9 3**
1999–2000 Birmingham C 1 0 **5 1**
1999–2000 Peterborough U 25 7
2000–01 Peterborough U 8 1
2001–02 Peterborough U 17 2 **50 10**

FORSYTH, Richard (M) 196 21
H: 5 11 W: 13 00 b.Dudley 3-10-70
Source: Kidderminster H.
1995–96 Birmingham C 26 2 **26 2**
1996–97 Stoke C 40 8
1997–98 Stoke C 37 7
1998–99 Stoke C 18 2 **95 17**
1999–2000 Blackpool 13 0 **13 0**
2000–01 Peterborough U 30 2
2001–02 Peterborough U 32 0 **62 2**

FRENCH, Daniel (M) 18 1
H: 5 11 W: 11 00 b.Peterborough 25-11-79
Source: Trainee.
1998–99 Peterborough U 0 0
1999–2000 Peterborough U 6 0
2000–01 Peterborough U 2 0
2001–02 Peterborough U 10 1 **18 1**

GILL, Matthew (M) 77 4
H: 5 11 W: 11 07 b.Cambridge 8-11-80
Source: Trainee.
1997–98 Peterborough U 2 0
1998–99 Peterborough U 26 0
1999–2000 Peterborough U 20 1
2000–01 Peterborough U 17 1
2001–02 Peterborough U 12 2 **77 4**

GREEN, Francis (F) 86 12
H: 5 9 W: 11 04 b.Derby 23-4-80
Source: Ilkeston T.
1997–98 Peterborough U 4 1
1998–99 Peterborough U 7 1
1999–2000 Peterborough U 20 1
2000–01 Peterborough U 32 6
2001–02 Peterborough U 23 3 **86 12**

HOOPER, Dean‡ (D) 121 2
H: 5 11 W: 12 06 b.Harefield 13-4-71
Source: Hayes.
1994–95 Swindon T 4 0
From Hayes
1995–96 Swindon T 0 0
1995–96 *Peterborough U* 4 0
1996–97 Swindon T 0 0
1997–98 Swindon T 0 0 **4 0**
From Kingstonian.
1998–99 Peterborough U 38 2
1999–2000 Peterborough U 29 0
2000–01 Peterborough U 33 0
2001–02 Peterborough U 13 0 **117 2**

JELLEYMAN, Gareth (D) 38 0
H: 5 10 W: 10 03 b.Holywell 14-11-80
Source: Trainee. *Honours:* Wales Youth, Under-21.
1998–99 Peterborough U 0 0
1999–2000 Peterborough U 20 0
2000–01 Peterborough U 8 0
2001–02 Peterborough U 10 0 **38 0**

JOSEPH, Marc (D) 197 2
H: 6 2 W: 10 07 b.Leicester 10-11-76
Source: Trainee.
1995–96 Cambridge U 12 0
1996–97 Cambridge U 8 0
1997–98 Cambridge U 41 0
1998–99 Cambridge U 29 0
1999–2000 Cambridge U 33 0
2000–01 Cambridge U 30 0 **153 0**
2001–02 Peterborough U 44 2 **44 2**

LAURIE, Steve (D) 0 0
H: 6 3 W: 13 00 b.Melbourne 30-10-82
1999–2000 West Ham U 0 0
2000–01 West Ham U 0 0
2001–02 West Ham U 0 0
2001–02 Peterborough U 0 0

LEE, Jason (F) 329 68
H: 6 3 W: 13 03 b.Newham 9-5-71
Source: Trainee.
1989–90 Charlton Ath 1 0
1990–91 Charlton Ath 0 0
1990–91 *Stockport Co* 2 0 **2 0**
1990–91 Lincoln C 17 3
1991–92 Lincoln C 35 6
1992–93 Lincoln C 41 12 **93 21**
1993–94 Southend U 24 3 **24 3**
1993–94 Nottingham F 13 2
1994–95 Nottingham F 22 3
1995–96 Nottingham F 28 8
1996–97 Nottingham F 13 1 **76 14**
1996–97 *Charlton Ath* 8 3 **9 3**
1996–97 *Grimsby T* 7 1 **7 1**
1997–98 Watford 36 10
1998–99 Watford 1 1 **37 11**
1998–99 Chesterfield 22 1
1999–2000 Chesterfield 6 0 **28 1**
1999–2000 Peterborough U 23 6
2000–01 Peterborough U 30 8
2001–02 Peterborough U 0 0 **53 14**

MACDONALD, Gary (M) 9 1
H: 6 1 W: 12 00 b.Germany 25-10-79
1998–99 Portsmouth 0 0
1999–2000 Portsmouth 0 0
2000–01 Portsmouth 0 0
From Havant & W.
2000–01 Peterborough U 1 0
2001–02 Peterborough U 8 1 **9 1**

McKENZIE, Leon (F) 162 46
H: 5 10 W: 10 03 b.Croydon 17-5-78
Source: Trainee.
1995–96 Crystal Palace 12 0
1996–97 Crystal Palace 21 2
1997–98 Crystal Palace 3 0
1997–98 *Fulham* 3 0 **3 0**
1998–99 Crystal Palace 16 1
1998–99 *Peterborough U* 14 8
1999–2000 Crystal Palace 25 4
2000–01 Crystal Palace 8 0 **85 7**
2000–01 Peterborough U 30 13
2001–02 Peterborough U 30 18 **74 39**

MURRAY, Dan (D) 5 0
H: 6 2 W: 12 12 b.Cambridge 16-5-82
Source: Scholar.
1999–2000 Peterborough U 2 0
2000–01 Peterborough U 3 0
2001–02 Peterborough U 0 0 **5 0**

OLDFIELD, David* (M) 520 71
H: 6 1 W: 13 04 b.Perth (Aus) 30-5-68
Source: Apprentice. *Honours:* England Under-21.
1986–87 Luton T 0 0
1987–88 Luton T 8 3
1988–89 Luton T 21 1
1988–89 Manchester C 11 3
1989–90 Manchester C 15 3 **26 6**
1989–90 Leicester C 20 5
1990–91 Leicester C 42 7
1991–92 Leicester C 41 4
1992–93 Leicester C 44 5
1993–94 Leicester C 27 4
1994–95 Leicester C 14 1 **188 26**
1994–95 *Millwall* 17 6 **17 6**
1995–96 Luton T 34 2
1996–97 Luton T 38 6
1997–98 Luton T 45 10 **146 22**
1998–99 Stoke C 46 6
1999–2000 Stoke C 19 1 **65 7**
1999–2000 Peterborough U 9 0
2000–01 Peterborough U 39 3
2001–02 Peterborough U 30 1 **78 4**

PEARCE, Dennis (D) 136 3
H: 6 0 W: 11 07 b.Wolverhampton 10-9-74
Source: Trainee.
1993–94 Aston Villa 0 0
1994–95 Aston Villa 0 0
1995–96 Wolverhampton W 5 0
1996–97 Wolverhampton W 4 0 **9 0**
1997–98 Notts Co 38 2
1998–99 Notts Co 33 1
1999–2000 Notts Co 20 0
2000–01 Notts Co 27 0 **118 3**
2000–01 Peterborough U 0 0
2001–02 Peterborough U 9 0 **9 0**

REA, Simon (D) 81 4
H: 6 1 W: 13 00 b.Coventry 20-9-76
Source: Trainee.
1994–95 Birmingham C 0 0
1995–96 Birmingham C 1 0
1996–97 Birmingham C 0 0
1997–98 Birmingham C 0 0
1998–99 Birmingham C 0 0
1999–2000 Birmingham C 0 0 **1 0**
1999–2000 Peterborough U 14 1
2000–01 Peterborough U 36 2
2001–02 Peterborough U 30 1 **80 4**

SHIELDS, Tony (M) 82 2
H: 5 8 W: 10 01 b.Derry 4-6-80
Source: Trainee.
1997–98 Peterborough U 1 0
1998–99 Peterborough U 9 0
1999–2000 Peterborough U 24 1
2000–01 Peterborough U 33 1
2001–02 Peterborough U 15 0 **82 2**

SHOWLER, Paul (M) 186 33
H: 5 10 W: 11 00 b.Doncaster 10-10-66
Source: Sheffield W, Sunderland, Colne Dynamoes, Altrincham.
1991–92 Barnet 39 7
1992–93 Barnet 32 5 **71 12**
1993–94 Bradford C 32 5
1994–95 Bradford C 23 2
1995–96 Bradford C 33 8 **88 15**
1996–97 Luton T 23 6
1997–98 Luton T 1 0
1998–99 Luton T 3 0 **27 6**
1999–2000 Peterborough U 0 0
2000–01 Peterborough U 0 0
2001–02 Peterborough U 0 0

TOLLEY, Shane (F) 0 0
H: 5 8 W: 10 00 b.Devon 18-2-85
Source: Scholar. *Honours:* England Youth.
2001–02 Peterborough U 0 0

TYLER, Mark (G) 197 0
H: 5 11 W: 12 00 b.Norwich 2-4-77
Source: Trainee. *Honours:* England Youth.
1994–95	Peterborough U	5	0
1995–96	Peterborough U	0	0
1996–97	Peterborough U	3	0
1997–98	Peterborough U	46	0
1998–99	Peterborough U	27	0
1999–2000	Peterborough U	32	0
2000–01	Peterborough U	40	0
2001–02	Peterborough U	44	0 197 0

Scholars
Bishop, James; Bowater, Graham J; Brennan, Killian E; Brewster, Jorden; Cobb, Stuart D; De'Ath, Frederick AB; Frew, Michael A; Fry, Adam G; Hutton, Rory N; Judge, Liam; Last, Guy D; Semple, Ryan D; St Ledger-Hall, Sean P; Thomas, Bradley M; Thompson, Craig
Player who does not hold a current contract but his registration has been retained by the club
Lehtinen, Tony

PLYMOUTH ARG

ADAMS, Steve (M) 64 2
H: 6 0 W: 12 01 b.Plymouth 25-9-80
Source: Trainee.
1999–2000	Plymouth Arg	1	0
2000–01	Plymouth Arg	17	0
2001–02	Plymouth Arg	46	2 64 2

BANCE, Danny§ (D) 1 0
H: 5 10 W: 11 07 b.Plymouth 27-9-82
Source: Scholar.
2000–01	Plymouth Arg	1	0
2001–02	Plymouth Arg	0	0 1 0

BASTOW, Darren (M) 42 3
H: 5 11 W: 12 00 b.Torquay 22-12-81
Source: Trainee.
1998–99	Plymouth Arg	29	2
1999–2000	Plymouth Arg	13	1
2000–01	Plymouth Arg	0	0
2001–02	Plymouth Arg	0	0 42 3

BENT, Jason (M) 79 5
H: 5 9 W: 11 11 b.Toronto 8-3-77
Honours: Canada 29 full caps.
1998	Colorado Rapids	14	0
1999	Colorado Rapids	20	0
2000	Colorado Rapids	24	2 58 2
2001–02	Plymouth Arg	21	3 21 3

BESWETHERICK, John# (D) 146 0
H: 5 11 W: 11 04 b.Liverpool 15-1-78
Source: Trainee.
1996–97	Plymouth Arg	0	0
1997–98	Plymouth Arg	2	0
1998–99	Plymouth Arg	22	0
1999–2000	Plymouth Arg	45	0
2000–01	Plymouth Arg	45	0
2001–02	Plymouth Arg	32	0 146 0

BROAD, Joseph (M) 7 0
H: 5 11 W: 12 07 b.Bristol 24-8-82
Source: Trainee.
2000–01	Plymouth Arg	0	0
2001–02	Plymouth Arg	7	0 7 0

CONNOLLY, Paul (D) 1 0
H: 6 0 W: 11 09 b.Liverpool 29-9-83
Source: Scholar.
2000–01	Plymouth Arg	1	0
2001–02	Plymouth Arg	0	0 1 0

COUGHLAN, Graham (D) 105 13
H: 6 2 W: 13 04 b.Dublin 18-11-74
Source: Bray Wanderers.
1995–96	Blackburn R	0	0
1996–97	Blackburn R	0	0
1996–97	*Swindon T*	3	0 3 0
1997–98	Blackburn R	0	0
1998–99	Livingston	6	0
1999–2000	Livingston	29	0
2000–01	Livingston	21	2 56 2
2001–02	Plymouth Arg	46	11 46 11

EVANS, Micky (F) 317 63
H: 6 0 W: 13 00 b.Plymouth 1-1-73
Source: Trainee. *Honours:* Eire 1 full cap.
1990–91	Plymouth Arg	4	0
1991–92	Plymouth Arg	13	0
1992–93	Plymouth Arg	23	1
1992–93	*Blackburn R*	0	0
1993–94	Plymouth Arg	22	9
1994–95	Plymouth Arg	23	4
1995–96	Plymouth Arg	45	12
1996–97	Plymouth Arg	33	12
1996–97	Southampton	12	4

1997–98	Southampton	10	0 22 4
1997–98	WBA	10	1
1998–99	WBA	20	2
1999–2000	WBA	33	3
2000–01	WBA	0	0 63 6
2000–01	Bristol R	21	4 21 4
2000–01	Plymouth Arg	10	4
2001–02	Plymouth Arg	38	7 211 49

EVERS, Sean (M) 84 6
H: 5 10 W: 9 07 b.Hitchin 10-10-77
Source: Trainee.
1995–96	Luton T	1	0
1996–97	Luton T	1	0
1997–98	Luton T	23	3
1998–99	Luton T	27	3 52 6
1998–99	Reading	1	0
1999–2000	Reading	17	0
2000–01	Reading	0	0 18 0
2000–01	Plymouth Arg	7	0
2001–02	Plymouth Arg	7	0 14 0

FRIIO, David (M) 67 13
H: 6 0 W: 11 07 b.Thionville 17-2-73
Source: Epinal, Nimes, ASOA Valence.
2000–01	Plymouth Arg	26	5
2001–02	Plymouth Arg	41	8 67 13

GRITTON, Martin (F) 44 7
H: 6 1 W: 12 02 b.Glasgow 1-6-78
Source: Porthleven.
1998–99	Plymouth Arg	2	0
1999–2000	Plymouth Arg	30	6
2000–01	Plymouth Arg	10	1
2001–02	Plymouth Arg	2	0 44 7

HEANEY, Neil (F) 167 15
H: 5 9 W: 11 06 b.Middlesbrough 3-11-71
Source: Trainee. *Honours:* England Youth, Under-21.
1989–90	Arsenal	0	0
1990–91	Arsenal	0	0
1990–91	*Hartlepool U*	3	0 3 0
1991–92	Arsenal	1	0
1991–92	*Cambridge U*	13	4 13 4
1992–93	Arsenal	5	0
1993–94	Arsenal	1	0 7 0
1993–94	Southampton	2	0
1994–95	Southampton	34	2
1995–96	Southampton	17	2
1996–97	Southampton	8	1 61 5
1996–97	Manchester C	15	1
1997–98	Manchester C	3	0
1997–98	*Charlton Ath*	6	0 6 0
1998–99	Manchester C	0	0 18 1
1998–99	*Bristol C*	3	0 3 0
1999–2000	Darlington	36	5 36 5
2000–01	Dundee U	12	0
2001–02	Dundee U	0	0 12 0
2001–02	Plymouth Arg	8	0 8 0

HODGES, Lee (M) 244 44
H: 6 0 W: 12 01 b.Epping 4-9-73
Source: Trainee.
1991–92	Tottenham H	0	0
1992–93	Tottenham H	4	0
1992–93	*Plymouth Arg*	7	2
1993–94	Tottenham H	0	0 4 0
1993–94	*Wycombe W*	4	0 4 0
1994–95	Barnet	34	4
1995–96	Barnet	40	17
1996–97	Barnet	31	5 105 26
1997–98	Reading	24	6
1998–99	Reading	1	0
1999–2000	Reading	25	2
2000–01	Reading	29	2
2001–02	Reading	0	0 79 10
2001–02	Plymouth Arg	45	6 52 8

KEITH, Marino (F) 110 43
H: 5 10 W: 12 12 b.Peterhead 16-12-74
Source: Fraserburgh.
1995–96	Dundee U	4	0
1996–97	Dundee U	0	0 4 0
1997–98	Falkirk	32	10
1998–99	Falkirk	29	17 61 27
1999–2000	Livingston	9	4
2000–01	Livingston	13	3 22 7
2001–02	Plymouth Arg	23	9 23 9

LARRIEU, Romain (G) 60 0
H: 6 2 W: 13 00 b.Mont-de-Marsan 31-8-76
Source: Montpellier, ASOA Valence.
2000–01	Plymouth Arg	15	0
2001–02	Plymouth Arg	45	0 60 0

MALONGA, Marly‡ (M) 0 0
b.Pointe Noire 20-8-81
2001–02	Plymouth Arg	0	0

McCORMICK, Luke§ (G) 1 0
H: 6 0 W: 13 12 b.Coventry 15-8-83
Source: Scholar.
2000–01	Plymouth Arg	1	0
2001–02	Plymouth Arg	0	0 1 0

McGLINCHEY, Brian (D) 78 3
H: 5 6 W: 10 02 b.Derry 26-10-77
Source: Trainee. *Honours:* Northern Ireland Youth, Under-21, B.
1995–96	Manchester C	0	0
1996–97	Manchester C	0	0
1997–98	Manchester C	0	0
1998–99	Port Vale	15	1 15 1
1999–2000	Gillingham	13	1
2000–01	Gillingham	1	0 14 1
2000–01	Plymouth Arg	20	0
2001–02	Plymouth Arg	29	1 49 1

PHILLIPS, Martin (M) 185 13
H: 5 6 W: 12 08 b.Exeter 13-3-76
Source: Trainee.
1992–93	Exeter C	6	0
1993–94	Exeter C	9	0
1994–95	Exeter C	24	2
1995–96	Exeter C	13	3
1995–96	Manchester C	11	0
1996–97	Manchester C	4	0
1997–98	Manchester C	0	0
1997–98	*Scunthorpe U*	3	0 3 0
1997–98	*Exeter C*	8	0 60 5
1998–99	Manchester C	0	0 15 0
1998–99	Portsmouth	17	1
1998–99	*Bristol R*	2	0 2 0
1999–2000	Portsmouth	7	0 24 1
2000–01	Plymouth Arg	42	1
2001–02	Plymouth Arg	39	6 81 7

STONEBRIDGE, Ian (F) 104 28
H: 6 0 W: 11 04 b.Lewisham 30-8-81
Source: Tottenham H Trainee. *Honours:* England Youth.
1999–2000	Plymouth Arg	31	9
2000–01	Plymouth Arg	31	11
2001–02	Plymouth Arg	42	8 104 28

STURROCK, Blair (M) 46 7
H: 6 0 W: 11 01 b.Dundee 25-8-81
Source: Dundee U.
2000–01	Brechin C	27	6 27 6
2001–02	Plymouth Arg	19	1 19 1

TAYLOR, Craig (D) 142 9
H: 6 1 W: 13 02 b.Plymouth 24-1-74
Source: Dorchester T.
1996–97	Swindon T	0	0
1997–98	Swindon T	32	2
1998–99	Swindon T	21	0
1998–99	*Plymouth Arg*	6	1
1999–2000	Swindon T	2	0 55 2
1999–2000	Plymouth Arg	41	3
2000–01	Plymouth Arg	39	3
2001–02	Plymouth Arg	1	0 87 7

TRUDGIAN, Ryan (M) 1 0
H: 6 0 W: 11 01 b.Truro 15-9-83
Source: Scholar.
2000–01	Plymouth Arg	0	0
2001–02	Plymouth Arg	0	0 1 0

WILLS, Kevin (M) 32 1
H: 5 9 W: 10 04 b.Torbay 15-10-80
Source: Trainee.
1998–99	Plymouth Arg	2	0
1999–2000	Plymouth Arg	2	0
2000–01	Plymouth Arg	10	1
2001–02	Plymouth Arg	18	0 32 1

WORRELL, David (D) 73 0
H: 5 11 W: 11 08 b.Dublin 12-1-78
Source: Trainee. *Honours:* Eire Youth, Under-21.
1994–95	Blackburn R	0	0
1995–96	Blackburn R	0	0
1996–97	Blackburn R	0	0
1997–98	Blackburn R	0	0
1998–99	Dundee U	4	0
1999–2000	Dundee U	13	0 17 0
2000–01	Plymouth Arg	14	0
2001–02	Plymouth Arg	42	0 56 0

WOTTON, Paul (D) 198 12
H: 5 11 W: 11 01 b.Plymouth 17-8-77
Source: Trainee.
1994–95	Plymouth Arg	7	0
1995–96	Plymouth Arg	1	0
1996–97	Plymouth Arg	9	1
1997–98	Plymouth Arg	34	1
1998–99	Plymouth Arg	36	1
1999–2000	Plymouth Arg	23	0
2000–01	Plymouth Arg	42	4
2001–02	Plymouth Arg	46	5 198 12

Scholars
Baker, Paul M; Bance, Daniel R; Barwick, Jake W; Coxon, Lee D; Curtis, Karl G; Edwards, Darren P; Fice, Ryan P; Guppy, Robert A; Martin, Marcus AP; McCormick, Luke M; McGowan, Jamie P; McGowan, Matthew J; Sawyer, Gary D; Steward, Benjamin L; Sundercombe, Thomas J; Teagle, Robin D; Yetton, Stewart D
Players who do not hold a current contract but their registration has been retained by the club
Bastow, Darren; Connolly, Paul; Trudgian, Ryan

PORTSMOUTH

ALLEN, Rory (F)   44 11
H: 5 11 W: 11 10 b.Beckenham 17-10-77
Source: Trainee. *Honours:* England Under-21.

1995–96	Tottenham H	0	0		
1996–97	Tottenham H	12	2		
1997–98	Tottenham H	4	0		
1997–98	Luton T	8	6	8	6
1998–99	Tottenham H	5	0	21	2
1999–2000	Portsmouth	15	3		
2000–01	Portsmouth	0	0		
2001–02	Portsmouth	0	0	15	3

BARRETT, Neil (M)   26 2
H: 5 10 W: 11 00 b.Tooting 24-12-81
Source: Chelsea. *Honours:* England Schools.

2001–02	Portsmouth	26	2	26	2

BEASANT, Dave* (G)   757 0
H: 6 4 W: 14 02 b.Willesden 20-3-59
Source: Edgware T. *Honours:* England B, 2 full caps.

1979–80	Wimbledon	2	0		
1980–81	Wimbledon	34	0		
1981–82	Wimbledon	46	0		
1982–83	Wimbledon	46	0		
1983–84	Wimbledon	46	0		
1984–85	Wimbledon	42	0		
1985–86	Wimbledon	42	0		
1986–87	Wimbledon	42	0		
1987–88	Wimbledon	40	0	340	0
1988–89	Newcastle U	20	0	20	0
1988–89	Chelsea	22	0		
1989–90	Chelsea	38	0		
1990–91	Chelsea	35	0		
1991–92	Chelsea	21	0		
1992–93	Chelsea	17	0		
1992–93	*Grimsby T*	6	0	6	0
1992–93	*Wolverhampton W*	4	0	4	0
1993–94	Chelsea	0	0	133	0
1993–94	Southampton	25	0		
1994–95	Southampton	13	0		
1995–96	Southampton	36	0		
1996–97	Southampton	14	0		
1997–98	Southampton	0	0	88	0
1997–98	Nottingham F	41	0		
1998–99	Nottingham F	26	0		
1999–2000	Nottingham F	27	0		
2000–01	Nottingham F	45	0	139	0
2001–02	Portsmouth	27	0	27	0

BIAGINI, Leo* (F)   176 26
H: 6 0 W: 11 11 b.Arroyo Seco 13-4-77

1993–94	Newell's Old Boys	10	1		
1994–95	Newell's Old Boys	23	4	33	5
1995–96	Atletico Madrid	26	4		
1996–97	Atletico Madrid	21	1	47	5
1997–98	Merida	27	1	27	1
1998–99	Mallorca	31	11		
1999–2000	Mallorca	8	1		
2000–01	Mallorca	13	1		
2001–02	Mallorca	9	0	61	13
2001–02	Portsmouth	8	2	8	2

BRADBURY, Lee (F)   243 63
H: 6 2 W: 13 10 b.Isle of Wight 3-7-75
Source: Cowes. *Honours:* England Under-21.

1995–96	Portsmouth	12	0		
1995–96	*Exeter C*	14	5	14	5
1996–97	Portsmouth	42	15		
1997–98	Manchester C	27	7		
1998–99	Manchester C	13	3	40	10
1998–99	Crystal Palace	22	4		
1998–99	*Birmingham C*	7	0	7	0
1999–2000	Crystal Palace	10	2	32	6
1999–2000	Portsmouth	35	10		
2000–01	Portsmouth	39	10		
2001–02	Portsmouth	22	7	150	42

BRADSHAW, Craig (M)   0 0
b.Chertsey 31-7-84
Source: Scholar.

2001–02	Portsmouth	0	0		

BRADY, Garry* (M)   40 0
H: 5 10 W: 11 02 b.Glasgow 7-9-76
Source: Trainee. *Honours:* Scotland Schools, Youth.

1993–94	Tottenham H	0	0		
1994–95	Tottenham H	0	0		
1995–96	Tottenham H	0	0		
1996–97	Tottenham H	0	0		
1997–98	Tottenham H	9	0	9	0
1998–99	Newcastle U	9	0		
1999–2000	Newcastle U	0	0		
1999–2000	*Norwich C*	6	0		
2000–01	Newcastle U	0	0	9	0
2000–01	*Norwich C*	2	0	8	0
2001–02	Portsmouth	8	0		
2001–02	Portsmouth	6	0	14	0

BURCHILL, Mark (F)   49 19
H: 5 8 W: 11 09 b.Broxburn 18-8-80
Source: Celtic BC. *Honours:* Scotland Schools, Under-21, 6 full caps.

1997–98	Celtic	0	0		
1998–99	Celtic	21	9		
1999–2000	Celtic	0	0		
2000–01	Celtic	2	1	23	10
2000–01	*Birmingham C*	13	4	13	4
2000–01	*Ipswich T*	7	1		
2001–02	Ipswich T	0	0	7	1
2001–02	Portsmouth	6	4	6	4

BUXTON, Lewis (D)   29 0
H: 6 1 W: 13 10 b.Newport (IW) 10-12-83
Source: School.

2000–01	Portsmouth	0	0		
2001–02	Portsmouth	29	0	29	0

CASEY, Mark (M)   0 0
b.Glasgow 9-10-82

2001–02	Portsmouth	0	0		

COOPER, Shaun (D)   7 0
H: 5 10 W: 10 07 b.Isle of Wight 5-10-83
Source: School.

2000–01	Portsmouth	0	0		
2001–02	Portsmouth	7	0	7	0

COURVILLE, Uliano (M)   2 0
H: 6 0 W: 12 06 b.Mantes La Jolie 8-8-78
Source: Ajaccio.

2000–01	Monaco	2	0	2	0
2001–02	Portsmouth	0	0		

CROWE, Jason (D)   87 1
H: 5 9 W: 11 02 b.Sidcup 30-9-78
Source: Trainee. *Honours:* England Schools, Youth.

1995–96	Arsenal	0	0		
1996–97	Arsenal	0	0		
1997–98	Arsenal	0	0		
1998–99	Arsenal	0	0		
1998–99	*Crystal Palace*	8	0	8	0
1999–2000	Portsmouth	25	0		
2000–01	Portsmouth	23	0		
2000–01	*Brentford*	9	0	9	0
2001–02	Portsmouth	22	1	70	1

CURTIS, Tom (M)   257 12
H: 5 10 W: 12 10 b.Exeter 1-3-73
Source: School.

1991–92	Derby Co	0	0		
1992–93	Derby Co	0	0		
1993–94	Chesterfield	36	3		
1994–95	Chesterfield	40	2		
1995–96	Chesterfield	46	0		
1996–97	Chesterfield	40	3		
1997–98	Chesterfield	36	1		
1998–99	Chesterfield	24	3		
1999–2000	Chesterfield	18	0	240	12
2000–01	Portsmouth	4	0		
2001–02	Portsmouth	9	0	13	0
2001–02	*Walsall*	4	0	4	0

DERRY, Shaun (M)   200 5
H: 5 10 W: 13 02 b.Nottingham 6-12-77
Source: Trainee.

1995–96	Notts Co	12	0		
1996–97	Notts Co	39	2		
1997–98	Notts Co	28	2	79	4
1997–98	Sheffield U	12	0		
1998–99	Sheffield U	26	0		
1999–2000	Sheffield U	34	0	72	0
1999–2000	Portsmouth	9	1		
2000–01	Portsmouth	28	0		
2001–02	Portsmouth	12	0	49	1

EDINBURGH, Justin‡ (D)   285 2
H: 5 10 W: 12 01 b.Basildon 18-12-69
Source: Trainee.

1988–89	Southend U	15	0		
1989–90	Southend U	22	0	37	0
1989–90	*Tottenham H*	0	0		
1990–91	Tottenham H	16	1		
1991–92	Tottenham H	23	0		
1992–93	Tottenham H	34	1		
1993–94	Tottenham H	25	0		
1994–95	Tottenham H	31	0		
1995–96	Tottenham H	22	0		
1996–97	Tottenham H	24	0		
1997–98	Tottenham H	16	0		
1998–99	Tottenham H	16	0		
1999–2000	Tottenham H	8	0	213	1
1999–2000	Portsmouth	11	0		
2000–01	Portsmouth	17	0		
2001–02	Portsmouth	7	1	35	1

GRIFFITHS, Ben* (D)   0 0
b.Bournemouth 27-11-81
Source: Trainee.

1999–2000	Portsmouth	0	0		
2000–01	Portsmouth	0	0		
2001–02	Portsmouth	0	0		

HARPER, Kevin (F)   212 22
H: 5 7 W: 12 00 b.Oldham 15-1-76
Source: Hutcheson Vale BC. *Honours:* Scotland Schools, Under-21, B.

1993–94	Hibernian	2	0		
1994–95	Hibernian	23	5		
1995–96	Hibernian	16	3		
1996–97	Hibernian	26	5		
1997–98	Hibernian	27	1		
1998–99	Hibernian	2	1	96	15
1998–99	Derby Co	27	1		
1999–2000	Derby Co	5	0	32	1
1999–2000	*Walsall*	9	1	9	1
1999–2000	Portsmouth	12	2		
2000–01	Portsmouth	24	2		
2001–02	Portsmouth	39	1	75	5

HILEY, Scott (D)   375 12
H: 5 8 W: 11 08 b.Plymouth 27-9-68
Source: Trainee.

1986–87	Exeter C	0	0		
1987–88	Exeter C	15	1		
1988–89	Exeter C	37	5		
1989–90	Exeter C	46	0		
1990–91	Exeter C	46	2		
1991–92	Exeter C	33	1		
1992–93	Exeter C	33	3	210	12
1992–93	Birmingham C	7	0		
1993–94	Birmingham C	28	0		
1994–95	Birmingham C	9	0		
1995–96	Birmingham C	5	0	49	0
1995–96	Manchester C	6	0		
1996–97	Manchester C	3	0		
1997–98	Manchester C	0	0	9	0
1998–99	Southampton	29	0		
1999–2000	Southampton	3	0	32	0
1999–2000	Portsmouth	8	0		
2000–01	Portsmouth	34	0		
2001–02	Portsmouth	33	0	75	0

HOWE, Eddie (D)   201 10
H: 5 9 W: 11 02 b.Amersham 29-11-77
Source: Trainee.

1995–96	Bournemouth	5	0		
1996–97	Bournemouth	13	0		
1997–98	Bournemouth	40	1		
1998–99	Bournemouth	45	2		
1999–2000	Bournemouth	28	1		
2000–01	Bournemouth	31	2		
2001–02	Bournemouth	38	4	200	10
2001–02	Portsmouth	1	0	1	0

HUNT, Warren (M)   0 0
b.Portsmouth 2-3-84
Source: Scholar.

2001–02	Portsmouth	0	0		

KAWAGUCHI, Yoshikatsu (G)   204 0
H: 5 10 W: 12 03 b.Shizuoka 15-8-75
Honours: Japan 52 full caps.

1995	Yokohama Flugels	14	0		
1996	Yokohama Flugels	15	0		
1997	Yokohama Flugels	22	0		
1998	Yokohama Flugels	34	0	112	0
1999	Yokohama Marinos	28	0		
2000	Yokohama Marinos	28	0		
2001	Yokohama Marinos	25	0	81	0
2001–02	Portsmouth	11	0	11	0

LOVELL, Stephen (F)   50 5
H: 5 11 W: 11 08 b.Amersham 6-12-80
Source: Trainee.

1998–99	Bournemouth	7	0		
1999–2000	Bournemouth	1	0	8	0
1999–2000	Bournemouth	3	0		
1999–2000	*Exeter C*	5	1	5	1
2000–01	Portsmouth	9	1		
2001–02	Portsmouth	20	2	32	3
2001–02	*Sheffield U*	5	1	5	1

MIGLIORANZI, Stefani* (M)   35 2
H: 6 1 W: 12 12 b.Pacos de Caldas 20-9-77
Source: St Johns Univ.

1998–99	Portsmouth	7	0		
1999–2000	Portsmouth	13	2		

2000–01	Portsmouth	12	0		
2001–02	Portsmouth	3	0	35	2

MOLYNEAUX, Lee (M)   **0 0**
b.Portsmouth 16-1-83
Source: Scholar.

2001–02	Portsmouth	0	0

NIGHTINGALE, Luke (F)   **45 4**
H: 5 11   W: 11 07   b.Portsmouth 22-12-80
Source: Trainee.

1998–99	Portsmouth	19	3		
1999–2000	Portsmouth	7	0		
2000–01	Portsmouth	19	1		
2001–02	Portsmouth	0	0	45	4

O'NEIL, Gary (M)   **44 2**
H: 5 10   W: 11 00   b.Beckenham 18-5-83
Source: Scholar. *Honours*: England Youth.

1999–2000	Portsmouth	1	0		
2000–01	Portsmouth	10	1		
2001–02	Portsmouth	33	1	44	2

PANOPOULOS, Mike‡ (M)   **76 10**
H: 6 1   W: 12 10   b.Melbourne 9-10-76
Source: Heidelberg 8 apps. *Honours*:
Australia Youth.

1998–99	Aris Salonika	22	3	22	3
1999–2000	Aris Salonika	22	1		
2000–01	Portsmouth	30	6		
2001–02	Portsmouth	2	0	54	7

(On loan to Dunfermline Ath, December 2001).

PETTEFER, Carl (M)   **3 0**
H: 5 7   W: 10 02   b.Taplow 22-3-81
Source: Trainee.

1998–99	Portsmouth	0	0		
1999–2000	Portsmouth	0	0		
2000–01	Portsmouth	1	0		
2001–02	Portsmouth	2	0	3	0

PITT, Courtney (M)   **39 3**
H: 5 7   W: 10 08   b.London 17-12-81
Source: Scholar.

2000–01	Chelsea	0	0		
2001–02	Portsmouth	39	3	39	3

PRIMUS, Linvoy (D)   **271 10**
H: 6 0   W: 12 04   b.Forest Gate 14-9-73
Source: Trainee.

1992–93	Charlton Ath	4	0		
1993–94	Charlton Ath	0	0	4	0
1994–95	Barnet	39	0		
1995–96	Barnet	42	4		
1996–97	Barnet	46	3	127	7
1997–98	Reading	36	1		
1998–99	Reading	31	0		
1999–2000	Reading	28	0	95	1
2000–01	Portsmouth	23	0		
2001–02	Portsmouth	22	2	45	2

PROSINECKI, Robert‡ (M)   **349 73**
H: 6 0   W: 11 13   b.Schweiningen 12-1-69
Honours: Yugoslavia 15 full caps, 4 goals.
Croatia 49 full caps, 10 goals.

1987–88	Red Star Belgrade	23	4		
1988–89	Red Star Belgrade	33	4		
1989–90	Red Star Belgrade	32	5		
1990–91	Red Star Belgrade	29	11	117	24
1991–92	Real Madrid	3	1		
1992–93	Real Madrid	29	3		
1993–94	Real Madrid	23	6	55	10
1994–95	Oviedo	30	5	30	5
1995–96	Barcelona	19	2	19	2
1996–97	Sevilla	20	4	20	4
1997–98	Dynamo Zagreb	16	5		
1998–99	Dynamo Zagreb	15	4		
1999–2000	Dynamo Zagreb	19	5	50	14
2000–01	Hrvatski Dragovoljac	4	1	4	1
2000–01	Standard Liege	21	4	21	4
2001–02	Portsmouth	33	9	33	9

QUASHIE, Nigel (M)   **167 12**
H: 5 9   W: 12 08   b.Nunhead 20-7-78
Source: Trainee. *Honours*: England Youth,
Under-21, B.

1995–96	QPR	11	0		
1996–97	QPR	13	0		
1997–98	QPR	33	3		
1998–99	QPR	0	0	57	3
1998–99	Nottingham F	16	0		
1999–2000	Nottingham F	28	2	44	2
2000–01	Portsmouth	31	5		
2001–02	Portsmouth	35	2	66	7

RUDONJA, Mladen‡ (M)   **220 51**
H: 5 9   W: 11 07   b.Slovenia 26-7-71
Honours: Slovenia 61 full caps, 1 goal.

1992–93	Izola	32	7		
1993–94	Izola	14	9	46	16
1993–94	Zagreb	6	0	6	0
1994–95	Koper	15	3	15	3
1994–95	Olimpija	11	1		
1995–96	Olimpija	15	1	26	2
1995–96	Marsonia	14	1	14	1
1996–97	HIT Gorica	16	4	16	4

From Lugano

1997–98	Primoje	9	4	9	4
1997–98	St Truiden	23	6		
1998–99	St Truiden	29	10		
1999–2000	St Truiden	22	5	74	21
2000–01	Portsmouth	11	0		
2001–02	Portsmouth	3	0	14	0

TARDIF, Chris (G)   **5 0**
H: 5 11   W: 12 07   b.Guernsey 10-9-79
Source: Trainee.

1998–99	Portsmouth	0	0		
1999–2000	Portsmouth	0	0		
2000–01	Portsmouth	4	0		
2001–02	Portsmouth	1	0	5	0

THOGERSEN, Thomas‡ (M)   **283 39**
H: 6 2   W: 13 01   b.Copenhagen 2-4-68

1989	Frem	2	0		
1990	Frem	17	0		
1991–92	Frem	20	5		
1992–93	Frem	18	2	57	7
1993–94	Brondby	32	11		
1994–95	Brondby	26	7		
1995–96	Brondby	21	1		
1996–97	Brondby	21	2		
1997–98	Brondby	11	1	111	22
1998–99	Portsmouth	34	0		
1999–2000	Portsmouth	35	5		
2000–01	Portsmouth	34	3		
2001–02	Walsall	7	2	7	2
2001–02	Portsmouth	5	0	108	8

TILER, Carl (D)   **261 11**
H: 6 2   W: 14 03   b.Sheffield 11-2-70
Source: Trainee. *Honours*: England Under-21.

1987–88	Barnsley	1	0		
1988–89	Barnsley	4	0		
1989–90	Barnsley	21	1		
1990–91	Barnsley	45	2	71	3
1991–92	Nottingham F	26	1		
1992–93	Nottingham F	37	0		
1993–94	Nottingham F	3	0		
1994–95	Nottingham F	3	0		
1994–95	Swindon T	2	0	2	0
1995–96	Nottingham F	0	0	69	1
1995–96	Aston Villa	1	0		
1996–97	Aston Villa	11	1	12	1
1996–97	Sheffield U	6	1		
1997–98	Sheffield U	17	1	23	2
1997–98	Everton	19	1		
1998–99	Everton	2	0	21	1
1998–99	Charlton Ath	27	1		
1999–2000	Charlton Ath	11	1		
2000–01	Charlton Ath	7	0	45	2
2000–01	Birmingham C	1	0	1	0
2001–02	Portsmouth	8	0	17	1

TODOROV, Svetoslav (F)   **100 41**
H: 6 0   W: 12 02   b.Dobrich 30-8-78
Honours: Bulgaria 27 full caps, 2 goals.

1996–97	Dobrudzha	12	2	12	2
1997–98	Litets Lovech	19	9		
1998–99	Litets Lovech	11	2		
1999–2000	Litets Lovech	26	19		
2000–01	Litets Lovech	15	7	71	37
2000–01	West Ham U	8	1		
2001–02	West Ham U	6	0	14	1
2001–02	Portsmouth	3	1	3	1

VINCENT, Jamie (M)   **245 8**
H: 5 10   W: 11 09   b.London 18-6-75
Source: Trainee.

1993–94	Crystal Palace	0	0		
1994–95	Crystal Palace	0	0		
1994–95	Bournemouth	8	0		
1995–96	Crystal Palace	25	0		
1996–97	Crystal Palace	0	0	25	0
1996–97	Bournemouth	29	0		
1997–98	Bournemouth	44	3		
1998–99	Bournemouth	32	2	113	5
1998–99	Huddersfield T	7	0		
1999–2000	Huddersfield T	36	2		
2000–01	Huddersfield T	16	0	59	2
2000–01	Portsmouth	14	0		
2001–02	Portsmouth	34	1	48	1

VINE, Rowan (F)   **13 0**
H: 6 1   W: 11 12   b.Basingstoke 21-9-82
Source: Scholar.

2000–01	Portsmouth	2	0		
2001–02	Portsmouth	11	0	13	0

WILSON, Scott (D)   **53 1**
H: 6 1   W: 11 04   b.Edinburgh 19-3-77
Source: Rangers BC. *Honours*: Scotland
Under-21.

1996–97	Rangers	1	0		
1997–98	Rangers	0	0		
1998–99	Rangers	12	1		
1999–2000	Rangers	9	0		
2000–01	Rangers	20	0		
2001–02	Rangers	6	0	48	1
2001–02	Portsmouth	5	0	5	0

WHITE, Tom (M)   **0 0**
b.Chichester 30-10-81
Source: Trainee.

2000–01	Portsmouth	0	0
2001–02	Portsmouth	0	0

ZAMPERINI, Alessandro (D)   **16 2**
H: 6 2   W: 12 08   b.Rome 15-8-82
Source: Roma.

2000–01	Roma	0	0		
2001–02	Portsmouth	16	2	16	2

Scholars
Clark, Christopher J; Crawford, James L;
Harfield, Matthew T; Hughes, Ryan; Moore,
Ben; Parker, Terry J; Pook, Robbie J; Pulis,
Anthony J; Silk, Gary L; Whitley, Luke

PORT VALE

ARMSTRONG, Ian (M)   **31 3**
H: 5 7   W: 10 01   b.Liverpool 16-11-81
Source: Trainee. *Honours*: England Schools,
Youth.

1998–99	Liverpool	0	0		
1999–2000	Liverpool	0	0		
2000–01	Liverpool	0	0		
2001–02	Port Vale	31	3	31	3

ATANGANA, Mvondo (F)   **13 0**
H: 5 9   W: 11 00   b.Yaounde 10-7-79
Source: Tonerre Kalara.

2000–01	Dundee U	11	0	11	0
2001–02	Port Vale	2	0	2	0

BIRCHALL, Christopher§ (M)   **1 0**
H: 5 9   W: 12 12   b.Liverpool 5-5-84
Source: Scholar.

2001–02	Port Vale	1	0	1	0

BRIDGE-WILKINSON, Marc (M)   **69 15**
H: 5 6   W: 11 03   b.Coventry 16-3-79
Source: Trainee.

1996–97	Derby Co	0	0		
1997–98	Derby Co	0	0		
1998–99	Derby Co	1	0		
1998–99	Carlisle U	7	0	7	0
1999–2000	Derby Co	0	0	1	0
2000–01	Port Vale	42	9		
2001–02	Port Vale	19	6	61	15

BRISCO, Neil (M)   **67 1**
H: 6 0   W: 13 02   b.Billinge 26-1-78
Source: Trainee.

1996–97	Manchester C	0	0		
1997–98	Manchester C	0	0		
1998–99	Port Vale	1	0		
1999–2000	Port Vale	12	0		
2000–01	Port Vale	17	1		
2001–02	Port Vale	37	0	67	1

BROOKER, Stephen (F)   **65 18**
H: 6 0   W: 13 13   b.Newport Pagnell 21-5-81
Source: Trainee.

1999–2000	Watford	1	0		
2000–01	Watford	0	0	1	0
2000–01	Port Vale	23	9		
2001–02	Port Vale	41	9	64	18

BURGESS, Richard‡ (F)   **3 0**
H: 5 8   W: 11 00   b.Bromsgrove 18-8-78
Source: Trainee.

1996–97	Aston Villa	0	0		
1997–98	Stoke C	0	0		
1998–99	Stoke C	0	0		
1999–2000	Stoke C	0	0		

From Bromsgrove R.

2000–01	Port Vale	1	0		
2001–02	Port Vale	2	0	3	0

BURNS, Liam (D)   **75 0**
H: 6 0   W: 13 06   b.Belfast 30-10-78
Source: Trainee. *Honours*: Northern Ireland
Youth, Under-21.

1997–98	Port Vale	1	0		
1998–99	Port Vale	4	0		
1999–2000	Port Vale	24	0		
2000–01	Port Vale	13	0		
2001–02	Port Vale	13	0	75	0

BURTON, Sagi* (D)   **120 3**
H: 6 2   W: 14 05   b.Birmingham 25-11-77
Source: Trainee.

1995–96	Crystal Palace	0	0		
1996–97	Crystal Palace	0	0		
1997–98	Crystal Palace	2	0		
1998–99	Crystal Palace	23	1	25	1

1999–2000 Colchester U 9 0 **9 0**
1999–2000 Sheffield U 0 0
1999–2000 Port Vale 20 2
2000–01 Port Vale 29 0
2001–02 Port Vale 37 0 **86 2**

BYRNE, Paul§ (M) **3 0**
H: 5 9 W: 11 00 b.Natal 26-11-82
Source: Scholar.
2000–01 Port Vale 1 0
2001–02 Port Vale 2 0 **3 0**

CARRAGHER, Matthew (D) **278 1**
H: 5 9 W: 11 08 b.Liverpool 14-1-76
Source: Trainee.
1993–94 Wigan Ath 32 0
1994–95 Wigan Ath 41 0
1995–96 Wigan Ath 28 0
1996–97 Wigan Ath 18 0 **119 0**
1997–98 Port Vale 26 0
1998–99 Port Vale 10 0
1999–2000 Port Vale 37 1
2000–01 Port Vale 45 0
2001–02 Port Vale 41 0 **159 1**

CUMMINS, Michael (M) **105 11**
H: 6 0 W: 12 13 b.Dublin 1-6-78
Source: Trainee. Honours: Eire Youth, Under-21.
1995–96 Middlesbrough 0 0
1996–97 Middlesbrough 0 0
1997–98 Middlesbrough 0 0
1998–99 Middlesbrough 1 0
1999–2000 Middlesbrough 1 0 **2 0**
1999–2000 Port Vale 12 1
2000–01 Port Vale 45 2
2001–02 Port Vale 46 8 **103 11**

DELANY, Dean (G) **12 0**
H: 6 0 W: 13 02 b.Dublin 15-9-80
Honours: Eire Under-21.
1997–98 Everton 0 0
1998–99 Everton 0 0
1999–2000 Everton 0 0
2000–01 Port Vale 8 0
2001–02 Port Vale 4 0 **12 0**

DODD, Ashley* (M) **12 1**
H: 5 10 W: 10 10 b.Stafford 7-1-82
1999–2000 Manchester U 0 0
2000–01 Manchester U 0 0
2000–01 Port Vale 3 0
2001–02 Port Vale 9 1 **12 1**

DONNELLY, Paul* (D) **11 0**
H: 5 9 W: 11 13 b.Newcastle under Lyme 16-2-81
Source: Trainee.
1999–2000 Port Vale 4 0
2000–01 Port Vale 1 0
2001–02 Port Vale 6 0 **11 0**

DURNIN, John‡ (M) **424 90**
H: 5 10 W: 12 05 b.Liverpool 18-8-65
Source: Waterloo Dock.
1985–86 Liverpool 0 0
1986–87 Liverpool 0 0
1987–88 Liverpool 0 0
1988–89 Liverpool 0 0
1988–89 WBA 5 2 **5 2**
1988–89 Oxford U 19 3
1989–90 Oxford U 42 13
1990–91 Oxford U 26 9
1991–92 Oxford U 37 8
1992–93 Oxford U 37 11 **161 44**
1993–94 Portsmouth 28 6
1994–95 Portsmouth 16 2
1995–96 Portsmouth 41 3
1996–97 Portsmouth 34 3
1997–98 Portsmouth 34 10
1998–99 Portsmouth 26 7
1999–2000 Portsmouth 2 0 **181 31**
1999–2000 Blackpool 5 1 **5 1**
1999–2000 Carlisle U 22 2
2000–01 Carlisle U 0 0 **22 2**
2000–01 Kidderminster H 31 9
2001–02 Kidderminster H 0 0 **31 9**
From Rhyl.
2001–02 Port Vale 19 1 **19 1**

GIBSON, Alex* (D) **1 0**
H: 5 9 W: 10 03 b.Plymouth 12-8-82
Source: Scholar.
2001–02 Stoke C 0 0
2001–02 Port Vale 1 0 **1 0**

GOODLAD, Mark (G) **87 0**
H: 6 1 W: 14 02 b.Barnsley 9-9-79
Source: Trainee.
1996–97 Nottingham F 0 0
1997–98 Nottingham F 0 0
1998–99 Nottingham F 0 0
1998–99 Scarborough 3 0 **3 0**

1999–2000 Nottingham F 0 0
1999–2000 Port Vale 1 0
2000–01 Port Vale 40 0
2001–02 Port Vale 43 0 **84 0**

HARDY, Phil* (M) **357 2**
H: 5 7 W: 12 00 b.Chester 9-4-73
Source: Trainee. Honours: Eire Under-21.
1989–90 Wrexham 1 0
1990–91 Wrexham 32 0
1991–92 Wrexham 42 0
1992–93 Wrexham 32 0
1993–94 Wrexham 25 0
1994–95 Wrexham 44 0
1995–96 Wrexham 42 0
1996–97 Wrexham 13 0
1997–98 Wrexham 34 0
1998–99 Wrexham 33 0
1999–2000 Wrexham 38 1
2000–01 Wrexham 13 0 **349 1**
2001–02 Port Vale 8 1 **8 1**

INGRAM, Rae (D) **150 1**
H: 5 11 W: 13 02 b.Manchester 6-12-74
Source: Trainee.
1993–94 Manchester C 0 0
1994–95 Manchester C 0 0
1995–96 Manchester C 5 0
1996–97 Manchester C 18 0
1997–98 Manchester C 0 0 **23 0**
1997–98 *Macclesfield T* 5 0
1998–99 *Macclesfield T* 29 0
1999–2000 Macclesfield T 36 0
2000–01 Macclesfield T 33 1 **103 1**
2001–02 Port Vale 24 0 **24 0**

MAYE, Daniel* (M) **2 0**
H: 5 9 W: 11 05 b.Leicester 14-7-82
Source: Scholar.
2001–02 Port Vale 2 0 **2 0**

McCLARE, Sean (M) **82 7**
H: 5 11 W: 12 10 b.Rotherham 12-1-78
Source: Trainee. Honours: Eire Under-21.
1996–97 Barnsley 0 0
1997–98 Barnsley 0 0
1998–99 Barnsley 30 3
1999–2000 Barnsley 10 2
1999–2000 *Rochdale* 9 0 **9 0**
2000–01 Barnsley 10 1
2001–02 Barnsley 0 0 **50 6**
2001–02 Port Vale 23 1 **23 1**

McPHEE, Stephen (F) **44 11**
H: 5 7 W: 11 08 b.Glasgow 5-6-81
Honours: Scotland Under-21.
1998–99 Coventry C 0 0
1999–2000 Coventry C 0 0
2000–01 Coventry C 0 0
2001–02 Port Vale 44 11 **44 11**

O'CALLAGHAN, George‡ (M) **34 4**
H: 6 1 W: 10 11 b.Cork 5-9-79
Source: Trainee.
1998–99 Port Vale 0 0
1999–2000 Port Vale 11 0
2000–01 Port Vale 8 1
2001–02 Port Vale 11 3 **34 4**

OLAOYE, Dolapo§ (M) **1 0**
H: 5 10 W: 12 04 b.Lagos 17-10-82
2000–01 Port Vale 1 0
2001–02 Port Vale 0 0 **1 0**

PAYNTER, Billy§ (F) **8 0**
H: 6 0 W: 12 04 b.Liverpool 13-7-84
Source: Schoolboy.
2000–01 Port Vale 1 0
2001–02 Port Vale 7 0 **8 0**

ROWLAND, Stephen (D) **25 1**
H: 5 10 W: 12 01 b.Wrexham 2-11-81
Source: Scholar.
2001–02 Port Vale 25 1 **25 1**

SIMPSON, Ben* (M) **0 0**
H: 5 8 W: 11 00 b.Liverpool 30-12-81
Source: Scholar.
2001–02 Port Vale 0 0

TAYLOR, Paul* (D) **0 0**
H: 6 0 W: 11 03 b.Stoke 16-9-80
Source: Trainee.
1999–2000 Port Vale 0 0
2000–01 Port Vale 0 0
2001–02 Port Vale 0 0

TORPEY, Steve‡ (F) **1 0**
H: 5 9 W: 10 08 b.Liverpool 16-9-81
Source: Trainee. Honours: England Youth.
1998–99 Liverpool 0 0
1999–2000 Liverpool 0 0
2000–01 Liverpool 0 0
2001–02 Port Vale 1 0 **1 0**

WALSH, Michael# (D) **201 4**
H: 6 0 W: 13 06 b.Rotherham 5-8-77
Source: Trainee.
1994–95 Scunthorpe U 3 0
1995–96 Scunthorpe U 25 0
1996–97 Scunthorpe U 36 0
1997–98 Scunthorpe U 39 1 **103 1**
1998–99 Port Vale 19 1
1999–2000 Port Vale 12 1
2000–01 Port Vale 39 1
2001–02 Port Vale 20 0 **98 3**

Scholars
Barker, Philip; Birchall, Christopher; Brown, Ryan A; Byrne, Paul; Doxey, Shaun G; Eldershaw, Simon; Fairbrother, Craig; Fairhurst, Neil A; Gowan, Christopher J; Kirkham, Shane M; Molloy, Jospeh M; O'Reilly, Graham; Olaoye, Dolapo; Orpe, Mark; Paynter, William P; Reid, Levi SJ; Robinson, Simon; Rowley, Christoper J; Stevenson, Matthew JR; Taylor, Andrew

PRESTON NE

ABBOTT, Pawel (F) **0 0**
H: 6 1 W: 11 07 b.York 2-12-81
Source: LKS Lodz.
2000–01 Preston NE 0 0
2001–02 Preston NE 0 0

ALEXANDER, Graham (D) **444 50**
H: 5 11 W: 12 04 b.Coventry 10-10-71
Source: Trainee. Honours: Scotland 4 full caps.
1989–90 Scunthorpe U 0 0
1990–91 Scunthorpe U 1 0
1991–92 Scunthorpe U 36 5
1992–93 Scunthorpe U 41 5
1993–94 Scunthorpe U 41 4
1994–95 Scunthorpe U 40 4 **159 18**
1995–96 Luton T 37 1
1996–97 Luton T 45 2
1997–98 Luton T 39 8
1998–99 Luton T 29 4 **150 15**
1998–99 Preston NE 10 0
1999–2000 Preston NE 46 6
2000–01 Preston NE 34 5
2001–02 Preston NE 45 6 **135 17**

ANDERSON, Iain (F) **203 28**
H: 5 5 W: 12 04 b.Glasgow 23-7-77
Source: X-Form. Honours: Scotland Under-21.
1994–95 Dundee 10 1
1995–96 Dundee 17 0
1996–97 Dundee 35 5
1997–98 Dundee 36 6
1998–99 Dundee 28 3 **126 15**
1999–2000 *Toulouse* 3 0 **3 0**
1999–2000 Preston NE 12 2
2000–01 Preston NE 31 6
2001–02 Preston NE 31 5 **74 13**

BAILEY, John (M) **0 0**
H: 5 5 W: 10 05 b.Manchester 2-7-84
Source: Scholar. Honours: England Youth.
2001–02 Preston NE 0 0

BARRY-MURPHY, Brian (M) **107 3**
H: 5 11 W: 13 03 b.Cork 27-7-78
Honours: Eire Under-21.
1995–96 Cork City 13 0
1996–97 Cork City 25 0
1997–98 Cork City 15 1
1998–99 Cork City 27 1 **80 2**
1999–2000 Preston NE 1 0
2000–01 Preston NE 14 0
2001–02 Preston NE 4 0 **19 0**
2001–02 *Southend U* 8 1 **8 1**

BASHAM, Steve* (F) **92 16**
H: 5 10 W: 11 03 b.Southampton 2-12-77
Source: Trainee.
1996–97 Southampton 6 0
1997–98 Southampton 9 0
1997–98 *Wrexham* 5 0 **5 0**
1998–99 Southampton 4 1 **19 1**
1998–99 Preston NE 17 10
1999–2000 Preston NE 24 2
2000–01 Preston NE 15 2
2001–02 Preston NE 16 1 **68 15**

CARTWRIGHT, Lee (M) **363 22**
H: 5 8 W: 11 05 b.Rossendale 19-9-72
Source: Trainee.
1990–91 Preston NE 14 1
1991–92 Preston NE 33 4
1992–93 Preston NE 34 3
1993–94 Preston NE 39 1
1994–95 Preston NE 36 1

1995–96	Preston NE	26	3		
1996–97	Preston NE	14	1		
1997–98	Preston NE	36	2		
1998–99	Preston NE	27	4		
1999–2000	Preston NE	30	1		
2000–01	Preston NE	38	0		
2001–02	Preston NE	36	1	**363**	**22**

CRESSWELL, Richard (F) **190** **39**
H: 6 0 W: 12 04 b.Bridlington 20-9-77
Source: Trainee. *Honours:* England Under-21.

1995–96	York C	16	1		
1996–97	York C	17	0		
1996–97	*Mansfield T*	5	1	**5**	**1**
1997–98	York C	26	4		
1998–99	York C	36	16	**95**	**21**
1998–99	Sheffield W	7	1		
1999–2000	Sheffield W	20	1		
2000–01	Sheffield W	4	0	**31**	**2**
2000–01	Leicester C	8	0	**8**	**0**
2000–01	*Preston NE*	11	2		
2001–02	Preston NE	40	13	**51**	**15**

EATON, Adam (D) **13** **0**
H: 5 10 W: 12 00 b.Liverpool 2-5-80
Source: Trainee.

1997–98	Everton	0	0		
1998–99	Everton	0	0		
1999–2000	Preston NE	0	0		
2000–01	Preston NE	1	0		
2001–02	Preston NE	12	0	**13**	**0**

EDWARDS, Rob (D) **383** **14**
H: 6 0 W: 13 03 b.Kendal 1-7-73
Source: Trainee. *Honours:* Wales Youth, Under-21, B, 4 full caps.

1989–90	Carlisle U	12	0		
1990–91	Carlisle U	36	5	**48**	**5**
1990–91	Bristol C	0	0		
1991–92	Bristol C	20	1		
1992–93	Bristol C	18	0		
1993–94	Bristol C	38	2		
1994–95	Bristol C	30	0		
1995–96	Bristol C	19	0		
1996–97	Bristol C	31	0		
1997–98	Bristol C	37	2		
1998–99	Bristol C	23	0	**216**	**5**
1999–2000	Preston NE	41	2		
2000–01	Preston NE	42	0		
2001–02	Preston NE	36	2	**119**	**4**

ETUHU, Dixon (M) **28** **3**
H: 6 2 W: 13 00 b.Kano 8-6-82
Source: Scholar.

1999–2000	Manchester C	0	0		
2000–01	Manchester C	0	0		
2001–02	Manchester C	12	0	**12**	**0**
2001–02	Preston NE	16	3	**16**	**3**

GREGAN, Sean (M) **348** **16**
H: 6 2 W: 14 11 b.Stockton 29-3-74
Source: Trainee.

1991–92	Darlington	17	0		
1992–93	Darlington	17	1		
1993–94	Darlington	23	1		
1994–95	Darlington	25	2		
1995–96	Darlington	38	0		
1996–97	Darlington	16	0	**136**	**4**
1996–97	Preston NE	21	1		
1997–98	Preston NE	35	2		
1998–99	Preston NE	41	3		
1999–2000	Preston NE	33	3		
2000–01	Preston NE	41	2		
2001–02	Preston NE	41	1	**212**	**12**

GUDJONSSON, Thordur‡ (M) **199** **60**
H: 5 10 W: 11 06 b.Reykjavik 23-1-73
Honours: Iceland 42 full caps, 11 goals.

1990	KA	16	2	**16**	**2**
1991	IA Akranes	0	0		
1992	IA Akranes	18	6		
1993	IA Akranes	18	19	**36**	**25**
1994–95	Bochum	16	3		
1995–96	Bochum	0	0		
1996–97	Bochum	13	1	**29**	**4**
1997–98	Genk	33	9		
1998–99	Genk	28	9		
1999–2000	Genk	33	10	**94**	**28**
2000–01	Las Palmas	7	0		
2000–01	Derby Co	10	1	**10**	**1**
2001–02	Las Palmas	0	0	**7**	**0**
2001–02	Preston NE	7	0	**7**	**0**

GUNNLAUGSSON, Bjarki‡ (F) **163** **39**
H: 5 10 W: 12 00 b.Reykjavik 6-3-73
Honours: Iceland 27 full caps, 7 goals.

1990	IA Akranes	7	1		
1991	IA Akranes	0	0		
1992	IA Akranes	17	5		
1992–93	Feyenoord	0	0		
1993–94	Feyenoord	0	0		
1994–95	Nuremberg	27	5	**27**	**5**
1995	IA Akranes	7	3	**31**	**9**
1996–97	Waldhof Mannheim	26	6	**26**	**6**
1997	Molde	10	4		
1998	Molde	8	2	**18**	**6**
1999	KR	16	11	**16**	**11**
1999–2000	Preston NE	26	1		
2000–01	Preston NE	19	1		
2001–02	Preston NE	0	0	**45**	**2**

HEALY, David (F) **83** **22**
H: 5 7 W: 10 09 b.Downpatrick 5-8-79
Source: Trainee. *Honours:* Northern Ireland Schools, Youth, Under-21, B, 18 full caps, 8 goals.

1997–98	Manchester U	0	0		
1998–99	Manchester U	0	0		
1999–2000	Manchester U	0	0		
1999–2000	*Port Vale*	16	3	**16**	**3**
2000–01	Manchester U	1	0	**1**	**0**
2000–01	Preston NE	22	9		
2001–02	Preston NE	44	10	**66**	**19**

JACKSON, Michael (D) **310** **25**
H: 6 0 W: 13 07 b.Chester 4-12-73
Source: Trainee.

1991–92	Crewe Alex	1	0		
1992–93	Crewe Alex	4	0	**5**	**0**
1993–94	Bury	39	0		
1994–95	Bury	24	2		
1995–96	Bury	31	4		
1996–97	Bury	31	3	**125**	**9**
1996–97	Preston NE	7	0		
1997–98	Preston NE	40	2		
1998–99	Preston NE	44	8		
1999–2000	Preston NE	46	5		
2000–01	Preston NE	30	1		
2001–02	Preston NE	13	0	**180**	**16**

KEANE, Michael (M) **22** **2**
H: 5 6 W: 11 05 b.Dublin 29-12-82
Source: Scholar.

2000–01	Preston NE	2	0		
2001–02	Preston NE	20	2	**22**	**2**

KIDD, Ryan‡ (D) **260** **9**
H: 6 1 W: 12 00 b.Radcliffe 6-10-71
Source: Trainee.

1990–91	Port Vale	0	0		
1991–92	Port Vale	1	0	**1**	**0**
1992–93	Preston NE	15	0		
1993–94	Preston NE	36	1		
1994–95	Preston NE	32	3		
1995–96	Preston NE	30	0		
1996–97	Preston NE	35	0		
1997–98	Preston NE	33	2		
1998–99	Preston NE	28	3		
1999–2000	Preston NE	29	0		
2000–01	Preston NE	15	0		
2001–02	Preston NE	6	0	**259**	**9**

LONERGAN, Andrew (G) **1** **0**
H: 6 2 W: 13 10 b.Preston 19-10-83
Source: Scholar. *Honours:* England Youth.

2000–01	Preston NE	1	0		
2001–02	Preston NE	0	0	**1**	**0**

LUCAS, David (G) **118** **0**
H: 6 0 W: 12 04 b.Preston 23-11-77
Source: Trainee. *Honours:* England Youth.

1995–96	Preston NE	1	0		
1995–96	*Darlington*	6	0		
1996–97	Preston NE	2	0		
1996–97	*Darlington*	7	0	**13**	**0**
1996–97	*Scunthorpe U*	6	0	**6**	**0**
1997–98	Preston NE	6	0		
1998–99	Preston NE	31	0		
1999–2000	Preston NE	6	0		
2000–01	Preston NE	29	0		
2001–02	Preston NE	24	0	**99**	**0**

LUCKETTI, Chris (D) **422** **13**
H: 6 1 W: 13 04 b.Littleborough 28-9-71
Source: Trainee.

1988–89	Rochdale	1	0		
1989–90	Rochdale	0	0	**1**	**0**
1990–91	Stockport Co	0	0		
1991–92	Halifax T	36	0		
1992–93	Halifax T	42	2	**78**	**2**
1993–94	Bury	27	1		
1994–95	Bury	39	3		
1995–96	Bury	42	1		
1996–97	Bury	38	0		
1997–98	Bury	46	2		
1998–99	Bury	43	1	**235**	**8**
1999–2000	Huddersfield T	26	0		
2000–01	Huddersfield T	40	1		
2001–02	Huddersfield T	2	0	**68**	**1**
2001–02	Preston NE	40	2	**40**	**2**

McKENNA, Paul (M) **152** **12**
H: 5 5 W: 13 03 b.Eccleston 29-10-77
Source: Trainee.

1995–96	Preston NE	0	0		
1996–97	Preston NE	5	1		
1997–98	Preston NE	5	0		
1998–99	Preston NE	36	0		
1999–2000	Preston NE	24	2		
2000–01	Preston NE	44	5		
2001–02	Preston NE	38	4	**152**	**12**

MOILANEN, Teuvo (G) **252** **0**
H: 6 3 W: 13 00 b.Oulu 12-12-73
Honours: Finland Under-21, 3 full caps.

1990	Ilves	3	0		
1991	Ilves	7	0		
1992	Ilves	29	0		
1993	Ilves	5	0		
1994	Ilves	19	0	**63**	**0**
1995	Jaro	26	0	**26**	**0**
1995–96	Preston NE	2	0		
1996–97	Preston NE	4	0		
1996–97	*Scarborough*	4	0	**4**	**0**
1996–97	*Darlington*	16	0	**16**	**0**
1997–98	Preston NE	40	0		
1998–99	Preston NE	15	0		
1999–2000	Preston NE	41	0		
2000–01	Preston NE	17	0		
2001–02	Preston NE	24	0	**143**	**0**

MURDOCK, Colin (D) **153** **6**
H: 6 3 W: 13 05 b.Belfast 12-7-76
Source: Trainee. *Honours:* Northern Ireland Schools, Youth, B, 14 full caps.

1992–93	Manchester U	0	0		
1993–94	Manchester U	0	0		
1994–95	Manchester U	0	0		
1995–96	Manchester U	0	0		
1996–97	Manchester U	0	0		
1997–98	Preston NE	27	1		
1998–99	Preston NE	33	1		
1999–2000	Preston NE	33	2		
2000–01	Preston NE	37	0		
2001–02	Preston NE	23	2	**153**	**6**

O'HANLON, Kelham† (G) **485** **0**
H: 6 1 W: 13 00 b.Saltburn 16-5-62
Source: Apprentice. *Honours:* Eire Under-21, 1 full cap.

1980–81	Middlesbrough	0	0		
1981–82	Middlesbrough	0	0		
1982–83	Middlesbrough	19	0		
1983–84	Middlesbrough	30	0		
1984–85	Middlesbrough	38	0	**87**	**0**
1985–86	Rotherham U	46	0		
1986–87	Rotherham U	40	0		
1987–88	Rotherham U	40	0		
1988–89	Rotherham U	46	0		
1989–90	Rotherham U	43	0		
1990–91	Rotherham U	33	0	**248**	**0**
1991–92	Carlisle U	42	0		
1992–93	Carlisle U	41	0	**83**	**0**
1993–94	Preston NE	23	0		
1994–95	Dundee U	29	0		
1995–96	Dundee U	1	0		
1996–97	Dundee U	0	0	**30**	**0**
1996–97	Preston NE	13	0		
1997–98	Preston NE	0	0		
1998–99	Preston NE	0	0		
1999–2000	Preston NE	0	0		
2000–01	Preston NE	1	0		
2001–02	Preston NE	0	0	**37**	**0**

O'NEILL, Joe§ (F) **0** **0**
H: 5 11 W: 11 04 b.Blackburn 28-10-82
Source: Scholar.

2001–02	Preston NE	0	0		

QUINN, Patrick* (M) **0** **0**
H: 6 0 W: 13 00 b.Dundalk 3-12-81

2000–01	Preston NE	0	0		
2001–02	Preston NE	0	0		

RANKINE, Mark (M) **510** **33**
H: 5 7 W: 12 01 b.Doncaster 30-9-69
Source: Trainee.

1987–88	Doncaster R	18	2		
1988–89	Doncaster R	46	11		
1989–90	Doncaster R	36	2		
1990–91	Doncaster R	40	2		
1991–92	Doncaster R	24	3	**164**	**20**
1991–92	Wolverhampton W	15	1		
1992–93	Wolverhampton W	27	0		
1993–94	Wolverhampton W	31	0		
1994–95	Wolverhampton W	27	0		
1995–96	Wolverhampton W	32	0		
1996–97	Wolverhampton W	0	0	**132**	**1**
1996–97	Preston NE	23	0		
1997–98	Preston NE	35	1		
1998–99	Preston NE	42	3		
1999–2000	Preston NE	44	0		
2000–01	Preston NE	44	4		
2001–02	Preston NE	26	4	**214**	**12**

REID, Paul (D)   20   1
H: 6 2   W: 11 04   b.Carlisle 18-2-82
Source: Trainee. *Honours:* England Youth, Under-20.

Season	Club	App	Gls	Tot	Tot
1998–99	Carlisle U	0	0		
1999–2000	Carlisle U	19	0		
2000–01	Carlisle U	0	0	19	0
2001–02	Rangers	0	0		
2001–02	*Preston NE*	1	1	1	1

ROBINSON, Steve (M)   272   53
H: 5 7   W: 11 03   b.Lisburn 10-12-74
Source: Trainee. *Honours:* Northern Ireland Schools, Youth, Under-21, B, 5 full caps.

Season	Club	App	Gls	Tot	Tot
1992–93	Tottenham H	0	0		
1993–94	Tottenham H	2	0		
1994–95	Tottenham H	0	0	2	0
1994–95	*Leyton Orient*	0	0		
1994–95	Bournemouth	32	5		
1995–96	Bournemouth	41	7		
1996–97	Bournemouth	40	7		
1997–98	Bournemouth	45	10		
1998–99	Bournemouth	42	13		
1999–2000	Bournemouth	40	9	240	51
2000–01	Preston NE	22	1		
2001–02	Preston NE	2	0	24	1
2001–02	Bristol C	6	1	6	1

SKORA, Eric (M)   4   0
H: 5 11   W: 12 05   b.France 20-8-81

Season	Club	App	Gls	Tot	Tot
2001–02	Preston NE	4	0	4	0

SOW, Sadio* (M)   1   0
H: 5 11   W: 11 00   b.Dakar 13-3-78
Source: Niort.

Season	Club	App	Gls	Tot	Tot
2001–02	Nancy	1	0	1	0
2001–02	Preston NE	0	0		

WIJNHARD, Clyde# (F)   192   59
H: 5 11   W: 12 04   b.Paramaribo 1-11-73

Season	Club	App	Gls	Tot	Tot
1992–93	Ajax	4	2		
1993–94	Groningen	23	3	23	3
1994–95	Ajax	0	0	4	2
1995–96	RKC	33	8		
1996–97	RKC	17	10	50	18
1997–98	Willem II	29	14	29	14
1998–99	Leeds U	18	3	18	3
1999–2000	Huddersfield T	45	15		
2000–01	Huddersfield T	0	0		
2001–02	Huddersfield T	13	1	62	16
2001–02	Preston NE	6	3	6	3

WRIGHT, Mark (F)   3   0
H: 5 10   W: 12 07   b.Chorley 4-9-81
Source: Schoolboy.

Season	Club	App	Gls	Tot	Tot
1998–99	Preston NE	1	0		
1999–2000	Preston NE	2	0		
2000–01	Preston NE	0	0		
2001–02	Preston NE	0	0	3	0

Scholars
Brown, Michael; Cromwell, Mark; Curwen, George E; Douglas, Adam M; Hallam, Anthony T; Keane, Graeme; Kempson, Darran K; Kewley, Michael; Langmead, Kelvin S; Mercer, Richard M; Nesa, Remo; O'Neill, Joseph
Non-Contract
O'Hanlon, Kelham G
Player who does not hold a current contract but his registration has been retained by the club
Wilkinson, Craig

QPR

AGOGO, Manuel‡ (M)   23   7
H: 5 11   W: 11 09   b.Accra 1-8-79
Source: Willesden.

Season	Club	App	Gls	Tot	Tot
1996–97	Sheffield W	0	0		
1997–98	Sheffield W	1	0		
1998–99	Sheffield W	0	0		
1999–2000	Sheffield W	0	0		
1999–2000	*Oldham Ath*	2	0	2	0
1999–2000	*Chester C*	10	6	10	6
1999–2000	*Chesterfield*	4	0	4	0
1999–2000	*Lincoln C*	3	1	3	1
2000–01	Sheffield W	0	0	2	0
From San Jose E.					
2001–02	QPR	2	0	2	0

BARR, Hamid* (M)   0   0
H: 5 11   W: 12 07   b.Lewisham 29-9-76
Source: Fisher Ath.

Season	Club	App	Gls	Tot	Tot
2001–02	QPR	0	0		

BEN ASKAR, Aziz‡ (D)   18   0
H: 6 2   W: 13 03   b.Chateau-Gontier 30-3-76

Season	Club	App	Gls	Tot	Tot
2001–02	QPR	18	0	18	0

BIGNOT, Marcus# (D)   175   2
H: 5 7   W: 11 04   b.Birmingham 22-8-74
Source: Kidderminster H.

Season	Club	App	Gls	Tot	Tot
1997–98	Crewe Alex	42	0		
1998–99	Crewe Alex	26	0		
1999–2000	Crewe Alex	27	0	95	0
2000–01	Bristol R	26	1	26	1
2000–01	QPR	9	1		
2001–02	QPR	45	0	54	1

BONNOT, Alex‡ (M)   38   1
H: 5 8   W: 11 05   b.Poissy 31-7-73
Source: Angers.

Season	Club	App	Gls	Tot	Tot
1998–99	Watford	4	0		
1999–2000	Watford	12	0		
2000–01	Watford	0	0	16	0
2001–02	QPR	22	1	22	1

BRADY, Richard (F)   0   0
H: 5 8   W: 10 04   b.Dartford 17-9-82
Source: Trainee.

Season	Club	App	Gls	Tot	Tot
1999–2000	QPR	0	0		
2000–01	QPR	0	0		
2001–02	QPR	0	0		

BROWN, Carlos‡ (D)   0   0
H: 6 0   W: 11 07   b.Edmonton 22-4-81
Source: Trainee.

Season	Club	App	Gls	Tot	Tot
1998–99	QPR	0	0		
1999–2000	QPR	0	0		
2000–01	QPR	0	0		
2001–02	QPR	0	0		

BROWNE, Rickey* (D)   0   0
H: 6 1   W: 12 05   b.Edmonton 19-10-81
Source: Scholar.

Season	Club	App	Gls	Tot	Tot
1999–2000	QPR	0	0		
2000–01	QPR	0	0		
2001–02	QPR	0	0		

BRUCE, Paul* (D)   41   3
H: 5 11   W: 12 01   b.London 18-2-78
Source: Trainee.

Season	Club	App	Gls	Tot	Tot
1996–97	QPR	0	0		
1997–98	QPR	5	1		
1998–99	QPR	0	0		
1998–99	*Cambridge U*	4	0	4	0
1999–2000	QPR	12	0		
2000–01	QPR	7	1		
2001–02	QPR	13	1	37	3

BULL, Nikki* (G)   0   0
H: 6 2   W: 12 08   b.Hastings 2-10-81
Source: Scholar.

Season	Club	App	Gls	Tot	Tot
1999–2000	QPR	0	0		
2000–01	QPR	0	0		
2001–02	QPR	0	0		

BURGESS, Oliver§ (M)   5   1
H: 5 10   W: 11 07   b.Ascot 12-10-81
Source: Scholar.

Season	Club	App	Gls	Tot	Tot
2000–01	QPR	1	0		
2001–02	QPR	4	1	5	1

CARLISLE, Clarke (D)   120   10
H: 6 3   W: 12 07   b.Preston 14-10-79
Source: Trainee. *Honours:* England Under-21.

Season	Club	App	Gls	Tot	Tot
1997–98	Blackpool	11	2		
1998–99	Blackpool	39	1		
1999–2000	Blackpool	43	4	93	7
2000–01	QPR	27	3		
2001–02	QPR	0	0	27	3

COCHRANE, Justin* (M)   1   0
H: 5 11   W: 11 07   b.Hackney 26-1-82
Source: Scholar.

Season	Club	App	Gls	Tot	Tot
1999–2000	QPR	0	0		
2000–01	QPR	1	0		
2001–02	QPR	0	0	1	0

CONNOLLY, Karl (F)   414   96
H: 5 10   W: 11 08   b.Prescot 9-2-70
Source: Napoli (Liverpool Sunday League).

Season	Club	App	Gls	Tot	Tot
1990–91	Wrexham	0	0		
1991–92	Wrexham	36	8		
1992–93	Wrexham	42	9		
1993–94	Wrexham	39	2		
1994–95	Wrexham	45	10		
1995–96	Wrexham	46	18		
1996–97	Wrexham	30	14		
1997–98	Wrexham	35	7		
1998–99	Wrexham	44	11		
1999–2000	Wrexham	41	9	358	88
2000–01	QPR	23	4		
2001–02	QPR	33	4	56	8

D'AUSTIN, Ryan (M)   0   0
H: 5 9   W: 10 13   b.Edgware 29-11-82
Source: Trainee.

Season	Club	App	Gls	Tot	Tot
1999–2000	QPR	0	0		
2000–01	QPR	0	0		
2001–02	QPR	0	0		

DALY, Wesley§ (M)   1   0
H: 5 9   W: 11 00   b.Hammersmith 7-3-84
Source: Scholar.

Season	Club	App	Gls	Tot	Tot
2001–02	QPR	1	0	1	0

DAY, Chris (G)   65   0
H: 6 2   W: 13 06   b.Whipps Cross 28-7-75
Source: Trainee. *Honours:* England Under-21.

Season	Club	App	Gls	Tot	Tot
1992–93	Tottenham H	0	0		
1993–94	Tottenham H	0	0		
1994–95	Tottenham H	0	0		
1995–96	Tottenham H	0	0		
1996–97	Crystal Palace	24	0	24	0
1997–98	Watford	0	0		
1998–99	Watford	0	0		
1999–2000	Watford	11	0		
2000–01	Watford	0	0	11	0
2000–01	*Lincoln C*	14	0	14	0
2001–02	QPR	16	0	16	0

DE ORNELAS, Fernando‡ (M)   11   0
H: 6 0   W: 11 07   b.Caracas 29-7-76
Source: Happy Valley. *Honours:* Venezuela 13 full caps, 2 goals.

Season	Club	App	Gls	Tot	Tot
1999–2000	Crystal Palace	9	0	9	0
1999–2000	Zaragoza	0	0		
2000–01	Zaragoza	0	0		
From Italchacao.					
2001–02	QPR	2	0	2	0

DIGBY, Fraser# (G)   492   0
H: 6 1   W: 12 12   b.Sheffield 23-4-67
Source: Apprentice. *Honours:* England Schools, Youth, Under-21.

Season	Club	App	Gls	Tot	Tot
1984–85	Manchester U	0	0		
1985–86	Manchester U	0	0		
1985–86	*Oldham Ath*	0	0		
1985–86	*Swindon T*	0	0		
1986–87	Manchester U	0	0		
1986–87	Swindon T	39	0		
1987–88	Swindon T	31	0		
1988–89	Swindon T	46	0		
1989–90	Swindon T	45	0		
1990–91	Swindon T	41	0		
1991–92	Swindon T	21	0		
1992–93	Swindon T	33	0		
1992–93	*Manchester U*	0	0		
1993–94	Swindon T	28	0		
1994–95	Swindon T	39	0		
1995–96	Swindon T	25	0		
1996–97	Swindon T	31	0		
1997–98	Swindon T	38	0	417	0
1998–99	Crystal Palace	18	0		
1999–2000	Crystal Palace	38	0		
2000–01	Crystal Palace	0	0	56	0
2001–02	Huddersfield T	0	0		
2001–02	QPR	19	0	19	0

DODOU, Ebeli M'bombo (F)   36   3
H: 5 5   W: 9 11   b.Kinshasa 11-9-80

Season	Club	App	Gls	Tot	Tot
2001–02	QPR	36	3	36	3

DUNCAN, Lyndon (D)   0   0
H: 5 8   W: 11 02   b.Ealing 12-1-83
Source: Trainee. *Honours:* England Youth.

Season	Club	App	Gls	Tot	Tot
1999–2000	QPR	0	0		
2000–01	QPR	0	0		
2001–02	QPR	0	0		

FITZGERALD, Brian (M)   1   0
H: 5 9   W: 12 00   b.Perivale 23-10-83
Source: School.

Season	Club	App	Gls	Tot	Tot
2000–01	QPR	0	0		
2001–02	QPR	1	0	1	0

FORBES, Terrell (D)   46   0
H: 6 0   W: 12 05   b.Southwark 17-8-81
Source: Trainee.

Season	Club	App	Gls	Tot	Tot
1999–2000	West Ham U	0	0		
1999–2000	*Bournemouth*	3	0	3	0
2000–01	West Ham U	0	0		
2001–02	QPR	43	0	43	0

GALLEN, Kevin (F)   243   55
H: 5 11   W: 13 05   b.Hammersmith 21-9-75
Source: Trainee. *Honours:* England Schools, Youth, Under-21.

Season	Club	App	Gls	Tot	Tot
1992–93	QPR	0	0		
1993–94	QPR	0	0		
1994–95	QPR	37	10		
1995–96	QPR	30	8		
1996–97	QPR	2	3		
1997–98	QPR	44	8		
1998–99	QPR	44	8		
1999–2000	QPR	0	0		
2000–01	Huddersfield T	38	10	38	10
2001–02	Barnsley	9	2	9	2
2001–02	QPR	25	7	196	43

GRADLEY, Patrick (M) 0 0
b.London 1-6-83
Source: Scholar.

2000-01	QPR	0	0
2001-02	QPR	0	0

GRAHAM, Richard‡ (M) 2 0
H: 5 8 W: 10 06 b.Newry 5-8-79
Source: Trainee. *Honours:* Northern Ireland Youth, Under-21.

1996-97	QPR	0	0		
1997-98	QPR	0	0		
1998-99	QPR	2	0		
1999-2000	QPR	0	0		
2000-01	QPR	0	0		
2001-02	QPR	0	0	2	0

GRIFFITHS, Leroy (F) 30 3
H: 5 11 W: 13 05 b.London 30-12-76
Source: Hampton & Richmond B.

2000-01	QPR	0	0		
2001-02	QPR	30	3	30	3

LANGLEY, Richard (M) 93 8
H: 6 0 W: 12 06 b.London 27-12-79
Source: Trainee. *Honours:* England Youth. Jamaica 1 full cap.

1996-97	QPR	0	0		
1997-98	QPR	0	0		
1998-99	QPR	8	1		
1999-2000	QPR	41	3		
2000-01	QPR	26	1		
2001-02	QPR	18	3	93	8

LEABURN, Carl‡ (F) 391 57
H: 6 3 W: 13 00 b.Lewisham 30-3-69
Source: Apprentice. *Honours:* England Youth.

1986-87	Charlton Ath	3	1		
1987-88	Charlton Ath	12	0		
1988-89	Charlton Ath	32	2		
1989-90	Charlton Ath	13	0		
1989-90	*Northampton T*	9	0	9	0
1990-91	Charlton Ath	20	1		
1991-92	Charlton Ath	39	11		
1992-93	Charlton Ath	39	5		
1993-94	Charlton Ath	39	10		
1994-95	Charlton Ath	27	3		
1995-96	Charlton Ath	40	9		
1996-97	Charlton Ath	44	8		
1997-98	Charlton Ath	14	3	322	53
1997-98	Wimbledon	16	4		
1998-99	Wimbledon	22	0		
1999-2000	Wimbledon	18	0		
2000-01	Wimbledon	3	0		
2001-02	Wimbledon	0	0	59	4
2001-02	QPR	1	0	1	0

LUSARDI, Mario‡ (F) 0 0
H: 5 9 W: 12 00 b.Islington 27-9-79
Source: Trainee.

1996-97	QPR	0	0
1997-98	QPR	0	0
1998-99	QPR	0	0
1999-2000	QPR	0	0
2000-01	QPR	0	0
2001-02	QPR	0	0

McEWEN, Dave‡ (F) 9 0
H: 6 0 W: 11 00 b.Westminster 2-11-77
Source: Dulwich H.

1999-2000	Tottenham H	1	0		
2000-01	Tottenham H	3	0	4	0
2001-02	QPR	5	0	5	0

MURPHY, Danny (D) 12 0
H: 5 6 W: 10 04 b.London 4-12-82
Source: Trainee.

1999-2000	QPR	0	0		
2000-01	QPR	0	0		
2001-02	QPR	12	0	12	0

NUGENT, Marcel‡ (M) 0 0
b.London 10-9-82
Source: Scholar.

2000-01	QPR	0	0
2001-02	QPR	0	0

OLI, Dennis† (F) 2 0
H: 6 0 W: 12 02 b.Newham 28-1-84

2001-02	QPR	2	0	2	0

PACQUETTE, Richard (F) 18 2
H: 5 11 W: 13 12 b.Paddington 28-1-83
Source: Trainee.

1999-2000	QPR	0	0		
2000-01	QPR	2	0		
2001-02	QPR	16	2	18	2

PALMER, Steve (D) 392 14
H: 6 1 W: 12 13 b.Brighton 31-3-68
Source: Cambridge Univ. *Honours:* England Schools.

1989-90	Ipswich T	5	0
1990-91	Ipswich T	23	1
1991-92	Ipswich T	23	0
1992-93	Ipswich T	7	0
1993-94	Ipswich T	36	1
1994-95	Ipswich T	12	0
1995-96	Ipswich T	5	0	111	2
1995-96	Watford	35	1
1996-97	Watford	41	2
1997-98	Watford	41	2
1998-99	Watford	41	2
1999-2000	Watford	38	0
2000-01	Watford	39	1	235	8
2001-02	QPR	46	4	46	4

PEACOCK, Gavin (M) 546 107
H: 5 9 W: 11 08 b.Eltham 18-11-67
Source: Apprentice. *Honours:* England Schools, Youth, Football League.

1984-85	QPR	0	0		
1985-86	QPR	0	0		
1986-87	QPR	12	1		
1987-88	QPR	5	0		
1987-88	Gillingham	26	2		
1988-89	Gillingham	44	9	70	11
1989-90	Bournemouth	41	4		
1990-91	Bournemouth	15	4	56	8
1990-91	Newcastle U	27	7		
1991-92	Newcastle U	46	16		
1992-93	Newcastle U	32	12	105	35
1993-94	Chelsea	37	8		
1994-95	Chelsea	38	4		
1995-96	Chelsea	28	5		
1996-97	Chelsea	0	0	103	17
1996-97	QPR	27	5		
1997-98	QPR	39	9		
1998-99	QPR	42	8		
1999-2000	QPR	30	8		
2000-01	QPR	32	3		
2001-02	QPR	20	2	207	36
2001-02	*Charlton Ath*	5	0	5	0

PERRY, Mark* (D) 66 1
H: 5 11 W: 13 03 b.Perivale 19-10-78
Source: Trainee. *Honours:* England Schools, Youth.

1995-96	QPR	0	0		
1996-97	QPR	2	1		
1997-98	QPR	8	0		
1998-99	QPR	1	0		
1999-2000	QPR	10	0		
2000-01	QPR	29	0		
2001-02	QPR	16	0	66	1

PLUMMER, Chris (D) 60 2
H: 6 2 W: 13 08 b.Isleworth 12-10-76
Source: Trainee. *Honours:* England Youth, Under-21.

1994-95	QPR	0	0		
1995-96	QPR	5	0		
1996-97	QPR	5	0		
1997-98	QPR	0	0		
1998-99	QPR	10	0		
1999-2000	QPR	18	0		
2000-01	QPR	25	2		
2001-02	QPR	1	0	60	2

ROSE, Matthew# (D) 145 4
H: 5 11 W: 12 02 b.Dartford 24-9-75
Source: Trainee. *Honours:* England Under-21.

1994-95	Arsenal	0	0		
1995-96	Arsenal	4	0		
1996-97	Arsenal	1	0	5	0
1997-98	QPR	16	0		
1998-99	QPR	29	0		
1999-2000	QPR	29	1		
2000-01	QPR	27	0		
2001-02	QPR	39	3	140	4

RUSTEM, Adam* (F) 0 0
H: 6 0 W: 11 07 b.Whipps Cross 18-9-81
Source: Scholar.

1999-2000	QPR	0	0
2000-01	QPR	0	0
2001-02	QPR	0	0

SHITTU, Dan (D) 44 4
H: 6 2 W: 16 03 b.Lagos 2-9-80
Honours: Nigeria 1 full cap.

1999-2000	Charlton Ath	0	0		
2000-01	Charlton Ath	0	0		
2000-01	*Blackpool*	17	2	17	2
2001-02	Charlton Ath	0	0		
2001-02	QPR	27	2	27	2

SODJE, Iroroakpeyere‡ (M) 0 0
b.Greenwich 31-1-81

2000-01	QPR	0	0
2001-02	QPR	0	0

THOMSON, Andy# (D) 433 167
H: 5 11 W: 11 11 b.Motherwell 1-4-71
Source: Jerviston BC.

1989-90	Q of S	26	6
1990-91	Q of S	37	11
1991-92	Q of S	39	26
1992-93	Q of S	38	21
1993-94	Q of S	35	29	175	93
1994-95	Southend U	39	11
1995-96	Southend U	33	6
1996-97	Southend U	17	5
1997-98	Southend U	33	6	122	28
1998-99	Oxford U	38	7	38	7
1999-2000	Gillingham	28	9
2000-01	Gillingham	24	5	52	14
2000-01	QPR	8	4
2001-02	QPR	38	21	46	25

WALSHE, Ben (M) 1 0
H: 5 11 W: 12 12 b.Hammersmith 24-5-83
Source: Scholar.

2000-01	QPR	1	0		
2001-02	QPR	0	0	1	0

WARREN, Christer* (D) 161 14
H: 5 11 W: 12 03 b.Dorchester 10-10-74
Source: Cheltenham T.

1994-95	Southampton	0	0		
1995-96	Southampton	7	0		
1995-96	Southampton	1	0		
1996-97	Brighton & HA	3	0	3	0
1996-97	*Fulham*	11	1	11	1
1997-98	Southampton	0	0	8	0
1997-98	Bournemouth	30	6		
1998-99	Bournemouth	32	5		
1999-2000	Bournemouth	41	2	103	13
2000-01	QPR	22	0		
2001-02	QPR	14	0	36	0

WATTLEY, David (M) 0 0
b.Enfield 5-9-83
Source: School.

2000-01	QPR	0	0
2001-02	QPR	0	0

WRIGHT, Danny* (M) 0 0
H: 5 7 W: 10 13 b.London 24-9-81
Source: Trainee.

1998-99	QPR	0	0
1999-2000	QPR	0	0
2000-01	QPR	0	0
2001-02	QPR	0	0

Scholars
Alexander, Irvin; Bean, Marcus T; Burgess, Oliver D; Butler, Kerry RJ; Daly, Wesley JP; Ifura, Marien M; Patrick-Heselton, Alistair; Ramsey, Matthew J; Scully, Samuel I
Non-Contract
Oli, Dennis C; Sheekey, Luke
Associated Schoolboy
Egan, Richard L

READING

ALLAWAY, Ricky (D) 0 0
H: 6 2 W: 12 05 b.Reading 16-2-83
Source: Trainee.

1999-2000	Reading	0	0
2000-01	Reading	0	0
2001-02	Reading	0	0

ASHDOWN, Jamie (G) 2 0
H: 6 1 W: 13 05 b.Reading 30-11-80

1999-2000	Reading	0	0		
2000-01	Reading	1	0		
2001-02	Reading	1	0	2	0
2001-02	*Arsenal*	0	0		

BOUCAUD, Andre (M) 0 0
b.Enfield 9-10-84
Source: Scholar.

2001-02	Reading	0	0

BUTLER, Martin (F) 256 79
H: 5 11 W: 12 00 b.Dudley 15-9-74
Source: Trainee.

1993-94	Walsall	15	3		
1994-95	Walsall	8	0		
1995-96	Walsall	28	4		
1996-97	Walsall	23	1	74	8
1997-98	Cambridge U	31	10		
1998-99	Cambridge U	46	17		
1999-2000	Cambridge U	26	14	103	41
1999-2000	Reading	17	4		
2000-01	Reading	45	24		
2001-02	Reading	17	2	79	30

CASPER, Chris‡ (D) 74 2
H: 6 0 W: 11 11 b.Burnley 28-4-75
Source: Trainee. *Honours:* England Youth, Under-21.

1992-93	Manchester U	0	0		
1993-94	Manchester U	0	0		
1994-95	Manchester U	0	0		
1995-96	Manchester U	0	0		
1995-96	*Bournemouth*	16	1	16	1

1996–97	Manchester U	2	0		
1997–98	Manchester U	0	0		
1997–98	*Swindon T*	9	1	9	1
1998–99	Manchester U	0	0	2	0
1998–99	Reading	32	0		
1999–2000	Reading	15	0		
2000–01	Reading	0	0		
2001–02	Reading	0	0	47	0

CURETON, Jamie (F) 289 119
H: 5 8 W: 10 07 b.Bristol 28-8-75
Source: Trainee. Honours: England Youth.

1992–93	Norwich C	0	0		
1993–94	Norwich C	0	0		
1994–95	Norwich C	17	4		
1995–96	Norwich C	12	2		
1995–96	*Bournemouth*	5	0	5	0
1996–97	Norwich C	0	0	29	6
1996–97	Bristol R	38	11		
1997–98	Bristol R	43	13		
1998–99	Bristol R	46	25		
1999–2000	Bristol R	46	22		
2000–01	Bristol R	1	1	174	72
2000–01	Reading	43	26		
2001–02	Reading	38	15	81	41

FORSTER, Nicky (F) 331 104
H: 5 8 W: 11 05 b.Caterham 8-9-73
Source: Horley T. Honours: England Under-21.

1992–93	Gillingham	26	6		
1993–94	Gillingham	41	18	67	24
1994–95	Brentford	46	24		
1995–96	Brentford	38	5		
1996–97	Brentford	25	10	109	39
1996–97	Birmingham C	7	3		
1997–98	Birmingham C	28	3		
1998–99	Birmingham C	33	5	68	11
1999–2000	Reading	36	10		
2000–01	Reading	9	1		
2001–02	Reading	42	19	87	30

GAMBLE, Joe (M) 7 0
H: 5 6 W: 11 02 b.Cork 14-1-82
Source: Cork C.

| 2000–01 | Reading | 1 | 0 | | |
| 2001–02 | Reading | 6 | 0 | 7 | 0 |

HARPER, James (M) 41 2
H: 5 9 W: 11 10 b.Chelmsford 9-11-80
Source: Trainee.

1999–2000	Arsenal	0	0		
2000–01	Arsenal	0	0		
2000–01	*Cardiff C*	3	0	3	0
2000–01	Reading	12	1		
2001–02	Reading	26	1	38	2

HENDERSON, Darius (F) 48 7
H: 6 1 W: 13 08 b.Doncaster 7-9-81
Source: Trainee.

1999–2000	Reading	6	0		
2000–01	Reading	4	0		
2001–02	Reading	38	7	48	7

HUGHES, Andy (M) 182 24
H: 6 0 W: 12 10 b.Manchester 2-1-78
Source: Trainee.

1995–96	Oldham Ath	15	1		
1996–97	Oldham Ath	8	0		
1997–98	Oldham Ath	10	0	33	1
1997–98	Notts Co	15	2		
1998–99	Notts Co	30	3		
1999–2000	Notts Co	35	7		
2000–01	Notts Co	30	5	110	17
2001–02	Reading	39	6	39	6

IGOE, Sammy (M) 232 18
H: 5 6 W: 10 00 b.Spelthorne 30-9-75
Source: Trainee.

1993–94	Portsmouth	0	0		
1994–95	Portsmouth	1	0		
1995–96	Portsmouth	22	0		
1996–97	Portsmouth	40	2		
1997–98	Portsmouth	31	3		
1998–99	Portsmouth	40	5		
1999–2000	Portsmouth	26	1	160	11
1999–2000	Reading	6	0		
2000–01	Reading	31	6		
2001–02	Reading	35	1	72	7

JONES, Keith* (M) 508 37
H: 5 8 W: 11 02 b.Dulwich 14-10-65
Source: Apprentice. Honours: England Schools, Youth.

1982–83	Chelsea	2	0		
1983–84	Chelsea	0	0		
1984–85	Chelsea	19	2		
1985–86	Chelsea	14	2		
1986–87	Chelsea	17	3		
1987–88	Chelsea	0	0	52	7
1987–88	Brentford	36	1		
1988–89	Brentford	40	3		

1989–90	Brentford	42	2		
1990–91	Brentford	45	6		
1991–92	Brentford	6	1	169	13
1991–92	Southend U	34	5		
1992–93	Southend U	29	1		
1993–94	Southend U	20	5		
1994–95	Southend U	9	0	90	11
1994–95	Charlton Ath	31	1		
1995–96	Charlton Ath	25	0		
1996–97	Charlton Ath	19	0		
1997–98	Charlton Ath	44	3		
1998–99	Charlton Ath	22	1		
1999–2000	Charlton Ath	17	1	158	6
2000–01	Reading	23	0		
2001–02	Reading	16	0	39	0

LOCKWOOD, Adam‡ (D) 0 0
H: 6 0 W: 12 00 b.Wakefield 26-10-81
Source: Trainee.

1998–99	Reading	0	0		
1999–2000	Reading	0	0		
2000–01	Reading	0	0		
2001–02	Reading	0	0		

MACKIE, John (D) 37 2
H: 6 1 W: 13 00 b.London 5-7-76
Source: Sutton U.

1999–2000	Reading	0	0		
2000–01	Reading	10	0		
2001–02	Reading	27	2	37	2

MURTY, Graeme (M) 209 8
H: 5 10 W: 11 10 b.Saltburn 13-11-74
Source: Trainee.

1992–93	York C	1	0		
1993–94	York C	20	2		
1994–95	York C	35	2		
1995–96	York C	27	2		
1996–97	York C	27	2		
1997–98	York C	34	1	117	7
1998–99	Reading	9	0		
1999–2000	Reading	17	0		
2000–01	Reading	23	1		
2001–02	Reading	43	0	92	1

NEWMAN, Ricky (D) 254 10
H: 5 10 W: 12 06 b.Guildford 5-8-70
Source: Trainee.

1987–88	Crystal Palace	0	0		
1988–89	Crystal Palace	0	0		
1989–90	Crystal Palace	0	0		
1990–91	Crystal Palace	0	0		
1991–92	Crystal Palace	0	0		
1991–92	*Maidstone U*	10	1	10	1
1992–93	Crystal Palace	2	0		
1993–94	Crystal Palace	11	0		
1994–95	Crystal Palace	35	3	48	3
1995–96	Millwall	36	1		
1996–97	Millwall	41	3		
1997–98	Millwall	35	1		
1998–99	Millwall	24	0		
1999–2000	Millwall	14	0	150	5
1999–2000	*Reading*	7	1		
2000–01	Reading	39	0		
2001–02	Reading	0	0	46	1

PARKINSON, Phil (M) 501 25
H: 6 0 W: 12 08 b.Chorley 1-12-67
Source: Apprentice.

1985–86	Southampton	0	0		
1986–87	Southampton	0	0		
1987–88	Southampton	0	0		
1987–88	Bury	8	1		
1988–89	Bury	39	0		
1989–90	Bury	22	2		
1990–91	Bury	44	2		
1991–92	Bury	32	0	145	5
1992–93	Reading	39	4		
1993–94	Reading	42	3		
1994–95	Reading	31	0		
1995–96	Reading	42	0		
1996–97	Reading	24	1		
1997–98	Reading	37	0		
1998–99	Reading	42	5		
1999–2000	Reading	22	1		
2000–01	Reading	44	4		
2001–02	Reading	33	2	356	20

ROBINSON, Matt* (D) 148 1
H: 5 11 W: 11 08 b.Exeter 23-12-74
Source: Trainee.

1993–94	Southampton	0	0		
1994–95	Southampton	1	0		
1995–96	Southampton	5	0		
1996–97	Southampton	7	0		
1997–98	Southampton	1	0	14	0
1997–98	Portsmouth	15	0		
1998–99	Portsmouth	29	1		
1999–2000	Portsmouth	25	0	69	1
1999–2000	Reading	19	0		
2000–01	Reading	32	0		
2001–02	Reading	14	0	65	0

ROUGIER, Tony (F) 206 17
H: 6 0 W: 14 01 b.Trinidad 17-7-71
Source: Trinity Pros. Honours: Trinidad & Tobago full caps.

1994–95	Raith R	4	0		
1995–96	Raith R	22	1		
1996–97	Raith R	30	1	56	2
1997–98	Hibernian	20	3		
1998–99	Hibernian	15	1	35	4
1998–99	Port Vale	13	0		
1999–2000	Port Vale	38	8	51	8
2000–01	Reading	31	2		
2001–02	Reading	33	1	64	3

SALAKO, John (F) 395 38
H: 5 9 W: 11 12 b.Nigeria 11-2-69
Source: Trainee. Honours: England 5 full caps.

1986–87	Crystal Palace	4	0		
1987–88	Crystal Palace	31	0		
1988–89	Crystal Palace	28	0		
1989–90	Crystal Palace	17	2		
1989–90	*Swansea C*	13	3	13	3
1990–91	Crystal Palace	35	6		
1991–92	Crystal Palace	10	2		
1992–93	Crystal Palace	13	0		
1993–94	Crystal Palace	38	8		
1994–95	Crystal Palace	39	4	215	22
1995–96	Coventry C	37	3		
1996–97	Coventry C	24	1		
1997–98	Coventry C	11	0	72	4
1997–98	Bolton W	7	0	7	0
1998–99	Fulham	10	1		
1999–2000	Fulham	0	0	10	1
1999–2000	Charlton Ath	27	2		
2000–01	Charlton Ath	17	0		
2001–02	Charlton Ath	3	0	47	2
2001–02	Reading	31	6	31	6

SAVAGE, Bas (F) 1 0
H: 6 3 W: 13 08 b.London 7-1-82
Source: Walton & Hersham.

| 2001–02 | Reading | 1 | 0 | 1 | 0 |

SHOREY, Nicky (D) 47 0
H: 5 9 W: 10 10 b.Romford 19-2-81
Source: Trainee.

1999–2000	Leyton Orient	7	0		
2000–01	Leyton Orient	8	0	15	0
2000–01	Reading	0	0		
2001–02	Reading	32	0	32	0

SMITH, Alex (M) 140 7
H: 5 8 W: 10 06 b.Liverpool 15-2-76
Source: Trainee.

1994–95	Everton	0	0		
1995–96	Everton	0	0		
1995–96	Swindon T	8	0		
1996–97	Swindon T	18	1		
1997–98	Swindon T	5	0	31	1
1997–98	Huddersfield T	6	0	6	0
1998–99	Chester C	32	2	32	2
1998–99	Port Vale	8	0		
1999–2000	Port Vale	13	0		
2000–01	Port Vale	37	2	58	2
2001–02	Reading	13	2	13	2

SMITH, Neil* (M) 350 14
H: 5 9 W: 12 12 b.Lambeth 30-9-71
Source: Trainee.

1990–91	Tottenham H	0	0		
1991–92	Tottenham H	0	0		
1991–92	Gillingham	26	2		
1992–93	Gillingham	39	3		
1993–94	Gillingham	35	2		
1994–95	Gillingham	33	1		
1995–96	Gillingham	37	1		
1996–97	Gillingham	42	1	212	10
1997–98	Fulham	44	0		
1998–99	Fulham	29	1		
1999–2000	Fulham	0	0	73	1
1999–2000	Reading	36	1		
2000–01	Reading	15	1		
2001–02	Reading	14	1	65	3

TALIA, Frank* (G) 141 0
H: 6 1 W: 13 06 b.Melbourne 20-7-72

1990–91	Sunshine	11	0		
1991–92	Sunshine	0	0	11	0
1992–93	Blackburn R	0	0		
1992–93	*Hartlepool U*	14	0	14	0
1993–94	Blackburn R	0	0		
1994–95	Blackburn R	0	0		
1995–96	Blackburn R	0	0		
1995–96	Swindon T	16	0		
1996–97	Swindon T	15	0		
1997–98	Swindon T	2	0		
1998–99	Swindon T	43	0		
1999–2000	Swindon T	31	0	107	0
2000–01	Wolverhampton W	0	0		
2000–01	Sheffield U	6	0	6	0

2001–02	Antwerp	3	0	3	0
2001–02	Reading	0	0		

TYSON, Nathan (F) 21 2
H: 6 0 W: 10 01 b.Reading 4-5-82
Source: Trainee.

1999–2000	Reading	1	0		
2000–01	Reading	0	0		
2001–02	Reading	1	0	.2	0
2001–02	Swansea C	11	1	11	1
2001–02	Cheltenham T	8	1	8	1

VIVEASH, Adrian (D) 327 19
H: 6 2 W: 12 13 b.Swindon 30-9-69
Source: Trainee.

1988–89	Swindon T	0	0		
1989–90	Swindon T	0	0		
1990–91	Swindon T	25	1		
1991–92	Swindon T	10	0		
1992–93	Swindon T	5	0		
1992–93	*Reading*	5	0		
1993–94	Swindon T	0	0		
1994–95	Swindon T	14	1		
1994–95	*Reading*	6	0		
1995–96	Swindon T	0	0	54	2
1995–96	*Barnsley*	2	1	2	1
1995–96	Walsall	31	0		
1996–97	Walsall	46	9		
1997–98	Walsall	42	3		
1998–99	Walsall	40	0		
1999–2000	Walsall	43	1	202	13
2000–01	Reading	40	2		
2001–02	Reading	18	1	69	3

WARREN, Steven (M) 0 0
b.London 27-9-83

2000–01	Crystal Palace	0	0		
2001–02	Crystal Palace	0	0		
2001–02	Reading	0	0		

WATSON, Kevin (M) 207 9
H: 5 10 W: 12 08 b.Hackney 3-1-74
Source: Trainee.

1991–92	Tottenham H	0	0		
1992–93	Tottenham H	5	0		
1993–94	Tottenham H	0	0		
1993–94	*Brentford*	3	0	3	0
1994–95	Tottenham H	0	0		
1994–95	*Bristol C*	2	0	2	0
1994–95	*Barnet*	13	0	13	0
1995–96	Tottenham H	0	0	5	0
1996–97	Swindon T	27	1		
1997–98	Swindon T	18	0		
1998–99	Swindon T	18	0	63	1
1999–2000	Rotherham U	44	1		
2000–01	Rotherham U	46	5		
2001–02	Rotherham U	19	1	109	7
2001–02	Reading	12	1	12	1

WHITBREAD, Adrian (D) 360 5
H: 6 0 W: 12 12 b.Epping 22-10-71
Source: Trainee.

1989–90	Leyton Orient	8	0		
1990–91	Leyton Orient	38	0		
1991–92	Leyton Orient	43	1		
1992–93	Leyton Orient	36	1	125	2
1993–94	Swindon T	35	1		
1994–95	Swindon T	1	0	36	1
1994–95	West Ham U	8	0		
1995–96	West Ham U	2	0		
1995–96	*Portsmouth*	13	0		
1996–97	West Ham U	0	0	10	0
1996–97	Portsmouth	24	0		
1997–98	Portsmouth	38	1		
1998–99	Portsmouth	33	0		
1999–2000	Portsmouth	39	1		
2000–01	Portsmouth	0	0	147	2
2000–01	*Luton T*	9	0	9	0
2000–01	*Reading*	19	0		
2001–02	Reading	14	0	33	0

WHITEHEAD, Phil (G) 412 0
H: 6 3 W: 15 10 b.Halifax 17-12-69
Source: Trainee.

1986–87	Halifax T	12	0		
1987–88	Halifax T	0	0		
1988–89	Halifax T	11	0		
1989–90	Halifax T	19	0		
1989–90	Barnsley	0	0		
1990–91	Barnsley	0	0		
1990–91	*Halifax T*	9	0	51	0
1991–92	Barnsley	3	0		
1991–92	*Scunthorpe U*	8	0		
1992–93	Barnsley	13	0		
1992–93	*Scunthorpe U*	8	0	16	0
1992–93	*Bradford C*	6	0	6	0
1992–93	Barnsley	0	0	16	0
1993–94	Oxford U	39	0		
1994–95	Oxford U	38	0		
1995–96	Oxford U	34	0		
1996–97	Oxford U	43	0		
1997–98	Oxford U	32	0		

1998–99	Oxford U	21	0	207	0
1998–99	WBA	26	0		
1999–2000	WBA	0	0	26	0
1999–2000	Reading	11	0		
2000–01	Reading	46	0		
2001–02	Reading	33	0	90	0

WILLIAMS, Adrian (D) 278 16
H: 6 2 W: 13 02 b.Reading 16-8-71
Source: Trainee. *Honours:* Wales 12 full caps, 1 goal.

1988–89	Reading	8	0		
1989–90	Reading	16	2		
1990–91	Reading	7	0		
1991–92	Reading	40	4		
1992–93	Reading	31	4		
1993–94	Reading	41	0		
1994–95	Reading	22	1		
1995–96	Reading	31	3		
1996–97	Wolverhampton W	6	0		
1997–98	Wolverhampton W	20	0		
1998–99	Wolverhampton W	0	0		
1999–2000	Wolverhampton W	1	0	27	0
1999–2000	*Reading*	15	1		
2000–01	Reading	5	0		
2001–02	Reading	35	1	251	16

Scholars
Alcott, Joseph D; Awbery, Jason S; Birnie, Matthew T; Boddy, Mark S; Cox, Simon P; Davies, Christopher; Earl, Callum T; Fashanu, Andre; Howell, Simieon; Kurton, Stuart M; Laidler, Stephen T; Middleton, Gary; O'Hara, Declan M; Soares, Louie; Stamp, Nathan; Stanley, Alex M; Theophanides, Adam; Williams, Scott; Young, Jamie I

ROCHDALE

ATKINSON, Graeme* (M) 317 35
H: 5 8 W: 11 07 b.Hull 11-11-71
Source: Trainee.

1989–90	Hull C	13	1		
1990–91	Hull C	16	0		
1991–92	Hull C	25	8		
1992–93	Hull C	46	6		
1993–94	Hull C	40	7		
1994–95	Hull C	9	1	149	23
1994–95	Preston NE	15	1		
1995–96	Preston NE	44	5		
1996–97	Preston NE	17	0		
1997–98	Preston NE	3	0	79	6
1997–98	*Rochdale*	6	0		
1997–98	Brighton & HA	9	0		
1998–99	Brighton & HA	7	0	16	0
1998–99	Scunthorpe U	1	0	1	0
1998–99	Scarborough	15	1	15	1
1999–2000	Rochdale	40	5		
2000–01	Rochdale	0	0		
2001–02	Rochdale	11	0	57	5

COLEMAN, Simon* (D) 390 27
H: 6 0 W: 12 03 b.Worksop 13-6-68
Source: Apprentice.

1985–86	Mansfield T	0	0		
1986–87	Mansfield T	2	0		
1987–88	Mansfield T	44	2		
1988–89	Mansfield T	45	5		
1989–90	Mansfield T	5	0	96	7
1989–90	Middlesbrough	36	1		
1990–91	Middlesbrough	19	1	55	2
1991–92	Derby Co	43	2		
1992–93	Derby Co	25	0		
1993–94	Derby Co	2	0	70	2
1993–94	Sheffield W	15	1		
1994–95	Sheffield W	1	0	16	1
1994–95	Bolton W	22	4		
1995–96	Bolton W	12	1		
1996–97	Bolton W	0	0	34	5
1997–98	Bolton W	0	0	4	0
1997–98	*Wolverhampton W*	4	0		
1997–98	Southend U	14	0		
1998–99	Southend U	42	4		
1999–2000	Southend U	43	5	99	9
2000–01	Rochdale	5	0		
2001–02	Rochdale	11	1	16	1

CONNOR, Paul (F) 85 23
H: 6 2 W: 11 08 b.Bishop Auckland 12-1-79
Source: Trainee.

1996–97	Middlesbrough	0	0		
1997–98	Middlesbrough	0	0		
1997–98	*Hartlepool U*	5	0	5	0
1998–99	Middlesbrough	0	0		
1998–99	*Stoke C*	3	2		
1999–2000	Stoke C	26	5		
2000–01	Stoke C	7	0	36	7
2000–01	*Cambridge U*	13	5	13	5

DOUGHTY, Matt (D) 69 2
H: 5 8 W: 11 00 b.Warrington 2-11-81
Source: Scholar.

1999–2000	Chester C	33	1	33	1
2001–02	Rochdale	36	1	36	1

DUFFY, Lee (D) 6 0
H: 5 7 W: 10 07 b.Oldham 24-7-82
Source: Scholar.

2001–02	Rochdale	6	0	6	0

DURKAN, Kieron (F) 254 21
H: 5 10 W: 12 09 b.Chester 1-12-73
Source: Trainee. *Honours:* Eire Under-21.

1991–92	Wrexham	1	0		
1992–93	Wrexham	1	0		
1993–94	Wrexham	10	1		
1994–95	Wrexham	30	2		
1995–96	Wrexham	8	0	50	3
1995–96	Stockport Co	16	0		
1996–97	Stockport Co	41	3		
1997–98	Stockport Co	7	1	64	4
1997–98	Macclesfield T	4	0		
1998–99	Macclesfield T	26	3		
1999–2000	Macclesfield T	42	6		
2000–01	Macclesfield T	31	4	103	13
2000–01	*York C*	7	0	7	0
2001–02	Rochdale	30	1	30	1

EDWARDS, Neil (G) 327 0
H: 5 8 W: 11 02 b.Aberdare 8-12-70
Source: Trainee.

1988–89	Leeds U	0	0		
1989–90	Leeds U	0	0		
1990–91	Leeds U	0	0		
1990–91	*Huddersfield T*	0	0		
1991–92	Stockport Co	39	0		
1992–93	Stockport Co	35	0		
1993–94	Stockport Co	26	0		
1994–95	Stockport Co	19	0		
1995–96	Stockport Co	45	0		
1996–97	Stockport Co	0	0		
1997–98	Stockport Co	0	0	164	0
1997–98	Rochdale	27	0		
1998–99	Rochdale	45	0		
1999–2000	Rochdale	40	0		
2000–01	Rochdale	44	0		
2001–02	Rochdale	7	0	163	0

EVANS, Wayne (D) 317 4
H: 5 10 W: 12 03 b.Welshpool 25-8-71
Source: Welshpool.

1993–94	Walsall	41	0		
1994–95	Walsall	36	0		
1995–96	Walsall	24	0		
1996–97	Walsall	28	0		
1997–98	Walsall	43	1		
1998–99	Walsall	11	0	183	1
1999–2000	Rochdale	46	1		
2000–01	Rochdale	45	0		
2001–02	Rochdale	43	0	134	3

FLITCROFT, David (M) 296 22
H: 5 11 W: 13 05 b.Bolton 14-1-74
Source: Trainee.

1991–92	Preston NE	0	0		
1992–93	Preston NE	8	2		
1993–94	Preston NE	0	0	8	2
1993–94	*Lincoln C*	2	0	2	0
1993–94	Chester C	8	1		
1994–95	Chester C	32	0		
1995–96	Chester C	9	1		
1996–97	Chester C	32	6		
1997–98	Chester C	44	4		
1998–99	Chester C	42	6	167	18
1999–2000	Rochdale	43	2		
2000–01	Rochdale	41	0		
2001–02	Rochdale	35	0	119	2

FORD, Tony‡ (M) 931 108
H: 5 9 W: 13 00 b.Grimsby 14-5-59
Source: Apprentice. *Honours:* England B.

1975–76	Grimsby T	15	0		
1976–77	Grimsby T	6	0		
1977–78	Grimsby T	34	2		
1978–79	Grimsby T	45	16		
1979–80	Grimsby T	37	5		
1980–81	Grimsby T	28	4		
1981–82	Grimsby T	35	7		
1982–83	Grimsby T	37	4		
1983–84	Grimsby T	42	8		
1984–85	Grimsby T	42	6		
1985–86	Grimsby T	34	3		
1985–86	*Sunderland*	9	1	9	1
1986–87	Stoke C	41	6		
1987–88	Stoke C	44	7		
1988–89	Stoke C	27	0	112	13
1988–89	WBA	11	1		
1989–90	WBA	42	8		
1990–91	WBA	46	5		

1991–92	WBA	15	0	114	14
1991–92	Grimsby T	22	1		
1992–93	Grimsby T	17	2		
1993–94	Grimsby T	29	0	423	58
1993–94	*Bradford C*	5	0	5	0
1994–95	Scunthorpe U	38	2		
1995–96	Scunthorpe U	38	7	76	9

From Barrow

1996–97	Mansfield T	27	2		
1997–98	Mansfield T	34	3		
1998–99	Mansfield T	42	2	103	7
1999–2000	Rochdale	34	2		
2000–01	Rochdale	38	2		
2001–02	Rochdale	17	2	89	6

GILKS, Matthew (G) 22 0
H: 6 0 W: 12 10 b.Rochdale 4-6-82
Source: Scholar.

2000–01	Rochdale	3	0		
2001–02	Rochdale	19	0	22	0

GRIFFITHS, Gareth (D) 194 10
H: 6 4 W: 14 00 b.Winsford 10-4-70
Source: Rhyl.

1992–93	Port Vale	0	0		
1993–94	Port Vale	4	2		
1994–95	Port Vale	20	0		
1995–96	Port Vale	41	2		
1996–97	Port Vale	26	0		
1997–98	Port Vale	3	0	94	4
1997–98	*Shrewsbury T*	6	0	6	0
1998–99	Wigan Ath	20	0		
1999–2000	Wigan Ath	16	1		
2000–01	Wigan Ath	17	1	53	2
2001–02	Rochdale	41	4	41	4

HICKS, Graham‡ (D) 1 0
H: 5 10 W: 13 05 b.Oldham 17-2-81
Source: Trainee.

1998–99	Rochdale	1	0		
1999–2000	Rochdale	0	0		
2000–01	Rochdale	0	0		
2001–02	Rochdale	0	0	1	0

JOBSON, Richard# (D) 572 40
H: 6 2 W: 12 12 b.Holderness 9-5-63
Source: Burton Alb. *Honours:* England B.

1982–83	Watford	13	1		
1983–84	Watford	13	2		
1984–85	Watford	2	0		
1984–85	Hull C	8	0		
1985–86	Hull C	36	7		
1986–87	Hull C	40	5		
1987–88	Hull C	44	2		
1988–89	Hull C	46	1		
1989–90	Hull C	45	2		
1990–91	Hull C	2	0	221	17
1990–91	Oldham Ath	44	1		
1991–92	Oldham Ath	36	2		
1992–93	Oldham Ath	40	2		
1993–94	Oldham Ath	37	5		
1994–95	Oldham Ath	20	0		
1995–96	Oldham Ath	12	0	189	10
1995–96	Leeds U	12	1		
1996–97	Leeds U	10	0		
1997–98	Leeds U	9	0	22	1
1997–98	*Southend U*	8	1	8	1
1997–98	Manchester C	6	1		
1998–99	Manchester C	1	0		
1999–2000	Manchester C	44	3		
2000–01	Manchester C	0	0	50	4
2000–01	*Watford*	2	0	30	4
2000–01	Tranmere R	16	0		
2001–02	Tranmere R	1	0	17	0
2001–02	Rochdale	35	3	35	3

McAULEY, Sean‡ (D) 260 3
H: 5 11 W: 12 02 b.Sheffield 23-6-72
Source: Trainee. *Honours:* Scotland Youth, Under-21.

1991–92	Manchester U	0	0		
1992–93	St Johnstone	26	0		
1993–94	St Johnstone	28	0		
1994–95	St Johnstone	8	0	62	0
1994–95	*Chesterfield*	1	1	1	1
1995–96	Hartlepool U	46	0		
1996–97	Hartlepool U	38	1	84	1
1996–97	Scunthorpe U	3	1		
1997–98	Scunthorpe U	35	1		
1998–99	Scunthorpe U	17	0		
1998–99	*Scarborough*	7	0	7	0
1999–2000	Scunthorpe U	8	0	69	1
1999–2000	Rochdale	13	0		
2000–01	Rochdale	1	0		
2001–02	Rochdale	0	0	37	0

McCOURT, Patrick (F) 23 4
H: 5 10 W: 11 00 b.Derry 16-12-83
Source: Scholar. *Honours:* Northern Ireland Under-21, 1 full cap.

2001–02	Rochdale	23	4	23	4

McEVILLY, Lee (F) 18 4
H: 6 0 W: 13 00 b.Liverpool 15-4-82
Source: Burscough. *Honours:* Northern Ireland 1 full cap.

2001–02	Rochdale	18	4	18	4

McLOUGHLIN, Alan* (M) 503 80
H: 5 8 W: 10 10 b.Manchester 20-4-67
Source: Local. *Honours:* Eire B, 42 full caps, 2 goals.

1984–85	Manchester U	0	0		
1985–86	Manchester U	0	0		
1986–87	Swindon T	9	0		
1986–87	Torquay U	16	1		
1987–88	Torquay U	8	3	24	4
1987–88	Swindon T	8	0		
1988–89	Swindon T	26	3		
1989–90	Swindon T	46	12		
1990–91	Swindon T	17	4	106	19
1990–91	Southampton	22	1		
1991–92	Southampton	2	0	24	1
1991–92	*Aston Villa*	0	0		
1991–92	Portsmouth	14	2		
1992–93	Portsmouth	46	9		
1993–94	Portsmouth	38	6		
1994–95	Portsmouth	38	6		
1995–96	Portsmouth	40	10		
1996–97	Portsmouth	36	5		
1997–98	Portsmouth	37	4		
1998–99	Portsmouth	41	7		
1999–2000	Portsmouth	19	5	309	54
1999–2000	Wigan Ath	15	1		
2000–01	Wigan Ath	4	0		
2001–02	Wigan Ath	3	0	22	1
2001–02	Rochdale	18	1	18	1

OLIVER, Michael (M) 256 22
H: 5 10 W: 11 04 b.Middlesbrough 2-8-75
Source: Trainee.

1992–93	Middlesbrough	0	0		
1993–94	Middlesbrough	0	0		
1994–95	Stockport Co	13	0		
1995–96	Stockport Co	9	1	22	1
1996–97	Darlington	39	9		
1997–98	Darlington	39	2		
1998–99	Darlington	36	1		
1999–2000	Darlington	37	2	151	14
2000–01	Rochdale	38	0		
2001–02	Rochdale	45	7	83	7

PLATT, Clive (F) 159 28
H: 6 3 W: 13 04 b.Wolverhampton 27-10-77
Source: Trainee.

1995–96	Walsall	4	2		
1996–97	Walsall	1	0		
1997–98	Walsall	20	1		
1998–99	Walsall	7	1		
1999–2000	Walsall	0	0	32	4
1999–2000	Rochdale	41	9		
2000–01	Rochdale	43	8		
2001–02	Rochdale	43	7	127	24

ROSE, Karl‡ (F) 5 0
H: 5 10 W: 11 00 b.Barnsley 12-10-78
Source: Trainee.

1995–96	Barnsley	0	0		
1996–97	Barnsley	0	0		
1997–98	Barnsley	0	0		
1998–99	Barnsley	4	0		
1998–99	*Mansfield T*	1	0	1	0
1999–2000	Barnsley	0	0		
2000–01	Barnsley	0	0	4	0
2001–02	Rochdale	0	0		

SIMPSON, Paul (F) 602 134
H: 5 7 W: 11 03 b.Carlisle 26-7-66
Source: Apprentice. *Honours:* England Youth, Under-21.

1982–83	Manchester C	3	0		
1983–84	Manchester C	0	0		
1984–85	Manchester C	10	6		
1985–86	Manchester C	37	8		
1986–87	Manchester C	32	3		
1987–88	Manchester C	38	1		
1988–89	Manchester C	7	0	121	18
1988–89	Oxford U	25	8		
1989–90	Oxford U	42	9		
1990–91	Oxford U	46	17		
1991–92	Oxford U	31	9	144	43
1991–92	Derby Co	16	7		
1992–93	Derby Co	35	12		
1993–94	Derby Co	34	9		
1994–95	Derby Co	42	8		
1995–96	Derby Co	39	10		
1996–97	Derby Co	1	0		
1996–97	*Sheffield U*	6	0	6	0
1997–98	Derby Co	1	0	186	48
1997–98	Wolverhampton W	28	4		
1998–99	Wolverhampton W	11	2		
1998–99	*Walsall*	10	1	10	1
1999–2000	Wolverhampton W	13	0		
2000–01	Wolverhampton W	0	0	52	6
2000–01	Blackpool	44	12		
2001–02	Blackpool	32	1	76	13
2001–02	Rochdale	7	5	7	5

TODD, Lee* (D) 301 5
H: 5 7 W: 11 01 b.Hartlepool 7-3-72
Source: Hartlepool U Trainee.

1990–91	Stockport Co	14	0		
1991–92	Stockport Co	19	0		
1992–93	Stockport Co	39	0		
1993–94	Stockport Co	33	0		
1994–95	Stockport Co	37	2		
1995–96	Stockport Co	42	0		
1996–97	Stockport Co	41	0	225	2
1997–98	Southampton	10	0	10	0
1998–99	Bradford C	15	0		
1999–2000	Bradford C	0	0	15	0
1999–2000	Walsall	1	0	1	0
2000–01	Rochdale	40	3		
2001–02	Rochdale	10	0	50	3

TOWNSON, Kevin (F) 44 14
H: 5 6 W: 10 07 b.Liverpool 19-4-83
Honours: England Youth.

2000–01	Rochdale	3	0		
2001–02	Rochdale	41	14	44	14

WARE, Paul* (M) 230 18
H: 5 9 W: 12 00 b.Congleton 7-11-70
Source: Trainee.

1987–88	Stoke C	1	0		
1988–89	Stoke C	11	1		
1989–90	Stoke C	16	0		
1990–91	Stoke C	34	2		
1991–92	Stoke C	24	3		
1992–93	Stoke C	28	4		
1993–94	Stoke C	1	0		
1994–95	Stoke C	0	0	115	10
1994–95	Stockport Co	19	1		
1995–96	Stockport Co	27	3		
1996–97	Stockport Co	8	0	54	4
1996–97	*Cardiff C*	5	0	5	0

From Hednesford T.

1999–2000	Macclesfield T	18	2	18	2
2000–01	Rochdale	30	2		
2001–02	Rochdale	8	0	38	2

Scholars
Baker, John D; Bell, Colin; Duffy, Matthew J; Ford, Joshua MA; Gartside, Karl; Gibbons, Joseph; Grand, Simon; Hamilton, Kiel; Hill, Stephen B; Murphy, Shane P; Patterson, Rory C; Ridings, A; Semmens, Christopher; Smith, Steven K; Taylor, Warren D; Waldron, Luke; Walsh, David A; Warner, Scott

ROTHERHAM U

ARTELL, David (D) 37 4
H: 6 3 W: 13 10 b.Rotherham 22-11-80
Source: Trainee.

1999–2000	Rotherham U	1	0		
2000–01	Rotherham U	36	4		
2001–02	Rotherham U	0	0	37	4

BARKER, Richard (F) 178 39
H: 6 0 W: 13 12 b.Sheffield 30-5-75
Source: Trainee. *Honours:* England Schools.

1993–94	Sheffield W	0	0		
1994–95	Sheffield W	0	0		
1995–96	Sheffield W	0	0		
1995–96	*Doncaster R*	6	0	6	0
1996–97	Sheffield W	0	0		

From Linfield

1997–98	Brighton & HA	17	2		
1998–99	Brighton & HA	43	10	60	12
1999–2000	Macclesfield T	35	16		
2000–01	Macclesfield T	23	7	58	23
2000–01	Rotherham U	19	1		
2001–02	Rotherham U	35	3	54	4

BEECH, Chris (D) 99 2
H: 5 9 W: 11 13 b.Congleton 5-11-75
Source: Trainee. *Honours:* England Schools, Youth.

1992–93	Manchester C	0	0		
1993–94	Manchester C	0	0		
1994–95	Manchester C	0	0		
1995–96	Manchester C	0	0		
1996–97	Manchester C	0	0		
1997–98	Cardiff C	46	1	46	1
1998–99	Rotherham U	24	0		
1999–2000	Rotherham U	6	0		
2000–01	Rotherham U	15	0		
2001–02	Rotherham U	8	1	53	1

BERRY, Trevor‡ (M) 179 21
H: 5 6 W: 11 00 b.Haslemere 1-8-74
Source: Bournemouth.

1991–92	Aston Villa	0	0		

1992–93	Aston Villa	0	0		
1993–94	Aston Villa	0	0		
1994–95	Aston Villa	0	0		
1995–96	Aston Villa	0	0		
1995–96	Rotherham U	36	7		
1996–97	Rotherham U	30	4		
1997–98	Rotherham U	42	3		
1998–99	Rotherham U	18	2		
1999–2000	Rotherham U	36	4		
2000–01	Rotherham U	11	0		
2000–01	Scunthorpe U	6	1	6	1
2001–02	Rotherham U	0	0	173	20

BRANSTON, Guy (D) 105 13
H: 6 1 W: 14 13 b.Leicester 9-1-79
Source: Trainee.

1997–98	Leicester C	0	0		
1997–98	Colchester U	12	1		
1998–99	Leicester C	0	0		
1998–99	Colchester U	1	0	13	1
1998–99	Plymouth Arg	7	1	7	1
1999–2000	Leicester C	0	0		
1999–2000	Lincoln C	4	0	4	0
1999–2000	Rotherham U	30	4		
2000–01	Rotherham U	41	6		
2001–02	Rotherham U	10	1	81	11

BRYAN, Marvin (D) 243 5
H: 5 11 W: 12 13 b.Paddington 2-8-75
Source: Trainee.

1992–93	QPR	0	0		
1993–94	QPR	0	0		
1994–95	QPR	0	0		
1994–95	Doncaster R	5	1	5	1
1995–96	Blackpool	46	1		
1996–97	Blackpool	34	1		
1997–98	Blackpool	43	1		
1998–99	Blackpool	41	1		
1999–2000	Blackpool	18	0	182	4
1999–2000	Bury	9	0	9	0
2000–01	Rotherham U	28	0		
2001–02	Rotherham U	19	0	47	0

BYFIELD, Darren (F) 105 17
H: 5 11 W: 13 06 b.Sutton Coldfield 29-9-76
Source: Trainee.

1993–94	Aston Villa	0	0		
1994–95	Aston Villa	0	0		
1995–96	Aston Villa	0	0		
1996–97	Aston Villa	0	0		
1997–98	Aston Villa	7	0		
1998–99	Aston Villa	0	0		
1998–99	Preston NE	5	1	5	1
1999–2000	Aston Villa	0	0	7	0
1999–2000	Northampton T	6	1	6	1
1999–2000	Cambridge U	4	0	4	0
1999–2000	Blackpool	3	0	3	0
2000–01	Walsall	40	9		
2001–02	Walsall	37	4	77	13
2001–02	Rotherham U	3	2	3	2

DAWS, Nick (M) 404 17
H: 5 11 W: 13 07 b.Salford 15-3-70
Source: Altrincham.

1992–93	Bury	36	1		
1993–94	Bury	37	1		
1994–95	Bury	34	2		
1995–96	Bury	37	1		
1996–97	Bury	46	2		
1997–98	Bury	46	2		
1998–99	Bury	46	2		
1999–2000	Bury	43	2		
2000–01	Bury	44	3	369	16
2001–02	Rotherham U	35	1	35	1

ESSON, Ryan (G) 46 0
H: 6 1 W: 12 06 b.Aberdeen 19-3-80

1999–2000	Aberdeen	1	0		
2000–01	Aberdeen	36	0		
2001–02	Aberdeen	9	0	46	0
2001–02	Rotherham U	0	0		

GARNER, Darren (M) 234 21
H: 5 10 W: 12 01 b.Plymouth 10-12-71
Source: Trainee.

1988–89	Plymouth Arg	1	0		
1989–90	Plymouth Arg	1	0		
1990–91	Plymouth Arg	5	1		
1991–92	Plymouth Arg	10	0		
1992–93	Plymouth Arg	10	0		
1993–94	Plymouth Arg	0	0	27	1

From Dorchester T.

1995–96	Rotherham U	31	1		
1996–97	Rotherham U	30	2		
1997–98	Rotherham U	40	3		
1998–99	Rotherham U	40	4		
1999–2000	Rotherham U	35	9		
2000–01	Rotherham U	31	1		
2001–02	Rotherham U	0	0	207	20

GRAY, Ian (G) 128 0
H: 6 2 W: 13 13 b.Manchester 25-2-75
Source: Trainee.

1993–94	Oldham Ath	0	0		
1994–95	Oldham Ath	0	0		
1994–95	Rochdale	12	0		
1995–96	Rochdale	20	0		
1996–97	Rochdale	46	0	78	0
1997–98	Stockport Co	3	0		
1998–99	Stockport Co	3	0		
1999–2000	Stockport Co	10	0	16	0
2000–01	Rotherham U	33	0		
2001–02	Rotherham U	1	0	34	0

HOLLOWAY, Chris* (M) 68 2
H: 5 5 W: 12 05 b.Swansea 5-2-80
Source: Trainee. Honours: Wales Under-21.

1997–98	Exeter C	6	0		
1998–99	Exeter C	34	1		
1999–2000	Exeter C	24	1		
2000–01	Exeter C	4	0	68	2
2001–02	Rotherham U	0	0		

HUDSON, Danny (M) 48 5
H: 5 9 W: 11 00 b.Mexborough 25-6-79
Source: Trainee.

1997–98	Rotherham U	10	0		
1998–99	Rotherham U	26	4		
1999–2000	Rotherham U	7	1		
2000–01	Rotherham U	5	0		
2001–02	Rotherham U	0	0	48	5

HURST, Paul (D) 268 11
H: 5 5 W: 9 12 b.Sheffield 25-9-74
Source: Trainee.

1993–94	Rotherham U	4	0		
1994–95	Rotherham U	13	0		
1995–96	Rotherham U	40	1		
1996–97	Rotherham U	30	3		
1997–98	Rotherham U	30	0		
1998–99	Rotherham U	32	2		
1999–2000	Rotherham U	30	2		
2000–01	Rotherham U	44	3		
2001–02	Rotherham U	45	0	268	11

JONES, Rhodri (D) 0 0
H: 5 11 W: 12 05 b.Cardiff 19-1-82
Source: Trainee.

1999–2000	Manchester U	0	0		
2000–01	Manchester U	0	0		
2001–02	Rotherham U	0	0		

LEE, Alan (F) 102 26
H: 6 2 W: 13 09 b.Galway 21-8-78
Source: Trainee. Honours: Éire Under-21.

1995–96	Aston Villa	0	0		
1996–97	Aston Villa	0	0		
1997–98	Aston Villa	0	0		
1998–99	Aston Villa	0	0		
1998–99	Torquay U	7	2	7	2
1998–99	Port Vale	11	2	11	2
1999–2000	Burnley	15	0		
2000–01	Burnley	0	0	15	0
2000–01	Rotherham U	31	13		
2001–02	Rotherham U	38	9	69	22

LOWNDES, Nathan (F) 94 17
H: 5 11 W: 10 11 b.Salford 2-6-77
Source: Trainee.

1994–95	Leeds U	0	0		
1995–96	Leeds U	0	0		
1995–96	Watford	0	0		
1996–97	Watford	3	0		
1997–98	Watford	4	0	7	0
1998–99	St Johnstone	29	2		
1999–2000	St Johnstone	25	10		
2000–01	St Johnstone	10	2	64	14
2001–02	Livingston	21	3	21	3
2001–02	Rotherham U	2	0	2	0

McINTOSH, Martin (D) 315 31
H: 6 2 W: 13 04 b.East Kilbride 19-3-71
Honours: Scotland B.

1988–89	St Mirren	2	0		
1989–90	St Mirren	2	0		
1990–91	St Mirren	0	0	4	0
1991–92	Clydebank	28	5		
1992–93	Clydebank	33	4		
1993–94	Clydebank	4	1	65	10
1993–94	Hamilton A	13	2		
1994–95	Hamilton A	30	2		
1995–96	Hamilton A	23	1		
1996–97	Hamilton A	33	7	99	12
1997–98	Stockport Co	38	2		
1998–99	Stockport Co	41	3		
1999–2000	Stockport Co	20	0	99	5
1999–2000	Hibernian	9	0		
2000–01	Hibernian	0	0		
2001–02	Hibernian	0	0	9	0
2001–02	Rotherham U	39	4	39	4

MIRANDA, Jose (M) 2 0
H: 5 7 W: 9 12 b.Lisbon 20-4-74

2001–02	Rotherham U	2	0	2	0

MONKHOUSE, Andy (M) 55 3
H: 6 2 W: 12 05 b.Leeds 23-10-80
Source: Trainee.

1998–99	Rotherham U	5	1		
1999–2000	Rotherham U	0	0		
2000–01	Rotherham U	12	0		
2001–02	Rotherham U	38	2	55	3

MULLIN, John (M) 177 16
H: 5 9 W: 12 09 b.Bury 11-8-75
Source: School.

1992–93	Burnley	0	0		
1993–94	Burnley	6	1		
1994–95	Burnley	12	1		
1995–96	Sunderland	10	1		
1996–97	Sunderland	10	1		
1997–98	Sunderland	6	0		
1997–98	Preston NE	7	0	7	0
1997–98	Burnley	6	0		
1998–99	Sunderland	9	2	35	4
1999–2000	Burnley	37	5		
2000–01	Burnley	36	3		
2001–02	Burnley	4	0	101	10
2001–02	Rotherham U	34	2	34	2

POLLITT, Mike (G) 333 0
H: 6 3 W: 14 10 b.Farnworth 29-2-72
Source: Trainee.

1990–91	Manchester U	0	0		
1990–91	Oldham Ath	0	0		
1991–92	Bury	0	0		
1992–93	Lincoln C	27	0		
1993–94	Lincoln C	30	0	57	0
1994–95	Darlington	40	0		
1995–96	Darlington	15	0	55	0
1995–96	Notts Co	8	0		
1996–97	Notts Co	8	0		
1997–98	Notts Co	2	0	10	0
1997–98	Oldham Ath	16	0	16	0
1997–98	Gillingham	6	0	6	0
1997–98	Brentford	5	0	5	0
1997–98	Sunderland	0	0		
1998–99	Rotherham U	46	0		
1999–2000	Rotherham U	46	0		
2000–01	Chesterfield	46	0	46	0
2001–02	Rotherham U	46	0	138	0

ROBINS, Mark (F) 301 88
H: 5 8 W: 11 10 b.Ashton-under-Lyne 22-12-69
Source: Apprentice. Honours: England Under-21.

1986–87	Manchester U	0	0		
1987–88	Manchester U	0	0		
1988–89	Manchester U	10	0		
1989–90	Manchester U	17	7		
1990–91	Manchester U	19	4		
1991–92	Manchester U	2	0	48	11
1992–93	Norwich C	37	15		
1993–94	Norwich C	13	1		
1994–95	Norwich C	17	4	67	20
1994–95	Leicester C	17	5		
1995–96	Leicester C	31	6		
1996–97	Leicester C	8	1		
1997–98	Leicester C	0	0	56	12
1997–98	Reading	5	0	5	0

From Panionios.

1998–99	Manchester C	2	0	2	0
1999–2000	Walsall	40	6	40	6
2000–01	Rotherham U	42	24		
2001–02	Rotherham U	41	15	83	39

SCOTT, Rob (D) 227 31
H: 6 1 W: 12 06 b.Epsom 15-8-73
Source: Sutton U.

1993–94	Sheffield U	0	0		
1994–95	Sheffield U	1	0		
1994–95	Scarborough	8	3	8	3
1995–96	Sheffield U	5	1	6	1
1995–96	Northampton T	5	0	5	0
1995–96	Fulham	21	5		
1996–97	Fulham	43	9		
1997–98	Fulham	17	3		
1998–99	Fulham	3	0	84	17
1998–99	Carlisle U	7	3	7	3
1998–99	Rotherham U	6	1		
1999–2000	Rotherham U	34	1		
2000–01	Rotherham U	39	2		
2001–02	Rotherham U	38	3	117	7

SEDGWICK, Chris (M) 140 12
H: 6 0 W: 12 03 b.Sheffield 28-4-80
Source: Trainee.

1997–98	Rotherham U	4	0		
1998–99	Rotherham U	33	4		
1999–2000	Rotherham U	38	5		
2000–01	Rotherham U	21	2		
2001–02	Rotherham U	44	1	140	12

SWAILES, Chris (D) 252 17
H: 6 2 W: 12 07 b.Gateshead 19-10-70
Source: Ipswich T Trainee, Peterborough U, Boston U, Birmingham C, Bridlington T.
1993-94	Doncaster R	17	0		
1994-95	Doncaster R	32	0	49	0
1995-96	Ipswich T	5	0		
1996-97	Ipswich T	23	1		
1997-98	Ipswich T	5	0	33	1
1997-98	Bury	13	1		
1998-99	Bury	43	3		
1999-2000	Bury	27	2		
2000-01	Bury	43	4	126	10
2001-02	Rotherham U	44	6	44	6

TALBOT, Stuart (M) 213 16
H: 6 0 W: 13 10 b.Birmingham 14-6-73
Source: Doncaster R, Moor Green.
1994-95	Port Vale	2	0		
1995-96	Port Vale	20	0		
1996-97	Port Vale	34	4		
1997-98	Port Vale	42	6		
1998-99	Port Vale	33	0		
1999-2000	Port Vale	6	0	137	10
2000-01	Rotherham U	38	5		
2001-02	Rotherham U	38	1	76	6

WARNE, Paul (F) 167 28
H: 5 9 W: 11 09 b.Norwich 8-5-73
Source: Wroxham.
1997-98	Wigan Ath	25	2		
1998-99	Wigan Ath	11	1	36	3
1998-99	Rotherham U	19	8		
1999-2000	Rotherham U	43	10		
2000-01	Rotherham U	44	7		
2001-02	Rotherham U	25	0	131	25

Scholars
Alabi, Stephen; Barker, Shaun; Barraclough, Simon D; Beggs, John A; Bowler, Kris PM; Boyd, Darren; Clarke, Leon K; Fells, Daniel D; Gregory, Benjamin D; Holyer, Ian D; Jones, Andrew S; Kerr, Aaron G; Lees, Scott; Letts, Scott D; McCoy, James TG; Middlebrook, Andrew; Smith, Thomas; Wright, Mark J

RUSHDEN & D

ANGELL, Brett* (F) 437 159
H: 6 2 W: 13 11 b.Marlborough 20-8-68
Source: Portsmouth, Cheltenham T.
1987-88	Derby Co	0	0		
1988-89	Stockport Co	26	5		
1989-90	Stockport Co	44	23		
1990-91	Southend U	42	15		
1991-92	Southend U	43	21		
1992-93	Southend U	13	5		
1993-94	Southend U	5	4		
1993-94	*Everton*	1	0		
1993-94	Southend U	12	2	115	47
1993-94	Everton	15	1		
1994-95	Everton	4	0	20	1
1994-95	Sunderland	8	0		
1995-96	Sunderland	2	0		
1995-96	*Sheffield U*	6	2	6	2
1995-96	WBA	3	0	3	0
1996-97	Sunderland	0	0	10	0
1996-97	Stockport Co	34	15		
1997-98	Stockport Co	45	18		
1998-99	Stockport Co	42	17		
1999-2000	Stockport Co	5	0	196	78
1999-2000	*Notts Co*	6	5	6	5
1999-2000	*Preston NE*	15	8	15	8
2000-01	Walsall	41	13		
2001-02	Walsall	20	3	61	16
2001-02	Rushden & D	5	2	5	2

BELL JNR, David‡ (M) 1 0
H: 5 10 W: 11 01 b.Buncrana 13-5-85
Source: Institute.
| 2001-02 | Rushden & D | 1 | 0 | 1 | 0 |

BELL, David (M) 0 0
H: 5 10 W: 11 06 b.Kettering 21-1-84
Source: Trainee.
| 2001-02 | Rushden & D | 0 | 0 | 0 | 0 |

BRADY, Jon* (M) 22 1
H: 5 8 W: 11 01 b.Newcastle, Australia 14-1-75
Source: Hayes.
| 2001-02 | Rushden & D | 22 | 1 | 22 | 1 |

BURGESS, Andy (M) 32 4
H: 6 2 W: 11 11 b.Bedford 10-8-81
| 2001-02 | Rushden & D | 32 | 4 | 32 | 4 |

BUTTERWORTH, Garry* (M) 153 5
H: 5 10 W: 11 13 b.Peterborough 8-6-69
1986-87	Peterborough U	1	0		
1987-88	Peterborough U	11	0		
1988-89	Peterborough U	8	0		
1989-90	Peterborough U	39	3		
1990-91	Peterborough U	46	0		
1991-92	Peterborough U	19	1	124	4
From Dagenham & R.
2001-02	Rushden & D	29	1	29	1

CAREY, Shaun‡ (M) 76 0
H: 5 9 W: 11 01 b.Kettering 13-5-76
Source: Trainee.
1994-95	Norwich C	0	0		
1995-96	Norwich C	9	0		
1996-97	Norwich C	14	0		
1997-98	Norwich C	14	0		
1998-99	Norwich C	10	0		
1999-2000	Norwich C	21	0		
2000-01	Norwich C	0	0	68	0
2001-02	Rushden & D	8	0	8	0

CARR, Darre‡ (D) 308 12
H: 6 2 W: 13 07 b.Bristol 4-9-68
Source: Trainee.
1985-86	Bristol R	1	0		
1986-87	Bristol R	20	0		
1987-88	Bristol R	9	0	30	0
1987-88	Newport Co	9	0	9	0
1987-88	Sheffield U	3	0		
1988-89	Sheffield U	10	1		
1989-90	Sheffield U	0	0		
1990-91	Sheffield U	0	0	13	1
1990-91	Crewe Alex	36	0		
1991-92	Crewe Alex	36	3		
1992-93	Crewe Alex	32	2	104	5
1993-94	Chesterfield	28	1		
1994-95	Chesterfield	35	2		
1995-96	Chesterfield	1	0		
1996-97	Chesterfield	12	0		
1997-98	Chesterfield	10	1	86	4
1998-99	Gillingham	30	2	30	2
1999-2000	Brighton & HA	19	0		
2000-01	Brighton & HA	2	0	21	0
2000-01	*Rotherham U*	1	0	1	0
2000-01	*Lincoln C*	3	0	3	0
2000-01	*Carlisle U*	10	0	10	0
2001-02	Rushden & D	1	0	1	0

DARBY, Duane (F) 269 69
H: 5 11 W: 14 00 b.Birmingham 17-10-73
Source: Trainee.
1991-92	Torquay U	14	2		
1992-93	Torquay U	34	12		
1993-94	Torquay U	36	8		
1994-95	Torquay U	24	4	108	26
1995-96	Doncaster R	17	4	17	4
1995-96	Hull C	8	1		
1996-97	Hull C	41	13		
1997-98	Hull C	29	13		
1998-99	Notts Co	0	0		
1998-99	*Hull C*	8	0	86	27
1999-2000	Notts Co	28	5		
2000-01	Notts Co	0	0	28	5
2001-02	Rushden & D	30	7	30	7

DAVIES, Alex‡ (G) 1 0
H: 6 1 W: 13 00 b.Swansea 2-11-82
Source: Scholar.
| 2000-01 | Swansea C | 1 | 0 | 1 | 0 |
| 2001-02 | Rushden & D | 0 | 0 | | |

DEMPSTER, John (D) 2 0
H: 6 0 W: 11 06 b.Kettering 1-4-83
Source: Trainee.
| 2001-02 | Rushden & D | 2 | 0 | 2 | 0 |

DOWELL, Adam (G) 0 0
H: 6 1 W: 12 10 b.Gateshead 6-12-82
Source: Scholar.
2000-01	Sunderland	0	0		
2001-02	Sunderland	0	0		
2001-02	Rushden & D	0	0		

DUFFY, Robert (F) 8 1
H: 6 1 W: 12 01 b.Swansea 2-12-82
Honours: Wales Under-18.
| 2001-02 | Rushden & D | 8 | 1 | 8 | 1 |

GRAY, Stuart (D) 92 3
H: 5 10 W: 13 05 b.Harrogate 18-12-73
Source: Giffnock N. *Honours:* Scotland Under-21.
1992-93	Celtic	1	0		
1993-94	Celtic	0	0		
1994-95	Celtic	11	0		
1995-96	Celtic	5	1		
1996-97	Celtic	11	0		
1997-98	Celtic	0	0	28	1
1997-98	Reading	7	0		
1998-99	Reading	27	2		
1999-2000	Reading	15	0		
2000-01	Reading	3	0	52	2
2001-02	Rushden & D	12	0	12	0

HALL, Paul (M) 392 57
H: 5 8 W: 10 02 b.Manchester 3-7-72
Source: Trainee. *Honours:* Jamaica 33 full caps.
1989-90	Torquay U	10	0		
1990-91	Torquay U	17	0		
1991-92	Torquay U	38	1		
1992-93	Torquay U	28	0	93	1
1992-93	Portsmouth	0	0		
1993-94	Portsmouth	28	4		
1994-95	Portsmouth	43	5		
1995-96	Portsmouth	46	10		
1996-97	Portsmouth	42	13		
1997-98	Portsmouth	29	5	188	37
1998-99	Coventry C	9	0		
1998-99	*Bury*	7	0	7	0
1999-2000	Coventry C	1	0	10	0
1999-2000	*Sheffield U*	4	1	4	1
1999-2000	WBA	4	0	4	0
1999-2000	Walsall	10	4		
2000-01	Walsall	42	6		
2001-02	Walsall	0	0	52	10
2001-02	Rushden & D	34	8	34	8

HANLON, Ritchie (M) 84 9
H: 6 1 W: 12 13 b.Kenton 25-5-78
Source: Chelsea Trainee.
| 1996-97 | Southend U | 2 | 0 | | |
| 1997-98 | Southend U | 0 | 0 | 2 | 0 |
From Rushden & D.
| 1998-99 | Peterborough U | 4 | 1 | | |
From Welling U.
1999-2000	Peterborough U	16	1		
2000-01	Peterborough U	26	1		
2001-02	Peterborough U	1	0	47	3
2001-02	Rushden & D	35	6	35	6

HUNTER, Barry# (D) 203 11
H: 6 4 W: 12 00 b.Coleraine 18-11-68
Source: Crusaders. *Honours:* Northern Ireland Youth, B, 15 full caps, 1 goal.
1993-94	Wrexham	23	1		
1994-95	Wrexham	37	0		
1995-96	Wrexham	31	3	91	4
1996-97	Reading	27	2		
1997-98	Reading	0	0		
1998-99	Reading	3	0		
1998-99	*Southend U*	5	2	5	2
1999-2000	Reading	31	1		
2000-01	Reading	23	1		
2001-02	Reading	0	0	84	4
2001-02	Rushden & D	23	1	23	1

JACKSON, Justin‡ (F) 49 5
H: 5 11 W: 11 09 b.Nottingham 10-12-74
Source: Woking.
1997-98	Notts Co	15	1		
1998-99	Notts Co	10	0	25	1
1998-99	*Rotherham U*	2	1	2	1
1998-99	Halifax T	16	3		
1999-2000	Halifax T	1	0		
2000-01	Halifax T	0	0	17	3
2001-02	Rushden & D	5	0	5	0

LEE, Christian‡ (F) 80 11
H: 6 2 W: 11 07 b.Aylesbury 8-10-76
Source: Doncaster R.
1995-96	Northampton T	5	0		
1996-97	Northampton T	29	7		
1997-98	Northampton T	6	0		
1998-99	Northampton T	19	1	59	8
1999-2000	Gillingham	3	0		
2000-01	Gillingham	0	0	3	0
2000-01	*Rochdale*	5	1	5	1
2000-01	*Leyton Orient*	3	0	3	0
2000-01	Bristol R	9	2	9	2
2001-02	Rushden & D	1	0	1	0

LOWE, Onandi (F) 30 20
H: 6 3 W: 14 07 b.Kingston, Jamaica 2-12-74
Honours: Jamaica full caps.
| 2000-01 | Port Vale | 5 | 1 | 5 | 1 |
From Kansas City W.
| 2001-02 | Rushden & D | 25 | 19 | 25 | 19 |

McELHATTON, Mike (M) 119 10
H: 5 11 W: 13 03 b.Killarney 16-4-75
Source: Trainee.
1992-93	Bournemouth	1	0		
1993-94	Bournemouth	10	0		
1994-95	Bournemouth	27	2		
1995-96	Bournemouth	4	0		
1996-97	Bournemouth	0	0	42	2
1996-97	Scarborough	28	1		
1997-98	Scarborough	42	6		
1998-99	Scarborough	0	0	70	7
2001-02	Rushden & D	7	1	7	1

MILLS, Gary (M) 9 0
H: 5 9 W: 11 04 b.Sheppey 20-5-81
| 2001-02 | Rushden & D | 9 | 0 | 9 | 0 |

MUSTAFA, Tarkan (D) 34 1
H: 5 11 W: 11 11 b.Islington 28-8-73
Source: Kettering T.

1997–98	Barnet	11	0	**11**	**0**

From Kingstonian.

2001–02	Rushden & D	23	1	**23**	**1**

NAYLOR, Stuart‡ (G) 541 0
H: 6 4 W: 13 12 b.Wetherby 6-12-62
Source: Yorkshire Amateur. *Honours:* England Youth, B.

1980–81	Lincoln C	0	0		
1981–82	Lincoln C	3	0		
1982–83	Lincoln C	1	0		
1982–83	*Peterborough U*	8	0	**8**	**0**
1983–84	Lincoln C	0	0		
1983–84	*Crewe Alex*	38	0		
1984–85	*Crewe Alex*	17	0	**55**	**0**
1984–85	Lincoln C	25	0		
1985–86	Lincoln C	20	0	**49**	**0**
1985–86	WBA	12	0		
1986–87	WBA	42	0		
1987–88	WBA	35	0		
1988–89	WBA	44	0		
1989–90	WBA	39	0		
1990–91	WBA	28	0		
1991–92	WBA	34	0		
1992–93	WBA	32	0		
1993–94	WBA	20	0		
1994–95	WBA	42	0		
1995–96	WBA	27	0	**355**	**0**
1996–97	Bristol C	35	0		
1997–98	Bristol C	2	0		
1998–99	Bristol C	0	0	**37**	**0**
1998–99	*Mansfield T*	6	0	**6**	**0**
1998–99	Walsall	0	0		
1999–2000	Exeter C	31	0		
2000–01	Exeter C	0	0	**31**	**0**
2001–02	Rushden & D	0	0		

PARTRIDGE, Scott (F) 281 51
H: 5 9 W: 11 02 b.Leicester 13-10-74
Source: Trainee.

1992–93	Bradford C	4	0		
1993–94	Bradford C	1	0	**5**	**0**
1993–94	Bristol C	9	4		
1994–95	Bristol C	33	2		
1995–96	Bristol C	9	1		
1995–96	*Torquay U*	5	2		
1995–96	*Plymouth Arg*	7	2	**7**	**2**
1995–96	*Scarborough*	7	0	**7**	**0**
1996–97	Bristol C	6	0	**57**	**7**
1996–97	Cardiff C	15	0		
1997–98	Cardiff C	22	2	**37**	**2**
1997–98	Torquay U	5	0		
1998–99	Torquay U	29	12	**39**	**14**
1998–99	Brentford	14	7		
1999–2000	Brentford	41	6		
2000–01	Brentford	36	8		
2001–02	Brentford	1	0	**92**	**21**
2001–02	Rushden & D	37	5	**37**	**5**

PATMORE, Warren‡ (F) 4 1
H: 6 3 W: 15 01 b.Kingsbury 14-8-71

2001–02	Rushden & D	4	1	**4**	**1**

PENNOCK, Tony (G) 5 0
H: 6 1 W: 12 10 b.Swansea 10-4-71

2001–02	Rushden & D	5	0	**5**	**0**

PETERS, Mark* (D) 167 9
H: 6 0 W: 13 03 b.St Asaph 6-7-72
Source: Trainee. *Honours:* Wales Under-21.

1991–92	Manchester C	0	0		
1992–93	Norwich C	0	0		
1993–94	Peterborough U	19	0		
1994–95	Peterborough U	0	0	**19**	**0**
1994–95	Mansfield T	26	4		
1995–96	Mansfield T	21	2		
1996–97	Mansfield T	0	0		
1997–98	Mansfield T	24	2		
1998–99	Mansfield T	37	1	**108**	**9**
2001–02	Rushden & D	40	0	**40**	**0**

RODWELL, Jim‡ (D) 9 0
H: 6 1 W: 14 02 b.Lincoln 20-11-70
Source: Halesowen T.

2001–02	Rushden & D	9	0	**9**	**0**

ROWLETT, Luke‡ (F) 0 0
H: 5 9 W: 10 09 b.Nottingham 20-10-82
Source: Nottingham F.

2001–02	Rushden & D	0	0		

SAMBROOK, Andrew (D) 27 0
H: 5 10 W: 11 08 b.Chatham 13-7-79
Source: Trainee.

1996–97	Gillingham	1	0		
1997–98	Gillingham	0	0		
1998–99	Gillingham	0	0	**1**	**0**
2001–02	Rushden & D	26	0	**26**	**0**

SETCHELL, Gary* (D) 22 1
H: 6 0 W: 13 06 b.Kings Lynn 8-5-75

2001–02	Rushden & D	22	1	**22**	**1**

SIGERE, Jean-Michel‡ (F) 7 1
H: 6 1 W: 13 05 b.Martinique 26-1-77

2001–02	Rushden & D	7	1	**7**	**1**

SOLKHON, Brett (D) 1 0
H: 5 11 W: 12 03 b.Canvey Island 12-9-82

2001–02	Rushden & D	1	0	**1**	**0**

TALBOT, Daniel (D) 3 0
H: 5 9 W: 10 07 b.Enfield 30-1-84

2001–02	Rushden & D	3	0	**3**	**0**

TILLSON, Andy# (D) 456 20
H: 6 2 W: 13 05 b.Huntingdon 30-6-66
Source: Kettering T.

1988–89	Grimsby T	45	2		
1989–90	Grimsby T	42	3		
1990–91	Grimsby T	18	0		
1990–91	QPR	19	2		
1991–92	QPR	10	0		
1992–93	QPR	0	0	**29**	**2**
1992–93	*Grimsby T*	4	0	**109**	**5**
1992–93	Bristol R	29	0		
1993–94	Bristol R	13	0		
1994–95	Bristol R	40	2		
1995–96	Bristol R	38	1		
1996–97	Bristol R	38	2		
1997–98	Bristol R	33	3		
1998–99	Bristol R	19	2		
1999–2000	Bristol R	43	1	**253**	**11**
2000–01	Walsall	42	1		
2001–02	Walsall	9	1	**51**	**2**
2001–02	Rushden & D	14	0	**14**	**0**

TURLEY, Billy (G) 85 0
H: 6 3 W: 15 06 b.Wolverhampton 15-7-73
Source: Evesham U.

1995–96	Northampton T	2	0		
1996–97	Northampton T	1	0		
1997–98	Northampton T	0	0		
1997–98	*Leyton Orient*	14	0	**14**	**0**
1998–99	Northampton T	25	0	**28**	**0**
2001–02	Rushden & D	43	0	**43**	**0**

UNDERWOOD, Paul (D) 40 0
H: 5 11 W: 12 08 b.Wimbledon 16-8-73
Source: Enfield.

2001–02	Rushden & D	40	0	**40**	**0**

WARBURTON, Ray‡ (D) 281 21
H: 6 0 W: 13 03 b.Rotherham 7-10-67
Source: Apprentice.

1984–85	Rotherham U	1	0		
1985–86	Rotherham U	0	0		
1986–87	Rotherham U	3	0		
1987–88	Rotherham U	0	0		
1988–89	Rotherham U	0	0	**4**	**0**
1989–90	York C	43	2		
1990–91	York C	22	4		
1991–92	York C	9	0		
1992–93	York C	10	3		
1993–94	York C	6	0	**90**	**9**
1993–94	*Northampton T*	17	1		
1994–95	Northampton T	39	3		
1995–96	Northampton T	44	3		
1996–97	Northampton T	35	4		
1997–98	Northampton T	39	0		
1998–99	Northampton T	12	1		
1999–2000	Northampton T	0	0		
2000–01	Northampton T	0	0		
2001–02	Northampton T	0	0	**186**	**12**
2001–02	Rushden & D	1	0	**1**	**0**

WARDLEY, Stuart (M) 105 18
H: 6 1 W: 13 11 b.Cambridge 10-9-75
Source: Saffron Walden T. *Honours:*

1999–2000	QPR	43	11		
2000–01	QPR	34	3		
2001–02	QPR	10	0	**87**	**14**
2001–02	Rushden & D	18	4	**18**	**4**

WORMULL, Simon‡ (M) 10 0
H: 5 10 W: 12 12 b.Crawley 1-12-76
Source: Trainee.

1995–96	Tottenham H	0	0		
1996–97	Tottenham H	0	0		
1997–98	Brentford	5	0	**5**	**0**
1997–98	Brighton & HA	0	0		
1998–99	Brighton & HA	0	0		
1999–2000	Brighton & HA	0	0		
2000–01	Brighton & HA	0	0		
2001–02	Rushden & D	5	0	**5**	**0**

SCUNTHORPE U

ANDERSON, Mark‡ (F) 1 0
H: 5 11 W: 12 08 b.Scunthorpe 7-10-81
Source: Scholar.

2001–02	Scunthorpe U	1	0	**1**	**0**

BARWICK, Terry§ (M) 11 0
H: 5 10 W: 10 12 b.Doncaster 11-1-83
Source: Scholar.

1999–2000	Scunthorpe U	1	0		
2000–01	Scunthorpe U	0	0		
2001–02	Scunthorpe U	10	0	**11**	**0**

BEAGRIE, Peter (M) 529 67
H: 5 9 W: 12 04 b.Middlesbrough 28-11-65
Source: Local. *Honours:* England Under-21, B.

1983–84	Middlesbrough	0	0		
1984–85	Middlesbrough	7	1		
1985–86	Middlesbrough	26	1	**33**	**2**
1986–87	Sheffield U	41	9		
1987–88	Sheffield U	43	2	**84**	**11**
1988–89	Stoke C	41	7		
1989–90	Stoke C	13	0	**54**	**7**
1989–90	Everton	19	0		
1990–91	Everton	17	2		
1991–92	Everton	27	3		
1991–92	*Sunderland*	5	1	**5**	**1**
1992–93	Everton	22	3		
1993–94	Everton	29	3		
1993–94	Manchester C	9	1		
1994–95	Manchester C	37	2		
1995–96	Manchester C	5	0		
1996–97	Manchester C	1	0	**52**	**3**
1997–98	Bradford C	34	0		
1997–98	*Everton*	6	0	**120**	**11**
1998–99	Bradford C	43	12		
1999–2000	Bradford C	35	7		
2000–01	Bradford C	19	1	**131**	**20**
2000–01	Wigan Ath	10	1	**10**	**1**
2001–02	Scunthorpe U	40	11	**40**	**11**

BENNION, Chris‡ (G) 0 0
H: 6 2 W: 12 05 b.Edinburgh 30-8-80
Source: Trainee.

1999–2000	Middlesbrough	0	0		
2000–01	Middlesbrough	0	0		
2001–02	Middlesbrough	0	0		
2001–02	Scunthorpe U	0	0		

BRADSHAW, Carl* (D) 396 27
H: 5 9 W: 12 04 b.Sheffield 2-10-68
Source: Apprentice. *Honours:* England Youth.

1986–87	Sheffield W	9	2		
1986–87	*Barnsley*	6	1	**6**	**1**
1987–88	Sheffield W	20	2		
1988–89	Sheffield W	3	0	**32**	**4**
1988–89	Manchester C	5	0		
1989–90	Manchester C	0	0	**5**	**0**
1989–90	Sheffield U	30	3		
1990–91	Sheffield U	27	1		
1991–92	Sheffield U	18	2		
1992–93	Sheffield U	32	1		
1993–94	Sheffield U	40	1	**147**	**8**
1994–95	Norwich C	26	1		
1995–96	Norwich C	21	1		
1996–97	Norwich C	17	0		
1997–98	Norwich C	1	0	**65**	**2**
1997–98	Wigan Ath	28	1		
1998–99	Wigan Ath	39	6		
1999–2000	Wigan Ath	26	1		
2000–01	Wigan Ath	27	3	**120**	**11**
2001–02	Scunthorpe U	21	1	**21**	**1**

BROUGH, Scott (M) 23 1
H: 5 5 W: 9 11 b.Doncaster 10-2-83

2000–01	Scunthorpe U	4	0		
2001–02	Scunthorpe U	19	1	**23**	**1**

CALVO-GARCIA, Alex# (M) 186 27
H: 5 9 W: 12 03 b.Ordizia 1-1-72
Source: Eibar.

1996–97	Scunthorpe U	13	1		
1997–98	Scunthorpe U	44	6		
1998–99	Scunthorpe U	43	9		
1999–2000	Scunthorpe U	18	1		
2000–01	Scunthorpe U	34	4		
2001–02	Scunthorpe U	34	6	**186**	**27**

CARRUTHERS, Martin (F) 309 82
H: 5 10 W: 11 13 b.Nottingham 7-8-72
Source: Trainee.

1990–91	Aston Villa	0	0		
1991–92	Aston Villa	3	0		
1992–93	Aston Villa	1	0	**4**	**0**
1992–93	*Hull C*	13	6	**13**	**6**
1993–94	Stoke C	34	5		
1994–95	Stoke C	32	5		
1995–96	Stoke C	24	3		

1996–97	Stoke C	1	0	91	13
1996–97	Peterborough U	14	4		
1997–98	Peterborough U	39	15		
1998–99	Peterborough U	14	2	67	21
1998–99	York C	6	0	6	0
1998–99	Darlington	11	2		
1999–2000	Darlington	6	0	17	2
1999–2000	Southend U	38	19		
2000–01	Southend U	32	7	70	26
2000–01	Scunthorpe U	8	1		
2001–02	Scunthorpe U	33	13	41	14

COLLINS, Neil§ (G)   0 0
H: 6 0 W: 12 02 b.Pontypridd 12-4-84
Source: Scholar.

2001–02	Scunthorpe U	0	0

COTTERILL, James (D)   14 0
H: 5 11 W: 12 04 b.Barnsley 3-8-82
Source: Scholar.

2000–01	Scunthorpe U	4	0		
2001–02	Scunthorpe U	10	0	14	0

DAWSON, Andy (D)   152 6
H: 5 9 W: 11 12 b.Northallerton 20-10-78
Source: Trainee.

1995–96	Nottingham F	0	0		
1996–97	Nottingham F	0	0		
1997–98	Nottingham F	0	0		
1998–99	Nottingham F	0	0		
1998–99	Scunthorpe U	24	0		
1999–2000	Scunthorpe U	43	2		
2000–01	Scunthorpe U	41	4		
2001–02	Scunthorpe U	44	0	152	6

EVANS, Tom (G)   145 0
H: 6 1 W: 13 11 b.Doncaster 31-12-76
Source: Trainee. *Honours:* Northern Ireland Youth.

1995–96	Sheffield U	0	0		
1996–97	Crystal Palace	0	0		
1996–97	Coventry C	0	0		
1997–98	Scunthorpe U	5	0		
1998–99	Scunthorpe U	24	0		
1999–2000	Scunthorpe U	28	0		
2000–01	Scunthorpe U	46	0		
2001–02	Scunthorpe U	42	0	145	0

GRANT, Kim‡ (F)   243 39
H: 5 10 W: 11 05 b.Ghana 25-9-72
Source: Trainee. *Honours:* Ghana full caps.

1990–91	Charlton Ath	12	2		
1991–92	Charlton Ath	4	0		
1992–93	Charlton Ath	21	2		
1993–94	Charlton Ath	30	1		
1994–95	Charlton Ath	26	6		
1995–96	Charlton Ath	30	7	123	18
1995–96	Luton T	10	3		
1996–97	Luton T	25	2		
1997–98	Luton T	0	0	35	5
1997–98	Millwall	39	8		
1998–99	Millwall	16	3	55	11
1998–99	Notts Co	6	1	6	1
1999–2000	Lommel	20	3	20	3
From FC Marco					
2001–02	Scunthorpe U	4	1	4	1

GRAVES, Wayne (M)   73 5
H: 5 7 W: 11 01 b.Scunthorpe 18-9-80
Source: Trainee.

1997–98	Scunthorpe U	3	0		
1998–99	Scunthorpe U	0	0		
1999–2000	Scunthorpe U	19	0		
2000–01	Scunthorpe U	34	2		
2001–02	Scunthorpe U	17	3	73	5

HODGES, Lee‡ (M)   159 21
H: 5 5 W: 11 00 b.Newham 2-3-78
Source: Trainee. *Honours:* England Schools.

1994–95	West Ham U	0	0		
1995–96	West Ham U	0	0		
1996–97	West Ham U	0	0		
1996–97	Exeter C	17	0	17	0
1996–97	Leyton Orient	3	0	3	0
1997–98	West Ham U	2	0		
1997–98	Plymouth Arg	9	0	9	0
1998–99	West Ham U	1	0	3	0
1998–99	Ipswich T	4	0	4	0
1998–99	Southend U	10	1	10	1
1999–2000	Scunthorpe U	40	6		
2000–01	Scunthorpe U	38	8		
2001–02	Scunthorpe U	35	6	113	20

JACKSON, Mark (D)   108 4
H: 5 11 W: 12 13 b.Leeds 30-9-77
Source: Trainee. *Honours:* England Youth.

1995–96	Leeds U	1	0		
1996–97	Leeds U	17	0		
1997–98	Leeds U	0	0		
1998–99	Leeds U	5	0		
1998–99	Huddersfield T	5	0	5	0
1999–2000	Leeds U	0	0	19	0
1999–2000	Barnsley	1	0	1	0
1999–2000	Scunthorpe U	6	0		
2000–01	Scunthorpe U	32	1		
2001–02	Scunthorpe U	45	3	83	4

KELL, Richard (M)   31 4
H: 6 1 W: 10 13 b.Bishop Auckland 15-9-79
Source: Trainee.

1998–99	Middlesbrough	0	0		
1999–2000	Middlesbrough	0	0		
2000–01	Middlesbrough	0	0		
2000–01	Torquay U	15	3		
2001–02	Torquay U	0	0	15	3
2001–02	Scunthorpe U	16	1	16	1

McCOMBE, Jamie (D)   17 0
H: 6 5 W: 12 05 b.Pontefract 1-1-83
Source: Scholar.

2001–02	Scunthorpe U	17	0	17	0

PARTON, Andy§ (M)   1 0
H: 5 10 W: 12 00 b.Doncaster 29-9-83
Source: Scholar.

2001–02	Scunthorpe U	1	0	1	0

PEPPER, Nigel (M)   361 53
H: 5 10 W: 13 12 b.Rotherham 5-4-68
Source: Apprentice.

1985–86	Rotherham U	7	0		
1986–87	Rotherham U	2	0		
1987–88	Rotherham U	15	0		
1988–89	Rotherham U	2	0		
1989–90	Rotherham U	19	1	45	1
1990–91	York C	39	3		
1991–92	York C	35	4		
1992–93	York C	34	8		
1993–94	York C	23	0		
1994–95	York C	35	4		
1995–96	York C	40	8		
1996–97	York C	29	12	235	39
1996–97	Bradford C	11	5		
1997–98	Bradford C	32	5		
1998–99	Bradford C	9	1	52	11
1998–99	Aberdeen	10	0		
1999–2000	Aberdeen	4	0	14	0
1999–2000	Southend U	12	2	12	2
2000–01	Scunthorpe U	2	0		
2001–02	Scunthorpe U	1	0	3	0

QUAILEY, Brian# (F)   91 18
H: 6 0 W: 13 04 b.Leicester 21-3-78
Source: Nuneaton B. *Honours:* St Kitts & Nevis full caps.

1997–98	WBA	5	0		
1998–99	WBA	2	0		
1998–99	Exeter C	12	2	12	2
1999–2000	WBA	0	0	7	0
1999–2000	Blackpool	1	0	1	0
1999–2000	Scunthorpe U	14	5		
2000–01	Scunthorpe U	27	3		
2001–02	Scunthorpe U	30	8	71	16

RIDLEY, Lee (D)   6 0
H: 5 9 W: 11 10 b.Scunthorpe 5-12-81
Source: Scholar.

2000–01	Scunthorpe U	2	0		
2001–02	Scunthorpe U	4	0	6	0

SHELDON, Gareth* (M)   87 6
H: 5 10 W: 12 10 b.Birmingham 31-1-80
Source: Scholar.

1997–98	Scunthorpe U	1	0		
1998–99	Scunthorpe U	11	1		
1999–2000	Scunthorpe U	22	2		
2000–01	Scunthorpe U	39	1		
2001–02	Scunthorpe U	14	2	87	6

SPARROW, Matthew (M)   46 5
H: 5 11 W: 10 06 b.London 3-10-81
Source: Scholar.

1999–2000	Scunthorpe U	11	0		
2000–01	Scunthorpe U	11	4		
2001–02	Scunthorpe U	24	1	46	5

STANTON, Nathan (D)   119 0
H: 5 9 W: 12 07 b.Nottingham 6-5-81
Source: Trainee. *Honours:* England Youth.

1997–98	Scunthorpe U	1	0		
1998–99	Scunthorpe U	4	0		
1999–2000	Scunthorpe U	34	0		
2000–01	Scunthorpe U	38	0		
2001–02	Scunthorpe U	42	0	119	0

THOM, Stuart* (D)   80 5
H: 6 2 W: 14 05 b.Dewsbury 27-12-76
Source: Trainee.

1993–94	Nottingham F	0	0		
1994–95	Nottingham F	0	0		
1995–96	Nottingham F	0	0		
1996–97	Nottingham F	0	0		
1997–98	Nottingham F	0	0		
1997–98	Mansfield T	5	0	5	0
1998–99	Nottingham F	2	0		
1998–99	Oldham Ath	25	1		
1999–2000	Oldham Ath	9	2		
2000–01	Oldham Ath	0	0	34	3
2000–01	Scunthorpe U	21	0		
2001–02	Scunthorpe U	20	2	41	2

TORPEY, Steve (F)   435 104
H: 6 3 W: 13 06 b.Islington 8-12-70
Source: Trainee.

1988–89	Millwall	0	0		
1989–90	Millwall	7	0		
1990–91	Millwall	0	0	7	0
1990–91	Bradford C	29	7		
1991–92	Bradford C	43	10		
1992–93	Bradford C	24	5	96	22
1993–94	Swansea C	40	9		
1994–95	Swansea C	41	11		
1995–96	Swansea C	42	15		
1996–97	Swansea C	39	9	162	44
1997–98	Bristol C	29	8		
1998–99	Bristol C	21	4		
1998–99	Notts Co	6	1	6	1
1999–2000	Bristol C	20	1	70	13
1999–2000	Scunthorpe U	15	1		
2000–01	Scunthorpe U	40	10		
2001–02	Scunthorpe U	39	13	94	24

WILCOX, Russ (D)   500 27
H: 6 0 W: 13 01 b.Hemsworth 25-3-64
Source: Apprentice.

1980–81	Doncaster R	1	0		
From Cambridge U, Frickley Ath					
1986–87	Northampton				
1987–88	Northampton T	46	4		
1988–89	Northampton T	11	1		
1989–90	Northampton T	46	3	138	9
1990–91	Hull C	31	1		
1991–92	Hull C	40	4		
1992–93	Hull C	29	2	100	7
1993–94	Doncaster R	40	2		
1994–95	Doncaster R	37	4		
1995–96	Doncaster R	4	0	82	6
1995–96	Preston NE	27	1		
1996–97	Preston NE	35	0	62	1
1997–98	Scunthorpe U	31	2		
1998–99	Scunthorpe U	28	1		
1999–2000	Scunthorpe U	14	0		
2000–01	Scunthorpe U	36	1		
2001–02	Scunthorpe U	9	0	118	4

Scholars
Barwick, Terence P; Baxter, Matthew; Burraway, David; Butler, Andrew P; Capp, Adam; Collins, Neil J; Hawcroft, Richard C; Hunt, Jonathan M; Masson, Daniel P; Morley, Craig C; Parton, Andrew; Ridley, Steven; Ridout, Aaron J; Singh, Sean; Smith, Fabian SM

SHEFFIELD U

ASABA, Carl (F)   215 83
H: 6 2 W: 13 04 b.London 28-1-73
Source: Dulwich Hamlet.

1994–95	Brentford	0	0		
1994–95	Colchester U	12	2	12	2
1995–96	Brentford	10	2		
1996–97	Brentford	44	23	54	25
1997–98	Reading	32	8		
1998–99	Reading	1	0	33	8
1998–99	Gillingham	41	20		
1999–2000	Gillingham	11	6		
2000–01	Gillingham	25	10	77	36
2000–01	Sheffield U	10	5		
2001–02	Sheffield U	29	7	39	12

BOUSSATTA, Dries‡ (M)   0 0
H: 5 8 W: 10 06 b.Amsterdam 23-12-72

2001–02	Sheffield U	0	0

BROWN, Michael R (M)   195 12
H: 5 9 W: 12 04 b.Hartlepool 25-1-77
Source: Trainee. *Honours:* England Under-21.

1994–95	Manchester C	0	0		
1995–96	Manchester C	21	0		
1996–97	Manchester C	11	0		
1996–97	Hartlepool U	6	1	6	1
1997–98	Manchester C	26	0		
1998–99	Manchester C	31	2		
1999–2000	Manchester C	10	0	89	2
1999–2000	Portsmouth	4	0	4	0
1999–2000	Sheffield U	24	3		
2000–01	Sheffield U	36	1		
2001–02	Sheffield U	36	5	96	9

BROWNE, Tom‡ (D)   0 0
H: b.Dublin 3-10-82
Source: Scholar.

2001–02	Sheffield U	0	0

BURLEY, Adam* (M) 3 1
H: 5 10 W: 12 06 b.Sheffield 27-11-80
Source: Trainee.

1999-2000	Sheffield U	2	1		
2000-01	Sheffield U	1	0		
2001-02	Sheffield U	0	0	3	1

COLVIN, David‡ (M) 0 0
b.Newcastle 6-8-82
Source: Scholar.

2001-02	Sheffield U	0	0

CROISSANT, Benoit (D) 0 0
H: 6 0 W: 12 06 b.Vitriy le Francois 9-8-80
Source: Troyes.

2001-02	Sheffield U	0	0

CRYAN, Colin (D) 2 0
H: 5 10 W: 13 00 b.Dublin 23-3-81
Source: Scholar.

1999-2000	Sheffield U	0	0		
2000-01	Sheffield U	1	0		
2001-02	Sheffield U	1	0	2	0

CURLE, Keith‡ (D) 680 34
H: 6 1 W: 12 05 b.Bristol 14-11-63
Source: Apprentice. *Honours:* England B, 3 full caps.

1981-82	Bristol R	20	2		
1982-83	Bristol R	12	2		
1983-84	Bristol R	0	0	32	4
1983-84	Torquay U	16	5	16	5
1983-84	Bristol C	6	0		
1984-85	Bristol C	40	0		
1985-86	Bristol C	44	1		
1986-87	Bristol C	28	0		
1987-88	Bristol C	3	0	121	1
1987-88	Reading	30	0		
1988-89	Reading	10	0	40	0
1988-89	Wimbledon	18	0		
1989-90	Wimbledon	38	2		
1990-91	Wimbledon	37	1	93	3
1991-92	Manchester C	40	5		
1992-93	Manchester C	39	3		
1993-94	Manchester C	29	1		
1994-95	Manchester C	31	2		
1995-96	Manchester C	32	0	171	11
1996-97	Wolverhampton W	21	2		
1997-98	Wolverhampton W	40	1		
1998-99	Wolverhampton W	44	4		
1999-2000	Wolverhampton W	45	2	150	9
2000-01	Sheffield U	25	0		
2001-02	Sheffield U	32	1	57	1

D'JAFFO, Laurent* (F) 187 39
H: 6 0 W: 14 00 b.Aquitane 5-11-70

1991-92	Montpellier	11	2		
1992-93	Montpellier	5	0		
1993-94	Montpellier	12	1		
1994-95	Montpellier	8	0	36	3

From Niort

1997-98	Ayr U	24	10	24	10
1998-99	Bury	37	8		
1999-2000	Bury	0	0	37	8
1999-2000	Stockport Co	21	7	21	7
1999-2000	Sheffield U	15	1		
2000-01	Sheffield U	22	5		
2001-02	Sheffield U	32	5	69	11

DE VOGT, Wilko (G) 21 0
H: 6 1 W: 12 08 b.Breda 17-9-75

1996-97	NAC Breda	1	0		
1997-98	NAC Breda	1	0		
1998-99	NAC Breda	7	0		
1999-2000	NAC Breda	6	0		
2000-01	NAC Breda	0	0	15	0
2001-02	Sheffield U	6	0	6	0

DOANE, Ben (D) 18 1
H: 5 10 W: 11 00 b.Sheffield 22-12-79
Source: Trainee.

1998-99	Sheffield U	0	0		
1999-2000	Sheffield U	1	0		
2000-01	Sheffield U	3	0		
2001-02	Sheffield U	14	1	18	1

FEATHERSTONE, Lee (M) 0 0
b.Chesterfield 20-7-83
Source: Scholar.

2001-02	Sheffield U	0	0

FORD, Bobby* (M) 271 13
H: 5 8 W: 10 06 b.Bristol 22-9-74
Source: Trainee.

1992-93	Oxford U	0	0		
1993-94	Oxford U	14	0		
1994-95	Oxford U	23	2		
1995-96	Oxford U	28	3		
1996-97	Oxford U	33	0		
1997-98	Oxford U	18	2	116	7
1997-98	Sheffield U	23	1		
1998-99	Sheffield U	30	0		
1999-2000	Sheffield U	41	2		
2000-01	Sheffield U	35	3		
2001-02	Sheffield U	26	0	155	6

GIJSBRECHTS, Davy‡ (D) 245 8
H: 6 1 W: 13 04 b.Heusden 20-9-72

1990-91	Mechelen	7	0		
1991-92	Mechelen	24	1		
1992-93	Mechelen	32	3		
1993-94	Mechelen	24	0		
1994-95	Mechelen	32	2		
1995-96	Mechelen	30	2		
1996-97	Mechelen	32	0	181	8
1997-98	Lokeren	33	0		
1998-99	Lokeren	14	0	47	0
1999-2000	Sheffield U	17	0		
2000-01	Sheffield U	0	0		
2001-02	Sheffield U	0	0	17	0

JAGIELKA, Philip (M) 39 3
H: 5 11 W: 13 01 b.Manchester 17-8-82
Source: Scholar. *Honours:* England Youth, Under-20.

1999-2000	Sheffield U	1	0		
2000-01	Sheffield U	15	0		
2001-02	Sheffield U	23	3	39	3

JAVARY, Jean-Philippe (M) 38 1
H: 5 10 W: 11 13 b.Montpellier 10-1-78

1995-96	Montpellier	3	0		
1996-97	Montpellier	7	0		
1997-98	Montpellier	0	0	10	0
1998-99	Espanyol	0	0		
1999-2000	Raith R	11	0	11	0
2000-01	Brentford	6	0	6	0
2000-01	Plymouth Arg	4	0		
2001-02	Plymouth Arg	0	0	4	0
2001-02	Sheffield U	7	1	7	1

JONES, Stuart‡ (D) 0 0
b.Doncaster 31-12-83

2001-02	Sheffield U	0	0

KILLEEN, Lewis (F) 1 0
b.Peterborough 23-9-82
Source: Scholar.

2001-02	Sheffield U	1	0	1	0

KOZLUK, Robert (D) 114 0
H: 5 8 W: 11 05 b.Sutton-in-Ashfield 5-8-77
Source: Trainee. *Honours:* England Under-21.

1995-96	Derby Co	0	0		
1996-97	Derby Co	0	0		
1997-98	Derby Co	9	0		
1998-99	Derby Co	7	0	16	0
1998-99	Sheffield U	30	0		
1999-2000	Sheffield U	39	0		
2000-01	Sheffield U	27	0		
2000-01	Huddersfield T	14	0	14	0
2001-02	Sheffield U	8	0	84	0

LITTLEJOHN, Adrian‡ (M) 346 61
H: 5 10 W: 11 00 b.Wolverhampton 26-9-71
Source: WBA Trainee.

1989-90	Walsall	11	0		
1990-91	Walsall	33	1	44	1
1991-92	Sheffield U	7	0		
1992-93	Sheffield U	27	8		
1993-94	Sheffield U	19	3		
1994-95	Sheffield U	16	1		
1995-96	Plymouth Arg	42	17		
1996-97	Plymouth Arg	30	3		
1997-98	Plymouth Arg	31	6	110	29
1997-98	Oldham Ath	5	3		
1998-99	Oldham Ath	16	2	21	5
1998-99	Bury	20	1		
1999-2000	Bury	42	9		
2000-01	Bury	37	4	99	14
2001-02	Sheffield U	3	0	72	12

MALLON, Ryan (F) 1 0
H: 5 9 W: 11 08 b.Sheffield 22-3-83
Source: Schoolboy.

2001-02	Sheffield U	1	0	1	0

MONTGOMERY, Nick (M) 58 2
H: 5 9 W: 11 08 b.Leeds 28-10-81
Source: Scholar.

2000-01	Sheffield U	27	0		
2001-02	Sheffield U	31	2	58	2

MURPHY, Shaun (D) 325 21
H: 6 1 W: 13 10 b.Sydney 5-11-70
Honours: Australia 18 full caps, 3 goals.

1989-90	Blacktown City	10	1		
1990-91	Blacktown City	0	0	10	1
1991-92	Heidelberg	9	0	9	0
1992-93	Notts Co	8	1		
1993-94	Notts Co	11	1		
1994-95	Notts Co	35	0		
1995-96	Notts Co	39	3		
1996-97	Notts Co	16	0	109	5
1996-97	WBA	17	2		
1997-98	WBA	17	1		
1998-99	WBA	37	4	71	7
1999-2000	Sheffield U	42	3		
2000-01	Sheffield U	46	5		
2001-02	Sheffield U	27	0	115	8
2001-02	Crystal Palace	11	0	11	0

NDLOVU, Peter (F) 350 71
H: 5 8 W: 10 02 b.Bulawayo 25-2-73
Source: Highlanders. *Honours:* Zimbabwe full caps.

1991-92	Coventry C	23	2		
1992-93	Coventry C	32	7		
1993-94	Coventry C	40	11		
1994-95	Coventry C	30	11		
1995-96	Coventry C	32	5		
1996-97	Coventry C	20	1	177	37
1997-98	Birmingham C	39	9		
1998-99	Birmingham C	43	10		
1999-2000	Birmingham C	13	1		
2000-01	Birmingham C	12	2	107	22
2000-01	Huddersfield T	6	4	6	4
2000-01	Sheffield U	15	4		
2001-02	Sheffield U	45	4	60	8

NICHOLSON, Shane (D) 385 13
H: 5 10 W: 12 02 b.Newark 3-6-70
Source: Trainee.

1986-87	Lincoln C	7	0		
1987-88	Lincoln C	0	0		
1988-89	Lincoln C	34	1		
1989-90	Lincoln C	23	0		
1990-91	Lincoln C	40	4		
1991-92	Lincoln C	29	1	133	6
1991-92	Derby Co	0	0		
1992-93	Derby Co	17	0		
1993-94	Derby Co	22	1		
1994-95	Derby Co	15	0		
1995-96	Derby Co	20	0	74	1
1995-96	WBA	18	0		
1996-97	WBA	18	0		
1997-98	WBA	16	0	52	0
1998-99	Chesterfield	24	0	24	0
1999-2000	Stockport Co	42	1		
2000-01	Stockport Co	35	2	77	3
2001-02	Sheffield U	25	3	25	3

NUGENT, Robert (D) 0 0
b.Manchester 27-12-82
Source: Scholar.

2001-02	Sheffield U	0	0

PAGE, Robert (D) 259 2
H: 6 0 W: 13 00 b.Tylorstown 3-9-74
Source: Trainee. *Honours:* Wales Schools, Youth, Under-21, B, 25 full caps.

1992-93	Watford	0	0		
1993-94	Watford	0	0		
1994-95	Watford	5	0		
1995-96	Watford	19	0		
1996-97	Watford	36	0		
1997-98	Watford	41	0		
1998-99	Watford	39	0		
1999-2000	Watford	36	1		
2000-01	Watford	36	1		
2001-02	Watford	0	0	216	2
2001-02	Sheffield U	43	0	43	0

PESCHISOLIDO, Paul (F) 302 87
H: 5 7 W: 10 12 b.Canada 25-5-71
Source: Toronto Blizzard. *Honours:* Canada 45 full caps, 9 goals.

1992-93	Birmingham C	19	7		
1993-94	Birmingham C	24	9		
1994-95	Stoke C	40	13		
1995-96	Stoke C	26	6	66	19
1995-96	Birmingham C	9	1	52	17
1996-97	WBA	37	15		
1997-98	WBA	8	3	45	18
1997-98	Fulham	32	13		
1998-99	Fulham	33	7		
1999-2000	Fulham	30	4		
2000-01	Fulham	0	0	95	24
2000-01	QPR	5	1	5	1
2000-01	Sheffield U	5	2		
2000-01	Norwich C	5	0	5	0
2001-02	Sheffield U	29	6	34	8

PHELAN, Terry‡ (D) 402 4
H: 5 6 W: 10 06 b.Manchester 16-3-67
Source: Trainee. *Honours:* Eire Youth, Under-21, Under-23, B, 42 full caps.

1984-85	Leeds U	0	0		
1985-86	Leeds U	14	0	14	0
1986-87	Swansea C	45	0	45	0
1987-88	Wimbledon	30	0		
1988-89	Wimbledon	29	0		
1989-90	Wimbledon	34	0		
1990-91	Wimbledon	29	0		
1991-92	Wimbledon	37	1		
1992-93	Wimbledon	0	0	159	1

1992–93	Manchester C	37	0		
1993–94	Manchester C	30	1		
1994–95	Manchester C	27	0		
1995–96	Manchester C	9	0	103	1
1995–96	Chelsea	12	0		
1996–97	Chelsea	3	0	15	0
1996–97	Everton	15	0		
1997–98	Everton	9	0		
1998–99	Everton	0	0		
1999–2000	Everton	1	0	25	0
1999–2000	*Crystal Palace*	14	0	14	0
1999–2000	Fulham	17	2		
2000–01	Fulham	2	0	19	2
2001–02	Sheffield U	8	0	8	0

PURKISS, Ben (D) 0 0
b.Sheffield 1-4-84

2001–02	Sheffield U	0	0		

QUINN, Gerry (M) 0 0
b.Dublin 16-9-83

2000–01	Sheffield U	0	0		
2001–02	Sheffield U	0	0		

SANDFORD, Lee (D) 493 13
H: 6 0 W: 14 04 b.Basingstoke 22-4-68
Source: Apprentice. Honours: England Youth.

1985–86	Portsmouth	7	0		
1986–87	Portsmouth	0	0		
1987–88	Portsmouth	21	1		
1988–89	Portsmouth	31	0		
1989–90	Portsmouth	13	0	72	1
1989–90	Stoke C	23	2		
1990–91	Stoke C	32	2		
1991–92	Stoke C	38	0		
1992–93	Stoke C	42	2		
1993–94	Stoke C	42	1		
1994–95	Stoke C	35	1		
1995–96	Stoke C	46	0	258	8
1996–97	Sheffield U	30	2		
1997–98	Sheffield U	15	0		
1997–98	*Reading*	5	0	5	0
1998–99	Sheffield U	35	0		
1999–2000	Sheffield U	43	1		
2000–01	Sheffield U	22	1		
2001–02	Sheffield U	6	0	151	4
2001–02	*Stockport Co*	7	0	7	0

SANTOS, Georges‡ (M) 116 8
H: 6 3 W: 14 02 b.Marseille 15-8-70
Source: Toulon.

1998–99	Tranmere R	37	1		
1999–2000	Tranmere R	10	1	47	2
1999–2000	WBA	8	0	8	0
2000–01	Sheffield U	31	4		
2001–02	Sheffield U	30	2	61	6

SCOTT, Ben (G) 0 0
b.Doncaster 16-11-83
Source: Schoolboy.

2001–02	Sheffield U	0	0		

SMITH, Andy‡ (F) 8 0
H: 5 11 W: 11 11 b.Lisburn 25-9-80

1999–2000	Sheffield U	0	0		
2000–01	Sheffield U	6	0		
2000–01	*Bury*	2	0	2	0
2001–02	Sheffield U	0	0	6	0

SMITH, Grant (M) 18 0
H: 5 11 W: 12 08 b.Irvine 5-5-80

1998–99	Reading	0	0		
1999–2000	Reading	0	0		
2000–01	Reading	0	0		
2001–02	*Halifax T*	11	0	11	0
2001–02	Sheffield U	7	0	7	0

SUFFO, Patrick‡ (F) 66 9
H: 5 11 W: 13 05 b.Ebolowa 17-1-78
Source: Tonnerre Yaounde. Honours: Cameroon 27 full caps, 6 goals.

1995–96	Nantes	0	0		
1996–97	Barcelona	0	0		
1997–98	Nantes	4	0		
1998–99	Nantes	21	4		
1999–2000	Nantes	5	0	30	4
2000–01	Sheffield U	16	1		
2001–02	Sheffield U	20	4	36	5

THOMPSON, Lee (M) 0 0
H: 5 7 W: 10 10 b.Sheffield 25-3-83
Honours: England Schools.

2000–01	Sheffield U	0	0		
2001–02	Sheffield U	0	0		

THOMPSON, Tyrone (F) 0 0
H: 5 9 W: 11 02 b.Sheffield 8-5-82
Source: Scholar.

2000–01	Sheffield U	0	0		
2001–02	Sheffield U	0	0		

TONGE, Michael (M) 32 3
H: 5 11 W: 12 04 b.Manchester 7-4-83
Source: Scholar.

2000–01	Sheffield U	2	0		
2001–02	Sheffield U	30	3	32	3

TRACEY, Simon (G) 338 0
H: 6 0 W: 14 01 b.Woolwich 9-12-67
Source: Apprentice.

1985–86	Wimbledon	0	0		
1986–87	Wimbledon	0	0		
1987–88	Wimbledon	1	0		
1988–89	Wimbledon	0	0		
1988–89	Sheffield U	7	0		
1989–90	Sheffield U	46	0		
1990–91	Sheffield U	31	0		
1991–92	Sheffield U	29	0		
1992–93	Sheffield U	10	0		
1993–94	Sheffield U	15	0		
1994–95	Sheffield U	5	0		
1994–95	*Manchester C*	3	0	3	0
1994–95	*Norwich C*	1	0	1	0
1995–96	Sheffield U	11	0		
1995–96	*Wimbledon*	1	0	2	0
1996–97	Sheffield U	7	0		
1997–98	Sheffield U	27	0		
1998–99	Sheffield U	18	0		
1999–2000	Sheffield U	45	0		
2000–01	Sheffield U	40	0		
2001–02	Sheffield U	41	0	332	0

TRAVERS, Mervyn‡ (G) 0 0
b.Dublin 22-11-82
Source: Trainee.

1999–2000	Leeds U	0	0		
2000–01	Sheffield U	0	0		
2001–02	Sheffield U	0	0		

UHLENBEEK, Gus* (D) 247 6
H: 5 10 W: 12 06 b.Paramaribo 20-8-70

1990–91	Ajax	2	0		
1991–92	Ajax	0	0	2	0
1992–93	Cambuur	24	0		
1993–94	Cambuur	15	0	39	0
1994–95	TOPS SV	22	3	22	3
1995–96	Ipswich T	40	4		
1996–97	Ipswich T	38	0		
1997–98	Ipswich T	11	0	89	4
1998–99	Fulham	23	1		
1999–2000	Fulham	16	0	39	1
2000–01	Sheffield U	31	0		
2001–02	Sheffield U	20	0	51	0
2001–02	*Walsall*	5	0	5	0

ULLATHORNE, Robert (D) 171 8
H: 5 8 W: 11 03 b.Wakefield 11-10-71
Source: Trainee.

1989–90	Norwich C	0	0		
1990–91	Norwich C	2	0		
1991–92	Norwich C	20	3		
1992–93	Norwich C	0	0		
1993–94	Norwich C	16	2		
1994–95	Norwich C	27	2		
1995–96	Norwich C	29	0	94	7
1996–97	Osasuna	18	0	18	0
1996–97	Leicester C	0	0		
1997–98	Leicester C	6	1		
1998–99	Leicester C	25	0		
1999–2000	Leicester C	0	0	31	1
2000–01	Sheffield U	14	0		
2001–02	Sheffield U	14	0	28	0

WARD, Mark‡ (F) 2 0
H: 6 1 W: 10 11 b.Sheffield 27-1-82
Source: Sheffield Colleges. Honours: England Schools.

2000–01	Sheffield U	1	0		
2001–02	Sheffield U	1	0	2	0

Scholars
Baum, Adam P; Crutchley, Steven J; Ellis, Nicky; Glarvey, Christopher; Harper, Adrian; Hazell, Rohan J; Hurrell, Paul J; Hurst, Kevan; Lindley, Thomas; Platel, Daniel; Sloane, Daniel; Tansley, Anthony D; Wood, Daniel, J

Non-Contract
Blackwell, Kevin P

SHEFFIELD W

ARMSTRONG, Craig (D) 198 5
H: 5 11 W: 12 10 b.South Shields 23-5-75
Source: Trainee.

1992–93	Nottingham F	0	0		
1993–94	Nottingham F	0	0		
1994–95	Nottingham F	0	0		
1994–95	*Burnley*	4	0	4	0
1995–96	*Bristol R*	14	0	14	0
1996–97	Nottingham F	0	0		
1996–97	*Gillingham*	10	0	10	0
1996–97	*Watford*	15	0	15	0
1997–98	Nottingham F	18	0		
1998–99	Nottingham F	22	0	40	0
1998–99	Huddersfield T	13	1		
1999–2000	Huddersfield T	39	0		
2000–01	Huddersfield T	44	3		
2001–02	Huddersfield T	11	1	107	5
2001–02	Sheffield W	8	0	8	0

BETTNEY, Scott‡ (M) 0 0
H: 5 9 W: 13 00 b.Hull 12-3-80
Source: Trainee.

1998–99	Sheffield W	0	0		
1999–2000	Sheffield W	0	0		
2000–01	Sheffield W	0	0		
2001–02	Sheffield W	0	0		

BONVIN, Pablo* (F) 23 4
H: 5 10 W: 11 11 b.Concepcion 15-4-81
Source: Boca Juniors.

2000–01	Newcastle U	0	0		
2001–02	Newcastle U	0	0		
2001–02	Sheffield U	23	4	23	4

BROMBY, Leigh (D) 54 2
H: 5 11 W: 11 06 b.Dewsbury 2-6-80
Honours: England Schools.

1998–99	Sheffield W	0	0		
1999–2000	Sheffield W	0	0		
1999–2000	*Mansfield T*	10	1	10	1
2000–01	Sheffield W	18	0		
2001–02	Sheffield W	26	1	44	1

BROOMES, Marlon* (D) 82 2
H: 6 1 W: 13 00 b.Meriden 28-11-77
Source: Trainee. Honours: England Schools, Youth, Under-21.

1994–95	Blackburn R	0	0		
1995–96	Blackburn R	0	0		
1996–97	Blackburn R	0	0		
1996–97	*Swindon T*	12	1	12	1
1997–98	Blackburn R	4	0		
1998–99	Blackburn R	13	0		
1999–2000	Blackburn R	13	1		
2000–01	Blackburn R	0	0		
2000–01	*QPR*	5	0	5	0
2001–02	Blackburn R	0	0	31	1
2001–02	*Grimsby T*	15	0	15	0
2001–02	Sheffield U	19	0	19	0

BURROWS, David* (D) 384 5
H: 5 8 W: 11 08 b.Dudley 25-10-68
Source: Apprentice. Honours: England Under-21, B.

1985–86	WBA	1	0		
1986–87	WBA	15	1		
1987–88	WBA	21	0		
1988–89	WBA	9	0	46	1
1988–89	Liverpool	21	0		
1989–90	Liverpool	26	0		
1990–91	Liverpool	35	0		
1991–92	Liverpool	30	1		
1992–93	Liverpool	30	2		
1993–94	Liverpool	4	0	146	3
1993–94	West Ham U	25	1		
1994–95	West Ham U	4	0	29	1
1994–95	Everton	19	0	19	0
1994–95	Coventry C	11	0		
1995–96	Coventry C	11	0		
1996–97	Coventry C	18	0		
1997–98	Coventry C	33	0		
1998–99	Coventry C	23	0		
1999–2000	Coventry C	15	0	111	0
2000–01	Birmingham C	13	0		
2001–02	Birmingham C	12	0	25	0
2001–02	Sheffield W	8	0	8	0

BYRNE, Michael (M) 0 0
b.Dublin 14-2-84
Source: Scholar.

2000–01	Nottingham F	0	0		
2001–02	Nottingham F	0	0		
2001–02	Sheffield W	0	0		

CAWLEY, Alan* (M) 0 0
H: 6 2 W: 10 00 b.Sligo 3-1-82
Source: Belvedere.

1998–99	Leeds U	0	0		
1999–2000	Leeds U	0	0		
2000–01	Leeds U	0	0		
2000–01	Sheffield W	0	0		
2001–02	Sheffield W	0	0		

CONNOLLY, Calem (F) 0 0
H: 5 8 W: 11 10 b.Leeds 12-2-82

2000–01	Sheffield W	0	0		
2001–02	Sheffield W	0	0		

CRANE, Tony (M) 30 2
H: 6 1 W: 12 06 b.Liverpool 8-9-82
Source: Trainee. Honours: England Youth.

1999–2000	Sheffield W	0	0		
2000–01	Sheffield W	15	2		

2001–02	Sheffield W	15	0	**30**	**2**

DI PIEDI, Michaelli (F) — **37 5**
H: 6 6 W: 13 05 b.Palermo 4-12-80

2000–01	Sheffield W	25	4		
2001–02	Sheffield W	12	1	**37**	**5**

DONNELLY, Simon (M) — **184 36**
H: 5 9 W: 10 06 b.Glasgow 1-12-74
Source: Celtic BC. *Honours:* Scotland Under-21, 10 full caps.

1993–94	Celtic	12	5		
1994–95	Celtic	17	0		
1995–96	Celtic	35	6		
1996–97	Celtic	29	4		
1997–98	Celtic	30	10		
1998–99	Celtic	23	5	**146**	**30**
1999–2000	Sheffield W	12	1		
2000–01	Sheffield W	3	1		
2001–02	Sheffield W	23	4	**38**	**6**

EKOKU, Efan (F) — **309 106**
H: 6 2 W: 12 00 b.Manchester 8-6-67
Source: Sutton U. *Honours:* Nigeria 5 full caps.

1990–91	Bournemouth	20	3		
1991–92	Bournemouth	28	11		
1992–93	Bournemouth	14	7	**62**	**21**
1992–93	Norwich C	4	3		
1993–94	Norwich C	27	12		
1994–95	Norwich C	6	0	**37**	**15**
1994–95	Wimbledon	24	9		
1995–96	Wimbledon	31	7		
1996–97	Wimbledon	30	11		
1997–98	Wimbledon	16	4		
1998–99	Wimbledon	22	6	**123**	**37**
1999–2000	Grasshoppers	21	16		
2000–01	Grasshoppers	7	3	**28**	**19**
2000–01	Sheffield W	32	7		
2001–02	Sheffield W	27	7	**59**	**14**

GALLACHER, Kevin‡ (F) — **423 106**
H: 5 8 W: 10 10 b.Clydebank 23-11-66
Source: Duntocher BC. *Honours:* Scotland Youth, Under-21, B, 53 full caps, 9 goals.

1983–84	Dundee U	0	0		
1984–85	Dundee U	0	0		
1985–86	Dundee U	20	3		
1986–87	Dundee U	37	10		
1987–88	Dundee U	26	4		
1988–89	Dundee U	31	9		
1989–90	Dundee U	17	1	**131**	**27**
1989–90	Coventry C	15	3		
1990–91	Coventry C	32	11		
1991–92	Coventry C	33	8		
1992–93	Coventry C	20	6	**100**	**28**
1992–93	Blackburn R	9	5		
1993–94	Blackburn R	30	7		
1994–95	Blackburn R	1	1		
1995–96	Blackburn R	16	2		
1996–97	Blackburn R	34	10		
1997–98	Blackburn R	33	16		
1998–99	Blackburn R	16	5		
1999–2000	Blackburn R	5	0	**144**	**46**
1999–2000	Newcastle U	20	2		
2000–01	Newcastle U	19	2	**39**	**4**
2001–02	Preston NE	5	1	**5**	**1**
2001–02	Sheffield W	4	0	**4**	**0**

GEARY, Derek (D) — **37 0**
H: 5 6 W: 10 08 b.Dublin 19-6-80

1997–98	Sheffield W	0	0		
1998–99	Sheffield W	0	0		
1999–2000	Sheffield W	0	0		
2000–01	Sheffield W	5	0		
2001–02	Sheffield W	32	0	**37**	**0**

GIBSON, Neil* (M) — **1 0**
H: 5 11 W: 11 08 b.St Asaph 11-10-79
Source: Trainee. *Honours:* Wales Under-21.

1997–98	Tranmere R	0	0		
1998–99	Tranmere R	1	0		
1999–2000	Tranmere R	0	0	**1**	**0**

From Rhyl.

2000–01	Sheffield W	0	0		
2001–02	Sheffield W	0	0		

HAMSHAW, Matthew (M) — **39 0**
H: 5 9 W: 11 09 b.Rotherham 1-1-82
Source: Trainee. *Honours:* England Youth, Under-20.

1998–99	Sheffield W	0	0		
1999–2000	Sheffield W	0	0		
2000–01	Sheffield W	18	0		
2001–02	Sheffield W	21	0	**39**	**0**

HARKNESS, Steve‡ (D) — **182 3**
H: 5 9 W: 11 09 b.Carlisle 27-8-71
Source: Trainee. *Honours:* England Youth.

1988–89	Carlisle U	13	0	**13**	**0**
1989–90	Liverpool	0	0		
1990–91	Liverpool	0	0		
1991–92	Liverpool	11	0		
1992–93	Liverpool	10	0		
1993–94	Liverpool	11	0		
1993–94	Huddersfield T	5	0	**5**	**0**
1994–95	Liverpool	8	1		
1994–95	Southend U	6	0	**6**	**0**
1995–96	Liverpool	24	1		
1996–97	Liverpool	7	0		
1997–98	Liverpool	25	0		
1998–99	Liverpool	6	0	**102**	**2**
1998–99	Benfica	9	0	**9**	**0**
1999–2000	Blackburn R	17	0		
2000–01	Blackburn R	0	0	**17**	**0**
2000–01	Sheffield W	30	1		
2001–02	Sheffield W	0	0	**30**	**1**

HASLAM, Steven (D) — **93 1**
H: 5 11 W: 10 10 b.Sheffield 6-9-79
Source: Trainee. *Honours:* England Schools, Youth.

1996–97	Sheffield W	0	0		
1997–98	Sheffield W	0	0		
1998–99	Sheffield W	2	0		
1999–2000	Sheffield W	23	0		
2000–01	Sheffield W	27	1		
2001–02	Sheffield W	41	0	**93**	**1**

HENDON, Ian (D) — **337 16**
H: 6 1 W: 13 08 b.Ilford 5-12-71
Source: Trainee. *Honours:* England Youth, Under-21.

1989–90	Tottenham H	0	0		
1990–91	Tottenham H	2	0		
1991–92	Tottenham H	2	0		
1991–92	Portsmouth	4	0	**4**	**0**
1991–92	Leyton Orient	6	0		
1992–93	Tottenham H	0	0	**4**	**0**
1992–93	Barnsley	6	0	**6**	**0**
1993–94	Leyton Orient	36	2		
1994–95	Leyton Orient	29	0		
1994–95	Birmingham C	4	0	**4**	**0**
1995–96	Leyton Orient	38	2		
1996–97	Leyton Orient	28	1	**137**	**5**
1996–97	Notts Co	12	0		
1997–98	Notts Co	38	0		
1998–99	Notts Co	32	6	**82**	**6**
1998–99	Northampton T	7	0		
1999–2000	Northampton T	44	2		
2000–01	Northampton T	9	1	**60**	**3**
2000–01	Sheffield W	31	2		
2001–02	Sheffield W	9	0	**40**	**2**

HINCHCLIFFE, Andy‡ (D) — **380 22**
H: 5 10 W: 13 07 b.Manchester 5-2-69
Source: Apprentice. *Honours:* England Youth, Under-21, 7 full caps.

1986–87	Manchester C	0	0		
1987–88	Manchester C	42	1		
1988–89	Manchester C	39	5		
1989–90	Manchester C	31	2	**112**	**8**
1990–91	Everton	21	1		
1991–92	Everton	18	0		
1992–93	Everton	25	1		
1993–94	Everton	26	0		
1994–95	Everton	29	2		
1995–96	Everton	28	2		
1996–97	Everton	18	1		
1997–98	Everton	17	0	**182**	**7**
1997–98	Sheffield W	15	1		
1998–99	Sheffield W	32	3		
1999–2000	Sheffield W	29	1		
2000–01	Sheffield W	9	2		
2001–02	Sheffield W	1	0	**86**	**7**

JOHNSON, Tommy‡ (F) — **303 106**
H: 5 11 W: 12 07 b.Newcastle 15-1-71
Source: Trainee. *Honours:* England Under-21.

1988–89	Notts Co	10	4		
1989–90	Notts Co	40	18		
1990–91	Notts Co	37	16		
1991–92	Notts Co	31	9	**118**	**47**
1991–92	Derby Co	12	2		
1992–93	Derby Co	35	8		
1993–94	Derby Co	37	13		
1994–95	Derby Co	14	7	**98**	**30**
1994–95	Aston Villa	14	4		
1995–96	Aston Villa	23	5		
1996–97	Aston Villa	20	4	**57**	**13**
1996–97	Celtic	4	1		
1997–98	Celtic	2	0		
1998–99	Celtic	3	3		
1999–2000	Celtic	10	9		
1999–2000	Everton	3	0	**3**	**0**
2000–01	Celtic	0	0		
2001–02	Celtic	0	0	**19**	**13**
2001–02	Sheffield W	8	3	**8**	**3**

KUQI, Shefki (F) — **174 45**
H: 6 2 W: 13 13 b.Kosovo 11-11-76
Source: Trepka, Miki. *Honours:* Albania 8 full caps, 1 goal; Finland 23 full caps, 4 goals.

1995	MP	24	3		
1996	MP	26	7	**50**	**10**
1997	HJK Helsinki	25	6		
1998	HJK Helsinki	22	1		
1999	HJK Helsinki	25	11	**72**	**18**

From Jokerit

2000–01	Stockport Co	17	6		
2001–02	Stockport Co	18	5	**35**	**11**
2001–02	Sheffield W	17	6	**17**	**6**

MADDIX, Danny* (D) — **332 14**
H: 5 11 W: 12 00 b.Ashford 11-10-67
Source: Apprentice. *Honours:* Jamaica 2 full caps.

1985–86	Tottenham H	0	0		
1986–87	Tottenham H	0	0		
1986–87	Southend U	2	0	**2**	**0**
1987–88	QPR	9	0		
1988–89	QPR	33	2		
1989–90	QPR	32	3		
1990–91	QPR	32	1		
1991–92	QPR	19	0		
1992–93	QPR	14	0		
1993–94	QPR	0	0		
1994–95	QPR	27	1		
1995–96	QPR	22	0		
1996–97	QPR	25	0		
1997–98	QPR	25	1		
1998–99	QPR	37	4		
1999–2000	QPR	17	1		
2000–01	QPR	2	0	**294**	**13**
2001–02	Sheffield W	36	1	**36**	**1**

McLAREN, Paul (M) — **202 6**
H: 6 1 W: 13 00 b.High Wycombe 17-11-76
Source: Trainee.

1993–94	Luton T	1	0		
1994–95	Luton T	0	0		
1995–96	Luton T	12	1		
1996–97	Luton T	24	0		
1997–98	Luton T	43	0		
1998–99	Luton T	23	0		
1999–2000	Luton T	29	1		
2000–01	Luton T	35	2	**167**	**4**
2001–02	Sheffield W	35	2	**35**	**2**

MORRISON, Owen (M) — **55 8**
H: 5 8 W: 11 12 b.Derry 8-12-81
Source: Trainee. *Honours:* Northern Ireland Schools, Youth, Under-21.

1998–99	Sheffield W	1	0		
1999–2000	Sheffield W	0	0		
2000–01	Sheffield W	30	6		
2001–02	Sheffield W	24	2	**55**	**8**

MULLER, Adam‡ (F) — **5 0**
H: 5 11 W: 12 02 b.Thackley 17-4-82

1999–2000	Sheffield W	0	0		
2000–01	Sheffield W	5	0		
2001–02	Sheffield W	0	0	**5**	**0**

O'DONNELL, Phil (M) — **234 30**
H: 5 10 W: 11 07 b.Bellshill 25-3-72
Source: X Form. *Honours:* Scotland Under-21, 1 full cap.

1990–91	Motherwell	12	0		
1991–92	Motherwell	42	4		
1992–93	Motherwell	32	4		
1993–94	Motherwell	35	7		
1994–95	Motherwell	3	0	**124**	**15**
1994–95	Celtic	27	6		
1995–96	Celtic	15	3		
1996–97	Celtic	19	2		
1997–98	Celtic	14	2		
1998–99	Celtic	15	2	**90**	**15**
1999–2000	Sheffield W	1	0		
2000–01	Sheffield W	11	0		
2001–02	Sheffield W	8	0	**20**	**0**

PRESSMAN, Kevin (G) — **349 0**
H: 6 1 W: 15 05 b.Fareham 6-11-67
Source: Apprentice. *Honours:* England Schools, Youth, Under-21, B.

1985–86	Sheffield W	0	0		
1986–87	Sheffield W	0	0		
1987–88	Sheffield W	11	0		
1988–89	Sheffield W	9	0		
1989–90	Sheffield W	15	0		
1990–91	Sheffield W	23	0		
1991–92	Sheffield W	1	0		
1991–92	Stoke C	4	0	**4**	**0**
1992–93	Sheffield W	3	0		
1993–94	Sheffield W	32	0		
1994–95	Sheffield W	34	0		
1995–96	Sheffield W	30	0		
1996–97	Sheffield W	38	0		
1997–98	Sheffield W	35	0		
1998–99	Sheffield W	15	0		
1999–2000	Sheffield W	19	0		
2000–01	Sheffield W	39	0		
2001–02	Sheffield W	40	0	**345**	**0**

QUINN, Alan (M) 96 7
H: 5 9 W: 10 02 b.Dublin 13-6-79
Source: Cherry Orchard. *Honours:* Eire Under-21.

Season	Club	Apps	Gls		
1997–98	Sheffield W	1	0		
1998–99	Sheffield W	1	0		
1999–2000	Sheffield W	19	3		
2000–01	Sheffield W	37	2		
2001–02	Sheffield W	38	2	96	7

RAND, Craig‡ (D) 0 0
H: 6 1 W: 11 00 b.Bishop Auckland 24-6-82
Source: Trainee.

Season	Club	Apps	Gls
1999–2000	Sheffield W	0	0
2000–01	Sheffield W	0	0
2001–02	Sheffield W	0	0

ROBERTS, Sean* (G) 1 0
H: 6 2 W: 12 08 b.Johannesburg 2-1-83

Season	Club	Apps	Gls		
2001–02	Sheffield W	1	0	1	0

SCOTT, Phil* (M) 143 28
H: 5 9 W: 11 01 b.Perth 14-11-74
Source: Scone Thistle. *Honours:* Scotland Under-21.

Season	Club	Apps	Gls		
1991–92	St Johnstone	0	0		
1992–93	St Johnstone	3	0		
1993–94	St Johnstone	24	3		
1994–95	St Johnstone	12	1		
1995–96	St Johnstone	28	8		
1996–97	St Johnstone	29	12		
1997–98	St Johnstone	22	1		
1998–99	St Johnstone	16	2	134	27
1998–99	Sheffield W	4	1		
1999–2000	Sheffield W	5	0		
2000–01	Sheffield W	0	0		
2001–02	Sheffield W	0	0	9	1

SHAW, Matthew (M) 0 0
b.Blackpool 7-5-84

Season	Club	Apps	Gls
2001–02	Sheffield W	0	0

SIBON, Gerald (F) 271 81
H: 6 3 W: 13 04 b.Emmen 19-4-74

Season	Club	Apps	Gls		
1993–94	Twente	3	0	3	0
1994–95	VVV	30	20		
1995–96	VVV	23	14	53	34
1996–97	Roda	34	13	34	13
1997–98	Ajax	12	2		
1998–99	Ajax	11	2	23	4
1999–2000	Sheffield W	28	5		
2000–01	Sheffield W	41	13		
2001–02	Sheffield W	35	12	104	30

SIDDALL, Richard‡ (G) 0 0
H: 6 1 W: 11 06 b.Sheffield 24-1-82
Source: Scholar.

Season	Club	Apps	Gls
1998–99	Barnsley	0	0
1999–2000	Barnsley	0	0
2000–01	Barnsley	0	0
2001–02	Scunthorpe U	0	0
2001–02	Sheffield W	0	0

SOLTVEDT, Trond Egil (M) 329 69
H: 6 1 W: 12 09 b.Voss 15-2-67
Source: Dale, Ny-Krohnborg. *Honours:* Norway 4 full caps.

Season	Club	Apps	Gls		
1988	Viking	21	3		
1989	Viking	11	3		
1990	Viking	20	3		
1991	Viking	13	1	65	10
1992	Brann	22	6		
1993	Brann	21	16		
1994	Brann	21	12	64	34
1995	Rosenborg	25	4		
1996	Rosenborg	26	10		
1997	Rosenborg	9	4	60	18
1997–98	Coventry C	30	1		
1998–99	Coventry C	27	2		
1999–2000	Coventry C	0	0	57	3
1999–2000	Southampton	24	1		
2000–01	Southampton	6	1	30	2
2000–01	Sheffield W	15	1		
2001–02	Sheffield W	38	1	53	2

STRINGER, Chris (G) 6 0
H: 6 6 W: 12 00 b.Grimsby 16-6-83
Source: Scholar.

Season	Club	Apps	Gls		
2000–01	Sheffield W	5	0		
2001–02	Sheffield W	1	0	6	0

U'DDIN, Anwar‡ (D) 0 0
b.London 1-11-81
Source: West Ham U Scholar.

Season	Club	Apps	Gls
2001–02	West Ham U	0	0
2001–02	Sheffield W	0	0

WESTWOOD, Ashley (D) 181 14
H: 5 11 W: 11 02 b.Bridgnorth 31-8-76
Source: Trainee. *Honours:* England Youth.

Season	Club	Apps	Gls		
1994–95	Manchester U	0	0		
1995–96	Crewe Alex	33	4		
1996–97	Crewe Alex	44	2		
1997–98	Crewe Alex	21	3	98	9
1998–99	Bradford C	19	2		
1999–2000	Bradford C	5	0		
2000–01	Bradford C	0	0	24	2
2000–01	Sheffield W	33	2		
2001–02	Sheffield W	26	1	59	3

Scholars
Barrett, Jamie J; Beadsley, Scott M; Byne, Nicholas F; Callery, Alex J; Cropper, Dene J; Doherty, Michael F; Hill, Matthew J; Jubb, Ryan G; Knowles, Alexander S; Lowe, Scott; McMahon, Lewis J; Quinn, Adam R; Shaw, Jon S; Stevenson, Lee C; Strutt, Luke M; Taylor, Robert J; Tevendale, James R; Wilson, Laurie J; Wood, Daniel G; Wood, Richard M; Young, Gregory J

SHREWSBURY T

AISTON, Sam (F) 138 4
H: 6 1 W: 12 00 b.Newcastle 21-11-76
Source: Newcastle U Trainee. *Honours:* England Schools.

Season	Club	Apps	Gls		
1995–96	Sunderland	14	0		
1996–97	Sunderland	2	0		
1996–97	Chester C	14	0		
1997–98	Sunderland	3	0		
1998–99	Sunderland	1	0		
1999–99	Chester C	11	0	25	0
1999–2000	Sunderland	0	0	20	0
1999–2000	Stoke C	6	0	6	0
1999–2000	Shrewsbury T	10	0		
2000–01	Shrewsbury T	42	2		
2001–02	Shrewsbury T	35	2	87	4

ATKINS, Mark# (M) 491 50
H: 6 0 W: 12 05 b.Doncaster 14-8-68
Honours: England Schools.

Season	Club	Apps	Gls		
1986–87	Scunthorpe U	26	0		
1987–88	Scunthorpe U	22	2	48	2
1988–89	Blackburn R	46	6		
1989–90	Blackburn R	41	7		
1990–91	Blackburn R	42	4		
1991–92	Blackburn R	44	6		
1992–93	Blackburn R	31	5		
1993–94	Blackburn R	15	1		
1994–95	Blackburn R	34	6		
1995–96	Blackburn R	4	0	257	35
1995–96	Wolverhampton W	32	3		
1996–97	Wolverhampton W	45	4		
1997–98	Wolverhampton W	34	2		
1998–99	Wolverhampton W	15	0	126	9
1999–2000	York C	10	2	10	2
2000–01	Doncaster R	0	0		
2000–01	Hull C	8	0	8	0
2001–02	Shrewsbury T	42	2	42	2

CARTWRIGHT, Mark# (G) 64 0
H: 6 2 W: 13 00 b.Chester 13-1-73
Source: York C.

Season	Club	Apps	Gls		
1994–95	Wrexham	0	0		
1995–96	Wrexham	0	0		
1996–97	Wrexham	3	0		
1997–98	Wrexham	4	0		
1998–99	Wrexham	30	0		
1999–2000	Wrexham	0	0		
2000–01	Wrexham	0	0	37	0
2000–01	Brighton & HA	13	0	13	0
2001–02	Shrewsbury T	14	0	14	0

DRYSDALE, Leon (D) 46 0
H: 5 9 W: 10 12 b.London 3-2-81
Source: Trainee.

Season	Club	Apps	Gls		
1998–99	Shrewsbury T	2	0		
1999–2000	Shrewsbury T	18	0		
2000–01	Shrewsbury T	26	0	46	0

DUNBAVIN, Ian (G) 63 0
H: 6 1 W: 13 00 b.Knowsley 27-5-80
Source: Trainee.

Season	Club	Apps	Gls		
1998–99	Liverpool	0	0		
1999–2000	Liverpool	0	0		
1999–2000	Shrewsbury T	7	0		
2000–01	Shrewsbury T	22	0		
2001–02	Shrewsbury T	34	0	63	0

FREESTONE, Chris‡ (F) 140 25
H: 5 11 W: 11 07 b.Nottingham 4-9-71
Source: Arnold T.

Season	Club	Apps	Gls		
1994–95	Middlesbrough	1	0		
1995–96	Middlesbrough	3	1		
1996–97	Middlesbrough	3	0		
1996–97	Carlisle U	5	2	5	2
1997–98	Middlesbrough	0	0		
1997–98	Northampton T	25	11		
1998–99	Northampton T	32	2	57	13
1998–99	Hartlepool U	10	3		
1999–2000	Hartlepool U	27	4	37	7
1999–2000	Cheltenham T	5	2	5	2
2000–01	Shrewsbury T	20	0		
2001–02	Shrewsbury T	7	0	27	0

GUINAN, Stephen‡ (F) 86 14
H: 6 1 W: 13 07 b.Birmingham 24-12-75
Source: Trainee.

Season	Club	Apps	Gls		
1992–93	Nottingham F	0	0		
1993–94	Nottingham F	0	0		
1994–95	Nottingham F	0	0		
1995–96	Nottingham F	2	0		
1995–96	Darlington	3	1	3	1
1996–97	Nottingham F	2	0		
1996–97	Burnley	6	0	6	0
1997–98	Nottingham F	2	0		
1997–98	Crewe Alex	3	0	3	0
1998–99	Nottingham F	0	0		
1998–99	Halifax T	12	2	12	2
1998–99	Plymouth Arg	11	7		
1999–2000	Nottingham F	1	0	7	0
1999–2000	Scunthorpe U	3	1	3	1
1999–2000	Cambridge U	6	0	6	0
1999–2000	Plymouth Arg	8	2		
2000–01	Plymouth Arg	22	1		
2001–02	Plymouth Arg	0	0	41	10
2001–02	Shrewsbury T	5	0	5	0

HEATHCOTE, Mick (D) 424 35
H: 6 2 W: 12 05 b.Durham 10-9-65
Source: Middlesbrough, Spennymoor U.

Season	Club	Apps	Gls		
1987–88	Sunderland	1	0		
1987–88	Halifax T	7	1	7	1
1988–89	Sunderland	0	0		
1989–90	Sunderland	8	0	9	0
1989–90	York C	3	0	3	0
1990–91	Shrewsbury T	39	6		
1991–92	Shrewsbury T	5	0		
1991–92	Cambridge U	22	5		
1992–93	Cambridge U	42	2		
1993–94	Cambridge U	40	5		
1994–95	Cambridge U	24	1	128	13
1995–96	Plymouth Arg	44	4		
1996–97	Plymouth Arg	42	1		
1997–98	Plymouth Arg	36	4		
1998–99	Plymouth Arg	43	3		
1999–2000	Plymouth Arg	29	1		
2000–01	Plymouth Arg	5	0	199	13
2001–02	Shrewsbury T	34	2	78	8

JAGIELKA, Steve (F) 142 14
H: 5 8 W: 11 03 b.Manchester 10-3-78
Source: Trainee.

Season	Club	Apps	Gls		
1996–97	Stoke C	0	0		
1997–98	Shrewsbury T	16	1		
1998–99	Shrewsbury T	31	1		
1999–2000	Shrewsbury T	33	1		
2000–01	Shrewsbury T	31	6		
2001–02	Shrewsbury T	31	5	142	14

JEMSON, Nigel (F) 368 93
H: 5 11 W: 13 00 b.Preston 10-8-69
Source: Trainee. *Honours:* England Under-21.

Season	Club	Apps	Gls		
1985–86	Preston NE	1	0		
1986–87	Preston NE	4	3		
1987–88	Preston NE	27	5		
1987–88	Nottingham F	0	0		
1988–89	Nottingham F	0	0		
1988–89	Bolton W	5	0	5	0
1988–89	Preston NE	9	2	41	10
1989–90	Nottingham F	18	4		
1990–91	Nottingham F	23	8		
1991–92	Nottingham F	6	1	47	13
1991–92	Sheffield W	20	4		
1992–93	Sheffield W	13	0		
1993–94	Sheffield W	18	5	51	9
1993–94	Grimsby T	6	2	6	2
1994–95	Notts Co	11	1		
1994–95	Watford	4	0	4	0
1994–95	Coventry C	0	0		
1995–96	Notts Co	3	0	14	1
1995–96	Rotherham U	16	5	16	5
1996–97	Oxford U	44	18		
1997–98	Oxford U	24	9		
1997–98	Bury	15	1		
1998–99	Bury	14	0		
1999–2000	Bury	0	0	29	1
1999–2000	Oxford U	18	0	86	27
2000–01	Shrewsbury T	41	15		
2001–02	Shrewsbury T	28	10	69	25

JENKINS, Iain‡ (D) 205 1
H: 5 9 W: 11 10 b.Whiston 24-11-72
Source: Trainee. *Honours:* Northern Ireland B, 6 full caps.

Season	Club	Apps	Gls		
1990–91	Everton	1	0		
1991–92	Everton	3	0		
1992–93	Everton	1	0	5	0
1992–93	Bradford C	6	0	6	0
1993–94	Chester C	34	0		
1994–95	Chester C	40	0		
1995–96	Chester C	13	0		
1996–97	Chester C	39	0		

1997–98	Chester C	34	1		
1997–98	Dundee U	7	0		
1998–99	Dundee U	6	0	13	0
1999–2000	Chester C	0	0	160	1
2000–01	Shrewsbury T	16	0		
2001–02	Shrewsbury T	5	0	21	0

LOWE, Ryan (F)   68 11
H: 5 11 W: 11 05 b.Liverpool 18-9-78
Source: Burscough.

| 2000–01 | Shrewsbury T | 30 | 4 | | |
| 2001–02 | Shrewsbury T | 38 | 7 | 68 | 11 |

MALESSA, Antony‡ (G)   1 0
H: 5 11 W: 11 12 b.Ascot 13-11-80

1999–2000	Bristol C	0	0		
2000–01	Bristol C	1	0	1	0
2001–02	Oxford U	0	0		
2001–02	Reading	0	0		
2001–02	Shrewsbury T	0	0		

MOSS, Darren (D)   73 2
H: 5 10 W: 11 00 b.Wrexham 24-5-81
Source: Trainee.

1998–99	Chester C	7	0		
1999–2000	Chester C	35	0		
2000–01	Chester C	0	0	42	0
2001–02	Shrewsbury T	31	2	31	2

MURPHY, Chris§ (F)   5 0
H: 5 6 W: 9 00 b.Leamington Spa 8-3-83
Source: Scholar.

| 2000–01 | Shrewsbury T | 1 | 0 | | |
| 2001–02 | Shrewsbury T | 4 | 0 | 5 | 0 |

MURRAY, Karl (D)   81 3
H: 5 10 W: 11 12 b.Islington 24-6-82
Source: Trainee.

1999–2000	Shrewsbury T	12	1		
2000–01	Shrewsbury T	35	0		
2001–02	Shrewsbury T	34	2	81	3

REDMILE, Matt (D)   215 12
H: 6 3 W: 14 10 b.Nottingham 12-11-76
Source: Trainee.

1995–96	Notts Co	0	0		
1996–97	Notts Co	23	2		
1997–98	Notts Co	34	3		
1998–99	Notts Co	41	1		
1999–2000	Notts Co	41	1		
2000–01	Notts Co	8	0	147	7
2000–01	Shrewsbury T	24	3		
2001–02	Shrewsbury T	44	2	68	5

RIOCH, Greg‡ (D)   217 14
H: 5 11 W: 12 10 b.Sutton Coldfield 24-6-75
Source: Trainee.

1993–94	Luton T	0	0		
1993–94	*Barnet*	3	0	3	0
1994–95	Luton T	0	0		
1995–96	Peterborough U	18	0	18	0
1996–97	Hull C	39	1		
1997–98	Hull C	39	5		
1998–99	Hull C	13	0	91	6
1999–2000	Macclesfield T	42	5		
2000–01	Macclesfield T	17	1	59	6
2000–01	Shrewsbury T	8	0		
2001–02	Shrewsbury T	38	2	46	2

RODGERS, Luke (F)   70 30
H: 5 8 W: 10 00 b.Birmingham 1-1-82
Source: Trainee.

1999–2000	Shrewsbury T	6	1		
2000–01	Shrewsbury T	26	7		
2001–02	Shrewsbury T	38	22	70	30

SEABURY, Kevin‡ (D)   229 7
H: 5 10 W: 12 00 b.Shrewsbury 24-11-73
Source: Trainee.

1992–93	Shrewsbury T	1	0		
1993–94	Shrewsbury T	0	0		
1994–95	Shrewsbury T	30	0		
1995–96	Shrewsbury T	34	0		
1996–97	Shrewsbury T	38	0		
1997–98	Shrewsbury T	39	2		
1998–99	Shrewsbury T	44	5		
1999–2000	Shrewsbury T	32	0		
2000–01	Shrewsbury T	11	0		
2001–02	Shrewsbury T	0	0	229	7

THOMPSON, Andy† (D)   517 48
H: 5 4 W: 10 11 b.Cannock 9-11-67
Source: Apprentice.

1985–86	WBA	15	1		
1986–87	WBA	9	0	24	1
1986–87	Wolverhampton W	29	8		
1987–88	Wolverhampton W	42	2		
1988–89	Wolverhampton W	46	6		
1989–90	Wolverhampton W	33	4		
1990–91	Wolverhampton W	44	3		
1991–92	Wolverhampton W	17	0		
1992–93	Wolverhampton W	20	0		
1993–94	Wolverhampton W	37	3		
1994–95	Wolverhampton W	31	9		
1995–96	Wolverhampton W	45	6		
1996–97	Wolverhampton W	32	2	376	43
1997–98	Tranmere R	44	3		
1998–99	Tranmere R	37	1		
1999–2000	Tranmere R	15	0	96	4
2000–01	Cardiff C	7	0		
2001–02	Cardiff C	0	0	7	0
2001–02	Shrewsbury T	14	0	14	0

TOLLEY, Jamie (M)   49 3
H: 6 1 W: 10 08 b.Shrewsbury 12-5-83
Source: Scholar. *Honours:* Wales Under-21.

1999–2000	Shrewsbury T	2	0		
2000–01	Shrewsbury T	24	2		
2001–02	Shrewsbury T	23	1	49	3

TRETTON, Andy‡ (D)   111 6
H: 6 0 W: 12 08 b.Derby 9-10-76
Source: Trainee.

1993–94	Derby Co	0	0		
1994–95	Derby Co	0	0		
1995–96	Derby Co	0	0		
1996–97	Derby Co	0	0		
1997–98	Chesterfield	0	0		
1997–98	Shrewsbury T	14	1		
1998–99	Shrewsbury T	23	0		
1999–2000	Shrewsbury T	33	3		
2000–01	Shrewsbury T	22	2		
2001–02	Shrewsbury T	19	0	111	6

WALKER, Josh‡ (M)   3 0
H: 6 1 W: 11 01 b.Birmingham 20-12-81
Source: Trainee.

1999–2000	Manchester U	0	0		
2000–01	Manchester U	0	0		
2001–02	Shrewsbury T	3	0	3	0

WILDING, Peter# (D)   160 4
H: 6 1 W: 12 09 b.Shrewsbury 28-11-68
Source: Telford U.

1997–98	Shrewsbury T	34	1		
1998–99	Shrewsbury T	42	0		
1999–2000	Shrewsbury T	41	2		
2000–01	Shrewsbury T	21	1		
2001–02	Shrewsbury T	22	0	160	4

WOAN, Ian‡ (F)   260 37
H: 6 1 W: 13 07 b.Wirral 14-12-67
Source: Runcorn.

1989–90	Nottingham F	0	0		
1990–91	Nottingham F	12	3		
1991–92	Nottingham F	21	5		
1992–93	Nottingham F	28	3		
1993–94	Nottingham F	24	5		
1994–95	Nottingham F	37	5		
1995–96	Nottingham F	33	8		
1996–97	Nottingham F	32	1		
1997–98	Nottingham F	21	1		
1998–99	Nottingham F	0	0		
1999–2000	Nottingham F	11	0	221	31
2000–01	Barnsley	3	0	3	0
2000–01	Swindon T	22	3	22	3
2001–02	Shrewsbury T	14	3	14	3

Scholars
Brooks-Courtney, Christian D; Corbett, Mark; Evans, Nicholas J; Griffin, Thomas B; Hart, Timothy J; Johnson, Mathew T; March, Daniel S; McCann, Neal; Morgan, Stephen J; Murphy, Christopher P; Murray, Liam J; Packer, Christopher; Rondel, Robert E; Silgram, James; Thompson, Darren M; Thompson, Neville E; Tolley, Glenn A; Walker, Richard
Non-Contract
Thompson, Andrew R

SOUTHAMPTON

BAIRD, Chris (D)   0 0
H: 5 10 W: 11 11 b.Ballymoney 25-2-82
Source: Scholar. *Honours:* Northern Ireland Under-21.

| 2000–01 | Southampton | 0 | 0 | | |
| 2001–02 | Southampton | 0 | 0 | | |

BEATTIE, James (F)   122 28
H: 6 1 W: 13 06 b.Lancaster 27-2-78
Source: Trainee. *Honours:* England Under-21.

1994–95	Blackburn R	0	0		
1995–96	Blackburn R	0	0		
1996–97	Blackburn R	1	0		
1997–98	Blackburn R	3	0	4	0
1998–99	Southampton	35	5		
1999–2000	Southampton	18	0		
2000–01	Southampton	37	11		
2001–02	Southampton	28	12	118	28

BENALI, Francis (D)   324 1
H: 5 9 W: 11 04 b.Southampton 30-12-68
Source: Apprentice. *Honours:* England Schools.

1986–87	Southampton	0	0		
1987–88	Southampton	0	0		
1988–89	Southampton	7	0		
1989–90	Southampton	27	0		
1990–91	Southampton	12	0		
1991–92	Southampton	22	0		
1992–93	Southampton	33	0		
1993–94	Southampton	37	0		
1994–95	Southampton	35	0		
1995–96	Southampton	29	0		
1996–97	Southampton	18	0		
1997–98	Southampton	33	1		
1998–99	Southampton	23	0		
1999–2000	Southampton	26	0		
2000–01	Southampton	4	0		
2000–01	*Nottingham F*	15	0	15	0
2001–02	Southampton	3	0	309	1

BEVAN, Scott (G)   0 0
H: 6 6 W: 15 10 b.Southampton 16-9-79
Source: Trainee.

1997–98	Southampton	0	0		
1998–99	Southampton	0	0		
1999–2000	Southampton	0	0		
2000–01	Southampton	0	0		
2001–02	Southampton	0	0		
2001–02	*Stoke C*	0	0		

BLAYNEY, Alan (G)   0 0
H: 6 2 W: 13 12 b.Belfast 9-10-81
Source: Scholar.

| 2001–02 | Southampton | 0 | 0 | | |

BLEIDELIS, Imants (M)   131 25
H: 5 10 W: 12 01 b.Latvia 16-8-75
Honours: Latvia 59 full caps, 5 goals.

1994	Interskonto Riga	11	1	11	1
1994	Skonto Riga	11	0		
1995	Skonto Riga	24	1		
1996	Skonto Riga	20	3		
1997	Skonto Riga	20	8		
1998	Skonto Riga	24	8		
1999	Skonto Riga	19	4	118	24
1999–2000	Southampton	0	0		
2000–01	Southampton	1	0		
2001–02	Southampton	1	0	2	0

BRIDGE, Wayne (D)   118 1
H: 5 10 W: 12 05 b.Southampton 5-8-80
Source: Trainee. *Honours:* England Youth, Under-21, 7 full caps.

1997–98	Southampton	0	0		
1998–99	Southampton	23	0		
1999–2000	Southampton	19	1		
2000–01	Southampton	38	0		
2001–02	Southampton	38	0	118	1

BYLES, Luke (D)   0 0
H: 5 11 W: 12 00 b.Southampton 8-1-84
Source: Scholar.

| 2001–02 | Southampton | 0 | 0 | | |

CHALA, Kleber (M)   0 0
H: 5 10 W: 12 07 b.Ibarra 29-6-71
Source: Nacional. *Honours:* Ecuador 69 full caps, 6 goals.

| 2001–02 | Southampton | 0 | 0 | | |

CROWELL, Matt (M)   0 0
H: 5 9 W: 10 09 b.Bridgend 3-7-84
Source: Scholar.

| 2001–02 | Southampton | 0 | 0 | | |

DAVIES, Kevin (F)   250 41
H: 6 0 W: 14 08 b.Sheffield 26-5-77
Source: Trainee. *Honours:* England Youth, Under-21.

1993–94	Chesterfield	24	4		
1994–95	Chesterfield	41	11		
1995–96	Chesterfield	30	4		
1996–97	Chesterfield	34	3	129	22
1996–97	Southampton	0	0		
1997–98	Southampton	25	9		
1998–99	Blackburn R	21	1		
1999–2000	Blackburn R	2	0	23	1
1999–2000	Southampton	23	6		
2000–01	Southampton	27	1		
2001–02	Southampton	2	0	98	18

DELAP, Rory (M)   196 20
H: 6 3 W: 13 00 b.Sutton Coldfield 6-7-76
Source: Trainee. *Honours:* Eire 7 full caps.

1992–93	Carlisle U	1	0		
1993–94	Carlisle U	1	0		
1994–95	Carlisle U	3	0		
1995–96	Carlisle U	19	3		
1996–97	Carlisle U	32	4		
1997–98	Carlisle U	9	0	65	7
1997–98	Derby Co	13	0		
1998–99	Derby Co	23	0		

1999–2000	Derby Co	34	8		
2000–01	Derby Co	33	3	103	11
2001–02	Southampton	28	2	28	2

DELGADO, Agustin (F) 155 73
H: 6 3 W: 13 08 b.Ibarra 23-12-74
Honours: Ecuador 49 full caps, 22 goals.

1996	Nacional	30	18	30	18
1997	Barcelona	25	12		
1998	Barcelona	9	3	34	15
1998–99	Cruz Azul	8	2	8	2
1998–99	Necaxa	15	5		
1999–2000	Necaxa	33	25		
2000–01	Necaxa	34	8	82	38
2001–02	Southampton	1	0	1	0

DODD, Jason (D) 350 9
H: 5 10 W: 12 11 b.Bath 2-11-70
Source: Bath C. Honours: England Under-21.

1988–89	Southampton	0	0		
1989–90	Southampton	22	0		
1990–91	Southampton	19	0		
1991–92	Southampton	28	0		
1992–93	Southampton	30	1		
1993–94	Southampton	10	0		
1994–95	Southampton	26	2		
1995–96	Southampton	37	2		
1996–97	Southampton	23	1		
1997–98	Southampton	36	1		
1998–99	Southampton	28	1		
1999–2000	Southampton	31	0		
2000–01	Southampton	31	1		
2001–02	Southampton	29	0	350	9

DRAPER, Mark (M) 405 53
H: 5 10 W: 12 02 b.Long Eaton 11-11-70
Source: Trainee. Honours: England Under-21.

1988–89	Notts Co	20	3		
1989–90	Notts Co	34	3		
1990–91	Notts Co	45	9		
1991–92	Notts Co	35	1		
1992–93	Notts Co	44	11		
1993–94	Notts Co	44	13	222	40
1994–95	Leicester C	39	5	39	5
1995–96	Aston Villa	36	2		
1996–97	Aston Villa	29	0		
1997–98	Aston Villa	31	3		
1998–99	Aston Villa	23	2		
1999–2000	Aston Villa	1	0	120	7
2000–01	Southampton	22	1		
2001–02	Southampton	2	0	24	1

EL KHALEJ, Tahar (D) 172 21
H: 6 2 W: 13 10 b.Morocco 16-6-68
Source: KAC Marrakesh. Honours: Morocco 69 full caps, 8 goals.

1994–95	Uniao Leiria	21	5		
1995–96	Uniao Leiria	22	3	43	8
1996–97	Benfica	25	1		
1997–98	Benfica	21	5		
1998–99	Benfica	22	4		
1999–2000	Benfica	4	0	72	10
1999–2000	Southampton	11	1		
2000–01	Southampton	32	1		
2001–02	Southampton	14	1	57	3

ELA-EYENE, Jacinto (M) 31 5
H: 5 7 W: 10 02 b.Equatorial Guinea 2-5-82

2000–01	Espanyol B	31	5	31	5
2001–02	Southampton	0	0		

FERNANDES, Fabrice (F) 81 7
H: 5 8 W: 10 07 b.Aubervilliers 29-10-79

1998–99	Rennes	15	2		
1999–2000	Rennes	17	1		
2000–01	Fulham	29	2	29	2
2000–01	Rangers	4	1	4	1
2001–02	Marseille	4	0	4	0
2001–02	Rennes	1	0	33	3
2001–02	Southampton	11	1	11	1

GRAY, Steven (D) 0 0
H: 6 2 W: 12 11 b.Dublin 17-10-81
Source: Cherry Orchard.

1999–2000	Southampton	0	0	
2000–01	Southampton	0	0	
2001–02	Southampton	0	0	

HASSLI, Eric* (F) 22 2
H: 6 3 W: 14 02 b.Sarreguemines 3-5-81

2000–01	Metz	18	2		
2001–02	Metz	4	0	22	2
2001–02	Southampton	0	0		

HOWARD, Brian (M) 0 0
H: 5 8 W: 11 01 b.Winchester 23-1-83
Source: Trainee. Honours: England Youth.

1999–2000	Southampton	0	0	
2000–01	Southampton	0	0	
2001–02	Southampton	0	0	

HUXLEY, Matthew (M) 0 0
b.Bristol 27-5-82
Source: Scholar.

2001–02	Southampton	0	0

JONES, Paul (G) 250 0
H: 6 3 W: 15 02 b.Chirk 18-4-67
Source: Bridgnorth, Kidderminster H.
Honours: Wales 25 full caps.

1991–92	Wolverhampton W	0	0		
1992–93	Wolverhampton W	16	0		
1993–94	Wolverhampton W	9	0		
1994–95	Wolverhampton W	9	0		
1995–96	Wolverhampton W	8	0	33	0
1996–97	Stockport Co	46	0	46	0
1997–98	Southampton	38	0		
1998–99	Southampton	31	0		
1999–2000	Southampton	31	0		
2000–01	Southampton	35	0		
2001–02	Southampton	36	0	171	0

JONES, Richard (M) 0 0
H: 5 10 W: 10 01 b.Swansea 6-1-85
Source: Scholar.

2001–02	Southampton	0	0

LE TISSIER, Matthew* (M) 443 161
H: 6 1 W: 13 12 b.Guernsey 14-10-68
Source: Trainee. Honours: England Youth, B, 8 full caps.

1986–87	Southampton	24	6		
1987–88	Southampton	19	0		
1988–89	Southampton	28	9		
1989–90	Southampton	35	20		
1990–91	Southampton	35	19		
1991–92	Southampton	32	6		
1992–93	Southampton	40	15		
1993–94	Southampton	38	25		
1994–95	Southampton	41	20		
1995–96	Southampton	34	7		
1996–97	Southampton	31	13		
1997–98	Southampton	26	11		
1998–99	Southampton	30	6		
1999–2000	Southampton	18	3		
2000–01	Southampton	8	1		
2001–02	Southampton	4	0	443	161

LUCAS, Jay (M) 7 0
H: 6 1 W: 13 03 b.Wollongong 14-1-85
Source: Scholar.

2000–01	Wollongong Wolves	7	0	7	0
2001–02	Southampton	0	0		

LUNDEKVAM, Claus (D) 245 1
H: 6 3 W: 13 05 b.Austevoll 22-2-73
Honours: Norway 12 full caps.

1993	Brann	3	0		
1994	Brann	20	0		
1995	Brann	14	0		
1996	Brann	16	1	53	1
1996–97	Southampton	29	0		
1997–98	Southampton	31	0		
1998–99	Southampton	33	0		
1999–2000	Southampton	27	0		
2000–01	Southampton	38	0		
2001–02	Southampton	34	0	192	0

MARSDEN, Chris (M) 365 21
H: 5 11 W: 12 08 b.Sheffield 3-1-69
Source: Trainee.

1986–87	Sheffield U	0	0		
1987–88	Sheffield U	16	1	16	1
1988–89	Huddersfield T	14	1		
1989–90	Huddersfield T	32	2		
1990–91	Huddersfield T	43	5		
1991–92	Huddersfield T	23	1		
1992–93	Huddersfield T	7	0		
1993–94	Huddersfield T	2	0	121	9
1993–94	Coventry C	7	0	7	0
1993–94	Wolverhampton W	8	0		
1994–95	Wolverhampton W	0		8	0
1994–95	Notts Co	7	0		
1995–96	Notts Co	3	0	10	0
1995–96	Stockport Co	20	1		
1996–97	Stockport Co	35	2		
1997–98	Stockport Co	10	0	65	3
1997–98	Birmingham C	32	1		
1998–99	Birmingham C	20	2	52	3
1998–99	Southampton	14	2		
1999–2000	Southampton	21	0		
2000–01	Southampton	23	0		
2001–02	Southampton	28	3	86	5

McDONALD, Scott (F) 5 0
H: 5 7 W: 12 07 b.Dandenong 21-8-83

1998–99	Eastern Pride	3	0	3	0
1999–2000	Southampton	0	0		
2000–01	Southampton	0	0		
2001–02	Southampton	2	0	2	0

MILLS, Jonathan (M) 0 0
H: 5 9 W: 11 03 b.Swindon 8-9-83
Source: Oxford U.

2000–01	Southampton	0	0	
2001–02	Southampton	0	0	

MONK, Garry (D) 28 0
H: 6 1 W: 13 10 b.Bedford 6-3-79
Source: Trainee.

1995–96	Torquay U	5	0		
1996–97	Southampton	0	0		
1997–98	Southampton	0	0		
1998–99	Southampton	4	0		
1998–99	Torquay U	6	0	11	0
1999–2000	Southampton	2	0		
1999–2000	Stockport Co	2	0	2	0
2000–01	Southampton	2	0		
2000–01	Oxford U	5	0	5	0
2001–02	Southampton	2	0	10	0

MOSS, Neil (G) 56 0
H: 5 10 W: 14 03 b.New Milton 10-5-75
Source: Trainee.

1992–93	Bournemouth	1	0		
1993–94	Bournemouth	6	0		
1994–95	Bournemouth	8	0		
1995–96	Bournemouth	7	0	22	0
1995–96	Southampton	0	0		
1996–97	Southampton	3	0		
1997–98	Southampton	0	0		
1997–98	Gillingham	10	0	10	0
1998–99	Southampton	7	0		
1999–2000	Southampton	9	0		
2000–01	Southampton	3	0		
2001–02	Southampton	2	0	24	0

OAKLEY, Matthew (M) 187 11
H: 5 10 W: 12 06 b.Peterborough 17-8-77
Source: Trainee. Honours: England Under-21.

1994–95	Southampton	1	0		
1995–96	Southampton	10	0		
1996–97	Southampton	28	3		
1997–98	Southampton	33	1		
1998–99	Southampton	22	2		
1999–2000	Southampton	31	3		
2000–01	Southampton	35	1		
2001–02	Southampton	27	1	187	11

ORMEROD, Brett (F) 146 46
H: 5 11 W: 11 12 b.Blackburn 18-10-76
Source: Blackburn R Trainee, Accrington S.

1996–97	Blackpool	4	0		
1997–98	Blackpool	9	2		
1998–99	Blackpool	40	8		
1999–2000	Blackpool	13	5		
2000–01	Blackpool	41	17		
2001–02	Blackpool	21	13	128	45
2001–02	Southampton	18	1	18	1

PAHARS, Marian (F) 224 90
H: 5 8 W: 10 08 b.Latvia 5-8-76
Honours: Latvia 53 full caps, 14 goals.

1994	Pardaugava Riga	17	3	17	3
1995	Skonto/Metals Riga	16	4	16	4
1995	Skonto Riga	9	8		
1996	Skonto Riga	28	12		
1997	Skonto Riga	22	5		
1998	Skonto Riga	26	19	85	44
1998–99	Southampton	6	3		
1999–2000	Southampton	33	13		
2000–01	Southampton	31	9		
2001–02	Southampton	36	14	106	39

PETRESCU, Dan (D) 413 58
H: 5 10 W: 11 06 b.Bucharest 22-12-67
Honours: Romania 95 full caps, 12 goals.

1985–86	Steaua	2	0		
1986–87	FC Olt	24	0	24	0
1987–88	Steaua	11	0		
1988–89	Steaua	28	4		
1989–90	Steaua	23	9		
1990–91	Steaua	31	13	95	26
1991–92	Foggia	25	4		
1992–93	Foggia	30	3	55	7
1993–94	Genoa	24	1	24	1
1994–95	Sheffield W	29	3		
1995–96	Sheffield W	8	0	37	3
1995–96	Chelsea	24	2		
1996–97	Chelsea	34	3		
1997–98	Chelsea	31	5		
1998–99	Chelsea	32	4		
1999–2000	Chelsea	29	4	150	18
2000–01	Bradford C	17	1	17	1
2001–02	Southampton	9	2		
2001–02	Southampton	2	0	11	2

RIPLEY, Stuart* (M) 510 43
H: 6 0 W: 13 08 b.Middlesbrough 20-10-67
Source: Apprentice. Honours: England Youth, Under-21, 2 full caps.

1984–85	Middlesbrough	1	0

1985–86	Middlesbrough	8	0		
1985–86	*Bolton W*	5	1	5	1
1986–87	Middlesbrough	44	4		
1987–88	Middlesbrough	43	8		
1988–89	Middlesbrough	36	4		
1989–90	Middlesbrough	39	1		
1990–91	Middlesbrough	39	6		
1991–92	Middlesbrough	39	3	249	26
1992–93	Blackburn R	40	7		
1993–94	Blackburn R	40	4		
1994–95	Blackburn R	37	0		
1995–96	Blackburn R	28	0		
1996–97	Blackburn R	13	0		
1997–98	Blackburn R	29	2	187	13
1998–99	Southampton	22	0		
1999–2000	Southampton	23	1		
2000–01	Southampton	3	0		
2000–01	*Barnsley*	10	1	10	1
2000–01	*Sheffield W*	6	1	6	1
2001–02	Southampton	5	0	53	1

RODRIGUES, Dani* (M)   15 0
H: 5 11 W: 11 07 b.Madeira 3-3-80
Source: Farense.

1998–99	Bournemouth	5	0	5	0
1998–99	Southampton	0	0		
1999–2000	Southampton	2	0		
2000–01	Southampton	0	0		
2000–01	*Bristol C*	4	0		
2001–02	Southampton	0	0	2	0
2001–02	*Bristol C*	4	0	8	0

ROSIER, Matthew* (M)   0 0
b.Australia 7-1-83

| 2000–01 | Southampton | 0 | 0 | | |
| 2001–02 | Southampton | 0 | 0 | | |

ROSLER, Uwe‡ (F)   367 91
H: 6 0 W: 12 09 b.Altenburg 15-11-68
Source: Traktor Starken, Lokomotiv Leipzig, Chemie Leipzig. *Honours:* East Germany 5 full caps.

1988–89	Magdeburg	12	3		
1989–90	Magdeburg	24	10		
1990–91	Magdeburg	26	9	62	22
1991–92	Dynamo Dresden	33	4		
1992–93	Nuremberg	28	0	28	0
1993–94	Dynamo Dresden	7	0	40	4
1993–94	Manchester C	12	5		
1994–95	Manchester C	31	15		
1995–96	Manchester C	36	9		
1996–97	Manchester C	44	15		
1997–98	Manchester C	29	6	152	50
1998–99	Kaiserslautern	28	8	28	8
1999–2000	Tennis Berlin	28	6	28	6
2000–01	Southampton	20	0		
2001–02	Southampton	4	0	24	0
2001–02	*WBA*	5	1	5	1

(Transferred to Unterhaching, January 2002.)

SVENSSON, Anders (M)   191 42
H: 5 10 W: 12 10 b.Gothenburg 17-7-76
Honours: Sweden 29 full caps, 7 goals.

1992	Hestrafors	2	0	2	0
1993	Elfsborg	0	0		
1994	Elfsborg	1	0		
1995	Elfsborg	26	3		
1996	Elfsborg	24	9		
1997	Elfsborg	26	3		
1998	Elfsborg	26	5		
1999	Elfsborg	20	3		
2000	Elfsborg	24	10		
2001	Elfsborg	8	5	155	38
2001–02	Southampton	34	4	34	4

TELFER, Paul (M)   363 26
H: 5 10 W: 11 13 b.Edinburgh 21-10-71
Source: Trainee. *Honours:* Scotland Under-21, B, 1 full cap.

1988–89	Luton T	0	0		
1989–90	Luton T	0	0		
1990–91	Luton T	1	0		
1991–92	Luton T	20	1		
1992–93	Luton T	32	2		
1993–94	Luton T	45	7		
1994–95	Luton T	46	9	144	19
1995–96	Coventry C	31	1		
1996–97	Coventry C	34	0		
1997–98	Coventry C	33	3		
1998–99	Coventry C	32	2		
1999–2000	Coventry C	30	0		
2000–01	Coventry C	31	0		
2001–02	Coventry C	0	0	191	6
2001–02	Southampton	28	1	28	1

TESSEM, Jo (M)   180 47
H: 6 2 W: 13 01 b.Norway 28-2-72
Honours: Norway 5 full caps.

1996	Lyn	22	15		
1997	Lyn	26	8	48	23
1998	Molde	26	8		
1999	Molde	26	6	52	14

1999–2000	Southampton	25	4		
2000–01	Southampton	33	4		
2001–02	Southampton	22	2	80	10

TRUEMAN, Daniel* (M)   0 0
b.Leeds 21-2-83

| 2001–02 | Southampton | 0 | 0 | | |

WILLIAMS, Gareth (G)   0 0
H: 6 1 W: 12 05 b.Pontypool 18-3-85
Source: Scholar.

| 2001–02 | Southampton | 0 | 0 | | |

WILLIAMS, Paul (D)   360 31
H: 5 11 W: 14 04 b.Burton 26-3-71
Source: Trainee. *Honours:* England Under-21.

1989–90	Derby Co	10	1		
1989–90	Lincoln C	3	0	3	0
1990–91	Derby Co	19	4		
1991–92	Derby Co	41	13		
1992–93	Derby Co	19	4		
1993–94	Derby Co	34	1		
1994–95	Derby Co	37	3	160	26
1995–96	Coventry C	32	2		
1996–97	Coventry C	32	2		
1997–98	Coventry C	20	0		
1998–99	Coventry C	22	0		
1999–2000	Coventry C	28	1		
2000–01	Coventry C	30	0		
2001–02	Coventry C	5	0	169	5
2001–02	Southampton	28	0	28	0

WILLIAMSON, Mike (D)   3 0
H: 6 4 W: 13 03 b.Stoke 8-11-83
Source: Trainee.

| 2001–02 | Torquay U | 3 | 0 | 3 | 0 |
| 2001–02 | Southampton | 0 | 0 | | |

Trainees
Davies, Arron R; Gleeson, Jamie B; Green, Michael J; Hunt, Stephen J; Poate, Brett; Robertson, Andrew J; Saunders, Shea

SOUTHEND U

ALDERTON, Rio† (M)   2 0
H: 6 0 W: 12 07 b.Colchester 12-8-82
Source: Scholar.

| 2001–02 | *Millwall* | 0 | 0 | | |
| 2001–02 | Southend U | 2 | 0 | 2 | 0 |

BEARD, Mark# (D)   183 3
H: 5 6 W: 10 07 b.Roehampton 8-10-74
Source: Trainee.

1992–93	Millwall	0	0		
1993–94	Millwall	14	1		
1994–95	Millwall	31	1	45	2
1995–96	Sheffield U	20	0		
1996–97	Sheffield U	16	0		
1997–98	Sheffield U	2	0	38	0
1997–98	*Southend U*	8	0		
1998–99	Southend U	37	0		
1999–2000	Southend U	41	1		
2000–01	Southend U	0	0		
2001–02	Southend U	14	0	100	1

BELGRAVE, Barrington (F)   49 5
H: 5 9 W: 13 00 b.Bedford 16-9-80
Source: Norwich C Trainee.

1999–2000	Plymouth Arg	15	0		
2000–01	Plymouth Arg	0	0	15	0
2001–02	Southend U	34	5	34	5

BRAMBLE, Tesfaye (F)   51 15
H: 6 2 W: 13 01 b.Ipswich 20-7-80
Source: Cambridge C.

| 2000–01 | Southend U | 16 | 6 | | |
| 2001–02 | Southend U | 35 | 9 | 51 | 15 |

BROAD, Stephen (D)   42 2
H: 6 0 W: 12 00 b.Epsom 10-6-80
Source: Trainee.

1997–98	Chelsea	0	0		
1998–99	Chelsea	0	0		
1999–2000	Chelsea	0	0		
2000–01	Chelsea	0	0		
2000–01	*Southend U*	10	0		
2001–02	Southend U	32	2	42	2

BYRNE, Paul (M)   125 11
H: 5 11 W: 13 00 b.Dublin 30-6-72
Source: Trainee. *Honours:* Eire Youth.

1989–90	Oxford U	3	0		
1990–91	Oxford U	2	0		
1991–92	Oxford U	1	0	6	0
From Bangor					
1993–94	Celtic	22	2		
1994–95	Celtic	6	2	28	4
1994–95	*Brighton & HA*	8	1	8	1
1995–96	Southend U	41	5		
1996–97	Southend U	32	1		
1997–98	Southend U	10	0		

1998–99	Southend U	0	0		
1999–2000	Southend U	0	0		
2000–01	Southend U	0	0		
2001–02	Southend U	0	0	83	6

CAPLETON, Mel‡ (G)   68 0
H: 6 1 W: 13 06 b.London 24-10-73
Source: Trainee.

1992–93	Southend U	0	0		
1993–94	Blackpool	0	0		
1994–95	Blackpool	10	0		
1995–96	Blackpool	1	0	11	0
1996–97	Leyton Orient	0	0		
1997–98	Leyton Orient	0	0		
1998–99	Leyton Orient	0	0		
From Grays Ath.					
1998–99	Southend U	14	0		
1999–2000	Southend U	42	0		
2000–01	Southend U	1	0		
2001–02	Southend U	0	0	57	0

CHIBOGU, Edmund‡ (F)   0 0
H: 5 6 W: 11 12 b.London 9-9-82
Source: Ipswich T scholar.

| 2001–02 | Southend U | 0 | 0 | | |

CLARK, Anthony§ (M)   2 0
H: 5 10 W: 9 0 b.Camden 5-10-84
Source: Scholar.

| 2001–02 | Southend U | 2 | 0 | 2 | 0 |

CLARK, Steve (M)   12 1
H: 6 0 W: 12 09 b.Mile End 10-2-82
Source: Scholar.

| 2001–02 | West Ham U | 0 | 0 | | |
| 2001–02 | Southend U | 12 | 1 | 12 | 1 |

CORT, Leon (D)   45 4
H: 6 4 W: 13 00 b.Southwark 11-9-79
Source: Dulwich H.

1997–98	Millwall	0	0		
1998–99	Millwall	0	0		
1999–2000	Millwall	0	0		
2000–01	Millwall	0	0		
2001–02	Southend U	45	4	45	4

DSANE, Roscoe‡ (M)   2 0
H: 5 4 W: 11 00 b.Epsom 16-10-80
Source: Trainee.

1999–2000	Crystal Palace	0	0		
2000–01	Crystal Palace	0	0		
2001–02	Southend U	2	0	2	0

FLAHAVAN, Darryl# (G)   70 0
H: 5 11 W: 12 05 b.Southampton 28-11-78
Source: Trainee.
From Woking.

| 2000–01 | Southend U | 29 | 0 | | |
| 2001–02 | Southend U | 41 | 0 | 70 | 0 |

FORBES, Scott* (M)   47 3
H: 5 7 W: 11 07 b.Canewdon 3-12-76
Source: Saffron Walden T. *Honours:*

| 2000–01 | Southend U | 34 | 3 | | |
| 2001–02 | Southend U | 13 | 0 | 47 | 3 |

GAY, Daniel (G)   6 0
H: 6 0 W: 12 13 b.Kings Lynn 5-8-82
Source: Norwich C Scholar.

| 2001–02 | Southend U | 6 | 0 | 6 | 0 |

HARRIS, Jason‡ (M)   127 19
H: 6 1 W: 13 13 b.Sutton 24-11-76
Source: Trainee.

1995–96	Crystal Palace	0	0		
1996–97	Crystal Palace	2	0		
1996–97	*Bristol R*	6	2	6	2
1997–98	Crystal Palace	0	0		
1997–98	*Lincoln C*	1	0	1	0
1997–98	Leyton Orient	35	6		
1998–99	Leyton Orient	2	1	37	7
1998–99	Preston NE	34	6	34	6
1999–2000	Hull C	29	4		
2000–01	Hull C	9	0	38	4
2000–01	*Shrewsbury T*	4	0	4	0
2001–02	Southend U	5	0	5	0

HOLNESS, Dean‡ (M)   2 0
H: 5 5 W: 10 13 b.Lewisham 25-7-76
Source: Dulwich Hamlet.

| 2001–02 | Southend U | 2 | 0 | 2 | 0 |

HUNTER, Leon (M)   0 0
H: 5 7 W: 11 06 b.London 27-8-81
Source: Scholar.

| 2001–02 | Southend U | 0 | 0 | | |

JOHNSON, Leon* (M)   48 3
H: 6 0 W: 12 00 b.London 10-5-81
Source: Scholar.

1999–2000	Southend U	0	0		
2000–01	Southend U	20	1		
2001–02	Southend U	28	2	48	3

KERRIGAN, Danny* (M)   15 0
H: 5 6   W: 11 10   b.Basildon 4-7-82
Source: Trainee.
1999–2000 Southend U   4   0
2000–01 Southend U   0   0
2001–02 Southend U   11   0   15   0

KING, Stuart‡ (M)   7   1
H: 5 11   W: 10 00   b.Derry 20-3-81
Source: Trainee.
1998–99 Preston NE   0   0
1999–2000 Preston NE   0   0
2000–01 *Ross C*   1   0   1   0
2000–01 Q of S   6   1   6   1
2000–01 Preston NE   0   0
2001–02 Southend U   0   0

LUNAN, Daniel§ (D)   1   0
H: 6 0   W: 13 00   b.Farnborough 14-3-84
Source: Scholar.
2001–02 Southend U   1   0   1   0

MAHER, Kevin (M)   153 12
H: 6 0   W: 12 13   b.Ilford 17-10-76
Source: Trainee.
1995–96 Tottenham H   0   0
1996–97 Tottenham H   0   0
1997–98 Tottenham H   0   0
1997–98 Southend U   18   1
1998–99 Southend U   34   4
1999–2000 Southend U   24   0
2000–01 Southend U   41   2
2001–02 Southend U   36   5   153 12

McSWEENEY, Dave (D)   32   0
H: 5 9   W: 12 00   b.Basildon 28-12-81
Source: Scholar.
2000–01 Southend U   11   0
2001–02 Southend U   21   0   32   0

NEWMAN, Rob† (M)   690 77
H: 6 1   W: 13 02   b.Bradford-on-Avon 13-12-63
Source: Apprentice.
1981–82 Bristol C   21   3
1982–83 Bristol C   43   3
1983–84 Bristol C   30   1
1984–85 Bristol C   34   3
1985–86 Bristol C   39   3
1986–87 Bristol C   45   6
1987–88 Bristol C   44 11
1988–89 Bristol C   46   6
1989–90 Bristol C   46   8
1990–91 Bristol C   46   8   394 52
1991–92 Norwich C   41   7
1992–93 Norwich C   18   2
1993–94 Norwich C   32   2
1994–95 Norwich C   23   1
1995–96 Norwich C   23   1
1996–97 Norwich C   44   1
1997–98 Norwich C   15   0   205 14
1997–98 *Motherwell*   11   0   11   0
1997–98 *Wigan Ath*   8   0   8   0
1998–99 Southend U   36   7
1999–2000 Southend U   19   0
2000–01 Southend U   6   2
2001–02 Southend U   11   2   72 11

RAWLE, Mark (F)   44   6
H: 5 11   W: 12 04   b.Leicester 27-4-79
Source: Boston U.
2000–01 Southend U   14   1
2001–02 Southend U   30   5   44   6

RICHARDS, Tony (F)   155 26
H: 6 1   W: 13 05   b.Newham 17-9-73
Source: West Ham U Trainee, Sudbury T.
1995–96 Cambridge U   19   1
1996–97 Cambridge U   23   4   42   5
1997–98 Leyton Orient   17   2
1998–99 Leyton Orient   29   7
1999–2000 Leyton Orient   17   2   63 11
2000–01 Barnet   33   8   33   8
2001–02 Southend U   17   2   17   2

RISBRIDGER, Gareth‡ (M)   1   0
H: 5 10   W: 11 05   b.High Wycombe 31-10-81
Source: Yeovil T.
2001–02 Southend U   1   0   1   0

SEARLE, Damon (D)   444   8
H: 5 10   W: 11 00   b.Cardiff 26-10-71
Source: Trainee. *Honours:* Wales Schools, Youth, Under-21, B.
1990–91 Cardiff C   35   0
1991–92 Cardiff C   42   1
1992–93 Cardiff C   42   1
1993–94 Cardiff C   42   0
1994–95 Cardiff C   32   0
1995–96 Cardiff C   41   1   234   3
1996–97 Stockport Co   10   0
1997–98 Stockport Co   31   0   41   0
1998–99 Carlisle U   45   2

1999–2000 Carlisle U   21   1   66   3
1999–2000 *Rochdale*   14   0   14   0
2000–01 Southend U   46   1
2001–02 Southend U   43   1   89   2

SMITH, Ben (M)   1   0
H: 5 10   W: 12 13   b.Chelmsford 23-11-78
Source: Yeovil T.
2001–02 Southend U   1   0   1   0

SZMID, Marek‡ (D)   2   0
H: 5 8   W: 11 06   b.Nuneaton 2-3-82
Source: Trainee.
1999–2000 Manchester U   0   0
2000–01 Manchester U   0   0
2001–02 Southend U   2   0   2   0

THURGOOD, Stuart (M)   52   0
H: 5 8   W: 11 10   b.Enfield 4-11-81
From Shimizu S-Pulse
2000–01 Southend U   13   1
2001–02 Southend U   39   0   52   1

WALLACE, Adam‡ (F)   2   0
H: 5 11   W: 12 00   b.Ashford 5-10-81
Source: Scholar.
2001–02 Southampton   0   0
2001–02 Southend U   2   0   2   0

WARDLEY, Shane‡ (D)   2   0
H: 5 5   W: 9 12   b.Ipswich 26-2-80
Source: Cambridge C.
2000–01 Southend U   2   0
2001–02 Southend U   0   0   2   0

WEBB, Daniel (F)   43   4
H: 6 1   W: 12 03   b.Poole 2-7-83
2000–01 Southend U   15   1
2001–02 Southend U   16   2   31   3
2001–02 *Brighton & HA*   12   1   12   1

WHELAN, Rob† (M)   257 15
H: 6 4   W: 14 05   b.Stockport 7-3-72
Honours: England Under-21.
1989–90 Ipswich T   0   0
1990–91 Ipswich T   0   0
1991–92 Ipswich T   8   2
1992–93 Ipswich T   32   0
1993–94 Ipswich T   29   0
1994–95 Ipswich T   13   0   82   2
1994–95 Middlesbrough   0   0
1995–96 Middlesbrough   13   1
1996–97 Middlesbrough   9   0   22   1
1997–98 Oxford U   8   0
1998–99 Oxford U   15   0
1998–99 *Rotherham U*   13   4   13   4
1999–2000 Oxford U   31   2   54   2
2000–01 Southend U   42   1
2001–02 Southend U   44   5   86   6

Scholars
Boot, Anthony RD; Brown, Jonathan P; Clark, Anthony C; Cleverly, Gareth FJ; Coburn, Sean; England, Gerald L; Fisher, James D; Ing, Martin P; Kawu-Zinga, Flory; Lunan, Daniel D; Plummer, Daryl O; Simmons, Michael K; Smith, Liam K
Non-Contract
Alderton, Rio; Newman, Robert N
Player who does not hold a current contract but his registration has been retained by the club
Byrne, Paul

STOCKPORT CO

BECKETT, Luke (F)   155 54
H: 5 11   W: 11 06   b.Sheffield 25-11-76
Source: Trainee.
1995–96 Barnsley   0   0
1996–97 Barnsley   0   0
1997–98 Barnsley   0   0
1998–99 Chester C   28 11
1999–2000 Chester C   46 14   74 25
2000–01 Chesterfield   4   0
2001–02 Chesterfield   21   6   62 22
2001–02 Stockport Co   19   7   19   7

BRIGGS, Keith (M)   39   1
H: 6 0   W: 11 00   b.Glossop 11-12-81
Source: Trainee.
1999–2000 Stockport Co   7   1
2000–01 Stockport Co   0   0
2001–02 Stockport Co   32   0   39   1

BRYNGELSSON, Fredrik‡ (D)   78   2
H: 6 2   W: 11 13   b.Sweden 10-4-75
1996 Norrby   13   0
1997 Norrby   23   1   36   1
1998 Hacken   2   0
1999 Hacken   24   1

2000 Hacken   8   0   34   1
2000–01 Stockport Co   5   0
2001–02 Stockport Co   3   0   8   0

BYRNE, Mark (F)   5   0
H: 5 10   W: 11 00   b.Billinge 8-5-83
Source: Blackburn R Scholar.
2001–02 Stockport Co   5   0   5   0

CARRATT, Phil* (F)   4   0
H: 5 9   W: 10 10   b.Stockport 22-10-81
Source: Scholar.
2000–01 Stockport Co   2   0
2001–02 Stockport Co   2   0   4   0

CARRIGAN, Brian‡ (F)   125 26
H: 5 8   W: 10 07   b.Glasgow 26-9-79
Source: Kilsyth R. *Honours:* Scotland Under-21.
1996–97 Clyde   14   1
1997–98 Clyde   34   3
1998–99 Clyde   31   3
1999–2000 Clyde   33 18   112 25
2000–01 Stockport Co   13   1
2001–02 Stockport Co   0   0   13   1

CHALLINOR, Dave (D)   158   6
H: 6 1   W: 12 00   b.Chester 2-10-75
Source: Brombrough Pool. *Honours:* England Schools.
1994–95 Tranmere R   0   0
1995–96 Tranmere R   0   0
1996–97 Tranmere R   5   0
1997–98 Tranmere R   32   1
1998–99 Tranmere R   34   2
1999–2000 Tranmere R   41   3
2000–01 Tranmere R   22   0
2001–02 Tranmere R   6   0   140   6
2001–02 Stockport Co   18   0   18   0

CLARE, Robert (D)   45   0
H: 6 2   W: 13 00   b.Belper 28-2-83
Source: Trainee.
1999–2000 Stockport Co   0   0
2000–01 Stockport Co   22   0
2001–02 Stockport Co   23   0   45   0

CLARK, Peter (D)   130   3
H: 6 1   W: 12 04   b.Romford 10-12-79
Source: Arsenal Trainee.
1998–99 Carlisle U   36   0
1999–2000 Carlisle U   43   1   79   1
2000–01 Stockport Co   37   2
2001–02 Stockport Co   14   0   51   2

DALY, Jon (F)   17   1
H: 6 3   W: 12 00   b.Dublin 8-1-83
Source: Trainee.
1999–2000 Stockport Co   4   0
2000–01 Stockport Co   0   0
2001–02 Stockport Co   13   1   17   1

DIBBLE, Andy* (G)   311   0
H: 6 2   W: 16 07   b.Cwmbran 8-5-65
Source: Apprentice. *Honours:* Wales Schools, Youth, Under-21, 3 full caps.
1981–82 Cardiff C   1   0
1982–83 Cardiff C   20   0
1983–84 Cardiff C   41   0   62   0
1984–85 Luton T   13   0
1985–86 Luton T   7   0
1985–86 *Sunderland*   12   0   12   0
1986–87 Luton T   1   0
1986–87 *Huddersfield T*   5   0   5   0
1987–88 Luton T   9   0
1988–89 Manchester C   38   0
1989–90 Manchester C   31   0
1990–91 Manchester C   3   0
1990–91 *Aberdeen*   5   0   5   0
1990–91 *Middlesbrough*   19   0
1991–92 Manchester C   2   0
1991–92 *Bolton W*   13   0   13   0
1991–92 *WBA*   9   0   9   0
1992–93 Manchester C   2   0
1992–93 *Oldham Ath*   0   0
1993–94 Manchester C   11   0
1994–95 Manchester C   15   0
1995–96 Manchester C   0   0
1996–97 Manchester C   13   0   115   0
1996–97 *Rangers*   7   0   7   0
1997–98 Luton T   1   0   31   0
1997–98 Middlesbrough   0   0
1998–99 Middlesbrough   0   0   21   0
From Altrincham
1998–99 Hartlepool U   0   0
1999–2000 Hartlepool U   6   0   6   0
1999–2000 *Carlisle U*   2   0   2   0
2000–01 Stockport Co   10   0
2001–02 Stockport Co   13   0   23   0

ELLISON, Kevin (F)   12   0
H: 6 0   W: 12 00   b.Liverpool 23-2-79
Source: Altrincham.
2000–01 Leicester C   1   0

2001–02	Leicester C	0	0	1	0
2001–02	Stockport Co	11	0	11	0

FRADIN, Karim (M) 253 13
H: 5 11 W: 12 00 b.Ste Martin d'Hyeres 2-2-72

1993–94	Niort	36	1		
1994–95	Niort	37	0		
1995–96	Niort	39	1		
1996–97	Niort	37	1		
1997–98	Niort	25	1	174	4
1998–99	Nice	7	0	7	0
1999–2000	Stockport Co	21	1		
2000–01	Stockport Co	31	6		
2001–02	Stockport Co	20	2	72	9

GIBB, Ali (M) 225 4
H: 5 9 W: 11 07 b.Salisbury 17-2-76

1994–95	Norwich C	0	0		
1995–96	Norwich C	0	0		
1995–96	Northampton T	23	2		
1996–97	Northampton T	18	1		
1997–98	Northampton T	35	1		
1998–99	Northampton T	41	0		
1999–2000	Northampton T	14	0	131	4
1999–2000	Stockport Co	14	0		
2000–01	Stockport Co	39	0		
2001–02	Stockport Co	41	0	94	0

HANCOCK, Glynn (D) 3 0
H: 6 0 W: 12 02 b.Biddulph 24-5-82
Source: Trainee.

1999–2000	Stockport Co	0	0		
2000–01	Stockport Co	2	0		
2001–02	Stockport Co	1	0	3	0

HARDIKER, John (D) 12 3
H: 5 11 W: 11 01 b.Preston 7-7-82
Source: Morecambe.

2001–02	Stockport Co	12	3	12	3

HARDY, Neil‡ (F) 10 2
H: 5 11 W: 12 00 b.Bury 29-12-73
Source: Crewe Alex, Northwich Vic, Hyde U, Altrincham, Radcliffe B.

2001–02	Stockport Co	10	2	10	2

HELIN, Petri (D) 274 16
H: 5 10 W: 11 03 b.Helsinki 13-12-69
Honours: Finland 24 full caps, 3 goals.

1988	PPT	12	2	12	2
1989	HJK Helsinki	18	0		
1990	HJK Helsinki	24	0		
1991	HJK Helsinki	30	4		
1992	HJK Helsinki	30	1		
1992–93	Ikast	0	0		
1993–94	Ikast	28	3		
1994–95	Ikast	18	0		
1995–96	Ikast	2	0	48	3
1996	HJK Helsinki	12	1		
1997	HJK Helsinki	10	1	124	7
1998	PK-35	27	2	27	2
1999	Jokerit	27	1	27	1
2000–01	Luton T	23	1	23	1
2001–02	Stockport Co	13	0	13	0

HOLT, David (F) 1 0
b.Gorton 18-11-84
Source: Trainee.

2001–02	Stockport Co	1	0	1	0

JONES, Lee (G) 133 0
H: 6 3 W: 14 10 b.Pontypridd 9-8-70
Source: Porth.

1993–94	Swansea C	0	0		
1994–95	Swansea C	2	0		
1995–96	Swansea C	1	0		
1995–96	Crewe Alex	0	0		
1996–97	Swansea C	1	0		
1997–98	Swansea C	2	0	6	0
1997–98	Bristol R	8	0		
1998–99	Bristol R	32	0		
1999–2000	Bristol R	36	0	76	0
2000–01	Stockport Co	27	0		
2001–02	Stockport Co	24	0	51	0

KIELTY, Anthony (D) 0 0
H: 6 0 W: 12 07 b.Manchester 6-4-83
Source: Trainee.

2001–02	Stockport Co	0	0		

LAMBERT, Ricky (M) 47 0
H: 6 2 W: 12 01 b.Liverpool 16-2-82
Source: Trainee.

1999–2000	Blackpool	3	0		
2000–01	Blackpool	0	0	3	0
2000–01	Macclesfield T	9	0		
2001–02	Macclesfield T	35	8	44	8
2001–02	Stockport Co	0	0		

LARSSON, Jonas‡ (M) 0 0
b.Vanersborg 1-4-82
Source: Trainee.

1999–2000	Stockport Co	0	0		
2000–01	Stockport Co	0	0		
2001–02	Stockport Co	0	0		

LESCOTT, Aaron (M) 59 0
H: 5 8 W: 10 10 b.Birmingham 2-12-78
Source: Trainee. *Honours:* England Schools.

1996–97	Aston Villa	0	0		
1997–98	Aston Villa	0	0		
1998–99	Aston Villa	0	0		
1999–2000	Aston Villa	0	0		
1999–2000	Lincoln C	5	0	5	0
2000–01	Aston Villa	0	0		
2000–01	Sheffield W	30	0		
2001–02	Sheffield W	7	0	37	0
2001–02	Stockport Co	17	0	17	0

MAGUIRE, Gary* (G) 0 0
H: 6 0 W: 12 00 b.Ormskirk 26-12-82
Source: Trainee.

2001–02	Stockport Co	0	0		

McLACHLAN, Fraser‡ (M) 11 1
H: 5 10 W: 12 07 b.Knutsford 9-11-82
Source: Scholar.

2001–02	Stockport Co	11	1	11	1

PALMER, Carlton (M) 567 31
H: 6 3 W: 13 00 b.Oldbury 5-12-65
Source: Trainee. *Honours:* England Under-21, B, 18 full caps, 1 goal.

1984–85	WBA	0	0		
1985–86	WBA	20	0		
1986–87	WBA	37	1		
1987–88	WBA	38	3		
1988–89	WBA	26	0	121	4
1988–89	Sheffield W	13	1		
1989–90	Sheffield W	34	0		
1990–91	Sheffield W	45	2		
1991–92	Sheffield W	42	5		
1992–93	Sheffield W	34	0		
1993–94	Sheffield W	37	5		
1994–95	Leeds U	39	3		
1995–96	Leeds U	35	2		
1996–97	Leeds U	28	0		
1997–98	Leeds U	0	0	102	5
1997–98	Southampton	26	3		
1997–98	Southampton	19	0	45	3
1998–99	Nottingham F	13	0		
1998–99	Nottingham F	3	1	16	1
1999–2000	Coventry C	15	1		
1999–2000	Coventry C	15	0		
2000–01	Coventry C	15	0		
2000–01	Watford	5	0	5	0
2000–01	Sheffield W	12	0		
2001–02	Coventry C	0	0	30	1
2001–02	Sheffield W	10	0	227	14
2001–02	Stockport Co	21	3	21	3

PEMBERTON, Martin (M) 106 7
H: 5 11 W: 11 08 b.Bradford 1-2-76
Source: Trainee.

1994–95	Oldham Ath	0	0		
1995–96	Oldham Ath	3	0		
1996–97	Oldham Ath	3	0	5	0
1996–97	Doncaster R	9	1		
1997–98	Doncaster R	26	1	35	2
1997–98	Scunthorpe U	6	0	6	0
1998–99	Hartlepool U	4	0		
1999–2000	Hartlepool U	0	0	4	0
From Bradford PA.					
2000–01	Mansfield T	18	1		
2001–02	Mansfield T	38	4	56	5
2001–02	Stockport Co	0	0		

ROGET, Leo‡ (D) 152 8
H: 6 1 W: 12 02 b.Ilford 1-8-77
Source: Trainee.

1995–96	Southend U	8	1		
1996–97	Southend U	25	0		
1997–98	Southend U	11	0		
1998–99	Southend U	14	0		
1999–2000	Southend U	36	2		
2000–01	Southend U	26	4	120	7
2000–01	Stockport Co	9	0		
2001–02	Stockport Co	22	1	31	1
2001–02	Reading	1	0	1	0

ROSS, Neil (F) 10 1
H: 6 1 W: 12 02 b.West Bromwich 10-8-82
Source: Birmingham C Trainee, Leeds U Trainee.

1999–2000	Leeds U	0	0		
1999–2000	Stockport Co	2	0		
2000–01	Stockport Co	0	0		
2001–02	Bristol R	5	0	5	0
2001–02	Stockport Co	3	1	5	1

SMITH, David‡ (M) 295 5
H: 5 10 W: 12 11 b.Liverpool 26-12-70
Source: Trainee.

1989–90	Norwich C	3	0		
1990–91	Norwich C	3	0		
1991–92	Norwich C	1	0		
1992–93	Norwich C	6	0		
1993–94	Norwich C	7	0	18	0
1994–95	Oxford U	42	0		
1995–96	Oxford U	45	1		
1996–97	Oxford U	45	0		
1997–98	Oxford U	44	1		
1998–99	Oxford U	22	0	198	2
1998–99	Stockport Co	17	1		
1999–2000	Stockport Co	9	1		
2000–01	Stockport Co	34	1		
2001–02	Stockport Co	11	0	71	3
2001–02	Macclesfield T	8	0	8	0

SPENCER, James (G) 2 0
H: 6 3 W: 15 04 b.Stockport 11-4-85
Source: Trainee.

2001–02	Stockport Co	2	0	2	0

THOMAS, Andy (D) 10 0
H: 5 7 W: 10 00 b.Stockport 2-12-82
Source: Trainee.

2001–02	Stockport Co	10	0	10	0

TURNER, Sam* (G) 6 0
H: 6 1 W: 12 05 b.Pontypool 9-9-80
Source: Trainee.

1998–99	Charlton Ath	0	0		
1999–2000	Charlton Ath	0	0		
2000–01	Stockport Co	0	0		
2001–02	Stockport Co	6	0	6	0

WELSH, Andy (F) 15 0
H: 5 8 W: 9 06 b.Manchester 24-11-83
Source: Scholar.

2001–02	Stockport Co	15	0	15	0

WILBRAHAM, Aaron (F) 116 20
H: 6 3 W: 12 04 b.Knutsford 21-10-79
Source: Trainee.

1997–98	Stockport Co	7	1		
1998–99	Stockport Co	26	0		
1999–2000	Stockport Co	26	4		
2000–01	Stockport Co	36	12		
2001–02	Stockport Co	21	3	116	20

WILD, Peter (F) 1 0
H: 5 9 W: 11 10 b.Bramhall 12-10-82
Source: Trainee.

2001–02	Stockport Co	1	0	1	0

WILLIAMS, Chris (F) 5 0
H: 5 7 W: 9 00 b.Manchester 2-2-85
Source: Scholar.

2001–02	Stockport Co	5	0	5	0

WISS, Jarkko‡ (M) 227 31
H: 6 0 W: 12 08 b.Finland 17-4-72
Honours: Finland 36 full caps, 2 goals.

1993	TPV Tampere	25	0		
1994	TPV Tampere	23	0		
1995	TPV Tampere	25	3	73	6
1996	Jaro	25	1	25	1
1997	HJK Helsinki	26	5		
1998	HJK Helsinki	26	3	52	8
1999	Molde	3	0	3	0
1999	Lillestrom	16	4	16	4
2000	Moss	17	6	17	6
2000–01	Stockport Co	30	6		
2001–02	Stockport Co	11	0	41	6

(Transferred to Hibernian, October 2001).

WOODTHORPE, Colin (D) 399 12
H: 6 0 W: 11 08 b.Ellesmere Pt 13-1-69
Source: Apprentice.

1986–87	Chester C	30	2		
1987–88	Chester C	35	0		
1988–89	Chester C	44	3		
1989–90	Chester C	46	1	155	6
1990–91	Norwich C	1	0		
1991–92	Norwich C	15	1		
1992–93	Norwich C	7	0		
1993–94	Norwich C	20	0	43	1
1994–95	Aberdeen	14	0		
1995–96	Aberdeen	15	1		
1996–97	Aberdeen	19	0	48	1
1997–98	Stockport Co	32	1		
1998–99	Stockport Co	37	2		
1999–2000	Stockport Co	26	0		
2000–01	Stockport Co	24	1		
2001–02	Stockport Co	34	0	153	4

Scholars
Baguley, Jamie; Budgen, Craig; Eames, Haydn T; Elderton, Ryan; Gollop, Wesley Q; Hilton, Oliver; Holt, David A; Lord, Alexander P; Myers, John; Norton, Blake A; Ogden, Michael A; Paterson, Daniel; Scragg, Jonathan R; Stanton, James; Walsh, Gareth; Warrender, Oliver J

STOKE C

ALBRIGTSEN, Ole# (F) 0 0
H: 5 9 W: 12 00 b.Sortland 21-4-75
Source: Vestealen.

2001–02	Stoke C	0	0	

ALCOCK, Danny§ (G) 0 0
H: 5 11 W: 11 03 b.Staffordshire 15-2-84
Source: Scholar.

2001–02	Stoke C	0	0	

BRIGHTWELL, Ian* (D) 406 18
H: 5 10 W: 12 04 b.Lutterworth 9-4-68
Source: Congleton T. *Honours:* England
Schools, Youth, Under-21.

1986–87	Manchester C	16	1	
1987–88	Manchester C	33	5	
1988–89	Manchester C	26	6	
1989–90	Manchester C	28	2	
1990–91	Manchester C	33	0	
1991–92	Manchester C	40	1	
1992–93	Manchester C	21	1	
1993–94	Manchester C	7	0	
1994–95	Manchester C	30	0	
1995–96	Manchester C	29	0	
1996–97	Manchester C	37	2	
1997–98	Manchester C	21	0	321 18
1998–99	Coventry C	0	0	
1999–2000	Coventry C	0	0	
1999–2000	Walsall	10	0	
2000–01	Walsall	44	0	
2001–02	Walsall	27	0	81 0
2001–02	Stoke C	4	0	4 0

BULLOCK, Matthew‡ (M) 10 0
H: 5 8 W: 11 00 b.Stoke 1-11-80
Source: Trainee.

1997–98	Stoke C	0	0	
1998–99	Stoke C	0	0	
1999–2000	Stoke C	7	0	
2000–01	Stoke C	0	0	
2001–02	Stoke C	0	0	7 0
2001–02	*Macclesfield T*	3	0	3 0

CLARKE, Clive (D) 108 2
H: 6 1 W: 12 02 b.Dublin 14-1-80
Source: Trainee. *Honours:* Eire Under-21.

1996–97	Stoke C	0	0	
1997–98	Stoke C	0	0	
1998–99	Stoke C	2	0	
1999–2000	Stoke C	42	1	
2000–01	Stoke C	21	0	
2001–02	Stoke C	43	1	108 2

COMMONS, Kris (D) 0 0
H: 5 6 W: 9 08 b.Nottingham 30-8-83
Source: Scholar.

2000–01	Stoke C	0	0	
2001–02	Stoke C	0	0	

COOKE, Andy (F) 228 67
H: 6 0 W: 12 07 b.Shrewsbury 20-1-74
Source: Newtown.

1994–95	Burnley	0	0	
1995–96	Burnley	23	5	
1996–97	Burnley	31	13	
1997–98	Burnley	34	16	
1998–99	Burnley	36	9	
1999–2000	Burnley	36	7	
2000–01	Burnley	11	2	171 52
2000–01	Stoke C	22	6	
2001–02	Stoke C	35	9	57 15

CUTLER, Neil (G) 77 0
H: 6 1 W: 12 00 b.Birmingham 3-9-76
Source: Trainee. *Honours:* England Schools,
Youth.

1993–94	WBA	0	0	
1994–95	WBA	0	0	
1995–96	WBA	0	0	
1995–96	*Coventry C*	0	0	
1995–96	*Chester C*	1	0	
1996–97	*Crewe Alex*	5	0	
1996–97	*Chester C*	5	0	
1997–98	*Chester C*	0	0	
1998–99	Chester C	23	0	
1999–2000	Chester C	0	0	29 0
1999–2000	Aston Villa	1	0	
2000–01	Aston Villa	0	0	
2000–01	*Oxford U*	11	0	11 0
2001–02	Aston Villa	0	0	1 0
2001–02	Stoke C	36	0	36 0

DADASON, Rikhardur (F) 240 110
H: 6 4 W: 12 00 b.Reykjavik 26-4-72
Honours: Iceland 40 full caps, 12 goals.

1990	Fram	17	5
1991	Fram	18	4
1992	Fram	12	2
1993	Fram	12	4
1994	Fram	16	9
1995	Fram	13	5	88	29
1996	KR	18	14		
1996–97	Kalamata	10	1	10	1
1997	KR	16	7	34	21
1998	Viking	25	15		
1999	Viking	21	17		
2000	Viking	23	17	69	49
2000–01	Stoke C	28	6		
2001–02	Stoke C	11	4	39	10

FOSTER, Ben (G) 0 0
b.Leamington 3-4-83
Source: Racing Club Warwick.

2000–01	Stoke C	0	0	
2001–02	Stoke C	0	0	

GOODFELLOW, Marc (F) 30 5
H: 5 10 W: 11 00 b.Swadlincote 20-9-81

1998–99	Stoke C	0	0	
1999–2000	Stoke C	0	0	
2000–01	Stoke C	7	0	
2001–02	Stoke C	23	5	30 5

GUDJONSSON, Bjarni (M) 135 25
H: 5 8 W: 11 02 b.Reykjavik 26-2-79
Honours: Iceland Under-21, 8 full caps, 1
goal.

1995	IA Akranes	2	0	
1996	IA Akranes	17	13	
1997	IA Akranes	6	2	25 15
1997–98	Newcastle U	0	0	
1998–99	Newcastle U	0	0	
1999–2000	Genk	14	0	14 0
1999–2000	Stoke C	8	1	
2000–01	Stoke C	42	6	
2001–02	Stoke C	46	3	96 10

GUNNARSSON, Brynjar (D) 146 14
H: 6 1 W: 12 01 b.Reykjavik 16-10-75
Honours: Iceland 29 full caps, 3 goals.

1995	KR	16	1	
1996	KR	18	0	
1997	KR	16	0	50 1
1998	Moss	5	2	5 2
1999–2000	Stoke C	22	1	
2000–01	Stoke C	46	5	
2001–02	Stoke C	23	5	91 11

GUNNLAUGSSON, Arnar* (F) 170 63
H: 5 11 W: 11 11 b.Akranes 6-3-73
Honours: Iceland 30 full caps, 3 goals.

1990	IA Akranes	12	3	
1991	IA Akranes	0	0	
1992	IA Akranes	18	15	
1992–93	Feyenoord	4	0	
1993–94	Feyenoord	5	0	9 0
1994–95	Nuremberg	28	8	28 8
1995	IA Akranes	7	15	
	From Sochaux.			
1997	IA Akranes	2	1	39 34
1997–98	Bolton W	15	0	
1998–99	Bolton W	27	13	42 13
1998–99	Leicester C	9	0	
1999–2000	Leicester C	2	0	
1999–2000	*Stoke C*	13	2	
2000–01	Leicester C	17	3	
2001–02	Leicester C	2	0	30 3
2001–02	Stoke C	9	3	22 5

HALL, Laurence§ (F) 0 0
H: 6 0 W: 12 00 b.Nottingham 26-3-84
Source: Scholar.

2001–02	Stoke C	0	0	

HANDYSIDE, Peter (D) 224 4
H: 6 2 W: 13 09 b.Dumfries 31-7-74
Source: Trainee. *Honours:* Scotland Under-
21.

1992–93	Grimsby T	11	0	
1993–94	Grimsby T	13	0	
1994–95	Grimsby T	35	0	
1995–96	Grimsby T	30	0	
1996–97	Grimsby T	9	1	
1997–98	Grimsby T	42	0	
1998–99	Grimsby T	31	2	
1999–2000	Grimsby T	0	0	
2000–01	Grimsby T	19	1	190 4
2001–02	Stoke C	34	0	34 0

HANSSON, Mikael‡ (D) 309 28
H: 5 11 W: 11 12 b.Norrkoping 15-3-68
Honours: Sweden 1 full cap.

1988	Soderkopings	21	3	
1989	Soderkopings	19	4	40 7
1990	Norrkoping	1	0	
1991	Norrkoping	19	4	
1992	Norrkoping	18	6	
1993	Norrkoping	25	1	
1994	Norrkoping	24	2	
1995	Norrkoping	26	2	
1996	Norrkoping	25	0	
1997	Norrkoping	20	0	
1998	Norrkoping	25	3	
1999	Norrkoping	21	1	204 19
1999–2000	Stoke C	27	0	
2000–01	Stoke C	38	2	
2001–02	Stoke C	0	0	65 2

HEATH, Robert‡ (M) 19 0
H: 5 9 W: 10 00 b.Newcastle-Under-Lyme
1-7-78

1996–97	Stoke C	0	0	
1997–98	Stoke C	6	0	
1998–99	Stoke C	10	0	
1999–2000	Stoke C	3	0	
2000–01	Stoke C	0	0	
2001–02	Stoke C	0	0	19 0

HENRY, Karl (M) 24 0
H: 6 0 W: 11 04 b.Wolverhampton 26-11-
82
Source: Trainee. *Honours:* England Youth,
Under-20.

1999–2000	Stoke C	0	0	
2000–01	Stoke C	0	0	
2001–02	Stoke C	24	0	24 0

HOEKSTRA, Peter (M) 196 39
H: 6 3 W: 12 03 b.Asser 4-4-73
Source: ACV. *Honours:* Holland 5 full caps.

1991–92	PSV Eindhoven	14	3	
1992–93	PSV Eindhoven	19	0	
1993–94	PSV Eindhoven	23	6	
1994–95	PSV Eindhoven	19	6	
1995–96	PSV Eindhoven	15	6	90 21
1995–96	Ajax	16	5	
1996–97	Ajax	8	0	
1997–98	Ajax	23	3	
1998–99	Ajax	21	6	
1999–2000	Ajax	0	0	68 14
2000–01	Groningen	14	1	14 1
2001–02	Stoke C	24	3	24 3

IWELUMO, Chris (F) 112 18
H: 6 4 W: 13 00 b.Coatbridge 1-8-79

1996–97	St Mirren	14	0	
1997–98	St Mirren	12	0	26 0
1998–99	Aarhus Fremad	27	4	27 4
1999–2000	Stoke C	3	0	
2000–01	Stoke C	2	1	
2000–01	*York C*	12	2	12 2
2000–01	*Cheltenham T*	4	1	4 1
2001–02	Stoke C	38	10	43 11

KOEJOE, Sammy‡ (F) 115 19
H: 6 2 W: 14 07 b.Surinam 17-8-74

1997–98	Lustenau	29	7	29 7
1998–99	Salzburg	34	7	
1999–2000	Salzburg	18	2	52 9
1999–2000	QPR	11	1	
2000–01	QPR	21	2	
2001–02	QPR	2	0	34 3
2001–02	Stoke C	0	0	

KRISTINSSON, Birkir‡ (G) 223 0
b.Vestmann 15-8-64
Honours: Iceland 70 full caps.

1987	IA	18	0	18 0
1988	Fram	18	0	
1989	Fram	18	0	
1990	Fram	18	0	
1991	Fram	18	0	
1992	Fram	18	0	
1993	Fram	18	0	
1994	Fram	18	0	
1995	Fram	18	0	144 0
1996	Brann	14	0	
1997	Brann	1	0	15 0
1997	Norrkoping	0	0	
1998	Norrkoping	3	0	3 0
1998–99	Bolton W	0	0	
1998	IBV	0	0	
1999	IBV	18	0	18 0
1999–2000	Lustenau	7	0	7 0
2000–01	Stoke C	18	0	
2001–02	Stoke C	0	0	18 0

MARTEINSSON, Petur (M) 168 3
H: 6 1 W: 12 02 b.Reykjavik 14-7-73
Honours: Iceland 24 full caps.

1994	Fram	16	0	
1995	Fram	16	0	32 0
1996	Hammarby	23	0	
1997	Hammarby	23	2	
1998	Hammarby	24	2	
1999	Hammarby	0	0	70 4
1999	Stabaek	18	0	
2000	Stabaek	21	2	
2001	Stabaek	24	2	63 4
2001–02	Stoke C	3	0	3 0

MILES, John‡ (F) 1 0
H: 5 10 W: 10 08 b.Fazackerley 28-9-81
Source: Trainee.

1998–99	Liverpool	0	0	
1999–2000	Liverpool	0	0	

2000–01	Liverpool	0	0		
2001–02	Liverpool	0	0		
2001–02	Stoke C	1	0	1	0

NEAL, Lewis (M) 12 0
H: 5 11 W: 10 11 b.Leicester 14-7-81

1998–99	Stoke C	0	0		
1999–2000	Stoke C	0	0		
2000–01	Stoke C	1	0		
2001–02	Stoke C	11	0	12	0

O'CONNOR, James (M) 133 16
H: 5 8 W: 11 00 b.Dublin 1-9-79
Source: Trainee. *Honours:* Eire Under-21.

1996–97	Stoke C	0	0		
1997–98	Stoke C	0	0		
1998–99	Stoke C	4	0		
1999–2000	Stoke C	42	6		
2000–01	Stoke C	44	8		
2001–02	Stoke C	43	2	133	16

OULARE, Souleymane (F) 155 57
H: 5 11 W: 12 09 b.Guinea 16-10-72
Honours: Guinea full caps.

1992–93	Beveren	14	5		
1993–94	Beveren	14	3	28	8
1994–95	Waregem	0	0		
1995–96	Waregem	14	3	14	3
1996–97	Genk	24	4		
1997–98	Genk	27	14		
1998–99	Genk	31	17		
1999–2000	Genk	2	2	84	37
1999–2000	Fenerbahce	11	5	11	5
2000–01	Las Palmas	17	4	17	4
2001–02	Stoke C	1	0	1	0

OWEN, Gareth (D) 0 0
H: 6 1 W: 11 07 b.Staffordshire 21-9-82
Source: Scholar.

| 2001–02 | Stoke C | 0 | 0 | 0 | 0 |

ROWSON, David (M) 108 7
H: 5 10 W: 11 09 b.Aberdeen 14-9-76
Source: FC Stoneywood. *Honours:* Scotland Under-21.

1994–95	Aberdeen	0	0		
1995–96	Aberdeen	9	0		
1996–97	Aberdeen	34	2		
1997–98	Aberdeen	30	5		
1998–99	Aberdeen	22	0		
1999–2000	Aberdeen	0	0		
2000–01	Aberdeen	0	0	95	7
2001–02	Stoke C	13	0	13	0

SHTANYUK, Sergei (D) 238 15
H: 6 3 W: 12 12 b.Minsk 11-1-72
Honours: Belarus 34 full caps.

1992–93	Belarus Minsk	30	3	30	3
1993–94	Dynamo 93 Minsk	30	0	30	0
1994–95	Dynamo Minsk	13	1		
1995	Dynamo Minsk	11	0	24	1
1996	Moscow Dynamo	28	3		
1997	Moscow Dynamo	33	2		
1998	Moscow Dynamo	27	2		
1999	Moscow Dynamo	2	0		
2000	Moscow Dynamo	40	2	114	9
2001–02	Stoke C	40	2	40	2

THOMAS, Wayne (D) 197 7
H: 5 11 W: 11 02 b.Gloucester 17-5-79
Source: Trainee.

1995–96	Torquay U	6	0		
1996–97	Torquay U	12	0		
1997–98	Torquay U	21	1		
1998–99	Torquay U	44	1		
1999–2000	Torquay U	40	3	123	5
2000–01	Stoke C	34	0		
2001–02	Stoke C	40	2	74	2

THORDARSON, Stefan (F) 51 8
H: 6 1 W: 12 02 b.Reykjavik 27-3-75
Honours: Iceland 5 full caps, 1 goal.

| 2000–01 | Stoke C | 30 | 4 | | |
| 2001–02 | Stoke C | 21 | 4 | 51 | 8 |

VAN DEURZEN, Jurgen (M) 40 4
H: 5 7 W: 11 00 b.Genk 26-1-74
Source: Turnhout.

| 2001–02 | Stoke C | 40 | 4 | 40 | 4 |

VIANDER, Jani (G) 157 0
H: 6 4 W: 13 04 b.Tuusula 18-8-75
Honours: Finland 11 full caps.

1994	FinnPa	25	0		
1995	FinnPa	14	0	39	0
1995	Ilves	6	0	6	0
1996	Jaro	27	0	27	0
1997	Jazz	2	0	2	0
From Kortrijk					
1998	HJK Helsinki	8	0		
1999	HJK Helsinki	27	0		
2000	HJK Helsinki	32	0		
2001	HJK Helsinki	16	0	83	0
2001–02	Stoke C	0	0		

WARD, Gavin* (G) 251 0
H: 6 3 W: 12 02 b.Sutton Coldfield 30-6-70
Source: Aston Villa Trainee.

1988–89	Shrewsbury T	0	0		
1989–90	WBA	0	0		
1989–90	Cardiff C	2	0		
1990–91	Cardiff C	1	0		
1991–92	Cardiff C	24	0		
1992–93	Cardiff C	32	0	59	0
1993–94	Leicester C	32	0		
1994–95	Leicester C	6	0	38	0
1995–96	Bradford C	36	0	36	0
1995–96	Bolton W	5	0		
1996–97	Bolton W	11	0		
1997–98	Bolton W	6	0		
1998–99	Bolton W	0	0	22	0
1998–99	*Burnley*	17	0	17	0
1998–99	Stoke C	6	0		
1999–2000	Stoke C	46	0		
2000–01	Stoke C	17	0		
2001–02	Stoke C	10	0	79	0

WHITE, Gary* (D) 0 0
H: 5 7 W: 12 07 b.Warwickshire 23-6-63

| 2001–02 | Stoke C | 0 | 0 | | |

WILKINSON, Andy§ (D) 0 0
H: 5 11 W: 11 00 b.Stone 6-8-84
Source: Scholar.

| 2001–02 | Stoke C | 0 | 0 | | |

WILSON, Brian (D) 1 0
H: 5 10 W: 11 00 b.Manchester 9-5-83
Source: Scholar.

| 2001–02 | Stoke C | 1 | 0 | 1 | 0 |

Scholars
Alcock, Daniel J; Armstrong, Matthew; Cromie, Mark; Gibbs, Dean P; Hall, Laurence W; Hemmings, Andrew P; Humphreys, Shaun J; Hutchinson, Ryan C; Rees, Oliver HW; Swift, Christopher; Wilkinson, Andrew G

SUNDERLAND

ARCA, Julio (M) 85 4
H: 6 2 W: 11 00 b.Quilmes 31-1-81

1999–2000	Argentinos Juniors	19	0		
2000–01	Argentinos Juniors	17	1	36	1
2000–01	Sunderland	27	2		
2001–02	Sunderland	22	1	49	3

BELLION, David (F) 9 0
H: 6 0 W: 11 09 b.Paris 27-11-82
Source: Cannes.

| 2001–02 | Sunderland | 9 | 0 | 9 | 0 |

BJORKLUND, Joachim (D) 287 1
H: 6 0 W: 12 06 b.Vaxjo 12-2-71
Honours: Sweden 78 full caps.

1988	Osters	6	0		
1989	Osters	0	0	6	0
1990	Brann	21	0		
1991	Brann	22	0		
1992	Brann	13	0	56	0
1993	IFK Gothenburg	19	0		
1994	IFK Gothenburg	16	0		
1995	IFK Gothenburg	11	0	46	0
1995–96	Vicenza	33	0	33	0
1996–97	Rangers	28	0		
1997–98	Rangers	31	0	59	0
1998–99	Valencia	24	1		
1999–2000	Valencia	23	0		
2000–01	Valencia	10	0	57	1
2001–02	Venezia	18	0	18	0
2001–02	Sunderland	12	0	12	0

BLACK, Christopher (M) 0 0
b.Ashington 7-9-82
Source: Scholar.

| 2000–01 | Sunderland | 0 | 0 | | |
| 2001–02 | Sunderland | 0 | 0 | | |

BUTLER, Thomas (M) 20 0
H: 5 7 W: 10 06 b.Ballymena 25-4-81
Source: Trainee.

1998–99	Sunderland	0	0		
1999–2000	Sunderland	1	0		
2000–01	Sunderland	4	0		
2000–01	*Darlington*	8	0	8	0
2001–02	Sunderland	7	0	12	0

BYRNE, Cliff (D) 0 0
H: 6 0 W: 12 11 b.Dublin 27-4-82

1999–2000	Sunderland	0	0		
2000–01	Sunderland	0	0		
2001–02	Sunderland	0	0		

CAPPER, Stephen (F) 0 0
b.Dublin 28-2-83
Source: Scholar.

| 2001–02 | Sunderland | 0 | 0 | | |

CLARK, Ben (D) 0 0
H: 6 2 W: 12 06 b.Shotley Bridge 24-1-83
Source: Manchester U Trainee. *Honours:* England Youth.

| 2000–01 | Sunderland | 0 | 0 | | |
| 2001–02 | Sunderland | 0 | 0 | | |

COLLINS, Patrick (M) 0 0
b.Oman 4-2-85
Source: Scholar. *Honours:* England Youth.

| 2001–02 | Sunderland | 0 | 0 | | |

CRADDOCK, Jody (D) 276 5
H: 6 2 W: 12 00 b.Bromsgrove 25-7-75
Source: Christchurch.

1993–94	Cambridge U	20	0		
1994–95	Cambridge U	38	0		
1995–96	Cambridge U	46	3		
1996–97	Cambridge U	41	1	145	4
1997–98	Sunderland	32	0		
1998–99	Sunderland	6	0		
1999–2000	Sunderland	19	0		
1999–2000	*Sheffield U*	10	0	10	0
2000–01	Sunderland	34	0		
2001–02	Sunderland	30	1	121	1

DICKMAN, Jonjo (M) 0 0
H: 5 8 W: 10 05 b.Hexham 22-9-81

1998–99	Sunderland	0	0		
1999–2000	Sunderland	0	0		
2000–01	Sunderland	0	0		
2001–02	Sunderland	0	0		

EMERSON (D) 125 3
H: 6 2 W: 13 04 b.Porto Alegre 30-3-72
Source: Benfica.

1997–98	Sheffield W	6	0		
1998–99	Sheffield W	38	1		
1999–2000	Sheffield W	17	0	61	1
1999–2000	Chelsea	20	0		
2000–01	Chelsea	1	0	21	0
2000–01	Sunderland	31	1		
2001–02	Sunderland	12	1	43	2

GRAY, Michael (D) 330 15
H: 5 9 W: 10 07 b.Sunderland 3-8-74
Source: Trainee. *Honours:* England 3 full caps.

1992–93	Sunderland	27	2		
1993–94	Sunderland	22	1		
1994–95	Sunderland	16	0		
1995–96	Sunderland	46	4		
1996–97	Sunderland	34	3		
1997–98	Sunderland	44	2		
1998–99	Sunderland	37	2		
1999–2000	Sunderland	33	0		
2000–01	Sunderland	36	1		
2001–02	Sunderland	35	2	330	15

GRAYDON, Keith (F) 0 0
b.Dublin 10-2-83

1999–2000	Sunderland	0	0		
2000–01	Sunderland	0	0		
2001–02	Sunderland	0	0		

HAAS, Bernt (D) 187 6
H: 6 1 W: 12 08 b.Vienna 8-4-78
Honours: Switzerland 14 full caps, 1 goal.

1994–95	Grasshoppers	2	0		
1995–96	Grasshoppers	20	0		
1996–97	Grasshoppers	29	1		
1997–98	Grasshoppers	27	2		
1998–99	Grasshoppers	28	1		
1999–2000	Grasshoppers	29	1		
2000–01	Grasshoppers	25	1	160	6
2001–02	Sunderland	27	0	27	0

HARRISON, Steve* (D) 0 0
b.Hexham 3-2-82
Source: Scholar.

1999–2000	Sunderland	0	0		
2000–01	Sunderland	0	0		
2001–02	Sunderland	0	0		

INGHAM, Michael (G) 25 0
H: 6 4 W: 13 10 b.Preston 7-9-80
Source: Malachians. *Honours:* Northern Ireland Under-21.

1998–99	Cliftonville	18	0	18	0
1999–2000	Sunderland	0	0		
1999–2000	*Carlisle U*	7	0	7	0
2000–01	Sunderland	0	0		
2001–02	Sunderland	0	0		
2001–02	*Stoke C*	0	0		

JAMES, Craig (D) 0 0
b.Middlesbrough 15-11-82
Source: Scholar.

| 2000–01 | Sunderland | 0 | 0 | | |
| 2001–02 | Sunderland | 0 | 0 | | |

KENNEDY, Jon (G) 6 0
H: 6 1 W: 14 03 b.Rotherham 30-11-80
Source: Worksop T.

| 1999–2000 | Sunderland | 0 | 0 | | |

2000–01 Sunderland 0 0
2000–01 *Blackpool* 6 0   6 0
2001–02 Sunderland 0 0

KILBANE, Kevin (M)   231 25
H: 6 0 W: 12 07 b.Preston 1-2-77
Source: Trainee. *Honours:* Eire Under-21, 37 full caps, 3 goals.
1993–94 Preston NE 0 0
1994–95 Preston NE 0 0
1995–96 Preston NE 11 1
1996–97 Preston NE 36 2 47 3
1997–98 WBA 43 4
1998–99 WBA 44 6
1999–2000 WBA 19 5 106 15
1999–2000 Sunderland 20 1
2000–01 Sunderland 30 4
2001–02 Sunderland 28 2 78 7

KYLE, Kevin (F)   24 1
H: 6 3 W: 13 00 b.Stranraer 7-6-81
Honours: Scotland 3 full caps, 1 goal.
1998–99 Sunderland 0 0
1999–2000 Sunderland 0 0
2000–01 Sunderland 0 0
2000–01 *Huddersfield T* 4 0 4 0
2000–01 *Darlington* 5 1 5 1
2000–01 *Rochdale* 6 0 6 0
2001–02 Sunderland 6 0 9 0

LACEY, Glenn* (M)   0 0
b.Dublin 5-6-83
Source: Scholar.
2000–01 Sunderland 0 0
2001–02 Sunderland 0 0

LASLANDES, Lilian (F)   289 104
H: 6 1 W: 13 05 b.Pauillac 4-9-71
Honours: France 7 full caps, 3 goals.
1991–92 Saint-Seurin 33 10 33 10
1992–93 Auxerre 19 9
1993–94 Auxerre 19 5
1994–95 Auxerre 26 11
1995–96 Auxerre 34 12
1996–97 Auxerre 27 10 125 47
1997–98 Bordeaux 33 14
1998–99 Bordeaux 33 15
1999–2000 Bordeaux 31 14
2000–01 Bordeaux 22 4 119 47
2001–02 Sunderland 12 0 12 0

MACHO, Jurgen (G)   9 0
H: 6 4 W: 13 12 b.Vienna 24-8-77
Source: Honda Havelka, First Vienna.
2000–01 Sunderland 5 0
2001–02 Sunderland 4 0 9 0

MALEY, Mark (D)   17 0
H: 6 0 W: 13 00 b.Newcastle 26-1-81
Source: Trainee. *Honours:* England Schools, Youth.
1997–98 Sunderland 0 0
1998–99 Sunderland 0 0
1999–2000 Sunderland 0 0
2000–01 Sunderland 0 0
2000–01 *Blackpool* 2 0 2 0
2000–01 *Northampton T* 2 0 2 0
2001–02 Sunderland 0 0
2001–02 *York C* 13 0 13 0

MARCHANT, Ross* (M)   0 0
b.Bournemouth 6-4-82
Source: Scholar.
2000–01 Sunderland 0 0
2001–02 Sunderland 0 0

MBOMA, Patrick‡ (F)   169 73
H: 6 1 W: 11 70 b.Douala 15-11-70
Honours: Cameroon 53 full caps, 26 goals.
1993–94 Paris St Germain 0 0
1993–94 Chateauroux 29 17 29 17
1994–95 Paris St Germain 8 1
1995–96 Metz 17 4 17 4
1996–97 Paris St Germain 8 1 16 2
1997 Gamba Osaka 28 25
1998 Gamba Osaka 6 4 34 29
1998–99 Cagliari 13 7
1999–2000 Cagliari 27 8 40 15
2000–01 Parma 20 5
2001–02 Parma 4 0 24 5
2001–02 Sunderland 9 1 9 1

McATEER, Jason (M)   312 17
H: 5 10 W: 11 12 b.Birkenhead 18-6-71
Source: Marine. *Honours:* Eire B, 49 full caps, 3 goals.
1991–92 Bolton W 0 0
1992–93 Bolton W 21 0
1993–94 Bolton W 46 3
1994–95 Bolton W 43 5
1995–96 Bolton W 4 0 114 8
1995–96 Liverpool 29 0
1996–97 Liverpool 37 1
1997–98 Liverpool 21 2

1998–99 Liverpool 13 0 100 3
1998–99 Blackburn R 13 1
1999–2000 Blackburn R 28 2
2000–01 Blackburn R 27 1
2001–02 Blackburn R 4 0 72 4
2001–02 Sunderland 26 2 26 2

McCANN, Gavin (M)   97 7
H: 6 1 W: 12 08 b.Blackpool 10-1-78
Source: Trainee. *Honours:* England 1 full cap.
1995–96 Everton 0 0
1996–97 Everton 0 0
1997–98 Everton 11 0
1998–99 Everton 0 0 11 0
1998–99 Sunderland 11 0
1999–2000 Sunderland 24 4
2000–01 Sunderland 22 3
2001–02 Sunderland 29 0 86 7

McCARTNEY, George (D)   20 0
H: 5 11 W: 10 10 b.Belfast 29-4-81
Source: Trainee. *Honours:* Northern Ireland Schools, Youth, Under-21, 5 full caps, 1 goal.
1998–99 Sunderland 0 0
1999–2000 Sunderland 0 0
2000–01 Sunderland 2 0
2001–02 Sunderland 18 0 20 0

McGILL, Brendan (M)   28 2
H: 5 8 W: 9 02 b.Dublin 22-3-81
1998–99 Sunderland 0 0
1999–2000 Sunderland 0 0
2000–01 Sunderland 0 0
2001–02 Sunderland 0 0
2001–02 *Carlisle U* 28 2 28 2

MEDINA, Nicolas (M)   47 1
H: 5 9 W: 10 04 b.Buenos Aires 17-2-82
1999–2000 Argentinos Jun 26 0
2000–01 Argentinos Jun 21 1 47 1
2001–02 Sunderland 0 0

MERCIMEK, Baki (D)   0 0
H: 6 1 W: 11 11 b.Amsterdam 17-9-82
Source: Haarlem.
2001–02 Sunderland 0 0

MORDEY, Gareth* (D)   0 0
b.Sunderland 21-8-83
Source: Scholar.
2000–01 Sunderland 0 0
2001–02 Sunderland 0 0

OSTER, John (M)   84 4
H: 5 9 W: 10 09 b.Boston 8-12-78
Source: Trainee. *Honours:* Wales Youth, Under-21, B, 4 full caps.
1996–97 Grimsby T 24 3 24 3
1997–98 Everton 31 1
1998–99 Everton 9 0 40 1
1999–2000 Sunderland 10 0
2000–01 Sunderland 8 0
2001–02 Sunderland 0 0 18 0
2001–02 *Barnsley* 2 0 2 0

PEETERS, Tom (M)   33 1
H: 5 10 W: 11 00 b.Bornem 25-9-78
Source: Ekeren.
1999–2000 Mechelen 33 1 33 1
2000–01 Sunderland 0 0
2001–02 Sunderland 0 0
(On loan to Antwerp, November 2001).

PHILLIPS, Kevin (F)   235 131
H: 5 8 W: 11 05 b.Hitchin 25-7-73
Source: Baldock T. *Honours:* England B, 8 full caps.
1994–95 Watford 16 9
1995–96 Watford 27 11
1996–97 Watford 16 4 59 24
1997–98 Sunderland 43 29
1998–99 Sunderland 26 23
1999–2000 Sunderland 36 30
2000–01 Sunderland 34 14
2001–02 Sunderland 37 11 176 107

PROCTOR, Michael (F)   53 18
H: 6 0 W: 11 08 b.Sunderland 3-10-80
Source: Trainee.
1997–98 Sunderland 0 0
1998–99 Sunderland 0 0
1999–2000 Sunderland 0 0
2000–01 *Halifax T* 12 4 12 4
2001–02 Sunderland 0 0
2001–02 *York C* 41 14 41 14

QUINN, Niall (F)   465 141
H: 6 5 W: 14 08 b.Dublin 6-10-66
Honours: Eire Youth, Under-21, Under-23, B, 91 full caps, 21 goals.
1983–84 Arsenal 0 0
1984–85 Arsenal 0 0
1985–86 Arsenal* 12 1
1986–87 Arsenal 35 8

1987–88 Arsenal 11 2
1988–89 Arsenal 3 1
1989–90 Arsenal 6 2 67 14
1989–90 Manchester C 9 4
1990–91 Manchester C 38 20
1991–92 Manchester C 35 12
1992–93 Manchester C 39 9
1993–94 Manchester C 15 5
1994–95 Manchester C 35 8
1995–96 Manchester C 32 8 203 66
1996–97 Sunderland 12 2
1997–98 Sunderland 35 14
1998–99 Sunderland 39 18
1999–2000 Sunderland 37 14
2000–01 Sunderland 34 7
2001–02 Sunderland 38 6 195 61

RAMSDEN, Simon (D)   0 0
H: 6 0 W: 12 04 b.Bishop Auckland 17-12-81
Source: Scholar.
2000–01 Sunderland 0 0
2001–02 Sunderland 0 0

REDDY, Michael (F)   33 9
H: 6 1 W: 11 07 b.Graignamanagh 24-3-80
Source: Kilkenny C. *Honours:* Eire Under-21.
1999–2000 Sunderland 8 1
2000–01 Sunderland 2 0
2000–01 *Swindon T* 18 4 18 4
2001–02 Sunderland 0 0 10 1
2001–02 *Hull C* 5 4 5 4
2001–02 *Barnsley* 0 0

REYNA, Claudio (M)   133 17
H: 5 9 W: 11 09 b.New Jersey 20-7-73
Source: Union County SC, Univ Virginia.
Honours: USA 92 full caps, 8 goals.
1996–97 Leverkusen 5 0 5 0
1997–98 Wolfsburg 28 4
1998–99 Wolfsburg 20 2 48 6
1998–99 Rangers 6 0
1999–2000 Rangers 29 5
2000–01 Rangers 18 2
2001–02 Rangers 10 1 63 8
2001–02 Sunderland 17 3 17 3

ROSSITER, Mark (M)   0 0
b.Sligo 27-5-83
Source: Scholar.
2000–01 Sunderland 0 0
2001–02 Sunderland 0 0

ROY, Eric‡ (M)   345 24
H: 6 2 W: 13 00 b.Nice 26-9-67
1988–89 Nice 4 0
1989–90 Nice 19 0
1990–91 Nice 36 2
1991–92 Nice 27 2 86 4
1992–93 Toulon 34 2 34 2
1993–94 Lyon 36 3
1994–95 Lyon 37 3
1995–96 Lyon 38 3 111 9
1996–97 Marseille 36 5
1997–98 Marseille 27 1
1998–99 Marseille 24 3 87 9
1999–2000 Marseille 24 0
2000–01 Sunderland 3 0
2001–02 Sunderland 0 0 27 0

RYAN, Richard (M)   0 0
b.Kilkenny 6-1-85
Source: Scholar.
2001–02 Sunderland 0 0

SCHWARZ, Stefan (M)   318 18
H: 6 0 W: 12 00 b.Malmo 18-4-69
Honours: Sweden 69 full caps, 6 goals.
1987 Malmo 0 0
1988 Malmo 10 0
1989 Malmo 15 0
1990 Malmo 7 0 32 0
1990–91 Benfica 9 3
1991–92 Benfica 16 0
1992–93 Benfica 29 3
1993–94 Benfica 23 1 77 7
1994–95 Arsenal 34 2 34 2
1995–96 Fiorentina 32 0
1996–97 Fiorentina 24 0
1997–98 Fiorentina 22 2 78 2
1998–99 Valencia 30 4 30 4
1999–2000 Sunderland 27 1
2000–01 Sunderland 20 1
2001–02 Sunderland 20 1 67 3

SHIELDS, Dene (F)   7 1
H: 5 9 W: 12 00 b.Edinburgh 16-9-82
Source: Granton BC.
1999–2000 Raith R 0 0
2000–01 Raith R 7 1 7 1
2000–01 Sunderland 0 0
2001–02 Sunderland 0 0

SHIPPEN, Carl (M) 0 0
b.Bishop Auckland 2-3-84
Source: Scholar.
2001–02 Sunderland 0 0

SORENSEN, Thomas (G) 150 0
H: 6 4 W: 13 08 b.Odense 12-6-76
Source: Odense. *Honours:* Denmark 19 full caps.
1998–99 Sunderland 45 0
1999–2000 Sunderland 37 0
2000–01 Sunderland 34 0
2001–02 Sunderland 34 0 150 0

STRAKER, Philip (M) 0 0
b.Middlesbrough 9-11-83
Source: Scholar.
2001–02 Sunderland 0 0

SULLIVAN, David (M) 0 0
b.Glasgow 7-9-76
2001–02 Sunderland 0 0

TEGGART, Neil (F) 0 0
b.Downpatrick 16-9-84
Source: Scholar.
2001–02 Sunderland 0 0

THIRLWELL, Paul (M) 41 0
H: 5 11 W: 11 04 b.Springwell Village 13-2-79
Source: Trainee. *Honours:* England Under-21.
1996–97 Sunderland 0 0
1997–98 Sunderland 0 0
1998–99 Sunderland 2 0
1999–2000 Sunderland 8 0
1999–2000 *Swindon T* 12 0 12 0
2000–01 Sunderland 5 0
2001–02 Sunderland 14 0 29 0

TURNS, Craig (G) 0 0
b.Easington 4-11-82
Source: Scholar.
2000–01 Sunderland 0 0
2001–02 Sunderland 0 0

VARGA, Stanislav (D) 187 23
H: 6 5 W: 14 09 b.Lipany 8-10-72
Honours: Slovakia 40 full caps.
1993–94 Tatran Presov 15 2
1994–95 Tatran Presov 25 2
1995–96 Tatran Presov 21 2
1996–97 Tatran Presov 22 3
1997–98 Tatran Presov 26 1 106 10
1998–99 Slovan Bratislava 28 3
1999–2000 Slovan Bratislava 28 9 56 12
2000–01 Sunderland 12 1
2001–02 Sunderland 9 0 21 1
2001–02 *WBA* 4 0 4 0

WILLIAMS, Darren (D) 173 4
H: 5 11 W: 12 00 b.Middlesbrough 28-4-77
Source: Trainee. *Honours:* England Under-21, B.
1994–95 York C 1 0
1995–96 York C 18 0
1996–97 York C 1 0 20 0
1996–97 Sunderland 11 2
1997–98 Sunderland 36 2
1998–99 Sunderland 25 0
1999–2000 Sunderland 25 0
2000–01 Sunderland 28 0
2001–02 Sunderland 28 0 153 4

Trainees
Atkinson, Mark; Brown, Christopher; Cronin, Christopher; Davidson, Iain; George, Lee; Scott, Christopher; Toft, John

SWANSEA C

BRODIE, Steve* (F) 154 30
H: 5 7 W: 10 06 b.Sunderland 14-1-73
Source: Trainee.
1991–92 Sunderland 0 0
1992–93 Sunderland 0 0
1993–94 Sunderland 4 0
1994–95 Sunderland 8 0
1995–96 Sunderland 0 0
1995–96 *Doncaster R* 5 1 5 1
1996–97 Sunderland 0 0 12 0
1996–97 Scarborough 24 5
1997–98 Scarborough 44 10
1998–99 Scarborough 43 12
1999–2000 Scarborough 0 0
2000–01 Scarborough 0 0
2001–02 Scarborough 0 0 111 27
2001–02 Swansea C 26 2 26 2

CASEY, Ryan* (M) 62 2
H: 6 1 W: 11 02 b.Coventry 3-1-79
Source: Trainee. *Honours:* Eire Under-21.
1996–97 Swansea C 10 0
1997–98 Swansea C 6 0
1998–99 Swansea C 10 1
1999–2000 Swansea C 11 0
2000–01 Swansea C 9 1
2001–02 Swansea C 16 0 62 2

COATES, Jonathan* (M) 250 23
H: 5 8 W: 10 04 b.Swansea 27-6-75
Source: Trainee. *Honours:* Wales Youth, B, Under-21.
1993–94 Swansea C 4 1
1994–95 Swansea C 5 0
1995–96 Swansea C 18 0
1996–97 Swansea C 40 3
1997–98 Swansea C 44 7
1998–99 Swansea C 33 0
1999–2000 Swansea C 42 6
2000–01 Swansea C 19 1
2001–02 Swansea C 45 5 250 23

CUSACK, Nick (M) 532 70
H: 6 0 W: 11 13 b.Maltby 24-12-65
Source: Alvechurch.
1987–88 Leicester C 16 1 16 1
1988–89 Peterborough U 44 10 44 10
1989–90 Motherwell 31 11
1990–91 Motherwell 29 4
1991–92 Motherwell 17 2 77 17
1991–92 Darlington 21 6 21 6
1992–93 Oxford U 39 4
1993–94 Oxford U 20 6
1993–94 Wycombe W 4 0 4 0
1994–95 Oxford U 2 0 61 10
1995–96 Fulham 27 7
1995–96 Fulham 42 5
1996–97 Fulham 45 2
1997–98 Fulham 2 0 116 14
1997–98 Swansea C 32 0
1998–99 Swansea C 43 1
1999–2000 Swansea C 43 7
2000–01 Swansea C 40 2
2001–02 Swansea C 35 2 193 12

DE-VULGT, Leigh (M) 19 0
H: 5 9 W: 11 02 b.Swansea 17-3-81
Source: Trainee. *Honours:* Wales Youth, Under-21.
1999–2000 Swansea C 2 0
2000–01 Swansea C 7 0
2001–02 Swansea C 10 0 19 0

DRAPER, Craig* (M) 2 0
H: 5 7 W: 9 02 b.Swansea 4-12-82
Source: Trainee.
2001–02 Swansea C 2 0 2 0

EVANS, Terry (D) 30 0
H: 5 7 W: 11 08 b.Pontypridd 8-1-76
Source: Trainee. *Honours:* Wales Under-21.
1993–94 Cardiff C 5 0
1994–95 Cardiff C 7 0
1995–96 Cardiff C 2 0
1996–97 Cardiff C 0 0
1997–98 Cardiff C 0 0
1998–99 Cardiff C 0 0 14 0
From Barry Town.
2001–02 Swansea C 16 0 16 0

FREESTONE, Roger (G) 559 3
H: 6 2 W: 12 02 b.Newport 19-8-68
Source: Trainee. *Honours:* Wales Schools, Youth, Under-21, 1 full cap.
1986–87 Newport Co 13 0 13 0
1986–87 Chelsea 6 0
1987–88 Chelsea 15 0
1988–89 Chelsea 21 0
1989–90 Chelsea 0 0
1989–90 *Swansea C* 14 0
1989–90 *Hereford U* 8 0 8 0
1990–91 Chelsea 0 0 42 0
1991–92 Swansea C 42 0
1992–93 Swansea C 46 0
1993–94 Swansea C 46 0
1994–95 Swansea C 45 1
1995–96 Swansea C 45 2
1996–97 Swansea C 45 0
1997–98 Swansea C 43 0
1998–99 Swansea C 38 0
1999–2000 Swansea C 46 0
2000–01 Swansea C 43 0
2001–02 Swansea C 43 0 496 3

HEALEY, Stephen* (D) 0 0
H: 6 0 W: 10 10 b.Cardiff 19-9-82
Source: Trainee.
2001–02 Swansea C 0 0

HOWARD, Mike (D) 165 2
H: 5 7 W: 10 07 b.Birkenhead 2-12-78
Source: Tranmere R Trainee.
1997–98 Swansea C 3 0
1998–99 Swansea C 39 1
1999–2000 Swansea C 40 0
2000–01 Swansea C 41 0
2001–02 Swansea C 42 1 165 2

JENKINS, Lee (M) 126 3
H: 5 9 W: 11 00 b.Pontypool 28-6-79
Source: Trainee. *Honours:* Wales Schools, Youth, Under-21.
1996–97 Swansea C 23 2
1997–98 Swansea C 21 0
1998–99 Swansea C 12 0
1999–2000 Swansea C 16 0
2000–01 Swansea C 39 0
2001–02 Swansea C 15 1 126 3

JONES, Jason* (G) 10 0
H: 6 2 W: 12 10 b.Wrexham 10-5-79
Source: Liverpool Trainee. *Honours:* Wales Youth, Under-21.
1997–98 Swansea C 3 0
1998–99 Swansea C 0 0
1999–2000 Swansea C 0 0
2000–01 Swansea C 3 0
2001–02 Swansea C 3 0 10 0

KEEGAN, Michael‡ (M) 10 0
H: 5 10 W: 11 00 b.Wallasey 12-5-81
Source: Trainee.
1999–2000 Swansea C 4 0
2000–01 Swansea C 4 0
2001–02 Swansea C 2 0 10 0

LACEY, Damien (M) 94 2
H: 5 9 W: 11 03 b.Bridgend 3-8-77
Source: Trainee.
1996–97 Swansea C 10 0
1997–98 Swansea C 22 1
1998–99 Swansea C 12 0
1999–2000 Swansea C 16 0
2000–01 Swansea C 18 0
2001–02 Swansea C 16 1 94 2

MAZZINA, Nicolas* (M) 3 0
H: 5 8 W: 11 01 b.Buenos Aires 31-1-79
Source: AC Kimberley.
2001–02 Swansea C 3 0 3 0

MUMFORD, Andrew (M) 38 5
H: 6 1 W: 12 03 b.Neath 18-6-81
Source: Llanelli. *Honours:* Schools, Youth.
2000–01 Swansea C 6 0
2001–02 Swansea C 32 5 38 5

O'LEARY, Kristian (D) 136 7
H: 5 11 W: 12 09 b.Port Talbot 30-8-77
Source: Trainee. *Honours:* Wales Youth.
1995–96 Swansea C 1 0
1996–97 Swansea C 12 1
1997–98 Swansea C 29 0
1998–99 Swansea C 19 2
1999–2000 Swansea C 20 0
2000–01 Swansea C 24 2
2001–02 Swansea C 31 2 136 7

O'SULLIVAN, Chris* (M) 0 0
H: 5 8 W: 9 04 b.Fishguard 16-2-83
Source: Trainee.
2001–02 Swansea C 0 0

PHILLIPS, Gareth (M) 61 2
H: 5 8 W: 9 08 b.Pontypridd 19-8-79
Source: Trainee. *Honours:* Wales Schools, Youth, Under-21.
1996–97 Swansea C 1 0
1997–98 Swansea C 6 0
1998–99 Swansea C 1 0
1999–2000 Swansea C 3 0
2000–01 Swansea C 15 0
2001–02 Swansea C 35 2 61 2

ROMO, David (M) 43 1
H: 5 11 W: 12 06 b.Nimes 7-8-78
Honours: France Youth.
2000–01 Swansea C 33 0
2001–02 Swansea C 10 1 43 1

SHARP, Neil# (D) 25 1
H: 6 1 W: 12 08 b.Hemel Hempstead 19-1-78
Source: Merthyr T.
2001–02 Swansea C *25 1 25 1

SIDIBE, Mamady (F) 31 7
H: 6 4 W: 12 10 b.Mali 18-12-79
Source: CA Paris.
2001–02 Swansea C 31 7 31 7

SMITH, Jason (D) 115 5
H: 6 3 W: 14 00 b.Bromsgrove 6-9-74
Source: Tiverton. *Honours:* England Schools.
1993–94 Coventry C 0 0

1994–95	Coventry C	0	0
1995–96	Coventry C	0	0
1996–97	Coventry C	0	0
1997–98	Coventry C	0	0

From Tiverton T

1998–99	Swansea C	42	4
1999–2000	Swansea C	43	1
2000–01	Swansea C	22	0
2001–02	Swansea C	8	0	115	5

TODD, Chris* (D)   43   4
H: 6 1 W: 12 01 b.Swansea 22-8-81
Source: Trainee.

2000–01	Swansea C	11	1
2001–02	Swansea C	32	3	43	4

WATKIN, Steve (F)   380   97
H: 5 10 W: 11 10 b.Wrexham 16-6-71
Source: School. *Honours:* Wales Schools, B.

1989–90	Wrexham	0	0
1990–91	Wrexham	1	0
1991–92	Wrexham	28	8
1992–93	Wrexham	33	18
1993–94	Wrexham	40	9
1994–95	Wrexham	32	4
1995–96	Wrexham	29	7
1996–97	Wrexham	26	7
1997–98	Wrexham	3	1	200	55
1997–98	Swansea C	32	3
1998–99	Swansea C	43	17
1999–2000	Swansea C	39	7
2000–01	Swansea C	35	7
2001–02	Swansea C	31	8	180	42

WILLIAMS, John (F)   381   66
H: 6 1 W: 13 12 b.Birmingham 11-5-68
Source: Cradley T.

1991–92	Swansea C	39	11
1992–93	Coventry C	41	8
1993–94	Coventry C	32	3
1994–95	Coventry C	7	0
1994–95	Notts Co	5	2	5	2
1994–95	Stoke C	4	0	4	0
1994–95	Swansea C	7	2
1995–96	Coventry C	0	0	80	11
1995–96	Wycombe W	29	8
1996–97	Wycombe W	19	1	48	9
1996–97	Hereford U	11	3	11	3
1997–98	Walsall	1	0	1	0
1997–98	Exeter C	36	4	36	4
1998–99	Cardiff C	43	12
1999–2000	Cardiff C	0	0	43	12
1999–2000	York C	36	3
2000–01	York C	6	0	42	3
2000–01	Darlington	24	5	24	5
2001–02	Swansea C	41	4	87	17

Scholars
Cole, Simon D; Corbisiero, Antonio; Davies, Peter B; Duffy, Richard M; Eames, Jonathan J; Jones, Stuart J; King, Jack A; Thompson, Jay K; Waters, Michael

SWINDON T

BRAYLEY, Bertie* (M)   7   0
H: 5 9 W: 12 07 b.Basildon 5-9-81

2000–01	QPR	0	0
2001–02	Swindon T	7	0	7	0

COBIAN, Juan (D)   16   0
H: 5 6 W: 12 10 b.Buenos Aires 11-9-75
Source: Boca Juniors.

1998–99	Sheffield W	9	0	9	0
1999–2000	Charlton Ath	0	0
1999–2000	Aberdeen	3	0	3	0
2000–01	Swindon T	3	0
2001–02	Swindon T	1	0	4	0

COLLINS, Christopher (M)   0   0
b.Merthyr 6-8-83
Source: Scholar.

2001–02	Swindon T	0	0

DAVIS, Sol (D)   117   0
H: 5 8 W: 11 00 b.Cheltenham 4-9-79
Source: Trainee.

1997–98	Swindon T	6	0
1998–99	Swindon T	25	0
1999–2000	Swindon T	29	0
2000–01	Swindon T	36	0
2001–02	Swindon T	21	0	117	0

DUKE, David (M)   74   3
H: 5 10 W: 11 01 b.Inverness 7-11-78
Source: Redby CA.

1997–98	Sunderland	0	0
1998–99	Sunderland	0	0
1999–2000	Sunderland	0	0
2000–01	Swindon T	32	1
2001–02	Swindon T	42	2	74	3

EDWARDS, Nathan§ (M)   7   0
b.Lincoln 8-4-83
Source: Scholar.

2001–02	Swindon T	7	0	7	0

EDWARDS, Paul (M)   20   0
H: 5 11 W: 10 12 b.Manchester 1-1-80
Source: Altrincham.

2001–02	Swindon T	20	0	20	0

GRAZIOLI, Giuliano* (F)   119   34
H: 5 11 W: 12 11 b.London 23-3-75
Source: Wembley.

1995–96	Peterborough U	3	1
1996–97	Peterborough U	4	0
1997–98	Peterborough U	0	0
1998–99	Peterborough U	34	15	41	16
1999–2000	Swindon T	19	8
2000–01	Swindon T	28	2
2001–02	Swindon T	31	8	78	18

GRIEMINK, Bart# (G)   152   0
H: 6 3 W: 15 02 b.Holland 29-3-72
Source: WKE.

1995–96	Birmingham C	20	0
1996–97	Birmingham C	0	0	20	0
1996–97	Barnsley	0	0
1996–97	Peterborough U	27	0
1997–98	Peterborough U	38	0
1998–99	Peterborough U	17	0
1999–2000	Peterborough U	14	0	58	0
1999–2000	Swindon T	4	0
2000–01	Swindon T	25	0
2001–02	Swindon T	45	0	74	0

GURNEY, Andy (D)   282   28
H: 5 8 W: 10 08 b.Bristol 25-1-74
Source: Trainee.

1992–93	Bristol R	0	0
1993–94	Bristol R	3	0
1994–95	Bristol R	38	1
1995–96	Bristol R	43	6
1996–97	Bristol R	24	2	108	9
1997–98	Torquay U	44	9
1998–99	Torquay U	20	1	64	10
1998–99	Reading	8	0
1999–2000	Reading	38	2
2000–01	Reading	21	1	67	3
2001–02	Swindon T	43	6	43	6

HERRING, Ian§ (M)   1   0
b.Swindon 14-2-84
Source: Scholar.

2001–02	Swindon T	1	0	1	0

HEWLETT, Matt# (M)   194   10
H: 6 2 W: 12 12 b.Bristol 25-2-76
Source: Trainee. *Honours:* England Youth.

1993–94	Bristol C	12	0
1994–95	Bristol C	1	0
1995–96	Bristol C	27	2
1996–97	Bristol C	36	2
1997–98	Bristol C	34	4
1998–99	Bristol C	10	1
1998–99	Burnley	2	0	2	0
1999–2000	Bristol C	7	0	127	9
2000–01	Swindon T	26	0
2001–02	Swindon T	39	1	65	1

HEYWOOD, Matthew (D)   78   5
H: 6 3 W: 14 00 b.Chatham 26-8-79
Source: Trainee.

1998–99	Burnley	13	0
1999–2000	Burnley	0	0
2000–01	Burnley	0	0	13	0
2000–01	Swindon T	21	2
2001–02	Swindon T	44	3	65	5

HOWE, Bobby* (M)   139   8
H: 5 7 W: 10 04 b.Annisford 6-11-73
Source: Trainee.

1991–92	Nottingham F	0	0
1992–93	Nottingham F	0	0
1993–94	Nottingham F	4	0
1994–95	Nottingham F	7	0
1995–96	Nottingham F	9	2
1996–97	Nottingham F	1	0
1996–97	Ipswich T	3	0	3	0
1997–98	Nottingham F	0	0	14	2
1997–98	Swindon T	10	0
1998–99	Swindon T	23	3
1999–2000	Swindon T	31	1
2000–01	Swindon T	19	1
2001–02	Swindon T	39	1	122	6

INVINCIBILE, Danny (M)   130   18
H: 6 0 W: 12 02 b.Australia 31-3-79

1997–98	Brisbane Strikers	5	1	5	1
1998–99	Marconi Stallions	7	0
1999–2000	Marconi Stallions	32	2	39	2
2000–01	West Ham U	0	0
2000–01	Swindon T	42	9
2001–02	Swindon T	44	6	86	15

McAREAVEY, Paul* (M)   24   1
H: 5 10 W: 11 00 b.Belfast 3-12-80
Source: Trainee. *Honours:* Northern Ireland Youth, Under-21.

1997–98	Swindon T	1	0
1998–99	Swindon T	1	0
1999–2000	Swindon T	0	0
2000–01	Swindon T	3	1
2001–02	Swindon T	19	0	24	1

McKINNEY, Richard* (G)   1   0
H: 6 3 W: 14 00 b.Ballymoney 18-5-79
Source: Ballymena U.

1999–2000	Manchester C	0	0
2000–01	Manchester C	0	0
2001–02	Swindon T	1	0	1	0

O'HALLORAN, Keith (D)   108   9
H: 5 9 W: 11 06 b.Ireland 10-11-75
Source: Cherry Orchard.

1994–95	Middlesbrough	1	0
1995–96	Middlesbrough	3	0
1995–96	Scunthorpe U	7	0	7	0
1996–97	Middlesbrough	0	0	4	0
1996–97	Cardiff C	8	0	8	0
1996–97	St Johnstone	5	0
1997–98	St Johnstone	22	1
1998–99	St Johnstone	16	1
1999–2000	St Johnstone	0	0	43	2
2000–01	Swindon T	40	5
2001–02	Swindon T	6	2	46	7

REEVES, Alan# (D)   372   23
H: 6 0 W: 12 00 b.Birkenhead 19-11-67
Source: Heswall.

1988–89	Norwich C	0	0
1988–89	Gillingham	18	0	18	0
1989–90	Chester C	30	2
1990–91	Chester C	10	0	40	2
1991–92	Rochdale	34	3
1992–93	Rochdale	41	3
1993–94	Rochdale	41	3
1994–95	Rochdale	5	0	121	9
1994–95	Wimbledon	31	3
1995–96	Wimbledon	24	1
1996–97	Wimbledon	2	0
1997–98	Wimbledon	0	0	57	4
1998–99	Swindon T	24	2
1999–2000	Swindon T	43	1
2000–01	Swindon T	44	3
2001–02	Swindon T	25	2	136	8

ROBINSON, Mark‡ (D)   433   10
H: 5 9 W: 12 04 b.Rochdale 21-11-68
Source: Trainee.

1985–86	WBA	1	0
1986–87	WBA	1	0	2	0
1987–88	Barnsley	3	0
1988–89	Barnsley	18	2
1989–90	Barnsley	24	0
1990–91	Barnsley	22	1
1991–92	Barnsley	41	2
1992–93	Barnsley	29	1	137	6
1992–93	Newcastle U	9	0
1993–94	Newcastle U	16	0	25	0
1994–95	Swindon T	40	0
1995–96	Swindon T	46	1
1996–97	Swindon T	43	1
1997–98	Swindon T	27	1
1998–99	Swindon T	29	0
1999–2000	Swindon T	42	0
2000–01	Swindon T	34	1
2001–02	Swindon T	8	0	269	4

ROBINSON, Steve (M)   144   2
H: 5 9 W: 11 00 b.Nottingham 17-10-75
Source: Trainee.

1993–94	Birmingham C	0	0
1994–95	Birmingham C	6	0
1995–96	Birmingham C	0	0
1995–96	Peterborough U	5	0	5	0
1996–97	Birmingham C	9	0
1997–98	Birmingham C	25	0
1998–99	Birmingham C	31	0
1999–2000	Birmingham C	6	0
2000–01	Birmingham C	4	0	81	0
2000–01	Swindon T	18	2
2001–02	Swindon T	40	0	58	2

RUDDOCK, Neil (D)   355   29
H: 6 2 W: 12 12 b.Wandsworth 9-5-68
Source: Apprentice. *Honours:* England Youth, Under-21, B, 1 full cap.

1985–86	Millwall	0	0
1985–86	Tottenham H	0	0
1986–87	Tottenham H	4	0
1987–88	Tottenham H	5	0
1988–89	Millwall	2	1	2	1
1988–89	Southampton	13	3
1989–90	Southampton	29	3
1990–91	Southampton	35	3
1991–92	Southampton	30	0	107	9

1992–93	Tottenham H	38	3	**47**	**3**
1993–94	Liverpool	39	3		
1994–95	Liverpool	37	2		
1995–96	Liverpool	20	5		
1996–97	Liverpool	17	1		
1997–98	Liverpool	2	0	**115**	**11**
1997–98	QPR	7	0	**7**	**0**
1998–99	West Ham U	27	2		
1999–2000	West Ham U	15	0	**42**	**2**
2000–01	Crystal Palace	20	2	**20**	**2**
2001–02	Swindon T	15	1	**15**	**1**

SABIN, Eric (F)   **62**   **8**
H: 6 0   W: 12 00   b.Sarcelles 22-1-75

2000–01	Wasquehal	28	3	**28**	**3**
2001–02	Swindon T	34	5	**34**	**5**

SMITH, Bryan§ (D)   **1**   **0**
H: 6 1   W: 12 00   b.Swindon 26-8-83
Source: Trainee.

1999–2000	Swindon T	1	0		
2000–01	Swindon T	0	0		
2001–02	Swindon T	0	0	**1**	**0**

WALTON, Graeme (M)   **0**   **0**
b.Newcastle 9-12-83
Source: Scholar.

2001–02	Swindon T	0	0		

WILLIAMS, James* (M)   **37**   **1**
H: 5 7   W: 10 08   b.Liverpool 15-7-82
Source: Trainee.

1998–99	Swindon T	3	0		
1999–2000	Swindon T	26	1		
2000–01	Swindon T	7	0		
2001–02	Swindon T	1	0	**37**	**1**

WILLIS, Adam# (D)   **87**   **1**
H: 6 1   W: 12 02   b.Nuneaton 21-9-76
Source: Trainee.

1995–96	Coventry C	0	0		
1996–97	Coventry C	0	0		
1997–98	Coventry C	0	0		
1997–98	Swindon T	0	0		
1998–99	Swindon T	11	0		
1998–99	*Mansfield T*	10	0	**10**	**0**
1999–2000	Swindon T	23	0		
2000–01	Swindon T	21	0		
2001–02	Swindon T	22	1	**77**	**1**

YOUNG, Alan (F)   **18**   **1**
H: 5 6   W: 10 00   b.Swindon 12-8-83
Source: Scholar. *Honours:* England Youth.

2000–01	Swindon T	4	0		
2001–02	Swindon T	14	1	**18**	**1**

Scholars
Andersen, Paul A; Bampton, David P; Bristow, Adrian G; Cheeseman, James; Collier, Adam J; Draycott, Mark R; Edwards, Nathan M; Farr, Craig J; Fenwick, Mark T; Halliday, Kevin J; Herring, Ian; Reed, Paul S; Scarlett, Philip J; Smith, Bryan J; Smith, Steven A; Taylor, Daniel S; Thomas, Joshua O

Non-Contract
Crosby, Neil; Hughes, Christopher WJ; Titcombe, Paul R

TORQUAY U

AGGREY, Jimmy‡ (D)   **95**   **2**
H: 6 3   W: 15 03   b.London 26-10-78
Source: Chelsea Trainee.

1997–98	Fulham	0	0		
1998–99	Torquay U	25	0		
1999–2000	Torquay U	27	0		
2000–01	Torquay U	41	2		
2001–02	Torquay U	2	0	**95**	**2**

ASHFORD, Ryan‡ (D)   **2**   **1**
H: 5 11   W: 12 07   b.Honiton 13-10-81
Source: Scholar.

2000–01	Southampton	0	0		
2001–02	Southampton	0	0		
2001–02	Torquay U	2	1	**2**	**1**

ASHINGTON, Ryan (F)   **14**   **0**
H: 5 10   W: 12 06   b.Torbay 28-3-83
Source: Scholar.

2000–01	Torquay U	14	0		
2001–02	Torquay U	0	0	**14**	**0**

BANGER, Nicky‡ (F)   **200**   **28**
H: 5 8   W: 11 03   b.Southampton 25-2-71
Source: Trainee.

1988–89	Southampton	0	0		
1989–90	Southampton	0	0		
1990–91	Southampton	6	0		
1991–92	Southampton	4	0		
1992–93	Southampton	27	6		
1993–94	Southampton	14	0		
1994–95	Southampton	2	2	**55**	**8**
1994–95	Oldham Ath	28	3		
1995–96	Oldham Ath	13	2		
1996–97	Oldham Ath	23	5	**64**	**10**
1997–98	Oxford U	28	3		
1998–99	Oxford U	32	5		
1999–2000	Oxford U	3	0	**63**	**8**
1999–2000	Dundee	6	0	**6**	**0**
2000–01	Scunthorpe U	1	0	**1**	**0**
2001–02	Plymouth Arg	10	2	**10**	**2**
2001–02	Torquay U	1	0	**1**	**0**

BEDEAU, Anthony (F)   **178**   **40**
H: 5 10   W: 12 03   b.Hammersmith 24-3-79
Source: Trainee.

1995–96	Torquay U	4	0		
1996–97	Torquay U	8	1		
1997–98	Torquay U	34	5		
1998–99	Torquay U	36	9		
1999–2000	Torquay U	38	16		
2000–01	Torquay U	34	5		
2001–02	Torquay U	21	4	**175**	**40**
2001–02	*Barnsley*	3	0	**3**	**0**

BENEFIELD, Jimmy (F)   **9**   **0**
H: 5 11   W: 11 05   b.Bristol 6-5-83
Source: Scholar.

2000–01	Torquay U	1	0		
2001–02	Torquay U	8	0	**9**	**0**

BRABIN, Gary‡ (M)   **234**   **25**
H: 5 11   W: 14 08   b.Liverpool 9-12-70
Source: Trainee.

1989–90	Stockport Co	1	0		
1990–91	Stockport Co	1	0	**2**	**0**
From Runcorn					
1994–95	Doncaster R	28	8		
1995–96	Doncaster R	31	3	**59**	**11**
1995–96	Bury	5	0	**5**	**0**
1996–97	Blackpool	32	2		
1997–98	Blackpool	24	3		
1998–99	Blackpool	7	0	**63**	**5**
1998–99	*Lincoln C*	4	0	**4**	**0**
1998–99	Hull C	21	4		
1999–2000	Hull C	37	3		
2000–01	Hull C	37	2	**95**	**9**
From Boston U.					
2001–02	Torquay U	6	0	**6**	**0**

BRANDON, Chris‡ (M)   **71**   **8**
H: 5 8   W: 11 02   b.Bradford 7-4-76
Source: Bradford PA.

1999–2000	Torquay U	42	5		
2000–01	Torquay U	2	0		
2001–02	Torquay U	27	3	**71**	**8**

BROWN, David‡ (F)   **133**   **23**
H: 5 10   W: 11 02   b.Bolton 2-10-78
Source: Trainee.

1995–96	Manchester U	0	0		
1996–97	Manchester U	0	0		
1997–98	Manchester U	0	0		
1997–98	*Hull C*	7	2		
1998–99	Hull C	42	11		
1999–2000	Hull C	45	6		
2000–01	Hull C	37	4		
2001–02	Hull C	0	0	**131**	**23**
2001–02	Torquay U	2	0	**2**	**0**

CANOVILLE, Lee (F)   **14**   **1**
H: 6 0   W: 11 04   b.Ealing 14-3-81
Source: Trainee. *Honours:* FA Schools, England Youth.

1998–99	Arsenal	0	0		
1999–2000	Arsenal	0	0		
2000–01	Arsenal	0	0		
2000–01	*Northampton T*	2	0	**2**	**0**
2001–02	Torquay U	12	1	**12**	**1**

DEARDEN, Kevin (G)   **384**   **0**
H: 5 11   W: 14 02   b.Luton 8-3-70
Source: Trainee.

1988–89	Tottenham H	0	0		
1988–89	*Cambridge U*	15	0	**15**	**0**
1989–90	Tottenham H	0	0		
1989–90	*Hartlepool U*	10	0	**10**	**0**
1989–90	*Oxford U*	0	0		
1989–90	*Swindon T*	1	0	**1**	**0**
1990–91	Tottenham H	0	0		
1990–91	*Peterborough U*	7	0	**7**	**0**
1990–91	*Hull C*	3	0	**3**	**0**
1991–92	Tottenham H	0	0		
1991–92	*Rochdale*	2	0	**2**	**0**
1991–92	*Birmingham C*	12	0	**12**	**0**
1992–93	Tottenham H	1	0		
1992–93	*Portsmouth*	0	0		
1993–94	Tottenham H	0	0	**1**	**0**
1993–94	Brentford	35	0		
1994–95	Brentford	43	0		
1995–96	Brentford	41	0		
1996–97	Brentford	44	0		
1997–98	Brentford	35	0		
1998–99	Brentford	7	0	**205**	**0**
1998–99	*Barnet*	1	0	**1**	**0**
1998–99	*Huddersfield T*	0	0		
1999–2000	Wrexham	45	0		
2000–01	Wrexham	36	0	**81**	**0**
2001–02	Torquay U	46	0	**46**	**0**

DOUGLIN, Troy (D)   **9**   **0**
H: 6 0   W: 12 03   b.Coventry 7-5-82
Source: Trainee.

2000–01	Torquay U	3	0		
2001–02	Torquay U	6	0	**9**	**0**

FOWLER, Jason (M)   **184**   **15**
H: 6 3   W: 12 07   b.Bristol 20-8-74
Source: Trainee.

1992–93	Bristol C	1	0		
1993–94	Bristol C	1	0		
1994–95	Bristol C	13	0		
1995–96	Bristol C	10	0	**25**	**0**
1996–97	Cardiff C	37	5		
1997–98	Cardiff C	38	5		
1998–99	Cardiff C	37	3		
1999–2000	Cardiff C	28	1		
2000–01	Cardiff C	5	0		
2001–02	Cardiff C	0	0	**145**	**14**
2001–02	Torquay U	14	1	**14**	**1**

GOODRIDGE, Greg* (F)   **192**   **21**
H: 5 8   W: 11 00   b.Barbados 10-7-71
Source: Lambada. *Honours:* Barbados full caps.

1993–94	Torquay U	8	1		
1994–95	Torquay U	30	3		
1995–96	QPR	7	1	**7**	**1**
1996–97	Bristol C	28	6		
1997–98	Bristol C	31	6		
1998–99	Bristol C	30	2		
1999–2000	Bristol C	21	0		
2000–01	Bristol C	7	0		
2000–01	*Cheltenham T*	11	1	**11**	**1**
2001–02	Bristol C	2	0	**119**	**14**
2001–02	Torquay U	17	1	**55**	**5**

GRAHAM, David (F)   **65**   **12**
H: 5 11   W: 12 01   b.Edinburgh 6-10-78
Source: Rangers SABC. *Honours:* Scotland Under-21.

1995–96	Rangers	0	0		
1996–97	Rangers	0	0		
1997–98	Rangers	0	0		
1998–99	Rangers	3	0	**3**	**0**
1998–99	Dunfermline Ath	21	2		
1999–2000	Dunfermline Ath	0	0		
2000–01	Dunfermline Ath	0	0	**21**	**2**
2000–01	Torquay U	5	2		
2001–02	Torquay U	36	8	**41**	**10**

GREYLING, Anton‡ (M)   **2**   **0**
H: 6 0   W: 11 09   b.Pretoria 5-12-77
Source: Supersport U.

2001–02	Torquay U	2	0	**2**	**0**

GUMMER, Sean‡ (M)   **0**   **0**
b.Derby 14-4-81
Source: Trainee.

1999–2000	Derby Co	0	0		
2000–01	Derby Co	0	0		
2001–02	Torquay U	0	0		

HALL, Daniel‡ (D)   **0**   **0**
H: 5 8   W: 10 06   b.Rugby 29-12-81
Source: Trainee. *Honours:* England Youth.

1998–99	Coventry C	0	0		
1999–2000	Coventry C	0	0		
2000–01	Coventry C	0	0		
2001–02	Torquay U	0	0		

HANKIN, Sean (M)   **28**   **0**
H: 5 11   W: 12 04   b.Camberley 28-2-81
Source: Trainee.

1999–2000	Crystal Palace	1	0		
2000–01	Crystal Palace	0	0		
2001–02	Crystal Palace	0	0	**1**	**0**
2001–02	Torquay U	27	0	**27**	**0**

HAZELL, Reuben (D)   **61**   **1**
H: 5 11   W: 11 11   b.Birmingham 24-4-79
Source: Trainee.

1996–97	Aston Villa	0	0		
1997–98	Aston Villa	0	0		
1998–99	Aston Villa	0	0		
1999–2000	Tranmere R	23	1		
2000–01	Tranmere R	13	0		
2001–02	Tranmere R	6	0	**42**	**1**
2001–02	Torquay U	19	0	**19**	**0**

HILL, Kevin (M)   **203**   **25**
H: 5 8   W: 10 06   b.Exeter 6-3-76
Source: Torrington.

1997–98	Torquay U	37	7		
1998–99	Torquay U	35	5		
1999–2000	Torquay U	43	2		
2000–01	Torquay U	44	9		
2001–02	Torquay U	44	2	**203**	**25**

HOCKLEY, Matthew (D) 18 1
H: 5 10 W: 11 11 b.Paignton 5-6-82
Source: Trainee.

2000–01	Torquay U	6	1	
2001–02	Torquay U	12	0	18 1

HOLMES, Paul (D) 401 8
H: 5 10 W: 12 05 b.Stocksbridge 18-2-68
Source: Apprentice.

1985–86	Doncaster R	5	1	
1986–87	Doncaster R	16	0	
1987–88	Doncaster R	26	0	47 1
1988–89	Torquay U	25	0	
1989–90	Torquay U	44	2	
1990–91	Torquay U	33	1	
1991–92	Torquay U	36	1	
1992–93	Birmingham C	12	0	12 0
1992–93	Everton	4	0	
1993–94	Everton	15	0	
1994–95	Everton	1	0	
1995–96	Everton	1	0	21 0
1995–96	WBA	18	0	
1996–97	WBA	38	1	
1997–98	WBA	30	0	
1998–99	WBA	17	0	
1999–2000	WBA	0	0	103 1
1999–2000	Torquay U	30	0	
2000–01	Torquay U	32	2	
2001–02	Torquay U	18	0	218 6

JAMES, John (D) 0 0
b.Plymouth 3-8-84
Source: Topsham T.

2001–02	Torquay U	0	0

JONES, Stuart‡ (G) 32 0
H: 6 2 W: 14 04 b.Bristol 24-10-77
Source: Weston-Super-Mare.

1997–98	Sheffield W	0	0	
1998–99	Sheffield W	0	0	
1998–99	*Crewe Alex*	0	0	
1999–2000	Sheffield W	0	0	
1999–2000	Torquay U	16	0	
2000–01	Torquay U	16	0	
2001–02	Torquay U	0	0	32 0

LAW, Gareth‡ (F) 15 1
H: 6 0 W: 11 05 b.Newton Abbot 20-8-82
Source: Scholar.

2000–01	Torquay U	10	1	
2001–02	Torquay U	5	0	15 1

LINCOLN, Greg‡ (M) 0 0
H: 6 0 W: 12 11 b.Enfield 23-3-80
Source: Trainee. Honours: England Youth.

1998–99	Arsenal	0	0
1999–2000	Arsenal	0	0
2000–01	Arsenal	0	0
2001–02	Torquay U	0	0

LYONS, Simon‡ (D) 9 1
H: 5 10 W: 11 09 b.Hamilton 2-12-82
Source: Arsenal Trainee.

2000–01	Torquay U	9	1	
2001–02	Torquay U	0	0	9 1

MARTIN, Andrew‡ (F) 27 2
H: 5 9 W: 10 04 b.Cardiff 28-2-80
Source: Trainee. Honours: Wales Youth, Under-21.

1996–97	Crystal Palace	0	0	
1997–98	Crystal Palace	0	0	
1998–99	Crystal Palace	3	0	
1999–2000	Crystal Palace	19	2	
2000–01	Crystal Palace	0	0	
2001–02	Crystal Palace	0	0	22 2
2001–02	Torquay U	5	0	5 0

McNEIL, Martin‡ (M) 57 0
H: 6 1 W: 13 05 b.Rutherglen 28-9-80
Source: Trainee.

1998–99	Cambridge U	6	0	
1999–2000	Cambridge U	29	0	
2000–01	Cambridge U	6	0	
2001–02	Cambridge U	0	0	41 0
2001–02	Torquay U	16	0	16 0

MORRIS, Jason (D) 0 0
H: 6 0 W: 12 07 b.Torquay 7-5-83
Source: Buckland Ath.

2001–02	Torquay U	0	0

2001–02	Torquay U	9	1	9 1

(Transferred to Hamilton A, October 2001).

NORTHMORE, Ryan (G) 28 0
H: 6 2 W: 13 00 b.Plymouth 5-9-80
Source: Trainee.

1999–2000	Torquay U	3	0	
2000–01	Torquay U	25	0	
2001–02	Torquay U	0	0	28 0

O'BRIEN, Mick‡ (M) 52 5
H: 5 6 W: 11 00 b.Liverpool 25-9-79
Source: Trainee. Honours: England Schools.

1997–98	Everton	0	0	
1998–99	Everton	0	0	
1999–2000	Torquay U	30	4	
2000–01	Torquay U	21	1	
2001–02	Torquay U	1	0	52 5

PARKER, Kevin‡ (F) 17 2
H: 5 9 W: 11 02 b.Plymouth 20-9-79
Source: Trainee.

1999–2000	Norwich C	0	0	
2000–01	Torquay U	15	2	
2001–02	Torquay U	2	0	17 2

PREECE, David‡ (M) 554 30
H: 5 6 W: 11 05 b.Bridgnorth 28-5-63
Source: Apprentice. Honours: England B.

1980–81	Walsall	8	0	
1981–82	Walsall	8	0	
1982–83	Walsall	42	2	
1983–84	Walsall	41	3	
1984–85	Walsall	12	0	111 5
1984–85	Luton T	21	2	
1985–86	Luton T	41	2	
1986–87	Luton T	14	0	
1987–88	Luton T	13	0	
1988–89	Luton T	26	0	
1989–90	Luton T	32	1	
1990–91	Luton T	37	1	
1991–92	Luton T	38	3	
1992–93	Luton T	43	3	
1993–94	Luton T	29	5	
1994–95	Luton T	42	4	336 21
1994–95	Derby Co	13	1	13 1
1995–96	Birmingham C	6	0	6 0
1995–96	Swindon T	7	1	7 1
1996–97	Cambridge U	25	0	
1997–98	Cambridge U	22	0	
1998–99	Cambridge U	14	2	
1999–2000	Cambridge U	12	0	
2000–01	Cambridge U	2	0	75 2
2001–02	Torquay U	6	0	6 0

REES, Jason (M) 312 11
H: 5 6 W: 10 11 b.Aberdare 22-12-69
Source: Trainee. Honours: Wales Schools, Youth, Under-21, B, 1 full cap.

1988–89	Luton T	0	0	
1989–90	Luton T	14	0	
1990–91	Luton T	21	0	
1991–92	Luton T	5	0	
1992–93	Luton T	32	0	
1993–94	Luton T	10	0	82 0
1993–94	*Mansfield T*	15	1	15 1
1994–95	Portsmouth	19	1	
1995–96	Portsmouth	21	1	
1996–97	Portsmouth	3	1	43 3
1996–97	Exeter C	7	0	
1997–98	Cambridge U	20	0	20 0
1998–99	Exeter C	44	1	
1999–2000	Exeter C	43	4	
2000–01	Exeter C	0	0	94 5
2000–01	Torquay U	25	2	
2001–02	Torquay U	33	0	58 2

RICHARDSON, Marcus‡ (F) 46 8
H: 6 2 W: 13 00 b.Reading 31-8-77
Source: Harrow B.

2000–01	Cambridge U	10	2	
2001–02	Cambridge U	0	0	16 2
2001–02	Torquay U	30	6	30 6

ROACH, Neville‡ (F) 45 4
H: 5 11 W: 12 00 b.Reading 29-9-78
Source: Trainee.

1996–97	Reading	3	1	
1997–98	Reading	8	0	
1998–99	Reading	5	0	16 1
1998–99	Southend U	8	1	
1999–2000	Southend U	8	1	
2000–01	Southend U	0	0	16 2
2000–01	Oldham Ath	1	0	1 0
2001–02	Torquay U	12	1	12 1

RUSSELL, Alex (M) 216 29
H: 5 10 W: 10 09 b.Crosby 17-3-73
Source: Burscough.

1994–95	Rochdale	7	1	
1995–96	Rochdale	25	0	
1996–97	Rochdale	39	9	
1997–98	Rochdale	31	4	102 14
1998–99	Cambridge U	37	6	
1999–2000	Cambridge U	15	0	
2000–01	Cambridge U	29	2	81 8
2001–02	Torquay U	33	7	33 7

RUSSELL, Lee‡ (D) 208 3
H: 5 11 W: 12 00 b.Southampton 3-9-69
Source: Trainee.

1988–89	Portsmouth	2	0	
1989–90	Portsmouth	3	0	
1990–91	Portsmouth	19	1	
1991–92	Portsmouth	9	0	
1992–93	Portsmouth	14	0	
1993–94	Portsmouth	10	0	
1994–95	Portsmouth	19	0	
1994–95	*Bournemouth*	3	0	3 0
1995–96	Portsmouth	19	0	
1996–97	Portsmouth	20	2	
1997–98	Portsmouth	8	0	
1998–99	Portsmouth	0	0	123 3
1998–99	*Torquay U*	9	0	
1999–2000	Torquay U	35	0	
2000–01	Torquay U	27	0	
2001–02	Torquay U	11	0	82 0

STEPHENS, Nicholas (M) 0 0
H: 6 2 W: 12 00 b.Plymouth 30-5-83
Source: Scholar.

2001–02	Torquay U	0	0

STOCCO, Tom‡ (F) 10 2
H: 6 1 W: 13 07 b.London 4-1-83
Source: Trainee.

1999–2000	Torquay U	8	2	
2000–01	Torquay U	2	0	
2001–02	Torquay U	0	0	10 2

TULLY, Stephen* (D) 106 3
H: 5 8 W: 11 02 b.Paignton 10-2-80
Source: Trainee.

1997–98	Torquay U	9	0	
1998–99	Torquay U	37	2	
1999–2000	Torquay U	13	0	
2000–01	Torquay U	29	1	
2001–02	Torquay U	18	0	106 3

WOODS, Steve (D) 102 2
H: 6 0 W: 13 00 b.Northwich 15-12-76
Source: Trainee.

1995–96	Stoke C	0	0	
1996–97	Stoke C	0	0	
1997–98	Stoke C	1	0	
1997–98	*Plymouth Arg*	5	0	5 0
1998–99	Stoke C	33	0	34 0
1999–2000	Chesterfield	25	0	
2000–01	Chesterfield	0	0	25 0
2001–02	Torquay U	38	2	38 2

WOOZLEY, David (D) 52 0
H: 6 0 W: 12 10 b.Berkshire 6-12-79
Source: Trainee.

1997–98	Crystal Palace	0	0	
1998–99	Crystal Palace	7	0	
1999–2000	Crystal Palace	23	0	
2000–01	Crystal Palace	0	0	
2000–01	*Bournemouth*	6	0	6 0
2001–02	Crystal Palace	0	0	30 0
2001–02	Torquay U	16	0	16 0

Scholars
Bevan, Lee W; Bond, Kain; Brimming, Robert G; Burgess, Lucas; Camara, Ben I; Carns, David; Gibbens, Jonathan D; Griffiths, Kenneth Y; Killoughery, Graham A; Kironde, Biju S; Maguire, Anthony E; Morris, John K; O'Donovan, Timothy J; Rosindale, Christopher A
Non-Contract
Hancox, Richard C

TOTTENHAM H

ACIMOVIC, Milenko (M) 136 41
H: 6 2 W: 12 08 b.Ljubljana 15-2-77
Honours: Slovenia 42 full caps, 10 goals.

1996–97	Olimpija	18	3	
1997–98	Olimpija	16	4	34 7
1997–98	Red Star Belgrade	9	1	
1998–99	Red Star Belgrade	22	8	
1999–2000	Red Star Belgrade	21	4	
2000–01	Red Star Belgrade	28	14	
2000–01	Red Star Belgrade	22	7	102 34
2001–02	Tottenham H	0	0	

ANDERTON, Darren (M) 321 40
H: 6 1 W: 12 11 b.Southampton 3-3-72
Source: Trainee. Honours: England Youth, Under-21, B, 30 full caps, 7 goals.

1989–90	Portsmouth	0	0	
1990–91	Portsmouth	20	0	
1991–92	Portsmouth	42	7	62 7
1992–93	Tottenham H	34	6	

Season	Club				
1993–94	Tottenham H	37	6		
1994–95	Tottenham H	37	5		
1995–96	Tottenham H	8	2		
1996–97	Tottenham H	16	3		
1997–98	Tottenham H	15	0		
1998–99	Tottenham H	32	3		
1999–2000	Tottenham H	22	3		
2000–01	Tottenham H	23	2		
2001–02	Tottenham H	35	3	259	33

ARMSTRONG, Chris* (F)   347 111
H: 6 0 W: 13 01 b.Newcastle 19-6-71
Source: Llay Welfare. Honours: England B.

Season	Club				
1988–89	Wrexham	0	0		
1989–90	Wrexham	22	3		
1990–91	Wrexham	38	10	60	13
1991–92	Millwall	25	4		
1992–93	Millwall	3	1	28	5
1992–93	Crystal Palace	35	15		
1993–94	Crystal Palace	43	22		
1994–95	Crystal Palace	40	8	118	45
1995–96	Tottenham H	36	15		
1996–97	Tottenham H	12	5		
1997–98	Tottenham H	19	5		
1998–99	Tottenham H	34	7		
1999–2000	Tottenham H	31	14		
2000–01	Tottenham H	9	2		
2001–02	Tottenham H	0	0	141	48

BOWDITCH, Ben (D)   0 0
b.Harlow 19-2-84
Source: Scholar. Honours: England Youth.

Season	Club		
2000–01	Tottenham H	0	0
2001–02	Tottenham H	0	0

BUNJEVCEVIC, Goran (D)   191 21
H: 6 1 W: 11 11 b.Karlovac 17-2-73
Honours: Yugoslavia 14 full caps.

Season	Club				
1994–95	Rad	17	0		
1995–96	Rad	13	2		
1996–97	Rad	30	3	60	5
1997–98	Red Star Belgrade	30	5		
1998–99	Red Star Belgrade	22	4		
1999–2000	Red Star Belgrade	40	7		
2000–01	Red Star Belgrade	33	0	125	16
2001–02	Tottenham H	6	0	6	0

CARR, Stephen (D)   164 6
H: 5 9 W: 12 04 b.Dublin 29-8-76
Source: Trainee. Honours: Eire Under-21, 18 full caps.

Season	Club				
1993–94	Tottenham H	1	0		
1994–95	Tottenham H	0	0		
1995–96	Tottenham H	0	0		
1996–97	Tottenham H	26	0		
1997–98	Tottenham H	38	0		
1998–99	Tottenham H	37	0		
1999–2000	Tottenham H	34	3		
2000–01	Tottenham H	28	3		
2001–02	Tottenham H	0	0	164	6

CLEMENCE, Stephen (M)   90 2
H: 6 0 W: 12 04 b.Liverpool 31-3-78
Source: Trainee. Honours: England Schools, Youth, Under-21.

Season	Club				
1994–95	Tottenham H	0	0		
1995–96	Tottenham H	0	0		
1996–97	Tottenham H	0	0		
1997–98	Tottenham H	17	0		
1998–99	Tottenham H	18	0		
1999–2000	Tottenham H	20	1		
2000–01	Tottenham H	29	1		
2001–02	Tottenham H	6	0	90	2

CONSORTI, Maurizio‡ (M)   0 0
H: 5 9 W: 11 02 b.Rome 6-3-82
Source: Trainee.

Season	Club		
1999–2000	Tottenham H	0	0
2000–01	Tottenham H	0	0
2001–02	Tottenham H	0	0

DAVIES, Simon (M)   112 12
H: 5 10 W: 11 07 b.Haverfordwest 23-10-79
Source: Trainee. Honours: Wales Youth, Under-21, B, 8 full caps.

Season	Club				
1997–98	Peterborough U	6	0		
1998–99	Peterborough U	43	4		
1999–2000	Peterborough U	16	2	65	6
1999–2000	Tottenham H	3	0		
2000–01	Tottenham H	13	2		
2001–02	Tottenham H	31	4	47	6

DOHERTY, Gary (D)   101 15
H: 6 1 W: 13 06 b.Carndonagh 31-1-80
Source: Trainee. Honours: Eire Under-21, 9 full caps, 1 goal.

Season	Club				
1997–98	Luton T	10	0		
1998–99	Luton T	20	6		
1999–2000	Luton T	40	6	70	12
1999–2000	Tottenham H	2	0		
2000–01	Tottenham H	22	3		
2001–02	Tottenham H	7	0	31	3

ETHERINGTON, Matthew (F)   86 7
H: 5 9 W: 10 12 b.Truro 14-8-81
Source: School. Honours: England Youth, Under-21.

Season	Club				
1996–97	Peterborough U	1	0		
1997–98	Peterborough U	2	0		
1998–99	Peterborough U	29	3		
1999–2000	Peterborough U	19	3	51	6
1999–2000	Tottenham H	5	0		
2000–01	Tottenham H	6	0		
2001–02	Bradford C	13	1	13	1
2001–02	Tottenham H	11	0	22	0

FERDINAND, Les (F)   365 166
H: 5 11 W: 13 02 b.Paddington 8-12-66
Source: Hayes. Honours: England B, 17 full caps, 5 goals.

Season	Club				
1986–87	QPR	2	0		
1987–88	QPR	1	0		
1987–88	Brentford	3	0	3	0
1988–89	QPR	0	0		
1988–89	Besiktas	24	14	24	14
1989–90	QPR	9	2		
1990–91	QPR	18	8		
1991–92	QPR	23	10		
1992–93	QPR	37	20		
1993–94	QPR	36	16		
1994–95	QPR	37	24	163	80
1995–96	Newcastle U	37	25		
1996–97	Newcastle U	31	16	68	41
1997–98	Tottenham H	21	5		
1998–99	Tottenham H	24	5		
1999–2000	Tottenham H	9	2		
2000–01	Tottenham H	28	10		
2001–02	Tottenham H	25	9	107	31

FERGUSON, Steven (F)   11 6
H: 5 10 W: 11 02 b.Dunfermline 1-4-82

Season	Club				
2000–01	East Fife	11	6	11	6
2000–01	Tottenham H	0	0		
2001–02	Tottenham H	0	0		

FREUND, Steffen (M)   286 9
H: 5 11 W: 12 08 b.Brandenburg 19-1-70
Source: Motor Sud, Stahl Brandenburg. Honours: Germany 21 full caps.

Season	Club				
1989–90	Brandenburg	9	0		
1990–91	Brandenburg	22	0	31	0
1991–92	Schalke	33	1		
1992–93	Schalke	20	2	53	3
1993–94	Borussia Dortmund	19	0		
1994–95	Borussia Dortmund	28	2		
1995–96	Borussia Dortmund	30	2		
1996–97	Borussia Dortmund	2	0		
1997–98	Borussia Dortmund	25	2		
1998–99	Borussia Dortmund	13	0	117	6
1998–99	Tottenham H	17	0		
1999–2000	Tottenham H	27	0		
2000–01	Tottenham H	21	0		
2001–02	Tottenham H	20	0	85	0

GARDNER, Anthony (D)   64 4
H: 6 3 W: 14 00 b.Stafford 19-9-80
Source: Trainee. Honours: England Under-21.

Season	Club				
1998–99	Port Vale	15	1		
1999–2000	Port Vale	26	3	41	4
1999–2000	Tottenham H	0	0		
2000–01	Tottenham H	8	0		
2001–02	Tottenham H	15	0	23	0

HUGHES, Mark (M)   0 0
b.Dungannon 16-9-83
Source: Scholar.

Season	Club		
2001–02	Tottenham H	0	0

IVERSEN, Steffen (F)   149 44
H: 6 1 W: 12 07 b.Oslo 10-11-76
Honours: Norway 31 full caps, 6 goals.

Season	Club				
1996	Rosenborg	25	10	25	10
1996–97	Tottenham H	16	6		
1997–98	Tottenham H	13	0		
1998–99	Tottenham H	27	8		
1999–2000	Tottenham H	36	14		
2000–01	Tottenham H	14	2		
2001–02	Tottenham H	18	4	124	34

JACKSON, Johnnie (M)   0 0
H: 6 1 W: 12 11 b.Camden 15-8-82
Source: Trainee. Honours: England Youth, Under-20.

Season	Club		
1999–2000	Tottenham H	0	0
2000–01	Tottenham H	0	0
2001–02	Tottenham H	0	0

JALAL, Shwan (G)   0 0
b.Baghdad 14-8-83
Source: Hastings T.

Season	Club		
2001–02	Tottenham H	0	0

KAMANAN, Yannick* (F)   0 0
H: 6 0 W: 11 08 b.Lille 5-10-81
Source: Le Mans.

Season	Club		
1999–2000	Tottenham H	0	0
2000–01	Tottenham H	0	0
2001–02	Tottenham H	0	0

KELLER, Kasey (G)   358 0
H: 6 2 W: 13 12 b.Washington 27-11-69
Source: Portland Univ. Honours: USA 60 full caps.

Season	Club				
1991–92	Millwall	1	0		
1992–93	Millwall	45	0		
1993–94	Millwall	44	0		
1994–95	Millwall	44	0		
1995–96	Millwall	42	0	176	0
1996–97	Leicester C	31	0		
1997–98	Leicester C	32	0		
1998–99	Leicester C	36	0	99	0
1999–2000	Rayo Vallecano	28	0		
2000–01	Rayo Vallecano	23	0		
2001–02	Rayo Vallecano	23	0	74	0
2001–02	Tottenham H	9	0	9	0

KELLY, Gavin (G)   0 0
H: 6 0 W: 13 07 b.Hammersmith 3-6-81
Source: Trainee.

Season	Club		
1999–2000	Tottenham H	0	0
2000–01	Tottenham H	0	0
2001–02	Tottenham H	0	0

KELLY, Stephen (D)   0 0
b.Dublin 6-9-83

Season	Club		
2000–01	Tottenham H	0	0
2001–02	Tottenham H	0	0

KING, Ledley (D)   54 1
H: 6 2 W: 14 05 b.Bow 12-10-80
Source: Trainee. Honours: England Youth, Under-21, 1 full cap.

Season	Club				
1998–99	Tottenham H	1	0		
1999–2000	Tottenham H	3	0		
2000–01	Tottenham H	18	1		
2001–02	Tottenham H	32	0	54	1

KORSTEN, Willem‡ (M)   105 17
H: 6 3 W: 13 00 b.Boxtel 21-1-75

Season	Club				
1992–93	NEC	4	0	4	0
1993–94	Vitesse	22	3		
1994–95	Vitesse	18	6		
1995–96	Vitesse	1	1		
1996–97	Vitesse	12	1		
1997–98	Vitesse	17	1		
1998–99	Vitesse	1	0	71	12
1998–99	Leeds U	7	2	7	2
1999–2000	Tottenham H	9	0		
2000–01	Tottenham H	14	3		
2001–02	Tottenham H	0	0	23	3

LEONHARDSEN, Oyvind (M)   294 56
H: 5 10 W: 11 07 b.Kristiansund 17-8-70
Source: Clausenengen. Honours: Norway 78 full caps, 18 goals.

Season	Club				
1989	Molde	22	5		
1990	Molde	21	2		
1991	Molde	21	2	64	9
1992	Rosenborg	22	6		
1993	Rosenborg	19	6		
1994	Rosenborg	22	8	63	20
1994–95	Wimbledon	20	˙4		
1995–96	Wimbledon	29	4		
1996–97	Wimbledon	27	5	76	13
1997–98	Liverpool	28	6		
1998–99	Liverpool	9	1	37	7
1999–2000	Tottenham H	22	4		
2000–01	Tottenham H	25	3		
2001–02	Tottenham H	7	0	54	7

McKIE, Marcel (D)   0 0
b.Edmonton 22-9-84
Source: Scholar. Honours: England Youth.

Season	Club		
2001–02	Tottenham H	0	0

O'DONOGHUE, Paul (D)   0 0
b.Lewisham 14-12-83
Source: Scholar.

Season	Club		
2001–02	Tottenham H	0	0

PERRY, Chris (D)   269 4
H: 5 8 W: 10 12 b.Carshalton 26-4-73
Source: Trainee.

Season	Club				
1991–92	Wimbledon	0	0		
1992–93	Wimbledon	0	0		
1993–94	Wimbledon	2	0		
1994–95	Wimbledon	22	0		
1995–96	Wimbledon	37	0		
1996–97	Wimbledon	37	1		
1997–98	Wimbledon	35	1		
1998–99	Wimbledon	34	0	167	2
1999–2000	Tottenham H	37	1		
2000–01	Tottenham H	32	1		
2001–02	Tottenham H	33	0	102	2

PIERCY, John (M)   8 0
H: 5 9 W: 11 13 b.Forest Gate 18-9-79
Source: Trainee. Honours: England Youth.

Season	Club		
1998–99	Tottenham H	0	0
1999–2000	Tottenham H	3	0

Season	Club	Apps	Gls		
2000–01	Tottenham H	5	0		
2001–02	Tottenham H	0	0	8	0

POYET, Gustavo (M) 378 109
H: 6 2   W: 13 00   b.Montevideo 15-11-67
Source: River Plate, Grenoble, Bella Vista.
Honours: Uruguay 25 full caps, 3 goals.

Season	Club	Apps	Gls		
1990–91	Zaragoza	31	7		
1991–92	Zaragoza	33	3		
1992–93	Zaragoza	33	6		
1993–94	Zaragoza	34	11		
1994–95	Zaragoza	34	11		
1995–96	Zaragoza	36	11		
1996–97	Zaragoza	38	14	239	63
1997–98	Chelsea	14	4		
1998–99	Chelsea	28	11		
1999–2000	Chelsea	33	10		
2000–01	Chelsea	30	11	105	36
2001–02	Tottenham H	34	10	34	10

REBROV, Sergei (F) 275 115
H: 5 7   W: 11 00   b.Gorlovka 3-6-74
Honours: Ukraine 49 full caps, 13 goals.

Season	Club	Apps	Gls		
1991	Shakhtor Donetsk	7	2		
1991–92	Shakhtor Donetsk	19	10	26	12
1992–93	Dynamo Kiev	23	5		
1993–94	Dynamo Kiev	10	2		
1994–95	Dynamo Kiev	25	8		
1995–96	Dynamo Kiev	31	9		
1996–97	Dynamo Kiev	30	20		
1997–98	Dynamo Kiev	29	22		
1998–99	Dynamo Kiev	22	9		
1999–2000	Dynamo Kiev	20	18	190	93
2000–01	Tottenham H	29	9		
2001–02	Tottenham H	30	1	59	10

REDKNAPP, Jamie (M) 250 30
H: 6 0   W: 13 04   b.Barton-on-Sea 25-6-73
Source: Tottenham H Schoolboy, Bournemouth Trainee. Honours: England Schools, Youth, B, Under-21, 17 full caps, 1 goal.

Season	Club	Apps	Gls		
1989–90	Bournemouth	4	0		
1990–91	Bournemouth	9	0	13	0
1990–91	Liverpool	6	1		
1991–92	Liverpool	6	1		
1992–93	Liverpool	29	2		
1993–94	Liverpool	35	4		
1994–95	Liverpool	41	3		
1995–96	Liverpool	23	3		
1996–97	Liverpool	23	2		
1997–98	Liverpool	20	3		
1998–99	Liverpool	34	8		
1999–2000	Liverpool	22	3		
2000–01	Liverpool	0	0		
2001–02	Liverpool	4	1	237	30
2001–02	Tottenham H	0	0		

RICHARDS, Dean (D) 299 16
H: 6 2   W: 13 12   b.Bradford 9-6-74
Source: Trainee. Honours: England Under-21.

Season	Club	Apps	Gls		
1991–92	Bradford C	7	1		
1992–93	Bradford C	3	0		
1993–94	Bradford C	46	2		
1994–95	Bradford C	30	1	86	4
1994–95	*Wolverhampton W*	10	2		
1995–96	*Wolverhampton W*	37	1		
1996–97	*Wolverhampton W*	21	1		
1997–98	*Wolverhampton W*	13	0		
1998–99	*Wolverhampton W*	41	3	122	7
1999–2000	Southampton	35	2		
2000–01	Southampton	28	1		
2001–02	Southampton	4	0	67	3
2001–02	Tottenham H	24	2	24	2

SHERINGHAM, Teddy (F) 571 223
H: 5 11   W: 12 05   b.Highams Park 2-4-66
Source: Apprentice. Honours: England Youth, 51 full caps, 11 goals.

Season	Club	Apps	Gls		
1983–84	Millwall	7	1		
1984–85	Millwall	0	0		
1984–85	*Aldershot*	5	0	5	0
1985–86	Millwall	18	4		
1986–87	Millwall	42	13		
1987–88	Millwall	43	22		
1988–89	Millwall	33	11		
1989–90	Millwall	31	9		
1990–91	Millwall	46	33	220	93
1991–92	Nottingham F	39	13		
1992–93	Nottingham F	3	1	42	14
1992–93	Tottenham H	38	21		
1993–94	Tottenham H	19	13		
1994–95	Tottenham H	42	18		
1995–96	Tottenham H	38	16		
1996–97	Tottenham H	32	7		
1997–98	Manchester U	31	9		
1998–99	Manchester U	29	2		
1999–2000	Manchester U	27	5		
2000–01	Manchester U	29	15	104	31
2001–02	Tottenham H	34	10	200	85

SHERWOOD, Tim (M) 442 49
H: 6 1   W: 13 03   b.St Albans 2-2-69
Source: Trainee. Honours: England Under-21, B, 3 full caps.

Season	Club	Apps	Gls		
1986–87	Watford	0	0		
1987–88	Watford	13	0		
1988–89	Watford	19	2	32	2
1989–90	Norwich C	27	3		
1990–91	Norwich C	37	7		
1991–92	Norwich C	7	0	71	10
1991–92	Blackburn R	11	0		
1992–93	Blackburn R	39	3		
1993–94	Blackburn R	38	2		
1994–95	Blackburn R	38	6		
1995–96	Blackburn R	33	3		
1996–97	Blackburn R	37	3		
1997–98	Blackburn R	31	5		
1998–99	Blackburn R	19	3	246	25
1998–99	Tottenham H	14	2		
1999–2000	Tottenham H	27	8		
2000–01	Tottenham H	33	2		
2001–02	Tottenham H	19	0	93	12

SLABBER, Jamie (F) 0 0
b.Enfield 31-12-84
Source: Scholar. Honours: England Youth.

Season	Club	Apps	Gls		
2001–02	Tottenham H	0	0		

SNEE, George (F) 0 0
b.Dublin 26-1-83
Source: Scholar.

Season	Club	Apps	Gls		
2000–01	Tottenham H	0	0		
2001–02	Tottenham H	0	0		

SULLIVAN, Neil (G) 246 0
H: 6 2   W: 15 02   b.Sutton 24-2-70
Source: Trainee. Honours: Scotland 27 full caps.

Season	Club	Apps	Gls		
1988–89	Wimbledon	0	0		
1989–90	Wimbledon	0	0		
1990–91	Wimbledon	1	0		
1991–92	Wimbledon	1	0		
1991–92	*Crystal Palace*	1	0	1	0
1992–93	Wimbledon	1	0		
1993–94	Wimbledon	2	0		
1994–95	Wimbledon	11	0		
1995–96	Wimbledon	16	0		
1996–97	Wimbledon	36	0		
1997–98	Wimbledon	38	0		
1998–99	Wimbledon	38	0		
1999–2000	Wimbledon	37	0	181	0
2000–01	Tottenham H	35	0		
2001–02	Tottenham H	29	0	64	0

SUTTON, John (F) 0 0
b.Norwich 26-12-83
Source: Scholar. Honours: England Youth.

Season	Club	Apps	Gls		
2001–02	Tottenham H	0	0		

TARICCO, Mauricio (D) 235 4
H: 5 8   W: 11 07   b.Buenos Aires 10-3-73
Honours: Argentina Under-23.

Season	Club	Apps	Gls		
1993–94	Argentinos Juniors	21	0	21	0
1994–95	Ipswich T	0	0		
1995–96	Ipswich T	39	0		
1996–97	Ipswich T	41	3		
1997–98	Ipswich T	41	0		
1998–99	Ipswich T	16	1	137	4
1998–99	Tottenham H	13	0		
1999–2000	Tottenham H	29	0		
2000–01	Tottenham H	5	0		
2001–02	Tottenham H	30	0	77	0

THATCHER, Ben (D) 200 1
H: 5 10   W: 12 06   b.Swindon 30-11-75
Source: Trainee. Honours: England Youth, Under-21.

Season	Club	Apps	Gls		
1992–93	Millwall	0	0		
1993–94	Millwall	8	0		
1994–95	Millwall	40	1		
1995–96	Millwall	42	0	90	1
1996–97	Wimbledon	9	0		
1997–98	Wimbledon	26	0		
1998–99	Wimbledon	31	0		
1999–2000	Wimbledon	20	0	86	0
2000–01	Tottenham H	12	0		
2001–02	Tottenham H	12	0	24	0

THELWELL, Alton (D) 18 0
H: 5 10   W: 12 02   b.Holloway 5-9-80
Source: Trainee.

Season	Club	Apps	Gls		
1998–99	Tottenham H	0	0		
1999–2000	Tottenham H	0	0		
2000–01	Tottenham H	16	0		
2001–02	Tottenham H	2	0	18	0

THOMAS, Walter (M) 0 0
b.Sierra Leone 19-11-83
Source: Scholar.

Season	Club	Apps	Gls		
2001–02	Tottenham H	0	0		

VEDEUX, Ghyslain* (F) 0 0
b.Yaounde 23-10-83

Season	Club	Apps	Gls		
2000–01	Tottenham H	0	0		
2001–02	Tottenham H	0	0		

ZIEGE, Christian (D) 283 57
H: 6 1   W: 12 13   b.Berlin 1-2-72
Honours: Germany 71 full caps, 9 goals.

Season	Club	Apps	Gls		
1990–91	Bayern Munich	13	1		
1991–92	Bayern Munich	26	2		
1992–93	Bayern Munich	28	9		
1993–94	Bayern Munich	29	3		
1994–95	Bayern Munich	29	10		
1995–96	Bayern Munich	20	9		
1996–97	Bayern Munich	27	7	172	41
1997–98	AC Milan	22	2		
1998–99	AC Milan	17	2	39	4
1999–2000	Middlesbrough	29	6		
2000–01	Middlesbrough	0	0	29	6
2000–01	Liverpool	16	1	16	1
2001–02	Tottenham H	27	5	27	5

Trainees
Barnard, Lee J; Barnett, Lee J; Black, Jonathan; Burch, Robert K; Ford, Timothy J; Foster, Danny; Galbraith, David J; Henry, Ronnie S; Marney, Dean E; Noto, Mario; Perry, Daniel M; Rutherford, Paul GE; Tyrie, David; Wettner, Nicholas T; Yeates, Mark S

Non-Contract
Hirschfeld, Lars

TRANMERE R

ACHTERBERG, John (G) 141 0
H: 6 1   W: 13 00   b.Utrecht 8-7-71
Source: VV RUC, Utrecht.

Season	Club	Apps	Gls		
1993–94	NAC	1	0		
1994–95	NAC	2	0		
1995–96	NAC	6	0	9	0
1996–97	Eindhoven	32	0	32	0

From Utrecht.

Season	Club	Apps	Gls		
1998–99	Tranmere R	24	0		
1999–2000	Tranmere R	26	0		
2000–01	Tranmere R	25	0		
2001–02	Tranmere R	25	0	100	0

ALLEN, Graham (D) 124 6
H: 6 0   W: 12 00   b.Bolton 8-4-77
Source: Trainee. Honours: England Youth.

Season	Club	Apps	Gls		
1994–95	Everton	0	0		
1995–96	Everton	0	0		
1996–97	Everton	1	0		
1997–98	Everton	5	0		
1998–99	Everton	0	0	6	0
1998–99	Tranmere R	41	5		
1999–2000	Tranmere R	24	0		
2000–01	Tranmere R	22	0		
2001–02	Tranmere R	31	1	118	6

ALLISON, Wayne* (F) 564 143
H: 6 0   W: 14 07   b.Huddersfield 16-10-68
Source: Trainee.

Season	Club	Apps	Gls		
1986–87	Halifax T	8	4		
1987–88	Halifax T	35	4		
1988–89	Halifax T	41	15	84	23
1989–90	Watford	7	0	7	0
1990–91	Bristol C	37	6		
1991–92	Bristol C	43	10		
1992–93	Bristol C	39	4		
1993–94	Bristol C	39	15		
1994–95	Bristol C	37	13	195	48
1995–96	Swindon T	44	17		
1996–97	Swindon T	41	11		
1997–98	Swindon T	16	3	101	31
1997–98	Huddersfield T	27	6		
1998–99	Huddersfield T	44	9		
1999–2000	Huddersfield T	3	0	74	15
1999–2000	Tranmere R	40	16		
2000–01	Tranmere R	36	6		
2001–02	Tranmere R	27	4	103	26

BAKER, Phillip (D) 0 0
H: 6 0   W: 11 10   b.Birkenhead 4-11-82
Source: Scholar.

Season	Club	Apps	Gls		
2001–02	Tranmere R	0	0		

BARLOW, Stuart (F) 312 97
H: 5 10   W: 11 03   b.Liverpool 16-7-68
Source: School.

Season	Club	Apps	Gls		
1990–91	Everton	2	0		
1991–92	Everton	7	0		
1991–92	*Rotherham U*	0	0		
1992–93	Everton	26	5		
1993–94	Everton	22	3		
1994–95	Everton	11	2		
1995–96	Everton	3	0	71	10
1995–96	Oldham Ath	26	7		
1996–97	Oldham Ath	35	12		
1997–98	Oldham Ath	32	12	93	31
1997–98	Wigan Ath	9	3		

1998–99	Wigan Ath	41	19	
1999–2000	Wigan Ath	33	18	83 40
2000–01	Tranmere R	27	2	
2001–02	Tranmere R	38	14	65 16

FLYNN, Sean* (M) 336 26
H: 5 8 W: 11 09 b.Birmingham 13-5-68
Source: Halesowen T.

1991–92	Coventry C	22	2	
1992–93	Coventry C	7	0	
1993–94	Coventry C	36	3	
1994–95	Coventry C	32	4	97 9
1995–96	Derby Co	42	2	
1996–97	Derby Co	17	1	59 3
1996–97	Stoke C	5	0	5 0
1997–98	WBA	35	2	
1998–99	WBA	38	2	
1999–2000	WBA	36	4	109 8
2000–01	Tranmere R	35	1	
2001–02	Tranmere R	31	5	66 6

HARRISON, Danny (M) 1 0
H: 5 10 W: 12 03 b.Liverpool 4-11-82
Source: Scholar.

2001–02	Tranmere R	1	0	1 0

HAWORTH, Simon (F) 177 58
H: 6 1 W: 14 02 b.Cardiff 30-3-77
Source: Trainee. *Honours:* Wales Youth, Under-21, B, 5 full caps.

1995–96	Cardiff C	13	0	
1996–97	Cardiff C	24	9	37 9
1997–98	Coventry C	10	0	
1998–99	Coventry C	1	0	11 0
1998–99	Wigan Ath	20	10	
1999–2000	Wigan Ath	40	13	
2000–01	Wigan Ath	30	11	
2001–02	Wigan Ath	27	10	117 44
2001–02	Tranmere R	12	5	12 5

HAY, Alexander (F) 3 0
H: 5 10 W: 11 05 b.Birkenhead 14-10-81
Source: Scholar.

1999–2000	Tranmere R	0	0	
2000–01	Tranmere R	0	0	
2001–02	Tranmere R	3	0	3 0

HENRY, Nick* (M) 386 21
H: 5 6 W: 10 12 b.Liverpool 21-2-69
Source: Trainee.

1987–88	Oldham Ath	5	0	
1988–89	Oldham Ath	18	0	
1989–90	Oldham Ath	41	0	
1990–91	Oldham Ath	43	4	
1991–92	Oldham Ath	42	6	
1992–93	Oldham Ath	32	6	
1993–94	Oldham Ath	22	0	
1994–95	Oldham Ath	34	2	
1995–96	Oldham Ath	14	0	
1996–97	Oldham Ath	22	1	273 19
1996–97	Sheffield U	9	0	
1997–98	Sheffield U	1	0	
1998–99	Sheffield U	6	0	16 0
1998–99	Walsall	8	0	8 0
1999–2000	Tranmere R	30	1	
2000–01	Tranmere R	20	0	
2001–02	Tranmere R	39	1	89 2

HILL, Clint (D) 140 16
H: 6 0 W: 11 06 b.Liverpool 19-10-78
Source: Trainee.

1997–98	Tranmere R	14	0	
1998–99	Tranmere R	33	4	
1999–2000	Tranmere R	29	5	
2000–01	Tranmere R	34	5	
2001–02	Tranmere R	30	2	140 16

HINDS, Richard (D) 47 0
H: 6 2 W: 12 00 b.Sheffield 22-8-80
Source: Schoolboy.

1998–99	Tranmere R	2	0	
1999–2000	Tranmere R	6	0	
2000–01	Tranmere R	29	0	
2001–02	Tranmere R	10	0	47 0

HUME, Iain (F) 27 0
H: 5 7 W: 11 02 b.Edinburgh 31-10-83

1999–2000	Tranmere R	3	0	
2000–01	Tranmere R	10	0	
2001–02	Tranmere R	14	0	27 0

KOUMAS, Jason (M) 123 23
H: 5 10 W: 11 06 b.Wrexham 25-9-79
Source: Trainee. *Honours:* Wales 2 full caps.

1997–98	Tranmere R	1	0	
1998–99	Tranmere R	23	3	
1999–2000	Tranmere R	23	2	
2000–01	Tranmere R	39	10	
2001–02	Tranmere R	38	8	123 23

LINWOOD, Paul (M) 0 0
b.Birkenhead 24-10-83
Source: Scholar.

2001–02	Tranmere R	0	0	

McGUIRE, Jamie (M) 0 0
b.Birkenhead 13-11-83
Source: Scholar.

2001–02	Tranmere R	0	0	

MELLON, Micky (M) 385 31
H: 5 10 W: 12 11 b.Paisley 18-3-72
Source: Trainee.

1989–90	Bristol C	9	0	
1990–91	Bristol C	0	0	
1991–92	Bristol C	16	0	
1992–93	Bristol C	10	1	35 1
1992–93	WBA	17	3	
1993–94	WBA	21	2	
1994–95	WBA	7	1	45 6
1994–95	Blackpool	26	4	
1995–96	Blackpool	45	6	
1996–97	Blackpool	43	4	
1997–98	Blackpool	10	0	124 14
1997–98	Tranmere R	33	2	
1998–99	Tranmere R	24	1	
1998–99	Burnley	20	2	
1999–2000	Burnley	42	3	
2000–01	Burnley	22	0	84 5
2000–01	Tranmere R	13	1	
2001–02	Tranmere R	27	1	97 5

MORGAN, Alan‡ (M) 65 1
H: 5 9 W: 11 00 b.Aberystwyth 2-11-73
Source: Trainee. *Honours:* Wales Schools, Youth, Under-21.

1991–92	Tranmere R	0	0	
1992–93	Tranmere R	0	0	
1993–94	Tranmere R	0	0	
1994–95	Tranmere R	0	0	
1995–96	Tranmere R	4	1	
1996–97	Tranmere R	1	0	
1997–98	Tranmere R	19	0	
1998–99	Tranmere R	6	0	
1999–2000	Tranmere R	26	0	
2000–01	Tranmere R	7	0	
2001–02	Tranmere R	2	0	65 1

MURPHY, Joe (G) 63 0
H: 6 2 W: 13 06 b.Dublin 21-8-81
Source: Trainee. *Honours:* Eire Under-21.

1999–2000	Tranmere R	21	0	
2000–01	Tranmere R	20	0	
2001–02	Tranmere R	22	0	63 0

N'DIAYE, Seyni (F) 87 16
H: 6 2 W: 13 06 b.Dakar 1-6-73

1997–98	Paris St Germain	0	0	
1998–99	Neuchatel Xamax	31	8	31 8
1999–2000	Caen	30	3	
2000–01	Caen	7	1	37 4
2000–01	Tranmere R	8	2	
2001–02	Tranmere R	11	2	19 4

NAVARRO, Alan (D) 36 2
H: 5 10 W: 11 07 b.Liverpool 31-5-81
Source: Trainee.

1998–99	Liverpool	0	0	
1999–2000	Liverpool	0	0	
2000–01	Liverpool	0	0	
2000–01	Crewe Alex	8	1	
2001–02	Liverpool	0	0	
2001–02	Crewe Alex	7	0	15 1
2001–02	Tranmere R	21	1	21 1

NIXON, Eric‡ (G) 521 0
H: 6 4 W: 14 00 b.Manchester 4-10-62
Source: Curzon Ashton.

1983–84	Manchester C	0	0	
1984–85	Manchester C	0	0	
1985–86	Manchester C	28	0	
1986–87	Manchester C	5	0	
1986–87	Wolverhampton W	16	0	16 0
1986–87	Bradford C	3	0	
1986–87	Southampton	4	0	4 0
1986–87	Carlisle U	16	0	16 0
1987–88	Manchester C	25	0	58 0
1987–88	Tranmere R	8	0	
1988–89	Tranmere R	45	0	
1989–90	Tranmere R	46	0	
1990–91	Tranmere R	43	0	
1991–92	Tranmere R	46	0	
1992–93	Tranmere R	45	0	
1993–94	Tranmere R	42	0	
1994–95	Tranmere R	41	0	
1995–96	Tranmere R	0	0	
1995–96	Blackpool	20	0	20 0
1996–97	Tranmere R	25	0	
1996–97	Bradford C	12	0	15 0
1997–98	Stockport Co	43	0	
1998–99	Stockport Co	0	0	43 0
1998–99	Wigan Ath	3	0	3 0
1999–2000	Tranmere R	2	0	
2000–01	Tranmere R	0	0	
2001–02	Kidderminster H	2	0	2 0
2001–02	Tranmere R	1	0	344 0

OLSEN, James (D) 1 0
H: 5 10 W: 12 00 b.Bootle 23-10-81
Source: Liverpool scholar.

2000–01	Tranmere R	1	0	
2001–02	Tranmere R	0	0	1 0

PARKINSON, Andy (F) 154 18
H: 5 8 W: 10 12 b.Liverpool 27-5-79
Source: Liverpool Trainee.

1996–97	Tranmere R	0	0	
1997–98	Tranmere R	18	1	
1998–99	Tranmere R	29	2	
1999–2000	Tranmere R	37	7	
2000–01	Tranmere R	39	6	
2001–02	Tranmere R	31	2	154 18

PRICE, Jason (M) 183 25
H: 6 2 W: 11 05 b.Pontypridd 12-4-77
Source: Aberaman Ath. *Honours:* Wales Under-21.

1995–96	Swansea C	0	0	
1996–97	Swansea C	2	0	
1997–98	Swansea C	34	3	
1998–99	Swansea C	28	4	
1999–2000	Swansea C	39	6	
2000–01	Swansea C	41	4	144 17
2001–02	Brentford	15	1	15 1
2001–02	Tranmere R	24	7	24 7

RIDEOUT, Paul* (F) 562 150
H: 5 11 W: 12 00 b.Bournemouth 14-8-64
Source: Apprentice. *Honours:* England Schools, Youth, Under-21.

1980–81	Swindon T	16	4	
1981–82	Swindon T	35	14	
1982–83	Swindon T	44	20	
1983–84	Aston Villa	25	5	
1984–85	Aston Villa	29	14	54 19
1985–86	Bari	28	6	
1986–87	Bari	34	10	
1987–88	Bari	37	7	99 23
1988–89	Southampton	24	6	
1989–90	Southampton	31	7	
1990–91	Southampton	16	6	
1990–91	Swindon T	9	1	104 39
1991–92	Southampton	4	0	75 19
1991–92	Notts Co	11	3	11 3
1991–92	Rangers	11	1	
1992–93	Rangers	1	0	12 1
1992–93	Everton	24	3	
1993–94	Everton	24	6	
1994–95	Everton	29	14	
1995–96	Everton	25	6	
1996–97	Everton	10	0	112 29
1997	Huan Dao Van	22	7	22 7
1998	Kansas City W	27	4	27 4
From Shengzhen				
2000–01	Tranmere R	31	2	
2001–02	Tranmere R	15	4	46 6

ROBERTS, Gareth* (D) 116 3
H: 5 8 W: 11 00 b.Wrexham 6-2-78
Source: Trainee. *Honours:* Wales Under-21, B, 4 full caps.

1995–96	Liverpool	0	0	
1996–97	Liverpool	0	0	
1997–98	Liverpool	0	0	
1998–99	Liverpool	0	0	
1999–2000	Tranmere R	37	1	
2000–01	Tranmere R	34	0	
2001–02	Tranmere R	45	2	116 3

SHARPS, Ian (D) 30 0
H: 6 3 W: 13 05 b.Warrington 23-10-80
Source: Trainee.

1998–99	Tranmere R	1	0	
1999–2000	Tranmere R	0	0	
2000–01	Tranmere R	0	0	
2001–02	Tranmere R	29	0	30 0

TAYLOR, Ryan (D) 0 0
b.Liverpool 19-8-84
Source: Scholar. *Honours:* England Youth.

2001–02	Tranmere R	0	0	

THORNTON, Sean§ (M) 11 1
H: 5 10 W: 11 00 b.Drogheda 18-5-83
Source: Scholar.

2001–02	Tranmere R	11	1	11 1

YATES, Steve‡ (D) 444 9
H: 5 10 W: 12 02 b.Bristol 29-1-70
Source: Trainee.

1986–87	Bristol R	2	0	
1987–88	Bristol R	0	0	
1988–89	Bristol R	35	0	
1989–90	Bristol R	42	0	
1990–91	Bristol R	34	0	
1991–92	Bristol R	39	0	
1992–93	Bristol R	44	0	
1993–94	Bristol R	1	0	197 0
1993–94	QPR	29	0	
1994–95	QPR	23	1	

1995–96	QPR	30	0		
1996–97	QPR	16	1		
1997–98	QPR	30	0		
1998–99	QPR	6	0	134	2
1999–2000	Tranmere R	33	2		
2000–01	Tranmere R	43	2		
2001–02	Tranmere R	37	3	113	7

Scholars
Ashton, Neil J; Brown, Paul; Carroll, Thomas; Climo, Daniel P; Dreves, Thomas; Dunbar, Karl A; Evans, Dylan T; Griffiths, Alan T; Hooper, Gareth P; Jennings, Steven J; Ralph, Andrew O; Rooney, Thomas; Sanna, Richard J; Thornton, Sean

WALSALL

ANDRE, Carlos* (M)   5   0
H: 5 10   W: 11 13   b.Portugal 28-11-71
Source: Guimaraes.

2001–02	Walsall	5	0	5	0

ARANALDE, Zigor# (D)   90   2
H: 6 1   W: 13 02   b.Ibarra 28-2-73
Source: Logrones.

2000–01	Walsall	45	0		
2001–02	Walsall	45	2	90	2

BARRAS, Tony (D)   379   27
H: 6 0   W: 13 00   b.Billingham 29-3-71
Source: Trainee.

1988–89	Hartlepool U	3	0		
1989–90	Hartlepool U	9	0	12	0
1990–91	Stockport Co	40	0		
1991–92	Stockport Co	42	5		
1992–93	Stockport Co	14	0		
1993–94	Stockport Co	3	0	99	5
1993–94	Rotherham U	5	1	5	1
1994–95	York C	31	1		
1995–96	York C	32	3		
1996–97	York C	46	1		
1997–98	York C	38	6		
1998–99	York C	24	0	171	11
1998–99	Reading	6	1	6	1
1999–2000	Walsall	24	4		
2000–01	Walsall	36	1		
2001–02	Walsall	26	4	86	9

BENNETT, Tom* (M)   314   15
H: 5 11   W: 11 08   b.Falkirk 12-12-69
Source: Trainee.

1987–88	Aston Villa	0	0		
1988–89	Wolverhampton W	2	0		
1989–90	Wolverhampton W	30	0		
1990–91	Wolverhampton W	26	0		
1991–92	Wolverhampton W	38	2		
1992–93	Wolverhampton W	1	0		
1993–94	Wolverhampton W	10	0		
1994–95	Wolverhampton W	8	0	115	2
1995–96	Stockport Co	24	1		
1996–97	Stockport Co	43	3		
1997–98	Stockport Co	27	1		
1998–99	Stockport Co	7	0		
1999–2000	Stockport Co	9	0	110	5
1999–2000	Walsall	11	3		
2000–01	Walsall	38	5		
2001–02	Walsall	40	0	89	8

BIANCALANI, Frederic (D)   196   9
H: 5 11   W: 12 01   b.France 21-7-74

1993–94	Nancy	28	3		
1994–95	Nancy	9	0		
1995–96	Nancy	14	0		
1996–97	Nancy	28	0		
1997–98	Nancy	37	1		
1998–99	Nancy	31	2		
1999–2000	Nancy	28	1		
2000–01	Nancy	3	0	178	7
2001–02	Walsall	18	2	18	2

BIRCH, Gary (F)   25   2
H: 6 0   W: 12 03   b.Birmingham 8-10-81
Source: Trainee.

1998–99	Walsall	0	0		
1999–2000	Walsall	0	0		
2000–01	Walsall	0	0		
2000–01	Exeter C	9	2		
2001–02	Exeter C	15	0	24	2
2001–02	Walsall	1	0	1	0

CARBON, Matt (D)   224   16
H: 6 2   W: 12 05   b.Nottingham 8-6-75
Source: Trainee. *Honours:* England Under-21.

1992–93	Lincoln C	1	0		
1993–94	Lincoln C	9	0		
1994–95	Lincoln C	33	7		
1995–96	Lincoln C	26	3	69	10
1995–96	Derby Co	6	0		
1996–97	Derby Co	10	0		
1997–98	Derby Co	4	0	20	0
1997–98	WBA	16	1		
1998–99	WBA	39	2		
1999–2000	WBA	34	2		
2000–01	WBA	24	0	113	5
2001–02	Walsall	22	1	22	1

CORICA, Steve* (F)   232   24
H: 5 8   W: 10 10   b.Cairns 24-3-73
Honours: Australia 31 full caps, 5 goals.

1990–91	Marconi Stallions	17	0		
1991–92	Marconi Stallions	17	2		
1992–93	Marconi Stallions	27	4		
1993–94	Marconi Stallions	24	5		
1994–95	Marconi Stallions	18	3	103	14
1995–96	Leicester C	16	2	16	2
1995–96	Wolverhampton W	17	0		
1996–97	Wolverhampton W	36	2		
1997–98	Wolverhampton W	1	0		
1998–99	Wolverhampton W	31	2		
1999–2000	Wolverhampton W	15	1		
2000–01	Wolverhampton W	0	0	100	5
2001–02	Walsall	13	3	13	3

GADSBY, Matt (D)   37   0
H: 6 1   W: 11 12   b.Sutton Coldfield 6-9-79
Source: Trainee.

1997–98	Walsall	1	0		
1998–99	Walsall	6	0		
1999–2000	Walsall	3	0		
2000–01	Walsall	5	0		
2001–02	Walsall	22	0	37	0

GARROCHO, Carlos* (M)   4   0
H: 5 11   W: 12 02   b.Angola 26-1-74
Source: Farense, Leca.

2001–02	Walsall	4	0	4	0

GOODMAN, Don# (F)   557   159
H: 5 10   W: 12 12   b.Leeds 9-5-66
Source: School.

1983–84	Bradford C	2	0		
1984–85	Bradford C	25	5		
1985–86	Bradford C	20	4		
1986–87	Bradford C	23	5	70	14
1986–87	WBA	10	2		
1987–88	WBA	40	7		
1988–89	WBA	36	15		
1989–90	WBA	39	21		
1990–91	WBA	22	8		
1991–92	WBA	11	7	158	60
1991–92	Sunderland	22	11		
1992–93	Sunderland	41	16		
1993–94	Sunderland	35	10		
1994–95	Sunderland	18	3	116	40
1994–95	Wolverhampton W	24	3		
1995–96	Wolverhampton W	44	16		
1996–97	Wolverhampton W	27	6		
1997–98	Wolverhampton W	30	8	125	33

From Hiroshima

1998–99	*Barnsley*	8	0	8	0
1998–99	Motherwell	8	1		
1999–2000	Motherwell	29	7		
2000–01	Motherwell	18	1	55	9
2000–01	Walsall	8	2		
2001–02	Walsall	17	1	25	3

HARPER, Lee (G)   122   0
H: 6 1   W: 13 11   b.Chelsea 30-10-71
Source: Sittingbourne.

1994–95	Arsenal	0	0		
1995–96	Arsenal	0	0		
1996–97	Arsenal	1	0	1	0
1997–98	QPR	36	0		
1998–99	QPR	15	0		
1999–2000	QPR	38	0		
2000–01	QPR	29	0	118	0
2001–02	QPR	3	0	3	0

HAWLEY, Karl (F)   1   0
H: 5 8   W: 12 02   b.Walsall 6-12-81
Source: Scholar.

2000–01	Walsall	0	0		
2001–02	Walsall	1	0	1	0

HERIVELTO, Harry (M)   24   4
H: 5 10   W: 11 06   b.Brazil 23-8-75
Source: Flamengo, Maritimo, Cruzeiro.

2001–02	Walsall	24	4	24	4

KEATES, Dean# (M)   159   9
H: 5 6   W: 10 10   b.Walsall 30-6-78
Source: Trainee.

1996–97	Walsall	2	0		
1997–98	Walsall	33	1		
1998–99	Walsall	43	2		
1999–2000	Walsall	35	1		
2000–01	Walsall	33	4		
2001–02	Walsall	1	1	159	9

LEITAO, Jorge (F)   82   26
H: 5 11   W: 13 05   b.Oporto 14-1-74
Source: Feirense.

2000–01	Walsall	44	18		
2001–02	Walsall	38	8	82	26

MARCELO* (F)   152   49
H: 6 0   W: 13 04   b.Niteroi 11-10-69
Source: Alaves.

1997–98	Sheffield U	21	6		
1998–99	Sheffield U	35	16		
1999–2000	Sheffield U	10	2	66	24
1999–2000	Birmingham C	25	5		
2000–01	Birmingham C	31	7		
2001–02	Birmingham C	21	12	77	24
2001–02	Walsall	9	1	9	1

MATIAS, Pedro (M)   141   22
H: 6 0   W: 12 00   b.Madrid 11-10-73

1998–99	Logrones	12	0	12	0
1998–99	Macclesfield T	22	2	22	2
1999–2000	Tranmere R	4	0	4	0
1999–2000	Walsall	33	6		
2000–01	Walsall	40	9		
2001–02	Walsall	30	5	103	20

O'CONNOR, Martin# (M)   324   42
H: 5 8   W: 10 08   b.Walsall 10-12-67
Source: Bromsgrove R. *Honours:* Cayman Islands 2 full caps.

1992–93	Crystal Palace	0	0		
1992–93	*Walsall*	10	1		
1993–94	Crystal Palace	2	0	2	0
1993–94	Walsall	14	2		
1994–95	Walsall	39	10		
1995–96	Walsall	41	9		
1996–97	Peterborough U	18	3	18	3
1997–98	Birmingham C	24	4		
1997–98	Birmingham C	33	1		
1998–99	Birmingham C	37	4		
1999–2000	Birmingham C	39	2		
2000–01	Birmingham C	30	5		
2001–02	Birmingham C	24	0	187	16
2001–02	Walsall	13	1	117	23

OFODILE, Adolf‡ (F)   1   0
H: 5 7   W: 12 01   b.Fungu 15-12-79
Source: Kapellen, Magdeburg.

2001–02	Walsall	1	0	1	0

ROPER, Ian (D)   155   2
H: 6 3   W: 13 04   b.Nuneaton 20-6-77
Source: Trainee.

1994–95	Walsall	0	0		
1995–96	Walsall	5	0		
1996–97	Walsall	11	0		
1997–98	Walsall	21	0		
1998–99	Walsall	32	1		
1999–2000	Walsall	34	1		
2000–01	Walsall	25	0		
2001–02	Walsall	27	0	155	2

SCOTT, Dion‡ (D)   2   0
H: 5 11   W: 11 00   b.Bearwood 24-12-80
Source: Trainee.

1999–2000	Walsall	0	0		
2000–01	Walsall	1	0		
2001–02	Walsall	1	0	2	0

SIMPSON, Fitzroy* (M)   383   26
H: 5 8   W: 10 08   b.Trowbridge 26-2-70
Source: Trainee. *Honours:* Jamaica 33 full caps.

1988–89	Swindon T	7	0		
1989–90	Swindon T	30	2		
1990–91	Swindon T	38	3		
1991–92	Swindon T	30	4	105	9
1991–92	Manchester C	11	1		
1992–93	Manchester C	29	1		
1993–94	Manchester C	15	0		
1994–95	Manchester C	16	2		
1994–95	*Bristol C*	4	0	4	0
1995–96	Manchester C	0	0	71	4
1995–96	Portsmouth	30	5		
1996–97	Portsmouth	41	4		
1997–98	Portsmouth	19	0		
1998–99	Portsmouth	41	1		
1999–2000	Portsmouth	17	0	148	10
1999–2000	Hearts	11	0		
2000–01	Hearts	6	0	17	0
2000–01	*Walsall*	10	1		
2001–02	Walsall	28	2	38	3

WALKER, James# (M)   319   0
H: 5 11   W: 13 05   b.Sutton-in-Ashfield 9-7-73
Source: Trainee.

1991–92	Notts Co	0	0		
1992–93	Notts Co	0	0		
1993–94	Walsall	31	0		
1994–95	Walsall	4	0		
1995–96	Walsall	26	0		
1996–97	Walsall	36	0		

Season	Club	Apps	Gls	Tot A	Tot G
1997–98	Walsall	46	0		
1998–99	Walsall	46	0		
1999–2000	Walsall	43	0		
2000–01	Walsall	44	0		
2001–02	Walsall	43	0	319	0

WRACK, Darren# (M) 204 27
H: 5 9 W: 12 10 b.Cleethorpes 5-5-76
Source: Trainee.

Season	Club	Apps	Gls	Tot A	Tot G
1994–95	Derby Co	16	1		
1995–96	Derby Co	10	0	26	1
1996–97	Grimsby T	12	1		
1996–97	*Shrewsbury T*	4	0	4	0
1997–98	Grimsby T	1	0	13	1
1998–99	Walsall	46	13		
1999–2000	Walsall	44	4		
2000–01	Walsall	28	4		
2001–02	Walsall	43	4	161	25

WRIGHT, Mark (M) 4 0
H: 5 11 W: 11 00 b.Wolverhampton 24-2-82
Source: Scholar.

Season	Club	Apps	Gls	Tot A	Tot G
2000–01	Walsall	4	0		
2001–02	Walsall	0	0	4	0

Scholars
Atieno, Taiwo L; Barrau, Xavier; Bennett, Julian; Bishop, Andrew J; Bissell, James; Caines, Gavin L; Fitzpatrick, Andrew J; Harris, Andrew; Jones, Craig R; Joseph, Andre P; Lloyd, Arron SD; Paschalis, Eliot D; Smith, Nicholas A; Stanley, Craig; Taylor, Daryl S; Teesdale, Richard C; Willetts, Ryan J; Worley, Andrew I

WATFORD

BAARDSEN, Espen (G) 64 0
H: 6 5 W: 13 03 b.San Rafael 7-12-77
Source: San Francisco All Blacks. *Honours:* USA Youth, Norway Under-21, 4 full caps.

Season	Club	Apps	Gls	Tot A	Tot G
1996–97	Tottenham H	2	0		
1997–98	Tottenham H	9	0		
1998–99	Tottenham H	12	0		
1999–2000	Tottenham H	0	0	23	0
2000–01	Watford	27	0		
2001–02	Watford	14	0	41	0

BLIZZARD, Dominic (M) 0 0
b.High Wycombe 2-9-83
Source: Scholar.

Season	Club	Apps	Gls	Tot A	Tot G
2001–02	Watford	0	0		

BLONDEAU, Patrick (D) 246 2
H: 5 9 W: 11 06 b.Marseille 27-1-68
Source: Septemes, Martigues. *Honours:* France 2 full caps.

Season	Club	Apps	Gls	Tot A	Tot G
1989–90	Monaco	13	0		
1990–91	Monaco	16	0		
1991–92	Monaco	4	0		
1992–93	Monaco	15	0		
1993–94	Monaco	14	0		
1994–95	Monaco	25	1		
1995–96	Monaco	31	0	148	2
1996–97	Sheffield W	6	0		
1997–98	Bordeaux	9	0	9	0
1998–99	Marseille	23	0		
1999–2000	Marseille	23	0		
2000–01	Monaco	12	0	58	0
2001–02	Watford	25	0	25	0

CHAMBERLAIN, Alec (G) 603 0
H: 6 2 W: 13 10 b.March 20-6-64
Source: Ramsey T.

Season	Club	Apps	Gls	Tot A	Tot G
1981–82	Ipswich T	0	0		
1982–83	Colchester U	0	0		
1983–84	Colchester U	46	0		
1984–85	Colchester U	46	0		
1985–86	Colchester U	46	0		
1986–87	Colchester U	46	0	184	0
1987–88	Everton	0	0		
1987–88	*Tranmere R*	15	0	15	0
1988–89	Luton T	6	0		
1989–90	Luton T	38	0		
1990–91	Luton T	38	0		
1991–92	Luton T	24	0		
1992–93	Luton T	32	0	138	0
1992–93	*Chelsea*	0	0		
1993–94	Sunderland	43	0		
1994–95	Sunderland	18	0		
1994–95	*Liverpool*	0	0		
1995–96	Sunderland	29	0	90	0
1996–97	Watford	4	0		
1997–98	Watford	46	0		
1998–99	Watford	46	0		
1999–2000	Watford	27	0		
2000–01	Watford	21	0		
2001–02	Watford	32	0	176	0

COOK, Lee (M) 14 0
H: 5 9 W: 11 04 b.Hammersmith 3-8-82
Source: Aylesbury U.

Season	Club	Apps	Gls	Tot A	Tot G
1999–2000	Watford	0	0		
2000–01	Watford	4	0		
2001–02	Watford	10	0	14	0

COX, Neil (D) 350 21
H: 6 0 W: 12 01 b.Scunthorpe 8-10-71
Source: Trainee. *Honours:* England Under-21.

Season	Club	Apps	Gls	Tot A	Tot G
1989–90	Scunthorpe U	0	0		
1990–91	Scunthorpe U	17	1	17	1
1990–91	Aston Villa	7	0		
1991–92	Aston Villa	7	0		
1992–93	Aston Villa	15	1		
1993–94	Aston Villa	20	2	42	3
1994–95	Middlesbrough	40	1		
1995–96	Middlesbrough	35	2		
1996–97	Middlesbrough	31	0	106	3
1997–98	Bolton W	21	1		
1998–99	Bolton W	44	4		
1999–2000	Bolton W	15	2	80	7
1999–2000	Watford	21	0		
2000–01	Watford	44	5		
2001–02	Watford	40	2	105	7

DOYLEY, Lloyd (D) 20 0
H: 5 10 W: 11 04 b.London 1-12-82
Source: Scholar.

Season	Club	Apps	Gls	Tot A	Tot G
2000–01	Watford	0	0		
2001–02	Watford	20	0	20	0

FISKEN, Gary (M) 17 1
H: 5 10 W: 12 08 b.Watford 27-10-81
Source: Scholar.

Season	Club	Apps	Gls	Tot A	Tot G
1999–2000	Watford	0	0.		
2000–01	Watford	0	0		
2001–02	Watford	17	1	17	1

FOLEY, Dominic (F) 60 8
H: 6 1 W: 12 08 b.Cork 7-7-76
Source: St James Gate. *Honours:* Eire 6 full caps, 2 goals.

Season	Club	Apps	Gls	Tot A	Tot G
1995–96	Wolverhampton W	5	0		
1996–97	Wolverhampton W	5	1		
1997–98	Wolverhampton W	5	0		
1997–98	Watford	8	1		
1998–99	Wolverhampton W	5	2	20	3
1998–99	Notts Co	2	0	2	0
1999–2000	Watford	12	1		
2000–01	Watford	5	1		
2001–02	Watford	1	0	26	3
2001–02	Swindon T	7	1	7	1
2001–02	QPR	5	1	5	1

FORDE, Fabian (F) 1 0
H: 5 11 W: 12 10 b.London 26-10-81
Source: Scholar.

Season	Club	Apps	Gls	Tot A	Tot G
2000–01	Watford	1	0		
2001–02	Watford	0	0	1	0

GALLI, Filippo* (D) 420 10
H: 6 0 W: 11 00 b.Monza 19-5-63

Season	Club	Apps	Gls	Tot A	Tot G
1981–82	AC Milan	0	0		
1982–83	Pescara	28	2	28	2
1983–84	AC Milan	28	1		
1984–85	AC Milan	28	0		
1985–86	AC Milan	22	2		
1986–87	AC Milan	21	0		
1987–88	AC Milan	30	0		
1988–89	AC Milan	10	0		
1989–90	AC Milan	14	0		
1990–91	AC Milan	20	0		
1991–92	AC Milan	8	0		
1992–93	AC Milan	1	0		
1993–94	AC Milan	8	0		
1994–95	AC Milan	19	0		
1995–96	AC Milan	6	0		
1996–97	AC Milan	2	0	217	3
1996–97	Reggiana	21	1		
1997–98	Reggiana	33	1	54	2
1998–99	Brescia	33	1		
1999–2000	Brescia	37	1		
2000–01	Brescia	23	0	93	2
2001–02	Watford	28	1	28	1

GAYLE, Marcus (F) 432 63
H: 6 3 W: 13 12 b.Hammersmith 28-9-70
Source: Trainee. *Honours:* England Youth. Jamaica 14 full caps.

Season	Club	Apps	Gls	Tot A	Tot G
1988–89	Brentford	3	0		
1989–90	Brentford	9	0		
1990–91	Brentford	33	6		
1991–92	Brentford	38	6		
1992–93	Brentford	38	4		
1993–94	Brentford	35	6	156	22
1993–94	Wimbledon	10	0		
1994–95	Wimbledon	23	2		
1995–96	Wimbledon	34	5		
1996–97	Wimbledon	36	8		
1997–98	Wimbledon	30	2		
1998–99	Wimbledon	35	10		
1999–2000	Wimbledon	36	7		
2000–01	Wimbledon	32	3	236	37
2000–01	Rangers	4	0	4	0
2001–02	Watford	36	4	36	4

GIBBS, Nigel* (D) 408 5
H: 5 7 W: 11 06 b.St Albans 20-11-65
Source: Apprentice. *Honours:* England Youth, Under-21.

Season	Club	Apps	Gls	Tot A	Tot G
1983–84	Watford	3	0		
1984–85	Watford	12	0		
1985–86	Watford	40	1		
1986–87	Watford	15	0		
1987–88	Watford	30	0		
1988–89	Watford	46	1		
1989–90	Watford	41	0		
1990–91	Watford	34	0		
1991–92	Watford	43	1		
1992–93	Watford	7	0		
1993–94	Watford	0	0		
1994–95	Watford	11	0		
1995–96	Watford	9	0		
1996–97	Watford	45	1		
1997–98	Watford	38	1		
1998–99	Watford	10	0		
1999–2000	Watford	17	0		
2000–01	Watford	6	0		
2001–02	Watford	1	0	408	5

GLASS, Stephen (M) 180 17
H: 5 9 W: 10 11 b.Dundee 23-5-76
Source: Crombie Sports. *Honours:* Scotland Schools, Under-21, B, 1 full cap.

Season	Club	Apps	Gls	Tot A	Tot G
1994–95	Aberdeen	19	1		
1995–96	Aberdeen	32	3		
1996–97	Aberdeen	24	1		
1997–98	Aberdeen	31	2	106	7
1998–99	Newcastle U	22	3		
1999–2000	Newcastle U	7	1		
2000–01	Newcastle U	14	3	43	7
2001–02	Watford	31	3	31	3

GODFREY, Elliott (M) 0 0
b.Toronto 22-2-83
Source: Scholar.

Season	Club	Apps	Gls	Tot A	Tot G
2000–01	Watford	0	0		
2001–02	Watford	0	0		

HAND, Jamie (M) 10 0
H: 6 0 W: 11 08 b.Uxbridge 7-2-84
Source: Scholar. *Honours:* England Youth.

Season	Club	Apps	Gls	Tot A	Tot G
2001–02	Watford	10	0	10	0

HELGUSON, Heidar (F) 127 38
H: 5 10 W: 12 04 b.Akureyri 22-8-77
Source: Throttur. *Honours:* Iceland 20 full caps, 1 goal.

Season	Club	Apps	Gls	Tot A	Tot G
1998	Lillestrom	19	2		
1999	Lillestrom	25	16	44	18
1999–2000	Watford	16	6		
2000–01	Watford	33	8		
2001–02	Watford	34	6	83	20

HUGHES, Stephen (M) 96 5
H: 6 0 W: 12 12 b.Wokingham 18-9-76
Source: Trainee. *Honours:* England Schools, Youth, Under-21.

Season	Club	Apps	Gls	Tot A	Tot G
1994–95	Arsenal	1	0		
1995–96	Arsenal	1	0		
1996–97	Arsenal	14	1		
1997–98	Arsenal	17	2		
1998–99	Arsenal	14	1		
1999–2000	Fulham	3	0	3	0
1999–2000	Everton	2	0	49	4
1999–2000	Everton	11	1		
2000–01	Everton	18	0	29	1
2001–02	Watford	15	0	15	0

HYDE, Micah (M) 290 32
H: 5 10 W: 11 07 b.Newham 10-11-74
Source: Trainee. *Honours:* Jamaica 5 full caps.

Season	Club	Apps	Gls	Tot A	Tot G
1993–94	Cambridge U	18	2		
1994–95	Cambridge U	27	0		
1995–96	Cambridge U	24	4		
1996–97	Cambridge U	38	7	107	13
1997–98	Watford	40	4		
1998–99	Watford	44	2		
1999–2000	Watford	34	3		
2000–01	Watford	26	6		
2001–02	Watford	39	4	183	19

IFIL, Jerel (D) 2 0
H: 6 1 W: 12 11 b.London 27-6-82
Source: Academy.

Season	Club	Apps	Gls	Tot A	Tot G
1999–2000	Watford	0	0		
2000–01	Watford	0	0		
2001–02	*Huddersfield T*	2	0	2	0

ISSA, Pierre (D)   61   1
H: 6 4   W: 14 00   b.Johannesburg 11-9-75
Source: Dunkerque. *Honours:* South Africa 45 full caps.

1996–97	Marseille	9	0	
1997–98	Marseille	4	0	
1998–99	Marseille	16	0	
1999–2000	Marseille	8	0	
2000–01	Marseille	9	0	46 0
2000–01	Chelsea	0	0	
2001–02	Chelsea	0	0	
2001–02	Watford	15	1	15 1

JOHNSON, Richard (M)   230   20
H: 5 10   W: 11 13   b.Kurri Kurri 27-4-74
Source: Trainee. *Honours:* Australia 1 full cap.

1991–92	Watford	2	0	
1992–93	Watford	1	0	
1993–94	Watford	27	0	
1994–95	Watford	35	3	
1995–96	Watford	20	1	
1996–97	Watford	37	2	
1997–98	Watford	42	7	
1998–99	Watford	40	4	
1999–2000	Watford	23	3	
2000–01	Watford	3	0	
2001–02	Watford	0	0	230 20

LANGSTON, Matthew (D)   0   0
H: 6 2   W: 12 04   b.Brighton 2-4-81
Source: Trainee.

1998–99	Watford	0	0
1999–2000	Watford	0	0
2000–01	Watford	0	0
2001–02	Watford	0	0

LEE, Richard (G)   0   0
H: 6 0   W: 12 07   b.Oxford 5-10-82
Source: Scholar.

2000–01	Watford	0	0
2001–02	Watford	0	0

MAHON, Gavin (M)   158   9
H: 6 0   W: 13 02   b.Birmingham 2-1-77
Source: Trainee.

1995–96	Wolverhampton W	0	0	
1996–97	Hereford U	11	1	
1997–98	Hereford U	0	0	
1998–99	Hereford U	0	0	11 1
1998–99	Brentford	29	4	
1999–2000	Brentford	37	3	
2000–01	Brentford	40	1	
2001–02	Brentford	35	0	141 8
2001–02	Watford	6	0	6 0

MATTHEWS, Barrie (M)   0   0
b.Forest of Dean 1-2-83
Source: Scholar.

2000–01	Watford	0	0
2001–02	Watford	0	0

McNAMEE, Anthony (M)   7   1
H: 5 5   W: 9 06   b.Lambeth 13-7-83
Source: Scholar.

2001–02	Watford	7	1	7 1

MEAD, Daniel (M)   0   0
b.Luton 19-9-84
Source: Scholar.

2001–02	Watford	0	0

NEILL, Thomas* (M)   0   0
b.Harrow 13-11-81
Source: Scholar.

2000–01	Watford	0	0
2001–02	Watford	0	0

NIELSEN, Allan (M)   295   53
H: 5 8   W: 11 02   b.Esbjerg 13-3-71
Source: Esbjerg. *Honours:* Denmark Under-21, 45 full caps, 7 goals.

1988–89	Bayern Munich	0	0	
1989–90	Bayern Munich	0	0	
1990–91	Bayern Munich	1	0	1 0
1991–92	Sion	0	0	
1991–92	Odense	8	2	
1992–93	Odense	30	4	
1993–94	Odense	17	3	55 9
1993–94	FC Copenhagen	18	3	
1994–95	FC Copenhagen	18	3	26 3
1994–95	Brondby	10	3	
1995–96	Brondby	28	6	
1996–97	Brondby	4	2	42 11
1996–97	Tottenham H	29	6	
1997–98	Tottenham H	28	3	
1998–99	Tottenham H	26	3	
1999–2000	Tottenham H	14	0	97 12
1999–2000	Wolverhampton W	7	2	7 2
2000–01	Watford	45	10	
2001–02	Watford	22	6	67 16

NOEL-WILLIAMS, Gifton (F)   153   33
H: 6 4   W: 14 00   b.Islington 21-1-80
Source: Trainee. *Honours:* England Youth.

1996–97	Watford	25	2	
1997–98	Watford	38	7	
1998–99	Watford	26	10	
1999–2000	Watford	3	0	
2000–01	Watford	32	8	
2001–02	Watford	29	6	153 33

NORVILLE, Jason (F)   2   0
H: 5 11   W: 10 07   b.Trinidad & Tobago 9-9-83
Source: Scholar.

2001–02	Watford	2	0	2 0

OKON, Paul* (M)   194   5
H: 5 10   W: 13 03   b.Sydney 5-4-72
Honours: Australia 25 full caps.

1989–90	Marconi Stallions	22	2	
1990–91	Marconi Stallions	27	2	49 4
1991–92	FC Brugge	0	0	
1992–93	FC Brugge	5	0	
1993–94	FC Brugge	27	0	
1994–95	FC Brugge	26	0	
1995–96	FC Brugge	14	1	72 1
1996–97	Lazio	14	0	
1997–98	Lazio	0	0	
1998–99	Lazio	5	0	19 0
1999–2000	Fiorentina	11	0	11 0
2000–01	Middlesbrough	24	0	
2001–02	Middlesbrough	4	0	28 0
2001–02	Watford	15	0	15 0

PANAYI, James* (D)   13   0
H: 6 1   W: 12 06   b.Hammersmith 24-1-80
Source: Trainee.

1998–99	Watford	0	0	
1999–2000	Watford	2	0	
2000–01	Watford	9	0	
2001–02	Watford	2	0	13 0

PATTERSON, Simon (M)   0   0
b.Northwick 4-9-82

2000–01	Watford	0	0
2001–02	Watford	0	0

ROBINSON, Paul (D)   172   5
H: 5 9   W: 11 11   b.Watford 14-12-78
Source: Trainee. *Honours:* England Under-21.

1996–97	Watford	12	0	
1997–98	Watford	22	2	
1998–99	Watford	29	0	
1999–2000	Watford	32	0	
2000–01	Watford	39	0	
2001–02	Watford	38	3	172 5

SAUNDERS, Neil (M)   0   0
b.Barking 7-5-83
Source: Scholar.

2001–02	Watford	0	0

SMITH, Jack (D)   0   0
b.Hemel Hempstead 14-10-83
Source: Scholar.

2001–02	Watford	0	0

SMITH, Tommy (F)   114   26
H: 5 9   W: 10 00   b.Hemel Hempstead 22-5-80
Source: Trainee. *Honours:* England Youth, Under-21.

1997–98	Watford	1	0	
1998–99	Watford	8	2	
1999–2000	Watford	22	2	
2000–01	Watford	43	11	
2001–02	Watford	40	11	114 26

SWONNELL, Sam (M)   0   0
H: 5 10   W: 11 10   b.Brentwood 13-9-82
Source: Scholar.

2000–01	Watford	0	0
2001–02	Watford	0	0

VEGA, Ramon (D)   279   23
H: 6 3   W: 14 00   b.Olten 14-6-71
Source: Trimbach. *Honours:* Switzerland 23 full caps, 2 goals.

1990–91	Grasshoppers	3	0	
1991–92	Grasshoppers	34	2	
1992–93	Grasshoppers	20	2	
1993–94	Grasshoppers	36	2	
1994–95	Grasshoppers	33	3	
1995–96	Grasshoppers	30	4	156 13
1996–97	Cagliari	14	0	14 0
1996–97	Tottenham H	8	1	
1997–98	Tottenham H	25	3	
1998–99	Tottenham H	16	2	
1999–2000	Tottenham H	5	1	
2000–01	Tottenham H	10	0	64 7
2000–01	Celtic	18	2	18 2
2001–02	Watford	27	1	27 1

VERNAZZA, Paulo (M)   58   3
H: 5 10   W: 10 13   b.Islington 1-11-79
Source: Trainee. *Honours:* England Youth, Under-21.

1997–98	Arsenal	1	0	
1998–99	Arsenal	0	0	
1998–99	Ipswich T	2	0	2 0
1999–2000	Arsenal	2	0	
1999–2000	Portsmouth	7	0	7 0
2000–01	Arsenal	2	1	5 1
2000–01	Watford	23	2	
2001–02	Watford	21	0	44 2

WILLIAMS, Nick (D)   0   0
H: 6 1   W: 12 10   b.Cheltenham 16-2-83

2000–01	Watford	0	0
2001–02	Watford	0	0

WOOTER, Nordin* (F)   154   10
H: 5 6   W: 10 08   b.Breda 24-8-76

1994–95	Ajax	5	1	
1995–96	Ajax	25	2	
1996–97	Ajax	28	3	58 6
1997–98	Zaragoza	15	1	
1998–99	Zaragoza	18	0	
1999–2000	Zaragoza	0	0	33 1
1999–2000	Watford	20	1	
2000–01	Watford	26	1	
2001–02	Watford	17	1	63 3

WRIGHT, Nick (F)   62   11
H: 5 10   W: 11 08   b.Derby 15-10-75
Source: Trainee.

1994–95	Derby Co	0	0	
1995–96	Derby Co	0	0	
1996–97	Derby Co	0	0	
1997–98	Derby Co	0	0	
1997–98	Carlisle U	25	5	25 5
1998–99	Watford	33	6	
1999–2000	Watford	4	0	
2000–01	Watford	0	0	
2001–02	Watford	0	0	37 6

Scholars
Buxton, Nicholas J; Collins, James E; Cowen, Joseph W; Deamer, William D; E'Beyer, Mark E; Hammond, Benjamin I; Herd, Ben; Hopton, Matthew A; Hughes, Bradley R; Martin, Robert; Walsh, Liam S; Watson, Liam J; Williams, Robert
Non-Contract
Hitchcock, Kevin

WBA

ADAMS, Ross§ (M)   0   0
b.Birmingham 11-3-83
Source: Scholar.

2001–02	WBA	0	0

ADAMSON, Chris (G)   22   0
H: 6 3   W: 12 00   b.Ashington 4-11-78
Source: Trainee.

1997–98	WBA	3	0	
1998–99	WBA	0	0	
1998–99	Mansfield T	2	0	2 0
1999–2000	WBA	9	0	
1999–2000	Halifax T	7	0	7 0
2000–01	WBA	0	0	
2001–02	WBA	0	0	12 0
2001–02	Plymouth Arg	1	0	1 0

APPLETON, Michael (M)   162   15
H: 5 8   W: 11 00   b.Salford 4-12-75
Source: Trainee.

1994–95	Manchester U	0	0	
1995–96	Manchester U	0	0	
1995–96	Lincoln C	4	0	4 0
1996–97	Manchester U	0	0	
1996–97	Grimsby T	10	3	10 3
1997–98	Preston NE	38	2	
1998–99	Preston NE	25	2	
1999–2000	Preston NE	26	3	
2000–01	Preston NE	26	5	115 12
2000–01	WBA	15	0	
2001–02	WBA	18	0	33 0

BALIS, Igor (D)   177   7
H: 5 11   W: 11 00   b.Czech Republic 5-1-70
Honours: Slovakia 41 full caps, 1 goal.

1995–96	Spartak Trnava	32	0	
1996–97	Spartak Trnava	26	4	
1997–98	Spartak Trnava	28	0	
1998–99	Spartak Trnava	26	1	
1999–2000	Spartak Trnava	24	0	136 5
2000–01	WBA	7	0	
2001–02	WBA	34	2	41 2

BRIGGS, Mark (M) — 0 0
H: 6 1 W: 11 01 b.Wolverhampton 16-2-82
Source: Scholar.

Season	Club				
2000–01	WBA	0	0		
2001–02	WBA	0	0		

BUTLER, Tony# (D) — 336 6
H: 6 2 W: 12 00 b.Stockport 28-9-72
Source: Trainee.

Season	Club				
1990–91	Gillingham	6	0		
1991–92	Gillingham	5	0		
1992–93	Gillingham	41	0		
1993–94	Gillingham	27	1		
1994–95	Gillingham	33	2		
1995–96	Gillingham	36	2	148	5
1996–97	Blackpool	42	0		
1997–98	Blackpool	37	0		
1998–99	Blackpool	20	0	99	0
1998–99	Port Vale	4	0		
1999–2000	Port Vale	15	0	19	0
1999–2000	WBA	7	0		
2000–01	WBA	44	1		
2001–02	WBA	19	0	70	1

CHAMBERS, Adam (D) — 43 1
H: 5 10 W: 11 08 b.Sandwell 20-11-80
Source: Trainee. Honours: England Youth.

Season	Club				
1998–99	WBA	0	0		
1999–2000	WBA	0	0		
2000–01	WBA	11	1		
2001–02	WBA	32	0	43	1

CHAMBERS, James (D) — 48 0
H: 5 10 W: 11 08 b.Sandwell 20-11-80
Source: Trainee. Honours: England Youth.

Season	Club				
1998–99	WBA	0	0		
1999–2000	WBA	12	0		
2000–01	WBA	31	0		
2001–02	WBA	5	0	48	0

CLEMENT, Neil (D) — 122 12
H: 6 0 W: 14 07 b.Reading 3-10-78
Source: Trainee. Honours: England Schools, Youth.

Season	Club				
1995–96	Chelsea	0	0		
1996–97	Chelsea	1	0		
1997–98	Chelsea	0	0		
1998–99	Chelsea	0	0		
1998–99	Reading	11	1	11	1
1998–99	Preston NE	4	0	4	0
1999–2000	Chelsea	0	0	1	0
1999–2000	Brentford	8	0	8	0
1999–2000	WBA	8	0		
2000–01	WBA	45	5		
2001–02	WBA	45	6	98	11

COLLINS, Matt‡ (M) — 0 0
H: 5 10 W: 10 12 b.Hitchin 10-2-82
Source: Scholar.

Season	Club				
2000–01	WBA	0	0		
2001–02	WBA	0	0		

DICHIO, Danny (F) — 191 43
H: 6 4 W: 13 10 b.Hammersmith 19-10-74
Source: Trainee. Honours: England Schools, Under-21.

Season	Club				
1993–94	QPR	0	0		
1993–94	Barnet	9	2	9	2
1994–95	QPR	9	3		
1995–96	QPR	29	10		
1996–97	QPR	37	7	75	20
1997–98	Sampdoria	0	0		
1997–98	Lecce	4	1	4	1
1997–98	Sunderland	13	0		
1998–99	Sunderland	36	10		
1999–2000	Sunderland	12	0		
2000–01	Sunderland	15	1		
2001–02	Sunderland	0	0	76	11
2001–02	WBA	27	9	27	9

DOBIE, Scott (F) — 185 34
H: 6 2 W: 12 09 b.Workington 10-10-78
Source: Trainee. Honours: Scotland 3 full caps, 1 goal.

Season	Club				
1996–97	Carlisle U	2	1		
1997–98	Carlisle U	23	0		
1998–99	Carlisle U	33	6		
1998–99	Clydebank	6	0	6	0
1999–2000	Carlisle U	34	7		
2000–01	Carlisle U	44	10	136	24
2001–02	WBA	43	10	43	10

DYER, Lloyd (M) — 0 0
b.Birmingham 13-9-82

Season	Club				
2001–02	WBA	0	0		

FOX, Ruel* (M) — 394 49
H: 5 6 W: 10 05 b.Ipswich 14-1-68
Source: Apprentice. Honours: England B.

Season	Club				
1985–86	Norwich C	0	0		
1986–87	Norwich C	3	0		
1987–88	Norwich C	34	2		
1988–89	Norwich C	4	0		
1989–90	Norwich C	7	3		
1990–91	Norwich C	28	4		
1991–92	Norwich C	37	2		
1992–93	Norwich C	34	4		
1993–94	Norwich C	25	7	172	22
1993–94	Newcastle U	14	2		
1994–95	Newcastle U	40	10		
1995–96	Newcastle U	4	0	58	12
1995–96	Tottenham H	26	6		
1996–97	Tottenham H	25	1		
1997–98	Tottenham H	32	3		
1998–99	Tottenham H	20	3		
1999–2000	Tottenham H	3	0		
2000–01	Tottenham H	0	0	106	13
2000–01	WBA	38	1		
2001–02	WBA	20	1	58	2

GILCHRIST, Phil (D) — 349 11
H: 6 0 W: 13 03 b.Stockton 25-8-73
Source: Trainee.

Season	Club				
1990–91	Nottingham F	0	0		
1991–92	Middlesbrough	0	0		
1992–93	Hartlepool U	24	0		
1993–94	Hartlepool U	35	0		
1994–95	Hartlepool U	23	0	82	0
1994–95	Oxford U	18	1		
1995–96	Oxford U	42	3		
1996–97	Oxford U	38	2		
1997–98	Oxford U	39	2		
1998–99	Oxford U	39	2		
1999–2000	Oxford U	1	0	177	10
1999–2000	Leicester C	27	1		
2000–01	Leicester C	12	0	39	1
2000–01	WBA	8	0		
2001–02	WBA	43	0	51	0

HOULT, Russell (G) — 252 0
H: 6 4 W: 14 01 b.Ashby 22-11-72
Source: Trainee.

Season	Club				
1990–91	Leicester C	0	0		
1991–92	Leicester C	0	0		
1991–92	Lincoln C	2	0		
1991–92	Blackpool	0	0		
1992–93	Leicester C	10	0		
1993–94	Leicester C	0	0		
1993–94	Bolton W	4	0	4	0
1994–95	Leicester C	0	0	10	0
1994–95	Lincoln C	15	0	17	0
1994–95	Derby Co	15	0		
1995–96	Derby Co	41	0		
1996–97	Derby Co	32	0		
1997–98	Derby Co	2	0		
1998–99	Derby Co	23	0		
1999–2000	Derby Co	10	0	123	0
1999–2000	Portsmouth	18	0		
2000–01	Portsmouth	22	0	40	0
2000–01	WBA	13	0		
2001–02	WBA	45	0	58	0

JENSEN, Brian (G) — 47 0
H: 6 1 W: 12 04 b.Copenhagen 8-6-75

Season	Club				
1997–98	AZ	0	0		
1998–99	AZ	1	0		
1999–2000	WBA	12	0		
2000–01	WBA	33	0		
2001–02	WBA	1	0	46	0

JOHNSON, Andy (M) — 217 26
H: 6 0 W: 13 03 b.Bristol 2-5-74
Source: Trainee. Honours: Wales 7 full caps.

Season	Club				
1991–92	Norwich C	2	1		
1992–93	Norwich C	2	1		
1993–94	Norwich C	2	0		
1994–95	Norwich C	7	0		
1995–96	Norwich C	27	5		
1996–97	Norwich C	27	5	66	13
1997–98	Nottingham F	34	4		
1998–99	Nottingham F	28	0		
1999–2000	Nottingham F	25	2		
2000–01	Nottingham F	31	3		
2001–02	Nottingham F	1	0	119	9
2001–02	WBA	32	4	32	4

JORDAO (M) — 247 18
H: 6 0 W: 12 07 b.Malanje 30-8-71

Season	Club				
1990–91	Amadora	0	0		
1991–92	Amadora	17	3		
1992–93	Amadora	3	0		
1993–94	Campomaiorense	9	0	9	0
1994–95	Leca	26	3	26	3
1995–96	Amadora	30	1		
1996–97	Amadora	31	3	81	7
1997–98	Benfica	6	0	6	0
1997–98	Braga	14	1		
1998–99	Braga	29	1		
1999–2000	Braga	22	0	65	2
2000–01	WBA	35	1		
2001–02	WBA	25	5	60	6

LYTTLE, Des# (D)
H: 5 9 W: 12 00 b.Wolverhampton 24-9-71
Source: Worcester C.

Season	Club				
1992–93	Swansea U	46	1	46	1

McINNES, Derek (M) — 330 24
H: 5 7 W: 11 04 b.Paisley 5-7-71
Source: Gleniffer Th.

Season	Club				
1987–88	Greenock Morton	2	0		
1988–89	Greenock Morton	23	1		
1989–90	Greenock Morton	23	1		
1990–91	Greenock Morton	31	3		
1991–92	Greenock Morton	42	7		
1992–93	Greenock Morton	40	2		
1993–94	Greenock Morton	16	1		
1994–95	Greenock Morton	26	3		
1995–96	Greenock Morton	12	1	221	19
1995–96	Rangers	0	0		
1996–97	Rangers	21	1		
1997–98	Rangers	0	0		
1998–99	Rangers	7	0	34	1
1998–99	Stockport Co	13	0	13	0
1999–2000	Toulouse	3	0	3	0
2000–01	WBA	14	1		
2001–02	WBA	45	3	59	4

MOORE, Darren (D) — 332 22
H: 6 3 W: 15 08 b.Birmingham 22-4-74
Source: Trainee. Honours: Jamaica 3 full caps.

Season	Club				
1991–92	Torquay U	5	1		
1992–93	Torquay U	31	2		
1993–94	Torquay U	37	2		
1994–95	Torquay U	30	3	103	8
1995–96	Doncaster R	35	2		
1996–97	Doncaster R	41	5	76	7
1997–98	Bradford C	18	0		
1998–99	Bradford C	44	3		
1999–2000	Bradford C	0	0	62	3
1999–2000	Portsmouth	25	1		
2000–01	Portsmouth	32	1		
2001–02	Portsmouth	2	0	59	2
2001–02	WBA	32	3	32	2

MORRIS, Elliott* (G) — 0 0
H: 5 11 W: 11 07 b.Belfast 4-5-81
Source: Trainee. Honours: Northern Ireland Under-21.

Season	Club				
1999–2000	WBA	0	0		
2000–01	WBA	0	0		
2001–02	WBA	0	0		

OLIVER, Adam (M) — 23 1
H: 5 9 W: 11 02 b.Sandwell 25-10-80
Source: Trainee. Honours: England Youth.

Season	Club				
1998–99	WBA	1	0		
1999–2000	WBA	15	1		
2000–01	WBA	7	0		
2001–02	WBA	0	0	23	1

PETTERSON, Andy* (G) — 145 0
H: 6 2 W: 15 02 b.Fremantle 29-9-69

Season	Club				
1988–89	Luton T	0	0		
1988–89	Swindon T	0	0		
1989–90	Luton T	0	0		
1990–91	Luton T	0	0		
1991–92	Luton T	0	0		
1991–92	Ipswich T	0	0		
1992–93	Luton T	14	0		
1992–93	Ipswich T	1	0		
1993–94	Luton T	5	0	19	0
1994–95	Charlton Ath	9	0		
1994–95	Bradford C	3	0	3	0
1995–96	Charlton Ath	9	0		
1995–96	Ipswich T	1	0	2	0
1995–96	Plymouth Arg	6	0	6	0
1995–96	Colchester U	5	0	5	0
1996–97	Charlton Ath	21	0		
1997–98	Charlton Ath	23	0		
1998–99	Charlton Ath	10	0	72	0
1998–99	Portsmouth	13	0		
1999–2000	Portsmouth	17	0		
1999–2000	Wolverhampton W	0	0		
2000–01	Portsmouth	2	0		
2000–01	Torquay U	6	0	6	0
2001–02	Portsmouth	0	0	32	0
2001–02	WBA	0	0		

QUINN, James* (M) — 282 50
H: 6 1 W: 12 10 b.Coventry 15-12-74
Source: Trainee. Honours: Northern Ireland Youth, Under-21, B, 25 full caps, 3 goals.

Season	Club				
1992–93	Birmingham C	4	0	4	0
1993–94	Blackpool	14	2		
1993–94	Stockport Co	1	0	1	0
1994–95	Blackpool	41	9		

1995–96	Blackpool	44	9		
1996–97	Blackpool	38	13		
1997–98	Blackpool	14	4	151	37
1997–98	WBA	13	2		
1998–99	WBA	43	6		
1999–2000	WBA	37	0		
2000–01	WBA	14	1		
2001–02	WBA	7	0	114	9
2001–02	*Notts Co*	6	3	6	3
2001–02	*Bristol R*	6	1	6	1

ROBERTS, Jason (F)   152 66
H: 6 1   W: 13 06   b.Park Royal 25-1-78
Source: Hayes. *Honours:* Grenada 6 full caps.

1997–98	Wolverhampton W	0	0		
1997–98	*Torquay U*	14	6	14	6
1997–98	*Bristol C*	3	1	3	1
1998–99	Bristol R	37	16		
1999–2000	Bristol R	41	22	78	38
2000–01	WBA	43	14		
2001–02	WBA	14	7	57	21

SCOTT, Mark (F)   0 0
H: 6 1   W: 12 02   b.Sandwell 16-7-82
Source: Scholar.

2000–01	WBA	0	0
2001–02	WBA	0	0

SIGURDSSON, Larus# (D)   282 8
H: 6 0   W: 13 11   b.Akureyri 4-6-73
Source: Thor. *Honours:* Iceland 35 full caps, 2 goals.

1994–95	Stoke C	23	1		
1995–96	Stoke C	46	0		
1996–97	Stoke C	45	0		
1997–98	Stoke C	43	1		
1998–99	Stoke C	38	4		
1999–2000	Stoke C	5	1	200	7
1999–2000	WBA	27	0		
2000–01	WBA	12	0		
2001–02	WBA	43	1	82	1

TAYLOR, Bob (F)   545 193
H: 5 11   W: 13 05   b.Easington 3-2-67
Source: Horden CW.

1985–86	Leeds U	2	0		
1986–87	Leeds U	2	0		
1987–88	Leeds U	32	9		
1988–89	Leeds U	6	0	42	9
1988–89	Bristol C	12	8		
1989–90	Bristol C	37	27		
1990–91	Bristol C	39	11		
1991–92	Bristol C	18	4	106	50
1991–92	WBA	19	8		
1992–93	WBA	46	30		
1993–94	WBA	42	18		
1994–95	WBA	42	11		
1995–96	WBA	42	17		
1996–97	WBA	32	10		
1997–98	WBA	15	2		
1997–98	*Bolton W*	12	3		
1998–99	Bolton W	38	15		
1999–2000	Bolton W	27	3	77	21
1999–2000	WBA	8	5		
2000–01	WBA	40	5		
2001–02	WBA	34	7	320	113

TURNER, Matt (M)   0 0
H: 5 9   W: 10 00   b.Nottingham 29-12-81
Source: Trainee. *Honours:* England Youth.

1998–99	Nottingham F	0	0
1999–2000	Nottingham F	0	0
2000–01	Nottingham F	0	0
2000–01	WBA	0	0
2001–02	WBA	0	0

Scholars
Adams, Richard; Adams, Ross I; Attewell, Stuart J; Brown, Simon A; Bruce, Kevin; Carey-Bertram, Daniel P; Crane, Daniel P; Cudworth, Jack R; Fox, James E; Gowling, Joshua AI; McHugh, Cameron J; Midworth, Philip; Meakamde, Tamika P; Nightingale, Peter E; Oakey, Paul E; Perry, Joshua; Sherwood, Lee; Warmer, Thomas E
Player who does not hold a current contract but his registration has been retained by the club
Blake, Mosiah N

WEST HAM U

ANDERSSON, Sven* (G)   508 0
H: 6 5   W: 14 08   b.Gothenburg 6-10-63

1980	Orgryte	11	0
1981	Orgryte	6	0
1982	Orgryte	24	0
1983	Orgryte	24	0
1984	Orgryte	22	0
1985	Orgryte	26	0
1986	Orgryte	22	0
1987	Orgryte	21	0
1988	Orgryte	24	0
1989	Orgryte	17	0
1990	Orgryte	22	0
1991	Orgryte	28	0	247	0
1992	Stromstad	28	0	28	0
1993	Helsingborg	26	0
1994	Helsingborg	26	0
1995	Helsingborg	26	0
1996	Helsingborg	26	0
1997	Helsingborg	26	0
1998	Helsingborg	26	0
1999	Helsingborg	26	0
2000	Helsingborg	26	0
2001	Helsingborg	25	0
2002	Helsingborg	0	0	233	0
2001–02	West Ham U	0	0

BRITTON, Leon (M)   0 0
b.South London 16-9-82
Source: Trainee. *Honours:* England Youth.

1999–2000	West Ham U	0	0
2000–01	West Ham U	0	0
2001–02	West Ham U	0	0

BYRNE, Shaun (D)   4 0
H: 5 9   W: 11 08   b.Taplow 21-1-81
Source: Trainee.

1999–2000	West Ham U	1	0		
1999–2000	*Bristol R*	2	0	2	0
2000–01	West Ham U	0	0		
2001–02	West Ham U	1	0	2	0

BYWATER, Steve (G)   11 0
H: 6 2   W: 12 00   b.Manchester 7-6-81
Source: Trainee. *Honours:* England Youth, Under-20, Under-21.

1997–98	Rochdale	0	0		
1998–99	West Ham U	4	0		
1999–2000	West Ham U	4	0		
1999–2000	*Wycombe W*	2	0	2	0
1999–2000	*Hull C*	4	0	4	0
2000–01	West Ham U	1	0		
2001–02	West Ham U	0	0	5	0
2001–02	*Wolverhampton W*	0	0		
2001–02	*Cardiff C*	0	0		

CAMARA, Titi (F)   258 47
H: 6 0   W: 13 00   b.Conakry 17-11-72
Honours: Guinea full caps.

1990–91	St Etienne	4	0		
1991–92	St Etienne	15	3		
1992–93	St Etienne	16	2		
1993–94	St Etienne	26	4		
1994–95	St Etienne	33	7	94	16
1995–96	Lens	36	8		
1996–97	Lens	27	6	63	14
1997–98	Marseille	31	2		
1998–99	Marseille	30	6	61	8
1999–2000	Liverpool	33	9		
2000–01	Liverpool	0	0	33	9
2000–01	West Ham U	6	0		
2001–02	West Ham U	1	0	7	0

CARRICK, Michael (M)   79 6
H: 6 1   W: 11 10   b.Wallsend 28-7-81
Source: Trainee. *Honours:* England Youth, Under-21, 2 full caps.

1998–99	West Ham U	0	0		
1999–2000	West Ham U	8	1		
1999–2000	*Swindon T*	6	2	6	2
1999–2000	*Birmingham C*	2	0	2	0
2000–01	West Ham U	33	1		
2001–02	West Ham U	30	2	71	4

CASCIONE, Emmanuel‡ (M)   0 0
b.Catanzaro 22-9-83
Source: Lucchese.

2000–01	West Ham U	0	0
2001–02	West Ham U	0	0

(Transferred to Pistoiese, January 2002).

CHARLES, Gary (D)   216 9
H: 5 9   W: 11 08   b.East London 13-4-70
Source: Trainee. *Honours:* England Under-21, 2 full caps.

1987–88	Nottingham F	0	0		
1988–89	Nottingham F	1	0		
1988–89	*Leicester C*	8	0	8	0
1989–90	Nottingham F	1	0		
1990–91	Nottingham F	10	0		
1991–92	Nottingham F	30	1		
1992–93	Nottingham F	14	0	56	1
1993–94	Derby Co	43	1		
1994–95	Derby Co	18	2	61	3
1994–95	Aston Villa	16	0		
1995–96	Aston Villa	34	1		
1996–97	Aston Villa	0	0		
1997–98	Aston Villa	18	1		
1998–99	Aston Villa	11	1	79	3
1998–99	Benfica	4	1	4	1
1999–2000	West Ham U	3	0		
2000–01	West Ham U	1	0		

2000–01	*Birmingham C*	3	0	3	0
2001–02	West Ham U	0	0	5	0

COLE, Joe (M)   90 6
H: 5 7   W: 9 08   b.Islington 8-11-81
Source: Trainee. *Honours:* England Schools, Youth, Under-21, 7 full caps.

1998–99	West Ham U	8	0		
1999–2000	West Ham U	22	1		
2000–01	West Ham U	30	5		
2001–02	West Ham U	30	0	90	6

COURTOIS, Laurent (M)   30 0
H: 5 7   W: 10 11   b.Lyon 11-9-78
Source: Lyon.

1998–99	Ajaccio	0	0		
1999–2000	Toulouse	0	0		
2000–01	Toulouse	23	0	23	0
2001–02	West Ham U	7	0	7	0

DAILLY, Christian (D)   328 26
H: 6 0   W: 12 10   b.Dundee 23-10-73
Source: 'S' Form. *Honours:* Scotland Schools, Youth, B, Under-21, 35 full caps, 3 goals.

1990–91	Dundee U	18	5		
1991–92	Dundee U	8	0		
1992–93	Dundee U	14	4		
1993–94	Dundee U	38	4		
1994–95	Dundee U	33	4		
1995–96	Dundee U	30	1	141	18
1996–97	Derby Co	36	3		
1997–98	Derby Co	30	1		
1998–99	Derby Co	1	0	67	4
1998–99	Blackburn R	17	0		
1999–2000	Blackburn R	43	4		
2000–01	Blackburn R	10	0	70	4
2000–01	West Ham U	12	0		
2001–02	West Ham U	38	0	50	0

DEFOE, Jermain (F)   65 28
H: 5 7   W: 10 04   b.Beckton 7-10-82
Source: Charlton Ath. *Honours:* England Youth, Under-21.

1999–2000	West Ham U	0	0		
1999–2000	*Bournemouth*	29	18	29	18
2000–01	West Ham U	35	10	36	10

DI CANIO, Paolo (F)   389 87
H: 5 9   W: 11 09   b.Rome 9-7-68
Source: Milan AC.

1985–86	Lazio	0	0		
1986–87	Ternana	27	2	27	2
1987–88	Lazio	0	0		
1988–89	Lazio	30	1		
1989–90	Lazio	24	3	54	4
1990–91	Juventus	23	3		
1991–92	Juventus	24	0		
1992–93	Juventus	31	3		
1993–94	Napoli	26	5	26	5
1994–95	Juventus	0	0	78	6
1994–95	AC Milan	15	1		
1995–96	AC Milan	22	5	37	6
1996–97	Celtic	26	12	26	12
1997–98	Sheffield W	35	12		
1998–99	Sheffield W	6	3	41	15
1998–99	West Ham U	13	3		
1999–2000	West Ham U	30	16		
2000–01	West Ham U	31	9		
2001–02	West Ham U	26	9	100	37

FERRANTE, Michael* (M)   0 0
H: 5 8   W: 10 10   b.Sydney 28-4-81
Source: Australia IOS.

1998–99	West Ham U	0	0
1999–2000	West Ham U	0	0
2000–01	West Ham U	0	0
2001–02	West Ham U	0	0

FORDE, David (G)   0 0
H: 6 2   W: 13 06   b.Galway 20-12-79
Source: Barry T.

2001–02	West Ham U	0	0

FORREST, Craig* (G)   307 0
H: 6 4   W: 14 04   b.Vancouver 20-9-67
Source: Apprentice. *Honours:* Canada 56 full caps.

1985–86	Ipswich T	0	0		
1986–87	Ipswich T	0	0		
1987–88	Ipswich T	0	0		
1987–88	*Colchester U*	11	0	11	0
1988–89	Ipswich T	28	0		
1989–90	Ipswich T	45	0		
1990–91	Ipswich T	43	0		
1991–92	Ipswich T	46	0		
1992–93	Ipswich T	11	0		
1993–94	Ipswich T	27	0		
1994–95	Ipswich T	36	0		
1995–96	Ipswich T	21	0		
1996–97	Ipswich T	6	0	263	0
1996–97	*Chelsea*	3	0	3	0
1997–98	West Ham U	13	0		

1998–99	West Ham U	2	0		
1999–2000	West Ham U	11	0		
2000–01	West Ham U	4	0		
2001–02	West Ham U	0	0	30	0

FOXE, Hayden (D)   53 5
H: 6 3 W: 13 05 b.Sydney 23-6-77
Honours: Australia 10 full caps, 2 goals.

1997–98	Arminia Bielefeld	1	0	1	0
1998	Sanfrecce	15	3		
1999	Sanfrecce	22	2	37	5
2000–01	Mechelen	4	0	4	0
2000–01	West Ham U	5	0		
2001–02	West Ham U	6	0	11	0

GARCIA, Richard (F)   26 4
H: 5 11 W: 12 00 b.Perth 9-4-81
Source: Trainee.

1998–99	West Ham U	0	0		
1999–2000	West Ham U	0	0		
2000–01	West Ham U	0	0		
2000–01	Leyton Orient	18	4	18	4
2001–02	West Ham U	8	0	8	0

HISLOP, Shaka* (G)   262 0
H: 6 4 W: 14 04 b.Hackney 22-2-69
Source: Howard Univ, USA. *Honours:* England Under-21. Trinidad & Tobago 7 full caps.

1992–93	Reading	12	0		
1993–94	Reading	46	0		
1994–95	Reading	46	0	104	0
1995–96	Newcastle U	24	0		
1996–97	Newcastle U	16	0		
1997–98	Newcastle U	13	0	53	0
1998–99	West Ham U	37	0		
1999–2000	West Ham U	22	0		
2000–01	West Ham U	34	0		
2001–02	West Ham U	12	0	105	0

HUTCHISON, Don (M)   315 44
H: 6 1 W: 11 08 b.Gateshead 9-5-71
Source: Trainee. *Honours:* Scotland B, 19 full caps, 6 goals.

1989–90	Hartlepool U	13	2		
1990–91	Hartlepool U	11	0	24	2
1990–91	Liverpool	3	0		
1991–92	Liverpool	11	0		
1992–93	Liverpool	31	7		
1993–94	Liverpool	10	0	45	7
1994–95	West Ham U	23	9		
1995–96	West Ham U	12	2		
1995–96	Sheffield U	13	0		
1996–97	Sheffield U	41	3		
1997–98	Sheffield U	18	0	78	5
1997–98	Everton	11	1		
1998–99	Everton	33	3		
1999–2000	Everton	31	6	75	10
2000–01	Sunderland	32	8		
2001–02	Sunderland	2	0	34	8
2001–02	West Ham U	24	1	59	12

IRIEKPEN, Ezomo (D)   0 0
H: 6 1 W: 12 02 b.East London 14-5-82
Source: Trainee. *Honours:* England Youth.

1998–99	West Ham U	0	0		
1999–2000	West Ham U	0	0		
2000–01	West Ham U	0	0		
2001–02	West Ham U	0	0		

JAMES, David (G)   396 0
H: 6 5 W: 14 02 b.Welwyn 1-8-70
Source: Trainee. *Honours:* England Youth, Under-21, B, 9 full caps.

1988–89	Watford	0	0		
1989–90	Watford	0	0		
1990–91	Watford	46	0		
1991–92	Watford	43	0	89	0
1992–93	Liverpool	29	0		
1993–94	Liverpool	14	0		
1994–95	Liverpool	42	0		
1995–96	Liverpool	38	0		
1996–97	Liverpool	38	0		
1997–98	Liverpool	27	0		
1998–99	Liverpool	26	0	214	0
1999–2000	Aston Villa	29	0		
2000–01	Aston Villa	38	0	67	0
2001–02	West Ham U	26	0	26	0

JOHNSON, Glen (D)   0 0
b.London 23-8-84
Source: Scholar. *Honours:* England Youth.

| 2001–02 | West Ham U | 0 | 0 | | |

KANOUTE, Frederic (F)   107 33
H: 6 3 W: 13 08 b.Ste. Foy-Les-Lyon 2-9-77

1997–98	Lyon	18	6		
1998–99	Lyon	9	2		
1999–2000	Lyon	13	1	40	9
1999–2000	West Ham U	8	2		
2000–01	West Ham U	32	11		
2001–02	West Ham U	27	11	67	24

KITSON, Paul* (F)   264 71
H: 5 11 W: 10 12 b.Murton 9-1-71
Source: Trainee. *Honours:* England Under-21.

1988–89	Leicester C	0	0		
1989–90	Leicester C	13	0		
1990–91	Leicester C	7	0		
1991–92	Leicester C	30	6	50	6
1991–92	Derby Co	12	4		
1992–93	Derby Co	44	17		
1993–94	Derby Co	41	13		
1994–95	Derby Co	8	2	105	36
1994–95	Newcastle U	26	8		
1995–96	Newcastle U	7	2		
1996–97	Newcastle U	3	0	36	10
1996–97	West Ham U	14	8		
1997–98	West Ham U	13	4		
1998–99	West Ham U	17	3		
1999–2000	West Ham U	10	0		
1999–2000	Charlton Ath	6	1	6	1
2000–01	West Ham U	2	0		
2000–01	Crystal Palace	4	0	4	0
2001–02	West Ham U	7	3	63	18

LABANT, Vladimir (D)   141 8
H: 6 0 W: 13 00 b.Zilina 8-6-74
Honours: Slovakia 19 full caps, 2 goals.

1996–97	Bystrica	28	3	28	3
1997–98	Slavia Prague	23	0		
1998–99	Slavia Prague	26	1	49	1
1999–2000	Sparta Prague	12	2		
2000–01	Sparta Prague	24	1		
2001–02	Sparta Prague	16	1	52	4
2001–02	West Ham U	12	0	12	0

LOMAS, Steve (M)   241 17
H: 6 0 W: 12 08 b.Hanover 14-3-72
Source: Trainee. *Honours:* Northern Ireland Schools, Youth, B, 40 full caps, 3 goals.

1991–92	Manchester C	0	0		
1992–93	Manchester C	0	0		
1993–94	Manchester C	23	0		
1994–95	Manchester C	20	2		
1995–96	Manchester C	33	3		
1996–97	Manchester C	35	3	111	8
1996–97	West Ham U	7	0		
1997–98	West Ham U	33	2		
1998–99	West Ham U	30	1		
1999–2000	West Ham U	25	1		
2000–01	West Ham U	30	1		
2001–02	West Ham U	15	4	130	9

McCANN, Grant (M)   36 3
H: 5 10 W: 11 00 b.Belfast 14-4-80
Source: Trainee. *Honours:* Northern Ireland Youth, Under-21, 3 full caps.

1998–99	West Ham U	0	0		
1999–2000	West Ham U	0	0		
2000–01	West Ham U	1	0		
2000–01	Notts Co	2	0	2	0
2000–01	Cheltenham T	30	3	30	3
2001–02	West Ham U	3	0	4	0

McMAHON, Daryl (M)   0 0
b.Dublin 10-10-83

| 2000–01 | West Ham U | 0 | 0 | | |
| 2001–02 | West Ham U | 0 | 0 | | |

MINTO, Scott (D)   304 11
H: 5 10 W: 11 00 b.Wirral 6-8-71
Source: Trainee. *Honours:* England Youth, Under-21.

1988–89	Charlton Ath	3	0		
1989–90	Charlton Ath	23	2		
1990–91	Charlton Ath	43	1		
1991–92	Charlton Ath	33	1		
1992–93	Charlton Ath	36	1		
1993–94	Charlton Ath	42	2	180	7
1994–95	Chelsea	19	0		
1995–96	Chelsea	10	0		
1996–97	Chelsea	25	4	54	4
1997–98	Benfica	21	0		
1998–99	Benfica	10	0	31	0
1998–99	West Ham U	15	0		
1999–2000	West Ham U	18	0		
2000–01	West Ham U	1	0		
2001–02	West Ham U	5	0	39	0

MONCUR, John (M)   273 13
H: 5 8 W: 9 10 b.Mile End 22-9-66
Source:

1984–85	Tottenham H	0	0		
1985–86	Tottenham H	0	0		
1986–87	Tottenham H	1	0		
1986–87	Cambridge U	4	0	4	0
1986–87	Doncaster R	4	0	4	0
1987–88	Tottenham H	5	0		
1988–89	Tottenham H	1	0		
1988–89	Portsmouth	7	0	7	0
1989–90	Brentford	5	1	5	1
1990–91	Tottenham H	9	0	21	1

1991–92	Ipswich T	6	0	6	0
1991–92	Nottingham F	0	0		
1991–92	Swindon T	3	0		
1992–93	Swindon T	14	1		
1993–94	Swindon T	41	4	58	5
1994–95	West Ham U	30	2		
1995–96	West Ham U	20	0		
1996–97	West Ham U	27	2		
1997–98	West Ham U	20	1		
1998–99	West Ham U	14	0		
1999–2000	West Ham U	22	1		
2000–01	West Ham U	16	0		
2001–02	West Ham U	19	0	168	6

NEWTON, Adam* (D)   35 2
H: 5 10 W: 11 00 b.Ascot 4-12-80
Source: West Ham U Trainee. *Honours:* England Under-21.

1999–2000	West Ham U	2	0		
1999–2000	Portsmouth	3	0	3	0
2000–01	West Ham U	0	0		
2000–01	Notts Co	20	1	20	1
2001–02	West Ham U	0	0	2	0
2001–02	Leyton Orient	10	1	10	1

PEARCE, Ian (D)   154 8
H: 6 3 W: 14 04 b.Bury St Edmunds 7-5-74
Source: School. *Honours:* England Youth, Under-21.

1990–91	Chelsea	1	0		
1991–92	Chelsea	2	0		
1992–93	Chelsea	1	0		
1993–94	Chelsea	0	0	4	0
1993–94	Blackburn R	5	1		
1994–95	Blackburn R	28	0		
1995–96	Blackburn R	12	1		
1996–97	Blackburn R	12	0		
1997–98	Blackburn R	5	0	62	2
1997–98	West Ham U	30	1		
1998–99	West Ham U	33	2		
1999–2000	West Ham U	1	0		
2000–01	West Ham U	15	1		
2001–02	West Ham U	9	2	88	6

POTTS, Steve* (D)   399 1
H: 5 7 W: 10 11 b.Hartford (USA) 7-5-67
Source: Apprentice. *Honours:* England Youth.

1984–85	West Ham U	1	0		
1985–86	West Ham U	1	0		
1986–87	West Ham U	8	0		
1987–88	West Ham U	8	0		
1988–89	West Ham U	28	0		
1989–90	West Ham U	32	0		
1990–91	West Ham U	37	1		
1991–92	West Ham U	34	0		
1992–93	West Ham U	46	0		
1993–94	West Ham U	41	0		
1994–95	West Ham U	42	0		
1995–96	West Ham U	34	0		
1996–97	West Ham U	20	0		
1997–98	West Ham U	23	0		
1998–99	West Ham U	19	0		
1999–2000	West Ham U	17	0		
2000–01	West Ham U	8	0		
2001–02	West Ham U	0	0	399	1

REPKA, Tomas (D)   278 9
H: 6 0 W: 12 04 b.Slavicin Zlin 2-1-74
Honours: Czechoslovakia 1 full cap.Czech Republic 46 full caps, 1 goal.

1991–92	Banik Ostrava	16	1		
1992–93	Banik Ostrava	19	0		
1993–94	Banik Ostrava	26	2		
1994–95	Banik Ostrava	16	0	77	3
1995–96	Sparta Prague	29	3		
1996–97	Sparta Prague	25	1		
1997–98	Sparta Prague	28	2	82	6
1998–99	Fiorentina	31	0		
1999–2000	Fiorentina	29	0		
2000–01	Fiorentina	28	0	88	0
2001–02	West Ham U	31	0	31	0

RIZA, Omer* (F)   22 7
H: 5 9 W: 11 00 b.Edmonton 8-11-79
Source: Trainee.

1998–99	Arsenal	0	0		
1999–2000	Arsenal	0	0		
1999–2000	West Ham U	0	0		
2000–01	West Ham U	0	0		
2000–01	Barnet	10	4	10	4
2000–01	Cambridge U	12	3	12	3
2001–02	West Ham U	0	0		

SCHEMMEL, Sebastian (D)   253 4
H: 5 8 W: 11 13 b.Nancy 2-6-75

1993–94	Nancy	1	0		
1994–95	Nancy	35	0		
1995–96	Nancy	33	0		
1996–97	Nancy	32	0		
1997–98	Nancy	40	1	146	1
1998–99	Metz	20	1		

1999–2000	Metz	21	1		
2000–01	Metz	19	0	60	2
2000–01	West Ham U	12	0		
2001–02	West Ham U	35	1	47	1

SINCLAIR, Trevor (M) 418 60
H: 5 10 W: 12 05 b.Dulwich 2-3-73
Source: Trainee. Honours: England Youth, Under-21, B, 9 full caps.

1989–90	Blackpool	9	0		
1990–91	Blackpool	31	1		
1991–92	Blackpool	27	3		
1992–93	Blackpool	45	11	112	15
1993–94	QPR	32	4		
1994–95	QPR	33	4		
1995–96	QPR	37	2		
1996–97	QPR	39	3		
1997–98	QPR	26	3	167	16
1997–98	West Ham U	14	7		
1998–99	West Ham U	36	7		
1999–2000	West Ham U	36	7		
2000–01	West Ham U	19	3		
2001–02	West Ham U	34	5	139	29

SOMA, Ragnvald (D) 57 5
H: 6 2 W: 12 02 b.Bryne 10-11-79

1999	Bryne	25	0		
2000	Bryne	25	5	50	5
2000–01	West Ham U	4	0		
2001–02	West Ham U	3	0	7	0

SONG, Rigobert (D) 185 4
H: 6 0 W: 13 00 b.Nkanglicock 1-7-76
Source: Tonnerre. Honours: Cameroon 69 full caps, 2 goals.

1994–95	Metz	24	2		
1995–96	Metz	37	0		
1996–97	Metz	34	0		
1997–98	Metz	28	1	123	3
1998–99	Salernitana	4	1	4	1
1998–99	Liverpool	13	0		
1999–2000	Liverpool	18	0		
2000–01	Liverpool	3	0	34	0
2000–01	West Ham U	19	0		
2001–02	West Ham U	5	0	24	0

(On loan to Cologne, November 2001).

WARD, Elliott (D) 0 0
b.Harrow 19-1-85
Source: Scholar.
| 2001–02 | West Ham U | 0 | 0 | | |

WINTERBURN, Nigel (D) 669 17
H: 5 8 W: 11 04 b.Coventry 11-12-63
Source: Local. Honours: England Youth, Under-21, B, 2 full caps.

1981–82	Birmingham C	0	0		
1982–83	Birmingham C	0	0		
1983–84	Oxford U	0	0		
1983–84	Wimbledon	43	1		
1984–85	Wimbledon	41	4		
1985–86	Wimbledon	39	1		
1986–87	Wimbledon	42	2	165	8
1987–88	Arsenal	17	0		
1988–89	Arsenal	38	3		
1989–90	Arsenal	36	0		
1990–91	Arsenal	38	0		
1991–92	Arsenal	41	1		
1992–93	Arsenal	29	1		
1993–94	Arsenal	34	0		
1994–95	Arsenal	39	0		
1995–96	Arsenal	36	2		
1996–97	Arsenal	38	0		
1997–98	Arsenal	36	1		
1998–99	Arsenal	30	0		
1999–2000	Arsenal	28	0	440	8
2000–01	West Ham U	33	1		
2001–02	West Ham U	31	0	64	1

Trainees
Akinsete, Ayo; Allen, James P; Carrick, Graeme; Eastwood; Freddy; Ferdinand, Anton J; Fletcher, Ronnie M; Jackson, Glenn G; Khan, Terence G; Lumsden, Philip; McClenahan, Trent J; Mehmet, Billy O; Morris, Daniel; Pearson, Gregory; Riddle, Louis S; Sealey, George; Tattam, Brent S
Non-Contract
Miklosko, Ludek

WIGAN ATH

ADAMCZUK, Dariusz (M) 136 9
H: 5 10 W: 12 00 b.Stettin 20-10-69
Source: Eintracht Frankfurt. Honours: Poland 11 full caps, 1 goal.

1993–94	Dundee	11	1		
1994–95	Pogon	0	0		
1995–96	Pogon	6	0	6	0
1995–96	Dundee	13	0		
1996–97	Dundee	30	1		

1997–98	Dundee	34	1		
1998–99	Dundee	26	6	114	9
1999–2000	Rangers	10	0		
2000–01	Rangers	3	0	13	0
2001–02	Wigan Ath	3	0	3	0

ASHCROFT, Lee (F) 358 57
H: 5 9 W: 13 04 b.Preston 7-9-72
Source: Trainee. Honours: England Under-21.

1990–91	Preston NE	14	1		
1991–92	Preston NE	38	5		
1992–93	Preston NE	39	7		
1993–94	WBA	21	3		
1994–95	WBA	38	10		
1995–96	WBA	26	4		
1995–96	Notts Co	6	0	6	0
1996–97	WBA	5	0	90	17
1996–97	Preston NE	27	8		
1997–98	Preston NE	37	14		
1998–99	Preston NE	0	0	155	35
1998–99	Grimsby T	27	3		
1999–2000	Grimsby T	34	12	61	15
2000–01	Wigan Ath	30	5		
2001–02	Wigan Ath	16	3	46	8

BRANNAN, Ged (M) 396 35
H: 6 0 W: 13 09 b.Liverpool 15-1-72
Source: Trainee.

1990–91	Tranmere R	18	1		
1991–92	Tranmere R	18	1		
1992–93	Tranmere R	38	1		
1993–94	Tranmere R	45	9		
1994–95	Tranmere R	41	2		
1995–96	Tranmere R	44	0		
1996–97	Tranmere R	34	6	238	20
1996–97	Manchester C	11	1		
1997–98	Manchester C	32	3		
1998–99	Manchester C	0	0	43	4
1998–99	Norwich C	11	1	11	1
1998–99	Motherwell	25	5		
1999–2000	Motherwell	33	5	58	10
2000–01	Wigan Ath	13	0		
2001–02	Wigan Ath	33	0	46	0

BUKRAN, Gabby‡ (M) 74 4
H: 5 11 W: 12 01 b.Eger 16-11-75
Source: Xerxes. Honours: Hungary 1 full cap.
1999–2000	Walsall	37	2		
2000–01	Walsall	36	2	73	4
2001–02	Wigan Ath	1	0	1	0

DALGLISH, Paul* (F) 101 5
H: 5 9 W: 10 00 b.Glasgow 18-2-77
Honours: Scotland Under-21.

1995–96	Celtic	0	0		
1996–97	Liverpool	0	0		
1997–98	Liverpool	0	0		
1997–98	Newcastle U	0	0		
1997–98	Bury	12	0	12	0
1998–99	Newcastle U	11	1	11	1
1998–99	Norwich C	5	0		
1999–2000	Norwich C	31	2		
2000–01	Norwich C	7	0	43	2
2001–02	Wigan Ath	6	0		
2001–02	Wigan Ath	29	2	35	2

DE VOS, Jason (D) 157 12
H: 6 4 W: 13 10 b.Ontario 2-1-74
Source: Montreal Impact. Honours: Canada 38 full caps.

1996–97	Darlington	8	0		
1997–98	Darlington	24	3		
1998–99	Darlington	12	2	44	5
1998–99	Dundee U	25	0		
1999–2000	Dundee U	35	2		
2000–01	Dundee U	33	0	93	2
2001–02	Wigan Ath	20	5	20	5

DE ZEEUW, Arjan# (D) 366 18
H: 6 1 W: 13 10 b.Castricum 16-4-70
Source: Vitesse 22.

1992–93	Telstar	30	1		
1993–94	Telstar	31	2		
1994–95	Telstar	29	1		
1995–96	Telstar	12	1	102	5
1995–96	Barnsley	31	1		
1996–97	Barnsley	43	2		
1997–98	Barnsley	26	0		
1998–99	Barnsley	38	4	138	7
1999–2000	Wigan Ath	39	3		
2000–01	Wigan Ath	45	1		
2001–02	Wigan Ath	42	2	126	6

DICKSON, Hugh‡ (D) 6 0
H: 6 0 W: 12 00 b.Down Patrick 28-8-81
Honours: Northern Ireland Under-21.
1999–2000	Glentoran	5	0	5	0
2000–01	Wigan Ath	1	0		
2001–02	Wigan Ath	0	0	1	0

DINNING, Tony (M) 264 36
H: 5 11 W: 12 00 b.Wallsend 12-4-75
Source: Trainee.

1993–94	Newcastle U	0	0		
1994–95	Stockport Co	40	1		
1995–96	Stockport Co	10	1		
1996–97	Stockport Co	20	2		
1997–98	Stockport Co	30	4		
1998–99	Stockport Co	41	5		
1999–2000	Stockport Co	44	12		
2000–01	Stockport Co	6	0	191	25
2000–01	Wolverhampton W	31	6		
2001–02	Wolverhampton W	4	0	35	6
2001–02	Wigan Ath	33	5	33	5
2001–02	Stoke C	5	0	5	0

ELLINGTON, Nathan (F) 119 37
H: 5 10 W: 13 06 b.Bradford 2-7-81
Source: Walton & Hersham. Honours:

1998–99	Bristol R	10	1		
1999–2000	Bristol R	37	4		
2000–01	Bristol R	42	15		
2001–02	Bristol R	27	15	116	35
2001–02	Wigan Ath	3	2	3	2

FILAN, John (G) 252 0
H: 6 2 W: 14 11 b.Sydney 8-2-70
Honours: Australia 2 full caps.

1989–90	St George	26	0		
1990–91	St George	26	0	52	0
1991–92	Wollongong	23	0		
	Wolves				
1992–93	Wollongong	6	0	29	0
	Wolves				
1992–93	Cambridge U	6	0		
1993–94	Cambridge U	46	0		
1994–95	Cambridge U	16	0	68	0
1994–95	Nottingham F	0	0		
1994–95	Coventry C	2	0		
1995–96	Coventry C	13	0		
1996–97	Coventry C	1	0	16	0
1997–98	Blackburn R	7	0		
1998–99	Blackburn R	26	0		
1999–2000	Blackburn R	16	0		
2000–01	Blackburn R	13	0		
2001–02	Blackburn R	0	0	62	0
2001–02	Wigan Ath	25	0	25	0

GREEN, Scott (D) 402 33
H: 5 10 W: 13 02 b.Walsall 15-1-70
Source: Trainee.

1988–89	Derby Co	0	0		
1989–90	Derby Co	0	0		
1989–90	Bolton W	5	2		
1990–91	Bolton W	41	6		
1991–92	Bolton W	37	2		
1992–93	Bolton W	41	6		
1993–94	Bolton W	22	4		
1994–95	Bolton W	31	1		
1995–96	Bolton W	31	3		
1996–97	Bolton W	12	1	220	25
1997–98	Wigan Ath	38	1		
1998–99	Wigan Ath	37	0		
1999–2000	Wigan Ath	33	2		
2000–01	Wigan Ath	35	2		
2001–02	Wigan Ath	39	3	182	8

JACKSON, Matt (D) 363 10
H: 6 0 W: 14 00 b.Leeds 19-10-71
Source: School. Honours: England Schools, Under-21.

1990–91	Luton T	0	0		
1990–91	Preston NE	4	0	4	0
1991–92	Luton T	9	0	9	0
1991–92	Everton	30	1		
1992–93	Everton	27	3		
1993–94	Everton	38	0		
1994–95	Everton	29	0		
1995–96	Everton	14	0		
1995–96	Charlton Ath	8	0	8	0
1996–97	Everton	0	0	138	4
1996–97	QPR	7	0	7	0
1996–97	Birmingham C	10	0	10	0
1996–97	Norwich C	19	2		
1997–98	Norwich C	41	3		
1998–99	Norwich C	37	1		
1999–2000	Norwich C	38	0		
2000–01	Norwich C	26	0		
2001–02	Norwich C	0	0	161	6
2001–02	Wigan Ath	26	0	26	0

JARRETT, Jason (M) 70 4
H: 6 0 W: 13 03 b.Bury 14-9-79
Source: Trainee.

1998–99	Blackpool	2	0		
1999–2000	Blackpool	0	0	2	0
1999–2000	Wrexham	1	0	1	0
2000–01	Bury	25	2		
2001–02	Bury	37	2	62	4
2001–02	Wigan Ath	5	0	5	0

JOHNSON, Ian* (M)   0   0
H: 5 11   W: 12 05   b.Liverpool 7-3-83
Source: Trainee.

Season	Club				
2001–02	Wigan Ath	0	0		

KAY, Ben* (M)   0   0
H: 5 10   W: 11 07   b.Wigan 22-9-82
Source: Trainee.

Season	Club				
2001–02	Wigan Ath	0	0		

KENNEDY, Peter (M)   168   18
H: 5 10   W: 11 12   b.Lisburn 10-9-73
Source: Portadown. *Honours:* Northern Ireland B, 13 full caps.

Season	Club				
1996–97	Notts Co	22	0	22	0
1997–98	Watford	34	11		
1998–99	Watford	46	6		
1999–2000	Watford	18	1		
2000–01	Watford	17	0	115	18
2001–02	Wigan Ath	31	0	31	0

KERR, Stewart (G)   40   0
H: 6 2   W: 14 08   b.Bellshill 13-11-74
Source: Celtic BC. *Honours:* Scotland Under-21.

Season	Club				
1993–94	Celtic	0	0		
1994–95	Celtic	0	0		
1994–95	*Brighton & HA*	2	0	2	0
1995–96	Celtic	0	0		
1996–97	Celtic	26	0		
1997–98	Celtic	0	0		
1998–99	Celtic	4	0		
1999–2000	Celtic	0	0		
2000–01	Celtic	0	0		
2001–02	Celtic	0	0	30	0
2001–02	Wigan Ath	8	0	8	0

KILFORD, Ian* (M)   222   32
H: 5 10   W: 11 06   b.Bristol 6-10-73
Source: Trainee.

Season	Club				
1991–92	Nottingham F	0	0		
1992–93	Nottingham F	0	0		
1993–94	Nottingham F	1	0	1	0
1993–94	*Wigan Ath*	8	3		
1994–95	Wigan Ath	35	5		
1995–96	Wigan Ath	25	3		
1996–97	Wigan Ath	35	8		
1997–98	Wigan Ath	30	10		
1998–99	Wigan Ath	23	0		
1999–2000	Wigan Ath	21	1		
2000–01	Wigan Ath	24	2		
2001–02	Wigan Ath	20	0	221	32

LIDDELL, Andy (F)   338   79
H: 5 8   W: 11 13   b.Leeds 28-6-73
Source: Trainee. *Honours:* Scotland Under-21.

Season	Club				
1990–91	Barnsley	0	0		
1991–92	Barnsley	0	0		
1992–93	Barnsley	21	2		
1993–94	Barnsley	22	1		
1994–95	Barnsley	39	13		
1995–96	Barnsley	43	9		
1996–97	Barnsley	38	8		
1997–98	Barnsley	26	1		
1998–99	Barnsley	8	0	198	34
1998–99	Wigan Ath	28	10		
1999–2000	Wigan Ath	41	8		
2000–01	Wigan Ath	37	9		
2001–02	Wigan Ath	34	18	140	45

McCULLOCH, Lee (F)   166   31
H: 6 1   W: 13 10   b.Bellshill 14-5-78
Source: Cumbernauld U. *Honours:* Scotland Under-18, Under-21.

Season	Club				
1995–96	Motherwell	1	0		
1996–97	Motherwell	15	0		
1997–98	Motherwell	25	2		
1998–99	Motherwell	26	3		
1999–2000	Motherwell	29	9		
2000–01	Motherwell	26	8	122	22
2000–01	Wigan Ath	10	3		
2001–02	Wigan Ath	34	6	44	9

McGIBBON, Pat* (D)   180   11
H: 6 2   W: 14 00   b.Lurgan 6-9-73
Source: Portadown. *Honours:* Northern Ireland Schools, Under-21, B, 7 full caps.

Season	Club				
1992–93	Manchester U	0	0		
1993–94	Manchester U	0	0		
1994–95	Manchester U	0	0		
1995–96	Manchester U	0	0		
1996–97	Manchester U	0	0		
1996–97	*Swansea C*	1	0	1	0
1996–97	*Wigan Ath*	10	1		
1997–98	Wigan Ath	35	0		
1998–99	Wigan Ath	36	5		
1999–2000	Wigan Ath	34	2		
2000–01	Wigan Ath	40	2		
2001–02	Wigan Ath	18	1	173	11
2001–02	*Scunthorpe U*	6	0	6	0

McMILLAN, Steve (D)   187   6
H: 5 8   W: 12 00   b.Edinburgh 19-1-76
Source: Troon Juniors. *Honours:* Scotland Under-21.

Season	Club				
1993–94	Motherwell	1	0		
1994–95	Motherwell	3	0		
1995–96	Motherwell	12	0		
1996–97	Motherwell	16	0		
1997–98	Motherwell	34	1		
1998–99	Motherwell	30	2		
1999–2000	Motherwell	31	3		
2000–01	Motherwell	25	0	152	6
2000–01	Wigan Ath	6	0		
2001–02	Wigan Ath	29	0	35	0

MITCHELL, Paul (D)   35   0
H: 5 9   W: 12 03   b.Manchester 26-8-81
Source: Trainee.

Season	Club				
2000–01	Wigan Ath	1	0		
2000–01	*Halifax T*	11	0	11	0
2001–02	Wigan Ath	23	0	24	0

NOLAN, Ian* (D)   282   5
H: 6 0   W: 12 01   b.Liverpool 9-7-70
Source: Preston NE Trainee, Northwich Vic, Marine. *Honours:* Northern Ireland 18 full caps.

Season	Club				
1991–92	Tranmere R	34	1		
1992–93	Tranmere R	14	0		
1993–94	Tranmere R	40	0	88	1
1994–95	Sheffield W	42	3		
1995–96	Sheffield W	29	0		
1996–97	Sheffield W	38	1		
1997–98	Sheffield W	27	0		
1998–99	Sheffield W	0	0		
1999–2000	Sheffield W	29	0	165	4
2000–01	Bradford C	21	0	21	0
2001–02	Wigan Ath	8	0	8	0

PENDLEBURY, Ian (D)   4   0
b.Bolton 3-9-83
Source: Trainee.

Season	Club				
2001–02	Wigan Ath	4	0	4	0

ROBERTS, Neil (F)   141   28
H: 5 10   W: 13 08   b.Wrexham 7-4-78
Source: Trainee. *Honours:* Wales Youth, Under-21, B, 1 full cap.

Season	Club				
1996–97	Wrexham	0	0		
1997–98	Wrexham	34	8		
1998–99	Wrexham	22	3		
1999–2000	Wrexham	19	6	75	17
1999–2000	Wigan Ath	9	1		
2000–01	Wigan Ath	34	6		
2001–02	*Hull C*	6	0	6	0
2001–02	Wigan Ath	17	4	60	11

SANTUS, Paul§ (M)   1   0
b.Billinge 8-9-83
Source: Trainee.

Season	Club				
2001–02	Wigan Ath	1	0	1	0

STILLIE, Derek* (G)   67   0
H: 6 0   W: 12 07   b.Cumnock 3-12-73
Source: Notts Co. *Honours:* Scotland Under-21.

Season	Club				
1991–92	Aberdeen	0	0		
1992–93	Aberdeen	0	0		
1993–94	Aberdeen	5	0		
1994–95	Aberdeen	0	0		
1995–96	Aberdeen	0	0		
1996–97	Aberdeen	8	0		
1997–98	Aberdeen	2	0		
1998–99	Aberdeen	8	0	23	0
1999–2000	Wigan Ath	13	0		
2000–01	Wigan Ath	18	0		
2001–02	Wigan Ath	13	0	44	0

TEALE, Gary (F)   167   22
H: 5 9   W: 12 04   b.Glasgow 21-7-78
Source: Ayr U.

Season	Club				
1996–97	Clydebank	33	6		
1997–98	Clydebank	27	6	60	12
1998–99	Ayr U	23	4		
1999–2000	Ayr U	32	0		
2000–01	Ayr U	29	5	84	9
2001–02	Wigan Ath	23	1	23	1

TRAYNOR, Greg§ (M)   1   0
b.Salford 17-10-84
Source: Scholar.

Season	Club				
2001–02	Wigan Ath	1	0	1	0

Trainees
Charnock, Kieran J; Clarke, Alistair A; Clegg, Michael J; Ishmael, Martin J; Lee, Paul K; Pendlebury, Ian D; Santus, Paul G

Scholars
Baines, Leighton J; Jones, Christopher; Kay, Robert P; Lynch, Christopher; Moore, David L; Roberts, Joseph; Thompson, Jonathan; Traynor, Greg

WIMBLEDON

AGYEMANG, Patrick (F)   74   8
H: 6 1   W: 12 00   b.Walthamstow 29-9-80
Source: Trainee.

Season	Club				
1998–99	Wimbledon	0	0		
1999–2000	Wimbledon	0	0		
1999–2000	*Brentford*	12	0	12	0
2000–01	Wimbledon	29	4		
2001–02	Wimbledon	33	4	62	8

AINSWORTH, Gareth* (M)   258   65
H: 5 6   W: 13 00   b.Blackburn 10-5-73
Source: Blackburn R Trainee.

Season	Club				
1991–92	Preston NE	5	0		
1992–93	Cambridge U	4	1	4	1
1992–93	Preston NE	2	0		
1993–94	Preston NE	38	11		
1994–95	Preston NE	16	1		
1995–96	Preston NE	2	0		
1995–96	Lincoln C	31	12		
1996–97	Lincoln C	46	22		
1997–98	Lincoln C	6	3	83	37
1997–98	Port Vale	40	5		
1998–99	Port Vale	15	5	55	10
1998–99	Wimbledon	8	0		
1999–2000	Wimbledon	2	2		
2000–01	Wimbledon	12	2		
2001–02	Wimbledon	2	0	24	4
2001–02	*Preston NE*	5	1	92	13

ANDERSEN, Trond (M)   213   9
H: 6 0   W: 11 06   b.Kristiansund 6-1-75
Source: Clausenengen. *Honours:* Norway 18 full caps.

Season	Club				
1995	Molde	18	1		
1996	Molde	21	0		
1997	Molde	25	0		
1998	Molde	24	2		
1999	Molde	17	1	105	4
1999–2000	Wimbledon	36	0		
2000–01	Wimbledon	42	5		
2001–02	Wimbledon	30	0	108	5

ARDLEY, Neal* (M)   245   18
H: 5 11   W: 11 09   b.Epsom 1-9-72
Source: Trainee. *Honours:* England Under-21.

Season	Club				
1990–91	Wimbledon	1	0		
1991–92	Wimbledon	8	0		
1992–93	Wimbledon	26	4		
1993–94	Wimbledon	16	1		
1994–95	Wimbledon	14	1		
1995–96	Wimbledon	6	0		
1996–97	Wimbledon	34	2		
1997–98	Wimbledon	34	2		
1998–99	Wimbledon	23	0		
1999–2000	Wimbledon	17	2		
2000–01	Wimbledon	37	3		
2001–02	Wimbledon	29	3	245	18

BERNI, Tommaso (G)   0   0
H: 6 0   W: 11 04   b.Florence 6-3-83
Source: Internazionale.

Season	Club				
2000–01	Wimbledon	0	0		
2001–02	Wimbledon	0	0		

BLACKWELL, Dean* (D)   212   1
H: 6 1   W: 12 10   b.Camden 5-12-69
Source: Trainee. *Honours:* England Under-21.

Season	Club				
1988–89	Wimbledon	0	0		
1989–90	Wimbledon	3	0		
1989–90	*Plymouth Arg*	7	0	7	0
1990–91	Wimbledon	35	0		
1991–92	Wimbledon	4	1		
1992–93	Wimbledon	24	0		
1993–94	Wimbledon	18	0		
1994–95	Wimbledon	0	0		
1995–96	Wimbledon	8	0		
1996–97	Wimbledon	27	0		
1997–98	Wimbledon	35	0		
1998–99	Wimbledon	28	0		
1999–2000	Wimbledon	17	0		
2000–01	Wimbledon	6	0		
2001–02	Wimbledon	0	0	205	1

BOLGER, Gavin* (M)   0   0
b.Dublin 7-8-82

Season	Club				
2000–01	Wimbledon	0	0		
2001–02	Wimbledon	0	0		

BURWOOD, John (D)   0   0
H: 5 10   W: 11 00   b.Newcastle 18-9-84
Source: Scholar.

Season	Club				
2001–02	Wimbledon	0	0		

BYRNE, Des (D)   18   0
H: 6 1   W: 12 07   b.Dublin 10-4-81
Source: Trainee.

Season	Club				
1998–99	Stockport Co	2	0	2	0
1999–2000	Sr Patrick's Ath	11	0	11	0

2000–01 Wimbledon 0 0
2001–02 *Cambridge U* 4 0 **4 0**
2001–02 Wimbledon 1 0 **1 0**

COATES, Craig* (F) **0 0**
H: 5 7 W: 10 11 b.Dryburn 26-10-82
Source: Trainee.
1999–2000 Manchester U 0 0
2000–01 Manchester U 0 0
2001–02 Wimbledon 0 0

CONNOLLY, David (F) **150 70**
H: 5 9 W: 10 09 b.Willesden 6-6-77
Source: Trainee. *Honours:* Eire 34 full caps, 8 goals.
1994–95 Watford 2 0
1995–96 Watford 11 8
1996–97 Watford 13 2 **26 10**
1997–98 Feyenoord 10 2
1998–99 Wolverhampton W 32 6 **32 6**
1999–2000 Excelsior 32 29 **32 29**
2000–01 Feyenoord 15 5 **25 7**
2001–02 Wimbledon 35 18 **35 18**

CUNNINGHAM, Kenny (D) **386 1**
H: 5 11 W: 11 04 b.Dublin 28-6-71
Source: Tolka R. *Honours:* Eire Under-21, B, 40 full caps.
1989–90 Millwall 5 0
1990–91 Millwall 23 0
1991–92 Millwall 17 0
1992–93 Millwall 37 0
1993–94 Millwall 39 1
1994–95 Millwall 15 0 **136 1**
1994–95 Wimbledon 28 0
1995–96 Wimbledon 33 0
1996–97 Wimbledon 36 0
1997–98 Wimbledon 32 0
1998–99 Wimbledon 35 0
1999–2000 Wimbledon 37 0
2000–01 Wimbledon 15 0
2001–02 Wimbledon 34 0 **250 0**

DARLINGTON, Jermaine (D) **100 2**
H: 5 9 W: 12 09 b.Hackney 11-4-74
Source: Aylesbury U.
1998–99 QPR 4 0
1999–2000 QPR 34 2
2000–01 QPR 33 0 **71 2**
2001–02 Wimbledon 29 0 **29 0**

DAVIS, Kelvin (G) **181 0**
H: 6 1 W: 11 04 b.Bedford 29-9-76
Source: Trainee. *Honours:* England Youth, Under-21.
1993–94 Luton T 1 0
1994–95 Luton T 9 0
1994–95 *Torquay U* 2 0 **2 0**
1995–96 Luton T 6 0
1996–97 Luton T 0 0
1997–98 Luton T 32 0
1997–98 *Hartlepool U* 2 0 **2 0**
1998–99 Luton T 44 0 **92 0**
1999–2000 Wimbledon 0 0
2000–01 Wimbledon 45 0
2001–02 Wimbledon 40 0 **85 0**

FEUER, Ian* (G) **167 0**
H: 6 6 W: 15 06 b.Las Vegas 20-5-71
Source: Los Angeles Salsa. *Honours:* USA full caps.
1993–94 West Ham U 0 0
1994–95 West Ham U 0 0
1994–95 *Peterborough U* 16 0 **16 0**
1995–96 West Ham U 0 0
1995–96 Luton T 38 0
1996–97 Luton T 46 0
1997–98 Luton T 13 0 **97 0**
1998 New England Rev 26 0 **26 0**
1999 Colorado Rapids 19 0 **19 0**
1999–2000 Cardiff C 0 0
1999–2000 West Ham U 3 0 **3 0**
2000–01 Wimbledon 0 0
2001–02 Wimbledon 4 0 **4 0**
2001–02 *Derby Co* 2 0 **2 0**

FRANCIS, Damien (M) **63 9**
H: 6 0 W: 10 10 b.Wandsworth 27-2-79
Source: Trainee.
1996–97 Wimbledon 0 0
1997–98 Wimbledon 2 0
1998–99 Wimbledon 0 0
1999–2000 Wimbledon 9 0
2000–01 Wimbledon 29 8
2001–02 Wimbledon 23 1 **63 9**

GIER, Robert (D) **17 0**
H: 5 10 W: 11 07 b.Ascot 6-1-80
Source: Trainee.
1998–99 Wimbledon 0 0
1999–2000 Wimbledon 0 0
2000–01 Wimbledon 14 0
2001–02 Wimbledon 3 0 **17 0**

GORE, Shane (G) **1 0**
H: 5 10 W: 11 02 b.Ashford 28-10-81
Source: Scholar.
2001–02 Wimbledon 1 0 **1 0**

GRAY, Wayne (F) **46 8**
H: 5 10 W: 11 07 b.South London 7-11-80
Source: Trainee.
1998–99 Wimbledon 0 0
1999–2000 Wimbledon 1 0
1999–2000 *Swindon T* 12 2 **12 2**
2000–01 Wimbledon 11 0
2000–01 *Port Vale* 3 0 **3 0**
2001–02 Wimbledon 0 0 **12 0**
2001–02 *Leyton Orient* 15 5 **15 5**
2001–02 *Brighton & HA* 4 1 **4 1**

HAARA, Heikki (D) **0 0**
H: 6 1 W: 11 04 b.Lahti 20-11-82
2000–01 Wimbledon 0 0
2001–02 Wimbledon 0 0

HARDING, Ben (M) **0 0**
H: 5 10 W: 11 02 b.Carshalton 6-9-84
Source: Scholar. *Honours:* England Youth.
2001–02 Wimbledon 0 0

HAWKINS, Peter (D) **73 0**
H: 6 0 W: 11 04 b.Maidstone 19-9-78
Source: Trainee.
1996–97 Wimbledon 0 0
1997–98 Wimbledon 0 0
1998–99 Wimbledon 0 0
1999–2000 Wimbledon 0 0
1999–2000 *York C* 14 0 **14 0**
2000–01 Wimbledon 30 0
2001–02 Wimbledon 29 0 **59 0**

HEALD, Paul* (G) **213 0**
H: 6 2 W: 12 05 b.Wath-on-Dearne 20-9-68
Source: Trainee.
1987–88 Sheffield U 0 0
1988–89 Sheffield U 0 0
1988–89 Leyton Orient 28 0
1989–90 Leyton Orient 37 0
1990–91 Leyton Orient 38 0
1991–92 Leyton Orient 2 0
1991–92 *Coventry C* 2 0 **2 0**
1992–93 Leyton Orient 26 0
1992–93 *Crystal Palace* 2 0
1993–94 Leyton Orient 0 0
1993–94 *Swindon T* 2 0 **2 0**
1994–95 Leyton Orient 45 0 **176 0**
1995–96 Wimbledon 18 0
1996–97 Wimbledon 2 0
1997–98 Wimbledon 0 0
1998–99 Wimbledon 0 0
1999–2000 Wimbledon 1 0
2000–01 Wimbledon 3 0
2001–02 Wimbledon 4 0 **28 0**
2001–02 *Sheffield W* 5 0 **5 0**

HERZIG, Denny* (M) **0 0**
b.Pobneck 13-11-84
2001–02 Wimbledon 0 0

HERZIG, Nico (M) **0 0**
H: 5 10 W: 11 00 b.Pobneck 10-12-83
Source: Carl Zeiss Jena.
2001–02 Wimbledon 0 0

HOLLOWAY, Darren (D) **130 0**
H: 6 0 W: 12 00 b.Crook 3-10-77
Source: Trainee. *Honours:* England Under-21.
1995–96 Sunderland 0 0
1996–97 Sunderland 0 0
1997–98 Sunderland 32 0
1997–98 *Carlisle U* 5 0 **5 0**
1998–99 Sunderland 6 0
1999–2000 Sunderland 15 0
1999–2000 *Bolton W* 4 0 **4 0**
2000–01 Sunderland 5 0 **58 0**
2000–01 Wimbledon 31 0
2001–02 Wimbledon 32 0 **63 0**

HUGHES, Michael (M) **310 28**
H: 5 6 W: 10 08 b.Larne 2-8-71
Source: Carrick R. *Honours:* Northern Ireland Schools, Youth, Under-21, Under-23, 63 full caps, 5 goals.
1988–89 Manchester C 1 0
1989–90 Manchester C 0 0
1990–91 Manchester C 1 0
1991–92 Manchester C 26 1 **26 1**
1992–93 Strasbourg 36 2
1993–94 Strasbourg 34 7
1994–95 Strasbourg 13 0 **83 9**
1994–95 West Ham U 17 2
1995–96 West Ham U 28 0
1996–97 West Ham U 33 3
1997–98 West Ham U 5 0 **83 5**
1997–98 Wimbledon 29 4
1998–99 Wimbledon 30 2

1999–2000 Wimbledon 20 2
2000–01 Wimbledon 10 1
2001–02 Wimbledon 26 4 **115 13**
2001–02 *Birmingham C* 3 0 **3 0**

JENKINS, Neil* (M) **0 0**
b.Carshalton 6-1-82
Source: Scholar. *Honours:* England Youth, Under-20.
2000–01 Wimbledon 0 0
2001–02 Wimbledon 0 0

JUPP, Duncan (D) **135 2**
H: 6 0 W: 12 04 b.Guildford 25-1-75
Source: Trainee. *Honours:* Scotland Under-21.
1992–93 Fulham 3 0
1993–94 Fulham 30 0
1994–95 Fulham 36 2
1995–96 Fulham 36 0 **105 2**
1996–97 Wimbledon 6 0
1997–98 Wimbledon 3 0
1998–99 Wimbledon 6 0
1999–2000 Wimbledon 9 0
2000–01 Wimbledon 4 0
2001–02 Wimbledon 2 0 **30 0**

KARLSSON, Par (M) **87 6**
H: 5 8 W: 10 11 b.Gothenburg 29-5-78
Source: Karlskoga.
1997 IFK Gothenburg 10 3
1998 IFK Gothenburg 13 0
1999 IFK Gothenburg 25 1
2000 IFK Gothenburg 16 2 **64 6**
2000–01 Wimbledon 16 0
2001–02 Wimbledon 7 0 **23 0**

KIMBLE, Alan* (D) **524 24**
H: 5 10 W: 12 04 b.Poole 6-8-66
1984–85 Charlton Ath 6 0
1985–86 Charlton Ath 0 0 **6 0**
1985–86 *Exeter C* 1 0 **1 0**
1986–87 Cambridge U 35 0
1987–88 Cambridge U 41 2
1988–89 Cambridge U 45 6
1989–90 Cambridge U 44 8
1990–91 Cambridge U 43 4
1991–92 Cambridge U 45 0
1992–93 Cambridge U 46 4 **299 24**
1993–94 Wimbledon 14 0
1994–95 Wimbledon 26 0
1995–96 Wimbledon 31 0
1996–97 Wimbledon 31 0
1997–98 Wimbledon 25 0
1998–99 Wimbledon 26 0
1999–2000 Wimbledon 28 0
2000–01 Wimbledon 25 0
2001–02 Wimbledon 9 0 **215 0**
2001–02 *Peterborough U* 3 0 **3 0**

LEIGERTWOOD, Mikele (D) **9 0**
H: 6 1 W: 11 04 b.Enfield 12-11-82
Source: Scholar.
2001–02 Wimbledon 1 0 **1 0**
2001–02 *Leyton Orient* 8 0 **8 0**

LUND, Andreas (F) **108 57**
H: 6 1 W: 11 07 b.Kristiansund 7-5-75
Honours: Norway 8 full caps, 4 goals.
1995 Start 22 9
1996 Start 15 4 **37 13**
1996 Molde 6 3
1997 Molde 4 2
1998 Molde 25 16
1999 Molde 24 21 **59 42**
1999–2000 Wimbledon 12 2
2000–01 Wimbledon 0 0
2001–02 Wimbledon 0 0 **12 2**

McANUFF, Joel (F) **38 4**
H: 5 11 W: 11 04 b.Edmonton 9-11-81
Source: Scholar. *Honours:* Jamaica 1 full cap.
2000–01 Wimbledon 0 0
2001–02 Wimbledon 38 4 **38 4**

MENSING, Simon‡ (M) **0 0**
H: 5 10 W: 11 06 b.Woifenbuttel 27-6-82
1999–2000 Wimbledon 0 0
2000–01 Wimbledon 0 0
2001–02 Wimbledon 0 0

MILD, Hakan (M) **250 19**
H: 5 11 W: 11 02 b.Trollhattan 14-6-71
Honours: Sweden 58 caps, 6 goals.
1989 IFK Gothenburg 0 0
1990 IFK Gothenburg 19 0
1991 IFK Gothenburg 28 2
1992 IFK Gothenburg 27 2
1993 IFK Gothenburg 21 5
1993–94 Servette 11 1
1994–95 Servette 10 0 **21 1**
1995 IFK Gothenburg 9 2
1996 IFK Gothenburg 12 3
1996–97 Real Sociedad 25 1

1997–98	Real Sociedad	25 0	**50**	**1**
1998	IFK Gothenburg	10 1		
1999	IFK Gothenburg	21 0		
2000	IFK Gothenburg	23 2	**170**	**17**
2001–02	Wimbledon	9 0	**9**	**0**

MORGAN, Lionel (F)   **16**   **1**
H: 5 11 W: 11 00 b.Tottenham 17-2-83
Source: Scholar. *Honours:* England Youth.

2000–01	Wimbledon	5 0		
2001–02	Wimbledon	11 1	**16**	**1**

NOWLAND, Adam (F)   **76**   **5**
H: 5 11 W: 11 06 b.Preston 6-7-81
Source: Trainee.

1997–98	Blackpool	1 0		
1998–99	Blackpool	37 2		
1999–2000	Blackpool	21 3		
2000–01	Blackpool	10 0	**69**	**5**
2001–02	Wimbledon	7 0	**7**	**0**

OKIKIOLU, Samuel* (D)   **0**   **0**
b.Hackney 15-1-82
Source: Scholar.

2001–02	Wimbledon	0	0

OWUSU, Ansah* (M)   **21**   **0**
H: 5 11 W: 11 02 b.Hackney 22-11-79
Source: Trainee.

1998–99	Wimbledon	0 0		
1999–2000	Wimbledon	0 0		
2000–01	Wimbledon	4 0		
2000–01	*Bristol R*	17 0	**17**	**0**
2001–02	Wimbledon	0 0	**4**	**0**

REMY, Ellis* (M)   **0**   **0**
b.London 13-2-84

2001–02	Wimbledon	0	0

REO-COKER, Nigel (M)   **1**   **0**
H: 5 8 W: 10 05 b.Southwark 14-5-84
Source: Scholar.

2001–02	Wimbledon	1 0	**1**	**0**

ROBERTS, Andy* (M)   **352**   **13**
H: 5 10 W: 13 00 b.Dartford 20-3-74
Source: Trainee. *Honours:* England Under-21.

1991–92	Millwall	7 0		
1992–93	Millwall	45 0		
1993–94	Millwall	42 2		
1994–95	Millwall	44 3	**138**	**5**
1995–96	Crystal Palace	38 0		
1996–97	Crystal Palace	45 2		
1997–98	Crystal Palace	25 0	**108**	**2**
1997–98	Wimbledon	12 1		
1998–99	Wimbledon	28 2		
1999–2000	Wimbledon	36 0		
2000–01	Wimbledon	27 2		
2001–02	Wimbledon	18 1	**101**	**6**
2001–02	*Norwich C*	5 0	**5**	**0**

ROBINSON, Paul (F)   **49**   **3**
H: 5 11 W: 12 00 b.Sunderland 20-11-78
Source: Trainee.

1995–96	Darlington	4 0		
1996–97	Darlington	3 0		
1997–98	Darlington	19 3	**26**	**3**
1997–98	Newcastle U	0 0		
1998–99	Newcastle U	0 0		
1999–2000	Newcastle U	11 0	**11**	**0**
2000–01	Wimbledon	2 0		
2000–01	*Burnley*	4 0	**4**	**0**
2001–02	Wimbledon	1 0	**3**	**0**
2001–02	*Grimsby T*	5 0	**5**	**0**

SELLEY, Ian (M)   **66**   **0**
H: 5 10 W: 10 11 b.Chertsey 14-6-74
Source: Trainee. *Honours:* England Youth, Under-21.

1992–93	Arsenal	9 0		
1993–94	Arsenal	18 0		
1994–95	Arsenal	13 0		
1995–96	Arsenal	0 0		
1996–97	Arsenal	1 0		
1996–97	*Southend U*	4 0		
1997–98	Arsenal	0 0	**41**	**0**
1997–98	Fulham	3 0		
1998–99	Fulham	0 0		
1999–2000	Fulham	0 0	**3**	**0**
2000–01	Wimbledon	4 0		
2001–02	Wimbledon	0 0	**4**	**0**
2001–02	*Southend U*	14 0	**18**	**0**

SHIPPERLEY, Neil (F)   **309**   **80**
H: 6 0 W: 13 11 b.Chatham 30-10-74
Source: Trainee. *Honours:* England Under-21.

1992–93	Chelsea	3 1		
1993–94	Chelsea	24 4		
1994–95	Chelsea	10 2	**37**	**7**
1994–95	*Watford*	6 1	**6**	**1**
1994–95	Southampton	19 4		
1995–96	Southampton	37 7		
1996–97	Southampton	10 1	**66**	**12**
1996–97	Crystal Palace	32 12		
1997–98	Crystal Palace	26 7		
1998–99	Crystal Palace	3 1	**61**	**20**
1998–99	Nottingham F	20 1	**20**	**1**
1999–2000	Barnsley	39 13		
2000–01	Barnsley	39 14	**78**	**27**
2001–02	Wimbledon	41 12	**41**	**12**

TAPP, Alex (M)   **0**   **0**
H: 5 8 W: 11 09 b.Redhill 7-6-82
Source: Trainee.

1999–2000	Wimbledon	0	0
2000–01	Wimbledon	0	0
2001–02	Wimbledon	0	0

THOMAS, Michael* (M)   **308**   **33**
H: 5 9 W: 12 06 b.Lambeth 24-8-67
Source: Apprentice. *Honours:* England Schools, Youth, Under-21, B, 2 full caps.

1985–86	Arsenal	0 0		
1986–87	Arsenal	12 0		
1986–87	*Portsmouth*	3 0	**3**	**0**
1987–88	Arsenal	37 9		
1988–89	Arsenal	37 7		
1989–90	Arsenal	36 5		
1990–91	Arsenal	32 2		
1991–92	Arsenal	10 1	**163**	**24**
1991–92	Liverpool	17 3		
1992–93	Liverpool	8 1		
1993–94	Liverpool	7 0		
1994–95	Liverpool	23 0		
1995–96	Liverpool	27 1		
1996–97	Liverpool	31 3		
1997–98	Liverpool	11 1		
1997–98	*Middlesbrough*	10 0	**10**	**0**
1998–99	Liverpool	0 0		
1999–2000	Liverpool	0 0	**124**	**9**
2000–01	Wimbledon	8 0		
2001–02	Wimbledon	0 0	**8**	**0**

WAEHLER, Kjetil (M)   **88**   **6**
H: 5 10 W: 11 04 b.Oslo 16-3-76

1992	Lyn	8 0		
1993	Lyn	20 2		
1994	Lyn	0 0		
1995	Lyn	0 0		
1996	Lyn	12 0		
1997	Lyn	26 3		
1998	Lyn	0 0		
1999	Lyn	22 1	**88**	**6**
1999–2000	Wimbledon	0 0		
2000–01	Wimbledon	0 0		
2001–02	Wimbledon	0 0		

WILLIAMS, Mark (D)   **339**   **22**
H: 6 0 W: 12 04 b.Stalybridge 28-9-70
Source: Newtown. *Honours:* Northern Ireland B, 19 full caps, 1 goal.

1991–92	Shrewsbury T	3 0		
1992–93	Shrewsbury T	28 1		
1993–94	Shrewsbury T	36 1		
1994–95	Shrewsbury T	35 1	**102**	**3**
1995–96	Chesterfield	42 3		
1996–97	Chesterfield	42 3		
1997–98	Chesterfield	44 3		
1998–99	Chesterfield	40 3	**168**	**12**
1999–2000	Watford	22 1	**22**	**1**
2000–01	Wimbledon	42 6		
2001–02	Wimbledon	5 0	**47**	**6**

WILLMOTT, Chris (D)   **62**   **2**
H: 5 11 W: 10 12 b.Bedford 30-9-77
Source: Trainee.

1995–96	Luton T	0 0		
1996–97	Luton T	0 0		
1997–98	Luton T	14 0	**14**	**0**
1998–99	Luton T	14 0		
1999–2000	Wimbledon	7 0		
2000–01	Wimbledon	14 1		
2001–02	Wimbledon	27 1	**48**	**2**

Scholars
Boyce, Jerome; Cook, Paul T; Deacons, James; Hallett, David JN; Innocent, Anton L; Kamara, Malvin G; Lewington, Dean S; Maclean-Daley, Kingslee J; Morgan, Daniel; Murphy, David C; Nolan, Robert D; Oyedele, Shola; Reo-Coker, Nigel SA; Sikora, Christopher J; Slater, Jamie R; Sloma, Samuel M; Small, Wade K; Suleymanoglu, Ahmet; Wallace, Dean; Worgan, Lee J

WOLVERHAMPTON W

ANDREWS, Keith (M)   **39**   **1**
H: 6 0 W: 13 05 b.Dublin 13-9-80
Source: Trainee.

1997–98	Wolverhampton W	0	0
1998–99	Wolverhampton W	0	0
1999–2000	Wolverhampton W	2	0
2000–01	Wolverhampton W	22	0
2000–01	*Oxford U*	4 1	**4** **1**
2001–02	Wolverhampton W	11 0	**35** **0**

BARRETT, Shane‡ (F)   **0**   **0**
H: 5 10 W: 11 00 b.Luton 23-11-81
Source: Trainee.

1999–2000	Wolverhampton W	0	0
2000–01	Wolverhampton W	0	0
2001–02	Wolverhampton W	0	0

BAZELEY, Darren (D)   **310**   **25**
H: 5 11 W: 11 09 b.Northampton 5-10-72
Source: Trainee. *Honours:* England Under-21.

1989–90	Watford	1 0		
1990–91	Watford	7 0		
1991–92	Watford	34 6		
1992–93	Watford	22 1		
1993–94	Watford	10 1		
1994–95	Watford	28 4		
1995–96	Watford	41 1		
1996–97	Watford	41 3		
1997–98	Watford	16 3		
1998–99	Watford	40 2	**240**	**21**
1999–2000	Wolverhampton W	46 3		
2000–01	Wolverhampton W	24 1		
2001–02	Wolverhampton W	0 0	**70**	**4**

BLAKE, Nathan (F)   **400**   **131**
H: 5 11 W: 13 12 b.Cardiff 27-1-72
Source: Chelsea Trainee. *Honours:* Wales Youth, B, Under-21, 22 full caps, 4 goals.

1989–90	Cardiff C	6 0		
1990–91	Cardiff C	40 4		
1991–92	Cardiff C	31 6		
1992–93	Cardiff C	34 11		
1993–94	Cardiff C	20 14	**131**	**35**
1993–94	Sheffield U	12 5		
1994–95	Sheffield U	35 17		
1995–96	Sheffield U	22 12	**69**	**34**
1995–96	Bolton W	18 1		
1996–97	Bolton W	42 19		
1997–98	Bolton W	35 12		
1998–99	Bolton W	12 6	**107**	**38**
1998–99	Blackburn R	11 3		
1999–2000	Blackburn R	28 3		
2000–01	Blackburn R	12 6		
2001–02	Blackburn R	3 1	**54**	**13**
2001–02	Wolverhampton W	39 11	**39**	**11**

BRANCH, Michael (F)   **119**   **13**
H: 5 10 W: 11 07 b.Liverpool 18-10-78
Source: Trainee. *Honours:* England Schools, Youth, Under-21.

1995–96	Everton	3 0		
1996–97	Everton	25 3		
1997–98	Everton	6 0		
1998–99	Everton	7 0		
1998–99	*Manchester C*	4 0	**4**	**0**
1999–2000	Everton	0 0	**41**	**3**
2000–01	Wolverhampton W	38 4		
1999–2000	Wolverhampton W	27 6		
2001–02	Wolverhampton W	7 0	**72**	**10**
2001–02	*Reading*	2 0	**2**	**0**

BUTLER, Paul (D)   **376**   **18**
H: 6 0 W: 14 09 b.Manchester 2-11-72
Source: Trainee. *Honours:* Eire 1 full cap.

1990–91	Rochdale	2 0		
1991–92	Rochdale	25 0		
1992–93	Rochdale	16 2		
1993–94	Rochdale	38 2		
1994–95	Rochdale	39 3		
1995–96	Rochdale	38 3	**158**	**10**
1996–97	Bury	41 2		
1997–98	Bury	43 2	**84**	**4**
1998–99	Sunderland	44 2		
1999–2000	Sunderland	32 1		
2000–01	Sunderland	3 0	**79**	**3**
2000–01	Wolverhampton W	12 0		
2001–02	Wolverhampton W	43 1	**55**	**1**

CAMARA, Mohammed (D)   **162**   **2**
H: 5 11 W: 11 09 b.Conakry 25-6-75

1993–94	Beauvais	19 0		
1994–95	Beauvais	0 0		
1995–96	Troyes	13 0	**13**	**0**
1996–97	Beauvais	35 0	**54**	**0**
1997–98	Le Havre	14 0		
1998–99	Lille	34 2	**34**	**2**
1999–2000	Le Havre	2 0	**16**	**0**
2000–01	Wolverhampton W	18 0		
2001–02	Wolverhampton W	27 0	**45**	**0**

CAMERON, Colin (M)   **245**   **50**
H: 5 8 W: 11 00 b.Kirkcaldy 23-10-72
Source: Lochore Welfare. *Honours:* Scotland B, 15 full caps, 2 goals.

1990–91	Raith R	0	0
1991–92	*Sligo R*	0	0
1992–93	Raith R	16	1
1993–94	Raith R	41	6

1994–95	Raith R	35	7		
1995–96	Raith R	30	9	122	23
1995–96	Hearts	4	2		
1996–97	Hearts	36	7		
1997–98	Hearts	31	8		
1998–99	Hearts	11	6		
1999–2000	Hearts	0	0		
2000–01	Hearts	0	0		
2001–02	Hearts	0	0	82	23
2001–02	Wolverhampton W	41	4	41	4

CLINGAN, Sammy (M)   0   0
H: 5 11   W: 11 06   b.Belfast 13-1-84
Source: Scholar.

2001–02	Wolverhampton W	0	0

CLYDE, Mark (D)   0   0
H: 6 1   W: 12 00   b.Limavady 27-12-82
Source: Scholar. *Honours:* Northern Ireland Under-21.

2001–02	Wolverhampton W	0	0

COLEMAN, Ken (D)   0   0
H: 6 0   W: 12 00   b.Cork 20-9-82
Source: Scholar.

2000–01	Wolverhampton W	0	0
2001–02	Wolverhampton W	0	0

CONNELLY, Sean (D)   316   6
H: 5 10   W: 11 10   b.Sheffield 26-6-70
Source: Hallam.

1991–92	Stockport Co	0	0		
1992–93	Stockport Co	7	0		
1993–94	Stockport Co	32	0		
1994–95	Stockport Co	39	0		
1995–96	Stockport Co	43	0		
1996–97	Stockport Co	45	2		
1997–98	Stockport Co	45	2		
1998–99	Stockport Co	35	1		
1999–2000	Stockport Co	43	3		
2000–01	Stockport Co	13	0	302	6
2000–01	Wolverhampton W	6	0		
2001–02	Wolverhampton W	8	0	14	0

COOPER, Kevin (M)   226   34
H: 5 8   W: 10 04   b.Derby 8-2-75
Source: Trainee.

1993–94	Derby Co	0	0		
1994–95	Derby Co	1	0		
1995–96	Derby Co	1	0		
1996–97	Derby Co	0	0	2	0
1996–97	*Stockport Co*	12	3		
1997–98	Stockport Co	38	8		
1998–99	Stockport Co	38	1		
1999–2000	Stockport Co	46	4		
2000–01	Stockport Co	34	5	168	21
2000–01	Wimbledon	11	3		
2001–02	Wimbledon	40	10	51	13
2001–02	Wolverhampton W	5	0	35	5

DICKSON, Andrew‡ (M)   0   0
b.Belfast 3-8-82
Source: Scholar.

2000–01	Wolverhampton W	0	0
2001–02	Wolverhampton W	0	0

GILMORE, Craig‡ (M)   0   0
b.Belfast 28-9-82
Source: Scholar.

2001–02	Wolverhampton W	0	0

KENNEDY, Mark (M)   189   24
H: 5 11   W: 11 09   b.Dublin 15-5-76
Source: Belvedere, Trainee. *Honours:* Eire Under-21, 34 full caps, 3 goals.

1992–93	Millwall	1	0		
1993–94	Millwall	12	4		
1994–95	Millwall	30	5	43	9
1994–95	Liverpool	6	0		
1995–96	Liverpool	4	0		
1996–97	Liverpool	5	0		
1997–98	Liverpool	1	0	16	0
1997–98	QPR	8	2	8	2
1997–98	Wimbledon	4	0		
1998–99	Wimbledon	17	0	21	0
1999–2000	Manchester C	41	8		
2000–01	Manchester C	25	0	66	8
2001–02	Wolverhampton W	35	5	35	5

KETSBAIA, Temuri‡ (F)   316   78
H: 5 8   W: 10 12   b.Gale 18-3-68
Source: Dynamo Sukhumi. *Honours:* Georgia 50 full caps, 17 goals.

1987	Dynamo Tbilisi	14	4		
1988	Dynamo Tbilisi	13	4		
1989	Dynamo Tbilisi	27	4		
1990	Dynamo Tbilisi	9	0	54	8
1991–92	Anorthosis	26	13		
1992–93	Anorthosis	24	4		
1993–94	Anorthosis	26	19	76	36
1994–95	AEK Athens	22	5		
1995–96	AEK Athens	32	14		
1996–97	AEK Athens	30	5	84	24
1997–98	Newcastle U	31	3		
1998–99	Newcastle U	26	4		
1999–2000	Newcastle U	21	0	78	7
2000–01	Wolverhampton W	22	3		
2001–02	Wolverhampton W	2	0	24	3

(Transferred to Dundee, October 2001).

LARKIN, Colin (F)   36   6
H: 5 9   W: 10 02   b.Dundalk 27-4-82
Source: Trainee.

1998–99	Wolverhampton W	0	0		
1999–2000	Wolverhampton W	1	0		
2000–01	Wolverhampton W	2	0		
2001–02	Wolverhampton W	0	0	3	0
2001–02	*Kidderminster H*	33	6	33	6

LESCOTT, Jolean (D)   81   7
H: 6 2   W: 14 00   b.Birmingham 16-8-82
Source: Trainee. *Honours:* England Youth, Under-20.

1999–2000	Wolverhampton W	0	0		
2000–01	Wolverhampton W	37	2		
2001–02	Wolverhampton W	44	5	81	7

McCHRYSTAL, Mark (D)   0   0
H: 6 1   W: 13 07   b.Derry 25-6-84
Source: Scholar.

2001–02	Wolverhampton W	0	0

McGRANE, Ian (M)   0   0
H: 5 10   W: 12 00   b.Dublin 4-8-84
Source: Scholar.

2001–02	Wolverhampton W	0	0

McQUADE, Scott‡ (M)   0   0
H: 5 7   W: 10 06   b.Dumfries 7-1-82
Source: Trainee.

2000–01	Wolverhampton W	0	0
2001–02	Wolverhampton W	0	0

McSTEA, Anthony‡ (M)   0   0
H: 5 10   W: 12 02   b.Gateshead 6-5-81
Source: Trainee.

1999–2000	Middlesbrough	0	0
2000–01	Middlesbrough	0	0

From Brandon U.

2001–02	Wolverhampton W	0	0

MELLIGAN, John (M)   8   0
H: 5 9   W: 11 02   b.Dublin 11-2-82
Source: Trainee.

2000–01	Wolverhampton W	0	0		
2001–02	Wolverhampton W	0	0		
2001–02	*Bournemouth*	8	0	8	0

MILLER, Kenny (F)   95   22
H: 5 10   W: 11 04   b.Edinburgh 23-12-79
Source: Hutchison Vale. *Honours:* Scotland Under-21.

1996–97	Hibernian	0	0		
1997–98	Hibernian	7	0		
1998–99	Hibernian	7	1		
1999–2000	Hibernian	31	11	45	12
2000–01	Rangers	27	8		
2001–02	Rangers	3	0	30	8
2001–02	Wolverhampton W	2	0	20	2

MURRAY, Matt (G)   0   0
H: 6 4   W: 13 10   b.Solihull 2-5-81
Source: Trainee. *Honours:* England Youth.

1997–98	Wolverhampton W	0	0
1998–99	Wolverhampton W	0	0
1999–2000	Wolverhampton W	0	0
2000–01	Wolverhampton W	0	0
2001–02	Wolverhampton W	0	0

MUSCAT, Kevin* (D)   333   22
H: 5 11   W: 11 07   b.Crawley 7-8-73
Honours: Australia 37 full caps, 10 goals.

1989–90	Sunshine	9	0		
1990–91	Sunshine	0	0	9	0
1991–92	Heidelberg	18	0	18	0
1992–93	South Melbourne	17	0		
1993–94	South Melbourne	24	2		
1994–95	South Melbourne	20	3		
1995–96	South Melbourne	12	1	73	6
1996–97	Crystal Palace	44	2		
1997–98	Crystal Palace	9	0	53	2
1997–98	Wolverhampton W	24	3		
1998–99	Wolverhampton W	37	4		
1999–2000	Wolverhampton W	45	4		
2000–01	Wolverhampton W	37	3		
2001–02	Wolverhampton W	37	0	180	14

NAYLOR, Lee (D)   142   4
H: 5 10   W: 12 00   b.Bloxwich 19-3-80
Source: Trainee. *Honours:* England Youth, Under-21.

1997–98	Wolverhampton W	16	0		
1998–99	Wolverhampton W	23	1		
1999–2000	Wolverhampton W	30	2		
2000–01	Wolverhampton W	46	1		
2001–02	Wolverhampton W	27	0	142	4

NDAH, George (F)   209   31
H: 6 1   W: 12 06   b.Dulwich 23-12-74
Source: Trainee.

1992–93	Crystal Palace	13	0		
1993–94	Crystal Palace	1	0		
1994–95	Crystal Palace	12	1		
1995–96	Crystal Palace	23	4		
1995–96	*Bournemouth*	12	2	12	2
1996–97	Crystal Palace	26	3		
1997–98	Crystal Palace	3	0	78	8
1997–98	*Gillingham*	4	0	4	0
1997–98	Swindon T	14	2		
1998–99	Swindon T	41	11		
1999–2000	Swindon T	12	1	67	14
1999–2000	Wolverhampton W	4	0		
2000–01	Wolverhampton W	29	6		
2001–02	Wolverhampton W	15	1	48	7

NEWTON, Shaun (M)   285   28
H: 5 8   W: 11 00   b.Camberwell 20-8-75
Source: Trainee. *Honours:* England Under-21.

1992–93	Charlton Ath	2	0		
1993–94	Charlton Ath	19	2		
1994–95	Charlton Ath	26	0		
1995–96	Charlton Ath	41	5		
1996–97	Charlton Ath	43	3		
1997–98	Charlton Ath	41	5		
1998–99	Charlton Ath	16	0		
1999–2000	Charlton Ath	42	5		
2000–01	Charlton Ath	10	0	240	20
2001–02	Wolverhampton W	45	8	45	8

NIESTROJ, Robert‡ (M)   6   0
H: 5 10   W: 11 03   b.Oppeln 2-12-74
Source: Fortuna Dusseldorf.

1998–99	Wolverhampton W	5	0		
1999–2000	Wolverhampton W	1	0		
2000–01	Wolverhampton W	0	0		
2001–02	Wolverhampton W	0	0	6	0

OAKES, Michael (G)   172   0
H: 6 2   W: 14 00   b.Northwich 30-10-73
Source: Trainee. *Honours:* England Under-21.

1991–92	Aston Villa	0	0		
1992–93	Aston Villa	0	0		
1993–94	Aston Villa	0	0		
1993–94	*Scarborough*	1	0	1	0
1993–94	*Tranmere R*	0	0		
1994–95	Aston Villa	0	0		
1995–96	Aston Villa	0	0		
1996–97	Aston Villa	20	0		
1997–98	Aston Villa	8	0		
1998–99	Aston Villa	23	0		
1999–2000	Aston Villa	0	0	51	0
1999–2000	Wolverhampton W	28	0		
2000–01	Wolverhampton W	46	0		
2001–02	Wolverhampton W	46	0	120	0

POLLET, Ludovic (D)   216   10
H: 5 11   W: 11 07   b.Vieux-conde 18-6-70

1991–92	Cannes	6	0		
1992–93	Cannes	6	0		
1993–94	Cannes	8	1		
1994–95	Cannes	15	2	38	3
1995–96	Le Havre	26	0		
1996–97	Le Havre	21	0		
1997–98	Le Havre	34	0		
1998–99	Le Havre	21	0	102	0
1999–2000	Wolverhampton W	39	5		
2000–01	Wolverhampton W	29	2		
2001–02	Wolverhampton W	8	0	76	7

PROUDLOCK, Adam (F)   61   15
H: 6 0   W: 13 07   b.Wellington 9-5-81
Source: Trainee.

1999–2000	Wolverhampton W	0	0		
2000–01	*Clyde*	4	4	4	4
2000–01	Wolverhampton W	35	8		
2001–02	Wolverhampton W	19	3	54	11
2001–02	*Nottingham F*	3	0	3	0

RAE, Alex (M)   451   102
H: 5 10   W: 11 09   b.Glasgow 30-9-69
Source: Bishopbriggs. *Honours:* Scotland Under-21, B.

1987–88	Falkirk	12	0		
1988–89	Falkirk	37	12		
1989–90	Falkirk	34	8	83	20
1990–91	Millwall	39	10		
1991–92	Millwall	38	11		
1992–93	Millwall	30	6		
1993–94	Millwall	36	13		
1994–95	Millwall	38	10		
1995–96	Millwall	37	13	218	63
1996–97	Sunderland	24	3		
1997–98	Sunderland	29	3		
1998–99	Sunderland	15	2		
1999–2000	Sunderland	26	3		

2000–01	Sunderland	18	2		
2001–02	Sunderland	3	0	114	12
2001–02	Wolverhampton W	36	7	36	7

ROBINSON, Carl* (M)   168 19
H: 5 11   W: 12 04   b.Llandrindod Wells 13-10-76
Source: Trainee. *Honours:* Wales Youth, Under-21, B, 8 full caps.

1995–96	Wolverhampton W	0	0		
1995–96	Shrewsbury T	4	0	4	0
1996–97	Wolverhampton W	2	0		
1997–98	Wolverhampton W	32	3		
1998–99	Wolverhampton W	34	8		
1999–2000	Wolverhampton W	33	3		
2000–01	Wolverhampton W	40	3		
2001–02	Wolverhampton W	23	2	164	19

ROUSSEL, Cedric (F)   100 21
H: 6 3   W: 13 12   b.Mons 6-1-78
Honours: La Louviere.

1998–99	Gent	31	8		
1999–2000	Gent	4	3	35	11
1999–2000	Coventry C	22	6		
2000–01	Coventry C	17	2	39	8
2000–01	Wolverhampton W	9	0		
2001–02	Wolverhampton W	17	2	26	2

SINTON, Andy* (M)   617 75
H: 5 6   W: 11 07   b.Newcastle 19-3-66
Source: Apprentice. *Honours:* England Schools, B, 12 full caps.

1982–83	Cambridge U	13	5		
1983–84	Cambridge U	34	6		
1984–85	Cambridge U	26	2		
1985–86	Cambridge U	20	0	93	13
1985–86	Brentford	26	3		
1986–87	Brentford	46	5		
1987–88	Brentford	46	11		
1988–89	Brentford	31	9	149	28
1988–89	QPR	10	3		
1989–90	QPR	38	6		
1990–91	QPR	38	3		
1991–92	QPR	38	3		
1992–93	QPR	36	7	160	22
1993–94	Sheffield W	25	3		
1994–95	Sheffield W	25	0		
1995–96	Sheffield W	10	0	60	3
1995–96	Tottenham H	9	0		
1996–97	Tottenham H	33	6		
1997–98	Tottenham H	19	0		
1998–99	Tottenham H	22	0	83	6
1999–2000	Wolverhampton W	35	0		
2000–01	Wolverhampton W	30	2		
2001–02	Wolverhampton W	7	1	72	3

STURRIDGE, Dean (F)   249 84
H: 5 8   W: 12 02   b.Birmingham 27-7-73
Source: Trainee.

1991–92	Derby Co	1	0		
1992–93	Derby Co	10	0		
1993–94	Derby Co	0	0		
1994–95	Derby Co	12	1		
1994–95	Torquay U	10	5	10	5
1995–96	Derby Co	39	20		
1996–97	Derby Co	30	11		
1997–98	Derby Co	30	9		
1998–99	Derby Co	29	5		
1999–2000	Derby Co	25	6		
2000–01	Derby Co	14	1	190	53
2000–01	Leicester C	13	3		
2001–02	Leicester C	9	3	22	6
2001–02	Wolverhampton W	27	20	27	20

WARD, Graham (M)   0 0
H: 5 8   W: 11 09   b.Dublin 25-2-83
Source: Scholar.

2000–01	Wolverhampton W	0	0		
2001–02	Wolverhampton W	0	0		

Scholars
Bampfield, Steve D; Brown, Scott; Clark, Nicholas E; Clarke, Leon M; Danks, Mark J; Fitter, John A; Flynn, Patrick J; Gobern, Lewis; Jones, Jimmi L; Mahon, Ryan; Morrow, Andrew J; Mulligan, Gary; Slater, Christopher J; Solly, Lewis A; Talbott, Nathan; Vincent, Ashley D; Walters, Marlon J; Watson, Matthew G; Willis, James R
Associated Schoolboys
Clark, David; Rollins, Mark

WREXHAM

BARRETT, Paul# (M)   67 2
H: 5 10   W: 11 04   b.Newcastle 13-4-78
Source: Trainee.

1996–97	Newcastle U	0	0		
1997–98	Newcastle U	0	0		
1998–99	Newcastle U	0	0		
1998–99	Wrexham	10	0		
1999–2000	Wrexham	18	2		
2000–01	Wrexham	24	0		
2001–02	Wrexham	15	0	67	2

BENNETT, Dan† (D)   6 0
H: 6 1   W: 12 05   b.Great Yarmouth 7-1-78
Source: Balestier Central, Tanjong Pagar.

2001–02	Wrexham	6	0	6	0

BLACKWOOD, Michael* (F)   55 4
H: 5 10   W: 11 04   b.Birmingham 30-9-79
Source: Trainee.

1998–99	Aston Villa	0	0		
1999–2000	Aston Villa	0	0		
1999–2000	Chester C	9	2	9	2
2000–01	Wrexham	15	0		
2001–02	Wrexham	31	2	46	2

CAREY, Brian (D)   285 11
H: 6 3   W: 13 02   b.Cork 31-5-68
Source: Cork C. *Honours:* Eire 3 full caps.

1989–90	Manchester U	0	0		
1990–91	Manchester U	0	0		
1990–91	Wrexham	3	0		
1991–92	Manchester U	0	0		
1991–92	Wrexham	13	1		
1992–93	Manchester U	0	0		
1993–94	Leicester C	27	0		
1994–95	Leicester C	12	0		
1995–96	Leicester C	19	1	58	1
1996–97	Wrexham	38	0		
1997–98	Wrexham	43	1		
1998–99	Wrexham	36	2		
1999–2000	Wrexham	43	1		
2000–01	Wrexham	33	3		
2001–02	Wrexham	18	2	227	10

CHALK, Martyn* (M)   234 20
H: 5 6   W: 11 03   b.Swindon 30-8-69
Source: Louth U.

1990–91	Derby Co	0	0		
1991–92	Derby Co	7	1		
1992–93	Derby Co	0	0		
1993–94	Derby Co	0	0	7	1
1994–95	Stockport Co	33	6		
1995–96	Stockport Co	10	0	43	6
1995–96	Wrexham	19	4		
1996–97	Wrexham	43	1		
1997–98	Wrexham	26	1		
1998–99	Wrexham	28	0		
1999–2000	Wrexham	20	0		
2000–01	Wrexham	24	4		
2001–02	Wrexham	24	3	184	13

EDWARDS, Carlos (M)   62 9
H: 5 11   W: 11 01   b.Trinidad 24-10-78
Honours: Trinidad & Tobago 15 full caps.

2000–01	Wrexham	36	4		
2001–02	Wrexham	26	5	62	9

EVANS, Mark§ (F)   4 0
H: 6 1   W: 11 02   b.Chester 16-9-82
Source: Scholar.

2001–02	Wrexham	4	0	4	0

FAULCONBRIDGE, Craig# (F)   134 32
H: 6 1   W: 13 00   b.Nuneaton 20-4-78
Source: Trainee.

1996–97	Coventry C	0	0		
1997–98	Coventry C	0	0		
1997–98	Dunfermline Ath	7	1		
1998–99	Dunfermline Ath	6	0	13	1
1998–99	Hull C	10	0	10	0
1999–2000	Wrexham	35	8		
2000–01	Wrexham	39	10		
2001–02	Wrexham	37	13	111	31

FERGUSON, Darren (M)   262 20
H: 5 10   W: 11 10   b.Glasgow 9-2-72
Source: Trainee. *Honours:* Scotland Youth, Under-21.

1990–91	Manchester U	5	0		
1991–92	Manchester U	4	0		
1992–93	Manchester U	15	0		
1993–94	Manchester U	3	0	27	0
1993–94	Wolverhampton W	14	0		
1994–95	Wolverhampton W	24	0		
1995–96	Wolverhampton W	33	1		
1996–97	Wolverhampton W	16	3		
1997–98	Wolverhampton W	26	0		
1998–99	Wolverhampton W	4	0		
1999–2000	Wolverhampton W	0	0	117	4
1999–2000	Wrexham	37	4		
2000–01	Wrexham	43	9		
2001–02	Wrexham	38	3	118	16

GIBSON, Robin* (F)   77 3
H: 5 7   W: 11 07   b.Crewe 15-11-79
Source: Trainee.

1998–99	Wrexham	7	1		
1999–2000	Wrexham	24	1		
2000–01	Wrexham	28	1		
2001–02	Wrexham	18	0	77	3

HOLMES, Shaun (D)   40 0
H: 5 9   W: 10 07   b.Derry 27-12-80
Source: Trainee. *Honours:* Northern Ireland Under-21, 1 full cap.

1997–98	Manchester C	0	0		
1998–99	Manchester C	0	0		
1999–2000	Manchester C	0	0		
2000–01	Manchester C	0	0		
2001–02	Wrexham	40	0	40	0

JONES, Lee‡ (F)   206 46
H: 5 8   W: 10 06   b.Wrexham 29-5-73
Source: Trainee. *Honours:* Wales Youth, Under-21, B, 2 full caps.

1990–91	Wrexham	18	5		
1991–92	Wrexham	21	5		
1991–92	Liverpool	0	0		
1992–93	Liverpool	0	0		
1993–94	Liverpool	0	0		
1993–94	Crewe Alex	8	1	8	1
1994–95	Liverpool	1	0		
1995–96	Liverpool	0	0		
1995–96	Wrexham	20	9		
1996–97	Liverpool	2	0	3	0
1996–97	Wrexham	6	0		
1996–97	Tranmere R	8	5		
1997–98	Tranmere R	34	9		
1998–99	Tranmere R	30	2		
1999–2000	Tranmere R	14	0	86	16
2000–01	Barnsley	27	5		
2001–02	Barnsley	13	0	40	5
From Oswestry T					
2001–02	Wrexham	4	5	69	24

LAWRENCE, Dennis (D)   35 2
H: 6 7   W: 11 13   b.Trinidad 1-8-74
Source: Defence Force. *Honours:* Trinidad & Tobago 30 full caps.

2000–01	Wrexham	3	0		
2001–02	Wrexham	32	2	35	2

MOODY, Adrian§ (D)   4 0
H: 6 0   W: 11 03   b.Birkenhead 29-9-82
Source: Scholar.

2000–01	Wrexham	3	0		
2001–02	Wrexham	1	0	4	0

MORGAN, Craig§ (D)   2 0
H: 6 0   W: 11 06   b.St Asaph 16-6-85
Source: Scholar.

2001–02	Wrexham	2	0	2	0

MORRELL, Andy# (F)   65 6
H: 5 11   W: 11 06   b.Doncaster 28-9-74
Source: Newcastle Blue Star.

1998–99	Wrexham	7	0		
1999–2000	Wrexham	13	1		
2000–01	Wrexham	20	3		
2001–02	Wrexham	25	2	65	6

PEJIC, Shaun§ (D)   13 0
H: 6 0   W: 11 07   b.Hereford 16-11-82

2000–01	Wrexham	1	0		
2001–02	Wrexham	12	0	13	0

PHILLIPS, Wayne# (M)   266 18
H: 5 11   W: 11 00   b.Bangor 15-12-70
Source: Trainee. *Honours:* Wales B.

1989–90	Wrexham	0	0		
1990–91	Wrexham	28	0		
1991–92	Wrexham	30	3		
1992–93	Wrexham	15	0		
1993–94	Wrexham	21	1		
1994–95	Wrexham	18	1		
1995–96	Wrexham	44	5		
1996–97	Wrexham	26	5		
1996–97	Wrexham	20	1		
1997–98	Stockport Co	13	0		
1998–99	Stockport Co	9	0	22	0
1999–2000	Wrexham	7	1		
2000–01	Wrexham	7	1		
2001–02	Wrexham	27	1	244	18

ROBERTS, Steve (D)   50 1
H: 6 2   W: 11 06   b.Wrexham 24-2-80
Source: Trainee. *Honours:* Wales Youth, Under-21.

1997–98	Wrexham	0	0		
1998–99	Wrexham	0	0		
1999–2000	Wrexham	19	0		
2000–01	Wrexham	0	0		
2001–02	Wrexham	24	1	50	1

ROGERS, Kristian (G)   33 0
H: 6 0   W: 11 12   b.Chester 2-10-80
Honours: England Schools.

1999–2000	Wrexham	1	0		
2000–01	Wrexham	5	0		
2001–02	Wrexham	27	0	33	0

ROVDE, Marius‡ (G)   12 0
H: 6 2   W: 13 10   b.Trondheim 26-6-72

2001–02	Wrexham	12	0	12	0

RUSSELL, Kevin* (M)   455 88
H: 5 9   W: 10 12   b.Portsmouth 6-12-66
Source: Brighton & HA Apprentice.
Honours: England Youth.

1984–85	Portsmouth	0	0	
1985–86	Portsmouth	1	0	
1986–87	Portsmouth	3	1	4 1
1987–88	Wrexham	38	21	
1988–89	Wrexham	46	22	
1989–90	Leicester C	10	0	
1990–91	Leicester C	13	5	
1990–91	*Peterborough U*	7	3	7 3
1990–91	*Cardiff C*	3	0	3 0
1991–92	Leicester C	20	5	43 10
1991–92	*Hereford U*	3	1	3 1
1991–92	Stoke C	5	1	
1992–93	Stoke C	40	5	45 6
1993–94	Burnley	28	6	28 6
1993–94	Bournemouth	17	1	
1994–95	Bournemouth	13	0	30 1
1994–95	Notts Co	11	0	11 0
1995–96	Wrexham	40	7	
1996–97	Wrexham	41	0	
1997–98	Wrexham	16	0	
1998–99	Wrexham	31	2	
1999–2000	Wrexham	33	4	
2000–01	Wrexham	26	4	
2001–02	Wrexham	10	0	281 60

SAM, Hector (F)   49 11
H: 5 9   W: 11 05   b.Trinidad 25-2-78
Source: San Juan Jabloteh. *Honours:* Trinidad & Tobago 10 full caps.

2000–01	Wrexham	20	6	
2001–02	Wrexham	29	5	49 11

SHARP, Kevin‡ (M)   210 10
H: 5 10   W: 11 04   b.Ontario 19-9-74
Source: Auxerre. *Honours:* England Schools, Youth.

1992–93	Leeds U	4	0	
1993–94	Leeds U	10	0	
1994–95	Leeds U	2	0	
1995–96	Leeds U	1	0	17 0
1995–96	Wigan Ath	20	6	
1996–97	Wigan Ath	35	2	
1997–98	Wigan Ath	38	0	
1998–99	Wigan Ath	31	2	
1999–2000	Wigan Ath	21	0	
2000–01	Wigan Ath	31	0	
2001–02	Wigan Ath	2	0	178 10
2001–02	Wrexham	15	0	15 0

THOMAS, Steve (M)   50 3
H: 5 10   W: 11 07   b.Hartlepool 23-6-79
Source: Trainee. *Honours:* Wales Youth, Under-21.

1997–98	Wrexham	0	0	
1998–99	Wrexham	4	0	
1999–2000	Wrexham	2	0	
2000–01	Wrexham	6	0	
2001–02	Wrexham	38	3	50 3

TRUNDLE, Lee (F)   50 16
H: 6 0   W: 11 11   b.Liverpool 10-10-76
Source: Rhyl.

2000–01	Wrexham	14	8	
2001–02	Wrexham	36	8	50 16

WALSH, Dave* (G)   14 0
H: 6 1   W: 12 05   b.Wrexham 29-4-79
Source: Trainee. *Honours:* Wales Under-21.

1997–98	Wrexham	0	0	
1998–99	Wrexham	0	0	
1999–2000	Wrexham	0	0	
2000–01	Wrexham	5	0	
2001–02	Wrexham	9	0	14 0

WARREN, David* (D)   6 0
H: 5 10   W: 11 05   b.Cork 28-2-81
Source: Mayfield U.

1999–2000	Wrexham	1	0	
2000–01	Wrexham	0	0	
2001–02	Wrexham	5	0	6 0

WHITFIELD, Paul (G)   0 0
b.St Asaph 6-5-82
Source: Scholar.

2001–02	Wrexham	0	0

WHITLEY, Jim# (D)   103 1
H: 5 9   W: 10 12   b.Zambia 14-4-75
Source: Trainee. *Honours:* Northern Ireland B, 3 full caps.

1993–94	Manchester C	0	0	
1994–95	Manchester C	0	0	
1995–96	Manchester C	0	0	
1996–97	Manchester C	0	0	
1997–98	Manchester C	19	0	
1998–99	Manchester C	18	0	
1999–2000	Manchester C	1	0	
1999–2000	*Blackpool*	8	0	8 0
2000–01	Manchester C	0	0	38 0
2000–01	*Norwich C*	8	1	8 1
2000–01	*Swindon T*	2	0	2 0
2000–01	*Northampton T*	13	0	13 0
2000–01	*Nottingham F*	0	0	
2001–02	Wrexham	34	0	34 0

Scholars
Arkell, Adam N; Campbell, Luke; Dabbs, Matthew S; Evans, Mark G; Hamill, Christopher D; Hughes, Robert A; Jackson, Mark G; Jones, Darren; Jones, Mark A; Jones, Osian L; Legrand, David A; McNulty, Jimmy; Moody, Adrian JH; Moody, Craig; Morgan, Craig; Owen, Dylan; Parry, Christopher D; Pejic, Shaun M; Redshaw, Mark; Stacey, Alec J; Sudlow, Gareth GL
Non-Contract
Bennett, Daniel M
Associated Schoolboys
Bates, Matthew J; Brand, Benjamin J; Cargill, Gary S; Entwistle, Mark R; Graham, Adam; Jones, Adam; O'Toole, Dominic; Taylor, Michael J

WYCOMBE W

BAIRD, Andy* (F)   79 13
H: 5 10   W: 11 13   b.East Kilbride 18-1-79
Source: Trainee.

1997–98	Wycombe W	2	0	
1998–99	Wycombe W	28	6	
1999–2000	Wycombe W	30	4	
2000–01	Wycombe W	13	3	
2001–02	Wycombe W	6	0	79 13

BROWN, Steve (M)   467 48
H: 5 10   W: 11 12   b.Northampton 6-7-66

1985–86	Northampton T	0	0	
From Irthlingborough D				
1989–90	Northampton T	21	1	
1990–91	Northampton T	40	2	
1991–92	Northampton T	35	3	
1992–93	Northampton T	38	9	
1993–94	Northampton T	24	4	158 19
1993–94	Wycombe W	9	2	
1994–95	Wycombe W	40	1	
1995–96	Wycombe W	38	0	
1996–97	Wycombe W	34	5	
1997–98	Wycombe W	40	3	
1998–99	Wycombe W	38	3	
1999–2000	Wycombe W	39	3	
2000–01	Wycombe W	32	4	
2001–02	Wycombe W	39	8	309 29

BULMAN, Dannie (M)   122 11
H: 5 9   W: 11 12   b.Ashford 24-1-79
Source: Ashford T.

1998–99	Wycombe W	11	1	
1999–2000	Wycombe W	29	1	
2000–01	Wycombe W	36	4	
2001–02	Wycombe W	46	5	122 11

CARROLL, Dave‡ (M)   302 41
H: 5 10   W: 11 12   b.Paisley 20-9-66
Source: Ruislip Manor. *Honours:* England Schools.

1993–94	Wycombe W	41	6	
1994–95	Wycombe W	41	6	
1995–96	Wycombe W	46	9	
1996–97	Wycombe W	43	9	
1997–98	Wycombe W	39	1	
1998–99	Wycombe W	32	6	
1999–2000	Wycombe W	36	2	
2000–01	Wycombe W	12	2	
2001–02	Wycombe W	12	0	302 41

CASTLEDINE, Stewart‡ (M)   52 7
H: 6 1   W: 12 00   b.Wandsworth 22-1-73
Source: Trainee.

1991–92	Wimbledon	2	0	
1992–93	Wimbledon	0	0	
1993–94	Wimbledon	3	1	
1994–95	Wimbledon	6	1	
1995–96	Wimbledon	4	1	
1995–96	*Wycombe W*	7	3	
1996–97	Wimbledon	6	1	
1997–98	Wimbledon	1	0	
1998–99	Wimbledon	1	0	
1999–2000	Wimbledon	0	0	28 4
2000–01	Wycombe W	17	0	
2001–02	Wycombe W	0	0	24 3

COUSINS, Jason* (D)   317 6
H: 5 10   W: 12 07   b.Hayes 4-10-70
Source: Trainee.

1989–90	Brentford	13	0	
1990–91	Brentford	8	0	21 0
From Wycombe W				
1993–94	Wycombe W	37	1	
1994–95	Wycombe W	41	2	
1995–96	Wycombe W	30	0	
1996–97	Wycombe W	37	0	
1997–98	Wycombe W	29	0	
1998–99	Wycombe W	34	2	
1999–2000	Wycombe W	37	1	
2000–01	Wycombe W	32	0	
2001–02	Wycombe W	19	0	296 6

CURRIE, Darren (M)   273 32
H: 5 10   W: 12 07   b.Hampstead 29-11-74
Source: Trainee.

1993–94	West Ham U	0	0	
1994–95	West Ham U	0	0	
1994–95	*Shrewsbury T*	17	2	
1995–96	West Ham U	0	0	
1995–96	*Leyton Orient*	10	0	10 0
1995–96	Shrewsbury T	13	2	
1996–97	Shrewsbury T	37	2	
1997–98	Shrewsbury T	16	4	83 10
1997–98	*Plymouth Arg*	7	0	7 0
1998–99	Barnet	38	4	
1999–2000	Barnet	44	5	
2000–01	Barnet	45	10	127 19
2001–02	Wycombe W	46	3	46 3

DEVINE, Sean (F)   197 83
H: 5 11   W: 13 00   b.Lewisham 6-9-72
Source: Omonia.

1995–96	Barnet	35	19	
1996–97	Barnet	31	11	
1997–98	Barnet	40	16	
1998–99	Barnet	21	1	126 47
1998–99	Wycombe W	12	8	
1999–2000	Wycombe W	39	23	
2000–01	Wycombe W	0	0	
2001–02	Wycombe W	20	5	71 36

EMBLEN, Paul* (M)   82 7
H: 5 9   W: 12 12   b.Bromley 3-4-76
Source: Tonbridge A.

1996–97	Charlton Ath	0	0	
1997–98	Charlton Ath	4	0	
1997–98	*Brighton & HA*	15	4	15 4
1998–99	Charlton Ath	0	0	4 0
1998–99	Wycombe W	35	2	
1999–2000	Wycombe W	16	0	
2000–01	Wycombe W	0	0	
2001–02	Wycombe W	12	1	63 3

HARRIS, Richard (F)   18 0
H: 5 11   W: 10 09   b.Croydon 23-10-80
Source: Trainee.

1997–98	Crystal Palace	0	0	
1998–99	Crystal Palace	1	0	
1999–2000	Crystal Palace	6	0	
2000–01	Crystal Palace	2	0	
2001–02	Crystal Palace	0	0	9 0
2001–02	*Mansfield T*	6	0	6 0
2001–02	Wycombe W	3	0	3 0

HOLLIGAN, Gavin (F)   25 4
H: 5 10   W: 13 00   b.Lambeth 30-6-80
Source: Kingstonian.

1998–99	West Ham U	1	0	
1999–2000	West Ham U	0	0	
1999–2000	*Leyton Orient*	1	0	1 0
2000–01	West Ham U	1	0	1 0
2000–01	*Exeter C*	3	0	3 0
2001–02	Wycombe W	20	4	20 4

JOHNSON, Roger (D)   9 1
H: 6 3   W: 11 00   b.Ashford 28-4-83
Source: Trainee.

1999–2000	Wycombe W	1	0	
2000–01	Wycombe W	1	0	
2001–02	Wycombe W	7	1	9 1

LEACH, Marc (D)   1 0
H: 6 1   W: 11 10   b.Hemel Hempstead 12-7-83
Source: Trainee.

2001–02	Wycombe W	1	0	1 0

LEE, Martyn (M)   40 3
H: 5 6   W: 9 00   b.Guildford 10-8-80
Source: Trainee.

1998–99	Wycombe W	3	0	
1999–2000	Wycombe W	4	0	
2000–01	Wycombe W	21	3	
2001–02	Wycombe W	7	0	35 3
2001–02	*Cheltenham T*	5	0	5 0

LOPEZ, Carlos‡ (D)   1 0
H: 6 1   W: 12 00   b.Mexico City 18-4-70
Source: Trainee.

2001–02	Wycombe W	1	0	1 0

McCARTHY, Paul (D)   369 14
H: 5 10   W: 13 10   b.Cork 4-8-71
Source: Trainee. *Honours:* Eire Youth, Under-21.

1989–90	Brighton & HA	3	0
1990–91	Brighton & HA	21	0
1991–92	Brighton & HA	20	0
1992–93	Brighton & HA	30	0
1993–94	Brighton & HA	37	3

1994–95	Brighton & HA	37	2		
1995–96	Brighton & HA	33	1	**181**	**6**
1996–97	Wycombe W	40	0		
1997–98	Wycombe W	31	1		
1998–99	Wycombe W	29	1		
1999–2000	Wycombe W	22	1		
2000–01	Wycombe W	38	2		
2001–02	Wycombe W	28	3	**188**	**8**

McSPORRAN, Jermaine (F) 116 22
H: 5 10 W: 10 12 b.Manchester 1-1-77
Source: Oxford C.

1998–99	Wycombe W	26	4		
1999–2000	Wycombe W	38	9		
2000–01	Wycombe W	20	2		
2001–02	Wycombe W	32	7	**116**	**22**

OSBORN, Mark (G) 1 0
H: 6 0 W: 14 01 b.Bletchley 19-6-81
Source: Trainee.

1998–99	Wycombe W	0	0		
1999–2000	Wycombe W	1	0		
2000–01	Wycombe W	0	0		
2001–02	Wycombe W	0	0	**1**	**0**

PHELAN, Leeyon* (F) 3 0
H: 5 11 W: 12 06 b.Hammersmith 6-10-82
Source: Scholar.

2000–01	Wycombe W	2	0		
2001–02	Wycombe W	1	0	**3**	**0**

RAMMELL, Andy (F) 376 101
H: 6 1 W: 13 12 b.Nuneaton 10-2-67
Source: Atherstone U.

1989–90	Manchester U	0	0		
1990–91	Barnsley	40	12		
1991–92	Barnsley	37	8		
1992–93	Barnsley	30	7		
1993–94	Barnsley	34	6		
1994–95	Barnsley	24	7		
1995–96	Barnsley	20	4	**185**	**44**
1995–96	Southend U	7	2		
1996–97	Southend U	36	9		
1997–98	Southend U	26	2	**69**	**13**
1998–99	Walsall	39	18		
1999–2000	Walsall	30	5		
2000–01	Walsall	0	0	**69**	**23**
2000–01	Wycombe W	26	10		
2001–02	Wycombe W	27	11	**53**	**21**

ROBERTS, Stuart (M) 118 14
H: 5 6 W: 9 08 b.Carmarthen 22-7-80
Source: Trainee. *Honours:* Wales Under-21.

1998–99	Swansea C	32	3		
1999–2000	Swansea C	11	1		
2000–01	Swansea C	36	5		
2001–02	Swansea C	13	5	**92**	**14**
2001–02	Wycombe W	26	0	**26**	**0**

ROGERS, Mark (D) 88 3
H: 5 11 W: 12 12 b.Geulph 3-11-75
Honours: Canada 5 full caps.

1998–99	Wycombe W	0	0		
1999–2000	Wycombe W	25	0		
2000–01	Wycombe W	22	1		
2001–02	Wycombe W	41	2	**88**	**3**

RYAN, Keith (M) 260 24
H: 5 10 W: 12 06 b.Northampton 25-6-70
Source: Berkhamsted T.

1993–94	Wycombe W	42	1		
1994–95	Wycombe W	24	4		
1995–96	Wycombe W	23	4		
1996–97	Wycombe W	0	0		
1997–98	Wycombe W	40	3		
1998–99	Wycombe W	28	1		
1999–2000	Wycombe W	38	6		
2000–01	Wycombe W	30	4		
2001–02	Wycombe W	35	1	**260**	**24**

SENDA, Danny (F) 107 3
H: 5 10 W: 10 02 b.Harrow 17-4-81
Source: Southampton Trainee. *Honours:* England Youth.

1998–99	Wycombe W	6	0		
1999–2000	Wycombe W	27	1		
2000–01	Wycombe W	31	2		
2001–02	Wycombe W	43	0	**107**	**3**

SIMPEMBA, Ian (M) 0 0
b.Dublin 28-3-83
Source: Scholar.

2001–02	Wycombe W	0	0		

SIMPSON, Michael (M) 266 12
H: 5 8 W: 11 07 b.Nottingham 28-2-74
Source: Trainee.

1992–93	Notts Co	0	0		
1993–94	Notts Co	6	1		
1994–95	Notts Co	19	2		
1995–96	Notts Co	23	0		
1996–97	Notts Co	1	0	**49**	**3**
1996–97	*Plymouth Arg*	12	0	**12**	**0**
1996–97	Wycombe W	20	1		
1997–98	Wycombe W	21	0		
1998–99	Wycombe W	33	4		
1999–2000	Wycombe W	43	0		
2000–01	Wycombe W	45	3		
2001–02	Wycombe W	43	1	**205**	**9**

TAYLOR, Martin (G) 348 0
H: 6 0 W: 13 11 b.Tamworth 9-12-66
Source: Mile Oak R.

1986–87	Derby Co	0	0		
1987–88	Derby Co	0	0		
1987–88	*Carlisle U*	10	0	**10**	**0**
1987–88	*Scunthorpe U*	8	0	**8**	**0**
1988–89	Derby Co	0	0		
1989–90	Derby Co	3	0		
1990–91	Derby Co	7	0		
1991–92	Derby Co	5	0		
1992–93	Derby Co	21	0		
1993–94	Derby Co	46	0		
1994–95	Derby Co	12	0		
1995–96	Derby Co	0	0		
1996–97	Derby Co	3	0	**97**	**0**
1996–97	*Crewe Alex*	6	0	**6**	**0**
1996–97	*Wycombe W*	4	0		
1997–98	Wycombe W	45	0		
1998–99	Wycombe W	44	0		
1999–2000	Wycombe W	42	0		
2000–01	Wycombe W	46	0		
2001–02	Wycombe W	46	0	**227**	**0**

THOMSON, Andy (D) 245 9
H: 6 3 W: 14 03 b.Swindon 28-3-74
Source: Trainee.

1992–93	Swindon T	0	0		
1993–94	Swindon T	1	0		
1994–95	Swindon T	21	0		
1995–96	Swindon T	0	0	**22**	**0**
1995–96	Portsmouth	16	0		
1996–97	Portsmouth	28	1		
1997–98	Portsmouth	35	2		
1998–99	Portsmouth	14	0	**93**	**3**
1998–99	Bristol R	21	1		
1999–2000	Bristol R	43	3		
2000–01	Bristol R	32	1		
2001–02	Bristol R	31	1	**127**	**6**
2001–02	Wycombe W	3	0	**3**	**0**

TOWNSEND, Ben (D) 13 0
H: 5 10 W: 11 03 b.Reading 8-10-81
Source: Scholar.

1999–2000	Wycombe W	1	0		
2000–01	Wycombe W	10	0		
2001–02	Wycombe W	2	0	**13**	**0**

VINNICOMBE, Chris (D) 317 7
H: 5 9 W: 10 12 b.Exeter 20-10-70
Source: Trainee. *Honours:* England Under-21.

1988–89	Exeter C	25	0		
1989–90	Exeter C	14	1	**39**	**1**
1989–90	Rangers	7	0		
1990–91	Rangers	10	1		
1991–92	Rangers	2	0		
1992–93	Rangers	0	0		
1993–94	Rangers	4	0	**23**	**1**
1994–95	Burnley	29	1		
1995–96	Burnley	35	2		
1996–97	Burnley	8	0		
1997–98	Burnley	23	0	**95**	**3**
1998–99	Wycombe W	41	0		
1999–2000	Wycombe W	35	0		
2000–01	Wycombe W	42	1		
2001–02	Wycombe W	42	1	**160**	**2**

WILLIAMS, Steven (G) 0 0
b.Oxford 21-4-83
Source: Scholar.

2001–02	Wycombe W	0	0		

Scholars
Cook, Lewis L; Dash, Scott; Dixon, Jonathan J; Gott, Tom P; Harding, Billy; Hole, Stuart M; Kelly, John P; Leach, Marc T; Lynott, Patrick J; McCullagh, Ryan; Parsons, Ryan D; Philo, Mark; Smillie, Jack; Sudheimer, Kai; Warner, Matthew J

YORK C

BASHAM, Mike (D) 160 7
H: 6 0 W: 13 09 b.Barking 27-9-73
Source: Trainee. *Honours:* England Schools.

1992–93	West Ham U	0	0		
1993–94	West Ham U	0	0		
1993–94	*Colchester U*	1	0	**1**	**0**
1993–94	Swansea C	5	0		
1994–95	Swansea C	13	0		
1995–96	Swansea C	11	1	**29**	**1**
1995–96	Peterborough U	14	1		
1996–97	Peterborough U	5	0	**19**	**1**
1997–98	Barnet	20	1		
1998–99	Barnet	32	1		
1999–2000	Barnet	15	0		
2000–01	Barnet	8	0	**75**	**2**
2000–01	York C	7	1		
2001–02	York C	29	2	**36**	**3**

BRACKSTONE, Stephen (M) 9 0
H: 5 11 W: 10 08 b.Hartlepool 19-9-82
Source: Scholar. *Honours:* England Youth.

2000–01	Middlesbrough	0	0		
2001–02	Middlesbrough	0	0		
2001–02	York C	9	0	**9**	**0**

BRASS, Chris (M) 198 4
H: 5 10 W: 11 11 b.Easington 24-7-75
Source: Trainee.

1993–94	Burnley	0	0		
1994–95	Burnley	5	0		
1994–95	*Torquay U*	7	0	**7**	**0**
1995–96	Burnley	9	0		
1996–97	Burnley	39	0		
1997–98	Burnley	40	1		
1998–99	Burnley	34	0		
1999–2000	Burnley	7	0		
2000–01	Burnley	0	0	**134**	**1**
2000–01	*Halifax T*	6	0	**6**	**0**
2000–01	York C	10	1		
2001–02	York C	41	2	**51**	**3**

BULLOCK, Lee (M) 97 11
H: 6 0 W: 12 12 b.Stockton 22-5-81
Source: Trainee.

1999–2000	York C	24	0		
2000–01	York C	33	3		
2001–02	York C	40	8	**97**	**11**

COOPER, Richard (M) 42 1
H: 5 8 W: 11 01 b.Nottingham 27-9-79
Source: Trainee. *Honours:* England Schools, Youth.

1996–97	Nottingham F	0	0		
1997–98	Nottingham F	0	0		
1998–99	Nottingham F	0	0		
1999–2000	Nottingham F	1	0		
2000–01	Nottingham F	2	0	**3**	**0**
2000–01	York C	14	0		
2001–02	York C	25	1	**39**	**1**

DARLOW, Kieran§ (D) 5 0
H: 6 0 W: 13 12 b.Bedford 9-11-82
Source: Trainee.

1999–2000	York C	2	0		
2000–01	York C	1	0		
2001–02	York C	2	0	**5**	**0**

DUFFIELD, Peter# (F) 303 104
H: 5 7 W: 10 13 b.Middlesbrough 4-2-69
Source: Apprentice.

1986–87	Middlesbrough	0	0		
1987–88	Sheffield U	11	1		
1987–88	*Halifax T*	12	6	**12**	**6**
1988–89	Sheffield U	38	11		
1989–90	Sheffield U	5	2		
1990–91	Sheffield U	2	0		
1990–91	*Rotherham U*	17	4	**17**	**4**
1991–92	Sheffield U	2	0		
1992–93	Sheffield U	0	0		
1992–93	*Blackpool*	5	1	**5**	**1**
1992–93	*Bournemouth*	0	0		
1992–93	*Stockport Co*	7	4	**7**	**4**
1992–93	*Crewe Alex*	2	0	**2**	**0**
1993–94	Sheffield U	0	0	**58**	**14**
1993–94	Hamilton A	36	19		
1994–95	Hamilton A	36	20	**72**	**39**
1995–96	Airdrieonians	24	6	**24**	**6**
1995–96	Raith R	9	5		
1996–97	Raith R	33	5		
1997–98	Raith R	0	0		
1998–99	Raith R	0	0	**42**	**10**
1998–99	Darlington	14	2		
1999–2000	Darlington	33	12	**47**	**14**
2000–01	York C	6	3		
2001–02	York C	11	3	**17**	**6**

EDMONDSON, Darren# (D) 321 9
H: 6 0 W: 12 07 b.Ulverston 4-11-71
Source: Trainee.

1990–91	Carlisle U	31	0		
1991–92	Carlisle U	27	2		
1992–93	Carlisle U	34	0		
1993–94	Carlisle U	22	3		
1994–95	Carlisle U	38	2		
1995–96	Carlisle U	42	1		
1996–97	Carlisle U	20	1	**214**	**9**
1996–97	Huddersfield T	10	0		
1997–98	Huddersfield T	19	0		
1998–99	Huddersfield T	3	0		
1998–99	*Plymouth Arg*	4	0	**4**	**0**
1999–2000	Huddersfield T	5	0	**37**	**0**
1999–2000	York C	7	0		
2000–01	York C	23	0		
2001–02	York C	36	0	**66**	**0**

EMMERSON, Scott§ (F)   14   1
H: 5 9 W: 12 07 b.Durham 10-10-82
Source: Scholar.
2000–01 York C 8 1
2001–02 York C 6 0 14 1

EVANS, Michael‡ (F)   2   0
H: 6 0 W: 12 02 b.Venlo 21-7-76
Source: Venlosche Boys.
2001–02 York C 2 0 2 0

FETTIS, Alan (G)   257   2
H: 6 0 W: 13 09 b.Newtownards 1-2-71
Source: Ards. *Honours:* Northern Ireland Schools, Youth, B, 25 full caps.
1991–92 Hull C 43 0
1992–93 Hull C 20 0
1993–94 Hull C 37 0
1994–95 Hull C 28 2
1995–96 Hull C 7 0 135 2
1995–96 WBA 3 0 3 0
1996–97 Nottingham F 4 0
1997–98 Nottingham F 0 0 4 0
1997–98 Blackburn R 8 0
1998–99 Blackburn R 2 0
1999–2000 Blackburn R 1 0 11 0
1999–2000 Leicester C 0 0
1999–2000 York C 13 0
2000–01 York C 46 0
2001–02 York C 45 0 104 0

FIELDING, John* (D)   9   1
H: 6 1 W: 14 07 b.Billingham 7-4-82
Source: Scholar.
2001–02 York C 9 1 9 1

FOX, Christian (M)   54   1
H: 5 10 W: 11 12 b.Auchenbrae 11-4-81
Source: Trainee.
1999–2000 York C 34 1
2000–01 York C 8 0
2001–02 York C 12 0 54 1

GRANT, Lee (D)   1   0
H: 6 0 W: 11 00 b.York 31-12-85
2001–02 York C 1 0 1 0

HOBSON, Gary (D)   287   2
H: 6 1 W: 13 04 b.North Ferriby 12-11-72
Source: Trainee.
1990–91 Hull C 4 0
1991–92 Hull C 16 0
1992–93 Hull C 21 0
1993–94 Hull C 36 0
1994–95 Hull C 36 0
1995–96 Hull C 29 0 142 0
1995–96 Brighton & HA 9 0
1996–97 Brighton & HA 37 1
1997–98 Brighton & HA 33 0
1998–99 Brighton & HA 13 0
1999–2000 Brighton & HA 6 0 98 1
1999–2000 Chester C 20 0 20 0
2000–01 York C 11 0
2001–02 York C 16 0 27 0

HOCKING, Matt* (D)   154   4
H: 6 0 W: 12 09 b.Boston 30-1-78
Source: Trainee.
1995–96 Sheffield U 0 0
1996–97 Sheffield U 0 0
1997–98 Sheffield U 0 0
1997–98 Hull C 31 1
1998–99 Hull C 26 1 57 2
1998–99 *York C* 6 0
1999–2000 York C 32 2
2000–01 York C 26 0
2001–02 York C 33 0 97 2

HOWARTH, Russell (G)   8   0
H: 6 2 W: 14 07 b.York 27-3-82
Source: Scholar. *Honours:* England Youth, Under-20.
1999–2000 York C 6 0

2000–01 York C 0 0
2001–02 York C 2 0 8 0

MATHIE, Alex (F)   310   82
H: 5 10 W: 12 00 b.Bathgate 20-12-68
Source: Celtic BC. *Honours:* Scotland Youth.
1987–88 Celtic 0 0
1988–89 Celtic 1 0
1989–90 Celtic 6 0
1990–91 Celtic 4 0 11 0
1991–92 Morton 42 18
1992–93 Morton 32 13 74 31
1992–93 *Port Vale* 3 0 3 0
1993–94 Newcastle U 16 3
1994–95 Newcastle U 9 1 25 4
1994–95 Ipswich T 13 2
1995–96 Ipswich T 39 18
1996–97 Ipswich T 12 4
1997–98 Ipswich T 37 13
1998–99 Ipswich T 8 1 109 38
1998–99 Dundee U 22 1
1999–2000 Dundee U 12 3 34 4
1999–2000 Preston NE 12 2 12 2
2000–01 York C 19 1
2001–02 York C 23 2 42 3

NOGAN, Lee (F)   476   101
H: 5 10 W: 11 09 b.Cardiff 21-5-69
Source: Apprentice. *Honours:* Wales Under-21, B, 2 full caps.
1986–87 *Oxford U* 0 0
1986–87 *Brentford* 11 2 11 2
1987–88 *Oxford U* 3 0
1987–88 *Southend U* 6 1
1988–89 *Oxford U* 3 0
1989–90 *Oxford U* 4 0
1990–91 *Oxford U* 32 5
1991–92 *Oxford U* 22 5 64 10
1991–92 *Watford* 23 5
1992–93 *Watford* 42 11
1993–94 *Watford* 26 3
1993–94 *Southend U* 5 0 11 1
1994–95 *Watford* 14 7 105 26
1994–95 Reading 20 10
1995–96 Reading 39 10
1996–97 Reading 32 6 91 26
1996–97 *Notts Co* 6 0 6 0
1997–98 Grimsby T 36 8
1998–99 Grimsby T 38 2 74 10
1999–2000 Darlington 31 2
2000–01 Darlington 18 4 49 6
2000–01 *Luton T* 7 1 7 1
2000–01 York C 16 6
2001–02 York C 42 13 58 19

O'KANE, Aiden (M)   40   6
H: 5 9 W: 11 03 b.Belfast 24-11-79
2000–01 Cliftonville 28 6 28 6
2001–02 York C 12 0 12 0

PARKIN, Jonathan (D)   29   2
H: 6 1 W: 15 00 b.Barnsley 30-12-81
Source: Scholar.
1998–99 Barnsley 2 0
1999–2000 Barnsley 0 0
2000–01 Barnsley 4 0
2001–02 Barnsley 4 0 10 0
2001–02 *Hartlepool U* 1 0 1 0
2001–02 York C 18 2 18 2

POTTER, Graham (D)   207   7
H: 5 11 W: 11 13 b.Solihull 20-5-75
Source: Trainee. *Honours:* England Youth, Under-21.
1992–93 Birmingham C 18 2
1993–94 Birmingham C 7 0 25 2
1993–94 *Wycombe W* 3 0 3 0
1993–94 Stoke C 3 0
1994–95 Stoke C 1 0
1995–96 Stoke C 41 1 45 1
1996–97 Southampton 8 0 8 0
1996–97 WBA 6 0

1997–98 WBA 5 0
1997–98 *Northampton T* 4 0 4 0
1998–99 WBA 22 0
1999–2000 WBA 10 0 43 0
1999–2000 Reading 4 0 4 0
2000–01 York C 38 2
2001–02 York C 37 2 75 4

RHODES, Benjamin§ (M)   1   0
H: 5 10 W: 11 12 b.York 2-5-83
Source: Scholar.
2001–02 York C 1 0 1 0

RICHARDSON, Nick* (M)   435   45
H: 6 0 W: 12 06 b.Halifax 11-4-67
Source: Local.
1988–89 Halifax T 7 0
1989–90 Halifax T 27 6
1990–91 Halifax T 26 3
1991–92 Halifax T 41 8 101 17
1992–93 Cardiff C 39 4
1993–94 Cardiff C 39 5
1994–95 Cardiff C 33 4 111 13
1994–95 Wrexham 4 2 4 2
1994–95 Chester C 6 1
1995–96 Bury 5 0 5 0
1995–96 Chester C 37 4
1996–97 Chester C 9 0
1997–98 Chester C 44 2
1998–99 Chester C 43 3
1999–2000 Chester C 36 2
2000–01 Chester C 0 0 175 12
2000–01 York C 17 1
2001–02 York C 22 0 39 1

SALVATI, Marc§ (M)   8   1
b.Middlesbrough 5-3-83
Source: Scholar.
2001–02 York C 8 1 8 1

SMITH, Christopher (D)   15   0
H: 5 11 W: 13 01 b.Derby 30-6-81
Source: Trainee.
1999–2000 Reading 0 0
2000–01 Reading 0 0
2001–02 York C 15 0 15 0

STAMP, Neville* (D)   21   0
H: 5 9 W: 13 01 b.Reading 7-7-81
Source: Trainee.
1998–99 Reading 1 0
1999–2000 Reading 0 0
2000–01 Reading 0 0 1 0
2000–01 York C 13 0
2001–02 York C 7 0 20 0

THOMPSON, Marc* (D)   22   0
H: 5 10 W: 13 05 b.York 15-1-82
1999–2000 York C 10 0
2000–01 York C 12 0
2001–02 York C 0 0 22 0

WISE, Stuart§ (M)   6   0
b.Middlesbrough 4-4-84
Source: Scholar.
2001–02 York C 6 0 6 0

WOOD, Leigh (M)   19   0
H: 5 11 W: 11 10 b.Selby 21-5-83
Source: Scholar.
2000–01 York C 5 0
2001–02 York C 14 0 19 0

Scholars
Barry, Daniel; Boyce, Marvin; Coad, Matthew P; Collinson, Jonathan E; Darlow, Kieran B; Davies, Sean G; Emmerson, Scott; Hampshire, Mark; Ibbetson, Luke G; Law, Graeme; Mackenzie, Michael; McCabe, Matthew D; Ormston, Gary; Rhodes, Benjamin; Salvati, Marc R; Vasey, Peter WJ; Wise, Stuart; Yalcin, Leven
Non-Contract
Batchelor, William J

TRANSFERS 2001–02

	From	To	Fee in £
June 2001	*From*	*To*	*Fee in £*
8 Alcide, Colin J.	York City	Cambridge United	Free
21 Alexander, Gary G.	Swindon Town	Hull City	160,000
4 Campbell, Stuart P.	Leicester City	Grimsby Town	200,000
25 Crichton, Paul A.	Burnley	Norwich City	150,000
19 Easton, Clint J.	Watford	Norwich City	200,000
14 Freeman, Mark W.	Cheltenham Town	Boston United	15,000
20 Glennon, Mathew W.	Bolton Wanderers	Hull City	50,000
27 Jeffers, Francis	Everton	Arsenal	10,000,000
27 Kerr, Scott A.	Bradford City	Hull City	undisclosed
11 McLaren, Paul A.	Luton Town	Sheffield Wednesday	Free
20 Pitcher, Geoffrey	Kingstonian	Brighton & Hove Albion	55,000
5 Pollitt, Michael F.	Chesterfield	Rotherham United	75,000
28 Rivers, Mark A.	Crewe Alexandra	Norwich City	600,000
1 Simpkins, Michael	Chesterfield	Cardiff City	Free
20 Vaesen, Nico	Huddersfield Town	Birmingham City	800,000
4 Warner, Philip	Southampton	Cambridge United	Free
23 Wise, Dennis F.	Chelsea	Leicester City	1,600,000
July 2001			
11 Bellamy, Craig D.	Coventry City	Newcastle United	6,000,000
27 Carroll, Roy E.	Wigan Athletic	Manchester United	2,500,000
20 Clarke, Darrell J.	Mansfield Town	Hartlepool United`	undisclosed
6 Conlon, Barry J.	York City	Darlington	60,000
18 Cresswell, Richard P.W.	Leicester City	Preston North End	500,000
11 Crouch, Peter J.	Queens Park Rangers	Portsmouth	1,250,000
14 Currie, Darren	Barnet	Wycombe Wanderers	200,000
16 Darlington, Jermaine C.	Queens Park Rangers	Wimbledon	200,000
21 Delap, Rory J.	Derby County	Southampton	4,000,000
11 Dobie, Scott R.	Carlisle United	West Bromwich Albion	150,000
7 Dudfield, Lawrie G.	Leicester City	Hull City	210,000
12 Emblen, Neil R.	Wolverhampton Wanderers	Norwich City	500,000
16 Euell, Jason J.	Wimbledon	Charlton Athletic	4,750,000
21 Fletcher, Gary	Northwich Victoria	Leyton Orient	150,000
16 Forbes, Adrian E.	Norwich City	Luton Town	60,000
24 Gorre, Dean	Huddersfield Town	Barnsley	50,000
10 Griffiths, Carl B.	Leyton Orient	Luton Town	65,000
16 Hackworth, Anthony	Leeds United	Notts County	120,000
9 Hadji, Moustapha	Coventry City	Aston Villa	2,250,000
16 Hughes, Andrew J.	Notts County	Reading	Free
19 Ireland, Craig	Dundee	Notts County	50,000
17 James, David B.	Aston Villa	West Ham United	3,500,000
26 Jevons, Philip	Everton	Grimsby Town	150,000
11 Joachim, Julian K.	Aston Villa	Coventry City	exch.
4 Jones, Stephen G.	Leigh RMI	Crewe Alexandra	75,000
6 Kavanagh, Graham A.	Stoke City	Cardiff City	1,000,000
7 Kennedy, Mark J.	Manchester City	Wolverhampton Wanderers	1,800,000
18 Kennedy, Peter H.J.	Watford	Wigan Athletic	300,000
3 Lampard, Frank J.	West Ham United	Chelsea	11,000,000
16 Mildenhall, Stephen J.	Swindon Town	Notts County	150,000
17 Miller, Thomas W.	Hartlepool United	Ipswich Town	800,000
17 Palmer, Stephen L.	Watford	Queens Park Rangers	Free
12 Peschisolido, Paul P.	Fulham	Sheffield United	150,000
10 Poyet, Gustavo D.A.	Chelsea	Tottenham Hotspur	2,250,000
3 Prior, Spencer J.	Manchester City	Cardiff City	650,000
16 Reddington, Stuart	Chelsea	Mansfield Town	20,000
24 Richards, Tony S.	Barnet	Southend United	36,000
31 Scowcroft, James B.	Ipswich Town	Leicester City	3,000,000
25 Shipperley, Neil J.	Barnsley	Wimbledon	750,000
14 Southgate, Gareth	Aston Villa	Middlesbrough	6,500,000
13 Stockley, Sam J.	Barnet	Oxford United	150,000
26 Walker, Ian M.	Tottenham Hotspur	Leicester City	2,500,000
9 Williams, Ryan N.	Chesterfield	Hull City	150,000
13 Williams, Thomas A.	West Ham United	Peterborough United	Free
13 Wright, Richard I.	Ipswich Town	Arsenal	6,000,000
27 Young, Luke P.	Tottenham Hotspur	Charlton Athletic	3,000,000
Temporary transfers			
17 Bywater, Stephen M.	West Ham United	Wolverhampton Wanderers	
9 Clarke, Matthew J.	Bradford City	Fulham	
25 Cummings, Warren	Chelsea	West Bromwich Albion	
10 Noble, David J.	Arsenal	Watford	
4 Parkin, Sam	Chelsea	Northampton Town	
4 Wolleaston, Robert A.	Chelsea	Northampton Town	
August 2001			
6 Alexander, Neil	Livingston	Cardiff City	200,000
2 Berkovic, Eyal	Celtic	Manchester City	1,500,000
10 Brammer, David	Port Vale	Crewe Alexandra	500,000
24 Burchill, Mark J.	Celtic	Portsmouth	600,000
24 Cameron, Colin	Heart of Midlothian	Wolverhampton Wanderers	1,750,000
9 Clements, Matthew	Mildenhall Town	Cambridge United	undisclosed
8 De Vos, Jason R.	Dundee United	Wigan Athletic	500,000
9 Evans, Gareth J.	Leeds United	Huddersfield Town	Free
9 Forbes, Adrian E.	Norwich City	Luton Town	60,000
8 Gayle, Marcus A.	Rangers	Watford	900,000
9 Greening, Jonathan	Manchester United	Middlesbrough	2,000,000
8 Harley, Jon	Chelsea	Fulham	3,500,000
2 Hartson, John	Coventry City	Celtic	6,500,000
9 Holmes, Shaun P.	Manchester City	Wrexham	Free
9 Hughes, Lee	West Bromwich Albion	Coventry City	5,000,000
31 Hutchison, Donald	Sunderland	West Ham United	5,000,000
15 Kelly, Leon M.	Atherstone United	Cambridge United	15,000
24 Kerr, James S.R.	Celtic	Wigan Athletic	undisclosed

31 Kirkland, Christopher	Coventry City	Liverpool	6,000,000
23 Lucketti, Christopher J.	Huddersfield Town	Preston North End	undisclosed
20 McNeil, Martin J.	Cambridge United	Torquay United	Free
10 Newton, Shaun O.	Charlton Athletic	Wolverhampton Wanderers	850,000
3 Nicholls, Kevin J.	Wigan Athletic	Luton Town	25,000
2 Nowland, Adam C.	Blackpool	Wimbledon	undisclosed
9 O'Neill, Keith P.	Middlesbrough	Coventry City	1,000,000
9 Perpetuini, David P.	Watford	Gillingham	100,000
10 Perrett, Russell	Cardiff City	Luton Town	Free
23 Wainwright, Neil	Sunderland	Darlington	50,000
9 Wilson, Mark A.	Manchester United	Middlesbrough	1,500,000
1 Ziege, Christian	Liverpool	Tottenham Hotspur	4,000,000

Temporary transfers

10 Adamczuk, Dariuz	Rangers	Wigan Athletic	
10 Beharall, David	Newcastle United	Grimsby Town	
18 Beresford, Marlon	Middlesbrough	Wolverhampton Wanderers	
25 Berkley, Austin J.	Barnet	Carlisle United	
10 Birch, Gary S.	Walsall	Exeter City	
16 Burgess, Benjamin K.	Blackburn Rovers	Brentford	
9 Byrne, Desmond	Wimbledon	Cambridge United	
31 Capleton, Melvin D.R.	Southend United	Grays Athletic	
17 Chillingworth, Daniel T.	Cambridge United	Cambridge City	
27 Constantine, Leon	Millwall	Leyton Orient	
16 Croudson, Steven D.	Grimsby Town	Scunthorpe United	
11 Crowe, Dean A.	Stoke City	Plymouth Argyle	
23 Dichio, Daniele S.E.	Sunderland	West Bromwich Albion	
18 Dorrian, Christopher S.	Leyton Orient	Dover Athletic	
10 Evatt, Ian R.	Derby County	Northampton Town	
15 Futcher, Benjamin P.	Oldham Athletic	Stalybridge Celtic	
31 Hammond, Elvis Z.	Fulham	Bristol Rovers	
18 Hillier, Ian M.	Tottenham Hotspur	Luton Town	
17 Hodgson, Steven G.	Macclesfield Town	Nuneaton Borough	
18 Hyde, Graham	Birmingham City	Chesterfield	
24 Kelly, Alan T.	Blackburn Rovers	Birmingham City	
17 McIntosh, Martin	Hibernian	Rotherham United	
9 McNeil, Martin J.	Cambridge United	Torquay United	
24 Myers, Peter W.	Halifax Town	Guiseley	
9 Navarro, Alan E.	Liverpool	Crewe Alexandra	
17 O'Flynn, John	Peterborough United	Cambridge City	
17 Okikiolu, Samuel K.	Wimbledon	Clyde	
18 Opara, Kelechi C.	Leyton Orient	Billericay Town	
24 Osei-Kuffour, Jonathan	Arsenal	Swindon Town	
8 Page, Robert J.	Watford	Sheffield United	
25 Parsons, David	Leyton Orient	Dover Athletic	
6 Peacock, Gavin K.	Queens Park Rangers	Charlton Athletic	
9 Proctor, Michael A.	Sunderland	York City	
10 Pullen, James	Ipswich Town	Blackpool	
7 Ramsay, Scott A.	Brighton & Hove Albion	Yeovil Town	
10 Richards, Marc J.	Blackburn Rovers	Crewe Alexandra	
24 Robinson, Paul M.J.	Millwall	Fisher Athletic	
25 Salt, Philip T.	Oldham Athletic	Leigh RMI	
17 Savic, Sinisa	Barnsley	Frickley Athletic	
14 Smart, Allan A.C.	Watford	Hibernian	
30 Taylor, Robert A.	Wolverhampton Wanderers	Queens Park Rangers	
21 Tod, Andrew	Dunfermline Athletic	Bradford City	
30 Tyson, Nathan	Reading	Swansea City	
17 Wainwright, Neil	Sunderland	Darlington	
24 Webb, Paul A.	Kidderminster Harriers	Hereford United	
16 Whitfield, Paul M.	Wrexham	Connah's Quay Nomads	
10 Wilkie, Lee	Dundee	Notts County	
23 Woozley, David J.	Crystal Palace	Torquay United	

September 2001

13 Belgrave, Barrington	Yeovil Town	Southend United	40,000
13 Blake, Nathan A.	Blackburn Rovers	Wolverhampton Wanderers	1,400,000
7 Clarke, Matthew J.	Bradford City	Crystal Palace	1,350,000
18 Coyne, Christopher J.	Dundee	Luton Town	50,000
10 Dinning, Tony	Wolverhampton Wanderers	Wigan Athletic	750,000
21 Goodhind, Warren	Barnet	Cambridge United	80,000
13 Hanlon, Ritchie K.	Peterborough United	Rushden & Diamonds	undisclosed
5 Jackson, Justin J.	Rushden & Diamonds	Doncaster Rovers	120,000
19 Johnson, Andrew J.	Nottingham Forest	West Bromwich Albion	200,000
6 Marsh, Christopher J.	Wycombe Wanderers	Northampton Town	10,000
24 Moody, Paul	Millwall	Oxford United	150,000
14 Moore, Darren M.	Portsmouth	West Bromwich Albion	750,000
7 Neill, Lucas E.	Millwall	Blackburn Rovers	1,000,000
14 Page, Robert J.	Watford	Sheffield United	350,000
13 Partridge, Scott M.	Brentford	Rushden & Diamonds	undisclosed
13 Patmore, Warren J.	Rushden & Diamonds	Woking	40,000
21 Rae, Alexander S.	Sunderland	Wolverhampton Wanderers	1,200,000
24 Richards, Dean I.	Southampton	Tottenham Hotspur	8,100,000
28 Richardson, Marcus G.	Cambridge United	Torquay United	undisclosed
13 Thorne, Peter L.	Stoke City	Cardiff City	1,700,000

Temporary transfers

7 Andrews, John H.	Mansfield Town	Hucknall Town	
24 Antony, Paul M.	Carlisle United	Newry Town	
29 Arphexad, Pegguy M.	Liverpool	Stockport County	
11 Barrett, Graham	Arsenal	Crewe Alexandra	
14 Beharall, David	Newcastle United	Grimsby Town	
21 Bennion, Christopher	Middlesbrough	Scunthorpe United	
7 Bettney, Scott	Sheffield Wednesday	Worksop Town	
7 Bragstad, Bjorn O.	Derby County	Birmingham City	
7 Broomes, Marlon C.	Blackburn Rovers	Grimsby Town	
14 Brown, Wayne L.	Ipswich Town	Wimbledon	
19 Burgess, Benjamin K.	Blackburn Rovers	Brentford	
7 Caceres, Adrian C.	Southampton	Brentford	
21 Capaldi, Anthony C.	Birmingham City	Hereford United	

17 Casey, Ryan P.	Swansea City	Merthyr Tydfil	
28 Castle, Stephen C.	Leyton Orient	Stevenage Borough	
25 Chettle, Stephen	Barnsley	Walsall	
16 Chillingworth, Daniel T.	Cambridge United	Cambridge City	
25 Cockrill, Dale	Cambridge United	Aylesbury United	
28 Constantine, Leon	Millwall	Leyton Orient	
29 Crowe, Dean	Stoke City	Luton Town	
20 Curtis, Thomas D.	Portsmouth	Walsall	
7 Dinning, Tony	Wolverhampton Wanderers	Wigan Athletic	
10 Evatt, Ian R.	Derby County	Northampton Town	
15 Futcher, Benjamin P.	Oldham Athletic	Stalybridge Celtic	
15 Gould, Ronny D.	Leyton Orient	Heybridge Swifts	
6 Grayson, Simon N.	Blackburn Rovers	Notts County	
14 Gregg, Matthew S.	Crystal Palace	Exeter City	
10 Hanlon, Ritchie K.	Peterborough United	Rushden & Diamonds	
28 Harris, Richard L.S.	Crystal Palace	Mansfield Town	
20 Hillier, Ian M.	Tottenham Hotspur	Luton Town	
14 Holmes, Derek	Ross County	AFC Bournemouth	
20 Hoolickin, Lee	Carlisle United	Gretna	
14 Hunter, Barry V.	Reading	Rushden & Diamonds	
19 Hyde, Graham	Birmingham City	Chesterfield	
7 Ilic, Sasa	Charlton Athletic	Portsmouth	
14 Kelly, Leon M.	Cambridge United	Stalybridge Celtic	
24 Killen, Christopher J.	Manchester City	Port Vale	
14 Larkin, Colin	Wolverhampton Wanderers	Kidderminster Harriers	
21 Lewis, Craig	Carlisle United	Workington	
12 Liddle, Graham	Darlington	Whitby Town	
18 Lockwood, Adam B.	Reading	Yeovil Town	
27 Maley, Mark	Sunderland	York City	
21 May, Kyle	Carlisle United	Gretna	
3 McCready, Christopher J.	Crewe Alexandra	Hyde United	
3 McElholm, Brendan A.	Leyton Orient	Chelmsford City	
7 McGill, Brendan	Sunderland	Carlisle United	
7 Miller, Kenneth	Rangers	Wolverhampton Wanderers	
18 Miller, William	Dundee	Wrexham	
21 Moody, Paul	Millwall	Oxford United	
18 Murphy, Danny	Queens Park Rangers	Hampton & Richmond Borough	
8 Murray, Jade A.	Leyton Orient	Sutton United	
17 Mustoe, Neil J.	Cambridge United	Cambridge City	
9 Navarro, Alan E.	Liverpool	Crewe Alexandra	
21 Nelson, Craig M.	Middlesbrough	Gateshead	
21 Ormerod, Anthony	Middlesbrough	Hartlepool United	
7 Palmer, Carlton L.	Coventry City	Sheffield Wednesday	
9 Proctor, Michael A.	Sunderland	York City	
10 Pullen, James	Ipswich Town	Blackpool	
21 Reddy, Michael	Sunderland	Hull City	
18 Richardson, Marcus G.	Cambridge United	Torquay United	
23 Robinson, Paul M.J.	Millwall	Fisher Athletic	
28 Rustem, Adam R.	Queens Park Rangers	Chertsey Town	
26 Salt, Philip T.	Oldham Athletic	Leigh RMI	
11 Singh, Harpal	Leeds United	Bury	
7 Smith, Grant G.	Sheffield United	Halifax Town	
5 Stamp, Philip L.	Middlesbrough	Millwall	
28 Summerbell, Mark	Middlesbrough	Bristol City	
8 Tate, Christopher D.	Leyton Orient	Stevenage Borough	
25 Uka, Niam	Leyton Orient	Wingate & Finchley	
20 Vickers, Stephen	Middlesbrough	Crystal Palace	
13 Walker, Richard M.	Aston Villa	Wycombe Wanderers	
28 Ward, Christopher	Birmingham City	Forest Green Rovers	
28 Webb, Paul A.	Kidderminster Harriers	Hereford United	
27 Wheatcroft, Paul M.	Bolton Wanderers	Rochdale	
22 White, Jason G.	Cheltenham Town	Mansfield Town	
7 Wilford, Aron L.	Middlesbrough	Scarborough	
21 Williams, Lee	Mansfield Town	Cheltenham Town	
23 Woozley, David J.	Crystal Palace	Torquay United	
28 Wright, Daniel J.	Queens Park Rangers	Chertsey Town	

October 2001

22 Armstrong, Christopher	Bury	Oldham Athletic	200,000
27 Crowe, Dean A.	Stoke City	Luton Town	Free
12 Gill, Wayne J.	Tranmere Rovers	Oldham Athletic	70,000
11 Grant, Anthony J.	Manchester City	Burnley	undisclosed
19 Green, Ryan M.	Wolverhampton Wanderers	Millwall	Free
19 Johnson, Seth A.M.	Derby County	Leeds United	7,000,000
19 McAteer, Jason W.	Blackburn Rovers	Sunderland	1,000,000
8 Mullin, John	Burnley	Rotherham United	150,000
19 Neilson, Alan B.	Fulham	Grimsby Town	undisclosed
19 Roberts, Stuart I.	Swansea City	Wycombe Wanderers	102,500
1 Sharpling, Christopher	Crystal Palace	Woking	60,000
3 Ward, Darren P.	Watford	Millwall	500,000
31 Williams, Paul D.	Coventry City	Southampton	undisclosed

Temporary transfers

19 Beharall, David	Newcastle United	Grimsby Town	
21 Bennion, Christopher	Middlesbrough	Scunthorpe United	
11 Betts, Robert	Coventry City	Lincoln City	
19 Boardman, Jonathan G.	Crystal Palace	Margate	
8 Broomes, Marlon C.	Blackburn Rovers	Grimsby Town	
16 Browne, Ricky D.	Queens Park Rangers	Enfield	
14 Brown, Wayne L.	Ipswich Town	Wimbledon	
22 Bullock, Matthew	Stoke City	Macclesfield Town	
2 Butterworth, Adam L.	Cambridge United	Heybridge Swifts	
12 Caldwell, Stephen	Newcastle United	Blackpool	
18 Carbone, Benito	Bradford City	Derby County	
12 Carlisle, Wayne T.	Crystal Palace	Swindon Town	
28 Castle, Stephen C.	Leyton Orient	Stevenage Borough	
19 Charles, Anthony D.	Crewe Alexandra	Hayes	
29 Charles, Julian	Brentford	Farnborough Town	
19 Clements, Matthew	Cambridge United	Stalybridge Celtic	

Player	From	To	Fee
26 De-Vulgt, Leigh S.	Swansea City	Merthyr Tydfil	
23 Douglas, Stuart A.	Luton Town	Oxford United	
23 Etherington, Matthew	Tottenham Hotspur	Bradford City	
12 Feuer, Anthony I.	Wimbledon	Derby County	
26 Flowers, Timothy D.	Leicester City	Stockport County	
5 Folan, Caleb C.	Leeds United	Rushden & Diamonds	
25 Foley, Dominic J.	Watford	Queens Park Rangers	
8 Ford, Ryan	Notts County	Gresley Rovers	
15 Futcher, Benjamin P.	Oldham Athletic	Stalybridge Celtic	
9 Gray, Philip	Oxford United	Boston United	
11 Grayson, Simon N.	Blackburn Rovers	Notts County	
27 Grimsdell, Daniel B.	Leyton Orient	Aveley	
12 Hahnemann, Marcus S.	Fulham	Rochdale	
4 Hammond, Elvis Z.	Fulham	Bristol Rovers	
15 Hankin, Sean A.	Crystal Palace	Torquay United	
11 Hill, Keith J.	Cheltenham Town	Wrexham	
26 Hillier, Ian M.	Tottenham Hotspur	Luton Town	
27 Hitzlsperger, Thomas	Aston Villa	Chesterfield	
12 Holden, Dean T.J.	Bolton Wanderers	Oldham Athletic	
18 Hoolickin, Lee	Carlisle United	Gretna	
19 Jackson, Matthew A.	Norwich City	Wigan Athletic	
29 Killen, Christopher J.	Manchester City	Port Vale	
23 Knight, Leon L.	Chelsea	Huddersfield Town	
14 Larkin, Colin	Wolverhampton Wanderers	Kidderminster Harriers	
24 Liddle, Gareth J.C.	Crewe Alexandra	Hyde United	
19 Lovett, Jay	Brentford	Crawley Town	
8 Lumsdon, Christopher	Sunderland	Barnsley	
26 Maley, Mark	Sunderland	York City	
19 May, Kyle	Carlisle United	Gretna	
20 McClare, Sean P.	Barnsley	Port Vale	
10 McGill, Brendan	Sunderland	Carlisle United	
27 Moore, Stefan	Aston Villa	Chesterfield	
5 Mullin, John	Burnley	Rotherham United	
9 Murray, Jade	Leyton Orient	Sutton United	
19 Nacca, Francesco	Cambridge United	Cambridge City	
22 Nelson, Craig M.	Middlesbrough	Gateshead	
5 O'Brien, Christopher T.	Liverpool	Chester City	
19 Odejayi, Olukayode	Bristol City	Forest Green Rovers	
4 O'Flynn, John	Peterborough United	Cambridge City	
27 Opara, Kelechi C.	Leyton Orient	Purfleet	
22 Ormerod, Anthony	Middlesbrough	Hartlepool United	
19 Oster, John	Sunderland	Barnsley	
26 O'Sullivan, Christopher	Swansea City	Aberystwyth Town	
9 Peacock, Gavin K.	Queens Park Rangers	Charlton Athletic	
26 Pearce, Alexander G.	Chesterfield	Ilkeston Town	
8 Proctor, Michael A.	Sunderland	York City	
10 Pullen, James	Ipswich Town	Blackpool	
12 Richards, Marc J.	Blackburn Rovers	Oldham Athletic	
5 Risbridger, Gareth	Southend United	Dover Athletic	
30 Rosler, Uwe	Southampton	West Bromwich Albion	
23 Ross, Neil J.	Stockport County	Bristol Rovers	
26 Rustem, Adam R.	Queens Park Rangers	Chertsey Town	
26 Samuel, J. Lloyd	Aston Villa	Gillingham	
11 Sandford, Lee R.	Sheffield United	Stockport County	
23 Shittu, Daniel O.	Charlton Athletic	Queens Park Rangers	
23 Sidwell, Steven J.	Arsenal	Brentford	
14 Singh, Harpal	Leeds United	Bury	
8 Skinner, Stephen K.	Gretna	Carlisle United	
9 Smith, Grant G.	Sheffield United	Halifax Town	
8 Taylor, Robert A.	Wolverhampton Wanderers	Gillingham	
26 Thogersen, Thomas	Portsmouth	Walsall	
22 Tudor, Shane A.	Wolverhampton Wanderers	Cambridge United	
5 Varty, John W.	Carlisle United	Workington	
14 Walker, Richard M.	Aston Villa	Wycombe Wanderers	
29 Wheatcroft, Paul M.	Bolton Wanderers	Rochdale	
16 White, Thomas J.C.	Portsmouth	Havant & Waterlooville	
7 Wilford, Aron L.	Middlesbrough	Scarborough	
26 Williams, Paul D.	Coventry City	Southampton	
26 Wright, Daniel J.	Queens Park Rangers	Chertsey Town	

November 2001

Player	From	To	Fee
23 Bent, Marcus N.	Blackburn Rovers	Ipswich Town	3,000,000
14 Clark, Ian D.	Hartlepool United	Darlington	10,000
30 Deane, Brian C.	Middlesbrough	Leicester City	150,000
30 Ellison, Kevin	Leicester City	Stockport County	55,000
7 Folan, Anthony S.	Brentford	Bohemians	Free
30 Fowler, Robert B.	Liverpool	Leeds United	11,000,000
20 Gallen, Kevin A.	Barnsley	Queens Park Rangers	Free
9 Hamilton, Ian R.	Notts County	Lincoln City	Free
6 Hillier, Ian M.	Tottenham Hotspur	Luton Town	Free
28 Holmes, Derek	Ross County	AFC Bournemouth	40,000
20 Jackson, Matthew A.	Norwich City	Wigan Athletic	Free
30 Jones, Gary R.	Rochdale	Barnsley	175,000
16 Jones, Mark A.	Chesterfield	Raith Rovers	Free
14 Lescott, Aaron A.	Sheffield Wednesday	Stockport County	75,000
29 McClare, Sean P.	Barnsley	Port Vale	Free
15 McIntosh, Martin	Hibernian	Rotherham United	125,000
16 Rogers, Alan	Nottingham Forest	Leicester City	300,000
30 Smart, Allan A.C.	Watford	Oldham Athletic	225,000
19 Tod, Andrew	Dunfermline Athletic	Bradford City	100,000
23 Tudor, Shane A.	Wolverhampton Wanderers	Cambridge United	undisclosed
2 Zhiyi, Fan	Crystal Palace	Dundee	300,000

Temporary transfers

Player	From	To
9 Appleby, Richard D.	Swansea City	Kidderminster Harriers
15 Armstrong, Joel	Chesterfield	Hucknall Town
19 Beharall, David	Newcastle United	Oldham Athletic
21 Bennion, Christopher	Middlesbrough	Scunthorpe United
13 Bloomfield, Daniel R.	Norwich City	King's Lynn

23 Broad, Joseph R.	Plymouth Argyle	Yeovil Town	
14 Broomes, Marlon C.	Blackburn Rovers	Grimsby Town	
12 Brown, Wayne L.	Ipswich Town	Wimbledon	
2 Burgess, Benjamin K.	Blackburn Rovers	Brentford	
28 Burns, John C.	Bristol City	Shelbourne	
20 Caldwell, Gary	Newcastle United	Darlington	
3 Capaldi, Anthony C.	Birmingham City	Hereford United	
21 Charles, Anthony D.	Crewe Alexandra	Hayes	
30 Charles, Julian	Brentford	Farnborough Town	
19 Chillingworth, Daniel T.	Cambridge United	Darlington	
1 Chilvers, Liam C.	Arsenal	Notts County	
19 Clark, Steven T.	West Ham United	Southend United	
30 Cook, Paul A.	Burnley	Wigan Athletic	
15 Delaney, Damien	Leicester City	Stockport County	
30 Dichio, Daniele S.E.	Sunderland	West Bromwich Albion	
27 Dryden, Richard A.	Luton Town	Scarborough	
29 Dunning, Darren	Blackburn Rovers	Rochdale	
16 Edwards, Christian N.H.	Nottingham Forest	Crystal Palace	
27 Etherington, Matthew	Tottenham Hotspur	Bradford City	
15 Evans, Rhys K.	Chelsea	Queens Park Rangers	
9 Evans, Stephen J.	Crystal Palace	Swansea City	
16 Fleming, Curtis	Middlesbrough	Birmingham City	
30 Folan, Caleb C.	Leeds United	Hull City	
9 Ford, Ryan	Notts County	Gresley Rovers	
23 Gordon, Dean D.	Middlesbrough	Cardiff City	
2 Grant, John A.C.	Crewe Alexandra	Rushden & Diamonds	
30 Gray, Wayne W.	Wimbledon	Leyton Orient	
20 Hadland, Philip J.	Leyton Orient	Carlisle United	
15 Hankin, Sean A.	Crystal Palace	Torquay United	
23 Hanson, Christian	Middlesbrough	Torquay United	
2 Hillier, Ian M.	Tottenham Hotspur	Luton Town	
27 Hitzlsperger, Thomas	Aston Villa	Chesterfield	
13 Holden, Dean T.J.	Bolton Wanderers	Oldham Athletic	
8 Kelly, Leon M.	Cambridge United	Nuneaton Borough	
2 Kenna, Jeffrey J.	Blackburn Rovers	Wigan Athletic	
16 Knight, Leon L.	Chelsea	Huddersfield Town	
14 Larkin, Colin	Wolverhampton Wanderers	Kidderminster Harriers	
19 Leigertwood, Mikele B.	Wimbledon	Leyton Orient	
16 Lovett, Jay	Brentford	Crawley Town	
9 Lumsdon, Christopher	Sunderland	Barnsley	
26 Maley, Mark	Sunderland	York City	
23 Marsh, Adam	Darlington	Whitby Town	
6 Marshall, Ian P.	Bolton Wanderers	Blackpool	
22 May, Kyle	Carlisle United	Gretna	
30 McSheffrey, Gary	Coventry City	Stockport County	
30 Melligan, John J.	Wolverhampton Wanderers	AFC Bournemouth	
28 Mills, Rowan L.	Portsmouth	Coventry City	
22 Nacca, Francesco	Cambridge United	Cambridge City	
9 Navarro, Alan E.	Liverpool	Tranmere Rovers	
18 Odejayi, Olukayode	Bristol City	Forest Green Rovers	
23 Oleksewycz, Stephen M.	Halifax Town	Frickley Athletic	
26 Pearce, Alexander G.	Chesterfield	Ilkeston Town	
23 Phelan, Leeyon	Wycombe Wanderers	Ashford Town (Middlesex)	
20 Piper, Matthew J.	Leicester City	Mansfield Town	
5 Proctor, Michael A.	Sunderland	York City	
6 Pullen, James	Ipswich Town	Blackpool	
30 Quinn, Stephen J.	West Bromwich Albion	Notts County	
23 Rachubka, Paul S.	Manchester United	Oldham Athletic	
12 Richards, Marc J.	Blackburn Rovers	Oldham Athletic	
9 Richardson, Leam N.	Bolton Wanderers	Notts County	
2 Salako, John A.	Charlton Athletic	Reading	
28 Samuel, J. Lloyd	Aston Villa	Gillingham	
2 Scott, Dion E.	Walsall	Boston United	
23 Shields, Dene	Sunderland	Scarborough	
26 Shittu, Daniel O.	Charlton Athletic	Queens Park Rangers	
22 Sidwell, Steven J.	Arsenal	Brentford	
19 Singh, Harpal	Leeds United	Bury	
6 Smart, Allan A.C.	Watford	Stoke City	
8 Smith, Andrew W.	Sheffield United	Glenavon	
23 Smith, Jeffrey	Bolton Wanderers	Macclesfield Town	
20 Street, Kevin	Crewe Alexandra	Luton Town	
23 Sturridge, Dean C.	Leicester City	Wolverhampton Wanderers	
5 Tait, Paul	Crewe Alexandra	Hull City	
5 Thomson, Peter D.	Luton Town	Rushden & Diamonds	
9 Trainer, Philip A.	Crewe Alexandra	Hednesford Town	
16 Vickers, Stephen	Middlesbrough	Birmingham City	
15 Walker, Richard M.	Aston Villa	Wycombe Wanderers	
23 Ward, Scott	Luton Town	Boreham Wood	
2 Watson, Kevin E.	Rotherham United	Reading	
23 Webber, Daniel V.	Manchester United	Port Vale	
7 Williams, Lee	Mansfield Town	Cheltenham Town	
24 Wright, Daniel J.	Queens Park Rangers	Chertsey Town	
23 Wright, Mark A.	Walsall	Nuneaton Borough	

December 2001

14 Appleby, Richard D.	Swansea City	Kidderminster Harriers	Free
14 Beckett, Luke J.	Chesterfield	Stockport County	undisclosed
13 Broomes, Marlon C.	Blackburn Rovers	Sheffield Wednesday	Free
29 Cole, Andrew A.	Manchester United	Blackburn Rovers	7,500,000
21 Coote, Adrian	Norwich City	Colchester United	50,000
13 Crosby, Andrew K.	Brighton & Hove Albion	Oxford United	Free
5 Dichio, Daniele S.E.	Sunderland	West Bromwich Albion	1,250,000
14 Filan, John R.	Blackburn Rovers	Wigan Athletic	450,000
31 Fleming, Curtis	Middlesbrough	Crystal Palace	100,000
28 Granville, Daniel P.	Manchester City	Crystal Palace	500,000
9 Hamilton, Ian R.	Notts County	Lincoln City	undisclosed
7 Hankin, Sean A.	Crystal Palace	Torquay United	20,000
14 Hurst, Glynn	Stockport County	Chesterfield	Free

12 Lumsdon, Christopher	Sunderland	Barnsley	350,000
24 McEvilly, Lee	Burscough	Rochdale	20,000
14 Miller, Kenneth	Rangers	Wolverhampton Wanderers	3,000,000
12 Murray, Paul	Southampton	Oldham Athletic	Free
24 O'Brien, Christopher T.	Liverpool	Chester City	undisclosed
7 Ormerod, Brett R.	Blackpool	Southampton	1,750,000
24 Sturridge, Dean C.	Leicester City	Wolverhampton Wanderers	375,000
7 Symons, Christopher J.	Fulham	Crystal Palace	400,000
14 Teale, Gary	Ayr United	Wigan Athletic	200,000
18 Vickers, Stephen	Middlesbrough	Birmingham City	400,000
21 Walker, Richard M.	Aston Villa	Blackpool	50,000

Temporary transfers

7 Aldridge, Paul J.	Tranmere Rovers	Vauxhall Motors
19 Allott, Mark S.	Oldham Athletic	Chesterfield
24 Artell, David J.	Rotherham United	Chesterfield
14 Banks, Steven	Bolton Wanderers	Rochdale
14 Barrett, Graham	Arsenal	Colchester United
3 Bart-Williams, Christopher G.	Nottingham Forest	Charlton Athletic
20 Benjamin, Trevor J.	Leicester City	Crystal Palace
22 Birch, Gary S.	Walsall	Nuneaton Borough
11 Bloomfield, Daniel	Norwich City	Kings Lynn
21 Bound, Matthew T.	Swansea City	Oxford United
15 Brown, Craig V.	Leyton Orient	Sutton United
7 Caldwell, Stephen	Newcastle United	Bradford City
14 Carey, Shaun P.	Rushden & Diamonds	Stevenage Borough
24 Clark, Steven T.	West Ham United	Southend United
10 Cleary, Sean J.	Derby County	Gresley Rovers
14 Clements, Matthew C.	Cambridge United	Kings Lynn
14 Cockrill, Dale	Cambridge United	Wisbech Town
28 Day, Rhys	Manchester City	Blackpool
20 Delaney, Damien	Leicester City	Stockport County
7 Djordjic, Bojan	Manchester United	Sheffield Wednesday
5 Dryden, Richard A.	Luton Town	Scarborough
18 Edwards, Christian	Nottingham Forest	Crystal Palace
14 Fallon, Rory M.	Barnsley	Shrewsbury Town
21 Fletcher, Gary	Leyton Orient	Grays Athletic
14 Ford, Ryan	Notts County	Gresley Rovers
29 Gough, Neil	Leyton Orient	Chelmsford City
14 Green, Stuart	Newcastle United	Carlisle United
7 Hadley, Stewart A.	Kidderminster Harriers	Worcester City
14 Hahnemann, Marcus S.	Fulham	Reading
21 Hanson, Christian	Middlesbrough	Torquay United
19 Ingham, Michael G.	Sunderland	Stoke City
24 Innes, Mark	Oldham Athletic	Chesterfield
24 Kenna, Jeffrey J.	Blackburn Rovers	Birmingham City
21 Larkin, Colin	Wolverhampton Wanderers	Kidderminster Harriers
18 Leigertwood, Mikele B.	Wimbledon	Leyton Orient
6 Liddle, Gareth J.C.	Crewe Alexandra	Hyde United
13 Logan, Richard J.	Ipswich Town	Torquay United
23 Lovell, Mark	Gillingham	St Leonards
15 Lovett, Jay	Brentford	Crawley Town
14 Macauley, Steven R.	Crewe Alexandra	Macclesfield Town
20 Maley, Mark	Sunderland	York City
5 Marshall, Ian P.	Bolton Wanderers	Blackpool
3 McGill, Brendan	Sunderland	Carlisle United
14 McSwegan, Gary J.	Heart of Midlothian	Barnsley
31 Melligan, John J.	Wolverhampton Wanderers	AFC Bournemouth
28 Mills, Rowan L.	Portsmouth	Coventry City
21 Milosevic, Dejan	Leeds United	Wolverhampton Wanderers
14 Morley, David T.	Carlisle United	Oxford United
28 Muggleton, Carl D.	Cheltenham Town	Bradford City
14 Murray, Frederick A.	Blackburn Rovers	Cambridge United
14 Nielsen, David	Wimbledon	Norwich City
24 Oleksewycz, Steven	Halifax Town	Worksop Town
28 Panopoulos, Michael	Portsmouth	Dunfermline Athletic
7 Parkin, Jonathan	Barnsley	Hartlepool United
6 Payton, Andrew P.	Burnley	Blackpool
22 Piper, Matthew J.	Leicester City	Mansfield Town
23 Rachubka, Paul S.	Manchester United	Oldham Athletic
21 Ramsay, Scott A.	Brighton & Hove Albion	Bognor Regis Town
19 Reeves, David	Chesterfield	Oldham Athletic
31 Rodrigues, Daniel F.	Southampton	Bristol City
24 Royce, Simon E.	Leicester City	Brighton & Hove Albion
14 Samuels, Anthony	Chelmsford City	Welling United
28 Scott, Dion E.	Walsall	Boston United
21 Shields, Dene	Sunderland	Scarborough
24 Smith, Jeff	Bolton Wanderers	Macclesfield Town
6 Thomson, Peter	Luton Town	Rushden & Diamonds
21 Toner, Ciaran	Tottenham Hotspur	Peterborough United
10 Trainer, Philip A.	Crewe Alexandra	Hednesford Town
21 Traore, Demba	Cambridge United	Aylesbury United
12 Webb, Daniel J.	Southend United	Brighton & Hove Albion
6 White, Ben	Gillingham	Dover Athletic
21 Wilkinson, Shaun F.	Brighton & Hove Albion	Havant & Waterlooville
6 Windass, Dean	Middlesbrough	Sheffield Wednesday
20 Wright, Mark A.	Walsall	Nuneaton Borough
19 Wright, Mark S.	Preston North End	Glentoran

January 2002

31 Bart-Williams, Christopher G.	Nottingham Forest	Charlton Athletic	Free
25 Blake, Robert J.	Bradford City	Burnley	1,000,000
12 Challinor, David P.	Tranmere Rovers	Stockport County	120,000
25 Clark, Steven T.	West Ham United	Southend United	12,000
24 Etuhu, Dickson	Manchester City	Preston North End	300,000
29 Hadley, Stewart	Kidderminster Harriers	Worcester City	undisclosed
28 Hardiker, John	Morecambe	Stockport County	150,000
29 Innes, Mark	Oldham Athletic	Chesterfield	Free
11 Kuqi, Shefki	Stockport County	Sheffield Wednesday	700,000

11 Lee, David J.F.	Hull City	Brighton & Hove Albion	exch.
7 Marshall, Ian P.	Bolton Wanderers	Blackpool	Free
16 Mills, Rowan L.	Portsmouth	Coventry City	Free
18 Morley, David T.	Carlisle United	Oxford United	Free
23 Navarro, Alan E.	Liverpool	Tranmere Rovers	225,000
9 Nielsen, David	Wimbledon	Norwich City	200,000
9 Reeves, David	Chesterfield	Oldham Athletic	Free
31 Salako, John A.	Charlton Athletic	Reading	75,000
8 Shittu, Daniel O.	Charlton Athletic	Queens Park Rangers	250,000
11 Wicks, Matthew J.	Brighton & Hove Albion	Hull City	exch.
30 Xavier, Abel	Everton	Liverpool	800,000

Temporary transfers

10 Adamson, Christopher	West Bromwich Albion	Plymouth Argyle
19 Allott, Mark S.	Oldham Athletic	Chesterfield
15 Appleby, Matthew W.	Barnsley	Oldham Athletic
15 Banks, Steven	Bolton Wanderers	Rochdale
11 Barrett, Daniel T.	Chesterfield	Matlock Town
2 Bart-Williams, Christopher G.	Nottingham Forest	Charlton Athletic
31 Beresford, Marlon	Middlesbrough	Burnley
18 Birch, Gary S.	Walsall	Nuneaton Borough
26 Bolland, Philip C.	Oxford United	Chester City
22 Bound, Matthew T.	Swansea City	Oxford United
30 Brown, Wayne L.	Ipswich Town	Watford
18 Bruce, Joseph M.	Luton Town	Wingate & Finchley
18 Burley, Adam G.	Sheffield United	Scarborough
11 Caldwell, Stephen	Newcastle United	Bradford City
7 Chilvers, Liam C.	Arsenal	Notts County
10 Cleary, Sean J.	Derby County	Gresley Rovers
13 Cockrill, Dale	Cambridge United	Wisbech Town
10 Constantine, Leon	Millwall	Partick Thistle
25 Coppinger, James	Newcastle United	Hartlepool United
19 Cowan, Thomas	Cambridge United	Peterborough United
17 Croft, Gary	Ipswich Town	Wigan Athletic
22 Delaney, Damien	Leicester City	Stockport County
21 De-Vulgt, Leigh S.	Swansea City	Llanelli
26 Douglas, Stuart A.	Luton Town	Rushden & Diamonds
31 Draper, Craig J.	Swansea City	Llanelli
3 Dunning, Darren	Blackburn Rovers	Rochdale
14 Fallon, Rory	Barnsley	Shrewsbury Town
12 Flynn, Michael A.	Stockport County	Stoke City
11 Foley, Dominic J.	Watford	Swindon Town
22 Ghent, Matthew I.	Barnsley	Doncaster Rovers
29 Gough, Neil	Leyton Orient	Chelmsford City
2 Gray, Wayne W.	Wimbledon	Leyton Orient
15 Green, Stuart	Newcastle United	Carlisle United
7 Hadley, Stewart	Kidderminster Harriers	Worcester City
18 Halls, John	Arsenal	Colchester United
25 Hay, Alexander N.	Tranmere Rovers	Morecambe
10 Hazell, Reuben	Tranmere Rovers	Torquay United
22 Heald, Paul A.	Wimbledon	Sheffield Wednesday
29 Healy, Colin	Celtic	Coventry City
18 Holdsworth, David G.	Birmingham City	Walsall
4 Jackson, Kirk S.S.	Darlington	Stevenage Borough
11 Jackson, Michael D.	Cheltenham Town	Weston-Super-Mare
29 Kelly, Leon M.	Cambridge United	Dover Athletic
14 Logan, Richard J.	Ipswich Town	Torquay United
14 Mann, Neil	Hull City	Scarborough
25 Marsh, Adam	Darlington	Hampton & Richmond Borough
10 Melligan, John J.	Wolverhampton Wanderers	AFC Bournemouth
18 Montgomery, Gary S.	Coventry City	Crewe Alexandra
15 Morley, David T.	Carlisle United	Oxford United
13 Murray, Frederick A.	Blackburn Rovers	Cambridge United
18 Mvondo Antangana, Simon P.	Dundee United	Port Vale
21 Myhill, Glyn O.	Aston Villa	Stoke City
29 Naylor, Richard A.	Ipswich Town	Millwall
25 O'Hare, Alan P.J.	Bolton Wanderers	Chesterfield
10 O'Neill, Paul D.	Macclesfield Town	Bangor
9 Parkin, Jonathan	Barnsley	Hartlepool United
18 Partridge, David W.	Dundee United	Leyton Orient
10 Pennant, Jermaine	Arsenal	Watford
24 Piper, Matthew J.	Leicester City	Mansfield Town
18 Pitcher, Geoffrey	Brighton & Hove Albion	Woking
24 Rachubka, Paul S.	Manchester United	Oldham Athletic
29 Reid, Paul M.	Rangers	Preston North End
24 Richards, Justin	Bristol Rovers	Newport County
28 Roberts, Andrew J.	Wimbledon	Norwich City
17 Roberts, Ben J.	Charlton Athletic	Reading
25 Roberts, Neil W.	Wigan Athletic	Hull City
18 Rodwell, James R.	Rushden & Diamonds	Dagenham & Redbridge
22 Rose, Richard A.	Gillingham	Longford Town
3 Salako, John A.	Charlton Athletic	Reading
28 Shandran, Anthony M.	Burnley	St Patrick's Athletic
24 Shields, Anthony G.	Peterborough United	Stevenage Borough
22 Spiller, Daniel	Gillingham	Longford Town
18 Taylor, Robert A.	Wolverhampton Wanderers	Grimsby Town
18 Thompson, Andrew R.	Cardiff City	Shrewsbury Town
11 Trainer, Philip A.	Crewe Alexandra	Hednesford Town
25 Wardley, Stuart J.	Queens Park Rangers	Rushden & Diamonds
9 White, Ben	Gillingham	Dover Athletic
4 Whitehead, Damien S.	Macclesfield Town	Drogheda
20 Wilkinson, Shaun F.	Brighton & Hove Albion	Havant & Waterlooville
18 Woodman, Andrew J.	Colchester United	Oxford United
25 Wright, Daniel J.	Queens Park Rangers	Wealdstone

February 2002

6 Akinbiyi, Adeola P.	Leicester City	Crystal Palace	2,200,000
20 Allott, Mark S.	Oldham Athletic	Chesterfield	Free
18 Appleby, Matthew W.	Barnsley	Oldham Athletic	Free

15	Armstrong, Steven C.	Huddersfield Town	Sheffield Wednesday	100,000
1	Barton, Warren D.	Newcastle United	Derby County	nominal
27	Brackstone, Stephen	Middlesbrough	York City	undisclosed
20	Clarke, Christopher E.	Halifax Town	Blackpool	120,000
19	Clegg, Michael J.	Manchester United	Oldham Athletic	Free
22	Dickov, Paul	Manchester City	Leicester City	nominal
28	Haworth, Simon O.	Wigan Athletic	Tranmere Rovers	undisclosed
10	Hazell, Reuben	Tranmere Rovers	Torquay United	Free
15	Howson, Stuart L.	Blackburn Rovers	Chesterfield	Free
8	Jenas, Jermaine A.	Nottingham Forest	Newcastle United	5,000,000
8	John, Stern	Nottingham Forest	Birmingham City	Free
1	Kenna, Jeffrey J.	Blackburn Rovers	Birmingham City	Free
7	Lee, Robert M.	Newcastle United	Derby County	250,000
8	Marcelo, Cipriano	Birmingham City	Walsall	Free
15	Mike, Leon J.	Manchester City	Aberdeen	50,000
1	N'Diaye, Seyni	Tranmere Rovers	Dunfermline Athletic	undisclosed
8	O'Connor, Martin J.	Birmingham City	Walsall	Free
18	Peters, Mark W.	Southampton	Brentford	Free
12	Reeves, David	Chesterfield	Oldham Athletic	undisclosed
14	Savage, Basir M.	Walton & Hersham	Reading	undisclosed
13	Thomas, Danny J.	Leicester City	AFC Bournemouth	undisclosed
13	Tipton, Matthew J.	Oldham Athletic	Macclesfield Town	Free
28	Uddin, Anwar	West Ham United	Sheffield Wednesday	Free

Temporary transfers

23	Armstrong, Joel	Chesterfield	Ilkeston Town
13	Austin, Neil J.	Barnsley	Gateshead
18	Banks, Steven	Bolton Wanderers	Rochdale
13	Barrett, Daniel	Chesterfield	Matlock Town
11	Barry-Murphy, Brian	Preston North End	Southend United
1	Bedeau, Anthony C.O.	Torquay United	Barnsley
8	Benjamin, Trevor J.	Leicester City	Norwich City
28	Betsy, Kevin E.L.	Fulham	Barnsley
1	Bevan, Scott	Southampton	Stoke City
14	Boardman, Jonathan G.	Crystal Palace	Woking
28	Brown, Wayne L.	Ipswich Town	Watford
22	Bruce, Joseph M.	Luton Town	Wingate & Finchley
22	Burton, Deon J.	Derby County	Stoke City
27	Cameron, Martin G.W.	Bristol Rovers	Partick Thistle
25	Campbell, Andrew P.	Middlesbrough	Cardiff City
8	Carbone, Benito	Bradford City	Middlesbrough
8	Carsley, Lee K.	Coventry City	Everton
11	Charles, Anthony D.	Crewe Alexandra	Hayes
6	Clements, Matthew C.	Cambridge United	Kings Lynn
1	Combe, Alan	Dundee United	Bradford City
17	Cowan, Thomas	Cambridge United	Peterborough United
15	Cudworth, Thomas J.S.	Coventry City	Evesham United
5	Deeney, Saul	Notts County	Gresley Rovers
8	Devlin, Paul J.	Sheffield United	Birmingham City
1	Dudley, Craig B.	Oldham Athletic	Scunthorpe United
7	Evans, Kevin	Cardiff City	Boston United
19	Flowers, Timothy D.	Leicester City	Coventry City
22	Fox, Christian	York City	Larne
8	Furlong, Paul A.	Birmingham City	Sheffield United
15	Grant, John A.C.	Crewe Alexandra	Northwich Victoria
3	Gray, Wayne W.	Wimbledon	Leyton Orient
15	Grayson, Simon N.	Blackburn Rovers	Bradford City
26	Heald, Paul A.	Wimbledon	Sheffield Wednesday
28	Hendry, Edward C.J.	Bolton Wanderers	Preston North End
19	Holdsworth, David G.	Birmingham City	Walsall
4	Hooper, Dean R.	Peterborough United	Dagenham & Redbridge
14	Jackman, Daniel J.	Aston Villa	Cambridge United
5	Johnson, David A.	Nottingham Forest	Sheffield Wednesday
5	Jones, Stephen G.	Crewe Alexandra	Rochdale
8	Lee, Andrew J.	Bradford City	Emley
8	Lewis, Karl J.	Leicester City	Brighton & Hove Albion
22	Liddle, Gareth J.C.	Crewe Alexandra	Leek Town
13	Logan, Richard J.	Ipswich Town	Torquay United
1	Lormor, Anthony	Hartlepool United	Shrewsbury Town
15	Macauley, Steven R.	Crewe Alexandra	Macclesfield Town
15	Macdonald, Charles L.	Charlton Athletic	Torquay United
5	Maddison, Lee R.	Carlisle United	Oxford United
25	Marsh, Adam	Darlington	Hampton & Richmond Borough
15	McAnespie, Kieran	Fulham	AFC Bournemouth
18	McElhatton, Michael T.	Rushden & Diamonds	Chester City
15	McGibbon, Patrick C.G.	Wigan Athletic	Scunthorpe United
15	McSweegan, Gary J.	Heart of Midlothian	Luton Town
1	Murphy, Shaun P.	Sheffield United	Crystal Palace
26	Murray, Adam D.	Derby County	Mansfield Town
15	Murray, Frederick A.	Blackburn Rovers	Cambridge United
15	Nicholls, Ashley	Ipswich Town	Canvey Island
19	Oleksewycz, Stephen M.	Halifax Town	Worksop Town
7	Parkin, Jonathan	Hartlepool United	York City
15	Pennock, Anthony	Rushden & Diamonds	Farnborough Town
21	Pringle, Ulf M.	Charlton Athletic	Grimsby Town
12	Richards, Marc J.	Blackburn Rovers	Halifax Town
14	Roget, Leo T.E.	Stockport County	Reading
13	Selley, Ian	Wimbledon	Southend United
19	Sheppard, Kyle D.	Bristol City	Merthyr Tydfil
19	Shields, Greg	Charlton Athletic	Walsall
1	Smith, David C.	Stockport County	Macclesfield Town
15	Stirling, Jude B.	Luton Town	Stevenage Borough
4	Strachan, Gavin D.	Coventry City	Motherwell
8	Thomas, Danny J.	Leicester City	AFC Bournemouth
21	Todd, Andrew J.J.	Charlton Athletic	Grimsby Town
26	Tuttle, David P.	Millwall	Wycombe Wanderers
7	Varty, John W.	Carlisle United	Workington
27	Wardley, Stuart	Queens Park Rangers	Rushden & Diamonds

8 Ward, Mark	Sheffield United	Aldershot Town	
26 Wheatcroft, Paul M.	Bolton Wanderers	Mansfield Town	
19 Woodman, Andrew J.	Colchester United	Oxford United	

March 2002

6 Beharall, David	Newcastle United	Oldham Athletic	undisclosed
28 Betsy, Kevin E.L.	Fulham	Barnsley	200,000
4 Bolland, Philip	Oxford United	Chester City	15,000
26 Campbell, Andrew P.	Middlesbrough	Cardiff City	950,000
15 Carsley, Lee K.	Coventry City	Everton	1,900,000
26 Cooper, Kevin L.	Wimbledon	Wolverhampton Wanderers	1,000,000
28 Crouch, Peter J.	Portsmouth	Aston Villa	4,000,000
28 Ellington, Nathan L.F.	Bristol Rovers	Wigan Athletic	750,000
7 Finnigan, John F.	Lincoln City	Cheltenham Town	Free
18 Gascoigne, Paul J.	Everton	Burnley	Free
15 Hall, Fitz	Chesham United	Oldham Athletic	20,000
28 Howe, Edward J.F.	AFC Bournemouth	Portsmouth	400,000
27 Jarrett, Jason L.M.	Bury	Wigan Athletic	75,000
8 Johnson, Damien M.	Blackburn Rovers	Birmingham City	nominal
21 Kearney, Thomas J.	Everton	Bradford City	Free
6 Macken, Jonathan P.	Preston North End	Manchester City	4,000,000
4 Mahon, Gavin A.	Brentford	Watford	150,000
8 Murray, Frederick A.	Blackburn Rovers	Cambridge United	Free
6 Parkin, Jonathan	Barnsley	York City	Free
26 Petterson, Andrew K.	Portsmouth	West Bromwich Albion	Free
26 Roberts, Christian J.	Exeter City	Bristol City	nominal
25 Simpson, Paul D.	Blackpool	Rochdale	Free
22 Tebily, Olivier	Celtic	Birmingham City	700,000
28 Thomson, Andrew J.	Bristol Rovers	Wycombe Wanderers	Free
20 Todorov, Svetoslav	West Ham United	Portsmouth	750,000
14 Watson, Kevin E.	Rotherham United	Reading	150,000
6 Williams, Eifion W.	Torquay United	Hartlepool United	30,000
13 Williams, Thomas A.	Peterborough United	Birmingham City	1,000,000
28 Woodman, Andrew J.	Colchester United	Oxford United	Free

Temporary transfers

20 Adebola, Bamberdele O.	Birmingham City	Oldham Athletic
28 Ainsworth, Gareth	Wimbledon	Preston North End
22 Armstrong, Joel	Chesterfield	Ilkeston Town
29 Armstrong, Joel	Chesterfield	Bradford Park Avenue
28 Ashdown, Jamie L.	Reading	Arsenal
9 Attwell, Jamie W.	Bristol City	Tiverton Town
15 Barrett, Daniel T.	Chesterfield	Matlock Town
27 Benjamin, Trevor J.	Leicester City	West Bromwich Albion
4 Beresford, Marlon	Middlesbrough	Burnley
15 Bevan, Scott	Southampton	Woking
22 Bloomer, Matthew B.	Hull City	Lincoln City
21 Branch, Paul M.	Wolverhampton Wanderers	Reading
19 Bruce, Joseph M.	Luton Town	Wingate & Finchley
22 Buchanan, Wayne B.	Bolton Wanderers	Chesterfield
25 Bull, Nikki	Queens Park Rangers	Hayes
1 Burrows, Mark	Exeter City	Merthyr Tydfil
25 Burton, Deon J.	Derby County	Stoke City
25 Bywater, Stephen M.	West Ham United	Cardiff City
22 Carbonari, Horacio A.	Derby County	Coventry City
2 Cole, Timothy	Dagenham & Redbridge	Billericay Town
8 Cooke, Stephen L.	Aston Villa	AFC Bournemouth
26 Coppinger, James	Newcastle United	Hartlepool United
28 Croft, Gary	Ipswich Town	Cardiff City
22 Davies, Gareth	Chesterfield	Matlock Town
29 Deeney, Saul	Notts County	Ilkeston Town
28 Delaney, Damien	Leicester City	Huddersfield Town
11 Devlin, Paul J.	Sheffield United	Birmingham City
27 Dinning, Tony	Wigan Athletic	Stoke City
28 Dublin, Dion	Aston Villa	Millwall
11 Duff, Shane	Cheltenham Town	Evesham United
28 Dunning, Darren	Blackburn Rovers	Blackpool
27 Esson, Ryan	Aberdeen	Rotherham United
28 Evers, Sean A.	Plymouth Argyle	Stevenage Borough
11 Flynn, Michael A.	Stockport County	Stoke City
28 Foley, Dominic J.	Watford	Queens Park Rangers
28 Galloway, Michael A.	Carlisle United	Gretna
18 Grant, John	Crewe Alexandra	Northwich Victoria
27 Gray, Wayne W.	Wimbledon	Brighton & Hove Albion
28 Halle, Gunnar	Bradford City	Wolverhampton Wanderers
1 Healey, Stephen J.	Swansea City	Llanelli
28 Hicks, Mark	Millwall	Farnborough Town
21 Holmes, Richard	Notts County	Hereford United
1 Hoolickin, Lee	Carlisle United	Gretna
5 Hooper, Dean R.	Peterborough United	Dagenham & Redbridge
14 Hopkins, Gareth	Cheltenham Town	Forest Green Rovers
28 Hore, John S.	Carlisle United	Workington
28 Hughes, Michael E.	Wimbledon	Birmingham City
28 Ifil, Jerel C.	Watford	Huddersfield Town
18 Jackman, Daniel J.	Aston Villa	Cambridge United
14 Jeffrey, Michael R.	Grimsby Town	Scunthorpe United
12 Johnson, David A.	Nottingham Forest	Burnley
28 Jones, Philip L.	Oswestry Town	Wrexham
26 Jones, Scott	Bristol Rovers	York City
7 Jones, Stephen G.	Crewe Alexandra	Rochdale
28 Joyce, Damien D.	Manchester City	Hyde United
28 Kabba, Steven	Crystal Palace	Luton Town
1 Kendall, Lee M.	Cardiff City	Haverfordwest
15 Kimble, Alan F.	Wimbledon	Peterborough United
28 Knight, Richard	Oxford United	Colchester United
27 Laursen, Jacob	Leicester City	Wolverhampton Wanderers
28 Lee, Martyn J.	Wycombe Wanderers	Cheltenham Town
4 Lewis, Craig	Carlisle United	Workington
20 Lightbourne, Kyle L.	Macclesfield Town	Hull City

19 Lovell, Stephen W.H.	Portsmouth	Sheffield United	
28 Lowndes, Nathan	St Johnstone	Rotherham United	
27 Macdonald, Charles L.	Charlton Athletic	Colchester United	
5 Macken, Jonathan P.	Preston North End	Manchester City	
8 Maddison, Lee R.	Carlisle United	Oxford United	
1 Mann, Neil	Hull City	Scarborough	
1 Marchant, Ross	Sunderland	Whitby Town	
25 Marsh, Adam	Darlington	Worksop Town	
18 McAnespie, Kieran	Fulham	AFC Bournemouth	
28 McCarthy, Jonathan D.	Birmingham City	Sheffield Wednesday	
25 McElhatton, Michael T.	Rushden & Diamonds	Chester City	
15 McPhail, Stephen J.P.	Leeds United	Millwall	
28 Montgomery, Gary S.	Coventry City	Kidderminster Harriers	
8 Murphy, Daryl	Luton Town	Harrow Borough	
5 Murphy, Shaun P.	Sheffield United	Crystal Palace	
26 Murray, Adam D.	Derby County	Mansfield Town	
4 Naylor, Richard A.	Ipswich Town	Barnsley	
8 Newton, Adam L.	West Ham United	Leyton Orient	
4 Norris, David M.	Bolton Wanderers	Hull City	
5 O'Hare, Alan	Bolton Wanderers	Chesterfield	
18 Pennock, Anthony	Rushden & Diamonds	Farnborough Town	
28 Pettinger, Paul A.	Lincoln City	Kettering Town	
22 Price, Michael D.	Hull City	North Ferriby United	
26 Proudlock, Adam D.	Wolverhampton Wanderers	Nottingham Forest	
22 Quinn, Stephen J.	West Bromwich Albion	Bristol Rovers	
28 Reddy, Michael	Sunderland	Barnsley	
28 Robinson, Paul D.	Wimbledon	Grimsby Town	
18 Robinson, Stephen	Preston North End	Bristol City	
18 Roget, Leo T.E.	Stockport County	Reading	
7 Ross, Brian S.	Hartlepool United	Harrogate Town	
15 Royce, Simon E.	Leicester City	Manchester City	
18 Russell, Samuel I.	Middlesbrough	Gateshead	
15 Selley, Ian	Wimbledon	Southend United	
28 Shandran, Anthony M.	Burnley	Stalybridge Celtic	
19 Shields, Greg	Charlton Athletic	Walsall	
8 Singh, Harpal	Leeds United	Bristol City	
4 Steel, Luke D.	Peterborough United	Manchester United	
28 Summerbell, Mark	Middlesbrough	Portsmouth	
4 Tate, Christopher D.	Leyton Orient	Chester City	
22 Thomas, James A.	Blackburn Rovers	Bristol Rovers	
27 Thomas, Jerome W.	Arsenal	Queens Park Rangers	
1 Thurston, Mark R.	Carlisle United	Gretna	
28 Tod, Andrew	Bradford City	Heart of Midlothian	
21 Todd, Andrew J.J.	Charlton Athletic	Grimsby Town	
28 Trainer, Philip A.	Crewe Alexandra	Stalybridge Celtic	
22 Tunnicliffe, Andrew J.	Manchester City	Altrincham	
22 Tyson, Nathan	Reading	Cheltenham Town	
28 Uhlenbeek, Gustav R.	Sheffield United	Walsall	
25 Varga, Stanislav	Sunderland	West Bromwich Albion	
8 Varty, John W.	Carlisle United	Workington	
26 Vaughan, Anthony J.	Nottingham Forest	Scunthorpe United	
28 Ward, Christopher	Birmingham City	Southport	
28 Wardley, Stuart	Queens Park Rangers	Rushden & Diamonds	
28 Waterman, David G.	Portsmouth	Oxford United	
28 Webber, Daniel V.	Manchester United	Watford	
28 Whalley, Gareth	Bradford City	Crewe Alexandra	
15 Whiteman, Marc C.	Bury	Altrincham	
21 Whitley, Jeffrey	Manchester City	Notts County	
12 Williams, Thomas A.	Peterborough United	Birmingham City	
28 Wilson, Scott P.	Rangers	Portsmouth	
29 Wright, Daniel J.	Queens Park Rangers	Molesey	

April 2002

4 Byfield, Darren	Walsall	Rotherham United	50,000
30 Lambert, Rickie L.	Macclesfield Town	Stockport County	300,000
18 Redknapp, Jamie F.	Liverpool	Tottenham Hotspur	Free
30 Walters, Jonathan R.	Blackburn Rovers	Bolton Wanderers	30,000
17 Waterman, David	Portsmouth	Oxford United	Free

Temporary transfers

28 Bull, Nikki	Queens Park Rangers	Hayes	
3 Deeney, Saul	Notts County	Ilkeston Town	
12 Devlin, Paul J.	Sheffield United	Birmingham City	
23 Dublin, Dion	Aston Villa	Millwall	
16 Duff, Shane	Cheltenham Town	Evesham United	
29 Galloway, Michael A.	Carlisle United	Gretna	
17 Grant, John	Crewe Alexandra	Northwich Victoria	
28 Hooper, Dean R.	Peterborough United	Dagenham & Redbridge	
15 Hopkins, Gareth	Cheltenham Town	Forest Green Rovers	
18 Jeffrey, Michael R.	Grimsby Town	Scunthorpe United	
9 Johnson, David A.	Nottingham Forest	Burnley	
28 Lee, Martyn J.	Wycombe Wanderers	Cheltenham Town	
5 Newton, Adam L.	West Ham United	Leyton Orient	
4 O'Hare, Alan	Bolton Wanderers	Chesterfield	
24 Osborn, Mark	Wycombe Wanderers	Farnborough Town	
17 Russell, Samuel I.	Middlesbrough	Gateshead	
2 Thurston, Mark R.	Carlisle United	Gretna	
22 Tyson, Nathan	Reading	Cheltenham Town	

THE NEW FOREIGN LEGION 2001–02

		From	To	Fee in £
June 2001	22 Van Bronckhorst, Giovanni	Rangers	Arsenal	8,500,000
July 2001	24 Inamoto, Junichi	Gamba Osaka	Arsenal	4,000,000
	9 Juan	Sao Paulo	Arsenal	undisclosed
	9 Paulinho	Sao Paulo	Arsenal	undisclosed
	11 Skulason, Olafur-Ingi	Fylkir	Arsenal	undisclosed
	25 Mellberg, Olof	Santander	Aston Villa	5,000,000
	20 Schmeichel, Peter	Sporting Lisbon	Aston Villa	Free
	12 Grabbi, Corrado	Ternana	Blackburn Rovers	6,750,000
	20 Tugay, Kerimoglu	Rangers	Blackburn Rovers	1,300,000
	16 Mahon, Alan	Sporting Lisbon	Blackburn Rovers	1,500,000
	17 Diawara, Djibril	Torino	Bolton Wanderers	loan
	11 Pedersen, Henrik	Silkeborg	Bolton Wanderers	650,000
	4 Gallas, William	Marseille	Chelsea	6,200,000
	23 Petit, Emmanuel	Barcelona	Chelsea	7,500,000
	19 Counago, Pablo	Celta Vigo	Ipswich Town	Free
	26 Riise, John Arne	Monaco	Liverpool	3,770,000
	5 Van Nistelrooy, Ruud	PSV Eindhoven	Manchester United	19,000,000
	13 Veron, Juan Sebastian	Lazio	Manchester United	28,100,000
	30 Nemeth, Szilard	Inter Bratislava	Middlesbrough	Free
	10 Ela-Eyene, Jacinto	Espanyol	Southampton	Free
	16 Svensson, Anders	Elfsborg	Southampton	750,000
	18 Laslandes, Lilian	Bordeaux	Sunderland	3,600,000
	2 Medina, Nicolas	Argentinos Juniors	Sunderland	3,500,000
	1 Mercimek, Baki	Haarlem	Sunderland	Free
	25 Bunjevcevic, Goran	Red Star Belgrade	Tottenham Hotspur	1,400,000
	20 Schemmel, Sebastien	Metz	West Ham United	465,000
August 2001	24 Balaban, Bosko	Dynamo Zagreb	Aston Villa	6,000,000
	8 Nishizawa, Akinori	Cerzo Osaka	Bolton Wanderers	loan
	10 Zenden, Boudewijn	Barcelona	Chelsea	7,500,000
	10 Daino, Daniele	AC Milan	Derby County	loan
	3 Ravanelli, Fabrizio	Lazio	Derby County	Free
	20 Radzinski, Tomasz	Anderlecht	Everton	4,500,000
	22 Legwinski, Sylvain	Bordeaux	Fulham	3,500,000
	14 Malbranque, Steed	Lyon	Fulham	5,000,000
	10 Ouaddou, Abdes	Nancy	Fulham	2,000,000
	10 Van der Sar, Edwin	Juventus	Fulham	7,000,000
	31 Gaardsoe, Thomas	Aalborg	Ipswich Town	1,300,000
	17 George, Finidi	Mallorca	Ipswich Town	3,100,000
	24 Peralta, Sixto	Torino	Ipswich Town	loan
	17 Sereni, Matteo	Sampdoria	Ipswich Town	undisclosed
	31 Dudek, Jerzy	Feyenoord	Liverpool	4,850,000
	10 Robert, Laurent	Paris St Germain	Newcastle United	10,500,000
	17 Bellion, David	Cannes	Sunderland	Free
	10 Haas, Bernt	Grasshoppers	Sunderland	750,000
	16 Keller, Kasey	Rayo Vallecano	Tottenham Hotspur	Free
	15 Courtois, Laurent	Toulouse	West Ham United	Free
September 2001	21 Tavlaridis, Efstathios	Iraklis	Arsenal	600,000
	19 Johnson, Jermaine	Tivoli Gardens	Bolton Wanderers	Free
	11 N'Gotty, Bruno	AC Milan	Bolton Wanderers	loan
	11 De Oliveira, Filipe	Porto	Chelsea	undisclosed
	3 Marlet, Steve	Lyon	Fulham	13,500,000
	3 Blanc, Laurent	Internazionale	Manchester United	Free
	14 Distin, Sylvain	Paris St Germain	Newcastle United	loan
	14 Repka, Tomas	Fiorentina	West Ham United	5,500,000
October 2001	5 Johansson, Nils-Eric	Nuremberg	Blackburn Rovers	2,700,000
	18 Ducrocq, Pierre	Paris St Germain	Derby County	loan
	19 Zavagno, Luciano	Troyes	Derby County	undisclosed
	12 Queudrue, Franck	Lens	Middlesbrough	loan
November 2001	16 Viander, Jani	HJK Helsinki	Bolton Wanderers	loan
	6 Grenet, Francois	Bordeaux	Derby County	3,000,000
	15 Le Pen, Ulrich	Lorient	Ipswich Town	1,400,000
	15 Chala, Kleber	El Nacional	Southampton	1,000,000
	13 Delgado, Agustin	Necxa	Southampton	3,500,000
December 2001	4 Costa, Jorge	Porto	Charlton Athletic	loan
	24 Baros, Milan	Banik Ostrava	Liverpool	3,400,000
	24 Anelka, Nicolas	Paris St Germain	Liverpool	loan
	27 Fernandes, Fabrice	Rennes	Southampton	1,100,000
	7 Reyna, Claudio	Rangers	Sunderland	4,500,000
	4 Andersson, Sven	Helsingborg	West Ham United	Free
	20 Bon, Jeremy	Bordeaux	Bolton Wanderers	250,000
January 2002	11 Bobic, Fredi	Borussia Dortmund	Bolton Wanderers	loan
	11 Laursen, Jacob	FC Copenhagen	Leicester City	400,000
	23 Forlan, Diego	Independiente	Manchester United	7,500,000
	11 Labant, Vladimir	Sparta Prague	West Ham United	900,000
February 2002	18 Toure, Kolo	ASEC Mimosas	Arsenal	undisclosed
	22 Yordi	Zaragoza	Blackburn Rovers	loan
	15 Djorkaeff, Youri	Kaiserslautern	Bolton Wanderers	loan
	22 Espartero, Mario	Metz	Bolton Wanderers	loan
	1 Forschelet, Gerald	Cannes	Bolton Wanderers	undisclosed
	8 Tofting, Stig	Hamburg	Bolton Wanderers	250,000
	22 Foletti, Patrick	Lucerne	Derby County	loan
	1 Linderoth, Tobias	Stabaek	Everton	2,500,000
	28 Debeve, Michael	Lens	Middlesbrough	Free
	1 Bjorklund, Joachim	Venezia	Sunderland	1,500,000
	15 Mboma, Patrick	Parma	Sunderland	loan
March 2002	1 Unsal, Hakan	Galatasaray	Blackburn Rovers	1,000,000
	27 Konstantinidis, Kostas	Hertha Berlin	Bolton Wanderers	loan
	18 Hassli, Eric	Metz	Southampton	loan
May 2002	14 Acimovic, Milenko	Red Star Belgrade	Tottenham Hotspur	undisclosed

Summer transfers to be found in Stop Press on page 991.

REFEREEING AND THE REFEREES

With this being a World Cup year it has become a convention that there are few if any Law changes during this period. As a result all we have had for the forthcoming season are some minor and inconsequential amendments to existing provisions. These include in Law 5, instructing the Referee to allow an injured player, who has gone off, to return *only after* the match has been restarted. In Law 12 the number of offences capable of being committed by the goalkeeper has been reduced from 5 to 4 owing to the 'keeper now being allowed more latitude. In players' equipment – specifying no advertising on any part of the playing equipment save shirts. Revealing slogans or adverts on undershirts will be sanctioned by the relevant competition. Referees are also reminded to be strict on simulation which is cautionable as unsporting behaviour and to likewise punish players guilty of delaying restarts, especially if players remove shirts for any length of time celebrating a goal.

Reverting to the World Cup, several different messages appear to have emerged. By and large the referees were considered to have done well in both applying the advantage rule and punishing simulation, whilst continuing to send off only when necessary. The major exception being Señor Lopez Nieto of Spain who set a new World Cup record of 16 cautions in the match between Cameroon and Germany. However, the criticism of the officials centred around the assistant referees who on many occasions failed to live up to the standards required, to the extent that prompted FIFA President Sepp Blatter to promise future changes to the format of selection. Furthermore, UEFA Chief Executive Gerhard Aigner called for the reintroduction of trials for the two referee system, where experiments involving this system, were abandoned by the International Board the season before last.

England's representatives at the World Cup were Graham Poll as referee and Philip Sharp who became the second ever English assistant referee to run the Line in a World Cup Final. There he supported referee Pierluigi Collina of Italy (voted the best referee in the world for the fourth successive year) with the other assistant being Sweden's Leif Lindberg. The fourth official was Scotland's Hugh Dallas.

On the domestic front a new organisation representing referees has been innovated. For many years referees have had as their main pro-active and protective organisation the Referees Association. Within the past year however, the Football Association, ever mindful of developing all aspects of the game, have initiated a further coalition for referees named The Football Association Match Officials Association (FAMOA). The aim is to be "a direct link between the FA and all connected with refereeing". Ten Regional Managers have been appointed who are to support their area County FAs and to look after the needs of an average 3,500 referees in their respective areas.

As to the National List of Referees, there are eight new entries to that list being Messrs Boyeson; Crossley; Evans; Ilderton; Mason; Penn; Thorpe and Williamson.

KEN GOLDMAN

NATIONAL LIST OF REFEREES FOR SEASON 2002–03

Indicates Select Group Referees

Armstrong, P. (Paul) Berkshire
Baines, S.J. (Steve) Chesterfield
Barber, G.P. (Graham) Hertfordshire*
Barry, N.S. (Neale) N. Lincolnshire*
Bates, A. (Tony) Stoke-on-Trent
Beeby, R.J. (Richard) Northampton
Bennett, S.G. (Steve) Kent*
Boyeson, C. (Carl) Hull
Butler, A.N. (Alan) Nottinghamshire
Cable, L.E. (Lee) Woking
Cain, G. (George) Merseyside
Clattenburg, M. (Mark) Chester-le-Street
Cooper, M.A. (Mark) Walsall
Cowburn, M.G. (Mark) Blackpool
Crick, D.R. (David) Surrey
Crossley, P.T. (Phil) Kent
Curson, B. (Brian) Leicestershire
Danson, P.S. (Paul) Leicester
Dean, M.L. (Mike) Wirral*
Dowd, P. (Phil) Stoke-on-Trent*
Dunn, S.W. (Steve) Bristol*
Durkin, P.A. (Paul) Dorset*
D'Urso, A.P. (Andy) Essex*
Elleray, D.R. (David) Harrow-on-the-Hill*
Evans, E.M. (Eddie) Manchester

Fletcher, M. (Mick) Worcestershire
Foy, C.J. (Chris) Merseyside*
Frankland, G.B. (Graham) Middlesbrough
Gallagher, D.J. (Dermot) Oxfordshire*
Hall, A.R. (Andy) Birmingham*
Halsey, M.R. (Mark) Lancashire*
Hegley, G.K. (Grant) Bishops Stortford
Hill, K.D. (Keith) Hertfordshire
Ilderton, E.L. (Eddie) Tyne & Wear
Jones, M.J. (Michael) Chester
Jordan, W.M. (Bill) Hertfordshire
Joslin, P.J. (Phil) Nottinghamshire
Kaye, A. (Alan) Wakefield
Knight, B. (Barry) Kent*
Laws, D. (David) Newcastle upon Tyne
Laws, G. (Graham) Whitley Bay
Leake, A.R. (Tony) Lancashire
Mason, L.S. (Lee) Bolton
Mathieson, S.W. (Scott) Stockport
Messias, M.D. (Matt) York*
Olivier, R.J. (Ray) Sutton Coldfield
Parkes, T.A. (Trevor) Birmingham
Pearson, R. (Roy) Durham
Penn, A.M. (Andy) West Midlands

Penton, C. (Clive) Sussex
Pike, M.S. (Mike) Barrow-in-Furness
Poll, G. (Graham) Hertfordshire*
Prosser, P.J. (Phil) Tewkesbury
Pugh, D. (David) Merseyside*
Rejer, P. (Paul) Worcestershire
Rennie, U.D. (Uriah) Sheffield*
Riley, M.A. (Mike) Leeds*
Robinson, J.P. (Paul) Hull
Ross, J.J. (Joe) London
Ryan, M. (Michael) Preston
Salisbury, G. (Graham) Preston
Stretton, F.G. (Frazer) Nottingham
Styles, R. (Rob) Hampshire*
Taylor, P. (Paul) Hertfordshire
Thorpe, M. (Mike) Ipswich*
Tomlin, S.G. (Steve) East Sussex
Walton, P. (Peter) Northants
Warren, M.R. (Mark) Walsall
Webb, H.M. (Howard) Rotherham
Webster, C.H. (Colin) Gateshead
Wiley, A.G. (Alan) Burntwood*
Wilkes, C.R. (Clive) Gloucester*
Williamson, I.G. (Iain) Reading
Winter, J.T. (Jeff) Stockton-on-Tees*
Wolstenholme, E.K. (Eddie) Blackburn*

ASSISTANT REFEREES

Ansell, I. (Ian) Exeter
Appleby, N.D. (Norman) St Albans
Artis, S.G. (Stephen) Norwich
Astley, M.A. (Mark) Stockport
Aston, G.A. (Glenn) Kingswinford
Barker, C. (Craig) Leeds
Barnes, K.G. (Kevin) Swindon
Beadle, J. (Jon) Gravesend
Bentley, I.F. (Ian) Kent
Birkett, D.J. (Dave) Gainsborough
Bratt, S.J. (Steve) Walsall
Buller, K.R. (Keith) Bridgwater
Cann, D.J. (Darren) Norwich
Carter, J.E. (John) Sunderland
Cassidy, M.T. (Martin) Weston-super-Mare
Castle, S. (Steve) Wolverhampton
Chapman, G.J. (Gary) Gloucestershire
Chittenden, S. (Steve) St Albans
Clyde, A.L. (Alex) Doncaster
Cockwill, N.R. (Nigel) North Devon
Conn, A.J. (Tony) Hertfordshire
Cooke, D.G. (Dave) West Midlands
Cordy, J.N. (Jon) Bristol
Coulson, D.H. (Des) Northallerton
Couzens, C. (Carl) Hitchin
Darlow, M. (Martin) Bedford
Deadman, D. (Darren) Hertfordshire
Denniff, A.P. (Andrew) Sheffield
Desmond, R.P. (Bob) Gloucester
Dewfield, A. (Adam) Leicestershire
Dexter, M.C. (Martin) Leicester
Dorr, S.J. (Steve) Worcester
East, R. (Roger) Wiltshire
Eastwood, P. (Peter) Manchester
Ebbage, M. (Martin) Hampshire
Enright, D.J. (Dave) Bolton
Evans, I.A. (Ian) Wolverhampton
Evans, R.J. (Russell) Kent
Evetts, G.S. (Gary) Hertfordshire
Faulkner, I.L. (Ian) Liverpool
Flynn, J. (John) Calne
Foster, D. (Dave) Newcastle-upon-Tyne
Foulkes, G.W. (Gary) Liverpool
Francis, C.J. (Chris) Cambridgeshire
Friend, K.A. (Kevin) Leicester
Gate, S. (Stan) Newcastle
Gibbs, P.N. (Phil) West Midlands
Gosling, I.J. (Ian) Kent
Graham, F. (Fred) Essex
Greaves, A.J. (Alan) Doncaster
Green, R.C. (Russell) Gloucestershire
Grove, P.J. (Peter) Stourbridge
Habgood, S.D. (Steve) Wiltshire
Haines, A. (Andy) Sunderland
Hambling, G.S. (Glenn) Norwich
Hancox, N. (Neil) West Midlands
Harris, I. (Ian) Cornwall
Harris, M.A. (Martin) Lincolnshire
Harwood, C.N. (Colin) Manchester
Hawken, M.A. (Mike) Cornwall
Hawkes, K.J. (Kevin) Gloucestershire
Haxby, M.D. (Mike) Wirral
Hayto, J.M. (John) Chelmsford
Haywood, M. (Mark) Wakefield
Hewitt, R.T. (Richard) Scarborough

Hilton, G. (Gary) Wigan
Hine, D.J. (David) Worcester
Hogg, A.S. (Andy) Sheffield
Hollick, S. (Simon) Plymouth
Horton, A.J. (Tony) Wolverhampton
Horwood, G.D. (Graham) Luton
Howes, T.P. (Tim) Norwich
Hubbard, J.R. (Jim) Leicester
Hughes, M.R. (Mike) London
Hutchinson, A.D. (Andrew) Flintshire
Hutchinson, S.M. (Mark) Notts
Ingram, K.R. (Kevin) Kingswinford
Ives, G.L. (Gary) Hornchurch
Ives, M. (Mark) Bedfordshire
James, R.G. (Ron) Milton Keynes
Jones, N.L. (Neil) Plymouth
Keane, P.J. (Patrick) Wolverhampton
Kellett, D.G. (Gary) Bradford
King, E.A. (Eddie) Northumberland
Kinseley, N. (Nick) Essex
Kirkup, P.J. (Peter) Northampton
Knight, M.T. (Matthew) Hove
Lawson, J. (John) Pontefract
Lawson, K.D. (Keith) Scunthorpe
Lee, R. (Ray) Essex
Lewis, G.J. (Gary) Cambridgeshire
Lockhart, R. (Bob) Newcastle upon Tyne
Lomas, W.D. (Wayne) Nr Worksop
McCallum, D.A. (Dave) Whitley Bay
McCoy, M.T. (Michael) Kent
McGee, A. (Tony) Merseyside
McIntosh, W.A. (Wayne) Lincoln
McPherson, M.W. (Michael) Ely
Mackrell, E.B. (Eric) Hampshire
Malone, B. (Brendan) Wiltshire
Marriner, A.M. (Andre) Birmingham
Martin, E.A.C. (Edward) Somerset
Martin, P.C. (Paul) Northants
Matadar, M. (Mo) Blackburn
Mattocks, K.J. (Kevin) Lancashire
Meads, C.J. (Colin) Wetherby
Melin, P.W. (Paul) Surrey
Mellor G. (Glyn) Derbyshire
Mellor, G.S. (Gary) Rotherham
Merchant, K. (Kevin) Surrey
Miller, P. (Patrick) Flitwick
Mullarkey, M. (Mike) Exeter
Murphy, M.E. (Michael) Coventry
Murphy, N. (Nigel) Mansfield
Naylor, D. (Dave) Notts
Nicholson, A.R. (Andy) Halifax
Nicholson, P.W. (Paul) Durham
Nolan, I. (Ian) Rochdale
Oliver, C.W. (Clive) Northumberland
Page, A. (Andy) Derbyshire
Palmer, R. (Richard) Bath
Parker, A.R. (Alan) Derby
Parry, B. (Brian) Peterlee
Pashley, R.A. (Rob) Chesterfield
Peacock, D. (David) Cleveland
Pearce, J.E. (John) Dagenham
Perkin, N.F. (Neil) Gravesend
Perlejewski, A.J. (Andy) Dorset
Pollard, T.J. (Trevor) Bury St Edmunds
Pollock, R.M. (Bob) Merseyside

Postles, M.D. (Martin) West Sussex
Powell, K. (Ken) Hartlepool
Probert, L.W. (Lee) Bristol
Pryme, G.D. (Greg) Colchester
Ramsay, W. (William) Coventry
Rawcliffe, A. (Allan) Manchester
Reeves, C.L. (Christopher) East Yorkshire
Richardson, D. (David) Halifax
Robinson, M.G. (Martin) Darlington
Rubery, S.P. (Steve) Ilford
Rushton, G.N. (Neale) Lancashire
Russell, G.R. (Geoff) Milton Keynes
Russell, M.P. (Mike) Herts
Sainsbury, A. (Andrew) Wiltshire
Sarginson, C.D. (Christopher) Staffordshire
Scarr, I.K. (Ian) Birmingham
Scholes, M.S. (Mark) Buckingham
Shaw, I.D. (Ian) Crewe
Shaw, M.A. (Mike) Macclesfield
Sheffield, J.A. (Alan) Staffordshire
Short, M. (Michael) Barnsley
Sim, T.J. (Tom) Burton-on-Trent
Simpson, G.H. (George) North Yorkshire
Singh, J. (Jarnail) Middlesex
Smith, A.N. (Andrew) West Yorkshire
Smith, R.G. (Robert) Chelmsford
Smith, R.H. (Richard) West Midlands
Snartt, S.P. (Simon) Bristol
Spicer, D.R. (Darren) Hampshire
Steans, R.J. (Rob) Loughborough
Stokes, J.D. (John) Merseyside
Storrie, D. (David) Leeds
Stott, G.T. (Gary) Manchester
Stroud, K.P. (Keith) Dorset
Sutton, G.J. (Gary) Lincoln
Swarbrick, N.D. (Neil) Lancashire
Sygmuta, B.C. (Barry) Northallerton
Tanner, S.J. (Steve) Bristol
Tarry, E.J. (Eddie) Manchester
Tattan, J.F. (James) Liverpool
Taylor, J.T. (Joe) Blackburn
Thiarra, S.S. (Sukhdev) Bedfordshire
Tiffin, R. (Russell) Houghton-le-Spring
Tilling, M.R. (Mark) Guisborough
Tincknell, S.W. (Steve) Watford
Tomlinson, S.D. (Stephen) Hampshire
Townsend, K.N. (Keith) West Midlands
Unsworth, D. (David) Bolton
Wade, B. (Barrie) Isle of Wight
Wallace, G. (Gary) Tyne & Wear
Ward, G.L. (Gavin) Beckenham
Warrent, G.J. (Graeme) Leeds
Weaver, M. (Mark) Birmingham
Webb, A.J. (Alf) Berkshire
West, M.G. (Malcolm) Cornwall
Whitby, D. (Dave) Liverpool
Whitestone, D. (Dean) Northampton
Wilkinson, K. (Keith) Blyth
Williams, M.A. (Andy) Hereford
Wilson, S.M. (Stuart) Wakefield
Wood, D. (David) West Yorkshire
Wood, P.M. (Paul) Lancashire
Woodward, I.J. (Irvine) East Sussex
Wright, K.K. (Kevin) Peterborough
Yates, N.A. (Neil) Blackburn
Young, G.R. (Gary) Bedfordshire

THE THINGS THEY SAID . . .

Boro chairman Steve Gibson after Bryan Robson ended his stint as manager at the Riverside Stadium:
"We are now the 9th biggest club in England and just outside the 20 biggest clubs in the world. That is Bryan's legacy."

Arsène Wenger on the future of star midfielder Patrick Vieira:
"I am beginning to feel like a parrot on the subject of Vieira. For me the subject is over."

Former Wombles boss Joe Kinnear:
"If they had listened to me the (Wimbledon) supporters would be sitting in a 70,000-seater stadium in Dublin and in the Premiership."

Wrexham's Brian Flynn praising his young side after twice coming from behind:
"There aren't many jock-straps to be found in our dressing-room, only nappies!"

Millwall's much-travelled striker-signing Steve Claridge:
"I've been given the No 35 shirt to reflect my age!"

PFA's Gordon Taylor reckons the Premier League is trying to crush his Union:
"They want us to be a nodding dog in the back of their car."

Rotherham's Ronnie Moore after a fruitless scouting visit to Norway:
"I went over and saw the standard but it's a million miles away from our First Division."

Jim Magilton preparing for his 50th Northern Ireland cap but reflecting on Southampton and international days under manager McMenemy:
"I knew malaria would have to set in before I would get a game under Lawrie. We had a good working relationship. He stayed away from the training ground –and I was chuffed!"

Jaap Stam on his quite sudden exit from Man U to Lazio:
"They sold me like a cow."

Ken Bates berating his anxious Chelsea players for revolting against a flight to Tel Aviv:
"If I had to choose between the Israelis or Tony Blair to protect me, then Israel wins every time."

FIFA ref assessor Keith Cooper commenting on Ashley Cole's role in dismissals for Bowyer and Mills:
"He was involved in both and spent so much time on the ground I was wondering when his funeral would be held."

Parma defender Antonio Benarrivo hinting that it might be grim on Teeside:
"My team-mates advised me to visit the city first. I went to have a look at Middlesbrough and decided I was better off in Parma."

Jimmy Case, a favourite of Seagull fans, on Peter Taylor's appointment:
"He's still got to prove himself, he's up and down the ladder very quickly. One minute he was at Dover, then the next he was in charge of England U21's."

Arsenal's Thierry Henry on the groin injury he picked up against Mallorca:
"I had to make a Michael Jackson-type move and it really hurt."

Graeme Souness on the stress of football management following the illness to Liverpool's Houllier:
"I was there the night Jock Stein died, and I want to go when I'm in bed with my beautiful young wife."

Another slightly confusing one from Hammers cult hero Paolo Di Canio:
"I scored at Liverpool on the opening day of the season – a 'big balls' goal."

Andy Goram, burly net-minder at a few clubs:
"People have got this preconceived idea of me as a fat bastard who can't move."

Excitable Celtic boss Martin O'Neill:
"I thought there were some immense performances against Rosenborg and I think Didier Agathe's gone from a £50,000 player to a £29m player."

Villa's John Gregory hailing veteran defender Steve Staunton as his 'Moanerator'.
"I've always said that when he's moaning, he's happy. That's a Liverpool thing, they are the world's biggest moaners."

Mick McCarthy after a dramatic Irish win which effectively ends Holland's World Cup interest.
"A technically brilliant team, great coach and great players end up battering balls into our box trying to break us down."

Southampton chairman Rupert Lowe on enticing Strachan while Stuart Gray was manager:
"He didn't know I was talking to Gordon, but what you are unaware of you don't worry about."

Danny Wilson fulsome in his praise for his Bristol City lads against Stoke:
"There were no hiding places out there, and I had players putting their family jewels in front of the ball."

Phil Thompson summing up Liverpool's effort at Charlton:
"We were caviar in the first half, cabbage in the second."

Real Madrid's McManaman after engine fire scare returning from Moscow:
"The Spanish are very superstitious and although we fly 3, 4, 5 times a week they are always blessing themselves on take-off. Quite often they sit in the cockpit to be reassured by the pilot."

Peter Reid on Don Hutchison's £5.2m exit back to West Ham:
"I would not say his representatives are people I'd like to go out to dinner with."

Keith Gillespie on Blackburn colleague Mark Hughes' physical presence at Southampton:
"He comes with his usual health warning for centre-halves."

Hapoel Tel Aviv skipper Shimon Gershon after 1-1 draw at Stamford Bridge:
"If we compare ourselves to Chelsea with the money, it is like the sky and the ground."

Graham Poll's reply to Boro boss Steve McClaren's criticism that foreign refs were better:
"Maybe I'll compare his squad of right-wingers with David Beckham and say none are as good."

Gordon Strachan's quip when a mobile phone goes off at his press conference:
"That will be the Samaritans, they usually call me this time of the day."

Ex Bradford striker Dean Windass joining Sheffield Wed on loan from Boro:
"I've been in the Premiership the last 3 and half seasons so I don't know too much about what it's like now in Division One – but I'm sure it's like riding a bike, you never forget."

Jimmy Floyd Hasselbaink's opinion of his current employers:
"Chelsea is a very nice, beautiful, great club but something is missing. Only small things need to be done to make this a top, top, top European club. It is a top club, but it's not a top, top, top club."

Incensed Darlington boss Tommy Taylor finishing with 9 players and a 7-1 hammering:
"I told the ref that if he booked any more I might as well take the players off."

Crystal Palace chairman Simon Jordan fearing Steve Bruce will be enticed to St Andrews:
"There has been no approach from Birmingham to me, but I wouldn't expect them to do anything above board. I expect they will do it on the tap and go straight to Steve."

PSV's president on an alleged approach for Kevin Hofland:
"I am not surprised at anything when that manager of Manchester Utd is involved – because he has a reputation for doing these things."

Sam Hammam stoking up the fires before the FA Cup 3rd round clash:
"Cardiff are a substantially bigger club than Leeds."

David O'Leary fed up with the bad publicity surrounding Leeds Utd after the infamous city centre incident:
"What did they think they were doing, boozed up and running through the streets? Was that not inviting trouble?"

Villa's chairman Doug Ellis, supporter of a rival Birmingham bid for a new national stadium:
"I believe Wembley is the next Millennium Dome. There will be a lot of tears if they continue this project."

Geoffrey Richmond vetting applications for the Bradford managerial post:
"I'd like to thank Stan (Collymore) for his interest, but we won't be taking it seriously."

Giles Smith, journalist, after Elton John complained about the new Watford strip:
"Apparently he finds the yellow and red a little too gaudy – which is pretty rich coming from someone who used to arrive on stage wearing a pink mohair jockstrap and a pair of angel's wings."

Ian Holloway contemplating freshening things up with new signings:
"When the water stands still in the pond, it starts to stink."

Paolo di Canio following his impetuous stamping on prostrate Morris of Chelsea:
"We were 3-0 down and what I did shows I am passionate about West Ham."

Rotherham's Ronnie Moore unhappy after FA Cup defeat by Crewe:
"The back four were like powder-puff girls, like the Tiller Girls."

Gary Mabbutt gives an insight into football in Afghanistan:
"The last time this ground was seen on worldwide television 'criminals' were being hung from the goalposts and shot in the centre circle."

John Smith, joint chairman of cash-strapped Bury:
"We are trapped in a one-way alley with bullets flying all around us. This isn't scaremongering, this is the truth. We have two weeks to save the Shakers."

New £11m Leeds striker Robbie Fowler:
"I'll never say a bad word about Liverpool."

A priceless gem from Bobby Robson following Newcastle's defeat by Arsenal:
"I'm glad we don't have to play them every week. Oh, we've got them again on Saturday in the FA Cup."

Manager Souness after Blackburn defeat at West Ham:
"We should be going home wearing pointed hats with the word 'dopes' written on them."

Leicester's Dave Bassett is obviously not a fan of Spurs' Argentine defender Taricco:
"He's got all the tricks – spitting, pushing you in the eye, falling over – and he gets away with it every week. He ought to be done away with, it's a shame he hasn't been topped before!"

Steve Parkin, Barnsley's boss after defeat and relegation:
"There's an unprofessional culture at this club and I've smelt it since the beginning."

Preston's caretaker manager Kelham O'Hanlon:
"I'll give you an Arsène Wenger answer – I didn't see the sending-off."

Kevin Keegan summing up Manchester City's championship win:
"Over 100 goals, over 50 conceded. I guess you could say that's my style."

Boss Ferguson winding-up relegation battlers Derby after Man U are held at Pride Park:
"They fought like tigers and you expect that, but I believe they will be knackered by Tuesday when they play Arsenal."

TV presenter Michael Parkinson on The Beautiful Game:
"It spends money it hasn't got on players who aren't worth it. What kind of business is that? A bankrupt one is the answer."

Reading's Alan Pardew picking things up fast:
"These days management isn't about throwing tea-cups about and shouting because players today won't accept that. They need a more intelligent approach."

Brentford's Steve Coppell reflecting on his impoverished team's adventures this season:
"Money. What's that?"

Jack Hayward vows to keep backing Wolves' bid for the Premiership after another promotion failure:
"The disappointment was we could see the Promised Land but like Moses things turned against us."

Burnley's new capture Paul Gascoigne 11 days after playing for Everton:
"It was hard. I haven't been playing or training for 5 weeks!"

Bobby Robson's thoughts about El Khalej's cynical challenge :
"A Moroccan wiped out Dyer and got applause from the home fans. They must be prats . . ."

Niall Quinn has seen countless changes since joining Arsenal 18 years ago:
"Back then, you were made if your photo and an interview appeared in Shoot. Now all some players want is to get into Hello magazine."

World Cup 66 hero Alan Ball's gripe about the club he started with and managed:
"There are no pictures or plaques of me at Blackpool, something that sticks in my throat."

Back-up goalie Dean Kiely trying to focus attention away from Roy Keane to Ireland's World Cup attempt:
"We didn't book this trip through Thomas Cook, you know. There's something going on out here."

A typical no-nonsense retort from Mick McCarthy when quizzed on his 'tetchy' first half rant against Saudi Arabia:
". . . You want to try it sometime. It's not that easy in that dug-out when your backside's on the bacon slicer!"

Diego Maradona after learning his previous drug problems had denied him early entry to Japan:
"It's not as if I've dropped a nuclear bomb on them. The Americans still get in don't they."

Teddy Sheringham remembering Argentine antics on a previous occasion:
"If we see them on their coach on the way home we will give them a wave."

FA CHARITY SHIELD WINNERS 1908–2001

1908	Manchester U v QPR	4-0 after 1-1 draw	1962	Tottenham H v Ipswich T	5-1
1909	Newcastle U v Northampton T	2-0	1963	Everton v Manchester U	4-0
1910	Brighton v Aston Villa	1-0	1964	Liverpool v West Ham U	2-2*
1911	Manchester U v Swindon T	8-4	1965	Manchester U v Liverpool	2-2*
1912	Blackburn R v QPR	2-1	1966	Liverpool v Everton	1-0
1913	Professionals v Amateurs	7-2	1967	Manchester U v Tottenham H	3-3*
1920	WBA v Tottenham H	2-0	1968	Manchester C v WBA	6-1
1921	Tottenham H v Burnley	2-0	1969	Leeds U v Manchester C	2-1
1922	Huddersfield T v Liverpool	1-0	1970	Everton v Chelsea	2-1
1923	Professionals v Amateurs	2-0	1971	Leicester C v Liverpool	1-0
1924	Professionals v Amateurs	3-1	1972	Manchester C v Aston Villa	1-0
1925	Amateurs v Professionals	6-1	1973	Burnley v Manchester C	1-0
1926	Amateurs v Professionals	6-3	1974	Liverpool† v Leeds U	1-1
1927	Cardiff C v Corinthians	2-1	1975	Derby Co v West Ham U	2-0
1928	Everton v Blackburn R	2-1	1976	Liverpool v Southampton	1-0
1929	Professionals v Amateurs	3-0	1977	Liverpool v Manchester U	0-0*
1930	Arsenal v Sheffield W	2-1	1978	Nottingham F v Ipswich T	5-0
1931	Arsenal v WBA	1-0	1979	Liverpool v Arsenal	3-1
1932	Everton v Newcastle U	5-3	1980	Liverpool v West Ham U	1-0
1933	Arsenal v Everton	3-0	1981	Aston Villa v Tottenham H	2-2*
1934	Arsenal v Manchester C	4-0	1982	Liverpool v Tottenham H	1-0
1935	Sheffield W v Arsenal	1-0	1983	Manchester U v Liverpool	2-0
1936	Sunderland v Arsenal	2-1	1984	Everton v Liverpool	1-0
1937	Manchester C v Sunderland	2-0	1985	Everton v Manchester U	2-0
1938	Arsenal v Preston NE	2-1	1986	Everton v Liverpool	1-1*
1948	Arsenal v Manchester U	4-3	1987	Everton v Coventry C	1-0
1949	Portsmouth v Wolverhampton W	1-1*	1988	Liverpool v Wimbledon	2-1
1950	World Cup Team v Canadian Touring Team	4-2	1989	Liverpool v Arsenal	1-0
1951	Tottenham H v Newcastle U	2-1	1990	Liverpool v Manchester U	1-1*
1952	Manchester U v Newcastle U	4-2	1991	Arsenal v Tottenham H	0-0*
1953	Arsenal v Blackpool	3-1	1992	Leeds U v Liverpool	4-3
1954	Wolverhampton W v WBA	4-4*	1993	Manchester U† v Arsenal	1-1
1955	Chelsea v Newcastle U	3-0	1994	Manchester U v Blackburn R	2-0
1956	Manchester U v Manchester C	1-0	1995	Everton v Blackburn R	1-0
1957	Manchester U v Aston Villa	4-0	1996	Manchester U v Newcastle U	4-0
1958	Bolton W v Wolverhampton W	4-1	1997	Manchester U† v Chelsea	1-1
1959	Wolverhampton W v Nottingham F	3-1	1998	Arsenal v Manchester U	3-0
1960	Burnley v Wolverhampton W	2-2*	1999	Arsenal v Manchester U	2-1
1961	Tottenham H v FA XI	3-2	2000	Chelsea v Manchester U	2-0

Each club retained shield for six months.   † Won on penalties.

ONE2ONE CHARITY SHIELD 2001

Manchester U (0) 1, Liverpool (2) 2

At Millennium Stadium, 12 August 2001, attendance 70,227

Manchester U: Barthez; Irwin, Silvestre, Neville G, Keane, Stam, Beckham, Butt (Yorke), Van Nistelrooy, Scholes, Giggs.
Scorer: Van Nistelrooy 51.

Liverpool: Westerveld; Babbel, Riise (Carragher), Hamann, Henchoz, Hyypia, Murphy (Berger), McAllister, Heskey, Owen, Barmby (Biscan).
Scorers: McAllister 2 (pen), Owen 16.
Referee: A. D'Urso (Billericay).

ENGLISH LEAGUE HONOURS 1888 TO 2002

FA PREMIER LEAGUE
Maximum points: a 126; b 114.

	First	Pts	Second	Pts	Third	Pts
1992–93a	Manchester U	84	Aston Villa	74	Norwich C	72
1993–94a	Manchester U	92	Blackburn R	84	Newcastle U	77
1994–95a	Blackburn R	89	Manchester U	88	Nottingham F	77
1995–96a	Manchester U	82	Newcastle U	78	Liverpool	71
1996–97b	Manchester U	75	Newcastle U*	68	Arsenal*	68
1997–98b	Arsenal	78	Manchester U	77	Liverpool	65
1998–99b	Manchester U	79	Arsenal	78	Chelsea	75
1999–2000b	Manchester U	91	Arsenal	73	Leeds U	69
2000–01	Manchester U	80	Arsenal	70	Liverpool	69
2001–02	Arsenal	87	Liverpool	80	Manchester U	77

FIRST DIVISION
Maximum points: 138

1992–93	Newcastle U	96	West Ham U*	88	Portsmouth††	88
1993–94	Crystal Palace	90	Nottingham F	83	Millwall††	74
1994–95	Middlesbrough	82	Reading††	79	Bolton W	77
1995–96	Sunderland	83	Derby Co	79	Crystal Palace††	75
1996–97	Bolton W	98	Barnsley	80	Wolverhampton W††	76
1997–98	Nottingham F	94	Middlesbrough	91	Sunderland††	90
1998–99	Sunderland	105	Bradford C	87	Ipswich T††	86
1999–2000	Charlton Ath	91	Manchester C	89	Ipswich T	87
2000–01	Fulham	101	Blackburn R	91	Bolton W	87
2001–02	Manchester C	99	WBA	89	Wolverhampton W††	86

SECOND DIVISION
Maximum points: 138

1992–93	Stoke C	93	Bolton W	90	Port Vale††	89
1993–94	Reading	89	Port Vale	88	Plymouth Arg*††	85
1994–95	Birmingham C	89	Brentford††	85	Crewe Alex††	83
1995–96	Swindon T	92	Oxford U	83	Blackpool††	82
1996–97	Bury	84	Stockport Co	82	Luton T††	78
1997–98	Watford	88	Bristol C	85	Grimsby T	72
1998–99	Fulham	101	Walsall	87	Manchester C	82
1999–2000	Preston NE	95	Burnley	88	Gillingham	85
2000–01	Millwall	93	Rotherham U	91	Reading††	86
2001–02	Brighton & HA	90	Reading	84	Brentford*††	83

THIRD DIVISION
Maximum points: a 126; b 138.

1992–93a	Cardiff C	83	Wrexham	80	Barnet	79
1993–94a	Shrewsbury T	79	Chester C	74	Crewe Alex	73
1994–95a	Carlisle U	91	Walsall	83	Chesterfield	81
1995–96b	Preston NE	86	Gillingham	83	Bury	79
1996–97b	Wigan Ath*	87	Fulham	87	Carlisle U	84
1997–98b	Notts Co	99	Macclesfield T	82	Lincoln C	72
1998–99b	Brentford	85	Cambridge U	81	Cardiff C	80
1999–2000b	Swansea C	85	Rotherham U	84	Northampton T	82
2000–01	Brighton & HA	92	Cardiff C	82	Chesterfield¶	80
2001–02	Plymouth Arg	102	Luton T	97	Mansfield T	79

††Not promoted after play-offs. ¶9pts deducted for irregularities.

FOOTBALL LEAGUE
Maximum points: a 44; b 60

	First	Pts	Second	Pts	Third	Pts
1888–89a	Preston NE	40	Aston Villa	29	Wolverhampton W	28
1889–90a	Preston NE	33	Everton	31	Blackburn R	27
1890–91a	Everton	29	Preston NE	27	Notts Co	26
1891–92b	Sunderland	42	Preston NE	37	Bolton W	36

FIRST DIVISION to 1991–92
Maximum points: a 44; b 52; c 60; d 68; e 76; f 84; g 126; h 120; k 114.

1892–93c	Sunderland	48	Preston NE	37	Everton	36
1893–94c	Aston Villa	44	Sunderland	38	Derby Co	36
1894–95c	Sunderland	47	Everton	42	Aston Villa	39
1895–96c	Aston Villa	45	Derby Co	41	Everton	39
1896–97c	Aston Villa	47	Sheffield U*	36	Derby Co	36
1897–98c	Sheffield U	42	Sunderland	37	Wolverhampton W*	35
1898–99d	Aston Villa	45	Liverpool	43	Burnley	39
1899–1900d	Aston Villa	50	Sheffield U	48	Sunderland	41
1900–01d	Liverpool	45	Sunderland	43	Notts Co	40
1901–02d	Sunderland	44	Everton	41	Newcastle U	37
1902–03d	The Wednesday	42	Aston Villa*	41	Sunderland	41
1903–04d	The Wednesday	47	Manchester C	44	Everton	43
1904–05d	Newcastle U	48	Everton	47	Manchester C	46
1905–06e	Liverpool	51	Preston NE	47	The Wednesday	44
1906–07e	Newcastle U	51	Bristol C	48	Everton*	45
1907–08e	Manchester U	52	Aston Villa*	43	Manchester C	43
1908–09e	Newcastle U	53	Everton	46	Sunderland	44
1909–10e	Aston Villa	53	Liverpool	48	Blackburn R*	45
1910–11e	Manchester U	52	Aston Villa	51	Sunderland*	45
1911–12e	Blackburn R	49	Everton	46	Newcastle U	44
1912–13e	Sunderland	54	Aston Villa	50	Sheffield W	49
1913–14e	Blackburn R	51	Aston Villa	44	Middlesbrough*	43
1914–15e	Everton	46	Oldham Ath	45	Blackburn R*	43

*Won or placed on goal average (ratio), goal difference or most goals scored.

	First	Pts	Second	Pts	Third	Pts
1919–20f	WBA	60	Burnley	51	Chelsea	49
1920–21f	Burnley	59	Manchester C	54	Bolton W	52
1921–22f	Liverpool	57	Tottenham H	51	Burnley	49
1922–23f	Liverpool	60	Sunderland	54	Huddersfield T	53
1923–24f	Huddersfield T*	57	Cardiff C	57	Sunderland	53
1924–25f	Huddersfield T	58	WBA	56	Bolton W	55
1925–26f	Huddersfield T	57	Arsenal	52	Sunderland	48
1926–27f	Newcastle U	56	Huddersfield T	51	Sunderland	49
1927–28f	Everton	53	Huddersfield T	51	Leicester C	48
1928–29f	Sheffield W	52	Leicester C	51	Aston Villa	50
1929–30f	Sheffield W	60	Derby Co	50	Manchester C*	47
1930–31f	Arsenal	66	Aston Villa	59	Sheffield W	52
1931–32f	Everton	56	Arsenal	54	Sheffield W	50
1932–33f	Arsenal	58	Aston Villa	54	Sheffield W	51
1933–34f	Arsenal	59	Huddersfield T	56	Tottenham H	49
1934–35f	Arsenal	58	Sunderland	54	Sheffield W	49
1935–36f	Sunderland	56	Derby Co*	48	Huddersfield T	48
1936–37f	Manchester C	57	Charlton Ath	54	Arsenal	52
1937–38f	Arsenal	52	Wolverhampton W	51	Preston NE	49
1938–39f	Everton	59	Wolverhampton W	55	Charlton Ath	50
1946–47f	Liverpool	57	Manchester U*	56	Wolverhampton W	56
1947–48f	Arsenal	59	Manchester U*	52	Burnley	52
1948–49f	Portsmouth	58	Manchester U*	53	Derby Co	53
1949–50f	Portsmouth*	53	Wolverhampton W	53	Sunderland	52
1950–51f	Tottenham H	60	Manchester U	56	Blackpool	50
1951–52f	Manchester U	57	Tottenham H*	53	Arsenal	53
1952–53f	Arsenal*	54	Preston NE	54	Wolverhampton W	51
1953–54f	Wolverhampton W	57	WBA	53	Huddersfield T	51
1954–55f	Chelsea	52	Wolverhampton W*	48	Portsmouth*	48
1955–56f	Manchester U	60	Blackpool*	49	Wolverhampton W	49
1956–57f	Manchester U	64	Tottenham H*	56	Preston NE	56
1957–58f	Wolverhampton W	64	Preston NE	59	Tottenham H	51
1958–59f	Wolverhampton W	61	Manchester U	55	Arsenal*	50
1959–60f	Burnley	55	Wolverhampton W	54	Tottenham H	53
1960–61f	Tottenham H	66	Sheffield W	58	Wolverhampton W	57
1961–62f	Ipswich T	56	Burnley	53	Tottenham H	52
1962–63f	Everton	61	Tottenham H	55	Burnley	54
1963–64f	Liverpool	57	Manchester U	53	Everton	52
1964–65f	Manchester U*	61	Leeds U	61	Chelsea	56
1965–66f	Liverpool	61	Leeds U*	55	Burnley	55
1966–67f	Manchester U	60	Nottingham F*	56	Tottenham H	56
1967–68f	Manchester C	58	Manchester U	56	Liverpool	55
1968–69f	Leeds U	67	Liverpool	61	Everton	57
1969–70f	Everton	66	Leeds U	57	Chelsea	55
1970–71f	Arsenal	65	Leeds U	64	Tottenham H*	52
1971–72f	Derby Co	58	Leeds U*	57	Liverpool*	57
1972–73f	Liverpool	60	Arsenal	57	Leeds U	53
1973–74f	Leeds U	62	Liverpool	57	Derby Co	48
1974–75f	Derby Co	53	Liverpool*	51	Ipswich T	51
1975–76f	Liverpool	60	QPR	59	Manchester U	56
1976–77f	Liverpool	57	Manchester C	56	Ipswich T	52
1977–78f	Nottingham F	64	Liverpool	57	Everton	55
1978–79f	Liverpool	68	Nottingham F	60	WBA	59
1979–80f	Liverpool	60	Manchester U	58	Ipswich T	52
1980–81f	Aston Villa	60	Ipswich T	56	Arsenal	53
1981–82g	Liverpool	87	Ipswich T	83	Manchester U	78
1982–83g	Liverpool	82	Watford	71	Manchester U	70
1983–84g	Liverpool	80	Southampton	77	Nottingham F*	74
1984–85g	Everton	90	Liverpool*	77	Tottenham H	77
1985–86g	Liverpool	88	Everton	86	West Ham U	84
1986–87g	Everton	86	Liverpool	77	Tottenham H	71
1987–88h	Liverpool	90	Manchester U	81	Nottingham F	73
1988–89k	Arsenal*	76	Liverpool	76	Nottingham F	64
1989–90k	Liverpool	79	Aston Villa	70	Tottenham H	63
1990–91k	Arsenal†	83	Liverpool	76	Crystal Palace	69
1991–92g	Leeds U	82	Manchester U	78	Sheffield W	75

No official competition during 1915–19 and 1939–46; Regional Leagues operated.
†2 pts deducted

SECOND DIVISION to 1991–92

Maximum points: a 44; b 56; c 60; d 68; e 76; f 84; g 126; h 132; k 138.

	First	Pts	Second	Pts	Third	Pts
1892–93a	Small Heath	36	Sheffield U	35	Darwen	30
1893–94b	Liverpool	50	Small Heath	42	Notts Co	39
1894–95c	Bury	48	Notts Co	39	Newton Heath*	38
1895–96c	Liverpool*	46	Manchester C	46	Grimsby T*	42
1896–97c	Notts Co	42	Newton Heath	39	Grimsby T	38
1897–98c	Burnley	48	Newcastle U	45	Manchester C	39
1898–99d	Manchester C	52	Glossop NE	46	Leicester Fosse	45
1899–1900d	The Wednesday	54	Bolton W	52	Small Heath	46
1900–01d	Grimsby T	49	Small Heath	48	Burnley	44
1901–02d	WBA	55	Middlesbrough	51	Preston NE*	42
1902–03d	Manchester C	54	Small Heath	51	Woolwich A	48
1903–04d	Preston NE	50	Woolwich A	49	Manchester U	48

Won or placed on goal average (ratio)/goal difference.

	First	Pts	Second	Pts	Third	Pts
1904–05d	Liverpool	58	Bolton W	56	Manchester U	53
1905–06e	Bristol C	66	Manchester U	62	Chelsea	53
1906–07e	Nottingham F	60	Chelsea	57	Leicester Fosse	48
1907–08e	Bradford C	54	Leicester Fosse	52	Oldham Ath	50
1908–09e	Bolton W	52	Tottenham H*	51	WBA	51
1909–10e	Manchester C	54	Oldham Ath*	53	Hull C*	53
1910–11e	WBA	53	Bolton W	51	Chelsea	49
1911–12e	Derby Co*	54	Chelsea	54	Burnley	52
1912–13e	Preston NE	53	Burnley	50	Birmingham	46
1913–14e	Notts Co	53	Bradford PA*	49	Woolwich A	49
1914–15e	Derby Co	53	Preston NE	50	Barnsley	47
1919–20f	Tottenham H	70	Huddersfield T	64	Birmingham	56
1920–21f	Birmingham*	58	Cardiff C	58	Bristol C	51
1921–22f	Nottingham F	56	Stoke C*	52	Barnsley	52
1922–23f	Notts Co	53	West Ham U*	51	Leicester C	51
1923–24f	Leeds U	54	Bury*	51	Derby Co	51
1924–25f	Leicester C	59	Manchester U	57	Derby Co	55
1925–26f	Sheffield W	60	Derby Co	57	Chelsea	52
1926–27f	Middlesbrough	62	Portsmouth*	54	Manchester C	54
1927–28f	Manchester C	59	Leeds U	57	Chelsea	54
1928–29f	Middlesbrough	55	Grimsby T	53	Bradford PA*	48
1929–30f	Blackpool	58	Chelsea	55	Oldham Ath	53
1930–31f	Everton	61	WBA	54	Tottenham H	51
1931–32f	Wolverhampton W	56	Leeds U	54	Stoke C	52
1932–33f	Stoke C	56	Tottenham H	55	Fulham	50
1933–34f	Grimsby T	59	Preston NE	52	Bolton W*	51
1934–35f	Brentford	61	Bolton W*	56	West Ham U	56
1935–36e	Manchester U	56	Charlton Ath	55	Sheffield U*	52
1936–37f	Leicester C	56	Blackpool	55	Bury	52
1937–38f	Aston Villa	57	Manchester U*	53	Sheffield U	53
1938–39f	Blackburn R	55	Sheffield U	54	Sheffield W	53
1946–47f	Manchester C	62	Burnley	58	Birmingham C	55
1947–48f	Birmingham C	59	Newcastle U	56	Southampton	52
1948–49f	Fulham	57	WBA	56	Southampton	55
1949–50f	Tottenham H	61	Sheffield W*	52	Sheffield U*	52
1950–51f	Preston NE	57	Manchester C	52	Cardiff C	50
1951–52f	Sheffield W	53	Cardiff C*	51	Birmingham C	51
1952–53f	Sheffield U	60	Huddersfield T	58	Luton T	52
1953–54f	Leicester C*	56	Everton	56	Blackburn R	55
1954–55f	Birmingham C*	54	Luton T*	54	Rotherham U	54
1955–56f	Sheffield W	55	Leeds U	52	Liverpool*	48
1956–57f	Leicester C	61	Nottingham F	54	Liverpool	53
1957–58f	West Ham U	57	Blackburn R	56	Charlton Ath	55
1958–59f	Sheffield W	62	Fulham	60	Sheffield U*	53
1959–60f	Aston Villa	59	Cardiff C	58	Liverpool*	50
1960–61f	Ipswich T	59	Sheffield U	58	Liverpool	52
1961–62f	Liverpool	62	Leyton Orient	54	Sunderland	53
1962–63f	Stoke C	53	Chelsea*	52	Sunderland	52
1963–64f	Leeds U	63	Sunderland	61	Preston NE	56
1964–65f	Newcastle U	57	Northampton T	56	Bolton W	50
1965–66f	Manchester C	59	Southampton	54	Coventry C	53
1966–67f	Coventry C	59	Wolverhampton W	58	Carlisle U	52
1967–68f	Ipswich T	59	QPR	58	Blackpool	58
1968–69f	Derby Co	63	Crystal Palace	56	Charlton Ath	50
1969–70f	Huddersfield T	60	Blackpool	53	Leicester C	51
1970–71f	Leicester C	59	Sheffield U	56	Cardiff C*	53
1971–72f	Norwich C	57	Birmingham C	56	Millwall	55
1972–73f	Burnley	62	QPR	61	Aston Villa	50
1973–74f	Middlesbrough	65	Luton T	50	Carlisle U	49
1974–75f	Manchester U	61	Aston Villa	58	Norwich C	53
1975–76f	Sunderland	56	Bristol C*	53	WBA	53
1976–77f	Wolverhampton W	57	Chelsea	55	Nottingham F	52
1977–78f	Bolton W	58	Southampton	57	Tottenham H*	56
1978–79f	Crystal Palace	57	Brighton & HA*	56	Stoke C	56
1979–80f	Leicester C*	55	Sunderland	54	Birmingham C*	53
1980–81f	West Ham U	66	Notts Co	53	Swansea C*	50
1981–82g	Luton T	88	Watford	80	Norwich C	71
1982–83g	QPR	85	Wolverhampton W	75	Leicester C	70
1983–84g	Chelsea*	88	Sheffield W	88	Newcastle U	80
1984–85g	Oxford U	84	Birmingham C	82	Manchester C	74
1985–86g	Norwich C	84	Charlton Ath	77	Wimbledon	76
1986–87g	Derby Co	84	Portsmouth	78	Oldham Ath††	75
1987–88h	Millwall	82	Aston Villa*	78	Middlesbrough	78
1988–89k	Chelsea	99	Manchester C	82	Crystal Palace	81
1989–90k	Leeds U*	85	Sheffield U	85	Newcastle U††	80
1990–91k	Oldham Ath	88	West Ham U	87	Sheffield W	82
1991–92k	Ipswich T	84	Middlesbrough	80	Derby Co	78

No official competition during 1915–19 and 1939–46; Regional Leagues operated.
*Won or placed on goal average (ratio)/goal difference.
††Not promoted after play-offs.

THIRD DIVISION to 1991–92
Maximum points: 92; 138 from 1981–82.

	First	Pts	Second	Pts	Third	Pts
1958–59	Plymouth Arg	62	Hull C	61	Brentford*	57
1959–60	Southampton	61	Norwich C	59	Shrewsbury T*	52
1960–61	Bury	68	Walsall	62	QPR	60
1961–62	Portsmouth	65	Grimsby T	62	Bournemouth*	59
1962–63	Northampton T	62	Swindon T	58	Port Vale	54
1963–64	Coventry C*	60	Crystal Palace	60	Watford	58
1964–65	Carlisle U	60	Bristol C*	59	Mansfield T	59
1965–66	Hull C	69	Millwall	65	QPR	57
1966–67	QPR	67	Middlesbrough	55	Watford	54
1967–68	Oxford U	57	Bury	56	Shrewsbury T	55
1968–69	Watford*	64	Swindon T	64	Luton T	61
1969–70	Orient	62	Luton T	60	Bristol R	56
1970–71	Preston NE	61	Fulham	60	Halifax T	56
1971–72	Aston Villa	70	Brighton & HA	65	Bournemouth*	62
1972–73	Bolton W	61	Notts Co	57	Blackburn R	55
1973–74	Oldham Ath	62	Bristol R*	61	York C	61
1974–75	Blackburn R	60	Plymouth Arg	59	Charlton Ath	55
1975–76	Hereford U	63	Cardiff C	57	Millwall	56
1976–77	Mansfield T	64	Brighton & HA	61	Crystal Palace*	59
1977–78	Wrexham	61	Cambridge U	58	Preston NE*	56
1978–79	Shrewsbury T	61	Watford*	60	Swansea C	60
1979–80	Grimsby T	62	Blackburn R	59	Sheffield W	58
1980–81	Rotherham U	61	Barnsley*	59	Charlton Ath	59
1981–82	Burnley*	80	Carlisle U	80	Fulham	78
1982–83	Portsmouth	91	Cardiff C	86	Huddersfield T	82
1983–84	Oxford U	95	Wimbledon	87	Sheffield U*	83
1984–85	Bradford C	94	Millwall	90	Hull C	87
1985–86	Reading	94	Plymouth Arg	87	Derby Co	84
1986–87	Bournemouth	97	Middlesbrough	94	Swindon T	87
1987–88	Sunderland	93	Brighton & HA	84	Walsall	82
1988–89	Wolverhampton W	92	Sheffield U*	84	Port Vale	84
1989–90	Bristol R	93	Bristol C	91	Notts Co	87
1990–91	Cambridge U	86	Southend U	85	Grimsby T*	83
1991–92	Brentford	82	Birmingham C	81	Huddersfield T	78

FOURTH DIVISION (1958–1992)
Maximum points: 92; 138 from 1981–82.

	First	Pts	Second	Pts	Third	Pts	Fourth	Pts
1958–59	Port Vale	64	Coventry C*	60	York C	60	Shrewsbury T	58
1959–60	Walsall	65	Notts Co*	60	Torquay U	60	Watford	57
1960–61	Peterborough U	66	Crystal Palace	64	Northampton T*	60	Bradford PA	60
1961–62†	Millwall	56	Colchester U	55	Wrexham	53	Carlisle U	52
1962–63	Brentford	62	Oldham Ath*	59	Crewe Alex	59	Mansfield T*	59
1963–64	Gillingham*	60	Carlisle U	60	Workington	59	Exeter C	58
1964–65	Brighton & HA	63	Millwall*	62	York C	62	Oxford U	61
1965–66	Doncaster R*	59	Darlington	59	Torquay U	58	Colchester U*	56
1966–67	Stockport Co	64	Southport*	59	Barrow	59	Tranmere R	58
1967–68	Luton T	66	Barnsley	61	Hartlepools U	60	Crewe Alex	58
1968–69	Doncaster R	59	Halifax T	57	Rochdale*	56	Bradford C	56
1969–70	Chesterfield	64	Wrexham	61	Swansea C	60	Port Vale	59
1970–71	Notts Co	69	Bournemouth	60	Oldham Ath	59	York C	56
1971–72	Grimsby T	63	Southend U	60	Brentford	59	Scunthorpe U	57
1972–73	Southport	62	Hereford U	58	Cambridge U	57	Aldershot*	56
1973–74	Peterborough U	65	Gillingham	62	Colchester U	60	Bury	59
1974–75	Mansfield T	68	Shrewsbury T	62	Rotherham U	59	Chester*	57
1975–76	Lincoln C	74	Northampton T	68	Reading	60	Tranmere R	58
1976–77	Cambridge U	65	Exeter C	62	Colchester U*	59	Bradford C	59
1977–78	Watford	71	Southend U	60	Swansea C*	56	Brentford	56
1978–79	Reading	65	Grimsby T*	61	Wimbledon*	61	Barnsley	61
1979–80	Huddersfield T	66	Walsall	64	Newport Co	61	Portsmouth*	60
1980–81	Southend U	67	Lincoln C	65	Doncaster R	56	Wimbledon	55
1981–82	Sheffield U	96	Bradford C*	91	Wigan Ath	91	Bournemouth	88
1982–83	Wimbledon	98	Hull C	90	Port Vale	88	Scunthorpe U	83
1983–84	York C	101	Doncaster R	85	Reading*	82	Bristol C	82
1984–85	Chesterfield	91	Blackpool	86	Darlington	85	Bury	84
1985–86	Swindon T	102	Chester C	84	Mansfield T	81	Port Vale	79
1986–87	Northampton T	99	Preston NE	90	Southend U	80	Wolverhampton W††	79
1987–88	Wolverhampton W	90	Cardiff C	85	Bolton W	78	Scunthorpe U††	77
1988–89	Rotherham U	82	Tranmere R	80	Crewe Alex	78	Scunthorpe U††	77
1989–90	Exeter C	89	Grimsby T	79	Southend U	75	Stockport Co††	74
1990–91	Darlington	83	Stockport Co*	82	Hartlepool U	82	Peterborough U	80
1991–92†*	Burnley	83	Rotherham U*	77	Mansfield T	77	Blackpool	76

* Won or placed on goal average (ratio)/goal difference.

†Maximum points: 88 owing to Accrington Stanley's resignation.   ††Not promoted after play-offs.

†*Maximum points: 126 owing to Aldershot being expelled (and only 23 teams started the competition).

THIRD DIVISION—SOUTH (1920–1958)
1920–21 season as Third Division.
Maximum points: a 84; b 92.

	First	Pts	Second	Pts	Third	Pts
1920–21a	Crystal Palace	59	Southampton	54	QPR	53
1921–22a	Southampton*	61	Plymouth Arg	61	Portsmouth	53
1922–23a	Bristol C	59	Plymouth Arg*	53	Swansea T	53
1923–24a	Portsmouth	59	Plymouth Arg	55	Millwall	54
1924–25a	Swansea T	57	Plymouth Arg	56	Bristol C	53
1925–26a	Reading	57	Plymouth Arg	56	Millwall	53
1926–27a	Bristol C	62	Plymouth Arg	60	Millwall	56
1927–28a	Millwall	65	Northampton T	55	Plymouth Arg	53
1928–29a	Charlton Ath*	54	Crystal Palace	54	Northampton T*	52
1929–30a	Plymouth Arg	68	Brentford	61	QPR	51
1930–31a	Notts Co	59	Crystal Palace	51	Brentford	50
1931–32a	Fulham	57	Reading	55	Southend U	53
1932–33a	Brentford	62	Exeter C	58	Norwich C	57
1933–34a	Norwich C	61	Coventry C*	54	Reading*	54
1934–35a	Charlton Ath	61	Reading	53	Coventry C	51
1935–36a	Coventry C	57	Luton T	56	Reading	54
1936–37a	Luton T	58	Notts Co	56	Brighton & HA	53
1937–38a	Millwall	56	Bristol C	55	QPR*	53
1938–39a	Newport Co	55	Crystal Palace	52	Brighton & HA	49
1939–46	Competition cancelled owing to war. Regional Leagues operated.					
1946–47a	Cardiff C	66	QPR	57	Bristol C	51
1947–48a	QPR	61	Bournemouth	57	Walsall	51
1948–49a	Swansea T	62	Reading	55	Bournemouth	52
1949–50a	Notts Co	58	Northampton T*	51	Southend U	51
1950–51b	Nottingham F	70	Norwich C	64	Reading*	57
1951–52b	Plymouth Arg	66	Reading*	61	Norwich C	61
1952–53b	Bristol R	64	Millwall*	62	Northampton T	62
1953–54b	Ipswich T	64	Brighton & HA	61	Bristol C	56
1954–55b	Bristol C	70	Leyton Orient	61	Southampton	59
1955–56b	Leyton Orient	66	Brighton & HA	65	Ipswich T	64
1956–57b	Ipswich T*	59	Torquay U	59	Colchester U	58
1957–58b	Brighton & HA	60	Brentford*	58	Plymouth Arg	58

THIRD DIVISION—NORTH (1921–1958)
Maximum points: a 76; b 84; c 80; d 92.

	First	Pts	Second	Pts	Third	Pts
1921–22a	Stockport Co	56	Darlington*	50	Grimsby T	50
1922–23a	Nelson	51	Bradford PA	47	Walsall	46
1923–24b	Wolverhampton W	63	Rochdale	62	Chesterfield	54
1924–25b	Darlington	58	Nelson*	53	New Brighton	53
1925–26b	Grimsby T	61	Bradford PA	60	Rochdale	59
1926–27b	Stoke C	63	Rochdale	58	Bradford PA	55
1927–28b	Bradford PA	63	Lincoln C	55	Stockport Co	54
1928–29b	Bradford C	63	Stockport Co	62	Wrexham	52
1929–30b	Port Vale	67	Stockport Co	63	Darlington*	50
1930–31b	Chesterfield	58	Lincoln C	57	Wrexham*	54
1931–32c	Lincoln C*	57	Gateshead	57	Chester	50
1932–33b	Hull C	59	Wrexham	57	Stockport Co	54
1933–34b	Barnsley	62	Chesterfield	61	Stockport Co	59
1934–35b	Doncaster R	57	Halifax T	55	Chester	54
1935–36b	Chesterfield	60	Chester*	55	Tranmere R	55
1936–37b	Stockport Co	60	Lincoln C	57	Chester	53
1937–38b	Tranmere R	56	Doncaster R	54	Hull C	53
1938–39b	Barnsley	67	Doncaster R	56	Bradford C	52
1939–46	Competition cancelled owing to war. Regional Leagues operated.					
1946–47b	Doncaster R	72	Rotherham U	60	Chester	56
1947–48b	Lincoln C	60	Rotherham U	59	Wrexham	50
1948–49b	Hull C	65	Rotherham U	62	Doncaster R	50
1949–50b	Doncaster R	55	Gateshead	53	Rochdale*	51
1950–51d	Rotherham U	71	Mansfield T	64	Carlisle U	62
1951–52d	Lincoln C	69	Grimsby T	66	Stockport Co	59
1952–53d	Oldham Ath	59	Port Vale	58	Wrexham	56
1953–54d	Port Vale	69	Barnsley	58	Scunthorpe U	57
1954–55d	Barnsley	65	Accrington S	61	Scunthorpe U*	58
1955–56d	Grimsby T	68	Derby Co	63	Accrington S	59
1956–57d	Derby Co	63	Hartlepools U	59	Accrington S*	58
1957–58d	Scunthorpe U	66	Accrington S	59	Bradford C	57

* *Won or placed on goal average (ratio).*

PROMOTED AFTER PLAY-OFFS
(Not accounted for in previous section)

1986–87 Aldershot to Division 3.
1987–88 Swansea C to Division 3.
1988–89 Leyton Orient to Division 3.
1989–90 Cambridge U to Division 3; Notts Co to Division 2; Sunderland to Division 1.
1990–91 Notts Co to Division 1; Tranmere R to Division 2; Torquay U to Division 3.
1991–92 Blackburn R to Premier League; Peterborough U to Division 1.
1992–93 Swindon T to Premier League; WBA to Division 1; York C to Division 2.
1993–94 Leicester C to Premier League; Burnley to Division 1; Wycombe W to Division 2.
1994–95 Huddersfield T to Division 1.
1995–96 Leicester C to Premier League; Bradford C to Division 1; Plymouth Arg to Division 2.
1996–97 Crystal Palace to Premier League; Crewe Alex to Division 1; Northampton T to Division 2.

1997–98 Charlton Ath to Premier League; Colchester U to Division 2.
1998–99 Watford to Premier League; Scunthorpe U to Division 2.
1999–2000 Peterborough U to Division 2
2000–01 Walsall to Division 1; Blackpool to Division 2
2001–02 Birmingham C to Premier League; Stoke C to Division 1; Cheltenham T to Division 2

LEAGUE TITLE WINS

FA PREMIER LEAGUE – Manchester U 6, Arsenal 2, Blackburn R 1.

LEAGUE DIVISION 1 – Liverpool 18, Arsenal 10, Everton 9, Sunderland 8, Manchester U 7, Aston Villa 7, Newcastle U 5, Sheffield W 4, Huddersfield T 3, Leeds U 3, Manchester C 3, Wolverhampton W 3, Blackburn R 2, Portsmouth 2, Preston NE 2, Burnley 2, Nottingham F 2, Tottenham H 2, Derby Co 2, Bolton W, Charlton Ath, Chelsea, Crystal Palace, Sheffield U, WBA, Ipswich T, Middlesbrough 1 each.

LEAGUE DIVISION 2 – Leicester C 6, Manchester C 6, Sheffield W 5, Birmingham C (one as Small Heath) 5, Derby Co 4, Liverpool 4, Preston NE 4, Ipswich T 3, Leeds U 3, Notts Co 3, Middlesbrough 3, Stoke C 3, Bury 2, Grimsby T 2, Norwich C 2, Nottingham F 2, Tottenham H 2, WBA 2, Aston Villa 2, Burnley 2, Chelsea 2, Manchester U 2, West Ham U 2, Wolverhampton W 2, Bolton W 2, Fulham 2, Swindon T, Huddersfield T, Bristol C, Brentford, Bradford C, Everton, Sheffield U, Newcastle U, Coventry C, Blackpool, Blackburn R, Brighton & HA, Sunderland, Crystal Palace, Luton T, QPR, Oxford U, Millwall, Oldham Ath, Reading, Watford 1 each.

LEAGUE DIVISION 3 – Portsmouth 2, Oxford U 2, Shrewsbury T 2, Carlisle U 2, Preston NE 2, Brentford 2, Plymouth Arg 2, Southampton, Bury, Northampton T, Coventry, Hull C, QPR, Watford, Leyton Orient, Aston Villa, Bolton W, Oldham Ath, Blackburn R, Hereford U, Mansfield T, Wrexham, Grimsby T, Rotherham U, Burnley, Bradford C, Bournemouth, Reading, Sunderland, Wolverhampton W, Bristol R, Cambridge U, Cardiff C, Swansea C, Wigan Ath, Notts Co 1 each.

LEAGUE DIVISION 4 – Chesterfield 2, Doncaster R 2, Peterborough U 2, Port Vale, Walsall, Millwall, Brentford, Gillingham, Brighton & HA, Stockport Co, Luton T, Notts Co, Grimsby T, Southport, Mansfield T, Lincoln C, Cambridge U, Watford, Reading, Huddersfield T, Southend U, Sheffield U, Wimbledon, York C, Swindon T, Northampton T, Wolverhampton W, Rotherham U, Exeter C, Darlington, Burnley 1 each.

To 1957–58

DIVISION 3 (South) – Bristol C 3; Charlton Ath, Ipswich T, Millwall, Notts Co, Plymouth Arg, Swansea T 2 each; Brentford, Bristol R, Cardiff C, Crystal Palace, Coventry C, Fulham, Leyton Orient, Luton T, Newport Co, Nottingham F, Norwich C, Portsmouth, QPR, Reading, Southampton, Brighton & HA 1 each.

DIVISION 3 (North) – Barnsley, Doncaster R, Lincoln C 3 each; Chesterfield, Grimsby T, Hull C, Port Vale, Stockport Co 2 each; Bradford PA, Bradford C, Darlington, Derby Co, Nelson, Oldham Ath, Rotherham U, Stoke C, Tranmere R, Wolverhampton W, Scunthorpe U 1 each.

RELEGATED CLUBS

1891–92 League extended. Newton Heath, Sheffield W and Nottingham F admitted. *Second Division formed* including Darwen.
1892–93 In Test matches, Sheffield U and Darwen won promotion in place of Notts Co and Accrington S.
1893–94 In Tests, Liverpool and Small Heath won promotion. Newton Heath and Darwen relegated.
1894–95 After Tests, Bury promoted, Liverpool relegated.
1895–96 After Tests, Liverpool promoted, Small Heath relegated.
1896–97 After Tests, Notts Co promoted, Burnley relegated.
1897–98 Test system abolished after success of Stoke C and Burnley. League extended. Blackburn R and Newcastle U elected to First Division. *Automatic promotion and relegation introduced.*

FA PREMIER LEAGUE TO DIVISION 1

1992–93 Crystal Palace, Middlesbrough, Nottingham F
1993–94 Sheffield U, Oldham Ath, Swindon T
1994–95 Crystal Palace, Norwich C, Leicester C, Ipswich T
1995–96 Manchester C, QPR, Bolton W
1996–97 Sunderland, Middlesbrough, Nottingham F

1997–98 Bolton W, Barnsley, Crystal Palace
1998–99 Charlton Ath, Blackburn R, Nottingham F
1999–2000 Wimbledon, Sheffield W, Watford
2000–01 Manchester C, Coventry C, Bradford C
2001–02 Ipswich T, Derby Co, Leicester C

DIVISION 1 TO DIVISION 2

1898–99 Bolton W and Sheffield W
1899–1900 Burnley and Glossop
1900–01 Preston NE and WBA
1901–02 Small Heath and Manchester C
1902–03 Grimsby T and Bolton W
1903–04 Liverpool and WBA
1904–05 League extended. Bury and Notts Co, two bottom clubs in First Division, re-elected.
1905–06 Nottingham F and Wolverhampton W
1906–07 Derby Co and Stoke C
1907–08 Bolton W and Birmingham C
1908–09 Manchester C and Leicester Fosse
1909–10 Bolton W and Chelsea
1910–11 Bristol C and Nottingham F
1911–12 Preston NE and Bury
1912–13 Notts Co and Woolwich Arsenal
1913–14 Preston NE and Derby Co
1914–15 Tottenham H and Chelsea*
1919–20 Notts Co and Sheffield W
1920–21 Derby Co and Bradford PA
1921–22 Bradford C and Manchester U
1922–23 Stoke C and Oldham Ath
1923–24 Chelsea and Middlesbrough
1924–25 Preston NE and Nottingham F
1925–26 Manchester C and Notts Co
1926–27 Leeds U and WBA
1927–28 Tottenham H and Middlesbrough
1928–29 Bury and Cardiff C
1929–30 Burnley and Everton

1930–31 Leeds U and Manchester U
1931–32 Grimsby T and West Ham U
1932–33 Bolton W and Blackpool
1933–34 Newcastle U and Sheffield U
1934–35 Leicester C and Tottenham H
1935–36 Aston Villa and Blackburn R
1936–37 Manchester U and Sheffield W
1937–38 Manchester C and WBA
1938–39 Birmingham C and Leicester C
1946–47 Brentford and Leeds U
1947–48 Blackburn R and Grimsby T
1948–49 Preston NE and Sheffield U
1949–50 Manchester C and Birmingham C
1950–51 Sheffield W and Everton
1951–52 Huddersfield T and Fulham
1952–53 Stoke C and Derby Co
1953–54 Middlesbrough and Liverpool
1954–55 Leicester C and Sheffield W
1955–56 Huddersfield T and Sheffield U
1956–57 Charlton Ath and Cardiff C
1957–58 Sheffield W and Sunderland
1958–59 Portsmouth and Aston Villa
1959–60 Luton T and Leeds U
1960–61 Preston NE and Newcastle U
1961–62 Chelsea and Cardiff C
1962–63 Manchester C and Leyton Orient
1963–64 Bolton W and Ipswich T
1964–65 Wolverhampton W and Birmingham C
1965–66 Northampton T and Blackburn R

1966–67 Aston Villa and Blackpool
1967–68 Fulham and Sheffield U
1968–69 Leicester C and QPR
1969–70 Sunderland and Sheffield W
1970–71 Burnley and Blackpool
1971–72 Huddersfield T and Nottingham F
1972–73 Crystal Palace and WBA
1973–74 Southampton, Manchester U, Norwich C
1974–75 Luton T, Chelsea, Carlisle U
1975–76 Wolverhampton W, Burnley, Sheffield U
1976–77 Sunderland, Stoke C, Tottenham H
1977–78 West Ham U, Newcastle U, Leicester C
1978–79 QPR, Birmingham C, Chelsea
1979–80 Bristol C, Derby Co, Bolton W
1980–81 Norwich C, Leicester C, Crystal Palace
1981–82 Leeds U, Wolverhampton W, Middlesbrough
1982–83 Manchester C, Swansea C, Brighton & HA
1983–84 Birmingham C, Notts Co, Wolverhampton W

1984–85 Norwich C, Sunderland, Stoke C
1985–86 Ipswich T, Birmingham C, WBA
1986–87 Leicester C, Manchester C, Aston Villa
1987–88 Chelsea**, Portsmouth, Watford, Oxford U
1988–89 Middlesbrough, West Ham U, Newcastle U
1989–90 Sheffield W, Charlton Ath, Millwall
1990–91 Sunderland and Derby Co
1991–92 Luton T, Notts Co, West Ham U
1992–93 Brentford, Cambridge U, Bristol R
1993–94 Birmingham C, Oxford U, Peterborough U
1994–95 Swindon T, Burnley, Bristol C, Notts Co
1995–96 Millwall, Watford, Luton T
1996–97 Grimsby T, Oldham Ath, Southend U
1997–98 Manchester C, Stoke C, Reading
1998–99 Bury, Oxford U, Bristol C
1999–2000 Walsall, Port Vale, Swindon T
2000–01 Huddersfield T, QPR, Tranmere R
2001–02 Crewe Alex, Barnsley, Stockport Co

**Relegated after play-offs.
*Subsequently re-elected to Division 1 when League was extended after the War.

DIVISION 2 TO DIVISION 3

1920–21 Stockport Co
1921–22 Bradford PA and Bristol C
1922–23 Rotherham Co and Wolverhampton W
1923–24 Nelson and Bristol C
1924–25 Crystal Palace and Coventry C
1925–26 Stoke C and Stockport Co
1926–27 Darlington and Bradford C
1927–28 Fulham and South Shields
1928–29 Port Vale and Clapton Orient
1929–30 Hull C and Notts Co
1930–31 Reading and Cardiff C
1931–32 Barnsley and Bristol C
1932–33 Chesterfield and Charlton Ath
1933–34 Millwall and Lincoln C
1934–35 Oldham Ath and Notts Co
1935–36 Port Vale and Hull C
1936–37 Doncaster R and Bradford C
1937–38 Barnsley and Stockport Co
1938–39 Norwich C and Tranmere R
1946–47 Swansea T and Newport Co
1947–48 Doncaster R and Millwall
1948–49 Nottingham F and Lincoln C
1949–50 Plymouth Arg and Bradford PA
1950–51 Grimsby T and Chesterfield
1951–52 Coventry C and QPR
1952–53 Southampton and Barnsley
1953–54 Brentford and Oldham Ath
1954–55 Ipswich T and Derby Co
1955–56 Plymouth Arg and Hull C
1956–57 Port Vale and Bury
1957–58 Doncaster R and Notts Co
1958–59 Barnsley and Grimsby T
1959–60 Bristol C and Hull C
1960–61 Lincoln C and Portsmouth
1961–62 Brighton & HA and Bristol R
1962–63 Walsall and Luton T
1963–64 Grimsby T and Scunthorpe U
1964–65 Swindon T and Swansea T
1965–66 Middlesbrough and Leyton Orient
1966–67 Northampton T and Bury
1967–68 Plymouth Arg and Rotherham U

1968–69 Fulham and Bury
1969–70 Preston NE and Aston Villa
1970–71 Blackburn R and Bolton W
1971–72 Charlton Ath and Watford
1972–73 Huddersfield T and Brighton & HA
1973–74 Crystal Palace, Preston NE, Swindon T
1974–75 Millwall, Cardiff C, Sheffield W
1975–76 Oxford U, York C, Portsmouth
1976–77 Carlisle U, Plymouth Arg, Hereford U
1977–78 Blackpool, Mansfield T, Hull C
1978–79 Sheffield U, Millwall, Blackburn R
1979–80 Fulham, Burnley, Charlton Ath
1980–81 Preston NE, Bristol C, Bristol R
1981–82 Cardiff C, Wrexham, Orient
1982–83 Rotherham U, Burnley, Bolton W
1983–84 Derby Co, Swansea C, Cambridge U
1984–85 Notts Co, Cardiff C, Wolverhampton W
1985–86 Carlisle U, Middlesbrough, Fulham
1986–87 Sunderland**, Grimsby T, Brighton & HA
1987–88 Huddersfield T, Reading, Sheffield U**
1988–89 Shrewsbury T, Birmingham C, Walsall
1989–90 Bournemouth, Bradford C, Stoke C
1990–91 WBA and Hull C
1991–92 Plymouth Arg, Brighton & HA, Port Vale
1992–93 Preston NE, Mansfield T, Wigan Ath, Chester C
1993–94 Fulham, Exeter C, Hartlepool U, Barnet
1994–95 Cambridge U, Plymouth Arg, Cardiff C,
          Chester C, Leyton Orient
1995–96 Carlisle U, Swansea C, Brighton & HA, Hull C
1996–97 Peterborough U, Shrewsbury T, Rotherham U,
          Notts Co
1997–98 Brentford, Plymouth Arg, Carlisle U, Southend U
1998–99 York C, Northampton T, Lincoln C,
          Macclesfield T
1999–2000 Cardiff C, Blackpool, Scunthorpe U,
          Chesterfield
2000–01 Bristol R, Luton T, Swansea C, Oxford U
2001–02 Bournemouth, Bury, Wrexham, Cambridge U

DIVISION 3 TO DIVISION 4

1958–59 Rochdale, Notts Co, Doncaster R, Stockport Co
1959–60 Accrington S, Wrexham, Mansfield T, York C
1960–61 Chesterfield, Colchester U, Bradford C,
          Tranmere R
1961–62 Newport Co, Brentford, Lincoln C, Torquay U
1962–63 Bradford PA, Brighton & HA, Carlisle U,
          Halifax T
1963–64 Millwall, Crewe Alex, Wrexham, Notts Co
1964–65 Luton T, Port Vale, Colchester U, Barnsley
1965–66 Southend U, Exeter C, Brentford, York C
1966–67 Doncaster R, Workington, Darlington, Swansea T
1967–68 Scunthorpe U, Colchester U, Grimsby T,
          Peterborough U (demoted)
1968–69 Oldham Ath, Crewe Alex, Hartlepool,
          Northampton T
1969–70 Bournemouth, Southport, Barrow, Stockport Co
1970–71 Reading, Bury, Doncaster R, Gillingham
1971–72 Mansfield T, Barnsley, Torquay U, Bradford C
1972–73 Rotherham U, Brentford, Swansea C,

          Scunthorpe U
1973–74 Cambridge U, Shrewsbury T, Southport,
          Rochdale
1974–75 Bournemouth, Tranmere R, Watford,
          Huddersfield T
1975–76 Aldershot, Colchester U, Southend U, Halifax T
1976–77 Reading, Northampton T, Grimsby T, York C
1977–78 Port Vale, Bradford C, Hereford U, Portsmouth
1978–79 Peterborough U, Walsall, Tranmere R, Lincoln C
1979–80 Bury, Southend U, Mansfield T, Wimbledon
1980–81 Sheffield U, Colchester U, Blackpool, Hull C
1981–82 Wimbledon, Swindon T, Bristol C, Chester
1982–83 Reading, Wrexham, Doncaster R, Chesterfield
1983–84 Scunthorpe U, Southend U, Port Vale, Exeter C
1984–85 Burnley, Orient, Preston NE, Cambridge U
1985–86 Lincoln C, Cardiff C, Wolverhampton W,
          Swansea C
1986–87 Bolton W**, Carlisle U, Darlington, Newport Co
1987–88 Doncaster R, York C, Grimsby T, Rotherham U**

1988–89 Southend U, Chesterfield, Gillingham, Aldershot   1990–91 Crewe Alex, Rotherham U, Mansfield T
1989–90 Cardiff C, Northampton T, Blackpool, Walsall   1991–92 Bury, Shrewsbury T, Torquay U, Darlington

** *Relegated after play-offs. N.B. Relegated clubs not featured in exact order of finishing.*

APPLICATIONS FOR RE-ELECTION
FOURTH DIVISION

Eleven: Hartlepool U.
Seven: Crewe Alex.
Six: Barrow (lost League place to Hereford U 1972), Halifax T, Rochdale, Southport (lost League place to Wigan Ath 1978), York C.
Five: Chester C, Darlington, Lincoln C, Stockport Co, Workington (lost League place to Wimbledon 1977).
Four: Bradford PA (lost League place to Cambridge U 1970), Newport Co, Northampton T.
Three: Doncaster R, Hereford U.
Two: Bradford C, Exeter C, Oldham Ath, Scunthorpe U, Torquay U.
One: Aldershot, Colchester U, Gateshead (lost League place to Peterborough U 1960), Grimsby T, Swansea C, Tranmere R, Wrexham, Blackpool, Cambridge U, Preston NE.
Accrington S resigned and Oxford U were elected 1962.
Port Vale were forced to re-apply following expulsion in 1968.
Aldershot expelled March 1992. Maidstone U resigned August 1992.

THIRD DIVISIONS NORTH & SOUTH

Seven: Walsall.
Six: Exeter C, Halifax T, Newport Co.
Five: Accrington S, Barrow, Gillingham, New Brighton, Southport.
Four: Rochdale, Norwich C.
Three: Crystal Palace, Crewe Alex, Darlington, Hartlepool U, Merthyr T, Swindon T.
Two: Aberdare Ath, Aldershot, Ashington, Bournemouth, Brentford, Chester, Colchester U, Durham C, Millwall, Nelson, QPR, Rotherham U, Southend U, Tranmere R, Watford, Workington.
One: Bradford C, Bradford PA, Brighton & HA, Bristol R, Cardiff C, Carlisle U, Charlton Ath, Gateshead, Grimsby T, Mansfield T, Shrewsbury T, Torquay U, York C.

LEAGUE STATUS FROM 1986–87

RELEGATED FROM LEAGUE		PROMOTED TO LEAGUE
1986–87	Lincoln C	Scarborough
1987–88	Newport Co	Lincoln C
1988–89	Darlington	Maidstone U
1989–90	Colchester U	Darlington
1990–91	—	Barnet
1991–92	—	Colchester U
1992–93	Halifax T	Wycombe W
1993–94	—	—
1994–95	—	—
1995–96	—	
1996–97	Hereford U	Macclesfield T
1997–98	Doncaster R	Halifax T
1998–99	Scarborough	Cheltenham T
1999–2000	Chester C	Kidderminster H
2000–01	Barnet	Rushden & D
2001–02	Halifax T	Boston U

FOOTBALL AWARDS 2002

FOOTBALLER OF THE YEAR

The Football Writers' Association Sir Stanley Matthews Trophy for the Footballer of the Year went to Robert Pires of Arsenal and France.

THE PFA AWARDS 2002

Player of the Year: Ruud Van Nistelrooy, Manchester United and Holland.
Young Player of the Year: Craig Bellamy, Newcastle United and Wales.
Merit Award: Niall Quinn, Sunderland and Republic of Ireland.

THE SCOTTISH FOOTBALL WRITERS' ASSOCIATION

Player of the Year: Paul Lambert, Celtic.

THE SCOTTISH PFA AWARDS 2001

Player of the Year: Lorenzo Amoruso, Rangers.
Young Player of the Year: Kevin McNaughton, Aberdeen.
First Division: Owen Coyle, Airdrieonians.
Second Division: John O'Neil, Queen of the South.
Third Division: Paul McManus, East Fife.

EUROPEAN FOOTBALLER OF THE YEAR 2001

Michael Owen, Liverpool and England.

WORLD PLAYER OF THE YEAR 2001

Luis Figo, Real Madrid and Portugal.

Ruud Van Nistelrooy. (ASP)

Robert Pires. (Colorsport)

LEAGUE ATTENDANCES SINCE 1946–47

Season	Matches	Total	Div. 1	Div. 2	Div. 3 (S)	Div. 3 (N)
1946–47	1848	35,604,606	15,005,316	11,071,572	5,664,004	3,863,714
1947–48	1848	40,259,130	16,732,341	12,286,350	6,653,610	4,586,829
1948–49	1848	41,271,414	17,914,667	11,353,237	6,998,429	5,005,081
1949–50	1848	40,517,865	17,278,625	11,694,158	7,104,155	4,440,927
1950–51	2028	39,584,967	16,679,454	10,780,580	7,367,884	4,757,109
1951–52	2028	39,015,866	16,110,322	11,066,189	6,958,927	4,880,428
1952–53	2028	37,149,966	16,050,278	9,686,654	6,704,299	4,708,735
1953–54	2028	36,174,590	16,154,915	9,510,053	6,311,508	4,198,114
1954–55	2028	34,133,103	15,087,221	8,988,794	5,996,017	4,051,071
1955–56	2028	33,150,809	14,108,961	9,080,002	5,692,479	4,269,367
1956–57	2028	32,744,405	13,803,037	8,718,162	5,622,189	4,601,017
1957–58	2028	33,562,208	14,468,652	8,663,712	6,097,183	4,332,661

Season	Matches	Total	Div. 1	Div. 2	Div. 3	Div. 4
1958–59	2028	33,610,985	14,727,691	8,641,997	5,946,600	4,276,697
1959–60	2028	32,538,611	14,391,227	8,399,627	5,739,707	4,008,050
1960–61	2028	28,619,754	12,926,948	7,033,936	4,784,256	3,874,614
1961–62	2015	27,979,902	12,061,194	7,453,089	5,199,106	3,266,513
1962–63	2028	28,885,852	12,490,239	7,792,770	5,341,362	3,261,481
1963–64	2028	28,535,022	12,486,626	7,594,158	5,419,157	3,035,081
1964–65	2028	27,641,168	12,708,752	6,984,104	4,436,245	3,512,067
1965–66	2028	27,206,980	12,480,644	6,914,757	4,779,150	3,032,429
1966–67	2028	28,902,596	14,242,957	7,253,819	4,421,172	2,984,648
1967–68	2028	30,107,298	15,289,410	7,450,410	4,013,087	3,354,391
1968–69	2028	29,382,172	14,584,851	7,382,390	4,339,656	3,075,275
1969–70	2028	29,600,972	14,868,754	7,581,728	4,223,761	2,926,729
1970–71	2028	28,194,146	13,954,337	7,098,265	4,377,213	2,764,331
1971–72	2028	28,700,729	14,484,603	6,769,308	4,697,392	2,749,426
1972–73	2028	25,448,642	13,998,154	5,631,730	3,737,252	2,081,506
1973–74	2027	24,982,203	13,070,991	6,326,108	3,421,624	2,163,480
1974–75	2028	25,577,977	12,613,178	6,955,970	4,086,145	1,992,684
1975–76	2028	24,896,053	13,089,861	5,798,405	3,948,449	2,059,338
1976–77	2028	26,182,800	13,647,585	6,250,597	4,152,218	2,132,400
1977–78	2028	25,392,872	13,255,677	6,474,763	3,332,042	2,330,390
1978–79	2028	24,540,627	12,704,549	6,153,223	3,374,558	2,308,297
1979–80	2028	24,623,975	12,163,002	6,112,025	3,999,328	2,349,620
1980–81	2028	21,907,569	11,392,894	5,175,442	3,637,854	1,701,379
1981–82	2028	20,006,961	10,420,793	4,750,463	2,836,915	1,998,790
1982–83	2028	18,766,158	9,295,613	4,974,937	2,943,568	1,552,040
1983–84	2028	18,358,631	8,711,448	5,359,757	2,729,942	1,557,484
1984–85	2028	17,849,835	9,761,404	4,030,823	2,667,008	1,390,600
1985–86	2028	16,488,577	9,037,854	3,551,968	2,490,481	1,408,274
1986–87	2028	17,379,218	9,144,676	4,168,131	2,350,970	1,715,441
1987–88	2030	17,959,732	8,094,571	5,341,599	2,751,275	1,772,287
1988–89	2036	18,464,192	7,809,993	5,887,805	3,035,327	1,791,067
1989–90	2036	19,445,442	7,883,039	6,867,674	2,803,551	1,891,178
1990–91	2036	19,508,202	8,618,709	6,285,068	2,835,759	1,768,666
1991–92	2064*	20,487,273	9,989,160	5,809,787	2,993,352	1,694,974

Season	Matches	Total	FA Premier	Div. 1	Div. 2	Div. 3
1992–93	2028	20,657,327	9,759,809	5,874,017	3,483,073	1,540,428
1993–94	2028	21,683,381	10,644,551	6,487,104	2,972,702	1,579,024
1994–95	2028	21,856,020	11,213,168	6,044,293	3,037,752	1,560,807
1995–96	2036	21,844,416	10,469,107	6,566,349	2,843,652	1,965,308
1996–97	2036	22,783,163	10,804,762	6,931,539	3,195,223	1,851,639
1997–98	2036	24,692,608	11,092,106	8,330,018	3,503,264	1,767,220
1998–99	2036	25,435,542	11,620,326	7,543,369	4,169,697	2,102,150
1999–2000	2036	25,341,090	11,668,497	7,810,208	3,700,433	2,161,952
2000–01	2036	26,030,167	12,472,094	7,909,512	3,488,166	2,160,395
2001–02	2036	27,756,977	13,043,118	8,352,128	3,963,153	2,398,578

*Figures include matches played by Aldershot.
Football League official total for their three divisions in 2001–02 was 14,716,162.

ENGLISH LEAGUE ATTENDANCES 2001–02

FA BARCLAYCARD PREMIERSHIP ATTENDANCES

	Average Gate			Season 2001/02	
	2000/01	2001/02	+/–%	Highest	Lowest
Arsenal	37,975	38,054	+0.21	38,240	37,898
Aston Villa	31,597	35,012	+10.81	42,632	27,701
Blackburn Rovers	20,740	25,984	+25.28	30,487	21,873
Bolton Wanderers	16,062	25,098	+56.26	27,351	20,747
Charlton Athletic	20,020	24,135	+20.56	26,551	20,451
Chelsea	34,698	39,033	+12.49	41,725	33,504
Derby County	28,551	29,818	+4.44	33,297	25,712
Everton	34,130	34,004	–0.37	39,948	29,503
Fulham	14,985	19,545	+30.43	21,159	15,885
Ipswich Town	22,524	24,396	+8.31	28,286	21,133
Leeds United	39,016	39,789	+1.98	40,287	38,337
Leicester City	20,453	19,835	–3.02	21,886	15,412
Liverpool	43,699	43,389	–0.71	44,371	37,163
Manchester United	67,544	67,586	+0.06	67,683	67,534
Middlesbrough	30,730	28,450	–7.42	34,358	24,041
Newcastle United	51,290	51,373	+0.16	52,130	49,185
Southampton	15,115	30,633	+102.66	31,973	26,794
Sunderland	45,069	44,108	–2.13	47,989	39,730
Tottenham Hotspur	35,216	34,878	–0.96	36,075	29,596
West Ham United	25,697	31,359	+22.04	35,546	24,517

TOTAL ATTENDANCES:	13,043,118 (380 games)
	Average 34,324 (+4.58%)
HIGHEST:	67,683 Manchester United v Middlesbrough
LOWEST:	15,412 Leicester City v Middlesbrough
HIGHEST AVERAGE:	67,586 Manchester United
LOWEST AVERAGE:	19,545 Fulham

NATIONWIDE FOOTBALL LEAGUE: DIVISION ONE ATTENDANCES

	Average Gate			Season 2001/02	
	2000/01	2001/02	+/–%	Highest	Lowest
Barnsley	14,465	13,292	–8.1	18,303	10,976
Birmingham City	21,283	21,854	+2.7	29,178	17,310
Bradford City	18,511	15,489	–16.3	20,209	12,846
Burnley	16,234	15,252	–6.0	21,823	13,162
Coventry City	20,535	15,436	–24.8	22,902	12,448
Crewe Alexandra	6,698	7,113	+6.2	10,092	5,419
Crystal Palace	17,061	17,177	+0.7	22,080	13,970
Gillingham	9,293	8,569	–7.8	10,477	6,575
Grimsby Town	5,646	6,430	+13.9	9,275	4,859
Manchester City	34,058	33,059	–2.9	34,657	30,238
Millwall	11,442	13,253	+15.8	17,058	10,021
Norwich City	16,525	18,738	+13.4	21,251	15,710
Nottingham Forest	20,615	21,701	+5.3	28,546	15,632
Portsmouth	13,533	15,117	+11.7	19,103	12,336
Preston North End	14,617	14,883	+1.8	21,014	11,371
Rotherham United	5,652	7,488	+32.5	11,426	5,586
Sheffield United	17,211	18,020	+4.7	29,364	14,180
Sheffield Wednesday	19,268	20,864	+8.3	29,772	15,592
Stockport County	7,031	6,244	–11.2	9,537	4,086
Walsall	5,632	6,816	+21.0	9,181	5,080
Watford	13,941	14,896	+6.9	18,911	12,160
West Bromwich Albion	17,657	20,691	+17.2	26,712	17,335
Wimbledon	7,901	6,958	–11.9	13,564	4,249
Wolverhampton Wanderers	19,258	23,796	+23.6	28,015	19,231

TOTAL ATTENDANCES:	8,352,128 (552 games)
	Average 15,131 (+5.6%)
HIGHEST:	34,657 Manchester City v Portsmouth
LOWEST:	4,086 Stockport County v Watford
HIGHEST AVERAGE:	33,059 Manchester City
LOWEST AVERAGE:	6,244 Stockport County

Nationwide attendance averages and highest crowd figures for 2001–02 supplied by Football League.
Other attendances unofficial.

NATIONWIDE FOOTBALL LEAGUE: DIVISION TWO ATTENDANCES

	Average Gate			Season 2001/02	
	2000/01	2001/02	+/–%	Highest	Lowest
Blackpool	4,457	5,682	+27.5	9,333	4,118
AFC Bournemouth	4,403	5,062	+15.0	8,147	2,908
Brentford	4,645	6,729	+44.9	11,303	4,561
Brighton & Hove Albion	6,603	6,559	–0.7	6,870	6,117
Bristol City	10,369	11,241	+8.4	15,609	8,299
Bury	3,444	3,914	+13.6	7,953	2,459
Cambridge United	4,403	3,505	–20.4	5,665	2,379
Cardiff City	7,962	12,523	+57.3	17,403	8,013
Chesterfield	4,846	4,305	–11.2	5,442	3,538
Colchester United	3,555	3,822	+7.5	5,186	2,835
Huddersfield Town	12,808	10,880	–15.1	16,041	7,179
Northampton Town	5,654	5,246	–7.2	6,723	3,909
Notts County	5,201	5,956	+14.5	15,618	3,140
Oldham Athletic	4,972	5,812	+16.9	8,859	3,970
Peterborough United	6,252	5,420	–13.3	8,656	3,445
Port Vale	4,458	5,214	+17.0	10,344	3,514
Queens Park Rangers	12,013	11,750	–2.2	18,346	8,519
Reading	12,647	14,115	+11.6	22,151	8,081
Stoke City	13,767	13,966	+1.4	23,019	9,515
Swindon Town	6,187	5,840	–5.6	9,264	3,821
Tranmere Rovers	9,045	8,656	–4.3	12,201	7,342
Wigan Athletic	6,774	5,651	–16.6	7,783	3,535
Wrexham	3,600	3,782	+5.1	5,832	2,470
Wycombe Wanderers	5,513	6,681	+21.2	9,250	5,400

TOTAL ATTENDANCES: 3,963,153 (552 games)
                                  Average 7,180 (+13.6%)
HIGHEST: 23,019 Stoke City v Port Vale
LOWEST: 2,379 Cambridge United v Port Vale
HIGHEST AVERAGE: 14,115 Reading
LOWEST AVERAGE: 3,505 Cambridge United

NATIONWIDE FOOTBALL LEAGUE: DIVISION THREE ATTENDANCES

	Average Gate			Season 2001/02	
	2000/01	2001/02	+/–%	Highest	Lowest
Bristol Rovers	7,275	6,565	–9.8	10,127	4,457
Carlisle United	3,670	3,214	–14.5	5,226	1,849
Cheltenham Town	3,695	4,052	+9.7	7,013	2,402
Darlington	3,844	3,842	–0.1	6,339	2,729
Exeter City	3,692	3,313	–10.3	5,756	2,038
Halifax Town	2,214	1,717	–22.4	3,400	1,227
Hartlepool United	3,423	3,566	+4.2	4,842	2,599
Hull City	6,684	9,506	+42.2	12,529	8,419
Kidderminster Harriers	3,422	2,984	–12.8	4,147	2,002
Leyton Orient	4,528	4,550	+0.5	6,540	3,284
Lincoln City	3,273	2,673	–18.3	5,849	1,935
Luton Town	5,754	7,413	+28.8	9,585	5,066
Macclesfield Town	2,064	2,128	+3.1	3,002	1,356
Mansfield Town	2,706	4,896	+80.9	8,638	2,681
Oxford United	5,148	6,258	+21.6	11,121	4,964
Plymouth Argyle	4,945	8,788	+77.7	18,517	3,850
Rochdale	3,249	3,412	+5.0	5,292	2,819
Rushden & Diamonds	3,876	4,404	+13.6	5,876	2,771
Scunthorpe United	3,446	3,800	+10.3	6,479	2,574
Shrewsbury Town	2,898	3,849	+32.8	7,858	2,576
Southend United	4,322	3,986	–7.8	5,973	2,477
Swansea City	4,913	3,693	–24.8	5,501	2,677
Torquay United	2,556	2,534	–0.9	4,217	1,702
York City	3,026	3,143	+3.9	6,495	1,840

TOTAL ATTENDANCES: 2,398,578 (552 games)
                                  Average 4,345 (+11.0%)
HIGHEST: 18,517 Plymouth Argyle v Cheltenham Town
LOWEST: 1,227 Halifax Town v Kidderminster Harriers
HIGHEST AVERAGE: 9,506 Hull City
LOWEST AVERAGE: 1,717 Halifax Town

LEAGUE CUP FINALISTS 1961–2002

Played as a two-leg final until 1966. All subsequent finals at Wembley until 2000, then at Millennium Stadium, Cardiff.

Year	Winners	Runners-up	Score
1961	Aston Villa	Rotherham U	0-2, 3-0 (aet)
1962	Norwich C	Rochdale	3-0, 1-0
1963	Birmingham C	Aston Villa	3-1, 0-0
1964	Leicester C	Stoke C	1-1, 3-2
1965	Chelsea	Leicester C	3-2, 0-0
1966	WBA	West Ham U	1-2, 4-1
1967	QPR	WBA	3-2
1968	Leeds U	Arsenal	1-0
1969	Swindon T	Arsenal	3-1 (aet)
1970	Manchester C	WBA	2-1 (aet)
1971	Tottenham H	Aston Villa	2-0
1972	Stoke C	Chelsea	2-1
1973	Tottenham H	Norwich C	1-0
1974	Wolverhampton W	Manchester C	2-1
1975	Aston Villa	Norwich C	1-0
1976	Manchester C	Newcastle U	2-1
1977	Aston Villa	Everton	0-0, 1-1 (aet), 3-2 (aet)
1978	Nottingham F	Liverpool	0-0 (aet), 1-0
1979	Nottingham F	Southampton	3-2
1980	Wolverhampton W	Nottingham F	1-0
1981	Liverpool	West Ham U	1-1 (aet), 2-1

MILK CUP

Year	Winners	Runners-up	Score
1982	Liverpool	Tottenham H	3-1 (aet)
1983	Liverpool	Manchester U	2-1 (aet)
1984	Liverpool	Everton	0-0 (aet), 1-0
1985	Norwich C	Sunderland	1-0
1986	Oxford U	QPR	3-0

LITTLEWOODS CUP

Year	Winners	Runners-up	Score
1987	Arsenal	Liverpool	2-1
1988	Luton T	Arsenal	3-2
1989	Nottingham F	Luton T	3-1
1990	Nottingham F	Oldham Ath	1-0

RUMBELOWS LEAGUE CUP

Year	Winners	Runners-up	Score
1991	Sheffield W	Manchester U	1-0
1992	Manchester U	Nottingham F	1-0

COCA-COLA CUP

Year	Winners	Runners-up	Score
1993	Arsenal	Sheffield W	2-1
1994	Aston Villa	Manchester U	3-1
1995	Liverpool	Bolton W	2-1
1996	Aston Villa	Leeds U	3-0
1997	Leicester C	Middlesbrough	1-1 (aet), 1-0 (aet)
1998	Chelsea	Middlesbrough	2-0 (aet)

WORTHINGTON CUP

Year	Winners	Runners-up	Score
1999	Tottenham H	Leicester C	1-0
2000	Leicester C	Tranmere R	2-1
2001	Liverpool	Birmingham C	1-1 (aet)
Liverpool won 5-4 on penalties			
2002	Blackburn R	Tottenham H	2-1

LEAGUE CUP WINS
Liverpool 6, Aston Villa 5, Nottingham F 4, Leicester C 3, Tottenham H 3, Arsenal 2, Chelsea 2, Manchester C 2, Norwich C 2, Wolverhampton W 2, Birmingham C 1, Blackburn R 1, Leeds U 1, Luton T 1, Manchester U 1, Oxford U 1, QPR 1, Sheffield W 1, Stoke C 1, Swindon T 1, WBA 1.

APPEARANCES IN FINALS
Liverpool 8, Aston Villa 7, Nottingham F 6, Arsenal 5, Tottenham H 5, Leicester C 5, Manchester U 4, Norwich C 4, Chelsea 3, Manchester C 3, WBA 3, Birmingham C 2, Everton 2, Leeds U 2, Luton T 2, Middlesbrough 2, QPR 2, Sheffield W 2, Stoke C 2, West Ham U 2, Wolverhampton W 2, Blackburn R 1, Bolton W 1, Newcastle U 1, Oldham Ath 1, Oxford U 1, Rochdale 1, Rotherham U 1, Southampton 1, Sunderland 1, Swindon T 1, Tranmere R 1.

APPEARANCES IN SEMI-FINALS
Aston Villa 11, Liverpool 11, Tottenham H 10, Arsenal 9, Chelsea 7, Manchester U 7, West Ham U 7, Nottingham F 6, Leeds U 5, Leicester C 5, Manchester C 5, Norwich C 5, Birmingham C 4 Middlesbrough 4, Sheffield W 4, WBA 4, Blackburn R 3, Bolton W 3, Burnley 3, Crystal Palace 3, Everton 3, Ipswich T 3, QPR 3, Sunderland 3, Swindon T 3, Wolverhampton W 3, Bristol C 2, Coventry C 2, Luton T 2, Oxford U 2, Plymouth Arg 2, Southampton 2, Stoke C 2, Tranmere R 2, Wimbledon 2, Blackpool 1, Bury 1, Cardiff C 1, Carlisle U 1, Chester C 1, Derby Co 1, Huddersfield T 1, Newcastle U 1, Oldham Ath 1, Peterborough U 1, Rochdale 1, Rotherham U 1, Shrewsbury T 1, Stockport Co 1, Walsall 1, Watford 1.

WORTHINGTON CUP 2001–02

FIRST ROUND

20 AUG

Darlington (0) 0
Sheffield U (0) 1 *(D'Jaffo 90)*   3983
Darlington: Collett; Harper, Betts, Liddle, Brightwell, Maddison, Hodgson, Convery, Conlon, Mellanby (Marsh), Ford (Jackson).
Sheffield U: Tracey; Kozluk, Phelan, Ford, Murphy, Santos, Devlin, Brown, Asaba (D'Jaffo), Peschisolido (Ndlovu), Jagielka.

Hartlepool U (0) 0
Nottingham F (1) 2 *(John 33, Bart-Williams 60)*   3938
Hartlepool U: Hollund; Bass, Clark, Barron, Lee, Westwood, Tinkler, Widdrington (Clarke), Humphreys, Henderson, Stephenson (Lormor).
Nottingham F: Ward; Louis-Jean, Brennan, Bart-Williams, Hjelde, Edwards, Johnson A, Jenas, Johnson D, John, Williams.

Scunthorpe U (0) 0
Rotherham U (2) 2 *(Lee 37, Robins 45)*   2589
Scunthorpe U: Croudson; Stanton, Dawson, Bradshaw, Jackson, Thom, Sheldon (Graves), Barwick (Brough), Carruthers, Grant (Wilcox), Beagrie.
Rotherham U: Pollitt; Scott, Beech, Daws, Swailes, McIntosh, Sedgwick (Bryan), Watson (Hudson), Lee, Robins (Barker), Monkhouse.

21 AUG

Barnsley (1) 2 *(Tinkler 27, Dyer 79)*
Halifax T (0) 0   5418
Barnsley: Miller; Regan, Barker, Morgan, Chettle, Neil (Sheron), Donovan, Tinkler, Gorre, Dyer (Rankin), Barnard.
Halifax T: Butler; Harsley, Jules, Woodward, Clarke C, Stoneman (Middleton), Swales, Redfearn, Kerrigan (Jones), Wood, Midgley (Wright).

Blackpool (0) 3 *(Ormerod 56, 67, 85)*
Wigan Ath (0) 2 *(Brannan 59, Haworth 69)*   4237
Blackpool: Barnes; Parkinson (Bullock), Jaszczun, O'Kane, Hughes, Thompson, Wellens, Simpson (Milligan J), Murphy J, Ormerod (Fenton), MacKenzie.
Wigan Ath: Stillie; Mitchell, Sharp, McGibbon, De Vos, De Zeeuw, Brannan, Adamczuk, Haworth, Moores, Traynor.

Bournemouth (0) 0
Torquay U (1) 2 *(Graham 45, Brandon 89)*   2556
Bournemouth: Stewart; Birmingham (Foyewa), Elliott, Howe, Maher, Purches (Broadhurst), Feeney, Hayter, O'Connor (Huck), Fletcher C, Ford.
Torquay U: Dearden; Tully, Douglin, Woods, McNeil, Russell A, Brandon, Rees, Roach (Williams), Graham, Hill.

Brentford (0) 1 *(O'Connor 90)*
Norwich C (0) 0   4111
Brentford: Gottskalksson; Dobson, Anderson (Hunt), Ingimarsson, Powell, Price, Evans, Mahon, Burgess (Partridge), O'Connor, Gibbs.
Norwich C: Green; McGovern, Drury, Mackay, Fleming, Holt, Mulryne, Russell, Libbra (Roberts), Abbey, McVeigh.

Brighton & HA (0) 2 *(Zamora 57, 65)*
Wimbledon (0) 1 *(Williams 52)*   6334
Brighton & HA: Kuipers; Watson, Jones, Morgan, Cullip, Carpenter, Hart (Pethick), Rogers, Lehmann (Steele), Zamora, Brooker (Melton).
Wimbledon: Feuer; Darlington, Kimble, Roberts, Williams (Jupp), Willmott, Ardley, Nielsen (Gier), Shipperley (Agyemang), Connolly, Cooper.

Bristol C (1) 2 *(Amankwaah 2, Jones 78)*
Cheltenham T (0) 1 *(Grayson 66)*   5367
Bristol C: Stowell; Amankwaah (Murray), Bell, Hill, Lever, Carey, Clist (Burnell), Brown A, Jones (Matthews), Thorpe, Tinnion.
Cheltenham T: Muggleton; Duff, Victory, Banks, Walker, Howarth (Griffin), Milton, Devaney (Alsop), Grayson (White), Naylor, Yates.

Burnley (0) 2 *(Moore A 55, McGregor 84)*
Rushden & D (1) 3 *(Peters 5, Mustafa 50, Darby 76)*
                                                                          4398
Burnley: Michopoulos; Gnohere, McGregor, Cox, Davis, Maylett (Moore I), Ball, Mullin (Cook), Taylor, Papadopoulos (Little), Moore A.
Rushden & D: Turley; Mustafa, Underwood, Carey (Mills), Peters, Rodwell, Brady, Butterworth, Patmore (Darby), Jackson, Gray.

Bury (0) 1 *(Reid 87 (pen))*
Sheffield W (1) 3 *(Ekoku 33, Maddix 53, McLaren 71)*
                                                                          3129
Bury: Kenny; Unsworth, Armstrong, Nelson, Collins, Redmond (Preece), Billy, Forrest (Jarrett), Newby, Seddon, Reid.
Sheffield W: Pressman; Hendon (Lescott), Geary, Soltvedt, Bromby, Maddix, Haslam, Sibon, Ekoku, McLaren (Bonvin), Quinn (Morrison).

Exeter C (0) 0
Walsall (0) 1 *(Herivelto 66)*   1993
Exeter C: Van Heusden; Whitworth (Tomlinson), Campbell, Kerr, Watson (McConnell), Curran, Flack (Breslan), Ampadu, McCarthy, Barlow, Roberts.
Walsall: Harper; Gadsby (Garrocho), Aranalde (Biancalani), Brightwell, Barras, Keates, Herivelto, Simpson, Goodman, Ofodile (Roper), Wrack.

Grimsby T (0) 2 *(Jevons 73, Rowan 90)*
Lincoln C (1) 1 *(Battersby 34)*   5906
Grimsby T: Coyne; McDermott, Gallimore, Chapman (Ford), Groves, Butterfield, Pouton, Willems, Jeffrey (Rowan), Jevons, Campbell.
Lincoln C: Marriott; Barnett (Cameron), Bimson, Morgan, Holmes, Finnigan, Black, Sedgemore, Battersby (Walker), Thorpe, Gain.

Huddersfield T (0) 0
Rochdale (1) 1 *(Ford 20)*   3995
Huddersfield T: Margetson; Jenkins, Evans, Irons (Thorrington), Heary, Gray, Beech (Macari), Holland, Booth, Hay, Armstrong (Mattis).
Rochdale: Edwards; Evans, Todd, Jones, Coleman, Griffiths (McAuley), Ford, Flitcroft (Ware), Platt, Oliver, Durkan.

Kidderminster H (2) 2 *(Bird 16, 37)*
Preston NE (0) 3 *(Macken 77, Gallacher 81, Jackson 99)*
                                                                          2227
Kidderminster H: Brock; Medou-Otye, Stamps, Blake, Hinton, Ayres, Bird, Davies, Broughton (Hadley), Foster (Doyle), Shilton.
Preston NE: Lucas; Alexander, Eaton, Murdock, Jackson, Gregan, Cartwright (Keane), Rankine (Gallacher), Macken, Healy, Anderson (Cresswell).
aet.

Leyton Orient (2) 2 *(Minton 28, Houghton 37)*
Crystal Palace (1) 4 *(Morrison 35, 83, Black 56, 86)* 4290
Leyton Orient: Bayes; Joseph, Lockwood, Smith, Downer, Harris, Oakes, Ibehre, Watts, Houghton (Hadland), Minton (Castle).
Crystal Palace: Kolinko; Austin, Gray, Popovic, Carlisle (Rubins), Riihilahti, Mullins, Rodger (Berhalter), Morrison, Thomson, Black.

Macclesfield T (0) 1 *(Glover 57)*
Bradford C (0) 2 *(Tod 76, McCall 115)* 2526
Macclesfield T: Martin; Hitchen, Adams, Keen, Tinson, Ridler, Tracey (McAvoy), Byrne (Munroe), Lightbourne, Glover, Eyre.
Bradford C: Davison; Halle, Sharpe, Emanuel (McCall), Bower, Tod, Jorgensen (Whalley), Lawrence, Grant, Blake, Jess (Molenaar).
aet.

Mansfield T (2) 3 *(Greenacre 18, 43, White 60)*
Notts Co (4) 4 *(Allsopp 20, 25, 31, Mildenhall 34)* 4553
Mansfield T: Pilkington; Hassell, Tankard, Robinson, Reddington, Williamson, Lawrence, Disley (Bacon), White, Greenacre, Corden.
Notts Co: Mildenhall; Fenton, Baraclough, Caskey (Jorgensen), Warren, Ireland, Owers, Cas (Liburd), Stallard, Allsopp, Nicholson (Heffernan).

Millwall (1) 2 *(Sadlier 24, Claridge 61 (pen))*
Cardiff C (1) 1 *(Earnshaw 45)* 5516
Millwall: Warner; Neill, Ryan, Cahill, Nethercott, Dyche, Livermore, Sadlier, Claridge, Reid (Bull), Ifill (Lawrence).
Cardiff C: Alexander; Simpkins, Legg, Weston, Hughes, Gabbidon, Boland, Kavanagh, Brayson (Low), Fortune-West (Gordon), Earnshaw.

Northampton T (0) 2 *(Forrester 90, McGregor 110)*
QPR (1) 1 *(Evatt 16 (og))* 4638
Northampton T: Sollitt; Lavin (Dempsey), Spedding, Frain, Evatt, Hope, Hunt, Parkin (Asamoah), Forrester, Gabbiadini (McGregor), Hargreaves.
QPR: Day; Forbes, Bruce, Palmer, Ben Askar, Perry, Bignot (Paquette), Bonnot, Doudou (McEwen), Wardley (Koejoe), Warren.
aet.

Oxford U (1) 1 *(Scott 41)*
Gillingham (0) 2 *(King 82 (pen), Onuora 120)* 5886
Oxford U: McCaldon; Stockley, Ricketts, Guyett, Hatswell, Bolland, Savage (Whitehead), Tait (Folland), Scott, Gray (Beauchamp), Thomas.
Gillingham: Bartram; Patterson, Edge, Hope, Ashby (Shaw), Pennock, Smith, Browning, Onuora, Ipoua (King), Gooden (Perpetuini).
aet.

Port Vale (2) 2 *(McPhee 14, 35)*
Chesterfield (1) 1 *(Rowland 4)* 2723
Port Vale: Goodlad; Cummins, Ingram, Carragher, Walsh, Burton, Hardy, O'Callaghan, McPhee, Brooker, Brisco.
Chesterfield: Abbey; Booty, Pearce, Ingledow, Breckin, Payne, Williams (Rushbury), Howard, Reeves, Rowland, Willis.

Portsmouth (0) 1 *(Crouch 77)*
Colchester U (0) 2 *(Stockwell 53, Izzet 82)* 7078
Portsmouth: Beasant; Panopoulos (Bradbury), Vincent (Harper), Hiley, Moore (Miglioranzi), Zamperini, O'Neil, Prosinecki, Crouch, Quashie, Pitt.
Colchester U: Woodman; Dunne (White), Keith, Pinault, Fitzgerald, Clark, Gregory, Izzet, Rapley, Stockwell (Bowry), McGleish.

Reading (2) 4 *(Henderson 38, 90, Parkinson 45, Smith A 51)*
Luton T (0) 0 5115
Reading: Whitehead; Murty, Shorey, Whitbread, Williams, Parkinson (Gamble), Igoe, Harper, Forster (Rougier), Henderson, Smith A (Tyson).
Luton T: Emberson; Boyce, Taylor, Forbes, Perrett (Dryden), Johnson, Nicholls, Mansell (Holmes), Howard, Griffiths (Douglas), Hughes.

Stockport Co (1) 3 *(Kuqi 21, Taylor 56, 83)*
Carlisle U (0) 0 2075
Stockport Co: Jones; Gibb, Van Blerk, Roget, Clare (Wiss), Woodthorpe (Helin), Flynn, Kuqi, Wilbraham (Hardy), Taylor, Smith.

Carlisle U: Weaver; Birch, Maddison (Berkley), Whitehead, Murphy, Morley, Harkin (Haddow), Hopper, Stevens (Allan), Elliott, Halliday.

Swansea C (0) 0
Peterborough U (1) 2 *(Fenn 45, Clarke A 82)* 2347
Swansea C: Freestone; Mazzina, Howard, O'Leary, Todd (Cusack), Romo (Appleby), Phillips, Jenkins, Williams, Watkin, Coates (Sidibe).
Peterborough U: Connor; Joseph, Williams T, Forsyth, Edwards, Cullen, Farrell (Fenn), Oldfield, Clarke A, Green, MacDonald.

Tranmere R (1) 3 *(Henry 16, Flynn 66, Barlow 74)*
Shrewsbury T (0) 1 *(Jemson 90)* 5549
Tranmere R: Murphy; Yates, Roberts, Henry, Hill, Challinor, Flynn, Parkinson (Hume), N'Diaye (Allison), Barlow, Mellon.
Shrewsbury T: Cartwright; Drysdale, Rioch, Redmile, Heathcote, Wilding (Walker), Murray (Freestone), Atkins, Rodgers, Jemson, Jagielka.

Watford (0) 1 *(Gayle 82)*
Plymouth Arg (0) 0 9230
Watford: Baardsen; Blondeau, Robinson (Panayi), Vernazza, Ward, Vega, Foley (Nielsen), Noel-Williams, Gayle, Wooter (Helguson), Hughes.
Plymouth Arg: Larrieu; Adams, Wills (Stonebridge), Friio (Broad), Wotton, Coughlan, Phillips, Hodges L, Evans (Gritton), Evers, McGlinchey.

Wrexham (0) 2 *(Faulconbridge 71, Russell 90)*
Hull C (1) 3 *(Whitmore 24, Greaves 64, Alexander 79)* 1761
Wrexham: Rogers; Warren (Edwards), Holmes, Lawrence, Carey, Thomas, Chalk, Ferguson, Sam (Russell), Blackwood, Faulconbridge.
Hull C: Glennon; Goodison, Edwards, Whittle, Greaves (Petty), Mohan, Whitmore, Johnsson, Alexander (Rowe), Dudfield (Lee), Beresford.

Wycombe W (0) 0
Bristol R (0) 1 *(Hillier 67)* 3166
Wycombe W: Taylor; Rogers, Vinnicombe, Bulman, Cousins (Marsh), McCarthy, Emblen, Simpson, Currie, Rammell (Ryan), Brown (McSporran).
Bristol R: Howie; Wilson, Jones, Foster, Thomson, Trought, Mauge, Gall, Ellington, Weare (Cameron), Hillier.

York C (1) 2 *(Bullock 32, Brass 108)*
Crewe Alex (1) 2 *(Little 5, Richards 112)* 1663
York C: Fettis; Edmondson, Potter, Fielding, Basham, Cooper, O'Kane (Emmerson), Brass, Proctor, Nogan, Bullock.
Crewe Alex: Ince; Navarro, Smith S, Sodje, Macauley, Brammer, Hulse, Collins, Jack, Little (Richards), Sorvel (Lunt).
aet; Crewe Alex won 6-5 on penalties.

22 AUG

Birmingham C (2) 3 *(Mooney 7, 90 (pen), Whelan 16 (og))*
Southend U (0) 0 12,015
Birmingham C: Vaesen; Gill, Grainger, Hughes, Purse, Johnson M, Eaden, Sonner (Woodhouse), Horsfield (Furlong), Mooney, Lazaridis (Marcelo).
Southend U: Flahavan; Broad (Bramble), Searle (Richards), Johnson, Cort, Whelan, Hutchings, Maher, Webb (McSweeney), Rawle, Thurgood.

Cambridge U (0) 1 *(Alcide 85)*
WBA (1) 1 *(Dobie 18)* 3363
Cambridge U: Perez; Fleming, Byrne (Duncan), Walling, Angus, Ashbee, Wanless, Richardson, Kitson, Alcide (Guttridge), Traore (Youngs).
WBA: Hoult; Lyttle (Balis), Clement, Sigurdsson, Butler, Gilchrist, Appleton, McInnes, Dobie, Taylor (Quinn), Chambers A.
aet; WBA won 4-3 on penalties.

Stoke C (0) 0
Oldham Ath (0) 0 5636
Stoke C: Cutler; Thomas, Van Deurzen, Handyside, Shtaniuk, Gudjonsson, Rowson (Clarke), Henry, Goodfellow (Cooke), Thordarson (Iwelumo), Hoekstra.
Oldham Ath: Kelly; McNiven, Sheridan D, Prenderville, Balmer, Duxbury, Rickers (Hotte), Carss, Tipton, Eyre (Dudley), Eyres (Innes).
aet; Oldham Ath won 6-5 on penalties.

Wolverhampton W (0) 1 *(Dinning 49)*
Swindon T (0) 2 *(Howe 48, O'Halloran 51 (pen))* 7598
Wolverhampton W: Oakes; Connelly (Sinton), Camara, Dinning, Pollet, Butler, Newton, Robinson, Ketsbaia (Roussel), Proudlock, Kennedy.
Swindon T: Griemink; Invincible (Grazioli), Davis, Heywood, Reeves, Gurney, O'Halloran, Hewlett, Sabin, Howe (Brayley), Duke.

SECOND ROUND
10 SEPT

Blackpool (0) 0
Leicester C (1) 1 *(Akinbiyi 21)* 4866
Blackpool: Pullen; Hills (Simpson), Jaszczun, O'Kane, Collins (MacKenzie), Reid, Wellens, Bullock, Murphy J, Ormerod, Coid.
Leicester C: Walker; Marshall, Stewart, Elliott, Sinclair, Davidson, Savage, Izzet, Akinbiyi (Impey), Lewis (Benjamin), Delaney (Jones).

11 SEPT

Bolton W (0) 4 *(Ricketts 68, Holdsworth 80, Nishizawa 90, Pedersen 97)*
Walsall (0) 3 *(Wrack 66, Byfield 84, Barras 86)* 5761
Bolton W: Banks; Holden, Richardson, Nishizawa, Hendry, Norris (Ricketts), Farrelly (Pedersen), Smith (Nolan), Marshall, Holdsworth, Southall.
Walsall: Harper (Walker); Gadsby, Aranalde, Brightwell, Barras, Roper, Herivelto, Simpson, Leitao (Byfield), Wrack, Matias (Hall).
aet.

Brighton & HA (0) 0
Southampton (1) 3 *(Beattie 44, Svensson 71, 85)* 6489
Brighton & HA: Kuipers; Watson, Jones (Mayo), Morgan, Wicks, Carpenter, Rogers (Hart), Oatway, Steele (Lehmann), Zamora, Brooker.
Southampton: Jones; Delap, Bridge, Oakley, Lundekvam, Richards, Svensson, McDonald (Draper), Beattie (Rosler), Davies (El Khalej), Tessem.

Bristol R (0) 0
Birmingham C (1) 3 *(Johnson A 45, Johnson M 62, Hughes 68)* 5582
Bristol R: Howie; Wilson, Jones, Foster, Thomson, Foran, Mauge, Gall, Ellington, Weare (Cameron), Hillier (Hammond).
Birmingham C: Poole; Gill, Grainger, Hughes (Burrows), Hutchinson, Johnson M, Eaden, Sonner, Horsfield (Marcelo), Johnson A (Furlong), Woodhouse.

Colchester U (0) 1 *(Keith 72)*
Barnsley (1) 3 *(Dyer 27, 90, Jones 88)* 3442
Colchester U: Woodman; Duguid, Keith, Pinault, Fitzgerald, Clark, Izzet (Bowry), Gregory, Rapley, Stockwell, McGleish.
Barnsley: Miller; Regan, Barker, Morgan, Crooks, Ward, Neil, Gorre (Donovan), Sheron (Jones), Dyer, Barnard.

Crewe Alex (0) 2 *(Walton 108, Smith S 112 (pen))*
Rushden & D (0) 0 4807
Crewe Alex: Ince; Navarro, Smith S, Thomas (Sodje), Walton, Collins (Barrett), Hulse, Lunt, Jack, Little (Charnock), Sorvel.
Rushden & D: Turley; Mustafa, Underwood, Carey, Peters, Rodwell, Mills (Hanlon), Brady, Sigere (Wormull), Patmore (Duffy), Burgess.
aet.

Gillingham (1) 2 *(King 5, Nethercott 90 (og))*
Millwall (0) 1 *(Moody 53)* 7511
Gillingham: Bartram; Patterson, Perpetuini, Hope, Ashby, Pennock, Smith, Browning (Shaw), Onuora (Ipoua), King, Gooden (Hessenthaler).
Millwall: Warner; Lawrence, Ryan, Cahill, Nethercott, Dyche (Tuttle), Ifill, Livermore, Moody (Claridge), Sadlier, Stamp (Kinet).

Grimsby T (1) 3 *(Broomes 29, Jeffrey 73, Allen 117)*
Sheffield U (0) 3 *(Devlin 51, Ndlovu 66, Suffo 104)* 5236
Grimsby T: Coyne; McDermott, Gallimore, Broomes, Groves, Butterfield, Pouton, Burnett (Allen), Rowan (Jeffrey), Jevons, Campbell.
Sheffield U: Tracey; Uhlenbeek, Nicholson, Ford, Murphy, Curle, Devlin, Brown, Asaba (Suffo), Peschisolido (D'Jaffo), Ndlovu (Santos).
aet; Grimsby T won 4-2 on penalties.

Middlesbrough (0) 3 *(Murphy 54, Nemeth 62, Wilson 82)*
Northampton T (0) 1 *(Parkin 79)* 3915
Middlesbrough: Schwarzer; Stockdale, Murphy (Cooper), Gavin, Ehiogu, Mustoe (Job), Wilson, Marinelli, Nemeth, Windass, Johnston (Ricard).
Northampton T: Sollitt; Dempsey, Hunter, Hope, Evatt (Asamoah) (Thompson), Spedding, Hunt, McGregor (Wolleaston), Forrester, Parkin, Hargreaves.

Notts Co (0) 2 *(Allsopp 68 (pen), Stallard 70)*
Manchester C (0) 4 *(Shuker 61, Goater 86, Dickov 92, Huckerby 103)* 5972
Notts Co: Mildenhall; Fenton, Baraclough, Caskey, Warren, Grayson (Hamilton), Owers, Cas, Stallard (Hackworth), Allsopp, Nicholson (Bolland).
Manchester C: Weaver; Colosimo, Grant, Dunne, Howey, Pearce (Huckerby), Horlock, Berkovic (Shuker), Wanchope, Goater (Dickov), Tiatto.
aet.

Peterborough U (0) 2 *(Forsyth 59, Hedman 89 (og))*
Coventry C (0) 2 *(Thompson 56, Carsley 90)* 5729
Peterborough U: Tyler; Joseph, MacDonald (Williams T), Forsyth, Rea, Edwards, Bullard, Danielsson (Green), Fenn (Clarke A), McKenzie, Farrell.
Coventry C: Hedman; Nilsson (Shaw), Hall, Breen, Konjic, Carsley, Thompson, Safri, Hughes, Joachim, Quinn (Bothroyd).
aet; Coventry C won 4-2 on penalties.

Reading (0) 0
West Ham U (0) 0 21,173
Reading: Whitehead; Murty, Robinson, Whitbread, Williams (Viveash), Parkinson, Igoe, Harper, Cureton (Henderson), Butler (Rougier), Smith A.
West Ham U: Hislop; Schemmel, Minto, Hutchison, Song, Dailly, Moncur (Courtois), Todorov (Garcia), Sinclair, Defoe, Carrick.
aet; Reading won 6-5 on penalties.

Rochdale (0) 2 *(Townson 74, 102)*
Fulham (1) 2 *(Boa Morte 17, Brevett 120)* 6303
Rochdale: Gilks; Evans, McAuley, Jones, Griffiths, Bayliss, Ford (Flitcroft), Connor (Townson), Platt, Oliver, Durkan (Doughty).
Fulham: Taylor; Finnan, Harley (Brevett), Knight (Melville), Ouaddou, Davis, Goldbaek (Legwinski), Clark, Hayles, Boa Morte, Malbranque.
aet; Fulham won 6-5 on penalties.

Rotherham U (0) 0
Bradford C (3) 4 *(Blake 4 (pen), 33, Tod 29, Lawrence 76)* 3539
Rotherham U: Pollitt; Hurst, Scott, Daws (Hudson), Swailes, McIntosh, Talbot, Watson, Lee, Robins (Branston), Barker (Miranda).
Bradford C: Davison; Emanuel, Makel, Myers, Molenaar, Wetherall (Halle), Lawrence, Blake, Grant, Tod, Jorgensen.

Tranmere R (2) 4 *(Flynn 8, Koumas 15, Barlow 83, Mellon 89)*
Preston NE (1) 1 *(Cresswell 31)* 5143
Tranmere R: Murphy; Yates, Roberts, Henry, Allen, Hazell, Flynn, Hay, Barlow, Mellon, Koumas.
Preston NE: Moilanen; Alexander, Edwards, Murdock, Lucketti, Kidd (Basham), McKenna, Gregan, Cresswell, Healy, Anderson (Robinson).

WBA (0) 2 *(Dobie 96, Jordao 110)*
Swindon T (0) 0 14,536
WBA: Hoult; Lyttle (Quinn), Clement (Cummings), Sigurdsson, Butler, Gilchrist, McInnes, Chambers A, Dobie (Jordao), Taylor, Appleton.
Swindon T: Griemink; Invincible, Davis (Grazioli), Heywood, Ruddock (Edwards P), Gurney, Robinson S, Howe, Osei-Kuffour (Reeves), Hewlett, Duke.
aet.

12 SEPT

Blackburn R (1) 2 *(Jansen 14, Dunning 77)*
Oldham Ath (0) 0 9559
Blackburn R: Friedel; Greer, Taylor (Hughes), Dunning, Berg, Tugay, Mahon, Hignett, Grabbi (Bent), Jansen, Johnson.
Oldham Ath: Kelly; McNiven, Sheridan D, Prenderville, Balmer (Hotte), Duxbury (Tipton), Rickers, Garnett, Allott (Corazzin), Eyre, Eyres.

Bristol C (0) 2 *(Clist 48, Thorpe 55)*
Watford (0) 3 *(Gayle 73 (pen), Vega 87, Hyde 90)* 7256
Bristol C: Stowell; Murray, Bell, Hill, Lever, Carey, Doherty (Amankwaah), Brown A, Jones (Matthews), Thorpe, Clist (Burnell).
Watford: Baardsen; Cox, Robinson, Noble (Helguson), Galli, Vega, Glass, Hyde, Noel-Williams (Smith), Wooter, Fisken (Gayle).

Charlton Ath (1) 2 *(Fortune 36, Konchesky 63)*
Port Vale (0) 0 7247
Charlton Ath: Kiely; Fortune, Powell, Young (Konchesky), Todd (Brown), Fish, Stuart, Euell, Bartlett, Parker (Salako), Robinson.
Port Vale: Goodlad; Cummins, Ingram, Carragher, Burns, Brisco (Birchall), O'Callaghan (Dodd), Osborn, McPhee, Brooker, Hardy.

Derby Co (1) 3 *(Burton 45, 90, Kinkladze 64)*
Hull C (0) 0 11,246
Derby Co: Oakes; Mawene, Boertien, Riggott, Higginbotham, Valakari (O'Neil), Burley (Daino), Kinkladze, Burton, Ravanelli, Murray.
Hull C: Glennon; Edwards, Holt (Price), Petty, Bloomer, Mohan, Whitmore, Johnsson, Alexander, Dudfield (Matthews), Beresford (Morley).

Everton (1) 1 *(Ferguson 6 (pen))*
Crystal Palace (1) 1 *(Freedman 10 (pen))* 21,128
Everton: Gerrard; Watson, Xavier, Stubbs, Weir, Tal, McLeod, Gascoigne, Campbell, Ferguson (Chadwick), Moore (Hibbert).
Crystal Palace: Clarke; Smith, Gray, Austin, Popovic, Berhalter (Riihilahti), Mullins, Rodger, Morrison, Freedman, Kirovski (Thomson).
aet; Crystal Palace won 5-4 on penalties.

Newcastle U (0) 4 *(Ameobi 59, Bellamy 108, 117, 120)*
Brentford (1) 1 *(Owusu 17)* 25,633
Newcastle U: Harper; Griffin, Quinn (Bellamy), O'Brien (Lua-Lua), Hughes (Elliott), Solano, Bassedas, Acuna, Shearer, Ameobi, Robert.
Brentford: Gottskalksson; Dobson (Williams), Anderson, Ingimarsson, Powell, Price (O'Connor), Evans, Mahon, Owusu, Burgess, Gibbs (Rowlands).
aet.

Nottingham F (1) 1 *(Lester 8)*
Stockport Co (1) 1 *(Taylor 36)* 5432
Nottingham F: Ward; Scimeca, Brennan, Williams, Hjelde, Doig, Prutton (Bopp), Jenas, Harewood, Lester, Reid (Gray).
Stockport Co: Jones; Helin, Gibb (Hurst), Roget, Flynn, Woodthorpe, Sneekes, Kuqi, Taylor (Dibble), Fradin, Hardy (Wiss).
aet; Nottingham F won 8-7 on penalties.

Sheffield W (2) 4 *(Ekoku 30, Morrison 45 (pen), Di Piedi 92, Bonvin 105)*
Sunderland (1) 2 *(Phillips 43, Laslandes 75)* 12,074
Sheffield W: Pressman; Haslam, Bromby, Soltvedt, Westwood, Maddix, Quinn, McLaren, Ekoku (Bonvin), Johnson (Hamshaw), Morrison (Di Piedi).
Sunderland: Ingham; Williams (Haas), Gray, Varga, McCartney, McCann, Thirlwell, Arca (Kyle), Bellion (Laslandes), Phillips, Kilbane.
aet.

13 SEPT

Tottenham H (0) 2 *(King 61, Ferdinand 69)*
Torquay U (0) 0 20,347
Tottenham H: Keller; Taricco, Ziege, King, Doherty (Bunjevcevic), Perry, Leonhardsen (Sheringham), Freund, Rebrov, Ferdinand (Etherington), Davies.
Torquay U: Dearden; Tully, Hill, Douglin, Woozley, McNeil, Brandon (Nicholls), Rees, Williams (Roach), Graham (Benefield), Russell A.

THIRD ROUND

8 OCT

Bolton W (1) 1 *(Wallace 3)*
Nottingham F (0) 0 6881
Bolton W: Jaaskelainen; Richardson, Charlton, Hendry, N'Gotty, Diawara (Norris), Wallace (Ricketts), Nolan, Hansen, Marshall (Holdsworth), Southall.
Nottingham F: Ward; Louis-Jean, Brennan, Bart-Williams, Hjelde, Scimeca, Prutton, Gray (Bopp), Johnson (Harewood), Lester, Rogers (Reid).

9 OCT

Barnsley (0) 0
Newcastle U (0) 1 *(Bellamy 79)* 14,493
Barnsley: Marriott; Crooks, Barker, Morgan, Parkin, Sand (Neil), Donovan, Jones (Barnard), Fallon (Gallen), Dyer, Lumsdon.
Newcastle U: Harper; Barton, Bernard, Distin, O'Brien, Solano, Lee, Speed, Shearer, Bellamy, Robert.

Coventry C (0) 0
Chelsea (0) 2 *(Gudjohnsen 56, Forssell 60)* 12,582
Coventry C: Montgomery; Edworthy, Shaw, Breen, Konjic, Carsley, Chippo, Safri, Bothroyd (Hughes), Martinez (McSheffrey), Thompson (Delorge).
Chelsea: Cudicini; Ferrer (Forssell), Le Saux, Gallas, Terry, Desailly, Morris, Petit, Gudjohnsen, Zola (Babayaro), Zenden (Dalla Bona).

Crewe Alex (1) 2 *(Hulse 8, Brammer 73)*
Ipswich T (2) 3 *(Reuser 4, 72, Armstrong 35)* 6116
Crewe Alex: Bankole; Foster, Smith S, Brammer, Walton, Charnock (Ashton), Hulse, Lunt, Jack, Sodje, Sorvel.
Ipswich T: Sereni; Makin, Clapham, Venus, McGreal, Reuser, Miller (Wilnis), Peralta, Stewart, Armstrong (Naylor), Wright.

Gillingham (0) 0
Southampton (1) 2 *(Beattie 9 (pen), Pahars 83)* 7948
Gillingham: Bartram; Patterson, Edge, Hope, Butters (Ipoua), Pennock, Smith, Hessenthaler (Browning), Onuora (Shaw), King, Saunders.
Southampton: Jones; Dodd, Bridge, Marsden, Lundekvam, Monk, Svensson (Tessem), Oakley, Beattie, Pahars (Ripley), Davies.

Leicester C (0) 0
Leeds U (3) 6 *(Keane 12, 16, 53, Bakke 40, Viduka 56,*
Kewell 64) 16,316
Leicester C: Walker; Piper, Jones, Elliott, Rowett,
Sinclair, Savage, Izzet, Sturridge (Davidson), Scowcroft,
Wise (Impey).
Leeds U: Martyn; Mills, Harte, Bakke (McPhail),
Ferdinand (Duberry), Woodgate, Dacourt, Keane
(Smith), Viduka, Kewell, Bowyer.

Liverpool (0) 1 *(McAllister 101 (pen))*
Grimsby T (0) 2 *(Broomes 113, Jevons 120)* 32,672
Liverpool: Kirkland; Vignal (Kippe), Carragher, Hamann
(Heskey), Wright, Hyypia, Murphy, Smicer, Litmanen
(Redknapp), McAllister, Barmby.
Grimsby T: Coyne; Butterfield, Gallimore, Beharall,
Groves, Broomes, Pouton, Chapman (Allen), Rowan
(Boulding), Jevons, Campbell.
aet.

Tranmere R (0) 0
Tottenham H (2) 4 *(Sheringham 21 (pen), Anderton 39,*
Poyet 49, Rebrov 81) 12,386
Tranmere R: Murphy; Sharps, Roberts, Henry (Hinds),
Allen, Yates, Flynn, Parkinson, N'Diaye (Hume),
Barlow, Mellon.
Tottenham H: Sullivan; Taricco, Thatcher, Freund
(Sherwood), King, Perry, Anderton, Poyet
(Leonhardsen), Ferdinand (Rebrov), Sheringham,
Davies.

WBA (0) 0
Charlton Ath (1) 1 *(Euell 19 (pen))* 17,734
WBA: Hoult; Lyttle (Chambers J), Clement, Sigurdsson,
Butler (Fox), Gilchrist, McInnes, Chambers A
(Cummings), Dobie, Taylor, Appleton.
Charlton Ath: Kiely; Young, Powell, Brown, Fortune,
Parker, Kinsella, Jensen (Konchesky), Euell, Johansson,
Robinson (Lisbie).

Watford (2) 4 *(Hyde 32, Noel-Williams 45, 67, Vega 51)*
Bradford C (0) 1 *(Ward 76 (pen))* 8613
Watford: Baardsen; Blondeau, Robinson, Cox, Noble,
Vega, Glass, Hyde (Fisken), Noel-Williams (Helguson),
Smith (Wooter), Hughes.
Bradford C: Davison; Halle, Jacobs (Whalley), Makel
(McCall), Wetherall, Myers, Locke, Blake (Tod), Ward,
Carbone, Jess.

10 OCT

Aston Villa (1) 1 *(Dublin 45)*
Reading (0) 0 23,431
Aston Villa: Schmeichel; Delaney (Dublin), Wright,
Staunton, Alpay, Boateng, Kachloul, Hendrie, Angel
(Balaban), Hadji, Ginola.
Reading: Whitehead; Whitbread (Robinson), Shorey,
Viveash, Williams, Parkinson (Henderson), Smith N,
Harper, Butler, Forster, Rougier (Cureton).

Blackburn R (1) 2 *(Hignett 31, Short 113)*
Middlesbrough (1) 1 *(Nemeth 39)* 9536
Blackburn R: Filan; Johnson, Bjornebye, Short, Curtis,
Mahon (Jansen), Flitcroft, Johansson, Hughes (Grabbi),
Hignett, Dunn (Tugay).
Middlesbrough: Crossley; Stockdale, Cooper (Gavin),
Southgate, Ehiogu, Murphy, Greening, Wilson (Mustoe),
Boksic (Marinelli), Nemeth, Ince.
aet.

Fulham (1) 5 *(Hayles 37, Legwinski 56, Collins 62, Saha*
71, Malbranque 81 (pen))
Derby Co (1) 2 *(Burley 19, Ravanelli 55)* 9217
Fulham: Taylor; Finnan, Brevett, Melville, Knight, Davis,
Legwinski (Boa Morte), Collins, Marlet (Malbranque),
Hayles, Clark (Saha).
Derby Co: Oakes; Daino, Johnson, Riggott, Mawene,
Higginbotham, Burley, Murray (Christie), Burton,
Ravanelli, Powell.

Manchester C (3) 6 *(Huckerby 10, 25, 81, 89, Luntala 15*
(og), Goater 54)
Birmingham C (0) 0 13,112
Manchester C: Weaver; Dunne, Granville, Wiekens
(Mettomo), Howey, Pearce, Benarbia (Wright-Phillips),
Etuhu, Huckerby, Goater, Tiatto (Berkovic).
Birmingham C: Vaesen; Burrows (Marcelo), Grainger,
Sonner, Holdsworth, Johnson M, Eaden, Luntala,
Horsfield, Johnson A (Lazaridis), Woodhouse
(O'Connor).

Sheffield W (0) 2 *(Westwood 68, Crane 114)*
Crystal Palace (1) 2 *(Rodger 11, Riihilahti 105)* 8796
Sheffield W: Pressman; Haslam, Geary, Bromby,
Westwood, Maddix, Soltvedt, Quinn, Di Piedi, Bonvin
(Crane), Morrison.
Crystal Palace: Clarke; Smith (Austin), Gray, Vickers,
Popovic, Riihilahti, Mullins, Rodger (Hopkin), Morrison,
Freedman (Black), Kirovski.
aet; Sheffield W won 3-1 on penalties.

5 NOV

Arsenal (3) 4 *(Wiltord 15, 31 (pen), 45, Kanu 66 (pen))*
Manchester U (0) 0 30,693
Arsenal: Wright; Luzhny, Tavlaridis, Edu, Stepanovs,
Grimandi (Itonga), Parlour, Pennant (Ricketts), Wiltord,
Kanu, Van Bronckhorst (Halls).
Manchester U: Carroll (Van der Gouw); Neville P,
Roche, Stewart, O'Shea, Wallwork (Clegg), Chadwick,
Djordjic (Nardiello), Davis, Yorke, Webber.

FOURTH ROUND

27 NOV

Arsenal (1) 2 *(Edu 4, Wiltord 74)*
Grimsby T (0) 0 16,917
Arsenal: Taylor; Edu, Juan, Tavlaridis, Keown,
Stepanovs, Van Bronckhorst (Svard), Pennant
(Aliadiere), Wiltord, Bergkamp, Inamoto (Halls).
Grimsby T: Coyne; Neilson, Chapman, Broomes, Groves,
Burnett, Butterfield, Willems, Allen (Boulding), Jevons,
Campbell.

Bolton W (0) 2 *(Holdsworth 55 (pen), Ricketts 110)*
Southampton (0) 2 *(Davies 80, El Khalej 111)* 8404
Bolton W: Jaaskelainen; Southall, Barness, Warhurst,
Hendry, Diawara, Farrelly, Johnson (N'Gotty), Hansen,
Holdsworth (Ricketts), Nishizawa (Wallace).
Southampton: Jones; Dodd, Bridge, Marsden, El Khalej,
Williams, Telfer, Oakley, Beattie, Pahars, Svensson
(Davies).
aet; Bolton W won 6-5 on penalties.

Newcastle U (4) 4 *(Robert 18, Ameobi 26, Shearer 37, 40)*
Ipswich T (0) 1 *(Bent D 77)* 32,576
Newcastle U: Harper; Hughes (O'Brien), Elliott, Dabizas,
Distin, Solano, Lee (Acuna), Speed, Shearer, Ameobi,
Robert (Lua-Lua).
Ipswich T: Sereni; Wilnis, Makin, Clapham, McGreal,
Hreidarsson, Miller (Gaardsoe), Holland, Counago
(Naylor), Armstrong (Bent D), Wright.

Watford (1) 3 *(Vernazza 17, Robinson 60, Helguson 99)*
Charlton Ath (1) 2 *(Brown 43, Robinson 90)* 12,621
Watford: Chamberlain; Doyley, Robinson, Cox, Issa,
Vega, Vernazza, Hyde, Noel-Williams (Helguson),
Smith, Gayle (Fisken).
Charlton Ath: Kiely; Young, Powell (MacDonald), Stuart
(Lisbie), Brown, Todd (Konchesky), Parker, Jensen,
Bartlett, Johansson, Robinson.
aet.

28 NOV

Aston Villa (0) 0
Sheffield W (1) 1 *(Ekoku 40)* 26,526
Aston Villa: Schmeichel; Stone, Staunton, Mellberg,
Alpay, Taylor (Ginola), Hadji (Boateng), Hendrie,
Dublin, Balaban (Vassell), Kachloul.
Sheffield W: Pressman; Haslam, Geary, Soltvedt,
Bromby, Maddix, O'Donnell, Sibon (Westwood),
Morrison (McLaren), Donnelly, Quinn (Ekoku).

Blackburn R (1) 2 *(Johansson 45, Johnson 90)*
Manchester C (0) 0 17,907
Blackburn R: Friedel; Curtis, Taylor, Tugay, Johansson,
Dunn (Mahon), Gillespie, Hignett (Ostenstad), Hughes,
Johnson, Duff.
Manchester C: Nash; Dunne, Pearce (Granville),
Wiekens, Mettomo, Negouai, Benarbia (Toure),
Berkovic (Ritchie), Huckerby, Horlock, Wright-Phillips.

Leeds U (0) 0
Chelsea (0) 2 *(Gudjohnsen 59, 80)* 33,841
Leeds U: Martyn; Mills, Harte, Batty, Ferdinand, Keane,
(Duberry), Dacourt, Keane, Smith, Bakke (McPhail),
Wilcox (Kelly).
Chelsea: Cudicini; Melchiot, Babayaro, Lampard, Terry,
Gallas, Jokanovic, Dalla Bona, Hasselbaink (Forssell),
Gudjohnsen (Zola), Le Saux (Zenden).

29 NOV

Fulham (1) 1 *(Hayles 45)*
Tottenham H (1) 2 *(Rebrov 15, Davies 86)* 17,006
Fulham: Taylor; Finnan, Harley, Ouaddou, Goma, Davis,
Goldbaek (Malbranque), Collins, Boa Morte (Zaha),
Hayles, Clark.
Tottenham H: Sullivan; Anderton, Ziege, King, Perry,
Bunjevcevic, Leonhardsen (Thatcher), Freund, Rebrov,
Sheringham, Davies.

FIFTH ROUND

11 DEC

Blackburn R (3) 4 *(Jansen 11, 15, 68, Hughes 21)*
Arsenal (0) 0 13,278
Blackburn R: Friedel; Curtis, Kenna, Tugay, Taylor,
Johansson, Gillespie, Jansen (Ostenstad), Hughes
(Grabbi), Dunn, Duff (Mahon).
Arsenal: Taylor; Tavlaridis (Halls), Edu, Grimandi,
Keown, Upson, Van Bronckhorst, Pennant (Aliadiere),
Kanu, Wiltord, Inamoto (Stepanovs).

Tottenham H (4) 6 *(Davies 21, Ferdinand 29, 30, 38,*
Barness 79 (og), Iversen 84)
Bolton W (0) 0 28,430
Tottenham H: Sullivan; Anderton, Taricco, Gardner,
King, Perry, Poyet (Sherwood), Freund, Ferdinand
(Rebrov), Sheringham (Iversen), Davies.
Bolton W: Jaaskelainen; N'Gotty (Whitlow), Southall,
Frandsen (Wallace), Hendry, Barness, Farrelly,
Pedersen, Holdsworth, Johnson, Nishizawa (Gardner).

12 DEC

Chelsea (0) 1 *(Hasselbaink 90)*
Newcastle U (0) 0 27,613
Chelsea: Cudicini; Melchiot, Babayaro, Lampard, Terry,
Gallas, Jokanovic (Stanic), Dalla Bona, Hasselbaink,
Gudjohnsen (Zola), Le Saux (Zenden).
Newcastle U: Given; Hughes, Elliott, Dabizas, O'Brien,
Solano (Lua-Lua), Lee (Ameobi), Speed, Shearer,
Bellamy, Bernard (Dyer).

19 DEC

Sheffield W (1) 4 *(Sibon 40, Hamshaw 73, O'Donnell 89,*
Soltvedt 90)
Watford (0) 0 20,319
Sheffield W: Pressman; Haslam, Geary, Soltvedt,
Westwood, Maddix, Hamshaw (O'Donnell), McLaren,
Ekoku (Bonvin), Sibon, Donnelly (Crane).
Watford: Chamberlain; Cox, Robinson, Vernazza, Issa,
Vega, Noble (Smith), Hyde (Nielsen), Gayle, Noel-
Williams, Fisken (Helguson).

SEMI-FINAL, FIRST LEG

8 JAN

Sheffield W (0) 1 *(Ekoku 52)*
Blackburn R (2) 2 *(Hignett 28, Cole 39)* 30,883
Sheffield W: Pressman; Haslam, Geary, O'Donnell
(Hinchcliffe), Westwood, Bromby (Morrison), Hamshaw,
McLaren, Ekoku, Bonvin (Crane), Quinn.
Blackburn R: Friedel; Curtis, Bjornebye, Short, Taylor,
Tugay, Hignett (Gillespie), Dunn, Cole, Mahon
(Hughes), Duff.

9 JAN

Chelsea (1) 2 *(Hasselbaink 10, 77)*
Tottenham H (0) 1 *(Ferdinand 65)* 37,264
Chelsea: Cudicini; Melchiot, Babayaro, Morris (Ferrer),
Terry, Desailly, Lampard, Zola (Jokanovic),
Hasselbaink, Gudjohnsen (Forssell), Dalla Bona.
Tottenham H: Keller; Taricco, Ziege, Gardner, King,
Perry, Anderton, Freund (Sherwood), Ferdinand
(Rebrov), Poyet, Davies.

SEMI-FINAL, SECOND LEG

22 JAN

Blackburn R (2) 4 *(Jansen 35, Duff 37, Cole 82, Hignett*
88)
Sheffield W (0) 2 *(Ekoku 59 (pen), Soltvedt 85)* 26,844
Blackburn R: Friedel; Curtis, Bjornebye, Tugay, Taylor,
Johansson, Hignett, Flitcroft, Cole, Jansen (Mahon),
Duff.
Sheffield W: Heald; Haslam, Geary (O'Donnell),
Soltvedt, Westwood, Bromby, Hamshaw (Bonvin),
McLaren, Ekoku, Sibon, Quinn.
Blackburn R won 6-3 on aggregate.

23 JAN

Tottenham H (2) 5 *(Iverson 2, Sherwood 33, Sheringham*
50, Davies 76, Rebrov 87)
Chelsea (0) 1 *(Forssell 90)* 36,100
Tottenham H: Sullivan; Gardner, Taricco, Sherwood,
King, Perry, Anderton, Poyet (Leonhardsen), Iversen
(Rebrov), Sheringham, Davies.
Chelsea: Cudicini; Melchiot (Zola), Gallas, Petit
(Forssell), Terry, Desailly, Stanic, Lampard, Hasselbaink,
Gudjohnsen, Zenden (Dalla Bona).
Tottenham H won 6-3 on aggregate.

FINAL (at Millennium Stadium)

24 FEB

Blackburn R (1) 2 *(Jansen 25, Cole 69)*
Tottenham H (1) 1 *(Ziege 33)* 72,500
Blackburn R: Friedel; Taylor, Bjornebye, Dunn, Berg,
Johansson, Gillespie (Hignett), Jansen (Yordi), Cole,
Hughes, Duff.
Tottenham H: Sullivan; Taricco (Davies), Ziege,
Thatcher, Perry, King, Anderton, Sherwood, Ferdinand,
Sheringham, Poyet (Iversen).
Referee: G. Poll.

FOOTBALL LEAGUE COMPETITION ATTENDANCES

LEAGUE CUP ATTENDANCES

Season	Attendances	Games	Average
1960/61	1,204,580	112	10,755
1961/62	1,030,534	104	9,909
1962/63	1,029,893	102	10,097
1963/64	945,265	104	9,089
1964/65	962,802	98	9,825
1965/66	1,205,876	106	11,376
1966/67	1,394,553	118	11,818
1967/68	1,671,326	110	15,194
1968/69	2,064,647	118	17,497
1969/70	2,299,819	122	18,851
1970/71	2,035,315	116	17,546
1971/72	2,397,154	123	19,489
1972/73	1,935,474	120	16,129
1973/74	1,722,629	132	13,050
1974/75	1,901,094	127	14,969
1975/76	1,841,735	140	13,155
1976/77	2,236,636	147	15,215
1977/78	2,038,295	148	13,772
1978/79	1,825,643	139	13,134
1979/80	2,322,866	169	13,745
1980/81	2,051,576	161	12,743
1981/82	1,880,682	161	11,681
1982/83	1,679,756	160	10,498
1983/84	1,900,491	168	11,312
1984/85	1,876,429	167	11,236
1985/86	1,579,916	163	9,693
1986/87	1,531,498	157	9,755
1987/88	1,539,253	158	9,742
1988/89	1,552,780	162	9,585
1989/90	1,836,916	168	10,934
1990/91	1,675,496	159	10,538

Season	Attendances	Games	Average
1991/92	1,622,337	164	9,892
1992/93	1,558,031	161	9,677
1993/94	1,744,120	163	10,700
1994/95	1,530,478	157	9,748
1995/96	1,776,060	162	10,963
1996/97	1,529,321	163	9,382
1997/98	1,484,297	153	9,701
1998/99	1,555,856	153	10,169
1999/2000	1,354,233	153	8,851
2000/01	1,501,304	154	9,749

WORTHINGTON CUP 2001-02

Round	Aggregate	Games	Average
One	156,909	35	4,483
Two	229,926	25	9,197
Three	230,526	16	14,408
Four	165,798	8	20,725
Five	89,640	4	22,410
Semi-finals	131,091	4	32,773
Final	72,500	1	72,500
Total	1,076,390	93	11,574

LDV VANS TROPHY 2001-02

Round	Aggregate	Games	Average
One	47,325	24	1,972
Two	40,532	16	2,533
Area Quarter-finals	22,787	8	2,848
Area Semi-finals	31,072	4	7,768
Area finals	28,043	4	7,011
Final	20,287	1	20,287
Total	190,046	57	3,334

FA CUP ATTENDANCES 1967–2002

	1st Round	2nd Round	3rd Round	4th Round	5th Round	6th Round	Semi-finals & Final	Total	No. of matches	Average per match
2001-02	198,369	119,781	566,284	330,434	249,190	173,757	171,278	1,809,093	148	12,224
2000-01	171,689	122,061	577,204	398,241	256,899	100,663	177,778	1,804,535	151	11,951
1999-2000	181,485	127,728	514,030	374,795	182,511	105,443	214,921	1,700,913	158	10,765
1998-99	191,954	132,341	609,486	431,613	359,398	181,005	202,150	2,107,947	155	13,599
1997-98	204,803	130,261	629,127	455,557	341,290	192,651	172,007	2,125,696	165	12,883
1996-97	209,521	122,324	651,139	402,293	199,873	67,035	191,813	1,843,998	151	12,211
1995-96	185,538	115,669	748,997	391,218	274,055	174,142	156,500	2,046,199	167	12,252
1994-95	219,511	125,629	640,017	438,596	257,650	159,787	174,059	2,015,249	161	12,517
1993-94	190,683	118,031	691,064	430,234	172,196	134,705	228,233	1,965,146	159	12,359
1992-93	241,968	174,702	612,494	377,211	198,379	149,675	293,241	2,047,670	161	12,718
1991-92	231,940	117,078	586,014	372,576	270,537	155,603	201,592	1,935,340	160	12,095
1990-91	194,195	121,450	594,592	530,279	276,112	124,826	196,434	2,038,518	162	12,583
1989-90	209,542	133,483	683,047	412,483	351,423	123,065	277,420	2,190,463	170	12,885
1988-89	212,775	121,326	690,199	421,255	206,781	176,629	167,353	1,966,318	164	12,173
1987-88	204,411	104,561	720,121	443,133	281,461	119,313	177,585	2,050,585	155	13,229
1986-87	209,290	146,761	593,520	349,342	263,550	119,396	195,533	1,877,400	165	11,378
1985-86	171,142	130,034	486,838	495,526	311,833	184,262	192,316	1,971,951	168	11,738
1984-85	174,604	137,078	616,229	320,772	269,232	148,690	242,754	1,909,359	157	12,162
1983-84	192,276	151,647	625,965	417,298	181,832	185,382	187,000	1,941,400	166	11,695
1982-83	191,312	150,046	670,503	452,688	260,069	193,845	291,162	2,209,625	154	14,348
1981-82	236,220	127,300	513,185	356,987	203,334	124,308	279,621	1,840,955	160	11,506
1980-81	246,824	194,502	832,578	534,402	320,530	288,714	339,250	2,756,800	169	16,312
1979-80	267,121	204,759	804,701	507,725	364,039	157,530	355,541	2,661,416	163	16,328
1978-79	243,773	185,343	880,345	537,748	243,683	263,213	249,897	2,604,002	166	15,687
1977-78	258,248	178,930	881,406	540,164	400,751	137,059	198,020	2,594,578	160	16,216
1976-77	379,230	192,159	942,523	631,265	373,330	205,379	258,216	2,982,102	174	17,139
1975-76	255,533	178,099	867,880	573,843	471,925	206,851	205,810	2,759,941	161	17,142
1974-75	283,956	170,466	914,994	646,434	393,323	268,361	291,369	2,968,903	172	17,261
1973-74	214,236	125,295	840,142	747,909	346,012	233,307	273,051	2,779,952	167	16,646
1972-73	259,432	169,114	938,741	735,825	357,386	241,934	226,543	2,928,975	160	18,306
1971-72	277,726	236,127	986,094	711,399	486,378	230,292	248,546	3,158,562	160	19,741
1970-71	229,687	230,942	956,683	757,852	360,687	304,937	279,644	3,220,432	162	19,879
1969-70	345,229	195,102	925,930	651,374	319,893	198,537	390,700	3,026,765	170	17,805
1968-69	331,858	252,710	1,094,043	883,675	464,915	188,121	216,232	3,431,554	157	21,857
1967-68	322,121	236,195	1,229,519	771,284	563,779	240,095	223,831	3,586,824	160	22,418

LDV VANS TROPHY 2001–02

FIRST ROUND

15 OCT

Stevenage Bor (0) 1 *(Sigere 55)*
Southend U (3) 4 *(Bramble 13, Rawle 22, Hutchings 26, Webb 86)*   1114
Stevenage Bor: Greygoose; Hamsher, Dreyer, Goodliffe, Sodje, Wormull (Scarlett), McMahon, Castle, Clarke, Williams, Sigere.
Southend U: Flahavan; McSweeney, Searle, Johnson, Cort, Whelan, Hutchings, Maher (Webb), Rawle (Kerrigan), Belgrave (Beard), Bramble.

16 OCT

Barnet (0) 2 *(Sawyers 54, Essandoh 98)*
Bournemouth (1) 1 *(Kandol 31)*   789
Barnet: Harrison; Gledhill, Flynn, Bell, Heald, Arber, Sawyers, Gower, Brown (Wiper), Essandoh, Purser.
Bournemouth: Menetrier; Broadhurst, Elliott, Howe, Smith (Tindall), Huck (Bernard), O'Connor, Stock, Hayter, Holmes, Kandol (Eribenne).
aet; Barnet won on sudden death.

Blackpool (1) 3 *(Parkinson 44, Caldwell 54, Murphy J 58)*
Stoke C (0) 2 *(Iwelumo 72, Neal 83 (pen))*   3561
Blackpool: Pullen; Parkinson, Coid, Reid, Caldwell, Milligan M, Milligan J, Clarkson, Murphy J, MacKenzie, Fenton (Ormerod).
Stoke C: Ward; Thomas, Clarke (Wilkinson), Henry, Wilson, Gunnarsson, Rowson, Commons, Goodfellow, Iwelumo, Neal.

Bristol C (0) 1 *(Peacock 92)*
Torquay U (0) 0   3407
Bristol C: Phillips; Burnell, Coles, Goodridge (Murray), Hill, Doherty, Hulbert, Clist (Brown M), Peacock, Thorpe (Correia), Woodman.
Torquay U: Dearden; Douglin, Hill, Williamson, Tully, Hankin, Brandon, Rees, Canoville (Benefield), Williams, Nicholls (Richardson).
aet; Bristol C won on sudden death.

Cardiff C (4) 7 *(Bonner 6, Gordon 12, 33, 41, 70, 80, Giles 79)*
Rushden & D (0) 1 *(Hall 73)*   2052
Cardiff C: Kendall; Thompson (Jones), Brazier, Hughes, Young, Hamilton, Low, Maxwell (Giles), Gordon, Nugent (Collins), Bonner.
Rushden & D: Turley; Sambrook, Underwood (Setchell), Rodwell, Peters, Hanlon, Hall, Mills, Folan (Bell), Lee (Burgess), Talbot.

Cheltenham T (0) 2 *(Victory 53, Alsop 63)*
Plymouth Arg (1) 1 *(Friio 16)*   1310
Cheltenham T: Book; Duff, Victory, Banks, Howarth, Milton, Howells, Williams, Alsop, Naylor, McAuley.
Plymouth Arg: Larrieu; Worrell, Beswetherick, Friio, Wotton, Coughlan, Adams (Wills), Hodges L, Stonebridge (Evans), Banger (McGlinchey), Bent.

Colchester U (0) 1 *(Izzet 49)*
Swindon T (0) 0   1251
Colchester U: Brown; Duguid, Johnson G, Pinault, Johnson R, Clark, Izzet, Bowry (Keith), Rapley, Stockwell (Morgan), McGleish.
Swindon T: Griemink; Edwards N (Halliday), Duke, Heywood, Reeves (Ruddock), Gurney, Edwards P, McAreavey, Osei-Kuffour, Grazioli (Brayley), Howe.

Dagenham & R (0) 3 *(Heffer 61, 90, Goodwin 102)*
Leyton Orient (1) 2 *(Smith 40, McLean 58)*   2642
Dagenham & R: Gothard; Rooney (Cole) (Broom), Vickers, Goodwin, Smith, McGavin, Heffer, Terry (Hill), Hayzelden, Shipp, Stein.

Leyton Orient: Morris; Herrera, McElholm (Canham), McGhee, Smith, Harris, Martin, McLean (Constantine), Watts (Ibehre), Beall, Minton.
aet; Dagenham & R won on sudden death.

Darlington (0) 2 *(Brumwell 59, Ridler 76 (og))*
Macclesfield T (1) 1 *(Glover 7 (pen))*   1591
Darlington: Van der Geest; Heckingbottom, Betts, Liddle, Jeannin, Pearson (Brumwell), Wainwright, Hodgson, Jackson (Marsh), Marcelle (Harper).
Macclesfield T: Wilson; Abbey, Hitchen, Keen, Tinson, Ridler, Eyre, Priest, Shuttleworth (Wooley), Glover, Lambert.

Doncaster R (0) 0
Kidderminster H (0) 1 *(Larkin 72)*   1750
Doncaster R: Richardson; Hawkins, Squires, Ryan, Barrick, Carden, Owen, Kelly (Barnes), Watson (Tierney), Campbell, Whitman (Jackson).
Kidderminster H: Nixon; Clarkson, Joy, Williams, Hinton, Shail, Bird (Larkin) (Hadley), Bennett, Broughton, Foster, Shilton (Blake).

Exeter C (1) 1 *(Fleming 45 (og))*
Cambridge U (1) 2 *(Chillingworth 15, One 104)*   1047
Exeter C: Van Heusden; McConnell, Power, Buckle, Campbell, Watson, Breslan, Birch, Barlow (Richardson), Roscoe (Cronin), Roberts.
Cambridge U: Perez; Goodhind, Warner (Angus), Walling, Duncan, Ashbee, Fleming, Guttridge (Prokas), Revell, Chillingworth (One), Youngs.
aet; Cambridge U won on sudden death.

Hartlepool U (0) 0
Bury (0) 1 *(Newby 114)*   2190
Hartlepool U: Williams; Arnison, Robinson, Barron, Lee, Sharp, Tinkler, Humphreys, Boyd, Watson, Widdrington.
Bury: Kenny; Forrest, Stuart, Nelson, Swailes, Redmond, Reid, Jarrett, Newby, Murphy, Singh.
aet; Bury won on sudden death.

Huddersfield T (0) 0
Halifax T (0) 0   3570
Huddersfield T: Margetson; Jenkins, Heary, Irons, Clarke, Gray, Thorrington, Holland, Booth (Hay), Schofield (Baldry) (Macari), Mattis.
Halifax T: Butler; Harsley (Midgley), Jules (Swales), Mitchell, Clarke M, Stoneman, Redfearn, Middleton, Kerrigan (Wood), Jones, Smith.
aet; Huddersfield T won 4-3 on penalties.

Leigh RMI (0) 2 *(Heald 76, Maamria 94 (pen))*
Scarborough (0) 1 *(Pounder 48)*   300
Leigh RMI: Westhead; Scott, Swan, Farrell, German, Black (Hallows), Fitzpatrick (Heald), Salt, Kielty, Fisher, Maamria.
Scarborough: Woods; Stoker (Newton), Wilford, Jones, Faure, Fitzsimmons, Blunt, Elliott, Pounder, Windross, Torpey (Atkinson).
aet; Leigh RMI won on sudden death.

Northampton T (2) 2 *(Hunt 34, McGregor 45)*
Oxford U (0) 0   2640
Northampton T: Welch; Dempsey, Hunter (Hodge), Frain, Burgess, Hope, McGregor, Hunt, Forrester (Asamoah), Rankin (Gabbiadini), Carruthers.
Oxford U: McCaldon; Stockley (Hackett), Ricketts (Powell), Guyett, Hatswell, Bolland, Savage, Whitehead, Brooks, Omoyimni, Folland.

Notts Co (0) 2 *(Allsopp 50, Hackworth 57 (pen))*
York C (0) 0   1128
Notts Co: Garden; Grayson, Baraclough, Caskey (Hamilton), Warren, Richardson I, Brough, Cas, Allsopp (Heffernan), Hackworth, Nicholson (Liburd).
York C: Howarth; Smith, Hocking, Fielding (Basham), Maley, Cooper, Brass, Fox, Nogan, Proctor, Stamp (Mathie).

Port Vale (0) 2 *(Armstrong 55, Brooker 61)*
Carlisle U (1) 1 *(Foran 19)* 2664
Port Vale: Goodlad; Cummins, Ingram, Gibson (Maye), Burns, Donnelly, Dodd, Brisco, McPhee, Brooker, Armstrong.
Carlisle U: Keen; Birch (Galloway), Rogers, McAughtrie, Winstanley, Morley, McGill, Soley (Skinner), Foran, Murphy, Halliday (Jack).

Rochdale (1) 2 *(Platt 37, Jones 88 (pen))*
Southport (0) 0 1411
Rochdale: Hahnemann; Evans, McAuley (Duffy), Jones, Jobson, Griffiths, Ford, Flitcroft, Platt, Townson (McCourt), Doughty.
Southport: Dickinson; Robertson, Clark, Teale, Lane, Jones B, Bauress, Elam, MacAuley, Parke, Eastwood.

Scunthorpe U (1) 3 *(Torpey 38, Beagrie 56, 76)*
Lincoln C (0) 1 *(Cameron 71)* 1662
Scunthorpe U: Evans; Stanton (Ridley), Dawson, Cotterill, Jackson, Hodges (Brough), Calvo-Garcia, Kell, Carruthers, Torpey, Beagrie.
Lincoln C: Marriott; Bailey (Barnett), Bimson, Walker, Holmes, Brown, Black, Sedgemore (Betts), Cameron, Thorpe, Gain (Buckley).

Shrewsbury T (0) 0
Chesterfield (0) 1 *(D'Auria 90)* 1915
Shrewsbury T: Dunbavin; Moss, Rioch, Redmile, Heathcote, Murray, Lowe, Atkins, Rodgers, Jemson, Jagielka.
Chesterfield: Abbey; Booty, Edwards, Ingledow, Breckin, Payne, Willis (Jones), Ebdon (D'Auria), Reeves, Beckett, Richardson.

Swansea C (1) 1 *(Coates 9)*
Brighton & HA (1) 2 *(Lehmann 45, Steele 89)* 2851
Swansea C: Freestone; De Vulgt, Howard, Bound, O'Leary, Todd, Phillips (Romo), Cusack, Sidibe (Appleby), Williams, Coates.
Brighton & HA: Kuipers; Watson, Jones, Pethick, Wicks, Crosby, Pitcher, Rogers, Lehmann, Steele, Melton.

Wrexham (1) 5 *(Trundle 31, 56, Morrell 64, 80, Thomas 90)*
Wigan Ath (1) 1 *(Hill 25 (og))* 1550
Wrexham: Rogers; Whitley, Hill, Thomas, Roberts, Holmes, Sam, Ferguson, Russell (Barrett), Trundle, Faulconbridge (Morrell).
Wigan Ath: Stillie; Green (Mitchell), Sharp, McLoughlin, McGibbon, De Zeeuw, Brannan (McCulloch), Kilford, Haworth, Roberts (Liddell), Kennedy.

Yeovil T (1) 3 *(Giles 37, 90, Grant 80)*
QPR (0) 0 2879
Yeovil T: Weale; Schram, Haveron, White, Tonkin, Crittenden, Johnson, Turner, McIndoe, Giles, Alford (Grant).
QPR: Day; Bignot (Dodou), Bruce, Palmer, Ben Askar, Perry, Rose, Bonnot (Barr), Thomson, Wardley (Pacquette), Connolly.

17 OCT

Wycombe W (0) 1 *(Emblen 69)*
Brentford (0) 0 2051
Wycombe W: Osborn; Senda, Townsend (Johnson), Bulman, Rogers, Ryan, Carroll, Lee, McSporran, Holligan, Emblen (Phelan).
Brentford: Smith P; Theobald, Anderson, Hutchinson, Ingimarsson, Price (Williams), Evans (Smith J), Hunt, Owusu (Gibbs), O'Connor, Burgess.

SECOND ROUND

30 OCT

Brighton & HA (1) 2 *(Pitcher 45, Melton 92)*
Wycombe W (0) 1 *(Holligan 66)* 3237
Brighton & HA: Kuipers; Pethick, Jones, Crosby, Wicks (Virgo), Melton, Pitcher, Rogers, Steele, Lehmann, Brooker (McPhee).

Wycombe W: Osborn; Johnson, Phelan (Roberts), Bulman, Cousins, Ryan, Carroll, Emblen, Holligan, Lee, Senda.
aet; Brighton & HA won on sudden death.

Bury (1) 2 *(Lawson 11, Swailes 62)*
Notts Co (1) 3 *(Caskey 32, Allsopp 59, 116)* 1197
Bury: Garner; Forrest, Stuart, Collins, Swailes, Nelson, Borley, Reid, Newby, Lawson (Clegg), Unsworth.
Notts Co: Mildenhall; Fenton, Baraclough, Caskey, Warren, Grayson, Owers (Bolland), Cas (Stone), Allsopp, Hackworth, Hamilton.
aet; Notts Co won on sudden death.

Cambridge U (1) 1 *(One 19)*
Cheltenham T (0) 1 *(Naylor 63)* 1511
Cambridge U: Perez; Duncan, Warner, Tudor, Angus, Ashbee, Wanless, Alcide (Revell), Kitson (Prokas), One (Chillingworth), Youngs.
Cheltenham T: Book; Duff, Victory, Banks, Howarth, Milton (McAuley), Howells, Williams (Grayson), Alsop, Naylor (Devaney), Yates.
aet; Cambridge U won 5-4 on penalties.

Cardiff C (0) 1 *(Nugent 90 (pen))*
Peterborough U (1) 3 *(Bullard 8 (pen), McKenzie 78, Green 83)* 2584
Cardiff C: Walton; Jones (Thompson), Low, Hughes, Young, McCulloch (Giles), Hamilton, Bonner, Fortune-West, Maxwell (Nugent), Collins.
Peterborough U: Tyler; Joseph, Williams T (French), Oldfield, Rea, Cullen, Bullard (Shields), Danielsson, McKenzie (Green), Fenn, Jelleyman.

Chesterfield (0) 1 *(Reeves 93)*
Kidderminster H (0) 0 1904
Chesterfield: Abbey; Booty, Edwards, Parrish, Breckin, Moore (Jones), Ingledow, D'Auria (Williams), Reeves, Hitzlsperger (Payne), Ebdon.
Kidderminster H: Brock; Clarkson, Stamps, Blake, Hinton, Sall, Bennett, Foster, Broughton, Larkin, Williams.
aet; Chesterfield won on sudden death.

Dagenham & R (0) 3 *(McGavin 50, Ovendale 76 (og), Vickers 94)*
Luton T (0) 2 *(Brennan 56, Thomson 68)* 2433
Dagenham & R: Gothard; Rooney, Vickers, Goodwin, Smith, Hill, McGavin (Broom), Terry, Hayzelden, McDougald (Lock), Shipp (Janney).
Luton T: Ovendale; Gillman, Holmes, Fraser, Dryden, Johnson, George, Mansell (Stirling), Thomson, Fotiadis, Brennan.
aet; Dagenham & R won on sudden death.

Hull C (1) 3 *(Alexander 11 (pen), 63, 67)*
Leigh RMI (0) 0 5226
Hull C: Glennon; Edwards, Holt (Price), Whitmore (Lee), Mohan, Petty, Williams (Matthews), Johnsson, Alexander, Dudfield, Beresford.
Leigh RMI: Westhead; Scott, Swan, Durkin, Farrell (Black), Heald, Fisher, Fitzpatrick, Kielty (Monk), Twiss, Maamria (Hallows).

Mansfield T (0) 0
Blackpool (1) 4 *(MacKenzie 32 (pen), 69, Ormerod 80, 90)* 3601
Mansfield T: Bingham; Hassell, Tankard (Jervis), Asher, Reddington, Williamson, Barrett, Pemberton, White J, Bradley, Corden (Lawrence).
Blackpool: Barnes; Parkinson, Jaszczun, Bullock, Thompson, Reid (Coid), Milligan J, Wellens (Ormerod), Fenton (Blinkhorn), MacKenzie, Hills.

Northampton T (0) 0
Barnet (0) 1 *(Flynn 57)* 2142
Northampton T: Welch; Marsh, Spedding, Frain, Burgess, Hope, Hunt, Parkin, McGregor (Hodge), Gabbiadini (Asamoah), Hargreaves.
Barnet: Naisbitt; Gledhill (Sawyers), Flynn, Niven, Heald, Arber, Berkley (Taylor), Bell, Midgley, Essandoh, Purser (Strevens).

Oldham Ath (1) 2 *(Eyre 18, Richards 90)*
Tranmere R (0) 0 2940
Oldham Ath: Kelly; Holden, Armstrong, McNiven, Balmer, Sheridan D, Rickers, Richards, Eyre (Dudley), Corazzin (Allott), Innes.
Tranmere R: Murphy; Sharps, Hazell, Hinds, Challinor, Harrison, Hay (N'Diaye), Hume (Thornton), Parkinson, Allison, Mellon (Henry).

Reading (1) 2 *(Smith N 45, Henderson 72)*
Colchester U (0) 1 *(Stockwell 77)* 2725
Reading: Ashdown; Murty, Shorey, Viveash, Mackie, Gamble, Hughes (Igoe), Smith N (Harper), Forster, Henderson, Smith A (Rougier).
Colchester U: Brown; Johnson G, Keith, Pinault (Hadrava), Fitzgerald, Clark, Izzet, Gregory (Opara), Morgan, Bowry (Stockwell), McGleish.

Rochdale (0) 1 *(Townson 49)*
Port Vale (0) 2 *(Burton 53 (pen), Armstrong 66)* 1639
Rochdale: Hahnemann; Duffy, McAuley, Rose (McCourt), Jobson, Bayliss, Durkan, Flitcroft, Townson, Oliver, Doughty.
Port Vale: Goodlad; Cummins, Rowland, Carragher, Burton, McClare, Killen, Brisco, McPhee, Brooker, Armstrong (Byrne).

Scunthorpe U (0) 3 *(Hodges 50, Carruthers 61, McCombe 79)*
Darlington (0) 0 1626
Scunthorpe U: Evans; Stanton, Dawson, Hodges (Brough), Jackson, McCombe, Calvo-Garcia, Kell (Barwick), Carruthers, Torpey (Quailey), Beagrie.
Darlington: Van der Geest; Heckingbottom, Betts, Brightwell, Jeannin, Maddison, Wainwright, Hodgson, Conlon (Sheeran), Jackson, Atkinson (Brumwell).

Southend U (0) 0
Bristol C (0) 2 *(Amankwaah 53, Peacock 81)* 1741
Southend U: Flahavan; Beard, Searle, Johnson (Thurgood), Broad, Whelan, Hutchings, Kerrigan, Rawle (Richards), Belgrave, Bramble (Webb).
Bristol C: Phillips; Amankwaah, Coles, Clist, Carey (Jones D), Brown M, Doherty, Hulbert, Peacock, Matthews (Goodridge), Woodman.

Wrexham (0) 0
Huddersfield T (1) 1 *(Holland 5)* 1725
Wrexham: Walsh; Whitley (Carey), Miller, Thomas, Roberts, Hill, Chalk (Morrell), Ferguson, Blackwood, Faulconbridge (Trundle), Sam.
Huddersfield T: Margetson; Moses, Heary, Irons, Clarke, Gray, Knight, Holland, Booth, Schofield, Mattis.

31 OCT

Bristol R (0) 1 *(Cameron 69 (pen))*
Yeovil T (1) 1 *(McIndoe 27)* 4301
Bristol R: Howie; Wilson, Jones, Foster, Thomson, Foran (Walters), Mauge (Bryant), Gall (Bubb), Cameron, Ross, Plummer.
Yeovil T: Weale; Skiverton, White, Schram (Way) (Thompson), Lockwood, Tonkin, Johnson, McIndoe, Crittenden, Grant, Alford (Giles).
aet; Bristol R won 5-4 on penalties.

QUARTER-FINALS

4 DEC

Barnet (2) 4 *(Strevens 15, 79, Arber 30, Berkley 90)*
Reading (1) 1 *(Henderson 16)* 1171
Barnet: Naisbitt; Gledhill, Flynn, Bell, Heald (Sawyers), Arber, Doolan, Toms (Berkley), Midgley, Strevens, Purser.
Reading: Ashdown; Gamble (Parkinson), Shorey (Mackie), Viveash, Williams, Harper, Igoe, Henderson, Rougier (Tyson), Forster, Salako.

Bristol C (1) 2 *(Murray 34, Thorpe 96)*
Peterborough U (1) 1 *(Bullard 24)* 3949
Bristol C: Phillips; Murray, Burnell (Fortune), Hulbert (Jones D), Coles, Hill, Clist (Matthews), Brown A, Peacock, Thorpe, Woodman.
Peterborough U: Tyler; Hooper, Jelleyman, Forsyth, Joseph, Edwards, Bullard, Danielsson (Oldfield), Clarke A (Clarke L), Fenn, Farrell.
aet; Bristol C won on sudden death.

Cambridge U (1) 2 *(Kitson 43, One 94)*
Brighton & HA (1) 1 *(Melton 35)* 2306
Cambridge U: Perez; Tann, Guttridge (Youngs), Duncan, Angus, Ashbee (Fleming), Wanless, Tudor, Kitson, One, Scully.
Brighton & HA: Kuipers; Virgo, Mayo, Crosby, Wicks, Pethick, Pitcher, Rogers, Steele, Lehmann (Ramsay), Melton.
aet; Cambridge U won on sudden death.

Chesterfield (0) 0
Blackpool (1) 3 *(Edwards 37 (og), Murphy J 48, Bullock 51)* 2373
Chesterfield: Abbey; Booty, Edwards, Parrish, Breckin, Payne, Howard, D'Auria, Reeves, Beckett (Williams), Richardson.
Blackpool: Barnes; Coid, Jaszczun, O'Kane (Milligan J), Reid (Hughes), Marshall, Collins, Bullock, Murphy J, MacKenzie, Hills.

Huddersfield T (1) 4 *(Schofield 23, 65, Hay 76, Booth 85)*
Scunthorpe U (0) 1 *(Torpey 63)* 3587
Huddersfield T: Margetson; Jenkins, Heary, Irons (Senior M), Moses, Gray, Baldry (Hay), Holland, Booth (Macari), Schofield, Knight.
Scunthorpe U: Evans; Bradshaw, Dawson, McCombe, Jackson (Stanton), Hodges, Calvo-Garcia, Kell, Carruthers, Torpey, Brough (Sheldon) (Quailey).

Hull C (1) 2 *(Whittle 26, Whitmore 66)*
Port Vale (1) 1 *(McPhee 14)* 5326
Hull C: Glennon; Edwards, Goodison, Whitmore (Sneekes), Whittle, Petty, Matthews (Williams), Johnsson, Alexander, Dudfield, Beresford (Holt).
Port Vale: Goodlad; Cummins, Ingram, Carragher (Webber), Burns, Burton, McClare, Brisco (Donnelly), McPhee, Brooker,Rowland.

Notts Co (0) 0
Oldham Ath (1) 1 *(Smart 41)* 1047
Notts Co: Garden; Fenton, Baraclough, Jorgensen, Stone, Riley, Brough, Holmes (Allsopp), Quinn, Hackworth (Heffernan), Nicholson (Caskey).
Oldham Ath: Rachubka; Holden (McNiven), Armstrong, Beharall, Balmer, Duxbury, Sheridan D, Eyre (Allott), Tipton, Smart, Innes (Rickers).

5 DEC

Bristol R (2) 4 *(Hogg 29, Ellington 30, 75, Ommel 81)*
Dagenham & R (0) 1 *(Charlery 80)* 3028
Bristol R: Howie; Astafjevs, Challis, Thomson, Foran, Trought, Mauge (Wilson), Hogg, Ellington (Gall), Cameron (Ommel), Plummer.
Dagenham & R: Gothard; Rooney, Goodwin, Heffer (Janney), Broom, Hill, Jones (Hayzelden), McDougald, Charlery, McGavin, Shipp (Forbes).

NORTHERN SEMI-FINALS

8 JAN

Hull C (0) 0
Huddersfield T (1) 1 *(Booth 39)* 7248
Hull C: Musselwhite; Petty, Goodison, Sneekes (Johnsson), Whittle, Holt, Whitmore, Williams, Alexander, Dudfield (Greaves), Beresford.
Huddersfield T: Margetson; Heary, Evans, Irons, Moses, Gray, Knight (Wijnhard), Hay (Holland), Booth, Schofield, Mattis.

9 JAN

Oldham Ath (1) 2 *(Duxbury 3, Eyres 46)*
Blackpool (2) 5 *(Walker 28, 36, 88, Murphy J 65, Bullock 80)*   3349
Oldham Ath: Kelly; Holden, Armstrong, Beharall (Eyre), Baudet, Duxbury, Sheridan D, Murray, Tipton (Dudley), Smart, Eyres (McNiven).
Blackpool: Barnes; Coid (O'Kane), Jaszczun (Simpson), Collins, Day, Reid, Wellens, Bullock, Fenton (Murphy J), Walker, Hills.

SOUTHERN SEMI-FINALS

5 JAN

Cambridge U (1) 2 *(Tudor 29, Guttridge 90)*
Barnet (0) 0   3108
Cambridge U: Perez; Tann, Murray, Duncan, Angus, Guttridge, Wanless (Taylor S), Tudor, Kitson (One), Chillingworth, Scully (Goodhind).
Barnet: Naisbitt; Sawyers, Gledhill, Niven, Heald, Arber, Toms (Purser), Bell, Strevens, Midgley (Brown), Berkley (Doolan).

9 JAN

Bristol C (2) 3 *(Matthews 31, 45, Bell 49)*
Bristol R (0) 0   17,367
Bristol C: Phillips; Murray (Rodrigues), Bell (Lever), Amankwaah, Coles, Hill, Doherty (Tinnion), Brown A, Peacock, Matthews, Burnell.
Bristol R: Howie; Smith, Challis, Gall (Bubb), Foran, Trought, Plummer, Hogg, Ellington, Ommel (Cameron), Shore.

NORTHERN FINAL, FIRST LEG

29 JAN

Blackpool (2) 3 *(Wellens 3, Murphy J 38, Taylor 70)*
Huddersfield T (0) 1 *(Schofield 56)*   4573
Blackpool: Barnes; Coid, Hills, O'Kane, Day, Marshall, Wellens, Bullock, Murphy J, Taylor, Simpson.
Huddersfield T: Margetson; Jenkins, Evans, Irons, Clarke, Gray, Knight, Holland (Armstrong), Booth, Schofield, Heary.

NORTHERN FINAL, SECOND LEG

12 FEB

Huddersfield T (2) 2 *(Wijnhard 5 (pen), Schofield 33)*
Blackpool (0) 1 *(Bullock 103)*   7736
Huddersfield T: Margetson; Jenkins, Evans, Armstrong, Clarke, Gray, Heary, Holland, Wijnhard, Schofield, Hay.
Blackpool: Barnes; Coid, Jaszczun, O'Kane (Collins), Day (Hughes), Marshall, Wellens, Bullock, Murphy J, Taylor, Hills.
3-3 on aggregate aet; Blackpool won on sudden death.

SOUTHERN FINAL, FIRST LEG

30 JAN

Cambridge U (0) 0
Bristol C (0) 0   3470
Cambridge U: Perez; Fleming, Murray, Duncan, Tann, Ashbee, Wanless (Mustoe), Tudor, Youngs (Revell), Chillingworth, One (Goodhind).
Bristol C: Phillips; Murray, Bell, Amankwaah, Coles, Hill, Burnell, Brown A, Peacock, Thorpe (Brown M), Tinnion (Hulbert).

SOUTHERN FINAL, SECOND LEG

19 FEB

Bristol C (0) 0
Cambridge U (1) 2 *(One 38, 60)*   12,264
Bristol C: Phillips; Carey, Bell, Burnell, Lever (Hill), Coles (Hulbert), Brown M (Jones), Brown A, Peacock, Thorpe, Tinnion.
Cambridge U: Perez; Angus, Austin, Tann, Duncan, Fleming, Wanless, Tudor, Jackman, One (Revell), Youngs.
Cambridge U won 2-0 on aggregate.

FINAL (at Millennium Stadium)

24 MAR

Blackpool (1) 4 *(Murphy J 6, Clarke 54, Hills 77, Taylor 82)*
Cambridge U (1) 1 *(Wanless 28 (pen))*   20,287
Blackpool: Barnes; O'Kane, Jaszczun, Collins, Clarke, Marshall (Hughes), Wellens (Simpson), Bullock, Murphy J, Taylor (Walker), Hills.
Cambridge U: Perez; Angus (Goodhind), Murray, Duncan, Tann, Ashbee, Wanless, Tudor (Jackman), Kitson (One), Youngs, Guttridge.
Referee: R. Furnandiz.

FA CUP FINALS 1872–2002

1872 and 1874–92	Kennington Oval
1873	Lillie Bridge
1886	Replay at Derby
	(Racecourse Ground)
1893	Fallowfield, Manchester
1894	Everton
1895–1914	Crystal Palace
1901	Replay at Bolton

1910	Replay at Everton
1911	Replay at Old Trafford
1912	Replay at Bramall Lane
1915	Old Trafford, Manchester
1920–22	Stamford Bridge
1923 to 2000	Wembley
1970	Replay at Old Trafford
2001 to date	Millennium Stadium, Cardiff

Year	Winners	Runners-up	Score
1872	Wanderers	Royal Engineers	1-0
1873	Wanderers	Oxford University	2-0
1874	Oxford University	Royal Engineers	2-0
1875	Royal Engineers	Old Etonians	2-0 (after 1-1 draw aet)
1876	Wanderers	Old Etonians	3-0 (after 1-1 draw aet)
1877	Wanderers	Oxford University	2-1 (aet)
1878	Wanderers*	Royal Engineers	3-1
1879	Old Etonians	Clapham R	1-0
1880	Clapham R	Oxford University	1-0
1881	Old Carthusians	Old Etonians	3-0
1882	Old Etonians	Blackburn R	1-0
1883	Blackburn Olympic	Old Etonians	2-1 (aet)
1884	Blackburn R	Queen's Park, Glasgow	2-1
1885	Blackburn R	Queen's Park, Glasgow	2-0
1886	Blackburn R†	WBA	2-0 (after 0-0 draw)
1887	Aston Villa	WBA	2-0
1888	WBA	Preston NE	2-1
1889	Preston NE	Wolverhampton W	3-0
1890	Blackburn R	Sheffield W	6-1
1891	Blackburn R	Notts Co	3-1
1892	WBA	Aston Villa	3-0
1893	Wolverhampton W	Everton	1-0
1894	Notts Co	Bolton W	4-1
1895	Aston Villa	WBA	1-0
1896	Sheffield W	Wolverhampton W	2-1
1897	Aston Villa	Everton	3-2
1898	Nottingham F	Derby Co	3-1
1899	Sheffield U	Derby Co	4-1
1900	Bury	Southampton	4-0
1901	Tottenham H	Sheffield U	3-1 (after 2-2 draw)
1902	Sheffield U	Southampton	2-1 (after 1-1 draw)
1903	Bury	Derby Co	6-0
1904	Manchester C	Bolton W	1-0
1905	Aston Villa	Newcastle U	2-0
1906	Everton	Newcastle U	1-0
1907	Sheffield W	Everton	2-1
1908	Wolverhampton W	Newcastle U	3-1
1909	Manchester U	Bristol C	1-0
1910	Newcastle U	Barnsley	2-0 (after 1-1 draw)
1911	Bradford C	Newcastle U	1-0 (after 0-0 draw)
1912	Barnsley	WBA	1-0 (aet, after 0-0 draw)
1913	Aston Villa	Sunderland	1-0
1914	Burnley	Liverpool	1-0
1915	Sheffield U	Chelsea	3-0
1920	Aston Villa	Huddersfield T	1-0 (aet)
1921	Tottenham H	Wolverhampton W	1-0
1922	Huddersfield T	Preston NE	1-0
1923	Bolton W	West Ham U	2-0
1924	Newcastle U	Aston Villa	2-0
1925	Sheffield U	Cardiff C	1-0
1926	Bolton W	Manchester C	1-0
1927	Cardiff C	Arsenal	1-0
1928	Blackburn R	Huddersfield T	3-1
1929	Bolton W	Portsmouth	2-0
1930	Arsenal	Huddersfield T	2-0
1931	WBA	Birmingham	2-1
1932	Newcastle U	Arsenal	2-1
1933	Everton	Manchester C	3-0
1934	Manchester C	Portsmouth	2-1
1935	Sheffield W	WBA	4-2
1936	Arsenal	Sheffield U	1-0
1937	Sunderland	Preston NE	3-1
1938	Preston NE	Huddersfield T	1-0 (aet)
1939	Portsmouth	Wolverhampton W	4-1
1946	Derby Co	Charlton Ath	4-1 (aet)
1947	Charlton Ath	Burnley	1-0 (aet)
1948	Manchester U	Blackpool	4-2
1949	Wolverhampton W	Leicester C	3-1
1950	Arsenal	Liverpool	2-0
1951	Newcastle U	Blackpool	2-0
1952	Newcastle U	Arsenal	1-0

Year	Winners	Runners-up	Score
1953	Blackpool	Bolton W	4-3
1954	WBA	Preston NE	3-2
1955	Newcastle U	Manchester C	3-1
1956	Manchester C	Birmingham C	3-1
1957	Aston Villa	Manchester U	2-1
1958	Bolton W	Manchester U	2-0
1959	Nottingham F	Luton T	2-1
1960	Wolverhampton W	Blackburn R	3-0
1961	Tottenham H	Leicester C	2-0
1962	Tottenham H	Burnley	3-1
1963	Manchester U	Leicester C	3-1
1964	West Ham U	Preston NE	3-2
1965	Liverpool	Leeds U	2-1 (aet)
1966	Everton	Sheffield W	3-2
1967	Tottenham H	Chelsea	2-1
1968	WBA	Everton	1-0 (aet)
1969	Manchester C	Leicester C	1-0
1970	Chelsea	Leeds U	2-1 (aet)
		(after 2-2 draw, after extra time)	
1971	Arsenal	Liverpool	2-1 (aet)
1972	Leeds U	Arsenal	1-0
1973	Sunderland	Leeds U	1-0
1974	Liverpool	Newcastle U	3-0
1975	West Ham U	Fulham	2-0
1976	Southampton	Manchester U	1-0
1977	Manchester U	Liverpool	2-1
1978	Ipswich T	Arsenal	1-0
1979	Arsenal	Manchester U	3-2
1980	West Ham U	Arsenal	1-0
1981	Tottenham H	Manchester C	3-2
		(after 1-1 draw, after extra time)	
1982	Tottenham H	QPR	1-0
		(after 1-1 draw, after extra time)	
1983	Manchester U	Brighton & HA	4-0
		(after 2-2 draw, after extra time)	
1984	Everton	Watford	2-0
1985	Manchester U	Everton	1-0 (aet)
1986	Liverpool	Everton	3-1
1987	Coventry C	Tottenham H	3-2 (aet)
1988	Wimbledon	Liverpool	1-0
1989	Liverpool	Everton	3-2 (aet)
1990	Manchester U	Crystal Palace	1-0
		(after 3-3 draw, after extra time)	
1991	Tottenham H	Nottingham F	2-1 (aet)
1992	Liverpool	Sunderland	2-0
1993	Arsenal	Sheffield W	2-1 (aet)
		(after 1-1 draw, after extra time)	
1994	Manchester U	Chelsea	4-0
1995	Everton	Manchester U	1-0
1996	Manchester U	Liverpool	1-0
1997	Chelsea	Middlesbrough	2-0
1998	Arsenal	Newcastle U	2-0
1999	Manchester U	Newcastle U	2-0
2000	Chelsea	Aston Villa	1-0
2001	Liverpool	Arsenal	2-1
2002	Arsenal	Chelsea	2-0

* *Won outright, but restored to the Football Association.*
† *A special trophy was awarded for third consecutive win.*

FA CUP WINS

Manchester U 10, Arsenal 8, Tottenham H 8, Aston Villa 7, Blackburn R 6, Liverpool 6, Newcastle U 6, Everton 5, The Wanderers 5, WBA 5, Bolton W 4, Manchester C 4, Sheffield U 4, Wolverhampton W 4, Chelsea 3, Sheffield W 3, West Ham U 3, Bury 2, Nottingham F 2, Old Etonians 2, Preston NE 2, Sunderland 2, Barnsley 1, Blackburn Olympic 1, Blackpool 1, Bradford C 1, Burnley 1, Cardiff C 1, Charlton Ath 1, Clapham R 1, Coventry C 1, Derby Co 1, Huddersfield T 1, Ipswich T 1, Leeds U 1, Notts Co 1, Old Carthusians 1, Oxford University 1, Portsmouth 1, Royal Engineers 1, Southampton 1, Wimbledon 1.

APPEARANCES IN FINALS

Arsenal 15, Manchester U 15, Newcastle U 13, Everton 12, Liverpool 12, Newcastle U 12, Aston Villa 10, WBA 10, Tottenham H 9, Blackburn R 8, Manchester C 8, Wolverhampton W 8, Bolton W 7, Chelsea 7, Preston NE 7, Old Etonians 6, Sheffield U 6, Sheffield W 6, Huddersfield T 5, *The Wanderers 5, Derby Co 4, Leeds U 4, Leicester C 4, Oxford University 4, Royal Engineers 4, Sunderland 4, West Ham U 4, Blackpool 3, Burnley 3, Nottingham F 3, Portsmouth 3, Southampton 3, Barnsley 2, Birmingham C 2, *Bury 2, Cardiff C 2, Charlton Ath 2, Clapham R 2, Notts Co 2, Queen's Park (Glasgow) 2, *Blackburn Olympic 1, *Bradford C 1, Brighton & HA 1, Bristol C 1, *Coventry C 1, Crystal Palace 1, Fulham 1, *Ipswich T 1, Luton T 4, Middlesbrough 1, *Old Carthusians 1, QPR 1, Watford 1, *Wimbledon 1.
* *Denotes undefeated.*

APPEARANCES IN SEMI-FINALS

Everton 23, Arsenal 22, Manchester U 22, Liverpool 21, Aston Villa 19, WBA 19, Tottenham H 17, Blackburn R 16, Newcastle U 16, Sheffield W 16, Chelsea 15, Wolverhampton W 14, Bolton W 13, Derby Co 13, Nottingham F 12, Sheffield U 12, Sunderland 11, Manchester C 10, Preston NE 10, Southampton 10, Birmingham C 9, Burnley 8, Leeds U 8, Leicester C 8, Huddersfield T 7, Old Etonians 6, Fulham 6, Oxford University 6, West Ham U 6, Notts Co 5, Portsmouth 5, The Wanderers 5, Luton T 4, Queen's Park (Glasgow) 4, Royal Engineers 4, Blackpool 3, Burnley 3, Nottingham F 3, Crystal Palace 3, Ipswich T 3, Millwall 3, Norwich C 3, Old Carthusians 3, Oldham Ath 3, Stoke C 3, The Swifts 3, Watford 3, Barnsley 2, Blackburn Olympic 2, Bristol C 2, Bury 2, Charlton Ath 2, Grimsby T 2, Middlesbrough 2, Swansea T 2, Swindon T 2, Wimbledon 2, Bradford C 1, Brighton & HA 1, Cambridge University 1, Chesterfield 1, Coventry C 1, Crewe Alex 1, Crystal Palace (amateur club) 1, Darwen 1, Derby Junction 1, Glasgow R 1, Hull C 1, Marlow 1, Old Harrovians 1, Orient 1, Plymouth Arg 1, Port Vale 1, QPR 1, Reading 1, Shropshire W 1, Wycombe W 1, York C 1.

FA CUP 2001–02

SPONSORED BY AXA

PRELIMINARY AND QUALIFYING ROUNDS

EXTRA PRELIMINARY ROUND

Newcastle Blue Star v Hebburn	5-0
Prescot Cables v Salford City	2-4
Brigg Town v Great Harwood Town	2-2, 1-0
Brandon United v St Helens Town	3-2
Clitheroe v Rossington Main	1-3
Flixton v Maine Road	0-0, 0-2
Marske United v Abbey Hey	8-1
Lymington & New Milton v Burgess Hill Town	0-6
Slade Green v Chipstead	5-1
Saltdean United v Walton Casuals	3-3, 0-7
Ramsgate v AFC Newbury	2-1
Street v Frome Town	1-2

PRELIMINARY ROUND

Warrington Town v Ashington	0-0, 0-3
Spennymoor United v Mossley	4-2
Hatfield Main v Salford City	0-2
Eccleshill United v Chester-Le-Street Town	3-1
Woodleigh Sports v Gretna	1-2
Yorkshire Amateur v Shildon	3-6
Ossett Town v Tadcaster Albion	5-1
Curzon Ashton v Louth United	3-4
Guisborough Town v Bacup Borough	1-0
Esh Winning v Ashton United	0-3
West Auckland Town v Harrogate Town	2-2, 1-4
Horden CW v Evenwood Town	2-0
Northallerton Town v Chorley	0-3
Shotton Comrades v Pickering Town	1-5
Selby Town v South Shields	3-2
Rossington Main v Stocksbridge Park Steels	1-5
Marske United v Maine Road	3-3, 0-0
Maine Road won 4-3 on penalties.	
Chadderton v Maltby Main	0-2
Billingham Synthonia v Tow Law Town	4-2
Squires Gate v Oldham Town	2-0
Brigg Town v Morpeth Town	3-1
Kendal Town v Consett	4-0
Farsley Celtic v Trafford	1-0
Radcliffe Borough v Atherton LR	3-3, 5-2
Skelmersdale United v Jarrow Roofing Boldon CA	2-0
Willington v Durham City	0-8
Sheffield v Dunston FB	1-1, 1-3
Fleetwood Freeport v Pontefract Collieries	4-0
Blackpool Mechanics v Ramsbottom United	0-2
Witton Albion v Atherton Collieries	4-0
Workington v Penrith	1-0
Liversedge v Darwen	2-2, 1-0
Garforth Town v Rossendale United	0-4
Parkgate v Crook Town	3-3, 0-1
Cheadle Town v North Ferriby United	4-1
Harrogate Railway v Bridlington Town	2-0
Peterlee Newtown v Castleton Gabriels	4-0
Hallam v Armthorpe Welfare	1-0
Easington Colliery v Denaby United	4-3
Glasshoughton Welfare v Winsford United	0-2
Seaham Red Star v Brandon United	0-7
Thornaby v Billingham Town	0-3
Ossett Albion v Bedlington Terriers	0-3
Newcastle Blue Star v Whitley Bay	0-8
Brodsworth v Guiseley	1-4
Thackley v Goole	1-0
Buxton v Atherstone United	1-3
Borrowash Victoria v Boston Town	2-2, 0-1
Willenhall Town v Solihull Borough	1-6
Bourne Town v Eastwood Town	1-2
Belper Town v Paget Rangers	1-0
Pelsall Villa v Knypersley Victoria	1-2
Stafford Town v Cradley Town	5-0
Oadby Town v Leek Town	0-3
Blackstone v Bromsgrove Rovers	0-1
Mickleover Sports v Stapenhill	1-0
Matlock Town v Holbeach United	3-1
Bloxwich United v Gresley Rovers	0-2
Halesowen Harriers v Redditch United	0-4

Leek CSOB v Nantwich Town	2-3
Leek CSOB reinstated; Nantwich Town fielded an ineligible player.	
Stamford v Congleton Town	3-2
Arnold Town v Kidsgrove Athletic	4-1
Corby Town v Alfreton Town	1-2
Bilston Town v Gedling Town	4-2
Halesowen Town v Chasetown	2-0
Grantham Town v Glapwell	3-2
Rocester v Boldmere St Michaels	2-1
Oldbury United v Bedworth United	0-4
Newcastle Town v Shepshed Dynamo	3-1
Glossop North End v Stourbridge	0-1
Shifnal Town v Rushall Olympic	0-4
Barwell v Racing Club Warwick	2-0
Stourport Swifts v Rugby United	5-1
Staveley MW v Stratford Town	1-0
Bridgnorth Town v Sutton Coldfield Town	2-3
Lincoln United v Spalding United	3-0
Clacton Town v Tiptree United	2-1
Hullbridge Sports v Concord Rangers	0-1
Rothwell Town v Hornchurch	2-2, 0-2
Burnham v Flackwell Heath	4-0
Northwood v Bishop's Stortford	3-3, 1-0
Witham Town v Saffron Walden Town	6-0
AFC Wallingford v Mildenhall Town	1-2
Stotfold v Harlow Town	0-2
Potters Bar Town v Staines Town	0-5
Romford v Southend Manor	1-2
Wivenhoe Town v Harwich & Parkeston	0-2
Leyton v Felixstowe & Walton United	2-1
Wroxham v Aveley	2-1
Ford United v Royston Town	3-2
Maldon Town v Buckingham Town	0-0, 4-2
Leighton Town v Dunstable Town	1-4
Aylesbury United v Brentwood	10-1
Long Buckby v Berkhamsted Town	0-9
London Colney v Soham Town Rangers	1-2
Wisbech Town v Bowers United	3-2
Woodbridge Town v Diss Town	1-2
Hertford Town v Harringey Borough	3-1
Kingsbury Town v Wootton Blue Cross	0-3
St Neots Town v Northampton Spencer	5-0
Wingate & Finchley v Barking & East Ham United	0-0, 2-1
Fakenham Town v Marlow	4-3
Yeading v Ilford	3-1
Clapton v Somersett Ambury V&E	0-5
Beaconsfield SYCOB v Brackley Town	2-3
Hemel Hempstead Town v Holmer Green	4-0
Burnham Ramblers v Leyton Pennant	0-2
Bedford United v Newmarket Town	0-1
Southall v Uxbridge	1-11
St Margaretsbury v Gorleston	3-1
Tilbury v Wealdstone	1-1, 1-2
Barton Rovers v Cheshunt	1-3
Bury Town v Great Wakering Rovers	1-2
Bugbrooke St Michaels v Histon	0-0, 1-3
Tring Town v Coggenhoe United	0-2
Arlesey Town v Chalfont St Peter	4-0
Stowmarket Town v Ruislip Manor	4-3
Desborough Town v Great Yarmouth Town	1-2
Yaxley v Raunds Town	2-1
Banbury United v Ware	4-0
Banbury United removed from competition; fielded a suspended player.	
Hoddesdon Town v Wellingborough Town	6-1
Brook House v Hanwell Town	2-1
Ipswich Wanderers v Kempston Rovers	3-1
Lowestoft Town v Wembley	3-4
East Thurrock United v Sawbridgeworth Town	3-0
Milton Keynes City v Edgware Town	2-0
Ford Sports Daventry v Stewart & Lloyds	0-1
Brockenhurst v Three Bridges	3-1
Fareham Town v Chessington United	2-0
Horsham v Dulwich Hamlet	2-0

Banstead Athletic v Carshalton Athletic 0-2
Fisher Athletic v Ashford Town (Middlesex) 3-0
Tooting & Mitcham United v Burgess Hill Town 0-0, 3-1
Walton Casuals v Horsham YMCA 0-4
Thamesmead Town v Corinthian Casuals 1-1, 1-3
Walton & Hersham v Slade Green 4-0
Lordswood v Hungerford Town 4-2
Hastings Town v Ringmer 3-0
Whyteleafe v Eastbourne United 2-0
Greenwich Borough v Cowes Sports 2-2, 3-0
Whitehawk v Leatherhead 2-2, 0-2
Chatham Town v Moneyfields 1-1, 0-4
Hillingdon Borough v BAT Sports 2-3
Egham Town v Cobham 3-0
Molesey v Arundel 2-1
Hassocks v Ashford Town 3-2
Hailsham Town v Peacehaven & Telscombe 0-1
Tonbridge Angels v AFC Totton 4-1
VCD Athletic v Chichester City United 1-3
Dartford v Eastbourne Town 3-1
Eastbourne Borough v Whitchurch United 3-1
Selsey v Littlehampton Town 0-2
Thame United v Worthing 3-2
Cove v Erith & Belvedere 1-3
Windsor & Eton v Fleet Town 3-1
Bracknell Town v Reading Town 5-0
Ramsgate v Andover 0-4
Croydon Athletic v Erith Town 6-2
Bedfont v Epsom & Ewell 5-0
Abingdon United v Lancing 2-1
Redhill v Oxford City 2-2, 0-4
Sandhurst Town v Deal Town 2-3
Lewes v Slough Town 3-0
Abingdon Town v Bognor Regis Town 1-3
Blackfield & Langley v Chertsey Town 2-5
Beckenham Town v Dorking 2-2, 0-1
Metropolitan Police v Carterton Town 2-1
Wick v Bashley 2-2, 2-3
Thatcham Town v North Leigh 3-1
Chessington & Hook United v Didcot Town 2-0
Whitstable Town v Merstham 4-0
Wokingham Town v Sittingbourne 0-4
Eastleigh v Tunbridge Wells 2-2, 3-2
Ash United v East Preston 3-0
Godalming & Guildford v Gosport Borough 0-3
Herne Bay v St Leonards 0-2
Bromley v Pagham 2-0
Hythe Town v Camberley Town 1-0
Cray Wanderers v Southwick 3-0
Torrington v Elmore 0-1
St Blazey v Bishop Sutton 4-2
Chard Town v Evesham United 0-4
Bournemouth v Dorchester Town 3-1
Frome Town v Melksham Town 2-0
Downton v Falmouth Town 0-3
Backwell United v Christchurch 0-1
Cinderford Town v Bideford 1-1, 1-3
Swindon Supermarine v Calne Town 1-1, 1-0
Yate Town v Shortwood United 1-3
Mangotsfield United v Clevedon Town 1-0
Weston-Super-Mare v Taunton Town 0-0, 3-1
Cirencester Town v Gloucester City 2-1
Clevedon United v Barnstaple Town 3-3, 1-2
Highworth Town v Welton Rovers 2-0
Devizes Town v Odd Down 0-3
Minehead Town v Bemerton Heath Harlequins 4-1
Bridgwater Town v Fairford Town 0-0, 2-1
Brislington v Paulton Rovers 3-1
Tuffley Rovers v Wimborne Town 2-5
Westbury United v Bristol Manor Farm 1-4
Shepton Mallet v Chippenham Town 1-1, 0-3

FIRST QUALIFYING ROUND
Spennymoor United v Cheadle Town 2-0
Horden CW v Witton Albion 1-2
Stocksbridge Park Steels v Easington Colliery 3-2
Rossendale United v Guisborough Town 3-2
Dunston FB v Hallam 3-1
Brandon United v Kendal Town 1-3
Louth United v Durham City 0-3
Squires Gate v Ossett Town 3-2
Crook Town v Pickering Town 1-1, 0-1
Farsley Celtic v Radcliffe Borough 3-1
Ramsbottom United v Ashington 6-1
Chorley v Maine Road 1-2
Whitley Bay v Workington 1-0

Ashton United v Skelmersdale United 4-2
Billingham Synthonia v Liversedge 0-2
Selby Town v Gretna 0-2
Guiseley v Eccleshill United 1-2
Bedlington Terriers v Peterlee Newtown 2-0
Shildon v Brigg Town 2-8
Salford City v Harrogate Town 2-3
Billingham Town v Fleetwood Freeport 7-0
Thackley v Maltby Main 2-1
Harrogate Railway v Winsford United 1-1, 4-1
Alfreton Town v Newcastle Town 0-2
Belper Town v Leek Town 1-1, 2-1
Matlock Town v Bilston Town 2-2, 2-4
Mickleover Sports v Bromsgrove Rovers 1-2
Halesowen Town v Staveley MW 2-0
Arnold Town v Rushall Olympic 2-2, 3-0
Gresley Rovers v Redditch United 1-1, 1-2
Stamford v Grantham Town 0-3
Lincoln United v Stourport Swifts 3-3, 0-1
Rocester v Barwell 1-2
Atherstone United v Bedworth United 1-1, 1-0
Stourbridge v Knypersley Victoria 3-2
Solihull Borough v Sutton Coldfield Town 4-1
Stafford Town v Boston Town 2-1
Eastwood Town v Leek CSOB 5-0
Great Yarmouth Town v Hoddesdon Town 0-1
Great Wakering Rovers v Northwood 2-3
Uxbridge v Wroxham 0-3
Hertford Town v St Margaretsbury 0-4
Mildenhall Town v Wingate & Finchley 1-5
Fakenham Town v Leyton 1-1, 0-3
Southend Manor v Diss Town 0-0, 2-1
Hornchurch v Wisbech Town 1-3
Wootton Blue Cross v Harwich & Parkeston 2-0
Somersett Ambury V&E v Stewart & Lloyds 3-0
Ware v Wealdstone 1-5
Clacton Town v Leyton Pennant 3-0
St Neots Town v Ipswich Wanderers 0-2
Burnham v Soham Town Rangers 4-3
Aylesbury United v AFC Sudbury 4-3
Brackley Town v Ford United 1-1, 2-4
Witham Town v Harlow Town 1-1, 2-7
Concord Rangers v Stowmarket Town 1-2
Yeading v Staines Town 1-1, 4-1
Dunstable Town v Coggenhoe United 1-1, 2-2
  Dunstable Town won 4-2 on penalties.
Berkhamsted Town v Brook House 3-2
Wembley v Maldon Town 2-1
Arlesey Town v Cheshunt 2-0
Histon v Yaxley 3-0
Newmarket Town v Hemel Hempstead Town 3-1
East Thurrock United v Milton Keynes City 2-1
Chessington & Hook United v Eastleigh 2-5
Chertsey Town v Fisher Athletic 0-6
Oxford City v Leatherhead 2-0
Dartford v Deal Town 1-1, 3-0
Horsham YMCA v Thame United 0-0, 0-2
Erith & Belvedere v Greenwich Borough 3-2
Hastings Town v Chichester City United 3-0
Horsham v Tonbridge Angels 2-0
Eastbourne Borough v Whyteleafe 3-1
Bracknell Town v Cray Wanderers 3-1
Sittingbourne v Lewes 1-1, 3-6
Brockenhurst v Bedfont 3-3, 3-2
Littlehampton Town v Gosport Borough 3-3, 0-3
Carshalton Athletic v Peacehaven & Telscombe 1-0
Molesey v Walton & Hersham 0-0, 1-0
Andover v Moneyfields 2-1
Tooting & Mitcham United v Corinthian Casuals 0-2
Fareham Town v Thatcham Town 2-1
Windsor & Eton v Lordswood 4-0
Egham Town v Metropolitan Police 0-0, 1-1
  Egham Town won 5-3 on penalties.
Hassocks v Ash United 1-1, 3-0
St Leonards v BAT Sports 3-0
Bashley v Bognor Regis Town 3-0
Dorking v Whitstable Town 1-2
Abingdon United v Croydon Athletic 0-5
Bromley v Hythe Town 1-0
Christchurch v Bristol Manor Farm 2-0
Bideford v Wimborne Town 1-0
Chippenham Town v Frome Town 3-0
Elmore v Swindon Supermarine 1-2
Cirencester Town v Bournemouth 5-0
Evesham United v Bridgwater Town 1-3
Weston-Super-Mare v Mangotsfield United 3-4

Falmouth Town v Odd Down	2-1
Highworth Town v Brislington	2-1
St Blazey v Shortwood United	5-0
Minehead Town v Barnstaple Town	0-2

SECOND QUALIFYING ROUND

Blyth Spartans v Eccleshill United	5-0
Barrow v Kendal Town	3-0
Maine Road v Marine	0-2
Durham City v Lancaster City	0-0, 1-2
Spennymoor United v Billingham Town	6-1
Gretna v Brigg Town	3-3, 1-2
Witton Albion v Whitley Bay	4-2
Gainsborough Trinity v Dunston FB	5-1
Whitby Town v Ramsbottom United	5-2
Emley v Bamber Bridge	1-0
Vauxhall Motors v Hyde United	2-1
Worksop Town v Bishop Auckland	3-1
Gateshead v Runcorn FC Halton	2-4
Ashton United v Stocksbridge Park Steels	1-1, 1-2
Harrogate Town v Burscough	1-1, 2-2
Harrogate Town won 5-4 on penalties.	
Liversedge v Harrogate Railway	3-3, 1-2
Thackley v Rossendale United	0-3
Squires Gate v Bedlington Terriers	2-2, 0-4
Pickering Town v Accrington Stanley	1-2
Bradford (Park Avenue) v Droylsden	3-2
Colwyn Bay v Farsley Celtic	2-2, 1-3
Altrincham v Frickley Athletic	4-1
Redditch United v Kettering Town	0-0, 0-2
Grantham Town v Ilkeston Town	2-1
Moor Green v Halesowen Town	0-2
Newcastle Town v Stafford Rangers	0-1
Stourport Swifts v Solihull Borough	2-0
Bromsgrove Rovers v Tamworth	2-2, 0-1
Bilston Town v Hinckley United	1-3
Stourbridge v Atherstone United	0-2
Arnold Town v Burton Albion	1-1, 0-4
Eastwood Town v Hucknall Town	0-1
Belper Town v Barwell	2-1
Hednesford Town v Stafford Town	4-3
Boreham Wood v Harlow Town	2-2, 0-0
Harlow Town won 4-2 on penalties.	
Bedford Town v Leyton	3-0
Clacton Town v Heybridge Swifts	3-2
Southend Manor v Hendon	1-2
Hoddesdon Town v Berkhamsted Town	0-2
Ford United v Yeading	1-2
Northwood v Ipswich Wanderers	5-1
Grays Athletic v Wingate & Finchley	4-1
Purfleet v Wealdstone	3-2
Chesham United v East Thurrock United	2-0
King's Lynn v Harrow Borough	1-0
St Albans City v Billericay Town	0-1
Hampton & Richmond Borough v Hitchin Town	1-1, 1-2
Burnham v Wroxham	1-3
Dunstable Town v Cambridge City	2-3
Aylesbury United v Arlesey Town	2-0
Wembley v St Margaretsbury	1-4
Wisbech Town v Stowmarket Town	0-2
Wootton Blue Cross v Histon	0-1
Braintree Town v Chelmsford City	0-1
Canvey Island v Somersett Ambury V&E	9-1
Newmarket Town v Enfield	1-3
Lewes v Gosport Borough	0-0, 2-0
Croydon Athletic v Dartford	2-2, 2-4
Windsor & Eton v Oxford City	0-4
Andover v Bashley	1-1, 2-0
Basingstoke Town v Corinthian Casuals	6-0
Bracknell Town v Horsham	1-3
Maidenhead United v Aldershot Town	1-1, 0-1
Brockenhurst v Kingstonian	2-1
Fareham Town v Crawley Town	1-1, 0-4
Hassocks v Bromley	2-0
Erith & Belvedere v Whitstable Town	3-0
Carshalton Athletic v Croydon	1-2
Thame United v Havant & Waterlooville	3-4
Welling United v Egham Town	1-0
Sutton United v Eastleigh	5-1
Molesey v Folkestone Invicta	1-3
Fisher Athletic v St Leonards	2-1
(Abandoned; waterlogged pitch)	
Gravesend & Northfleet v Eastbourne Borough	1-0
Hastings Town v Newport (IW)	0-2
Christchurch v Cirencester Town	1-3
Salisbury City v Tiverton Town	3-3, 1-3

Bath City v Bideford	1-3
Merthyr Tydfil v Bridgwater Town	4-1
Barnstaple Town v Worcester City	0-5
Mangotsfield United v Falmouth Town	10-1
Highworth Town v Weymouth	0-3
St Blazey v Chippenham Town	3-1
Swindon Supermarine v Newport County	1-1, 1-3

THIRD QUALIFYING ROUND

Farsley Celtic v Brigg Town	2-2, 3-4
Vauxhall Motors v Harrogate Town	3-1
Lancaster City v Stocksbridge Park Steels	2-1
Emley v Accrington Stanley	1-0
Worksop Town v Gainsborough Trinity	4-0
Altrincham v Witton Albion	4-1
Barrow v Rossendale United	1-1, 3-3
Barrow won 5-3 on penalties.	
Whitby Town v Spennymoor United	3-0
Runcorn FC Halton v Bedlington Terriers	2-2, 1-4
Marine v Bradford (Park Avenue)	4-2
Blyth Spartans v Harrogate Railway	1-2
Chesham United v Cambridge City	0-1
King's Lynn v Clacton Town	3-2
Halesowen Town v Canvey Island	0-2
St Margaretsbury v Stafford Rangers	0-3
Belper Town v Stowmarket Town	2-1
Bedford Town v Hednesford Town	2-0
Burton Albion v Berkhamsted Town	2-1
Enfield v Yeading	3-4
Hucknall Town v Stourport Swifts	2-0
Billericay Town v Grantham Town	2-1
Kettering Town v Northwood	3-0
Hendon v Hitchin Town	0-0, 1-3
Tamworth v Wroxham	3-1
Aylesbury United v Atherstone United	3-1
Chelmsford City v Harlow Town	1-1, 0-3
Purfleet v Grays Athletic	1-1, 2-3
Histon v Hinckley United	3-3, 0-2
Aldershot Town v Sutton United	3-0
Basingstoke Town v Bideford	3-1
Merthyr Tydfil v Mangotsfield United	3-3, 1-4
Welling United v Newport (IW)	3-0
Horsham v Folkestone Invicta	1-2
Fisher Athletic v Erith & Belvedere	4-0
Andover v Newport County	0-4
Dartford v Gravesend & Northfleet	0-2
Cirencester Town v Brockenhurst	2-0
Croydon v Havant & Waterlooville	0-1
Weymouth v Crawley Town	3-1
Lewes v Hassocks	3-1
St Blazey v Worcester City	2-3
Tiverton Town v Oxford City	3-1

FOURTH QUALIFYING ROUND

Stalybridge Celtic v Bedlington Terriers	2-1
Harrogate Railway v Morecambe	2-3
Telford United v Northwich Victoria	1-1, 1-2
Doncaster Rovers v Emley	3-2
Boston United v Brigg Town	0-1
Leigh RMI v Worksop Town	2-4
Barrow v Chester City	1-0
Altrincham v Nuneaton Borough	3-0
Marine v Southport	1-1, 1-2
Whitby Town v Scarborough	3-1
Lancaster City v Vauxhall Motors	2-2, 1-0
King's Lynn v Farnborough Town	0-4
Dover Athletic v Hereford United	0-1
Harlow Town v Bedford Town	1-2
Havant & Waterlooville v Barnet	1-1, 0-3
Grays Athletic v Margate	2-0
Belper Town v Worcester City	2-2, 1-3
Yeading v Aylesbury United	0-5
Hayes v Yeovil Town	3-1
Hucknall Town v Cambridge City	1-1, 1-3
Woking v Newport County	0-0, 1-3
Folkestone Invicta v Welling United	1-1, 1-5
Mangotsfield United v Lewes	0-0, 0-2
Stevenage Borough v Kettering Town	0-0, 1-2
Burton Albion v Gravesend & Northfleet	0-2
Fisher Athletic v Forest Green Rovers	1-3
Aldershot Town v Hitchin Town	2-1
Billericay Town v Tiverton Town	2-1
Basingstoke Town v Dagenham & Redbridge	2-2, 0-3
Weymouth v Hinckley United	1-2
Tamworth v Cirencester Town	2-1
Canvey Island v Stafford Rangers	5-1

FA CUP 2001–02
SPONSORED BY AXA

COMPETITION PROPER

FIRST ROUND

16 NOV

Hayes (2) 3 *(Warner K 36, Clark 41 (pen), Warner D 85)*
Wycombe W (2) 4 *(Rammell 24, 73, Currie 45, 82)* 3475
Hayes: Bossu; Spencer, Gallen, Charles, Sterling, Gray, Clark, Dyer, Hodge (Currie), Molesley (Warner D), Warner K.
Wycombe W: Taylor; Senda (Cousins), Vinnicombe, Brown (Bulman), Rogers, McCarthy, Roberts, Simpson, Currie, Rammell, Holligan (Carroll).

17 NOV

Aldershot T (0) 0
Bristol R (0) 0 5059
Aldershot T: Howells; Coll, Chewins, Kirby, Adedeji, Harford (Protheroe), Graham, Bentley, Browne (Forrester), Watson, Parker.
Bristol R: Howie; Wilson, Challis, Foster, Thomson, Foran (Trought), Astafjevs, Gall (Bubb), Cameron, Plummer, Hillier.

Altrincham (1) 1 *(Thornley 6 (pen))*
Lancaster C (1) 1 *(Whittaker 12)* 2076
Altrincham: Coburn; Scott, Adams, Maddox, Sertori, Hawes, Hulme, Craney, Murphy, Gallacher (Swanick), Thornley.
Lancaster C: Thornley; Haddow, Lyons, Kilbarne, Mayers, Clitheroe L, Martin, Butler, Potts (Holliday), Whittaker (Rigby), Brown (Clitheroe S).

Barnet (0) 0
Carlisle U (0) 0 2277
Barnet: Harrison; Sawyers, Flynn, Niven, Heald, Arber, Gledhill, Gower, Strevens, Purser, Bell (Midgley).
Carlisle U: Keen; Birch, Rogers, Andrews, Winstanley, Morley, McGill, Hopper, Foran, Murphy (Jack), Halliday.

Bedford T (0) 0
Peterborough U (0) 0 2626
Bedford T: Heeps; Haley, Jackman, Harvey, Covington (Wilson), Miller, Turner, Dyer, Adams, Slinn, Paul.
Peterborough U: Tyler; Joseph, Pearce (Williams), Shields, Rea, Edwards, Farrell, Green (Forinton), Clarke A, Fenn, Oldfield.

Blackpool (1) 2 *(Jaszczun 36, MacKenzie 78 (pen))*
Newport Co (2) 2 *(Hughes 20 (og), Clark 40)* 5005
Blackpool: Pullen; Hills, Jaszczun, O'Kane, Hughes (MacKenzie), Bullock, Milligan J, Simpson, Murphy J, Ormerod, Coid.
Newport Co: Mountain; Robison, Clark, Eckhardt, Benton, James (Walker), Davies, Perry, Rose, Ryan, Shephard (Cowe).

Bournemouth (2) 3 *(Hughes 14, Hayter 26, Fletcher S 77)*
Worksop T (0) 0 4414
Bournemouth: Stewart; Broadhurst, Elliott (O'Connor), Howe, Tindall, Purches, Feeney, Stock (Kandol), Hayter, Fletcher C (Fletcher S), Hughes.
Worksop T: Holmshaw; Smith G, Davis, Bradshaw, Bennett (Ludlum), Kotylo, Smith C (Smith A), Whitehead, Gray (Waddle), Townsend, Cropper.

Brentford (0) 1 *(Gibbs 77)*
Morecambe (0) 0 4026
Brentford: Gottskalksson; Dobson, Anderson (Hutchinson), Ingimarsson, Powell, Mahon, Sidwell, O'Connor (Rowlands), Owusu, Burgess (McCammon), Gibbs.
Morecambe: Mawson; Fensome, Hardiker, McGuire, Colkin (Murphy), Rigoglioso, Drummond, Perkins, Thompson, Talbot, Arnold (Curtis).

Brighton & HA (1) 1 *(Zamora 31)*
Shrewsbury T (0) 0 5450
Brighton & HA: Kuipers; Watson, Mayo, Morgan, Cullip, Carpenter, Pethick, Oatway, Steele, Zamora, Jones (Brooker).
Shrewsbury T: Dunbavin; Drysdale, Rioch (Jenkins), Heathcote, Tretton, Murray (Tolley), Moss (Aiston), Atkins, Rodgers, Jemson, Jagielka.

Bristol C (0) 0
Leyton Orient (1) 1 *(Watts 31)* 6343
Bristol C: Stowell; Murray (Goodridge), Bell, Hill, Lever (Clist), Carey, Doherty, Brown A, Peacock, Thorpe, Coles (Brown M).
Leyton Orient: Barrett; Joseph, Jones, Smith, McGhee, Harris, Dorrian, Martin (Herrera), Watts (Hatcher), Ibehre (McLean), Minton.

Cambridge U (0) 1 *(Tudor 61)*
Notts Co (1) 1 *(Allsopp 15)* 3061
Cambridge U: Perez; Fleming, Ashbee, Walling, Duncan, Scully, Wanless, Alcide (Revell), Kitson (One), Tudor, Youngs (Warner).
Notts Co: Mildenhall; Fenton (Jorgensen), Baraclough, Caskey, Richardson I, Chilvers, Bolland (Brough), Cas, Stallard, Allsopp (Hackworth), Richardson L.

Colchester U (0) 0
York C (0) 0 3350
Colchester U: Woodman; Duguid, Keith, Pinault, Fitzgerald, Johnson R, Izzet (Dunne), Johnson G, Rapley, Stockwell (Morgan), McGleish.
York C: Fettis; Hocking, Potter, Smith, Hobson, Maley (Richardson), Brass, Bullock, Nogan, Proctor, Cooper.

Dagenham & R (1) 1 *(Stein 26 (pen))*
Southport (0) 0 1736
Dagenham & R: Roberts; Vickers, Goodwin, Smith, Janney, Terry, Shipp, Heffer, Hayzelden, McDougall, Stein (Charlery).
Southport: Dickinson; MacAuley, Grayston, Teale, Clark, Robertson (Whittaker), Bauress (Sullivan), Jones S, Elam, Parke, Whitehall (Leadbeater).

Doncaster R (1) 2 *(Tierney 21, Watson 49)*
Scunthorpe U (2) 3 *(Hodges 42, Carruthers 45, Calvo-Garcia 62)* 6222
Doncaster R: Richardson; Marples, Miller, Hawkins, Barrick, Tierney, Kelly, Owen, Watson (Sall), Barnes (Whitman), Jackson.
Scunthorpe U: Evans; Stanton, Dawson, McCombe, Jackson, Hodges, Calvo-Garcia, Kell, Carruthers (Quailey), Torpey, Beagrie.

Exeter C (1) 3 *(Curran 44, Tomlinson 62, Roscoe 90)*
Cambridge C (0) 0   2849
Exeter C: Van Heusden; McConnell, Power, Buckle, Curran, Watson, Roscoe, Ampadu (Cronin), McCarthy (Flack), Tomlinson (Afful), Barlow.
Cambridge C: Nurse; Nacca (Taylor), Holden, Wignall, Fox, Challinor (Pope), Nightingale, Wenlock, Wilde, Wilkin, Hann.

Grays Ath (0) 1 *(Lock 53)*
Hinckley U (0) 2 *(Hunter 49, Lenton 67)*   1133
Grays Ath: Lunan; Robinson, Halle, O'Sullivan (Abraham), Sussex, Fiddes (Morgan), McCloud, Rainford, Thomas, Edwards, Lock.
Hinckley U: Beattie; Cartwright, Lenton, Hadland, Penney, Eustace, Storer, Coates, Hunter, Lucas (Gordon), Wilkes.

Halifax T (1) 2 *(Middleton 35, Wood 52)*
Farnborough T (0) 1 *(Piper C 51)*   1914
Halifax T: Butler; Harsley, Mitchell, Redfearn, Clarke M, Clarke C, Swales, Wood, Jones (Jules), Fitzpatrick, Middleton.
Farnborough T: Bonfield; Bunce (Dublin), Patterson, Laker (Harper), Warner, Annon, Piper C, Watson, Taggart, Baptiste, Piper L.

Huddersfield T (0) 2 *(Moses 63, Knight 90)*
Gravesend & N (1) 1 *(Clarke 2 (og))*   6112
Huddersfield T: Margetson; Moses, Heary (Baldry), Irons, Clarke, Gray, Knight, Holland, Booth, Schofield, Mattis.
Gravesend & N: Turner; Lee, Martin, Barnett, Duke, Jackson, Lye (McKimm), Owen, Smith, Wilkins (Hatch), Stadhart (Booth).

Kettering T (1) 1 *(Norman 4)*
Cheltenham T (2) 6 *(Naylor 39, 63, Alsop 44, 74, Howells 87, Devaney 89)*   2942
Kettering T: Bowling; Hughes (Inman), Matthews, Perkins, Norman, Piercewright (Lenagh), Butcher, Fear, Murray, Watkins, Collins.
Cheltenham T: Book; Duff, Victory, Banks, Howarth, Williams, Howells, Milton (McAuley), Alsop (Grayson), Naylor (Devaney), Yates.

Kidderminster H (0) 0
Darlington (0) 1 *(Campbell 54)*   2471
Kidderminster H: Brock; Clarkson, Stamps, Blake (Ducros), Hinton, Sall, Bird, Bennett, Henriksen, Appleby (Shilton), Williams.
Darlington: Collett; Betts, Heckingbottom, Brightwell, Reed (McGurk), Brumwell, Wainwright, Healy, Jackson (Convery), Hodgson, Campbell.

Lincoln C (0) 1 *(Holmes 90)*
Bury (0) 1 *(Seddon 48)*   2925
Lincoln C: Marriott; Bailey, Bimson, Buckley (Gain), Holmes, Brown, Black (Camm), Sedgemore (Walker), Battersby, Cameron, Hamilton.
Bury: Kenny; Unsworth, Singh (Stuart), Nelson, Swailes, Redmond, Forrest, Jarrett (Reid), Newby, Seddon, Borley (Siros).

Macclesfield T (1) 2 *(Lambert 17, 76)*
Forest Green R (1) 2 *(Meechan 45, Cooper 82 (pen))*
                                                        1520
Macclesfield T: Wilson; Abbey, Adams, Byrne, Tinson, Ridler, Keen, Priest, McAvoy (Whitehead), Glover, Lambert.
Forest Green R: Perrin; Cousins, Jenkins, Impey, Howey, Travis, Cooper, Langan, Foster (Daley), Odejayi, Meechan.

Mansfield T (1) 1 *(Greenacre 7)*
Oxford U (0) 0   4201
Mansfield T: Pilkington; Hassell, Tankard, Robinson, Barrett, Williamson, Lawrence, Disley, Bacon (White A), Greenacre, Corden.
Oxford U: McCaldon; Stockley, Powell, Guyett, Hatswell, Bolland, Savage, Whitehead, Moody, Brooks (Hackett), Omoyimni.

Northwich Vic (0) 2 *(Blundell 73, Mike 80)*
Hull C (3) 5 *(Johnsson 13, Matthews 39, Dudfield 42, Alexander 79, Barnard 83 (og))*   2285
Northwich Vic: Gibson; Bardsley (Quinn), Barnard, Talbot, Burke, Norris, Garvey, Collins (Skinner), Ingram, Mike, Blundell.
Hull C: Glennon; Edwards, Goodison, Whitmore, Whittle, Petty, Williams, Johnsson (Lee), Alexander (Bradshaw), Dudfield, Matthews.

Oldham Ath (1) 1 *(Duxbury 33)*
Barrow (1) 1 *(Housham 3)*   5795
Oldham Ath: Kelly; McNiven, Armstrong, Sheridan D, Balmer, Duxbury, Rickers, Sheridan J, Allott (Dudley), Corazzin, Eyres (Tipton).
Barrow: Bishop; Shaw, Hall, Hume, Maxfield, Housham, Anthony, Gaughan, Warren, Peverell (Waters), Holt.

Port Vale (0) 3 *(Burgess 54, Cummins 71, Brooker 90)*
Aylesbury U (0) 0   4956
Port Vale: Goodlad; Cummins, Ingram (Burns), Carragher, Rowland, Burton, Dodd, Brisco, Brooker, McPhee (Burgess), Armstrong.
Aylesbury U: Wheeler; Williams, Risley (Clark), Clarke (Joe), Honeyball, Stanbridge, Maynard, Gordon, Silvestri, Marshall (Clifford), Bangura.

Reading (0) 1 *(Cureton 61)*
Welling U (0) 0   5338
Reading: Whitehead; Murty, Shorey, Viveash, Whitbread, Smith N (Igoe), Hughes, Gamble, Cureton, Forster (Mackie), Smith A (Henderson).
Welling U: Knight; Hone, Edwards, Watts, Riviere, Lindsey, Rutherford, Overton, Barnes, Abbott (Flemming), Powell (Standen).

Southend U (1) 3 *(Rawle 45, Bramble 56, 85)*
Luton T (1) 2 *(Forbes 34, Brkovic 75)*   6526
Southend U: Flahavan; McSweeney, Searle, Johnson, Cort, Whelan, Thurgood, Maher, Rawle, Belgrave, Bramble.
Luton T: Emberson; Skelton, Taylor, Brennan (George), Dryden, Hillier, Holmes (Fotiadis), Brkovic, Crowe, Forbes, Spring.

Stalybridge C (0) 0
Chesterfield (2) 3 *(Beckett 20, Scott 27 (og), D'Auria 70)*
                                                        3503
Stalybridge C: Batty; Woods, Crooks (Clements), Beesley, Murphy, Bushell (Parr), Wood, Pickford, Scott, Courtney, Peacock.
Chesterfield: Abbey; Booty, Edwards, Ingledow (Howard), Breckin, Payne, Ebdon, D'Auria, Reeves (Willis), Beckett, Parrish.

Swindon T (2) 3 *(Ruddock 36 (pen), Invincible 37, Heywood 74)*
Hartlepool U (1) 1 *(Clarke 39)*   4766
Swindon T: Griemink; Robinson M, Duke, Heywood, Ruddock, Gurney, Invincible, Robinson S, Sabin (Brayley), Grazioli (McAreavey), Hewlett.
Hartlepool U: Williams; Bass, Simms (Lee), Barron, Westwood, Clarke, Widdrington, Tinkler, Humphreys, Watson, Smith.

Tamworth (1) 1 *(Wilson 43)*
Rochdale (1) 1 *(Doughty 5)*   3119
Tamworth: Acton; Warner, Mutchell, Gould, Grocutt, Colley, Turner, Foy, Mills (Hatton), Bailey (Rickards), Wilson.
Rochdale: Gilks; Evans, McAuley, Jones, Jobson, Bayliss, Durkan, Townson (Connor), Platt, Oliver, Doughty (Flitcroft).

Tiverton T (0) 1 *(Nancekivell 82)*
Cardiff C (1) 3 *(Brayson 34, Hamilton 55, Earnshaw 74)*
6638
Tiverton T: Edwards; Winter, Saunders (Chenoweth), Tatterton, Marker, Leonard, Steele, Rogers, Nancekivell, Pears (Mudge), Everett (Owens).
Cardiff C: Alexander; Weston, Legg, Boland, Prior, Gabbidon, Hamilton (Bonner), Kavanagh, Brayson, Fortune-West (Collins), Earnshaw (Maxwell).
at Cardiff.

Torquay U (0) 1 *(Hill 82)*
Northampton T (2) 2 *(Gabbiadini 28, 35)*   2241
Torquay U: Dearden; Hockley (Law), Hill, Woods, Douglin, Hankin (Russell L), Brandon, Brown (Benefield), Richardson, Graham, Brabin.
Northampton T: Welch; Frain, Spedding, Sampson, Burgess, Hope, Hunt, Hunter, Forrester (McGregor), Gabbiadini (Parkin), Hargreaves.

Tranmere R (1) 4 *(Navarro 20, Price 64, 77, Flynn 87)*
Brigg T (0) 1 *(Leech 78)*   7693
Tranmere R: Murphy; Yates, Roberts, Henry, Allen, Hill, Flynn, Navarro, Rideout (N'Diaye), Barlow, Price.
Brigg T: Jordan; Raspin, Hope, Blanchard (Cadman), Nethers, Rowland, Thompson, Stones (Leech), Carter, Roach, Drayton (Wilby).

Whitby T (1) 1 *(Gildea 42)*
Plymouth Arg (0) 1 *(Phillips 72)*   2202
Whitby T: Naisbett; Rennison, Dixon, Goodchild, Logan, Gildea (Veart), Williams I, Williams G, Ure (Ingram), Robinson, Burt (Key).
Plymouth Arg: Larrieu; Worrell, Beswetherick, Friio, Wotton, Coughlan, Phillips (Bent), Hodges, Stonebridge, Evans (Keith), Adams (Wills).

Wigan Ath (0) 0
Canvey Island (0) 1 *(Gregory 88)*   3671
Wigan Ath: Stillie; Green, Kenna, Dinning, McGibbon, De Zeeuw, Dalglish (Kilford), Liddell, Ashcroft, McCulloch, Kennedy.
Canvey Island: Harrison; Dicks, Bodley, Chenery, Smith, Duffy, Knight (Boylan), Miller, Bennett (Vaughan), Kennedy, Gregory.

Worcester C (0) 0
Rushden & D (0) 1 *(Hanlon 67)*   3313
Worcester C: McDonnell; Weir, Heeley, Carty, Jukes, Davies, Ellis, Bullock (Burrow), Hyde, Shepherd, Stant (McFarlane).
Rushden & D: Turley; Sambrook, Underwood (Setchell), Hanlon, Peters, Hunter, Hall, Butterworth, Darby (Duffy), Burgess (Brady), Partridge.

18 NOV

Hereford U (1) 1 *(Wright 9)*
Wrexham (0) 0   4107
Hereford U: Baker; Shirley, James T, Wright, Capaldi, Quiggin, Robinson, Snape, Parry, Williams G, Voice (Elmes).
Wrexham: Rogers; Whitley, Holmes, Ferguson, Roberts, Hill, Gibson, Sam (Lawrence), Faulconbridge, Blackwood (Morrell), Chalk.

Lewes (0) 0
Stoke C (1) 2 *(Handyside 19, Gunnarsson 57)*   7081
Lewes: Standen; Harris (Beeston), Johnson C, McCallum, Hack, Cable, Venables (Shepherd), Thomsett, Stokes, Dicker (Johnson A), Francis.
Stoke C: Ward; Thomas, Clarke (Goodfellow), Handyside, Shtanyuk, Gunnarsson, Gudjonsson (Neal), O'Connor, Iwelumo (Cooke), Van Deurzen, Hoekstra.
at Stoke.

Swansea C (2) 4 *(Williams 6, Cusack 39, Sidibe 80, Watkin 90)*
QPR (0) 0   4784
Swansea C: Freestone; Evans T, Evans S, Cusack, O'Leary, Smith, Lacey, Bound, Sidibe, Williams (Watkin), Coates (Phillips).
QPR: Digby; Forbes, Warren (Bruce), Palmer, Plummer, Perry (Burgess), Bignot, Bonnot, Dodou, Griffiths (Pacquette), Connolly.

FIRST ROUND REPLAYS

27 NOV

Barrow (0) 0
Oldham Ath (1) 1 *(Eyres 5)*   4368
Barrow: Bishop; Shaw, Maxfield, Hall, Hume, Anthony, Housham, Gaughan, Warren, Peverell, Holt.
Oldham Ath: Kelly; McNiven, Armstrong, Baudet, Balmer, Duxbury, Sheridan D, Sheridan J (Innes), Tipton (Rickers), Corazzin (Eyre), Eyres.

Bristol R (0) 1 *(Astafjevs 85)*
Aldershot T (0) 0   4848
Bristol R: Howie; Smith, Challis, Foster, Thomson, Trought, Mauge, Plummer, Ellington, Weare (Cameron), Hillier (Astafjevs).
Aldershot T: Howells; Coll, Chewins, Kirby, Adedeji, Harford (Watson), Graham, Bentley, Browne (Payne), Parker (Gell), Protheroe.

Bury (0) 1 *(Singh 64)*
Lincoln C (1) 1 *(Cameron 34)*   2194
Bury: Garner; Stuart, Singh, Nelson, Swailes, Redmond, Reid, Jarrett (Connell), Newby, Lawson (Clegg), Borley.
Lincoln C: Marriott; Bailey (Camm), Buckley (Battersby), Hamilton, Holmes (Mayo), Brown, Walker, Sedgemore, Cameron, Thorpe, Gain.
aet; Lincoln C won 3-2 on penalties.

Carlisle U (0) 1 *(Soley 57)*
Barnet (0) 0   1470
Carlisle U: Keen; Birch, Rogers, Andrews, Winstanley, Murphy, McGill, Soley, Foran, Stevens, Jack.
Barnet: Harrison; Sawyers, Flynn, Niven (Midgley), Heald, Arber, Gledhill, Gower, Strevens, Purser, Bell (Toms).

Lancaster C (1) 1 *(Mayers 22)*
Altrincham (1) 4 *(Poland 41, 106, 120 (pen), Thornley 119 (pen))*   1800
Lancaster C: Thornley; Haddow, Kilbane, Mayers, Lyons, Clitheroe L (Holliday), Martin, Butler, Potts, Whittaker, Brown.
Altrincham: Coburn; Scott, Adams, Maddox, Sertori, Hawes, Hulme (Hargreaves), Craney, Murphy (Swanick), Gallagher (Poland), Thornley.
aet.

Notts Co (1) 2 *(Allsopp 29, Owers 54)*
Cambridge U (0) 0   2661
Notts Co: Mildenhall; Fenton, Baraclough, Caskey, Richardson I (Stone), Chilvers, Owers, Cas, Allsopp, Hackworth, Brough (Jorgensen).
Cambridge U: Perez; Guttridge, Warner, Walling, Angus, Ashbee, Duncan, Tudor (One), Kitson (Revell), Youngs, Scully.

Peterborough U (1) 2 *(Clarke A 19, Fenn 59)*
Bedford T (0) 1 *(Slinn 54)*   5751
Peterborough U: Tyler; Hooper, Williams, Forsyth, Joseph, Edwards, Bullard, Green (Oldfield), Clarke A, Fenn, Farrell.
Bedford T: Heeps; Haley (Lawley), Wilson, Jackman, Harvey, Turner, Dyer, Adams, Miller, Slinn, Paul.

Plymouth Arg (3) 3 *(Bent 16, Stonebridge 39, Phillips 44)*
Whitby T (0) 2 *(Burt 70, Robinson 72)* 5914
Plymouth Arg: Larrieu; Worrell, McGlinchey, Friio, Wotton, Coughlan, Phillips, Hodges (Beswetherick), Stonebridge, Evans, Bent (Adams).
Whitby T: Naisbett; Rennison, Dixon, Goodchild, Logan, Key, Williams G, Gildea (Allen), Ure (Anderson), Burt, Robinson.

Rochdale (0) 1 *(Oliver 90)*
Tamworth (0) 0 2709
Rochdale: Edwards; Evans, McAuley, Jones, Jobson, Griffiths, Durkan, Connor (Townson), Platt, Oliver, Doughty (McCourt).
Tamworth: Acton; Gould, Mutchell, Grocutt, Warner, Mills, Foy, Turner, Colley, Hallam, Bailey (Hatton).

York C (1) 2 *(Brass 8, Potter 84)*
Colchester U (0) 2 *(McGleish 81, Duguid 90)* 2014
York C: Fettis; Edmondson, Potter, Smith, Hocking, Cooper, Brass, Stamp (Maley), Nogan (Mathie) (Bullock), Proctor, Richardson.
Colchester U: Woodman; Duguid, Keith (Morgan), Pinault, Fitzgerald, Johnson R, Johnson G, Bowry, Rapley (White), Stockwell (Opara), McGleish.
aet; York C won 3-2 on penalties.

28 NOV

Forest Green R (1) 1 *(Cooper 29)*
Macclesfield T (1) 1 *(Keen 33)* 1714
Forest Green R: Perrin; Cousins, Impey, Howey, Jenkins, Travis, Foster, Cooper, Langan, Odejayi (Heggs), Meechan.
Macclesfield T: Wilson; Hitchen, Adams, Byrne, Tinson, Ridler, Keen, Priest, Tracey (Shuttleworth), McAvoy (Glover), Lambert.
aet; Macclesfield T won 11-10 on penalties.

Newport Co (1) 1 *(Rose 24)*
Blackpool (0) 4 *(Ormerod 65, 116, Murphy J 91, Benton 115 (og))* 3721
Newport Co: Mountain; Robison, Clark, Eckhardt, Benton, Davies, Perry (Cowe), Ryan, Rose, James, Shepherd (Paul).
Blackpool: Barnes; Coid, Hills, O'Kane (Milligan J), Hughes, Reid, Wellens, Simpson (MacKenzie), Murphy J, Ormerod, Bullock.
aet.

SECOND ROUND
8 DEC

Altrincham (0) 1 *(Maddox 69)*
Darlington (1) 2 *(Chillingworth 22, Wainwright 73)* 3302
Altrincham: Coburn; Scott, Swanick, Sertori, Maddox, Hawes, Craney, Hulme (Hargreaves) (Taylor), Murphy, Poland (Furlong), Thornley.
Darlington: Collett; Betts, Heckingbottom, Brightwell, Clark, Brumwell, Wainwright, Hodgson (Maddison), Chillingworth (Jackson), Mellanby, Atkinson.

Blackpool (2) 2 *(Murphy J 22, Simpson 39)*
Rochdale (0) 0 5191
Blackpool: Barnes; Coid, Jaszczun, Collins, Hughes, Reid (Thompson), Bullock, Simpson, Murphy J, MacKenzie, Hills.
Rochdale: Gilks; Evans, McAuley, Flitcroft, Jobson, Griffiths, Durkan (McCourt), Connor, Platt, Oliver, Doughty (Atkinson).

Brighton & HA (1) 2 *(Zamora 6, Cullip 51)*
Rushden & D (0) 1 *(Hanlon 60 (pen))* 5647
Brighton & HA: Kuipers; Watson, Mayo, Morgan, Cullip, Carpenter, Hart (Steele), Oatway, Brooker, Zamora, Jones.
Rushden & D: Turley; Sambrook (Thomson), Underwood, Hanlon, Peters, Hunter, Hall, Butterworth, Lowe, Partridge, Brady (Burgess).

Cardiff C (1) 3 *(Earnshaw 26, Gordon G 49, Fortune-West 74)*
Port Vale (0) 0 9650
Cardiff C: Alexander; Gabbidon, Legg (Weston), Bonner, Prior, Young, Bowen (Brayson), Kavanagh, Earnshaw, Gordon G (Fortune-West), Boland.
Port Vale: Goodlad; Cummins, Ingram, Carragher, Burns (Paynter), Burton, O'Callaghan (Dodd), McClare, Brooker, McPhee, Rowland.

Chesterfield (0) 1 *(Beckett 89)*
Southend U (0) 1 *(Bramble 75)* 4522
Chesterfield: Abbey; Booty, Edwards, Parrish, Breckin, Willis, Howard, D'Auria (Williams), Reeves, Beckett, Richardson.
Southend U: Flahavan; Broad, Searle, Hutchings, Cort, Newman, Thurgood, Maher, Rawle (Beard), Bramble, Forbes (Johnson).

Exeter C (0) 0
Dagenham & R (0) 0 4082
Exeter C: Van Heusden; McConnell, Power, Buckle, Campbell, Watson, Roscoe (Flack), Ampadu, Tomlinson, Barlow, Roberts (Breslan).
Dagenham & R: Roberts; Vickers, Smith, Rooney, Janney, Heffer, Shipp, Terry (Hill), Stein (McDougald), Charlery, Broom (Hayzelden).

Halifax T (0) 1 *(Harsley 85)*
Stoke C (1) 1 *(Cooke 27)* 3335
Halifax T: Butler; Harsley, Mitchell, Woodward, Clarke M, Clarke C, Ludden (Herbert), Redfearn (Wright), Kerrigan, Fitzpatrick, Midgley (Jones).
Stoke C: Cutler; Thomas (Rowson), Clarke, Handyside, Shtanyuk, Gunnarsson, Gudjonsson, O'Connor, Cooke, Van Deurzen, Hoekstra (Iwelumo).

Hinckley U (0) 0
Cheltenham T (1) 2 *(Naylor 5, Alsop 49)* 2661
Hinckley U: Beattie; Penney, Eustace, Storer, Cartwright, Titterton (Hadland), Coates (Gordon), Wilkes, Lenton, Hunter (Jenkins), Lucas.
Cheltenham T: Book; Griffin, Victory, Williams, Banks (Brough), Duff, Howells, Grayson, Alsop, Naylor, Yates.

Hull C (1) 2 *(Dudfield 15, Alexander 64)*
Oldham Ath (1) 3 *(Sheridan J 32, Eyres 48, Duxbury 50)* 9422
Hull C: Glennon; Edwards, Goodison (Williams), Whitmore, Whittle, Petty, Matthews (Sneekes), Johnsson, Alexander, Dudfield, Beresford.
Oldham Ath: Kelly; Holden, Armstrong, Beharall, Balmer, Duxbury, Sheridan D, Sheridan J (Baudet), Tipton (Allott), Eyre, Eyres (Innes).

Leyton Orient (0) 2 *(Ibehre 58, Watts 66)*
Lincoln C (1) 1 *(Hamilton 26)* 4195
Leyton Orient: Barrett; Joseph, Jones, Smith, McGhee, Harris, Martin, Ibehre, Watts (McLean), Leigertwood, Minton.
Lincoln C: Marriott; Camm (Finnigan), Gain, Mayo (Bimson), Brown, Walker, Hamilton, Sedgemore (Black), Cameron, Thorpe, Buckley.

Macclesfield T (0) 4 *(Byrne 60, 68, Glover 61, 66)*
Swansea C (0) 1 *(Cusack 86)* 2025
Macclesfield T: Wilson; Hitchen, Adams, Byrne, Tinson, Ridler, Keen, Priest, Tracey (Askey), Glover, Lambert.
Swansea C: Freestone; Evans T, Evans S, Cusack, Todd (Phillips), Bound, Howard (Duffy), Brodie (Romo), Sidibe, Williams, Coates.

Mansfield T (2) 4 *(Greenacre 27, 68, 81, Corden 45)*
Huddersfield T (0) 0 6836
Mansfield T: Pilkington; Hassell, Tankard, Robinson, Barrett, Williamson, Lawrence, Disley, Bradley (White A), Greenacre (Asher), Corden (Pemberton).
Huddersfield T: Margetson; Jenkins, Heary, Irons (Hay), Dyson (Moses), Gray, Knight, Holland, Booth, Schofield, Mattis.

Peterborough U (1) 1 *(Danielsson 39)*
Bournemouth (0) 0   4773
Peterborough U: Tyler; Hooper, Jelleyman, Forsyth (Cullen), Rea, MacDonald, Bullard, Danielsson, Clarke A, Fenn (Forinton), Oldfield.
Bournemouth: Stewart; Broadhurst, Elliott (Holmes), Howe, Tindall, Purches (Kandol), Feeney, Stock (Fletcher C), Hayter, Melligan, Hughes.

Plymouth Arg (1) 1 *(Wotton 27)*
Bristol R (0) 1 *(Walters 60)*   6141
Plymouth Arg: Larrieu; Worrell, McGlinchey, Friio, Wotton, Coughlan, Phillips (Adams), Hodges (Beswetherick), Stonebridge, Evans (Sturrock), Bent.
Bristol R: Howie; Astafjevs (Walters), Wilson, Thomson, Foran, Trought, Mauge, Hogg, Ellington (Gall), Cameron, Plummer (Challis).

Scunthorpe U (2) 3 *(Carruthers 14, 73, Calvo-Garcia 34)*
Brentford (1) 2 *(Dobson 39, Burgess 52)*   3457
Scunthorpe U: Evans; Stanton, Dawson, McCombe, Jackson, Hodges, Calvo-Garcia, Kell, Carruthers, Torpey, Beagrie.
Brentford: Gottskalksson; Dobson, Gibbs, Ingimarsson, Powell, Sidwell (O'Connor), Evans, Mahon, Owusu, Burgess, Hunt (Williams).

Swindon T (1) 3 *(Invincible 11, Edwards P 53, Howe 76)*
Hereford U (2) 2 *(Williams G 14, Wright 27)*   7699
Swindon T: Griemink; Duke (Robinson M), Edwards P, Heywood, Willis, Ruddock, Carlisle, Howe, Sabin, Invincible, Robinson S.
Hereford U: Baker; Clarke, James T, Wright, Capaldi, Quiggin (Davidson), Snape, Goodwin, Parry, Elmes (Kevan), Williams G.

Tranmere R (4) 6 *(Price 9, Koumas 17, 18, 45, Barlow 70 (pen), Yates 77)*
Carlisle U (0) 1 *(Foran 71)*   7428
Tranmere R: Achterberg; Yates, Roberts, Henry (Thornton), Allen, Hill, Flynn, Navarro, Price (Barlow), Allison, Koumas.
Carlisle U: Keen; Birch, Rogers (Winstanley), McDonagh, Andrews, Murphy, McGill, Jack, Foran, Stevens, Hadland (Allan).

Wycombe W (0) 3 *(Bulman 52, Walker 60, Currie 80)*
Notts Co (0) 0   4725
Wycombe W: Taylor; Senda, Vinnicombe, Bulman, Rogers, McCarthy, Roberts (Carroll), Simpson, Currie (Brown), Walker, Holligan (Emblen).
Notts Co: Mildenhall; Fenton, Baraclough, Caskey, Richardson I, Stone, Brough (Nicholson), Heffernan, Allsopp, Hackworth, Bolland (Holmes).

York C (2) 2 *(Richardson 4, Potter 41)*
Reading (0) 0   3161
York C: Fettis; Edmondson, Potter, Smith, Basham, Maley, Brass, Bullock, Proctor, Richardson, Cooper.
Reading: Ashdown; Murty, Shorey, Viveash (Mackie), Williams, Jones, Hughes (Tyson), Harper, Cureton, Henderson, Rougier (Igoe).

9 DEC

Canvey Island (0) 1 *(Gregory 48)*
Northampton T (0) 0   3232
Canvey Island: Harrison; Kennedy, Dicks, Duffy, Chenery, Smith, Stimson (Bennett), Gregory, Vaughan (Boylan), Miller, Parmenter (Ward).
Northampton T: Welch; Marsh (McGregor), Spedding, Sampson, Burgess, Hope, Hunt (Parkin), Hunter, Forrester (Asamoah), Gabbiadini, Frain.

SECOND ROUND REPLAYS

12 DEC

Stoke C (2) 3 *(Gudjonsson 22, Iwelumo 27, Gunnarsson 47)*
Halifax T (0) 0   4356
Stoke C: Cutler; Henry, Neal (Goodfellow), Handyside, Shtanyuk, Gunnarsson, Gudjonsson, O'Connor (Rowson), Cooke, Iwelumo (Dadason), Van Deurzen.
Halifax T: Butler; Harsley, Jules (Wright), Woodward, Clarke M, Clarke C, Mitchell, Redfearn (Herbert), Kerrigan, Fitzpatrick, Midgley (Jones).

18 DEC

Bristol R (0) 3 *(Ommel 56, Hogg 71, Ellington 87)*
Plymouth Arg (0) 2 *(Friio 76, 86)*   5763
Bristol R: Howie; Wilson, Challis, Foran, Thomson, Trought, Astafjevs, Hogg, Ellington, Cameron (Ommel), Hillier (Walters) (Smith).
Plymouth Arg: Larrieu; Worrell, McGlinchey, Friio, Wotton, Coughlan, Phillips (Keith), Hodges (Evers), Stonebridge (Sturrock), Wills, Adams.

Southend U (1) 2 *(Whelan 2, Belgrave 85)*
Chesterfield (0) 0   5518
Southend U: Flahavan; Broad, Searle, Newman, Cort, Whelan, Hutchings (Johnson), Maher, Rawle (Belgrave), Bramble, Thurgood.
Chesterfield: Abbey; Booty, Edwards, Parrish, Breckin, Payne, Willis (Rushbury), D'Auria, Reeves, Howard, Richardson (Williams).

19 DEC

Dagenham & R (3) 3 *(Janney 6, McDougald 21, Charlery 43)*
Exeter C (0) 0   2660
Dagenham & R: Roberts; Rooney, Smith, Heffer, Vickers, Janney, Terry, Shipp, Hayzelden, Charlery, Stein (McDougald).
Exeter C: Van Heusden; McConnell, Power, Roscoe, Curran (Campbell), Watson, Flack (Read), Ampadu, Tomlinson, Barlow (Cronin), Roberts.

THIRD ROUND

5 JAN

Barnsley (0) 1 *(Barnard 76)*
Blackburn R (0) 1 *(Hignett 82)*   12,314
Barnsley: Miller; Mulligan, Barker, Morgan, Chettle, Crooks, Lumsdon, Donovan, Sheron (Bertos), Dyer, Barnard.
Blackburn R: Friedel; Neill, Bjornebye (Taylor), Short, Berg, Tugay, Hignett, Jansen (Hughes), Ostenstad (Gillespie), Mahon, Dunn.

Burnley (2) 4 *(Little 24, Moore I 45, 78, 84)*
Canvey Island (0) 1 *(Boylan 67)*   11,496
Burnley: Michopoulos; West, Briscoe, Grant, Cox, Gnohere, Ball, Taylor (Weller), Moore I, Little (Cook), Moore A (Papadopoulos).
Canvey Island: Harrison; Bennett, Duffy, Stimson, Ward, Chenery, Kennedy, Miller, Boylan, Knight, Parmenter (Cobb).

Charlton Ath (0) 2 *(Stuart 74 (pen), Euell 75)*
Blackpool (1) 1 *(Hills 19)*   17,525
Charlton Ath: Kiely; Young, Powell, Costa, Fortune, Konchesky (Bartlett), Stuart, Euell, Lisbie (Johansson), Bart-Williams (Brown), Robinson.
Blackpool: Barnes; Coid, Jaszczun, Collins, Reid, Marshall, Wellens (Day), Simpson (O'Kane), Fenton (MacKenzie), Bullock, Hills.

Dagenham & R (1) 1 *(McDougald 18)*
Ipswich T (2) 4 *(Peralta 30, 66, Magilton 45, Stewart 81)*
5949

Dagenham & R: Roberts; Rooney, Smith, Vickers, Goodwin; Heffer, Terry (Brennan), Janney (McGavin), Shipp, McDougald, Hayzelden (Broom).
Ipswich T: Marshall; Makin, Hreidarsson, Bramble, Brown, Reuser, Magilton, Wright, Stewart (Counago), Bent M (Naylor), Peralta (Miller).

Grimsby T (0) 0
York C (0) 0 5052
Grimsby T: Coyne; Butterfield, Chapman, Coldicott, Groves, Gallimore, Burnett, Willems, Thompson (Jeffrey), Jevons (Boulding), Ford.
York C: Fettis; Edmondson, Potter, Hocking, Basham, Hobson, Brass (Cooper), Bullock, Nogan, Proctor, Richardson.

Leicester C (1) 2 *(Scowcroft 24, 62)*
Mansfield T (1) 1 *(Greenacre 38)* 14,466
Leicester C: Walker; Marshall (Akinbiyi), Impey, Stewart (Heath), Sinclair, Savage, Wise, Izzet, Deane, Scowcroft, Rogers.
Mansfield T: Pilkington; Hassell, Tankard, Robinson, Barrett, Williamson, Lawrence (White A), Pemberton (Asher), Bradley, Greenacre, Corden.

Liverpool (2) 3 *(Owen 17, 25, Anelka 86)*
Birmingham C (0) 0 40,875
Liverpool: Dudek; Carragher, Riise, Hamann, Henchoz, Hyypia, Gerrard, Smicer (Berger), Anelka, Owen (Heskey), Murphy.
Birmingham C: Bennett; Gill, Burrows, Vickers, Purse, Woodhouse (Marcelo), Bak, O'Connor (Hughes), Horsfield, Johnson A, Mooney.

Manchester C (1) 2 *(Wanchope 8, Horlock 62)*
Swindon T (0) 0 21,581
Manchester C: Nash; Edghill (Pearce), Ritchie, Dunne, Howey, Horlock, Benarbia, Berkovic (Haaland), Wanchope (Goater), Huckerby, Wright-Phillips.
Swindon T: Griemink; Invincible, Duke, Heywood, Reeves, Gurney, Robinson S, Howe (Grazioli), Sabin, McAreavey (Davis), Carlisle.

Millwall (1) 2 *(Sadlier 14, 63)*
Scunthorpe U (1) 1 *(McCombe 20)* 9244
Millwall: Warner; Lawrence, Ryan, Cahill (Kinet), Nethercott, Dyche, Bircham, Livermore, Harris (Claridge), Sadlier, Reid.
Scunthorpe U: Evans; Stanton, Ridley, McCombe (Thom), Jackson, Hodges, Calvo-Garcia, Sparrow, Graves (Quailey), Torpey, Beagrie.

Newcastle U (1) 2 *(Shearer 40, Acuna 76)*
Crystal Palace (0) 0 38,089
Newcastle U: Given; Hughes, Elliott, Dabizas, Distin, Solano (Lua-Lua), Dyer (O'Brien), Speed (Acuna), Shearer, Bernard.
Crystal Palace: Kolinko; Gray, Granville, Symons, Popovic, Riihilahti, Hopkin (Rodger), Mullins, Morrison, Thomson, Kirovski.

Norwich C (0) 0
Chelsea (0) 0 21,017
Norwich C: Green; Kenton, Drury, Mackay, Fleming, Holt, Nedergaard (Rivers), Mulryne (Russell), Libbra (Llewellyn), Notman, McVeigh.
Chelsea: Cudicini; Ferrer (Melchiot), Babayaro, Dalla Bona, Gallas, Desailly (Terry), Jokanovic, Forssell (Lampard), Hasselbaink, Zola, Le Saux.

Portsmouth (1) 1 *(Smith 12 (og))*
Leyton Orient (0) 4 *(Smith 48, Watts 66, Gray 77, Christie 90)* 12,936
Portsmouth: Kawaguchi; Harper, Pitt, Hiley (Crowe), Primus, Tiler, O'Neil (Derry), Prosinecki, Crouch, Lovell, Quashie.

Leyton Orient: Barrett; Dorrian (Barnard), Jones, Smith, McGhee, Harris, Martin, Gray (Ibehre), Watts (Christie), Leigertwood, Minton.

Sheffield U (0) 1 *(Brown 80)*
Nottingham F (0) 0 14,696
Sheffield U: De Vogt; Uhlenbeek, Ullathorne, Tonge, Curle, Page, Devlin (Sandford), Brown, Asaba (D'Jaffo), Ford, Ndlovu.
Nottingham F: Ward; Vaughan, Brennan, Williams, Hjelde, Scimeca, Prutton, Jenas (Johnson), John, Lester, Summerbee.

Stoke C (0) 0
Everton (0) 1 *(Stubbs 53)* 28,218
Stoke C: Cutler; Rowson, Clarke, Thomas, Shtanyuk, Van Deurzen, Gudjonsson, O'Connor, Goodfellow (Hoekstra), Iwelumo (Cooke), Henry (Dadason).
Everton: Simonsen; Unsworth, Naysmith, Stubbs, Weir, Xavier, Blomqvist, Gascoigne, Moore, Ferguson, Gemmill.

Sunderland (1) 1 *(Phillips 12)*
WBA (1) 2 *(Clement 21 (pen), Johnson 61)* 29,133
Sunderland: Sorensen; Haas (Kyle), McCartney, McCann, Williams (Craddock), Varga, McAteer, Arca (Kilbane), Quinn, Phillips, Thirlwell.
WBA: Hoult; Lyttle, Clement, Sigurdsson, Moore, Gilchrist, McInnes, Johnson, Dichio (Dobie), Roberts, Chambers A.

Watford (1) 2 *(Noel-Williams 13, Gayle 90)*
Arsenal (2) 4 *(Henry 8, Ljungberg 10, Kanu 63, Bergkamp 85)* 20,105
Watford: Chamberlain; Blondeau, Cox, Vernazza (Hand), Issa, Vega, Nielsen, Noel-Williams, Gayle, Smith, Fisken (Helguson).
Arsenal: Taylor; Luzhny, Cole, Vieira, Campbell, Keown, Van Bronckhorst, Ljungberg, Kanu (Wiltord), Henry (Bergkamp), Pires.

Wolverhampton W (0) 0
Gillingham (0) 1 *(Shaw 53)* 15,271
Wolverhampton W: Oakes; Muscat (Roussel), Camara, Pollet, Butler, Cameron, Newton, Rae, Blake (Miller), Sturridge, Kennedy.
Gillingham: Bartram; Nosworthy, Perpetuini, Hope, Ashby, Browning, Smith, Osborn, Onuora (Ipoua), King, Shaw (Gooden).

6 JAN

Aston Villa (0) 2 *(Taylor 52, Neville P 54 (og))*
Manchester U (0) 3 *(Solskjaer 77, Van Nistelrooy 80, 82)*
38,444
Aston Villa: Schmeichel; Samuel, Wright (Stone), Mellberg, Staunton, Boateng (Barry), Taylor, Hendrie, Angel, Vassell, Merson (Hadji).
Manchester U: Carroll; Neville P, Silvestre, Neville G, Keane, Blanc, Beckham, Butt (Chadwick) (Van Nistelrooy), Solskjaer, Veron, Scholes.

Cardiff C (1) 2 *(Kavanagh 21, Young 87)*
Leeds U (1) 1 *(Viduka 12)* 22,009
Cardiff C: Alexander; Gabbidon, Legg, Bonner, Prior, Young, Brayson, Kavanagh, Gordon G (Fortune-West), Earnshaw, Boland.
Leeds U: Martyn; Mills, Harte, Batty, Ferdinand (Duberry), Woodgate, Kelly, Smith, Viduka, Fowler, Bowyer.

Cheltenham T (1) 2 *(Naylor 25, 60)*
Oldham Ath (1) 1 *(Eyres 43)* 5801
Cheltenham T: Book; Griffin, Victory, Williams, Banks, Duff, Howells, Milton, Alsop, Naylor (Grayson), Yates.
Oldham Ath: Kelly; McNiven (Baudet), Sheridan D, Beharall, Balmer, Duxbury, Murray, Sheridan J, Eyre (Tipton), Smart (Dudley), Eyres.

Derby Co (0) 1 *(Ravanelli 88)*
Bristol R (2) 3 *(Ellington 14, 40, 62)*   18,549
Derby Co: Poom; Grenet, Zavagno, Mawene (Morris), Higginbotham, Carbonari, Bolder, Carbone, Christie, Ravanelli, Boertien.
Bristol R: Howie; Wilson, Challis, Gall (Walters), Foran, Smith, Plummer, Hogg, Ellington, Ommel, Hillier.

Macclesfield T (0) 0
West Ham U (1) 3 *(Defoe 45, 72, Cole 85)*   5706
Macclesfield T: Wilson; Hitchen, Adams, Byrne, Tinson, Macauley, Tracey (McAvoy), Priest (Ridler), Lambert, Glover, Keen.
West Ham U: James; Schemmel, Winterburn, Hutchison (Foxe), Repka, Dailly, Sinclair, Cole, Kitson, Defoe, Moncur.

8 JAN

Southend U (0) 1 *(Belgrave 76)*
Tranmere R (0) 3 *(Allison 64, Price 74, Flynn 80)*   8164
Southend U: Flahavan; Broad (Rawle), Searle, Newman (Forbes), Cort, Whelan, Hutchings (Richards), Maher, Belgrave, Bramble, Thurgood.
Tranmere R: Achterberg; Yates, Roberts, Henry, Allen, Hill, Flynn (Barlow), Mellon, Price, Allison, Koumas.

Walsall (0) 2 *(Bennett 47, Angell 56)*
Bradford C (0) 0   4509
Walsall: Walker; Brightwell, Aranalde, Tillson, Roper, Bennett (Keates), Wrack, Biancalani, Angell, Byfield (Matias), Andre (Leitao).
Bradford C: Muggleton; Locke, Jacobs, McCall, Molenaar (Bower), Tod, Juanjo (Emanuel), Blake (Grant), Ward, Sharpe, Jess.

Wimbledon (0) 0
Middlesbrough (0) 0   6885
Wimbledon: Feuer; Holloway, Hawkins, Andersen, Cunningham, Francis, Ardley, Hughes, Shipperley (Agyemang), Connolly, Cooper (McAnuff).
Middlesbrough: Crossley; Stockdale, Queudrue, Southgate, Festa, Mustoe, Greening, Gavin (Stamp), Ricard (Nemeth), Whelan (Windass), Ince.

Wycombe W (0) 2 *(Brown 57 (pen), McSporran 66)*
Fulham (0) 2 *(Legwinski 47, Marlet 88)*   9921
Wycombe W: Taylor; Senda, Vinnicombe, Bulman, Rogers, McCarthy (Cousins), Currie (Carroll), Simpson, McSporran, Rammell (Ryan), Brown.
Fulham: Taylor; Finnan, Brevett, Melville, Goma, Knight (Davis), Legwinski, Collins (Hayles), Saha, Marlet, Malbranque.

15 JAN

Brighton & HA (0) 0
Preston NE (1) 2 *(Skora 16, Macken 63)*   6548
Brighton & HA: Packham; Watson, Mayo, Morgan, Cullip, Carpenter, Hart, Oatway (Jones), Webb (Steele), Zamora, Brooker.
Preston NE: Lucas; Alexander, Edwards, Murdock, Lucketti, Skora, McKenna, Keane, Macken (Basham), Healy (Robinson), Anderson (Barry-Murphy).

Crewe Alex (1) 2 *(Rix 12, Foster 68)*
Sheffield W (1) 1 *(Hamshaw 23)*   6271
Crewe Alex: Bankole; Wright, Smith, Foster, Sodje, Brammer (Thomas), Hulse, Lunt, Jack, Rix (Ashton), Sorvel.
Sheffield W: Pressman; Haslam, Geary (Crane), Broomes, Westwood, Bromby, Hamshaw, McLaren, Ekoku, Sibon, Quinn (Bonvin).

Darlington (1) 2 *(Wainwright 43, Conlon 59)*
Peterborough U (0) 2 *(Farrell 67, Bullard 82 (pen))* 6832
Darlington: Collett; Betts, Heckingbottom, Ford, Brightwell, Brumwell, Wainwright (Convery), Hodgson, Conlon, Mellanby (Clark), Atkinson (Maddison).

Peterborough U: Tyler; Joseph (Hooper), Williams, Toner (Clarke A), Rea, Edwards, Bullard, Oldfield, McKenzie, Fenn (Cullen), Farrell.

16 JAN

Coventry C (0) 0
Tottenham H (1) 2 *(Poyet 23, Ferdinand 52)*   20,758
Coventry C: Hedman; Edworthy, Antonelius (Martinez), Breen, Konjic, Shaw, Thompson, Carsley (Quinn), Joachim, Bothroyd (Delorge), Betts.
Tottenham H: Sullivan; Anderton (Leonhardsen), Taricco, King, Perry, Richards, Poyet, Sherwood, Rebrov, Ferdinand (Iversen), Davies.

Rotherham U (1) 2 *(Barker 39, Mullin 55)*
Southampton (0) 1 *(Pahars 70 (pen))*   8464
Rotherham U: Pollitt; Scott, Hurst, Sedgwick (Daws), Swailes, McIntosh, Watson, Monkhouse (Talbot), Barker, Warne, Mullin.
Southampton: Jones; Dodd, Bridge, Marsden, Lundekvam, Williams, Telfer, Fernandes (Davies), Delgado (Le Tissier), Pahars, Svensson.

Stockport Co (0) 1 *(Daly 90 (pen))*
Bolton W (2) 4 *(Bergsson 36, Norris 42, Pedersen 73, Ricketts 85)*   5821
Stockport Co: Dibble; Gibb, Woodthorpe, Lescott, Palmer, Clare, Briggs, Ellison (Taylor), Welsh (Helin), Daly, Fradin (Williams).
Bolton W: Viander; Southall, Barness, Norris (Taylor), Bergsson (Nolan), Johnson, Farrelly, Pedersen, Hansen, Wallace (Ricketts), Gardner.

THIRD ROUND REPLAYS

15 JAN

Fulham (0) 1 *(Hayles 68)*
Wycombe W (0) 0   11,984
Fulham: Taylor; Finnan, Brevett, Melville, Goma, Knight (Stolcers), Malbranque, Davis, Saha (Marlet), Hayles, Boa Morte.
Wycombe W: Taylor; Ryan, Vinnicombe, Bulman, Rogers, Cousins, Carroll (Roberts), Simpson, McSporran (Devine), Currie, Brown (Lee).

Middlesbrough (1) 2 *(Whelan 3, Cunningham 81 (og))*
Wimbledon (0) 0   9687
Middlesbrough: Crossley; Stockdale, Queudrue, Southgate, Festa, Mustoe, Stamp (Johnston), Marinelli (Greening), Nemeth (Windass), Whelan, Ince.
Wimbledon: Feuer; Holloway, Hawkins, Andersen, Cunningham, Francis, Ardley, Hughes, Shipperley (Agyemang), Connolly, Cooper (McAnuff).

York C (1) 1 *(Neilson 17 (og))*
Grimsby T (0) 0   6638
York C: Fettis; Edmondson, Potter, Hocking, Basham, Hobson, Richardson, Bullock, Nogan, Proctor, Cooper.
Grimsby T: Coyne; Neilson, Chapman (Boulding), Ford, Groves, Gallimore, Butterfield, Burnett, Thompson (Raven), Jevons, Campbell (Smith D).

16 JAN

Blackburn R (2) 3 *(Grabbi 30, Dunn 45 (pen), Johansson 49)*
Barnsley (0) 1 *(Dyer 65)*   10,203
Blackburn R: Kelly; Curtis, Neill, Dunn, Taylor, Johansson, Gillespie (Hignett), Mahon, Grabbi, Hughes, Johnson (Tugay).
Barnsley: Miller; Mulligan, Barker, Morgan, Chettle, Ward (Sand), Donovan (Christie), Neil, Sheron (Jones L), Dyer, Barnard.

Chelsea (1) 4 *(Stanic 11, Lampard 56, Zola 63, Forssell 89)*
Norwich C (0) 0   24,231
Chelsea: Cudicini; Melchiot, Le Saux, Stanic, Gallas (Zenden), Desailly, Lampard, Dalla Bona, Gudjohnsen (Forssell), Zola, Morris (Jokanovic).
Norwich C: Green; Kenton, Sutch, Mackay, Fleming, Holt, Nedergaard, Russell, Notman (Rivers), Libbra (Easton), McVeigh (Llewellyn).

21 JAN

Peterborough U (0) 2 *(McKenzie 52, Clarke A 90)*
Darlington (0) 0   10,892
Peterborough U: Tyler; Joseph, Williams, Forsyth, Rea, Edwards, Bullard, McKenzie, Clarke A, Fenn, Farrell.
Darlington: Collett; Betts, Heckingbottom, Liddle (Campbell), Brightwell (Pearson), Kilty (Wainwright), Atkinson, Ford, Mellanby, Maddison, Clark.

FOURTH ROUND

26 JAN

Charlton Ath (0) 1 *(Stuart 69)*
Walsall (1) 2 *(Leitao 5, 59)*   18,573
Charlton Ath: Kiely; Brown, Powell (Lisbie), Stuart, Costa (Kishishev), Fortune, Konchesky, Bart-Williams, Euell, Johansson (Svensson), Robinson.
Walsall: Walker; Brightwell, Aranalde, Bennett, Holdsworth, Carbon, Wrack, Andre (Keates), Leitao (Angell), Byfield (Herivelto), Matias.

Chelsea (1) 1 *(Hasselbaink 21)*
West Ham U (0) 1 *(Kanoute 83)*   33,443
Chelsea: Cudicini; Ferrer, Melchiot, Petit (Jokanovic), Terry, Desailly, Lampard, Forssell (Gudjohnsen), Hasselbaink (Dalla Bona), Zola, Le Saux.
West Ham U: James; Schemmel, Winterburn (Labant), Soma (Defoe), Repka, Dailly, Hutchison (Lomas), Cole, Kanoute, Di Canio, Carrick.

Everton (3) 4 *(McGhee 12 (og), Ferguson 32, Campbell 45, 80)*
Leyton Orient (1) 1 *(Canham 36)*   35,851
Everton: Simonsen; Hibbert, Unsworth, Stubbs, Weir, Gemmill, Alexandersson (Moore), Gascoigne, Campbell, Ferguson, Naysmith (Tal).
Leyton Orient: Barrett; Joseph, Lockwood (Jones), Smith, McGhee, Partridge (Martin), Harris, Gray, Watts (McLean), Canham, Minton.

Middlesbrough (0) 2 *(Whelan 85, Campbell 89)*
Manchester U (0) 0   17,624
Middlesbrough: Crossley; Stockdale, Queudrue, Southgate, Cooper, Mustoe, Greening, Marinelli (Wilson) (Campbell), Whelan, Windass, Johnston (Gavin).
Manchester U: Barthez; Neville P, Silvestre, Neville G, Keane, Blanc, Wallwork (Giggs), Butt, Solskjaer (Yorke), Scholes, Chadwick (Van Nistelrooy).

Millwall (0) 0
Blackburn R (0) 1 *(Cole 87)*   15,004
Millwall: Gueret; Lawrence, Ryan, Ward, Nethercott, Dyche, Ifill (Braniff), Livermore, Harris, Cahill, Reid.
Blackburn R: Friedel; Neill, Bjornebye (Duff), Tugay, Taylor, Johansson, Johnson, Flitcroft, Cole, Jansen (Grabbi), Mahon.

Preston NE (0) 2 *(Cresswell 53, Alexander 71 (pen))*
Sheffield U (1) 1 *(Ndlovu 14)*   13,068
Preston NE: Moilanen; Alexander, Edwards, Murdock (Cartwright), Lucketti, Skora (Macken), Gregan, Keane, Basham (Cresswell), Healy, Anderson.
Sheffield U: De Vogt; Uhlenbeek, Ullathorne, Ford (Santos), Page, Sandford, Tonge, Brown, Asaba (Montgomery), D'Jaffo, Ndlovu.

Rotherham U (2) 2 *(Mullin 3, Warne 37)*
Crewe Alex (1) 4 *(Thomas 32, Ashton 60, 65, Vaughan 78)*   8477
Rotherham U: Pollitt; Scott, Hurst, Sedgwick (Lee), Swailes, McIntosh, Talbot, Watson (Monkhouse), Barker, Warne, Mullin.
Crewe Alex: Bankole; Wright, Charnock, Foster, Sodje, Brammer, Vaughan (Rix), Lunt, Jack, Ashton, Thomas.

WBA (0) 1 *(Clement 80 (pen))*
Leicester C (0) 0   26,820
WBA: Hoult; Balis (Lyttle), Clement, Sigurdsson, Moore, Gilchrist, McInnes, Johnson, Dichio (Dobie), Roberts, Chambers A (Fox).
Leicester C: Walker; Marshall, Rogers (Davidson), Elliott, Stewart, Jones (Piper), Impey, Izzet, Akinbiyi, Benjamin, Oakes.

York C (0) 0
Fulham (1) 2 *(Malbranque 26, Marlet 85)*   7563
York C: Fettis; Edmondson, Potter, Hocking, Basham, Hobson (Duffield), Brass, Bullock, Nogan (Mathie), Proctor, Cooper.
Fulham: Van der Sar; Finnan, Brevett, Melville, Goma, Knight, Legwinski, Collins (Goldbaek), Saha, Marlet, Malbranque.

27 JAN

Arsenal (1) 1 *(Bergkamp 28)*
Liverpool (0) 0   38,092
Arsenal: Wright; Luzhny, Cole, Vieira, Campbell, Keown, Van Bronckhorst (Grimandi), Wiltord (Upson), Henry, Bergkamp, Pires (Parlour).
Liverpool: Dudek; Wright (Murphy), Carragher, Hamann, Henchoz, Hyypia, Gerrard, Anelka (Litmanen), Heskey, Owen, Riise.

Cheltenham T (2) 2 *(Milton 23, Alsop 28)*
Burnley (1) 1 *(Moore A 29)*   7300
Cheltenham T: Book; Griffin, Victory, Williams, Banks, Duff, Howells, Milton, Alsop, Naylor (Grayson), Yates.
Burnley: Michopoulos (Cennamo); West, Briscoe,Grant, Cox, Gnohere, Little (Branch), Ball, Moore I (Maylet), Taylor, Moore A.

Ipswich T (0) 1 *(Bent M 83)*
Manchester C (1) 4 *(Berkovic 43, Goater 65, 86, Huckerby 90)*   21,199
Ipswich T: Marshall; Wilnis (Armstrong), Hreidarsson (Le Pen), Bramble, McGreal, Reuser (Clapham), Peralta, Holland, Stewart, Bent M, Wright.
Manchester C: Weaver; Wright-Phillips, Jensen, Wiekens, Dunne, Pearce, Benarbia, Berkovic, Huckerby, Goater, Horlock.

Peterborough U (0) 2 *(O'Brien 52 (og), Farrell 69)*
Newcastle U (2) 4 *(O'Brien 14, McClen 43, Shearer 84 (pen), Hughes 85)*   13,841
Peterborough U: Tyler; Joseph, Williams, Forsyth (Oldfield), Rea (Hooper), Edwards, Bullard, McKenzie, Clarke A, Fenn (Forinton), Farrell.
Newcastle U: Given; Hughes, Elliott, Distin, O'Brien, Solano, McClen (Kerr), Acuna, Shearer, Bellamy, Bernard (Quinn).

Tranmere R (1) 3 *(Rideout 23, Flynn 53, Koumas 79)*
Cardiff C (1) 1 *(Kavanagh 21 (pen))*   9442
Tranmere R: Achterberg; Yates, Roberts, Henry, Sharps, Hill, Flynn, Mellon, Rideout, Price, Koumas.
Cardiff C: Alexander; Hamilton (Bowen), Legg, Weston, Young, Gabbidon, Bonner, Kavanagh, Brayson (Collins), Fortune-West, Boland (Low).

5 FEB

Gillingham (1) 1 *(Jones 32 (og))*
Bristol R (0) 0   9772
Gillingham: Bartram; Patterson, Perpetuini, Hope, Ashby, Browning (Nosworthy), Smith, Shaw (Osborn), Onuora (Ipoua), King, Gooden.
Bristol R: Howie; Smith, Challis (Walters), Mauge, Jones, Wilson, Astafjevs, Hogg (McKeever), Ellington, Ommel, Lopez R.

Tottenham H (2) 4 *(Anderton 22 (pen), Iversen 35, Etherington 56, Barness 73 (og))*
Bolton W (0) 0   27,093
Tottenham H: Sullivan; Thatcher, Taricco (Leonhardsen), Sherwood, King, Richards, Anderton (Thelwell), Poyet, Rebrov, Iversen, Etherington.
Bolton W: Jaaskelainen; Southall, Gardner, Barness, Bergsson, Whitlow (Buchanan), Nolan (Johnson), Hansen, Pedersen (Holdsworth), Ricketts, Farrelly.

FOURTH ROUND REPLAY

6 FEB

West Ham U (1) 2 *(Defoe 38, 50)*
Chelsea (1) 3 *(Hasselbaink 43, Forssell 65, Terry 90)*
                                                           27,272
West Ham U: James; Schemmel, Winterburn, Hutchison (Labant), Repka, Dailly, Sinclair, Cole, Kitson (Todorov), Defoe, Lomas.
Chelsea: Cudicini; Ferrer, Le Saux, Petit, Terry, Desailly, Stanic, Lampard, Hasselbaink, Gudjohnsen (Forssell), Dalla Bona (Zola).

FIFTH ROUND

16 FEB

Arsenal (1) 5 *(Wiltord 38, 81, Kanu 50, Adams 67, Parlour 88)*
Gillingham (0) 2 *(King 47, Gooden 54)*   38,003
Arsenal: Wright; Dixon, Juan, Vieira, Campbell, Adams, Wiltord, Edu (Henry), Kanu (Grimandi), Jeffers (Pires), Parlour.
Gillingham: Bartram; Patterson, Perpetuini, Hope, Ashby, Osborn (Hessenthaler), Smith, Shaw, Onuora (Ipoua), King, Gooden (Browning).

Middlesbrough (0) 1 *(Ehiogu 87)*
Blackburn R (0) 0   20,921
Middlesbrough: Schwarzer; Stockdale, Queudrue, Southgate, Ehiogu, Mustoe, Wilson (Nemeth), Marinelli (Murphy), Whelan, Windass (Boksic), Ince.
Blackburn R: Friedel; Neill, Taylor, Short, Berg (Douglas), Johansson, Gillespie (Hughes), Hignett, Cole, Tugay, Duff (Jansen).

WBA (0) 1 *(Dichio 64)*
Cheltenham T (0) 0   27,179
WBA: Hoult; Balis, Clement, Sigurdsson, Moore (Butler), Gilchrist, McInnes, Johnson, Dichio, Roberts, Chambers A (Dobie).
Cheltenham T: Book; Griffin, Victory, Williams (Devaney), Banks, Duff, Howells, Milton (Brough), Alsop, Naylor (Grayson), Yates.

Walsall (0) 1 *(Byfield 49)*
Fulham (1) 2 *(Bennett 43 (og), Hayles 61)*   8766
Walsall: Walker; Bennett (Corica), Aranalde, Keates, Holdsworth, Carbon (Roper), Wrack, Biancalani, Leitao, Heriveito (Byfield), Matias.
Fulham: Van der Sar; Finnan, Brevett, Ouaddou (Melville), Goma, Davis, Legwinski, Collins (Harley), Marlet (Saha), Hayles, Malbranque.

17 FEB

Chelsea (2) 3 *(Gudjohnsen 16, Hasselbaink 26, Forssell 90)*
Preston NE (1) 1 *(Cresswell 9)*   28,133
Chelsea: Cudicini; Babayaro, Le Saux, Lampard, Desailly (Morris), Petit, Stanic, Gudjohnsen (Forssell), Hasselbaink, Zola (Keenan), Dalla Bona.
Preston NE: Moilanen; Alexander, Edwards, Keane, Lucketti, Gregan, Cartwright (Gudjonsson), McKenna, Macken, Cresswell, Anderson (Healy).

Everton (0) 0
Crewe Alex (0) 0   29,399
Everton: Simonsen; Clarke, Naysmith, Stubbs, Weir, Linderoth (Pembridge), Alexandersson (Gascoigne), Gemmill, Campbell, Ginola, Blomqvist (Moore).
Crewe Alex: Ince; Wright, Smith, Walton, Sodje, Brammer, Vaughan (Rix), Lunt, Hulse (Foster), Ashton (Jack), Sorvel.

Newcastle U (0) 1 *(Solano 59)*
Manchester C (0) 0   51,020
Newcastle U: Given; Hughes, Elliott, Distin, O'Brien, Solano, McClen (Acuna), Speed, Shearer, Bellamy, Robert (Lua-Lua).
Manchester C: Weaver; Wright-Phillips, Jensen, Dunne, Howey, Ritchie, Horlock, Berkovic, Huckerby (Edghill), Wanchope, Tiatto (Negouai).

Tottenham H (2) 4 *(Ziege 9, Poyet 36, 90, Sheringham 64)*
Tranmere R (0) 0   35,696
Tottenham H: Sullivan; Taricco, Ziege (Etherington), Thatcher, Perry, Richards, Poyet, Sherwood, Ferdinand (Iversen), Sheringham, Davies.
Tranmere R: Achterberg; Sharps, Roberts, Henry (Mellon), Allen, Hill, Navarro, Parkinson, Rideout (Barlow), Price, Koumas.

FIFTH ROUND REPLAY

26 FEB

Crewe Alex (1) 1 *(Ashton 24)*
Everton (1) 2 *(Radzinski 45, Campbell 70)*   10,073
Crewe Alex: Ince; Wright, Smith, Walton, Sodje, Brammer (Sorvel), Collins (Rix), Lunt, Hulse, Ashton, Vaughan (Jack).
Everton: Simonsen; Clarke, Naysmith (Unsworth), Stubbs, Weir, Pembridge, Alexandersson, Gemmill, Campbell (Linderoth), Radzinski, Ginola (Gravesen).

SIXTH ROUND

9 MAR

Newcastle U (0) 1 *(Robert 52)*
Arsenal (1) 1 *(Edu 14)*   51,027
Newcastle U: Given; Hughes, Distin, Dabizas, O'Brien, Solano, McClen, Acuna, Shearer, Cort (Ameobi), Robert.
Arsenal: Wright; Dixon, Lauren, Vieira, Campbell, Stepanovs, Edu (Bergkamp), Grimandi, Kanu, Wiltord, Ljungberg (Pires).

10 MAR

Middlesbrough (3) 3 *(Whelan 35, Nemeth 37, Ince 42)*
Everton (0) 0   26,950
Middlesbrough: Schwarzer; Stockdale, Queudrue, Southgate, Festa, Mustoe, Greening, Nemeth (Marinelli), Boksic (Debeve), Whelan (Windass), Ince.
Everton: Simonsen; Pistone, Unsworth, Stubbs, Weir, Clarke, Linderoth (Alexandersson), Gascoigne, Moore (Chadwick), Radzinski, Gemmill (Blomqvist).

Ray Parlour comes out on top over former colleague Emmanuel Petit during the FA Cup Final at the Millennium Stadium, Cardiff. A brilliant second half strike from Parlour set Arsenal on their way to a comfortable 2-0 victory over London rivals Chelsea. (Colorsport)

Tottenham H (0) 0
Chelsea (1) 4 *(Gallas 12, Gudjohnsen 48, 66, Le Saux 54)*
32,896
Tottenham H: Sullivan; Davies, Ziege, Gardner, King, Richards (Rebrov), Anderton (Taricco), Sherwood, Ferdinand, Sheringham, Poyet.
Chelsea: Cudicini; Melchiot, Babayaro, Petit, Gallas, Desailly, Gronkjaer (Dalla Bona), Lampard, Hasselbaink (Forssell), Gudjohnsen (Jokanovic), Le Saux.

WBA (0) 0
Fulham (0) 1 *(Marlet 47)* 24,811
WBA: Hoult; Balis, Clement, Sigurdsson, Moore, Gilchrist, McInnes, Johnson, Dichio, Dobie (Fox), Chambers A (Taylor).
Fulham: Van der Sar; Finnan, Brevett, Melville, Goma, Malbranque (Hayles), Legwinski, Collins, Saha (Goldbaek), Marlet, Boa Morte (Ouaddou).

SIXTH ROUND REPLAY

23 MAR

Arsenal (2) 3 *(Pires 2, Bergkamp 9, Campbell 50)*
Newcastle U (0) 0 38,073
Arsenal: Wright; Luzhny, Cole, Vieira, Campbell, Adams, Ljungberg, Edu (Jeffers), Wiltord (Dixon), Bergkamp, Pires (Grimandi).
Newcastle U: Given; Hughes, Distin (Elliott), Dabizas, O'Brien, Solano, Dyer, Acuna (Kerr), Shearer, Cort (Lua-Lua), Robert.

SEMI-FINALS

14 APR

Fulham (0) 0
Chelsea (1) 1 *(Terry 42)* 36,147
Fulham: Van der Sar; Finnan, Brevett, Melville, Goma, Davis, Legwinski (Hayles), Collins (Boa Morte), Saha, Marlet, Malbranque.
Chelsea: Cudicini; Melchiot, Le Saux (Ferrer), Petit, Terry, Desailly, Gronkjaer, Lampard, Hasselbaink (Jokanovic), Gudjohnsen, Stanic (Zenden).

Middlesbrough (0) 0
Arsenal (1) 1 *(Festa 39 (og))* 61,168
Middlesbrough: Schwarzer; Stockdale, Queudrue, Southgate, Ehiogu (Festa), Mustoe, Wilkshire (Stamp), Debeve, Boksic, Windass, Johnston (Marinelli).
Arsenal: Wright; Lauren, Luzhny (Dixon), Vieira, Campbell (Parlour), Keown, Wiltord, Edu, Henry, Bergkamp (Kanu), Ljungberg.

FINAL (at Millennium Stadium)

4 MAY

Arsenal (0) 2 *(Parlour 70, Ljungberg 80)*
Chelsea (0) 0 73,963
Arsenal: Seaman; Lauren, Cole, Vieira, Campbell, Adams, Wiltord (Keown), Parlour, Henry (Kanu), Bergkamp (Edu), Ljungberg.
Chelsea: Cudicini; Melchiot (Zenden), Babayaro (Terry), Petit, Gallas, Desailly, Gronkjaer, Lampard, Hasselbaink (Zola), Gudjohnsen, Le Saux.
Referee: M. Riley (Leeds).

THE SCOTTISH SEASON 2001–02

This has been a season of change.

After a valiant but unsuccessful attempt to lead Scotland into the World Cup Finals, Craig Brown decided to call it a day. He has done extremely well with very little, and has made the most of the limited talent available. It has not helped that some players who might well have made telling contributions in the international side were not given games in their club teams. Some players had little option but to descend into England; others bore it without much of a grin. The mantle is now being held by the German Berti Vogts.

The Bell's League Challenge Cup comes early in the season, and gets it off to a good start. There were many close encounters. Brechin City swept all ahead of them, finally losing on penalties in the semi-final to the ultimate winners; Alloa again reached the final, and matched their opponents blow for blow till the last quarter of an hour, when the division of three goals went against them. So it was Airdrieonians who again triumphed – it was good for their fans to have something to cheer about in what was to prove this historic club's swansong.

The CIS Cup holds its own in a competitive world, and not much was heard this year about its being a waste of time for the top clubs. In fact, here were some intriguing results: the first round went pretty well by the book, though East Fife did win against Arbroath; later on Motherwell lost to Airdrie, and Hearts to Ross County, and Livingston demolished Aberdeen at Pittodrie – an interesting one in view of their later proximity in the league. A cracking semi-final saw Rangers into the final at the expense of Celtic, and Ayr United defeated Hibernian in a rather lack-lustre game the following night. Rangers won a comfortable final.

The Tennent's Scottish Cup is always likely to turn up giant-killers. A one-off game can somehow make for a more level pitch. The cream, they say, always comes to the top: there are some teams which, perhaps without too much cream, always seem to manage to make progress. When it comes to cup games, there are few teams to equal Ayr United. Gordon Dalziel, their shrewd manager, is a master of tactics, and it took the combined efforts of the Old Firm to oust his teams from the Scottish and CIS Cups, the one in a semi-final and the other in the final. Hearts had trouble with the northern fringes, whilst Hibs, at the other end of the country, took two games to dislodge Stranraer from the Scottish Cup. Partick Thistle and Inverness took each other on frequently in cup matches, with the honours perhaps just shading to the former; Berwick Rangers entertained the mighty Rangers in the Scottish Cup, and there were memories of a former such encounter. Rangers were, indeed, held to a draw, and the Wee Rangers thus earned a replay visit to Ibrox. The Highland League clubs made their presence felt: Deveronvale, in the third round, could not hold Ayr United, but Forres Mechanics put the wind up Dundee United before finally succumbing.

The final of the Scottish Cup at Hampden was one of the better finals. Who but the Old Firm could have graced this occasion? It was a game to remember. There was not much in it, but Rangers deserved their win.

The Cup Final should have ended the season on a high note; but there was a touch of anti-climax in the full round of Premier games the following week-end when nothing much remained to be settled. It was a pity that it was so, but the fixture list is no easy one to compile, and the final a week later would have been far too close to that other great game at Hampden this year, the final of the European Cup. This was a high profile game which came fully up to expectation. Not only was it a spectacle *per se*, but the whole event passed off as a great occasion, and UEFA were delighted with their hosts.

In Europe hopes were raised of a Scottish club reaching the later stages: it was not to be, although Celtic had some notable results over good opposition.

The Premier League was rather remarkably uninteresting. For all the talk, it was quite apparent that Celtic were virtually uncatchable even before the end of December. It is easy enough to say this in retrospect, but many of the experts (and the bookmakers, of course) required little retrospect to state the obvious. Rangers fiddled about at times and had some poor results; this made it all the easier for their rivals. It was not until the appointment of Alex McLeish that the story began to look different, and by then it was too late in the League. Martin O'Neill is again to be highly commended for continuing to lead a dominating team. The shock of the year came from Livingston: confidently recommended in most publications as certain to return to the First Division at the end of the season, they surprised all, including – I suspect – themselves. This, of course, does not apply to their ebullient manager, Jim Leishman, who takes enthusiasm to the point of disbelief! Livingston did produce some excellent performances. For the first time in some years, Aberdeen, too, did well. Ebbe Skovdahl, their manager, knows what he wants, and is not to be hurried; his team made a real challenge for third place. There was some interest when the split into two groups was imminent, but later games in the lower half did not attract many fans. St Johnstone were already doomed. Bobby Williamson started to gather some better results for Hibernian, whilst Jim Jefferies at Kilmarnock, after just failing to remain in the top half, finished on a strong note.

The First Division was far more interesting. For a long while Airdrie held the lead. However, their off-stage troubles cannot have helped the team, and gradually they were overtaken by the efficient Partick Thistle. Once the latter reached the top, they stayed there to some purpose. With a fine ground, a large band of dedicated fans, and sound management and back-room teams, they are now all set to take their place in the top group. Ayr United were third, never quite challenging for top place,

and Ross County, who had been in the depths at the end of the year, soon caught up when the weather relented in their highland fastnesses and they could play some of their postponed games. Arbroath had a sound campaign, and finished comfortably clear of trouble. In the end, Falkirk and Raith Rovers occupied the two relegation spots, but the former were relieved of the descent by the demise of Airdrieonians. It is sad to see the passing of this fine and ancient club after a hundred and twenty years or so. They could not weather the financial storm. Various other clubs must have been shaken by the finality, for they too are in precarious positions. Now the latest news is that a new Airdrie team is to take the place of Clydebank in the League. Clydebank, who have never been comfortable since they lost their ground, are to lose their identity; it will be a great disappointment to many in that area.

Queen of the South won the Second Division, in the end by a comfortable margin. They had had to work for it, but in the last phase went ahead confidently. Clydebank did well in the early stages, but faltered, and finished fourth. Alloa Athletic held their nerve, and took the second place; leaving the wholehearted Forfar Athletic to rue one or two seemingly needless defeats. However, they did have memories of a home cup tie against Rangers. Stenhousemuir and Morton brought up the rear, and Morton go down; Stenhousemuir take advantage of the goings on above, and remain in this division.

The Third Division was dominated by Brechin City. They started the season with a bang, both in the League and in the cups, and never looked like failing. There was the odd careless result, but in general they knew what they were required to do, and did it. The rest were left trailing, but some trailed more than others. Queen's Park looked to be better than their results suggested, but it was not a good season for them; nor for Stirling Albion. Elgin City looked a good deal more settled, and Peterhead for a long while were in the running for promotion. A poor spell left them with too much to do. East Fife and East Stirlingshire had mixed results, with occasional high spots, and Montrose, after a sound start, fell away. In the end, the race for the second promotion place was between Dumbarton and Albion Rovers. Dumbarton, in their attractive new home, succeeded when it mattered.

Management changes continue at frequent intervals, and there are not many who stay for long at one club. A manager's job does not hold much hope of security. Success has to be continuous, but a few adverse results can soon lead to the call for a change. To make ends meet, clubs must sell, and any good player is soon snapped up – often by a bigger club, where he may not even get many games. Financial issues loom large, and the result of trying to keep up with the rest, both in ground improvements and escalating wages, often lands a club in tricky circumstances. All this emphasis on money has led to Scottish football being the loser. The authorities in the Leagues have a difficult time, too, and at times they have to face last-minute changes when a club cannot honour its fixture commitments.

It all sounds rather gloomy, but there are plenty of signs which are encouraging. The Tartan Army, for example, was welcomed wherever it went, and congratulations to Hugh Dallas for representing us at the World Cup finals. There are young players coming through now in many teams, and training schemes and academies can provide the material for a revival. We are not downhearted.

ALAN ELLIOTT

AIRDRIE UNITED Second Division

Year Formed: 2002. *Ground & Address:* Shyberry Excelsior Stadium, Broomfield Park, Craigneuk Avenue, Airdrie ML6 8QZ.
Ground Capacity: all seated: 10,000. *Size of Pitch:* 112yd × 76yd.
Chairman: James Ballantyne.
Manager: Sandy Stewart.
Airdrie United replace Clydebank.

GRETNA Third Division

Year Formed: 1946. *Ground & Address:* Raydale Park, Dominion Rd, Gretna DG16 5AP. *Telephone:* 01461 337602.
Ground Capacity: 2200.
Club Shop: Alan Watson, 01387 251550.
President: Thomas Kerr.
Chairman: Brian Fulton.
Secretary: Ron MacGregor.
Manager: Rowan Alexander.
Assistant Manager: Derek Frye.
Physio: William Bentley.
Record Attendance: 2307 v Rochdale, FA Cup: 16 Nov 1991.
Record Victory: 20-0 v Silloth, 9 Feb 1923.
Record Defeat: 0-6 v Worksop Town, 1994–95 and 0-6 v Bradford (Park Avenue) 1999–2000.

ABERDEEN   Premier League

Year Formed: 1903. *Ground & Address:* Pittodrie Stadium, Pittodrie St, Aberdeen AB24 5QH. *Telephone:* 01224 650400. *Fax:* 01224 644173.
Ground Capacity: all seated: 22,199. *Size of Pitch:* 110yd × 72yd.
Chairman: Stewart Milne. *Chief Executive:* Keith Wyness. *Secretary:* Roy Johnston. *Operations Manager:* John Morgan.
Manager: Ebbe Skovdahl. *Assistant Manager:* Gardner Speirs. *Physios:* David Wylie, John Sharp.
Managers since 1975: Ally MacLeod, Billy McNeill, Alex Ferguson, Ian Porterfield, Alex Smith and Jocky Scott, Willie Miller, Roy Aitken, Alex Miller, Paul Hegarty. *Club Nicknames(s):* The Dons. *Previous Grounds:* None.
Record Attendance: 45,061 v Hearts, Scottish Cup 4th rd; 13 Mar, 1954.
Record Transfer Fee received: £1.75 million for Eoin Jess to Coventry City (February 1996).
Record Transfer Fee paid: £1m+ for Paul Bernard from Oldham Athletic (September 1995).
Record Victory: 13-0 v Peterhead, Scottish Cup; 9 Feb, 1923.
Record Defeat: 0-8 v Celtic, Division 1; 30 Jan, 1965.
Most Capped Players: Alex McLeish, 77, Scotland.
Most League Appearances: 556: Willie Miller, 1973-90.
Most League Goals in Season (Individual): 38: Benny Yorston, Division I; 1929-30.
Most Goals Overall (Individual): 199: Joe Harper.

ABERDEEN 2001–02 LEAGUE RECORD

Match No.	Date	Venue	Opponents	Result	H/T Score	Lg. Pos.	Goalscorers	Attendance
1	Jul 28	H	Rangers	L	0-3	0-0	—	17,757
2	Aug 4	A	Hearts	L	0-1	0-1	11		12,696
3	11	A	Hibernian	L	0-2	0-2	11		13,150
4	18	H	Motherwell	W	4-2	2-2	10	Thornley [19], Winters [33], Mackie [54], Zerouali [74]	10,988
5	25	A	St Johnstone	D	1-1	1-0	10	McGuire [21]	5459
6	Sept 8	H	Kilmarnock	W	2-0	0-0	9	Thornley 2 [53, 66]	10,832
7	15	H	Dundee U	W	2-1	0-0	7	Winters (pen) [51], Zerouali [67]	12,946
8	22	A	Celtic	L	0-2	0-0	8		59,386
9	29	A	Dundee	W	4-1	1-1	6	Zerouali 3 [25, 49, 69], Mackie [80]	8359
10	Oct 13	A	Livingston	D	2-2	0-1	5	Mackie 2 [60, 70]	5894
11	20	H	Dunfermline Ath	W	3-2	3-0	5	Winters 2 (1 pen) [20, 40 lp], Solberg [22]	11,516
12	27	H	Hearts	W	3-2	2-1	4	Dadi [17], Winters (pen) [32], Young Dk [67]	13,935
13	Nov 4	A	Rangers	L	0-2	0-2	4		49,739
14	10	H	Motherwell	W	1-0	1-0	4	Dadi [6]	11,497
15	17	H	Hibernian	W	2-0	0-0	4	Winters [88], Zerouali [89]	12,504
16	24	A	Motherwell	L	2-3	1-2	4	Winters [39], Zerouali [79]	7302
17	Dec 1	H	St Johnstone	W	1-0	1-0	4	Winters [23]	17,369
18	8	A	Kilmarnock	L	1-3	0-1	4	Zerouali [59]	7611
19	15	A	Dundee U	D	1-1	0-1	4	Winters (pen) [56]	9129
20	22	H	Celtic	W	2-0	0-0	4	Winters (pen) [59], Mackie [90]	18,610
21	29	A	Dunfermline Ath	L	0-1	0-1	4		7774
22	Jan 2	H	Livingston	L	0-3	0-1	—		15,709
23	12	A	Hearts	L	1-3	1-1	5	Bisconti [45]	12,902
24	19	H	Rangers	L	0-1	0-1	5		17,846
25	23	A	Hibernian	W	4-3	2-2	—	Dadi [9], Winters [27], Guntweit [47], Mackie [88]	10,555
26	29	H	Dundee	D	0-0	0-0	—		11,027
27	Feb 2	A	St Johnstone	W	1-0	1-0	4	Dadi [44]	4305
28	9	H	Kilmarnock	D	1-1	0-0	4	McGuire [55]	13,004
29	16	H	Dundee U	W	4-0	2-0	4	Winters [2], Young Dk 2 [7, 48], Mike [81]	13,612
30	Mar 2	A	Celtic	L	0-1	0-1	4		59,584
31	9	A	Dundee	W	3-2	0-2	4	Young Dn [55], Anderson [73], Mackie [76]	8906
32	16	H	Dunfermline Ath	W	1-0	1-0	3	Mike [6]	13,764
33	23	A	Livingston	D	0-0	0-0	3		8603
34	Apr 6	A	Dunfermline Ath	D	0-0	0-0	3		7339
35	13	H	Hearts	L	2-3	1-1	3	Rutkiewicz [7], Winters [78]	12,467
36	20	H	Livingston	W	3-0	3-0	3	Mike [7], McGuire [10], Mackie [38]	14,109
37	27	A	Rangers	L	0-2	0-1	3		48,878
38	May 12	H	Celtic	L	0-1	0-0	4		15,332

Final League Position: 4

Honours
League Champions: Division I 1954-55. Premier Division 1979-80, 1983-84, 1984-85; *Runners-up:* Division I 1910-11, 1936-37, 1955-56, 1970-71, 1971-72. Premier Division 1977-78, 1980-81, 1981-82, 1988-89, 1989-90, 1990-91, 1992-93, 1993-94.
Scottish Cup Winners: 1947, 1970, 1982, 1983, 1984, 1986, 1990; *Runners-up:* 1937, 1953, 1954, 1959, 1967, 1978, 1993, 2000.
League Cup Winners: 1955-56, 1976-77, 1985-86, 1989-90, (Coca Cola cup) 1995-96; *Runners-up:* 1946-47, 1978-79, 1979-80, 1987-88, 1988-89, 1992-93, 1999-2000.
Drybrough Cup Winners: 1971, 1980.

European: *European Cup:* 12 matches (1980-81, 1984-85, 1985-86); *Cup Winners' Cup:* 39 matches (1967-68, 1970-71, 1978-79, 1982-83 winners, 1983-84 semi-finals, 1986-87, 1990-91, 1993-94); *UEFA Cup:* 44 matches (*Fairs Cup:* 1968-69. *UEFA Cup:* 1971-72, 1972-73, 1973-74, 1977-78, 1979-80, 1981-82, 1987-88, 1988-89, 1989-90, 1991-92, 1994-95, 1996-97, 2000-01).

Club colours: Shirt, Shorts, Stockings: Red with white trim.

Goalscorers: *League* (51): Winters 13 (5 pens), Mackie 8, Zerouali 8, Dadi 4, McGuire 3, Mike 3, Thornley 3, Derek Young 3, Anderson 1, Bisconti 1, Guntweit 1, Rutkiewicz 1, Solberg 1, Darren Young 1.
Scottish Cup (4): McAllister 1, Thornley 1, Winters 1, Darren Young 1.
CIS Cup (3): Dadi 1, Mackie 1, Thornley 1.

Preece D 7+1	McGuire P 38	McNaughton K 33+1	Whyte D 30+1	Solberg T 10+5	Young D n 32	Bisconti R 31	Guntweit C 16+2	Winters R 34	Young Dk 23+9	Mackie D 28+7	Rutkiewicz K 1+3	Belabed R —+1	Clark C 1+7	McAllister J 26+3	Thornley B 15+9	Tiernan F 11+12	Bett C 1+2	Zerouali H 6+12	Dadi E 20+8	Esson R 7+2	Anderson R 17+7	Kjaer R 23	Mike L 7+2	O'Donoghue R —+1	Peat M 1	Match No.
1	2	3	4	5	6	7²	8	9²	10	11¹	12	13	14													1
1	2	5	4		6	7	8²		10¹	9¹	14			3	11	12	13									2
1	2	3	4	5¹	6	7		9	10					12	11		8²	13								3
1	2	5	4		6	7	8	9²		10				3	11¹	13	12									4
1	2	5	4		6	7	8		10²	9¹				3	11		12	13								5
1	2	5²	4	13	6	7	14	9	10					3³	11		12	8¹								6
1	2	5	4	14	6	7		9	10¹	13				3³	11		12	8²								7
	2	5	4	6²	7			9		11				3¹	13	8	10	1	12							8
	2	3	4	5	6	7		9¹	12	8³				11	14	10²	13	1								9
	2	13	4	5	6	7		9¹		11				3³	12	8²	10	1	14							10
	2	3	4	5	6	7		9	12	10				11²	8¹	1	13									11
	2	3	4	5	6			9	12	10¹				11	7³	13	8²	14	1							12
	2	5	4	6¹	7			9²	13	10			14	3	8	11²	12	1								13
	2	3	4		6			9	10	11				7	12	8¹	5	1								14
	2	3	4		6	7²		9	13	10				11²	14	12	8¹	5	1							15
	2	3	4			7	12	9²	10	11				6	14	8¹	15	5	1ᵘ							16
	2	3	4		7³	8¹		9	13	6			14	11²	12	10		5	1							17
	2	3³	4		6	7	8	9²	10¹				13	14	11	12	5	1								18
	2	3	4		6	7³		9	13	10				11²	14	12	8¹	5	1							19
	2		4		6	7	8	9	10¹	12				3		11	5	1								20
	2			4	6	7	8	9	13	10¹				3	12	11¹	5	1								21
	2		4		6	7	8	9	14	13				3	11²	10³	15	5	1ᵘ							22
	2	3	4		6	7	8	9		10²				5	13	11¹	1	12								23
2²	3	4		6		7		9	10	11³			14	5	12	8¹	13	1								24
	2	3		4	6	7	8	9¹	10²	12				5	13	11	1									25
	2	3	4		6		8	9	10	12				5	7	11¹	1									26
	2	3	4		7	8		9	10¹	13				5	12	6	11²	1								27
	2	3	4	13		6	8	9	10	14				5²	7¹	12	11³	1								28
	2	3	4	14		6	7²	9	10	11³				5	13	8¹	1	12								29
	2	3	4		6	8		9		11				5	12	10¹	7	1								30
	2	3		6		9¹	11				8²	5	13	7	10¹			4	1	12	14					31
	2	3		6	7		9	10¹	11			12	5	13			4	1	8²							32
	2	3	4		6	7		9	10	11				12	13		5	1	8²							33
15	2	3		6		9³	10	11				5	14	7	12		4	1ᵘ	8¹							34
	2	3		6	7		9	10	11	4			5	12	8¹	1								1		35
	2	3		6²	7		9	10	11³			14	5	12	13		4	1	8¹							36
2²	3	13		6	7		10	11			12	5	9³	14		1	4	8¹								37
	2		4		6	7³		10²	11	12			14	3¹	9	13		1	5	8						38

AIRDRIEONIANS   Withdrawn from League

Year Formed: 1878. *Ground & Address:* Shyberry Excelsior Stadium, Broomfield Park, Craigneuk Avenue, Airdrie
ML6 8QZ.
Ground Capacity: all seated: 10,000. *Size of Pitch:* 112yd × 76yd.
Manager: Ian McCall.
Managers since 1975: I. McMillan, J. Stewart, R. Watson, W. Munro, A. MacLeod, D. Whiteford, G. McQueen, J. Bone,
A. MacDonald, G. Mackay, I. McCall. *Club Nickname(s):* The Diamonds or The Waysiders. *Previous Grounds:*
Mavisbank, Broomfield Park.
Record Attendance: 26,000 v Hearts, Scottish Cup; 8 Mar, 1952 (at Broomfield Park). 8762 v Celtic, League Cup 3rd rd,
19 Aug 1998 (at Shyberry Excelsior Stadium).
Record Transfer Fee received: £200,000 for Sandy Clark to West Ham U (May 1982).
Record Transfer Fee paid: £175,000 for Owen Coyle from Clydebank (February 1990).
Record Victory: 15-1 v Dundee Wanderers, Division II; 1 Dec, 1894.
Record Defeat: 1-11 v Hibernian, Division I; 24 Oct, 1959.
Most Capped Player: Jimmy Crapnell, 9, Scotland.
Most League Appearances: 523: Paul Jonquin, 1962-79.
Most League Goals in Season (Individual): 53, Hugh Baird, Division II, 1954-55. *Most Goals Overall (Individual):* —

AIRDRIEONIANS 2001–02 LEAGUE RECORD

Match No.	Date	Venue	Opponents	Result	H/T Score	Lg. Pos.	Goalscorers	Attendance
1	Aug 4	H	Raith R	D 2-2	2-0	—	McPherson [30], Coyle [40]	1229
2	11	A	Arbroath	W 6-0	2-0	2	McPherson [10], Roberts [12], Coyle [54], Smith [62], Taylor [63], McDonald C [85]	926
3	18	H	Ayr U	W 2-1	1-1	1	Roberts 2 [30, 63]	2019
4	25	A	Ross Co	W 1-0	1-0	1	Coyle [4]	2022
5	Sept 8	A	St Mirren	D 0-0	0-0	9		2657
6	15	H	Falkirk	W 2-1	1-1	1	Macfarlane [43], Coyle [52]	2108
7	18	A	Clyde	W 3-0	3-0	—	Coyle 2 [12, 25], Roberts [20]	908
8	22	H	Inverness CT	W 6-0	5-0	1	Macfarlane [13], Coyle 3 (1 pen) [19, 26 ipi, 38], Gardner [34], Armstrong [86]	1197
9	29	A	Partick Th	D 1-1	0-1	1	Coyle [90]	5061
10	Oct 6	H	Raith R	D 2-2	2-1	1	James [29], Macfarlane [42]	2077
11	20	H	Arbroath	W 3-1	2-1	1	Taylor 2 [3, 55], Roberts [29]	1324
12	27	A	St Mirren	D 0-0	0-0	1		4121
13	Nov 3	A	Ross Co	D 1-1	0-1	1	Coyle [55]	1516
14	10	H	Clyde	L 1-2	0-0	2	Roberts [55]	1629
15	17	A	Falkirk	W 2-1	1-1	1	McPherson [26], Roberts [65]	2586
16	24	H	Partick Th	W 1-0	1-0	1	Coyle [18]	4132
17	Dec 1	A	Inverness CT	W 2-1	1-0	1	Smith [18], Coyle (pen) [59]	1591
18	8	H	Ayr U	W 3-1	0-0	1	Taylor [53], Roberts [56], Coyle [90]	2656
19	15	H	Raith R	D 1-1	0-1	1	Coyle [90]	1566
20	Jan 12	A	Clyde	W 1-0	1-0	2	Taylor [28]	1637
21	19	A	Inverness CT	W 3-0	0-0	2	Taylor 2 [49, 64], Coyle [89]	1506
22	22	H	St Mirren	L 2-3	2-1	—	Coyle [10], Roberts [34]	1803
23	Feb 2	A	Partick Th	D 1-1	1-0	2	McPherson [22]	6253
24	9	H	Ayr U	L 1-2	0-1	2	Coyle (pen) [59]	1771
25	16	A	Arbroath	L 1-2	1-1	2	Coyle [3]	885
26	Mar 2	H	Ross Co	L 0-2	0-0	2		1337
27	9	A	St Mirren	L 1-2	0-1	2	Coyle [59]	3040
28	12	H	Falkirk	W 1-0	0-0	—	Christie (og) [51]	1812
29	16	H	Clyde	D 2-2	1-1	2	Coyle [17], Roberts [58]	1551
30	23	A	Falkirk	D 2-2	1-0	2	Roberts [14], Taylor [72]	2601
31	26	A	Ross Co	L 1-4	1-1	—	Roberts [42]	2087
32	30	A	Inverness CT	L 0-1	0-0	2		1709
33	Apr 6	H	Partick Th	D 1-1	0-0	—	Coyle [60]	5746
34	13	A	Raith R	L 1-2	1-1	2	Coyle [12]	1138
35	20	H	Arbroath	W 2-0	2-0	2	Vareille 2 [6, 45]	1143
36	27	A	Ayr U	L 0-1	0-0	2		2793

Final League Position: 2

Honours
League Champions: Division II 1902-03, 1954-55, 1973-74; *Runners-up:* Division I 1922-23, 1923-24, 1924-25, 1925-26. First Division 1979-80, 1989-90, 1990-91, 1996-97, 2001-02. Division II 1900-01, 1946-47, 1949-50, 1965-66.
Scottish Cup Winners: 1924; *Runners-up:* 1975, 1992, 1995. *Scottish Spring Cup Winners:* 1976.
League Cup semi-finalists: 1991-92, 1994-95, 1998-99.
B&Q Cup Winners: 1994-95.
Bell's League Challenge Winners: 2000-01, 2001-02.

European: *Cup Winners' Cup:* 2 matches (1992-93).

Club colours: Shirt: White with red diamond. Shorts: White. Stockings: Red.

Goalscorers: *League* (59): Coyle 23 (3 pens), Roberts 12, Taylor 8, McPherson 4, Macfarlane 3, Smith 2, Vareille 2, Armstrong 1, Gardner 1, James 1, McDonald C 1, own goal 1.
Scottish Cup (0):
CIS Cup (5): Coyle 1, James 1, Macfarlane 1, Roberts 1, own goal 1.
Challenge Cup (11): Coyle 3, Roberts 3, McPherson 2, Taylor 2, James 1.

Bennett N 10 + 1	Armstrong P 30 + 2	McPherson C 29 + 3	Stewart A 25 + 3	McManus A 28	James K 34	Macfarlane N 28	Taylor S 24 + 8	Coyle O 36	Roberts M 34 + 2	Smith A 26 + 6	McAlpine J — + 1	Dunn R — + 14	Beasley D 4 + 6	Docherty S 11 + 8	McDonald C — + 4	Ferguson A 26	Gardner L 8 + 14	Macdonald S 4 + 6	Henry J 21 + 1	Reilly M 6	Ronald P — + 6	Vareille J 9 + 3	McCulloch S 3	Lawrence A — + 1	Match No.
1	2	3	4	5	6	7	8	9	10^2	11^1	12	13													1
1	2	3	4	5	6		8^2	12	9	11^3	10			7	13	14									2
	2^1	3	4	5	6		8	12	9	11	10			7^2	13	1									3
	2	3		5	6	8	13	9	11^3	10^2	14		7^1	4		1	12								4
	2	3^4	4	5	6		8^1	12	9	11	10			7^1	14	1									5
	2	3	4	5	6	8	12	9^3	11	10^1		14		13		1	7^2								6
	2	3	4	5	6^1	8	12	9	11^2	10		13	14			1	7^2								7
	2	3	4	5	6^1	8	12	9^1	11	10		13		14		1	7^2								8
	2	3	4^2	5	6	8	10^1	9	11		12	13				1	7^3	14							9
	2	3	4	5	6	8	10	9	11		12	13				1	7^2								10
	2	3	4	5	6	8	10^2	9	11		12	13				1			7^1						11
	2	3	4	5	6	8	10^1	9	11		12					1			7						12
	2	3	4	5	6	8	10^2	9	11^3	13	14					1	12		7^1						13
	2^1	3	4		6	8	5	9	11^2	10	13					1	7^3	14	12						14
	2	3	4		6	8	5	9^2	11^3	10	14		13		1	12	7^1								15
	2	3	4		6	8	5	9^2	11	10			13		1	12	7^1								16
	2	3			6	8	5	9	11^2	10			12		1	13	4	7^1							17
	2	3		4	6	8	5	9	11^1	10			12		1	13	7^2								18
	2	3	4^1	5	6	8		9	11^2	10^3	14	13			1	12	7^2								19
1	2	3		5	6	8	10	9	11^2	12	13					4^1	7								20
1	2^3	3		5	6^1	8	7	9	11	10			13	14			4^2	12							21
1	2	3	12	5	6^1		7	9	11	10			14	8^2			4^3	13							22
1	2^2	3^1	13	5	6	8	7	9	11^3	12			10	4	14										23
1			13	5	6	8	7^3	9	11	3	12	2		10^2	4	14									24
	2			5		6^1	8	7	9	14	3		13		12	10	4^3		11^2						25
1	2		4	5		8	12	9	11	13		14		7	6^3		10^1			3^2					26
	2		4	5	6	8	7	9	13	12						1	10^2		11		3^1				27
	13		4	5	6	8	7	9	11^3	12	2					1	10^2		11		3^1				28
15	14	10^2	4	5	6	8	7	9	11	3		2^3		1^9					13						29
1	5	12	4		6		7	9	11	3		2					8		10^1						30
1		13	4^1	6		7	9	11	3	5	12	2		8^2			10								31
	2^3	10^2	4	6		7	9	11	3	5	1	13		8^1			12					14			32
	2	3	5	6		7	9	11^1	10	4	1	12					8								33
	2	3	4^2	6			9	11	10^1	5	1	12	13	8^3			14	7							34
12	10		4	6^1			9	11^2	3	5	1	13	2^3	8			14	7							35
	10	7	5				9	11	3	4	1		2	6			8								36

ALBION ROVERS   Third Division

Year Formed: 1882. *Ground & Address:* Cliftonhill Stadium, Main St, Coatbridge ML5 3RB. *Telephone/Fax:* 01236 606334.
Ground capacity: total: 2496, seated: 538. *Size of Pitch:* 110yd × 72yd.
Chairman: Andrew Dick, *Company Secretary:* David Shanks BSc. *General Manager:* John Reynolds.
Commercial Manager: Chris Fahey.
Manager: Peter Hetherston. *Assistant Manager:* Jock McStay. *Youth Development:* Jimmy Lindsay. *Physio:* Dan Young.
Managers since 1975: G. Caldwell, S. Goodwin, H. Hood, J. Baker, D. Whiteford, M. Ferguson, W. Wilson, B. Rooney,
A. Ritchie, T. Gemmell, D. Provan, M. Oliver, B. McLaren, T. Gemmell, T Spence, J. Crease, V. Moore, B. McLaren,
J. McVeigh.
Club Nickname(s): The Wee Rovers. *Previous Grounds:* Cowheath Park, Meadow Park, Whifflet.
Record Attendance: 27,381 v Rangers, Scottish Cup 2nd rd; 8 Feb, 1936.
Record Transfer Fee received: £40,000 from Motherwell for Bruce Cleland.
Record Transfer Fee paid: £7000 for Gerry McTeague to Stirling Albion, September 1989.
Record Victory: 12-0 v Airdriehill, Scottish Cup; 3 Sept, 1887.
Record Defeat: 1-11 v Partick T, League Cup, 11 August 1993.
Most Capped Player: Jock White, 1 (2), Scotland.
Most League Appearances: 399, Murdy Walls, 1921-36.
Most League Goals in Season (Individual): 41: Jim Renwick, Division II; 1932-33.
Most Goals Overall (Individual): 105: Bunty Weir, 1928-31.

ALBION ROVERS 2001–02 LEAGUE RECORD

Match No.	Date	Venue	Opponents	Result	H/T Score	Lg. Pos.	Goalscorers	Atten- dance
1	Aug 4	A	East Fife	D 0-0	0-0	—		465
2	11	H	Stirling A	L 1-3	0-3	6	Bonar [81]	444
3	18	A	Elgin C	L 0-2	0-1	9		623
4	25	A	Brechin C	L 1-4	0-3	9	Stirling (pen) [48]	517
5	Sept 8	H	Queen's Park	W 2-1	0-1	8	McCormick [52], Booth (pen) [86]	377
6	15	A	Dumbarton	D 1-1	0-0	8	Booth [53]	581
7	18	H	East Stirling	L 0-4	0-1	—		159
8	22	A	Montrose	W 2-1	0-0	8	Harty [48], Diack [51]	354
9	29	H	Peterhead	W 1-0	0-0	7	Waldie [81]	296
10	Oct 13	H	East Fife	W 3-0	2-0	7	Booth 2 (1 pen) [16, 42 (p)], Smith [65]	303
11	20	A	Stirling A	D 2-2	1-2	6	Booth 2 [30, 81]	489
12	27	A	Queen's Park	W 2-1	1-1	4	Harty [19], McLean [81]	518
13	Nov 3	H	Brechin C	L 1-2	1-1	6	Silvestro [37]	262
14	10	H	Dumbarton	L 0-2	0-0	8		278
15	27	A	East Stirling	W 2-1	2-1	—	Bonar [27], McLean [63]	196
16	Dec 1	H	Montrose	D 0-0	0-0	5		246
17	15	A	Peterhead	D 0-0	0-0	5		485
18	Jan 12	A	Brechin C	D 0-0	0-0	5		457
19	19	H	East Stirling	W 5-1	4-0	5	McLean 3 (1 pen) [7, 14, 82 (p)], McKenzie J 2 [18, 29]	253
20	26	A	Dumbarton	L 0-2	0-0	6		686
21	Feb 2	H	Peterhead	W 2-1	2-1	6	Donnelly [9], McLean [45]	297
22	9	A	Montrose	L 0-2	0-2	6		310
23	12	A	East Fife	W 3-2	1-0	—	Diack [14], Harty 2 [78, 83]	301
24	16	H	Stirling A	W 2-0	2-0	4	Diack [19], McKenna [38]	420
25	26	H	Elgin C	D 4-4	3-0	—	Diack 2 [18, 35], Smith [31], McLean [78]	249
26	Mar 2	H	Brechin C	L 0-1	0-1	5		304
27	5	H	Queen's Park	W 2-0	0-0	—	McLean 2 [75, 82]	293
28	9	A	Queen's Park	W 3-0	1-0	4	McLean [9], Booth [66], Silvestro [77]	547
29	16	H	Dumbarton	D 1-1	1-1	5	Harty [22]	503
30	23	A	East Stirling	W 2-1	0-1	4	Booth [62], Diack [74]	212
31	26	A	Elgin C	D 0-0	0-0	—		652
32	30	H	Montrose	D 0-0	0-0	4		353
33	Apr 6	A	Peterhead	W 2-0	0-0	3	McMullan 2 [84, 90]	789
34	13	A	East Fife	W 2-1	1-1	3	Carr [27], Diack (pen) [85]	442
35	20	A	Stirling A	W 3-0	2-0	3	Hamilton [30], Carr [74], Nugent (og) [69]	516
36	27	H	Elgin C	D 2-2	0-1	3	McLean [84], McKenzie J [86]	767

Final League Position: 3

Honours
League Champions: Division II 1933-34, Second Division 1988-89; *Runners-up:* Division II 1913-14, 1937-38, 1947-48. *Scottish Cup Runners-up:* 1920. *League Cup:* —.

Club colours: Shirt: Scarlet and yellow. Shorts: Scarlet. Stockings: Yellow.

Goalscorers: *League* (51): McLean 11 (1 pen), Booth 8 (2 pens), Diack 7 (1 pen), Harty 5, McKenzie 3, Bonar 2, Carr 2, McMullan 2, Silvestro 2, Smith 2, Donnelly 1, Hamilton 1, McCormick 1, McKenna 1, Stirling 1 (pen), Waldie 1, own goal 1.
Scottish Cup (3): McLean 2, Harty 1.
CIS Cup (0):
Challenge Cup (3): Bonar 1, Hamilton 1, McMullan 1.

Fahey C 27	McKenzie J 18+5	Stirling J 4	Smith J 20	Tait T 15	Silvestro C 15+3	Waldie C 35+1	Easton S 25+2	McMullan R 8+20	McCormick S 11+6	McKenna G 25+9	Bonar P 19+2	Hamilton S 32+1	McLean C 19+8	Booth M 31	Harty M 23+4	Carr D 5+9	Struthers W 1	Coulter J 1	Lumsden T 22	Ingram S —+2	Shearer S 9+1	Diack J 19+7	Rankin I —+3	McLees J —+2	Murdoch S —+3	Coulter R 10+2	Donnelly K 2+2	Rodden P —+2	Match No.
1	2	3	4	5	6	7	8²	9³	10	11¹	12	13	14																1
1	2	3	4	5	13	7	14	12	10²		11	8	9¹	6³															2
1	2	3	4	5	12	7¹	8	9	14	11³		6	10²	13															3
1		3	4	5	11¹	14		2	13	10	12		6	9²					7³	8									4
1			4	5	11	7	8	9	10	13		2¹		6	12				3²										5
1			4	5	11	7	8²	9	10¹	13		2		6	12				3²	14									6
			4	5	11	7	8	2	13			9³	12	6				1	3²	14		10¹							7
1	2		8³	7	14			5	11	4		6	9¹	13	3				10²	12									8
1	2			8	7		13	11	3	4		6	9		5¹				10²	12									9
1⁸	5	2	3²	8	7		14	13	11	4		6	9						15	10³									10
	5²	2	8	7	12		14	11	4	13		6	9¹		3				1	10³									11
	5	2	8³	7	12		13	11	4			6	9¹		3²				1	10¹									12
	5	2	8	7	12		11	4	13			6	9¹		3				1	10²									13
1	5²	2	8	7³	12		14	11	4	13		6	9		3					10¹									14
1	12			7	5	8¹		2	11	4		9	6	10	3														15
1	8¹			7	5		2	11	4	9		6	10		3					12									16
1				7	5	8²	13	2	11	4		9¹	6	10	3					12									17
1	8¹			7	5	12	10³	2	11	4		9²	6		3					14			13						18
1	8			7	5	14	10³	2	11²	4		9	6		3¹								13	12					19
1	8²			7	5	14	10¹	2	11	4		9	6²	12	3							13							20
				7	5	13		3	11	4		9²	6	12					1	10¹					2	8			21
	12			7	5	13		3	11	4		9²	6³	14					1	10					2	8¹			22
	8	2		7	5	13		11		4		9	6	12					1	10¹	14				3²				23
	8	2		7	5			11		4		9	6	12					1	10¹					3				24
	8¹	2		7	5			11		4		9	6	12					1	10					3				25
1	8		12	7	5	13		2		4		9²	6	11					3	10¹									26
1			4	8	7	5	13	3	11³	12		6	9²						10¹			2	14						27
1	13		4	11	7	5		2	8²	9¹	6	10³			3				12								14		28
1			4	11²	7	5		3		9¹	6	8							10³	12			2	14	13				29
1	2¹		4	7		12	13	5		8	9²	6	11	14					10³				3						30
1	4³			7	5	12	13	3		8	9	6¹	11	14					10²				2						31
1	4³			7		12	14	3		8	9²	6¹	11	10		5			13				2						32
1	2			7	5	12	10³		8			6¹	11	9²	4				13				14						33
1	14		4³	7	5	6¹	10²	2	8	12		11	9		3				13										34
1	6²		4	7	5	14	10¹	2	13	8		11	9³		3				12										35
1	14		4	7	5	12		2	11¹	8	13	6	9		3³				10²										36

ALLOA ATHLETIC　　　　　　　First Division

Year Formed: 1878. *Ground & Address:* Recreation Park, Clackmannan Rd, Alloa FK10 1RY. *Telephone:* 01259 722695.
Ground Capacity: total: 3100, seated: 400. *Size of Pitch:* 110yd × 75yd.
Chairman/Secretary: Ewen G. Cameron. *Commercial Director:* Willie McKie.
Manager: Terry Christie. *Assistant Manager:* Graeme Armstrong. *Physio:* Jim Law.
Managers since 1975: H. Wilson, A. Totten, W. Garner, J. Thomson, D. Sullivan, G. Abel, B. Little, H. McCann, W. Lamont, P. McAuley, T. Hendrie. *Club Nickname(s):* The Wasps. *Previous Grounds:* None.
Record Attendance: 13,000 v Dunfermline Athletic, Scottish Cup 3rd rd replay; 26 Feb, 1939.
Record Transfer Fee received: £100,000 for Martin Cameron to Bristol Rovers.
Record Transfer Fee paid: £26,000 for Ross Hamilton from Stenhousemuir.
Record Victory: 9-2 v Forfar Ath, Division II; 18 Mar, 1933.
Record Defeat: 0-10 v Dundee, Division II; 8 Mar, 1947: v Third Lanark, League Cup, 8 Aug, 1953.
Most Capped Player: Jock Hepburn, 1, Scotland.
Most League Appearances: —.
Most League Goals in Season (Individual): 49: 'Wee' Willie Crilley, Division II; 1921-22.
Most Goals Overall (Individual): —.

ALLOA ATHLETIC 2001–02 LEAGUE RECORD

Match No.	Date		Venue	Opponents	Result	H/T Score	Lg. Pos.	Goalscorers	Atten- dance
1	Aug	4	A	Berwick R	W 4-0	1-0	—	Seaton [31], Knox 2 [74, 80], Hamilton [90]	649
2		11	H	Morton	D 1-1	1-0	0	Knox [12]	972
3		18	A	Stranraer	D 1-1	1-1	2	Hutchison [11]	444
4		25	A	Cowdenbeath	W 2-1	1-0	2	Raeside (pen) [36], Hamilton [59]	416
5	Sept	2	A	Forfar Ath	W 1-0	1-0	—	Hutchison [18]	469
6		8	H	Stenhousemuir	L 0-1	0-0	2		632
7		15	H	Clydebank	W 1-0	1-0	1	Fisher [15]	626
8		22	H	Hamilton A	W 2-1	2-1	1	Walker [19], Hamilton [31]	645
9		29	A	Queen of the S	L 1-2	1-1	1	Hutchison [28]	1320
10	Oct	6	H	Berwick R	D 2-2	1-2	1	Seaton [28], Hutchison [82]	492
11		20	A	Morton	D 1-1	0-0	3	Curran [56]	1243
12		27	H	Stenhousemuir	D 1-1	1-0	3	Seaton [24]	568
13	Nov	3	H	Cowdenbeath	W 5-1	2-1	1	Hutchison [30], Hamilton [39], Donnachie [59], Curran [76], Little [81]	618
14		10	A	Clydebank	L 0-1	0-0	2		247
15		24	H	Forfar Ath	L 1-2	1-0	3	Watson [15]	458
16	Dec	1	A	Hamilton A	L 0-1	0-1	5		1833
17		15	H	Queen of the S	W 2-0	1-0	2	Fisher [44], Walker [66]	472
18	Jan	12	A	Cowdenbeath	W 2-1	0-0	2	Hutchison 2 [50, 71]	390
19		19	A	Forfar Ath	L 1-4	0-2	3	Little [71]	442
20	Feb	2	A	Queen of the S	W 1-0	1-0	4	Raeside [30]	1367
21		9	H	Hamilton A	D 2-2	2-1	2	Knox [24], Hutchison [42]	626
22		16	H	Morton	W 4-0	2-0	2	Hutchison 3 [7, 23, 70], Little [57]	657
23		23	A	Stranraer	W 2-0	1-0	2	Hamilton [2], Little [70]	320
24	Mar	2	H	Cowdenbeath	D 0-0	0-0	3		560
25		5	A	Berwick R	W 1-0	0-0	—	Raeside [49]	637
26		9	A	Stenhousemuir	L 0-1	0-1	3		507
27		12	H	Clydebank	D 2-2	1-2	—	Walker [5], Donnachie [90]	474
28		16	A	Clydebank	D 1-1	1-0	3	Brown [25]	260
29		19	H	Stranraer	D 2-2	0-2	—	Knox [62], Seaton (pen) [75]	378
30		23	H	Forfar Ath	W 2-1	0-0	2	Seaton (pen) [65], Curran [75]	462
31		30	A	Hamilton A	D 1-1	1-0	2	Curran [32]	1963
32	Apr	2	H	Stenhousemuir	W 4-0	1-0	—	Thomson [3], Hutchison 2 [53, 80], Hamilton [58]	571
33		6	H	Queen of the S	W 4-1	2-0	2	Hutchison [16], Christie [38], Hamilton (pen) [62], Seaton [63]	1442
34		13	A	Berwick R	D 1-1	0-1	2	Little [60]	675
35		20	A	Morton	D 0-0	0-0	2		928
36		27	H	Stranraer	D 0-0	0-0	2		613

Final League Position: 2

Honours
League Champions: Division II 1921-22; Third Division 1997-98. *Runners-up:* Division II 1938-39. Second Division 1976-77, 1981-82, 1984-85, 1988-89, 1999-2000, 2001-02.
Bell's League Challenge Winners: 1999-2000. *Runners-up:* 2001-02.
Scottish Cup: —.
League Cup: —.

Club colours: Shirt: Gold with black trim. Shorts: Black with gold stripe. Stockings: Gold, black hoop on top.

Goalscorers: *League* (55): Hutchison 14, Hamilton 7 (1 pen), Seaton 6 (1 pen), Knox 5, Little 5, Curran 4, Raeside 3 (1 pen), Walker 3, Donnachie 2, Fisher 2, Brown 1, Christie 1, Thomson 1, Watson 1.
Scottish Cup (4): Evans 2, Hutchison 1, Little 1.
CIS Cup (4): Curran 1, Little 1, Thomson 1, Walker 1.
Challenge Cup (10): Evans 2, Hamilton 2, Little 2, Curran 1, Fisher 1, Hutchison 1, Irvine 1.

Soutar D 31	Knox K 28	Seaton A 21+6	Watson G 17	Raeside R 22+1	Anderson D 7+3	Curran H 19+12	Fisher J 26+4	Walker R 23+9	Irvine W 2+5	Hutchison G 32+3	Hamilton R 24+10	Little I 29+5	Thomson S 31+1	Valentine C 33	Evans G 7+4	Christie M 16+6	Donnachie S 2+11	Kerr C	Evans J 5+1	Cowan M 8+2	Whalen S 5	Brown T 7+3	Match No.
1	2	3	4	5	6	7^2	8	9	10^1	11	12	13											1
1	2	3	4	5^1	6	13	8^2	11^3	10	14	9	7	12										2
1	2	3	4	8^1	12	10	7	13	11	14				5^1	6	9^3							3
1	2		4	3		10	8^1	13		11	9^2	7	5	6	12								4
1	2^1	3	4	7			8	13		10	12	11	5	6	9^2								5
1		3	4	2^1		13	8^1	14	12	10	7	11	5	6	9^3								6
1		3		12	4	8^1	2	9^3	14	10	7^2	11	5	6	13								7
1	2		4		8	3	13			9^1	10^2	7	11	5	6	12							8
1	2		4		3	12	7	13	14	10	9^2	11	5	6^1		8^3							9
1	2	3	4		5^2	8	7	9^3	13	10	12	11		6									10
1	2	3^1	4			7	8			10	9	11	5	6		12							11
1		3	4		8	12	13			10	7^3	11	5	2	9^2	6^1	14						12
1	3^2	12	5		13	4	8	14		10	7	11		2	6^1	9^3							13
1		13	4		8	6^1	12			10	7	11	5	2	14	9^2	3^3						14
			4		3	8	6	14		10^2	7^3	11	5	2	9^1	13	12	1					15
			4			7	8			10	9^1	11	5	2	13	6	12	1	3^2				16
			4		14	13	3	12		10	7	11^2		2	9^1	6^3		1	5	8			17
1^6	2	11		4		8		7^1		10	12		5	6			13	15	3	9^1			18
	2^2	11		4		8^1	13	9		10	7	12	5	6					1	3			19
1	3		8			7				10		11	5	2		6	12			4	9^1		20
1	3		8		13	7^2				10		11	5	2		6	12			4	9^1		21
1	5	13	8		12	3^3	7^2			10	14	11	4	2		6^1					9		22
1	3	12	6			8	7			10	9	11	5	2						4^1			23
1	3	13		4^3		12	8^2	7		10	9	11^3	5	2		6	14						24
1	3	11		4		13	8^2	7		10	12	9	5	2		6^1							25
1	6	3^1		4		10	8	7		12	9^2	11^3	5	2			14					13	26
1	3			4		8	11^1	7		10	12	13	5	2		6^2	14					9^1	27
1	6	3		4			7			10^2	8	11	5	2		13	12					9^1	28
1	3	13		4^2		12	6^1	7		10	8	11	5	2		14						9^1	29
1	3	11		4		10		7		8^1	9	5	2		6							12	30
1	4	3				10	13	7		8	12	11	5	2		6^2						9^1	31
1	4	3				10^1	6	7^2		8	11	12	5	2		13	14					9^2	32
1	4	3					8	7		10	9	11	5	2		6							33
1	4^2	3				12	8^1	7		10	9^2	11	5	2		6		13	14				34
1	4^3	3	8^1			13	12			10	7^2	11	5	2		6			14			9	35
	3	2	6^8			8	11	7^3		12	14	13	5		10^1			1	4			9	36

ARBROATH

First Division

Year Formed: 1878. *Ground & Address:* Gayfield Park, Arbroath DD11 1QB. *Telephone and Fax:* 01241 431125.
Ground Capacity: 4020, seated: 715. *Size of Pitch:* 115yd × 71yd.
President: John D. Christison. *Secretary:* Charles Kinnear. *Administrator:* Mike Cargill. *Commercial Manager:* G. Cant.
Manager: John Brownlie. *Assistant Manager:* Steve Kirk. *Coach:* Jake Ferrier. *Physio:* Jim Crosby.
Managers since 1975: A. Henderson, I. J. Stewart, G. Fleming, J. Bone, J. Young, W. Borthwick, M. Lawson, D. McGrain MBE, J. Scott, J. Brogan, T. Campbell, G. Mackie, D. Baikie.
Club Nickname(s): The Red Lichties. *Previous Grounds:* None.
Record Attendance: 13,510 v Rangers, Scottish Cup 3rd rd; 23 Feb, 1952.
Record Transfer Fee received: £120,000 for Paul Tosh to Dundee (Aug 1993).
Record Transfer Fee paid: £20,000 for Douglas Robb from Montrose (1981).
Record Victory: 36-0 v Bon Accord, Scottish Cup 1st rd; 12 Sept, 1885.
Record Defeat: 1-9 v Celtic, League Cup 3rd rd; 25 Aug 1993.
Most Capped Player: Ned Doig, 2 (5), Scotland.
Most League Appearances: 445: Tom Cargill, 1966-81.
Most League Goals in Season (Individual): 45: Dave Easson, Division II; 1958-59.
Most Goals Overall (Individual): 120: Jimmy Jack; 1966-71.

ARBROATH 2001–02 LEAGUE RECORD

Match No.	Date		Venue	Opponents	Result		H/T Score	Lg. Pos.	Goalscorers	Atten- dance
1	Aug	4	A	Ross Co	W	2-0	2-0	—	Mallan [30], Heenan [36]	2682
2		11	H	Airdrieonians	L	0-6	0-2	6		926
3		18	A	Clyde	L	0-1	0-0	8		831
4		25	H	Partick Th	L	1-3	0-0	8	Bayne [88]	1510
5	Sept	8	A	Inverness CT	L	1-5	0-2	10	Mallan [88]	1505
6		15	A	Raith R	L	1-3	1-0	10	Bayne [10]	1698
7		18	H	Ayr U	W	3-2	2-2	—	Ritchie 2 [16, 35], McGlashan [50]	452
8		22	H	Falkirk	W	1-0	0-0	7	McKinnon [88]	1072
9		29	A	St Mirren	L	0-1	0-1	10		2733
10	Oct	13	H	Ross Co	W	2-1	1-0	8	Cargill 2 [41, 52]	765
11		20	A	Airdrieonians	L	1-3	1-2	10	McGlashan [26]	1324
12		27	H	Inverness CT	W	3-2	1-1	7	Cusick [17], Bayne [46], McKinnon [76]	773
13	Nov	3	A	Partick Th	L	1-4	0-2	8	Cusick [57]	3253
14		10	A	Ayr U	W	1-0	1-0	5	Cargill [24]	1977
15		17	H	Raith R	D	1-1	1-0	6	McGlashan [24]	1034
16		24	H	St Mirren	L	0-2	0-1	8		1392
17	Dec	1	A	Falkirk	L	2-3	0-1	8	Bayne [50], McKinnon [70]	2047
18		8	H	Clyde	W	2-1	1-0	8	Bayne [40], Ritchie [88]	813
19		15	A	Ross Co	W	1-0	0-0	7	Mallan [69]	2056
20		22	A	Inverness CT	L	2-3	1-2	8	McGlashan [42], Mallan (pen) [56]	1173
21	Jan	12	H	Ayr U	L	0-2	0-0	8		700
22		19	H	Falkirk	L	0-1	0-1	8		964
23		26	A	Raith R	D	0-0	0-0	8		1737
24	Feb	2	A	St Mirren	W	3-2	2-0	7	McKinnon [2], Brownlie [6], Rowe [90]	2472
25		9	A	Clyde	L	0-1	0-1	8		941
26		16	H	Airdrieonians	W	2-1	1-1	7	Rowe [34], McKinnon [86]	885
27		26	H	Partick Th	W	1-0	1-0	—	McGlashan [42]	1074
28	Mar	2	A	Partick Th	D	2-2	2-0	5	Ritchie [23], Cusick [40]	3729
29		9	H	Inverness CT	W	1-0	0-0	4	Ritchie [87]	738
30		23	H	Raith R	D	2-2	2-1	6	Bayne [30], McGlashan [36]	1185
31		26	A	Ayr U	D	0-0	0-0	—		2249
32		30	A	Falkirk	W	3-1	1-1	4	Rowe [16], McAulay [76], Cargill [77]	2634
33	Apr	6	H	St Mirren	L	0-3	0-1	7		1312
34		13	H	Ross Co	D	1-1	0-1	6	Mallan (pen) [62]	826
35		20	A	Airdrieonians	L	0-2	0-2	7		1143
36		27	H	Clyde	W	2-0	2-0	7	Mallan [28], Cusick [37]	859

Final League Position: 7

Honours
League Champions Runners-up: Division II 1934-35, 1958-59, 1967-68, 1971-72; Second Division 2000-01; Third Division 1997-98.
Scottish Cup: Quarter-finals: 1993.
League Cup: —.

Club colours: Shirt: Maroon with white trim. Shorts: White. Stockings: Maroon.

Goalscorers: *League* (42): Bayne 6, McGlashan 6, Mallan 6 (2 pens), McKinnon 5, Ritchie 5, Cargill 4, Cusick 4, Rowe 3, Brownlie 1, Heenan 1, McAulay 1.
Scottish Cup (0):
CIS Cup (0):
Challenge Cup (1): Brownlie 1.

Hinchcliffe C 35	Fallon S 3	Florence S 25 + 2	Cusick J 23 + 6	McKinnon C 20 + 9	Mackay D 5	Heenan K 9 + 12	McGlashan J 32	Mallan S 14 + 9	Mercer J 6 + 12	McInally D 17 + 2	McAulay J 7 + 13	Brownlie P 26 + 5	Cargill A 29 + 3	Bayne G 33 + 1	Rowe G 31	Gardner J 3 + 6	Wight C 1	Ritchie J 31	Tait J 31	Swankie G 3 + 6	Arbuckle D — + 3	Moffat S 6 + 2	Roddie A 3 + 1	Henslee G 2 + 1	Graham E 1	Durno P — + 1	Match No
1	2	3	4	5	6	7^2	8	9	10^3	11^1	12	13	14														1
1	2^3	3		5	4	7	10	9	6	11^1	14	8^2	13	12													2
1		3^2	4	10^1	5	7	11	9^2	6			13	12	8	2	14											3
1		3	4	10^2	5	7	6	13	8^1	12	14			9	2			11^3									4
1		3	4	5		7	8	10	12	14		13	6^2	9	11^3		1	2									5
1		3	6				12		10	13	11^1	7	8^2	9	4			5	2								6
1		3	6				12		10		11	7	8^1	9	4			5	2								7
1		3	6^2	13			10^2	11^1			14	7	8	9	4	12		5	2								8
1		3	6^2				10			13	11^1	7	8^3	9	4	12		5	2	14							9
1		3	12	6^1			13		10		11^3	7^2	8	9	4			5	2	14							10
1		3	14	6^3			12		10		11^3	7	8^2	9	4			5	2		13						11
1		3	6	13			12		10		11^1	7^3	8	9^2	4	14		5	2								12
1			6	13		7^1	10			3	11^1		8^2	9	4	12		5	2	14							13
1			6				10		12	3	11		8	9	4			5	2	7^1							14
1			12	6			10		13	3			8	9	4	11^3		5	2	7^1							15
1			6^1			7	10	11^2		3	13		8	9^3	4			5	2	12	14						16
1				11^1	6		12		10			7	8	9	4			5	2								17
1		3	6^1	11			13		10^3	14	12	7^2	8	9	4			5	2								18
1		3	6^1				10	11^2		13	12	7	8	9	4			5	2								19
1		3	6				10	11	12		13	7^1	8^2	9	4			5	2								20
1		3^2	6				13	11^1	10			7^2	8	9	4	14		5	2	12							21
1		13	6	11	14		12			3^2	10		8	9	4			5	2^3	7^1							22
1		3	6^1	13			10		12		11^2	7	8	9	4			5	2								23
1		3	6^1	13			10		12	14	11^2	7	8	9	4			5	2								24
1		3	12	6^3			10		14		11	7^1	8	9	4			5	2^2				13				25
1		3	6	13	14		10		12		11^1	7	8^2	9^3	4			5	2								26
1		3	6				12		10		11	7	8^1	9	4				2						5		27
1		3	6^1	13			10	11^3	12			7	8	9	4			5	2	14							28
1			6	12			13	10^1	11^2	14		7^3	8	9	4			5	2			3					29
1			6	13		7^1	10	11^2	12	14			8^3	9	4			5	2			3					30
1			6^2				10	11^1	12		13		8	9	4			5	2			3	7				31
1		14	6^1	11^3			10	13	12			7	8	9	4			5	2			3^3					32
1		3	6^1			7	12		10		11^3		8	9	4			5	2^3					13	14		33
1		3	6^3				12	11	10		13	7^1		9	4			5	2				14	8^2			34
1		3	6^3	12			10	11	14		13			9				5	2			4		8^2	7^1		35
1		3	6^1			7^1	10	9	12		11							5	2	13		8^2			4	14	36

AYR UNITED

First Division

Year Formed: 1910. *Ground & Address:* Somerset Park, Tryfield Place, Ayr KA8 9NB. *Telephone:* 01292 263435.
Ground Capacity: 10,185, seated: 1549. *Size of Pitch:* 110yd × 72yd.
Chairman: W. J. Barr. *Administrator:* Brian Caldwell. *Secretary:* J. E. Eyley. *Lottery Manager:* Andrew Downie.
Manager: Gordon Dalziel. *Youth Coach:* Campbell Money. *Physio:* John Kerr.
Managers since 1975: Alex Stuart, Ally MacLeod, Willie McLean, George Caldwell, Ally MacLeod, George Burley,
Simon Stainrod. *Club Nickname(s):* The Honest Men. *Previous Grounds:* None.
Record Attendance: 25,225 v Rangers, Division I; 13 Sept, 1969.
Record Transfer Fee received: £300,000 for Steven Nicol to Liverpool (Oct 1981).
Record Transfer Fee paid: £80,000 for Mark Campbell from Stranraer (March 1999).
Record Victory: 11-1 v Dumbarton, League Cup; 13 Aug, 1952.
Record Defeat: 0-9 in Division I v Rangers (1929); v Hearts (1931): B Division v Third Lanark (1954).
Most Capped Player: Jim Nisbet, 3, Scotland.
Most League Appearances: 459, John Murphy, 1963-78.
Most League League and Cup Goals in Season (Individual): 66, Jimmy Smith, 1927-28.
Most League and Cup Goals Overall (Individual): 213, Peter Price, 1955-61.

AYR UNITED 2001–02 LEAGUE RECORD

Match No.	Date		Venue	Opponents	Result	H/T Score	Lg. Pos.	Goalscorers	Attendance
1	Aug	4	A	Falkirk	W 2-1	0-1	—	Grady (pen) [47], Annand (pen) [54]	2828
2		11	H	Ross Co	W 2-0	1-0	1	Annand 2 [34, 61]	2457
3		18	A	Airdrieonians	L 1-2	1-1	3	Lovering [32]	2019
4		25	H	Raith R	D 1-1	1-0	3	Robertson [17]	2410
5	Sept	8	A	Partick Th	L 1-1	1-1	4	Annand [11]	3820
6		15	H	St Mirren	W 4-2	2-1	3	Annand 2 (2 pens) [2, 24], Sheerin [71], Robertson [85]	3645
7		18	A	Arbroath	L 2-3	2-2	—	Teale [18], Wilson [24]	452
8		23	H	Clyde	W 2-1	2-0	3	Annand 2 [16, 28]	2278
9		29	A	Inverness CT	L 1-3	0-0	3	Grady [70]	1533
10	Oct	13	H	Falkirk	D 2-2	1-1	5	McLaughlin [2], Annand (pen) [84]	2439
11		20	A	Ross Co	L 2-3	0-1	5	Sheerin [58], Grady [59]	1991
12		27	H	Partick Th	L 0-2	0-0	8		3447
13	Nov	3	A	Raith R	D 1-1	0-1	7	Moss [59]	1781
14		10	H	Arbroath	L 0-1	0-0	9		1977
15		17	A	St Mirren	W 1-0	0-0	7	McGinley [81]	3897
16		24	H	Inverness CT	W 3-0	1-0	6	Sheerin [11], Crabbe [55], Teale [67]	1999
17	Dec	1	A	Clyde	D 2-2	1-1	6	McEwan [7], Teale [50]	1314
18		8	H	Airdrieonians	L 1-3	0-0	7	Teale [47]	2656
19		15	A	Falkirk	W 2-0	0-0	5	Crabbe [60], Grady [87]	2148
20		26	H	Partick Th	L 1-2	1-0	—	Grady [18]	4611
21		29	H	Raith R	W 3-1	0-0	3	Annand 2 [61, 87], McGinley [83]	2033
22	Jan	12	A	Arbroath	W 2-0	0-0	3	Annand (pen) [65], Sheerin [78]	700
23		19	H	Clyde	L 0-1	0-1	3		2151
24	Feb	2	A	Inverness CT	D 1-1	0-1	3	Crabbe [60]	1409
25		9	A	Airdrieonians	W 2-1	1-0	3	Wilson [21], Scally [83]	1771
26		16	H	Ross Co	D 0-0	0-0	3		2186
27		26	H	St Mirren	W 4-1	2-0	—	McGinley 2 [15, 86], Grady 2 [34, 65]	1932
28	Mar	2	A	Raith R	D 3-3	3-2	3	Sheerin [11], Grady [17], Kean [39]	2010
29		9	H	Partick Th	D 1-1	0-0	3	Sheerin [65]	3624
30		26	H	Arbroath	D 0-0	0-0	—		2249
31		30	A	Clyde	D 2-2	1-0	3	McGinley [37], Annand [77]	1084
32	Apr	2	A	St Mirren	D 1-1	0-1	—	Hughes [61]	3002
33		6	H	Inverness CT	W 1-0	0-0	3	Annand (pen) [65]	1818
34		13	H	Falkirk	D 0-0	0-0	3		2473
35		20	A	Ross Co	D 1-1	0-1	3	Kean [81]	2822
36		27	H	Airdrieonians	W 1-0	0-0	3	Kean [21]	2793

Final League Position: 3

Honours
League Champions: Division II 1911-12, 1912-13, 1927-28, 1936-37, 1958-59, 1965-66. Second Division 1987-88, 1996-97;
Runners-up: Division II 1910-11, 1955-56, 1968-69.
Scottish Cup: Semi-final 2002.
League Cup: (CIS) Runners-up: 2001-02.
B&Q Cup Runners-up: 1990-91, 1991-92.

Club colours: Shirt: White with black trim. Shorts: Black. Stockings: White with black.

Goalscorers: *League* (53): Annand 14 (6 pens), Grady 8 (1 pen), Sheerin 6, McGinlay 5, Teale 4, Crabbe 3, Kean 3, Robertson 2, Wilson 2, Hughes 1, Lovering 1, McEwan 1, McLaughlin 1, Moss 1, Scally 1
Scottish Cup (13): Crabbe 3, Annand 2, Grady 2, McGinlay 2, Sheerin 2, Robertson 1, own goal 1.
CIS Cup (10): Annand 4, Grady 2, McGinlay 1, Robertson 1, Sheerin 1, Teale 1.
Challenge Cup (5): Annand 1, Bradford 1, McGinlay 1, Sheerin 1, Teale 1.

Nelson C 35	Robertson J 36	Sharp L 9 + 12	Duffy C 21 + 1	Hughes J 30	Craig D 27 + 1	Teale G 18	McGinlay P 27	Annand E 21 + 7	Grady J 24 + 7	Sheerin P 33 + 1	Wilson M 20 + 6	Bradford J — + 10	Lovering P 27 + 5	McEwan C 15 + 7	McLaughlin B 8 + 11	Scally N 5 + 2	Chaplain S 4 + 4	Kean S 4 + 4	Crabbe S 20	Moss D 5	Twaddle K 1	Stevenson C — + 1	Smyth M 4	Dunlop M 1	Molloy T — + 1	Latta J — + 1	Bruce R — + 1	Dodds J 1	Match No.
1	2	3	4	5	6	7	8	9^1	10^2	11^3	12	13	14																1
1	2	13	4	5	6	7^3	8	9		11^1	10	12		3^1	14														2
1			4	5	6	7	8	9		10^2		13	3	2	11^1	12													3
1	2	13	4	5	6^2	7^3	11	9	12	14	8			3		10^1													4
1	2	13	4^3	5		7	11	9	10^1	6^2	8	12		3	14														5
1	2	11		5		7	8^1	9	10^2	6	12		3	13			4												6
1	2	11		5		7		9	10	6	8	12	3				4^1												7
1	2	12	4	5		7		9^3	10	6^2	8	14	3^1	13	11														8
1	2	12	4	5		7		9^2	10	6	8	13	3^3	14	11^1	11													9
1	2	6	4	5		7		9	10^3		8	13	3^1	11^2	12	14													10
1	2	3	4	5		7		9^3	10	6	8	12		11															11
1	2	4^2	5	13		7	8	9^3	10	6	12	14	3	11^1															12
1	5	12		6		7	11	9		4			3	2				8	10^1										13
1	2		5	6		7^3	11	9^1	12	4			3	13	14		8	10^2											14
1	4	3		5	6	7^3	8	14	13	11	12		2					9^3	10^1										15
1	4	3^3		5	6	7	8		13	11^1	10	12	2	14				9^2											16
1	4	13		5	6	7^3	8	14	12	11			3^2	2	10			9^1											17
1	4	13		5	6	7	8	12	14	11			3^2	2	10^1			9^3											18
1	4	12		5	6		8	9	13	11^3	14		3^1	2				7^2	10										19
1	3		4	5	6		8^2	14	9	11			12	2^3	13			7^3	10										20
1	4	13		5	6		8	9	10^1	11^2	12		3	2				7											21
1	4	12		5	6		8	9	10	11			3	2				7^1											22
1	4	12	6	5			8	9	10	11			3	2^2	13			7^2											23
1	2		4	5	6		9^1		11	7		3		8						12	10								24
1	2	3^3	4	5	6			10	11^2	7		14	12	13	8					9^1									25
1	2		5	6	4			10	11^2	8		3	12	13						9		7^1							26
1	5		4		6		8	10	11	7^2		3	2	12		13	9^1												27
1	2	4^3	5	6			8	10	11	7^1		3	14	13		12^2	9												28
1	4^1		5	6			8	10^3	11	7^2		3	2	9		13	14				12								29
1	2	12		5	6		8	13	10	11	7		3	4^1				9^2											30
1	4		5	6			8	12	10	11	7		3		13			9^2					2^1						31
1	2		4	5	6		8	9	10	7			3					11											32
1	2		4	5	6		8	10^2	11^1	7			3	13				9											33
1	4		5	6			8	9^2		11	12		7	13	10								2^3		3^1	14			34
1	4	3^2	5	6				10^1	11	7				9	8								2			12	13		35
	4		5	6				10	11	8			3		7	9							2					1	36

BERWICK RANGERS Second Division

Year Formed: 1881. *Ground & Address:* Shielfield Park, Tweedmouth, Berwick-upon-Tweed TD15 2EF. *Telephone:* 01289 307424. *Fax:* 01289 307424. Club 24 hour hotline 09068 800697. *Ground Capacity:* 4131, seated: 1366. *Size of Pitch:* 110yd × 70yd.
Chairman: James G. Curle. *Vice-chairman:* Moray McLaren. *Club Secretary:* Dennis McCleary. *Treasurer:* J. N. Simpson.
Manager: Paul Smith. *Assistant Manager:* Greg Shaw. *Coaches:* Ian Oliver, Ian Smith, Brian Cordery. *Physios:* Rev. Glyn Jones, Ian Oliver and Ian Smith.
Managers since 1975: H. Melrose, G. Haig, W. Galbraith, D. Smith, F. Connor, J. McSherry, E. Tait, J. Thomson, J. Jefferies, R. Callachan, J. Anderson, J. Crease, T. Hendrie, I. Ross, J. Thomson.
Club Nickname(s): The Borderers. *Previous Grounds:* Bull Stob Close, Pier Field, Meadow Field, Union Park, Old Shielfield.
Record Attendance: 13,365 v Rangers, Scottish Cup 1st rd; 28 Jan, 1967.
Record Victory: 8-1 v Forfar Ath. Division II; 25 Dec, 1965; v Vale of Leithen, Scottish Cup; Dec, 1966.
Record Defeat: 1-9 v Hamilton A, First Division; 9 Aug, 1980.
Most Capped Player: —.
Most League Appearances: 435: Eric Tait, 1970-87.
Most League Goals in Season (Individual): 38: Ken Bowron, Division II; 1963-64.
Most Goals Overall (Individual): 115: Eric Tait, 1970-87.

BERWICK RANGERS 2001–02 LEAGUE RECORD

Match No.	Date	Venue	Opponents	Result	H/T Score	Lg. Pos.	Goalscorers	Attendance
1	Aug 4	H	Alloa Ath	L	0-4	0-1	—	649
2	11	A	Cowdenbeath	L	1-2	1-1	0	Duthie [24]	326
3	18	H	Clydebank	L	0-2	0-1	10		420
4	25	A	Stenhousemuir	L	0-3	0-3	10		505
5	Sept 2	H	Morton	W	2-0	1-0	—	Anthony [1], Brannigan [81]	647
6	8	H	Hamilton A	L	0-2	0-2	10		475
7	15	A	Stranraer	W	2-0	2-0	9	Neill A [24], Wood [34]	379
8	22	H	Queen of the S	L	0-4	0-1	10		460
9	29	A	Forfar Ath	L	1-2	0-0	10	Glancy [60]	380
10	Oct 6	A	Alloa Ath	D	2-2	2-1	10	Robertson [6], Smith [15]	492
11	20	H	Cowdenbeath	L	2-5	1-3	10	Wood 2 [21, 62]	472
12	27	A	Hamilton A	W	1-0	1-0	10	Anthony [36]	2441
13	Nov 3	H	Stenhousemuir	D	1-1	1-0	10	Wood [12]	387
14	10	H	Stranraer	D	2-2	1-1	10	Anthony [44], Bennett (pen) [64]	382
15	24	A	Morton	W	2-1	2-0	9	Forrest [29], Thomas [45]	1193
16	Dec 1	A	Queen of the S	D	2-2	0-2	9	Forrest [70], Wood [88]	1113
17	15	H	Forfar Ath	D	1-1	1-1	9	Anthony [38]	518
18	Jan 12	A	Stenhousemuir	W	3-1	1-1	10	Smith [44], Feroz 2 [47, 49]	406
19	19	H	Morton	D	0-0	0-0	9		690
20	26	A	Stranraer	D	2-2	0-1	8	Bennett [77], Neil M [89]	370
21	Feb 2	A	Forfar Ath	D	0-0	0-0	9		1066
22	9	H	Queen of the S	W	1-0	1-0	7	Feroz [15]	552
23	16	A	Cowdenbeath	D	1-1	0-1	7	Bennett [78]	366
24	19	H	Hamilton A	W	2-0	1-0	—	Wood [8], Feroz [73]	576
25	23	H	Clydebank	L	1-2	0-1	7	McDowell [76]	535
26	Mar 2	H	Stenhousemuir	W	2-1	1-0	7	Smith [10], Bennett [82]	420
27	5	A	Alloa Ath	L	0-1	0-0	—		637
28	9	A	Hamilton A	L	1-3	1-2	7	Anthony [33]	1868
29	16	H	Stranraer	W	4-1	0-0	6	Wood 2 [68, 70], McDowell 2 [73, 81]	424
30	23	A	Morton	L	2-3	2-1	7	McDowell [5], Smith A [40]	1011
31	30	A	Queen of the S	D	0-0	0-0	8		2758
32	Apr 3	A	Clydebank	W	2-0	2-0	—	Bennett [9], Neil M [14]	175
33	6	H	Forfar Ath	L	0-2	0-0	8		356
34	13	A	Alloa Ath	D	1-1	1-0	8	Wood [44]	675
35	20	A	Cowdenbeath	W	1-0	1-0	7	McDowell [25]	631
36	27	A	Clydebank	W	2-1	2-1	6	McDowell 2 [18, 25]	209

Final League Position: 6

Honours
League Champions: Second Division 1978-79; *Runners-up:* Second Division 1993-94. Third Division 1999-2000.
Scottish Cup: Quarter-finals: 1953-54, 1979-80.
League Cup: Semi-finals: 1963-64.

Club colours: Shirt: Black with 4 inch gold stripes. Shorts: Black with white trim. Stockings: Gold with black trim.

Goalscorers: *League* (44): Wood 9, McDowell 7, Anthony 5, Bennett 5 (1 pen), Feroz 4, Smith D 3, Forrest 2, Neil M 2, Brannigan 1, Duthie 1, Glancy 1, Neill A 1, Robertson 1, Smith A 1, Thomas 1.
Scottish Cup (1): Feroz 1.
CIS Cup (0):
Challenge Cup (3): Glancy 1, Ritchie 1, Wood 1.

McCulloch W 24	Ritchie I 4	McNicoll G 13+4	Murie D 35	Neill A 36	Forrest G 25+6	Bradley M 17+11	Whelan J 6+4	Ronald P 2+3	Glancy M 6+3	Bennett N 25+2	Crawford D 1+2	Duthie M 1	Rae D -+2	Anthony M 23+4	Farrell G 21+1	Neil M 19+4	Wood G 28	Smith D 19+8	O'Connor G 6	Brannigan K 5	Gray D 1+3	Robertson A 8	Harvey J 1+3	Thomas K 3+2	Feroz C 20+2	Huxford R 11+3	McDonald C 7+4	McDowell M 10+6	May E 3+3	Smith A 5	Mathers P 6	Match No.
1	2	3	4	5	6	7	8	9¹	10	11	12																					1
1	2	3	4	5	6¹	7	8	9	10²		12	11	13																			2
1	2	3	4	5	6²	7	13	12	10	9¹							8	11														3
1	5	2¹	4	3	6	7		14	10²				13	12		8¹	9	11														4
			4	5		7	11						3¹	10	2	8¹	9	12	1		6											5
			4²	5		7	11¹	13					3	10	2	8	9	12	1			6³	14									6
		2	4	5	6	7	11¹	12					3	9		8			1			10										7
		2	4	5	6	7	14	11¹	12				3	8²			9³		1			13	10									8
		2²	4	6²	7			10	3				14	12	9	11¹			1	5	13	8										9
			4²	5	12	13	7	9	8³	3				2		11			1	6					10¹	14						10
1			4²	5	12	13	7		14	3				8³	2		9	11		6					10¹							11
1		2	5	6	7	12	10¹			3				11	4		8	9														12
1		2	5	6	7	13	10¹			3				11²	4		8	9							12							13
1		2	5	6						3				11	4		8	9	13						7²	10¹	12					14
1		2	5	6						3				8	4		9	12							10	13	11¹	7²				15
1	12	2	5	6						3				8	4³		9	13							10²	11¹	7	14				16
1		2	5	6	12					3				8	4		9	10								11	7					17
1	7	4	5	6	14					3				8¹	2	12		11³							13	10		9²				18
1	7	4	5	6	14					3				8²	2	13		11³							10			9¹				19
1	7	4³	5	6	14					3				9¹	2²	10	9								13	11	12					20
1		4	5	6						3				8	2	7		11²							9	10¹	12	13				21
1		4	5	6	13					3				8²		7	14								9³	2	10¹	12	11			22
1	14	4³	5	6										8	13	7									9	2	10¹	12	11²			23
1		4	5	6	11					3				8		7	13								9	2	12					24
1		4	5	6	11¹					3²				12	8	7	13								9	2	10					25
1		4	5		11					12				2	8	7	3								9	6¹	13	10²				26
1		4	5	6	11¹					3				13	2¹	8	7	12							9	14	10²					27
1	13	3³	4	6										7²	2¹	8	10	11							9	5	14	12				28
1	13	3	5	6	14					10³				2	8	7	11								9¹	12		4²				29
1		3	5	6²	14					12				10¹	2	8	7	11³							13	9		4				30
		4	3	5	12					6				8		7	11	10							2			9¹			1	31
		4	3	5	12					6¹				8		7	11	10							2	13		9²			1	32
		4		5	6									8		7	11	10							2			9	3		1	33
		2	4	3	12									8		10	7	11							6			9²	5		1	34
		3	5	12	14					10³				8		7²	11								6	2	13	9¹	4		1	35
		3	5	14	7					13				6³		11¹	4					12			2	10	9²	8			1	36

BRECHIN CITY

Second Division

Year Formed: 1906. *Ground & Address:* Glebe Park, Trinity Rd, Brechin, Angus DD9 6BJ. *Telephone:* 01356 622856.
Fax (to Secretary): 01356 625524.
Ground Capacity: total: 3980, seated: 1518. *Size of Pitch:* 110yd × 67yd.
Chairman: David Birse. *Vice-Chairman:* Hugh Campbell Adamson. *Secretary:* Ken Ferguson.
Manager: Dick Campbell. *Assistant Manager:* Ian Campbell. *Youth Coach:* George Shields. *Physio:* Tom Gilmartin.
Managers since 1975: C. Dunn, I. Stewart, D. Houston, I. Fleming, J. Ritchie, I. Redford, J. Young.
Club Nickname(s): The City. *Previous Grounds:* Nursery Park.
Record Attendance: 8122 v Aberdeen, Scottish Cup 3rd rd; 3 Feb, 1973.
Record Transfer Fee received: £100,000 for Scott Thomson to Aberdeen (1991).
Record Transfer Fee paid: £16,000 for Sandy Ross from Berwick Rangers (1991).
Record Victory: 12-1 v Thornhill, Scottish Cup 1st rd; 28 Jan, 1926.
Record Defeat: 0-10 v Airdrieonians, Albion R and Cowdenbeath, all in Division II; 1937-38.
Most Capped Player: —.
Most League Appearances: 459: David Watt, 1975-89.
Most League Goals in Season (Individual): 26: W. McIntosh, Division II; 1959-60.
Most Goals Overall (Individual): 131: Ian Campbell.

BRECHIN CITY 2001–02 LEAGUE RECORD

Match No.	Date	Venue	Opponents	Result	H/T Score	Lg. Pos.	Goalscorers	Atten-dance
1	Aug 4	A	Dumbarton	W 2-1	1-1	—	Bain [28], King [47]	837
2	11	H	East Fife	W 6-0	2-0	1	Grant 2 [15, 83], Templeman 3 [38, 46, 51], Leask [82]	472
3	18	A	Stirling A	W 3-1	1-1	1	Grant 2 [43, 47], Templeman [55]	626
4	25	H	Albion R	W 4-1	3-0	1	Fotheringham [10], Bain (pen) [17], Campbell [26], Honeyman [85]	517
5	Sept 8	A	Montrose	W 1-0	1-0	1	Templeman [17]	859
6	15	H	Queen's Park	W 3-1	1-0	1	Templeman [23], Honeyman 2 [54, 82]	423
7	22	A	Peterhead	L 2-4	0-3	1	Grant [47], Smith J [79]	643
8	29	H	East Stirling	L 1-2	0-1	1	Grant [70]	422
9	Oct 7	H	Elgin C	W 1-0	0-0	1	Bain [80]	501
10	13	A	Dumbarton	W 3-2	2-2	1	Grant [17], Fotheringham [39], Clark [90]	439
11	20	A	East Fife	L 1-3	0-0	1	King [71]	434
12	27	H	Montrose	D 0-0	0-0	1		865
13	Nov 3	A	Albion R	W 2-1	1-1	1	Bain [20], Black [71]	262
14	10	H	Queen's Park	W 2-1	0-1	1	O'Boyle [75], Bain (pen) [79]	436
15	24	A	East Stirling	W 4-3	1-2	1	O'Boyle [11], Smith J [49], Templeman 2 [71, 72]	228
16	27	H	Elgin C	W 1-0	1-0	—	Clark [37]	415
17	Dec 1	H	Peterhead	W 4-3	3-2	1	Clark [7], Templeman 2 [39, 42], Smith J [90]	511
18	Jan 12	H	Albion R	D 0-0	0-0	1		457
19	19	H	Elgin C	W 1-0	0-0	1	Smith D [85]	438
20	26	A	Queen's Park	D 0-0	0-0	1		646
21	Feb 2	H	East Stirling	W 2-0	2-0	1	King [9], Templeman [33]	383
22	9	A	Peterhead	W 3-1	2-1	1	Smith J [33], King [45], Miller [59]	796
23	16	H	East Fife	D 1-1	1-0	1	Templeman [38]	452
24	27	A	Dumbarton	L 1-2	1-0	—	Fotheringham [29]	533
25	Mar 2	A	Albion R	W 1-0	1-0	1	Smith J [5]	304
26	5	A	Montrose	D 0-0	0-0	—		748
27	9	H	Montrose	W 2-0	0-0	1	Smith J [52], Fotheringham [78]	738
28	12	H	Stirling A	W 3-1	0-0	1	Grant 2 [48, 51], Bain [75]	398
29	16	A	Queen's Park	W 5-0	5-0	1	King [1], Grant [4], Clark [13], Fotheringham [18], Templeman [40]	471
30	19	A	Stirling A	W 3-1	0-1	1	Templeman [48], King [64], Fotheringham [67]	315
31	23	A	Elgin C	L 1-3	0-2	1	Templeman [62]	652
32	30	H	Peterhead	D 1-1	1-0	1	Bain [43]	1186
33	Apr 6	A	East Stirling	L 0-2	0-0	1		237
34	13	H	Dumbarton	L 0-1	0-1	1		714
35	20	A	East Fife	D 1-1	0-1	1	Miller [60]	356
36	27	H	Stirling A	W 2-1	2-0	1	King [37], Campbell [44]	449

Final League Position: 1

Honours
League Champions: C Division 1953-54. Second Division 1982-83, 1989-90. Third Division 2001-02. *Runners-up:* Second Division 1992-93. Third Division 1995-96.
Scottish Cup: —.
League Cup: —.
Bell's League Challenge: Semi-finalists 2001-02.

Club colours: Shirt, Shorts, Stockings: Red with white trimmings.

Goalscorers: *League* (67): Templeman 15, Grant 10, Bain 7 (2 pens), King 7, Fotheringham 6, Smith J 6, Clark 4, Honeyman 3, Campbell 2, Miller 2, O'Boyle 2, Black 1, Leask 1, Smith D 1.
Scottish Cup (4): O'Boyle 2, Fotheringham 1, Grant 1.
CIS Cup (0):
Challenge Cup (11): Fotheringham 3 (1 pen), Smith 3, Grant 2, Bain 1, Kernaghan 1, Templeman 1.

Cairns M 26	Smith D 17+15	Fotheringham K 32	Bain K 29+2	Carney H 32	Kernaghan A 3	King C 36	Miller G 26	Grant R 23+2	Black R 29+5	Templeman C 34+1	Honeyman B 6+13	Leask M 1+7	Craig D 2+3	Riley P 13+9	Dewar G —+3	Campbell P 11+11	McAllister S 1+1	Henderson R —+6	Smith J 30	Donachie B 3+4	Clark D 24+3	Ewart J 4+2	O'Boyle G 4+1	McKeown K 10	Match No.
1	2	3^1	4	5	6	7	8	9	10^2	11^1	12	13	14												1
1	2	6	4	5		7^1	8^3	9	3	10	11^2	13		12	14										2
1	2^1	3	4	5	6	7	8	9	10^2	12	13			11^3	14										3
1	2^2	3	4	5	6	7	11^3	9	13	10^2	12	14							8						4
1	2	3	4	5		7^3	8	9	11	10^1	12	14							13		6^2				5
1	12	3	4	5		7	8	9^3	6	10^2	11					2^1	13	14							6
1	12	3	4	5		7	8^1	9	6	10^2	11^3		14			13				2					7
1	12		4	5		7		9	6	10^3	11^2	3		8^1	13				2	14					8
1	2		4	5		7		9^1	8	10	12		3						6		11				9
1	8	3		5^1		7		9	6	10^2	13	12	4						2		11				10
1	2	3	4			7		9	6^2	10				8^1	14	12			5		11^3	13			11
1		3	4			7		6	9	10^1	12		8						2		11	5			12
1	14	3	4			7^3		6	13	9^1			12	8^2					2		11	5	10		13
1	13	3	4			7		6	9				12	8^1					2		11	5^2	10		14
1	2	11	4	5		7^2		3	9	13			8^1						6		12		10		15
1	2	3	4	5		7^1	12	8^3	9^2	13						6	14	11					10		16
1	2	8	4	5		7		9^1	3	10						6		11					12		17
1		3	4^1	5		7	8	9	11^3	10^2	14	13	12			6	2								18
1	12	6		5		7^1	8	9	3	10				4^2				13	2		11				19
1	13	6	4	5		10	7^2	9^1	3	8								12	2		11				20
1	8^1	6	4	5		7	10		3	9^2	12							13	2		11				21
1	8	6	4^1	5		7	10^3		3	9^2		13				14		12^2	2		11				22
1	8^1	6	4^2	5		7	10^3	12	3	9		13				14		13	2		11				23
1		6	4	5		7	8^1	9	3	10		13				12			2		11^2				24
	14	6	12	5		11^3	3^1	9^2	13	7					8	10			4		2			1	25
	14	6	13	5		11	3	9	12	10					7^3	8^2			4		2^1			1	26
		6	4	5		7	11	9	3	10					8^1				2		12			1	27
	14	6	4^3	5		11	7^1	9	3	10					8^2				2	13	12			1	28
	13	6	4^3	5		7	11	9^2		10					8^1	12			2	14	3			1	29
	13	6	4	5		7	11^3	9	14	10					8^1	12			2		3^2			1	30
	13	6	4	5		7	11^3	9	12	10					8^1	14			2		3^2			1	31
	13	6	4	5		10	7^2	3	9^1	12					8				2		11			1	32
	7			5		11	6	3	9						4				2	10	8			1	33
	7^2	6	4	5		10	8^1	3	9	13					12				2		11			1	34
1	2^1			5		7	10	3	9	12		14			8^2				6		4	11^3	13		35
1	12	6^1		5		7	8^3	3	9	13					10^2	14			4		2	11			36

CELTIC
Premier League

Year Formed: 1888. *Ground & Address:* Celtic Park, Glasgow G40 3RE. *Telephone:* 0141 556 2611. *Fax:* 0141 551 8106.
Ground Capacity: all seated: 60,832. *Size of Pitch:* 110m × 68m.
Chairman: Brian Quinn. *Chief Executive:* Ian McLeod. *Secretary:* Robert Howat.
Manager: Martin O'Neill. *Assistant Manager:* John Robertson. *First Team Coach:* Steve Walford. *Youth Development Manager:* Tommy Burns. *Head Youth Coach:* Willie McStay. *Physio:* Brian Scott. *Assistant Physio:* Neil McLeod.
Kit Manager: John Clark.
Managers since 1975: Jock Stein, Billy McNeill, David Hay, Billy McNeill, Liam Brady, Lou Macari, Tommy Burns, Wim Jansen, Dr Jozef Venglos, John Barnes (Head Coach). *Club Nickname(s):* The Bhoys. *Previous Grounds:* None.
Record Attendance: 92,000 v Rangers, Division I; 1 Jan, 1938.
Record Transfer Fee received: £4,700,000 for Paolo Di Canio to Sheffield W (August 1997).
Record Transfer Fee paid: £6,000,000 for Chris Sutton from Chelsea (July 2000).
Record Victory: 11-0 Dundee, Division I; 26 Oct, 1895.
Record Defeat: 0-8 v Motherwell, Division I; 30 Apr, 1937.
Most Capped Player: Paddy Bonner, 80, Republic of Ireland.
Most League Appearances: 486: Billy McNeill 1957-75.
Most League Goals in Season (Individual): 50: James McGrory, Division I; 1935-36.
Most Goals Overall (Individual): 397: James McGrory; 1922-39.

Honours
League Champions: (38 times) Division I 1892-93, 1893-94, 1895-96, 1897-98, 1904-05, 1905-06, 1906-07, 1907-08, 1908-09, 1909-10, 1913-14, 1914-15, 1915-16, 1916-17, 1918-19, 1921-22, 1925-26, 1935-36, 1937-38, 1953-54, 1965-66, 1966-67, 1967-68, 1968-69, 1969-70, 1970-71, 1971-72, 1972-73, 1973-74. Premier Division 1976-77, 1978-79, 1980-81, 1981-82, 1985-86, 1987-88, 1997-98, 2000-01, 2001-02. *Runners-up:* 26 times.

CELTIC 2001–02 LEAGUE RECORD

Match No.	Date	Venue	Opponents	Result	H/T Score	Lg. Pos.	Goalscorers	Attendance
1	Jul 28	H	St Johnstone	W 3-0	1-0	—	Mjällby [36], Lambert 2 [63, 72]	57,933
2	Aug 4	A	Kilmarnock	W 1-0	0-0	2	Larsson [75]	13,201
3	11	H	Hearts	W 2-0	1-0	1	Larsson 2 [45, 64]	57,715
4	18	H	Livingston	D 0-0	0-0	1		10,024
5	25	A	Hibernian	W 4-1	4-0	1	Moravcik [15], Sutton 2 [16, 19], Larsson [31]	14,701
6	Sept 8	H	Dunfermline Ath	W 3-1	2-0	1	Moravcik 2 [8, 72], Sutton [45]	58,004
7	15	A	Dundee	W 4-0	1-0	1	Larsson 2 [1, 59], Petrov [69], Maloney [87]	9842
8	22	H	Aberdeen	W 2-0	0-0	1	Larsson [65], Petrov [80]	59,386
9	30	H	Rangers	W 2-0	1-0	1	Petrov [13], Thompson [90]	50,097
10	Oct 13	A	Motherwell	W 2-1	1-0	1	Moravcik [14], Larsson (pen) [88]	9922
11	20	H	Dundee U	W 5-1	2-0	1	Hartson 3 [7, 60, 82], Balde [44], Maloney [86]	58,873
12	27	A	Kilmarnock	W 1-0	0-0	1	Valgaeren [89]	58,845
13	Nov 3	A	St Johnstone	W 2-1	1-1	1	Dods (og) [20], Larsson [89]	9041
14	17	A	Hearts	W 1-0	1-0	1	Larsson (pen) [43]	15,570
15	25	H	Rangers	W 2-1	0-0	1	Valgaeren [58], Larsson [70]	59,633
16	Dec 1	A	Hibernian	W 3-0	2-0	1	Hartson 2 [10, 39], Lennon [71]	59,220
17	9	A	Dunfermline Ath	W 4-0	2-0	1	Balde [8], Hartson 2 [19, 58], Thompson [60]	8207
18	15	H	Dundee	W 3-1	0-1	1	Sutton [49], Larsson [56], Hartson [65]	57,559
19	22	A	Aberdeen	L 0-2	0-0	1		18,610
20	26	H	Livingston	W 3-2	1-1	—	Moravcik [12], Larsson 2 [50, 89]	58,407
21	29	A	Dundee U	W 4-0	2-0	1	Hartson [3], Petrov [27], Thompson [47], Larsson [70]	12,165
22	Jan 2	H	Motherwell	W 2-0	0-0	—	Larsson [80], Hartson [87]	58,105
23	12	A	Kilmarnock	W 2-0	0-0	1	Hartson (pen) [50], Lambert [60]	11,689
24	19	H	St Johnstone	W 2-1	2-1	1	Larsson [8], Thompson [11]	58,516
25	23	H	Hearts	W 2-0	0-0	—	Larsson 2 [76, 86]	57,177
26	30	A	Livingston	W 3-1	0-1	1	Moravcik [57], Larsson [60], Hartson [72]	8437
27	Feb 2	A	Hibernian	D 1-1	0-1	1	Hartson [50]	12,313
28	9	H	Dunfermline Ath	W 5-0	4-0	1	Larsson 3 [12, 36, 42], Hartson [31], Agathe [72]	58,987
29	17	A	Dundee	W 3-0	2-0	1	Larsson [19], Mjällby [42], Hartson [76]	10,642
30	Mar 2	H	Aberdeen	W 1-0	1-0	1	Thompson (pen) [45]	59,584
31	10	A	Rangers	D 1-1	1-0	1	Petrov [23]	49,765
32	16	H	Dundee U	W 1-0	1-0	1	Petrov [40]	58,392
33	19	A	Motherwell	W 4-0	1-0	—	Lambert [9], Larsson 2 [52, 66], Mjällby [77]	10,134
34	Apr 6	H	Livingston	W 5-1	4-0	1	Larsson 3 [2, 32, 59], Hartson 2 [18, 24]	59,510
35	13	A	Dunfermline Ath	W 5-0	2-0	1	Hartson 2 [19, 70], Lambert [39], Smith [59], Sylla [76]	56,715
36	21	H	Rangers	D 1-1	1-1	1	Thompson [42]	59,034
37	28	A	Hearts	W 4-1	2-1	1	Lynch 2 [12, 41], Maloney 2 [50, 65]	13,288
38	May 12	A	Aberdeen	W 1-0	0-0	1	Maloney [70]	15,332

Final League Position: 1

Scottish Cup Winners: (31 times) 1892, 1899, 1900, 1904, 1907, 1908, 1911, 1912, 1914, 1923, 1925, 1927, 1931, 1933, 1937, 1951, 1954, 1965, 1967, 1969, 1971, 1972, 1974, 1975, 1977, 1980, 1985, 1988, 1989, 1995, 2001. *Runners-up:* 18 times.
League Cup Winners: (12 times) 1956-57, 1957-58, 1965-66, 1966-67, 1967-68, 1968-69, 1969-70, 1974-75, 1982-83, 1997-98, 1999-2000, 2000-01. *Runners-up:* 10 times.

European: *European Cup:* 90 matches (1966-67 winners, 1967-68, 1968-69, 1969-70 runners-up, 1970-71, 1971-72 semi-finals, 1972-73, 1973-74 semi-finals, 1974-75, 1977-78, 1979-80, 1981-82, 1982-83, 1986-87, 1988-89, 1998-99, 2001-02). *Cup Winners' Cup:* 39 matches (1963-64 semi-finals, 1965-66 semi-finals, 1975-76, 1980-81, 1984-85, 1985-86, 1989-90, 1995-96). *UEFA Cup:* 56 matches (*Fairs Cup:* 1962-63, 1964-65). *UEFA Cup:* 1976-77, 1983-84, 1987-88, 1991-92, 1992-93, 1993-94, 1996-97, 1997-98, 1998-99, 1999-2000, 2000-01, 2001-02).

Club colours: Shirt: Emerald green and white hoops. Shorts: White with emerald trim. Stockings: White.

Goalscorers: *League* (94): Larsson 29 (2 pens), Hartson 19 (1 pen), Moravcik 6, Petrov 6, Thompson 6 (1 pen), Lambert 5, Maloney 5, Sutton 4, Mjällby 3, Balde 2, Lynch 2, Valgaeren 2, Agathe 1, Lennon 1, Smith 1, Sylla 1, own goal 1.
Scottish Cup (14): Balde 2, Hartson 2, Larsson 2, Thompson 2, Maloney 1, Petrov 1, Petta 1, Sylla 1, Wieghorst 1, own goal 1.
CIS Cup (11): Maloney 4, Hartson 3, Balde 2, Healy 1, Tebily 1.

Douglas R 35	Mjällby J 35	Valgaeren J 19	Tebily O 8 + 3	Thompson A 22 + 3	Lennon N 32 + 1	Lambert P 33 + 1	Sutton C 18	Larsson H 33	Agathe D 21	McNamara J 9 + 11	Moravcik L 17 + 7	Crainey S 10 + 5	Hartson J 26 + 5	Maloney S 3 + 13	Guppy S 10 + 6	Boyd T 9	Sylla M 7 + 1	Kharine D 2 + 1	Balde B 22	Petrov S 25 + 2	Healy C 2 + 2	Smith J 3 + 9	Wieghorst M 2 + 1	Gould J 1	Kennedy J 1	Lynch S 1	Match No.
1	2³	3	4	5¹	6	7	8	9	10	11³	12	13	14														1
1	2	3	4³	5¹	6¹	7	8	9	10	11	13		14 12														2
1	2		4		5²	3	8	9	10¹	6		7		11	12	13											3
1	2¹		12	13		6	8	9	10		5		11		7²	3	4										4
1⁸	2²			4	5		6¹	8	9	10	11		7		12		13	3		15							5
	3²	2	5¹		6		9	10	11		7	12	13					1	4	8³	14						6
1	2	3		5		6³	8	9²	10	11		7¹			13	14			4	12							7
1	2		3	5	7		8		10¹				11	12		6			4	9²	13						8
1	2	3		5			7	8	9	10	11		12						4	6¹							9
1	2	3			7			10			9¹		11	12	8		5		4	6							10
1	2	3	14	5		6¹	8		10²	9	12	7		11	13				4³								11
	2	3	4¹		6	12	8	9		11		7		10²	13		1		5								12
1	2	3		5¹	7²	6	13	9	10	8				11	12				4								13
1	2			12	7	6	8	9	10	11¹			3						4	5							14
1	2	3			6	7	8		10		13	9¹		11²	12				4	5							15
1	2	3¹		12	6¹	7³	8	9	10				13	11	14		4			5							16
1	2	3		5		7³	8¹	10		13			11	12	9				4	6¹		14					17
1	2			5		7	8	3	10	6		9¹		11					4								18
1	2	3		5	13	7	8²	9	10		12			11¹					4	6							19
1	2	3		5		7	8	11¹	10		13	9²		12					4	6							20
1	2		12	9	13	7²	8³		10		5		3¹	11	14				4	6							21
1	2	3		9	13	7	8		10		5	12		11					4²	6¹							22
1	2	3		9	12	7¹	8		10		5			11					4	6							23
1	2	3	4	7	12		8		10		5	9¹		11						6							24
1	2	3		9	6¹	7	8		10		5	12		11					4								25
1	2	3		6³	7	8		10		5¹	12		11			14			4	9²		13					26
1	2			6²	7	8		10			9¹	3	11	13	12				4			5					27
1	2¹		5		7¹	8	3	10	6		9²	14	11	13					4			12					28
1	2		5		7	8²	3	10¹	9²		12		11		13				4	6		14					29
1	2		5		7	8²		11	13	9¹	4		10		3				6			12					30
1	2			7	8		10	9	12		3	11		5¹					4	6							31
1	2			7	8		10	11		9¹	3			5	4				6	12							32
1	2			8¹		10	7¹	13	9²	3	3	11		5	4	12			6	14							33
1	2			7	8²	4	10	9	13	12	3³	11		5¹					6	14							34
1	2³		13	7¹	8		11²				3	10		9	4	5			6	12		14					35
1	2		5	7	8¹		10	6		9²	3	11		13	4				12								36
					5						10	9	4	3							8	7	6	1	2	11	37
1					5						10	11	2	3					4	8	9	7	6				38

CLYDE

First Division

Year Formed: 1878. *Ground & Address:* Broadwood Stadium, Cumbernauld, G68 9NE. *Telephone:* 01236 451511.
Ground Capacity: all seated: 8200. *Size of Pitch:* 112yd × 76yd.
Chairman: W. B. Carmichael. *Secretary:* John D. Taylor.
Manager: Alan Kernaghan. *Assistant Manager:* Billy Reid. *First Team Coach:* Denis McDaid. *Physio:* Ian McKinlay.
Managers since 1975: S. Anderson, C. Brown, J. Clark, A. Smith, G. Speirs, A. Maitland.
Club Nickname(s): The Bully Wee. *Previous Grounds:* Barrowfield & Shawfield Stadium.
Record Attendance: 52,000 v Rangers, Division I; 21 Nov, 1908.
Record Transfer Fee received: £175,000 for Scott Howie to Norwich City (Aug 1993).
Record Transfer Fee paid: £14,000 for Harry Hood from Sunderland (1966).
Record Victory: 11-1 v Cowdenbeath, Division II; 6 Oct, 1951.
Record Defeat: 0-11 v Dumbarton, Scottish Cup 4th rd, 22 Nov, 1879; v Rangers, Scottish Cup 4th rd, 13 Nov, 1880.
Most Capped Player: Tommy Ring, 12, Scotland.
Most League Appearances: 428: Brian Ahern.
Most League Goals in Season (Individual): 32: Bill Boyd, 1932-33.
Most Goals Overall (Individual): —.

CLYDE 2001–02 LEAGUE RECORD

Match No.	Date	Venue	Opponents	Result	H/T Score	Lg. Pos.	Goalscorers	Attendance
1	Aug 4	H	Inverness CT	D	1-1	1-0	—	Crawford [35]	975
2	11	A	St Mirren	L	1-4	1-2	9	Crawford [45]	3668
3	18	H	Arbroath	W	1-0	0-0	6	Cusick (og) [72]	831
4	25	A	Falkirk	D	1-1	1-0	6	Mitchell [26]	2618
5	Sept 8	H	Ross Co	W	3-0	2-0	3	Keogh 2 [23, 35], Millen [65]	888
6	15	A	Partick Th	L	0-3	0-2	5		4226
7	18	H	Airdrieonians	L	0-3	0-3	—		908
8	23	A	Ayr U	L	1-2	0-2	10	Hinds [62]	2278
9	29	H	Raith R	W	3-2	2-0	8	Hagen [1], Millen [19], Convery [71]	1222
10	Oct 13	A	Inverness CT	L	1-5	0-2	9	McCusker (pen) [88]	1653
11	20	H	St Mirren	D	1-1	1-0	9	Keogh [7]	2481
12	27	A	Ross Co	L	0-4	0-3	10		2311
13	Nov 3	H	Falkirk	D	1-1	1-0	10	Keogh (pen) [41]	2013
14	10	A	Airdrieonians	W	2-1	0-0	8	Convery [71], Mitchell [73]	1629
15	17	H	Partick Th	W	3-1	2-0	5	Mitchell 2 [5, 47], Keogh [40]	3551
16	24	A	Raith R	W	2-1	1-1	5	Kernaghan [33], Mensing [82]	1556
17	Dec 1	A	Ayr U	D	2-2	1-1	5	Keogh [10], McLaughlin [64]	1314
18	8	A	Arbroath	L	1-2	0-1	6	Keogh [63]	813
19	15	H	Inverness CT	W	1-0	0-0	4	Hinds [61]	782
20	Jan 2	A	Partick Th	L	1-2	0-1	—	Hagen [83]	5005
21	12	A	Airdrieonians	L	0-1	0-1	6		1637
22	19	A	Ayr U	W	1-0	1-0	6	Hinds [29]	2151
23	Feb 2	H	Raith R	L	1-2	0-1	6	Hinds [77]	1095
24	9	H	Arbroath	W	1-0	1-0	5	Keogh (pen) [29]	941
25	16	A	St Mirren	D	2-2	1-1	6	Hinds [3], Mitchell (pen) [89]	2827
26	Mar 2	H	Falkirk	L	2-3	0-3	7	Carrigan (pen) [73], Ross [82]	1719
27	5	A	Falkirk	W	6-1	1-1	—	Carrigan 3 [16, 61, 82], Hinds 3 [47, 64, 70]	1817
28	9	A	Ross Co	L	1-2	0-0	7	Hinds [84]	2145
29	12	H	Ross Co	D	0-0	0-0	—		703
30	16	A	Airdrieonians	D	2-2	1-1	7	Hinds [29], Millen [84]	1551
31	27	H	Partick Th	W	2-1	0-0	—	Hinds [54], Ross [60]	2541
32	30	A	Ayr U	D	2-2	0-1	7	Ross [60], Potter [62]	1084
33	Apr 6	A	Raith R	W	1-0	1-0	5	Keogh [39]	1626
34	13	A	Inverness CT	D	1-1	0-0	5	Fraser [78]	1525
35	20	H	St Mirren	W	3-1	1-1	5	Fraser 2 [19, 65], Keogh [62]	1480
36	27	A	Arbroath	L	0-2	0-2	5		859

Final League Position: 5

Honors
League Champions: Division II 1904-05, 1951-52, 1956-57, 1961-62, 1972-73. Second Division 1977-78, 1981-82, 1992-93, 1999-2000.
Runners-up: Division II 1903-04, 1905-06, 1925-26, 1963-64.
Scottish Cup Winners: 1939, 1955, 1958; *Runners-up:* 1910, 1912, 1949.
League Cup: —

Club colours: Shirt: White with red and black trim. Shorts: Black. Stockings: Black with red and white tops.

Goalscorers: *League* (51): Hinds 11, Keogh 10 (2 pens), Mitchell 5 (1 pen), Carrigan 4 (1 pen), Fraser 3, Millen 3, Ross 3, Convery 2, Crawford 2, Hagen 2, Kernaghan 1, McCusker 1 (pen), McLaughlin 1, Mensing 1, Potter 1, own goal 1.
Scottish Cup (2): Fraser 1, Mensing 1.
CIS Cup (3): Crawford 2, Kane A 1.
Challenge Cup (9): Kane A 2, Keogh 2, Ross 2, Convery 1, McCusker 1, Mitchell 1.

Halliwell B 24 + 1	Murray D 9	Dunn D 22 + 5	Smith B 25 + 1	Keogh P 28 + 3	Ross J 27	Mitchell J 31	Millen A 31	Hinds L 24 + 8	McClay A 3 + 1	Convery S 13 + 15	Crawford B 8 + 9	Aitken C 2 + 3	Kane A 1 + 9	Budinauckas K 10 + 2	Bingham C 10 + 6	Cranmer C 8 + 5	Okikiolu S 2 + 1	Hagen O 16 + 12	Kernaghan A 15	McPhee B 4	McCusker R — + 1	Grant A — + 1	Mensing S 23	Fraser J 22	De Gregorio R 4 + 5	McDowell M 1 + 3	McLaughlin M 12 + 2	Carrigan B 9	Potter J 6	Kane P 4 + 1	Graham M 2	Match No.
1	2	3	4	5	6	7	8	9¹	10²	11³	12	13	14																			1
15	2	3	4	5	6	7	8			11²	9	13	12	1⁹	10¹																	2
1⁹	2	3	4	9	6	7	8	11²	13	12			10¹		15	5																3
	2	3	4	9¹	6	7	8			10²	14	11¹	12	1				5	13													4
	2	10	4	9²	6²	7	8	13		14				1	12			3¹	5	11												5
	2		4	9	6	7	8			10¹	13	12		1				3	5	11²												6
		3	4	9	6	7	8							1				12	2	10¹	5	11										7
		3	4		6	7	8	11				13	12	1				5²	2	10¹			9									8
	2	13	4	9		7	8	10		12	11³		14	1	6	5¹		3³														9
	12		4	9		7					5	10	6	2¹¹	11¹	8²		3					13	14								10
1	2	13	4¹	9		7	8				10³	11²	14		6	12		3	5													11
1	2¹	13		9		7	8²				10³	12	14		6	5		11	4				3									12
1	8			9		7					10¹	11²	13		12	6		5	3				4	2								13
1	3			9	6¹	7	4				10²	11	13		12			5					2	8³			14					14
1	3			9	6¹	7	4				10³	11³	13		12			5					2	8			14					15
1	3			9	6²	7	4				10¹	11³			13			5					2	8			12	14				16
1	3³			9		7	4	14				11¹			6³			13					2	8	10		13					17
1				9		7	4	14				11¹			6	12		11	5¹				2	8	10³	13		3²				18
				9		7	4	13		11¹	14			1	12	5		3					2	8	6²	10³						19
	12			9		7	4	10³		11¹				1	6²			13	5				2	8			14	3				20
1	3¹	4			6²	7	8	9		11					13				5				2	10	12							21
1		4		6²	7		9³	14							12	13		3	5				2	8	10¹		11					22
1				9	6	7	13										5	10³	4				2	8	12		3¹	11				23
1⁹		6	4	5	10	7		9²		14			15					13					2	8			3	11³				24
1		6	4	5	10	7		9										12					2	8			3	11¹				25
1	10	4		6		8	9	12	14					7¹				13					2	5			3	11³				26
1	10	4		6		8	9	7¹	12						13			14					2	5			3²	11³				27
1	10²	4		6		7³	8	9		12	13							14					2	5			3	11¹				28
1	10¹	4	12	6		7	8³	9²		14	13												2	5			3	11¹				29
1	10	4	5²	6		7	8	9		13								12					2				3	11¹				30
1	11	4	9²	6		7	8	10¹		13								12					2	5					3			31
1	11²	4	9	6¹		7	8	10³		13								14					2	5					3	12		32
1	13	4	9	6²		7	11¹	10³		14								12						5	3		2	8				33
1		4	9	6			11	10¹		12								7						5	3		2	8				34
		4	12	11		6	13	10¹	9²									5					2	8				3	7	1	35
		4	13	6		7	12³	11	10¹									9²					2	5			14	3	8	1	36

CLYDEBANK   Replaced by Airdrie United

Year Formed: 1965. *Club Address:* c/o West of Scotland RFC, Burnbrae, Milngavie, G62 6HX. *Telephone:* 0141 955 9048.
Fax: 0141 955 9049. *Telephone (Match days only):* 01475 723571. *Ground:* (sharing with Morton) Cappielow Park, Sinclair
St, Greenock PA15 2TY. *Ground Capacity:* total: 14,891, seated: 5741. *Size of Pitch:* 110yd × 71yd.
Chairman: Dr John Hall. *Secretary:* Billy Hall.
Manager: Kenneth Brannigan. *Managers since 1975:* D. Ferguson.
Club Nickname(s): The Bankies. *Previous Ground:* Kilbowie Park.
Record Attendance: 14,900 v Hibernian, Scottish Cup 1st rd; 10 Feb, 1965.
Record Transfer Fee received: £175,000 for Owen Coyle from Airdrieonians (Feb 1990).
Record Transfer Fee paid: £50,000 for Gerry McCabe from Clyde.
Record Victory: 8-1 Arbroath, First Division; 3 Jan 1977.
Record Defeat: 1-9 v Gala Fairydean, Scottish Cup qual rd; 15 Sept, 1965.
Most Capped Player: —.
Most League Appearances: 620: Jim Fallon; 1968-86.
Most League Goals in Season (Individual): 29: Ken Eadie, First Division, 1990-91.
Most League Goals Overall (Individual): 138, Ken Eadie 1988-95.

CLYDEBANK 2001–02 LEAGUE RECORD

Match No.	Date	Venue	Opponents	Result	H/T Score	Lg. Pos.	Goalscorers	Attendance
1	Aug 4	A	Forfar Ath	W 2-1	1-1	—	McGrillen [27], Graham [89]	460
2	11	H	Hamilton A	W 3-2	1-2	1	Potter (og) [22], Ferguson [80], Burke (pen) [90]	367
3	18	A	Berwick R	W 2-0	1-0	1	Paton [45], Neill (og) [47]	420
4	25	A	Queen of the S	L 0-1	0-0	1		1108
5	Sept 8	H	Morton	W 3-2	0-1	1	Lavety [62], Burke (pen) [65], McGrillen [90]	1142
6	15	A	Alloa Ath	L 0-1	0-1	3		626
7	19	H	Cowdenbeath	W 3-2	1-1	—	Burke (pen) [41], Lavety [67], Paton [90]	154
8	22	A	Stenhousemuir	D 2-2	2-0	2	Lavety [8], McGrillen [17]	389
9	29	H	Stranraer	L 1-3	0-2	4	Paton [76]	201
10	Oct 13	A	Forfar Ath	D 1-1	0-1	3	Paton [89]	161
11	20	A	Hamilton A	L 0-3	0-0	4		1975
12	27	A	Morton	W 2-0	1-0	4	Burke [12], McColligan [86]	1311
13	Nov 3	H	Queen of the S	W 3-0	3-0	2	McGrillen [9], Paton [26], Burke [37]	392
14	10	H	Alloa Ath	W 1-0	1-0	1	Burke [2]	247
15	24	A	Cowdenbeath	D 1-1	0-0	1	Burke [47]	333
16	Dec 1	H	Stenhousemuir	W 3-2	2-2	1	O'Neill [16], Burke 2 [43, 50]	235
17	15	A	Stranraer	W 1-0	0-0	1	O'Neill [49]	398
18	Jan 8	H	Morton	L 1-2	1-0	—	O'Neill [43]	940
19	12	A	Queen of the S	L 0-1	0-0	1		1161
20	19	H	Cowdenbeath	W 1-0	1-0	1	Jackson [15]	245
21	Feb 2	H	Stranraer	L 1-2	1-0	1	Jackson [33]	231
22	9	A	Stenhousemuir	D 0-0	0-0	1		379
23	16	H	Hamilton A	D 1-1	1-1	1	Shields [27]	421
24	23	A	Berwick R	W 2-1	1-0	1	Paton (pen) [18], Shields [80]	535
25	Mar 5	A	Queen of the S	L 0-1	0-1	2		402
26	5	A	Forfar Ath	W 2-1	1-1	—	Shields [43], Henry (og) [89]	373
27	9	A	Morton	L 1-3	0-1	2	McKinnon [90]	1145
28	12	A	Alloa Ath	D 2-2	2-1	—	O'Neill [6], McGrillen [18]	474
29	16	H	Alloa Ath	D 1-1	0-1	2	McGrillen [77]	260
30	23	A	Cowdenbeath	L 1-2	0-1	3	McGrillen [65]	344
31	30	H	Stenhousemuir	D 0-0	0-0	3		208
32	Apr 3	H	Berwick R	L 0-2	0-2	—		175
33	6	A	Stranraer	D 1-1	0-0	4	Graham [50]	365
34	13	H	Forfar Ath	W 1-0	0-0	4	Paton (pen) [72]	166
35	20	A	Hamilton A	L 0-2	0-1	4		2030
36	27	H	Berwick R	L 1-2	1-2	4	Paton [30]	209

Final League Position: 4

Honours
League Champions: Second Division 1975-76; *Runners-up:* 1997-98; *Runners-up:* First Division 1976-77, 1984-85.
Scottish Cup: Semi-finalists 1990. *League Cup:* —.

Club colours: Shirt: Vertical red and white stripes. Shorts: Black. Stockings: Black.

Goalscorers: *League* (44): Burke 9 (2 pens), Paton 8 (2 pens), McGrillen 7, O'Neill 4, Lavety 3, Shields 3, Graham 2, Jackson 2, Ferguson 1, McColligan 1, McKinnon 1, own goals 3.
Scottish Cup (1): Paton 1
CIS Cup (0):
Challenge Cup (1): Burke 1

Smith H 26	Bossy F 27+3	McNally M 18+1	McGowan N 31+1	Ferguson D 28	Hamilton B 27	Paton E 31+5	McVey W 5+2	Falconer W 1	Burke A 17+10	McGrillen P 19+16	Mooney G 2+1	Kinnard P —+4	Graham A 9+12	McKinnon R 20	Shaw G 1	Brannigan K —+1	Robertson S 9+2	Klein D 1	Whiteford A 10+4	McColligan B 25+4	Gow A 3+2	Stirling J 1	Dick J 4+5	Carrigan B 7+3	Lavety B 7+1	Nicholls M 5+4	O'Neill M 19	McKinlay W 8	McPeak A 3	Jackson D 7+7	Miller J 1+2	Shields P 13+2	Vella S 9	George L 2	Match No.
1	2	3	4	5^1	6	7	8^2	9	10	11^3	12	13	14																						1
1^3	2	3		6	5	8	7		13	11^2			9						4^1	10	12	15													2
	2		4	8	6	7			10^1	11^3	9	12	3					1	5^2	13	14														3
1	4	5^1	3		7	2	12		10	11^3		8^1	14	9	6					13															4
1	4			6	7	2			11^3				14	9^1			5			13			3	8	10^2	12									5
1	4	5			7^1	8	2			11^2			14	13			3						12	6	10^3		9								6
1	4	5	12		7^1	2				11				13			3^1						14	6	8		10^2	9							7
1	4	3	7	5		2			11^2					10^1			12						6	8	13		9								8
	4	3	7	6^2		2			10^2	11	12			5				1		14			8	13			9^1								9
1	4	13	6	7	5	2			3^2	11^1	12		14										8		10^3		9								10
1	4	5	3	7	6	2			10^2	11	13	12					8^1										9								11
1	4	3	7	5	6					11	12		10^3				2		8				13	14			9^1								12
1	4	3	7	5	6				10	11			9^1				2		8				12												13
1	4	3	7^2	5	6				10	11			9^1				2		8				13	12											14
1	4	3	6	5		2			10	14	12		11										13	9^3			7^1	8^2							15
1	4	3	7	5		2			9^1	12			11						8								10	6							16
1	4	3	7^1	14	12	5			2	11													13	10			6^2	9^3							17
1	4	3	7^1	2	12	13			8	5			11														10	6	9^2						18
1			3^1	7	4	8			12	5			2														10	6	9						19
1	4	5	3	7		2			11^2	12			6^1	14													10^3	8	9	13					20
1	2^3	4	3	7	12				13	9^1	5																8^2	6		10	14	11			21
	4	3^3	7	6		2			13	14			5						8								10			9^1		11^2			22
1	2	3	7	8	4				13	12			5						6								10			9^2		11^1			23
1	2	4	7	5	8				12	13			3														10^2	6		9		11			24
1	4		7	5		2			12	14			3						6^1								10	8		13		11^1	9^2		25
1	13	5	3	7	2^2				11				12	4						6^1							10^3			14		9			26
1	13	4	3	7	2				11				5						6^1								10			12		9			27
	2	4	3	7	8	14			11^2							1	12		6^2								10			13		9^1	5		28
	2	4	3	7	8^2	13			11							1			6								14	10		12			5	9	29
	2^3	4	3	7		6			13	11^2						1											14	10		12		9	5	8^1	30
		5	3	7	6				11^1	9	12					1	2										10			8^2		13	4		31
		5	3	7	6				11^2	9	14					1	2										13	10		8^1		12	4	4^1	32
		3	7^1	12					11	9	5					1	2		6								10			13		8^2	4		33
	2	3		8		13				12	4					1	6		11						10^2		7					9^1	5		34
	2	3		8	13	14				12	4^2					1	6		11						10^3		7					9^1	5		35
1^4	12		4		8	3				13			9			15	2		6^1	10							7					11^2	5		36

COWDENBEATH

Second Division

Year Formed: 1881. *Ground & Address:* Central Park, Cowdenbeath KY4 9EY. *Telephone:* 01383 610166. *Fax:* 01383 512132.
Ground Capacity: total: 5268, seated: 1622. *Size of Pitch:* 107yd × 66yd.
Chairman: Gordon McDougall. *Secretary:* Tom Ogilvie. *General Manager:* Joe McNamara.
Manager: Keith Wright. *Assistant Manager:* Mickey Weir. *Physio:* Derek Campbell.
Managers since 1975: D. McLindon, F. Connor, P. Wilson, A. Rolland, H. Wilson, W. McCulloch, J. Clark, J. Craig, R. Campbell, J. Blackley, J. Brownlie, A. Harrow, J. Reilly, P Dolan, T. Steven, S. Conn, C. Levein, G. Kirk. *Previous Grounds:* North End Park, Cowdenbeath.
Record Attendance: 25,586 v Rangers, League Cup quarter-final; 21 Sept, 1949.
Record Transfer Fee received: £30,000 for Nicky Henderson to Falkirk (March 1994).
Record Transfer Fee paid: —
Record Victory: 12-0 v Johnstone, Scottish Cup 1st rd; 21 Jan, 1928.
Record Defeat: 1-11 v Clyde, Division II; 6 Oct, 1951.
Most Capped Player: Jim Paterson, 3, Scotland.
Most League and Cup Appearances: 491 Ray Allan 1972-75, 1979-89.
Most League Goals in Season (Individual): 54, Rab Walls, Division II, 1938-39.
Most Goals Overall (Individual): 127, Willie Devlin, 1922-26, 1929-30.

COWDENBEATH 2001–02 LEAGUE RECORD

Match No.	Date	Venue	Opponents	Result	H/T Score	Lg. Pos.	Goalscorers	Attendance
1	Aug 4	A	Stranraer	L 0-3	0-1	—		473
2	11	H	Berwick R	W 2-1	1-1	0	Ritchie (og) [6], Brown [90]	326
3	18	A	Hamilton A	L 0-1	0-0	8		2131
4	25	H	Alloa Ath	L 1-2	0-1	9	Wright [69]	416
5	Sept 8	A	Forfar Ath	L 1-2	0-2	9	Mauchlen [46]	403
6	15	H	Queen of the S	D 1-1	1-1	10	King [41]	364
7	19	A	Clydebank	L 2-3	1-1	—	White 2 [21, 76]	154
8	22	A	Morton	W 2-0	1-0	8	Lawrence 2 [41, 55]	1184
9	29	H	Stenhousemuir	D 1-1	0-0	8	Swift [49]	354
10	Oct 13	A	Stranraer	D 2-2	0-1	9	Brown [70], French [90]	277
11	20	A	Berwick R	W 5-2	3-1	8	Wright 4 [5, 39, 53, 68], Brown [27]	472
12	27	H	Forfar Ath	W 3-2	0-1	7	Swift [54], Wright [76], Brown [85]	316
13	Nov 3	A	Alloa Ath	L 1-5	1-2	8	Wright [29]	618
14	10	A	Queen of the S	W 3-1	1-0	7	Brown 3 [38, 55, 61]	1321
15	24	H	Clydebank	D 1-1	0-0	7	Brown [70]	333
16	Dec 1	H	Morton	D 1-1	0-1	7	Brown [88]	501
17	15	A	Stenhousemuir	W 3-0	1-0	6	Brown [42], Dixon [52], Wright [90]	312
18	29	A	Stranraer	L 1-2	0-1	6	Brown [65]	385
19	Jan 12	H	Alloa Ath	L 1-2	0-0	6	Young [54]	390
20	19	A	Clydebank	L 0-1	0-1	7		245
21	26	H	Queen of the S	L 1-2	1-1	7	White (pen) [42]	420
22	Feb 2	A	Stenhousemuir	L 2-4	2-0	8	Brown 2 [10, 32]	259
23	16	H	Berwick R	D 1-1	1-0	9	French [3]	366
24	23	A	Hamilton A	W 2-0	1-0	8	Brown [16], Elliot [83]	1284
25	26	A	Hamilton A	W 2-1	1-0	—	Wilson K [34], Wright [74]	283
26	Mar 2	A	Alloa Ath	D 0-0	0-0	8		560
27	9	H	Forfar Ath	L 1-2	1-0	8	Brown [44]	321
28	12	A	Forfar Ath	D 0-0	0-0	—		444
29	16	A	Queen of the S	L 1-2	0-1	9	Brown [90]	2028
30	23	H	Clydebank	W 2-1	1-0	8	Mauchlen [43], Vella (og) [51]	344
31	26	A	Morton	D 0-0	0-0	—		1171
32	30	H	Morton	D 2-2	1-1	7	Brown [20], French [77]	635
33	Apr 6	A	Stenhousemuir	W 1-0	0-0	6	Mauchlen [80]	466
34	13	A	Stranraer	D 1-1	1-0	6	Mauchlen [36]	309
35	20	A	Berwick R	L 0-1	0-1	8		631
36	27	H	Hamilton A	W 2-1	1-0	8	French [44], Crabbe [50]	412

Final League Position: 8

Honours
League Champions: Division II 1913-14, 1914-15, 1938-39; *Runners-up:* Division II 1921-22, 1923-24, 1969-70. Second Division 1991-92. *Runners-up:* Third Division 2000-01.
Scottish Cup: Quarter-finals: 1931.
League Cup: Semi-finals: 1959-60, 1970-71.

Club colours: Shirt: Royal blue with white cuffs and collar. Shorts: White. Stockings: White.

Goalscorers: *League* (49): Brown 17, Wright 9, French 4, Mauchlen 4, White 3 (1 pen), Lawrence 2, Swift 2, Crabbe 1, Dixon 1, Elliot 1, King 1, Wilson K 1, Young 1, own goals 2
Scottish Cup (0):
CIS Cup (2): Wilson K 1, Wright 1
Challenge Cup (0):

Martin J 4	Lawrence A 21 + 2	Raynes S 12 + 3	Welsh B 1 + 1	Wilson K 32	Swift S 31 + 2	King T 9	Moffat A 3	Brown G 35	French H 33 + 1	Burns J 1 + 1	Mauchlen I 13 + 9	White D 30	Boyle J 34 + 1	McMillan C — + 5	Wright K 13 + 12	Young C 7 + 8	Robertson A 1	Winter C 25	Gordon C 13	Neeson C 11 + 3	Kwik Ajet W 1	Campbell A 12 + 2	Gibb S 1	Dixon J 5 + 5	O'Connor G 19	Milne K 9	Byle K 1 + 2	Miller C — + 1	Huggon R 2 + 3	Elliot J 6 + 6	Sullivan V 2 + 2	Wilson P 1	Renwick M 7	Crabbe G 1 + 1	Match No.
1	2	3	4	5	6	7	8	9	10	11[1]	12																								1
1	6[1]	3		5	2	11	7[2]	10	8		9	4	12	13																					2
1	10[2]	3[1]		4	6[1]	11	8		7		9	5	2	12	13	14																			3
1		3	13	4				9[1]	8		11[2]	5	2		10	12		6	7																4
				4	6	11		10[1]	8		12	5	2		9			7	1	3															5
6	12			5		11		9	8			4	2		10			7	1	3[1]															6
6				5	3	10[1]		9	8		11[2]	4	2	12	13			7	1															7
6	12			5	11			9[1]	8			4	2[1]	13	10	14		7	1	3[2]															8
6	3			5	11			9[1]	8		14	4	2[2]		10[1]	12		7	1	13															9
6[2]	3			5	11			9	8	13		4	2		12			7	1		10[1]														10
6[2]	3[1]			5	11			9[3]	8		13	4	2		10	14		7	1	12														11
6[1]	3			5	11			9[2]	8			4	2		10	13		7	1	12														12
12	3				6			9	8	13		4	2		10[3]	14		7[2]	1	11[1]		5												13
6	3				11			9				4	2		10			7	1			5	8											14
6	3			5	11	8		9				4	2		10			7	1															15
6[1]	3			5	11[2]	8		9	12			4	2		10			7	1		13													16
	12			5	6			9	8		11[1]	4	2		13			7	1	3		10[3]												17
12				5	6[3]	7		9	8		11[1]	4	2		13					3		14	10[2]	1										18
				5	6			9	7		12		2		10	8[2]				3[1]		4	13	1	11									19
6[1]				5	11			9	7		12		2		13	10[3]						4		1	3	8[2]	14							20
				5	6			9	8		12	4	2			10[1]		7		3				1	11									21
				5	6			9	8			4	2		13	10[3]		7		3				1	11[1]	12								22
6[2]					11			9	8		12	4	2		13	10[1]		7						1	5			3						23
7[2]				5	13			9	6			4	2			10[1]		8				12		1	11			3[3]	14					24
6[2]				5	13			9	7			4	2		12	10[1]		8						1	3			14	11[3]					25
6[1]				4	11			9	7			5	2					8						1	3			13	12	10[2]				26
6[1]				5	11			9	7			4	2	14		13		8						1				12	10[2]	3[3]				27
7					11			9	6			4	2					8				5		10	1	3								28
7[1]				5	11			9	6			4	2					8				3		10[2]	1				12	13				29
				5	7			9	8	11		4	2					8				3		1				10[1]	12		6			30
				5	7			9	6	11			2					8				3		12	1			10[1]			4			31
				5	7			9	6	11		4	2		13					3[2]		4		10[1]	1			12			8			32
				5				9[1]	8	7		2		10[2]							4	3		12	1			13	11		6			33
				5	11			9	8	7		4	2									3		12	1				10[1]		6			34
				5	11			9	8	7		4	2		13					3[1]				1					10[2]		6	12		35
				5	3[1]			9	11	7		4	2		13			8[2]						1		14			12		6	10[3]		36

DUMBARTON   Second Division

Year Formed: 1872. *Ground:* Strathclyde Homes Stadium, Dumbarton G82 1JJ. *Telephone:* 01389 762569/767864.
Fax: 01389 762629
Ground Capacity: total: 2050. *Size of Pitch:* 110yd × 75yd.
Chairman: D. Dalglish. *Club Secretary:* David Prophet. *Company Secretary:* John Benn.
Manager: David Winnie. *Assistant Manager:* Jim Denny. *Physio:* Linda McIllwraith.
Managers since 1975: A. Wright, D. Wilson, S. Fallon, W. Lamont, D. Wilson, D. Whiteford, A. Totten, M. Clougherty,
R. Auld, J. George, W. Lamont, M. MacLeod, J. Fallon, I. Wallace, T. Carson. *Club Nickname(s):* The Sons. *Previous
Grounds:* Broadmeadow, Ropework Lane, Townend Ground, Boghead Park.
Record Attendance: 18,000 v Raith Rovers, Scottish Cup; 2 Mar, 1957.
Record Transfer Fee received: £125,000 for Graeme Sharp to Everton (March 1982).
Record Transfer Fee paid: £50,000 for Charlie Gibson from Stirling Albion (1989).
Record Victory: 13-1 v Kirkintilloch Central. 1st rd; 1 Sept, 1888.
Record Defeat: 1-11 v Albion Rovers, Division II; 30 Jan, 1926: v Ayr United, League Cup; 13 Aug, 1952.
Most Capped Player: James McAulay, 9, Scotland.
Most League Appearances: 297: Andy Jardine, 1957-67.

DUMBARTON 2001–02 LEAGUE RECORD

Match No.	Date		Venue	Opponents	Result	H/T Score	Lg. Pos.	Goalscorers	Attendance
1	Aug	4	H	Brechin C	L 1-2	1-1	—	Flannery [14]	837
2		11	A	Peterhead	W 3-0	1-0	5	McKeown [3], Flannery [50], Robertson [84]	528
3		18	H	Queen's Park	W 2-1	0-0	3	Brown [82], Robertson [84]	823
4		25	A	Montrose	L 0-1	0-0	6		751
5	Sept	8	A	East Stirling	W 4-2	1-1	3	Flannery [11], O'Neill [62], Robertson [71], Bonar [77]	212
6		15	H	Albion R	D 1-1	0-0	4	Flannery [77]	581
7		19	A	Stirling A	W 5-4	3-2	—	Robertson 2 [4, 35], Flannery 2 [38, 65], Crilly [87]	446
8		22	H	Elgin C	D 2-2	1-1	3	Lynes [10], Crilly [71]	749
9		29	A	East Fife	L 1-4	0-0	3	Crilly [47]	392
10	Oct	13	H	Brechin C	L 2-3	2-2	6	Brown [20], Flannery [31]	439
11		20	H	Peterhead	L 0-3	0-2	7		715
12		27	A	East Stirling	D 2-2	1-1	8	Flannery 2 [8, 60]	591
13	Nov	3	A	Montrose	W 3-1	2-0	5	Flannery [39], Stewart [52], Crilly [57]	503
14		10	A	Albion R	W 2-0	0-0	4	Crilly [67], Brown [78]	278
15		24	A	Stirling A	W 4-1	2-0	4	O'Neill [10], Flannery [36], Crilly [70], Brittain [89]	861
16	Dec	8	A	Elgin C	W 3-0	1-0	3	Brittain [35], Robertson [58], Brown [72]	511
17		15	H	East Fife	W 1-0	0-0	2	Flannery [62]	821
18	Jan	12	H	Montrose	L 0-5	0-2	4		742
19		19	A	Stirling A	L 1-2	0-1	4	Flannery [59]	554
20		26	H	Albion R	W 2-0	0-0	4	Robertson 2 [63, 78]	686
21	Feb	2	A	East Fife	L 0-1	0-1	3		369
22		9	H	Elgin C	W 3-1	2-0	2	Flannery [26], Lauchlan [33], Crilly [68]	690
23		16	A	Peterhead	L 0-4	0-2	3		589
24		23	A	Queen's Park	D 0-0	0-0	3		725
25		27	H	Brechin C	W 2-1	0-1	—	Brown [53], Crilly [67]	533
26	Mar	2	A	Montrose	D 1-1	0-0	4	McCann [52]	435
27		9	H	East Stirling	W 2-1	1-1	2	Crilly [18], McCann [69]	715
28		16	A	Albion R	D 1-1	1-1	3	Flannery [4]	503
29		19	A	Queen's Park	W 2-0	1-0	—	Dunn 2 [32, 90]	411
30		23	H	Stirling A	W 2-0	0-0	2	Flannery [48], Dunn [79]	792
31		30	A	Elgin C	L 0-2	0-0	2		709
32	Apr	2	A	East Stirling	L 0-1	0-0	—		317
33		6	H	East Fife	W 2-0	1-0	2	Flannery (pen) [26], Crilly [84]	716
34		13	A	Brechin C	W 1-0	1-0	2	Brown [39]	714
35		20	H	Peterhead	W 3-0	0-0	2	Dunn [61], Brown [65], Dillon [84]	1636
36		27	H	Queen's Park	D 1-1	0-0	2	Flannery (pen) [46]	1959

Final League Position: 2

Most Goals in Season (Individual): 38: Kenny Wilson, Division II; 1971-72. *(League and Cup):* 46 Hughie Gallacher, 1955-56.
Most Goals Overall (Individual): 169: Hughie Gallacher, 1954-62 (including C Division 1954-55). *(League and Cup):* 202 Hughie Gallacher, 1954-62.

Honours
League Champions: Division I 1890-91 (shared with Rangers), 1891-92. Division II 1910-11, 1971-72. Second Division 1991-92; *Runners-up:* First Division 1983-84. Division II 1907-08. Third Division 2001-02.
Scottish Cup Winners: 1883; *Runners-up:* 1881, 1882, 1887, 1891, 1897. *League Cup:* —.

Club colours: Shirt: Yellow with black facing. Shorts: Yellow with black stripe. Stockings: Yellow.

Goalscorers: *League* (59): Flannery 18 (2 pens), Crilly 10, Robertson 8, Brown 7, Dunn 4, Brittain 2, McCann 2, O'Neill 2, Bonar 1, Dillon 1, Lauchlan 1, Lynes 1, McKeown 1, Stewart 1
Scottish Cup (1): McKeown 1.
CIS Cup (2): Brown 1, Flannery 1.
Challenge Cup (0):

Hillcoat J 12	Dickie M 23	Stewart D 17	Murdoch S 5	McKeown J 23	Jack S 25+3	Bonar S 19+13	O'Neill M 26+3	Flannery P 32+1	Brown A 35	Dillon J 15+18	Brittain C 27+5	Lynes C 5+15	McKelvie D 2+20	McCann K 19	Robertson J 28+6	Crilly M 29+1	Bruce J 10	Wight J 22	Lauchlan M 9+2	Dunn R 11+2	Connolly J 2	Match No.
1	2	3	4^3	5	6	7^2	8	9	10	11^1	12	13	14									1
1	2	6		5^1	4	13	8	9	10	3^2	12	11^3			7	14						2
1	2			5^3	4	13	8	9	10	3^2	6	11^1	14		7	12						3
1	2	6		5^3	4	13	8	9	10	3^1		11^2	14		7	12						4
1		3	4		5	2	8^1	9	10^3	13	12		14	6	11^2	7						5
1	2		4		5		7	9	10^2	3^1	12	13	14	6	11^2	8						6
1		3	4	6	5	2	8^1	9	10^2		12	13			11	7						7
1		3^2	4	6^1	5	2		9	10	13	12	7^1	14		11	8						8
1			4	6	5	2	8^2	9	10^3	3	12	13	14		11^1	7						9
1	2	6			5		7^1	9	10	3	12	13			11^1	8	4					10
1	2	6			5		7^1	9	10	3	12	13	14		11	8^1	4					11
1	2	6			5		8	9	10	3					11	7	4					12
	2	3			4	13	8^1	9	10		12		14	6	11^3	7^2	5	1				13
	2	3			4		8^1	9^1	10		12	13	14	6	11^3	7	5	1				14
	2	6			4		8^3	9	10	3	12	13	14		11^2	7	5	1				15
	2	6^2			4		8^2	9	10	3	12	13	14		11	7^1	5	1				16
	2	6			4		8^2	9	10^3	3	12		14		11^1	7	5	1	13			17
	2^1	6			4^3		8	9	10	3	12	13	14		11^2		5	1	7			18
	2	6			4		8	9	10^3	3	12		14		11^1		5	1	13	7^2		19
	2			5		13	8	9	10^1	3	12		14	6^3	11	4		1		7^2		20
	2			5		13	8	9	10	3	12			6^1	11	4		1		7^2		21
	2			5			8	9	10	3	12			6	11	4		1		7		22
	2			5		13	8	9^1	10	3			14	6	11^2	4		1	12	7^3		23
	2			5^2			8	9	10	3	4	12	13	6	11^3	7			14		1	24
	2			5			8	9^1	10	3	4	12	13	6^1	11^2	7			14		1	25
	2						8	9	10	3	4	12	13		11^2	7	5	1		6		26
	2						8	9^1	10	3	4	12	13		11	7	5	1		6^2		27
	2						8^1	9	10	3	4	12			11	7	5	1		6		28
	2						8^2	9^1	10	3	4	12	13		11	7	5	1		6		29
	2						8^2	9	10^1	3	4	12	13		11	7	5	1		6		30
	2						8	9^2	10	3	4	12	13		11^1	7	5	1		6		31
	2			5			8	9^1	10	3	4	12	13		11	7		1		6		32
	2			5			8	9	10^2	3	4	12	13	6^1	11	7		1		6		33
	2			5			8^1	9	10	3	4	12	13		11	7		1		6^1		34
	2			5			8^2	9	10^3	3	4	12	13	14	11	7		1		6		35
	2			5			8	9	10	3^1	4	12	13		11	7		1		6^2		36

DUNDEE   Premier League

Year Formed: 1893. *Ground & Address:* Dens Park Stadium, Sandeman St, Dundee DD3 7JY. *Telephone:* 01382 889966.
Fax: 01382 832284.
Ground Capacity: all seated: 11,760. *Size of Pitch:* 101m × 66m.
Chairman: Jim Marr. *Chief Executive:* Peter Marr.
Manager: Jim Duffy. *Coach:* Billy Thomson. *Physio:* John McCreadie.
Under 21 Coach: Ray Farningham. *Under 18 Coach:* Steve Campbell. *Goalkeeping Coach:* Paul Mathers.
Youth Development Coach: Kenny Cameron. *Community Coach:* Kevin Lee.
Managers since 1975: David White, Tommy Gemmell, Donald Mackay, Archie Knox, Jocky Scott, Dave Smith, Gordon
Wallace, Iain Munro, Simon Stainrod, Jim Duffy, John McCormack, John Scott, Ivano Bonetti.
Club Nickname(s): The Dark Blues or The Dee. *Previous Grounds:* Carolina Port 1893-98.
Record Attendance: 43,024 v Rangers, Scottish Cup; 1953.
Record Transfer Fee received: £500,000 for Tommy Coyne to Celtic (March 1989).
Record Transfer Fee paid: £200,000 for Jim Leighton (Feb 1992).
Record Victory: 10-0 Division II v Alloa; 9 Mar, 1947 and v Dunfermline Ath; 22 Mar, 1947.
Record Defeat: 0-11 v Celtic, Division I; 26 Oct, 1895.
Most Capped Player: Alex Hamilton, 24, Scotland. *Most League Appearances:* 341: Doug Cowie 1945-61.
Most League Goals in Season (Individual): 52: Alan Gilzean, 1963-64.
Most Goals Overall (Individual): 113: Alan Gilzean.

DUNDEE 2001–02 LEAGUE RECORD

Match No.	Date		Venue	Opponents	Result	H/T Score	Lg. Pos.	Goalscorers	Atten-dance
1	Jul	28	A	Dundee U	D 2-2	1-1	—	Sara [33], Rae [55]	13,237
2	Aug	4	H	Hibernian	W 2-1	1-0	4	Sara [8], Caballero [62]	9447
3		11	H	Livingston	W 1-0	1-0	3	Sara [24]	7712
4		18	A	Hearts	L 1-3	0-3	4	Nemsadze [66]	12,259
5		26	A	Rangers	L 0-2	0-1	6		48,038
6	Sept	8	H	St Johnstone	D 1-1	1-0	7	Milne [2]	7050
7		15	H	Celtic	L 0-4	0-1	9		9842
8		23	A	Kilmarnock	W 1-0	1-0	6	Rae [37]	7052
9		29	H	Aberdeen	L 1-4	1-1	8	Caballero [31]	8359
10	Oct	13	A	Dunfermline Ath	L 0-1	0-1	9		5094
11		27	A	Hibernian	W 2-1	1-1	8	Rae [18], Milne [90]	11,185
12		30	H	Motherwell	W 3-1	1-1	—	Sara [31], Ketsbaia [54], Caballero [61]	6863
13	Nov	3	H	Dundee U	D 1-1	1-1	6	Carranza (pen) [41]	11,751
14		10	A	Hearts	L 0-2	0-0	6		10,374
15		17	A	Livingston	L 0-1	0-0	8		5391
16		24	H	Hearts	D 1-1	0-1	6	Mackay [79]	7219
17	Dec	1	H	Rangers	D 0-0	0-0	6		11,085
18		8	A	St Johnstone	W 2-0	1-0	6	Sara [20], Ketsbaia [54]	5299
19		15	A	Celtic	L 1-3	1-0	6	Zhiyi [18]	57,559
20		22	H	Kilmarnock	L 1-2	0-1	6	Rae [47]	6342
21	Jan	9	A	Motherwell	L 2-4	1-2	—	Sara [34], Kemas [90]	3563
22		12	H	Hibernian	W 1-0	0-0	8	Zhiyi [65]	7326
23		19	A	Dundee U	L 0-1	0-0	9		12,851
24		29	A	Aberdeen	D 0-0	0-0	—		11,027
25	Feb	2	A	Rangers	L 1-2	0-0	9	Rae [71]	48,861
26		9	H	St Johnstone	W 1-0	1-0	10	Torres [32]	6344
27		13	H	Dunfermline Ath	D 2-2	2-0	—	Rae [3], Caballero [6]	6043
28		17	H	Celtic	L 0-3	0-2	9		10,642
29	Mar	2	A	Kilmarnock	L 2-3	1-1	9	Sara [43], Ketsbaia [53]	6890
30		9	H	Aberdeen	L 2-3	2-0	11	Sara (pen) [14], Ketsbaia [39]	8906
31		13	H	Livingston	W 2-0	0-0	—	Sara 2 [57, 90]	5506
32		16	H	Motherwell	W 2-0	2-0	8	Ketsbaia 2 [4, 25]	5785
33		23	A	Dunfermline Ath	L 0-2	0-1	8		7299
34	Apr	6	A	Kilmarnock	W 2-0	1-0	8	Sara [42], Milne [48]	5579
35		13	A	St Johnstone	W 1-0	0-0	8	Milne [79]	2768
36		20	H	Dundee U	L 0-1	0-1	9		10,087
37		27	A	Hibernian	D 2-2	1-1	9	Caballero [32], Milne [87]	8852
38	May	12	A	Motherwell	L 1-2	0-2	9	Caballero (pen) [64]	6574

Final League Position: 9

Honours
League Champions: Division I 1961-62. First Division 1978-79, 1991-92, 1997-98. Division II 1946-47; *Runners-up:* Division I 1902-03, 1906-07, 1908-09, 1948-49, 1980-81.
Scottish Cup Winners: 1910; *Runners-up:* 1925, 1952, 1964.
League Cup Winners: 1951-52, 1952-53, 1973-74; *Runners-up:* 1967-68, 1980-81. *(Coca-Cola Cup):* 1995-96.
B&Q (Centenary) Cup Winners: 1990-91; *Runners-up:* 1994-95.

European: *European Cup:* 8 matches (1962-63 semi-finals). *Cup Winners' Cup:* 2 matches: (1964-65).
UEFA Cup: 18 matches: (*Fairs Cup;* 1967-68 semi-finals. *UEFA Cup:* 1971-72, 1973-74, 1974-75).

Club colours: Shirt: Navy with red, blue and white stripes on front. Shorts: White with navy/red piping. Stockings: Red with blue and white tops.

Goalscorers: *League* (41): Sara 11 (1 pen), Caballero 6 (1 pen), Ketsbaia 6, Rae 6, Milne 5, Zhiyi 2, Carranza 1, Kemas 1, Mackay 1, Nemsadze 1, Torres 1.
Scottish Cup (4): Milne 1, Sara 1, Torres 1, Zhiyi 1.
CIS Cup (3): Boylan 1, Caballero 1, Milne 1.

Langfield J 21	Smith B 36 + 2	Marrocco M 12	Khizanishvili Z 18	Del Rio W 31 + 2	Romano A 17 + 4	Nemsadze G 10 + 1	Carranza A 23 + 3	Rae G 36	Milne S 15 + 15	Sara J 25 + 3	Caballero F 28 + 4	Garrido B 8 + 10	Robertson M 7 + 9	Coyne C — + 2	Boylan C — + 1	Robb S — + 1	Mackay D 13 + 4	Gatti L — + 4	Naveda B — + 2	Forbes B 2 + 2	Beghetto M 21	Ketsbaia T 22	Zhiyi F 14	Artero J 12 + 9	Torres E 19	Kemas K 2 + 10	Speroni J 17	Baith G 1 + 2	Wilkie L 8	Traverso G — + 2	Match No.
1	2	3	4	5	6	7	8	9	10	11																					1
1	2	3	4	5	6	7¹	8²	9	14	11	10³	12	13																		2
1	2	3¹	4	5	6	7	8	9	13	11²	10³	12		14																	3
1	2		4	3	5	7	8	9	12	11	10	6¹																			4
1	2	3	4	5	6	7²	8	9	12	11¹	10		13																		5
1	2	3	4	5	6¹	7		9	11	13	10	8²	12																		6
1	2	3	4	6²	7		9	11			10	8¹	13	12²	14																7
1	2	3	4		5¹		8³	9	11²		10	7	6			12	13	14													8
1	2	3	4³	5	6	7²	8¹	9	11		10	12			14	13															9
1	2		4	5			9	12	11¹	10	7	6			3		8														10
1	2		4	5	6		8³	9	13	12	10²	7				14			3	11¹											11
1	2		4	5	6		8	9	12	11³	10¹					14		13	3	7²											12
1	14		4	5	12		8	9	13³	11	10²	6¹							3	7	2										13
1	2		4	5			8²	9	12	11			6¹					13	3	7		10									14
1	2		4	5			8¹	9	10²	11	13		6						3	7		12									15
1	2		4				8	9	14	11³	10	6²	12				5		3¹	7		13									16
1	2		4				8³	9	13	11¹	10¹		14				5			7	3	12	6								17
1	2						8²	9	11	10¹		13				4			7	3	12	6									18
1	12		4¹	5			13	9		11	10								3	7	2	8²	6								19
1	2		5				8	9	12		10							13	3	7	4²	11¹	6								20
1	2		5	6²			8¹		10	11³		13							3	7	4	12	9	14							21
	2		5	6				11¹		10²	13								3	7	4	9	12	1	8						22
	2		5	6			8³	9¹	10²	11	13						14		3		4	12	7		1						23
	2		5	13				9	10²		12						4		3³	7	6		8	11¹	1	14					24
	2		5	6¹			8	9	13		10²						4			7²	3	14	11	12	1						25
	2		5					9	12	11²	10¹		6				4			7	3	6	8		1						26
	2		5					9	11¹		10		12				4			7	3	6	8		1						27
	2		5	6				9	11³	14	10²						4¹			7	8	3	12		13	1					28
	2		5					9		11¹	10		6							4	8	3	7		1						29
	2		5	12				9		11²	10						3			4	8	6¹	7	13	1						30
	2		5					9		11²	10¹	13								4	8	6	7	12	1		3				31
	2		5					9		11	10²	14	12							4	8	6¹	7		1		3	13³			32
	2		5		12		9		11	10³						13				4¹	8	6²	7	14	1		3				33
2	3						8¹	9	10²	11¹		12				5					6	7	13	1		4	14				34
2	3			7¹			8³	9	10	11¹		12	14			5					6		13	1		4					35
	2		5		12		8³	9	10	11³	13	14					4				6¹	7		1		3					36
	2	3¹		14	13	11²	8¹	9	12		10						4			6		7		1		5					37
	2	3¹		14		11	13	9		10							4			8¹		7²	6	1	12	5					38

DUNDEE UNITED   Premier League

Year Formed: 1909 (1923). *Ground & Address:* Tannadice Park, Tannadice St, Dundee DD3 7JW. *Telephone:* 01382
833166. *Fax:* 01382 889398. *Ground Capacity:* total: 14,223 all seated: stands: east 2868, west 2096, south 2201, Fair Play
1601, George Fox 5151, executive boxes 292.
Size of Pitch: 110yd × 72yd.
Chairman: Scott Carnegie. *Secretary:* Spence Anderson. *General Manager:* Bill Campbell. *Community Development
Officer:* John Holt.
Manager: Alex Smith. *Assistant Manager:* John Blackley. *Coaches:* Maurice Malpas and Paul Hegarty. *Physio:* David Rankine.
Managers since 1975: J. McLean, I. Golac, W. Kirkwood, T. McLean, P. Sturrock. *Club Nickname(s):* The Terrors. *Previous
Grounds:* None.
Record Attendance: 28,000 v Barcelona, Fairs Cup; 16 Nov, 1966.
Record Transfer Fee received: £4,000,000 for Duncan Ferguson from Rangers (July 1993).
Record Transfer Fee paid: £750,000 for Steven Pressley from Coventry C (July 1995).
Record Victory: 14-0 v Nithsdale Wanderers, Scottish Cup 1st rd; 17 Jan, 1931.
Record Defeat: 1-12 v Motherwell, Division II; 23 Jan, 1954.
Most Capped Player: Maurice Malpas, 55, Scotland.
Most League Appearances: 612, Dave Narey; 1973-94.
Most Appearances in European Matches: 76, Dave Narey (record for Scottish player).
Most League Goals in Season (Individual): 41: John Coyle, Division II; 1955-56.
Most Goals Overall (Individual): 158: Peter McKay.

DUNDEE UNITED 2001–02 LEAGUE RECORD

Match No.	Date	Venue	Opponents	Result	H/T Score	Lg. Pos.	Goalscorers	Attendance
1	Jul 28	H	Dundee	D 2-2	1-1	—	Miller [30], Hamilton [89]	13,237
2	Aug 4	A	Motherwell	D 0-0	0-0	7		5057
3	11	A	St Johnstone	W 1-0	1-0	5	Griffin [39]	5162
4	18	H	Dunfermline Ath	W 3-2	2-0	3	McIntyre [12], Lilley [27], Hamilton (pen) [79]	7260
5	26	H	Kilmarnock	L 0-2	0-1	5		7404
6	Sept 8	A	Livingston	L 0-2	0-0	8		5496
7	15	A	Aberdeen	L 1-2	0-0	7	McIntyre [46]	12,946
8	22	H	Rangers	L 1-6	1-1	9	McIntyre [33]	11,117
9	29	A	Hearts	W 2-1	0-0	7	McIntyre [49], Thompson [89]	11,034
10	Oct 13	H	Hibernian	W 3-1	0-1	7	Hamilton 2 [64, 71], Griffin [84]	7950
11	20	A	Celtic	L 1-5	0-2	7	McIntyre [75]	58,873
12	27	H	Motherwell	D 1-1	1-0	6	Easton [22]	6343
13	Nov 3	A	Dundee	D 1-1	1-1	7	Miller [11]	11,751
14	10	H	Dunfermline Ath	L 0-2	0-1	8		6214
15	17	H	St Johnstone	W 2-1	0-0	5	Aljofree [62], Hamilton [74]	6624
16	24	A	Dunfermline Ath	D 1-1	0-0	5	McConalogue [86]	4891
17	Dec 1	A	Kilmarnock	L 0-2	0-1	7		6130
18	8	H	Livingston	D 0-0	0-0	7		6312
19	15	A	Aberdeen	D 1-1	1-0	7	Easton [25]	9129
20	22	A	Rangers	L 2-3	1-2	8	Thompson 2 [28, 56]	47,315
21	26	H	Hearts	L 0-2	0-1	—		8762
22	29	A	Celtic	L 0-4	0-2	10		12,165
23	Jan 2	A	Hibernian	W 1-0	0-0	—	Paterson [87]	11,155
24	12	A	Motherwell	L 0-2	0-0	9		4631
25	19	H	Dundee	W 1-0	0-0	8	McIntyre [88]	12,851
26	22	A	St Johnstone	W 4-0	3-0	—	Lilley 3 [28, 44, 51], Miller [36]	3401
27	Feb 2	H	Kilmarnock	L 0-2	0-1	8		5774
28	9	A	Livingston	D 1-1	0-0	8	Lilley [76]	4497
29	16	A	Aberdeen	L 0-4	0-2	8		13,612
30	Mar 3	H	Rangers	L 0-1	0-0	8		9383
31	9	A	Hearts	W 2-1	2-0	8	Aljofree (pen) [10], Miller [35]	10,893
32	16	A	Celtic	L 0-1	0-1	9		58,392
33	23	H	Hibernian	L 1-2	0-1	9	Thompson [76]	5801
34	Apr 7	A	Hibernian	W 2-1	1-0	9	Venetis [44], Lilley [59]	5417
35	13	H	Motherwell	W 1-0	0-0	9	Thompson [66]	5108
36	20	A	Dundee	W 1-0	1-0	8	Paterson [39]	10,087
37	27	H	St Johnstone	D 0-0	0-0	8		5190
38	May 12	A	Kilmarnock	D 2-2	0-1	8	Thompson [64], Easton [83]	6142

Final League Position: 8

Honours
League Champions: Premier Division 1982-83. Division II 1924-25, 1928-29; *Runners-up:* Division II 1930-31, 1959-60. First Division Runners-up 1995-96.
Scottish Cup Winners: 1994; *Runners-up:* 1974, 1981, 1985, 1987, 1988, 1991.
League Cup Winners: 1979-80, 1980-81; *Runners-up:* 1981-82, 1984-85, 1997-98.
Summer Cup Runners-up: 1964-65. *Scottish War Cup Runners-up:* 1939-40.

European: *European Cup:* 8 matches (1983-84, semi-finals). *Cup Winners' Cup:* 10 matches (1974-75, 1988-89, 1994-95). *UEFA Cup:* 84 matches (*Fairs Cup:* 1966-67, 1969-70, 1970-71. *UEFA Cup:* 1975-76, 1977-78, 1978-79, 1979-80, 1980-81, 1981-82, 1982-83, 1984-85, 1985-86, 1986-87 runners-up, 1987-88, 1989-90, 1990-91, 1993-94, 1997-98).

Club colours: Shirts: Tangerine. Shorts: Black. Stockings: Tangerine with black hoop.

Goalscorers: *League* (38): Lilley 6, McIntyre 6, Thompson 6, Hamilton 5 (1 pen), Miller 4, Easton 3, Aljofree 2 (1 pen), Griffin 2, Paterson 2, McConalogue 1, Venetis 1.
Scottish Cup (9): Aljofree 3, Thompson 2, Winters 2, Easton 1, Miller 1.
CIS Cup (6): Thompson 2, Easton 1, Griffin 1, Hamilton 1, Paterson 1.

Gallacher P 38	Partridge D 13	Lauchlan J 33	Buchan J 6 + 1	Griffin D 29	Venetis A 14 + 10	McCunnie J 27 + 1	Miller C 31 + 3	Hannah D 16 + 4	McIntyre J 16 + 3	Lilley D 19 + 7	Paterson J 12 + 15	Hamilton J 20 + 4	Thompson S 20 + 12	Easton C 33 + 3	Aljofree H 27	McCracken D 16 + 3	Carson S 6 + 7	Wright S 8 + 1	O'Brien R 2 + 6	Fullarton J 11	McConalogue S 5 + 7	Duff S 9	Cocozza M 1 + 1	Wilson M 1	Winters D 4 + 9	O'Donnell S 1 + 5	Ogunmade D — + 2	Jarvie P — + 1	Match No
1	2	3	4	5	6^1	7	8^3	9	10^2	11	12	13	14																1
1	2^1	3	12	5		4	8	6	10	11^{13}	7^2	13	14	9															2
1		3	2	5	14	4	8^2	6^1	12	11^1		10		9	7	13													3
1		3	2	5	14	4	8^3	6	9^1	11^2	12	10			7	13													4
1		3	2	5		4	8^2	6	9^1	11	12	10			13	7^2	14												5
1		3	2^2	5	12	4	8^3	6^1		11		10	14	9	7	13													6
1	2	3		5	14	4	8^3		11	13		10^1	9^2	7		6	12												7
1	2	4^1		5			8		9	11		10^2	13	7		6	3	12											8
1	2			5		4	8^1		9	11^2	13	10^2	14	7	6	3		12											9
1	2			5		4	8^1	12	9	13	14	10^1	11^2	7	6			13											10
1	2	3		5		4^2			8	9	14	12	10^1	11^2	7	6		13											11
1		3		5		12	6^1	9	11^2	13	10		8	7	2	4													12
1		3		5		4	8		11^1		12	10^3	14	13	7	2			6^2	9									13
1	2^1		5		4^3	8		11		10	13	12	7	3	14			6^2	9										14
1		3		5	12	4	8^1	6		10	11	7	2			9													15
1^6		3		5		4^1	8	6^2		13	10	11	7	2	12			9^1	14										16
1		3		5	6	12	8^1		7^3	10	14	9	2	13					11	4^2									17
1	2	3		5	12	4		7	10^3	13	9	6		8^1					11										18
1	2	3		5	12	4	13		7^2	10	14	9	6^1		8^3				11										19
1	2	3		5	10^2	4	8	12		7^3		11	9			6^1	13		14										20
1	2	3		5^1	14	4	8	12		7^3	13	11^2	9		6				10										21
1	2	3		9^3		8	6		13	10^1	12	11^2	7		4		14			5									22
1	3			4	8^1	6	13	11^2	12	10		7	5			2	9												23
1	3			4	13	6	12	11	9^1	10^3	14	7	5		8^2	2													24
1	3			4	8	14	9^3	11^2		10^1	13	7			2		6				5	12							25
1	3		13		4	8	6	9^2	11^1		10^3	7			2		5^1	12			14								26
1	3			4	8^3	6	9^2	11	13		10^1	7			2		5^1	14			12								27
1	3		5^3	14	4			12	13		11	7	6		8^2	2	9				10^1								28
1	3		5	9	4^3			11^2	8^1		10	7	2	13			6			14	12								29
1	3		5	9^3	4	8	2			11	7		12	13			6^1	14			10^2								30
1	3		5	9		8				11	7	6	4		12			2			10^1								31
1	3		5	9^2	6	8			13	12		11^3	7	10	4			2^1			14								32
1	3		5	9^3		8			12	13		11	7	6	4^2			2			10^1	14							33
1	3		6		8^1			11	12		10	7	5^3	4			14^2			2	13^9								34
1	3		5^1	9	8^3			11^2			10	7	6	4						2	13	12	14						35
1	3		9^1	8				11^2	6		10	7	5	4			13	2			12								36
1	3		9^2	8				11^3	6			7	5	4			10^1	2			14	12	13						37
1^1			5	9	8^3		10^2	6	McIntyre	11	7	3	4					2			14	13	15						38

DUNFERMLINE ATHLETIC Premier League

Year Formed: 1885. *Ground & Address:* East End Park, Halbeath Rd, Dunfermline KY12 7RB. *Telephone:* 01383 724295. *Fax:* 01383 723468. *Ticket office telephone:* 01383 726863. *e-mail:* pars@dunfermline-ath.com
Ground Capacity: all seated: 12,500. *Size of Pitch:* 115yd × 71yd.
Chairman: John Yorkston. *Secretary:* Mrs Elaine Cromwell. *Commercial Manager:* Karen McNeil.
Manager: Jim Calderwood. *Assistant Manager:* Jimmy Nichol. *Physio:* Philip Yeates, MCSP.
Coach and Youth Development Officer: John Ritchie.
Managers since 1975: G. Miller, H. Melrose, P. Stanton, T. Forsyth, J. Leishman, I. Munro, J. Scott, B. Paton, R. Campbell. *Club Nickname(s):* The Pars. *Previous Grounds:* None.
Record Attendance: 27,816 v Celtic, Division I, 30 April, 1968.
Record Transfer Fee received: £650,000 for Jackie McNamara to Celtic (Oct 1995).
Record Transfer Fee paid: £540,000 for Istvan Kozma from Bordeaux (Sept 1989).
Record Victory: 11-2 v Stenhousemuir, Division II, 27 Sept, 1930.
Record Defeat: 1-11 v Hibernian, Scottish Cup, 3rd rd replay, 26 Oct, 1889.
Most Capped Player: Colin Miller 16(61), Canada.
Most League Appearances: 497: Norrie McCathie, 1981-96.
Most League Goals in Season (Individual): 53: Bobby Skinner, Division II, 1925-26.
Most Goals Overall (Individual): 154: Charles Dickson.

DUNFERMLINE ATHLETIC 2001–02 LEAGUE RECORD

Match No.	Date	Venue	Opponents	Result	H/T Score	Lg. Pos.	Goalscorers	Atten-dance
1	Jul 28	H	Motherwell	W 5-2	1-1	—	de Gier 2 [7, 58], Nicholson 2 [44, 69], Bullen [55]	4825
2	Aug 4	A	St Johnstone	W 2-0	1-0	1	Nicholson [6], Nicholls [54]	4702
3	11	H	Rangers	L 1-4	0-2	4	Klos (og) [52]	10,405
4	18	A	Dundee U	L 2-3	0-2	5	Thomson SM 2 (1 pen) [61 (p), 77]	7260
5	25	H	Hearts	L 0-1	0-0	7		6992
6	Sept 8	A	Celtic	L 1-3	0-2	10	Crawford [35]	58,004
7	16	A	Hibernian	L 1-5	1-3	10	Mason [37]	11,035
8	22	H	Livingston	L 1-2	1-0	10	Crawford [8]	4516
9	30	A	Kilmarnock	L 0-2	0-1	11		3983
10	Oct 13	H	Dundee	W 1-0	1-0	10	Hampshire [23]	5094
11	20	A	Aberdeen	L 2-3	0-3	11	Crawford [69], de Gier [77]	11,516
12	27	H	St Johnstone	W 2-1	0-1	10	de Gier 2 [62, 76]	4449
13	Nov 3	A	Motherwell	L 0-1	0-1	11		4578
14	10	A	Dundee U	W 2-0	1-0	10	Petrie [12], Crawford [62]	6214
15	17	A	Rangers	L 0-4	0-1	10		48,554
16	24	A	Dundee U	D 1-1	0-0	10	Petrie [69]	4891
17	Dec 1	A	Hearts	D 1-1	0-0	10	Nicholson [72]	11,086
18	9	H	Celtic	L 0-4	0-2	10		8207
19	15	H	Hibernian	W 1-0	0-0	10	Nicholson [74]	6617
20	22	A	Livingston	D 0-0	0-0	10		4588
21	26	A	Kilmarnock	D 0-0	0-0	—		6873
22	29	H	Aberdeen	W 1-0	1-0	7	Bullen [21]	7774
23	Jan 12	A	St Johnstone	W 1-0	1-0	7	Mason [80]	3459
24	19	A	Motherwell	W 3-1	1-0	7	Skerla [24], Mason [49], Bullen [58]	4280
25	23	H	Rangers	L 2-4	2-0	7	Thomson SM 2 [17, 32]	8795
26	Feb 2	H	Hearts	D 1-1	0-0	7	Thomson SM [53]	5527
27	9	A	Celtic	L 0-5	0-4	7		58,987
28	13	A	Dundee	D 2-2	0-2	—	Thomson SM [47], Nicholson [88]	6043
29	16	A	Hibernian	D 1-1	0-0	7	Hampshire [59]	9788
30	Mar 2	H	Livingston	W 1-0	0-0	7	Bullen [50]	5032
31	9	H	Kilmarnock	W 2-0	0-0	6	N'Diaye [66], Hampshire [75]	5518
32	16	A	Aberdeen	L 0-1	0-1	7		13,764
33	23	H	Dundee	W 2-0	1-0	5	Nicholson [33], Crawford [51]	7299
34	Apr 6	H	Aberdeen	D 0-0	0-0	5		7339
35	13	A	Celtic	L 0-5	0-2	6		56,715
36	20	H	Hearts	L 0-2	0-0	6		10,108
37	28	A	Livingston	L 1-4	1-1	6	Dair [42]	8749
38	May 12	H	Rangers	D 1-1	0-1	6	Crawford [85]	8716

Final League Position: 6

Honours
League Champions: First Division 1988-89, 1995-96. Division II 1925-26. Second Division 1985-86; *Runners-up:* First Division 1986-87, 1993-94, 1994-95, 1999-2000. Division II 1912-13, 1933-34, 1954-55, 1957-58, 1972-73. Second Division 1978-79.
Scottish Cup Winners: 1961, 1968; *Runners-up:* 1965.
League Cup Runners-up: 1949-50, 1991-92.

European: *Cup Winners' Cup:* 14 matches (1961-62, 1968-69 semi-finals). *UEFA Cup:* 28 matches (*Fairs Cup:* 1962-63, 1964-65, 1965-66, 1966-67, 1969-70).

Club colours: Shirt: Black and white vertical stripes. Shorts: White with black piping. Stockings: White with black band at top.

Goalscorers: *League* (41): Nicholson 7, Crawford 6, Thomson SM 6 (1 pen), de Gier 5, Bullen 4, Hampshire 3, Mason 3, Petrie 2, Dair 1, N'Diaye 1, Nicholls 1, Skerla 1, own goal 1.
Scottish Cup (3): Crawford 2, Thomson SM 1.
CIS Cup (4): Mason 2, Hampshire 1, Nicholson 1.

Ruitenbeek M 29	Potter J 2+2	McGroarty C 17+5	Mason G 33+2	Skerla A 36	Nicholls D 12+11	Nicholson B 36+1	Hampshire S 13+10	Bullen L 25+6	Crawford S 36	de Gier J 12	Dair J 17+11	Petrie S 14+9	Thomson SM 32	Skinner J 18+8	Nish C 2+12	Doesburg M 4+5	MacPherson A 22+2	Rossi Y 9+1	Thomson SY 9	Ferguson I 20	McLeish K 1+1	Kilgannon S 3+7	Panopoulos M 7+2	N'Diaye S 6+3	Karnebeek A 3+2	McGarry M —+2	Blair B —+1	Match No.
1	2	3	4	5	6	7	8¹	9	10	11²	12	13																1
1		2	6	5	8	7	12	9	10³	11¹	13		3²	4	14													2
1		2	6	5²	8¹	7	13	9²	10	11	12		3	4	14													3
1		2	8	5	9	7	12	13	10¹	11	6		3				4²											4
1	2		5		8¹	7		9²	10	11		6³	3	13	14	4	12											5
1		8	9	13		7			10	11		6¹	3				4²	2	5									6
1	12		6	5	8³	7	13	9	10	11¹			3	14			4	2²										7
				5²	12	7	13	9	10	11		6	3				4	2	1	8¹								8
		4		5	13	7	8³	9	10	6		11²	3	12				2¹	1		14							9
	13	2		5	12	7²	6¹	9	10	11			3	14			4		1	8³								10
	13	2		5	7³	6	10	9	12	11			3¹	14			4		1	8⁶								11
1	3¹			5	7	11²	12	10	9³	6	13		4	14			2			8								12
1		7		5	12	11²	9	10	6	13			4¹	14			2	3		8³								13
1			5	13	7	12	9	10	6	11			3²	4			2¹			8								14
1	9		5		7¹	12	11	10	6²	13			3	4	14		2			8¹								15
1	12	2	5	14	7	9	10	6²	11¹		3		4				13			8⁶								16
1		2	5		7	6¹	9	10	11		3	4		12						8								17
1	14	4²	5		7	6	9	10	13	11³	3		12				2¹			8								18
1	4	14	5		7	6³	9	10	12	11¹	3²		13				2			8								19
1		6	5	13	7		9	10	12	11¹	3		4				2			8²								20
1	3	8	5		7		9	10	11²		6		4	12			2¹					13						21
1	4²	6	5		7		9	10	11		3	12	14	2³								13	8¹					22
1	3³	9	5	12	7	13	11	10²			14	6	4	2									8¹					23
1	13	6	5	12	7		9	10	11²		3	4		2									8¹					24
1		6	5	14	7		9	10	12	13	3	4³		2	1								11¹	8²				25
	4	14	5		7	13	10		6		2		3	1			8⁴					12		9²	11¹			26
	14	8	5		7	12	10	4	6	13	2³	3¹	1										9	11²				27
1	4	6	5	9	7	12	10	13			3	2¹	1	8									14	11²				28
1	3	2	5	6	7	11¹	10³	9			4	13	1	8²									14	12				29
1	3²	2	5	6	7	11¹	10	9			4	14	8³									13	12					30
1	4		5		7	11	9	10	13		3	14		8³				6¹	2²	12								31
1	4	2	5		7	11²	9³	10	13		3		12	8⁴	14	6												32
1	3	6	5		7	13	11	10²	9		4		2	8¹									12					33
1		6	5		7	9³	10	8		3	4²	14	2	12								11¹	13					34
1		2	5	8²	7		9	10	4	13	3	12	2									11¹	6³	14				35
1		4	5	8²	7	11³	10	9		14	3	12	2²									13	6					36
1		4	5	14	7	13	10	9³		12	3	11	2									8²	6¹					37
1		2	5	6¹	7		10	11	3		9			8²	4³	12						13	14					38

EAST FIFE
Third Division

Year Formed: 1903. *Ground & Address:* Bayview Stadium, Harbour View, Methil, Fife KY8 3RW. *Telephone:* 01333 426323. *Fax:* 01333 426376.
Ground Capacity: all seated: 2000. *Size of Pitch:* 115yd × 75yd.
Chairman: W. Bruce Black. *Secretary:* Derrick Brown.
Manager: James Moffat. *Assistant Manager:* Craig Robertson.
Managers since 1975: Frank Christie, Roy Barry, David Clarke, Gavin Murray, Alex Totten, Steve Archibald, James Bone, Steve Kirk, Rab Shannon, Dave Clarke. *Club Nickname(s):* The Fifers. *Previous Ground:* Bayview Park.
Record Attendance: 22,515 v Raith Rovers, Division I; 2 Jan, 1950.
Record Transfer Fee received: £150,000 for Paul Hunter from Hull C (March 1990).
Record Transfer Fee paid: £70,000 for John Sludden from Kilmarnock (July 1991).
Record Victory: 13-2 v Edinburgh City, Division II; 11 Dec, 1937.
Record Defeat: 0-9 v Hearts, Division I; 5 Oct, 1957.
Most Capped Player: George Aitken, 5 (8), Scotland.
Most League Appearances: 517: David Clarke, 1968-86.
Most League Goals in Season (Individual): 41: Jock Wood, Division II; 1926-27 and Henry Morris, Division II; 1947-48.
Most Goals Overall (Individual): 225: Phil Weir (215 in League).

EAST FIFE 2001–02 LEAGUE RECORD

Match No.	Date	Venue	Opponents	Result	H/T Score	Lg. Pos.	Goalscorers	Attendance
1	Aug 4	H	Albion R	D 0-0	0-0	—		465
2	11	A	Brechin C	L 0-6	0-2	8		472
3	18	H	East Stirling	L 0-4	0-3	10		299
4	25	H	Peterhead	L 0-1	0-0	10		331
5	Sept 8	A	Stirling A	L 1-2	0-0	10	McManus [72]	553
6	15	A	Elgin C	D 1-1	1-1	9	Nairn [44]	543
7	18	H	Montrose	L 1-2	0-1	—	McManus [51]	237
8	22	A	Queen's Park	W 2-1	2-1	9	Gibson 2 [28, 43]	825
9	29	A	Dumbarton	W 4-1	0-0	9	Allan 2 [58, 59], McManus 2 [71, 89]	392
10	Oct 13	A	Albion R	L 0-3	0-2	9		303
11	20	H	Brechin C	W 3-1	0-0	9	Bailey [62], Gibson [64], Wilson [74]	434
12	27	H	Stirling A	D 1-1	1-0	9	Graham [10]	495
13	Nov 3	A	Peterhead	W 3-1	2-1	9	McManus [2], Simpson (og) [24], Gallagher [89]	753
14	10	H	Elgin C	W 3-0	1-0	7	Cunningham [17], McManus [57], Munro [77]	418
15	24	A	Montrose	L 1-2	0-1	7	McManus [54]	453
16	Dec 1	H	Queen's Park	L 1-4	0-2	9	Bailey [55]	442
17	15	A	Dumbarton	L 0-1	0-0	9		821
18	Jan 12	H	Peterhead	L 2-3	1-1	9	Bailey [38], Mortimer [85]	444
19	19	H	Montrose	W 2-0	2-0	8	McManus 2 [8, 24]	325
20	26	A	Elgin C	L 0-2	0-0	8		538
21	Feb 2	H	Dumbarton	W 1-0	1-0	8	Mortimer [38]	369
22	9	A	Queen's Park	L 0-2	0-0	8		553
23	12	H	Albion R	L 2-3	0-1	—	Gallagher [65], Herkes [81]	301
24	16	A	Brechin C	D 1-1	0-1	8	Cunningham [64]	452
25	23	H	East Stirling	W 1-0	0-0	8	Bailey [75]	357
26	Mar 2	A	Peterhead	D 1-1	1-0	8	Bailey [24]	672
27	6	A	Stirling A	W 1-0	1-0	—	McManus [12]	361
28	9	H	Stirling A	D 1-1	1-0	8	Oliver [44]	477
29	16	A	Elgin C	L 0-1	0-1	8		321
30	23	A	Montrose	W 1-0	1-0	7	Mortimer [11]	358
31	30	H	Queen's Park	L 0-3	0-2	7		449
32	Apr 6	A	Dumbarton	L 0-2	0-1	8		716
33	13	A	Albion R	L 1-2	1-1	9	Cunningham [43]	442
34	16	A	East Stirling	L 1-2	0-1	—	McManus [88]	223
35	20	H	Brechin C	D 1-1	1-0	8	Gilbert [2]	356
36	27	A	East Stirling	W 2-1	0-0	8	Herkes [57], Graham [69]	236

Final League Position: 8

Honours
League Champions: Division II 1947-48; *Runners-up:* Division II 1929-30, 1970-71. Second Division 1983-84, 1995-96.
Scottish Cup Winners: 1938; *Runners-up:* 1927, 1950.
League Cup Winners: 1947-48, 1949-50, 1953-54.

Club colours: Shirt: Gold and black. Shorts: White. Stockings: Black.

Goalscorers: *League* (39): McManus 11, Bailey 5, Cunningham 3, Gibson 3, Mortimer 3, Allan 2, Gallagher 2, Graham 2, Herkes 2, Gilbert 1, Munro 1, Nairn 1. Oliver 1, Wilson 1, own goal 1.
Scottish Cup (4): McManus 3, Bailey 1.
CIS Cup (1): McManus 1.
Challenge Cup (2): Graham 1, McManus 1.

Godfrey R 36	Wilson W 36	Gallagher J 35	Gibson K 24	Mortimer P 35	Ovenstone J 6 + 2	Herkes J 19 + 11	Graham R 12 + 4	McManus P 32 + 2	Munro K 33	Allan J 18 + 15	Nairn J 13 + 8	Cunningham G 28 + 4	Macdonald A — + 1	Tejero A 1	Coulston D 4	Oliver N 15	Bailey L 27 + 3	Clyde R 1	Courts C — + 1	Lofting A 2 + 8	Rae J 3 + 1	Spink D 1 + 2	Thomson J 12	Geisler M — + 1	Gilbert G 3 + 2	Brown S — + 1	Match No.
1	2	3	4	5	6	7^1	8^2	9	10	11	12	13															1
1	2	3	4	5	6^2		8	9	7	12	10	11^1	13														2
1	2	3	4	5	6			9	7	10	8			11													3
1	2	3	4	5	6			8	9	7^1	12	10			11												4
1	2	3	4		6			9		7	12	10^1	11			5	8										5
1	2	3	4		6	12		9^2	7	13	10	11				5	8^1										6
1	2	3	4		6	14	13	9	5	12	10	7^3		11^1			8^2										7
1	2	3	4		6	14		9	7	13	10^1	12		11^2		5	8^3										8
1	2	3	4			14	13	9	6	12	10^3	7^2		11^1		5	8										9
1	2	3	4		6	12	14	9	7	11^2	10^1	13				5	8^3										10
1	2	3	4		6	12		9	5	11	10^1	7					8										11
1	2	3	4		6	12	7	10	9	5	11						8^1										12
1	2	3	4	5		10		9	7	12	11						8^1	6									13
1	2	3	4		6	10		9	7	12		11^2				5	8^1		13								14
1	2	3	4		6	14	10	9	7^1	12^2		11^3				5	8				13						15
1	2	3	4		6	12	10^1	9	5			7					8			11							16
1	2	3	4		6	12	7	9	5			8^1	10				11										17
1	2	3^2	4		6	7^1	10	9	5	12		11					8		13								18
1	2	3	8^1	5	12	6		9	4	11^2	7						10		13								19
1	2	3^1		5	12	6^3		9	4	11	13	7					8			14		10^2					20
1	2	3	10^1	5	7			9	4	11	12	6					8^2					13					21
1	2	3	10	5	7			9	4	11		6					8										22
1	2	3	10	5	12	7		9	4^1	11		6					8										23
1	2	3	10	5	7			9		11		6					8						4				24
1	2	3	10	5	7	12		9^1		11		6					8^2					13	4				25
1	2	3	4		7			9	6	11		10					8						5				26
1	2	3	4		7			9	6^2	11	13	10					8^1			12			5				27
1	2	3	8		7			9		11	12	6				4^1	10^2						5	13			28
1	2	3	8		7			9	6^2	12	13	11^1				4	10^3				14		5				29
1	2	3	8		7			10^2	6	12	14					4	9^3		13		11^1		5				30
1	2	3	8		7^3			10	6	9^1	12	13				4			14		11^2		5				31
1	2	3	5	8				9^2	7	12		6				4	10^3					13			11^1	14	32
1	2	8	3	10						11	7^1	6				4			13			9^2	5		12		33
1	2	3	8	10						12	6^3	11^2				7			4			14	5	9^1	11^1		34
1	2	3	8	10				9			7^2	12				6	4		13				5		11^1		35
1	2	8	4	3	10	12		9	7			6^1				5	11										36

EAST STIRLINGSHIRE   Third Division

Year Formed: 1880. *Ground & Address:* Firs Park, Firs St, Falkirk FK2 7AY. *Telephone:* 01324 623583. *Fax:* 01324 637 862
Ground Capacity: total: 1880, seated: 200. *Size of Pitch:* 112yd × 72yd.
Chairman: A. Mackin. *Vice Chairman:* Douglas Morrison. *Chief Executive/Secretary:* Leslie G. Thomson.
Head Coach: Danny Diver. *Physio:* Laura Gillogley.
Managers since 1975: I. Ure, D. McLinden, W. P. Lamont, A. Ferguson, W. Little, D. Whiteford, D. Lawson,
J. D. Connell, A. Mackin, D. Sullivan, B. McCulley, B. Little, J. Brownlie, H. McCann, G. Fairley, B. Ross.
Club Nickname(s): The Shire. *Previous Grounds:* Burnhouse, Randyford Park, Merchiston Park, New Kilbowie Park.
Record Attendance: 12,000 v Partick T, Scottish Cup 3rd rd; 21 Feb 1921.
Record Transfer Fee received: £35,000 for Jim Docherty to Chelsea (1978).
Record Transfer Fee paid: £6,000 for Colin McKinnon from Falkirk (March 1991).
Record Victory: 11-2 v Vale of Bannock, Scottish Cup 2nd rd; 22 Sept, 1888.
Record Defeat: 1-12 v Dundee United, Division II; 13 Apr, 1936.
Most Capped Player: Humphrey Jones, 5 (14), Wales.
Most League Appearances: 415: Gordon Russell, 1983-2001.
Most League Goals in Season (Individual): 36: Malcolm Morrison, Division II; 1938-39.
Most Goals Overall (Individual): —.

EAST STIRLINGSHIRE 2001–02 LEAGUE RECORD

Match No.	Date		Venue	Opponents	Result		H/T Score	Lg. Pos.	Goalscorers	Attendance
1	Aug	4	A	Elgin C	L	1-2	0-1	—	Lyle [67]	731
2		11	H	Montrose	L	0-1	0-1	9		191
3		18	A	East Fife	W	4-0	3-0	6	Lyle [30], Menelaws 3 (1 pen) [42, 45, 66 (p)]	299
4		25	A	Queen's Park	W	3-2	2-0	5	Maughan [15], Ferguson [19], Lyle [72]	502
5	Sept	8	H	Dumbarton	L	2-4	1-1	7	Menelaws 2 [35, 56]	212
6		15	H	Peterhead	L	2-3	0-1	7	McKechnie 2 [74, 77]	171
7		18	A	Albion R	W	4-0	1-0	—	Maughan [14], McKechnie [75], Lyle [80], Gordon [85]	159
8		22	H	Stirling A	D	1-1	0-1	6	Gordon [87]	403
9		29	A	Brechin C	W	2-1	1-0	5	Gordon [11], McAuley [77]	422
10	Oct	13	H	Elgin C	W	2-1	1-1	4	Lyle 2 [24, 60]	214
11		20	A	Montrose	L	0-2	0-1	4		321
12		27	A	Dumbarton	D	2-2	1-1	5	Lorimer [24], Lyle [48]	591
13	Nov	3	H	Queen's Park	L	0-1	0-1	7		301
14		10	A	Peterhead	L	2-3	2-2	9	Lyle 2 [19, 21]	482
15		24	H	Brechin C	L	3-4	2-1	9	Lyle [16], Gordon 2 (1 pen) [24, 89 (p)]	228
16		27	H	Albion R	L	1-2	1-2	—	Gordon [4]	196
17	Dec	1	A	Stirling A	D	1-1	1-1	8	McGhee [29]	438
18	Jan	12	A	Queen's Park	L	0-1	0-1	8		477
19		19	A	Albion R	L	1-5	0-4	9	Ure [73]	253
20	Feb	2	A	Brechin C	L	0-2	0-2	9		383
21		9	H	Stirling A	W	3-0	1-0	9	Ure [19], Gordon [71], McKechnie [83]	389
22		16	H	Montrose	W	2-1	0-1	9	Hall [62], Ferguson (og) [68]	203
23		23	A	East Fife	L	0-1	0-0	10		357
24	Mar	2	A	Queen's Park	W	3-1	2-1	9	McKechnie 2 [2, 48], Gordon [8]	254
25		5	A	Elgin C	D	2-2	1-1	—	McCheyne [32], McAuley [67]	309
26		9	A	Dumbarton	L	1-2	1-1	9	Lorimer [11]	715
27		16	H	Peterhead	L	1-2	0-0	9	McDonald [69]	503
28		23	H	Albion R	L	1-2	1-0	9	Gordon [31]	212
29		30	A	Stirling A	L	0-1	0-1	10		436
30	Apr	2	H	Dumbarton	W	1-0	0-0	—	Ure [88]	317
31		6	H	Brechin C	W	2-0	0-0	9	Gordon [81], Scott [88]	237
32		9	H	Peterhead	W	1-0	1-0	—	Todd D [25]	258
33		13	H	Elgin C	L	0-3	0-1	7		187
34		16	H	East Fife	W	2-1	1-0	—	Lorimer [29], Gordon [55]	223
35		20	A	Montrose	L	0-2	0-1	7		316
36		27	H	East Fife	L	1-2	0-0	7	McCheyne [81]	236

Final League Position: 7

Honours
League Champions: Division II 1931-32; C Division 1947-48. *Runners-up:* Division II 1962-63. Second Division 1979-80. Division Three 1923-24.
Scottish Cup: —.
League Cup: —.

Club colours: Shirt: Black with white hoop. Shorts: Black with white and red stripes. Stockings: Red with black tops and 3 white hoops.

Goalscorers: *League* (51): Gordon 11 (1 pen), Lyle 10, McKechnie 6, Menelaws 5 (1 pen), Lorimer 3, Ure 3, McAuley 2, McCheyne 2, Maughan 2, Ferguson 1, Hall 1, McDonald 1, McGhee 1, Scott 1, Todd D 1, own goal 1.
Scottish Cup (2): Lyle 1, McDonald 1.
CIS Cup (0):
Challenge Cup (0):

Hay D 27	Maughan R 29+3	McGhee R 24+2	Russell G 30	McDonald I 25+2	Scott A 19+4	Ferguson B 22+2	McAuley S 31+2	Menelaws D 7	Todd D 24+6	Lyle D 16+1	Gordon K 23+9	Aitken A —+2	McCheyne G 28	McKechnie G 16+4	Lorimer D 23+5	Wood D —+2	Todd C 8+1	Robertson S 1	Tolland M 4+2	Hall M 21+2	Hunter M 1+8	Kristjansson T 1	Ure D 13+5	McLaren G 1+4	Gilbert G —+1	McLaughlin P 2	Match No.
1	2	3	4	5	6²	7	8	9¹	10	11	12	13															1
1	7	4	6	3	11	2²	9¹	8	10				5	12	13												2
1	7	4	2	3	11¹	8	9³	6	10²	13			5	12	14												3
1	7	4	2	3	11¹	8	9³	6	10²				5	14	12												4
	7	6	4	3	11²	2	14	9	8³	10¹			5	12	13			1									5
1	8	5²		3	2	6	9	11	10¹		4		12							7	13						6
1	7	4	3	2	11	9¹	8	12			13		5²		10					6							7
1	7	4¹	5	3	2	8	6		9		13		10							11²	12						8
1		6		3	2	7	8		10	11¹			5		9					12	4						9
1	12			3	2	8	6		10	11			5¹		9²	7				4	13						10
1	7	12		3	2	6	9			11²		14	5		8³		10			4¹	13						11
1	2	6	4	3⁴	5	7	12		9	11¹				10	8³					13	14						12
1	7	6	4	3	2	10	8						5		9					12			11¹				13
1	7	6	4	3	2²	11	8		9¹				5		10					12			13				14
1		6	5	3	2	7	8		9¹				10							4			11	12			15
1	7	6		3	2	8¹	4		9				10		5					11			12				16
1		6	4	3	2	12	8		9	11¹			5		10					7							17
1	7	4	3	11²	2	8	6		10						9¹					5			12	13			18
1	7	4	3	11	2	6¹			10						8²					5	12		9	13			19
1	7	2	3	11¹	6	12			10				5		8²					4			9	13			20
1	2	5	3	11³	6	13	12		8		10				7²					4			9¹	14			21
1	2	5	3	11	6²	13	12		8		10				7					4			9¹				22
1	2	5	3	11²	6³	13	12		8		10				7					4			9¹	14			23
1	7	4	3	11	6				10				5		8					2			9				24
1	7	2	4	12	11³	6			10			14	5		9					13			8²	3¹			25
1	2	6¹	4	12	9²	7			10				5		11³					8	3		13	14			26
1	14	3	6	12	2³	8	7		10		4				11²					9¹			5	13			27
1	2²	3	11	14	13	7	6³		9		12				8					5			10¹		4		28
	8¹	3	2	12	13	7	11		10²				5							6			9	14		4²	29
		3	4	9	2	7	11						6		8		1						5	10			30
	12	3	4	9	2¹	7	11						6		8		1						5	10			31
	2	3	4	9		7	6		11						8		1						5	10			32
	2	12	4	9		7	6		11¹				3		8		1						5	10			33
	2¹	3	4	12		7	6		11				9		8		1						5	10			34
		3	4	2		7	6		11				9		8¹		1						5	10	12		35
	2	3	4			7	6		11				9		8		1						5	10			36

ELGIN CITY   Third Division

Year Formed: 1893. *Ground and Address:* Borough Briggs, Borough Briggs Road, Elgin IV30 1AP.
Telephone: 01343 551114. *Fax:* 01343 547921.
Ground Capacity: 3927, seated 478, standing 3449. *Size of pitch:* 111yd × 72yd.
Chairman: Dennis J. Miller. *General Manager:* Harry McFadden. *Secretary:* John A. Milton.
Manager: Alex Caldwell. *Coach:* Neil MacLennan. *Physio:* Maurice O'Donnell.
Managers since 1975: McHardy, Wilson, McHardy, Dickson, Shewan, Tedcastle, Grant, Cochran, Cumming, Cowie,
Paterson, Winton, Black, Teasdale, Fleming, McHardy, Tatters.
Previous names: 1893-1900 Elgin City, 1900-03 Elgin City United, 1903- Elgin City.
Club Nickname(s): City or Black & Whites. *Previous Grounds:* Association Park 1893-95; Milnfield Park 1895-1909;
Station Park 1909-19; Cooper Park 1919-21.
Record Attendance: 12,608 v Arbroath, Scottish Cup, 17 Feb 1968.
Record Transfer Fee received: £32,000 for Michael Teasdale to Dundee (Jan 1994).
Record Transfer Fee paid: £10,000 to Fraserburgh for Russell McBride (July 2001).
Record Victory: 18-1 v Brora Rangers, North of Scotland Cup, 6 Feb 1960.
Record Defeat: 1-14 v Hearts, Scottish Cup, 4 Feb 1939.
Most League Appearances: 67: Martin Pirie, 2000-02.
Most League Goals in Season (Individual): 12, Ian Gilzean, 2001-02.
Most Goals Overall (Individual): Ian Gilzean, 13.

ELGIN CITY 2001–02 LEAGUE RECORD

Match No.	Date		Venue	Opponents	Result	H/T Score	Lg. Pos.	Goalscorers	Attendance
1	Aug	4	H	East Stirling	W 2-1	1-0	—	Gilzean [44], Rutherford [75]	731
2		11	A	Queen's Park	D 0-0	0-0	4		691
3		18	H	Albion R	W 2-0	1-0	2	Gilzean [45], Craig D [83]	623
4		25	H	Stirling A	L 2-3	1-1	4	Morrison (og) [24], Mailer [54]	769
5	Sept	8	A	Peterhead	D 1-1	1-0	5	Gilzean [21]	564
6		15	H	East Fife	D 1-1	1-1	6	Gilzean [36]	543
7		22	A	Dumbarton	D 2-2	1-1	7	Hind [8], Kelly (pen) [50]	749
8		29	H	Montrose	L 1-2	1-2	8	Gilzean [26]	665
9	Oct	7	A	Brechin C	L 0-1	0-0	8		501
10		13	A	East Stirling	L 1-2	1-1	8	Gilzean [26]	214
11		20	H	Queen's Park	W 2-0	0-0	8	Kelly [61], MacDonald S [88]	581
12		27	H	Peterhead	W 4-1	0-1	7	Tully 2 [61, 79], Kelly [85], Gilzean [90]	974
13	Nov	3	A	Stirling A	W 1-0	1-0	4	Campbell [28]	524
14		10	A	East Fife	L 0-3	0-1	5		418
15		27	H	Brechin C	L 0-1	0-1	—		415
16	Dec	8	H	Dumbarton	L 0-3	0-1	6		511
17		15	A	Montrose	W 2-0	2-0	6	Tully (pen) [4], Kelly [43]	394
18	Jan	5	A	Peterhead	L 0-1	0-0	6		798
19		12	H	Stirling A	W 2-1	0-0	5	Campbell [37], Rae [45]	564
20		19	A	Brechin C	L 0-1	0-0	6		438
21		26	H	East Fife	W 2-0	0-0	5	Gilzean [53], Kelly [88]	538
22	Feb	2	H	Montrose	W 1-0	1-0	4	Mackay S [45]	601
23		9	A	Dumbarton	L 1-3	0-2	5	Gilzean [75]	690
24		16	A	Queen's Park	L 0-3	0-2	6		533
25		26	A	Albion R	D 4-4	0-3	—	Ross [47], Mackay S [55], Kelly [79], Tully [84]	249
26	Mar	2	H	Stirling A	L 1-3	0-1	6	Sanderson [55]	355
27		5	H	East Stirling	D 2-2	1-1	—	Gilzean [17], Dlugonski [64]	309
28		16	A	East Fife	W 1-0	1-0	6	James [5]	321
29		19	H	Peterhead	L 0-3	0-1	—		530
30		23	H	Brechin C	W 3-1	2-0	6	James 2 [20, 43], Campbell [87]	652
31		26	H	Albion R	D 0-0	0-0	—		652
32		30	H	Dumbarton	W 2-0	0-0	6	McBride [82], Gilzean [90]	709
33	Apr	6	A	Montrose	L 0-1	0-1	6		301
34		13	A	East Stirling	W 3-0	1-0	6	James [45], Teasdale [67], Ross [89]	187
35		20	A	Queen's Park	L 0-1	0-0	6		627
36		27	A	Albion R	D 2-2	1-0	6	Hind [18], Gilzean [66]	767

Final League Position: 6

Honours
Scottish Cup, Quarter Finals 1968.
Highland League Champions: winners 15 times.
Scottish Qualifying Cup (North): winners 7 times.
North of Scotland Cup: winners 17 times.
Highland League Cup: winners 5 times.
Inverness Cup: winners twice.

Club colours: Shirt: Black and white vertical stripes. Shorts: Black. Stockings: Red.

Goalscorers: *League* (45): Gilzean 12, Kelly 6 (1 pen), James 4, Tully 4 (1 pen), Campbell 3, Hind 2, Mackay S 2, Ross 2, Craig D 1, Dlugonski 1, McBride 1, MacDonald S 1, Mailer 1, Rae D 1, Rutherford 1, Sanderson 1, Teasdale 1, own goal 1.
Scottish Cup (0):
CIS Cup (2): Gilzean 1, McGlashan 1.
Challenge Cup (0):

Pirie M 33	Mailer C 17+2	McBride R 25+1	Furphy W 12+1	MacDonald S 22+1	Tully C 34	Ross D 28+1	Craig R 4+7	McGlashan C 11+3	Gilzean J 33+1	Craig D 11+17	Rutherford R 4+5	MacDonald J 14+8	Hind D 23+4	Campbell C 22+6	Kelly J 12+7	Morrison M 6	Dlugonski B 22	Bremner F 1+1	Rae D 5+1	Sanderson M 15+1	Mackay D 8	Mackay S 12	Rae M 1	Hamilton G 2	Teasdale M 10	James R 9	Match No.
1	2	3	4	5	6	7	8¹	9	10	11	12																1
1	2	3	4	5	6	7	12	9¹	10				8	11													2
1	2	3	4¹	5	6	7	13	9	10³	11	8²	12	14														3
1	3	4		5	6	7	12	9²	10	11	8¹		2	13													4
1	4	3		5	6	7		9	10	11			2		8												5
1	4	3		5	6	7		9	10	11¹		13	2²	12	8												6
1	2	3		5	6	7	12		10	11			4	9¹	8												7
1	2¹	3		5	6	7	12	9²	10	11¹		4	14	13	8												8
1		3		5	4	7		9	10	12		11	2	8¹	6												9
1	11	14		5	4	7	12	9¹	10	13		3²	2	8	6³												10
1	3	4	5	11	2		10	13	7¹		12	8¹	9				6										11
1	3¹	4	5	11	2²		10	12	13		7	8	9				6										12
1	3	4	5¹	11		14	10	2	13	12	7	8²	9³				6										13
1	3	4	11		7¹	13	10	5	14	12	2	8³	9²				6										14
1		4	5	6	7	11	9					3	2	8	10												15
1		4	5	6	8	7²	9³	10	14			2	11	12			3¹	13									16
1		4		5	8	12	10¹	11				3	2	7	9		6										17
1		4		5	8	12	10	11				3	2	7	9¹		6										18
1		4		5	8		9¹	12	13			3	2	7²			6		10	11¹							19
1				5	9¹		12	13				3	2	7			6		10	11²	4	8					20
1	3¹				8		9³	13				12	2	7	14		5		10	11²	4	6					21
1	3				8		9	12				2	7	13			5		10	11¹	4	6					22
1			14	5	8		9	12				2¹	7	13			3		10²	11³	4	6					23
1	12	3¹		2	6	8²	9	13				7					5		14	11	4	10³					24
12	3			5	6	7	9²					14	2¹	13	8	10³				4	11	1					25
2	3²			5	6	7		11³				13	14	8	9		4		12		10¹	1					26
2	9		5¹	6	7			10	13			3		12			8		11¹			1	4				27
1	5	2		6	7¹		10²	13				14	12				8		11		3			4	9³		28
1	5			2	6		10	11¹				12	7				8				3			4	9		29
1	5	2			6		10	12				13	7				3		11²		8			4	9¹		30
1	5	2			6		10	12					7				3		11		8			4	9¹		31
1	2				6		10	12				5	7				3		11		8			4	9¹		32
1	2¹			6	13		10	12²				5	7				3		11	8				4	9		33
1	2				6		10					3	7				11		5					4	9		34
1	2			5	6	8	10					3	12				7¹		11					4	9		35
1	2	12		5	6		10¹					3	8	7			11							4	9		36

FALKIRK   First Division

Year Formed: 1876. *Ground & Address:* Brockville Park, Hope St, Falkirk FK1 5AX. *Telephone:* 01324 624121.
Fax: 01324 612418.
Ground Capacity: total: 9706, seated: 2661. *Size of Pitch:* 110yd × 72yd.
Chairman: Campbell Christie. *Secretary:* Alex Blackwood. *General Manager:* Crawford Baptie.
Manager: Ian McCall. *Assistant Manager:* Gordon Chisholm. *Coach:* Tony Docherty. *Physio:* Alec McQueen.
Director of Football: Alex Totten.
Managers since 1975: J. Prentice, G. Miller, W. Little, J. Hagart, A. Totten, G. Abel, W. Lamont, D. Clarke, J. Duffy,
W. Lamont, J. Jefferies, J. Lambie E. Bannon, A. Totten. *Club Nickname(s):* The Bairns. *Previous Grounds:* Randyford
1876-81; Blinkbonny Grounds 1881-83; Brockville Park 1883 to present.
Record Attendance: 23,100 v Celtic, Scottish Cup 3rd rd; 21 Feb, 1953.
Record Transfer Fee received: £380,000 for John Hughes to Celtic (Aug 1995).
Record Transfer Fee paid: £225,000 to Chelsea for Kevin McAllister (Aug 1991).
Record Victory: 12-1 v Laurieston, Scottish Cup 2nd rd; 23 Sept, 1893.
Record Defeat: 1-11 v Airdrieonians, Division I; 28 Apr, 1951.
Most Capped Player: Alex Parker, 14 (15), Scotland.
Most League Appearances: (post-war): 353, George Watson, 1975-87.
Most League Goals in Season (Individual): 43: Evelyn Morrison, Division I; 1928-29.
Most Goals Overall (Individual): Dougie Moran, 86, 1957-61 and 1964-67.

FALKIRK 2001–02 LEAGUE RECORD

Match No.	Date		Venue	Opponents	Result	H/T Score	Lg. Pos.	Goalscorers	Attendance
1	Aug	4	H	Ayr U	L 1-2	1-0	—	Henry [17]	2828
2		11	A	Inverness CT	W 2-1	1-1	5	Watson [31], Wright (pen) [78]	2281
3		18	H	St Mirren	W 3-2	0-1	4	McQuilken [57], Christie [81], Kerr [90]	3748
4		25	H	Clyde	D 1-1	0-1	4	Waddell [55]	2618
5	Sept	8	A	Raith R	L 2-5	1-3	5	Lawrie [29], Craig [83]	2279
6		15	A	Airdrieonians	L 1-2	1-1	6	Christie [7]	2108
7		18	H	Partick Th	D 1-1	0-0	—	McAllister [73]	2633
8		22	A	Arbroath	L 0-1	0-0	9		1072
9		29	H	Ross Co	W 4-2	0-2	7	Henry [63], Rennie [65], Lawrie [69], Waddell [76]	1805
10	Oct	13	A	Ayr U	D 2-2	1-1	7	Miller [34], Kerr [51]	2439
11		20	H	Inverness CT	L 1-2	1-0	7	Rennie [28]	2075
12		27	H	Raith R	W 1-0	1-0	5	Miller [37]	2393
13	Nov	3	A	Clyde	D 1-1	0-1	5	Morris [65]	2013
14		10	A	Partick Th	L 1-5	0-1	7	Wright (pen) [54]	4245
15		17	H	Airdrieonians	L 1-2	1-1	8	Miller [13]	2586
16		24	A	Ross Co	W 2-1	1-0	7	McQuilken [31], Rodgers [85]	2184
17	Dec	1	A	Arbroath	W 3-2	1-0	7	Rowe (og) [43], Craig (pen) [65], Christie [90]	2047
18		8	A	St Mirren	W 5-1	1-0	4	Morris 2 [28, 73], Miller 2 [56, 76], Wilkie [83]	3852
19		15	H	Ayr U	L 0-2	0-0	6		2148
20	Jan	12	H	Partick Th	L 1-4	0-3	7	Morris [78]	3890
21		19	A	Arbroath	W 1-0	1-0	7	Craig [36]	964
22	Feb	2	H	Ross Co	L 1-4	0-3	8	Wilkie [85]	1834
23		9	H	St Mirren	D 0-0	0-0	7		2386
24		16	A	Inverness CT	L 2-3	1-1	8	Deuchar [43], Waddell [76]	1803
25		23	A	Raith R	L 1-5	1-2	9	Morris [36]	2511
26	Mar	2	A	Clyde	W 3-2	3-0	9	Kerr [14], Rennie [27], Miller [42]	1719
27		5	H	Clyde	L 1-6	1-1	—	Christie [26]	1817
28		9	H	Raith R	W 2-1	0-0	8	Miller 2 [54, 63]	2680
29		12	A	Airdrieonians	L 0-1	0-0	—		1812
30		16	A	Partick Th	L 0-3	0-1	9		4222
31		23	H	Airdrieonians	D 2-2	0-1	9	Brown [58], Miller [81]	2601
32		30	H	Arbroath	L 1-3	1-1	9	Miller [14]	2634
33	Apr	6	A	Ross Co	L 2-4	2-1	9	Miller [6], Craig [37]	2715
34		13	A	Ayr U	D 0-0	0-0	9		2473
35		20	H	Inverness CT	D 0-0	0-0	9		1965
36		27	A	St Mirren	D 0-0	0-0	9		3006

Final League Position: 9

Honours
League Champions: Division II 1935-36, 1969-70, 1974-75. First Division 1990-91, 1993-94. Second Division 1979-80; *Runners-up:* Division I 1907-08, 1909-10. First Division 1985-86, 1988-89. Division II 1904-05, 1951-52, 1960-61.
Scottish Cup Winners: 1913, 1957; *Runners-up:* 1997. *League Cup Runners-up:* 1947-48. *B&Q Cup Winners:* 1993-94.
League Challenge Cup Winners: 1997-98.

Club colours: Shirt: Navy blue with white. Shorts: White. Stockings: White.

Goalscorers: *League* (49): Miller 11, Morris 5, Christie 4, Craig 4 (1 pen), Kerr 3, Rennie 3, Waddell 3, Henry 2, Lawrie 2, McQuilken 2, Wilkie 2, Wright 2 (pens), Brown 1, Deuchar 1, McAllister 1, Rodgers 1, Watson 1, own goal 1.
Scottish Cup (1): Rodgers 1.
CIS Cup (2): Craig 1, Lawrie 1.
Challenge Cup (4): Watson 2 (1 pen), Craig 1, Kerr 1.

Hogarth M 31	Lawrie A 34	McQuilken J 35	Rennie S 28+2	Denham G 9	Christie K 29	McAllister K 21+7	Kerr M 28+2	Deuchar K 3+10	Watson S 4+2	Henry J 9	Mair L 19+1	Morris I 18+16	Waddell R 17+12	Wright P 12+2	Craig S 19+10	Miller J 27	McStay G 8+9	Oponga C 3	Wilkie L 9	Rodgers A 4+10	Pearson C 1+1	Murray N 8	Convery D 3	Hill D 5	Brown K 5	Moss D 3	Tano P 4+2	Match No.
1	2	3	4^2	5	6	7	8	9^5	10^3	11	12	13	14															1
1	5	3	4		10	7^1	8	6		11^2	2	14	12	9^1	13													2
1	5	3	4		10	7^2	8	6^1		11^2	2	14	12	9	13													3
1	5	3	4		10	7^3	8	6^2		11^1	2	12	13	9	14													4
1	5	3	4		6	7	8	10^1		2	12	11		9	13													5
1	4	3	13	5	6	12	8	14		11^1	2	7^3		9^2	10													6
1	4	3		5	6	7^1	8	13	10		2	12	11^2	9														7
1	4	3		5	6^2	7^2	8	13	12	10^1	2	14	11	9														8
1	4	3	6	5		8	13	14	10	2^1	12		11^2	9	7													9
1	2	3	4	5		7^1	8	6		11		13		9^2	10	12												10
1	2	3	4	5		7	8	6^1	14	11^2		13		9^2	10	12												11
1	2	3	4			7^1	8	6		10		11		12	9	5												12
1	2	3^4	4			7	8	6		10		11		12	9	13	5											13
1	2	3	4			7	8	6		11		10^1		12	9	5												14
1		3	4		6	7	12	2	8	10		11^1		9	5													15
1	2	3	4		6^1	7^2	8	10	14	11				9^3	12	5	13											16
1	2	3	4		6	12	8			11		7		9	5	10												17
1	2	3	4^1		6	13	8			7		11		9	12	5	10^2											18
1	2	3			6	7^1	8^3	10	13	14		11^2		9	4	5	12											19
1	2	3	4^1		6	13^3	12	8		7		11		9	10^2	5	14											20
1	2	3			6	8	13	10		11^1		7		9^2	4	5	12											21
1	2	3	12		6	8		10^3		11		7^2		9	4	5	13											22
1	4	3			6	13	10^3	2		8		11^2		7	12	5	14	9^1										23
1	5	3	4		6	12	10	2		7^2		13		11^1	9^3		8	14										24
1		3	2		6	7^2	8^1		11	12		9		10	13	4	5											25
1	2	3	4		6	7^1	8^2	14		12		9		13	11^3	10	5											26
1	2	3	4		6	7^3	8	12		13		14		9	11^1	10	5^2											27
	2	3	4	5		7^2	8	12		11		10^1		9	13		6				1							28
	2	3	4	5		7^2	8	13		12		11		10^1	9		6				1							29
	2	3	4		6	7^1	8	13		11		12		9	10^2		1				5							30
	4	3	2			8	13			7		11^2		9		6	1			5	10	12						31
	4	3	2		6^3		14			11^1		7		9	12	13	1			5	10	8^2						32
1	2	3				8	13			10		12		7^1	9		6			4		11^2						33
1	2		4	5		8	12			13		11		9	14		6^2			3^3	10^1	7						34
1	2	3	4	5	6	8	13			7		11^2		10	9		12											35
1	2	3	4	5	6^1	8	12	14		7^3		9		10	13		11^2											36

FORFAR ATHLETIC   Second Division

Year Formed: 1885. *Ground & Address:* Station Park, Carseview Road, Forfar. *Telephone:* 01307 463576/462259.
Fax: 01307 466956.
Ground Capacity: total: 4640, seated: 739. *Size of Pitch:* 115yd × 69yd.
Chairman and Secretary: David McGregor.
Manager: Neil Cooper. *Assistant Manager:* Phil Bonnyman. *Coaches:* Peter Castle, Derek Mitchell, Donald Ritchie.
Physio: Jim Barrett.
Managers since 1975: Jerry Kerr, Archie Knox, Alex Rae, Doug Houston, Henry Hall, Bobby Glennie, Paul Hegarty,
Tommy Campbell. *Club Nickname(s):* Loons. *Previous Grounds:* None.
Record Attendance: 10,780 v Rangers, Scottish Cup 2nd rd; 2 Feb, 1970.
Record Transfer Fee received: £65,000 for David Bingham to Dunfermline Ath (September 1995).
Record Transfer Fee paid: £50,000 for Ian McPhee from Airdrieonians (1991).
Record Victory: 14-1 v Lindertis, Scottish Cup 1st rd; 1 Sept 1988.
Record Defeat: 2-12 v King's Park, Division II; 2 Jan, 1930.
Most Capped Player: —.
Most League Appearances: 484: Ian McPhee, 1978-88 and 1991-98.
Most League Goals in Season (Individual): 45: Dave Kilgour, Division II; 1929-30.
Most Goals Overall (Individual): 124, John Clark.

FORFAR ATHLETIC 2001–02 LEAGUE RECORD

Match No.	Date	Venue	Opponents	Result	H/T Score	Lg. Pos.	Goalscorers	Attendance
1	Aug 4	H	Clydebank	L 1-2	1-1	—	Tosh (pen) [8]	460
2	11	A	Queen of the S	W 2-1	1-0	0	Moffat [44], Tosh [68]	1149
3	18	H	Stenhousemuir	L 1-2	1-0	7	Sellars [39]	415
4	25	A	Hamilton A	D 1-1	0-1	8	Tosh (pen) [70]	2191
5	Sept 2	H	Alloa Ath	L 0-1	0-1	—		469
6	8	H	Cowdenbeath	W 2-1	2-0	7	White (og) [30], Tosh [41]	403
7	15	A	Morton	W 3-1	1-1	5	Horn [37], Byers [66], Christie [82]	1231
8	22	A	Stranraer	L 0-2	0-0	6		360
9	29	H	Berwick R	W 2-1	0-0	6	Tosh 2 [66, 69]	380
10	Oct 13	A	Clydebank	D 1-1	1-0	6	Byers [41]	161
11	20	H	Queen of the S	L 0-3	0-1	7		407
12	27	A	Cowdenbeath	L 2-3	1-0	8	White (og) [41], Sellars [67]	316
13	Nov 3	H	Hamilton A	W 3-0	0-0	5	Moffat [65], Byers [82], Christie [85]	498
14	10	H	Morton	W 2-1	2-0	5	Byers [9], Moffat [28]	570
15	24	A	Alloa Ath	W 2-1	0-1	5	Byers [65], Sellars [88]	458
16	Dec 1	H	Stranraer	D 1-1	1-0	4	Sellars [2]	420
17	15	A	Berwick R	D 1-1	1-1	4	Tosh [23]	518
18	Jan 12	A	Hamilton A	L 0-2	0-1	5		1693
19	19	A	Alloa Ath	W 4-1	2-0	5	Tosh [30], Yardley 3 [41, 55, 86]	442
20	Feb 2	H	Berwick R	D 0-0	0-0	5		1066
21	9	A	Stranraer	W 3-0	2-0	5	Stewart [26], Sellars [32], Tosh [75]	366
22	16	A	Queen of the S	L 1-3	0-2	5	Tosh [72]	1141
23	27	A	Stenhousemuir	D 1-1	1-0	—	Byers [16]	227
24	Mar 2	H	Hamilton A	L 1-4	1-3	5	Byers [28]	471
25	5	H	Clydebank	L 1-2	1-1	5	Tosh [29]	373
26	9	A	Cowdenbeath	W 2-1	0-1	5	Tosh 2 [69, 72]	321
27	12	H	Cowdenbeath	D 0-0	0-0	—		444
28	16	H	Morton	W 2-1	0-0	5	Tosh [50], Byers [90]	524
29	23	A	Alloa Ath	L 1-2	0-0	5	Tosh [71]	462
30	26	H	Stenhousemuir	W 2-0	0-0	—	Christie [47], McCulloch [66]	340
31	30	H	Stranraer	W 3-2	0-2	4	Stewart [63], Tosh 2 [73, 85]	427
32	Apr 6	A	Berwick R	W 2-0	0-0	3	Byers [82], Tosh [89]	356
33	9	A	Morton	W 4-1	2-1	—	Christie 2 [41, 70], Tosh [44], Stewart [79]	681
34	13	A	Clydebank	L 0-1	0-0	3		166
35	20	H	Queen of the S	L 0-3	0-1	3		1022
36	27	A	Stenhousemuir	D 0-0	0-0	3		442

Final League Position: 3

Honours
League Champions: Second Division 1983-84. Third Division 1994-95; *Runners-up:* 1996-97. C Division 1948-49.
Scottish Cup: Semi-finals 1982; Quarter-finals 2002.
League Cup: Semi-finals 1977-78.

Club colours: Shirt: Sky blue with navy flashes. Shorts: Navy. Stockings: Navy.

Goalscorers: *League* (51): Tosh 19 (2 pens), Byers 9, Christie 5, Sellars 5, Moffat 3, Stewart 3, Yardley 3, Horn 1, McCulloch 1, own goals 2.
Scottish Cup (9): Sellars 3, Tosh 3, Byers 2, Yardley 1.
CIS Cup (1): Tosh 1.
Challenge Cup (2): Moffat 1, own goal 1

Brown M 36	Rattray A 29	Milne K 23+1	Horn R 20+1	Good I 26	Bowman D 11+1	Sellars B 24	Henry J 18+4	Tosh P 30	Moffat B 17+8	Byers K 34+1	Christie S 12+19	Stewart W 22+10	Farnan C 1+8	Morris R 12+7	McCloy B 25+1	Williams D 5+7	Lunan P 16+9	Walker D —+3	Mallan S 3	Taylor S 1+3	Yardley M 4	Bett C 8	Donaldson E 10+5	McCulloch S 9	Match No.
1	2²	3	4	5	6	7	8¹	9	10²	11	12	13	14												1
1		3	4	5	8	7		9	10³	11¹²			14	13	2	6	12								2
1		3	4¹	5	8	7		9	10	11¹³			14	12	6³	2	13								3
1		3	4¹	5	8	7		9	10	6²	11³	13		12	2	14									4
1	5	3	4		8	6		9	10	11¹		7		12	2										5
1	5	3	4			6¹	8	7²	9	10²	12	11	14		2		13								6
1	5	3	4				8	9	10¹	6	12	7²			2	11¹³	14	13							7
1	5	3	4			6		9	10²	8	12	7¹	14		2	11¹³	13								8
1	6	3	4			7	4	9	12	8	10²	13		2	5	11¹									9
1	5	3	4			7	6	10³	8	9¹	12			2	11¹²	13	14								10
1	5	3	4			7	6	10²	8	9	12			2¹	11	13									11
1	5	3	4			7	8¹	9²	6	11	10			2	13	12									12
1	6		5	3		7	4	9²	10	12	11			2¹		8	13								13
1	2	3	4	5		7	8	9¹	11	13	12			6					10²						14
1	2	3	4	5		8	13	9¹	11	12	7²			6²			10	14							15
1	2³	3	4	5		8	13	7³	9¹	11	12			6			10	14							16
1	2	3	4	5		8		10		11	12	7¹		6					9						17
1	2	3¹	4	5		8		9	14	11	13	7³		12		6			10²						18
1	4			5		8	13	9	14	11¹²		2		3	12	6¹			10	7³					19
1	4	3		5¹		8		9		11		13		2		6			10²	7	12				20
1	4	3		5		8		9	12	11		10¹		2		6²				7	13				21
1	4	3	12	5²		8		9		11	14	10		2		6²				7¹	13				22
1	2	3	4	5		8¹		9		6²	13	10		12						7	11				23
1	2	3¹	4¹	5		8		9	14	6	13	10		12						7³	11				24
1	4²	13		5			8	9¹	12	10		7		2	3		6				11				25
1	4			5		8	6	9		11¹²	12	10¹		2	3					7	13				26
1	4²			5	14	8¹	6	9		10		12		2	3	13				7³	11				27
1	2¹			5	4		7	9	10²	8	13	14		12	6								11¹³	3	28
1				5	6		8²	9	10¹	11	12	7		2	4								13	3	29
1				5	6¹		2	9	13	8	10²	7	14	12	4								11	3³	30
1	2			5			6	9		8	10¹	7	13		4²		12						11	3	31
1	2			5			7²	9		8	12	10	13	14	4		6³						11¹³	3	32
1	5				7		9	13	8	11¹²	10	12	2¹	4		6								3	33
1	2¹			5			12	9		10	11	7	8		4		6							3	34
1		4²	5			7	9		8	10¹		14		2³	13	6		12					11	3	35
1	3¹					9		8	13	7		2	4	12	6			10²			11	5			36

HAMILTON ACADEMICAL   Second Division

Year Formed: 1874. *Ground:* New Douglas Park, Cadzow Avenue, Hamilton ML3 0FT. *Telephone:* 01698 286103. *Fax:* 01698 285422.
Ground Capacity: 5330. *Size of Pitch:* 115yd × 75yd.
Secretary: Scott A. Struthers BA. *Commercial Manager:* Chris Norris.
Manager: Ally Dawson. *Assistant Manager:* Chris Hillcoat. *Physio:* John Queen.
Managers since 1975: J. Eric Smith, Dave McParland, John Blackley, Bertie Auld, John Lambie, Jim Dempsey, John Lambie, Billy McLaren, Iain Munro, Sandy Clark, Colin Miller. *Club Nickname(s):* The Accies. *Previous Grounds:* Bent Farm, South Avenue, South Haugh, Douglas Park, Cliftonhill Stadium, Firhill Stadium.
Record Attendance: 28,690 v Hearts, Scottish Cup 3rd rd; 3 Mar, 1937.
Record Transfer Fee received: £380,000 for Paul Hartley to Millwall (July 1996).
Record Transfer Fee paid: £60,000 for Paul Martin from Kilmarnock (Oct 1988) and for John McQuade from Dumbarton (Aug 1993).
Record Victory: 11-1 v Chryston, Lanarkshire Cup; 28 Nov, 1885.
Record Defeat: 1-11 v Hibernian, Division I; 6 Nov, 1965.
Most Capped Player: Colin Miller, 29, Canada, 1988-94.
Most League Appearances: 452: Rikki Ferguson, 1974-88.
Most League Goals in Season (Individual): 35: David Wilson, Division I; 1936-37.
Most Goals Overall (Individual): 246: David Wilson, 1928-39.

HAMILTON ACADEMICAL 2001–02 LEAGUE RECORD

Match No.	Date		Venue	Opponents	Result		H/T Score	Lg. Pos.	Goalscorers	Atten-dance
1	Aug	4	H	Queen of the S	D	1-1	0-1	—	Gaughan [54]	3047
2		11	A	Clydebank	L	2-3	2-1	0	Moore [5], Russell [18]	367
3		18	H	Cowdenbeath	W	1-0	0-0	5	Sherry [73]	2131
4		25	H	Forfar Ath	D	1-1	1-0	6	Callaghan [30]	2191
5	Sept	8	A	Berwick R	W	2-0	2-0	5	Callaghan [30], Moore [41]	475
6		15	A	Stenhousemuir	L	0-2	0-0	6		547
7		18	H	Stranraer	L	0-1	0-0	—		1539
8		22	A	Alloa Ath	L	1-2	1-2	7	Moore [43]	645
9		29	H	Morton	D	2-2	2-1	7	Callaghan [16], Moore [45]	3035
10	Oct	13	A	Queen of the S	W	1-0	0-0	7	Moore [57]	1552
11		20	H	Clydebank	W	3-0	0-0	5	McNiven [50], Moore 2 [54, 85]	1975
12		27	H	Berwick R	L	0-1	0-1	6		2441
13	Nov	3	A	Forfar Ath	L	0-3	0-0	7		498
14		10	H	Stenhousemuir	L	2-3	0-1	8	Nicholls 2 [84, 87]	1563
15		24	A	Stranraer	L	1-2	1-2	8	Moore [13]	436
16	Dec	1	H	Alloa Ath	W	1-0	1-0	8	Martin [33]	1833
17		15	A	Morton	D	1-1	0-0	83	McFarlane D [83]	1145
18	Jan	12	A	Forfar Ath	W	2-0	1-0	7	Moore [3], Graham [51]	1693
19		19	H	Stranraer	W	2-0	1-0	6	Sweeney [19], Bonnar [63]	1808
20	Feb	2	H	Morton	W	2-1	2-0	6	Bonnar [1], Martin [15]	2142
21		9	A	Alloa Ath	D	2-2	1-2	6	Moore [3], Bonnar [61]	626
22		16	A	Clydebank	D	1-1	1-1	6	McNiven [7]	421
23		19	A	Berwick R	L	0-2	0-1	—		576
24		23	H	Cowdenbeath	L	0-2	0-1	6		1284
25		26	A	Cowdenbeath	L	1-2	0-1	—	McFarlane D [85]	283
26	Mar	2	A	Forfar Ath	W	4-1	3-1	6	McFarlane D 2 [2, 70], Good (og) [19], McPhee [36]	471
27		5	H	Queen of the S	W	3-1	2-1	—	Callaghan 2 [33, 76], McNiven [42]	1592
28		9	H	Berwick R	W	3-1	2-1	4	McPhee 2 [2, 31], McFarlane D [80]	1868
29		16	A	Stenhousemuir	D	0-0	0-0	4		1910
30		19	A	Stenhousemuir	W	3-0	1-0	—	Callaghan [36], McFarlane D [74], McNiven [85]	344
31		23	A	Stranraer	L	2-3	0-1	4	McNiven 2 [53, 63]	453
32		30	H	Alloa Ath	D	1-1	0-1	5	McFarlane D [66]	1963
33	Apr	6	A	Morton	D	0-0	0-0	5		907
34		13	A	Queen of the S	L	1-3	0-0	5	Moore [88]	3062
35		20	H	Clydebank	W	2-0	1-0	5	Moore [30], Callaghan (pen) [63]	2030
36		27	A	Cowdenbeath	L	1-2	0-1	5	Armstrong [58]	412

Final League Position: 5

Honours
League Champions: First Division 1985-86, 1987-88; Third Division 2000-01. *Runners-up:* Division II 1903-04, 1952-53, 1964-65; Second Division 1996-97.
Scottish Cup Runners-up: 1911, 1935. *League Cup:* Semi-finalists three times.
B&Q Cup Winners: 1991-92, 1992-93.

Club colours: Shirt: Red and white hoops. Shorts: White. Stockings: White.

Goalscorers: *League* (49): Moore 12, Callaghan 7 (1 pen), McFarlane D 7, McNiven 6, Bonnar 3, McPhee 3, Martin 2, Nicholls 2, Armstrong 1, Gaughan 1, Graham 1, Russell 1, Sherry 1, Sweeney 1, own goal 1.
Scottish Cup (5): McPhee 2, Callaghan 1, McFarlane D 1, McNiven 1.
CIS Cup (1): Moore 1
Challenge Cup (0):

Goram A 1	Renicks S 29 + 1	Cunnington E 19	MacLaren R 11 + 4	Gaughan R 17 + 1	Bonnar M 26 + 1	Russell A 7 + 5	Sherry J 13 + 3	Moore M 25 + 5	McFarlane D 12 + 4	Callaghan S 32	O'Neil K 3 + 13	Graham A 25 + 7	Potter G 14 + 3	Kwik Ajet W 2 + 3	Stewart C 2	Martin M 18 + 5	Nelson M 27 + 4	McDonald P 15 + 4	Sweeney S 24 + 2	Walker J — + 3	Macfarlane I 14	Armstrong G 5 + 2	McCreadie 16 + 1	McNiven D 25 + 1	Lurinsky A 1 + 2	Nicholls M 2	McPhee B 15 + 2	Miller D — + 1	Herbet M 5	Elfallah M 1 + 3	McLaughlin S — + 2	Davidson S — + 1	Match No
1	2	3	4	5	6	7	8	9[1]	10	11[2]	12	13																					1
	2	3	4	5	6	7[1]	8	9[2]	10[3]	11	14	12	1	13																			2
	2		4[1]	5	6	8	13	10	11[3]			7		9[1]	1	3	12	14															3
	2	3		5	6	8	12	10	11[2]			7[3]		9[1]	1	4	13	14															4
	2	3		5	6[1]	12	8	9	10[2]	11		7	15	13		4						1[6]											5
	2	3		5	6[2]	13	8	9				7			1	12	11[1]	4						10									6
	2	3		5	6	8		9		11		7[2]			1	13	12	4[1]						10									7
	2	3		5	6	8[1]		9		11	14				1	13	4	7[2]	12					10[3]									8
	2	3		5	6	8		9[2]		11[3]		7[1]			1	13	12	14	4					10									9
	2			5		8		9		11		7			1	3	4						6	10									10
	2			5		8[1]		9		11		7			1	3	4		12	13			6	10[2]									11
	2			5	6[2]			9		11		7[1]			1	3[1]	4	14		13			8	10			12						12
	2			5	6			9				7			1	3[1]	4	11					12	10			8						13
	2			5				9[1]		11[2]	14	7			1	13	4	12					6	10	3[1]		8						14
	2[2]			5[1]	6		13	9		11	12	7			1	3	4			14				10			8[1]						15
	2			5	6		13	9		11	12	7[2]			1	3	4							10			8[1]						16
	2			5[1]				9		11	12	7	13	15		3	4					1[6]	6	10			8[2]						17
	2				6			9		11[1]		7				3	4	12	5		1			10			8						18
	2				6			9		11	12					3	4		5		1		7	10			8[1]						19
	2				6	7		9		11	12					3	4		5		1			10			8[1]						20
	2	3			6	7		9[1]		11	12						4		5	13	1			10			8[2]						21
	2	3			6	7		9[1]		11	12						4		5		1			10			8						22
	2				6	7		9		11	12					3[2]	4		5	13	1			10			8[1]						23
	2		4		6[1]	8	13	9		11	12	7[3]				3			5	14	1			10[2]									24
	2[3]	3	4		6	8	13	9		11	12	7[1]							5	14	1			10[2]									25
	2	3[2]	13	14	6[1]			9[3]		11	12	7					4		5		1			10			8						26
	2	3	14		6		13	9[2]		11[1]	12	7					4		5					10[3]			8						27
	2	3	13		6			9		11[2]	12	7					4		5		1			10[1]			8						28
	2	3			6			9[2]		11[1]	12	7					4		5					10			8			13			29
	2[4]	3			6		13	9[2]		11	12						4		5		1			10			8						30
	2	3			6		13	9[2]		11[1]		7					4		5		1			10			8			12			31
	2	3	14		6[3]		13	9		11[2]		7[1]					4		5					10			8			12			32
	2[3]	3			6[1]		13	9		11[2]	12						4		5		1			10			8			14	7		33
	2[1]	3			6			9		11[2]		7		15			4	14	5		1[6]			10			8			12			34
	2	3			6			9		11[2]	12						4	14	5		1			10			8[3]				7[1]	13	35
	2[1]	3						9		11		7					4		5		1		6[2]	10			8	-		12		13	36

HEART OF MIDLOTHIAN   Premier League

Year Formed: 1874. *Ground & Address:* Tynecastle Stadium, Gorgie Rd, Edinburgh EH11 2NL. *Telephone:* 0131 200 7200. *Fax:* 0131 200 7222. *Website:* www.heartsfc.co.uk
Ground Capacity: 18,000. *Size of Pitch:* 108yd × 73yd.
Chairman: Douglas Smith. *Chief Executive:* Christopher Robinson. *Sales and Marketing Manager:* Kenny Wittmann.
Manager: Craig Levein. *Assistant Coach:* Peter Houston. *Coach:* John McGlynn. *Physio:* Alan Rae.
Managers since 1975: J. Hagart, W. Ormond, R. Moncur, T. Ford, A. MacDonald, A. MacDonald & W. Jardine, A. MacDonald, J. Jordan, S. Clark, T. McLean, J. Jefferies.
Club Nickname(s): Hearts, Jambo's. *Previous Grounds:* The Meadows 1874, Powderhall 1878, Old Tynecastle 1881, (Tynecastle Park, 1886).
Record Attendance: 53,396 v Rangers, Scottish Cup 3rd rd; 13 Feb, 1932.
Record Transfer Fee received: £2,100,000 for Alan McLaren from Rangers (October 1994).
Record of Transfer paid: £750,000 for Derek Ferguson to Rangers (July 1990).
Record Victory: 21-0 v Anchor, EFA Cup 30th October 1880.
Record Defeat: 1-8 v Vale of Leven, Scottish Cup, 1888.
Most Capped Player: Bobby Walker, 29, Scotland.
Most League Appearances: 515: Gary Mackay, 1980-97.
Most League Goals in Season (Individual): 44: Barney Battles.
Most Goals Overall (Individual): 214: John Robertson, 1983-98.

HEART OF MIDLOTHIAN 2001–02 LEAGUE RECORD

Match No.	Date	Venue	Opponents	Result		H/T Score	Lg. Pos.	Goalscorers	Attendance
1	Jul 28	A	Livingston	L	1-2	0-1	—	Cameron [86]	8325
2	Aug 4	H	Aberdeen	W	1-0	1-0	6	Cameron [19]	12,696
3	11	A	Celtic	L	0-2	0-1	8		57,715
4	18	H	Dundee	W	3-1	3-0	6	Cameron [11], Wales 2 [13, 17]	12,259
5	25	A	Dunfermline Ath	W	1-0	0-0	3	Severin [74]	6992
6	Sept 8	H	Rangers	D	2-2	1-1	3	McKenna [9], Simmons [82]	14,014
7	16	A	Kilmarnock	L	0-1	0-0	6		7566
8	22	A	Motherwell	L	0-2	0-1	7		4808
9	29	H	Dundee U	L	1-2	0-0	9	Simmons [69]	11,034
10	Oct 13	H	St Johnstone	W	3-0	2-0	8	Juanjo 2 [25, 60], Adam [38]	10,735
11	21	A	Hibernian	L	1-2	0-2	8	Simmons [64]	13,774
12	27	A	Aberdeen	L	2-3	1-2	9	Fulton [16], Adam [54]	13,935
13	Nov 3	H	Livingston	L	1-3	0-2	9	McKenna [75]	12,173
14	10	H	Dundee	W	2-0	0-0	7	McKenna [55], Fuller [72]	10,374
15	17	H	Celtic	L	0-1	0-1	9		15,570
16	24	A	Dundee	D	1-1	1-0	9	Webster [29]	7219
17	Dec 1	H	Dunfermline Ath	D	1-1	0-0	9	Simmons (pen) [85]	11,086
18	9	A	Rangers	L	1-3	1-2	9	McKenna [40]	47,891
19	15	H	Kilmarnock	W	2-0	2-0	8	Simmons (pen) [7], Fuller [24]	10,027
20	22	H	Motherwell	W	3-1	0-1	6	Fuller 2 [52, 79], McKenna [60]	10,674
21	26	A	Dundee U	W	2-0	1-0	—	Wales [33], Fuller [47]	8762
22	29	H	Hibernian	D	1-1	1-0	6	McKenna [10]	17,474
23	Jan 2	A	St Johnstone	W	2-0	1-0	—	Wales [37], Fuller [72]	5413
24	12	H	Aberdeen	W	3-1	1-1	4	Grönlund [38], Fulton [55], Wales [62]	12,902
25	19	A	Livingston	L	0-2	0-0	4		7474
26	23	A	Celtic	L	0-2	0-0	—		57,177
27	Feb 2	A	Dunfermline Ath	D	1-1	0-0	6	Adam [88]	5527
28	9	H	Rangers	L	0-2	0-0	6		14,511
29	16	A	Kilmarnock	D	3-3	1-0	6	Mahe [39], Pressley (pen) [82], Grönlund [85]	7138
30	Mar 2	A	Motherwell	W	2-1	1-0	6	Severin [22], Sloan [82]	7223
31	9	H	Dundee U	L	1-2	0-2	7	McKenna [80]	10,893
32	16	A	Hibernian	W	2-1	1-1	5	Severin [39], Pressley (pen) [86]	13,240
33	23	H	St Johnstone	L	1-3	0-3	6	Wales [50]	10,762
34	Apr 7	A	Rangers	L	0-2	0-1	6		47,492
35	13	A	Aberdeen	W	3-2	1-1	5	Tod [3], Mahe [86], McKenna [88]	12,467
36	20	H	Dunfermline Ath	W	2-0	0-0	5	McKenna [59], Kirk [79]	10,108
37	28	H	Celtic	L	1-4	1-2	5	Fuller [32]	13,288
38	May 12	H	Livingston	L	2-3	0-0	5	Fuller [50], Fulton (pen) [88]	10,223

Final League Position: 5

Honours
League Champions: Division I 1894-95, 1896-97, 1957-58, 1959-60. First Division 1979-80; *Runners-up:* Division I 1893-94, 1898-99, 1903-04, 1905-06, 1914-15, 1937-38, 1953-54, 1956-57, 1958-59, 1964-65. Premier Division 1985-86, 1987-88, 1991-92. First Division 1977-78, 1982-83.
Scottish Cup Winners: 1891, 1896, 1901, 1906, 1956, 1998; *Runners-up:* 1903, 1907, 1968, 1976, 1986, 1996.
League Cup Winners: 1954-55, 1958-59, 1959-60, 1962-63; *Runners-up:* 1961-62, 1996-97.

European: *European Cup:* 4 matches (1958-59, 1960-61). *Cup Winners' Cup:* 10 matches (1976-77, 1996-97, 1998-99).
UEFA Cup: 37 matches (*Fairs Cup:* 1961-62, 1963-64, 1965-66. *UEFA Cup:* 1984-85, 1986-87, 1988-89, 1990-91, 1992-93, 1993-94, 2000-01).

Club colours: Shirt: Maroon. Shorts: White. Stockings: Maroon.

Goalscorers: *League* (52): McKenna 9, Fuller 8, Wales 6, Simmons 5 (2 pens), Adam 3, Cameron 3, Fulton 3 (1 pen), Severin 3, Grönlund 2, Juanjo 2, Mahe 2, Pressley 2 (pens), Kirk 1, Sloan 1, Tod 1, Webster 1.
Scottish Cup (3): Fuller 2, Wales 1.
CIS Cup (0):

Niemi A 32	Pressley S 30	Neilson R 2	McCann A 4+2	McKenna K 31+2	Tomaschek R 6+1	Severin S 24+3	Fulton S 27+8	Cameron C 4	Adam S 12+7	Wales G 21+11	McSwegan G 1+4	Boyack S 6+13	Simmons S 24+9	Mahe S 35	Webster A 25+2	Juanjo 5+4	Flögel T 29+3	Kirk A 4+16	Sloan R 4+2	Maybury A 27	Fuller R 27	Weir G 3+6	Grönlund T 22+1	Davidson R —+2	McKenzie R 6	McMullan P —+1	Milne K 3+1	Tod A 3	Hamill J 1+2	Match No.
1	2	3²	4³	5	6	7	8	9	10	11¹	12	13	14																	1
1	2	3	4	5²	6	7	8	9	10	11³	12	13	14																	2
1	2	3	4	12	6¹	7²	8³	9	10	11		13	14		5															3
1	2	3	4	14	6³	7	8¹	9	10	11²	12	13			5															4
1	2	3	4		6	7	8	9	11¹	13					5	10²	12													5
1	2	3	4		6	7²	8	9	10	11¹		13			5	6	11¹													6
1		3	4			7	8	12	14	11²	10		9¹		6³	3	2	13	5											7
1	2	3	4	5²	6	7	8	9	10³	11¹	13		14		2	6	12													8
1	2	6¹	4			7	9¹	14		8	13	3			5	12	10	11³												9
1	2					7²			10	12					8	3	5	11	6	9¹	13	4								10
1	2		13			7	12		10²	14					8	3	5¹	9	6			4	11³							11
1	2		6				8²		10³	12	13				9	3	5		7			4	11¹	14						12
1	2		6				8		10	12					9²	3	5					4	11¹		7	13				13
1	2		6				8		10¹	12					9	3	5				13	4	11²		7					14
1	2		6				8		10¹	12					9	3	5				13	4	11		7²					15
1	2		6				8²		10¹	12						3	5	9				4	11		7	13				16
1	2		6				8³			10		13			9	3	5	12				4	11	14	7²					17
1	2		6¹				8²			13		12			9	3	5	10	14			4	11		7³					18
1	2		5				12			10		8			9¹	3		6²	13			4	11³	14	7					19
1	2		5				12			10²		8			9¹	3		6	13			4	11	14	7³					20
	2		6				8			10¹		13				3	5	9²	12			4	11		7	1				21
	2	3	6		14		8³			10		13	12		9¹		5					4	11		7²	1				22
	2		6		12		8			10						3	5	9	13			4	11²		7¹	1				23
	2		6				8²			10		13				3	5	9	12			4	11¹		7	1				24
	2					7	8	13	10³						12	3	5	9				4	11		6²	1				25
1	2					7	8	12	10¹	13					9	3	5					4	14	11	6²					26
1	2					7	8¹	14	10³	13					9	3	5					12	4	11	6²					27
1	2		4			7	8		12	10¹					9²	3		5	13			4	11	6		1				28
1	2		6			7			10¹	11³					9	3	5²		8		4	14	12				13			29
1	2		5			7						12	13		3		8			9¹	4	11	10²	6						30
1	2		5			7	12				13					3	14		8¹		9	4	11	10³	6²					31
1	2		5			7	8			13					10¹	3			12		9¹	4	11		6					32
1	2¹		12			7	8			10			14		3		5				9²	4	11		6		13			33
1			5	13		7	12			10³						3			8			4	11	14	6¹		9²	2		34
1			5	6¹		7	13						8²		9	3	14		12			4	11	10¹				2		35
1			5	6³		7	12						9²		3¹	2				8	13	4	11				10		14	36
1				6¹		7	8³					14			9	3	2		5	13		4	11				10²		12	37
		3	5			7	12			10²	13				14				8³		4	11		6¹		1		2	9	38

HIBERNIAN   Premier League

Year Formed: 1875. *Ground & Address:* Easter Road Stadium, Albion Rd, Edinburgh EH7 5QG. *Telephone:* 0131 661 2159. *Fax:* 0131 659 6488.
Ground Capacity: total: 17,500. *Size of Pitch:* 112yd × 74yd.
Managing Director: Rod Petrie. *Commercial Director:* Steven Powell.
Manager: Bobby Williamson. *Assistant Managers:* Gerry McCabe, Jim Clarke.
Physio: Malcolm Colquhoun.
Managers since 1975: Eddie Turnbull, Willie Ormond, Bertie Auld, Pat Stanton, John Blackley, Alex Miller, Jim Duffy, Alex McLeish, Frank Sauzee. *Club Nickname(s):* Hibees. *Previous Grounds:* Meadows 1875-78, Powderhall 1878-79, Mayfield 1879-80, First Easter Road 1880-92, Second Easter Road 1892-.
Record Attendance: 65,860 v Hearts, Division I; 2 Jan, 1950.
Record Victory: 22-1 v 42nd Highlanders; 3 Sept, 1881.
Record Defeat: 0-10 v Rangers; 24 Dec, 1898.
Most Capped Player: Lawrie Reilly, 38, Scotland.
Most League Appearances: 446: Arthur Duncan.
Most League Goals in Season (Individual): 42: Joe Baker.
Most Goals Overall (Individual): 364: Gordon Smith.

HIBERNIAN 2001–02 LEAGUE RECORD

Match No.	Date		Venue	Opponents	Result	H/T Score	Lg. Pos.	Goalscorers	Attendance
1	Jul	28	H	Kilmarnock	D 2-2	1-2	—	Sauzee (pen) [38], Laursen [81]	12,725
2	Aug	4	A	Dundee	L 1-2	0-1	8	Luna [60]	9447
3		11	H	Aberdeen	W 2-0	2-0	6	Sauzee (pen) [5], McManus [45]	13,150
4		18	A	Rangers	D 2-2	1-1	7	McManus [18], Orman [58]	45,940
5		25	H	Celtic	L 1-4	0-4	9	Fenwick [85]	14,701
6	Sept	8	A	Motherwell	W 3-1	1-1	5	Sauzee 2 (1 pen) [17 (p), 50], Fenwick [66]	5784
7		16	A	Dunfermline Ath	W 5-1	3-1	5	Brewster 2 [17, 22], McManus [44], Luna 2 [73, 81]	11,035
8		23	H	St Johnstone	W 4-0	1-0	3	Luna [25], Fenwick [56], Brebner [59], Smart [71]	10,398
9		30	A	Livingston	L 0-1	0-0	4		8863
10	Oct	13	A	Dundee U	L 1-3	1-0	4	Brebner [3]	7950
11		21	H	Hearts	W 2-1	2-0	4	de la Cruz 2 [1, 23]	13,774
12		27	H	Dundee	L 1-2	1-1	5	Brewster [45]	11,185
13	Nov	3	A	Kilmarnock	D 0-0	0-0	5		7460
14		17	A	Aberdeen	L 0-2	0-0	6		12,504
15		24	H	Livingston	L 0-3	0-2	7		11,146
16	Dec	1	A	Celtic	L 0-3	0-2	8		59,220
17		8	H	Motherwell	D 1-1	1-0	8	O'Neil [6]	11,158
18		12	A	Rangers	D 1-1	1-0	—	Luna [22]	46,179
19		15	A	Dunfermline Ath	L 0-1	0-0	9		6617
20		22	A	St Johnstone	D 0-0	0-0	9		4056
21		26	H	Rangers	L 0-3	0-1	—		14,021
22		29	A	Hearts	D 1-1	1-1	9	O'Neil [88]	17,474
23	Jan	2	A	Dundee U	L 0-1	0-0	—		11,155
24		12	A	Dundee	L 0-1	0-0	11		7326
25		19	H	Kilmarnock	D 2-2	1-0	11	Hurtado [11], O'Connor [62]	9592
26		23	H	Aberdeen	L 3-4	2-2	—	Luna 2 [17, 68], Townsley [36]	10,555
27	Feb	2	H	Celtic	D 1-1	1-0	11	O'Connor [21]	12,313
28		9	A	Motherwell	L 0-4	0-0	11		5374
29		16	H	Dunfermline Ath	D 1-1	1-0	11	Townsley [79]	9788
30	Mar	2	H	St Johnstone	W 3-0	2-0	11	Murray 2 [2, 37], O'Connor [67]	13,731
31		9	A	Livingston	W 3-0	2-0	10	O'Connor [15], O'Neil [44], Petersen (og) [77]	6463
32		16	H	Hearts	L 1-2	1-1	11	O'Connor [4]	13,240
33		23	A	Dundee U	W 2-1	1-0	10	Arpinon [38], O'Connor [72]	5801
34	Apr	7	A	Dundee U	L 1-2	0-1	10	O'Connor [64]	5417
35		13	A	Kilmarnock	L 0-1	0-1	10		6236
36		21	H	Motherwell	W 4-0	2-0	10	Townsley [27], Arpinon [44], O'Connor 2 [80, 84]	7701
37		27	H	Dundee	D 2-2	1-1	10	Townsley [14], O'Connor [75]	8852
38	May	12	A	St Johnstone	W 1-0	1-0	10	Townsley [42]	3372

Final League Position: 10

Honours
League Champions: Division I 1902-03, 1947-48, 1950-51, 1951-52. First Division 1980-81, 1998-99. Division II 1893-94, 1894-95, 1932-33; *Runners-up:* Division I 1896-97, 1946-47, 1949-50, 1952-53, 1973-74, 1974-75.
Scottish Cup Winners: 1887, 1902; *Runners-up:* 1896, 1914, 1923, 1924, 1947, 1958, 1972, 1979, 2001.
League Cup Winners: 1972-73, 1991-92; *Runners-up:* 1950-51, 1968-69, 1974-75, 1993-94.

European: *European Cup:* 6 matches (1955-56 semi-finals). *Cup Winners' Cup:* 6 matches (1972-73). *UEFA Cup:* 61 matches (*Fairs Cup:* 1960-61 semi-finals, 1961-62, 1962-63, 1965-66, 1967-68, 1968-69, 1970-71. *UEFA Cup:* 1973-74, 1974-75, 1975-76, 1976-77, 1978-79, 1989-90, 1992-93, 2001-02).

Club colours: Shirt: Green with white sleeves and collar. Shorts: White with green stripe. Stockings: White with green trim.

Goalscorers: *League* (51): O'Connor 10, Luna 7, Townsley 5, Sauzee 4 (3 pens), Brewster 3, Fenwick 3, McManus 3, O'Neil 3, Arpinon 2, Brebner 2, de la Cruz 2, Murray 2, Hurtado 1, Laursen 1, Orman 1, Smart 1, own goal 1.
Scottish Cup (5): Brebner 1, Hurtado 1, Luna 1, Smith 1, Zitelli 1.
CIS Cup (4): Brewster 2, Luna 1, McManus 1.

Colgan N 30	de la Cruz U 25+7	Smith G 30	Sauzee F 10	Laursen U 23+1	Jack M 28+3	Murray I 30+2	Luna F 16+9	O'Neil J 32	Brewster C 23+2	Orman A 30	Zitelli D 7+14	O'Connor G 14+5	Brebner G 23+5	Townsley D 7+11	Fenwick P 22	McManus T 14+7	Smart A 2+3	Arpinon F 16+4	Andrews L —+2	Carg A 8	Hurtado E 4+8	Riordan D 1+5	Wiss J 6+5	Caldwell G 10+1	Martin L 1	Dempsie A 2+1	Hilland P 3	Raid A —2	Nicol K —+2	Daquin F 1+1	Whittaker S —+1	Match No.
1	2	3	4	5	6	7	8¹	9	10²	11	12	13																				1
1	2	3	4	5	6	7	11¹	9	10²		12	13³	8	14																		2
1			4	5	3²	7	14	9	10³	11	12		6	13		2	8¹															3
1	14		4	5	3	7	12	9	10²	11³	13		6			2	8¹															4
1	12		4	5	3¹	7		9	10	11			6			2	8²	13														5
1	7	3	4	5	6		12	9	10²	11						2	8¹	13														6
1	7		4³	5	6	14	13	9	10²	11	12					2	8¹															7
1	3		5	4²	7	10	9¹		11	12		6	13³		2	14	8															8
1	3		5	4	7	12	9	13	11			6			2	10²	8¹															9
1	3		5	6²	7	11¹	9	10	11	12		6			2	12																10
1	3	4	5		7	8²	9	10¹	11	13		6			2	12																11
1	3	4	5		7		9	10	11²	12		6			2	8¹	13														12
1	3		5	4³	7		10¹	11	9			6	14		2	8²	12	13														13
1	12	3	5	4	7	8²	9	10	11				13		2¹																	14
	2	3	5	4³	7	11¹	9	10		12		8	14		13	6²		1														15
	2	3	5	4	7	10	9		11²	8	12	13			6¹			1														16
1	2	3	5	4	7	8	9		11¹	10			13	12		6²																17
1	12	3		4	7	8²	9		11	10³		5	2	6¹	14		13															18
1	13	3	14	4	7³	8	9		11	10¹		5	2	6²			12															19
1	13	3		5	4²	14		9	11	10¹		7	2	8		6³		12														20
1	4¹	3		5		7³	10	9	11	14			8		2	12		6²			13											21
1	2	3			12	5		9	11¹	8²	10	4	13			6		7³	14													22
1	2	3	5	4	7		9		13	10	8		11¹			6²		12														23
1	4³	3		5	13	7	12	9⁴		14	10	8		2	11¹		6															24
1	12	3		5	4	7	10²		11¹		13	8	6	2				9³	14													25
1	6	3		5	4	7	10			8	9¹	2						11²	13	12												26
1	5	3			7	10³			14	11²	8	9²		2			12		13	6	4											27
1		3			7		9	10		12		8	6	2	13			11²	5¹	4												28
1	2¹	3			5		10³	9	11²	12		7			14	13	6	4	8													29
1	2	3	6	5		9	10³	8		12	13	7¹		14		4																30
1	2	3	5¹	6		9	10³	8		11	13	7²		14		12		4														31
1	2³	3		5	6	12	9	10	8		11¹	13	14		7²			4														32
	2³	3		5	6	13	9	10²	8		11	12			7¹		14	4														33
1	2³	3		5	12		9	10	8¹		11		14		7³		13	4				6										34
	2²	3		5¹		10³	9	14	8		11		13		7		1	12	4			6										35
		3				9	10	2		11		6²				7³			1		5	4	12	8¹	13	14						36
		3	14			9²	10	5		11		8¹	2		7			1			6³	13	4						12			37
		3	5			10²	9	11		8		2	1					6¹			4	13	12	7³	14							38

INVERNESS CALEDONIAN THISTLE
First Division

Year Formed: 1994. *Ground & Address:* Caledonian Stadium, East Longman, Inverness IV1 1FF. *Telephone:* 01463 222880.
Ground Capacity: 6500, seated: 2200. *Size of Pitch:* 115yd × 75yd.
Chairman: Kenneth Mackie. *Hon. Presidents:* John S. McDonald and Norman Miller. *Secretary:* Jim Falconer.
Manager: Steven W. Paterson. *Assistant Manager:* Duncan Shearer. *Coach:* John Docherty. *Physio:* Emily Goodlad.
Record Attendance: 6290 v Aberdeen, Scottish Cup, 20 February 2000.
Record Victory: 8-1, v Annan Ath, Scottish Cup 3rd rd, 24 January 1998.
Record Defeat: 1-5, v Morton, First Division, 12 November 1999 and v Airdrieonians, First Division, 15 April 2000.
Most League Appearances: 264, Charlie Christie, 1995-2002.
Most League Goals in Season: 27, Ian Stewart, 1996-97.
Most Goals Overall (Individual): 70, Ian Stewart, 1995-2001.

INVERNESS CALEDONIAN THISTLE 2001–02 LEAGUE RECORD

Match No.	Date	Venue	Opponents	Result	H/T Score	Lg. Pos.	Goalscorers	Attendance
1	Aug 4	A	Clyde	D 1-1	0-1	—	Mann (pen) [48]	975
2	11	H	Falkirk	L 1-2	1-1	8	Mann (pen) [45]	2281
3	18	A	Partick Th	L 0-1	0-1	10		3314
4	25	A	St Mirren	D 1-1	0-0	10	Mann [88]	3492
5	Sept 8	H	Arbroath	W 5-1	2-0	7	Wyness 3 [5, 60, 89], Mann [14], McBain [70]	1505
6	15	A	Ross Co	L 1-2	0-0	9	Robson [77]	3870
7	19	H	Raith R	W 5-2	3-0	—	Wyness 4 [7, 16, 42, 71], Ritchie [84]	984
8	22	A	Airdrieonians	L 0-6	0-5	8		1197
9	29	H	Ayr U	W 3-1	0-0	6	Christie [49], Ritchie 2 [51, 63]	1533
10	Oct 13	H	Clyde	W 5-1	2-0	4	Wyness 2 [31, 48], Ritchie [42], Bavidge [72], Duncan [89]	1653
11	20	A	Falkirk	W 2-1	0-1	3	Mann [58], Ritchie [81]	2075
12	27	A	Arbroath	L 2-3	1-1	3	Ritchie 2 [38, 50]	773
13	Nov 3	H	St Mirren	L 1-2	1-1	4	Wyness [31]	2343
14	10	A	Raith R	W 5-1	2-1	—	Mann (pen) [11], Christie [21], Ritchie [64], Tokely [71], Robson [86]	1468
15	17	H	Ross Co	W 3-0	1-0	3	McCormick (og) [15], Wyness 2 [59, 73]	4513
16	24	A	Ayr U	L 0-3	0-1	4		1999
17	Dec 1	H	Airdrieonians	L 1-2	0-1	4	Ritchie [61]	1591
18	8	H	Partick Th	L 1-2	0-0	5	Wyness [58]	1926
19	15	A	Clyde	L 0-1	0-0	8		782
20	22	H	Arbroath	W 3-2	2-1	4	Ritchie [25], Wyness [35], Bavidge [64]	1173
21	29	A	St Mirren	D 0-0	0-0	5		3613
22	Jan 12	H	Raith R	W 5-0	2-0	4	Tokely [7], McBain [36], Bavidge [46], Mann [57], Bagan [77]	1822
23	19	A	Airdrieonians	L 0-3	0-0	4		1506
24	Feb 2	H	Ayr U	D 1-1	1-0	5	Wyness [28]	1409
25	9	A	Partick Th	L 1-4	0-2	6	Ritchie [85]	3969
26	16	H	Falkirk	W 3-2	1-1	4	Munro [13], Wyness 2 [69, 73]	1803
27	Mar 2	H	St Mirren	W 4-2	1-1	4	Bagan [38], Ritchie 3 [55, 57, 80]	1866
28	9	A	Arbroath	L 0-1	0-0	5		738
29	16	A	Raith R	D 0-0	0-0	5		1590
30	19	A	Ross Co	D 0-0	0-0	—		4679
31	23	H	Ross Co	D 1-1	0-0	4	Tokely [57]	4185
32	30	H	Airdrieonians	W 1-0	0-0	5	Bavidge [50]	1709
33	Apr 6	A	Ayr U	L 0-1	0-0	8		1818
34	13	H	Clyde	D 1-1	0-0	7	Macdonald [89]	1525
35	20	A	Falkirk	D 0-0	0-0	6		1965
36	27	H	Partick Th	W 3-0	3-0	6	Stewart [10], Ritchie [13], Wyness [21]	2526

Final League Position: 6

Honours
Scottish Cup: Quarter-finals 1996.
League Champions: Third Division 1996-97; *Runners-up:* Second Division 1998-99.
Bell's League Challenge Cup runners-up: 1999-2000.

Club colours: Shirts: Royal blue with red stripes. Shorts: Royal blue. Stockings: Royal blue.

Goalscorers: *League* (60): Wyness 18, Ritchie 15, Mann 7 (3 pens), Bavidge 4, Tokely 3, Bagan 2, Christie 2, McBain 2, Robson 2, Duncan 1, Macdonald 1, Munro 1, Stewart 1, own goal 1.
Scottish Cup (7): Wyness 3, Bagan 1, Ritchie 1, Robson 1, Tokely 1.
CIS Cup (7): Ritchie 2, Robson 2, Bavidge 1, Teasdale 1, Tokely 1.
Challenge Cup (5): Ritchie 2, Bavidge 1, Christie 1, Wyness 1.

Calder J 9+1	Teasdale M 14+3	Golabek S 5+10	Mann R 34	McCaffrey S 32	Bradshaw P 2	Tokely R 34	Bavidge M 23+11	Wyness D 35+1	Christie C 30+3	McBain R 33	Duncan R 25+6	Ritchie P 29+5	Robson B 33+1	Walker J 27	Stewart G 3+17	Munro G 18	Macdonald N —+11	Bagan D 10+7	Match No.
1	2¹	3	4	5	6	7	8	9¹	10	11	12	13							1
1	2	3	4	5	6	7	8¹	9	10	11		12							2
1	2	3	4	5		7	12	8	10	6		9¹	11						3
			4	5		2	6	9	10	3	7	8¹	1		12				4
	14	12	4	5		2	7	8	10²	3	6³	9	11¹	1	13				5
1	12		4	5		2	7	8	10	3	6	9¹	11						6
1		12		5		2	7	8²	10¹	3	6	9³	11		13	4	14		7
	13	12	4	5		2	7	8	10²	3	6¹	9	11	1					8
	6		4	5		2	7¹	8	10	3		9²	11	1	12		13		9
	6	12	4	5		2³	7²	8	10	3	14	9	11¹	1	13				10
	6	12	4	5		2	7	8²	10	3	13	9	11¹	1					11
	6		4	5		2¹	7²	8	10	3	12	9	11	1	13				12
	6	13	4	5		2²	7	8	10	3	12	9¹	11³	1	14				13
15	6		4	5		2	14	8	10¹	3	7	9³	11	1	12				14
1	6		4	5		2	13	8²	12	3	7	9	11³		14			10¹	15
1	6²		4	5		2	13	8	12	3	7	9	11					10¹	16
	2		4	5			12	8	10	3	7	9	11	1				6¹	17
	6		4	5		2		8	10	3	7	9	11	1					18
	2¹	13	4	5			12	8	10³	3²	7	9	11	1		6		14	19
			4	5		2	7²	8	10	3	12	9	11³	1	14	6¹		13	20
			4	5		2	7	8	10	3		9	11	1		6			21
	14		4	5		2¹	7	8	10	3²	9		11³	1	13	6		12	22
	14		4	5		2	9	8	10²	3³	7		11	1	13	6¹		12	23
			4	5		2¹	12	8		3	7	9	11	1		6		10	24
				5		2	4²	8		3	7	9	11¹	1	12	6	13	10	25
	14		4	5		2¹	12	8	10	3	7²	9	11³	1		6		14	26
	3		4	5¹		2	13	8¹	10		7	9²	12	1		6	14	11	27
			4			2	12	8	10	3	7	9¹	11	1	5	6			28
	5¹		4			2	9³	8	10²	3	7	13	11¹	1	12	6		14	29
			4	5		2		8	10	3	7	9	11	1					30
			4	5		2	13	8	10	3	7¹	9²	11³	1		6	14	12	31
			4			2	9²	8¹	10	3	5	12	11	1	14	6	13	7¹	32
			4			2	9	8¹	10	3	5²	12	11³	1	13	6	14	7	33
			4	5		2³	8	12	10	3		9¹	11	1	13	6	14	7²	34
1			4	5		2	7	8		3		9¹	11		10	6¹	13	12	35
1			4	5		2	7²	8	12	3		9	11		10		13	6¹	36

KILMARNOCK   Premier League

Year Formed: 1869. *Ground & Address:* Rugby Park, Kilmarnock KA1 2DP. *Telephone:* 01563 545300. *Fax:* 01563
522181. *Website:* www.kilmarnockfc.co.uk
Ground Capacity: all seated: 18,128. *Size of Pitch:* 114yd × 72yd.
Chairman: J. Orr. *Secretary:* Derek Porter.
Manager: Jim Jefferies. *Assistant Manager:* Billy Brown. *Physio:* A. MacFie.
Managers since 1975: W. Fernie, D. Sneddon, J. Clunie, E. Morrison, J. Fleeting, T. Burns, A. Totten, B. Brown.
Club Nickname(s): Killie. *Previous Grounds:* Rugby Park (Dundonald Road); The Grange; Holm Quarry; Present
ground since 1899.
Record Attendance: 35,995 v Rangers, Scottish Cup; 10 March, 1962.
Record Transfer Fee received: £300,000 for Shaun McSkimming to Motherwell (1995).
Record Transfer Fee paid: £300,000 for Paul Wright from St Johnstone (1995).
Record Victory: 11-1 v Paisley Academical, Scottish Cup; 18 Jan, 1930 (15-0 v Lanemark, Ayrshire Cup; 15 Nov, 1890).
Record Defeat: 1-9 v Celtic, Division I; 13 Aug, 1938.
Most Capped Player: Joe Nibloe, 11, Scotland.
Most League Appearances: 481: Alan Robertson, 1972-88.
Most League Goals in Season (Individual): 34: Harry 'Peerie' Cunningham 1927-28 and Andy Kerr 1960-61.
Most Goals Overall (Individual): 148: W. Culley; 1912-23.

KILMARNOCK 2001–02 LEAGUE RECORD

Match No.	Date	Venue	Opponents	Result	H/T Score	Lg. Pos.	Goalscorers	Attendance
1	Jul 28	A	Hibernian	D 2-2	2-1	—	Ngonge [3], Cocard [44]	12,725
2	Aug 4	H	Celtic	L 0-1	0-0	9		13,201
3	12	A	Motherwell	D 2-2	0-0	9	Ngonge [7], Mitchell [82]	5188
4	18	H	St Johnstone	W 2-1	2-0	8	Di Giacomo [11], Pizzo [23]	6486
5	26	A	Dundee U	W 2-0	1-0	4	Di Giacomo [12], McLaren [62]	7404
6	Sept 8	A	Aberdeen	L 0-2	0-0	6		10,832
7	16	H	Hearts	W 1-0	0-0	4	Dargo [77]	7566
8	23	H	Dundee	L 0-1	0-1	5		7052
9	30	A	Dunfermline Ath	W 2-0	1-0	5	McLaren [28], Dargo [80]	3983
10	Oct 13	A	Rangers	L 1-3	0-2	6	Calderon [65]	49,351
11	20	H	Livingston	L 1-5	1-2	6	Santini (og) [4]	7346
12	27	A	Celtic	L 0-1	0-0	7		58,845
13	Nov 3	H	Hibernian	D 0-0	0-0	8		7460
14	10	H	St Johnstone	L 0-1	0-1	9		6008
15	17	A	Motherwell	W 2-0	1-0	7	Boyd [39], Di Giacomo [79]	6813
16	24	A	St Johnstone	L 0-1	0-1	5		3711
17	Dec 1	H	Dundee U	W 2-0	1-0	5	Mahood [31], Lauchlan (og) [56]	6130
18	8	H	Aberdeen	W 3-1	1-0	5	Dindeleux [13], Boyd [83], Mahood [87]	7611
19	15	A	Hearts	L 0-2	0-2	5		10,027
20	22	A	Dundee	W 2-1	1-0	5	Mitchell [21], Murray [57]	6342
21	26	A	Dunfermline Ath	D 0-0	0-0	—		6873
22	29	A	Livingston	W 1-0	1-0	5	Canero [34]	4972
23	Jan 12	H	Celtic	L 0-2	0-0	5		11,689
24	19	A	Hibernian	D 2-2	0-1	6	Johnson [64], McGowne [89]	9592
25	23	A	Motherwell	L 0-2	0-2	—		4342
26	30	H	Rangers	D 2-2	0-1	—	Boyd [84], Johnson [89]	11,589
27	Feb 2	A	Dundee U	W 2-0	1-0	5	Dargo [3], McGowne [64]	5774
28	9	A	Aberdeen	D 1-1	0-0	5	Johnson (pen) [50]	13,004
29	16	H	Hearts	D 3-3	0-1	5	Dargo [46], Johnson [51], Murray [65]	7138
30	Mar 2	H	Dundee	W 3-2	1-1	5	Dargo [9], McLaren 2 [72, 89]	6890
31	9	A	Dunfermline Ath	L 0-2	0-0	5		5518
32	16	H	Livingston	D 1-1	1-1	—	Dargo [36]	6936
33	20	A	Rangers	L 0-5	0-3	—		47,678
34	Apr 6	A	Dundee	L 0-2	0-1	7		5579
35	13	H	Hibernian	W 1-0	1-0	7	Ngonge [18]	6236
36	20	A	St Johnstone	W 3-0	0-0	7	Johnson 2 [49, 59], Boyd [84]	2245
37	27	H	Motherwell	L 1-4	0-1	7	Johnson [68]	5642
38	May 12	H	Dundee U	D 2-2	1-0	7	Mitchell [43], Innes [47]	6142

Final League Position: 7

Honours
League Champions: Division I 1964-65. Division II 1897-98, 1898-99; *Runners-up:* Division I 1959-60, 1960-61, 1962-63, 1963-64. First Division 1975-76, 1978-79, 1981-82, 1992-93. Division II 1953-54, 1973-74. Second Division 1989-90.
Scottish Cup Winners: 1920, 1929, 1997; *Runners-up:* 1898, 1932, 1938, 1957, 1960.
League Cup Runners-up: 1952-53, 1960-61, 1962-63, 2000-01.

European: *European Cup:* 4 matches (1965-66). *Cup Winners' Cup:* 4 matches (1997-98). *UEFA Cup:* 24 matches (*Fairs Cup:* 1964-65, 1966-67, 1969-70, 1970-71, *UEFA Cup:* 1998-99, 1999-2000, 2001-02).

Club colours: Shirt: Blue and white vertical stripes. Shorts: White. Stockings: White with blue tops.

Goalscorers: *League* (44): Johnson 7 (1 pen), Dargo 6, Boyd 4, McLaren 4, Di Giacomo 3, Mitchell 3, Ngonge 3, McGowne 2, Mahood 2, Murray 2, Calderon 1, Canero 1, Cocard 1, Dindeleux 1, Innes 1, Pizzo 1, own goals 2.
Scottish Cup (3): Canero 1, Mitchell 1, Sanjuan 1.
CIS Cup (0):

Marshall G 36	Canero P 31+1	Hay G 26	Innes C 20	Dindeleux F 27	Sanjuan J 18+2	Mahood A 33	Mitchell A 33+1	Calderon A 9+8	Cocard C 4+6	Ngonge M 7+2	Pizzo M 10+3	Di Giacomo P 15+8	Boyd K 11+17	Hessey S 13+2	McLaren A 13+15	Reilly M —+1	Fowler J 22+7	Dargo C 25+4	Baker M 6	McCutcheon G 2+1	McGowne K 22	Vareille J 3	McDonald G 1+5	Murray S 16+3	Jaconelli E —+3	Johnson T 7+3	Meldrum C 2+1	Shields G 5	Dillon S 1+1	Canning M —+1	Durrant I —+1	Match No.
1	2	3	4	5	6	7	8	9^2	10^3	11^1	12	13	14																			1
1	2	3		6	5	9^1	7	8	14	10^2	11^3		13		4		12															2
1	2	3		6	5	7^3	8			11		9^1	10^2		4	13	12	14														3
1	2	3	6	5		7	8	14	12		9^1	11^2		4	10^1		13															4
1		3	6	5		7	8	13		11^1		9^2	10	4	12		2															5
1		3	6	5	9	7		14	13		8^1	11		4^3	10^2		2	12														6
1		3	4	5	6^2	7	8	9^1	12		13	11		14			10															7
1	2	3	4	5		7	8^3	9^2	13	12	6	11^1		14			10															8
1	2		4	5	6	7	8				12		9		13	10^1	3	11^1														9
1	2		4	5	6^1	7	8	13					11^2	12	9		10^3	3	14													10
1	2		4		13	7	8	6^2					12	14	5	9^1		10	3	11^3												11
1	2		4		9	7	8						6^1	13			12	10			3	5	11^2									12
1	2		4^1		9	7	8						6^3	13	10		12				3	5	11^2	14								13
1	2				5	9	7	8	13				6^2		12			10			3		4^1	11^1								14
1	2				5	8	7				9^2		6	12	11^1		13				3		10^3		4	14						15
1	2				5	8	7				9^3		6	13	11^2		12				3		10^1		4	14						16
1		3			5		7	8	9				11	13			12				2		10^2		4			6^1				17
1		3			5		7	8	6	14			11^3	12			13				2		10^1		4			9^2				18
1	13	3			5		7	8	6	14			11^3	10							2^2		12		4			9^1				19
1	2	3			5		7	8	13				11^1	12			6	10							4			9^2				20
1	2	3			5		7	8	13				11	12			6	10^1							4			9^2				21
1	2	3			5		7	8					11	10			6								4			9^1	12			22
1	2	3			5		7	8	9^3				11	10^1			13								4			6^2	14	12		23
1	2	3			5^1		7	8					11	14	13		6	12							4			9^3	10			24
1	2	3			5		7	8	9^3				13		14		6^1	10^2							4			12	11			25
1	2	3			5^1		7	8					13	14	10^1		6	12							4			9^3	11			26
1	2	3					7	8					9^1	5	12		6	10							4				11			27
1	2	3					7	8					9^1	5	13		6	10							4			12	11^2			28
1	2	3					7	8					12	5	13		6	10							4			9^2	11^1			29
1	2	3					12	7	8				11^1	5	13		6^2	10							4			9				30
1	2	3	4			9	7	8^1				12	13	5	11^2		6	10														31
10	3	2		9^2			8						14	5	11^3		6	10			4	13	7			15						32
	2	3	6			7^1	8						12	5	11^2		14	10			4	9^3	13			1						33
1	2	3^1		5	9		14		13				11^2		12		6	10^3			4		8				7					34
1	2			5	7^1		8				11^2				9			10			4	12	3		13	6						35
1	2		4	5		7	8^1						11	14	9^3			10					3^2		12		6	13				36
1	2		4	5			8^1						12	14	9^2		3^1	10					13		11	6						37
	2		4			9	7	8					11		10			3^2								1	6	5^1	12	13		38

LIVINGSTON

Premier League

Year Formed: 1974. *Ground:* West Lothian Courier Stadium, Alderton Road, Livingston EH54 7DN. *Telephone:* 01506 417000. *Fax:* 01506 418888. *Email:* info@livingstonfc.co.uk
Ground Capacity: 10,024 (all seated). *Size of Pitch:* 105yd × 72yd.
Chairman: Dominic Keane. *Secretary:* J. R. S. Renton.
Team Manager: Jim Leishman. *Head Coach:* David Hay. *First Team Coach:* John Robertson. *Physios:* Michael McBride and Arthur Duncan.
Managers since 1975: John Bain, Alec Ness, Willie MacFarlane, Terry Christie, Michael Lawson. *Club Nickname:* Livi Lions. *Previous Grounds:* None.
Record Attendance: 10,024 v Celtic, Premier League; 18 Aug, 2001.
Record Transfer Fee received: £1,000,000 for D. Fernandez to Celtic (June 2002).
Record Transfer Fee paid: £60,000 for Barry Wilson from Inverness CT (May 2000).
Record Victory: 7-0 v Queen of the South, Scottish Cup; 29 Jan, 2000.
Record Defeat: 0-8 v Hamilton A. Division II; 14 Dec, 1974.
Most Capped Player (under 18): I. Little.
Most League Appearances: 446: Walter Boyd, 1979-89.
Most League Goals in Season (Individual): 21: John McGachie, 1986-87. *(Team):* 69; Second Division, 1986-87.
Most Goals Overall (Individual): 64: David Roseburgh, 1986-93.

LIVINGSTON 2001–02 LEAGUE RECORD

Match No.	Date	Venue	Opponents	Result	H/T Score	Lg. Pos.	Goalscorers	Attendance
1	Jul 28	H	Hearts	W 2-1	1-0	—	Quino [33], Fernandez [62]	8325
2	Aug 4	A	Rangers	D 0-0	0-0	5		47,805
3	11	A	Dundee	L 0-1	0-1	7		7712
4	18	H	Celtic	D 0-0	0-0	9		10,024
5	25	A	Motherwell	D 0-0	0-0	8		4828
6	Sept 8	H	Dundee U	W 2-0	0-0	4	Lowndes [57], Lovell [84]	5496
7	15	A	St Johnstone	D 2-2	2-1	5	Quino [24], Bingham [28]	3417
8	22	A	Dunfermline Ath	W 2-1	0-1	4	Bingham [74], Wilson [82]	4516
9	30	H	Hibernian	W 1-0	0-0	3	Quino [64]	8863
10	Oct 13	A	Aberdeen	D 2-2	1-0	3	Wilson (pen) [11], Tosh [78]	5894
11	20	A	Kilmarnock	W 5-1	2-1	3	Bingham [7], Andrews [19], Fernandez [68], Xausa [77], Aurellio (pen) [90]	7346
12	27	H	Rangers	L 0-2	0-1	3		9309
13	Nov 3	A	Hearts	W 3-1	2-0	3	Fernandez 2 [21, 25], Wilson [71]	12,173
14	17	A	Dundee	W 1-0	0-0	3	Wilson [56]	5391
15	24	A	Hibernian	W 3-0	2-0	3	Xausa 2 [7, 33], Lowndes [86]	11,146
16	Dec 1	H	Motherwell	W 3-1	3-0	3	Xausa 2 [20, 40], Wilson [21]	4895
17	8	A	Dundee U	D 0-0	0-0	3		6312
18	15	H	St Johnstone	W 2-1	0-0	3	Fernandez [53], Lowndes [79]	3739
19	22	H	Dunfermline Ath	D 0-0	0-0	3		4588
20	26	A	Celtic	L 2-3	1-1	—	Rubio [37], Quino [58]	58,407
21	29	H	Kilmarnock	L 0-1	0-1	3		4972
22	Jan 2	A	Aberdeen	W 3-0	1-0	—	Tosh [38], Brinquin [57], Andrews [66]	15,709
23	12	A	Rangers	L 0-3	0-2	3		48,044
24	19	H	Hearts	W 2-0	0-0	3	Bingham [53], Fernandez [65]	7474
25	30	H	Celtic	L 1-3	1-0	—	Quino [4]	8437
26	Feb 2	A	Motherwell	W 2-1	1-1	3	Andrews [44], Quino [70]	4458
27	9	H	Dundee U	D 1-1	0-0	3	Bingham [51]	4497
28	16	A	St Johnstone	L 0-3	0-1	3		3784
29	Mar 2	A	Dunfermline Ath	L 0-1	0-0	3		5032
30	9	H	Hibernian	L 0-3	0-2	3		6463
31	13	A	Dundee	L 0-2	0-0	—		5506
32	16	A	Kilmarnock	D 1-1	1-1	4	Wilson [22]	6936
33	23	H	Aberdeen	D 0-0	0-0	4		8603
34	Apr 6	A	Celtic	L 1-5	0-4	4	Wilson [72]	59,510
35	13	H	Rangers	W 2-1	1-1	4	Wilson [42], Lovell [84]	10,019
36	20	A	Aberdeen	L 0-3	0-3	4		14,109
37	28	A	Dunfermline Ath	W 4-1	1-1	4	Lovell [34], Xausa 2 [61, 75], Quino [83]	8749
38	May 12	A	Hearts	W 3-2	0-0	3	Quino [52], Bingham [71], Wilson [86]	10,223

Final League Position: 3

Honours
League Champions: First Division: Champions: 2000-01. Second Division 1986-87, 1998-99. Third Division 1995-96;
Runners-up: Second Division 1982-83. First Division 1987-88.
Scottish Cup: —. *League Cup:* Semi-finals 1984-85. *B&Q Cup:* Semi-finals 1992-93, 1993-94, 2001.
Bell's League Challenge Runners-up: 2000-01.

Club colours: Shirt: Gold, black and white trim, black band. Shorts: Black, gold and white trim. Stockings: Gold.

Goalscorers: *League* (50): Wilson 9 (1 pen), Quino 8, Xausa 7, Bingham 6, Fernandez 6, Andrews 3, Lovell 3, Lowndes 3, Tosh 2, Aurellio 1 (pen), Brinquin 1, Rubio 1.
Scottish Cup (4): Bingham 2, Fernandez 1, Wilson 1.
CIS Cup (9): Caputo 4, Wilson 2, Bingham 1, Lovell 1, Tosh 1.

Broto J 17	Brinquin P 23	Bollan G 20 + 1	Rubio O 33	Andrews M 35	Quino R 34 + 2	Lovell S 26 + 1	Wilson B 32 + 5	Xausa D 19 + 9	Fernandez D 30 + 3	Bingham D 31 + 6	Tosh S 21 + 10	Keith M — 1	Caputo M 4 + 17	Lowndes N 7 + 14	Hart M 14 + 7	Anderson J 10 + 1	Deas P 1	Aurellio D 5 + 9	McCulloch M — + 2	McEwan D — + 1	Culkin N 21	Santini D 21	Del Nero S — + 1	Toure-Mamman C 3 + 6	Makel L 9 + 4	Brittain R — + 2	Petersen M 2 + 1	Jokovic N — + 3	Match No.
1	2	3	4	5	6	7	8^1	9^2	10^3	11	12	13	14																1
1	2	3	4	5	6	7	8^1	9^2	10	11^2	13		14	12															2
1	2	3	4	5	6^1	7	8^3	9^2	10	11	12		13	14															3
1		3	4	5	6	7	8^1	9^2	10^3	11	14		12	2	13														4
1			4	5	6^3	7	8^1	9^2	10	11	14		12	13	2		3												5
1		3	4	5	6	7	8	13	10^3	11^2	12			9^2	2			14											6
1		3	4	5	6	7	8^1	13	10^3	11	12		14	9^2	2														7
1		3	4	5		7	13	9^2		11	8		12	10^1	2	6^2		14											8
1		3	4	5	6	7	8^2	12		11	9		10^1					13	15										9
		3	4				8^2	12	14	11^3	9		10^1	13	2	5					1								10
	2		4	5	6^1	7	8		10	12	11^3		9					14	13		1	3							11
	2		4	5	6^1	7	8		10^2	12	11		9								1	3		13					12
	2		4		12	7	8^1		10^2	11	9		14	13		5		6^1			1	3							13
	2	14		5	13	7	8^2		10^1	11	9^3	12				4		6			1	3							14
	2		4	5	6	7	8^2	9^1	10^3	11	14		13								1	3		12					15
	2		4	5	6^2	7	8^1	9^3	10	11	14		12								1	3		13					16
	2		4	5	6	7	8	9^1	10	11			12								1	3							17
	2		4	5	6^1	7	8^2	9^3	10	11	13		12								1	3		14					18
	2		4	5	6^3	14	10^2	12	9	13	11							8			1	3		7^1					19
	2		4	5	6^2		8^1		10^1	11	9		12	13	7			14			1	3							20
	2		4	5		7	8	9	10^1		14		12	13	7						1	3^1							21
	2	3	4	5		7	8^1	14	10^1	11^2	9		12		6						1			13					22
	2	3	4	5			8^1	12	10	11	7		9^2	13	14						1			6^1					23
	2	3	4			7	8		10^1	11	9		12			5^2		6			1			13					24
		3	4	5		7	8^1		10	11^2	9		13	9^2	2			6			1					13			25
		3	4	5		7	8		10	11^1			13	9^2	2			6			1			12					26
	2	3	4	5		7	8	12	10^2	11	9^1							6			1			13					27
	2	3		5		7	8^3	9^1	10	11^2			12	14	13			6			1				4				28
		3^1		5	6	14	8^2		10	11^3	9		13	12	2	6					1				4				29
		3^1		5	6	7	13	14	10	11	8^2				2^3			9			1				4	12			30
1		3		5	6	7^2	12		10	14	13		11		2							4		9^1	8^3				31
1		3		5	6^2	7	8	12	10	11^1					2							4		13	9				32
1		3		5	6	7	8	12	10	11^3	14											4		13	9^1		2		33
1		3	4	5	6^1	7	8		10^1	11^2														12	9	14	2	13	34
1	2		4	5	6	12	8^2		10^3	11	14											3		7^1	9			13	35
1	2		4	5	6	7^2	8^3	12	10	11^1	13											3			9	14			36
1	2		4	5	6	7	8^1	12	10^3	11^2	13		14									3			9				37
1	2		4	5	6	7	8	12	10^3	11^1	13		14									3			9^2				38

MONTROSE

Third Division

Year Formed: 1879. *Ground & Address:* Links Park, Wellington St, Montrose DD10 8QD. *Telephone:* 01674 673200.
Ground Capacity: total: 3292, seated: 1338. *Size of Pitch:* 113yd × 70yd.
Chairman: John F. Paton. *Secretary:* Malcolm J. Watters.
Manager: John Sheran. *Assistant Manager:* David Larter.
Managers since 1975: A. Stuart, K. Cameron, R. Livingstone, S. Murray, D. D'Arcy, I. Stewart, C. McLelland, D. Rougvie,
J. Leishman, J Holt, A. Dornan, D. Smith, T. Campbell, K. Drinkell.
Club Nickname(s): The Gable Endies. *Previous Grounds:* None.
Record Attendance: 8983 v Dundee, Scottish Cup 3rd rd; 17 Mar, 1973.
Record Transfer Fee received: £50,000 for Gary Murray to Hibernian (Dec 1980).
Record Transfer Fee paid: £17,500 for Jim Smith from Airdrieonians (Feb 1992).
Record Victory: 12-0 v Vale of Leithen, Scottish Cup 2nd rd; 4 Jan, 1975.
Record Defeat: 0-13 v Aberdeen; 17 Mar, 1951.
Most Capped Player: Alexander Keillor, 2 (6), Scotland.
Most League Appearances: 426: David Larter, 1987-98.
Most League Goals in Season (Individual): 28: Brian Third, Division II; 1972-73.

MONTROSE 2001–02 LEAGUE RECORD

Match No.	Date	Venue	Opponents	Result	H/T Score	Lg. Pos.	Goalscorers	Attendance
1	Aug 4	H	Queen's Park	W 3-1	2-0	—	McKellar [13], Brand [26], Laidlaw [51]	384
2	11	A	East Stirling	W 1-0	1-0	3	Stewart [15]	191
3	18	H	Peterhead	L 0-3	0-1	5		438
4	25	A	Dumbarton	W 1-0	0-0	3	Brand [65]	751
5	Sept 8	H	Brechin C	L 0-1	0-1	4		859
6	15	H	Stirling A	W 4-0	3-0	2	Magee [12], Johnson [31], Kerrigan [33], Laidlaw [90]	400
7	18	A	East Fife	W 2-1	1-0	—	Kerrigan [20], Laidlaw [47]	237
8	22	H	Albion R	L 1-2	0-0	2	Laidlaw [74]	354
9	29	A	Elgin C	W 2-1	2-1	2	Kerrigan [23], Laidlaw [36]	665
10	Oct 13	A	Queen's Park	D 2-2	1-2	2	Conway 2 [29, 65]	407
11	20	H	East Stirling	W 2-0	1-0	2	Laidlaw [29], Kerrigan [66]	321
12	27	A	Brechin C	D 0-0	0-0	2		865
13	Nov 3	H	Dumbarton	L 1-3	0-2	2	Sharp R [77]	503
14	10	A	Stirling A	D 1-1	0-0	2	Laidlaw [87]	392
15	24	H	East Fife	W 2-1	1-0	2	McKinnon [21], Kerrigan [81]	453
16	Dec 1	A	Albion R	D 0-0	0-0	2		246
17	15	H	Elgin C	L 0-2	0-2	3		394
18	22	H	Peterhead	L 0-4	0-2	4		441
19	Jan 12	A	Dumbarton	W 5-0	2-0	3	Laidlaw 3 (1 pen) [8, 64 (p), 79], Kerrigan [12], Ferguson [58]	742
20	19	A	East Fife	L 0-2	0-2	3		325
21	26	H	Stirling A	L 1-3	1-0	4	Sharp R [38]	348
22	Feb 2	A	Elgin C	L 0-1	0-1	5		601
23	9	H	Albion R	W 2-0	2-0	4	McKinnon [1], Conway [31]	310
24	16	A	East Stirling	L 1-2	1-0	5	McKellar [18]	203
25	23	H	Peterhead	W 2-1	1-0	4	Christie [40], Johnson [62]	617
26	26	H	Queen's Park	W 3-1	3-0	—	Mitchell [4], Laidlaw [11], Ferguson [15]	250
27	Mar 2	H	Dumbarton	D 1-1	0-0	3	Christie [89]	435
28	5	H	Brechin C	D 0-0	0-0	—		748
29	9	A	Brechin C	L 0-2	0-0	5		738
30	16	A	Stirling A	W 1-0	0-0	4	Allison [80]	385
31	23	H	East Fife	L 0-1	0-1	5		358
32	30	A	Albion R	D 0-0	0-0	5		353
33	Apr 6	H	Elgin C	W 1-0	1-0	5	Kerrigan [6]	301
34	13	A	Queen's Park	W 1-0	0-0	5	Laidlaw [47]	416
35	20	H	East Stirling	W 2-0	1-0	4	Ferguson [39], Leask [88]	316
36	27	A	Peterhead	L 1-3	0-1	5	Laidlaw [68]	652

Final League Position: 5

Honours
League Champions: Second Division 1984-85: *Runners-up:* 1990-91. Third Division, *Runners-up:* 1994-95.
Scottish Cup: Quarter-finals 1973, 1976.
League Cup: Semi-finals 1975-76.
B&Q Cup: Semi-finals 1992-93.
League Challenge Cup: Semi-finals 1996-97.

Club colours: Shirt: Royal blue. Shorts: Royal blue. Stockings: White.

Goalscorers: *League* (43): Laidlaw 13 (1 pen), Kerrigan 7, Conway 3, Ferguson 3, Brand 2, Christie 2, Johnson 2, McKellar 2, McKinnon 2, Sharp R 2, Allison 1, Leask 1, Magee 1, Mitchell 1, Stewart 1.
Scottish Cup (4): Laidlaw 3 (1 pen), Lowe 1
CIS Cup (0):
Challenge Cup (0):

McGlynn G 32 + 2	McQuillan J 27	Ferguson S 34 + 2	Muirhead D 1 + 1	Christie G 33	Craib M 10 + 1	McKellar J 12 + 11	Brand R 22 + 4	Kerrigan S 23 + 2	Laidlaw S 18 + 14	Stewart S 4	Mitchell J 6 + 13	Hutcheon A 3 + 23	Sharp R 25	Conway F 20 + 1	Johnson G 31	Magee K 5 + 4	Allison J 26 + 5	Craig D 26 + 3	Lowe B 1 + 6	Butler J 4	McKinnon R 21	Yates M 2 + 2	Thomas K 3	Leask M 6 + 1	Webster K 1	Sharp G — + 1	Match No
1	2	3	4	5	6	7	8[1]	9	10[2]	11	12	13															1
1	2	12		5	6	7[1]	9[2]		10	11	13			3	4		8										2
1	2	14		5	6	7[2]	9		10[1]	11[3]			12	3	4		8	13									3
1	2	3		5	6	12	7[3]	9		11[1]			10[2]		4		8	14	13								4
1	2	3			6[1]	14	7	9			13	10[2]	5		4	8		12	11[3]								5
1	4	11		5			9[2]	10[3]	14	13			3		8	7[1]	6	2	12								6
1	4	11		5		14	9[1]	10	12			3		8	7[1]	6	2[2]	13									7
1	4	11		5			9[2]	10	13	14		3	12	8	7	6[1]	2[3]										8
1	4	11		5			13	10[2]	9[1]	12	3	6	8	2[3]	7	14											9
1	4	11		5			10	9[1]	12	3	6	8	2[2]	7	13												10
1	4	11		5		10[1]	9	12	13	3	6	8	7[2]	2													11
1	4	11		5		10	9[1]	12	13	3	6	8	7[2]	2													12
1	4	11[2]		5	7[3]	10[1]	12	9	14	3	6	8	13	2													13
	3	13	5		10[3]	9	14	12	6	8	11[1]	2[2]	7		1	4											14
15	11[1]	5		7	9	10	3	6	8	12	2	1[0]	4														15
1	3	5	13	11[2]	10[3]	9	14	6	8	7	2[1]	12	4														16
10	5	13	9	14	3	6	8	11	12	2[3]	1	4	7														17
12	11	5	8[1]	7	10[3]	14	13	3	6	4	2	1	9[2]														18
1	11	5	14	7	10	9[2]	3	6	8	2[3]	12	4[1]	13														19
1	11[2]	5	12	7[1]	10	9	13	3	6	8	2	4															20
1	3	11[2]	14	10[1]	9	13	5	6	8	7[3]	2	4	12														21
1	11	5	12	14	9[2]	13	7[3]	3[1]	6	8	2	10	4														22
1	4	3	5	2[1]	11	13	6	8	12	7	10	9[2]															23
1	4	3	5	2[1]	11[2]	14	13	6	8	12	7	10	9[3]														24
1	4	10	5	13	12	11[2]	3	6	8	2	7	9[1]															25
1	4	10	5	12	13	9[3]	11	14	3[2]	8	2	7	6														26
1	3	10	5	7	12	9[1]	11	13	8	6[2]	2	4															27
1	6	3	5	7	9[2]	13	11	12	8	4	2	10															28
1	6	3	5	7[1]	9[2]	13	11	12	8	4	2	10															29
1	6	11	5	12	8[1]	14	9[2]	13	3	2	7	4	10[3]														30
1	6	3	5	11[2]	10[3]	13	14	12	8	2	7[1]	4	9														31
1	4	6	5	3[2]	13	11[3]	10	14	12	8	2	7	9[1]														32
1	4	3	6	7	10[3]	12	14	13	5[2]	8	2	11	9[1]														33
1	4	3	5	6[2]	7	10[1]	12	14	8	2	13	11	9[3]														34
1	4	6	5	7[2]	10[3]	9[1]	12	3	8	2	13	11	14														35
1	4	6	5	10[2]	13	3	8	2[2]	12	11	9	7[1]	14														36

MORTON   Third Division

Year Formed: 1874. *Ground & Address:* Cappielow Park, Sinclair St, Greenock. *Telephone:* 01475 723571. *Fax:* 01475 781084
Ground Capacity: total: 14,891, seated: 5741. *Size of Pitch:* 110yd × 71yd.
Manager: Dave McPherson. *Managers since 1975:* Joe Gilroy, Benny Rooney, Alex Miller, Tommy McLean, Willie McLean, Allan McGraw, Billy Stark, Ian McCall, Allan Evans, Peter Cormack.
Club Nickname(s): The Ton. *Previous Grounds:* Grant Street 1874, Garvel Park 1875, Cappielow Park 1879, Ladyburn Park 1882, (Cappielow Park 1883).
Record Attendance: 23,500 v Celtic; 29 April, 1922.
Record Transfer Fee received: £350,000 for Neil Orr to West Ham U.
Record Transfer Fee paid: £150,000 for Allan Mahood from Nottingham Forest.
Record Victory: 11-0 v Carfin Shamrock, Scottish Cup 1st rd; 13 Nov, 1886.
Record Defeat: 1-10 v Port Glasgow Ath, Division II; 5 May, 1894 and v St Bernards, Division II; 14 Oct, 1933.
Most Capped Player: Jimmy Cowan, 25, Scotland.
Most League Appearances: 358: David Hayes, 1969-84.
Most League Goals in Season (Individual): 58: Allan McGraw, Division II; 1963-64.

MORTON 2001–02 LEAGUE RECORD

Match No.	Date	Venue	Opponents	Result	H/T Score	Lg. Pos.	Goalscorers	Attendance
1	Aug 4	H	Stenhousemuir	W 4-1	1-0		Bannerman 2 [25, 90], Reid [63], Miller (pen) [69]	2050
2	11	A	Alloa Ath	D 1-1	0-1	0	Bannerman (pen) [71]	972
3	18	H	Queen of the S	D 2-2	0-1	3	Gibson [53], Reid [88]	1827
4	25	H	Stranraer	D 1-1	1-0	4	O'Connor [10]	1727
5	Sept 1	A	Berwick R	L 0-2	0-1	—		647
6	8	A	Clydebank	L 2-3	1-0	8	McPherson [37], O'Connor [73]	1142
7	15	H	Forfar Ath	L 1-3	1-1	8	Bannerman [12]	1231
8	22	H	Cowdenbeath	L 0-2	0-1	9		1184
9	29	A	Hamilton A	D 2-2	1-2	9	Moore [27], O'Connor [54]	3035
10	Oct 13	A	Stenhousemuir	W 3-0	2-0	8	Tweedie [21], Miller [24], O'Connor [88]	664
11	20	H	Alloa Ath	D 1-1	0-0	9	Bottiglieri [73]	1243
12	27	H	Clydebank	L 0-2	0-1	9		1311
13	Nov 3	A	Stranraer	W 4-1	1-0	9	Bottiglieri [45], Tweedie [84], O'Connor 2 [88, 89]	523
14	10	A	Forfar Ath	L 1-2	0-2	9	Miller [83]	570
15	24	H	Berwick R	L 1-2	0-2	10	Votinen [56]	1193
16	Dec 1	A	Cowdenbeath	D 1-1	0-0	10	Miller [39]	501
17	15	H	Hamilton A	D 1-1	0-0	10	Bannerman [82]	1145
18	Jan 8	A	Clydebank	W 2-1	0-1	—	O'Connor [68], Wright [72]	940
19	12	H	Stranraer	D 2-2	1-2	9	Bannerman [22], Tweedie [64]	1368
20	19	A	Berwick R	D 0-0	0-0	8		690
21	Feb 2	A	Hamilton A	L 1-2	0-2	10	Aitken [78]	2142
22	16	A	Alloa Ath	L 0-4	0-2	10		657
23	26	A	Queen of the S	L 5-6	3-6	—	Wright [2], McPherson [33], O'Connor [35], Redmond [87], Hawke [90]	1242
24	Mar 2	A	Stranraer	D 0-0	0-0	10		421
25	9	H	Clydebank	W 3-1	1-0	10	Hawke [19], McPherson [50], Wright (pen) [82]	1145
26	12	H	Stenhousemuir	L 0-1	0-0	—		1038
27	16	A	Forfar Ath	L 1-2	0-0	10	Kerr [77]	524
28	23	H	Berwick R	W 3-2	1-2	10	Tweedie 2 [44, 60], Bannerman (pen) [78]	1011
29	26	H	Cowdenbeath	D 0-0	0-0	—		1171
30	30	A	Cowdenbeath	D 2-2	1-1	10	Wright [42], Cannie [62]	635
31	Apr 2	H	Queen of the S	L 0-3	0-1	—		1344
32	6	H	Hamilton A	D 0-0	0-0	10		907
33	9	H	Forfar Ath	L 1-4	1-2	—	Kerr [39]	681
34	13	A	Stenhousemuir	W 3-2	1-0	10	Bannerman [29], Cannie [77], McPherson [90]	559
35	20	H	Alloa Ath	D 0-0	0-0	9		928
36	27	A	Queen of the S	L 0-4	0-2	10		6158

Final League Position: 10

Honours
League Champions: First Division 1977-78, 1983-84, 1986-87. Division II 1949-50, 1963-64, 1966-67. Second Division 1994-95. *Runners-up:* Division 1 1916-17, Division II 1899-1900, 1928-29, 1936-37.
Scottish Cup Winners: 1922; *Runners-up:* 1948. *League Cup Runners-up:* 1963-64.
B&Q Cup Runners-up: 1992-93.

European: *UEFA Cup:* 2 matches (*Fairs Cup:* 1968-69).

Club colours: Shirt: Royal blue and white 4" Hoops. Shorts: White with royal blue panel down side. Stockings: Royal blue and white hoops.

Goalscorers: *League* (48): Bannerman 8 (2 pens), O'Connor 8, Tweedie 5, McPherson 4, Miller 4 (1 pen), Wright 4 (1 pen), Bottiglieri 2, Cannie 2, Hawke 2, Kerr 2, Reid 2, Aitken 1, Gibson 1, Moore 1, Redmond 1, Votinen 1.
Scottish Cup (1): Aitken 1.
CIS Cup (0):
Challenge Cup (1): O'Connor 1.

Coyle C 33	Bannerman S 31	Bottiglieri E 15+11	Greacen S 15	Frail S 24	MacGregor D 32	Moore A 11+4	Gibson J 14+8	Miller S 16+4	Reid A 9	Correia A 1+1	O'Connor S 20+1	Kearney D 2+4	Tweedie G 19+12	McPherson D 16	McMillan A —+2	Redmond G 2+16	McAneny P 5	Collins D 32	Renwick M 2	Riddle S 1+3	Kerr D 21+1	Mapes C 1+1	Aitken C 7+12	Votinen J 1	Hawke W 19	Wright P 13	Compston M —+2	Maisano M 11	Curran S 9+1	Moffat C 2+1	Carmichael D 1+3	Cannie P 8	Ross K 3+1	Match No.
1	2	3²	4	5	6	7¹	8⁵	9	10	11	12	13	14																					1
1	2			5	8	6	11¹		7	10	13	9³	3³		4	12	14																	2
1	2		4	8	3	7	11	10¹	9			5	12		6																			3
1	2		5	8	11	14	12	7²	10		9¹	13		4		6	3³																	4
1	2			8	6¹	7²	12²		10		9	11	13	5		14	4	3																5
1	2		5	8		12		14	10³		9	13		4	11¹	6	3	7²																6
1	2		5	8		7¹		11²	10		9	14	13	4		12		3	6²															7
1	2		5	8		7⁴		12	10		9		13	4		6	3	11¹																8
1	2	13	5	8		7		11	10²		9		12	4¹		6		3																9
1	2	12	5	8	4	7²	11		9		10¹			6	13	3																		10
1	2	3		8	5	7¹	12	11	9		10²			6	13	4																		11
1	2	3		8	5	7²		11	9		10¹		12	6	13	4																		12
1	2	3		8	5	12	6	10	9		13			11¹		4	7²																	13
1	2	3		8	5	7¹	6²	11	9		10			4	12	13																		14
1	7	12		2³	5	13	6²		10		14			4		3	11¹	8	9															15
1	10	11³		2	5	7	6²		9		14		13	4		3	12	8¹																16
1	7	11²	5	2	4	8¹		10³	13		14		6	3		12	9																	17
1	7	11³	5	2	4	12		9	13				3			6²		8	10															18
1	7	12	5	2	4			9	11		13		3			6²		8	10²															19
1	7	12	5	2	4	13	14	9	11				3			6²		8¹	10³															20
1		7	5¹	2	4	6	9¹				11²		14			3		13	12	8														21
1	7	12	5		4	6¹					11²		13			2		3	8³		9	10	14											22
1			6	4	11	7³		9²		12	5		14			2¹		3	13	8	10													23
1	7			2	4	12			9		5			6		3			8¹	10		11												24
1	7			4	13	9¹			2		5	12		6		3			8	10		11²												25
1	7	13		2	4	14	9¹				3¹	5		12		6			8	10		11³												26
1	2	14		4	8³			11	5		10		6			3		13					7²	9¹	12									27
1	2	14		4				11	5¹				6			3		7²		8	9³		10	12	13									28
1		5		4				11			12		6			3		13		8	9²	10	2	8¹				7²						29
1⁹	14			4				11	5				6			3		13		8	9²	10	2³				7	15						30
1	2	5		4				12			13		6			3		13		8	9²	10	11¹				7							31
1	7	5		4	10			11²			12		6			3		13		8¹		2						10	7¹	12	9			32
1	2	5¹		4				11			12		6			3		13		8		10	7¹					12	9					33
	7	12		4	14			11¹	5				6			3		13		8		10²	2³						9			1		34
	2	3		4	5			11¹			6							12		8²		10	7		13				9			1		35
	5			4	7			3¹			12		6							11²		13	10	2				8	9			1		36

MOTHERWELL Premier League

Year Formed: 1886. *Ground & Address:* Fir Park Stadium, Motherwell ML1 2QN. *Telephone:* 01698 333333. *Fax:* 01698 338001.
Ground Capacity: all seated: 13,742. *Size of Pitch:* 110yd × 75yd.
Chairman: John Boyle. *General Manager/Secretary:* Alisdair Barron. *Commercial Manager:* Karen Paterson. *Director of Football:* Pat Nevin.
Manager: Terry Butcher. *First Team Coach:* Miodrag Krivokapic. *Physio:* John Porteous.
Managers since 1975: Ian St. John, Willie McLean, Rodger Hynd, Ally MacLeod, David Hay, Jock Wallace, Bobby Watson, Tommy McLean, Alex McLeish, Harri Kampman, Billy Davies, Eric Black.
Club Nickname(s): The Well. *Previous Grounds:* Roman Road, Dalziel Park.
Record Attendance: 35,632 v Rangers, Scottish Cup 4th rd replay: 12 Mar, 1952.
Record Transfer Fee received: £1,750,000 for Phil O'Donnell to Celtic (September 1994).
Record Transfer Fee paid: £500,000 for John Spencer from Everton (Jan 1999).
Record Victory: 12-1 v Dundee U, Division II: 23 Jan, 1954.
Record Defeat: 0-8 v Aberdeen, Premier Division: 26 Mar, 1979.
Most Capped Player: Tommy Coyne, 13, Republic of Ireland.
Most League Appearances: 626: Bobby Ferrier, 1918-37.

MOTHERWELL 2001–02 LEAGUE RECORD

Match No.	Date	Venue	Opponents	Result	H/T Score	Lg. Pos.	Goalscorers	Attendance
1	Jul 28	A	Dunfermline Ath	L 2-5	1-1	—	Kelly (pen) [24], Adams [78]	4825
2	Aug 4	H	Dundee U	D 0-0	0-0	10		5057
3	12	H	Kilmarnock	D 2-2	0-0	10	Dow [13], Elliott [90]	5188
4	18	A	Aberdeen	L 2-4	2-2	11	Ready [26], Kelly [30]	10,988
5	25	H	Livingston	D 0-0	0-0	11		4828
6	Sept 8	H	Hibernian	L 1-3	1-1	11	Kelly (pen) [14]	5784
7	16	A	Rangers	L 0-3	0-1	11		47,137
8	22	H	Hearts	W 2-0	1-0	11	Kelly [36], Elliott [72]	4808
9	29	A	St Johnstone	W 3-2	1-1	10	Nicholas 2 [44, 88], Elliott [79]	3983
10	Oct 13	H	Celtic	L 1-2	0-1	11	Strong [68]	9922
11	27	A	Dundee U	D 1-1	0-1	11	Kelly [50]	6343
12	30	A	Dundee	L 1-3	1-1	—	Ready [44]	6863
13	Nov 3	H	Dunfermline Ath	W 1-0	1-0	10	Strong [16]	4578
14	10	A	Aberdeen	L 0-1	0-1	11		11,497
15	17	A	Kilmarnock	L 0-2	0-1	11		6813
16	24	A	Aberdeen	W 3-2	2-1	11	Pearson [7], Elliott [17], McFadden [83]	7302
17	Dec 1	A	Livingston	L 1-3	0-3	11	McFadden [78]	4895
18	8	A	Hibernian	D 1-1	0-1	11	Elliott [82]	11,158
19	15	H	Rangers	D 2-2	1-1	11	Lasley [15], Kelly (pen) [80]	9894
20	22	H	Hearts	L 1-3	1-0	11	Elliott [20]	10,674
21	26	A	St Johnstone	L 1-2	0-2	—	McFadden [89]	4659
22	Jan 2	A	Celtic	L 0-2	0-0	—		58,105
23	9	H	Dundee	W 4-2	2-1	—	McFadden 2 [8, 85], Ready [36], Elliott [70]	3563
24	12	H	Dundee U	W 2-0	0-0	10	McFadden [53], Hammell [80]	4631
25	19	A	Dunfermline Ath	L 1-3	0-1	10	McFadden [76]	4280
26	23	H	Kilmarnock	W 2-0	2-0	—	McFadden [13], Lehmann [27]	4342
27	Feb 2	H	Livingston	L 1-2	1-1	10	Soloy [38]	4458
28	9	H	Hibernian	W 4-0	0-0	9	Ferrere 3 [52, 65, 80], Lehmann [72]	5374
29	16	A	Rangers	L 0-3	0-2	10		49,284
30	Mar 2	H	Hearts	L 1-2	0-1	10	Lasley [55]	7223
31	9	A	St Johnstone	W 2-0	1-0	9	McFadden (pen) [9], Lehmann [61]	3282
32	16	A	Dundee	L 0-2	0-2	10		5785
33	19	H	Celtic	L 0-4	0-1	—		10,134
34	Apr 6	H	St Johnstone	D 1-1	0-1	11	Elliott [69]	3418
35	13	A	Dundee U	L 0-1	0-0	11		5108
36	21	A	Hibernian	L 0-4	0-2	11		7701
37	27	A	Kilmarnock	W 4-1	1-0	11	Adams [20], McFadden [70], Elliott [72], Pearson [73]	5642
38	May 12	H	Dundee	W 2-1	2-0	11	Lehmann [14], Elliott [44]	6574

Final League Position: 11

Most League Goals in Season (Individual): 52: Willie McFadyen, Division I: 1931-32.
Most Goals Overall (Individual): 283: Hugh Ferguson, 1916-25.

Honours
League Champions: Division I 1931-32. First Division 1981-82, 1984-85. Division II 1953-54, 1968-69: *Runners-up:* Premier Division 1994-95. Division I 1926-27, 1929-30, 1932-33, 1933-34. Division II 1894-95, 1902-03. *Scottish Cup:* 1952, 1991: *Runners-up:* 1931, 1933, 1939, 1951.
League Cup: 1950-51. *Runners-up:* 1954-55. *Scottish Summer Cup:* 1944, 1965.

Club colours: Shirt: Amber with claret hoop and trimmings. Shorts: White. Stockings: Claret.

European: *Cup Winners' Cup:* 2 matches (1991-92). *UEFA Cup:* 6 matches (1994-95, 1995-96).

Goalscorers: *League* (49): Elliott 10, McFadden 10 (1 pen), Kelly 6 (3 pens), Lehmann 4, Ferrere 3, Ready 3, Adams 2, Lasley 2, Nicholas 2, Pearson 2, Strong 2, Dow 1, Hammell 1, Soloy 1.
Scottish Cup (1): Elliott 1.
CIS Cup (1): Kelly 1.

Brown M 19	Corrigan M 26 + 4	Ready K 35 + 1	Hammell S 37 + 1	Strong G 31 + 1	Dow A 7 + 2	Martinez R 8 + 9	Twaddle K 7 + 5	Elliott S 30 + 7	Adams D 19 + 9	Kelly D 19	Tarrant N 2 + 3	Nicholas S 5 + 11	Lasley K 25 + 3	Leitch S 26	Harvey P — + 2	Cosgrove S — + 2	Forrest E 9 + 5	McFadden J 20 + 4	Pearson S 19 + 8	Deloumeaux E 22 + 1	Soloy Y 11 + 1	Woods S 15 + 1	Lehmann D 10 + 1	Ferrere D 7 + 2	Dubourdeau F 4	Bernhard F 2 + 1	Fagan S — + 2	Ramsay D 2	Clarkson D — + 1	Kinniburgh W 1	Clarke D — + 1	MacDonald K — + 1	Match No
1	2	3	4¹	5	6	7³	8²	9	10	11	12	13	14																				1
1	2	3	4	5	6	7	8³	12		11	10¹			9²	13	14																	2
1	2	3¹	4	5	6	7	8	14	13	11	10³			9²				12															3
1	2	3	4	5³	6	7¹	8	10		11	12			9²			13	14															4
1	2	3	4¹		6	14	13	10	11				8	9³				12	5	7²													5
1	2	3	12	4		7¹	9	10²	11³	14	13		8						5	6													6
1	2	3	4	5		7¹	10	14	11³	12		9²	13					6	8														7
1	2	3	4	12		14	9³	13	11²	10	7	8						5	6¹														8
1	2	3	4	13		8¹	10	14	11	12	7³	9						5	6²														9
1	14	3	4¹	5		13	9	12	11	10²	7³	8						2	6														10
1	2	3	4	5		12		9	10	11¹	8							6	7														11
1	2	3	4²	5			9	10	11	8¹	12							6	13	7													12
1	2	3	4	5		12	9	10¹	11³	14	6²	8						13	7														13
1	2	3	4	5		8²	11	10	13	6	9							7¹	12														14
1	2	3	4	5		12	11	10	9¹	6²	8							13	7														15
1	2	3	4	5¹			11	10		6	9⁴	13	12	7	8																		16
1	2	3	4	14		13	9	10	11²	12	7¹	5						12	7¹	5													17
1		3	4	5		10	12	11¹	6	8								9		2	7												18
1	12	3	4	5		10		11		6²	8							9	13	2	7¹												19
	12		4	5		10	13	11²		6	8			3	9³	14		2	7¹		1												20
		3	4	5		13		9	10¹		6	8³		12	14			2	7¹		1												21
	2	3	4	5	10		12		11			7¹			9			6	8	1													22
		3	4	5		12		10³		13	6	8²		11	7			2	9	1													23
		3	4	5		12		10		13	6	8¹		11²	7			2	9	1													24
		3	4	5				10		13	6	8²		11	7¹			2	9²	1	12												25
	12	3	4	5	13			10			6	8²			9¹	14		2	7¹	1	1												26
		3	4	5				10		12		8			9	6	2	7¹	1	11													27
	2	3	4	5				9	10	13	7	8¹			6		1	11²	12														28
		3	4	5				10²	9			6			7¹	13	2	1	11	12													29
	2	3	4	5				12	9			6			8³	7		1	11	10¹													30
	2	3	4	5	8			12				7			11²	13	6	1	10	9¹													31
	2	3	4	5	8¹			12	14			7			6	13	1	10³	9²														32
	2	3	4	5				10²	13			7¹			12	11	8	6	9		1												33
	2	12	4	5	8¹			10	9		13				11		3			7²	1	6											34
	2	3	4		12			9	8			11			5		15	10¹	7	1⁶	6												35
	2	3¹	4	5				10²	9						11	8	6			7	1	12	13										36
	2	3	4	5	14			12	9³						11	8		1	10²	7¹			6	13									37
		4						9	7			6¹			11³	8	5	1	10²			12	3			2	13	14					38

PARTICK THISTLE   Premier League

Year Formed: 1876. *Ground & Address:* Firhill Stadium, 80 Firhill Rd, Glasgow G20 7AL. *Telephone:* 0141 579 1971. *Fax:* 0141 945 1525
Ground Capacity: total: 14,538, seated: 8397. *Size of Pitch:* 110yd × 75yd.
Chairman: T. Brown McMaster. *Chief Executive Secretary:* Alan C. Dick. *Commercial Manager:* Amanda Stark.
Manager: John Lambie. *Assistant Manager:* Gerry Collins. *Physio:* Walter Cannon.
Managers since 1975: R. Auld, P. Cormack, B. Rooney, R. Auld, D. Johnstone, W. Lamont, S. Clark, J. Lambie, M. MacLeod, J. McVeigh, T. Bryce. *Club Nickname(s):* The Jags. *Previous Grounds:* Jordanvale Park; Muirpark; Inchview; Meadowside Park.
Record Attendance: 49,838 v Rangers, Division I; 18 Feb, 1922. *Ground Record:* 54,728, Scotland v Ireland, 25 Feb 1928.
Record Transfer Fee received: £200,000 for Mo Johnston to Watford.
Record Transfer Fee paid: £85,000 for Andy Murdoch from Celtic (Feb 1991).
Record Victory: 16-0 v Royal Albert, Scottish Cup 1st rd; 17 Jan, 1931.
Record Defeat: 0-10 v Queen's Park, Scottish Cup; 3 Dec, 1881.
Most Capped Player: Alan Rough, 51 (53), Scotland.
Most League Appearances: 410: Alan Rough, 1969-82.
Most League Goals in Season (Individual): 41: Alec Hair, Division I; 1926-27.

PARTICK THISTLE 2001–02 LEAGUE RECORD

Match No.	Date	Venue	Opponents	Result	H/T Score	Lg. Pos.	Goalscorers	Atten-dance
1	Aug 4	H	St Mirren	D 3-3	2-2	—	McLean (pen) [21], Elliot [38], Lennon [86]	6603
2	11	A	Raith R	W 2-1	1-0	4	Britton 2 [44, 49]	3118
3	18	H	Inverness CT	W 1-0	1-0	2	Fleming [35]	3314
4	25	A	Arbroath	W 3-1	1-0	2	McLean [57], Archibald 2 [72, 75]	1510
5	Sept 8	A	Ayr U	W 2-1	1-1	1	Dolan [40], Britton [63]	3820
6	15	H	Clyde	W 3-0	2-0	1	Britton 2 [11, 79], McKinstrey [34]	4226
7	18	A	Falkirk	D 1-1	0-0	—	Britton [83]	2633
8	22	A	Ross Co	L 2-3	2-2	2	Fleming [2], Britton [4]	2656
9	29	H	Airdrieonians	D 1-1	1-0	2	Dolan [16]	5061
10	Oct 13	A	St Mirren	L 0-1	0-0	2		5244
11	20	H	Raith R	W 2-1	1-0	2	Fleming [14], Britton [71]	3129
12	27	A	Ayr U	W 2-0	0-0	2	Lennon [68], Walker [70]	3447
13	Nov 3	A	Arbroath	W 4-1	2-0	2	Walker 2 [2, 69], Fleming [44], Hardie [89]	3253
14	10	H	Falkirk	W 5-1	1-0	1	Walker [37], Oponga (og) [50], Britton 2 (2 pens) [59, 75], McKinstry [69]	4245
15	17	A	Clyde	L 1-3	0-2	2	Hardie [63]	3551
16	24	A	Airdrieonians	L 0-1	0-1	2		4132
17	Dec 1	H	Ross Co	D 0-0	0-0	2		3589
18	8	A	Inverness CT	W 2-1	0-0	2	Hardie 2 [82, 90]	1926
19	15	H	St Mirren	W 1-0	0-0	2	Hardie [84]	4750
20	26	H	Ayr U	W 2-1	0-1	—	McLean [57], Hardie [77]	4611
21	Jan 2	A	Clyde	W 2-1	1-0	2	McLean [4], Fleming [46]	5005
22	12	A	Falkirk	W 4-1	3-0	1	McLean 2 [12, 39], Lennon [26], Hardie [48]	3890
23	19	A	Ross Co	W 1-0	1-0	1	Hardie [30]	3043
24	Feb 2	H	Airdrieonians	D 1-1	0-1	1	Burns [70]	6253
25	9	H	Inverness CT	W 4-1	2-0	1	Hardie [11], Lennon [23], Britton [75], McLean [81]	3969
26	16	A	Raith R	L 0-2	0-2	1		2729
27	26	A	Arbroath	L 0-1	0-1	—		1074
28	Mar 2	A	Arbroath	D 2-2	0-2	1	McLean [60], Hardie [82]	3729
29	9	A	Ayr U	D 1-1	0-0	1	Fleming [69]	3624
30	16	H	Falkirk	W 3-0	1-0	1	Burns 2 [36, 46], McLean [72]	4222
31	27	A	Clyde	L 1-2	0-0	—	Cameron [78]	2541
32	30	H	Ross Co	D 1-1	0-0	1	Hardie [79]	4013
33	Apr 6	A	Airdrieonians	D 1-1	0-0	1	Burns [81]	5746
34	13	A	St Mirren	W 2-0	1-0	1	McCulloch [22], Fleming [52]	7118
35	20	H	Raith R	W 1-0	0-0	1	Britton [61]	6208
36	27	A	Inverness CT	L 0-3	0-3	1		2526

Final League Position: 1

Honours
League Champions: First Division 1975-76, 2001-02. Division II 1896-97, 1899-1900, 1970-71; Second Division 2000-01;
Runners-up: First Division 1991-92. Division II 1901-02.
Scottish Cup Winners: 1921; *Runners-up:* 1930; *Semi-finals:* 2002.
League Cup Winners: 1971-72; *Runners-up:* 1953-54, 1956-57, 1958-59.

European: *Fairs Cup:* 4 matches (1963-64). *UEFA Cup:* 2 matches (1972-73). *Inter Toto Cup:* 4 matches 1995-96.

Club colours: Shirt: Red and yellow stripes. Shorts: Red. Stockings: Red with yellow hoops.

Goalscorers: *League* (61): Britton 12 (2 pens), Hardie 11, McLean 9 (1 pen), Fleming 7, Burns 4, Lennon 4, Walker 4,
Archibald 2, Dolan 2, McKinstry 2, Cameron 1, Elliot 1, McCulloch 1, own goal 1.
Scottish Cup (10): Hardie 2, McLean 2, Paterson 2, Walker 2, Britton 1, Gibson 1.
CIS Cup (6): Lennon 2, McLean 2, Hardie 1, McDowell 1
Challenge Cup (10): Britton 2, Fleming 2, Hardie 2, Lennon 2, McCallum 1, McDowell 1.

Gow G 5	Huxford R 2 + 4	Archibald A 31 + 2	Craigan S 31 + 1	Paterson S 36	Connaghan D 8	Kelly P 9 + 1	Lennon D 32 + 3	McLean S 23 + 6	Hardie M 22 + 9	Elliot B 2 + 6	Britton G 24 + 9	McKinstry J 21 + 2	Dolan J 19 + 7	Howie W — + 2	Smith J — + 1	Nicholls M 1	Fleming D 24 + 5	McDowell M — + 4	Arthur K 22 + 1	Walker P 12 + 16	Klein D 5	Watson S 1	Deas P 25	Javary J — + 1	McCulloch M 14 + 2	Gibson A 1 + 3	Lyle D — + 2	Constantine L 2	Burns A 13	Roddie A 1 + 2	Cameron M 6 + 2	Budinauckas K 4	McAnespie S — + 1	Match No.
1	2	3	4	5	6	7³	8	9¹	10²	11	12	13	14																					1
1		3¹	4	5	6		8	9	10	11¹	12	2⁵	7	13	14																			2
1		3	4	5	6		14	12	10		9²	2	8³				7¹	11	13															3
1⁴	10	3	4	5	6		8	9²			7	2		14			11³	13	15															4
1	12	3	4	5	6		8	9³	13		7	2¹	10				11²			14														5
14		3	4	5	6		8	9¹	13		7	2³	10				11²			12	1													6
		3	4	5	6		8	9¹	13		7	2³	10				11			12	1													7
		3	4	5	6¹		8	9²	12	14	7	2³	10				11			13	1													8
		3	4	5			8	9¹	6	12	7	2	10				11			1														9
12		3	4	5			8	9³			7	2	10¹				11	14		13	1	6²												10
		3	4	5			8	9¹			7	2	10				11	12	1			6												11
14		3	4	5			8			13	7	2	10³				11¹		1	9²		6	12											12
		3	4	5			8²	14	13		7	2	10¹				11	1	9³			6	12											13
			4	5			12	13	10	14	7²	2	6¹				11		1	9³			3	8										14
				5			8	13	10	12	7¹	2	6²				11		1	9			3	4										15
		3	4	5				14	11²	13	7	2³	10¹				12		1	9			6	8										16
		3	4	5			12	13	10¹		7²	2³	14				11		1	9			6	8										17
		3	4	5			8	9	12		13		10¹				11		1	7²			6	2										18
		3	4	5			8	9¹	13		12		10				11³		1	7²			6	2	14									19
		3	4	5			8	9	12		7¹						11²		1	13			6	2										20
		3	4	5			8	9¹	10		7²						11		1	12			6	2		13								21
		3	4	5			8	9²	10		12						11		1				6	2		13	7¹							22
		3	4	5			8	9	10²		12		13				11		1				6	2			7¹							23
		3	4	5			8	9¹	10		7	2					13	1	12				6					11²						24
		3	4	5			8	9	10		13		12				14	1	7²				6					11						25
		3¹	4	5			2¹	8	9	10		13	12				14	1	12				6					11¹	13					26
		3	4	5			7³	8		10	9²		2¹					1	13				6		12			11	14					27
		3	4	5			12	8	7	10		2¹					14	1	13									6²	11³	9				28
		3	4	5			2	8		10	7²	13					3	1	12				6					11³		9¹				29
	14	4	5				2	8	9³	10		12	14				3		13				6					11³		7¹	1			30
		13		5			2	8		10		7					3²		1	9⁵			6	4				11		12				31
		3	4	5			2	8	9¹	10									12				6					11		7	1			32
		3	4	5			2¹	8	10²		9³								14				6	12				11		7	1	13		33
		3		5				8	9²		13	2	12				10¹		14				6	4				11		7³	1			34
		3	14	5				8		10²		7	2³						9¹				6	4	13			11		12				35
		3		5			2¹	8		13			12	10²					1	9				6	4	7			11					36

PETERHEAD

Third Division

Year Formed: 1891. *Ground and Address:* Balmoor Stadium, Lord Catto Park, Peterhead AB42 1EU.
Telephone: 01779 478256. *Fax:* 01779 490682. *Ground Capacity:* 3250, seated 1000.
Chairman: Roger Taylor. *General Manager:* Dave Watson. *Secretary:* George Moore.
Manager: Ian Wilson. *Assistant Manager:* Alan Lyons. *Physio:* Jennifer Johnson.
Managers since 1975: C. Grant, D. Darcy, I. Taylor, J. Harper, D. Smith, J. Hamilton, G. Adams, J. Guyan, I. Wilson,
D. Watson, R. Brown, D. Watson, I. Wilson. *Club Nickname(s):* Blue Toon. *Previous Ground:* Recreation Park.
Record Attendance: 6310 friendly v Celtic, 1948.
Record Victory: 17-0 v Fort William, 1998-99 (in Highland League).
Record Defeat: 0-13 v Aberdeen, Scottish Cup 1923-24.
Most League Appearances: 70, Martin Johnston, 2000-02.
Most League Goals in Season (Individual): 19, Ian Stewart, 2001-02.
Most Goals Overall (Individual): 30, Ian Stewart, 2000-02.

PETERHEAD 2001–02 LEAGUE RECORD

Match No.	Date	Venue	Opponents	Result	H/T Score	Lg. Pos.	Goalscorers	Attendance
1	Aug 4	A	Stirling A	L 1-2	1-1	—	Johnston 40	588
2	11	H	Dumbarton	L 0-3	0-1	10		528
3	18	A	Montrose	W 3-0	1-0	7	Johnston 8, Findlay 67, Tindal 88	438
4	25	A	East Fife	W 1-0	0-0	7	Stewart 55	331
5	Sept 8	H	Elgin C	D 1-1	0-1	6	Johnston 60	564
6	15	A	East Stirling	W 3-2	1-0	5	Yeats 2 7, 80, Bisset 62	171
7	22	H	Brechin C	W 4-2	3-0	5	Stewart 3 5, 32, 44, Bisset 50	643
8	29	A	Albion R	L 0-1	0-0	6		296
9	Oct 6	H	Queen's Park	W 2-1	1-1	3	Yeats 35, Stewart 52	533
10	13	H	Stirling A	D 3-3	2-1	3	Livingstone 15, Stewart 33, Clark S 69	642
11	20	A	Dumbarton	W 3-0	2-0	3	Johnston 1, Mackay 34, Stewart 50	715
12	27	A	Elgin C	L 1-4	1-0	3	Yeats 43	974
13	Nov 3	H	East Fife	L 1-3	1-2	3	Johnston 31	753
14	10	H	East Stirling	W 3-2	2-2	3	Johnston 2 30, 55, Cooper (pen) 40	482
15	24	A	Queen's Park	W 1-0	0-0	3	Johnston 76	524
16	Dec 1	A	Brechin C	L 3-4	2-3	3	Tindal 19, Johnston 27, Cooper 87	511
17	15	H	Albion R	D 0-0	0-0	4		485
18	22	H	Montrose	W 4-0	2-0	3	Stewart 3 (1 pen) 32, 45 (pl, 50, Wood 89	441
19	Jan 5	H	Elgin C	W 1-0	0-0	2	Stewart (pen) 79	798
20	12	A	East Fife	W 3-2	1-1	2	Wood 7, Johnston 74, Stewart 85	444
21	19	A	Queen's Park	L 0-2	0-1	2		567
22	Feb 2	A	Albion R	L 1-2	1-2	2	McSkimming 44	297
23	9	H	Brechin C	L 1-3	1-2	3	Johnston 39	796
24	16	H	Dumbarton	W 4-0	2-0	2	Stewart 2 25, 70, Tindal 35, Robertson 89	589
25	23	A	Montrose	L 1-2	0-1	2	Mackay 57	617
26	Mar 2	A	Stirling A	W 2-0	1-0	—	Stewart 31, Yeats 55	335
27	Mar 2	H	East Fife	D 1-1	0-1	2	Johnston 79	672
28	16	H	East Stirling	W 2-1	0-0	2	Robertson 2 53, 87	503
29	19	A	Elgin C	W 3-0	1-0	—	Stewart 18, Johnston 2 75, 80	530
30	23	A	Queen's Park	L 1-2	1-1	3	Stewart 30	666
31	30	A	Brechin C	D 1-1	0-1	3	Johnston 85	1186
32	Apr 6	H	Albion R	L 0-2	0-0	4		789
33	9	A	East Stirling	L 0-1	0-1	—		258
34	13	H	Stirling A	W 5-1	1-1	4	Stewart 44, Johnston 2 51, 70, Cooper (pen) 68, Mackay 85	523
35	20	A	Dumbarton	L 0-3	0-0	5		1636
36	27	H	Montrose	W 3-1	1-0	4	Tindal 15, Stewart 46, Johnston 55	652

Final League Position: 4

Honours
Scottish Cup: Quarter Finals 2001.
Highland League Champions: winners 5 times.
Scottish Qualifying Cup (North): winners 6 times.
North of Scotland Cup: winners 5 times.
Aberdeenshire Cup: winners 20 times.

Club colours: Shirt: Royal blue with white; Shorts: Royal blue; Stockings: Royal blue tops with white hoops.

Goalscorers: *League* (63): Stewart 19 (2 pens), Johnston 18, Yeats 5, Tindal 4, Cooper 3 (2 pens), Mackay 3, Robertson 3, Bisset 2, Wood 2, Clark S 1, Findlay 1, Livingstone 1, McSkimming 1.
Scottish Cup (0):
CIS Cup (0):
Challenge Cup (2): Stewart 2.

Pirie I	Slater M	Smith G	Duffy J	Simpson M	Brown S	Mackay S	Stewart I	Findlay C	Johnston M	Livingstone R	Cooper C	Bisset K	Yeats C	Buchanan R	Tindal K	King S	Murray I	Clark S	Canning M	Clark G	Mathers P	Wood M	McQuade J	McSkimming S	Robertson K	Rennie K	Marrs V	Match No.
1	2	3	4³	5	6¹	7	8	9²	10	11	12	13	14															1
	2	3	4¹	5		10³	8	9	12	11	7	14	13	1	6²													2
1	2	4	14	5		7³	8²	9	10	12	11¹		13		6	3												3
1	2¹	4	12	5		7	8	9³	10	11²		14			6	3		13										4
1	2¹	4		5		7	8	9³	10	11²	13	12	14		6	3												5
1		3		5		4	8	12	10¹	11	7	6²	9		2		13											6
1		3		5		6	8	13		11	7¹	10	9²		4		12	2										7
1		3		5		4	8	13	12	11	7	10¹	9²		6²		14	2										8
1		3		5		4	8	13	12	11	7¹	10	9²		6			2										9
1		3		5		4	8	13	12	11		10¹	9²		6		7	2										10
1		3		5		4	8²	12	9	11		10¹			6		7	2	13									11
1	3¹	5				4		14	9	11		10¹	8²		6	12	7	2	13									12
1		5²				4¹	8	13	10	11	7	9	12		6	3	2											13
		5				4		12	10	11	7	8	9¹		6	3	2		1									14
	3	5				4			11²		7	12	9		6	13	8	2	1									15
	3¹	5				4³	12		10	11	7	13	9¹		6	14	8	2	1									16
	3	5				4	8		10	11²		9¹	12		6	13	7	2	1									17
	3	5				4³	8²		10			13	12		6	11	7	2	1	9								18
	3	5				4¹	8		10			13	12		6²	11	7	2	1	9								19
	3	5				12	8		10						6	11²	7	2	1	9¹		4	13					20
	3	5				6	8		10			14	13			11	7³	2	1	9²		4¹	12					21
	3¹	5				6²	8		10			14	13			11	7	2	1	12		4²	9					22
		5				8²			10	14	12		13		6	3		4	2		1	9	7¹	11¹				23
1		5				4	8		10¹	11	7³	14			6	3		12	2			9²			13			24
1		5				4	8		10	11	7³		12		6	3¹		14	2			9²			13			25
1		5				4	8²		12	11		13	10		6	3	7		2						9¹			26
1	12	5¹				4³	8		14	11²		13	10		6	3	7		2						9			27
1	4	5				12	8		11	13	7		10¹		6	3²	2								9			28
1	3					4	8		10		7		5		6	11¹	2							12	9			29
1	13	3¹	14			4²	8		10		7		5		6	11	2¹							12	9			30
1	2	5				4	8		10	13	7³	14	9		6	11²								3	12			31
1	2	5				13	8		10	12	7	14	4²		6	11								3¹	9³			32
1	2²	5				4	8		10	11	7	13	12		6	3									9¹			33
1	2	5				4	8		10	11	7	13	9²		6¹	3		12										34
1	2¹	5				4³	8		10	11	7²	14			6	3	9	13							12			35
1		5				4	8		10	11²	7	9¹			6	3	2									12	13	36

QUEEN OF THE SOUTH — First Division

Year Formed: 1919. *Ground & Address:* Palmerston Park, Dumfries DG2 9BA. *Telephone and Fax:* 01387 254853.
Ground Capacity: total: 8352, seated: 3549. *Size of Pitch:* 112yd × 73yd.
Chairman: Ronald Bradford. *Secretary:* Richard Shaw MBE. *Commercial Manager:* Margaret Heuchan.
Manager: John Connolly. *Assistant Manager:* Ian Scott.
Managers since 1975: M. Jackson, W. Hunter, B. Little, G. Herd, H. Hood, A. Busby, R. Clark, M. Jackson, D. Wilson, W. McLaren, F. McGarvey, A. MacLeod, D. Frye, W. McLaren, M. Shanks, R. Alexander. *Club Nickname(s):* The Doonhamers. *Previous Grounds:* None.
Record Attendance: 24,500 v Hearts, Scottish Cup 3rd rd: 23 Feb, 1952.
Record Transfer Fee received: £250,000 for Andy Thomson to Southend U (1994).
Record Transfer Fee paid: £30,000 for Jim Butter from Alloa Athletic (1995).
Record Victory: 11-1 v Stranraer, Scottish Cup 1st rd: 16 Jan, 1932.
Record Defeat: 2-10 v Dundee, Division I: 1 Dec, 1962.
Most Capped Player: Billy Houliston, 3, Scotland.
Most League Appearances: 731: Allan Ball, 1963-82.
Most League Goals in Season (Individual): 37: Jimmy Gray, Division II: 1927-28.

QUEEN OF THE SOUTH 2001–02 LEAGUE RECORD

Match No.	Date	Venue	Opponents	Result	H/T Score	Lg. Pos.	Goalscorers	Attendance
1	Aug 4	A	Hamilton A	D	1-1	1-0	—	Weatherson [20]	3047
2	11	H	Forfar Ath	L	1-2	0-1	8	O'Neil [72]	1149
3	18	A	Morton	D	2-2	1-0	9	O'Neil 2 (2 pens) [40, 86]	1827
4	25	H	Clydebank	W	1-0	0-0	7	Atkinson [86]	1108
5	Sept 2	H	Stenhousemuir	W	2-0	1-0	—	O'Neil 2 [21, 82]	1153
6	8	A	Stranraer	D	2-2	1-2	4	Atkinson [7], O'Neil [77]	696
7	15	A	Cowdenbeath	D	1-1	1-1	4	O'Neil (pen) [37]	364
8	22	A	Berwick R	W	4-0	1-0	4	Neill A (og) [30], O'Neil 2 (2 pens) [50, 74], Connelly G [85]	460
9	29	H	Alloa Ath	W	2-1	1-1	2	McAlpine [29], Feroz [46]	1320
10	Oct 13	A	Hamilton A	L	0-1	0-0	4		1552
11	20	A	Forfar Ath	W	3-0	1-0	2	Weatherson 2 [1, 59], O'Neil [65]	407
12	27	H	Stranraer	W	1-0	0-0	1	O'Neil [49]	3083
13	Nov 3	A	Clydebank	L	0-3	0-3	3		392
14	10	H	Cowdenbeath	L	1-3	0-1	3	Weatherson [71]	1321
15	24	A	Stenhousemuir	D	1-1	1-0	4	Davidson [27]	460
16	Dec 1	H	Berwick R	D	2-2	2-0	3	Atkinson [6], O'Neil [15]	1113
17	15	A	Alloa Ath	L	0-2	0-1	5		472
18	Jan 12	H	Clydebank	W	1-0	0-0	4	Weatherson [88]	1161
19	19	H	Stenhousemuir	W	1-0	0-0	2	O'Boyle [77]	1224
20	26	A	Cowdenbeath	W	2-1	1-1	2	O'Boyle 2 [29, 89]	420
21	Feb 2	H	Alloa Ath	L	0-1	0-1	3		1367
22	9	A	Berwick R	L	0-1	0-1	4		552
23	16	H	Forfar Ath	W	3-1	2-0	3	Lyle [15], O'Neil 2 (2 pens) [36, 90]	1141
24	26	H	Morton	W	6-5	6-3	—	McAlpine 2 [1, 45], Weatherson 2 [14, 18], Bowey [16], Lyle [42]	1242
25	Mar 2	A	Clydebank	W	1-0	1-0	1	Weatherson [38]	402
26	5	A	Hamilton A	L	1-3	1-2	1	Lyle [32]	1592
27	9	H	Stranraer	W	3-1	0-0	1	McAlpine 2 [50, 62], O'Neil [72]	2094
28	12	A	Stranraer	W	2-1	1-1	—	O'Neil [19], McAlpine [64]	895
29	16	H	Cowdenbeath	W	2-1	1-0	1	Weatherson 2 [42, 72]	2028
30	23	A	Stenhousemuir	W	4-1	3-1	1	Lyle 2 [6, 42], Davidson [16], Weatherson [62]	577
31	30	H	Berwick R	D	0-0	0-0	1		2758
32	Apr 2	A	Morton	W	3-0	1-0	—	O'Connor [8], O'Neil 2 [53, 58]	1344
33	6	A	Alloa Ath	L	1-4	0-2	1	Gray [70]	1442
34	13	H	Hamilton A	W	3-1	0-0	1	Sweeney (og) [48], Weatherson [55], Lyle [57]	3062
35	20	A	Forfar Ath	W	3-0	1-0	1	Weatherson 2 [31, 50], O'Connor [85]	1022
36	27	H	Morton	W	4-0	2-0	1	Weatherson [7], Moore [14], O'Neil [73], O'Connor [86]	6158

Final League Position: 1

Most Goals in Season: 41: Jimmy Rutherford, 1931-32.
Most Goals Overall (Individual): 250: Jim Patterson, 1949-63.

Honours
League Champions: Division II 1950-51. Second Division 2001-02. *Runners-up:* Division II 1932-33, 1961-62, 1974-75.
Second Division 1980-81, 1985-86.
Scottish Cup: semi-finalists 1949-50.
League Cup: semi-finalists 1950-51, 1960-61.
B&Q Cup: semi-finalists 1991-92. *League Challenge Cup:* runners-up 1997-98.

Club colours: Shirt: Royal blue with white sleeves. Shorts: White with blue piping. Stockings: Royal blue.

Goalscorers: *League* (64): O'Neil 19 (7 pens), Weatherson 15, Lyle 6, McAlpine 6, Atkinson 3, O'Boyle 3, O'Connor 3,
Davidson 2, Bowey 1, Connelly 1, Feroz 1, Gray 1, Moore 1, own goals 2.
Scottish Cup (2): O'Neil 2.
CIS Cup (4): Feroz 4.
Challenge Cup (0):

Campbell J 3+1	Atkinson P 23+4	McKeown D 2+1	Gray A 34+1	Thomson J 32+1	Crawford J 16+3	Sunderland J 2+6	Aitken A 25+1	Weatherson P 26+7	Hogg A 2	Hawke W 6	Connelly G 27+4	McGhie G —+1	Connolly S 1+2	Scott C 33	Allan D 11+2	Connell G 26+6	O'Neil J 27+5	Feroz C 8	Patterson M 1+1	Davidson S 7+9	McAlpine J 27+3	Armstrong G —+2	Hollier P —+3	McDowell M 2	Glancy M 2+1	Moore A 2+10	Donald B 6+5	O'Boyle G 7	McMahon D —+1	Burns G —+1	Anderson D 15+1	Bowey S 5+3	Lyle D 13	Walker L —+2	Poston T 1	O'Connor S 4+4	Dawson S —+1	Match No
	2	3	4	5	6	7³	8²	9	10¹	11	12	13	14	1																								1
15	3		2	5	6	13		9	10²	11	7			1	1⁹	4	8³	14																				2
	3		4	5	6		9		11²	7				1	8	7	10	12																				3
2	3¹		4	5	6	12		9		7				1	8	10	11¹²	13																				4
2¹			4	5	6		9		11	13	1	12	8	7	10²		3																					5
11			4	5	6		10		2	1	8	7	9	3																								6
			4	5	6	11		2	10¹	1	8	7	9	3	12																							7
	13	2		6		5	10¹	11	1	4	8	7³	9	14	3²	12																						8
		2	13	6		5	10	11	1	4	8²	7¹	9	12	3																							9
14		2	5	6¹		10²	11	1	4	8¹	7	9	12	3	13																							10
		2	5	6	14	12	9³	10¹	11	1	4	8	7	13	3²																							11
1	13		2	5	6		10¹	11	4	8	7³	12	3²	14	9																							12
1	2	12	5	6¹	13		10	11³	4	7	8	3	14	9²																								13
12		2	5	6³	13		9	11²	1	4	8¹	7	14	3	10																							14
	3	2	5¹		8	9²	11	1	4	12	7	6	10	13																								15
	3	2		14	5	9²	6	1	4	13	7	8³	11¹	10	12																							16
	3	2	6		5	9¹	11	1	4	7³		12	8²	10	13	14																						17
	3	2	6		5	12	11	1	8²	7¹	9	13	4	10																								18
9³		2	6		5	12	11	1	8	7¹	14	13	4²	10	3																							19
9		2	6		5	12	11	1	14	8	7¹	13	4²	10³	3																							20
11¹		2	6		5	9	7³	1	8	14	12	13	4²	10	3																							21
		2	6		5	9¹	11	1	8³	7	13	12	4²	14	10	3																						22
	3	2	6		5	12	11²	1	14	7	8	13	10¹	4	9²																							23
	3¹	2	6		5	10	11	1	8	7²	13	12	4	9³	14																							24
11³		2	6	13	5	10	14	1	8²	7	3	4	9																									25
		2	6		5	10	12	1	8³	13	7²	4	14	3	9	11¹																						26
12		2	6		5	10	11¹	1	8	7²	4	13	3	9³	14																							27
4		2	6		5	10		1	8	7¹	11	12	3	9																								28
4		2	6		5	10²		1	12	7¹	13	11	8	3	9																							29
11	2²		6		5	12	13	1	8	7	4³	14	3	9	10¹																							30
		2	6		5	10³	4	1⁹	8	13	7³	11	3	9	14	15																						31
		2	6	3	5	13	11¹	1	14	7	8³	12	4	9	10²																							32
		2	6		5	13	11²	1	12	7	8	3	4	9	10																							33
4		2	6		5	10²		1	8	7¹	11	14	3	12	9³	13																						34
4	2²		6	14	5	10		1	8	7	11³	3	13	9¹	12																							35
	2		6	14	5	10		1	8	7	11²	4¹	3	12	9²	13																						36

QUEEN'S PARK
Third Division

Year Formed: 1867. *Ground & Address:* Hampden Park, Mount Florida, Glasgow G42 9BA. *Telephone:* 0141 632 1275. *Fax:* 0141 636 1612.
Ground Capacity: all seated: 52,000. *Size of Pitch:* 115yd × 75yd.
President: Kenneth Harvey. *Secretary:* Alistair Mackay. *Commercial Director:* Garry Templeman.
Coach/Player: John McCormack. *Physio:* R. C. Findlay.
Coaches since 1975: D. McParland, J. Gilroy, E. Hunter, H. McCann. *Club Nickname(s):* The Spiders. *Previous Grounds:* 1st Hampden (Recreation Ground); (Titwood Park was used as an interim measure between 1st & 2nd Hampdens); 2nd Hampden (Cathkin); 3rd Hampden.
Record Attendance: 95,772 v Rangers, Scottish Cup, 18 Jan, 1930.
Record for Ground: 149,547 Scotland v England, 1937.
Record Transfer Fee received: Not applicable due to amateur status.
Record Transfer Fee paid: Not applicable due to amateur status.
Record Victory: 16-0 v St. Peters, Scottish Cup 1st rd; 29 Aug, 1885.
Record Defeat: 0-9 v Motherwell, Division I; 26 Apr, 1930.
Most Capped Player: Walter Arnott, 14, Scotland.
Most League Appearances: 532: Ross Caven.

QUEEN'S PARK 2001–02 LEAGUE RECORD

Match No.	Date	Venue	Opponents	Result	H/T Score	Lg. Pos.	Goalscorers	Attendance
1	Aug 4	A	Montrose	L	1-3	0-2	—	Martin [75]	384
2	11	H	Elgin C	D	0-0	0-0	7		691
3	18	A	Dumbarton	L	1-2	0-0	83	Marshall [51]	823
4	25	H	East Stirling	L	2-3	0-2	9	Miller G [46], Caven (pen) [69]	502
5	Sept 8	A	Albion R	L	1-2	1-0	9	Caven (pen) [41]	377
6	15	H	Brechin C	L	1-3	0-1	10	Jackson [69]	423
7	22	H	East Fife	L	1-2	1-2	10	Wilson (og) [36]	825
8	29	A	Stirling A	D	0-0	0-0	10		584
9	Oct 6	A	Peterhead	L	1-2	1-1	10	Jackson [20]	533
10	13	H	Montrose	D	2-2	2-1	10	Quinn [25], Jackson [37]	407
11	20	A	Elgin C	L	0-2	0-0	10		581
12	27	A	Albion R	L	1-2	1-1	10	Quinn [25]	518
13	Nov 3	A	East Stirling	W	1-0	1-0	10	Gemmell [23]	301
14	10	A	Brechin C	L	1-2	1-0	10	Jackson [17]	436
15	24	H	Peterhead	L	0-1	0-0	10		524
16	Dec 1	A	East Fife	W	4-1	2-0	10	Gemmell 2 [10, 69], Jackson [41], Fisher [73]	442
17	15	H	Stirling A	D	2-2	1-1	10	Canning 2 [5, 62]	558
18	Jan 12	H	East Stirling	W	1-0	1-0	10	Whelan [43]	477
19	19	H	Peterhead	W	2-0	1-0	10	Canning [24], Fisher [90]	567
20	26	H	Brechin C	D	0-0	0-0	10		646
21	Feb 2	A	Stirling A	L	2-3	1-2	10	Canning [26], Martin [90]	564
22	9	H	East Fife	W	2-0	0-0	10	Proudfoot [53], Gallagher M [78]	553
23	16	H	Elgin C	W	3-0	2-0	10	Quinn [25], Marshall [37], Ferry [47]	533
24	23	H	Dumbarton	D	0-0	0-0	9		725
25	26	A	Montrose	L	1-3	0-3	—	Martin [75]	250
26	Mar 2	A	East Stirling	L	1-3	1-2	10	Dunning [15]	254
27	5	A	Albion R	L	0-2	0-0	—		293
28	9	H	Albion R	L	0-3	0-1	10		547
29	16	A	Brechin C	L	0-5	0-5	10		471
30	19	H	Dumbarton	L	0-2	0-1	—		411
31	23	A	Peterhead	W	2-1	1-1	10	Gallagher M [14], Canning [63]	666
32	30	A	East Fife	W	3-0	2-0	9	Fisher [31], Dunning [35], Whelan (pen) [83]	449
33	Apr 6	H	Stirling A	D	0-0	0-0	10		496
34	13	H	Montrose	L	0-1	0-0	10		416
35	20	A	Elgin C	W	1-0	0-0	10	Whelan [87]	627
36	27	A	Dumbarton	D	1-1	0-0	10	Whelan [79]	1959

Final League Position: 10

Most League Goals in Season (Individual): 30: William Martin, Division I; 1937-38.
Most Goals Overall (Individual): 163: J. B. McAlpine.

Honours
League Champions: Division II 1922-23. B Division 1955-56. Second Division 1980-81. Third Division 1999-2000.
Scottish Cup Winners: 1874, 1875, 1876, 1880, 1881, 1882, 1884, 1886, 1890, 1893; *Runners-up:* 1892, 1900.
League Cup: —.
FA Cup runners-up: 1884, 1885.

Club colours: Shirt: White and black hoops. Shorts: White. Stockings: Black with white tops.

Goalscorers: *League* (38): Canning 5, Jackson 5, Whelan 4 (1 pen), Fisher 3, Gemmell 3, Martin 3, Quinn 3, Caven 2 (pens), Dunning 2, Gallagher M 2, Marshall 2, Ferry 1, Miller G 1, Proudfoot 1, own goal 1.
Scottish Cup (2): Jackson 2.
CIS Cup (0):
Challenge Cup (0):

Smith G 24	Ferry D 26 + 1	Borland P 21	White J 7	Collins N 28	Sinclair R 11 + 1	Canning S 27 + 9	Marshall S 22 + 2	Brown J 7 + 11	McPhee G 2 + 2	Carberry A 2 + 1	Martin W 9 + 16	Quinn A 33 + 2	Ewing C 5 + 2	Cunningham J 7 + 1	Caven R 16	Miller G 7 + 1	Miller B 2 + 4	Jackson R 18 + 11	Miller K 3	Gallagher P 4 + 3	Bruce J 11 + 1	Orr S 1 + 3	Stevenson C 18	Patterson P 9 + 5	Rae D 5 + 1	Mitchell A 12	Gemmell J 7 + 5	Clark R — + 2	Gallagher M 10 + 2	Dunning A 7 + 4	Fisher C 6 + 10	Whelan J 21	Proudfoot K 2 + 1	McVey W 6 + 1	Match No.
1	2	3	4	5^2	6	7	8	9	10^3	11^1	12	13	14																						1
1	2	3				7	8^2		13	11^1	9^3	4	14	5	6	10	12																		2
1	2	3				14	8		13		9^3	4	11^1	5	6	10	7^2	12																	3
1	2	3^1				12	8	13			9	4	11	5^3	6	10	7^2	14																	4
1						2	3	7			13	4	9	5^2	6	8		12	10^3	11^1	14														5
1		2				3		9^1			12	4		5	6^3	8	14	11	10	13	7^2														6
1	8	3^1		2		6	12	5^2			4	9	14		11		10	13			7^3														7
1	2			6	14	3					4	9^1		8	13	12		11^3			5	7^2	10												8
1	2			6	14	3				12	4			8	13	9^3		11^2			5	7^1	10												9
1	2		8			12	3^1	11^2			4		6		9	14				7^3	10			5											10
1		3	2			12	8	11	14	10^1	4		6		9^3	13	5	7^2																	11
	2	3	5			14	11	12				4		6	9^3		8	7^1	10^3	1	13														12
	2		4			3	11	12				8		6	9	13	5	7^1	1	10^1															13
	2	3	8		5^1	11	12					4		6	10	7^2	13	1	9^3	14															14
	2		4	10^3	3	8						6		7	14	5	1	9^2	11^1	12	13														15
	2	3^2	4		11		8					6		12	5	14	1	9^3	7^1	13	10														16
	2	3	4	7	14							8^3		6	12	5	1	9^2	13	11^1	10														17
1	2	3	4	11	10^3						13	12		6	7^1	5	14	9^2	8																18
1	2	3	4	11^2	10						12	6		5	7		9^1	13	8																19
1	2		4	11	10	12					9	6		5	7		3^1	8																	20
1^1	2^2	3	4	11	10						12	6^3		5	7		9	13	8	14															21
1	2^2	3	4	10^1	11	13					7			12	5		9^2	14	8	6															22
1^2	2	3	4	6	10	11					12	7		9^1	5		13	8																	23
1	2	3	4	6	10	11^1	14				13	7^3		9^2	5		12	8																	24
1	2		4	6	10		12				11	7^3		9^2	5^1	14	13	8																	25
1	2			6	10		5	14			7	12		9^2	13			11^3	8	4^1	3														26
			4	10	2		7	6^2					5	12	9^1	11	13	8	3																27
1			4	10	12		2	5^1		7		6		13	9^2	11^3	14	8	3																28
1			4	10	13		11^1	5		9^3		2	6^2	7	12	14	8	3																	29
1			4	10	2^2		13	7		5		12	5		9^3	11^1	14	8	3																30
	3	5	4	10	13	12	6						2		1		9^3	7^1	11^2	8	14														31
	3^1	5	4	10	14	13	6				12		2		1		9	7^1	11^3	8															32
14	3	5	4	10	13		6						2		1		12^3	7^2	9^1	11	8														33
7		5	4	13	10		3^3	12	6				2		14	1	9^2			11^1	8														34
7	3^1	5	4		10^3	11		9	6				13		2^3	14	1			12	8														35
7	3^2	5	4		13	11		9^1	6^2				10		2		1	14		12	8														36

RAITH ROVERS   Second Division

Year Formed: 1883. *Ground & Address:* Stark's Park, Pratt St, Kirkcaldy KY1 1SA. *Telephone:* 01592 263514. *Fax:* 01592 642833.
Ground Capacity: all seated: 10,104. *Size of Pitch:* 113yd × 70yd.
Chairman: Danny Smith. *Office Manager:* Carrie Sommerville.
Manager: Antonio Calderon. *Assistant Manager:* Francisco Ortez. *Physio:* Paul Green.
Managers since 1975: R. Paton, A. Matthew, W. McLean, G. Wallace, R. Wilson, F. Connor, J. Nicholl, J. Thomson, T. McLean, I. Munro, J. Nicholl, J. McVeigh, P. Hetherston, J. Scott.
Club Nickname: Rovers. *Previous Grounds:* Robbie's Park.
Record Attendance: 31,306 v Hearts, Scottish Cup 2nd rd: 7 Feb, 1953.
Record Transfer Fee received: £900,000 for S. McAnespie to Bolton Wanderers (Sept 1995).
Record Transfer Fee paid: £225,000 for Paul Harvey from Airdrieonians (1996).
Record Victory: 10-1 v Coldstream, Scottish Cup 2nd rd: 13 Feb, 1954.
Record Defeat: 2-11 v Morton, Division II: 18 Mar, 1936.
Most Capped Player: David Morris, 6, Scotland.
Most League Appearances: 430: Willie McNaught.
Most League Goals in Season (Individual): 38: Norman Haywood, Division II: 1937-38.
Most Goals Overall (Individual): 154: Gordon Dalziel (League), 1987-94.

RAITH ROVERS 2001–02 LEAGUE RECORD

Match No.	Date	Venue	Opponents	Result	H/T Score	Lg. Pos.	Goalscorers	Atten- dance
1	Aug 4	A	Airdrieonians	D	2-2	0-2	—	Novo [56], Henderson [62]	1229
2	11	H	Partick Th	L	1-2	0-1	7	Crabbe [56]	3118
3	18	A	Ross Co	L	0-1	0-1	9		2060
4	25	A	Ayr U	D	1-1	0-1	9	Crabbe [80]	2410
5	Sept 8	H	Falkirk	W	5-2	3-1	8	Crabbe 2 [11, 33], Stein [13], Novo 2 (1 pen) [53, 85 (p)]	2279
6	15	H	Arbroath	W	3-1	0-1	4	Novo 2 [66, 85], Crabbe [72]	1698
7	19	A	Inverness CT	L	2-5	0-3	—	Crabbe [55], Smith [82]	984
8	22	H	St Mirren	W	3-0	1-0	3	Stein (pen) [45], Novo 2 [87, 89]	2465
9	29	A	Clyde	L	2-3	0-2	5	Novo [65], Smith [66]	1222
10	Oct 6	H	Airdrieonians	D	2-2	1-2	4	Novo [31], Smith [52]	2077
11	20	A	Partick Th	L	1-2	0-1	6	Smith [58]	3129
12	27	A	Falkirk	L	0-1	0-1	9		2393
13	Nov 3	H	Ayr U	D	1-1	1-0	9	Dennis [17]	1781
14	10	H	Inverness CT	L	1-5	1-2	10	Novo (pen) [2]	1468
15	17	A	Arbroath	D	1-1	0-1	10	Novo (pen) [60]	1034
16	24	H	Clyde	L	1-2	1-1	10	Smith [30]	1556
17	Dec 1	A	St Mirren	D	1-1	1-1	10	Miller J [10]	3360
18	8	H	Ross Co	L	1-3	0-3	10	Clark A [38]	1449
19	15	A	Airdrieonians	D	1-1	1-0	10	Jones [4]	1566
20	29	A	Ayr U	L	1-3	0-0	10	Queseda [78]	2033
21	Jan 12	A	Inverness CT	L	0-5	0-2	10		1822
22	19	H	St Mirren	W	1-0	0-0	10	Novo [89]	1849
23	26	H	Arbroath	D	0-0	0-0	10		1737
24	Feb 2	A	Clyde	W	2-1	1-0	10	Smith 2 [34, 66]	1095
25	9	A	Ross Co	L	2-4	1-1	10	Henderson D [38], Novo [65]	2592
26	16	H	Partick Th	W	2-0	2-0	10	Novo [3], Henderson D [24]	2729
27	23	H	Falkirk	W	5-1	2-1	8	Novo 2 [1, 77], Davidson [28], Smith [67], Rivas [79]	2511
28	Mar 2	A	Ayr U	D	3-3	2-3	10	Smith 2 [38, 43], Novo [60]	2010
29	9	A	Falkirk	L	1-2	0-0	10	Smith [72]	2680
30	16	H	Inverness CT	D	0-0	0-0	10		1590
31	23	A	Arbroath	D	2-2	1-2	10	Dennis [22], Novo [90]	1185
32	30	A	St Mirren	L	0-1	0-1	10		4014
33	Apr 6	H	Clyde	L	0-1	0-1	10		1626
34	13	H	Airdrieonians	W	2-1	1-1	10	Novo [35], Jones [67]	1138
35	20	A	Partick Th	L	0-1	0-0	10		6208
36	27	H	Ross Co	L	0-1	0-0	10		1216

Final League Position: 10

Honours
League Champions: First Division: 1992-93, 1994-95. Division II 1907-08, 1909-10 (shared), 1937-38, 1948-49;
Runners-up: Division II 1908-09, 1926-27, 1966-67. Second Division 1975-76, 1977-78, 1986-87.
Scottish Cup Runners-up: 1913. *League Cup Winners: (Coca-Cola Cup):* 1994-95. *Runners-up:* 1948-49.

European: *UEFA Cup:* 6 matches (1995-96).

Club colours: Shirt: Navy blue, white trim. Shorts: White with navy blue edges. Stockings: Navy blue with white turnover.

Goalscorers: *League* (50): Novo 19 (3 pens), Smith A 11, Crabbe 6, Henderson D 3, Dennis 2, Jones 2, Stein 2 (1 pen), Clark A 1, Davidson H 1, Miller J 1, Queseda 1, Rivas 1.
Scottish Cup (0):
CIS Cup (3): Henderson D 1, Novo 1, Smith A 1.
Challenge Cup (6): Novo 3, Dennis 1, Matheson 1, Zoco 1.

Monin S 27	McCulloch G 25+1	Ellis L 19+2	Dennis S 26	Browne P 34+1	Zoco J 18+1	Nanou W 13+9	Matheson R 13+2	Novo I 33	O'Boyle G 2+3	Stein J 22+6	Henderson D 28+1	Crabbe S 11	Miotto S 9	Clark J 1+2	Clark A 1+11	Smith A 32	Queseda A 14+3	Hampshire P 4+3	Javary P 8	Rivas F 14+1	Jones M 8+7	Miller J 2+3	Henderson R 8	McGarty M 3+5	Davidson H 10+1	Miller M 8	Miller W 3	Match No.
1	2	3	4	5	6[1]	7	8	9	10	11	12																	1
1		3	4	5	2[1]	12	8	7	10	11	6	9																2
	2[1]	3	4	5[2]	7	8	10				13	11	9	1	6	12												3
	2		4	5	3[1]	8	7			11	6	10		1		12	9											4
	2	14	4[3]	5	3	8	7	12		11	6	10[2]		1	13		9[1]											5
	2		4	5	3	8	7			11	6	10		1			9											6
	2		4	5	3	8[1]	7			11	6	10		1		12	9											7
1		4	3[1]	5	2	8	7[2]			11	6	10			12	13	9											8
1		4	3	5[1]	2	8	7			11	6	10			12		9											9
1		4	3	5	2	12	8[2]	7[1]		11	6	10				13	9											10
1		3	4	5	2[1]	8	7	14		11	6[1]	10				9	13	12										11
1		3	4	5	2[1]	8[3]	7	14		11	6[2]	10				9	12	13										12
1	2		4	5		8	10	7		11						9	3	6										13
1	2		4	5		8[1]	12	10[2]	7	11		13				9	3	6										14
1	2	12	4	5	14		7					11[1]				9	3	6	8[2]	10[2]	13							15
1	2		4	5			7					11				9	3	6	8	10[1]	12							16
1	2		4	5			13					11			12	9	3	6	8	10[1]	7[2]							17
1	2[1]		5	4		12	10					11			13	9	3	6	8		7[2]							18
1	2		5	4		13	7[2]					11			12	9	3	6	8	10								19
	2		4	5		7[1]						11		1		9	3	6	8	10	12							20
	2		4	5		12						11	8	1	10[2]	9	3		7[1]		13		6					21
1		5	4		2		7					11				9	3		8	10[1]			6	12				22
1			4	5	2		7		10							9	3						6	8	11			23
1	2	5	4				10					11				9	3						6	7	8			24
1	2	5	4			12	10	14				11				9	3[3]				13		6	7[1]	8[2]			25
1			4	5	6		10					11				9	3						8[1]	12	7	2		26
1			4	5	6		10[3]	12				11				9	3				13		8	14	7[2]	2		27
1		12	4	5	6		10					11				9	3[1]				13		8[2]		7	2		28
1			4	5	6		10	13				11				9	3[2]				14		8[3]	12	7[1]	2		29
1	2	3[2]	4[1]	5	6		10					11				9	13						8	12	7			30
1		3	4	5	6[1]		10					11				9	12						8		7	2		31
1		6	4	5			10	12				11[1]				9	3[2]				13		8		7	2		32
1		3	4	5	6[2]	14	10	12				11				9	7[1]				13		8				2[2]	33
1		3	4	5	6		7					11				9	8						10[1]	12			2	34
		5	3	4	13	12	8[2]		10			11		1	6	9					14				7[2]	2[1]		35
	2	3	4	5			8	13	10			11		1	6	9[1]	12								7[2]			36

RANGERS   Premier League

Year Formed: 1873. *Ground & Address:* Ibrox Stadium, 150 Edmiston Drive, Glasgow G51 2XD.
Telephone: 0870 600 1972. *Fax:* 0870 600 1978. *Website:* www.rangers.co.uk
Ground Capacity: all seated: 50,444. *Size of Pitch:* 114.5m × 81.5m.
Chairman: John McClelland. *Hon. Chairman:* David Murray. *Secretary:* R. C. Ogilvie. *Commercial & Marketing Manager:* Martin Bain. *Director of Football:* Dick Advocaat.
Manager: Alex McLeish. *Assistant Manager:* Andy Watson. *First Team Coach:* Jan Wouters. *Physio:* Grant Downie.
Reserve team coaches: John McGregor, John Brown.
Managers since 1975: Jock Wallace, John Greig, Jock Wallace, Graeme Souness, Walter Smith, Dick Advocaat.
Club Nickname(s): The Gers. *Previous Grounds:* Flesher's Haugh, Burnbank, Kinning Park, Old Ibrox.
Record Attendance: 118,567 v Celtic, Division I; 2 Jan, 1939.
Record Transfer Fee received: £8,500,000 for G. Van Bronckhorst to Arsenal (2001).
Record Transfer Fee paid: £12 million for Tore Andre Flo from Chelsea (November 2000).
Record Victory: 14-2 v Blairgowrie, Scottish Cup 1st rd; 20 Jan, 1934. *Record Defeat:* 2-10 v Airdrieonians; 1886.
Most Capped Player: Ally McCoist, 60, Scotland. *Most League Appearances:* 496: John Greig, 1962-78.
Most League Goals in Season (Individual): 44: Sam English, Division I; 1931-32.
Most Goals Overall (Individual): 355: Ally McCoist; 1985-98.

Honours
League Champions: (49 times) Division I 1890-91 (shared), 1898-99, 1899-1900, 1900-01, 1901-02, 1910-11, 1911-12, 1912-13, 1917-18, 1919-20, 1920-21, 1922-23, 1923-24, 1924-25, 1926-27, 1927-28, 1928-29, 1929-30, 1930-31, 1932-33, 1933-34, 1934-35, 1936-37, 1938-39, 1946-47, 1948-49, 1949-50, 1952-53, 1955-56, 1956-57, 1958-59, 1960-61, 1962-63, 1963-64, 1974-75. Premier Division: 1975-76, 1977-78, 1986-87, 1988-89, 1989-90, 1990-91, 1991-92, 1992-93, 1993-94, 1994-95, 1995-96, 1996-97, 1998-99, 1999-2000; *Runners-up:* 24 times.

RANGERS 2001–02 LEAGUE RECORD

Match No.	Date	Venue	Opponents	Result	H/T Score	Lg. Pos.	Goalscorers	Attendance
1	Jul 28	A	Aberdeen	W 3-0	0-0	—	Nerlinger [54], Latapy (pen) [68], Caniggia [73]	17,757
2	Aug 4	H	Livingston	D 0-0	0-0	3		47,805
3	11	A	Dunfermline Ath	W 4-1	2-0	2	Latapy [12], Flo [16], Konterman 2 [46, 82]	10,405
4	18	H	Hibernian	D 2-2	1-1	2	Konterman [25], Mols [48]	45,940
5	26	H	Dundee	W 2-0	1-0	2	Mols [25], Ricksen [68]	48,038
6	Sept 8	A	Hearts	D 2-2	1-1	2	Latapy [14], Flo [57]	14,014
7	16	H	Motherwell	W 3-0	1-0	2	Flo [36], de Boer [89], Caniggia [89]	47,137
8	22	A	Dundee U	W 6-1	1-1	2	Buchan (og) [2], Flo 3 [49, 72, 80], de Boer [65], McCann [90]	11,117
9	30	H	Celtic	L 0-2	0-1	2		50,097
10	Oct 13	H	Kilmarnock	W 3-1	2-0	2	Arveladze [9], Caniggia [39], Flo [52]	49,351
11	21	A	St Johnstone	W 2-0	0-0	2	Arveladze [47], Flo [68]	8351
12	27	A	Livingston	W 2-0	1-0	2	Reyna 2 [23, 58]	9309
13	Nov 4	H	Aberdeen	W 2-0	2-0	2	Flo 2 [4, 20]	49,739
14	17	H	Dunfermline Ath	W 4-0	1-0	2	Arveladze 2 [5, 58], Flo 2 [49, 54]	48,554
15	25	A	Celtic	L 1-2	0-0	2	Lovenkrands [76]	59,633
16	Dec 1	A	Dundee	D 0-0	0-0	2		11,085
17	9	H	Hearts	W 3-1	2-1	2	de Boer [7], Latapy [20], Arveladze [70]	47,891
18	12	H	Hibernian	D 1-1	0-1	—	Ricksen [59]	46,179
19	15	A	Motherwell	D 2-2	1-1	2	Arveladze [37], McCann [63]	9894
20	22	H	Dundee U	W 3-2	2-1	2	Arveladze 2 [20, 54], Amoruso [43]	47,315
21	26	A	Hibernian	W 3-0	1-0	—	Moore [15], Flo [85], Arveladze [87]	14,021
22	29	H	St Johnstone	W 1-0	1-0	2	Mols [2]	48,827
23	Jan 12	H	Livingston	W 3-0	2-0	2	Flo [29], Caniggia 2 [34, 86]	48,044
24	19	A	Aberdeen	W 1-0	1-0	2	Amoruso [33]	17,846
25	23	A	Dunfermline Ath	W 4-2	0-2	—	Vidmar [47], de Boer 2 [53, 62], Arveladze [80]	8795
26	30	A	Kilmarnock	D 2-2	1-0	2	de Boer [33], Flo [54]	11,589
27	Feb 2	H	Dundee	W 2-1	0-0	2	Arveladze [73], Moore [76]	48,861
28	9	A	Hearts	W 2-0	0-0	2	de Boer [60], McCann [82]	14,511
29	16	H	Motherwell	W 3-0	2-0	2	Latapy [14], Flo [41], Ricksen [84]	49,284
30	Mar 3	A	Dundee U	W 1-0	0-0	2	Amoruso [66]	9383
31	6	A	St Johnstone	W 2-0	1-0	—	Flo [45], Ricksen [60]	6382
32	10	H	Celtic	D 1-1	0-1	2	Numan [59]	49,765
33	20	H	Kilmarnock	W 5-0	3-0	—	McCann 3 [24, 40, 60], Kanchelskis [33], Burke [80]	47,678
34	Apr 7	H	Hearts	W 2-0	1-0	2	Dodds 2 [38, 70]	47,492
35	13	A	Livingston	L 1-2	1-1	2	Amoruso [3]	10,019
36	21	A	Celtic	D 1-1	1-1	2	Lovenkrands [2]	59,034
37	27	H	Aberdeen	W 2-0	1-0	2	McCann [41], Ferguson [80]	48,878
38	May 12	A	Dunfermline Ath	D 1-1	1-0	2	Moore [27]	8716

Final League Position: 2

Scottish Cup Winners: (29 times) 1894, 1897, 1898, 1903, 1928, 1930, 1932, 1934, 1935, 1936, 1948, 1949, 1950, 1953, 1960, 1962, 1963, 1964, 1966, 1973, 1976, 1978, 1979, 1981, 1992, 1993, 1996, 1999, 2000, 2002: *Runners-up:* 17 times.
League Cup Winners: (22 times) 1946-47, 1948-49, 1960-61, 1961-62, 1963-64, 1964-65, 1970-71, 1975-76, 1977-78, 1978-79, 1981-82, 1983-84, 1984-85, 1986-87, 1987-88, 1988-89, 1990-91, 1992-93, 1993-94, 1996-97, 1998-99, 2001-02; *Runners-up:* 6 times.

European: *European Cup:* 109 matches (1956-57, 1957-58, 1959-60 semi-finals, 1961-62, 1963-64, 1964-65, 1975-76, 1976-77, 1978-79, 1987-88, 1989-90, 1990-91, 1991-92, 1992-93 final pool, 1993-94, 1994-95, 1995-96; 1996-97, 1997-98, 1999-2000, 2000-01). *Cup Winners' Cup:* 54 matches (1960-61 runners-up, 1962-63, 1966-67 runners-up, 1969-70, 1971-72 winners, 1973-74, 1977-78, 1979-80, 1981-82, 1983-84). *UEFA Cup:* 54 matches (*Fairs Cup:* 1967-68, 1968-69 semi-finals, 1970-71. *UEFA Cup:* 1982-83, 1984-85, 1985-86, 1986-87, 1988-89, 1997-98, 1998-99, 1999-2000, 2000-01).

Club colours: Shirt: Royal blue with red and white collar trim and red piping at front. Shorts: White with royal blue trim. Stockings: Black with red tops.

Goalscorers: *League* (82): Flo 17, Arveladze 11, de Boer 7, McCann 7, Caniggia 5, Latapy 5, Amoruso 4, Ricksen 4, Konterman 3, Mols 3, Moore 3, Dodds 2, Lovenkrands 2, Reyna 2, Burke 1, Ferguson 1, Kanchelskis 1, Nerlinger 1, Numan 1, Vidmar 1, own goal 1.
Scottish Cup (19): Dodds 4, Arveladze 3, Lovenkrands 3, Ferguson 2, Flo 2, Nerlinger 2, Amoruso 1, Kanchelskis 1, Konterman 1.
CIS Cup (11): Arveladze 3, Caniggia 2, Ferguson 1 (pen), Flo 1, Konterman 1, Lovenkrands 1, Numan 1, Reyna 1.

Klos S 36	Ricksen F 31	Moore C 18	Vidmar T 23+2	Numan A 28+2	Reyna C 10	Konterman B 26	Nerlinger C 7+1	Latapy R 14+2	Mols M 8+7	Caniggia C 16+7	Miller K —+3	Hughes S 12+5	McCann N 13+12	Wilson S 6	Johnston A 1	Flo T 25+5	Kanchelskis A 6+4	Ross M 19+2	de Boer R 19+5	Dodds W 5+6	Amoruso L 28	Christiansen J —+1	Lovenkrands P 10+8	Ferguson B 21+1	Ball M 5+2	Arveladze S 21+1	Malcolm R 6+1	Penttila T —+1	Burke C 1+1	McGregor A 2	Brighton T 1	Gibson J —+1	Dowie A —+1	Match No.
1	2	3	4	5¹	6	7	8	9	10¹	11³	12	13	14																					1
1	5	3	4			7			12	11³	14			6	9	2	8²	10¹	13															2
1	2		4	5		6		9	11²			8¹			3	10³	12	7	13	14													3
1	2	13	5	7	6²		9	11			8¹				4	10			3	12														4
1	2		4	5		6		9¹	10²	11	13	8	12			7	3																	5
1	2		4	5		6		9		8				10	7	3	11¹¹	13		12²														6
1	2	3	4	5		6		9		13		8³		10		7¹	11²		14	12														7
1	2		4		5	6		9		8				10³	13	11¹	3	12	7															8
1	2	4		5	8¹	6		11²	12	14	13			10		12		7	8	9	13													9
1	2	3		5	6²	4		11				10¹		12			7	8	9	13														10
1	2		5	6¹	4			14		12			10³	13	11	3	7¹	8	9															11
1	2	4		5	8¹	6		11³				10²		12		3	13	7	14	9														12
1	2	4		5²	8	6		12				10¹		11	3	12	7	13	9															13
1	2		5	6	4			11				10¹		3	12	7	8	9																14
1			5	6	4			12				10	2¹	9	14	3	13	7	8²	11¹¹														15
1	3		5¹	6	4			14	11²			10³	2	13		12	7	8	9															16
1	6		7	5				9	11²	12	13	4		2	8¹	3				10														17
1	6	3	7	5				9³		14	13	12	4²	10¹	2	8		11																18
1	2	3	4	5		6		9¹		12	11				8			7	10															19
1	2		8	5		6			12			10¹	4	9		3		7	11															20
1	8	2³	14	5		6			11¹		12	13	4		3	9²	7	10																21
1	2		5	6				10²	11¹		12	13	4	8	3		7	9																22
1	2	5				6		12	11	7	13	10¹	4	8	3	9²																		23
1	2	4	5				6		11			10		8	3	7	9																	24
1	2	4	5				6		11¹		12			8	3	10	7	9																25
1	2	4	5							6	12			10	8²	13	3	11¹	7	9														26
1	2	4	5	12					11²			6	13	10			3	8	7	9¹														27
1	2		5		4						6	11		10	8	3		7	9															28
1	2		4	5		6		8	12					10¹	14	13	3	11³	7²	9														29
1	2		4	5				8²	10¹			6	9	12	14	7	13	3	11³															30
1	2¹		6	5		12			8	11	4			10	7	9	3																	31
1	2		4	5		6		9¹		11				10		3	8	7	12															32
1			5¹	8				6	11			7²	4	10	3	9					2	12	13											33
1	4			8	14	13			11			6	5	9¹⁰	3	7²			2										12³					34
1			5¹	12				8	7	9³			11	13	6	4	10²	3	14				2											35
1	2		5					8	9¹	13				10²	7	6	12	3	11				4											36
	3	5		8					10¹			6	12	4	9			7	11	2		1												37
	4²	5						8³	13	12			11		6	10	3		2		7	1	9¹	14										38

ROSS COUNTY

First Division

Year Formed: 1929. *Ground & Address:* Victoria Park, Dingwall IV15 9QW. *Telephone:* 01349 860860. *Fax:* 01349 866277.
Website: www.rosscountyfootballclub.co.uk
Ground Capacity: 6700. *Size of Ground:* 110×75yd.
Chairman: Roy McGregor. *Secretary:* Donnie MacBean. *Facilities Manager:* Brian Campbell.
Manager: Neale Cooper. *Assistant Manager:* Danny MacDonald. *Physio:* Douglas Sim.
Record Attendance: 6600, benefit match v Celtic, 31 August 1970.
Record Transfer Fee Received: £200,000 for Neil Tarrant to Aston Villa (April 1999).
Record Transfer Fee Paid: £25,000 for Barry Wilson from Southampton (Oct. 1992).
Record Victory: 11-0 v St Cuthbert Wanderers, Scottish Cup, Dec. 1993.
Record Defeat: 1-10 v Inverness Thistle, Highland League.
Most League Appearances: 157: David Mackay, 1995-2001.
Most League Goals in Season: 22: D. Adams, 1996-97.
Most League Goals (Overall): 44: Steven Ferguson, 1996-2002.

ROSS COUNTY 2001–02 LEAGUE RECORD

Match No.	Date		Venue	Opponents	Result	H/T Score	Lg. Pos.	Goalscorers	Atten- dance
1	Aug	4	H	Arbroath	L	0-2	0-2	—	2682
2		11	A	Ayr U	L	0-2	0-1	10	2457
3		18	H	Raith R	W	1-0	1-0	7	Robertson [12]	2060
4		25	H	Airdrieonians	L	0-1	0-1	7		2022
5	Sept	8	A	Clyde	L	0-3	0-2	9		888
6		15	H	Inverness CT	W	2-1	0-0	8	Ferguson [63], Bone [67]	3870
7		18	A	St Mirren	L	0-1	0-1	—		2264
8		22	H	Partick Th	W	3-2	2-2	6	Bone [21], Hislop 2 [39, 50]	2656
9		29	A	Falkirk	L	2-4	2-0	9	Bone 2 [28, 29]	1805
10	Oct	13	A	Arbroath	L	1-2	0-1	10	Hislop [65]	765
11		20	H	Ayr U	W	3-2	1-0	8	Hislop 2 [20, 59], Prest [82]	1991
12		27	H	Clyde	W	4-0	3-0	6	Gethins 2 [21, 34], Hislop [37], Ferguson [69]	2311
13	Nov	3	A	Airdrieonians	D	1-1	1-0	6	Hislop [29]	1516
14		10	H	St Mirren	L	0-1	0-0	6		3578
15		17	A	Inverness CT	L	0-3	0-1	9		4513
16		24	H	Falkirk	L	1-2	0-1	9	Boukraa [71]	2184
17	Dec	1	A	Partick Th	D	0-0	0-0	9		3589
18		8	A	Raith R	W	3-1	3-0	9	Robertson [18], Hislop [28], McCormick [33]	1449
19		15	H	Arbroath	L	0-1	0-0	9		2056
20	Jan	12	A	St Mirren	D	1-1	1-0	9	Bone [27]	2648
21		19	A	Partick Th	L	0-1	0-1	9		3043
22	Feb	2	A	Falkirk	W	4-1	3-0	9	Robertson [11], Hislop 2 [41, 45], Boukraa [88]	1834
23		9	H	Raith R	W	4-2	1-1	9	Irvine [3], Henderson R (og) [56], Gethins [60], Bone [61]	2592
24		16	A	Ayr U	D	0-0	0-0	9		2186
25	Mar	2	A	Airdrieonians	W	2-0	0-0	9	Robertson [62], Bone [74]	1337
26		9	H	Clyde	W	2-1	0-0	9	Gilbert [75], Gethins [80]	2145
27		12	A	Clyde	D	0-0	0-0	—		703
28		16	H	St Mirren	W	4-1	2-1	6	Ferguson [24], McGowan (og) [32], Gethins [48], Hislop [77]	2957
29		19	H	Inverness CT	D	0-0	0-0	—		4679
30		23	A	Inverness CT	D	1-1	0-0	5	Hislop [55]	4185
31		26	H	Airdrieonians	W	4-1	1-1	—	Bone (pen) [45], McCormick 2 [59, 81], Irvine [69]	2087
32		30	A	Partick Th	D	1-1	0-0	3	Robertson [78]	4013
33	Apr	6	H	Falkirk	W	4-2	1-2	4	Bone (pen) [17], Robertson [59], Gethins [77], Ferguson [81]	2715
34		13	A	Arbroath	D	1-1	1-0	4	Hislop [20]	826
35		20	A	Ayr U	D	1-1	1-0	4	Hislop [44]	2822
36		27	A	Raith R	W	1-0	0-0	4	Campbell [84]	1216

Final League Position: 4

Honours
League Champions: Third Division: 1998-99.

Club colours: Navy blue, white and red.

Goalscorers: *League* (51): Hislop 14, Bone 9 (2 pens), Gethins 6, Robertson 6, Ferguson 4, McCormick 3, Boukraa 2, Irvine 2, Campbell 1, Gilbert 1, Prest 1, own goals 2.
Scottish Cup (1): Perry 1.
CIS Cup (6): Bone 2, Boukraa 2, Irvine 1, Mackay 1.
Challenge Cup (4): Hislop 3, McQuade 1.

Bullock A 33	Perry M 36	Robertson H 36	Maxwell I 35	Irvine B 29 + 1	Ferguson S 26 + 2	McCormick M 11 + 9	Hislop S 29 + 4	Holmes D 2 + 1	Cowie D 14 + 4	Prest M 2 + 6	Mackay S 3 + 10	McQuade J 5 + 2	Fraser J 4	Hastings R 26 + 2	Webb S 15 + 4	Bone A 27 + 4	Boukraa K 10 + 6	Dlugonski B 3	Blackley D — + 1	Gethins C 11 + 13	MacDonald K — + 1	Tarrant N 2 + 5	Anselin C 7 + 4	Lilley D 5 + 1	Gonzales R 2 + 1	Gilbert K 15	Jack D — + 1	Canning M 7	Kuyper N — + 1	Campbell C — + 2	Fridge L 1	Match No.
1	2	3	4	5	6	7	8¹	9	10	11²	12	13																				1
1	2	3	4	5	6	12	13	9		10¹	11	7⁴	8																			2
1	2	11	4		12		8²	13	10	14		7¹	6	3	5	9³																3
1	2	11	4		6	8	9²		12			7¹		3	5	13	10															4
1	2	11	4		6	12	8¹		13			7²		3	5	9	10															5
1	2	11	4	5	8	7	12							3	6	9	10¹															6
1	2	11	4	5	8	7¹	12			13	10²			3	6	9																7
1	2	11	4	5	8		10²			13	7¹			3	6	9	12															8
1	2	11	4	5			10	8²		3³	13			6	9	12	7¹	14														9
1	2	11	4	5	8	7	10		13			3¹			9	12	6²															10
1	2	11	4	5	8		10¹	3	13					6	9	7²			12													11
1	2	11	4	5	8²		10³	7	14					3	6	12	13		9¹													12
1	2	11	4	5	8¹		10	7		14				3	6				9²	12³	13											13
1	2²	11³	4			13	10	7		14				3	6	9	8¹				12											14
1	2	11	4	5²		8	10¹	7						3	6	14			9³		12	13										15
1	2²	11	4			6¹	10³	7		12				3	5	9	8		13	14												16
1	2	11	4	5		14	10²			6				3		9³	8¹		12	13	7											17
1	2	11	4	5		6	10¹							3	12	9			13	8	7²											18
1	2	11	4	5	13		10	6		12				3		9³			14	8¹	7²											19
1	2	11	4	5	8		10	12						3	13	9			7¹			6²										20
1⁹	2	11	4	5¹	8		10	6						9	13	7			12	3³	15											21
	5	3	4		8	7¹	10							9²	12			13		11	2	1	6									22
	2	3	4	5	8	13	10		14					9³	7²			12		11¹		1	6									23
1	2	3	4	5	8	12	10				14			9²	7¹			13		11³			6									24
1	2	3	4	5	8	14	10²				7			9³				13		11¹	12		6									25
1	2	3	4	5	8									11²		9³	10¹			12		13	7		6	14						26
1	5	3	4	13	8²		10	14						11	9			7¹			12	2³	6									27
1	2	3	4	5	8		10							11	12			9¹					6	7								28
1	2	3	4	5	8		10							11	9								6	7								29
1	2	3	4	5	8	12	10							11				9¹					6	7								30
1	2	3	4	5	8	10²								11	9¹			12					6	7	13							31
1	2	3	4	5	8	10¹	12							11	14	9²			13				6	7³								32
1	2	3	4	5	8	13			14		12			11	7¹	9³			10²				6									33
1	2	3	4	5			10		8		12			11¹		9²			7				6			13						34
1	2	3	4¹	5			10		8					11	12	9²			13				6	7								35
	2	3			8		10		11		13			12	5¹		4²		9³				6		7		14	1				36

ST JOHNSTONE   First Division

Year Formed: 1884. *Ground & Address:* McDiarmid Park, Crieff Road, Perth PH1 2SJ. *Telephone:* 01738 459090. *Fax:*
01738 625 771. *Clubcall:* 0898 121559. *Website:* www.stjohnstonefc.co.uk
Ground Capacity: all seated: 10,673. *Size of Pitch:* 115yd × 75yd.
Chairman: G.S. Brown. *Secretary and Managing Director:* Stewart Duff. *Sales Executive:* Susan Weir.
Manager: Billy Stark. *Coach:* Billy Kirkwood. *Physio:* Nick Summersgill. *Youth Development Officer:* Alistair Stevenson.
Managers since 1975: J. Stewart, J. Storrie, A. Stuart, A. Rennie, I. Gibson, A. Totten, J. McClelland, P. Sturrock,
S. Clark.
Club Nickname(s): Saints. *Previous Grounds:* Recreation Grounds, Muirton Park.
Record Attendance: (McDiarmid Park): 10,545 v Dundee, Premier Division; 23 May, 1999.
Record Transfer Fee received: £1,750,000 for Calum Davidson to Blackburn R (March 1998).
Record Transfer Fee paid: £300,000 for Billy Dodds from Dundee (1994).
Record Victory: 9-0 v Albion R, League Cup: 9 March, 1946.
Record Defeat: 1-10 v Third Lanark, Scottish Cup: 24 January, 1903.
Most Capped Player: Nick Dasovic, 17, Canada.
Most League Appearances: 298: Drew Rutherford.

ST JOHNSTONE 2001–02 LEAGUE RECORD

Match No.	Date		Venue	Opponents	Result		H/T Score	Lg. Pos.	Goalscorers	Atten- dance
1	Jul	28	A	Celtic	L	0-3	0-1	—		57,933
2	Aug	4	H	Dunfermline Ath	L	0-2	0-1	12		4702
3		11	H	Dundee U	L	0-1	0-1	12		5162
4		18	A	Kilmarnock	L	1-2	0-2	12	Falconer [89]	6486
5		25	A	Aberdeen	D	1-1	0-1	12	Weir [46]	5459
6	Sept	8	A	Dundee	D	1-1	0-1	12	Jackson (pen) [73]	7050
7		15	H	Livingston	D	2-2	1-2	12	Falconer [16], MacDonald [49]	3417
8		23	A	Hibernian	L	0-4	0-1	12		10,398
9		29	H	Motherwell	L	2-3	1-1	12	Connolly [11], MacDonald [54]	3983
10	Oct	13	A	Hearts	L	0-3	0-2	12		10,735
11		21	H	Rangers	L	0-2	0-0	12		8351
12		27	A	Dunfermline Ath	L	1-2	1-0	12	Hartley [3]	4449
13	Nov	3	H	Celtic	L	1-2	1-1	12	Dods [26]	9041
14		10	A	Kilmarnock	W	1-0	1-0	12	Falconer [38]	6008
15		17	A	Dundee U	L	1-2	0-0	12	Hartley [65]	6624
16		24	H	Kilmarnock	W	1-0	1-0	12	Russell [13]	3711
17	Dec	1	A	Aberdeen	L	0-1	0-1	12		17,369
18		8	H	Dundee	L	0-2	0-1	12		5299
19		15	A	Livingston	L	1-2	0-0	12	Hartley [48]	3739
20		22	H	Hibernian	D	0-0	0-0	12		4056
21		26	A	Motherwell	W	2-1	2-0	—	Murray [9], MacDonald [37]	4659
22		29	A	Rangers	L	0-1	0-1	12		48,827
23	Jan	2	H	Hearts	L	0-2	0-1	—		5413
24		12	H	Dunfermline Ath	L	0-1	0-0	12		3459
25		19	A	Celtic	L	1-2	1-2	12	Dods [6]	58,516
26		22	H	Dundee U	L	1-4	0-3	—	Youssouf [65]	3401
27	Feb	2	H	Aberdeen	L	0-1	0-1	12		4305
28		9	A	Dundee	L	0-1	0-1	12		6344
29		16	H	Livingston	W	3-0	1-0	12	Hartley [43], Parker [79], Jones [89]	3784
30	Mar	2	A	Hibernian	L	0-3	0-2	12		13,731
31		6	H	Rangers	L	0-2	0-1	—		6382
32		9	H	Motherwell	L	0-2	0-1	12		3282
33		23	A	Hearts	W	3-1	3-0	12	Lovenkrands 2 [20, 30], McBride (pen) [38]	10,762
34	Apr	6	A	Motherwell	D	1-1	1-0	12	Hartley [22]	3418
35		13	H	Dundee	L	0-1	0-0	12		2768
36		20	H	Kilmarnock	L	0-3	0-0	12		2245
37		27	A	Dundee U	D	0-0	0-0	12		5190
38	May	12	H	Hibernian	L	0-1	0-1	12		3372

Final League Position: 12

Most League Goals in Season (Individual): 36: Jimmy Benson, Division II: 1931-32.
Most Goals Overall (Individual): 140: John Brogan, 1977-83.

Honours
League Champions: First Division 1982-83, 1989-90, 1996-97. Division II 1923-24, 1959-60, 1962-63; *Runners-up:* Division II 1931-32. Second Division 1987-88.
Scottish Cup: Semi-finals 1934, 1968, 1989, 1991.
League Cup Runners-up: 1969, 1998.
League Challenge Cup Runners-up: 1996-97.

European: *UEFA Cup:* 10 matches (1971-72, 1999-2000).

Club colours: Shirt: Royal blue with white trim. Shorts: White. Stockings: Royal blue with white hoops.

Goalscorers: *League* (24): Hartley 5, Falconer 3, MacDonald 3, Dods 2, Lovenkrands 2, Connolly 1, Jackson 1 (pen), Jones 1, McBride 1 (pen), Murray 1, Parker 1, Russell 1, Weir 1, Youssouf 1.
Scottish Cup (0):
CIS Cup (4): MacDonald 2, Dods 1, Hartley 1.

Main A 7	Kemble B 14	Forsyth R 15+1	Dods D 32	Murray G 38	Sylla M 1	McBride J 15+6	Kane P 15	Hartley P 32	Parker K 14+7	Lovenkrands T 28+1	Djebali R 4+9	Connolly P 21+8	MacDonald P 12+16	Jackson D 6+3	Fotheringham M 2+4	Weir J 17	Dasovic N 22+2	Falconer W 16+9	McCluskey S 19+4	Cuthbert K 11+1	Miller A 18	Lynch M 20	Russell C 7+6	Jones G 7+6	McClune D 5+2	McCulloch M 4+2	Youssof S 5	Maher M 4+6	Roy L 2	Panther E 5+2	Ferry M —+2	Match No.
1	2	3	4	5	6	7^2	8	9	10^1	11	12	13																				1
1	2	3	4	5		7	8^1	9	10^2	6		11^3	12	13	14																	2
1	2	3		5		7	8		13	12		14	9^1	11^1		4		6^3	10													3
1	2	3		5			8	9^1				7	12	13	11		4^3	6^2	10	14												4
1	2	3	6	5			14	8^1		12		9^3	11			4^2	7	10	13													5
1	2		3	5		7	8	9^2		14		13	11			4^1	6	10	12^3													6
	2	3^1	5			7		12	8			13	9	11^2		6	10	4	1													7
	2	3^1	5			7			8			13	12	11		4	9	10^2	6	1												8
1^9		3	2	5		14		8	10	11		9^2	4			7^3	13	6	15													9
4	3	2	5				12	8^1	10			11^1	9	13		7		6	15	1												10
		2	5				4^2	8	10	6		11	12		13		7	9^1	3		1											11
		2	5				8^1		9	10^3	6	11^2	14			7	12	3		1	4	13										12
	2	3	5				8	10^1	6	12		11^2	13			7	9			1	4											13
	2	3	5				14	8	6			11^1	10^2			7	9			1	4	12	13^3									14
	2	3	5				8		6	12		11^2	10^1			7	9			1	4	13										15
	2	3	5				9	8	6			13	11^2	12		7				1	4	10^1										16
	2^1		5				3^2	8		6		13	11	14		7^2	9			1	4	10^3		12								17
		3	5					8				11	12		13	7^2	9			1	4	10		2^2	6							18
	2	3	5				8^3	9				10	11^2		14	4	7	13		1		6^1	12									19
	2	3	5				8^3	7				6^2	10	12	13	9		14		4	1	11^1										20
	2	3	5				8	9				6	13	11^2	10^1		7	12	4	1												21
	3	5	13				8					2	9^2		10	6^1	7	11	4	1			12									22
	2	3	5				13	8^2	9			6	12	11	10^3		7^1	14	4	1												23
		3	5				6^1	8				13	12	11^2		7^3	9			1		4	10	14								24
		3	5				8^3	7				9	13			11	2			1	4	10^2	14	12	6^1							25
		3	5				8	7	12			9	13			11	2			1	4^3	14	11^1	6	10	13						26
		3	5				8	11	7			9^1				4			2	1	6	13			10^2	12						27
		3	5				8	9	10^1	7						4	13			1	2	12			11^2	6						28
		3	5				8	9	10^3	8						4^1	14	12	1		2	13			11^2	6						29
	2^3	3	5				8	9	10			4	13	14			6		12			11^1	7^2	1								30
		3	5				8^1	10	9			12		4	7	13				2		11^2			6	1						31
	2		5^2				7^1	8	10	9				4			3	1		6		11			13	12						32
		2	5				7		9			10^2	13		4		3	1	2			11^3			14			8^1	12			33
		3	5				7^1	9^1	8			10^2	12		4		6	1	2			13			14	13						34
	14	3^3	5				7^1	9	12	8		10			4		1	2				11			13	6^2						35
		3	5				8	9^1	7			10	12		4					11	2^2	13				6						36
		3	5				9	12	8			10	13		4	1			11^1		2	6				7^2						37
		3	5^2				9	12	8^3			10	11^1	14		4	1				2	6				7	13					38

ST MIRREN

First Division

Year Formed: 1877. *Ground & Address:* St Mirren Park, Love St, Paisley PA3 2EJ. *Telephone:* 0141 889 2558/0141 840 1337. *Fax:* 0141 848 6444.
Ground Capacity: 10,866 (all seated). *Size of Pitch:* 112yd × 73yd.
Chairman: Stewart Gilmour. *Vice-Chairman:* George Campbell. *Secretary:* Allan Marshall.
Manager: Tom Hendrie. *Youth Development Officer:* Arthur Bell.
Managers since 1975: Alex Ferguson, Jim Clunie, Rikki MacFarlane, Alex Miller, Alex Smith, Tony Fitzpatrick, David Hay, Jimmy Bone, Tony Fitzpatrick. *Club Nickname(s):* The Buddies. *Previous Grounds:* Short Roods 1877-79, Thistle Park Greenhill 1879-83, Westmarch 1883-94.
Record Attendance: 47,438 v Celtic, League Cup, 20 Aug, 1949.
Record Transfer Fee received: £850,000 for Ian Ferguson to Rangers (1988).
Record Transfer Fee paid: £400,000 for Thomas Stickroth from Bayer Uerdingen (1990).
Record Victory: 15-0 v Glasgow University, Scottish Cup 1st rd; 30 Jan, 1960.
Record Defeat: 0-9 v Rangers, Division I; 4 Dec, 1897.
Most Capped Player: Godmundor Torfason, 29, Iceland.
Most League Appearances: 351: Tony Fitzpatrick, 1973-88.

ST MIRREN 2001–02 LEAGUE RECORD

Match No.	Date		Venue	Opponents	Result		H/T Score	Lg. Pos.	Goalscorers	Attendance
1	Aug	4	A	Partick Th	D	3-3	2-2		McLaughlin [16], Quitongo [25], Burns [64]	6603
2		11	H	Clyde	W	4-1	2-1	3	Yardley 2 [2,7], Kerr [64], Walker [80]	3668
3		18	A	Falkirk	L	2-3	1-0	5	McQuilken (og) [33], McGarry [59]	3748
4		25	H	Inverness CT	D	1-1	0-0	5	McGarry [50]	3492
5	Sept	8	A	Airdrieonians	D	0-0	0-0	6		2657
6		15	H	Ayr U	L	2-4	1-2	7	Yardley [18], Gillies (pen) [60]	3645
7		18	H	Ross Co	W	1-0	1-0	—	Gillies [2]	2264
8		22	A	Raith R	L	0-3	0-1	5		2465
9		29	H	Arbroath	W	1-0	1-0	4	Baltacha [17]	2733
10	Oct	13	H	Partick Th	W	1-0	0-0	3	Quitongo [67]	5244
11		20	A	Clyde	D	1-1	0-1	4	Gillies (pen) [64]	2481
12		27	A	Airdrieonians	D	0-0	0-0	4		4121
13	Nov	3	A	Inverness CT	W	2-1	1-1	3	Ross [14], Walker [50]	2343
14		10	A	Ross Co	W	1-0	0-0	3	McLaughlin [47]	3578
15		17	H	Ayr U	L	0-1	0-0	4		3897
16		24	A	Arbroath	W	2-0	1-0	3	Walker [27], Quitongo [87]	1392
17	Dec	1	H	Raith R	D	1-1	1-1	3	Quitongo [45]	3360
18		8	H	Falkirk	L	1-5	0-1	3	McLaughlin [64]	3852
19		15	A	Partick Th	L	0-1	0-0	3		4750
20		29	H	Inverness CT	D	0-0	0-0	4		3613
21	Jan	12	A	Ross Co	D	1-1	0-1	5	Gillies [60]	2648
22		19	A	Raith R	L	0-1	0-0	5		1849
23		22	A	Airdrieonians	W	3-2	1-2	—	Ross [32], McGinty 2 [64,77]	1803
24	Feb	2	H	Arbroath	L	2-3	0-2	4	Quitongo [56], McGinty (pen) [57]	2472
25		9	A	Falkirk	D	0-0	0-0	4		2386
26		16	H	Clyde	D	2-2	1-1	5	McGinty (pen) [44], Nicolson [55]	2827
27		26	A	Ayr U	L	1-4	0-2	—	McGinty [46]	1932
28	Mar	2	A	Inverness CT	L	2-4	1-1	6	Gillies (pen) [10], Ross [72]	1866
29		9	H	Airdrieonians	W	2-1	1-0	6	McGinty [17], Yardley [83]	3040
30		16	A	Ross Co	L	1-4	1-2	6	Ross [28]	2957
31		30	H	Raith R	W	1-0	1-0	8	McGowan [16]	4014
32	Apr	2	H	Ayr U	D	1-1	1-0	—	Gillies [25]	3002
33		6	A	Arbroath	W	3-0	1-0	6	Nicolson [10], McLaughlin 2 [54,61]	1312
34		13	H	Partick Th	L	0-2	0-1	8		7118
35		20	A	Clyde	L	1-3	1-1	8	Ross [20]	1480
36		27	H	Falkirk	D	0-0	0-0	8		3006

Final League Position: 8

Most League Goals in Season (Individual): 45: Dunky Walker, Division I; 1921-22.
Most Goals Overall (Individual): 221: David McCrae, 1923-34.

Honours
League Champions: First Division 1976-77, 1999-2000. Division II 1967-68; *Runners-up:* 1935-36.
Scottish Cup Winners: 1926, 1959, 1987. *Runners-up:* 1908, 1934, 1962.
League Cup Runners-up: 1955-56.
B&Q Cup Runners-up: 1993-94. *Victory Cup:* 1919-20. *Summer Cup:* 1943-44. *Anglo-Scottish Cup:* 1979-80.

European: *Cup Winners' Cup:* 4 matches (1987-88). *UEFA Cup:* 10 matches (1980-81, 1983-84, 1985-86).

Club colours: Shirt: Black and white vertical stripes. Shorts: White with black trim. Stockings: White with 2 black hoops. Change colours: Predominantly red.

Goalscorers: *League* (43): Gillies 6 (3 pens), McGinty 6 (2 pens), McLaughlin 5, Quitongo 5, Ross 5, Yardley 4, Walker 3, Nicolson 2, McGarry 2, Baltacha 1, Burns 1, Kerr 1, McGowan 1, own goal 1.
Scottish Cup (0):
CIS Cup (1): Quitongo 1.
Challenge Cup (1): Yardley 1.

Roy L 25	Baltacha S 9 + 4	Bowman G 17 + 2	McGowan J 24	McLaughlin B 31	Walker S 34	Quitongo J 33 + 1	Mackenzie S 26 + 2	McGarry S 11 + 10	Gillies R 27 + 4	Yardley M 16 + 7	Rudden P 2 + 5	Burns A 16 + 6	Murray H 27 + 5	Kerr C 11 + 5	Turner T 8 + 1	Nicolson I 17 + 6	Ross J 23 + 2	Wreh C — + 5	McKnight P 6 + 8	McGinty B 20 + 1	Robinson R — + 1	Robertson K 1 + 2	Hillcoat J 9	Strang S 1	McCann R — + 1	Dempster J — + 1	Keogh L — + 1	Lowing D 2	Lapping S — + 1	Guy G — + 1	Match No.
1	2	3	4¹	5	6	7	8	9²	10	11³	12	13	14																		1
1	14	10³		5	6	7²	2	9	8¹	11		13	12	3	4																2
1		10		5	6		2	9	8	11		7	4	3																	3
1	3²			5	6	7³	2	9¹	10	11	14	12	8	13	4																4
1	3¹			5	6	7	2	9	10	11		13	8²	12	4																5
1	3			5	6	7	2²	9³	10	11		12	8	4		13															6
1	3			5	6	7⁴		9³	10	11	2		8	4¹		12	13	14													7
1		4	5	6	7¹			10³	11		12	8	3²		2	13	14														8
1	2¹	4	5	6	9	7	13	10	11²			8	12		3																9
1		4	5	6	9²	7¹		10	11			8	12		2	3		13													10
1	3¹	4	5	6	9²	7		10	11			8		12	2		13														11
1	2	4	5	6	9	7		10¹	11²			8		13	3		13														12
1	2	4	5	6	9³	7	14		11¹			8	10²		13	3		12													13
1	2	4	5	6	9²	7	12		14			8	10²		13	3		11¹													14
1	2	4	5	6	9²	7	12		14			8	10³			3		13	11¹												15
1	2	4	5	6	9²	7		12				8¹	10			3		13	11												16
1	2²	4	5	6	9¹	7						8	10		13	3		12	11												17
1	2	4³	5	6	9¹	7²						8	10		14	3	13	12	11												18
1		4	5	6	7	8	9	13				10²	2			3	12	11													19
1	6		5	4	7	8²	12	2³				10			13	3		11¹	9	14											20
1	12	4	5¹	6	11²		13	8				10	7			2	3		9												21
1		5		6	12			8				10	7		4	2	3		11¹	9											22
1		5		6	7	2	13					10	8²		4	3	12	11¹	9												23
		5		6	7	10		12				8	4		2	3		11¹	9												24
1	12	3	5		6	7	10¹		11	13	2		4	8					9²												25
1⁰	6	4		5	7²		10	13				8	3		2	11			9	15											26
12	6		5	4	7		10	13				8²			2	3	11¹	9		1											27
13	3²	4	5	6		8	11	7				12	2¹	10				9		1											28
1		4	5	6	7	13		10	11			8²			2	3			9	15	16										29
	13	4³	5	6	9	7²		10	11			8			2¹	3				1				12	14						30
	3	4	5	6	7²	12	11¹	10				8	14		2				9		1					13³					31
	4²	5	6	11¹	7	12	10					8	3	13	2				9		1										32
	4		5	6²	7¹		12	10		13		8	3		2	11			9		1										33
	4		5	6	7¹	2²	13	10	12			8	3			11			9		1										34
	4¹		5		7²	8	14	10	13³	12			3		2	11			9		1							6			35
			5			8	11	10		13			7	3	4³	2²			9⁵		1							6	12	14	36

STENHOUSEMUIR
Second Division

Year Formed: 1884. *Ground & Address:* Ochilview Park, Gladstone Rd, Stenhousemuir FK5 5QL. *Telephone:* 01324 562992. *Fax:* 01324 562980.
Ground Capacity: total: 2374, seated: 626. *Size of Pitch:* 110yd × 72yd.
Chairman: Mike Laing. *Secretary:* David O. Reid. *General Manager:* George W. Peat. *Commercial Manager:* Jock Rolland.
Manager: John McVeigh. *Assistant Manager:* Andy Smith. *Physio:* John Watson.
Managers since 1975: H. Glasgow, J. Black, A. Rose, W. Henderson, A. Rennie, J. Meakin, D. Lawson, T. Christie, G. Armstrong, Brian Fairley.
Club Nickname(s): The Warriors. *Previous Grounds:* Tryst Ground 1884-86, Goschen Park 1886-90.
Record Attendance: 12,500 v East Fife, Scottish Cup 4th rd: 11 Mar, 1950.
Record Transfer Fee received: £70,000 for Euan Donaldson to St Johnstone (May 1995).
Record Transfer Fee paid: £20,000 to Livingston for Ian Little (June 1995).
Record Victory: 9-2 v Dundee U, Division II: 19 Apr, 1937.
Record Defeat: 2-11 v Dunfermline Ath. Division II: 27 Sept, 1930.
Most Capped Player: —.
Most League Appearances: 360: Archie Rose.

STENHOUSEMUIR 2001–02 LEAGUE RECORD

Match No.	Date	Venue	Opponents	Result	H/T Score	Lg. Pos.	Goalscorers	Attendance
1	Aug 4	A	Morton	L	1-4	0-1	—	English [85]	2050
2	11	H	Stranraer	D	0-0	0-0	0		341
3	18	A	Forfar Ath	W	2-1	0-1	6	Donald 2 [65, 88]	415
4	25	H	Berwick R	W	3-0	3-0	3	Ferguson 2 (1 pen) [10, 24 (p)], Donald G [36]	505
5	Sept 2	A	Queen of the S	L	0-2	0-1	—		1153
6	8	A	Alloa Ath	W	1-0	0-0	3	Mooney [58]	632
7	15	H	Hamilton A	W	2-0	0-0	2	Mooney [60], English [88]	547
8	22	H	Clydebank	D	2-2	0-2	3	Ferguson [64], Jackson [67]	389
9	29	A	Cowdenbeath	D	1-1	0-0	5	English [70]	354
10	Oct 13	H	Morton	L	0-3	0-2	5		664
11	20	A	Stranraer	L	1-6	0-1	6	Stone [83]	357
12	27	H	Alloa Ath	D	1-1	0-1	6	Graham D [70]	568
13	Nov 3	A	Berwick R	D	1-1	0-1	6	Irvine (pen) [80]	387
14	10	A	Hamilton A	W	3-2	1-0	6	Irvine 3 (1 pen) [25, 50, 70 (p)]	1563
15	24	H	Queen of the S	D	1-1	0-1	6	Irvine (pen) [74]	460
16	Dec 1	A	Clydebank	L	2-3	2-2	6	Storrar [1], Ferguson [10]	235
17	15	H	Cowdenbeath	L	0-3	0-1	7		312
18	Jan 12	H	Berwick R	L	1-3	1-1	8	Ferguson [20]	406
19	19	A	Queen of the S	L	0-1	0-0	10		1224
20	Feb 2	A	Cowdenbeath	W	4-2	0-2	7	Irvine 2 (2 pens) [69, 80], Ferguson [72], Graham D [86]	259
21	9	H	Clydebank	D	0-0	0-0	8		379
22	16	H	Stranraer	D	0-0	0-0	8		365
23	H	Forfar Ath	D	1-1	0-1	—	English [88]	227
24	Mar 2	A	Berwick R	L	1-2	0-1	9	Donald G [85]	420
25	9	H	Alloa Ath	W	1-0	1-0	9	English [43]	507
26	12	A	Morton	W	1-0	0-0	—	Milne [70]	1038
27	16	A	Hamilton A	D	0-0	0-0	8		1910
28	19	H	Hamilton A	L	0-3	0-1	—		344
29	23	H	Queen of the S	L	1-4	1-3	9	Wood [10]	577
30	26	A	Forfar Ath	L	0-2	0-0	—		340
31	30	A	Clydebank	D	0-0	0-0	9		208
32	Apr 2	A	Alloa Ath	L	0-4	0-1	—		571
33	6	H	Cowdenbeath	L	0-1	0-0	9		466
34	13	H	Morton	L	2-3	0-1	9	English [51], Donald G [67]	559
35	20	A	Stranraer	L	0-1	0-0	10		391
36	27	H	Forfar Ath	D	0-0	0-0	9		442

Final League Position: 9

Most League Goals in Season (Individual): 32: Robert Taylor, Division II: 1925-26.
Most Goals Overall (Individual): —.

Honours
League Champions: Third Division runners-up: 1998-99. *Scottish Cup:* Semi-finals 1902-03. Quarter-finals 1948-49, 1949-50, 1994-95. *League Cup:* Quarter-finals 1947-48, 1960-61, 1975-76. *League Challenge Cup:* Winners 1995-96.

Club colours: Shirt: Maroon. Shorts: White. Stockings: Maroon.

Goalscorers: *League* (33): Irvine 7 (5 pens), English 6, Ferguson 6 (1 pen), Donald G 5, Graham D 2, Mooney 2, Jackson 1, Milne 1, Stone 1, Storrar 1, Wood 1.
Scottish Cup (0):
CIS Cup (2): Abbott 1, Ferguson 1.
Challenge Cup (1): Mooney 1.

Graham M 10	Storrar A 27 + 6	Donaldson E 13 + 2	Davidson G 10	Stone M 35	Sandison J 8 + 1	Jackson C 32	Donald B 4 + 7	Ferguson J 24	Donald G 20 + 3	English I 25 + 6	Abbott G 8 + 1	Mooney M 11 + 6	McGurk R 4	Vella S 10 + 2	Shanks P 1 + 1	Cormack P 13 + 3	Graham D 16 + 9	Milne D 20 + 1	Murphy S 3 + 2	Shearer G — + 4	Miller P — + 3	McKeown D 25	Wood C 15 + 6	Forrest F 2 + 1	Connaghan D 4	Irvine W 11 + 11	Jarvie P 5	Clyde R 1 + 1	Wilson M 15	Carlin A 17	Dick J 1	Harvey P 2 + 1	Taggart C — + 2	Grant M 4 + 2	Black G — + 1	Match No
1	2	3	4	5	6	7	8	9²	10¹	11	12	13																								1
	2	3		5²		8	12	9¹	6	10	11³	7		1	4	13	14																			2
1	2	3	4	6		7	12	9	8	11	10¹			5																						3
1	2	3	4	6		7	13	9	8	12	11²	10¹		5																						4
1	2	3	4	6¹		7	12	9	8	13	11	10²		5																						5
1	2	3	4	6			7	9	8	12	11	10¹		5																						6
	2	3	4	6		7	8	9¹		12	11	10	1	5																						7
	2	3	4¹	6		7	8²	9		13	11	10	1	5		12																				8
1	2	3		6		7	12	9	8²	11	10		5			4¹	13																			9
1	2	3		6		7		9		11			5			10	4²	8¹	12	13																10
1	2	3	4			7				11			5¹			9²	8		13		6	10	12													11
	2¹		4	5	7				11		1					9²	8	14	12	13	3	10³	6													12
	2³	3	4	5	7¹	12			11¹				14			9	8	13			6	10														13
1	2	3	4	5	7	12			9¹				14			8²		13³	11		6	10														14
	2		4	5	7	9										11	8				3	6	10	1												15
	2	13	6¹	4	5²	7		9								11	8				3		10	1	12											16
	2		4	5¹	7	9²			12	13						11	8²				3	14	10	1	6											17
	2	13	6	5		9		11		7¹						12	4				3	8²	10	1												18
	2¹		6	5	13	9		11³		12						14	4				3	8	10²	1	7											19
	7		4		8	9	12	11¹		10³						5	14				3	6	13		2²	1										20
	7		4		8	12	9	10								5					3	11¹			2	1	6									21
	7²		4	6		13	9	12								5	10¹	8²			3	11	14		2	1										22
	12		4	8		6	9									5¹	13	7			3	11²	10		2	1										23
	7²		4	10		6	9									5	11	8¹			3	12	13		2	1										24
	14		4	8		9	6	10¹								5	7¹	13			3	11²	12		2	1										25
			4	8		9	6	10²								5	13	7			3	11	12		2¹	1										26
	2		4	8		6	10	13								5	9²				3	11	12		1			7¹								27
	2¹		4	8		6	10²	14								5	13	7¹			3	11	12		1											28
	2			8		9	4	10³								5	13	6¹			3	11²	7		1			12	14						29
	14		4	6	8		9	7¹								5³					3	11	10		2²	1		13	12						30
	14		4		8		9¹	5	11²							10	6				3	13	12		2	1			7³						31
			4	8		6¹										5	10	7	13		3	12	9		2	1		11²							32
	14		4	6			9²	5	11							10	8¹				3	13	12		2	1		7²							33
	14		4	6			9¹	5	11							10	9³				3	13	12		2	1		7²							34
	7		4²	10			6	9¹								13	11³	8			3	5			2	1		12				14			35
			4				6	9²						10		12	8				3	11¹	5		13			2	1		7				36

STIRLING ALBION Third Division

Year Formed: 1945. *Ground & Address:* Forthbank Stadium, Springkerse Industrial Estate, Stirling FK7 7UJ.
Telephone: 01786 450399. *Fax:* 01786 448592.
Ground Capacity: 3808, seated: 2508. *Size of Pitch:* 110yd × 74yd.
Chairman: Peter McKenzie. *Secretary:* Mrs Marlyn Hallam.
Manager: To be appointed. *Assistant Manager:* To be appointed. *Player-Coach:* Allan Moore. *Physio:* George Cameron.
Managers since 1975: A. Smith, G. Peebles, J. Fleeting, J. Brogan, K. Drinkell, J. Philliben. *Club Nickname(s):* The Binos.
Previous Grounds: Annfield 1945-92.
Record Attendance: 26,400 (at Annfield) v Celtic, Scottish Cup 4th rd; 14 Mar, 1959. 3808 v Aberdeen, Scottish Cup
4th rd, 15 February 1996 (Forthbank).
Record Transfer Fee received: £70,000 for John Philliben to Doncaster R (Mar 1984).
Record Transfer Fee paid: £25,000 for Craig Taggart from Falkirk (Aug 1994).
Record Victory: 20-0 v Selkirk, Scottish Cup 1st rd; 8 Dec, 1984.
Record Defeat: 0-9 v Dundee U, Division I; 30 Dec, 1967.
Most Capped Player: —.
Most League Appearances: 504: Matt McPhee, 1967-81.

STIRLING ALBION 2001–02 LEAGUE RECORD

Match No.	Date	Venue	Opponents	Result	H/T Score	Lg. Pos.	Goalscorers	Atten-dance
1	Aug 4	H	Peterhead	W 2-1	1-1	—	Henderson 22, Higgins 57	588
2	11	A	Albion R	W 3-1	3-0	2	Geraghty 11, Henderson (pen) 43, Devine 44	444
3	18	H	Brechin C	L 1-3	1-1	4	Geraghty 24	626
4	25	A	Elgin C	W 3-2	1-1	2	Mailer (og) 45, Devine 71, Williams 85	769
5	Sept 8	H	East Fife	W 2-1	0-0	2	Williams 47, Devine 89	553
6	15	A	Montrose	L 0-4	0-3	3		400
7	19	H	Dumbarton	L 4-5	2-3	—	Henderson 41, Williams 3 43, 54, 61	446
8	22	A	East Stirling	D 1-1	1-0	5	Devine 1	403
9	29	H	Queen's Park	D 0-0	0-0	4		584
10	Oct 13	A	Peterhead	D 3-3	1-2	5	Hay 4, Williams 52, Henderson (pen) 85	642
11	20	H	Albion R	D 2-2	2-1	5	Williams 20, Goldie 24	489
12	27	A	East Fife	D 1-1	0-1	6	Geraghty 53	495
13	Nov 3	H	Elgin C	L 0-1	0-1	8		524
14	10	H	Montrose	D 1-1	0-0	6	Higgins 60	392
15	24	A	Dumbarton	L 1-4	0-2	6	Williams 55	861
16	Dec 1	H	East Stirling	D 1-1	1-1	7	Higgins 31	438
17	15	A	Queen's Park	D 2-2	1-1	7	Ross 16, Cremin 82	558
18	Jan 12	A	Elgin C	L 1-2	0-2	7	Williams (pen) 79	564
19	19	H	Dumbarton	W 2-1	1-0	7	Brannigan 41, Williams 90	554
20	26	A	Montrose	W 3-1	0-1	7	Nugent 79, Williams 86, Ross 90	348
21	Feb 2	H	Queen's Park	W 3-2	2-1	7	Geraghty 12, Devine 43, Ross 77	564
22	9	A	East Stirling	L 0-3	0-1	7		389
23	16	A	Albion R	L 0-2	0-2	7		420
24	27	H	Peterhead	L 0-2	0-1	—		335
25	Mar 2	H	Elgin C	W 3-1	1-0	7	Geraghty 34, Williams 2 66, 90	355
26	6	H	East Fife	L 0-1	0-1	—		361
27	9	A	East Fife	D 1-1	0-1	7	Williams 65	477
28	12	A	Brechin C	L 1-3	0-0	7	Williams 59	398
29	16	H	Montrose	L 0-1	0-0	7		385
30	19	H	Brechin C	L 1-3	1-0	—	Geraghty 30	315
31	23	A	Dumbarton	L 0-2	0-0	8		792
32	30	H	East Stirling	W 1-0	1-0	8	Williams 37	436
33	Apr 6	A	Queen's Park	D 0-0	0-0	7		496
34	13	A	Peterhead	L 1-5	1-1	8	Crozier 20	523
35	20	A	Albion R	L 0-3	0-2	9		516
36	27	A	Brechin C	L 1-2	0-2	9	Williams 63	449

Final League Position: 9

Most League Goals in Season (Individual): 27: Joe Hughes, Division II; 1969-70.
Most Goals Overall (Individual): 129: Billy Steele, 1971-83.

Honours
League Champions: Division II 1952-53, 1957-58, 1960-61, 1964-65. Second Division 1976-77, 1990-91, 1995-96;
Runners-up: Division II 1948-49, 1950-51.
Scottish Cup: —. *League Cup:* —.

Club colours: Shirt: Red and white halves. Shorts: Red with white piping. Stockings: Red with 2 white hoops at top.

Goalscorers: *League* (45): Williams 17 (1 pen), Geraghty 6. Devine 5, Henderson 4 (2 pens), Higgins 3, Ross 3, Brannigan 1, Cremin 1, Crozier 1, Goldie 1, Hay 1, Nugent 1, own goal 1.
Scottish Cup (2): Munro 1, Williams 1.
CIS Cup (5): Williams 4, Munro 1.
Challenge Cup (1): Henderson 1.

Reid C 33	Hay P 29+3	Devine S 24+1	Reilly S 27	Morrison G 16+3	McLellan K 21+5	Moriarty T 13	Henderson N 14	Geraghty M 24+2	Higgins G 9+4	McCallion K 13+9	Bailey L —+1	Stuart W 6+11	Munro G 11+12	Ross D 4+19	Edwards C 4+2	Williams A 29+3	Goldie D 12	Kelly G 2+2	Davies D 1	Raeside R 6	Middleton G 2	De Gregorio R 1	Nugent P 22	Kearney D 9+1	Cremin B 2+3	Brannigan K 19	Crozier B 13	Cosgrove S 9+1	Heighton H 3	O'Brien D 9+3	Butler D 3+1	Zujovic G 2+1	Hutchison S 3+2	Wilson D —+1	Beveridge R 1+1	Match No.
1	2	3	4	5	6^2	7	8	9	10^1	11^3	12	13	14																							1
1	2	3	4	5	6	7^3	8	9	10^2	11^1	12	13	14																							2
1	2^3		4	5	6^1	7	8	9	10^2	11		3	14	12	13																					3
1	2	11	4	5	6^1	7	8	9^2	10		12	13				3																				4
1	2	11	4	5	6	7^1	8	9			12	13	10^2			3																				5
1	2	3		5	6	4	8	9			12	7^2	14	10^3	11^1	13																				6
1		3	2^1	5	6	7^1	8	9			13	12	14	10	4	11^2																				7
1		3	2^2		6^1	4	8	9	11			12		13	10	5		7																		8
1	7	3	2	4	6		8	9				12	11^1	13	10	5																				9
1	11	3	2	4	6^2	7^1	8	9^3			13		12	14		10	5																			10
1	11	3	2^1	4	6^2	7	8^3	9			13		12	14		10	5																			11
1	2			4	6	7^1	8	9			12			10	3					5	11															12
1	2			4	14	7^1	8^3	9^3	13		12			10	3					5	11	6														13
1		2				8	9^2	10	6		12	7		13	3^1					4					5	11										14
1	8							10^1	3		7	11	12		9^2	5	13			4					2	6										15
1	7						9	8		12	11	13	5	10^2		6^1				4					2	3										16
1	7	3^1			6^2			12		14	11	10^2	4	9						5					2	8	13									17
1	7	3	4	13	6^1			12		14	8^2	9								2	11	10^3	5													18
1	2	3	4	13			14	8	7^2		10^1	9								6^3	11	12	5													19
1	2	3	4	12			10^1	11		13	9	7								6^1			5	8												20
1	2	3	4	13			10^1	11^2		12	9	7								6			5	8												21
1	2	3		8^2			10^1	6		13	12	4^3	9							7	11	14	5													22
1	2	3	4	13			10	11^2		12	9									7^1			5	8	6											23
	3	4				2^2				13	8^1	12	11^2	10		9							7^1		5	8	6	1	14							24
14	3	6	4					10^1	12^2		11^2			9							2		5	7	8	1	13									25
12	3	6	4					10^2				11^1	13	9							2		5	7	8	1										26
1	6	3^1	8	4							14			9							2		5	7	10^2	12	11^3	13								27
1	6		8	4								13		9							2		5	7	$7^1$2	3	11^2	10								28
1	7		4		6			9	12	13		11^1		9							2		5		8	3^2		10								29
1	6		4		11^1			10		13	12			9							2		5	7	8	3^2										30
1	7		4	13	8^2				10					9^3							2		5	6		3	12	11^1	14							31
1	3^4		4	14					10^1					9							2		5	7	9^2	11		6								32
1	3	12	4	8					10^2			13		9							2		5	7		11		6^1								33
1	8	3	4^1	6^3					10^2			13	14	9							2		5	7		11		12								34
1	2	3			8^2						4		14	9							6	12	10^3	5	7^1		11							13		35
1	13	3									6	7^1	12	4	9						2			5^9		8	11^2		14		10					36

STRANRAER
Second Division

Year Formed: 1870. *Ground & Address:* Stair Park, London Rd, Stranraer DG9 8BS. *Telephone:* 01776 703271.
Ground Capacity: 5600. *Size of Pitch:* 110yd × 70yd.
Chairman: R. J. Clanachan. *Secretary:* Graham Rodgers. *Commercial Manager:* T. L. Sutherland.
Manager: Billy McLaren.
Managers since 1975: J. Hughes, N. Hood, G. Hamilton, D. Sneddon, J. Clark, R. Clark, A. McAnespie, C. Money.
Club Nickname(s): The Blues. *Previous Grounds:* None.
Record Attendance: 6500 v Rangers, Scottish Cup 1st rd: 24 Jan, 1948.
Record Transfer Fee received: £90,000 for Mark Campbell to Ayr Utd, 1999.
Record Transfer Fee paid: £15,000 for Colin Harkness from Kilmarnock (Aug 1989).
Record Victory: 7-0 v Brechin C, Division II: 6 Feb, 1965.
Record Defeat: 1-11 v Queen of the South, Scottish Cup 1st rd: 16 Jan, 1932.
Most Capped Player: —.
Most League Appearances: 301, Keith Knox, 1986-90: 1999-2001.
Most League Goals in Season (Individual): 59, Tommy Sloan.
Most Goals Overall (Individual): —.

STRANRAER 2001–02 LEAGUE RECORD

Match No.	Date	Venue	Opponents	Result		H/T Score	Lg. Pos.	Goalscorers	Attendance
1	Aug 4	H	Cowdenbeath	W	3-0	1-0	—	Harty 3 [15, 49, 88]	473
2	11	A	Stenhousemuir	D	0-0	0-0	0		341
3	18	H	Alloa Ath	D	1-1	1-1	4	Wright [45]	444
4	25	A	Morton	L	1-1	0-1	5	Gaughan [87]	1727
5	Sept 8	H	Queen of the S	D	2-2	2-1	6	Harty (pen) [25], Shaw [36]	696
6	15	H	Berwick R	L	0-2	0-2	7		379
7	18	A	Hamilton A	W	1-0	0-0	—	Jenkins [89]	1539
8	22	H	Forfar Ath	W	2-0	0-0	5	Harty 2 (1 pen) [49, 84 (p)]	360
9	29	A	Clydebank	W	3-1	2-0	3	Wright [5], Macdonald [37], Aitken [88]	201
10	Oct 13	A	Cowdenbeath	D	2-2	1-0	2	Wingate [40], Finlayson [56]	277
11	20	H	Stenhousemuir	W	6-1	1-0	1	Harty 3 [3, 52, 79], Finlayson [47], Aitken [51], Grace [66]	357
12	27	A	Queen of the S	L	0-1	0-0	2		3083
13	Nov 3	H	Morton	L	1-4	0-1	4	Finlayson [59]	523
14	10	A	Berwick R	D	2-2	1-1	4	Finlayson [8], Farrell [77]	382
15	24	H	Hamilton A	W	2-1	2-1	2	Hodge [6], Shaw [32]	436
16	Dec 1	A	Forfar Ath	D	1-1	0-1	2	Finlayson [57]	420
17	15	H	Clydebank	L	0-1	0-0	3		398
18	29	H	Cowdenbeath	W	2-1	1-0	2	Shaw 2 [42, 69]	385
19	Jan 12	A	Morton	D	2-2	2-1	3	Harty [23], Bradford [28]	1368
20	19	A	Hamilton A	L	0-2	0-1	4		1808
21	26	H	Berwick R	D	2-2	1-0	3	Blair [45], Harty [47]	370
22	Feb 2	A	Clydebank	W	2-1	0-1	2	Finlayson 2 [53, 75]	231
23	9	H	Forfar Ath	L	0-3	0-2	3		366
24	16	A	Stenhousemuir	D	0-0	0-0	4		365
25	23	H	Alloa Ath	L	0-2	0-1	4		320
26	Mar 2	H	Morton	D	0-0	0-0	4		421
27	9	A	Queen of the S	L	1-3	0-0	6	Wright [47]	2094
28	12	A	Queen of the S	L	1-2	1-1	—	Wingate [42]	895
29	16	A	Berwick R	L	1-4	0-0	7	Smith A (og) [74]	424
30	19	A	Alloa Ath	D	2-2	2-0	—	Grace [2], Kerr [9]	378
31	23	H	Hamilton A	W	3-2	1-0	6	Kerr [44], Wright [76], Harty (pen) [80]	453
32	30	A	Forfar Ath	L	2-3	2-0	6	Harty 2 [39, 45]	427
33	Apr 6	H	Clydebank	D	1-1	0-0	7	Harty [64]	365
34	13	A	Cowdenbeath	D	1-1	0-1	7	Aitken [89]	309
35	20	H	Stenhousemuir	W	1-0	0-0	6	Harty [88]	391
36	27	A	Alloa Ath	D	0-0	0-0	7		613

Final League Position: 7

Honours
League Champions: Second Division 1993-94, 1997-98.
Qualifying Cup Winners: 1937.
League Challenge Cup Winners: 1996-97.

Club colours: Shirt: Blue with white side panels. Shorts: Blue with white side panels. Stockings: Blue with two white hoops.

Goalscorers: *League* (48): Harty 16 (3 pens), Finlayson 7, Shaw 4, Wright 4, Aitken 3, Grace 2, Kerr 2, Wingate 2, Blair 1, Bradford 1, Farrell 1, Gaughan 1, Hodge 1, Jenkins 1, Macdonald 1, own goal 1.
Scottish Cup (1): Harty 1.
CIS Cup (3): Finlayson 1, Harty 1, Shaw 1.
Challenge Cup (10): Gallagher M 3, Wright 2, Finlayson 1, Gaughan 1, Harty 1, Jenkins 1, Johnstone 1.

McGeown M 35	Wingate D 34	Hodge A 21+3	Gaughan K 15+4	Johnstone D 8	Macdonald W 32	Finlayson K 24+6	Aitken S 36	Harty I 28+2	Shaw G 27+2	Jenkins A 13+11	Weir M 1+7	Gallagher M 2+6	Farrell D 21+2	Sherry M 1+1	Wright F 31+2	George D 3+3	Duthie M 2	Blair P 11+10	Paterson A 10+3	Grace A 16+5	O'Neill S —+1	Stewart C 1	Rodosthenous M —+1	Bradford J 3	Gallagher P —+2	Stirling J 11+2	Glancy M 5+1	Kerr P 2	Dempster J 3+2	Match No.
1	2	3	4	5	6^2	7	8	9	10	11^1	12	13																		1
1	2	13	5	3	8	10	6	9		7^1			12	4	11^2															2
1	7		4	2	8^2	11	6	9	10	12		13	3		5^1															3
1	5	14	2	4	8^2	11	6	12	10^3	7			9^1		3			13												4
1	5		2	4	6	7^1	8	9	10^2				12	13	3			11												5
1	5			3		12	8	9	10				11^2	4	13			6	2	7^1										6
1	5		2	3	6^1	7	8	9	10	12			4					11												7
1	4		2	5	6^2	7^3	8	9	10^1	3	13	12			14^2			11												8
1	4	5	2	3^1	7	11	8	9	10	12			6																	9
1	4	3	2		10	7	8	9				12			11	5		6^1												10
1	11	2			8	10	6	9^3		14			4		3^1			12	7	5	15									11
1	2	5^1			11	7	8	9			13		4		10			12	3^2	6										12
	5	11			9	10	8			7^1			4^2		3			12	2	6		1	15							13
1	3^1	5	2		10^2	9	8			11			4		6			12	13	7										14
1	2		5		13	9	11	6	10^3	14			4		3			12	7^2	8^1										15
1	2^1		5	3		11	7	8	9				4		10			12	13	6^2										16
1	2		5		12	11^2	7	8	9	6			4		10			3	13											17
1	2	11			12	7	10	8	13	9			4^1		3			14	5^2	6^3										18
1	4	3^1	13		12		6	9		7			2		8^1			5	11	10										19
1	3	5	2^3		7	12	6	9	10				4					13	14	8^1				11^2						20
1	4	3			8^1	11	6	9	13	12			5		7			2		10^3										21
1	2	3			8	11	6	9	10				4					7		5										22
1	2^2	3			8	11	6	9	10^3	12			4					7^1	13	5					14					23
1	2^2	3			7^3	10	8	9		12			4					6		13					14	5^1	11			24
1		3	5		7^2	10	8	9	13				4^2					2	12	6^1						14	11			25
1	2	3^3			8^2		6	9^1	14	12			4					7		5						13	11		10	26
1	2	12			8^3		6	9	10	13			4					3	11							14	5^1	7^2		27
1	2	3^2			8	11	6	9	7^1	12			4					5								13	10			28
1	2	11			8	10^1	6	9	13	12			4^1					5								14	3		7^2	29
1	4				8		6	9	10				2					3	7^1	5						12	11			30
1	4				8		6^1	9	10				2					3	12	7						5	11			31
1	4		5		12		6	9	10				2					3	8^1							11		7		32
1	4				8		6	9	10	13			2^1					3	12	5						7		11^1		33
1	2		5		12		6	9	8				4					3	10	7^2						11^1			13	34
1	4		5		12		6	9	8				2					3	7	11^2						13			10^1	35
1	3	2^2	5		12		6	9	10				4					7	8							11^1			13	36

SCOTTISH LEAGUE TABLES 2001–02

Premier Division

	P	W	D	L	F	A	W	D	L	F	A	Pts	GD
		Home			*Goals*		*Away*			*Goals*			
Celtic	38	18	1	0	51	9	15	3	1	43	9	103	76
Rangers	38	14	4	1	42	11	11	6	2	40	16	85	55
Livingston	38	9	5	4	23	17	7	5	8	27	30	58	3
Aberdeen	38	12	2	5	31	19	4	5	10	20	30	55	2
Hearts	38	8	3	8	30	27	6	3	10	22	30	48	−5
Dunfermline Ath	38	9	4	6	25	24	3	5	11	16	40	45	−23
Kilmarnock	38	7	6	6	24	26	6	4	9	20	28	49	−10
Dundee U	38	6	5	8	18	30	6	5	8	20	29	46	−21
Dundee	38	8	5	6	23	24	4	3	12	18	31	44	−14
Hibernian	38	6	6	7	35	30	4	5	10	16	26	41	−5
Motherwell	38	8	5	6	30	25	3	2	14	19	44	40	−20
St Johnstone	38	2	3	15	11	32	3	3	12	13	30	21	−38

First Division

	P	W	D	L	F	A	W	D	L	F	A	Pts	GD
		Home			*Goals*		*Away*			*Goals*			
Partick T	36	12	6	0	38	15	7	3	8	23	23	66	23
Airdrieonians	36	8	6	4	31	19	7	5	6	28	21	56	19
Ayr U	36	8	6	4	25	16	5	7	6	28	28	52	9
Ross Co	36	10	2	6	33	21	4	8	6	18	22	52	8
Clyde	36	8	6	4	27	21	5	4	9	24	35	49	−5
Inverness CT	36	11	3	4	47	22	2	6	10	13	29	48	9
Arbroath	36	9	3	6	22	28	5	3	10	20	31	48	−17
St Mirren	36	6	8	4	19	19	5	4	9	24	34	45	−10
Falkirk	36	5	5	8	24	36	5	4	9	25	37	39	−24
Raith R	36	7	5	6	31	25	1	6	11	19	37	35	−12

Second Division

	P	W	D	L	F	A	W	D	L	F	A	Pts	GD
		Home			*Goals*		*Away*			*Goals*			
Queen of the S	36	12	2	4	33	19	8	5	5	31	23	67	22
Alloa Ath	36	8	8	2	35	17	7	6	5	20	16	59	22
Forfar Ath	36	8	3	7	25	25	7	5	6	26	22	53	4
Clydebank	36	8	4	6	25	23	6	5	7	19	22	51	−1
Hamilton A	36	9	5	4	26	15	4	4	10	23	29	48	5
Berwick R	36	6	4	8	19	28	6	7	5	25	24	47	−8
Stranraer	36	7	5	6	27	25	3	10	5	21	26	45	−3
Cowdenbeath	36	5	8	5	27	28	6	3	9	22	23	44	−2
Stenhousemuir	36	3	8	7	15	25	5	4	9	18	32	36	−24
Morton	36	3	8	7	20	28	4	6	8	28	35	35	−15

Third Division

	P	W	D	L	F	A	W	D	L	F	A	Pts	GD
		Home			*Goals*		*Away*			*Goals*			
Brechin C	36	12	4	2	38	14	10	3	5	29	24	73	29
Dumbarton	36	10	4	4	30	22	8	3	7	29	26	61	11
Albion R	36	8	5	5	28	23	8	6	4	23	19	59	9
Peterhead	36	9	4	5	36	26	8	1	9	27	26	56	11
Montrose	36	9	2	7	25	20	7	5	6	18	19	55	4
Elgin C	36	9	3	6	26	20	4	5	9	19	27	47	−2
East Stirlingshire	36	8	1	9	27	27	4	3	11	24	31	40	−7
East Fife	36	6	4	8	23	26	5	3	10	16	30	40	−17
Stirling Albion	36	6	4	8	23	29	3	6	9	22	39	37	−23
Queen's Park	36	4	6	8	17	21	5	2	11	21	32	35	−15

SCOTTISH LEAGUE HONOURS 1890 to 2002

*On goal average (ratio)/difference.   †Held jointly after indecisive play-off.   ‡Won on deciding match.
††Held jointly.   ¶Two points deducted for fielding ineligible player.
Competition suspended 1940–45 during war: Regional Leagues operating.   ‡‡Two points deducted for registration irregularities.

PREMIER LEAGUE

Maximum points: 108

	First	Pts	Second	Pts	Third	Pts
1998–99	Rangers	77	Celtic	71	St Johnstone	57
1999–2000	Rangers	90	Celtic	69	Hearts	54

Maximum points: 114

2000–01	Celtic	97	Rangers	82	Hibernian	66
2001–02	Celtic	103	Rangers	85	Livingston	58

PREMIER DIVISION

Maximum points: 72

1975–76	Rangers	54	Celtic	48	Hibernian	43
1976–77	Celtic	55	Rangers	46	Aberdeen	43
1977–78	Rangers	55	Aberdeen	53	Dundee U	40
1978–79	Celtic	48	Rangers	45	Dundee U	44
1979–80	Aberdeen	48	Celtic	47	St Mirren	42
1980–81	Celtic	56	Aberdeen	49	Rangers*	44
1981–82	Celtic	55	Aberdeen	53	Rangers	43
1982–83	Dundee U	56	Celtic*	55	Aberdeen	55
1983–84	Aberdeen	57	Celtic	50	Dundee U	47
1984–85	Aberdeen	59	Celtic	52	Dundee U	47
1985–86	Celtic*	50	Hearts	50	Dundee U	47

Maximum points: 88

1986–87	Rangers	69	Celtic	63	Dundee U	60
1987–88	Celtic	72	Hearts	62	Rangers	60

Maximum points: 72

1988–89	Rangers	56	Aberdeen	50	Celtic	46
1989–90	Rangers	51	Aberdeen*	44	Hearts	44
1990–91	Rangers	55	Aberdeen	53	Celtic*	41

Maximum points: 88

1991–92	Rangers	72	Hearts	63	Celtic	62
1992–93	Rangers	73	Aberdeen	64	Celtic	60
1993–94	Rangers	58	Aberdeen	55	Motherwell	54

Maximum points: 108

1994–95	Rangers	69	Motherwell	54	Hibernian	53
1995–96	Rangers	87	Celtic	83	Aberdeen*	55
1996–97	Rangers	80	Celtic	75	Dundee U	60
1997–98	Celtic	74	Rangers	72	Hearts	67

FIRST DIVISION

Maximum points: 52

1975–76	Partick T	41	Kilmarnock	35	Montrose	30

Maximum points: 78

1976–77	St Mirren	62	Clydebank	58	Dundee	51
1977–78	Morton*	58	Hearts	58	Dundee	57
1978–79	Dundee	55	Kilmarnock*	54	Clydebank	54
1979–80	Hearts	53	Airdrieonians	51	Ayr U*	44
1980–81	Hibernian	57	Dundee	52	St Johnstone	51
1981–82	Motherwell	61	Kilmarnock	51	Hearts	50
1982–83	St Johnstone	55	Hearts	54	Clydebank	50
1983–84	Morton	54	Dumbarton	51	Partick T	46
1984–85	Motherwell	50	Clydebank	48	Falkirk	45
1985–86	Hamilton A	56	Falkirk	45	Kilmarnock	44

Maximum points: 88

1986–87	Morton	57	Dunfermline Ath	56	Dumbarton	53
1987–88	Hamilton A	56	Meadowbank T	52	Clydebank	49

Maximum points: 78

1988–89	Dunfermline Ath	54	Falkirk	52	Clydebank	48
1989–90	St Johnstone	58	Airdrieonians	54	Clydebank	44
1990–91	Falkirk	54	Airdrieonians	53	Dundee	52

Maximum points: 88

1991–92	Dundee	58	Partick T*	57	Hamilton A	57
1992–93	Raith R	65	Kilmarnock	54	Dunfermline Ath	52
1993–94	Falkirk	66	Dunfermline Ath	65	Airdrieonians	54

Maximum points: 108

1994–95	Raith R	69	Dunfermline Ath*	68	Dundee	68
1995–96	Dunfermline Ath	71	Dundee U*	67	Morton	67
1996–97	St Johnstone	80	Airdieonians	60	Dundee*	58
1997–98	Dundee	70	Falkirk	65	Raith R*	60
1998–99	Hibernian	89	Falkirk	66	Ayr U	62
1999–2000	St Mirren	76	Dunfermline Ath	71	Falkirk	68
2000–01	Livingston	76	Ayr U	69	Falkirk	56
2001–02	Partick T	66	Airdrieonians	56	Ayr U	52

SECOND DIVISION

	First	Pts	Second	Pts	Third	Pts
			Maximum points: 52			
1975–76	Clydebank*	40	Raith R	40	Alloa	35
			Maximum points: 78			
1976–77	Stirling A	55	Alloa	51	Dunfermline Ath	50
1977–78	Clyde*	53	Raith R	53	Dunfermline Ath	48
1978–79	Berwick R	54	Dunfermline Ath	52	Falkirk	50
1979–80	Falkirk	50	East Stirling	49	Forfar Ath	46
1980–81	Queen's Park	50	Queen of the S	46	Cowdenbeath	45
1981–82	Clyde	59	Alloa*	50	Arbroath	50
1982–83	Brechin C	55	Meadowbank T	54	Arbroath	49
1983–84	Forfar Ath	63	East Fife	47	Berwick R	43
1984–85	Montrose	53	Alloa	50	Dunfermline Ath	49
1985–86	Dunfermline Ath	57	Queen of the S	55	Meadowbank T	49
1986–87	Meadowbank T	55	Raith R*	52	Stirling A*	52
1987–88	Ayr U	61	St Johnstone	59	Queen's Park	51
1988–89	Albion R	50	Alloa	45	Brechin C	43
1989–90	Brechin C	49	Kilmarnock	48	Stirling A	47
1990–91	Stirling A	54	Montrose	46	Cowdenbeath	45
1991–92	Dumbarton	52	Cowdenbeath	51	Alloa	50
1992–93	Clyde	54	Brechin C*	53	Stranraer	53
1993–94	Stranraer	56	Berwick R	48	Stenhousemuir*	47
			Maximum points: 108			
1994–95	Morton	64	Dumbarton	60	Stirling A	58
1995–96	Stirling A	81	East Fife	67	Berwick R	60
1996–97	Ayr U	77	Hamilton A	74	Livingston	64
1997–98	Stranraer	61	Clydebank	60	Livingston	59
1998–99	Livingston	77	Inverness CT	72	Clyde	53
1999–2000	Clyde	65	Alloa Ath	64	Ross Co	62
2000–01	Partick T	75	Arbroath	58	Berwick R*	54
2001–02	Queen of the S	67	Alloa	59	Forfar Ath	53

THIRD DIVISION

	First	Pts	Second	Pts	Third	Pts
			Maximum points: 108			
1994–95	Forfar Ath	80	Montrose	67	Ross Co	60
1995–96	Livingston	72	Brechin C	63	Caledonian T	57
1996–97	Inverness CT	76	Forfar Ath*	67	Ross Co	67
1997–98	Alloa Ath	76	Arbroath	68	Ross Co	67
1998–99	Ross Co	77	Stenhousemuir	64	Brechin C	59
1999–2000	Queen's Park	69	Berwick R	66	Forfar Ath	61
2000–01	Hamilton A*	76	Cowdenbeath	76	Brechin C	72
2001–02	Brechin C	73	Dumbarton	61	Albion R	59

FIRST DIVISION to 1974–75

Maximum points: a 36; b 44; c 40; d 52; e 60; f 68; g 76; h 84.

	First	Pts	Second	Pts	Third	Pts
1890–91a	Dumbarton††	29	Rangers††	29	Celtic	21
1891–92b	Dumbarton	37	Celtic	35	Hearts	34
1892–93a	Celtic	29	Rangers	28	St Mirren	20
1893–94a	Celtic	29	Hearts	26	St Bernard's	23
1894–95a	Hearts	31	Celtic	26	Rangers	22
1895–96a	Celtic	30	Rangers	26	Hibernian	24
1896–97a	Hearts	28	Hibernian	26	Rangers	25
1897–98a	Celtic	33	Rangers	29	Hibernian	22
1898–99a	Rangers	36	Hearts	26	Celtic	24
1899–1900a	Rangers	32	Celtic	25	Hibernian	24
1900–01c	Rangers	35	Celtic	29	Hibernian	25
1901–02a	Rangers	28	Celtic	26	Hearts	22
1902–03b	Hibernian	37	Dundee	31	Rangers	29
1903–04d	Third Lanark	43	Hearts	39	Celtic*	38
1904–05d	Celtic‡	41	Rangers	41	Third Lanark	35
1905–06e	Celtic	49	Hearts	43	Airdrieonians	38
1906–07f	Celtic	55	Dundee	48	Rangers	45
1907–08f	Celtic	55	Falkirk	51	Rangers	50
1908–09f	Celtic	51	Dundee	50	Clyde	48
1909–10f	Celtic	54	Falkirk	52	Rangers	46
1910–11f	Rangers	52	Aberdeen	48	Falkirk	44
1911–12f	Rangers	51	Celtic	45	Clyde	42
1912–13f	Rangers	53	Celtic	49	Hearts*	41
1913–14g	Celtic	65	Rangers	59	Hearts*	54
1914–15g	Celtic	65	Hearts	61	Rangers	50
1915–16g	Celtic	67	Rangers	56	Morton	51
1916–17g	Celtic	64	Morton	54	Rangers	53
1917–18f	Rangers	56	Celtic	55	Kilmarnock*	43
1918–19f	Celtic	58	Rangers	57	Morton	47
1919–20h	Rangers	71	Celtic	68	Motherwell	57
1920–21h	Rangers	76	Celtic	66	Hearts	50
1921–22h	Celtic	67	Rangers	66	Raith R	51
1922–23g	Rangers	55	Airdrieonians	50	Celtic	46
1923–24g	Rangers	59	Airdrieonians	50	Celtic	46
1924–25g	Rangers	60	Airdrieonians	57	Hibernian	52

	First	Pts	Second	Pts	Third	Pts
1925–26g	Celtic	58	Airdrieonians*	50	Hearts	50
1926–27g	Rangers	56	Motherwell	51	Celtic	49
1927–28g	Rangers	60	Celtic*	55	Motherwell	55
1928–29g	Rangers	67	Celtic	51	Motherwell	50
1929–30g	Rangers	60	Motherwell	55	Aberdeen	53
1930–31g	Rangers	60	Celtic	58	Motherwell	56
1931–32g	Motherwell	66	Rangers	61	Celtic	48
1932–33g	Rangers	62	Motherwell	59	Hearts	50
1933–34g	Rangers	66	Motherwell	62	Celtic	47
1934–35g	Rangers	55	Celtic	52	Hearts	50
1935–36g	Celtic	66	Rangers*	61	Aberdeen	61
1936–37g	Rangers	61	Aberdeen	54	Celtic	52
1937–38g	Celtic	61	Hearts	58	Rangers	49
1938–39g	Rangers	59	Celtic	48	Aberdeen	46
1946–47e	Rangers	46	Hibernian	44	Aberdeen	39
1947–48e	Hibernian	48	Rangers	46	Partick T	36
1948–49e	Rangers	46	Dundee	45	Hibernian	39
1949–50e	Rangers	50	Hibernian	49	Hearts	43
1950–51e	Hibernian	48	Rangers*	38	Dundee	38
1951–52e	Hibernian	45	Rangers	41	East Fife	37
1952–53e	Rangers*	43	Hibernian	43	East Fife	39
1953–54e	Celtic	43	Hearts	38	Partick T	35
1954–55e	Aberdeen	49	Celtic	46	Rangers	41
1955–56f	Rangers	52	Aberdeen	46	Hearts*	45
1956–57f	Rangers	55	Hearts	53	Kilmarnock	42
1957–58f	Hearts	62	Rangers	49	Celtic	46
1958–59f	Rangers	50	Hearts	48	Motherwell	44
1959–60f	Hearts	54	Kilmarnock	50	Rangers*	42
1960–61f	Rangers	51	Kilmarnock	50	Third Lanark	42
1961–62f	Dundee	54	Rangers	51	Celtic	46
1962–63f	Rangers	57	Kilmarnock	48	Partick T	46
1963–64f	Rangers	55	Kilmarnock	49	Celtic*	47
1964–65f	Kilmarnock*	50	Hearts	50	Dunfermline Ath	49
1965–66f	Celtic	57	Rangers	55	Kilmarnock	45
1966–67f	Celtic	58	Rangers	55	Clyde	46
1967–68f	Celtic	63	Rangers	61	Hibernian	45
1968–69f	Celtic	54	Rangers	49	Dunfermline Ath	45
1969–70f	Celtic	57	Rangers	45	Hibernian	44
1970–71f	Celtic	56	Aberdeen	54	St Johnstone	44
1971–72f	Celtic	60	Aberdeen	50	Rangers	44
1972–73f	Celtic	57	Rangers	56	Hibernian	45
1973–74f	Celtic	53	Hibernian	49	Rangers	48
1974–75f	Rangers	56	Hibernian	49	Celtic	45

SECOND DIVISION to 1974–75

Maximum points: a 76; b 72; c 68; d 52; e 60; f 36; g 44.

	First	Pts	Second	Pts	Third	Pts
1893–94f	Hibernian	29	Cowlairs	27	Clyde	24
1894–95f	Hibernian	30	Motherwell	22	Port Glasgow	20
1895–96f	Abercorn	27	Leith Ath	23	Renton	21
1896–97f	Partick T	31	Leith Ath	27	Kilmarnock*	21
1897–98f	Kilmarnock	29	Port Glasgow	25	Morton	22
1898–99f	Kilmarnock	32	Leith Ath	27	Port Glasgow	25
1899–1900f	Partick T	29	Morton	28	Port Glasgow	20
1900–01f	St Bernard's	25	Airdrieonians	23	Abercorn	21
1901–02g	Port Glasgow	32	Partick T	31	Motherwell	26
1902–03g	Airdrieonians	35	Motherwell	28	Ayr U*	27
1903–04g	Hamilton A	37	Clyde	29	Ayr U	28
1904–05g	Clyde	32	Falkirk	28	Hamilton A	27
1905–06g	Leith Ath	34	Clyde	31	Albion R	27
1906–07g	St Bernard's	32	Vale of Leven*	27	Arthurlie	27
1907–08g	Raith R	30	Dumbarton*‡‡	27	Ayr U	27
1908–09g	Abercorn	31	Raith R*	28	Vale of Leven	28
1909–10g	Leith Ath‡	33	Raith R	33	St Bernard's	27
1910–11g	Dumbarton	31	Ayr U	27	Albion R	25
1911–12g	Ayr U	35	Abercorn	30	Dumbarton	27
1912–13d	Ayr U	34	Dunfermline Ath	33	East Stirling	32
1913–14g	Cowdenbeath	31	Albion R	27	Dunfermline Ath*	26
1914–15d	Cowdenbeath*	37	St Bernard's*	37	Leith Ath	37
1921–22a	Alloa	60	Cowdenbeath	47	Armadale	45
1922–23a	Queen's Park	57	Clydebank¶	50	St Johnstone¶	45
1923–24a	St Johnstone	56	Cowdenbeath	55	Bathgate	44
1924–25a	Dundee U	50	Clydebank	48	Clyde	47
1925–26a	Dunfermline Ath	59	Clyde	53	Ayr U	52
1926–27a	Bo'ness	56	Raith R	49	Clydebank	45
1927–28a	Ayr U	54	Third Lanark	45	King's Park	44
1928–29b	Dundee U	51	Morton	50	Arbroath	47
1929–30a	Leith Ath*	57	East Fife	57	Albion R	54
1930–31a	Third Lanark	61	Dundee U	50	Dunfermline Ath	47
1931–32a	East Stirling*	55	St Johnstone	55	Raith R*	46
1932–33c	Hibernian	54	Queen of the S	49	Dunfermline Ath	47

	First	Pts	Second	Pts	Third	Pts
1933–34c	Albion R	45	Dunfermline Ath*	44	Arbroath	44
1934–35c	Third Lanark	52	Arbroath	50	St Bernard's	47
1935–36c	Falkirk	59	St Mirren	52	Morton	48
1936–37c	Ayr U	54	Morton	51	St Bernard's	48
1937–38c	Raith R	59	Albion R	48	Airdrieonians	47
1938–39c	Cowdenbeath	60	Alloa*	48	East Fife	48
1946–47d	Dundee	45	Airdrieonians	42	East Fife	31
1947–48e	East Fife	53	Albion R	42	Hamilton A	40
1948–49e	Raith R*	42	Stirling A	42	Airdrieonians*	41
1949–50e	Morton	47	Airdrieonians	44	Dunfermline Ath*	36
1950–51e	Queen of the S*	45	Stirling A	45	Ayr U*	36
1951–52e	Clyde	44	Falkirk	43	Ayr U	39
1952–53e	Stirling A	44	Hamilton A	43	Queen's Park	37
1953–54e	Motherwell	45	Kilmarnock	42	Third Lanark*	36
1954–55e	Airdrieonians	46	Dunfermline Ath	42	Hamilton A	39
1955–56b	Queen's Park	54	Ayr U	51	St Johnstone	49
1956–57b	Clyde	64	Third Lanark	51	Cowdenbeath	45
1957–58b	Stirling A	55	Dunfermline Ath	53	Arbroath	47
1958–59b	Ayr U	60	Arbroath	51	Stenhousemuir	46
1959–60b	St Johnstone	53	Dundee U	50	Queen of the S	49
1960–61b	Stirling A	55	Falkirk	54	Stenhousemuir	50
1961–62b	Clyde	54	Queen of the S	53	Morton	44
1962–63b	St Johnstone	55	East Stirling	49	Morton	48
1963–64b	Morton	67	Clyde	53	Arbroath	46
1964–65b	Stirling A	59	Hamilton A	50	Queen of the S	45
1965–66b	Ayr U	53	Airdrieonians	50	Queen of the S	47
1966–67a	Morton	69	Raith R	58	Arbroath	57
1967–68b	St Mirren	62	Arbroath	53	East Fife	49
1968–69b	Motherwell	64	Ayr U	53	East Fife*	48
1969–70b	Falkirk	56	Cowdenbeath	55	Queen of the S	50
1970–71b	Partick T	56	East Fife	51	Arbroath	46
1971–72b	Dumbarton*	52	Arbroath	52	Stirling A	50
1972–73b	Clyde	56	Dumfermline Ath	52	Raith R*	47
1973–74b	Airdrieonians	60	Kilmarnock	58	Hamilton A	55
1974–75a	Falkirk	54	Queen of the S*	53	Montrose	53

Elected to First Division: 1894 Clyde: 1895 Hibernian: 1896 Abercorn: 1897 Partick T: 1899 Kilmarnock: 1900 Morton and Partick T: 1902 Port Glasgow and Partick T: 1903 Airdrieonians and Motherwell: 1905 Falkirk and Aberdeen: 1906 Clyde and Hamilton A: 1910 Raith R: 1913 Ayr U and Dumbarton.

RELEGATED FROM PREMIER LEAGUE

1998–99 Dunfermline Ath
1999–2000 *No relegation due to League reorganization*

2000–01 St Mirren
2001–02 St Johnstone

RELEGATED FROM PREMIER DIVISION

1974–75 *No relegation due to League reorganization*
1975–76 Dundee, St Johnstone
1976–77 Hearts, Kilmarnock
1977–78 Ayr U, Clydebank
1978–79 Hearts, Motherwell
1979–80 Dundee, Hibernian
1980–81 Kilmarnock, Hearts
1981–82 Partick T, Airdrieonians
1982–83 Morton, Kilmarnock
1983–84 St Johnstone, Motherwell
1984–85 Dumbarton, Morton
1985–86 *No relegation due to League reorganization*
1986–87 Clydebank, Hamilton A
1987–88 Falkirk, Dunfermline Ath, Morton
1988–89 Hamilton A
1989–90 Dundee
1990–91 *None*
1991–92 St Mirren, Dunfermline Ath
1992–93 Falkirk, Airdrieonians
1993–94 *See footnote*
1994–95 Dundee U
1995–96 Partick T, Falkirk
1996–97 Raith R
1997–98 Hibernian

RELEGATED FROM DIVISION 1

1974–75 *No relegation due to League reorganization*
1975–76 Dunfermline Ath, Clyde
1976–77 Raith R, Falkirk
1977–78 Alloa Ath, East Fife
1978–79 Montrose, Queen of the S
1979–80 Arbroath, Clyde
1980–81 Stirling A, Berwick R
1981–82 East Stirling, Queen of the S
1982–83 Dunfermline Ath, Queen's Park
1983–84 Raith R, Alloa
1984–85 Meadowbank T, St Johnstone
1985–86 Ayr U, Alloa
1986–87 Brechin C, Montrose
1987–88 East Fife, Dumbarton
1988–89 Kilmarnock, Queen of the S
1989–90 Albion R, Alloa
1990–91 Clyde, Brechin C
1991–92 Montrose, Forfar Ath
1992–93 Meadowbank T, Cowdenbeath
1993–94 *See footnote*
1994–95 Ayr U, Stranraer
1995–96 Hamilton A, Dumbarton
1996–97 Clydebank, East Fife
1997–98 Partick T, Stirling A
1998–99 Hamilton A, Stranraer
1999–2000 Clydebank
2000–01 Morton, Alloa
2001–02 Raith R

RELEGATED FROM DIVISION 2

1994–95 Meadowbank T, Brechin C
1995–96 Forfar Ath, Montrose
1996–97 Dumbarton, Berwick R
1997–98 Stenhousemuir, Brechin C

1998–99 East Fife, Forfar Ath
1999–2000 Hamilton A**
2000–01 Queen's Park, Stirling A
2001–02 Morton

RELEGATED FROM DIVISION 1 (TO 1973–74)

1921–22 *Queen's Park, Dumbarton, Clydebank	1951–52 Morton, Stirling A
1922–23 Albion R, Alloa Ath	1952–53 Motherwell, Third Lanark
1923–24 Clyde, Clydebank	1953–54 Airdrieonians, Hamilton A
1924–25 Third Lanark, Ayr U	1954–55 *No clubs relegated*
1925–26 Raith R, Clydebank	1955–56 Stirling A, Clyde
1926–27 Morton, Dundee U	1956–57 Dunfermline Ath, Ayr U
1927–28 Dunfermline Ath, Bo'ness	1957–58 East Fife, Queen's Park
1928–29 Third Lanark, Raith R	1958–59 Queen of the S, Falkirk
1929–30 St Johnstone, Dundee U	1959–60 Arbroath, Stirling A
1930–31 Hibernian, East Fife	1960–61 Ayr U, Clyde
1931–32 Dundee U, Leith Ath	1961–62 St Johnstone, Stirling A
1932–33 Morton, East Stirling	1962–63 Clyde, Raith R
1933–34 Third Lanark, Cowdenbeath	1963–64 Queen of the S, East Stirling
1934–35 St Mirren, Falkirk	1964–65 Airdrieonians, Third Lanark
1935–36 Airdrieonians, Ayr U	1965–66 Morton, Hamilton A
1936–37 Dunfermline Ath, Albion R	1966–67 St Mirren, Ayr U
1937–38 Dundee, Morton	1967–68 Motherwell, Stirling A
1938–39 Queen's Park, Raith R	1968–69 Falkirk, Arbroath
1946–47 Kilmarnock, Hamilton A	1969–70 Raith R, Partick T
1947–48 Airdrieonians, Queen's Park	1970–71 St Mirren, Cowdenbeath
1948–49 Morton, Albion R	1971–72 Clyde, Dunfermline Ath
1949–50 Queen of the S, Stirling A	1972–73 Kilmarnock, Airdrieonians
1950–51 Clyde, Falkirk	1973–74 East Fife, Falkirk

*Season 1921–22 – only 1 club promoted, 3 clubs relegated. **15pts deducted for failing to field a team.*

Scottish League championship wins: Rangers 49, Celtic 38, Aberdeen 4, Hearts 4, Hibernian 4, Dumbarton 2, Dundee 1, Dundee U 1, Kilmarnock 1, Motherwell 1, Third Lanark 1.

At the end of the 1993–94 season four divisions were created assisted by the admission of two new clubs Ross County and Caledonian Thistle. Only one club was promoted from Division 1 and Division 2. The three relegated from the Premier joined with teams finishing second to seventh in Division 1 to form the new Division 1. Five relegated from Division 1 combined with those who finished second to sixth to form a new Division 2 and the bottom eight in Division 2 linked with the two newcomers to form a new Division 3. At the end of the 1997–98 season the nine clubs remaining in the Premier Division plus the promoted team from Division 1 formed a breakaway Premier League. At the end of the 1999–2000 season two teams were added to the Scottish League. There was no relegation from the Premier League but two promoted from the First Division and three from each of the Second and Third Divisions. One team was relegated from the First Division and one from the Second Division, leaving 12 teams in each division.

Rangers Tore Andre Flo is crowded out by Bobo Balde, Paul Lambert and Johan Mjallby of Celtic during the 1-1 draw in the Scottish Premier League at Ibrox in March. (Actionimages)

SCOTTISH LEAGUE CUP FINALS 1946–2002

Season	Winners	Runners-up	Score
1946–47	Rangers	Aberdeen	4-0
1947–48	East Fife	Falkirk	4-1 after 0-0 draw
1948–49	Rangers	Raith R	2-0
1949–50	East Fife	Dunfermline Ath	3-0
1950–51	Motherwell	Hibernian	3-0
1951–52	Dundee	Rangers	3-2
1952–53	Dundee	Kilmarnock	2-0
1953–54	East Fife	Partick T	3-2
1954–55	Hearts	Motherwell	4-2
1955–56	Aberdeen	St Mirren	2-1
1956–57	Celtic	Partick T	3-0 after 0-0 draw
1957–58	Celtic	Rangers	7-1
1958–59	Hearts	Partick T	5-1
1959–60	Hearts	Third Lanark	2-1
1960–61	Rangers	Kilmarnock	2-0
1961–62	Rangers	Hearts	3-1 after 1-1 draw
1962–63	Hearts	Kilmarnock	1-0
1963–64	Rangers	Morton	5-0
1964–65	Rangers	Celtic	2-1
1965–66	Celtic	Rangers	2-1
1966–67	Celtic	Rangers	1-0
1967–68	Celtic	Dundee	5-3
1968–69	Celtic	Hibernian	6-2
1969–70	Celtic	St Johnstone	1-0
1970–71	Rangers	Celtic	1-0
1971–72	Partick T	Celtic	4-1
1972–73	Hibernian	Celtic	2-1
1973–74	Dundee	Celtic	1-0
1974–75	Celtic	Hibernian	6-3
1975–76	Rangers	Celtic	1-0
1976–77	Aberdeen	Celtic	2-1
1977–78	Rangers	Celtic	2-1
1978–79	Rangers	Aberdeen	2-1
1979–80	Dundee U	Aberdeen	3-0 after 0-0 draw
1980–81	Dundee U	Dundee	3-0
1981–82	Rangers	Dundee U	2-1
1982–83	Celtic	Rangers	2-1
1983–84	Rangers	Celtic	3-2
1984–85	Rangers	Dundee U	1-0
1985–86	Aberdeen	Hibernian	3-0
1986–87	Rangers	Celtic	2-1
1987–88	Rangers	Aberdeen	3-3
		(Rangers won 5-3 on penalties)	
1988–89	Rangers	Aberdeen	3-2
1989–90	Aberdeen	Rangers	2-1
1990–91	Rangers	Celtic	2-1
1991–92	Hibernian	Dunfermline Ath	2-0
1992–93	Rangers	Aberdeen	2-1
1993–94	Rangers	Hibernian	2-1
1994–95	Raith R	Celtic	2-2
		(Raith R won 6-5 on penalties)	
1995–96	Aberdeen	Dundee	2-0
1996–97	Rangers	Hearts	4-3
1997–98	Celtic	Dundee U	3-0
1998–99	Rangers	St Johnstone	2-1
1999–2000	Celtic	Aberdeen	2-0
2000–01	Celtic	Kilmarnock	3-0
2001–02	Rangers	Ayr U	4-0

SCOTTISH LEAGUE CUP WINS

Rangers 22, Celtic 12, Aberdeen 5, Hearts 4, Dundee 3, East Fife 3, Dundee U 2, Hibernian 2, Motherwell 1, Partick T 1, Raith R 1.

APPEARANCES IN FINALS

Rangers 28, Celtic 24, Aberdeen 12, Hibernian 7, Dundee 6, Hearts 6, Dundee U 5, Kilmarnock 4, Partick T 4, East Fife 3, Dunfermline Ath 2, Motherwell 2, Raith R 2, St Johnstone 2, Ayr U 1, Falkirk 1, Morton 1, St Mirren 1, Third Lanark 1.

CIS SCOTTISH LEAGUE CUP 2001–02

FIRST ROUND

2 SEPT

Elgin C (1) 2 *(McGlashan 14, Gilzean 59)*
Stranraer (1) 3 *(Shaw 3, Harty 48, Finlayson 80)*   566
Elgin C: Pirie; Hind, MacDonald J, McBride, MacDonald S,
Tully, Ross, Morrison (Rutherford), McGlashan, Gilzean,
Craig D.
Stranraer: McGeown; Paterson, Wright, Wingate, Gaughan,
Aitken, Finlayson, George, Harty, Shaw, Jenkins (Weir).

11 SEPT

Airdrieonians (1) 3 *(James 12, Roberts 58, Macfarlane 60)*
Morton (0) 0   864
Airdrieonians: Ferguson; Armstrong, McPherson, Stewart
(McDonald C), McManus, James, Gardner, Macfarlane
(Beasley), Coyle, Smith (Docherty), Roberts.
Morton: Coyle; Bannerman, Collins, McAneny, Greacen,
Renwick, Moore (Tweedie), Frail, O'Connor, Reid
(Redmond), Miller (Kearney).

Albion R (0) 0
Inverness CT (0) 2 *(Ritchie 77, 84)*   123
Albion R: Fahey; Hamilton, Lumsden, Smith, Tait, Booth,
Waldie (Carr), Easton, McMullan, McCormick, Silvestro.
Inverness CT: Calder; Tokely, Golabek, Mann, McCaffrey,
Duncan, Bavidge, Wyness (MacDonald), Ritchie, Stewart
(Robson), McBain.

Alloa Ath (2) 4 *(Little 25, Curran 44, Walker 55, Thomson 80)*
Peterhead (0) 0   298
Alloa Ath: Soutar; Clark, Anderson, Watson, Thomson,
Valentine, Hamilton (Evans G), Curran, Walker, Irvine, Little
(Hutchison).
Peterhead: Pirie; Bisset, King (Slater), Smith, Simpson, Tindal,
Mackay, Stewart, Yeats (Findlay), Johnston, Livingstone
(Cooper).

Berwick R (0) 0
Partick T (2) 3 *(Lennon 8, McLean 17, McDowell 76)*   416
Berwick R: O'Connor; Murie, Bennett, Gray, Neill A, Farrell
(Smith), Bradley, Neil M, Wood (Glancy), Robertson, Ronald
(Forrest).
Partick T: Klein; Huxford, Archibald, Craigan, Paterson,
Connaghan, Britton (McDowell), Lennon, McLean (Walker),
Dolan (Hardie), Fleming.

Clyde (0) 2 *(Crawford 55, 93)*
Stenhousemuir (1) 2 *(Abbott 17, Ferguson 98)*   612
Clyde: Halliwell; Murray (Ross), Hagen, Smith, Kernaghan,
Okikiolu (Dunn), Mitchell, Millen, Hinds, Bingham
(Crawford), McPhee.
Stenhousemuir: Graham M (McGurk); Storrar, Donaldson,
Davidson, Vella, Donald B, Jackson, Donald G, Ferguson,
English (Wood), Abbott.
aet; Clyde won 4-2 on penalties.

Dumbarton (1) 2 *(Brown 38, Flannery 59)*
Clydebank (0) 0   695
Dumbarton: Hillcoat; Bonar, Dillon (Brittain), Stewart,
McKeown, McCann, Crilly, O'Neill (Lynes), Flannery
(McKelvie), Brown, Robertson.
Clydebank: Smith; Paton, Stirling, Bossy, McKinnon,
McGowan, Hamilton, Dick (Kinnaird), Graham (McGrillen),
Burke, Carrigan (Lavety).

East Fife (0) 1 *(McManus 68)*
Arbroath (0) 0   388
East Fife: Godfrey; Wilson, Gallagher, Gibson, Oliver,
Mortimer, Munro (Allen), Bailey (Graham), McManus, Nairn,
Cunningham.
Arbroath: Hinchcliffe; Rowe, Florence (Mackay), McAulay
(Cargill), Ritchie, Fallon, Heenan (Gardner), Mercer, Mallan,
McKinnon, Brownlie.

East Stirling (0) 0
Queen of the S (1) 3 *(Feroz 17, 57, 68)*   208
East Stirling: Hay; Ferguson, McDonald, Russell, McCheyne,
McGhee (Hall), Maughan (Todd D), McAuley, Menelaws,
McKechnie, Lorimer (Gordon).

Queen of the S: Scott; Connelly G, McAlpine, Gray, Thomson,
Crawford, O'Neil, Connell, Feroz (Connolly S), Weatherson,
Atkinson (Sunderland).

Forfar Ath (0) 1 *(Tosh 84)*
Falkirk (1) 2 *(Lawrie 38, Craig 69)*   511
Forfar Ath: Brown; McCloy, Milne, Horn, Rattray, Bowman
(Lunan), Byers (Williams), Sellars, Tosh, Moffat, Christie
(Stewart).
Falkirk: Hogarth; Mair, McQuilken, Lawrie, Denham,
Christie, McAllister (Morris), Kerr, Wright, Craig, Waddell.

Raith R (1) 1 *(Henderson 10)*
Montrose (0) 0   .   1004
Raith R: Miotto; McCulloch, Zoco, Dennis, Browne,
Henderson, Novo, Matheson (O'Boyle), Smith A (Clark A),
Crabbe, Stein.
Montrose: McGlynn; McQuillan, Ferguson, Conway
(McKellar), Lowe, Allison, Mitchell, Johnson, Brand,
Kerrigan (Laidlaw), Craig (Magee).

Ross Co (0) 3 *(Boukraa 50, Bone 51, 79)*
Brechin C (0) 0   499
Ross Co: Bullock; Perry, Hastings, Maxwell, Irvine, Webb,
McCormick, Ferguson, Bone, Boukraa (Hislop), Robertson.
Brechin C: Cairns; Smith, Fotheringham, Bayne, Cairney,
McAllister (Honeyman), King, Miller, Grant, Templeman
(Leask), Black (Craig).

12 SEPT

Queen's Park (0) 0
Hamilton A (1) 1 *(Moore 13)*   614
Queen's Park: Smith; Collins, Canning, Quinn, Marshall
(Cunningham), Caven, Miller B, Miller G, Ewing (Brown),
Miller K (Martin), Jackson.
Hamilton A: Potter; Renicks, Cunnington, Sweeney, Gaughan,
Bonnar, Graham, Russell, Moore, McFarlane D (Ajet)
(Martin), Callaghan (McDonald).

Stirling Albion (2) 3 *(Williams 13, 44, 56)*
Cowdenbeath (1) 2 *(Wilson 23, Wright 89)*   447
Stirling Albion: Reid; Hay, Devine, Moriarty, Morrison,
McLellan, Munro, Henderson, Geraghty, Williams (Butler),
Stuart (Kelly).
Cowdenbeath: Gordon; Boyle (Wright), Neeson, Wilson,
White, Swift, Winter (Burns), French, Brown, Mauchlen
(Young), King.

SECOND ROUND

25 SEPT

Airdrieonians (1) 2 *(Coyle 12 (pen), Lasley 85 (og))*
Motherwell (0) 1 *(Kelly 57)*   3369
Airdrieonians: Ferguson; Armstrong, McPherson, Stewart,
McManus, James, Gardner (Beasley), Macfarlane, Coyle,
Smith (Taylor), Roberts.
Motherwell: Brown; Corrigan, Ready, Hammell, Forrest,
Pearson, Lasley, Leitch (Cosgrove), Kelly (Tarrant), Nicholas,
Elliott (Adams).

Ayr U (1) 4 *(Grady 35, Teale 72, Sharp 74, Annand 82)*
Stranraer (0) 0   1410
Ayr U: Nelson; Robertson, Lovering, Duffy, Hughes, Sheerin
(Sharp), Teale, Wilson, Annand (Smyth), Grady (Bradford),
Scally.
Stranraer: McGeown; Gaughan (Hodge), Wright, Wingate,
Johnstone (Gallagher), Macdonald, Jenkins (Paterson),
Aitken, Harty, Shaw, Finlayson.

Dundee U (2) 3 *(Thompson 1, Easton 34, Griffin 51)*
Dumbarton (0) 0   3702
Dundee U: Gallacher; McCracken, Lauchlan, McCunnie,
Griffin, Aljofree, Easton (O'Brien), Miller (Paterson),
McIntyre, Hamilton (Carson), Thompson.
Dumbarton: Hillcoat; Bonar, Dillon (Brittain), Stewart, Jack,
McKeown, Crilly, McCann, Flannery, Brown (McKelvie),
Robertson (Lynes).

Falkirk (0) 0
Raith R (1) 2 *(Novo 20, Smith A 70)*   1600
Falkirk: Hogarth; Mair (Waddell), McQuilken, Lawrie, Denham, Rennie, McAllister (Watson), Kerr, Wright, Christie, Craig (Deuchar).
Raith R: Monin; Zoco (Hampshire), Ellis, McCulloch, Browne, Henderson, Novo (Clark A), Matheson (Nanou), Smith A, Crabbe, Stein.

Queen of the S (0) 1 *(Feroz 64)*
Aberdeen (2) 2 *(Dadi 2, Thornley 22)*   3418
Queen of the S: Scott; Gray, McAlpine, Allan, Aitken, Crawford, O'Neill, Connell (Davidson), Feroz, Weatherson, Connelly (Sunderland).
Aberdeen: Esson; McGuire, McNaughton, Whyte, Solberg, Darren Young, Tiernan, Dadi (Mackie), Winters, Thornley (Derek Young), Zerouali.

Ross Co (0) 0
Hearts (0) 0   2657
Ross Co: Bullock; Perry, Hastings (Mackay S), Maxwell, Irvine, Webb, Boukraa (McQuade), Cowie, Bone, Hislop, Robertson.
Hearts: Niemi; Pressley, Mahe, McKenna (Simmons), Webster, Neilson, Severin, Fulton (Juanjo), Flögel, Boyack, Adam (Kirk).
aet; Ross Co won 5-4 on penalties.

26 SEPT

Clyde (0) 1 *(Kane A 90)*
St Johnstone (1) 2 *(MacDonald 25, 86)*   911
Clyde: Halliwell; Murray, Dunn, Keogh, Cranmer, Ross, Mitchell, Millen, Hinds (Okikiolu), Bingham (Kane A), Convery (Crawford).
St Johnstone: Cuthbert; Dods, McCluskey, Weir, Forsyth, Murray, Dasovic, McBride (Hartley), MacDonald, Connolly (Parker), Falconer.

Dunfermline Ath (1) 3 *(Nicholson 36, Mason 58, 76)*
Alloa Ath (0) 0   2798
Dunfermline Ath: Thomson SY; Doesburg, McGroarty, Mason, Skerla, Nicholls, Nicholson, Ferguson (Dair), Crawford (Potter), de Gier, Petrie (Bullen).
Alloa Ath: Soutar; Clark, Seaton, Watson, Thomson, Valentine, Hamilton, Curran, Walker (Christie), Irvine (Hutchison), Raeside (Little).

Hamilton A (0) 0
Dundee (0) 2 *(Milne 67, Boylan 81)*   2104
Hamilton A: Potter; Renicks, Martin, Nelson, Gaughan, Bonnar, Graham, Walker (McCreadie), Moore, Armstrong (O'Neil), Callaghan.
Dundee: Langfield; Smith, Del Rio, Khizanishvili, Marrocco, Robertson (Forbes), Garrido, Gatti (Boylan), Rae, Carranza (Fatello), Milne.

Inverness CT (1) 3 *(Teasdale 12, Robson 63, 120)*
Partick T (1) 3 *(Hardie 26, Lennon 68, McLean 114)*   1034
Inverness CT: Walker; Tokely, Golabek (Stewart), Mann, McCaffrey, Teasdale, Bavidge, Wyness, Ritchie (MacDonald), McBain, Robson.
Partick T: Klein; Huxford, Archibald, Craigan, Paterson, Hardie (McKinstry), Britton (McLean), Lennon, Walker (Elliot), Dolan, Fleming.
aet; Inverness CT won 4-2 on penalties.

Livingston (2) 3 *(Caputo 3, 20, Tosh 82)*
East Fife (0) 0   1951
Livingston: Broto; Hart, Bollan, Deas, Andrews, Quino, Wilson, Tosh (Sullivan), Caputo, Aurellio (Keith), Bingham (Brady).
East Fife: Godfrey; Wilson (Cunningham), Gallagher, Gibson (Graham), Oliver, Mortimer (Herkes), Munro, Bailey, McManus, Nairn, Coulston.

Stirling Albion (1) 2 *(Williams 10, Munro 89)*
St Mirren (1) 1 *(Quitongo 6)*   983
Stirling Albion: Reid; Reilly, Devine, Morrison, Goldie, McLellan, Munro, Henderson, Geraghty, Williams, McCallum (Hay).
St Mirren: Roy; Nicolson, Bowman, McGowan, McLaughlin, Walker, Quitongo, Murray (Baltacha), McGarry, MacKenzie (Ross), Yardley.

THIRD ROUND

9 OCT

Aberdeen (0) 1 *(Mackie 50)*
Livingston (4) 6 *(Wilson 10, 33, Caputo 11, 28, Lovell 55, Bingham 58)*   9049
Aberdeen: Esson; McGuire, McNaughton, Whyte, Solberg, Darren Young, Bisconti, Clark, Zerouali (Dadi), Thornley (Tiernan), Mackie (McAllister).
Livingston: Culkin; Hart, Bollan, Rubio, Anderson, Quino, Lovell, Wilson (Xausa), Tosh (McCulloch), Caputo (Lowndes), Bingham.

Ayr U (0) 0
Kilmarnock (0) 0   7219
Ayr U: Nelson; Robertson, Lovering (McLaughlin), Duffy, Hughes, Sheerin, Teale (Bradford), Wilson, Annand, Grady (McEwan), Sharp.
Kilmarnock: Marshall; Canero, Baker, Innes, Dindeleux, Calderon (Pizzo), Mahood, Mitchell, McLaren, Dargo, McCutcheon (Boyd).
aet; Ayr U won 5-4 on penalties.

Dundee U (1) 3 *(Thompson 23, Hamilton 89, Paterson 99)*
St Johnstone (2) 2 *(Hartley 9, Dods 36)*   5851
Dundee U: Gallacher; Partridge (Aljofree), Lauchlan, McCunnie, Griffin, McCracken, Easton (Hamilton), Miller, McIntyre, Thompson, Lilley (Paterson).
St Johnstone: Cuthbert; Dods, McCluskey, Weir, Forsyth, Murray, Dasovic, Hartley, Connolly (McBride), Parker (Jackson), MacDonald (Falconer).
aet

Dunfermline Ath (0) 1 *(Hampshire 63)*
Inverness CT (1) 1 *(Bavidge 15)*   1929
Dunfermline Ath: Thomson SY; Rossi (Potter), Mason, Dair, Skerla, Nicholls, Nicholson, Hampshire (Matthaei), de Gier, Crawford, Petrie (Doesburg).
Inverness CT: Walker; Tokely, McBain, Mann, McCaffrey, Teasdale, Bavidge, Wyness, Ritchie, Christie, Robson.
aet; Inverness CT won 4-1 on penalties.

Raith R (0) 0
Hibernian (0) 2 *(Brewster 70, 75)*   4587
Raith R: Monin; Zoco, Ellis, McCulloch, Browne (Dennis), Henderson, Nanou, Matheson (Clark A), Smith A, Crabbe, Stein.
Hibernian: Caig; Fenwick, Laursen, Murray, Orman, Townsley, McManus, Brebner, O'Neil, Brewster, Luna.

Rangers (2) 3 *(Arveladze 5, 37, Numan 90)*
Airdrieonians (0) 0   34.073
Rangers: Klos; Ricksen, Moore, Amoruso, Numan, Ball, McCann (Vidmar), Latapy, de Boer (Gibson), Caniggia, Arveladze (Mols).
Airdrieonians: Ferguson; Armstrong, McPherson, Stewart (Dunn), McManus, James, Gardner (MacDonald S), Macfarlane, Coyle, Smith (Taylor), Roberts.

Ross Co (1) 2 *(Irvine 10, Boukraa 67)*
Dundee (0) 1 *(Caballero 54)*   2427
Ross Co: Bullock; Perry, Fraser (Boukraa), Maxwell, Irvine, Webb, McCormick, Ferguson, Bone, Hislop (Prest), Robertson.
Dundee: Langfield; Smith, Khizanishvili, Del Rio, Garrido, Robertson (Naveda), Romano, Gatti (Forbes), Rae, Caballero, Milne.

6 NOV

Celtic (3) 8 *(Hartson 22, 74, Maloney 28, 41, 53, 68, Tebily 72, Healy 78)*
Stirling Albion (0) 0   29.933
Celtic: Kharine (Gould); Crainey, Tebily, Balde (Petrov), McNamara, Wieghorst, Guppy, Healy, Moravcik (Smith), Hartson, Maloney.
Stirling Albion: Reid; Hay, Goldie, Morrison (Higgins), Moriarty (McCallion), McLellan, Reilly, Henderson, Williams (Geraghty), Munro, Nugent.

QUARTER-FINALS

27 NOV

Hibernian (1) 2 *(McManus 1, Luna 70)*
Dundee U (0) 0 8825

Hibernian: Caig; De la Cruz, Smith, Laursen, Jack (Brebner), Murray, Orman, O'Neil, McManus (O'Connor), Luna (Arpinon), Zitelli.
Dundee U: Gallacher; Aljofree, Lauchlan, McCracken (McConalogue), Griffin, Fullarton, Easton, Miller, Hannah (Venetis), Hamilton, Thompson (Paterson).

28 NOV

Ayr U (2) 5 *(Grady 10, Robertson 15, McGinlay 56, Annand 77, 81)*
Inverness CT (1) 1 *(Tokely 9)* 2638

Ayr U: Nelson; McEwan, Lovering, Robertson, Hughes, Craig, Teale, McGinlay, Grady (Annand), Moss (Wilson), Sheerin (McLaughlin).
Inverness CT: Walker; Tokely, McBain, Mann, McCaffrey, Teasdale, Duncan, Wyness, Ritchie, Christie, Robson.

Ross Co (0) 1 *(Mackay S 90)*
Rangers (2) 2 *(Arveladze 24, Reyna 32)* 5972

Ross Co: Bullock; Perry (Mackay S), Hastings, Maxwell, Irvine, Webb, Cowie, Boukraa (McCormick), Bone (Gethins), Hislop, Robertson.
Rangers: Klos; Wilson, Amoruso, Ross, Ball, Reyna, Ferguson, de Boer (Mols), Caniggia (Konterman), Arveladze, Lovenkrands (Latapy).

19 DEC

Livingston (0) 0
Celtic (1) 2 *(Balde 36, Hartson 80)* 8395

Livingston: Culkin; Brinquin, Santini, Rubio, Andrews, Quino, Toure-Maman, Wilson, Xausa (Aurellio), Fernandez (Lowndes), Bingham (Tosh).
Celtic: Douglas; Mjällby, Valgaeren, Balde, McNamara, Sylla, Petrov, Guppy, Moravcik (Lennon), Sutton, Hartson.

SEMI-FINALS (at Hampden Park)

5 FEB

Rangers (1) 2 *(Lovenkrands 45, Konterman 104)*
Celtic (0) 1 *(Balde 73)* 43,457

Rangers: Klos; Ricksen, Moore (Vidmar), Amoruso, Numan, Konterman, Ferguson, de Boer (Flo), Caniggia, Arveladze (Hughes), Lovenkrands.
Celtic: Douglas; Mjällby, Valgaeren, Balde, Thompson, Petrov (Petta), Lennon, Lambert (Moravcik), Agathe, Larsson, Hartson (Sutton).
aet

6 FEB

Hibernian (0) 0
Ayr U (0) 1 *(Annand 99 (pen))* 11,779

Hibernian: Colgan; Fenwick, Smith, Caldwell, De la Cruz (Orman), Murray, Wiss, Brebner, O'Neil, Zitelli (Hurtado), O'Connor (Riordan).
Ayr U: Nelson; Robertson, Lovering (Sharp), Duffy, Hughes, Craig, Wilson (Scally), McGinlay, Annand (McLaughlin), Grady, Sheerin.
aet

FINAL (at Hampden Park)

17 MAR

Rangers (1) 4 *(Flo 43, Ferguson 48 (pen), Caniggia 74, 89)*
Ayr U (0) 0 50,049

Rangers: Klos; Ricksen, Vidmar (Hughes), Amoruso, Numan, Konterman, Ferguson, Latapy (Dodds), Caniggia, Flo, Lovenkrands (McCann).
Ayr U: Nelson; Robertson, Lovering, Duffy, Hughes, Craig, Wilson (Chaplain), McGinlay, McLaughlin (Kean), Grady, Sheerin.
Referee: Hugh Dallas.

Two-goal hero Claudio Caniggia watched closely by Ayr United's Marvyn Wilson during the 4–0 win by Rangers in the CIS Scottish League Cup Final at Hampden Park. (Actionimages)

BELL'S LEAGUE CHALLENGE 2001–02

FIRST ROUND

7 AUG

Airdrieonians (0) 2 *(McPherson 61, Taylor 63)*
Queen of the South (0) 0   563
Airdrieonians: Bennett; Armstrong, McPherson, Stewart, Macfarlane, James, Beasley, Taylor (Docherty), Coyle (Dunn), Smith, Roberts (McDonald C).
Queen of the South: Scott; Connelly G, McGhie, Gray, Thomson, Crawford, O'Neil (Sunderland), Connell, Connolly S, Hawke, Patterson (Davidson).

Albion R (0) 2 *(Hamilton 108, McMullan 117)*
Montrose (0) 0   142
Albion R: Fahey; McKenzie, Stirling, Smith, Tait, Booth (Silvestro), Waldie, Hamilton, McLean (Carr), McCormick (McMullan), Bonar.
Montrose: McGlynn; McQuillan, Ferguson, Muirhead (Craib), Christie, Sharp, McKellar (Magee), Brand, Kerrigan (Stewart), Laidlaw, Johnson.
aet

Berwick R (1) 3 *(Ritchie 36, Glancy 56, Wood 80)*
Elgin C (0) 0   227
Berwick R: McCulloch; Ritchie, McNicoll, Murie, Neill A, Forrest, Bradley, Anthony (Whelan), Wood, Glancy (Ronald), Bennett (Crawford).
Elgin C: Pirie; Hind, McBride, Furphy, MacDonald S, Tully (Mailer), Ross, Craig R (Rutherford), Campbell (McGlashan), Gilzean, MacDonald J.

Brechin C (3) 4 *(Templeman 3, Fotheringham 15, 71 (pen), Smith 43)*
Stirling Albion (0) 1 *(Henderson 46 (pen))*   376
Brechin C: Cairns; Smith (Black), Fotheringham (Leask), Kernaghan (Donachie), Cairney, Campbell, King, Miller, Templeman, Honeyman, Riley.
Stirling Albion: Reid; Hay (Stuart), Devine, Reilly, Morrison, McLellan, Moriarty, Henderson (Bailey), Geraghty (Ross), Higgins, McCallion.

Cowdenbeath (0) 0
Ross Co (0) 2 *(Hislop 96, 106)*   243
Cowdenbeath: Martin; Swift, Raynes, Wilson, White, Lawrence (Boyle), Winter, French, Mauchlen, Brown, King (Moffat).
Ross Co: Bullock; Perry, Robertson, Maxwell, Irvine, Ferguson, McCormick (Hislop), Holmes (McQuade), Bone, Cowie (Mackay S), Fraser.
aet

East Fife (2) 2 *(McManus 23, Graham 42)*
Raith R (0) 3 *(Novo 52, 89, Dennis 66)*   1085
East Fife: Godfrey; Wilson, Gallagher, Cunningham, Mortimer, Ovenstone, Munro, McManus, Graham, Gibson (Lofting), Allan (Herkes).
Raith R: Monin; Clark J, Ellis (Hampshire), Dennis, Zoco, Henderson, Novo, Matheson, Smith A, Crabbe, Stein.

East Stirling (0) 0
Alloa Ath (0) 1 *(Hamilton 81)*   271
East Stirling: Hay; McCheyne, McGhee, Russell, McDonald, Scott, Maughan, Ferguson, Menelaws, Todd D, Scott (McAuley).
Alloa Ath: Soutar; Clark, Seaton, Watson, Thomson, Valentine, Curran, Little, Hamilton, Evans (Irvine), Hutchison.

Falkirk (2) 4 *(Kerr 10, Watson 29, 59 (pen), Craig 64)*
Arbroath (1) 1 *(Brownlie 19)*   1002
Falkirk: Hogarth; Mair, McQuilken, Lawrie, Denham (Rennie), Watson, Morris, Kerr (Craig), Deuchar (McAllister), Henry, Waddell.

Arbroath: Hinchcliffe; Fallon, McInally, Cusick (McAulay), McKinnon, Mackay, Heenan, Cargill, Mallan (Bayne), Brownlie, Gardner.

Inverness CT (2) 3 *(Christie 7, Bavidge 16, Ritchie 115)*
Forfar Ath (1) 2 *(Tokely 22 (og), Moffat 61)* 876
Inverness CT: Calder; Teasdale (Duncan), Golabek, Mann, McCaffrey, Bradshaw, Tokely, Bavidge, Wyness (Ritchie), Christie, Robson.
Forfar Ath: Brown; Morris, Milne (Williams), Horn, Good, Bowman, Stewart (Christie), Sellars, Tosh, Moffat, Byers (Farnan).
aet

Morton (0) 1 *(O'Connor 44)*
Clyde (2) 3 *(Ross 8, 84, Convery 15)*   1558
Morton: Ross; Bannerman, Correia (Moore), Greacen, Frail, McGregor, Gibson (McAneny), Miller, O'Connor (Redmond), Reid, Kearney.
Clyde: Budinauckas; Murray, Dunn, Smith, Keogh, Ross, Mitchell (Bingham), Millen, Crawford, McClay, Convery (Kane A).

Partick T (3) 5 *(Lennon 8, 14, Britton 39, 50, Hardie 85)*
Queen's Park (0) 0   1810
Partick T: Gow; McKinstry, Archibald (McCallum), Smith, Craigan (Paterson), Connaghan, Britton, Lennon (Hardie), McLean, Dolan, Fleming.
Queen's Park: Smith; Ferry, Borland, Bruce (Carberry), Quinn, Sinclair, Canning, Marshall, Martin (Miller G), Brown, Orr (McPhee).

Peterhead (1) 2 *(Stewart 42, 84)*
Hamilton A (0) 0   518
Peterhead: Buchanan; Slater, Smith, Duffy, Simpson, Tindal, Cooper, Stewart (Bisset), Findlay, Mackay, Livingstone.
Hamilton A: Potter; Renicks, Cunnington, Nelson, Gaughan, Walker (Graham), Russell, Sherry, O'Neil (Ajet), McFarlane D, McDonald.

St Mirren (0) 1 *(Yardley 58)*
Ayr U (1) 3 *(Teale 16, Sheerin 48, Annand 71)* 2272
St Mirren: Roy; Baltacha, Kerr, Turner T, McLaughlin, Walker, McKnight (Gillies), Murray, McGarry (Quitongo), Bowman (Yardley), Burns.
Ayr U: Nelson; Robertson, Lovering, Duffy, Hughes, Craig, Teale, McGinlay, Annand, Grady (McEwan), Sheerin (Wilson).

Stenhousemuir (1) 1 *(Mooney 44)*
Stranraer (1) 4 *(Gaughan 42, Wright 79, Johnstone 83, Gallagher 90)* 233
Stenhousemuir: Graham M (McGurk); Storrar, Donaldson, Davidson (Sandison), Stone, Donald B, Abbott, Jackson, English, Mooney, Wood.
Stranraer: McGeown; Wingate, Sherry, Johnstone, Gaughan, Aitken, Jenkins (Gallagher), Macdonald, Harty (Farrell), Wright, Finlayson.

SECOND ROUND

14 AUG

Albion R (0) 1 *(Bonar 66)*
Airdrieonians (2) 4 *(Taylor 35, Roberts 45, Coyle 65, James 88)* 1023
Albion R: Shearer; Lumsden (Booth), Stirling, Smith, Tait, Silvestro, Waldie, Hamilton, McMullan, Carr (McLean), Bonar.
Airdrieonians: Bennett; Armstrong, McPherson, Stewart, McManus, James, Taylor (Docherty), Macfarlane, Coyle, Smith (Beasley), Roberts (McDonald C).

Alloa Ath (1) 3 *(Evans G 36, Irvine 112, Little 116)*
Inverness CT (1) 2 *(Ritchie 78, Wyness 91)* 394
Alloa Ath: Soutar; Clark, Seaton, Watson, Thomson, Valentine, Fisher, Raeside (Irvine), Evans G (Little), Curran, Hutchison (Hamilton).
Inverness CT: Calder; Teasdale (Duncan), Golabek (McBain), Mann, McCaffrey, Bradshaw, Tokely, Bavidge (Wyness), Ritchie, Christie, Robson.
aet

Brechin C (1) 4 *(Grant 2, Smith 65, 82, Bain 71)*
Peterhead (0) 0 394
Brechin C: Cairns; Smith, Fotheringham, Bain, Cairney, Kernaghan, King, Miller, Grant (Honeyman), Templeman (Leask), Black (Riley).
Peterhead: Buchanan; Slater, Smith, Tindal, Simpson, Mackay, Cooper, Stewart (Yeats), Findlay, Johnston (Bisset), Livingstone (King).

Clyde (3) 5 *(Kane A 30, 36, Mitchell 45, Keogh 60, McCusker 70)*
Berwick R (0) 0 593
Clyde: Halliwell; Murray, Dunn (Tolland), Smith, Cranmer, Ross, Mitchell (Crawford), Millen (McCusker), Keogh, Aitken, Kane A.
Berwick R: O'Connor; Gray, McNicoll, Murie (Farrell), Neill A, Forrest, Bradley, Anthony (Ronald), Wood, Whelan, Crawford (McCulloch).

Dumbarton (0) 0
Ross Co (0) 2 *(McQuade 47, Hislop 67)* 370
Dumbarton: Wight; Dickie, Brittain, Jack, McCann, Dillon, Bonar, Lynes (O'Neill), McKelvie, Brown (Melvin), Robertson (Stewart).
Ross Co: Bullock; Perry, Robertson, Maxwell, Webb, Ferguson (Cowie), McCormick (McQuade), Holmes (Hislop), Bone, Fraser, Mackay S.

Falkirk (0) 0
Clydebank (0) 0 1128
Falkirk: Hogarth; Mair, McQuilken, Rennie, Lawrie, Watson, Morris, Craig (McAllister), Wright, Christie (Henry) (Kerr), Waddell.
Clydebank: Smith; Bossy, McKinnon, Brannigan (McGowan), Hamilton, Ferguson (Whiteford), McVey, Paton, Graham (Mooney), Burke, McGrillen.
aet; Clydebank won 5-4 on penalties.

Raith R (2) 3 *(Matheson 13, Novo 45, Zoco 120)*
Partick T (1) 5 *(McDowell 36, McCallum 73, Fleming 100, 104, Hardie 112)* 1585
Raith R: Miotto; McCulloch, Zoco, Dennis, Browne, Henderson (O'Boyle), Novo, Matheson, Smith A, Crabbe (Hampshire), Stein.
Partick T: Gow; Huxford (Howie), Archibald, Craigan, Paterson, Connaghan, McDowell (McCallum) (McKinstry), Hardie, Britton, Dolan, Fleming.
aet

Stranraer (1) 3 *(Finlayson 36, Harty 57, Wright 58)*
Ayr U (1) 2 *(Bradford 7, McGinlay 82)* 1055
Stranraer: McGeown; Farrell (Jenkins), Wright, Gaughan, Johnstone, Macdonald, Aitken, George, Harty (Gallagher), Wingate, Finlayson.
Ayr U: Nelson; Robertson, Sharp, Duffy (McEwan), Hughes, Craig, Teale, McGinlay, Annand, Bradford (Scally), Wilson (Sheerin).

QUARTER-FINALS

21 AUG

Alloa Ath (3) 4 *(Fisher 16, Little 35, Hamilton 44, Curran 119)*
Stranraer (1) 3 *(Gallagher 33, 71, Jenkins 57)* 450
Alloa Ath: Soutar; Clark, Seaton, Watson, Anderson, Valentine, Little (Curran), Fisher, Hamilton, Irvine (Hutchison), Walker (Raeside).

Stranraer: McGeown; Gaughan, Wright, Johnstone (Gallagher M), Hodge (Weir), Wingate, Finlayson (George), Aitken, Jenkins, Shaw, Macdonald.
aet

Clyde (0) 1 *(Keogh 58)*
Partick T (0) 0 2838
Clyde: Budinauckas; Murray, Dunn, Smith, Cranmer, Ross, Okikiolu (Bingham), Millen, Keogh (Crawford), McClay, Hinds (Convery).
Partick T: Gow; Huxford (McKinstry), Archibald, Craigan, Paterson, Connaghan, Walker (McLean), Lennon, Britton, Dolan (Kelly), Hardie.

Clydebank (1) 1 *(Burke 41)*
Airdrieonians (2) 2 *(McPherson 10, Coyle 31)* 469
Clydebank: Smith; Bossy, McKinnon (McVey), McNally, Whiteford (Mooney), Paton, McGowan, Hamilton, Kinnaird (Gilliland), Burke, McGrillen.
Airdrieonians: Ferguson; Docherty, McPherson, Stewart, McManus, James, Taylor (Armstrong), Macfarlane, Coyle, Smith (Beasley), Roberts (Dunn).

Ross Co (0) 0
Brechin C (1) 2 *(Grant 17, Kernaghan 83)* 730
Ross Co: Bullock; Perry, Hastings (Prest), Maxwell, Webb, Fraser (Ferguson), Mackay S, Hislop (Holmes), Bone, Cowie, Robertson.
Brechin C: Cairns; Smith, Fotheringham, Bain, Cairney, Kernaghan, King, Riley, Grant, Templeman, Miller.

SEMI-FINALS

28 AUG

Airdrieonians (1) 1 *(Roberts 23)*
Brechin C (0) 1 *(Fotheringham 87)* 1655
Airdrieonians: Ferguson; Armstrong, McPherson (Taylor), Docherty, McManus, James, Beasley (Gardner), Macfarlane, Coyle, Smith, Roberts (Dunn).
Brechin C: Cairns; Smith (Leask), Fotheringham, Bain, Cairney, Kernaghan, King, Miller, Grant (McAllister), Templeman, Honeyman (Black).
aet; Airdrieonians won 4-3 on penalties.

Clyde (0) 0
Alloa Ath (0) 1 *(Hutchison 55)* 1197
Clyde: Budinauckas; Murray, Dunn (Convery), Smith, Cranmer, Ross, Mitchell, Millen, Keogh (Hinds), Okikiolu (McClay), McPhee.
Alloa Ath: Soutar; Knox, Seaton, Watson, Thomson, Valentine, Hamilton, Fisher, Evans (Irvine), Hutchison, Little

FINAL (at Broadwood Stadium)

14 OCT

Airdrieonians (0) 2 *(Coyle 76, Roberts 86)*
Alloa Ath (0) 1 *(Evans 90)* 4548
Airdrieonians: Ferguson; Armstrong, McPherson, Stewart, McManus, James, Gardner (Dunn), Macfarlane, Coyle, Taylor, Roberts.
Alloa Ath: Soutar; Knox (Curran), Seaton, Watson, Thomson, Valentine, Hamilton, Fisher (Christie), Walker (Evans), Hutchison, Little.
Referee: Michael McCurry.

SCOTTISH CUP FINALS 1874–2002

Year	Winners	Runners-up	Score
1874	Queen's Park	Clydesdale	2-0
1875	Queen's Park	Renton	3-0
1876	Queen's Park	Third Lanark	2-0 after 1-1 draw
1877	Vale of Leven	Rangers	3-2 after 0-0 and 1-1 draws
1878	Vale of Leven	Third Lanark	1-0
1879	Vale of Leven*	Rangers	
1880	Queen's Park	Thornlibank	3-0
1881	Queen's Park†	Dumbarton	3-1
1882	Queen's Park	Dumbarton	4-1 after 2-2 draw
1883	Dumbarton	Vale of Leven	2-1 after 2-2 draw
1884	Queen's Park‡	Vale of Leven	
1885	Renton	Vale of Leven	3-1 after 0-0 draw
1886	Queen's Park	Renton	3-1
1887	Hibernian	Dumbarton	2-1
1888	Renton	Cambuslang	6-1
1889	Third Lanark§	Celtic	2-1
1890	Queen's Park	Vale of Leven	2-1 after 1-1 draw
1891	Hearts	Dumbarton	1-0
1892	Celtic¶	Queen's Park	5-1
1893	Queen's Park	Celtic	2-1
1894	Rangers	Celtic	3-1
1895	St Bernard's	Renton	2-1
1896	Hearts	Hibernian	3-1
1897	Rangers	Dumbarton	5-1
1898	Rangers	Kilmarnock	2-0
1899	Celtic	Rangers	2-0
1900	Celtic	Queen's Park	4-3
1901	Hearts	Celtic	4-3
1902	Hibernian	Celtic	1-0
1903	Rangers	Hearts	2-0 after 1-1 and 0-0 draws
1904	Celtic	Rangers	3-2
1905	Third Lanark	Rangers	3-1 after 0-0 draw
1906	Hearts	Third Lanark	1-0
1907	Celtic	Hearts	3-0
1908	Celtic	St Mirren	5-1
1909	••		
1910	Dundee	Clyde	2-1 after 2-2 and 0-0 draws
1911	Celtic	Hamilton A	2-0 after 0-0 draw
1912	Celtic	Clyde	2-0
1913	Falkirk	Raith R	2-0
1914	Celtic	Hibernian	4-1 after 0-0 draw
1920	Kilmarnock	Albion R	3-2
1921	Partick T	Rangers	1-0
1922	Morton	Rangers	1-0
1923	Celtic	Hibernian	1-0
1924	Airdrieonians	Hibernian	2-0
1925	Celtic	Dundee	2-1
1926	St Mirren	Celtic	2-0
1927	Celtic	East Fife	3-1
1928	Rangers	Celtic	4-0
1929	Kilmarnock	Rangers	2-0
1930	Rangers	Partick T	2-1 after 0-0 draw
1931	Celtic	Motherwell	4-2 after 2-2 draw
1932	Rangers	Kilmarnock	3-0 after 1-1 draw
1933	Celtic	Motherwell	1-0
1934	Rangers	St Mirren	5-0
1935	Rangers	Hamilton A	2-1
1936	Rangers	Third Lanark	1-0
1937	Celtic	Aberdeen	2-1
1938	East Fife	Kilmarnock	4-2 after 1-1 draw
1939	Clyde	Motherwell	4-0
1947	Aberdeen	Hibernian	2-1
1948	Rangers	Morton	1-0 after 1-1 draw
1949	Rangers	Clyde	4-1
1950	Rangers	East Fife	3-0
1951	Celtic	Motherwell	1-0
1952	Motherwell	Dundee	4-0
1953	Rangers	Aberdeen	1-0 after 1-1 draw
1954	Celtic	Aberdeen	2-1
1955	Clyde	Celtic	1-0 after 1-1 draw
1956	Hearts	Celtic	3-1
1957	Falkirk	Kilmarnock	2-1 after 1-1 draw
1958	Clyde	Hibernian	1-0
1959	St Mirren	Aberdeen	3-1
1960	Rangers	Kilmarnock	2-0
1961	Dunfermline Ath	Celtic	2-0 after 0-0 draw
1962	Rangers	St Mirren	2-0
1963	Rangers	Celtic	3-0 after 1-1 draw
1964	Rangers	Dundee	3-1
1965	Celtic	Dunfermline Ath	3-2
1966	Rangers	Celtic	1-0 after 0-0 draw
1967	Celtic	Aberdeen	2-0
1968	Dunfermline Ath	Hearts	3-1
1969	Celtic	Rangers	4-0
1970	Aberdeen	Celtic	3-1

Year	Winners	Runners-up	Score
1971	Celtic	Rangers	2-1 after 1-1 draw
1972	Celtic	Hibernian	6-1
1973	Rangers	Celtic	3-2
1974	Celtic	Dundee U	3-0
1975	Celtic	Airdrieonians	3-1
1976	Rangers	Hearts	3-1
1977	Celtic	Rangers	1-0
1978	Rangers	Aberdeen	2-1
1979	Rangers	Hibernian	3-2 after 0-0 and 0-0 draws
1980	Celtic	Rangers	1-0
1981	Rangers	Dundee U	4-1 after 0-0 draw
1982	Aberdeen	Rangers	4-1 (aet)
1983	Aberdeen	Rangers	1-0 (aet)
1984	Aberdeen	Celtic	2-1 (aet)
1985	Celtic	Dundee U	2-1
1986	Aberdeen	Hearts	3-0
1987	St Mirren	Dundee U	1-0 (aet)
1988	Celtic	Dundee U	2-1
1989	Celtic	Rangers	1-0
1990	Aberdeen	Celtic	0-0 (aet)

(Aberdeen won 9-8 on penalties)

Year	Winners	Runners-up	Score
1991	Motherwell	Dundee U	4-3 (aet)
1992	Rangers	Airdrieonians	2-1
1993	Rangers	Aberdeen	2-1
1994	Dundee U	Rangers	1-0
1995	Celtic	Airdrieonians	1-0
1996	Rangers	Hearts	5-1
1997	Kilmarnock	Falkirk	1-0
1998	Hearts	Rangers	2-1
1999	Rangers	Celtic	1-0
2000	Rangers	Aberdeen	4-0
2001	Celtic	Hibernian	3-0
2002	Rangers	Celtic	3-2

*Vale of Leven awarded cup, Rangers failing to appear for replay after 1-1 draw.
†After Dumbarton protested the first game, which Queen's Park won 2-1.
‡Queen's Park awarded cup, Vale of Leven failing to appear.
§Replay by order of Scottish FA because of playing conditions in first match, won 3-0 by Third Lanark.
¶After mutually protested game which Celtic won 1-0.
••Owing to riot, the cup was withheld after two drawn games – between Celtic and Rangers 2-2 and 1-1.

SCOTTISH CUP WINS

Celtic 31, Rangers 30, Queen's Park 10, Aberdeen 7, Hearts 6, Clyde 3, Kilmarnock 3, St Mirren 3, Vale of Leven 3, Dunfermline Ath 2, Falkirk 2, Hibernian 2, Motherwell 2, Renton 2, Third Lanark 2, Airdrieonians 1, Dumbarton 1, Dundee 1, Dundee U 1, East Fife 1, Morton 1, Partick T 1, St Bernard's 1.

APPEARANCES IN FINAL

Celtic 50, Rangers 47, Aberdeen 15, Queen's Park 12, Hearts 12, Hibernian 11, Kilmarnock 8, Vale of Leven 7, Clyde 6, Dumbarton 6, Dundee U 7, Motherwell 6, St Mirren 6, Third Lanark 6, Renton 5, Airdrieonians 4, Dundee 4, Dunfermline Ath 3, East Fife 3, Falkirk 3, Hamilton A 2, Morton 2, Partick T 2, Albion R 1, Cambuslang 1, Clydesdale 1, Raith R 1, St Bernard's 1, Thornliebank 1.

Here we go! Rangers players celebrate a famous last minute Scottish Cup Final win over arch rivals Celtic. Peter Lovenkrands second goal of the game sealed victory after being 2-1 down. (Colorsport)

TENNENT'S SCOTTISH CUP 2001–02

FIRST ROUND

17 NOV

Albion R (0) 0
Elgin C (0) 0   257
Albion R: Fahey: Smith J, Lumsden, Hamilton, Easton, Booth, Waldie, McKenzie, McLean, McMullan, Bonnar.
Elgin C: Pirie: Hind, MacDonald, Furphy, McBride, Dlugonski, Ross, Campbell, Kelly, Gilzean, Tully.

Alloa A (2) 3 *(Little 11, Evans 38, Hutchison 79)*
Dumbarton (0) 1 *(McKeown 83)*   539
Alloa A: Soutar: Valentine, Anderson, Watson, Thomson, Fisher, Hamilton, Curran, Evans G, Hutchison, Little (Walker).
Dumbarton: Wight: Dickie, Stewart, McKeown, Bruce, Brittain (Dillon), Crilly, O'Neil (McCann), Robertson, McKelvie, Bonar.

Brechin C (0) 4 *(Fotheringham 59, O'Boyle 61, 70, Grant 72)*
Stenhousemuir (0) 0   408
Brechin C: Cairns: Smith D, Black, Bain (Templeman), Cairney, Smith J, King, Riley, Grant, O'Boyle, Fotheringham.
Stenhousemuir: Graham M: Storrar, Donaldson, Stone, Sandison (Ferguson), Vella (Donald B), Jackson, Milne, Graham D, Irvine, McKeown.

Morton (1) 1 *(Aitken 33)*
Queen of the S (2) 2 *(O'Neil 7, 29)*   1380
Morton: Coyle: Bannerman, Bottiglieri (Moore), Collins, McGregor, Kerr, Tweedie, Frail, O'Connor, Aitken, Miller.
Queen of the S: Scott: Gray, Atkinson, Allan, Thomson, Davidson, O'Neil (Connell), Aitken, Weatherson, McAlpine, Connelly S.

Stirling Albion (0) 2 *(Williams 55, Munro 90)*
Buckie Thistle (1) 1 *(Holmes 4)*   676
Stirling Albion: Reid: Hay, McCallion, Nugent, Morrison, Edwards, Munro, Henderson, Williams, Higgins (Ross), Stuart.
Buckie Thistle: Rae: Grant, Lamberton, Anderson, Davidson, Rattray, Holmes, Stephen, Thomson (Rowley), Bruce (Catto), Reid (Green).

Tarff Rovers (0) 1 *(Lamont 56)*
Montrose (2) 4 *(Laidlaw 19, 45, 53, Lowe 84)*   324
Tarff Rovers: Whiting: McCall, McCluskie (Rogerson), Milligan, Brown, Paterson, Eeles (Beattie), Kerr (Sloan), Lamont, Montgomery, Clelland.
Montrose: Butter: Craig, Ferguson, Muirhead, Christie, Conway, Allison, Johnson, Laidlaw (Lowe), Kerrigan (Brand), Hutcheon (McGee).

Wick Academy (0) 2 *(MacDonald 56, Mackenzie N 90)*
Threave Rovers (2) 3 *(Cochrane 22, Hudson 32, Adams 68)*   929
Wick Academy: Strong: MacLeod, Mowat, Sinclair, Gunn, Shearer, Mackenzie N, Sutherland (Murray), Mackenzie J, MacDonald (Ross), Manson (Makhouli).
Threave Rovers: McWilliam: Smith (Tuchewicz), Fraser, Allen, Gordon, Cochrane (Docherty), Kirkpatrick, McGinley, Adams (True), Hudson, Armstrong.

18 NOV

Clydebank (0) 1 *(Paton 68)*
Peterhead (0) 0   303
Clydebank: Smith: Whiteford (Dick), McGowan, Bossy, Hamilton, Paton, Ferguson, McColligan, Carrigan (Kinnaird), Burke (Graham), McGrillen.

Peterhead: Mathers: Clark, Smith, Mackay, Simpson, Tindal, Cooper, Bissett (Findlay), Yeats, Johnston, Livingstone.

FIRST ROUND REPLAY

24 NOV

Elgin C (0) 0
Albion R (1) 1 *(McLean 21)*   640
Elgin C: Pirie: Hinds, McBride, Furphy, MacDonald S, Dlugonski, Ross, Campbell (Craig R), Kelly (Morrison), Gilzean (McGlashan), Tully.
Albion R: Fahey: McKenna, Lumsden, Hamilton, Easton, Booth, Waldie, McMullan, McLean (Rankin), Harty (Silvesto) (McCormick), Bonnar.

SECOND ROUND

8 DEC

Alloa Ath (1) 1 *(Evans G 5)*
Queen of the S (0) 0   586
Alloa Ath: Evans J: Valentine, Cowan, Watson, Thomson, Christie, Hamilton (Walker), Fisher, Evans G, Hutchison, Little.
Queen of the S: Scott: Gray, Crawford, Allan, Aitken, Sunderland, O'Neil, Connell, Weatherson, Glancy (Armstrong), Atkinson (McAlpine).

Berwick R (1) 1 *(Feroz 6)*
Cowdenbeath (0) 0   412
Berwick R: McCulloch: Murie, Bennett, Farrell, Neill A, Forrest, Feroz (Harvey), Anthony, Wood, Smith (Neil M), Thomas (Bradley).
Cowdenbeath: Carver: Boyle, Raynes, Campbell, Wilson, Lawrence (Fleming), Winter, King, Brown (Mauchlen), Wright, Swift (Duff).

Brechin C (0) 0
Albion R (1) 1 *(Harty 2)*   412
Brechin C: Cairns: Riley (Millar), Black (Leask), Bain, Cairney, Smith J, King, Honeyman (Smith D), Grant, Templeman, Fotheringham.
Albion R: Fahey: McKenna, Lumsden, Hamilton, Easton, Booth, Waldie, McMullan (Diack) (McLees), McLean (McCormick), Harty, Bonnar.

Clydebank (0) 0
Stranraer (0) 1 *(Harty 48)*   314
Clydebank: Smith: Whiteford, McGowan, Bossy, Hamilton, McKinlay, Ferguson (McGrillen), Nicholls (Carrigan), Burke (Graham), Paton, McColligan.
Stranraer: McGeown: Jenkins, Wright, Farrell, Wingate, Macdonald, Finlayson, Aitken, Harty, Shaw (Blair), Hodge.

Deveronvale (0) 0
Spartans (0) 0   654
Deveronvale: Thompson: Dolan, Kinghorn, Chisholm, Henderson, Montgomery, More (McAllister), Pressley, Watt, Murray (McKenzie), Urquhart.
Spartans: Brown: McLaren, Rae, Gowrie, Burns, Irvine, Hughes, Samuel, Hobbins, Manson (Middlemist), Bird.

East Stirlingshire (0) 1 *(Lyle 73)*
Forres Mechanics (1) 1 *(Brown 37)*   427
East Stirlingshire: Hay: Ferguson, McDonald, Russell, McCheyne, McGhee, McAuley, Todd D, Lyle, Gordon, Lorimer (Hunter).
Forres Mechanics: Ridgers: Reid, Main (McIntosh), Bradshaw, MacLean, Sanderson, Whyte, MacLeod (Cameron), Brown, Connelly, Ross.

Forfar Ath (2) 2 *(Byers 8, Sellars 21)*
Threave Rovers (0) 0 545
Forfar Ath: Brown; Rattray, Milne, Horn, Good, Lunan, Sellars, Byers, Tosh, Moffat (Stewart), Christie (Henry).
Threave Rovers: McWilliam; Smith (Docherty), Fraser, Allen, McGinnlay P, McGinley A, Kirkpatrick, Cochrane, Adams, Hudson, Tuchewicz.

Gala Fairydean (1) 1 *(Lindsay 41)*
Stirling Albion (0) 0 444
Gala Fairydean: Lumsden; Green (Peters), Reid, Montgomery, Sneddon, Rose, Cochrane, Ballantyne, Martin, Clark (McGinlay), Lindsay.
Stirling Albion: Reid; Nugent (Ross), McCallion, Morrison, Edwards, Stuart (McLellan), Hay, Kearney (Moriarty), Higgins, Williams, Munro.

Hamilton A (3) 4 *(Callaghan 17, McPhee 23, McNiven 24, McFarlane 67)*
Montrose (0) 0 1079
Hamilton A: Macfarlane; Renicks, Martin, Nelson, Gaughan, Sweeney, Bonnar (Russell), McNiven (McFarlane), Moore (O'Neil), McPhee, Callaghan.
Montrose: McGlynn; Craig, Sharp, Lowe (McKellar), Christie, Conway, Allison, Johnston, Laidlaw (Mitchell), Kerrigan (Brand), Ferguson.

Queen's Park (0) 0
East Fife (0) 0 701
Queen's Park: Mitchell; Ferry, Borland, Collins, Stevenson, Caven, Jackson, Quinn, Gemmell (Brown), Canning, Fisher.
East Fife: Godfrey; Wilson, Gallagher, Gibson, Munro, Mortimer, Graham, Nairn (Allen) (Rae), McManus, Cunningham, Bailey (Herkes).

SECOND ROUND REPLAYS

15 DEC

Forres Mechanics (1) 3 *(Main 29, 60, Ross 78)*
East Stirling (1) 1 *(McDonald 15)* 522
Forres Mechanics: Ridgers; Reid, Main, Bradshaw, MacLean, Sanderson, Whyte (Cameron), MacLeod, Brown, Connelly (McIntosh), Ross.
East Stirling: Hay; Ferguson, McDonald, Russell, McGhee, Todd D, Mauchan, Lorimer, Gordon, Hunter (Hall), Scott (Tolland).

18 DEC

Spartans (0) 1 *(Samuel 73)*
Deveronvale (0) 2 *(Brown 49, Chisholm 72)* 228
Spartans: Brown; McLaren, Rae (Middlemist), Gowrie, Burns, Jardine, Hughes, Samuel, Hobbins, Manson, Bird.
Deveronvale: Thompson; Dolan, Kinghorn, Chisholm (Murray), Henderson, Montgomery, More (McAllister), Pressley, Watt, Mackenzie (Craigie), Brown.

East Fife (1) 2 *(McManus 44, 50)*
Queen's Park (1) 2 *(Jackson 5, 90)* 534
East Fife: Godfrey; Wilson, Gallagher, Gibson (Nairn), Munro, Mortimer, Herkes, Bailey (Rae), McManus, Graham (Lofting), Cunningham.
Queen's Park: Mitchell; Ferry, Borland (Gallagher) (Patterson), Collins, Stevenson, Caven, Jackson, Quinn, Gemmell, Canning, Fisher (Brown).
aet; East Fife won 4-2 on penalties.

THIRD ROUND

5 JAN

Deveronvale (0) 0
Ayr U (4) 6 *(Annand 5, 11, Sheerin 34, McGinlay 44, Crabbe 53, Grady 72)* 1648
Deveronvale: Thompson; Dolan, Kinghorn, Chisholm (Urquhart), Henderson, Montgomery, More (McAllister), Brown (McKenzie), Murray, Watt, Pressley.

Ayr U: Nelson; McEwan, Lovering, Robertson, Hughes, Craig (Sharp), Crabbe, McGinlay, Annand (McLaughlin), Grady, Sheerin (Wilson).

Dundee U (0) 3 *(Aljofree 51, 59, Miller 86)*
Forres Mechanics (0) 0 5904
Dundee U: Gallacher; Wright, Lauchlan, McCunnie, Aljofree, Carson, Fullarton (Wilson), Paterson, Easton, Hamilton (Miller), Lilley (McIntyre).
Forres Mechanics: McRitchie; Grigor, Main, Bradshaw, MacLean, McIntosh (Cameron), Whyte, MacLeod (Murphy), Brown, Connelly (Maguire), Ross.

Dunfermline Ath (2) 3 *(Crawford 20, 46, Thomson SM 37)*
Motherwell (0) 1 *(Elliott 80)* 5131
Dunfermline Ath: Ruitenbeek; MacPherson (Dair), Thomson SM, Skinner, Skerla, Mason, Nicholson, Ferguson (Kilgannon), Bullen, Crawford, Petrie (McGroarty).
Motherwell: Woods; Corrigan (Elliott), Deloumeaux, Hammell, Strong, Dow (Pearson), Lasley, Soloy (Forrest), Kelly, Adams, McFadden.

Hearts (0) 2 *(Fuller 51, 78)*
Ross Co (0) 1 *(Perry 89)* 9908
Hearts: McKenzie; Pressley, Mahe, Maybury, Webster, McKenna, Grönlund, Fulton, Flögel (Simmons), Fuller, Wales.
Ross Co: Bullock; Perry, Hastings, Maxwell, Irvine, Anselin (Cowie), McCormick (Hislop), Ferguson, Bone, Boukraa (Prest), Robertson.

Kilmarnock (3) 3 *(Mitchell 11, Sanjuan 20, Canero 33)*
Airdrieonians (0) 0 6849
Kilmarnock: Marshall; Canero, Hay, McGowne, Dindeleux, Calderon (McDonald), Murray (Johnson), Mitchell, Sanjuan, Boyd (Jaconelli), Di Giacomo.
Airdrieonians: Ferguson (Bennett); Armstrong (McDonald), McPherson, Stewart, Taylor, James, Henry, McFarlane, Coyle, Smith (Gardner), Roberts.

Stranraer (0) 0
Hibernian (0) 0 1910
Stranraer: McGeown; Gaughan, Wright, Wingate, Hodge, Aitken, Finlayson, Macdonald, Harty, Shaw (Jenkins), Grace.
Hibernian: Colgan; Fenwick, Smith, De La Cruz (Townsley), Laursen, Murray, Arpinon (Riordan), Brebner, O'Neil, McManus (Zitelli), O'Connor.

6 JAN

Dundee (0) 1 *(Milne 81)*
Falkirk (0) 1 *(Rodges 88)* 5517
Dundee: Speroni; Smith, Del Rio, Zhiyi, Beghetto, Garrido (Artero), Ketsbaia, Torres, Carranza (Romano), Milne, Sara (Caballero).
Falkirk: Hogarth; Lawrie, McQuilken, Rennie, Mair, McStay, Craig (Deuchar), Morris, Miller, Pearson (Rodgers), Waddell.

8 JAN

Albion R (0) 0
Livingston (0) 0 1116
match abandoned at half-time; floodlighting failure
Albion R: Fahey; McKenna, Lumsden, Hamilton, Easton, Booth, Waldie, McKenzie, McLean, McCormick, Bonnar.
Livingston: McEwan; Brinquin, Bollan, Rubio, Andrews, Anderson, Quino, Wilson, Tosh, Fernandez, Bingham.

Alloa Ath (0) 0
Celtic (2) 5 *(Balde 19, Wieghorst 42, Maloney 55, Petta 74, Sylla 81)* 5763
Alloa Ath: Soutar; Valentine, Cowan, Watson (Walker), Thomson, Christie, Hamilton, Fisher, Whalen (Evans G), Hutchison (Curran), Little.
Celtic: Gould; Boyd, Balde (Healy), Tebily, McNamara, Sylla, Petrov (Smith), Petta, Guppy, Wieghorst, Maloney.

Arbroath (0) 0
Inverness CT (1) 2 *(Robson 40, Ritchie 51)* 921
Arbroath: Hinchcliffe; Tait, Florence, Rowe, Ritchie, Cusick, Heenan (Swankie), McKinnon (McAulay), Bayne, McGlashan (Mallan), McInally.
Inverness CT: Walker; Tokely, McBain, Duncan, McCaffrey, Munro, Bavidge (Stewart), Wyness, Ritchie (MacDonald), Christie, Robson.

Berwick R (0) 0
Rangers (0) 0 4280
Berwick R: McCulloch; Farrell, Bennett, Murie, Neill A, Forrest, Wood, Anthony, McDonald (Bradley), Feroz (Huxford), Smith (Neil M).
Rangers: Klos; Wilson, Amoruso, Vidmar, Ross, Hughes, McCann, Latapy, Caniggia (Kanchelskis), Flo (Arveladze), Mols (de Boer).

Clyde (0) 1 *(Fraser 78)*
St Mirren (0) 0 2235
Clyde: Halliwell; Mensing, Dunn, Smith, Kernighan, De Gregorio (Bingham), Mitchell, Millen, Hinds (Cranmer), Fraser, McDowall (Convery).
St Mirren: Roy; Murray, Ross, McGowan, McLaughlin, Walker, Quitongo, Gillies, McGarry (Wreh), Burns, McGinty (Nicolson).

East Fife (1) 2 *(McManus 19, Bailey 56)*
Partick T (3) 4 *(Walker 22, 69, McLean 40, Hardie 44)* 1658
East Fife: Godfrey; Wilson, Gallagher, Gibson, Munro, Mortimer, Herkes, Bailey (Allan), McManus, Graham (Lofting), Cunningham.
Partick T: Arthur; McCulloch (McKinstry), Archibald, Craigan, Paterson, Deas, Walker, Lennon, McLean (Britton), Hardie, Fleming (Dolan).

Hamilton A (0) 1 *(McPhee 77)*
Raith R (0) 0 1727
Hamilton A: Macfarlane; Renicks, Martin (MacLaren), Nelson, Sweeney, Bonnar, Graham, McNiven, Moore, McPhee, Callaghan.
Raith R: Miotto; McCulloch, Quesada, Ellis, Browne, Javary, Zoco (Novo), Nanou (Clark), Smith A, Jones (Hampshire), Stein.

St Johnstone (0) 0
Aberdeen (0) 2 *(Thornley 58, Darren Young 89)* 4267
St Johnstone: Miller; Forsyth, McCluskey, Murray, Dods, Djebeili (Russell), Dasovic, Kane (McBride), Hartley, Connolly (Falconer), MacDonald.
Aberdeen: Esson; McAllister, McGuire, Whyte, McNaughton, Bisconti (Thornley), Darren Young, Guntweit, Dadi, Winters (Anderson), Derek Young.

16 JAN

Gala Fairydean (0) 0
Forfar Ath (3) 5 *(Tosh 12, 54, Yardley 36, Sellars 42, Byers 52)* 892
Gala Fairydean: Lumsden; Green (Brown), Reid, Sneddon, Montgomery, Rose, Cochrane, Ballantyne, Martin, Clark, Lindsay.
Forfar Ath: Brown; McCloy, Milne (Williams), Horn, Good, Lunan (Moffat), Stewart, Sellars, Tosh, Yardley (Taylor), Byers.

THIRD ROUND REPLAYS

14 JAN

Albion R (1) 1 *(McLean 42)*
Livingston (2) 4 *(Wilson 1, Bingham 29, 89, Fernandez 84)* 2234
Albion R: Fahey; McKenna, Lumsden, Hamilton, Easton, Booth, Waldie (McMullan), McKenzie, McLean, Harty (McCormick), Bonnar.
Livingston: Culkin; Brinquin, Bollan, Anderson, Rubio, Tosh, Quino, Wilson (Brittain), Hart (Lowndes), Fernandez, Bingham.
at New Broomfield, Airdrie

15 JAN

Hibernian (2) 4 *(Luna 5, Zitelli 15 (pen), Smith 47, Hurtado 87)*
Stranraer (0) 0 8536
Hibernian: Colgan; Fenwick, Smith, Jack, Laursen, Murray, Orman (Hurtado), Brebner (De la Cruz), Townsley, Luna, Zitelli (O'Connor).
Stranraer: McGeown; Gaughan (Blair), Wright, Wingate, Hodge, Macdonald, Finlayson, Aitken, Harty (Jenkins), Shaw, Grace.

16 JAN

Falkirk (0) 0
Dundee (1) 1 *(Zhiyi 11)* 4739
Falkirk: Hogarth; Lawrie, McQuilken, Mair, Christie, McStay (Deuchar), Morris, Kerr, Miller, Rodgers (Waddell), Craig.
Dundee: Speroni; Smith, Zhiyi, Del Rio, Artero (Beith), Romano, Rae, Beghetto, Carranza, Caballero (Kemas), Sara (Ketsbaia).

21 JAN

Rangers (0) 3 *(Amoruso 57, Konterman 65, Arveladze 69)*
Berwick R (0) 0 17,662
Rangers: Klos; Ross, Amoruso, Vidmar (de Boer), Konterman, Hughes, Ferguson, Latapy (Lovenkrands), McCann, Arveladze, Mols (Dodds).
Berwick R: McCulloch; Farrell (McNicoll), Bennett, Murie, Neill A, Forrest, Wood, Anthony (Bradley), McDonald (Neil M), Feroz, Smith.

FOURTH ROUND

26 JAN

Aberdeen (2) 2 *(Winters 6, McAllister 18)*
Livingston (0) 0 10,261
Aberdeen: Kjaer; McGuire, McAllister, Whyte, McNaughton, Darren Young, Bisconti, Guntweit, Dadi (Mackie), Winters (Thornley), Derek Young.
Livingston: Culkin; Brinquin (Lowndes), Bollan, Rubio, Hart (Aurellio), Anderson, Quino, Wilson, Tosh, Fernandez, Bingham.

Ayr U (2) 3 *(Grady 30, MacPherson 38 (og), Robertson 58)*
Dunfermline Ath (0) 0 3627
Ayr U: Nelson; Robertson, Lovering, Duffy, Hughes, Craig, Wilson, McGinlay, Crabbe (Annand), Grady, Sheerin (Scally).
Dunfermline Ath: Thomson SY; MacPherson, Thomson SM, Skinner (Panoploulos), Skerla, Mason, Nicholson, Ferguson (Hampshire), Bullen, Crawford, Petrie.

Clyde (1) 1 *(Mensing 32)*
Forfar Ath (1) 2 *(Tosh 11, Sellars 57)* 1289
Clyde: Halliwell; Mensing, McLaughlin (Convery), Smith, Kernighan, Ross (Bingham), Mitchell, Fraser, Keogh, Hinds (Crawford), Hagen.
Forfar Ath: Brown; McCloy, Milne, Rattray, Good, Lunan, Stewart, Sellars, Tosh, Yardley (Christie), Byers.

Hearts (1) 1 *(Wales 45)*
Inverness CT (1) 3 *(Tokely 25, Wyness 58, Bagan 73)* 12,516
Hearts: Niemi; McCann (Simmons), Mahe, Maybury, Webster (Kirk), Flögel, Severin, Fulton, Grönlund, Fuller, Wales (Adam).
Inverness CT: Walker; Tokely, McBain, Mann, McCaffrey, Munro, Duncan, Wyness, Ritchie, Christie (Bagan), Robson.

Kilmarnock (0) 0
Celtic (0) 2 *(Hay 50 (og), Larsson 62)* 11,249
Kilmarnock: Marshall; Canero, McGowne, Hay, Dindeleux, Murray (Dargo), Mahood, Fowler, Mitchell, McLaren (Boyd), Johnson.
Celtic: Douglas; Mjällby, Valgaeren, Balde, Thompson (Petta), McNamara, Lennon, Lambert (Sylla), Petrov, Larsson, Hartson.

Partick T (0) 1 *(McLean 51)*

Dundee (0) 1 *(Torres 52)*   7025

Partick T: Arthur; McCulloch (McKinstry), Archibald, Craigan, Paterson, Dolan, Constantine (Britton), Lennon, McLean, Hardie, Fleming (Walker).
Dundee: Speroni; Smith, Zhiyi, Del Rio, Artero (Carranza), Beghetto, Torres, Romano, Robertson, Sara (Kemas), Caballero (Beith).

Rangers (2) 4 *(Flo 23, 64, Lovenkrands 45, Dodds 85)*

Hibernian (1) 1 *(Brebner 28)*   25,636

Rangers: Klos; Ricksen, Moore, Amoruso, Vidmar, Konterman, Ferguson, de Boer (Dodds), Lovenkrands, Flo, Arveladze.
Hibernian: Colgan; Fenwick, Smith, Jack, Laursen, De la Cruz, Murray, Brebner, Townsley (Arpinon), Hurtado (Riordan), Luna (O'Connor).

4 FEB

Dundee U (0) 4 *(Winters 83, Thompson 84, 89, Aljofree 86)*

Hamilton A (0) 0   4999

Dundee U: Gallacher; Wright, Lauchlan, McCunnie, Aljofree, Easton, Fullarton, Miller, McIntyre (Carson), McConalogue (Thompson), Lilley (Winters).
Hamilton A: Macfarlane; Renicks, Cunnington, Nelson, Sweeney, MacLaren, Bonnar (O'Neil), McNiven (McCreadie), Moore, Graham, Callaghan.

FOURTH ROUND REPLAY

6 FEB

Dundee (0) 1 *(Sara 55)*

Partick T (1) 2 *(Britton 24, Gibson 87)*   5913

Dundee: Speroni; Smith, Del Rio, Mackay, Zhiyi, Torres, Ketsbaia, Rae, Carranza (Robertson), Kemas (Sara), Milne (Caballero).
Partick T: Arthur; McKinstry (Gibson), Archibald, Craigan, Kelly, Deas, Britton, Lennon, Walker, Hardie, Fleming.

QUARTER-FINALS

23 FEB

Dundee U (2) 2 *(Winters 6, Easton 23)*

Ayr U (1) 2 *(Crabbe 8, McGinlay 73)*   5584

Dundee U: Gallacher; McCracken, Lauchlan, McCunnie, Griffin, Aljofree, Fullarton (Lilley), Miller, Easton, Winters, Thompson (Carson).
Ayr U: Nelson; Robertson, Lovering, Duffy, Hughes, Craig, Wilson, McGinlay, Crabbe (Scally), Grady, Sheerin.

Partick T (0) 2 *(Hardie 59, Paterson 74)*

Inverness CT (1) 2 *(Wyness 6, 61)*   8730

Partick T: Arthur; Dolan (McKinstry), Archibald, Craigan, Paterson, Deas, Britton (McLean), Lennon, Walker, Hardie, Fleming (Gibson).
Inverness CT: Walker; Tokely, McBain, Mann, McCaffrey, Munro, Duncan, Wyness, Ritchie (Bavidge), Christie, Robson.

24 FEB

Aberdeen (0) 0

Celtic (1) 2 *(Hartson 5, Petrov 52)*   17,082

Aberdeen: Kjaer; McGuire, McAllister, Whyte, McNaughton, Darren Young, Bisconti, Dadi, Winters, Derek Young (Zerouali), Mackie.
Celtic: Douglas; Mjällby, Sutton (Crainey), Balde, Thompson, Petrov, Lennon, Lambert, Moravcik (Maloney), Hartson, Agathe.

Forfar Ath (0) 0

Rangers (4) 6 *(Dodds 45sec, 60, 90, Arveladze 30, 39, Kanchelskis 42)*   4504

Forfar Ath: Brown; Rattray, Milne (Christie), Horn, Good, Lunan (Henry), Bett (Moffat), Sellars, Tosh, Stewart, Byers.
Rangers: Klos (McGregor); Ricksen (Ross), Amoruso, Vidmar, Numan, Hughes, Ferguson, McCann, Kanchelskis, Dodds, Arveladze (Latapy).

QUARTER-FINAL REPLAYS

5 MAR

Inverness CT (0) 0

Partick T (0) 1 *(Paterson 67)*   4935

Inverness CT: Walker; Tokely, McBain, Mann, McCaffrey (Bavidge), Munro, Duncan, Wyness, Ritchie, Christie, Bagan.
Partick T: Arthur; Kelly, Dolan, Cragan, Paterson, Deas, Britton, Lennon, McLean, Hardie, Fleming.

6 MAR

Ayr U (1) 2 *(Crabbe 16, Sheerin 80)*

Dundee U (0) 0   4445

Ayr U: Nelson; Robertson, Lovering, Duffy (McEwan), Hughes, Craig, Wilson, McGinlay, Crabbe (Kean), Grady (Sharp), Sheerin.
Dundee U: Gallacher; McCunnie, Lauchlan, McCracken, Griffin, Hannah (Aljofree), Venetis (Carson), Miller, Easton, Thompson, Lilley (Winters).

SEMI-FINALS (at Hampden Park)

23 MAR

Ayr U (0) 0

Celtic (0) 3 *(Larsson 49, Thompson 80, 87)* 26,774

Ayr U: Nelson; Robertson, Lovering, Duffy, Hughes, Craig, Wilson (McLaughlin), McGinlay, Crabbe (Annand), Grady, Sheerin.
Celtic: Douglas; Mjällby, Crainey, Balde, Guppy (Thompson), Petrov (McNamara), Lennon, Lambert, Agathe, Larsson, Hartson.

24 MAR

Rangers (1) 3 *(Nerlinger 10, 72, Ferguson 78)*

Partick T (0) 0   31,969

Rangers: Klos; Ricksen, Amoruso, Vidmar, Malcolm, Kanchelskis, Ferguson (Hughes), Nerlinger, McCann, Caniggia (Lovenkrands), Flo.
Partick T: Arthur; Kelly, Archibald, Craigan, Paterson, Deas, Walker, Lennon, McLean (Cameron), McCulloch (McAnespie), Britton (McKinstry).

FINAL (at Hampden Park)

4 MAY

Celtic (1) 2 *(Hartson 18, Balde 50)*

Rangers (1) 3 *(Lovenkrands 20, 90, Ferguson 69)* 51,138

Celtic: Douglas; Mjällby, Sutton, Balde, Thompson, Petrov, Lennon, Lambert (McNamara), Agathe, Larsson, Hartson.
Rangers: Klos; Ricksen, Amoruso, Moore, Numan, Ross, Ferguson, Lovenkrands, de Boer, Caniggia (Arveladze), McCann.
Referee: Hugh Dallas.

WELSH FOOTBALL 2001–02

It was the stuff of fantasy football. A 21-year-old local lad scoring the winner on his international debut in one of the game's finest stadiums against a team with an unrivalled World Cup track record. Indeed, Robert Earnshaw could hardly believe it himself.

'It's like a dream really,' he said immediately after Wales had beaten Germany 1-0 at the Millennium Stadium in the Welsh capital in May. 'I don't really know what to say.'

Fortunately for the diminutive and dashing Cardiff City striker, plenty of other people weren't lost for words following his breathtaking left-foot volley just 15 seconds into the second half of another historic victory over Germany.

Mark Hughes, who played in the 1-0 win over the then World Champions in 1991, described the result as the biggest victory of his managerial career. 'Before the game,' he said, 'Germany didn't know anything about Robert Earnshaw – they do now.' And that result, after impressive displays against the Czech Republic and Argentina in Cardiff, also meant that Wales too were a force to be reckoned with. Germany may not have been the team they once were – as well as winning the World Cup three times, they have lost two finals and three semi-finals – but it was a fully deserved victory which confirmed the Welsh resurgence under Hughes. Too many draws blunted their hopes of reaching Japan and Korea but a well-organised and hard-working side – supplemented by the flair of Ryan Giggs, Craig Bellamy and now Earnshaw – will surely pose problems for Italy, Yugoslavia, Finland and Azerbaijan in the Euro 2004 qualifiers.

Although the international season ended on a high, there wasn't too much to celebrate on the domestic front. Cardiff City's expensively assembled squad under-performed until Lennie Lawrence replaced Alan Cork as manager in late February. A fantastic 14-match unbeaten run took The Bluebirds to within a minute of the Division Two play-off final but Stoke refused to give up, scored a late equaliser and then an extra-time winner to deprive Cardiff and owner Sam Hammam of a second successive promotion. As some had suspected all along, the team weren't quite good enough. Their remarkable 2-1 FA Cup win over the then Premiership leaders, Leeds United, at Ninian Park in January was sadly overshadowed by some disgraceful crowd scenes during and after the tie – behaviour which incredibly earned the club a derisory £20,000 fine from the Welsh FA. If Hammam is serious about taking Cardiff into the Premiership on the back of a new stadium, he needs to clean up his act and completely disown the hooligans who are threatening to destroy the club. As rehabilitation has clearly failed, it's time for the former Wimbledon owner to take a personal lead. It's not only racism that needs to be kicked out of football.

As Cardiff went very close at one end of the table, Wrexham made it perfectly clear that they would struggle to stay in Division Two. After narrowly missing out on the play-offs for three years, a hat-trick of indifferent seasons was followed by relegation as The Robins paid the price for investing more in their stadium than their team by finishing next to bottom. Long-serving manager Brian Flynn resigned but his successor Denis Smith was powerless to stop the rot.

Wrexham's problems were as nothing compared to those of Swansea who, during a traumatic and often tempestuous season, managed to retain their place in Division Three. It all started to go wrong when manager John Hollins and his assistant, Alan Curtis, were prematurely sacked after just six league games and replaced by another old hand, Colin Addison, and the former Barry manager, Peter Nicholas. Boardroom shenanigans led to the club being briefly owned by the Australian-based businessman Tony Petty who succeeded in upsetting virtually everyone by threatening to sack some players and reduce the contracts of others. Stability was restored by the Professional Footballer's Association who stepped in to pay their members' wages but after steering The Swans to safety, Addison and Nicholas were then summarily sacked by a consortium of enthusiastic, well-meaning but naive local businessmen. They then attempted to recruit Flynn before finally settling on PFA chairman Nick Cusack as player-coach who, after the club had finished 20th – in the end 15 points ahead of relegated Halifax – immediately, and inevitably, began to wield the axe.

The three Welsh teams playing in the English pyramid had a mixed season. While Newport finished 5th, their highest position, in the Premier Division of the Dr Martens League, Merthyr were relegated but Colwyn Bay managed to stay in the Unibond League's top flight.

As usual, the League of Wales clubs who qualified for Europe struggled to make an impact. Carmarthen Town performed gallantly in their Intertoto Cup home leg before going down 3-0 to AIK Solna but TNS Llansantffraid and Cwmbran lost heavily to Polonia Warsaw and Slovan Bratislava respectively in the qualifying round of the UEFA Cup. Barry Town became the first Welsh club to win a Champions League tie after beating Shamkir from Azerbaijan 3-0 on aggregate in the first qualifying round but were then thumped 8-0 in Porto. Pride was restored with a 3-1 home win and after completing a second successive 'double' under Nicholas's replacement Kenny Brown, Barry will fly the Welsh flag in Europe again this season. TNS Llansantffraid and Bangor City, who Barry beat in the Welsh Cup Final, will be the UEFA Cup representatives while Caersws make their European debut in the Intertoto Cup. Mention must be made of the semi-professional Welsh team who upset the form book by winning the non-league Four Nations tournament in May under the astute management of Carmarthen's Tomi Morgan and Bangor City striker Marc Lloyd-Williams who finished as Europe's top scorer with 47 league goals. After their play-off anti-climax, Cardiff won the FAW Premier Cup by beating arch-rivals Swansea 1-0 at Ninian Park.

As the Wembley replacement row rumbled on, the magnificent Millennium Stadium successfully staged all the domestic game's finals for the second successive season with Mark Hughes helping Blackburn to lift the Worthington Cup in his first appearance on the famous turf before being released by the Premiership club. Like Earnshaw, Hughes made a spectacular Welsh debut – scoring the winner against England in 1984 – and he'll now be hoping that 'Earnie' enjoys an equally successful international career – particularly after his sensational goal ensured that Wales did, after all, reach one of the most extraordinary World Cups ever staged. A photograph of Earnshaw's trademark celebration – a double somersault – was featured on the front page of the *Korean Herald* and was later used to both launch the World Cup and help explain football's appeal to a mainly baseball-loving nation. 'This player's enthusiasm sums up the excitement of soccer' read the accompanying article: let's hope a few more stunning somersaults will mean Wales spending a month in Portugal in the summer of 2004.

GRAHAME LLOYD

LEAGUE OF WALES 2001-02

Home \ Away	Aberystwyth Town	Afan Lido	Bangor City	Barry Town	Caernarfon	Caersws	Carmarthen Town	Connah's Quay Nomads	Cwmbran Town	Flexsys Cefn Druids	Haverfordwest County	Llanelli	Newtown	Oswestry Town	Port Talbot Town	Rhayader Town	Rhyl	Total Network Solutions
Aberystwyth Town	—	2-0	2-1	2-2	0-0	1-3	1-1	2-0	3-0	1-1	0-0	3-1	2-2	3-0	4-1	1-0	1-1	1-3
Afan Lido	0-1	—	1-0	1-1	3-0	2-1	1-0	0-2	2-0	0-0	3-0	2-1	1-0	3-0	2-1	4-1	2-1	0-2
Bangor City	2-0	1-0	—	2-2	3-3	1-1	3-0	2-1	1-3	6-0	3-0	2-0	2-1	2-1	3-1	1-0	3-0	3-0
Barry Town	4-1	3-2	1-1	—	2-0	0-3	0-0	0-1	2-1	6-0	5-0	2-0	3-0	7-1	3-0	5-0	1-0	3-1
Caernarfon	4-1	2-1	1-3	1-5	—	3-3	1-2	2-1	0-2	4-2	6-0	4-5	0-0	4-1	1-2	2-0	3-2	0-1
Caersws	2-1	6-0	2-1	1-4	2-1	—	1-1	1-2	2-0	0-0	3-0	2-1	1-0	2-3	2-1	3-0	2-0	1-2
Carmarthen Town	2-1	3-0	0-0	1-2	5-1	3-0	—	2-2	1-2	0-2	1-2	0-0	3-1	3-2	0-1	5-0	1-0	3-1
Connah's Quay Nomads	1-2	2-0	4-2	2-2	1-2	1-2	0-0	—	4-2	2-1	2-2	0-6	2-2	5-1	0-0	4-0	2-1	0-0
Cwmbran Town	2-0	0-1	3-6	1-2	3-2	3-2	1-1	2-1	—	5-1	2-2	6-1	0-1	8-2	0-0	4-2	0-3	0-4
Flexsys Cefn Druids	1-2	1-2	3-7	0-2	1-3	2-1	0-4	1-2	2-4	—	2-2	0-1	1-0	1-2	0-0	4-2	2-0	2-2
Haverfordwest County	2-3	0-1	2-4	0-1	2-2	2-4	0-3	0-3	2-0	2-2	—	2-1	2-0	4-1	1-1	3-3	4-2	3-3
Llanelli	3-2	0-1	2-6	1-1	1-0	2-0	1-0	1-1	0-3	1-1	3-4	—	1-1	2-2	1-2	1-1	3-3	1-3
Newtown	1-1	1-3	2-1	0-1	3-3	1-0	1-0	1-0	1-1	0-5	2-1	1-0	—	1-1	1-3	2-0	1-1	0-1
Oswestry Town	2-5	0-3	0-1	0-2	1-1	1-3	1-1	1-0	0-2	0-2	3-2	0-1	0-0	—	2-3	1-2	0-3	1-5
Port Talbot Town	1-1	1-1	1-1	2-3	1-4	1-0	1-0	0-2	1-2	6-2	1-1	3-2	3-1	2-3	—	1-1	2-2	1-0
Rhayader Town	0-2	0-0	0-7	0-3	0-1	2-6	2-4	1-1	0-3	3-4	3-2	3-0	0-3	1-2	1-1	—	2-3	0-1
Rhyl	3-0	1-0	0-3	3-1	3-1	1-3	3-1	0-4	1-0	1-2	2-1	2-0	1-0	2-0	3-1	1-1	—	1-1
Total Network Solutions	2-1	2-0	1-1	1-1	2-2	1-0	3-0	5-1	0-1	2-1	2-1	1-0	3-2	1-0	4-0	4-0	1-2	—

LEAGUE OF WALES

	P	W	*Home* D	L	*Goals* F	A	W	*Away* D	L	*Goals* F	A	GD	Pts
Barry Town	34	13	2	2	47	11	10	6	1	35	18	53	77
Total Network Solutions.	34	12	3	2	35	13	9	4	4	30	20	32	70
Bangor City	34	13	3	1	40	13	8	3	6	43	25	45	69
Caersws	34	11	2	4	33	17	7	2	8	32	27	21	58
Afan Lido	34	12	2	3	27	11	6	2	9	15	25	6	58
Rhyl	34	11	2	4	28	19	6	3	8	25	26	8	56
Cwmbran Town	34	8	3	6	40	31	9	1	7	26	22	13	55
Connah's Quay Nomads	34	7	6	4	32	25	7	3	7	24	21	10	51
Aberystwyth Town	34	8	7	2	29	16	6	2	9	24	32	5	51
Carmarthen Town	34	9	3	5	33	17	4	6	7	18	20	14	48
Caernarfon Town	34	8	2	7	38	31	4	6	7	26	33	0	44
Port Talbot Town	34	7	3	7	28	27	5	4	8	16	28	−11	43
Newtown	34	7	6	4	21	19	2	5	10	14	25	−9	38
Flexsys Cefn Druids	34	4	2	11	23	38	4	6	7	26	41	−30	32
Llanelli	34	4	6	7	21	31	4	1	12	20	33	−23	31
Oswestry Town	34	4	4	9	17	33	4	2	11	22	51	−45	30
Haverfordwest County	34	4	5	8	27	33	2	5	10	20	43	−29	28
Rhayader Town	34	2	3	12	17	43	1	3	13	12	46	−60	15

WELSH CUP 2001–02

Preliminary Round (played Saturday 25th August 2001)
Caerau Ely v Troedyrhiw	3-0
RTB Ebbw Vale v Pontypool Town	4-0

First Round (played Saturday 15th September 2001)
Aberaman Athletic v Abercynon Athletic	5-1
Ammanford v Pontardawe Town	3-5
Bala Town v Mold Alexandra	1-5
Bettws v Ely Rangers	2-1
(aet)	
Brickfield Rangers v Brymbo Broughton	1-2
Briton Ferry Athletic v Pontlottyn Blast Furnace	4-2
Buckley Town v Gresford Athletic	0-1
Caerleon v Caerau Ely	2-2
(aet; Caerleon won 6-5 on penalties)	
Cemaes Bay v Lex XI	2-3
Corwen Amateurs v Llandudno	0-6
Flint Town United v Denbigh Town	1-2
Garden Village v Seven Sisters	3-1
Goytre United v Dinas Powys	1-3
Guilsfield v CPD Penrhyncoch	0-5
Gwynfi United v Bridgend Town	6-2
Holyhead Hotspur v Prestatyn Town	7-4
Llandyrnog United v Halkyn United	1-2
Llanfairpwll v Caersws	2-0
Meifod v Llanidloes Town	2-3
Merthyr Saints v Garw Athletic	2-4
Neath v Porth Tywyn Suburbs	4-3
Newcastle Emlyn v Llanrhaeadr	0-2
Penrhiwceiber Rangers v AFC Rhondda	3-1
Pontyclun v Taffs Well	1-0
Pontypridd Town v AFC Llwydcoed	3-1
Porthcawl Town v Newport YMCA	3-3
(aet; Newport YMCA won 5-4 on penalties)	
CPD Porthmadog v Conwy United	2-1
Portos Grange Quins v Cardiff Corinthians	1-3
Presteigne St Andrews v Llandrindod Wells	5-0
Risca & Gelli United v Fields Park Pontllanfraith	2-4
Ruthin Town v Rhos Aelwyd	2-0
Skewen Athletic v Morriston Town	5-0
Tredegar Town v RTB Ebbw Vale	0-1
Treharris Athletic v Cardiff Civil Service	0-2
Treowen Stars v Blaenrhondda	1-3
Welshpool Town v Chirk AAA	3-0

Second Round
Bettws v Garw Athletic	5-2
Blaenrhondda v UWIC Inter Cardiff	7-3
(aet)	
Brymbo Broughton v Llandudno	1-4
Caerleon v Aberaman Athletic	1-3
Caernarfon Town v Caersws	1-4
Cardiff Civil Service v Pontyclun	2-1
Fields Park Pontllanfraith v Afan Lido	2-4
Flexsys Cefn Druids v Llangefni/Glantraeth	6-2
Gresford Athletic v Lex XI	1-2
Halkyn United v Holyhead Hotspur	5-1
Haverfordwest County v Neath	3-2
Llanelli v Cardiff Corinthians	8-1

Llanfairpwll v Presteigne St Andrews	7-2
Llanrhaeadr v Newtown	1-7
Llanidloes Town v Ruthin Town	1-2
Newport YMCA v Garden Village	4-4
(aet; Newport YMCA won 5-3 on penalties)	
Oswestry Town v Rhayader Town	1-3
Penrhyncoch v Connah's Quay Nomads	1-5
Pontardawe Town v Dinas Powys	2-0
Pontypridd Town v Briton Ferry Athletic	2-3
(aet)	
CPD Porthmadog v Denbigh Town	3-1
Rhyl v Bangor City	1-2
RTB Ebbw Vale v Gwynfi United	2-3
Skewen Athletic v Port Talbot Town	0-3
Ton Pentre v Penrhiwceiber Rangers	7-0
Welshpool Town v Mold Alexandra	2-0

Third Round
Blaenrhondda v Cwmbran Town	1-3
Cardiff Civil Service v Llanelli	2-1
Afan Lido v Carmarthen Town	0-2
Ton Pentre v Briton Ferry Athletic	2-1
Aberystwyth Town v Aberaman Athletic	0-1
Haverfordwest County v Pontardawe Town	0-2
Bettws v Newport YMCA	1-0
Maesteg Park v Gwynfi United	2-3
Connah's Quay Nomads v Newtown	3-2
Flexsys Cefn Druids v Ruthin Town	2-1
CPD Porthmadog v Bangor City	1-5
Halkyn United v Rhayader Town	2-1
Caersws v Lex XI	5-1
Welshpool Town v Llanfairpwll	3-2
Total Network Solutions v Llandudno	1-0
Port Talbot v Barry Town	1-2

Fourth Round
Bangor City v Cardiff Civil Service	9-1
Barry Town v Caersws	4-3
Bettws v Ton Pentre	0-3
Carmarthen Town v Connah's Quay Nomads	2-1
Cwmbran Town v Aberaman Athletic	8-1
Flexsys Cefn Druids v Halkyn United	1-0
Gwynfi United v Total Network Solutions	0-1
(aet)	
Pontardawe Town v Welshpool Town	0-1

Fifth Round
Barry Town v Total Network Solutions	3-0
Carmarthen Town v Bangor City	0-4
Ton Pentre v Cwmbran Town	3-2
(aet)	
Welshpool Town v Flexsys Cefn Druids	0-4

Semi-finals
Flexsys Cefn Druids v Bangor City	0-5
(at Rhyl)	
Ton Pentre v Barry Town	0-2
(aet; at Llanelli)	

Final

Barry Town (2) 4 Bangor City (1) 1

(At Park Avenue, Aberystwyth)

Barry Town: Rayner; Jarman, Lloyd, Kennedy, Morgan, Phillips (Toomey 28), York, French, Moralee, Flynn, Ramasut (Pratt 84).
Scorers: French 8, Flynn 35, Moralee 51, 90.
Bangor City: Priestley; Jones (Cooper 70), Goodall, Short, Rowlands (C. Roberts 70), Griffiths, Lloyd-Williams, Blackmore, P. Roberts, Davies, Burgess.
Scorers: Griffiths 41.
Referee: R. J. Ellingham (Cardiff).
Attendance: 2256

FAW PREMIER CUP

Group A	P	W	D	L	F	A	GD	Pts
Caersws	6	4	2	0	12	2	10	14
Newtown	6	2	1	3	9	9	0	7
TNS	6	2	1	3	7	10	–3	7
Aberystwyth	6	2	0	4	6	13	–7	6

Group B	P	W	D	L	F	A	GD	Pts
Newport	6	4	2	0	8	3	5	14
Carmarthen	6	4	1	1	6	2	4	13
Rhyl	6	1	2	3	6	9	–3	5
Cwmbran	6	0	1	5	5	11	–6	1

Quarter-finals

Caersws v Barry Town	0-3
Newport County v Swansea City	0-3
Carmarthen Town v Wrexham	2-4
Newtown v Cardiff City	0-3

Semi-finals

Swansea City v Barry Town	2-0
Wrexham v Cardiff City	1-1
(Cardiff City won 4-3 on penalties)	

Final

Cardiff City v Swansea City	1-0

C.C. SPORTS WELSH LEAGUE

Division One

	P	W	D	L	F	A	GD	Pts
Ton Pentre	36	26	6	4	81	22	59	84
Pontardawe	36	27	2	7	94	36	58	83
UWIC	36	23	7	6	81	45	36	76
Garw	36	18	10	8	74	49	25	64
Neath	36	19	7	10	64	47	17	64
Maesteg Park	36	18	6	12	61	53	8	60
Goytre United	36	14	13	9	61	49	12	55
Ely Rangers	36	15	9	12	69	52	17	54
Llanwern	36	13	8	15	76	62	14	47
Gwynfi United*	36	14	6	16	66	69	–3	45
Caerleon	36	12	6	18	48	55	–7	42
Penrhiwceiber	36	12	6	18	69	100	–31	42
Cardiff Corries	36	12	5	19	54	66	–12	41
Milford United	36	10	9	17	43	64	–21	39
Cardiff Civil Service	36	10	7	19	54	62	–8	37
Fields Park Pontllanfraith	36	10	7	19	50	76	–26	37
AFC Rhondda	36	9	4	23	30	80	–50	31
Ammanford	36	8	5	23	40	85	–45	29
Bridgend Town	36	7	7	22	50	93	–43	28

*3 points deducted for fielding an ineligible player.

HUWS GRAY – FITLOCK CYMRU ALLIANCE LEAGUE

	P	W	D	L	F	A	GD	Pts
Welshpool Town	34	25	5	4	101	29	72	80
Llangefni/Glantraeth	34	24	3	7	76	36	40	75
Cemaes Bay	34	23	4	7	81	45	36	73
Porthmadog	34	20	8	6	88	45	43	68
Buckley Town	34	21	4	9	72	38	34	67
Ruthin Town	34	17	7	10	76	51	25	58
Halkyn United	34	17	7	10	58	43	15	58
Airbus UK	34	16	6	12	55	55	0	54
Holyhead Hotspur	34	15	4	15	72	78	–6	49
Llandudno	34	12	3	19	55	80	–25	39
Gresford Athletic	34	10	7	17	47	59	–12	37
Llanfairpwll	34	10	6	18	59	81	–22	36
Flint Town United	34	8	7	19	40	58	–18	31
Lex XI**	34	13	4	17	67	87	–20	31
Guilsfield	34	8	6	20	49	82	–33	30
Holywell Town	34	8	5	21	50	85	–35	29
Brymbo Broughton	34	6	5	23	40	80	–40	23
Denbigh Town*	34	5	5	24	29	83	–54	17

*3 points deducted for non-fulfilment of fixture.
**12 points deducted for fielding an ineligible player in 4 games.

NORTHERN IRISH FOOTBALL 2001–02

Northern Ireland football finds itself at the cross-roads – domestically and internationally. What the future holds is anybody's guess but radical changes will have to be made otherwise the consequences could be dire.

Currently the Irish FA and Irish League are studying a Government report initiated by the Minister of Sport, Michael McGimpsey to examine the acute problems facing the game – low attendances, the poor state of the grounds and the financial difficulties of clubs. "Measures need to be taken to develop and secure soccer as a flourishing sport for the long term," he said.

Among the recommendations being assessed is one advocating the Irish League coming under the administrative aegis of the Irish FA provided the necessary Government funding is made available and another proposing a revamping of the IFA Constitution including the establishing of an Executive Committee. There is growing opposition to this, particularly from juniors. Just what will be the outcome, if any, arising from the report remains to be seen.

A £330,000 loss was made on the season by the Irish FA and a £1.3m accumulated deficit over three years. Sponsorship is still being sort for the Northern Ireland national squad but a major step forward was the signing of a new agreement with UFA Sports, the television and advertising partners, which will operate until 2008. "It will guarantee income, removing uncertainty from the World Cup and European championship draws," said David Bowen, the Irish FA general secretary. "In tandem with our BBCTV television agreement, it provides essential financial security in these uncertain times."

The Nationwide Building Society have approved a new four year sponsorship of the Irish Cup, CIS Insurance are commercially backing the League Cup, but Smirnoff has ended its support of the Irish League after 20 years of outstanding success. Avenues are being explored to find a replacement, but so far without success. Funding has, however, been obtained to stage the 2005 UEFA youth championships in Northern Ireland, a prestigious event which will coincide with the IFA's 125th anniversary.

While Northern Ireland had a disappointing World Cup qualifying series, finishing second bottom of Group Three – eleven points behind Denmark, the winners – there were alleviating circumstances for manager Sammy McIlroy who was plagued by injury withdrawals.

In fact, on one occasion there were no fewer than 10 regulars missing, either injured, suspended or simply not made available on the most feeble excuses by their clubs. "Our squad is so numerically limited we just cannot cope with a situation like that," said McIlroy. "For the European Championship matches against Ukraine, Spain, Greece and Armenia, another formidable challenge, I intend strictly applying the FIFA rule prohibiting players appearing in their club sides five days before internationals."

On the domestic front, Portadown proved the most accomplished and consistent team, winning the Premiership and Ronnie McFall deservedly given the Manager of the Year accolade. It was a remarkable achievement considering that a year ago the team struggled to avoid a relegation play-off and in August only five professionals had been re-signed. Shrewd transfer deals involving high-class players and coaching expertise produced the transformation.

Glentoran, who appeared in the early stages as if they would be the dominant force, suffered a mid-season form dip to be pipped at the championship post by Portadown, and, while Linfield failed to retain the title for the third successive year, they won the Irish Cup. At last manager David Jeffrey collected a winners' medal which had eluded him for more than 20 years as a distinguished player and coach.

Lisburn Distillery and Institute, first and second in the First Division, gained promotion to the Premiership in which relegation did not apply this season, but it is re-introduced with promotion in the new campaign. The fixture format has also been altered to include a "split" similar to that operated in Scotland.

Women's soccer is flourishing in Northern Ireland, the fastest growing sport. So, too, is mini-soccer, the schools programmes, the scheme for people with learning difficulties and the IFA's "Football For All" project has made an impact with aid from the Community Relations Council, the Sports Council and the University of Ulster.

"Get the Irish League right and the rest will fall into place," says IFA President Jim Boyce. That is a commendable theory but many hurdles will have to be overcome before it can be achieved. That is the reality of life in Northern Ireland football these days.

DR MALCOLM BRODIE

SMIRNOFF IFL PREMIERSHIP

	P	W	D	L	F	A	GD	Pts
Portadown	36	22	9	5	75	34	+41	75
Glentoran	36	21	11	4	63	23	+40	74
Linfield	36	17	11	8	64	35	+29	62
Coleraine	36	19	2	15	64	58	+6	59
Omagh Town	36	15	9	12	55	55	0	54
Cliftonville	36	9	11	16	37	46	–9	38
Glenavon	36	9	9	18	37	57	–20	36
Newry Town	36	8	12	16	40	62	–22	36
Crusaders	36	9	7	20	41	65	–24	34
Ards	36	6	9	21	30	71	–41	27

First Division

	P	W	D	L	F	A	GD	Pts
Lisburn Distillery	36	24	4	8	64	26	+38	76
Institute	36	22	8	6	76	35	+41	74
Dungannon Swifts	36	17	8	11	55	42	+13	59
Larne	36	14	11	11	51	42	+9	53
Ballymena United	36	14	11	11	59	56	+3	53
Bangor	36	10	12	14	40	45	–5	42
Limavady United	36	10	7	19	49	67	–18	37
Carrick Rangers	36	9	9	18	34	55	–21	36
Ballyclare Comrades	36	7	12	17	40	73	–33	33
Armagh City	36	8	8	20	40	67	–27	32

Second Division

	P	W	D	L	F	A	GD	Pts
Moyola Park	24	20	2	2	55	20	+35	62
Dundela	24	16	4	4	65	30	+35	52
HW Welders	24	15	3	6	48	28	+20	48
Tobermore United	24	11	5	8	42	43	–1	38
Loughgall	24	10	5	9	42	25	+17	35
Banbridge Town	24	9	8	7	48	37	+11	35
Portstewart	24	9	7	8	28	37	–9	34
Brantwood	24	9	4	11	38	44	–6	31
Ballymoney United	24	8	6	10	40	44	–4	30
Coagh United	24	8	5	11	40	38	+2	29
Ballinamallard United	24	8	4	12	31	40	–9	28
PSNI	24	2	4	18	21	72	–51	10
Chimney Corner	24	2	1	21	27	67	–40	7

IFL Reserve League

	P	W	D	L	F	A	GD	Pts
Glentoran II	36	30	4	2	107	25	+82	94
Linfield Swifts	36	26	2	8	93	35	+58	80
Cliftonville Olympic	36	23	7	6	83	34	+49	76
Institute II	36	20	8	8	72	45	+27	68
Newry Town Res	36	18	7	11	70	51	+19	61
Dungannon Swifts Res	36	19	4	13	68	56	+12	61
Coleraine Res	36	16	6	14	72	77	–5	54
Ards II	36	14	7	15	52	54	–2	49
Omagh Town Res	36	14	7	15	66	69	–3	49
Carrick Rangers Res	36	11	11	14	79	80	–1	44
Glenavon Res	36	12	8	16	64	72	–8	44
Crusaders Res	36	12	8	16	48	57	–9	44
Lisburn Distillery II	36	11	9	16	52	66	–14	42
Bangor Res	36	10	8	18	43	73	–30	38
Ballymena United Res	36	10	7	19	57	78	–21	37
Portadown Res	36	9	8	19	39	61	–22	35
Limavady United Res	36	9	6	21	50	91	–41	33
Larne Olympic	36	8	6	22	42	94	–52	30
Armagh City Res	36	7	3	26	43	82	–39	24

IFL Youth League

	P	W	D	L	F	A	GD	Pts
Institute Academy	22	16	3	3	69	39	+30	51
Cliftonville Strollers	22	15	4	3	69	30	+39	49
Glentoran Colts	22	15	2	5	70	29	+41	47
Newry Town Wanderers	22	11	4	7	49	34	+15	37
Linfield Rangers	22	11	3	8	61	38	+23	36
Lisburn Distillery III	22	10	6	6	65	53	+12	36
Ballyclare Comrades Colts	22	8	5	9	66	48	+18	29
Glenavon III	22	7	5	10	47	51	–4	26
Crusaders Colts	22	7	2	13	45	61	–16	23
Ballymena United III	22	6	2	14	42	76	–34	20
Coleraine Colts	22	5	4	13	41	70	–29	19
Portadown III	22	1	0	21	24	119	–95	3

IRISH LEAGUE CHAMPIONSHIP WINNERS

1891	Linfield	1911	Linfield	1936	Belfast Celtic	1964	Glentoran	1985	Linfield
1892	Linfield	1912	Glentoran	1937	Belfast Celtic	1965	Derry City	1986	Linfield
1893	Linfield	1913	Glentoran	1938	Belfast Celtic	1966	Linfield	1987	Linfield
1894	Glentoran	1914	Linfield	1939	Belfast Celtic	1967	Glentoran	1988	Glentoran
1895	Linfield	1915	Belfast Celtic	1940	Belfast Celtic	1968	Glentoran	1989	Linfield
1896	Distillery	1920	Belfast Celtic	1948	Belfast Celtic	1969	Linfield	1990	Portadown
1897	Glentoran	1921	Glentoran	1949	Linfield	1970	Glentoran	1991	Portadown
1898	Linfield	1922	Linfield	1950	Linfield	1971	Linfield	1992	Glentoran
1899	Distillery	1923	Linfield	1951	Glentoran	1972	Glentoran	1993	Linfield
1900	Belfast Celtic	1924	Queen's Island	1952	Glenavon	1973	Crusaders	1994	Linfield
1901	Distillery	1925	Glentoran	1953	Glentoran	1974	Coleraine	1995	Crusaders
1902	Linfield	1926	Belfast Celtic	1954	Linfield	1975	Linfield	1996	Portadown
1903	Distillery	1927	Belfast Celtic	1955	Linfield	1976	Crusaders	1997	Crusaders
1904	Linfield	1928	Belfast Celtic	1956	Linfield	1977	Glentoran	1998	Cliftonville
1905	Glentoran	1929	Belfast Celtic	1957	Glentoran	1978	Linfield	1999	Glentoran
1906	Cliftonville	1930	Linfield	1958	Ards	1979	Linfield	2000	Linfield
	Distillery	1931	Glentoran	1959	Linfield	1980	Linfield	2001	Linfield
1907	Linfield	1932	Linfield	1960	Glenavon	1981	Glentoran	2002	Portadown
1908	Linfield	1933	Belfast Celtic	1961	Linfield	1982	Linfield		
1909	Linfield	1934	Linfield	1962	Linfield	1983	Linfield		
1910	Cliftonville	1935	Linfield	1963	Distillery	1984	Linfield		

FIRST DIVISION

1996	Coleraine	1999	Distillery	2002	Lisburn Distillery
1997	Ballymena United	2000	Omagh Town		
1998	Newry Town	2001	Ards		

ULSTER CUP WINNERS

1949	Linfield	1960	Linfield	1971	Linfield	1982	Glentoran	1993	Crusaders
1950	Larne	1961	Ballymena U	1972	Coleraine	1983	Glentoran	1994	Bangor
1951	Glentoran	1962	Linfield	1973	Ards	1984	Linfield	1995	Portadown
1952		1963	Crusaders	1974	Linfield	1985	Coleraine	1996	Portadown
1953	Glentoran	1964	Linfield	1975	Coleraine	1986	Coleraine	1997	Coleraine
1954	Crusaders	1965	Coleraine	1976	Glentoran	1987	Larne	1998	Ballyclare Comrades
1955	Glenavon	1966	Glentoran	1977	Linfield	1988	Glentoran	1999	Distillery
1956	Linfield	1967	Linfield	1978	Linfield	1989	Glentoran	2000	*No competition*
1957	Linfield	1968	Coleraine	1979	Linfield	1990	Portadown		
1958	Distillery	1969	Coleraine	1980	Ballymena U	1991	Bangor		
1959	Glenavon	1970	Linfield	1981	Glentoran	1992	Linfield		

NATIONWIDE IRISH CUP 2001–02

Fifth Round

Limavady v Ards	1-2
Armagh City v Dungannon Swifts	2-5
Linfield v Portstewart	3-0
Glentoran v Newry Town	1-0
Cliftonville v Portadown	1-1, 1-2
Institute v Ards Rangers	4-1
Bangor v Crusaders	0-2
Glenavon v Lurgan Celtic	0-0, 0-1*, 1-1

*abandoned 28 minutes; rain
(Glenavon won 3-2 on penalties).

Tobermore United v Dunmurray Rec	1-2
Brantwood v Moyola Park	1-1, 0-1
Omagh Town v Ballymena United	0-0, 0-1
Ballyclare Comrades v Barn United	4-1
Killyleagh YC v Ballinamallard	4-1
Loughall v Larne	2-2, 1-1

(Larne won 4-2 on penalties).

Coleraine v Donegal Celtic	5-3
Carrick Rangers v Lisburn Distillery	4-3

Sixth Round

Ballyclare Comrades v Dunmurray Rec	3-1
Ballymena United v Glenavon	0-3
Portadown v Institute	3-1
Carrick Rangers v Linfield	0-7
Ards v Glentoran	0-5
Crusaders v Dungannon Swifts	1-1, 0-1
Moyola Park v Coleraine	3-3, 1-5
Larne v Killyleagh YC	0-0, 1-2

Quarter-finals

Coleraine v Dungannon Swifts	2-0
Killyleagh YC v Ballyclare Comrades	1-0
Glentoran v Portadown	1-1, 3-4
Linfield v Glenavon	3-0

Semi-finals

Linfield v Killyleagh YC	5-0 *(at The Oval)*
Portadown v Coleraine	2-0 *(at Windsor Park)*

Final

Linfield 2 Portadown 1
(at Windsor Park)

Linfield: Mannus; Collier, McShane (Kelly N), Hunter A, King (Murphy D), Kelly R, Morgan (McBride), Gorman, Ferguson, Marks, Bailie.
Scorer: Morgan 2
Portadown: Keenan; Douglas, O'Hara, McCann, Feeney (Ogden), Major, Clarke (Hamilton A), Collins, Hamilton M, Arkins, Neill.
Scorer: Neill.
Referee: M. Ross (Carrickfergus).
Attendance: 11,129.
Prize money: Winners £11,000; Runners-up £6000.
Man of the Match: Noel Bailie (Linfield).
Player of the Tournament: Chris Morgan (Linfield) who scored in every round.

IRISH CUP FINALS (from 1946–47)

1946–47	Belfast Celtic 1, Glentoran 0	
1947–48	Linfield 3, Coleraine 0	1976–77
1948–49	Derry City 3, Glentoran 1	1977–78
1949–50	Linfield 2, Distillery 1	1978–79
1950–51	Glentoran 3, Ballymena U 1	
1951–52	Ards 1, Glentoran 0	1980–81
1952–53	Linfield 5, Coleraine 0	1981–82
1953–54	Derry City 1, Glentoran 0	1982–83
1954–55	Dundela 3, Glenavon 0	1983–84
1955–56	Distillery 1, Glentoran 0	1984–85
1956–57	Glenavon 2, Derry City 0	1985–86
1957–58	Ballymena U 2, Linfield 0	1986–87
1958–59	Glenavon 2, Ballymena U 0	
1959–60	Linfield 5, Ards 1	1988–89
1960–61	Glenavon 5, Linfield 1	1989–90
1961–62	Linfield 4, Portadown 0	1990–91
1962–63	Linfield 2, Distillery 1	1991–92
1963–64	Derry City 2, Glentoran 0	1992–93
1964–65	Coleraine 2, Glenavon 1	1993–94
1965–66	Glentoran 2, Linfield 0	1994–95
1966–67	Crusaders 3, Glentoran 1	1995–96
1967–68	Crusaders 2, Linfield 0	1996–97
1968–69	Ards 4, Distillery 2	1997–98
1969–70	Linfield 2, Ballymena U 1	1998–99
1970–71	Distillery 3, Derry City 0	
1971–72	Coleraine 2, Portadown 1	
1972–73	Glentoran 3, Linfield 2	1999–2000
1973–74	Ards 2, Ballymena U 1	2000–01
1974–75	Coleraine 1:0:1, Linfield 1:0:0	

1975–76	Carrick Rangers 2, Linfield 1	
	Coleraine 4, Linfield 1	
	Linfield 3, Ballymena U 1	
	Cliftonville 3, Portadown 2	
1979–80	Linfield 2, Crusaders 0	
	Ballymena U 1, Glenavon 0	
	Linfield 2, Coleraine 1	
	Glentoran 1:2, Linfield 1:1	
	Ballymena U 4, Carrick Rangers 1	
	Glentoran 1:1, Linfield 1:0	
	Glentoran 2, Coleraine 1	
	Glentoran 1, Larne 0	
1987–88	Glentoran 1, Glenavon 0	
	Ballymena U 1, Larne 0	
	Glentoran 3, Portadown 0	
	Portadown 2, Glenavon 1	
	Glenavon 2, Linfield 1	
	Bangor 1:1:1, Ards 1:1:0	
	Linfield 2, Bangor 0	
	Linfield 3, Carrick Rangers 1	
	Glentoran 1, Glenavon 0	
	Glenavon 1, Cliftonville 0	
	Glentoran 1, Glenavon 0	

Portadown awarded trophy after Cliftonville were eliminated for using an ineligible player in semi-final.

	Glentoran 1, Portadown 0	
	Glentoran 1, Linfield 0	
2001–02	Linfield 2, Portadown 1	

COUNTY ANTRIM SHIELD

Semi-final

Glentoran v Cliftonville	1-0 *(at Windsor Park)*
Linfield v Ballymena United	4-0 *(at Seaview)*

Final

Glentoran 2, Linfield 0

Glentoran: Gough; Nixon, Glendinning, Halliday, Leeman, Smyth, Tim McCann, Armour, Smith, Batey (Hunter), Wright.
Scorers: Batey, Armour.

Linfield: Robinson; Collier, McShane (Arthur), Hunter A, Murphy D, Kelly N (Picking), Morgan, King, McBride (McConnell), Marks, Bailie.
Referee: A. Snoddy (Carryduff).
Attendance: 4500.
Man of the Match: Darren Armour (Glentoran).

CIS INSURANCE IRISH LEAGUE CUP

First Phase

Northern	P	W	D	L	F	A	GD	Pts
Institute	4	4	0	0	7	0	+7	12
Coleraine	4	3	0	1	8	2	+6	9
Ballymena United	4	2	0	2	4	9	–5	6
Limavady United	4	1	0	3	2	6	–4	3
Omagh Town	4	0	0	4	1	5	–4	0

Southern	P	W	D	L	F	A	GD	Pts
Newry Town	4	3	0	1	8	5	+3	9
Glenavon	4	2	1	1	6	5	+1	7
Armagh City	4	1	2	1	3	2	+1	5
Portadown	4	1	1	2	3	6	–3	4
Dungannon Swifts	4	0	2	2	3	5	–2	2

Eastern	P	W	D	L	F	A	GD	Pts
Carrick Rangers	4	3	1	0	8	1	+7	10
Crusaders	4	3	0	1	5	3	+2	9
Cliftonville	4	2	1	1	5	3	+2	7
Ballyclare Comrades	4	1	0	3	3	8	–5	3
Larne	4	0	0	4	1	7	–6	0

Greater Belfast	P	W	D	L	F	A	GD	Pts
Linfield	4	2	2	0	11	3	+8	8
Glentoran	4	2	2	0	4	0	+4	8
Lisburn Distillery	4	0	4	0	4	4	0	4
Ards	4	1	1	2	3	8	–5	4
Bangor	4	0	1	3	3	10	–7	1

Group winners and runners-up qualified for quarter-finals.

Quarter-finals

Carrick Rangers v Institute	2-0
Crusaders v Coleraine	1-3
Glenavon v Glentoran	2-3
Linfield v Newry Town	3-1

Semi-finals

Carrick Rangers v Glentoran	1-3, 0-5
Coleraine v Linfield	2-1, 0-2

Final

Glentoran 1, Linfield 3 *(at Windsor Park)*
Glentoran: Gough; Nixon, Leeman, Smyth, Glendinning, Tim McCann, Batey (Ferguson), Hunter M (Halliday), Timothy McCann, Haylock, Armour (Russell).
Scorer: Haylock.
Linfield: Robinson; Collier, Hunter A, Bailie, McShane, Scates, Gorman, Murphy D (Arthur), Picking (Parker), Morgan, McBride (Kelly R).
Scorers: Morgan, Gorman, Russell.
Referee: A. Snoddy (Carryduff).

WHERE THE TROPHIES WENT

	Winners	Runners-up
Smirnoff Irish League		
Premier Division	Portadown	Glentoran
First Division	Lisburn Distillery	Institute
Irish League Second Division	Moyola Park	Dundela
Irish Reserve League	Glentoran II	Linfield Swifts
Smirnoff Irish League Knock Out Cup	H & W Welders	Banbridge Town
Irish League Youth Cup	Linfield Rangers	Glentoran Colts
Irish Youth League	Institute Academy	Cliftonville Strollers
Nationwide Irish Cup	Linfield	Portadown
CIS Insurance Irish League Cup	Linfield	Glentoran
County Antrim Shield	Glentoran	Linfield
Steel and Sons Cup	Glentoran II	Dundela
County Antrim Junior Shield	Raceview Rangers	Downpatrick Hospitals
Belfast Telegraph Intermediate Cup	Linfield Swifts	Donegal Celtic
Irish Junior Cup Final	NFC Kesh	Derryhirk United
Mid Ulster Cup	*Final postponed until new season*	
North West Senior Cup	Coleraine	Omagh Town
Harry Cavan Youth Cup	Ballinamallard United III	Balymena United III
George Wilson Memorial Cup	Glentoran II	Linfield Swifts
Wilkinson Sword Charity Shield	*Not played*	

Ulster Footballer of Year
(Castlereagh Glentoran Supporters Club) — Michael Keenan (Portadown)
Northern Ireland Player of the Year (NIFWA) — Vinny Arkins (Portadown)
Young Footballer of Year — Peter McCann (Portadown)
Premier Division Manager of Year — Ronnie McFall (Portadown)
Outstanding Non Senior Team — Glentoran II
Irish League First Division Manager of Year — Paul Kee (Institute)
Irish League First Division Player of Year — Mark Holland (Lisburn Distillery)
Irish League Merit Award — Billy Hamilton (ex-Northern Ireland international)

Sunday Life Leading Scorers Award:
Premier Division — Vinnie Arkins (Portadown) — 35 goals
First Division — Mark Holland (Lisburn Distillery) — 23 goals

EUROPEAN CUP

EUROPEAN CUP FINALS 1956–2002

Year	Winners	Runners-up	Venue	Attendance	Referee
1956	Real Madrid 4	Reims 3	Paris	38,000	Ellis (E)
1957	Real Madrid 2	Fiorentina 0	Madrid	124,000	Horn (Ho)
1958	Real Madrid 3	AC Milan 2 *(aet)*	Brussels	67,000	Alsteen (Bel)
1959	Real Madrid 2	Reims 0	Stuttgart	80,000	Dutsch (WG)
1960	Real Madrid 7	Eintracht Frankfurt 3	Glasgow	135,000	Mowat (S)
1961	Benfica 3	Barcelona 2	Berne	28,000	Dienst (Sw)
1962	Benfica 5	Real Madrid 3	Amsterdam	65,000	Horn (Ho)
1963	AC Milan 2	Benfica 1	Wembley	45,000	Holland (E)
1964	Internazionale 3	Real Madrid 1	Vienna	74,000	Stoll (A)
1965	Internazionale 1	Benfica 0	Milan	80,000	Dienst (Sw)
1966	Real Madrid 2	Partizan Belgrade 1	Brussels	55,000	Kreitlein (WG)
1967	Celtic 2	Internazionale 1	Lisbon	56,000	Tschenscher (WG)
1968	Manchester U 4	Benfica 1 *(aet)*	Wembley	100,000	Lo Bello (I)
1969	AC Milan 4	Ajax 1	Madrid	50,000	Ortiz (Sp)
1970	Feyenoord 2	Celtic 1 *(aet)*	Milan	50,000	Lo Bello (I)
1971	Ajax 2	Panathinaikos 0	Wembley	90,000	Taylor (E)
1972	Ajax 2	Internazionale 0	Rotterdam	67,000	Helies (F)
1973	Ajax 1	Juventus 0	Belgrade	93,500	Guglovic (Y)
1974	Bayern Munich 1	Atletico Madrid 1	Brussels	49,000	Loraux (Bel)
Replay	Bayern Munich 4	Atletico Madrid 0	Brussels	23,000	Delcourt (Bel)
1975	Bayern Munich 2	Leeds U 0	Paris	50,000	Kitabdjian (F)
1976	Bayern Munich 1	St Etienne 0	Glasgow	54,864	Palotai (H)
1977	Liverpool 3	Moenchengladbach 1	Rome	57,000	Wurtz (F)
1978	Liverpool 1	FC Brugge 0	Wembley	92,000	Corver (Ho)
1979	Nottingham F 1	Malmo 0	Munich	57,500	Linemayr (A)
1980	Nottingham F 1	Hamburg 0	Madrid	50,000	Garrido (P)
1981	Liverpool 1	Real Madrid 0	Paris	48,360	Palotai (H)
1982	Aston Villa 1	Bayern Munich 0	Rotterdam	46,000	Konrath (F)
1983	Hamburg 1	Juventus 0	Athens	80,000	Rainea (R)
1984	Liverpool 1	Roma 1	Rome	69,693	Fredriksson (Se)
	(aet; Liverpool won 4–2 on penalties)				
1985	Juventus 1	Liverpool 0	Brussels	58,000	Daina (Sw)
1986	Steaua Bucharest 0	Barcelona 0	Seville	70,000	Vautrot (F)
	(aet; Steaua won 2–0 on penalties)				
1987	Porto 2	Bayern Munich 1	Vienna	59,000	Ponnet (Bel)
1988	PSV Eindhoven 0	Benfica 0	Stuttgart	70,000	Agnolin (I)
	(aet; PSV won 6–5 on penalties)				
1989	AC Milan 4	Steaua Bucharest 0	Barcelona	97,000	Tritschler (WG)
1990	AC Milan 1	Benfica 0	Vienna	57,500	Kohl (A)
1991	Red Star Belgrade 0	Marseille 0	Bari	56,000	Lanese (I)
	(aet; Red Star won 5–3 on penalties)				
1992	Barcelona 1	Sampdoria 0 *(aet)*	Wembley	70,827	Schmidhuber (G)
1993	Marseille* 1	AC Milan 0	Munich	64,400	Rothlisberger (Sw)
1994	AC Milan 4	Barcelona 0	Athens	70,000	Don (E)
1995	Ajax 1	AC Milan 0	Vienna	49,730	Craciunescu (Ro)
1996	Juventus 1	Ajax 1	Rome	67,000	Vega (Sp)
	(aet; Juventus won 4–2 on penalties)				
1997	Borussia Dortmund 3	Juventus 1	Munich	59,000	Puhl (H)
1998	Real Madrid 1	Juventus 0	Amsterdam	47,500	Krug (G)
1999	Manchester U 2	Bayern Munich 1	Barcelona	90,000	Collina (I)
2000	Real Madrid 3	Valencia 0	Paris	78,759	Braschi (I)
2001	Bayern Munich 1	Valencia 1	Milan	71,500	Jol (Ho)
	(aet; Bayern Munich won 5–4 on penalties)				
2002	Real Madrid 2	Leverkusen 1	Glasgow	52,000	Meier (Sw)

Subsequently stripped of title.

EUROPEAN CUP 2001–02

FIRST QUALIFYING ROUND, FIRST LEG
Araks (0) 0, Serif (0) 1 *(Barburos 62)* 8500
Barry Town (0) 2 *(York 54, French 68)*,
  Shamkir (0) 0 1992
Bohemians (2) 3 *(Maher 1, Crowe 9, 57 (pen))*,
  Levadia (0) 0 3832
F91 Dudelange (1) 1 *(Cicchirillo 44)*,
  Skonto Riga (1) 6 *(Verpakovskis 1, Miholaps 60, 75,*
  Kolesnicenko 66, 85, Zemlinskis 72 (pen)) 1100
KR Reykjavik (0) 2 *(Benediktsson 62, Olafsson S 78)*,
  Vllaznia (1) 1 *(Duro 16)* 2000
Levski (3) 4 *(Terziev 8, Ivanov 21, 75 (pen), Markov 28)*,
  Zeljeznicar (0) 0 15,000
Linfield (0) 0, Torpedo Kutaisi (0) 0 2699
Sloga (0) 0, Kaunas (0) 0 3000
Valletta (0) 0, Haka (0) 0 6000
VB Vagur (0) 0, Slavia Mozyr (0) 0 480

FIRST QUALIFYING ROUND, SECOND LEG
Haka (4) 5 *(Torkkeli 4, Kovacs 16, 23, 29, Pogioli 90)*,
  Valletta (0) 0 2423
Kaunas (0) 1 *(Papeckys 65)*, Sloga (0) 1 *(Nuhiji 52)* 1400
Levadia (0) 0, Bohemians (0) 0 1034
Serif (1) 2 *(Comlenoc 12, Dadu 90)*, Araks (0) 0 6000
Shamkir (0) 0, Barry Town (0) 1 *(Phillips 57)* 12,000
Skonto Riga (0) 0, F91 Dudelange (0) 1
  (Cicchirillo 77) 1500
Slavia Mozyr (5) 5 *(Jacobsen 4 (og), Stripeikis 12, 29*
  (pen), 32, Rybakov 24), VB Vagur (0) 0 4000
Torpedo Kutaisi (0) 1 *(Ashvetia 68)*, Linfield (0) 0 7130
Vllaznia (0) 1 *(Duro 62)*, KR Reykjavik (0) 0 5000
Zeljeznicar (0) 0, Levski (0) 0 6000

SECOND QUALIFYING ROUND, FIRST LEG
Anderlecht (2) 4 *(Crasson 18, 81, De Boeck 41, 65)*,
  Serif (0) 0 21,055
Bohemians (1) 1 *(Crowe 23)*, Halmstad (1) 2
  (Jonsson 31, Selakovic 55) 4225
Ferencvaros (0) 0, Hajduk Split (0) 0 9259
Galatasaray (1) 2 *(Karan 18, Kaya 90)*,
  Vllaznia (0) 0 14,804
Haka (0) 0, Maccabi Haifa (1) 1 *(Zano 28)* 3350
Levski (0) 0, Brann (0) 0 13,780
Maribor (0) 0, Rangers (1) 3 *(Flo 38, 73,*
  Nerlinger 56) 6100
Omonia (0) 1 *(Thiebaut 70)*, Red Star Belgrade (1) 1
  (Pjanovic 30) 16,756
Porto (5) 8 *(Pena 12, 51, 72, Deco 22, 23, 43,*
  Sodestrom 41, Capucho 52), Barry Town (0) 0 43,050
Shakhtjor Donetsk (1) 3 *(Bakharev 21,*
  Tymoschuk 57, Vorobei 65), Lugano (0) 0 31,714
Skonto Riga (0) 0, Wisla (0) 2
  (Glowacki 48, Zurawski 80) 2000
Slavia Mozyr (0) 0, Inter Bratislava (1) 1 *(Kunzo 43)* 2420
Steaua (2) 3 *(Raducanu 1, 19, Trica 82)*, Sloga (0) 0 9200
Torpedo Kutaisi (0) 1 *(Ashvetia 77)*,
  FC Copenhagen (1) 1 *(Zuma 43)* 11,500

SECOND QUALIFYING ROUND, SECOND LEG
Barry Town (2) 3 *(Phillips 37, Flynn 38, Lloyd 90 (pen))*,
  Porto (1) 1 *(Dias 18)* 2377
Brann (1) 1 *(Walltin 16)*, Levski (1) 1 *(Ivanov 5)* 10,902
FC Copenhagen (1) 3 *(Zuma 45, Lonstrup 59,*
  Fernandez 74), Torpedo Kutaisi (0) 1
  (Kutateladze 90) 14,345
Hajduk Split (0) 0, Ferencvaros (0) 0 26,400
  (aet; Hajduk Split won 5-4 on penalties)
Halmstad (0) 2 *(Jonsson 57, Selakovic 68)*,
  Bohemians (0) 0 3643
Inter Bratislava (0) 1 *(Lembakoali 73)*,
  Slavia Mozyr (0) 0 2500
Lugano (0) 2 *(Gaspoz 53, Rossi 66)*,
  Shakhtjor Donetsk (1) 1 *(Aghahowa 13)* 4000
Maccabi Haifa (1) 4 *(Rosso 39, Katan 57, 78, 90)*,
  Haka (0) 0 8000
  (Match awarded 3-0 to Haka; Maccabi Haifa fielded
  an ineligible player)
Rangers (0) 3 *(Flo 54, Caniggia 58, 73)*, Maribor (1) 1
  (Starcevic 17) 50,045

Red Star Belgrade (0) 2 *(Lerinc 53, Acimovic 79)*,
  Omonia (0) 1 *(Kaiafas 71)* 18,145
Serif (1) 1 *(Boret 4)*, Anderlecht (1) 2 *(Iachtchouk 28,*
  De Boeck 59) 4498
Sloga (0) 1 *(Nuhiji 86)*, Steaua (2) 2 *(N'Gassam 18,*
  Raducanu 41) 462
Vllaznia (1) 1 *(Sinani 33)*, Galatasaray (1) 4
  (Umit 38, Arif 49, Hasan Sas 73, Serkan 80) 4600
Wisla (0) 1 *(Zurawski 85)*, Skonto Riga (0) 0 4500

THIRD QUALIFYING ROUND, FIRST LEG
Ajax (1) 1 *(Arveladze 40)*, Celtic (2) 3 *(Petta 7,*
  Agathe 20, Sutton 55) 51,859
FC Copenhagen (0) 2 *(Laursen 72 (pen)*,
  Fernandez 85), Lazio (1) 1 *(Crespo 56)* 37,516
Galatasaray (1) 2 *(Karan 9, Bulent K 69)*,
  Levski (0) 0 *(Ivanov 78)* 17,000
Hajduk Split (1) 1 *(Bilic 21)*, Mallorca (0) 0 40,000
Haka (0) 0, Liverpool (1) 5 *(Heskey 32,*
  Owen 56, 66, 88, Hyypia 87) 33,217
Halmstad (1) 2 *(Svensson M 13, Selakovic 75)*,
  Anderlecht (0) 3 *(Seol 56, Hasi 66, Mornar 85)* 3876
Inter Bratislava (0) 3 *(Lembakoali 49, 62,*
  Drobnjak 68), Rosenborg (1) 3 *(Brattbakk 10,*
  Skammelsrud 77 (pen), Kunzo 90 (og)) 5150
Lokomotiv Moscow (2) 3 *(Lekgetho 2, Izmailov 37,*
  Ignashevich 79), Tirol Innsbruck (1) 1
  (Kirchler 19) 14,000
Parma (0) 0, Lille (0) 2 *(Bassir 47, Ecker 80)* 14,974
Porto (1) 2 *(Paredes 7, Helder 59)*,
  Grasshoppers (0) 2 *(Nunez 51, Petric 57)* 46,142
Rangers (0) 0, Fenerbahce (0) 0 49,472
Red Star Belgrade (0) 0, Leverkusen (0) 0 45,000
Shakhtjor Donetsk (0) 0, Borussia Dortmund (1) 2
  (Ricken 35, Oliseh 72) 32,000
Slavia Prague (0) 1 *(Kuka 70)*, Panathinaikos (1) 2
  (Liberopoulos 26, Karagounis 56) 14,707
Steaua (1) 2 *(Trica 30, 53)*, Dynamo Kiev (3) 4
  (Belkevich 9 (pen), 20, Idahor 43,
  Melashchenko 64) 20,000
Wisla (3) 3 *(Pater 21, 30, Frankowski 38)*,
  Barcelona (2) 4 *(Rivaldo 29 (pen), 32, 71,*
  Kluivert 54) 10,000

THIRD QUALIFYING ROUND, SECOND LEG
Anderlecht (0) 1 *(De Boeck 82)*, Halmstad (1) 1
  (Jonsson 12) 16,853
Barcelona (0) 1 *(Luis Enrique 72)*, Wisla (0) 0 58,233
Borussia Dortmund (0) 3 *(Koller 49, 68, Amoroso 64)*,
  Shakhtjor Donetsk (1) 1 *(Aghahowa 7)* 47,000
Celtic (0) 0, Ajax (1) 1 *(Wamberto 30)* 60,000
Dynamo Kiev (0) 1 *(Melashchenko 46)*, Steaua (1) 1
  (Neaga 30) 16,800
Fenerbahce (1) 2 *(Revivo 3, Serhat 71)*, Rangers (0) 1
  (Ricksen 73) 30,000
Grasshoppers (0) 2 *(Petric 77, Chapuisat 86)*,
  Porto (2) 3 *(Clayton 13, Capucho 43, Deco 79)* 16,066
Lazio (0) 4 *(Crespo 48, 63, Lopez 64, Fiore 90)*,
  FC Copenhagen (0) 1 *(Zuma 81)* 37,133
Leverkusen (2) 3 *(Neuville 13, 59, Kirsten 31)*,
  Red Star Belgrade (0) 0 22,500
Levski (0) 1 *(Pantelic 79)*, Galatasaray (0) 1
  (Aykut 50) 27,000
Lille (0) 0, Parma (1) 1 *(Sensini 27)* 14,358
Liverpool (1) 4 *(Fowler 37, Redknapp 50, Heskey 56,*
  Wilson 83 (og)), Haka (1) 1 *(Kovacs 45)* 31,602
Mallorca (1) 2 *(Eto'o 25, Luque 92)*,
  Hajduk Split (0) 0 23,500
Panathinaikos (1) 1 *(Basinas 26 (pen))*,
  Slavia Prague (0) 0 16,500
Rosenborg (3) 4 *(Johnsen 11, Rushfeldt 15,*
  Skammelsrud 42, Strand 84), Inter Bratislava (0) 0 17,000
Tirol Innsbruck (0) 0, Lokomotiv Moscow (0) 1
  (Maminov 51)
  (result annulled; referee Van der Ende wrongly booked
  Maminov instead of Pimenov already on a yellow card)
Tirol Innsbruck (1) 1 *(Brzeczek 30)*, Lokomotiv Moscow
  (0) 0 15,500

CHAMPIONS LEAGUE

GROUP A

Lokomotiv Moscow (1) 1 *(Maminov 18)*,
  Anderlecht (1) 1 *(Hendrikx 15)*   15,500
Roma (0) 1 *(Totti 73 (pen))*, Real Madrid (0) 2
  (Figo 50, Guti 63)   70,000
Anderlecht (0) 0, Roma (0) 0   24,000
Real Madrid (1) 4 *(Munitis 39, Figo 64 (pen)*,
  Roberto Carlos 81, Savio 87), Lokomotiv
  Moscow (0) 0   70,000
Real Madrid (0) 4 *(Celades 49, Raul 50, 68, Solari 79)*,
  Anderlecht (1) 1 *(Dindane 33)*   65,000
Roma (0) 2 *(Chugainov 69 (og), Totti 79)*,
  Lokomotiv Moscow (0) 1 *(Obradovic 59)*   38,472
Anderlecht (0) 0, Real Madrid (2) 2 *(Raul 19,*
  McManaman 35)   21,992
Lokomotiv Moscow (0) 0, Roma (0) 1 *(Cafu 78)*   20,000
Anderlecht (1) 1 *(Ilic 2)*, Lokomotiv Moscow (2) 5
  (Izmailov 13, Sennikov 28, Pimenov 58,
  Buznikin 63, 69)   26,000
Real Madrid (0) 1 *(Figo 75 (pen))*, Roma (1) 1
  (Totti 34)   63,000
Lokomotiv Moscow (1) 2 *(Buznikin 30, Cherevchenko*
  50), Real Madrid (0) 0   22,400
Roma (1) 2 *(Delvecchio 52)*, Anderlecht (1) 1
  (Mornar 11)   20,000

FINAL TABLE	P	W	D	L	F	A	Pts
Real Madrid	6	4	1	1	13	5	13
Roma	6	2	3	1	6	5	9
Lokomotiv Moscow	6	2	1	3	9	9	7
Anderlecht	6	0	3	3	4	13	3

GROUP B

Dynamo Kiev (2) 2 *(Melashchenko 15, Idahor 45)*,
  Borussia Dortmund (0) 2 *(Koller 55, Amoroso 74)*
   60,000
Liverpool (1) 1 *(Owen 29)*, Boavista (1) 1 *(Silva 3)*   30,015
Boavista (3) 3 *(Sanchez 4, Silva 11, Duda 30)*,
  Dynamo Kiev (1) 1 *(Gioane 5)*   20,000
Borussia Dortmund (0) 0, Liverpool (0) 0   46,000
Boavista (2) 2 *(Silva 24, Sanchez 39)*,
  Borussia Dortmund (0) 1 *(Amoroso 75)*   7000
Liverpool (1) 1 *(Litmanen 24)*, Dynamo Kiev (0) 0   33,513
Borussia Dortmund (0) 2 *(Ricken 50, Koller 68)*,
  Boavista (1) 1 *(Goulart 33)*   42,000
Dynamo Kiev (0) 1 *(Gioane 59)*, Liverpool (1) 2
  (Murphy 43, Gerrard 67)   50,000
Boavista (0) 1 *(Silva 60)*, Liverpool (1) 1
  (Murphy 17)   6000
Borussia Dortmund (1) 1 *(Rosicky 35)*,
  Dynamo Kiev (0) 0   41,500
Dynamo Kiev (0) 1 *(Melashchenko 49)*,
  Boavista (0) 0   30,000
Liverpool (1) 2 *(Smicer 15, Wright 82)*,
  Borussia Dortmund (0) 0   41,507

FINAL TABLE	P	W	D	L	F	A	Pts
Liverpool	6	3	3	0	7	3	12
Boavista	6	2	2	2	8	7	8
Borussia Dortmund	6	2	2	2	6	7	8
Dynamo Kiev	6	1	1	4	5	9	4

Boavista qualified on better head-to-head record.

GROUP C

Mallorca (1) 1 *(Engonga 11 (pen))*, Arsenal (0) 0   22,000
Schalke (0) 0, Panathinaikos (0) 2 *(Vlaovic 75,*
  Basinas 80)   52,300
Arsenal (2) 3 *(Ljungberg 33, Henry 35, 47 (pen))*,
  Schalke (1) 3 *(Van Hoogdalem 43, Mpenza 59)*   35,361
Panathinaikos (2) 2 *(Vlaovic 25, Konstantinou 28)*,
  Mallorca (0) 0   30,000
Panathinaikos (1) 1 *(Karagounis 24)*, Arsenal (0) 0   17,200
Schalke (0) 0, Mallorca (0) 1 *(Eto'o 65)*   52,300
Arsenal (1) 2 *(Henry 23, 52 (pen))*, Panathinaikos (0) 1
  (Olisadebe 50)   35,432
Mallorca (0) 0, Schalke (2) 4 *(Van Hoogdalem 15,*
  Hajto 22 (pen), Asamoah 77, Sand 84)   20,000
Arsenal (0) 3 *(Pires 61, Bergkamp 63, Henry 90)*,
  Mallorca (0) 1 *(Novo 74)*   34,764
Panathinaikos (1) 2 *(Olisadebe 31, Konstantinou 60)*,
  Schalke (0) 0   16,250
Mallorca (0) 1 *(Biagini 55)*, Panathinaikos (0) 0   10,000

Schalke (1) 3 *(Mulder 2, Vermant 60, Moller 64)*,
  Arsenal (0) 1 *(Wiltord 71)*   52,500

FINAL TABLE	P	W	D	L	F	A	Pts
Panathinaikos	6	4	0	2	8	3	12
Arsenal	6	3	0	3	9	9	9
Mallorca	6	3	0	3	4	9	9
Schalke	6	2	0	4	9	9	6

Arsenal qualified on better head-to-head record.

GROUP D

Galatasaray (0) 1 *(Karan 79)*, Lazio (0) 0   20,000
Nantes (3) 4 *(Andre 5, Quint 10 (pen), Dalmat 43,*
  Vahirua 75), PSV Eindhoven (0) 1 *(De Jong 90)*   28,000
Lazio (1) 1 *(Couto 7)*, Nantes (1) 3 *(Fabbri 3,*
  Armand 63, Ziani 82)   30,000
PSV Eindhoven (1) 3 *(Bruggink 38, Faber 53,*
  Kezman 90), Galatasaray (0) 1 *(Karan 68)*   20,000
Nantes (0) 0, Galatasaray (0) 1 *(Yalcin 79)*   28,000
PSV Eindhoven (1) 1 *(Hofland 39)*, Lazio (0) 0   30,000
Galatasaray (0) 0, Nantes (0) 0   20,000
Lazio (1) 2 *(Fiore 38, Lopez 55 (pen))*,
  PSV Eindhoven (0) 1 *(Kezman 56)*   30,000
Lazio (0) 1 *(Stankovic 76)*, Galatasaray (0) 0   17,500
PSV Eindhoven (0) 0, Nantes (0) 0   31,500
Galatasaray (1) 2 *(Yalcin 26, Arif 50)*,
  PSV Eindhoven (0) 0   22,000
Nantes (0) 1 *(Andre 72)*, Lazio (0) 0   38,337

FINAL TABLE	P	W	D	L	F	A	Pts
Nantes	6	3	2	1	8	3	11
Galatasaray	6	3	1	2	5	4	10
PSV Eindhoven	6	2	1	3	6	9	7
Lazio	6	2	0	4	4	7	6

GROUP E

Juventus (1) 3 *(Trezeguet 43, 55, Amoruso 90 (pen))*,
  Celtic (0) 2 *(Petrov 67, Larsson 85 (pen))*   39,945
Rosenborg (0) 1 *(Rushfeldt 90)*, Porto (1) 2
  (Pena 10, Deco 60)   20,007
Celtic (1) 1 *(Larsson 36)*, Porto (0) 0   54,664
Rosenborg (0) 1 *(Skammelsrud 88 (pen))*,
  Juventus (0) 1 *(Del Piero 85)*   20,578
Celtic (1) 1 *(Thompson 21)*, Rosenborg (0) 0   54,664
Porto (0) 0, Juventus (0) 0   40,228
Porto (2) 3 *(Clayton 1, 61, Mario Silva 45)*,
  Celtic (0) 0   30,303
Juventus (1) 1 *(Trezeguet 25)*, Rosenborg (0) 0   38,000
Juventus (1) 3 *(Del Piero 32, Montero 47,*
  Trezeguet 73), Porto (1) 1 *(Clayton 13)*   38,328
Rosenborg (2) 2 *(Brattbakk 19, 36)*, Celtic (0) 0   21,500
Celtic (2) 4 *(Valgaeren 24, Sutton 45, 64,*
  Larsson 57 (pen)), Juventus (1) 3 *(Del Piero 19,*
  Trezeguet 51, 77)   57,717
Porto (1) 1 *(Pena 37)*, Rosenborg (0) 0   30,000

FINAL TABLE	P	W	D	L	F	A	Pts
Juventus	6	3	2	1	11	8	11
Porto	6	3	1	2	7	5	10
Celtic	6	3	0	3	8	11	9
Rosenborg	6	1	1	4	4	6	4

GROUP F

Fenerbahce (0) 0, Barcelona (2) 3 *(Kluivert 25,*
  Saviola 66, Andersson 28)   21,000
Lyon (0) 0, Leverkusen (0) 1 *(Kirsten 75)*   32,000
Fenerbahce (0) 0, Lyon (0) 1 *(Delmotte 89)*   16,000
Leverkusen (0) 2 *(Basturk 52, Neuville 69)*,
  Barcelona (1) 1 *(Luis Enrique 21)*   22,500
Barcelona (0) 2 *(Kluivert 79, Rivaldo 87 (pen))*,
  Lyon (0) 0   60,000
Leverkusen (1) 2 *(Lucio 36, Ballack 59)*,
  Fenerbahce (1) 1 *(Revivo 6)*   22,500
Barcelona (2) 2 *(Kluivert 12, Luis Enrique 38)*,
  Leverkusen (1) 1 *(Ramelow 32)*   70,000
Lyon (1) 3 *(Govou 45, Carriere 56, Delmotte 69)*,
  Fenerbahce (1) 1 *(Derelioglu 39)*   37,773
Fenerbahce (1) 1 *(Derelioglu 40)*, Leverkusen (2) 2
  (Schneider 21, Kirsten 34)   13,000
Lyon (0) 2 *(Luyindula 66, Carriere 88)*, Barcelona (2) 3
  (Kluivert 9, Rivaldo 18, Gerard 90)   37,000
Barcelona (0) 1 *(Rivaldo 90)*, Fenerbahce (0) 0   44,100
Leverkusen (1) 2 *(Sebescen 45, Berbatov 52)*,
  Lyon (2) 4 *(Carriere 32, 38, Nee 64, Govou 81)*   22,500

FINAL TABLE

	P	W	D	L	F	A	Pts
Barcelona	6	5	0	1	12	5	15
Leverkusen	6	4	0	2	10	9	12
Lyon	6	3	0	3	10	9	9
Fenerbahce	6	0	0	6	3	12	0

GROUP G

La Coruna (1) 2 *(Fran 21, Valeron 90)*,
Olympiakos (0) 2 *(Giannakopoulos 79,*
  Oforiquaye 82) — 22,000
Manchester United (0) 1 *(Beckham 90)*, Lille (0) 0 64,827
La Coruna (0) 2 *(Pandiani 86, Naybet 89)*,
  Manchester United (1) 1 *(Scholes 40)* — 28,000
Lille (2) 3 *(Bakari 33, Cheyrou 43, Tafforeau 79)*,
  Olympiakos (0) 1 *(Giannakopoulos 90)* — 22,000
Lille (0) 1 *(Olufade 87)*, La Coruna (0) 1
  (Valeron 49) — 37,033
Olympiakos (0) 0, Manchester United (0) 2
  (Beckham 66, Cole 82) — 73,537
Manchester United (2) 2 *(Van Nistelrooy 7, 40)*,
  La Coruna (2) 3 *(Sergio 37, Diego Tristan 38, 60)* 65,585
Olympiakos (0) 2 *(Alexandris 53, Niniadis 64)*,
  Lille (1) 1 *(Bassir 37)* — 30,000
La Coruna (1) 1 *(Diego Tristan 13 (pen))*,
  Lille (1) 1 *(Cheyrou 19 (pen))* — 28,000
Manchester United (0) 3 *(Solskjaer 79, Giggs 88,*
  Van Nistelrooy 90), Olympiakos (0) 0 66,769
Lille (0) 1 *(Cheyrou 65)*, Manchester United (1) 1
  (Solskjaer 6) — 37,400
Olympiakos (0) 1 *(Alexandris 51)*, La Coruna (0) 1
  (Capdevila 84) — 28,000

FINAL TABLE

	P	W	D	L	F	A	Pts
La Coruna	6	2	4	0	10	8	10
Manchester United	6	3	1	2	10	6	10
Lille	6	1	3	2	7	7	6
Olympiakos	6	1	2	3	6	12	5

La Coruna finished top on better head-to-head record.

GROUP H

Bayern Munich (0) 0, Sparta Prague (0) 0 16,000
Spartak Moscow (0) 2 *(Robson 63, Bestchastnykh 69)*,
  Feyenoord (1) 2 *(Bosvelt 12, Tomasson 58)* 25,000
Sparta Prague (2) 4 *(Hartig 24, Labant 38 (pen), Kinci 71,*
  Michalik 74), Feyenoord (0) 0 15,150
Spartak Moscow (0) 1 *(Baranov 64)*, Bayern Munich (2)
  3 *(Salihamidzic 16, Elber 41, 74)* 30,000
Feyenoord (2) 2 *(Van Hooijdonk 40, Tomasson 45)*,
  Bayern Munich (1) 2 *(Elber 12, 50)* 40,000
Sparta Prague (0) 2 *(Kinci 57, Sionko 88)*, Spartak
  Moscow (0) 0 17,221
Bayern Munich (3) 5 *(Pisarro 7, 23, Elber 34, 52, Zickler*
  90), Spartak Moscow (0) 1 *(Bestchastnykh 58)* 19,000
Feyenoord (0) 0, Sparta Prague (1) 2 *(Jarosik 43,*
  Novotny 77) — 37,500
Bayern Munich (2) 3 *(Van Gobbel 12 (og), Santa Cruz*
  30, 90), Feyenoord (1) 1 *(Elmander 25)* 40,000
Spartak Moscow (2) 2 *(Robson 5, Bestchastnykh 34)*,
  Sparta Prague (1) 2 *(Holub 29, Babnic 90)* 2000
Feyenoord (2) 2 *(Tomasson 5, Elmander 17)*,
  Spartak Moscow (1) 1 *(Bestchastnykh 13)* 40,000
Sparta Prague (0) 0, Bayern Munich (1) 1
  (Novotny 41 (og)) — 19,369

FINAL TABLE

	P	W	D	L	F	A	Pts
Bayern Munich	6	4	2	0	14	5	14
Sparta Prague	6	3	2	1	10	3	11
Feyenoord	6	1	2	3	7	14	5
Spartak Moscow	6	0	2	4	7	16	2

SECOND STAGE

GROUP A

Bayern Munich (0) 1 *(Sergio 87)*, Manchester United (0)
  1 *(Van Nistelrooy 74)* — 59,000
Boavista (1) 1 *(Sanchez 24)*, Nantes (0) 0 21,000
Manchester United (1) 3 *(Van Nistelrooy 31, 62,*
  Blanc 55), Boavista (0) 0 66,274
Nantes (0) 0, Bayern Munich (0) 1 *(Sergio 65)* 19,500
Boavista (0) 0, Bayern Munich (0) 0 11,000
Nantes (1) 1 *(Moldovan 9)*, Manchester United (0) 1
  (Van Nistelrooy 90 (pen)) — 38,285
Bayern Munich (0) 1 *(Santa Cruz 81)*,
  Boavista (0) 0 — 24,000
Manchester United (3) 5 *(Beckham 19,*
  Solskjaer 31, 78, Silvestre 38, Van Nistelrooy 64 (pen)),
  Nantes (1) 1 *(Da Rocha 17)* — 66,492

Manchester United (0) 0, Bayern Munich (0) 0 66,818
Nantes (1) 1 *(Moldovan 43)*, Boavista (0) 1
  (Martelinho 79) — 28,000
Bayern Munich (0) 2 *(Jeremies 57, Pizarro 87)*,
  Nantes (0) 1 *(Ahamada 53)* — 32,000
Boavista (0) 0, Manchester United (2) 3 *(Blanc 14,*
  Solskjaer 29, Beckham 51 (pen)) — 13,223

FINAL TABLE

	P	W	D	L	F	A	Pts
Manchester United	6	3	3	0	13	3	12
Bayern Munich	6	3	3	0	5	2	12
Boavista	6	1	2	3	2	8	5
Nantes	6	0	2	4	4	11	2

Manchester United finished top on better head-to-head record.

GROUP B

Galatasaray (1) 1 *(Perez 22)*, Roma (0) 1
  (Emerson 90) — 22,000
Liverpool (1) 1 *(Owen 27)*, Barcelona (1) 3
  (Kluivert 41, Rochemback 65, Overmars 84) 41,521
Barcelona (2) 2 *(Saviola 49, 66)*, Galatasaray (2) 2
  (Karan 5, Fleurquin 41) — 49,300
Roma (0) 0, Liverpool (0) 0 — 57,819
Barcelona (0) 1 *(Kluivert 82)*, Roma (0) 1
  (Panucci 57) — 75,000
Liverpool (0) 0, Galatasaray (0) 0 41,605
Galatasaray (0) 1 *(Niculescu 71)*, Liverpool (0) 1
  (Heskey 79) — 39,362
Roma (0) 3 *(Emerson 61, Montella 74, Tommasi 90)*,
  Barcelona (0) 0 — 70,000
Barcelona (0) 0, Liverpool (0) 0 75,362
Roma (1) 1 *(Cafu 50)*, Galatasaray (1) 1
  (Karan 44) — 58,000
Galatasaray (0) 0, Barcelona (0) 1
  (Luis Enrique 58) — 39,500
Liverpool (1) 2 *(Litmanen 7 (pen), Heskey 64)*,
  Roma (0) 0 — 41,794

FINAL TABLE

	P	W	D	L	F	A	Pts
Barcelona	6	2	3	1	7	7	9
Liverpool	6	1	4	1	4	4	7
Roma	6	1	4	1	6	5	7
Galatasaray	6	0	5	1	5	6	5

Liverpool qualified on better head-to-head record.

GROUP C

Panathinaikos (0) 0, Porto (0) 0 17,200
Sparta Prague (1) 2 *(Michalik 30, Sionko 72)*,
  Real Madrid (2) 3 *(Zidane 20, Morientes 36, 74)* 20,482
Porto (0) 0, Sparta Prague (0) 1 *(Sionko 76)* 25,766
Real Madrid (1) 3 *(Helguera 40, Raul 67, 71)*,
  Panathinaikos (0) 0 — 60,000
Real Madrid (0) 1 *(Solari 83)*, Porto (0) 0 64,855
Sparta Prague (0) 0, Panathinaikos (1) 2
  (Karagounis 39, Konstantinou 71) 15,557
Panathinaikos (1) 2 *(Konstantinou 15, 47)*,
  Sparta Prague (0) 1 *(Klein 90)* 17,500
Porto (1) 1 *(Capucho 28)*, Real Madrid (2) 2
  (Solari 7, Helguera 20) — 37,000
Porto (1) 2 *(Deco 12, Pena 54)*, Panathinaikos (0) 1
  (Kolkka 65) — 12,835
Real Madrid (0) 3 *(Solari 60, Guti 64, Savio 70)*,
  Sparta Prague (0) 0 — 40,000
Panathinaikos (1) 2 *(Liberopoulos 9, Goumas 64)*,
  Real Madrid (1) 2 *(Morientes 11, Portillo 80)* 17,000
Sparta Prague (0) 2 *(Sionko 63, Jarosik 71)*,
  Porto (0) 0 — 10,521

FINAL TABLE

	P	W	D	L	F	A	Pts
Real Madrid	6	5	1	0	14	5	16
Panathinaikos	6	2	2	2	7	8	8
Sparta Prague	6	2	0	4	6	10	6
Porto	6	1	1	4	3	7	4

GROUP D

Juventus (3) 4 *(Trezeguet 8, 60, Del Piero 37, Tudor 44)*,
  Leverkusen (0) 0 — 5000
La Coruna (2) 2 *(Makaay 9, Diego Tristan 25)*,
  Arsenal (0) 0 — 32,800
Arsenal (2) 3 *(Ljungberg 21, 88, Henry 27)*,
  Juventus (1) 1 *(Taylor 51 (og))* — 35,421
Leverkusen (0) 3 *(Ze Roberto 64, Neuville 67,*
  Ballack 79), La Coruna (0) 0 — 22,500
Juventus (0) 0, La Coruna (0) 0 9836

Leverkusen (0) 1 *(Kirsten 90)*, Arsenal (0) 1
(*Pires 56*)   22,200
Arsenal (2) 4 *(Pires 5, Henry 7, Vieira 48,*
Bergkamp 83), Leverkusen (0) 1 *(Sebescen 86)*   35,019
La Coruna (1) 2 *(Diego Tristan 8, Djalminha 78)*,
Juventus (0) 0   30,000
Arsenal (0) 0, La Coruna (2) 2 *(Valeron 30,*
Naybet 40)   35,392
Leverkusen (1) 3 *(Butt 24 (pen), Brdaric 71, Babic 90)*,
Juventus (0) 1 *(Tudor 61)*   22,500
La Coruna (0) 1 *(Diego Tristan 74)*, Leverkusen (1) 3
(Ballack 33, Schneider 53, Neuville 85)   23,000
Juventus (0) 1 *(Zalayeta 76)*, Arsenal (0) 0   . 8652

FINAL TABLE	P	W	D	L	F	A	Pts
Leverkusen	6	3	1	2	11	11	10
La Coruna	6	3	1	2	7	6	10
Arsenal	6	2	1	3	8	8	7
Juventus	6	2	1	3	7	8	7

Leverkusen finished top on better head-to-head record.

QUARTER-FINALS, FIRST LEG
Bayern Munich (0) 2 *(Effenberg 81, Pizarro 87)*, Real
Madrid (1) 1 *(Geremi 12)*   60,000
La Coruna (0) 0, Manchester United (2) 2
(Beckham 15, Van Nistelrooy 41)   32,351
Liverpool (1) 1 *(Hyypia 44)*, Leverkusen (0) 0   42,454
Panathinaikos (0) 1 *(Basinas 78 (pen))*,
Barcelona (0) 0   15,800

QUARTER-FINALS, SECOND LEG
Barcelona (1) 3 *(Luis Enrique 22, 49, Saviola 61)*,
Panathinaikos (1) 1 *(Konstantinou 7)*   82,000
Leverkusen (1) 4 *(Ballack 15, 63, Berbatov 68, Lucio 84)*,
Liverpool (1) 2 *(Xavier 42, Litmanen 79)*   22,500
Manchester United (1) 3 *(Solskjaer 23, 56, Giggs 69)*,
La Coruna (1) 2 *(Blanc 44 (og), Djalminha 90)* 65,875
Real Madrid (0) 2 *(Helguera 68, Guti 84)*,
Bayern Munich (0) 0   75,000

SEMI-FINALS, FIRST LEG
Barcelona (0) 0, Real Madrid (0) 2 *(Zidane 55,*
McManaman 90)   98,000
Manchester United (1) 2 *(Zivkovic 30 (og),*
Van Nistelrooy 67 (pen)), Leverkusen (0) 2
(Ballack 62, Neuville 75)   66,534

SEMI-FINALS, SECOND LEG
Leverkusen (1) 1 *(Neuville 45)*, Manchester United (1) 1
(Keane 28)   22,500
Real Madrid (1) 1 *(Raul 43)*, Barcelona (0) 1
(Helguera 48 (og))   75,000

FINAL

Leverkusen (1) 1, Real Madrid (2) 2

(at Hampden Park, 15 May 2002, 52,000)

Leverkusen: Butt; Sebescen (Kirsten 65), Placente, Ramelow, Zivkovic, Lucio (Babic 90), Schneider, Ballack, Neuville,
Basturk, Brdaric (Berbatov 39).
Scorer: Lucio 14.
Real Madrid: Cesar (Casillas 68); Michel Salgado, Roberto Carlos, Makelele (Conceicao 73), Hierro, Helguera, Figo
(McManaman 61), Morientes, Raul, Zidane, Solari.
Scorers: Raul 8, Zidane 45.
Referee: Meier (Switzerland).

Zinedine Zidane in action during Real Madrid's European Champions League Final win. His spectacular left-foot shot
condemned Leverkusen to another runners-up spot. (Colorsport)

EUROPEAN CUP 2001–02 – BRITISH AND IRISH CLUBS

FIRST QUALIFYING ROUND, FIRST LEG

11 JULY

Barry Town (0) 2 *(York 54, French 68)*
Shamkir (0) 0   1992
Barry Town: Clarke; Evans, Lloyd, York, Phillips, Brown (Jenkins 60), French, Moralee (Davies 85), Flynn, Staton, Morgan.
Shamkir: Mahammadov; Karimov, Yunusov, Azer Mammadov, Mardonov, Kurbanov E (Isayev 73), Kurbanov M, Mammadov I, Yadullayev (Kulikov 70), Mammadov K (Kvaratsckhelia 70), Rzayev.

Bohemians (2) 3 *(Maher 1, Crowe 9, 57 (pen))*
Levadia (0) 0   3832
Bohemians: Russell; Shelly (O'Connor 88), Webb, Hunt, Maher, John, Byrne, Caffrey, Nesovic (Harkin 82), Crowe (O'Neill 84), Rutherford.
Levadia: Martinsons; Leitan J (Lepik 74), Tatarinov, Kulikov, Rotskov, Fenin (Olumets 87), Bragin, Krasnopjorov, Kalimullin, Krom (Leitan V 58), Tselnokov.

Linfield (0) 0
Torpedo Kutaisi (0) 0   2699
Linfield: Robinson; Collier (Kelly N 87), Murphy D, Picking, Murphy W, Kelly R, Larmour, Gorman (Scates 82), Ferguson, McBride (Marks 10), Bailie.
Torpedo Kutaisi: Gvaramadze; Makhviladze (Isiani 32), Didava, Todua, Kemoklidze, Kutateladze (Akhalkatsi 46), Ashvetia (Gancharov 82), Abramidze, Asatiani, Akofian, Khvadagiani.

FIRST QUALIFYING ROUND, SECOND LEG

18 JULY

Levadia (0) 0
Bohemians (0) 0   1034
Levadia: Martinsons; Tatarinov, Kulikov, Rotskov, Leitan V (Olumets 77), Fenin, Bragin, Krasnopjorov, Kalimullin, Krom, Tselnokov.
Bohemians: Russell; Shelly, Webb, Hunt, Maher, John, Byrne, Caffrey, Nesovic (Harkin 75), Crowe (O'Neill 85), Rutherford.

Shamkir (0) 0
Barry Town (0) 1 *(Phillips 57)*   12,000
Shamkir: Mahammadov; Karimov, Yunusov, Azer Mammadov, Kurbanov M, Mardanov, Mammadov I, Kvaratsckhelia, Isayev (Kurbanov E 46), Kulikov (Agil Mammadov 77), Rzayev (Mammadov K 70).
Barry Town: Clarke; Evans, Lloyd, Jenkins, York, Phillips (Sharp 82), Brown (Kennedy 76), French, Moralee (Davies 79), Flynn, Staton.

Torpedo Kutaisi (0) 1 *(Ashvetia 68)*
Linfield (0) 0   7130
Torpedo Kutaisi: Gvaramadze; Didava, Todua, Kemoklidze, Kutateladze (Makhviladze 72), Ashvetia (Gancharov 83), Abramidze, Akhalkatsi (Paramonovi 46), Asatiani, Akofian, Khvadagiani.
Linfield: Robinson; Collier, McShane, Picking, Murphy W, Kelly R (Larmour 75), Marks (Scates 65), Gorman, Ferguson, Kelly N (Murphy D 65), Bailie.

SECOND QUALIFYING ROUND, FIRST LEG

25 JULY

Bohemians (1) 1 *(Crowe 23)*
Halmstad (1) 2 *(Jonsson 31, Selakovic 55)*   4225
Bohemians: Russell; Shelly, Webb, Hunt, Maher, John, Byrne (Harkin 62), Caffrey, Nesovic (Morrison 62), Crowe (O'Neill 81), Rutherford.

Halmstad: Svensson H; Arvidsson, Jonsson, Vennberg, Nilsson, Hansson (Gustafson 46), Andersson R, Wowoah, Selakovic (Karlsson 88), Andersson F (Jensen 57), Svensson M.

Maribor (0) 0   6100
Rangers (1) 3 *(Flo 38, 73, Nerlinger 56)*
Maribor: Simeunovic; Duro, Krizan, Seslar (Golob 58), Dvorsak, Sztipanovics, Filekovic, Balajic (Znuderl 88), Sarkezi, Cipot (Kvas 73), Snofl.
Rangers: Klos; Ricken, Moore, Amoruso (Ferguson 46), Numan, Caniggia (Mols 69), Nerlinger (McCann 64), Flo, Reyna, Konterman, Latapy.

Porto (5) 8 *(Pena 12, 51, 72, Deco 22, 23, 43, Sodestrom 41, Capucho 52)*
Barry Town (0) 0   43,050
Porto: Ovchinnikov; Jorge Costa, Paredes, Secretario (Ricardo Carvalho 69), Deco (Alenichev 73), Jorge Andrade, Sodestrom, Capucho (Candido 61), Clayton, Mario Silva, Pena.
Barry Town: Clarke; Evans (Kennedy 50), Lloyd, Jenkins (Morgan 50), York, Phillips, Brown (Davies 65), French, Moralee, Flynn, Staton.

SECOND QUALIFYING ROUND, SECOND LEG

1 AUG

Barry Town (2) 3 *(Phillips 37, Flynn 38, Lloyd 90 (pen))*
Porto (1) 1 *(Dias 18)*   2377
Barry Town: Clarke; Evans, Lloyd, York, Phillips (Sharp 82), Brown, French, Moralee, Flynn (Jenkins 51), Staton (Davies 74), Kennedy.
Porto: Espinha; Jorge Costa, Ricardo Carvalho, Francisco Costa, Rubens Junior, Oliviera, Ibarra (Helder 53), Dias (Alenichev 62), Victor (Santos 68), Candido, Ricardo Silva.

Halmstad (0) 2 *(Jonsson 57, Selakovic 68)*
Bohemians (0) 0   3643
Halmstad: Svensson H; Arvidsson (Ekstrom 88), Jonsson, Nilsson, Hansson, Andersson F, Wowoah (Karlsson 84), Selakovic, Andersson R (Bertilsson 74), Svensson M, Jensen.
Bohemians: Russell; Shelly, Webb, Hunt, Maher (O'Neill 64), John, Byrne (Morrison 70), Caffrey, Molloy (Hill 76), Crowe, Rutherford.

Rangers (0) 3 *(Flo 54, Caniggia 58, 73)*
Maribor (1) 1 *(Starcevic 17)*   50,045
Rangers: Klos; Ricksen, Moore, Ferguson, Caniggia (Dodds 73), Nerlinger (McCann 38), Flo, Konterman, Latapy (Wilson 50), Vidmar, Hughes.
Maribor: Simeunovic (Murko 73); Duro, Krizan, Seslar, Kvas (Golob 60), Filekovic, Znuderl, Balajic, Starcevic (Ihtijarevic 77), Snofl, Vuksanovic.

THIRD QUALIFYING ROUND, FIRST LEG

8 AUG

Ajax (1) 1 *(Arveladze 40)*   51,859
Celtic (2) 3 *(Petta 7, Agathe 20, Sutton 55)*
Ajax: Grim; Trabelsi, Chivu, Cruz, Pasanen, Yakuba, Van der Vaart (Van der Meyde 74), Ikeida (Ibrahimovic 46), Machlas, Arveladze, Hossam.
Celtic: Douglas; Agathe, Petta (Guppy 86), Mjallby, Boyd, Valgaeren, Lennon, McNamara, Sutton, Larsson (Hartson 83), Lambert.

Haka (0) 0 33,217
Liverpool (1) 5 *(Heskey 32, Owen 56, 66, 88, Hyypia 87)*
Haka: Vilnrotter; Kangaskorpi, Aalto, Makela, Okkonen, Vaisanen, Wilson, Karjalainen (Ivanov 84), Popovitch (Ruhanen 71), Kovacs, Torkkeli (Pasanen 73).
Liverpool: Arphexad; Babbel, Carragher, Hamann, Henchoz, Hyypia, Gerrard (Murphy 66), Litmanen (McAllister 59), Heskey (Fowler 73), Owen, Berger.

Rangers (0) 0
Fenerbahce (0) 0 49,472
Rangers: Klos; Vidmar, Numan, Moore, Wilson, Konterman, Ricksen, McCann, Caniggia (Mols 46), Flo, Hughes.
Fenerbahce: Recber; Meric, Ercan, Ozat, Mirkovic, Dogan (Akin 77), Lazetic, Temizkanoglu, Revivo (Andersson K 86), Johnson, Rapajic.

THIRD QUALIFYING ROUND, SECOND LEG
21 AUG
Liverpool (1) 4 *(Fowler 37, Redknapp 50, Heskey 56, Wilson 83 (og))*
Haka (1) 1 *(Kovacs 45)* 31,602
Liverpool: Arphexad; Wright, Vignal, Redknapp (Gerrard 72), Traore, Hyypia (Babbel 66), Barmby, Diomede, Heskey (Litmanen 60), Fowler, Biscan.
Haka: Vilnrotter; Kangaskorpi, Aalto, Pogioli (Ivanov 78), Karjalainen, Okkonen, Bajic (Koivuranta 81), Wilson, Kovacs, Ruhanen (Innanen 66), Torkkeli.

22 AUG
Celtic (0) 0
Ajax (1) 1 *(Wamberto 30)* 60,000
Celtic: Douglas; Agathe, Guppy, Mjallby, Boyd, Valgaeren, Lennon, McNamara (Moravcik 71), Sutton, Larsson, Lambert.
Ajax: Grim; Trabelsi, Maxwell, Vierklau (Knopper 71), Chivu, Bergdolmo (Mido 76), Yakubu, Van der Vaart, Machlas (Ibrahimovic 65), Arveladze, Wamberto.

Fenerbahce (1) 2 *(Revivo 3, Serhat 71)*
Rangers (0) 1 *(Ricksen 73)* 30,000
Fenerbahce: Recber; Meric, Ercan, Mirkovic, Ogun, Dogan, Lazetic (Ugar 90), Johnson, Revivo (Serhat 69), Rapajic (Andersson K 77), Ozat.
Rangers: Klos; Ricksen, Vidmae (Ross 46), Reyna (Hughes 36), Wilson, Amoruso, Kanchelskis (Caniggia 72), Konterman, Flo, Numan, De Boer.

CHAMPIONS LEAGUE
GROUP B
11 SEPT
Liverpool (1) 1 *(Owen 29)*
Boavista (1) 1 *(Silva 3)* 30,015
Liverpool: Dudek; Carragher, Vignal, Hamann, Henchoz, Hyypia, Gerrard, McAllister, Heskey, Owen, Murphy (Riise 71).
Boavista: Ricardo; Frechaut, Erivan, Petit, Turra, Emanuel, Duda (Bosingwa 85), Sanchez (Santos 58), Goulart, Silva (Serginho 79), Glauber.

19 SEPT
Borussia Dortmund (0) 0
Liverpool (0) 0 46,000
Borussia Dortmund: Lehmann; Evanilson, Dede, Kohler, Reuter, Worns, Stevic, Sorensen (Bobic 87), Rosicky, Koller, Amoroso (Ricken 87).
Liverpool: Dudek; Carragher, Vignal, Hamann, Henchoz, Hyypia, Gerrard, Riise (McAllister 75), Heskey, Owen, Murphy.

26 SEPT
Liverpool (1) 1 *(Litmanen 24)*
Dynamo Kiev (0) 0 33,513
Liverpool: Dudek; Carragher, Vignal, Hamann, Henchoz, Hyypia, Gerrard, Riise (McAllister 79), Heskey, Litmanen (Fowler 65), Barmby (Murphy 62).

Dynamo Kiev: Filimonov; Gioane, Nesmachnyi, Fedorov, Vashchuk, Golovko, Gavrancic, Belkevich (Serebrennikov 81), Melashchenko, Idahor, Cernat (Peev 68).

16 OCT
Dynamo Kiev (0) 1 *(Gioane 59)*
Liverpool (1) 2 *(Murphy 43, Gerrard 67)* 50,000
Dynamo Kiev: Reva; Bodnar (Gusin 56), Nesmachnyi, Gioane, Vashchuk, Golovko, Gavrancic, Khatksevich, Belkevich, Melashchenko (Idahor 79), Cernat.
Liverpool: Dudek; Carragher, Riise, McAllister, Henchoz, Hyypia, Gerrard, Smicer (Redknapp 79), Heskey, Barmby (Berger 62), Murphy.

24 OCT
Boavista (0) 1 *(Silva 60)*
Liverpool (1) 1 *(Murphy 17)* 6000
Boavista: Ricardo; Rui Oscar (Martelinho 26), Erivan, Frechaut, Emanuel, Turra, Petit, Duda (Bosingwa 57), Silva, Goulart (Glauber 57), Sanchez.
Liverpool: Dudek; Carragher, Riise, Hamann, Henchoz, Hyypia (Wright 6), Murphy, Smicer, Heskey, Fowler, McAllister (Berger 76).

30 OCT
Liverpool (1) 2 *(Smicer 15, Wright 82)*
Borussia Dortmund (0) 0 41,507
Liverpool: Dudek; Wright, Riise, Hamann, Henchoz, Carragher, Gerrard (Redknapp 85), Smicer (Berger 64), Heskey, Owen (Fowler 76), Murphy.
Borussia Dortmund: Lehmann; Evanilson, Dede, Worns, Reuter, Metzelder, Oliseh (Bobic 69), Sorensen, Rosicky, Koller, Ricken.

GROUP C
11 SEPT
Mallorca (1) 1 *(Engonga 11 (pen))*
Arsenal (0) 0 22,000
Mallorca: Franco; Olaizola, Soler, Campano, Nino, Nadal, Marcos, Engonga (Vicente 67), Eto'o, Luque (Paunovic 76), Ibagaza (Novo 44).
Arsenal: Seaman; Lauren, Cole, Vieira, Campbell, Keown, Van Bronckhorst, Ljungberg (Jeffers 75), Wiltord (Kanu 71), Henry, Pires (Parlour 79).

19 SEPT
Arsenal (2) 3 *(Ljungberg 33, Henry 35, 47 (pen))*
Schalke (1) 2 *(Van Hoogdalem 43, Mpenza 59)* 35,361
Arsenal: Seaman; Lauren, Van Bronckhorst, Vieira, Keown, Grimandi, Parlour, Ljungberg, Wiltord (Bergkamp 71), Henry (Upson 90), Pires (Inamoto 76).
Schalke: Reck; Vermant (Asamoah 53), Bohme (Mulder 82), Hajto, Waldoch, Van Kerckhoven, Kamphuis, Van Hoogdalem, Moller (Djordjevic 71), Mpenza, Agali.

26 SEPT
Panathinaikos (1) 1 *(Karagounis 24)*
Arsenal (0) 0 17,200
Panathinaikos: Nikopolidis; Kirgiakos, Fissas, Henriksen, Vokolos, Michaelsen, Paulo Sousa, Karagounis (Saric 84), Vlaovic (Konstantinou 64), Olisadebe (Kolkka 69), Basinas.
Arsenal: Seaman; Lauren, Cole, Vieira, Keown, Upson, Parlour (Van Bronckhorst 53), Ljungberg (Kanu 68), Wiltord (Jeffers 68), Henry, Pires.

16 OCT
Arsenal (1) 2 *(Henry 23, 52 (pen))*
Panathinaikos (0) 1 *(Olisadebe 50)* 35,432
Arsenal: Wright; Lauren, Cole, Vieira, Campbell, Upson, Van Bronckhorst, Ljungberg, Wiltord (Bergkamp 71), Henry (Grimandi 89), Pires (Parlour 71).
Panathinaikos: Nikopolidis; Michaelsen, Fissas, Kirgiakos, Henriksen, Vokolos, Karagounis (Kolkka 77), Paulo Sousa (Seitaridis 77), Olisadebe, Konstantinou (Vlaovic 77), Basinas.

24 OCT

Arsenal (0) 3 *(Pires 61, Bergkamp 63, Henry 90)*
Mallorca (0) 1 *(Novo 74)* 34,764
Arsenal: Wright; Lauren, Van Bronckhorst, Vieira, Campbell, Keown, Grimandi (Parlour 85), Ljungberg (Kanu 79), Henry, Bergkamp (Wiltord 72), Pires.
Mallorca: Franco; Fatih (Biagini 66), Soler, Olaizola, Nadal, Campano, Marcos (Robles 72), Paunovic, Novo, Luque (Carlos 80), Diaz.

30 OCT

Schalke (1) 3 *(Mulder 2, Vermant 60, Moller 64)*
Arsenal (0) 1 *(Wiltord 71)* 52,500
Schalke: Reck; Van Hoogdalem (Knetsch 63), Nemec (Thon 67), Hajto, Waldoch, Matellan, Vermant (Djordjevic 74), Sand, Mulder, Moller, Bohme.
Arsenal: Wright; Luzhny, Cole, Edu, Campbell (Keown 67), Upson (Stepanovs 66), Parlour, Grimandi, Wiltord, Kanu (Pennant 78), Pires.

GROUP E

18 SEPT

Juventus (1) 3 *(Trezeguet 43, 55, Amoruso 90 (pen))*
Celtic (0) 2 *(Petrov 67, Larsson 85 (pen))* 39,945
Juventus: Buffon; Zenoni, Pessotto (Birindelli 64), Thuram, Montero, Iuliano, Del Piero (Amoruso 88), Tacchinardi, Trezeguet, Salas (O'Neill 69), Davids.
Celtic: Douglas; Agathe, Thompson (Petta 59), Balde, Mjallby, Valgaeren, Lennon, Petrov, Sutton, Larsson, Lambert.

25 SEPT

Celtic (1) 1 *(Larsson 36)*
Porto (0) 0 54,664
Celtic: Douglas; Agathe, Petta (Thompson 68), Balde, Mjallby, Valgaeren, Lennon, Petrov (McNamara 88), Sutton, Larsson, Lambert.
Porto: Ovchinnikov; Ibarra (Helder 76), Mario Silva (Rubens Junior 46), Jorge Costa, Andrade, Carvalho, Costinha (Alenichev 46), Deco, Capucho, Pena, Paredes.

10 OCT

Celtic (1) 1 *(Thompson 21)*
Rosenborg (0) 0 54,664
Celtic: Douglas; Agathe, Thompson (Guppy 66), Balde, Mjallby, Valgaeren, Lennon, Petrov, Sutton, Larsson, Lambert.
Rosenborg: Arason; Johnsen B, Saarinen, Skammelsrud, Basma, Hoftun, Strand (Winsnes 82), Olsen (Johnsen F 86), Rushfeldt, Brattbakk (George 74), Berg.

17 OCT

Porto (2) 3 *(Clayton 1, 61, Mario Silva 45)*
Celtic (0) 0 30,303
Porto: Ovchinnikov; Ibarra, Mario Silva, Andrade, Carvalho, Deco, Costinha (Fredrick 82), Clayton (Rubens Junior 75), Capucho (Paulo Costa 87), Pena, Paredes.
Celtic: Douglas; Agathe, Thompson (Moravcik 56), Balde, Mjallby, Valgaeren, Lennon, Petrov (Sylla 68), Hartson (Maloney 89), Larsson, Lambert.

23 OCT

Rosenborg (2) 2 *(Brattbakk 19, 36)*
Celtic (0) 0 21,500
Rosenborg: Arason; Olsen, Saarinen, Skammelsrud, Basma, Hoftun, Strand, Brattbakk, Rushfeldt, George (Johnsen B 82), Berg (Winsnes 73).
Celtic: Douglas; Agathe, Thompson (Hartson 77), Balde, Mjallby, Valgaeren, Lennon, Petrov (Moravcik 66), Sutton, Larsson, Lambert.

31 OCT

Celtic (2) 4 *(Valgaeren 24, Sutton 45, 64, Larsson 57 (pen))*
Juventus (1) 3 *(Del Piero 19, Trezeguet 51, 77)* 57,717
Celtic: Douglas; Agathe, Petta, Balde, Mjallby, Valgaeren, Lennon, Moravcik (Petrov 65), Sutton, Larsson, Lambert.
Juventus: Carini; Birindelli, Paramatti, Zenoni, Ferrara, Iuliano, Maresca (Frara 81), Tacchinardi, Del Piero (Trezeguet 46), Amoruso (Pessotto 67), Nedved.

GROUP G

18 SEPT

Manchester United (0) 1 *(Beckham 90)*
Lille (0) 0 64,827
Manchester United: Barthez; Neville G (Silvestre 12), Irwin, Brown, Keane, Blanc, Beckham, Scholes, Van Nistelrooy, Veron, Giggs (Solskjaer 74).
Lille: Wimbee; Pichot, Tafforeau (Schmitz 85), Fahmi, Cygan, Ecker, Sterjovski (Olufade 90), N'Diaye, Cheyrou (Boutoille 74), Bakari, D'Amico.

25 SEPT

La Coruna (0) 2 *(Pandiani 86, Naybet 89)*
Manchester United (1) 1 *(Scholes 40)* 28,000
La Coruna: Molina; Manuel Pablo, Romero, Naybet, Donato, Emerson (Valeron 46), Mauro Silva, Makaay (Pandiani 60), Sergio (Scaloni 60), Diego Tristan, Fran.
Manchester United: Barthez; Neville G, Irwin, Johnsen, Keane, Blanc, Beckham (Cole 90), Scholes, Van Nistelrooy (Solskjaer 90), Veron, Giggs.

10 OCT

Olympiakos (0) 0
Manchester United (0) 2 *(Beckham 66, Cole 82)* 73,537
Olympiakos: Eleftheropoulos; Patsatzoglou, Venetidis, Kostoulas (Oforiquaye 69), Bermudez, Anatolakis, Karembeu, Giannakopoulos, Djordjevic (Alexandris 80), Giovanni, Zetterberg (Niniadis 65).
Manchester United: Barthez; Neville G, Irwin (Silvestre 87), Johnsen, Keane, Blanc, Beckham, Scholes, Van Nistelrooy (Solskjaer 84), Veron (Cole 80), Giggs.

17 OCT

Manchester United (2) 2 *(Van Nistelrooy 7, 40)*
La Coruna (2) 3 *(Sergio 37, Diego Tristan 38, 60)* 65,585
Manchester United: Barthez; Neville G, Irwin (Solskjaer 85), Johnsen (Brown 7), Keane, Blanc, Beckham, Scholes (Cole 63), Van Nistelrooy, Veron, Giggs.
La Coruna: Molina (Nuno 46); Hector, Romero (Capdevila 79), Sergio, Naybet, Donato, Victor, Dusher, Tristan (Pandiani 83), Valeron, Amavisca.

23 OCT

Manchester United (0) 3 *(Solskjaer 79, Giggs 88, Van Nistelrooy 90)*
Olympiakos (0) 0 66,769
Manchester United: Barthez; Neville G, Irwin, Brown, Butt (Solskjaer 72), Blanc, Beckham, Scholes, Van Nistelrooy, Veron, Giggs.
Olympiakos: Eleftheropoulos; Mavrogenidis (Poursanidis 46), Kontis, Patsatzoglou, Amanatidis, Anatolakis, Karembeu, Giannakopoulos (Roberts 83), Oforiquaye, Djordjevic, Alexandris (Alvez 62).

31 OCT

Lille (0) 1 *(Cheyrou 65)*
Manchester United (1) 1 *(Solskjaer 6)* 37,400
Lille: Wimbee; Pichot, Ecker, Fahmi, Cygan, Boutoille (Beck 58), N'Diaye (Landrin 86), D'Amico, Cheyrou, Bassir (Murati 78), Sterjovski.
Manchester United: Carroll; Neville P, Irwin, May (O'Shea 69), Butt, Silvestre, Beckham, Scholes, Cole (Yorke 76), Solskjaer, Fortune.

SECOND STAGE

20 NOV

GROUP A

Bayern Munich (0) 1 *(Sergio 87)*

Manchester United (0) 1 *(Van Nistelrooy 74)* 59,000

Bayern Munich: Kahn; Sagnol, Lizarazu, Salihamidzic (Zickler 72), Kuffour, Kovac, Hargreaves, Effenberg (Sforza 68), Pizarro, Elber (Jancker 68), Sergio.
Manchester United: Barthez; Neville G, Irwin (Silvestre 46), Brown, Keane, Blanc, Beckham, Scholes, Van Nistelrooy (Yorke 84), Veron, Fortune.

5 DEC

Manchester United (1) 3 *(Van Nistelrooy 31, 62, Blanc 55)*

Boavista (0) 0 66,274

Manchester United: Barthez; Neville P, Silvestre, Neville G (O'Shea 77), Keane, Blanc, Veron, Butt, Van Nistelrooy (Solskjaer 88), Yorke, Scholes (Fortune 86).
Boavista: Ricardo; Frechaut, Erivan, Pedro Emanuel, Paulo Turra, Jorge Silva (Martelinho 61), Petit, Goulart, Duda, Silva (Marcio Santos 58), Sanchez (Pedro Santos 69).

20 FEB

Nantes (1) 1 *(Moldovan 9)*

Manchester United (0) 1 *(Van Nistelrooy 90 (pen))* 38,285

Nantes: Landreau; Cetto, Armand, Ziani, Yepes, Fabbri, Savinaud, Berson, Moldovan (Andre 75), Vahirua (Da Rocha 61), Quint (Bilayi Ateba 77).
Manchester United: Barthez; Neville P (Forlan 77), Silvestre, Neville G, Keane, Blanc, Beckham, Scholes, Van Nistelrooy, Veron (Solskjaer 63), Giggs.

26 FEB

Manchester United (3) 5 *(Beckham 19, Solskjaer 31, 78, Silvestre 38, Van Nistelrooy 64 (pen))*

Nantes (1) 1 *(Da Rocha 17)* 66,492

Manchester United: Barthez; Irwin, Silvestre, Neville G, Keane (Butt 75), Blanc (Johnsen 68), Beckham, Veron, Van Nistelrooy (Forlan 68), Solskjaer, Giggs.
Nantes: Landreau; Deroff, Bilayi Ateba (Vahirua 63), Cetto, Fabbri, Armand, Da Rocha, Berson, Djemba-Djemba (Savinaud 57), Andre, Ziani (Quint 78).

13 MAR

Manchester United (0) 0

Bayern Munich (0) 0 66,818

Manchester United: Barthez; Neville G, Silvestre, Johnsen, Keane, Blanc, Beckham, Veron, Van Nistelrooy, Solskjaer (Forlan 78), Giggs.
Bayern Munich: Kahn; Kuffour, Lizarazu, Jeremies (Fink 72), Linke, Kovac, Hargreaves, Effenberg, Santa Cruz (Zickler 77), Pizarro, Sergio (Elber 83).

19 MAR

Boavista (0) 0 13,223

Manchester United (2) 3 *(Blanc 14, Solskjaer 29, Beckham 51 (pen))*

Boavista: Ricardo; Frechaut, Mario Loja, Jorge Silva (Martelinho 34), Paulo Turra, Pedro Emanuel, Petit, Duda, Serginho, Sanchez, Silva (Goulart 21) (Marcio Santos 77).
Manchester United: Barthez; Neville G, Silvestre, Johnsen (Neville P 73), Scholes (Stewart 59), Blanc (O'Shea 73), Beckham, Butt, Solskjaer, Forlan, Giggs.

20 NOV

GROUP B

Liverpool (1) 1 *(Owen 27)*

Barcelona (1) 3 *(Kluivert 41, Rochemback 65, Overmars 84)* 41,521

Liverpool: Dudek; Carragher, Riise, McAllister (Berger 69), Henchoz, Hyypia, Gerrard, Smicer (Litmanen 80), Heskey (Fowler 65), Owen, Murphy.
Barcelona: Bonano; Christanval, Coco, Andersson, Frank de Boer, Cocu, Gabri (Rochemback 58), Rivaldo, Kluivert (Reiziger 89), Luis Enrique (Overmars 18), Xavi.

5 DEC

Roma (0) 0

Liverpool (0) 0 57,819

Roma: Antonioli; Zebina, Aldair, Guigou (Assuncao 46), Candela, Samuel, Tommasi' (Fuser 79), Totti, Batistuta, Emerson, Lima.
Liverpool: Dudek; Carragher, Riise, Hamann, Henchoz, Hyypia, Gerrard (Biscan 83), Smicer (McAllister 63), Heskey, Owen, Murphy (Berger 61).

20 FEB

Liverpool (0) 0

Galatasaray (0) 0 41,605

Liverpool: Kirkland; Xavier, Carragher (Smicer 67), Hamann, Henchoz, Hyypia, Gerrard (McAllister 73), Murphy, Heskey, Owen, Riise.
Galatasaray: Mondragon; Perez, Victoria, Emre, Bulent K, Bulent A, Fleurquin, Hasan Sas (Sozkesen 80) (Niculescu 90), Berkant, Umit K, Ergun.

26 FEB

Galatasaray (0) 1 *(Niculescu 71)*

Liverpool (0) 1 *(Heskey 79)* 39,362

Galatasaray: Mondragon; Perez, Victoria, Fleurquin, Bulent K, Goktan, Hasan Sas, Ayhan, Ergun, Erdem, Niculescu (Serkan 79).
Liverpool: Kirkland; Xavier, Carragher, Hamann, Henchoz, Hyypia, Murphy, Smicer (Litmanen 74), Heskey, Owen, Riise.

13 MAR

Barcelona (0) 0

Liverpool (0) 0 75,362

Barcelona: Bonano; Puyol, Coco, Cocu, Christanval, De Boer, Luis Enrique (Gerard 77), Motta, Kluivert, Rivaldo, Saviola (Geovanni 87).
Liverpool: Dudek; Xavier, Carragher, Hamann, Henchoz, Hyypia, Gerrard (Barmby 80), Murphy, Heskey (Baros 74), Litmanen (Smicer 70), Riise.

19 MAR

Liverpool (1) 2 *(Litmanen 7 (pen), Heskey 64)*

Roma (0) 0 41,794

Liverpool: Dudek; Xavier, Carragher, Gerrard, Henchoz, Hyypia, Murphy, Smicer (McAllister 90), Heskey, Litmanen (Biscan 88), Riise.
Roma: Antonioli; Panucci, Samuel, Aldair, Tommasi, Emerson, Assuncao (Cassano 68), Lima (Delvecchio 46), Totti, Batistuta (Montella 46), Candela.

21 NOV

GROUP D

La Coruna (2) 2 *(Makaay 9, Diego Tristan 25)*

Arsenal (0) 0 32,800

La Coruna: Molina; Scaloni, Romero, Donato, Naybet, Mauro Silva, Valeron (Djalminha 74), Emerson, Makaay (Pandiani 50), Diego Tristan (Amavisca 28), Victor.
Arsenal: Wright (Taylor 46); Lauren, Cole, Vieira, Campbell, Upson, Van Bronckhorst (Edu 79), Ljungberg, Wiltord (Kanu 74), Henry, Pires.

4 DEC

Arsenal (2) 3 *(Ljungberg 21, 88, Henry 27)*

Juventus (0) 1 *(Taylor 51 (og))* 35,421

Arsenal: Taylor; Lauren, Cole (Keown 88), Vieira, Campbell, Upson, Ljungberg, Parlour, Kanu (Bergkamp 69), Henry (Grimandi 84), Pires.
Juventus: Buffon; Birindelli, Pessotto (Paramatti 77), Tacchinardi, Montero, Thuram, Zambrotta, Tudor (Davids 22), Del Piero, Trezeguet, Nedved (Amoruso 71).

19 FEB

Leverkusen (0) 1 *(Kirsten 90)*

Arsenal (0) 1 *(Pires 56)* 22,200

Leverkusen: Butt; Zivkovic, Placente (Berbatov 73), Nowotny (Vranjes 60), Lucio, Basturk, Schneider, Ballack, Kirsten, Neuville, Ze Roberto.
Arsenal: Seaman; Lauren, Van Bronckhorst, Vieira, Campbell, Stepanovs, Parlour, Wiltord (Grimandi 70), Kanu (Edu 74), Henry, Pires.

27 FEB

Arsenal (2) 4 *(Pires 5, Henry 7, Vieira 48, Berkamp 83)*
Leverkusen (0) 1 *(Sebescen 86)*   35,019
Arsenal: Seaman; Dixon, Lauren (Inamoto 83), Vieira,
Campbell, Stepanovs, Wiltord (Pennant 89), Grimandi
(Edu 66), Henry, Bergkamp, Pires.
Leverkusen: Butt; Zivkovic (Sebescen 73), Placente,
Nowotny, Lucio, Ramelow, Neuville, Ballack, Kirsten
(Berbatov 46), Schneider (Basturk 46), Ze Roberto.

12 MAR

Arsenal (0) 0

La Coruna (2) 2 *(Valeron 30, Naybet 40)*   35,392
Arsenal: Seaman; Lauren, Luzhny, Vieira, Campbell,
Stepanovs, Wiltord (Kanu 64), Grimandi (Ljungberg 64),
Henry, Bergkamp, Pires.
La Coruna: Molina; Scaloni, Romero, Mauro Silva,
Naybet, Cesar, Victor, Valeron (Duscher 80), Diego
Tristan (Makaay 85), Fran (Capdevila 72), Sergio.

20 MAR

Juventus (0) 1 *(Zalayeta 76)*

Arsenal (0) 0   8652
Juventus: Carini; Zenoni, Conte, Zambrotta (Amoruso
69), Birindelli, Iuliano, Paramatti (Pessotto 23), Maresca,
Davids, Guzman (Pericard 60), Zalayeta.
Arsenal: Seaman; Dixon, Lauren (Cole 81), Vieira,
Campbell, Luzhny, Ljungberg, Edu (Wiltord 78), Kanu,
Henry, Pires.

QUARTER-FINALS, FIRST LEG

2 APR

La Coruna (0) 0

Manchester United (2) 2 *(Beckham 15, Van Nistelrooy
41)*   32,351
La Coruna: Molina; Scaloni, Romero, Mauro Silva,
Cesar, Naybet, Victor (Duscher 80), Valeron (Djalminha
68), Diego Tristan, Fran (Makaay 60), Sergio.
Manchester United: Barthez; Neville G, Silvestre,
Johnsen, Keane (Fortune 44), Blanc, Beckham (Neville P
90), Butt, Van Nistelrooy (Solskjaer 74), Scholes, Giggs.

3 APR

Liverpool (1) 1 *(Hyppia 44)*

Leverkusen (0) 0   42,454
Liverpool: Dudek; Carragher, Riise, Hamann, Henchoz,
Hyypia, Gerrard, Smicer (Berger 74), Heskey, Owen
(Litmanen 69), Murphy.

Leverkusen: Butt; Sebescen, Placente, Schneider,
Ramelow, Lucio, Neuville (Kirsten 73), Ballack,
Berbatov (Zivkovic 65), Basturk, Ze Roberto.

QUARTER-FINALS, SECOND LEG

9 APR

Leverkusen (1) 4 *(Ballack 15, 63, Berbatov 68, Lucio 84)*
Liverpool (1) 2 *(Xavier 42, Litmanen 79)*   22,500
Leverkusen: Butt; Sebescen (Neuville 46), Placente,
Schneider, Nowotny, Lucio, Basturk, Ballack, Kirsten
(Berbatov 46), Brdaric (Zivkovic 70), Ze Roberto.
Liverpool: Dudek; Xavier (Berger 75), Carragher,
Hamann (Smicer 61), Henchoz, Hyypia, Gerrard,
Murphy, Heskey (Litmanen 42), Owen, Riise.

10 APR

Manchester United (1) 3 *(Solskjaer 23, 56, Giggs 69)*
La Coruna (1) 2 *(Blanc 44 (og), Djalminha 90)*   65,875
Manchester United: Barthez; Neville G, Silvestre, Johnsen
(Brown 36), Butt, Blanc, Beckham (Solskjaer 22), Veron
(Neville P 73), Van Nistelrooy, Fortune, Giggs.
La Coruna: Molina; Scaloni, Romero, Duscher, Naybet,
Hector, Victor (Makaay 50), Valeron, Diego Tristan
(Pandani 72), Fran (Capdevila 62), Djalminha.

SEMI-FINALS, FIRST LEG

24 APR

Manchester United (1) 2 *(Zivkovic 30 (og), Van
Nistelrooy 67 (pen))*   66,534
Leverkusen (0) 2 *(Ballack 62, Neuville 75)*
Manchester United: Barthez; Neville G (Neville P 17)
(Irwin 89), Silvestre, Brown, Scholes (Keane 81), Blanc,
Veron, Butt, Van Nistelrooy, Solskjaer, Giggs.
Leverkusen: Butt; Zivkovic, Ramelow, Schneider,
Nowotny (Sebescen 46), Lucio, Placente, Basturk
(Vranjes 77), Ballack, Berbatov (Neuville 71), Ze
Roberto.

SEMI-FINALS, SECOND LEG

30 APR

Leverkusen (1) 1 *(Neuville 45)*

Manchester United (1) 1 *(Keane 28)*   22,500
Leverkusen: Butt; Zivkovic, Ramelow, Schneider,
Nowotny (Sebescen 9), Lucio, Placente, Basturk (Vranjes
79), Ballack, Neuville (Kirsten 84), Ze Roberto.
Manchester United: Barthez; Brown (Forlan 80),
Silvestre, Johnsen (Irwin 59), Keane, Blanc, Veron, Butt
(Solskjaer 59), Van Nistelrooy, Scholes, Giggs.

Mikael Silvestre of Manchester United watches his shot go just wide in the semi-final first leg against Leverkusen.
United twice led in the first leg, and were ahead in the second only to be pegged back and eventually exit on the
away goals rule. (Actionimages)

EUROPEAN CUP-WINNERS' CUP
FINALS 1961–99

Year	Winners		Runners-up		Venue	Attendance	Referee
1961	Fiorentina	2	Rangers	0 *(1st Leg)*	Glasgow	80,000	Steiner (A)
	Fiorentina	2	Rangers	1 *(2nd Leg)*	Florence	50,000	Hernadi (H)
1962	Atletico Madrid	1	Fiorentina	1	Glasgow	27,389	Wharton (S)
Replay	Atletico Madrid	3	Fiorentina	0	Stuttgart	38,000	Tschenscher (WG)
1963	Tottenham Hotspur	5	Atletico Madrid	1	Rotterdam	49,000	Van Leuwen (Ho)
1964	Sporting Lisbon	3	MTK Budapest	3 *(aet)*	Brussels	3000	Van Nuffel (Bel)
Replay	Sporting Lisbon	1	MTK Budapest	0	Antwerp	19,000	Versyp (Bel)
1965	West Ham U	2	Munich 1860	0	Wembley	100,000	Szolt (H)
1966	Borussia Dortmund	2	Liverpool	1 *(aet)*	Glasgow	41,657	Schwinte (F)
1967	Bayern Munich	1	Rangers	0 *(aet)*	Nuremberg	69,480	Lo Bello (I)
1968	AC Milan	2	Hamburg	0	Rotterdam	53,000	Ortiz (Sp)
1969	Slovan Bratislava	3	Barcelona	2	Basle	19,000	Van Ravens (Ho)
1970	Manchester C	2	Gornik Zabrze	1	Vienna	8,000	Schiller (A)
1971	Chelsea	1	Real Madrid	1 *(aet)*	Athens	42,000	Scheurer (Sw)
Replay	Chelsea	2	Real Madrid	1 *(aet)*	Athens	35,000	Bucheli (Sw)
1972	Rangers	3	Moscow Dynamo	2	Barcelona	24,000	Ortiz (Sp)
1973	AC Milan	1	Leeds U	0	Salonika	45,000	Mihas (Gr)
1974	Magdeburg	2	AC Milan	0	Rotterdam	4000	Van Gemert (Ho)
1975	Dynamo Kiev	3	Ferencvaros	0	Basle	13,000	Davidson (S)
1976	Anderlecht	4	West Ham U	2	Brussels	58,000	Wurtz (F)
1977	Hamburg	2	Anderlecht	0	Amsterdam	65,000	Partridge (E)
1978	Anderlecht	4	Austria/WAC	0	Paris	48,679	Adlinger (WG)
1979	Barcelona	4	Fortuna Dusseldorf	3 *(aet)*	Basle	58,000	Palotai (H)
1980	Valencia	0	Arsenal	0	Brussels	36,000	Christov (Cz)
	(aet; Valencia won 5-4 on penalties)						
1981	Dynamo Tbilisi	2	Carl Zeiss Jena	1	Dusseldorf	9000	Lattanzi (I)
1982	Barcelona	2	Standard Liege	1	Barcelona	100,000	Eschweiler (WG)
1983	Aberdeen	2	Real Madrid	1 *(aet)*	Gothenburg	17,804	Menegali (I)
1984	Juventus	2	Porto	1	Basle	60,000	Prokop (EG)
1985	Everton	3	Rapid Vienna	1	Rotterdam	50,000	Casarin (I)
1986	Dynamo Kiev	3	Atletico Madrid	0	Lyon	39,300	Wohrer (A)
1987	Ajax	1	Lokomotiv Leipzig	0	Athens	35,000	Agnolin (I)
1988	Mechelen	1	Ajax	0	Strasbourg	39,446	Pauly (WG)
1989	Barcelona	2	Sampdoria	0	Berne	45,000	Courtney (E)
1990	Sampdoria	2	Anderlecht	0	Gothenburg	20,103	Galler (Sw)
1991	Manchester U	2	Barcelona	1	Rotterdam	42,000	Karlsson (Se)
1992	Werder Bremen	2	Monaco	0	Lisbon	16,000	D'Elia (I)
1993	Parma	3	Antwerp	1	Wembley	37,393	Assenmacher (G)
1994	Arsenal	1	Parma	0	Copenhagen	33,765	Krondl (Czr)
1995	Zaragoza	2	Arsenal	1	Paris	42,424	Ceccarini (I)
1996	Paris St Germain	1	Rapid Vienna	0	Brussels	37,500	Pairetto (I)
1997	Barcelona	1	Paris St Germain	0	Rotterdam	45,000	Merk (G)
1998	Chelsea	1	Stuttgart	0	Stockholm	30,216	Braschi (I)
1999	Lazio	2	Mallorca	1	Villa Park	33,021	Benko (A)

INTER-CITIES FAIRS CUP FINALS 1958–71

(Winners in italics)

Year	First Leg	Attendance	Second Leg	Attendance
1958	London 2 Barcelona 2	45,466	*Barcelona* 6 London 0	62,000
1960	Birmingham C 0 Barcelona 0	40,500	*Barcelona* 4 Birmingham C 1	70,000
1961	Birmingham C 2 Roma 2	21,005	*Roma* 2 Birmingham C 0	60,000
1962	Valencia 6 Barcelona 2	65,000	Barcelona 1 *Valencia* 1	60,000
1963	Dynamo Zagreb 1 Valencia 2	40,000	*Valencia* 2 Dynamo Zagreb 0	55,000
1964	*Zaragoza* 2 Valencia 1	50,000	(in Barcelona)	
1965	*Ferencvaros* 1 Juventus 0	25,000	(in Turin)	
1966	Barcelona 0 Zaragoza 1	70,000	Zaragoza 2 *Barcelona* 4	70,000
1967	Dynamo Zagreb 2 Leeds U 0	40,000	Leeds U 0 *Dynamo Zagreb* 0	35,604
1968	Leeds U 1 Ferencvaros 0	25,368	Ferencvaros 0 *Leeds U* 0	70,000
1969	Newcastle U 3 Ujpest Dozsa 0	60,000	Ujpest Dozsa 2 *Newcastle U* 3	37,000
1970	Anderlecht 3 Arsenal 1	37,000	*Arsenal* 3 Anderlecht 0	51,612
1971	Juventus 0 Leeds U 0 *(abandoned 51 minutes)*	42,000		
	Juventus 2 Leeds U 2	42,000	*Leeds U* 1* Juventus 1	42,483

UEFA CUP FINALS 1972–97

(Winners in italics)

Year	First Leg	Attendance	Second Leg	Attendance
1972	Wolverhampton W 1 Tottenham H 2	45,000	*Tottenham H* 1 Wolverhampton W 1	48,000
1973	Liverpool 0 Moenchengladbach 0			
	(abandoned 27 minutes)	44,967		
	Liverpool 3 Moenchengladbach 0	41,169	Moenchengladbach 2 *Liverpool* 0	35,000
1974	Tottenham H 2 Feyenoord 2	46,281	*Feyenoord* 2 Tottenham H 0	68,000
1975	Moenchengladbach 0 Twente 0	45,000	Twente 1 *Moenchengladbach* 5	24,500
1976	Liverpool 3 FC Brugge 2	56,000	FC Brugge 1 *Liverpool* 1	32,000
1977	Juventus 1 Athletic Bilbao 0	75,000	Athletic Bilbao 2 *Juventus* 1*	43,000
1978	Bastia 0 PSV Eindhoven 0	15,000	*PSV Eindhoven* 3 Bastia 0	27,000
1979	Red Star Belgrade 1 Moenchengladbach 1	87,500	*Moenchengladbach* 1 Red Star Belgrade 0	45,000
1980	Moenchengladbach 3 Eintracht Frankfurt 2	25,000	*Eintracht Frankfurt* 1* Moenchengladbach 0	60,000
1981	Ipswich T 3 AZ 67 Alkmaar 0	27,532	AZ 67 Alkmaar 4 *Ipswich T* 2	28,500
1982	Gothenburg 1 Hamburg 0	42,548	Hamburg 0 *Gothenburg* 3	60,000
1983	Anderlecht 1 Benfica 0	45,000	Benfica 1 *Anderlecht* 1	80,000
1984	Anderlecht 1 Tottenham H 1	40,000	*Tottenham H* 1[1] Anderlecht 1	46,258
1985	Videoton 0 Real Madrid 3	30,000	*Real Madrid* 0 Videoton 1	98,300
1986	Real Madrid 5 Cologne 1	80,000	Cologne 2 *Real Madrid* 0	15,000
1987	Gothenburg 1 Dundee U 0	50,023	Dundee U 1 *Gothenburg* 1	20,911
1988	Espanol 3 Bayer Leverkusen 0	42,000	*Bayer Leverkusen* 3[2] Espanol 0	22,000
1989	Napoli 2 Stuttgart 1	83,000	Stuttgart 3 *Napoli* 3	67,000
1990	Juventus 3 Fiorentina 1	45,000	Fiorentina 0 *Juventus* 0	32,000
1991	Internazionale 2 Roma 0	68,887	Roma 1 *Internazionale* 0	70,901
1992	Torino 2 Ajax 2	65,377	*Ajax* 0* Torino 0	40,000
1993	Borussia Dortmund 1 Juventus 3	37,000	*Juventus* 3 Borussia Dortmund 0	62,781
1994	Salzburg 0 Internazionale 1	47,500	*Internazionale* 1 Salzburg 0	80,326
1995	Parma 1 Juventus 0	23,000	Juventus 1 *Parma* 1	80,750
1996	Bayern Munich 2 Bordeaux 0	62,000	Bordeaux 1 *Bayern Munich* 3	36,000
1997	Schalke 1 Internazionale 0	56,824	Internazionale 1 *Schalke* 0[3]	81,670

UEFA CUP FINALS 1998–2002

Year	Winners	Runners-up	Venue	Attendance	Referee
1998	Internazionale 3	Lazio 0	Paris	42,938	Nieto (Sp)
1999	Parma 3	Marseille 0	Moscow	61,000	Dallas (S)
2000	Galatasaray 0	Arsenal 0	Copenhagen	38,919	Nieto (Sp)
(aet; Galatasaray won 4-1 on penalties)					
2001	Liverpool 5¶	Alaves 4	Dortmund	65,000	Veissiere (F)
2002	Feyenoord 3	Borussia Dortmund 2	Rotterdam	45,000	Pereira (P)

*won on away goals   [1]*Tottenham H won 4-3 on penalties aet*   [2]*Bayer Leverkusen won 3-2 on penalties aet*
[3]*Schalke won 4-1 on penalties aet*   ¶*won on sudden death*

UEFA CUP 2001–02

QUALIFYING ROUND, FIRST LEG

AEK Athens (2) 6 *(Tsartas 39, Zagorakis 42,*
Lakis 54, Nikolaidis 66, 90, Konstantinidis 70),
Grevenmacher (0) 0   6082
Ararat Erevan (0) 0, Hapoel Tel Aviv (2) 2
(Toema 38, Osterc 43)   4500
Atlantas (0) 0, Rapid Bucharest (1) 4 *(Schumacher 18,*
Pancu 46, Nita 66, Sumudica 90)   3111
Birkirkara (0) 0, Lokomotiv Tbilisi (0) 0   495
Brasov (3) 5 *(Buga 21, Sandor 23, 27, Isaila 47,*
Badea 61), Mika (0) 1 *(Nazaryan 57)*   6200
Brondby (1) 2 *(Jonson 16, Bagger 80),*
Shelbourne (0) 0   8011
FC Brugge (0) 4 *(Lange 62, 85, Lembi 77, Mendoza 88),*
IA Akranes (0) 0   2925
Cosmos (0) 0, Rapid Vienna (1) 1 *(Wallner 10)*   1132
CSKA Kiev (1) 2 *(Kostyshyn 23, Maltsev 49),*
Jokerit (0) 0   2000
Cwmbran Town (0) 0, Slovan Bratislava (2) 4
(Mojic 40, Obzera 45, Vittek 83, Sobona 87)   496
Debrecen (2) 3 *(Bajzat 26, Ulveczki 36, Tiber 83),*
Otaci (0) 0   3200
Dinaburg (0) 2 *(Sorosh 60, Pucinskas 80),* Osijek (0) 1
(Vuka 53)   2000
Dinamo Bucharest (1) 1 *(Niculescu 34),*
Dinamo Tirana (0) 0   8000
Dynamo Tbilisi (1) 2 *(Daraselia 22, Mikuchadze 86),*
BATE Borisov (0) 1 *(Hancharyk 88)*   4500
Dynamo Zagreb (0) 1 *(Gondzic 53),* Flora (0) 0   5480
Etzella (0) 0, Legia (3) 4 *(Magiera 12, Kucharski 15,*
Wroblewski 26, Mierzejewski 72)   1000
Fylkir (2) 2 *(McFarlane 8, Stigsson 41),* Pogon (0) 1
(Dzwigala 71)   1319
Glenavon (0) 0, Kilmarnock (0) 1 *(Innes 90)*   3200
HB Torshavn (0) 2 *(Mortansson 50, 58),* Graz (0) 2
(Akwuegbu 60, 90)   500
HJK Helsinki (1) 2 *(Kallio 37, Jensen 75),*
Ventspils (0) 1 *(Rimkus 62)*   2751
Longford Town (1) 1 *(O'Connor 15),* Liteks (0) 1
(Yurukov 84)   2922
Maccabi Tel Aviv (3) 6 *(Ben Dayan 7, Dago 21, 45, 77,*
Banin 51, Biton 80), Zalgiris (0) 0   6726
Maritimo (1) 1 *(Dinda 5),* Sarajevo (0) 0   2000
Matador (1) 3 *(Breska 10, Pernis 66, Belak 72),*
Sliema Wanderers (0) 0   4200
Midtjylland (1) 1 *(Pimpong 15),* Glentoran (0) 1
(Glendinning 83)   1550
MyPa (0) 1 *(Lindberg 50),* Helsingborg (1) 3
(Eklund 26, Prica 47, Lindstrom 86)   1702
Neftchi (0) 0, Gorica (0) 0   8000
Obilic (2) 4 *(Simonovic 22, Zoric 45, Mladenovic 48,*
Filipovic 65), GI Gotu (0) 0   850
Olimpija (1) 4 *(Komac 28, Tiganj 58, Tigank 59,*
Calleja 74), Shafa (0) 0   500
Olympiakos (0) 2 *(Themistocleous 49, Kozlej 78),*
Dunaferr (1) 2 *(Sowunmi 15, Tokoli 50)*   3000
Pelister (0) 0, St Gallen (1) 2 *(Pereira 4,*
Dal Santo 89)   1664
Polonia (0) 4 *(Tarachulski 70, 78, Moskal 89, 90),*
TNS (0) 0   300
Ruzomberok (2) 3 *(Fabula 22, 83, Oravec 42),*
Belshina (0) 1 *(Rak 58)*   2756
Shakhter (0) 1 *(Padrez 81),* CSKA Sofia (0) 2
(Mantchev 65, Giglio 78)   1650
SK Tirana (0) 3 *(Fortuzi 56, 81, Helezei 74),*
Apollon (1) 2 *(Zoumparis 4, 47)*   1500
Santa Coloma (0) 0, Partizan Belgrade (1) 1
(Cakar 12)   900
Trans (0) 1 *(Gruznov 40),* Elfsborg (2) 3
(Lundstrom 33, Andreasson 36, 61)   350
Vaduz (1) 3 *(Niederhauser 41, Merenda 53, 75),*
Varteks (0) 3 *(Bjelanovic 49, 85, 86)*   1065
Vardar (0) 0, Standard Liege (1) 3 *(Meyssen 30,*
Blay 50, Walem 69)   1560
Viking (0) 1 *(Fuglestad 82 (pen)),* Brotnjo (0) 0   2900
Zimbru Chisinau (0) 0, Gaziantep (0) 0   4000

QUALIFYING ROUND, SECOND LEG

Apollon (0) 3 *(Miserdovski 57, Kavazis 60,*
Spoljaric 80), SK Tirana (1) 1 *(Fortuzi 26)*   2000

BATE Borisov (2) 4 *(Lisovsky 22, Kutuzov 44 (pen),*
Loshankov 48, Grigorov 90),
Dynamo Tbilisi (0) 0   5000
Belshina (0) 0, Ruzomberok (0) 0   2000
Brotnjo (1) 1 *(Jerkovic 32),* Viking (1) 1
(Tihinen 29)   2500
CSKA Sofia (1) 3 *(Mantchev 33, 62, Giglio 67),*
Shakhter (0) 1 *(Bezborodov 89)*   8000
Dinamo Tirana (0) 1 *(Dhembi 87),*
Dinamo Bucharest (2) 3 *(Niculescu 20,*
Mihalcea 43, Dragan 76)   2500
Dunaferr (0) 2 *(Sowunmi 46, Tokoli 59),*
Olympiakos (2) 4 *(Kozlej 25, Radosavljevic 38,*
Themistocleous 57, Aristocleous 63)   8000
Elfsborg (1) 5 *(Andreasson 27, 46, 79,*
Klarstrom 50, 54), Trans (0) 0   3000
Flora (0) 0, Dynamo Zagreb (1) 1 *(Allas 44 (og))*   2000
Gaziantep (2) 4 *(Fatih 2, Romashenko 30,*
Hasan Ozer 60, Mustafa 81), Zimbru Chisinau (1) 1
(Cebotariu 44)   2500
GI Gotu (1) 1 *(Jarnskor 33 (pen)),* Obilic (1) 1
(Simonovic 19)   500
Glentoran (0) 0, Midtjylland (1) 4 *(Skoubo 13, 82,*
From 66, Pimpong 86)   5231
Gorica (0) 1 *(Tezacki 80),* Neftchi (0) 0   1500
Graz (2) 4 *(Brunmayr 13, 30, Tokic 70, Milinkovic 90),*
HB Torshavn (0) 0   6245
Grevenmacher (0) 0, AEK Athens (1) 2 *(Lakis 26,*
Konstantinidis 54)   750
Hapoel Tel Aviv (2) 3 *(Osterc 7, Domb 16, Udi 90),*
Ararat (0) 0   10,000
Helsingborg (1) 2 *(Prica 44, Eklund 82),* MyPa (1) 1
(Puhakainen 25)   3738
IA Akranes (1) 1 *(Karvelsson 3),* FC Brugge (1) 6
(Lembi 25, 55, Englebert 65, Van der Heyden 72,
Mendoza 83, Martens 90)   900
Jokerit (0) 0, CSKA Kiev (0) 2 *(Zakarlyuka 60,*
Kossyrin 82)   2500
Kilmarnock (0) 1 *(Mitchell 66),* Glenavon (0) 0   7454
Legia (1) 2 *(Mierzejewski 43, Karwan 72),*
Etzella (0) 1 *(Leweck 48)*   4000
Liteks (0) 2 *(Jankovic 89, 90 (pen)),*
Longford Town (0) 0   4000
Lokomotiv Tbilisi (0) 1 *(Anchabadze 88),*
Birkirkara (1) 1 *(Zahra 22)*   5550
Mika (0) 0, Brasov (1) 2 *(Sandor 38, Buga 89)*   500
Osijek (1) 1 *(Balatinac 45 (pen)),* Dinaburg (0) 0   5000
Otaci (0) 1 *(Samkov 54 (pen)),* Debrecen (0) 0   2000
Partizan Belgrade (2) 7 *(Ivic 11, 60, Delibasic 21,*
Cakar 68, 86 (pen), Vukic 78, Iliev 90), Santa Coloma
(1) 1 *(Ariaz 37 (pen)*   10,000
Pogon (1) 1 *(Dzwigala 6),* Fylkir (0) 1 *(Jonsson 89)* 2500
Rapid Bucharest (2) 8 *(Nita 23, 82, Sumudica 29, 53*
(pen), Schumacher 60, Bogdanovic 68, 89, Bratu 74),
Atlantas (0) 0   5000
Rapid Vienna (1) 2 *(Lagonikakis 30, 89),*
Cosmos (0) 0   5000
Sarajevo (0) 0, Maritimo (0) 1 *(Bruno 90)*   5000
Shafa (0) 0, Olimpija (1) 3 *(Kosic 29, Komac 70,*
Jolic 82)   5000
Shelbourne (0) 0, Brondby (1) 3 *(Bagger 11,*
Jorgensen 53, Madsen 78)   4000
Sliema Wanderers (0) 2 *(Busuttil 6, Said 78),*
Matador (1) 1 *(Pernis 60 (pen))*   2500
Slovan Bratislava (0) 1 *(Meszaros 80),* Cwmbran Town
(0) 0   2439
St Gallen (0) 2 *(Gane 57, 61),* Pelister (0) 3 *(Dal*
Santo 65 (og), Deliovski 72, Stojmenovski 75)   9000
Standard Liege (0) 3 *(Lukunku 58, 68, Walem 60),*
Vardar (0) 1 *(Abazi 62)*   8000
TNS (0) 0, Polonia (1) 2 *(Bak 43, Bartczak 53)*   1000
(at Wrexham).
Varteks (3) 6 *(Mumiek 9 (pen), Bjelanovic 20,*
Andricevic 25, Drobne 71, 75, Rezic 86),
Vaduz (1) 1 *(Merenda 50)*   6000
Ventspils (0) 0, HJK Helsinki (1) 1 *(Roiha 8)*   2500
Zalgiris (0) 0, Maccabi Tel Aviv (0) 1 *(Goldberg 58)* 1000

FIRST ROUND, FIRST LEG

AEK Athens (0) 2 *(Tsartas 54 (pen), Nikolaidis 66),*
Hibernian (0) 0   15,525

Ajax (1) 2 *(Ibrahimovic 4, Machlas 59)*,
  Apollon (0) 0   20,000
Aston Villa (0) 2 *(Angel 54, 70)*, Varteks (1) 3
  (Bjelanovic 44, 86, Karic 64)   27,132
BATE Borisov (0) 0, AC Milan (0) 2 *(Shevchenko 65,*
  Javi Moreno 88)   10,000
Bordeaux (2) 5 *(Pauleta 13, 77, Christian 42,*
  Dugarry 52, 53), Debrecen (1) 1 *(Tiber 38)*   13,958
Celta Vigo (1) 4 *(Karpin 41, 88, Edu 67,*
  Katanha 63 (pen), Olomouc (0) 0   12,000
Chelsea (1) 3 *(Gudjohnsen 45, 74, Lampard 90)*,
  Levski (0) 0   20,812
Chernomorets (0) 0, Valencia (0) 1 *(Mista 55)*   10,000
CSKA Kiev (1) 3 *(Kachenko 44, Kostyshyn 51,*
  Tkachenko 64), Red Star Belgrade (1) 2
  (Pjanovic 33, Acimovic 66 (pen))   10,000
CSKA Sofia (2) 3 *(Mantchev 28, 80, Panev 41)*,
  Shakhtjor Donetsk (0) 0   8000
Dinamo Bucharest (0) 1 *(Mihalcea 84 (pen))*,
  Grasshoppers (1) 3 *(Chapuisat 31, Nunez 68,*
  Mwaruwaru 79)   5000
Dnepr (0) 0, Fiorentina (0) 0   12,000
Dynamo Moscow (1) 1 *(Khazov 22)*,
  Birkirkara (0) 0   5000
Dynamo Zagreb (0) 2 *(Agic 55, Sedlovski 71)*,
  Maccabi Tel Aviv (2) 2 *(Goldberg 22, Dago 41)*   5000
FC Copenhagen (1) 2 *(Fernandez 8, 70)*,
  Obilic (0) 0   5000
Genclerbirligi (0) 1 *(Zdebel 79)*, Halmstad (1) 1
  (Selakovic 8)   5000
Gorica (0) 1 *(Tezacki 58)*, Osijek (0) 2
  (Turkovic 54, Besirevic 75)   1700
Hajduk Split (1) 2 *(Deranja 21, Srna 88)*,
  Wisla (0) 2 *(Zurawski 52, Moskalewicz 90)*   20,000
Haka (1) 1 *(Vaisanen 13 (pen))*, Union Berlin (0) 1
  (Ristic 70)   2000
Hapoel Tel Aviv (0) 1 *(Ryndziuk (og) 89)*,
  Gaziantep (0) 0   10,000
Inter Bratislava (0) 1 *(Kratochvil 54)*, Liteks (0) 0   3000
Internazionale (3) 3 *(Dalmat 24, Kallon 30, Di Biagio*
  42), Brasov (0) 0   6439
  (in Trieste).
Ipswich Town (0) 1 *(Bramble 85)*,
  Torpedo Moscow (1) 1 *(Vyazmikin 14)*   21,201
Karnten (0) 0, PAOK Salonika (0) 0   2000
Kilmarnock (0) 1 *(Dargo 73)*, Viking (1) 1
  (Sanne 45)   6322
Legia (1) 4 *(Karwan 22, Vukovic 58, Kucharski 71, 81)*,
  Elfsborg (1) 1 *(Lundstrom 41)*   5000
Liberec (1) 2 *(Baffour 7, Nezmar 88)*,
  Slovan Bratislava (0) 0   8000
Maritimo (1) 1 *(Bruno 33)*, Leeds United (0) 0   10,500
Matador (0) 0, Freiburg (0) 0   5500
Midtjylland (0) 0, Sporting Lisbon (0) 3
  (Babb 48, Beto 61, Jardel 89)   2000
Odd Grenland (2) 2 *(Fevang 10, Van Ankeren 32)*,
  Helsingborg (1) 2 *(Hansson 28, Dos Santos 58)*   2000
Olimpija (1) 2 *(Zioncar 1, 60)*, Brondby (1) 4
  (Bagger 32, Johansen 53 (pen), Niznik 70,
  73 (pen))   2500
Olympiakos (1) 2 *(Aristocleous 3, Radosavljevic 78)*,
  FC Brugge (1) 2 *(Verheyen 30, Clement 66)*   1500
Paris St Germain (0) 0, Rapid Bucharest (0) 0   19,200
Parma (1) 1 *(Milosevic 22 (pen))*,
  HJK Helsinki (0) 0   2670
Partizan Belgrade (0) 1 *(Bajic 90)*,
  Rapid Vienna (0) 0   10,000
Polonia (0) 1 *(Bak 76)*, Twente (0) 2 *(Kollmann 60,*
  Van der Laan 85)   2000
Pribram (1) 4 *(Kulic 15, 60, 70, Otepka 68)*,
  Sedan (0) 0   4552
Roda (1) 3 *(Nygaard 27, Anastasiou 65, 70)*,
  Fylkir (0) 0   5000
Servette (0) 1 *(Oruma 76)*, Slavia Prague (0) 0   3000
St Gallen (1) 2 *(Jefferson 33, Mokoena 58)*,
  Steaua (1) 1 *(Neaga 38)*   12,000
Standard Liege (1) 2 *(Moriera 40, 89)*,
  Strasbourg (0) 0   17,000
Troyes (3) 6 *(Loko 21, 84, Boutal 27, 29, 57,*
  Meniri 51), Ruzomberok (0) 1 *(Kurty 77)*   6011
Utrecht (2) 3 *(Van den Bergh 21, Tanghe 35,*
  Gluscevic 49), Graz (0) 0   13,500
Viktoria Zizkov (0) 0, Tirol Innsbruck (0) 0   1300
Westerlo (0) 0, Hertha Berlin (1) 2 *(Schmidt 4,*
  Beinlich 87)   4500

Zaragoza (0) 3 *(Yordi 49, Juanele 83, Jose Ignacio 83)*,
  Silkeborg (0) 0   15,000

FIRST ROUND, SECOND LEG

Apollon (0) 0, Ajax (1) 3 *(Van der Vaart 35,*
  Ibrahimovic 66, Wamberto 79)   1000
Birkirkara (0) 0, Dynamo Moscow (0) 0   2000
Brasov (0) 0, Internazionale (2) 3 *(Ventola 13, 79,*
  Guglielminpietro 35)   5000
Brondby (0) 0, Olimpija (0) 0   5000
FC Brugge (2) 7 *(Lange 22, 87, Sillah 27, Martens 47,*
  Englebert 57, Simons 70, Ceh 90), Olympiakos (0) 1
  (Themistocleous 88)   3000
Debrecen (1) 3 *(Plokai 44, Kerekes 58 (pen), 68)*,
  Bordeaux (0) 1 *(Pauleta 79)*   7000
Elfsborg (2) 3 *(Karlsson 55)*, Legia (1) 6 *(Yahaya 35,*
  Sokokowski 65, 90, Skaw 75, Kucharski 80,
  Kielbowicz 89)   2602
Fiorentina (0) 2 *(Adani 75, Chiesa 77)*, Dnepr (0) 1
  (Slabishev 88)   10,150
Freiburg (1) 2 *(Coulibaly 20, Tanko 88)*,
  Matador (0) 1 *(Pernis 51)*   18,855
Fylkir (0) 1 *(Johannesson 54)*, Roda (0) 3
  (Zafarin 55, Berglund 77, Anastasiou 88)   500
Gaziantep (0) 1 *(Ryndziuk 51)*, Hapoel Tel Aviv (1) 1
  (Osterc 19)   2500
Grasshoppers (2) 3 *(Baturina 18, Chapuisat 21,*
  Morales 87), Dinamo Bucharest (0) 1
  (Mihalcea 52 (pen))   5000
Graz (3) 3 *(Bazina 4, Brunmayr 20, Akwuegbu 36)*,
  Utrecht (0) 3 *(Kuijt 46, Zwaanswijk 55,*
  Jochemsen 69)   5000
Halmstad (1) 1 *(Arvidsson 21)*, Genclerbirligi (0) 0   2500
Helsingborg (1) 1 *(Alvaro 3)*, Odd Grenland (1) 1
  (Fevang 43)   3000
Hertha Berlin (0) 1 *(Marcelinho 85)*, Westerlo (0) 0   9000
Hibernian (0) 3 *(Luna 52, 82, Zitelli 114)*,
  AEK Athens (0) 2 *(Tsartas 92, 105)* aet   16,647
HJK Helsinki (0) 0, Parma (0) 2 *(Marchionni 79,*
  Bonazzoli 90)   7588
Leeds United (2) 3 *(Keane 20, Kewell 37, Bakke 62)*,
  Maritimo (0) 0   38,125
Levski (0) 0, Chelsea (2) 2 *(Terry 32,*
  Gudjohnsen 45)   10,000
Liteks (2) 3 *(Jankovic 43, 45, Petrov 84)*,
  Inter Bratislava (0) 0   4000
Maccabi Tel Aviv (1) 1 *(Nimni 41 (pen))*,
  Dynamo Zagreb (1) 1 *(Agic 32)*   5000
AC Milan (2) 4 *(Rui Costa 20, Javi Moreno 45,*
  Sarr 55, Inzaghi 73 (pen)), BATE Borisov (0) 0   12,000
Obilic (1) 2 *(Vujosevic 32, 47)*, FC Copenhagen (0) 2
  (Fernandez 75, 85)   6000
Olomouc (0) 4 *(Siegl 47, Kotrys 57, Mucha 58, 64)*, Celta
  Vigo (2) 3 *(McCarthy 2, Caceres 32, Coira 89)*   6000
Osijek (0) 1 *(Fuka 64)*, Gorica (0) 0   6000
PAOK Salonika (1) 4 *(Konstantinidis 25, 52,*
  Kafes 50, Luciano 75), Karnten (0) 0   20,000
Rapid Bucharest (0) 0, Paris St Germain (0) 1
  (Alosio 93)   15,000
  (abandoned after 113 minutes; floodlight failure. Game
  awarded 3-0 to PSG as Rapid failed to have necessary
  back-up generator).
Rapid Vienna (2) 5 *(Wallner 15, 60, Taument 33, Wagner*
  65, 75), Partizan Belgrade (0) 1 *(Cakar 55)*   5500
Red Star Belgrade (0) 0, CSKA Kiev (0) 0   30,000
Ruzomberok (0) 1 *(Oravec 56)*, Troyes (0) 0   200
Sedan (1) 3 *(N'Diefi 29, Brogno 52, 55 (pen))*,
  Pribram (0) 1 *(Siegl 47)*   18,000
Shakhtjor Donetsk (1) 2 *(Zubov 31, Vorobei 51)*,
  CSKA Sofia (0) 1 *(Okoronkwo 89 (og))*   25,000
Silkeborg (1) 1 *(Larsen 39)*, Zaragoza (1) 2
  (Yordi 24, Jamelli 90)   800
Slavia Prague (0) 1 *(Petros 89)*, Servette (1) 1
  (Oruma 13)   4500
Slovan Bratislava (0) 1 *(Mojic 22)*, Liberec (0) 0   4500
Sporting Lisbon (3) 3 *(Jardel 4, 45, Skriver 86 (og))*,
  Midtjylland (0) 2 *(Lindqvist 54, Souko 55)*   30,000
Steaua (1) 1 *(Raducanu 11)*, St Gallen (0) 1
  (Guido 59)   5000
Strasbourg (2) 2 *(Ljuboja 4, 37)*, Standard Liege (0) 2
  (Goossens 55, Vandooren 59)   12,227
Tirol Innsbruck (0) 1 *(Glieder 49)*,
  Viktoria Zizkov (0) 0   6500

Torpedo Moscow (0) 1 *(Viazmikin 66)*,
Ipswich Town (0) 2 *(George 47,
Stewart 54 (pen))*   10,500
Twente (0) 2 *(Kollmann 70, Booth 71)*,
Polonia (0) 0   13,000
Union Berlin (2) 3 *(Djurkovic 36, Chifon 44, Koilov 89)*,
Haka (0) 0   12,111
Valencia (3) 5 *(Sanchez 6, 22, Ilie 18, Salva 52,
Rufete 68)*, Chernomorets (0) 0   20,000
Varteks (0) 0, Aston Villa (0) 1 *(Hadji 90)*   12,100
Viking (2) 2 *(Sanne 1, Nevland 17)*,
Kilmarnock (0) 0   4599
Wisla (1) 1 *(Frankowski 22)*, Hajduk Split (0) 0   7500
Anzhi 0 (0), Rangers (0) 1 *(Konterman 84)*   3700
(Tie decided over one match played in Warsaw).

SECOND ROUND, FIRST LEG
Bordeaux (2) 2 *(Pauleta 4, Christian 32)*,
Standard Liege (0) 0   12,000
Celta Vigo (1) 3 *(Mostovoi 34, 76, 89)*,
Liberec (0) 1 *(Edu 66 (og))*   15,000
FC Copenhagen (0) 0, Ajax (0) 0   20,067
CSKA Kiev (0) 0, FC Brugge (1) 2
(Verheyen 33, 48)   2750
Fiorentina (0) 2 *(Morfeo 47, Nuno Gomes 85)*,
Tirol Innsbruck (0) 0   10,418
Freiburg (0) 0, St Gallen (0) 1 *(Mokoena 90)*   18,855
Grasshoppers (2) 4 *(Nunez 30, 35, 90, Petric 53)*,
Twente (0) 1 *(Polak 64)*   5500
Halmstad (0) 0, Sporting Lisbon (0) 1 *(Niculae 55)*   3141
Hapoel Tel Aviv (0) 2 *(Gershon 89 (pen),
Kleschenco 90)*, Chelsea (0) 0   11,500
Internazionale (0) 2 *(Kallon 61, 63)*, Wisla (0) 0   4934
Ipswich Town (0) 0, Helsingborg (0) 0   22,254
Leeds United (3) 4 *(Viduka 6, 44, Bowyer 23, 46)*,
Troyes (1) 2 *(Loko 31, 81)*   40,015
Legia (1) 1 *(Karwan 12)*, Valencia (0) 1
(Ilie 61 (pen))   11,000
AC Milan (1) 2 *(Rui Costa 19, Shevchenko 50)*,
CSKA Sofia (0) 0   6759
Osijek (0) 1 *(Mijatovic 72)*, AEK Athens (1) 2
(Zagorakis 13, Nikolaidis 71)   8000
PAOK Salonika (3) 6 *(Yasemakis 22, 28,
Okkas 38, 87, Konstantinidis 50, De Souza 75)*,
Pribram (0) 1 *(Siegl 56)*   20,000
Paris St Germain (2) 4 *(Ronaldinho 16, 58,
Mendy 28, Anelka 55)*, Rapid Vienna (0) 0   30,000
Rangers (1) 3 *(Amoruso 9, Ball 61, De Boer 80)*,
Dynamo Moscow (0) 1 *(Gusev 90)*   45,008
Roda (2) 4 *(Soetaers 4, 36, Berglund 54, Sonkaya 81)*,
Maccabi Tel Aviv (0) 1 *(Horvath 78)*   7000
Union Berlin (0) 0, Liteks (0) 2 *(Boumosusov 49,
Petrov 90)*   11,300
Utrecht (0) 1 *(Jochemsen 75)*, Parma (1) 3
(Di Vaio 20, 69, Bonazzoli 55)   13,500
Varteks (0) 3 *(Bjelanovic 65, Murniek 78,
Karic 83 (pen))*, Brondby (0) 1 *(Niznik 81)*   9000
Viking (0) 0, Hertha Berlin (1) 1 *(Preetz 6)*   3750
Zaragoza (0) 0, Servette (0) 0   15,000

SECOND ROUND, SECOND LEG
AEK Athens (2) 3 *(Lakis 31, Tsartas 39,
Konstantinidis 80)*, Osijek (2) 2 *(Feruzem 14 (og),
Mitu 44)*   12,300
Ajax (0) 0, FC Copenhagen (0) 1 *(Jensen 83)*   31,500
Brondby (2) 5 *(Borovic 1 (og), Bagger 31,
Jonson 53, 76, 83)*, Varteks (0) 0   8160
FC Brugge (3) 5 *(Martens 6, 73, 86, Verheyen 9,
Mendoza 40)*, CSKA Kiev (0) 0   7788
Chelsea (0) 1 *(Zola 64)*, Hapoel Tel Aviv (1) 1
(Osterc 36)   28,433
CSKA Sofia (0) 0, AC Milan (0) 1 *(Inzaghi 62)*   20,000
Dynamo Moscow (1) 1 *(Gusev 27)*, Rangers (3) 4
*(De Boer 8, Khomutovsky 16 (og), Flo 43,
Lovenkrands 79)*   5000
Helsingborg (1) 1 *(Eklund 36)*, Ipswich Town (0) 3
(Hreidarsson 69, Stewart 81, 88)   9484
Hertha Berlin (2) 2 *(Alves 17, Sverrisson 28)*,
Viking (0) 0   19,864
Liberec (1) 3 *(Stajner 38, Nezmar 71, 90)*,
Celta Vigo (0) 0   6052
Liteks (0) 0, Union Berlin (0) 0   3000
Maccabi Tel Aviv (1) 2 *(Biton 37, 57)*, Roda (1) 1
(Lawal 6)   8500
Parma (0) 0, Utrecht (0) 0   8560

Pribram (1) 2 *(Cizek 36, Kucera 63)*, PAOK
Salonika (1) 2 *(De Souza 15, Yasemakis 61)*   2225
Rapid Vienna (2) 2 *(Wallner 10, 16)*,
Paris St Germain (0) 2 *(Potillon 53, Leal 89)*   10,400
St Gallen (1) 1 *(Zellweger 8)*, Freiburg (2) 4
(Zkitischwili 11, Sellimi 37, But 75, Kehl 82)   16,066
Servette (0) 1 *(Oruma 87)*, Zaragoza (0) 0   9000
Sporting Lisbon (2) 6 *(Jardel 30 (pen), 76, 90,
Joao Pinto 38, Niculae 62, Paulo Bento 70)*,
Halmstad (1) 1 *(Nordstrand 39)*   17,800
Standard Liege (0) 0, Bordeaux (0) 2
(Dugarry 57, Pauleta 84)   18,000
Tirol Innsbruck (1) 2 *(Gilewicz 24, 75)*,
Fiorentina (2) 2 *(Nuno Gomez 26, Morfeo 40)*   14,500
Troyes (2) 3 *(Anzine 8, Hamed 38, Rothen 59)*,
Leeds United (1) 2 *(Viduka 14, Keane 78)*   15,000
Twente (2) 4 *(Van der Laan 36, 79, Cairo 44,
El Brazi 61)*, Grasshoppers (0) 2 *(Chapuisat 70,
Mwaruwari 85)*   6000
Valencia (4) 6 *(Albelda 13, Ilie 15, Djukic 32,
Aimar 39 (pen), Sanchez 70, Angulo 77)*,
Legia (0) 1 *(Svitlica 76)*   32,000
Wisla (1) 1 *(Zurawski 4)*, Internazionale (0) 0   7000

THIRD ROUND, FIRST LEG
AEK Athens (3) 3 *(Tsartas 9 (pen), Zagorakis 17,
Konstantinidis 22)*, Liteks (1) 2 *(Yankovich 28,
Rakita 71)*   23,400
Bordeaux (0) 1 *(Miranda 49)*, Roda (0) 0   14,000
FC Brugge (1) 4 *(Englebert 5, Van der Heyden 53,
Mendoza 75, De Brul 90)*, Lyon (0) 1
(Luyindula 83)   14,670
FC Copenhagen (0) 0, Borussia Dortmund (0) 1
(Herrlich 90)   18,620
Feyenoord (0) 1 *(Ono 82)*, Freiburg (0) 0   28,000
Fiorentina (0) 0, Lille (1) 1 *(Bakari 23)*   7699
Grasshoppers (1) 1 *(Chapuisat 17)*,
Leeds United (0) 2 *(Harte 73, Smith 79)*   15,000
Hapoel Tel Aviv (1) 2 *(Osterc 41, Domb 89)*,
Lokomotiv Moscow (0) 1 *(Izmailov 55)*   14,000
Ipswich Town (0) 1 *(Armstrong 81)*,
Internazionale (0) 0   24,569
Liberec (2) 3 *(Lukas 3, Johana 21, Jun 50)*,
Mallorca (0) 1 *(Biagini 60)*   6678
AC Milan (1) 2 *(Shevchenko 39, Inzaghi 76)*,
Sporting Lisbon (0) 0   10,132
PAOK Salonika (2) 3 *(Yasemakis 35, 69, Udeze 39)*,
PSV Eindhoven (1) 2 *(De Jong 20, Bruggink 81)* 28,200
Parma (1) 1 *(Johansen 1 (og))*, Brondby (0) 1
(Nordin 90 (pen))   4582
Rangers (0) 0, Paris St Germain (0) 0   49,223
Servette (0) 0, Hertha Berlin (0) 0   8412
Valencia (0) 1 *(Vicente 75)*, Celtic (0) 0   38,000

THIRD ROUND, SECOND LEG
Borussia Dortmund (0) 1 *(Sorensen 89)*,
FC Copenhagen (0) 0   42,500
Brondby (0) 0, Parma (1) 3 *(Mboma 43, Nakata 57,
Lamouchi 84)*   20,628
Celtic (1) 1 *(Larsson 45)*, Valencia (0) 0   57,299
(aet; Valencia won 5-4 on penalties).
Freiburg (1) 2 *(Kehl 22, Kobiashvili 49 (pen))*,
Feyenoord (0) 2 *(Van Hooijdonk 57,
Leonardo 86)*   18,600
Hertha Berlin (0) 0, Servette (1) 3 *(Hilton 17,
Frei 50, Obradovic 70)*   10,000
Internazionale (2) 4 *(Vieri 18, 34, 70, Kallon 46)*,
Ipswich Town (0) 1 *(Armstrong 79 (pen))*   25,358
Leeds United (2) 2 *(Kewell 19, Keane 45)*,
Grasshoppers (1) 2 *(Nunez 45, 90)*   40,014
Lille (1) 2 *(Cheyrou 33, Sterjovski 79)*,
Fiorentina (0) 0   17,000
Liteks (0) 1 *(Yurukov 90)*, AEK Athens (1) 1
(Gamarra 17)   5000
Lokomotiv Moscow (0) 0, Hapoel Tel Aviv (0) 1
(Osterc 49)   10,000
Lyon (2) 3 *(Anderson 18, 22, 90)*, FC Brugge (0) 0 39,583
Mallorca (0) 1 *(Eto'o 80 (pen))*, Liberec (0) 2
(Baffour 55, Stajner 67)   16,000
Paris St Germain (0) 0, Rangers (0) 0   35,000
(aet; Rangers won 4-3 on penalties).
PSV Eindhoven (2) 4 *(Vennegoor of Hesselink 2, 59,
Gakhokidze 33, Van Bommel 90 (pen))*,
PAOK Salonika (1) 1 *(De Souza 59)*   26,000
Roda (0) 2 *(Anastasiou 56 (pen), Lawal 65)*,
Bordeaux (0) 0   12,000

Sporting Lisbon (0) 1 *(Niculae 50)*, AC Milan (0) 1
(Javi Moreno 90)   38,000

FOURTH ROUND, FIRST LEG
Hapoel Tel Aviv (0) 0, Parma (0) 0   17,000
Internazionale (2) 3 *(Zanetti 13, Kallon 36,*
Ventola 56), AEK Athens (1) 1 *(Zagorakis 7)*   14,000
Lille (0) 1 *(Bassir 74)*, Borussia Dortmund (0) 1
(Ewerthon 68)   16,500
Lyon (1) 1 *(Govou 89)*, Liberec (1) 1
(Stajner 15 (pen))   26,069
PSV Eindhoven (0) 0, Leeds United (0) 0   32,000
Rangers (0) 1 *(Ferguson 80 (pen))*,
Feyenoord (0) 1 *(Ono 72)*   49,041
Roda (0) 0, AC Milan (1) 1 *(Jose Mari 29)*   19,800
Valencia (1) 3 *(Hilton 3 (og), Aimar 47, Salva 58)*,
Servette (0) 0   24,380

FOURTH ROUND, SECOND LEG
AC Milan (0) 0, Roda (0) 1 *(Luypers 71)*   7219
(aet; AC Milan won 3-2 on penalties).
AEK Athens (1) 2 *(Konstantinidis 23, Nikolaidis 56)*,
Internazionale (1) 2 *(Gresko 21, Ventola 57)*   28,000
Borussia Dortmund (0) 0, Lille (0) 0   43,000
Feyenoord (2) 3 *(Van Hooijdonk 37, 45, Kalou 46)*,
Rangers (1) 2 *(McCann 26,*
Ferguson B 54 (pen))   43,000
Leeds United (0) 0, PSV Eindhoven (0) 1
(Vennegoor of Hesselink 89)   39,755
Liberec (1) 4 *(Nezmar 1, 82, Stajner 74,*
Neumann 85), Lyon (1) 1 *(Muller 17)*   15,000
Parma (0) 1 *(Bonazzoli 85)*, Hapoel Tel Aviv (1) 2
(Osterc 31, Pisont 53)   6000
Servette (1) 2 *(Robert 37, Frei 67)*, Valencia (2) 2
(Sanchez 12, Angulo 45)   8125

QUARTER-FINALS, FIRST LEG
Hapoel Tel Aviv (1) 1 *(Clescenko 32)*,
AC Milan (0) 0   4000
(in Nicosia).
Internazionale (0) 1 *(Materazzi 52)*,
Valencia (0) 1 *(Rufete 65)*   25,184
Liberec (0) 0, Borussia Dortmund (0) 0   14,458
(in Prague).
PSV Eindhoven (0) 1 *(Kezman 47)*,
Feyenoord (1) 1 *(Van Hooijdonk 45)*   31,000

QUARTER-FINALS, SECOND LEG
Borussia Dortmund (0) 4 *(Amoroso 51, Koller 57,*
Ricken 71, Ewerthon 90), Slovan Liberec (0) 0   36,500
Feyenoord (0) 1 *(Van Hooijdonk 90)*,
PSV Eindhoven (1) 1 *(Van Bommel 76)*   43,000
(aet; Feyenoord won 5-4 on penalties).
AC Milan (2) 2 *(Rui Costa 5, Gershon 45 (og))*,
Hapoel Tel Aviv (0) 0   23,184
Valencia (0) 0, Internazionale (1) 1 *(Ventola 2)*   51,000

SEMI-FINALS, FIRST LEG
Borussia Dortmund (3) 4 *(Amoroso 8 (pen), 34, 39,*
Heinrich 62), AC Milan (0) 0   52,000
Internazionale (0) 0, Feyenoord (0) 1
(Cordoba 50 (og))   40,000

SEMI-FINALS, SECOND LEG
Feyenoord (2) 2 *(Van Hooijdonk 17, Tomasson 34)*,
Internazionale (0) 2 *(Zanetti 82, Kallon 90 (pen))*   45,000
AC Milan (2) 3 *(Inzaghi 11, Chamot 19, Serginho 89*
(pen)), Borussia Dortmund (0) 1 *(Ricken 90)*   15,301

FINAL

Feyenoord (2) 3, Borussia Dortmund (0) 2

(in Rotterdam, 8 May 2002, 45,000)

Feyenoord: Zoetebier; Gyan, Rzasa, Ono (De Haan 75), Van Wonderen, Paauwe, Bosvelt, Kalou (Elmander 75), Van Hooijdonk, Van Persie (Leonardo 62), Tomasson.
Scorers: Van Hooijdonk 33 (pen), 40, Tomasson 50.
Borussia Dortmund: Lehmann; Evanilson, Dede, Ricken (Heinrich 69), Worns, Kohler, Reuter, Ewerthon (Addo 61), Koller, Amoroso, Rosicky.
Scorers: Amoroso 47 (pen), Koller 58.
Referee: Pereira (Portugal).

Feyenoord players celebrate UEFA Cup Final win over Borussia Dortmund in Rotterdam. Pierre Van Hooijdonk scored twice and Jon Dahl Tomasson once as the Dutch team lifted the trophy for the second time. (ASP).

UEFA CUP 2001–02 – BRITISH AND IRISH CLUBS

QUALIFYING ROUND, FIRST LEG

9 AUG

Brondby (1) 2 *(Jonson 14, Bagger 80)*
Shelbourne (0) 0   8011
Brondby: Krogh M; Rasmussen, Nordin, Nielsen, Niznik (Jensen R 78), Jonson, Jorgensen (Krogh S 89), Bagger, Skarbalius, Lindrup, Riebers (Johansen 46).
Shelbourne: Williams; Heary, Mimmock, McCarthy, Hutton, Baker D, Byrne B (Fitzpatrick 76), Baker B, Crawford, Byrne D, Foran (Geoghegan 84).

Cwmbran Town (0) 0   496
Slovan Bratislava (2) 4 *(Mojic 40, Obzera 45, Vittek 83, Sobona 87)*
Cwmbran Town: Wager; Carter, Wile, Watkins, Philpott, James, Wigg, Wharton, Griffiths (Pattimore 46), Brown, Cotterrall (Mainwaring 78).
Slovan Bratislava: Prole; Sobona, Mojic, Kljestan, Petrus, Pecko, Necas, Ujlaky, Vittek (Meszaros 83), Obzera (Pancik 66), Hrncar (Bednar 46).

Glenavon (0) 0
Kilmarnock (0) 1 *(Innes 90)*   3200
Glenavon: Addis; Wright, Mallon, Montgomery, Rafferty (O'Kane 74), Keegan (Campbell 72), McMahon, Collins, McCann, Smith (Forker 76), McAree.
Kilmarnock: Marshall; Canero, Hay, Mahood, Innes, Dindeleux, McLaren (Fowler 79), Ngonge, Merdy (Cocard 56), Calderon (Pizzo 64), Mitchell.

Longford Town (1) 1 *(O'Connor 15)*
Liteks (0) 1 *(Yurukov 84)*   2922
Longford Town: O'Brien; Murphy, Byrne W, Reynolds, Smith, McNally, Kirby, Byrne S, Lavine, O'Connor (Lynch 79), Prunty.
Liteks: Vutov; Zhelev, Kirilov (Karadaliev 53), Yurukov, Bogdanov (Jelenkovic 46), Yovov, Dimitrov (Bornosouzov 46), Nikolov, Rachita, Hidiouad, Yankovich.

Midtjylland (1) 1 *(Pimpong 15)*
Glentoran (0) 1 *(Glendinning 83)*   1550
Midtjylland: Skov-Jensen; Nielsen, Sand, Skriver, Thomasberg, From A, Mikkelsen, Jessen (Pedersen 74), Skoubo, Kristensen, Pimpong (From K 70).
Glentoran: Gough; Nixon, Glendinning, Walker, Leeman, Young, McCann T, Fitzgerald (Hunter 87), Armour (Halliday 76), Batey, McCann A.

Polonia (0) 4 *(Tarachulski 70, 78, Moskal 89, 90)*
TNS (0) 0   300
Polonia: Krzysztalowicz; Zvirgzdauskas (Tarachulski 56), Kaliszan, Bykowski (Moskal 78), Golaszewski, Ekwuene, Bak, Dziewicki, Kaczorowski, Dabrowski (Bartczak 67), Szymanek.
TNS: Deegan; Powell A, Morgan, Edwards, Alexander (Toner 88), Powell G (Welton 81), Anthrobus, Jenkins, Ward, Coathup, Bridgewater (Evans 76).

QUALIFYING ROUND, SECOND LEG

23 AUG

Glentoran (0) 0   5231
Midtjylland (1) 4 *(Skoubo 13, 82, From 66, Pimpong 86)*
Glentoran: Gough; Nixon, Glendinning, Walker, Leeman (Smyth 59), Young, McCann (Hunter 46), Fitzgerald, Armour (Armstrong 50), Batey, Lockhart.
Midtjylland: Skov-Jensen; Nielsen, Sand, Skriver, Pedersen (Mikkelsen 74), Thomasberg (Pimpong 84), From, Jessen (Laursen 74), Rooba, Kristensen, Skoubo.

Kilmarnock (0) 1 *(Mitchell 66)*
Glenavon (0) 0   7454
Kilmarnock: Marshall; Fowler, Hay, Pizzo, Innes, Dindeleux, Cocard (Canning 84), Ngonge (Di Giacomo 78), Boyd (McLaren 12), Mahood, Mitchell.
Glenavon: Addis; Wright, Mallon (O'Kane 88), Montgomery, Rafferty, Keegan (Forker 63), McMahon, McKinstry, Collins, McCann (Smith 63), McAree.

Liteks (0) 2 *(Jankovic 89, 90 (pen))*
Longford Town (0) 0   4000
Liteks: Vutov; Zhelev, Patrascu, Kirilov, Yurukov (Bogdanov 55), Voyov (Bornosouzov 90), Nikolov (Petrov 69), Rachita, Hidiouad, Jankovic, Jelenkovic.
Longford Town: O'Brien; Murphy, Byrne W, Reynolds (Holt 86), Smith, McNally, Kirby (Gavin 60), Byrne S, Lavine, O'Connor (Kenny 68), Prunty.

Shelbourne (0) 0   4000
Brondby (1) 3 *(Bagger 11, Jorgensen 53, Madsen 78)*
Shelbourne: Williams; Heary, Mimmock, McCarthy, Hutton, Gannon, Byrne B (Fenlon 46), Baker R (Dempsey 73), Byrne D, Haylock (Fitzpatrick 46), Foran.
Brondby: Krogh; Rasmussen, Nordin, Nielsen, Johansen, Madsen (Degn 82), Niznik (Lindrup 62), Jonson (Jensen 75), Jorgensen, Bagger, Skarbalius.

Slovan Bratislava (0) 1 *(Meszaros 80)*
Cwmbran Town (0) 0   2439
Slovan Bratislava: Prole; Kozmer, Sobona, Mojic (Cifranic 88), Petrus, Pecko, Pancik (Obzera 58), Necas, Ujlaky (Bednar 65), Sedlak, Meszaros.
Cwmbran Town: O'Hagan (Wager 62); Carter, Smothers, James, Wharton, David, Wigg, Moore (Pattimore 70), Brown, Watkins (Wile 82), Cotterall.

TNS (0) 0
Polonia (1) 2 *(Bak 43, Bartczak 53)*   1000
(at Wrexham)
TNS: Deegan; Powell, Coathup, Taylor, Edwards, Alexander (Graves 77), Evans (Edge 59), Bridgewater, Anthrobus, Jenkins (Welton 66), Toner.
Polonia: Liberda; Szymanek, Dziewicki, Malinowski, Kaczorowski, Bartczak (Golaszewski 82), Ekwuene, Bak, Mazurkiewicz (Keska 75), Tarachulski (Moskal 75), Bykowski.

FIRST ROUND, FIRST LEG

20 SEPT

AEK Athens (0) 2 *(Tsartas 54 (pen), Nikolaidis 66)*
Hibernian (0) 0   *aet* 15,525
AEK Athens: Atmatsidis; Georgeas, Gamarra, Ramos, Zikos, Zagorakis, Tsartas (Petkov 87), Maladenis (Lakis 46), Konstantinidis, Nikolaidis (Mielcarski 89).
Hibernian: Colgan; De la Cruz, Fenwick, Smith, Laursen, Murray, O'Neil, Jack, Orman, Brewster (Zitelli 74), McManus (Luna 63).

Aston Villa (0) 2 *(Angel 54, 70)*
Varteks (1) 3 *(Bjelanovic 44, 86, Karic 64)*   27,132
Aston Villa: Schmeichel; Delaney, Wright, Mellberg, Alpay, Boateng, Stone (Ginola 64), Hadji, Angel, Vassell, Kachloul (Barry 76).
Varteks: Madaric; Sabolcki, Hrman (Balajic 90), Kristic, Granic, Rezic, Mukaj, Mumlek, Karic, Bjelanovic, Kastel.

Chelsea (1) 3 *(Gudjohnsen 45, 74, Lampard 90)*
Levski (0) 0   20,812
Chelsea: De Goey; Melchiot, Le Saux, Petit (Morris 30), Terry, Gallas, Jokanovic, Lampard, Gudjohnsen, Zola, Zenden.
Levski: Petkov; Stankov, Stoyanov (Angelov 80), Markov, Stoilov, Topuzakov, Ivanov, Golovskoy (Telkiyski 54), Chilikov (Pantelic 46), Botelho, Genchev.

Ipswich Town (0) 1 *(Bramble 85)*
Torpedo Moscow (1) 1 *(Vyazmikin 14)*   21,201
Ipswich Town: Sereni; Makin (Reuser 67), Hreidarsson, Bramble, McGreal (Clapham 46), Wright, Magilton, Holland, Stewart, Counago (Naylor 57), George.
Torpedo Moscow: Berezovski; Sadjaia, Zyryanov, Malai, Dayev, Jolovic, Leonchenko, Lukhvich, Vyazmikin (Kamoltsev 89), Shirko (Semshov 82), Kormyltsev.

Kilmarnock (0) 1 *(Dargo 73)*
Viking (1) 1 *(Sanne 45)*   6322
Kilmarnock: Marshall; Fowler, Dindeleux, Innes, Hay (Canero 79), Sanjuan (Pizzo 67), Calderon (Cocard 80), Mahood, Mitchell, Di Giacomo, Dargo.
Viking: Snorteland; Dahl, Tihinen, Kuivasto, Pereira, Sanne, Hangeland, Nygaard, Fuglestad, Berre, Nevland (Berland 82).

Maritimo (1) 1 *(Bruno 33)*
Leeds United (0) 0   10,500
Maritimo: Nelson; Albertino, Briguel, Bruno, Paulo Sergio, Van der Gaag, Zeca, Dinda, Andre (Alan 75), Quim (Gaucho 61), Kenedy.
Leeds United: Martyn; Kelly, Harte, Batty, Ferdinand, Matteo, Mills, Keane, Viduka, Kewell, McPhail (Wilcox 57).

FIRST ROUND

27 SEPT

Anzhi (0) 0   *(in Warsaw)*
Rangers (0) 1 *(Konterman 85)*   3700
Anzhi: Zhidkov; Gordeyev, Akayev (Nikolic 87), Ramazanov, Yaskovic, Bilong, Agalarov, Adiyev, Edu, Sirkhayev, Tsymbalar.
Rangers: Klos; Ricksen, Numan, Ferguson B, Amoruso, Moore, Latapy (Hughes 90), McCann (Lovenkrands 63), Flo (Caniggia 58), De Boer, Konterman.
Tie decided over single leg played in Warsaw.

FIRST ROUND, SECOND LEG

Hibernian (0) 3 *(Luna 52, 82, Zitelli 114)*
AEK Athens (0) 2 *(Tsartas 92, 105)*   16,647
Hibernian: Colgan; Fenwick, Sauzee (Brebner 80), Murray, Orman, De la Cruz, Jack, O'Neil (Zitelli 91), Laursen, Brewster (McManus 69), Luna.
AEK Athens: Chiotis; Marica (Mielcarski 63), Ramos, Gamarra, Kassapis, Lakis (Kappos 118), Zagorakis, Zikos, Kostenoglou, Konstantinidis (Tsartas 58), Nikolaidis.

Leeds United (2) 3 *(Keane 20, Kewell 37, Bakke 62)*
Maritimo (0) 0   38,125
Leeds United: Martyn; Mills, Harte, Batty, Ferdinand, Matteo, Dacourt, Keane, Viduka, Kewell, Bakke.
Maritimo: Nelson; Lino, Briguel, Bruno (Andre 59), Paulo Sergio, Van der Gaag, Zeca, Dinda (Santos 15) (Gaucho 46), Quim, Albertino, Kenedy.

Levski (0) 0
Chelsea (2) 2 *(Terry 33, Gudjohnsen 45)*   10,000
Levski: Petkov; Stankov, Angelov, Markov (Dragich 56),

Ivanov, Topuzakov, Telkiyski, Golovskoy, Chilikov (Genchev 71), Pantelic (Stoilov 46), Botelho.
Chelsea: De Goey; Gallas, Babayaro, Petit, Terry, Desailly, Melchiot, Lampard, Gudjohnsen (Forssell 45), Zola (Knight 61), Jokanovic (Dalla Bona 63).

Torpedo Moscow (0) 1 *(Vyazmikin 66)*
Ipswich Town (0) 2 *(George 47, Stewart 54(pen))* 10,500
Torpedo Moscow: Berezovski; Sadjaia (Gashkin 56), Zyryanov, Malai, Jolovic (Lakic 80), Dayev, Leonchenko, Kormyltsev (Semshov 42), Vyazmikin, Shirko, Lukhvich.
Ipswich Town: Sereni; Makin, Hreidarsson, Venus, McGreal, Clapham (Miller 87), Magilton, Holland, Stewart, Armstrong (Naylor 84), George (Wright 70).

Varteks (0) 0
Aston Villa (0) 1 *(Hadji 90)*   12,100
Varteks: Madaric; Sobolcki, Mumlek (Balajic 58), Rezic, Granic, Kristic, Mukaj, Hrman (Andricevic 90), Karic (Drobne 90), Bjelanovic, Kastel.
Aston Villa: Schmeichel; Delaney, Wright, Mellberg (Stone 45), Alpay, Boateng, Hadji, Hendrie, Balaban (Angel 46), Ginola, Kachloul (Dublin 62).

Viking (2) 2 *(Sanne 1, Nevland 17)*
Kilmarnock (0) 0   4599
Viking: Andersen; Dahl, Tihinen, Kuivasto, Pereira, Sanne, Hangeland, Berre (Nygaard 84), Nevland (Berland 72), Tengesdal (Wright 89).
Kilmarnock: Marshall; Canero, Innes, Dindeleux, Hay (Fowler 78), Mahood, Pizzo (McLaren 57), Sanjuan, Mitchell, Ngonge (Dargo 54), Di Giacomo.

SECOND ROUND, FIRST LEG

18 OCT

Hapoel Tel Aviv (0) 2 *(Gershon 89 (pen), Kleschenco 90)*
Chelsea (0) 0   11,500
Hapoel Tel Aviv: Elimelech; Bachr, Antebi, Onischenko, Domb, Gershon, Abuksis, Pishant (Knafo 75), Osterc (Afek 89), Kleschenco, Halmai (Luz 86).
Chelsea: Bosnich; Melchiot, Babayaro, Stanic, Terry, Kitamirike, Jokanovic, Lampard, Hasselbaink (Forssell 81), Zola, Zenden (Dalla Bona 55).

Ipswich Town (0) 0
Helsingborg (0) 0   22,254
Ipswich Town: Sereni; Wilnis (Clapham 85), Hreidarsson, Venus, McGreal, Reuser (Counago 54), Magilton (Peralta 75), Holland, Stewart, George, Wright.
Helsingborg: Andersson S; Gustavsson; Matovac, Eklund, Nilsson, Jansson J, Hansson, Bakkerud, Santos, Andersson C (Lindstrom 57), Prica (Jansson U 83).

Leeds United (3) 4 *(Viduka 6, 44, Bowyer 23, 46)*
Troyes (1) 2 *(Loko 31, 81)*   40,015
Leeds United: Martyn; Mills, Harte, Bakke (Batty 66), Ferdinand, Matteo, Dacourt, Keane (Smith 70), Viduka, Kewell, Bowyer.
Troyes: Heurtebis; Thomas, Bradga, Anzine, Danjou, Meniri, Rothen, Leroy, Boutal (Niang 77), Loko (Djukic 86), Gousse (Hamed 58).

Rangers (1) 3 *(Amoruso 9, Ball 61, De Boer 80)*
Dynamo Moscow (0) 1 *(Gusev 90)*   45,008
Rangers: Klos; Ricksen, Numan, Amoruso, Moore (Ball 46), Konterman, Reyna, Ferguson B, Flo (McCann 67), De Boer, Caniggia.
Dynamo Moscow: Khomutovski; Hornyak, Semberas, Tochilin (Kharlachev 81), Zharinov, Zutautas, Gusev, Bystrov, Bulykin, Grishin (Dyatel 87), Nemov (Medvedev 46).

SECOND ROUND, SECOND LEG

1 NOV

Chelsea (0) 1 *(Zola 64)*
Hapoel Tel Aviv (1) 1 *(Osterc 36)*   26,433
Chelsea: Bosnich; Gallas, Le Saux, Stanic (Forssell 46), Terry, Desailly, Lampard, Petit (Dalla Bona 46), Hasselbaink, Gudjohnsen, Zenden (Zola 46).
Hapoel Tel Aviv: Elimelech; Bachar, Antebi, Onischenko, Domb, Gershon, Abuksis (Toema 54), Halmai, Osterc (Hillel 69), Kleschenko, Luz (Pishont 17).

Dynamo Moscow (1) 1 *(Gusev 27)*
Rangers (3) 4 *(De Boer 8, Khomutovsky 16 (og), Flo 43, Lovenkrands 79)*   5000
Dynamo Moscow: Khomutovsky; Semberas, Hornyak, Dyatel (Cesnauskis 46), Novikov, Zutautas, Gusev, Tochilin, Bulykin (Shapovalov 46), Bystrov (Nemov 85), Grishin.
Rangers: Klos; Ricksen, Numan, Amoruso, Moore, Konterman, Reyna, Ferguson B, Flo (Mols 79), De Boer (Lovenkrands 72), Caniggia (Latapy 72).

Helsingborg (1) 1 *(Eklund 8)*
Ipswich Town (0) 3 *(Hreidarsson 69, Stewart 81, 88)* 9484
Helsingborg: Andersson S; Gustavsson, Matovac, Eklund (Johansen 31), Nilsson, Jansson J, Hansson, Bakkerud, Santos, Andersson C, Prica.
Ipswich Town: Sereni; Wilnis (Makin 38), Clapham, Bramble, Hreidarsson, Venus, Magilton, Holland, Stewart, Naylor (Bent 72), Peralta (Miller 89).

Troyes (2) 3 *(Anzine 8, Hamed 38, Rothen 59)*
Leeds United (1) 2 *(Viduka 14, Keane 78)*   15,000
Troyes: Heurtebis; Thomas, Bradja (Adam 80), Anzine, Danjou, Hamed, Rothen, Saifi (Gousse 74), Boutal, Loko, Tourenne.
Leeds United: Martyn; Mills, Harte, Batty, Duberry, Matteo, Dacourt, Keane, Viduka, Kewell (Wilcox 46), Bakke.

THIRD ROUND, FIRST LEG

22 NOV

Grasshoppers (1) 1 *(Chapuisat 17)*
Leeds United (0) 2 *(Harte 73, Smith 79)*   15,000
Grasshoppers: Jehle; Schwegler, Smiljanic, Diop, Hodei, Castillo, Cabanas (Baturina 74), Mwaruwari (Gerber 80), Chapuisat, Nunez, Tararache (Petric 88).
Leeds United: Martyn; Mills, Harte, Batty, Ferdinand, Matteo, Dacourt, Smith, Keane, Bakke, Wilcox.

Ipswich Town (0) 1 *(Armstrong 81)*
Internazionale (0) 0   24,569
Ipswich Town: Sereni; Makin, Hreidarsson, Venus, Bramble, Clapham (Gaardsoe 90), Peralta (Reuser 85), Holland, Counago, Naylor (Armstrong 77), Wright.
Internazionale: Toldo; Zanetti J, Gresko, Seedorf, Di Biagio (Georgatos 77), Cordoba, Zanetti C, Farinos, Ventola (Adriano 57), Kallon, Emre (Conceicao 69).

Rangers (0) 0
Paris St Germain (0) 0   49,223
Rangers: Klos; Amoruso, Ricksen, Konterman, Ball (Lovenkrands 55), Ferguson, Numan, de Boer (Ross 86), Flo, Caniggia (Latapy 72), Reyna.
Paris St Germain: Letizi; Heinze, Parralo (Llacer 46), Pochettino, Dehu, Potillon, Arteta, Leal, Ogbeche (Alex 81), Ronaldinho, Leroy (Cisse 67).

Valencia (0) 1 *(Vicente 75)*
Celtic (0) 0   38,000
Valencia: Canizares; Pellegrino, Ayala (Djukic 44), Albelda, Vicente, Angulo, Carboni, Sanchez (Mista 64), Carew, Aimar (Salva 85), Curro.
Celtic: Douglas; Mjallby, Balde, Petrov, Crainey, Lennon, Lambert, Moravcik (Petta 57), Hartson (Sylla 80), Larsson, McNamara.

THIRD ROUND, SECOND LEG

6 DEC

Celtic (1) 1 *(Larsson 45)*
Valencia (0) 0   57,299
Celtic: Douglas; Mjallby, Petrov, Balde, Valgaeren, Petta (Thompson 85), Lennon, Moravcik (Sylla 55) (Hartson 110), Sutton, Larsson, Lambert.
Valencia: Canizares; Ayala, Djukic, Pellegrino, Curro (Angloma 46), De los Santos, Vicente, Aurelio (Mista 67), Carew, Aimar (Sanchez 84), Carboni.
aet; Valencia won 5-4 on penalties.

Internazionale (2) 4 *(Vieri 18, 34, 70, Kallon 46)*
Ipswich Town (0) 1 *(Armstrong 79 (pen))*   25,358
Internazionale: Toldo; Zanetti J, Gresko, Guly, Di Biagio, Cordoba, Okan, Farinos, Emre (Conceicao 90), Vieri (Ronaldo 80), Kallon.
Ipswich Town: Sereni; Makin, Hreidarsson, Venus, Bramble, Clapham, Magilton (Peralta 71), Holland, Naylor (Armstrong 46), George (Counago 61), Wright.

Leeds United (2) 2 *(Kewell 19, Keane 45)*
Grasshoppers (1) 2 *(Nunez 45, 90)*   40,014
Leeds United: Martyn; Kelly, Harte, Batty, Ferdinand, Mills, Dacourt, Smith, Keane, Viduka, Kewell.
Grasshoppers: Jehle; Schwegler, Smiljanic (Morales 74), Diop, Hodei, Castillo, Gerber (Mwaruwari 59), Cabanas (Ippoliti 66), Chapuisat, Nunez, Tararache.

Paris St Germain (0) 0
Rangers (0) 0   35,000
Paris St Germain: Letizi; Cristobal, Heinze, Arteta, Karkouri, Pochettino, Ogbeche (Okocha 56), Aloisio, Leroy (Anelka 62), Cisse (Mendy 78), Ronaldinho.
Rangers: Klos; Moore, Numan, Ferguson, Konterman, Amoruso, de Boer, Lovenkrands (Caniggia 30), Flo (Latapy 78), Ross (Vidmar 109), Reyna.
aet: Rangers won 4-3 on penalties.

FOURTH ROUND, FIRST LEG

21 FEB

PSV Eindhoven (0) 0
Leeds United (0) 0   32,000
PSV Eindhoven: Lodewijks; Bogelund, Bouma, Vogel, Ooijer, Holland (Nikiforov 68), Van Bommel, Rommedahl, Gakhokidze, Vennegoor of Hesselink (Kezman 60), Bruggink (De Jong 36).
Leeds United: Martyn; Mills, Harte, Bakke, Ferdinand, Matteo, Dacourt, Smith, Viduka, Kewell, Bowyer.

Rangers (0) 1 *(Ferguson 80 (pen))*
Feyenoord (0) 1 *(Ono 72)*   49,041
Rangers: Klos; Ricksen, Numan, Ferguson B, Amoruso, Vidmar, Hughes (Latapy 81), Konterman, Caniggia, Flo (Mols 59), Lovenkrands.
Feyenoord: Zoetebier; Emerton, Rzasa, Bosvelt, Loovens, Paauwe, Kalou (Van Persie 56), Ono, Tomasson, Van Hooijdonk, Van Wonderen.

FOURTH ROUND, SECOND LEG

28 FEB

Feyenoord (2) 3 *(Van Hooijdonk 37, 45, Kalou 46)*
Rangers (1) 2 *(McCann 26, Ferguson B 54 (pen))* 43,000
Feyenoord: Zoetebier; Emerton, Rzasa, Loovens, Paauwe, Bosvelt, Kalou (Smolarek 76), Van Wonderen, Van Hooijdonk, Van Persie, Ono.
Rangers: Klos; Vidmar (Flo 74), Numan, Amoruso, Wilson, Ferguson B, Konterman, De Boer (Mols 38), Cannigia, McCann, Lovenkrands.

Leeds United (0) 0 39,755
PSV Eindhoven (0) 1 *(Vennegoor of Hesselink 89)*
Leeds United: Martyn; Mills, Harte, Bakke, Ferdinand, Matteo, Kelly, Smith, Viduka, Kewell, Bowyer.
PSV Eindhoven: Lodewijks; Bogelund, Bouma, Vogel, Hofland, Ooijer, Rommedahl, Van Bommel, Kezman, Vennegoor of Hesselink (Gakhokidze 90), Lucius.

EUROPEAN CHAMPIONS LEAGUE 2002–03

DRAW 2002–03

FIRST QUALIFYING ROUND
To be played July 17 and 24

Tampere United v FC Pyunik	0-4
Skonto v Barry Town	5-0
Portadown v Belshina Bobruisk	0-0
F91 Dudelange v Vardar	1-1
FBK Kaunas v Dinamo Tirana	2-3
Flora v Apoel Nicosia	0-0
FK Zeljeznikar v IA Akranes	3-0
Hibernians v Shelbourne	2-2
Torpedo Kutaisi v B36 Torshavn	5-2
Sheriff Tiraspol v Zhenis Aspana.	2-1

First leg results only.

SECOND QUALIFYING ROUND
To be played July 31 and August 7
Zalaegerszegi TE v NK Zagreb
Club Brugge v Dinamo Bucharest
MSK Zilina v FC Basel
Skonto or Barry v PFC Levski Sofia.
Dynamo Kiev v Tampere United or FC Pyunik
Brondby IF v FBK Kaunas or Dinamo Tirana
NK Maribor v Flora or Apoel Nicosia
F91 Dudelange or Vardar v Legia Warsaw
Boavista v Hibernians or Shelbourne
Maccabi Haifa v Portadown or Belshina Bobruisk
Lillestrom v FK Zeljeznikar v IA Akranes
Hammarby v FK Partizan
Sparta Prague v Torpedo Kutaisi v B36 Torshavn
Sheriff Tiraspol v Zhenis Aspana v Grazer AK

SEEDINGS:
Pot 1: Real Madrid, Bayern Munich*, Manchester United*, Barcelona*, Valencia, Juventus, Arsenal, Internazionale*.
Pot 2: Deportivo La Coruna, Bayer Leverkusen, Liverpool, Galatasaray, Roma, Lyon, Borussia Dortmund, Feyenoord*.
Pot 3: AC Milan*, PSV Eindhoven, Dinamo Kiev*, Spartak Moscow, Lokomotiv Moscow*, Olympiakos, AEK Athens*, Sparta Prague*.
Pot 4: Ajax, Rosenborg*, Lens, Newcastle*, Brugge*, Sturm Graz*, Boavista*, Celtic*.
* denotes team has to pre-qualify.
Teams from the same pot cannot be drawn to face each other.
Draw for the first round proper will take place on August 29, with the eight groups consisting of one team from each pot.

SUMMARY OF APPEARANCES

EUROPEAN CUP (1955–2002)

English clubs
13 Liverpool, Manchester U
6 Arsenal
4 Leeds U
3 Nottingham F
2 Derby Co, Wolverhampton W, Everton, Aston Villa
1 Burnley, Tottenham H, Ipswich T, Manchester C,
Blackburn R, Newcastle U, Chelsea

Scottish clubs
22 Rangers
17 Celtic
3 Aberdeen
2 Hearts
1 Dundee, Dundee U, Kilmarnock, Hibernian

Welsh clubs
4 Barry T
1 Cwmbran T, TNS

Northern Ireland clubs
20 Linfield
9 Glentoran
3 Crusaders
2 Portadown
1 Glenavon, Ards, Distillery, Derry C, Coleraine,
Cliftonville

Eire clubs
7 Shamrock R, Dundalk
6 Waterford
3 Bohemians, Drumcondra, St Patrick's Ath,
Shelbourne
2 Sligo R, Limerick, Athlone T, Derry C*
1 Cork Hibs, Cork Celtic, Cork City

**Winners: Celtic 1966–67; Manchester U 1967–68,
1998–99; Liverpool 1976–77, 1977–78, 1980–81, 1983–84;
Nottingham F 1978–79, 1979–80; Aston Villa 1981–82**

**Finalists: Celtic 1969–70; Leeds U 1974–75; Liverpool
1984–85**

EUROPEAN CUP-WINNERS' CUP (1960–99)

English clubs
6 Tottenham H
5 Manchester U, Liverpool, Chelsea
4 West Ham U
3 Arsenal, Everton
2 Manchester C
1 Wolverhampton W, Leicester C, WBA, Leeds U,
Sunderland, Southampton, Ipswich T, Newcastle U

Scottish clubs
10 Rangers
8 Aberdeen, Celtic
3 Hearts
2 Dunfermline Ath, Dundee U
1 Dundee, Hibernian, St Mirren, Motherwell,
Airdrieonians, Kilmarnock

Welsh clubs
14 Cardiff C
8 Wrexham
7 Swansea C
3 Bangor C
1 Borough U, Newport Co, Merthyr Tydfil, Barry T,
Llansantfraid, Cwmbran T

Northern Ireland clubs
9 Glentoran
5 Glenavon
4 Ballymena U, Coleraine
3 Crusaders, Linfield
2 Ards, Bangor
1 Derry C, Distillery, Portadown, Carrick Rangers,
Cliftonville

Eire clubs
6 Shamrock R
4 Shelbourne
3 Limerick, Waterford, Dundalk, Bohemians
2 Cork Hibs, Galway U, Derry C*, Cork City
1 Cork Celtic, St Patrick's Ath, Finn Harps, Home
Farm, University College Dublin, Bray W, Sligo R

**Winners: Tottenham H 1962–63; West Ham U 1964–65;
Manchester C 1969–70; Chelsea 1970–71, 1997–98;
Rangers 1971–72; Aberdeen 1982–83; Everton 1984–85;
Manchester U 1990–91; Arsenal 1993–94**

**Finalists: Rangers 1960–61, 1966–67; Liverpool 1965–66;
Leeds U 1972–73; West Ham U 1975–76; Arsenal
1979–80, 1994–95**

EUROPEAN FAIRS CUP & UEFA CUP (1955–2002)

English clubs
12 Leeds U
11 Liverpool
10 Aston Villa
9 Arsenal, Ipswich T
7 Manchester U, Newcastle U
6 Everton, Tottenham H
5 Chelsea, Southampton, Nottingham F
4 Manchester C, Birmingham C, Wolverhampton W, WBA
3 Sheffield W
2 Stoke C, Derby Co, QPR, Blackburn R, Leicester C
1 Burnley, Coventry C, Norwich C, London Rep XI,
Watford, West Ham U

Scottish clubs
18 Dundee U
15 Hibernian
14 Aberdeen, Celtic
12 Rangers
10 Hearts
7 Kilmarnock
5 Dunfermline Ath
4 Dundee
3 St Mirren
2 Partick T, Motherwell, St Johnstone
1 Morton, Raith R

Welsh Clubs
3 Inter Cardiff (formerly Inter Cable-Tel), Bangor C
2 Newtown, Barry T, Cwmbran
1 Afan Lido, TNS

Northern Ireland clubs
13 Glentoran
8 Coleraine
7 Linfield
5 Portadown, Glenavon
3 Crusaders
1 Ards, Ballymena U, Bangor

Eire clubs
11 Bohemians
5 Dundalk, Shelbourne
4 Shamrock R, Cork City
3 Finn Harps, St Patrick's Ath
2 Drumcondra, Derry C*
1 Cork Hibs, Athlone T, Limerick, Drogheda U,
Galway U, Bray Wanderers, Longford T

**Winners: Leeds U 1967–68, 1970–71; Newcastle U
1968–69; Arsenal 1969–70; Tottenham H 1971–72,
1983–84; Liverpool 1972–73, 1975–76, 2000–01; Ipswich T
1980–81**

**Finalists: London 1955–58, Birmingham C 1958–60,
1960–61; Leeds U 1966–67; Wolverhampton W 1971–72;
Tottenham H 1973–74; Dundee U 1986–87**

Now play in League of Ireland

INTERTOTO CUP 2001

FIRST ROUND

Carmarthen Town v AIK Stockholm 0-0, 0-3
Dundee v Sartid 0-0, 2-5
Cork City v Metalurgs 0-1, 1-2
Anorthosis v Slaven Belupo 0-2, 0-7
WIT v Ried 1-0, 1-2
Aarhus v Publikum 1-0, 1-7
St Julia v Lausanne 1-3, 0-6
Tatabanya v Shirak 2-3, 3-1
B68 v Lokeren 2-4, 0-0
Uni Craiova v Bylis 3-3, 1-0
Dynamo Minsk v Hobscheid 6-0, 1-1
Groclin v Spartak Varna 1-0, 0-4
Jazz v Gloria 1-0, 1-2
Grindavik v Vilash 1-0, 2-1
Tiligul v Cliftonville 1-0, 3-1
Celik v Denizli 1-0, 5-3
Ekranas v Artmedia 1-1, 1-1
   Artmedia won on penalties.
NK Zagreb v Pobeda 1-2, 1-1
Hapoel Haifa v VMK 2-0, 3-0
Zaglebie v Hibernians 4-0, 0-1

SECOND ROUND

Sturm Graz v Lausanne 0-1, 3-3
Celik v Gent 1-0, 0-2
Slaven Belupo v Bastia 1-0, 1-0
Dynamo Minsk v Hapoel Haifa 2-0, 1-0
Pobeda v Rize 2-1, 2-0
Basle v Grindavik 3-0, 2-0
Troyes v WIT 6-0, 1-1
Spartak Varna v Tavriya 0-3, 2-2
Tiligul v Tatabanya 1-1, 0-4
Odense v AIK Stockholm 2-2, 0-2
Zaglebie v Lokeren 2-2, 1-2
Paris St Germain v Jazz 3-0, 4-1
1860 Munich v Sartid 3-1, 3-2
Metalurgs v Heerenveen 3-2, 1-6
Synot v Uni Craiova 3-2, 2-2
Publikum v Artmedia 5-0, 1-1

THIRD ROUND

Chmel v Pobeda 0-0, 1-0
Lokeren v Newcastle United 0-4, 0-1
Publikum v Lausanne 1-1, 0-0
Slaven Belupo v Aston Villa 2-1, 0-2
Basle v Heerenveen 2-1, 3-2
Werder Bremen v Gent 2-3, 1-0
Wolfsburg v Dynamo Minsk 4-3, 0-0
Brescia v Tatabanya 2-1, 1-1
Tavriya v Paris St Germain 0-1, 0-4
RKC v 1860 Munich 1-2, 1-3
Troyes v AIK Stockholm 2-1, 2-1
Rennes v Synot 5-0, 2-4

SEMI-FINALS

Gent v Paris St Germain 0-0, 1-7
Troyes v Wolfsburg 1-0, 2-2
Rennes v Aston Villa 2-1, 0-1
1860 Munich v Newcastle United 2-3, 1-3
Basle v Lausanne 3-0, 2-2
Chmel v Brescia 1-2, 2-2

FINALS

Troyes v Newcastle United 0-0, 4-4
   Troyes won on away goals.
Basle v Aston Villa 1-1, 1-4
Paris St Germain v Brescia 0-0, 1-1

Slaven Belupo (0) 2 *(Crnac 60, Gersak 90)*
Aston Villa (0) 1 *(Ginola 89)*   3000
Aston Villa: Enckelman; Delaney, Wright, Boateng, Alpay, Barry (Ginola 74), Stone (Samuel 80), Merson, Dublin (Vassell 55), Hendrie, Staunton.

Lokeren (0) 0   2425
Newcastle United (3) 4 *(Quinn 13, Ameobi 23, 39, Lua-Lua 85)*
Newcastle United: Given; Barton, Elliott, Dabizas, Hughes (Caldwell S 61), Solano, Bassedas (McClen 78), Speed, Ameobi (Lua-Lua 70), Bellamy, Quinn.

Aston Villa (2) 2 *(Hendrie 19, 41)*
Slaven Belupo (0) 0   21,412
Aston Villa: Schmeichel (Enckleman 46); Delaney, Wright, Boateng, Alpay, Barry, Stone, Merson, Dublin (Angel 55), Hendrie, Kachloul (Hadji 74).

Newcastle United (0) 1 *(Bellamy 60)*
Lokeren (0) 0   29,021
Newcastle United: Given; Barton, Elliott, Dabizas, Hughes, Solano, Bassedas (McClen 62), Speed, Ameobi, Bellamy (Lua-Lua 72), Quinn (Bernard 72).

Rennes (1) 2 *(Lucas 19, Chapuis 66)*
Aston Villa (0) 1 *(Vassell 90)*   15,753
Aston Villa: Enckelman; Delaney, Wright, Boateng, Alpay, Barry, Stone (Ginola 52), Merson, Dublin (Vassell 78), Hendrie, Kachloul (Hadji 61).

1860 Munich (0) 2 *(Agostino 56, Tapalovic 66)*   15,000
Newcastle United (1) 3 *(Solano 10, 55, Hughes 84)*
Newcastle United: Given; Barton, Elliott, Dabizas, Hughes, Solano, Bassedas (Caldwell S 85), Speed, Ameobi (Lua-Lua 85), Bellamy, Quinn (Bernard 85).

Aston Villa (1) 1 *(Dublin 5)*
Rennes (0) 0   30,782
Aston Villa: Enckelman; Delaney, Wright, Boateng, Alpay, Barry, Kachloul, Merson (Hadji 56), Dublin, Hendrie (Stone 75), Ginola (Vassell 84).

Newcastle United (1) 3 *(Speed 5, Lua-Lua 80, Solano 90 (pen)*
1860 Munich (1) 1 *(Schroth 42)*   36,635
Newcastle United: Given; Barton, Elliott, Dabizas, Hughes, Solano, Lee (Caldwell S 82), Speed (Acuna 78), Ameobi, Bellamy (Lua-Lua 78), Quinn.

Basle (0) 1 *(Gimenez 75)*
Aston Villa (0) 1 *(Merson 59)*   29,879
Aston Villa: Enckelman; Delaney, Wright, Barry, Alpay, Boateng, Hadji, Merson (Vassell 65), Dublin (Stone 80), Hendrie, Kachloul.

Troyes (0) 0
Newcastle U (0) 0   10,414
Newcastle U: Given; Barton, Elliott, Dabizas, Hughes, Solano, Lee, Speed, Ameobi (Bassedas 90), Bellamy (Lua-Lua 88), Quinn.

Aston Villa (1) 4 *(Vassell 45, Angel 55, 79, Ginola 83)*
Basle (1) 1 *(Chipperfield 30)*   39,593
Aston Villa: Schmeichel; Delaney, Staunton (Samuel 68), Barry, Alpay, Boateng, Stone, Hendrie (Kachloul 65), Angel (Dublin 80), Vassell, Ginola.

Newcastle U (1) 4 *(Solano 2, Ameobi 65, Speed 69 (pen), Hughes 90)*
Troyes (2) 4 *(Leroy 25, Gousse 28, Boutal 47, 61)*   36,577
Newcastle U: Given; Barton (O'Brien 66), Elliott, Dabizas, Hughes, Solano (Lua-Lua 66), Lee, Speed, Ameobi, Bellamy, Quinn (Bernard 66).

WORLD CLUB CHAMPIONSHIP

Played annually up to 1974 and intermittently since then between the winners of the European Cup and the winners of the South American Champions Cup — known as the Copa Libertadores. In 1980 the winners were decided by one match arranged in Tokyo in February 1981 and the venue has been the same since. AC Milan replaced Marseille who had been stripped of their European Cup title in 1993.

1960	Real Madrid beat Penarol 0-0, 5-1
1961	Penarol beat Benfica 0-1, 5-0, 2-1
1962	Santos beat Benfica 3-2, 5-2
1963	Santos beat AC Milan 2-4, 4-2, 1-0
1964	Inter-Milan beat Independiente 0-1, 2-0, 1-0
1965	Inter-Milan beat Independiente 3-0, 0-0
1966	Penarol beat Real Madrid 2-0, 2-0
1967	Racing Club beat Celtic 0-1, 2-1, 1-0
1968	Estudiantes beat Manchester United 1-0, 1-1
1969	AC Milan beat Estudiantes 3-0, 1-2
1970	Feyenoord beat Estudiantes 2-2, 1-0
1971	Nacional beat Panathinaikos* 1-1, 2-1
1972	Ajax beat Independiente 1-1, 3-0
1973	Independiente beat Juventus* 1-0
1974	Atlético Madrid* beat Independiente 0-1, 2-0
1975	Independiente and Bayern Munich could not agree dates; no matches.
1976	Bayern Munich beat Cruzeiro 2-0, 0-0
1977	Boca Juniors beat Borussia Moenchengladbach* 2-2, 3-0
1978	Not contested
1979	Olimpia beat Malmö* 1-0, 2-1
1980	Nacional beat Nottingham Forest 1-0
1981	Flamengo beat Liverpool 3-0

1982	Penarol beat Aston Villa 2-0
1983	Gremio Porto Alegre beat SV Hamburg 2-1
1984	Independiente beat Liverpool 1-0
1985	Juventus beat Argentinos Juniors 4-2 on penalties after a 2-2 draw
1986	River Plate beat Steaua Bucharest 1-0
1987	FC Porto beat Penarol 2-1 after extra time
1988	Nacional (Uru) beat PSV Eindhoven 7-6 on penalties after 1-1 draw
1989	AC Milan beat Atletico Nacional (Col) 1-0 after extra time
1990	AC Milan beat Olimpia 3-0
1991	Red Star Belgrade beat Colo Colo 3-0
1992	Sao Paulo beat Barcelona 2-1
1993	Sao Paulo beat AC Milan 3-2
1994	Velez Sarsfield beat AC Milan 2-0
1995	Ajax beat Gremio Porto Alegre 4-3 on penalties after 0-0 draw
1996	Juventus beat River Plate 1-0
1997	Borussia Dortmund beat Cruzeiro 2-0
1998	Real Madrid beat Vasco da Gama 2-1
1999	Manchester U beat Palmeiras 1-0
2000	Boca Juniors beat Real Madrid 2-1

*European Cup runners-up; winners declined to take part.

2001

27 November in Tokyo

Bayern Munich (0) 1

Boca Juniors (0) 0 *aet*   51,360

Bayern Munich: Kahn; Sagnol, Lizarazu, Kovac R, Kuffour, Fink, Hargreaves (Sforza 76), Kovac N (Jancker 76), Sergio, Elber, Pizarro (Thiam 118).
Scorer: Kuffour 110.
Boca Juniors: Cordoba; Burdisso, Martinez (Calvo 19) (Carreno 112), Schiavi, Rodriguez, Serna, Villarreal (Pinto 100), Traverso, Riquelme, Delgardo, Schelotto.
Referee: Nielsen (Denmark).

EUROPEAN SUPER CUP

Played annually between the winners of the European Champions' Cup and the European Cup-Winners' Cup (UEFA Cup from 2000). AC Milan replaced Marseille in 1993–94.

1972	Ajax beat Rangers 3-1, 3-2
1973	Ajax beat AC Milan 0-1, 6-0
1974	Not contested
1975	Dynamo Kiev beat Bayern Munich 1-0, 2-0
1976	Anderlecht beat Bayern Munich 4-1, 1-2
1977	Liverpool beat Hamburg 1-1, 6-0
1978	Anderlecht beat Liverpool 3-1, 1-2
1979	Nottingham F beat Barcelona 1-0, 1-1
1980	Valencia beat Nottingham F 1-0, 1-2
1981	Not contested
1982	Aston Villa beat Barcelona 0-1, 3-0
1983	Aberdeen beat Hamburg 0-0, 2-0
1984	Juventus beat Liverpool 2-0
1985	Juventus v Everton not contested due to UEFA ban on English clubs
1986	Steaua Bucharest beat Dynamo Kiev 1-0

1987	FC Porto beat Ajax 1-0, 1-0
1988	KV Mechelen beat PSV Eindhoven 3-0, 0-1
1989	AC Milan beat Barcelona 1-1, 1-0
1990	AC Milan beat Sampdoria 1-1, 2-0
1991	Manchester U beat Red Star Belgrade 1-0
1992	Barcelona beat Werder Bremen 1-1, 2-1
1993	Parma beat AC Milan 0-1, 2-0
1994	AC Milan beat Arsenal 0-0, 2-0
1995	Ajax beat Zaragoza 1-1, 4-0
1996	Juventus beat Paris St. Germain 6-1, 3-1
1997	Barcelona beat Borussia Dortmund 2-0, 1-1
1998	Chelsea beat Real Madrid 1-0
1999	Lazio beat Manchester U 1-0
2000	Galatasaray beat Real Madrid 2-1

2001

24 August 2001, Monaco

Bayern Munich (0) 2 *(Salihamidzic 57, Jancker 81)*

Liverpool (2) 3 *(Riise 22, Heskey 45, Owen 46)*   15,000

Bayern Munich: Kahn; Sagnol, Lizarazu, Kovac R, Thiam, Linke, Hargreaves, Sforza (Kovac N 65), Elber, Pizarro (Jancker 65), Salihamidzic (Santa Cruz 71).
Liverpool: Westerveld; Babbel, Carragher, Hamann, Henchoz, Hyypia, Gerrard (Biscan 65), McAllister, Heskey, Owen (Fowler 82), Riise (Murphy 68).
Referee: Pereira (Portugal).

INTERNATIONAL DIRECTORY

The latest available information has been given regarding numbers of clubs and players registered with FIFA, the world governing body. Where known, official colours are listed. With European countries, League tables show a number of signs. * indicates relegated teams, + play-offs, *+ relegated after play-offs, ++ promoted.

There are 197 member associations and one provisional member, Palestine. The four home countries, England, Scotland, Northern Ireland and Wales, are dealt with elsewhere in the Yearbook; but basic details appear in this directory.

EUROPE

ALBANIA

The Football Association of Albania, Rruga Dervish Hima Nr. 31, Tirana.
Founded: 1930; *Number of Clubs:* 49; *Number of Players:* 5,192; *National Colours:* All red.
Telephone: 00–355–42 27 877; *Cable:* ALBSPORT TIRANA; *Telex:* 2228 bfssh ab. *Fax:* 00 355–42 50 275.

International matches 2001
Germany (a) 1-2, England (h) 1-3, Turkey (a) 2-0, Greece (a) 0-1, Germany (h) 0-2, Finland (h) 0-2, England (a) 0-2.

League Championship wins (1930–37; 1945–2002)
SK Tirana 19 (including 17 Nentori 8); Dinamo Tirana 16; Partizani Tirana 15; Vllaznia 9; Flamurtari 1; Elbasan 2 (including Labinoti 1); Skenderbeu 1; Teuta 1.

Cup wins (1948–2001)
Partizani Tirana 14; Dinamo Tirana 12; SK Tirana 9 (including 17 Nentori 6); Vllaznia 5; Teuta 3; Elbasan 3 (including Labintoti 1); Flamurtari 2; Apolonia 1.

Final League Table 2001–02

	P	W	D	L	F	A	Pts
Dinamo	26	19	6	1	55	15	63
SK Tirana	26	19	5	2	52	15	62
Partizani	26	13	7	6	41	24	46
Teuta	26	12	6	8	31	19	42
Vllaznia	26	11	5	10	43	28	38
Shkumbini	26	10	3	13	32	36	33
Lushnja	26	8	7	11	32	32	31
Flamurtari	26	8	5	13	26	32	29
Apolonia	26	9	2	15	22	48	29
Beselidhja	26	6	10	10	20	25	28
Bylis	26	7	7	12	28	42	28
Erzeni	26	9	1	16	31	54	28
Luftetari	26	8	4	14	25	49	28
Tomori	26	7	4	15	29	48	25

ANDORRA

Federacio Andorrana de Futbol, C/Sant Salvador, 10-2-5, Edifici Galerias Plaza, Andorra la Vella, Principat d'Andorra.
Founded: 1994; *Number of Clubs:* 12; *Number of Players:* 300; *National Colours:* Yellow shirts, red shorts, yellow stockings.
Telephone: 00376 862003; *Fax:* 00376 862006.

International matches 2001
Portugal (a) 0-3, Holland (h) 0-5, Republic of Ireland (h) 0-3, Republic of Ireland (a) 1-3, Portugal (h) 1-7, Holland (a) 0-4.

League Championship wins (1996–2002)
Principat 3; Dicoansa 1; Constelacio 1; St Julia 1; Encamp 1.

Cup wins (1996–2000)
Principat 4; Constelacio 1.

Qualifying Table 2001–02

	P	W	D	L	F	A	Pts
Encamp	14	11	1	2	34	12	34
St Julia	14	10	2	2	35	13	32
Santa Coloma	14	9	4	1	43	17	31
Rangers	14	5	4	5	23	20	19
Principat	14	5	2	7	28	28	17
Lusitanos	14	3	3	8	19	30	12
Inter	14	2	1	11	15	39	7
Sporting	14	1	3	10	11	49	6

Final League Table 2001–02

	P	W	D	L	F	A	Pts
Encamp	20	14	2	4	43	18	44
St Julia	20	13	4	3	51	21	43
Santa Coloma	20	12	6	2	57	23	42
Rangers	20	6	5	9	28	36	23

Relegation Table 2001–02

	P	W	D	L	F	A	Pts
Lusitanos	20	6	4	10	32	34	22
Principat	20	6	4	10	32	40	22
Inter	20	6	2	12	23	42	20
Sporting	20	2	3	15	15	62	9

ARMENIA

Football Federation of Armenia, 9, Abovian Str. 375001 Erevan, Armenia.
Founded: 1992; *Number of Clubs:* 32; *Number of Players:* 15,000; *National Colours:* Red shirts, blue shorts, orange stockings.
Telephone: 00374 2/589480; *Telex:* 243337 minor su; *Fax:* 00374 2/151573.

International matches 2001
Uzbekistan (a) 2-0, Wales (h) 2-2, Poland (a) 0-4, Belarus (h) 0-0, Poland (h) 1-1, Wales (a) 0-0, Ukraine (a) 0-3, Norway (h) 1-4.

League Championship wins (1992–2001)
Shirak Gyumri 4*; Pyunik 3; Ararat Erevan 2*; Homenmen 1; FC Erevan 1; Tsement 1; Araks 1.
*Includes one unofficial title.

Cup wins (1992–2002)
Ararat Erevan 5; Tsement 2; Pyunik 2; Banants 1; Mika 1.

Final League Table 2001

	P	W	D	L	F	A	Pts
Pyunik	22	17	2	3	77	23	53
Zvartnots	22	16	0	6	52	21	48
Spartak (ex Araks)	22	15	3	4	57	13	48
Shirak	22	14	5	3	52	19	47
Ararat	22	13	3	6	42	22	42
Mika	22	12	5	5	44	20	41
Banants	22	10	4	8	46	28	34
Lemagorts	22	5	3	14	25	63	18
Dinamo	22	4	4	14	18	48	16
Kotaik	22	3	3	16	19	65	12
Karabach	22	2	6	14	19	63	12
Lori*	22	1	2	19	17	83	5

Kilikia expelled after one match.
Cup Final: Pyunik 2, Zvartnots 0.

AUSTRIA

Oesterreichischer Fussball-Bund, Ernst-Happel Stadion, Postfach 340, Meierestrasse, A-1021 Wien.
Founded: 1904; *Number of Clubs:* 2,081; *Number of Players:* 253,576; *National Colours:* White shirts, black shorts, white stockings.
Telephone: 0043 1 727 180; *Cable:* FOOTBALL WIEN; *Telex:* 111919 oefb a; *Fax:* 0043 1 728 1632.

International matches 2001
Croatia (a) 0-1, Bosnia (a) 1-1, Israel (h) 2-1, Liechtenstein (h) 2-0, Switzerland (h) 1-2, Spain (a) 0-4, Bosnia (h) 2-0, Israel (a) 1-1, Turkey (h) 0-1, Turkey (a) 0-5.

League Championship wins (1912–2002)
Rapid Vienna 30; FK Austria 22; Tirol-Svarowski-Innsbruck 10; Admira-Energie-Wacker 9; First Vienna 6; Wiener Sportklub 3; Austria Salzburg 3; Sturm Graz 2; FAC 1; Hakoah 1; Linz ASK 1; WAF 1; Voest Linz 1.

Cup wins (1919-2002)
FK Austria 25; Rapid Vienna 14; TS Innsbruck (formerly Wacker Innsbruck) 7; Admira-Energie-Wacker (formerly Sportklub Admira & Admira-Energie) 5; First Vienna 3; Sturm Graz 3; Graz 3; Linz ASK 1; Wacker Vienna 1; WAF 1; Wiener Sportklub 1; Stockerau 1; Ried 1; Karnten 1.

Final League Table 2001-02

	P	W	D	L	F	A	Pts
Innsbruck	36	23	6	7	63	20	75
Sturm Graz	36	18	11	7	68	42	65
Graz	36	17	12	7	69	39	63
FK Austria	36	14	11	11	53	38	53
Karnten	36	14	8	14	40	52	50
Salzburg	36	13	10	13	42	40	49
Bregenz	36	12	9	15	51	70	45
Rapid	36	11	10	15	37	49	43
Ried	36	9	9	18	37	54	36
Admira*	36	3	6	27	25	81	15

Top scorer: Brunmayr (Graz) 27.
Cup Final: Graz 3, Sturm Graz 2.

AZERBAIJAN

Association of Football Federations of Azerbaijan, Husu Haciyev kuc., 42, 370009 Baku, Azerbaijan.
Founded: 1992; *Number of Clubs:* 1,500;. *Number of Players:* 95,000; *National Colours:* White shirts with blue stripes, blue shorts, white stockings.
Telephone: 00994 12 94 49 16; *Cable:* FOOTBALL ASSOCIATION, AZ; *Fax:* 00994 12 98 93 93.

International matches 2001
Uzbekistan (a) 1-2, Belarus (h) 1-0, Moldova (h) 0-0, Slovakia (a) 1-3, Georgia (a) 0-1, Turkey (a) 0-3, Slovakia (h) 2-0, Moldova (a) 0-2, Macedonia (h) 1-1, Sweden (a) 0-3.

League Championship wins (1992-2002)
Kopaz 3; Shamkir 3; Karabach 2; Neftchi 2; Turan 1.

Cup wins (1992-2001)
Kopaz 4; Neftchi 3; Karabach 1; Inshatchi 1; Shafa 1.

Final League Table 2001-02

	P	W	D	L	F	A	Pts
Shamkir	22	15	5	2	54	14	50
Shafa	22	13	5	4	40	13	44
Neftchi	22	13	5	4	35	8	44
Karabach	22	13	1	8	41	27	40
Kopaz	22	12	2	8	37	31	38
Khazar	22	11	3	8	33	24	36
Turan	22	10	5	7	27	27	35
Araz	22	6	6	10	25	43	24
Tefekkur	22	6	4	12	23	47	22
Shahdagh	22	5	5	12	16	39	20
OIK*	22	4	3	15	15	35	15
Dinamo Baku*	22	0	4	18	10	48	4

BELARUS

Belarus Football Association, 8-2 Kyrov Str. 220600 Minsk, Belarus.
Founded: 1989; *Number of Clubs:* 455; *Number of Players:* 120,000; *National Colours:* All green.
Telephone: 007 0172 375 272325; *Telex:*252175 athlet su; *Fax:* 007 0172 27 29 20.

International matches 2001
Uzbekistan (a) 0-2, Azerbaijan (a) 0-1, Ukraine (a) 0-0, Norway (h) 2-1, Armenia (a) 0-0, Norway (a) 1-1, Ukraine (h) 0-2, Poland (h) 4-1, Wales (a) 0-1.

League Championship wins (1992-2001)
Dynamo Minsk 6; Slavia Mozyr (formerly MPKC Mozyr) 2; Dnepr Mogilev 1; BATE Borisov 1; Belshina 1.

Cup wins (1992-2002)
Belshina 3; Dynamo Minsk 2; Slavia Mozyr (formerly MPKC Mozyr) 2; Neman 1; Dynamo 93 Minsk 1; Lokomotiv 96 1; Gomel 1.

Final League Table 2001

	P	W	D	L	F	A	Pts
Belshina	26	17	4	5	43	20	55
Dynamo Minsk	26	16	5	5	52	21	53
BATE Borisov	26	16	3	7	54	31	51
Neman	26	14	8	4	44	20	50
Shakhter	26	13	7	6	43	24	46
Gomel	26	13	5	8	36	24	44
Slavia	26	13	5	8	49	27	44
Torpedo Minsk	26	10	7	9	31	32	37
Dnepr Mogilev	26	8	7	11	29	37	31
Molodechno	26	8	5	13	23	47	29
Dynamo Brest	26	8	5	13	26	38	29
Lokomotiv 96	26	4	7	15	18	51	19
Naftan*	26	4	2	20	18	51	14
Vedrich 97*	26	2	2	22	17	60	8

Cup Final: Gomel 2, BATE Borisov 0

BELGIUM

Union Royale Belge Des Societes De Football Association, 145 Avenue Houba de Strooper, B-1020 Bruxelles.
Founded: 1895; *Number of Clubs:* 2,120; *Number of Players:* 390,468; *National Colours:* All red.
Telephone: 0032 2 477 12 11; *Cable:* URBSFA BRUXELLES; *Telex:* 23257 bvbfbf b; *Fax:* 0032 2 478 23 91.

International matches 2001
San Marino (h) 10-1, Scotland (a) 2-2, Czech Republic (a) 1-1, Latvia (h) 3-1, San Marino (a) 4-1, Finland (a) 1-4, Scotland (h) 2-0, Croatia (a) 0-1, Czech Republic (h) 1-0, Czech Republic (a) 1-0.

League Championship wins (1896-2002)
Anderlecht 26; Union St Gilloise 11; FC Brugge 11; Standard Liege 8; Beerschot 7; RC Brussels 6; FC Liege 5; Daring Brussels 5; Antwerp 4; Mechelen 4; Lierse SK 4; SV Brugge 3; Beveren 2; Genk 2; RWD Molenbeek 1.

Cup wins (1954-2002)
Anderlecht 8; FC Brugge 8; Standard Liege 5; Beerschot 2; Waterschei 2; Beveren 2; Gent 2; Antwerp 2; Lierse SK 2; Genk 2; Racing Doornik 1; Waregem 1; SV Brugge 1; Mechelen 1; FC Liege 1; Ekeren 1; Westerlo 1.

Final League Table 2001-02

	P	W	D	L	F	A	Pts
Genk	34	20	12	2	85	43	72
FC Brugge	34	22	4	8	74	41	70
Anderlecht	34	18	12	4	71	37	66
Gent	34	16	10	8	62	51	58
Standard Liege	34	15	12	7	57	38	57
Mouscron	34	17	5	12	68	40	56
Lokeren	34	15	10	9	43	33	55
St Truiden	34	16	5	13	52	47	53
Beerschot	34	11	16	7	68	51	49
Molenbeek	34	13	5	16	50	59	44
La Louviere	34	12	8	14	41	52	44
Charleroi	34	11	6	17	40	63	39
Lommel	34	10	9	15	54	66	39
Westerlo	34	9	9	16	49	61	36
Lierse	34	9	8	17	55	65	35
Royal Antwerp	34	7	10	17	47	67	31
Aalst*	34	4	9	21	32	73	21
Beveren*	34	2	8	24	30	91	14

Top scorer: Sonck (Genk) 30.
Cup Final: Mouscron 1, FC Brugge 3.

BOSNIA HERZEGOVINA

Bosnia & Herzegovina Football Federation, Sime Milutinovico, 12/1 71000 Sarajevo.
Founded: 1992; *National Colours:* White shirts, blue shorts, white stockings.
Telephone: 00387 71/213881; *Fax:* 00387 71/444332.

International matches 2001
Bangladesh (h) 2-0, Hungary (h) 1-1, Austria (h) 1-1, Liechtenstein (a) 3-0, Spain (a) 1-4, Iran (h) 2-2, South Africa (h) 4-2, Iran (a) 0-4, Malta (h) 2-0, Israel (h) 0-0, Austria (a) 0-2, Liechtenstein (h) 5-0.

League Championship wins (1996-2002)
Zeljeznicar 3; Celik 2; Sarajevo 1; Brotnjo 1.

Cup wins (1996-2002)
Sarajevo 3; Zeljeznicar 2; Bosna 1; Celik 1.

Muslim Final League Table 2001–02

	P	W	D	L	F	A	Pts
Zeljeznicar	30	19	5	6	59	26	62
Siroki	30	14	9	7	43	24	51
Brotnjo	30	14	5	11	45	27	47
Sarajevo	30	13	8	9	50	34	47
Zrinjski	30	13	7	10	35	38	46
Celik	30	12	7	11	39	30	43
Orasje	30	13	4	13	38	38	43
Velez	30	13	3	14	44	46	42
Jedinstvo	30	12	5	13	33	39	41
Sloboda	30	11	7	12	32	28	40
Posusje	30	12	4	14	30	38	40
Bosna	30	11	6	13	33	46	39
Olimpik	30	11	5	14	40	46	38
Troglav	30	8	8	14	33	49	32
Grude*	30	8	7	15	23	43	31
Iskra*	30	7	8	15	25	48	29

Croatian Final League Table 2001–02

	P	W	D	L	F	A	Pts
Leotar	30	20	2	8	67	25	62
Kozara	30	17	5	8	58	35	56
Borac	30	16	7	7	45	25	55
Glasinac	30	17	3	10	49	39	54
Mladost	30	16	4	10	45	29	52
Rudar Ugljevik	30	14	8	8	38	31	50
Slavija	30	13	5	12	34	40	44
Ljubic	30	12	6	12	34	26	42
Modrica	30	11	7	12	31	38	40
Omladinac	30	11	6	13	40	40	39
Radnik	30	12	1	17	33	42	37
Boksit	30	10	6	14	41	43	36
Sloboda	30	10	5	15	25	49	35
Polet	30	9	2	19	28	56	29
BSK*	30	7	7	16	29	45	28
Jedinstvo*	30	6	4	20	25	59	22

Cup Final: Sarajevo 2, Zeljeznicar 1.

There are three separate leagues in Bosnia, Muslim, Serbian and Croatian. An agreement was reached on play-offs for an overall winner between Muslim and Croatian League in 2000.

BULGARIA

Bulgarian Football Union, Karnigradska 19, BG-1000 Sofia.
Founded: 1923; *Number of Clubs:* 376; *Number of Players:* 48,240; *National Colours:* White shirts, green shorts, white stockings.
Telephone: 00359 2 987 74 90; *Cable:* BULFUTBOL SOFIA; *Telex:* 23145 bfs bg; *Fax:* 00359 2 986 2538.

International matches 2001
Mexico (a) 2-0, Jamaica (a) 0-0, Jordan (a) 2-0, Iceland (h) 2-1, Northern Ireland (h) 4-3, Norway (a) 1-2, Northern Ireland (a) 1-0, Iceland (a) 1-1, Macedonia (h) 1-0, Malta (a) 2-0, Denmark (h) 0-2, Czech Republic (a) 0-6.

League Championship wins (1925–2002)
CSKA Sofia 28; Levski Sofia 22; Slavia Sofia 7; Vladislav Varna 3; Lokomotiv Sofia 3; Litets 2; Trakia Plovdiv 2; AC 23 Sofia 1; Botev Plovdiv 1; SC Sofia 1; Sokol Varna 1; Spartak Plovdiv 1; Tichka Varna 1; JSZ Sofia 1; Beroe Stara Zagora 1; Etur 1.

Cup wins (1946–2002)
Levski Sofia 21; CSKA Sofia 16; Slavia Sofia 7; Lokomotiv Sofia 4; Botev Plovdiv 1; Spartak Plovdiv 1; Spartak Sofia 1; Marek Stanke 1; Trakia Plovdiv 1; Spartak Varna 1; Sliven 1; Litets 1.

Qualifying League Table 2001–02

	P	W	D	L	F	A	Pts
Levski Sofia	26	20	5	1	58	21	65
Litets	26	16	7	3	50	27	55
Lokomotiv Plovdiv	26	16	5	5	42	23	53
CSKA Sofia	26	15	7	4	48	17	52
Neftochimik	26	12	6	8	35	25	42
Slavia Sofia	26	10	7	9	30	32	37
Spartak Pleven	26	10	3	13	40	44	33
Lokomotiv Sofia	26	7	8	11	33	32	29
Spartak Varna	26	5	11	10	29	39	26
Chernomorets	26	7	5	14	24	54	26
Cherno Varna	26	6	6	14	28	36	24
Marek	26	6	6	14	22	42	24
Belasitsa	26	6	5	15	21	35	23
Beroe	26	3	5	18	13	46	14

Championship Table 2001–02

	P	W	D	L	F	A	Pts
Levski Sofia	10	7	2	1	19	6	56
Litets	10	7	1	2	16	7	50
CSKA Sofia	10	4	0	6	12	11	38
Lokomotiv Plovdiv	10	2	1	7	6	18	34
Slavia Sofia	10	4	1	5	11	16	32
Neftochimik	10	2	3	5	9	15	30

Promotion/Relegation Table 2001–02

	P	W	D	L	F	A	Pts
Marek	14	8	2	4	25	16	38
Lokomotiv Sofia	14	7	1	6	16	16	37
Spartak Varna	14	7	2	5	21	12	36
Cherno Varna	14	6	5	3	19	15	35
Chernomorets	14	6	4	4	17	15	35
Spartak Plovdiv+	14	5	1	8	18	22	33
Belasitsa*	14	6	2	6	13	15	32
Beroe*	14	1	3	10	7	25	13

Cup Final: Levski Sofia 3, CSKA Sofia 1.

CROATIA

Croatian Football Federation, Illica 31, CRO-10000 Zagreb, Croatia.
Founded: 1912; *Number of Clubs:* 1,221; *Number of Players:* 78,127; *National Colours:* Red/white shirts, white shorts, blue stockings.
Telephone: 00385 1/4554100. *Fax:* 00385 1 42 46 39.

International matches 2001
Romania (h) 2-2, Austria (h) 1-0, Latvia (h) 4-1, Greece (h) 2-2, San Marino (h) 4-0, Latvia (a) 1-0, Republic of Ireland (a) 2-2, Scotland (a) 0-0, San Marino (a) 4-0, Belgium (h) 1-0, South Korea (a) 0-2, South Korea (a) 1-1.

League Championship wins (1941–44; 1992–2002)
Dynamo Zagreb (formerly Croatia Zagreb) 6; Hajduk Split 4; Gradanski 3; Concordia 1; Zagreb 1.

Cup wins (1993–2002)
Dynamo Zagreb (formerly Croatia Zagreb) 6; Hajduk Split 3; Osijek 1.

Final League Table 2001–02

	P	W	D	L	F	A	Pts
Zagreb	30	20	7	3	71	24	67
Hajduk Split	30	20	5	5	61	28	65
Dynamo Zagreb	30	18	5	7	58	30	59
Varteks	30	17	6	7	58	40	57
Rijeka	30	15	6	9	46	37	51
Slaven	30	11	9	10	34	36	42
Pomorac	30	12	4	14	36	41	40
Osijek	30	11	4	15	45	48	37
Zadar	30	9	9	12	43	47	36
Cibalia	30	9	9	12	34	37	36
Sibenik	30	10	6	14	33	36	36
Kamen	30	9	8	13	28	46	35
Dragovoljac*	30	9	7	14	34	45	34
Cakovec*	30	9	5	16	31	44	32
Marsonia*	30	8	6	16	37	46	30
TSK*	30	4	2	24	31	95	14

Cup Final: Dynamo Zagreb 1, 1, Varteks 1, 0.

CYPRUS

Cyprus Football Association, 1 Stasinos Str., Engomi, P.O. Box 5071, CY-2404 Nicosia.
Founded: 1934; *Number of Clubs:* 85; *Number of Players:* 6,000; *National Colours:* Blue shirts, white shorts, blue stockings.
Telephone: 00357 2 /352341; *Cable:* FOOTBALL CYPRUS; *Telex:* 3880 football cy; *Fax:* 00357 2/590544.

International matches 2001
Lithuania (h) 1-2, Ukraine (h) 4-3, Republic of Ireland (h) 0-4, Estonia (h) 2-2, Holland (a) 0-4, Portugal (a) 0-6, Estonia (a) 2-2, Portugal (h) 1-3, Republic of Ireland (a) 0-4, Greece (a) 2-1.

League Championship wins (1935–2002)
Omonia 18; Apoel 17; Anorthosis 11; AEL 5; EPA 3; Olympiakos 3; Apollon 2; Pezoporikos 2; Chetin Kayal 1; Trast 1.

Cup wins (1935–2002)
Apoel 17; Omonia 11; AEL 6; Anorthosis 6; EPA 5; Apollon 5; Trast 3; Chetin Kayal 2; Olympiakos 1; Pezoporikos 1; Salamina 1.

Final League Table 2001–02

	P	W	D	L	F	A	Pts
Apoel	26	18	5	3	66	22	59
Anorthosis	26	18	4	4	71	31	58
AEL	26	17	3	6	47	27	54
Omonia	26	17	2	7	56	35	53
Olympiakos	26	13	3	10	53	45	42
Ethnikos Ahnas	26	13	3	10	46	38	42
AEK	26	13	2	11	56	42	41
Paralimni	26	11	6	9	42	38	39
Apollon	26	10	6	10	56	48	36
Evagoras	26	10	6	10	54	46	36
Alki	26	8	7	11	37	37	31
Ethnikos Ashia*	26	5	3	18	40	70	18
Doxa*	26	2	3	21	30	84	9
Ermis*	26	0	1	25	16	107	1

Cup Final: Anorthosis 1, Ethnikos Ahnas 0.

CZECH REPUBLIC

Football Association of Czech Republic, Diskarska 100, 169 00 Prague 6 - Strahov, Czech Republic.
Founded: 1901; *Number of Clubs:* 3,836; *Number of Players:* 319,500; *National Colours:* Red shirts, white shorts, blue stockings.
Telephone: 00422 20513575; *Cable:* SPORTSVAZ PRAHA; *Telex:* 122650 cstv c; *Fax:* 004202 3335 3107.

International matches 2001
Macedonia (a) 1-1, Northern Ireland (a) 1-0, Denmark (h) 0-0, Belgium (h) 1-1, Denmark (a) 1-2, Northern Ireland (h) 3-1, South Korea (h) 5-0, Iceland (a) 1-3, Malta (h) 3-2, Bulgaria (h) 6-0, Belgium (a) 0-1, Belgium (h) 0-1.

League Championship wins (1926–93)
Sparta Prague 19; Slavia Prague 12; Dukla Prague (prev. UDA) 11; Slovan Bratislava 7; Spartak Trnava 5; Banik Ostrava 3; Inter-Bratislava 1; Spartak Hradec Kralove 1; Viktoria Zizkov 1; Zbrojovka Brno 1; Bohemians 1; Vitkovice 1.

Cup wins (1961–93)
Dukla Prague 8; Sparta Prague 8; Slovan Bratislava 5; Spartak Trnava 4; Banik Ostrava 3; Lokomotiv Kosice 3; TJ Gottwaldov 1; Dunajska Streda 1.
From 1993–94, there were two separate countries; the Czech Republic and Slovakia.

League Championship wins (1994–2002)
Sparta Prague 7; Slavia Prague 1; Slovan Liberec 1.

Cup wins (1994–2002)
Slavia Prague 3; Viktoria Zizkov 2; Spartak Hradec Kralove 1; Sparta Prague 1; Jablonec 1; Slovan Liberec 1.

Final League Table 2001–02

	P	W	D	L	F	A	Pts
Slovan Liberec	30	19	7	4	55	26	64
Sparta Prague	30	20	3	7	55	19	63
Viktoria Zizkov	30	19	6	5	42	20	63
Bohemians	30	14	6	10	40	35	48
Slavia Prague	30	12	11	7	45	34	47
Banik Ostrava	30	12	8	10	43	36	44
Teplice	30	12	5	13	37	41	41
Jablonec	30	10	10	10	35	33	40
Artikel Brno	30	10	10	10	34	42	40
Sigma Olomouc	30	9	10	11	29	31	37
Synot	30	10	6	14	31	38	36
Hredec Kralove	30	9	8	13	28	42	35
Marila Pribram	30	9	7	14	27	39	34
Chmel Blsany	30	8	5	17	35	51	29
Petra Drnovice*	30	7	5	18	31	45	26
Opava*	30	5	3	22	23	58	18

Cup Final: Slavia Prague 2, Sparta Prague 1.

DENMARK

Danish Football Association, Idraettens Hus, Brondby Stadion 20, DK-2605, Brondby.
Founded: 1889; *Number of Clubs:* 1,555; *Number of Players:* 268,517; *National Colours:* Red shirts, white shorts, red stockings.
Telephone: 0045 43/262222; *Cable:* DANSKBOLDSPIL COPENHAGEN; *Telex:* 15545 dbu dk; *Fax:* 0045 43/262245.

International matches 2001
Malta (a) 5-0, Czech Republic (a) 0-0, Slovenia (h) 3-0, Czech Republic (h) 2-1, Malta (h) 2-1, France (a) 0-1,

Northern Ireland (h) 1-1, Bulgaria (a) 2-0, Iceland (h) 6-0, Holland (h) 1-1.

League Championship wins (1913–2002)
KB Copenhagen 15; B 93 Copenhagen 10; AB (Akademisk) 9; Brondby 9; B 1903 Copenhagen 7; Frem 6; Esbjerg BK 5; Vejle BK 5; AGF Aarhus 5; Hvidovre 3; Odense BK 3; AaB Aalborg 2; B 1909 Odense 2; Koge BK 2; Lyngby 2; FC Copenhagen 2; Silkeborg 1; Herfolge 1.

Cup wins (1955–2002)
Aarhus GF 9; Vejle BK 6; OB Odense 4; Randers Freja 3; Lyngby 3; Brondby 3; B1909 Odense 2; Aalborg BK 2; Esbjerg BK 2; Frem 2; B 1903 Copenhagen 2; FC Copenhagen 2; B 93 Copenhagen 1; KB Copenhagen 1; Vanlose 1; Hvidovre 1; B1913 Odense 1, AB Copenhagen 1, Viborg 1; Silkeborg 1.

Final League Table 2001–02

	P	W	D	L	F	A	Pts
Brondby	33	20	9	4	74	28	69
FC Copenhagen	33	20	9	4	62	25	69
Midtjylland	33	16	9	8	47	27	57
Aalborg	33	16	6	11	52	45	54
AB Copenhagen	33	13	11	9	48	38	50
Odense	33	13	10	10	56	51	49
Esbjerg	33	13	6	14	42	44	45
Viborg	33	10	11	12	46	45	41
Silkeborg	33	8	17	8	41	50	32
Aarhus	33	7	10	16	42	56	31
Vejle*	33	6	10	17	38	72	28
Lyngby*	33	2	9	22	25	92	15

Top scorers: Madsen (Brondby) 22, Dalgas (Odense) 22.
Cup Final: FC Copenhagen 1, Odense 2.

ENGLAND

The Football Association, 25 Soho Square, London W1D 4FA.
Founded: 1863; *Number of Clubs:* 42,000; *Number of Players:* 2,250,000; *National Colours:* White shirts with vertical red stripe, navy shorts, white stockings.
Telephone: 020 7745 4545, 020 7402 7151; *Fax:* 020 7745 4546; *Website:* www.the-fa.org

ESTONIA

Estonian Football Association, Voidu 16, Tallinn EE 0012.
Founded: 1921; *Number of Clubs:* 40; *Number of Players:* 12,000; *National Colours:* Blue shirts, black shorts, white stockings.
Telephone: 00372 6/542715, 542716, 542717; *Fax:* 00372 6/542719.

International matches 2001
Egypt (a) 3-3, Cyprus (a) 2-2, Moldova (a) 0-0, Finland (h) 1-1, Holland (h) 2-4, Republic of Ireland (h) 0-2, Latvia (a) 1-3, Lithuania (h) 2-5, Cyprus (h) 2-2, Holland (a) 0-5, Portugal (a) 0-5, Greece (a) 2-4, Kazakhstan (h) 0-0.

League Championship wins (1922–40; 1992–2001)
Sport 8; Estonia 5; Flora Tallinn 5; Norma Tallinn 2; Tallinn JK 2; Kalev 2; Levadia 2; LFLS 1; Olimpia 1; Lantana 1.

Cup wins (1992–2001)
Levadia (merged with Sadam) 4; VMV Tallinn 1; Nikol Tallinn 1; Norma Tallinn 1; Lantana 1; Flora Tallinn 1; Trans 1.

Final League Table 2001

	P	W	D	L	F	A	Pts
Flora	28	21	5	2	62	18	68
VMK	28	16	8	4	77	30	56
Levadia	28	16	7	5	72	35	55
Trans	28	16	3	9	79	35	51
Tulevik	28	11	6	11	41	37	39
Levadia Tallinn	28	6	5	17	30	78	23
Lootus+	28	5	4	19	21	53	17
Kuressaare*	28	2	1	25	18	114	7

Relegation/promotion play-off: Valga 2, 0, Lootus 1, 1.
Lootus remain; Valga stay in Division 2.
Top scorer: Gruznov (Trans) 37.

FAEROE ISLANDS

Fotboltssamband Foroya, The Faeroes' Football Assn., Gundalur, P.O. Box 3028, FR-110, Torshavn.
Founded: 1979; *Number of Clubs:* 16; *Number of Players:* 1,014; *National Colours:* White shirts, blue shorts, white stockings.
Telephone: 00298 31 6707/457607; *Telex:* 81328 nspkkl fa; *Fax:* 00298 31 9079.

International matches 2001
Sweden (a) 0-0, Luxembourg (a) 2-0, Russia (a) 0-1, Switzerland (h) 0-1, Yugoslavia (h) 0-6, Yugoslavia (a) 0-2, Luxembourg (h) 1-0, Russia (h) 0-3, Slovenia (a) 0-3.

League Championship wins (1942–2001)
KI Klaksvik 16; HB Torshavn 15; TB Tvoroyri 7; GI Gotu 7; B36 Torshavn 7; B68 Toftir 3; SI Sorvag 1; IF Fuglafjordur 1; B71 Sandur 1; VB 1.

Cup wins (1955–2001)
HB Torshavn 25; KI Klaksvik 5; GI Gotu 5; TB Tvoroyri 4; B36 Torshavn 2; VB Vagur 1; NSI Runavik 1; B71 Sandur 1.

Final League Table 2001

	P	W	D	L	F	A	Pts
B36	18	15	1	2	55	15	46
GI	18	13	3	2	53	20	42
B68	18	9	4	5	39	25	31
VB	18	9	3	6	43	24	30
NSI	18	8	4	6	23	21	28
KI	18	8	1	9	27	38	25
HB	18	7	2	9	32	25	23
EB/Streymur	18	5	1	12	20	34	16
B71*+	18	3	1	14	17	52	10
Vagar*	18	3	0	15	19	76	9

Relegation/promotion play-off: Skala 0, 4, B71 1, 1.
Skala promoted; B71 relegated.
Cup Final: B36 1, KI 0.

FINLAND

Suomen Palloliitto Finlands Bollfoerbund, Lantinen Brahenkatu 2, P.O. Box 179, SF-00511 Helsinki.
Founded: 1907; *Number of Clubs:* 1,135; *Number of Players:* 66,100; *National Colours:* White shirts, blue shorts, white stockings.
Telephone: 00358 0 9701 01 01; *Cable:* SUOMIFOT-BOLL HELSINKI; *Telex:* 126033 spl sf; *Fax:* 00358 0 9701 01 099.

International matches 2001
Sweden (a) 1-0, Kuwait (a) 3-4, Oman (a) 2-1, Oman (a) 2-0, Luxembourg (a) 1-0, England (a) 1-2, Hungary (a) 0-0, Estonia (a) 1-1, Germany (h) 2-2, Belgium (h) 4-1, Albania (a) 2-0, Greece (h) 5-1, Germany (a) 0-0.

League Championship wins (1949–2001)
HJK Helsinki 10; Valkeakosken Haka 8; Turun Palloseura 5; Kuopion Palloseura 5; Kuusysi 4; Lahden Reipas 3; IF Kamraterna 3; Ilves-Kissat 2; Jazz Pori 2; Kotkan TP 2; OPS Oulu 2; Torun Pyrkiva 1; IF Kronohagens 1; Helsinki PS 1; Kokkolan PV 1; Vasa 1; TPV Tampere 1; Tampere U 1.

Cup wins (1955–2001)
Valkeakosken Haka 10; Lahden Reipas 7; HJK Helsinki 7; Kotkan TP 4; Mikkeli 2; Kuusysi 2; Kuopion Palloseura 2; Ilves Tampere 2; TPS Turku 2; MyPa 2; IFK Abo 1; Drott 1; Helsinki PS 1; Pallo-Peikot 1; Rovaniemi PS 1; Jokerit 1 (formerly PK-35); Atlantis 1.

Final League Table 2001

	P	W	D	L	F	A	Pts
Tampere U	33	21	5	7	47	31	68
HJK Helsinki	33	19	10	4	64	19	67
MyPa	33	17	11	5	45	23	62
Haka	33	14	10	9	44	29	52
Inter	33	15	4	14	46	47	49
VPS	33	14	3	16	50	52	45
Atlantis	33	12	9	12	45	47	45
KuPS	33	9	10	14	37	48	37
Lahti	33	9	9	15	38	48	36
Jazz Pori	33	7	11	15	36	52	32
Jokerit*+	33	7	7	19	31	56	28
RoPS Rovaniemi*	33	5	9	19	25	56	24

Relegation/promotion play-off: Jaro 1, 4, Jokerit 1, 3.
Jaro promoted; Jokerit relegated.
Cup Final: Atlantis 1, Tampere U 0.

FRANCE

Federation Francaise De Football, 60 Bis Avenue D'Iena, F-75783 Paris, Cedex 16.
Founded: 1919; *Number of Clubs:* 21,629; *Number of Players:* 1,692,205; *National Colours:* Blue shirts, white shorts, red stockings.
Telephone: 0033 1 44 31 73 00; *Cable:* CEFI PARIS 034; *Telex:* 640000 fedfoot f; *Fax:* 0033 1 47 20 82 96.

International matches 2001
Germany (h) 1-0, Japan (h) 5-0, Spain (a) 1-2, Portugal (h) 4-0, South Korea (h) 5-0, Australia (a) 0-1, Mexico (h) 4-0, Brazil (h) 2-1, Japan (a) 1-0, Denmark (h) 1-0, Chile (a) 1-2, Algeria (h) 4-1, Australia (a) 1-1.

League Championship wins (1933–2002)
Saint Etienne 10; Olympique Marseille 8; Nantes 8; AS Monaco 7; Stade de Reims 6; Girondins Bordeaux 5; OGC Nice 4; Lille OSC 3; Paris St Germain 2; FC Sete 2; Sochaux 2; Racing Club Paris 1; Roubaix-Tourcoing 1; Strasbourg 1; Auxerre 1; Lens 1; Lyon 1.

Cup wins (1918–2002)
Olympique Marseille 10; Saint Etienne 6; AS Monaco 6; Lille OSC 5; Racing Club Paris 5; Red Star 5; Paris St Germain 4; Olympique Lyon 3; Girondins Bordeaux 3; OGC Nice 3; Nantes 3; Racing Club Strasbourg 3; CAS Genereaux 2; Nancy 2; Sedan 2; FC Sete 2; Stade de Reims 2; SO Montpellier 2; Stade Rennes 2; Auxerre 2; AS Cannes 1; Club Français 1; Excelsior Roubaix 1; Le Havre 1; Olympique de Pantin 1; CA Paris 1; Sochaux 1; Toulouse 1; Bastia 1; Metz 1; Lorient 1.

Final League Table 2001–02

	P	W	D	L	F	A	Pts
Lyon	34	20	6	8	62	32	66
Lens	34	18	10	6	55	30	64
Auxerre	34	16	11	7	48	38	59
Paris St Germain	34	15	13	6	43	24	58
Lille	34	15	11	8	39	32	56
Bordeaux	34	14	8	12	34	31	50
Troyes	34	13	8	13	40	35	47
Sochaux	34	12	10	12	41	40	46
Marseille	34	11	11	12	34	39	44
Nantes	34	12	7	15	35	41	43
Bastia	34	12	5	17	38	44	41
Rennes	34	11	8	15	40	51	41
Montpellier	34	9	13	12	28	31	40
Sedan	34	8	15	11	35	39	39
Monaco	34	9	12	13	36	41	39
Guingamp	34	9	8	17	34	57	35
Metz*	34	9	6	19	31	47	33
Lorient*	34	7	10	17	43	64	31

Top scorers: Cisse (Auxerre) 22, Pauleta (Bordeaux) 22.
Cup Final: Bastia 0, Lorient 1.

GEORGIA

Georgian Football Federation, 5 Shota Iamanidze Str, Tbillisi 380012, Georgia.
Founded: 1990; *Number of Clubs:* 4050. *Number of Players:* 115,000; *National Colours:* White shirts, black shorts, cherry stockings.
Telephone: 00995 32/960750; *Fax:* 00995 32/001128.

International matches 2001
Ukraine (h) 0-0, Romania (h) 0-2, Israel (h) 3-2, Azerbaijan (h) 1-0, Italy (h) 1-2, Hungary (a) 1-4, Luxembourg (a) 3-0, Hungary (h) 3-1, Lithuania (h) 2-0, Romania (a) 1-1.

League Championship wins (1990–2002)
Dynamo Tbilisi 10; Torpedo Kutaisi 3.

Cup wins (1992–2001)
Dynamo Tbilisi 7; Torpedo Kutaisi 2; Dynamo Batumi 1; Lokomotivi 1.

Qualifying Table 2001–02

	P	W	D	L	F	A	Pts
Torpedo Kutaisi	22	16	4	2	51	13	52
Lokomotivi	22	15	4	3	38	12	49
Dynamo Tbilisi	22	11	5	6	37	19	38
Dynamo Batumi	22	11	4	7	31	19	37
Kolkheti	22	10	5	7	32	29	35
Merani 91	22	10	4	8	34	28	34
WIT	22	9	6	7	33	28	33
Sioni	22	9	4	11	17	30	25
Metalurgi	22	4	8	10	17	34	20
Guria	22	3	6	13	14	44	15
Gorda	22	3	5	14	16	37	14
Samgurrali	22	3	5	14	14	41	14

Championship Table 2001–02

	P	W	D	L	F	A	Pts
Torpedo Kutaisi	10	7	1	2	12	5	48
Lokomotivi	10	7	1	2	18	6	47
Dynamo Tbilisi	10	8	1	1	20	1	44
Kolkheti	10	2	2	6	9	16	25
Dynamo Batumi	10	1	1	8	5	19	23
Merani 91	10	2	0	8	7	24	23

Relegation Table 2001–02

	P	W	D	L	F	A	Pts
WIT	10	5	3	2	18	8	35
Sioni	10	5	1	4	18	13	29
Metalurgi	10	5	2	3	16	10	27
Gorda	10	5	3	2	20	11	25
Samgurrali*	10	5	1	4	11	10	23
Guria*	10	0	0	10	4	29	8

GERMANY

Deutscher Fussball-Bund, Postfach 710265, D-60492, Frankfurt Am Main.
Founded: 1900; *Number of Clubs:* 26,760; *Number of Players:* 5,260,320; *National Colours:* White shirts, black shorts, white stockings.
Telephone: 0049 69 678 80; *Telex:* 416815 dfb d; *Fax:* 0049 69 678 82 66.

International matches 2001
France (a) 0-1, Albania (h) 2-1, Greece (a) 4-2, Slovakia (h) 2-0, Finland (a) 2-2, Albania (a) 2-0, Hungary (a) 5-2, England (h) 1-5, Finland (h) 0-0, Ukraine (a) 1-1, Ukraine (h) 4-1.

League Championship wins (1903–2002)
Bayern Munich 17; IFC Nuremberg 9; Schalke 04 7; Borussia Dortmund 6; SV Hamburg 6; Borussia Moenchengladbach 5; VfB Stuttgart 4; IFC Kaiserslautern 4; VfB Leipzig 3; SpVgg Furth 3; IFC Cologne 3; Werder Bremen 3; Viktoria Berlin 2; Hertha Berlin 2; Hanover 96 2; Dresden SC 2; Munich 1860 1; Union Berlin 1; FC Freiburg 1; Phoenix Karlsruhe 1; Karlsruher FV 1; Holstein Kiel 1; Fortuna Dusseldorf 1; Rapid Vienna 1; VfR Mannheim 1; Rot-Weiss Essen 1; Eintracht Frankfurt 1; Eintracht Brunswick 1.

Cup wins (1935–2002)
Bayern Munich 10; IFC Cologne 4; Eintracht Frankfurt 4; Werder Bremen 4; Schalke 04 4; IFC Nuremberg 3; SV Hamburg 3; Moenchengladbach 3; VfB Stuttgart 3; Dresden SC 2; Fortuna Dusseldorf 2; Karlsruhe SC 2; Munich 1860 2; Borussia Dortmund 2; Kaiserslautern 2; First Vienna 1; VfB Leipzig 1; Kickers Offenbach 1; Rapid Vienna 1; Rot-Weiss Essen 1; SW Essen 1; Bayer Uerdingen 1; Hannover 96 1; Leverkusen 1.

Final League Table 2001–02

	P	W	D	L	F	A	Pts
Borussia Dortmund	34	21	7	6	62	33	70
Leverkusen	34	21	6	7	77	38	69
Bayern Munich	34	20	8	6	65	25	68
Hertha	34	18	7	9	61	38	61
Schalke	34	18	7	9	52	36	61
Werder Bremen	34	17	5	12	54	43	56
Kaiserslautern	34	17	5	12	62	53	56
Stuttgart	34	13	11	10	47	43	50
Munich 1860	34	15	5	14	59	59	50
Wolfsburg	34	13	7	14	57	49	46
Hamburg	34	10	10	14	51	57	40
Moenchengladbach	34	9	12	13	41	53	39
Cottbus	34	9	8	17	36	60	35
Hansa Rostock	34	9	7	18	35	54	34
Nuremburg	34	10	4	20	34	57	34
Freiburg*	34	7	9	18	37	64	30
Cologne*	34	7	8	19	26	61	29
St Pauli*	34	4	10	20	37	70	22

Top scorers: Amoroso (Borussia Dortmund) 18, Max (Munich 1860) 18.
Cup Final: Schalke 4, Leverkusen 2.

GREECE

Federation Hellenique De Football, Singrou Avenue 137, 17121 Athens.
Founded: 1926; *Number of Clubs:* 4,050; *Number of Players:* 180,000; *National Colours:* White shirts, blue shorts, white stockings.
Telephone: 0030 1 933 88 50; *Cable:* FOOTBALL ATHENS; *Telex:* 215328 epo gr; *Fax:* 0030 1 935 96 66.

International matches 2001
Russia (h) 3-3, Germany (h) 2-4, Croatia (a) 2-2, Albania (h) 1-0, England (h) 0-2, Russia (a) 0-0, Finland (a) 1-5, England (a) 2-2, Estonia (h) 4-2, Cyprus (h) 1-2.

League Championship wins (1928–2002)
Olympiakos 31; Panathinaikos 18; AEK Athens 11; Aris Salonika 3; PAOK Salonika 2; Larissa 1.

Cup wins (1932–2002)
Olympiakos 21; Panathinaikos 16; AEK Athens 13; PAOK Salonika 3; Panionios 2; Aris Salonika 1; Ethnikos 1; Iraklis 1; Kastoria 1; Larissa 1; Ofi Crete 1.

Final League Table 2001–02

	P	W	D	L	F	A	Pts
Olympiakos	26	17	7	2	69	30	58
AEK Athens	26	19	1	6	65	28	58
Panathinaikos	26	16	7	3	53	25	55
PAOK Salonika	26	14	6	6	55	45	48
Xanthi	26	12	6	8	34	26	42
Iraklis	26	9	9	8	32	35	36
Panionios	26	8	11	7	37	33	35
Ofi Crete	26	9	6	11	32	35	33
Aris	26	7	8	11	25	34	29
Aigaleo	26	7	5	14	27	46	26
Akratitos	26	6	5	15	29	41	23
Ionikos	26	5	7	14	21	47	22
Panachaiki	26	3	9	14	26	55	18
Ethnikos*	26	4	5	17	19	44	17

Cup Final: AEK Athens 2, Olympiakos 1.

HOLLAND

Koninklijke Nederlandsche Voetbalbond, Woudenbergseweg 56-58, Postbus 515, NL-3700 AM, Zeist.
Founded: 1889; *Number of Clubs:* 3,097; *Number of Players:* 962,397; *National Colours:* Orange shirts, white shorts, orange stockings.
Telephone: 0031343 499211; *Cable:* VOETBAL ZEIST; *Telex:* 40497 knvb nl; *Fax:* 0031343 499189.

International matches 2001
Turkey (h) 0-0, Andorra (a) 5-0, Portugal (a) 2-2, Cyprus (h) 4-0, Estonia (a) 4-2, England (a) 2-0, Republic of Ireland (a) 0-1, Estonia (h) 5-0, Andorra (h) 4-0, Denmark (a) 1-1.

League Championship wins (1898–2002)
Ajax Amsterdam 28; PSV Eindhoven 16; Feyenoord 14; HVV The Hague 8; Sparta Rotterdam 6; Go Ahead Deventer 4; HBS The Hague 3; Willem II Tilburg 3; RAP 2; Heracles 2; ADO The Hague 2; Quick The Hague 1; BVV Den Bosch 1; NAC Breda 1; Eindhoven 1; Enschede 1; Volewijckers Amsterdam 1; Limburgia 1; Rapid JC Heerlen 3; DOS Utrecht 1; DWS Amsterdam 1; Haarlem 1; Be Quick Groningen 1; AZ 67 Alkmaar 1.

Cup wins (1899–2002)
Ajax Amsterdam 15; Feyenoord 10; PSV Eindhoven 7; Quick The Hague 4; AZ 67 Alkmaar 3; Rotterdam 3; DFC 2; Fortuna Geleen 2; Haarlem 2; HBS The Hague 2; RCH Haarlem 2; Roda 2; VOC 2; Wageningen 2; Willem II Tilburg 2; FC Den Haag 2; Twente Enschede 2; Concordia Rotterdam 1; CVV 1; Eindhoven 1; HVV The Hague 1; Longa 1; Quick Nijmegen 1; RAP 1; Roermond 1; Schoten 1; Velocitas Breda 1; Velocitas Groningen 1; VSV 1; VUC 1; VVV Groningen 1; ZFC 1; NAC Breda 1; Utrecht 1.

Final League Table 2001–02

	P	W	D	L	F	A	Pts
Ajax	34	22	7	5	73	30	73
PSV Eindhoven	34	20	8	6	77	32	68
Feyenoord	34	19	7	8	68	29	64
Heerenveen	34	17	9	8	57	27	60
Vitesse	34	16	12	6	45	34	60
NAC Breda	34	15	9	10	55	52	54
Utrecht	34	14	9	11	60	51	51
RKC Waalwijk	34	14	6	14	49	44	48
NEC Nijmegen	34	13	6	15	38	59	45
AZ	34	12	7	15	43	45	43
Willem II	34	10	13	11	54	61	43
Twente	34	10	12	12	41	41	42
Roda JC	34	11	8	15	33	45	41
De Graafschap	34	10	7	17	43	55	37

Groningen	34	10	7	17	40	59	37
Den Bosch*	34	8	9	17	40	55	33
Sparta*	34	4	12	18	26	75	24
Fortuna Sittard*	34	3	8	23	27	71	17

Top scorer: Van Hooijdonk (Feyenoord) 24.
Cup Final: Utrecht 2, Ajax 3.

HUNGARY

Hungarian Football Federation, Magyar Labdarugo Szovetseg, Istvanmezei ut. 3-5, Nepstadion (Toronyepulet), H-1146 Budapest. For correspondence: Pf. 106H-1581 Budapest.
Founded: 1901; *Number of Clubs:* 1944; *Number of Players* 95,986; *National Colours:* Red shirts, white shorts, green stockings.
Telephone: 0036 1 222 0343; *Telex:* 225782 misz h; *Fax:* 0036 1 222 0324/222 0344.

International matches 2001
Bosnia (a) 1-1, Jordan (a) 1-1, Lithuania (h) 1-1, Finland (h) 0-0, Romania (a) 0-2, Georgia (h) 4-1, Germany (h) 2-5, Georgia (a) 1-3, Romania (h) 0-2, Italy (a) 0-1, Macedonia (h) 5-0.

League Championship wins (1901–2002)
Ferencvaros 26; MTK-VM Budapest 21; Ujpest Dozsa 20; Honved 13; Vasas Budapest 6; Csepel 4; Raba Gyor 3; BTC 2; Nagyvarad 1; Vac 1; Dunaferr 1; Zalaegerszeg 1.

Cup wins (1910–2002)
Ferencvaros 17; MTK-VM Budapest 12; Ujpest Dozsa 9; Raba Gyor 4; Kispest Honved 4; Vasas Budapest 3; Diösgyör 2; ; Debrecen 2; Bocskai 1; III Ker 1; Kispesti AC 1; Soroksar 1; Szolnoki MAV 1; Siofok Banyasz 1; Bekescsaba 1; Pecs 1.
Cup not regularly held until 1964.

Qualifying League Table 2001–02
	P	W	D	L	F	A	Pts
MTK	33	20	4	9	56	34	64
Zalaegerszeg	33	18	7	8	65	40	61
Ferencvaros	33	18	5	10	58	34	59
Dunaferr	33	15	8	10	62	38	53
Videoton	33	12	10	11	45	47	46
Ujpest	33	12	8	13	58	57	44
Matav	33	10	10	13	47	51	40
Gyor	33	9	11	13	45	57	38
Kispest Honved	33	10	8	15	40	63	38
Debrecen	33	7	15	11	34	45	36
Haladas	33	8	11	14	41	62	35
Vasas	33	6	9	18	42	65	27

Final Championship Table 2001–02
	P	W	D	L	F	A	Pts
Zalaegerszeg	5	3	1	1	76	47	71
Ferencvaros	5	3	1	1	66	39	69
MTK	5	1	0	4	62	47	67
Dunaferr	5	2	0	3	71	47	59
Videoton	5	3	0	2	56	53	55
Ujpest	5	2	0	3	65	69	50

Promotion/Relegation Table 2001–02
	P	W	D	L	F	A	Pts
Kispest Honved	5	2	3	0	51	70	47
Matav	5	0	4	1	54	60	44
Debrecen	5	2	2	1	47	53	44
Gyor	5	1	3	1	51	64	44
Haladas*	5	1	2	2	48	71	40
Vasas*	5	1	2	2	51	78	32

Cup Final: Haladas 1, Ujpest 2.

ICELAND

Knattspyrnusamband Island, Laugardal, 104 Reykjavik.
Founded: 1929; *Number of Clubs:* 73; *Number of Players:* 23,673; *National Colours:* All blue.
Telephone: 00354 5102900; *Cable* KSI REYKJAVIK; *Telex:* 2314 isi is; *Fax:* 00354 75689793.

International matches 2001
India (a) 3-0, Bulgaria (a) 1-2, Malta (a) 4-1, Malta (h) 3-0, Bulgaria (h) 1-1, Poland (h) 1-1, Czech Republic (h) 3-1, Northern Ireland (a) 0-3, Denmark (a) 0-6.

League Championship wins (1912–2001)
KR 22; Valur 19; Fram 18; IA Akranes 18; Vikingur 5; IBV Vestmann 4; IBK Keflavik 3; KA Akureyri 1.

Cup wins (1960–2001)
KR 10; Valur 8; Fram 7; IA Akranes 7; IBV Vestmann 4; IBK Keflavik 2; IBA Akureyri 1; Vikingur 1; Fylkir 1.

Final League Table 2001
	P	W	D	L	F	A	Pts
IA	18	11	3	4	29	16	36
IBV	18	11	3	4	23	15	36
FH	18	9	5	4	23	16	32
Grindavik	18	9	0	9	27	29	27
Fylkir	18	7	4	7	26	23	25
Keflavik	18	6	5	7	27	30	23
KR	18	6	4	8	16	20	22
Fram	18	6	2	10	28	28	20
Valur*	18	5	4	9	19	26	19
Breidablik*	18	4	2	12	17	32	14

Cup Final: Fylkir 2, KA 2.
Fylkir won 5-4 on penalties.

REPUBLIC OF IRELAND

The Football Association of Ireland (Cumann Peile Na H-Eireann), 80 Merrion Square, South Dublin 2.
Founded: 1921; *Number of Clubs:* 3,190; *Number of Players:* 124,615; *National Colours:* Green shirts, white shorts, green and white stockings.
Telephone: 00353 1 676 68 64; *Telex:* 91397 fai ei; *Fax:* 00353 1 661 09 31.

International matches 2001
Cyprus (a) 4-0, Andorra (a) 3-0, Andorra (h) 3-1, Portugal (h) 1-1, Estonia (a) 2-0, Croatia (h) 2-2, Holland (h) 1-0, Cyprus (h) 4-0, Iran (h) 2-0, Iran (a) 0-1.

League Championship wins (1922–2002)
Shamrock Rovers 15; Shelbourne 10; Dundalk 9; St Patrick's Athletic 8; Bohemians 8; Waterford 6; Cork United 5; Drumcondra 5; St James's Gate 2; Cork Athletic 2; Sligo Rovers 2; Limerick 2; Athlone Town 2; Derry City 2; Dolphin 1; Cork Hibernians 1; Cork Celtic 1; Cork City 1.

Cup wins (1922–2002)
Shamrock Rovers 24; Dundalk 9; Shelbourne 6; Bohemians 6; Drumcondra 5; Cork Athletic 2; Cork United 2; St James's Gate 2; St Patrick's Athletic 2; Cork Hibernians 2; Limerick 2; Waterford 2; Derry City 2; Athlone Town 2; Sligo 2; Bray Wanderers 2; Alton United 1; Cork 1; Fordsons 1; Transport 1; Finn Harps 1; Home Farm 1; UCD 1; Galway United 1; Cork City 1.

Final League Table 2001–02
	P	W	D	L	F	A	Pts
Shelbourne	33	19	6	8	50	28	63
Shamrock Rovers	33	17	6	10	54	32	57
St Patrick's Athletic	33	20	8	5	59	29	53
Bohemians	33	14	10	9	57	32	52
Derry City	33	14	9	10	42	30	51
Cork City	33	14	7	12	48	39	49
UCD	33	12	12	9	40	39	48
Bray Wanderers	33	12	10	11	54	45	48
Longford Town+	33	10	10	13	41	51	40
Dundalk*	33	9	12	12	37	46	39
Galway United*	33	5	4	24	28	73	19
Monaghan United*	33	2	6	25	19	85	12

St Patrick's Athletic had nine points deducted for fielding an ineligible player. The points were later reinstated. They then had a further 15 points deducted for fielding another ineligible player.

Cup Final: Bohemians 1, Dundalk 2.

ISRAEL

Israel Football Association, Ramat-Gan Stadium, 299 Aba Hilell Street, Ramat-Gan 52594.
Founded: 1948; *Number of Clubs:* 544; *Number of Players:* 30,449; *National Colours:* Blue shirts, white shorts, blue stockings.
Telephone: 00972 3 570 59 99; *Cable:* CADUREGEL RAMAT-GAN; *Telex:* 361353 fa; *Fax:* 00972 3 570 20 44.

International matches 2001
Uzbekistan (h) 2-0, Moldova (h) 1-0, Austria (a) 1-2, Georgia (a) 2-3, Liechtenstein (a) 3-0, Spain (h) 1-1, Lithuania (a) 3-2, Bosnia (a) 0-0, Austria (h) 1-1.

League Championship wins (1932–2002)
Maccabi Tel Aviv 18; Hapoel Tel Aviv 13; Maccabi Haifa 7; Hapoel Petah Tikva 6; Maccabi Netanya 5; Beitar Jerusalem 4; Hakoah Ramat Gan 2; Hapoel Beersheba 2; Bnei Yehouda 1; British Police 1; Hapoel Kfar Sava 1; Hapoel Ramat Gan 1; Hapoel Haifa 1.

Cup wins (1928–2002)
Maccabi Tel Aviv 21; Hapoel Tel Aviv 11; Beitar Jerusalem 5; Maccabi Haifa 5; Hapoel Haifa 3; Hapoel Kfar Sava 3; Beitar Tel Aviv 2; Bnei Yehouda 2; Hakoah Ramat Gan 2; Hapoel Petah Tikva 2; Maccabi Petah Tikva 2; British Police 1; Hapoel Jerusalem 1; Hapoel Lod 1; Maccabi Netanya 1; Hapoel Beersheba 1.

Final League Table 2001–02

	P	W	D	L	F	A	Pts
Maccabi Haifa	33	22	9	2	72	32	75
Hapoel Tel Aviv	33	20	7	6	55	32	67
Maccabi Tel Aviv	33	15	12	6	43	24	57
Ashdod	33	14	7	12	47	52	49
Hapoel Beersheba	33	14	6	13	44	48	48
Hapoel Petah Tikva	33	13	8	12	40	36	47
Maccabi Netanya	33	11	7	15	41	44	40
Maccabi Petah Tikva	33	8	12	13	34	46	36
Rishon	33	10	5	18	39	53	35
Beitar Jerusalem	33	7	12	14	39	48	33
Hapoel Haifa*	33	7	9	17	35	50	30
Maccabi Kiriat*	33	7	6	20	34	58	27

Cup Final: Maccabi Tel Aviv 0, Maccabi Haifa 0
Maccabi Tel Aviv won 5-4 on penalties.

ITALY

Federazione Italiana Giuoco Calcio, Via Gregorio Allegri 14, C.P. 2450, I-00198, Roma.
Founded: 1898; *Number of Clubs:* 20,961; *Number of Players:* 1,420,160; *National Colours:* Blue shirts, white shorts, blue stockings with white trim.
Telephone: 0039 6 849 11; *Cable:* FEDERCALCIO ROMA; *Telex:* 624132 calcio i; *Fax:* 0039 6 849 12 526.

International matches 2001
Argentina (h) 1-2, Romania (a) 2-0, Lithuania (h) 4-0, South Africa (h) 1-0, Georgia (a) 2-1, Lithuania (a) 0-0, Morocco (h) 1-0, Hungary (h) 1-0, Japan (a) 1-1.

League Championship wins (1898–2002)
Juventus 26; AC Milan 16; Inter-Milan 13; Genoa 9; Torino 8; Pro Vercelli 7; Bologna 7; AS Roma 3; Fiorentina 2; Lazio 2; Napoli 2; Casale 1; Novese 1; Cagliari 1; Verona 1; Sampdoria 1.

Cup wins (1922–2002)
Juventus 9; AS Roma 8; Fiorentina 6; Torino 4; AC Milan 4; Sampdoria 4; Lazio 3; Inter-Milan 3; Napoli 3; Parma 3; Bologna 2; Atalanta 1; Genoa 1; Vado 1; Venezia 1; Vicenza 1.

Final League Table 2001–02

	P	W	D	L	F	A	Pts
Juventus	34	20	11	3	64	23	71
Roma	34	19	13	2	58	24	70
Internazionale	34	20	9	5	62	35	69
AC Milan	34	14	13	7	47	33	55
Chievo	34	14	12	8	57	52	54
Lazio	34	14	11	9	50	37	53
Bologna	34	15	7	12	40	40	52
Perugia	34	13	7	14	38	46	46
Atalanta	34	12	9	13	41	50	45
Parma	34	12	8	14	43	47	44
Torino	34	10	13	11	37	39	43
Piacenza	34	11	9	14	49	43	42
Brescia	34	9	13	12	43	52	40
Udinese	34	11	7	16	41	52	40
Verona*	34	11	6	17	41	53	39
Lecce*	34	6	10	18	36	56	28
Fiorentina*	34	5	7	22	29	63	22
Venezia*	34	3	9	22	30	61	18

Top scorers: Hubner (Piacenza) 24, Trezeguet (Juventus) 24.
Cup Final: Juventus 2, 0, Parma 1, 1.

KAZAKHSTAN

The Football Association of the Republic of Kazakhstan, 44 Abai Street, 480072 Almaty, Kazakhstan.
Founded: 1914; *Number of Clubs:* 5,793; *Number of Players:* 260,000.
Telephone: 0073272 671885; *Telex:* 251347 TREK SU; *Fax:* 0073272 671885.

LATVIA

Latvian Football Federation, Augsiela, 1, LV-1009, Riga.
Founded: 1921; *Number of Clubs:* 50; *Number of Players:* 12,000; *National Colours:* Carmine red shirts, white shorts, carmine red stockings.
Telephone: 00371 2 29 29 88; *Fax:* 00371 7828331.

International matches 2001
Romania (a) 0-2, Liechtenstein (a) 2-0, Croatia (a) 1-4, San Marino (h) 1-1, Belgium (a) 1-3, Croatia (h) 0-1, Estonia (h) 3-1, Lithuania (h) 4-1, Ukraine (h) 0-1, Scotland (a) 1-2, Russia (h) 1-3.

League Championship wins (1922–2001)
Skonto Riga 11; ASK Riga 9; RFK Riga 8; Olympia Liepaya 7; Sarkanais Metalurgs Liepaya 7; VEF Riga 6; Energija Riga 4; Elektrons Riga 3; Torpedo Riga 3; Daugava Liepaya 2; ODO Riga 2; Khimikis Daugavpils 2; RAF Yelgava 2; Keisermezhs Riga 2; Dinamo Riga 1; Zhmilyeva Team 1; Darba Rezervi 1; REZ Riga 1; Start Brotseni 1; Venta Ventspils 1; Yurnieks Riga 1; Alfa Riga 1; Gauya Valmiera 1.

Cup wins (1937–2001)
Elektrons Riga 7; Skonto Riga 6; Sarkanais Metalurgs Liepaya 5; ODO Riga 3; VEF Riga 3; ASK Riga 3; Tseltnieks Riga 3; RAF Yelgava 3; RFK Riga 2; Daugava Liepaya 2; Start Brotseni 2; Selmash Liepaya 2; Yurnieks Riga 2; Khimikis Daugavpils 2; Rigas Vilki 1; Dinamo Liepaya 1; Dinamo Riga 1; REZ Riga 1; Voulkan Kouldiga 1; Baltija Liepaya 1; Venta Ventspils 1; Pilot Riga 1; Lielupe Yurmala 1; Energija Riga 1; Torpedo Riga 1; Daugava SKIF Riga 1; Tseltnieks Daugavpils 1; Olympia Riga 1; FK Riga 1.

Final League Table 2001

	P	W	D	L	F	A	Pts
Skonto Riga	28	22	2	4	94	26	68
FK Ventspils	28	22	1	5	69	21	67
Metalurgs Liepaya	28	20	4	4	60	24	64
Dinaburg Daugavpils	28	15	5	8	60	29	50
PFK/Daugava#	28	12	2	14	37	38	38
FK Valmiera	28	5	4	19	28	56	19
FK Riga	28	3	5	20	25	72	14
Zemessardze*	28	1	1	26	11	118	4

 # Police FK and LU Daugava Riga combined.
Top scorers: Mikholap (Skonto Riga), Katasonov (Metalurgs Liepaya) 23.

LIECHTENSTEIN

Liechtensteiner Fussball-Verband, Malbuner Huus Altenbach 11, Postfach 165, 9490 Vaduz.
Founded: 1934; *Number of Clubs:* 7; *Number of Players:* 1,247; *National Colours:* Blue shirts, red shorts, blue stockings.
Telephone: 004175 237 4747; *Cable:* FUSSBALLVER-BAND VADUZ; *Fax:* 004175 237 4748.

International matches 2001
Latvia (h) 0-2, Spain (a) 0-5, Bosnia (h) 0-3, Austria (a) 0-2, Israel (h) 0-3, Spain (h) 0-2, Bosnia (a) 0-5.

Liechtenstein has no national league. Teams compete in Swiss regional leagues.

Cup wins (1946–2001)
Vaduz 30; Balzers 11; Triesen 8; Eschen/Mauren 4; Schaan 3.
Cup Final: Vaduz 9, Ruggell 0.

LITHUANIA

Lithuanian Football Federation, Seimyniskiu str. 15, 2005 Vilnius.
Founded: 1922; *Number of Clubs:* 152; *Number of Players:* 16,600; *National Colours:* Yellow shirts, green shorts, yellow stockings.
Telephone: 00370 2/723654; *Fax:* 00370 2/723651.

International matches 2001
Cyprus (a) 2-1, Romania (h) 0-3, Hungary (a) 1-1, Italy (a) 0-4, Romania (a) 1-2, Estonia (a) 5-2, Latvia (a) 1-4, Israel (h) 2-3, Italy (h) 0-0, Georgia (a) 0-2.

League Championship wins (1922–2001)
Kovas Kaunas 6; KSS Klaipeda 6; LFLS Kaunas 4; Zalgiris Vilnius 4; FBK Kaunas 3; LGSF Kaunas 2; Kareda 2; MSK Kaunas 1; Ekranas Panevezys 1; Romar Mazeikiai 1; Inkaras Grifas 1.

Cup wins (1992–2002)
Zalgiris Vilnius 3; Kareda 2; Ekranas 2; Inkaras 1; Atlantas 1; Kaunas 1.

Final League Table 2001

	P	W	D	L	F	A	Pts
FBK Kaunas	36	26	7	3	76	13	85
Atlantas	36	19	12	5	66	29	69
Zalgiris	36	20	9	7	64	39	69
Ekranas	36	15	10	10	58	38	55
Inkaras#	36	11	12	13	50	44	44
Gelezinis##	36	10	6	20	42	69	36
Nevezis	36	8	11	17	33	54	35
Sakalas###	36	7	13	16	32	61	34
Vetra*	36	7	11	18	32	57	32
Dainava*	36	7	9	20	34	83	30

Formerly Atletas.
Formerly Klevas.
Promoted after relegation of Kareda and Polonija, nursery clubs of FBK Kaunas and Zalgiris.

Top scorer: Pocius (FBK Kaunas) 22.
Cup Final: FBK Kaunas 3, Suduva 1.

LUXEMBOURG

Federation Luxembourgeoise De Football (F.L.F.), 50, Rue De Strasbourg, L-2560, Luxembourg.
Founded: 1908; *Number of Clubs:* 126; *Number of Players:* 21,684; *National Colours:* All red.
Telephone: 00352 48 86 65; *Cable:* FOOTBALL LUXEMBOURG; *Telex:* 2426 flf l; *Fax:* 00352 40 02 01.

International matches 2001
Finland (h) 0-1, Faeroes (h) 0-2, Switzerland (a) 0-5, Slovenia (a) 0-2, Russia (h) 1-2, Georgia (h) 0-3, Faeroes (a) 0-1, Switzerland (h) 0-3, Yugoslavia (a) 2-6.

League Championship wins (1910–2002)
Jeunesse Esch 26; Spora Luxembourg 11; Stade Dudelange 10; Avenir Beggen 7; Red Boys Differdange 6; US Hollerich-Bonnevoie 5; Fola Esch 5; US Luxembourg 5; Aris Bonnevoie 3; Progres Niedercorn 3; F91 Dudelange 3.

Cup wins (1922–2002)
Red Boys Differdange 16; Jeunesse Esch 12; US Luxembourg 10; Spora Luxembourg 8; Avenir Beggen 7; Stade Dudelange 4; Progres Niedercorn 4; Fola Esch 3; Alliance Dudelange 2; US Rumelange 2; Grevenmacher 2; Aris Bonnevoie 1; US Dudelange 1; Jeunesse Hautcharage 1; National Schiffige 1; Racing Luxembourg 1; SC Tetange 1; Hesperange 1; Etzella 1.

Qualifying Table 2001–02

	P	W	D	L	F	A	Pts
Grevenmacher	22	15	6	1	45	14	51
F91 Dudelange	22	15	5	2	56	18	50
Jeunesse Esch	22	12	5	5	38	22	41
Union	22	11	4	7	38	35	37
Mondercange	22	10	3	9	42	39	33
Hesperange	22	8	6	8	44	37	30
Avenir Beggen	22	6	8	8	30	39	26
Sporting Mertzig	22	6	6	10	24	41	24
Rumelange	22	4	8	10	28	42	20
Niedercorn	22	5	5	12	29	51	20
Hobscheid	22	4	6	12	34	52	18
Etzella	22	3	4	15	33	51	13

Championship Table 2001–02

	P	W	D	L	F	A	Pts
F91 Dudelange	6	4	0	2	64	23	62
Grevenmacher	6	2	1	3	52	22	58
Union	6	3	1	2	42	39	47
Jeunesse Esch	6	1	2	3	45	31	46

Promotion Table 2001–02

	P	W	D	L	F	A	Pts
Monnerich	6	2	2	2	10	12	41
Rumelange	6	4	0	2	19	13	32
Avenir Beggen	6	1	3	2	10	11	32
Hobscheid*	6	2	1	3	10	13	25

Relegation Table 2001–02

	P	W	D	L	F	A	Pts
Hesperange	6	2	0	4	12	10	36
Sporting Mertzig	6	3	1	2	9	9	34
Progres	6	2	2	2	9	11	28
Etzella*	6	3	1	2	14	14	23

Cup Final: Avenir Beggen 1, F91 Dudelange 0.

MACEDONIA

Football Association of the Former Yugoslav Republic of Macedonia, VIII-ma Udarna Brigada 31A, PO Box 84, MAC-91000 Skopje.
Founded: 1948; *Number of Clubs:* 598; *Number of Players:* 15,165; *National Colours:* All red.
Telephone: 00389 1 22 90 42; *Fax:* 00389 1 23 54 48.

International matches 2001
Czech Republic (h) 1-1, Sweden (a) 0-1, Turkey (h) 1-2, Moldova (h) 2-2, Turkey (a) 3-3, Qatar (a) 0-1, Saudi Arabia (a) 1-1, Bulgaria (a) 0-1, Sweden (h) 1-2, Azerbaijan (a) 1-1, Slovakia (h) 0-5, Hungary (a) 0-5.

League Championship wins (1993–2002)
Vardar 4; Sileks 3; Sloga 3.

Cup wins (1993–2002)
Vardar 4; Sileks 1; Sloga 1; Pellister 1; Pobeda 1.

Qualifying Table 2001–02

	P	W	D	L	F	A	Pts
Pobeda	22	14	2	6	41	23	44
Belasica	22	14	2	6	36	19	44
Vardar	22	13	2	7	29	18	41
Rabotnicki	22	12	3	7	40	25	39
Cement	22	10	5	7	32	19	35
Sloga	22	9	8	5	32	22	35
Sileks	22	10	3	9	44	35	33
Kumanovo	22	10	2	10	27	42	32
Napredak	22	7	3	12	17	33	24
Pelister	22	5	4	13	24	40	19
Osogovo*	22	5	1	16	18	40	16
Makedonia*	22	4	3	15	14	38	15

Championship Table 2001–02

	P	W	D	L	F	A	Pts
Vardar	10	6	3	1	28	16	37
Belasica	10	6	1	3	28	22	36
Cement	10	3	2	5	33	33	27
Pobeda	10	3	3	4	28	28	25
Sloga	10	3	1	6	18	25	23
Rabotnicki	10	3	2	5	30	41	21

Promotion/Relegation Table 2001–02

	P	W	D	L	F	A	Pts
Sileks	10	4	0	6	48	35	35
Napredak	10	5	2	3	34	34	35
Kumanovo	10	5	1	4	34	36	32
Pelister	10	5	2	3	34	34	27
Makedonia	10	3	4	3	27	28	22
Osogovo	10	1	5	4	23	36	18

Cup Final: Pobeda 8, Cement 1.

MALTA

Malta Football Association, 280 St. Paul Street, Valletta VLT07.
Founded: 1900; *Number of Clubs:* 252; *Number of Players:* 5,544; *National Colours:* Red shirts, white shorts, red stockings.
Telephone: 00356 22 26 97; *Cable:* FOOTBALL MALTA VALLETTA; *Fax:* 00356 24 51 36.

International matches 2001
Sweden (h) 0-3, Denmark (h) 0-5, Iceland (h) 1-4, Iceland (a) 0-3, Denmark (a) 1-2, Bosnia (a) 0-2, Bulgaria (h) 0-2, Czech Republic (a) 2-3, Northern Ireland (h) 0-1, Canada (h) 2-1.

League Championship wins (1910–2002)
Floriana 25; Sliema Wanderers 23; Valletta 18; Hibernians 9; Hamrun Spartans 7; Rabat Ajax 2; St George's 1; KOMR 1; Birkirkara 1.

Cup wins (1935–2002)
Floriana 18; Sliema Wanderers 18; Valletta 10; Hamrun Spartans 6; Hibernians 6; Gzira United 1; Melita 1; Zurrieq 1; Rabat Ajax 1; Birkirkara 1.

Qualifying League Table 2001–02

	P	W	D	L	F	A	Pts
Birkirkara	18	12	4	2	46	16	40
Hibernians	18	12	4	2	41	22	40
Sliema Wanderers	18	12	2	4	48	16	36
Valletta	18	10	5	3	40	21	35
Hamrun Spartans	18	7	2	9	23	33	23
Floriana	18	6	4	8	27	24	22
Marsa	18	6	4	8	32	38	22
Pieta Hotspurs	18	4	3	11	20	36	15
Naxxar Lions	18	4	0	14	24	54	12
Lija	18	2	2	14	14	55	8

Championship Table 2001–02

	P	W	D	L	F	A	Pts
Hibernians	10	7	2	1	67	34	43
Sliema Wanderers	10	5	2	3	67	30	36
Birkirkara	10	5	3	2	60	29	31
Valletta	10	3	3	4	52	33	30
Floriana	10	4	2	4	39	38	25
Hamrun Spartans	10	1	2	7	26	54	17

Promotion/Relegation Table 2001–02

	P	W	D	L	F	A	Pts
Marsa	6	3	1	2	43	47	21
Pieta Hotspurs	6	3	0	3	28	43	17
Naxxar Lions	6	2	2	2	37	62	14
Lija	6	2	1	3	21	70	11

Cup Final: Birkirkara 1, Sliema Wanderers 0.

MOLDOVA

Moldavian Football Federation, 39 Tricolorului Str, 2012, Chisinau.
Founded: 1990; *Number of Clubs:* 143; *Number of Players:* 75,000; *National Colours:* Blue shirts, red shorts, yellow stockings.
Telephone: 00373 2 247878. *Fax:* 00373 2 247890.

International matches 2001
Israel (a) 0-1, Azerbaijan (a) 0-0, Sweden (h) 0-2, Estonia (h) 0-0, Macedonia (a) 2-2, Sweden (a) 0-6, Portugal (a) 0-3, Azerbaijan (h) 2-0, Slovakia (a) 2-4, Turkey (h) 0-3.

League Championship wins (1992–2002)
Zimbru Chisinau 8; Serif 2; Constructorul 1.

Cup wins (1992–2002)
Tiligul 4; Serif 3; Zimbru Chisinau 2; Combat 1; Constructorul 1.

Final League Table 2001–02

	P	W	D	L	F	A	Pts
Serif	28	20	7	1	62	18	67
Otaci	28	14	10	4	40	19	52
Zimbru Chisinau	28	12	10	6	52	20	46
Constructorul	28	11	6	11	36	42	39
Hincesti	28	7	11	10	30	40	32
Agro	28	8	5	15	25	38	29
Tiligul	28	6	7	15	24	46	25
Happy End*	28	3	6	19	23	69	15

Cup Final: Serif 3, Otaci 2.

NORTHERN IRELAND

Irish Football Association Ltd, 20 Windsor Avenue, Belfast BT9 6EG.
Founded: 1880; *Number of Clubs:* 1,555; *Number of Players:* 24,558; *National Colours:* Green shirts, white shorts, green stockings.
Telephone: 01232 66 94 58; *Cable:* FOOTBALL BELFAST; *Telex:* 747317 ifa ni g; *Fax:* 01232 66 76 20.

NORWAY

Norges Fotballforbund, Ullevaal Stadion, Postboks 3823, Ulleval Hageby, 0805 Oslo 8.
Founded: 1902; *Number of Clubs:* 1,810; *Number of Players:* 300,000; *National Colours:* Red shirts, white shorts, blue stockings.
Telephone: 0047 22/024500 ; *Cable* FOTBALLFOR-BUND OSLO; *Telex:* 71722 nff n; *Fax:* 0047 22 95 10 10.

International matches 2001
South Korea (a) 3-2, Republic of Ireland (a) 4-0, Poland (h) 2-3, Belarus (a) 1-2, Bulgaria (h) 2-1, Ukraine (a) 0-0, Belarus (h) 1-1, Turkey (h) 1-1, Poland (a) 0-3, Wales (h) 3-2, Armenia (a) 4-1.

League Championship wins (1938–2001)
Rosenborg Trondheim 15; Fredrikstad 9; Viking Stavanger 8; Lillestroem 6; Valerengen 4; Larvik Turn 3; Brann Bergen 2; Lyn Oslo 2; IK Start 2; Friedig 1; Skeid Oslo 1; Strömsgodset Drammen 1; Moss 1.

Cup wins (1902–2001)
Odds Bk Skien 11; Fredrikstad 10; Lyn Oslo 8; Skeid Oslo 8; Rosenborg Trondheim 7; Sarpsborg FK 6; Brann Bergen 5; Viking Stavanger 5; Orn F Horten 4; Lillestroem 4; Strömsgodset Drammen 4; Frigg 3; Mjondalens F 3; Bodo-Glimt 2; Mercantile 2; Tromso 2; Valerengen 2; Grane Nordstrand 1; Kvik Halden 1; Sparta 1; Gjovik 1; Moss 1; Byrne 1; Molde 1; Stabaek 1; Odd Grenland 1.
(Known as the Norwegian Championship for HM The King's Trophy).

Final League Table 2001

	P	W	D	L	F	A	Pts
Rosenborg	26	17	6	3	71	30	57
Lillestrom	26	17	5	4	64	33	56
Viking	26	14	7	5	43	29	49
Stabaek	26	14	3	9	45	39	45
Molde	26	13	5	8	54	41	44
Odd	26	12	6	8	50	40	42
Brann	26	12	5	9	63	48	41
Sogndal	26	9	5	12	45	61	32
Bodo-Glimt	26	7	8	11	45	47	29
Moss	26	9	2	15	35	48	29
Lyn	26	6	8	12	40	49	26
Bryne+	26	6	4	16	33	61	22
Strömsgodset*	26	3	10	13	40	73	19
Tromso*	26	4	4	18	23	52	16

Relegation/Promotion Play-off: Bryne 3, 0, Hamark 0, 0. *Bryne remain; Hamark stay in Division 2.*
Cup Final: Viking 3, Bryne 0.

POLAND

Federation Polonaise De Foot-Ball, Al. Ujazdowskie 22, 00-478 Warszawa.
Founded: 1919; *Number of Clubs:* 5,881; *Number of Players:* 317,442; *National Colours:* White shirts, red shorts, white and red stockings.
Telephone: 0048 22 6223398; *Cable:* PEZETPEEN WARSZAWA; *Telex:* 825320 pzpn pl; *Fax:* 0048 22 629 24 89.

International matches 2001
Switzerland (a) 4-0, Norway (a) 3-2, Armenia (h) 4-0, Scotland (h) 1-1, Wales (a) 2-1, Armenia (a) 1-1, Iceland (a) 1-1, Norway (h) 3-0, Belarus (a) 1-4, Ukraine (h) 1-1, Cameroon (h) 0-0.

League Championship wins (1921–2002)
Gornik Zabrze 14; Ruch Chorzow 13; Wisla Krakow 8; Legia Warsaw 7; Widzew Lodz 6; Lech Poznan 5; Pogon Lwow 4; Cracovia 3; Warta Poznan 2; Polonia Bytom 2; Stal Mielec 2; LKS Lodz 2; Polonia Warsaw 2; Garbarnia Krakow 1; Slask Wroclaw 1; Szombierki Bytom 1; Zaglebie Lubin 1.

Cup wins (1951–2002)
Legia Warsaw 12; Gornik Zabrze 6; Zaglebie Sosnowiec 4; Lech Poznan 3; GKS Katowice 3; Ruch Chorzow 3; Amica Wronki 3; Slask Wroclaw 2; Polonia Warsaw 2; Wisla Krakow 2; Gwardia Warsaw 1; LKS Lodz 1; Stal Rzeszow 1; Arka Gdynia 1; Lechia Gdansk 1; Widzew Lodz 1; Miedz Legnica 1.

Group A Qualifying Table 2001–02

	P	W	D	L	F	A	Pts
Odra	14	10	1	3	28	14	31
Wisla	14	9	1	4	28	15	28
Polonia	14	7	4	3	25	13	25
Zaglebie Lubin	14	5	3	6	23	28	18
Katowice	14	5	3	6	17	23	18
KSZO	14	4	3	7	14	18	15
Gornik Zabrze	14	2	5	7	13	22	11
Widzew	14	3	2	9	9	24	11

Group B Qualifying Table 2001–02

	P	W	D	L	F	A	Pts
Legia	14	8	3	3	31	14	27
Amica	14	6	6	2	26	16	24
Pogon	14	7	3	4	20	16	24
Ruch	14	5	4	5	16	18	19
Slask	14	5	3	6	21	25	18
Radomsko	14	4	4	6	10	16	16
Groclin	14	4	3	7	18	23	15
Stomil	14	2	4	8	10	24	10

Championship Table 2001–02

	P	W	D	L	F	A	Pts
Legia	14	7	7	0	19	10	42
Wisla	14	8	3	3	22	14	41
Amica	14	7	3	4	21	11	36
Polonia	14	5	4	5	16	19	32
Odra	14	2	5	7	12	19	27
Katowice	14	4	5	5	10	15	26
Ruch	14	3	4	7	14	18	23
Pogon	14	2	5	7	9	17	23

Promotion/Relegation Table 2001–02

	P	W	D	L	F	A	Pts
Gornik Zabrze	14	8	4	2	23	11	34
Widzew	14	6	7	1	19	8	31
Zaglebie	14	5	5	4	16	16	29
Groclin	14	6	2	6	18	15	28
KSZO	14	4	5	5	14	19	25
Radomsko*	14	3	6	5	13	16	23
Slask*	14	2	4	8	14	22	19
Stomil*	14	2	7	5	11	21	18

Cup Final: Amica 2, 0, Wisla 4, 4.

PORTUGAL

Federacao Portuguesa De Futebol, Praca De Alegria N.25, Apartado 21.100, P-1127, Lisboa Codex.
Founded: 1914; *Number of Clubs:* 204; *Number of Players:* 79,235; *National Colours:* Red shirts, green shorts, red stockings.
Telephone: 00351 1 342 8207/8/9/0; *Cable:* FUTEBOL LISBOA; *Telex:* 13489 fpf p; *Fax:* 00351 1 346 72 31.

International matches 2001

Andorra (h) 3-0, Holland (h) 2-2, France (a) 0-4, Republic of Ireland (a) 1-1, Cyprus (h) 6-0, Moldova (h) 3-0, Andorra (a) 7-1, Cyprus (a) 3-1, Estonia (h) 5-0, Angola (h) 5-1.

League Championship wins (1935–2002)

Benfica 30; FC Porto 18; Sporting Lisbon 18; Belenenses 1; Boavista 1.

Cup wins (1939–2002)

Benfica 23; Sporting Lisbon 13; FC Porto 11; Boavista 5; Belenenses 3; Vitoria Setubal 2; Academica Coimbra 1; Leixoes Porto 1; Sporting Braga 1; Amadora 1; Beira Mar 1.

Final League Table 2001–02

	P	W	D	L	F	A	Pts
Sporting Lisbon	34	22	9	3	74	25	75
Boavista	34	21	7	6	53	20	70
Porto	34	21	5	8	66	34	68
Benfica	34	17	12	5	66	37	63
Belenenses	34	17	6	11	54	44	57
Maritimo	34	17	5	12	48	35	56
Uniao Leiria	34	15	10	9	52	35	55
Pacos	34	12	10	12	41	44	46
Guimaraes	34	11	9	14	35	41	42
Braga	34	10	12	12	43	43	42
Beira Mar	34	10	9	15	48	56	39
Gil Vicente	34	10	8	16	42	56	38
Setubal	34	9	11	14	40	46	38
Santa Clara	34	9	10	15	32	46	37
Varzin	34	8	8	18	27	55	32
Salgueiros*	34	8	6	20	29	71	30
Farense*	34	7	7	20	29	63	28
Alverca*	34	7	6	21	39	67	27

Top scorer: Jardel (Sporting Lisbon) 42.
Cup Final: Leixoes 0, Sporting Lisbon 1.

ROMANIA

Federatia Romana De Fotbal, Str. Poligrafiei 3, Sector 1, 71556 Bucharest.
Founded: 1909; *Number of Clubs:* 414; *Number of Players:* 22,920; *National Colours:* All yellow.
Telephone: 0040 1 224 1993/224 2983; *Cable:* SPORTROM BUCURESTI-FOTBAL; *Telex:* 10097 frf r; *Fax:* 0040 1 224 0661.

International matches 2001

Croatia (a) 2-2, Latvia (h) 2-0, Ukraine (h) 1-0, Lithuania (a) 3-0, Italy (h) 0-2, Georgia (a) 2-0, Slovakia (h) 0-0, Hungary (h) 2-0, Lithuania (a) 2-1, Slovenia (a) 2-2, Hungary (a) 2-0, Georgia (h) 1-1, Slovenia (a) 1-2, Slovenia (h) 1-1.

League Championship wins (1910–2002)

Steaua Bucharest 21; Dinamo Bucharest 16; Venus Bucharest 8; Chinezul Timisoara 6; UT Arad 6; Ripensia Temesvar 4; Uni Craiova 4; Petrolul Ploesti 3; Olimpia Bucharest 2; Colentina Bucharest 2; Arges Pitesti 2; ICO Oradea 2; Rapid Bucharest 2; Soc RA Bucharest 1; Prahova Ploesti 1; Coltea Brasov 1; Juventus Bucharest 1; Metalochimia Resita 1; Ploesti United 1; Unirea Tricolor 1.

Cup wins (1934–2002)

Steaua Bucharest 20; Rapid Bucharest 11; Dinamo Bucharest 9; Uni Craiova 6; UT Arad 2; Ripensia Temesvar 2; Politehnica Timisoara 2; Petrolul Ploesti 2; ICO Oradeo 1; Metalochimia Resita 1; Stinta Cluj 1; CFR Turnu Severin 1; Chimia Ramnicu Vilcea 1; Jiul Petroseni 1; Progresul Bucharest 1; Progresul Oradea 1; Gloria Bistrita 1.

Final League Table 2001–02

	P	W	D	L	F	A	Pts
Dinamo	30	17	9	4	64	32	60
National	30	16	10	4	44	20	58
Rapid	30	15	6	9	50	31	50
Steaua	30	15	5	10	47	31	50
Otelul	30	14	7	9	34	24	49
Bacau	30	14	4	12	43	40	46
Uni Craiova	30	12	8	10	40	35	44
Arges	30	12	6	12	36	38	42
Gloria	30	13	2	15	29	41	41
Ceahlaul	30	12	4	14	33	39	40
Brasov	30	10	9	11	32	34	39
Astra	30	9	10	11	29	28	37
Sportul	30	9	7	14	40	53	34
Farul	30	8	7	15	31	44	31
Petrolul*	30	5	10	15	30	48	25
Timisoara*	30	4	6	20	25	69	18

Cup Final: Dinamo 1, Rapid 2.

RUSSIA

Football Union of Russia; Luzhnetskaya Naberezyhnaja, 8. SU-119871 Moscow.
Founded: 1912; *Number of Clubs:* 43,700; *Number of Players:* 785,000; *National Colours:* White shirts, blue shorts, red stockings.
Telephone: 0070 95 2011637; *Telex:* 411287 priz su; *Fax:* 0070 95 2011303.

International matches 2001

Greece (a) 3-3, Slovenia (h) 1-1, Faeroes (h) 1-0, Yugoslavia (h) 1-0, Yugoslavia (h) 1-1, Luxembourg (a) 2-1, Greece (h) 0-0, Slovenia (a) 1-2, Faeroes (a) 3-0, Switzerland (h) 4-0, Latvia (a) 3-1.

League Championship wins (1945–2001)

Spartak Moscow 20; Dynamo Kiev 13; Dynamo Moscow 11; CSKA Moscow 7; Torpedo Moscow 3; Dynamo Tbilisi 2; Dnepr Dnepropetrovsk 2; Saria Voroshilovgrad 1; Ararat Erevan 1; Dynamo Minsk 1; Zenit Leningrad 1; Spartak Vladikavkaz 1.

Cup wins (1936–2002)

Spartak Moscow 12; Dynamo Kiev 10; Torpedo Moscow 7; Dynamo Moscow 6; CSKA Moscow 6; Dynamo Tbilisi 2; Ararat Erevan 2; Zenit Leningrad 2; Karpaty Lvov 1; SKA Rostov 1; Metallist Kharkov 1; Dnepr 1.

Final League Table 2001

	P	W	D	L	F	A	Pts
Spartak Moscow	30	17	9	4	56	30	60
Lokomotiv Moscow	30	16	8	6	53	24	56
Zenit	30	16	8	6	52	35	56
Torpedo Moscow	30	15	7	8	53	42	52
Krylia Sovekov	30	14	7	9	38	23	49
Saturn	30	13	8	9	45	22	47
CSKA Moscow	30	12	11	7	39	30	47
Sokol	30	12	5	13	31	42	41
Dynamo Moscow	30	10	8	12	43	51	38
Volgograd	30	8	8	14	38	42	32
Vladikavkaz	30	8	8	14	31	47	32
Rostelmash	30	8	8	14	29	43	32
Anzhi	30	7	11	12	28	34	32
Torpedo ZIL	30	7	10	13	22	35	31
Fakel*	30	8	4	18	30	53	28
Chernomorets*	30	5	8	17	19	54	23

Cup Final: CSKA Moscow 2, Zenit 0.

SAN MARINO

Federazione Sammarinese Giuoco Calcio, Viale Campo dei Giudei, 14; 47031-Rep. San Marino.
Founded: 1931; *Number of Clubs:* 17; *Number of Players:* 1,033; *National Colours:* All light blue.
Telephone: 00378 9990515; *Telex:* 0505284 cosmar so; *Fax:* 00378 9992348.

International matches 2001
Belgium (a) 1-10, Scotland (a) 0-4, Latvia (a) 1-1, Croatia (a) 0-4, Belgium (h) 1-4, Croatia (h) 0-4.

League Championship wins (1986–2002)
Tre Fiori 4; Faetano 3; Folgore 3; Fiorita 2; Domagnano 2; Montevito 1; Libertas 1; Cosmos 1.

Cup wins (1986–2001)
Domagnano 5; Libertas 3; Faetano 3; Cosmos 2; Fiorita 1; Tre Penne 1; Murata 1.

Qualifying Table 2001–02

	P	W	D	L	F	A	Pts
Cosmos	20	14	5	1	45	16	47
Pennarossa	20	14	5	1	41	18	47
Libertas	20	13	3	4	38	18	42
Cailungo	21	11	7	3	31	18	40
Domagnano	21	10	6	5	36	27	36
Virtus	21	10	5	6	40	24	35
Faetano	21	10	5	6	27	22	35
Murata	20	10	3	7	40	27	33
Folgore	21	8	4	9	37	37	28
San Giovanni	21	6	6	9	27	35	24
Tre Fiore	20	5	3	12	21	30	18
Montevito	20	4	6	10	27	38	18
Tre Penne	20	1	7	12	16	40	10
La Fiorita	21	1	6	14	12	42	9
Juvenes/Dogana	21	0	3	18	13	59	3

Play-Offs: Preliminary Round: Pennarossa 1, Faetano 2; Domagnano 4, Libertas 2; Cailungo 3, Faetano 0; Cosmos 1, Domagnano 0; Faetano 1, Libertas 2; Domagnano 1, Pennarossa 0; Cailungo 2, Cosmos 1.
Semi-Finals: Libertas 1, Domagnano 3; Domagnano 1, Cosmos 0.
Final: Cailungo 0, Domagnano 1.

SCOTLAND

The Scottish Football Association Ltd, Hampden Park, Glasgow G42 9AY.
Founded: 1873; *Number of Clubs:* 6,148; *Number of Players:* 135,474; *National Colours:* Dark blue shirts, white shorts, red stockings with dark blue tops.
Telephone: 0141 616 6000; *Cable:* EXECUTIVE GLASGOW; *Telex:* 778904 sfa g; *Fax:* 0141 616 6001.

SLOVAKIA

Slovak Football Association, Junacka 6, 83280 Bratislava, Slovakia.
Founded: 1993; *Number of Clubs:* 2,140; *Number of Players:* 141,000; *National Colours:* All blue.
Telephone: 00421 75049151/5; *Fax:* 00421 75 049554.

International matches 2001
Algeria (a) 1-1, Turkey (a) 1-1, Azerbaijan (h) 3-1, Romania (a) 0-0, Germany (a) 0-2, Sweden (a) 0-2, Azerbaijan (a) 0-2, Iran (h) 3-4, Turkey (h) 0-1, Moldova (h) 4-2, Macedonia (a) 5-0.

League Championship wins (1939–44; 1994–2002)
Slovan Bratislava 8; Kosice 2; Inter 2; Bystrica 1; OAP Bratislava 1; Zilina 1.

Cup wins (1994–2002)
Inter 3; Slovan Bratislava 2; Tatran Presov 1; Humenne 1; Spartak Trnava 1; Koba 1.

Final League Table 2001–02

	P	W	D	L	F	A	Pts
Zilina	36	21	6	9	62	37	69
Matador	36	18	8	10	48	33	62
Inter	36	16	8	12	53	39	56
Ruzomberok	36	15	9	12	49	41	54
Trencin	36	15	9	12	45	43	54
Slovan Bratislava	36	14	9	13	42	39	51
Petrzalka	36	11	14	11	51	45	47
Dubnica	36	9	11	16	38	48	38
Kosice	36	6	13	17	30	62	31
Tatran Presov*	36	8	7	21	35	66	31

Cup Final: Matador 1, Koba 1.
Koba won 4-2 on penalties.

SLOVENIA

Football Association of Slovenia, P.P. 3986, 1001 Ljubljana, Slovenia.
Founded: 1920; *Number of Clubs:* 375; *Number of Players:* 20,117; *National Colours:* White shirts, green shorts, white stockings.
Telephone: 00386 1 5300400; *Fax:* 00386 1 5300410.

International matches 2001
Uruguay (h) 0-2, Russia (a) 1-1, Yugoslavia (h) 1-1, Denmark (a) 0-3, Luxembourg (h) 2-0, Switzerland (a) 1-0, Romania (h) 2-2, Russia (h) 2-1, Yugoslavia (a) 1-1, Faeroes (h) 3-0, Romania (h) 2-1, Romania (a) 1-1.

League Championship wins (1992–2002)
Maribor 6; SCT Olimpija 4; Gorica 1.

Cup wins (1992–2002)
Maribor 4; SCT Olimpija 3; Gorica 2; Mura 1; Rudar 1.

Final League Table 2001–02

	P	W	D	L	F	A	Pts
Maribor Teatanic	33	19	9	5	64	23	66
Primorje	33	18	6	9	57	26	60
Koper	33	15	11	7	45	26	56
Gorica	33	14	9	10	38	40	51
Olimpija	33	15	6	12	39	42	51
Publikum	33	14	6	13	50	39	48
Mura	33	14	6	13	36	35	48
Rudar	33	11	9	13	46	52	42
Era	33	9	13	11	41	40	40
Korotan	33	10	7	16	28	46	37
Zivila*	33	9	5	19	34	60	32
Domzale*	33	3	7	23	26	75	16

Cup Final: Gorica 4, 2, Aluminij 0, 1.

SPAIN

Real Federacion Espanola De Futbol, Calle Alberto Bosch 13, Apartado Postal 347, E-28014 Madrid.
Founded: 1913; *Number of Clubs:* 10,240; *Number of Players:* 408,135; *National Colours:* Red shirts, blue shorts, blue stockings with red, blue and yellow border.
Telephone: 0034 91 420 1362; *Cable:* FUTBOL MADRID; *Fax:* 0034 91 420 2094.

International matches 2001
England (a) 0-3, Liechtenstein (h) 5-0, France (h) 2-1, Japan (h) 1-0, Bosnia (h) 4-1, Israel (h) 1-1, Austria (h) 4-0, Liechtenstein (a) 2-0, Mexico (h) 1-0.

League Championship wins (1929–36; 1940–2002)
Real Madrid 28; Barcelona 16; Atletico Madrid 9; Athletic Bilbao 8; Valencia 5; Real Sociedad 2; Real Betis 1; Seville 1; La Coruna 1.

Cup wins (1902–2002)
Barcelona 24; Athletic Bilbao 23; Real Madrid 17; Atletico Madrid 9; Valencia 6; Real Zaragoza 5; Real Union de Irun 3; Seville 3; Espanyol 3; La Coruna 2; Arenas 1; Ciclista Sebastian 1; Racing de Irun 1; Vizcaya Bilbao 1; Real Betis 1; Real Sociedad 1.

Final League Table 2001–02

	P	W	D	L	F	A	Pts
Valencia	38	21	12	5	51	27	75
La Coruna	38	20	8	10	65	41	68
Real Madrid	38	19	9	10	69	44	66
Barcelona	38	18	10	10	65	37	64
Celta	38	16	12	10	64	46	60
Betis	38	15	14	9	42	34	59
ABaves	38	17	3	18	41	44	54
Sevilla	38	14	11	13	51	40	53
Athletic Bilbao	38	14	11	13	54	66	53
Malaga	38	13	14	11	44	44	53
Rayo Vallecano	38	13	10	15	46	52	49
Valladolid	38	13	9	16	45	58	48
Real Sociedad	38	13	8	17	48	54	47
Espanyol	38	13	8	17	47	56	47
Villarreal	38	11	10	17	46	55	43
Mallorca	38	11	10	17	40	52	43
Osasuna	38	10	12	16	36	49	42
Las Palmas*	38	9	13	16	40	50	40
Tenerife*	38	10	8	20	32	58	38
Zaragoza*	38	9	10	19	35	54	37

Top scorer: Diego Tristan (La Coruna) 21.
Cup Final: Real Madrid 1, La Coruna 2.

SWEDEN

Svenska Fotbollfoerbundet, Box 1216, S-17123 Solna.
Founded: 1904; *Number of Clubs:* 3,250; *Number of Players:* 485,000; *National Colours:* Yellow shirts, blue shorts, yellow stockings.
Telephone: 0046 8 735 09 00; *Cable:* FOOTBALL-S; *Fax:* 0046 8 27 51 47.

International matches 2001
Faeroes (h) 0-0, Finland (h) 0-1, Thailand (n) 4-1, China (n) 2-2, Qatar (n) 0-0, China (n) 3-0, Malta (a) 3-0, Macedonia (h) 1-0, Moldova (a) 2-0, Switzerland (a) 2-0, Slovakia (h) 2-0, Moldova (h) 6-0, South Africa (h) 3-0, Macedonia (a) 2-1, Turkey (a) 2-1, Azerbaijan (h) 3-0, England (a) 1-1.

League Championship wins (1896–2001)
IFK Gothenburg 18; Oergryte IS Gothenburg 14; Malmo FF 14; IFK Norrköping 11; AIK Stockholm 10; Djurgaarden 8; GAIS Gothenburg 6; IF Helsingborg 6; Boras IF Elfsborg 4; Oster Vaxjo 4; Halmstad 4; Atvidaberg 2; IFK Ekilstune 1; IF Gavic Brynas 1; IF Gothenburg 1; Fassbergs 1; Norrköping IK Sleipner 1; Hammarby 1.

Cup wins (1941–2001)
Malmo FF 13; AIK Stockholm 8; IFK Norrköping 6; IFK Gothenburg 4; Atvidaberg 2; Kalmar 2; Helsingborg 2; GAIS Gothenburg 1; IF Raa 1; Landskrona 1; Oster Vaxjo 1; Djurgaarden 1; Degerfors 1; Halmstad 1; Orgryte 1.

Final League Table 2001

	P	W	D	L	F	A	Pts
Hammarby	26	14	6	6	45	28	48
Djurgaarden	26	13	8	5	36	24	47
AIK	26	12	9	5	45	29	45
IFK Gothenburg	26	12	8	6	41	31	44
Helsingborg	26	11	9	6	47	29	42
Orgryte	26	10	9	7	36	33	39
Halmstad	26	10	8	8	50	31	38
Orebro	26	8	9	9	48	44	33
Malmo	26	9	5	12	39	46	32
Elfsborg	26	9	3	14	31	51	30
Sundsvall	26	7	8	11	28	37	29
Norrköping	26	7	8	11	29	40	29
Hacken*	26	5	9	12	35	50	24
Trelleborg*	26	3	5	18	25	62	14

Top scorer: Selakovic (Halmstad) 15.

SWITZERLAND

Schweizerisher Fussballverband, Postfach 3000 Berne 15.
Founded: 1895; *Number of Clubs:* 1,473; *Number of Players:* 185,286; *National Colours:* Red shirts, white shorts, red stockings.
Telephone: 0041 31 950 81 11; *Cable:* SWISSFOOT BERNE; *Fax:* 0041 31 950 81 81.

International matches 2001
Poland (h) 0-4, Yugoslavia (a) 1-1, Luxembourg (h) 5-0, Sweden (h) 0-2, Faeroes (a) 1-0, Slovenia (h) 0-1, Austria (a) 2-1, Yugoslavia (h) 1-2, Luxembourg (a) 3-0, Russia (a) 0-4.

League Championship wins (1898–2002)
Grasshoppers 25; Servette 17; Young Boys Berne 11; FC Zurich 9; FC Basle 9; Lausanne 7; La Chaux-de-Fonds 3; FC Lugano 3; Winterthur 3; FX Aarau 3; Neuchatel Xamax 3; Sion 2; St Gallen 2; FC Anglo-American 1; FC Brühl 1; Cantonal-Neuchatel 1; Biel 1; Bellinzona 1; FC Etoile La Chaux-de-Fonds 1; Lucerne 1.

Cup wins (1926–2002)
Grasshoppers 18; FC Sion 9; Lausanne 9; Servette 7; La Chaux-de-Fonds 6; Young Boys Berne 6; FC Zurich 6; FC Basle 6; Lucerne 2; FC Lugano 2; FC Granges 1; St Gallen 1; Urania Geneva 1; Young Fellows Zurich 1; Aarau 1.

Qualifying Table 2001–02

	P	W	D	L	F	A	Pts
Basle	22	13	4	5	52	37	43
Lugano	22	11	5	6	39	33	38
Grasshoppers	22	11	4	7	50	33	37
St Gallen	22	9	8	5	38	32	35
Servette	22	9	7	6	36	29	34
Sion	22	10	3	9	40	29	33
Young Boys	22	8	7	7	35	28	31
Zurich	22	7	9	6	24	27	30
Aarau	22	7	6	9	28	25	27
Neuchatel Xamax	22	6	7	9	28	36	25
Lausanne	22	4	4	14	24	49	16
Lucerne	22	3	4	15	23	59	13

Championship Table 2001–02

	P	W	D	L	F	A	Pts
Basle	14	11	0	3	36	16	55
Grasshoppers	14	7	5	2	27	17	44
Lugano	14	7	2	5	23	19	42
Servette	14	6	3	5	25	23	38
Zurich	14	6	2	6	14	17	35
St Gallen	14	4	4	6	18	20	34
Young Boys	14	4	3	7	18	25	31
Sion	14	1	1	12	10	34	21

Promotion/Relegation Table 2001–02

	P	W	D	L	F	A	Pts
Neuchatel Xamax	14	8	4	2	26	12	28
Lausanne	14	8	2	4	21	14	26
Wil	14	6	5	3	17	13	23
Thun	14	6	3	5	19	18	21
Aarau*	14	6	3	5	20	20	21
Delemont*	14	4	4	6	14	20	16
Lucerne*	14	2	5	7	26	28	11
Winterthur*	14	1	4	9	11	29	7

Top scorers: Gimenez (Lugano/Basle) 28, Nunez (Grasshoppers) 28.
Cup Final: Basle 2, Grasshoppers 1.

TURKEY

Turkiye Futbol Federasyonu, Konaklar Mah. Ihlamurlu Sok. 9, 80620 4 Levent, Istanbul.
Founded: 1923; *Number of Clubs:* 230; *Number of Players:* 64,521; *National Colours:* White shirts, white shorts, red and white stockings.
Telephone: 0090 212 282 70 10; *Cable:* ISTANBUL FUTBOL SPOR; *Telex:* 46308 btff tr; *Fax:* 0090 212 282 70 15.

International matches 2001
Holland (a) 0-0, Slovakia (h) 1-1, Macedonia (a) 2-1, Albania (h) 0-2, Azerbaijan (h) 3-0, Macedonia (h) 3-3, Norway (a) 1-1, Slovakia (a) 1-0, Sweden (h) 1-2, Moldova (a) 3-0, Austria (a) 1-0, Austria (h) 5-0.

League Championship wins (1960–2002)
Galatasaray 15; Fenerbahce 14; Besiktas 10; Trabzonspor 6.

Cup wins (1963–2002)
Galatasaray 13; Besiktas 6; Trabzonspor 5; Fenerbahce 4; Goztepe Izmir 2; Altay Izmir 2; Ankaragucu 2; Genclerbirligi 2; Kocaeli 2; Eskisehirspor 1; Bursapor 1; Sakaryaspor 1.

Final League Table 2001–02

	P	W	D	L	F	A	Pts
Galatasaray	34	24	6	4	75	31	78
Fenerbahce	34	24	3	7	70	31	75
Besiktas	34	18	8	8	69	39	62
Ankaragucu	34	15	8	11	72	58	53
Denizli	34	12	12	10	65	52	48
Gaziantep	34	13	9	12	57	52	48
Goztepe	34	12	9	13	38	56	45
Genclerbirligi	34	11	12	11	47	51	45
Istanbul	34	12	8	14	33	38	44
Bursa	34	13	5	16	48	60	44
Kocaeli	34	12	7	15	45	60	43
Diyarbakir	34	10	10	14	41	50	40
Malatya	34	11	7	16	34	50	40
Trabzonspor	34	11	7	16	49	60	40
Samsun	34	10	8	16	32	43	38
Rize*	34	9	10	15	43	51	37
Antalya*	34	9	10	15	46	61	37
Yozgat*	34	6	9	19	46	67	27

Cup Final: Kocaeli 4, Besiktas 0.

UKRAINE

Football Federation of Ukraine, Ulianovyh Street 1, P.O. Box 503, 252150 Kiev, Ukraine.
Founded: 1991; *Number of Clubs:* 1500; *Number of Players:* 759,500; *National Colours:* Yellow and blue shirts, blue shorts, yellow stockings.
Telephone: 00380 44 2528498; *Fax:* 00380 44 2528513 (or) 2692550; *Telex:* 631461 uff ux.

International matches 2001
Georgia (a) 0-0, Romania (a) 0-1, Cyprus (a) 3-4, Belarus (h) 0-0, Wales (a) 1-1, Norway (h) 0-0, Wales (h) 1-1, Latvia (a) 1-0, Belarus (a) 2-0, Armenia (h) 3-0, Poland (a) 1-1, Germany (h) 1-1, Germany (a) 1-4.

League Championship wins (1992–2002)
Dynamo Kiev 8; Tavriya Simferopol 1; Shakhtjor Donetsk 1.

Cup wins (1992–2002)
Dynamo Kiev 5; Shakhtjor Donetsk 4; Chernomorets 2.

Final League Table 2001–02

	P	W	D	L	F	A	Pts
Shakhtjor Donetsk	26	20	6	0	49	10	66
Dynamo Kiev	26	20	5	1	62	9	65
Metalurg Donetsk	26	12	6	8	38	28	42
Dnepr	26	11	7	8	30	20	40
Metalurg Zapor	26	11	7	8	25	22	40
Metallist Charkov	26	11	7	8	35	36	40
Tavriya	26	8	6	12	27	36	30
Karpaty	26	7	8	11	19	31	29
Krivbas	26	6	10	10	28	40	28
Metalurg Mariupol	26	6	7	13	28	42	25
Vorskla	26	6	7	13	19	33	25
CSKA Kiev	26	6	5	15	18	28	23
Olexandriya*	26	5	8	13	21	39	23
Zakarpattya*	26	6	5	15	23	48	23

Cup Final: Dynamo Kiev 2, Shakhtjor Donetsk 3.

ARGENTINA

Asociacion Del Futbol Argentina, Viamonte 1366/76, 1053 Buenos Aires.
Founded: 1893; *Number of Clubs:* 3,035; *Number of Players:* 306,365; *National Colours:* Light blue and white striped shirts, black shorts, white stockings.
Telephone: 00541 371 4276; *Cable:* FUTBOL BUENOS AIRES; *Telex:* 17848 AFA AR; *Fax:* 00541 375 4410.

International matches 2001
Italy (a) 2-1, Venezuela (h) 5-0, Bolivia (a) 3-3, Colombia (h) 3-0, Ecuador (a) 2-0, Brazil (h) 2-1, Paraguay (a) 2-2, Peru (h) 2-0, Uruguay (a) 1-1.

BOLIVIA

Federacion Boliviana De Futbol, Av. Libertador Bolivar No. 1168, Casilla de Correo 484, Cochabamba, Bolivia.
Founded: 1925; *Number of Clubs:* 305; *Number of Players:* 15,290; *National Colours:* Green shirts with white borders, white shorts with green borders, green stockings.
Telephone: 0059142 44982; *Cable:* FEDFUTBOL COCHABAMBA; *Telex:* 6239 FEDBOL; *Fax:* 0059142 82132.

WALES

The Football Association of Wales Limited, Plymouth Chambers, 3 Westgate Street, Cardiff, South Glamorgan CF1 1DD.
Founded: 1876; *Number of Clubs:* 2,326; *Number of Players:* 53,926; *National Colours:* All red.
Telephone: 01222 372325; *Telex:* 497 363 faw g; *Cable:* WELSOCCER CARDIFF; *Fax:* 01222 343961.

YUGOSLAVIA

Yugoslav Football Association, P.O. Box 263, Terazije 35, 11000 Beograd.
Founded: 1919; *Number of Clubs:* 6,532; *Number of Players:* 229,024; *National Colours:* Blue shirts, white shorts, red stockings.
Telephone: 00381 11 323 3447; *Cable:* JUGOFUDBAL BEOGRAD; *Telex:* 11666 fsj yu; *Fax:* 00381 11 323 3433.

International matches 2001
Switzerland (h) 1-1, Slovenia (a) 1-1, Russia (h) 0-1, Russia (a) 1-1, Faeroes (a) 6-0, Paraguay (n) 0-2, Japan (n) 0-1, Faeroes (h) 2-0, Switzerland (a) 2-1, Slovenia (h) 1-1, Luxembourg (h) 6-2.

League Championship wins (1923–2002)
Red Star Belgrade 22; Partizan Belgrade 17; Hajduk Split 9; Gradjanski Zagreb 5; BSK Belgrade 5; Dynamo Zagreb 4; Jugoslavija Belgrade 2; Concordia Zagreb 2; FC Sarajevo 2; Vojvodina Novi Sad 2; HASK Zagreb 1; Zeljeznicar 1; Obilic 1.

Cup wins (1947–2002)
Red Star Belgrade 19; Hajduk Split 9; Partizan Belgrade 9; Dynamo Zagreb 8; BSK Belgrade 2; OFK Belgrade 2; Rijeka 2; Velez Mostar 2; Vardar Skopje 1; Borac Banjaluka 1.

Final League Table 2001–02

	P	W	D	L	F	A	Pts
Partizan Belgrade	34	25	6	3	82	33	81
Red Star Belgrade	34	18	12	4	54	28	66
Sartid 1913	34	17	7	10	46	36	58
Obilic	34	16	8	10	52	41	56
Zeta	34	15	7	12	48	50	52
Zeleznik	34	14	7	13	41	42	48
Rudar	34	13	8	13	35	33	47
Vojvodina	34	10	16	8	34	26	46
OFK Belgrade	34	12	10	12	44	37	46
Rad	34	13	7	14	45	40	46
Sutjeska	34	14	4	16	32	45	46
Zemun	34	12	9	13	48	43	45
Hajduk Rodic	34	12	9	13	38	42	45
Cukaricki	34	12	7	15	40	40	43
Mladost Lucani*	34	12	6	16	42	42	42
Zvezdara*	34	7	8	19	34	63	29
Mladost Apatin*	34	4	12	18	26	62	24
Radnicki Kragujevac*	34	6	5	23	25	63	23

Cup Final: Red Star Belgrade 1, Sartid 1913 0.

SOUTH AMERICA

International matches 2001
Jamaica (a) 0-3, Colombia (a) 0-2, Argentina (h) 3-3, Venezuela (h) 5-0, Uruguay (n) 0-1, Honduras (n) 0-2, Costa Rica (n) 0-4, Chile (a) 2-2, Paraguay (a) 1-5, Ecuador (h) 1-5, Brazil (h) 3-1, Peru (a) 1-1.

BRAZIL

Confederacao Brasileira De Futebol, Rua Da Alfandega, 70, P.O. Box 1078, 20.070 Rio De Janeiro.
Founded: 1914; *Number of Clubs:* 12,987; *Number of Players:* 551,358; *National Colours:* Yellow shirts with green collar/cuffs, blue shorts, white stockings with green-yellow border.
Telephone: 005521 509 5937; *Cable:* DESPORTOS RIO DE JANEIRO; *Telex:* 21509 CBDS BR; *Fax:* 005521 252 9294.

International matches 2001
USA (a) 2-1, Mexico (a) 3-3, Ecuador (a) 0-1, Peru (h) 1-1, Cameroon (n) 2-0, Canada (n) 0-0, Japan (n) 0-0, France (n) 1-2, Australia (n) 0-1, Uruguay (a) 0-1, Mexico (n) 0-1, Peru (n) 2-0, Paraguay (n) 3-1, Honduras (n) 0-2, Panama (h) 5-0, Paraguay (h) 2-0, Argentina (a) 1-2, Chile (h) 2-0, Bolivia (h) 1-3, Venezuela (h) 3-0.

CHILE

Federacion De Futbol De Chile, Avda. Quillin No. 5635, Casilla postal 3733, Correo Central, Santiago de Chile. *Founded:* 1895; *Number of Clubs:* 4,598; *Number of Players:* 609,724; *National Colours:* Red shirts with white collar and cuffs, blue shorts, white stockings. *Telephone:* 00562 2849000; *Cable:* FEDFUTBOL SANTIAGO DE CHILE; *Fax:* 00562 2843510.

International matches 2001
Honduras (a) 1-3, Peru (a) 1-3, Mexico (a) 0-1, Uruguay (h) 0-1, Paraguay (a) 0-1, Ecuador (n) 4-1, Venezuela (n) 1-0, Colombia (n) 0-2, Mexico (n) 0-2, Bolivia (h) 2-2, France (h) 2-1, Venezuela (h) 0-2, Brazil (a) 0-2, Colombia (a) 1-3, Ecuador (h) 0-0.

COLOMBIA

Federacion Colombiana De Futbol, Avenida 32, No. 16-22 piso 40. Apartado Aereo 17602, Santafe de Bogota. *Founded:* 1924; *Number of Clubs:* 3,685; *Number of Players:* 188,050; *National Colours:* Yellow shirts with tricolour borders, blue shorts, red stockings with tricolour borders. *Telephone:* 00571 2853320; *Cable:* COLFUTBOL BOGOTA; *Fax:* 00571 2889740.

International matches 2001
Mexico (a) 3-2, USA (a) 1-0, Australia (h) 3-2, Bolivia (h) 2-0, Venezuela (a) 2-2, Argentina (a) 0-3, Venezuela (h) 2-0, Ecuador (h) 1-0, Chile (h) 2-0, Peru (h) 3-0, Honduras (h) 2-0, Mexico (h) 1-0, Liberia (h) 2-1, Peru (h) 0-1, Ecuador (h) 0-0, Uruguay (a) 1-1, Chile (h) 3-1, Paraguay (a) 4-0.

ECUADOR

Federacion Ecuatoriana del Futbol, km 4 via a la Costa (Avda. del Bombero), Guayaquil. *Founded:* 1925; *Number of Clubs:* 170; *Number of Players:* 15,700; *National Colours:* Yellow shirts with blue and red fringes, blue shorts, red stockings. *Telephone:* 005934 352 372/3; *Cable:* ECUAFUTBOL GUAYAQUIL; *Fax:* 005934 352 116.

International matches 2001
Brazil (h) 1-0, Paraguay (h) 2-1, Peru (a) 2-1, USA (a) 0-0, El Salvador (a) 1-0, Honduras (a) 1-1, Chile (n) 1-4, Colombia (n) 0-1, Venezuela (n) 4-0, Argentina (h) 0-2, Colombia (a) 0-0, Bolivia (a) 5-1, Uruguay (h) 1-1, Chile (a) 0-0.

PARAGUAY

Asociacion Paraguaya de Futbol, Estadio De Sajonia, Calles Mayor Martinez Y Alejo Garcia, Asuncion. *Founded:* 1906; *Number of Clubs:* 1,500; *Number of Players:* 140,000; *National Colours:* Red and white shirts, blue shorts, blue stockings. *Telephone:* 0059521 480120; *Telex:* 38009 PY FUTBOL; *Fax:* 0059521 480124.

International matches 2001

South Korea (a) 1-1, Uruguay (a) 1-0, Ecuador (a) 1-2, Chile (h) 1-0, Yugoslavia (n) 2-0, Japan (n) 0-2, Peru (n) 3-3, Mexico (n) 0-0, Brazil (n) 1-3, Brazil (a) 0-2, Bolivia (h) 5-1, Argentina (h) 2-2, Venezuela (a) 1-3, Colombia (h) 0-4.

PERU

Federacion Peruana De Futbol, Av. Aviacion Cdra. 20 s/n, San Luis, Lima. *Founded:* 1922; *Number of Clubs:* 10,000; *Number of Players:* 325,650; *National Colours:* White shirts with red stripe, white shorts with red lines, white stockings with red line. *Telephone:* 00511 2258236-9; *Cable* FEPEFUTBOL LIMA; *Fax:* 00511 2258240; *Telex:* 20066 FEPEFUT PE.

International matches 2001
Honduras (a) 0-0, Chile (h) 3-1, Brazil (a) 1-1, Ecuador (h) 1-2, Paraguay (n) 3-3, Bolivia (n) 0-2, Mexico (n) 1-0, Colombia (n) 0-3, Colombia (a) 1-0, Uruguay (h) 0-2, Venezuela (a) 0-3, Argentina (a) 0-2, Bolivia (h) 1-1.

URUGUAY

Asociacion Uruguaya De Futbol, Guayabo 1531, 11200 Montevideo. *Founded:* 1900; *Number of Clubs:* 1,091; *Number of Players:* 134,310; *National Colours:* Sky blue shirts with white collar/cuffs, black shorts, black stockings with sky blue borders. *Telephone:* 005982 4007101/06; *Cable:* FOOTBALL MONTEVIDEO; *Fax:* 005982 4090550; *Telex:* AUF UY 22607.

International matches 2001
Slovenia (a) 2-0, Paraguay (h) 0-1, Chile (a) 1-0, Brazil (h) 1-0, Bolivia (n) 1-0, Costa Rica (n) 1-1, Honduras (n) 0-1, Costa Rica (n) 2-1, Mexico (n) 1-2, Honduras (n) 2-2, Venezuela (a) 0-2, Peru (a) 2-0, Colombia (h) 1-1, Ecuador (a) 1-1, Argentina (h) 1-1, Australia (a) 0-1, Australia (h) 3-0.

VENEZUELA

Federacion Venezolana De Futbol, Avda S. Erminy, Torre Mega II Pent House B, e/Sabana Gr. y la Solano, Parroquia el Recreo, Caracas. *Founded:* 1926; *Number of Clubs:* 1,753; *Number of Players:* 63,175; *National Colours:* Dark red shirts, white shorts, white stockings with black border. *Telephone:* 00582 7620362; *Cable:* FEVEFUTBOL CARACAS; *Telex:* 26140 FVFCS VC; *Fax:* 00582 7620596.

International matches 2001
Argentina (a) 0-5, Costa Rica (a) 2-2, Colombia (h) 2-2, Bolivia (a) 0-5, Colombia (n) 0-2, Chile (n) 0-1, Ecuador (n) 0-4, Uruguay (h) 2-0, Chile (a) 2-0, Peru (h) 3-0, Paraguay (h) 3-1, Brazil (a) 0-3.

ASIA

AFGHANISTAN

Afghanistan Football Federation, c/o Afghanistan Olympic Committee, P.O. Box 1824, Kabul. *Founded:* 1933; Number of Clubs: 30; Number of Players: 3,300; National Colours: All white with red lines. *Telephone:* 0093 11420579; *Cable:* OLYMPIC KABUL.

BAHRAIN

Bahrain Football Association, P.O. Box 5464, Manama. *Founded:* 1957; *Number of Clubs:* 25; *Number of Players:* 2,030; *National Colours:* All red. *Telephone:* 00973 252929; *Cable:* BAHKORA BAHRAIN; *Telex:* 9040 FAB BN; *Fax:* 00973 255560.

BANGLADESH

Bangladesh Football Federation, National Stadium-1, Dhaka 1000. *Founded:* 1972; *Number of Clubs:* 1,265; *Number of Players:* 30,385; *National Colours:* Orange shirts, white shorts, green stockings. *Telephone:* 008802 9556072; *Cable:* FOOTBALFED DHAKA; *Fax:* 008802 9563419.

BHUTAN

Bhutan Football Federation, P.O. Box 365, Thimphu. *Telephone:* 009752 322350; *Fax:* 009752 321131.

BRUNEI

The Football Association of Brunei Darussalam, P.O. Box 2010, 1920 Bandar Seri Begawan. *Founded:* 1959; *Number of Clubs:* 22; *Number of Players:* 830; *National Colours:* Yellow shirts, black shorts, yellow stockings. *Telephone:* 006732 383883; *Cable:* BAFA BRUNEI; *Telex:* BU 2575 Attn; BAFA; *Fax:* 006732 382900.

CAMBODIA

Cambodian Football Federation, PO Box 2327 PTT, Phnom-Penh 3. *Founded:* 1933; *Number of Clubs:* 30; *Number of Players:* 650; *National Colours:* Blue, red and white shirts, white and blue shorts, red, white and blue stockings. *Telephone:* 0085523 364889; *Cable:* CFF PHNOM PENH; *Fax:* 0088523 367191.

CHINA PR

Football Association of The People's Republic of China, 9 Tiyuguan Road, Beijing 100763. *Founded:* 1924; *Number of Clubs:* 1,045; *Number of Players:* 2,250,000; *National Colours:* All white. *Telephone:* 008610 67117019; *Cable:* SPORTSCHINE BEIJING; *Telex:* 22034 ACSF CN; *Fax:* 008610 67142533.

CHINA TAIPEI

Chinese Taipei Football Association, 100, Kuang-Fu South Road, Taipei, Taiwan.
Founded: 1936; *Number of Players:* 17,000; *National Colours:* Blue shirts, white shorts, red stockings.
Telephone: 008862 27117710; *Cable:* CTFA Taipei; *Fax:* 008862 27117713.

GUAM

Guam Soccer Association, P.O.Box 5093, Agana, Guam 96932.
Founded: 1975; *National Colours:* Blue shirts, white shorts, blue stockings.
Telephone: 00671 472 1824, 646 9609; *Fax:* 00671 4775424.

HONG KONG

The Hong Kong Football Association Ltd, 55 Fat Kwong Street, Homantin, Kowloon, Hong Kong.
Founded: 1914; *Number of Clubs:* 69; *Number of Players:* 3,274; *National Colours:* All red.
Telephone: 00852 27129122; *Cable:* FOOTBALL HONG KONG; *Telex:* 40518 FAHKG HX; *Fax:* 00852 27604303.

INDIA

All India Football Federation , Mr KN Mour, Gen. Secretary, Youth Hostel Complex, Paltan Bazar, Guwahati - 781 008, Assam.
Founded: 1937; *Number of Clubs:* 2,000; *Number of Players:* 56,000; *National Colours:* Orange shirts, white shorts, green stockings.
Telephone: 0091361 525109; *Fax:* 0091 361525110.

INDONESIA

All Indonesia Football Federation, Wisma Karsa Pemuda, Jl.Gerbang Pemuda No. 3, PO Box 2305, Jakarta 10023.
Founded: 1930; *Number of Clubs:* 2,880; *Number of Players:* 97,000; *National Colours:* Red shirts, white shorts, red and white stockings.
Telephone: 006221 5722948; *Cable:* PSSI JAKARTA; *Telex:* 65739 PSSI IA; *Fax:* 006221 5734386.

IRAN

IR Iran Football Federation, Shahid Keshvari Sports Complex, Mirdamad Ave., Razan Jonoobi Str., PO Box 15875-6967 Tehran 15875.
Founded: 1920; *Number of Clubs:* 6,326; *Number of Players:* 306,000; *National Colours:* All white.
Telephone: 009821 2258116; *Cable:* FOOTBALL IRAN - TEHRAN; *Telex:* 212691 NOC IR; *Fax:* 009821 2258123.

IRAQ

Iraqi Football Association, Olympic Committee Building, Palestine Street, PO Box 484, Baghdad.
Founded: 1948; *Number of Clubs:* 155; *Number of Players:* 4,400; *National Colours:* All black.
Telephone: 009641 7729990; *Cable:* BALL BAGHDAD; *Telex:* 213409 IRFA IK; *Fax:* 009641 7744475.

JAPAN

Japan Football Association, 2nd Floor, Gotoh Ikueikai Bldg, 1-10-7 Dogenzaka, Shibuya-Ku, Tokyo 150, Japan.
Founded: 1921; *Number of Clubs:* 13,047; *Number of Players:* 358,989; *National Colours:* Blue shirts, white shorts, blue stockings.
Telephone: 00813 34762011; *Cable:* SOCCERJAPAN TOKYO; *Telex:* 2422975 FOTJPN J; *Fax:* 00813 34762291.

JORDAN

Jordan Football Association, P.O. Box 962024 Al. Hussein Sports City, 11196 Amman.
Founded: 1949; *Number of Clubs:* 98; *Number of Players:* 4,305; *National Colours:* All white and red.
Telephone: 009626 5657662/3/4/5; *Cable:* JORDAN FOOTBALL ASSN AMMAN; *Fax:* 009626 5657660.

KOREA, NORTH

Football Association of The Democratic People's Rep. of Korea, Kumsong-dong 2, Mangyongdae Distr, Pyongyang.
Founded: 1945; *Number of Clubs:* 90; *Number of Players:* 3,420; *National Colours:* All white.
Telephone: 008502 3814164; *Cable:* DPR KOREA

FOOTBALL PYONGYANG; *Telex:* 5472 KP; *Fax:* 008502 3814403.

KOREA, SOUTH

Korea Football Association, 110-39, Kyeonji-Dong, Chongro-Ku, Seoul.
Founded: 1928; *Number of Clubs:* 476; *Number of Players:* 2,047; *National Colours:* Red shirts, black shorts, red stockings.
Telephone: 00822 7336764; *Cable:* FOOTBALLKOREA SEOUL; *Telex:* KFASEL K 25373; *Fax:* 00822 7352755.

KUWAIT

Kuwait Football Association, P.O. Box 2029 Safat, 13021 Safat.
Founded: 1952; *Number of Clubs:* 14 (senior); *Number of Players:* 1,526; *National Colours:* Blue shirts, white shorts, blue stockings.
Telephone: 00965 2555851; *Cable:* FOOT KUWAIT; *Fax:* 00965 2549955.

KYRGYZSTAN

Football Association of Kyrgyz Republic, Frunze Street, 503 Bishkek 720040, Kyrgyzstan.
Founded: 1992; *Number of Players:* 20,000; *National Colours:* Red shirts, white shorts, red stockings.
Telephone: 00331 2223507; *Fax:* 00331 2225492.

LAOS

Federation Lao de Football, National Stadium, Vientiane, Laos.
Founded: 1951; *Number of Clubs:* 76; *Number of Players:* 2,060; *National Colours:* Red shirts, white shorts, blue stockings.
Telephone: 0085621 216008/9; *Cable:* FOOTBALL VIENTIANE; *Fax:* 0085621 216008.

LEBANON

Federation Libanaise De Football-Association, P.O. Box 4732, Verdun Street, Bristol, Radwan Centre Building, Beirut.
Founded: 1933; *Number of Clubs:* 105; *Number of Players:* 8,125; *National Colours:* Red shirts, white shorts, red stockings.
Telephone: 009611 347157; *Cable:* FOOTBALL BEIRUT; *Telex:* 21404 LIBALL; *Fax:* 009611 349529; Internet: http://www.lebanon-online.com/lfa; E-mail: lfa@lebanon-online.com.lb.

MACAO

Associacao De Futebol De Macau (AFM), P.O. Box 920, Macau.
Founded: 1939; *Number of Clubs:* 52; *Number of Players:* 800; *National Colours:* Green shirts, black shorts, green stockings.
Telephone: 00853 71996; *Cable:* FOOTBALL MACAU; *Fax:* 00853 260148.

MALAYSIA

Football Association of Malaysia, Wisma Fam, Tingkat 3, Jalan SS5A/9, Kelana Jaya, 47301 Petaling Jaya, Selangor.
Founded: 1933; *Number of Clubs:* 450; *Number of Players:* 11,250; *National Colours:* All yellow and black.
Telephone: 00603 7763766; *Cable:* FOOTB. PETALING JAYA SELANGO; *Telex:* FAM PJ MA 36701; *Fax:* 00603 7757984.

MALDIVES REPUBLIC

Football Association of Maldives, National Stadium Ghalolhu, Male 20-04.
Founded: 1982; *Number of Clubs: Number of Players: National Colours:* Green shirts, white shorts, red stockings.
Telephone: 0096031 7006; *Fax:* 0096031 7005.

MONGOLIA

Mongolia Football Federation, R413, Mongolia Youth Association Building, Baga Toiruu 10, Ulaanbaatar 10.
Telephone & fax: 009761 313145.

MYANMAR

Myanmar Football Federation, Attn Maj. Naw Tawng, Gen. Secr. Youth Training Centre, Thuwunna, Yangon.
Founded: 1947; *Number of Clubs:* 600; *Number of Players:* 21,000; *National Colours:* Red shirts, white shorts, red stockings.
Telephone: 00951 577366; *Cable:* FOOTBALL YANGON; *Telex:* 21253 SPED BM; *Fax:* 00951 571253.

NEPAL

All-Nepal Football Association, Dasharath Rangashala, Tripureshwor, PO Box 2090, Kathmandu.
Founded: 1951; *Number of Clubs:* 85; *Number of Players:* 2,550; *National Colours:* All red.
Telephone: 009771 241367; *Cable:* ANFA KATHMANDU; *Telex:* 2390 NSC NP; *Fax:* 009771 241365.

OMAN

Oman Football Association, P.O. Box 3462, Ruwi Postal Code 112.
Founded: 1978; *Number of Clubs:* 47; *Number of Players:* 2,340; *National Colours:* Red shirts with white sleeves, red/white shorts and stockings.
Telephone: 00968 787638/9; *Cable:* FOOTBALL MUSCAT; *Telex:* FOOTBALL 3223 ON; *Fax:* 00968 787632/33.

PAKISTAN

Pakistan Football Federation, 183, Abu Bakar Block, New Garden Town, Lahore, Pakistan.
Founded: 1948; *Number of Clubs:* 882; *Number of Players:* 21,000; *National Colours:* Green shirts, white shorts, green stockings.
Telephone: 009242 5832786; *Cable:* FOOTBALL LAHORE; *Telex:* 47643 PFF PK; *Fax:* 009242 7281541.

PALESTINE

Palestinian Football Federation, Al-Yarmouk, Gaza.
Telephone: 009727 829433; *Fax:* 009727 857020.

PHILIPPINES

Philippine Football Federation, Room 207 PSC, Administration Building, Rizal Memorial Sports Complex, P. Ocampo Street, Manila.
Founded: 1907; *Number of Clubs:* 650; *Number of Players:* 45,000; *National Colours:* Blue and red shirts, blue shorts, white stockings.
Telephone: 00632 5256502; *Cable:* FOOTBALL MANILA; *Telex:* 65014 POC PACA PN; *Fax:* 00632 5233741.

QATAR

Qatar Football Association, P.O. Box 5333, Doha.
Founded: 1960; *Number of Clubs:* 8 (senior); *Number of Players:* 1,380; *National Colours:* All white.
Telephone: 00974 434455; *Cable:* FOOTQATAR DOHA; *Telex:* 4749 QATFOT DH; *Fax:* 00974 411660.

SAUDI ARABIA

Saudi Arabian Football Federation, Al Mather Quarter (Olympic Complex), P.O. Box 5844, Riyadh 11432.
Founded: 1959; *Number of Clubs:* 120; *Number of Players:* 9,600; *National Colours:* White shirts, green shorts, white stockings.
Telephone: 009661 4822240; *Cable:* KURA RIYADH; *Telex:* 404300 SAFOTB SJ; *Fax:* 009661 4821215.

SINGAPORE

Football Association of Singapore, Jalan Besar Stadium, Tyrwhitt Road, Singapore 207542.
Founded: 1892; *Number of Clubs:* 250; *Number of Players:* 8,000; *National Colours:* All red.
Telephone: 0065 2931477; *Fax:* 0065 2933728.

SRI LANKA

Football Federation of Sri Lanka, No. 2, Old Grand Stand, Race Course, Reid Avenue, Colombo 7.
Founded: 1939; *Number of Clubs:* 600; *Number of Players:* 18,825; *National Colours:* Maroon and gold shirts, white shorts and stockings.
Telephone: 00941 696179; *Cable:* SOCCER COLOMBO; *Telex:* 21537 METALIX CE; *Fax:* 00941 682471.

SYRIA

Syrian Football Federation, Maysaloon St., PO Box 421, Damascus.
Founded: 1936; *Number of Clubs:* 102; *Number of Players:* 30,600; *National Colours:* All white.
Telephone: 0096311 3335866; *Cable:* FOOTBALL DAMASCUS; *Telex:* 411578 SPOFED SY; *Fax:* 0096311 3331511.

TAJIKISTAN

Tajikistan National Football Federation, 44, Rudaki Ave., PO Box 26, 734025 Dushanbe, Tajikistan.
Founded: 1991; *Number of Clubs:* 1,804; *Number of Players:* 71,400; *National Colours:* Green shirts, white shorts, green stockings.
Telephone: 0073772 212363; *Telex:* 116286 SHAKH; *Fax:* 00992 372212447 (or) 212953.

THAILAND

The Football Association of Thailand, National Stadium, Rama I Road, Bangkok.
Founded: 1916; *Number of Clubs:* 168; *Number of Players:* 15,000; *National Colours:* All red.
Telephone: 00662 2141058; *Cable:* FOOTBALL BANGKOK; *Telex:* 20211 FAT TH; *Fax:* 00662 2154494.

TURKMENISTAN

Turkmenistan Football Federation, 10 Turkmenbashi Avenue, 744005 Ashgabat, Turkmenistan.
Founded: 1992; *Number of Players:* 75,000; *National Colours:* Green shirts, white shorts, green stockings.
Telephone: 00363 2353739; *Fax:* 00363 2355327; *Telex:* 116175 TINTO SU.

UNITED ARAB EMIRATES

United Arab Emirates Football Association, P.O. Box 916, Abu Dhabi.
Founded: 1971; *Number of Clubs:* 23 (senior); *Number of Players:* 1,787; *National Colours:* All white.
Telephone: 00971 2444 5600; *Cable:* FOOTBALL EMIRATES ABU DHABI; *Telex:* 22121 UAEFA EM; *Fax:* 00971 2444 8558.

UZBEKISTAN

Uzbekistan Football Federation, Massiv Almazar Furkat Street 15/1, 700003 Tashkent, Uzbekistan.
Founded: 1946; *Number of Clubs:* 15,000; *Number of Players:* 217,000; *National Colours:* Blue shirts, white shorts, green stockings.
Telephone: 0073712 457106; *Telex:* 116108 PTB SU; *Fax:* 0073712 454948.

VIETNAM

Vietnam Football Federation, 141 Nguyen Thai Hoc Str., Dis Dongda, Hanoi.
Founded: 1962; *Number of Clubs:* 55 (senior); *Number of Players:* 16,000; *National Colours:* All red.
Telephone: 008448 452480; *Cable:* AFBVN, 141 NGUYEN THAI HOC STR.; *Fax:* 008448 233119.

YEMEN

Yemen Football Association, P.O. Box 908, Sana'a.
Founded: 1962; *Number of Clubs:* 26; *Number of Players:* 1750; *National Colours:* All green.
Telephone: 009671 269066. *Cable:* SANA'A FOOTBALL; *Telex:* 2710 YOUTH YE; *Fax:* 009671 276067.

CONCACAF

ANGUILLA

Anguilla Football Association, P.O. Box 608, The Valley, Anguilla, BWI.
National Colours: All blue.
Telephone: 001264 4975214/4972416; *Fax:* 001264 4972326.

ANTIGUA & BARBUDA

The Antigua Football Association, P.O. Box 773, St John's.
Founded: 1928; *Number of Clubs:* 60; *Number of Players:* 1,008; *National Colours:* Gold shirts, black shorts and stockings.
Telephone: 001268 4624863; *Cable:* AFA ANTIGUA; *Fax:* 001268 4624864.

ARUBA

Arubaanse Voetbal Bond, P.O. Box 376, Oranjestad, Aruba.
Founded: 1932; *Number of Clubs:* 50; *Number of Players:* 1,000; *National Colours:* Yellow shirts, blue shorts, yellow and blue stockings.
Telephone: 00297 829550; *Cable:* AVB ARUBA; *Fax:* 00297 820624.

BAHAMAS

Bahamas Football Association, P.O. Box N 8434, Nassau, NP.
Founded: 1967; *Number of Clubs:* 14; *Number of Players:* 700; *National Colours:* Yellow shirts, black shorts, yellow stockings.
Telephone: 001809 3233426; *Cable:* BAHSOCA NASSAU; *Fax:* 001809 3288006.

BARBADOS

Barbados Football Association, P.O. Box 1362, Bridgetown, Barbados.
Physical address: Hadley Court, Upper Collymore Rock, St Michael.
Founded: 1910; *Number of Clubs:* 92; *Number of Players:* 1,100; *National Colours:* Royal blue and gold shirts, gold shorts, white, gold and blue stockings.
Tel: 001246 2281707; *Cable:* FOOTBALL BRIDGETOWN; *Fax:* 001246 2286484.

BELIZE

Belize National Football Association, P.O. Box 1742, Belize City.
Founded: 1980; *National Colours:* Red, white and blue shirts and shorts, red stockings.
Telephone: 005012 36563; *Fax:* 005012 36564.

BERMUDA

The Bermuda Football Association, P.O. Box HM 745, Hamilton HM CX.
Founded: 1928; *Number of Clubs:* 30; *Number of Players:* 1,947; *National Colours:* Royal blue shirts, white shorts and stockings.
Telephone: 001809 2952199; *Cable:* FOOTBALL BERMUDA; *Telex:* 3441 BFA BA; *Fax:* 001809 2950773.

BRITISH VIRGIN ISLANDS

British Virgin Islands Football Association, P.O. Box 29, Road Town, Tortola, BVI.
Telephone: 001284 4945655; *Fax:* 001284 4948968.

US VIRGIN ISLANDS

V.I. Soccer Federation, P.O. Box 2618, Kingshill, St Croix, USVI 00851-2618.
Telephone: 001 340 7737216; *Fax:* 001 340 7739686.

CANADA

The Canadian Soccer Association, Place Soccer Canada, 237 Metcalfe Street, Ottawa, ONT K2P 1R2.
Founded: 1912; *Number of Clubs:* 1,600; *Number of Players:* 224,290; *National Colours:* All red.
Telephone: 001613 2377678; *Cable:* SOCCANADA OTTAWA; *Fax:* 001613 2371516.

CAYMAN ISLANDS

Cayman Islands Football Association, PO Box 178 GT, George Town, Grand Cayman, Cayman Islands WI.
Founded: 1966; *Number of Clubs:* 25; *Number of Players:* 875; *National Colours:* Red shirts, blue shorts, white stockings.
Telephone: 001345 9497822328. *Fax:* 001345 945 7673.

COSTA RICA

Federacion Costarricense De Futbol, Apartado 670-1000, Calle 40, Avda CTL & I, San Jose.
Founded: 1921; *Number of Clubs:* 431; *Number of Players:* 12,429; *National Colours:* Red and white shirts, blue shorts, white stockings.
Telephone: 00506 2221544; *Cable:* FEDEFUTBOL SAN JOSE; *Telex:* 3394 DIDER CR; *Fax:* 00506 2552674.

CUBA

Federacion Cubana De Futbol, c/o Comite Olimpico Cubano, Calle 13 No. 601, Esq. C. Vedado, La Habana, ZP 4.
Founded: 1924; *Number of Clubs:* 70; *Number of Players:* 12,900; *National Colours:* White shirts with red collar and cuffs, dark blue shorts, white and red stockings.
Telephone: 00537 403581; *Cable:* FOOTBALL HABANA; *Telex:* 511332 INDER CU; *Fax:* 00537 409037.

DOMINICA

Dominica Football Association, P.O. Box 372, Roseau, Commonwealth of Dominica.
Founded: 1970; *Number of Clubs:* 30; *Number of Players:* 500; *National Colours:* Emerald green shirts, green shorts, yellow stockings.
Telephone & fax: 001767 4492173.

DOMINICAN REPUBLIC

Federacion Dominicana De Futbol, Apartado De Correos No. 1953, Santo Domingo.
Founded: 1953; *Number of Clubs:* 128; *Number of Players:* 10,706; *National Colours:* Navy blue shirts, white shorts, red stockings.
Telephone: 001809542 6923. *Cable:* FEDOFUTBOL SANTO DOMINGO; *Telex:* 817240; *Fax:* 001809547 5363.

EL SALVADOR

Federacion Salvadorena De Futbol, Av. J.M. Delgado, Col. Escalon, Frente Ctro Espanol, Apartado 1029, San Salvador.
Founded: 1935; *Number of Clubs:* 944; *Number of Players:* 21,294; *National Colours:* Blue shirts, white shorts, blue stockings.
Telephone: 00503 2637525/6; *Cable:* FESFUT SAN SALVADOR; *Fax:* 00503 2637583.

GRENADA

Grenada Football Association, P.O. Box 326, St Juilles Street, St George's, Grenada, West Indies.
Founded: 1924; *Number of Clubs:* 15; *Number of Players:* 200; *National Colours:* Green and yellow striped shirts, red shorts, yellow stockings.
Telephone & fax: 001473 4404850; *Cable:* GRENBALL GRENADA; *Telex:* 3431 CW BUR.

GUATEMALA

Federacion Nacional de Futbol de Guatemala, 7a Avenida 12-23 Zona 9, Edificio Etisa 6. Nivel, Guatemala City.
Founded: 1946; *Number of Clubs:* 1,611; *Number of Players:* 43,516; *National Colours:* Blue shirts, white shorts, blue stockings.
Telephone: 005023 322424; *Cable:* FEDFUTBOL GUATEMALA C.A.; *Fax:* 005023 320406.

GUYANA

Guyana Football Association, Lot 65 King Street, P.O. Box 10727, Georgetown.
Founded: 1902; *Number of Clubs:* 103; *Number of Players:* 1,665; *National Colours:* Green shirts and shorts, yellow stockings.
Telephone: 0059222 78758, 63226; *Telex:* 2266 RICEBRD GY; *Fax:* 0059222 52096, 62641.

HAITI

Federation Haitienne De Football, P.O. Box 2258, Port-Au-Prince.
Founded: 1904; *Number of Clubs:* 40; *Number of Players:* 4,000; *National Colours:* Blue and red shirts, blue shorts, blue and red stockings.
Telephone: 00509 464509; *Cable:* FEDHAFOOB PORT-AU-PRINCE; *Fax:* 00509 573001.

HONDURAS

Federacion Nacional Autonoma De Futbol De Honduras, Apartado Postal 827, Costa Oeste Del Est. Nac, Tegucigalpa, D.C.
Founded: 1951; *Number of Clubs:* 1,050; *Number of Players:* 15,300; *National Colours:* Blue shirts, white shorts, blue stockings.
Telephone: 00504 235 4236 (or) 235 4246; *Cable* FENAFUTH TEGUCIGALPA; *Fax:* 00504 235 4237.

JAMAICA

Jamaica Football Federation, General Secretariat, Room 8, Nat. Arena, Institue of Sports, Independence Park, Kingston 6.
Founded: 1910; *Number of Clubs:* 266; *Number of Players:* 45,200; *National Colours:* Gold shirts, black shorts, gold stockings.
Telephone: 001809 9290484; *Cable:* FOOTBALL JAMAICA KINGSTON; *Telex:* 2224 FEDLASCO JA; *Fax:* 001809 9290483.

MEXICO

Federacion Mexicana De Futbol Asociacion, A.C., Abraham Gonzales 74, Col. Juarez, C.P. 06600, Mexico 6, D.F.
Founded: 1927; *Number of Clubs:* 77 (senior); *Number of Players:* 1,402,270; *National Colours:* Green shirts with white collar, white shorts, red stockings.
Telephone: 00525 5662155; *Cable:* MEXFUTBOL MEXICO; *Fax:* 00525 5667580.

MONSERRAT

Monserrat Football Association, P.O. Box 46, Church Road, Plymouth, Monserrat.
Telephone: 001664 4912346; *Fax:* 001664 4912719.

NETHERLANDS ANTILLES

Nederlands Antiliaanse Voetbal Unie, P.O. Box 341, Curacao, NA.
Founded: 1921; *Number of Clubs:* 85; *Number of Players:* 4,500; *National Colours:* white shirts with red and blue stripes, white shorts, red, white and blue stockings.
Telephone: 005999 4627222/4343862; *Cable:* NAVU CURACAO; *Telex:* 1046 ENNIA NA; *Fax:* 005999 4627087/4343837.

NICARAGUA

Federacion Nicaraguense De Futbol, Estadio Futbol Camilo Ortega (Cranshaw), Apdo Postal 976, Managua.
Founded: 1931; *Number of Clubs:* 31; *Number of Players:* 160 (senior); *National Colours:* Blue and white striped shirts, blue shorts, blue and white striped stockings.
Telephone: 005052 680006/7/8; *Cable:* FENIFUT MANAGUA; *Fax:* 005052 664134.

PANAMA

Federacion Panamena De Futbol, Apartado Postal 8-391, Zona 8, Panama.
Founded: 1937; *Number of Clubs:* 65; *Number of Players:* 4,225; *National Colours:* Red shirts, blue shorts, white stockings.
Telephone & fax: 00507 2282238.

PUERTO RICO

Federacion Puertorriquena De Futbol, Coliseo Roberto Clemente, P.O. Box 1944355, Hato Rey, P.R. 00919-4355.
Founded: 1940; *Number of Clubs:* 175; *Number of Players:* 4,200; *National Colours:* Blue shirts, blue and white shorts and stockings.
Telephone & fax: 001787 7642025.

SAINT LUCIA

St Lucia National Football Association, PO Box 255, Castries, St Lucia.
Founded: 1979; *Number of Clubs:* 100; *Number of Players:* 4,000; *National Colours:* Blue and white shirts, black shorts, blue stockings.
Telephone: 001758 0689; *Cable:* NFU ST. LUCIA; *Telex:* 6394 FOR AFF LC; *Fax:* 001758 2506.

SAINT KITTS & NEVIS

St Kitts-Nevis Football Association, P.O. Box 465, Basseterre, St Kitts, WI.
Founded: 1932; *Number of Clubs:* 36; *Number of Players:* 600; *National Colours:* Green and yellow shirts, red shorts, yellow stockings.
Telephone: 001869 465 6809; *Cable:* HORSFORD ST. KITTS; *Telex:* 6822 HORSFDSKB KC; *Fax:* 001869 465 1190; *Internet:* www.skbee.com/sknfa; *E-mail:* sknfa@skbee.com.

SAINT VINCENT & THE GRENADINES

St Vincent & The Grenadines Football Federation, PO Box 1278, Kingstown, St Vincent, WI.
Founded: 1979; *Number of Clubs:* 500; *Number of Players:* 5,000; *National Colours:* Green shirts with yellow border, blue shorts, yellow stockings.
Telephone: 001784 4561659; *Fax:* 001784 4571659.

SURINAM

Surinaamse Voetbal Bond, Letitia Vriesde Laan 7, P.O. Box 1223, Paramaribo.
Founded: 1920; *Number of Clubs:* 168; *Number of Players:* 4,430; *National Colours:* Red green and white shirts, white or green shorts and stockings.
Telephone: 00597 473112; *Cable:* SVB Paramaribo; *Fax:* 00597 479718.

TRINIDAD & TOBAGO

Trinidad & Tobago Football Federation, Petrotrin Savannah Building, 9 Queen's Park West, P.O. Box 400, Port of Spain.
Founded: 1908; *Number of Clubs:* 124; *Number of Players:* 5,050; *National Colours:* Red shirts, black shorts, white stockings.
Telephone: 001809 6271011; *Fax:* 001809 6271007.

TURKS & CAICOS

Turks & Caicos Football Association, P.O. Box 180, Providenciales, Turks & Caicos Islands, BWI.
Telephone: 001649 9464650; *Fax:* 001649 9464663.

USA

US Soccer, Soccer House, 1801-1811 S. Prairie Avenue, Chicago, Illinois 60616.
Founded: 1913; *Number of Clubs:* 7,000; *Number of Players:* 1,411,500; *National Colours:* All white.
Telephone: 001312 8081300; *Telex:* 450024 US SOCCER FED; *Fax:* 001312 8081301.

OCEANIA

AMERICAN SAMOA

American Samoa Football Association, P.O. Box 282, Pago Pago.
Telephone: 00684 6882290; *Fax:* 00684 6882291.

AUSTRALIA

Soccer Australia, Sydney Football Stadium, Driver Avenue, P.O. Box 175, Paddington NSW 2021.
Founded: 1961; *Number of Clubs:* 6,816; *Number of Players:* 433,957; *National Colours:* Gold shirts with green trim, gold shorts, gold and green stockings.
Telephone: 0061 293806099; *Cable:* FOOTBALL SYDNEY; *Fax:* 0061 293806155.

COOK ISLANDS

Cook Islands Football Federation, P.O. Box 29, Avarua, Rarotonga, Cook Islands.
Founded: 1971; *Number of Clubs:* 9; *National Colours:* Green shirts and shorts with gold stripes, gold and green stockings.
Telephone: 00682 21231; *Fax:* 00682 25912.

FIJI

Fiji Football Association, Bob S. Kumar, Hon. Secretary, Government Bldgs, P.O.Box 2514, Suva.
Founded: 1938; *Number of Clubs:* 140; *Number of Players:* 21,300; *National Colours:* White shirts, blue shorts and stockings.
Telephone: 00679 300453; *Fax:* 00679 304642.

NEW ZEALAND

Soccer New Zealand, 51 O'Rorke Road, Penrose, Auckland, New Zealand.
Founded: 1891; *Number of Clubs:* 312; *Number of Players:* 52,969; *National Colours:* White shirts with black trim, white shorts and stockings.
Telephone: 00649 5256120; *Fax:* 00649 5256123.

PAPUA NEW GUINEA

Papua New Guinea Football (Soccer) Association, c/o National Sports Institute, P.O. Box 337, Goroka, EHP 441.

Founded: 1962; *Number of Clubs:* 350; *Number of Players:* 8,250; *National Colours:* Red shirts, black shorts, red stockings.
Telephone: 00675 7321699; *Telex:* TOTOTRA NE 23436; *Fax:* 00675 7321941.

SOLOMON ISLANDS

Solomon Islands Football Federation, PO Box 854, Honiara, Solomon Islands.
Founded: 1978; *Number of Players:* 4,000; *National Colours:* Green, yellow and blue shirts and shorts, white stockings.
Telephone: 00677 26496; *Telex:* HQ 66349; *Fax:* 00677 26497.

TAHITI

Federation Tahitienne de Football (F.T.F.), B.P.50 358, Pirae, Tahiti, French Polynesia.
Founded: 1989; *National Colours:* White shirts, red shorts, white stockings.
Telephone: 00689 540954; *Cable:* FOOTBALL TAHITI; *Fax:* 00689 419629.

TONGA

Tonga Football Association, P.O. Box 852, Nuku'Alofa, Tonga.
Founded: 1965; *Number of Clubs:* 23; *Number of Players:* 350; *National Colours:* Red shirts, white shorts, red and white stockings.
Telephone: 00676 24442; *Cable:* SOCCER NUKU'ALOFA; *Fax:* 00676 23340; E-mail: tfa@kalianet.to.

VANUATU

Vanuatu Football Federation, P.O. Box 226, Port Vila, Vanuatu.
Founded: 1934; *National Colours:* Gold and black shirts, black shorts, gold and black stockings.
Telephone: 00678 25236; *Cable:* FUTBOL BLONG VANUATU; *Fax:* 00678 25236.

WESTERN SAMOA

Samoa Football (Soccer) Association, P.O. Box 960, Apia.
Founded: 1968; *National Colours:* Royal blue shirts, white shorts, royal blue and white stockings.
Telephone: 00685 22822; *Telex:* 233 TREASURY SX; *Fax:* 00685 21312.

AFRICA

ALGERIA

Federation Algerienne De Foot-ball, Chemin Ahmed Ouaked, Boite Postale No. 39, Dely-Ibrahim-Alger.
Founded: 1962; *Number of Clubs:* 780; *Number of Players:* 58,567; *National Colours:* Green shirts, white shorts, green stockings.
Telephone: 002132 365938; *Cable:* FAFOOT ALGER; *Telex:* 61378. *Fax:* 002132 365949.

ANGOLA

Federation Angolaise De Football, Compl. da Cidadela Desportiva, B.P. 3449, Luanda.
Founded: 1979; *Number of Clubs:* 276; *Number of Players:* 4,269; *National Colours:* Red shirts, black shorts, red stockings.
Telephone: 002442 261331, 264948, 265936; *Cable:* FUTANGOLA; *Telex:* 2580 PALANCA AN; *Fax:* 002442 260566.

BENIN

Federation Beninoise De Football, B.P. 965, Cotonou.
Founded: 1962; *Number of Clubs:* 117; *Number of Players:* 6,700; *National Colours:* Yellow shirts, green shorts, red stockings.
Telephone & fax: 00229 330537; *Cable:* FEBEFOOT COTONOU; *Telex:* 5245 SONACOP COTONOU.

BOTSWANA

Botswana Football Association, P.O. Box 1396, Gabarone.
Founded: 1970; *National Colours:* Blue and white shirts, blue, white and black shorts, blue, white and black striped stockings.
Telephone: 00267 300279; *Cable:* BOTSBALL GABARONE; *Telex:* 2977 BD; *Fax:* 00267 300280.

BURKINA FASO

Federation Burkinabe De Foot-Ball, 01 B.P. 57, Ouagadougou 01.
Founded: 1960; *Number of Clubs:* 57; *Number of Players:* 4,672; *National Colours:* Red shirts, green shorts with yellow star, red stockings.
Telephone: 00226 318815; *Cable:* FEDEFOOT OUAGADOUGOU; *Fax:* 00226 318843.

BURUNDI

Federation De Football Du Burundi, B.P. 3426, Bujumbura.
Founded: 1948; *Number of Clubs:* 132; *Number of Players:* 3,930; *National Colours:* Red shirts, white shorts, green stockings.
Telephone & fax: 00257 212891; *Cable:* FFB BUJA.

CAMEROON

Federation Camerounaise De Football, B.P. 1116, Yaounde.
Founded: 1959; *Number of Clubs:* 200; *Number of Players:* 9,328; *National Colours:* Green shirts, red shorts, yellow stockings.
Telephone: 00237 216662; *Cable:* FECAFOOT YAOUNDE; *Telex:* 8568 JEUNESPO KN; *Fax:* 00237 210012.

CAPE VERDE ISLANDS

Federacao Cabo-Verdiana De Futebol, P.O. Box 234, Praia.
Founded: 1982; *National Colours:* All green.
Telephone & fax: 00238 611362; *Cable:* FUTEBOL PRAIA CV; *Telex:* 6005 ACAS CV.

CENTRAL AFRICAN REPUBLIC

Federation Centrafricaine De Football Amateur, B.P. 344, Bangui.
Founded: 1937; *Number of Clubs:* 256; *Number of Players:* 7,200; *National Colours:* Grey and blue shirts with national emblem and star, white shorts, red stockings with yellow trim.
Telephone: 00236 612433; *Cable:* FOOTBANGUI BANGUI; *Fax:* 00236 615660.

CHAD

Federation Tchadienne de Football, B.P. 886, N'Djamena.
Founded: 1962; *National Colours:* Blue shirts, yellow shorts, red stockings.
Telephone: 00235/519204; *Telex:* 5248 kd; *Fax:* 00235/518648.

CONGO

Federation Congolaise De Football, B.P. 4041, Brazzaville.
Founded: 1962; *Number of Clubs:* 250; *Number of Players:* 5,940; *National Colours:* All red.
Telephone: 00242 834885; *Cable:* FECOFOOT BRAZZAVILLE; *Telex:* 5210 KG; *Fax:* 00242 836199.

CONGO DR

Federation Congolaise De Football-Association (FECOFA), P.O. Box 1284, Av. De L'Enseignem. 210, Z/Kasa-Vubu, Kinshasa 1.
Founded: 1919; *Number of Clubs:* 3,800; *Number of Players:* 64,627; *National Colours:* Green shirts, yellow shorts, red stockings.
Telephone & fax: 001212 3769411; *Cable:* FECOFA KINSHASA.

DJIBOUTI

Federation Djiboutienne de Football, B.P. 2694, Djibouti.
Founded: 1977; *Number of Players:* 2,000; *National Colours:* Green shirts, white shorts, blue stockings.
Telephone: 00253 342049; *Fax:* 00253 356793.

EGYPT

Egyptian Football Association, 5, Shareh Gabalaya, Guezira, Al Borg Post Office, Cairo.
Founded: 1921; *Number of Clubs:* 247; *Number of Players:* 19,735; *National Colours:* Red shirts, white shorts, black stockings.
Telephone: 00202 3401793; *Cable:* KORA CAIRO; *Telex:* 93506 KORA UN; *Fax:* 00202 3417817.

ERITREA

The Eritrean National Football Federation, P.O. Box 3665, Asmara.
Telephone & fax: 002911 126821.

ETHIOPIA

Ethiopia Football Federation, Addis Ababa Stadium, P.O. Box 1080, Addis Ababa.
Founded: 1943; *Number of Clubs:* 767; *Number of Players:* 20,594; *National Colours:* Green shirts, yellow shorts, red stockings.
Telephone: 002511 514453; *Cable:* FOOTBALL ADDIS ABABA; *Telex:* 21377 NESCO ET; *Fax:* 002511 513345.

GABON

Federation Gabonaise De Football, B.P. 181, Libreville.
Founded: 1962; *Number of Clubs:* 320; *Number of Players:* 10,000; *National Colours:* Green, yellow and blue shirts, blue and yellow shorts, white stockings with tri-colour trims.
Telephone: 00241 730460; *Cable:* FEGAFOOT LIBRE-VILLE; *Telex:* 5526 GO; *Fax:* 00241 746047.

GAMBIA

Gambia Football Association, Independence Stadium, Bakau, P.O. Box 523, Banjul.
Founded: 1952; *Number of Clubs:* 30; *Number of Players:* 860; *National Colours:* White shirts with striped band, white shorts, white stockings with red tops.
Telephone: 00220 496980; *Cable:* SPORTS GAMBIA BANJUL; *Telex:* 2262 FISCO GV.

GHANA

Ghana Football Association, P.O. Box 1272, Accra.
Founded: 1957; *Number of Clubs:* 347; *Number of Players:* 11,275; *National Colours:* All yellow.
Telephone: 0023321 666697; *Cable:* GFA ACCRA; *Telex:* 2519 SPORTS GH; *Fax:* 0023321 668590.

GUINEA

Federation Guineenne De Football, P.O. Box 3645, Conakry.
Founded: 1959; *Number of Clubs:* 351; *Number of Players:* 10,000; *National Colours:* Red shirts, yellow shorts, green stockings.
Telephone: 00224 461159; *Cable:* GUINEFOOT CONAKRY; *Telex:* 22302 MJ GE; *Fax:* 00224 411926.

GUINEA-BISSAU

Federacao De Football Da Guinea-Bissau, Rua 4 No. 10-C, Apartado 375, 1035 Bissau- Codex.
Founded: 1974; *National Colours:* All red.
Telephone & fax: 00245 201918; *Cable:* FUTEBOL BISSAU.

GUINEA, EQUATORIAL

Federacion Ecuatoguineana De Futbol, Malabo.
Founded: 1986; *National Colours:* All red.
Telephone: 002409 2392; *Cable:* FEGUIFUT MALABO; *Telex:* 9991111 EG; *Fax:* 002409 3353.

IVORY COAST

Federation Ivoirienne De Football, Av. 1 Treichville, 01 B.P. 1202, Abidjan 01.
Founded: 1960; *Number of Clubs:* 84 (senior); *Number of Players:* 3,655; *National Colours:* Orange shirts, white shorts, green stockings.
Telephone: 00225 242301; *Cable:* FIF ABIDJAN; *Telex:* 42344 FIF CI; *Fax:* 00225 257111.

KENYA

Kenya Football Federation, Nyayo National Stadium, P.O. Box 40234, Nairobi.
Founded: 1960; *Number of Clubs:* 351; *Number of Players:* 8,880; *National Colours:* Red, green and white shirts, red, green and black shorts and stockings.
Telephone: 002542 501825/35; *Cable:* KEFF NAIROBI; *Telex:* 24069 SPICERS KE; *Fax:* 002542 501120.

LESOTHO

Lesotho Football Association, P.O. Box 756, Maseru-100, Lesotho.
Founded: 1932; *Number of Clubs:* 88; *Number of Players:* 2,076; *National Colours:* Blue shirts, green shorts, white stockings.
Telephone: 00266 311879; *Cable:* LEFA MASERU; *Telex:* 4493, 4228; *Fax:* 00266 310586.

LIBERIA

Liberia Football Association, 110 Camp Johnson Road, P.O. Box 10-1066, 1000 Monrovia 10.
Founded: 1936; *National Colours:* Red shirts, white shorts, blue stockings.
Telephone: 00231 226284; *Cable:* LIBFOTASS MON-ROVIA; *Telex:* 44220 EXM IBR. *Fax:* 00231 225217.

LIBYA

Libyan Arab Football Federation, 7th October Stadium, P.O. Box 5137, Tripoli.
Founded: 1963; *Number of Clubs:* 89; *Number of Players:* 2,941; *National Colours:* Green shirts, white shorts, green stockings.
Telephone & fax: 0021821 4446610/3339150; *Telex:* 20896 LY.

MADAGASCAR

Federation Malagasy de Football, Immeuble Preservatrice Vie-Lot IBF-9B, Rue Rabearivelo-Antsahavola, Antananarivo 101.
Founded: 1961; *Number of Clubs:* 775; *Number of Players:* 23,536; *National Colours:* Red shirts, white shorts, green stockings.
Telephone: 0026120 2268374; *Telex:* 22265 AROSUR MG; *Fax:* 0026120 2268373.

MALAWI

Football Association of Malawi, P.O. Box 865, Blantyre.
Founded: 1966; *Number of Clubs:* 465; *Number of Players:* 12,500; *National Colours:* Red shirts, red and green shorts, green stockings.
Telephone & fax: 00265 674290; *Cable:* FOOTBALL BLANTYRE; *Telex:* 4526 SPORTS MI.

MALI

Federation Malienne De Football, Stade Mamdou Konate, B.P. 1020, Bamako.
Founded: 1960; *Number of Clubs:* 128; *Number of Players:* 5,480; *National Colours:* Green shirts, yellow shorts, red stockings.
Telephone: 00223 224254; *Cable:* MALIFOOT BAMAKO; Telex: 0985 1200 MJ; *Fax:* 00356 245136.

MAURITANIA

Federation De Foot-Ball De La Rep. Islamique. De Mauritanie, B.P. 566, Nouakchott.
Founded: 1961; *Number of Clubs:* 59; *Number of Players:* 1,930; *National Colours:* Green and yellow shirts, yellow shorts, green stockings.
Telephone: 00222 291032 (or) 50424; *Cable:* FOOTRIM NOUAKCHOTT; *Telex:* 577 MTN NKTT RIM; *Fax:* 00222 291031 (or) 250424 (or) 291077.

MAURITIUS

Mauritius Football Association, Chancery House, 2nd Floor Nos. 303-305, 14 Lislet Geoffroy Street, Port Louis.
Founded: 1952; *Number of Clubs:* 397; *Number of Players:* 29,375; *National Colours:* Red shirts, white shorts, red stockings with white tops.
Telephone: 00230 2121418; *Cable:* MFA PORT LOUIS; *Fax:* 00230 2084100.

MOROCCO

Federation Royale Marocaine De Football, Av. Ibn Sina, C.N.S. Bellevue, B.P. 51, Rabat.
Founded: 1955; *Number of Clubs:* 350; *Number of Players:* 19,768; *National Colours:* All red.
Telephone: 002127 672706/08; *Cable:* FERMAFOOT RABAT; *Telex:* 32940 FERMFOOT M. *Fax:* 002127 671070.

MOZAMBIQUE

Federacao Mocambicana De Futebol, Av. Samora Machel, 11-2, Caixa Postal 1467, Maputo.
Founded: 1978; *Number of Clubs:* 144; *National Colours:* Red shirts, black shorts, black and red stockings.
Telephone: 002581 300366; *Cable:* MOCAMBOLA MAPUTO; *Telex:* 6-747 MCID MO; *Fax:* 002581 300367.

NAMIBIA

Namibia Football Federation, Abraham Mashego Street 8521, Katurua Council of Churches in Namibia, P.O. Box 1345, Windhoek, Namibia.
Founded: 1990; *Number of Clubs:* 244; *Number of Players:* 7320; *National Colours:* All blue, red, green, yellow and white.
Telephone: 0026461 217621; *Fax:* 0026461 265693.

NIGER

Federation Nigerienne De Football (Fenifoot), Stade du 29 Juillet, B.P. 10299, Niamey.
Founded: 1967; *Number of Clubs:* 64; *Number of Players:* 1,525; *National Colours:* Orange shirts, white shorts, green stockings.
Telephone: 00227 725127/722147; *Cable:* FEDERFOOT NIGER NIAMEY; *Telex:* 5527; *Fax:* 00227 722147/ 734694.

NIGERIA

Nigeria Football Association, Plot 2033, Olusegun Obasanjo Way, Wuse Zone 7, Abuja, Nigeria.
Founded: 1945; *Number of Clubs:* 326; *Number of Players:* 80,190; *National Colours:* Green shirts, white shorts, green stockings.
Telephone: 002349 5237326; *Cable:* FOOTBALL ABUJA; *Telex:* 26570 NFA NG; *Fax:* 002349 5237327.

RWANDA

Federation Rwandaise De Football Amateur, B.P. 2000, Kigali.
Founded: 1972; *Number of Clubs:* 167; *National Colours:* Red, green and yellow shirts, green shorts, red stockings.
Telephone: 00250 84999; *Cable:* FERWAFA KIGALI; *Telex:* 22504 PUBLIC RW; *Fax:* 00250 76574.

SENEGAL

Federation Senegalaise De Football, Stade L.S. Senghor, Route De L'Aeroport De Yoff, B.P. 130 21, Dakar.
Founded: 1960; *Number of Clubs:* 75 (senior); *Number of Players:* 3,977; *National Colours:* Green shirts, yellow shorts, red stockings.
Telephone & fax: 00221 8273524; *Cable:* SENEFOOT DAKAR ; *Telex:* 13048 PUBLIDK SG.

SEYCHELLES

Seychelles Football Federation, P.O. Box 843, People's Stadium, Victoria-Mahe, Seychelles.
Founded: 1979; *National Colours:* Red and blue shirts, blue and red shorts, white stockings.
Telephone: 00248 323908 ext. 244; *Fax:* 00248 225468.

ST THOMAS AND PRINCIPE

Federation Santomense De Futebol, P.O. Box 42, Sao Tome.
Founded: 1975; *National Colours:* All green and yellow.
Telephone: 0023912 23431; *Telex:* 213 PUBLICO STP; *Fax:* 0023912 21365.

SIERRA LEONE

Sierra Leone Football Association, P.O. Box 672, National Stadium, Brookfields, Freetown.
Founded: 1967; *Number of Clubs:* 104; *Number of Players:* 8,120; *National Colours:* Green, white and blue shirts, white shorts, blue stockings with white tops.
Telephone: 00232 2224 1872; *Fax:* 00232 2222 7771.

SOMALIA

Somali Football Federation, c/o Conf. Afric. de Football, 5 Gabalaya Street, 11567, El Borg, Cairo, Egypt.
Founded: 1951; *Number of Clubs:* 46 (senior); *Number of Players:* 1,150; *National Colours:* All sky blue and white.
Telephone: 0020 2/3412497; *Cable:* SOMALIA FOOTBALL CAIRO; *Telex:* 93162 CAF UN; *Fax:* 0020 2/3420114 (CAF).

SOUTH AFRICA

South African Football Association, First National Bank Stadium, Nasrec/PO Box 910, Johannesburg 2000, South Africa.
Founded: 1991; *Number of Teams:* 51,944; *Number of Players:* 1,039,880; *National Colours:* Gold and black shirts, green shorts, white stockings.
Telephone: 002711 4943522; *Fax:* 002711 4943013.

SUDAN

Sudan Football Association, P.O. Box 437, Khartoum.
Founded: 1936; *Number of Clubs:* 750; *Number of Players:* 42,200; *National Colours:* Green shirts, white shorts, green stockings.
Telephone & fax: 0024911 776633; *Cable:* ALKOURA KHARTOUM; *Telex:* 23007 KORA SD.

SWAZILAND

National Football Association of Swaziland, P.O. Box 641, Mbabane.
Founded: 1968; *Number of Clubs:* 136; *National Colours:* Blue shirts, gold shorts, white stockings.
Telephone: 00268 46852; *Telex:* 2245 EXP WD; *Fax:* 00268 46206.

TANZANIA

Football Association of Tanzania, Uhuru/Shaurimoyo Road, Karume Memorial Stadium, P.O. Box 1574, Ilala/Dar Es Salaam.
Founded: 1930; *Number of Clubs:* 51; *National Colours:* Yellow shirts with black stripes, yellow shorts, yellow and black stockings with horizontal stripe.
Telephone: 0025551 117931; *Cable:* FAT DAR-ES-SALAAM; *Telex:* 41873 TZ; *Fax:* 0025551 117930.

TOGO

Federation Togolaise De Football, C.P. 5, Lome.
Founded: 1960; *Number of Clubs:* 144; *Number of Players:* 4,346; *National Colours:* White shirts, green shorts, red and yellow stockings with green stripes.
Telephone: 00228 221412; *Cable:* TOGOFOOT LOME; *Telex:* 5015 CNOT TG. *Fax:* 00228 221413.

TUNISIA

Federation Tunisienne De Football, 16 Rue de la Ligue Arabe, El-Menzah VI, Tunis 1004.
Founded: 1956; *Number of Clubs:* 215; *Number of Players:* 18,300; *National Colours:* Red shirts, white shorts, red stockings.
Telephone: 002161 233303; *Cable:* FOOTBALL TUNIS; *Telex:* 14783 FTFOOT TN; *Fax:* 002161 767929.

UGANDA

Federation of Uganda Football Associations, P.O. Box 22518, Kampala, Uganda.
Founded: 1924; *Number of Clubs:* 400; *Number of Players:* 1,518; *National Colours:* Yellow shirts with black stripes, black shorts with yellow stripes, yellow and red stockings.
Telephone: 0025641 342731; *Cable:* FUFA LUGOGO STADIUM, KAMPALA; *Telex:* 61605; *Fax:* 0025641 342731.

ZAMBIA

Football Association of Zambia, P.O. Box 34751, Lusaka.
Founded: 1929; *Number of Clubs:* 20 (senior); *Number of Players:* 4,100; *National Colours:* Copper shirts, black shorts, copper stockings.
Telephone: 002601 750254; *Cable:* FOOTBALL LUSAKA; *Fax:* 002601 225046.

ZIMBABWE

Zimbabwe Football Association, P.O. Box CY 114, Causeway, Harare.
Founded: 1965; *National Colours:* Green shirts, gold shorts, green and gold stockings.
Telephone: 002634 731262; *Cable:* SOCCER HARARE; *Telex:* 22299 SOCCER ZW; *Fax:* 002634 731265.

THE WORLD CUP 1930–2002

Year	Winners		Runners-up		Venue	Attendance	Referee
1930	Uruguay	4	Argentina	2	Montevideo	90,000	Langenus (B)
1934	Italy	2	Czechoslovakia	1	Rome	50,000	Eklind (Se)
	(after extra time)						
1938	Italy	4	Hungary	2	Paris	45,000	Capdeville (F)
1950	Uruguay	2	Brazil	1	Rio de Janeiro	199,854	Reader (E)
1954	West Germany	3	Hungary	2	Berne	60,000	Ling (E)
1958	Brazil	5	Sweden	2	Stockholm	49,737	Guigue (F)
1962	Brazil	3	Czechoslovakia	1	Santiago	68,679	Latychev (USSR)
1966	England	4	West Germany	2	Wembley	93,802	Dienst (Sw)
	(after extra time)						
1970	Brazil	4	Italy	1	Mexico City	107,412	Glockner (EG)
1974	West Germany	2	Holland	1	Munich	77,833	Taylor (E)
1978	Argentina	3	Holland	1	Buenos Aires	77,000	Gonella (I)
	(after extra time)						
1982	Italy	3	West Germany	1	Madrid	90,080	Coelho (Br)
1986	Argentina	3	West Germany	2	Mexico City	114,580	Filho (Br)
1990	West Germany	1	Argentina	0	Rome	73,603	Codesal (Mex)
1994	Brazil	0	Italy	0	Los Angeles	94,194	Puhl (H)
	(Brazil won 3-2 on penalties aet)						
1998	France	3	Brazil	0	St-Denis	75,000	Belqola (Mor)
2002	Brazil	2	Germany	0	Yokohama	69,029	Collina (I)

GOALSCORING AND ATTENDANCES IN WORLD CUP FINAL ROUNDS

Venue	Matches	Goals (av)	Attendance (av)
1930, Uruguay	18	70 (3.9)	434,500 (24,138)
1934, Italy	17	70 (4.1)	395,000 (23,235)
1938, France	18	84 (4.6)	483,000 (26,833)
1950, Brazil	22	88 (4.0)	1,337,000 (60,772)
1954, Switzerland	26	140 (5.4)	943,000 (36,270)
1958, Sweden	35	126 (3.6)	868,000 (24,800)
1962, Chile	32	89 (2.8)	776,000 (24,250)
1966, England	32	89 (2.8)	1,614,677 (50,458)
1970, Mexico	32	95 (2.9)	1,673,975 (52,311)
1974, West Germany	38	97 (2.5)	1,774,022 (46,684)
1978, Argentina	38	102 (2.7)	1,610,215 (42,374)
1982, Spain	52	146 (2.8)	2,064,364 (38,816)
1986, Mexico	52	132 (2.5)	2,441,731 (46,956)
1990, Italy	52	115 (2.2)	2,515,168 (48,368)
1994, USA	52	141 (2.7)	3,567,415 (68,604)
1998, France	64	171 (2.6)	2,775,400 (43,366)
2002, Japan/S. Korea	64	161 (2.5)	2,705,566 (42,274)

LEADING GOALSCORERS

Year	Player	Goals
1930	Guillermo Stabile (Argentina)	8
1934	Angelo Schiavio (Italy), Oldrich Nejedly (Czechoslovakia), Edmund Conen (Germany)	4
1938	Leonidas da Silva (Brazil)	8
1950	Ademir (Brazil)	9
1954	Sandor Kocsis (Hungary)	11
1958	Just Fontaine (France)	13
1962	Valentin Ivanov (USSR), Leonel Sanchez (Chile), Garrincha, Vava (both Brazil), Florian Albert (Hungary), Drazen Jerkovic (Yugoslavia)	4
1966	Eusebio (Portugal)	9
1970	Gerd Muller (West Germany)	10
1974	Grzegorz Lato (Poland)	7
1978	Mario Kempes (Argentina)	6
1982	Paolo Rossi (Italy)	6
1986	Gary Lineker (England)	6
1990	Salvatore Schillaci (Italy)	6
1994	Oleg Salenko (Russia), Hristo Stoichkov (Bulgaria)	6
1998	Davor Suker (Croatia)	6
2002	Ronaldo (Brazil)	8

A brilliant finish by Michael Owen, leaving Brazilian goalkeeper Marcos stranded, sends the country into World Cup dreamland. The dream wouldn't last for long. (Colorsport)

2002 FIFA WORLD CUP – QUALIFYING COMPETITION

EUROPE
(Members 51, Entries 51)

Fifteen teams qualified: Belgium, Croatia, Denmark, England, France (holders), Germany, Italy, Poland, Portugal, Republic of Ireland, Russia, Slovenia, Spain, Sweden and Turkey.

GROUP 1

Zurich, 2 September 2000, 14,500

Switzerland (0) 0
Russia (0) 1 *(Bestchastnykh 74)*

Switzerland: Pascolo; Lubamba, Henchoz, Muller P, Mazzarelli (Buhlmann 72), Cantaluppi (Wicky 64), Vogel, Sforza, Comisetti, Rey, Yakin H (N'Kufo 64).
Russia: Nigmatullin; Khlestov, Chugainov, Smertin, Gusev (Alenichev 52), Drozdov, Onopko, Karpin, Titov (Panov 46) (Semak 88), Mostovoi, Bestchastnykh.
Referee: Nielsen (Denmark).

Toftir, 3 September 2000, 3200

Faeroes (0) 2 *(Arge 87, Hansen O 90)*
Slovenia (1) 2 *(Udovic 25, Osterc 86)*

Faeroes: Mikkelsen; Hansen HF, Johannesen O, Hansen JK, Morkore A, Joensen S, Petersen (Joensen J 78), Johnsson, Hansen O, Arge, Jonsson T (Morkore K 57).
Slovenia: Simeunovic; Bulajic, Vugdalic, Milinovic, Novak, Karic, Ceh A, Pavlin, Zahovic, Rudonja (Zlogar 89), Udovic (Osterc 71).
Referee: Vuorela (Finland).

Luxembourg, 3 September 2000, 3305

Luxembourg (0) 0
Yugoslavia (2) 2 *(Milosevic 4, Jokanovic 26)*

Luxembourg: Besic; Vanek, Schauls, Funck, Strasser, Deville L, Saibene, Alverdi (Theis 84), Holtz (Ferron 89), Schneider, Zaritski (Huss 62).
Yugoslavia: Cicovic; Mirkovic, Dudic (Sakic 62), Jokanovic, Bunjevcevic, Djordjevic, Lazetic, Stankovic D (Ilic I 73), Drulovic, Mijatovic (Kovacevic 70), Milosevic.
Referee: Smolik (Belarus).

Luxembourg, 7 October 2000, 1788

Luxembourg (0) 1 *(Strasser 46)*
Slovenia (2) 2 *(Zahovic 39, Milinovic 41)*

Luxembourg: Besic; Vanek, Schauls, Funck, Strasser (Posing 88), Saibene, Peters, Holtz, Schneider, Cardoni (Zaritski 80), Huss (Braun 73).
Slovenia: Dabanovic; Milinovic, Vugdalic, Karic, Knavs, Novak, Ceh A, Siljak (Udovic 80), Zahovic, Pavlin (Pavlovic 67), Acimovic.
Referee: Benes (Czech Republic).

Zurich, 7 October 2000, 9500

Switzerland (4) 5 *(Zwyssig 26, Fournier 35, Turkyilmaz 43 (pen), 45 (pen), 53 (pen))*
Faeroes (1) 1 *(Petersen 4)*

Switzerland: Zuberbuhler; Lubamba (Wicky 66), Henchoz, Zwyssig, Fournier, Sesa, Vogel (Celestini 66), Sforza, Comisetti, Chapuisat, Turkyilmaz (Cantaluppi 76).
Faeroes: Mikkelsen; Morkore A, Johannesen O, Hansen JK, Hansen HF, Petersen (Jacobsen R 63), Joensen S (Joensen J 63), Johnsson, Hansen O, Hansen JB, Arge.
Referee: Kapitanis (Cyprus).

Moscow, 11 October 2000, 12,000

Russia (1) 3 *(Buznikin 19, Khokhlov 57, Titov 90)*
Luxembourg (0) 0

Russia: Nigmatullin; Khlestov, Khokhlov, Smertin, Tetradze, Buznikin, Onopko, Karpin, Titov, Mostovoi, Bestchastnykh.
Luxembourg: Gillet; Funck (Ferron 86), Schauls, Vanek, Strasser, Saibene, Peters, Holtz, Schneider (Posing 77), Cardoni, Huss (Zaritski 61).
Referee: Ferry (Northern Ireland).

Ljubljana, 11 October 2000, 7000

Slovenia (1) 2 *(Siljak 44, Acimovic 78)*
Switzerland (1) 2 *(Turkyilmaz 20, 66)*

Slovenia: Dabanovic; Milinovic, Vugdalic, Knavs, Novak, Ceh A, Pavlin (Acimovic 69), Karic, Udovic (Tavcar 46), Zahovic, Siljak (Osterc 59).
Switzerland: Zuberbuhler; Zellweger, Mazzarelli, Zwyssig, Fournier (Magnin 64) (Muller P 72), Wicky (Cantaluppi 46), Comisetti, Vogel, Chapuisat, Sforza, Turkyilmaz.
Referee: Durkin (England).

Luxembourg, 24 March 2001, 2380

Luxembourg (0) 0
Faeroes (0) 2 *(Jacobsen C 75, Morkore K 82)*

Luxembourg: Besic; Deville L, Schauls, Posing, Strasser, Saibene, Peters (Huss 46), Holtz, Zaritski, Cardoni, Schneider (Braun 77).
Faeroes: Mikkelsen; Johannesen O, Hansen M, Borg (Olsen 84), Hansen HF, Hansen O, Benjaminsen (Jacobsen R 73), Johnsson, Morkore K, Jonsson T (Jacobsen C 20), Petersen J.
Referee: Hanacsek (Hungary).

Moscow, 24 March 2001, 35,000

Russia (1) 1 *(Khlestov 8)*
Slovenia (1) 1 *(Knavs 22)*

Russia: Nigmatulin; Khlestov, Nikiforov, Kovtun, Tetradze, Karpin, Smertin (Bestchastnykh 46), Onopko, Alenichev (Semak 66), Titov, Buznikin.
Slovenia: Simeunovic; Gajser, Milinovic, Knavs, Bulajic, Novak, Ceh A, Pavlin, Rudonja (Pavlovic 88), Zahovic, Osterc (Cimerotic 66).
Referee: Dallas (Scotland).

Belgrade, 24 March 2001, 36,000

Yugoslavia (0) 1 *(Mihajlovic 68)*
Switzerland (0) 1 *(Chapuisat 84)*

Yugoslavia: Kocic; Duljaj, Djukic, Mihajlovic, Obradovic, Lazetic (Stefanovic 78), Jugovic, Stankovic D (Ivic 56), Djordjevic (Kovacevic 70), Kezman, Milosevic.
Switzerland: Pascolo; Zellweger, Henchoz, Muller P, Quentin, Lombardo (Buhlmann 72), Vogel, Fournier, Lonfat, Yakin H (Frei 58), Chapuisat (Vega 86).
Referee: Nilsson (Sweden).

Moscow, 28 March 2001, 10,500

Russia (1) 1 *(Mostovoi 19)*
Faeroes (0) 0

Russia: Nigmatulin; Tetradze (Alenichev 46), Nikiforov, Kovtun, Karpin, Gusev (Drozdov 46), Onopko, Khokhlov, Mostovoi, Titov, Buznikin (Bestchastnykh 67).
Faeroes: Mikkelsen; Johannesen O, Thorsteinsson, Borg, Hansen O, Hansen HF, Benjaminsen, Johnsson, Morkore K (Joensen S 75), Jacobsen C, Petersen J.
Referee: Irvine (Republic of Ireland).

Ljubljana, 28 March 2001, 10,000

Slovenia (0) 1 *(Zahovic 90)*
Yugoslavia (1) 1 *(Milosevic 32)*

Slovenia: Simeunovic; Gajser (Acimovic 37), Vugdalic, Bulajic, Knavs, Novak, Ceh A, Osterc (Cimerotic 46), Pavlin (Pavlovic 62), Zahovic, Rudonja.
Yugoslavia: Kocic; Obradovic, Djukic, Mihajlovic, Krstajic, Stefanovic, Jokanovic (Duljaj 68), Lazetic, Djordjevic, Milosevic (Ivic 79), Kezman (Drulic 57).
Referee: Jol (Holland).

Zurich, 28 March 2001, 8600
Switzerland (2) 5 *(Frei 9, 31, 90, Lonfat 64, Chapuisat 72)*
Luxembourg (0) 0
Switzerland: Pascolo; Zellweger, Henchoz, Muller P, Quentin, Lonfat (Buhlmann 74), Vogel, Fournier, Lombardo (Muller S 86), Frei, Chapuisat (Yakin H 79).
Luxembourg: Besic; Schauls, Saibene, Deville L, Peters (Reiter 77), Cardoni, Strasser, Posing, Holtz, Schneider (Schaack 53), Huss (Zaritski 68).
Referee: Larsen (Denmark).

Belgrade, 25 April 2001, 48,000
Yugoslavia (0) 0
Russia (0) 1 *(Bestchastnykh 72)*
Yugoslavia: Ilic II; Dudic, Djukic, Bunjevcevic, Krstajic (Stefanovic 84), Jokanovic, Mihajlovic, Lazetic, Tomic, Drulic (Stankovic D 73), Kezman (Djordjevic 63).
Russia: Nigmatullin; Tugaynov, Onopko, Drozdov (Tetradze 47), Kovtun, Alenichev, Mostovoi, Khokhlov, Gusev (Semak 87), Titov, Fedkov (Bestchastnykh 46).
Referee: Plautz (Austria).

Toftir, 2 June 2001, 4000
Faeroes (0) 0
Switzerland (0) 1 *(Frei 81)*
Faeroes: Mikkelsen; Hansen HF, Johannesen O, Hansen JB, Borg, Benjaminsen, Petersen J (Petersen H 87), Johnsson, Hansen O, Arge (Jacobsen J 78), Jacobsen C.
Switzerland: Pascolo; Zellweger, Henchoz, Muller P, Quentin, Wicky, Vogel, Sforza (Lonfat 69), Lombardo, Sesa (N'Kufo 58), Frei (Magnin 87).
Referee: McDonald (Scotland).

Moscow, 2 June 2001, 70,000
Russia (1) 1 *(Kovtun 25)*
Yugoslavia (1) 1 *(Mijatovic 38)*
Russia: Nigmatullin; Smertin, Chugainov, Onopko, Kovtun, Karpin, Titov, Mostovoi, Khokhlov, Alenichev, Bestchastnykh (Buznikin 71).
Yugoslavia: Radakovic; Obradovic, Djukic, Mihajlovic, Djorovic, Mirkovic (Bunjevcevic 85), Lazetic (Drulovic 71), Dmitrovic, Tomic, Mijatovic (Kezman 65), Milosevic.
Referee: Fandel (Germany).

Ljubljana, 2 June 2001, 5000
Slovenia (1) 2 *(Zahovic 35, 65 (pen))*
Luxembourg (0) 0
Slovenia: Simeunovic; Galic, Milinovic, Knavs, Novak, Ceh A, Pavlin, Cimerotic (Osterc 80), Karic (Rudonja 46), Zahovic, Acimovic (Pavlovic 62).
Luxembourg: Gillet; Deville L, Schauls, Theis, Strasser, Saibene, Peters, Holtz, Huss (Mischo 46), Cardoni (Braun 82), Schneider.
Referee: Brugger (Austria).

Toftir, 6 June 2001, 4371
Faeroes (0) 0
Yugoslavia (2) 6 *(Stankovic D 20, 55, Kezman 29, 87, 90, Milosevic 68)*
Faeroes: Mikkelsen; Hansen HF, Benjaminsen, Hansen JB, Borg, Hansen O, Joensen S (Jacobsen R 88), Johnsson (Morkore A 75), Jacobsen C (Petersen H 75), Arge, Petersen J.
Yugoslavia: Radakovic; Mirkovic (Bunjevcevic 46), Mihajlovic, Djorovic, Dmitrovic, Lazetic (Obradovic 46), Stankovic D, Drulovic (Ilic I 74), Mijatovic, Milosevic, Kezman.
Referee: Jara (Czech Republic).

Luxembourg, 6 June 2001, 2200
Luxembourg (0) 1 *(Schneider 48)*
Russia (1) 2 *(Alenichev 16, Semak 76)*
Luxembourg: Gillet; Schauls, Deville L, Theis, Strasser, Peters (Reiter 89), Saibene, Holtz, Cardoni, Schneider (Braun 83), Huss (Christophe 64).
Russia: Nigmatullin; Smertin (Popov 52), Nikiforov, Alenichev (Semak 61), Karpin, Titov, Mostovoi, Khokhlov, Bestchastnykh (Fedkov 66).
Referee: Skjervold (Norway).

Basle, 6 June 2001, 26,000
Switzerland (0) 0
Slovenia (0) 1 *(Cimerotic 83)*
Switzerland: Pascolo; Zellweger, Henchoz, Muller P, Quentin, Wicky (Lonfat 66), Vogel, Fournier, Lombardo (Sforza 56), N'Kufo, Frei (Sesa 79).
Slovenia: Simeunovic; Galic, Milinovic, Knavs, Novak, Ceh A, Pavlin, Rudonja, Karic (Cimerotic 32), Zahovic, Osterc (Acimovic 46).
Referee: Granat (Poland).

Belgrade, 15 August 2001, 20,000
Yugoslavia (1) 2 *(Mihajlovic 23, Djukic 85)*
Faeroes (0) 0
Yugoslavia: Kralj; Mirkovic, Djukic, Mihajlovic, Djorovic, Tomic, Dmitrovic (Djordjevic 68), Drulovic (Lazetic 62), Mijatovic, Kezman, Milosevic (Kovacevic 46).
Faeroes: Mikkelsen; Hansen JB, Hansen HF, Johannesen O, Hansen JK, Borg, Benjaminsen (Jacobsen R 90), Johnsson, Hansen O, Petersen J (Olsen 84), Jacobsen C.
Referee: Pratas (Portugal).

Toftir, 1 September 2001, 1470
Faeroes (0) 1 *(Hansen JK 85 (pen))*
Luxembourg (0) 0
Faeroes: Mikkelsen; Hansen HF, Johannesen O, Hansen JK, Hansen JB, Olsen (Lakjuni 59), Borg, Benjaminsen, Petersen J, Johnsson J, Jacobsen C.
Luxembourg: Gillet; Schauls, Schaack, Reiter, Saibene (Schneider 46), Strasser, Peters, Holtz, Braun (Huss 67), Cardoni, Posing.
Referee: Siric (Croatia).

Ljubljana, 1 September 2001, 8000
Slovenia (0) 2 *(Osterc 62, Acimovic 90 (pen))*
Russia (0) 1 *(Titov 73)*
Slovenia: Simeunovic; Karic, Milinovic, Galic, Knavs, Novak, Ceh A, Pavlin, Rudonja (Pavlovic 78), Cimerotic (Osterc 46), Acimovic.
Russia: Nigmatullin; Khokhlov (Izmailov 46), Dayev, Tugaynov, Gusev (Semak 65), Kovtun, Onopko, Karpin, Titov, Mostovoi, Bestchastnykh (Shirko 79).
Referee: Poll (England).

Basle, 1 September 2001, 28,190
Switzerland (1) 1 *(Yakin H 24)*
Yugoslavia (1) 2 *(Milosevic 39, Krstajic 74)*
Switzerland: Pascolo; Zellweger (Frei 75), Yakin M, Muller P, Berner, Sesa (Chapuisat 75), Vogel, Fournier, Comisetti (Sforza 69), Yakin H, Turkyilmaz.
Yugoslavia: Kralj; Mirkovic, Djukic, Krstajic, Lazetic (Drulovic 67), Jokanovic, Djordjevic, Dmitrovic, Mijatovic (Stankovic D 80), Kezman, Milosevic (Kovacevic 69).
Referee: Colombo (France).

Torshavn, 5 September 2001, 2927
Faeroes (0) 0
Russia (2) 3 *(Bestchastnykh 20, 31, Shirko 88)*
Faeroes: Mikkelsen; Johannesen O, Hansen JK, Hansen JB, Hansen HF, Hansen O, Benjaminsen, Johnsson, Borg (Olsen 81), Petersen J, Jacobsen C (Morkore K 46).
Russia: Nigmatullin; Drozdov, Nikiforov, Semak (Khokhlov 53), Alenichev (Koriaka 83), Kovtun, Onopko, Karpin, Titov, Izmailov, Bestchastnykh (Shirko 46).
Referee: Byrne (Republic of Ireland).

Luxembourg, 5 September 2001, 2312
Luxembourg (0) 0
Switzerland (1) 3 *(Frei 12, Turkyilmaz 57, 84)*
Luxembourg: Gillet; Schauls, Schaack, Posing, Strasser, Saibene, Peters (Rohmann 89), Holtz (Mischo 46), Braun (Huss 66), Cardoni, Christophe.
Switzerland: Stiel; Haas, Yakin M, Muller P, Quentin, Sesa (Lonfat 46), Vogel (Mazzarelli 67), Sforza, Comisetti (Fournier 46), Frei, Turkyilmaz.
Referee: Corpodean (Romania).

Belgrade, 5 September 2001, 22,000
Yugoslavia (0) 1 *(Djordjevic 52)*
Slovenia (1) 1 *(Milinovic 11)*
Yugoslavia: Kralj; Djorovic, Djukic, Krstajic (Gvozdenovic 65), Lazetic (Stankovic D 73), Jokanovic, Djordjevic, Dmitrovic, Mijatovic, Kezman (Kovacevic 76), Milosevic.
Slovenia: Simeunovic (Dabanovic 81); Milinovic, Galic, Knavs, Gajser, Ceh A, Pavlin, Zahovic (Acimovic 56), Karic, Rudonja (Cimerotic 37), Osterc.
Referee: Nieto (Spain).

Moscow, 6 October 2001, 20,000
Russia (3) 4 *(Bestchastnykh 14 (pen), 18, 38, Titov 83)*
Switzerland (0) 0
Russia: Nigmatullin; Smertin (Khokhlov 88), Drozdov (Dayev 25), Tugaynov, Alenichev, Kovtun, Onopko, Gusev (Semak 74), Titov, Izmailov, Bestchastnykh.
Switzerland: Stiel; Zellweger, Quentin, Yakin M (Zwyssig 46), Mazzarelli, Sesa, Comisetti (Lonfat 79), Yakin H, Sforza, Di Jorio (Lombardo 46).
Referee: Fisker (Denmark).

Ljubljana, 6 October 2001, 10,000
Slovenia (2) 3 *(Ceh N 13, 31, Tiganj 82)*
Faeroes (0) 0
Slovenia: Simeunovic; Milinovic, Galic, Knavs, Novak, Osterc (Tiganj 67), Ceh N (Bulajic 90), Rakovic (Tavcar 53), Rudonja, Gajser, Pavlovic.
Faeroes: Mikkelsen; Johannesen O, Hansen JK, Hansen JB (Danielsen 80), Hansen HF, Hansen O (Olsen 73), Jacobsen R, Morkore K, Borg, Petersen J, Jacobsen C (Jacobsen JR 74).
Referee: Kasnaferis (Greece).

Belgrade, 6 October 2001, 1758
Yugoslavia (1) 6 *(Jokanovic 19, Mijatovic 58, Kezman 61, 71, Milosevic 62, 68)*
Luxembourg (1) 2 *(Peters 38, Christophe 52)*
Yugoslavia: Stevanovic; Mirkovic, Djorovic (Ilic I 56), Jokanovic, Krstajic, Djordjevic, Mijatovic, Milosevic, Kezman (Tomic 73), Stankovic D, Lazetic (Drulovic 44).
Luxembourg: Gillet; Ferron, Schauls, Deville F, Strasser, Saibene, Peters (Reiter 85), Posing, Christophe, Cardoni (Deville L 15), Schneider (Theis 75).
Referee: Irvine (Northern Ireland).

Group 1 Table	P	W	D	L	F	A	Pts
Russia	10	7	2	1	18	5	23
Slovenia	10	5	5	0	17	9	20
Yugoslavia	10	5	4	1	22	8	19
Switzerland	10	4	2	4	18	12	14
Faeroes	10	2	1	7	6	23	7
Luxembourg	10	0	0	10	4	28	0

GROUP 2

Tallinn, 16 August 2000, 1695
Estonia (0) 1 *(Reim 64 (pen))*
Andorra (0) 0
Estonia: Tohver; Allas, Lemsalu, Stepanovs, Rooba U, Piiroja (Jurisson 73), Reim, Alonen (Anniste 67), Terehhov, Oper, Zelinski (Ustritski 87).
Andorra: Koldo; Felix Alvarez (Soria 71), Jonas, Txema, Lima I, Escura, Sonejee, Emiliano (Pujol 74), Jimenez, Ruiz, Sanchez J.
Referee: Arsic (Yugoslavia).

La Vella, 2 September 2000, 1000
Andorra (1) 2 *(Emiliano 45, Lima I 51)*
Cyprus (1) 3 *(Constantinou M 25 (pen), 90, Agathocleous 77)*
Andorra: Koldo; Ramirez, Txema, Jonas, Sonejee, Lima I, Emiliano (Lucendo 89), Escura, Ruiz, Jimenez, Sanchez J.
Cyprus: Panayiotou N; Theodotou, Charalambous C (Agathocleous 54), Ioannou D, Charalambous M, Ioakim, Engomitis, Aristocleous (Yiasonmi 71), Christodolou M, Okkas (Kotsonis 85), Constantinou M.
Referee: Yarmenchuk (Ukraine).

Amsterdam, 2 September 2000, 50,000
Holland (0) 2 *(Talan 71, Van Bronckhorst 84)*
Republic of Ireland (1) 2 *(Robbie Keane 21, McAteer 65)*
Holland: Van der Sar; Reiziger (Seedorf 46), Konterman (Talan 66), Frank de Boer, Van Bronckhorst, Witschge (Bruggink 59), Ronald de Boer, Bosvelt, Cocu, Bouma, Kluivert.
Republic of Ireland: Kelly A; Carr, Harte, Dunne, Breen, Roy Keane, McAteer (Kelly G 75), Kinsella, Quinn (Connolly 71), Robbie Keane, Kilbane (Staunton 79).
Referee: Michel (Slovakia).

Tallinn, 3 September 2000, 4700
Estonia (0) 1 *(Oper 84)*
Portugal (1) 3 *(Rui Costa 15, Figo 49, Sa Pinto 57)*
Estonia: Poom; Allas, Stepanovs, Lemsalu, Rooba U, Jurisson (Haavistu 71), Alonen (Anniste 36), Reim, Terehhov, Zelinski (Viikmae 67), Oper.
Portugal: Quim; Nelson (Costinha 64), Fernando Couto, Jorge Costa, Rui Jorge, Figo, Rui Costa, Paulo Sousa, Simao (Vidigal 71), Sa Pinto, Joao Pinto (Pauleta 74).
Referee: Agius (Malta).

La Vella, 7 October 2000, 800
Andorra (0) 1 *(Ruiz 90 (pen))*
Estonia (0) 2 *(Reim 54, Oper 65)*
Andorra: Koldo; Ramirez, Txema, Jonas, Lima A, Lima I, Emiliano, Sonejee (Lucendo 60), Sanchez J, Jimenez (Soria 83), Ruiz.
Estonia: Poom; Allas, Rooba U, Lemsalu, Stepanovs, Viikmae (Haavistu 80), Terehhov, Oper, Kristal (Anniste 58), Reim, Zelinski (Ustritski 46).
Referee: Koren (Israel).

Nicosia, 7 October 2000, 12,000
Cyprus (0) 0
Holland (0) 4 *(Seedorf 69, 78, Overmars 81, Kluivert 90)*
Cyprus: Panayiotou N; Theodotou, Charalambous C, Ioannou D, Charalambous M (Poyiatzis 62), Pounnas (Gjurev 80), Melanarkitis, Spoljaric, Ioakim, Malekkos (Okkas 77), Agathocleous.
Holland: Van der Sar; Bosvelt (Van Bommel 75), Reiziger, Frank de Boer, Van Bronckhorst, Cocu, Talan (Seedorf 58), Davids, Kluivert, Ronald de Boer (Bouma 80), Overmars.
Referee: Cesari (Italy).

Lisbon, 7 October 2000, 65,000
Portugal (0) 1 *(Conceicao 57)*
Republic of Ireland (0) 1 *(Holland 72)*
Portugal: Quim; Beto, Fernando Couto, Jorge Costa, Dimas (Capucho 88), Conceicao, Rui Costa, Vidigal, Figo, Sa Pinto (Pauleta 76), Joao Pinto (Simao 76).
Republic of Ireland: Kelly A; Carr, Harte, Dunne, Breen, Roy Keane, McAteer (Duff 69), Kinsella, Quinn (Holland 46), Robbie Keane (Finnan 83), Kilbane.
Referee: Ouzounov (Bulgaria).

Rotterdam, 11 October 2000, 48,000
Holland (0) 0
Portugal (2) 2 *(Conceicao 11, Pauleta 44)*
Holland: Van der Sar; Melchiot, Frank de Boer, Cocu, Reiziger, Van Bommel (Bosvelt 72), Overmars (Talan 46), Davids, Kluivert (Vennegoor of Hesselink 65), Seedorf, Bouma.
Portugal: Quim; Jorge Costa, Dimas, Secretario, Fernando Couto, Vidigal (Fernando Meira 90), Figo, Bino, Pauleta (Simeo 90), Rui Costa (Sa Pinto 87), Conceicao.
Referee: Poll (England).

Dublin, 11 October 2000, 34,562
Republic of Ireland (1) 2 *(Kinsella 25, Dunne 50)*
Estonia (0) 0
Republic of Ireland: Kelly A; Carr, Harte, Dunne, Breen, Roy Keane, McAteer (Duff 46), Kinsella, Quinn, Robbie Keane (Foley 87), Kilbane (Finnan 87).
Estonia: Poom; Allas, Stepanovs, Lemsalu, Saviauk, Viikmae (Haavistu 68), Reim, Anniste, Terehhov, Oper, Zelinski (Ustritski 68).
Referee: Hauge (Norway).

Nicosia, 15 November 2000, 8000

Cyprus (3) 5 *(Okkas 10, 18, Agathocleous 42, Christodoulou M 74, Spoljaric 90 (pen))*

Andorra (0) 0

Cyprus: Panayiotou N; Konnafis, Charalambous C, Ioannou D (Nicolaou N 82), Charalambous M, Pounnas, Ioakim, Spoljaric, Okkas, Agathocleous (Neophytou 74), Constantinou M (Christodoulou M 46).
Andorra: Koldo; Txema, Marc, Jonas, Sonejee, Lima I (Soria 88), Emiliano (Ramirez 59), Sanchez J, Lucendo, Jimenez, Ruiz (Escura 78).
Referee: Johansson (Sweden).

Madeira, 28 February 2001, 12,000

Portugal (2) 3 *(Figo 1, 48, Pauleta 36)*

Andorra (0) 0

Portugal: Quim; Xavier, Rui Jorge, Fernando Couto (Capucho 46), Beto, Paulo Bento (Joao Pinto 63), Rui Costa, Conceicao, Figo, Nuno Gomes (Tomas 75), Pauleta.
Andorra: Koldo; Pol, Ramirez, Jonas, Lucendo (Soria 89), Txema, Emiliano (Escura 61), Sonejee, Ruiz, Marc, Sanchez J (Garcia 89).
Referee: Allaerts (Belgium).

Barcelona, 24 March 2001, 1000

Andorra (0) 0

Holland (2) 5 *(Kluivert 9, Hasselbaink 36, Van Hooijdonk 60, 71, Van Bommel 85)*

Andorra: Sanchez A; Pol, Jonas, Sonejee, Lima I, Ramirez, Emiliano (Escura 85), Txema, Lucendo (Jimenez 64), Ruiz (Fernandez 90), Sanchez J.
Holland: Van der Sar; Bosvelt, Stam (Bouma 72), Frank de Boer, Cocu, Van Bommel, Davids (Paauwe 46), Zenden, Hasselbaink, Kluivert (Van Hooijdonk 58), Overmars.
Referee: Trivkovic (Croatia).

Nicosia, 24 March 2001, 13,000

Cyprus (0) 0

Republic of Ireland (2) 4 *(Roy Keane 32, 89, Harte 42 (pen), Kelly 81)*

Cyprus: Panayiotou N; Melanarkitis (Filippou 56), Konnafis, Charalambous M, Christodolou M, Theodotou, Pounnas (Malekkos 43), Ioakim, Spoljaric, Constandinou M, Okkas (Agathocleous 75).
Republic of Ireland: Given; Kelly G, Harte, Roy Keane, Breen, Cunningham, McAteer (Holland 78), Kinsella, Connolly, Robbie Keane (Doherty 89), Kilbane (Duff 82).
Referee: De Bleeckere (Belgium).

Barcelona, 28 March 2001, 5000

Andorra (0) 0

Republic of Ireland (1) 3 *(Harte 33 (pen), Kilbane 76, Holland 80)*

Andorra: Sanchez A; Pol, Jonas (Soria 90), Lima A, Lucendo, Lima I, Sonejee, Txema, Sanchez J (Jimenez 87), Emiliano (Escura 80), Ruiz.
Republic of Ireland: Given; Kelly G, Harte, Roy Keane, Breen, Cunningham, Holland, Kilbane (Finnan 84), Connolly (Doherty 25), Robbie Keane, Duff.
Referee: Ishchenko (Ukraine).

Limassol, 28 March 2001, 5000

Cyprus (0) 2 *(Constantinou M 48, Okkas 66)*

Estonia (0) 2 *(Kristal 77, Piiroja 79)*

Cyprus: Panayiotou; Ioakim, Germanou, Charalambous M, Theodotou, Konnafis, Agathocleous (Christodolou M 63), Engomitis (Melanarkitis 69), Malekkos (Spoljaric 46), Okkas, Constantinou M.
Estonia: Kaalma; Rooba M, Stepanovs, Piiroja, Rooba U, Novikov (Alonen 81), Reim, Kristal, Haavistu (Terehhov 54), Zelinski (Viikmae 59), Oper.
Referee: Mikulski (Poland).

Oporto, 28 March 2001, 45,000

Portugal (0) 2 *(Pauleta 83, Figo 90 (pen))*

Holland (1) 2 *(Hasselbaink 17 (pen), Kluivert 47)*

Portugal: Quim; Secretario, Litos, Fernando Couto, Rui Jorge, Costinha, Paulo Bento (Capucho 32), Conceicao (Nuno Gomes 57), Figo, Rui Costa, Pauleta.
Holland: Van der Sar; Reiziger, Frank de Boer, Stam, Cocu, Zenden (Makaay 72), Davids, Van Bommel (Bosvelt 68), Overmars, Kluivert, Hasselbaink (Van Hooijdonk 80).
Referee: Meier (Switzerland).

Eindhoven, 25 April 2001, 30,000

Holland (3) 4 *(Hasselbaink 29, Overmars 35, Kluivert 44, Van Nistelrooy 82)*

Cyprus (0) 0

Holland: Van der Sar; Melchiot, Hofland, Frank de Boer, Cocu, Zenden, Seedorf (Van Nistelrooy 71), Van Bommel, Overmars (Sikora 83), Kluivert, Hasselbaink (Van Hooijdonk 71).
Cyprus: Morphis; Konnafis, Filippou, Charalambous M, Germanou, Melanarkitis, Engomitis (Kaiafas 89), Christodolou M (Yiasoumi 76), Satsias, Okkas (Agathocleous 84), Constandinou M.
Referee: Baskakov (Russia).

Dublin, 25 April 2001, 34,000

Republic of Ireland (2) 3 *(Kilbane 34, Kinsella 36, Breen 76)*

Andorra (1) 1 *(Lima I 32)*

Republic of Ireland: Given; Kelly G, Harte, Breen (Staunton 84), Dunne, Holland, Kennedy (Carr 66), Kinsella (Finnan 79), Connolly, Doherty, Kilbane.
Andorra: Sanchez A; Escura, Lima I, Lima A, Jonas, Txema, Emiliano (Soria 86), Ruiz, Sonejee, Jimenez (Pujol 81), Sanchez J (Fernandez 90).
Referee: Jakobsson (Iceland).

Tallinn, 2 June 2001, 9500

Estonia (0) 2 *(Oper 65, Zelinski 78)*

Holland (0) 4 *(Frank de Boer 68, Van Nistelrooy 82, 90, Kluivert 89)*

Estonia: Kaalma; Saviauk, Stepanovs, Piiroja, Rooba U, Viikmae (Zelinski 29), Reim, Haavistu (Rahn 70), Novikov, Kristal, Oper.
Holland: Van der Sar; Reiziger, Melchiot, Frank de Boer, Cocu, Paauwe (Landzaat 60), Zenden, Makaay (Van Hooijdonk 69), Hasselbaink (Van Nistelrooy 60), Kluivert, Overmars.
Referee: Richards (Wales).

Dublin, 2 June 2001, 34,000

Republic of Ireland (0) 1 *(Roy Keane 65)*

Portugal (0) 1 *(Figo 79)*

Republic of Ireland: Given; Carr, Harte, Kelly G, Dunne, Staunton, Kinsella (Doherty 79), Roy Keane, Quinn (Holland 75), Robbie Keane (Duff 60), Kilbane.
Portugal: Ricardo; Frechaut, Litos (Boa Morte 87), Jorge Costa, Rui Jorge (Joao Pinto 74), Beto, Petit, Barbosa (Capucho 71), Figo, Rui Costa, Pauleta.
Referee: Fisker (Denmark).

Tallinn, 6 June 2001, 9000

Estonia (0) 0

Republic of Ireland (2) 2 *(Dunne 9, Holland 39)*

Estonia: Kaalma; Saviauk, Stepanovs, Piiroja, Rooba U (Allas 69), Reim, Novikov (Ustritski 72), Haavistu (Terehhov 49), Kristal, Oper, Zelinski.
Republic of Ireland: Given; Carr, Harte, Kelly G, Dunne, Staunton, Kinsella, Holland, Quinn (Doherty 37), Kilbane, Duff (O'Brien 89).
Referee: Mircea (Romania).

Lisbon, 6 June 2001, 35,000

Portugal (1) 6 *(Pauleta 36, 71, Barbosa 55, 59, Joao Pinto 76, 81)*

Cyprus (0) 0

Portugal: Ricardo; Frechaut, Jorge Costa (Nuno Gomes 82), Beto, Rui Jorge, Petit (Paulo Bento 87), Rui Costa, Barbosa (Sa Pinto 72), Capucho, Pauleta, Joao Pinto.
Cyprus: Morphis; Theodotou, Filippou, Charalambous M, Ioakim, Satsias, Engomitis (Yiasoumi 69), Christodoulou M (Melanarkitis 61), Germanou, Okkas (Stavrou 83), Constantinou M.
Referee: Farina (Italy).

Tallinn, 15 August 2001, 5000

Estonia (0) 2 *(Zelinski 51, Novikov 86)*

Cyprus (1) 2 *(Constantinou M 39 (pen), 69)*

Estonia: Kaalma; Allas, Lemsalu (Rooba U 79), Piiroja, Saviauk, Reim, Viikmae (Svets 75), Novikov, Zelinski, Kristal, Oper.
Cyprus: Petrides; Konnafis, Georgiou, Melanarkitis, Charalambous M, Nicolaou C, Theodotou, Kaiafas (Agathocleous 75), Okkas, Christodoulou M (Yiasemakis 90), Constantinou M.
Referee: Chikun (Belarus).

Lleida, 1 September 2001, 4876

Andorra (1) 1 *(Jonas 41)*

Portugal (5) 7 *(Nuno Gomes 36, 40, 44, 90, Pauleta 39, Rui Jorge 45, Conceicao 58)*

Andorra: Koldo; Ramirez, Lucendo (Txema 60), Jonas, Lima A, Sonejee, Emiliano (Jimenez 76), Sanchez J, Escura, Pol, Ruiz (Garcia 90).
Portugal: Ricardo; Frechaut, Beto, Jorge Costa, Rui Jorge (Nuno Gomes 32), Petit (Fernando Meira 61), Figo, Capucho (Simao 46), Conceicao, Joao Pinto, Pauleta.
Referee: Hauge (Norway).

Dublin, 1 September 2001, 49,000

Republic of Ireland (0) 1 *(McAteer 67)*

Holland (0) 0

Republic of Ireland: Given; Kelly G, Harte, Dunne, Staunton, Holland, McAteer (O'Brien 90), Roy Keane, Robbie Keane (Finnan 58), Kilbane, Duff (Quinn 88).
Holland: Van der Sar; Melchiot, Numan (Van Hooijdonk 63), Cocu, Stam, Hofland, Zenden (Hasselbaink 55), Van Bommel, Kluivert, Van Nistelrooy, Overmars (Van Bronckhorst 71).
Referee: Krug (Germany).

Larnaca, 5 September 2001, 6000

Cyprus (1) 1 *(Constantinou M 24)*

Portugal (0) 3 *(Nuno Gomes 48, Pauleta 63, Conceicao 71)*

Cyprus: Petrides; Theodotou, Konnafis, Charalambous M, Ioakim, Georgiou, Satsias (Themistocleous 88), Engomitis (Nicolaou N 58), Christodoulou M, Okkas (Agathocleous 58), Constantinou M.
Portugal: Ricardo; Frechaut, Beto, Jorge Costa (Capucho 34), Rui Jorge, Petit, Fernando Meira, Figo, Conceicao, Joao Pinto (Nuno Gomes 34), Pauleta (Simao 80).
Referee: Nilsson (Sweden).

Eindhoven, 5 September 2001, 28,500

Holland (5) 5 *(Zenden 15, Van Bommel 26, 39, Cocu 30, Van Nistelrooy 43)*

Estonia (0) 0

Holland: Van der Sar; Melchiot, Numan, Cocu, Stam, Hofland, Zenden, Van Bommel, Kluivert, Van Nistelrooy (Hasselbaink 46), Overmars (Makaay 46) (Van Hooijdonk 63).
Estonia: Kaalma; Rooba U, Piiroja, Stepanovs, Saviauk, Novikov, Kristal, Reim, Oper, Zelinski, Viikmae (Anniste 46).
Referee: Vassaras (Greece).

Arnhem, 6 October 2001, 20,000

Holland (2) 4 *(Van Hooijdonk 4 (pen), Seedorf 45, Van Nistelrooy 54, 90)*

Andorra (0) 0

Holland: Van der Sar; Melchiot (Numan 72), Landzaat, Seedorf, Hofland, Van Bronckhorst, Sikora (Van der Vaart 67), Davids, Van Hooijdonk, Van Nistelrooy, Zenden.
Andorra: Koldo; Escura, Txema, Jonas, Lima A, Fernandez, Emiliano (Gil 90), Sonejee, Jimenez, Ferron (Benet 90), Ruiz.
Referee: Erdemir (Turkey).

Lisbon, 6 October 2001, 80,000

Portugal (1) 5 *(Joao Pinto 29, Nuno Gomes 49, 64, Pauleta 58, Figo 78)*

Estonia (0) 0

Portugal: Ricardo; Frechaut (Nuno Gomes 39), Fernando Couto, Jorge Costa, Rui Jorge, Figo, Petit, Rui Costa, Capucho (Paulo Sousa 66), Joao Pinto (Simao 46), Pauleta.
Estonia: Kaalma; Saviauk (Allas 55), Stepanovs, Piiroja, Rooba U, Kristal, Reim, Novikov (Anniste 68), Haavistu (Alonen 68), Oper, Zelinski.
Referee: Strampe (Germany).

Dublin, 6 October 2001, 35,000

Republic of Ireland (2) 4 *(Harte 3, Quinn 11, Connolly 63, Roy Keane 68)*

Cyprus (0) 0

Republic of Ireland: Given; Finnan, Harte, Breen, Staunton, Holland, Kennedy (Carsley 65), Roy Keane, Quinn (Morrison 70), Connolly, Kilbane (McPhail 85).
Cyprus: Panayiotou N; Konnafis (Louka 70), Kotsonis, Theodotou, Melanarkitis, Daskalakis, Nicolaou N, Okkas (Themistocleous 85), Satsias, Christodoulou M, Yiasoumi (Kontolefterou 90).
Referee: Roca (Spain).

Group 2 Table	P	W	D	L	F	A	Pts
Portugal	10	7	3	0	33	7	24
Republic of Ireland	10	7	3	0	23	5	24
Holland	10	6	2	2	30	9	20
Estonia	10	2	2	6	10	26	8
Cyprus	10	2	2	6	13	31	8
Andorra	10	0	0	10	5	36	0

GROUP 3

Sofia, 2 September 2000, 15,000

Bulgaria (0) 0

Czech Republic (0) 1 *(Poborsky 73 (pen))*

Bulgaria: Zdravkov; Peev, Markov, Ivanov B, Kirilov (Topuzakov 76), Petrov S, Todorov (Ivanov G 63), Stoyanov, Yovov (Petrov M 33), Balakov, Iliev.
Czech Republic: Srnicek; Repka, Rada, Nedved, Fukal, Horvath (Rosicky 77), Tyce, Poborsky, Koller (Lokvenc 63), Smicer (Vicek 90), Bejbl.
Referee: Marin (Spain).

Reykjavik, 2 September 2000, 7072

Iceland (1) 1 *(Sverrisson E 12)*

Denmark (1) 2 *(Tomasson 26, Bisgaard 49)*

Iceland: Arason; Helgason A (Gunnarsson B 29), Hreidarsson, Marteinsson, Kolvidsson, Kristinsson R, Gudmundsson (Helguson 70), Sverrisson E, Gudjohnsen E, Gudjonsson T (Sigurdsson H 70), Dadason.
Denmark: Schmeichel; Goldbaek (Nielsen A 76), Henriksen, Gravesen, Heintze, Helveg, Steen-Nielsen, Rommedahl (Michaelsen 81), Tomasson, Bisgaard (Jensen C 70), Sand.
Referee: Bre (France).

Belfast, 2 September 2000, 8227
Northern Ireland (0) 1 *(Gray 70)*
Malta (0) 0
Northern Ireland: Carroll; Nolan, Hughes, Murdock, Taggart, Horlock, Johnson, Magilton, Healy, Elliott (Gray 61), Lomas.
Malta: Barry; Dimech, Debono, Said, Carabott, Sylla (Brincat 46), Thuma, Camilleri (Veselji 78), Chetcuti, Busuttil, Mallia (Turner 58).
Referee: Bezubiak (Russia).

Sofia, 7 October 2000, 4000
Bulgaria (1) 3 *(Ivanov G 39, 65, Todorov 90)*
Malta (0) 0
Bulgaria: Zdravkov; Markov, Pazin, Petrov S, Hristov, Stoyanov (Petkov M 59), Ivanov G (Todorov 88), Balakov, Iliev (Petkov I 70), Peev, Petrov M.
Malta: Barry; Carabott, Chetcuti, Said, Debono, Dimech (Holland 67), Busuttil (Mallia 60), Giglio, Nwoko, Brincat (Agius 75), Zahra.
Referee: Caljia (Bosnia).

Teplice, 7 October 2000, 9843
Czech Republic (3) 4 *(Koller 17, 41, Nedved 44, 90)*
Iceland (0) 0
Czech Republic: Srnicek; Repka, Rada, Nedved, Fukal, Horvath (Rosicky 79), Tyce, Poborsky (Latal 68), Koller (Lokvenc 75), Sionko, Bejbl.
Iceland: Kristinsson B; Helgason A, Hreidarsson, Marteinsson (Gudmundsson 46), Kolvidsson, Kristinsson R (Gretarsson 85), Jonsson S, Sverrisson E, Gudjohnsen E, Helguson, Dadason (Gudjonsson T 46).
Referee: Vassaros (Greece).

Belfast, 7 October 2000, 11,823
Northern Ireland (1) 1 *(Healy 38)*
Denmark (0) 1 *(Rommedahl 60)*
Northern Ireland: Carroll; Lomas, Hughes, Murdock, Taggart, Horlock, Magilton, Jeff Whitley (Mulryne 72), Healy, Elliott (Gray 84), Lennon.
Denmark: Schmeichel; Helveg, Henriksen, Gravesen, Heintze, Steen-Nielsen, Tofting, Rommedahl, Tomasson, Sand (Jensen C 82), Gronkjaer (Bisgaard 63).
Referee: Pereira (Portugal).

Copenhagen, 11 October 2000, 39,847
Denmark (0) 1 *(Sand 73)*
Bulgaria (0) 1 *(Berbatov 82)*
Denmark: Schmeichel; Helveg, Henriksen, Gravesen, Heintze, Rommedahl, Tofting, Steen-Nielsen (Jensen C 46), Gronkjaer (Mikaelsen 55), Tomasson (Nielsen A 79), Sand.
Bulgaria: Zdravkov; Kishishev, Petkov M (Todorov 77), Kirilov, Pazin, Petrov S, Hristov (Peev 68), Ivanov B, Balakov, Ivanov G (Berbatov 64), Petrov M.
Referee: Sarvan (Turkey).

Reykjavik, 11 October 2000, 5415
Iceland (0) 1 *(Gudjonsson T 89)*
Northern Ireland (0) 0
Iceland: Kristinsson B; Helgason A, Hreidarsson, Sverrisson E, Vidarsson, Helguson, Gunnarsson B, Kristinsson R (Gretarsson 46), Gudjonsson T, Gudjohnsen E, Dadason (Sigurdsson H 64).
Northern Ireland: Carroll; Lomas, Hughes, Murdock, Taggart (Williams 46), Horlock, Lennon, Johnson, Healy, Magilton, Elliott (Gray 82).
Referee: Merk (Germany).

Valletta, 11 October 2000, 4000
Malta (0) 0
Czech Republic (0) 0
Malta: Muscat; Said, Chetcuti (Camilleri 61), Spiteri, Debono, Agius, Busuttil, Giglio (Turner 75), Brincat (Theuma 63), Nwoko, Zahra.
Czech Republic: Srnicek; Fukal (Latal 46), Rada, Repka, Tyce, Poborsky, Nedved, Bejbl, Horvath (Vicek 65), Koller, Sionko (Lokvenc 82).
Referee: Siric (Croatia).

Sofia, 24 March 2001, 20,000
Bulgaria (1) 2 *(Chamokov 36, Berbatov 78)*
Iceland (1) 1 *(Hreidarsson 24)*
Bulgaria: Zdravkov; Kishishev (Peev 63), Pazin, Chomakov, Markov, Kirilov (Todorov 77), Petkov M, Balakov, Hristov, Ivanov G (Berbatov 63), Petrov.
Iceland: Arason; Sigurdsson L, Hreidarsson, Vidarsson, Gunnarsson B, Kristinsson R, Helguson (Gudmundsson 76), Sverrisson E, Gudjonsson T (Gretarsson 59), Gudjohnsen E (Sigthorsson 61), Dadason.
Referee: Riley (England).

Valletta, 24 March 2001, 2500
Malta (0) 0
Denmark (1) 5 *(Sand 8, 65, 80, Heintze 50, Jensen C 76)*
Malta: Muscat; Turner (Okoh 46), Carabott, Dimech (Holland 65), Zahra, Debono, Giglio (Camilleri 65), Busuttil, Saliba, Nwoko, Brincat.
Denmark: Sorensen; Tofting, Henriksen, Laursen, Heintze, Helveg (Goldbaek 68), Gravesen (Steen-Nielsen 63), Gronkjaer, Rommedahl, Sand, Martin Jorgensen (Jensen C 75).
Referee: McCurry (Scotland).

Belfast, 24 March 2001, 10,368
Northern Ireland (0) 0
Czech Republic (0) 1 *(Nedved 11)*
Northern Ireland: Carroll; Griffin, Hughes A, Elliott (Gray 78), Williams, Murdock, Gillespie, Lennon, Healy (Ferguson 78), Magilton, Hughes M.
Czech Republic: Srnicek; Fukal, Votava, Ujfalusi, Tyce, Poborsky, Bejbl, Rosicky (Jarosik 81), Nedved, Smicer (Nemec 90), Koller (Lokvenc 73).
Referee: Gonzalez (Spain).

Sofia, 28 March 2001, 20,000
Bulgaria (2) 4 *(Balakov 10, Petrov M 17, 78, Chomakov 72)*
Northern Ireland (1) 3 *(Williams 14, Elliott 83, Healy 90 (pen))*
Bulgaria: Zdravkov; Kishishev, Petkov M (Stoilov 58), Markov, Chomakov, Pazin, Ivanov B, Hristov (Petrov Sv 67), Berbatov (Ivanov G 81), Balakov, Petrov M.
Northern Ireland: Carroll; Griffin, Nolan (McCarthy 90), Elliott, Williams, Murdock, Gillespie (Johnson 85), Lennon (Kennedy 85), Healy, Magilton, Hughes M.
Referee: Hrinak (Slovakia).

Prague, 28 March 2001, 16,354
Czech Republic (0) 0
Denmark (0) 0
Czech Republic: Srnicek; Fukal, Votava, Ujfalusi, Poborsky, Rosicky (Jarosik 86), Bejbl, Nedved, Nemec, Smicer (Kuka 67), Koller (Lokvenc 89).
Denmark: Sorensen; Helveg, Henriksen, Laursen, Heintze (Nygaard 88), Rommedahl (Jensen C 78), Tofting, Gravesen, Gronkjaer (Martin Jorgensen 46), Tomasson, Sand.
Referee: Barber (England).

Valletta, 25 April 2001, 1500
Malta (1) 1 *(Mifsud 14)*
Iceland (2) 4 *(Gudmundsson 42, Sigurdsson H 45, Gudjohnsen E 83, Gudjonsson T 90)*
Malta: Muscat; Debono, Said, Carabott, Spiteri, Giglio (Theuma 63), Busuttil, Mifsud, Zahra (Mallia 70), Nwoko, Brincat (Turner 56).
Iceland: Arason; Vidarsson, Sverrisson E (Marteinsson 67), Hreidarsson, Kristinsson R, Gudmundsson, Gretarsson, Gunnarsson B, Sigurdsson H (Gudjonsson T 84), Gudjohnsen E, Sigthorsson (Dadason 84).
Referee: Zotta (Romania).

Copenhagen, 2 June 2001, 41,669
Denmark (1) 2 *(Sand 6, Tomasson 82)*
Czech Republic (1) 1 *(Tyce 40)*
Denmark: Sorensen; Helveg, Henriksen, Laursen, Heintze, Tofting, Tomasson, Steen-Nielsen (Jensen C 58), Rommedahl (Gronkjaer 74), Sand, Martin Jorgensen (Nielsen A 87).
Czech Republic: Srnicek; Johana, Ujfalusi, Votava, Tyce (Rada 60), Poborsky (Kuka 85), Nedved, Galasek, Berger, Lokvenc (Koller 68), Smicer.
Referee: Merk (Germany).

Reykjavik, 2 June 2001, 3554
Iceland (2) 3 *(Gudmundsson 7, Dadason 38, Gudjohnsen E 68)*
Malta (0) 0
Iceland: Arason; Helgason, Vidarsson, Gretarsson, Gunnarsson B, Kristinsson R (Kolvidsson 74), Gudmundsson, Sverrisson E (Marteinsson 74), Gudjohnsen E, Sigurdsson H, Dadason (Helguson 74).
Malta: Muscat; Said, Turner, Spiteri, Theuma, Dimech, Agius, Giglio (Suda 74), Mifsud, Brincat (Camilleri 46), Mallia (Nwoko 69).
Referee: Lajuks (Latvia).

Belfast, 2 June 2001, 7663
Northern Ireland (0) 0
Bulgaria (0) 1 *(Ivanov G 52)*
Northern Ireland: Taylor; Nolan (Quinn 86), Griffin, Murdock, Hughes A, Lennon (Mulryne 79), Gillespie, Johnson, Healy, Elliott (Ferguson 79), Hughes M.
Bulgaria: Zdravkov; Ivanov B, Markov, Pazin, Kishishev (Peev 23), Hristov (Stoilov 87), Petrov M (Kirilov 77), Balakov, Chomakov, Petkov M, Ivanov G.
Referee: Busacca (Switzerland).

Teplice, 6 June 2001, 14,850
Czech Republic (1) 3 *(Kuka 40, 88, Baros 90)*
Northern Ireland (1) 1 *(Mulryne 45)*
Czech Republic: Srnicek; Repka, Votava (Bejbl 46), Tyce, Poborsky (Lokvenc 83), Nedved, Galasek, Rosicky, Berger, Koller (Baros 65), Kuka.
Northern Ireland: Taylor; Nolan, Hughes A, Murdock, Williams, Griffin, Johnson (Ferguson 76), Mulryne (Kennedy 81), Healy, Elliott (Quinn 65), Hughes M.
Referee: Sundell (Sweden).

Copenhagen, 6 June 2001, 38,499
Denmark (1) 2 *(Sand 43, 83)*
Malta (1) 1 *(Mallia 8)*
Denmark: Sorensen; Helveg, Henriksen, Heintze, Tofting (Nielsen A 75), Tomasson (Nygaard 68), Gravesen, Jensen C, Rommedahl (Gronkjaer 55), Sand, Martin Jorgensen.
Malta: Barry; Debono, Said, Theuma, Camilleri, Turner, Brincat (Holland 73), Mallia (Nwoko 65), Dimech, Agius (Okoh 78), Mifsud.
Referee: Shmolik (Belarus).

Reykjavik, 6 June 2001, 4316
Iceland (1) 1 *(Dadason 43)*
Bulgaria (0) 1 *(Berbatov 81)*
Iceland: Arason; Helgason, Vidarsson, Gretarsson, Gunnarsson B, Kristinsson R, Hreidarsson, Sverrisson E, Gudjohnsen E, Sigurdsson H, Dadason (Helguson 46).
Bulgaria: Zdravkov; Pazin (Petrov Sv 54), Markov, Ivanov B, Stoilov, Chomakov (Petrov M 65), Balakov (Todorov 73), Kirilov, Peev, Ivanov G, Berbatov.
Referee: Gallagher (England).

Copenhagen, 1 September 2001, 41,500
Denmark (1) 1 *(Rommedahl 3)*
Northern Ireland (0) 1 *(Mulryne 73)*
Denmark: Sorensen (Kjaer 11); Helveg, Heintze, Tofting, Laursen, Henriksen, Rommedahl, Nielsen P (Frandsen 68), Tomasson (Nygaard 78), Sand, Gronkjaer.
Northern Ireland: Taylor; Griffin, Kennedy, Murdock, Hughes A, Horlock, Gillespie, Magilton, Healy, Mulryne, Hughes M (Elliott 70).
Referee: Wojcik (Poland).

Reykjavik, 1 September 2001, 6011
Iceland (1) 3 *(Sverrisson E 45, 77, Sigthorsson 65)*
Czech Republic (0) 1 *(Jankulovski 88)*
Iceland: Arason; Helgason, Sverrisson E, Hreidarsson, Vidarsson, Gretarsson, Marteinsson (Sigurdsson L 83), Gudjonsson J, Sigurdsson H (Helguson 73), Sigthorsson, Gudjohnsen E (Baldvinsson 73).
Czech Republic: Srnicek; Grygera (Horvath 66), Novotny, Johana, Tyce, Poborsky (Lokvenc 66), Jarosik (Jankulovski 46), Rosicky, Nedved, Koller, Baros.
Referee: Messina (Italy).

Valletta, 1 September 2001, 409
Malta (0) 0
Bulgaria (0) 2 *(Berbatov 75, 80)*
Malta: Muscat; Said, Turner, Spiteri, Theuma, Carabott, Agius (Zahra 36), Giglio (Ciantar 67), Mifsud, Debono, Nwoko (Licari 87).
Bulgaria: Zdravkov; Pazin, Markov, Ivanov B, Petrov S, Peev, Chomakov (Balakov 54) (Stoilov 82), Alexandrov (Yanchev 70), Petkov M, Ivanov G, Berbatov.
Referee: Strampe (Germany).

Sofia, 5 September 2001, 21,500
Bulgaria (0) 0
Denmark (0) 2 *(Tomasson 47, 90)*
Bulgaria: Zdravkov; Markov, Pazin, Ivanov B, Petkov M (Todorov 76), Petrov S (Yanchev 62), Balakov, Peev, Petkov I, Ivanov G (Petrov M 62), Berbatov.
Denmark: Kjaer; Tofting, Henriksen, Laursen, Heintze, Helveg, Nielsen P (Nielsen A 46) (Steen-Nielsen 78), Gronkjaer (Michaelsen 73), Tomasson, Rommedahl, Sand.
Referee: Wegereef (Holland).

Teplice, 5 September 2001, 9218
Czech Republic (2) 3 *(Jankulovski 20, Lokvenc 37, Baros 68)*
Malta (1) 2 *(Carabott 22 (pen), Agius 55)*
Czech Republic: Srnicek; Grygera, Jankulovski, Novotny, Johana, Jarosik (Horvath 66), Baranek, Rosicky, Poborsky, Kuka (Baros 54), Lokvenc (Velkoborsky 90).
Malta: Muscat; Said (Dimech 79), Carabott, Spiteri, Debono, Agius, Giglio, Mifsud (Licari 74), Turner, Zahra (Ciantar 88), Nwoko.
Referee: Mammedov (Azerbaijan).

Belfast, 5 September 2001, 6625
Northern Ireland (0) 3 *(Healy 48, Hughes M 58, McCartney 60)*
Iceland (0) 0
Northern Ireland: Taylor; Griffin, Kennedy, Horlock, Hughes A, McCartney, Gillespie (McVeigh 88), Magilton, Healy, Mulryne, Hughes M.
Iceland: Arason; Helgason (Helguson 62), Vidarsson, Sverrisson E, Hreidarsson, Marteinsson, Gudjonsson J, Gretarsson, Gudjohnsen E, Sigurdsson H (Baldvinsson 86), Sigthorsson.
Referee: Hanacsek (Hungary).

Prague, 6 October 2001, 15,020
Czech Republic (3) 6 *(Rosicky 5, 70, Nedved 16, 76, Baros 28, Lokvenc 66)*
Bulgaria (0) 0
Czech Republic: Srnicek; Grygera, Novotny, Repka, Tyce (Hasek 26), Jankulovski, Poborsky (Baranek 78), Rosicky, Nedved, Lokvenc (Smicer 68), Baros.
Bulgaria: Zdravkov; Pazin, Markov, Ivanov B, Petrov S, Petkov M (Peev 72), Balakov, Zhelev, Yanchev (Berbatov 20), Ivanov G (Manchev 65), Petrov M.
Referee: Colombo (France).

Copenhagen, 6 October 2001, 42,000

Denmark (4) 6 *(Rommedahl 12, Sand 14, 67, Gravesen 30, 35, Michaelsen 90)*

Iceland (0) 0

Denmark: Sorensen; Helveg, Laursen, Henriksen, Heintze, Tofting, Gravesen, Tomasson (Mads Jorgensen 80), Rommedahl (Michaelsen 55), Martin Jorgensen, Sand (Madsen 68).

Iceland: Arason; Sigurdsson L (Vidarsson 69), Marteinsson, Sverrisson E, Hreidarsson, Gudjonsson J, Gretarsson, Gunnarsson B, Kristinsson R, Baldvinsson (Sigthorsson 74), Gudjohnsen E.

Referee: Ibanez (Spain).

Valletta, 6 October 2001, 3223

Malta (0) 0

Northern Ireland (0) 1 *(Healy 57 (pen))*

Malta: Muscat; Said, Spiteri, Debono, Carabott, Agius, Theuma (Mallia 65), Zahra (Suda 80), Chetcuti, Mifsud, Nwoko.

Northern Ireland: Taylor; Griffin, Kennedy, Horlock, Murdock, McCartney, Johnson, Magilton, Healy (McCann 80), Elliott (Quinn J 80), Hughes M.

Referee: Schuttengruber (Austria).

Group 3 Table	P	W	D	L	F	A	Pts
Denmark	10	6	4	0	22	6	22
Czech Republic	10	6	2	2	20	8	20
Bulgaria	10	5	2	3	14	15	17
Iceland	10	4	1	5	14	20	13
Northern Ireland	10	3	2	5	11	12	11
Malta	10	0	1	9	4	24	1

GROUP 4

Baku, 2 September 2000, 20,000

Azerbaijan (0) 0

Sweden (1) 1 *(Svensson A 10)*

Azerbaijan: Kramarenko; Kuliyev E, Agayev, Akhmedov, Yadullayev, Kuliyev K, Mamedov R (Imamaliev 86), Tagizade, Musayev B (Kurbanov M 65), Vasilyev, Kvaratskhelia.

Sweden: Hedman; Nilsson R, Andersson P, Bjorklund, Mellberg, Mjallby, Alexandersson, Svensson A (Mild 75), Ljungberg, Andersson K, Larsson.

Referee: Luinge (Holland).

Istanbul, 2 September 2000, 22,000

Turkey (1) 2 *(Okan 45, Emre 70)*

Moldova (0) 0

Turkey: Rustu; Umit D, Ogun, Fatih, Emre, Bulent K, Okan (Tayfur 60), Suat (Tayfun 65), Hakan Sukur, Cenk (Umit K 84), Unsal.

Moldova: Dinov; Covalenco, Sosnovschi, Testimitanu, Rebeja, Stroenco, Curtianu (Sischin 46), Oprea (Tanurkov 77), Catinsus, Epureanu (Stratulat 34), Rogaciov.

Referee: Benko (Austria).

Bratislava, 3 September 2000, 4011

Slovakia (1) 2 *(Lazarevski 3 (og), Demo 74)*

Macedonia (0) 0

Slovakia: Konig; Dzurik, Karhan, Timko, Leitner, Balis, Kratochvil, Moravcik (Nemeth P 46), Ujlaky (Demo 46), Jancula (Meszaros 76), Nemeth S.

Macedonia: Filevski; Veselinovski, Stojanovski (Lazarevski 64), Sedloski, Nikolovski, Stavrevski, Serafimovski, Micevski (Gerasimovski 69), Hristov, Ciric (Beciri 77), Savevski.

Referee: Hamer (Luxembourg).

Skopje, 6 October 2000, 4000

Macedonia (2) 3 *(Hristov 35, 42, Beciri 75)*

Azerbaijan (0) 0

Macedonia: Filevski; Lazarevski (Veselinovski 70), Stavrevski, Sedloski, Nikolovski (Gerasimovski 20), Serafimovski, Sainovski, Micevski, Hristov, Sakiri, Beciri (Miserdovski 80).

Azerbaijan: Kramarenko; Asadov, Yadullayev, Akhmedov, Agayev, Kuliyev K (Kvaratskhelia 55), Kurbanov M (Musayev R 65), Tagizade, Musayev B, Vasilyev (Lychkin 75), Kuliyev E.

Referee: Fisker (Denmark).

Chisinau, 7 October 2000, 5000

Moldova (0) 0

Slovakia (0) 1 *(Nemeth S 79)*

Moldova: Dinov; Covalenco, Catinsus, Testimitanu, Rebeja, Stroenco, Curtianu, Sischin (Rogaciov 60), Sosnovschi (Epureanu 82), Gaidamasciuc (Stratulat 72), Clescenco.

Slovakia: Konig; Dzurik, Sobona, Suchancok, Karhan, Demo (Nemeth P 74), Valachovic, Leitner, Pinte, Nemeth S (Prohaszka 88), Moravcik (Meszaros 53).

Referee: Stuchlik (Austria).

Gothenburg, 7 October 2000, 42,152

Sweden (0) 1 *(Larsson 68)*

Turkey (0) 1 *(Tayfur 90 (pen))*

Sweden: Hedman; Nilsson R, Andersson P, Bjorklund, Alexandersson (Corneliusson 55), Jonsson (Svensson A 63), Mjallby, Ljungberg, Mild, Andersson K, Larsson (Osmanovski 90).

Turkey: Rustu; Ogun, Fatih, Bulent K, Arif, Ergun (Abdullah 80), Suat (Tayfur 64), Hakan Sukur, Nihat, Izzet (Hasan Sas 75), Unsal.

Referee: Krug (Germany).

Baku, 11 October 2000, 40,000

Azerbaijan (0) 0

Turkey (0) 1 *(Hakan Sukur 72)*

Azerbaijan: Kramarenko; Agayev, Yadullayev, Akhmedov, Lychkin (Mamedov R 85), Kuliyev K, Kurbanov M, Tagizade (Gambarov 72), Musayev B (Kerimov 58), Vasilyev, Kuliyev E.

Turkey: Rustu; Nihat (Fatih 46), Ogun, Bulent K, Alpay, Arif (Tayfur 90), Ergun, Suat, Hakan Sukur, Izzet (Hasan Sas 62), Unsal.

Referee: Snoddy (Northern Ireland).

Chisinau, 11 October 2000, 4000

Moldova (0) 0

Macedonia (0) 0

Moldova: Hmaruc; Stratulat, Catinsus, Testimitanu, Rebeja (Epureanu 46), Stroenco, Curtianu (Boret 65), Sischin (Rogaciov 56), Sosnovschi, Gaidamasciuc, Clescenco.

Macedonia: Filevski; Stavrevski, Lazarevski, Sedloski, Gerasimovski, Serafimovski (Veselinovski 70), Sainovski (Karanfilovski 76), Micevski, Hristov, Ciric (Miserdovski 85), Sakiri.

Referee: Ibanez (Spain).

Bratislava, 11 October 2000, 11,227

Slovakia (0) 0

Sweden (0) 0

Slovakia: Konig; Dzurik, Sobona, Timko, Karhan, Suchancok, Balis, Leitner, Meszaros (Prohaszka 86), Nemeth S, Moravcik (Gresko 58).

Sweden: Hedman; Nilsson R, Andersson P, Bjorklund, Mellberg, Mjallby, Svensson A (Osmanovski 70), Jonsson (Mild 47), Ljungberg, Andersson K (Andersson D 82), Larsson.

Referee: Dallas (Scotland).

Baku, 24 March 2001, 20,000

Azerbaijan (0) 0

Moldova (0) 0

Azerbaijan: Kramarenko; Agayev, Akhmedov, Kuliyev E (Getman 68), Yadullayev, Niftaliyev (Ismailov 46), Kuliyev K, Tagizade, Rzayev, Lychkin (Kuliyev R 80), Vasiliev.

Moldova: Hmaruc; Covalenco, Rebeja, Testimitanu (Romanenco 13), Sosnovschi, Catinsus, Epureanu, Gaidamasciuc, Sischin, Rogaciov (Oprea 46), Clescenco (Pogreban 61).

Referee: Stark (Germany).

Gothenburg, 24 March 2001, 22,106
Sweden (1) 1 *(Svensson A 43)*
Macedonia (0) 0
Sweden: Hedman; Mellberg, Andersson P, Matovac, Corneliusson, Linderoth (Andersson D 64), Schwarz (Selakovic 80), Svensson A (Mild 66), Ljungberg, Osmanovski, Larsson.
Macedonia: Milosevski; Mitrevski, Stavrevski, Sedloski, Zdravevski (Krstev S 68), Veselinovski, Serafimovski, Micevski, Lazarevski, Sakiri, Beciri (Sainovski 82).
Referee: Wegereef (Holland).

Istanbul, 24 March 2001, 23,000
Turkey (0) 1 *(Hakan Sukur 53 (pen))*
Slovakia (0) 1 *(Tomaschek 68)*
Turkey: Rustu; Bulent K, Ogun, Fatih, Alpay, Okan (Arif 77) (Tayfun 83), Umit, Ergun (Tayfun 83), Abdullah, Hakan Sukur, Hasan Sas.
Slovakia: Konig; Karhan, Valachovic, Varga, Dzurik, Demo (Nemeth P 89), Labant, Tomaschek, Gresko, Nemeth S, Pinte.
Referee: Wojcik (Poland).

Chisinau, 28 March 2001, 8000
Macedonia (1) 1 *(Micevski 20)*
Turkey (0) 2 *(Mitrevski 68 (og), Umit D 69)*
Macedonia: Milosevski; Stavrevski, Zdravevski (Krstev S 82), Sedloski, Mitrevski, Serafimovski (Georgieski 75), Micevski (Krsevski 75), Hristov, Beciri, Sakiri, Lazarevski.
Turkey: Rustu; Fatih, Alpay, Tayfur, Okan (Tayfun 82), Umit D, Ogun (Umit O 37), Ergun (Ozer 59), Abdullah, Hakan Sukur, Hasan Sas.
Referee: Colombo (France).

Skopje, 28 March 2001, 7000
Moldova (0) 0
Sweden (0) 2 *(Allback 89, 90)*
Moldova: Romanenco; Covalenco, Rebeja, Catinsus, Sosnovschi, Gaidamasciuc, Rogaciov (Pogreban 67), Oprea (Berco 72), Cebotari (Lungu 55), Sischin, Clescenco.
Sweden: Hedman; Mellberg, Andersson P, Matovac, Corneliusson, Selakovic (Andersson D 55), Schwarz, Mild (Jonsson 44), Ljungberg, Larsson, Svensson A (Allback 78).
Referee: Duhamel (France).

Trnava, 28 March 2001, 10,000
Slovakia (2) 3 *(Nemeth S 1, 10, Meszaros 57)*
Azerbaijan (1) 1 *(Vasilyev 3 (pen))*
Slovakia: Konig; Varga, Karhan, Meszaros, Tomaschek, Labant, Pinte, Dzurik (Ujlaky 64), Demo (Jancula 78), Gresko, Nemeth S (Valachovic 68).
Azerbaijan: Kramarenko; Agayev, Yadullayev, Akhmedov, Kuliyev E, Kuliyev K, Kurbanov M, Imamaliev, Niftaliyev, Vasilyev (Musayev S 82), Lychkin (Aliev 46).
Referee: Kapitanis (Cyprus).

Skopje, 2 June 2001, 3000
Macedonia (1) 2 *(Sakiri 20 (pen), Krstev M 65)*
Moldova (1) 2 *(Pogreban 10, Barburos 72)*
Macedonia: Zekir; Stavrevski, Stojanov, Guzelov, Nikolovski (Trajanov 46), Jovanovski Z, Serafimovski (Jovanovski G 70), Krstev M, Krstev S, Sakiri, Beciri (Nacevski 46).
Moldova: Romanenco; Covalenco, Rebeja, Testimitanu (Osipenco 65), Sosnovschi, Stroenco, Sischin (Barburos 70), Catinsus, Pogreban (Epureanu 46), Gaidamasciuc, Clescenco.
Referee: Van Hulten (Holland).

Stockholm, 2 June 2001, 34,327
Sweden (1) 2 *(Allback 45, 51)*
Slovakia (0) 0
Sweden: Hedman; Mellberg, Andersson P, Saarenpaa, Lucic, Alexandersson (Jonsson 73) Linderoth (Svensson A 90), Magnus Svensson, Allback (Andersson D 88), Larsson, Ljungberg.

Slovakia: Konig; Karhan, Timko, Varga, Dzurik, Tomaschek, Demo (Janocko 58), Nemeth S (Vittek 58), Gresko (Babnic 82), Labant, Pinte.
Referee: Aranda (Spain).

Istanbul, 2 June 2001, 25,000
Turkey (3) 3 *(Tayfun 2, Oktay 29, Hakan Sukur 33)*
Azerbaijan (0) 0
Turkey: Rustu; Umit D, Alpay, Bulent K, Abdullah, Tayfun, Okan (Basturk 61), Tugay, Emre (Ergun 80), Hakan Sukur, Oktay (Ozer 37).
Azerbaijan: Gasanadze; Yunusov, Mamedov A (Niftaliyev 68), Akhmedov, Mamedov R, Kurbanov K, Kuliyev K, Tagizade (Kuliyev R 80), Rzayev (Orudzev 50), Kurbanov M, Mardanov.
Referee: Roca (Spain).

Baku, 6 June 2001, 20,000
Azerbaijan (1) 2 *(Vasilyev 26, Tagizade 55)*
Slovakia (0) 0
Azerbaijan: Gasanzade; Yunusov, Akhmedov, Mamedov R, Niftaliyev, Kurbanov M, Yadullayev, Tagizade (Kuliyev R 82), Kurbanov K (Ismailov 89), Getman, Vasilyev (Rzayev 75).
Slovakia: Konig; Dzurik, Vittek (Bencik 69), Varga, Karhan, Tomaschek, Janocko, Nemeth S, Labant, Gresko, Pinte (Babnic 62).
Referee: Vollquartz (Denmark).

Gothenburg, 6 June 2001, 30,233
Sweden (1) 6 *(Larsson 38 (pen), 58, 68 (pen), 79 (pen), Alexandersson 74, Allback 77)*
Moldova (0) 0
Sweden: Hedman; Mellberg, Andersson P, Saarenpaa (Andersson C 34), Lucic, Alexandersson, Linderoth, Magnus Svensson (Mathias Svensson 83), Svensson A (Andersson D 71), Allback, Larsson.
Moldova: Romanenco; Covalenco, Stroenco, Rebeja (Osipenco 63), Catinsus, Gaidamasciuc, Epureanu, Testimitanu, Oprea, Pogreban (Barburos 46), Clescenco (Sischin 78).
Referee: Dunn (England).

Bursa, 6 June 2001, 20,000
Turkey (1) 3 *(Alpay 43, 58, 70)*
Macedonia (2) 3 *(Sakiri 7, Serafimovski 20, Nikolovski 62)*
Turkey: Rustu; Umit D, Bulent K, Alpay, Abdullah, Tayfun (Fatih 84), Okan (Basturk 69), Tugay, Emre, Hakan Sukur, Oktay (Ozer 46).
Macedonia: Filevski; Stavrevski, Nikolovski, Mitreveski, Stojanov, Serafimovski (Trajanov 72), Krstev M, Guzelov, Sakiri, Nacevski (Lazarevski 48), Beciri (Pandev 66).
Referee: Rodomonti (Italy).

Skopje, 1 September 2001, 8000
Macedonia (0) 1 *(Nacevski 63)*
Sweden (2) 2 *(Larsson 27, Andersson P 32)*
Macedonia: Gruevski; Nikolovski, Guzelov, Mitrevski, Jovanovski Z, Stavrevski, Trajanov (Stojanov 61), Serafimovski (Ignjatov 83), Sakiri, Beciri (Nacevski 46), Maznov.
Sweden: Hedman; Mellberg, Andersson P, Mjallby (Andersson C 66), Kaamark (Saarenpaa 83), Linderoth, Alexandersson, Svensson A (Andersson D 64), Ljungberg, Allback, Larsson.
Referee: Levnikov (Russia).

Chisinau, 1 September 2001, 4000
Moldova (1) 2 *(Clescenco 15, Covalciuc 85)*
Azerbaijan (0) 0
Moldova: Romanenco; Olexic, Rebeja, Berco, Sosnovschi, Catinsus, Curtianu (Boret 68), Comleonoc, Sischin (Andronic 54), Rogaciov (Covalciuc 83), Clescenco.
Azerbaijan: Gasanzade; Getman (Kuliyev R 66), Yunusov, Niftaliyev (Mamedov A 72), Mamedov R, Kuliyev K, Kurbanov M, Tagizade, Ismailov (Vasilyev 69), Aliyev, Kuliyev E.
Referee: Melnychuk (Ukraine).

Bratislava, 1 September 2001, 8783
Slovakia (0) 0
Turkey (1) 1 *(Hakan Sukur 34)*
Slovakia: Bucek; Kozak, Varga, Timko (Labant 78), Balis (Pinte 46), Karhan, Janocko, Demo, Gresko, Nemeth S (Vittek 46), Oravec.
Turkey: Rustu; Fatih, Alpay, Umit O, Umit D, Basturk (Nihat 61), Tayfur, Ogun (Tayfun 87), Hasan Sas (Arif 78), Abdullah, Hakan Sukur.
Referee: Pereira (Portugal).

Baku, 5 September 2001, 7000
Azerbaijan (0) 1 *(Ismailov 90)*
Macedonia (1) 1 *(Trajanov 12)*
Azerbaijan: Gasanzade; Yadullayev, Yunusov, Mamedov A, Kuliyev E, Kuliyev K, Kurbanov, Tagizade, Vasilyev (Ismailov 71), Kuliyev R (Aliyev 58), Mamedov.
Macedonia: Gruevski; Stojanov, Guzelov (Pikolavski 25), Nikolovski, Stavrevski, Serafimovski, Ivanovski, Trajanov (Ignjatov 81), Sakiri, Maznov, Baciri (Nacevski 71).
Referee: Ross (Northern Ireland).

Trencin, 5 September 2001, 2789
Slovakia (0) 4 *(Nemeth P 54, Nemeth S 59, 73, Demo 65)*
Moldova (1) 2 *(Clescenco 11, Rebeja 76)*
Slovakia: Hyll, Karhan, Kozak (Demo 22), Varga, Labant, Janocko, Nemeth P, Dzurik, Gresko (Balis 80), Oravec (Nemeth S 46), Vittek.
Moldova: Romanenco; Sosnovschi, Catinsus, Rebeja, Olexic, Berco, Sischin (Covalciuc 46), Curtianu (Boret 46), Comleonoc (Andronic 88), Rogaciov, Clescenco.
Referee: Vuorela (Finland).

Istanbul, 5 September 2001, 22,000
Turkey (0) 1 *(Hakan Sukur 51)*
Sweden (0) 2 *(Larsson 87, Andersson A 90)*
Turkey: Rustu; Fatih, Alpay, Umit O, Umit D, Emre (Arif 46), Tayfur, Basturk (Tayfun 63), Abdullah, Hasan Sas (Ergun 88), Hakan Sukur.
Sweden: Hedman; Mellberg, Saarenpaa, Andersson P, Kaamark (Andersson A 64), Linderoth, Alexandersson (Jonsson 80), Ljungberg, Andersson D (Svensson A 64), Allback, Larsson.
Referee: Braschi (Italy).

Skopje, 7 October 2001, 5000
Macedonia (0) 0
Slovakia (1) 5 *(Reiter 27, Dzurik 57, Nemeth P 72, Pinte 81, Oravec 90)*
Macedonia: Gruevski; Stavrevski, Stojanov (Kapinkovski 66), Sedloski, Mitreveski, Jovanovski G (Beciri 64), Lazarevski, Trajanov, Maznov, Sakiri (Ignjatov 64), Nacevski.
Slovakia: Bucek; Karhan, Kozak, Hornyak, Varga, Nemeth P, Dzurik (Soitis 84), Reiter (Janocko 75), Gresko, Nemeth S (Oravec 66), Pinte.
Referee: Riley (England).

Chisinau, 7 October 2001, 3000
Moldova (0) 0
Turkey (1) 3 *(Emre 5, Nihat 75, Ilhan 83)*
Moldova: Romanenco; Andronic, Olexic, Ivanov, Cebotari, Catinsus, Epureanu, Sischin (Covalciuc 72), Miterev (Pogreban 76), Gaidamasciuc, Berco.
Turkey: Rustu; Mehmet, Emre, Umit O, Unsal, Okan, Tugay, Nihat, Hasan Sas (Ergun 84), Arif (Ilhan 75), Umit K (Basturk 68).
Referee: De Bleeckere (Belgium).

Stockholm, 7 October 2001, 32,786
Sweden (0) 3 *(Svensson A 53, Larsson 61 (pen), Ibrahimovic 69)*
Azerbaijan (0) 0
Sweden: Hedman; Saarenpaa, Andersson P (Michael Svensson 36), Mjallby, Andersson C, Linderoth, Alexandersson, Andersson D (Svensson A 46), Ljungberg, Allback (Ibrahimovic 66), Larsson.

Azerbaijan: Gasanzade; Yadullayev, Sadykhov, Mamedov A, Asadov, Kuliyev E (Getman 77), Akhmedov, Tagizade, Kurbanov M, Kurbanov K (Vasilyev 83), Guseynov (Aliev 75).
Referee: Wojcik (Poland).

Group 4 Table	P	W	D	L	F	A	Pts
Sweden	10	8	2	0	20	3	26
Turkey	10	6	3	1	18	8	21
Slovakia	10	5	2	3	16	9	17
Macedonia	10	1	4	5	11	18	7
Moldova	10	1	3	6	6	20	6
Azerbaijan	10	1	2	7	4	17	5

GROUP 5

Minsk, 2 September 2000, 35,000
Belarus (1) 2 *(Khatskevich 40, Belkevich 56)*
Wales (0) 1 *(Speed 89)*
Belarus: Tumilovich; Lukhvich, Yakhimovich, Shtanyuk, Gurenko, Khatskevich, Yaskovich (Shuneiko 71), Orlovski (Skripchenko 85), Vasilyuk, Romashchenko M (Ryndyuk 28), Belkevich.
Wales: Jones P; Page, Roberts G, Savage, Coleman, Melville, Robinson, Speed, Bellamy, Roberts I (Blake 73), Giggs.
Referee: Trentalange (Italy).

Oslo, 2 September 2000, 19,201
Norway (0) 0
Armenia (0) 0
Norway: Olsen F; Bergdolmo, Hoftun, Berg, Riseth (Basma 49), Mykland, Leonhardsen, Iversen, Flo T (Helstad 85), Solskjaer, Skammelsrud (Strand R 70).
Armenia: Berezovski; Soukiassian, Hovsepian, Khodgoyan, Vardanian, Khachatrian, Art Petrossian (Minasian 90), Voskanian, Dokhoyan K, Shahgeldian (Demirchian 65), Movsissian (Arm Karamian 85).
Referee: Young (Scotland).

Kiev, 2 September 2000, 50,000
Ukraine (1) 1 *(Shevchenko 13)*
Poland (2) 3 *(Olisadebe 3, 33, Kaluzny 57)*
Ukraine: Kernozenko; Luzhny, Tymoschuk (Zubov 46), Golovko, Vashchuk, Dmitrulin, Gusin, Popov (Kossovski V 75), Vorobei (Yashkin 61), Shevchenko, Rebrov.
Poland: Dudek; Klos (Hajto 85), Zielinski, Michal Zewlakow, Waldoch, Kozminski (Krzynowek 89), Swierczewski, Iwan, Juskowiak (Gilewicz 70), Kaluzny, Olisadebe.
Referee: Aranda (Spain).

Erevan, 7 October 2000, 14,000
Armenia (2) 2 *(Art Petrossian 17, 44)*
Ukraine (1) 3 *(Shevchenko 45, 59, Gusin 55)*
Armenia: Berezovski; Soukiassian, Khodgoyan (Arm Karamian 63), Hovsepian, Vardanian, Khachatrian, Art Petrossian, Voskanian, Dokhoyan K, Shahgeldian (Aram Hakopian 77), Movsissian (Art Karamian 63).
Ukraine: Shovkovskyi; Luzhny, Nesmachni, Golovko, Vashchuk, Dmitrulin, Shevchenko, Gusin, Vorobei (Mikhailenko 67), Tymoschuk (Yashkin 46), Rebrov.
Referee: Larsen (Denmark).

Lodz, 7 October 2000, 7000
Poland (1) 3 *(Kaluzny 24, 62, 73)*
Belarus (1) 1 *(Ryndyuk 37)*
Poland: Dudek; Klos, Zielinksi, Michal Zewlakow, Waldoch, Krzynowek, Swierczewski, Karwan (Iwan 81), Juskowiak (Kryszalowicz 46), Kaluzny, Olisadebe.
Belarus: Varivonchik; Yakhimovich, Ostrovski, Lukhvich, Shtanyuk, Gurenko, Baranov (Lavrik 74), Belkevich, Romashchenko M, Vasilyuk (Ryndyuk 30), Skripchenko (Orlovski 68).
Referee: Frisk (Sweden).

Cardiff, 7 October 2000, 51,000
Wales (0) 1 *(Blake 60)*
Norway (0) 1 *(Helstad 80)*
Wales: Jones P; Delaney, Savage, Page, Coleman, Melville, Robinson, Speed, Hartson (Roberts I 86), Blake, Giggs.
Norway: Olsen F; Basma, Bjornebye, Leonhardsen, Berg, Johnsen R, Bakke (Helstad 78), Mykland, Iversen (Flo T 59), Solskjaer, Strand R.
Referee: Strampe (Germany).

Minsk, 11 October 2000, 20,000
Belarus (2) 2 *(Khatskevich 23, Ryndyuk 34)*
Armenia (0) 1 *(Khodgoyan 50)*
Belarus: Tumilovich; Yakhimovich, Ostrovski, Lukhvich, Lavrik, Gurenko, Khatskevich, Belkevich, Romashchenko M (Skripchenko 89), Vasilyuk (Shuneiko 60), Ryndyuk.
Armenia: Abramian; Soukiassian, Khodgoyan (Art Karamian 61), Hovsepian, Vardanian, Khachatrian, Art Petrossian (Arm Karamian 85), Voskanian, Dokhoyan K, Shahgeldian, Movsissian.
Referee: Corpodean (Romania).

Oslo, 11 October 2000, 23,612
Norway (0) 0
Ukraine (0) 1 *(Shevchenko 49)*
Norway: Olsen F; Basma, Johnsen R, Berg, Bergdolmo, Bakke (Helstad 75), Mykland, Iversen, Solskjaer, Leonhardsen (Flo T 54), Strand R.
Ukraine: Shovkovskyi; Luzhny (Fedorov 80), Nesmachni, Golovko, Vashchuk, Dmitrulin, Shevchenko, Gusin, Vorobei, Popov (Yashkin 50), Rebrov.
Referee: Meier (Switzerland).

Warsaw, 11 October 2000, 14,000
Poland (0) 0
Wales (0) 0
Poland: Dudek; Klos, Zielinski, Waldoch, Michal Zewlakow, Karwan, Kaluzny, Swierczewski, Krzynowek (Rzasa 70), Gilewicz (Kryszalowicz 56), Juskowiak (Olisabede 75).
Wales: Jones P; Delaney, Savage, Page, Coleman, Melville, Robinson, Speed, Hartson (Jones N 75), Blake, Giggs.
Referee: Cortez (Portugal).

Erevan, 24 March 2001, 12,000
Armenia (1) 2 *(Minasian 32, Movsissian 71)*
Wales (1) 2 *(Hartson 41, 48)*
Armenia: Abramian; Vardanian, Hovsepian, Khodgoyan (Art Karamian 58), Sargsyan, Art Petrossian, Voskanian (Aram Hakopian 70), Dokhoyan K, Minasian (Demirchian 39), Shahgeldian, Movsissian.
Wales: Jones P; Delaney, Legg, Melville, Page, Pembridge (Jones M 46), Saunders (Robinson C 70), Speed, Bellamy, Hartson (Roberts I 79), Robinson J.
Referee: Kasnaferis (Greece).

Oslo, 24 March 2001, 15,077
Norway (0) 2 *(Carew 58, Solskjaer 66)*
Poland (2) 3 *(Olisadebe 23, 29, Karwan 80)*
Norway: Myhre; Bergdolmo, Berg, Lundekvam, Stensaas (Flo T 84), Winsnes, Larsen T, Tessem, Solskjaer, Carew, Helstad (Iversen 60).
Poland: Matysek (Dudek 64); Klos, Hajto, Zielinski, Michal Zewlakow, Iwan (Karwan 64), Kaluzny, Swierczewski (Zdebel 88), Kozminski, Kryszalowicz, Olisadebe.
Referee: Dougal (Scotland).

Kiev, 24 March 2001, 75,000
Ukraine (0) 0
Belarus (0) 0
Ukraine: Shovkovskyi; Luzhny, Golovko, Vashchuk, Nesmachni, Popov (Vorobei 61), Dmitrulin (Tymoshchuk 78), Kardash, Yashkin, Shevchenko, Rebrov.

Belarus: Tumilovich; Shuneiko, Ostrovski, Shtanyuk, Yaskovich, Gurenko, Khatskevich, Belkevich, Vasilyuk, Milevski, Romashchenko M (Lavrik 73).
Referee: Marin (Spain).

Minsk, 28 March 2001, 39,000
Belarus (1) 2 *(Khatskevich 19, Vasilyuk 90)*
Norway (0) 1 *(Solskjaer 68)*
Belarus: Tumilovich; Shuneiko, Yakhimovich, Shtanyuk, Lukhvich, Gurenko, Khatskevich, Belkevich, Vasilyuk, Milevski (Lavrik 46), Romashchenko M.
Norway: Myhre; Riseth, Berg, Eggen, Bergdolmo, Tessem (Helstad 87), Larsen T, Winsnes, Solskjaer, Carew, Iversen (Flo T 46).
Referee: Vassaras (Greece).

Warsaw, 28 March 2001, 11,000
Poland (2) 4 *(Michal Zewlakow 15 (pen), Olisadebe 41, Marcin Zewlakow 81, Karwan 88)*
Armenia (0) 0
Poland: Dudek; Klos, Zielinski, Hajto, Michal Zewlakow (Krzynowek 76), Swierczewski, Iwan (Karwan 67), Kaluzny, Kozminski, Kryszalowicz (Marcin Zewlakow 79), Olisadebe.
Armenia: Abramian; Mkrchian, Demirchian, Hovsepian, Vardanian, Khachatrian, Art Petrossian, Voskanian (Art Karamian 66), Dokhoyan K, Shahgeldian (Arm Karamian 73), Movsissian.
Referee: Poulat (France).

Cardiff, 28 March 2001, 46,750
Wales (1) 1 *(Hartson 12)*
Ukraine (0) 1 *(Shevchenko 52)*
Wales: Jones P; Delaney, Barnard, Melville, Page, Jones M (Davies 55), Robinson C, Speed, Bellamy, Hartson (Saunders 70), Giggs.
Ukraine: Shovkovskyi; Luzhny, Golovko, Vashchuk, Nesmachni, Tymoshchuk, Popov (Melashchenko 70), Yashkin, Rebrov (Kardash 46), Vorobei, Shevchenko.
Referee: Romain (Belgium).

Erevan, 2 June 2001, 10,000
Armenia (0) 0
Belarus (0) 0
Armenia: Abramian; Soukiassian, Khodgoyan, Demirchian (Dokhoyan A 65), Vardanian A, Khachatrian, Art Petrossian, Minasian (Art Karamian 36), Sargsyan, Arm Karamian (Gevorgian 69), Dokhoyan K.
Belarus: Tumilovic; Yakhimovich, Ostrovski, Lukhvich, Shtanyuk (Kulchi 84), Gurenko, Khatskevich, Belkevich, Shuneiko, Vasilyuk (Tarlovski 79), Milevski (Yaskovich 72).
Referee: Guenov (Bulgaria).

Kiev, 2 June 2001, 42,000
Ukraine (0) 0
Norway (0) 0
Ukraine: Shovkovskyi; Starostyak, Golovko, Vashchuk, Dmitrulin, Parfenov, Tymoshchuk, Zubov, Vorobei (Spivak 68), Shevchenko, Yashkin (Rebrov 46).
Norway: Myhre; Basma, Hoftun, Berg, Riseth, Rudi, Leonhardsen, Andersen T, Bakke, Strand R (Helstad 78), Carew.
Referee: Maric (Croatia).

Cardiff, 2 June 2001, 48,500
Wales (1) 1 *(Blake 13)*
Poland (1) 2 *(Olisadebe 32, Kryszalowicz 72)*
Wales: Jones P; Page (Jenkins 84), Barnard (Jones M 79), Melville, Symons, Pembridge, Savage, Speed, Hartson, Blake, Giggs.
Poland: Dudek; Klos, Bak J, Hajto, Michal Zewlakow, Iwan, Zdebel (Krynowek 62), Bak A, Kozminski, Juskowiak (Kryszalowicz 54), Olisadebe (Marcin Zewlakow 90).
Referee: Ersoy (Turkey).

Erevan, 6 June 2001, 10,000
Armenia (1) 1 *(Art Petrossian 11)*
Poland (1) 1 *(Kaluzny 4)*

Armenia: Abramian; Soukiassian, Khodgoyan, Hovsepian, Vardanian (Demirchian 41), Khachatrian, Art Petrossian, Dokhoyan A (Ara Hakopian 33) (Gevorgian 66), Dokhoyan K, Sargsyan, Art Karamian.
Poland: Dudek; Kukielka, Hajto, Bak J, Michal Zewlakow, Swierczewski, Bak A, Kaluzny (Krzynowek 36), Kozminski (Zdebel 84), Juskowiak (Marcin Zewlakow 64), Kryszalowicz.
Referee: Romain (Belgium).

Oslo, 6 June 2001, 17,164
Norway (0) 1 *(Carew 80)*
Belarus (1) 1 *(Belkevich 23)*

Norway: Myhre; Basma (Aas 90), Hoftun, Berg, Riseth, Johnsen F, Leonhardsen, Andersen T, Bakke (Rudi 69), Strand R (Nevland 69), Carew.
Belarus: Tumilovich; Yakhimovich, Ostrovski (Tarlovski 85), Lukhvich, Shtanyuk, Gurenko, Khatskevich, Belkevich, Shuneiko, Vasilyuk (Khomutovsky 81), Milevski (Yaskovich 50).
Referee: Radoman (Yugoslavia).

Kiev, 6 June 2001, 33,000
Ukraine (1) 1 *(Zubov 44)*
Wales (0) 1 *(Pembridge 74)*

Ukraine: Shovkovskyi (Levytsky 90); Starostiak (Luzhny 46), Golovko, Vashchuk, Dmitrulin (Nesmachni 46), Parfenov, Tymoshchuk, Zubov, Vorobei, Shevchenko, Rebrov.
Wales: Jones P; Delaney (Jenkins 38), Barnard, Page, Melville, Pembridge, Davies, Speed, Hartson, Blake (Koumas 73), Giggs.
Referee: Gomes (Portugal).

Minsk, 1 September 2001, 44,000
Belarus (0) 0
Ukraine (1) 2 *(Shevchenko 45, 56)*

Belarus: Khomutovsky; Yakhimovich, Ostrovski (Yaskovich 53), Lukhvich, Shtanyuk, Gurenko, Khatskevich (Tarlovski 46), Belkevich (Romashchenko M 60), Shuneiko, Volodenkov, Katchuro.
Ukraine: Virt; Luzhny, Golovko, Vashchuk, Nesmachni, Tymoshchuk, Parfenov, Zubov, Shevchenko, Vorobei (Melaschenko 71), Rebrov.
Referee: Sars (France).

Chorzow, 1 September 2001, 42,500
Poland (1) 3 *(Kryszalowicz 45, Olisadebe 77, Marcin Zewlakow 88)*
Norway (0) 0

Poland: Dudek; Klos, Hajto, Waldoch, Michal Zewlakow, Karwan, Kaluzny, Swierczewski (Bak A 90), Kozminski (Krzynowek 81), Kryszalowicz (Marcin Zewlakow 74), Olisadebe.
Norway: Myhre; Basma, Johnsen R, Berg, Bergdolmo, Strand R (Riise 62), Rudi, Sorensen, Leonhardsen (Rushfeldt 80), Iversen (Strand P 89), Solskjaer.
Referee: Liba (Czech Republic).

Cardiff, 1 September 2001, 18,000
Wales (0) 0
Armenia (0) 0

Wales: Jones P; Delaney, Jenkins (Barnard 80), Robinson C (Jones M 80), Symons, Melville, Savage, Davies, Roberts I, Bellamy, Giggs.
Armenia: Berezovski; Soukiassian, Hovsepian, Vardanian, Dokhoyan A, Art Petrossian (Demirchian 80), Khachatrian, Voskanian (Harutyunian 67), Dokhoyan K, Shahgeldian (Simonian 75), Movsissian.
Referee: Attard (Malta).

Minsk, 5 September 2001, 24,302
Belarus (1) 4 *(Vasilyuk 8, 46, 51, 62)*
Poland (0) 1 *(Marcin Zewlakow 77)*

Belarus: Tumilovich; Yakhimovich, Milevski (Yaskovich 61), Lukhvich, Shtanyuk, Gurenko, Romashchenko M, Kulchi, Shuneiko, Kachuro, Vasilyuk (Ryndyuk 70) (Ostrovski 83).
Poland: Dudek; Klos, Karwan, Michal Zewlakow, Waldoch, Kukielka, Swierczewski, Kozminski (Krzynowek 46), Kryszalowicz (Marcin Zewlakow 46), Bak A, Olisadebe (Gilewicz 61).
Referee: Plautz (Austria).

Oslo, 5 September 2001, 18,211
Norway (1) 3 *(Johnsen R 17, Carew 65, Johnsen F 83)*
Wales (2) 2 *(Savage 10, Bellamy 27)*

Norway: Myhre; Basma, Johnsen R, Berg, Riise, Sorensen (Johnsen F 46), Strand R, Rudi, Leonhardsen (Strand P 90), Iversen (Carew 5), Solskjaer.
Wales: Jones P; Delaney, Jenkins, Robinson C (Jones M 84), Symons, Page, Savage, Davies (Robinson J 77), Hartson (Blake 83), Bellamy, Giggs.
Referee: Stuchlik (Austria).

Lviv, 5 September 2001, 27,000
Ukraine (1) 3 *(Shevchenko 13, Vorobei 84, 90)*
Armenia (0) 0

Ukraine: Virt; Luzhny, Nesmachni, Golovko, Vashchuk, Serebrennikov (Shyshchenko 65), Shevchenko, Parfenov, Zubov (Popov 46), Melaschenko (Vorobei 74), Rebrov.
Armenia: Berezovski; Soukiassian, Dokhoyan K, Hovsepian, Vardanian, Khachatrian, Art Petrossian, Dokhoyan A (Harutyunian 82), Sarkissian, Shahgeldian (Hakopian H 70), Movsissian.
Referee: Loizou (Cyprus).

Erevan, 6 October 2001, 10,000
Armenia (0) 1 *(Hakopian H 71)*
Norway (0) 4 *(Borgersen 50, 80, Carew 70, 89)*

Armenia: Berezovski; Khodgoyan (Art Karamian 63), Dokhoyan A (Minasian 74), Hovsepian, Vardanian, Khachatrian, Art Petrossian, Dokhoyan K, Sarkissian, Voskanian (Hakopian H 59), Arm Karamian.
Norway: Myhre; Bergdolmo, Johnsen R (Borgersen 46), Basma, Riise, Sorensen (Riseth 83), Bakke, Strand R, Rudi, Johnsen F (Flo T 90), Carew.
Referee: Schluchter (Switzerland).

Chorzow, 6 October 2001, 20,900
Poland (1) 1 *(Olisadebe 40)*
Ukraine (0) 1 *(Shevchenko 81)*

Poland: Dudek; Klos, Hajto, Waldoch, Michal Zewlakow, Swierczewski (Bak J 77), Karwan, Bak A, Kozminski (Krzynowek 65), Marcin Zewlakow (Kryszalowicz 46), Olisadebe.
Ukraine: Reva; Luzhny, Golovko, Vashchuk (Fedorov 79), Nesmachni (Zadorozhni 84), Zubov, Popov, Melaschenko (Shyshchenko 46), Tymoshchuk, Shevchenko, Vorobei.
Referee: Dallas (Scotland).

Cardiff, 6 October 2001, 12,000
Wales (0) 1 *(Hartson 47)*
Belarus (0) 0

Wales: Jones P; Delaney, Speed, Jones M (Robinson C 65), Symons (Page 17), Melville, Robinson J, Davies, Hartson (Roberts I 90), Bellamy, Pembridge.
Belarus: Tumilovich; Lukhvich, Yakhimovich, Shtanyuk, Gurenko, Shuneiko, Kulchi, Yaskovich, Baranov (Gleb 67), Vasilyuk (Ryndyuk 44), Katchuro.
Referee: Rodomonti (Italy).

Group 5 Table	P	W	D	L	F	A	Pts
Poland	10	6	3	1	21	11	21
Ukraine	10	4	5	1	13	8	17
Belarus	10	4	3	3	12	11	15
Norway	10	2	4	4	12	14	10
Wales	10	1	6	3	10	12	9
Armenia	10	0	5	5	7	19	5

GROUP 6

Brussels, 2 September 2000, 40,000
Belgium (0) 0
Croatia (0) 0
Belgium: De Vlieger; Deflandre, Valgaeren, Van Meir, Van Kerckhoven, Vanderhaeghe, Wilmots, Goor (Hendrikx 88), Mpenza E (Mpenza M 74), Strupar (Peeters 60), Verheyen.
Croatia: Pletikosa; Kovac R, Jarni, Soldo, Stimac, Simic, Vugrinec (Biscan 46), Jurcic, Suker, Kovac N, Balaban (Tudor 90).
Referee: Levnikov (Russia).

Riga, 2 September 2000, 9500
Latvia (0) 0
Scotland (0) 1 *(McCann 89)*
Latvia: Kolinko; Laizans, Lobanyov, Stepanovs, Blagonadezhdin, Bleidelis, Ivanov, Astafjevs, Rubins, Pahars, Stolcers.
Scotland: Sullivan; Boyd, Davidson (Naysmith 46), Weir (Cameron 46), Hendry, Dailly, Ferguson B, Elliott, Dodds (Holt 90), Hutchison, McCann.
Referee: Schluchter (Switzerland).

Riga, 7 October 2000, 9000
Latvia (0) 0
Belgium (2) 4 *(Wilmots 5, Peeters 13, Cavens 82, Verheyen 90)*
Latvia: Kolinko; Stepanovs, Laizans, Lobanyov (Zemlinsky 75), Blagonadezhdin (Polyakov 63), Astafjevs, Bleidelis, Ivanov, Pahars, Rubins, Stolcers (Peltsis 68).
Belgium: De Vlieger; Deflandre, Valgaeren, Van Meir, Van Kerckhoven, Vanderhaeghe, Wilmots (Goossens 88), Goor, Peeters (Cavens 80), Walem (Boffin 85), Verheyen.
Referee: Irvine (Northern Ireland).

Serravalle, 7 October 2000, 4377
San Marino (0) 0
Scotland (0) 2 *(Elliott 71, Hutchison 73)*
San Marino: Gasperoni F; Gennari, Gobbi, Matteoni (Valentini V 74), Bacciocchi, Marani, Gasperoni B, Zonzini (Della Valle 80), Manzaroli, Muccioli, Montagna (De Luigi 60).
Scotland: Sullivan; McNamara, Naysmith, Elliott, Hendry, Dailly (Weir 36), Cameron, Gallacher (Dickov 65), Dodds, Hutchison, McCann (Johnston 46).
Referee: Orrason (Iceland).

Zagreb, 11 October 2000, 30,000
Croatia (1) 1 *(Boksic 16)*
Scotland (1) 1 *(Gallacher 24)*
Croatia: Pavlovic; Kovac R, Stimac, Simic, Saric, Kovac N, Soldo (Biscan 46), Jarni (Zivkovic 46), Prosinecki, Balaban, Boksic (Vugrinec 75).
Scotland: Sullivan; Boyd, Naysmith, Elliott, Hendry, Weir, Cameron, Burley, Gallacher, Hutchison, Johnston (Dickov 46) (Holt 90).
Referee: Veissiere (France).

Serravalle, 15 November 2000, 537
San Marino (0) 0
Latvia (1) 1 *(Yeliseyev 9)*
San Marino: Gasperoni F; Gennari, Marani, Valentini V, Matteoni, Bacciocchi, Muccioli, Zonzoni (Selva R 84), Montagna (De Luigi 78), Manzaroli (Bugli 74), Selva A.
Latvia: Kolinko; Stepanovs, Laizans, Zemlinsky, Blagonadezhdin, Bleidelis, Troitsky, Astafjevs, Pahars, Rubins (Verpakovsky 66), Yeliseyev (Ivanov 84).
Referee: Cheferin (Slovakia).

Brussels, 28 February 2001, 40,104
Belgium (3) 10 *(Vanderhaeghe 10, 50, Mpenza E 13, Goor 26, 60, Baseggio 64, Wilmots 72, Peeters 76, 84, 88)*
San Marino (0) 1 *(Selva A 90)*
Belgium: De Vlieger; Deflandre (Crasson 67), Van Meir, Van Buyten, Dheedene, Englebert (Peeters 59), Vanderhaeghe, Baseggio (Vermant 75), Goor, Mpenza E, Wilmots.
San Marino: Gasperoni F; Gennari, Gobbi, Della Balda (Manzaroli 69), Marani, Matteoni, Muccioli, Selva A, Valentini, Zonzini (Vannucci 78), De Luigi (Bugli 87).
Referee: Kaldma (Estonia).

Osijek, 24 March 2001, 18,000
Croatia (3) 4 *(Balaban 8, 43, 45, Vugrinec 89)*
Latvia (0) 1 *(Stolcers 60)*
Croatia: Pletikosa; Simic, Tudor, Kovac R (Vranjes 77), Jarni, Zivkovic, Stanic (Cvitanovic 46), Prosinecki (Bjelica 63), Balaban, Suker, Vugrinec.
Latvia: Kolinko; Troitsky, Stepanovs, Zemlinsky, Blagonadezhdin, Bleidelis (Verpakovsky 39), Astafjevs, Laizans, Rubins (Rimkus 73), Pahars, Yeliseyev (Stolcers 54).
Referee: Ingvarsson (Sweden).

Glasgow, 24 March 2001, 37,480
Scotland (2) 2 *(Dodds 1, 28 (pen))*
Belgium (0) 2 *(Wilmots 58, Van Buyten 90)*
Scotland: Sullivan; Weir, Boyd, Elliott, Hendry, Ferguson B, Burley, Lambert, Dodds (Gallacher 88), Hutchison, Matteo.
Belgium: De Vlieger; Mpenza E, Wilmots, Goor, Vanderhaege, Baseggio (Vermant 79), Hendrikx (Peeters 46), Dheedene, De Boeck, Valgaeren (Van Buyten 57), Deflandre.
Referee: Nielsen (Denmark).

Glasgow, 28 March 2001, 27,313
Scotland (3) 4 *(Hendry 22, 33, Dodds 34, Cameron 65)*
San Marino (0) 0
Scotland: Sullivan; Johnston, Matteo (Gallacher 64), Elliott (Boyd 46), Hendry, Weir, Burley, Lambert, Dodds, Hutchison, Cameron (Gemmill 82).
San Marino: Gasperoni F; Della Balda (Albani 90), Marani, Gobbi, Matteoni, Bacciocchi, Manzaroli (Selva R 80), Zonzini, Muccioli, Vannucci (Bugli 69), Selva A.
Referee: Kari (Finland).

Riga, 25 April 2001, 4000
Latvia (1) 1 *(Pahars 1)*
San Marino (0) 1 *(Albani 59)*
Latvia: Kolinko; Astafjevs, Stepanovs, Zemlinsky, Kolesnichenko (Mikholap 46), Ivanov (Zakreshevski 77), Blagonadezhdin, Rubins, Rimkus (Yeliseyev 66), Pahars, Stolcers.
San Marino: Gasperoni F; Albani, Vannucci, Della Balda, Matteoni, Bugli (Selva R 80), Bacciocchi, Muccioli, Zonzini, Manzaroli (Nanni 90), Selva A (Montagna 83).
Referee: Nalbandian (Albania).

Brussels, 2 June 2001, 30,000
Belgium (2) 3 *(Wilmots 2, Mpenza E 12, Zemlinsky 49 (og))*
Latvia (0) 1 *(Pahars 51)*
Belgium: De Vlieger; Crasson, Valgaeren, Van Meir, Van der Heyden, Simons, Wilmots (Vermant 83), Goor (Boffin 68), Mpenza E (Sonck 78), Walem, Verheyen.
Latvia: Kolinko; Stepanovs, Astafjevs (Stolcers 67), Zemlinsky, Laizans, Blagonadezhdin (Zakreshevsky 68), Ivanov, Bleidelis, Pahars (Mikholap 71), Rubins, Isakov.
Referee: Dobrinov (Bulgaria).

Varazdin, 2 June 2001, 15,000

Croatia (2) 4 *(Vlaovic 3, Balaban 29, Suker 54 (pen), Vugrinec 61)*
San Marino (0) 0

Croatia: Pletikosa; Saric, Tudor, Simic, Jarni, Kovac R, Kovac N (Agic 64), Prosinecki, Vugrinec (Vucko 76), Vlaovic, Balaban (Suker 46).
San Marino: Gasperoni F; Albani, Della Balda, Matteoni (Manzaroli 26), Bacciocchi, Marani, Gennari, Vannucci, Gasperoni B (Ugolini 86), Zonzini (Selva R 76), Selva A.
Referee: Timofejev (Estonia).

Riga, 6 June 2001, 5000

Latvia (0) 0
Croatia (1) 1 *(Balaban 40)*

Latvia: Kolinko; Stepanovs, Astafjevs (Mikholap 71), Zemlinsky, Laizans, Blagonadezhdin, Zakreshevsky, Bleidelis (Dobretsov 88), Isakov, Rubins (Verpakovsky 61), Stolcers.
Croatia: Pletikosa; Saric, Jarni, Tomas, Simic, Rapaic (Vugrinec 75), Prosinecki, Suker, Kovac N (Agic 90), Balaban (Vlaovic 65).
Referee: McDermott (Republic of Ireland).

Serraville, 6 June 2001, 1000

San Marino (1) 1 *(Selva A 11)*
Belgium (1) 4 *(Wilmots 10, 89 (pen), Verheyen 60, Sonck 68)*

San Marino: Gasperoni F; Albani (Selva R 69), Della Balda, Bacciocchi, Marani, Gennari, Muccioli, Vannucci, Zonzini (Ugolini 82), Selva A, Gasperoni B (Bugli 74).
Belgium: De Vlieger; Deflandre, Van Meir, Valgaeren, Van Kerckhoven (Boffin 79), Verheyen, Vanderhaeghe, Walem, Goor (Vermant 75), Peeters (Sonck 52), Wilmots.
Referee: Yakov (Israel).

Glasgow, 1 September 2001, 47,384

Scotland (0) 0
Croatia (0) 0

Scotland: Sullivan; Weir, Naysmith (Gemmill 84), Elliott, Matteo, Dailly, Burley, Hutchison, Booth (Dodds 72), Lambert, McCann (Cameron 52).
Croatia: Pletikosa; Tudor, Stimac, Kovac R, Zivkovic, Soldo, Tomas (Biscan 84), Jarni, Prosinecki (Vugrinec 78), Stanic (Suker 71), Balaban.
Referee: Michel (Slovakia).

Brussels, 5 September 2001, 48,500

Belgium (1) 2 *(Van Kerckhoven 28, Goor 90)*
Scotland (0) 0

Belgium: De Vlieger; Deflandre, De Boeck, Van Meir, Van Kerckhoven, Verheyen, Vanderhaeghe, Walem (Simons 89), Goor, Wilmots, Sonck (Peeters 82).
Scotland: Sullivan; Weir (Cameron 66), Boyd (Booth 57), Elliott, Matteo, Dailly, Burley (McNamara 82), Hutchison, Dodds, Lambert, Naysmith.
Referee: Gonzalez (Spain).

Serravalle, 5 September 2001, 1500

San Marino (0) 0
Croatia (1) 4 *(Kovac N 40, Prosinecki 49 (pen), 90, Soldo 77)*

San Marino: Gasperoni F; Della Balda, Matteoni, Gobbi, Gennari, Marani (Bugli 49), Gasperoni B, Zonzini (Nanni 88), Muccioli, Selva A, Montagna (Ugolini 62).
Croatia: Butina; Zivkovic, Jarni, Stimac, Simic, Soldo, Stanic (Suker 78), Kovac N, Prosinecki, Vlaovic (Balaban 63), Vugrinec (Saric 63).
Referee: Stadsgaard (Denmark).

Zagreb, 6 October 2001, 36,077

Croatia (0) 1 *(Boksic 75)*
Belgium (0) 0

Croatia: Pletikosa; Simic, Tudor, Kovac R, Zivkovic, Tomas, Soldo (Rapajic 72), Jarni, Prosinecki (Vranjes 79), Vlaovic (Balaban 63), Boksic.

Belgium: De Vlieger; Deflandre (Peeters 83), Van Meir, De Boeck, Van Kerckhoven, Verheyen, Vanderhaeghe, Baseggio, Goor (Hendrikx 81), Wilmots (Sonck 71), Mpenza E.
Referee: Krug (Germany).

Glasgow, 6 October 2001, 23,228

Scotland (1) 2 *(Freedman 44, Weir 53)*
Latvia (1) 1 *(Rubins 21)*

Scotland: Sullivan; Nicholson B (Booth 63), Davidson, Weir, Dailly (Rae 71), Elliott, Burley, Hutchison (Severin 76), Freedman, Cameron, McCann.
Latvia: Kolinko; Isakov, Zakreshevsky, Stepanovs, Blagonadezhdin, Bleidelis (Kolesnichenko 76), Laizans, Astafjevs, Rubins (Dobretsov 82), Pahars, Verpakovsky.
Referee: Hauge (Norway).

Group 6 Table	P	W	D	L	F	A	Pts
Croatia	8	5	3	0	15	2	18
Belgium	8	5	2	1	25	6	17
Scotland	8	4	3	1	12	6	15
Latvia	8	1	1	6	5	16	4
San Marino	8	0	1	7	3	30	1

GROUP 7

Sarajevo, 2 September 2000, 35,000

Bosnia (1) 1 *(Baljic 41)*
Spain (1) 2 *(Gerard 39, Etxeberria 72)*

Bosnia: Guso; Akrapovic, Hujdurovic, Mujcin (Topic 79), Varesanovic, Hibic, Bolic, Sabic (Muratovic 86), Barbarez, Salihamidzic, Baljic.
Spain: Casillas; Manuel Pablo, Sergi, Paco, Abelardo, Mendieta, Helguera, Gerard (Guerrero 85), Urzaiz (Celades 70), Raul, Munitis (Etxeberria 58).
Referee: Fandel (Germany).

Ramat Gan, 3 September 2000, 14,000

Israel (1) 2 *(Mizrahi A 1, Balili 79)*
Liechtenstein (0) 0

Israel: Davidovich; Talker (Benayoun 66), Shelach, Gershon, Harazi A, Keissi, Berkovic (Zohar 82), Tal (Balili 77), Nimny, Mizrahi A, Banin.
Liechtenstein: Jehle; Ospelt, Zech, Hasler D, Frick C (Gigon 76), Martin Stocklasa (Hanselmann 85), Michael Stocklasa (Burgmeier 85), Hefti, Telser, Frick M, Beck T.
Referee: O'Hanlon (Republic of Ireland).

Vaduz, 7 October 2000, 3500

Liechtenstein (0) 0
Austria (1) 1 *(Flogel 20)*

Liechtenstein: Jehle; Ospelt, Hasler D, Telser, Martin Stocklasa, Hanselmann, Hefti, Michael Stocklasa (Nigg 74), Gigon, Beck T, Frick M.
Austria: Wohlfahrt; Martin Hiden, Baur, Stranzl, Schopp (Hortnagl 67), Kuhbauer, Herzog, Flogel, Kirchler, Brunmayr (Kitzbichler 46), Mayrleb.
Referee: Rowbotham (Scotland).

Madrid, 7 October 2000, 80,000

Spain (1) 2 *(Gerard 22, Hierro 53)*
Israel (0) 0

Spain: Casillas; Hierro, Manuel Pablo, Abelardo, Sergi, Helguera, Gerard (Baraja 31), Mendieta, Munitis, Raul (Guerrero 85), Urzaiz (Catanha 75).
Israel: Davidovich; Halfon, Talker, Shelach, Benado, Keissi, Tal, Nimny (Benayoun 65), Badir (Berkovic 75), Revivo, Mizrahi A.
Referee: Colombo (France).

Vienna, 11 October 2000, 48,000

Austria (1) 1 *(Baur 21)*
Spain (1) 1 *(Baraja 27)*

Austria: Wohlfahrt; Hatz, Baur, Martin Hiden, Stranzl (Hortnagl 46), Flogel, Cerny, Kuhbauer (Schopp 75), Mayrleb, Herzog, Kocijan (Kirchler 54).
Spain: Casillas; Hierro, Abelardo, Sergi, Baraja, Helguera, Mendieta, Urzaiz (Catanha 60), Raul (Guerrero 88), Victor Sanchez (Rufete 46), Manuel Pablo.
Referee: Ivanov (Russia).

Tel Aviv, 11 October 2000, 30,000

Israel (1) 3 *(Berkovic 12, Abuksis 62, Katan 76)*
Bosnia (0) 1 *(Akrapovic 48)*

Israel: Davidovich; Benado, Talker, Shelach, Gershon, Keissi (Ben-Dayan 86), Tal, Revivo, Abuksis, Berkovic (Benayoun 60), Mizrahi A (Katan 73).
Bosnia: Guso; Akrapovic, Music, Hujdurovic (Krupinac 79), Varesanovic, Hibic, Bolic, Demirovich (Joldic 73), Barbarez, Salihamidzic, Baljic.
Referee: Jol (Holland).

Sarajevo, 24 March 2001, 25,000

Bosnia (1) 1 *(Barbarez 42)*
Austria (0) 1 *(Baur 61)*

Bosnia: Piplica; Varesanovic, Hujdurovic, Hibic, Rizvic (Hota 70), Sabic, Akrapovic, Barbarez, Music, Bolic, Baljic (Topic 83).
Austria: Wohlfahrt; Baur, Martin Hiden, Neukirchner (Prilasnig 54), Cerny (Schopp 46), Kuhbauer, Stranzl, Herzog (Haas 71), Flogel, Vastic, Mayrleb.
Referee: Ovrebo (Norway).

Alicante, 24 March 2001, 29,900

Spain (2) 5 *(Helguera 20, Mendieta 36, 81, Hierro 54 (pen), Raul 68)*
Liechtenstein (0) 0

Spain: Casillas; Manuel Pablo, Hierro, Nadal, Romero, Mendieta, Guardiola (Sergio 82), Helguera (Baraja 67), Raul, Javi Moreno, Munitis (Etxeberria 39).
Liechtenstein: Jehle; Ospelt, Zech, Hefti, Hasler D, Gigon, Beck T (Buchel R 88), Martin Stocklasa (Gerster 90), Telser, Michael Stocklasa, Frick M.
Referee: Ceferin (Slovakia).

Vienna, 28 March 2001, 21,000

Austria (2) 2 *(Baur 9, Herzog 41 (pen))*
Israel (1) 1 *(Baur 6 (og))*

Austria: Wohlfahrt; Baur, Martin Hiden, Prilasnig, Schopp, Kuhbauer, Herzog (Kitzbichler 90), Stranzl, Flogel, Vastic (Hortnagl 57), Mayrleb (Haas 63).
Israel: Davidovich; Benado (Mizrahi A 57), Talker, Shelach (Brumer 46), Gershon, Banin (Tal 72), Keissi, Nimny, Berkovic, Zeituni, Benayoun.
Referee: Trentalange (Italy).

Vaduz, 28 March 2001, 3400

Liechtenstein (0) 0
Bosnia (1) 3 *(Barbarez 10, 72, Hota 89)*

Liechtenstein: Jehle; Ospelt, Hefti, Zech, Martin Stocklasa, Hasler D, Beck T (Nigg 73), Telser (Buchel R 46), Michael Stocklasa (Ritter 90), Gigon, Frick M.
Bosnia: Piplica; Varesanovic, Hujdurovic, Hibic, Music, Salihamidzic, Akrapovic, Sabic (Rivzic 90), Barbarez, Bolic (Topic 63), Baljic (Hota 81).
Referee: Sipailo (Latvia).

Innsbruck, 25 April 2001, 13,000

Austria (1) 2 *(Glieder 43, Flogel 75)*
Liechtenstein (0) 0

Austria: Manninger; Prilasnig, Baur, Martin Hiden, Kitzbichler (Ibertsberger 75), Kirchler, Flogel, Herzog (Wallner 89), Hortnagl, Vastic (Weissenberger 61), Glieder.
Liechtenstein: Jehle; Ospelt (Buchel R 66), Hefti, Ritter, Zech, Beck T (D'Elia 52), Hasler D, Telser, Martin Stocklasa, Gigon, Frick M (Michael Stocklasa 81).
Referee: Malcolm (Northern Ireland).

Vaduz, 2 June 2001, 1500

Liechtenstein (0) 0
Israel (3) 3 *(Revivo 2, Tal 6, Nimny 17)*

Liechtenstein: Jehle; Ospelt, Ritter, Zech, Martin Stocklasa, Michael Stocklasa, Beck T (Gerster 85), Buchel R (Beck M 71), Telser, Gigon, Hasler H (D'Elia 65).
Israel: Davidovich; Ben-Dayan (Badir 65), Talker, Benado, Gershon, Keissi, Zeituni, Revivo (Mizrahi A 74), Nimny, Berkovic (Benayoun 65), Tal.
Referee: Isaksen (Faeroes).

Oviedo, 2 June 2001, 27,000

Spain (1) 4 *(Hierro 26, Javi Moreno 75, Raul 88, Diego Tristan 90)*
Bosnia (1) 1 *(Beslija 41)*

Spain: Canizares; Manuel Pablo, Hierro, Nadal, Juanfran, Mendieta (Munitis 55), Guardiola, Helguera (Valeron 46), Luis Enrique (Javi Moreno 75), Raul, Diego Tristan.
Bosnia: Piplica; Hujdurovic, Varesanovic, Hibic, Beslija, Akrapovic, Mujcin, Barbarez, Music (Hota 70), Baljic, Bolic (Demirovic 82).
Referee: Olsen (Norway).

Tel Aviv, 6 June 2001, 25,000

Israel (1) 1 *(Revivo 4)*
Spain (0) 1 *(Raul 63)*

Israel: Davidovich (Auat 46); Brumer, Talker, Benado, Gershon, Keissi, Zeituni, Berkovic (Benayoun 87), Tal, Nimny, Revivo (Banin 70).
Spain: Canizares; Manuel Pablo, Hierro, Nadal, Sergi, Valeron (Helguera 76), Guardiola (Diego Tristan 60), Baraja, Luis Enrique (Puyol 83), Javi Moreno, Raul.
Referee: Frisk (Sweden).

Sarajevo, 1 September 2001, 7700

Bosnia (0) 0
Israel (0) 0

Bosnia: Piplica; Beslija, Music, Konjic, Akrapovic, Hibic, Sabic, Salihamidzic, Topic (Muharemovic 74), Mujcin (Hota 82), Baljic (Saranovic 79).
Israel: Auat; Talker (Harazi 46), Shelach, Gershon, Benado, Keissi, Zeituni, Banin, Tal, Nimny, Revivo (Katan 70).
Referee: Schoch (Switzerland).

Valencia, 1 September 2001, 35,000

Spain (1) 4 *(Diego Tristan 44, Morientes 78, 83, Mendieta 90)*
Austria (0) 0

Spain: Canizares; Manuel Pablo, Hierro, Nadal, Aranzabal, Victor Sanchez (Mendieta 79), Valeron, Xavi, Vicente (Luis Enrique 83), Raul, Diego Tristan (Morientes 71).
Austria: Wohlfahrt; Baur, Prilasnig, Martin Hiden, Kogler, Flogel, Herzog, Ibertsberger (Winklhofer 69), Hortnagl, Vastic (Brunmayr 65), Weissenberger (Kitzbichler 57).
Referee: Elizondo (Argentina).

Vienna, 5 September 2001, 23,200

Austria (1) 2 *(Herzog 38, 86)*
Bosnia (0) 0

Austria: Wohlfahrt; Baur, Kogler, Martin Hiden, Ibertsberger (Winklhofer 83), Kuhbauer, Prilasnig, Herzog (Kitzbichler 88), Flogel, Vastic, Haas (Weissenberger 81).
Bosnia: Piplica; Beslija, Ikanovic (Hota 68), Konjic, Hibic, Salihamidzic, Sabic, Mujcin, Music, Baljic, Barbarez (Topic 71).
Referee: Barber (England).

Vaduz, 5 September 2001, 4648

Liechtenstein (0) 0
Spain (1) 2 *(Raul 17, Nadal 77)*

Liechtenstein: Jehle; Telser, Ospelt, Zech, Michael Stocklasa, Gigon, Beck T (Nigg 88), Martin Stocklasa, Gerster, Beck M (Burgmeier 67), Buchel R (Buchel M 82).
Spain: Casillas; Puyol, Tellez, Hierro (Nadal 46), Aranzabal, Etxeberria, Mendieta, Albelda, Luis Enrique (Diego Tristan 72), Raul (Jose Ignacio 46), Morientes.
Referee: Dobrinov (Bulgaria).

Zenica, 7 October 2001, 7000

Bosnia (2) 5 *(Konjic 34, Baljic 45 (pen), 82 (pen), Sabic 69, Dodik 86)*
Liechtenstein (0) 0

Bosnia: Piplica; Beslija (Hota 72), Music, Konjic, Hibic, Akrapovic (Biscevic 71), Sabic, Salihamidzic (Ikanovic 58), Dodik, Muharemovic, Baljic.

Liechtenstein: Jehle; Ospelt, Martin Stocklasa, Hefti, Michael Stocklasa, Gerster, Telser, Buchel R (D'Elia 76), Beck T (Nigg 46), Burgmeier (Beck M 71), Gigon.
Referee: McDermott (Republic of Ireland).

Tel Aviv, 27 October 2001, 41,000
Israel (0) 1 *(Gershon 56 (pen))*
Austria (0) 1 *(Herzog 90)*

Israel: Auat; Ben Dayan, Benado, Gershon, Talker, Keissi, Banin (Tal 26), Berkovic, Nimny, Revivo (Katan 52), Abuksis.
Austria: Wohlfahrt; Strafner (Wallner 69), Winklhofer, Prilasnig, Vukovic, Schopp (Lexa 60), Kitzbichler (Kocijan 74), Markus Hiden, Herzog, Vastic, Haas.
Referee: Pereira (Portugal).

Group 7 Table	P	W	D	L	F	A	Pts
Spain	8	6	2	0	21	4	20
Austria	8	4	3	1	10	8	15
Israel	8	3	3	2	11	7	12
Bosnia	8	2	2	4	12	12	8
Liechtenstein	8	0	0	8	0	23	0

GROUP 8

Budapest, 3 September 2000, 57,000
Hungary (1) 2 *(Horvath 29, 78)*
Italy (1) 2 *(Inzaghi F 26, 35)*

Hungary: Kiraly; Korsos G, Sebok V, Matyus (Peto 46), Feher C, Halmai, Hamar (Lendvai 89), Illes, Lisztes, Horvath, Tokoli (Dombi 75).
Italy: Toldo; Cannavaro, Nesta, Iuliano, Zambrotta, Albertini, Maldini, Fiore (Gattuso 80), Totti, Inzaghi F, Del Piero (Delvecchio 73).
Referee: Barber (England).

Bucharest, 3 September 2000, 4500
Romania (0) 1 *(Ganea 89)*
Lithuania (0) 0

Romania: Stelea; Ciobotariu (Mutu 49), Filipescu, Belodedici, Contra (Petre 58), Petrescu, Munteanu C, Munteanu D, Chivu, Moldovan (Ganea 67), Vladoiu.
Lithuania: Padimanskas; Kancelskis, Gleveckas, Skerla, Zvirgzdauskas, Zutautas D, Danilevicius, Semberas, Preiksaitis (Buitkus 46), Maciulevicius (Mikalajunas 46), Fomenka (Radzius 80).
Referee: Norman (Sweden).

Milan, 7 October 2000, 54,297
Italy (3) 3 *(Inzaghi F 13, Delvecchio 17, Totti 42)*
Romania (0) 0

Italy: Toldo; Cannavaro, Nesta, Maldini, Di Livio, Albertini, Fiore (Pancaro 55), Coco, Totti, Inzaghi F (Del Piero 81), Delvecchio (Gattuso 71).
Romania: Stelea; Petrescu (Contra 46), Belodedici, Filipescu, Chivu, Rosu, Galca, Lupescu, Munteanu D (Munteanu C 62), Moldovan (Mutu 58), Ganea.
Referee: Wegereef (Holland).

Vilnius, 7 October 2000, 5000
Lithuania (0) 0
Georgia (2) 4 *(Ketsbaia 18, 33, Kinkladze 46, Arveladze A 84)*

Lithuania: Padimanskas; Skerla, Gleveckas, Graziunas (Maciulevicius 39), Zutatas D, Buitkus, Semberas, Ivanauskas (Morinas 46), Fomenka (Zvinglas 55), Danilevicius, Jankauskas.
Georgia: Gvaramadze; Silagadze, Kobiashvili, Rekhviashvili, Khizanishvili, Kaladze, Nemsadze, Kavelashvili, Ketsbaia (Menteshashvili 67), Kinkladze (Jamarauli 70), Demetradze (Arveladze A 56).
Referee: Wojcik (Poland).

Ancona, 11 October 2000, 26,000
Italy (0) 2 *(Del Piero 47 (pen), 88 (pen))*
Georgia (0) 0

Italy: Toldo; Cannavaro, Nesta, Bertotto, Di Livio, Albertini, Fiore (Pancaro 76), Coco, Totti (Montella 83), Delvecchio (Gattuso 52), Del Piero.

Georgia: Gvaramadze; Silagadze, Kobiashvili, Rekhviashvili, Khizanishvili, Kaladze, Nemsadze, Kavelashvili, Ketsbaia (Menteshashvili 68), Kinkladze (Jamarauli 61), Arveladze A (Demetradze 61).
Referee: Nilsson (Sweden).

Vilnius, 11 October 2000, 2000
Lithuania (0) 0 *(Buitkus 71)*
Hungary (2) 6 *(Illes 24, Feher M 36, 62, 72, Horvath 66, Lisztes 84 (pen))*

Lithuania: Padimanskas; Skerla, Gleveckas, Radzius, Kancelskis (Graziunas 69), Buitkus, Semberas, Ivanauskas (Maciulevicius 70), Preiksaitis, Morinas (Danielvicius 83), Jankauskas.
Hungary: Kiraly; Korsos G (Bodnar 84), Feher C (Juhar 78), Matyus (Dombi 73), Sebok V, Peto, Feher M, Lisztes, Horvath, Illes, Hamar.
Referee: Erdemir (Turkey).

Budapest, 24 March 2001, 20,000
Hungary (0) 1 *(Sebok V 70 (pen))*
Lithuania (0) 1 *(Razanauskas 74)*

Hungary: Kiraly; Feher C, Sebok V, Korsos G, Juhar, Miriuta, Dardai, Illes, Hamar (Egressy 46), Horvath, Feher M (Dombi 64).
Lithuania: Stauce; Skarbalius, Dedura (Dziaukstas 35), Gleveckas, Zvirgzdauskas, Razanauskas (Joksas 89), Zutautas R, Poskus, Morinas, Semberas, Mikalajunas.
Referee: Melnischuk (Ukraine).

Bucharest, 24 March 2001, 24,500
Romania (0) 0
Italy (2) 2 *(Inzaghi F 29, 32)*

Romania: Stelea; Radoi (Serban 71), Filipescu, Prodan, Contra, Codrea, Galca (Munteanu C 59), Munteanu D, Moldovan (Ganea 78), Niculae, Ilie A.
Italy: Buffon; Cannavaro, Nesta, Maldini, Zambrotta, Tommasi, Fiore (Tacchinardi 62), Albertini, Pancaro, Inzaghi F (Montella 86), Del Piero.
Referee: Fandel (Germany).

Tbilisi, 28 March 2001, 27,000
Georgia (0) 0
Romania (0) 2 *(Munteanu D 68, Contra 81)*

Georgia: Gvaramadze; Silagadze, Rekhviashvili (Iashvili 73), Kobiashvili, Khizanishvili, Nemsadze, Kaladze, Kavelashvili (Janashia 52), Ketsbaia (Kemoklidze 62), Arveladze S, Kinkladze.
Romania: Stelea; Contra, Filipescu, Prodan, Radoi (Galca 58), Munteanu C, Codrea, Chivu, Munteanu D, Moldovan (Stoica 82), Ilie A (Niculae 21).
Referee: Pedersen (Norway).

Trieste, 28 March 2001, 14,800
Italy (1) 4 *(Inzaghi F 17, 63, Del Piero 49, 79)*
Lithuania (0) 0

Italy: Buffon; Cannavaro, Nesta, Maldini, Zambrotta, Tommasi, Tacchinardi, Coco, Totti (Fiore 75), Inzaghi F (Montella 69), Del Piero (Di Livio 83).
Lithuania: Stauce; Zvirgzdauskas, Skarbalius, Joksas, Dziaukstas, Razanauskas (Danilevicius 50), Zutautas R, Semberas, Morinas, Poskus (Zvingilas 77), Mikalajunas (Jankauskas 65).
Referee: Shmolik (Belarus).

Tbilisi, 2 June 2001, 28,000
Georgia (0) 1 *(Gakhokidze 80)*
Italy (1) 2 *(Delvecchio 45, Totti 66)*

Georgia: Zoidze; Silagadze, Abramidze, Kaladze, Kobiashvili, Khizanishvili (Gakhokidze 79), Nemsadze (Arveladze S 80), Rekhviashvili, Menteshashvili (Arveladze A 60), Ketsbaia, Kavelashvili.
Italy: Buffon; Cannavaro, Nesta (Materazzi 74), Maldini, Zambrotta, Tommasi, Tacchinardi, Pancaro, Totti, Delvecchio (Montella 79), Del Piero (Di Livio 58).
Referee: Iturralde (Spain).

Bucharest, 2 June 2001, 22,000

Romania (1) 2 *(Niculae 4, 54)*

Hungary (0) 0

Romania: Stelea; Contra, Radoi (Prodan 64), Ciobotariu, Chivu, Munteanu D, Codrea, Ilie A (Munteanu C 75), Dumitru, Moldovan (Ganea 72), Niculae.

Hungary: Kiraly; Feher C, Korsos G, Sebok V, Matyus, Peto, Lisztes, Sowunmi (Kabat 73), Dardai, Horvath (Korsos A 46), Hamar (Dombi 41).

Referee: Poulat (France).

Budapest, 6 June 2001, 10,000

Hungary (2) 4 *(Matyus 40, Sebok V 45 (pen), Korsos A 55, 62)*

Georgia (0) 1 *(Kobiashvili 77)*

Hungary: Kiraly; Korsos G, Sebok V, Peto, Matyus, Lisztes (Lendvai 80), Halmai (Dardai 70), Illes, Korsos A (Dombi 77), Horvath, Kabat.

Georgia: Zoidze; Abramidze, Kaladze (Todua 67), Arveladze A, Kobiashvili, Nemsadze (Kemoklidze 67), Rekhviashvili, Khizanishvili, Ketsbaia, Arveladze S, Kavelashvili (Kinkladze 53).

Referee: Strampe (Germany).

Kaunas, 6 June 2001, 7000

Lithuania (0) 1 *(Fomenka 87)*

Romania (1) 2 *(Ilie A 31, Moldovan 49)*

Lithuania: Stauce; Zvirgzdauskas, Dedura, Skarbalius, Graziunas, Morinas (Fomenka 46), Zutautas R, Mikalajunas, Semberas, Razanauskas (Buitkus 73), Poskus.

Romania: Stelea; Contra (Ganea 54), Radoi, Filipescu, Chivu, Dumitru, Niculae, Kodrea, Munteanu D, Moldovan (Prodan 57), Ilie A (Mutu 63).

Referee: Stredak (Slovakia).

Tbilisi, 1 September 2001, 8000

Georgia (1) 3 *(Arveladze S 34, Jamarauli 49, Iashvili 64)*

Hungary (1) 1 *(Matyus 44)*

Georgia: Gvaramadze; Kobiashvili, Khizanishvili, Rekhviashvili, Kaladze, Tskitishvili (Sajala 78), Nemsadze, Kavelashvili (Iashvili 46), Jamarauli, Kinkladze, Arveladze S (Demetradze 62).

Hungary: Kiraly; Korsos G, Peto, Matyus, Sebok V, Halmai (Dardai 53), Kabat, Lisztes, Horvath (Tokoli 62), Illes (Lendvai 66), Korsos A.

Referee: Kos (Slovenia).

Kaunas, 1 September 2001, 5500

Lithuania (0) 0

Italy (0) 0

Lithuania: Stauce; Skarbalius, Stankevicius, Gleveckas, Dziaukstas, Razanauskas (Narbekovas 88), Zutautas R, Morinas, Mikalajunas, Jankauskas, Poskus (Semberas 85).

Italy: Buffon; Cannavaro, Nesta, Maldini, Zambrotta (Coco 82), Tommasi, Tacchinardi, Pancaro, Totti (Fiore 88), Vieri, Del Piero (Inzaghi F 61).

Referee: Van der Ende (Holland).

Tbilisi, 5 September 2001, 18,000

Georgia (0) 2 *(Iashvili 85, 87)*

Lithuania (0) 0

Georgia: Gvaramadze; Kobiashvili, Khizanishvili, Sajala, Kaladze, Tskitishvili, Nemsadze, Kavelashvili (Demetradze 46), Alexidze (Burduli 74), Kinkladze, Iashvili (Arveladze S 90).

Lithuania: Stauce; Stankevicius, Dziaukstas, Gleveckas, Skarbalius, Morinas, Zutautas R, Mikalajunas (Jankausas 86), Semberas, Razanauskas, Poskus.

Referee: Yakov (Israel).

Budapest, 5 September 2001, 8000

Hungary (0) 0

Romania (2) 2 *(Ilie A 10, Niculae 26)*

Hungary: Kiraly; Korsos G (Kabat 46), Sebok V, Juhar, Matyus, Dardai, Lisztes, Lendvai (Gyori 63), Korsos A (Fuzi 55), Tokoli, Horvath.

Romania: Lobont; Filipescu (Kirita 73), Popescu G, Radoi, Chivu, Contra, Sabau, Munteanu D, Mutu, Ilie A (Rosu 75), Niculae (Ganea 80).

Referee: Dallas (Scotland).

Parma, 6 October 2001, 20,805

Italy (1) 1 *(Del Piero 45)*

Hungary (0) 0

Italy: Buffon; Cannavaro, Materazzi, Maldini, Zambrotta (Di Livio 80), Tommasi, Albertini (Di Biagio 73), Coco, Totti, Del Piero (Gattuso 57), Inzaghi F.

Hungary: Kiraly; Bodnar, Kuttor, Juhar, Matyus, Peto, Sebok V, Halmai (Lisztes 55), Dardai, Tokoli (Egressy 77), Kabat (Ferenczi 66).

Referee: Chavez (Paraguay).

Bucharest, 6 October 2001, 16,500

Romania (0) 1 *(Popescu G 88)*

Georgia (0) 1 *(Iashvili 54)*

Romania: Lobont; Kirita, Lacusta, Miu, Parvu (Mihalcea 61), Popescu G, Dumitru, Munteanu D, Niculae, Mutu (Rosu 46), Ilie A (Pancu 70).

Georgia: Gvaramadze; Kobiashvili, Khizanishvili, Rekhviashvili, Sajala, Tskitishvili, Kaladze, Jamarauli, Iashvili (Alexidze 80), Kinkladze (Ketsbaia 63), Kavelashvili (Burduli 75).

Referee: Michel (Slovakia).

Group 8 Table	P	W	D	L	F	A	Pts
Italy	8	6	2	0	16	3	20
Romania	8	5	1	2	10	7	16
Georgia	8	3	1	4	12	12	10
Hungary	8	2	2	4	14	13	8
Lithuania	8	0	2	6	3	20	2

GROUP 9

Helsinki, 2 September 2000, 10,770

Finland (1) 2 *(Litmanen 45, Riihilahti 67)*

Albania (0) 1 *(Murati 63)*

Finland: Jaaskelainen; Saarinen, Turpeinen, Hyypia, Tihinen, Nurmela (Johansson 57), Koppinen (Riihilahti 46), Valakari, Forssell (Ylonen 77), Litmanen, Kolkka.

Albania: Strakosha; Lala, Cipi, Xhumba, Vata R, Murati (Bushi 76), Haxhi, Muka (Skela 46), Kola, Rraklli, Tare.

Referee: Timmink (Holland).

Hamburg, 2 September 2000, 48,500

Germany (1) 2 *(Deisler 17, Ouzounidis 75 (og))*

Greece (0) 0

Germany: Kahn; Rehmer, Nowotny, Heinrich (Linke 46), Deisler, Ramelow, Ballack, Bode, Scholl, Jancker, Zickler (Rink 71).

Greece: Eleftheropoulos; Ouzounidis, Goumas, Amanatidis, Georgatos, Poursanidis (Choutos 66), Mavrogenidis (Patsatzoglou 23), Tsartas, Zagorakis, Liberopoulos, Georgiadis (Lakis 76).

Referee: Nieto (Spain).

Wembley, 7 October 2000, 76,377

England (0) 0

Germany (1) 1 *(Hamann 14)*

England: Seaman; Neville G (Dyer 46), Le Saux (Barry 77), Southgate, Keown, Adams, Beckham (Parlour 82), Barmby, Cole, Scholes.

Germany: Kahn; Rehmer, Nowotny, Linke, Deisler, Ramelow, Hamann, Ballack, Bode (Ziege 86), Scholl, Bierhoff.

Referee: Braschi (Italy).

Athens, 7 October 2000, 14,800

Greece (0) 1 *(Liberopoulos 59)*

Finland (0) 0

Greece: Nikopolidis; Georgatos (Venetidis 72), Patsatzoglou, Amanatidis, Ouzounidis, Karagounis (Lakis 76), Zagorakis, Basinas, Liberopoulos, Georgiadis, Choutos (Antzas 83).

Finland: Niemi; Reini, Helin, Hyypia, Tihinen, Nurmela, Wiss (Kottila 81), Valakari, Johansson (Kuqi 64), Litmanen, Kolkka (Forssell 46).

Referee: Collina (Italy).

Tirana, 11 October 2000, 11,000
Albania (0) 2 *(Bushi 50, Fakaj 90)*
Greece (0) 0
Albania: Strakosha; Muka, Cipi, Xhumba (Fakaj 75), Vata R, Vata F (Basha 78), Skela, Kola, Haxhi, Bushi, Tare (Bogdani 86).
Greece: Nikopolidis; Basinas, Venetidis (Kyparissis 72), Patsatzogolou, Ouzounidis, Zagorakis (Lakis 70), Georgiadis, Karagounis, Choutos, Liberopoulos, Zikos (Poursanidis 70).
Referee: Pedersen (Norway).

Helsinki, 11 October 2000, 36,210
Finland (0) 0
England (0) 0
Finland: Niemi; Helin (Reini 36), Tihinen, Hyypia, Saarinen (Salli 66), Nurmela, Wiss, Valakari, Johansson, Litmanen, Forssell (Kuqi 76).
England: Seaman; Neville P, Barry (Brown 69), Southgate, Keown, Wise, Parlour, Scholes, Cole, Sheringham (McManaman 69), Heskey.
Referee: Sars (France).

Liverpool, 24 March 2001, 44,262
England (1) 2 *(Owen 43, Beckham 50)*
Finland (1) 1 *(Neville G 26 (og))*
England: Seaman; Neville G, Powell, Ferdinand R, Campbell, Scholes, Beckham, Gerrard, Cole (Fowler 82), Owen (Butt 90), McManaman (Heskey 72).
Finland: Niemi; Pasanen, Hyypia, Tihinen, Ylonen (Helin 89), Wiss, Nurmela (Forssell 63), Riihilahti, Litmanen, Kolkka (Kuqi 63), Johansson.
Referee: Ivanov (Russia).

Leverkusen, 24 March 2001, 22,500
Germany (0) 2 *(Deisler 50, Klose 88)*
Albania (0) 1 *(Kola 65)*
Germany: Kahn; Nowotny, Worns, Jeremies, Ramelow, Deisler, Hamann (Rehmer 46), Bode, Neuville (Klose 73), Bierhoff (Jancker 46), Scholl.
Albania: Strakosha; Cipi, Vata R, Lala, Xhumba, Vata F (Skela 79), Hasi (Fakaj 86), Kola, Murati, Tare, Bushi (Rraklli 67).
Referee: Cesari (Italy).

Tirana, 28 March 2001, 18,000
Albania (0) 1 *(Rraklli 90)*
England (0) 3 *(Owen 73, Scholes 85, Andy Cole 90)*
Albania: Strakosha; Cipi, Fakaj, Lala, Xhumba, Hasi, Vata F (Rraklli 88), Kola (Muka 82), Bellai, Tare (Skela 90), Bushi.
England: Seaman; Neville G, Ashley Cole, Ferdinand R, Campbell (Brown 29), Butt, Beckham, Scholes, Andy Cole, Owen (Sheringham 84), McManaman (Heskey 46).
Referee: Hamer (Luxembourg).

Athens, 28 March 2001, 53,000
Greece (2) 2 *(Haristeas 21, Georgiadis 44)*
Germany (2) 4 *(Rehmer 6, Ballack 25 (pen), Klose 82, Bode 90)*
Greece: Eleftheropoulos; Patsatzoglou, Kostoulas (Mavrogenidis 35), Goumas, Basinas, Karagounis (Niniadis 75), Zagorakis, Georgiadis, Haristeas (Alexandris 64), Liberopoulos, Georgatos.
Germany: Kahn; Worns, Nowotny, Heinrich, Rehmer, Jeremies (Ramelow 90), Deisler, Ballack, Ziege, Jancker (Bode 78), Neuville (Klose 67).
Referee: Pereira (Portugal).

Helsinki, 2 June 2001, 35,774
Finland (2) 2 *(Forssell 28, 43)*
Germany (0) 2 *(Ballack 68 (pen), Jancker 72)*
Finland: Niemi; Pasanen, Nylund, Hyypia, Tihinen, Nurmela (Johansson 71), Riihilahti (Gronlund 80), Litmanen, Rantanen, Forssell, Kolkka (Kuqi 85).
Germany: Kahn; Rehmer, Nowotny, Linke, Asamoah, Ramelow, Ballack, Bode (Ziege 69), Ricken, Neuville (Klose 62), Jancker (Bierhoff 83).
Referee: Jol (Holland).

Iraklion, 2 June 2001, 4000
Greece (1) 1 *(Mahlas 72)*
Albania (0) 0
Greece: Nikopolidis; Patsatzogolou, Dabizas, Venetidis, Zagorakis, Goumas, Ouzounidis, Georgiadis (Basinas 85), Karagounis, Alexandris (Haristeas 62), Liberopoulos (Mahlas 46).
Albania: Strakosha; Cipi, Vata R, Lala, Xhumba, Hasi, Haxhi (Skela 76), Bushi, Vata F, Murati, Tare (Bogdani 71).
Referee: Levnikov (Russia).

Tirana, 6 June 2001, 18,000
Albania (0) 0
Germany (1) 2 *(Rehmer 28, Ballack 68)*
Albania: Strakosha; Vata R, Cipi, Xhumba (Bellai 46), Lala, Vata F, Murati, Hasi (Skela 61), Haxhi (Muka 81), Bushi, Tare.
Germany: Kahn; Rehmer, Nowotny, Linke, Asamoah (Ricken 70), Ramelow, Ballack, Ziege, Deisler (Baumann 84), Jancker, Neuville (Zickler 46).
Referee: Veissiere (France).

Athens, 6 June 2001, 46,000
Greece (0) 0
England (0) 2 *(Scholes 64, Beckham 87)*
Greece: Nikopolidis; Goumas, Ouzounidis, Dabizas, Mavrogenidis (Giannakopoulos 70), Basinas, Zagorakis, Fyssas, Karagounis (Liberopoulos 24), Mahlas (Alexandris 64), Vryzas.
England: Seaman; Neville P, Ashley Cole, Gerrard, Keown, Ferdinand, Beckham, Scholes (Butt 88), Fowler (Smith 79), Owen, Heskey (McManaman 74).
Referee: Pedersen (Norway).

Tirana, 1 September 2001, 6400
Albania (0) 0
Finland (0) 2 *(Tainio 57, Kuqi 90)*
Albania: Beqaj; Lala, Cipi, Xhumba, Bellai, Muka (Vata R 62), Haxhi, Vata F, Bushi, Rraklli (Bogdani 64), Tare (Fortuzi 64).
Finland: Niemi; Helin, Saarinen, Hyypia, Kuivasto, Riihilahti, Nurmela (Kuqi 78), Tainio, Forssell (Johansson 66) Litmanen (Ilola 86), Kolkka.
Referee: Ersoy (Turkey).

Munich, 1 September 2001, 63,000
Germany (1) 1 *(Jancker 6)*
England (2) 5 *(Owen 13, 48, 66, Gerrard 45, Heskey 74)*
Germany: Kahn; Worns (Asamoah 46), Nowotny, Linke, Rehmer, Hamann, Ballack (Klose 67), Bohme, Deisler, Jancker, Neuville (Kehl 78).
England: Seaman; Neville G, Ashley Cole, Gerrard (Hargreaves 78), Ferdinand, Campbell, Beckham, Scholes (Carragher 83), Heskey, Owen, Barmby (McManaman 65).
Referee: Collina (Italy).

Newcastle, 5 September 2001, 51,046
England (1) 2 *(Owen 44, Fowler 88)*
Albania (0) 0
England: Seaman; Neville G, Ashley Cole, Gerrard (Carragher 81), Ferdinand, Campbell, Beckham, Scholes, Heskey (Fowler 53), Owen, Barmby (McManaman 62).
Albania: Strakosha; Dede, Fakaj, Cipi, Xhumba, Murati, Vata F, Bellai, Hasi (Bushi 46), Bogdani (Tare 55), Rraklli (Muka 61).
Referee: Marin (Spain).

Helsinki, 5 September 2001, 27,216
Finland (4) 5 *(Forssell 13, 44, Riihilahti 22, Kolkka 40, Litmanen 53 (pen))*
Greece (1) 1 *(Karagounis 32)*
Finland: Niemi; Helin, Saarinen, Hyypia, Tihinen, Riihilahti, Nurmela, Tainio (Wiss 62), Forssell (Johansson 79), Litmanen (Kuqi 72), Kolkka.
Greece: Eleftheropoulos; Basinas (Zikos 46), Dabizas, Georgatos, Amanatidis, Konstantinidis (Georgiadis 25), Haristeas, Zagorakis (Fyssas 82), Vryzas, Mahlas, Karagounis.
Referee: Allaerts (Belgium).

Manchester, 6 October 2001, 66,009
England (0) 2 *(Sheringham 68, Beckham 90)*
Greece (1) 2 *(Haristeas 36, Nikolaidis 70)*
England: Martyn; Neville G, Ashley Cole (McManaman 78), Gerrard, Ferdinand, Keown, Beckham, Scholes, Heskey, Fowler (Sheringham 67), Barmby (Andy Cole 46).
Greece: Nikopolidis; Patsatzoglou, Dabizas, Konstantinidis, Vokolos, Fyssas, Haristeas (Lakis 73), Zagorakis (Basinas 57), Karagounis, Kassapis, Nikolaidis (Mahlas 86).
Referee: Jol (Holland).

Gelsenkirchen, 6 October 2001, 52,000
Germany (0) 0
Finland (0) 0
Germany: Kahn; Rehmer, Worns, Nowotny, Ziege, Ballack, Ramelow, Deisler, Bohme (Asamoah 46), Bierhoff, Neuville (Klose 76).
Finland: Niemi; Reini (Helin 78), Tihinen, Saarinen, Hyypia, Nurmela, Tainio (Gronlund 83), Riihilahti, Johansson (Kuqi 66), Litmanen, Forssell.
Referee: Frisk (Sweden).

Group 9 Table	P	W	D	L	F	A	Pts
England	8	5	2	1	16	6	17
Germany	8	5	2	1	14	10	17
Finland	8	3	3	2	12	7	12
Greece	8	2	1	5	7	17	7
Albania	8	1	0	7	5	14	3

SOUTH AMERICA
(Members 10, Entries 10)

Five teams qualified: Argentina, Brazil, Ecuador, Paraguay and Uruguay.

Bogota, 28 March 2000, 42,493
Colombia (0) 0
Brazil (0) 0
Colombia: Cordoba O; Bermudez, Cordoba I, Yepes, Martinez, Viveros, Dinas, Rincon, Oviedo (Moreno 74), Angel, Ricard (Maturana 60).
Brazil: Dida; Evanilson, Aldair, Zago, Roberto Carlos, Emerson, Ze Roberto, Vampeta, Alex (Ricardinho 46), Elber (Ronaldinho 68), Jardel (Edilson 46).
Referee: Mendez (Uruguay).

Buenos Aires, 29 March 2000, 50,000
Argentina (2) 4 *(Batistuta 9, Veron 33, 71 (pen), Lopez C 88)*
Chile (1) 1 *(Tello 29)*
Argentina: Bonano; Pochettino, Ayala, Samuel, Zanetti, Simeone, Kily Gonzalez, Veron, Ortega (Sensini 85), Batistuta (Crespo 89), Lopez C (Lopez G 89).
Chile: Ramirez Ma; Maldonado, Reyes, Margas, Contreras, Ormazabal (Aros 83), Acuna, Tello, Pizarro (Sierra 70), Zamorano, Salas.
Referee: Moreno (Ecuador).

Quito, 29 March 2000, 50,000
Ecuador (1) 2 *(Delgado 17, Aguinaga A 51)*
Venezuela (0) 0
Ecuador: Cevallos; De la Cruz, Jacome, Montano, Guagua (Ayovi M 49), Blandon, Tenorio (Chala 73), Aguinaga A, Obregon, Graziani (Poroso 38), Delgado.
Venezuela: Dudamel; Alvarez, Villafraz (Mea Vitali M 62), Becerra, Rey, Urdaneta, Rojas (Arango 55), Bidoglio, Vera J, Casseres, Garcia (Ochoa 55).
Referee: Gamboa (Chile).

Lima, 29 March 2000, 45,000
Peru (0) 2 *(Solano 55 (pen), Palacios 60)*
Paraguay (0) 0
Peru: Ibanez; Jorge Soto, Rebosio, Pajuelo, Olivares (Huaman 72), Jayo, Palacios, Del Solar, Solano, Pizarro (Ciurlizza 81), Zuniga (Holsen 59).
Paraguay: Chilavert; Arce, Ayala, Gamarra, Caniza, Enciso (Struway 68), Paredes (Gavilan 74), Acuna, Campos, Santa Cruz, Jose Cardozo (Gonzalez G 68).
Referee: Elizondo (Argentina).

Montevideo, 29 March 2000, 55,000
Uruguay (1) 1 *(Pablo Garcia 26)*
Bolivia (0) 0
Uruguay: Carini; Mendez, Lopez, Montero, Rodriguez, Coelho, Pablo Garcia, O'Neill, Cedres (Olivera 58), Alonso (Zalayeta 76), Recoba (Poyet 89).
Bolivia: Fernandez; Ribera, Pena, Oscar Sanchez, Sandy (Rimba 75), Ivan Castillo, Cristaldo, Justiniano, Erwin Sanchez, Gutierrez L (Suarez 59), Moreno (Botero 70).
Referee: Pereira (Argentina).

La Paz, 26 April 2000, 20,000
Bolivia (1) 1 *(Erwin Sanchez 16)*
Colombia (1) 1 *(Castillo J 32)*
Bolivia: Fernandez; Ribeiro, Pena, Sandy (Rimba 33), Ivan Castillo, Cristaldo, Soria, Gutierrez R (Galindo 63), Erwin Sanchez, Antelo (Suarez 46), Moreno.
Colombia: Cordoba O; Cordoba I, Bermudez, Yepes, Viveros, Martinez (Cardona 79), Dinas, Oviedo (Ortegon 82), Rincon, Ricard (Angel 74), Castillo J.
Referee: Arana (Peru).

Sao Paulo, 26 April 2000, 65,000
Brazil (2) 3 *(Rivaldo 18, 51, Zago 42)*
Ecuador (1) 2 *(Aguinaga A 12, De la Cruz 76)*
Brazil: Dida; Cafu, Zago, Aldair, Roberto Carlos (Athirson 68), Cesar Sampaio, Vampeta, Rivaldo, Ze Roberto (Alex 68), Amoroso, Edilson.
Ecuador: Cevallos; De la Cruz, Poroso, Capurro, Hurtado I, Tenorio, Obregon, Aguinaga A (Ayovi M 40) (Kaviedes 88), Blandon, Delgado, Graziani (Hurtado E 66).
Referee: Cervantes (Colombia).

Santiago, 26 April 2000, 45,000
Chile (1) 1 *(Margas 42)*
Peru (1) 1 *(Jayo 38)*
Chile: Tapia N; Vargas, Reyes, Margas, Maldonado (Nunez C 70), Acuna, Rojas F (Nunez R 70), Pizarro (Sierra 58), Tello, Zamorano, Salas.
Peru: Ibanez; Jorge Soto, Rebosio, Pajuelo, Olivares, Jayo, Soria (Zuniga 58), Del Solar, Palacios, Solano, Pizarro.
Referee: Rojas (Paraguay).

Asuncion, 26 April 2000, 15,000
Paraguay (1) 1 *(Ayala 35)*
Uruguay (0) 0
Paraguay: Chilavert; Espinola, Gamarra, Ayala, Caniza, Quintana (Gonzalez G 59), Paredes, Struway, Acuna (Enciso 68), Santa Cruz, Baez (Benitez 82).
Uruguay: Carini; Mendez, Ramos, Lembo, Tabare Silva (Guigou 67), Coelho, Pablo Garcia, De los Santos, Poyet (Olivera 63), Recoba, Dario Silva (Alvez 75).
Referee: Sanchez (Argentina).

Maracaibo, 26 April 2000, 27,000
Venezuela (0) 0
Argentina (2) 4 *(Ayala 7, Ortega 23, 76, Crespo 88)*
Venezuela: Dudamel; Rojas, Rey, Villafraz (Luzardo 46), Gonzalez, Mea Vitali M, Bidoglio, Urdaneta, Vera J, Garcia (Martinez 70), Castellin.
Argentina: Bonano; Ayala, Samuel, Sensini, Kily Gonzalez, Zanetti, Simeone, Veron, Ortega (Gallardo 78), Lopez C (Lopez G 68), Crespo.
Referee: Amarilla (Paraguay).

Ascunion, 3 June 2000, 22,000
Paraguay (2) 3 *(Toledo 11, Brizuela 43, 64)*
Ecuador (0) 1 *(Graziani 87)*
Paraguay: Chilavert; Caniza, Gamarra, Ayala, Toledo, Paredes, Struway (Enciso 82), Quintana, Acuna, Brizuela (Gonzalez G 76), Baez (Benitez 66).
Ecuador: Cevallos; De la Cruz, Poroso (Kaviedes 66), Montano, Capurro, Blandon, Hurtado I, Tenorio (Chala 46), Aguinaga A, Juarez, Delgado (Graziani 61).
Referee: Gallesio (Uruguay).

Montevideo, 3 June 2000, 60,000
Uruguay (2) 2 *(Dario Silva 35, Montero 41)*
Chile (1) 1 *(Zamorano 39 (pen))*
Uruguay: Carini; Mendez, Montero, Lembo, Rodriguez, Pablo Garcia, Guigou, O'Neill, Olivera, Recoba (Giacomazzi 89), Dario Silva (Alonso 81).
Chile: Tapia N; Rojas R, Vargas, Reyes, Olarra (Rozental 68), Galdames, Estay (Nunez C 87), Villaseca, Tello, Zamorano, Salas.
Referee: Troxler (Paraguay).

Buenos Aires, 4 June 2000, 50,669
Argentina (0) 1 *(Lopez G 83)*
Bolivia (0) 0
Argentina: Bonano; Sensini, Ayala, Samuel, Zanetti (Lopez G 71), Simeone, Kily Gonzalez, Veron, Ortega (Aimar 83), Batistuta, Lopez C (Almeyda 88).
Bolivia: Fernandez; Carballo, Pena, Sandy, Ivan Castillo, Ribera, Baldivieso, Cristaldo, Etcheverry (Galindo 78), Suarez (Garcia 65), Botero (Coimbra 83).
Referee: Rezende (Brazil).

Bogota, 4 June 2000, 22,000
Colombia (2) 3 *(Viveros 27, Cordoba I 42 (pen), Valenciano 88)*
Venezuela (0) 0
Colombia: Cordoba O; Martinez, Cordoba I,Ortegon, Bedoya, Rincon, Bolano, Oviedo (Candelo 70), Viveros (Dinas 77), Angel, Castillo J (Valenciano 81).
Venezuela: Dudamel; Filosa, Gonzalez, Alvarado, Echenausi, Arango, Vera J (Farias 55), Mea Vitali M, Bidoglio (De Ornelas 67), Castellin (Savarese 52), Moran.
Referee: Godoi (Brazil).

Lima, 4 June 2000, 45,000
Peru (0) 0
Brazil (1) 1 *(Zago 35)*
Peru: Miranda; Jorge Soto, Pajuelo, Olivares, Rebosio, Palacios, Del Solar, Jayo (Serrano 49), Zuniga, Holsen (Ciurlizza 46), Huaman (Maldonado 46).
Brazil: Dida; Cafu, Roberto Carlos, Aldair, Zago, Cesar Sampaio, Alex (Denilson 65), Emerson, Edmundo, Rivaldo (Vampeta 90), Franca (Ze Roberto 77).
Referee: Giminez (Argentina).

Rio, 28 June 2000, 47,715
Brazil (0) 1 *(Rivaldo 85 (pen))*
Uruguay (1) 1 *(Dario Silva 6)*
Brazil: Dida; Cafu, Zago, Aldair, Roberto Carlos, Emerson, Vampeta (Ze Roberto 70), Rivaldo, Ronaldinho (Guilherme 46), Franca, Savio (Alex 46).
Uruguay: Carini; Tais, Lembo, Montero, Rodriguez, Pablo Garcia, O'Neill (Giacomazzi 82), Recoba (Coelho 59), Olivera, Dario Silva, Guigou.
Referee: Acosta (Colombia).

Santiago, 28 June 2000, 60,000
Chile (2) 3 *(Caniza 18 (og), Salas 35, Zamorano 78 (pen))*
Paraguay (0) 1 *(Jose Cardozo 71)*
Chile: Tapia N; Fuentes, Rojas R, Reyes, Villarroel, Maldonado, Tello, Estay, Nunez C (Pizarro 68), Zamorano, Salas.
Paraguay: Chilavert; Caniza, Zelaya, Ayala, Toledo, Quintana, Struway (Gonzalez G 46), Paredes, Acuna (Gavilan 37), Santa Cruz (Jose Cardozo 76), Brizuela.
Referee: Martin (Argentina).

Bogota, 28 June 2000, 50,000
Colombia (1) 1 *(Oviedo 27)*
Argentina (2) 3 *(Batistuta 24, 45, Crespo 75)*
Colombia: Cordoba O; Cordoba I, Bermudez, Yepes, Bolano, Oviedo, Rincon, Dinas (Grisales 51) (Candelo 85), Viveros, Angel, Castillo J (Valenciano 58).
Argentina: Bonano; Sensini, Ayala, Samuel, Zanetti, Veron (Lopez G 70), Kily Gonzalez, Ortega (Sorin 86), Simeone, Lopez C, Batistuta (Crespo 70).
Referee: Larrionda (Uruguay).

San Cristobal, 28 June 2000, 7000
Venezuela (2) 4 *(Mea Vitali M 23, Moran 38, Savarese 61, Tortolero 67 (pen))*
Bolivia (0) 2 *(Moreno 49, Baldivieso 59)*
Venezuela: Angelucci; Jimenez, Gonzalez, Alvarado, Martinez, Urdaneta (Echenausi 90), Farias, Tortolero, Mea Vitali M, Moran, Savarese (Galan 72).
Bolivia: Fernandez; Ribera, Etcheverry (Galindo 80), Pena, Sandy, Ivan Castillo, Cristaldo, Erwin Sanchez, Baldivieso, Suarez (Garcia 73), Botero (Moreno 46).
Referee: Zambrano (Ecuador).

Quito, 29 June 2000, 45,000
Ecuador (1) 2 *(Chala 16, Hurtado E 51)*
Peru (0) 1 *(Pajuelo 76)*
Ecuador: Cevallos; De la Cruz, Hurtado I, Poroso, Ayovi M, Obregon, Blandon, Chala, Aguinaga A (Burbano 70), Delgado (Graziani 70), Hurtado E (Kaviedes 74).
Peru: Ibanez; Jorge Soto, Rebosio, Pajuelo, Olivares (Zuniga 75), Solano, Del Solar, Jayo (Ciurlizza 75), Serrano (Soria 20), Palacios, Pizarro.
Referee: Simon (Brazil).

Asuncion, 18 July 2000, 36,000
Paraguay (1) 2 *(Paredes 6, Campos 84)*
Brazil (0) 1 *(Rivaldo 75)*
Paraguay: Chilavert; Sarabia, Ayala, Gamarra, Caniza, Gavilan (Quintana 72), Enciso, Acuna, Paredes (Campos 63), Jose Cardozo, Santa Cruz (Avalos 79).
Brazil: Dida; Cafu, Roque Junior, Edmilson, Roberto Carlos, Cesar Sampaio, Flavio Conceicao, Rivaldo, Ze Roberto (Marques 70), Djalminha (Vampeta 60), Franca (Guilherme 46).
Referee: Larrionda (Uruguay).

Montevideo, 18 July 2000, 62,000
Uruguay (1) 3 *(Olivera 29, 89, Rodriguez 52)*
Venezuela (1) 1 *(Noriega 23)*
Uruguay: Carini; Tais, Lembo, Montero (Ramos 81), Rodriguez, O'Neill, Pablo Garcia, Olivera, Guigou, Recoba, Dario Silva.
Venezuela: Angelucci; Jimenez, Gonzalez, Alvarado, Martinez, Urdaneta, Farias (Vera J 63), Tortolero, Mea Vitali M, Savarese (Perez 73), Noriega (Alvarez 63).
Referee: Ortube (Bolivia).

Buenos Aires, 19 July 2000, 50,000
Argentina (1) 2 *(Crespo 23, Lopez C 50)*
Ecuador (0) 0
Argentina: Bonano; Ayala, Sensini, Samuel, Zanetti, Simeone, Kily Gonzalez (Sorin 76), Veron, Ortega, Crespo (Aimar 76), Lopez C.
Ecuador: Cevallos; De la Cruz, Hurtado I, Poroso, Ayovi M, Tenorio, Blandon, Obregon, Aguinaga A (Chala 88), Hurtado E, Delgado (Graziani 73).
Referee: Bello (Uruguay).

La Paz, 19 July 2000, 35,000
Bolivia (0) 1 *(Suarez 84)*
Chile (0) 0
Bolivia: Soria M; Ribeiro, Pena, Sandy, Carballo (Rimba 38), Galindo (Colque 65), Garcia, Calustro, Baldivieso, Botero (Gutierrez T 55), Suarez.
Chile: Tapia N; Villarroel, Reyes, Fuentes, Rojas R, Maldonado, Cornejo, Tello, Estay (Tapia H 69), Zamorano (Navia 84), Rozental (Pizarro 69).
Referee: Toro (Colombia).

Lima, 19 July 2000, 45,000
Peru (0) 0
Colombia (0) 1 *(Angel 48)*
Peru: Vegas; Jorge Soto (Carlos Flores 57), Rebosio, Pajuela, Olivares, Jayo, Solano, Del Solar, Palacios, Pizarro, Zuniga (Lobaton 57).
Colombia: Cordoba O; Martinez, Cordoba I, Yepes, Bolano, Candelo (Hernandez 66), Viveros, Luis Garcia (Dinas 77), Bedoya, Angel, Valenciano (Restrepo 46).
Referee: Sanchez (Chile).

Quito, 25 July 2000, 43,000
Ecuador (0) 0
Colombia (0) 0
Ecuador: Cevallos; De la Cruz, Hurtado I, Poroso, Ayovi M, Obregon, Chala (Herrera 68), Aguinaga A, Hurtado Ed, Graziani (Delgado 68), Hurtado E (Juarez 76).
Colombia: Cordoba O; Martinez, Cordoba I, Yepes, Bolano, Candelo (Hurtado 46), Viveros, Luis Garcia, Bedoya, Moreno (Restrepo 46), Preciado (Dinas 78).
Referee: Aquino (Paraguay).

San Cristobal, 25 July 2000, 23,000
Venezuela (0) 0
Chile (0) 2 *(Tapia H 69, Zamorano 90)*
Venezuela: Angelucci; Alvarez, Alvarado, Ornella, Martinez, Mea Vitali M (Arango 72), Farias, Tortolero, Urdaneta, Moran, Savarese (Perez 85).
Chile: Tapia N; Fuentes, Rojas R, Margas, Rojas F, Maldonado, Tello, Estay (Cornejo 72), Sierra (Pizarro 65), Zamorano, Rozental (Tapia H 46).
Referee: Baldassi (Argentina).

Sao Paulo, 26 July 2000, 80,000
Brazil (2) 3 *(Alex 4, Vampeta 44, 50)*
Argentina (1) 1 *(Almeyda 45)*
Brazil: Dida; Evanilson, Zago, Roque Junior, Roberto Carlos, Emerson, Vampeta, Ze Roberto (Marques 60), Alex (Cesar Sampaio 75), Ronaldinho, Rivaldo.
Argentina: Bonano; Sensini, Ayala, Samuel, Zanetti (Almeyda 39), Simeone, Veron, Kily Gonzalez (Sorin 73), Ortega (Lopez G 73), Crespo, Lopez C.
Referee: Mendez (Uruguay).

Montevideo, 26 July 2000, 60,000
Uruguay (0) 0
Peru (0) 0
Uruguay: Carini; Tais, Lembo, Montero, Rodriguez, O'Neill, Pablo Garcia, Olivera, Guigou (Zalayeta 56), Recoba (Coelho 69), Magallanes.
Peru: Vegas; Jorge Soto, Rebosio, Pajuelo, Olivares, Serrano (Torres 81), Jayo, Ciurlizza, Solano, Palacios, Pizarro.
Referee: Godoi (Brazil).

La Paz, 27 July 2000, 40,000
Bolivia (0) 0
Paraguay (0) 0
Bolivia: Soria M; Ribeiro, Pena, Sandy, Rimba (Paz Garcia 38), Calustro (Cardenas 71), Garcia, Colque, Baldivieso, Botero (Gutierrez L 52), Suarez.
Paraguay: Chilavert; Caballero, Ayala, Gamarra, Da Silva, Esteche, Enciso, Acuna (Ortiz 85), Paredes (Struway 55), Gonzalez G (Benitez 58), Jose Cardozo.
Referee: Almeida (Brazil).

Santiago, 15 August 2000, 65,000
Chile (2) 3 *(Estay 26, Zamorano 43, Salas 75)*
Brazil (0) 0
Chile: Tapia N; Fuentes, Rojas R, Reyes, Villaseca (Pizarro 13), Rojas F, Galdames, Tello, Estay, Salas (Villarroel 80), Zamorano (Tapia H 87).
Brazil: Dida; Evanilson, Edmilson, Zago, Roberto Carlos, Assuncao (Djalminha 46), Emerson, Alex (Marques 61), Ricardinho, Rivaldo, Amoroso (Luizao 46).
Referee: Gonzalez (Paraguay).

Bogota, 15 August 2000, 32,000
Colombia (0) 1 *(Castillo J 72)*
Uruguay (0) 0
Colombia: Cordoba O; Martinez, Cordoba I, Yepes, Bedoya, Luis Garcia (Morantes 64), Bolano, Oviedo, Aristizabal (Dinas 88), Angel, Castillo J (Bezerra 90).
Uruguay: Carini; Mendez, Lembo, Sorondo, Rodriguez, O'Neill, Pablo Garcia, Guigou (Giacomazzi 56), Olivera, Otero (Ruben Da Silva 51), Dario Silva (Magallanes 85).
Referee: Gimenez (Argentina).

Buenos Aires, 16 August 2000, 55,000
Argentina (0) 1 *(Aimar 67)*
Paraguay (0) 1 *(Acuna 61)*
Argentina: Bonano; Sensini, Ayala, Samuel, Veron, Simeone (Vivas 71), Kily Gonzalez (Sorin 46), Aimar, Ortega, Crespo, Lopez G (Saviola 75).
Paraguay: Tavarelli; Sarabia, Ayala, Gamarra, Caniza, Esteche, Struway (Quintana 78), Enciso, Acuna, Santa Cruz (Campos 55), Jose Cardozo (Benitez 85).
Referee: Pereira (Brazil).

Quito, 16 August 2000, 25,000
Ecuador (1) 2 *(Delgado 17, 59)*
Bolivia (0) 0
Ecuador: Ibarra; De la Cruz, Hurtado I, Poroso, Ayovi M (Reascos 46), Obregon, Chala, Aguinaga A, Ed Hurtado, Graziani (Juarez 62), Delgado.
Bolivia: Soria M; Paz Garcia, Ribera, Sandy, Arana, Garcia, Calustro (Vaca 76), Castillo S, Galindo, Baldivieso (Coimbra 46), Suarez.
Referee: Solorzano (Venezuela).

Lima, 16 August 2000, 40,000
Peru (0) 1 *(Palacios 70)*
Venezuela (0) 0
Peru: Ibanez; Jorge Soto, Jose Soto, Pajuelo (Marengo 40), Soria (Maldonado 67), Jayo, Palacios, Del Solar, Pizarro, Zuniga.
Venezuela: Angelucci; Jimenez, Alvarado, Gonzalez, Martinez, Mea Vitali M (De Ornelas 82), Farias, Tortolero, Urdaneta, Moran, Savarese (Casseres 71).
Referee: Moreno (Ecuador).

Santiago, 2 September 2000, 60,000
Chile (0) 0
Colombia (0) 1 *(Castillo J 66)*
Chile: Tapia N; Fuentes, Rojas R (Contreras 30), Reyes, Rojas F, Galdames, Tello, Estay (Cornejo 63), Sierra (Valencia 63), Zamorano, Salas.
Colombia: Cordoba O; Martinez, Cordoba I, Yepes, Mazziri, Luis Garcia (Viveros 46), Bolano, Grisales, Aristizabal, Castillo J (Dinas 86), Angel.
Referee: Gallesio (Uruguay).

Asuncion, 2 September 2000, 40,000
Paraguay (3) 3 *(Gonzalez G 30, Jose Cardozo 35, Paredes 44)*
Venezuela (0) 0
Paraguay: Chilavert; Gamarra (Gonzalez G 21), Sarabia, Arce, Ayala, Caniza, Acuna, Enciso, Paredes, Santa Cruz (Caceres 87), Jose Cardozo (Campos 77).
Venezuela: Angelucci; Jimenez, Alvarado, Gonzalez (Rey 46), Martinez, Mea Vitali M (Garcia 55), Tortolero (Paez 67), Farias, Urdaneta, De Ornelas, Moran.
Referee: Arandia (Bolivia).

Rio de Janeiro, 3 September 2000, 55,000
Brazil (1) 5 *(Romario 11 (pen), 78, 81, Rivaldo 46, Marques 88)*
Bolivia (0) 0
Brazil: Rogerio Ceni; Cafu, Zago, Emerson Carvalho, Roque Junior (Athirson 64), Vampeta, Flavio Conceicao, Alex (Juninho Paulista 59), Rivaldo, Ronaldinho (Marques 80), Romario.
Bolivia: Soria M; Ribeiro, Oscar Sanchez, Paz Garcia (Gutierrez L 73), Sandy, Garcia, Baldivieso, Alvarez, Cristaldo, Etcheverry, Moreno (Lider Paz 28).
Referee: Aros (Chile).

Lima, 3 September 2000, 45,000

Peru (0) 1 *(Samuel 69 (og))*
Argentina (2) 2 *(Crespo 25, Veron 38)*

Peru: Vegas; Solano, Pajuelo, Jose Soto, Olivares (Zuniga 78), Pereda, Jayo, Del Solar (Tempone 46), Palacios, Mendoza, Pizarro.
Argentina: Bonano; Sensini, Ayala, Samuel, Veron, Simeone (Vivas 80), Sorin, Aimar, Ortega (Husain 73), Crespo, Lopez C (Lopez G 84).
Referee: Ruiz (Colombia).

Montevideo, 3 September 2000, 60,000

Uruguay (2) 4 *(Magallanes 14, Dario Silva 37, Olivera 55, Cedres 87)*
Ecuador (0) 0

Uruguay: Carini; Tais, Lembo, Rodriguez, Mendez, Pablo Garcia (Fleurquin 68), Cedres, Olivera, Guigou, Dario Silva (Recoba 73), Magallanes (Abreu 63).
Ecuador: Cevallos; De la Cruz, Poroso, Hurtado I, Capurro, Tenorio (Burbano 56), Obregon, Chala (Candelario 46), Aguinaga A, Juarez, Graziani.
Referee: Jimenez (Colombia).

Bogota, 7 October 2000, 46,000

Colombia (0) 0
Paraguay (1) 2 *(Santa Cruz 4, Chilavert 90)*

Colombia: Cordoba O; Cordoba I, Yepes, Mazziri (Grisales 46), Martinez, Dinas, Bolano, Oviedo (Morantes 59), Aristizabal, Bonilla (Castro 67), Angel.
Paraguay: Chilavert; Arce, Sarabia, Ayala, Da Silva, Struway, Quintana (Alvarengo 66), Paredes, Acuna, Santa Cruz (Yegros 66) (Esteche 90), Jose Cardozo.
Referee: Gallesio (Uruguay).

Buenos Aires, 8 October 2000, 60,000

Argentina (2) 2 *(Gallardo 28, Batistuta 42)*
Uruguay (0) 1 *(Magallanes 48)*

Argentina: Burgos; Vivas, Ayala, Samuel, Sorin, Simeone, Husain, Gallardo (Delgado 80), Kily Gonzalez, Lopez C (Lopez G 73), Batistuta.
Uruguay: Carini; Pablo Garcia, Tais, Lembo, Rodriguez, Sorondo, Cedres (Reguero 45), Olivera, Guigou, Recoba (Abreu 70), Magallanes (Alonso 87).
Referee: Rezende (Brazil).

La Paz, 8 October 2000, 25,000

Bolivia (1) 1 *(Suarez 4)*
Peru (0) 0

Bolivia: Soria M; Ribeiro, Oscar Sanchez, Pena, Paz Garcia, Colque, Calustro, Garcia, Vaca (Gutierrez R 66), Lider Paz (Moreno 46), Suarez (Galindo 80).
Peru: Ibanez; Zeballos, Rebosio, Pajuelo, Soria, Jayo, Solano (Carmona 46), Bernales, Palacios, Pizarro (Lobaton 57), Zuniga (Alba 57).
Referee: Guevara (Ecuador).

Quito, 8 October 2000, 45,000

Ecuador (0) 1 *(Delgado 76)*
Chile (0) 0

Ecuador: Cevallos; De la Cruz, Espinoza, Hurtado I, Guerron, Obregon, Tenorio (Fernandez 63), Aguinaga A, Chala (Sanchez 59), Kaviedes (Ordonez 76), Delgado.
Chile: Tapia N; Alvarez, Contreras, Vargas, Olarra, Pizarro (Valencia 85), Maldonado, Tello, Estay (Rozental 78), Navia (Nunez C 46), Zamorano.
Referee: Rendon (Colombia).

San Cristobal, 8 October 2000, 20,000

Venezuela (0) 0
Brazil (5) 6 *(Euller 21, Juninho Paulista 29, Romario 31, 36 (pen), 39, 64)*

Venezuela: Angelucci; Gonzalez, Martinez, Rey, Alvarado, Farias, De Ornelas, Jimenez, Echenausi (Arango 46), Moran (Paez 66), Garcia (Savarese 77).
Brazil: Rogerio Ceni; Cafu, Zago, Cleber, Silvinho, Donizete, Vampeta, Juninho Pernambucano (Ze Roberto 66), Juninho Paulista (Ricardinho 81), Euller (Marques 70), Romario.
Referee: Aquino (Paraguay).

La Paz, 15 November 2000, 29,112

Bolivia (0) 0
Uruguay (0) 0

Bolivia: Soria M; Oscar Sanchez, Sandy, Paz Garcia (Vaca 80), Ribeiro, Calustro, Garcia, Erwin Sanchez, Colque, Menacho, Suarez (Lider Paz 66).
Uruguay: Carini; Varela, Lembo, Sorondo, Rodriguez, Pablo Garcia, Romero, Coelho (Callejas 64), Regueiro, Magallanes (Dario Silva 56), Franco (Cedres 76).
Referee: Elizondo (Argentina).

Sao Paulo, 15 November 2000, 56,213

Brazil (0) 1 *(Roque Junior 90)*
Colombia (0) 0

Brazil: Rogerio Ceni; Cafu, Lucio, Roque Junior, Junior, Cesar Sampaio, Vampeta (Juninho Permanbucano 71), Rivaldo, Juninho Paulista, Franca (Adriano 79), Edmundo (Marques 67).
Colombia: Calero; Martinez, Dinas, Yepes, Bedoya, Bolano, Serna, Viveros, Aristizabal, Angel (Bonilla 67), Castillo J.
Referee: Larrionda (Uruguay).

Santiago, 15 November 2000, 56,529

Chile (0) 0
Argentina (1) 2 *(Ortega 26, Husain 90)*

Chile: Tapia N; Reyes, Rojas R, Contreras (Navia 79), Galdames, Maldonado (Villarroel 74), Rojas F, Pizarro, Estay (Valencia 64), Salas, Zamorano.
Argentina: Burgos (Bonano 74); Vivas, Ayala, Samuel, Almeyda, Husain, Sorin, Veron (Aimar 52), Kily Gonzalez, Cruz (Berizzo 84), Ortega.
Referee: Amarilla (Paraguay).

Asuncion, 15 November 2000, 30,000

Paraguay (3) 5 *(Santa Cruz 15, Del Solar 25 (og), Jose Cardozo 44, Paredes 65, Chilavert 84 (pen))*
Peru (0) 1 *(Garcia 78)*

Paraguay: Chilavert; Arce, Sarabia, Ayala, Caniza, Paredes, Enciso, Acuna, Jose Cardozo (Brizuela 76), Alvarenga (Campos 86), Santa Cruz (Ferreira 70).
Peru: Ibanez; Zeballos (Garcia 60), Pajuelo (Velasquez 16), Rebosio, Soria, Bernales, Del Solar, Pereda (Lobaton 46), Palacios, Muchotrigo, Alva.
Referee: Gimenez (Argentina).

Maracaibo, 15 November 2000, 11,000

Venezuela (0) 1 *(Arango 65)*
Ecuador (2) 2 *(Kaviedes 4, Sanchez 21)*

Venezuela: Angelucci; De Ornelas, Alvarado, Gonzalez, Vallenilla (Paez 86), Mea Vitali M (Luzardo 46), Farias, Urdaneta, Arango, Castellin (Perez 64), Garcia.
Ecuador: Cevallos; De la Cruz, Poroso, Hurtado I, Guerron, Burbano, Chala, Mendez (Zamora 72), Sanchez, Kaviedes (Fernandez 67), Delgado (Espinoza 88).
Referee: Betancourt (Peru).

Bogota, 27 March 2001, 45,000

Colombia (0) 2 *(Angel 53, 73 (pen))*
Bolivia (0) 0

Colombia: Cordoba O; Gonzalez, Dinas, Yepes, Bedoya, Serna, Grisales, Aristizabal (Viveros 46), Asprilla, Bonilla (Ferreira 46), Angel (Quintana 84).
Bolivia: Fernandez; Ribeiro, Pena, Sandy, Arana, Colque, Justiniano, Rojas, Vaca, Coimbra (Lider Paz 79), Cardenas (Suarez 57).
Referee: Souza (Brazil).

Lima, 27 March 2001, 45,000

Peru (0) 3 *(Maestri 54, Mendoza 73, Pizarro 81)*
Chile (0) 1 *(Navia 62)*

Peru: Miranda; Solano, Rebosio, Pajuela, Olivares (Hidalgo 42), Jayo, Palacios, Del Solar (Maestri 46), Muchotrigo (Ciurlizza 75), Mendoza, Pizarro.
Chile: Tapia N; Vargas, Rojas R, Mi Ramirez, Ponce, Parraguez (Mirosevic 25) (Ruiz 65), Maldonado, Osorio, Tello (Tapia H 46), Zamorano, Navia.
Referee: Sanchez (Argentina).

Buenos Aires, 28 March 2001, 32,000
Argentina (2) 5 *(Crespo 13, Sorin 31, Veron 51, Gallardo 60, Samuel 85)*
Venezuela (0) 0
Argentina: Burgos; Vivas, Pochettino, Samuel, Sorin (Zanetti 61), Simeone, Veron, Ortega (Lopez G 70), Kily Gonzalez, Gallardo (Lopez C 76), Crespo.
Venezuela: Dudamel; Alvarado, Rey, Vallenilla, De Ornelas (Perez 51), Urdaneta, Vera J (Mea Vitali M 74), Vera L, Rojas (Martinez 65), Noriega, Paez.
Referee: Zamora (Peru).

Quito, 28 March 2001, 40,800
Ecuador (0) 1 *(Delgado 49)*
Brazil (0) 0
Ecuador: Cevallos; De la Cruz, Hurtado I, Poroso, Guerron, Tenorio (Sanchez 69), Burbano, Mendez, Aguinaga A, Kaviedes (Obregon 90), Delgado.
Brazil: Rogerio Ceni; Belletti, Lucio, Roque Junior, Silvinho (Cesar Aparecido 59), Emerson, Vampeta, Juninho Paulista, Rivaldo (Luizao 64), Ronaldinho (Euller 46), Romario.
Referee: Rizo (Mexico).

Montevideo, 28 March 2001, 60,000
Uruguay (0) 0
Paraguay (0) 1 *(Alvarenga 64)*
Uruguay: Carini; Varela, Sorondo, Montero, Rodriguez, De los Santos, Fleurquin (O'Neill 69), Olivera, Guigou (Pandiani 49), Dario Silva (Zalayeta 76), Recoba.
Paraguay: Chilavert; Ayala, Gamarra, Sarabia, Quintana (Alvarenga 46), Struway, Paredes, Acuna, Caniza, Caceres (Cuevas 83), Jose Cardozo (Esteche 88).
Referee: Aranda (Spain).

Santiago, 24 April 2001, 51,000
Chile (0) 0
Uruguay (1) 1 *(Diaz 12 (og))*
Chile: Vargas S; Diaz (Valdes 57), Reyes, Contreras, Tello, Maldonado, Galdames, Osorio (Gonzalez 74), Estay, Tapia H (Nunez C 46), Zamorano.
Uruguay: Carini; Mendez, Lembo, Sorondo, Rodriguez, Pablo Garcia, Guigou, Olivera (Regueiro 84), Magallanes, Recoba (Romero 72), Dario Silva (Varela 76).
Referee: Elizondo (Argentina).

Quito, 24 April 2001, 40,000
Ecuador (1) 2 *(Delgado 45, 54)*
Paraguay (1) 1 *(Jose Cardozo 26)*
Ecuador: Cevallos; De la Cruz, Hurtado I, Poroso, Guerron, Burbano (Espinoza 46), Chala (Sanchez 68), Aguinaga A (Mendez 46), Tenorio, Kaviedes, Delgado.
Paraguay: Tavarelli; Espinola, Gamarra, Ayala, Da Silva (Quintana 73), Esteche, Struway, Paredes, Alvarenga (Gonzalez G 62), Cuevas (Brizuela 46), Jose Cardozo.
Referee: Sanchez (Argentina).

San Cristobal, 24 April 2001, 35,000
Venezuela (1) 2 *(Rondon 22, Arango 81)*
Colombia (0) 2 *(Bedoya 83, Bonilla 88)*
Venezuela: Dudamel; Vallenilla, Mea Vitali R, Rey, Rojas, Vera L, Arango, Mea Vitali M (De Ornelas 61), Urdaneta (Paez 70), Savarese (Vera J 55), Rondon.
Colombia: Calero; Martinez, Bermudez, Dinas, Bedoya, Grisales, Viveros (Quintana 70), Bolano (Gonzalez 61), Restrepo (Ferreira 46), Bonilla, Angel.
Referee: Alvaredo (Chile).

La Paz, 25 April 2001, 35,000
Bolivia (1) 3 *(Lider Paz 41, Colque 55, Botero 81)*
Argentina (3) 3 *(Crespo 44, 89, Sorin 90)*
Bolivia: Fernandez; Ribeiro, Pena, Paz Garcia, Sandy, Colque, Justiniano, Baldivieso, Vaca (Rojas 59), Lider Paz (Cardenas 74), Botero.
Argentina: Burgos; Vivas, Ayala, Samuel, Zanetti (Ortega 62), Simeone, Veron, Sorin, Aimar (Gallardo 57); Crespo, Lopez G (Lopez C 46).
Referee: Ruiz (Colombia).

Sao Paolo, 25 April 2001, 40,000
Brazil (0) 1 *(Romario 66)*
Peru (0) 1 *(Pajuelo 79)*
Brazil: Rogerio Ceni; Alessandro, Edmilson, Lucio, Cesar Aparecido, Leomar, Vampeta (Washington 80), Ricardinho (Mineiro 77), Marcelinho Carioca (Juninho Paulista 46), Ewerthon, Romario.
Peru: Miranda; Rebosio, Pajuelo, Hidalgo, Solano, Jayo, Ciurlizza, Muchotrigo (Mendoza 46), Palacios, Olivares (Tempone 75), Maestri (Pizarro 46).
Referee: Al-Zaid (Saudi Arabia).

Asuncion, 2 June 2001, 45,000
Paraguay (0) 1 *(Paredes 90)*
Chile (0) 0
Paraguay: Chilavert; Arce, Sarabia, Ayala, Caniza, Quintana (Amarilla 77), Paredes, Acuna, Alvarenga, Santa Cruz (Cuevas 66), Brizuela (Julio Gonzalez 46).
Chile: Vargas S; Reyes, Vargas, Contreras, Pozo, Osorio, Villaseca, Perez (Valenzuela 78), Tello, Montecinos, Navia (Neira 63).
Referee: Badilla (Costa Rica).

Lima, 2 June 2001, 60,000
Peru (1) 1 *(Pizarro 2)*
Ecuador (1) 2 *(Mendez 12, Delgado 90)*
Peru: Miranda; Pajuelo, Rebosio, Olivares (Hidalgo 62), Solano, Jayo, Palacios, Ciurlizza, Mendoza (Muchotrigo 74), Pizarro, Maestri (Silva 46).
Ecuador: Cevallos; De la Cruz, Hurtado I, Espinoza, Guerron, Obregon (Guagua 71), Tenorio, Chala (Aguinaga J 86), Mendez, Delgado, Kaviedes (Fernandez 81).
Referee: Marrufo (Mexico).

Buenos Aires, 3 June 2001, 40,000
Argentina (3) 3 *(Kily Gonzalez 23, Lopez C 35, Crespo 38)*
Colombia (0) 0
Argentina: Cavallero; Vivas, Ayala, Pochettino, Simeone, Zanetti, Veron (Gallardo 84), Sorin, Kily Gonzalez, Lopez C (Aimar 82), Crespo (Delgado 48).
Colombia: Cordoba O; Martinez, Dinas, Yepes, Bedoya, Serna, Rincon, Viveros (Gonzalez 46), Asprilla (Ferreira 46), Castillo J, Angel (Murillo 77).
Referee: Sanchez (Chile).

La Paz, 3 June 2001, 20,000
Bolivia (3) 5 *(Baldivieso 32, 68, Botero 35, 51, Justiniano 38)*
Venezuela (0) 0
Bolivia: Arias; Raldes, Pena, Paz Garcia, Ribeiro (Rojas 85), Justiniano, Baldivieso (Pena D 90), Calustro, Colque, Lider Paz (Cardenas 73), Botero.
Venezuela: Sanhouse; Vallenilla, Rey, Mea Vitali R, Martinez, Vera L, Mea Vitali M, Arango (Casseres 67), Gonzalez (Alvarado 54), Paez (Jimenez 42), Rondon.
Referee: Carpio (Ecuador).

Montevideo, 1 July 2001, 62,000
Uruguay (1) 1 *(Magallanes 32 (pen))*
Brazil (0) 0
Uruguay: Carini; Mendez, Montero, Sorondo, Guigou, De los Santos, Pablo Garcia, Romero, Recoba (Lembo 76), Dario Silva (Regueiro 62), Magallanes (Giacomazzi 71).
Brazil: Marcos; Cris, Zago (Jardel 76), Roque Junior, Cafu, Emerson, Rivaldo, Juninho Paulista, Roberto Carlos, Elber (Euller 60), Romario.
Referee: Dallas (Scotland).

Santiago, 14 August 2001, 30,000
Chile (1) 2 *(Salas 35 (pen), 77)*
Bolivia (1) 2 *(Baldivieso 11 (pen), Coimbra 73)*
Chile: Vargas S; Pozo (Solis 33), Reyes, Vargas J, Aros, Chavarria, Valencia (Ahumada 82), Villaseca, Nunez C (Castillo 46), Salas, Montecinos.
Bolivia: Soria M; Raldes, Pena, Oscar Sanchez, Carballo, Justiniano, Rojas, Lider Paz (Colque 84), Baldivieso, Galindo, Coimbra.
Referee: Gimenez (Argentina).

Maracaibo, 14 August 2001, 25,000
Venezuela (0) 2 *(Moran 53, Rondon 90)*
Uruguay (0) 0
Venezuela: Dudamel; Vallenilla, Rey, Alvarado, Rojas, Mea Vitali M, Vera L, Arango, Paez (Perez 87), Noriega (Rondon 66), Moran (Jimenez 76).
Uruguay: Carini; Mendez, Sorondo, Montero, Guigou, De los Santos, Giacomazzi (Regueiro 54), Romero (Morales 65), Olivera, Recoba, Dario Silva (Zalayeta 69).
Referee: Mendoza (Mexico).

Porto Alegre, 15 August 2001, 48,000
Brazil (1) 2 *(Marcelinho Carioca 4, Rivaldo 69)*
Paraguay (0) 0
Brazil: Marcos; Roque Junior, Cris, Juan, Belletti, Tinga, Eduardo Costa, Rivaldo (Vampeta 85), Roberto Carlos, Marcelinho Carioca (Denilson 63), Edilson (Leonardo 66).
Paraguay: Chilavert; Arce, Sarabia, Cacares, Morel, Struway (Campos 73), Paredes, Acuna, Gavilan, Santa Cruz (Ferreira 58), Jose Cardozo.
Referee: Krug (Germany).

Quito, 15 August 2001, 45,000
Ecuador (0) 0
Argentina (2) 2 *(Veron 19, Crespo 31 (pen))*
Ecuador: Ibarra; De la Cruz, Hurtado I, Espinoza, Guerron, Burbano (Aguinaga J 46), Chala, Guagua (Fernandez 51), Sanchez (Aguinaga A 46), Delgado, Kaviedes.
Argentina: Burgos; Vivas, Ayala, Samuel, Zanetti, Simeone (Almeyda 67), Veron, Sorin, Aimar (Ortega 60), Crespo, Kily Gonzalez (Lopez C 84).
Referee: Braschi (Italy).

Bogota, 16 August 2001, 33,875
Colombia (0) 0
Peru (0) 1 *(Solano 47)*
Colombia: Cordoba O; Cordoba I, Yepes, Serna, Oviedo (Arriaga 54), Hernandez, Aristizabal, Lopez, Murillo (Ramirez 65), Grisales (Castillo J 65), Bedoya.
Peru: Miranda; Rebosio, Hidalgo, Pajuelo, Solano, Jayo (Salazar 73), Pizarro (Jose Soto 82), Palacios, Jorge Soto, Mendoza (Holsen 87), Del Solar.
Referee: Rizo (Mexico).

Santiago, 4 September 2001, 30,000
Chile (0) 0
Venezuela (0) 2 *(Paez 56, Arango 62)*
Chile: Tapia N; Rojas F, Fuentes, Acuna, Navia, Vargas, Tello, Montecinos, Nunez C (Valencia 63), Galdames, Aros (Perez 72).
Venezuela: Dudamel; Vallenilla, Mea Vitali R, Alvarado, Mea Vitali M, Noriega (Jimenez 75), Vera L, Arango, Paez (Martinez 79), Rojas, Moran (Rondon 86).
Referee: Betancourt (Bolivia).

Lima, 4 September 2001, 45,000
Peru (0) 0
Uruguay (2) 2 *(Dario Silva 12, Recoba 45)*
Peru: Miranda; Jorge Soto, Jose Soto, Pajuelo, Hidalgo, Solano, Jayo, Del Solar (Pereda 72), Palacios, Pizarro (Maestri 46), Mendoza.
Uruguay: Carini; Bizera, Lembo, Rodriguez, Tais, Pablo Garcia, De los Santos, Gigou, Recoba (Perez 89), Dario Silva (Regueiro 72), Chevanton (Magallanes 65).
Referee: Frisk (Sweden).

Buenos Aires, 5 September 2001, 51,000
Argentina (0) 2 *(Gellardo 76, Cris 84 (og))*
Brazil (1) 1 *(Ayala 2 (og))*
Argentina: Burgos; Ayala, Piacente (Ortega 46), Vivas, Samuel, Lopez C (Almeyda 87), Zanetti, Crespo, Simeone, Aimar (Gellardo 64), Kily Gonzalez.
Brazil: Marcos; Cafu, Lucio, Roque Junior, Cris, Roberto Carlos, Eduardo Costa (Denilson 89), Mauro Silva (Vampeta 70), Marcelinho Carioca, Rivaldo, Elber (Euller 65).
Referee: Meier (Switzerland).

Bogota, 5 September 2001, 46,000
Colombia (0) 0
Ecuador (0) 0
Colombia: Cordoba O; Lopez, Cordoba I, Yepes, Bedoya (Cortes 80), Ramirez, Serna, Hernandez, Murillo (Molina 68), Aristizabal (Arriaga 80), Angel.
Ecuador: Cevallos; De la Cruz, Espinoza, Hurtado I, Guerron, Tenorio, Obregon, Gomez (Aguinaga J 68), Mendez, Kaviedes (Fernandez 58), Delgado.
Referee: Al-Aqily (Saudi Arabia).

Asuncion, 5 September 2001, 30,000
Paraguay (2) 5 *(Paredes 33, Jose Cardozo 45, 89, Chilavert 48, Santa Cruz 70)*
Bolivia (1) 1 *(Lider Paz 15)*
Paraguay: Chilavert; Sarabia, Ayala, Gamarra, Paredes (Quintana 56), Arce, Rodriguez, Struway (Morinigo 70), Ferreira (Gavilan 65), Santa Cruz, Jose Cardozo.
Bolivia: Arias; Reyes, Paz Garcia, Raldes, Pena, Rojas, Justiniano, Galindo, Baldivieso, Castillo A (Andaveriz 66), Lider Paz (Calustro 79).
Referee: Solorzano (Venezuela).

La Paz, 6 October 2001, 5000
Bolivia (0) 1 *(Galindo 60)*
Ecuador (2) 5 *(De la Cruz 13, Delgado 23, Kaviedes 58, Fernandez 89, Gomez 90)*
Bolivia: Arias; Raldes, Jiguchi, Carballo, Reyes, Castillo S (Vaca 33), Calustro, Justiniano, Galindo, Lider Paz, Andaveris (Castillo A 46).
Ecuador: Cevallos; De la Cruz, Hurtado I, Espinoza, Guerron, Tenorio (Gomez 90), Obregon (Burbano 90), Mendez, Chala, Kaviedes (Fernandez 77), Delgado.
Referee: Sanchez (Argentina).

San Cristobal, 6 October 2001, 30,000
Venezuela (0) 3 *(Alvarado 49, 67, Moran 78)*
Peru (0) 0
Venezuela: Angelucci; Vallenilla, Mea Vitali R, Alvarado, Rojas, Vera L (Jimenez 10), Mea Vitali M, Arango, Paez (Urdaneta 67), Noriega (Martinez 60), Moran.
Peru: Miranda; Huaman (Mi Ramirez 57), Pajuela, Rebosio, Hidalgo, Jorge Soto, Ciurlizza, Jayo, Palacios, Maestri (Garcia 70), Mendoza (Arakaki 46).
Referee: Sanchez (Chile).

Curitiba, 7 October 2001, 52,000
Brazil (0) 2 *(Edilson 53, Rivaldo 67)*
Chile (0) 0
Brazil: Marcos; Lucio, Juan, Edmilson, Cafu, Emerson, Vampeta, Rivaldo (Juninho Paulista 89), Roberto Carlos (Belleti 84), Marcelinho Carioca (Denilson 46), Edilson.
Chile: Toro; Vargas, Robles, Munoz, Cancino, Villaseca, Ormazabal, Perez (Melendez 61), Pizarro, Salas, Valenzuela (Navia 55).
Referee: Elizondo (Argentina).

Asuncion, 7 October 2001, 43,000
Paraguay (0) 2 *(Chilavert 52 (pen), Morinigo 70)*
Argentina (0) 2 *(Pochettino 86, Batistuta 73)*
Paraguay: Chilavert; Arce, Ayala (Caceres 80), Caniza, Gamarra, Alvarenga, Morinigo, Quintana (Rodriguez 71), Struway, Jose Cardozo (Caballero 79), Santa Cruz.
Argentina: Cavellero; Ayala, Pochettino, Samuel, Almeyda, Sorin (Lopez C 63), Veron, Zanetti, Batistuta (Cruz 90), Kily Gonzalez, Ortega (Aimar 80).
Referee: Zamora (Peru).

Montevideo, 7 October 2001, 65,000
Uruguay (1) 1 *(Magallanes 35 (pen))*
Colombia (0) 1 *(Valentierra 68)*
Uruguay: Munua; Lembo, Montero, Rodriguez, Tais, De los Santos, Pablo Garcia, Guigou (Canobbio 83), Recoba, Dario Silva (Morales 75), Magallanes (Chevanton 46).
Colombia: Cordoba O; Lopez, Cordoba I, Yepes, Bedoya (Cortes 46), Grisales, Restrepo, Bolano, Valentierra, Aristizabal (Murillo 71), Asprilla.
Referee: Collina (Italy).

La Paz, 7 November 2001, 32,574
Bolivia (1) 3 *(Lider Paz 41, Baldivieso 69, 89 (pen))*
Brazil (1) 1 *(Edilson 26)*
Bolivia: Soria M; Pena, Paz Garcia, Colque (Oscar Sanchez 68), Olivares, Ribeiro, Rojas, Botero, Baldivieso, Lider Paz (Castillo A 76), Galindo (Gutierrez L 56).
Brazil: Marcos; Cafu, Lucio, Juan (Juninho Paulista 76), Edmilson, Serginho, Emerson, Vampeta (Gilberto 62), Ze Roberto (Denilson 56), Rivaldo, Edilson.
Referee: Torres (Venezuela).

Bogota, 7 November 2001, 16,050
Colombia (1) 3 *(Grisales 17, Angel 68, Gonzalez 70)*
Chile (1) 1 *(Riveros 40)*
Colombia: Cordoba O; Cordoba I, Yepes, Cortes, Bolano (Castillo J 46), Valentierra (Mina 74), Angel, Asprilla (Castro 59), Gonzalez, Restrepo, Grisales.
Chile: Vargas S; Munoz, Ormazabal, Riveros (Medina 72), Navia (Martel 73), Vargas, Villarroel, Robles, Villaseca, Cancino, Norambuela (Almendra 77).
Referee: Gimenez (Argentina).

Quito, 7 November 2001, 40,000
Ecuador (0) 1 *(Kaviedes 73)*
Uruguay (1) 1 *(Olivera 44 (pen))*
Ecuador: Cevallos; Hurtado I, De la Cruz, Obregon, Guerron (Fernandez 68), Kaviedes (Gomez 77), Delgado, Chala (Aguinaga A 58), Espinoza, Mendez, Tenorio.
Uruguay: Carini; Tais, Lembo, Montero, Pablo Garcia, Guigou, Romero, De los Santos, Dario Silva (Morales 74), Olivera (Sanchez 52), Recoba (Perez 84).
Referee: Rizo (Mexico).

Buenos Aires, 8 November 2001, 18,901
Argentina (0) 2 *(Samuel 46, Lopez C 85)*
Peru (0) 0
Argentina: Burgos; Pochettino, Ayala, Samuel, Zanetti, Almeyda, Sorin, Veron, Ortega (Aimar 74), Cruz (Lopez C 46), Kily Gonzalez (Romeo 87).
Peru: Miranda; Jorge Soto, Salazar, Pajuelo, Hidalgo (Huaman 62), Ciurlizza, Del Solar (Mendoza 59), Jayo, Palacios, Pizarro, Maestri.
Referee: Larrionda (Uruguay).

San Cristobal, 8 November 2001, 22,500
Venezuela (3) 3 *(Moran 2, Noriega 22, Gonzalez 40)*
Paraguay (1) 1 *(Arce 27 (pen))*
Venezuela: Angelucci; Gonzalez, Alvarado, Mea Vitali R, Rojas, Vera L, Mea Vitali M, Urdaneta, Paez (Martinez 72), Noriega (Rondon 61), Moran (Perez 79).
Paraguay: Bobadilla; Arce, Gamarra, Caceres, Morel, Acuna, Struway (Alvarenga 46), Paredes, Morinigo (Quintana 46), Brizuela (Masi 72), Jose Cardozo.
Referee: Elizondo (Argentina).

Sao Luis, 14 November 2001, 65,000
Brazil (3) 3 *(Luizao 12, 19, Rivaldo 35)*
Venezuela (0) 0
Brazil: Marcos; Lucio, Roque Junior, Edmilson, Belletti, Roberto Carlos, Emerson, Juninho Paulista (Ronaldinho 68), Rivaldo, Luizao (Denilson 58), Edilson (Marcelinho Carioca 75).
Venezuela: Dudamel; Gonzalez, Rey, Mea Vitali R, Rojas, Mea Vitali M, Vera L, Urdaneta (Vallenilla 58), Paez (Martinez 32), Noriega, Moran (Jimenez 51).
Referee: Gimenez (Argentina).

Santiago, 14 November 2001, 19,237
Chile (0) 0
Ecuador (0) 0
Chile: Vargas S; Robles, Torres, Gomez (Almendra 65), Perez, Sanhueza (Ormeno 46), Medina (Ahumada 46), Munoz, Riveros, Martel, Gutierrez.
Ecuador: Cevallos; De la Cruz, Hurtado I, Espinoza, Ayovi M, Obregon, Burbano, Gomez, Mendez, Fernandez, Kaviedes (Tenorio 70).
Referee: Arandia (Bolivia).

Asuncion, 14 November 2001, 25,000
Paraguay (0) 0
Colombia (2) 4 *(Aristizabal 24, 33 (pen), 62, Castillo J 83)*
Paraguay: Bobadilla; Arce (Masi 71), Sanabria, Gamarra, Ayala, Caniza, Quintana (Struway 83), Paredes, Acuna, Gimenez (Brizuela 56), Jose Cardozo.
Colombia: Cordoba O; Vallejo, Cordoba I, Yepes, Bedoya, Serna, Restrepo, Grisales (Castillo J 83), Morantes, Aristizabal (Castro 85), Asprilla.
Referee: Poll (England).

Lima, 14 November 2001, 2374
Peru (1) 1 *(Alva 9)*
Bolivia (0) 1 *(Castillo A 88)*
Peru: Miranda; Huaman, Hidalgo, Pajuelo, Jayo, Palacios, Mendoza, Jorge Soto (Palomino 46), Salazar, Ciurlizza (Ferrari 69), Alva (Carty 76).
Bolivia: Fernandez; Reyes, Paz Garcia, Oscar Sanchez (Ribeiro 54), Olivares, Rojas, Botero (Castillo A 63), Coimbra, Lider Paz (Justiniano 90), Pena D, Galindo.
Referee: Baldassi (Argentina).

Montevideo, 14 November 2001, 45,000
Uruguay (1) 1 *(Dario Silva 19)*
Argentina (1) 1 *(Lopez C 45)*
Uruguay: Carini; Tais (Morales R 64), Lembo, Montero, Rodriguez (Regueiro 83), Guigou, Pablo Garcia, De los Santos, Recoba, Magallanes, Dario Silva (Alonso 46).
Argentina: Burgos; Pochettino, Ayala, Samuel, Zanetti, Sorin, Almeyda, Veron, Aimar (Piacente 84), Ortega (Cruz 46), Lopez C.
Referee: Merk (Germany).

SOUTH AMERICA

Table

	P	W	D	L	F	A	Pts
Argentina	18	13	4	1	42	15	43
Ecuador	18	9	4	5	23	20	31
Brazil	18	9	3	6	31	17	30
Paraguay	18	9	3	6	29	23	30
Uruguay	18	7	6	5	19	13	27
Colombia	18	7	6	5	20	15	27
Bolivia	18	4	6	8	21	33	18
Peru	18	4	4	10	14	25	16
Venezuela	18	5	1	12	18	44	16
Chile	18	3	3	12	15	27	12

PLAY-OFFS, FIRST LEG

Vienna, 10 November 2001, 48,500
Austria (0) 0
Turkey (0) 1 *(Okan 60)*
Austria: Wohlfahrt; Flogel, Vukovic, Winklhofer, Baur, Schopp (Lexa 54), Strafner, Herzog, Markus Hiden (Kitzbichler 72), Haas, Wallner (Weissenberger 61).
Turkey: Rustu; Umit O, Alpay, Emre, Umit D, Okan (Tayfur 88), Tugay, Ergun (Arif 62), Abdullah, Basturk (Fatih 70), Hakan Sukur.
Referee: Gonzalez (Spain).

Brussels, 10 November 2001, 44,000
Belgium (0) 1 *(Verheyen 29)*
Czech Republic (0) 0
Belgium: De Vlieger; Deflandre, Van Meir (De Boeck 46), Clement, Van Kerckhoven, Verheyen, Simons, Vermant, Walem, Goor, Sonck (Van Houdt 79).
Czech Republic: Srnicek; Grygera (Ujfalusi 32), Repka, Novotny, Jankulovski, Poborsky, Hasek, Jarosik, Smicer (Hubschmann 46), Nedved, Baros (Lokvenc 65).
Referee: Meier (Switzerland).

Ljubljana, 10 November 2001, 9000
Slovenia (1) 2 *(Acimovic 41, Osterc 70)*
Romania (1) 1 *(Niculae 26)*
Slovenia: Simeunovic; Milinovic, Galic, Vugdalic, Karic (Ceh N 40), Pavlin, Ceh A, Novak, Acimovic (Pavlovic 66), Osterc, Rudonja.
Romania: Stelea; Contra, Iencsi, Popescu, Chivu, Sabau (Rosu 84), Miu (Pancu 90), Mutu, Munteanu D, Ilie A (Ghioane 84), Niculae.
Referee: Nielsen (Denmark).

Kiev, 10 November 2001, 85,000

Ukraine (1) 1 *(Zoubov 18)*
Germany (1) 1 *(Ballack 30)*

Ukraine: Levytsky; Luzhny, Vashchuk, Golovko, Nesmachni, Zoubov, Tymoshchuk (Parfenov 73), Shevchenko, Vorobei (Melaschenko 76), Gusin, Rebrov (Chitchenko 56).
Germany: Kahn; Rehmer, Nowotny, Linke, Schneider (Ricken 80), Ramelow, Ballack, Hamann, Ziege, Asamoah, Zickler (Jancker 68).
Referee: Braschi (Italy).

PLAY-OFFS, SECOND LEG

Prague, 14 November 2001, 18,996

Czech Republic (0) 0
Belgium (0) 1 *(Wilmots 86 (pen))*

Czech Republic: Srnicek; Johana (Jarosik 58), Hubschmann, Novotny, Jankulovski, Poborsky (Sionko 46), Hasek (Smicer 67), Rosicky, Nedved, Baros, Lokvenc.
Belgium: De Vlieger; Deflandre, Clement, De Boeck, Van Kerckhoven, Vermant (Vanderhaeghe 90), Simons, Goor, Walem (Boffin 84), Verheyen, Sonck (Wilmots 63).
Referee: Frisk (Sweden).

Dortmund, 14 November 2001, 52,000

Germany (3) 4 *(Ballack 3, 50, Neuville 10, Rehmer 14)*
Ukraine (0) 1 *(Shevchenko 90)*

Germany: Kahn; Rehmer (Baumann 87), Nowotny, Linke, Schneider, Ramelow, Hamann, Ziege, Ballack, Neuville (Ricken 70), Jancker (Bierhoff 58).
Ukraine: Levytsky; Luzhny, Vashchuk, Golovko, Nesmachni (Chitchenko 55), Skrypnyk, Zubov, Tymoshchuk (Gusin 24), Parfenov, Shevchenko, Vorobei (Rebrov 70).
Referee: Pereira (Portugal).

Bucharest, 14 November 2001, 24,500

Romania (0) 1 *(Contra 65)*
Slovenia (0) 1 *(Rudonja 57)*

Romania: Lobont; Contra, Popescu, Ghioane (Ganea 58), Chivu, Sabau, Miu (Mihalcea 78), Munteanu D, Mutu (Pancu 58), Niculae, Ilie A.
Slovenia: Simeunovic; Milinovic, Vugdalic, Galic, Novak, Ceh A, Gajser, Pavlin, Acimovic (Sankovic 62), Osterc (Pavlovic 89), Rudonja.
Referee: Krug (Germany).

Istanbul, 14 November 2001, 22,000

Turkey (3) 5 *(Basturk 21, Hakan Sukur 30, Okan 45, Arif 61, 86)*
Austria (0) 0

Turkey: Rustu; Umit D, Emre, Alpay, Abudullah, Okan (Sergen 63), Umit O, Tugay, Basturk (Arif 42), Hasan Sas (Ilhan 87), Hakan Sukur.
Austria: Wohlfahrt; Winklhofer, Vukovic, Strafner, Lexa (Schopp 54), Markus Hiden, Prilasnig (Kitzbichler 46), Herzog, Flogel, Vastic (Weissenberger 75), Haas.
Referee: Collina (Italy).

ASIA/EURO PLAY-OFF, FIRST LEG

Dublin, 10 November 2001, 35,000

Republic of Ireland (1) 2 *(Harte 45 (pen), Robbie Keane 50)*
Iran (0) 0

Republic of Ireland: Given; Finnan, Harte, Breen, Staunton (Cunningham 75), Holland, McAteer (Kelly G 84), Roy Keane, Robbie Keane, Quinn, Kilbane.
Iran: Mirzapour; Mahdavikia, Vahedinikbakht (Khaziravi 46), Peyrovani, Golmohammadi, Rezaei, Kavianpour, Bagheri, Karimi, Daei, Minavand.
Referee: Da Silva (Brazil).

ASIA/EURO PLAY-OFF, SECOND LEG

Teheran, 15 November 2001, 110,000

Iran (0) 1 *(Golmohammadi 90)*
Republic of Ireland (0) 0

Iran: Mirzapour; Mahdavikia, Minavand, Golmohammadi, Rezaei, Kavianpour, Karimi, Bagheri, Daei, Vahedinikbakht, Peyrovani.
Republic of Ireland: Given; Finnan, Harte, Holland, Staunton, Breen, McAteer, Kinsella, Robbie Keane (Morrison 75), Connolly, Kilbane (Kelly G 79).
Referee: Vega (Costa Rica).

STH AMERICA/OCEANIA PLAY-OFFS

Melbourne, 20 November 2001, 84,656

Australia (0) 1 *(Muscat 78 (pen))*
Uruguay (0) 0

Australia: Schwarzer; Muscat, Moore, Murphy, Okon, Vidmar, Emerton, Skoko, Viduka, Kewell, Lazaridis (Agostino 46).
Uruguay: Carini; Tais, Montero, Rodriguez, Lembo, Guigou, Pablo Garcia, Recoba, De los Santos, Chevanton (Regueiro 77), Magallanes (Giacomazza 72).
Referee: Cesari (Italy).

Montevideo, 25 November 2001, 62,000

Uruguay (1) 3 *(Dario Silva 14, Morales R 70, 90)*
Australia (0) 0

Uruguay: Carini; Tais, Lembo, Montero, Rodriguez, Guigou, Pablo Garcia, Regueiro (De los Santos 64), Recoba, Dario Silva (Sorondo 81), Magallanes (Morales R 65).
Australia: Schwarzer; Muscat (Agostino 62), Moore, Okon, Vidmar, Emerton, Skoko, Viduka, Murphy (Aloisi 81), Kewell, Lazaridis.
Referee: Bujsaim (UAE).

OCEANIA
(Members 11, Entries 10)

Group 1: Australia, Tonga, Fiji, American Samoa, Samoa.

Samoa 0, Tonga 1; Fiji 13, American Samoa 0; Tonga 0, Australia 22; American Samoa 0, Samoa 8; Samoa 1, Fiji 6; Australia 31, American Samoa 0; Fiji 0, Australia 2; American Samoa 0, Tonga 5; Australia 11, Samoa 0; Tonga 1, Fiji 8.

Group 2: New Zealand, Tahiti, Solomon Islands, Vanuatu, Cook Islands.

Vanuatu 1, Tahiti 6; Solomon Islands 9, Cook Islands 1; Tahiti 0, New Zealand 5; Cook Islands 1, Vanuatu 8; Vanuatu 2, Solomon Islands 7; New Zealand 2, Cook Islands 0; Solomon Islands 1, New Zealand 5; Cook Islands 0, Tahiti 6; New Zealand 7, Vanuatu 0; Tahiti 2, Solomon Islands 0.

Final Round, First Leg: New Zealand 0, Australia 2.

Final Round, Second Leg: Australia 4, New Zealand 1.
Australia lost to Uruguay in play-off.

ASIA
(Members 44, Entries 42)

Four teams qualified: China, Japan (hosts), Saudi Arabia and South Korea (hosts).

Group 1: Laos, Oman, Philippines, Syria.
Oman 12, Laos 0; Syria 12, Philippines 0; Philippines 1, Syria 5; Laos 0, Oman 7; Oman 7, Philippines 0; Syria 11, Laos 0; Philippines 0, Oman 2; Laos 0, Syria 9; Syria 3, Oman 3; Laos 2, Philippines 0; Oman 2, Syria 0; Philippines 1, Laos 1.

Group 2: Guam, Iran, Tajikistan.
Iran 19, Guam 0; Tajikistan 16, Guam 0; Iran 2, Tajikistan 0.
(all ties played in Iran)

Group 3: Hong Kong, Malaysia, Palestine, Qatar.
Qatar 5, Malaysia 1; Hong Kong 1, Palestine 1; Palestine 1, Qatar 2; Malaysia 2, Hong Kong 0; Palestine 1, Malaysia 0; Qatar 2, Hong Kong 0; Palestine 1, Hong Kong 0; Malaysia 0, Qatar 0; Qatar 2, Palestine 1; Hong Kong 2, Malaysia 1; Hong Kong 0, Qatar 3; Malaysia 4, Palestine 3.

Group 4: Bahrain, Kuwait, Kyrgyzstan, Singapore.
Bahrain 1, Kuwait 2; Singapore 0, Kyrgyzstan 1; Bahrain 1, Kyrgyzstan 0; Kuwait 1, Singapore 1; Kyrgyzstan 0, Kuwait 3; Singapore 1, Bahrain 2; Kyrgyzstan 1, Bahrain 2; Singapore 0, Kuwait 1; Kuwait 2, Kyrgyzstan 0; Bahrain 2, Singapore 0; Kyrgyzstan 1, Singapore 1; Kuwait 0, Bahrain 1.

Group 5: Lebanon, Pakistan, Sri Lanka, Thailand.
Thailand 4, Sri Lanka 2; Lebanon 6, Pakistan 0; Thailand 3, Pakistan 0; Lebanon 4, Sri Lanka 0; Pakistan 3, Sri Lanka 1; Lebanon 1, Thailand 2; Pakistan 1, Lebanon 8; Sri Lanka 0, Thailand 3; Sri Lanka 0, Lebanon 5; Pakistan 0, Thailand 6; Sri Lanka 3, Pakistan 1; Thailand 2, Lebanon 2.

Group 6: Iraq, Kazakhstan, Macao, Nepal.
Nepal 0, Kazakhstan 6; Iraq 8, Macao 0; Kazakhstan 3, Macao 0; Nepal 1, Iraq 9; Nepal 4, Macao 1; Kazakhstan 1, Iraq 1; Kazakhstan 4, Nepal 0; Macao 0, Iraq 5; Macao 0, Kazakhstan 5; Iraq 4, Nepal 2; Macao 1, Nepal 6; Iraq 1, Kazakhstan 1.

Group 7: Uzbekistan, Jordan, Turkmenistan, Taiwan.
Turkmenistan 2, Jordan 0; Uzbekistan 7, Taiwan 0; Taiwan 0, Jordan 2; Uzbekistan 1, Turkmenistan 0; Taiwan 0, Turkmenistan 5; Uzbekistan 2, Jordan 2; Jordan 6, Taiwan 0; Turkmenistan 2, Uzbekistan 5; Taiwan 0, Uzbekistan 4; Jordan 1, Turkmenistan 2; Turkmenistan 1, Taiwan 0; Jordan 1, Uzbekistan 1.

Group 8: Brunei, India, UAE, Yemen.
Brunei 0, Yemen 5; India 1, UAE 0; Brunei 0, UAE 12; India 1, Yemen 1; UAE 1, India 0; Yemen 1, Brunei 0; Yemen 3, India 3; UAE 4, Brunei 0; Yemen 2, UAE 1; Brunei 0, India 1; UAE 3, Yemen 2; India 5, Brunei 0.

Group 9: Cambodia, China, Indonesia, Maldives.
Maldives 6, Cambodia 0; Indonesia 5, Maldives 0; Cambodia 1, Maldives 1; China 10, Maldives 1; Indonesia 6, Cambodia 0; Maldives 0, China 1; Cambodia 0, Indonesia 2; Cambodia 0, China 4; Maldives 0, Indonesia 2; China 5, Indonesia 1; China 3, Cambodia 1; Indonesia 0, China 2.

Group 10: Bangladesh, Mongolia, Saudi Arabia, Vietnam.
Vietnam 0, Bangladesh 0; Saudi Arabia 6, Mongolia 0; Mongolia 0, Vietnam 1; Bangladesh 0, Saudi Arabia 3; Mongolia 0, Bangladesh 3; Saudi Arabia 5, Vietnam 0; Mongolia 0, Saudi Arabia 6; Bangladesh 0, Vietnam 4; Vietnam 4, Mongolia 0; Saudi Arabia 6, Bangladesh 0; Bangladesh 2, Mongolia 2; Vietnam 0, Saudi Arabia 4.

Second Round
Group A: Iraq 4, Thailand 0; Saudi Arabia 1, Bahrain 1; Bahrain 2, Iraq 2; Saudi Arabia 0; Saudi Arabia 1, Iraq 0; Thailand 0, Iran 0; Bahrain 1, Thailand 1; Iraq 1, Iran 2; Iran 0, Bahrain 0; Thailand 1, Saudi Arabia 3; Bahrain 0, Saudi Arabia 4; Thailand 1, Iraq 1; Iraq 1, Saudi Arabia 2; Iran 1, Thailand 0; Iraq 1, Saudi Arabia 2; Iran 2, Iraq 1; Thailand 1, Bahrain 1; Bahrain 3, Iran 1; Saudi Arabia 4, Thailand 1.

Group B: Qatar 0, Oman 0; UAE 4, Uzbekistan 1; China 3, UAE 0; Uzbekistan 2, Qatar 1; UAE 0, Qatar 2; Oman 0, China 2; Qatar 1, China 1; Uzbekistan 5, Oman 0; Oman 1, UAE 1; China 2, Uzbekistan 0; Oman 0, Qatar 3; Uzbekistan 0, UAE 1; UAE 0, China 1; Qatar 2, Uzbekistan 2; Qatar 1, UAE 2; China 1, Oman 0; Oman 4, Uzbekistan 2; China 3, Qatar 0; UAE 2, Oman 2; Uzbekistan 1, China 0.

Asian Play-offs: Iran 1, UAE 0; UAE 0, Iran 3.
Saudi Arabia and China qualified for finals.
Iran lost to Republic of Ireland in play-off.

CONCACAF
(Members 35, Entries 35)

Three teams qualified: Costa Rica, Mexico and the USA.

Caribbean Zone
First Round

Group 1: Barbados 2, Grenada 2; Grenada 2, Barbados 3; Cuba 4, Cayman Islands 0; Cayman Islands 0, Cuba 0; St Lucia 1, Surinam 0; Surinam 1, St Lucia 0 (Surinam won 3-1 on penalties); Aruba 4, Puerto Rico 2; Puerto Rico 4, Aruba 2.

Group 2: St Vincent & Grenadines 9, US Virgin Islands 0; US Virgin Islands 1, St Vincent & Grenadines 5; British Virgin Islands 1, Bermuda 5; Bermuda 9, British Virgin Islands 0; St Kitts & Nevis 8, Turks & Caicos Islands 0; Turks & Caicos Islands 0, St Kitts & Nevis 6; Guyana suspended, Antigua and Barbuda w.o.

Group 3: Trinidad & Tobago 5, Netherlands Antilles 0; Netherlands Antilles 1, Trinidad & Tobago 1; Anguilla 1, Bahamas 3; Bahamas 2, Anguilla 1; Dominican Republic 3, Montserrat 0; Montserrat 1, Dominican Republic 3; Haiti 4, Dominica 0; Dominica 1, Haiti 3.

Caribbean Zone
Second Round

Group 1: Cuba 1, Surinam 0; Surinam 0, Cuba 0; Aruba 1, Barbados 3; Barbados 4, Aruba 0.

Group 2: St Vincent & the Grenadines 1, St Kitts & Nevis 0; St Kitts & Nevis 1, St Vincent & the Grenadines 2; Antigua & Barbuda 0, Bermuda 0; Bermuda 1, Antigua & Barbuda 1.

Group 3: Trinidad & Tobago 3, Dominican Republic 0; Dominican Republic 0, Trinidad & Tobago 1; Haiti 9, Bahamas 0; Bahamas 0, Haiti 4.

Caribbean Zone Finals

Group 1: Cuba 1, Barbados 1, Barbados 1, Cuba 1 (*Barbados won 5-4 on penalties*).

Group 2: Antigua & Barbuda 2, St Vincent & the Grenadines 1; St Vincent & the Grenadines 4, Antigua & Barbuda 0.

Group 3: Trinidad & Tobago 3, Haiti 1; Haiti 1, Trinidad & Tobago 1.

Central American Zone

Group A: El Salvador 5, Belize 0; Belize 1, Guatemala 2; Guatemala 0, El Salvador 1; Belize 1, El Salvador 3; El Salvador 1, Guatemala 1; Guatemala 0, Belize 0.

Group B: Honduras 3, Nicaragua 0; Nicaragua 0, Panama 2; Panama 1, Honduras 0; Nicaragua 0, Honduras 1; Honduras 3, Panama 1; Panama 4, Nicaragua 0

Inter zone round
Group 1: Cuba 0, Canada 1; Canada 0, Cuba 0.

Group 2: Antigua & Barbuda 0, Guatemala 1; Guatemala 8, Antigua & Barbuda 1.

Group 3: Honduras 4, Haiti 0; Haiti 1, Honduras 3.

Semi-final Round
Costa Rica, Jamaica, Mexico and USA qualified.

Group C: Canada, Mexico, Panama, Trinidad & Tobago.

Canada 0, Trinidad & Tobago 2; Panama 0, Mexico 1; Panama 0, Canada 0; Trinidad & Tobago 1, Mexico 0; Mexico 2, Canada 0; Trinidad & Tobago 6, Panama 0; Mexico 7, Panama 1; Trinidad & Tobago 4, Canada 0; Mexico 7, Trinidad & Tobago 0; Canada 1, Panama 0; Canada 0, Mexico 0; Panama 0, Trinidad & Tobago 1.

Group D: El Salvador, Honduras, Jamaica, St Vincent & the Grenadines.

El Salvador 2, Honduras 5; St Vincent & the Grenadines 0, Jamaica 1; El Salvador 7, St Vincent & the Grenadines 1; Jamaica 3, Honduras 1; Honduras 6, St Vincent & the Grenadines 0; Jamaica 1, El Salvador 0; Honduras 5, El Salvador 0; Jamaica 2, St Vincent & the Grenadines 0; Honduras 1, Jamaica 0; St Vincent & the Grenadines 1, El Salvador 2; St Vincent & the Grenadines 0, Honduras 7; El Salvador 2, Jamaica 0.

Group E: Barbados, Costa Rica, Guatemala, USA.

Barbados 2, Costa Rica 1; Guatemala 1, USA 1; Guatemala 2, Barbados 0; Costa Rica 2, USA 1; Costa Rica 2, Guatemala 1; USA 7, Barbados 0; Costa Rica 3, Barbados 0; USA 1, Guatemala 0; Barbados 1, Guatemala 3; USA 0, Costa Rica 0; Barbados 0, USA 4; Guatemala 2, Costa Rica 1.

Play-off: Costa Rica 5, Guatemala 0.

Final Round: Costa Rica, Honduras, Jamaica, Mexico, Trinidad & Tobago, USA.

USA 2, Mexico 0; Jamaica 1, Trinidad & Tobago 0; Costa Rica 2, Honduras 2; Mexico 4, Jamaica 0; Costa Rica 3, Trinidad & Tobago 0; Honduras 1, USA 2; Jamaica 1, Honduras 1; Trinidad & Tobago 1, Mexico 1; USA 1, Costa Rica 0; Mexico 1, Costa Rica 2; Trinidad & Tobago 2, Honduras 4; Jamaica 0, USA 2; Trinidad & Tobago 0; Honduras 3, Mexico 1; Costa Rica 2, Jamaica 1; Trinidad & Tobago 1, Jamaica 2; Mexico 1, USA 0; Honduras 2, Costa Rica 3; Trinidad & Tobago 0, Costa Rica 2; USA 2, Honduras 3; Jamaica 1, Mexico 2; Costa Rica 2, USA 0; Honduras 1, Jamaica 0; Mexico 3, Trinidad & Tobago 0; Costa Rica 0, Mexico 0; Honduras 0, Trinidad & Tobago 1; USA 2, Jamaica 1; Jamaica 0, Costa Rica 1; Mexico 3, Honduras 0; Trinidad & Tobago 0, USA 0.

Costa Rica, Mexico and USA qualified.

AFRICA
(Members 52, Entries 50)

Five teams qualified: Cameroon, Nigeria, Senegal, South Africa and Tunisia.

First Round

Group A: Mauritania 1, Tunisia 2; Tunisia 3, Mauritania 0; Guinea Bissau 0, Togo 0; Togo 3, Guinea Bissau 0; Benin 1, Senegal 1; Senegal 1, Benin 0; Cape Verde Islands 0, Algeria 0; Algeria 4, Cape Verde Islands 0; Gambia 0, Morocco 1; Morocco 2, Gambia 0.

Group B: Botswana 0, Zambia 1; Zambia 1, Botswana 0; Madagascar 2, Gabon 0; Gabon 1, Madagascar 0; Lesotho 0, South Africa 2; South Africa 1, Lesotho 0; Sudan 1, Mozambique 0; Mozambique 2, Sudan 1; Swaziland 0, Angola 1; Angola 7, Swaziland 1.

Group C: Sao Tome e Principe 2, Sierra Leone 0; Sierra Leone 4, Sao Tome e Principe 0; Central African Republic 0, Zimbabwe 3; Zimbabwe 3, Central African Republic 1; Equatorial Guinea 1, Congo 3; Congo 2, Equatorial Guinea 1; Libya 3, Mali 0; Mali 3, Libya 1; Rwanda 2, Ivory Coast 2; Ivory Coast 2, Rwanda 0.

Group D: Djibouti 1, Congo DR 1; Congo DR 9, Djibouti 1; Seychelles 1, Namibia 1; Namibia 3, Seychelles 0; Eritrea 0, Nigeria 0; Nigeria 4, Eritrea 0; Mauritius 0, Egypt 2; Egypt 4, Mauritius 0; Somalia 0, Cameroon 3; Cameroon 3, Somalia 0.

Group E: Malawi 2, Kenya 0; Kenya v Malawi abandoned 0-0 after 88 minutes; result stands; Tanzania 0, Ghana 1; Ghana 3, Tanzania 2; Uganda 4, Guinea 4; Guinea 3, Uganda 0; Chad 0, Liberia 1; Liberia 0, Chad 0; Ethiopia 2, Burkina Faso 1; Burkina Faso 3, Ethiopia 0.

Second Round

Group A: Angola, Cameroon, Libya, Togo, Zambia.

Angola 2, Zambia 1; Libya 0, Cameroon 3; Zambia 2, Togo 0; Cameroon 3, Angola 0; Angola 3, Libya 1; Togo 0, Cameroon 2; Libya 3, Togo 1; Cameroon 1, Zambia 0; Zambia 2, Libya 0; Togo 1, Angola 1; Cameroon 1, Libya 0; Togo 3, Zambia 2; Angola 2, Cameroon 0; Libya 1, Angola 1; Cameroon 2, Togo 0; Zambia 2, Cameroon 2; Togo 2, Libya 0; Libya 2, Zambia 4; Angola 1, Togo 1.
Cameroon qualified for finals.

Group B: Ghana, Liberia, Nigeria, Sierra Leone, Sudan.

Nigeria 3, Sierra Leone 0; Sudan 2, Liberia 0; Ghana 5, Sierra Leone 0; Liberia 2, Nigeria 1; Nigeria 3, Sudan 0;

Salvador 0; Jamaica 2, St Vincent & the Grenadines 0; Honduras 1, Jamaica 0; St Vincent & the Grenadines 1, El Salvador 2; St Vincent & the Grenadines 0, Honduras 7; El Salvador 2, Jamaica 0.

Ghana 1, Liberia 3; Sudan 1, Ghana 0; Liberia 1, Sierra Leone 0; Sierra Leone 0, Sudan 2; Ghana 0, Nigeria 0; Sierra Leone 1, Nigeria 0; Liberia 2, Sudan 0; Sierra Leone 1, Ghana 1; Nigeria 2, Liberia 0; Nigeria 4; Liberia 1, Ghana 2; Sierra Leone 0, Liberia 1; Ghana 1, Sudan 0; Nigeria 3, Ghana 0; Sudan 3, Sierra Leone 0.
Nigeria qualified for finals.

Group C: Algeria, Egypt, Morocco, Namibia, Senegal.

Algeria 1, Senegal 1; Namibia 0, Morocco 0; Morocco 2, Algeria 1; Senegal 0, Egypt 0; Algeria 1, Namibia 0; Egypt 0, Morocco 0; Namibia 1, Egypt 1; Morocco 0, Senegal 0; Senegal 4, Namibia 0; Egypt 5, Algeria 2; Senegal 3, Algeria 0; Morocco 3, Namibia 0; Algeria 1, Morocco 2; Egypt 1, Senegal 0; Morocco 1, Egypt 0; Namibia 0, Algeria 4; Egypt 8, Namibia 2; Senegal 1, Morocco 0; Algeria 1, Egypt 1; Namibia 0, Senegal 5.
Senegal qualified for finals.

Group D: Congo, Congo DR, Ivory Coast, Madagascar, Tunisia.

Ivory Coast 2, Tunisia 2; Madagascar 3, Congo DR 0; Tunisia 1, Madagascar 0; Congo DR 2, Congo 0; Congo 1, Tunisia 2; Madagascar 1, Ivory Coast 3; Tunisia 6, Congo DR 0; Congo DR 1, Ivory Coast 2; Congo DR 1, Madagascar 0; Ivory Coast 2, Congo 0; Congo 2, Madagascar 0; Madagascar 0, Tunisia 2; Congo 1, Congo DR 1; Tunisia 6, Congo 0; Ivory Coast 1, Tunisia 6, Congo 0; Ivory Coast 6, Madagascar 0; Congo 1, Ivory Coast 1; Congo DR 0, Tunisia 3; Ivory Coast 1, Congo DR 2; Madagascar 1, Congo 0.
Tunisia qualified for finals.

Group E: Burkina Faso, Guinea*, Malawi, South Africa, Zimbabwe.

Malawi 1, Burkina Faso 1; Guinea 3, Zimbabwe 0; Burkina Faso 2, Guinea 3; Zimbabwe 0, South Africa 2 (abandoned 82 minutes; result stands); South Africa 1, Burkina Faso 0; Guinea 1, Malawi 1; Burkina Faso 1, Zimbabwe 0; Malawi 1, South Africa 2; Zimbabwe 2, Malawi 0; Burkina Faso 4, Malawi 2; South Africa 2, Zimbabwe 1; Burkina Faso 1, South Africa 1; South Africa 2, Malawi 0; Zimbabwe 1, Burkina Faso 0; Malawi 0, Zimbabwe 0.
Guinea subsequently suspended; results expunged.
South Africa qualified for finals.

WORLD CUP FINALS REVIEW

It would be extremely churlish to say that the World Cup finals in South Korea and Japan were dull and boring. There was no feeling of ennui, but once the shocks and upsets were taken out, the standard of football which remained was disappointing.

Much of this was due to the below performances of three of the favourites, Argentina, France and Italy, the first two named even failing to survive their groups. Yet Germany with what was universally considered to be their poorest World Cup squad, managed to reach the final itself.

The two most pleasant surprises were South Korea and Turkey who appropriately enough reached the semi-finals and then disputed third place between themselves. The Koreans, most of whom were locally based, surprised everyone and their Dutch coach Guus Hiddink was arguably the tournament's most shrewd manager.

Other surprise early exits included Portugal and Poland in a group which stood on its head as the Koreans and the USA emerged into the second round. Russia missed out first time, but Mexico unexpectedly topped their section.

The Republic of Ireland gave a spirited display before failing with penalty kicks against Spain, those perennial underachievers and Senegal the early victors over France reached the quarter-finals though they should have lost to Uruguay at the group stage. Uruguay even gave them three goals start in what was the best game of the finals before drawing level and missing a chance to win.

The United States knocked Mexico out, Turkey beat Japan and England took full advantage of Denmark's defensive errors. Italy had chances to beat South Korea before losing in sudden death and all the time Germany and Brazil were still there.

However the Germans were fortunate to beat the USA 1-0 and after having two perfectly good goals ruled out, Spain were beaten in a penalty shoot-out by Korea. Turkey needed extra time to beat Senegal, who had flattered to deceive and England were unable to sufficiently trouble ten-man Brazil.

The final was more entertaining than expected. The Germans took the game initially to their opponents, who gradually imposed themselves on the game and scored twice through Ronaldo in the closing stages. Their coach Luiz Felipe Scolari had resurrected the team after an indifferent qualification in which three other coaches had been axed.

Unsavoury incidents were few and far between. However, the reaction of German manager Rudi Voller after Michael Ballack's yellow card preventing a possible South Korea attempt on goal in condoning the professional foul, was scarcely in the spirit of the game. It also kept the midfield player and match-winner out of the final because of a previous booking.

Also Rivaldo let himself down badly when in the group game with Turkey, he clutched his head when the ball had clearly been kicked against his leg. Hakan Unsal received a second caution for this and departed. The Brazilian was fined by FIFA.

Uruguay scored two of the best goals: by Rodriguez against Denmark and Diego Forlan against Senegal. Arguably the best save was Marcos' finger-tip onto the post from Oliver Neuville's blistering free-kick in the final itself.

Much criticism of assistant referees and occasionally of the man in charge. But Pierluigi Collina of Italy again demonstrated his prowess with an almost faultless control of the final.

Seventeen players received red cards: Diao (Senegal), Henry (France), Nastija Ceh (Slovenia), Paredes and Acuna (Paraguay), Alpay and Hakan Unsal (Turkey), Joao Pinto and Beto (Portugal), Jiayi (China), Suffo (Cameroon), Ramelow (Germany), Zivkovic (Croatia), Marquez (Mexico), Totti (Italy), Ronaldinho (Brazil) and Caniggia (Argentina) as a non-playing substitute!

Managers Jerzy Engel (Poland), Srecko Katanec (Slovenia), Bora Milutinovic (China), Victor Pua (Uruguay), Winfried Schafer (Cameroon), Jomo Sono (South Africa), Cesar Maldini (Paraguay) and Oleg Romantsev (Russia) either left their positions or were asked to go. Hiddink was expected to return to club football and Roger Lemarre (France) was another casualty of his team's failure. Others were likely to follow.

Milutinovic had become the first to coach different teams at five finals: Mexico 1986, Costa Rica 1990, USA 1994, Nigeria 1998 and China 2002.

Overall average attendance at 42,274 was the lowest since 1982 but was hampered by poor ticket distribution, the one black mark on an otherwise well-organised competition. A record world-wide TV audience of 45 billion was reported to have tuned in. The squad of the finals was announced before the last match as follows: Kahn (Germany), Rustu (Turkey); Alpay (Turkey), Campbell (England), Hierro (Spain), Hong (South Korea), Roberto Carlos (Brazil); Ballack (Germany), Reyna (USA), Rivaldo (Brazil), Ronaldinho (Brazil); Yoo (South Korea), Diouf (Senegal), Hasan Sas (Turkey), Klose (Germany), Ronaldo (Brazil).

After four years of World Cup frustration, Brazil's Ronaldo strikes for the second time in the match to win the World Cup Final against Germany. His eighth goal of the competition won him the Golden Boot. (Colorsport)

2002 WORLD CUP FINALS

GROUP A

Seoul, 31 May 2002, 62,561
France (0) 0
Senegal (1) 1 *(Diop PB 30)*
France: Barthez; Thuram, Lizarazu, Vieira, Leboeuf, Desailly, Wiltord (Cisse 80), Petit, Trezeguet, Henry, Djorkaeff (Dugarry 59).
Senegal: Sylva; Coly, Daf, Diao, Diatta, Diop PM, Ndiaye, Diop PB, Hadji Diouf, Cisse, Fadiga.
Referee: Bujsaim (UAE).

Ulsan, 1 June 2002, 30,157
Uruguay (0) 1 *(Rodriguez 47)*
Denmark (1) 2 *(Tomasson 45, 83)*
Uruguay: Carini; Mendez, Rodriguez (Magallanes 87), Garcia, Montero, Sorondo, Varela, Guigou, Abreu (Morales 88), Dario Silva, Recoba (Regueiro 80).
Denmark: Sorensen; Helveg, Heintze (Jensen N 58), Graversen, Laursen, Henriksen, Rommedahl, Tofting, Sand (Poulsen 89), Tomasson, Gronkjaer (Jorgensen 70).
Referee: Mane (Kuwait).

Daegu, 6 June 2002, 43,500
Denmark (1) 1 *(Tomasson 16 (pen))*
Senegal (0) 1 *(Diao 52)*
Denmark: Sorensen; Helveg, Heintze, Graversen (Poulsen 82), Laursen, Henriksen, Gronkjaer (Jorgensen 49), Tofting, Tomasson, Sand, Rommedahl (Lovenkrands 86).
Senegal: Sylva; Coly, Sarr (Camara S 46) (Beye 82), Diaye (Camara H 46), Diop PM, Diatta, Diao, Diop PB, Daf, Diouf, Fadiga.
Referee: Batres (Guatemala).

Busan, 6 June 2002, 38,070
France (0) 0
Uruguay (0) 0
France: Barthez; Thuram, Lizarazu, Petit, Leboeuf (Candela 16), Desailly, Wiltord (Dugarry 90), Vieira, Trezeguet (Cisse 81), Henry, Micoud.
Uruguay: Carini; Varela, Rodriguez (Guigou 73), Lembo, Sorondo, Montero, Romero (De Los Santos 71), Garcia, Dario Silva (Magallanes 60), Abreu, Recoba.
Referee: Rizo (Mexico).

Incheon, 11 June 2002, 48,100
Denmark (1) 2 *(Rommedahl 22, Tomasson 67)*
France (0) 0
Denmark: Sorensen; Helveg, Jensen N, Graversen, Laursen, Henriksen, Poulsen (Bogelund 75), Tofting (Steen-Nielsen 80), Tomasson, Jorgensen (Gronkjaer 46), Rommedahl.
France: Barthez; Candela, Lizarazu, Vieira (Micoud 71), Thuram, Desailly, Makelele, Wiltord (Djorkaeff 84), Trezeguet, Zidane, Dugarry (Cisse 54).
Referee: Pereira (Portugal).

Suwon, 11 June 2002, 33,681
Senegal (3) 3 *(Fadiga 20 (pen), Diop PB 26, 38)*
Uruguay (0) 3 *(Morales 46, Forlan 69, Recoba 88 (pen))*
Senegal: Sylva; Coly (Beye 63), Daf, Ndour (Faye 76), Diatta, Diop PM, Camara (Moussa Ndiaye 66), Cisse, Diouf, Diop PB, Fadiga.
Uruguay: Carini; Varela, Rodriguez, Lembo, Montero, Sorondo (Regueiro 31), Garcia, Romero (Forlan 46), Abreu (Morales 46), Dario Silva, Recoba.
Referee: Wegereef (Holland).

GROUP B

Busan, 2 June 2002, 25,186
Paraguay (1) 2 *(Santa Cruz 39, Arce 55)*
South Africa (0) 2 *(Struway 63 (og), Fortune 90 (pen))*
Paraguay: Tavarelli; Alvarenga (Gavilan 66), Arce, Ayala, Gamarra, Caniza, Struway (Franco 86), Acuna, Campos (Morinigo 72), Santa Cruz, Caceres.
South Africa: Arendse; Nzama, Carnell, Sibaya, Radebe, Issa (MacDonald 27), Mokoena T, Mokoena A, McCarthy (Koumantarakis 78), Zuma, Fortune.
Referee: Michel (Slovakia).

Gwangju, 2 June 2002, 25,598
Spain (1) 3 *(Raul 44, Valeron 74, Hierro 88 (pen))*
Slovenia (0) 1 *(Cimerotic 81)*
Spain: Casillas; Puyol, Juanfran (Romero 83), Baraja, Hierro, Nadal, Luis Enrique (Helguera 73), Valeron, Diego Tristan (Morientes 66), Raul, De Pedro.
Slovenia: Simeunovic; Novak (Gajser 77), Karic, Milinovic, Galic, Knavs, Ceh A, Pavlin, Osterc (Cimerotic 56), Rudonja, Zahovic (Acimovic 62).
Referee: Guezzaz (Morocco).

Jeonju, 7 June 2002, 24,000
Spain (0) 3 *(Morientes 53, 69, Hierro 83 (pen))*
Paraguay (1) 1 *(Puyol 10 (og))*
Spain: Casillas; Puyol, Juanfran, Baraja, Hierro, Nadal, Luis Enrique (Helguera 46), Valeron (Xavi 85), Diego Tristan (Morientes 46), Raul, De Pedro.
Paraguay: Chilavert; Arce, Caniza (Struway 78), Caceres, Ayala, Gamarra, Acuna, Paredes, Santa Cruz, Gavilan, Cardozo (Campos 63).
Referee: Ghandour (Egypt).

Daegu, 8 June 2002, 47,226
South Africa (1) 1 *(Nomvethe 4)*
Slovenia (0) 0
South Africa: Arendse; Nzama, Carnell, Sibaya, Mokoena A, Radebe, Zuma, Mokoena T, Nomvethe (Buckley 71), McCarthy (Koumantarakis 80), Fortune (Pule 83).
Slovenia: Simeunovic; Novak, Karic, Milinovic, Vugdalic, Knavs (Bulajic 60), Acimovic (Ceh N 60), Ceh A, Cimerotic (Osterc 41), Rudonja, Pavlin.
Referee: Sanchez (Argentina).

Seogwipo, 12 June 2002, 30,136
Slovenia (1) 1 *(Acimovic 45)*
Paraguay (0) 3 *(Cuevas 66, 84, Campos 73)*
Slovenia: Dabanovic; Bulajic, Tavcar, Ceh A, Milinovic, Karic, Novak, Pavlin (Rudonja 40), Cimirotic, Osterc (Tiganj 78), Acimovic (Ceh N 63).
Paraguay: Chilavert; Arce, Caniza, Caceres, Ayala, Gamarra, Paredes, Acuna, Cardozo (Cuevas 61) (Franco 90), Santa Cruz, Alvarenga (Campos 54).
Referee: Rizo (Mexico).

Daejeon, 12 June 2002, 31,024
Spain (2) 3 *(Raul 4, 56, Mendieta 45)*
South Africa (1) 2 *(McCarthy 31, Radebe 53)*
Spain: Casillas; Torres, Romero, Albelda, Helguera, Nadal, Joaquin, Xavi, Morientes (Luque 75), Raul (Luis Enrique 82), Mendieta.
South Africa: Arendse; Nzama, Carnell, Sibaya, Mokoena A, Radebe (Molefe 79), Zuma, Mokoena T, Nomvethe (Koumantarakis 74), McCarthy, Fortune (Lekgetho 83).
Referee: Mane (Kuwait).

Group A – Table	P	W	D	L	F	A	Pts
Denmark	3	2	1	0	5	2	7
Senegal	3	1	2	0	5	4	5
Uruguay	3	0	2	1	4	5	2
France	3	0	1	2	0	3	1

Group B – Table	P	W	D	L	F	A	Pts
Spain	3	3	0	0	9	4	9
Paraguay	3	1	1	1	6	6	4
South Africa	3	1	1	1	5	5	4
Slovenia	3	0	0	3	2	7	0

GROUP C

Ulsan, 3 June 2002, 33,842

Brazil (0) 2 *(Ronaldo 50, Rivaldo 87 (pen))*

Turkey (1) 1 *(Hasan Sas 45)*

Brazil: Marcos; Cafu, Roberto Carlos, Gilberto Silva, Edmilson, Lucio, Roque Junior, Juninho (Vampeta 73), Ronaldo (Luizao 73), Rivaldo, Ronaldinho (Denilson 67).
Turkey: Rustu; Alpay, Hakan Unsal, Tugay (Arif 88), Bulent K (Ilhan 65), Umit O, Fatih, Emre B, Hakan Sukur, Basturk (Umit D 65), Hasan Sas.
Referee: Young-joo (South Korea).

Gwangju, 4 June 2002, 27,217

China (0) 0

Costa Rica (0) 2 *(Gomez 61, Wright 65)*

China: Jin; Yunlong, Chengying, Xiaopeng, Zhiyi (Genwei 75), Weifeng, Jihai (Bo 26), Tie, Chen (Maozhen 65), Haidong, Mingyu.
Costa Rica: Lonnis; Wallace (Bryce 70), Castro, Marin, Wright, Martinez, Solis, Centeno, Wanchope (Lopez 80), Gomez, Fonseca (Medford 57).
Referee: Vassaras (Greece).

Seogwipo, 8 June 2002, 36,750

Brazil (3) 4 *(Roberto Carlos 15, Rivaldo 32, Ronaldinho 45 (pen), Ronaldo 55)*

China (0) 0

Brazil: Marcos; Cafu, Roberto Carlos, Lucio, Roque Junior, Anderson Polga, Gilberto Silva, Juninho (Ricardinho 70), Ronaldo (Edilson 71), Rivaldo, Ronaldinho (Denilson 46).
China: Jin; Yunlong, Chengying, Junzhe, Wei, Weifeng, Xiaopeng, Tie, Haidong (Bo 75), Hong (Jiayi 66), Mingyu (Pu 62).
Referee: Frisk (Sweden).

Incheon, 9 June 2002, 42,299

Costa Rica (0) 1 *(Parks 86)*

Turkey (0) 1 *(Emre B 56)*

Costa Rica: Lonnis; Wallace (Bryce 77), Castro, Martinez, Wright, Marin, Solis, Centeno (Medford 67), Wanchope, Lopez (Parks 77), Gomes.
Turkey: Rustu; Fatih, Ergun, Tugay (Arif 88), Umit O, Emre A, Umit D, Emre B, Basturk (Nihat 79), Hakan Sukur (Ilhan 75), Hakan Sas.
Referee: Codjia (Benin).

Suwon, 13 June 2002, 38,524

Costa Rica (1) 2 *(Wanchope 39, Gomez 56)*

Brazil (3) 5 *(Ronaldo 10, 13, Edmilson 38, Rivaldo 62, Junior 64)*

Costa Rica: Lonnis; Wallace (Bryce 46), Castro, Martinez (Parks 74), Wright, Marin, Solis (Fonseca 65), Lopez, Wanchope, Gomez, Centeno.
Brazil: Marcos; Cafu, Gilberto Silva, Lucio, Edmilson, Anderson Polga, Junior, Juninho (Ricardinho 60), Ronaldo, Rivaldo (Kaka 72), Edilson (Kleberson 57).
Referee: Ghandour (Egypt).

Seoul, 13 June 2002, 43,605

Turkey (2) 3 *(Hasan Sas 6, Bulent K 9, Umit D 85)*

China (0) 0

Turkey: Rustu (Catkic 35); Fatih, Hakan Unsal, Tugay (Havutgu 84), Bulent K, Emre A, Umit D, Emre B, Hasan Sas, Hakan Sukur, Basturk (Ilhan 70).
China: Jin; Yunlong, Chengying (Jiayi 46), Junzhe, Wei, Weifeng, Xiaopeng, Tie, Chen (Genwei 73), Haidong (Bo 73), Pu.
Referee: Ruiz (Colombia).

Group C – Table	P	W	D	L	F	A	Pts
Brazil	3	3	0	0	11	3	9
Turkey	3	1	1	1	5	3	4
Costa Rica	3	1	1	1	5	6	4
China	3	0	0	3	0	9	0

GROUP D

Busan, 4 June 2002, 55,982

South Korea (1) 2 *(Hwang SH 26, Yoo SC 53)*

Poland (0) 0

South Korea: Lee WJ; Song CG, Lee EY, Choi JC, Hong MB, Kim TY, Kim NI, Yoo SC (Lee CS 62), Park JS, Hwang SH (Ahn JH 50), Seol KH (Cha DR 90).
Poland: Dudek; Hajto, Michal Zewlakow, Kaluzny (Marcin Zewlakow 65), Bak J (Klos 51), Waldoch, Kozminski, Swierczewski, Olisadebe, Zurawski (Kryszalowicz 46), Krzynowek.
Referee: Ruiz (Colombia).

Suwon, 5 June 2002, 37,306

USA (3) 3 *(O'Brien 4, Jorge Costa 30 (og), McBride 36)*

Portugal (1) 2 *(Beto 40, Agoos 71 (og))*

USA: Friedel; Agoos, Sanneh, Beasley, Pope (Liamosa 79), Mastroeni, Hejduk, O'Brien, Stewart (Jones 46), McBride, Donovan (Moore 75).
Portugal: Vitor Baia; Jorge Costa (Andrade 73), Conceicao, Beto, Fernando Couto, Rui Jorge (Paulo Bento 68), Rui Costa, Petit, Joao Pinto, Pauleta, Figo.
Referee: Moreno (Ecuador).

Jeonju, 10 June 2002, 31,000

Portugal (1) 4 *(Pauleta 14, 65, 77, Rui Costa 87)*

Poland (0) 0

Portugal: Vitor Baia; Frechaut (Beto 63), Rui Jorge, Petit, Fernando Couto, Jorge Costa, Conceicao (Capucho 69), Paulo Bento, Pauleta, Joao Pinto (Rui Costa 60), Figo.
Poland: Dudek; Kozminski, Kaluzny (Bak A 16), Krzynowek, Hajto, Waldoch, Zurawski (Marcin Zewlakow 56), Swierczewski, Kryszalowicz, Olisadebe, Michal Zewlakow (Rzasa 71).
Referee: Dallas (Scotland).

Daegu, 10 June 2002, 60,778

South Korea (0) 1 *(Ahn JH 79)*

USA (1) 1 *(Mathis 24)*

South Korea: Lee WJ; Song CG, Park JS (Lee CS 37), Choi JC, Hong MB, Kim TY, Kim NI, Yoo SC (Choi YS 69), Seol KH, Hwang SH (Ahn JH 55), Lee EY.
USA: Friedel; Sanneh, Hejduk, Reyna, Pope, Agoos, Donovan, O'Brien, Mathis (Wolff 82), McBride, Beasley (Lewis 74).
Referee: Meier (Switzerland).

Daejon, 14 June 2002, 26,482

Poland (2) 3 *(Olisadebe 3, Kryszalowicz 5, Marcin Zewlakow 66)*

USA (0) 1 *(Donovan 83)*

Poland: Majdan; Klos (Waldoch 89), Kozminski, Kucharski (Marcin Zewlakow 65) Glowacki, Zielinski, Zurawski, Murawski, Kryszalowicz, Olisadebe (Sibik 86), Krzynowek.
USA: Friedel; Sanneh, Hejduk, Reyna, Pope, Agoos (Beasley 36), Mathis, Stewart (Jones 68), McBride (Moore 58), Donovan, O'Brien.
Referee: Lu (China).

Incheon, 14 June 2002, 50,239

Portugal (0) 0

South Korea (0) 1 *(Park JS 70)*

Portugal: Vitor Baia; Beto, Rui Jorge (Xavier 73), Petit (Gomes 77), Fernando Couto, Jorge Costa, Conceicao, Paulo Bento, Joao Pinto (Andrade 68), Pauleta, Figo.
South Korea: Lee WJ; Yoo SC, Lee YP, Song CG, Choi JC, Hong MB, Kim TY, Kim NI, Park JS, Seol KH, Ahn JH (Lee CS 90).
Referee: Sanchez (Argentina).

Group D – Table	P	W	D	L	F	A	Pts
South Korea	3	2	1	0	4	1	7
USA	3	1	1	1	5	6	4
Portugal	3	1	0	2	6	4	3
Poland	3	1	0	2	3	7	3

GROUP E

Sapporo, 1 June 2002, 32,218

Germany (4) 8 *(Klose 20, 25, 69, Ballack 40, Jancker 45, Linke 73, Bierhoff 84, Schneider 90)*

Saudi Arabia (0) 0

Germany: Kahn; Frings, Ziege, Hamann, Metzelder, Ramelow (Jeremies 46), Linke, Schneider, Jancker (Bierhoff 67), Klose (Neuville 77), Ballack.
Saudi Arabia: Al-Deayea; Tukar, Ahmed Al-Dossari, Zubromawi, Noor, Sulimani, Abdullah Al-Shahrani, Khamis Al-Dossari (Ibrahim Al-Shahrani 46), Temyat (Al-Khathran 46), Al-Jaber, Al-Yami (Abdallah Al-Dossari 77).
Referee: Aquino (Paraguay).

Niigata, 1 June 2002, 33,679

Republic of Ireland (0) 1 *(Holland 52)*

Cameroon (1) 1 *(Mboma 39)*

Republic of Ireland: Given; Kelly G, Harte (Reid 77), Breen, Staunton, Kinsella, McAteer (Finnan 46), Holland, Robbie Keane, Duff, Kilbane.
Cameroon: Alioum; Geremi, Wome, Kalla, Song, Tchato, Lauren, Foe, Mboma (Suffo 69), Eto'o, Olembe.
Referee: Kamikawa (Japan).

Ibaraki, 5 June 2002, 35,854

Germany (1) 1 *(Klose 19)*

Republic of Ireland (0) 1 *(Robbie Keane 90)*

Germany: Kahn; Frings, Ziege, Linke, Ramelow, Metzelder, Schneider (Jeremies 90), Hamann, Klose (Bode 86), Jancker (Bierhoff 74), Ballack.
Republic of Ireland: Given; Kelly G (Quinn 72), Harte (Reid 72), Breen, Staunton (Cunningham 88), Kinsella, Finnan, Holland, Robbie Keane, Kilbane, Duff.
Referee: Nielsen (Denmark).

Saitama, 6 June 2002, 52,328

Cameroon (0) 1 *(Eto'o 65)*

Saudi Arabia (0) 0

Cameroon: Alioum; Wome (Njanka 80), Kalla, Foe, Song, Tchato, Geremi, Lauren, Eto'o, Mboma (Ndiefi 63), Ngom Kome (Olembe 46).
Saudi Arabia: Al-Deayea; Al-Shehri, Temyat, Al-Jahani, Tukar, Zubromawi (Abdullah Al-Dossari 62), Ibrahim Al-Shahrani, Sulimani, Obeid Al-Dossari (Al-Yami 35), Abdullah Al-Shahrani, Al-Khathran (Noor 81).
Referee: Hauge (Norway).

Shizuoka, 11 June 2002, 47,085

Cameroon (0) 0

Germany (0) 2 *(Bode 50, Klose 79)*

Cameroon: Alioum; Wome, Kalla, Foe, Song, Tchato (Suffo 53), Geremi, Lauren, Eto'o, Mboma (Job 80), Olembe (Kome 64).
Germany: Kahn; Ramelow, Frings, Linke, Metzelder, Ziege, Schneider (Jeremies 80), Hamann, Jancker (Bode 46), Klose (Neuville 84), Ballack.
Referee: Nieto (Spain).

Yokohama, 11 June 2002, 65,320

Saudi Arabia (0) 0

Republic of Ireland (1) 3 *(Robbie Keane 7, Breen 61, Duff 87)*

Saudi Arabia: Al-Deayea; Al-Jahani (Ahmed Al-Dossari 78), Sulimani, Tukar, Zubromawi (Abdullah Al-Dossari 67), Al-Shehri, Ibrahim Al-Shahrani, Al-Temyat, Al-Yami, Khamis Al-Dossari, Al-Khathran (Al-Shalhoub 66).
Republic of Ireland: Given; Finnan, Harte (Quinn 46), Kinsella (Carsley 88), Breen, Staunton, Kelly G (McAteer 79), Holland, Robbie Keane, Kilbane, Duff.
Referee: Ndoye (Senegal).

GROUP F

Ibaraki, 2 June 2002, 34,050

Argentina (0) 1 *(Batistuta 63)*

Nigeria (0) 0

Argentina: Cavallero; Zanetti, Sorin, Pochettino, Samuel, Placente, Simeone, Ortega, Veron (Aimar 78), Batistuta (Crespo 81), Lopez C (Kily Gonzalez 46).
Nigeria: Shorunmu; Sodje (Christopher 73), Babayaro, Yobo, West, Okoronkwo, Okocha, Kanu (Ikedia 48), Ogbeche, Aghahowa, Lawal.
Referee: Veissiere (France).

Saitama, 2 June 2002, 52,271

England (1) 1 *(Campbell 24)*

Sweden (0) 1 *(Alexandersson 59)*

England: Seaman; Mills, Ashley Cole, Scholes, Campbell, Ferdinand, Beckham (Dyer 63), Hargreaves, Vassell (Cole J 73), Owen, Heskey.
Sweden: Hedman; Mellberg, Lucic, Linderoth, Mjallby, Jakobsson, Alexandersson, Ljungberg, Allback (Andersson A 80), Larsson, Magnus Svensson (Svensson A 55).
Referee: Simon (Brazil).

Sapporo, 7 June 2002, 35,927

Argentina (0) 0

England (1) 1 *(Beckham 44 (pen))*

Argentina: Cavallero; Zanetti, Kily Gonzalez (Lopez C 65), Pochettino, Samuel, Placente, Simeone, Veron (Aimar 46), Batistuta (Crespo 59), Ortega, Sorin.
England: Seaman; Mills, Ashley Cole, Butt, Campbell, Ferdinand, Beckham, Scholes, Heskey (Sheringham 55), Owen (Bridge 80), Hargreaves (Sinclair 19).
Referee: Collina (Italy).

Kobe, 7 June 2002, 36,194

Sweden (1) 2 *(Larsson 35, 62 (pen))*

Nigeria (1) 1 *(Aghahowa 27)*

Sweden: Hedman; Mellberg, Lucic, Linderoth, Mjallby, Jakobsson, Alexandersson, Svensson A (Magnus Svensson 84), Allback (Andersson A 64), Larsson, Ljungberg.
Nigeria: Shorunmu; Yobo, Udeze, Okocha, West, Okoronkwo, Christopher, Utaka, Ogbeche (Ikedia 71), Aghahowa, Babayaro (Kanu 66).
Referee: Ortube (Bolivia).

Miyagi, 12 June 2002, 45,777

Argentina (0) 1 *(Crespo 88)*

Sweden (0) 1 *(Svensson A 59)*

Argentina: Cavallero; Sorin (Veron 63), Almeyda (Kily Gonzalez 63), Pochettino, Samuel, Chamot, Aimar, Zanetti, Batistuta (Crespo 58), Lopez C, Ortega.
Sweden: Hedman; Lucic, Jakobsson, Linderoth, Mellberg, Mjallby, Alexandersson, Magnus Svensson, Allback (Andersson A 46), Larsson (Ibrahimovic 88), Svensson A (Jonsson 68).
Referee: Bujsaim (UAE).

Osaka, 12 June 2002, 44,864

Nigeria (0) 0

England (0) 0

Nigeria: Enyeama; Sodje, Udeze, Christopher, Yobo, Okoronkwo, Okocha, Obiorah, Aghahowa, Akwuegbu, Opabunmi (Ikedia 86).
England: Seaman; Mills, Ashley Cole (Bridge 85), Butt, Campbell, Ferdinand, Beckham, Scholes, Heskey (Sheringham 69), Owen (Vassell 77), Sinclair.
Referee: Hall (USA).

Group E – Table	P	W	D	L	F	A	Pts
Germany	3	2	1	0	11	1	7
Republic of Ireland	3	1	2	0	5	2	5
Cameroon	3	1	1	1	2	3	4
Saudi Arabia	3	0	0	3	0	12	0

Group F – Table	P	W	D	L	F	A	Pts
Sweden	3	1	2	0	4	3	5
England	3	1	2	0	2	1	5
Argentina	3	1	1	1	2	2	4
Nigeria	3	0	1	2	1	3	1

GROUP G

Niigata, 3 June 2002, 32,239

Croatia (0) 0

Mexico (0) 1 *(Blanco 60 (pen))*

Croatia: Pletikosa; Zivkovic, Soldo, Kovac R, Simunic, Jarni, Tomas, Prosinecki (Rapaic 46), Suker (Saric 64), Boksic (Stanic 67), Kovac N.
Mexico: Perez; Mercado, Luna, Vidrio, Marquez, Carmona, Caballero, Torrado, Blanco (Palencia 79), Borgetti (Hernandez 68), Morales.
Referee: Jun Lu (China).

Sapporo, 3 June 2002, 31,081

Italy (2) 2 *(Vieri 7, 27)*

Ecuador (0) 0

Italy: Buffon; Panucci, Maldini, Tommasi, Nesta, Cannavaro, Zambrotta, Di Biagio (Gattuso 70), Totti (Del Piero 74), Vieri, Doni (Di Livio 65).
Ecuador: Cevallos; De la Cruz, Guerron, Tenorio E (Ayovi M 60), Hurtado I, Porozo, Chala, Obregon, Aguinaga (Tenorio C 46), Delgado, Mendez.
Referee: Hall (USA).

Ibaraki, 8 June 2002, 36,472

Italy (0) 1 *(Vieri 55)*

Croatia (0) 2 *(Olic 73, Rapaic 76)*

Italy: Buffon; Panucci, Maldini, Tommasi, Nesta (Materazzi 24), Cannavaro, Zambrotta, Zanetti, Vieri, Totti, Doni (Inzaghi 79).
Croatia: Pletikosa; Saric, Jarni, Tomas, Kovac R, Simunic, Kovac N, Soldo (Vranjes 63), Boksic, Vugrinec (Olic 57), Rapaic (Simic 79).
Referee: Poll (England).

Miyagi, 9 June 2002, 45,610

Mexico (1) 2 *(Borgetti 28, Torrado 57)*

Ecuador (1) 1 *(Delgado 5)*

Mexico: Perez; Vidrio, Morales, Rodriguez (Cabellero 86), Marquez, Carmona, Arellano, Torrado, Borgetti (Hernandez 76), Blanco (Mercado 90), Luna.
Ecuador: Cevallos; De la Cruz, Guerron, Mendez, Hurtado I, Poroso, Obregon (Aguinaga 58), Tenorio E (Ayovi M 34), Delgado, Kaviedes (Tenorio C 48), Chala.
Referee: Daami (Tunisia).

Yokohama, 13 June 2002, 65,862

Ecuador (0) 1 *(Mendez 48)*

Croatia (0) 0

Ecuador: Cevallos; De la Cruz, Guerron, Ayovi M, Hurtado I, Porozo, Mendez, Obregon (Aguinaga 40), Tenorio C (Kaviedes 75), Delgado, Chala.
Croatia: Pletikosa; Saric (Stanic 67), Jarni, Simic (Vugrinec 52), Kovac N (Vranjes 59), Simunic, Tomas, Rapaic, Olic, Boksic, Kovac R.
Referee: Mattus (Costa Rica).

Oita, 13 June 2002, 39,291

Mexico (1) 1 *(Borgetti 34)*

Italy (0) 1 *(Del Piero 85)*

Mexico: Perez; Arellano, Morales (Garcia 75), Vidrio, Marquez, Carmona, Rodriguez (Caballero 75), Torrado, Borgetti (Palencia 80), Blanco, Luna.
Italy: Buffon; Zambrotta, Panucci (Coco 63), Cannavaro, Nesta, Maldini, Tomassi, Zanetti, Vieri, Totti (Del Piero 78), Inzaghi (Montella 56).
Referee: Simon (Brazil).

Group G – Table	P	W	D	L	F	A	Pts
Mexico	3	2	1	0	4	2	7
Italy	3	1	1	1	4	3	4
Croatia	3	1	0	2	2	3	3
Ecuador	3	1	0	2	2	4	3

GROUP H

Saitama, 4 June 2002, 55,256

Japan (0) 2 *(Suzuki 59, Inamoto 69)*

Belgium (0) 2 *(Wilmots 57, Van der Heyden 75)*

Japan: Narazaki; Ichikawa, Ono (Alex 64), Matsuda, Morioka (Miyamoto 72), Nakata K, Inamoto, Toda, Suzuki (Morishima 70), Yanagisawa, Nakata H.
Belgium: De Vlieger; Peeters, Goor, Van Buyten, Van Meir, Van der Heyden, Vanderhaeghe, Simons, Wilmots, Verheyen (Strupar 83), Walem (Sonck 70).
Referee: Vega (Costa Rica).

Kobe, 5 June 2002, 30,957

Russia (0) 2 *(Titov 59, Karpin 64 (pen))*

Tunisia (0) 0

Russia: Nigmatullin; Solomatin, Izmailov (Alenichev 78), Kovtun, Onopko, Nikiforov, Semshov (Khokhlov 78), Karpin, Bestchastnykh (Sychev 55), Pimenov, Titov.
Tunisia: Boumnijel; Badra (Zitouni 84), Jaidi, Mkacher, Trabelsi, Bouzaiane, Gabsi (Mhadhebi 67), Bouazizi, Jaziri, Sellimi (Baya 67), Achour.
Referee: Prendergast (Jamaica).

Yokohama, 9 June 2002, 66,108

Japan (0) 1 *(Inamoto 51)*

Russia (0) 0

Japan: Narazaki; Myojin, Ono (Hattori 75), Matsuda, Miyamoto, Nakata K, Toda, Nakata H, Suzuki (Nakayana 72), Yanagisawa, Inamoto (Fukunishi 85).
Russia: Nigmatullin; Solomatin, Semshov, Sonck, Nikiforov, Onopko, Karpin, Smertin (Bestchastnykh 57), Izmailov (Khokhlov 52), Pimenov (Sychev 46), Titov.
Referee: Merk (Germany).

Oita, 10 June 2002, 37,900

Tunisia (1) 1 *(Bouzaine 17)*

Belgium (1) 1 *(Wilmots 13)*

Tunisia: Boumnijel; Trabelsi, Bouzaine, Ghodhbane, Jaidi, Badra, Gabsi (Sellini 67), Bouazizi, Jaziri (Zitouni 78), Ben Achour, Melki (Baya 89).
Belgium: De Vlieger; Deflandre, Van der Heyden, Simons (Mpenza M 74), De Boeck, Van Buyten, Vanderhaeghe, Goor, Wilmots, Strupar (Sonck 46), Verheyen (Vermant 46).
Referee: Shield (Australia).

Shizuoka, 14 June 2002, 46,640

Belgium (1) 3 *(Walem 7, Sonck 78, Wilmots 82)*

Russia (0) 2 *(Bestchastnykh 52, Sychev 88)*

Belgium: De Vlieger; Peeters, Van Kerckhoven, Walem, De Boeck (Van Meir 90), Van Buyten, Mpenza M (Sonck 71), Vanderhaeghe, Verheyen (Simons 79), Wilmots, Goor.
Russia: Nigmatullin; Karpin (Kerzhakov 83), Alenichev, Nikiforov (Sennikov 44), Onopko, Kovtun, Solomatin, Smertin (Sychev 35), Khokhlov, Bestchastnykh, Titov.
Referee: Nielsen (Denmark).

Osaka, 14 June 2002, 45,213

Tunisia (0) 0

Japan (0) 2 *(Morishima 48, Nakata H 75)*

Tunisia: Boumnijel; Badra, Jaidi, Bouazizi, Trabelsi, Bouzaiane (Zitouni 77), Clayton (Mhadhebi 60), Ben Achour, Jaziri, Jhodhbane, Melki (Baya 46).
Japan: Narazaki; Myojin, Ono, Matsuda, Miyamoto, Nakata K, Inamoto (Ichikawa 46), Toda, Suzuki, Yanagisawa (Morishima 46), Nakata H (Ogasawara 84).
Referee: Veissiere (France).

Group H – Table	P	W	D	L	F	A	Pts
Japan	3	2	1	0	5	2	7
Belgium	3	1	2	0	6	5	5
Russia	3	1	0	2	4	4	3
Tunisia	3	0	1	2	1	5	1

SECOND ROUND

Niigata, 15 June 2002, 40,582
Denmark (0) 0
England (3) 3 *(Ferdinand 5, Owen 22, Heskey 44)*
Denmark: Sorensen; Helveg (Bogelund 7), Jensen N, Gravesen, Laursen, Henriksen, Rommedahl, Tofting (Jensen C 58), Sand, Tomasson, Gronkjaer.
England: Seaman; Mills, Ashley Cole, Butt, Campbell, Ferdinand, Beckham, Scholes (Dyer 49), Heskey (Sheringham 69), Owen (Fowler 46), Sinclair.
Referee: Merk (Germany).

Seogwipo, 15 June 2002, 25,176
Germany (0) 1 *(Neuville 88)*
Paraguay (0) 0
Germany: Kahn; Frings, Metzelder (Baumann 60), Jeremies, Rehmer (Kehl 46), Linke, Schneider, Ballack, Neuville (Asamoah 90), Klose, Bode.
Paraguay: Chilavert; Arce, Caniza, Gamarra, Ayala, Caceres, Bonet (Gavilan 84), Acuna, Cardozo, Santa Cruz (Campos 29), Struway (Cuevas 90).
Referee: Batres (Guatemala).

Suwon, 16 June 2002, 38,926
Spain (1) 1 *(Morientes 8)*
Republic of Ireland (0) 1 *(Robbie Keane 90 (pen))*
Spain: Casillas; Puyol, Juanfran, Baraja, Hierro, Helguera, Luis Enrique, Valeron, Morientes (Albelda 71), Raul (Luque 80), De Pedro (Mendieta 65).
Republic of Ireland: Given; Finnan, Harte (Connolly 82), Kinsella, Breen, Staunton (Cunningham 49), Kelly G (Quinn 54), Holland, Robbie Keane, Duff, Kilbane.
aet; Spain won 3-2 on penalties. Keane (scored), Hierro (scored), Holland (missed), Baraja (scored), Connolly (saved), Juanfran (missed), Kilbane (saved), Valeron (missed), Finnan (scored), Mendieta (scored).
Referee: Frisk (Sweden).

Oita, 16 June 2002, 39,747
Sweden (1) 1 *(Larsson 11)*
Senegal (1) 2 *(Camara 37, 104)*
Sweden: Hedman; Lucic, Jakobsson, Magnus Svensson (Jonsson 99), Mellberg, Mjallby, Alexandersson (Ibrahimovic 76), Linderoth, Allback (Andersson A 65), Larsson, Svensson A.
Senegal: Sylva; Daf, Coly, Cisse, Diop PM (Beye 66), Diatta, Faye, Diouf, Camara, Thiaw, Diop PB.
aet; Senegal won on sudden death.
Referee: Aquino (Paraguay).

Kobe, 17 June 2002, 40,440
Brazil (0) 2 *(Rivaldo 67, Ronaldo 87)*
Belgium (0) 0
Brazil: Marcos; Cafu, Roberto Carlos, Lucio, Roque Junior, Edmilson, Juninho (Denilson 57), Gilberto Silva, Ronaldo, Rivaldo (Ricardinho 90), Ronaldinho (Kleberson 81).
Belgium: De Vlieger; Verheyen, Goor, Van Kerckhoven, Van Buyten, Peeters (Sonck 73), Simons, Vanderhaeghe, Mpenza M, Wilmots, Walem.
Referee: Prendergast (Jamaica).

Jeonju, 17 June 2002, 36,380
Mexico (0) 0
USA (1) 2 *(McBride 8, Donovan 65)*
Mexico: Perez; Arellano, Morales, Vidrio (Mercado 46), Mastroeni, Carmona, Rodriguez, Torrado (Garcia Aspe 78), Borgetti, Blanco, Luna.
USA: Friedel; Reyna, Lewis, Sanneh, Pope, Berhalter, Mastroeni (Llamosa 90), Donovan, Wolff (Stewart 59), McBride (Jones 79), O'Brien.
Referee: Pereira (Portugal).

Miyagi, 18 June 2002, 45,666
Japan (0) 0
Turkey (1) 1 *(Umit D 12)*
Japan: Narazaki; Myojin, Ono, Matsuda, Miyamoto, Nakata K, Toda, Inamoto (Ichikawa 46) (Morishima 86), Alex (Suzuki 46), Nishizawa, Nakata H.

Turkey: Rustu; Fatih, Hakan Unsal, Tugay, Bulent K, Alpay, Ergun, Basturk (Ilhan 90), Umit D (Nihat 74), Hakan Sukur, Hasan Sas (Tayfur 85).
Referee: Collina (Italy).

Daejeon, 18 June 2002, 38,588
South Korea (0) 2 *(Seol KH 88, Ahn JH 116)*
Italy (1) 1 *(Vieri 18)*
South Korea: Lee WJ; Song CG, Lee YP, Choi JC, Hong MB (Cha DR 82), Kim TY (Hwang SH 63), Yoo SC, Kim NI (Lee CS 68), Park JS, Ahn JH, Seol KH.
Italy: Buffon; Panucci, Coco, Tommasi, Iuliano, Maldini, Zambrotta (Di Livio 72), Del Piero (Gattuso 61), Vieri, Totti, Zanetti.
aet; South Korea won on sudden death.
Referee: Moreno (Ecuador).

QUARTER-FINALS

Shizuoka, 21 June 2002, 47,436
England (1) 1 *(Owen 23)*
Brazil (1) 2 *(Rivaldo 45, Ronaldinho 50)*
England: Seaman; Mills, Ashley Cole (Sheringham 80), Butt, Campbell, Ferdinand, Beckham, Scholes, Heskey, Owen (Vassell 79), Sinclair (Dyer 56).
Brazil: Marcos; Cafu, Roberto Carlos, Lucio, Roque Junior, Edmilson, Kleberson, Gilberto Silva, Ronaldo (Edilson 70), Rivaldo, Ronaldinho.
Referee: Rizo (Mexico).

Ulsan, 21 June 2002, 37,337
Germany (1) 1 *(Ballack 39)*
USA (0) 0
Germany: Kahn; Frings, Ziege, Kehl, Linke, Metzelder, Schneider (Jeremies 61), Hamann, Neuville (Bode 79), Klose (Bierhoff 88), Ballack.
USA: Friedel; Hejduk (Jones 65), Lewis, Sanneh, Pope, Berhalter, Mastroeni (Stewart 79), Reyna, Donovan, McBride (Mathis 58), O'Brien.
Referee: Dallas (Scotland).

Osaka, 22 June 2002, 44,233
Senegal (0) 0
Turkey (0) 1 *(Ilhan 94)*
Senegal: Sylva; Daf, Coly, Cisse, Diatta, Diop PM, Camara, Fadiga, Diop PB, Diouf, Diao.
Turkey: Rustu; Ergun, Umit D, Alpay, Bulent K, Fatih, Basturk, Tugay, Hakan Sukur (Ilhan 67), Emre B (Arif 90), Hasan Sas.
aet; Turkey won on sudden death.
Referee: Ruiz (Colombia).

Gwangju, 22 June 2002, 42,114
Spain (0) 0
South Korea (0) 0
Spain: Casillas; Puyol, Romero, Helguera (Xavi 93), Hierro, Nadal, Joaquin, Baraja, Morientes, Valeron (Luis Enrique 80), De Pedro (Mendieta 70).
South Korea: Lee WJ; Song CG, Lee YP, Choi JC, Hong MB, Kim TY (Hwang SH 90), Kim NI (Lee EY 32), Park JS, Ahn JH, Seol KH, Yoo SC (Lee CS 60).
aet; South Korea won 5-3 on penalties. Hwang SH (scored), Hierro (scored) Park JS (scored), Baraja (scored), Seol KH (scored), Xavi (scored), Ahn JH (scored, Joaquin (saved), Hong MB (scored).
Referee: Ghandour (Egypt).

SEMI-FINALS

Seoul, 25 June 2002, 65,256
Germany (0) 1 *(Ballack 75)*
South Korea (0) 0
Germany: Kahn; Frings, Metzelder, Hamann, Ramelow, Linke, Schneider (Jeremies 85), Ballack, Neuville (Asamoah 88), Klose (Bierhoff 70), Bode.
South Korea: Lee WJ; Song CG, Lee YP, Choi JC (Lee MS 56), Hong MB (Seol KH 80), Kim TY, Yoo SC, Park JS, Cha DR, Hwang SH (Ahn JH 54), Lee CS.
Referee: Meier (Switzerland).

Saitama, 26 June 2002, 61,058
Brazil (0) 1 *(Ronaldo 49)*
Turkey (0) 0
Brazil: Marcos; Cafu, Roberto Carlos, Lucio, Edmilson, Roque Junior, Edilson (Denilson 75), Kleberson (Belletti 85), Gilberto Silva, Ronaldo (Luizao 68), Rivaldo.
Turkey: Rustu; Fatih, Ergun, Tugay, Bulent K, Alpay, Umit D (Izzet 74), Basturk (Arif 88), Emre B (Ilhan 62), Hakan Sukur, Hasan Sas.
Referee: Nielsen (Denmark).

MATCH FOR THIRD PLACE

Daegu, 29 June 2002, 63,483
South Korea (1) 2 *(Lee EY 9, Song CG 90)*
Turkey (3) 3 *(Hakan Sukur 1, Ilhan 13, 32)*
South Korea: Lee WJ; Song CG, Lee CS (Cha DR 64), Lee MS, Hong MB (Kim TY 46), Lee EY, Yoo SC, Park JS, Lee YP, Ahn JH, Seol KH (Choi TU 79).
Turkey: Rustu; Fatih, Ergun, Tugay, Alpay, Bulent K, Umit D (Okan 75), Basturk (Tayfur 85), Hakan Sukur, Ilhan, Emre B (Hakan Unsal 41).
Referee: Mane (Kuwait).

FINAL

Yokohama, 30 June 2002, 69,029

Germany (0) 0,
Brazil (0) 2 *(Ronaldo 67, 79)*
Germany: Kahn; Frings, Bode (Ziege 84), Linke, Ramelow, Metzelder, Jeremies (Asamoah 77), Hamann, Neuville, Klose (Bierhoff 74), Schneider.
Brazil: Marcos; Cafu, Roberto Carlos, Lucio, Edmilson, Roque Junior, Kleberson, Gilberto Silva, Ronaldo (Denilson 90), Rivaldo, Ronaldinho (Juninho 85).
Referee: Collina (Italy).

WORLD CUP FINAL TOURNAMENT STATISTICS

Average goals per game 2.52
Fastest individual goal: Hakan Sukur, Turkey v South Korea 10.8 secs
Top scoring team: Brazil 18 goals
Top marksman Ronaldo (Brazil) 8 goals
Yellow cards 267
Red cards 17
Cafu, the Brazilian captain, became the first player to figure in the final match of three World Cup tournaments.

Brazil's Ronaldo with the World Cup.

EURO 2004 – FIXTURES

Group 1
Cyprus, France, Israel, Malta, Slovenia.

07.09.02	Slovenia v Malta
07.09.02	Cyprus v France
12.10.02	France v Slovenia
12.10.02	Malta v Israel
16.10.02	Israel v Cyprus
16.10.02	Malta v France
20.11.02	Cyprus v Malta
29.03.03	Cyprus v Israel
29.03.03	France v Malta
02.04.03	Slovenia v Cyprus
02.04.03	Israel v France
30.04.03	Malta v Slovenia
07.06.03	Israel v Slovenia
07.06.03	Malta v Cyprus
06.09.03	France v Cyprus
06.09.03	Slovenia v Israel
10.09.03	Israel v Malta
10.09.03	Slovenia v France
11.10.03	Cyprus v Slovenia
11.10.03	France v Israel

Group 2
Denmark, Luxembourg, Norway, Romania, Bosnia.

07.09.02	Norway v Denmark
07.09.02	Bosnia v Romania
12.10.02	Denmark v Luxembourg
12.10.02	Romania v Norway
16.10.02	Norway v Bosnia
16.10.02	Luxembourg v Romania
29.03.03	Bosnia v Luxembourg
29.03.03	Romania v Denmark
02.04.03	Luxembourg v Norway
02.04.03	Denmark v Bosnia
07.06.03	Denmark v Norway
07.06.03	Romania v Bosnia
11.06.03	Luxembourg v Denmark
11.06.03	Norway v Romania
06.09.03	Bosnia v Norway
06.09.03	Romania v Luxembourg
10.09.03	Luxembourg v Bosnia
10.09.03	Denmark v Romania
11.10.03	Norway v Luxembourg
11.10.03	Bosnia v Denmark

Group 3
Austria, Holland, Belarus, Moldova, Czech Republic.

07.09.02	Austria v Moldova
07.09.02	Holland v Belarus
12.10.02	Belarus v Austria
13.10.02	Moldova v Czech Republic
16.10.02	Austria v Holland
16.10.02	Czech Republic v Belarus
29.03.03	Belarus v Moldova
29.03.03	Holland v Czech Republic
02.04.03	Czech Republic v Austria
02.04.03	Moldova v Holland
07.06.03	Moldova v Austria
07.06.03	Belarus v Holland
11.06.03	Czech Republic v Moldova
11.06.03	Austria v Belarus
06.09.03	Holland v Austria
06.09.03	Belarus v Czech Republic
10.09.03	Czech Republic v Holland
10.09.03	Moldova v Belarus
11.10.03	Austria v Czech Republic
11.10.03	Holland v Moldova

Group 4
Hungary, Poland, Sweden, San Marino, Latvia.

07.09.02	San Marino v Poland
07.09.02	Latvia v Sweden
12.10.02	Sweden v Hungary
12.10.02	Poland v Latvia
16.10.02	Hungary v San Marino
20.11.02	San Marino v Latvia
29.03.03	Poland v Hungary
02.04.03	Poland v San Marino
02.04.03	Hungary v Sweden
30.04.03	Latvia v San Marino
07.06.03	Hungary v Latvia
07.06.03	San Marino v Sweden
11.06.03	Sweden v Poland
11.06.03	San Marino v Hungary
06.09.03	Latvia v Poland
06.09.03	Sweden v San Marino
10.09.03	Poland v Sweden
10.09.03	Latvia v Hungary
11.10.03	Sweden v Latvia
11.10.03	Hungary v Poland

Group 5
Germany, Iceland, Scotland, Faeroes, Lithuania.

07.09.02	Lithuania v Germany
07.09.02	Faeroes v Scotland
12.10.02	Lithuania v Faeroes
12.10.02	Iceland v Scotland
16.10.02	Germany v Faeroes
16.10.02	Iceland v Lithuania
29.03.03	Germany v Lithuania
29.03.03	Scotland v Iceland
02.04.03	Lithuania v Scotland
07.06.03	Scotland v Germany
07.06.03	Iceland v Faeroes
11.06.03	Faeroes v Germany
11.06.03	Lithuania v Iceland
20.08.03	Faeroes v Iceland
06.09.03	Scotland v Faeroes
06.09.03	Iceland v Germany
10.09.03	Germany v Scotland
10.09.03	Faeroes v Lithuania
11.10.03	Scotland v Lithuania
11.10.03	Germany v Iceland

Group 6
Greece, Northern Ireland, Spain, Ukraine, Armenia.

07.09.02	Greece v Spain
07.09.02	Armenia v Ukraine
12.10.02	Spain v Northern Ireland
12.10.02	Ukraine v Greece
16.10.02	Greece v Armenia
16.10.02	Northern Ireland v Ukraine
29.03.03	Armenia v Northern Ireland
29.03.03	Ukraine v Spain
02.04.03	Northern Ireland v Greece
02.04.03	Spain v Armenia
07.06.03	Spain v Greece
07.06.03	Ukraine v Armenia
11.06.03	Northern Ireland v Spain
11.06.03	Greece v Ukraine
06.09.03	Armenia v Greece
06.09.03	Ukraine v Northern Ireland
10.09.03	Northern Ireland v Armenia
10.09.03	Spain v Ukraine
11.10.03	Greece v Northern Ireland
11.10.03	Armenia v Spain

Group 7
England, Liechtenstein, Turkey, Slovakia, Macedonia.
07.09.02	Turkey v Slovakia
07.09.02	Liechtenstein v Macedonia
12.10.02	Slovakia v England
12.10.02	Macedonia v Turkey
16.10.02	Turkey v Liechtenstein
16.10.02	England v Macedonia
29.03.03	Liechtenstein v England
29.03.03	Macedonia v Slovakia
02.04.03	England v Turkey
02.04.03	Slovakia v Liechtenstein
07.06.03	Slovakia v Turkey
07.06.03	Macedonia v Liechtenstein
11.06.03	England v Slovakia
11.06.03	Turkey v Macedonia
06.09.03	Liechtenstein v Turkey
06.09.03	Macedonia v England
10.09.03	England v Liechtenstein
10.09.03	Slovakia v Macedonia
11.10.03	Turkey v England
11.10.03	Liechtenstein v Slovakia

Group 8
Belgium, Bulgaria, Croatia, Estonia, Andorra.
07.09.02	Belgium v Bulgaria
07.09.02	Croatia v Estonia
12.10.02	Andorra v Belgium
12.10.02	Bulgaria v Croatia
16.10.02	Estonia v Belgium
16.10.02	Bulgaria v Andorra
29.03.03	Croatia v Belgium
02.04.03	Estonia v Bulgaria
02.04.03	Croatia v Andorra
30.04.03	Andorra v Estonia
07.06.03	Bulgaria v Belgium
07.06.03	Estonia v Andorra
11.06.03	Estonia v Croatia
11.06.03	Belgium v Andorra
06.09.03	Bulgaria v Estonia
06.09.03	Andorra v Croatia
10.09.03	Belgium v Croatia
10.09.03	Andorra v Bulgaria
11.10.03	Croatia v Bulgaria
11.10.03	Belgium v Estonia

Group 9
Finland, Italy, Wales, Yugoslavia, Azerbaijan.
07.09.02	Azerbaijan v Italy
07.09.02	Finland v Wales
12.10.02	Italy v Yugoslavia
12.10.02	Finland v Azerbaijan
16.10.02	Wales v Italy
16.10.02	Yugoslavia v Finland
20.11.02	Azerbaijan v Wales
29.03.03	Italy v Finland
29.03.03	Wales v Azerbaijan
02.04.03	Yugoslavia v Wales
30.04.03	Azerbaijan v Yugoslavia
07.06.03	Finland v Yugoslavia
11.06.03	Finland v Italy
11.06.03	Yugoslavia v Azerbaijan
06.09.03	Italy v Wales
06.09.03	Azerbaijan v Finland
10.09.03	Wales v Finland
10.09.03	Yugoslavia v Italy
11.10.03	Italy v Azerbaijan
11.10.03	Wales v Yugoslavia

Group 10
Albania, Republic of Ireland, Switzerland, Georgia, Russia.
07.09.02	Russia v Republic of Ireland
07.09.02	Switzerland v Georgia
12.10.02	Albania v Switzerland
12.10.02	Georgia v Russia
16.10.02	Republic of Ireland v Switzerland
16.10.02	Russia v Albania
29.03.03	Georgia v Republic of Ireland
29.03.03	Albania v Russia
02.04.03	Albania v Republic of Ireland
02.04.03	Georgia v Switzerland
07.06.03	Switzerland v Russia
07.06.03	Republic of Ireland v Albania
11.06.03	Republic of Ireland v Georgia
11.06.03	Switzerland v Albania
06.09.03	Republic of Ireland v Russia
06.09.03	Georgia v Albania
10.09.03	Russia v Switzerland
10.09.03	Albania v Georgia
11.10.03	Russia v Georgia
11.10.03	Switzerland v Republic of Ireland

Play-offs
15/19.11.03

Group matches
12/19.06.04

Quarter-finals
30.06.04

Semi-finals
01.07.04

Final
04.07.04

EUROPEAN FOOTBALL CHAMPIONSHIP
(formerly EUROPEAN NATIONS' CUP)

Year	Winners		Runners-up		Venue	Attendance
1960	USSR	2	Yugoslavia	1	Paris	17,966
1964	Spain	2	USSR	1	Madrid	120,000
1968	Italy	2	Yugoslavia	0	Rome	60,000
	After 1-1 draw					75,000
1972	West Germany	3	USSR	0	Brussels	43,437
1976	Czechoslovakia	2	West Germany	2	Belgrade	45,000
	(Czechoslovakia won on penalties)					
1980	West Germany	2	Belgium	1	Rome	47,864
1984	France	2	Spain	0	Paris	48,000
1988	Holland	2	USSR	0	Munich	72,308
1992	Denmark	2	Germany	0	Gothenburg	37,800
1996	Germany	2	Czech Republic	1	Wembley	73,611
	(Germany won on sudden death)					
2000	France	2	Italy	1	Rotterdam	50,000
	(France won on sudden death)					

BRITISH AND IRISH INTERNATIONAL RESULTS 1872–2002

Note: In the results that follow, wc=World Cup, ec=European Championship, ui=Umbro International Trophy. tf = Tournoi de France. For Ireland, read Northern Ireland from 1921.

ENGLAND v SCOTLAND

Played: 110; England won 45, Scotland won 41, Drawn 24. *Goals:* England 192, Scotland 169.

Year	Date	Venue	E	S	Year	Date	Venue	E	S
1872	30 Nov	Glasgow	0	0	1932	9 Apr	Wembley	3	0
1873	8 Mar	Kennington Oval	4	2	1933	1 Apr	Glasgow	1	2
1874	7 Mar	Glasgow	1	2	1934	14 Apr	Wembley	3	0
1875	6 Mar	Kennington Oval	2	2	1935	6 Apr	Glasgow	0	2
1876	4 Mar	Glasgow	0	3	1936	4 Apr	Wembley	1	1
1877	3 Mar	Kennington Oval	1	3	1937	17 Apr	Glasgow	1	3
1878	2 Mar	Glasgow	2	7	1938	9 Apr	Wembley	0	1
1879	5 Apr	Kennington Oval	5	4	1939	15 Apr	Glasgow	2	1
1880	13 Mar	Glasgow	4	5	1947	12 Apr	Wembley	1	1
1881	12 Mar	Kennington Oval	1	6	1948	10 Apr	Glasgow	2	0
1882	11 Mar	Glasgow	1	5	1949	9 Apr	Wembley	1	3
1883	10 Mar	Sheffield	2	3	wc1950	15 Apr	Glasgow	1	0
1884	15 Mar	Glasgow	0	1	1951	14 Apr	Wembley	2	3
1885	21 Mar	Kennington Oval	1	1	1952	5 Apr	Glasgow	2	1
1886	31 Mar	Glasgow	1	1	1953	18 Apr	Wembley	2	2
1887	19 Mar	Blackburn	2	3	wc1954	3 Apr	Glasgow	4	2
1888	17 Mar	Glasgow	5	0	1955	2 Apr	Wembley	7	2
1889	13 Apr	Kennington Oval	2	3	1956	14 Apr	Glasgow	1	1
1890	5 Apr	Glasgow	1	1	1957	6 Apr	Wembley	2	1
1891	6 Apr	Blackburn	2	1	1958	19 Apr	Glasgow	4	0
1892	2 Apr	Glasgow	4	1	1959	11 Apr	Wembley	1	0
1893	1 Apr	Richmond	5	2	1960	9 Apr	Glasgow	1	1
1894	7 Apr	Glasgow	2	2	1961	15 Apr	Wembley	9	3
1895	6 Apr	Everton	3	0	1962	14 Apr	Glasgow	0	2
1896	4 Apr	Glasgow	1	2	1963	6 Apr	Wembley	1	2
1897	3 Apr	Crystal Palace	1	2	1964	11 Apr	Glasgow	0	1
1898	2 Apr	Glasgow	3	1	1965	10 Apr	Wembley	2	2
1899	8 Apr	Birmingham	2	1	1966	2 Apr	Glasgow	4	3
1900	7 Apr	Glasgow	1	4	ec1967	15 Apr	Wembley	2	3
1901	30 Mar	Crystal Palace	2	2	ec1968	24 Jan	Glasgow	1	1
1902	3 Mar	Birmingham	2	2	1969	10 May	Wembley	4	1
1903	4 Apr	Sheffield	1	2	1970	25 Apr	Glasgow	0	0
1904	9 Apr	Glasgow	1	0	1971	22 May	Wembley	3	1
1905	1 Apr	Crystal Palace	1	0	1972	27 May	Glasgow	1	0
1906	7 Apr	Glasgow	1	2	1973	14 Feb	Glasgow	5	0
1907	6 Apr	Newcastle	1	1	1973	19 May	Wembley	1	0
1908	4 Apr	Glasgow	1	1	1974	18 May	Glasgow	0	2
1909	3 Apr	Crystal Palace	2	0	1975	24 May	Wembley	5	1
1910	2 Apr	Glasgow	0	2	1976	15 May	Glasgow	1	2
1911	1 Apr	Everton	1	1	1977	4 June	Wembley	1	2
1912	23 Mar	Glasgow	1	1	1978	20 May	Glasgow	1	0
1913	5 Apr	Chelsea	1	0	1979	26 May	Wembley	3	1
1914	14 Apr	Glasgow	1	3	1980	24 May	Glasgow	2	0
1920	10 Apr	Sheffield	5	4	1981	23 May	Wembley	0	1
1921	9 Apr	Glasgow	0	3	1982	29 May	Glasgow	1	0
1922	8 Apr	Aston Villa	0	1	1983	1 June	Wembley	2	0
1923	14 Apr	Glasgow	2	2	1984	26 May	Glasgow	1	1
1924	12 Apr	Wembley	1	1	1985	25 May	Glasgow	0	1
1925	4 Apr	Glasgow	0	2	1986	23 Apr	Wembley	2	1
1926	17 Apr	Manchester	0	1	1987	23 May	Glasgow	0	0
1927	2 Apr	Glasgow	2	1	1988	21 May	Wembley	1	0
1928	31 Mar	Wembley	1	5	1989	27 May	Glasgow	2	0
1929	13 Apr	Glasgow	0	1	ec1996	15 June	Wembley	2	0
1930	5 Apr	Wembley	5	2	ec1999	13 Nov	Glasgow	2	0
1931	28 Mar	Glasgow	0	2	ec1999	17 Nov	Wembley	0	1

ENGLAND v WALES

Played: 97; England won 62, Wales won 14, Drawn 21. *Goals:* England 239, Wales 90.

Year	Date	Venue	E	W	Year	Date	Venue	E	W
1879	18 Jan	Kennington Oval	2	1	1882	13 Mar	Wrexham	3	5
1880	15 Mar	Wrexham	3	2	1883	3 Feb	Kennington Oval	5	0
1881	26 Feb	Blackburn	0	1	1884	17 Mar	Wrexham	4	0

Year	Date	Venue	E	W		Year	Date	Venue	E	W
1885	14 Mar	Blackburn	1	1		1934	29 Sept	Cardiff	4	0
1886	29 Mar	Wrexham	3	1		1936	5 Feb	Wolverhampton	1	2
1887	26 Feb	Kennington Oval	4	0		1936	17 Oct	Cardiff	1	2
1888	4 Feb	Crewe	5	1		1937	17 Nov	Middlesbrough	2	1
1889	23 Feb	Stoke	4	1		1938	22 Oct	Cardiff	2	4
1890	15 Mar	Wrexham	3	1		1946	13 Nov	Manchester	3	0
1891	7 May	Sunderland	4	1		1947	18 Oct	Cardiff	3	0
1892	5 Mar	Wrexham	2	0		1948	10 Nov	Aston Villa	1	0
1893	13 Mar	Stoke	6	0		wc1949	15 Oct	Cardiff	4	1
1894	12 Mar	Wrexham	5	1		1950	15 Nov	Sunderland	4	2
1895	18 Mar	Queen's Club, Kensington	1	1		1951	20 Oct	Cardiff	1	1
1896	16 Mar	Cardiff	9	1		1952	12 Nov	Wembley	5	2
1897	29 Mar	Sheffield	4	0		wc1953	10 Oct	Cardiff	4	1
1898	28 Mar	Wrexham	3	0		1954	10 Nov	Wembley	3	2
1899	20 Mar	Bristol	4	0		1955	27 Oct	Cardiff	1	2
1900	26 Mar	Cardiff	1	1		1956	14 Nov	Wembley	3	1
1901	18 Mar	Newcastle	6	0		1957	19 Oct	Cardiff	4	0
1902	3 Mar	Wrexham	0	0		1958	26 Nov	Aston Villa	2	2
1903	2 Mar	Portsmouth	2	1		1959	17 Oct	Cardiff	1	1
1904	29 Feb	Wrexham	2	2		1960	23 Nov	Wembley	5	1
1905	27 Mar	Liverpool	3	1		1961	14 Oct	Cardiff	1	1
1906	19 Mar	Cardiff	1	0		1962	21 Oct	Wembley	4	0
1907	18 Mar	Fulham	1	1		1963	12 Oct	Cardiff	4	0
1908	16 Mar	Wrexham	7	1		1964	18 Nov	Wembley	2	1
1909	15 Mar	Nottingham	2	0		1965	2 Oct	Cardiff	0	0
1910	14 Mar	Cardiff	1	0		EC1966	16 Nov	Wembley	5	1
1911	13 Mar	Millwall	3	0		EC1967	21 Oct	Cardiff	3	0
1912	11 Mar	Wrexham	2	0		1969	7 May	Wembley	2	1
1913	17 Mar	Bristol	4	3		1970	18 Apr	Cardiff	1	1
1914	16 Mar	Cardiff	2	0		1971	19 May	Wembley	0	0
1920	15 Mar	Highbury	1	2		1972	20 May	Cardiff	3	0
1921	14 Mar	Cardiff	0	0		wc1972	15 Nov	Cardiff	1	0
1922	13 Mar	Liverpool	1	0		wc1973	24 Jan	Wembley	1	1
1923	5 Mar	Cardiff	2	2		1973	15 May	Wembley	3	0
1924	3 Mar	Blackburn	1	2		1974	11 May	Cardiff	2	0
1925	28 Feb	Swansea	2	1		1975	21 May	Wembley	2	2
1926	1 Mar	Crystal Palace	1	3		1976	24 Mar	Wrexham	2	1
1927	12 Feb	Wrexham	3	3		1976	8 May	Cardiff	1	0
1927	28 Nov	Burnley	1	2		1977	31 May	Wembley	0	1
1928	17 Nov	Swansea	3	2		1978	3 May	Cardiff	3	1
1929	20 Nov	Chelsea	6	0		1979	23 May	Wembley	0	0
1930	22 Nov	Wrexham	4	0		1980	17 May	Wrexham	1	4
1931	18 Nov	Liverpool	3	1		1981	20 May	Wembley	0	1
1932	16 Nov	Wrexham	0	0		1982	27 Apr	Cardiff	1	0
1933	15 Nov	Newcastle	1	2		1983	23 Feb	Wembley	2	1
						1984	2 May	Wrexham	0	1

ENGLAND v IRELAND

Played: 96; England won 74, Ireland won 6, Drawn 16. *Goals:* England 319, Ireland 80.

Year	Date	Venue	E	I		Year	Date	Venue	E	I
1882	18 Feb	Belfast	13	0		1903	14 Feb	Wolverhampton	4	0
1883	24 Feb	Liverpool	7	0		1904	12 Mar	Belfast	3	1
1884	23 Feb	Belfast	8	1		1905	25 Feb	Middlesbrough	1	1
1885	28 Feb	Manchester	4	0		1906	17 Feb	Belfast	5	0
1886	13 Mar	Belfast	6	1		1907	16 Feb	Everton	1	0
1887	5 Feb	Sheffield	7	0		1908	15 Feb	Belfast	3	1
1888	31 Mar	Belfast	5	1		1909	13 Feb	Bradford	4	0
1889	2 Mar	Everton	6	1		1910	12 Feb	Belfast	1	1
1890	15 Mar	Belfast	9	1		1911	11 Feb	Derby	2	1
1891	7 Mar	Wolverhampton	6	1		1912	10 Feb	Dublin	6	1
1892	5 Mar	Belfast	2	0		1913	15 Feb	Belfast	1	2
1893	25 Feb	Birmingham	6	1		1914	14 Feb	Middlesbrough	0	3
1894	3 Mar	Belfast	2	2		1919	25 Oct	Belfast	1	1
1895	9 Mar	Derby	9	0		1920	23 Oct	Sunderland	2	0
1896	7 Mar	Belfast	2	0		1921	22 Oct	Belfast	1	1
1897	20 Feb	Nottingham	6	0		1922	21 Oct	West Bromwich	2	0
1898	5 Mar	Belfast	3	2		1923	20 Oct	Belfast	1	2
1899	18 Feb	Sunderland	13	2		1924	22 Oct	Everton	3	1
1900	17 Mar	Dublin	2	0		1925	24 Oct	Belfast	0	0
1901	9 Mar	Southampton	3	0		1926	20 Oct	Liverpool	3	3
1902	22 Mar	Belfast	1	0		1927	22 Oct	Belfast	0	2

			E	I				E	I
1928	22 Oct	Everton	2	1	1962	20 Oct	Belfast	3	1
1929	19 Oct	Belfast	3	0	1963	20 Nov	Wembley	8	3
1930	20 Oct	Sheffield	5	1	1964	3 Oct	Belfast	4	3
1931	17 Oct	Belfast	6	2	1965	10 Nov	Wembley	2	1
1932	17 Oct	Blackpool	1	0	EC1966	20 Oct	Belfast	2	0
1933	14 Oct	Belfast	3	0	EC1967	22 Nov	Wembley	2	0
1935	6 Feb	Everton	2	1	1969	3 May	Belfast	3	1
1935	19 Oct	Belfast	3	1	1970	21 Apr	Wembley	3	1
1936	18 Nov	Stoke	3	1	1971	15 May	Belfast	1	0
1937	23 Oct	Belfast	5	1	1972	23 May	Wembley	0	1
1938	16 Nov	Manchester	7	0	1973	12 May	Everton	2	1
1946	28 Sept	Belfast	7	2	1974	15 May	Wembley	1	0
1947	5 Nov	Everton	2	2	1975	17 May	Belfast	0	0
1948	9 Oct	Belfast	6	2	1976	11 May	Wembley	4	0
wc1949	16 Nov	Manchester	9	2	1977	28 May	Belfast	2	1
1950	7 Oct	Belfast	4	1	1978	16 May	Wembley	1	0
1951	14 Nov	Aston Villa	2	0	EC1979	7 Feb	Wembley	4	0
1952	4 Oct	Belfast	2	2	1979	19 May	Belfast	2	0
wc1953	11 Nov	Everton	3	1	EC1979	17 Oct	Belfast	5	1
1954	2 Oct	Belfast	2	0	1980	20 May	Wembley	1	1
1955	2 Nov	Wembley	3	0	1982	23 Feb	Wembley	4	0
1956	10 Oct	Belfast	1	1	1983	28 May	Belfast	0	0
1957	6 Nov	Wembley	2	3	1984	24 Apr	Wembley	1	0
1958	4 Oct	Belfast	3	3	wc1985	27 Feb	Belfast	1	0
1959	18 Nov	Wembley	2	1	wc1985	13 Nov	Wembley	0	0
1960	8 Oct	Belfast	5	2	EC1986	15 Oct	Wembley	3	0
1961	22 Nov	Wembley	1	1	EC1987	1 Apr	Belfast	2	0

SCOTLAND v WALES

Played: 102; Scotland won 60, Wales won 19, Drawn 23. *Goals:* Scotland 238, Wales 112.

			S	W				S	W
1876	25 Mar	Glasgow	4	0	1921	12 Feb	Aberdeen	2	1
1877	5 Mar	Wrexham	2	0	1922	4 Feb	Wrexham	1	2
1878	23 Mar	Glasgow	9	0	1923	17 Mar	Paisley	2	0
1879	7 Apr	Wrexham	3	0	1924	16 Feb	Cardiff	0	2
1880	3 Apr	Glasgow	5	1	1925	14 Feb	Tynecastle	3	1
1881	14 Mar	Wrexham	5	1	1925	31 Oct	Cardiff	3	0
1882	25 Mar	Glasgow	5	0	1926	30 Oct	Glasgow	3	0
1883	12 Mar	Wrexham	3	0	1927	29 Oct	Wrexham	2	2
1884	29 Mar	Glasgow	4	1	1928	27 Oct	Glasgow	4	2
1885	23 Mar	Wrexham	8	1	1929	26 Oct	Cardiff	4	2
1886	10 Apr	Glasgow	4	1	1930	25 Oct	Glasgow	1	1
1887	21 Mar	Wrexham	2	0	1931	31 Oct	Wrexham	3	2
1888	10 Mar	Edinburgh	5	1	1932	26 Oct	Edinburgh	2	5
1889	15 Apr	Wrexham	0	0	1933	4 Oct	Cardiff	2	3
1890	22 Mar	Paisley	5	0	1934	21 Nov	Aberdeen	3	2
1891	21 Mar	Wrexham	4	3	1935	5 Oct	Cardiff	1	1
1892	26 Mar	Edinburgh	6	1	1936	2 Dec	Dundee	1	2
1893	18 Mar	Wrexham	8	0	1937	30 Oct	Cardiff	1	2
1894	24 Mar	Kilmarnock	5	2	1938	9 Nov	Edinburgh	3	2
1895	23 Mar	Wrexham	2	2	1946	19 Oct	Wrexham	1	3
1896	21 Mar	Dundee	4	0	1947	12 Nov	Glasgow	1	2
1897	20 Mar	Wrexham	2	2	wc1948	23 Oct	Cardiff	3	1
1898	19 Mar	Motherwell	5	2	1949	9 Nov	Glasgow	2	0
1899	18 Mar	Wrexham	6	0	1950	21 Oct	Cardiff	3	1
1900	3 Feb	Aberdeen	5	2	1951	14 Nov	Glasgow	0	1
1901	2 Mar	Wrexham	1	1	wc1952	18 Oct	Cardiff	2	1
1902	15 Mar	Greenock	5	1	1953	4 Nov	Glasgow	3	3
1903	9 Mar	Cardiff	1	0	1954	16 Oct	Cardiff	1	0
1904	12 Mar	Dundee	1	1	1955	9 Nov	Glasgow	2	0
1905	6 Mar	Wrexham	1	3	1956	20 Oct	Cardiff	2	2
1906	3 Mar	Edinburgh	0	2	1957	13 Nov	Glasgow	1	1
1907	4 Mar	Wrexham	0	1	1958	18 Oct	Cardiff	3	0
1908	7 Mar	Dundee	2	1	1959	4 Nov	Glasgow	1	1
1909	1 Mar	Wrexham	2	3	1960	20 Oct	Cardiff	0	2
1910	5 Mar	Kilmarnock	1	0	1961	8 Nov	Glasgow	2	0
1911	6 Mar	Cardiff	2	2	1962	20 Oct	Cardiff	3	2
1912	2 Mar	Tynecastle	1	0	1963	20 Nov	Glasgow	2	1
1913	3 Mar	Wrexham	0	0	1964	3 Oct	Cardiff	2	3
1914	28 Feb	Glasgow	0	0	EC1965	24 Nov	Glasgow	4	1
1920	26 Feb	Cardiff	1	1	EC1966	22 Oct	Cardiff	1	1

			S	W				S	W
1967	22 Nov	Glasgow	3	2	wc1977	12 Oct	Liverpool	2	0
1969	3 May	Wrexham	5	3	1978	17 May	Glasgow	1	1
1970	22 Apr	Glasgow	0	0	1979	19 May	Cardiff	0	3
1971	15 May	Cardiff	0	0	1980	21 May	Glasgow	1	0
1972	24 May	Glasgow	1	0	1981	16 May	Swansea	0	2
1973	12 May	Wrexham	2	0	1982	24 May	Glasgow	1	0
1974	14 May	Glasgow	2	0	1983	28 May	Cardiff	2	0
1975	17 May	Cardiff	2	2	1984	28 Feb	Glasgow	2	1
1976	6 May	Glasgow	3	1	wc1985	27 Mar	Glasgow	0	1
wc1976	17 Nov	Glasgow	1	0	wc1985	10 Sept	Cardiff	1	1
1977	28 May	Wrexham	0	0	1997	27 May	Kilmarnock	0	1

SCOTLAND v IRELAND

Played: 93; Scotland won 61, Ireland won 16, Drawn 16. *Goals:* Scotland 254, Ireland 84.

			S	I				S	I
1884	26 Jan	Belfast	5	0	1934	20 Oct	Belfast	1	2
1885	14 Mar	Glasgow	8	2	1935	13 Nov	Edinburgh	2	1
1886	20 Mar	Belfast	7	2	1936	31 Oct	Belfast	3	1
1887	19 Feb	Glasgow	4	1	1937	10 Nov	Aberdeen	1	1
1888	24 Mar	Belfast	10	2	1938	8 Oct	Belfast	2	0
1889	9 Mar	Glasgow	7	0	1946	27 Nov	Glasgow	0	0
1890	29 Mar	Belfast	4	1	1947	4 Oct	Belfast	0	2
1891	28 Mar	Glasgow	2	1	1948	17 Nov	Glasgow	3	2
1892	19 Mar	Belfast	3	2	1949	1 Oct	Belfast	8	2
1893	25 Mar	Glasgow	6	1	1950	1 Nov	Glasgow	6	1
1894	31 Mar	Belfast	2	1	1951	6 Oct	Belfast	3	0
1895	30 Mar	Glasgow	3	1	1952	5 Nov	Glasgow	1	1
1896	28 Mar	Belfast	3	3	1953	3 Oct	Belfast	3	1
1897	27 Mar	Glasgow	5	1	1954	3 Nov	Glasgow	2	2
1898	26 Mar	Belfast	3	0	1955	8 Oct	Belfast	1	2
1899	25 Mar	Glasgow	9	1	1956	7 Nov	Glasgow	1	0
1900	3 Mar	Belfast	3	0	1957	5 Oct	Belfast	1	1
1901	23 Feb	Glasgow	11	0	1958	5 Nov	Glasgow	2	2
1902	1 Mar	Belfast	5	1	1959	3 Oct	Belfast	4	0
1902	9 Aug	Belfast	0	3	1960	9 Nov	Glasgow	5	2
1903	21 Mar	Glasgow	0	2	1961	7 Oct	Belfast	6	1
1904	26 Mar	Dublin	1	1	1962	7 Nov	Glasgow	5	1
1905	18 Mar	Glasgow	4	0	1963	12 Oct	Belfast	1	2
1906	17 Mar	Dublin	1	0	1964	25 Nov	Glasgow	3	2
1907	16 Mar	Glasgow	3	0	1965	2 Oct	Belfast	2	3
1908	14 Mar	Dublin	5	0	1966	16 Nov	Glasgow	2	1
1909	15 Mar	Glasgow	5	0	1967	21 Oct	Belfast	0	1
1910	19 Mar	Belfast	0	1	1969	6 May	Glasgow	1	1
1911	18 Mar	Glasgow	2	0	1970	18 Apr	Belfast	1	0
1912	16 Mar	Belfast	4	1	1971	18 May	Glasgow	0	1
1913	15 Mar	Dublin	2	1	1972	20 May	Glasgow	2	0
1914	14 Mar	Belfast	1	1	1973	16 May	Glasgow	1	2
1920	13 Mar	Glasgow	3	0	1974	11 May	Glasgow	0	1
1921	26 Feb	Belfast	2	0	1975	20 May	Glasgow	3	0
1922	4 Mar	Glasgow	2	1	1976	8 May	Glasgow	3	0
1923	3 Mar	Belfast	1	0	1977	1 June	Glasgow	3	0
1924	1 Mar	Glasgow	2	0	1978	13 May	Glasgow	1	1
1925	28 Feb	Belfast	3	0	1979	22 May	Glasgow	1	0
1926	27 Feb	Glasgow	4	0	1980	17 May	Belfast	0	1
1927	26 Feb	Belfast	2	0	wc1981	25 Mar	Glasgow	1	1
1928	25 Feb	Glasgow	0	1	1981	19 May	Glasgow	2	0
1929	23 Feb	Belfast	7	3	wc1981	14 Oct	Belfast	0	0
1930	22 Feb	Glasgow	3	1	1982	28 Apr	Belfast	1	1
1931	21 Feb	Belfast	0	0	1983	24 May	Glasgow	0	0
1931	19 Sept	Glasgow	3	1	1983	13 Dec	Belfast	0	2
1932	12 Sept	Belfast	4	0	1992	19 Feb	Glasgow	1	0
1933	16 Sept	Glasgow	1	2					

WALES v IRELAND

Played: 90; Wales won 42, Ireland won 27, Drawn 21. *Goals:* Wales 181, Ireland 127.

			W	I				W	I
1882	25 Feb	Wrexham	7	1	1886	27 Feb	Wrexham	5	0
1883	17 Mar	Belfast	1	1	1887	12 Mar	Belfast	1	4
1884	9 Feb	Wrexham	6	0	1888	3 Mar	Wrexham	11	0
1885	11 Apr	Belfast	8	2	1889	27 Apr	Belfast	3	1

			W	I
1890	8 Feb	Shrewsbury	5	2
1891	7 Feb	Belfast	2	7
1892	27 Feb	Bangor	1	1
1893	8 Apr	Belfast	3	4
1894	24 Feb	Swansea	4	1
1895	16 Mar	Belfast	2	2
1896	29 Feb	Wrexham	6	1
1897	6 Mar	Belfast	3	4
1898	19 Feb	Llandudno	0	1
1899	4 Mar	Belfast	0	1
1900	24 Feb	Llandudno	2	0
1901	23 Mar	Belfast	1	0
1902	22 Mar	Cardiff	0	3
1903	28 Mar	Belfast	0	2
1904	21 Mar	Bangor	0	1
1905	18 Apr	Belfast	2	2
1906	2 Apr	Wrexham	4	4
1907	23 Feb	Belfast	3	2
1908	11 Apr	Aberdare	0	1
1909	20 Mar	Belfast	3	2
1910	11 Apr	Wrexham	4	1
1911	28 Jan	Belfast	2	1
1912	13 Apr	Cardiff	2	3
1913	18 Jan	Belfast	1	0
1914	19 Jan	Wrexham	1	2
1920	14 Feb	Belfast	2	2
1921	9 Apr	Swansea	2	1
1922	4 Apr	Belfast	1	1
1923	14 Apr	Wrexham	0	3
1924	15 Mar	Belfast	1	0
1925	18 Apr	Wrexham	0	0
1926	13 Feb	Belfast	0	3
1927	9 Apr	Cardiff	2	2
1928	4 Feb	Belfast	2	1
1929	2 Feb	Wrexham	2	2
1930	1 Feb	Belfast	0	7
1931	22 Apr	Wrexham	3	2
1931	5 Dec	Belfast	0	4
1932	7 Dec	Wrexham	4	1
1933	4 Nov	Belfast	1	1
1935	27 Mar	Wrexham	3	1

			W	I
1936	11 Mar	Belfast	2	3
1937	17 Mar	Wrexham	4	1
1938	16 Mar	Belfast	0	1
1939	15 Mar	Wrexham	3	1
1947	16 Apr	Belfast	1	2
1948	10 Mar	Wrexham	2	0
1949	9 Mar	Belfast	2	0
wc1950	8 Mar	Wrexham	0	0
1951	7 Mar	Belfast	2	1
1952	19 Mar	Swansea	3	0
1953	15 Apr	Belfast	3	2
wc1954	31 Mar	Wrexham	1	2
1955	20 Apr	Belfast	3	2
1956	11 Apr	Cardiff	1	1
1957	10 Apr	Belfast	0	0
1958	16 Apr	Cardiff	1	1
1959	22 Apr	Belfast	1	4
1960	6 Apr	Wrexham	3	2
1961	12 Apr	Belfast	5	1
1962	11 Apr	Cardiff	4	0
1963	3 Apr	Belfast	4	1
1964	15 Apr	Cardiff	2	3
1965	31 Mar	Belfast	5	0
1966	30 Mar	Cardiff	1	4
EC1967	12 Apr	Belfast	0	0
EC1968	28 Feb	Wrexham	2	0
1969	10 May	Belfast	0	0
1970	25 Apr	Swansea	1	0
1971	22 May	Belfast	0	1
1972	27 May	Wrexham	0	0
1973	19 May	Everton	0	1
1974	18 May	Wrexham	1	0
1975	23 May	Belfast	0	1
1976	14 May	Swansea	1	0
1977	3 June	Belfast	1	1
1978	19 May	Wrexham	1	0
1979	25 May	Belfast	1	1
1980	23 May	Cardiff	0	1
1982	27 May	Wrexham	3	0
1983	31 May	Belfast	1	0
1984	22 May	Swansea	1	1

OTHER BRITISH INTERNATIONAL RESULTS 1908–2002
ENGLAND

v ALBANIA

			E	A
wc1989	8 Mar	Tirana	2	0
wc1989	26 Apr	Wembley	5	0
wc2001	28 Mar	Tirana	3	1
wc2001	5 Sept	Newcastle	2	0

v ARGENTINA

			E	A
1951	9 May	Wembley	2	1
1953	17 May	Buenos Aires	0	0
(abandoned after 21 mins)				
wc1962	2 June	Rancagua	3	1
1964	6 June	Rio de Janeiro	0	1
wc1966	23 July	Wembley	1	0
1974	22 May	Wembley	2	2
1977	12 June	Buenos Aires	1	1
1980	13 May	Wembley	3	1
wc1986	22 June	Mexico City	1	2
1991	25 May	Wembley	2	2
wc1998	30 June	St Etienne	2	2
2000	23 Feb	Wembley	0	0
wc2002	7 June	Sapporo	1	0

v AUSTRALIA

			E	A
1980	31 May	Sydney	2	1
1983	11 June	Sydney	0	0
1983	15 June	Brisbane	1	0
1983	18 June	Melbourne	1	1
1991	1 June	Sydney	1	0

v AUSTRIA

			E	A
1908	6 June	Vienna	6	1
1908	8 June	Vienna	11	1
1909	1 June	Vienna	8	1
1930	14 May	Vienna	0	0
1932	7 Dec	Chelsea	4	3
1936	6 May	Vienna	1	2
1951	28 Nov	Wembley	2	2
1952	25 May	Vienna	3	2
wc1958	15 June	Boras	2	2
1961	27 May	Vienna	1	3
1962	4 Apr	Wembley	3	1
1965	20 Oct	Wembley	2	3
1967	27 May	Vienna	1	0
1973	26 Sept	Wembley	7	0
1979	13 June	Vienna	3	4

v BELGIUM

			E	B
1921	21 May	Brussels	2	0
1923	19 Mar	Highbury	6	1
1923	1 Nov	Antwerp	2	2
1924	8 Dec	West Bromwich	4	0
1926	24 May	Antwerp	5	3
1927	11 May	Brussels	9	1
1928	19 May	Antwerp	3	1
1929	11 May	Brussels	5	1
1931	16 May	Brussels	4	1
1936	9 May	Brussels	2	3
1947	21 Sept	Brussels	5	2

			E	B
1950	18 May	Brussels	4	1
1952	26 Nov	Wembley	5	0
wc1954	17 June	Basle	4	4*
1964	21 Oct	Wembley	2	2
1970	25 Feb	Brussels	3	1
EC1980	12 June	Turin	1	1
wc1990	27 June	Bologna	1	0*
1998	29 May	Casablanca	0	0
1999	10 Oct	Sunderland	2	1

*After extra time

v BOHEMIA

			E	B
1908	13 June	Prague	4	0

v BRAZIL

			E	B
1956	9 May	Wembley	4	2
wc1958	11 June	Gothenburg	0	0
1959	13 May	Rio de Janeiro	0	2
wc1962	10 June	Vina del Mar	1	3
1963	8 May	Wembley	1	1
1964	30 May	Rio de Janeiro	1	5
1969	12 June	Rio de Janeiro	1	2
wc1970	7 June	Guadalajara	0	1
1976	23 May	Los Angeles	0	1
1977	8 June	Rio de Janeiro	0	0
1978	19 Apr	Wembley	1	1
1981	12 May	Wembley	0	1
1984	10 June	Rio de Janeiro	2	0
1987	19 May	Wembley	1	1
1990	28 Mar	Wembley	1	0
1992	17 May	Wembley	1	1
1993	13 June	Washington	1	1
UI1995	11 June	Wembley	1	3
TF1997	10 June	Paris	0	1
2000	27 May	Wembley	1	1
wc2002	21 June	Shizuoka	1	2

v BULGARIA

			E	B
wc1962	7 June	Rancagua	0	0
1968	11 Dec	Wembley	1	1
1974	1 June	Sofia	1	0
EC1979	6 June	Sofia	3	0
EC1979	22 Nov	Wembley	2	0
1996	27 Mar	Wembley	1	0
EC1998	10 Oct	Wembley	0	0
EC1999	9 June	Sofia	1	1

v CAMEROON

			E	C
wc1990	1 July	Naples	3	2*
1991	6 Feb	Wembley	2	0
1997	15 Nov	Wembley	2	0
2002	26 May	Kobe	2	2

*After extra time

v CANADA

			E	C
1986	24 May	Burnaby	1	0

v CHILE

			E	C
wc1950	25 June	Rio de Janeiro	2	0
1953	24 May	Santiago	2	1
1984	17 June	Santiago	0	0
1989	23 May	Wembley	0	0
1998	11 Feb	Wembley	0	2

v CHINA

			E	C
1996	23 May	Beijing	3	0

v CIS

			E	C
1992	29 Apr	Moscow	2	2

v COLOMBIA

			E	C
1970	20 May	Bogota	4	0
1988	24 May	Wembley	1	1
1995	6 Sept	Wembley	0	0
wc1998	26 June	Lens	2	0

v CROATIA

			E	C
1996	24 Apr	Wembley	0	0

v CYPRUS

			E	C
EC1975	16 Apr	Wembley	5	0
EC1975	11 May	Limassol	1	0

v CZECHOSLOVAKIA

			E	C
1934	16 May	Prague	1	2
1937	1 Dec	Tottenham	5	4
1963	29 May	Bratislava	4	2
1966	2 Nov	Wembley	0	0
wc1970	11 June	Guadalajara	1	0
1973	27 May	Prague	1	1
EC1974	30 Oct	Wembley	3	0
EC1975	30 Oct	Bratislava	1	2
1978	29 Nov	Wembley	1	0
wc1982	20 June	Bilbao	2	0
1990	25 Apr	Wembley	4	2
1992	25 Mar	Prague	2	2

v CZECH REPUBLIC

			E	C
1998	18 Nov	Wembley	2	0

v DENMARK

			E	D
1948	26 Sept	Copenhagen	0	0
1955	2 Oct	Copenhagen	5	1
wc1956	5 Dec	Wolverhampton	5	2
wc1957	15 May	Copenhagen	4	1
1966	3 July	Copenhagen	2	0
EC1978	20 Sept	Copenhagen	4	3
EC1979	12 Sept	Wembley	1	0
EC1982	22 Sept	Copenhagen	2	2
EC1983	21 Sept	Wembley	0	1
1988	14 Sept	Wembley	1	0
1989	7 June	Copenhagen	1	1
1990	15 May	Wembley	1	0
EC1992	11 June	Malmo	0	0
1994	9 Mar	Wembley	1	0
wc2002	15 June	Niigata	3	0

v ECUADOR

			E	Ec
1970	24 May	Quito	2	0

v EGYPT

			E	Eg
1986	29 Jan	Cairo	4	0
wc1990	21 June	Cagliari	1	0

v FIFA

			E	FIFA
1938	26 Oct	Highbury	3	0
1953	21 Oct	Wembley	4	4
1963	23 Oct	Wembley	2	1

v FINLAND

			E	F
1937	20 May	Helsinki	8	0
1956	20 May	Helsinki	5	1
1966	26 June	Helsinki	3	0
wc1976	13 June	Helsinki	4	1
wc1976	13 Oct	Wembley	2	1
1982	3 June	Helsinki	4	1
wc1984	17 Oct	Wembley	5	0
wc1985	22 May	Helsinki	1	1
1992	3 June	Helsinki	2	1
wc2000	11 Oct	Helsinki	0	0
wc2001	24 Mar	Liverpool	2	1

v FRANCE

			E	F
1923	10 May	Paris	4	1
1924	17 May	Paris	3	1
1925	21 May	Paris	3	2
1927	26 May	Paris	6	0
1928	17 May	Paris	5	1
1929	9 May	Paris	4	1
1931	14 May	Paris	2	5
1933	6 Dec	Tottenham	4	1
1938	26 May	Paris	4	2
1947	3 May	Highbury	3	0
1949	22 May	Paris	3	1

			E	F
1951	3 Oct	Highbury	2	2
1955	15 May	Paris	0	1
1957	27 Nov	Wembley	4	0
EC1962	3 Oct	Sheffield	1	1
EC1963	27 Feb	Paris	2	5
wc1966	20 July	Wembley	2	0
1969	12 Mar	Wembley	5	0
wc1982	16 June	Bilbao	3	1
1984	29 Feb	Paris	0	2
1992	19 Feb	Wembley	2	0
EC1992	14 June	Malmo	0	0
TF1997	7 June	Montpellier	1	0
1999	10 Feb	Wembley	0	2
2000	2 Sept	Paris	1	1

v GEORGIA			E	G
wc1996	9 Nov	Tbilisi	2	0
wc1997	30 Apr	Wembley	2	0

v GERMANY			E	G
1930	10 May	Berlin	3	3
1935	4 Dec	Tottenham	3	0
1938	14 May	Berlin	6	3
1991	11 Sept	Wembley	0	1
1993	19 June	Detroit	1	2
EC1996	26 June	Wembley	1	1*
EC2000	17 June	Charleroi	1	0
wc2000	7 Oct	Wembley	0	1
wc2001	1 Sept	Munich	5	1

v EAST GERMANY			E	EG
1963	2 June	Leipzig	2	1
1970	25 Nov	Wembley	3	1
1974	29 May	Leipzig	1	1
1984	12 Sept	Wembley	1	0

v WEST GERMANY			E	WG
1954	1 Dec	Wembley	3	1
1956	26 May	Berlin	3	1
1965	12 May	Nuremberg	1	0
1966	23 Feb	Wembley	1	0
wc1966	30 July	Wembley	4	2*
1968	1 June	Hanover	0	1
wc1970	14 June	Leon	2	3*
EC1972	29 Apr	Wembley	1	3
EC1972	13 May	Berlin	0	0
1975	12 Mar	Wembley	2	0
1978	22 Feb	Munich	1	2
wc1982	29 June	Madrid	0	0
1982	13 Oct	Wembley	1	2
1985	12 June	Mexico City	3	0
1987	9 Sept	Dusseldorf	1	3
wc1990	4 July	Turin	1	1*

*After extra time

v GREECE			E	G
EC1971	21 Apr	Wembley	3	0
EC1971	1 Dec	Piraeus	2	0
EC1982	17 Nov	Salonika	3	0
EC1983	30 Mar	Wembley	0	0
1989	8 Feb	Athens	2	1
1994	17 May	Wembley	5	0
wc2001	6 June	Athens	2	0
wc2001	6 Oct	Old Trafford	2	2

v HOLLAND			E	H
1935	18 May	Amsterdam	1	0
1946	27 Nov	Huddersfield	8	2
1964	9 Dec	Amsterdam	1	1
1969	5 Nov	Amsterdam	1	0
1970	14 Jun	Wembley	0	0
1977	9 Feb	Wembley	0	2
1982	25 May	Wembley	2	0
1988	23 Mar	Wembley	2	2
EC1988	15 June	Dusseldorf	1	3
wc1990	16 June	Cagliari	0	0
wc1993	28 Apr	Wembley	2	2
wc1993	13 Oct	Rotterdam	0	2
EC1996	18 June	Wembley	4	1
2001	15 Aug	Tottenham	0	2
2002	13 Feb	Amsterdam	1	1

v HUNGARY			E	H
1908	10 June	Budapest	7	0
1909	29 May	Budapest	4	2
1909	31 May	Budapest	8	2
1934	10 May	Budapest	1	2
1936	2 Dec	Highbury	6	2
1953	25 Nov	Wembley	3	6
1954	23 May	Budapest	1	7
1960	22 May	Budapest	0	2
wc1962	31 May	Rancagua	1	2
1965	5 May	Wembley	1	0
1978	24 May	Wembley	4	1
wc1981	6 June	Budapest	3	1
wc1982	18 Nov	Wembley	1	0
EC1983	27 Apr	Wembley	2	0
EC1983	12 Oct	Budapest	3	0
1988	27 Apr	Budapest	0	0
1990	12 Sept	Wembley	1	0
1992	12 May	Budapest	1	0
1996	18 May	Wembley	3	0
1999	28 Apr	Budapest	1	1

v ICELAND			E	I
1982	2 June	Reykjavik	1	1

v REPUBLIC OF IRELAND			E	RI
1946	30 Sept	Dublin	1	0
1949	21 Sept	Everton	0	2
wc1957	8 May	Wembley	5	1
wc1957	19 May	Dublin	1	1
1964	24 May	Dublin	3	1
1976	8 Sept	Wembley	1	1
EC1978	25 Oct	Dublin	1	1
EC1980	6 Feb	Wembley	2	0
1985	26 Mar	Wembley	2	1
EC1988	12 June	Stuttgart	0	1
wc1990	11 June	Cagliari	1	1
EC1990	14 Nov	Dublin	1	1
EC1991	27 Mar	Wembley	1	1
1995	15 Feb	Dublin	0	1

(abandoned after 27 mins)

v ISRAEL			E	I
1986	26 Feb	Ramat Gan	2	1
1988	17 Feb	Tel Aviv	0	0

v ITALY			E	I
1933	13 May	Rome	1	1
1934	14 Nov	Highbury	3	2
1939	13 May	Milan	2	2
1948	16 May	Turin	4	0
1949	30 Nov	Tottenham	2	0
1952	18 May	Florence	1	1
1959	6 May	Wembley	2	2
1961	24 May	Rome	3	2
1973	14 June	Turin	0	2
1973	14 Nov	Wembley	0	1
1976	28 May	New York	3	2
wc1976	17 Nov	Rome	0	2
wc1977	16 Nov	Wembley	2	0
EC1980	15 June	Turin	0	1
1985	6 June	Mexico City	1	2
1989	15 Nov	Wembley	0	0
wc1990	7 July	Bari	1	2
wc1997	12 Feb	Wembley	0	1
TF1997	4 June	Nantes	2	0
wc1997	11 Oct	Rome	0	0
2000	15 Nov	Turin	0	1
2002	27 Mar	Leeds	1	2

v JAPAN			E	J
UI1995	3 June	Wembley	2	1

v KUWAIT			E	K
wc1982	25 June	Bilbao	1	0

v LUXEMBOURG			E	L
1927	21 May	Esch-sur-Alzette	5	2
wc1960	19 Oct	Luxembourg	9	0
wc1961	28 Sept	Highbury	4	1
wc1977	30 Mar	Wembley	5	0
wc1977	12 Oct	Luxembourg	2	0
EC1982	15 Dec	Wembley	9	0
EC1983	16 Nov	Luxembourg	4	0
EC1998	14 Oct	Luxembourg	3	0
EC1999	4 Sept	Wembley	6	0

v MALAYSIA			E	M
1991	12 June	Kuala Lumpur	4	2

v MALTA			E	M
EC1971	3 Feb	Valletta	1	0
EC1971	12 May	Wembley	5	0
2000	3 June	Valletta	2	1

v MEXICO			E	M
1959	24 May	Mexico City	1	2
1961	10 May	Wembley	8	0
wc1966	16 July	Wembley	2	0
1969	1 Jan	Mexico City	0	0
1985	9 June	Mexico City	0	1
1986	17 May	Los Angeles	3	0
1997	29 Mar	Wembley	2	0
2001	25 May	Derby	4	0

v MOLDOVA			E	M
wc1996	1 Sept	Chisinau	3	0
wc1997	10 Sept	Wembley	4	0

v MOROCCO			E	M
wc1986	6 June	Monterrey	0	0
1998	27 May	Casablanca	1	0

v NEW ZEALAND			E	NZ
1991	3 June	Auckland	1	0
1991	8 June	Wellington	2	0

v NIGERIA			E	N
1994	16 Nov	Wembley	1	0
wc2002	12 June	Osaka	0	0

v NORWAY			E	N
1937	14 May	Oslo	6	0
1938	9 Nov	Newcastle	4	0
1949	18 May	Oslo	4	1
1966	29 June	Oslo	6	1
wc1980	10 Sept	Wembley	4	0
wc1981	9 Sept	Oslo	1	2
wc1992	14 Oct	Wembley	1	1
wc1993	2 June	Oslo	0	2
1994	22 May	Wembley	0	0
1995	11 Oct	Oslo	0	0

v PARAGUAY			E	P
wc1986	18 June	Mexico City	3	0
2002	17 Apr	Liverpool	4	0

v PERU			E	P
1959	17 May	Lima	1	4
1962	20 May	Lima	4	0

v POLAND			E	P
1966	5 Jan	Everton	1	1
1966	5 July	Chorzow	1	0
wc1973	6 June	Chorzow	0	2
wc1973	17 Oct	Wembley	1	1
wc1986	11 June	Monterrey	3	0
wc1989	3 June	Wembley	3	0
wc1989	11 Oct	Katowice	0	0
EC1990	17 Oct	Wembley	2	0
EC1991	13 Nov	Poznan	1	1
wc1993	29 May	Katowice	1	1
wc1993	8 Sept	Wembley	3	0
wc1996	9 Oct	Wembley	2	1
wc1997	31 May	Katowice	2	0
EC1999	27 Mar	Wembley	3	1
EC1999	8 Sept	Warsaw	0	0

v PORTUGAL			E	P
1947	25 May	Lisbon	10	0
1950	14 May	Lisbon	5	3
1951	19 May	Everton	5	2
1955	22 May	Oporto	1	3
1958	7 May	Wembley	2	1
wc1961	21 May	Lisbon	1	1
wc1961	25 Oct	Wembley	2	0
1964	17 May	Lisbon	4	3
1964	4 June	São Paulo	1	1
wc1966	26 July	Wembley	2	1
1969	10 Dec	Wembley	1	0
1974	3 Apr	Lisbon	0	0
EC1974	20 Nov	Wembley	0	0
EC1975	19 Nov	Lisbon	1	1
wc1986	3 June	Monterrey	0	1
1995	12 Dec	Wembley	1	1
1998	22 Apr	Wembley	3	0
EC2000	12 June	Eindhoven	2	3

v ROMANIA			E	R
1939	24 May	Bucharest	2	0
1968	6 Nov	Bucharest	0	0
1969	15 Jan	Wembley	1	1
wc1970	2 June	Guadalajara	1	0
wc1980	15 Oct	Bucharest	1	2
wc1981	29 April	Wembley	0	0
wc1985	1 May	Bucharest	0	0
wc1985	11 Sept	Wembley	1	1
1994	12 Oct	Wembley	1	1
wc1998	22 June	Toulouse	1	2
EC2000	20 June	Charleroi	2	3

v SAN MARINO			E	SM
wc1992	17 Feb	Wembley	6	0
wc1993	17 Nov	Bologna	7	1

v SAUDI ARABIA			E	SA
1988	16 Nov	Riyadh	1	1
1998	23 May	Wembley	0	0

v SOUTH AFRICA			E	SA
1997	24 May	Old Trafford	2	1

v SOUTH KOREA			E	SK
2002	21 May	Seoguipo	1	1

v SPAIN			E	S
1929	15 May	Madrid	3	4
1931	9 Dec	Highbury	7	1
wc1950	2 July	Rio de Janeiro	0	1
1955	18 May	Madrid	1	1
1955	30 Nov	Wembley	4	1
1960	15 May	Madrid	0	3
1960	26 Oct	Wembley	4	2
1965	8 Dec	Madrid	2	0
1967	24 May	Wembley	2	0
EC1968	3 Apr	Wembley	1	0
EC1968	8 May	Madrid	2	1
1980	26 Mar	Barcelona	2	0
EC1980	18 June	Naples	2	1
1981	25 Mar	Wembley	1	2
wc1982	5 July	Madrid	0	0
1987	18 Feb	Madrid	4	2
1992	9 Sept	Santander	0	1
EC 1996	22 June	Wembley	0	0
2001	28 Feb	Villa Park	3	0

v SWEDEN			E	S
1923	21 May	Stockholm	4	2
1923	24 May	Stockholm	3	1
1937	17 May	Stockholm	4	0
1947	19 Nov	Highbury	4	2
1949	13 May	Stockholm	1	3
1956	16 May	Stockholm	0	0
1959	28 Oct	Wembley	2	3
1965	16 May	Gothenburg	2	1
1968	22 May	Wembley	3	1
1979	10 June	Stockholm	0	0
1986	10 Sept	Stockholm	0	1
wc1988	19 Oct	Wembley	0	0
wc1989	6 Sept	Stockholm	0	0
EC1992	17 June	Stockholm	1	2

			E	S
ut1995	8 June	Leeds	3	3
EC1998	5 Sept	Stockholm	1	2
EC1999	5 June	Wembley	0	0
2001	10 Nov	Old Trafford	1	1
wc2002	2 June	Saitama	1	1

v SWITZERLAND			E	S
1933	20 May	Berne	4	0
1938	21 May	Zurich	1	2
1947	18 May	Zurich	0	1
1948	2 Dec	Highbury	6	0
1952	28 May	Zurich	3	0
wc1954	20 June	Berne	2	0
1962	9 May	Wembley	3	1
1963	5 June	Basle	8	1
EC1971	13 Oct	Basle	3	2
EC1971	10 Nov	Wembley	1	1
1975	3 Sept	Basle	2	1
1977	7 Sept	Wembley	0	0
wc1980	19 Nov	Wembley	2	1
wc1981	30 May	Basle	1	2
1988	28 May	Lausanne	1	0
1995	15 Nov	Wembley	3	1
EC1996	8 June	Wembley	1	1
1998	25 Mar	Berne	1	1

v TUNISIA			E	T
1990	2 June	Tunis	1	1
wc1998	15 June	Marseilles	2	0

v TURKEY			E	T
wc1984	14 Nov	Istanbul	8	0
wc1985	16 Oct	Wembley	5	0
EC1987	29 Apr	Izmir	0	0
EC1987	14 Oct	Wembley	8	0
EC1991	1 May	Izmir	1	0
EC1991	16 Oct	Wembley	1	0
wc1992	18 Nov	Wembley	4	0
wc1993	31 Mar	Izmir	2	0

v UKRAINE			E	U
2000	31 May	Wembley	2	0

v URUGUAY			E	U
1953	31 May	Montevideo	1	2
wc1954	26 June	Basle	2	4
1964	6 May	Wembley	2	1

			E	U
wc1966	11 July	Wembley	0	0
1969	8 June	Montevideo	2	1
1977	15 June	Montevideo	0	0
1984	13 June	Montevideo	0	2
1990	22 May	Wembley	1	2
1995	29 Mar	Wembley	0	0

v USA			E	USA
wc1950	29 June	Belo Horizonte	0	1
1953	8 June	New York	6	3
1959	28 May	Los Angeles	8	1
1964	27 May	New York	10	0
1985	16 June	Los Angeles	5	0
1993	9 June	Foxboro	0	2
1994	7 Sept	Wembley	2	0

v USSR			E	USSR
1958	18 May	Moscow	1	1
wc1958	8 June	Gothenburg	2	2
wc1958	17 June	Gothenburg	0	1
1958	22 Oct	Wembley	5	0
1967	6 Dec	Wembley	2	2
EC1968	8 June	Rome	2	0
1973	10 June	Moscow	2	1
1984	2 June	Wembley	0	2
1986	26 Mar	Tbilisi	1	0
EC1988	18 June	Frankfurt	1	3
1991	21 May	Wembley	3	1

v YUGOSLAVIA			E	Y
1939	18 May	Belgrade	1	2
1950	22 Nov	Highbury	2	2
1954	16 May	Belgrade	0	1
1956	28 Nov	Wembley	3	0
1958	11 May	Belgrade	0	5
1960	11 May	Wembley	3	3
1965	9 May	Belgrade	1	1
1966	4 May	Wembley	2	0
EC1968	5 June	Florence	0	1
1972	11 Oct	Wembley	1	1
1974	5 June	Belgrade	2	2
EC1986	12 Nov	Wembley	2	0
EC1987	11 Nov	Belgrade	4	1
1989	13 Dec	Wembley	2	1

SCOTLAND

v ARGENTINA			S	A
1977	18 June	Buenos Aires	1	1
1979	2 June	Glasgow	1	3
1990	28 Mar	Glasgow	1	0

v AUSTRALIA			S	A
wc1985	20 Nov	Glasgow	2	0
wc1985	4 Dec	Melbourne	0	0
1996	27 Mar	Glasgow	1	0
2000	15 Nov	Glasgow	0	2

v AUSTRIA			S	A
1931	16 May	Vienna	0	5
1933	29 Nov	Glasgow	2	2
1937	9 May	Vienna	1	1
1950	13 Dec	Glasgow	0	1
1951	27 May	Vienna	0	4
wc1954	16 June	Zurich	0	1
1955	19 May	Vienna	4	1
1956	2 May	Glasgow	1	1
1960	29 May	Vienna	1	4
1963	8 May	Glasgow	4	1
(abandoned after 79 mins)				
wc1968	6 Nov	Glasgow	2	1
wc1969	5 Nov	Vienna	0	2
EC1978	20 Sept	Vienna	2	3
EC1979	17 Oct	Glasgow	1	1
1994	20 Apr	Vienna	2	1
wc1996	31 Aug	Vienna	0	0
wc1997	2 Apr	Celtic Park	2	0

v BELARUS			S	B
wc1997	8 June	Minsk	1	0
wc1997	7 Sept	Aberdeen	4	1

v BELGIUM			S	B
1947	18 May	Brussels	1	2
1948	28 Apr	Glasgow	2	0
1951	20 May	Brussels	5	0
EC1971	3 Feb	Liège	0	3
EC1971	10 Nov	Aberdeen	1	0
1974	2 June	Brussels	1	2
EC1979	21 Nov	Brussels	0	2
EC1979	19 Dec	Glasgow	1	3
EC1982	15 Dec	Brussels	2	3
EC1983	12 Oct	Glasgow	1	1
EC1987	1 Apr	Brussels	1	4
EC1987	14 Oct	Glasgow	2	0
wc2001	24 Mar	Glasgow	2	2
wc2001	5 Sept	Brussels	0	2

v BOSNIA			S	B
EC1999	4 Sept	Sarajevo	2	1
EC1999	5 Oct	Glasgow	1	0

v BRAZIL			S	B
1966	25 June	Glasgow	1	1
1972	5 July	Rio de Janeiro	0	1
1973	30 June	Glasgow	0	1
wc1974	18 June	Frankfurt	0	0
1977	23 June	Rio de Janeiro	0	2

			S	B
wc1982	18 June	Seville	1	4
1987	26 May	Glasgow	0	2
wc1990	20 June	Turin	0	1
wc1998	10 June	Sant-Denis	1	2

v BULGARIA			S	B
1978	22 Feb	Glasgow	2	1
EC1986	10 Sept	Glasgow	0	0
EC1987	11 Nov	Sofia	1	0
EC1990	14 Nov	Sofia	1	1
EC1991	27 Mar	Glasgow	1	1

v CANADA			S	C
1983	12 June	Vancouver	2	0
1983	16 June	Edmonton	3	0
1983	20 June	Toronto	2	0
1992	21 May	Toronto	3	1

v CHILE			S	C
1977	15 June	Santiago	4	2
1989	30 May	Glasgow	2	0

v CIS			S	C
EC1992	18 June	Norrkoping	3	0

v COLOMBIA			S	C
1988	17 May	Glasgow	0	0
1996	30 May	Miami	0	1
1998	23 May	New York	2	2

v COSTA RICA			S	CR
wc1990	11 June	Genoa	0	1

v CROATIA			S	C
wc2000	11 Oct	Zagreb	1	1
wc2001	1 Sept	Glasgow	0	0

v CYPRUS			S	C
wc1968	17 Dec	Nicosia	5	0
wc1969	11 May	Glasgow	8	0
wc1989	8 Feb	Limassol	3	2
wc1989	26 Apr	Glasgow	2	1

v CZECHOSLOVAKIA			S	C
1937	22 May	Prague	3	1
1937	8 Dec	Glasgow	5	0
wc1961	14 May	Bratislava	0	4
wc1961	26 Sept	Glasgow	3	2
wc1961	29 Nov	Brussels	2	4*
1972	2 July	Porto Alegre	0	0
wc1973	26 Sept	Glasgow	2	1
wc1973	17 Oct	Prague	0	1
wc1976	13 Oct	Prague	0	2
wc1977	21 Sept	Glasgow	3	1

*After extra time

v CZECH REPUBLIC			S	C
EC1999	31 Mar	Glasgow	1	2
EC1999	9 June	Prague	2	3

v DENMARK			S	D
1951	12 May	Glasgow	3	1
1952	25 May	Copenhagen	2	1
1968	16 Oct	Copenhagen	1	0
EC1970	11 Nov	Glasgow	1	0
EC1971	9 June	Copenhagen	0	1
wc1972	18 Oct	Copenhagen	4	1
wc1972	15 Nov	Glasgow	2	0
EC1975	3 Sept	Copenhagen	1	0
EC1975	29 Oct	Glasgow	3	1
wc1986	4 June	Nezahualcayotl	0	1
1996	24 Apr	Copenhagen	0	2
1998	25 Mar	Glasgow	0	1

v ECUADOR			S	E
1995	24 May	Toyama	2	1

v EGYPT			S	E
1990	16 May	Aberdeen	1	3

v ESTONIA			S	E
wc1993	19 May	Tallinn	3	0
wc1993	2 June	Aberdeen	3	1
wc1997	11 Feb	Monaco	0	0
wc1997	29 Mar	Kilmarnock	2	0

			S	E
EC1998	10 Oct	Edinburgh	3	2
EC1999	8 Sept	Tallinn	0	0

v FAEROES			S	F
EC1994	12 Oct	Glasgow	5	1
EC1995	7 June	Toftir	2	0
EC1998	14 Oct	Aberdeen	2	1
EC1999	5 June	Toftir	1	1

v FINLAND			S	F
1954	25 May	Helsinki	2	1
wc1964	21 Oct	Glasgow	3	1
wc1965	27 May	Helsinki	2	1
1976	8 Sept	Glasgow	6	0

			S	F
1992	25 Mar	Glasgow	1	1
EC1994	7 Sept	Helsinki	2	0
EC1995	6 Sept	Glasgow	1	0
1998	22 Apr	Edinburgh	1	1

v FRANCE			S	F
1930	18 May	Paris	2	0
1932	8 May	Paris	3	1
1948	23 May	Paris	0	3
1949	27 Apr	Glasgow	2	0
1950	27 May	Paris	1	0
1951	16 May	Glasgow	1	0
wc1958	15 June	Orebro	1	2
1984	1 June	Marseilles	0	2
wc1989	8 Mar	Glasgow	2	0
wc1989	11 Oct	Paris	0	3
1997	12 Nov	St Etienne	1	2
2000	29 Mar	Glasgow	0	2
2002	27 Mar	Paris	0	5

v GERMANY			S	G
1929	1 June	Berlin	1	1
1936	14 Oct	Glasgow	2	0
EC1992	15 June	Norrkoping	0	2
1993	24 Mar	Glasgow	0	1
1998	28 Apr	Bremen	1	0

v EAST GERMANY			S	EG
1974	30 Oct	Glasgow	3	0
1977	7 Sept	East Berlin	0	1
EC1982	13 Oct	Glasgow	2	0
EC1983	16 Nov	Halle	1	2
1985	16 Oct	Glasgow	0	0
1990	25 Apr	Glasgow	0	1

v WEST GERMANY			S	WG
1957	22 May	Stuttgart	3	1
1959	6 May	Glasgow	3	2
1964	12 May	Hanover	2	2
wc1969	16 Apr	Glasgow	1	1
wc1969	22 Oct	Hamburg	2	3
1973	14 Nov	Glasgow	1	1
1974	27 Mar	Frankfurt	1	2
wc1986	8 June	Queretaro	1	2

v GREECE			S	G
EC1994	18 Dec	Athens	0	1
EC1995	16 Aug	Glasgow	1	0

v HOLLAND			S	H
1929	4 June	Amsterdam	2	0
1938	21 May	Amsterdam	3	1
1959	27 May	Amsterdam	2	1
1966	11 May	Glasgow	0	3
1968	30 May	Amsterdam	0	0
1971	1 Dec	Rotterdam	1	2
wc1978	11 June	Mendoza	3	2
1982	23 Mar	Glasgow	2	1
1986	29 Apr	Eindhoven	0	0
EC1992	12 June	Gothenburg	0	1
1994	23 Mar	Glasgow	0	1
1994	27 May	Utrecht	1	3
EC1996	10 June	Birmingham	0	0
2000	26 Apr	Arnhem	0	0

v HONG KONG XI

			S	HK
†2002	23 May	Hong Kong	4	0

v HUNGARY

			S	H
1938	7 Dec	Glasgow	3	1
1954	8 Dec	Glasgow	2	4
1955	29 May	Budapest	1	3
1958	7 May	Glasgow	1	1
1960	5 June	Budapest	3	3
1980	31 May	Budapest	1	3
1987	9 Sept	Glasgow	2	0

v ICELAND

			S	I
wc1984	17 Oct	Glasgow	3	0
wc1985	28 May	Reykjavik	1	0

v IRAN

			S	I
wc1978	7 June	Cordoba	1	1

v REPUBLIC OF IRELAND

			S	RI
wc1961	3 May	Glasgow	4	1
wc1961	7 May	Dublin	3	0
1963	9 June	Dublin	0	1
1969	21 Sept	Dublin	1	1
EC1986	15 Oct	Dublin	0	0
EC1987	18 Feb	Glasgow	0	1
2000	30 May	Dublin	2	1

v ISRAEL

			S	I
wc1981	25 Feb	Tel Aviv	1	0
wc1981	28 Apr	Glasgow	3	1
1986	28 Jan	Tel Aviv	1	0

v ITALY

			S	I
1931	20 May	Rome	0	3
wc1965	9 Nov	Glasgow	1	0
wc1965	7 Dec	Naples	0	3
1988	22 Dec	Perugia	0	2
wc1992	18 Nov	Glasgow	0	0
wc1993	13 Oct	Rome	1	3

v JAPAN

			S	J
1995	21 May	Hiroshima	0	0

v LATVIA

			S	L
wc1996	5 Oct	Riga	2	0
wc1997	11 Oct	Glasgow	2	0
wc2000	2 Sept	Riga	1	0
wc2001	6 Oct	Glasgow	2	1

v LITHUANIA

			S	L
EC1998	5 Sept	Vilnius	0	0
EC1999	9 Oct	Glasgow	3	0

v LUXEMBOURG

			S	L
1947	24 May	Luxembourg	6	0
EC1986	12 Nov	Glasgow	3	0
EC1987	2 Dec	Esch	0	0

v MALTA

			S	M
1988	22 Mar	Valletta	1	1
1990	28 May	Valletta	2	1
wc1993	17 Feb	Glasgow	3	0
wc1993	17 Nov	Valletta	2	0
1997	1 June	Valletta	3	2

v MOROCCO

			S	M
wc1998	23 June	St Etienne	0	3

v NEW ZEALAND

			S	NZ
wc1982	15 June	Malaga	5	2

v NIGERIA

			S	N
2002	17 Apr	Aberdeen	1	2

v NORWAY

			S	N
1929	28 May	Oslo	7	3
1954	5 May	Glasgow	1	0
1954	19 May	Oslo	1	1
1963	4 June	Bergen	3	4
1963	7 Nov	Glasgow	6	1
1974	6 June	Oslo	2	1
EC1978	25 Oct	Glasgow	3	2
EC1979	7 June	Oslo	4	0
wc1988	14 Sept	Oslo	2	1
wc1989	15 Nov	Glasgow	1	1
1992	3 June	Oslo	0	0
wc1998	16 June	Bordeaux	1	1

v PARAGUAY

			S	P
wc1958	11 June	Norrkoping	2	3

v PERU

			S	P
1972	26 Apr	Glasgow	2	0
wc1978	3 June	Cordoba	1	3
1979	12 Sept	Glasgow	1	1

v POLAND

			S	P
1958	1 June	Warsaw	2	1
1960	4 June	Glasgow	2	3
wc1965	23 May	Chorzow	1	1
wc1965	13 Oct	Glasgow	1	2
1980	28 May	Poznan	0	1
1990	19 May	Glasgow	1	1
2001	25 Apr	Bydgoszcz	1	1

v PORTUGAL

			S	P
1950	21 May	Lisbon	2	2
1955	4 May	Glasgow	3	0
1959	3 June	Lisbon	0	1
1966	18 June	Glasgow	0	1
EC1971	21 Apr	Lisbon	0	2
EC1971	13 Oct	Glasgow	2	1
1975	13 May	Glasgow	1	0
EC1978	29 Nov	Lisbon	0	1
EC1980	26 Mar	Glasgow	4	1
wc1980	15 Oct	Glasgow	0	0
wc1981	18 Nov	Lisbon	1	2
wc1992	14 Oct	Glasgow	0	0
wc1993	28 Apr	Lisbon	0	5

v ROMANIA

			S	R
EC1975	1 June	Bucharest	1	1
EC1975	17 Dec	Glasgow	1	1
1986	26 Mar	Glasgow	3	0
EC1990	12 Sept	Glasgow	2	1
EC1991	16 Oct	Bucharest	0	1

v RUSSIA

			S	R
EC1994	16 Nov	Glasgow	1	1
EC1995	29 Mar	Moscow	0	0

v SAN MARINO

			S	SM
EC1991	1 May	Serravalle	2	0
EC1991	13 Nov	Glasgow	4	0
EC1995	26 Apr	Serravalle	2	0
EC1995	15 Nov	Glasgow	5	0
wc2000	7 Oct	Serravalle	2	0
wc2001	28 Mar	Glasgow	4	0

v SAUDI ARABIA

			S	SA
1988	17 Feb	Riyadh	2	2

v SOUTH AFRICA

			S	SA
2002	20 May	Hong Kong	0	2

v SOUTH KOREA

			S	SK
2002	16 May	Busan	1	4

v SPAIN

			S	Sp
wc1957	8 May	Glasgow	4	2
wc1957	26 May	Madrid	1	4
1963	13 June	Madrid	6	2
1965	8 May	Glasgow	0	0
EC1974	20 Nov	Glasgow	1	2
EC1975	5 Feb	Valencia	1	1
1982	24 Feb	Valencia	0	3
wc1984	14 Nov	Glasgow	3	1
wc1985	27 Feb	Seville	0	1
1988	27 Apr	Madrid	0	0

v SWEDEN

			S	Sw
1952	30 May	Stockholm	1	3

			S	Sw
1953	6 May	Glasgow	1	2
1975	16 Apr	Gothenburg	1	1
1977	27 Apr	Glasgow	3	1
wc1980	10 Sept	Stockholm	1	0
wc1981	9 Sept	Glasgow	2	0
wc1990	16 June	Genoa	2	1
1995	11 Oct	Stockholm	0	2
wc1996	10 Nov	Glasgow	1	0
wc1997	30 Apr	Gothenburg	1	2

v SWITZERLAND

			S	Sw
1931	24 May	Geneva	3	2
1948	17 May	Berne	1	2
1950	26 Apr	Glasgow	3	1
wc1957	19 May	Basle	2	1
wc1957	6 Nov	Glasgow	3	2
1973	22 June	Berne	0	1
1976	7 Apr	Glasgow	1	0
EC1982	17 Nov	Berne	0	2
EC1983	30 May	Glasgow	2	2
EC1990	17 Oct	Glasgow	2	1
EC1991	11 Sept	Berne	2	2
wc1992	9 Sept	Berne	1	3
wc1993	8 Sept	Aberdeen	1	1
EC1996	18 June	Birmingham	1	0

v TURKEY

			S	T
1960	8 June	Ankara	2	4

†match not recognised by FIFA

v URUGUAY

			S	U
wc1954	19 June	Basle	0	7
1962	2 May	Glasgow	2	3
1983	21 Sept	Glasgow	2	0
wc1986	13 June	Nezahualcoyotl	0	0

v USA

			S	USA
1952	30 Apr	Glasgow	6	0
1992	17 May	Denver	1	0
1996	26 May	New Britain	1	2
1998	30 May	Washington	0	0

v USSR

			S	USSR
1967	10 May	Glasgow	0	2
1971	14 June	Moscow	0	1
wc1982	22 June	Malaga	2	2
1991	6 Feb	Glasgow	0	1

v YUGOSLAVIA

			S	Y
1955	15 May	Belgrade	2	2
1956	21 Nov	Glasgow	2	0
wc1958	8 June	Vasteras	1	1
1972	29 June	Belo Horizonte	2	2
wc1974	22 June	Frankfurt	1	1
1984	12 Sept	Glasgow	6	1
wc1988	19 Oct	Glasgow	1	1
wc1989	6 Sept	Zagreb	1	3

v ZAIRE

			S	Z
wc1974	14 June	Dortmund	2	0

WALES

v ALBANIA

			W	A
EC1994	7 Sept	Cardiff	2	0
EC1995	15 Nov	Tirana	1	1

v ARGENTINA

			W	A
1992	3 June	Tokyo	0	1
2002	13 Feb	Cardiff	1	1

v ARMENIA

			W	A
wc2001	24 Mar	Erevan	2	2
wc2001	1 Sept	Cardiff	0	0

v AUSTRIA

			W	A
1954	9 May	Vienna	0	2
EC1955	23 Nov	Wrexham	1	2
EC1974	4 Sept	Vienna	1	2
1975	19 Nov	Wrexham	1	0
1992	29 Apr	Vienna	1	1

v BELARUS

			W	B
EC1998	14 Oct	Cardiff	3	2
EC1999	4 Sept	Minsk	2	2
wc2000	2 Sept	Minsk	1	2
wc2001	6 Oct	Cardiff	1	0

v BELGIUM

			W	B
1949	22 May	Liège	1	3
1949	23 Nov	Cardiff	5	1
EC1990	17 Oct	Cardiff	3	1
EC1991	27 Mar	Brussels	1	1
wc1992	18 Nov	Brussels	0	2
wc1993	31 Mar	Cardiff	2	0
wc1997	29 Mar	Cardiff	1	2
wc1997	11 Oct	Brussels	2	3

v BRAZIL

			W	B
wc1958	19 June	Gothenburg	0	1
1962	12 May	Rio de Janeiro	1	3
1962	16 May	São Paulo	1	3
1966	14 May	Rio de Janeiro	1	3
1966	18 May	Belo Horizonte	0	1
1983	12 June	Cardiff	1	1
1991	11 Sept	Cardiff	1	0
1997	12 Nov	Brasilia	0	3
2000	23 May	Cardiff	0	3

v BULGARIA

			W	B
EC1983	27 Apr	Wrexham	1	0
EC1983	16 Nov	Sofia	0	1
EC1994	14 Dec	Cardiff	0	3
EC1995	29 Mar	Sofia	1	3

v CANADA

			W	C
1986	10 May	Toronto	0	2
1986	20 May	Vancouver	3	0

v CHILE

			W	C
1966	22 May	Santiago	0	2

v COSTA RICA

			W	CR
1990	20 May	Cardiff	1	0

v CYPRUS

			W	C
wc1992	14 Oct	Limassol	1	0
wc1993	13 Oct	Cardiff	2	0

v CZECHOSLOVAKIA

			W	C
wc1957	1 May	Cardiff	1	0
wc1957	26 May	Prague	0	2
EC1971	21 Apr	Swansea	1	3
EC1971	27 Oct	Prague	0	1
wc1977	30 Mar	Wrexham	3	0
wc1977	16 Nov	Prague	0	1
wc1980	19 Nov	Cardiff	1	0
EC1981	9 Sept	Prague	0	2
EC1987	29 Apr	Wrexham	1	1
EC1987	11 Nov	Prague	0	2
wc1993	28 Apr	Ostrava†	1	1
wc1993	8 Sept	Cardiff†	2	2

†Czechoslovakia played as RCS (Republic of Czechs and Slovaks).

v CZECH REPUBLIC

			W	CR
2002	27 Mar	Cardiff	0	0

v DENMARK

			W	D
wc1964	21 Oct	Copenhagen	0	1
wc1965	1 Dec	Wrexham	4	2
EC1987	9 Sept	Cardiff	1	0
EC1987	14 Oct	Copenhagen	0	1
1990	11 Sept	Copenhagen	0	1
EC1998	10 Oct	Copenhagen	2	1
EC1999	9 June	Liverpool	0	2

v ESTONIA — W E

			W	E
1994	23 May	Tallinn	2	1

v FINLAND — W F

			W	F
EC1971	26 May	Helsinki	1	0
EC1971	13 Oct	Swansea	3	0
EC1987	10 Sept	Helsinki	1	1
EC1987	1 Apr	Wrexham	4	0
wc1988	19 Oct	Swansea	2	2
wc1989	6 Sept	Helsinki	0	1
2000	29 Mar	Cardiff	1	2

v FAEROES — W F

			W	F
wc1992	9 Sept	Cardiff	6	0
wc1993	6 June	Toftir	3	0

v FRANCE — W F

			W	F
1933	25 May	Paris	1	1
1939	20 May	Paris	1	2
1953	14 May	Paris	1	6
1982	2 June	Toulouse	1	0

v GEORGIA — W G

			W	G
EC1994	16 Nov	Tbilisi	0	5
EC1995	7 June	Cardiff	0	1

v GERMANY — W G

			W	G
EC1995	26 Apr	Dusseldorf	1	1
EC1995	11 Oct	Cardiff	1	2
2002	14 May	Cardiff	1	0

v EAST GERMANY — W EG

			W	EG
wc1957	19 May	Leipzig	1	2
wc1957	25 Sept	Cardiff	4	1
wc1969	16 Apr	Dresden	1	2
wc1969	22 Oct	Cardiff	1	3

v WEST GERMANY — W WG

			W	WG
1968	8 May	Cardiff	1	1
1969	26 Mar	Frankfurt	1	1
1976	6 Oct	Cardiff	0	2
1977	14 Dec	Dortmund	1	1
EC1979	2 May	Wrexham	0	2
EC1979	17 Oct	Cologne	1	5
wc1989	31 May	Cardiff	0	0
wc1989	15 Nov	Cologne	1	2
EC1991	5 June	Cardiff	1	0
EC1991	16 Oct	Nuremberg	1	4

v GREECE — W G

			W	G
wc1964	9 Dec	Athens	0	2
wc1965	17 Mar	Cardiff	4	1

v HOLLAND — W H

			W	H
wc1988	14 Sept	Amsterdam	0	1
wc1989	11 Oct	Wrexham	1	2
1992	30 May	Utrecht	0	4
wc1996	5 Oct	Cardiff	1	3
wc1996	9 Nov	Eindhoven	1	7

v HUNGARY — W H

			W	H
wc1958	8 June	Sanviken	1	1
wc1958	17 June	Stockholm	2	1
1961	28 May	Budapest	2	3
EC1962	7 Nov	Budapest	1	3
EC1963	20 Mar	Cardiff	1	1
EC1974	30 Oct	Cardiff	2	0
EC1975	16 Apr	Budapest	2	1
1985	16 Oct	Cardiff	0	3

v ICELAND — W I

			W	I
wc1980	2 June	Reykjavik	4	0
wc1981	14 Oct	Swansea	2	2
wc1984	12 Sept	Reykjavik	0	1
wc1984	14 Nov	Cardiff	2	1
1991	1 May	Cardiff	1	0

v IRAN — W I

			W	I
1978	18 Apr	Teheran	1	0

v REPUBLIC OF IRELAND — W RI

			W	RI
1960	28 Sept	Dublin	3	2
1979	11 Sept	Swansea	2	1
1981	24 Feb	Dublin	3	1
1986	26 Mar	Dublin	1	0
1990	28 Mar	Dublin	0	1
1991	6 Feb	Wrexham	0	3
1992	19 Feb	Dublin	1	0
1993	17 Feb	Dublin	1	2
1997	11 Feb	Cardiff	0	0

v ISRAEL — W I

			W	I
wc1958	15 Jan	Tel Aviv	2	0
wc1958	5 Feb	Cardiff	2	0
1984	10 June	Tel Aviv	0	0
1989	8 Feb	Tel Aviv	3	3

v ITALY — W I

			W	I
1965	1 May	Florence	1	4
wc1968	23 Oct	Cardiff	0	1
wc1969	4 Nov	Rome	1	4
1988	4 June	Brescia	1	0
1996	24 Jan	Terni	0	3
EC1998	5 Sept	Liverpool	0	2
EC1999	5 June	Bologna	0	4

v JAMAICA — W J

			W	J
1998	25 Mar	Cardiff	0	0

v JAPAN — W J

			W	J
1992	7 June	Matsuyama	1	0

v KUWAIT — W K

			W	K
1977	6 Sept	Wrexham	0	0
1977	20 Sept	Kuwait	0	0

v LUXEMBOURG — W L

			W	L
EC1974	20 Nov	Swansea	5	0
EC1975	1 May	Luxembourg	3	1
EC1990	14 Nov	Luxembourg	1	0
EC1991	13 Nov	Cardiff	1	0

v MALTA — W M

			W	M
EC1978	25 Oct	Wrexham	7	0
EC1979	2 June	Valletta	2	0
1988	1 June	Valletta	3	2
1998	3 June	Valletta	3	0

v MEXICO — W M

			W	M
wc1958	11 June	Stockholm	1	1
1962	22 May	Mexico City	1	2

v MOLDOVA — W M

			W	M
EC1994	12 Oct	Kishinev	2	3
EC1995	6 Sept	Cardiff	1	0

v NORWAY — W N

			W	N
EC1982	22 Sept	Swansea	1	0
EC1983	21 Sept	Oslo	0	0
1984	6 June	Trondheim	0	1
1985	26 Feb	Wrexham	1	1
1985	5 June	Bergen	2	4
1994	9 Mar	Cardiff	1	3
wc2000	7 Oct	Cardiff	1	1
wc2001	5 Sept	Oslo	2	3

v POLAND — W P

			W	P
wc1973	28 Mar	Cardiff	2	0
wc1973	26 Sept	Katowice	0	3
1991	29 May	Radom	0	0
wc2000	11 Oct	Warsaw	0	0
wc2001	2 June	Cardiff	1	2

v PORTUGAL — W P

			W	P
1949	15 May	Lisbon	2	3
1951	12 May	Cardiff	2	1
2000	2 June	Chaves	0	3

v QATAR — W Q

			W	Q
2000	23 Feb	Doha	1	0

		v ROMANIA	W	R
EC1970	11 Nov	Cardiff	0	0
EC1971	24 Nov	Bucharest	0	2
1983	12 Oct	Wrexham	5	0
wc1992	20 May	Bucharest	1	5
wc1993	17 Nov	Cardiff	1	2

		v SAN MARINO	W	SM
wc1996	2 June	Serravalle	5	0
wc1996	31 Aug	Cardiff	6	0

		v SAUDI ARABIA	W	SA
1986	25 Feb	Dahran	2	1

		v SPAIN	W	S
wc1961	19 Apr	Cardiff	1	2
wc1961	18 May	Madrid	1	1
1982	24 Mar	Valencia	1	1
wc1984	17 Oct	Seville	0	3
wc1985	30 Apr	Wrexham	3	0

		v SWEDEN	W	S
wc1958	15 June	Stockholm	0	0
1988	27 Apr	Stockholm	1	4
1989	26 Apr	Wrexham	0	2
1990	25 Apr	Stockholm	2	4
1994	20 Apr	Wrexham	0	2

		v SWITZERLAND	W	S
1949	26 May	Berne	0	4
1951	16 May	Wrexham	3	2
1996	24 Apr	Lugano	0	2
EC1999	31 Mar	Zurich	0	2
EC1999	9 Oct	Wrexham	0	2

		v TUNISIA	W	T
1998	6 June	Tunis	0	4

		v TURKEY	W	T
EC1978	29 Nov	Wrexham	1	0
EC1979	21 Nov	Izmir	0	1
wc1980	15 Oct	Cardiff	4	0
wc1981	25 Mar	Ankara	1	0
wc1996	14 Dec	Cardiff	0	0
wc1997	20 Aug	Istanbul	4	6

		v REST OF UNITED KINGDOM	W	UK
1951	5 Dec	Cardiff	3	2
1969	28 July	Cardiff	0	1

		v UKRAINE	W	U
wc2001	28 Mar	Cardiff	1	1
wc2001	6 June	Kiev	1	1

		v URUGUAY	W	U
1986	21 Apr	Wrexham	0	0

		v USSR	W	USSR
wc1965	30 May	Moscow	1	2
wc1965	27 Oct	Cardiff	2	1
wc1981	30 May	Wrexham	0	0
wc1981	18 Nov	Tbilisi	0	3
1987	18 Feb	Swansea	0	0

		v YUGOSLAVIA	W	Y
1953	21 May	Belgrade	2	5
1954	22 Nov	Cardiff	1	3
EC1976	24 Apr	Zagreb	0	2
EC1976	22 May	Cardiff	1	1
EC1982	15 Dec	Titograd	4	4
EC1983	14 Dec	Cardiff	1	1
1988	23 Mar	Swansea	1	2

NORTHERN IRELAND

		v ALBANIA	NI	A
wc1965	7 May	Belfast	4	1
wc1965	24 Nov	Tirana	1	1
EC1982	15 Dec	Tirana	0	0
EC1983	27 Apr	Belfast	1	0
wc1992	9 Sept	Belfast	3	0
wc1993	17 Feb	Tirana	2	1
wc1996	14 Dec	Belfast	2	0
wc1997	10 Sept	Zurich	0	1

		v ALGERIA	NI	A
wc1986	3 June	Guadalajara	1	1

		v ARGENTINA	NI	A
wc1958	11 June	Halmstad	1	3

		v ARMENIA	NI	A
wc1996	5 Oct	Belfast	1	1
wc1997	30 Apr	Erevan	0	0

		v AUSTRALIA	NI	A
1980	11 June	Sydney	2	1
1980	15 June	Melbourne	1	1
1980	18 June	Adelaide	2	1

		v AUSTRIA	NI	A
wc1982	1 July	Madrid	2	2
EC1982	13 Oct	Vienna	0	2
EC1983	21 Sept	Belfast	3	1
EC1990	14 Nov	Vienna	0	0
EC1991	16 Oct	Belfast	2	1
EC1994	12 Oct	Vienna	2	1
EC1995	15 Nov	Belfast	5	3

		v BELGIUM	NI	B
wc1976	10 Nov	Liège	0	2
wc1977	16 Nov	Belfast	3	0
1997	11 Feb	Belfast	3	0

		v BRAZIL	NI	B
wc1986	12 June	Guadalajara	0	3

		v BULGARIA	NI	B
wc1972	18 Oct	Sofia	0	3
wc1973	26 Sept	Sheffield	0	0
EC1978	29 Nov	Sofia	2	0
EC1979	2 May	Belfast	2	0
wc2001	28 Mar	Sofia	3	4
wc2001	2 June	Belfast	0	1

		v CANADA	NI	C
1995	22 May	Edmonton	0	2
1999	27 Apr	Belfast	1	1

		v CHILE	NI	C
1989	26 May	Belfast	0	1
1995	25 May	Edmonton	1	2

		v COLOMBIA	NI	C
1994	4 June	Boston	0	2

		v CYPRUS	NI	C
EC1971	3 Feb	Nicosia	3	0
EC1971	21 Apr	Belfast	5	0
wc1973	14 Feb	Nicosia	0	1
wc1973	8 May	London	3	0

		v CZECHOSLOVAKIA	NI	C
wc1958	8 June	Halmstad	1	0
wc1958	17 June	Malmo	2	1*

*After extra time

		v CZECH REPUBLIC	NI	C
wc2001	24 Mar	Belfast	0	1
wc2001	6 June	Teplice	1	3

		v DENMARK	NI	D
EC1978	25 Oct	Belfast	2	1
EC1979	6 June	Copenhagen	0	4
1986	26 Mar	Belfast	1	1
EC1990	17 Oct	Belfast	1	1
EC1991	13 Nov	Odense	1	2
wc1992	18 Nov	Belfast	0	1
wc1993	13 Oct	Copenhagen	0	1

			NI	D
wc2000	7 Oct	Belfast	1	1
wc2001	1 Sept	Copenhagen	1	1

v FAEROES			NI	F
EC1991	1 May	Belfast	1	1
EC1991	11 Sept	Landskrona	5	0

v FINLAND			NI	F
wc1984	27 May	Pori	0	1
wc1984	14 Nov	Belfast	2	1
EC1998	10 Oct	Belfast	1	0
EC1998	9 Oct	Helsinki	1	4

v FRANCE			NI	F
1928	21 Feb	Paris	0	4
1951	12 May	Belfast	2	2
1952	11 Nov	Paris	1	3
wc1958	19 June	Norrkoping	0	4
1982	24 Mar	Paris	0	4
wc1982	4 July	Madrid	1	4
1986	26 Feb	Paris	0	0
1988	27 Apr	Belfast	0	0
1999	18 Aug	Belfast	0	1

v GERMANY			NI	G
1992	2 June	Bremen	1	1
1996	29 May	Belfast	1	1
wc1996	9 Nov	Nuremberg	1	1
wc1997	20 Aug	Belfast	1	3
EC1999	27 Mar	Belfast	0	3
EC1999	8 Sept	Dortmund	0	4

v WEST GERMANY			NI	WG
wc1958	15 June	Malmo	2	2
wc1960	26 Oct	Belfast	3	4
wc1961	10 May	Hamburg	1	2
1966	7 May	Belfast	0	2
1977	27 Apr	Cologne	0	5
EC1982	17 Nov	Belfast	1	0
EC1983	16 Nov	Hamburg	1	0

v GREECE			NI	G
wc1961	3 May	Athens	1	2
wc1961	17 Oct	Belfast	2	0
1988	17 Feb	Athens	2	3

v HOLLAND			NI	H
1962	9 May	Rotterdam	0	4
wc1965	17 Mar	Belfast	2	1
wc1965	7 Apr	Rotterdam	0	0
wc1976	13 Oct	Rotterdam	2	2
wc1977	12 Oct	Belfast	0	1

v HONDURAS			NI	H
wc1982	21 June	Zaragoza	1	1

v HUNGARY			NI	H
wc1988	19 Oct	Budapest	0	1
wc1989	6 Sept	Belfast	1	2
2000	26 Apr	Belfast	0	1

v ICELAND			NI	I
wc1977	11 June	Reykjavik	0	1
wc1977	21 Sept	Belfast	2	0
wc2000	11 Oct	Reykjavik	0	1
wc2001	5 Sept	Belfast	3	0

v REPUBLIC OF IRELAND			NI	RI
EC1978	20 Sept	Dublin	0	0
EC1979	21 Nov	Belfast	1	0
wc1988	14 Sept	Belfast	0	0
wc1989	11 Oct	Dublin	0	3
wc1993	31 Mar	Dublin	0	3
wc1993	17 Nov	Belfast	1	1
EC1994	16 Nov	Belfast	0	4
EC1995	29 Mar	Dublin	1	1
1999	29 May	Dublin	1	0

v ISRAEL			NI	I
1968	10 Sept	Jaffa	3	2
1976	3 Mar	Tel Aviv	1	1
wc1980	26 Mar	Tel Aviv	0	0
wc1981	18 Nov	Belfast	1	0
1984	16 Oct	Belfast	3	0
1987	18 Feb	Tel Aviv	1	1

v ITALY			NI	I
wc1957	25 Apr	Rome	0	1
1957	4 Dec	Belfast	2	2
wc1958	15 Jan	Belfast	2	1
1961	25 Apr	Bologna	2	3
1997	22 Jan	Palermo	0	2

v LATVIA			NI	L
wc1993	2 June	Riga	2	1
wc1993	8 Sept	Belfast	2	0
EC1995	26 Apr	Riga	1	0
EC1995	7 June	Belfast	1	2

v LIECHTENSTEIN			NI	L
EC1994	20 Apr	Belfast	4	1
EC1995	11 Oct	Eschen	4	0
2002	27 Mar	Vaduz	0	0

v LITHUANIA			NI	L
wc1992	28 Apr	Belfast	2	2
wc1993	25 May	Vilnius	1	0

v LUXEMBOURG			NI	L
2000	23 Feb	Luxembourg	3	1
wc2000	2 Sept	Belfast	1	0

v MALTA			NI	M
wc1988	21 May	Belfast	3	0
wc1989	26 Apr	Valletta	2	0
2000	28 Mar	Valletta	3	0
wc2000	2 Sept	Belfast	1	0
wc2001	6 Oct	Valletta	1	0

v MEXICO			NI	M
1966	22 June	Belfast	4	1
1994	11 June	Miami	0	3

v MOLDOVA			NI	M
EC1998	18 Nov	Belfast	2	2
EC1999	31 Mar	Chisinau	0	0

v MOROCCO			NI	M
1986	23 Apr	Belfast	2	1

v NORWAY			NI	N
1922	25 May	Bergen	1	2
EC1974	4 Sept	Oslo	1	2
EC1975	29 Oct	Belfast	3	0
1990	27 Mar	Belfast	2	3
1996	27 Mar	Belfast	0	2
2001	28 Feb	Belfast	0	4

v POLAND			NI	P
EC1962	10 Oct	Katowice	2	0
EC1962	28 Nov	Belfast	2	0
1988	23 Mar	Belfast	1	1
1991	5 Feb	Belfast	3	1
2002	13 Feb	Limassol	1	4

v PORTUGAL			NI	P
wc1957	16 Jan	Lisbon	1	1
wc1957	1 May	Belfast	3	0
wc1973	28 Mar	Coventry	1	1
wc1973	14 Nov	Lisbon	1	1
wc1980	19 Nov	Lisbon	0	1
wc1981	29 Apr	Belfast	1	0
EC1994	7 Sept	Belfast	1	2
EC1995	3 Sept	Lisbon	1	1
wc1997	29 Mar	Belfast	0	0
wc1997	11 Oct	Lisbon	0	1

v ROMANIA			NI	R
wc1984	12 Sept	Belfast	3	2
wc1985	16 Oct	Bucharest	1	0
1994	23 Mar	Belfast	2	0

v SLOVAKIA			NI	S
1998	25 Mar	Belfast	1	0

v SOUTH AFRICA			NI	SA
1924	24 Sept	Belfast	1	2

v SPAIN			NI	S
1958	15 Oct	Madrid	2	6
1963	30 May	Bilbao	1	1
1963	30 Oct	Belfast	0	1
EC1970	11 Nov	Seville	0	3
EC1972	16 Feb	Hull	1	1
wc1982	25 June	Valencia	1	0
1985	27 Mar	Palma	0	0
wc1986	7 June	Guadalajara	1	2
wc1988	21 Dec	Seville	0	4
wc1989	8 Feb	Belfast	0	2
wc1992	14 Oct	Belfast	0	0
wc1993	28 Apr	Seville	1	3
1998	2 June	Santander	1	4
2002	17 Apr	Belfast	0	5

v SWEDEN			NI	S
EC1974	30 Oct	Solna	2	0
EC1975	3 Sept	Belfast	1	2
wc1980	15 Oct	Belfast	3	0
wc1981	3 June	Solna	0	1
1996	24 Apr	Belfast	1	2

v SWITZERLAND			NI	S
wc1964	14 Oct	Belfast	1	0
wc1964	14 Nov	Lausanne	1	2
1998	22 Apr	Belfast	1	0

v THAILAND			NI	T
1997	21 May	Bangkok	0	0

v TURKEY			NI	T
wc1968	23 Oct	Belfast	4	1
wc1968	11 Dec	Istanbul	3	0
EC1983	30 Mar	Belfast	2	1
EC1983	12 Oct	Ankara	0	1
wc1985	1 May	Belfast	2	0
wc1985	11 Sept	Izmir	0	0
EC1986	12 Nov	Izmir	0	0
EC1987	11 Nov	Belfast	1	0
EC1998	5 Sept	Istanbul	0	3
EC1999	4 Sept	Belfast	0	3

v UKRAINE			NI	U
wc1996	31 Aug	Belfast	0	1
wc1997	2 Apr	Kiev	1	2

v URUGUAY			NI	U
1964	29 Apr	Belfast	3	0
1990	18 May	Belfast	1	0

v USSR			NI	USSR
wc1969	19 Sept	Belfast	0	0
wc1969	22 Oct	Moscow	0	2
EC1971	22 Sept	Moscow	0	1
EC1971	13 Oct	Belfast	1	1

v YUGOSLAVIA			NI	Y
EC1975	16 Mar	Belfast	1	0
EC1975	19 Nov	Belgrade	0	1
wc1982	17 June	Zaragoza	0	0
EC1987	29 Apr	Belfast	1	2
EC1987	14 Oct	Sarajevo	0	3
EC1990	12 Sept	Belfast	0	2
EC1991	27 Mar	Belgrade	1	4
2000	16 Aug	Belfast	1	2

REPUBLIC OF IRELAND

v ALBANIA			RI	A
wc1992	26 May	Dublin	2	0
wc1993	26 May	Tirana	2	1

v ALGERIA			RI	A
1982	28 Apr	Algiers	0	2

v ANDORRA			RI	A
wc2001	28 Mar	Barcelona	3	0
wc2001	25 Apr	Dublin	3	1

v ARGENTINA			RI	A
1951	13 May	Dublin	0	1
1979	29 May	Dublin	0	0*
1980	16 May	Dublin	0	1
1998	22 Apr	Dublin	0	2

*Not considered a full international

v AUSTRIA			RI	A
1952	7 May	Vienna	0	6
1953	25 Mar	Dublin	4	0
1958	14 Mar	Vienna	1	3
1962	8 Apr	Dublin	2	3
EC1963	25 Sept	Vienna	0	0
EC1963	13 Oct	Dublin	3	2
1966	22 May	Vienna	0	1
1968	10 Nov	Dublin	2	2
EC1971	30 May	Dublin	1	4
EC1971	10 Oct	Linz	0	6
EC1995	11 June	Dublin	1	3
EC1995	6 Sept	Vienna	1	3

v BELGIUM			RI	B
1928	12 Feb	Liège	4	2
1929	30 Apr	Dublin	4	0
1930	11 May	Brussels	3	1
wc1934	25 Feb	Dublin	4	4
1949	24 Apr	Dublin	0	2
1950	10 May	Brussels	1	5
1965	24 Mar	Dublin	0	2
1966	25 May	Liège	3	2

			RI	B
wc1980	15 Oct	Dublin	1	1
wc1981	25 Mar	Brussels	0	1
EC1986	10 Sept	Brussels	2	2
EC1987	29 Apr	Dublin	0	0
wc1997	29 Oct	Dublin	1	1
wc1997	16 Nov	Brussels	1	2

v BOLIVIA			RI	B
1994	24 May	Dublin	1	0
1996	15 June	New Jersey	3	0

v BRAZIL			RI	B
1974	5 May	Rio de Janeiro	1	2
1982	27 May	Uberlandia	0	7
1987	23 May	Dublin	1	0

v BULGARIA			RI	B
wc1977	1 June	Sofia	1	2
wc1977	12 Oct	Dublin	0	0
EC1979	19 May	Sofia	0	1
EC1979	17 Oct	Dublin	3	0
wc1987	1 Apr	Sofia	1	2
wc1987	14 Oct	Dublin	2	0

v CAMEROON			RI	C
wc2002	1 June	Niigata	1	1

v CHILE			RI	C
1960	30 Mar	Dublin	2	0
1972	21 June	Recife	1	2
1974	12 May	Santiago	2	1
1982	22 May	Santiago	0	1
1991	22 May	Dublin	1	1

v CHINA			RI	C
1984	3 June	Sapporo	1	0

v CROATIA			RI	C
1996	2 June	Dublin	2	2
EC1998	5 Sept	Dublin	2	0
EC1999	4 Sept	Zagreb	0	1
2001	15 Aug	Dublin	2	2

v CYPRUS

			RI	C
wc1980	26 Mar	Nicosia	3	2
wc1980	19 Nov	Dublin	6	0
wc2001	24 Mar	Nicosia	4	0
wc2001	6 Oct	Dublin	4	0

v CZECHOSLOVAKIA

			RI	C
1938	18 May	Prague	2	2
EC1959	5 Apr	Dublin	2	0
EC1959	10 May	Bratislava	0	4
wc1961	8 Oct	Dublin	1	3
wc1961	29 Oct	Prague	1	7
EC1967	21 May	Dublin	0	2
EC1967	22 Nov	Prague	2	1
wc1969	4 May	Dublin	1	2
wc1969	7 Oct	Prague	0	3
1979	26 Sept	Prague	1	4
1981	29 Apr	Dublin	3	1
1986	27 May	Reykjavik	1	0

v CZECH REPUBLIC

			RI	C
1994	5 June	Dublin	1	3
1996	24 Apr	Prague	0	2
1998	25 Mar	Olomouc	1	2
2000	23 Feb	Dublin	3	2

v DENMARK

			RI	D
wc1956	3 Oct	Dublin	2	1
wc1957	2 Oct	Copenhagen	2	0
wc1968	4 Dec	Dublin	1	1
(abandoned after 51 mins)				
wc1969	27 May	Copenhagen	0	2
wc1969	15 Oct	Dublin	1	1
EC1978	24 May	Copenhagen	3	3
EC1979	2 May	Dublin	2	0
wc1984	14 Nov	Copenhagen	0	3
wc1985	13 Nov	Dublin	1	4
wc1992	14 Oct	Copenhagen	0	0
wc1993	28 Apr	Dublin	1	1
2002	27 Mar	Dublin	3	0

v ECUADOR

			RI	E
1972	19 June	Natal	3	2

v EGYPT

			RI	E
wc1990	17 June	Palermo	0	0

v ENGLAND

			RI	E
1946	30 Sept	Dublin	0	1
1949	21 Sept	Everton	2	0
wc1957	8 May	Wembley	1	5
wc1957	19 May	Dublin	1	1
1964	24 May	Dublin	1	3
1976	8 Sept	Wembley	1	1
EC1978	25 Oct	Dublin	1	1
EC1980	6 Feb	Wembley	0	2
1985	26 Mar	Wembley	1	2
EC1988	12 June	Stuttgart	1	0
wc1990	11 June	Cagliari	1	1
EC1990	14 Nov	Dublin	1	1
EC1991	27 Mar	Wembley	1	1
1995	15 Feb	Dublin	1	0
(abandoned after 27 mins)				

v ESTONIA

			RI	E
wc2000	11 Oct	Dublin	2	0
wc2001	6 June	Tallinn	2	0

v FINLAND

			RI	F
wc1949	8 Sept	Dublin	3	0
wc1949	9 Oct	Helsinki	1	1
1990	16 May	Dublin	1	1
2000	15 Nov	Dublin	3	0

v FRANCE

			RI	F
1937	23 May	Paris	2	0
1952	16 Nov	Dublin	1	1
wc1953	4 Oct	Dublin	3	5
wc1953	25 Nov	Paris	0	1
wc1972	15 Nov	Dublin	2	1
wc1973	19 May	Paris	1	1

(v FRANCE continued)

			RI	F
wc1976	17 Nov	Paris	0	2
wc1977	30 Mar	Dublin	1	0
wc1980	28 Oct	Paris	0	2
wc1981	14 Oct	Dublin	3	2
1989	7 Feb	Dublin	0	0

v GERMANY

			RI	G
1935	8 May	Dortmund	1	3
1936	17 Oct	Dublin	5	2
1939	23 May	Bremen	1	1
1994	29 May	Hanover	2	0
wc2002	5 June	Ibaraki	1	1

v WEST GERMANY

			RI	WG
1951	17 Oct	Dublin	3	2
1952	4 May	Cologne	0	3
1955	28 May	Hamburg	1	2
1956	25 Nov	Dublin	3	0
1960	11 May	Dusseldorf	1	0
1966	4 May	Dublin	0	4
1970	9 May	Berlin	1	2
1975	1 Mar	Dublin	1	0†
1979	22 May	Dublin	1	3
1981	21 May	Bremen	0	3†
1989	6 Sept	Dublin	1	1

†v West Germany 'B'

v GREECE

			RI	G
2000	26 Apr	Dublin	0	1

v HOLLAND

			RI	N
1932	8 May	Amsterdam	2	0
1934	8 Apr	Amsterdam	2	5
1935	8 Dec	Dublin	3	5
1955	1 May	Dublin	1	0
1956	10 May	Rotterdam	4	1
wc1980	10 Sept	Dublin	2	1
wc1981	9 Sept	Rotterdam	2	2
EC1982	22 Sept	Rotterdam	1	2
EC1983	12 Oct	Dublin	2	3
EC1988	18 June	Gelsenkirchen	0	1
wc1990	21 June	Palermo	1	1
1994	20 Apr	Tilburg	1	0
wc1994	4 July	Orlando	0	2
EC1995	13 Dec	Liverpool	0	2
1996	4 June	Rotterdam	1	3
wc2000	2 Sept	Amsterdam	2	2
wc2001	1 Sept	Dublin	1	0

v HUNGARY

			RI	H
1934	15 Dec	Dublin	2	4
1936	3 May	Budapest	3	3
1936	6 Dec	Dublin	2	3
1939	19 Mar	Cork	2	2
1939	18 May	Budapest	2	2
wc1969	8 June	Dublin	1	2
wc1969	5 Nov	Budapest	0	4
wc1989	8 Mar	Budapest	0	0
wc1989	4 June	Dublin	2	0
1991	11 Sept	Gyor	2	1

v ICELAND

			RI	I
EC1962	12 Aug	Dublin	4	2
EC1962	2 Sept	Reykjavik	1	1
EC1982	13 Oct	Dublin	2	0
EC1983	21 Sept	Reykjavik	3	0
1986	25 May	Reykjavik	2	1
wc1996	10 Nov	Dublin	0	0
wc1997	6 Sept	Reykjavik	4	2

v IRAN

			RI	I
1972	18 June	Recife	2	1
wc2001	10 Nov	Dublin	2	0
wc2001	15 Nov	Tehran	0	1

v N. IRELAND

			RI	NI
EC1978	20 Sept	Dublin	0	0
EC1979	21 Nov	Belfast	0	1
wc1988	14 Sept	Belfast	0	0
wc1989	11 Oct	Dublin	3	0
wc1993	31 Mar	Dublin	3	0

			RI	NI
wc1993	17 Nov	Belfast	1	1
EC1994	16 Nov	Belfast	4	1
EC1995	29 Mar	Dublin	1	1
1999	29 May	Dublin	0	1

	v ISRAEL		RI	I
1984	4 Apr	Tel Aviv	0	3
1985	27 May	Tel Aviv	0	0
1987	10 Nov	Dublin	5	0

	v ITALY		RI	I
1926	21 Mar	Turin	0	3
1927	23 Apr	Dublin	1	2
EC1970	8 Dec	Rome	0	3
EC1971	10 May	Rome	1	2
1985	5 Feb	Dublin	1	2
wc1990	30 June	Rome	0	1
1992	4 June	Foxboro	0	2
wc1994	18 June	New York	1	0

	v LATVIA		RI	L
wc1992	9 Sept	Dublin	4	0
wc1993	2 June	Riga	2	1
EC1994	7 Sept	Riga	3	0
EC1995	11 Oct	Dublin	2	1

	v LIECHTENSTEIN		RI	L
EC1994	12 Oct	Dublin	4	0
EC1995	3 June	Eschen	0	0
wc1996	31 Aug	Eschen	5	0
wc1997	21 May	Dublin	5	0

	v LITHUANIA		RI	L
wc1993	16 June	Vilnius	1	0
wc1993	8 Sept	Dublin	2	0
wc1997	20 Aug	Dublin	0	0
wc1997	10 Sept	Vilnius	2	1

	v LUXEMBOURG		RI	I
1936	9 May	Luxembourg	5	1
wc1953	28 Oct	Dublin	4	0
wc1954	7 Mar	Luxembourg	1	0
EC1987	28 May	Luxembourg	2	0
EC1987	9 Sept	Dublin	2	1

	v MACEDONIA		RI	M
wc1996	9 Oct	Dublin	3	0
wc1997	2 Apr	Skopje	2	3
EC1999	9 June	Dublin	1	0
EC1999	9 Oct	Skopje	1	1

	v MALTA		RI	M
EC1983	30 Mar	Valletta	1	0
EC1983	16 Nov	Dublin	8	0
wc1989	28 May	Dublin	2	0
wc1989	15 Nov	Valletta	2	0
1990	2 June	Valletta	3	0
EC1998	14 Oct	Dublin	5	0
EC1999	8 Sept	Valletta	3	2

	v MEXICO		RI	M
1984	8 Aug	Dublin	0	0
wc1994	24 June	Orlando	1	2
1996	13 June	New Jersey	2	2
1998	23 May	Dublin	0	0
2000	4 June	Chicago	2	2

	v MOROCCO		RI	M
1990	12 Sept	Dublin	1	0

	v NIGERIA		RI	N
2002	16 May	Dublin	1	2

	v NORWAY		RI	N
wc1937	10 Oct	Oslo	2	3
wc1937	7 Nov	Dublin	3	3
1950	26 Nov	Dublin	2	2
1951	30 May	Oslo	3	2
1954	8 Nov	Dublin	2	1
1955	25 May	Oslo	3	1
1960	6 Nov	Dublin	3	1
1964	13 May	Oslo	4	1
1973	6 June	Oslo	1	1
1976	24 Mar	Dublin	3	0

			RI	N
1978	21 May	Oslo	0	0
wc1984	17 Oct	Oslo	0	1
wc1985	1 May	Dublin	0	0
1988	1 June	Oslo	0	0
wc1994	28 June	New York	0	0

	v PARAGUAY		RI	P
1999	10 Feb	Dublin	2	0

	v POLAND		RI	P
1938	22 May	Warsaw	0	6
1938	13 Nov	Dublin	3	2
1958	11 May	Katowice	2	2
1958	5 Oct	Dublin	2	2
1964	10 May	Kracow	1	3
1964	25 Oct	Dublin	3	2
1968	15 May	Dublin	2	2
1968	30 Oct	Katowice	0	1
1970	6 May	Dublin	1	2
1970	23 Sept	Dublin	0	2
1973	16 May	Wroclaw	0	2
1973	21 Oct	Dublin	1	0
1976	26 May	Poznan	2	0
1977	24 Apr	Dublin	0	0
1978	12 Apr	Lodz	0	3
1981	23 May	Bydgoszcz	0	3
1984	23 May	Dublin	0	0
1986	12 Nov	Warsaw	0	1
1988	22 May	Dublin	3	1
EC1991	1 May	Dublin	0	0
EC1991	16 Oct	Poznan	3	3

	v PORTUGAL		RI	P
1946	16 June	Lisbon	1	3
1947	4 May	Dublin	0	2
1948	23 May	Lisbon	0	2
1949	22 May	Dublin	1	0
1972	25 June	Recife	1	2
1992	7 June	Boston	2	0
EC1995	26 Apr	Dublin	1	0
EC1995	15 Nov	Lisbon	0	3
1996	29 May	Dublin	0	1
wc2000	7 Oct	Lisbon	1	1
wc2001	2 June	Dublin	1	1

	v ROMANIA		RI	R
1988	23 Mar	Dublin	2	0
wc1990	25 June	Genoa	0	0*
wc1997	30 Apr	Bucharest	0	1
wc1997	11 Oct	Dublin	1	1

*After extra time

	v RUSSIA		RI	R
1994	23 Mar	Dublin	0	0
1996	27 Mar	Dublin	0	2
2002	13 Feb	Dublin	2	0

	v SAUDI ARABIA		RI	SA
wc2002	11 June	Yokohama	3	0

	v SCOTLAND		RI	S
wc1961	3 May	Glasgow	1	4
wc1961	7 May	Dublin	0	3
1963	9 June	Dublin	1	0
1969	21 Sept	Dublin	1	1
EC1986	15 Oct	Dublin	0	0
EC1987	18 Feb	Glasgow	1	0
2000	30 May	Dublin	1	2

	v SOUTH AFRICA		RI	SA
2000	11 June	New Jersey	2	1

	v SPAIN		RI	S
1931	26 Apr	Barcelona	1	1
1931	13 Dec	Dublin	0	5
1946	23 June	Madrid	1	0
1947	2 Mar	Dublin	3	2
1948	30 May	Barcelona	1	2
1949	12 June	Dublin	1	4
1952	1 June	Madrid	0	6
1955	27 Nov	Dublin	2	2

			RI	S
EC1964	11 Mar	Seville	1	5
EC1964	8 Apr	Dublin	0	2
wc1965	5 May	Dublin	1	0
wc1965	27 Oct	Seville	1	4
wc1965	10 Nov	Paris	0	1
EC1966	23 Oct	Dublin	0	0
EC1966	7 Dec	Valencia	0	2
1977	9 Feb	Dublin	0	1
EC1982	17 Nov	Dublin	3	3
EC1983	27 Apr	Zaragoza	0	2
1985	26 May	Cork	0	0
wc1988	16 Nov	Seville	0	2
wc1989	26 Apr	Dublin	1	0
wc1992	18 Nov	Seville	0	0
wc1993	13 Oct	Dublin	1	3
wc2002	16 June	Suwon	1	1

		v SWEDEN	RI	S
wc1949	2 June	Stockholm	1	3
wc1949	13 Nov	Dublin	1	3
1959	1 Nov	Dublin	3	2
1960	18 May	Malmo	1	4
EC1970	14 Oct	Dublin	1	1
EC1970	28 Oct	Malmo	0	1
1999	28 Apr	Dublin	2	0

		v SWITZERLAND	RI	S
1935	5 May	Basle	0	1
1936	17 Mar	Dublin	1	0
1937	17 May	Berne	1	0
1938	18 Sept	Dublin	4	0
1948	5 Dec	Dublin	0	1
EC1975	11 May	Dublin	2	1
EC1975	21 May	Berne	0	1
1980	30 Apr	Dublin	2	0
wc1985	2 June	Dublin	3	0
wc1985	11 Sept	Berne	0	0
1992	25 Mar	Dublin	2	1

		v TRINIDAD & TOBAGO	RI	TT
1982	30 May	Port of Spain	1	2

		v TUNISIA	RI	T
1988	19 Oct	Dublin	4	0

		v TURKEY	RI	T
EC1966	16 Nov	Dublin	2	1
EC1967	22 Feb	Ankara	1	2
EC1974	20 Nov	Izmir	1	1

			RI	T
EC1975	29 Oct	Dublin	4	0
1976	13 Oct	Ankara	3	3
1978	5 Apr	Dublin	4	2
1990	26 May	Izmir	0	0
EC1990	17 Oct	Dublin	5	0
EC1991	13 Nov	Istanbul	3	1
EC2000	13 Nov	Dublin	1	1
EC2000	17 Nov	Bursa	0	0

		v URUGUAY	RI	U
1974	8 May	Montevideo	0	2
1986	23 Apr	Dublin	1	1

		v USA	RI	USA
1979	29 Oct	Dublin	3	2
1991	1 June	Boston	1	1
1992	29 Apr	Dublin	4	1
1992	30 May	Washington	1	3
1996	9 June	Boston	1	2
2000	6 June	Boston	1	1
2002	17 Apr	Dublin	2	1

		v USSR	RI	USSR
wc1972	18 Oct	Dublin	1	2
wc1973	13 May	Moscow	0	1
EC1974	30 Oct	Dublin	3	0
EC1975	18 May	Kiev	1	2
wc1984	12 Sept	Dublin	1	0
wc1985	16 Oct	Moscow	0	2
EC1988	15 June	Hanover	1	1
1990	25 Apr	Dublin	1	0

		v WALES	RI	W
1960	28 Sept	Dublin	2	3
1979	11 Sept	Swansea	1	2
1981	24 Feb	Dublin	1	3
1986	26 Mar	Dublin	0	1
1990	28 Mar	Dublin	1	0
1991	6 Feb	Wrexham	3	0
1992	19 Feb	Dublin	0	1
1993	17 Feb	Dublin	2	1
1997	11 Feb	Cardiff	0	0

		v YUGOSLAVIA	RI	Y
1955	19 Sept	Dublin	1	4
1988	27 Apr	Dublin	2	0
EC1998	18 Nov	Belgrade	0	1
EC1999	1 Sept	Dublin	2	1

OTHER BRITISH AND IRISH INTERNATIONAL MATCHES 2001–02

FRIENDLIES

Tottenham, 15 August 2001, 35,238
England (0) 0
Holland (2) 2 *(Van Bommel 30, Van Nistelrooy 39)*
England: Martyn (James 46) (Wright 49); Neville G (Mills 46), Ashley Cole (Powell 46), Carragher, Brown (Southgate 46), Keown (Ehiogu 49), Beckham (Lampard 46), Scholes (Carrick 46), Andy Cole (Smith 69), Fowler (Owen 46), Hargreaves (Barmby 46).
Holland: Van der Sar (Walerrius 46); Reiziger, Van Bronckhorst, Cocu (Kamphuis 80), Stam (Melchiot 46), Hofland, Overmars (Davids 46), Van Bommel (Landzaat 72), Kluivert (Van Hooijdonk 89), Van Nistelrooy (Hasselbaink 46), Zenden (Makaay 46).
Referee: Frisk (Sweden).

Old Trafford, 10 November 2001, 64,413
England (1) 1 *(Beckham 28 (pen))*
Sweden (1) 1 *(Mild 44)*
England: Martyn; Neville G (Mills 57), Carragher (Neville P 86), Butt (Murphy 57), Southgate, Ferdinand, Beckham, Scholes (Lampard 86), Heskey (Sheringham 57), Phillips (Fowler 57), Sinclair (Anderton 57).
Sweden: Hedman (Kihlstedt 46); Andersson C, Mjallby (Jakobsson 62), Edman (Andersson D 46), Linderoth, Magnus Svensson (Svensson A 46), Alexandersson (Soderstrom 85), Mild, Michael Svensson, Allback, Ibrahimovic (Osmanovski 74).
Referee: Colombo (France).

Amsterdam, 13 February 2002, 48,500
Holland (1) 1 *(Kluivert 26)*
England (0) 1 *(Vassell 61)*
Holland: Van der Sar; Ricksen, Van Bronckhorst, Cocu (Boateng 46), Reiziger, Frank de Boer (Paauwe 67), Ronald de Boer (Sikora 59), Van Bommel (Davids 46), Kluivert, Van Nistelrooy (Hasselbaink 64), Overmars (Makaay 88).
England: Martyn (James 46); Neville G (Neville P 77), Bridge (Powell 46), Gerrard (Lampard 77), Campbell (Southgate 46), Ferdinand, Beckham, Scholes (Butt 77), Vassell (Cole J 77), Ricketts (Phillips 46), Heskey.
Referee: Duhamel (France).

Leeds, 27 March 2002, 36,635
England (0) 1 *(Fowler 63)*
Italy (0) 2 *(Montella 67, 90 (pen))*
England: Martyn (James 46); Mills (Neville P 46), Bridge (Neville G 87), Lampard (Cole J 46), Southgate (Ehiogu 46), Campbell (King 46), Beckham (Murphy 46), Butt (Hargreaves 46), Heskey (Fowler 46), Owen (Vassell 46), Sinclair (Sheringham 70).
Italy: Buffon; Zambrotta, Panucci (Coco 74), Cannavaro, Nesta (Adani 82), Materazzi (Iuliano 57), Di Biagio (Gattuso 57), Zanetti (Albertini 57), Delvecchio (Maccarone 74), Totti (Montella 46), Doni (Tommasi 74).
Referee: Fandel (Germany).

Anfield, 17 April 2002, 42,713
England (1) 4 *(Owen 4, Murphy 47, Vassell 55, Ayala 81 (og))*
Paraguay (0) 0
England: Seaman; Neville G (Lampard 68); Bridge (Neville P 68), Butt (Hargreaves 46), Southgate (Carragher 68), Keown (Mills 46), Gerrard (Sinclair 46), Scholes (Murphy 46), Vassell (Sheringham 68), Owen (Fowler 46), Dyer (Cole J 46).
Paraguay: Tavarelli; Arce, Caniza, Gavilan (Sanabria 55), Ayala, Gamarra (Caceres 80), Struway, Paredes, Cardozo (Baez 46), Santa Cruz, Bonet (Moringo 80).
Referee: Boignino (Italy).

Seoguipo, 21 May 2002, 39,876
South Korea (0) 1 *(Park JS 52)*
England: (1) 1 *(Owen 26)*
South Korea: Lee WJ; Song CG, Lee YP, Yoo SC, Choi JC, Hong MB, Kim NI (Lee MS 89), Choi TU (Cha DR 76), Seol KH (Ahn JH 56), Lee CS, Park JS.
England: Martyn (James 46); Mills (Brown 68), Ashley Cole (Bridge 46), Murphy (Sinclair 46), Campbell (Keown 46), Ferdinand (Southgate 46), Hargreaves, Scholes (Cole J 46), Vassell, Owen (Sheringham 46), Heskey.
Referee: Supian (Malaysia).

Kobe, 26 May 2002, 42,000
Cameroon (1) 2 *(Eto'o 5, Geremi 58)*
England (1) 2 *(Vassell 12, Fowler 90)*
Cameroon: Alioum (Songo'o 77); Song (Ndo 68),Tchato,Geremi (Ainoudji 65), Kalla (Mettomo 55), Lauren (Epalle 59), Foe (Djemba-Djemba 53), Wome (Njanka 61), Eto'o (Suffo 59), Mboma (Ndiefi 65), Olembe (Ngom Kome 53).
England: Martyn (James 46); Brown, Bridge, Cole J, Campbell (Keown 46), Ferdinand (Southgate 46), Hargreaves, Scholes (Mills 46), Vassell (Fowler 76), Owen (Sheringham 46), Heskey (Sinclair 46).
Referee: Katayama (Japan).

Paris, 27 March 2002, 80,000
France (4) 5 *(Zidane 12, Trezeguet 23, 42, Henry 32, Marlet 87)*
Scotland (0) 0
France: Barthez; Candela (Karembeu 56), Lizarazu, Vieira (Makelele 46), Leboeuf (Christanval 63), Desailly (Silvestre 46), Wiltord (Marlet 56), Petit, Trezeguet (Carriere 74), Zidane (Djorkaeff 81), Henry.
Scotland: Sullivan; Weir, Crainey, Cameron (Holt 46) (McNamara 74), Caldwell G, Dailly, Lambert, Matteo, Freedman (Gemmill 46), Crawford (Thompson 63), McCann.

Aberdeen, 17 April 2002, 20,465
Scotland (1) 1 *(Dailly 7)*
Nigeria (1) 2 *(Aghahowa 40, 69)*
Scotland: Douglas; Stockdale (Alexander 46), Crainey, Lambert, Weir, Dailly, Williams (Stewart 64), McNaughton, Thompson (O'Connor 74), McCann (Johnston 78), Gemmill (Caldwell G 46).
Nigeria: Ejide (Bankole 46); Sodje (Ifeajigwa 85), Christopher (Adepoju 78), Yobo, Okoronkwo, Ejiofor, Okocha, Utaka, Aghahowa, Kanu, Ogbeche.
Referee: Ovredo (Norway).

Busan, 16 May 2002, 60,000
South Korea (1) 4 *(Lee CS 15, Ahn JH 57, 87, Yoon JH 67)*
Scotland (0) 1 *(Dobie 74)*
South Korea: Kim BJ; Lee CS (Cha DR 72), Hong MB (Yoon JH 65), Choi JC (Lee MS 46), Kim TY, Lee YP, Yoo SC, Hwang SH (Ahn JH 46), Park JS (Choi TU 72), Lee EY, Song CG.
Scotland: Sullivan; Ross, Alexander (Stockdale 62), Caldwell G, Weir, Dailly, Johnston (Kyle 66), O'Connor (Williams 46), Stewart (Severin 46), Dobie, Gemmill.
Referee: Santhan (Singapore).

Hong Kong, 20 May 2002, 3007
South Africa (1) 2 *(Mokoena T 32, Koumantarakis 90)*
Scotland (0) 0
South Africa: Vonk; Mokoena A (Nzama 62), Carnell, Sibaya, Radebe, Issa, Zuma (Koumantarakis 82), Pule (Arendse 69), McCarthy, Mokoena T, Fortune (Buckley 84).

Scotland: Douglas; Stockdale (Alexander 69), Ross, Caldwell G (Wilkie 46), Weir, Dailly, Williams (Severin 78), Kyle, Dobie, Gemmill (Stewart 86), Johnston (McFadden 62).
Referee: Chan SK (Hong Kong).

Hong Kong, 23 May 2002, 5000
Hong Kong (0) 0
Scotland (0) 4 *(Kyle, Thompson, Dailly, Gemmill)*

Scotland: Douglas (Gallacher 76); Ross (Cummings 46), Stockdale, Weir, Dailly, Wilkie, Johnston (Williams 62), Severin, Thompson (Dobie 46), Kyle (O'Connor 81), Gemmill (Alexander 88).

(Caps awarded by Scotland; match not considered a full international by FIFA).

Millennium Stadium, 13 February 2002, 65,000
Wales (1) 1 *(Bellamy 34)*
Argentina (0) 1 *(Cruz 61)*

Wales: Jones P (Crossley 46); Delaney, Speed, Melville, Page, Pembridge (Robinson C 90), Davies, Savage, Hartson, Bellamy, Giggs (Robinson J 61).
Argentina: Saja; Kily Gonzalez, Hussain, Placente, Chamot, Vivas, Sorin, Veron, Caniggia (Galletti 90), Cruz (Saviola 74), Riquelme (Aimar 74).
Referee: McKeown (Ireland).

Ninian Park, 27 March 2002, 22,000
Wales (0) 0
Czech Republic (0) 0

Wales: Ward (Coyne 46); Delaney, Gabbidon, Savage (Evans P 73), Melville, Page, Davies, Robinson J, Hartson (Taylor 73), Blake (Trollope 62), Koumas.
Czech Republic: Cech (Vaniak 46); Fukal, Jankulovski (Holenak 82), Galasek (Koldusek 62), Ujifalusi, Novotny (Johana 46), Poborsky, Rosicky (Sionko 46), Lokvenc (Koller 46), Stajner (Hubschman 46), Smicer.

Referee: Larsen (Denmark).

Millennium Stadium, 14 May 2002, 36,920
Wales (0) 1 *(Earnshaw 46)*
Germany (0) 0

Wales: Crossley; Delaney, Speed, Melville, Page, Savage, Davies, Earnshaw (Coleman 90), Hartson, Pembridge, Giggs.
Germany: Kahn; Heinrich, Ziege (Bode 63), Deisler (Asamoah 63), Linke, Metzelder, Jeremies, Hamann (Kehl 73), Bierhoff (Jancker 72), Klose, Frings.
Referee: Olsen (Norway).

Limassol, 13 February 2002, 221
Poland (2) 4 *(Kryszalowicz 6, 67, Kaluzny 11, Marcin Zewlakow 69)*
Northern Ireland (1) 1 *(Lomas 18)*

Poland: Majdan (Bledzewski 90); Krzynowek, Waldoch, Iwan (Smolarek 46), Bak J, Michal Zewlakow (Rzasa 60), Kozminski, Swierczewski (Zdebel 46), Kryszalowicz (Zielinski 82), Kaluzny (Bak A 46), Olisadebe (Marcin Zewlakow 46).
Northern Ireland: Taylor; Griffin (McCartney 46), Kennedy (McCann 82), Mulryne (Lennon 46), Hughes A, Lomas, Gillespie, Magilton (Duff 82), Johnson (McVeigh 66), Healy (Elliott 60), Hughes M.
Referee: Papaioannou (Cyprus).

Vaduz, 27 March 2002, 1080
Liechtenstein (0) 0
Northern Ireland (0) 0

Liechtenstein: Jehle; Hasler, Gigon, Martin Stocklasa, Zech, Michael Stocklasa, Telser, Beck M, Nigg (Burgmeier 73), Buchel, Beck T.
Northern Ireland: Taylor (Carroll 46); Lomas, McCann (Holmes 69), Mulryne, Williams M, McCartney, Gillespie, Magilton, Johnson, Healy (Elliott 84), Feeney (Hughes M 58).
Referee: Rogalla (Switzerland).

Belfast, 17 April 2002, 11,100
Northern Ireland (0) 0
Spain (1) 5 *(Raul 23, 54, Baraja 47, Puyol 69, Morientes 78)*

Northern Ireland: Taylor (Carroll 46); Nolan, McCartney, Horlock, Hughes A, Williams M, Gillespie (McCourt 77), Elliott, Feeney (McEvilly 63), Johnson, Healy.
Spain: Canizares (Casillas 74); Puyol, Juanfran, Albelda (Mendieta 46), Hierro (Sergio 74), Nadal (Torres 46), Joaquin (Helguera 46), Baraja, Morientes, Raul, De Pedro (Valeron 46).
Referee: Clark (Scotland).

Dublin, 15 August 2001, 27,000
Republic of Ireland (1) 2 *(Duff 21, Morrison 77)*
Croatia (0) 2 *(Vugrinec 80, Suker 90 (pen))*

Republic of Ireland: Given (Kelly A 46); Kelly G (O'Shea 84), Harte (McPhail 46), Carsley, Dunne (O'Brien 46), Staunton, Reid (Finnan 46), Roy Keane (McAteer 46), Robbie Keane (Morrison 52), Duff (Connolly 52), Kennedy (Kilbane 46).
Croatia: Pletikosa; Soldo (Prosinecki 74), Jarni (Saric 62), Kovac R, Tudor, Simic (Tomas 74), Stanic (Biscan 46), Kovac N (Bjelica 82), Balaban (Vugrinec 46), Boksic (Suker 74), Rapaic (Zivkovic 46).
Referee: Schluchter (Switzerland).

Dublin, 13 February 2002, 44,000
Republic of Ireland (2) 2 *(Reid 3, Robbie Keane 20)*
Russia (0) 0

Republic of Ireland: Given (Kiely 46); Finnan (McAteer 72) (Quinn 90), Harte (Staunton 72), Roy Keane (Holland 86), O'Brien (Dunne 46), Cunningham (Breen 46), Reid (Kelly G 46), Healy (Carsley 46), Robbie Keane (Sadlier 72), Duff (Morrison 46), Kilbane (Kennedy 46).
Russia: Nigmatullin; Khlestov (Daev 90), Kovtun, Khokhlov (Izmailov 53), Nikiforov (Chugainov 66), Onopko, Karpin, Mostovoi, Alenichev (Semak 72), Bestchastnykh, Titov.
Referee: Gallacher (England).

Dublin, 27 March 2002, 42,000
Republic of Ireland (1) 3 *(Harte 19, Robbie Keane 54, Morrison 90)*
Denmark (0) 0

Republic of Ireland: Kiely (Colgan 65); Kelly G, Harte, Holland, Cunningham, Staunton, McAteer (Reid 65), Kinsella (Healy 63), Robbie Keane (Connolly 75), Morrison, Duff (Dunne 83).
Denmark: Sorensen (Kjaer 46); Rytter, Heintze (Jensen N 80), Steen-Nielsen, Laursen, Henriksen, Poulsen, Nielsen A (Madsen 46), Rommedahl (Lovenkrands 67), Sand, Gronkjaer.
Referee: Lawlor (Wales).

Dublin, 17 April 2002, 39,000
Republic of Ireland (1) 2 *(Kinsella 6, Doherty 83)*
USA (1) 1 *(Pope 34)*

Republic of Ireland: Given; Finnan (Kelly G 46), Harte (Staunton 46), Kinsella (Holland 46), O'Brien (Cunningham 46), Breen (Doherty 71), Delap, Healy, Robbie Keane (Morrison 83), Duff (Connolly 46), Kilbane (Reid 46).
USA: Friedel (Keller 46); Sanneh, Agoos, Armas, Pope, Berhalter (Vanney 46), Reyna (Hejduk 71), O'Brien (Lewis 46), McBride (Moore 46), Mathis (Wolff 63), Stewart (Donovan 46).
Referee: Leuba (Switzerland).

Dublin, 16 May 2002, 42,652
Republic of Ireland (0) 1 *(Reid 69)*
Nigeria (1) 2 *(Aghahowa 13, Sodje 47)*

Republic of Ireland: Given; Finnan, Harte, Holland, Cunningham, Staunton, McAteer (Reid 46), Roy Keane (Kinsella 63), Robbie Keane (Morrison 61), Duff (Connolly 61), Kilbane (Kelly G 61).
Nigeria: Shorunmu; Yobo, West, Opabunmi, Udeze, Sodje, Ikedia, Okocha (Oruma 65), Kanu, Aghahowa, Ogbeche.
Referee: Dos Santos (Portugal).

INTERNATIONAL APPEARANCES 1872–2002

This is a list of full international appearances by Englishmen, Irishmen, Scotsmen and Welshmen in matches against the Home Countries and against foreign nations. It does not include unofficial matches against Commonwealth and Empire countries. The year indicated refers to the season; ie 2002 is the 2001–02 season.

Explanatory code for matches played by all five countries: A represents Austria; Alb, Albania; Alg, Algeria; An, Angola; And, Andorra; Arg, Argentina; Arm, Armenia; Aus, Australia; B, Bohemia; Bel, Belgium; Bl, Belarus; Bol, Bolivia; Bos, Bosnia; Br, Brazil; Bul, Bulgaria; C,CIS; Ca, Canada; Cam, Cameroon; Ch, Chile; Chn, China; Co, Colombia; Cr, Costa Rica; Cro, Croatia; Cy, Cyprus; Cz, Czechoslovakia; CzR, Czech Republic; D, Denmark; E, England; Ec, Ecuador; Ei, Republic of Ireland; EG, East Germany; Eg, Egypt; Es, Estonia; F, France; Fa, Faeroes; Fi, Finland; G, Germany; Ge, Georgia; Gr, Greece; H, Hungary; Hk, Hong Kong; Ho, Holland; Hon, Honduras; I, Italy; Ic, Iceland; Ir, Iran; Is, Israel; J, Japan; Jam, Jamaica; K, Kuwait; L, Luxembourg; La, Latvia; Li, Lithuania; Lie, Liechtenstein; M, Mexico; Ma, Malta; Mac, Macedonia; Mal, Malaysia; Mol, Moldova; Mor, Morocco; N, Norway; Ng, Nigeria; Ni, Northern Ireland; Nz, New Zealand; P, Portugal; Para, Paraguay; Pe, Peru; Pol, Poland; R, Romania; RCS, Republic of Czechs and Slovaks; R of E, Rest of Europe; R of UK, Rest of United Kingdom; R of W, Rest of World; Ru, Russia; S.Af, South Africa; S.Ar, Saudi Arabia; S, Scotland; Se, Sweden; Sk, South Korea; Slo, Slovakia; Slv, Slovenia; Sm, San Marino; Sp, Spain; Sw, Switzerland; T, Turkey; Th, Thailand; Tr, Trinidad & Tobago; Tun, Tunisia; U, Uruguay; Uk, Ukraine; US, United States of America; USSR, Soviet Union; W, Wales; WG, West Germany; Y, Yugoslavia; Z, Zaire.
As at July 2002.

ENGLAND

Abbott, W. (Everton), 1902 v W (1)

A'Court, A. (Liverpool), 1958 v Ni, Br, A, USSR; 1959 v W (5)

Adams, T. A. (Arsenal), 1987 v Sp, T, Br; 1988 v WG, T, Y, Ho, H, S, Co, Sw, Ei, Ho, USSR; 1989 v D, Se, S.Ar.; 1991 v Ei (2); 1993 v N, T, Sm, T, Ho, Pol, N; 1994 v Pol, Ho, D, Gr, N; 1995 v US, R, Ei, U; 1996 v Co, N, Sw, P, Chn, Sw, S, Ho, Sp, G; 1997 v Ge (2); 1998 v I, Ch, P, S.Ar, Tun, R, Co, Arg; 1999 v Se, F; 2000 v L, Pol, Bel, S (2), Uk, P; 2001 v F, G (66)

Adcock, H. (Leicester C), 1929 v F, Bel, Sp; 1930 v Ni, W (5)

Alcock, C. W. (Wanderers), 1875 v S (1)

Alderson, J. T. (C Palace), 1923 v F (1)

Aldridge, A. (WBA), 1888 v Ni; (with Walsall Town Swifts), 1889 v Ni (2)

Allen, A. (Stoke C) 1960 v Se, W, Ni (3)

Allen, A. (Aston Villa), 1888 v Ni (1)

Allen, C. (QPR), 1984 v Br (sub), U, Ch; (with Tottenham H), 1987 v T; 1988 v Is (5)

Allen, H. (Wolverhampton W), 1888 v S, W, Ni; 1889 v S; 1890 v S (5)

Allen, J. P. (Portsmouth), 1934 v Ni, W (2)

Allen, R. (WBA), 1952 v Sw; 1954 v Y, S; 1955 v WG, W (5)

Alsford, W. J. (Tottenham H), 1935 v S (1)

Amos, A. (Old Carthusians), 1885 v S; 1886 v W (2)

Anderson, R. D. (Old Etonians), 1879 v W (1)

Anderson, S. (Sunderland), 1962 v A, S (2)

Anderson, V. (Nottingham F), 1979 v Cz, Se; 1980 v Bul, Sp; 1981 v N, R, W, S; 1982 v Ni, Ic; 1984 v Ni; (with Arsenal), 1985 v T, Ni, Ei, R, Fi, S, M, US; 1986 v USSR, M; 1987 v Se, Ni (2), Y, Sp, T; (with Manchester U), 1988 v WG, H, Co (30)

Anderton, D. R. (Tottenham H), 1994 v D, Gr, N; 1995 v US, Ei, U, J, Se, Br; 1996 v H, Chn, Sw, S, Ho, Sp, G; 1998 v S.Ar, Mor, Tun, R, Co, Arg; 1999 v Se, Bul, L, CzR, F; 2001 v F, I (sub); 2002 v Se (sub) (30)

Angus, J. (Burnley), 1961 v A (1)

Armfield, J. C. (Blackpool), 1959 v Br, Pe, M, US; 1960 v Y, Sp, H, S; 1961 v L, P, Sp, M, I, A, W, Ni, S; 1962 v A, Sw, Pe, W, Ni, S, L, P, H, Arg, Bul, Br; 1963 v F (2), Br, EG, Se, Ni, W, S; 1964 v R of W, W, Ni, S; 1966 v Y, Fi (43)

Armitage, G. H. (Charlton Ath), 1926 v Ni (1)

Armstrong, D. (Middlesbrough), 1980 v Aus; (with Southampton), 1982 v WG; 1984 v W (3)

Armstrong, K. (Chelsea), 1955 v S (1)

Arnold, J. (Fulham), 1933 v S (1)

Arthur, J. W. H. (Blackburn R), 1885 v S, W, Ni; 1886 v S, W; 1887 v W, Ni (7)

Ashcroft, J. (Woolwich Arsenal), 1906 v Ni, W, S (3)

Ashmore, G. S. (WBA), 1926 v Bel (1)

Ashton, C. T. (Corinthians), 1926 v Ni (1)

Ashurst, W. (Notts Co), 1923 v Se (2); 1925 v S, W, Bel (5)

Astall, G. (Birmingham C), 1956 v Fi, WG (2)

Astle, J. (WBA), 1969 v W; 1970 v S, P, Br (sub), Cz (5)

Aston, J. (Manchester Utd), 1949 v S, W, D, Sw, Se, N, F; 1950 v S, W, Ni, Ei, I, P, Bel, Ch, US; 1951 v Ni (17)

Athersmith, W. C. (Aston Villa), 1892 v Ni, 1897 v S, W, Ni; 1898 v S, W, Ni; 1899 v S, W, Ni; 1900 v S, W (12)

Atyeo, P. J. W. (Bristol C), 1956 v Br, Se, Sp; 1957 v D, Ei (2) (6)

Austin, S. W. (Manchester C), 1926 v Ni (1)

Bach, P. (Sunderland), 1899 v Ni (1)

Bache, J. W. (Aston Villa), 1903 v W; 1904 v W, Ni; 1905 v S; 1907 v Ni; 1910 v Ni; 1911 v S (7)

Baddeley, T. (Wolverhampton W), 1903 v S, Ni; 1904 v S, W, Ni (5)

Bagshaw, J. J. (Derby Co), 1920 v Ni (1)

Bailey, G. R. (Manchester U), 1985 v Ei, M (2)

Bailey, H. P. (Leicester Fosse), 1908 v W, A (2), H, B (5)

Bailey, M. A. (Charlton Ath), 1964 v US; 1965 v W (2)

Bailey, N. C. (Clapham Rovers), 1878 v S; 1879 v S, W; 1880 v S; 1881 v S; 1882 v S, W; 1883 v S, W; 1884 v S, W, Ni; 1885 v S, W, Ni; 1886 v S, W; 1887 v S, W (19)

Baily, E. F. (Tottenham H), 1950 v Sp; 1951 v Y, Ni, W; 1952 v A (2), Sw, W; 1953 v Ni (9)

Bain, J. (Oxford University), 1887 v S (1)

Baker, A. (Arsenal), 1928 v W (1)

Baker, B. H. (Everton), 1921 v Bel; (with Chelsea), 1926 v Ni (2)

Baker, J. H. (Hibernian), 1960 v Y, Sp, H, Ni, S; (with Arsenal) 1966 v Sp, Pol, S (8)

Ball, A. J. (Blackpool), 1965 v Y, WG, Se; 1966 v S, Sp, Fi, D, U, Arg, P, WG (2), Pol (2); (with Everton), 1967 v W, S, Ni, A, Cz, Sp; 1968 v W, S, USSR, Sp (2), Y, WG; 1969 v Ni, W, S, R (2), M, Br; U; 1970 v P, Co, Ec, R, Br, Cz (sub), WG, W, S, Bel; 1971 v Ma, EG, Gr, Ma (sub), Ni, S; 1972 v Sw, Gr; (with Arsenal) WG (2), S; 1973 v W (3), Y, S (2), Cz, Ni, Pol; 1974 v P (sub); 1975 v WG, Cy (2), Ni, W, S (72)

Ball, J. (Bury), 1928 v Ni (1)

Ball, M. J. (Everton), 2001 v Sp (sub) (1)

Balmer, W. (Everton), 1905 v Ni (1)

Bamber, J. (Liverpool), 1921 v W (1)

Bambridge, A. L. (Swifts), 1881 v W; 1883 v W; 1884 v Ni (3)

Bambridge, E. C. (Swifts), 1879 v S; 1880 v S; 1881 v S; 1882 v S, W, Ni; 1883 v W; 1884 v S, W, Ni; 1885 v S, W, Ni; 1886 v S, W; 1887 v S, W, Ni (18)

Bambridge, E. H. (Swifts), 1876 v S (1)

Banks, G. (Leicester C), 1963 v S, Br, Cz, EG; 1964 v W, Ni, S, R of W, U, P (2), US, Arg; 1965 v Ni, S, H, Y, WG, Se; 1966 v Ni, S, Sp, Pol (2), WG (2), Y, Fi, U, M, F, Arg, P; 1967 v Ni, W, S, Cz; (with Stoke C), 1968 v W, Ni, S, USSR (2), Sp, WG, Y; 1969 v Ni, S, R (2), F, U, Br; 1970 v W, Ni, S, Ho, Bel, Co, Ec, R, Br, Cz; 1971 v Gr, Ma (2), Ni, S; 1972 v Sw, Gr, WG (2), W, S (73)

Banks, H. E. (Millwall), 1901 v Ni (1)

Banks, T. (Bolton W), 1958 v USSR (3), Br, A; 1959 v Ni (6)

Bannister, W. (Burnley), 1901 v W; (with Bolton W), 1902 v Ni (2)

Barclay, R. (Sheffield U), 1932 v S; 1933 v Ni; 1936 v S (3)

Bardsley, D. J. (QPR), 1993 v Sp (sub), Pol (2)

Barham, M. (Norwich C), 1983 v Aus (2) (2)

Barkas, S. (Manchester C), 1936 v Bel; 1937 v S; 1938 v W, Ni, Cz (5)

Barker, J. (Derby Co), 1935 v I, Ho, S, W, Ni; 1936 v G, A, S, W, Ni; 1937 v W (11)

Barker, R. (Herts Rangers), 1872 v S (1)

Barker, R. R. (Casuals), 1895 v W (1)

Barlow, R. J. (WBA), 1955 v Ni (1)

Barmby, N. J. (Tottenham H), 1995 v U (sub), Se (sub); (with Middlesbrough), 1996 v Co, N, P, Chn, Sw (sub), Ho (sub), Sp (sub); 1997 v Mol; (with Everton), 2000 v Br (sub), Uk (sub), Ma, G (sub), R (sub); (with Liverpool), 2001 v F, G, I, Sp; 2002 v Ho (sub), G, Alb, Gr (23)

Barnes, J. (Watford), 1983 v Ni (sub), Aus (sub), Aus (2); 1984 v D, L (sub), F (sub), S, USSR, Br, U, Ch; 1985 v EG, Fi, T, Ni, R, Fi, S, I (sub), M, WG (sub), US (sub); 1986 v R (sub), Is (sub), M (sub), Ca (sub), Arg (sub); 1987 v Se, T (sub), Br; (with Liverpool), 1988 v WG, T, Y, Is, Ho, S, Co, Sw, Ei, Ho, USSR; 1989 v Se, Gr, Alb, Pol, D; 1990 v Se, I, Br, D, U, Tun, Ei, Ho, Eg, Bel, Cam; 1991 v H, Pol, Cam, Ei, T, USSR, Arg; 1992 v Cz, Fi; 1993 v Sm, T, Ho, Pol, US, G; 1995 v US, R, Ng, U, Se; 1996 v Co (sub) (79)

Barnes, P. S. (Manchester C), 1978 v I, WG, Br, W, S, H; 1979 v D, Ei, Cz, Ni (2), S, Bul, A; (with WBA), 1980 v D, W; 1981 v Sp (sub), Br, W, Sw (sub); (with Leeds U), 1982 v N (sub), Ho (sub) (22)

Barnet, H. H. (Royal Engineers), 1882 v Ni (1)

Barrass, M. W. (Bolton W), 1952 v W, Ni; 1953 v S (3)

Barrett, A. F. (Fulham), 1930 v Ni (1)

Barrett, E. D. (Oldham Ath), 1991 v Nz; 1993 v Br, G (3)

Barrett, J. W. (West Ham U), 1929 v Ni (1)

Barry, G. (Aston Villa), 2000 v Uk (sub), Ma (sub); 2001 v F, G (sub), Fi, I (6)

Barry, L. (Leicester C), 1928 v F, Bel; 1929 v F, Bel, Sp (5)

Barson, F. (Aston Villa), 1920 v W (1)

Barton, J. (Blackburn R), 1890 v Ni (1)

Barton, P. H. (Birmingham), 1921 v Bel; 1922 v Ni; 1923 v F; 1924 v Bel, S, W; 1925 v Ni (7)

Barton, W. D. (Wimbledon), 1995 v Ei; (with Newcastle U), Se, Br (sub) (3)

Bassett, W. I. (WBA), 1888 v Ni, 1889 v S, W; 1890 v S, W; 1891 v S, Ni; 1892 v S; 1893 v S, W; 1894 v S; 1895 v S, Ni; 1896 v S, W, Ni (16)

Bastard, S. R. (Upton Park), 1880 v S (1)

Bastin, C. S. (Arsenal), 1932 v W; 1933 v I, Sw; 1934 v S, Ni, W, H, Cz; 1935 v S, Ni, I; 1936 v S, W, G, A; 1937 v W, Ni; 1938 v S, G, Sw, F (21)

Batty, D. (Leeds U), 1991 v USSR (sub), Arg, Aus, Nz, Mal; 1992 v G, T, H (sub), F, Se; 1993 v N, Sm, US, Br; (with Blackburn R), 1994 v D (sub); 1995 v J, Br; (with Newcastle U), 1997 v Mol (sub), Ge, I, M, Ge, S.Af (sub), Pol (sub), F; 1998 v Mol, I, Ch, Sw (sub), P, S.Ar, Tun, R, Co (sub), Arg (sub); 1999 v Bul (sub), L; (with Leeds U), H, Se, Bul; 2000 v L, Pol (42)

Baugh, R. (Stafford Road), 1886 v Ni; (with Wolverhampton W) 1890 v Ni (2)

Bayliss, A. E. J. M. (WBA), 1891 v Ni (1)

Baynham, R. L. (Luton T), 1956 v Ni, D, Sp (3)

Beardsley, P. A. (Newcastle U), 1986 v Eg (sub), Is, USSR, M, Ca (sub), P (sub), Pol, Para, Arg; 1987 v Ni (2), Y, Sp, Br, S; (with Liverpool), 1988 v WG, T, Y, Is, Ho, H, S, Co, Sw, Ei, Ho; 1989 v D, Se, S.Ar, Gr (sub), Alb (sub+1), Pol, D; 1990 v Se, Pol, I, Br, U (sub), Tun (sub), Ei, Eg (sub), Cam (sub), WG, I; 1991 v Pol (sub), Ei (), USSR (sub); (with Newcastle U), 1994 v D, Gr, N; 1995 v Ng, Ei, U, J, Se; 1996 v P (sub), Chn (sub) (59)

Beasant, D. J. (Chelsea), 1990 v I (sub), Y (sub) (2)

Beasley, A. (Huddersfield T), 1939 v S (1)

Beats, W. E. (Wolverhampton W), 1901 v W; 1902 v S (2)

Beattie, T. K. (Ipswich T), 1975 v Cy (2), S; 1976 v Sw, P; 1977 v Fi, I (sub), Ho; 1978 v L (sub) (9)

Beckham, D. R. J. (Manchester U), 1997 v Mol, Pol, Ge, I, Ge, S.Af (sub), Pol, I, F; 1998 v Mol, I, Cam, P, S.Ar, Bel (sub), R (sub), Co, Arg; 1999 v L, CzR, F, Pol, Se; 2000 v L, Pol, S(2), Arg, Br, Uk, Ma, P, G, R; 2001 v F, I, Sp, Fi, Alb, M, Gr; 2002 v Ho, G, Alb, Gr, Se, Ho, I, Se, Arg, Ng, D, Br (54)

Becton, F. (Preston NE), 1895 v Ni; (with Liverpool), 1897 v W (2)

Bedford, H. (Blackpool), 1923 v Se; 1925 v Ni (2)

Bell, C. (Manchester C), 1968 v Se, WG; 1969 v W, Bul, F, U, Br; 1970 v Ni (sub), Ho (2), P, Br (sub), Cz, WG (sub); 1972 v Gr, WG (2), W, Ni, S; 1973 v W (3), Y, S (2), Cz, Pol; 1974 v A, Pol, I, W, Ni, S, Arg, EG, Bul, Y; 1975 v Cz, P, WG, Cy (2), Ni, S; 1976 v Sw, Cz (48)

Bennett, W. (Sheffield U), 1901 v S, W (2)

Benson, R. W. (Sheffield U), 1913 v Ni (1)

Bentley, R. T. F. (Chelsea), 1949 v Se; 1950 v S, P, Bel, Ch, USA; 1953 v W, Bel; 1955 v W, WG, Sp, P (12)

Beresford, J. (Aston Villa), 1934 v Cz (1)

Berry, A. (Oxford University), 1909 v Ni (1)

Berry, J. J. (Manchester U), 1953 v Arg, Ch, U; 1956 v Se (4)

Bestall, J. G. (Grimsby T), 1935 v Ni (1)

Betmead, H. A. (Grimsby T), 1937 v Fi (1)

Betts, M. P. (Old Harrovians), 1877 v S (1)

Betts, W. (Sheffield W), 1889 v W (1)

Beverley, J. (Blackburn R), 1884 v S, W, Ni (3)

Birkett, R. H. (Clapham Rovers), 1879 v S (1)

Birkett, R. J. E. (Middlesbrough), 1936 v Ni (1)

Birley, F. H. (Oxford University), 1874 v S; (with Wanderers), 1875 v S (2)

Birtles, G. (Nottingham F), 1980 v Arg (sub), I; 1981 v R (3)

Bishop, S. M. (Leicester C), 1927 v S, Bel, L, F (4)

Blackburn, F. (Blackburn R), 1901 v S; 1902 v Ni; 1904 v S (3)

Blackburn, G. F. (Aston Villa), 1924 v F (1)

Blenkinsop, E. (Sheffield W), 1928 v F, Bel; 1929 v S, W, Ni, F, Bel, Sp; 1930 v S, W, Ni, G, A; 1931 v S, W, Ni, F, Bel; 1932 v S, W, Ni, Sp; 1933 v S, W, Ni, A (26)

Bliss, H. (Tottenham H), 1921 v S (1)

Blissett, L. (Watford), 1983 v WG (sub), L, W, Gr (sub), H, Ni, S (sub), Aus (1+1 sub); (with AC Milan), 1984 v D (sub), H, W (sub), S, USSR (14)

Blockley, J. P. (Arsenal), 1973 v Y (1)

Bloomer, S. (Derby Co), 1895 v S, Ni; 1896 v W, Ni; 1897 v S, W, Ni; 1898 v S; 1899 v S, W, Ni; 1900 v S; 1901 v S, W; 1902 v S, W, Ni; 1904 v S; 1905 v S, W, Ni; (with Middlesbrough), 1907 v S, W (23)

Blunstone, F. (Chelsea), 1955 v W, S, F, P; 1957 v Y (5)

Bond, R. (Preston NE), 1905 v Ni, W; 1906 v S, W, Ni; (with Bradford C), 1910 v S, W, Ni (8)

Bonetti, P. P. (Chelsea), 1966 v D; 1967 v Sp, A; 1968 v Sp; 1970 v Ho, P, WG (7)

Bonsor, A. G. (Wanderers), 1873 v S; 1875 v S (2)

Booth, F. (Manchester C), 1905 v Ni (1)

Booth, T. (Blackburn R), 1898 v W; (with Everton), 1903 v S (2)

Bould, S. A. (Arsenal), 1994 v Gr, N (2)

Bowden, E. R. (Arsenal), 1935 v W, I; 1936 v W, Ni, A; 1937 v H (6)

Bower, A. G. (Corinthians), 1924 v Ni, Bel; 1925 v W, Bel; 1927 v W (5)

Bowers, J. W. (Derby Co), 1934 v S, Ni, W (3)

Bowles, S. (QPR), 1974 v P, W, Ni; 1977 v I, Ho (5)

Bowser, S. (WBA), 1920 v Ni (1)

Boyer, P. J. (Norwich C), 1976 v W (1)

Boyes, W. (WBA), 1935 v Ho; (with Everton), 1939 v W, R of E (3)

Boyle, T. W. (Burnley), 1913 v Ni (1)

Brabrook, P. (Chelsea), 1958 v USSR; 1959 v Ni; 1960 v Sp (3)

Bracewell, P. W. (Everton), 1985 v WG (sub), US; 1986 v Ni (3)

Bradford, G. R. W. (Bristol R), 1956 v D (1)

Bradford, J. (Birmingham), 1924 v Ni; 1925 v Bel; 1928 v S; 1929 v Ni, W, F, Sp; 1930 v S, Ni, G, A; 1931 v W (12)

Bradley, W. (Manchester U), 1959 v I, US, M (sub) (3)

Bradshaw, F. (Sheffield W), 1908 v A (1)

Bradshaw, T. H. (Liverpool), 1897 v Ni (1)

Bradshaw, W. (Blackburn R), 1910 v W, Ni; 1912 v Ni; 1913 v W (4)

Brann, G. (Swifts), 1886 v S, W; 1891 v W (3)

Brawn, W. F. (Aston Villa), 1904 v W, Ni (2)

Bray, J. (Manchester C), 1935 v W; 1936 v S, W, Ni, G; 1937 v S (6)

Brayshaw, E. (Sheffield W), 1887 v Ni (1)

Bridge W. M. (Southampton), 2002 v Ho, I, Para, Sk (sub), Cam, Arg (sub), Ng (sub) (7)

Bridges, B. J. (Chelsea), 1965 v S, H, Y; 1966 v A (4)

Bridgett, A. (Sunderland), 1905 v S; 1908 v S, A (2), H, B; 1909 v Ni, W, H (2), A (11)

Brindle, T. (Darwen), 1880 v S, W (2)

Brittleton, J. T. (Sheffield W), 1912 v S, W, Ni; 1913 v S; 1914 v W (5)

Britton, C. S. (Everton), 1935 v S, W, Ni, I; 1937 v S, Ni, H, N, Se (9)

Broadbent, P. F. (Wolverhampton W), 1958 v USSR; 1959 v S, W, Ni, I, Br; 1960 v S (7)

Broadis, I. A. (Manchester C), 1952 v S, A, I; 1953 v S, Arg, Ch, U, US; (with Newcastle U), 1954 v S, H, Y, Bel, Sw, U (14)

Brockbank, J. (Cambridge University), 1872 v S (1)

Brodie, J. B. (Wolverhampton W), 1889 v S, Ni; 1891 v Ni (3)

Bromilow, T. G. (Liverpool), 1921 v W; 1922 v S, W; 1923 v Bel; 1926 v Ni (5)

Bromley-Davenport, W. E. (Oxford University), 1884 v S, W (2)

Brook, E. F. (Manchester C), 1930 v Ni; 1933 v Sw: 1934 v S, W, Ni, F, H, Cz; 1935 v S, W, Ni, I; 1936 v S, W, Ni; 1937 v H; 1938 v W, Ni (18)

Brooking, T. D. (West Ham U), 1974 v P, Arg, EG, Bul, Y; 1975 v Cz (sub), P; 1976 v P, W, Br, I, Fi; 1977 v Ei, Fi, I, Ho, Ni, W; 1978 v I, WG, W, S (sub); 1979 v D, Ei, Ni, W (sub), S, Bul, Se (sub), A; 1980 v D, Ni, Arg (sub), W, Ni, S, Bel, Sp; 1981 v Sw, Sp, R, H; 1982 v H, S, Fi, Sp (sub) (47)

Brooks, J. (Tottenham H), 1957 v W, Y, D (3)

Broome, F. H. (Aston Villa), 1938 v G, Sw, F; 1939 v N, I, R, Y (7)

Brown, A. (Aston Villa), 1882 v S, W, Ni (3)
Brown, A. S. (Sheffield U), 1904 v W; 1906 v Ni (2)
Brown, A. (WBA), 1971 v W (1)
Brown, G. (Huddersfield T), 1927 v S, W, Ni, Bel, L, F; 1928 v W; 1929 v S; (with Aston Villa), 1933 v W (9)
Brown, J. (Blackburn R), 1881 v W; 1882 v Ni; 1885 v S, W, Ni (5)
Brown, J. H. (Sheffield W), 1927 v S, W, Bel, L, F; 1930 v Ni (6)
Brown, K. (West Ham U), 1960 v Ni (1)
Brown, W. (West Ham U), 1924 v Bel (1)
Brown, W. M. (Manchester U), 1999 v H; 2001 v Fi (sub), Alb (sub); 2002 v Ho, Sk (sub), Cam (6)
Bruton, J. (Burnley), 1928 v F, Bel; 1929 v S (3)
Bryant, W. I. (Clapton), 1925 v F (1)
Buchan, C. M. (Sunderland), 1913 v Ni; 1920 v W; 1921 v W, Bel; 1923 v F; 1924 v S (6)
Buchanan, W. S. (Clapham R), 1876 v S (1)
Buckley, F. C. (Derby Co), 1914 v Ni (1)
Bull, S. G. (Wolverhampton W), 1989 v S (sub), D (sub); 1990 v Y, Cz, D (sub), U (sub), Tun (sub), Ei (sub), Ho (sub), Eg, Bel (sub); 1991 v H, Pol (13)
Bullock, F. E. (Huddersfield T), 1921 v Ni (1)
Bullock, N. (Bury), 1923 v Bel; 1926 v W; 1927 v Ni (3)
Burgess, H. (Manchester C), 1904 v S, W, Ni; 1906 v S (4)
Burgess, H. (Sheffield W), 1931 v S, Ni, F, Bel (4)
Burnup, C. J. (Cambridge University), 1896 v S (1)
Burrows, H. (Sheffield W), 1934 v H, Cz; 1935 v Ho (3)
Burton, F. E. (Nottingham F), 1889 v Ni (1)
Bury, L. (Cambridge University), 1877 v S; (with Old Etonians), 1879 v W (2)
Butcher, T. (Ipswich T), 1980 v Aus; 1981 v Sp; 1982 v W, S, F, Cz, WG, Sp; 1983 v D, WG, L, W, Gr, H, Ni, S, Aus (3); 1984 v D, H, L, F, Ni; 1985 v EG, Fi, T, Ni, Ei, R, Fi, S, I, WG, US; 1986 v Is, USSR, S, M, Ca, P, Mor, Pol, Para, Arg; (with Rangers), 1987 v Se, Ni (2), Y, Sp, Br, S; 1988 v T, Y; 1989 v D, Se, Gr, Alb (2), Ch, S, Pol, D; 1990 v Se, Pol, I, Y, Br, Cz, D, U, Tun, Ei, Ho, Bel, Cam, WG (77)
Butler, J. D. (Arsenal), 1925 v Bel (1)
Butler, W. (Bolton W), 1924 v S (1)
Butt, N. (Manchester U), 1997 v M (sub), S.Af (sub); 1998 v Mol (sub), I (sub), Ch, Bel, CzR; 1999 v H; 2001 v I, Sp, Fi (sub), Alb, M (sub), Gr (sub); 2002 v Se, Ho (sub), I, Para, Arg, Ng, D, Br (22)
Byrne, J. (Liverpool), 1963 v S; 1966 v N (2)
Byrne, J. J. (C Palace), 1962 v Ni; (with West Ham U), 1963 v Sw; 1964 v S, U, P (2), Ei, Br, Arg; 1965 v W, S (11)
Byrne, R. W. (Manchester U), 1954 v S, H, Y, Bel, Sw, U; 1955 v S, W, Ni, WG, F, Sp, P; 1956 v S, W, Ni, Br, Se, Fi, WG, D, Sp; 1957 v S, W, Ni, Y, D (2), Ei (2); 1958 v W, Ni, F (33)

Callaghan, I. R. (Liverpool), 1966 v Fi, F; 1978 v Sw, L (4)
Calvey, J. (Nottingham F), 1902 v Ni (1)
Campbell, A. F. (Blackburn R), 1929 v W, Ni; (with Huddersfield T), 1931 v W, S, Ni; 1932 v W, Ni, Sp (8)
Campbell, S. (Tottenham H), 1996 v H (sub), S (sub); 1997 v Ge, I, Ge, S.Af (sub), Pol, F, Br; 1998 v Mol, I, Cam, Ch, P, Mor, Bel, Tun, R, Co, Arg; 1999 v Se, Bul, L, CzR, Pol, Se, Bul; 2000 v S (2), Arg, Br, Uk, Ma, P, G, R; 2001 v F, Sp, Fi, Alb; (with Arsenal), 2002 v G, Alb, Ho, I, Sk, Cam, Se, Arg, Ng, D, Br (51)
Camsell, G. H. (Middlesbrough), 1929 v F, Bel; 1930 v Ni, W; 1934 v F; 1936 v S, G, A, Bel (9)
Capes, A. J. (Stoke C), 1903 v S (1)
Carr, J. (Middlesbrough), 1920 v Ni; 1923 v W (2)
Carr, J. (Newcastle U), 1905 v Ni; 1907 v Ni (2)
Carr, W. H. (Owlerton, Sheffield), 1875 v S (1)
Carragher, J. L. (Liverpool), 1999 v H (sub); 2001 v I (sub), M (sub); 2002 v Ho, G (sub), Alb (sub), Se, Para (sub) (8)
Carrick, M. (West Ham U), 2001 v M (sub); 2002 v Ho (2)
Carter, H. S. (Sunderland), 1934 v S, H; 1936 v G; 1937 v S, Ni, H; (with Derby Co), 1947 v S, W, Ni, Ei, Ho, F, Sw (13)
Carter, J. H. (WBA), 1926 v Bel; 1929 v Bel, Sp (3)
Catlin, A. E. (Sheffield W), 1937 v W, Ni, H, N, Se (5)
Chadwick, A. (Southampton), 1900 v S, W (2)
Chadwick, E. (Everton), 1891 v S, W; 1892 v S; 1893 v S; 1894 v S; 1896 v Ni; 1897 v S (7)
Chamberlain, M. (Stoke C), 1983 v L (sub); 1984 v D (sub), S, USSR, Br, U, Ch; 1985 v Fi (sub) (8)
Chambers, H. (Liverpool), 1921 v S, W, Bel; 1923 v S, W, Ni, Bel; 1924 v Ni (8)
Channon, M. R. (Southampton), 1973 v Y, S (2), Ni, W, Cz, USSR, I; 1974 v A, Pol, I, P, W, Ni, S, Arg, EG, Bul, Y; 1975 v Cz, P, WG, Cy (2), Ni (sub), W, S; 1976 v Sw, Cz, P,

W, Ni, S, Br, I, Fi; 1977 v Fi, I, L, Ni, W, S, Br (sub), Arg, U; (with Manchester C), 1978 v Sw (46)
Charles, G. A. (Nottingham F), 1991 v Nz, Mal (2)
Charlton, J. (Leeds U), 1965 v S, H, Y, WG, Se; 1966 v W, Ni, S, A, Sp, Pol (2), WG (2), Y, Fi, D, U, M, F, Arg; 1967 v W, S, Ni, Cz; 1968 v W, Sp; 1969 v W, R, F; 1970 v Ho (2), P, Cz (35)
Charlton, R. (Manchester U), 1958 v S, P, Y; 1959 v S, W, Ni, USSR, I, Br, Pe, M, US; 1960 v W, S, Se, Y, Sp, H; 1961 v Ni, W, S, L, P, Sp, M, I, A; 1962 v W, Ni, S, A, Sw, Pe, L, P, H, Arg, Bul, Br; 1963 v S, F, Br, Cz, EG, Sw; 1964 v S, W, Ni, R of W, U, P, Ei, Br, Arg, US (sub); 1965 v Ni, S, Ho; 1966 v W, Ni, S, A, Sp, WG (2), Y, Fi, N, Pol, U, M, F, Arg, P; 1967 v Ni, W, S, Cz; 1968 v W, Ni, S, USSR (2), Sp (2), Se, Y; 1969 v S, W, Ni, R (2), Bul, M, Br; 1970 v W, Ni, Ho (2), P, Co, Ec, Cz, R, Br, WG (106)
Charnley, R. O. (Blackpool), 1963 v F (1)
Charsley, C. C. (Small Heath), 1893 v Ni (1)
Chedgzoy, S. (Everton), 1920 v W; 1921 v W, S, Ni; 1922 v Ni; 1923 v S; 1924 v W; 1925 v Ni (8)
Chenery, C. J. (C Palace), 1872 v S; 1873 v S; 1874 v S (3)
Cherry, T. J. (Leeds U), 1976 v W, S (sub), Br, Fi; 1977 v Ei, I, L, Ni, S (sub), Br, Arg, U; 1978 v Sw, L, I, Br, W; 1979 v Cz, W, Se; 1980 v Ei, Arg (sub), W, Ni, S, Aus, Sp (sub) (27)
Chilton, A. (Manchester U), 1951 v Ni; 1952 v F (2)
Chippendale, H. (Blackburn R), 1894 v Ni (1)
Chivers, M. (Tottenham H), 1971 v Ma (2), Gr, Ni, S; 1972 v Sw (1+1 sub), W, EG, Y, WG (2), Ni (sub), S; 1973 v W (3), S (2), Ni, Cz, Pol, USSR, I; 1974 v A, Pol (24)
Christian, E. (Old Etonians), 1879 v S (1)
Clamp, E. (Wolverhampton W), 1958 v USSR (2), Br, A (4)
Clapton, D. R. (Arsenal), 1959 v W (1)
Clare, T. (Stoke C), 1889 v Ni; 1892 v Ni; 1893 v W; 1894 v S (4)
Clarke, A. J. (Leeds U), 1970 v Cz; 1971 v EG, Ma, Ni, W (sub), S (sub); 1973 v S (2), W, Cz, Pol, USSR, I; 1974 v A, Pol, I; 1975 v P; 1976 v Cz, P (sub) (19)
Clarke, H. A. (Tottenham H), 1954 v S (1)
Clay, T. (Tottenham H), 1920 v W; 1922 v W, S, Ni (4)
Clayton, R. (Blackburn R), 1956 v Ni, Br, Se, Fi, WG, Sp; 1957 v S, W, Ni, Y, D (2), Ei (2); 1958 v S, W, Ni, F, P, Y, USSR; 1959 v S, W, Ni, USSR, I, Br, Pe, M, US; 1960 v W, Ni, S, Se, Y (35)
Clegg, J. C. (Sheffield W), 1872 v S (1)
Clegg, W. E. (Sheffield W), 1873 v S; (with Sheffield Albion), 1879 v W (2)
Clemence, R. N. (Liverpool), 1973 v W (2); 1974 v EG, Bul, Y; 1975 v Cz, P, WG, Cy, Ni, W, S; 1976 v Sw, Cz, P, W (2), Ni, S, Br, Fi; 1977 v Ei, Fi, I, Ho, L, S, Br, Arg, U; 1978 v Sw, L, I, WG, Ni, S; 1979 v D, Ei, Ni (2), S, Bul, A (sub); 1980 v D, Bul, Ei, Arg, W, S, Bel, Sp; 1981 v R, Sp, Br, Sw, H; (with Tottenham H), 1982 v Ni, Ni, Fi; 1983 v L; 1984 v L (61)
Clement, D. T. (QPR), 1976 v W (sub+1), I; 1977 v I, Ho (5)
Clough, B. H. (Middlesbrough), 1960 v W, Se (2)
Clough, N. H. (Nottingham F), 1989 v Ch; 1991 v Arg (sub), Aus, Mal; 1992 v F, Cz, C; 1993 v Sp, T (sub), Pol (sub), N (sub), US, Br, G (14)
Coates, R. (Burnley), 1970 v Ni; 1971 v Gr (sub); (with Tottenham H), Ma, W (4)
Cobbold, W. N. (Cambridge University), 1883 v S, Ni; 1885 v S, Ni; 1886 v S, W; (with Old Carthusians), 1887 v S, W, Ni (9)
Cock, J. G. (Huddersfield T), 1920 v Ni; (with Chelsea), v S (2)
Cockburn, H. (Manchester U), 1947 v W, Ni, Ei; 1948 v S, I; 1949 v S, Ni, D, Sw, Se; 1951 v Arg, P; 1952 v F (13)
Cohen, G. R. (Fulham), 1964 v U, P, Ei, US, Br; 1965 v W, S, Ni, Bel, H, Ho, Y, WG, Se; 1966 v W, S, Ni, A, Sp, Pol (2), WG (2), N, D, U, M, F, Arg, P; 1967 v W, S, Ni, Cz, Se; 1968 v W, Ni (37)
Cole, A. (Manchester U), 1995 v U (sub); 1997 v I (sub); 1999 v F (sub), Pol, Se; 2000 v S (sub), Arg (sub); 2001 v F, G, Fi, Sp, Fi, Alb; 2002 v Ho, Gr (sub) (15)
Cole, A. (Arsenal), 2001 v Alb, M, Gr; 2002 v Ho, G, Alb, Gr, Sk, Se, Arg, Ng, D, Br (13)
Cole, J. J. (West Ham U), 2001 v M (sub); 2002 v Ho (sub), I (sub), Para (sub), Sk (sub), Cam, Se (sub) (7)
Colclough, H. (C Palace), 1914 v W (1)
Coleman, E. H. (Dulwich Hamlet), 1921 v W (1)
Coleman, J. (Woolwich Arsenal), 1907 v Ni (1)
Collymore, S. V. (Nottingham F), 1995 v J, Br (sub); (with Aston Villa), 1998 v Mol (sub) (3)
Common, A. (Sheffield U), 1904 v W, Ni; (with Middlesbrough), 1906 v W (3)
Compton, L. H. (Arsenal), 1951 v W, Y (2)
Conlin, J. (Bradford C), 1906 v S (1)

Connelly, J. M. (Burnley), 1960 v W, N, S, Se; 1962 v W, A, Sw, P; 1963 v W, F; (with Manchester U), 1965 v H, Y, Se; 1966 v W, Ni, S, A, N, D, U (20)
Cook, T. E. R. (Brighton), 1925 v W (1)
Cooper, C. T. (Nottingham F), 1995 v Se, Br (2)
Cooper, N. C. (Cambridge University), 1893 v Ni (1)
Cooper, T. (Derby Co), 1928 v Ni; 1929 v W, Ni, S, F, Bel, Sp; 1931 v F; 1932 v W, Sp; 1933 v S; 1934 v S, H, Cz; 1935 v W (15)
Cooper, T. (Leeds U), 1969 v W, S, F, M; 1970 v Ho, Bel, Co, Ec, R, Cz, Br, WG; 1971 v EG, Ma, Ni, W, S; 1972 v Sw (2); 1975 v P (20)
Coppell, S. J. (Manchester U), 1978 v I, WG, Br, W, Ni, S, H; 1979 v D, Ei, Cz, Ni (2), W (sub), S, Bul, A; 1980 v D, Ni, Ei (sub), Sp, Arg, W, S, Bel, I; 1981 v R (sub), Sw, R, Br, W, S, Sw, H; 1982 v H, S, Fi, F, Cz, K, WG; 1983 v L, Gr (42)
Copping, W. (Leeds U), 1933 v I, Sw; 1934 v S, Ni, W, F; (with Arsenal), 1935 v Ni, I; 1936 v A, Bel; 1937 v N, Se, Fi; 1938 v S, W, Ni, Cz; 1939 v W, R of E; (with Leeds U), R (20)
Corbett, B. O. (Corinthians), 1901 v W (1)
Corbett, R. (Old Malvernians), 1903 v W (1)
Corbett, W. S. (Birmingham), 1908 v A, H, B (3)
Corrigan, J. T. (Manchester C), 1978 v I (sub), Br; 1979 v W; 1980 v Ni, Aus; 1981 v W, S; 1982 v W, Ic (9)
Cottee, A. R. (West Ham U), 1987 v Se (sub), Ni (sub); 1988 v H (sub); (with Everton) 1989 v D (sub), Se (sub), Ch (sub), S (7)
Cotterill, G. H. (Cambridge University), 1891 v Ni; (with Old Brightonians), 1892 v W; 1893 v S, Ni (4)
Cottle, J. R. (Bristol C), 1909 v Ni (1)
Cowan, S. (Manchester C), 1926 v Bel; 1930 v A; 1931 v Bel (3)
Cowans, G. (Aston Villa), 1983 v W, H, Ni, S, Aus (3); (with Bari), 1986 v Eg, USSR; (with Aston Villa), 1991 v Ei (10)
Cowell, A. (Blackburn R), 1910 v Ni (1)
Cox, J. (Liverpool), 1901 v Ni; 1902 v S; 1903 v S (3)
Cox, J. D. (Derby Co), 1892 v Ni (1)
Crabtree, J. W. (Burnley), 1894 v Ni; 1895 v Ni, S; (with Aston Villa), 1896 v W, S, Ni; 1899 v S, W, Ni; 1900 v S, W, Ni; 1901 v W; 1902 v W (14)
Crawford, J. F. (Chelsea), 1931 v S (1)
Crawford, R. (Ipswich T), 1962 v Ni, A (2)
Crawshaw, T. H. (Sheffield W), 1895 v Ni; 1896 v S, W, Ni; 1897 v S, W; 1901 v Ni; 1904 v W, Ni (10)
Crayston, W. J. (Arsenal), 1936 v S, W, G, A, Bel; 1938 v W, Ni, Cz (8)
Creek, F. N. S. (Corinthians), 1923 v F (1)
Cresswell, W. (South Shields), 1921 v W; (with Sunderland), 1923 v F; 1924 v Bel; 1925 v Ni; 1926 v W; 1927 v Ni; (with Everton), 1930 v Ni (7)
Crompton, R. (Blackburn R), 1902 v S, W, Ni; 1903 v S, W; 1904 v S, W, Ni; 1906 v S, W, Ni; 1907 v S, W, Ni; 1908 v S, W, Ni, A (2), H, B; 1909 v S, W, Ni, H (2), A; 1910 v S, W; 1911 v S, W, Ni; 1912 v S, W, Ni; 1913 v S, W, Ni; 1914 v S, W, Ni (41)
Crooks, S. D. (Derby Co), 1930 v S, G, A; 1931 v S, W, Ni, F, Bel; 1932 v S, W, Ni, Sp; 1933 v Ni, W, A; 1934 v S, Ni, W, F, H, Cz; 1935 v Ni; 1936 v S, W; 1937 v W, H (26)
Crowe, C. (Wolverhampton W), 1963 v F (1)
Cuggy, F. (Sunderland), 1913 v Ni; 1914 v Ni (2)
Cullis, S. (Wolverhampton W), 1938 v S, W, Ni, F, Cz; 1939 v S, Ni, R of E, N, I, R, Y (12)
Cunliffe, A. (Blackburn R), 1933 v Ni, W (2)
Cunliffe, D. (Portsmouth), 1900 v Ni (1)
Cunliffe, J. N. (Everton), 1936 v Bel (1)
Cunningham, L. (WBA), 1979 v W, Se, A (sub); (with Real Madrid), 1980 v Ei, Sp (sub); 1981 v R (sub) (6)
Curle, K. (Manchester C), 1992 v C (sub), H, D (3)
Currey, E. S. (Oxford University), 1890 v S, W (2)
Currie, A. W. (Sheffield U), 1972 v Ni; 1973 v USSR, I; 1974 v A, Pol, I; 1976 v Sw; (with Leeds U), 1978 v Br, W (sub), Ni, S, H (sub); 1979 v Cz, Ni (2), W, Se (17)
Cursham, A. W. (Notts Co), 1876 v S; 1877 v S; 1878 v S; 1879 v W; 1883 v S, W (6)
Cursham, H. A. (Notts Co), 1880 v W; 1882 v S, W, Ni; 1883 v S, W, Ni; 1884 v Ni (8)

Daft, H. B. (Notts Co), 1889 v Ni; 1890 v S, W; 1891 v Ni; 1892 v Ni (5)
Daley, A. M. (Aston Villa), 1992 v Pol (sub), C, H, Br, Fi (sub), D (sub), Se (7)
Danks, T. (Nottingham F), 1885 v S (1)
Davenport, P. (Nottingham F), 1985 v Ei (sub) (1)
Davenport, J. K. (Bolton W), 1885 v W; 1890 v Ni (2)
Davis, G. (Derby Co), 1904 v W, Ni (2)
Davis, H. (Sheffield W), 1903 v S, W, Ni (3)
Davison, J. E. (Sheffield W), 1922 v W (1)

Dawson, J. (Burnley), 1922 v S, Ni (2)
Day, S. H. (Old Malvernians), 1906 v Ni, W, S (3)
Dean, W. R. (Everton), 1927 v S, W, F, Bel, L; 1928 v S, W, Ni, F, Bel; 1929 v S, W, Ni; 1931 v S; 1932 v Sp; 1933 v Ni (16)
Deane, B. C. (Sheffield U), 1991 v Nz (sub + 1); 1993 v Sp (sub) (3)
Deeley, N. V. (Wolverhampton W), 1959 v Br, Pe (2)
Devey, J. H. G. (Aston Villa), 1892 v Ni; 1894 v Ni (2)
Devonshire, A. (West Ham U), 1980 v Aus (sub), Ni; 1982 v Ho, Ic; 1983 v WG, W, Gr; 1984 v L (8)
Dewhurst, F. (Preston NE), 1886 v W, Ni; 1887 v S, W, Ni; 1888 v S, W, Ni; 1889 v W (9)
Dewhurst, G. P. (Liverpool Ramblers), 1895 v W (1)
Dickinson, J. W. (Portsmouth), 1949 v N, F; 1950 v S, W, Ei, P, Bel, Ch, US, Sp; 1951 v Ni, W, Y; 1952 v W, Ni, S, A (2), I, Sw; 1953 v W, Ni, S, Bel, Arg, Ch, U, US; 1954 v W, Ni, S, R of E, H (2), Y, Bel, Sw, U; 1955 v Sp, P; 1956 v W, Ni, S, D, Sp; 1957 v W, Y, D (48)
Dimmock, J. H. (Tottenham H), 1921 v S; 1926 v W, Bel (3)
Ditchburn, E. G. (Tottenham H), 1949 v Sw, Se; 1953 v US; 1957 v W, Y, D (6)
Dix, R. W. (Derby Co), 1939 v N (1)
Dixon, J. A. (Notts Co), 1885 v W (1)
Dixon, K. M. (Chelsea), 1985 v M (sub), WG, US; 1986 v Ni, Is, M (sub), Pol (sub); 1987 v Se (8)
Dixon, L. M. (Arsenal), 1990 v Cz; 1991 v H, Pol, Ei (2), Cam, T, Arg; 1992 v G, T, Pol, Cz (sub); 1993 v Sp, N, T, Sm, T, Ho, N, US; 1994 v Sm; 1999 v F (22)
Dobson, A. T. C. (Notts Co), 1882 v Ni; 1884 v S, W, Ni (4)
Dobson, C. F. (Notts Co), 1886 v Ni (1)
Dobson, J. M. (Burnley), 1974 v P, EG, Bul, Y; (with Everton), 1975 v Cz (5)
Doggart, A. G. (Corinthians), 1924 v Bel (1)
Dorigo, A. R. (Chelsea), 1990 v Y (sub), Cz (sub), D (sub), I; 1991 v H (sub), USSR; (with Leeds U), 1992 v G, Cz (sub), H, Br; 1993 v Sm, Pol, US, Br; 1994 v H (15)
Dorrell, A. R. (Aston Villa), 1925 v W, Bel, F; 1926 v Ni (4)
Douglas, B. (Blackburn R), 1958 v S, W, Ni, F, P, Y, USSR (2), Br, A; 1959 v S, USSR; 1960 v Y, H; 1961 v Ni, W, S, L, P, Sp, M, I, A; 1962 v W, Ni, S, Pe, L, P, H, Arg, Bul, Br; 1963 v S, Br, Sw (36)
Downs, R. W. (Everton), 1921 v Ni (1)
Doyle, M. (Manchester C), 1976 v W, S (sub), Br, I; 1977 v Ho (5)
Drake, E. J. (Arsenal), 1935 v Ni, I; 1936 v W; 1937 v H; 1938 v F (5)
Dublin, D. (Coventry C), 1998 v Ch, Mor, Bel (sub); (with Aston Villa), 1999 v CzR (4)
Ducat, A. (Woolwich Arsenal), 1910 v S, W, Ni; (with Aston Villa), 1920 v S, W; 1921 v Ni (6)
Dunn, A. T. B. (Cambridge University), 1883 v Ni; 1884 v Ni; (with Old Etonians), 1892 v S, W (4)
Duxbury, M. (Manchester U), 1984 v L, F, W, S, USSR, Br, U, Ch; 1985 v EG, Fi (10)
Dyer, K. C. (Newcastle U), 2000 v L, Pol (sub), Bel, Arg, Uk (sub); 2001 v F (sub), G (sub), I; 2002 v Para, Se (sub), D (sub), Br (sub) (12)

Earle, S. G. J. (Clapton), 1924 v F; (with West Ham U), 1928 v Ni (2)
Eastham, G. (Arsenal), 1963 v Br, Cz, EG; 1964 v W, Ni, S, R of W, U, P, Ei, US, Br, Arg; 1965 v H, WG, Se; 1966 v Sp, Pol, D (19)
Eastham, G. R. (Bolton W), 1935 v Ho (1)
Eckersley, W. (Blackburn R), 1950 v Sp; 1951 v S, Y, Arg, P; 1952 v A (2), Sw; 1953 v Ni, Arg, Ch, U, US; 1954 v W, Ni, R of E, H (17)
Edwards, D. (Manchester U), 1955 v S, F, Sp, P; 1956 v S, Br, Se, Fi, WG; 1957 v S, Ni, Ei (2), D (2); 1958 v W, Ni, F (18)
Edwards, J. H. (Shropshire Wanderers), 1874 v S (1)
Edwards, W. (Leeds U), 1926 v S, W; 1927 v W, Ni, S, F, Bel, L; 1928 v S, F, Bel; 1929 v S, W, Ni; 1930 v W, Ni (16)
Ehiogu, U. (Aston Villa), 1996 v Chn (sub); (with Middlesbrough), 2001 v Sp (sub); 2002 v Ho (sub), I (sub) (4)
Ellerington, W. (Southampton), 1949 v N, F (2)
Elliott, G. W. (Middlesbrough), 1913 v Ni; 1914 v Ni; 1920 v W (3)
Elliott, W. H. (Burnley), 1952 v I, A; 1953 v Ni, W, Bel (5)
Evans, R. E. (Sheffield U), 1911 v S, W, Ni; 1912 v W (4)
Ewer, F. H. (Casuals), 1924 v F; 1925 v Bel (2)

Fairclough, P. (Old Foresters), 1878 v S (1)
Fairhurst, D. (Newcastle U), 1934 v F (1)
Fantham, J. (Sheffield W), 1962 v L (1)
Fashanu, J. (Wimbledon), 1989 v Ch, S (2)

Felton, W. (Sheffield W), 1925 v F (1)
Fenton, M. (Middlesbrough), 1938 v S (1)
Fenwick, T. (QPR), 1984 v W (sub), S, USSR, Br, U, Ch; 1985 v Fi, S, M, US; 1986 v R, T, Ni, Eg, M, P, Mor, Pol, Arg; (with Tottenham H), 1988 v Is (sub) (20)
Ferdinand, L. (QPR), 1993 v Sm, Ho, N, US; 1994 v Pol, Sm; 1995 v US (sub); (with Newcastle U), 1996 v P, Bul, H; 1997 v Pol, Ge, I (sub); (with Tottenham H), 1998 v Mol, S.Ar (sub), Mor (sub), Bel (17)
Ferdinand, R. G. (West Ham U), 1998 v Cam (sub), Sw, Bel (sub); 1999 v L, CzR, F (sub), H, Se (sub); 2000 v Arg (sub); 2001 v I; (with Leeds U), Sp, Fi, Alb, M, Gr; 2002 v G, Alb, Gr, Se, Ho, Sk, Cam, Se, Arg, Ng, D, Br (27)
Field, E. (Clapham Rovers), 1876 v S; 1881 v S (2)
Finney, T. (Preston NE), 1947 v W, Ni, Ei, Ho, F, P; 1948 v S, W, Ni, Bel, Se, I; 1949 v S, W, Ni, Se, N, F; 1950 v S, W, Ni, Ei, I, P, Bel, Ch, US, Sp; 1951 v S, Arg, P; 1952 v W, Ni, S, F, I, Sw, A; 1953 v W, Ni, S, Bel, Arg, Ch, U, US; 1954 v W, S, Bel, Sw, U, H, Y; 1955 v W(2); 1956 v S, W, Ni, D, Sp; 1957 v W, S, W, Y, D (2), Ei (2); 1958 v W, S, F, P, Y, USSR (2); 1959 v Ni, USSR (76)
Fleming, H. J. (Swindon T), 1909 v S, H (2); 1910 v W, Ni; 1911 v W, Ni; 1912 v Ni; 1913 v S, W; 1914 v S (11)
Fletcher, A. (Wolverhampton W), 1889 v W; 1890 v W (2)
Flowers, R. (Wolverhampton W), 1955 v F; 1959 v S, W, I, Br, Pe, US, M (sub); 1960 v W, Ni, S, Se, Y, Sp, H; 1961 v Ni, W, S, L, P, Sp, M, I, A; 1962 v W, Ni, S, A, Sw, Pe, L, P, H, Arg, Bul, Br; 1963 v Ni, W, S, F (2), Sw; 1964 v Ei, US, P; 1965 v W, Ho, W; 1966 v N (49)
Flowers, T. D. (Southampton), 1993 v Br; (with Blackburn R), 1994 v Gr; 1995 v Ng, U, J, Se, Br; 1996 v Chn; 1997 v I; 1998 v Sw, Mor (11)
Forman, Frank (Nottingham F), 1898 v S, Ni; 1899 v S, W, Ni; 1901 v S; 1902 v S, Ni; 1903 v W (9)
Forman, F. R. (Nottingham F), 1899 v S, W, Ni (3)
Forrest, J. H. (Blackburn R), 1884 v W; 1885 v S, W, Ni; 1886 v S, W; 1887 v S, W, Ni; 1889 v S; 1890 v Ni (11)
Fort, J. (Millwall), 1921 v Bel (1)
Foster, R. E. (Oxford University), 1900 v W; (with Corinthians), 1901 v W, Ni, S; 1902 v W (5)
Foster, S. (Brighton & HA), 1982 v Ni, Ho, K (3)
Foulke, W. J. (Sheffield U), 1897 v W (1)
Foulkes, W. A. (Manchester U), 1955 v Ni (1)
Fowler, R. B. (Liverpool), 1996 v Bul (sub), Cro, Chn (sub), Ho (sub), Sp (sub); 1997 v M; 1998 v Cam; 1999 v CzR (sub), Bul; 2000 v I, Pol, Br (sub), Uk, Ma (sub); 2001 v I (sub), Fi (sub), M, Gr; 2002 v Ho, Alb (sub), Gr, Se (sub); (with Leeds U), I (sub), Para (sub), Cam (sub), D (sub) (26)
Fox, F. S. (Millwall), 1925 v F (1)
Francis, G. C. J. (QPR), 1975 v Cz, P, W, S; 1976 v Sw, Cz, P, W, Ni, S, Br, Fi (12)
Francis, T. (Birmingham C), 1977 v Ho, L, S, Br; 1978 v Sw, L, I (sub) USSR (sub), Br, W, S, H; (with Nottingham F), 1979 v Bul (sub), Se, A (sub); 1980 v Ni, Bul, Sp; 1981 v Sp, R, S (sub), Sw; (with Manchester C), 1982 v N, Ni, W, S (sub), Fi (sub), F, Cz, K, WG, Sp; (with Sampdoria), 1983 v D, Gr, H, Ni, S, Aus (3); 1984 v D, Ni, USSR; 1985 v EG (sub), T (sub), Ni (sub), R, Fi, S, I, M; 1986 v S (52)
Franklin, C. F. (Stoke C), 1947 v S, W, Ni, Ei, Ho, F, Sw, P; 1948 v S, W, Ni, Bel, Se, I; 1949 v S, W, Ni, D, Sw, N, F, Se; 1950 v W, S, Ni, Ei, I (27)
Freeman, B. C. (Everton), 1909 v S, W; (with Burnley), 1912 v S, W, Ni (5)
Froggatt, J. (Portsmouth), 1950 v Ni, I; 1951 v S; 1952 v S, A (2), I, Sw; 1953 v Ni, W, S, Bel, US (13)
Froggatt, R. (Sheffield U), 1953 v W, S, Bel, US (4)
Fry, C. B. (Corinthians), 1901 v Ni (1)
Furness, W. I. (Leeds U), 1933 v I (1)

Galley, T. (Wolverhampton W), 1937 v N, Se (2)
Gardner, T. (Aston Villa), 1934 v Cz; 1935 v Ho (2)
Garfield, B. (WBA), 1898 v Ni (1)
Garratty, W. (Aston Villa), 1903 v W (1)
Garrett, T. (Blackpool), 1952 v S, I; 1954 v W (3)
Gascoigne, P. J. (Tottenham H), 1989 v D (sub), S.Ar (sub), Alb (sub), Ch, S (sub); 1990 v Se (sub), Br (sub), Cz, D, U, Tun, Ei, Ho, Eg, Bel, Cam, WG; 1991 v H, Pol, Cam; (with Lazio), 1993 v N, T, Sm, T, Ho, Pol, N; 1994 v Pol, D; 1995 v J (sub), Se (sub), Br (sub); (with Rangers), 1996 v Co, Sw, P, Bul, Cro, Chn, Sw, S, Ho, Sp, G; 1997 v Mol, Pol, Ge, S.Af, Pol, I (sub), F, Br; 1998 v Mol, I, Cam; (with Middlesbrough), S.Ar (sub), Mor (sub), Bel (57)
Gates, E. (Ipswich T), 1981 v N, R (2)
Gay, L. H. (Cambridge University), 1893 v S; (with Old Brightonians), 1894 v S, W (3)
Geary, F. (Everton), 1890 v Ni; 1891 v S (2)
Geaves, R. L. (Clapham Rovers), 1875 v S (1)

Gee, C. W. (Everton), 1932 v W, Sp; 1937 v Ni (3)
Geldard, A. (Everton), 1933 v I, Sw; 1935 v S; 1938 v Ni (4)
George, C. (Derby Co), 1977 v Ei (1)
George, W. (Aston Villa), 1902 v S, W, Ni (3)
Gerrard, S. G. (Liverpool), 2000 v Uk, G (sub); 2001 v Fi, M, Gr; 2002 v G, Alb, Gr, Ho, Para (10)
Gibbins, W. V. T. (Clapton), 1924 v F; 1925 v F (2)
Gidman, J. (Aston Villa), 1977 v L (1)
Gillard, I. T. (QPR), 1975 v WG, W; 1976 v Cz (3)
Gilliat, W. E. (Old Carthusians), 1893 v Ni (1)
Goddard, P. (West Ham U), 1982 v Ic (sub) (1)
Goodall, F. R. (Huddersfield T), 1926 v S; 1927 v S, F, Bel, L; 1928 v S, W, F, Bel; 1930 v S, G, A; 1931 v S, W, Ni, Bel; 1932 v Ni; 1933 v W, Ni, A, I, Sw; 1934 v W, Ni, F (25)
Goodall, J. (Preston NE), 1888 v S, W; 1889 v S, W; (with Derby Co), 1891 v S, W; 1892 v S; 1893 v W; 1894 v S; 1895 v S, Ni; 1896 v S, W; 1898 v W (14)
Goodhart, H. C. (Old Etonians), 1883 v S, W, Ni (3)
Goodwyn, A. G. (Royal Engineers), 1873 v S (1)
Goodyer, A. C. (Nottingham F), 1879 v S (1)
Gosling, R. C. (Old Etonians), 1892 v W; 1893 v S; 1894 v W; 1895 v W, S (5)
Gosnell, A. A. (Newcastle U), 1906 v Ni (1)
Gough, H. C. (Sheffield U), 1921 v S (1)
Goulden, L. A. (West Ham U), 1937 v Se, N; 1938 v W, Ni, Cz, G, Sw, F; 1939 v S, W, R of E, I, R, Y (14)
Graham, L. (Millwall), 1925 v S, W (2)
Graham, T. (Nottingham F), 1931 v F; 1932 v Ni (2)
Grainger, C. (Sheffield U), 1956 v Br, Se, Fi, WG; 1957 v W, Ni; (with Sunderland), 1957 v S (7)
Gray, A. A. (C Palace), 1992 v Pol (1)
Gray, M. (Sunderland), 1999 v H (sub), Se (sub), Bul (3)
Greaves, J. (Chelsea), 1959 v Pe, M, US; 1960 v W, Se, Y, Sp; 1961 v Ni, W, S, L, P, Sp, I, A; (with Tottenham H), 1962 v S, Sw, Pe, H, Arg, Bul, Br; 1963 v Ni, W, S, F (2), Br, Cz, Sw; 1964 v Ni, R of W, P (2). Ei, Br, U, Arg; 1965 v Ni, S, Bel, Ho, H, Y; 1966 v W, A, Y, N, D, Pol, U, M, F; 1967 v S, Sp, A (57)
Green, F. T. (Wanderers), 1876 v S (1)
Green, G. H. (Sheffield U), 1925 v F; 1926 v S, Bel, W; 1927 v W, Ni; 1928 v F, Bel (8)
Greenhalgh, E. H. (Notts Co), 1872 v S; 1873 v S (2)
Greenhoff, B. (Manchester U), 1976 v W, Ni; 1977 v Ei, Fi, I, Ho, Ni, W, S, Br, Arg, U; 1978 v Br, W, Ni, S (sub), H (sub); (with Leeds U), 1980 v Aus (sub) (18)
Greenwood, D. H. (Blackburn R), 1882 v S, Ni (2)
Gregory, J. (QPR), 1983 v Aus (3); 1984 v D, H, W (6)
Grimsdell, A. (Tottenham H), 1920 v S, W; 1921 v S, Ni; 1923 v W, Ni (6)
Grosvenor, A. T. (Birmingham), 1934 v Ni, W, F (3)
Gunn, W. (Notts Co), 1884 v S, W (2)
Guppy, S. (Leicester C), 2000 v Bel (1)
Gurney, R. (Sunderland), 1935 v S (1)

Hacking, J. (Oldham Ath), 1929 v S, W, Ni (3)
Hadley, N. (WBA), 1903 v Ni (1)
Hagan, J. (Sheffield U), 1949 v D (1)
Haines, J. T. W. (WBA), 1949 v Sw (1)
Hall, A. E. (Aston Villa), 1910 v Ni (1)
Hall, G. W. (Tottenham H), 1934 v F; 1938 v S, W, Ni, Cz; 1939 v S, Ni, R of E, I, Y (10)
Hall, J. (Birmingham C), 1956 v S, W, Ni, Br, Se, Fi, WG, D, Sp; 1957 v W, Ni, Y, D (2), Ei (2) (17)
Halse, H. J. (Manchester U), 1909 v A (1)
Hammond, H. E. D. (Oxford University), 1889 v S (1)
Hampson, J. (Blackpool), 1931 v Ni, W; 1933 v A (3)
Hampton, H. (Aston Villa), 1913 v S, W; 1914 v S, W (4)
Hancocks, J. (Wolverhampton W), 1949 v Sw; 1950 v W; 1951 v Y (3)
Hapgood, E. (Arsenal), 1933 v I, Sw; 1934 v S, Ni, W, H, Cz; 1935 v S, Ni, W, I, Ho; 1936 v S, Ni, W, G, A, Bel; 1937 v Fi; 1938 v S, G, Sw, F; 1939 v S, W, Ni, R of E, N, I, Y (30)
Hardinge, H. T. W. (Sheffield U), 1910 v S (1)
Hardman, H. P. (Everton), 1905 v W; 1907 v S, Ni; 1908 v W (4)
Hardwick, G. F. M. (Middlesbrough), 1947 v S, W, Ni, Ei, Ho, F, Sw, P; 1948 v S, W, Ni, Bel, Se (13)
Hardy, H. (Stockport Co), 1925 v Bel (1)
Hardy, S. (Liverpool), 1907 v S, W, Ni; 1908 v S; 1909 v S, W, Ni, H (2), A; 1910 v S, W, Ni; 1912 v Ni; (with Aston Villa), 1913 v S; 1914 v Ni, W, S; 1920 v S, W, Ni (21)
Harford, M. G. (Luton T), 1988 v Is (sub); 1989 v D (2)
Hargreaves, F. W. (Blackburn R), 1880 v W; 1881 v W; 1882 v Ni (3)
Hargreaves, J. (Blackburn R), 1881 v S, W (2)
Hargreaves, O. (Bayern Munich) 2002 v Ho, G (sub), I (sub), Para (sub), Sk, Cam, Se, Arg (8)

Harper, E. C. (Blackburn R), 1926 v S (1)
Harris, G. (Burnley), 1966 v Pol (1)
Harris, P. P. (Portsmouth), 1950 v Ei; 1954 v H (2)
Harris, S. S. (Cambridge University), 1904 v S; (with Old Westminsters), 1905 v Ni, W; 1906 v S, W, Ni (6)
Harrison, A. H. (Old Westminsters), 1893 v S, Ni (2)
Harrison, G. (Everton), 1921 v Bel; 1922 v Ni (2)
Harrow, J. H. (Chelsea), 1923 v Ni, Se (2)
Hart, E. (Leeds U), 1929 v W; 1930 v W, Ni; 1933 v S, A; 1934 v S, H, Cz (8)
Hartley, F. (Oxford C), 1923 v F (1)
Harvey, A. (Wednesbury Strollers), 1881 v W (1)
Harvey, J. C. (Everton), 1971 v Ma (1)
Hassall, H. W. (Huddersfield T), 1951 v S, Arg, P; 1952 v F; (with Bolton W), 1954 v Ni (5)
Hateley, M. (Portsmouth), 1984 v USSR (sub), Br, U, Ch; (with AC Milan), 1985 v EG (sub), Fi, Ni, Ei, Fi, S, I, M; 1986 v R, T, Eg, S, M, Ca, P, Mor, Para (sub); 1987 v T (sub), Br (sub), S; (with Monaco), 1988 v WG (sub), Ho (sub), H (sub), Co (sub), Ei (sub), Ho (sub), USSR (sub); (with Rangers), 1992 v Cz (32)
Hawkes, R. M. (Luton T), 1907 v Ni; 1908 v A (2), H, B (5)
Haworth, G. (Accrington), 1887 v Ni, W, S; 1888 v S; 1890 v S (5)
Hawtrey, J. P. (Old Etonians), 1881 v S, W (2)
Haygarth, E. B. (Swifts), 1875 v S (1)
Haynes, J. N. (Fulham), 1955 v Ni; 1956 v S, Ni, Br, Se, Fi, WG, Sp; 1957 v W, Y, D, Ei (2); 1958 v W, Ni, S, F, P, Y, USSR (3), Br, A; 1959 v S, Ni, USSR, I, Br, Pe, M, US; 1960 v Ni, Y, Sp, H; 1961 v Ni, W, S, L, P, Sp, M, I, A; 1962 v W, Ni, S, A, Sw, Pe, P, H, Arg, Bul, Br (56)
Healless, H. (Blackburn R), 1925 v Ni; 1928 v S (2)
Hector, K. J. (Derby Co), 1974 v Pol (sub), I (sub) (2)
Hedley, G. A. (Sheffield U), 1901 v Ni (1)
Hegan, K. E. (Corinthians), 1923 v Bel, F; 1924 v Ni, Bel (4)
Hellawell, M. S. (Birmingham C), 1963 v Ni, F (2)
Hendrie, L. A. (Aston Villa), 1999 v CzR (sub) (1)
Henfrey, A. G. (Cambridge University), 1891 v Ni; (with Corinthians), 1892 v W; 1895 v W; 1896 v S, W (5)
Henry, R. P. (Tottenham H), 1963 v F (1)
Heron, F. (Wanderers), 1876 v S (1)
Heron, G. H. H. (Uxbridge), 1873 v S; 1874 v S; (with Wanderers), 1875 v S; 1876 v S; 1878 v S (5)
Heskey, E. W. (Leicester C), 1999 v H (sub), Bul (sub); 2000 v Bel (sub), S (sub), Arg; (with Liverpool), Uk (sub), Ma (sub), P (sub), R (sub); 2001 v Fi, I, Sp (sub), Fi (sub), Alb (sub), M, Gr; 2002 v G, Alb, Gr, Se, Ho, I, Sk, Cam, Se, Arg, Ng, D, Br (29)
Hibbert, W. (Bury), 1910 v S (1)
Hibbs, H. E. (Birmingham), 1930 v S, W, A, G; 1931 v S, W, Ni; 1932 v W, Ni, Sp; 1933 v S, W, Ni, A, I, Sw; 1934 v Ni, W, F; 1935 v S, W, Ni, Ho; 1936 v G, W (25)
Hill, F. (Bolton W), 1963 v Ni, W (2)
Hill, G. A. (Manchester U), 1976 v I; 1977 v Ei (sub), Fi (sub), L; 1978 v Sw (sub), L (6)
Hill, J. H. (Burnley), 1925 v W; 1926 v S; 1927 v S, Ni, Bel, F; 1928 v Ni, W; (with Newcastle U), 1929 v F, Bel, Sp (11)
Hill, R. (Luton T), 1983 v D (sub), WG; 1986 v Eg (sub) (3)
Hill, R. H. (Millwall), 1926 v Bel (1)
Hillman, J. (Burnley), 1899 v Ni (1)
Hills, A. F. (Old Harrovians), 1879 v S (1)
Hilsdon, G. R. (Chelsea), 1907 v Ni; 1908 v S, W, Ni, A, H, B; 1909 v Ni (8)
Hinchcliffe, A. G. (Everton), 1997 v Mol, Pol, Ge; 1998 v Cam; (with Sheffield W), Sw, S,Ar; 1999 v Bul (7)
Hine, E. W. (Leicester C), 1929 v W, Ni; 1930 v W, Ni; 1932 v W, Ni (6)
Hinton, A. T. (Wolverhampton W), 1963 v F; (with Nottingham F), 1965 v W, Bel (3)
Hirst, D. E. (Sheffield W), 1991 v Aus, Nz (sub); 1992 v F (3)
Hitchens, G. A. (Aston Villa), 1961 v M, I, A; (with Inter-Milan), 1962 v Sw, Pe, H, Br (7)
Hobbis, H. H. F. (Charlton Ath), 1936 v A, Bel (2)
Hoddle, G. (Tottenham H), 1980 v Bul, W, Aus, Sp; 1981 v Sp, W, S; 1982 v N, Ni, W, Ic, Cz (sub), K; 1983 v L (sub), Ni, S; 1984 v H, L, F; 1985 v Ei (sub), S, I (sub), M, WG, US; 1986 v R, T, Ni, Is, USSR, S, M, Ca, P, Mor, Pol, Para, Arg; 1987 v Se, Ni, Y, Sp, T, S; (with Monaco), 1988 v WG, T (sub), Y (sub), Ho (sub), H (sub), Co (sub), Ei (sub), Ho, USSR (53)
Hodge, S. B. (Aston Villa), 1986 v USSR (sub), S, Ca, P (sub), Mor (sub), Pol, Para, Arg; 1987 v Se, Ni, Y; (with Tottenham H), Sp, Ni, T, S; (with Nottingham F), 1989 v D; 1990 v I (sub), Y (sub), Cz, D, U, Tun; 1991 v Cam (sub), T (sub) (24)
Hodgetts, D. (Aston Villa), 1888 v S, W, Ni; 1892 v S, Ni; 1894 v Ni (6)

Hodgkinson, A. (Sheffield U), 1957 v S, Ei (2), D; 1961 v W (5)
Hodgson, G. (Liverpool), 1931 v S, Ni, W (3)
Hodkinson, J. (Blackburn R), 1913 v W, S; 1920 v Ni (3)
Hogg, W. (Sunderland), 1902 v S, W, Ni (3)
Holdcroft, G. H. (Preston NE), 1937 v W, Ni (2)
Holden, A. D. (Bolton W), 1959 v S, I, Br, Pe, M (5)
Holden, G. H. (Wednesbury OA), 1881 v S; 1884 v S, W, Ni (4)
Holden-White, C. (Corinthians), 1888 v W, S (2)
Holford, T. (Stoke), 1903 v Ni (1)
Holley, G. H. (Sunderland), 1909 v S, W, H (2), A; 1910 v W; 1912 v S, W, Ni; 1913 v S (10)
Holliday, E. (Middlesbrough), 1960 v W, Ni, Se (3)
Hollins, J. W. (Chelsea), 1967 v Sp (1)
Holmes, R. (Preston NE), 1888 v Ni; 1891 v S; 1892 v S; 1893 v S, W; 1894 v Ni; 1895 v Ni (7)
Holt, J. (Everton), 1890 v W; 1891 v S, W; 1892 v S, Ni; 1893 v S; 1894 v S, Ni; 1895 v S; (with Reading), 1900 v Ni (10)
Hopkinson, E. (Bolton W), 1958 v W, Ni, S, F, P, Y; 1959 v S, I, Br, Pe, M, US; 1960 v W, Se (14)
Hossack, A. H. (Corinthians), 1892 v W; 1894 v W (2)
Houghton, W. E. (Aston Villa), 1931 v Ni, W, F, Bel; 1932 v S, Ni; 1933 v A (7)
Houlker, A. E. (Blackburn R), 1902 v S; (with Portsmouth), 1903 v S, W; (with Southampton), 1906 v W, Ni (5)
Howarth, R. H. (Preston NE), 1887 v Ni; 1888 v S, W; 1891 v S; (with Everton), 1894 v S (5)
Howe, D. (WBA), 1958 v S, W, H, F, P, Y, USSR (3), Br, A; 1959 v S, W, Ni, USSR, I, Br, Pe, M, US; 1960 v W, Ni, Se (23)
Howe, J. R. (Derby Co), 1948 v I; 1949 v S, Ni (3)
Howell, L. S. (Wanderers), 1873 v S (1)
Howell, R. (Sheffield U), 1895 v Ni; (with Liverpool) 1899 v S (2)
Howey, S. N. (Newcastle U), 1995 v Ng; 1996 v Co, P, Bul (4)
Hudson, A. A. (Stoke C), 1975 v WG, Cy (2)
Hudson, J. (Sheffield), 1883 v Ni (1)
Hudspeth, F. C. (Newcastle U), 1926 v Ni (1)
Hufton, A. E. (West Ham U), 1924 v Bel; 1928 v S, Ni; 1929 v F, Bel, Sp (6)
Hughes, E. W. (Liverpool), 1970 v W, Ni, S, Ho, P, Bel; 1971 v EG, Ma (2), Gr, W; 1972 v Sw, Gr, WG (2), W, Ni, S; 1973 v W (3, S (2), Pol, USSR, I; 1974 v A, Pol, I, W, Ni, S, Arg, EG, Bul, Y; 1975 v Cz, P, Cy (sub), Ni; 1977 v I, L, W, S, Br, Arg, U; 1978 v Sw, L, I, WG, Ni, S, H; 1979 v D, Ei, Ni, W, Se; (with Wolverhampton W), 1980 v Sp (sub), Ni, S (sub) (62)
Hughes, L. (Liverpool), 1950 v Ch, US, Sp (3)
Hulme, J. H. A. (Arsenal), 1927 v S, Bel, F; 1928 v S, Ni, W; 1929 v W; 1933 v S (9)
Humphreys, P. (Notts Co), 1903 v S (1)
Hunt, G. S. (Tottenham H), 1933 v I, Sw, S (3)
Hunt, Rev K R. G. (Leyton), 1911 v S, W (2)
Hunt, R. (Liverpool), 1962 v A; 1963 v EG; 1964 v S, US, P; 1965 v W; 1966 v S, Sp, Pol (2), WG (2), Fi, N, U, M, F, Arg, P; 1967 v Ni, W, Cz, Sp, A; 1968 v W, Ni, USSR (2), Sp (2), Se, Y; 1969 v R (2) (34)
Hunt, S. (WBA), 1984 v S (sub), USSR (sub) (2)
Hunter, J. (Sheffield Heeley), 1878 v S; 1880 v S, W; 1881 v S, W; 1882 v S, W (7)
Hunter, N. (Leeds U), 1966 v WG, Y, Fi, Sp (sub); 1967 v A; 1968 v Sp, Se, Y, WG, USSR; 1969 v R, W; 1970 v Ho, WG (sub); 1971 v Ma; 1972 v WG (2), W, Ni, S; 1973 v W (2) USSR (sub); 1974 v A, Pol, Ni (sub), S; 1975 v Cz (28)
Hurst, G. C. (West Ham U), 1966 v S, WG (2), Y, Fi, D, Arg, P; 1967 v Ni, W, S, Cz, Sp, A; 1968 v W, Ni, S, Se (sub), WG, USSR (2); 1969 v Ni, S, R (2), Bul, F, M, U, Br; 1970 v W, Ni, S, Ho (1+1 sub), Bel, Co, Ec, R, Br, WG; 1971 v EG, Gr, W, S; 1972 v Sw (2), Gr, WG (49)
Ince, P. E. C. (Manchester U), 1993 v Sp, N, T (2), Ho, Pol, US, Br; 1994 v Pol, Ho, Sm, D, N; 1995 v R, Ei; (with Internazionale), 1996 v Bul, Cro, H, Sw, S, Ho, G; 1997 v Mol, Pol, Ge, I, M, Ge, Pol, I, F (sub), Br; (with Liverpool), 1998 v I, Cam, Ch (sub), Sw, P, Mor, Tun, R, Co, Arg; 1999 v Se, F; (with Middlesbrough), 2000 v Bel, S (2), Br, Ma (sub), P, G, R (53)
Iremonger, J. (Nottingham F), 1901 v S; 1902 v Ni (2)

Jack, D. N. B. (Bolton W), 1924 v S, W; 1928 v F, Bel; (with Arsenal), 1930 v S, G, A; 1933 v W, A (9)
Jackson, E. (Oxford University), 1891 v W (1)
James, D. B. (Liverpool), 1997 v M; (with Aston Villa), 2001 v I, Sp, M (sub); (with West Ham U), 2002 v Ho (sub + sub), I (sub), Sk (sub), Cam (sub) (9)

Jarrett, B. G. (Cambridge University), 1876 v S; 1877 v S; 1878 v S (3)
Jefferis, F. (Everton), 1912 v S, W (2)
Jezzard, B. A. G. (Fulham), 1954 v H; 1956 v Ni (2)
Johnson, D. E. (Ipswich T), 1975 v W, S; 1976 v Sw; (with Liverpool), 1980 v Ei, Arg, Ni, S, Bel (8)
Johnson, E. (Saltley College), 1880 v W; (with Stoke C), 1884 v Ni (2)
Johnson, J. A. (Stoke C), 1937 v N, Se, Fi, S, Ni (5)
Johnson, S. A. M. (Derby Co), 2001 v I (sub) (1)
Johnson, T. C. F. (Manchester C), 1926 v Bel; 1930 v W; (with Everton), 1932 v S, Sp; 1933 v Ni (5)
Johnson, W. H. (Sheffield U), 1900 v S, W, Ni; 1903 v S, W, Ni (6)
Johnston, H. (Blackpool), 1947 v S, Ho; 1951 v S; 1953 v Arg, Ch, U, US; 1954 v W, Ni, H (10)
Jones, A. (Walsall Swifts), 1882 v S, W; (with Great Lever), 1883 v S (3)
Jones, H. (Blackburn R), 1927 v S, Bel, L, F; 1928 v S, Ni (6)
Jones, H. (Nottingham F), 1923 v F (1)
Jones, M. D. (Sheffield U), 1965 v WG, Se; (with Leeds U), 1970 v Ho (3)
Jones, R. (Liverpool), 1992 v F; 1994 v Pol, Gr, N; 1995 v US, R, Ng, U (8)
Jones, W. (Bristol C), 1901 v Ni (1)
Jones, W. H. (Liverpool), 1950 v P, Bel (2)
Joy, B. (Casuals), 1936 v Bel (1)

Kail, E. I. L. (Dulwich Hamlet), 1929 v F, Bel, Sp (3)
Kay, A. H. (Everton), 1963 v Sw (1)
Kean, F. W. (Sheffield W), 1923 v S, Bel; 1924 v W; 1925 v Ni; 1926 v Ni, Bel; 1927 v L; (with Bolton W), 1929 v F, Sp (9)
Keegan, J. K. (Liverpool), 1973 v W (2); 1974 v W, Ni, Arg, EG, Bul, Y; 1975 v Cz, WG, Cy (2), Ni, S; 1976 v Sw, Cz, P, W (2), Ni, S, Br, Fi; 1977 v Ei, Fi, I, Ho, L; (with SV Hamburg), W, Br, Arg, U; 1978 v Sw, I, WG, Br, H; 1979 v D, Ei, Cz, Ni, W, S, Bul, Se, A; 1980 v D, Ni, Ei, Sp (2), Arg, Bel, I; (with Southampton), 1981 v Sp, Sw, H; 1982 v N, H, Ni, S, Fi, Sp (sub) (63)
Keen, E. R. L. (Derby Co), 1933 v A; 1937 v W, Ni, H (4)
Kelly, R. (Burnley), 1920 v S; 1921 v S, W, Ni; 1922 v S, W; 1923 v S; 1924 v Ni; 1925 v W, Ni, S; (with Sunderland), 1926 v W; (with Huddersfield T), 1927 v L; 1928 v S (14)
Kennedy, A. (Liverpool), 1984 v Ni, W (2)
Kennedy, R. (Liverpool), 1976 v W (2), Ni, S; 1977 v L, W, S, Br (sub), Arg (sub); 1978 v Sw, L; 1980 v Bul, Sp, Arg, W, Bel (sub), I (17)
Kenyon-Slaney, W. S. (Wanderers), 1873 v S (1)
Keown, M. R. (Everton), 1992 v F, Cz, C, H, Br, Fi, D, Fe, Se; (with Arsenal), 1993 v Ho, G (sub); 1997 v M, S.Af, I, Br; 1998 v Sw, Mor, Bel; 1999 v CzR, F, Pol, H, Se; 2000 v L, Pol, Bel, S, Arg, Br, Ma, P (sub), G; 2001 v F, G, Fi, M, Gr; 2002 v Ho, Gr, Para, Sk (sub), Cam (sub) (43)
Kevan, D. T. (WBA), 1957 v S; 1958 v W, Ni, S, P, Y, USSR (3), Br, A; 1959 v M, US; 1961 v M (14)
Kidd, B. (Manchester U), 1970 v Ni, Ec (sub) (2)
King, L. B. (Tottenham H), 2002 v I (sub) (1)
King, R. S. (Oxford University), 1882 v Ni (1)
Kingsford, R. K. (Wanderers), 1874 v S (1)
Kingsley, M. (Newcastle U), 1901 v W (1)
Kinsey, G. (Wolverhampton W), 1892 v W; 1893 v S; (with Derby Co), 1896 v W, Ni (4)
Kirchen, A. J. (Arsenal), 1937 v N, Se, Fi (3)
Kirton, W. J. (Aston Villa), 1922 v Ni (1)
Knight, A. E. (Portsmouth), 1920 v Ni (1)
Knowles, C. (Tottenham H), 1968 v USSR, Sp, Se, WG (4)

Labone, B. L. (Everton), 1963 v Ni, W, F; 1967 v Sp, A; 1968 v S, Sp, Se, Y, USSR, WG; 1969 v Ni, S, R, Bul, M, U, Br; 1970 v W, Bel, Co, Ec, R, Br, WG (26)
Lampard, F. J. (West Ham U), 2000 v Bel; 2001 v Sp (sub); (with Chelsea), 2002 v Ho (sub), Se (sub), Ho (sub), I, Para (sub) (7)
Lampard, F. R. G. (West Ham U), 1973 v Y; 1980 v Aus (2)
Langley, E. J. (Fulham), 1958 v S, P, Y (3)
Langton, R. (Blackburn R), 1947 v W, Ni, Ei, Ho, F, Sw; 1948 v Se; (with Preston NE), 1949 v D, Se; (with Bolton W), 1950 v S; 1951 v Ni (11)
Latchford, R. D. (Everton), 1978 v I, Br, W; 1979 v D, Ei, Cz (sub), Ni (2), W, S, Bul, A (12)
Latheron, E. G. (Blackburn R), 1913 v W; 1914 v Ni (2)
Lawler, C. (Liverpool), 1971 v Ma, W, S; 1972 v Sw (4)
Lawton, T. (Everton), 1939 v S, W, Ni, R of E, N, I, R, Y; (with Chelsea), 1947 v S, W, Ni, Ei, Ho, F, Sw, P; 1948 v W, Ni, Bel; (with Notts Co), 1948 v S, Se, I; 1949 v D (23)
Leach, T. (Sheffield W), 1931 v W, Ni (2)
Leake, A. (Aston Villa), 1904 v S, Ni; 1905 v S, W, Ni (5)

Lee, E. A. (Southampton), 1904 v W (1)
Lee, F. H. (Manchester C), 1969 v Ni, W, S, Bul, F, M, U; 1970 v W, Ho (2), P, Bel, Co, Ec, R, Br, WG; 1971 v EG, Gr, Ma, Ni, W, S; 1972 v Sw (2), Gr, WG (27)
Lee, J. (Derby Co), 1951 v Ni (1)
Lee, R. M. (Newcastle U), 1995 v R, Ng; 1996 v Co (sub), N, Sw, Bul (sub), H; 1997 v M, Ge, S.Af, Pol, F (sub), Br (sub); 1998 v Cam (sub), Ch, Sw, Bel, Co (sub); 1999 v Se (sub), Bul, L (sub) (21)
Lee, S. (Liverpool), 1983 v Gr, L, W, Gr, H, S, Aus; 1984 v D, H, L, F, Ni, W, Ch (sub) (14)
Leighton, J. E. (Nottingham F), 1886 v Ni (1)
Le Saux, G. P. (Blackburn R), 1994 v D, Gr, N; 1995 v US, R, Ng, Ei, U, Se, Br; 1996 v Co, P (sub); 1997 v I, M, Ge, S.Af, Pol, I, F, Br; (with Chelsea), 1998 v I, Ch (sub), P, Mor, Bel, Tun, R, Co, Arg; 1999 v Se, Bul (sub), CzR, F, Pol, Se; 2001 v G (36)
Le Tissier, M. P. (Southampton), 1994 v D (sub), Gr (sub), N (sub); 1995 v R, Ng (sub), Ei; 1997 v Mol (sub), I (8)
Lilley, H. E. (Sheffield U), 1892 v W (1)
Linacre, H. J. (Nottingham F), 1905 v W, S (2)
Lindley, T. (Cambridge University), 1886 v S, W, Ni; 1887 v S, W, Ni; 1888 v S, W, Ni; (with Nottingham F), 1889 v S; 1890 v S, W; 1891 v Ni (13)
Lindsay, A. (Liverpool), 1974 v Arg, EG, Bul, Y (4)
Lindsay, W. (Wanderers), 1877 v S (1)
Lineker, G. (Leicester C), 1984 v S (sub); 1985 v Ei, R (sub), S (sub), I (sub), WG, US; (with Everton), 1986 v R, T, Ni, Eg, USSR, Ca, P, Mor, Para, Arg; (with Barcelona), 1987 v Ni (2), Y, Sp, T, Br; 1988 v WG, T, Y, Ho, H, S, Co, Sw, Ei, Ho, USSR; 1989 v Se, S.Ar, Gr, Alb (2), Pol, D; (with Tottenham H) 1990 v Se, Pol, I, Y, Br, Cz, D, U, Tun, Ei, Ho, Eg, Bel, Cam, WG, I; 1991 v H, Pol, Ei (2), Cam, T, Arg, Aus, Nz, Mal; 1992 v G, T, Pol, F (sub), Cz (sub), C, H, Br, Fi, D, F, Se (80)
Lintott, E. H. (QPR), 1908 v S, W, Ni; (with Bradford C), 1909 v S, Ni, H (2) (7)
Lipsham, H. B. (Sheffield U), 1902 v W (1)
Little, B. (Aston Villa), 1975 v W (sub) (1)
Lloyd, L. V. (Liverpool), 1971 v W; 1972 v Sw, Ni; (with Nottingham F), 1980 v W (4)
Lockett, A. (Stoke C), 1903 v Ni (1)
Lodge, L. V. (Cambridge University), 1894 v W; 1895 v S, W; (with Corinthians), 1896 v S, Ni (5)
Lofthouse, J. M. (Blackburn R), 1885 v S, W, Ni; 1887 v S, W; (with Accrington), 1889 v Ni; (with Blackburn R), 1890 v Ni (7)
Lofthouse, N. (Bolton W), 1951 v Y; 1952 v W, Ni, S, A (2), I, Sw; 1953 v W, Ni, S, Bel, Arg, Ch, U, US; 1954 v W, Ni, R of E, Bel, U; 1955 v Ni, S, F, Sp, P; 1956 v W, S, Sp, D, Fi (sub); 1959 v W, USSR (33)
Longworth, E. (Liverpool), 1920 v S; 1921 v Bel; 1923 v S, W, Bel (5)
Lowder, A. (Wolverhampton W), 1889 v W (1)
Lowe, E. (Aston Villa), 1947 v F, Sw, P (3)
Lucas, T. (Liverpool), 1922 v Ni; 1924 v F; 1926 v Bel (3)
Luntley, E. (Nottingham F), 1880 v S, W (2)
Lyttelton, Hon. A. (Cambridge University), 1877 v S (1)
Lyttelton, Hon. E. (Cambridge University), 1878 v S (1)

McCall, J. (Preston NE), 1913 v S, W; 1914 v S; 1920 v S; 1921 v Ni (5)
McCann, G. P. (Sunderland), 2001 v Sp (sub) (1)
McDermott, T. (Liverpool), 1978 v Sw, L; 1979 v Ni, W, Se; 1980 v D, Ni (sub), Ei, Ni, S, Bel (sub), Sp; 1981 v N, R, Sw, R (sub), Br, Sw (sub), H; 1982 v N, H, W (sub), Ho, S (sub), Ic (25)
McDonald, C. A. (Burnley), 1958 v USSR (3), Br, A; 1959 v W, Ni, USSR (8)
McFarland, R. L. (Derby Co), 1971 v Gr, Ma (2), Ni, S; 1972 v Sw, Gr, WG, W, S; 1973 v W (3), Ni, S, Cz, Pol, USSR, I; 1974 v A, Pol, I, W, Ni; 1976 v Cz, S; 1977 v Ei, I (28)
McGarry, W. H. (Huddersfield T), 1954 v Sw, U; 1956 v W, D (4)
McGuinness, W. (Manchester U), 1959 v Ni, M (2)
McInroy, A. (Sunderland), 1927 v Ni (1)
McMahon, S. (Liverpool), 1988 v Is, H, Co, USSR; 1989 v D (sub); 1990 v Se, Pol, I, Y (sub), Br, Cz (sub), D, Ei (sub), Eg, Bel, I; 1991 v Ei (17)
McManaman, S. (Liverpool), 1995 v Ng (sub), U (sub), I (sub); 1996 v Co, N, Sw, P (sub), Bul, Cro, Chn, Sw, S, Ho, Sp, G; 1997 v Pol, I, M; 1998 v Cam, Sw, Mor, Co (sub); 1999 v Pol, H; (with Real Madrid), 2000 v L, Pol, Uk, Ma (sub), P; 2001 v F (sub), Fi (sub+1), Alb, Gr (sub); 2002 v G (sub), Alb (sub), Gr (sub) (37)
McNab, R. (Arsenal), 1969 v Ni, Bul, R (1+1 sub) (4)
McNeal, R. (WBA), 1914 v S, W (2)

McNeil, M. (Middlesbrough), 1961 v W, Ni, S, L, P, Sp, M, I; 1962 v L (9)

Mabbutt, G. (Tottenham H), 1983 v WG, Gr, L, W, Gr, H, Ni, S (sub); 1984 v H; 1987 v Y, Ni, T; 1988 v WG; 1992 v T, Pol, Cz (16)

Macaulay, R. H. (Cambridge University), 1881 v S (1)

Macdonald, M. (Newcastle U), 1972 v W, Ni, S (sub); 1973 v USSR (sub); 1974 v P, S (sub), Y (sub); 1975 v WG, Cy (2), Ni; 1976 v Sw (sub), Cz, P (14)

Macrae, S. (Notts Co), 1883 v S, W, Ni; 1884 v S. Ni (5)

Maddison, F. B. (Oxford University), 1872 v S (1)

Madeley, P. E. (Leeds U), 1971 v Ni; 1972 v Sw (2), Gr, WG (2), W, S; 1973 v S, Cz, Pol, USSR, I; 1974 v A, Pol, I; 1975 v Cz, P, Cy; 1976 v Cz, P, Fi; 1977 v Ei, Ho (24)

Magee, T. P. (WBA), 1923 v W, Se; 1925 v S, Bel, F (5)

Makepeace, H. (Everton), 1906 v S; 1910 v S; 1912 v S, W (4)

Male, C. G. (Arsenal), 1935 v S, Ni, I, Ho; 1936 v S, W, Ni, G, A, Bel; 1937 v S, Ni, H, N, Se, Fi; 1939 v I, R, Y (19)

Mannion, W. J. (Middlesbrough), 1947 v S, W, Ni, Ei, Ho, F, Sw, P; 1948 v W, Ni, Bel, Se, I; 1949 v N, F; 1950 v S, Ei, P, Bel, Ch, US; 1951 v Ni, W, S, Y; 1952 v F (26)

Mariner, P. (Ipswich T), 1977 v L (sub), Ni; 1978 v L, W (sub), S; 1980 v W, Ni (sub), S, Aus, I (sub), Sp (sub); 1981 v N, Sw, Sp, Sw, H; 1982 v N, H, Ho, S, Fi, F, Cz, K, WG, Sp; 1983 v D, WG, Gr, W; 1984 v D, H, L; (with Arsenal), 1985 v EG, R (35)

Marsden, J. T. (Darwen), 1891 v Ni (1)

Marsden, W. (Sheffield W), 1930 v W, S, G (3)

Marsh, R. W. (QPR), 1972 v Sw (sub); (with Manchester C), WG (sub+1), W, Ni, S; 1973 v W (2), Y (9)

Marshall, T. (Darwen), 1880 v W; 1881 v W (2)

Martin, A. (West Ham U), 1981 v Br, S (sub); 1982 v H, Fi; 1983 v Gr, L, W, Gr, H; 1984 v H, L, W; 1985 v Ni; 1986 v Is, Ca, Para; 1987 v Se (17)

Martin, H. (Sunderland), 1914 v Ni (1)

Martyn, A. N. (C Palace), 1992 v C (sub), H; 1993 v G; (with Leeds U), 1997 v S.Af; 1998 v Cam, Ch, Bel; 1999 v CzR, F (sub); 2000 v L, Pol, Bel (sub), Uk, R; 2001 v Sp (sub), M; 2002 v Ho, Gr, Se, Ho, I, Sk, Cam (23)

Marwood, B. (Arsenal), 1989 v S.Ar (sub) (1)

Maskrey, H. M. (Derby Co), 1908 v Ni (1)

Mason, C. (Wolverhampton W), 1887 v Ni; 1888 v W; 1890 v Ni (3)

Matthews, R. D. (Coventry C), 1956 v S, Br, Se, WG; 1957 v Ni (5)

Matthews, S. (Stoke C), 1935 v W, I; 1936 v G; 1937 v S; 1938 v S, W, Cz, G, Sw, F; 1939 v S, W, Ni, R of E, N, I, Y; 1947 v S; (with Blackpool), 1947 v Sw, P; 1948 v S, W, Ni, Bel, I; 1949 v S, W, Ni, D, Sw; 1950 v Sp; 1951 v Ni, S; 1954 v Ni, R of E, H, Bel, U; 1955 v Ni, W, S, S, F, WG, Sp, P; 1956 v W, Br; 1957 v S, W, Ni, Y, D (2), Ei (54)

Matthews, V. (Sheffield U), 1928 v F, Bel (2)

Maynard, W. J. (1st Surrey Rifles), 1872 v S; 1876 v S (2)

Meadows, J. (Manchester C), 1955 v S (1)

Medley, L. D. (Tottenham H), 1951 v F, W; 1952 v F, A, W, Ni (6)

Meehan, T. (Chelsea), 1924 v Ni (1)

Melia, J. (Liverpool), 1963 v S, Sw (2)

Mercer, D. W. (Sheffield U), 1923 v Ni, Bel (2)

Mercer, J. (Everton), 1939 v S, Ni, I, R, Y (5)

Merrick, G. H. (Birmingham C), 1952 v Ni, S, A (2), I, Sw; 1953 v Ni, S, Bel, Arg, Ch, U; 1954 v W, Ni, S, R of E, H (2), Y, Bel, Sw, U (23)

Merson, P. C. (Arsenal), 1992 v G (sub), Cz, H, Br (sub), Fi (sub), D, Se (sub); 1993 v Sp (sub), N (sub), Ho (sub), Br (sub), G; 1994 v Ho, Gr; 1997 v I (sub); (with Middlesbrough), 1998 v Sw, P (sub), Bel, Arg (sub); 1999 v Se (sub); (with Aston Villa), CzR (21)

Metcalfe, V. (Huddersfield T), 1951 v Arg, P (2)

Mew, J. W. (Manchester U), 1921 v Ni (1)

Middleditch, B. (Corinthians), 1897 v Ni (1)

Milburn, J. E. T. (Newcastle U), 1949 v S, W, Ni, Sw; 1950 v W, P, Bel, Sp; 1951 v W, Arg, P; 1952 v F; 1956 v D (13)

Miller, B. G. (Burnley), 1961 v A (1)

Miller, H. S. (Charlton Ath), 1923 v Se (1)

Mills, D. J. (Leeds U), 2001 v M (sub); 2002 v Ho (sub), Se (sub), I, Para (sub), Sk, Cam (sub), Se, Arg, Ng, D, Br (12)

Mills, G. R. (Chelsea), 1938 v W, Ni, Cz (3)

Mills, M. D. (Ipswich T), 1973 v Y; 1976 v W (2), Ni, S, Br, I (sub), Fi; 1977 v Fi (sub), I, Ni, W, S; 1978 v WG, Br, W, Ni, S, H; 1979 v D, Ei, Ni (2), S, Bul, A; 1980 v D, Ni, Sp (2); 1981 v Sp (2), H; 1982 v N, H, S, Fi, F, Cz, K, WG, Sp (42)

Milne, G. (Liverpool), 1963 v Br, Cz, EG; 1964 v W, Ni, S, R of W, U, P, Ei, Br, Arg; 1965 v Ni, Bel (14)

Milton, C. A. (Arsenal), 1952 v A (1)

Milward, A. (Everton), 1891 v S, W; 1897 v S, W (4)

Mitchell, C. (Upton Park), 1880 v W; 1881 v S; 1883 v S, W; 1885 v W (5)

Mitchell, J. F. (Manchester C), 1925 v Ni (1)

Moffat, H. (Oldham Ath), 1913 v W (1)

Molyneux, G. (Southampton), 1902 v S; 1903 v S, W, Ni (4)

Moon, W. R. (Old Westminsters), 1888 v S, W; 1889 v S, W; 1890 v S, W; 1891 v S (7)

Moore, H. T. (Notts Co), 1883 v Ni; 1885 v W (2)

Moore, J. (Derby Co), 1923 v Se (1)

Moore, R. F. (West Ham U), 1962 v Pe, H, Arg, Bul, Br; 1963 v W, Ni, S, F (2), Br, Cz, EG, Sw; 1964 v W, Ni, S, R of W, U, P (2), Ei, Br, Arg; 1965 v Ni, S, Bel, H, Y, WG, Se; 1966 v W, Ni, S, A, Sp, Pol (2), WG (2), N, D, U, M, F, Arg, P; 1967 v W, Ni, S, Cz, Sp, A; 1968 v W, Ni, S, USSR (2), Sp (2), Se, Y, WG; 1969 v Ni, W, S, R, Bul, F, M, U, Br; 1970 v W, Ni, S, Ho, P, Bel, Co, Ec, R, Br, Cz, WG; 1971 v EG, Gr, Ma, Ni, S; 1972 v Sw (2), Gr, WG (2), W, S; 1973 v W (3), Y, S (2), Ni, Cz, Pol, USSR, I; 1974 v I (108)

Moore, W. G. B. (West Ham U), 1923 v Se (1)

Mordue, J. (Sunderland), 1912 v Ni; 1913 v Ni (2)

Morice, C. J. (Barnes), 1872 v S (1)

Morley, A. (Aston Villa), 1982 v H (sub), Ni, W, Ic; 1983 v D, Gr (6)

Morley, H. (Notts Co), 1910 v Ni (1)

Morren, T. (Sheffield U), 1898 v Ni (1)

Morris, F. (WBA), 1920 v S; 1921 v Ni (2)

Morris, J. (Derby Co), 1949 v N, F; 1950 v Ei (3)

Morris, W. W. (Wolverhampton W), 1939 v S, Ni, R (3)

Morse, H. (Notts Co), 1879 v S (1)

Mort, T. (Aston Villa), 1924 v W, F; 1926 v S (3)

Morten, A. (C Palace), 1873 v S (1)

Mortensen, S. H. (Blackpool), 1947 v P; 1948 v W, S, Ni, Bel, Se, I; 1949 v S, W, Ni, Se, N; 1950 v S, W, Ni, I, P, Bel, Ch, US, Sp; 1951 v S, Arg; 1954 v R of E, H (25)

Morton, J. R. (West Ham U), 1938 v Cz (1)

Mosforth, W. (Sheffield W), 1877 v S; (with Sheffield Albion), 1878 v S; 1879 v S, W; 1880 v S, W; (with Sheffield W), 1881 v W; 1882 v S, W (9)

Moss, F. (Arsenal), 1934 v S, H, Cz; 1935 v I (4)

Moss, F. (Aston Villa), 1922 v S, Ni; 1923 v Ni; 1924 v S, Bel (5)

Mosscrop, E. (Burnley), 1914 v S, W (2)

Mozley, B. (Derby Co), 1950 v W, Ni, Ei (3)

Mullen, J. (Wolverhampton W), 1947 v S; 1949 v N, F; 1950 v Bel; Ch, US; 1954 v W, Ni, S, R of E, Y, Sw (12)

Mullery, A. P. (Tottenham H), 1965 v Ho; 1967 v Sp, A; 1968 v W, Ni, S, USSR, Sp (2), Se, Y; 1969 v Ni, S, R, Bul, F, M, U, Br; 1970 v W, Ni, S (sub), Ho (sub), Bel, P, Co, Ec, R, Cz, WG, Br; 1971 v Ma, EG, Gr; 1972 v Sw (35)

Murphy, D. B. (Liverpool), 2002 v Se (sub), I (sub), Para (sub), Sk (4)

Neal, P. G. (Liverpool), 1976 v W, I; 1977 v W, S, Br, Arg, U; 1978 v Sw, I, WG, Ni, S, H; 1979 v D, Ei, Ni (2), S, Bul, A; 1980 v D, Ni, Sp, Arg, W, Bel, I; 1981 v R, Sw, Sp, Br, H; 1982 v N, H, W, Ho, Ic, F (sub); K; 1983 v D, Gr, L, W, Gr, H, Ni, S, Aus (2); 1984 v D (50)

Needham, E. (Sheffield U), 1894 v S; 1895 v S; 1897 v S, W, Ni; 1898 v S, W; 1899 v S, W, Ni; 1900 v S, Ni; 1901 v S, W, Ni; 1902 v W (16)

Neville, G. A. (Manchester U), 1995 v J, Br; 1996 v Co, N, Sw, P, Bul, Cro, H, Chn, Sw, S, Ho, Sp; 1997 v Mol, Pol, I, Ge, Pol, I (sub), F, Br (sub); 1998 v Mol, Ch, P, S.Ar, Bel, R, Co, Arg; 1999 v Bul, Pol; 2000 v L (sub), Pol, Br, Ma, P, G, R; 2001 v G, I, Sp (sub), Fi, Alb; 2002 v Ho, G, Alb, Gr, Se, Ho, I (sub), Para (52)

Neville, P. J. (Manchester U), 1996 v Chn; 1997 v S.Af, Pol (sub), I, F, Br; 1998 v Mol, Cam, Ch, P (sub), S.Ar (sub), Bel; 1999 v L, Pol (sub), H, Se, Bul; 2000 v L (sub), Pol (sub), Bel (sub), S (2), Arg (sub); Br, Uk, Ma, P, G, R; 2001 v Fi, Sp, M, Gr; 2002 v Se (sub), Ho (sub), I (sub), Para (sub) (37)

Newton, K. R. (Blackburn R), 1966 v S, WG; 1967 v Sp, A; 1968 v W, S, Sp, Se, Y, WG; 1969 v Ni, W, S, R, Bul, M, U, Br, F; (with Everton), 1970 v Ni, S, Ho, Co, Ec, R, Cz, WG (27)

Nicholls, J. (WBA), 1954 v S, Y (2)

Nicholson, W. E. (Tottenham H), 1951 v P (1)

Nish, D. J. (Derby Co), 1973 v Ni; 1974 v P, W, Ni, S (5)

Norman, M. (Tottenham H), 1962 v Pe, H, Arg, Bul, Br; 1963 v S, F, Br, Cz, EG; 1964 v W, Ni, S, R of W, U, P (2), US, Br, Arg; 1965 v Ni, Bel, Ho (23)

Nuttall, H. (Bolton W), 1928 v W, Ni; 1929 v S (3)

Oakley, W. J. (Oxford University), 1895 v W; 1896 v S, W, Ni; (with Corinthians), 1897 v S, W, Ni; 1898 v S, W, Ni; 1900 v S, W, Ni; 1901 v S, W, Ni (16)

O'Dowd, J. P. (Chelsea), 1932 v S; 1933 v Ni, Sw (3)

O'Grady, M. (Huddersfield T), 1963 v Ni; (with Leeds U), 1969 v F (2)

Ogilvie, R. A. M. M. (Clapham R), 1874 v S (1)

Oliver, L. F. (Fulham), 1929 v Bel (1)

Olney, B. A. (Aston Villa), 1928 v F, Bel (2)

Osborne, F. R. (Fulham), 1923 v Ni, F; (with Tottenham H), 1925 v Bel; 1926 v Bel (4)

Osborne, R. (Leicester C), 1928 v W (1)

Osgood, P. L. (Chelsea), 1970 v Bel, R (sub), Cz (sub); 1974 v I (4)

Osman, R. (Ipswich T), 1980 v Aus; 1981 v Sp, R, Sw; 1982 v N, Ic; 1983 v D, Aus (3); 1984 v D (11)

Ottaway, C. J. (Oxford University), 1872 v S; 1874 v S (2)

Owen, J. R. B. (Sheffield), 1874 v S (1)

Owen, M. J. (Liverpool), 1998 v Ch, Sw, P (sub), Mor (sub), Bel (sub), Tun (sub), R (sub), Co, Arg; 1999 v Se, Bul, L, F; 2000 v L (sub), Pol (sub), Bel (sub), S (2), Br, P, G, R; 2001 v F (sub), G, Sp, Fi, Alb, M, Gr; 2002 v Ho (sub), G, Alb, I, Para, Sk, Cam, Se, Arg, Ng, D, Br (41)

Owen, S. W. (Luton T), 1954 v H, Y, Bel (3)

Page, L. A. (Burnley), 1927 v S, W, Bel, L, F; 1928 v W, Ni (7)

Paine, T. L. (Southampton), 1963 v Cz, EG; 1964 v W, Ni, S, R of W, U, US, P; 1965 v H, Y, WG, Se; 1966 v W, A, Y, N, M (19)

Pallister, G. A. (Middlesbrough), 1988 v H; 1989 v S.Ar; (with Manchester U), 1991 v Cam (sub), T; 1992 v G; 1993 v N, US, Br, G; 1994 v Pol, Ho, Sm, D; 1995 v US, R, Ei, U, Se; 1996 v N, Sw; 1997 v Mol, Pol (sub) (22)

Palmer, C. L. (Sheffield W), 1992 v C, H, Br, Fi (sub), D, F, Se; 1993 v Sp (sub), N (sub), T, Sm, T, Ho, Pol, N, US, Br (sub); 1994 v Ho (18)

Pantling, H. H. (Sheffield U), 1924 v Ni (1)

Paravacini, P. J. de (Cambridge University), 1883 v S, W, Ni (3)

Parker, P. A. (QPR), 1989 v Alb (sub), Ch, D; 1990 v Y, U, Ho, Eg, Bel, Cam, WG, I; 1991 v H, Pol, USSR, Aus, Nz; (with Manchester U), 1992 v G; 1994 v Ho, D (19)

Parker, T. R. (Southampton), 1925 v F (1)

Parkes, P. B. (QPR), 1974 v P (1)

Parkinson, J. (Liverpool), 1910 v S, W (2)

Parlour, R. (Arsenal), 1999 v Pol (sub), Se (sub), Bul (sub); 2000 v L, S (sub), Arg (sub), Br (sub); 2001 v G (sub), Fi, I (10)

Parr, P. C. (Oxford University), 1882 v W (1)

Parry, E. H. (Old Carthusians), 1879 v W; 1882 v W, S (3)

Parry, R. A. (Bolton W), 1960 v Ni, S (2)

Patchitt, B. C. A. (Corinthians), 1923 v Se (2) (2)

Pawson, F. W. (Cambridge University), 1883 v Ni; (with Swifts), 1885 v Ni (2)

Payne, J. (Luton T), 1937 v Fi (1)

Peacock, A. (Middlesbrough), 1962 v Arg, Bul; 1963 v Ni, W; (with Leeds U), 1966 v W, Ni (6)

Peacock, J. (Middlesbrough), 1929 v F, Bel, Sp (3)

Pearce, S. (Nottingham F), 1987 v Br, S; 1988 v WG (sub), Is, H; 1989 v S.Ar, Se, S.Ar, Gr, Alb (2), Ch, S, Pol, D; 1990 v Se, Pol, I, Y, Br, Cz, D, U, Tun, Ei, Ho, Eg, Bel, Cam, WG; 1991 v H, Pol, Ei (2), Cam, T, Arg, Aus, Nz (2), Mal; 1992 v T, Pol, F, Cz, Br (sub), Fi, D, F, Se; 1993 v Sp, N, T; 1994 v Pol, Sm, Gr (sub); 1995 v R (sub), J, Br; 1996 v N, Sw, P, Bul, Cro, H, Sw, S, Ho, Sp, G; 1997 v Mol, Pol, I, M, S.Af, I; (with West Ham U), 2000 v L, Pol (78)

Pearson, H. F. (WBA), 1932 v S (1)

Pearson, J. H. (Crewe Alex), 1892 v Ni (1)

Pearson, J. S. (Manchester U), 1976 v W, Ni, S, Br, Fi; 1977 v Ei, Ho (sub), W, S, Br, Arg, U; 1978 v I (sub), WG, Ni (15)

Pearson, S. C. (Manchester U), 1948 v S; 1949 v S, Ni; 1950 v Ni, I; 1951 v P; 1952 v S, I (8)

Pease, W. H. (Middlesbrough), 1927 v W (1)

Pegg, D. (Manchester U), 1957 v Ei (1)

Pejic, M. (Stoke C), 1974 v P, W, Ni, S (4)

Pelly, F. R. (Old Foresters), 1893 v Ni; 1894 v S, W (3)

Pennington, J. (WBA), 1907 v S, W; 1908 v S, W, Ni, A; 1909 v S, W, H (2), A; 1910 v S, W; 1911 v S, W, Ni; 1912 v S, W, Ni; 1913 v S, W; 1914 v S, Ni; 1920 v S, W (25)

Pentland, F. B. (Middlesbrough), 1909 v S, W, H (2), A (5)

Perry, C. (WBA), 1890 v Ni; 1891 v Ni; 1893 v W (3)

Perry, T. (WBA), 1898 v W (1)

Perry, W. (Blackpool), 1956 v Ni, S, Sp (3)

Perryman, S. (Tottenham H), 1982 v Ic (sub) (1)

Peters, M. (West Ham U), 1966 v Y, Fi, Pol, M, F, Arg, P, WG; 1967 v Ni, W, S, Cz; 1968 v W, Ni, S, USSR (2), Sp (2), Se, Y; 1969 v Ni, S, R, Bul, F, M, U, Br; 1970 v Ho (2), P (sub), Bel; (with Tottenham H), W, Ni, S, Co, Ec, R, Br, Cz, WG; 1971 v EG, Gr, Ma (2), Ni, W, S; 1972 v Sw, Gr, WG (1+1 sub), Ni (sub); 1973 v S (2), Ni, W, Cz, Pol, USSR, I; 1974 v A, Pol, I, P, S (67)

Phelan, M. C. (Manchester U), 1990 v I (sub) (1)

Phillips, K. (Sunderland), 1999 v H; 2000 v Bel, Arg (sub), Br (sub), Ma; 2001 v I (sub); 2002 v Se, Ho (sub) (8)

Phillips, L. H. (Portsmouth), 1952 v Ni; 1955 v W, WG (3)

Pickering, F. (Everton), 1964 v US; 1965 v Ni, Bel (3)

Pickering, J. (Sheffield U), 1933 v S (1)

Pickering, N. (Sunderland), 1983 v Aus (1)

Pike, T. M. (Cambridge University), 1886 v Ni (1)

Pilkington, B. (Burnley), 1955 v Ni (1)

Plant, J. (Bury), 1900 v S (1)

Platt, D. (Aston Villa), 1990 v I (sub), Y (sub), Br, D (sub), Tun (sub), Ho (sub), Eg (sub), Bel (sub), Cam, WG, I; 1991 v H, Pol, Ei (2), T, USSR, Arg, Aus, Nz (2), Mal; (with Bari), 1992 v G, T, Pol, Cz, C, Br, Fi, D, F, Se; (with Juventus), 1993 v Sp, N, T, Sm, T, Ho, Pol, N, Br (sub), G; (with Sampdoria), 1994 v Pol, Ho, Sm, D, Gr, N; 1995 v US, Ng, Ei, U, J, Se, Br; (with Arsenal), 1996 v Bul (sub), Cro, H, Sw (sub), Ho (sub), Sp, G (62)

Plum, S. L. (Charlton Ath), 1923 v F (1)

Pointer, R. (Burnley), 1962 v W, L, P (3)

Porteous, T. S. (Sunderland), 1891 v W (1)

Powell, C. G. (Charlton Ath), 2001 v Sp, Fi, M (sub); 2002 v Ho (sub+sub) (5)

Priest, A. E. (Sheffield U), 1900 v Ni (1)

Prinsep, J. F. M. (Clapham Rovers), 1879 v S (1)

Puddefoot, S. C. (Blackburn R), 1926 v S, Ni (2)

Pye, J. (Wolverhampton W), 1950 v Ei (1)

Pym, R. H. (Bolton W), 1925 v S, W; 1926 v W (3)

Quantrill, A. (Derby Co), 1920 v S, W; 1921 v W, Ni (4)

Quixall, A. (Sheffield W), 1954 v W, Ni, R of E; 1955 v Sp, P (sub) (5)

Radford, J. (Arsenal), 1969 v R; 1972 v Sw (sub) (2)

Raikes, G. B. (Oxford University), 1895 v W; 1896 v W, Ni, S (4)

Ramsey, A. E. (Southampton), 1949 v Sw; (with Tottenham H), 1950 v S, I, P, Bel, Ch, US, Sp; 1951 v S, Ni, W, Y, Arg, P; 1952 v S, W, Ni, F, A (2), I, Sw; 1953 v Ni, W, S, Bel, Arg, Ch, U, US; 1954 v R of E, H (32)

Rawlings, A. (Preston NE), 1921 v Bel (1)

Rawlings, W. E. (Southampton), 1922 v S, W (2)

Rawlinson, J. F. P. (Cambridge University), 1882 v Ni (1)

Rawson, H. E. (Royal Engineers), 1875 v S (1)

Rawson, W. S. (Oxford University), 1875 v S; 1877 v S (2)

Read, A. (Tufnell Park), 1921 v Bel (1)

Reader, J. (WBA), 1894 v Ni (1)

Reaney, P. (Leeds U), 1969 v Bul (sub); 1970 v P; 1971 v Ma (3)

Redknapp, J. F. (Liverpool), 1996 v Co, N, Sw, Chn, S (sub); 1997 v M (sub), Ge (sub), S.Af; 1999 v Se, Bul, F, Pol (sub), H (sub), Bul; 2000 v Bel, S (2) (17)

Reeves, K. (Norwich C), 1980 v Bul; (with Manchester C), Ni (2)

Regis, C. (WBA), 1982 v Ni (sub), W (sub), Ic; 1983 v WG; (with Coventry C), 1988 v T (sub) (5)

Reid, P. (Everton), 1985 v Ni, WG, US (sub); 1986 v R, S (sub), Ca (sub), Pol, Para, Arg; 1987 v Br; 1988 v WG, Y (sub), Sw (sub) (13)

Revie, D. G. (Manchester C), 1955 v Ni, S, F; 1956 v W, D; 1957 v Ni (6)

Reynolds, J. (WBA), 1892 v S; 1893 v S, W; (with Aston Villa), 1894 v S, Ni; 1895 v S; 1897 v S, W (8)

Richards, C. H. (Nottingham F), 1898 v Ni (1)

Richards, G. H. (Derby Co), 1909 v A (1)

Richards, J. P. (Wolverhampton W), 1973 v Ni (1)

Richardson, J. R. (Newcastle U), 1933 v I, Sw (2)

Richardson, K. (Aston Villa), 1994 v Gr (1)

Richardson, W. G. (WBA), 1935 v Ho (1)

Rickaby, S. (WBA), 1954 v Ni (1)

Ricketts, M. B. (Bolton W), 2002 v Ho (1)

Rigby, A. (Blackburn R), 1927 v S, Bel, L, F; 1928 v W (5)

Rimmer, E. J. (Sheffield W), 1930 v S, G, A; 1932 v Sp (4)

Rimmer, J. J. (Arsenal), 1976 v I (1)

Ripley, S. E. (Blackburn R), 1994 v Sm; 1998 v Mol (sub) (2)

Rix, G. (Arsenal), 1981 v N, R, Sw (sub), Br, W, S; 1982 v Ho (sub), Fi (sub), F, Cz, WG, Sp; 1983 v D, WG (sub), Gr (sub); 1984 v Ni (17)

Robb, G. (Tottenham H), 1954 v H (1)

Roberts, C. (Manchester U), 1905 v Ni, W, S (3)

Roberts, F. (Manchester C), 1925 v S, W, Bel, F (4)

Roberts, G. (Tottenham H), 1983 v Ni, S; 1984 v F, Ni, S, USSR (6)

Roberts, H. (Arsenal), 1931 v S (1)

Roberts, H. (Millwall), 1931 v Bel (1)

Roberts, R. (WBA), 1887 v S; 1888 v Ni; 1890 v Ni (3)

Roberts, W. T. (Preston NE), 1924 v W, Bel (2)

Robinson, J. (Sheffield W), 1937 v Fi; 1938 v G, Sw; 1939 v W (4)

Robinson, J. W. (Derby Co), 1897 v S, Ni; (with New Brighton Tower), 1898 v S, W, Ni; (with Southampton), 1899 v W, S; 1900 v S, W, Ni; 1901 v Ni (11)

Robson, B. (WBA), 1980 v Ei, Aus; 1981 v N, R, Sw, Sp, R, Br, W, S, Sw, H; 1982 v N; (with Manchester U), H, Ni, W, Ho, S, Fi, F, Cz, WG, Sp; 1983 v D, Gr, L, S; 1984 v H, L, F, Ni, S, USSR, Br, U, Ch; 1985 v EG, Fi, T, Ei, R, Fi, S, M, I, WG, US; 1986 v R, T, Is, M, P, Mor; 1987 v Ni (2), Sp, T, Br, S; 1988 v T, Y, Ho, H, S, Co, Sw, Ei, Ho, USSR; 1989 v S, Se, S.Ar, Gr, Alb (2), Ch, S, Pol, D; 1990 v Pol, I, Y, Cz, U, Tun, Ei, Ho; 1991 v Cam, Ei; 1992 v T (90)

Robson, R. (WBA), 1958 v F, USSR (2), Br, A; 1960 v Sp, H; 1961 v Ni, W, S, L, P, Sp, M, I; 1962 v W, Ni, Sw, L, P (20)

Rocastle, D. (Arsenal), 1989 v D, S.Ar, Gr, Alb (2), Pol (sub), D; 1990 v Se (sub), Pol, Y, D (sub); 1992 v Pol, Cz, Br (sub) (14)

Rose, W. C. (Wolverhampton W), 1884 v S, W, Ni; (with Preston NE), 1886 v Ni; (with Wolverhampton W), 1891 v Ni (5)

Rostron, T. (Darwen), 1881 v S, W (2)

Rowe, A. (Tottenham H), 1934 v F (1)

Rowley, J. F. (Manchester U), 1949 v Sw, Se, F; 1950 v Ni, I; 1952 v S (6)

Rowley, W. (Stoke C), 1889 v Ni; 1892 v Ni (2)

Royle, J. (Everton), 1971 v Ma; 1973 v Y; (with Manchester C), 1976 v Ni (sub), I; 1977 v Fi, L (6)

Ruddlesdin, H. (Sheffield W), 1904 v W, Ni; 1905 v S (3)

Ruddock, N. (Liverpool), 1995 v Ng (1)

Ruffell, J. W. (West Ham U), 1926 v S; 1927 v Ni; 1929 v S, W, Ni; 1930 v W (6)

Russell, B. B. (Royal Engineers), 1883 v W (1)

Rutherford, J. (Newcastle U), 1904 v S; 1907 v S, Ni, W; 1908 v S, Ni, W, A (2), H, B (11)

Sadler, D. (Manchester U), 1968 v Ni, USSR; 1970 v Ec (sub); 1971 v EG (4)

Sagar, C. (Bury), 1900 v Ni; 1902 v W (2)

Sagar, E. (Everton), 1936 v S, Ni, A, Bel (4)

Salako, J. A. (C Palace), 1991 v Aus (sub), Nz (sub + 1), Mal; 1992 v G (5)

Sandford, E. A. (WBA), 1933 v W (1)

Sandilands, R. R. (Old Westminsters), 1892 v W; 1893 v Ni; 1894 v W; 1895 v W; 1896 v W (5)

Sands, J. (Nottingham F), 1880 v W (1)

Sansom, K. (C Palace), 1979 v W; 1980 v Bul, Ei, Arg, W (sub), Ni, S, Bel, I; (with Arsenal), 1981 v N, R, Sw, Sp, R, Br, W, S, Sw; 1982 v Ni, W, Ho, S, Fi, F, Cz, WG, Sp; 1983 v D, WG, Gr, L, Gr, H, Ni, S; 1984 v D, H, L, F, S, USSR, Br, U, Ch; 1985 v EG, Fi, T, Ni, Ei, R, Fi, S, I, M, WG, US; 1986 v R, T, Ni, Eg, Is, USSR, S, M, Ca, P, Mor, Pol, Para, Arg; 1987 v Se, Ni (2), Y, Sp, T; 1988 v WG, T, Y, Ho, S, Co, Sw, Ei, Ho, USSR (86)

Saunders, F. E. (Swifts), 1888 v W (1)

Savage, A. H. (C Palace), 1876 v S (1)

Sayer, J. (Stoke C), 1887 v Ni (1)

Scales, J. R. (Liverpool), 1995 v J, Se (sub), Br (3)

Scattergood, E. (Derby Co), 1913 v W (1)

Schofield, J. (Stoke C), 1892 v W; 1893 v W; 1895 v Ni (3)

Scholes, P. (Manchester U), 1997 v S.Af (sub), I, Br; 1998 v Mol, Cam, P, S.Ar, Tun, R, Co, Arg; 1999 v Se, Bul, L, F (sub), Pol, Se; 2000 v Pol, S (2), Arg, Br, Uk, Ma, P, G, R; 2001 v F, G, Fi, Sp, Fi, Alb, M, Gr; 2002 v Ho, G, Alb, Gr, Se, Ho, Para, Sk, Cam, Se, Arg, Ng, D, Br (49)

Scott, L. (Arsenal), 1947 v S, W, Ni, Ei, Ho, F, Sw, P; 1948 v S, W, Ni, Bel, Se, I; 1949 v W, Ni, D (17)

Scott, W. R. (Brentford), 1937 v W (1)

Seaman, D. A. (QPR), 1989 v S.Ar, D (sub); 1990 v Cz (sub); (with Arsenal), 1991 v Cam, Ei, T, Arg; 1992 v Cz, H (sub); 1994 v Pol, Ho, Sm, D, N; 1995 v US, R, Ei; 1996 v Co, N, Sw, P, Bul, Cro, H, Sw, S, Ho, Sp, G; 1997 v Mol, Pol, Ge (2), Pol, F, Br; 1998 v Mol, I, P, S.Ar, Tun, R, Co, Arg; 1999 v Se, Bul, L, F, Pol, H, Se, Bul; 2000 v Bel, S (2), Arg, Br, P, G; 2001 v F, G, Fi (2), Alb, Gr; 2002 v G, Alb, Para, Se, Arg, Ng, D, Br (73)

Seddon, J. (Bolton W), 1923 v F, Se (2); 1924 v Bel; 1927 v W; 1929 v S (6)

Seed, J. M. (Tottenham H), 1921 v Bel; 1923 v W, Ni, Bel; 1925 v S (5)

Settle, J. (Bury), 1899 v S, W, Ni; (with Everton), 1902 v S, Ni; 1903 v Ni (6)

Sewell, J. (Sheffield W), 1952 v Ni, A, Sw; 1953 v Ni; 1954 v H (2) (6)

Sewell, W. R. (Blackburn R), 1924 v W (1)

Shackleton, L. F. (Sunderland), 1949 v W, D; 1950 v W; 1955 v W, WG (5)

Sharp, J. (Everton), 1903 v Ni; 1905 v S (2)

Sharpe, L. S. (Manchester U), 1991 v Ei (sub); 1993 v T (sub), N, US, Br, G; 1994 v Pol, Ho (8)

Shaw, G. E. (WBA), 1932 v S (1)

Shaw, G. L. (Sheffield U), 1959 v S, W, USSR, I; 1963 v W (5)

Shea, D. (Blackburn R), 1914 v W, Ni (2)

Shearer, A. (Southampton), 1992 v F, C, F; (with Blackburn R), 1993 v Sp, N, T; 1994 v Ho, D, Gr, N; 1995 v US, R, Ng, Ei, J, Se, Br; 1996 v Co, N, Sw, P, H (sub), Cro, Sw, Ho, Sp, G; (with Newcastle U), 1997 v Mol, Pol, I, Ge, Pol, F, Br; 1998 v Ch (sub), Sw, P, S.Ar, Tun, R, Co, Arg; 1999 v Se, Bul, L, F, Pol, H, Se, Bul; 2000 v L, Pol, Bel, S (2), Arg, Br, Uk, Ma, P, G, R (63)

Shellito, K. J. (Chelsea), 1963 v Cz (1)

Shelton A. (Notts Co), 1889 v Ni; 1890 v S, W; 1891 v S, W; 1892 v S (6)

Shelton, C. (Notts Rangers), 1888 v Ni (1)

Shepherd, A. (Bolton W), 1906 v S; (with Newcastle U), 1911 v Ni (2)

Sheringham, E. P. (Tottenham H), 1993 v Pol, N; 1995 v US, R (sub), Ng (sub), U, J (sub), Se, Br; 1996 v Co (sub), N (sub), Sw, Bul, Cro, H, Sw, S, Ho, Sp, G; 1997 v Ge, M, Ge, S.Af, Pol, I, F (sub), Br; (with Manchester U), 1998 v I, Ch, Sw (sub), P, S.Ar, Tun, R; 1999 v Se (sub), Bul (sub), Bul; 2001 v Fi, Alb (sub), M (sub); (with Tottenham H), 2002 v Gr (sub), Se (sub), I (sub), Para (sub), Sk (sub), Cam (sub), Arg (sub), Ng (sub), D (sub), Br (sub) (51)

Sherwood, T. A. (Tottenham H), 1999 v Pol, H, Se (3)

Shilton, P. L. (Leicester C), 1971 v EG, W; 1972 v Sw, Ni; 1973 v Y, S (2), Ni, W, Cz, Pol, USSR, I; 1974 v A, Pol, I, W, Ni, S, Arg; (with Stoke C), 1975 v Cy; 1977 v Ni, W; (with Nottingham F), 1978 v W, H; 1979 v Cz, Se, A; 1980 v Ni, Sp, I; 1981 v N, Sw, R; 1982 v H, Ho, S, F, Cz, K, WG, Sp; (with Southampton), 1983 v D, WG, Gr, W, Gr, H, Ni, S, Aus (3); 1984 v D, H, F, Ni, W, S, USSR, Br, U, Ch; 1985 v EG, Fi, T, Ni, R, Fi, S, I, WG; 1986 v R, T, Ni, Eg, Is, USSR, S, M, Ca, P, Mor, Pol, Para, Arg; 1987 v Se, Ni (2), Sp, Br; (with Derby Co), 1988 v WG, T, Y, Ho, S, Co, Sw, Ei, Ho; 1989 v D, Se, Gr, Alb (2), Ch, S, Pol, D; 1990 v Se, Pol, I, Y, Br, Cz, D, U, Tun, Ei, Ho, Eg, Bel, Cam, WG, I (125)

Shimwell, E. (Blackpool), 1949 v Se (1)

Shutt, G. (Stoke C), 1886 v Ni (1)

Silcock, J. (Manchester U), 1921 v S, W; 1923 v Se (3)

Sillett, R. P. (Chelsea), 1955 v F, Sp, P (3)

Simms, E. (Luton T), 1922 v Ni (1)

Simpson, J. (Blackburn R), 1911 v S, W, Ni; 1912 v S, W, Ni; 1913 v S; 1914 v W (8)

Sinclair, T. (West Ham U), 2002 v Se, I, Para (sub), Sk (sub), Cam (sub), Ng, D, Br (9)

Sinton, A. (QPR), 1992 v Pol, C, H (sub), Br, F, Se; 1993 v Sp, T, Br, G; (with Sheffield W), 1994 v Ho (sub), Sm (12)

Slater, W. J. (Wolverhampton), 1955 v W, WG; 1958 v S, P, Y, USSR (3), Br, A; 1959 v USSR; 1960 v S (12)

Smalley, T. (Wolverhampton W), 1937 v W (1)

Smart, T. (Aston Villa), 1921 v S; 1924 v S, W; 1926 v Ni; 1930 v W (5)

Smith, A. (Nottingham F), 1891 v S, W; 1893 v Ni (3)

Smith, A. (Leeds U), 2001 v M (sub), Gr (sub); 2002 v Ho (sub) (3)

Smith, A. K. (Oxford University), 1872 v S (1)

Smith, A. M. (Arsenal), 1989 v S.Ar (sub), Gr, Alb (sub), Pol (sub); 1991 v T, USSR, Arg; 1992 v G, T, Pol (sub), H (sub), D, Se (sub) (13)

Smith, B. (Tottenham H), 1921 v S; 1922 v W (2)

Smith, C. E. (C Palace), 1876 v S (1)

Smith, G. O. (Oxford University), 1893 v Ni; 1894 v W, S; 1895 v W; 1896 v Ni, W, S; (with Old Carthusians), 1897 v Ni, W, S; 1898 v Ni, W, S; (with Corinthians), 1899 v Ni, W, S; 1899 v Ni, W, S; 1901 v S (20)

Smith, H. (Reading), 1905 v W, S; 1906 v W, Ni (4)

Smith, J. (WBA), 1920 v Ni; 1923 v Ni (2)

Smith, Joe (Bolton W), 1913 v Ni; 1914 v S, W; 1920 v W, Ni (5)

Smith, J. C. R. (Millwall), 1939 v Ni, N (2)

Smith, J. W. (Portsmouth), 1932 v Ni, W, Sp (3)

Smith, Leslie (Brentford), 1939 v R (1)

Smith, Lionel (Arsenal), 1951 v W; 1952 v W, Ni; 1953 v W, S, Bel (6)

Smith, R. A. (Tottenham H), 1961 v Ni, W, S, L, P, Sp; 1962 v S; 1963 v S, F, Br, Cz, EG; 1964 v W, Ni, R of W (15)

Smith, S. (Aston Villa), 1895 v S (1)

Smith, S. C. (Leicester C), 1936 v Ni (1)

Smith, T. (Birmingham C), 1960 v W, Se (2)

Smith, T. (Liverpool), 1971 v W (1)

Smith, W. H. (Huddersfield T), 1922 v W, S; 1928 v S (3)

Sorby, T. H. (Thursday Wanderers, Sheffield), 1879 v W (1)

Southgate, G. (Aston Villa), 1996 v P (sub), Bul, H (sub), Chn, Sw, S, Ho, Sp, G; 1997 v Mol, Pol, Ge, M, Ge (sub), S.Af, Pol, I, F, Br; 1998 v Mol, I, Cam, Sw, S.Ar, Mor, Tun, Arg (sub); 1999 v Se, Bul, L, Bul; 2000 v Bel, S, Arg, Uk, Ma (sub), R (sub); 2001 v F (sub), G, Fi, I, M (sub); (with Middlesbrough), 2002 v Ho (sub), Se, Ho (sub), I, Para, Sk (sub), Cam (sub) (49)

Southworth, J. (Blackburn R), 1889 v W; 1891 v W; 1892 v S (3)

Sparks, F. J. (Herts Rangers), 1879 v S; (with Clapham Rovers), 1880 v S, W (3)

Spence, J. W. (Manchester U), 1926 v Bel; 1927 v Ni (2)

Spence, R. (Chelsea), 1936 v A, Bel (2)

Spencer, C. W. (Newcastle U), 1924 v S; 1925 v W (2)

Spencer, H. (Aston Villa), 1897 v S, W; 1900 v W; 1903 v Ni; 1905 v W, S (6)

Spiksley, F. (Sheffield W), 1893 v S; 1894 v S, Ni; 1896 v Ni; 1898 v S, W (7)

Spilsbury, B. W. (Cambridge University), 1885 v Ni; 1886 v Ni, S (3)

Spink, N. (Aston Villa), 1983 v Aus (sub) (1)

Spouncer, W. A. (Nottingham F), 1900 v W (1)

Springett, R. D. G. (Sheffield W), 1960 v Ni, S, Y, Sp, H; 1961 v Ni, S, L, P, Sp, M, I, A; 1962 v W, Ni, S, A, Sw, Pe, L, P, H, Arg, Bul, Br; 1963 v Ni, W, F (2); Sw; 1966 v W, A, N (33)

Sproston, B. (Leeds U), 1937 v W; 1938 v S, W, Ni, Cz, G, Sw, F; (with Tottenham H), 1939 v W, R of E; (with Manchester C), N (11)

Squire, R. T. (Cambridge University), 1886 v S, W, Ni (3)

Stanbrough, M. H. (Old Carthusians), 1895 v W (1)

Staniforth, R. (Huddersfield T), 1954 v S, H, Y, Bel, Sw, U; 1955 v W, WG (8)

Starling, R. W. (Sheffield W), 1933 v S; (with Aston Villa), 1937 v S (2)

Statham, D. (WBA), 1983 v W, Aus (2) (3)

Steele, F. C. (Stoke C), 1937 v S, W, Ni, N, Se, Fi (6)

Stein, B. (Luton T), 1984 v F (1)

Stephenson, C. (Huddersfield T), 1924 v W (1)

Stephenson, G. T. (Derby Co), 1928 v F, Bel; (with Sheffield W), 1931 v F (3)

Stephenson, J. E. (Leeds U), 1938 v S; 1939 v Ni (2)

Stepney, A. C. (Manchester U), 1968 v Se (1)

Sterland, M. (Sheffield W), 1989 v S.Ar (1)

Steven, T. M. (Everton), 1985 v Ni, Ei, R, Fi, I, US (sub); 1986 v T (sub), Eg, USSR (sub), M (sub); Pol, Para, Arg; 1987 v Se, Y (sub), Sp (sub); 1988 v T, Y, Ho, H, S, Sw, Ho, USSR; 1989 v S; (with Rangers), 1990 v Cz, Cam (sub), WG (sub), I; 1991 v Cam; (with Marseille), 1992 v G, C, Br, Fi, D, F (36)

Stevens, G. A. (Tottenham H), 1985 v Fi (sub), T (sub), Ni; 1986 v S (sub), M (sub), Mor (sub), Para (sub) (7)

Stevens, M. G. (Everton), 1985 v I, WG; 1986 v R, T, Ni, Eg, Is, S, Ca, P, Mor, Pol, Para, Arg; 1987 v Br, S; 1988 v T, Y, Is, Ho, H (sub), S, Sw, Ei, Ho, USSR; (with Rangers), 1989 v D, Se, Gr, Alb (2), S, Pol; 1990 v Se, Pol, I, Br, D, Tun, Ei, I; 1991 v USSR; 1992 v C, H, Br, Fi (46)

Stewart, J. (Sheffield W), 1907 v S, W; (with Newcastle U), 1911 v S (3)

Stewart, P. A. (Tottenham H), 1992 v G (sub), Cz (sub), C (sub) (3)

Stiles, N. P. (Manchester U), 1965 v S, H, Y, Se; 1966 v W, Ni, S, A, Sp, Pol (2), WG (2), N, D, U, M, F, Arg, P; 1967 v Ni, W, S, Cz; 1968 v USSR; 1969 v R; 1970 v Ni, S (28)

Stoker, J. (Birmingham), 1933 v W; 1934 v S, H (3)

Stone, S. B. (Nottingham F), 1996 v N (sub), Sw (sub), P, Bul, Cro, Chn (sub), Sw (sub), S (sub), Sp (sub) (9)

Storer, H. (Derby Co), 1924 v F; 1928 v Ni (2)

Storey, P. E. (Arsenal), 1971 v Gr, Ni, S; 1972 v Sw, WG, W, Ni, S; 1973 v W (3), Y, S (2), Ni, Cz, Pol, USSR, I (19)

Storey-Moore, I. (Nottingham F), 1970 v Ho (1)

Strange, A. H. (Sheffield W), 1930 v S, A, G; 1931 v S, W, Ni, F, Bel; 1932 v S, W, Ni, Sp; 1933 v S, Ni, A, I, Sw; 1934 v Ni, W, F (20)

Stratford, A. H. (Wanderers), 1874 v S (1)

Streten, B. (Luton T), 1950 v Ni (1)

Sturgess, A. (Sheffield U), 1911 v Ni; 1914 v S (2)

Summerbee, M. G. (Manchester C), 1968 v S, Sp, WG; 1972 v Sw, WG (sub), W, Ni; 1973 v USSR (sub) (8)

Sunderland, A. (Arsenal), 1980 v Aus (1)

Sutcliffe, J. W. (Bolton U), 1893 v W; 1895 v S, Ni; 1901 v S; (with Millwall), 1903 v W (5)

Sutton, C. R. (Blackburn R), 1998 v Cam (sub) (1)

Swan, P. (Sheffield W), 1960 v Y, Sp, H; 1961 v Ni, W, S, L, P, Sp, M, I, A; 1962 v W, Ni, S, A, Sw, L, P (19)

Swepstone, H. A. (Pilgrims), 1880 v S; 1882 v S, W; 1883 v S, W, Ni (6)

Swift, F. V. (Manchester C), 1947 v S, W, Ni, Ei, Ho, F, Sw, P; 1948 v S, W, Ni, Bel, Se, I; 1949 v S, W, Ni, D, N (19)

Tait, G. (Birmingham Excelsior), 1881 v W (1)

Talbot, B. (Ipswich T), 1977 v Ni (sub), S, Br, Arg, U; (with Arsenal), 1980 v Aus (6)

Tambling, R. V. (Chelsea), 1963 v W, F; 1966 v Y (3)

Tate, J. T. (Aston Villa), 1931 v F, Bel; 1933 v W (3)

Taylor, E. (Blackpool), 1954 v H (1)

Taylor, E. H. (Huddersfield T), 1923 v S, W, Ni, Bel; 1924 v S, Ni, F; 1926 v S (8)

Taylor, J. G. (Fulham), 1951 v Arg, P (2)

Taylor, P. H. (Liverpool), 1948 v W, Ni, Se (3)

Taylor, P. J. (C Palace), 1976 v W (sub+1), Ni, S (4)

Taylor, T. (Manchester U), 1953 v Arg, Ch, U; 1954 v Bel, Sw; 1956 v S, Br, Se, Fi, WG; 1957 v Ni, Y (sub), D (2), Ei (2); 1958 v W, Ni, F (19)

Temple, D. W. (Everton), 1965 v WG (1)

Thickett, H. (Sheffield U), 1899 v S, W (2)

Thomas, D. (Coventry C), 1983 v Aus (1+1 sub) (2)

Thomas, D. (QPR), 1975 v Cz (sub), P, Cy (sub+1), W, S (sub); 1976 v Cz (sub), P (sub) (8)

Thomas, G. R. (C Palace), 1991 v T, USSR, Arg, Aus, Nz (2), Mal; 1992 v Pol, F (9)

Thomas, M. L. (Arsenal), 1989 v S.Ar; 1990 v Y (2)

Thompson, P. (Liverpool), 1964 v P (2), Ei, US, Br, Arg; 1965 v Ni, W, S, Bel, Ho; 1966 v Ni; 1968 v Ni, WG; 1970 v S, Ho (sub) (16)

Thompson, P. B. (Liverpool), 1976 v W (2), Ni, S, Br, I, Fi; 1977 v Fi; 1979 v Ei (sub), Cz, Ni, S, Bul, Se (sub), A; 1980 v D, Ni, Bul, Ei, Sp (2), Arg, W, S, Bel, I; 1981 v N, R, H; 1982 v N, H, W, Ho, S, Fi, F, Cz, K, WG, Sp; 1983 v WG, Gr (42)

Thompson T. (Aston Villa), 1952 v W; (with Preston NE), 1957 v S (2)

Thomson, R. A. (Wolverhampton W), 1964 v Ni, US, P, Arg; 1965 v Bel, Ho, Ni, W (8)

Thornewell, G. (Derby Co), 1923 v Se (2); 1924 v F; 1925 v F (4)

Thornley, I. (Manchester C), 1907 v W (1)

Tilson, S. F. (Manchester C), 1934 v H, Cz; 1935 v W; 1936 v Ni (4)

Titmuss, F. (Southampton), 1922 v W; 1923 v W (2)

Todd, C. (Derby Co), 1972 v Ni; 1974 v P, W, Ni, S, Arg, EG, Bul, Y; 1975 v P (sub), WG, Cy (2), Ni, W, S; 1976 v Sw, Cz, P, Ni, S, Br, Fi; 1977 v Ei, Fi, Ho (sub), Ni (27)

Toone, G. (Notts Co), 1892 v S, W (2)

Topham, A. G. (Casuals), 1894 v W (1)

Topham, R. (Wolverhampton W), 1893 v Ni; (with Casuals) 1894 v W (2)

Towers, M. A. (Sunderland), 1976 v W, Ni (sub), I (3)

Townley, W. J. (Blackburn R), 1889 v W; 1890 v Ni (2)

Townrow, J. E. (Clapton Orient), 1925 v S; 1926 v W (2)

Tremelling, D. R. (Birmingham), 1928 v W (1)

Tresadern, J. (West Ham U), 1923 v S, Se (2)

Tueart, D. (Manchester C), 1975 v Cy (sub), Ni; 1977 v Fi, Ni, W (sub), S (sub) (6)

Tunstall, F. E. (Sheffield U), 1923 v S; 1924 v S, W, Ni, F; 1925 v Ni, S (7)

Turnbull, R. J. (Bradford), 1920 v Ni (1)

Turner, A. (Southampton), 1900 v Ni; 1901 v Ni (2)

Turner, H. (Huddersfield T), 1931 v F, Bel (2)

Turner, J. A. (Bolton R), 1893 v W; (with Stoke C) 1895 v Ni; (with Derby Co) 1898 v Ni (3)

Tweedy, G. J. (Grimsby T), 1937 v H (1)

Ufton, D. G. (Charlton Ath), 1954 v R of E (1)

Underwood A. (Stoke C), 1891 v Ni; 1892 v Ni (2)

Unsworth, D. G. (Everton), 1995 v J (1)

Urwin, T. (Middlesbrough), 1923 v Se (2); 1924 v Bel; (with Newcastle U), 1926 v W (4)

Utley, G. (Barnsley), 1913 v Ni (1)

Vassell, D. (Aston Villa), 2002 v Ho, I (sub), Para, Sk, Cam, Se, Ng (sub), Br (sub) (8)

Vaughton, O. H. (Aston Villa), 1882 v S, W, Ni; 1884 v S, W (5)

Veitch, C. C. M. (Newcastle U), 1906 v S, W, Ni; 1907 v S, W; 1909 v W (6)

Veitch, J. G. (Old Westminsters), 1894 v W (1)

Venables, T. F. (Chelsea), 1965 v Ho, Bel (2)

Venison, B. (Newcastle U), 1995 v US, U (2)

Vidal, R. W. S. (Oxford University), 1873 v S (1)

Viljoen, C. (Ipswich T), 1975 v Ni, W (2)

Viollet, D. S. (Manchester U), 1960 v H; 1962 v L (2)

Von Donop (Royal Engineers), 1873 v S; 1875 v S (2)

Wace, H. (Wanderers), 1878 v S; 1879 v S, W (3)
Waddle, C. R. (Newcastle U), 1985 v Ei, R (sub), Fi (sub), S (sub), I, M (sub), WG, US; (with Tottenham H), 1986 v R, T, Ni, Is, USSR, S, M, Ca, P, Mor, Pol (sub), Arg (sub); 1987 v Se (sub), Ni (2), Y, Sp, T, Br, S; 1988 v WG, Is, H, S (sub), Co, Sw (sub), Ei, Ho (sub); 1989 v Se, S.Ar, Alb (2), Ch, S, Pol, D (sub); (with Marseille), 1990 v Se, Pol, I, Y, Br, D, U, Tun, Ei, Ho, Eg, Bel, Cam, WG, I (sub); 1991 v H (sub), Pol (sub); 1992 v T (62)
Wadsworth, S. J. (Huddersfield T), 1922 v S; 1923 v S, Bel; 1924 v S, Ni; 1925 v S, Ni; 1926 v W; 1927 v Ni (9)
Wainscoat, W. R. (Leeds U), 1929 v S (1)
Waiters, A. K. (Blackpool), 1964 v Ei, Br; 1965 v W, Bel, Ho (5)
Walden, F. I. (Tottenham H), 1914 v S; 1922 v W (2)
Walker, D. S. (Nottingham F), 1989 v D (sub), Se (sub), Gr, Alb (2), Ch, S, Pol, D; 1990 v Se, Pol, I, Y, Br, Cz, D, U, Tun, Ei, Ho, Eg, Bel, Cam, WG, I; 1991 v H, Pol, Ei (2), Cam, T, Arg, Aus, Nz (2), Mal; 1992 v T, Pol, F, Cz, C, H, Br, Fi, D, F, Se; (with Sampdoria), 1993 v Sp, N, T, Sm, T, Ho, Pol, N, US (sub), Br, G; (with Sheffield W), 1994 v Sm (59)
Walker, I. M. (Tottenham H), 1996 v H (sub), Chn (sub); 1997 v I (3)
Walker, W. H. (Aston Villa), 1921 v Ni; 1922 v Ni, W, S; 1923 v Se (2); 1924 v S; 1925 v Ni, W, S, Bel, F; 1926 v Ni, W, S; 1927 v Ni, W; 1933 v A (18)
Wall, G. (Manchester U), 1907 v W; 1908 v Ni; 1909 v S; 1910 v W, S; 1912 v S; 1913 v Ni (7)
Wallace, C. W. (Aston Villa), 1913 v W; 1914 v Ni; 1920 v S (3)
Wallace, D. L. (Southampton), 1986 v Eg (1)
Walsh, P. (Luton T), 1983 v Aus (2 + 1 sub); 1984 v F, W (5)
Walters, A. M. (Cambridge University), 1885 v S, N; 1886 v S; 1887 v S, W; (with Old Carthusians), 1889 v S, W; 1890 v S, W (9)
Walters, K. M. (Rangers), 1991 v Nz (1)
Walters, P. M. (Oxford University), 1885 v S, Ni; (with Old Carthusians), 1886 v S, W, Ni; 1887 v S, W; 1888 v S, Ni; 1889 v S, W; 1890 v S, W (13)
Walton, N. (Blackburn R), 1890 v Ni (1)
Ward, J. T. (Blackburn Olympic), 1885 v W (1)
Ward, P. (Brighton & HA), 1980 v Aus (sub) (1)
Ward, T. V. (Derby Co), 1948 v Bel; 1949 v W (2)
Waring, T. (Aston Villa), 1931 v F, Bel; 1932 v S, W, Ni (5)
Warner, C. (Upton Park), 1878 v S (1)
Warren, B. (Derby Co), 1906 v S, W, Ni; 1907 v S, W, Ni; 1908 v S, W, Ni, A (2), H, B; (with Chelsea), 1909 v S, Ni, W, H (2), A; 1911 v S, Ni, W (22)
Waterfield, G. S. (Burnley), 1927 v W (1)
Watson, D. (Norwich C), 1984 v Br, U, Ch; 1985 v M, US (sub); 1986 v S; (with Everton), 1987 v Ni; 1988 v Is, Ho, S, Sw (sub), USSR (12)
Watson, D. V. (Sunderland), 1974 v P, S (sub), Arg, EG, Bul, Y; 1975 v Cz, P, WG, Cy (2), Ni, W, S; (with Manchester C), 1976 v Sw, Cz (sub), P; 1977 v Ho, L, Ni, W, S, Br, Arg, U; 1978 v Sw, L, I, WG, Br, W, Ni, S, H; 1979 v D, Ei, Cz, Ni (2), W, S, Bul, Se, A; (with Werder Bremen), 1980 v D; (with Southampton), Ni, Bul, Ei, Sp (2), Arg, Ni, S, Bel, I; 1981 v N, R, Sw, R, W, S, Sw, H; (with Stoke C), 1982 v Ni, Ic (65)
Watson, V. M. (West Ham U), 1923 v W, S; 1930 v S, G, A (5)
Watson, W. (Burnley), 1913 v S; 1914 v Ni; 1920 v Ni (3)
Watson, W. (Sunderland), 1950 v Ni, I; 1951 v W, Y (4)
Weaver, S. (Newcastle U), 1932 v S, 1933 v S, Ni (3)
Webb, G. W. (West Ham U), 1911 v S, W (2)
Webb, N. J. (Nottingham F), 1988 v WG (sub), T, Y, Is, Ho, S, Sw, Ei, USSR; 1989 v D, Se, Gr, Alb (2), Ch, S, Pol, D; (with Manchester U), 1990 v Se, I (sub); 1992 v F, H, Br (sub), Fi, D (sub), Se (26)
Webster, M. (Middlesbrough), 1930 v S, A, G (3)
Wedlock, W. J. (Bristol C), 1907 v S, Ni, W; 1908 v S, Ni, W, A (2), H, B; 1909 v S, W, Ni, H (2), A; 1910 v S, W, Ni; 1911 v S, W, Ni; 1912 v S, W, Ni; 1914 v W (26)
Weir, D. (Bolton W), 1889 v S, Ni (2)
Welch, R. de C. (Wanderers), 1872 v S; (with Harrow Chequers), 1874 v S (2)
Weller, K. (Leicester C), 1974 v W, Ni, S, Arg (4)
Welsh, D. (Charlton Ath), 1938 v G, Sw; 1939 v R (3)
West, G. (Everton), 1969 v W, Bul, M (3)
Westwood, R. W. (Bolton W), 1935 v S, W, Ho; 1936 v Ni, G; 1937 v W (6)
Whateley, O. (Aston Villa), 1883 v S, Ni (2)
Wheeler, J. E. (Bolton W), 1955 v Ni (1)
Wheldon, G. F. (Aston Villa), 1897 v Ni; 1898 v S, W, Ni (4)
White, D. (Manchester C), 1993 v Sp (1)

White, T. A. (Everton), 1933 v I (1)
Whitehead, J. (Accrington), 1893 v W; (with Blackburn R), 1894 v Ni (2)
Whitfield, H. (Old Etonians), 1879 v W (1)
Whitham, M. (Sheffield U), 1892 v Ni (1)
Whitworth, S. (Leicester C), 1975 v WG, Cy, Ni, W, S; 1976 v Sw, P (7)
Whymark, T. J. (Ipswich T), 1978 v L (sub) (1)
Widdowson, S. W. (Nottingham F), 1880 v S (1)
Wignall, F. (Nottingham F), 1965 v W, Ho (2)
Wilcox, J. M. (Blackburn R), 1996 v H; 1999 v F (sub); (with Leeds U), 2000 v Arg (3)
Wilkes, A. (Aston Villa), 1901 v S, W; 1902 v S, W, Ni (5)
Wilkins, R. G. (Chelsea), 1976 v I; 1977 v Ei, Fi, Ni, Br, Arg, U; 1978 v Sw (sub), L, I, WG, W, Ni, S, H; 1979 v D, Ei, Cz, Ni, W, S, Bul, Se (sub), A; (with Manchester U), 1980 v D, Ni, Bul, Sp (2), Arg, W (sub), Ni, S, Bel, I; 1981 v Sp (sub), R, Br, W, S, Sw, H (sub); 1982 v Ni, W, Ho, S, Fi, F, Cz, K, WG, Sp; 1983 v D, WG; 1984 v D, Ni, W, S, USSR, Br, U, Ch; (with AC Milan), 1985 v EG, Fi, T, Ni, Ei, R, Fi, S, I, M; 1986 v T, Ni, Is, Eg, USSR, S, M, Ca, P, Mor; 1987 v Se, Y (sub) (84)
Wilkinson, B. (Sheffield U), 1904 v S (1)
Wilkinson, L. R. (Oxford University), 1891 v W (1)
Williams, B. F. (Wolverhampton W), 1949 v F; 1950 v S, W, Ei, I, P, Bel, Ch, US, Sp; 1951 v Ni, W, S, Y, Arg, P; 1952 v W, F; 1955 v S, WG, F, Sp, P; 1956 v W (24)
Williams, O. (Clapton Orient), 1923 v W, Ni (2)
Williams, S. (Southampton), 1983 v Aus (1+1 sub); 1984 v F; 1985 v EG, Fi, T (6)
Williams, W. (WBA), 1897 v Ni; 1898 v W, Ni, S; 1899 v W, Ni (6)
Williamson, E. C. (Arsenal), 1923 v Se (2) (2)
Williamson, R. G. (Middlesbrough), 1905 v Ni; 1911 v Ni, S, W; 1912 v S, W; 1913 v Ni (7)
Willingham, C. K. (Huddersfield T), 1937 v Fi; 1938 v S, G, Sw, F; 1939 v S, W, Ni, R of E, N, I, Y (12)
Willis, A. (Tottenham H), 1952 v F (1)
Wilshaw, D. J. (Wolverhampton W), 1954 v W, Sw, U; 1955 v S, F, Sp, P; 1956 v W, Ni, Fi, WG; 1957 v Ni (12)
Wilson, C. P. (Hendon), 1884 v S, W (2)
Wilson, C. W. (Oxford University), 1879 v W; 1881 v S (2)
Wilson, G. (Sheffield W), 1921 v S, W, Bel; 1922 v S, Ni; 1923 v S, W, Ni, Bel; 1924 v W, Ni, F (12)
Wilson, G. P. (Corinthians), 1900 v S, W (2)
Wilson, R. (Huddersfield T), 1960 v S, Y, Sp, H; 1962 v W, Ni, S, A, Sw, Pe, P, H, Arg, Bul, Br; 1963 v Ni, F, Br, Cz, EG, Sw; 1964 v W, S, R of W, U, P (2), Ei, Br, Arg; (with Everton), 1965 v S, H, Y, WG, Se; 1966 v WG (sub), W, Ni, A, Sp, Pol (2), Y, Fi, D, U, M, F, Arg, P, WG; 1967 v Ni, W, S, Cz, A; 1968 v Ni, S, USSR (2), Sp (2), Y (63)
Wilson, T. (Huddersfield T), 1928 v S (1)
Winckworth, W. N. (Old Westminsters), 1892 v W; 1893 v Ni (2)
Windridge, J. E. (Chelsea), 1908 v S, W, Ni, A (2), H, B; 1909 v Ni (8)
Wingfield-Stratford, C. V. (Royal Engineers), 1877 v S (1)
Winterburn, N. (Arsenal), 1990 v I (sub); 1993 v G (sub) (2)
Wise, D. F. (Chelsea), 1991 v T, USSR, Aus (sub), Nz (2); 1994 v N; 1995 v R (sub), Ng; 1996 v Co, N, P, H (sub); 2000 v Bel (sub), Arg, Br, Ma, P (sub), G, R; 2001 v F, Fi (21)
Withe, P. (Aston Villa), 1981 v Br, W, S; 1982 v N (sub), W, Ic; 1983 v H, Ni, S; 1984 v H (sub); 1985 v T (11)
Wollaston, C. H. R. (Wanderers), 1874 v S; 1875 v S; 1877 v S; 1880 v S (4)
Wolstenholme, S. (Everton), 1904 v S; (with Blackburn R), 1905 v W, Ni (3)
Wood, H. (Wolverhampton W), 1890 v S, W; 1896 v S (3)
Wood, R. E. (Manchester U), 1955 v Ni, W; 1956 v Fi (3)
Woodcock, A. S. (Nottingham F), 1978 v Ei; 1979 v Ei (sub), Cz, Bul (sub), Se; 1980 v Ni; (with Cologne), Bul, Ei, Sp (2), Arg, Bel, I; 1981 v N, R, Sw, R, W (sub), S; 1982 v N (sub), Ho, Fi (sub), WG (sub), Sp; (with Arsenal), 1983 v WG (sub), Gr, L, Gr; 1984 v L, F (sub), Ni, W, S, Br, U (sub); 1985 v EG, Fi, T, Ni; 1986 v R (sub), T (sub), Is (sub) (42)
Woodgate, J. S. (Leeds U), 1999 v Bul (1)
Woodger, G. (Oldham Ath), 1911 v Ni (1)
Woodhall, G. (WBA), 1888 v S, W (2)
Woodley, V. R. (Chelsea), 1937 v S, N, Se, Fi; 1938 v S, W, Ni, Cz, G, Sw, F; 1939 v S, W, Ni, R of E, N, I, R, Y (19)
Woods, C. C. E. (Norwich C), 1985 v US; 1986 v Eg (sub), Is (sub), Ca (sub); (with Rangers), 1987 v Y, Sp (sub), Ni (sub), T, S; 1988 v Is, H, Sw (sub), USSR; 1989 v D (sub); 1990 v Br (sub), D (sub); 1991 v H, Pol, Ei, USSR, Aus, Nz (2), Mal; (with Sheffield W), 1992 v G, T, Pol, F, C, Br, D, F, Se; 1993 v Sp, N, T, Sm, T, Ho, Pol, N, US (43)

Woodward, V. J. (Tottenham H), 1903 v S, W, Ni; 1904 v S, Ni; 1905 v S, W, Ni; 1907 v S; 1908 v S, W, Ni, A (2), H, B; 1909 v W, Ni, H (2), A; (with Chelsea), 1910 v Ni; 1911 v W (23)

Woosnam, M. (Manchester C), 1922 v W (1)

Worrall, F. (Portsmouth), 1935 v Ho; 1937 v Ni (2)

Worthington, F. S. (Leicester C), 1974 v Ni (sub), S, Arg, EG, Bul, Y; 1975 v Cz, P (sub) (8)

Wreford-Brown, C. (Oxford University), 1889 v Ni; (with Old Carthusians), 1894 v W; 1895 v W; 1898 v S (4)

Wright, E, G. D. (Cambridge University), 1906 v W (1)

Wright, I. E. (C Palace), 1991 v Cam, Ei (sub), USSR, Nz; (with Arsenal), 1992 v H (sub); 1993 v N, T (2), Pol (sub), N (sub), US (sub), Br, G (sub); 1994 v Pol, Ho (sub), Sm, Gr (sub), N (sub); 1995 v US (sub), R; 1997 v Ge (sub), I (sub), M (sub), S.Af, I, F, Br (sub); 1998 v Mol, I, S.Ar (sub), Mor; (with West Ham U), 1999 v L (sub), CzR (33)

Wright, J. D. (Newcastle U), 1939 v N (1)

Wright, M. (Southampton), 1984 v W; 1985 v EG, Fi, T, Ei, R, I, WG; 1986 v R, T, Ni, Eg, USSR; 1987 v S, W; (with Derby Co), 1988 v Is, Ho (sub), Co, Sw, Ei, Ho; 1990 v Cz (sub), Tun (sub), Ho, Eg, Bel, Cam, WG, I; 1991 v H, Pol, Ei (2), Cam, USSR, Arg, Aus, Nz, Mal; (with Liverpool), 1992 v F, Fi; 1993 v Sp; 1996 v Cro, H (45)

Wright, R. I. (Ipswich T), 2000 v Ma; (with Arsenal), 2002 v Ho (sub) (2)

Wright, T. J. (Everton), 1968 v USSR; 1969 v R (2), M (sub), U, Br; 1970 v W, Ho, Bel, R (sub), Br (11)

Wright, W. A. (Wolverhampton W), 1947 v S, W, Ni, Ei, Ho, F, Sw, P; 1948 v S, W, Ni, Bel, Se, I; 1949 v S, W, Ni, D, Sw, Se, N, F; 1950 v S, W, Ni, Ei, I, P, Bel, Ch, US, Sp; 1951 v Ni, S, Arg; 1952 v W, Ni, S, F, A (2), I, Sw; 1953 v Ni, W, S, Bel, Arg, Ch, U, US; 1954 v W, Ni, S, R of E, H (2), Y, Bel, Sw, U; 1955 v W, Ni, S, WG, F, Sp, P; 1956 v Ni, W, S, Br, Se, Fi, WG, D, Sp; 1957 v S, W, Ni, Y, D (2), Ei (2); 1958 v W, Ni, S, P, Y, USSR (3), Br, A, F; 1959 v W, Ni, S, USSR, I, Br, Pe, M, US (105)

Wylie, J. G. (Wanderers), 1878 v S (1)

Yates, J. (Burnley), 1889 v Ni (1)

York, R. E. (Aston Villa), 1922 v S; 1926 v S (2)

Young, A. (Huddersfield T), 1933 v W; 1937 v S, H, N, Se; 1938 v G, Sw, F; 1939 v W (9)

Young, G. M. (Sheffield W), 1965 v W (1)

R. E. Evans also played for Wales against E, Ni, S; J. Reynolds also played for Ireland against E, W, S.

NORTHERN IRELAND

Addis, D. J. (Cliftonville), 1922 v N (1)

Aherne, T. (Belfast C), 1947 v E; 1948 v S; 1949 v W; (with Luton T), 1950 v W (4)

Alexander, T. E. (Cliftonville), 1895 v S (1)

Allan, C. (Cliftonville), 1936 v E (1)

Allen, J. (Limavady), 1887 v E (1)

Anderson, J. (Distillery), 1925 v S.Af (1)

Anderson, T. (Manchester U), 1973 v Cy, E, S, W; 1974 v Bul, P; (with Swindon T), 1975 v S (sub); 1976 v Is; 1977 v Ho, Bel, WG, E, S, W, Ic; 1978 v Ic, Ho, Bel; (with Peterborough U), S, E, W; 1979 v D (sub) (22)

Anderson, W. (Linfield), 1898 v W, E, S; (with Cliftonville), 1899 v S (4)

Andrews, W. (Glentoran), 1908 v S; (with Grimsby T), 1913 v E, S (3)

Armstrong, G. J. (Tottenham H), 1977 v WG, E, W (sub), Ic (sub); 1978 v Bel, S, E, W; 1979 v Ei, D, Bul, E, Bul, E, S, W, D; 1980 v E, Ei, Is, S, E, W, Aus (3); 1981 v Se; (with Watford), P, S, P, S, Se; 1982 v S, Is, E, F, W, Y, Hon, Sp, A, F; 1983 v A, T, Alb, S, E, W; (with Real Mallorca), 1984 v A, WG, E, W, Fi; 1985 v R, Fi, E, Sp; (with WBA), 1986 v T, R (sub), E (sub), F (sub); (with Chesterfield), D (sub), Br (sub) (63)

Baird, G. (Distillery), 1896 v S, E, W (3)

Baird, H. C. (Huddersfield T), 1939 v E (1)

Balfe, J. (Shelbourne), 1909 v E; 1910 v W (2)

Bambrick, J. (Linfield), 1929 v W, S, E; 1930 v W, S, E; 1932 v W; (with Chelsea), 1935 v W; 1936 v E, S; 1938 v W (11)

Banks, S. J. (Cliftonville), 1937 v W (1)

Barr, H. H. (Linfield), 1962 v E; (with Coventry C), 1963 v E, Pol (3)

Barron, J. H. (Cliftonville), 1894 v E, W, S; 1895 v S; 1896 v S; 1897 v E, W (7)

Barry, J. (Cliftonville), 1888 v W, S; 1889 v E (3)

Barry, J. (Bohemians), 1900 v S (1)

Baxter, R. A. (Distillery), 1887 v S (1)

Baxter, S. N. (Cliftonville), 1887 v W (1)

Bennett, L. V. (Dublin University), 1889 v W (1)

Best, G. (Manchester U), 1964 v W, U; 1965 v E, Ho (2), S, Sw (2), Alb; 1966 v S, E, Alb; 1967 v E; 1968 v S; 1969 v E, S, W, T; 1970 v S, E, W, USSR; 1971 v Cy (2), Sp, E, S, W; 1972 v USSR, Sp; 1973 v Bul; 1974 v P; (with Fulham), 1977 v Ho, Bel, WG; 1978 v Ic, Ho (37)

Bingham, W. L. (Sunderland), 1951 v F; 1952 v E, S, W; 1953 v E, S, F, W; 1954 v E, S, W; 1955 v E, S, W; 1956 v E, S, W; 1957 v E, S, W, P (2), I; 1958 v E, S, W, I (2), Arg, Cz (2), WG, F; (with Luton T), 1959 v E, S, W, Sp; 1960 v S, E, W; (with Everton), 1961 v E, S, WG (2), Gr, I; 1962 v E, Gr; 1963 v E, S, Pol (2), Sp; (with Port Vale), 1964 v S, E, Sp (56)

Black, K. T. (Luton T), 1988 v Fr (sub), Ma (sub); 1989 v Ei, H, Sp (2), Ch (sub); 1990 v H, N, U; 1991 v Y (2), D, A, Pol, Fa; (with Nottingham F), 1992 v Fa, A, D, S, Li, G; 1993 v Sp, D (sub), Alb, Ei (sub), Sp; 1994 v D (sub), Ei (sub), R (sub) (30)

Black, T. (Glentoran), 1901 v E (1)

Blair, H. (Portadown), 1928 v F; 1931 v S; 1932 v S; (with Swansea), 1934 v S (4)

Blair, J. (Cliftonville), 1907 v W, E, S; 1908 v E, S (5)

Blair, R. V. (Oldham Ath), 1975 v Se (sub), S (sub), W; 1976 v Se, Is (5)

Blanchflower, J. (Manchester U), 1954 v W; 1955 v E, S; 1956 v S, W; 1957 v S, E, P; 1958 v S, E, I (2) (12)

Blanchflower, R. D. (Barnsley), 1950 v S, W; 1951 v E, S; (with Aston Villa), F; 1952 v W; 1953 v E, S, W, F; 1954 v E, S, W; 1955 v E, S (with Tottenham H), W; 1956 v E, S, W; 1957 v E, S, W, I, P (2); 1958 v E, S, W, I (2), Cz (2), Arg, F, WG; 1959 v E, S, W, Sp; 1960 v E, S, W; 1961 v E, S, W, WG (2); 1962 v E, S, W, Gr, Ho; 1963 v E, S, Pol (2) (56)

Bookman, L. J. O. (Bradford C), 1914 v W; (with Luton T), 1921 v S, W; 1922 v E (4)

Bothwell, A. W. (Ards), 1926 v S, E, W; 1927 v E, W (5)

Bowler, G. C. (Hull C), 1950 v E, S, W (3)

Boyle, P. (Sheffield U), 1901 v E; 1902 v E; 1903 v S, W; 1904 v E (5)

Braithwaite, R. M. (Linfield), 1962 v W; 1963 v P, Sp; (with Middlesbrough), 1964 v W, U; 1965 v E, S, Sw (2), Ho (10)

Breen, T. (Belfast C), 1935 v E, W; 1937 v E, S; (with Manchester U), 1937 v W; 1938 v E, S; 1939 v W, S (9)

Brennan, B. (Bohemians), 1912 v W (1)

Brennan, R. A. (Luton T), 1949 v W; (with Birmingham C), 1950 v E, S, W; (with Fulham), 1951 v E (5)

Briggs, W. R. (Manchester U), 1962 v W; (with Swansea T), 1965 v Ho (2)

Brisby, D. (Distillery), 1891 v S (1)

Brolly, T. H. (Millwall), 1937 v W; 1938 v W; 1939 v E, W (4)

Brookes, E. A. (Shelbourne), 1920 v S (1)

Brotherston, N. (Blackburn R), 1980 v S, E, W, Aus (3); 1981 v Se, P; 1982 v S, Is, E, F, S, W, Hon (sub), A (sub); 1983 v A (sub), WG, Alb, T, Alb, S (sub), E (sub), W; 1984 v T; 1985 v Is (sub), T (27)

Brown, J. (Glenavon), 1921 v W; (with Tranmere R), 1924 v E, W (3)

Brown, J. (Wolverhampton W), 1935 v E, W; 1936 v E; (with Coventry C), 1937 v E, W; 1938 v S, W; (with Birmingham C), 1939 v E, S, W (10)

Brown, N. M. (Limavady), 1887 v E (1)

Brown, W. G. (Glenavon), 1926 v W (1)

Browne, F. (Cliftonville), 1887 v E, S, W; 1888 v E, S (5)

Browne, R. J. (Leeds U), 1936 v E, W; 1938 v E, W; 1939 v E, S (6)

Bruce, A. (Belfast C), 1925 v S.Af (1)

Bruce, W. (Glentoran), 1961 v S; 1967 v W (2)

Buckle, H. R. (Cliftonville), 1903 v S; (with Sunderland), 1904 v E; (with Bristol R), 1908 v W (3)

Buckle, J. (Cliftonville), 1882 v E (1)

Burnett, J. (Distillery), 1894 v E, W, S; (with Glentoran), 1895 v E, W (5)

Burnison, J. (Distillery), 1901 v E, W (2)

Burnison, S. (Distillery), 1908 v E; 1910 v E, S; (with Bradford), 1911 v E, S, W; (with Distillery), 1912 v E; 1913 v W (8)

Burns, J. (Glenavon), 1923 v E (1)

Burns, W. (Glentoran), 1925 v S.Af (1)
Butler, M. P. (Blackpool), 1939 v W (1)

Campbell, A. C. (Crusaders), 1963 v W; 1965 v Sw (2)
Campbell, D. A. (Nottingham F), 1986 v Mor (sub), Br; 1987 v E (2), T, Y; (with Charlton Ath), 1988 v Y, T (sub), Gr (sub), Pol (sub) (10)
Campbell, James (Cliftonville), 1897 v E, S, W; 1898 v E, S, W; 1899 v E; 1900 v E, S; 1901 v S, W; 1902 v S; 1903 v E; 1904 v S (14)
Campbell, John (Cliftonville), 1896 v W (1)
Campbell, J. P. (Fulham), 1951 v E, S (2)
Campbell, R. M. (Bradford C), 1982 v S, W (sub) (2)
Campbell, W. G. (Dundee), 1968 v S, E; 1969 v T; 1970 v S, W, USSR (6)
Carey, J. J. (Manchester U), 1947 v E, S, W; 1948 v E; 1949 v E, S, W (7)
Carroll, E. (Glenavon), 1925 v S (1)
Carroll, R. E. (Wigan Ath), 1997 v Th (sub); 1999 v Ei (sub); 2000 v L, Ma; 2001 v Ma, D, Ic, CzR, Bul; (with Manchester U), 2002 v Lie (sub), Sp (sub) (11)
Casey, T. (Newcastle U), 1955 v W; 1956 v W; 1957 v E, S, W, I, P (2); 1958 v WG, F; (with Portsmouth), 1959 v E, Sp (12)
Caskey, W. (Derby Co), 1979 v Bul, E, Bul, E, S (sub), D (sub); 1980 v E (sub); (with Tulsa R), 1982 v F (sub) (8)
Cassidy, T. (Newcastle U), 1971 v E (sub); 1972 v USSR (sub); 1974 v Bul (sub), S, E, W; 1975 v N; 1976 v S, E, W; 1977 v WG (sub); 1980 v E, Ei (sub), Is, S, E, W, Aus (3); (with Burnley), 1981 v Se, P; 1982 v Is, Sp (sub) (24)
Caughey, M. (Linfield), 1986 v F (sub), D (sub) (2)
Chambers, R. J. (Distillery), 1921 v W; (with Bury), 1928 v E, S, W; 1929 v E, S, W; 1930 v S, W; (with Nottingham F), 1932 v E, S, W (12)
Chatton, H. A. (Partick T), 1925 v E, S; 1926 v E (3)
Christian, J. (Linfield), 1889 v S (1)
Clarke, C. J. (Bournemouth), 1986 v F, D, Mor, Alg (sub), Sp, Br; (with Southampton), 1987 v E, T, Y; 1988 v Y, T, Gr, Pol, F, Ma; 1989 v Ei, H, Sp (1+1 sub); (with QPR), Ma, Ch; 1990 v H, Ei, N; (with Portsmouth), 1991 v Y (sub), D, A, Pol, Y (sub), Fa; 1992 v Fa, D, S, G; 1993 v Alb, Sp, D (38)
Clarke, R. (Belfast C), 1901 v E, S (2)
Cleary, J. (Glentoran), 1982 v S, W; 1983 v W (sub); 1984 v T (sub); 1985 v Is (5)
Clements, D. (Coventry C), 1965 v W, Ho; 1966 v M; 1967 v S, W; 1968 v S, E; 1969 v T (2), S, W; 1970 v S, E, W, USSR (2); 1971 v Sp, E, S, W, Cy; (with Sheffield U), 1972 v USSR (2), Sp, E, S, W; 1973 v Bul, Cy (2), P, E, S, W; (with Everton), 1974 v Bul, P, S, E, W; 1975 v N, Y, E, S, W; 1976 v Se, Y; (with New York Cosmos), E, W (48)
Clugston, J. (Cliftonville), 1888 v W; 1889 v W, S, E; 1890 v E, S; 1891 v E, W; 1892 v E, S, W; 1893 v E, S, W (14)
Cochrane, D. (Leeds U), 1939 v E, W; 1947 v E, S, W; 1948 v E, S, W; 1949 v S, W; 1950 v S, E (12)
Cockrane, G. (Cliftonville), 1903 v S (1)
Cochrane, G. T. (Coleraine), 1976 v N (sub); (with Burnley), 1978 v S (sub), E (sub), W (sub); 1979 v Ei (sub); (with Middlesbrough), D, Bul, E, Bul, E; 1980 v Is, E (sub), W (sub), Aus (1+2 sub); 1981 v Se (sub), P (sub), S, P, S, Se; 1982 v E (sub), F; (with Gillingham), 1984 v S, Fi (sub) (26)
Cochrane, M. (Distillery), 1898 v S, W, E; 1899 v E; 1900 v E, S, W; (with Leicester Fosse), 1901 v S (8)
Collins, F. (Celtic), 1922 v S (1)
Collins, R. (Cliftonville), 1922 v N (1)
Condy, J. (Distillery), 1882 v W; 1886 v E, S (3)
Connell, T. E. (Coleraine), 1978 v W (sub) (1)
Connor, J. (Glentoran), 1901 v S, E; (with Belfast C), 1905 v E, S, W; 1907 v E, S; 1908 v E, S; 1909 v W; 1911 v S, E, W (13)
Connor, M. J. (Brentford), 1903 v S, W; (with Fulham), 1904 v E (3)
Cook, W. (Celtic), 1933 v E, W, S; (with Everton), 1935 v E; 1936 v S, W; 1937 v E, W; 1938 v E, S, W; 1939 v E, S, W (15)
Cooke, S. (Belfast YMCA), 1889 v E; (with Cliftonville), 1890 v E, S (3)
Coote, A. (Norwich C), 1999 v Ca, Ei (sub); 2000 v Fi (sub), L (sub), Ma (sub), H (sub) (6)
Coulter, J. (Belfast C), 1934 v E, S, W; (with Everton), 1935 v E, S, W; 1937 v S, W; (with Grimsby T), 1938 v S, W; (with Chelmsford C), 1939 v S (11)
Cowan, J. (Newcastle U), 1970 v E (sub) (1)
Cowan, T. S. (Queen's Island), 1925 v W (1)
Coyle, F. (Coleraine), 1956 v E, S; 1957 v P; (with Nottingham F), 1958 v Arg (4)
Coyle, L. (Derry C), 1989 v Ch (sub) (1)
Coyle, R. I. (Sheffield W), 1973 v P, Cy (sub), W (sub); 1974 v Bul (sub), P (sub) (5)

Craig, A. B. (Rangers), 1908 v E, S, W; 1909 v S; (with Morton), 1912 v S, W; 1914 v E, S, W (9)
Craig, D. J. (Newcastle U), 1967 v W; 1968 v W; 1969 v T (2), E, S, W; 1970 v E, S, W, USSR; 1971 v Cy (2), Sp, S (sub); 1972 v USSR, S (sub); 1973 v Cy (2), E, S, W; 1974 v Bul, P; 1975 v N (25)
Crawford, A. (Distillery), 1889 v E, W; (with Cliftonville), 1891 v E, S, W; 1893 v E, W (7)
Croft, T. (Queen's Island), 1922 v N; 1924 v E; 1925 v S.Af (3)
Crone, R. (Distillery), 1889 v S; 1890 v E, S, W (4)
Crone, W. (Distillery), 1882 v W; 1884 v E, S, W; 1886 v E, S, W; 1887 v E; 1888 v E, W; 1889 v S; 1890 v W (12)
Crooks, W. J. (Manchester U), 1922 v W (1)
Crossan, E. (Blackburn R), 1950 v S; 1951 v E; 1955 v W (3)
Crossan, J. A. (Sparta-Rotterdam), 1960 v E; (with Sunderland), 1963 v W, P, Sp; 1964 v E, S, W, U, Sp; 1965 v E, S, Sw (2); (with Manchester C), W, Ho (2), Alb; 1966 v S, E, Alb, WG; 1967 v E, S; (with Middlesbrough), 1968 v S (24)
Crothers, C. (Distillery), 1907 v W (1)
Cumming, L. (Huddersfield T), 1929 v W, S; (with Oldham Ath), 1930 v E (3)
Cunningham, W. (Ulster), 1892 v S, E, W; 1893 v E (4)
Cunningham, W. E. (St Mirren), 1951 v W; 1953 v E; 1954 v S; 1955 v S; (with Leicester C), 1956 v E, S, W; 1957 v E, S, W, I, P (2); 1958 v W, I, Cz (2), Arg, WG, F; 1959 v E, S, W; 1960 v E, S, W; (with Dunfermline Ath), 1961 v W; 1962 v W, Ho (30)
Curran, S. (Belfast C), 1926 v S, W; 1928 v F, S (4)
Curran, J. J. (Glenavon), 1922 v W, N; (with Pontypridd), 1923 v E, S; (with Glenavon), 1924 v E (5)
Cush, W. W. (Glenavon), 1951 v E, S; 1954 v S, E; 1957 v W, I, P (2); (with Leeds U), 1958 v I (2), W, Cz (2), Arg, WG, F; 1959 v E, S, W, Sp; 1960 v E, S, W; (with Portadown), 1961 v WG, Gr; 1962 v Gr (26)

Dalrymple, J. (Distillery), 1922 v N (1)
Dalton, W. (YMCA), 1888 v S; (with Linfield), 1890 v S, W; 1891 v S, W; 1892 v E, S, W; 1894 v E, S, W (11)
D'Arcy, S. D. (Chelsea), 1952 v W; 1953 v E; (with Brentford), 1953 v S, W, F (5)
Darling, J. (Linfield), 1897 v E, S; 1900 v S; 1902 v E, S, W; 1903 v E, S (2), W; 1905 v E, S, W; 1906 v E, S, W; 1908 v W; 1909 v E; 1910 v E, S, W; 1912 v S (22)
Davey, H. H. (Reading), 1926 v E; 1927 v E, S; 1928 v E; (with Portsmouth), 1928 v W (5)
Davis, T. L. (Oldham Ath), 1937 v E (1)
Davison, A. J. (Bolton W), 1996 v Se; (with Bradford C), 1997 v Th; (with Grimsby T), 1998 v G (3)
Davison, J. R. (Cliftonville), 1882 v E, W; 1883 v E, W; 1884 v E, W, S; 1885 v E (8)
Dennison, R. (Wolverhampton W), 1988 v F, Ma; 1989 v H, Sp Ch (sub); 1990 v Ei, U; 1991 v Y (2), A, Pol, Fa (sub); 1992 v Fa, A, D (sub); 1993 v Sp (sub); 1994 v Co (sub); 1997 v I (sub) (18)
Devine, A. O. (Limavady), 1886 v E, W; 1887 v W; 1888 v W (4)
Devine, J. (Glentoran), 1990 v U (sub) (1)
Dickson, D. (Coleraine), 1970 v S (sub), W; 1973 v Cy, P (4)
Dickson, T. A. (Linfield), 1957 v S (1)
Dickson, W. (Chelsea), 1951 v W, F; 1952 v E, S; 1953 v E, S, W, F; (with Arsenal), 1954 v E, W; 1955 v E (12)
Diffin, W. J. (Belfast C), 1931 v W (1)
Dill, A. H. (Knock), 1882 v E, W; (with Down Ath), 1883 v W; (with Cliftonville), 1884 v E, S, W; 1885 v E, S, W (9)
Doherty, I. (Belfast C), 1901 v E (1)
Doherty, J. (Portadown), 1928 v F (1)
Doherty, J. (Cliftonville), 1933 v E, W (2)
Doherty, L. (Linfield), 1985 v Is; 1988 v T (sub) (2)
Doherty, M. (Derry C), 1938 v S (1)
Doherty, P. D. (Blackpool), 1935 v E, W; 1936 v E, S; (with Manchester C), 1937 v E, W; 1938 v E, S; 1939 v E, W; (with Derby Co), 1947 v E; (with Huddersfield T), 1947 v W; 1948 v E, W; 1949 v S; (with Doncaster R), 1951 v S (16)
Donaghey, B. (Belfast C), 1903 v S (1)
Donaghy, M. M. (Luton T), 1980 v S, E, W; 1981 v Se, P, S (sub); 1982 v S, Is, E, F, S, W, Y, Hon, Sp, F; 1983 v A, WG, Alb, T, Alb, S, E, W; 1984 v A, T, WG, S, E, W, Fi; 1985 v R, Fi, E, Sp, T; 1986 v T, R, E, F, D, Mor, Alg, Sp, Br; 1987 v E (2), T, Is, Y; 1988 v Y, T, Gr, Pol, F, Ma; 1989 v Ei, H; (with Manchester U), Sp (2), Ma, Ch; 1990 v Ei, N; 1991 v Y (2), D, A, Pol, Fa; 1992 v Fa, A, D, S, Li, G; (with Chelsea), 1993 v Alb, Sp, D, Alb, Ei, Sp, Li, La; 1994 v La, D, Ei, R, Lie, Co, M (91)
Donnelly, L. (Distillery), 1913 v W (1)
Doran, J. F. (Brighton), 1921 v E; 1922 v E, W (3)

Dougan, A. D. (Portsmouth), 1958 v Cz; (with Blackburn R), 1960 v S; 1961 v E, W, I, Gr; (with Aston Villa), 1963 v S, Pol (2); (with Leicester C), 1966 v S, E, W, M, Alb, WG; 1967 v E, S; (with Wolverhampton W), 1967 v W; 1968 v S, W,; 1969 v Is, T (2), E, S, W; 1970 v S, E, USSR (2); 1971 v Cy (2), Sp, E, S, W; 1972 v USSR (2), E, S, W; 1973 v Bul, Cy (43)

Douglas, J. P. (Belfast C), 1947 v E (1)

Dowd, H. O. (Glenavon), 1974 v W; (with Sheffield W), 1975 v N (sub), Se (3)

Dowie, I. (Luton T), 1990 v N (sub), U; 1991 v Y, D, A (sub), (with West Ham U), Y, Fa; (with Southampton) 1992 v Fa, A, D (sub), S (sub), Li; 1993 v Alb (2), Ei, Sp (sub), Li, La; 1994 v La, D, Ei (sub), R (sub), Lie, Co, M (sub); 1995 v A, Ei; (with C Palace) Ei, La, Ca, Ch, La; 1996 v P; (with West Ham U), A, N, G; 1997 v Uk, Arm, G, Alb, P, Uk, Arm, Th; 1998 v Alb, P; (with QPR), Slo, Sw, Sp; 1999 v T, Fi, Mol, G, Mol, Ca, Ei; 2000 v F, T, G (59)

Duff, M. J. (Cheltenham T), 2002 v Pol (sub) (1)

Duggan, H. A. (Leeds U), 1930 v E; 1931 v E, W; 1933 v E; 1934 v E; 1935 v S, W; 1936 v S (8)

Dunlop, G. (Linfield), 1985 v Is; 1987 v E, Y; 1990 v Ei (4)

Dunne, J. (Sheffield U), 1928 v W; 1931 v W, E; 1932 v E, S; 1933 v E, W (7)

Eames, W. L. E. (Dublin U), 1885 v E, S, W (3)

Eglington, T. J. (Everton), 1947 v S, W; 1948 v E, S, W; 1949 v E (6)

Elder, A. R. (Burnley), 1960 v W; 1961 v S, E, W, WG (2), Gr; 1962 v E, S, Gr; 1963 v E, S, W, Pol (2), Sp; 1964 v W, U; 1965 v E, S, W, Sw (2), Ho (2), Alb; 1966 v E, S, W, M, Alb; 1967 v E, S, W; (with Stoke C), 1968 v E, W; 1969 v E (sub), S, W; 1970 v USSR (40)

Elleman, A. R. (Cliftonville), 1889 v W; 1890 v E (2)

Elliott, S. (Motherwell), 2001 v Ma, D, Ic, N (sub), CzR, Bul (2), CzR; 2002 v D (sub), Ma, Pol (sub), Lie (sub), Sp (13)

Elwood, J. H. (Bradford), 1929 v W; 1930 v E (2)

Emerson, W. (Glentoran), 1920 v E, S, W; 1921 v E; 1922 v E, S; (with Burnley), 1922 v W; 1923 v E, S, W; 1924 v E (11)

English, S. (Rangers), 1933 v W, S (2)

Enright, J. (Leeds C), 1912 v S (1)

Falloon, E. (Aberdeen), 1931 v S; 1933 v S (2)

Farquharson, T. G. (Cardiff C), 1923 v E, W; 1924 v E, S, W; 1925 v E, S (7)

Farrell, P. (Distillery), 1901 v S, W (2)

Farrell, P. (Hibernian), 1938 v W (1)

Farrell, P. D. (Everton), 1947 v S, W; 1948 v E, S, W; 1949 v E, W (7)

Feeney, J. M. (Linfield), 1947 v S; (with Swansea T), 1950 v E (2)

Feeney, W. (Glentoran), 1976 v Is (1)

Feeney, W. J. (Bournemouth), 2002 v Lie, Sp (2)

Ferguson, G. (Linfield), 1999 v Ca (sub); 2001 v N, CzR (sub), Bul (sub), CzR (sub) (5)

Ferguson, W. (Linfield), 1966 v M; 1967 v E (2)

Ferris, J. (Belfast C), 1920 v E, W; (with Chelsea), 1921 v S, E; (with Belfast C), 1928 v F, S (6)

Ferris, R. O. (Birmingham C), 1950 v S; 1951 v F; 1952 v S (3)

Fettis, A. W. (Hull C), 1992 v D, Li; 1993 v D; 1994 v M; 1995 v P, Ei, La, Ca, Ch, La; 1996 v P, Lie, A; (with Nottingham F), v N, G; 1997 v Uk, Arm (2); (with Blackburn R), 1998 v P, Slo, Sw, Sp; 1999 v T, Fi, Mol (25)

Finney, T. (Sunderland), 1975 v N, E (sub), S, W; 1976 v N, Y, S; (with Cambridge U), 1980 v E, Is, S, E, W, Aus (2) (14)

Fitzpatrick, J. C. (Bohemians), 1896 v E, S (2)

Flack, H. (Burnley), 1929 v S (1)

Fleming, J. G. (Nottingham F), 1987 v E (2), Is, Y; 1988 v T, Gr, Pol; 1989 v Ma, Ch; (with Manchester C), 1990 v H, Ei; (with Barnsley), 1991 v Y; 1992 v Li (sub), G; 1993 v Alb, Sp, D, Alb, Sp, Li, La; 1994 v La, D, Ei, R, Lie, Co, M; 1995 v P, A, Ei (31)

Forbes, G. (Limavady), 1888 v W; (with Distillery), 1891 v E, S (3)

Forde, J. T. (Ards), 1959 v Sp; 1961 v E, S, WG (4)

Foreman, T. A. (Cliftonville), 1899 v S (1)

Forsyth, J. (YMCA), 1888 v S, E (2)

Fox, W. T. (Ulster), 1887 v E, S (2)

Frame, T. (Linfield), 1925 v S.Af (1)

Fulton, R. P. (Larne), 1928 v F; (Belfast C), 1930 v W; 1931 v E, S, W; 1932 v W, E; 1933 v E, S; 1934 v E, W, S; 1935 v E, W, S; 1936 v S, W; 1937 v E, S, W; 1938 v W (21)

Gaffikin, G. (Linfield Ath), 1890 v S, W; 1891 v S, W; 1892 v E, S, W; 1893 v E, S, W; 1894 v E, S, W; 1895 v E, W (15)

Galbraith, W. (Distillery), 1890 v W (1)

Gallagher, P. (Celtic), 1920 v E, S; 1922 v S; 1923 v S, W; 1924 v S, W; 1925 v S, W, E; (with Falkirk), 1927 v S (11)

Gallogly, C. (Huddersfield T), 1951 v E, S (2)

Gara, A. (Preston NE), 1902 v E, S, W (3)

Gardiner, A. (Cliftonville), 1930 v S, W; 1931 v S; 1932 v E, S (5)

Garrett, J. (Distillery), 1925 v W (1)

Gaston, R. (Oxford U), 1969 v Is (sub) (1)

Gaukrodger, G. (Linfield), 1895 v W (1)

Gaussen, A. D. (Moyola Park), 1884 v E, S; (with Magherafelt), 1888 v E, W; 1889 v E, W (6)

Geary, J. (Glentoran), 1931 v S; 1932 v S (2)

Gibb, J. T. (Wellington Park) 1884 v S, W; 1885 v S, E, W; 1886 v S; 1887 v S, E, W; (with Cliftonville), 1889 v S (10)

Gibb, T. J. (Cliftonville), 1936 v W (1)

Gibson W. K. (Cliftonville), 1894 v S, W, E; 1895 v S; 1897 v W; 1898 v S, W, E; 1901 v S, W, E; 1902 v S, W; 1903 v S (14)

Gillespie, K. R. (Manchester U), 1995 v P, A, Ei; (with Newcastle U) Ei, La, Ca, Ch (sub), La (sub); 1996 v P, A, N, G; 1997 v Uk, Arm, Bel, P, Uk; 1998 v G, Alb, Slo, Sw; 1999 v T, Fi, Mol; (with Blackburn R), G, Mol; 2000 v F (sub), T (sub), G (sub), L, Ma, H; 2001 v Y (sub), CzR, Bul (2); 2002 v D, Ic, Pol, Lie, Sp (41)

Gillespie, S. (Hertford), 1886 v E, S, W; 1887 v E, S, W (6)

Gillespie, W. (Sheffield U), 1913 v E, S; 1914 v E, W; 1920 v S, W; 1921 v E; 1922 v E, S, W; 1923 v E, S, W; 1924 v E, S, W; 1925 v E, S; 1926 v S, W; 1927 v E, W; 1928 v E; 1929 v E; 1931 v E (25)

Gillespie, W. (West Down), 1889 v W (1)

Goodall, A. L. (Derby Co), 1899 v S, W; 1900 v E, S, W; 1901 v E; 1902 v S; 1903 v E, W; (with Glossop), 1904 v E, W (10)

Goodbody, M. F. (Dublin University), 1889 v E; 1891 v W (2)

Gordon, H. (Linfield), 1895 v E; 1896 v E, S (3)

Gordon R. W. (Linfield), 1891 v S; 1892 v W, E, S; 1893 v E, S, W (7)

Gordon, T. (Linfield), 1894 v W; 1895 v E (2)

Gorman, W. C. (Brentford), 1947 v E, S, W; 1948 v W (4)

Gough, J. (Queen's Island), 1925 v S.Af (1)

Gowdy, J. (Glentoran), 1920 v E; (with Queen's Island), 1924 v W; (with Falkirk), 1926 v E, S; 1927 v E, S (6)

Gowdy, W. A. (Hull C), 1932 v S; (with Sheffield W), 1933 v S; (with Linfield), 1935 v E, S, W; (with Hibernian), 1936 v W (6)

Graham, W. G. L. (Doncaster R), 1951 v W, F; 1952 v E, S, W; 1953 v S, F; 1954 v E, W; 1955 v S, W; 1956 v E, S; 1959 v E (14)

Gray, P. (Luton T), 1993 v D (sub), Alb, Ei, Sp; (with Sunderland), 1994 v La, D, Ei, R, Lie (sub); 1995 v P, A, Ei, Ca, Ch (sub); 1996 v P (sub), Lie, A; (with Nancy), 1997 v Uk, Arm, G (sub); (with Luton T), 1999 v Mol (sub); (with Burnley), 2001 v Ma (sub), D (sub), Ic (sub); (with Oxford U), N (sub), CzR (sub) (26)

Greer, W. (QPR), 1909 v E, S, W (3)

Gregg, H. (Doncaster R), 1954 v W; 1957 v E, S, W, I, P (2); 1958 v I; (with Manchester U), 1958 v Cz, Arg, WG, F, W; 1959 v E, W; 1960 v S, E, W; 1961 v E, S; 1962 v S, Gr; 1964 v S, E (25)

Griffin, D. J. (St Johnstone), 1996 v G; 1997 v Uk, I, Bel (sub), Th; 1998 v G (sub), Alb; 1999 v Mol, Ei (sub); 2000 v L, Ma, H; (with Dundee U), 2001 v Y (sub), N (sub), CzR, Bul (2), CzR; 2002 v D, Ic, Ma, Pol (22)

Hall, G. (Distillery), 1897 v E (1)

Halligan, W. (Derby Co), 1911 v W; (with Wolverhampton W), 1912 v E (2)

Hamill, M. (Manchester U), 1912 v E; 1914 v E, S; (with Belfast C), 1920 v E, S, W; (with Manchester C), 1921 v S (7)

Hamill, R. (Glentoran), 1999 v Ca (sub) (1)

Hamilton, B. (Linfield), 1969 v T; 1971 v Cy (2), E, S, W; (with Ipswich T), 1972 v USSR (1+1 sub), Sp; 1973 v Bul, Cy (2), P, E, S, W; 1974 v Bul, S, E, W; 1975 v N, Se, Y, E; 1976 v Se, N, Y; (with Everton), Is, S, E, W; 1977 v Ho, Bel, WG, E, S, W, Ic; (with Millwall), 1978 v S, E, W; 1979 v Ei (sub); (with Swindon T), Bul (2), E, S, W, D; 1980 v Aus (2 sub) (50)

Hamilton, J. (Knock), 1882 v E, W (2)

Hamilton, R. (Rangers), 1928 v S; 1929 v E; 1930 v S, E; 1932 v S (5)

Hamilton, W. D. (Dublin Association), 1885 v W (1)

Hamilton, W. J. (Distillery), 1908 v W (1)

Hamilton, W. J. (Dublin Association), 1885 v W (1)

Hamilton, W. R. (QPR), 1978 v S (sub); (with Burnley), 1980 v S, E, W, Aus (2); 1981 v Se, P, S, P, S, Se; 1982 v S, Is, E, W, Y, Hon, Sp, A, F; 1983 v A, WG, Alb (2), S, E, W; 1984

v A, T, WG, S, E, W, Fi; (with Oxford U), 1985 v R, Sp;
1986 v Mor (sub), Alg, Sp (sub), Br (sub) (41)

Hampton, H. (Bradford C), 1911 v E, S, W; 1912 v E, W; 1913
v E, S, W; 1914 v E (9)

Hanna, J. (Nottingham F), 1912 v S, W (2)

Hanna, J. D. (Royal Artillery, Portsmouth), 1899 v W (1)

Hannon, D. J. (Bohemians), 1908 v E, S; 1911 v E, S; 1912 v
W; 1913 v E (6)

Harkin, J. T. (Southport), 1968 v W; 1969 v T; (with
Shrewsbury T), W (sub); 1970 v USSR; 1971 v Sp (5)

Harland, A. I. (Linfield), 1922 v N; 1923 v E (2)

Harris, J. (Cliftonville), 1921 v W; (with Glenavon), 1925 v
S.Af (2)

Harris, V. (Shelbourne), 1906 v E; 1907 v E, W; 1908 v E, W,
S; (with Everton), 1909 v E, W, S; 1910 v E, S, W; 1911 v E,
S, W; 1912 v E; 1913 v E, S; 1914 v S, W (20)

Harvey, M. (Sunderland), 1961 v I; 1962 v Ho; 1963 v W, Sp;
1964 v S, E, W, U, Sp; 1965 v E, S, W, Sw (2), Ho (2), Alb;
1966 v S, E, W, M, Alb, WG; 1967 v E, S; 1968 v E, W; 1969
v Is, T (2), E; 1970 v USSR; 1971 v Cy, W (sub) (34)

Hastings, J. (Knock), 1882 v E, W; (with Ulster), 1883 v W;
1884 v E, S; 1886 v E, S (7)

Hatton, S. (Linfield), 1963 v S, Pol (2)

Hayes, W. E. (Huddersfield T), 1938 v E, S; 1939 v E, S (4)

Healy, D. J. (Manchester U), 2000 v L, Ma, H; 2001 v Y, Ma,
D, Ic; (with Preston NE), N, CzR, Bul (2); CzR; 2002 v D,
Ic, Ma, Pol, Lie, Sp (18)

Healy, P. J. (Coleraine), 1982 v S, W, Hon (sub); (with
Glentoran), 1983 v A (sub) (4)

Hegan, D. (WBA), 1970 v USSR; (with Wolverhampton W),
1972 v USSR, E, S, W; 1973 v Bul, Cy (7)

Henderson, J. (Ulster), 1885 v E, S, W (3)

Hewison, G. (Moyola Park), 1885 v E, S (2)

Hill, C. F. (Sheffield U), 1990 v N, U; 1991 v Pol, Y; 1992 v A,
D; (with Leicester C) 1995 v Ei, La; 1996 v P, Lie, A, N, Se,
G; 1997 v Uk, Arm, G, Alb, P, Uk, Arm, Th; (with
Trelleborg), 1998 v G, Alb, P; (with Northampton T), Slo;
1999 v T (27)

Hill, M. J. (Norwich C), 1959 v W; 1960 v W; 1961 v WG; 1962
v S; (with Everton), 1964 v S, E, Sp (7)

Hinton, E. (Fulham), 1947 v S, W; 1948 v S, E, W; (with
Millwall), 1951 v W, F (7)

Holmes, S. P. (Wrexham), 2002 v Lie (sub) (1)

Hopkins, J. (Brighton), 1926 v E (1)

Horlock, K. (Swindon T), 1995 v La, Ca; 1997 v G, Alb, I;
(with Manchester C), v Bel, Uk, Arm, Th; 1998 v G, Alb, P;
1999 v T, Fi, G, Mol, Ca; 2000 v F, T, G, Ma (sub); 2001 v Y,
Ma, D, Ic; 2002 v D, Ic, Ma, Sp (29)

Houston, J. (Linfield), 1912 v S, W; 1913 v W; (with Everton),
1913 v E, S; 1914 v S (6)

Houston, W. (Linfield), 1933 v W (1)

Houston, W. J. (Moyola Park), 1885 v E, S (2)

Hughes, A. W. (Newcastle U), 1998 v Slo, Sw, Sp (sub); 1999 v
T, Fi, Mol (sub), Ca, Ei; 2000 v F, T, L, H; 2001 v Y, Ma, D,
Ic, N, CzR, Bul, CzR; 2002 v D, Ic, Pol, Sp (24)

Hughes, M. E. (Manchester C), 1992 v D, S, Li, G; (with
Strasbourg), 1993 v Alb, Sp, D, Ei, Sp, Li, La; 1994 v La, D,
Ei, R, Lie, Co, M; 1995 v P, A, Ei (2) La, Ca, Ch, La; 1996 v
P, Lie, A, N, G; (with West Ham U), 1997 v Uk, Arm, G,
Alb, I, Uk; 1998 v G; (with Wimbledon), P, Slo, Sw, Sp;
1999 v T, Fi, Mol, G, Mol; 2000 v F, T, G, Fi, L (sub), Ma,
H; 2001 v CzR, Bul (2), CzR; 2002 v D, Ic, Ma, Pol, Lie
(sub) (63)

Hughes, P. A. (Bury), 1987 v E, T, Is (3)

Hughes, W. (Bolton W), 1951 v W (1)

Humphries, W. M. (Ards), 1962 v W; (with Coventry C), 1962
v Ho; 1963 v S, W, Pol, Sp; 1964 v S, E, Sp; 1965 v S, Ho;
(with Swansea T), 1965 v W, Alb (14)

Hunter, A. (Distillery), 1905 v W; 1906 v W, E, S; (with
Belfast C), 1908 v W; 1909 v W, E, S (8)

Hunter, A. (Blackburn R), 1970 v USSR; 1971 v Cy (2), E, S,
W; (with Ipswich T), 1972 v USSR (2), Sp, E, S, W; 1973 v
Bul, Cy (2), P, E, S, W; 1974 v Bul, S, E, W; 1975 v N, Se, Y,
E, S, W; 1976 v Se, N, Y, Is, S, E, W; 1977 v Ho, Bel, WG,
E, S, W, Ic; 1978 v Ic, Ho, Bel; 1979 v Ei, D, S, W, D; 1980 v
E, Ei (53)

Hunter, B. V. (Wrexham), 1995 v La; 1996 v P, Lie, A, Se, G;
(with Reading), 1997 v Arm, G, Alb, I, Bel; 1999 v Ca, Ei;
2000 v F, T (15)

Hunter, R. J. (Cliftonville), 1884 v E, S, W (3)

Hunter, V. (Coleraine), 1962 v E; 1964 v Sp (2)

Irvine, R. J. (Linfield), 1962 v Ho; 1963 v E, S, W, Pol (2), Sp;
(with Stoke C), 1965 v W (8)

Irvine, R. W. (Everton), 1922 v S; 1923 v E, W; 1924 v E, S;
1925 v E; 1926 v E; 1927 v E, W; 1928 v E, S; (with

Portsmouth), 1929 v E; 1930 v S; (with Connah's Quay),
1931 v E; (with Derry C), 1932 v W (15)

Irvine, W. J. (Burnley), 1963 v W, Sp; 1965 v S, W, Sw, Ho (2),
Alb; 1966 v S, E, W, M, Alb; 1967 v E, S; 1968 v E, W; (with
Preston NE), 1969 v Is, T, E; (with Brighton), 1972 v E, S,
W (23)

Irving, S. J. (Dundee), 1923 v S, W; 1924 v S, E, W; 1925 v S,
E, W; 1926 v S, W; (with Cardiff C), 1927 v S, E, W; 1928 v
S, E, W; (with Chelsea), 1929 v E; 1931 v W (18)

Jackson, T. A. (Everton), 1969 v Is, E, S, W; 1970 v USSR
(1+1 sub); (with Nottingham F), 1971 v Sp; 1972 v E, S, W;
1973 v Cy, E, S, W; 1974 v Bul, P, S (sub), E (sub), W (sub);
1975 v N (sub), Se, Y, E, S, W; (with Manchester U); 1976 v
Se, N, Y; 1977 v Ho, Bel, WG, E, S, W, Ic (35)

Jamison, J. (Glentoran), 1976 v N (1)

Jenkins, I. (Chester C), 1997 v Arm, Th; 1998 v Slo; (with
Dundee U), Sw, Sp; 2000 v Fi (6)

Jennings, P. A. (Watford), 1964 v W, U; (with Tottenham H),
1965 v E, S, Sw (2), Ho, Alb; 1966 v S, E, W, Alb, WG; 1967
v E, S; 1968 v S, E, W; 1969 v Is, T (2), E, S, W; 1970 v S, E,
USSR; 1971 v Cy (2), E, S, W; 1972 v USSR, Sp, S, E,
W; 1973 v Bul, Cy, P, E, S, W; 1974 v P, S, E, W; 1975 v N,
Se, Y, E, S, W; 1976 v Se, N, Y, Is, S, E, W; 1977 v Ho, Bel,
WG, E, S, W, Ic; (with Arsenal), 1978 v Ic, Ho, Bel; 1979 v
Ei, D, Bul, E, Bul, E, S, W, D; 1980 v Ei, Is; 1981 v S, P,
S, Se; 1982 v S, Is, E, W, Y, Hon, Sp, F; 1983 v Alb, S, E, W;
1984 v A, T, WG, S, W, Fi; 1985 v R, Fi, E, Sp, T; (with
Tottenham H), 1986 v T, R, E, F, D, (with Everton), Mor;
(with Tottenham H), Alg, Sp, Br (119)

Johnson, D. M. (Blackburn R), 1999 v Ei (sub); 2000 v Fi
(sub), L, Ma (sub), H (sub); 2001 v Y, Ma, Ic, N (sub), Bul
(sub+1); CzR; 2002 v Ma, Pol, (with Birmingham C), Lie,
Sp (16)

Johnston, H. (Portadown), 1927 v W (1)

Johnston, R. S. (Distillery), 1882 v W; 1884 v E; 1886 v E, S (4)

Johnston, R. S. (Distillery), 1905 v W (1)

Johnston, S. (Linfield), 1890 v W; 1893 v S, W; 1894 v E (4)

Johnston, W. (Oldpark), 1885 v S, W (2)

Johnston, W. C. (Glenavon), 1962 v W; (with Oldham Ath),
1966 v M (sub) (2)

Jones, J. (Linfield), 1930 v S, W; 1931 v S, W, E; 1932 v S, E;
1933 v S, E, W; 1934 v S, E, W; 1935 v S, E, W; 1936 v E, S;
(with Hibernian), 1936 v W; 1937 v E, W, S; (with
Glenavon), 1938 v E (23)

Jones, J. (Glenavon), 1956 v W; 1957 v E, W (3)

Jones, S. (Distillery), 1934 v E; (with Blackpool), 1934 v W (2)

Jordan, T. (Linfield), 1895 v E, W (2)

Kavanagh, P. J. (Celtic), 1930 v E (1)

Keane, T. R. (Swansea T), 1949 v S (1)

Kearns, A. (Distillery), 1900 v E, S, W; 1902 v E, S, W (6)

Kee, P. V. (Oxford U), 1990 v N; 1991 v Y (2), D, A, Pol, Fa;
(with Ards), 1995 v A, Ei (9)

Keith, R. M. (Newcastle U), 1958 v E, W, Cz (2), Arg, I, WG,
F; 1959 v E, S, W, Sp; 1960 v S, E; 1961 v S, E, W, I, WG (2),
Gr; 1962 v W, Ho (23)

Kelly, H. R. (Fulham), 1950 v E, W; (with Southampton), 1951
v E, S (4)

Kelly, J. (Glentoran), 1896 v E (1)

Kelly, J. (Derry C), 1932 v E, W; 1933 v E, W, S; 1934 v W;
1936 v E, S, W; 1937 v S, E (11)

Kelly, P. J. (Manchester C), 1921 v E (1)

Kelly, P. M. (Barnsley), 1950 v S (1)

Kennedy, A. L. (Arsenal), 1923 v W; 1925 v E (2)

Kennedy, P. H. (Watford), 1999 v Mol, G (sub); 2000 v F, T,
G, Fi; 2001 v N, Bul (sub), CzR (sub); (with Wigan Ath),
2002 v D, Ic, Ma, Pol (13)

Kernaghan, N. (Belfast C), 1936 v W; 1937 v S; 1938 v E (3)

Kirk, A. (Hearts), 2000 v H; 2001 v N (sub) (2)

Kirkwood, H. (Cliftonville), 1904 v W (1)

Kirwan, J. (Tottenham H), 1900 v W; 1902 v E, S, W; 1903 v E, S,
W; 1904 v E, S, W; 1905 v E, S, W; (with Chelsea), 1906 v E,
S, W; 1907 v W; (with Clyde), 1909 v S (17)

Lacey, W. (Everton), 1909 v E, S, W; 1910 v E, S, W; 1911 v E,
S, W; 1912 v E; (with Liverpool), 1913 v W; 1914 v E, S, W;
1920 v E, S, W; 1921 v E, S, W; 1922 v E, S; (with New
Brighton), 1925 v E (23)

Lawther, R. (Glentoran), 1888 v E, S (2)

Lawther, W. I. (Sunderland), 1960 v W; 1961 v I; (with
Blackburn R), 1962 v S, Ho (4)

Leatham, J. (Belfast C), 1939 v W (1)

Ledwidge, J. J. (Shelbourne), 1906 v S, W (2)

Lemon, J. (Glentoran), 1886 v W; (with Belfast YMCA), 1888
v S; 1889 v W (3)

Lennon, N. F. (Crewe Alex), 1994 v M (sub); 1995 v Ch; 1996 v P, Lie, A; (with Leicester C), v N; 1997 v Uk, Arm, G, Alb, Bel, P, Uk, Arm, Th; 1998 v G, Alb, P, Slo, Sw, Sp; 1999 v T, Fi, Mol, G, Mol, Ei; 2000 v F, T, G, Fi, Ma, H; 2001 v D, Ic; (with Celtic), N, CzR, Bul (2); 2002 v Pol (sub) (40)

Leslie, W. (YMCA), 1887 v E (1)

Lewis, J. (Glentoran), 1899 v S, E, W; (with Distillery), 1900 v S (4)

Lockhart, H. (Russell School), 1884 v W (1)

Lockhart, N. H. (Linfield), 1947 v E; (with Coventry C), 1950 v W; 1951 v W; 1952 v W; (with Aston Villa), 1954 v S, E; 1955 v W; 1956 v W (8)

Lomas, S. M. (Manchester C), 1994 v R, Lie, Co (sub), M; 1995 v P, A; 1996 v P, Lie, A, N, Se, G; 1997 v Uk, Arm, G, Alb, I, Bel; (with West Ham U), P, Uk, Arm, Th; 1998 v Alb, P, Slo, Sw; 1999 v Mol, G, Mol, Ca; 2000 v F, T, G, L, Ma; 2001 v Ma, D, Ic; 2002 v Pol, Lie (40)

Loyal, J. (Clarence), 1891 v S (1)

Lutton, R. J. (Wolverhampton W), 1970 v S, E; (with West Ham U), 1973 v Cy (sub), S (sub), W (sub); 1974 v P (6)

Lynas, R. (Cliftonville), 1925 v S.Af (1)

Lyner, D. R. (Glentoran), 1920 v E, W; 1922 v S, W; (with Manchester U), 1923 v E; (with Kilmarnock), 1923 v W (6)

Lytle, J. (Glentoran), 1898 W (1)

McAdams, W. J. (Manchester C), 1954 v W; 1955 v S; 1957 v E; 1958 v S, I; (with Bolton W), 1961 v E, S, W, I, WG (2), Gr; 1962 v E, Gr; (with Leeds U), Ho (15)

McAlery, J. M. (Cliftonville), 1882 v E, W (2)

McAlinden, J. (Belfast C), 1938 v S; 1939 v S; (with Portsmouth), 1947 v E; (with Southend U), 1949 v E (4)

McAllen, J. (Linfield), 1898 v E; 1899 v E, S, W; 1900 v E, S, W; 1901 v W; 1902 v S (9)

McAlpine, S. (Cliftonville), 1901 v S (1)

McArthur, A. (Distillery), 1886 v W (1)

McAuley, J. L. (Huddersfield T), 1911 v E, W; 1912 v E, S; 1913 v E, S (6)

McAuley, P. (Belfast C), 1900 v S (1)

McBride, S. D. (Glenavon), 1991 v D (sub); Pol (sub); 1992 v Fa (sub), D (4)

McCabe, J. J. (Leeds U), 1949 v S, W; 1950 v E; 1951 v W; 1953 v W; 1954 v S (6)

McCabe, W. (Ulster), 1891 v E (1)

McCambridge, J. (Ballymena), 1930 v S, W; (with Cardiff C), 1931 v W; 1932 v E (4)

McCandless, J. (Bradford), 1912 v W; 1913 v W; 1920 v W, S; 1921 v E (5)

McCandless, W. (Linfield), 1920 v E, W; 1921 v E; (with Rangers), 1921 v W; 1922 v S; 1924 v W, S; 1925 v S; 1929 v W (9)

McCann, G. S. (West Ham U), 2002 v Ma (sub), Pol (sub), Lie (3)

McCann, P. (Belfast C), 1910 v E, S, W; 1911 v E; (with Glentoran), 1911 v S; 1912 v E; 1913 v W (7)

McCarthy, J. D. (Port Vale), 1996 v Se; 1997 v I, Arm, Th; (with Birmingham C), 1998 v P (sub), Slo (sub), Sp; 1999 v Fi (sub), Mol (sub), G (sub), Ca, Ei; 2000 v F, T, G, Fi; 2001 v N, Bul (sub) (18)

McCartney, A. (Ulster), 1903 v S, W; (with Linfield), 1904 v S, W; (with Everton), 1905 v E, S; (with Belfast C), 1907 v E, S, W; 1908 v E, S, W; (with Glentoran), 1909 v E, S, W (15)

McCartney, G. (Sunderland), 2002 v Ic, Ma, Pol (sub), Lie, Sp (5)

McCashin, J. W. (Cliftonville), 1896 v W; 1898 v S, W; 1899 v S; 1903 v S (5)

McCavana, W. T. (Coleraine), 1955 v S; 1956 v E, S (3)

McCaw, D. (Malone), 1882 v S (1)

McCaw, J. H. (Linfield), 1927 v W; 1928 v F; 1930 v S; 1931 v E, S, W (6)

McClatchey, J. (Distillery), 1886 v E, S, W (3)

McClatchey, T. (Distillery), 1895 v S (1)

McCleary, J. W. (Cliftonville), 1955 v W (1)

McCleery, W. (Cliftonville), 1922 v N; (Linfield), 1930 v E, W; 1931 v E, S, W; 1932 v S, W; 1933 v E, W (10)

McClelland, J. (Mansfield T), 1980 v S (sub), Aus (3); 1981 v Se, S; (with Rangers), S, Se (sub); 1982 v S, W, Y, Hon, Sp, A, F; 1983 v A, WG, Alb, T, Alb, S, E, W; 1984 v A, T, WG, S, E, W, Fi; 1985 v R, Is; (with Watford), Fi, E, Sp, T; 1986 v T, F (sub); 1987 v E (2), T, Is, Y; 1988 v T, Gr, F, Ma; 1989 v Ei, H, Sp (2), Ma; (with Leeds U), 1990 v N (53)

McClelland, J. T. (Arsenal), 1961 v W, I, WG (2), Gr; (with Fulham), 1966 v M (6)

McCluggage, A. (Cliftonville), 1922 v N; (Bradford), 1924 v E; (with Burnley), 1927 v S, W; 1928 v S, E, W; 1929 v S, E, W; 1930 v W; 1931 v E, W (13)

McClure, G. (Cliftonville), 1907 v S, W; 1908 v E; (with Distillery), 1909 v E (4)

McConnell, E. (Cliftonville), 1904 v S, W; (with Glentoran), 1905 v S; (with Sunderland), 1906 v E; 1907 v E; 1908 v S, W; (with Sheffield W), 1909 v S, W; 1910 v S, W, E (12)

McConnell, P. (Doncaster R), 1928 v W; (with Southport), 1932 v E (2)

McConnell, W. G. (Bohemians), 1912 v W; 1913 v E, S; 1914 v E, S, W (6)

McConnell, W. H. (Reading), 1925 v W; 1926 v E, W; 1927 v E, S, W; 1928 v E, W (8)

McCourt, F. J. (Manchester C), 1952 v E, W; 1953 v E, S, W, F (6)

McCourt, P. J. (Rochdale), 2002 v Sp (sub) (1)

McCoy, R. K. (Coleraine), 1987 v Y (sub) (1)

McCoy, S. (Distillery), 1896 v W (1)

McCracken, E. (Barking), 1928 v F (1)

McCracken, R. (C Palace), 1921 v E; 1922 v E, S, W (4)

McCracken, R. (Linfield), 1922 v N (1)

McCracken, W. R. (Distillery), 1902 v E, W; 1903 v S, E; 1904 v E, S, W; (with Newcastle U), 1905 v E, S, W; 1907 v E; 1920 v E; 1922 v E, S, W; (with Hull C), 1923 v S (16)

McCreery, D. (Manchester U), 1976 v S (sub), E, W; 1977 v Ho, Bel, WG, E, S, W, Ic; 1978 v Ic, Ho, Bel, S, E, W; 1979 v Ei, D, Bul, E, Bul, W, D; (with QPR), 1980 v E, Ei, S (sub), E (sub), W (sub), Aus (1+1 sub); 1981 v Se (sub), P (sub); (with Tulsa R), S, P, Se; 1982 v S, Is, E (sub), F, Y, Hon, Sp, A, F; (with Newcastle U), 1983 v A; 1984 v T (sub); 1985 v R, Sp (sub); 1986 v T (sub), R, E, F, D, Alg, Sp, Br; 1987 v T, E, Y; 1988 v Y; 1989 v Sp, Ma, Ch; (with Hearts), 1990 v H, Ei, N, U (sub) (67)

McCrory, S. (Southend U), 1958 v E (1)

McCullough, K. (Belfast C), 1935 v W; 1936 v E; (with Manchester C), 1936 v S; 1937 v E, S (5)

McCullough, W. J. (Arsenal), 1961 v I; 1963 v Sp; 1964 v S, E, W, U, Sp; 1965 v E, Sw; (with Millwall), 1967 v E (10)

McCurdy, C. (Linfield), 1980 v Aus (sub) (1)

McDonald, A. (QPR), 1986 v R, E, F, D, Mor, Alg, Sp, Br; 1987 v E (2), T, Is, Y; 1988 v Y, T, Pol, F, Ma; 1989 v Ei, H, Sp, Ch; 1990 v H, Ei, U; 1991 v Y, D, A, Fa; 1992 v Fa, S, Li, G; 1993 v Alb, Sp, D, Alb, Ei, Sp, Li, La; 1994 v D, Ei; 1995 v P, A, Ei, La, Ca, Ch, La; 1996 v A (sub), N (52)

McDonald, R. (Rangers), 1930 v S; 1932 v E (2)

McDonnell, J. (Bohemians), 1911 v E, S; 1912 v W; 1913 v W (4)

McElhinney, G. M. A. (Bolton W), 1984 v WG, S, E, W, Fi; 1985 v R (6)

McEvilly, L. R. (Rochdale), 2002 v Sp (sub) (1)

McFaul, W. S. (Linfield), 1967 v E (sub); (with Newcastle U), 1970 v W; 1971 v Sp; 1972 v USSR; 1973 v Cy; 1974 v Bul (6)

McGarry, J. K. (Cliftonville), 1951 v W, F, S (3)

McGaughey, M. (Linfield), 1985 v Is (sub) (1)

McGibbon, P. C. G. (Manchester U), 1995 v Ca (sub), Ch, La; 1996 v Lie (sub); 1997 v Th; (with Wigan Ath), 1998 v Alb; 2000 v L (sub) (7)

McGrath, R. C. (Tottenham H), 1974 v S, E, W; 1975 v N; 1976 v Is (sub); 1977 v; (with Manchester U), Ho, Bel, WG, E, S, W, Ic; 1978 v Ic, Ho, Bel, S, E, W; 1979 v Bul (sub), E (2 sub) (21)

McGregor, S. (Glentoran), 1921 v S (1)

McGrillen, J. (Clyde), 1924 v S; (with Belfast C), 1927 v S (2)

McGuire, E. (Distillery), 1907 v S (1)

McGuire, J. (Linfield), 1928 v F (1)

McIlroy, H. (Cliftonville), 1906 v E (1)

McIlroy, J. (Burnley), 1952 v E, S, W; 1953 v E, S, W; 1954 v E, S, W; 1955 v E, S, W; 1956 v S, W; 1957 v E, S, W, I, P (2); 1958 v E, S, W, I (2), Cz (2), Arg, WG, F; 1959 v E, S, W, Sp; 1960 v E, S, W; 1961 v E, W, WG (2), Gr; 1962 v E, S, Gr, Ho; 1963 v E, S, Pol (2); (with Stoke C), 1963 v W; 1966 v S, E, Alb (55)

McIlroy, S. B. (Manchester U), 1972 v Sp, S (sub); 1974 v S, E, W; 1975 v N, Se, Y, E, S, W; 1976 v Se, N, Y, S, E, W; 1977 v Ho, Bel, E, S, W, Ic; 1978 v Ic, Ho, Bel, S, E, W; 1979 v Ei, D, Bul, E, Bul, E, S, W, D; 1980 v E, Ei, Is, S, E, W; 1981 v Se, P, S, P, S, Se; 1982 v S, Is; (with Stoke C), E, F, S, W, Y, Hon, Sp, A, F; 1983 v A, WG, Alb, T, Alb, S, E, W; 1984 v A, T, S, E, W, Fi; 1985 v Fi, E, T; (with Manchester C), 1986 v T, R, E, F, D, Mor, Alg, Sp, Br; 1987 v E (sub) (88)

McIlvenny, P. (Distillery), 1924 v W (1)

McIlvenny, R. (Distillery), 1890 v E; (with Ulster), 1891 v E (2)

McKeag, W. (Glentoran), 1968 v S, W (2)

McKeague, T. (Glentoran), 1925 v S.Af (1)

McKee, F. W. (Cliftonville), 1906 v S, W; (with Belfast C), 1914 v E, S, W (5)

McKelvey, H. (Glentoran), 1901 v W; 1903 v S (2)

McKenna, J. (Huddersfield), 1950 v E, S, W; 1951 v E, S, F; 1952 v E (7)

McKenzie, H. (Distillery), 1922 v N; 1923 v S (2)

McKenzie, R. (Airdrie), 1967 v W (1)

McKeown, N. (Linfield), 1892 v E, S, W; 1893 v S, W; 1894 v S, W (7)

McKie, H. (Cliftonville), 1895 v E, S, W (3)

McKinney, D. (Hull C), 1921 v S; (with Bradford C), 1924 v S (2)

McKinney, V. J. (Falkirk), 1966 v WG (1)

McKnight, A. D. (Celtic), 1988 v Y, T, Gr, Pol, F, Ma; (with West Ham U) 1989 v Ei, H, Sp (2) (10)

McKnight, J. (Preston NE), 1912 v S; (with Glentoran), 1913 v S (2)

McLaughlin, J. C. (Shrewsbury T), 1962 v E, S, W, Gr; 1963 v W; (with Swansea T), 1964 v W, U; 1965 v E, W, Sw (2); 1966 v W (12)

McLean, T. (Limavady), 1885 v S (1)

McMahon, G. J. (Tottenham H), 1995 v Ca (sub), Ch, La; 1996 v Lie, N (sub), Se, G; (with Stoke C), 1997 v Arm (sub), Alb (sub), Bel, P (sub), Uk (sub), Arm (sub), Th (sub); 1998 v G (sub), Alb (sub), P (sub) (17)

McMahon, J. (Bohemians), 1934 v S (1)

McMaster, G. (Glentoran), 1897 v E, S, W (3)

McMichael, A. (Newcastle U), 1950 v E, S; 1951 v E, S, F; 1952 v E, S, W; 1953 v E, S, W, F; 1954 v E, S, W; 1955 v E, W; 1956 v W; 1957 v E, S, W, I, P (2); 1958 v E, S, W, I (2), Cz (2), Arg, WG, F; 1959 v S, W, Sp; 1960 v E, S, W (40)

McMillan, G. (Distillery), 1903 v C; 1905 v W (2)

McMillan, S. T. (Manchester U), 1963 v E, S (2)

McMillen, W. S. (Manchester U), 1934 v E; 1935 v S; 1937 v S; (with Chesterfield), 1938 v S, W; 1939 v E, S (7)

McMordie, A. S. (Middlesbrough), 1969 v Is, T (2), E, S, W; 1970 v E, S, W, USSR; 1971 v Cy (2), E, S, W; 1972 v USSR, Sp, E, S, W; 1973 v Bul (21)

McMullan, D. (Liverpool), 1926 v E, W; 1927 v S (3)

McNally, B. A. (Shrewsbury T), 1986 v Mor; 1987 v T (sub); 1988 v Y, Gr, Ma (sub) (5)

McNinch, J. (Ballymena), 1931 v S; 1932 v S, W (3)

McParland, P. J. (Aston Villa), 1954 v W; 1955 v E, S; 1956 v E, S; 1957 v E, S, W, P; 1958 v E, S, W, I (2), Cz (2), Arg, WG, F; 1959 v E, S, W, Sp; 1960 v E, S, W; 1961 v E, S, W, I, WG (2), Gr; (with Wolverhampton W), 1962 v Ho (34)

McShane, J. (Cliftonville), 1899 v S; 1900 v E, S, W (4)

McVeigh, P. (Tottenham H), 1999 v Ca (sub); (with Norwich C), 2002 v Ic (sub), Pol (sub) (3)

McVicker, J. (Linfield), 1888 v E; (with Glentoran), 1889 v S (2)

McWha, W. B. R. (Knock), 1882 v E, W; (with Cliftonville), 1883 v E, W; 1884 v E; 1885 v E, W (7)

Mackie, J. (Arsenal), 1923 v W; (with Portsmouth), 1935 v S, W (3)

Madden, O. (Norwich C), 1938 v E (1)

Magee, G. (Wellington Park), 1885 v E, S, W (3)

Magill, E. J. (Arsenal), 1962 v E, S, Gr; 1963 v E, S, W, Pol (2), Sp; 1964 v E, S, W, U, Sp; 1965 v E, S, Sw (2), Ho, Alb; 1966 v S, (with Brighton), E, Alb, W, WG, M (26)

Magilton, J. (Oxford U), 1991 v Pol, Y, Fa; 1992 v Fa, A, D, S, Li, G; 1993 v Alb, D, Alb, Ei, Li, La; 1994 v La, D, Ei;(with Southampton), R, Lie, Co, M; 1995 v P, A, Ei (2), Ca, Ch, La; 1996 v P, N, G; 1997 v Uk (sub), Arm (sub), Bel, P; 1998 v G; (with Sheffield W), P, Sp; (with Ipswich T), 2000 v L; 2001 v Y, Ma, D, Ic, N, CzR, Bul; 2002 v D, Ic, Ma, Pol, Lie (52)

Maginnis, H. (Linfield), 1900 v E, S, W; 1903 v S, W; 1904 v E, S, W (8)

Mahood, J. (Belfast C), 1926 v S; 1928 v E, S, W; 1929 v E, S, W; 1930 v W; (with Ballymena), 1934 v S (9)

Manderson, R. (Rangers), 1920 v S, W; 1925 v S, E; 1926 v S (5)

Mansfield, J. (Dublin Freebooters), 1901 v E (1)

Martin, C. (Cliftonville), 1882 v E, W; 1883 v E (3)

Martin, C. (Bo'ness), 1925 v S (1)

Martin, C. J. (Glentoran), 1947 v S; (with Leeds U), 1948 v E, S, W; (with Aston Villa), 1949 v E; 1950 v W (6)

Martin, D. K. (Belfast C), 1934 v E, S, W; 1935 v S; (with Wolverhampton W), 1935 v E; 1936 v W; (with Nottingham F), 1937 v S; 1938 v E, S; 1939 v S (10)

Mathieson, A. (Luton T), 1921 v W; 1922 v E (2)

Maxwell, J. (Linfield), 1902 v W; 1903 v W, E; (with Glentoran), 1905 v W, S; (with Belfast C), 1906 v W; 1907 v S (7)

Meek, H. L. (Glentoran), 1925 v W (1)

Mehaffy, J. A. C. (Queen's Island), 1922 v W (1)

Meldon, P. A. (Dublin Freebooters), 1899 v S, W (2)

Mercer, H. V. A. (Linfield), 1908 v E (1)

Mercer, J. T. (Distillery), 1898 v E, S, W; 1899 v E; (with Linfield), 1902 v E, W; (with Distillery), 1903 v S (2), W; (with Derby Co), 1904 v E, W; 1905 v S (12)

Millar, W. (Barrow), 1932 v W; 1933 v S (2)

Miller, J. (Middlesbrough), 1929 v W, S; 1930 v E (3)

Milligan, D. (Chesterfield), 1939 v W (1)

Milne, R. G. (Linfield), 1894 v E, S, W; 1895 v E, W; 1896 v E, S, W; 1897 v E, S; 1898 v E, S, W; 1899 v E, W; 1901 v W; 1902 v E, S, W; 1903 v E, S (2); 1904 v E, S, W; 1906 v E, S, W (28)

Mitchell, E. J. (Cliftonville), 1933 v S; (with Glentoran), 1934 v W (2)

Mitchell, W. (Distillery), 1932 v E, W; 1933 v E, W; (with Chelsea), 1934 v W, S; 1935 v S, E; 1936 v S, E; 1937 v E, S, W; 1938 v E, S (15)

Molyneux, T. B. (Ligoniel), 1883 v E, W; (with Cliftonville), 1884 v S; 1885 v E, W; 1886 v E, W, S; 1888 v S (11)

Montgomery, F. J. (Coleraine), 1955 v E (1)

Moore, C. (Glentoran), 1949 v W (1)

Moore, P. (Aberdeen), 1933 v E (1)

Moore, R. (Linfield Ath), 1891 v E, S, W (3)

Moore, R. L. (Ulster), 1887 v S, W (2)

Moore, W. (Falkirk), 1923 v S (1)

Moorhead, F. W. (Dublin University), 1885 v E (1)

Moorhead, G. (Linfield), 1923 v S; 1928 v F, S; 1929 v S (4)

Moran, J. (Leeds C), 1912 v S (1)

Moreland, V. (Derby Co), 1979 v Bul (2 sub), E, S; 1980 v E, Ei (6)

Morgan, G. F. (Linfield), 1922 v N; 1923 v E; (with Nottingham F), 1924 v S; 1927 v E; 1928 v E, S, W; 1929 v E (8)

Morgan, S. (Port Vale), 1972 v Sp; 1973 v Bul (sub), P, Cy, E, S, W; (with Aston Villa), 1974 v Bul, P, S, E; 1975 v Se; 1976 v Se (sub), N, Y; (with Brighton & HA), S, W (sub); (with Sparta Rotterdam), 1979 v D (18)

Morrison, R. (Linfield Ath), 1891 v E, W (2)

Morrison, T. (Glentoran), 1895 v E, S, W; (with Burnley), 1899 v W; 1900 v W; 1902 v E, S (7)

Morrogh, D. (Bohemians), 1896 v S (1)

Morrow, S. J. (Arsenal), 1990 v U (sub); 1991 v A (sub), Pol, Y; 1992 v Fa, S (sub), G (sub); 1993 v Sp (sub), Alb, Ei; 1994 v R, Co, M (sub); 1995 v P, Ei (2), La; 1996 v P, Se; 1997 v Uk, G, Alb, I, Bel; (with QPR), P, Uk, Arm; 1998 v G, P, Slo, Sw, Sp; 1999 v T, Fi, Mol, G, Mol; 2000 v G, Fi (39)

Morrow, W. J. (Moyola Park), 1883 v E, W; 1884 v S (3)

Muir, R. (Oldpark), 1885 v S, W (2)

Mulholland, S. (Celtic), 1906 v S, E (2)

Mullan, G. (Glentoran), 1983 v S, E, W, Alb (sub) (4)

Mulligan, J. (Manchester C), 1921 v S (1)

Mulryne, P. P. (Manchester U), 1997 v Bel (sub), Arm (sub), Th; 1998 v Alb (sub), Sp (sub); 1999 v T, Fi; (with Norwich C), Ca; 2001 v Y, D (sub), Bul (sub), CzR; 2002 v D, Ic, Pol, Lie (16)

Murdock, C. J. (Preston NE), 2000 v L (sub), Ma, H (sub); 2001 v Y, Ma, D, Ic, N, CzR, Bul (2), CzR; 2002 v D, Ma (14)

Murphy, J. (Bradford C), 1910 v E, S, W (3)

Murphy, N. (QPR), 1905 v E, S, W (3)

Murray, J. M. (Motherwell), 1910 v E, S; (with Sheffield W), 1910 v W (3)

Napier, R. J. (Bolton W), 1966 v WG (1)

Neill, W. J. T. (Arsenal), 1961 v I, Gr, WG; 1962 v E, S, W, Gr; 1963 v E, W, Pol, Sp; 1964 v S, E, W, U, Sp; 1965 v E, S, W, Sw, Ho (2), Alb; 1966 v S, E, W, Alb, WG, M; 1967 v S, W; 1968 v S, E; 1969 v E, S, W, Is, T (2); 1970 v S, E, W, USSR (2); (with Hull C), 1971 v Cy, Sp; 1972 v USSR (2), Sp, S, E, W; 1973 v Bul, Cy (2), P, E, S, W (59)

Nelis, P. (Nottingham F), 1923 v E (1)

Nelson, S. (Arsenal), 1970 v W, E (sub); 1971 v Cy, Sp, E, S, W; 1972 v USSR (2), Sp, E, S, W; 1973 v Bul, Cy, P; 1974 v S, E; 1975 v Se, Y; 1976 v Se, N, Is, E; 1977 v Bel (sub), WG, W, Ic; 1978 v Ic, Ho, Bel; 1979 v Ei, D, Bul, E, Bul, E, S, W, D; 1980 v E, Ei, Is; 1981 v S, P, S, Se; (with Brighton & HA), 1982 v E, S, Sp (sub), A (51)

Nicholl, C. J. (Aston Villa), 1975 v Se, Y, E, S, W; 1976 v Se, N, Y, S, E, W; 1977 v W; (with Southampton), 1978 v Bel (sub), S, E, W; 1979 v Ei, Bul, E, Bul, E, W; 1980 v Ei, Is, S, E, W, Aus (3); 1981 v Se, P, S, P, S, Se; 1982 v S, Is, E, F, W, Y, Hon, Sp, A, F; 1983 v S (sub), E, W; (with Grimsby T), 1984 v A, T (51)

Nicholl, H. (Belfast C), 1902 v E, W; 1905 v E (3)

Nicholl, J. M. (Manchester U), 1976 v Is, W (sub); 1977 v Ho, Bel, E, S, W, Ic; 1978 v Ic, Ho, Bel, S, E, W; 1979 v Ei, D, Bul, E, Bul, E, S, W, D; 1980 v E, Ei, Is, S, E, W, Aus (3); 1981 v Se, P, S, P, S, Se; 1982 v S, Is, E; (with Toronto B), F, W, Y, Hon, Sp, A, F; (with Sunderland), 1983 v A, WG, Alb, T, Alb; (with Toronto B), S, E, W; 1984 v T; (with Rangers), WG, S, E; (with Toronto B), Fi; 1985 v R; (with WBA), Fi, E, Sp, T; 1986 v T, R, E, F, Alg, Sp, Br (73)

Nicholson, J. J. (Manchester U), 1961 v S, W; 1962 v E, W, Gr, Ho; 1963 v E, S, Pol (2); (with Huddersfield T), 1965 v W, Ho (2), Alb; 1966 v S, E, W, Alb, M; 1967 v S, W; 1968 v S, E, W; 1969 v S, E, W, T (2); 1970 v S, E, W, USSR (2); 1971 v Cy (2), E, S, W; 1972 v USSR (2) (41)

Nixon, R. (Linfield), 1914 v S (1)

Nolan, I. R. (Sheffield W), 1997 v Arm, G, Alb, P, Uk; 1998 v G, P; 2000 v G, Fi, L, Ma, H; (with Bradford C), 2001 v Y, Ma, Bul (2), CzR; (with Wigan Ath), 2002 v Sp (18)

Nolan-Whelan, J. V. (Dublin Freebooters), 1901 v E, W; 1902 v S, W; 1903 v S (5)

O'Boyle, G. (Dunfermline Ath), 1994 v Co (sub), M; (with St Johnstone), 1995 v P (sub), La (sub), Ca (sub), Ch (sub); 1996 v Se (sub), G (sub); 1997 v I (sub), Bel (sub); 1998 v Slo (sub), Sw (sub); 1999 v Fi (sub) (13)

O'Brien, M. T. (QPR), 1921 v S; (with Leicester C), 1922 v S, W; 1924 v S, W; (with Hull C), 1925 v S, E, W; 1926 v W; (with Derby Co), 1927 v W (10)

O'Connell, P. (Sheffield W), 1912 v E, S; (with Hull C), 1914 v E, S, W (5)

O'Doherty, A. (Coleraine), 1970 v E, W (sub) (2)

O'Driscoll, J. F. (Swansea T), 1949 v E, S, W (3)

O'Hagan, C. (Tottenham H), 1905 v S, W; 1906 v S, W, E; (with Aberdeen), 1907 v E, S, W; 1908 v S, W; 1909 v E (11)

O'Hagan, W. (St Mirren), 1920 v E, W (2)

O'Hehir, J. C. (Bohemians), 1910 v W (1)

O'Kane, W. J. (Nottingham F), 1970 v E, W, S (sub); 1971 v Sp, E, S, W; 1972 v USSR (2); 1973 v P, Cy; 1974 v Bul, P, S, E, W; 1975 v N, Se, E, S (20)

O'Mahoney, M. T. (Bristol R), 1939 v S (1)

O'Neill, C. (Motherwell), 1989 v Ch (sub); 1990 v Ei (sub); 1991 v D (3)

O'Neill, J. (Sunderland), 1962 v W (1)

O'Neill, J. P. (Leicester C), 1980 v Is, S, E, W, Aus (3); 1981 v P, S, P, S, Se; 1982 v S, Is, E, F, S, F (sub); 1983 v A, WG, Alb, T, Alb, S; 1984 v S (sub); 1985 v Is, Fi, E, Sp, T; 1986 v T, R, E, F, D, Mor, Alg, Sp, Br (39)

O'Neill, M. A. M. (Newcastle U), 1988 v Gr, Pol, F, Ma; 1989 v Ei, H, Sp (sub), Sp (sub), Ma (sub), Ch; (with Dundee U), 1990 v H (sub), Ei; 1991 v Pol; 1992 v Fa (sub), G (sub); 1993 v Alb (sub + 1), Ei, Sp, Li, La; (with Hibernian), 1994 v Lie (sub); 1995 v A (sub), Ei (sub), Lie, A, N, Se; (with Coventry C), 1997 v Uk (sub), Arm (sub) (31)

O'Neill, M. H. M. (Distillery), 1972 v USSR (sub), (with Nottingham F), Sp (sub), W (sub); 1973 v P, Cy, E, S, W; 1974 v Bul, P, E (sub); 1975 v Se, Y, E, S; 1976 v Y (sub); 1977 v E (sub), S; 1978 v Ic, Ho, S, E, W; 1979 v Ei, D, Bul, E, Bul, D; 1980 v E, Is, Aus (3); 1981 v Se, P; (with Norwich C), P, S, Se; (with Manchester C), 1982 v S; (with Norwich C), E, F, S, Y, Hon, Sp, A, F; 1983 v A, WG, Alb, T, Alb, S, E; (with Notts Co), 1984 v A, T, WG, E, W, Fi; 1985 v R, Fi (64)

O'Reilly, H. (Dublin Freebooters), 1901 v S, W; 1904 v S (3)

Parke, J. (Linfield), 1964 v S; (with Hibernian), 1964 v E, Sp; (with Sunderland), 1965 v Sw, S, W, Ho (2), Alb; 1966 v WG; 1967 v S; 1968 v S, E (14)

Patterson, D. J. (C Palace), 1994 v Co (sub), M (sub); 1995 v Ei (sub+1), La, Ca, Ch (sub), La (sub); (with Luton T), 1996 v N (sub), Se; 1998 v Sw, Sp; (with Dundee U), 1999 v Fi, Mol, G, Mol, Ei (17)

Peacock, R. (Celtic), 1952 v S; 1953 v F; 1954 v W; 1955 v E, S; 1956 v E, S; 1957 v W, I, P; 1958 v S, E, W, I (2), Arg, Cz (2), WG; 1959 v E, S, W; 1960 v S, E; 1961 v E, S, I, WG (2), Gr; (with Coleraine), 1962 v S (31)

Peden, J. (Distillery), 1887 v S, W; 1888 v W, E; 1889 v S, E; 1890 v W, S; 1891 v W, E; 1892 v W, E; 1893 v E, S, W; 1896 v W, E, S; 1897 v W, S; 1898 v W, E, S; 1899 v W (24)

Penney, S. (Brighton & HA), 1985 v Is; 1986 v T, R, E, F, D, Mor, Alg, Sp; 1987 v E, T, Is; 1988 v Pol, F, Ma; 1989 v Ei, Sp (17)

Percy, J. C. (Belfast YMCA), 1889 v W (1)

Platt, J. A. (Middlesbrough), 1976 v Is (sub); 1978 v S, E, W; 1980 v S, E, W, Aus (3); 1981 v Se, P; 1982 v F, S, W (sub), A; 1983 v A, WG, Alb, T; (with Ballymena U), 1984 v E, W (sub); (with Coleraine), 1986 v Mor (23)

Pollock, W. (Belfast C), 1928 v F (1)

Ponsonby, J. (Distillery), 1895 v S, W; 1896 v E, S, W; 1897 v E, S, W; 1899 v E (9)

Potts, R. M. C. (Cliftonville), 1883 v E, W (2)

Priestley, T. J. M. (Coleraine), 1933 v S; (with Chelsea), 1934 v E (2)

Pyper, Jas. (Cliftonville), 1897 v S, W; 1898 v S, E, W; 1899 v S; 1900 v E (7)

Pyper, John (Cliftonville), 1897 v S, W; 1899 v E, W; 1900 v E, W, S; 1902 v S (9)

Pyper, M. (Linfield), 1932 v W (1)

Quinn, J. M. (Blackburn R), 1985 v Is, Fi, E, Sp, T; 1986 v T, R, E, F, D (sub), Mor (sub); 1987 v E (sub), T; (with Swindon T), 1988 v Y (sub), T, Gr, Pol, F (sub), Ma; (with Leicester C), 1989 v Ei, H (sub), Sp (sub+1); (with Bradford C), Ma, Ch; 1990 v H, (with West Ham U), N; 1991 v Y (sub); (with Bournemouth), 1992 v Li; (with Reading), 1993 v Sp, D, Alb (sub), Ei (sub), La (sub); 1994 v La, D (sub), Ei, R, Lie, Co, M; 1995 v P, A (sub), La (sub); 1996 v Lie, A (sub) (46)

Quinn, S. J. (Blackpool), 1996 v Se (sub); 1997 v Alb (sub), I, Bel, P, Uk (sub), Arm, Th (sub); 1998 v G, Alb; (with WBA), Slo, Sw; 1999 v T (sub), Fi (sub), Ei; 2000 v F (sub), T (sub), G (sub), Fi, L, Ma; 2001 v Y (sub), Bul (sub), CzR (sub); 2002 v Ma (sub) (25)

Rafferty, P. (Linfield), 1980 v E (sub) (1)

Ramsey, P. C. (Leicester C), 1984 v A, WG, S; 1985 v Is, E, Sp, T; 1986 v T, Mor; 1987 v Is, E, Y (sub); 1988 v Y; 1989 v Sp (14)

Rankine, J. (Alexander), 1883 v E, W (2)

Rattray, D. (Avoniel), 1882 v E; 1883 v E, W (3)

Rea, R. (Glentoran), 1901 v E (1)

Redmond, R. (Cliftonville), 1884 v W (1)

Reid, G. H. (Cardiff C), 1923 v S (1)

Reid, J. (Ulster), 1883 v E; 1884 v W; 1887 v S; 1889 v W; 1890 v S, W (6)

Reid, S. E. (Derby Co), 1934 v E, W; 1936 v E (3)

Reid, W. (Hearts), 1931 v E (1)

Reilly, M. M. (Portsmouth), 1900 v E; 1902 v E (2)

Renneville, W. T. J. (Leyton), 1910 v S, E, W; (with Aston Villa), 1911 v W (4)

Reynolds, J. (Distillery), 1890 v E, W; (with Ulster), 1891 v E, S, W (5)

Reynolds, R. (Bohemians), 1905 v W (1)

Rice, P. J. (Arsenal), 1969 v Is; 1970 v USSR; 1971 v E, S, W; 1972 v USSR, Sp, E, S, W; 1973 v Bul, Cy, E, S, W; 1974 v Bul, P, S, E, W; 1975 v N, Y, E, S, W; 1976 v Se, N, Y, Is, S, E, W; 1977 v Ho, Bel, WG, E, S, Ic; 1978 v Ic, Ho, Bel; 1979 v Ei, D, E (2), S, W, D; 1980 v E (49)

Roberts, F. C. (Glentoran), 1931 v S (1)

Robinson, P. (Distillery), 1920 v S; (with Blackburn R), 1921 v W (2)

Robinson, S. (Bournemouth), 1997 v Th (sub); 1999 v Mol, Ei; 2000 v L (sub), H (sub) (5)

Rogan, A. (Celtic), 1988 v Y (sub), Gr, Pol (sub); 1989 v Ei (sub), H, Sp (sub), Ma (sub), Ch; 1990 v H, N (sub), U; 1991 v Y (2), D, A; (with Sunderland), 1992 v Li (sub); (with Millwall), 1997 v G (sub) (18)

Rollo, D. (Linfield), 1912 v W; 1913 v W; 1914 v W, E; (with Blackburn R), 1920 v S, W; 1921 v E, S, W; 1922 v E; 1923 v E; 1924 v S, W; 1925 v W; 1926 v E; 1927 v E (16)

Roper, E. O. (Dublin University), 1886 v W (1)

Rosbotham, A. (Cliftonville), 1887 v E, S, W; 1888 v E, S, W; 1889 v E (7)

Ross, W. E. (Newcastle U), 1969 v Is (1)

Rowland, K. (West Ham U), 1994 v La (sub); 1995 v Ca, Ch, La; 1996 v P (sub), Lie (sub), N (sub), Se, G (sub); 1997 v Uk, Arm, I (sub); 1998 v Alb; (with QPR), 1999 v T, Fi, Mol, G, Ca, Ei (19)

Rowley, R. W. M. (Southampton), 1929 v S, W; 1930 v W, E; (with Tottenham H), 1931 v W; 1932 v S (6)

Rushe, F. (Distillery),1925 v S.Af (1)

Russell, A. (Linfield), 1947 v E (1)

Russell, S. R. (Bradford C), 1930 v E, S; (with Derry C), 1932 v E (3)

Ryan, R. A. (WBA), 1950 v W (1)

Sanchez, L. P. (Wimbledon), 1987 v T (sub); 1989 v Sp, Ma (3)

Scott, E. (Liverpool), 1920 v S; 1921 v E, S, W; 1922 v E; 1925 v W; 1926 v E, S, W; 1927 v E, S, W; 1928 v E, S, W; 1929 v E, S, W; 1930 v E; 1931 v E; 1932 v W; 1933 v E, S, W; 1934 v E, S, W; (with Belfast C), 1935 v S; 1936 v E, S, W (31)

Scott, J. (Grimsby), 1958 v Cz, F (2)

Scott, J. E. (Cliftonville), 1901 v S (1)

Scott, L. J. (Dublin University), 1895 v S, W (2)

Scott, P. W. (Everton), 1975 v W; 1976 v Y; (with York C), Is, S, E (sub), W; 1978 v S, E, W; (with Aldershot), 1979 v S (sub) (10)
Scott, T. (Cliftonville), 1894 v E, S; 1895 v S, W; 1896 v S, E, W; 1897 v E, W; 1898 v E, S, W; 1900 v W (13)
Scott, W. (Linfield), 1903 v E, S, W; 1904 v E, S, W; (with Everton), 1905 v E, S; 1907 v E, S; 1908 v E, S, W; 1909 v E, S, W; 1910 v E, S; 1911 v E, S, W; 1912 v E; (with Leeds City), 1913 v E, S, W (25)
Scraggs, M. J. (Glentoran), 1921 v W; 1922 v E (2)
Seymour, H. C. (Bohemians), 1914 v W (1)
Seymour, J. (Cliftonville), 1907 v W; 1909 v W (2)
Shanks, T. (Woolwich Arsenal), 1903 v S; 1904 v W; (with Brentford), 1905 v E (3)
Sharkey, P. G. (Ipswich T), 1976 v S (1)
Sheehan, Dr G. (Bohemians), 1899 v S; 1900 v E, W (3)
Sheridan, J. (Everton), 1903 v W, E, S; 1904 v E, S; (with Stoke C), 1905 v E (6)
Sherrard, J. (Limavady), 1885 v S; 1887 v W; 1888 v W (3)
Sherrard, W. C. (Cliftonville), 1895 v E, W, S (3)
Sherry, J. J. (Bohemians), 1906 v E; 1907 v W (2)
Shields, R. J. (Southampton), 1957 v S (1)
Silo, M. (Belfast YMCA), 1888 v E (1)
Simpson, W. J. (Rangers), 1951 v W, F; 1954 v E, S; 1955 v E; 1957 v I P; 1958 v S, E, W, I; 1959 v S (12)
Sinclair, J. (Knock), 1882 v E, W (2)
Slemin, J. C. (Bohemians), 1909 v W (1)
Sloan, A. S. (London Caledonians), 1925 v W (1)
Sloan, D. (Oxford U), 1969 v Is; 1971 v Sp (2)
Sloan, H. A. de B. (Bohemians), 1903 v E; 1904 v S; 1905 v E; 1906 v W; 1907 v E, W; 1908 v W; 1909 v S (8)
Sloan, J. W. (Arsenal), 1947 v W (1)
Sloan, T. (Manchester U), 1979 v S, W (sub), D (sub) (3)
Sloan, T. (Cardiff C), 1926 v S, W, E; 1927 v W, S; 1928 v E, W; 1929 v E; (with Linfield), 1930 v W, S; 1931 v S (11)
Small, J. M. (Clarence), 1887 v E; (with Cliftonville), 1893 v E, S, W (4)
Smith, E. E. (Cardiff C), 1921 v S; 1923 v W, E; 1924 v E (4)
Smith, J. E. (Distillery), 1901 v S, W (2)
Smyth, R. H. (Dublin University), 1886 v W (1)
Smyth, S. (Wolverhampton W), 1948 v E, S, W; 1949 v S, W; 1950 v E, S, W; (with Stoke C), 1952 v E (9)
Smyth, W. (Distillery), 1949 v E, S; 1954 v S, E (4)
Snape, A. (Airdrie), 1920 v E (1)
Sonner, D. J. (Ipswich T), 1998 v Alb (sub); (with Sheffield W), 1999 v G (sub), Ca (sub); 2000 v L (sub), Ma (sub), H; (with Birmingham C), 2001 v N (sub) (7)
Spence, D. W. (Bury), 1975 v Y, E, S, W; 1976 v Se, Is, E, W, S (sub); (with Blackpool), 1977 v Ho (sub), WG (sub), E (sub), S (sub), W (sub), Ic (sub); 1979 v Ei, D (sub), E (sub), Bul (sub), E (sub), S, W, D; 1980 v Ei; (with Southend U), Is (sub), Aus (sub); 1981 v S (sub), Se (sub); 1982 v F (sub) (29)
Spencer, S. (Distillery), 1890 v E, S; 1892 v E, S, W; 1893 v E (6)
Spiller, E. A. (Cliftonville), 1883 v E, W; 1884 v E, W, S (5)
Stanfield, O. M. (Distillery), 1887 v E, S, W; 1888 v E, S, W; 1889 v E, S, W; 1890 v E, S; 1891 v E, S; 1892 v E, S, W; 1893 v E, W; 1894 v E, S, W; 1895 v E, S; 1896 v E, S, W; 1897 v E, S, W (30)
Steele, A. (Charlton Ath), 1926 v W, S; (with Fulham), 1929 v W, S (4)
Stevenson, A. E. (Rangers), 1934 v E, S, W; (with Everton), 1935 v E, S; 1936 v S, W; 1937 v E, W; 1938 v E, W; 1939 v E, S, W; 1947 v S, W; 1948 v S (17)
Stewart, A. (Glentoran), 1967 v W; 1968 v S, E; (with Derby Co), 1968 v W; 1969 v Is, T (1+1 sub) (7)
Stewart, D. C. (Hull C), 1978 v Bel (1)
Stewart, I. (QPR), 1982 v F (sub); 1983 v A, WG, Alb, T, Alb, S, E, W; 1984 v A, T, WG, S, E, W, Fi; 1985 v R, Fi, Is, E, Sp, T; (with Newcastle U), 1986 v R, E, D, Mor, Alg (sub), Sp (sub), Br; 1987 v E, Is (sub) (31)
Stewart, R. K. (St Columb's Court), 1890 v E, S, W; (with Cliftonville), 1892 v E, S, W; 1893 v E, W; 1894 v E, S, W (11)
Stewart, T. C. (Linfield), 1961 v W (1)
Swan, S. (Linfield), 1899 v S (1)

Taggart, G. P. (Barnsley), 1990 v N, U; 1991 v Y, D, A, Pol, Fa; 1992 v Fa, A, D, S, Li, G; 1993 v Alb, Sp, D, Alb, Ei, Sp, Li, La; 1994 v La, D, Ei, R, Lie, Co, M; 1995 v P (sub), A, Ei (2), Ca, Ch, La; (with Bolton W), 1997 v G, Alb, I, Bel, P, Uk, Arm; 1998 v G, P, Sp; (with Leicester C), 2000 v H; 2001 v Ma, D, Ic, N (50)
Taggart, J. (Walsall), 1899 v W (1)

Taylor, M. S. (Fulham), 1999 v G, Mol, Ca, Ei; 2000 v F, T, G, Fi, L (sub), Ma (sub), H; 2001 v Y, N, Bul, CzR; 2002 v D, Ic, Ma, Pol, Lie, Sp (21)
Thompson, F. W. (Cliftonville), 1910 v E, S, W; (with Linfield), 1911 v W; (with Bradford C), 1911 v E; 1912 v E, W; 1913 v E, S, W; (with Clyde), 1914 v E, S (12)
Thompson, J. (Distillery), 1897 v S (1)
Thompson, R. (Queen's Island), 1928 v F (1)
Thompson, W. (Belfast Ath), 1889 v S (1)
Thunder, P. J. (Bohemians), 1911 v W (1)
Todd, S. J. (Burnley), 1966 v M (sub); 1967 v E; 1968 v W; 1969 v E, S, W; 1970 v S, USSR; (with Sheffield W), 1971 v Cy (2), Sp (sub) (11)
Toner, J. (Arsenal), 1922 v W; 1923 v W; 1924 v W, E; 1925 v E, S; (with St Johnstone), 1927 v E, S (8)
Torrans, R. (Linfield), 1893 v S (1)
Torrans, S. (Linfield), 1889 v S; 1890 v S, W; 1891 v S, W; 1892 v E, S, W; 1893 v E, S; 1894 v E, S, W; 1895 v E; 1896 v E, S, W; 1897 v E, S, W; 1898 v E, S; 1899 v E, W; 1901 v S, W (26)
Trainor, D. (Crusaders), 1967 v W (1)
Tully, C. P. (Celtic), 1949 v E; 1950 v E; 1952 v S; 1953 v E, S, W, F; 1954 v S; 1956 v E; 1959 v Sp (10)
Turner, A. (Cliftonville), 1896 v W (1)
Turner, E. (Cliftonville), 1896 v E (1)
Turner, W. (Cliftonville), 1886 v E, S; 1888 v S (3)
Twoomey, J. F. (Leeds U), 1938 v W; 1939 v E (2)
Uprichard, W. N. M. C. (Swindon T), 1952 v E, S, W; 1953 v E, S; (with Portsmouth), 1953 v W, F; 1955 v E, S, W; 1956 v E, S, W; 1958 v S, I, Cz; 1959 v S, Sp (18)

Vernon, J. (Belfast C), 1947 v E, S; (with WBA), 1947 v W; 1948 v E, S, W; 1949 v E, S, W; 1950 v E, S; 1951 v E, S, W, F; 1952 v S, E (17)

Waddell, T. M. R. (Cliftonville), 1906 v S (1)
Walker, J. (Doncaster R), 1955 v W (1)
Walker, T. (Bury), 1911 v S (1)
Walsh, D. J. (WBA), 1947 v S, W; 1948 v E, S, W; 1949 v E, S, W; 1950 v W (9)
Walsh, W. (Manchester C), 1948 v E, S, W; 1949 v E, S (5)
Waring, J. (Cliftonville), 1899 v E (1)
Warren, P. (Shelbourne), 1913 v E, S (2)
Watson, J. (Ulster), 1883 v E, W; 1886 v E, S, W; 1887 v S, W; 1889 v E, W (9)
Watson, P. (Distillery), 1971 v Cy (sub) (1)
Watson, T. (Cardiff C), 1926 v S (1)
Wattie, J. (Distillery), 1899 v E (1)
Webb, C. G. (Brighton), 1909 v S, W; 1911 v S (3)
Weir, E. (Clyde), 1939 v W (1)
Welsh, E. (Carlisle U), 1966 v W, WG, M; 1967 v W (4)
Whiteside, N. (Manchester U), 1982 v Y, Hon, Sp, A, F; 1983 v WG, Alb, T; 1984 v A, T, WG, S, E, W, Fi; 1985 v R, Fi, Is, E, Sp, T; 1986 v R, E, F, D, Mor, Alg, Sp, Br; 1987 v E (2), Is, Y; 1988 v T, Pol, F; (with Everton), 1990 v H, Ei (38)
Whiteside, T. (Distillery), 1891 v E (1)
Whitfield, E. R. (Dublin University), 1886 v W (1)
Whitley, Jeff (Manchester C), 1997 v Bel (sub), Th (sub); 1998 v Sp (sub); 2000 v Fi; 2001 v Y, D, N (7)
Whitley, Jim (Manchester C), 1998 v Sp; 1999 v T (sub); 2000 v Fi (sub) (3)
Williams, J. R. (Ulster), 1886 v E, S (2)
Williams, M. S. (Chesterfield), 1999 v G, Mol, Ca, Ei; (with Watford), 2000 v F, T, G, Fi, L, Ma, H (sub); 2001 v Y, Ic (sub), N (sub), CzR, Bul, CzR; (with Wimbledon), 2002 v Lie, Sp (19)
Williams, P. A. (WBA), 1991 v Fa (sub) (1)
Williamson, J. (Cliftonville), 1890 v E; 1892 v S; 1893 v S (3)
Willighan, T. (Burnley), 1933 v W; 1934 v S (2)
Willis, G. (Linfield), 1906 v S, W; 1907 v S; 1912 v S (4)
Wilson, D. J. (Brighton & HA), 1987 v T, Is, E (sub); (with Luton T), 1988 v Y, T, Gr, Pol, F, Ma; 1989 v Ei, H, Sp, Ma, Ch; 1990 v H, N, U; (with Sheffield W), 1991 v Y, D, A, Fa; 1992 v A (sub), S (24)
Wilson, H. (Linfield), 1925 v W, S.Af (2)
Wilson, K. J. (Ipswich T), 1987 v Is, E, Y; (with Chelsea), 1988 v Y, T, Gr (sub), Pol (sub), F (sub); 1989 v H (sub), Sp (2), Ma, Ch; 1990 v Ei (sub), N, U; 1991 v Y (2), A, Pol, Fa; 1992 v Fa, A, D, S; (with Notts Co), Li, G; 1993 v Alb, Sp, D, Sp, Li, La; 1994 v La, D, Ei, R, Lie, Co, M; (with Walsall), 1995 v Ei (sub), La (42)
Wilson, M. (Distillery), 1884 v E, S, W (3)
Wilson, R. (Cliftonville), 1888 v S (1)
Wilson, S. J. (Glenavon), 1962 v S; 1964 v S; (with Falkirk), 1964 v E, W, U, Sp; 1965 v E, Sw; (with Dundee), 1966 v W, WG; 1967 v S; 1968 v E (12)

Wilton, J. M. (St Columb's Court), 1888 v E, W; 1889 v S, E; (with Cliftonville), 1890 v E; (with St Columb's Court); 1893 v W, S (7)
Wood, T. J. (Walsall), 1996 v Lie (sub) (1)
Worthington, N. (Sheffield W), 1984 v W, Fi (sub); 1985 v Is, Sp (sub); 1986 v T, R (sub), E (sub), D, Alg, Sp; 1987 v E (2), T, Is, Y; 1988 v Y, T, Gr, Pol, F, Ma; 1989 v Ei, H, Sp, Ma; 1990 v H, Ei, U; 1991 v Y, D, A, Fa; 1992 v A, D, S, Li, G; 1993 v Alb, Sp, D, Ei, Sp, Li, La; 1994 v La, D, Ei, Lie, Co, M; (with Leeds U), 1995 v P, A, Ei (2), La, Ca (sub), Ch, La; 1996 v P, Lie, A, N, Se, G; (with Stoke C), 1997 v I, Bel (sub) (66)

Wright, J. (Cliftonville), 1906 v E, S, W; 1907 v E, S, W (6)
Wright, T. J. (Newcastle U), 1989 v Ma, Ch; 1990 v H, U; 1992 v Fa, A, S, G; 1993 v Alb, Sp, Alb, Ei, Sp, Li, La; 1994 v La; (with Nottingham F), D, Ei, R, Lie, Co, M (sub); 1997 v G, Alb, I, Bel; (with Manchester C), P, Uk; 1998 v Alb; 1999 v Ca (sub); 2000 v F (sub) (31)

Young, S. (Linfield), 1907 v E, S; 1908 v E, S; (with Airdrie), 1909 v E; 1912 v S; (with Linfield), 1914 v E, S, W (9)

SCOTLAND

Adams, J. (Hearts), 1889 v Ni; 1892 v W; 1893 v Ni (3)
Agnew, W. B. (Kilmarnock), 1907 v Ni; 1908 v W, Ni (3)
Aird, J. (Burnley), 1954 v N (2), A, U (4)
Aitken, A. (Newcastle U), 1901 v E; 1902 v E; 1903 v E, W; 1904 v E; 1905 v E, W; 1906 v E; (with Middlesbrough), 1907 v E, W; 1908 v E; (with Leicester Fosse), 1910 v E; 1911 v E, Ni (14)
Aitken, G. G. (East Fife), 1949 v E, F; 1950 v W, Ni, Sw; (with Sunderland), 1953 v W, Ni; 1954 v E (8)
Aitken, R. (Dumbarton), 1886 v E; 1888 v Ni (2)
Aitken, R. (Celtic), 1980 v Pe (sub), Bel, W (sub), E, Pol; 1983 v Bel, Ca (1+1 sub); 1984 v Bel (sub), Ni, W (sub); 1985 v E, Ic; 1986 v W, EG, Aus (2), Is, R, E, D, WG, U; 1987 v Bul, Ei (2), L, Bel, E, Br; 1988 v H, Bel, Bul, L, S.Ar, Ma, Sp, Co, E; 1989 v N, Y, I, Cy, F, Cy, E, Ch; 1990 v Y, F, N; (with Newcastle U), Arg (sub), Pol, Ma, Cr, Se, Br; (with St Mirren), 1992 v R (sub) (57)
Aitkenhead, W. A. C. (Blackburn R), 1912 v Ni (1)
Albiston, A. (Manchester U), 1982 v Ni; 1984 v U, Bel, EG, W, E; 1985 v Y, Ic, Sp (2), W; 1986 v EG, Ho, U (14)
Alexander, D. (East Stirlingshire), 1894 v W, Ni (2)
Alexander, G. (Preston NE), 2002 v Ng (sub), Sk, S.Af (sub), Hk (sub) (4)
Allan, D. S. (Queen's Park), 1885 v E, W; 1886 v W (3)
Allan, G. (Liverpool), 1897 v E (1)
Allan, H. (Hearts), 1902 v W (1)
Allan, J. (Queen's Park), 1887 v E, W (2)
Allan, T. (Dundee), 1974 v WG, N (2)
Ancell, R. F. D. (Newcastle U), 1937 v W, Ni (2)
Anderson, A. (Hearts), 1933 v E; 1934 v A, E, W, Ni; 1935 v E, W, Ni; 1936 v E, W, Ni; 1937 v G, E, W, Ni, A; 1938 v E, W, Ni, Cz, Ho; 1939 v W, Ni (23)
Anderson, F. (Clydesdale), 1874 v E (1)
Anderson, G. (Kilmarnock), 1901 v Ni (1)
Anderson, H. A. (Raith R), 1914 v W (1)
Anderson, J. (Leicester C), 1954 v Fi (1)
Anderson, K. (Queen's Park), 1896 v Ni; 1898 v E, Ni (3)
Anderson, W. (Queen's Park), 1882 v E; 1883 v E, W; 1884 v E; 1885 v E, W (6)
Andrews, P. (Eastern), 1875 v E (1)
Archibald, A. (Rangers), 1921 v W; 1922 v W, E; 1923 v Ni; 1924 v E, W; 1931 v E; 1932 v E (8)
Archibald, S. (Aberdeen), 1980 v P (sub); (with Tottenham H), Ni, Pol, H; 1981 v Se (sub), Is, Ni, S, Ni, E; 1982 v Ni, P, Sp (sub), Ho, Nz (sub), Br, USSR; 1983 v EG, Sw (sub), Bel; 1984 v EG, E, F; (with Barcelona), 1985 v Sp, E, Ic (sub); 1986 v WG (27)
Armstrong, M. W. (Aberdeen), 1936 v W, Ni; 1937 v G (3)
Arnott, W. (Queen's Park), 1883 v W; 1884 v E, Ni; 1885 v E, W; 1886 v E; 1887 v E, W; 1888 v E; 1889 v E; 1890 v E; 1891 v E; 1892 v E; 1893 v E (14)
Auld, J. R. (Third Lanark), 1887 v E, W; 1889 v W (3)
Auld, R. (Celtic), 1959 v H, P; 1960 v W (3)

Baird, A. (Queen's Park), 1892 v Ni; 1894 v W (2)
Baird, D. (Hearts), 1890 v Ni; 1891 v E; 1892 v W (3)
Baird, H. (Airdrieonians), 1956 v A (1)
Baird, J. C. (Vale of Leven), 1876 v E; 1878 v W; 1880 v E (3)
Baird, S. (Rangers), 1957 v Y, Sp (2), Sw, WG; 1958 v F, Ni (7)
Baird, W. U. (St Bernard), 1897 v Ni (1)
Bannon, E. (Dundee U), 1980 v Bel; 1983 v Ni, W, E, Ca; 1984 v EG; 1986 v Is, R, E, D (sub), WG (11)
Barbour, A. (Renton), 1885 v Ni (1)
Barker, J. B. (Rangers), 1893 v W; 1894 v W (2)
Barrett, F. (Dundee), 1894 v Ni; 1895 v W (2)
Battles, B. (Celtic), 1901 v E, W, Ni (3)
Battles, B. jun. (Hearts), 1931 v W (1)
Bauld, W. (Hearts), 1950 v E, Sw, P (3)

Baxter, J. C. (Rangers), 1961 v Ni, Ei (2), Cz; 1962 v Ni, W, E, Cz (2), U; 1963 v W, Ni, E, A, N, Ei, Sp; 1964 v W, E, N, WG; 1965 v W, Ni, Fi; (with Sunderland), 1966 v P, Br, Ni, W, E, I; 1967 v W, E, USSR; 1968 v W (34)
Baxter, R. D. (Middlesbrough), 1939 v E, W, H (3)
Beattie, A. (Preston NE), 1937 v E, A, Cz; 1938 v E; 1939 v W, Ni, H (7)
Beattie, R. (Preston NE), 1939 v W (1)
Begbie, I. (Hearts), 1890 v Ni; 1891 v E; 1892 v W; 1894 v E (4)
Bell, A. (Manchester U), 1912 v Ni (1)
Bell, J. (Dumbarton), 1890 v Ni; 1892 v E; (with Everton), 1896 v E; 1897 v E; 1898 v E; (with Celtic), 1899 v E, W, Ni; 1900 v E, W (10)
Bell, M. (Hearts), 1901 v W (1)
Bell, W. J. (Leeds U), 1966 v P, Br (2)
Bennett, A. (Celtic), 1904 v W; 1907 v Ni; 1908 v W; (with Rangers), 1909 v W, Ni, E; 1910 v E, W; 1911 v E, W; 1913 v Ni (11)
Bennie, R. (Airdrieonians), 1925 v W, Ni; 1926 v Ni (3)
Bernard, P. R. J. (Oldham Ath), 1995 v J (sub), Ec (2)
Berry, D. (Queen's Park), 1894 v W; 1899 v W, Ni (3)
Berry, W. H. (Queen's Park), 1888 v E; 1889 v E; 1890 v E; 1891 v E (4)
Bett, J. (Rangers), 1982 v Ho; 1983 v Bel; (with Lokeren), 1984 v Bel, W, E, F; 1985 v Y, Ic, Sp (2), W, E, Ic; (with Aberdeen), 1986 v W, Is, Ho; 1987 v Bel; 1988 v H (sub); 1989 v Y; 1990 v F (sub), N, Arg, Eg, Ma, Cr (25)
Beveridge, W. W. (Glasgow University), 1879 v E, W; 1880 v W (3)
Black, A. (Hearts), 1938 v Cz, Ho; 1939 v H (3)
Black, D. (Hurlford), 1889 v Ni (1)
Black, E. (Metz), 1988 v H (sub), L (sub) (2)
Black, I. H. (Southampton), 1948 v E (1)
Blackburn, J. E. (Royal Engineers), 1873 v E (1)
Blacklaw, A. S. (Burnley), 1963 v N, Sp; 1966 v I (3)
Blackley, J. (Hibernian), 1974 v Cz, E, Bel, Z; 1976 v Sw; 1977 v W, Se (7)
Blair, D. (Clyde), 1929 v W, Ni; 1931 v E, A, I; 1932 v W, Ni; (with Aston Villa), 1933 v W (8)
Blair, J. (Sheffield W), 1920 v E, Ni; (with Cardiff C), 1921 v E; 1922 v E; 1923 v E, W, Ni; 1924 v W (8)
Blair, J. (Motherwell), 1934 v W (1)
Blair, J. A. (Blackpool), 1947 v W (1)
Blair, W. (Third Lanark), 1896 v W (1)
Blessington, J. (Celtic), 1894 v E, Ni; 1896 v E, Ni (4)
Blyth, J. A. (Coventry C), 1978 v Bul, W (2)
Bone, J. (Norwich C), 1972 v Y (sub); 1973 v D (2)
Booth, S. (Aberdeen), 1993 v G (sub), Es (2 subs); 1994 v Sw, Ma (sub); 1995 v Fa, Ru; 1996 v Fi, Sm, Aus (sub), US, Ho, Sw (sub); (with Borussia Dortmund), 1998 v D, Fi, Co (sub), Mor (sub); (with Twente), 2001 v Pol; 2002 v Cro, Bel (sub), La (sub) (21)
Bowie, J. (Rangers), 1920 v E, Ni (2)
Bowie, W. (Linthouse), 1891 v Ni (1)
Bowman, D. (Dundee U), 1992 v Fi, US (sub); 1993 v G, Es; 1994 v Sw, I (6)
Bowman, G. A. (Montrose), 1892 v Ni (1)
Boyd, J. M. (Newcastle U), 1934 v Ni (1)
Boyd, R. (Mossend Swifts), 1889 v Ni; 1891 v W (2)
Boyd, T. (Motherwell), 1991 v R (sub), Sw, Bul, USSR; (with Chelsea), 1992 v Sw, R; (with Celtic), Fi, Ca, N, C; 1993 v Sw, P, I, Ma, G, Es (2); 1994 v I, Ma (sub), Ho (sub), A; 1995 v Fi, Fa, Ru, Gr, Ru, Sm; 1996 v Gr, Fi, Se, Sm, Aus, D, US, Co, Ho, E, Sw; 1997 v A, La, Se, Es (2), A, Sw, Ma, Bl; 1998 v Bl, La, F, D, Fi (sub), Co, US, Br, N, Mor; 1999 v Li, Es, Fa, CzR, G, Fa, CzR; 2001 v La, Cro, Aus, Bel, Sm (sub), Pol; 2002 v Bel (72)
Boyd, W. G. (Clyde), 1931 v I, Sw (2)

Brackenbridge, T. (Hearts), 1888 v Ni (1)

Bradshaw, T. (Bury), 1928 v E (1)

Brand, R. (Rangers), 1961 v Ni, Cz, Ei (2); 1962 v Ni, W, Cz, U (8)

Branden, T. (Blackburn R), 1896 v E (1)

Brazil, A. (Ipswich T), 1980 v Pol (sub), H; 1982 v Sp, Ho (sub), Ni, W, E, Nz, USSR (sub); 1983 v EG, Sw, (with Tottenham H), W, E (sub) (13)

Bremner, D. (Hibernian), 1976 v Sw (sub) (1)

Bremner, W. J. (Leeds U), 1965 v Sp; 1966 v E, Pol, P, Br, I (2); 1967 v W, Ni, E; 1968 v W, E; 1969 v W, E, Ni, D, A, WG, Cy (2); 1970 v Ei, WG, A; 1971 v W, E; 1972 v P, Bel, Ho, Ni, W, E, Y, Cz, Br; 1973 v D (2), E (2), Ni (sub), Sw, Br; 1974 v Cz, WG, Ni, W, E, Bel, N, Z, Br, Y; 1975 v Sp (2); 1976 v D (54)

Brennan, F. (Newcastle U), 1947 v W, Ni; 1953 v W, Ni, E; 1954 v Ni, E (7)

Breslin, B. (Hibernian), 1897 v W (1)

Brewster, G. (Everton), 1921 v E (1)

Brogan, J. (Celtic), 1971 v W, Ni, P, E (4)

Brown, A. (St Mirren), 1890 v W; 1891 v W (2)

Brown, A. (Middlesbrough), 1904 v E (1)

Brown, A. D. (East Fife), 1950 v Sw, P, F; (with Blackpool), 1952 v USA, D, Se; 1953 v W; 1954 v W, E, N (2), Fi, A, U (14)

Brown, G. C. P. (Rangers), 1931 v W; 1932 v E, W, Ni; 1933 v E; 1934 v a; 1935 v E; 1936 v E, W; 1937 v G, E, W, Ni, Cz; 1938 v E, W, Cz, Ho (19)

Brown, H. (Partick T), 1947 v W, Ni, E, Bel, L (3)

Brown, J. (Cambuslang), 1890 v W (1)

Brown, J. B. (Clyde), 1939 v W (1)

Brown, J. G. (Sheffield U), 1975 v R (1)

Brown, R. (Dumbarton), 1884 v W, Ni (2)

Brown, R. (Rangers), 1947 v Ni; 1949 v Ni; 1952 v E (3)

Brown, R. jun. (Dumbarton), 1885 v W (1)

Brown, W. D. F. (Dundee), 1958 v F; 1959 v E, W, Ni; (with Tottenham H), 1960 v W, Ni, Pol, A, H, T; 1962 v Ni, W, E, Cz; 1963 v W, Ni, E, A; 1964 v Ni, W, N; 1965 v E, Fi, Pol, Sp; 1966 v Ni, Pol, I (28)

Browning, J. (Celtic), 1914 v W (1)

Brownlie, J. (Third Lanark), 1909 v E, Ni; 1910 v E, W, Ni; 1911 v W, Ni; 1912 v W, Ni, E; 1913 v W, Ni, E; 1914 v W, Ni, E (16)

Brownlie, J. (Hibernian), 1971 v USSR; 1972 v Pe, Ni, E; 1973 v D (2); 1976 v R (7)

Bruce, D. (Vale of Leven), 1890 v W (1)

Bruce, R. F. (Middlesbrough), 1934 v A (1)

Buchan, M. M. (Aberdeen), 1972 v P (sub), Bel; (with Manchester U), W, Y, Cz, Br; 1973 v D (2), E; 1974 v WG, Ni, W, N, Br, Y; 1975 v EG, Sp, P; 1976 v D, R; 1977 v Fi, Cz, Ch, Arg, Br; 1978 v EG, W (sub), Ni, Pe, Ir, Ho; 1979 v A, N, P (34)

Buchanan, J. (Cambuslang), 1889 v Ni (1)

Buchanan, J. (Rangers), 1929 v E; 1930 v E (2)

Buchanan, P. S. (Chelsea), 1938 v Cz (1)

Buchanan, R. (Abercorn), 1891 v W (1)

Buckley, P. (Aberdeen), 1954 v N; 1955 v W, Ni (3)

Buick, A. (Hearts), 1902 v W, Ni (2)

Burchill, M. J. (Celtic), 2000 v Bos (sub), Li, E (sub + sub), F (sub), Ho (sub) (6)

Burley, C. W. (Chelsea), 1995 v J, Ec, Fa; 1996 v Gr, Se, Aus, D, US, Co (sub), Ho (sub), E (sub), Sw; 1997 v A, La, Se, Es, A, Se, Ma, Bl; (with Celtic), 1998 v Bl, La, F, Co, US (sub); Br, Mor; 1999 v Fa, CzR; 2000 v Bos, Es, Bos, Li, E (2); (with Derby Co), Ho, Ei; 2001 v Cro, Aus, Bel, Sm; 2002 v Cro, Bel, La (45)

Burley, G. (Ipswich T), 1979 v W, Ni, E, Arg, N; 1980 v P, Ni, E (sub), Pol; 1982 v W (sub), E (11)

Burns, F. (Manchester U), 1970 v A (1)

Burns, K. (Birmingham C), 1974 v WG; 1975 v EG (sub), Sp (2); 1977 v Cz (sub), W, Se, W (sub); (with Nottingham F), 1978 v Ni (sub), W, E, Pe, Ir; 1979 v N; 1980 v Pe, A, Bel; 1981 v Is, Ni, W (20)

Burns, T. (Celtic), 1981 v Ni; 1982 v Ho (sub), W; 1983 v Bel (sub), Ni, Ca (1 + 1 sub); 1988 v E (sub) (8)

Busby, M. W. (Manchester C), 1934 v W (1)

Cairns, T. (Rangers), 1920 v W; 1922 v E; 1923 v E, W; 1924 v Ni; 1925 v W, E, Ni (8)

Calderhead, D. (Q of S Wanderers), 1889 v Ni (1)

Calderwood, C. (Tottenham H), 1995 v Ru, Sm, J, Ec, Fa; 1996 v Gr, Fi, Se, Sm, US, Co, Ho, E, Sw; 1997 v A, La, Se, Es (2), A, Se; 1998 v Bl, La, F, D, Fi, Co, US, Br, N; 1999 v Li, Es; (with Aston Villa) Fa, CzR; 2000 v Bos (1 + sub) (36)

Calderwood, R. (Cartvale), 1885 v Ni, E, W (3)

Caldow, E. (Rangers), 1957 v Sp (2), Sw, WG, E; 1958 v Ni, W, Sw, Par, H, Pol, Y, F; 1959 v E, W, Ni, WG, Ho, P; 1960 v E, W, Ni, A, H, T; 1961 v E, W, Ni, Ei (2), Cz; 1962 v Ni, W, E, Cz (2), U; 1963 v W, Ni, E (40)

Caldwell, G. (Newcastle U), 2002 v F, Ng (sub), Sk, S.Af (4)

Caldwell, S. (Newcastle U), 2001 v Pol (sub) (1)

Callaghan, P. (Hibernian), 1900 v Ni (1)

Callaghan, W. (Dunfermline Ath), 1970 v Ei (sub), W (2)

Cameron, C. (Hearts), 1999 v G (sub), Fa (sub); 2000 v Li (sub), F, Ei (sub); 2001 v La (sub), Sm, Cro, Aus, Sm, Pol; (with Wolverhampton W), 2002 v Cro (sub), Bel (sub), La, F (15)

Cameron, J. (Rangers), 1886 v Ni (1)

Cameron, J. (Queen's Park), 1896 v Ni (1)

Cameron, J. (St Mirren), 1904 v Ni; (with Chelsea), 1909 v E (2)

Campbell, C. (Queen's Park), 1874 v E; 1876 v W; 1877 v E, W; 1878 v E; 1879 v E; 1880 v E; 1881 v E; 1882 v E, W; 1884 v E; 1885 v E; 1886 v E (13)

Campbell, H. (Renton), 1889 v W (1)

Campbell, Jas (Sheffield W), 1913 v W (1)

Campbell, J. (South Western), 1880 v W (1)

Campbell, J. (Kilmarnock), 1891 v Ni; 1892 v W (2)

Campbell, John (Celtic), 1893 v E, Ni; 1898 v E, Ni; 1900 v E, Ni; 1901 v E, W, Ni; 1902 v W, Ni; 1903 v W (12)

Campbell, John (Rangers), 1899 v E, W, Ni; 1901 v Ni (4)

Campbell, K. (Liverpool), 1920 v E, W, Ni; (with Partick T), 1921 v W, Ni; 1922 v W, Ni, E (8)

Campbell, P. (Rangers), 1878 v W; 1879 v W (2)

Campbell, P. (Morton), 1898 v W (1)

Campbell, R. (Falkirk), 1947 v Bel, L; (with Chelsea), 1950 v Sw, P, F (5)

Campbell, W. (Morton), 1947 v Ni; 1948 v E, Bel, Sw, F (5)

Carabine, J. (Third Lanark), 1938 v Ho; 1939 v E, Ni (3)

Carr, W. M. (Coventry C), 1970 v Ni, W, E; 1971 v D; 1972 v Pe; 1973 v D (sub) (6)

Cassidy, J. (Celtic), 1921 v W, Ni; 1923 v Ni; 1924 v W (4)

Chalmers, S. (Celtic), 1965 v W, Fi; 1966 v P (sub), Br; 1967 v Ni (5)

Chalmers, W. (Rangers), 1885 v Ni (1)

Chalmers, W. S. (Queen's Park), 1929 v Ni (1)

Chambers, T. (Hearts), 1894 v W (1)

Chaplin, G. D. (Dundee), 1908 v W (1)

Cheyne, A. G. (Aberdeen), 1929 v E, N, G, Ho; 1930 v F (5)

Christie, a. J. (Queen's Park), 1898 v W; 1899 v E, Ni (3)

Christie, R. M. (Queen's Park), 1884 v E (1)

Clark, J. (Celtic), 1966 v Br; 1967 v W, Ni, USSR (4)

Clark, R. B. (Aberdeen), 1968 v W, Ho; 1970 v Ni; 1971 v W, Ni, E, D, P, USSR; 1972 v Bel, Ni, W, E, Cz, Br; 1973 v D, E (17)

Clarke, S. (Chelsea), 1988 v H, Bel, Bul, S.Ar, Ma; 1994 v Ho (6)

Cleland, J. (Royal Albert), 1891 v Ni (1)

Clements, R. (Leith Ath), 1891 v Ni (1)

Clunas, W. L. (Sunderland), 1924 v E; 1926 v W (2)

Collier, W. (Raith R), 1922 v W (1)

Collins, J. (Hibernian), 1988 v S.Ar; 1990 v EG, Pol (sub), Ma (sub); (with Celtic), 1991 v Sw (sub), Bul (sub); 1992 v Ni (sub), Fi; 1993 v P, Ma, G, P, Es (2); 1994 v Sw, Ho (sub), A, Ho; 1995 v Fi, Fa, Ru, Gr, Ru, Sm, Fa; 1996 v Gr, Fi, Se, Sm, Aus, D, US (sub), Co, Ho, E, Sw; (with Monaco), 1997 v A, La, Se, Es, A, Se, Ma; 1998 v Bl, La, F, Fi, Co, US, Br, N, Mor; (with Everton), 1999 v Li; 2000 v Bos, Es, Bos, E (2) (58)

Collins, R. Y. (Celtic), 1951 v W, Ni, A; 1955 v Y, A, H; 1956 v Ni, W; 1957 v E, W, Sp (2), Sw, WG; 1958 v Ni, W, Sw, H, Pol, Y, F, Par; (with Everton), 1959 v E, W, Ni, WG, Ho, P; (with Leeds U), 1965 v E, Pol, Sp (31)

Collins, T. (Hearts), 1909 v W (1)

Colman, D. (Aberdeen), 1911 v E, W, Ni; 1913 v Ni (4)

Colquhoun, E. P. (Sheffield U), 1972 v P, Ho, Pe, Y, Cz, Br; 1973 v D (2), E (9)

Colquhoun, J. (Hearts), 1988 v S.Ar (sub), Ma (sub) (1)

Combe, J. R. (Hibernian), 1948 v E, Bel, Sw (3)

Conn, A. (Hearts), 1956 v A (1)

Conn, A. (Tottenham H), 1975 v Ni (sub), E (2)

Connachan, E. D. (Dunfermline Ath), 1962 v Cz, U (2)

Connelly, G. (Celtic), 1974 v Cz, WG (2)

Connolly, J. (Everton), 1973 v Sw (1)

Connor, J. (Airdrieonians), 1886 v Ni (1)

Connor, J. (Sunderland), 1930 v F; 1932 v Ni; 1934 v E; 1935 v Ni (4)

Connor, R. (Dundee), 1986 v Ho; (with Aberdeen), 1988 v S.Ar (sub); 1989 v E; 1991 v R (4)

Cook, W. L. (Bolton W), 1934 v E; 1935 v W, Ni (3)

Cooke, C. (Dundee), 1966 v W, I; (with Chelsea), P, Br; 1968 v E, Ho; 1969 v W, Ni, A, WG (sub), Cy (2); 1970 v A; 1971 v Bel; 1975 v Sp, P (16)

Cooper, D. (Rangers), 1980 v Pe, A (sub); 1984 v W, E; 1985 v Y, Ic, Sp (2), W; 1986 v W (sub), EG, Aus (2), Ho, WG (sub), U (sub); 1987 v Bul, L, Ei, Br; (with Motherwell), 1990 v N, Eg (22)

Cormack, P. B. (Hibernian), 1966 v Br; 1969 v D (sub); 1970 v Ei, WG; (with Nottingham F), 1971 v D (sub), W, P, E; 1972 v Ho (sub) (9)

Cowan, J. (Aston Villa), 1896 v E; 1897 v E; 1898 v E (3)

Cowan, J. (Morton), 1948 v Bel, Sw; F; 1949 v E, W, F; 1950 v E, W, Ni, Sw, P, F; 1951 v E, W, Ni, A (2), D, F, Bel; 1952 v Ni, W, USA, D, Se (25)

Cowan, W. D. (Newcastle U), 1924 v E (1)

Cowie, D. (Dundee), 1953 v E, Se; 1954 v Ni, W, Fi, N, A, U; 1955 v W, Ni, A, H; 1956 v W, A; 1957 v Ni, W; 1958 v H, Pol, Y, Par (20)

Cox, C. J. (Hearts), 1948 v F (1)

Cox, S. (Rangers), 1949 v E, F; 1950 v E, F, W, Ni, Sw, P; 1951 v E, D, F, Bel, A; 1952 v Ni, W, USA, D, Se; 1953 v Ni, E; 1954 v W, Ni, E (24)

Craig, A. (Motherwell), 1929 v N, Ho; 1932 v E (3)

Craig, J. (Celtic), 1977 v Se (sub) (1)

Craig, J. P. (Celtic), 1968 v W (1)

Craig, T. (Rangers), 1927 v Ni; 1928 v Ni; 1929 v N, G, Ho; 1930 v Ni, E, W (8)

Craig, T. B. (Newcastle U), 1976 v Sw (1)

Crainey, S. (Celtic), 2002 v F, Ng (2)

Crapnell, J. (Airdrieonians), 1929 v E, N, G; 1930 v F; 1931 v Ni, Sw; 1932 v E, F; 1933 v Ni (9)

Crawford, D. (St Mirren), 1894 v W, Ni; 1900 v W (3)

Crawford, J. (Queen's Park), 1932 v F, Ni; 1933 v E, W, Ni (5)

Crawford, S. (Raith R), 1995 v Ec (sub); (with Dunfermline Ath), 2001 v Pol (sub); 2002 v F (3)

Crerand, P. T. (Celtic), 1961 v Ei (2), Cz; 1962 v Ni, W, E, Cz (2), U; 1963 v W, Ni; (with Manchester U), 1964 v Ni; 1965 v E, Pol, Fi; 1966 v Pol (16)

Cringan, W. (Celtic), 1920 v W; 1922 v E, Ni; 1923 v W, E (5)

Crosbie, J. A. (Ayr U), 1920 v W; (with Birmingham), 1922 v E (2)

Croal, J. A. (Falkirk), 1913 v Ni; 1914 v E, W (3)

Cropley, A. J. (Hibernian), 1972 v P, Bel (2)

Cross, J. H. (Third Lanark), 1903 v Ni (1)

Cruickshank, J. (Hearts), 1964 v WG; 1970 v W, E; 1971 v D, Bel; 1976 v R (6)

Crum, J. (Celtic), 1936 v E; 1939 v Ni (2)

Cullen, M. J. (Luton T), 1956 v A (1)

Cumming, D. S. (Middlesbrough), 1938 v E (1)

Cumming, J. (Hearts), 1955 v E, H, P, Y; 1960 v E, Pol, A, H, T (9)

Cummings, G. (Partick T), 1935 v E; 1936 v W, Ni; (with Aston Villa), E; 1937 v G; 1938 v W, Ni, Cz; 1939 v E (9)

Cummings, W. (Chelsea), 2002 v Hk (sub) (1)

Cunningham, A. N. (Rangers), 1920 v Ni; 1921 v W, E; 1922 v Ni; 1923 v E, W; 1924 v Ni; 1926 v E, Ni; 1927 v E, W (12)

Cunningham, W. C. (Preston NE), 1954 v N (2), U, Fi, A; 1955 v W, E, H (8)

Curran, H. P. (Wolverhampton W), 1970 v A; 1971 v Ni, E, D, USSR (sub) (5)

Dailly, C. (Derby Co), 1997 v W, Ma, Bl; 1998 v Bl, La, F, D, Fi, Co, US, Br, N, Mor; (with Blackburn R), 1999 v Li; 2000 v Bos (sub), Es, Bos, Li, E (2), F, Ho, Ei; 2001 v La, Sm, Aus; (with West Ham U), Pol; 2002 v Cro, Bel, La, F, Ng, Sk, S.Af, Hk (35)

Dalglish, K. (Celtic), 1972 v Bel (sub), Ho; 1973 v D (1+1 sub), E (2), W, Ni, Sw, Br; 1974 v Cz (2), WG (2), Ni, W, E, Bel, N (sub), Z, Br, Y; 1975 v EG, Sp (sub+1), Se, P, W, Ni, E, R; 1976 v D (2), R, Sw, Ni, E; 1977 v Fi, Cz, W (2), Se, Ni, E, Ch, Arg, Br; (with Liverpool), 1978 v EG, Cz, W, Bul, Ni (sub), W, E, Pe, Ir, Ho; 1979 v A, N, P, W, Ni, E, Arg, N; 1980 v Pe, A, Bel (2), P, Ni, W, E, Pol, H; 1981 v Se, P, Is; 1982 v Se, Ni, P (sub), Sp, Ho, Ni, W, E, Nz, Br (sub); 1983 v Bel, Sw; 1984 v U, Bel, EG; 1985 v Y, Ic, Sp, W; 1986 v EG, Aus, R; 1987 v Bul (sub), L (102)

Davidson, C. I. (Blackburn R), 1999 v Li (sub), Es, Fa, CzR, G, Fa, CzR; 2000 v Es, Bos, Li, E, F; (with Leicester C), 2001 v La, Pol; 2002 v La (15)

Davidson, D. (Queen's Park), 1878 v W; 1879 v W; 1880 v W; 1881 v E, W (5)

Davidson, J. A. (Partick T), 1954 v N (2), A, U; 1955 v W, Ni, E, H (8)

Davidson, S. (Middlesbrough), 1921 v E (1)

Dawson, A. (Rangers), 1980 v Pol (sub), H; 1983 v Ni, Ca (2) (5)

Dawson, J. (Rangers), 1935 v Ni; 1936 v E; 1937 v G, E, W, Ni, A, Cz; 1938 v W, Ho, Ni; 1939 v E, Ni, H (14)

Deans, J. (Celtic), 1975 v EG, Sp (2)

Delaney, J. (Celtic), 1936 v W, Ni; 1937 v G, E, A, Cz; 1938 v Ni; 1939 v W, Ni; (with Manchester U), 1947 v E; 1948 v E, W, Ni (13)

Divine, A. (Falkirk), 1910 v W (1)

Dewar, G. (Dumbarton), 1888 v Ni; 1889 v E (2)

Dewar, N. (Third Lanark), 1932 v E, F; 1933 v W (3)

Dick, J. (West Ham U), 1959 v E (1)

Dickie, M. (Rangers), 1897 v Ni; 1899 v Ni; 1900 v W (3)

Dickov, P. (Manchester C), 2001 v Sm (sub), Cro (sub), Aus (sub) (3)

Dickson, W. (Dumbarton), 1888 v Ni (1)

Dickson, W. (Kilmarnock), 1970 v Ni, W, E; 1971 v D, USSR (5)

Divers, J. (Celtic), 1895 v W (1)

Divers, J. (Celtic), 1939 v Ni (1)

Dobie, R. S. (WBA), 2002 v Sk, S.Af, Hk (sub) (3)

Docherty, T. H. (Preston NE), 1952 v W; 1953 v E, Se; 1954 v N (2), A, U; 1955 v W, E, H (2), A; 1957 v E, Y, Sp (2), Sw, WG; 1958 v Ni, W, E, Sw; (with Arsenal), 1959 v W, E, Ni (25)

Dodds, D. (Dundee U), 1984 v U (sub), Ni (2)

Dodds, J. (Celtic), 1914 v E, W, Ni (3)

Dodds, W. (Aberdeen), 1997 v La (sub), W, Bl (sub); 1998 v Bl (sub); (with Dundee U), 1999 v Es (sub), Fa, G, Fa, CzR; 2000 v Bos, Es, Bos, Li (sub), E (2); (with Rangers), F, Ho, Ei; 2001 v La, Sm, Aus, Bel, Sm, Pol; 2002 v Cro (sub), Bel (26)

Doig, J. E. (Arbroath), 1887 v Ni; 1889 v Ni; (with Sunderland), 1896 v E; 1899 v E; 1903 v E (5)

Donachie, W. (Manchester C), 1972 v Pe, Ni, E, Y, Cz, Br; 1973 v D, E, W, Ni; 1974 v Ni; 1976 v R, Ni, W, E; 1977 v Fi, Cz, W (2), Se, Ni, E, Ch, Arg, Br; 1978 v EG, W, Bul, W, E, Ir, Ho; 1979 v A, N, P (sub) (35)

Donaldson, A. (Bolton W), 1914 v E, Ni, W; 1920 v E, Ni; 1922 v Ni (6)

Donnachie, J. (Oldham Ath), 1913 v E; 1914 v E, Ni (3)

Donnelly, S. (Celtic), 1997 v W (sub), Ma (sub); 1998 v La (sub), F (sub), D (sub), Fi (sub), Co (sub), US (sub); 1999 v Es (sub), Fa (10)

Dougall, C. (Birmingham C), 1947 v W (1)

Dougall, J. (Preston NE), 1939 v E (1)

Dougan, R. (Hearts), 1950 v Sw (1)

Douglas, A. (Chelsea), 1911 v Ni (1)

Douglas, J. (Renfrew), 1880 v W (1)

Douglas, R. (Celtic), 2002 v Ng, S.Af, Hk (3)

Dowds, P. (Celtic), 1892 v Ni (1)

Downie, R. (Third Lanark), 1892 v W (1)

Doyle, D. (Celtic), 1892 v E; 1893 v W; 1894 v E; 1895 v E, Ni; 1897 v E; 1898 v E, Ni (8)

Doyle, J. (Ayr U), 1976 v R (1)

Drummond, J. (Falkirk), 1892 v Ni; (with Rangers), 1894 v Ni; 1895 v Ni; E; 1896 v E, Ni; 1897 v Ni; 1898 v E; 1900 v E; 1901 v E; 1902 v E, W, Ni; 1903 v Ni (14)

Dunbar, M. (Cartvale), 1886 v Ni (1)

Duncan, A. (Hibernian), 1975 v P (sub), W, Ni, E, R; 1976 v D (sub) (6)

Duncan, D. (Derby Co), 1933 v E, W; 1934 v A, W; 1935 v E, W; 1936 v E, W, Ni; 1937 v G, E, W, Ni; 1938 v W (14)

Duncan, D. M. (East Fife), 1948 v Bel, Sw, F (3)

Duncan, J. (Alexandra Ath), 1878 v W; 1882 v W (2)

Duncan, J. (Leicester C), 1926 v W (1)

Duncanson, J. (Rangers), 1947 v Ni (1)

Dunlop, J. (St Mirren), 1890 v W (1)

Dunlop, W. (Liverpool), 1906 v E (1)

Dunn, J. (Hibernian), 1925 v W, Ni; 1927 v Ni; 1928 v Ni, E; (with Everton), 1929 v W (6)

Durie, G. S. (Chelsea), 1988 v Bul (sub); 1989 v I (sub), Cy; 1990 v Y, EG, Eg, Se; 1991 v Sw (sub), Bul (2), USSR (sub), Sm; (with Tottenham H), 1992 v Sw, R, Sm, Ni (sub), Fi, Ca, N (sub), Ho, G; 1993 v Sw, I; 1994 v Sw, I; (with Rangers), Ho (2); 1996 v US, Ho, E, Sw; 1997 v A (sub), Se (sub), Ma (sub), Bl; 1998 v Bl, La, F, Fi (sub), Co, Br, N, Mor (43)

Durrant, I. (Rangers), 1988 v H, Bel, Ma, Sp; 1989 v N (sub); 1993 v Sw (sub), P (sub), I, P (sub); 1994 v I (sub), Ma; (with Kilmarnock), 1999 v Es, Fa (sub), G, Fa, CzR; 2000 v Bos (sub), Es, Ho (sub), Ei (sub) (20)

Dykes, J. (Hearts), 1938 v Ho; 1939 v Ni (2)

Easson, J. F. (Portsmouth), 1931 v A, Sw; 1934 v W (3)

Elliott, M. S. (Leicester C), 1998 v F (sub), D, Fi; 1999 v Li, Fa, CzR, Fa; 2000 v Ho, Ei; 2001 v La, Sm, Cro, Aus (sub), Bel, Sm; 2002 v Cro, Bel, La (18)

Ellis, J. (Mossend Swifts), 1892 v Ni (1)

Evans, A. (Aston Villa), 1982 v Ho, Ni, E, Nz (4)

Evans, R. (Celtic), 1949 v E, W, Ni, F; 1950 v W, Ni, Sw, P; 1951 v E, A; 1952 v Ni; 1953 v Se; 1954 v Ni, W, E, N, Fi; 1955 v Ni, P, Y, A, H; 1956 v E, Ni, W, A; 1957 v WG, Sp; 1958 v Ni, W, E, Sw, H, Pol, Y, Par, F; 1959 v E, WG, Ho, P; 1960 v E, Ni, W, Pol; (with Chelsea), 1960 v A, H, T (48)

Ewart, J. (Bradford C), 1921 v E (1)

Ewing, T. (Partick T), 1958 v W, E (2)

Farm, G. N. (Blackpool), 1953 v W, Ni, E, Se; 1954 v Ni, W, E; 1959 v WG, Ho, P (10)

Ferguson, B. (Rangers), 1999 v Li; 2000 v Bos, Es (sub), E (2), F, Ei; 2001 v La, Aus, Bel (10)

Ferguson, D. (Rangers), 1988 v Ma, Co (sub) (2)

Ferguson, D. (Dundee U), 1992 v US (sub), Ca, Ho (sub); 1993 v G; (with Everton) 1995 v Gr; 1997 v A, Es (7)

Ferguson, I. (Rangers), 1989 v I, Cy (sub), F; 1993 v Ma (sub), Es; 1994 v Ma, A (sub), Ho (sub); 1997 v Es (sub) (9)

Ferguson, J. (Vale of Leven), 1874 v E; 1876 v E, W; 1877 v E, W; 1878 v W (6)

Ferguson, R. (Kilmarnock), 1966 v W, E, Ho, P, Br; 1967 v W, Ni (7)

Fernie, W. (Celtic), 1954 v Fi, A, U; 1955 v W, Ni; 1957 v E, Ni, W, Y; 1958 v W, Sw, Par (12)

Findlay, R. (Kilmarnock), 1898 v W (1)

Fitchie, T. T. (Woolwich Arsenal), 1905 v W; 1906 v W, Ni; (with Queen's Park), 1907 v W (4)

Flavell, R. (Airdrieonians), 1947 v Bel, L (2)

Fleck, R. (Norwich C), 1990 v Arg, Se, Br (sub); 1991 v USSR (4)

Fleming, C. (East Fife), 1954 v Ni (1)

Fleming, J. W. (Rangers), 1929 v G, Ho; 1930 v E (3)

Fleming, R. (Morton), 1886 v Ni (1)

Forbes, A. R. (Sheffield U), 1947 v Bel, L, E; 1948 v W, Ni; (with Arsenal), 1950 v E, P, F; 1951 v W, Ni, A; 1952 v W, D, Se (14)

Forbes, J. (Vale of Leven), 1884 v E, N; 1887 v W, E (5)

Ford, D. (Hearts), 1974 v Cz (sub), WG (sub), W (3)

Forrest, J. (Rangers), 1966 v W, I; (with Aberdeen), 1971 v Bel (sub), D, USSR (5)

Forrest, J. (Motherwell), 1958 v E (1)

Forsyth, A. (Partick T), 1972 v Y, Cz, Br; 1973 v D; (with Manchester U), E; 1975 v Sp, Ni (sub), R, EG; 1976 v D (10)

Forsyth, C. (Kilmarnock), 1964 v E; 1965 v W, Ni, Fi (4)

Forsyth, T. (Motherwell), 1971 v D; (with Rangers), 1974 v Cz; 1976 v Sw, Ni, W; 1977 v Fi, Se, W, Ni, E, Ch, Arg, Br; 1978 v Cz, W, Ni, W (sub), E, Pe, Ir (sub), Ho (22)

Foyers, R. (St Bernards), 1893 v W; 1894 v W (2)

Fraser, D. M. (WBA), 1968 v Ho; 1969 v Cy (2)

Fraser, J. (Moffat), 1891 v Ni (1)

Fraser, M. J. E. (Queen's Park), 1880 v W; 1882 v W, E; 1883 v W, E (5)

Fraser, J. (Dundee), 1907 v Ni (1)

Fraser, W. (Sunderland), 1955 v W, Ni (2)

Freedman, D. A. (C Palace), 2002 v La, F (2)

Fulton, W. (Abercorn), 1884 v Ni (1)

Fyfe, J. H. (Third Lanark), 1895 v W (1)

Gabriel, J. (Everton), 1961 v W; 1964 v N (sub) (2)

Gallacher, J. (Airdrieonians), 1924 v Ni; 1925 v E, W, Ni; 1926 v W; (with Newcastle U), 1926 v E, Ni; 1927 v E, W, Ni; 1928 v E, W; 1929 v E, W, Ni; 1930 v W, Ni, F; (with Chelsea), 1934 v E; (with Derby Co), 1935 v E (20)

Gallacher, K. W. (Dundee U), 1988 v Co, E (sub); 1989 v N, I; (with Coventry C), 1991 v Sm; 1992 v R (sub), Sm (sub), Ni (sub), N (sub), Ho (sub), G (sub), C; 1993 v Sw (sub), P; (with Blackburn R), P, Es (2); 1994 v I, Ma; 1996 v Aus (sub), D, Co (sub), Ho; 1997 v Se (sub), Es (2), A, Se, W, Ma, Bl; 1998 v Bl, La, F, Fi (sub), US, Br, N, Mor; 1999 v Li, Es, Fa, CzR; 2000 v Bos (sub); (with Newcastle U), Bos, Li (sub), E, F, Ei (sub); 2001 v Sm, Cro, Bel (sub), Sm (sub) (53)

Gallacher, P. (Sunderland), 1935 v Ni (1)

Gallacher, P. (Dundee U), 2002 v Hk (sub) (1)

Galloway, M. (Celtic), 1992 v R (1)

Galt, J. H. (Rangers), 1908 v W, Ni (2)

Gardiner, I. (Motherwell), 1958 v W (1)

Gardner, D. R. (Third Lanark), 1897 v W (1)

Gardner, R. (Queen's Park), 1872 v E; 1873 v E; (with Clydesdale), 1874 v E; 1875 v E; 1878 v E (5)

Gemmell, T. (St Mirren), 1955 v P, Y (2)

Gemmell, T. (Celtic), 1966 v E; 1967 v W, Ni, E, USSR; 1968 v Ni, E; 1969 v W, Ni, E, D, A, WG, Cy; 1970 v E, Ei, WG; 1971 v Bel (18)

Gemmill, A. (Derby Co), 1971 v Bel; 1972 v P, Ho, Pe, Ni, W, E; 1976 v D, R, Ni, W, E; 1977 v Fi, Cz, W (2), Ni (sub), E (sub), Ch (sub), Arg, Br; 1978 v EG (sub); (with Nottingham F), Bul, Ni, W, E (sub), Pe (sub), Ir, Ho; 1979 v A, N, P, N; (with Birmingham C), 1980 v A, P, Ni, W, E, H; 1981 v Se, P, Is, Ni (43)

Gemmill, S. (Nottingham F), 1995 v J, Ec, Fa (sub); 1996 v Sm, D (sub), US; 1997 v Es, Se (sub), W, Ma (sub), Bl (sub); 1998 v D, Fi; (with Everton), 1999 v G, Fa (sub); 2001 v Sm (sub), Pol (sub); 2002 v Cro (sub), F (sub), Ng, Sk, S.Af, Hk (23)

Gibb, W. (Clydesdale), 1873 v E (1)

Gibson, D. W. (Leicester C), 1963 v A, N, Ei, Sp; 1964 v Ni; 1965 v W, Fi (7)

Gibson, J. D. (Partick T), 1926 v E; 1927 v E, W, Ni; (with Aston Villa), 1928 v E, W; 1930 v W, Ni (8)

Gibson, N. (Rangers), 1895 v E, Ni; 1896 v E, Ni; 1897 v E, Ni; 1898 v E; 1899 v E, W, Ni; 1900 v E, Ni; 1901 v W; (with Partick T), 1905 v Ni (14)

Gilchrist, J. E. (Celtic), 1922 v E (1)

Gilhooley, M. (Hull C), 1922 v W (1)

Gillespie, G. (Rangers), 1880 v W; 1881 v E, W; 1882 v E; (with Queen's Park), 1886 v W; 1890 v W; 1891 v Ni (7)

Gillespie, G. T. (Liverpool), 1988 v Bel, Bul, Sp; 1989 v N, F, Ch; 1990 v Y, EG, Eg, Pol, Ma, Br (sub); 1991 v Bul (13)

Gillespie, Jas (Third Lanark), 1898 v W (1)

Gillespie, John (Queen's Park), 1896 v W (1)

Gillespie, R. (Queen's Park), 1927 v W; 1931 v W; 1932 v F; 1933 v E (4)

Gillick, T. (Everton), 1937 v A, Cz; 1939 v W, Ni, H (5)

Gilmour, J. (Dundee), 1931 v W (1)

Gilzean, A. J. (Dundee), 1964 v W, E, N, WG; 1965 v Ni, (with Tottenham H), Sp; 1966 v Ni, W, Pol, I; 1968 v W; 1969 v W, E, WG, Cy (2), A (sub); 1970 v Ni, E (sub), WG, A; 1971 v P (22)

Glass, S. (Newcastle U), 1999 v Fa (sub) (1)

Glavin, R. (Celtic), 1977 v Se (1)

Glen, A. (Aberdeen), 1956 v E, Ni (2)

Glen, R. (Renton), 1895 v W; 1896 v W; (with Hibernian), 1900 v Ni (3)

Goram, A. L. (Oldham Ath), 1986 v EG (sub), R, Ho; 1987 v Br; (with Hibernian) 1989 v Y, I; 1990 v EG, Pol, Ma; 1991 v R, Sw, Bul (2), USSR, Sm; (with Rangers), 1992 v Sw, R, Sm, Fi, N, Ho, G, C; 1993 v Sw, P, I, Ma, P; 1994 v Ho; 1995 v Fi, Fa, Ru, Gr; 1996 v Se (sub), D (sub), Co, Ho, E, Sw; 1997 v A, La, Es; 1998 v D (sub) (43)

Gordon, J. E. (Rangers), 1912 v E, Ni; 1913 v E, Ni, W; 1914 v E, Ni; 1920 v W, E, Ni (10)

Gossland, J. (Rangers), 1884 v Ni (1)

Goudie, J. (Abercorn), 1884 v Ni (1)

Gough, C. R. (Dundee U), 1983 v Sw, Ni, W, E, Ca (3); 1984 v U, Bel, EG, Ni, W, E, F; 1985 v Sp, E, Ic; 1986 v W, EG, Aus, Is, R, E, D, WG, U; (with Tottenham H), 1987 v Bul, L, Ei (2), Bel, E, Br; 1988 v H; (with Rangers), S.Ar, Sp, Co, E; 1989 v Y, I, Cy, F, Cy; 1990 v F, Arg, EG, Eg, Pol, Ma, Cr; 1991 v USSR, Bul; 1992 v Sm, Ni, Ca, N, Ho, G, C; 1993 v Sw, P (61)

Gould, J. (Celtic), 2000 v Li; 2001 v Aus (2)

Gourlay, J. (Cambuslang), 1886 v Ni; 1888 v W (2)

Govan, J. (Hibernian), 1948 v E, W, Bel, Sw, F; 1949 v Ni (6)

Gow, D. R. (Rangers), 1888 v E (1)

Gow, J. J. (Queen's Park), 1885 v E (1)

Gow, J. R. (Rangers), 1888 v Ni (1)

Graham, A. (Leeds U), 1978 v EG (sub); 1979 v A (sub), N, W, Ni, E, Arg, N; 1980 v A; 1981 v W (10)

Graham, G. (Arsenal), 1972 v P, Ho, Ni, Y, Cz, Br; 1973 v D (2); (with Manchester U), E, W, Ni, Br (sub) (12)

Graham, J. (Annbank), 1884 v Ni (1)

Graham, J. A. (Arsenal), 1921 v Ni (1)

Grant, J. (Hibernian), 1959 v W, Ni (2)

Grant, P. (Celtic), 1989 v E (sub), Ch (2)

Gray, A. (Hibernian), 1903 v Ni (1)

Gray, A. M. (Aston Villa), 1976 v R, Sw; 1977 v Fi, Cz; 1979 v A, N; (with Wolverhampton W), 1980 v P, E (sub); 1981 v Se, P, Is (sub), Ni; 1982 v Se (sub), Ni; 1983 v Ni, W, E, Ca (1+1 sub); (with Everton), 1985 v Ic (20)

Gray, D. (Rangers), 1929 v W, Ni, G, Ho; 1930 v W, E, Ni; 1931 v W; 1933 v W, Ni (10)

Gray, E. (Leeds U), 1969 v E, Cy; 1970 v WG, A; 1971 v W, Ni; 1972 v Bel, Ho; 1976 v W, E; 1977 v Fi, W (12)

Gray, F. T. (Leeds U), 1976 v Sw; 1979 v N, P, W, Ni, E, Arg (sub); (with Nottingham F), 1980 v Bel (sub); 1981 v Se, P, Is, Ni, Is, W; (with Leeds U), Ni, E; 1982 v Se, P, Sp, Ho, W, Nz, Br, USSR; 1983 v EG, Sw, Bel, Sw, W, E, Ca (32)

Gray, W. (Pollokshields Ath), 1886 v E (1)

Green, A. (Blackpool), 1971 v Bel (sub), P (sub), Ni, E; (with Newcastle U), 1972 v W, E (sub) (6)

Greig, J. (Rangers), 1964 v E, WG; 1965 v W, Ni, E, Fi (2), Sp, Pol; 1966 v Ni, W, E, Pol, I (2), P, Ho, Br; 1967 v W, Ni, E; 1968 v Ni, W, E, Ho; 1969 v W, Ni, E, D, A, WG, Cy (2); 1970 v W, E, Ei, WG, A; 1971 v D, Bel, W (sub), Ni, E; 1976 v D (44)

Groves, W. (Hibernian), 1888 v W; (with Celtic), 1889 v Ni; 1890 v E (3)

Guilliland, W. (Queen's Park), 1891 v W; 1892 v Ni; 1894 v E; 1895 v E (4)

Gunn, B. (Norwich C), 1990 v Eg; 1993 v Es (2); 1994 v Sw, I, Ho (sub) (6)

Haddock, H. (Clyde), 1955 v E, H (2), P, Y; 1958 v E (6)
Haddow, D. (Rangers), 1894 v E (1)
Haffey, F. (Celtic), 1960 v E; 1961 v E (2)
Hamilton, A. (Queen's Park), 1885 v E, W; 1886 v E; 1888 v E (4)
Hamilton, A. W. (Dundee), 1962 v Cz, U, W, E; 1963 v W, Ni, E, A, N, Ei; 1964 v Ni, W, E, N, WG; 1965 v Ni, W, E, Fi (2), Pol, Sp; 1966 v Pol, Ni (24)
Hamilton, G. (Aberdeen), 1947 v Ni; 1951 v Bel, A; 1954 v N (2) (5)
Hamilton, G. (Port Glasgow Ath), 1906 v Ni (1)
Hamilton, J. (Queen's Park), 1892 v W; 1893 v E, Ni (3)
Hamilton, J. (St Mirren), 1924 v Ni (1)
Hamilton, R. C. (Rangers), 1899 v E, W, Ni; 1900 v W; 1901 v E, Ni; 1902 v W, Ni; 1903 v E; 1904 v Ni; (with Dundee), 1911 v W (11)
Hamilton, T. (Hurlford), 1891 v Ni (1)
Hamilton, T. (Rangers), 1932 v E (1)
Hamilton, W. M. (Hibernian), 1965 v Fi (1)
Hannah, A. B. (Renton), 1888 v W (1)
Hannah, J. (Third Lanark), 1889 v W (1)
Hansen, A. D. (Liverpool), 1979 v W, Arg; 1980 v Bel, P; 1981 v Se, P, Is; 1982 v Se, Ni, P, Sp, Ni (sub), W, E, Nz, Br, USSR; 1983 v EG, Sw, Bel, Sw; 1985 v W (sub); 1986 v R (sub); 1987 v Ei (2), L (26)
Hansen, J. (Partick T), 1972 v Bel (sub), Y (sub) (2)
Harkness, J. D. (Queen's Park), 1927 v E, Ni; 1928 v E; (with Hearts), 1929 v W, E, Ni; 1930 v E, W; 1932 v W, F; 1934 v Ni, W (12)
Harper, J. M. (Aberdeen), 1973 v D (1+1 sub); (with Hibernian), 1976 v D; (with Aberdeen), 1978 v Ir (sub) (4)
Harper, W. (Hibernian), 1923 v E, Ni, W; 1924 v E, Ni, W; 1925 v E, Ni, W; (with Arsenal), 1926 v E, Ni (11)
Harris, J. (Partick T), 1921 v W, Ni (2)
Harris, N. (Newcastle U), 1924 v E (1)
Harrower, W. (Queen's Park), 1882 v E; 1884 v Ni; 1886 v W (3)
Hartford, R. A. (WBA), 1972 v Pe, W (sub), E, Y, Cz, Br; (with Manchester C), 1976 v D, R, Ni (sub); 1977 v Cz (sub), W (sub), Se, W, Ni, E, Ch, Arg, Br; 1978 v EG, Cz, W, Bul, W, E, Pe, Ir, Ho; 1979 v A, N, P, W, Ni, E, Arg, N; (with Everton), 1980 v Pe, Bel; 1981 v Ni (sub); Is, W, Ni, E; 1982 v Se; (with Manchester C), Ni, P, Sp, Ni, W, E, Br (50)
Harvey, D. (Leeds U), 1973 v D; 1974 v Cz, WG, Ni, W, E, Bel, Z, Br, Y; 1975 v EG, Sp (2); 1976 v D (2); 1977 v Fi (sub) (16)
Hastings, A. C. (Sunderland), 1936 v Ni; 1938 v Ni (2)
Haughney, M. (Celtic), 1954 v E (1)
Hay, D. (Celtic), 1970 v Ni, W, E; 1971 v D, Bel, W, P, Ni; 1972 v P, Bel, Ho; 1973 v W, Ni, E, Sw, Br; 1974 v Cz (2), WG, Ni, W, E, Bel, N, Z, Br, Y (27)
Hay, J. (Celtic), 1905 v Ni; 1909 v Ni; 1910 v W, Ni, E; 1911 v Ni, E; (with Newcastle U), 1912 v E, W; 1914 v E, Ni (11)
Hegarty, P. (Dundee U), 1979 v W, Ni, E, Arg, N (sub); 1980 v W, E; 1983 v Ni (8)
Heggie, C. (Rangers), 1886 v Ni (1)
Henderson, G. H. (Rangers), 1904 v Ni (1)
Henderson, J. G. (Portsmouth), 1953 v Se; 1954 v Ni, E, N; 1956 v W; (with Arsenal), 1959 v W, Ni (7)
Henderson, W. (Rangers), 1963 v W, Ni, E, A, N, Ei, Sp; 1964 v W, Ni, E, N, WG; 1965 v Fi, Pol, E, Sp; 1966 v Ni, W, Pol, I, Ho; 1967 v W, Ni; 1968 v Ho; 1969 v Ni, E, Cy; 1970 v Ei; 1971 v P (29)
Hendry, E. C. J. (Blackburn R), 1993 v Es (2); 1994 v Ma, Ho, A, Ho; 1995 v Fi, Fa, Gr, Ru, Sm; 1996 v Fi, Se, Sm, Aus, D, US, Co, Ho, E, Sw; 1997 v A, Se, Es (2), A, Se; 1998 v La, D, Fi, Co, US, Br, N, Mor; (with Rangers), 1999 v Li, Es, Fa, G; 2000 v Bos, Es, Bos, E (2); (with Coventry C), F; 2001 v La, Sm, Cro, Aus (sub); (with Bolton W), Bel, Sm (51)
Hepburn, J. (Alloa Ath), 1891 v W (1)
Hepburn, R. (Ayr U), 1932 v Ni (1)
Herd, A. C. (Hearts), 1935 v Ni (1)
Herd, D. G. (Arsenal), 1959 v E, W, Ni; 1961 v Ei, Cz (5)
Herd, G. (Clyde), 1958 v E; 1960 v H, T; 1961 v W, Ni (5)

Herriot, J. (Birmingham C), 1969 v Ni, E, D, Cy (2), W (sub); 1970 v Ei (sub), WG (8)
Hewie, J. D. (Charlton Ath), 1956 v E, A; 1957 v E, Ni, W, Y, Sp (2), Sw, WG; 1958 v H, Pol, Y, F; 1959 v Ho, P; 1960 v Ni, W, Pol (19)
Higgins, A. (Kilmarnock), 1885 v Ni (1)
Higgins, A. (Newcastle U), 1910 v E, Ni; 1911 v E, Ni (4)
Highet, T. C. (Queen's Park), 1875 v E; 1876 v E, W; 1878 v E (4)
Hill, D. (Rangers), 1881 v E, W; 1882 v W (3)
Hill, D. A. (Third Lanark), 1906 v Ni (1)
Hill, F. R. (Aberdeen), 1930 v F; 1931 v W, Ni (3)
Hill, J. (Hearts), 1891 v E; 1892 v W (2)
Hogg, G (Hearts), 1896 v E, Ni (2)
Hogg, J. (Ayr U), 1922 v Ni (1)
Hogg, R. M. (Celtic), 1937 v Cz (1)
Holm, A. H. (Queen's Park), 1882 v W; 1883 v E, W (3)
Holt, D. D. (Hearts), 1963 v A, N, Ei, Sp; 1964 v WG (sub) (5)
Holt, G. J. (Kilmarnock), 2001 v La (sub), Cro (sub); (with Norwich C), 2002 v F (sub) (3)
Holton, J. A. (Manchester U), 1973 v W, Ni, E, Sw, Br; 1974 v Cz, WG, Ni, W, E, N, Z, Br, Y; 1975 v EG (15)
Hope, R. (WBA), 1968 v Ho; 1969 v D (2)
Hopkin, D. (Crystal Palace), 1997 v Ma, Bl; (with Leeds U), 1998 v Bl (sub), F (sub); 1999 v CzR; 2000 v Bos (2) (7)
Houliston, W. (Queen of the South), 1949 v E, Ni, F (3)
Houston, S. M. (Manchester U), 1976 v D (1)
Howden, W. (Partick T), 1905 v Ni (1)
Howe, R. (Hamilton A), 1929 v N, Ho (2)
Howie, H. (Hibernian), 1949 v W (1)
Howie, J. (Newcastle U), 1905 v E; 1906 v Ni, E; 1908 v E (3)
Howieson, J. (St Mirren), 1927 v Ni (1)
Hughes, J. (Celtic), 1965 v Pol, Sp; 1966 v Ni, I (2); 1968 v E; 1969 v A; 1970 v Ei (8)
Hughes, W. (Sunderland), 1975 v Se (sub) (1)
Humphries, W. (Motherwell), 1952 v Se (1)
Hunter, A. (Kilmarnock), 1972 v Pe, Y; (with Celtic), 1973 v E; 1974 v Cz (4)
Hunter, J. (Dundee), 1909 v W (1)
Hunter, J. (Third Lanark), 1874 v E; (with Eastern), 1875 v E; (with Third Lanark), 1876 v E; 1877 v W (4)
Hunter, R. (St Mirren), 1890 v Ni (1)
Hunter, W. (Motherwell), 1960 v H, T; 1961 v W (3)
Husband, J. (Partick T), 1947 v W (1)
Hutchison, D. (Everton), 1999 v CzR (sub), G; 2000 v Bos, Es, Li, E (2), F, Ho, Ei; (with Sunderland), 2001 v La, Sm, Cro, Aus, Bel, Sm; (with West Ham U), 2002 v Cro, Bel, La (19)
Hutchison, T. (Coventry C), 1974 v Cz (2), WG (2), Ni, W, Bel (sub), N, Z (sub), Y (sub); 1975 v EG, Sp (2), P, E (sub), R (sub); 1976 v D (17)
Hutton, J. (Aberdeen), 1923 v E, W, Ni; 1924 v Ni; 1926 v W, E, Ni; (with Blackburn R), 1927 v Ni; 1928 v W, Ni (10)
Hutton, J. (St Bernards), 1887 v Ni (1)
Hyslop, T. (Stoke C), 1896 v E; (with Rangers), 1897 v E (2)

Imlach, J. J. S. (Nottingham F), 1958 v H, Pol, Y, F (4)
Imrie, W. N. (St Johnstone), 1929 v N, G (2)
Inglis, J. (Rangers), 1883 v E, W (2)
Inglis, J. (Kilmarnock Ath), 1884 v Ni (1)
Irons, J. H. (Queen's Park), 1900 v W (1)
Irvine, B. (Aberdeen), 1991 v R; 1993 v G, Es (2); 1994 v Sw, I, Ma, A, Ho (9)

Jackson, A. (Cambuslang), 1886 v W; 1888 v Ni (2)
Jackson, A. (Aberdeen), 1925 v E, W, Ni; (with Huddersfield T), 1926 v E, W, Ni; 1927 v W, Ni; 1928 v E, W; 1929 v E, W, Ni; 1930 v E, W, Ni, F (17)
Jackson, C. (Rangers), 1975 v Se, P (sub), W; 1976 v D, R, Ni, W, E (8)
Jackson, D. (Hibernian), 1995 v Ru, Sm, J, Ec, Fa; 1996 v Gr, Fi (sub), Se (sub), Sm (sub), Aus (sub), D (sub), US; 1997 v La, Se, Es, A, Se, W, Ma, Bl; (with Celtic), 1998 v D, Fi, Co, US, Br, N; 1999 v Li, Es (sub) (28)
Jackson, J. (Partick T), 1931 v A, I, Sw; 1933 v E; (with Chelsea), 1934 v E; 1935 v E; 1936 v W, Ni (8)
Jackson, T. A. (St Mirren), 1904 v W, E, Ni; 1905 v W; 1907 v W, Ni (6)
James, A. W. (Preston NE), 1926 v W; 1928 v E; 1929 v E, Ni; (with Arsenal), 1930 v E, W, Ni; 1933 v W (8)
Jardine, A. (Rangers), 1971 v D (sub); 1972 v P, Bel, Ho; 1973 v E, Sw, Br; 1974 v Cz (2), WG (2), Ni, W, E, Bel, N, Z, Br, Y; 1975 v EG, Sp (2), Se, P, W, Ni, E; 1977 v Se (sub), Ch (sub), Br (sub); 1978 v Cz, W, Ni, Ir; 1980 v Pe, A, Bel (2) (38)
Jarvie, A. (Airdrieonians), 1971 v P (sub), Ni (sub), E (sub) (3)
Jenkinson, T. (Hearts), 1887 v Ni (1)

Jess, E. (Aberdeen), 1993 v I (sub); Ma; 1994 v Sw (sub), I, Ho (sub), A, Ho (sub); 1995 v Fi (sub); 1996 v Se (sub), Sm; (with Coventry C), US, Co (sub), E (sub); (with Aberdeen), 1998 v D (sub); 1999 v CzR, G (sub), Fa (sub), CzR (sub) (18)

Johnston, A. (Sunderland), 1999 v Es, Fa, CzR (sub), G, Fa, CzR; 2000 v Es, F (sub), Ei (sub); (with Rangers), 2001 v Sm (sub), Cro, Sm; (with Middlesbrough), 2002 v Ng (sub), Sk, S.Af, Hk (16)

Johnston, L. H. (Clyde), 1948 v Bel, Sw (2)

Johnston, M. (Watford), 1984 v W (sub), E (sub), F; 1985 v Y; (with Celtic), Ic, Sp (2), W; 1986 v EG; 1987 Bul, Ei (2), L; (with Nantes), 1988 v H, Bel, L, S.Ar, Sp, Co, E; 1989 v N, Y, I, Cy, F, Cy, E, Ch (sub); (with Rangers), 1990 v F, N, EG, Pol, Ma, Cr, Se, Br; 1992 v Sw, Sm (sub) (38)

Johnston, R. (Sunderland), 1938 v Cz (1)

Johnston, W. (Rangers), 1966 v W, E, Pol, Ho; 1968 v W, E; 1969 v Ni (sub); 1970 v Ni; 1971 v D; (with WBA), 1977 v Se, W (sub), Ni, E, Ch, Arg, Br; 1978 v EG, Cz, W (2), E, Pe (22)

Johnstone, D. (Rangers), 1973 v W, Ni, E, Sw, Br; 1975 v EG (sub), Se (sub); 1976 v Sw, Ni (sub), E (sub); 1978 v Bul (sub), Ni, W; 1980 v Bel (14)

Johnstone, J. (Abercorn), 1888 v W (1)

Johnstone, J. (Celtic), 1965 v W, Fi; 1966 v E; 1967 v W, USSR; 1968 v W; 1969 v A, WG; 1970 v E, WG; 1971 v D, E; 1972 v P, Bel, Ho, Ni, E (sub); 1974 v W, E, Bel, N; 1975 v EG, Sp (23)

Johnstone, Jas (Kilmarnock), 1894 v W (1)

Johnstone, J. A. (Hearts), 1930 v W; 1933 v W, Ni (3)

Johnstone, R. (Hibernian), 1951 v E, D, F; 1952 v Ni, E; 1953 v E, Se; 1954 v W, E, N, Fi; 1955 v Ni, H; (with Manchester C), 1955 v E; 1956 v E, Ni, W (17)

Johnstone, W. (Third Lanark), 1887 v Ni; 1889 v W; 1890 v E (3)

Jordan, J. (Leeds U), 1973 v E (sub), Sw (sub), Br; 1974 v Cz (sub+1), WG (sub), Ni (sub), W, E, Bel, N, Z, Br, Y; 1975 v EG, Sp (2); 1976 v Ni, W, E; 1977 v Cz, W, Ni, E; 1978 v EG, Cz, W; (with Manchester U), Bul, Ni, E, Pe, Ir, Ho; 1979 v A, P, W (sub), Ni, E, N; 1980 v Bel, Ni (sub), W, E, Pol; 1981 v Is, W, E; (with AC Milan), 1982 v Se, Ho, W, E, USSR (52)

Kay, J. L. (Queen's Park), 1880 v E; 1882 v E, W; 1883 v E, W; 1884 v W (6)

Keillor, A. (Montrose), 1891 v W; 1892 v Ni; (with Dundee), 1894 v Ni; 1895 v W; 1896 v W; 1897 v W (6)

Keir, L. (Dumbarton), 1885 v W; 1886 v Ni; 1887 v E, W; 1888 v E (5)

Kelly, H. T. (Blackpool), 1952 v USA (1)

Kelly, J. (Renton), 1888 v E; (with Celtic), 1889 v E; 1890 v E; 1892 v E; 1893 v E, Ni; 1894 v W; 1896 v Ni (8)

Kelly, J. C. (Barnsley), 1949 v W, Ni (2)

Kelso, R. (Renton), 1885 v W, Ni; 1886 v W; 1887 v E, W; 1888 v E, Ni; (with Dundee), 1898 v Ni (8)

Kelso, T. (Dundee), 1914 v W (1)

Kennaway, J. (Celtic), 1934 v A (1)

Kennedy, A. (Eastern), 1875 v E; 1876 v E, W; (with Third Lanark), 1878 v E; 1882 v W; 1884 v W (6)

Kennedy, J. (Hibernian), 1897 v W (1)

Kennedy, J. (Celtic), 1964 v W, E, WG; 1965 v W, Ni, Fi (6)

Kennedy, S. (Aberdeen), 1978 v Bul, W, E, Pe, Ho; 1979 v A, P; 1982 v P (sub) (8)

Kennedy, S. (Partick T), 1905 v W (1)

Kennedy, S. (Rangers), 1975 v Se, P, W, Ni, E (5)

Ker, G. (Queen's Park), 1880 v E; 1881 v E, W; 1882 v W, E (5)

Ker, W. (Granville), 1872 v E; (with Queen's Park), 1873 v E (2)

Kerr, A. (Partick T), 1955 v A, H (2)

Kerr, P. (Hibernian), 1924 v Ni (1)

Key, G. (Hearts), 1902 v Ni (1)

Key, W. (Queen's Park), 1907 v Ni (1)

King, A. (Hearts), 1896 v E, W; (with Celtic), 1897 v Ni; 1898 v Ni; 1899 v Ni, W (6)

King, J. (Hamilton A), 1933 v Ni; 1934 v Ni (2)

King, W. S. (Queen's Park), 1929 v W (1)

Kinloch, J. D. (Partick T), 1922 v Ni (1)

Kinnaird, A. F. (Wanderers), 1873 v E (1)

Kinnear, D. (Rangers), 1938 v Cz (1)

Kyle, K. (Sunderland), 2002 v Sk (sub), S.Af, Hk (3)

Lambert, P. (Motherwell), 1995 v J, Ec (sub); (with Borussia Dortmund), 1997 v La (sub), Se (sub), A, Se, Bl; 1998 v Bl, La; (with Celtic), Fi (sub), Co, US, Br, N, Mor; 1999 v Li, CzR, G, Fa, CzR; 2000 v Bos, Li, Ho, Ei; 2001 v Bel, Sm; 2002 v Cro, Bel, F, Ng (30)

Lambie, J. A. (Queen's Park), 1886 v Ni; 1887 v Ni; 1888 v E (3)

Lambie, W. A. (Queen's Park), 1892 v Ni; 1893 v W; 1894 v E; 1895 v E, Ni; 1896 v E, Ni; 1897 v E, Ni (9)

Lamont, D. (Pilgrims), 1885 v Ni (1)

Lang, A. (Dumbarton), 1880 v W (1)

Lang, J. J. (Clydesdale), 1876 v W; (with Third Lanark), 1878 v W (2)

Latta, A. (Dumbarton), 1888 v W; 1889 v E (2)

Law, D. (Huddersfield T), 1959 v W, Ni, Ho, P; 1960 v Ni, W; (with Manchester C), 1960 v E, Pol, A; 1961 v E, Ni; (with Torino), 1962 v Cz (2), E; (with Manchester U), 1963 v W, Ni, E, A, N, Ei, Sp; 1964 v W, E, N, WG; 1965 v W, Ni, E, Fi (2), Pol, Sp; 1966 v Ni, E, Pol; 1967 v W, E, USSR; 1968 v Ni; 1969 v Ni, A, WG; 1972 v Pe, Ni, W, E, Y, Cz, Br; (with Manchester C), 1974 v Cz (2), WG (2), Ni, Z (55)

Law, G. (Rangers), 1910 v E, Ni, W (3)

Law, T. (Chelsea), 1928 v E; 1930 v E (2)

Lawrence, J. (Newcastle U), 1911 v E (1)

Lawrence, T. (Liverpool), 1963 v Ei; 1969 v W, WG (3)

Lawson, D. (St Mirren), 1923 v E (1)

Leckie, R. (Queen's Park), 1872 v E (1)

Leggat, G. (Aberdeen), 1956 v E; 1957 v W; 1958 v Ni, H, Pol, Y, Par; (with Fulham), 1959 v E, W, Ni, WG, Ho; 1960 v E, Ni, W, Pol, A, H (18)

Leighton, J. (Aberdeen), 1983 v EG, Sw, Bel, Sw, W, E, Ca (2); 1984 v U, Bel, Ni, W, E, F; 1985 v Y, Ic, Sp (2), W, E, Ic; 1986 v W, EG, Aus (2), Is, D, WG, U; 1987 v Bul, Ei (2), L, Bel, E; 1988 v H, Bel, Bul, L, S.Ar, Ma, Sp; (with Manchester U), Co, E; 1989 v N, Cy, F, Cy, E, Ch; 1990 v Y, F, N, Arg, Ma (sub), Cr, Se, Br; (with Hibernian), 1994 v Ma, A, Ho; 1995 v Gr (sub), Ru, Sm, J, Ec, Fa; 1996 v Gr, Fi, Se, Sm, Aus, D, US; 1997 v Se, Es, A, Se, W (sub), Ma, Bl; (with Aberdeen), 1998 v Bl, La, D, Fi, US, Br, N, Mor; 1999 v Li, Es (91)

Lennie, W. (Aberdeen), 1908 v W, Ni (2)

Lennox, R. (Celtic), 1967 v Ni, E, USSR; 1968 v W, L; 1969 v D, A, WG, Cy (sub); 1970 v W (sub) (10)

Leslie, L. G. (Airdrieonians), 1961 v W, Ni, Ei (2), Cz (5)

Levein, C. (Hearts), 1990 v Arg, EG, Eg (sub), Pol, Ma (sub), Se; 1992 v R, Sm; 1993 v P, G, P; 1994 v Sw, Ho (sub); 1995 v Fi, Fa, Ru (16)

Liddell, W. (Liverpool), 1947 v W, Ni; 1948 v E, W, Ni; 1950 v E, W, P, F; 1951 v W, Ni, E, A; 1952 v W, Ni, E, USA, D, Se; 1953 v W, Ni, E; 1954 v Ni, E; 1955 v P, Y, A, H; 1956 v W (28)

Liddle, D. (East Fife), 1931 v A, I, Sw (3)

Lindsay, D. (St Mirren), 1903 v Ni (1)

Lindsay, J. (Dumbarton), 1880 v W; 1881 v W, E; 1884 v W, E; 1885 v W, E; 1886 v E (8)

Lindsay, J. (Renton), 1888 v E; 1893 v E, Ni (3)

Linwood, A. B. (Clyde), 1950 v W (1)

Little, R. J. (Rangers), 1953 v Se (1)

Livingstone, G. T. (Manchester C), 1906 v E; (with Rangers), 1907 v W (2)

Lochhead, A. (Third Lanark), 1889 v W (1)

Logan, J. (Ayr U), 1891 v W (1)

Logan, T. (Falkirk), 1913 v Ni (1)

Logie, J. T. (Arsenal), 1953 v Ni (1)

Loney, W. (Celtic), 1910 v W, Ni (2)

Long, H. (Clyde), 1947 v Ni (1)

Longair, W. (Dundee), 1894 v Ni (1)

Lorimer, P. (Leeds U), 1970 v A (sub); 1971 v W, Ni; 1972 v Ni (sub), E; 1973 v D (2), E (2); 1974 v WG (sub), E, Bel, N, Z, Br, Y; 1975 v Sp (sub); 1976 v D (2), R (sub) (21)

Love, A. (Aberdeen), 1931 v A, I, Sw (3)

Low, A. (Falkirk), 1934 v Ni (1)

Low, T. P. (Rangers), 1897 v Ni (1)

Low, W. L. (Newcastle U), 1911 v E, W; 1912 v Ni; 1920 v E, Ni (5)

Lowe, J. (St Bernards), 1887 v Ni (1)

Lowe, J. (Cambuslang), 1891 v Ni (1)

Lundie, J. (Hibernian), 1886 v W (1)

Lyall, J. (Sheffield W), 1905 v W (1)

McAdam, J. (Third Lanark), 1880 v W (1)

McAllister, B. (Wimbledon), 1997 v W, Ma, Bl (sub) (3)

McAllister, G. (Leicester C), 1990 v EG, Pol, Ma (sub); (with Leeds U), 1991 v R, Sw, Bul, USSR (sub), Sm; 1992 v Sw (sub), Sm, Ni, Fi (sub), US, Ca, N, Ho, G, C; 1993 v Sw, P, I, Ma; 1994 v Sw, I, Ma, Ho, A, Ho; 1995 v Fi, Ru, Gr, Ru, Sm; 1996 v Gr, Fi, Se, Sm, Aus, D, US (sub), Co, Ho, E, Sw; (with Coventry C), 1997 v A, La, Es (2), A, Se, W, Ma, Bl; 1998 v Bl, La, F; 1999 v CzR (57)

McArthur, D. (Celtic), 1895 v E, Ni; 1899 v W (3)

McAtee, A. (Celtic), 1913 v W (1)

McAulay, J. (Arthurlie), 1884 v Ni (1)
McAulay, J. D. (Dumbarton), 1882 v W; 1883 v E, W; 1884 v E; 1885 v E, W; 1886 v E; 1887 v E, W (9)
McAuley, R. (Rangers), 1932 v Ni, W (2)
McAvennie, F. (West Ham U), 1986 v Aus (2), D (sub), WG (sub); (with Celtic), 1988 v S.Ar (5)
McBain, E. (St Mirren), 1894 v W (1)
McBain, N. (Manchester U), 1922 v E; (with Everton), 1923 v Ni; 1924 v W (3)
McBride, J. (Celtic), 1967 v W, Ni (2)
McBride, P. (Preston NE), 1904 v E; 1906 v E; 1907 v E, W; 1908 v E; 1909 v W (6)
McCall, J. (Renton), 1886 v W; 1887 v E, W; 1888 v E; 1890 v E (5)
McCall, S. M. (Everton), 1990 v Arg, EG, Eg (sub), Pol, Ma, Cr, Se, Br; 1991 v Sw, USSR, Sm; (with Rangers), 1992 v Sw, R, Sm, US, Ca, N, Ho, G, C; 1993 v Sw, P (2); 1994 v I, Ho, A (sub), Ho; 1995 v Fi (sub), Ru, Gr; 1996 v Gr, D, US (sub), Co, Ho, E, Sw; 1997 v A, La; 1998 v D (40)
McCalliog, J. (Sheffield W), 1967 v E, USSR; 1968 v Ni; 1969 v D; (with Wolverhampton W), 1971 v P (5)
McCallum, N. (Renton), 1888 v Ni (1)
McCann, N. (Hearts), 1999 v Li (sub); (with Rangers), CzR; 2000 v Bos, Es (sub), E, F (sub), Ho, Ei; 2001 v La, Sm, Aus (sub); 2002 v Cro, La, F, Ng (15)
McCann, R. J. (Motherwell), 1959 v WG; 1960 v E, Ni, W; 1961 v E (5)
McCartney, W. (Hibernian), 1902 v Ni (1)
McClair, B. (Celtic), 1987 v L, Ei, E, Br (sub); (with Manchester U), 1988 v Bul, Ma (sub), Sp (sub); 1989 v N, Y, I (sub), Cy, F (sub); 1990 v N (sub), Arg (sub); 1991 v Bul (2), Sm; 1992 v Sw (sub), R, Ni, US, Ca (sub), N, Ho, G, C; 1993 v Sw, P (sub), Es (2) (30)
McClory, A. (Motherwell), 1927 v W; 1928 v Ni; 1935 v W (3)
McCloy, P. (Ayr U), 1924 v E; 1925 v E (2)
McCloy, P. (Rangers), 1973 v W, Ni, Sw, Br (4)
McCoist, A. (Rangers), 1986 v Ho; 1987 v L (sub), Ei (sub), Bel, E, Br; 1988 v H, Bel, Ma, Sp, Co, E; 1989 v Y (sub), F, Cy, E; 1990 v Y, F, N, EG (sub), Eg, Pol, Ma (sub), Cr (sub), Se (sub), Br; 1991 v R, Sw, Bul (2), USSR; 1992 v Sw, Sm, Ni, Fi (sub), US, Ca, N, Ho, G, C; 1993 v Sw, P, I, Ma, P; 1996 v Gr (sub), Fi (sub), Sm (sub), Aus, D (sub), Co, E (sub), Sw; 1997 v A, Se (sub), Es (sub), A (sub); 1998 v Bl (sub); (with Kilmarnock), 1999 v Li, Es (61)
McColl, A. (Renton), 1888 v Ni (1)
McColl, I. M. (Rangers), 1950 v E, F; 1951 v W, Ni, Bel; 1957 v E, Ni, W, Y, Sp, Sw, WG; 1958 v Ni, E (14)
McColl, R. S. (Queen's Park), 1896 v W, Ni; 1897 v Ni; 1898 v Ni; 1899 v Ni, E, W; 1900 v E, W; 1901 v E, W; (with Newcastle U), 1902 v E; (with Queen's Park), 1908 v Ni (13)
McColl, W. (Renton), 1895 v W (1)
McCombie, A. (Sunderland), 1903 v E, W; (with Newcastle U), 1905 v E, W (4)
McCorkindale, J. (Partick T), 1891 v W (1)
McCormick, R. (Abercorn), 1886 v W (1)
McCrae, D. (St Mirren), 1929 v N, G (2)
McCreadie, E. G. (Chelsea), 1965 v E, Sp, Fi, Pol; 1966 v P, Ni, W, Pol, I; 1967 v E, USSR; 1968 v Ni, W, E, Ho; 1969 v W, Ni, E, D, A, WG, Cy (2) (23)
McCulloch, D. (Hearts), 1935 v W; (with Brentford), 1936 v E; 1937 v W, Ni; 1938 v Cz; (with Derby Co), 1939 v H, W (7)
MacDonald, A. (Rangers), 1976 v Sw (1)
McDonald, J. (Edinburgh University), 1886 v E (1)
McDonald, J. (Sunderland), 1956 v W, Ni (2)
MacDougall, E. J. (Norwich C) 1975 v Se, P, W, Ni, E; 1976 v D, R (sub) (7)
McDougall, J. (Vale of Leven), 1877 v E, W; 1878 v E; 1879 v E, W (5)
McDougall, J. (Airdrieonians), 1926 v Ni (1)
McDougall, J. (Liverpool), 1931 v I, A (2)
McFadden, J. (Motherwell), 2002 v S.Af (sub) (1)
McFadyen, W. (Motherwell), 1934 v A, W (2)
Macfarlane, A. (Dundee), 1904 v W; 1906 v W; 1908 v W; 1909 v Ni; 1911 v W (5)
Macfarlane, H. (Hearts), 1947 v L (1)
McFarlane, R. (Greenock Morton), 1896 v W (1)
McGarr, E. (Aberdeen), 1970 v Ei, A (2)
McGarvey, F. P. (Liverpool), 1979 v Ni (sub), Arg; (with Celtic), 1984 v U, Bel (sub), EG (sub), Ni, W (7)
McGeoch, A. (Dumbreck), 1876 v E, W; 1877 v E, W (4)
McGhee, J. (Hibernian), 1886 v W (1)
McGhee, M. (Aberdeen), 1983 v Ca (1+1 sub); 1984 v Ni (sub), E (4)

McGinlay, J. (Bolton W), 1994 v A, Ho; 1995 v Fa, Ru, Gr, Ru, Sm, Fa; 1996 v Se; 1997 v Se, Es (1 + sub), A (sub) (13)
McGonagle, W. (Celtic), 1933 v E; 1934 v A, E, Ni; 1935 v Ni, W (6)
McGrain, D. (Celtic), 1973 v W, Ni, E, Sw, Br; 1974 v Cz (2), WG, W (sub), E, Bel, N, Z, Br, Y; 1975 v Sp, Se, P, W, Ni, E, R; 1976 v Z (sub), Sw, Ni, W, E; 1977 v Fi, Cz, W (2), Se, Ni, E, Ch, Arg, Br; 1978 v EG, Cz; 1980 v Bel, P, Ni, W, E, Pol, H; 1981 v Se, P, Is, Ni, Is, W (sub), Ni, E; 1982 v Se, Sp, Ho, Ni, E, Nz, USSR (sub) (62)
McGregor, J. C. (Vale of Leven), 1877 v E, W; 1878 v E; 1880 v E (4)
McGrory, J. (Celtic), 1928 v Ni; 1931 v E; 1932 v Ni, W; 1933 v E, Ni; 1934 v Ni (7)
McGrory, J. E. (Kilmarnock), 1965 v Ni, Fi; 1966 v P (3)
McGuire, W. (Beith), 1881 v E, W (2)
McGurk, F. (Birmingham), 1934 v W (1)
McHardy, H. (Rangers), 1885 v Ni (1)
McInally, A. (Aston Villa), 1989 v Cy (sub), Ch; (with Bayern Munich), 1990 v Y (sub), F (sub), Arg, Pol (sub), Ma, Cr (8)
McInally, J. (Dundee U), 1987 v Bel, Br; 1988 v Ma (sub); 1991 v Bul (2); 1992 v US (sub), N (sub), C (sub); 1993 v G, P (10)
McInally, T. B. (Celtic), 1926 v Ni; 1927 v W (2)
McInnes, T. (Cowlairs), 1889 v Ni (1)
McIntosh, W. (Third Lanark), 1905 v Ni (1)
McIntyre, A. (Vale of Leven), 1878 v E; 1882 v E (2)
McIntyre, H. (Rangers), 1880 v W (1)
McIntyre, J. (Rangers), 1884 v W (1)
MacKay, D. (Celtic), 1959 v E, WG, Ho, P; 1960 v E, Pol, A, H, T; 1961 v W, Ni; 1962 v Ni, Cz, U (sub) (14)
Mackay, D. C. (Hearts), 1957 v Sp; 1958 v F; 1959 v W, Ni; (with Tottenham H), 1959 v WG, E; 1960 v W, Ni, A, Pol, H, T; 1961 v W, Ni, E; 1963 v E, A, N; 1964 v Ni, W, N; 1966 v Ni (22)
Mackay, G. (Hearts), 1988 v Bul (sub), L (sub), S.Ar (sub), Ma (1)
McKay, J. (Blackburn R), 1924 v W (1)
McKay, R. (Newcastle U), 1928 v W (1)
McKean, R. (Rangers), 1976 v Sw (sub) (1)
McKenzie, D. (Brentford), 1938 v Ni (1)
Mackenzie, J. A. (Partick T), 1954 v W, E, N, Fi, A, U; 1955 v E, H; 1956 v A (9)
McKeown, M. (Celtic), 1889 v Ni; 1890 v E (2)
McKie, J. (East Stirling), 1898 v W (1)
McKillop, T. R. (Rangers), 1938 v Ho (1)
McKimmie, S. (Aberdeen), 1989 v E, Ch; 1990 v Arg, Eg, Cr (sub), Br; 1991 v R, Sw, Bul, Sm; 1992 v Sw, R, Ni, Fi, US, Ca (sub), N (sub), Ho, G, C; 1993 v P, Es (sub); 1994 v Sw, I, Ho, A, Ho; 1995 v Fi, Fa, Ru, Gr, Ru, Fa; 1996 v Gr, Fi, Se, D, Co, Ho, E (40)
McKinlay, D. (Liverpool), 1922 v W, Ni (2)
McKinlay, T. (Celtic), 1996 v Gr, Fi, D, Co, E, Sw; 1997 v A, La, Se, Es (sub + 1), A, Se, W, Ma, Bl; 1998 v Bl, La (sub), F (sub), US, Br (sub), Mor (sub) (22)
McKinlay, W. (Dundee U), 1994 v Ma, Ho (sub), A, Ho; 1995 v Fa (sub), Ru, Gr, Ru (sub), Sm (sub), J, Ec, Fa; 1996 v Fi (sub), Se (sub); (with Blackburn R), Sm (sub), Aus, D (sub), Ho (sub); 1997 v Se, Es (sub); 1998 v La (sub), F, D, Fi, Co (sub), US, Br (sub); 1999 v Es, Fa (29)
McKinnon, A. (Queen's Park), 1874 v V (1)
McKinnon, R. (Rangers), 1966 v W, E, I (2), Ho, Br; 1967 v W, Ni, E; 1968 v Ni, W, E, Ho; 1969 v D, A, WG, Cy; 1970 v Ni, W, E, Ei, WG, A; 1971 v D, Bel, P, USSR, D (28)
McKinnon, R. (Motherwell), 1994 v Ma; 1995 v J, Fa (3)
MacKinnon, W. (Dumbarton), 1883 v E, W; 1884 v E, W (4)
MacKinnon, W. W. (Queen's Park), 1872 v E; 1873 v E; 1874 v E; 1875 v E; 1876 v E, W; 1877 v E; 1878 v E; 1879 v E (9)
McLaren, A. (Preston NE), 1947 v E, Bel, L; 1948 v W (4)
McLaren, A. (Hearts), 1992 v US, Ca, N; 1993 v I, Ma, G, Es (sub + 1); 1994 v I, Ma, Ho, A; 1995 v Fi, Fa; (with Rangers), Ru, Gr, Ru, Sm, J, Ec, Fa; 1996 v Fi, Se, Sm (24)
McLaren, A. (Kilmarnock), 2001 v Pol (sub) (1)
McLaren, J. (Hibernian), 1888 v W; (with Celtic), 1889 v E; 1890 v E (3)
McLean, A. (Celtic), 1926 v W, Ni; 1927 v W, E (4)
McLean, D. (St Bernards), 1896 v W; 1897 v Ni (2)
McLean, D. (Sheffield W), 1912 v E (1)
McLean, G. (Dundee), 1968 v Ho (1)
McLean, T. (Kilmarnock), 1969 v D, Cy, W; 1970 v Ni, W; 1971 v D (6)
McLeish, A. (Aberdeen), 1980 v P, Ni, W, E, Pol, H; 1981 v Se, Is, Ni, Is, Ni, E; 1982 v Se, Sp, Ni, Br (sub); 1983 v Bel, Sw (sub), W, E, Ca (3); 1984 v U, Bel, EG, Ni, W, E, F; 1985 v Y, Ic, Sp (2), W, E, Ic; 1986 v W, EG, Aus (2), E, Ho, D;

1987 v Bel, E, Br; 1988 v Bel, Bul, L, S.Ar (sub), Ma, Sp, Co, E; 1989 v N, Y, I, Cy, F, Cy, E, Ch; 1990 v Y, F, N, Arg, EG, Eg, Cr, Se, Br; 1991 v R, Sw, USSR, Bul; 1993 v Ma (77)

McLeod, D. (Celtic), 1905 v Ni; 1906 v E, W, Ni (4)

McLeod, J. (Dumbarton), 1888 v Ni; 1889 v W; 1890 v Ni; 1892 v E; 1893 v W (5)

MacLeod, J. M. (Hibernian), 1961 v E, Ei (2), Cz (4)

MacLeod, M. (Celtic), 1985 v Co; 1987 v Ei, L, E, Br; (with Borussia Dortmund), 1988 v Co, E; 1989 v I, Ch; 1990 v Y, F, N, Arg, EG, Pol, Se Br; (with Hibernian), 1991 v R, Sw, USSR (sub) (20)

McLeod, W. (Cowlairs), 1886 v Ni (1)

McLintock, A. (Vale of Leven), 1875 v E; 1876 v E; 1880 v E (3)

McLintock, F. (Leicester C), 1963 v N (sub), Ei, Sp; (with Arsenal), 1965 v Ni; 1967 v USSR; 1970 v Ni; 1971 v W, Ni, E (9)

McLuckie, J. S. (Manchester C), 1934 v W (1)

McMahon, A. (Celtic), 1892 v E; 1893 v E, Ni; 1894 v E; 1901 v Ni; 1902 v W (6)

McMenemy, J. (Celtic), 1905 v Ni; 1909 v Ni; 1910 v E, W; 1911 v Ni, W, E; 1912 v W; 1914 v W, Ni, E; 1920 v Ni (12)

McMenemy, J. (Motherwell), 1934 v W (1)

McMillan, I. L. (Airdrieonians), 1952 v E, USA, D; 1955 v E; 1956 v E; (with Rangers), 1961 v Cz (6)

McMillan, J. (St Bernards), 1897 v W (1)

McMillan, T. (Dumbarton), 1887 v Ni (1)

McMullan, J. (Partick T), 1920 v W; 1921 v W, Ni, E; 1924 v E, Ni; 1925 v E; 1926 v W; (with Manchester C), 1926 v E; 1927 v E, W; 1928 v E, W; 1929 v W, E, Ni (16)

McNab, A. (Morton), 1921 v E, Ni (2)

McNab, A. (Sunderland), 1937 v A; 1939 v E (2)

McNab, C. D. (Dundee), 1931 v E, W, A, I, Sw; 1932 v E (6)

McNab, J. S. (Liverpool), 1923 v W (1)

McNair, A. (Celtic), 1906 v W; 1907 v Ni; 1908 v E, W; 1909 v E; 1910 v W; 1912 v E, W, Ni; 1913 v E; 1914 v Ni; 1920 v E, W, Ni (15)

McNamara, J. (Celtic), 1997 v La (sub), Se, Es, W (sub); 1998 v D, Co, US (sub), N (sub), Mor; 2000 v Ho; 2001 v Sm; 2002 v Bel (sub), F (sub) (13)

McNaught, W. (Raith R), 1951 v A, W, Ni; 1952 v E; 1955 v Ni (5)

McNaughton, K. (Aberdeen), 2002 v Ng (1)

McNiel, H. (Queen's Park), 1874 v E; 1875 v E; 1876 v E, W; 1877 v W; 1878 v E; 1879 v E, W; 1881 v E, W (10)

McNiel, M. (Rangers), 1876 v W; 1880 v E (2)

McNeill, W. (Celtic), 1961 v E, Ei (2), Cz; 1962 v Ni, E, Cz, U; 1963 v Ei, Sp; 1964 v W, E, WG; 1965 v E, Fi, Pol, Sp; 1966 v Ni, Pol; 1967 v USSR; 1968 v E; 1969 v Cy, W, E, Cy (sub); 1970 v WG; 1972 v Ni, W, E (29)

McPhail, J. (Celtic), 1950 v W; 1951 v W, Ni, A; 1954 v Ni (5)

McPhail, R. (Airdrieonians), 1927 v E; (with Rangers), 1929 v W; 1931 v E, Ni; 1932 v W, Ni, F; 1933 v E, Ni; 1934 v A, Ni; 1935 v E; 1937 v G, E, Cz; 1938 v W, Ni (17)

McPherson, D. (Kilmarnock), 1892 v Ni (1)

McPherson, D. (Hearts), 1989 v Cy, E; 1990 v N, Ma, Cr, Se, Br; 1991 v Sw, Bul (2), USSR (sub), Sm; 1992 v Sw, R, Sm, Ni, Fi, US, Ca, N, Ho, G, C; (with Rangers), 1993 v Sw, I, Ma, P (27)

McPherson, J. (Clydesdale), 1875 v E (1)

McPherson, J. (Vale of Leven), 1879 v E, W; 1880 v E; 1881 v W; 1883 v E; 1884 v E; 1885 v Ni (8)

McPherson, J. (Kilmarnock), 1888 v W; (with Cowlairs), 1889 v E; 1890 v Ni, E; (with Rangers), 1892 v W; 1894 v E; 1895 v E, Ni; 1897 v Ni (9)

McPherson, J. (Hearts), 1891 v E (1)

McPherson, R. (Arthurlie), 1882 v E (1)

McQueen, G. (Leeds U), 1974 v Bel; 1975 v Sp (2), P, W, Ni, E, R; 1976 v D; 1977 v Cz, W (2), Ni, E; 1978 v EG, Cz, W; (with Manchester U), Bul, Ni, W; 1979 v A, N, P, Ni, E, N; 1980 v Pe, A, Bel; 1981 v W (30)

McQueen, M. (Leith Ath), 1890 v W; 1891 v W (2)

McRorie, D. M. (Morton), 1931 v W (1)

McSpadyen, A. (Partick T), 1939 v E, Ni (2)

McStay, P. (Celtic), 1984 v U, Bel, EG, Ni, E (sub); 1985 v Y, Ic, Sp (2), W; 1986 v EG (sub), Aus, Is, U; 1987 v Bul, Ei (1+1 subs), L (sub), Bel, E, Br; 1988 v H, Bel, Bul, L, S.Ar, Sp, Co, E; 1989 v N, Y, I, Cy, F, Cy, E, Ch; 1990 v Y, F, N, Arg, EG (sub), Eg, Pol (sub), Ma, Cr, Se (sub); Br; 1991 v R, USSR, Bul; 1992 v Sm, Fi, US, Ca, N, Ho, G, C; 1993 v Sw, P, I, Ma, P, Es (2); 1994 v I (sub), Ho; 1995 v Fi, Fa, Ru; 1996 v Aus; 1997 v Es (sub), A (sub) (76)

McStay, W. (Celtic), 1921 v W, Ni; 1925 v E, Ni, W; 1926 v E, Ni, W; 1927 v E, Ni, W; 1928 v W, Ni (13)

McSwegan, G. (Hearts), 2000 v Bos (sub), Li (2)

McTavish, J. (Falkirk), 1910 v Ni (1)

McWattie, G. C. (Queen's Park), 1901 v W, Ni (2)

McWilliam, P. (Newcastle U), 1905 v E; 1906 v E; 1907 v E, W; 1909 v W; 1910 v E; 1911 v W (8)

Macari, L. (Celtic), 1972 v W (sub), E, Y, Cz, Br; 1973 v D; (with Manchester U), E (2), W (sub), Ni (sub); 1975 v Se, P (sub), W, E (sub), R; 1977 v Ni (sub), E (sub), Ch, Arg; 1978 v EG, W, Bul, Pe (sub), Ir (24)

Macauley, A. R. (Brentford), 1947 v E; (with Arsenal), 1948 v E, W, Ni, Bel, Sw, F (7)

Madden, J. (Celtic), 1893 v W; 1895 v W (2)

Main, F. R. (Rangers), 1938 v W (1)

Main, J. (Hibernian), 1909 v Ni (1)

Maley, W. (Celtic), 1893 v E, Ni (2)

Malpas, M. (Dundee U), 1984 v F; 1985 v E, Ic; 1986 v W, Aus (2), Is, R, E, Ho, D, WG; 1987 v Bul, Ei, Bel; 1988 v Bel, Bul, L, S.Ar, Ma; 1989 v N, Y, I, Cy, F, Cy, E, Ch; 1990 v Y, F, N, Eg, Pol, Ma, Cr, Se, Br; 1991 v R, Bul (2), USSR, Sm; 1992 v Sw, R, Sm, Ni, Fi, US, Ca (sub), N, Ho, G; 1993 v Sw, P, I (55)

Marshall, G. (Celtic), 1992 v US (1)

Marshall, H. (Celtic), 1899 v W; 1900 v Ni (2)

Marshall, J. (Third Lanark), 1885 v Ni; 1886 v W; 1887 v E, W (4)

Marshall, J. (Middlesbrough), 1921 v E, W, Ni; 1922 v E, W, Ni; (with Llanelly), 1924 v W (7)

Marshall, J. (Rangers), 1932 v E; 1933 v E; 1934 v E (3)

Marshall, R. W. (Rangers), 1892 v Ni; 1894 v Ni (2)

Martin, B. (Motherwell), 1995 v J, Ec (2)

Martin, F. (Aberdeen), 1954 v N (2), A, U; 1955 v E, H (6)

Martin, N. (Hibernian), 1965 v Fi, Pol; (with Sunderland), 1966 v I (3)

Martis, J. (Motherwell), 1961 v W (1)

Mason, J. (Third Lanark), 1949 v E, W, Ni; 1950 v W; 1951 v Ni, Bel, A (7)

Massie, A. (Hearts), 1932 v Ni, W, F; 1933 v Ni; 1934 v E, Ni; 1935 v E, Ni, W; 1936 v W, Ni; (with Aston Villa), 1936 v E; 1937 v G, E, W, Ni, A; 1938 v W (18)

Masson, D. S. (QPR), 1976 v Ni, W, E; 1977 v Fi, Cz, W, Ni, E, Ch, Arg, Br; 1978 v EG, Cz, W; (with Derby Co), Ni, E, Pe (17)

Mathers, D. (Partick T), 1954 v Fi (1)

Matteo, D. (Leeds U), 2001 v Aus, Bel, Sm; 2002 v Cro, Bel, F (6)

Maxwell, W. S. (Stoke C), 1898 v E (1)

May, J. (Rangers), 1906 v W, Ni; 1908 v E, Ni; 1909 v W (5)

Meechan, P. (Celtic), 1896 v Ni (1)

Meiklejohn, D. D. (Rangers), 1922 v W; 1924 v W; 1925 v W, Ni, E; 1928 v W, Ni; 1929 v E, Ni; 1930 v E, Ni; 1931 v E; 1932 v W, Ni; 1934 v A (15)

Menzies, A. (Hearts), 1906 v E (1)

Mercer, R. (Hearts), 1912 v W; 1913 v Ni (2)

Middleton, R. (Cowdenbeath), 1930 v Ni (1)

Millar, A. (Hearts), 1939 v W (1)

Millar, J. (Rangers), 1897 v E; 1898 v E, W (3)

Millar, J. (Rangers), 1963 v A, Ei (2)

Miller, C. (Dundee U), 2001 v Pol (1)

Miller, J. (St Mirren), 1931 v E, I, Sw; 1932 v F; 1934 v E (5)

Miller, K. (Rangers), 2001 v Pol (sub) (1)

Miller, P. (Dumbarton), 1882 v E; 1883 v E, W (3)

Miller, T. (Liverpool), 1920 v E; (with Manchester U), 1921 v E, Ni (3)

Miller, W. (Third Lanark), 1876 v E (1)

Miller, W. (Celtic), 1947 v E, W, Bel, L; 1948 v W, Ni (6)

Miller, W. (Aberdeen), 1975 v P; 1978 v Bul; 1980 v Bel, W, E, Pol, H; 1981 v Se, P, Is (sub), Ni, W, Ni, E; 1982 v Ni, P, Ho, Br, USSR; 1983 v EG, Sw (2), W, E, Ca (3); 1984 v U, Bel, EG, W, E, F; 1985 v Y, Ic, Sp (2), W, E, Ic; 1986 v W, EG, Aus (2), Is, R, E, Ho, D, WG, U; 1987 v Bul, E, Br; 1988 v H, L, S.Ar, Ma, Sp, Co, E; 1989 v N, Y; 1990 v N (65)

Mills, W. (Aberdeen), 1936 v W, Ni; 1937 v W (3)

Milne, J. V. (Middlesbrough), 1938 v E; 1939 v E (2)

Mitchell, D. (Rangers), 1890 v Ni; 1892 v E; 1893 v E, Ni; 1894 v E (5)

Mitchell, J. (Kilmarnock), 1908 v Ni; 1910 v Ni, W (3)

Mitchell, R. C. (Newcastle U), 1951 v D, F (2)

Mochan, N. (Celtic), 1954 v N, A, U (3)

Moir, W. (Bolton W), 1950 v E (1)

Moncur, R. (Newcastle U), 1968 v Ho; 1970 v Ni, W, E, Ei; 1971 v D, Bel, W, P, Ni, E, D; 1972 v Pe, Ni, W, E (16)

Morgan, H. (St Mirren), 1898 v W; (with Liverpool), 1899 v E (2)

Morgan, W. (Burnley), 1968 v Ni; (with Manchester U), 1972 v Pe, Y, Cz, Br; 1973 v D (2), E (2), W, Ni, Sw, Br; 1974 v Cz (2), WG (2), Ni, Bel (sub), Br, Y (21)

Morris, D. (Raith R), 1923 v Ni; 1924 v E, Ni; 1925 v E, W, Ni (6)

Morris, H. (East Fife), 1950 v Ni (1)

Morrison, T. (St Mirren), 1927 v E (1)
Morton, A. L. (Queen's Park), 1920 v W, Ni; (with Rangers), 1921 v E; 1922 v E, W; 1923 v E, W, Ni; 1924 v E, W, Ni; 1925 v E, W, Ni; 1927 v E, Ni; 1928 v E, W, Ni; 1929 v E, W, Ni; 1930 v E, W, Ni; 1931 v E, W, Ni; 1932 v E, W, F (31)
Morton, H. A. (Kilmarnock), 1929 v G, Ho (2)
Mudie, J. K. (Blackpool), 1957 v W, Ni, E, Y, Sw, Sp (2), WG; 1958 v Ni, E, W, Sw, H, Pol, Y, Par, F (17)
Muir, W. (Dundee), 1907 v Ni (1)
Muirhead, T. A. (Rangers), 1922 v Ni; 1923 v E; 1924 v W; 1927 v Ni; 1928 v Ni; 1929 v W, Ni; 1930 v W (8)
Mulhall, G. (Aberdeen), 1960 v Ni; (with Sunderland), 1963 v Ni; 1964 v Ni (3)
Munro, A. D. (Hearts), 1937 v W, Ni; (with Blackpool), 1938 v Ho (3)
Munro, F. M. (Wolverhampton W), 1971 v Ni (sub), E (sub), D, USSR; 1975 v Se, W (sub), Ni, E, R (9)
Munro, I. (St Mirren), 1979 v Arg, N; 1980 v Pe, A, Bel, W, E (7)
Munro, N. (Abercorn), 1888 v W; 1889 v E (2)
Murdoch, J. (Motherwell), 1931 v Ni (1)
Murdoch, R. (Celtic), 1966 v W, E, I (2); 1967 v Ni; 1968 v Ni; 1969 v W, Ni, E, WG, Cy; 1970 v A (12)
Murphy, F. (Celtic), 1938 v Ho (1)
Murray, J. (Renton), 1895 v W (1)
Murray, J. (Hearts), 1958 v E, H, Pol, Y, F (5)
Murray, J. W. (Vale of Leven), 1890 v W (1)
Murray, P. (Hibernian), 1896 v Ni; 1897 v W (2)
Murray, S. (Aberdeen), 1972 v Bel (1)
Mutch, G. (Preston NE), 1938 v E (1)

Napier, C. E. (Celtic), 1932 v E; 1935 v E, W; (with Derby Co), 1937 v Ni, A (5)
Narey, D. (Dundee U), 1977 v Se (sub); 1979 v P, Ni (sub), Arg; 1980 v P, Ni, Pol, H; 1981 v W, E (sub); 1982 v Ho, W, E, Nz (sub), Br, USSR; 1983 v EG, Sw, Bel, Ni, W, E, Ca (3); 1986 v Is, R, Ho, WG, U; 1987 v Bul, E, Bel; 1989 v I, Cy (35)
Naysmith, G. A. (Hearts), 2000 v Ei; 2001 v La (sub), Sm, Cro; (with Everton), 2002 v Cro, Bel (6)
Neil, R. G. (Hibernian), 1896 v W; (with Rangers), 1900 v W (2)
Neill, R. W. (Queen's Park), 1876 v W; 1877 v E, W; 1878 v W; 1880 v E (5)
Nellies, P. (Hearts), 1913 v Ni; 1914 v W (2)
Nelson, J. (Cardiff C), 1925 v W, Ni; 1928 v E; 1930 v F (4)
Nevin, P. K. F. (Chelsea), 1986 v R (sub), E (sub); 1987 v L, Ei, Bel (sub); 1988 v L; (with Everton), 1989 v Cy, E; 1991 v R (sub), Bul (sub), Sm (sub); 1992 v US, G (sub), C (sub); (with Tranmere R), 1993 v Ma, P (sub), Es; 1994 v Sw, Ma, Ho, A (sub), Ho; 1995 v Fa, Ru (sub), Sm; 1996 v Se (sub), Sm, Aus (sub) (28)
Niblo, T. D. (Aston Villa), 1904 v E (1)
Nibloe, J. (Kilmarnock), 1929 v E, N, Ho; 1930 v W; 1931 v E, Ni, A, I, Sw; 1932 v E, F (11)
Nicholas, C. (Celtic), 1983 v Sw, Ni, E, Ca (3); (with Arsenal), 1984 v Bel, F (sub); 1985 v Y (sub), Ic (sub), Sp (sub), W (sub); 1986 v Is, R (sub), E, D, U (sub); 1987 v Bul, E (sub); (with Aberdeen), 1989 v Cy (sub) (20)
Nicholson, B. (Dunfermline Ath), 2001 v Pol; 2002 v La (2)
Nicol, S. (Liverpool), 1985 v Y, Ic, Sp, W; 1986 v W, EG, Aus, E, D, WG, U; 1988 v H, Bul, S.Ar, Sp, Co, E; 1989 v N, Y, Cy, F; 1990 v Y, F; 1991 v N, G, Ho (3)
Nisbet, J. (Ayr U), 1929 v N, G, Ho (3)
Niven, J. B. (Moffatt), 1885 v Ni (1)

O'Connor, G. (Hibernian), 2002 v Ng (sub), Sk, Hk (sub) (3)
O'Donnell, F. (Preston NE), 1937 v E, A, Cz; 1938 v W; (with Blackpool), E, Ho (6)
O'Donnell, P. (Motherwell), 1994 v Sw (sub) (1)
Ogilvie, D. H. (Motherwell), 1934 v A (1)
O'Hare, J. (Derby Co), 1970 v W, Ni, E; 1971 v D, Bel, W, Ni; 1972 v P, Bel, Ho (sub), Pe, Ni, W (13)
O'Neil, B. (Celtic), 1996 v Aus; (with Wolfsburg), 1999 v G (sub); 2000 v Li, Ho (sub), Ei; (with Derby Co), 2001 v Aus (6)
O'Neil, J. (Hibernian), 2001 v Pol (1)
Ormond, W. E. (Hibernian), 1954 v E, N, Fi, A, U; 1959 v E (6)
O'Rourke, F. (Airdrieonians), 1907 v Ni (1)
Orr, J. (Kilmarnock), 1892 v W (1)
Orr, R. (Newcastle U), 1902 v E; 1904 v E (2)
Orr, T. (Morton), 1952 v Ni, W (2)
Orr, W. (Celtic), 1900 v Ni; 1903 v Ni; 1904 v W (3)
Orrock, R. (Falkirk), 1913 v W (1)
Oswald, J. (Third Lanark), 1889 v E; (with St Bernards), 1895 v E; (with Rangers), 1897 v W (3)

Parker, A. H. (Falkirk), 1955 v P, Y, A; 1956 v E, Ni, W, A; 1957 v Ni, W, Y; 1958 v Ni, W, E, Sw; (with Everton), Par (15)
Parlane, D. (Rangers), 1973 v W, Sw, Br; 1975 v Sp (sub), Se, P, W, Ni, E, R; 1976 v D (sub); 1977 v W (12)
Parlane, R. (Vale of Leven), 1878 v W; 1879 v E, W (3)
Paterson, G. D. (Celtic), 1939 v Ni (1)
Paterson, J. (Leicester C), 1920 v E (1)
Paterson, J. (Cowdenbeath), 1931 v A, I, Sw (3)
Paton, A. (Motherwell), 1952 v D, Se (2)
Paton, D. (St Bernards), 1896 v W (1)
Paton, M. (Dumbarton), 1883 v E; 1884 v W; 1885 v W, E; 1886 v E (5)
Paton, R. (Vale of Leven), 1879 v E, W (2)
Patrick, J. (St Mirren), 1897 v E, W (2)
Paul, H. McD. (Queen's Park), 1909 v E, W, Ni (3)
Paul, W. (Partick T), 1888 v W; 1889 v W; 1890 v W (3)
Paul, W. (Dykebar), 1891 v Ni (1)
Pearson, T. (Newcastle U), 1947 v E, Bel (2)
Penman, A. (Dundee), 1966 v Ho (1)
Pettigrew, W. (Motherwell), 1976 v Sw, Ni, W; 1977 v W (sub), Se (5)
Phillips, J. (Queen's Park), 1877 v E, W; 1878 v W (3)
Plenderleith, J. B. (Manchester C), 1961 v Ni (1)
Porteous, W. (Hearts), 1903 v Ni (1)
Pressley, S. J. (Hearts), 2000 v F (sub), Ei (sub) (2)
Pringle, C. (St Mirren), 1921 v W (1)
Provan, D. (Rangers), 1964 v Ni; 1966 v I (2), Ho (5)
Provan, D. (Celtic), 1980 v Bel (2 sub), P (sub), Ni (sub); 1981 v Is, W, E; 1982 v Se, P, Ni (10)
Pursell, P. (Queen's Park), 1914 v W (1)

Quinn, J. (Celtic), 1905 v Ni; 1906 v Ni, W; 1908 v Ni, E; 1909 v E; 1910 v E, Ni, W; 1912 v E, W (11)
Quinn, P. (Motherwell), 1961 v E, Ei (2); 1962 v U (4)

Rae, G. (Dundee), 2001 v Pol; 2002 v La (sub) (2)
Rae, J. (Third Lanark), 1889 v W; 1890 v Ni (2)
Raeside, J. S. (Third Lanark), 1906 v W (1)
Raisbeck, A. G. (Liverpool), 1900 v E; 1901 v E; 1902 v E; 1903 v E, W; 1904 v E; 1906 v E; 1907 v E (8)
Rankin, G. (Vale of Leven), 1890 v Ni; 1891 v E (2)
Rankin, R. (St Mirren), 1929 v N, G, Ho (3)
Redpath, W. (Motherwell), 1949 v W, Ni; 1951 v E, D, F, Bel, A; 1952 v Ni, E (9)
Reid, J. G. (Airdrieonians), 1914 v W; 1920 v W; 1924 v Ni (3)
Reid, R. (Brentford), 1938 v E, Ni (2)
Reid, W. (Rangers), 1911 v E, W, Ni; 1912 v Ni; 1913 v E, W, Ni; 1914 v E, Ni (9)
Reilly, L. (Hibernian), 1949 v E, W, F; 1950 v W, Ni, Sw, F; 1951 v W, E, D, F, Bel, A; 1952 v Ni, W, E, USA, D, Se; 1953 v Ni, W, E, Se; 1954 v W; 1955 v H (2), P, Y, A, E; 1956 v E, W, Ni, A; 1957 v E, Ni, W, Y (38)
Rennie, H. G. (Hearts), 1900 v E, Ni; (with Hibernian), 1901 v E; 1902 v E, Ni, W; 1903 v W, Ni; 1904 v Ni; 1905 v W; 1906 v Ni; 1908 v Ni, W (13)
Renny-Tailyour, H. W. (Royal Engineers), 1873 v E (1)
Rhind, A. (Queen's Park), 1872 v E (1)
Richmond, A. (Queen's Park), 1906 v W (1)
Richmond, J. T. (Clydesdale), 1877 v E; (with Queen's Park), 1878 v E; 1882 v W (3)
Ring, T. (Clyde), 1953 v Se; 1955 v W, Ni, E, H; 1957 v E, Sp (2), Sw, WG; 1958 v Ni, Sw (12)
Rioch, B. D. (Derby Co), 1975 v P, W, Ni, E, R; 1976 v D (2), R, Ni, W, E; 1977 v Fi, Cz, W; (with Everton), W, Ni, E, Ch, Br; 1978 v Cz; (with Derby Co), Ni, E, Pe, Ho (24)
Ritchie, A. (East Stirlingshire), 1891 v W (1)
Ritchie, H. (Hibernian), 1923 v W; 1928 v Ni (2)
Ritchie, J. (Queen's Park), 1897 v W (1)
Ritchie, P. S. (Hearts), 1999 v G (sub), CzR; 2000 v Li, E; (with Bolton W), F, Ho (6)
Ritchie, W. (Rangers), 1962 v U (sub) (1)
Robb, D. T. (Aberdeen), 1971 v W, E, P, D (sub), USSR (5)
Robb, W. (Rangers), 1926 v W; (with Hibernian), 1928 v W (2)
Robertson, A. (Clyde), 1955 v P, A, H; 1958 v Sw, Par (5)
Robertson, D. (Rangers), 1992 v Ni; 1994 v Sw, Ho (3)
Robertson, G. (Motherwell), 1910 v W; (with Sheffield W), 1912 v W; 1913 v E, Ni (4)
Robertson, G. (Kilmarnock), 1938 v Cz (1)
Robertson, H. (Dundee), 1962 v Cz (1)
Robertson, J. (Dundee), 1931 v A, I (2)
Robertson, J. (Hearts), 1991 v R, Sw, Bul (sub), Sm (sub); 1992 v Sm, Ni (sub), Fi (sub), Ma (sub), G, Es; 1995 v J (sub), Ec, Fa (sub); 1996 v Gr (sub), Se (16)
Robertson, J. N. (Nottingham F), 1978 v Ni, W (sub), Ir; 1979 v P, N; 1980 v Pe, A, Bel (2), P; 1981 v Se, P, Is, Ni, Is, Ni, E;

1982 v Se, Ni (2), E (sub), Nz, Br, USSR; 1983 v EG, Sw; (with Derby Co), 1984 v U, Bel (28)

Robertson, J. G. (Tottenham H), 1965 v W (1)

Robertson, J. T. (Everton), 1898 v E; (with Southampton), 1899 v E; (with Rangers), 1900 v E, W, Ni, E; 1902 v W, Ni, E; 1903 v E, W; 1904 v E, W, Ni; 1905 v W (16)

Robertson, P. (Dundee), 1903 v Ni (1)

Robertson, T. (Queen's Park), 1889 v Ni; 1890 v E; 1891 v W; 1892 v Ni (4)

Robertson, T. (Hearts), 1898 v Ni (1)

Robertson, W. (Dumbarton), 1887 v E, W (2)

Robinson, R. (Dundee), 1974 v WG (sub); 1975 v Se, Ni, R (sub) (4)

Ross, M. (Rangers), 2002 v Sk, S.Af, Hk (3)

Rough, A. (Partick T), 1976 v Sw, Ni, W, E; 1977 v Fi, Cz, W (2), Se, Ni, E, Ch, Arg, Br; 1978 v Cz, W, Ni, E, Pe, Ir, Ho; 1979 v A, P, W, Arg, N; 1980 v Pe, A, Bel (2), P, W, E, Pol, H; 1981 v Se, P, Is, Ni, Is, W, E; 1982 v Se, Ni, Sp, Ho, W, E, Nz, Br, USSR; (with Hibernian), 1986 v W (sub), E (53)

Rougvie, D. (Aberdeen), 1984 v Ni (1)

Rowan, A. (Caledonian), 1880 v E; (with Queen's Park), 1882 v W (2)

Russell, D. (Hearts), 1895 v E, Ni; (with Celtic), 1897 v W; 1898 v Ni; 1901 v W, Ni (6)

Russell, J. (Cambuslang), 1890 v Ni (1)

Russell, W. F. (Airdrieonians), 1924 v W; 1925 v E (2)

Rutherford, E. (Rangers), 1948 v F (1)

St John, I. (Motherwell), 1959 v WG; 1960 v E, Ni, W, Pol, A; 1961 v E; (with Liverpool), 1962 v Ni, W, E, Cz (2), U; 1963 v W, Ni, E, N, Ei (sub); Sp; 1964 v Ni; 1965 v E (21)

Sawers, W. (Dundee), 1895 v W (1)

Scarff, P. (Celtic), 1931 v Ni (1)

Schaedler, E. (Hibernian), 1974 v WG (1)

Scott, A. S. (Rangers), 1957 v Ni, Y, WG; 1958 v W, Sw; 1959 v P; 1962 v Ni, W, E, Cz, U; (with Everton), 1964 v W, N; 1965 v Fi; 1966 v P, Br (16)

Scott, J. (Hibernian), 1966 v Ho (1)

Scott, J. (Dundee), 1971 v D (sub), USSR (2)

Scott, M. (Airdrieonians), 1898 v W (1)

Scott, R. (Airdrieonians), 1894 v Ni (1)

Scoular, J. (Portsmouth), 1951 v D, F, A; 1952 v E, USA, D, Se; 1953 v W, Ni (9)

Sellar, W. (Battlefield), 1885 v E; 1886 v E; 1887 v E, W; 1888 v E; (with Queen's Park), 1891 v E; 1892 v E; 1893 v E, Ni (9)

Semple, W. (Cambuslang), 1886 v W (1)

Severin, S. (Hearts), 2002 v La (sub), Sk (sub), S.Af (sub), Hk (4)

Shankly, W. (Preston NE), 1938 v E; 1939 v E, W, Ni, H (5)

Sharp, G. M. (Everton), 1985 v Ic; 1986 v W, Aus (2 sub), Is, R, U; 1987 v Ei; 1988 v Bel (sub), Bul, L, Ma (12)

Sharp, J. (Dundee), 1904 v W; (with Woolwich Arsenal), 1907 v W, E; 1908 v E; (with Fulham), 1909 v W (5)

Shaw, D. (Hibernian), 1947 v W, Ni; 1948 v E, Bel, Sw, F; 1949 v W, Ni (8)

Shaw, F. W. (Pollokshields Ath), 1884 v E, W (2)

Shaw, J. (Rangers), 1947 v E, Bel, L; 1948 v Ni (4)

Shearer, D. (Aberdeen), 1994 v A (sub), Ho (sub); 1995 v Fi, Ru (sub), Sm, Fa; 1996 v Gr (7)

Shearer, R. (Rangers), 1961 v E, Ei (2), Cz (4)

Sillars, D. C. (Queen's Park), 1891 v E; 1892 v E; 1893 v W; 1894 v E; 1895 v W (5)

Simpson, J. (Third Lanark), 1895 v E, W, Ni (3)

Simpson, J. (Rangers), 1935 v E, W, Ni; 1936 v E, W, Ni; 1937 v G, E, W, Ni, A, Cz; 1938 v W, Ni (14)

Simpson, N. (Aberdeen), 1983 v Ni; 1984 v U (sub), F (sub); 1987 v E; 1988 v E (5)

Simpson, R. C. (Celtic), 1967 v E, USSR; 1968 v Ni, E; 1969 v A (5)

Sinclair, G. L. (Hearts), 1910 v Ni; 1912 v W, Ni (3)

Sinclair, J. W. E. (Leicester C), 1966 v P (1)

Skene, L. H. (Queen's Park), 1904 v W (1)

Sloan, T. (Third Lanark), 1904 v W (1)

Smellie, R. (Queen's Park), 1887 v Ni; 1888 v W; 1889 v E; 1891 v E; 1893 v E, Ni (6)

Smith, A. (Rangers), 1898 v E; 1900 v E, Ni, W; 1901 v E, Ni, W; 1902 v E, Ni, W; 1903 v E, Ni, W; 1904 v Ni; 1905 v W; 1906 v E, Ni; 1907 v W; 1911 v E, Ni (20)

Smith, D. (Aberdeen), 1966 v Ho; (with Rangers), 1968 v Ho (2)

Smith, G. (Hibernian), 1947 v E, Ni; 1948 v W, Bel, Sw, F; 1952 v E, USA; 1955 v P, Y, A, H; 1956 v E, Ni, W; 1957 v Sp (2), Sw (18)

Smith, H. G. (Hearts), 1988 v S.Ar (sub); 1992 v Ni, Ca (3)

Smith, J. (Ayr U), 1924 v E (1)

Smith, J. (Rangers), 1935 v Ni; 1938 v Ni (2)

Smith, J. (Aberdeen), 1968 v Ho (sub); (with Newcastle U), 1974 v WG, Ni (sub), W (sub) (4)

Smith, J. E. (Celtic), 1959 v H, P (2)

Smith, Jas (Queen's Park), 1872 v E (1)

Smith, John (Mauchline), 1877 v E, W; 1879 v E, W; (with Edinburgh University), 1880 v E; (with Queen's Park), 1881 v W, E; 1883 v E, W; 1884 v E (10)

Smith, N. (Rangers), 1897 v E; 1898 v W; 1899 v E, W, Ni; 1900 v E, W, Ni; 1901 v Ni, W; 1902 v E, Ni (12)

Smith, R. (Queen's Park), 1872 v E; 1873 v E (2)

Smith, T. M. (Kilmarnock), 1934 v E; (with Preston NE), 1938 v E (2)

Somers, P. (Celtic), 1905 v E, Ni; 1907 v Ni; 1909 v W (4)

Somers, W. S. (Third Lanark), 1879 v E, W; (with Queen's Park), 1880 v W (3)

Somerville, G. (Queen's Park), 1886 v E (1)

Souness, G. J. (Middlesbrough), 1975 v EG, Sp, Se; (with Liverpool), 1978 v Bul, W, E (sub), Ho; 1979 v A, N, W, Ni, E; 1980 v Pe, A, Bel, P, Ni; 1981 v P, Is (2); 1982 v Ni, P, Sp, W, E, Nz, Br, USSR; 1983 v EG, Sw, Bel, Sw, W, E, Ca (2 + 1 sub); 1984 v U, Ni, W; (with Sampdoria), 1985 v Y, Ic, Sp (2), W, E, Ic; 1986 v EG, Aus (2), R, E, D, WG (54)

Speedie, D. R. (Chelsea), 1985 v E; 1986 v W, EG (sub), Aus, E; (with Coventry C), 1989 v Y (sub), I (sub), Cy (1+1 sub), Ch (10)

Speedie, F. (Rangers), 1903 v E, W, Ni (3)

Speirs, J. H. (Rangers), 1908 v W (1)

Spencer, J. (Chelsea), 1995 v Ru (sub), Gr (sub), Sm (sub), J; 1996 v Fi, Aus, D, US (sub), Co, Ho (sub), E, Sw (sub); 1997 v La; (with QPR), W (sub) (14)

Stanton, P. (Hibernian), 1966 v Ho; 1969 v Ni; 1970 v Ei, A; 1971 v D, Bel, P, USSR, D; 1972 v P, Bel, Ho, W; 1973 v W, Ni; 1974 v WG (16)

Stark, J. (Rangers), 1909 v E, Ni (2)

Steel, W. (Morton), 1947 v E, Bel, L; (with Derby Co), 1948 v F, E, W, Ni; 1949 v E, W, Ni, F; 1950 v E, W, Ni, Sw, P, F; (with Dundee), 1951 v W, Ni, E, A (2), D, F, Bel; 1952 v W; 1953 v W, E, Ni, Se (30)

Steele, D. M. (Huddersfield), 1923 v E, W, Ni (3)

Stein, C. (Rangers), 1969 v W, Ni, D, E, Cy (2); 1970 v A (sub), Ni (sub), W, E, Ei, WG; 1971 v D, USSR, Bel, D; 1972 v Cz (sub); (with Coventry C), 1973 v E (2 sub), W (sub), Ni (21)

Stephen, J. F. (Bradford), 1947 v W; 1948 v W (2)

Stevenson, G. (Motherwell), 1928 v W, Ni; 1930 v Ni, E, F; 1931 v E, W; 1932 v W, Ni; 1933 v Ni; 1934 v E; 1935 v Ni (12)

Stewart, A. (Queen's Park), 1888 v Ni; 1889 v W (2)

Stewart, A. (Third Lanark), 1894 v W (1)

Stewart, D. (Dumbarton), 1888 v Ni (1)

Stewart, D. (Queen's Park), 1893 v W; 1894 v Ni; 1897 v Ni (3)

Stewart, D. S. (Leeds U), 1978 v EG (1)

Stewart, G. (Hibernian), 1906 v W, E; (with Manchester C), 1907 v E, W (4)

Stewart, J. (Kilmarnock), 1977 v Ch (sub); (with Middlesbrough), 1979 v N (2)

Stewart, M. J. (Manchester U), 2002 v Ng (sub), Sk, S.Af (sub) (3)

Stewart, R. (West Ham U), 1981 v W, Ni, E; 1982 v Ni, P, W; 1984 v F; 1987 v Ei (2), L (10)

Stewart, W. E. (Queen's Park), 1898 v Ni; 1900 v Ni (2)

Stockdale, R. K. (Middlesbrough), 2002 v Ng, Sk (sub), S.Af, Hk (4)

Storrier, D. (Celtic), 1899 v E, W, Ni (3)

Strachan, G. (Aberdeen), 1980 v Ni, W, E, Pol, H (sub); 1981 v Se, P; 1982 v Ni, P, Sp, Ho (sub), Nz, Br, USSR; 1983 v EG, Sw, Bel, Sw (sub), W, E, Ca (2 + 1 sub); 1984 v EG, Ni, E, F; (with Manchester U), 1985 v Sp (sub), E, Ic; 1986 v W, Aus, R, D, WG, U; 1987 v Bul, Ei (2); 1988 v H; 1989 v F (sub); (with Leeds U), 1990 v F; 1991 v USSR, Bul, Sm; 1992 v Sw, R, Ni, Fi (50)

Sturrock, P. (Dundee U), 1981 v W (sub), Ni, E (sub); 1982 v P, Ni (sub), W (sub), E (sub); 1983 v W, EG (sub), Sw, Bel (sub), Ca (3); 1984 v W; 1985 v Y (sub); 1986 v Is (sub), Ho, D, U; 1987 v Bel (20)

Sullivan, N. (Wimbledon), 1997 v W; 1998 v F, Co; 1999 v Fa, CzR, G, Fa, CzR; 2000 v Bos, Es, Bos, E (2), F, Ho, Ei; (with Tottenham H), 2001 v La, Sm, Cro, Bel, Sm, Pol; 2002 v Cro, Bel, La, F, Sk (27)

Summers, W. (St Mirren), 1926 v E (1)

Symon, J. S. (Rangers), 1939 v H (1)

Tait, T. S. (Sunderland), 1911 v W (1)

Taylor, J. (Queen's Park), 1872 v E; 1873 v E; 1874 v E; 1875 v E; 1876 v E, W (6)

Taylor, J. D. (Dumbarton), 1892 v W; 1893 v W; 1894 v Ni; (with St Mirren), 1895 v Ni (4)
Taylor, W. (Hearts), 1892 v E (1)
Telfer, P. N. (Coventry C), 2000 v F (1)
Telfer, W. (Motherwell), 1933 v Ni; 1934 v Ni (2)
Telfer, W. D. (St Mirren), 1954 v W (1)
Templeton, R. (Aston Villa), 1902 v E; (with Newcastle U), 1903 v E, W; 1904 v E; (with Woolwich Arsenal), 1905 v W; (with Kilmarnock), 1908 v Ni; 1910 v E, Ni; 1912 v E, Ni; 1913 v W (11)
Thompson, S. (Dundee U), 2002 v F (sub), Ng, Hk (3)
Thomson, A. (Arthurlie), 1886 v Ni (1)
Thomson, A. (Third Lanark), 1889 v W (1)
Thomson, A. (Airdrieonians), 1909 v Ni (1)
Thomson, A. (Celtic), 1926 v E; 1932 v F; 1933 v W (3)
Thomson, C. (Hearts), 1904 v Ni; 1905 v E, Ni, W; 1906 v W, Ni; 1907 v E, W, Ni; 1908 v E, W, Ni; (with Sunderland), 1909 v W; 1910 v E; 1911 v Ni; 1912 v E, W; 1913 v E, W; 1914 v E, Ni (21)
Thomson, C. (Sunderland), 1937 v Cz (1)
Thomson, D. (Dundee), 1920 v W (1)
Thomson, J. (Celtic), 1930 v F; 1931 v E, W, Ni (4)
Thomson, J. J. (Queen's Park), 1872 v E; 1873 v E; 1874 v E (3)
Thomson, J. R. (Everton), 1933 v W (1)
Thomson, R. (Celtic), 1932 v W (1)
Thomson, R. W. (Falkirk), 1927 v E (1)
Thomson, S. (Rangers), 1884 v W, Ni (2)
Thomson, W. (Dumbarton), 1892 v W; 1893 v W; 1898 v Ni, W (4)
Thomson, W. (Dundee), 1896 v W (1)
Thomson, W. (St Mirren), 1980 v Ni; 1981 v Ni (sub+1) 1982 v P; 1983 v Ni, Ca; 1984 v EG (7)
Thornton, W. (Rangers), 1947 v W, Ni; 1948 v E, Ni; 1949 v F; 1952 v D, Se (7)
Toner, W. (Kilmarnock), 1959 v W, Ni (2)
Townsley, T. (Falkirk), 1926 v W (1)
Troup, A. (Dundee), 1920 v E; 1921 v W, Ni; 1922 v Ni; (with Everton), 1926 v E (5)
Turnbull, E. (Hibernian), 1948 v Bel, Sw; 1951 v A; 1958 v H, Pol, Y, Par, F (8)
Turner, T. (Arthurlie), 1884 v W (1)
Turner, W. (Pollokshields Ath), 1885 v Ni; 1886 v Ni (2)

Ure, J. F. (Dundee), 1962 v W, Cz; 1963 v W, Ni, E, A, N, Sp; (with Arsenal), 1964 v Ni, N; 1968 v Ni (11)
Urquhart, D. (Hibernian), 1934 v W (1)

Vallance, T. (Rangers), 1877 v E, W; 1878 v E; 1879 v E, W; 1881 v E, W (7)
Venters, A. (Cowdenbeath), 1934 v Ni; (with Rangers), 1936 v E; 1939 v E (3)

Waddell, T. S. (Queen's Park), 1891 v Ni; 1892 v E; 1893 v E, Ni; 1895 v E, Ni (6)
Waddell, W. (Rangers), 1947 v W; 1949 v E, W, Ni, F; 1950 v E, Ni; 1951 v E, D, F, Bel, A; 1952 v Ni, W; 1954 v Ni; 1955 v W, Ni (17)
Wales, H. M. (Motherwell), 1933 v W (1)
Walker, A. (Celtic), 1988 v Co (sub); 1995 v Fi, Fa (sub) (3)
Walker, F. (Third Lanark), 1922 v W (1)
Walker, G. (St Mirren), 1930 v F; 1931 v Ni, A, Sw (4)
Walker, J. (Hearts), 1895 v Ni; 1897 v W; 1898 v Ni; (with Rangers), 1904 v W, Ni (5)
Walker, J. (Swindon T), 1911 v E, W, Ni; 1912 v E, W, Ni; 1913 v E, W, Ni (9)
Walker, J. N. (Hearts), 1993 v G; (with Partick T), 1996 v US (sub) (2)
Walker, R. (Hearts), 1900 v E, Ni; 1901 v E, W; 1902 v E, W, Ni; 1903 v E, W, Ni; 1904 v E, W, Ni; 1905 v E, W, Ni; 1906 v Ni; 1907 v E, Ni; 1908 v E, W, Ni; 1909 v E, W; 1912 v E, W, Ni; 1913 v E, W (29)
Walker, T. (Hearts), 1935 v E, W; 1936 v E, W, Ni; 1937 v G, E, W, Ni, A, Cz; 1938 v E, W, Ni, Cz, Ho; 1939 v E, W, Ni, H (20)
Walker, W. (Clyde), 1909 v Ni; 1910 v Ni (2)
Wallace, I. A. (Coventry C), 1978 v Bul (sub); 1979 v P (sub), W (3)
Wallace, W. S. B. (Hearts), 1965 v Ni; 1966 v E, Ho; (with Celtic), 1967 v E, USSR (sub); 1968 v Ni; 1969 v E (sub) (7)
Wardhaugh, J. (Hearts), 1955 v H; 1957 v Ni (2)
Wark, J. (Ipswich T), 1979 v W, Ni, E, Arg, N (sub); 1980 v Pe, A, Bel (2); 1981 v Is, Ni; 1982 v Se, Sp, Ho, Ni, Nz, Br, USSR; 1983 v EG, Sw (2), Ni, E (sub); 1984 v U, Bel, EG; (with Liverpool), E, F; 1985 v Y (29)
Watson, A. (Queen's Park), 1881 v E, W; 1882 v E (3)

Watson, J. (Sunderland), 1903 v E, W; 1904 v E; 1905 v E; (with Middlesbrough), 1909 v E, Ni (6)
Watson, J. (Motherwell), 1948 v Ni; (with Huddersfield T), 1954 v Ni (2)
Watson, J. A. K. (Rangers), 1878 v W (1)
Watson, P. R. (Blackpool), 1934 v A (1)
Watson, R. (Motherwell), 1971 v USSR (1)
Watson, W. (Falkirk), 1898 v W (1)
Watt, F. (Kilbirnie), 1889 v W, Ni; 1890 v W; 1891 v E (4)
Watt, W. W. (Queen's Park), 1887 v Ni (1)
Waugh, W. (Hearts), 1938 v Cz (1)
Weir, A. (Motherwell), 1959 v WG; 1960 v E, P, A, H, T (6)
Weir, D. G. (Hearts), 1997 v W, Ma (sub); 1998 v F, D (sub) Fi (sub), N (sub), Mor; 1999 v Es, Fa; (with Everton) CzR G, Fa, CzR; 2000 v Bos, Es, Bos, Li, E (2), Ho; 2001 v La Sm (sub), Cro, Aus, Bel, Sm, Pol (sub); 2002 v Cro, Bel, La F, Ng, Sk, S.Af, Hk (35)
Weir, J. (Third Lanark), 1887 v Ni (1)
Weir, J. B. (Queen's Park), 1872 v E; 1874 v E; 1875 v E; 1878 v W (4)
Weir, P. (St Mirren), 1980 v Ni, W, Pol (sub), H; (with Aberdeen), 1983 v Sw; 1984 v Ni (6)
White, John (Albion R), 1922 v W; (with Hearts), 1923 v Ni (2)
White, J. A. (Falkirk), 1959 v WG, Ho, P; 1960 v Ni; (with Tottenham H), 1960 v W, Pol, A, T; 1961 v W; 1962 v Ni, W, E, Cz (2); 1963 v W, Ni, E; 1964 v Ni, W, E, N, WG (22)
White, W. (Bolton W), 1907 v E; 1908 v E (2)
Whitelaw, A. (Vale of Leven), 1887 v Ni; 1890 v W (2)
Whyte, D. (Celtic), 1988 v Bel (sub), L; 1989 v Ch (sub); 1992 v US (sub); (with Middlesbrough), 1993 v P, I; 1995 v J (sub), Ec; 1996 v US; 1997 v La; (with Aberdeen), 1998 v Fi 1999 v G (sub) (12)
Wilkie, L. (Dundee), 2002 v S.Af (sub), Hk (2)
Williams, G. (Nottingham F), 2002 v Ng, Sk (sub), S.Af, Hk (sub) (4)
Wilson, A. (Sheffield W), 1907 v E; 1908 v E; 1912 v E; 1913 v E, W; 1914 v Ni (6)
Wilson, A. (Portsmouth), 1954 v Fi (1)
Wilson, A. N. (Dunfermline), 1920 v E, W, Ni; 1921 v E, W, Ni; (with Middlesbrough), 1922 v E, W, Ni; 1923 v E, W, Ni (12)
Wilson, D. (Queen's Park), 1900 v W (1)
Wilson, D. (Oldham Ath), 1913 v E (1)
Wilson, D. (Rangers), 1961 v E, W, Ni, Ei (2), Cz; 1962 v Ni W, E, Cz, U; 1963 v W, E, A, N, Ei, Sp; 1964 v E, WG; 1965 v Ni, E, Fi (22)
Wilson, G. W. (Hearts), 1904 v W; 1905 v E, Ni; 1906 v W (with Everton), 1907 v E; (with Newcastle U), 1909 v E (6)
Wilson, Hugh, (Newmilns), 1890 v W; (with Sunderland), 1897 v E; (with Third Lanark), 1902 v W; 1904 v Ni (4)
Wilson, I. A. (Leicester C), 1987 v E, Br; (with Everton), 1988 v Bel, Bul, L (5)
Wilson, J. (Vale of Leven), 1888 v W; 1889 v E; 1890 v E; 1891 v E (4)
Wilson, P. (Celtic), 1926 v Ni; 1930 v F; 1931 v Ni; 1933 v E (4)
Wilson, P. (Celtic), 1975 v Sp (sub) (1)
Wilson, R. P. (Arsenal), 1972 v P, Ho (2)
Winters, R. (Aberdeen), 1999 v G (sub) (1)
Wiseman, W. (Queen's Park), 1927 v W; 1930 v Ni (2)
Wood, G. (Everton), 1979 v Ni, E, Arg (sub); (with Arsenal) 1982 v W (4)
Woodburn, W. A. (Rangers), 1947 v E, Bel, L; 1948 v W, Ni 1949 v E, F; 1950 v E, W, Ni, P, F; 1951 v E, W, Ni, A (2), D F, Bel; 1952 v E, W, Ni, USA (24)
Wotherspoon, D. N. (Queen's Park), 1872 v E; 1873 v E (2)
Wright, K. (Hibernian), 1992 v Ni (1)
Wright, S. (Aberdeen), 1993 v G, Es (2)
Wright, T. (Sunderland), 1953 v W, Ni, E (3)
Wylie, T. G. (Rangers), 1890 v Ni (1)

Yeats, R. (Liverpool), 1965 v W; 1966 v I (2)
Yorston, B. C. (Aberdeen), 1931 v Ni (1)
Yorston, H. (Aberdeen), 1955 v W (1)
Young, A. (Everton), 1905 v E; 1907 v W (2)
Young, A. (Hearts), 1960 v E, A (sub), H, T; 1961 v W, Ni (with Everton), Ei; 1966 v P (8)
Young, G. L. (Rangers), 1947 v E, Ni, Bel, L; 1948 v E, Ni Bel, Sw, F; 1949 v E, W, Ni, F; 1950 v E, W, Ni, Sw, P, F 1951 v E, W, Ni, A (2), D, F, Bel; 1952 v E, W, Ni, USA, D Se; 1953 v W, E, Ni, Se; 1954 v Ni, W; 1955 v W, Ni, P, Y 1956 v Ni, W, E, A; 1957 v E, Ni, W, Y, Sp, Sw (53)
Young, J. (Celtic), 1906 v Ni (1)
Younger, T. (Hibernian), 1955 v P, Y, A, H; 1956 v E, Ni, W A; (with Liverpool), 1957 v E, Ni, W, Y, Sp (2), Sw, WG 1958 v Ni, W, E, Sw, H, Pol, Y, Par (24)

WALES

Adams, H. (Berwyn R), 1882 v Ni, E; (with Druids), 1883 v Ni, E (4)

Aizlewood, M. (Charlton Ath), 1986 v S.Ar, Ca (2); 1987 v Fi; (with Leeds U), USSR, Fi (sub); 1988 v D (sub), Se, Ma, I; 1989 v Ho, Se (sub), WG; (with Bradford C), 1990 v Fi, WG, Ei, Cr; (with Bristol C), 1991 v D, Bel (2), L, Ei, Ic, Pol, WG; 1992 v Br, L, Ei, A, R, Ho, Arg, J; 1993 v Ei, Bel, Fa; 1994 v RCS, Cy; (with Cardiff C) 1995v Bul (39)

Allchurch, I. J. (Swansea T), 1951 v E, Ni, P, Sw; 1952 v E, S, Ni, R of UK; 1953 v S, E, Ni, F, Y; 1954 v S, E, Ni, A; 1955 v S, E, Ni, Y; 1956 v E, S, Ni, A; 1957 v E, S; 1958 v Ni, Is (2), H (2), M, Sw, Br; (with Newcastle U), 1959 v E, S, Ni; 1960 v E, S; 1961 v Ni, H, Sp (2); 1962 v E, S, Br (2), M; (with Cardiff C), 1963 v S, E, Ni, H (2); 1964 v E; 1965 v S, E, Ni, Gr, I, USSR; (with Swansea T), 1966 v USSR, E, S, D, Br (2), Ch (68)

Allchurch, L. (Swansea T), 1955 v Ni; 1956 v A; 1958 v S, Ni, EG, Is; 1959 v S; (with Sheffield U), 1962 v S, Ni, Br; 1964 v E (11)

Allen, B. W. (Coventry C), 1951 v S, E (2)

Allen, M. (Watford), 1986 v S.Ar (sub), Ca (1 + 1 sub); (with Norwich C), 1989 v Is (sub); 1990 v Ho, WG; (with Millwall), Ei, Se, Cr (sub); 1991 v L (sub), Ei (sub); 1992 v A; 1993 v Ei (sub); (with Newcastle U), 1994 v R (sub) (14)

Arridge, S. (Bootle), 1892 v S, Ni; (with Everton), 1894 v Ni; 1895 v Ni; 1896 v E; (with New Brighton Tower), 1898 v E, Ni; 1899 v E (8)

Astley, D. J. (Charlton Ath), 1931 v Ni; (with Aston Villa), 1932 v E; 1933 v E, S, Ni; 1934 v E, S; 1935 v S; 1936 v E, Ni; (with Derby Co), 1939 v E, S; (with Blackpool), F (13)

Atherton, R. W. (Hibernian), 1899 v E, Ni; 1903 v E, S, Ni; (with Middlesbrough), 1904 v E, S, Ni; 1905 v Ni (9)

Bailiff, W. E. (Llanelly), 1913 v E, S, Ni; 1920 v Ni (4)

Baker, C. W. (Cardiff C), 1958 v M; 1960 v S, Ni; 1961 v S, E, Ei; 1962 v S (7)

Baker, W. G. (Cardiff C), 1948 v Ni (1)

Bamford, T. (Wrexham), 1931 v E, S, Ni; 1932 v Ni; 1933 v F (5)

Barnard, D. S. (Barnsley), 1998 v Jam; 1999 v I, D, Bl, I, D; 2000 v Bl, Sw, Q, Fi, Br (sub), P; 2001 v Uk, Pol, Uk; 2002 v Arm (sub) (16)

Barnes, W. (Arsenal), 1948 v E, S, Ni; 1949 v E, S, Ni; 1950 v E, S, Ni, Bel; 1951 v E, S, Ni, P; 1952 v E, S, Ni, R of UK; 1954 v E, S; 1955 v S, Y (22)

Bartley, T. (Glossop NE), 1898 v E (1)

Bastock, A. M. (Shrewsbury), 1892 v Ni (1)

Beadles, G. H. (Cardiff C), 1925 v E, S (2)

Bell, W. S. (Shrewsbury Engineers), 1881 v E, S; (with Crewe Alex), 1886 v E, S, Ni (5)

Bellamy, C. D. (Norwich C), 1998 v Jam (sub), Ma, Tun); 1999 v D (sub), Sw (sub), I, D (sub); 2000 v Br (sub), P; (with Coventry C), 2001 v Bl, Arm, Uk; (with Newcastle U), 2002 v Arm, N, Bl, Arg (16)

Bennion, S. R. (Manchester U), 1926 v S; 1927 v S; 1928 v S, E, Ni; 1929 v S, E, Ni; 1930 v S; 1932 v Ni (10)

Berry, G. F. (Wolverhampton W), 1979 v WG; 1980 v Ei, WG (sub); T; (with Stoke C), 1983 v E (sub) (5)

Blackmore, C. G. (Manchester U), 1985 v N (sub); 1986 v S (sub), H (sub), S.Ar, Ei, U; 1987 v Fi (sub), USSR, Cz; 1988 v D (2), Cz, Y, Se, Ma, I; 1989 v Ho, Fi, Is, WG; 1990 v F; Ho, WG, Cr; 1991 v Bel, L; 1992 v Ei (sub), A, R (sub), Ho, Arg, J; 1993 v Fa, Cy, Bel, RCS; 1994 v Se (sub); (with Middlesbrough), 1997 v Bel (39)

Blake, N. A. (Sheffield U), 1994 v N, Se (sub); 1995 v Alb, Mol; 1996 v G (with Bolton W), I (sub); 1998 v T; 1999 v I, D, Bl; (with Blackburn R) Sw; 2000 v Bl, Sw, Q, Fi; 2001 v Bl (sub), N, Pol (2), Uk; 2002 v N (sub); (with Wolverhampton W), CzR (22)

Blew, H. (Wrexham), 1899 v E, S, Ni; 1902 v S, Ni; 1903 v E, S; 1904 v E, S, Ni; 1905 v S, Ni; 1906 v E, S, Ni; 1907 v S; 1908 v E, S, Ni; 1909 v E, S; 1910 v E (22)

Boden, T. (Wrexham), 1880 v E (1)

Bodin, P. J. (Swindon T), 1990 v Cr; 1991 v D, Bel, L, Ei; (with C Palace), Bel, Ic, Pol, WG; 1992 v Br, G, L (sub); (with Swindon T), Ei, (sub), Ho, Arg; 1993 v Ei, Bel, RCS, Fa; 1994 v R, Se, Es (sub); 1995 v Alb (23)

Boulter, L. M. (Brentford), 1939 v Ni (1)

Bowdler, H. E. (Shrewsbury), 1893 v S (1)

Bowdler, J. C. H. (Shrewsbury), 1890 v Ni; (with Wolverhampton W), 1891 v S; 1892 v Ni; (with Shrewsbury), 1894 v E (4)

Bowen, D. L. (Arsenal), 1955 v S, Y; 1957 v Ni, Cz, EG; 1958 v E, S, Ni, EG, Is (2), H (2), M, Se, Br; 1959 v E, S, Ni (19)

Bowen, E. (Druids), 1880 v S; 1883 v S (2)

Bowen, J. P. (Swansea C), 1994 v Es; (with Birmingham C), 1997 v Ho (2)

Bowen, M. R. (Tottenham H), 1986 v Ca (2 sub); (with Norwich C), 1988 v Y (sub); 1989 v Fi (sub), Is, Se, WG (sub); 1990 v Fi (sub), Ho, WG, Se; 1992 v Br (sub), G, L, Ei, A, R, Ho (sub), J; 1993 v Fa, Cy, Bel (1 + sub), RCS (sub); 1994 v RCS, Se; 1995 v Mol, Ge, Bul (2), G, Ge; 1996 v Mol, G, Alb, Sw, Sm; (with West Ham U), 1997 v Sm, Ho (2), Ei (sub) (41)

Bowsher, S. J. (Burnley), 1929 v Ni (1)

Boyle, T. (C Palace), 1981 v Ei, S (sub) (2)

Britten, T. J. (Parkgrove), 1878 v S; (with Presteigne), 1880 v S (2)

Brookes, S. J. (Llandudno), 1900 v E, Ni (2)

Brown, A. I. (Aberdare Ath), 1926 v Ni (1)

Browning, M. T. (Bristol R), 1996 v I (sub), Sm; 1997 v Sm, Ho (with Huddersfield T), S (sub) (5)

Bryan, T. (Oswestry), 1886 v E, Ni (2)

Buckland, T. (Bangor), 1899 v E (1)

Burgess, W. A. R. (Tottenham H), 1947 v E, S, Ni; 1948 v E, S; 1949 v E, S, Ni, P, Bel, Sw; 1950 v E, S, Ni, Bel; 1951 v S, Ni, P, Sw; 1952 v E, S, Ni, R of UK; 1953 v S, E, Ni, F, Y; 1954 v S, E, Ni, A (32)

Burke, T. (Wrexham), 1883 v E; 1884 v S; 1885 v E, S, Ni; (with Newton Heath), 1887 v E, S; 1888 v S (8)

Burnett, T. B. (Ruabon), 1877 v S (1)

Burton, A. D. (Norwich C), 1963 v Ni, H; (with Newcastle U), 1964 v S; 1969 v S, E, Ni, I, EG; 1972 v Cz (9)

Butler, J. (Chirk), 1893 v E, S, Ni (3)

Butler, W. T. (Druids), 1900 v S, Ni (2)

Cartwright, L. (Coventry C), 1974 v E (sub), S, Ni; 1976 v S (sub); 1977 v WG (sub); (with Wrexham), 1978 v Ir (sub); 1979 v Ma (7)

Carty, T. [s] See McCarthy [s] (Wrexham).

Challen, J. B. (Corinthians), 1887 v E, S; 1888 v E; (with Wellingborough GS), 1890 v E (4)

Chapman, T. (Newtown), 1894 v E, S, Ni; 1895 v S, Ni; (with Manchester C), 1896 v E; 1897 v E (7)

Charles, J. M. (Swansea C), 1981 v Cz, T (sub), S (sub), USSR (sub); 1982 v Ic; 1983 v N (sub), Y (sub), Bul (sub), S, Ni, Br; 1984 v Bul (sub); (with QPR), Y (sub), S; (with Oxford U), 1985 v Ic (sub), Sp, Ic; 1986 v Ei; 1987 v Fi (19)

Charles, M. (Swansea T), 1955 v Ni; 1956 v E, S, A; 1957 v E, Ni, Cz (2), EG; 1958 v E, S, EG, Is (2), H (2), M, Se, Br; 1959 v S; (with Arsenal), 1961 v Ni, H, Sp (2); 1962 v E, S; (with Cardiff C), 1962 v Br, Ni; 1963 v S, H (31)

Charles, W. J. (Leeds U), 1950 v Ni; 1951 v Sw; 1953 v Ni, F, Y; 1954 v E, S, Ni, A; 1955 v S, E, Ni, Y; 1956 v E, S, A, Ni; 1957 v E, S, Ni, Cz (2), EG; (with Juventus), 1958 v Is (2), H (2) M, Se; 1960 v S; 1962 v E, Br (2), M; (with Leeds U), 1963 v S; (with Cardiff C), 1964 v S; 1965 v S, USSR (38)

Clarke, R. J. (Manchester C), 1949 v E; 1950 v S, Ni, Bel; 1951 v E, S, Ni, P, Sw; 1952 v E, S, Ni, R of UK; 1953 v S, E; 1954 v E, S, Ni; 1955 v Y, S, E; 1956 v Ni (22)

Coleman, C. (C Palace), 1992 v A (sub); 1993 v Ei (sub); 1994 v N, Es; 1995 v Alb, Mol, Ge, Bul (2), G; 1996 v Mol; (with Blackburn R), I, Sw, Sm; 1997 v Sm; 1998 v Br; (with Fulham), Jam, Ma, Tun; 1999 v I, D, Bl, Sw, D; 2000 v Bl, Sw, Q, Fi; 2001 v Bl, N, Pol; 2002 v G (sub) (32)

Collier, D. J. (Grimsby T), 1921 v S (1)

Collins, W. S. (Llanelly), 1931 v S (1)

Conde, C. (Chirk), 1884 v E, S, Ni (3)

Cook, F. C. (Newport Co), 1925 v E, S; (with Portsmouth), 1928 v E, S; 1930 v E, S, Ni; 1932 v E (8)

Cornforth, J. M. (Swansea C), 1995 v Bul (sub), Ge (2)

Coyne, D. (Tranmere R), 1996 v Sw; (with Grimsby T), 2002 v CzR (sub) (2)

Crompton, W. (Wrexham), 1931 v E, S, Ni (3)

Cross, E. A. (Wrexham), 1876 v S; 1877 v S (2)

Crosse, K. (Druids), 1879 v S; 1881 v E, S (3)

Crossley, M. G. (Nottingham F), 1997 v Ei; 1999 v Sw (sub); 2000 v Fi; (with Middlesbrough), 2002 v Arg (sub), G (5)

Crowe, V. H. (Aston Villa), 1959 v E, Ni; 1960 v E, Ni; 1961 v S, E, Ni, Ei, H, Sp (2); 1962 v E, S, Br, M; 1963 v H (14)

Cumner, R. H. (Arsenal), 1939 v E, S, Ni (3)

Curtis, A. (Swansea C), 1976 v E, Y (sub), S, Ni, Y (sub), E; 1977 v WG, S (sub), Ni (sub); 1978 v WG, E, S; 1979 v WG, S; (with Leeds U), S; 1980 v Ei, WG, T; (with Swansea C), 1982 v Cz, Ic, USSR, Sp, E, S, Ni; 1983 v N; 1984 v R (sub); (with Southampton), S; 1985 v Sp, N (1 + 1 sub); 1986 v H; (with Cardiff C), 1987 v USSR (35)

Curtis, E. R. (Cardiff C), 1928 v S; (with Birmingham), 1932 v S; 1934 v Ni (3)

Daniel, R. W. (Arsenal), 1951 v E, Ni, P; 1952 v E, S, Ni, R of UK; 1953 v S, E, Ni, F, Y; (with Sunderland), 1954 v E, S, Ni; 1955 v E, Ni; 1957 v S, E, Ni, Cz (21)
Darvell, S. (Oxford University), 1897 v S, Ni (2)
Davies, A. (Manchester U), 1983 v Ni, Br; 1984 v E, Ni; 1985 v Ic (2), N; (with Newcastle U), 1986 v H; (with Swansea C), 1988 v Ma, I; 1989 v Ho; (with Bradford C), 1990 v Fi, Ei (13)
Davies, A. (Wrexham), 1876 v S; 1877 v S (2)
Davies, A. (Druids), 1904 v S; (with Middlesbrough), 1905 v S (2)
Davies, A. O. (Barmouth), 1885 v Ni; 1886 v E, S; (with Swifts), 1887 v S; 1888 v E, Ni; (with Wrexham), 1889 v S; (with Crewe Alex), 1890 v E (9)
Davies, A. T. (Shrewsbury), 1891 v Ni (1)
Davies, C. (Charlton Ath), 1972 v R (sub) (1)
Davies, D. (Bolton W), 1904 v S, Ni; 1908 v E (sub) (3)
Davies, D. C. (Brecon), 1899 v Ni; (with Hereford); 1900 v Ni (2)
Davies, D. W. (Treharris), 1912 v Ni; (with Oldham Ath), 1913 v Ni (2)
Davies, E. Lloyd (Stoke C), 1904 v E; 1907 v E, S, Ni; (with Northampton T), 1908 v S; 1909 v Ni; 1910 v Ni; 1911 v E, S; 1912 v E, S; 1913 v E, S; 1914 v Ni, E, S (16)
Davies, E. R. (Newcastle U), 1953 v S, E; 1954 v E, S; 1958 v E, EG (6)
Davies, G. (Fulham), 1980 v T, Ic; 1982 v Sp (sub), F (sub); 1983 v E, Bul, S, Ni, Br; 1984 v R (sub), S (sub), E, Ni; 1985 v Ic; (with Manchester C), 1986 v S.Ar, Ei (16)
Davies, Rev. H. (Wrexham), 1928 v Ni (1)
Davies, Idwal (Liverpool Marine), 1923 v S (1)
Davies, J. E. (Oswestry), 1885 v E (1)
Davies, Jas (Wrexham), 1878 v S (1)
Davies, John (Wrexham), 1879 v S (1)
Davies, Jos (Newton Heath), 1888 v E, S, Ni; 1889 v S; 1890 v E; (with Wolverhampton W), 1892 v E; 1893 v E (7)
Davies, Jos (Everton), 1889 v S, Ni; (with Chirk), 1891 v Ni; (with Ardwick), v E, S; (with Sheffield U), 1895 v E, S, Ni; (with Manchester C), 1896 v E; (with Millwall), 1897 v E; (with Reading), 1900 v E (11)
Davies, J. P. (Druids), 1883 v E, Ni (2)
Davies, Ll. (Wrexham), 1907 v Ni; 1910 v Ni, S, E; (with Everton), 1911 v S, Ni; (with Wrexham), 1912 v Ni, S, E; 1913 v Ni, S, E; 1914 v Ni (13)
Davies, L. S. (Cardiff C), 1922 v E, S, Ni; 1923 v E, S, Ni; 1924 v E, S, Ni; 1925 v S, Ni; 1926 v E, Ni; 1927 v E, Ni; 1928 v S, Ni, E; 1929 v S, Ni, E; 1930 v E, S (23)
Davies, O. (Wrexham), 1890 v S (1)
Davies, R. (Wrexham), 1883 v Ni; 1884 v Ni; 1885 v Ni (3)
Davies, R. (Druids), 1885 v E (1)
Davies, R. O. (Wrexham), 1892 v Ni, E (2)
Davies, R. T. (Norwich C), 1964 v Ni; 1965 v E; 1966 v Br (2), Ch; (with Southampton), 1967 v S, E, Ni; 1968 v S, Ni, WG; 1969 v S, E, Ni, I, WG, R of UK; 1970 v S, Ni; 1971 v Cz, S, E, Ni; 1972 v R, E, S, N; (with Portsmouth), 1974 v E (29)
Davies, R. W. (Bolton W), 1964 v E; 1965 v E, S, Ni, D, Gr, USSR; 1966 v E, S, Ni, USSR, D, Br (2), Ch (sub); 1967 v S; (with Newcastle U), E; 1968 v S, Ni, WG; 1969 v S, E, Ni, I; 1970 v EG; 1971 v R, Cz; (with Manchester C), 1972 v E, S, Ni; (with Manchester U), 1973 v E, S (sub), Ni; (with Blackpool), 1974 v Pol (34)
Davies, S. (Tottenham H), 2001 v Uk (sub+1); 2002 v Arm, N, Bl, Arg, CzR, G (8)
Davies, S. I. (Manchester U), 1996 v Sw (sub) (1)
Davies, Stanley (Preston NE), 1920 v E, S, Ni; (with Everton), 1921 v E, S, Ni; (with WBA), 1922 v E, S, Ni; 1923 v S; 1925 v S, Ni; 1926 v S, E, Ni; 1927 v S; 1928 v S; (with Rotherham U), 1930 v Ni (18)
Davies, T. (Oswestry), 1886 v E (1)
Davies, T. (Druids), 1903 v E, Ni, S; 1904 v S (4)
Davies, W. (Wrexham), 1884 v Ni (1)
Davies, W. (Swansea T), 1924 v E, S, Ni; (with Cardiff C), 1925 v E, S, Ni; 1926 v E, S, Ni; 1927 v S; 1928 v Ni; (with Notts Co), 1929 v E, S, Ni; 1930 v E, S, Ni (17)
Davies, William (Wrexham), 1903 v Ni; 1905 v Ni; (with Blackburn R), 1908 v E, S; 1909 v E, S, Ni; 1911 v E, S, Ni; 1912 v Ni (11)
Davies, W. C. (C Palace), 1908 v S; (with WBA), 1909 v E; 1910 v S; (with C Palace), 1914 v E (4)
Davies, W. D. (Everton), 1975 v H, L, S, E, Ni; 1976 v Y (2), E, Ni; 1977 v WG, S (2), Cz, E, Ni; 1978 v K; (with Wrexham), S, Cz, WG, Ir, E, S, Ni; 1979 v Ma, T, WG, S, E, Ni, Ma; 1980 v Ei, WG, T, E, S, Ni, Ic; 1981 v T, Cz, Ei, T, S,

E, USSR; (with Swansea C), 1982 v Cz, Ic, USSR, Sp, E, S, F; 1983 v Y (52)
Davies, W. H. (Oswestry), 1876 v S; 1877 v S; 1879 v E; 1880 v E (4)
Davies, W. O. (Millwall Ath), 1913 v E, S, Ni; 1914 v S, Ni (5)
Davis, G. (Wrexham), 1978 v Ir, E (sub), Ni (3)
Day, A. (Tottenham H), 1934 v Ni (1)
Deacy, N. (PSV Eindhoven), 1977 v Cz, S, E, Ni; 1978 v K (sub), S (sub), Cz (sub), WG, Ir, S (sub), Ni; (with Beringen), 1979 v T (12)
Dearson, D. J. (Birmingham), 1939 v S, Ni, F (3)
Delaney, M. A. (Aston Villa), 2000 v Sw, Q, Br, P; 2001 v N, Pol, Arm, Uk (2); 2002 v Arm, N, Bl, Arg, CzR, G (15)
Derrett, S. C. (Cardiff C), 1969 v S, WG; 1970 v I; 1971 v Fi (4)
Dewey, F. T. (Cardiff Corinthians), 1931 v E, S (2)
Dibble, A. (Luton T), 1986 v Ca (1+1 sub); (with Manchester C), 1989 v Is (3)
Doughty, J. (Druids), 1886 v S; (with Newton Heath), 1887 v S, Ni; 1888 v E, S, Ni; 1889 v S; 1890 v E (8)
Doughty, R. (Newton Heath and Druids), 1888 v S, Ni (2)
Durban, A. (Derby Co), 1966 v Br (sub); 1967 v Ni; 1968 v E, S, Ni, WG; 1969 v EG, S, E, Ni, WG; 1970 v E, S, Ni, EG, I; 1971 v R, S, E, Ni, Cz, Fi; 1972 v Fi, Cz, E, S, Ni (27)
Dwyer, P. (Cardiff C), 1978 v Ir, E, S, Ni; 1979 v T, S, E, Ni, Ma (sub); 1980 v WG (10)

Earnshaw, R. (Cardiff C), 2002 v G (1)
Edwards, C. (Wrexham), 1878 v S (1)
Edwards, C. N. H. (Swansea C), 1996 v Sw (sub) (1)
Edwards, G. (Birmingham C), 1947 v E, S, Ni; 1948 v E, S, Ni; (with Cardiff C), 1949 v Ni, P, Bel, Sw; 1950 v E, S (12)
Edwards, H. (Wrexham Civil Service), 1878 v Ni; 1880 v E, S; 1882 v E, S; 1883 v S; 1884 v Ni; 1887 v Ni (8)
Edwards, J. H. (Wanderers), 1876 v S (1)
Edwards, J. H. (Oswestry), 1895 v Ni; 1897 v E, Ni (3)
Edwards, J. H. (Aberystwyth), 1898 v Ni (1)
Edwards, L. T. (Charlton Ath), 1957 v Ni, EG (2)
Edwards, R. I. (Chester), 1978 v K (sub); 1979 v Ma, WG; (with Wrexham), 1980 v T (sub) (4)
Edwards, R. W. (Bristol C), 1998 v T (sub), Bel, Ma (sub), Tun (sub) (4)
Edwards, T. (Linfield), 1932 v S (1)
Egan, W. (Chirk), 1892 v S (1)
Ellis, B. (Motherwell), 1932 v E; 1933 v E, S; 1934 v S; 1936 v E; 1937 v S (6)
Ellis, E. (Nunhead), 1931 v S; (with Oswestry), E; 1932 v Ni (3)
Emanuel, W. J. (Bristol C), 1973 v E (sub), Ni (sub) (2)
England, H. M. (Blackburn R), 1962 v Ni, Br, M; 1963 v Ni, H; 1964 v E, S, Ni; 1965 v E, D, Gr (2), USSR, Ni; 1966 v E, S, Ni, USSR, D; (with Tottenham H), 1967 v S, E; 1968 v E, Ni, WG; 1969 v EG; 1970 v R of UK, EG, E, S, Ni, I; 1971 v R; 1972 v Fi, E, S, Ni; 1973 v E (3), S; 1974 v Pol; 1975 v H, L (44)
Evans, B. C. (Swansea C), 1972 v Fi, Cz; 1973 v E (2), Pol, S; (with Hereford U), 1974 v Pol (7)
Evans, D. G. (Reading), 1926 v Ni; 1927 v Ni, E; (with Huddersfield T), 1929 v S (4)
Evans, H. P. (Cardiff C), 1922 v E, S, Ni; 1924 v E, S, Ni (6)
Evans, I. (C Palace), 1976 v A, E, Y (2), E, Ni; 1977 v WG, S (2), Cz, Ni; 1978 v K (13)
Evans, J. (Oswestry), 1893 v Ni; 1894 v E, Ni (3)
Evans, J. (Cardiff C), 1912 v Ni; 1913 v Ni; 1914 v S; 1920 v S, Ni; 1922 v Ni; 1923 v E, Ni (8)
Evans, J. H. (Southend U), 1922 v E, S, Ni; 1923 v S (4)
Evans, Len (Aberdare Ath), 1927 v Ni; (with Cardiff C), 1931 v E, S; (with Birmingham), 1934 v Ni (4)
Evans, M. (Oswestry), 1884 v E (1)
Evans, P. S. (Brentford), 2002 v CzR (sub) (1)
Evans, R. (Clapton), 1902 v Ni (1)
Evans, R. E. (Wrexham), 1906 v E, S; (with Aston Villa), Ni; 1907 v E; 1908 v E, S; (with Sheffield U), 1909 v S; 1910 v E, S, Ni (10)
Evans, R. O. (Wrexham), 1902 v Ni; 1903 v E, S, Ni; (with Blackburn R), 1908 v Ni; (with Coventry C), 1911 v E, Ni; 1912 v E, S, Ni (10)
Evans, R. S. (Swansea T), 1964 v Ni (1)
Evans, T. J. (Clapton Orient), 1927 v S; 1928 v E, S; (with Newcastle U), Ni (4)
Evans, W. (Tottenham H), 1933 v Ni; 1934 v E, S; 1935 v E; 1936 v E, Ni (6)
Evans, W. A. W. (Oxford University), 1876 v S; 1877 v S (2)
Evans, W. G. (Bootle), 1890 v E; 1891 v E; (with Aston Villa), 1892 v S (3)
Evelyn, E. C. (Crusaders), 1887 v E (1)
Eyton-Jones, J. A. (Wrexham), 1883 v Ni; 1884 v Ni, E, S (4)

Farmer, G. (Oswestry), 1885 v E, S (2)
Felgate, D. (Lincoln C), 1984 v R (sub) (1)
Finnigan, R. J. (Wrexham), 1930 v Ni (1)
Flynn, B. (Burnley), 1975 v L (2 sub), H (sub), S, E, Ni; 1976 v A, E, Y (2), E, Ni; 1977 v WG (sub), S (2), Cz, E, Ni; 1978 v K (2), S; (with Leeds U), Cz, WG, Ir (sub), E, S, Ni; 1979 v Ma, T, S, E, Ni, Ma; 1980 v Ei, WG, E, S, Ni, Ic; 1981 v T, Cz, Ei, T, S, E, USSR; 1982 v Cz, USSR, E, S, Ni, F; 1983 v N; (with Burnley), Y, E, Bul, S, Ni, Br; 1984 v N, R, Bul, Y, S, N, Is (66)
Ford, T. (Swansea T), 1947 v S; (with Aston Villa), 1947 v Ni; 1948 v S, Ni; 1949 v E, S, Ni, P, Bel, Sw; 1950 v E, S, Ni, Bel; 1951 v S; (with Sunderland), 1951 v E, Ni, P, Sw; 1952 v E, S, Ni, R of UK; 1953 v S, E, Ni, F, Y; (with Cardiff C), 1954 v A; 1955 v S, E, Ni, Y; 1956 v S, Ni, E, A; 1957 v S (38)
Foulkes, H. E. (WBA), 1932 v Ni (1)
Foulkes, W. I. (Newcastle U), 1952 v E, S, Ni, R of UK; 1953 v E, S, F, Y; 1954 v E, S, Ni (11)
Foulkes, W. T. (Oswestry), 1884 v Ni; 1885 v S (2)
Fowler, J. (Swansea T), 1925 v E; 1926 v E, Ni; 1927 v S; 1928 v S; 1929 v E (6)
Freestone, R. (Swansea C), 2000 v Br (1)

Gabbidon, D. L. (Cardiff C), 2002 v CzR (1)
Garner, J. (Aberystwyth), 1896 v S (1)
Giggs, R. J. (Manchester U), 1992 v G (sub), L (sub), R (sub); 1993 v Fa (sub), Bel (sub + 1), RCS, Fa; 1994 v RCS, Cy, R; 1995 v Alb, Bul; 1996 v G, Alb, Sm; 1997 v Sm, T, Bel; 1998 v T, Bel; 1999 v I (2), D; 2000 v Bl, Fi; 2001 v Bl, N, Pol, Uk, Pol, Uk; 2002 v Arm, N, Arg, G (36)
Giles, D. (Swansea C), 1980 v E, S, Ni, Ic; 1981 v T, Cz, T (sub), E, USSR (sub); (with C Palace), 1982 v Sp (sub); 1983 v Ni (sub), Br (12)
Gillam, S. G. (Wrexham), 1889 v S (sub), Ni; (with Shrewsbury), 1890 v E, Ni; (with Clapton), 1894 v S (5)
Glascodine, G. (Wrexham), 1879 v E (1)
Glover, E. M. (Grimsby T), 1932 v S; 1934 v Ni; 1936 v S; 1937 v E, S, Ni; 1939 v Ni (7)
Godding, G. (Wrexham), 1923 v S, Ni (2)
Godfrey, B. C. (Preston NE), 1964 v Ni; 1965 v D, I (3)
Goodwin, U. (Ruthin), 1881 v E (1)
Goss, J. (Norwich C), 1991 v Ic, Pol (sub); 1992 v A; 1994 v Cy (sub), R (sub), Se; 1995 v Alb; 1996 v Sw (sub), Sm (sub) (9)
Gough, R. T. (Oswestry White Star), 1883 v S (1)
Gray, A. (Oldham Ath), 1924 v E, S, Ni; 1925 v E, S, Ni; 1926 v E, S; 1927 v S; (with Manchester C), 1928 v E, S; 1929 v E, S, Ni; (with Manchester Central), 1930 v S; (with Tranmere R), 1932 v E, S, Ni; (with Chester), 1937 v E, S, Ni; 1938 v E, S, Ni (24)
Green, A. W. (Aston Villa), 1901 v Ni; (with Notts Co), 1903 v E; 1904 v S, Ni; 1906 v Ni, E; (with Nottingham F), 1907 v E; 1908 v S (8)
Green, C. R. (Birmingham C), 1965 v USSR, I; 1966 v E, S, USSR, Br (2); 1967 v E; 1968 v E, S, Ni, WG; 1969 v S, I, Ni (sub) (15)
Green, G. H. (Charlton Ath), 1938 v Ni; 1939 v E, Ni, F (4)
Green, R. M. (Wolverhampton W), 1998 v Ma, Tun (2)
Grey, Dr W. (Druids), 1876 v S; 1878 v S (2)
Griffiths, A. T. (Wrexham), 1971 v Cz (sub); 1975 v A, H (2), L (2), E, Ni; 1976 v A, E, S, E (sub), Ni, Y (2); 1977 v WG, S (17)
Griffiths, F. J. (Blackpool), 1900 v E, S (2)
Griffiths, G. (Chirk), 1887 v Ni (1)
Griffiths, J. H. (Swansea T), 1953 v Ni (1)
Griffiths, L. (Wrexham), 1902 v S (1)
Griffiths, M. W. (Leicester C), 1947 v Ni; 1949 v P, Bel; 1950 v E, S, Bel; 1951 v E, Ni, P, Sw; 1954 v A (11)
Griffiths, P. (Chirk), 1884 v E, Ni; 1888 v E; 1890 v S, Ni; 1891 v Ni (6)
Griffiths, P. H. (Everton), 1932 v S (1)
Griffiths, T. P. (Everton), 1927 v E, Ni; 1929 v E; 1930 v E; 1931 v Ni; 1932 v Ni, S, E; (with Bolton W), 1933 v E, S, Ni; (with Middlesbrough), F; 1934 v E, S; 1935 v E, Ni; 1936 v S; (with Aston Villa), Ni; 1937 v E, S, Ni (21)

Hall, G. D. (Chelsea), 1988 v Y (sub), Ma, I; 1989 v Ho, Fi, Is; 1990 v Ei; 1991 v Ei; 1992 v A (sub) (9)
Hallam, J. (Oswestry), 1889 v E (1)
Hanford, H. (Swansea T), 1934 v Ni; 1935 v S; 1936 v E; (with Sheffield W), 1936 v Ni; 1938 v E, S; 1939 v F (7)
Harrington, A. C. (Cardiff C), 1956 v Ni; 1957 v E, S; 1958 v S, Ni, Is (2); 1961 v S, E; 1962 v E, S (11)
Harris, C. S. (Leeds U), 1976 v E, S; 1978 v WG, Ir, E, S, Ni; 1979 v Ma, T, WG, E (sub), Ma; 1980 v Ni (sub), Ic (sub); 1981 v T, Cz (sub), Ei, T, S, E, USSR; 1982 v Cz, Ic, E (sub) (24)

Harris, W. C. (Middlesbrough), 1954 v A; 1957 v EG, Cz; 1958 v E, S, EG (6)
Harrison, W. C. (Wrexham), 1899 v E; 1900 v E, S, Ni; 1901 v Ni (5)
Hartson, J. (Arsenal), 1995 v Bul, G (sub), Ge (sub); 1996 v Mol (sub), Sw; 1997 v Ho, T (sub), Ei; (with West Ham U), Bel (sub), S; 1998 v Bel, Jam, Ma, Tun; (with Wimbledon), 1999 v Sw (sub), I (sub), D; 2000 v Sw (sub); 2001 v N, Pol; (with Coventry C), Arm, Uk, Pol, Uk; (with Celtic), 2002 v N, Bl, Arg, CzR, G (29)
Haworth, S. O. (Cardiff C), 1997 v S (sub); (with Coventry C), 1998 v Br, Jam (sub), Ma (sub), Tun (sub) (5)
Hayes, A. (Wrexham), 1890 v Ni; 1894 v Ni (2)
Hennessey, W. T. (Birmingham C), 1962 v Ni, Br (2); 1963 v S, E, H (2); 1964 v E, S; 1965 v S, E, D, Gr, USSR; 1966 v E, USSR; (with Nottingham F), 1966 v S, Ni, D, Br (2), Ch; 1967 v S, E; 1968 v E, S, Ni; 1969 v WG, EG, R of UK; 1970 v EG; (with Derby Co), E, S, Ni; 1972 v Fi, Cz, E, S; 1973 v E (39)
Hersee, A. M. (Bangor), 1886 v S, Ni (2)
Hersee, R. (Llandudno), 1886 v Ni (1)
Hewitt, R. (Cardiff C), 1958 v Ni, Is, Se, H, Br (5)
Hewitt, T. J. (Wrexham), 1911 v E, S, Ni; (with Chelsea), 1913 v E, S, Ni; (with South Liverpool), 1914 v E, S (8)
Heywood, D. (Druids), 1879 v E (1)
Hibbott, H. (Newtown Excelsior), 1880 v E, S; (with Newtown), 1885 v S (3)
Higham, G. G. (Oswestry), 1878 v S; 1879 v E (2)
Hill, M. R. (Ipswich T), 1972 v Cz, R (2)
Hockey, T. (Sheffield U), 1972 v Fi, R; 1973 v E (2); (with Norwich C), Pol, S, E, Ni; (with Aston Villa), 1974 v Pol (9)
Hoddinott, T. F. (Watford), 1921 v E, S (2)
Hodges, G. (Wimbledon), 1984 v N (sub), Is (sub); 1987 v USSR, Fi, Cz; (with Newcastle U), 1988 v D; (with Watford), D (sub), Cz (sub), Se, Ma (sub), I (sub); 1990 v Se, Cr; (with Sheffield U), 1992 v Br (sub), Ei (sub), A; 1996 v G (sub), I (18)
Hodgkinson, A. V. (Southampton), 1908 v Ni (1)
Holden, A. (Chester C), 1984 v Is (sub) (1)
Hole, B. G. (Cardiff C), 1963 v Ni; 1964 v Ni; 1965 v S, E, Ni, D, Gr (2), USSR, I; 1966 v E, S, Ni, USSR, D, Br (2), Ch; (with Blackburn R), 1967 v S, E, Ni; 1968 v E, S, Ni, WG; (with Aston Villa), 1969 v I, WG, EG; 1970 v I; (with Swansea C), 1971 v R (30)
Hole, W. J. (Swansea T), 1921 v Ni; 1922 v E; 1923 v E, Ni; 1928 v E, S, Ni; 1929 v E, S (9)
Hollins, D. M. (Newcastle U), 1962 v Br (sub), M; 1963 v Ni, H; 1964 v E; 1965 v Ni, Gr, I; 1966 v S, D, Br (11)
Hopkins, I. J. (Brentford), 1935 v S, Ni; 1936 v E, Ni; 1937 v E, S, Ni; 1938 v E, Ni; 1939 v E, S, Ni (12)
Hopkins, J. (Fulham), 1983 v Ni, Br; 1984 v N, R, Bul, Y, S, E, Ni, N, Is; 1985 v Ic (1 + 1 sub), N; (with C Palace), 1990 v Ho, Cr (16)
Hopkins, M. (Tottenham H), 1956 v Ni; 1957 v Ni, S, E, Cz (2), EG; 1958 v E, S, Ni, EG, Is (2), H (2), M, Se, Br; 1959 v E, S, Ni; 1960 v E, S; 1961 v Ni, H, Sp (2); 1962 v Ni, Br (2), M; 1963 v S, Ni, H (34)
Horne, B. (Portsmouth), 1988 v D (sub), Y, Se (sub), Ma, I; 1989 v Ho, Fi, Is; (with Southampton), Se, WG; 1990 v WG (sub), Ei, Se, Cr; 1991 v D, Bel (2), L, Ei, Ic, Pol, WG; 1992 v Br, G, L, Ei, A, Ho, Arg, J; (with Everton), 1993 v Fa, Cy, Bel, Ei, Bel, RCS, Fa; 1994 v RCS, Cy, R, N, Se, Es; 1995 v Mol, Ge, Bul, G, Ge; 1996 v Mol, G, I, Sw, Sm; (with Birmingham C), 1997 v Sm, Ho, T, Ei, Bel (59)
Howell, E. G. (Builth), 1888 v Ni; 1890 v E; 1891 v E (3)
Howells, R. G. (Cardiff C), 1954 v E, S (2)
Hugh, A. R. (Newport Co), 1930 v Ni (1)
Hughes, A. (Rhos), 1894 v E, S (2)
Hughes, A. (Chirk), 1907 v Ni (1)
Hughes, C. M. (Luton T), 1992 v Ho (sub); 1994 v N (sub), Se (sub), Es; 1996 v Alb; 1997 v Ei (sub); (with Wimbledon), 1998 v T, Bel (8)
Hughes, E. (Everton), 1899 v S, Ni; (with Tottenham H), 1901 v E, S; 1902 v Ni; 1904 v E, Ni, S; 1905 v E, Ni, S; 1906 v E, Ni; 1907 v E (14)
Hughes, E. (Wrexham), 1906 v S; (with Nottingham F), 1906 v Ni; 1908 v S, E; 1910 v Ni, E, S; 1911 v Ni, E, S; (with Wrexham), 1912 v Ni, E, S; (with Manchester C), 1913 v E, S; 1914 v N (16)
Hughes, F. W. (Northwich Victoria), 1882 v E, Ni; 1883 v E, Ni, S; 1884 v S (6)
Hughes, I. (Luton T), 1951 v E, Ni, P, Sw (4)
Hughes, J. (Cambridge University), 1877 v S; (with Aberystwyth), 1879 v S (2)
Hughes, J. (Liverpool), 1905 v Ni, E, S (3)
Hughes, J. I. (Blackburn R), 1935 v Ni (1)

Hughes, L. M. (Manchester U), 1984 v E, Ni; 1985 v Ic, Sp, Ic, N, S, Sp, N; 1986 v S, H, U; (with Barcelona), 1987 v USSR, Cz; 1988 v D (2), Cz, Se, Ma, I; (with Manchester U), 1989 v Ho, Fi, Is, Se, WG; 1990 v Fi, WG, Cr; 1991 v D, Bel (2), L, Ic, Pol, WG; 1992 v Br, G, L, Ei, R, Ho, Arg, J; 1993 v Fa, Cy, Bel, Ei, Bel, RCS, Fa; 1994 v RCS, Cy, N; 1995 v Ge, Bul, G, Ge; (with Chelsea), 1996 v Mol, I, Sm; 1997 v Sm, Ho, T, Ei, Bel; 1998 v T; (with Southampton), 1999 v I, D, Bl, Sw, I, D (72)

Hughes, P. W. (Bangor), 1887 v Ni; 1889 v Ni, E (3)

Hughes, W. (Bootle), 1891 v E; 1892 v S, Ni (3)

Hughes, W. A. (Blackburn R), 1949 v E, Ni, P, Bel, Sw (5)

Hughes, W. M. (Birmingham), 1938 v E, Ni, S; 1939 v E, Ni, S, F; 1947 v E, S, Ni (10)

Humphreys, J. V. (Everton), 1947 v Ni (1)

Humphreys, R. (Druids), 1888 v Ni (1)

Hunter, A. H. (FA of Wales Secretary), 1887 v Ni (1)

Jackett, K. (Watford), 1983 v N, Y, E, Bul, S; 1984 v N, R, Y, S, Ni, N, Is; 1985 v Ic, Sp, Ic, N, S, Sp, N; 1986 v S, H, S.Ar, Ei, Ca (2); 1987 v Fi (2); 1988 v D, Cz, Y, Se (31)

Jackson, W. (St Helens Rec), 1899 v Ni (1)

James, E. (Chirk), 1893 v E, Ni; 1894 v E, S, Ni; 1898 v S, E; 1899 v Ni (8)

James, E. G. (Blackpool), 1966 v Br (2), Ch; 1967 v Ni; 1968 v S; 1971 v Cz, S, E, Ni (9)

James, L. (Burnley), 1972 v Cz, R, S (sub); 1973 v E (3), Pol, S, Ni; 1974 v Pol, E, S, Ni; 1975 v A, H (2), L (2), S, E, Ni; 1976 v A; (with Derby Co), S, E, Y (2), Ni; 1977 v WG, S (2), Cz, E, Ni; 1978 v K (2); (with QPR), WG; (with Burnley), 1979 v T; (with Swansea C), 1980 v E, S, Ni, Ic; 1981 v T, Ei, T, S, E; 1982 v Cz, Ic, USSR, E (sub), S, Ni, F; (with Sunderland), 1983 v E (sub) (54)

James, R. M. (Swansea C), 1979 v Ma, WG (sub), S, E, Ni, Ma; 1980 v WG; 1982 v Cz (sub), Ic, Sp, E, S, Ni, F; 1983 v N, Y, E, Bul; (with Stoke C), 1984 v N, R, Bul, Y, S, E, Ni, N, Is; 1985 v Ic, Sp, Ic; (with QPR), N, S, Sp, N; 1986 v S, S.Ar, Ei, U, Ca (2); 1987 v Fi (2), USSR, Cz; (with Leicester C), 1988 v D (2); (with Swansea C), Y (47)

James, W. (West Ham U), 1931 v Ni; 1932 v Ni (2)

Jarrett, R. H. (Ruthin), 1889 v Ni; 1890 v S (2)

Jarvis, A. L. (Hull C), 1967 v S, E, Ni (3)

Jenkins, E. (Lovell's Ath), 1925 v E (1)

Jenkins, J. (Brighton), 1924 v Ni, E, S; 1925 v S, Ni; 1926 v E, S; 1927 v S (8)

Jenkins, R. W. (Rhyl), 1902 v Ni (1)

Jenkins, S. R. (Swansea C), 1995 v Ge, G; (with Huddersfield T), Alb, I; 1997 v Ho (sub), T, S; 1998 v T, Bel, Br, Jam; 1999 v I (sub), D; 2001 v Pol (sub), Uk (sub); 2002 v Arm, N (16)

Jenkyns, C. A. L. (Small Heath), 1892 v E, S, Ni; 1895 v E; (with Woolwich Arsenal), 1896 v S; (with Newton Heath), 1897 v Ni; (with Walsall), 1898 v S, E (8)

Jennings, W. (Bolton W), 1914 v E, S; 1920 v S; 1923 v Ni, E; 1924 v E, S, Ni; 1927 v S, Ni; 1929 v S (11)

John, R. F. (Arsenal), 1923 v E, Ni; 1925 v Ni; 1926 v E; 1927 v E; 1928 v E, Ni; 1930 v E, S; 1932 v E; 1933 v F, Ni; 1935 v Ni; 1936 v S; 1937 v E (15)

John, W. R. (Walsall), 1931 v Ni; (with Stoke C), 1933 v E, S, Ni, F; 1934 v E, S; (with Preston NE), 1935 v E, S; (with Sheffield U), 1936 v E, S, Ni; (with Swansea T), 1939 v E, S (14)

Johnson, A. J. (Nottingham F), 1999 v I, D, Bl, Sw; 2000 v Fi (sub), Br (sub), P (sub) (7)

Johnson, M. G. (Swansea T), 1964 v Ni (1)

Jones, A. (Port Vale), 1987 v Fi, Cz (sub); 1988 v D, (with Charlton Ath), D (sub), Cz (sub); 1990 v Hol (sub) (6)

Jones, A. E. (Oxford University), 1877 v S (1)

Jones, A. T. (Nottingham F), 1905 v E; (with Notts Co), 1906 v E (2)

Jones, Bryn (Wolverhampton W), 1935 v Ni; 1936 v E, S, Ni; 1937 v E, S, Ni; 1938 v E, S, Ni; (with Arsenal), 1939 v E, S, Ni; 1947 v S, Ni; 1948 v E; 1949 v S (17)

Jones, B. S. (Swansea C), 1963 v S, E, Ni, H (2); 1964 v S, Ni; (with Plymouth Arg), (with Cardiff C), 1969 v S, E, Ni, I (sub), WG, EG, R of UK (15)

Jones, Charlie (Nottingham F), 1926 v E; 1927 v S, Ni; 1928 v E; (with Arsenal), 1930 v E, S; 1932 v E; 1933 v F (8)

Jones, Cliff (Swansea T), 1954 v A; 1956 v E, Ni, S, A; 1957 v E, S, Ni, Cz (2), EG; 1958 v EG, E, S, Ni (2); (with Tottenham H), 1958 v Ni, H (2), M, Se, Br; 1959 v Ni; 1960 v E, S, Ni; 1961 v S, E, Ni, Sp, H, Ei; 1962 v E, Ni, S, Br (2), M; 1963 v S, Ni, H; 1964 v E, S, Ni; 1965 v E, S, Ni, D, Gr (2), USSR, I; 1967 v S, E; 1968 v E, S, WG; (with Fulham), 1969 v I, R of UK (59)

Jones, C. W. (Birmingham), 1935 v Ni; 1939 v F (2)

Jones, D. (Chirk), 1888 v S, Ni; (with Bolton W), 1889 v E, S, Ni; 1890 v E; 1891 v S; 1892 v Ni; 1893 v E; 1894 v E; 1895 v E; 1898 v S; (with Manchester C), 1900 v E, Ni (14)

Jones, D. E. (Norwich C), 1976 v S, E (sub); 1978 v S, Cz, WG, Ir, E; 1980 v E (8)

Jones, D. O. (Leicester C), 1934 v E, Ni; 1935 v E, S; 1936 v E, Ni; 1937 v Ni (7)

Jones, Evan (Chelsea), 1910 v S, Ni; (with Oldham Ath), 1911 v E, S; 1912 v E, S; (with Bolton W), 1914 v Ni (7)

Jones, F. R. (Bangor), 1885 v E, Ni; 1886 v S (3)

Jones, F. W. (Small Heath), 1893 v S (1)

Jones, G. P. (Wrexham), 1907 v S, Ni (2)

Jones, H. (Aberaman), 1902 v Ni (1)

Jones, Humphrey (Bangor), 1885 v E, Ni, S; 1886 v E, Ni, S; (with Queen's Park), 1887 v E; (with East Stirlingshire), 1889 v E, Ni; 1890 v E, S, Ni; (with Queen's Park), 1891 v E, S (14)

Jones, Ivor (Swansea T), 1920 v S, Ni; 1921 v Ni, E; 1922 v S, Ni; (with WBA), 1923 v E, Ni; 1924 v S; 1926 v Ni (10)

Jones, Jeffrey (Llandrindod Wells), 1908 v Ni; 1909 v Ni; 1910 v S (3)

Jones, J. (Druids), 1876 v S (1)

Jones, J. (Berwyn Rangers), 1883 v S, Ni; 1884 v S (3)

Jones, J. (Wrexham), 1925 v Ni (1)

Jones, J. L. (Sheffield U), 1895 v E, S, Ni; 1896 v Ni, S, E; 1897 v Ni, S, E; (with Tottenham H), 1898 v Ni, E, S; 1899 v S, Ni; 1900 v S; 1902 v Ni; 1904 v E, S, Ni (21)

Jones, J. Love (Stoke C), 1906 v S; (with Middlesbrough), 1910 v Ni (2)

Jones, J. O. (Bangor), 1901 v S, Ni (2)

Jones, J. P. (Liverpool), 1976 v A, E, S; 1977 v WG, S (2), Cz, E, Ni; 1978 v K (2), S, Cz, WG, Ir, E, S, Ni; (with Wrexham), 1979 v Ma, T, WG, S, E, Ni, Ma; 1980 v Ei, WG, T, E, S, Ni, Ic; 1981 v T, Ei, T, S, E, USSR; 1982 v Cz, Ic, USSR, Sp, E, S, Ni, F; 1983 v N; (with Chelsea), Y, E, Bul, S, Ni, Br; 1984 v N, R, Bul, Y, S, E, Ni, N, Is; 1985 v Ic, N, S, N; (with Huddersfield T), 1986 v S, H, Ei, U, Ca (2) (72)

Jones, J. T. (Stoke C), 1912 v E, S, Ni; 1913 v E, Ni; 1914 v S, Ni; 1920 v E, S, Ni; (with C Palace), 1921 v E, S; 1922 v E, S, Ni (15)

Jones, K. (Aston Villa), 1950 v S (1)

Jones, Leslie J. (Cardiff C), 1933 v F; (with Coventry C), 1935 v Ni; 1936 v S; 1937 v E, S, Ni; (with Arsenal), 1938 v E, S, Ni; 1939 v E, S (11)

Jones, M. G. (Leeds U), 2000 v Sw (sub), Q, Br, P; 2001 v Pol (sub); (with Leicester C), Arm (sub), Uk, Pol (sub); 2002 v Arm (sub), N (sub), Bl (11)

Jones, P. L. (Liverpool), 1997 v S (sub); (with Tranmere R), 1998 v T (sub) (2)

Jones, P. S. (Stockport Co), 1997 v S (sub); (with Southampton), 1998 v T (sub), Br, Jam, Ma; 1999 v I, D, Bl, Sw, I, D; 2000 v Bl, Sw, Q; 2001 v Bl, N, Pol, Arm, Uk, Pol, Uk; 2002 v Arm, N, Bl, Arg (25)

Jones, P. W. (Bristol R), 1971 v Fi (1)

Jones, R. (Bangor), 1887 v S; 1889 v E; (with Crewe Alex), 1890 v E (3)

Jones, R. (Leicester Fosse), 1898 v S (1)

Jones, R. (Druids), 1899 v S (1)

Jones, R. (Bangor), 1900 v S, Ni (2)

Jones, R. (Millwall), 1906 v S, Ni (2)

Jones, R. A. (Druids), 1884 v E, Ni, S; 1885 v S (4)

Jones, R. A. (Sheffield W), 1994 v Es (1)

Jones, R. S. (Everton), 1894 v Ni (1)

Jones, S. (Wrexham), 1887 v Ni; (with Chester), 1890 v S (2)

Jones, S. (Wrexham), 1893 v S, Ni; (with Burton Swifts), 1895 v S; 1896 v E, Ni; (with Druids), 1899 v E (6)

Jones, T. (Manchester U), 1926 v Ni; 1927 v E, Ni; 1930 v Ni (4)

Jones, T. D. (Aberdare), 1908 v Ni (1)

Jones, T. G. (Everton), 1938 v Ni; 1939 v E, S, Ni; 1947 v E, S; 1948 v E, S, Ni; 1949 v E, Ni, P, Bel, Sw; 1950 v E, S, Bel (17)

Jones, T. J. (Sheffield W), 1932 v Ni; 1933 v F (2)

Jones, V. P. (Wimbledon), 1995 v Bul (2), G, Ge; 1996 v Sw; 1997 v Ho, T, Ei, Bel (9)

Jones, W. E. A. (Swansea T), 1947 v E, S; (with Tottenham H), 1949 v E, S (4)

Jones, W. J. (Aberdare), 1901 v E, S; (with West Ham U), 1902 v S (4)

Jones, W. Lot (Manchester C), 1905 v E, Ni; 1906 v E, S, Ni; 1907 v E, S, Ni; 1908 v S; 1909 v E, S, Ni; 1910 v E; 1911 v E; 1913 v E, S; 1914 v S, Ni; (with Southend U), 1920 v E, Ni (20)

Jones, W. P. (Druids), 1889 v E, Ni; (with Wynstay), 1890 v S, Ni (4)

Jones, W. R. (Aberystwyth), 1897 v S (1)

Keenor, F. C. (Cardiff C), 1920 v E, Ni; 1921 v E, Ni, S; 1922 v Ni; 1923 v E, Ni, S; 1924 v E, Ni, S; 1925 v E, Ni, S; 1926 v S; 1927 v E, Ni, S; 1928 v E, Ni, S; 1929 v E, Ni, S; 1930 v E, Ni, S; 1931 v E, Ni, S; (with Crewe Alex), 1933 v S (32)

Kelly, F. C. (Wrexham), 1899 v S, Ni; (with Druids), 1902 v Ni (3)

Kelsey, A. J. (Arsenal), 1954 v Ni, A; 1955 v S, Ni, Y; 1956 v E, Ni, S, A; 1957 v E, Ni, S, Cz (2); EG; 1958 v E, S, Ni, Is (2), H (2), M, Se, Br; 1959 v E, S; 1960 v E, Ni, S; 1961 v E, Ni, S, H, Sp (2); 1962 v E, S, Ni, Br (2) (41)

Kenrick, S. L. (Druids), 1876 v S; 1877 v S; (with Oswestry), 1879 v E, S; (with Shropshire Wanderers), 1881 v E (5)

Ketley, C. F. (Druids), 1882 v Ni (1)

King, J. (Swansea T), 1955 v E (1)

Kinsey, N. (Norwich C), 1951 v Ni, P, Sw; 1952 v E; (with Birmingham C), 1954 v Ni; 1956 v E, S (7)

Knill, A. R. (Swansea C), 1989 v Ho (1)

Koumas, J. (Tranmere R), 2001 v Uk (sub); 2002 v CzR (2)

Krzywicki, R. L. (WBA), 1970 v EG, I; (with Huddersfield T), Ni, E, S; 1971 v R, Fi; 1972 v Cz (sub) (8)

Lambert, R. (Liverpool), 1947 v S; 1948 v E; 1949 v P, Bel, Sw (5)

Latham, G. (Liverpool), 1905 v E, S; 1906 v S; 1907 v E, S, Ni; 1908 v E; 1909 v Ni; (with Southport Central), 1910 v E; (with Cardiff C), 1913 v Ni (10)

Law, B. J. (QPR), 1990 v Se (1)

Lawrence, E. (Clapton Orient), 1930 v Ni; (with Notts Co), 1932 v S (2)

Lawrence, S. (Swansea T), 1932 v Ni; 1933 v F; 1934 v S, E, Ni; 1935 v E, S; 1936 v S (8)

Lea, A. (Wrexham), 1889 v E; 1891 v S, Ni; 1893 v Ni (4)

Lea, C. (Ipswich T), 1965 v Ni, I (2)

Leary, P. (Bangor), 1889 v Ni (1)

Leek, K. (Leicester C), 1961 v S, E, Ni, H, Sp (2); (with Newcastle U), 1962 v S; (with Birmingham C), v Br (sub), M; 1963 v E; 1965 v S, Gr; (with Northampton T), 1965 v Gr (13)

Legg, A. (Birmingham C), 1996 v Sw, Sm (sub); 1997 v Ho (sub), Ei; (with Cardiff C), 1999 v D (sub); 2001 v Arm (6)

Lever, A. R. (Leicester C), 1953 v S (1)

Lewis, B. (Chester), 1891 v Ni; (with Wrexham), 1892 v S, E, Ni; (with Middlesbrough), 1893 v S, E; (with Wrexham), 1894 v S, E, Ni; 1895 v S (10)

Lewis, D. (Arsenal), 1927 v E; 1928 v Ni; 1930 v E (3)

Lewis, D. (Swansea C), 1983 v Br (sub) (1)

Lewis, D. J. (Swansea T), 1933 v E, S (2)

Lewis, D. M. (Bangor), 1890 v Ni, S (2)

Lewis, J. (Bristol R), 1906 v E (1)

Lewis, J. (Cardiff C), 1926 v S (1)

Lewis, T. (Wrexham), 1881 v E, S (2)

Lewis, W. (Bangor), 1885 v E; 1886 v E, S; 1887 v E, S; 1888 v E; 1889 v E, Ni, S; (with Crewe Alex), 1890 v E; 1891 v E, S; 1892 v E, S, Ni; 1894 v E, S, Ni; (with Chester), 1895 v S, Ni, E; 1896 v E, S, Ni; (with Manchester C), 1897 v E, S; (with Chester), 1898 v Ni (27)

Lewis, W. L. (Swansea T), 1927 v E, Ni; 1928 v E, Ni; 1929 v S; (with Huddersfield T), 1930 v E (6)

Llewellyn, C. M. (Norwich C), 1998 v Ma (sub), Tun (sub) (2)

Lloyd, B. W. (Wrexham), 1976 v A, E, S (3)

Lloyd, J. W. (Wrexham), 1879 v S; (with Newtown), 1885 v S (2)

Lloyd, R. A. (Ruthin), 1891 v Ni; 1895 v S (2)

Lockley, A. (Chirk), 1898 v Ni (1)

Lovell, S. (C Palace), 1982 v USSR (sub); (with Millwall), 1985 v N; 1986 v S (sub), H (sub), Ca (1+1 sub) (6)

Lowrie, G. (Coventry C), 1948 v S, Ni; (with Newcastle U), 1949 v P (4)

Lowndes, S. (Newport Co), 1983 v S (sub), Br (sub); (with Millwall), 1985 v N (sub); 1986 v S.Ar (sub), Ei, U, Ca (2); (with Barnsley), 1987 v Fi (sub); 1988 v Se (sub) (10)

Lucas, P. M. (Leyton Orient), 1962 v Ni, M; 1963 v E, S (4)

Lucas, W. H. (Swansea T), 1949 v S, Ni, P, Bel, Sw; 1950 v E; 1951 v E (7)

Lumberg, A. (Wrexham), 1929 v Ni; 1930 v E, S; (with Wolverhampton W), 1932 v S (4)

McCarthy, T. P. (Wrexham), 1899 v Ni (1)

McMillan, R. (Shrewsbury Engineers), 1881 v E, S (2)

Maguire, G. T. (Portsmouth), 1990 v Fi (sub), Ho, WG, Ei, Se; 1992 v Br (sub), G (7)

Mahoney, J. F. (Stoke C), 1968 v E; 1969 v EG; 1971 v Cz; 1973 v E (3), Pol, S, Ni; 1974 v Pol, E, S, Ni; 1975 v A, H (2), L (2), S, E, Ni; 1976 v A, Y (2), E, Ni; 1977 v WG, Cz, S, E, Ni; (with Middlesbrough), 1978 v K (2), S, Cz, Ir, E (sub), S, Ni; 1979 v WG, S, E, Ni, Ma; (with Swansea C), 1980 v Ei, WG, T (sub); 1982 v Ic, USSR; 1983 v Y, E (51)

Mardon, P. J. (WBA), 1996 v G (sub) (1)

Marriott, A. (Wrexham), 1996 v Sw (sub); 1997 v S; 1998 v Bel, Br (sub), Tun (5)

Martin, T. J. (Newport Co), 1930 v Ni (1)

Marustik, C. (Swansea C), 1982 v Sp, E, S, Ni, F; 1983 v N (6)

Mates, J. (Chirk), 1891 v Ni; 1897 v E, S (3)

Mathews, R. W. (Liverpool), 1921 v Ni; (with Bristol C), 1923 v E; (with Bradford), 1926 v Ni (3)

Matthews, W. (Chester), 1905 v Ni; 1908 v E (2)

Matthias, J. S. (Brymbo), 1896 v S, Ni; (with Shrewsbury), 1897 v E, S; (with Wolverhampton W), 1899 v S (5)

Matthias, T. J. (Wrexham), 1914 v S, E; 1920 v Ni, S, E; 1921 v S, E, Ni; 1922 v S, E, Ni; 1923 v S (12)

Mays, A. W. (Wrexham), 1929 v Ni (1)

Medwin, T. C. (Swansea T), 1953 v Ni, F, Y; (with Tottenham H), 1957 v E, S, Ni, Cz (2), EG; 1958 v E, S, Ni, Is (2), H (2), M, Br; 1959 v E, S, Ni; 1960 v E, S; 1961 v S, Ei, E, Sp; 1963 v E, H (30)

Melville, A. K. (Swansea C), 1990 v WG, Ei, Se, Cr (sub); (with Oxford U), 1991 v Ic, Pol, WG; 1992 v Br, G, L, R, Ho, J (sub); 1993 v RCS, Fa (sub); (with Sunderland), 1994 v RCS (sub), R, N, Se, Es; 1995 v Alb, Mol (sub), Ge, Bul; 1996 v G, Alb, Sm; 1997 v Sm, Ho (2), T; 1998 v T; (with Fulham), 1999 v I, D; 2000 v Bl, Q, Fi, Br, P; 2001 v Bl, N, Pol, Arm, Uk, Pol, Uk; 2002 v Arm, Bl, Arg, CzR, G (51)

Meredith, S. (Chirk), 1900 v S; 1901 v S, E, Ni; (with Stoke C), 1902 v E; 1903 v Ni; 1904 v E; (with Leyton), 1907 v E (8)

Meredith, W. H. (Manchester C), 1895 v E, Ni; 1896 v E, Ni; 1897 v E, Ni, S; 1898 v E, Ni; 1899 v E; 1900 v E, Ni; 1901 v E, Ni; 1902 v E, S; 1903 v E, S, Ni; 1904 v E; 1905 v E, S; (with Manchester U), 1907 v E, S, Ni; 1908 v E, Ni; 1909 v E, S, Ni; 1910 v E, S, Ni; 1911 v E, S, Ni; 1912 v E, S, Ni; 1913 v E, S, Ni; 1914 v E, S, Ni; 1920 v E, S, Ni (48)

Mielczarek, R. (Rotherham U), 1971 v Fi (1)

Millership, H. (Rotherham Co), 1920 v E, S, Ni; 1921 v E, S, Ni (6)

Millington, A. H. (WBA), 1963 v S, E, H; (with C Palace), 1965 v E, USSR; (with Peterborough U), 1966 v Ch, Br; 1967 v E, Ni; 1968 v Ni, WG; 1969 v I, EG; (with Swansea T), 1970 v E, S, Ni; 1971 v Cz, Fi; 1972 v Fi (sub), Cz, R (21)

Mills, T. J. (Clapton Orient), 1934 v E, Ni; (with Leicester C), 1935 v E, S (4)

Mills-Roberts, R. H. (St Thomas' Hospital), 1885 v E, S, Ni; 1886 v E; 1887 v E; (with Preston NE), 1888 v E, Ni; (with Llanberis), 1892 v E (8)

Moore, G. (Cardiff C), 1960 v E, S, Ni; 1961 v Ei, Sp; (with Chelsea), 1962 v Br; 1963 v Ni, H; (with Manchester U), 1964 v S, Ni; (with Northampton T), 1966 v Ni, Ch; (with Charlton Ath), 1969 v S, E, Ni, R of UK; 1970 v E, S, Ni, I; 1971 v R (21)

Morgan, J. R. (Cambridge University), 1877 v S; (with Swansea T), 1879 v S; (with Derby School Staff), 1880 v E, S; 1881 v E, S; 1882 v E, S, Ni; (with Swansea T), 1883 v E (10)

Morgan, J. T. (Wrexham), 1905 v Ni (1)

Morgan-Owen, H. (Oxford University), 1902 v S; 1906 v E, Ni; (with Welshpool), 1907 v S (5)

Morgan-Owen, M. M. (Oxford University), 1897 v S, Ni; 1898 v E, S; 1899 v S; 1900 v E; (with Corinthians), 1901 v S, E; 1903 v S; 1906 v S, E, Ni; 1907 v E (13)

Morley, E. J. (Swansea T), 1925 v E; (with Clapton Orient), 1929 v E, S, Ni (4)

Morris, A. G. (Aberystwyth), 1896 v E, Ni, S; (with Swindon T), 1897 v E; 1898 v S; (with Nottingham F), 1899 v E, S; 1903 v S; 1905 v E, S; 1907 v E, S; 1908 v E; 1910 v E, S, Ni; 1911 v E, S, Ni; 1912 v E (21)

Morris, C. (Chirk), 1900 v E, S, Ni; (with Derby Co), 1901 v E, S, Ni; 1902 v E; 1903 v E, S, Ni; 1904 v Ni; 1905 v E, S, Ni; 1906 v S; 1907 v S; 1908 v E, S; 1909 v E, S, Ni; 1910 v E, S, Ni; (with Huddersfield T), 1911 v E, S, Ni (27)

Morris, E. (Chirk), 1893 v E, S, Ni (3)

Morris, H. (Sheffield U), 1894 v S; (with Manchester C), 1896 v E; (with Grimsby T), 1897 v E (3)

Morris, J. (Oswestry), 1887 v S (1)

Morris, J. (Chirk), 1898 v Ni (1)

Morris, R. (Chirk), 1900 v E, Ni; 1901 v Ni; 1902 v S; (with Shrewsbury T), 1903 v E, Ni (6)

Morris, R. (Druids), 1902 v E, S; (with Newtown), Ni; (with Liverpool), 1903 v S, Ni; 1904 v E, S, Ni; (with Leeds C), 1906 v S; (with Grimsby T), 1907 v Ni; (with Plymouth Arg), 1908 v Ni (11)

Morris, S. (Birmingham), 1937 v E, S; 1938 v E, S; 1939 v F (5)

Morris, W. (Burnley), 1947 v Ni; 1949 v E; 1952 v S, Ni, R of UK (5)

Moulsdale, J. R. B. (Corinthians), 1925 v Ni (1)

Murphy, J. P. (WBA), 1933 v F, E, Ni; 1934 v E, S; 1935 v E, S, Ni; 1936 v E, S, Ni; 1937 v S, Ni; 1938 v E, S (15)

Nardiello, D. (Coventry C), 1978 v Cz, WG (sub) (2)
Neal, J. E. (Colwyn Bay), 1931 v E, S (2)
Neilson, A. B. (Newcastle U), 1992 v Ei; 1994 v Se, Es; 1995 v Ge; (with Southampton), 1997 v Ho (5)
Newnes, J. (Nelson), 1926 v Ni (1)
Newton, L. F. (Cardiff Corinthians), 1912 v Ni (1)
Nicholas, D. S. (Stoke C), 1923 v S; (with Swansea T), 1927 v E, Ni (3)
Nicholas, P. (C Palace), 1979 v S (sub), Ni (sub), Ma; 1980 v Ei, WG, T, E, S, Ni, Ic; 1981 v T, Cz, E; (with Arsenal), T, S, E, USSR; 1982 v Cz, Ic, USSR, Sp, E, S, Ni, F; 1983 v Y, Bul, S, Ni; 1984 v N, Bul, N, Is; (with C Palace), 1985 v Sp; (with Luton T), N, S, Sp, N; 1986 v S, H, S.Ar, Ei, U, Ca (2); 1987 v Fi (2) USSR, Cz; (with Aberdeen), 1988 v D (2), Cz, Y, Se; (with Chelsea), 1989 v Ho, Fi, Is, Se, WG; 1990 v Fi, Ho, WG, Ei, Se, Cr; 1991 v D (sub), Bel, L, Ei; (with Watford), Bel, Pol, WG; 1992 v L (73)
Nicholls, J. (Newport Co), 1924 v E, Ni; (with Cardiff C), 1925 v E, S (4)
Niedzwiecki, E. A. (Chelsea), 1985 v N (sub); 1988 v D (2)
Nock, W. (Newtown), 1897 v Ni (1)
Nogan, L. M. (Watford), 1992 v A (sub); (with Reading), 1996 v Mol (2)
Norman, A. J. (Hull C), 1986 v Ei (sub), U, Ca; 1988 v Ma, I (5)
Nurse, M. T. G. (Swansea T), 1960 v E, Ni; 1961 v S, E, H, Ni, Ei, Sp (2); (with Middlesbrough), 1963 v E, H; 1964 v S (12)

O'Callaghan, E. (Tottenham H), 1929 v Ni; 1930 v S; 1932 v S, E; 1933 v Ni, S, E; 1934 v Ni, S, E; 1935 v E (11)
Oliver, A. (Blackburn R), 1905 v E; (with Bangor), S (2)
Oster, J. M. (Everton), 1998 v Bel (sub), Br, Jam; (with Sunderland), 2000 v Sw (4)
O'Sullivan, P. A. (Brighton), 1973 v S (sub); 1976 v S; 1979 v Ma (sub) (3)
Owen, D. (Oswestry), 1879 v E (1)
Owen, E. (Ruthin Grammar School), 1884 v E, Ni, S (3)
Owen, G. (Chirk), 1888 v S; (with Newton Heath), 1889 v S, Ni; 1893 v Ni (4)
Owen, J. (Newton Heath), 1892 v E (1)
Owen, Trevor (Crewe Alex), 1899 v E, S (2)
Owen, T. (Oswestry), 1879 v E (1)
Owen, W. (Chirk), 1884 v E; 1885 v Ni; 1887 v E; 1888 v E; 1889 v E, Ni, S; 1890 v S, Ni; 1891 v E, S, Ni; 1892 v E, S; 1893 v S, Ni (16)
Owen, W. P. (Ruthin), 1880 v E, S; 1881 v E, S; 1882 v E, S, Ni; 1883 v E, S; 1884 v E, S, Ni (12)
Owens, J. (Wrexham), 1902 v S (1)

Page, M. E. (Birmingham C), 1971 v Fi; 1972 v S, Ni; 1973 v E (1+1 sub), Ni; 1974 v S, Ni; 1975 v H, L, S, E, Ni; 1976 v E, Y (2), E, Ni; 1977 v WG, S; 1978 v K (sub+1), WG, Ir, E, S; 1979 v Ma, WG (28)
Page, R. J. (Watford), 1997 v T, Bel, S; 1998 v T, Bel (sub), Br, I; 2000 v Bl, Sw, Q, Fi, Br, P; 2001 v Bl, N, Pol, Arm, Uk, Pol, Uk; (with Sheffield U), 2002 v N, Bl (sub), Arg, CzR, G (25)
Palmer, D. (Swansea T), 1957 v Cz; 1958 v E, EG (3)
Parris, J. E. (Bradford), 1932 v Ni (1)
Parry, B. J. (Swansea T), 1951 v S (1)
Parry, C. (Everton), 1891 v E, S; 1893 v E; 1894 v E; 1895 v E, S; (with Newtown), 1896 v E, S, Ni; 1897 v Ni; 1898 v E, S, Ni (13)
Parry, E. (Liverpool), 1922 v S; 1923 v E, Ni; 1925 v Ni; 1926 v Ni (5)
Parry, M. (Liverpool), 1901 v E, S, Ni; 1902 v E, S, Ni; 1903 v E, S; 1904 v E, Ni; 1906 v E; 1908 v E, S, Ni; 1909 v E, S (16)
Parry, T. D. (Oswestry), 1900 v E, S, Ni; 1901 v E, S, Ni; 1902 v E (7)
Parry, W. (Newtown), 1895 v Ni (1)
Pascoe, C. (Swansea C), 1984 v N, Is; (with Sunderland), 1989 v Fi, Is, WG (sub); 1990 v Ho (sub), WG (sub); 1991 v Ei, Ic (sub); 1992 v Br (10)
Paul, R. (Swansea T), 1949 v E, S, Ni, P, Sw; 1950 v E, S, Ni, Bel; (with Manchester C), 1951 v S, E, Ni, P, Sw; 1952 v E, S, Ni, R of UK; 1953 v S, E, Ni, F, Y; 1954 v S, E, Ni; 1955 v S, E, Y; 1956 v E, Ni, S, A (33)
Peake, E. (Aberystwyth), 1908 v Ni; (with Liverpool), 1909 v Ni, S, E; 1910 v S, Ni; 1911 v Ni; 1912 v E; 1913 v E, Ni; 1914 v Ni (11)
Peers, E. J. (Wolverhampton W), 1914 v Ni, S, E; 1920 v E, S; 1921 v S, Ni, E; (with Port Vale), 1922 v E, S, Ni; 1923 v E (12)
Pembridge, M. A. (Luton T), 1992 v Br, Ei, R (with Derby Co), Ho, J (sub); 1993 v Bel (sub); Ei 1994 v N (sub); 1995 v Alb (sub), Mol, Ge (sub); (with Sheffield W), 1996 v Mol, G, Alb, Sw, Sm; 1997 v Sm, Ho (2), T, Ei, Bel, S; 1998 v Bel,

Br, Jam, Ma, Tun; (with Benfica), 1999 v D (sub), Bl, Sw, (sub), D (sub); (with Everton), 2000 v Bl, Q, Fi; 2001 v Arm, Pol, Uk; 2002 v Bl, Arg, G (42)
Perry, E. (Doncaster R), 1938 v E, S, Ni (3)
Perry, J. (Cardiff C), 1994 v N (1)
Phennah, E. (Civil Service), 1878 v S (1)
Phillips, C. (Wolverhampton W), 1931 v Ni; 1932 v E; 1933 v S 1934 v E, S, Ni; 1935 v E, S, Ni; 1936 v S; (with Aston Villa) 1936 v E, Ni; 1938 v S (13)
Phillips, D. (Plymouth Arg), 1984 v E, Ni, N; (with Manchester C), 1985 v Sp, Ic, S, Sp, N; 1986 v S, H, S.Ar, Ei U; (with Coventry C), 1987 v Fi, Cz; 1988 v D (2), Cz, Y, Se 1989 v Se, WG; (with Norwich C), 1990 v Fi, Ho, WG, Ei Se; 1991 v D, Bel, Ic, Pol, WG; 1992 v L, Ei, A, R, Ho (sub) Arg, J; 1993 v Fa, Cy, Bel, Ei, Bel, RCS, Fa; (with Nottingham F), 1994 v RCS, Cy, R, N, Se, Es; 1995 v Alb Mol, Ge, Bul (2), G, Ge; 1996 v Mol (sub), Alb, I (62)
Phillips, L. (Cardiff C), 1971 v Cz, S, E, Ni; 1972 v Cz, R, S, Ni 1973 v E; 1974 v Pol (sub), Ni; 1975 v A; (with Aston Villa) H (2), L (2), S, E, Ni; 1976 v A, E, Y (2), E, Ni; 1977 v WG S (2), Cz, E; 1978 v K (2), S, Cz, WG, E, S; 1979 v Ma; (with Swansea C), T, WG, S, E, Ni, Ma; 1980 v Ei, WG, S, T, Ni (sub), Ni, Ic; 1981 v T, Cz, T, S, E, USSR; (with Charlton Ath), 1982 v Cz, USSR (58)
Phillips, T. J. S. (Chelsea), 1973 v E; 1974 v E; 1975 v H (sub) 1978 v K (4)
Phoenix, H. (Wrexham), 1882 v S (1)
Poland, G. (Wrexham), 1939 v Ni, F (2)
Pontin, K. (Cardiff C), 1980 v E (sub), S (2)
Powell, A. (Leeds U), 1947 v E, S; 1948 v E, S, Ni; (with Everton), 1949 v E; 1950 v Bel; (with Birmingham C), 1951 v S (8)
Powell, D. (Wrexham), 1968 v WG; (with Sheffield U), 1969 v S, E, Ni, I, WG; 1970 v E, S, Ni, EG; 1971 v R (11)
Powell, I. V. (QPR), 1947 v E; 1948 v E, S, Ni; (with Aston Villa), 1949 v Bel; 1950 v S, Bel; 1951 v S (8)
Powell, J. (Druids), 1878 v S; 1880 v E, S; 1882 v E, S, Ni; 1883 v E, S, Ni; (with Bolton W), 1884 v E; (with Newton Heath), 1887 v E, S; 1888 v E, S, Ni (15)
Powell, Seth (WBA), 1885 v S; 1886 v E, Ni; 1891 v E, S; 1892 v E, S (7)
Price, H. (Aston Villa), 1907 v S; (with Burton U), 1908 v Ni; (with Wrexham), 1909 v S, E, Ni (5)
Price, J. (Wrexham), 1877 v S; 1878 v S; 1879 v E; 1880 v E, S; 1881 v E, S; (with Druids), 1882 v S, E, Ni; 1883 v S, Ni (12)
Price, P. (Luton T), 1980 v E, S, Ni, Ic; 1981 v T, Cz, Ei, T, S, E, USSR; (with Tottenham H), 1982 v USSR, Sp, F; 1983 v N, Y, E, Bul, S, Ni; 1984 v N, R, Bul, Y, S (sub) (25)
Pring, K. D. (Rotherham U), 1966 v Ch, D; 1967 v Ni (3)
Pritchard, H. K. (Bristol C), 1985 v N (sub) (1)
Pryce-Jones, A. W. (Newtown), 1895 v E (1)
Pryce-Jones, W. E. (Cambridge University), 1887 v S; 1888 v S, E, Ni; 1890 v Ni (5)
Pugh, A. (Rhostyllen), 1889 v S (sub) (1)
Pugh, D. H. (Wrexham), 1896 v S, Ni; 1897 v S, Ni; (with Lincoln C), 1900 v S; 1901 v S, E (7)
Pugsley, J. (Charlton Ath), 1930 v Ni (1)
Pullen, W. J. (Plymouth Arg), 1926 v E (1)

Rankmore, F. E. J. (Peterborough), 1966 v Ch (sub) (1)
Ratcliffe, K. (Everton), 1981 v Cz, Ei, T, S, E, USSR; 1982 v Cz, Ic, USSR, Sp, E; 1983 v Y, E, Bul, S, Ni, Br; 1984 v N, R, Bul, Y, S, E, Ni, N, Is; 1985 v Ic, Sp, Ic, N, S, Sp; 1986 v S, H, S.Ar, U; 1987 v Fi (2), USSR, Cz; 1988 v D (2), Cz; 1989 v Fi, Is, Se, WG; 1990 v Fi; 1991 v D, Bel (2), L, Ei, Ic, Pol, WG; 1992 v Br, G; (with Cardiff C), 1993 v Bel (59)
Rea, J. C. (Aberystwyth), 1894 v Ni, S, E; 1895 v S; 1896 v S, Ni; 1897 v S, Ni; 1898 v Ni (9)
Ready, K. (QPR), 1997 v Ei; 1998 v Bel, Br, Ma, Tun (5)
Reece, G. I. (Sheffield U), 1966 v E, S, Ni, USSR; 1967 v S; 1969 v R of UK (sub); 1970 v I (sub); 1971 v S, E, Ni, Fi; 1972 v Fi, R, E (sub), S, Ni; (with Cardiff C), 1973 v E (sub), Ni; 1974 v Pol (sub), E, S, Ni; 1975 v A, H (2), L (2), S, Ni (29)
Reed, W. G. (Ipswich T), 1955 v S, Y (2)
Rees, A. (Birmingham C), 1984 v N (sub) (1)
Rees, J. M. (Luton T), 1992 v A (sub) (1)
Rees, R. R. (Coventry C), 1965 v S, E, Ni, D, Gr (2), I, R; 1966 v E, S, Ni, R, D, Br (2), Ch; 1967 v E, Ni; 1968 v E, S, Ni; (with WBA), WG; 1969 v I; (with Nottingham F), 1969 v WG, EG, S (sub), R of UK; 1970 v E, S, Ni, EG, I; 1971 v Cz, R, E (sub), Ni (sub), Fi; 1972 v Cz (sub), R (39)
Rees, W. (Cardiff C), 1949 v Ni, Bel, Sw; (with Tottenham H), 1950 v Ni (4)
Richards, A. (Barnsley), 1932 v S (1)

Richards, D. (Wolverhampton W), 1931 v Ni; 1933 v E, S, Ni; 1934 v E, S, Ni; 1935 v S, Ni; 1936 v S; (with Brentford), 1936 v E, Ni; 1937 v S, E; (with Birmingham), Ni; 1938 v E, S, Ni; 1939 v E, S (21)

Richards, G. (Druids), 1899 v E, S, Ni; (with Oswestry), 1903 v Ni; (with Shrewsbury), 1904 v S; 1905 v Ni (6)

Richards, R. W. (Wolverhampton W), 1920 v E, S; 1921 v Ni; 1922 v E, S; (with West Ham U), 1924 v E, S, Ni; (with Mold), 1926 v S (9)

Richards, S. V. (Cardiff C), 1947 v E (1)

Richards, W. E. (Fulham), 1933 v Ni (1)

Roach, J. (Oswestry), 1885 v Ni (1)

Robbins, W. W. (Cardiff C), 1931 v E, S; 1932 v Ni, E, S; (with WBA), 1933 v F, E, S, Ni; 1934 v S; 1936 v S (11)

Roberts, A. M. (QPR), 1993 v Ei (sub); 1997 v Sm (sub) (2)

Roberts, D. F. (Oxford U), 1973 v Pol, E (sub), Ni; 1974 v E, S; 1975 v A; (with Hull C), L, Ni; 1976 v S, Ni, Y; 1977 v E (sub), Ni; 1978 v K (1+1 sub), S, Ni (17)

Roberts, G. W. (Tranmere R), 2000 v Fi (sub), Br, P; 2001 v Bl (4)

Roberts, I. W. (Watford), 1990 v Ho; (with Huddersfield T), 1992 v A, Arg, J; (with Leicester C), 1994 v Se; 1995 v Alb (sub), Mol; (with Norwich C), 2000 v Fi (sub), Br, P; 2001 v Bl, N (sub), Arm (sub); 2002 v Arm, Bl (sub) (15)

Roberts, Jas (Wrexham), 1913 v S, Ni (2)

Roberts, J. (Corwen), 1879 v S; 1880 v E, S; 1882 v E, S, Ni; (with Berwyn R), 1883 v E (7)

Roberts, J. (Ruthin), 1881 v S; 1882 v S (2)

Roberts, J. (Bradford C), 1906 v Ni; 1907 v Ni (2)

Roberts, J. G. (Arsenal), 1971 v S, E, Ni, Fi; 1972 v E, Ni; (with Birmingham C), 1973 v E (2), Pol, S, Ni; 1974 v Pol, E, S, Ni; 1975 v A, H, S, E; 1976 v E, S (22)

Roberts, J. H. (Bolton), 1949 v Bel (1)

Roberts, N. W. (Wrexham), 2000 v Sw (sub) (1)

Roberts, P. S. (Portsmouth), 1974 v E; 1975 v A, H, L (4)

Roberts, R. (Druids), 1884 v S; (with Bolton W), 1887 v S; 1888 v S, E; 1889 v S, E; 1890 v S; 1892 v Ni; (with Preston NE), S (9)

Roberts, R. (Wrexham), 1886 v Ni; 1887 v Ni; 1891 v Ni (3)

Roberts, R. (Rhos), 1891 v Ni; (with Crewe Alex), 1893 v E (2)

Roberts, R. L. (Chester), 1890 v Ni (1)

Roberts, W. (Llangollen), 1879 v E, S; 1880 v E, S; (with Berwyn R), 1881 v S; 1883 v S (6)

Roberts, W. (Wrexham), 1886 v E, S, Ni; 1887 v Ni (4)

Roberts, W. H. (Ruthin), 1882 v E, S; 1883 v E, S, Ni; (with Rhyl), 1884 v S (6)

Robinson, C. P. (Wolverhampton W), 2000 v Bl (sub), P (sub); 2001 v Arm (sub), Uk; 2002 v Arm, N, Bl (sub), Arg (sub) (8)

Robinson, J. R. C. (Charlton Ath), 1996 v Alb (sub), Sw, Sm; 1997 v Sm, Ho (1 + sub), Ei, S; 1998 v Bel, Br; 1999 v I, D (sub), Bl, Sw, I, D; 2000 v Bl, Sw, Q, Fi, Br, P; 2001 v Bl, N, Pol, Arm; 2002 v N (sub), Bl, Arg (sub), CzR (30)

Rodrigues, P. J. (Cardiff C), 1965 v Ni, USSR, E, S, D; (with Leicester C), Ni, Br (2), Ch; 1967 v S; 1968 v E, S, Ni; 1969 v E, Ni, EG, R of UK; 1970 v E, S, Ni, EG; (with Sheffield W), 1971 v R, E, S, Cz, Ni; 1972 v Fi, Cz, E, Ni (sub); 1973 v E (3), Pol, S, Ni; 1974 v Pol (40)

Rogers, J. P. (Wrexham), 1896 v E, S, Ni (3)

Rogers, W. (Wrexham), 1931 v E, S (2)

Roose, L. R. (Aberystwyth), 1900 v Ni; (with London Welsh), 1901 v E, S, Ni; (with Stoke C), 1902 v E, S; 1904 v E; (with Everton), 1905 v S, E; (with Stoke C), 1906 v E, S, Ni; 1907 v E, S, Ni; (with Sunderland), 1908 v E, S; 1909 v E, S, Ni; 1910 v E, S, Ni; 1911 v S (24)

Rouse, R. V. (C Palace), 1959 v Ni (1)

Rowlands, A. C. (Tranmere R), 1914 v E (1)

Rowley, T. (Tranmere R), 1959 v Ni (1)

Rush, I. (Liverpool), 1980 v S (sub), Ni; 1981 v E (sub); 1982 v Ic (sub), USSR, E, S, Ni, F; 1983 v N, Y, E, Bul; 1984 v N, R, Bul, Y, S, E, Ni; 1985 v Ic, N, S, Sp; 1986 v S, S.Ar, Ei, U; 1987 v Fi (2), USSR, Cz; (with Juventus), 1988 v D, Cz, Y, Se, Ma, I; (with Liverpool), 1989 v Ho, Fi, Se, WG; 1990 v Fi, Ei; 1991 v D, Bel (2), L, Ei, Pol, WG; 1992 v G, L, R; 1993 v Fa, Cy, Bel (2), RCS, Fa; 1994 v RCS, Cy, R, N, Se, Es; 1995 v Alb, Ge, Bul, G, Ge; 1996 v Mol, I (73)

Russell, M. R. (Merthyr T), 1912 v S, Ni; 1914 v E; (with Plymouth Arg), 1920 v E, S, Ni; 1921 v E, S, Ni; 1922 v E, Ni; 1923 v E, S, Ni; 1924 v E, S, Ni; 1925 v E, S, Ni; 1926 v E, S; 1928 v S; 1929 v E (23)

Sabine, H. W. (Oswestry), 1887 v Ni (1)

Saunders, D. (Brighton & HA), 1986 v Ei (sub), Ca (2); 1987 v Fi, USSR (sub); (with Oxford U), 1988 v Y, Se, Ma, I (sub); 1989 v Ho (sub), Fi; (with Derby Co), Is, Se, WG; 1990 v Fi, Ho, WG, Se, Cr; 1991 v D, Bel (2), L, Ei, Ic, Pol, WG; (with

Liverpool), 1992 v Br, G, Ei, R, Ho, Arg, J; 1993 v Fa; (with Aston Villa), Cy, Bel (2), RCS, Fa; 1994 v RCS, Cy, R, N (sub); 1995 v Ge, Bul (2), G, Ge; (with Galatasaray), 1996 v G, Alb, Sm; (with Nottingham F), 1997 v Sm, Ho (2), T, Bel, S; 1998 v T, Bel, Br; (with Sheffield U), Ma, Tun; 1999 v I (sub), D, Bl; (with Benfica) Sw, I, D; (with Bradford C), 2000 v Bl, Sw, Fi (sub), Br; 2001 v Arm, Uk (sub) (75)

Savage, R. W. (Crewe Alex), 1996 v Alb (sub), Sw (sub), Sm (sub); 1997 v Ei (sub), S; (with Leicester C), 1998 v T, Bel, Jam, Tun; 1999 v I (sub), D, Bl, Sw; 2000 v Sw, Fi, Br; 2001 v Bl, N, Pol (2); 2002 v Arm, N, Arg, CzR, Q (25)

Savin, G. (Oswestry), 1878 v S (1)

Sayer, P. (Cardiff C), 1977 v Cz, S, E, Ni; 1978 v K (2), S (7)

Scrine, F. H. (Swansea T), 1950 v E, Ni (2)

Sear, C. R. (Manchester C), 1963 v E (1)

Shaw, E. G. (Oswestry), 1882 v Ni; 1884 v S, Ni (3)

Sherwood, A. T. (Cardiff C), 1947 v E, Ni; 1948 v S, Ni; 1949 v E, S, Ni, P, Sw; 1950 v E, S, Ni, Bel; 1951 v E, S, Ni, P, Sw; 1952 v E, S, Ni, R of UK; 1953 v S, E, Ni, F, Y; 1954 v E, S, Ni, A; 1955 v S, E, Y, Ni; 1956 v E, S, Ni, A; (with Newport Co), 1957 v E, S (41)

Shone, W. W. (Oswestry), 1879 v E (1)

Shortt, W. W. (Plymouth Arg), 1947 v Ni; 1950 v Ni, Bel; 1952 v E, S, Ni, R of UK; 1953 v S, E, Ni, F, Y (12)

Showers, D. (Cardiff C), 1975 v E (sub), Ni (2)

Sidlow, C. (Liverpool), 1947 v E, S; 1948 v E, S, Ni; 1949 v S; 1950 v E (7)

Sisson, H. (Wrexham Olympic), 1885 v Ni; 1886 v S, Ni (3)

Slatter, N. (Bristol R), 1983 v S; 1984 v N (sub), Is; 1985 v Ic, Sp, Ic, N, S, Sp, N; (with Oxford U), 1986 v H (sub), S.Ar, Ca (2); 1987 v Fi (sub), Cz; 1988 v D (2), Cz, Ma, I; 1989 v Is (sub) (22)

Smallman, D. P. (Wrexham), 1974 v E (sub), S (sub), Ni; (with Everton), 1975 v H (sub), E, Ni (sub); 1976 v A (7)

Southall, N. (Everton), 1982 v Ni; 1983 v N, E, Bul, S, Ni, Br; 1984 v N, R, Bul, Y, S, E, Ni, N, Is; 1985 v Ic, Sp, Ic, N, S, Sp, N; 1986 v S, H, S.Ar, Ei; 1987 v USSR, Fi, Cz; 1988 v D, Cz, Y, Se; 1989 v Ho, Fi, Se, WG; 1990 v Fi, Ho, WG, Ei, Se, Cr; 1991 v D, Bel (2), L, Ei, Ic, Pol, WG; 1992 v Br, G, L, Ei, A, R, Ho, Arg, J; 1993 v Fa, Cy, Bel, Ei, Bel, RCS, Fa; 1994 v RCS, Cy, R, N, Se, Es; 1995 v Alb, Mol, Ge, Bul (2), G, Ge; 1996 v Mol, G, Alb, I, Sm; 1997 v Sm, Ho (2), T, Bel; 1998 v T (92)

Speed, G. A. (Leeds U), 1990 v Cr (sub); 1991 v D, L (sub), Ei (sub), Ic, WG (sub); 1992 v Br, G (sub), L, Ei, R, Ho,Arg,J; 1993 v Fa, Cy, Bel, Ei, Bel, Fa (sub); 1994 v RCS (sub), Cy, R, N, Se; 1995 v Alb, Mol, Ge, Bul (2), G; 1996 v Mol, G, I, Sw (sub); (with Everton), 1997 v Sm (sub), Ho (2), T, Ei, Bel, S; 1998 v T, Br; (with Newcastle U), Jam, Ma, Tun; 1999 v I, D, Sw, I, D; 2000 v Bl, Sw, Q, Fi, Br, P; 2001 v Bl, N, Pol, Arm, Uk, Pol, Uk; 2002 v Bl, Arg, G (66)

Sprake, G. (Leeds U), 1964 v S, Ni; 1965 v S, D, Gr; 1966 v E, Ni, USSR; 1967 v S; 1968 v E, S; 1969 v S, E, Ni, WG, R of UK; 1970 v EG, I; 1971 v R, S, E, Ni; 1972 v Fi, E, S, Ni; 1973 v E (2), Pol, S, Ni; 1974 v Pol; (with Birmingham C), S, Ni; 1975 v A, H, L (37)

Stansfield, F. (Cardiff C), 1949 v S (1)

Stevenson, B. (Leeds U), 1978 v Ni; 1979 v Ma, T, S, E, Ni, Ma; 1980 v WG, T, Ic (sub); 1982 v Cz; (with Birmingham C), Sp, S, Ni, F (15)

Stevenson, N. (Swansea C), 1982 v E, S, Ni; 1983 v N (4)

Stitfall, R. F. (Cardiff C), 1953 v E; 1957 v Cz (2)

Sullivan, D. (Cardiff C), 1953 v Ni, F, Y; 1954 v Ni; 1955 v E, Ni; 1957 v E, S; 1958 v Ni, H (2), Se, Br; 1959 v S, Ni; 1960 v E, S (17)

Symons, C. J. (Portsmouth), 1992 v Ei, Ho, Arg, J; 1993 v Fa, Cy, Bel, Ei, RCS, Fa; 1994 v RCS, Cy, R; 1995 v Mol, Ge (sub), Bul, G, Ge; (with Manchester C), 1996 v Mol, G, I, Sw; 1997 v Ho (2), Ei, Bel, S; (with Fulham), 1999 v I, D, Bl, Sw; 2000 v Q (sub); 2001 v Pol; 2002 v Arm, N, Bl (36)

Tapscott, D. R. (Arsenal), 1954 v A; 1955 v S, E, Ni, Y; 1956 v E, Ni, S, A; 1957 v Ni, Cz, EG; (with Cardiff C), 1959 v E, Ni (14)

Taylor, G. K. (C Palace), 1996 v Alb, I (sub); (with Sheffield U), Sw; 1997 v Sm (sub), Ho (sub), Ei (sub); 1998 v Bel (sub), Jam; (with Burnley), 2002 v CzR (sub) (9)

Taylor, J. (Wrexham), 1898 v E (1)

Taylor, O. D. S. (Newtown), 1893 v S, Ni; 1894 v S, Ni (4)

Thomas, C. (Druids), 1899 v Ni; 1900 v S (2)

Thomas, D. A. (Swansea T), 1957 v Cz; 1958 v EG (2)

Thomas, D. S. (Fulham), 1948 v E, S, Ni; 1949 v S (4)

Thomas, E. (Cardiff Corinthians), 1925 v E (1)

Thomas, G. (Wrexham), 1885 v E, S (2)

Thomas, H. (Manchester U), 1927 v E (1)

Thomas, M. (Wrexham), 1977 v WG, S (1+1 sub), Ni (sub); 1978 v K (sub), S, Cz, Ir, E, Ni (sub); 1979 v Ma; (with Manchester U), T, WG, Ma (sub); 1980 v Ei, WG (sub), T, E, S, Ni; 1981 v Cz, S, E, USSR; (with Everton), 1982 v Cz; (with Brighton & HA), USSR (sub), Sp, E, S (sub), Ni (sub); 1983 (with Stoke C), v N, Y, E, Bul, S, Ni, Br; 1984 v R, Bul, Y; (with Chelsea), S, E; 1985 v Ic, Sp, Ic, S, Sp, N; 1986 v S; (with WBA), H, S.Ar (sub) (51)

Thomas, M. R. (Newcastle U), 1987 v Fi (1)

Thomas, R. J. (Swindon T), 1967 v Ni; 1968 v WG; 1969 v E, Ni, I, WG, R of UK; 1970 v S, Ni, EG, I; 1971 v S, E, Ni, R, Cz; 1972 v Fi, Cz, R, E, S, Ni; 1973 v E (3), Pol, S, Ni; 1974 v Pol; (with Derby Co), E, S, Ni; 1975 v H (2), L (2), S, E, Ni; 1976 v A, Y, E; 1977 v Cz, S, E, Ni; 1978 v K, S; (with Cardiff C), Cz (50)

Thomas, T. (Bangor), 1898 v S, Ni (2)

Thomas, W. R. (Newport Co), 1931 v E, S (2)

Thomson, D. (Druids), 1876 v S (1)

Thomson, G. F. (Druids), 1876 v S; 1877 v S (2)

Toshack, J. B. (Cardiff C), 1969 v S, E, Ni, WG, EG, R of UK; 1970 v EG, I; (with Liverpool), 1971 v S, E, Ni, Fi; 1972 v Fi, E; 1973 v E (3), Pol, S; 1975 v A, H (2), L (2), S, E; 1976 v Y (2), E; 1977 v S; 1978 v K (2), S, Cz; (with Swansea C), 1979 v WG (sub), S, E, Ni, Ma; 1980 v WG (40)

Townsend, W. (Newtown), 1887 v Ni; 1893 v Ni (2)

Trainer, H. (Wrexham), 1895 v E, S, Ni (3)

Trainer, J. (Bolton W), 1887 v S; (with Preston NE), 1888 v S; 1889 v E; 1890 v S; 1891 v S; 1892 v Ni, S; 1893 v E; 1894 v Ni, E; 1895 v Ni, E; 1896 v S; 1897 v Ni, S, E; 1898 v S, E; 1899 v Ni, S (20)

Trollope, P. J. (Derby Co), 1997 v S; 1998 v Br (sub); (with Fulham), Jam (sub), Ma, Tun; (with Coventry C), 2002 v CzR (sub) (6)

Turner, H. G. (Charlton Ath), 1937 v E, S, Ni; 1938 v E, S, Ni; 1939 v Ni, F (8)

Turner, J. (Wrexham), 1892 v E (1)

Turner, R. E. (Wrexham), 1891 v E, Ni (2)

Turner, W. H. (Wrexham), 1887 v E, Ni; 1890 v S; 1891 v E, S (5)

Van Den Hauwe, P. W. R. (Everton), 1985 v Sp; 1986 v S, H; 1987 v USSR, Fi, Cz; 1988 v D (2), Cz, Y, I; 1989 v Fi, Se (13)

Vaughan, Jas (Druids), 1893 v E, S, Ni; 1899 v E (4)

Vaughan, John (Oswestry), 1879 v S; 1880 v S; 1881 v E, S; 1882 v E, S, Ni; 1883 v E, S, Ni; (with Bolton W), 1884 v E (11)

Vaughan, J. O. (Rhyl), 1885 v Ni; 1886 v Ni, E, S (4)

Vaughan, N. (Newport Co), 1983 v Y (sub), Br; 1984 v N; (with Cardiff C), R, Bul, Y, Ni (sub), N, Is; 1985 v Sp (sub) (10)

Vaughan, T. (Rhyl), 1885 v E (1)

Vearncombe, G. (Cardiff C), 1958 v EG; 1961 v Ei (2)

Vernon, T. R. (Blackburn R), 1957 v Ni, Cz (2), EG; 1958 v E, S, EG, Se; 1959 v S; (with Everton), 1960 v Ni; 1961 v S, E, Ei; 1962 v Ni, Br (2), M; 1963 v S, E, H; 1964 v E, S; (with Stoke C), 1965 v Ni, Gr, I; 1966 v E, S, Ni, USSR, D; 1967 v Ni; 1968 v E (32)

Villars, A. K. (Cardiff C), 1974 v E, S, Ni (sub) (3)

Vizard, E. T. (Bolton W), 1911 v E, S, Ni; 1912 v E, S; 1913 v S; 1914 v E, Ni; 1920 v E; 1921 v E, S, Ni; 1922 v E, S; 1923 v E, Ni; 1924 v E, S, Ni; 1926 v E, S; 1927 v S (22)

Walley, J. T. (Watford), 1971 v Cz (1)

Walsh, I. (C Palace), 1980 v Ei, T, E, S, Ic; 1981 v T, Cz, Ei, T, S, E, USSR; 1982 v Cz (sub), Ic; (with Swansea C), Sp, S (sub), Ni (sub), F (18)

Ward, D. (Bristol R), 1959 v E; (with Cardiff C), 1962 v E (2)

Ward, D. (Notts Co), 2000 v P; (with Nottingham F), 2002 v CzR (2)

Warner, J. (Swansea T), 1937 v E; (with Manchester U), 1939 v F (2)

Warren, F. W. (Cardiff C), 1929 v Ni; (with Middlesbrough), 1931 v Ni; 1933 v F, E; (with Hearts), 1937 v Ni; 1938 v Ni (6)

Watkins, A. E. (Leicester Fosse), 1898 v E, S; (with Aston Villa), 1900 v E, S; (with Millwall), 1904 v Ni (5)

Watkins, W. M. (Stoke C), 1902 v E; 1903 v E, S; (with Aston Villa); 1904 v E, S, Ni; (with Sunderland), 1905 v E, S, Ni; (with Stoke C), 1908 v Ni (10)

Webster, C. (Manchester U), 1957 v Cz; 1958 v H, M, Br (4)

Weston, R. D. (Arsenal), 2000 v P (sub) (1)

Whatley, W. J. (Tottenham H), 1939 v E, S (2)

White, P. F. (London Welsh), 1896 v Ni (1)

Wilcock, A. R. (Oswestry), 1890 v Ni (1)

Wilding, J. (Wrexham Olympians), 1885 v E, S, Ni; 1886 v E, Ni; (with Bootle), 1887 v E; 1888 v S, Ni; (with Wrexham), 1892 v S (9)

Williams, A. (Reading), 1994 v Es; 1995 v Alb, Mol, G (sub), Ge; 1996 v Mol, I; (with Wolverhampton W), 1998 v Br (sub), Jam; 1999 v I, D, I (12)

Williams, A. L. (Wrexham), 1931 v E (1)

Williams, A. P. (Southampton), 1998 v Br (sub), Ma (2)

Williams, B. (Bristol C), 1930 v Ni (1)

Williams, B. D. (Swansea T), 1928 v Ni, E; 1930 v E, S; (with Everton), 1931 v Ni; 1932 v E; 1933 v E, S, Ni; 1935 v N (10)

Williams, D. G. (Derby Co), 1988 v Cz, Y, Se, Ma, I; 1989 v Ho, I, Se, WG; 1990 v Fi, Ho; (with Ipswich T), 1993 v Ei; 1996 v G (sub) (13)

Williams, D. M. (Norwich C), 1986 v S.Ar (sub), U, Ca (2); 1987 v Fi (5)

Williams, D. R. (Merthyr T), 1921 v E, S; (with Sheffield W), 1923 v S; 1926 v S; 1927 v E, Ni; (with Manchester U), 1929 v E, S (8)

Williams, E. (Crewe Alex), 1893 v E, S (2)

Williams, E. (Druids), 1901 v E, Ni, S; 1902 v E, Ni (5)

Williams, G. (Chirk), 1893 v S; 1894 v S; 1895 v E, S, Ni; 1898 v Ni (6)

Williams, G. E. (WBA), 1960 v Ni; 1961 v S, E, Ei; 1963 v Ni, H; 1964 v E, S, Ni; 1965 v S, E, Ni, D, Gr (2), USSR, I; 1966 v Ni, Br (2), Ch; 1967 v S, E, Ni; 1968 v Ni; 1969 v I (26)

Williams, G. G. (Swansea T), 1961 v Ni, H, Sp (2); 1962 v E, S (5)

Williams, G. J. J. (Cardiff C), 1951 v Sw (1)

Williams, G. O. (Wrexham), 1907 v Ni (1)

Williams, H. J. (Swansea), 1965 v Gr (2); 1972 v R (3)

Williams, H. T. (Newport Co), 1949 v Ni, Sw; (with Leeds U) 1950 v Ni; 1951 v S (4)

Williams, J. H. (Oswestry), 1884 v E (1)

Williams, J. J. (Wrexham), 1939 v F (1)

Williams, J. T. (Middlesbrough), 1925 v Ni (1)

Williams, J. W. (C Palace), 1912 v S, Ni (2)

Williams, R. (Newcastle U), 1935 v S, E (2)

Williams, R. P. (Caernarvon), 1886 v S (1)

Williams, S. G. (WBA), 1954 v A; 1955 v E, Ni; 1956 v E, S, A; 1958 v E, S, Ni, Is (2), H (2), M, Se, Br; 1959 v E, S, Ni; 1960 v E, S, Ni; 1961 v Ni, Ei, H, Sp (2); 1962 v E, S, Ni, Br (2), M; (with Southampton), 1963 v S, E, H (2); 1964 v E, S; 1965 v S, E, D; 1966 v D (43)

Williams, W. (Druids), 1876 v S; 1878 v S; (with Oswestry), 1879 v E, S; (with Druids), 1880 v E; 1881 v E, S; 1882 v E, S, Ni; 1883 v Ni (11)

Williams, W. (Northampton T), 1925 v S (1)

Witcomb, D. F. (WBA), 1947 v E, S; (with Sheffield W), 1947 v Ni (3)

Woosnam, A. P. (Leyton Orient), 1959 v S; (with West Ham U), E; 1960 v E, S, Ni; 1961 v S, E, Ni, Ei, Sp, H; 1962 v E, S, Ni, Br; (with Aston Villa), 1963 v Ni, H (17)

Woosnam, G. (Newton White Star), 1879 v S (1)

Worthington, T. (Newtown), 1894 v S (1)

Wynn, G. A. (Wrexham), 1909 v E, S, Ni; (with Manchester C), 1910 v E; 1911 v Ni; 1912 v E, S; 1913 v E, S; 1914 v E, S (11)

Wynn, W. (Chirk), 1903 v Ni (1)

Yorath, T. C. (Leeds U), 1970 v I; 1971 v S, E, Ni; 1972 v Cz, E, S, Ni; 1973 v E, Pol, S; 1974 v Pol, E, S, Ni; 1975 v A, H (2), L (2), S; 1976 v A, E, S, Y (2), E, Ni; (with Coventry C), 1977 v WG, S (2), Cz, E, Ni; 1978 v K (2), S, Cz, WG, Ir, E, S, Ni; 1979 v T, WG, S, E, Ni; (with Tottenham H), 1980 v Ei, T, E, S, Ni, Ic; 1981 v T, Cz; (with Vancouver W), Ei, T, USSR (59)

Young, E. (Wimbledon), 1990 v Cr; (with C Palace), 1991 v D, Bel (2), L, Ei; 1992 v G, L, Ei, A; 1993 v Fa, Cy, Bel, Ei, Bel, Fa; 1994 v RCS, Cy, R, N; (with Wolverhampton W) 1996 v Alb (21)

REPUBLIC OF IRELAND

Aherne, T. (Belfast C), 1946 v P, Sp; (with Luton T), 1950 v Fi, E, Fi, Se, Bel; 1951 v N, Arg, N; 1952 v WG (2), A, Sp; 1953 v F; 1954 v F (16)

Aldridge, J. W. (Oxford U), 1986 v W, U, Ic, Cz; 1987 v Bel, S, Pol; (with Liverpool), S, Bul, Bel, Br, L; 1988 v Bul, Pol, N, E, USSR, Ho; 1989 v Ni, Tun, Sp, F (sub), H, Ma (sub), H; 1990 v WG; (with Real Sociedad), Ni, Ma, Fi (sub), H; Eg, Ho, R, I; 1991 v T, E (2), Pol; (with Tranmere R), 1992 v H (sub), T, W (sub), Sw (sub), US (sub), Alb, I, P (sub); 1993 v La, D, Sp, D, Alb, La, Li; 1994 v Li, Ni, CzR, I (sub), M (sub), N; 1995 v La, Ni, P, Lie; 1996 v La, P, Ho, Ru; 1997 v Mac (sub) (69)

Ambrose, P. (Shamrock R), 1955 v N, Ho; 1964 v Pol, N, E (5)

Anderson, J. (Preston NE), 1980 v Cz (sub), US (sub); 1982 v Ch, Br, Tr; (with Newcastle U), 1984 v Chn; 1986 v W, Ic, Cz; 1987 v Bul, Bel, Br, L; 1988 v R (sub), Y (sub); 1989 v Tun (16)

Andrews, P. (Bohemians), 1936 v Ho (1)

Arrigan, T. (Waterford), 1938 v N (1)

Babb, P. A. (Coventry C), 1994 v Ru, Ho, Bol, G, CzR (sub), I, M, N, Ho; (with Liverpool), 1995 v La, Lie, Ni (2), P, Lie, A; 1996 v La, P, Ho, CzR; 1997 v Ic; 1998 v Li (sub), R, Arg (sub), M; 1999 v Cro, Para (sub), Se (sub), Ni; 2000 v CzR (sub), S, M (sub), US, S.Af (34)

Bailham, E. (Shamrock R), 1964 v E (1)

Barber, E. (Shelbourne), 1966 v Sp; (with Birmingham C), 1966 v Bel (2)

Barry, P. (Fordsons), 1928 v Bel; 1929 v Bel (2)

Beglin, J. (Liverpool), 1984 v Chn; 1985 v M, D, I, Is, E, N, Sw; 1986 v Sw, USSR, D, W; 1987 v Bel (sub), S, Pol (15)

Bermingham, J. (Bohemians), 1929 v Bel (1)

Bermingham, P. (St James' Gate), 1935 v H (1)

Braddish, S. (Dundalk), 1978 v T (sub), Pol (2)

Bonner, P. (Celtic), 1981 v Pol; 1982 v Alg; 1984 v Ma, Is, Chn; 1985 v I, Is, E, N; 1986 v U, Ic; 1987 v Bel (2), S (2), Pol, Bul, Br, L; 1988 v Bul, R, Y, N, E, USSR, Ho; 1989 v Sp, F, H, Sp, Ma, H; 1990 v WG, Ni, Ma, W, Fi, T, E, Eg, Ho, R, I; 1991 v Mor, T, E (2), W, Pol, US; 1992 v H, Pol, T, W, Sw, Alb, I; 1993 v La, D, Sp, W, Ni, D, Alb, La, Li; 1994 v Li, Sp, Ni, Ru, Ho, Bol, CzR, I, M, N, Ho; 1995 v Lie; 1996 v M, Bol (sub) (80)

Bradshaw, P. (St James' Gate), 1939 v Sw, Pol, H (2), G (5)

Brady, F. (Fordsons), 1926 v I; 1927 v I (2)

Brady, T. R. (QPR), 1964 v A (2), Sp (2), Pol, N (6)

Brady, W. L. (Arsenal), 1975 v USSR, T, Sw, USSR, Sw, WG; 1976 v T, N, Pol; 1977 v E, T, F (2), Sp, Bul; 1978 v Bul, N; 1979 v Ni, E, D, Bul, WG; 1980 v W, Bul, E, Cy; (with Juventus), 1981 v Ho, Bel, F, Cy, Bel; 1982 v Ho, F, Ch, Br, Tr; (with Sampdoria), 1983 v Ho, Sp, Ic, Ma; 1984 v Ic, Ho, Ma, Pol, Is; (with Internazionale), 1985 v USSR, N, D, I, E, N, Sp, Sw; 1986 v Sw, USSR, D, W; (with Ascoli), 1987 v Bel, S (2), Pol; (with West Ham U), Bul, Bel, Br, L; 1988 v L, Bul; 1989 v F, H (sub), H (sub) (72)

Branagan, K. G. (Bolton W), 1997 v W (1)

Breen, G. (Birmingham C), 1996 v P (sub), Cro, Ho, US, M, Bol (sub); 1997 v Lie, Mac, Ic; (with Coventry C), v Mac; 1998 v Li (sub), R, CzR, Arg, M; 1999 v Ma, Y, Para, Se, Mac; 2000 v Y, Cro, Ma, Mac, T (2), Gr, S, M, US, S.Af; 2001 v Ho, P, Es, Fi, Cy, And (2); 2002 v Cy, Ir (2), Ru (sub), US, Cam, G, S.Ar, Sp (47)

Breen, T. (Manchester U), 1937 v Sw, F; (with Shamrock R), 1947 v E, Sp, P (5)

Brennan, F. (Drumcondra), 1965 v Bel (1)

Brennan, S. A. (Manchester U), 1965 v Sp; 1966 v Sp, A, Bel; 1967 v Sp, T, Sp; 1969 v Cz, D, H; 1970 v S, Cz, D, H, Pol (sub), WG; (with Waterford), 1971 v Pol, Se, I (19)

Brown, J. (Coventry C), 1937 v Sw, F (2)

Browne, M. (Bohemians), 1964 v A, Sp, E (3)

Buckley, L. (Shamrock R), 1984 v Pol (sub); (with Waregem), 1985 v M (2)

Burke, F. (Cork Ath), 1952 v WG (1)

Burke, J. (Shamrock R), 1929 v Bel (1)

Burke, J. (Cork), 1934 v Bel (1)

Butler, P. J. (Sunderland), 2000 v CzR (1)

Byrne, A. B. (Southampton), 1970 v D, Pol, WG; 1971 v Pol, Se (2), I (2), A; 1973 v F, USSR (sub), F, N; 1974 v Pol (14)

Byrne, D. (Shelbourne), 1929 v Bel; (with Shamrock R), 1932 v Sp; (with Coleraine), 1934 v Bel (3)

Byrne, J. (Bray Unknowns), 1928 v Bel (1)

Byrne, J. (QPR), 1985 v I, Is (sub), E (sub), Sp (sub); 1987 v S (sub), Bel (sub), Br, L (sub); 1988 v L, Bul, Is, R, Y (sub), Pol (sub); (with Le Havre), 1990 v WG (sub), W, Fi,

T (sub), Ma; (with Brighton & HA), 1991 v W; (with Sunderland), 1992 v T, W; (with Millwall), 1993 v W (23)

Byrne, P. (Dolphin), 1931 v Sp; 1932 v Ho; (with Drumcondra), 1934 v Ho (3)

Byrne, P. (Shamrock R), 1984 v Pol, Chn; 1985 v M; 1986 v D (sub), W (sub), U (sub), Ic (sub), Cz (8)

Byrne, S. (Bohemians), 1931 v Sp (1)

Campbell, A. (Santander), 1985 v I (sub), Is, Sp (3)

Campbell, N. (St Patrick's Ath), 1971 v A (sub); (with Fortuna, Cologne), 1972 v Ir, Ec, Ch, P; 1973 v USSR, F (sub); 1975 v WG; 1976 v N; 1977 v Sp, Bul (sub) (11)

Cannon, H. (Bohemians), 1926 v I; 1928 v Bel (2)

Cantwell, N. (West Ham U), 1954 v L; 1956 v Sp, Ho; 1957 v D, WG, E (2); 1958 v D, Pol, A; 1959 v Pol, Cz (2); 1960 v Se, Ch, Se; 1961 v N; (with Manchester U), S (2); 1962 v Cz (2), A; 1963 v Ic (2), S; 1964 v A, Sp, E; 1965 v Pol, Sp; 1966 v Sp (2), A, Bel; 1967 v Sp, T (36)

Carey, B. P. (Manchester U), 1992 v US (sub); 1993 v W; (with Leicester C), 1994 v Ru (3)

Carey, J. J. (Manchester U), 1938 v N, Cz, Pol; 1939 v Sw, Pol, H (2), G; 1946 v P, Sp; 1947 v E, Sp, P; 1948 v P, Sp; 1949 v Sw, Bel, P, Se, Sp; 1950 v Fi, E, Fi, Se; 1951 v N, Arg, N; 1953 v F, A (29)

Carolan, J. (Manchester U), 1960 v Se, Ch (2)

Carr, S. (Tottenham H), 1999 v Se, Ni, Mac; 2000 v Y (sub), Cro, Ma, T (2), S, M, US, S.Af; 2001 v Ho, P, Es, And (sub), P, Es (18)

Carroll, B. (Shelbourne), 1949 v Bel; 1950 v Fi (2)

Carroll, T. R. (Ipswich T), 1968 v Pol; 1969 v Pol, A, D; 1970 v Cz, Pol, WG; 1971 v Se; (with Birmingham C), 1972 v Ir, Ec, Ch, P; 1973 v USSR, Pol, F, N (17)

Carsley, L. K. (Derby Co), 1998 v R, Bel (1 + sub), CzR, Arg, M; 1999 v Cro (sub), Ma (sub), Para (sub); (with Blackburn R) Ni, Mac; 2000 v Y (sub), Cro, Ma, T; 2001 v Fi (sub); (with Coventry C), 2002 v Cro, Cy (sub), Ru (sub); (with Everton), S.Ar (sub) (20)

Cascarino, A. G. (Gillingham), 1986 v Sw, USSR, D; (with Millwall), 1988 v Pol, N (sub), USSR (sub), Ho (sub); 1989 v Ni, Tun, Sp, F, H, Sp, Ma, H; 1990 v WG (sub), Ni, Ma; (with Aston Villa), W, Fi, T, E, Eg, Ho (sub), R (sub), I (sub); 1991 v Mor (sub), T(sub), E (2 sub), Pol (sub), Ch (sub), US; (with Celtic), 1992 v Pol, T; (with Chelsea), W, Sw, US (sub); 1993 v W, Ni (sub), D (sub), Alb (sub), La (sub); 1994 v Li (sub), Sp (sub), Ni (sub), Ru, Bol (sub), G, CzR, Ho (sub); (with Marseille), 1995 v La (sub), Ni (sub), P (sub), Lie (sub), A (sub); 1996 v A (sub), P (sub), Ho, Ru (sub), P, Cro (sub), Ho; 1997 v Lie (sub), Mac, Ic; (with Nancy), v W, Mac, R (sub), Lie (sub); 1998 v Li (sub), Ic (sub), Li, R, Bel (2); 1999 v Cro (sub), Ma (sub), Y (sub), Para (sub), Se (sub), Ni (sub), Mac (sub); 2000 v Y (sub), Cro, Mac (sub), T (1 + sub) (88)

Chandler, J. (Leeds U), 1980 v Cz (sub), US (2)

Chatton, H. A. (Shelbourne), 1931 v Sp; (with Dumbarton), 1932 v Sp; (with Cork), 1934 v Ho (3)

Clarke, J. (Drogheda U), 1978 v Pol (sub) (1)

Clarke, K. (Drumcondra), 1948 v P, Sp (2)

Clarke, M. (Shamrock R), 1950 v Bel (1)

Clinton, T. J. (Everton), 1951 v N; 1954 v F, L (3)

Coad, P. (Shamrock R), 1947 v E, Sp, P; 1948 v P, Sp; 1949 v Sw, Bel, P, Se; 1951 v N (sub); 1952 v Sp (11)

Coffey, T. (Drumcondra), 1950 v Fi (1)

Colfer, M. D. (Shelbourne), 1950 v Bel; 1951 v N (2)

Colgan, N. (Hibernian), 2002 v D (sub) (1)

Collins, F. (Jacobs), 1927 v I (1)

Conmy, O. M. (Peterborough U), 1965 v Bel; 1967 v Cz; 1968 v Cz, Pol; 1970 v Cz (5)

Connolly, D. J. (Watford), 1996 v P, Ho, US, M; 1997 v R, Lie; (with Feyenoord), 1998 v Li, Ic, Li, Bel (1 + sub), CzR, M; (with Wolverhampton W), 1999 v Y, Para (sub). Se, Ni (sub), Mac (sub); (with Excelsior), 2000 v T (1 + sub), CzR (sub), Gr; 2001 v Ho (sub), Fi (sub), Cy, And; (with Feyenoord), And; (with Wimbledon), 2002 v Cro (sub), Cy, Ir, D (sub), US (sub), Ng (sub), Sp (sub) (34)

Connolly, H. (Cork), 1937 v G (1)

Connolly, J. (Fordsons), 1926 v I (1)

Conroy, G. A. (Stoke C), 1970 v Cz, D, H, Pol, WG; 1971 v Pol, Se (2), I; 1973 v USSR, F, USSR, N; 1974 v Pol, Br, U, Ch; 1975 v T, Sw, USSR, Sw, WG (sub); 1976 v T (sub), Pol; 1977 v E, T, Pol (27)

Conway, J. P. (Fulham), 1967 v Sp, T, Sp; 1968 v Cz; 1969 v A (sub), H; 1970 v S, Cz, D, H, Pol, WG; 1971 v I, A; 1974 v U, Ch; 1975 v WG (sub); 1976 v N, Pol; (with Manchester C), 1977 v Pol (20)

Corr, P. J. (Everton), 1949 v P, Sp; 1950 v E, Se (4)

Courtney, E. (Cork U), 1946 v P (1)

Coyle, O. C. (Bolton W), 1994 v Ho (sub) (1)

Coyne, T. (Celtic), 1992 v Sw, US, Alb (sub), US (sub), I (sub), P (sub); 1993 v W (sub), La (sub); (with Tranmere R), Ni; (with Motherwell), 1994 v Ru (sub), Ho, Bol, G (sub), CzR (sub), I, M, Ho; 1995 v Lie, Ni (sub), A; 1996 v Ru (sub); 1998 v Bel (sub) (22)

Cummins, G. P. (Luton T), 1954 v L (2); 1955 v N (2), WG; 1956 v Y, Sp; 1958 v D, Pol, A; 1959 v Pol, Cz (2); 1960 v Se, Ch, WG, Se; 1961 v S (2) (19)

Cuneen, T. (Limerick), 1951 v N (1)

Cunningham, K. (Wimbledon), 1996 v CzR, P, Cro, Ho (sub), US, Bol; 1997 v Ic (sub), W, R, Lie; 1998 v Li, Ic, Li, Bel (2), CzR; 1999 v Cro, Ma, Y, Para, Se, Ni, Mac; 2000 v Y, Cro, Ma, Mac, T (2), CzR, Gr; 2001 v Cy, And; 2002 v Ir (sub), Ru, D, US (sub), Ng, G (sub), Sp (sub) (40)

Curtis, D. P. (Shelbourne), 1957 v D, WG; (with Bristol C), 1957 v E (2); 1958 v D, Pol, A; (with Ipswich T), 1959 v Pol; 1960 v Se, Ch, WG, Se; 1961 v N, S; 1962 v A; 1963 v Ic; (with Exeter C), 1964 v A (17)

Cusack, S. (Limerick), 1953 v F (1)

Daish, L. S. (Cambridge U), 1992 v W, Sw (sub); (with Coventry C), 1996 v CzR (sub), Cro, M (5)

Daly, G. A. (Manchester U), 1973 v Pol (sub), N; 1974 v Br (sub), U (sub); 1975 v Sw (sub), WG; 1977 v E, T, F; (with Derby Co), F, Bul; 1978 v Bul, T, D; 1979 v Ni, E, D, Bul; 1980 v Ni, E, Cy, Sw, Arg; (with Coventry C), 1981 v WG 'B', Ho, Bel, Cy, W, Bel, Cz, Pol (sub); 1982 v Alg, Ch, Br, Tr; 1983 v Ho, Sp (sub); 1984 v Is (sub), Ma; (with Birmingham C), 1985 v M (sub), N, Sp, Sw; 1986 v Sw; (with Shrewsbury T), U, Ic (sub), Cz (sub); 1987 v S (sub) (48)

Daly, J. (Shamrock R), 1932 v Ho; 1935 v Sw (2)

Daly, M. (Wolverhampton W), 1978 v T, Pol (2)

Daly, P. (Shamrock R), 1950 v Fi (sub) (1)

Davis, T. L. (Oldham Ath), 1937 v G, H; (with Tranmere R), 1938 v Cz, Pol (4)

Deacy, E. (Aston Villa), 1982 v Alg (sub), Ch, Br, Tr (4)

Delap, R. J. (Derby Co), 1998 v CzR (sub), Arg (sub), M (sub); 2000 v T (2), Gr (sub); (with Southampton), 2002 v US (7)

De Mange, K. J. P. P. (Liverpool), 1987 v Br (sub); (with Hull C), 1989 v Tun (sub) (2)

Dempsey, J. T. (Fulham), 1967 v Sp, Cz; 1968 v Cz, Pol; 1969 v Pol, A, D; (with Chelsea), 1969 v Cz, D; 1970 v H, WG; 1971 v Pol, Se (2), I; 1972 v Ir, Ec, Ch, P (19)

Dennehy, J. (Cork Hibernians), 1972 v Ec (sub), Ch; (with Nottingham F), 1973 v USSR (sub), Pol, F, N; 1974 v Pol (sub); 1975 v T (sub), WG (sub); (with Walsall), 1976 v Pol (sub); 1977 v Pol (sub) (11)

Desmond, P. (Middlesbrough), 1950 v Fi, E, Fi, Se (4)

Devine, J. (Arsenal), 1980 v Cz, Ni; 1981 v WG 'B', Cz; 1982 v Ho, Alg; 1983 v Sp, Ma; (with Norwich C), 1984 v Ic, Ho, Is; 1985 v USSR, N (13)

Doherty, G. M. T. (Luton T), 2000 v Gr (sub); (with Tottenham H), US, S.Af (sub); 2001 v Cy (sub), And (sub+1), P (sub), Es (sub); 2002 v US (sub) (9)

Donnelly, J. (Dundalk), 1935 v H, Sw, G; 1936 v Ho, Sw, H, L; 1937 v G, H; 1938 v N (10)

Donnelly, T. (Drumcondra), 1938 v N; (Shamrock R), 1939 v Sw (2)

Donovan, D. C. (Everton), 1955 v N, Ho, N, WG; 1957 v E (5)

Donovan, T. (Aston Villa), 1980 v Cz; 1981 v WG 'B'(sub) (2)

Dowdall, C. (Fordsons), 1928 v Bel; (with Barnsley), 1929 v Bel; (with Cork), 1931 v Sp (3)

Doyle, C. (Shelbourne), 1959 v Cz (1)

Doyle, D. (Shamrock R), 1926 v I (1)

Doyle, L. (Dolphin), 1932 v Sp (1)

Duff, D. A. (Blackburn R), 1998 v CzR, M; 1999 v Cro, Ma, Y, Para, Se (sub), Ni, Mac; 2000 v Cro, Ma (sub), T (sub + sub), S (sub); 2001 v P (sub), Es (sub), Cy (sub), And, P (sub), Es; 2002 v Cro, Ho, Ru, D, US, Ng, Cam, G, S.Ar, Sp (30)

Duffy, B. (Shamrock R), 1950 v Bel (1)

Duggan, H. A. (Leeds U), 1927 v I; 1930 v Bel; 1936 v H, L; (with Newport Co), 1938 v N (5)

Dunne, A. P. (Manchester U), 1962 v A; 1963 v Ic, S; 1964 v A, Sp, Pol, N, E; 1965 v Pol, Sw; 1966 v Sp (2), A, Bel; 1967 v Sp, T, Sp; 1969 v Pol, D, H; 1970 v H; 1971 v Se, I, A; (with Bolton W), 1974 v Br (sub), U, Ch; 1975 v T, Sw, USSR, Sw, WG (sub) v T (33)

Dunne, J. (Sheffield U), 1930 v Bel; (with Arsenal), 1936 v Sw, H, L; (with Southampton), 1937 v Sw, F; (with Shamrock R), 1938 v N (2), Cz, Pol; 1939 v Sw, Pol, H (2), G (15)

Dunne, J. C. (Fulham), 1971 v A (1)

Dunne, L. (Manchester C), 1935 v Sw, G (2)

Dunne, P. A. J. (Manchester U), 1965 v Sp; 1966 v Sp (2), WG; 1967 v T (5)

Dunne, R. P. (Everton), 2000 v Gr, S (sub), M; 2001 v Ho, P, Es; (with Manchester C), Fi, And, P, Es; 2002 v Cro, Ho, Ru (sub), D (sub) (14)

Dunne, S. (Luton T), 1953 v F, A; 1954 v F, L; 1956 v Sp, Ho; 1957 v D, WG, E; 1958 v D, Pol, A; 1959 v Pol; 1960 v WG, Se (15)

Dunne, T. (St Patrick's Ath), 1956 v Ho; 1957 v D, WG (3)

Dunning, P. (Shelbourne), 1971 v Se, I (2)

Dunphy, E. M. (York C), 1966 v Sp; (with Millwall), 1966 v WG; 1967 v T, Sp, T, Cz; 1968 v Cz, Pol; 1969 v Pol, A, D (2), H; 1970 v D, H, Pol, WG (sub); 1971 v Pol, Se (2), I (2), A (23)

Dwyer, N. M. (West Ham U), 1960 v Se, Ch, WG, Se; (with Swansea T), 1961 v W, N, S (2); 1962 v Cz (2); 1964 v Pol (sub), N, E; 1965 v Pol (14)

Eccles, P. (Shamrock R), 1986 v U (sub) (1)

Egan, R. (Dundalk), 1929 v Bel (1)

Eglington, T. J. (Shamrock R), 1946 v P, Sp; (with Everton), 1947 v E, Sp, P; 1948 v P; 1949 v Sw, P, Se; 1951 v N, Arg; 1952 v WG (2), A, Sp; 1953 v F, A; 1954 v F, L, F; 1955 v N, Ho, WG; 1956 v Sp (24)

Ellis, P. (Bohemians), 1935 v Sw, G; 1936 v Ho, Sw, L; 1937 v G, H (7)

Evans, M. J. (Southampton), 1998 v R (sub) (1)

Fagan, E. (Shamrock R), 1973 v N (sub) (1)

Fagan, F. (Manchester C), 1955 v N; 1960 v Se; (with Derby Co), 1960 v Ch, WG, Se; 1961 v W, N, S (8)

Fagan, J. (Shamrock R), 1926 v I (1)

Fairclough, M. (Dundalk), 1982 v Ch (sub), Tr (sub) (2)

Fallon, S. (Celtic), 1951 v N; 1952 v WG (2), A, Sp; 1953 v F; 1955 v N, WG (8)

Fallon, W. J. (Notts Co), 1935 v H; 1936 v H; 1937 v H, Sw, F; 1939 v Sw, Pol; (with Sheffield W), 1939 v H, G (9)

Farquharson, T. G. (Cardiff C), 1929 v Bel; 1930 v Bel; 1931 v Sp; 1932 v Sp (4)

Farrell, P. (Hibernian), 1937 v Sw, F (2)

Farrell, P. D. (Shamrock R), 1946 v P, Sp; (with Everton), 1947 v Sp, P; 1948 v P, Sp; 1949 v Sw, P (sub), Sp; 1950 v E, Fi, Se; 1951 v Arg, N; 1952 v WG (2), A, Sp; 1953 v F, A; 1954 v F (2); 1955 v N, Ho, WG; 1956 v Y, Sp; 1957 E (28)

Farrelly, G. (Aston Villa), 1996 v P, US, Bol; (with Everton), 1998 v CzR, M; (with Bolton W), 2000 v US (6)

Feenan, J. J. (Sunderland), 1937 v Sw, F (2)

Finnan, S. (Fulham), 2000 v Gr, S; 2001 v P (sub), Es (sub), Fi, And (sub+sub); 2002 v Cro (sub), Ho (sub), Cy, Ir (2), Ru, US, Ng, Cam (sub), G, S.Ar, Sp (19)

Finucane, A. (Limerick), 1967 v T, Cz; 1969 v Cz, D, H; 1970 v S, Cz; 1971 v Se, I (1+sub); 1972 v A (11)

Fitzgerald, F. J. (Waterford), 1955 v Ho; 1956 v Ho (2)

Fitzgerald, P. J. (Leeds U), 1961 v W, N, S; (with Chester), 1962 v Cz (2) (5)

Fitzpatrick, K. (Limerick), 1970 v Cz (1)

Fitzsimons, A. G. (Middlesbrough), 1950 v Fi, Bel; 1952 v WG (2), A, Sp; 1953 v F, A; 1954 v F, L, F; 1955 v Ho, N, WG; 1956 v Y, Sp, Ho; 1957 v D, WG, E (2); 1958 v D, Pol, A; 1959 v Pol; (with Lincoln C), 1959 v Cz (26)

Fleming, C. (Middlesbrough), 1996 v CzR (sub), P, Cro (sub), Ho (sub), US (sub), M, Bol; 1997 v Lie (sub); 1998 v R (sub), M (10)

Flood, J. J. (Shamrock R), 1926 v I; 1929 v Bel; 1930 v Bel; 1931 v Sp; 1932 v Sp (5)

Fogarty, A. (Sunderland), 1960 v WG, Se; 1961 v S; 1962 v Cz (2); 1963 v Ic (2), S (sub); 1964 v A (2); (with Hartlepools U), Sp (11)

Foley, D. J. (Watford), 2000 v S (sub), M (sub), US, S.Af; 2001 v Es (sub), Fi (6)

Foley, J. (Cork), 1934 v Bel, Ho; (with Celtic), 1935 v H, Sw, G; 1937 v G, H (7)

Foley, M. (Shelbourne), 1926 v I (1)

Foley, T. C. (Northampton T), 1964 v Sp, Pol, N; 1965 v Pol, Bel; 1966 v Sp (2), WG; 1967 v Cz (9)

Foy, T. (Shamrock R), 1938 v N; 1939 v H (2)

Fullam, J. (Preston NE), 1961 v N; (with Shamrock R), 1964 v Sp, Pol, N; 1966 v A, Bel; 1968 v Pol; 1969 v Pol, A, D; 1970 v Cz (sub) (11)

Fullam, R. (Shamrock R), 1926 v I; 1927 v I (2)

Gallagher, C. (Celtic), 1967 v T, Cz (2)

Gallagher, M. (Hibernian), 1954 v L (1)

Gallagher, P. (Falkirk), 1932 v Sp (1)

Galvin, A. (Tottenham H), 1983 v Ho, Ma; 1984 v Ho (sub), Is (sub); 1985 v M, USSR, N, D, I, N, Sp; 1986 v U, Ic, Cz;

1987 v Bel (2), S, Bul, L; (with Sheffield W), 1988 v L, Bul, R, Pol, N, E, USSR, Ho; 1989 v Sp; (with Swindon T), 1990 v WG (29)

Gannon, E. (Notts Co), 1949 v Sw; (with Sheffield W), 1949 v Bel, P, Se, Sp; 1950 v Fi; 1951 v N; 1952 v WG, A; 1954 v L, F; 1955 v N; (with Shelbourne), 1955 v N, WG (14)

Gannon, M. (Shelbourne), 1972 v A (1)

Gaskins, P. (Shamrock R), 1934 v Bel, Ho; 1935 v H, Sw, G; (with St James' Gate), 1938 v Cz, Pol (7)

Gavin, J. T. (Norwich C), 1950 v Fi (2); 1953 v F; 1954 v L; (with Tottenham H), 1955 v Ho, WG; (with Norwich C), 1957 v D (7)

Geoghegan, M. (St James' Gate), 1937 v G; 1938 v N (2)

Gibbons, A. (St Patrick's Ath), 1952 v WG; 1954 v L; 1956 v Y, Sp (4)

Gilbert, R. (Shamrock R), 1966 v WG (1)

Giles, C. (Doncaster R), 1951 v N (1)

Giles, M. J. (Manchester U), 1960 v Se, Ch; 1961 v W, N, S (2); 1962 v Cz (2), A; 1963 v Ic, S; (with Leeds U), 1964 v A (2), Sp (2), Pol, N, E; 1965 v Sp; 1966 v Sp (2), A, Bel; 1967 v Sp, T (2); 1969 v A, D, Cz; 1970 v S, Pol, WG; 1971 v I; 1973 v F, USSR; 1974 v Br, U, Ch; 1975 v USSR, T, Sw, USSR, Sw; (with WBA), 1976 v T; 1977 v E, T, F (2), Pol, Bul; (with Shamrock R), 1978 v Bul, T, Pol, N, D; 1979 v Ni, D, Bul, WG (59)

Given, S. J. J. (Blackburn R), 1996 v Ru, CzR, P, Cro, Ho, US, Bol; 1997 v Lie (2); (with Newcastle U), 1998 v Li, Ic, Li, Bel (2), CzR, Arg, M; 1999 v Cro, Ma, Y, Para, Se, Ni; 2000 v Gr, S.Af; 2001 v Fi, Cy, And (2), P, Es; 2002 v Cro, Ho, Cy, Ir (2), Ru, US, Ng, Cam, G, S.Ar, Sp (43)

Givens, D. J. (Manchester U), 1969 v D, H; 1970 v S, Cz, D, H; (with Luton), 1970 v Pol, WG; 1971 v Se, I (2), A; 1972 v Ir, E, C; (with QPR), 1973 v F, USSR, Pol, F, N; 1974 v Pol, Br, U, Ch; 1975 v USSR, T, Sw, USSR, Sw, WG; 1976 v T, N, Pol; 1977 v E, T, F (2), Sp, Bul; 1978 v Bul, N, D; (with Birmingham C), 1979 v Ni (sub), E, D, Bul, WG; 1980 v US (sub), Ni (sub), Sw, Arg; 1981 v Ho, Bel, Cy (sub), W; (with Neuchatel X), 1982 v F (sub) (56)

Glen, W. (Shamrock R), 1927 v I; 1929 v Bel; 1930 v Bel; 1932 v Sp; 1936 v Ho, Sw, H, L (8)

Glynn, D. (Drumcondra), 1952 v WG; 1955 v N (2)

Godwin, T. F. (Shamrock R), 1949 v P, Se, Sp; 1950 v Fi, E; (with Leicester C), 1950 v Fi, Se, Bel; 1951 v N; (with Bournemouth), 1956 v Ho; 1957 v E; 1958 v D, Pol (13)

Golding, J. (Shamrock R), 1928 v Bel; 1930 v Bel (2)

Goodman, J. (Wimbledon), 1997 v W, Mac, R (sub), Lie (sub) (4)

Gorman, W. C. (Bury), 1936 v Sw, H, L; 1937 v G, H; 1938 v N, Cz, Pol; 1939 v Sw, Pol (with Brentford) H; 1947 v E, P (13)

Grace, J. (Drumcondra), 1926 v I (1)

Grealish, A. (Orient), 1976 v N, Pol; 1978 v N, D; 1979 v Ni, E, WG; (with Luton T), 1980 v W, Cz, Bul, US, Ni, E, Cy, Sw, Arg; 1981 v WG 'B', Ho, Bel, F, Cy, W, Bel, Pol; (with Brighton & HA), 1982 v Ho, Alg, Ch, Br, Tr; 1983 v Ho, Sp, Ic, Sp; 1984 v Ic, Ho; (with WBA), Pol, Chn; 1985 v M, USSR, N, D, Sp (sub), Sw; 1986 v USSR, D (45)

Gregg, E. (Bohemians), 1978 v Pol, D (sub); 1979 v E (sub), D, Bul, WG; 1980 v W, Cz (8)

Griffith (Walsall), 1935 v H (1)

Grimes, A. A. (Manchester U), 1978 v T, Pol, N (sub); 1980 v Bul, US, Ni, E, Cy; 1981 v WG 'B' (sub), Cz, Pol; 1982 v Alg; 1983 v Sp (2); (with Coventry C), 1984 v Pol, Is; (with Luton T), 1988 v L, R (18)

Hale, A. (Aston Villa), 1962 v A; (with Doncaster R), 1963 v Ic; 1964 v Sp (2); (with Waterford), 1967 v Sp; 1968 v Pol (sub); 1969 v Pol, A, D; 1970 v S, Cz; 1971 v Pol (sub); 1972 v A (1); 1974 v Pol (sub) (14)

Hamilton, T. (Shamrock R), 1959 v Cz (2) (2)

Hand, E. K. (Portsmouth), 1969 v Cz (sub); 1970 v Pol, WG; 1971 v Pol, A; 1973 v USSR, F, USSR, Pol, F; 1974 v Pol, Br, U, Ch; 1975 v T, Sw, USSR, Sw, WG; 1976 v T (20)

Harrington, M. (Cork), 1936 v Ho, Sw, H, L; 1938 v Pol (sub) (5)

Harte, I. P. (Leeds U), 1996 v Cro (sub), Ho, M, Bol; 1997 v Lie, Mac, Ic (sub), W, Mac (sub), R, Lie; 1998 v Li, Ic, Li, Bel (2), Arg, M; 1999 v Para; 2000 v Cro (sub), Ma (sub), CzR; 2001 v Ho, P, Es, Fi, Cy, And (2), P, Es; 2002 v Cro, Ho, Cy, Ir (2), Ru, D, US, Ng, Cam, G, S.Ar, Sp (44)

Hartnett, J. B. (Middlesbrough), 1949 v Sp; 1954 v L (2)

Haverty, J. (Arsenal), 1956 v Ho; 1957 v D, WG, E (2); 1958 v D, Pol, A; 1959 v Cz; 1960 v Se, Ch; 1961 v W, N, S (2); (with Blackburn R), 1962 v Cz (2); (with Millwall), 1963 v S; 1964 v A, Sp, Pol, N, E; (with Celtic), 1965 v Pol; (with Bristol R), 1965 v Sp; (with Shelbourne), 1966 v Sp (2), WG, A, Bel; 1967 v T, Sp (32)

Hayes, A. W. P. (Southampton), 1979 v D (1)

Hayes, W. E. (Huddersfield T), 1947 v E, P (2)

Hayes, W. J. (Limerick), 1949 v Bel (1)

Healey, R. (Cardiff C), 1977 v Pol; 1980 v E (sub) (2)

Healy, C. (Celtic), 2002 v Ru, D (sub), US (3)

Heighway, S. D. (Liverpool), 1971 v Pol, Se (2), I, A; 1973 v USSR; 1975 v USSR, T, USSR, WG; 1976 v T, N; 1977 v E, F (2), Sp, Bul; 1978 v Bul, N, D; 1979 v Ni, Bul; 1980 v Pol, US, Ni, E, Cy, Arg; 1981 v Bel, F, Cy, W, Bel; (with Minnesota K), 1982 v Ho (34)

Henderson, B. (Drumcondra), 1948 v P, Sp (2)

Hennessy, J. (Shelbourne), 1965 v Pol, Bel, Sp; 1966 v WG; (with St Patrick's Ath), 1969 v A (5)

Herrick, J. (Cork Hibernians), 1972 v A, Ch (sub); (with Shamrock R), 1973 v F (sub) (3)

Higgins, J. (Birmingham C), 1951 v Arg (1)

Holland, M. R. (Ipswich T), 2000 v Mac (sub), M, US, S.Af; 2001 v P (sub), Fi, Cy (sub), And (2), P (sub), Es; 2002 v Ho, Cy, Ir (2), Ru (sub), D, US (sub), Ng, Cam, G, S.Ar, Sp (23)

Holmes, J. (Coventry C), 1971 v A (sub); 1973 v F, USSR, Pol, F, N; 1974 v Pol, Br; 1975 v USSR, Sw; 1976 v T, N, Pol; 1977 v E, T, F, Sp; (with Tottenham H), F, Pol, Bul; 1978 v Bul, T, Pol, N, D; 1979 v Ni, E, D, Bul; (with Vancouver W), 1981 v W (30)

Horlacher, A. F. (Bohemians), 1930 v Bel; 1932 v Sp, Ho; 1934 v Ho (sub); 1935 v H;1936 v Ho, Sw (7)

Houghton, R. J. (Oxford U), 1986 v W, U, Ic, Cz; 1987 v Bel (2), S (2), Pol, L; 1988 v L, Bul; (with Liverpool), Is, Y, N, E, USSR, Ho; 1989 v Ni, Tun, Sp, F, H, Sp, Ma, H; 1990 v Ni, Ma, Fi, E, Eg, Ho, R, I; 1991 v Mor, T, E (2), Pol, Ch, US; 1992 v H, Alb, US, I, P; (with Aston Villa), 1993 v D, Sp, Ni, D, Alb, La, Li; 1994 v Li, Sp, Ni, Bol, G (sub), I, M, N, Ho; (with C Palace), 1995 v P, A; 1996 v A, CzR; 1997 v Lie, R, Lie; (with Reading), 1998 v Li, R, Bel (1 + sub) (73)

Howlett, G. (Brighton & HA), 1984 v Chn (sub) (1)

Hoy, M. (Dundalk), 1938 v N; 1939 v Sw, Pol, H (2), G (6)

Hughton, C. (Tottenham H), 1980 v US, E, Sw, Arg; 1981 v Ho, Bel, F, Cy, W, Bel, Pol; 1982 v F; 1983 v Ho, Sp, Ma, Sp; 1984 v Ic, Ho, Ma; 1985 v M (sub), USSR, N, I, Is, E, Sp; 1986 v Sw, USSR, U, Ic; 1987 v Bel, Bul; 1988 v Is, Y, Pol, N, E, USSR, Ho; 1989 v Ni, F, H, Sp, Ma, H; 1990 v W (sub), USSR, Fi, T (sub), Ma; 1991 v T; (with West Ham U), Ch; 1992 v T (53)

Hurley, C. J. (Millwall), 1957 v E; (with Sunderland), 1958 v D, Pol, A; 1959 v Cz (2); 1960 v Se, Ch, WG, Se; 1961 v W, N, S (2); 1962 v Cz (2), A; 1963 v Ic (2), S; 1964 v A (2), Sp (2), Pol, N; 1965 v Sp; 1966 v WG, A, Bel; 1967 v T, Sp, T, Cz; 1968 v Cz, Pol; 1969 v Pol, D, Cz, (with Bolton W), H (40)

Hutchinson, F. (Drumcondra), 1935 v Sw, G (2)

Irwin, D. J. (Manchester U), 1991 v Mor, T, W, E, Pol, US; 1992 v H, Pol, W, US, Alb, US (sub), I; 1993 v La, D, Sp, Ni, D, Alb, La, Li; 1994 v Li, Sp, Ni, Bol, G, I, M; 1995 v La, Lie, Ni, E, Ni, P, Lie, A; 1996 v A, P, Ho, CzR; 1997 v Lie, Mac, Ic, Mac, R; 1998 v Li, Bel, Arg (sub); 1999 v Cro, Y, Para, Mac; 2000 v Y, Mac, T (2) (56)

Jordan, D. (Wolverhampton W), 1937 v Sw, F (2)

Jordan, W. (Bohemians), 1934 v Ho; 1938 v N (2)

Kavanagh, G. A. (Stoke C), 1998 v CzR (sub); 1999 v Se (sub), Ni (sub) (3)

Kavanagh, P. J. (Celtic), 1931 v Sp; 1932 v Sp (2)

Keane, R. D. (Wolverhampton W), 1998 v CzR (sub), Arg, M; 1999 v Cro, Ma, Para, Se (sub), Ni, Mac; (with Coventry C), 2000 v Y, Ma, Mac, T, CzR, Gr, S, M, S.Af; (with Internazionale), 2001 v Ho, P, Es, Fi, Cy, And, P; (with Leeds U), 2002 v Cro, Ho, Ir (2), Ru, D, US, Ng, Cam, G, S.Ar, Sp (37)

Keane, R. M. (Nottingham F), 1991 v Ch; 1992 v H, Pol, W, Sw, Alb, US; 1993 v La, D, Sp, W, Ni, D, Alb, La, Li; (with Manchester U), 1994 v Li, Sp, Ni, Bol, G, CzR (sub), I, M, N, Ho; 1995 v Ni (2); 1996 v A, Ru; 1997 v Ic, W, Mac, R, Lie; 1998 v Li, Ic, Li; 1999 v Cro, Ma, Y, Para; 2000 v Y, T (2), CzR; 2001 v Ho, P, Es, Cy, And, P; 2002 v Cro, Ho, Cy, Ir, Ru, Ng (58)

Keane, T. R. (Swansea T), 1949 v Sw, P, Se, Sp (4)

Kearin, M. (Shamrock R), 1972 v A (1)

Kearns, F. T. (West Ham U), 1954 v L (1)

Kearns, M. (Oxford U), 1971 v Pol (sub); (with Walsall), 1974 v Pol (sub), U, Ch; 1976 v N, Pol; 1977 v E, T, F (2), Sp, Bul; 1978 v N, D; 1979 v Ni, E; (with Wolverhampton W), 1980 v US, Ni (18)

Kelly, A. T. (Sheffield U), 1993 v W (sub); 1994 v Ru (sub), G; 1995 v La, Ni, E, Ni, P, Lie, A; 1996 v A, La, P, Ho; 1997 v Mac, Ic, Mac, R; 1998 v R, Arg (sub); 1999 v Para (sub), Mac; (with Blackburn R), 2000 v Y, Cro, Ma, Mac, T, CzR, S, US; 2001 v Ho, P, Es; 2002 v Cro (sub) (34)

Kelly, D. T. (Walsall), 1988 v Is, R, Y; (with West Ham U), 1989 v Tun (sub); (with Leicester C), 1990 v USSR, Ma; 1991 v Mor, W (sub), Ch, US; 1992 v H; (with Newcastle U), I (sub), P; 1993 v Sp (sub), Ni; (with Wolverhampton W), 1994 v Ru, N (sub); 1995 v E, Ni; (with Sunderland), 1996 v La (sub); 1997 v Ic, W (sub), Mac (sub); (with Tranmere R), 1998 v Li (sub), R (sub), Bel (sub) (26)

Kelly, G. (Leeds U), 1994 v Ru, Ho, Bol (sub), G (sub), CzR, N, Ho; 1995 v La, Lie, Ni (2), P, Lie, A; 1996 v A, La, P, Ho; 1997 v W (sub), R, Lie; 1998 v Ic, Li, Bel (2), CzR, Arg, M; 2000 v Cro, Mac, CzR; 2001 v Ho (sub), Fi, Cy, And (2), P, Es; 2002 v Cro, Ho, Ir (sub+sub), Ru (sub), D, US (sub), Ng (sub), Cam, G, S.Ar, Sp (50)

Kelly, J. (Derry C), 1932 v Ho; 1934 v Bel; 1936 v Sw, L (4)

Kelly, J. A. (Drumcondra), 1957 v WG, E; (with Preston NE), 1962 v A; 1963 v Ic (2), S; 1964 v A (2), Sp (2), Pol; 1965 v Bel; 1966 v A, Bel; 1967 v Sp (2), T, Cz; 1968 v Pol, Cz; 1969 v Pol, A, D, Cz, D, H; 1970 v S, D, H, Pol, WG; 1971 v Pol, Se (2), I (2), A; 1972 v Ir, Ec, Ch, P; 1973 v USSR, F, USSR, Pol, F, N (47)

Kelly, J. P. V. (Wolverhampton W), 1961 v W, N, S; 1962 v Cz (2) (5)

Kelly, M. J. (Portsmouth), 1988 v Y, Pol (sub); 1989 v Tun; 1991 v Mor (4)

Kelly, N. (Nottingham F), 1954 v L (1)

Kendrick, J. (Everton), 1927 v I; (with Dolphin) 1934 v Bel, Ho; 1936 v Ho (4)

Kenna, J. J. (Blackburn R), 1995 v P (sub), Lie (sub), A (sub); 1996 v La, P, Ho, Ru (sub), CzR, P, Cro, Ho, US; 1997 v Lie, Mac, Ic, R (sub), Lie; 1998 v Li, Ic, R, Bel (1 + sub), CzR, Arg; 1999 v Cro (sub), Ma; 2000 v T (sub) (27)

Kennedy, M. F. (Portsmouth), 1986 v Ic, Cz (sub) (2)

Kennedy, M. J. (Liverpool), 1996 v A, La (sub), P, Ru, CzR, Cro, Ho (sub), US (sub), M, Bol (sub); 1997 v R, Lie; 1998 v Li, R (sub), Bel (2), (with Wimbledon), M (sub); 1999 v Ma (sub), Se, Ni, Mac; (with Manchester C), 2000 v Y, Ma, Mac, CzR, S, M, US (sub), S.Af (sub); 2001 v And; (with Wolverhampton W), 2002 v Cro, Cy, Ru (sub) (34)

Kennedy, W. (St James' Gate), 1932 v Ho; 1934 v Bel, Ho (3)

Keogh, J. (Shamrock R), 1966 v WG (sub) (1)

Keogh, S. (Shamrock R), 1959 v Pol (1)

Kernaghan, A. N. (Middlesbrough), 1993 v La, D (2), Alb, La, Li; 1994 v Li; (with Manchester C), Sp, Ni, Bol (sub), CzR; 1995 v Lie, E; 1996 v A, P (sub), Ho (sub), Ru, P, Cro (sub), Ho, US, Bol (22)

Kiely, D. L. (Charlton Ath), 2000 v T (sub + 1), Gr (sub); M; 2002 v Ru (sub), D (6)

Kiernan, F. W. (Shamrock R), 1951 v Arg, N; (with Southampton), 1952 v WG (2), A (5)

Kilbane, K. D. (WBA), 1998 v Ic, CzR (sub), Arg; 1999 v Se (sub), Mac (sub); 2000 v Y, Cro (sub), Ma, T (2); (with Sunderland), CzR, Gr, S, M (sub), US, S.Af (sub); 2001 v Ho, P, Es, Fi, Cy, And (2), P, Es; 2002 v Cro (sub), Ho, Cy, Ir (2), Ru, US, Ng, Cam, G, S.Ar, Sp (37)

Kinnear, J. P. (Tottenham H), 1967 v T; 1968 v Cz, Pol; 1969 v A; 1970 v Cz, D, H, Pol; 1971 v Se (sub); I; 1972 v Ir, Ec, Ch, P; 1973 v USSR, F; 1974 v Pol, Br, U, Ch; 1975 v USSR, T, Sw, USSR, WG; (with Brighton & HA), 1976 v T (sub) (26)

Kinsella, J. (Shelbourne), 1928 v Bel (1)

Kinsella, M. A. (Charlton Ath), 1998 v CzR, Arg; 1999 v Cro, Ma, Y, Para, Se, Ni, Mac; 2000 v Y, Cro, Ma, Mac, T, CzR, Gr; 2001 v Ho, P, Es, Fi, Cy, And, P, Es; 2002 v T, D, US, Ng (sub), Cam, G, S.Ar, Sp (32)

Kinsella, O. (Shamrock R), 1932 v Ho; 1938 v N (2)

Kirkland, A. (Shamrock R), 1927 v I (1)

Lacey, W. (Shelbourne), 1927 v I; 1928 v Bel; 1930 v Bel (3)

Langan, D. (Derby Co), 1978 v T, N; 1980 v Sw, Arg; (with Birmingham C), 1981 v WG 'B', Ho, Bel, F, Cy, W, Bel, Cz, Pol; 1982 v Ho, F; (with Oxford U), 1985 v N, Sp, Sw; 1986 v W, U; 1987 v Bel, S, Pol, Br (sub), L (sub); 1988 v L (26)

Lawler, J. F. (Fulham), 1953 v A; 1954 v L, F; 1955 v N, H, N, WG; 1956 v Y (8)

Lawlor, J. C. (Drumcondra), 1949 v Bel; (with Doncaster R), 1951 v N, Arg (3)

Lawlor, M. (Shamrock R), 1971 v Pol, Se (2), I (sub); 1973 v Pol (5)

Lawrenson, M. (Preston NE), 1977 v Pol; (with Brighton), 1978 v Bul, Pol, N (sub); 1979 v Ni, E; 1980 v E, Cy, Sw; 1981 v Ho, Bel, F, Cy, Pol; (with Liverpool), 1982 v Ho, F; 1983 v Ho, Sp, Ic, Ma, Sp; 1984 v Ic, Ho, Ma, Is; 1985 v

USSR, N, D, I, E, N; 1986 v Sw, USSR, D; 1987 v Bel, S; 1988 v Bul, Is (38)

Leech, M. (Shamrock R), 1969 v Cz, D, H; 1972 v A, Ir, Ec, P; 1973 v USSR (sub) (8)

Lennon, C. (St James' Gate), 1935 v H, Sw, G (3)

Lennox, G. (Dolphin), 1931 v Sp; 1932 v Sp (2)

Lowry, D. (St Patrick's Ath), 1962 v A (sub) (1)

Lunn, R. (Dundalk), 1939 v Sw, Pol (2)

Lynch, J. (Cork Bohemians), 1934 v Bel (1)

McAlinden, J. (Portsmouth), 1946 v P, Sp (2)

McAteer, J. W. (Bolton W), 1994 v Ru, Ho (sub), Bol (sub), G, CzR (sub), I (sub), M (sub), N, Ho (sub); 1995 v La, Lie, Ni (2 sub), Lie; (with Liverpool), 1996 v La, P, Ho (sub), Ru; 1997 v Mac, Ic, W, Mac; 1998 v Ic (sub), Li, R; 1999 v Cro, Ma, Y; (with Blackburn R), Para, Se; 2000 v CzR (sub), S, M, US (sub), S.Af; 2001 v Ho, P, Es, Fi (sub), Cy; 2002 v Cro (sub), Ho; (with Sunderland), Ir (2), Ru (sub), D, Ng, Cam, S.Ar (sub) (49)

McCann, J. (Shamrock R), 1957 v WG (1)

McCarthy, J. (Bohemians), 1926 v I; 1928 v Bel; 1930 v Bel (3)

McCarthy, M. (Shamrock R), 1932 v Ho (1)

McCarthy, M. (Manchester C), 1984 v Pol, Chn; 1985 v M, D, I, Is, E, Sp, Sw; 1986 v Sw, USSR, W (sub), U, Ic, Cz; 1987 v S (2), Pol, Bul, Bel (with Celtic), Br, L; 1988 v Bul, Is, R, Y, N, E, USSR, Ho; 1989 v Ni, Tun, Sp, F, H, Sp; (with Lyon), 1990 v WG, Ni (with Millwall), W, USSR, Fi, T, E, Eg, Ho, R, I; 1991 v Mor, T, E, US; 1992 v H, T, Alb (sub), US, I, P (57)

McConville, T. (Dundalk), 1972 v A; (with Waterford), 1973 v USSR, F, USSR, Pol, F (6)

McDonagh, Jacko (Shamrock R), 1984 v Pol (sub), Ma (sub); 1985 v M (sub) (3)

McDonagh, J. (Everton), 1981 v WG 'B', W, Bel, Cz; (with Bolton W), 1982 v Ho, F, Ch, Br; 1983 v Ho, Sp, Ic, Ma, Sp; (with Notts Co), 1984 v Ic, Ho, Pol; 1985 v M, USSR, N, D, Sp, Sw; 1986 v Sw, USSR; (with Wichita Wings) D (25)

McEvoy, M. A. (Blackburn R), 1961 v S (2); 1963 v S; 1964 v A, Sp (2), Pol, N, E; 1965 v Pol, Bel, Sp; 1966 v Sp (2); 1967 v Sp, T, Cz (17)

McGee, P. (QPR), 1978 v T, N (sub), D (sub); 1979 v Ni, E, D (sub), Bul (sub); 1980 v Cz, Bul; (with Preston NE), US, Ni, Cy, Sw, Arg; 1981 v Bel (sub) (15)

McGoldrick, E. J. (C Palace), 1992 v Sw, US, I, P (sub); 1993 v D, W, Ni (sub), D; (with Arsenal), 1994 v Ni, Ru, Ho, CzR; 1995 v La (sub), Lie, E (15)

McGowan, D. (West Ham U), 1949 v P, Se, Sp (3)

McGowan, J. (Cork U), 1947 v Sp (1)

McGrath, M. (Blackburn R), 1958 v A; 1959 v Pol, Cz (2); 1960 v Sw, WG, Se; 1961 v W; 1962 v Cz (2); 1963 v S; 1964 v A (2), E; 1965 v Pol, Bel, Sp; 1966 v Sp; (with Bradford), 1966 v WG, A, Bel; 1967 v T (22)

McGrath, P. (Manchester U), 1985 v I (sub), Is, E, N (sub), Sw (sub); 1986 v Sw (sub), D, W, Ic, Cz; 1987 v Bel (2), S (2), Pol, Bul, Br, L; 1988 v L, Bul, Y, Pol, N, E, Ho; 1989 v Ni, F, H, Sp, Ma, H; (with Aston Villa), 1990 v WG, Ma, USSR, Fi, T, E, Eg, Ho, R, I; 1991 v E (2), W, Pol, Ch (sub), US; 1992 v Pol, T, Sw, US, Alb, US, I, P; 1993 v La, Sp, Ni, D, La, Li; 1994 v Sp, Ni, G, CzR, I, M, N, Ho; 1995 v La, Ni, E, Ni, P, Lie, A; 1996 v A, La, P, Ho, Ru, CzR; (with Derby Co), 1997 v W (83)

McGuire, W. (Bohemians), 1936 v Ho (1)

McKenzie, G. (Southend U), 1938 v N (2), Cz, Pol; 1939 v Sw, Pol, H (2), G (9)

Mackey, G. (Shamrock R), 1957 v D, WG, E (3)

McLoughlin, A. F. (Swindon T), 1990 v Ma, E (sub), Eg (sub); 1991 v Mor (sub), E (sub); (with Southampton), W, Ch (sub); 1992 v H (sub), W (sub); (with Portsmouth), US (1 + sub), I (sub), P; 1993 v W; 1994 v Ni (sub), Ru, Ho (sub); 1995 v Lie (sub); 1996 v P, Cro, Ho, US, M, Bol (sub); 1997 v Lie, Mac, Ic, W, Mac; 1998 v Li (sub), Ic, Li, R, Bel, CzR (sub); 1999 v Y, Para (sub), Se, Ni (sub); 2000 v Cro, Ma (sub), Mac (42)

McLoughlin, F. (Fordsons), 1930 v Bel; (with Cork), 1932 v Sp (2)

McMillan, W. (Belfast Celtic), 1946 v P, Sp (2)

McNally, J. B. (Luton T), 1959 v Cz; 1961 v S; 1963 v Ic (3)

McPhail, S. (Leeds U), 2000 v S, US, S.Af; 2002 v Cro (sub), Cy (sub) (5)

Macken, A. (Derby Co), 1977 v Sp (1)

Madden, O. (Cork), 1936 v H (1)

Maguire, J. (Shamrock R), 1929 v Bel (1)

Mahon, A. J. (Tranmere R), 2000 v Gr (sub), S.Af (2)

Malone, G. (Shelbourne), 1949 v Bel (1)

Mancini, T. J. (QPR), 1974 v Pol, Br, U, Ch; (with Arsenal), 1975 v USSR (5)

Martin, C. (Bo'ness), 1927 v I (1)

Martin, C. J. (Glentoran), 1946 v P (sub), Sp; 1947 v E; (with Leeds U), 1947 v Sp; 1948 v P, Sp; (with Aston Villa), 1949 v Sw, Bel, P, Se, Sp; 1950 v Fi, E, Fi, Se, Bel; 1951 v Arg; 1952 v WG, A, Sp; 1954 v F (2), L; 1955 v N, Ho, N, WG; 1956 v Y, Sp, Ho (30)

Martin, M. P. (Bohemians), 1972 v A, Ir, Ec, Ch, P; 1973 v USSR; (with Manchester U), 1973 v USSR, Pol, F, N; 1974 v Pol, Br, U, Ch; 1975 v USSR, T, Sw, USSR, Sw, WG; (with WBA), 1976 v T, N, Pol; 1977 v E, T, F (2), Sp, Pol, Bul; (with Newcastle U), 1979 v D, Bul, WG; 1980 v W, Cz, Bul, US, Ni; 1981 v WG 'B', F, Bel, Cz; 1982 v Ho, F, Alg, Ch, Br, Tr; 1983 v Ho, Sp, Ma, Sp (52)

Maybury, A. (Leeds U), 1998 v CzR; 1999 v Ni (2)

Meagan, M. K. (Everton), 1961 v S; 1962 v A; 1963 v Ic; 1964 v Sp; (with Huddersfield T), 1965 v Bel; 1966 v Sp (2), A, Bel; 1967 v Sp, T, Sp, T, Cz; 1968 v Cz, Pol; (with Drogheda), 1970 v S (17)

Meehan, P. (Drumcondra), 1934 v Ho (1)

Milligan, M. J. (Oldham Ath), 1992 v US (sub) (1)

Monahan, P. (Sligo R), 1935 v Sw, G (2)

Mooney, J. (Shamrock R), 1965 v Pol, Bel (2)

Moore, A. (Middlesbrough), 1996 v CzR, Cro (sub), Ho, M, Bol; 1997 v Lie (sub), Mac (sub), Ic (sub) (8)

Moore, P. (Shamrock R), 1931 v Sp; 1932 v Ho; (with Aberdeen), 1934 v Bel, Ho; 1935 v H, G; (with Shamrock R), 1936 v Ho; 1937 v G, H (9)

Moran, K. (Manchester U), 1980 v Sw, Arg; 1981 v WG 'B', Bel, F, Cy, W (sub), Bel, Cz, Pol; 1982 v F, Alg; 1983 v Ic; 1984 v Ic, Ho, Ma, Is; 1985 v M; 1986 v D, Ic, Cz; 1987 v Bel (2), S (2), Pol, Bul, Br, L; 1988 v L, Bul, Is, R, Y, Pol, N, E, USSR, Ho; (with Sporting Gijon), 1989 v Ni, Sp, H, Ma, H; 1990 v Ni, Ma; (with Blackburn R), W, USSR (sub), Ma, E, Eg, Ho, R, I; 1991 v T (sub), W, E, Pol, Ch, US; 1992 v Pol, US; 1993 v D, Sp, Ni, Alb; 1994 v Li, Sp, Ho, Bol (71)

Moroney, T. (West Ham U), 1948 v Sp; 1949 v P, Se, Sp; 1950 v Fi, E, Fi, Bel; 1951 v N (2); 1952 v WG; (with Evergreen U), 1954 v F (12)

Morris, C. B. (Celtic), 1988 v Is, R, Y, Pol, N, E, USSR, Ho; 1989 v Ni, Tun, Sp, F, H (1+sub); 1990 v WG, Ni, Ma (sub), W, USSR, Fi (sub), T, E, Eg, Ho, R, I; 1991 v E; 1992 v H (sub), Pol, W, Sw, US (2), P; (with Middlesbrough), 1993 v W (35)

Morrison, C. H. (C Palace), 2002 v Cro (sub), Cy (sub), Ir (sub), Ru (sub), D, US (sub), Ng (sub) (7)

Moulson, C. (Lincoln C), 1936 v H, L; (with Notts Co), 1937 v H, Sw, F (5)

Moulson, G. B. (Lincoln C), 1948 v P, Sp; 1949 v Sw (3)

Mucklan, C. (Drogheda U), 1978 v Pol (1)

Muldoon, T. (Aston Villa), 1927 v I (1)

Mulligan, P. M. (Shamrock R), 1969 v Cz, D, H; 1970 v S, Cz, D; (with Chelsea), 1970 v H, Pol, WG; 1971 v Pol, Se, I; 1972 v A, Ir, Ec, Ch, P; (with C Palace), 1973 v F, USSR, Pol, F, N; 1974 v Pol, Br, U, Ch; 1975 v USSR, T, Sw, USSR, Sw; (with WBA), 1976 v T, Pol; 1977 v E, T, F (2), Pol, Bul; 1978 v Bul, N, D; 1979 v E, D, Bul (sub), WG; (with Shamrock R), 1980 v W, Cz, Bul, US (sub) (50)

Munroe, L. (Shamrock R), 1954 v L (1)

Murphy, A. (Clyde), 1956 v Y (1)

Murphy, B. (Bohemians), 1986 v U (1)

Murphy, J. (C Palace), 1980 v W, US, Cy (3)

Murray, T. (Dundalk), 1950 v Bel (1)

Newman, W. (Shelbourne), 1969 v D (1)

Nolan, R. (Shamrock R), 1957 v D, WG, E; 1958 v Pol; 1960 v Ch, WG, Se; 1962 v Cz (2); 1963 v Ic (10)

O'Brien, A. J. (Newcastle U), 2001 v Es (sub); 2002 v Cro (sub), Ho (sub), Ru, US (5)

O'Brien, F. (Philadelphia F), 1980 v Cz, E, Cy (sub) (3)

O'Brien, L. (Shamrock R), 1986 v U; (with Manchester U), 1987 v Br; 1988 v Is (sub), R (sub), Y (sub), Pol (sub); 1989 v Tun; (with Newcastle U), Sp (sub); 1992 v Sw (sub); 1993 v W; (with Tranmere R), 1994 v Ru; 1996 v Cro, Ho, US, Bol; 1997 v Mac (sub) (16)

O'Brien, M. T. (Derby Co), 1927 v I; (with Walsall), 1929 v Bel; (with Norwich C), 1930 v Bel; (with Watford), 1932 v Ho (4)

O'Brien, R. (Notts Co), 1976 v N, Pol; 1977 v Sp, Pol; 1980 v Arg (sub) (5)

O'Byrne, L. B. (Shamrock R), 1949 v Bel (1)

O'Callaghan, B. R. (Stoke C), 1979 v WG (sub); 1980 v W, US; 1981 v W; 1982 v Br, Tr (6)

O'Callaghan, K. (Ipswich T), 1981 v WG 'B', Cz, Pol; 1982 v Alg, Ch, Br, Tr (sub); 1983 v Sp, Ic (sub), Ma (sub), Sp (sub); 1984 v Ic, Ho, Ma; 1985 v M (sub), N (sub), D (sub), (with Portsmouth) E (sub); 1986 v Sw (sub), USSR (sub); 1987 v Br (21)

O'Connell, A. (Dundalk), 1967 v Sp; (with Bohemians), 1971 v Pol (sub) (2)

O'Connor, T. (Shamrock R), 1950 v Fi, E, Fi, Se (4)

O'Connor, T. (Fulham), 1968 v Cz; (with Dundalk), 1972 v A, Ir (sub), Ec (sub), Ch; (with Bohemians), 1973 v F (sub), Pol (sub) (7)

O'Driscoll, J. F. (Swansea T), 1949 v Sw, Bel, Se (3)

O'Driscoll, S. (Fulham), 1982 v Ch, Br, Tr (sub) (3)

O'Farrell, F. (West Ham U), 1952 v A; 1953 v A; 1954 v F; 1955 v Ho, N; 1956 v Y, Ho; (with Preston NE), 1958 v D; 1959 v Cz (9)

O'Flanagan, K. P. (Bohemians), 1938 v N, Cz, Pol; 1939 v Pol, H (2), G; (with Arsenal), 1947 v E, Sp, P (10)

O'Flanagan, M. (Bohemians), 1947 v E (1)

O'Hanlon, K. G. (Rotherham U), 1988 v Is (1)

O'Kane, P. (Bohemians), 1935 v H, Sw, G (3)

O'Keefe, E. (Everton), 1981 v W; (with Port Vale), 1984 v Chn; 1985 v M, USSR (sub), E (5)

O'Keefe, T. (Cork), 1934 v Bel; (with Waterford), 1938 v Cz, Pol (3)

O'Leary, D. (Arsenal), 1977 v E, F (2), Sp, Bul; 1978 v Bul, N, D; 1979 v E, Bul, WG; 1980 v W, Bul, Ni, E, Cy; 1981 v WG 'B',Ho, Cz, Pol; 1982 v Ho, F; 1983 v Ho, Ic, Sp; 1984 v Pol, Is, Chn; 1985 v USSR, N, D, Is, E (sub), N, Sp, Sw; 1986 v Sw, USSR, D, W; 1989 v Sp, Ma, H; 1990 v WG, Ni (sub), Ma, W (sub), USSR, Fi, T, Ma, R (sub); 1991 v Mor, T, E (2), Pol, Ch; 1992 v H, Pol, T, W, Sw, US, Alb, I, P; 1993 v W (68)

O'Leary, P. (Shamrock R), 1980 v Bul, US, Ni, E (sub), Cz, Arg; 1981 v Ho (7)

O'Mahoney, M. T. (Bristol R), 1938 v Cz, Pol; 1939 v Sw, Pol, H, G (6)

O'Neill, F. S. (Shamrock R), 1962 v Cz (2); 1965 v Pol, Bel, Sp; 1966 v Sp (2), WG, A; 1967 v Sp, T, Sp, T; 1969 v Pol, A, D, Cz, D (sub), H (sub); 1972 v A (20)

O'Neill, J. (Everton), 1952 v Sp; 1953 v F, A; 1954 v F, L, F; 1955 v N, Ho, N, WG; 1956 v Y, Sp; 1957 v D; 1958 v A; 1959 v Pol, Cz (2) (17)

O'Neill, J. (Preston NE), 1961 v W (1)

O'Neill, K. P. (Norwich C), 1996 v P (sub), Cro, Ho (sub), US (sub), M, Bol; 1997 v Lie, Mac (1 + sub); 1999 v Cro, Y (sub); (with Middlesbrough), Ni (sub); 2000 v Mac (sub) (13)

O'Neill, W. (Dundalk), 1936 v Ho, Sw, H, L; 1937 v G, H, Sw, F; 1938 v N; 1939 v H, G (11)

O'Regan, K. (Brighton & HA), 1984 v Ma, Pol; 1985 v M, Sp (sub) (4)

O'Reilly, J. (Brideville), 1932 v Ho; (with Aberdeen), 1934 v Bel, Ho; (with Brideville), 1936 v Ho; Sw, H, L; (with St James' Gate), 1937 v G, H, Sw, F; 1938 v N (2), Cz, Pol; 1939 v Sw, Pol, H (2), G (20)

O'Reilly, J. (Cork U), 1946 v P, Sp (2)

O'Shea, J. F. (Manchester U), 2002 v Cro (sub) (1)

Peyton, G. (Fulham), 1977 v Sp (sub); 1978 v Bul, T, Pol; 1979 v D, Bul, WG; 1980 v W, Cz, Bul, E, Cy, Sw, Arg; 1981 v Ho, Bel, F, Cy; 1982 v Tr; 1985 v M; 1986 v W, Cz; (with Bournemouth), 1988 v L, Pol; 1989 v Ni, Tun; 1990 v USSR, Ma; 1991 v Ch; (with Everton) 1992 v US (2), I (sub), P (33)

Peyton, N. (Shamrock R), 1957 v WG; (with Leeds U), 1960 v WG, Se (sub); 1961 v W; 1963 v Ic, S (6)

Phelan, T. (Wimbledon), 1992 v H, Pol (sub), T, W, Sw, US, I (sub), P; (with Manchester C), 1993 v La (sub), D, Sp, Ni, Alb, La, Li; 1994 v Li, Sp, Ni, Ho, Bol, G, CzR, I, M, Ho; 1995 v E; 1996 v La; (with Chelsea), Ho, Ru, P, Cro, Ho, US, M (sub), Bol; (with Everton), 1997 v W, Mac; 1998 v R; (with Fulham), 2000 v S (sub), M, US, S.Af (42)

Quinn, B. S. (Coventry C), 2000 v Gr, M, US (sub), S.Af (sub) (4)

Quinn, N. J. (Arsenal), 1986 v Ic (sub), Cz; 1987 v Bul (sub), Br (sub); 1988 v L (sub), Bul (sub), Is, R (sub), Pol (sub), E (sub); 1989 v Tun (sub), Sp (sub), H (sub); (with Manchester C), 1990 v USSR, Ma, Eg (sub), Ho, R, I; 1991 v Mor, T, E(2), W, Pol; 1992 v H, W (sub), US, I (sub), P; 1993 v La, D, Sp, Ni, D, Alb, La, Li; 1994 v Li, Sp, Ni; 1995 v La, Lie, Ni, E, Ni, P, Lie, A; 1996 v A, La, P, Ru, CzR, P (sub), Cro, Ho (sub), US; (with Sunderland), 1997 v Lie; 1998 v Li, Arg; 1999 v Ma, Y, Para, Se, Ni, Mac; 2000 v Y, Cro (sub), Ma, Mac, T, CzR, S, M, US (sub), S.Af; 2001 v Ho, P, Es, P, Es; 2002 v Ho (sub), Cy, Ir, Ru (sub), G (sub), S.Ar (sub), Sp (sub) (91)

Reid, C. (Brideville), 1931 v Sp (1)

Reid, S. J. (Millwall), 2002 v Cro, Ru, D (sub), US (sub), Ng (sub), Cam (sub), G (sub) (7)

Richardson, D. J. (Shamrock R), 1972 v A (sub); (with Gillingham), 1973 v N (sub); 1980 v Cz (3)

Rigby, A. (St James' Gate), 1935 v H, Sw, G (3)

Ringstead, A. (Sheffield U), 1951 v Arg, N; 1952 v WG (2), A, Sp; 1953 v A; 1954 v F; 1955 v N; 1956 v Y, Sp, Ho; 1957 v E (2); 1958 v D, Pol, A; 1959 v Pol, Cz (2) (20)

Robinson, J. (Bohemians), 1928 v Bel; (with Dolphin), 1931 v Sp (2)

Robinson, M. (Brighton & HA), 1981 v WG 'B', F, Cy, Bel, Pol; 1982 v Ho, F, Alg, Ch; 1983 v Ho, Sp, Ic, Ma; (with Liverpool), 1984 v Ic, Ho, Is; 1985 v USSR, N; (with QPR), N, Sp, Sw; 1986 v D (sub), W, Cz (24)

Roche, P. J. (Shelbourne), 1972 v A; (with Manchester U), 1975 v USSR, T, Sw, USSR, Sw, WG; 1976 v T (8)

Rogers, E. (Blackburn R), 1968 v Cz, Pol; 1969 v Pol, A, D, Cz, D, H; 1970 v S, D, H; 1971 v I (2), A; (with Charlton Ath), 1972 v Ir, Ec, Ch, P; 1973 v USSR (19)

Ryan, G. (Derby Co), 1978 v T; (with Brighton & HA), 1979 v E, WG; 1980 v W, Cy (sub), Sw, Arg (sub); 1981 v WG 'B' (sub), F (sub), Pol (sub); 1982 v Br (sub), Ho (sub), Alg (sub), Ch (sub); Tr; 1984 v Pol, Chn; 1985 v M (18)

Ryan, R. A. (WBA), 1950 v Se, Bel; 1951 v N, Arg, N; 1952 v WG (2), A, Sp; 1953 v F, A; 1954 v F, L, F; 1955 v N; (with Derby Co), 1956 v Sp (16)

Sadlier, R. T. (Millwall), 2002 v Ru (sub) (1)

Savage, D. P. T. (Millwall), 1996 v P (sub), Cro (sub), US (sub), M, Bol (5)

Saward, P. (Millwall), 1954 v L; (with Aston Villa), 1957 v E (2); 1958 v D, Pol, A; 1959 v Pol, Cz; 1960 v Se, Ch, WG, Se; 1961 v W, N; (with Huddersfield T), 1961 v S; 1962 v A; 1963 v Ic (2) (18)

Scannell, T. (Southend U), 1954 v L (1)

Scully, P. J. (Arsenal), 1989 v Tun (sub) (1)

Sheedy, K. (Everton), 1984 v Ho (sub), Ma; 1985 v D, I, Is, Sw; 1986 v Sw, D; 1987 v S, Pol; 1988 v Is, R, Pol, E (sub), USSR; 1989 v Ni, Tun, H, Sp, Ma, H; 1990 v Ni, Ma, W (sub), USSR, Fi (sub), T, E, Eg, Ho, R, I; 1991 v W, E, Pol, Ch, US; 1992 v H, Pol, T, W; (with Newcastle U), Sw (sub), Alb; 1993 v La, W (sub) (45)

Sheridan, J. J. (Leeds U), 1988 v R, Y, Pol, N (sub); 1989 v Sp; (with Sheffield W), 1990 v W, T (sub), Ma, I (sub); 1991 v Mor (sub), T, Ch, US (sub); 1992 v H; 1993 v La; 1994 v Sp (sub), Ho, Bol, G, CzR, I, M, N, Ho; 1995 v La, Lie, Ni, E, Ni, P, Lie, A; 1996 v A, Ho (34)

Slaven, B. (Middlesbrough), 1990 v W, Fi, T (sub), Ma; 1991 v W, Pol (sub); 1993 v W (7)

Sloan, J. W. (Arsenal), 1946 v P, Sp (2)

Smyth, M. (Shamrock R), 1969 v Pol (sub) (1)

Squires, J. (Shelbourne), 1934 v Ho (1)

Stapleton, F. (Arsenal), 1977 v T, F, Sp, Bul; 1978 v Bul, N, D; 1979 v Ni, E (sub), D, WG; 1980 v W, Bul, Ni, E, Cy; 1981 v WG 'B', Ho, Bel, F, Cy, Bel, Cz, Pol; (with Manchester U), 1982 v Ho, F, Alg; 1983 v Ho, Sp, Ic, Ma, Sp; 1984 v Ic, Ho, Ma, Pol, Is, Chn; 1985 v N, D, I, Is, E, N, Sw; 1986 v Sw, USSR, D, U, Ic, Cz (sub); 1987 v Bel (2), S (2), Pol, Bul, L; (with Ajax), 1988 v L, Bul, R, Y, N, E, USSR, Ho; (with Le Havre), 1989 v F, Sp, Ma; (with Blackburn R), 1990 v WG, Ma (sub) (71)

Staunton, S. (Liverpool), 1989 v Tun, Sp (2), Ma, H; 1990 v WG, Ni, Ma, W, USSR, Fi, T, Ma, E, Eg, Ho, R, I; 1991 v Mor, T, E (2), W, Pol, Ch, US; (with Aston Villa), 1992 v Pol, T, Sw, US, Alb, US, I, P; 1993 v La, Sp, Ni, D, Alb, La, Li; 1994 v Li, Sp, Ho, Bol, G, CzR, I, M, N, Ho; 1995 v La, Lie, Ni, E, Ni, P, Lie, A; 1996 v La, P, Ru; 1997 v Lie, Mac (2), W, R, Lie; 1998 v Li, Ic, Li, Bel (2), Arg; (with Liverpool), 1999 v Cro, Ma, Y, Se; 2000 v Y, Cro, Ma, Mac, CzR (sub), Gr; 2001 v Ho (sub), Fi (sub); (with Aston Villa), And (sub), P, Es; 2002 v Cro, Ho, Cy, Ir (2), Ru (sub), D, US (sub), Ng, Cam, G, S.Ar, Sp (102)

Stevenson, A. E. (Dolphin), 1932 v Ho; (with Everton), 1947 v E, Sp, P; 1948 v P, Sp; 1949 v Sw (7)

Strahan, F. (Shelbourne), 1964 v Pol, N, E; 1965 v Pol; 1966 v WG (5)

Sullivan, J. (Fordsons), 1928 v Bel (1)

Swan, M. M. G. (Drumcondra), 1960 v Se (sub) (1)

Synnott, N. (Shamrock R), 1978 v T, Pol; 1979 v Ni (3)

Taylor, T. (Waterford), 1959 v Pol (sub) (1)

Thomas, P. (Waterford), 1974 v Pol, Br (2)

Townsend, A. D. (Norwich C), 1989 v F, Sp (sub), Ma (sub), H; 1990 v WG (sub), Ni, Ma, W, USSR, Fi (sub), T, Ma (sub), E, Eg, Ho, R, I; (with Chelsea), 1991 v Mor, T, E (2), W, Pol, Ch, US; 1992 v Pol, W, US, Alb, US, I; 1993 v La, D, Sp, Ni, D, Alb, La, Li; (with Aston Villa), 1994 v Li, Ni, Ho, Bol, G, CzR, I, M, N, Ho; 1995 v La, Ni, E, Ni, P; 1996 v A, La, Ho, Ru, CzR, P; 1997 v Lie, Mac (2), Ic, R, Lie; 1998 v Li; (with Middlesbrough), Ic, Bel (2) (70)

Traynor, T. J. (Southampton), 1954 v L; 1962 v A; 1963 v Ic (2), S; 1964 v A (2), Sp (8)

Treacy, R. C. P. (WBA), 1966 v WG; 1967 v Sp, Cz; 1968 v Cz; (with Charlton Ath), 1968 v Pol; 1969 v Pol, Cz, D; 1970 v S, D, H (sub), Pol (sub), WG (sub); 1971 v Pol, Se (sub+1), I, A; (with Swindon T), 1972 v Ir, Ec, Ch, P; 1973 v USSR, F, USSR, Pol, F, N; 1974 v Pol; (with Preston NE), Br; 1975 v USSR, Sw (2), WG; 1976 v T, N (sub), Pol (sub); (with WBA), 1977 v F, Pol; (with Shamrock R), 1978 v T, Pol; 1980 v Cz (sub) (42)

Tuohy, L. (Shamrock R), 1956 v Y; 1959 v Cz (2); (with Newcastle U), 1962 v A; 1963 v Ic (2); (with Shamrock R), 1964 v A; 1965 v Bel (8)

Turner, C. J. (Southend U), 1936 v Sw; 1937 v G, H, Sw, F; 1938 v N (2), (with West Ham U) Cz, Pol; 1939 v H (10)

Turner, P. (Celtic), 1963 v S; 1964 v Sp (2)

Vernon, J. (Belfast C), 1946 v P, Sp (2)

Waddock, G. (QPR), 1980 v Sw, Arg; 1981 v W, Pol (sub); 1982 v Alg; 1983 v Ic, Ma, Sp, Ho (sub); 1984 v Ma (sub), Ic, Ho, Is; 1985 v I, Is, E, N, Sp; 1986 v USSR; (with Millwall), 1990 v USSR, T (21)

Walsh, D. J. (Linfield), 1946 v P, Sp; (with WBA), 1947 v Sp, P; 1948 v P, Sp; 1949 v Sw, P, Se, Sp; 1950 v E, Fi, Se; 1951 v N; (with Aston Villa), Arg, N; 1952 v Sp; 1953 v A; 1954 v F (2) (20)

Walsh, J. (Limerick), 1982 v Tr (1)

Walsh, M. (Blackpool), 1976 v N, Pol; 1977 v F (sub), Pol; (with Everton), 1979 v Ni (sub); (with QPR), D (sub), Bul, WG (sub); (with Porto), 1981 v Bel (sub), Cz; 1982 v Alg (sub); 1983 v Sp, Ho (sub), Sp (sub); 1984 v Ic (sub), Ma, Pol, Chn; 1985 v USSR, N (sub), D (21)

Walsh, M. (Everton), 1982 v Ch, Br, Tr; 1983 v Ic (4)

Walsh, W. (Manchester C), 1947 v E, Sp, P; 1948 v P, Sp; 1949 v Bel; 1950 v E, Se, Bel (9)

Waters, J. (Grimsby T), 1977 v T; 1980 v Ni (sub) (2)

Watters, F. (Shelbourne), 1926 v I (1)

Weir, E. (Clyde), 1939 v H (2), G (3)

Whelan, R. (St Patrick's Ath), 1964 v A, E (sub) (2)

Whelan, R. (Liverpool), 1981 v Cz (sub); 1982 v Ho (sub), F; 1983 v Ic, Ma, Sp; 1984 v Is; 1985 v USSR, N, I (sub), Is, E, N (sub), Sw (sub); 1986 v USSR (sub), W; 1987 v Bel (sub), S, Bul, Bel, Br, L; 1988 v L, Bul, Pol, N, E, USSR, Ho; 1989 v Ni, F, H, Sp, Ma; 1990 v WG, Ni, Ma, W, Ho (sub); 1991 v Mor, E; 1992 v Sw; 1993 v La, W (sub), Li (sub); 1994 v Li (sub), Sp, Ru, Ho, G (sub), N (sub); (with Southend U), 1995 v Lie, A (53)

Whelan, W. (Manchester U), 1956 v Ho; 1957 v D, E (2) (4)

White, J. J. (Bohemians), 1928 v Bel (1)

Whittaker, R. (Chelsea), 1959 v Cz (1)

Williams, J. (Shamrock R), 1938 v N (1)

BRITISH AND IRISH INTERNATIONAL GOALSCORERS SINCE 1872

Where two players with the same surname and initials have appeared for the same country, and one or both have scored, they have been distinguished by reference to the club which appears *first* against their name in the international appearances section.

ENGLAND

Name	
A'Court, A.	1
Adams, T. A.	5
Adcock, H.	1
Alcock, C. W.	1
Allen, A.	3
Allen, R.	2
Amos, A.	1
Anderson, V.	2
Anderton, D. R.	7
Astall, G.	1
Athersmith, W. C.	3
Atyeo, P. J. W.	5
Bache, J. W.	4
Bailey, N. C.	2
Baily, E. F.	5
Baker, J. H.	3
Ball, A. J.	8
Bambridge, A. L.	1
Bambridge, E. C.	11
Barclay, R.	2
Barmby, N. J.	4
Barnes, J.	11
Barnes, P. S.	4
Barton, J.	1
Bassett, W. I.	8
Bastin, C. S.	12
Beardsley, P. A.	9
Beasley, A.	1
Beattie, T. K.	1
Beckham, D. R. J.	7
Becton, F.	2
Bedford, H.	1
Bell, C.	9
Bentley, R. T. F.	9
Bishop, S. M.	1
Blackburn, F.	1
Blissett, L.	3
Bloomer, S.	28
Bond, R.	2
Bonsor, A. G.	1
Bowden, E. R.	1
Bowers, J. W.	2
Bowles, S.	1
Bradford, G. R. W.	1
Bradford, J.	7
Bradley, W.	2
Bradshaw, F.	3
Brann, G.	1
Bridges, B. J.	1
Bridgett, A.	3
Brindle, T.	1
Britton, C. S.	1
Broadbent, P. F.	2
Broadis, I. A.	8
Brodie, J. B.	1
Bromley-Davenport, W.	2
Brook, E. F.	10
Brooking, T. D.	5
Brooks, J.	2
Broome, F. H.	3
Brown, A.	4
Brown, A. S.	1
Brown, G.	5
Brown, J.	3
Brown, W.	1
Buchan, C. M.	4
Bull, S. G.	4
Bullock, N.	2
Burgess, H.	4
Butcher, T.	3
Byrne, J. J.	8
Campbell, S. J.	1
Camsell, G. H.	18
Carter, H. S.	7
Carter, J. H.	4
Chadwick, E.	3
Chamberlain, M.	1
Chambers, H.	5
Channon, M. R.	21
Charlton, J.	6
Charlton, R.	49
Chenery, C. J.	1
Chivers, M.	13
Clarke, A. J.	10
Cobbold, W. N.	6
Cock, J. G.	2
Cole, A.	1
Common, A.	2
Connelly, J. M.	7
Coppell, S. J.	7
Cotterill, G. H.	2
Cowans, G.	2
Crawford, R.	1
Crawshaw, T. H.	1
Crayston, W. J.	1
Creek, F. N. S.	1
Crooks, S. D.	7
Currey, E. S.	2
Currie, A. W.	3
Cursham, A. W.	2
Cursham, H. A.	5
Daft, H. B.	3
Davenport, J. K.	2
Davis, G.	1
Davis, H.	1
Day, S. H.	2
Dean, W. R.	18
Devey, J. H. G.	1
Dewhurst, F.	11
Dix, W. R.	1
Dixon, K. M.	4
Dixon, L. M.	1
Dorrell, A. R.	1
Douglas, B.	11
Drake, E. J.	6
Ducat, A.	1
Dunn, A. T. B.	2
Eastham, G.	2
Edwards, D.	5
Ehiogu, U.	1
Elliott, W. H.	3
Evans, R. E.	1
Ferdinand, L.	5
Ferdinand, R. G.	1
Finney, T.	30
Fleming, H. J.	9
Flowers, R.	10
Forman, Frank	1
Forman, Fred	3
Foster, R. E.	3
Fowler, R. B.	7
Francis, G. C. J.	3
Francis, T.	12
Freeman, B. C.	3
Froggatt, J.	2
Froggatt, R.	2
Galley, T.	1
Gascoigne, P. J.	10
Geary, F.	3
Gerrard, S. G.	1
Gibbins, W. V. T.	3
Gilliatt, W. E.	3
Goddard, P.	1
Goodall, J.	12
Goodyer, A. C.	1
Gosling, R. C.	2
Goulden, L. A.	4
Grainger, C.	3
Greaves, J.	44
Grovesnor, A. T.	2
Gunn, W.	1
Haines, J. T. W.	2
Hall, G. W.	9
Halse, H. J.	2
Hampson, J.	5
Hampton, H.	2
Hancocks, J.	2
Hardman, H. P.	1
Harris, S. S.	2
Hassall, H. W.	4
Hateley, M.	9
Haynes, J. N.	18
Hegan, K. E.	4
Henfrey, A. G.	2
Heskey, E. W.	4
Hilsdon, G. R.	14
Hine, E. W.	4
Hinton, A. T.	1
Hirst, D. E.	1
Hitchens, G. A.	5
Hobbis, H. H. F.	1
Hoddle, G.	8
Hodgetts, D.	1
Hodgson, G.	1
Holley, G. H.	8
Houghton, W. E.	5
Howell, R.	1
Hughes, E. W.	1
Hulme, J. H. A.	4
Hunt, G. S.	1
Hunt, R.	18
Hunter, N.	2
Hurst, G. C.	24
Ince, P. E. C.	2
Jack, D. N. B.	3
Johnson, D. E.	6
Johnson, E.	2
Johnson, J. A.	2
Johnson, T. C. F.	5
Johnson, W. H.	1
Kail, E. I. L.	2
Kay, A. H.	1
Keegan, J. K.	21
Kelly, R.	8
Kennedy, R.	3
Kenyon-Slaney, W. S.	2
Keown, M. R.	2
Kevan, D. T.	8
Kidd, B.	1
Kingsford, R. K.	1
Kirchen, A. J.	2
Kirton, W. J.	1
Langton, R.	1
Latchford, R. D.	5
Latherton, E. G.	1
Lawler, C.	1
Lawton, T.	22
Lee, F.	10
Lee, J.	1
Lee, R. M.	2
Lee, S.	2
Le Saux, G. P.	1
Lindley, T.	14
Lineker, G.	48
Lofthouse, J. M.	3
Lofthouse, N.	30
Hon. A. Lyttelton	1
Mabbutt, G.	1
Macdonald, M.	6
Mannion, W. J.	11
Mariner, P.	13
Marsh, R. W.	1
Matthews, S.	11
Matthews, V.	1
McCall, J.	1
McDermott, T.	3
McManaman, S.	3
Medley, L. D.	1
Melia, J.	1
Mercer, D. W.	1
Merson, P. C.	3
Milburn, J. E. T.	10
Miller, H. S.	1
Mills, G. R.	3
Milward, A.	3
Mitchell, C.	5
Moore, J.	1
Moore, R. F.	2
Moore, W. G. B.	2
Morren, T.	1
Morris, F.	1
Morris, J.	3
Mortensen, S. H.	23
Morton, J. R.	1
Mosforth, W.	3
Mullen, J.	6
Mullery, A. P.	1
Murphy, D. B	1
Neal, P. G.	5
Needham, E.	3
Nicholls, J.	1
Nicholson, W. E.	1
O'Grady, M.	3
Osborne, F. R.	3
Owen, M. J.	18
Own goals	24
Page, L. A.	1
Paine, T. L.	7
Palmer, C. L.	1
Parry, E. H.	1
Parry, R. A.	1
Pawson, F. W.	1
Payne, J.	2
Peacock, A.	3

Name		Name		Name		Name	
Pearce, S.	5	Wall, G.	2	Doherty, L.	1	McIlroy, S. B.	5
Pearson, J. S.	5	Wallace, D.	1	Doherty, P. D.	3	McKnight, J.	2
Pearson, S. C.	5	Walsh, P.	1	Dougan, A. D.	8	McLaughlin, J. C.	6
Perry, W.	2	Waring, T.	4	Dowie, I.	12	McMahon, G. J.	2
Peters, M.	20	Warren, B.	2	Dunne, J.	4	McMordie, A. S.	3
Pickering, F.	5	Watson, D. V.	4			McMorran, E. J.	4
Platt, D.	27	Watson, V. M.	4	Elder, A. R.	1	McParland, P. J.	10
Pointer, R.	2	Webb, G. W.	1	Elliott, S.	1	McWha, W. B. R.	1
		Webb, N.	4	Emerson, W.	1	Meldon, J.	1
Quantrill, A.	1	Wedlock, W. J.	2	English, S.	1	Mercer, J. T.	1
		Weller, K.	1			Millar, W.	1
Ramsay, A. E.	3	Welsh, D.	1	Feeney, W	1	Milligan, D.	1
Revie, D. G.	4	Whateley, O.	2	Ferguson, W.	1	Milne, R. G.	1
Redknapp, J. F.	1	Wheldon, G. F.	6	Ferris, J.	1	Molyneux, T. B.	1
Reynolds, J.	3	Whitfield, H.	1	Ferris, R. O.	1	Moreland, V.	1
Richardson, J. R.	2	Wignall, F.	2	Finney, T.	2	Morgan, S.	3
Rigby, A.	3	Wilkes, A.	1			Morrow, S. J.	1
Rimmer, E. J.	2	Wilkins, R. G.	3	Gaffkin, J.	4	Morrow, W. J.	1
Roberts, F.	2	Willingham, C. K.	1	Gara, A.	3	Mulryne, P. P.	3
Roberts, H.	1	Wilshaw, D. J.	10	Gaukrodger, G.	1	Murphy, N.	1
Roberts, W. T.	2	Wilson, G. P.	1	Gibb, J. T.	2		
Robinson, J.	3	Winckworth, W. N.	1	Gibb, T. J.	1	Neill, W. J. T.	2
Robson, B.	26	Windridge, J. E.	7	Gillespie, K. R.	1	Nelson, S.	1
Robson, R.	4	Wise, D. F.	1	Gillespie, W.	12	Nicholl, C. J.	3
Rowley, J. F.	6	Withe, P.	1	Goodall, A. L.	2	Nicholl, J. M.	1
Royle, J.	2	Wollaston, C. H. R.	1	Griffin, D. J.	1	Nicholson, J. J.	6
Rutherford, J.	3	Wood, H.	1	Gray, P.	6		
		Woodcock, T.	16			O'Boyle, G.	1
Sagar, C.	1	Woodhall, G.	1	Halligan, W.	1	O'Hagan, C.	2
Sandilands, R. R.	3	Woodward, V. J.	29	Hamill, M.	1	O'Kane, W. J.	1
Sansom, K.	1	Worrall, F.	2	Hamilton, B.	4	O'Neill, J.	2
Schofield, J.	1	Worthington, F. S.	2	Hamilton, W. R.	5	O'Neill, M. A.	4
Scholes, P.	13	Wright, I. E.	9	Hannon, D. J.	1	O'Neill, M. H.	8
Seed, J. M.	1	Wright, M.	1	Harkin, J. T.	2	Own goals	6
Settle, J.	6	Wright, W. A.	3	Harvey, M.	3		
Sewell, J.	3	Wylie, J. G.	1	Healy, D. J.	8	Patterson, D. J.	1
Shackleton, L. F.	1			Hill, C. F.	1	Peacock, R.	2
Sharp, J.	1	Yates, J.	3	Hughes, M. E.	5	Peden, J.	7
Shearer, A.	30			Humphries, W.	1	Penney, S.	2
Shelton, A.	1	**NORTHERN IRELAND**		Hunter, A. (*Distillery*)	1	Pyper, James	2
Shepherd, A.	2	Anderson, T.	4	Hunter, A.		Pyper, John	1
Sheringham, E. P.	11	Armstrong, G.	12	(*Blackburn R*)	1		
Simpson, J.	1			Hunter, B. V.	1	Quinn, J. M.	12
Smith, A. M.	2	Bambrick, J.	12			Quinn, S. J.	3
Smith, G. O.	11	Barr, H. H.	1	Irvine, R. W.	3		
Smith, Joe	1	Barron, H.	3	Irvine, W. J.	8	Reynolds, J.	1
Smith, J. R.	2	Best, G.	9			Rowland, K.	1
Smith, J. W.	4	Bingham, W. L.	10	Johnston, H.	2	Rowley, R. W. M.	2
Smith, R.	13	Black, K.	1	Johnston, S.	2		
Smith, S.	1	Blanchflower, D.	2	Johnston, W. C.	1	Sheridan, J.	2
Sorby, T. H.	1	Blanchflower, J.	1	Jones, S.	1	Sherrard, J.	1
Southgate, G.	1	Brennan, B.	1	Jones, J.	1	Sherrard, W. C.	2
Southworth, J.	3	Brennan, R. A.	1			Simpson, W. J.	5
Sparks, F. J.	3	Brotherston, N.	3	Kelly, J.	4	Sloan, H. A. de B.	4
Spence, J. W.	1	Brown, J.	1	Kernaghan, N.	2	Smyth, S.	5
Spiksley, F.	5	Browne, F.	2	Kirwan, J.	2	Spence, D. W.	3
Spilsbury, B. W.	5					Stanfield, O. M.	11
Steele, F. C.	8	Campbell, J.	1	Lacey, W.	3	Stevenson, A. E.	5
Stephenson, G. T.	2	Campbell, W. G.	1	Lemon, J.	2	Stewart, I.	2
Steven, T. M.	4	Casey, T.	2	Lennon, N. F.	2		
Stewart, J.	2	Caskey, W.	1	Lockhart, N.	3	Taggart, G. P.	7
Stiles, N. P.	1	Cassidy, T.	1	Lomas, S. M.	3	Thompson, F. W.	2
Storer, H.	1	Chambers, J.	3			Torrans, S.	1
Stone, S. B.	2	Clarke, C. J.	13	Magilton, J.	5	Tully, C. P.	1
Summerbee, M. G.	1	Clements, D.	2	Mahood, J.	2	Turner, E.	1
		Cochrane, T.	1	Martin, D. K.	3		
Tambling, R. V.	1	Condy, J.	1	Maxwell, J.	2	Walker, J.	1
Taylor, P. J.	2	Connor, M. J.	1	McAdams, W. J.	7	Walsh, D. J.	5
Taylor, T.	16	Coulter, J.	1	McAllen, J.	1	Welsh, E.	1
Thompson, P. B.	1	Croft, T.	1	Mcauley, J. L.	1	Whiteside, N.	9
Thornewell, G.	1	Crone, W.	1	McCartney, G.	1	Whiteside, T.	1
Tilson, S. F.	6	Crossan, E.	1	McCandless, J.	3	Whitley, Jeff	1
Townley, W. J.	2	Crossan, J. A.	10	McCaw, J. H.	1	Williams, J. R.	1
Tueart, D.	2	Curran, S.	2	McClelland, J.	1	Williams, M. S.	1
		Cush, W. W.	5	McCluggage, A.	2	Williamson, J.	1
Vassell, D.	3			McCracken, W.	1	Wilson, D. J.	1
Vaughton, O. H.	6	Dalton, W.	4	McCrory, S.	1	Wilson, K. J.	6
Veitch, J. G.	3	D'Arcy, S. D.	1	McCurdy, C.	1	Wilson, S. J.	1
Violett, D. S.	1	Darling, F.	1	McDonald, A.	3	Wilton, J. M.	2
		Davey, H. H.	1	McGarry, J. K.	1		
Waddle, C. R.	6	Davis, T. L.	1	McGrath, R. C.	4	Young, S.	2
Walker, W. H.	9	Dill, A. H.	1	McIlroy, J.	10		

SCOTLAND

Name	
Aitken, R. (*Celtic*)	1
Aitken, R. (*Dumbarton*)	1
Aitkenhead, W. A. C.	2
Alexander, D.	1
Allan, D. S.	4
Allan, J.	2
Anderson, F.	1
Anderson, W.	4
Andrews, P.	1
Archibald, A.	1
Archibald, S.	4
Baird, D.	2
Baird, J. C.	2
Baird, S.	2
Bannon, E.	1
Barbour, A.	1
Barker, J. B.	4
Battles, B. Jr	1
Bauld, W.	2
Baxter, J. C.	3
Bell, J.	5
Bennett, A.	2
Berry, D.	1
Bett, J.	1
Beveridge, W. W.	1
Black, A.	3
Black, D.	1
Bone, J.	1
Booth, S.	6
Boyd, R.	2
Boyd, T.	1
Boyd, W. G.	1
Brackenridge, T.	1
Brand, R.	8
Brazil, A.	1
Bremner, W. J.	3
Brown, A. D.	6
Buchanan, P. S.	1
Buchanan, R.	1
Buckley, P.	1
Buick, A.	2
Burley, C. W.	3
Burns, K.	1
Cairns, T.	1
Calderwood, C.	1
Calderwood, R.	2
Caldow, E.	4
Cameron, C.	2
Campbell, C.	1
Campbell, John (*Celtic*)	5
Campbell, John (*Rangers*)	4
Campbell, P.	2
Campbell, R.	1
Cassidy, J.	1
Chalmers, S.	3
Chambers, T.	1
Cheyne, A. G.	4
Christie, A. J.	1
Clunas, W. L.	1
Collins, J.	12
Collins, R. Y.	10
Combe, J. R.	1
Conn, A.	1
Cooper, D.	6
Craig, J.	1
Craig, T.	1
Crawford, S.	1
Cunningham, A. N.	5
Curran, H. P.	1
Dailly, C.	3
Dalglish, K.	30
Davidson, D.	1
Davidson, J. A.	1
Delaney, J.	3
Devine, A.	1
Dewar, G.	1
Dewar, N.	4
Dickson, W.	4
Divers, J.	1
Dobie, R. S.	1
Docherty, T. H.	1
Dodds, D.	1
Dodds, W.	7
Donaldson, A.	1
Donnachie, J.	1
Dougall, J.	1
Drummond, J.	2
Dunbar, M.	1
Duncan, D.	7
Duncan, D. M.	1
Duncan, J.	1
Dunn, J.	2
Durie, G. S.	7
Easson, J. F.	1
Elliott, M. S.	1
Ellis, J.	1
Ferguson, B.	1
Ferguson, J.	6
Fernie, W.	1
Fitchie, T. T.	1
Flavell, R.	2
Fleming, C.	2
Fleming, J. W.	3
Fraser, M. J. E.	3
Freedman, D. A.	1
Gallacher, H. K.	23
Gallacher, K. W.	9
Gallacher, P.	1
Galt, J. H.	1
Gemmell, T. (*St Mirren*)	1
Gemmell, T. (*Celtic*)	1
Gemmill, A.	8
Gemmill, S.	1
Gibb, W.	1
Gibson, D. W.	3
Gibson, J. D.	1
Gibson, N.	1
Gillespie, Jas.	3
Gillick, T.	3
Gilzean, A. J.	12
Gossland, J.	2
Goudie, J.	1
Gough, C. R.	6
Gourlay, J.	1
Graham, A.	2
Graham, G.	3
Gray, A.	6
Gray, E.	3
Gray, F.	1
Greig, J.	3
Groves, W.	4
Hamilton, G.	4
Hamilton, J. (*Queen's Park*)	3
Hamilton, R. C.	14
Harper, J. M.	2
Harrower, W.	5
Hartford, R. A.	4
Heggie, C.	5
Henderson, J. G.	1
Henderson, W.	5
Hendry, E. C. J.	3
Herd, D. G.	3
Herd, G.	1
Hewie, J. D.	2
Higgins, A. (*Newcastle U*)	1
Higgins, A. (*Kilmarnock*)	4
Highet, T. C.	1
Holton, J. A.	2
Hopkin, D.	2
Houliston, W.	1
Howie, H.	1
Howie, J.	2
Hughes, J.	1
Hunter, W.	1
Hutchison, D.	6
Hutchison, T.	1
Hutton, J.	1
Hyslop, T.	1
Imrie, W. N.	1
Jackson, A.	8
Jackson, C.	1
Jackson, D.	4
James, A. W.	4
Jardine, A.	1
Jenkinson, T.	1
Jess, E.	2
Johnston, A.	2
Johnston, L. H.	1
Johnston, M.	14
Johnstone, D.	2
Johnstone, J.	4
Johnstone, Jas.	1
Johnstone, R.	9
Johnstone, W.	1
Jordan, J.	11
Kay, J. L.	5
Keillor, A.	3
Kelly, J.	1
Kelso, J.	1
Ker, G.	10
King, A.	1
King, J.	1
Kinnear, D.	1
Kyle, K.	1
Lambie, J.	1
Lambie, W. A.	5
Lang, J. J.	1
Law, D.	30
Leggat, G.	8
Lennie, W.	1
Lennox, R.	3
Liddell, W.	6
Lindsay, J.	6
Linwood, A. B.	1
Logan, J.	1
Lorimer, P.	4
Love, A.	1
Lowe, J. (*Cambuslang*)	1
Lowe, J. (*St Bernards*)	1
Macari, L.	5
MacDougall, E. J.	3
MacLeod, M.	1
Mackay, D. C.	4
Mackay, G.	1
MacKenzie, J. A.	1
MacKinnon, W. W.	6
Madden, J.	5
Marshall, H.	1
Marshall, J.	1
Mason, J.	4
Massie, A.	1
Masson, D. S.	5
McAdam, J.	1
McAllister, G.	5
McAulay, J. D.	1
McAvennie, F.	1
McCall, J.	1
McCall, S. M.	1
McCalliog, J.	1
McCallum, N.	1
McCann, N.	1
McClair, B. J.	2
McCoist, A.	19
McColl, R. S.	13
McCulloch, D.	3
McDougall, J.	4
McFarlane, A.	1
McFadyen, W.	2
McGhee, M.	2
McGinlay, J.	4
McGrory, J.	6
McGuire, W.	1
McInally, A.	3
McInnes, T.	2
McKie, J.	2
McKimmie, S.	1
McKinlay, W.	4
McKinnon, A.	1
McKinnon, R.	1
McLaren, A.	4
McLaren, J.	1
McLean, A.	1
McLean, T.	1
McLeish, A.	1
McLintock, F.	1
McMahon, A.	6
McMenemy, J.	5
McMillan, I. L.	2
McNeil, H.	5
McNeill, W.	3
McPhail, J.	3
McPhail, R.	7
McPherson, J.	8
McPherson, R.	1
McQueen, G.	5
McStay, P.	9
McSwegan, G.	1
Meiklejohn, D. D.	3
Millar, J.	2
Miller, T.	2
Miller, W.	1
Mitchell, R. C.	1
Morgan, W.	1
Morris, D.	1
Morris, H.	3
Morton, A. L.	5
Mudie, J. K.	9
Mulhall, G.	1
Munro, A. D.	1
Munro, N.	1
Murdoch, R.	5
Murphy, F.	1
Murray, J.	1
Napier, C. E.	3
Narey, D.	1
Neil, R. G.	2
Nevin, P. K. F.	5
Nicholas, C.	5
Nisbet, J.	2
O'Donnell, F.	2
O'Hare, J.	5
Ormond, W. E.	1
O'Rourke, F.	1
Orr, R.	1
Orr, T.	1
Oswald, J.	1
Own goals	15
Parlane, D.	1
Paul, H. McD.	2
Paul, W.	6
Pettigrew, W.	2
Provan, D.	1
Quinn, J.	7
Quinn, P.	1
Rankin, G.	2
Rankin, R.	2
Reid, W.	4
Reilly, L.	22
Renny-Tailyour, H. W.	1
Richmond, J. T.	1
Ring, T.	2
Rioch, B. D.	6
Ritchie, J.	1
Ritchie, P. S.	1
Robertson, A.	2
Robertson, J.	2

Robertson, J. N.	9	Butler, W. T.	1	Jones, J. O.	1	Tapscott, D. R.	4
Robertson, J. T.	2			Jones, J. P.	1	Thomas, M.	4
Robertson, T.	1	Chapman, T.	2	Jones, Leslie J.	1	Thomas, T.	1
Robertson, W.	1	Charles, J.	1	Jones, R. A.	2	Toshack, J. B.	12
Russell, D.	1	Charles, M.	6	Jones, W. L.	6	Trainer, H.	2
		Charles, W. J.	15				
Scott, A. S.	5	Clarke, R. J.	5	Keenor, F. C.	2	Vaughan, John	2
Sellar, W.	4	Coleman, C.	4	Krzywicki, R. L.	1	Vernon, T. R.	8
Sharp, G.	1	Collier, D. J.	1			Vizard, E. T.	1
Shaw, F. W.	1	Crosse, K.	1	Leek, K.	5		
Shearer, D.	2	Cumner, R. H.	1	Lewis, B.	4	Walsh, I.	7
Simpson, J.	1	Curtis, A.	6	Lewis, D. M.	2	Warren, F. W.	3
Smith, A.	5	Curtis, E. R.	3	Lewis, W.	8	Watkins, W. M.	4
Smith, G.	4			Lewis, W. L.	3	Wilding, J.	4
Smith, J.	1	Davies, D. W.	1	Lovell, S.	1	Williams, A.	1
Smith, John	13	Davies, E. Lloyd	1	Lowrie, G.	2	Williams, D. R.	1
Somerville, G.	1	Davies, G.	2			Williams, G. E.	1
Souness, G. J.	4	Davies, L. S.	6	Mahoney, J. F.	1	Williams, G. G.	1
Speedie, F.	2	Davies, R. T.	9	Mays, A. W.	1	Williams, W.	1
St John, I.	9	Davies, R. W.	6	Medwin, T. C.	6	Woosnam, A. P.	3
Steel, W.	12	Davies, S.	5	Melville, A. K	3	Wynn, G. A.	1
Stein, C.	10	Davies, W.	6	Meredith, W. H.	11		
Stevenson, G.	4	Davies, W. H.	1	Mills, T. J.	1	Yorath, T. C.	2
Stewart, A.	1	Davies, William	5	Moore, G.	1	Young, E.	1
Stewart, R.	1	Davis, W. O.	1	Morgan, J. R.	2		
Stewart, W. E.	1	Deacy, N.	4	Morgan-Owen, H.	1	**REPUBLIC OF**
Strachan, G.	5	Doughty, J.	6	Morgan-Owen, M. M.	2	**IRELAND**
Sturrock, P.	3	Doughty, R.	2	Morris, A. G.	9	Aldridge, J.	19
		Durban, A.	2	Morris, H.	2	Ambrose, P.	1
Taylor, J. D.	1	Dwyer, P.	2	Morris, R.	1	Anderson, J.	1
Templeton, R.	1			Morris, S.	2		
Thompson, S.	1	Earnshaw, R.	1			Bermingham, P.	1
Thomson, A.	1	Edwards, G.	2	Nicholas, P.	2	Bradshaw, P.	4
Thomson, C.	4	Edwards, R. I.	4			Brady, L.	9
Thomson, R.	1	England, H. M.	4	O'Callaghan, E.	3	Breen, G.	6
Thomson, W.	1	Evans, I.	1	O'Sullivan, P. A.	1	Brown, D.	1
Thornton, W.	1	Evans, J.	1	Owen, G.	2	Byrne, J. (*Bray*)	1
		Evans, R. E.	2	Owen, W.	4	Byrne, J. (*QPR*)	4
Waddell, T. S.	1	Evans, W.	1	Owen, W. P.	6		
Waddell, W.	6	Eyton-Jones, J. A.	1	Own goals	13	Cantwell, J.	14
Walker, J.	2					Carey, J.	3
Walker, R.	7	Flynn, B.	7	Palmer, D.	3	Carroll, T.	1
Walker, T.	9	Ford, T.	23	Parry, T. D.	3	Cascarino, A.	19
Wallace, I. A.	1	Foulkes, W. I.	1	Paul, R.	1	Coad, P.	3
Wark, J.	7	Fowler, J.	3	Peake, E.	1	Connolly, D. J.	8
Watson, J. A. K.	1			Pembridge, M.	6	Conroy, T.	2
Watt, F.	2	Giles, D.	2	Perry, E.	1	Conway, J.	3
Watt, W. W.	1	Giggs, R. J.	7	Phillips, C.	5	Coyne, T.	6
Weir, A.	1	Glover, E. M.	7	Phillips, D.	2	Cummins, G.	5
Weir, D.	1	Godfrey, B. C.	2	Powell, A.	1	Curtis, D.	8
Weir, J. B.	2	Green, A. W.	3	Powell, D.	1		
White, J. A.	3	Griffiths, A. T.	6	Price, J.	4	Daly, G.	13
Wilson, A.	2	Griffiths, M. W.	2	Price, P.	1	Davis, T.	4
Wilson, A. N.	13	Griffiths, T. P.	3	Pryce-Jones, W. E.	3	Dempsey, J.	1
Wilson, D. (*Queen's Park*)	2			Pugh, D. H.	2	Dennehy, M.	2
		Harris, C. S.	1			Doherty, G. M. T.	1
Wilson, D. (*Rangers*)	9	Hartson, J.	6	Reece, G. I.	2	Donnelly, J.	4
Wilson, H.	1	Hersee, R.	1	Rees, R. R.	3	Donnelly, T.	1
Wylie, T. G.	1	Hewitt, R.	1	Richards, R. W.	1	Duff, D. A.	2
		Hockey, T.	1	Roach, J.	2	Duffy, B.	1
Young, A.	5	Hodges, G.	2	Robbins, W. W.	4	Duggan, H.	1
		Hole, W. J.	1	Roberts, J. (*Corwen*)	1	Dunne, J.	13
WALES		Hopkins, I. J.	2	Roberts, Jas.	1	Dunne, L.	1
Allchurch, I. J.	23	Horne, B.	2	Roberts, P. S.	1	Dunne, R. P.	3
Allen, M.	3	Howell, E. G.	3	Roberts, R. (*Druids*)	1		
Astley, D. J.	12	Hughes, L. M.	16	Roberts, W. (*Llangollen*)	2	Eglington, T.	2
Atherton, R. W.	2			Roberts, W. (*Wrexham*)	1	Ellis, P.	2
		James, E.	2	Roberts, W. H.	1		
Bamford, T.	1	James, L.	10	Robinson, J. R. C.	3	Fagan, F.	5
Barnes, W.	1	James, R.	7	Rush, I.	28	Fallon, S.	2
Bellamy, C. D.	4	Jarrett, R. H.	3	Russell, M. R.	1	Fallon, W.	2
Blackmore, C. G.	1	Jenkyns, C. A.	1			Farrell, P.	3
Blake, N. A.	4	Jones, A.	1	Sabine, H. W.	1	Finnan, S.	1
Bodin, P. J.	3	Jones, Bryn	6	Saunders, D.	22	Fitzgerald, P.	2
Boulter, L. M.	1	Jones, B. S.	2	Savage, R. W.	2	Fitzgerald, J.	1
Bowdler, J. C. H.	3	Jones, Cliff	16	Shaw, E. G.	2	Fitzsimmons, A.	7
Bowen, D. L.	1	Jones, C. W.	1	Sisson, N.	4	Flood, J. J.	4
Bowen, M.	3	Jones, D. E.	1	Slatter, N.	2	Fogarty, A.	3
Boyle, T.	1	Jones, Evan	1	Smallman, D. P.	1	Foley, D.	2
Bryan, T.	1	Jones, H.	1	Speed, G. A.	4	Fullam, J.	1
Burgess, W. A. R.	1	Jones, I.	1	Symons, C. J.	2	Fullam, R.	1
Burke, T.	1	Jones, J. L.	1			Galvin, A.	1

Gavin, J.	2	Keane, R. M.	9	Moore, P.	7	Ryan, G.	1
Geoghegan, M.	2	Kelly, D.	9	Moran, K.	6	Ryan, R.	3
Giles, J.	5	Kelly, G.	2	Morrison, C. H.	2		
Givens, D.	19	Kelly, J.	2	Moroney, T.	1	Sheedy, K.	9
Glynn, D.	1	Kennedy, M.	3	Mulligan, P.	1	Sheridan, J.	5
Grealish, T.	8	Kernaghan, A. N.	1			Slaven, B.	1
Grimes, A. A.	1	Kilbane, K. D	3	O'Callaghan, K.	1	Sloan, W.	1
		Kinsella, M. A.	3	O'Connor, T.	2	Squires, J.	1
Hale, A.	2			O'Farrell, F.	2	Stapleton, F.	20
Hand, E.	2	Lacey, W.	1	O'Flanagan, K.	3	Staunton, S.	7
Harte, I. P.	8	Lawrenson, M.	5	O'Keefe, E.	1	Strahan, J.	1
Haverty, J.	3	Leech, M.	2	O'Leary, D. A.	1	Sullivan, J.	1
Holland, M. R.	4			O'Neill, F.	1		
Holmes, J.	1	McAteer, J. W.	3	O'Neill, K. P.	4		
Horlacher, A.	2	McCann, J.	1	O'Reilly, J. (*Brideville*)	2	Townsend, A. D.	7
Houghton, R.	6	McCarthy, M.	2	O'Reilly, J. (*Cork*)	1	Treacy, R.	5
Hughton, C.	1	McEvoy, A.	6	Own goals	8	Touhy, L.	4
Hurley, C.		McGee, P.	4				
		McGrath, P.	8	Quinn, N.	21	Waddock, G.	3
Irwin, D.	4	McLoughlin, A. F.	2			Walsh, D.	5
		McPhail, S. J. P.	1	Reid, S. J.	2	Walsh, M.	3
Jordan, D.	1	Mancini, T.	1			Waters, J.	1
		Martin, C.	6	Ringstead, A.	7	White, J. J.	2
Kavanagh, G. A.	1	Martin, M.	4	Robinson, M.	4	Whelan, R.	3
Keane, R. D.	13	Mooney, J.	1	Rogers, E.	5		

BRITISH & IRISH INTERNATIONAL MANAGERS

England
Walter Winterbottom 1946–1962 (after period as coach); Alf Ramsey 1963–1974; Joe Mercer (caretaker) 1974; Don Revie 1974–1977; Ron Greenwood 1977–1982; Bobby Robson 1982–1990; Graham Taylor 1990–1993; Terry Venables (coach) 1994–1996; Glenn Hoddle 1996–1999; Kevin Keegan 1999–2000; Sven-Goran Eriksson from January 2001.

Northern Ireland
Peter Doherty 1951–1952; Bertie Peacock 1962–1967; Billy Bingham 1967–1971; Terry Neill 1971–1975; Dave Clements (player-manager) 1975–1976; Danny Blanchflower 1976–1979; Billy Bingham 1980–1994; Bryan Hamilton 1994–1998; Lawrie McMenemy 1998–1999; Sammy McIlroy from January 2000.

Scotland (since 1967)
Bobby Brown 1967–1971; Tommy Docherty 1971–1972; Willie Ormond 1973–1977; Ally MacLeod 1977–1978; Jock Stein 1978–1985; Alex Ferguson (caretaker) 1985–1986 Andy Roxburgh (coach) 1986–1993; Craig Brown 1993–2001; Berti Vogts from March 2002–

Wales (since 1974)
Mike Smith 1974–1979; Mike England 1980–1988; David Williams (caretaker) 1988; Terry Yorath 1988–1993; John Toshack 1994 for one match; Mike Smith 1994–1995; Bobby Gould 1995–1999; Mark Hughes from November 1999.

Republic of Ireland
Liam Tuohy 1971–1972; Johnny Giles 1973–1980 (after period as player-manager); Eoin Hand 1980–1985; Jack Charlton 1986–1996; Mick McCarthy from February 1996.

SOUTH AMERICA

COPA LIBERTADORES 2001

GROUP 1

	P	W	D	L	F	A	Pts
Sao Caetano	6	4	0	2	14	4	12
Cobreloa	6	4	0	2	12	8	12
Cerro Porteno	6	3	1	2	7	6	10
Alianza	6	0	1	5	1	16	1

GROUP 2

	P	W	D	L	F	A	Pts
Gremio	6	4	0	2	11	7	12
Clenciano	6	3	0	3	8	7	9
12 de Octubre	6	3	0	3	5	7	9
Oriente	6	2	0	4	10	13	6

GROUP 3

	P	W	D	L	F	A	Pts
Penarol	6	4	0	2	11	7	12
El Nacional	6	4	0	2	10	6	12
San Lorenzo	6	2	0	4	6	8	6
Real Potosi	6	2	0	4	10	16	6

GROUP 4

	P	W	D	L	F	A	Pts
America (Col)	6	3	2	1	10	3	11
Olmedo	6	3	0	3	7	7	9
Bolivar	6	2	2	2	11	13	8
Piranaense	6	1	2	3	10	15	5

GROUP 5

	P	W	D	L	F	A	Pts
At Morelia	6	4	2	0	15	7	14
Nacional	6	3	2	1	13	12	11
Velez Sarsfield	6	2	2	2	8	8	8
Sporting Cristal	6	0	0	6	5	14	0

GROUP 6

	P	W	D	L	F	A	Pts
Boca Juniors	6	4	1	1	7	2	13
Montevideo W	6	3	1	2	8	7	10
Santiago W	6	2	3	1	6	6	9
Emelec	6	0	1	5	4	10	1

GROUP 7

	P	W	D	L	F	A	Pts
America (Mex)	6	5	1	0	9	2	16
River Plate	6	2	3	1	8	4	9
Talleres	6	1	2	3	5	9	5
Tulua	6	1	0	5	9	16	3

GROUP 8

	P	W	D	L	F	A	Pts
Olimpia	6	3	2	1	8	5	11
Univ Catolica	6	3	1	2	9	8	10
Once	6	3	0	3	10	11	9
Flamengo	6	1	1	4	6	9	4

Second Round, First Leg
Clenciano 0, America (Mex) 1
Cobreloa 1, Olimpia 1
abandoned half-time – objects thrown from stands; match awarded 2-0 to Olimpia.
Nacional 1, America (Col) 0
Montevideo W 2, Penarol 2
Olmedo 0, At Morelia 5
River Plate 1, Gremio 2
El Nacional 0, Boca Juniors 0
Univ Catolica 1, Sao Caetano 1

Second Round, Second Leg
At Morelia 3, Olmedo 2
Penarol 2, Montevideo W 2
Penarol won 3-0 on penalties.
America (Mex) 4, Clenciano 1
Boca Juniors 2, El Nacional 0
Sao Caetano 1, Univ Catolica 1
Sao Caetano won 4-2 on penalties.
America (Col) 0, Nacional 0
Gremio 4, River Plate 0
Olimpia 2, Cobreloa 1

Quarter-Finals, First Leg
At Morelia 1, America (Mex) 2
Boca Juniors 1, Olimpia 1
Gremio 1, Nacional 0
Penarol 1, Sao Caetano 0

Quarter-Finals, Second Leg
Sao Caetano 2, Penarol 1
Sao Caetano won 3-1 on penalties.
Nacional 1, Gremio 1
America (Mex) 2, At Morelia 1
Olimpia 1, Boca Juniors 0
Competition still being played.

MERCONORTE CUP

GROUP A

	P	W	D	L	F	A	Pts
Necaxa	6	5	0	1	12	5	15
America	6	3	1	2	7	7	10
Alianza	6	1	2	3	8	10	5
Aucas	6	1	1	4	6	11	4

GROUP B

	P	W	D	L	F	A	Pts
Millonarios	6	4	0	2	10	7	12
Italchacao	6	4	0	2	9	8	12
NY MetroStars	6	3	0	3	8	5	9
Guadalajara	6	1	0	5	3	10	3

GROUP C

	P	W	D	L	F	A	Pts
Santos Laguna	6	5	0	1	15	6	15
Sporting Cristal	6	3	2	1	10	10	11
Kansas City	6	1	1	4	8	12	4
Barcelona	6	0	3	3	9	14	3

GROUP D

	P	W	D	L	F	A	Pts
Emelec	6	3	3	0	8	1	12
Atletico Nacional	6	3	1	2	7	5	10
Universitario	6	3	1	2	7	7	10
Blooming	6	0	1	5	3	12	1

Semi-Finals, First Leg
Necaxa 3, Millonarios 2
Santos Laguna 4, Emelec 1

Semi-Finals, Second Leg
Millonarios 3, Necaxa 2
Millonarios won 3-1 on penalties.
Emelec 4, Santos Laguna 1
Emelec won 4-2 on penalties.

Final, First Leg
Millonarios 1, Emelec 1

Final, Second Leg
Emelec 1, Millonarios 1
Millonarios won 3-1 on penalties.

MERCOSUR CUP

GROUP A	P	W	D	L	F	A	Pts
Cerro Porteno	6	3	1	2	8	6	10
Univ Catolica	6	3	0	3	8	9	9
Vasco da Gama	6	2	2	2	11	11	8
Boca Juniors	6	1	3	2	9	10	6

GROUP B	P	W	D	L	F	A	Pts
Flamengo	6	5	0	1	11	6	15
San Lorenzo	6	3	1	2	9	4	10
Nacional	6	3	1	2	8	5	10
Olimpia	6	0	0	6	0	13	0

GROUP C	P	W	D	L	F	A	Pts
Corinthians	6	3	1	2	8	6	10
Independiente	6	3	0	3	8	8	9
Cruzeiro	6	2	2	2	9	8	8
Colo Colo	6	1	3	2	3	6	6

GROUP D	P	W	D	L	F	A	Pts
Talleres	6	2	4	0	10	5	10
Velez Sarsfield	6	2	2	2	12	11	8
Sao Paulo	6	1	4	1	7	6	7
Penarol	6	1	2	3	5	12	5

GROUP E	P	W	D	L	F	A	Pts
Gremio	6	4	2	0	11	4	14
River Plate	6	2	2	2	13	10	8
Palmeiras	6	1	3	2	11	10	6
Univ de Chile	6	1	1	4	3	14	4

Quarter-Finals, First Leg
Independiente 0, Flamengo 0
Univ Catolica 2, Corinthians 1
Gremio 0, Talleres 0
San Lorenzo 4, Cerro Porteno 2

Quarter-Finals, Second Leg
Flamengo 4, Independiente 0
Corinthians 2, Univ Catolica 0
Talleres 0, Gremio 2
Cerro Porteno 1, San Lorenzo 2

Semi-Finals, First Leg
Corinthians 2, San Lorenzo 1
Flamengo 2, Gremio 2

Semi-Finals, Second Leg
San Lorenzo 4, Corinthians 1
Gremio 0, Flamengo 0
Flamengo won 4-2 on penalties.

Final, First Leg
Flamengo 0, San Lorenzo 0

Final, Second Leg
San Lorenzo 1, Flamengo 1
San Lorenzo won 4-3 on penalties.

AFRICA

AFRICAN NATIONS' CUP 2002

(Finals in Mali)

FIRST ROUND

GROUP A
Mali 1, Liberia 1
Algeria 0, Nigeria 1
Mali 0, Nigeria 0
Algeria 2, Liberia 2
Mali 2, Algeria 0
Liberia 0, Nigeria 1

GROUP B
Burkina Faso 0, South Africa 0
Ghana 0, Morocco 0
Ghana 0, South Africa 0
Burkina Faso 1, Morocco 2
Morocco 1, South Africa 3
Burkina Faso 1, Ghana 2

GROUP C
Cameroon 1, DR Congo 0
Ivory Coast 0, Togo 0
Cameroon 1, Ivory Coast 0
DR Congo 0, Togo 0
Cameroon 3, Togo 0
DR Congo 3, Ivory Coast 1

GROUP D
Egypt 0, Senegal 1
Tunisia 0, Zambia 0
Egypt 1, Tunisia 0
Senegal 1, Zambia 0
Egypt 2, Zambia 1
Senegal 0, Tunisia 0

QUARTER-FINALS
South Africa 0, Mali 2
Nigeria 1, Ghana 0
Cameroon 1, Egypt 0
Senegal 2, DR Congo 0

SEMI-FINALS
Senegal 2, Nigeria 1
Mali 0, Cameroon 3

THIRD PLACE
Mali 0, Nigeria 1

FINAL
Cameroon 0, Senegal 0
Cameroon won 3-2 on penalties.

UEFA UNDER-21 CHAMPIONSHIP 2000–02

GROUP 1
Switzerland 3, Russia 1
Luxembourg 0, Yugoslavia 3
Luxembourg 1, Slovenia 5
Slovenia 0, Switzerland 0
Russia 2, Luxembourg 0
Yugoslavia 3, Switzerland 3
Russia 0, Slovenia 0
Slovenia 1, Yugoslavia 2
Switzerland 6, Luxembourg 0
Yugoslavia 2, Russia 2
Slovenia 1, Luxembourg 0
Russia 2, Yugoslavia 0
Switzerland 2, Slovenia 1
Luxembourg 0, Russia 10
Switzerland 2, Yugoslavia 2
Slovenia 1, Russia 3
Luxembourg 0, Switzerland 3
Yugoslavia 2, Slovenia 1
Russia 3, Switzerland 3
Yugoslavia 8, Luxembourg 0

GROUP 2
Holland 2, Republic of Ireland 0
Estonia 1, Portugal 3
Portugal 3, Republic of Ireland 1
Cyprus 0, Holland 1
Holland 1, Portugal 1
Republic of Ireland 1, Estonia 0
Cyprus 0, Republic of Ireland 1
Cyprus 3, Estonia 1
Portugal 3, Holland 0
Holland 4, Cyprus 2
Estonia 0, Holland 5
Republic of Ireland 0, Portugal 1
Estonia 0, Republic of Ireland 3
Portugal 7, Cyprus 0
Estonia 0, Cyprus 3
Republic of Ireland 1, Holland 1
Cyprus 1, Portugal 0
Holland 6, Estonia 0
Portugal 4, Estonia 0
Republic of Ireland 3, Cyprus 0

GROUP 3
Bulgaria 1, Czech Republic 0
Iceland 0, Denmark 0
N Ireland 3, Malta 0
Czech Republic 2, Iceland 1
N Ireland 0, Denmark 3
Bulgaria 2, Malta 0
Iceland 2, N Ireland 5
Malta 0, Czech Republic 1
Denmark 2, Bulgaria 2
Bulgaria 1, Iceland 0
Malta 0, Denmark 0
N Ireland 0, Czech Republic 2
Bulgaria 2, N Ireland 1
Czech Republic 3, Denmark 0
Malta 1, Iceland 1
Iceland 3, Malta 0
Denmark 3, Czech Republic 4
N Ireland 1, Bulgaria 1
Denmark 3, Malta 0
Iceland 3, Bulgaria 2
Czech Republic 4, N Ireland 0
Malta 2, Bulgaria 2
Iceland 0, Czech Republic 1
Denmark 2, N Ireland 0
Bulgaria 3, Denmark 1
Czech Republic 3, Malta 0
N Ireland 1, Iceland 3
Czech Republic 8, Bulgaria 0
Malta 2, N Ireland 2
Denmark 4, Iceland 0

GROUP 4
Turkey 1, Moldova 0
Azerbaijan 0, Sweden 5
Slovakia 2, Macedonia 0
Sweden 0, Turkey 0
Macedonia 1, Azerbaijan 2
Moldova 0, Slovakia 3
Slovakia 1, Sweden 1
Moldova 3, Macedonia 0
Azerbaijan 1, Turkey 2
Sweden 2, Macedonia 0
Turkey 0, Slovakia 1

Azerbaijan 0, Moldova 0
Macedonia 1, Turkey 4
Slovakia 5, Azerbaijan 0
Moldova 0, Sweden 2
Sweden 4, Slovakia 0
Turkey 3, Azerbaijan 0
Macedonia 2, Moldova 0
Azerbaijan 0, Slovakia 0
Sweden 3, Moldova 0
Turkey 2, Macedonia 0
Moldova 1, Azerbaijan 0
Slovakia 0, Turkey 1
Macedonia 1, Sweden 1
Azerbaijan 1, Macedonia 0
Slovakia 0, Moldova 0
Turkey 4, Sweden 1
Moldova 2, Turkey 2
Macedonia 1, Slovakia 1
Sweden 0, Azerbaijan 0

GROUP 5
Belarus 4, Wales 1
Norway 5, Armenia 1
Ukraine 2, Poland 2
Armenia 1, Ukraine 2
Poland 0, Belarus 4
Wales 0, Norway 2
Belarus 5, Armenia 0
Poland 2, Wales 1
Norway 3, Ukraine 1
Armenia 1, Wales 0
Ukraine 1, Belarus 0
Norway 1, Poland 2
Belarus 1, Norway 0
Poland 1, Armenia 1
Wales 0, Ukraine 3
Armenia 1, Belarus 0
Ukraine 1, Norway 3
Wales 0, Poland 4
Armenia 2, Poland 0
Ukraine 1, Wales 0
Norway 5, Belarus 1
Belarus 1, Ukraine 2
Poland 3, Norway 0
Wales 1, Armenia 1
Belarus 3, Poland 3
Norway 2, Wales 0
Ukraine 1, Armenia 0
Armenia 0, Norway 0
Poland 3, Ukraine 0
Wales 1, Belarus 2

GROUP 6
Latvia 1, Scotland 3
Belgium 2, Croatia 1
Latvia 0, Belgium 2
Croatia 3, Scotland 1
Croatia 2, Latvia 1
Scotland 0, Belgium 1
Belgium 3, Latvia 0
Latvia 1, Croatia 1
Scotland 1, Croatia 1
Belgium 0, Scotland 0
Croatia 1, Belgium 0
Scotland 1, Latvia 0

GROUP 7
France 3, Israel 0
Bosnia 0, Spain 2
France 2, Austria 0
Spain 1, Israel 0
Austria 2, Spain 1
Israel 2, Bosnia 1
Bosnia 0, France 1
Israel 3, France 4
Bosnia 0, Austria 0
Spain 1, France 1
Austria 0, Israel 2
Austria 1, France 1
Spain 5, Bosnia 1
Israel 0, Spain 1
Spain 2, Austria 0
Bosnia 2, Israel 4
Austria 2, Bosnia 1
France 3, Spain 0
France 1, Bosnia 0
Israel 5, Austria 1

GROUP 8
Romania 3, Lithuania 0
Hungary 0, Italy 3
Lithuania 2, Georgia 1
Italy 1, Romania 1
Lithuania 0, Hungary 1
Italy 3, Georgia 2
Hungary 4, Lithuania 1
Romania 0, Italy 1
Georgia 0, Romania 3
Italy 1, Lithuania 0
Romania 1, Hungary 0
Georgia 0, Italy 2
Lithuania 1, Romania 0
Hungary 2, Georgia 1
Georgia 0, Hungary 2
Lithuania 0, Italy 3
Georgia 4, Lithuania 1
Hungary 1, Romania 3
Italy 0, Hungary 2
Romania 2, Georgia 1

GROUP 9
Finland 3, Albania 0
Germany 2, Greece 1
Greece 3, Finland 1
England 1, Germany 1
Albania 0, Greece 1
Finland 2, England 2
Germany 8, Albania 0
England 4, Finland 0
Albania 0, England 1
Greece 2, Germany 0
Finland 1, Germany 3
Greece 0, Albania 0
Greece 3, England 1
Albania 0, Germany 1
Albania 3, Finland 0
Germany 1, England 2
England 5, Albania 0
Finland 0, Greece 3
England 2, Greece 1
Germany 2, Finland 0

PLAY-OFFS FIRST LEG
Croatia 1, Czech Republic 1
Greece 3, Turkey 0
Holland 2, England 2
Poland 2, Italy 5
Romania 0, France 1
Spain 2, Portugal 1
Sweden 3, Belgium 2
Ukraine 1, Switzerland 2

PLAY-OFFS SECOND LEG
Belgium 2, Sweden 0
Czech Republic 0, Croatia 0
England 1, Holland 0
France 4, Romania 0
Italy 0, Poland 0
Portugal 1, Spain 0
Switzerland 2, Ukraine 1
Turkey 2, Greece 1

FINALS (in Switzerland)
GROUP A
England 2, Switzerland 1
Italy 1, Portugal 1
Italy 2, England 1
Portugal 0, Switzerland 2
Portugal 3, England 1
Switzerland 0, Italy 0

GROUP B
Belgium 0, France 2
Czech Republic 1, Greece 1
France 2, Czech Republic 0
Greece 1, Belgium 2
Greece 1, France 3
Belgium 0, Czech Republic 1

SEMI-FINALS
Czech Republic 3, Italy 2
France 2, Switzerland 0

FINAL
Czech Republic 0, France 0
*aet; Czech Republic won 3-1 on
penalties.*

WORLD UNDER-17 CHAMPIONSHIP

(Finals in Trinidad & Tobago)

GROUP A
Croatia 2, Trinidad & Tobago 1
Australia 0, Brazil 1
Croatia 1, Brazil 3
Trinidad & Tobago 0, Australia 1
Australia 4, Croatia 0
Brazil 6, Trinidad & Tobago 1

GROUP B
USA 0, Japan 1
France 1, Nigeria 2
Japan 0, Nigeria 4
USA 3, France 5
Nigeria 2, USA 0
France 5, Japan 1

GROUP C
Oman 1, Spain 2
Burkina Faso 2, Argentina 2
Spain 0, Burkina Faso 1
Oman 0, Argentina 3
Argentina 4, Spain 2
Burkina Faso 1, Oman 1

GROUP D
Mali 1, Paraguay 2
Iran 0, Costa Rica 2
Paraguay 0, Costa Rica 3
Mali 1, Iran 0
Mali 2, Costa Rica 0
Paraguay 3, Iran 2

QUARTER-FINALS
Brazil 1, France 2
Nigeria 5, Australia 1
Argentina 2, Mali 1
Costa Rica 0, Burkina Faso 2

SEMI-FINALS
Nigeria 1, Burkina Faso 0
Argentina 1, France 2

MATCH FOR 3RD PLACE
Argentina 0, Burkina Faso 2

FINAL
Nigeria 0, France 3

18TH UEFA UNDER-18 CHAMPIONSHIP

(Finals in Finland)

GROUP A
Finland 1, Ukraine 1
Czech Republic 1, Yugoslavia 0
Finland 1, Czech Republic 4
Ukraine 1, Yugoslavia 2
Yugoslavia 8, Finland 4
Ukraine 2, Czech Republic 3

GROUP B
Poland 4, Spain 1
Belgium 2, Denmark 0
Poland 1, Belgium 1
Spain 1, Denmark 0
Denmark 2, Poland 3
Spain 3, Belgium 1

MATCH FOR 3RD PLACE
Yugoslavia 2, Spain 6

FINAL
Czech Republic 1, Poland 3

UNDER-19 CHAMPIONSHIP

GROUP 1	P	W	D	L	F	A	Pts
Germany	4	3	1	0	11	4	10
Turkey	4	1	1	2	7	8	4
Sweden	4	1	0	3	5	11	3

GROUP 2	P	W	D	L	F	A	Pts
Poland	2	2	0	0	4	0	6
Wales	2	1	0	1	6	2	3
Estonia	2	0	0	2	1	9	0

GROUP 3	P	W	D	L	F	A	Pts
Lithuania	2	2	0	0	3	0	6
Russia	2	1	0	1	3	2	3
Cyprus	2	0	0	2	1	5	0

GROUP 4	P	W	D	L	F	A	Pts
England	2	2	0	0	7	2	6
Hungary	2	0	1	1	2	4	1
Georgia	2	0	1	1	2	5	1

GROUP 5	P	W	D	L	F	A	Pts
Macedonia	2	2	0	0	5	3	6
Finland	2	1	0	1	4	3	3
Azerbaijan	2	0	0	2	4	0	0

GROUP 6	P	W	D	L	F	A	Pts
Spain	4	4	0	0	17	1	12
Switzerland	4	2	0	2	8	6	6
Armenia	4	0	0	4	1	19	0

GROUP 7	P	W	D	L	F	A	Pts
Czech Republic	3	2	1	0	18	3	7
Iceland	3	2	1	0	10	2	7
Ukraine	3	1	0	2	4	4	3
Andorra	3	0	0	3	0	23	0

GROUP 8	P	W	D	L	F	A	Pts
Bulgaria	3	2	1	0	7	3	7
Denmark	3	1	1	1	3	3	4
Malta	3	1	0	2	2	5	3
Luxembourg	3	0	2	1	2	3	2

GROUP 9	P	W	D	L	F	A	Pts
Slovakia	3	2	1	0	5	1	7
Bosnia	3	1	1	1	2	2	4
Northern Ireland	3	1	1	1	2	2	4
Liechtenstein	3	0	1	2	1	5	1

GROUP 10	P	W	D	L	F	A	Pts
Portugal	3	2	0	1	5	2	6
Italy	3	2	0	1	6	2	6
Belarus	3	1	1	1	2	3	4
Moldova	3	0	1	2	0	6	1

GROUP 11	P	W	D	L	F	A	Pts
Belgium	6	3	1	2	10	5	10
Romania	6	2	3	1	9	6	9
Yugoslavia	5	2	1	2	6	9	7
Israel	5	1	1	3	4	9	4

GROUP 12	P	W	D	L	F	A	Pts
Greece	3	2	0	1	9	4	6
Slovenia	3	2	0	1	7	4	6
Scotland	3	2	0	1	5	4	6
Faeroes	3	0	0	3	1	10	0

GROUP 13	P	W	D	L	F	A	Pts
Holland	3	3	0	0	17	2	9
France	3	2	0	1	10	2	6
Albania	3	0	1	2	2	13	1
San Marino	3	0	1	2	1	13	1

GROUP 14	P	W	D	L	F	A	Pts
Republic of Ireland	3	3	0	0	8	1	9
Croatia	3	2	0	1	6	4	6
Austria	3	1	0	2	2	3	3
Latvia	3	0	0	3	1	9	0

INTERMEDIATE ROUND

GROUP 1
Germany 0, Poland 0; Poland 2, Germany 2.

GROUP 2
Lithuania 1, England 1; England 2, Lithuania 1.

GROUP 3
Macedonia 1, Spain 3; Spain 4, Macedonia 0.

GROUP 4
Czech Republic 1, Bulgaria 1; Bulgaria 1, Czech Republic 3.

GROUP 5
Slovakia 1, Portugal 1; Portugal 0, Slovakia 1.

GROUP 6
Belgium 4, Greece 1; Greece 1, Belgium 2

GROUP 7
Holland 1, Republic of Ireland 2; Republic of Ireland 0, Holland 0.
Competition still being played.

ENGLAND UNDER-21 RESULTS 1976–2002

EC UEFA Competition for Under-21 Teams

Year	Date		Venue	Eng	Alb
			v ALBANIA	**Eng**	**Alb**
EC1989	Mar	7	Shkroda	2	1
EC1989	April	25	Ipswich	2	0
EC2001	Mar	27	Tirana	1	0
EC2001	Sept	4	Middlesbrough	5	0
			v ANGOLA	**Eng**	**Ang**
1995	June	10	Toulon	1	0
1996	May	28	Toulon	0	2
			v ARGENTINA	**Eng**	**Arg**
1998	May	18	Toulon	0	2
2000	Feb	22	Fulham	1	0
			v AUSTRIA	**Eng**	**Aus**
1994	Oct	11	Kapfenberg	3	1
1995	Nov	14	Middlesbrough	2	1
			v BELGIUM	**Eng**	**Bel**
1994	June	5	Marseille	2	1
1996	May	24	Toulon	1	0
			v BRAZIL	**Eng**	**B**
1993	June	11	Toulon	0	0
1995	June	6	Toulon	0	2
1996	June	1	Toulon	1	2
			v BULGARIA	**Eng**	**Bul**
EC1979	June	5	Pernik	3	1
EC1979	Nov	20	Leicester	5	0
1989	June	5	Toulon	2	3
EC1998	Oct	9	West Ham	1	0
EC1999	June	8	Vratsa	1	0
			v CROATIA	**Eng**	**Cro**
1996	Apr	23	Sunderland	0	1
			v CZECHOSLOVAKIA	**Eng**	**Cz**
1990	May	28	Toulon	2	1
1992	May	26	Toulon	1	2
1993	June	9	Toulon	1	1
			v CZECH REPUBLIC	**Eng**	**CzR**
1998	Nov	17	Ipswich	0	1
			v DENMARK	**Eng**	**Den**
EC1978	Sept	19	Hvidovre	2	1
EC1979	Sept	11	Watford	1	0
EC1982	Sept	21	Hvidovre	4	1
EC1983	Sept	20	Norwich	4	1
EC1986	Mar	12	Copenhagen	1	0
EC1986	Mar	26	Manchester	1	1
1988	Sept	13	Watford	0	0
1994	Mar	8	Brentford	1	0
1999	Oct	8	Bradford	4	1
			v EAST GERMANY	**Eng**	**EG**
EC1980	April	16	Sheffield	1	2
EC1980	April	23	Jena	0	1
			v FINLAND	**Eng**	**Fin**
EC1977	May	26	Helsinki	1	0
EC1977	Oct	12	Hull	8	1
EC1984	Oct	16	Southampton	2	0
EC1985	May	21	Mikkeli	1	3
EC2000	Oct	10	Valkeakoski	2	2
EC2001	Mar	23	Barnsley	4	0
			v FRANCE	**Eng**	**Fra**
EC1984	Feb	28	Sheffield	6	1
EC1984	Mar	28	Rouen	1	0
1987	June	11	Toulon	0	2
EC1988	April	13	Besancon	2	4
EC1988	April	27	Highbury	2	2
1988	June	12	Toulon	2	4
1990	May	23	Toulon	7	3
1991	June	3	Toulon	1	0
1992	May	28	Toulon	0	0
1993	June	15	Toulon	1	0
1994	May	31	Aubagne	0	3
1995	June	10	Toulon	0	2
1998	May	14	Toulon	1	1
1999	Feb	9	Derby	2	1
			v GEORGIA	**Eng**	**Geo**
EC1996	Nov	8	Batumi	1	0
EC1997	April	29	Charlton	0	0
2000	Aug	31	Middlesbrough	6	1
			v GERMANY	**Eng**	**Ger**
1991	Sept	10	Scunthorpe	2	1
EC2000	Oct	6	Derby	1	1
EC2001	Aug	31	Frieburg	2	1

Year	Date		Venue	Eng	Gre
			v GREECE	**Eng**	**Gre**
EC1982	Nov	16	Piraeus	0	1
EC1983	Mar	29	Portsmouth	2	1
1989	Feb	7	Patras	0	1
EC1997	Nov	13	Heraklion	0	2
EC1997	Dec	17	Norwich	4	2
EC2001	June	5	Athens	1	3
EC2001	Oct	5	Ewood Park	2	1
			v HOLLAND	**Eng**	**H**
EC1993	April	27	Portsmouth	3	0
EC1993	Oct	12	Utrecht	1	1
2001	Aug	14	Reading	4	0
EC2001	Nov	9	Utrecht	2	2
EC2001	Nov	13	Derby	1	0
			v HUNGARY	**Eng**	**Hun**
EC1981	June	5	Keszthely	2	1
EC1981	Nov	17	Nottingham	2	0
EC1983	April	26	Newcastle	1	0
EC1983	Oct	11	Nyiregyhaza	2	0
1990	Sept	11	Southampton	3	1
1992	May	12	Budapest	2	2
1999	April	27	Budapest	2	2
			v ITALY	**Eng**	**Italy**
EC1978	Mar	8	Manchester	2	1
EC1978	April	5	Rome	0	0
EC1984	April	18	Manchester	3	1
EC1984	May	2	Florence	0	1
EC1986	April	9	Pisa	0	2
EC1986	April	23	Swindon	1	1
EC1997	Feb	12	Bristol	1	0
EC1997	Oct	10	Rieti	1	0
EC2000	May	27	Bratislava	0	2
2000	Nov	14	Monza*	0	0
2002	Mar	26	Valley Parade	1	1
EC2002	May	20	Basle	1	2

*Abandoned 11 mins; fog.

Year	Date		Venue	Eng	Isr
			v ISRAEL	**Eng**	**Isr**
1985	Feb	27	Tel Aviv	2	1
			v LATVIA	**Eng**	**Lat**
1995	April	25	Riga	1	0
1995	June	7	Burnley	4	0
			v LUXEMBOURG	**Eng**	**Lux**
EC1998	Oct	13	Greven Macher	5	0
EC1999	Sept	3	Reading	5	0
			v MALAYSIA	**Eng**	**Mal**
1995	June	8	Toulon	2	0
			v MEXICO	**Eng**	**Mex**
1988	June	5	Toulon	2	1
1991	May	29	Toulon	6	0
1992	May	25	Toulon	1	1
2001	May	24	Leicester	3	0
			v MOLDOVA	**Eng**	**Mol**
EC1996	Aug	31	Chisinau	2	0
EC1997	Sept	9	Wycombe	1	0
			v MOROCCO	**Eng**	**Mor**
1987	June	7	Toulon	2	0
1988	June	9	Toulon	1	0
			v NORWAY	**Eng**	**Nor**
EC1977	June	1	Bergen	2	1
EC1977	Sept	6	Brighton	6	0
1980	Sept	9	Southampton	3	0
1981	Sept	8	Drammen	0	0
EC1992	Oct	13	Peterborough	0	2
EC1993	June	1	Stavanger	1	1
1995	Oct	10	Stavanger	2	2
			v POLAND	**Eng**	**Pol**
EC1982	Mar	17	Warsaw	2	1
EC1982	April	7	West Ham	2	2
EC1989	June	2	Plymouth	2	1
EC1989	Oct	10	Jastrzebie	3	1
EC1990	Oct	16	Tottenham	0	1
EC1991	Nov	12	Pila	1	2
EC1993	May	28	Zdroj	4	1
EC1993	Sept	7	Millwall	1	2
EC1996	Oct	8	Wolverhampton	0	0
EC1997	May	30	Katowice	1	1
EC1999	Mar	26	Southampton	5	0
EC1999	Sept	7	Plock	1	3

v PORTUGAL

			Eng	Por
1987	June	13	Toulon	0	0
1990	May	21	Toulon	0	1
1993	June	7	Toulon	2	0
1994	June	7	Toulon	2	0
EC1994	Sept	6	Leicester	0	0
1995	Sept	2	Lisbon	0	2
1996	May	30	Toulon	1	3
2000	Apr	16	Stoke	0	1
EC2000	May	22	Zurich	1	3

v REPUBLIC OF IRELAND

			Eng	RoI
1981	Feb	25	Liverpool	1	0
1985	Mar	25	Portsmouth	3	2
1989	June	9	Toulon	0	0
EC1990	Nov	13	Cork	3	0
EC1991	Mar	26	Brentford	3	0
1994	Nov	15	Newcastle	1	0
1995	Mar	27	Dublin	2	0

v ROMANIA

			Eng	Rom
EC1980	Oct	14	Ploesti	0	4
EC1981	April	28	Swindon	3	0
EC1985	April	30	Brasov	0	0
EC1985	Sept	10	Ipswich	3	0

v RUSSIA

			Eng	Rus
1994	May	30	Bandol	2	0

v SAN MARINO

			Eng	SM
EC1993	Feb	16	Luton	6	0
EC1993	Nov	17	San Marino	4	0

v SENEGAL

			Eng	Sen
1989	June	7	Toulon	6	1
1991	May	27	Toulon	2	1

v SCOTLAND

			Eng	Sco
1977	April	27	Sheffield	1	0
EC1980	Feb	12	Coventry	2	1
EC1980	Mar	4	Aberdeen	0	0
EC1982	April	19	Glasgow	1	0
EC1982	April	28	Manchester	1	1
EC1988	Feb	16	Aberdeen	1	0
EC1988	Mar	22	Nottingham	1	0
1993	June	13	Toulon	1	0

v SLOVAKIA

			Eng	Slo
EC2002	June	1	Bratislava	0	2

v SLOVENIA

			Eng	Slo
2000	Feb	1	Nova Gorica	1	0

v SOUTH AFRICA

			Eng	SA
1998	May	16	Toulon	3	1

v SPAIN

			Eng	Spa
EC1984	May	17	Seville	1	0
EC1984	May	24	Sheffield	1	0
1987	Feb	18	Burgos	2	1
1992	Sept	8	Burgos	1	0
2001	Feb	27	Birmingham	0	4

v SWEDEN

			Eng	Swe
1979	June	9	Vasteras	2	1
1986	Sept	9	Ostersund	1	1
EC1988	Oct	18	Coventry	1	1
EC1989	Sept	5	Uppsala	0	1
EC1998	Sept	4	Sundvall	2	0
EC1999	June	4	Huddersfield	3	0

v SWITZERLAND

			Eng	Swit
EC1980	Nov	18	Ipswich	5	0
EC1981	May	31	Neuenburg	0	0
1988	May	28	Lausanne	1	1
1996	April	1	Swindon	0	0
1998	Mar	24	Brugglifeld	0	2
EC2002	May	17	Zurich	2	1

v USA

			Eng	USA
1989	June	11	Toulon	0	2
1994	June	2	Toulon	3	0

v TURKEY

			Eng	Tur
EC1984	Nov	13	Bursa	0	0
EC1985	Oct	15	Bristol	3	0
EC1987	April	28	Izmir	0	0
EC1987	Oct	13	Sheffield	1	1
EC1991	April	30	Izmir	2	2
1991	Oct	15	Reading	2	0
EC1992	Nov	17	Orient	0	1
EC1993	Mar	30	Izmir	0	0
EC2000	May	29	Bratislava	6	0

v USSR

			Eng	USSR
1987	June	9	Toulon	0	0
1988	June	7	Toulon	1	0
1990	May	25	Toulon	2	1
1991	May	31	Toulon	2	1

v WALES

			Eng	Wales
1976	Dec	15	Wolverhampton	0	0
1979	Feb	6	Swansea	1	0
1990	Dec	5	Tranmere	0	0

v WEST GERMANY

			Eng	WG
EC1982	Sept	21	Sheffield	3	1
EC1982	Oct	12	Bremen	2	3
1987	Sept	8	Ludenscheid	0	2

v YUGOSLAVIA

			Eng	Yugo
EC1978	April	19	Novi Sad	1	2
EC1978	May	2	Manchester	1	1
EC1986	Nov	11	Peterborough	1	1
EC1987	Nov	10	Zemun	5	1
EC2000	Mar	29	Barcelona	3	0

ENGLAND B RESULTS 1949–2002

Year	Date		Venue	Eng	Alg
			v ALGERIA	Eng	Alg
1990	Dec	11	Algiers	0	0
			v AUSTRALIA	Eng	Aust
1980	Nov	17	Birmingham	1	0
			v AUSTRIA	Eng	Aus
1979[†]	June	12	Klagenfurt	1	0

†*Abandoned 60 mins; waterlogged pitch.*

			v CHILE	Eng	Ch
1998	Feb	10	West Bromwich	1	2
			v CIS	Eng	CIS
1992	April	28	Moscow	1	1
			v CZECHOSLOVAKIA	Eng	Cz
1978	Nov	28	Prague	1	0
1990	April	24	Sunderland	2	0
1992	Mar	24	Budejovice	1	0
			v FINLAND	Eng	Fin
1949	May	15	Helsinki	4	0
			v FRANCE	Eng	Fra
1952	May	22	Le Havre	1	7
1992	Feb	18	Loftus Road	3	0
			v WEST GERMANY	Eng	WG
1954	Mar	24	Gelsenkirchen	4	0
1955	Mar	23	Sheffield	1	1
1978	Feb	21	Augsburg	2	1

			v HOLLAND	Eng	Hol
1949	May	18	Amsterdam	4	0
1950	Feb	22	Newcastle	1	0
1952	Mar	26	Amsterdam	1	0
			v ICELAND	Eng	Ice
1989	May	19	Reykjavik	2	0
1991	April	27	Watford	1	0
			v ITALY	Eng	Italy
1950	May	11	Milan	0	5
1989	Nov	14	Brighton	1	1
			v LUXEMBOURG	Eng	Lux
1950	May	21	Luxembourg	2	1
			v MALAYSIA	Eng	Mal
1978	May	30	Kuala Lumpur	1	1
			v MALTA	Eng	Mal
1987	Oct	14	Ta'Qali	2	0
			v NEW ZEALAND	Eng	NZ
1978	June	7	Christchurch	4	0
1978	June	11	Wellington	3	1
1978	June	14	Auckland	4	0
1979	Oct	15	Leyton	4	1
1984	Nov	13	Nottingham	2	0
			v NORTHERN IRELAND	Eng	NI
1994	May	10	Sheffield	4	2

			v NORWAY	Eng	Nor
1989	May	22	Stavanger	1	0
			v REPUBLIC OF IRELAND	Eng	RoI
1990	Mar	27	Cork	1	4
1994	Dec	13	Liverpool	2	0
			v RUSSIA	Eng	Rus
1998	Apr	21	Loftus Road	4	1
			v SCOTLAND	Eng	Sco
1953	Mar	11	Edinburgh	2	2
1954	Mar	3	Sunderland	1	1
1956	Feb	29	Dundee	2	2
1957	Feb	6	Birmingham	4	1
			v SINGAPORE	Eng	Sin
1978	June	18	Singapore	8	0
			v SPAIN	Eng	Sp
1980	Mar	26	Sunderland	1	0
1981	Mar	25	Granada	2	3
1991*	Dec	18	Castellon	1	0

Spanish Olympic XI

			v SWITZERLAND	Eng	Swit
1950	Jan	18	Sheffield	5	0
1954	May	22	Basle	0	2
1956	Mar	21	Southampton	4	1
1989	May	16	Winterthur	2	0
1991	May	20	Walsall	2	1
			v USA	Eng	USA
1980	Oct	14	Manchester	1	0
			v WALES	Eng	Wales
1991	Feb	5	Swansea	1	0
			v YUGOSLAVIA	Eng	Yugo
1954	May	16	Ljubljana	1	2
1955	Oct	19	Manchester	5	1
1989	Dec	12	Millwall	2	1

BRITISH AND IRISH UNDER-21 TEAMS 2001–02

ENGLAND UNDER-21 INTERNATIONALS

14 Aug

England (1) 4 *(Vassell 6, Christie 87, Defoe 50, 90)*

Holland (0) 0   19,467

England: Taylor (Bywater 64); Young (Wright 46), Bridge (Johnson S 46), Dunn (Prutton 43), Terry (Riggott 64), Barry (Bramble 46), Greening (Pennant 67), Davis (Parker 46), Vassell (Defoe 48), Jeffers (Christie 46), Chadwick (Wilson 64).

31 Aug

Germany (0) 1 *(Metzelder 90)*   21,400

England (0) 2 *(Cole J 55, Jeffers 90)*

England: Taylor; Wright, Bridge, Davis, King, Barry, Greening, Prutton, Vassell (Jeffers 57), Cole J (Parker 75), Chadwick (Defoe 70).

4 Sept

England (1) 5 *(Jeffers 17, 59, 90, Defoe 71, Greening 89)*

Albania (0) 0   23,118

England: Taylor; Wright, Bridge, Davis (Wilson 75), King, Barry, Greening, Parker (Pennant 70), Jeffers, Defoe, Chadwick (Johnson S 63).

5 Oct

England (1) 2 *(Defoe 10, Christie 85)*

Greece (0) 1 *(Papadopoulos 90 (pen))*   29,164

England: Kirkland; Young, Bridge, Dunn, King, Barry, Pennant, Carrick, Vassell, Defoe (Christie 73), Greening (Prutton 73).

9 Nov

Holland (2) 2 *(Van der Vaart 21, Kuyt 37)*

England (1) 2 *(Davis 45, Dunn 57)*   14,500

England: Kirkland; Young, Bridge, Davis, Terry (Barry 80), King, Pennant, Carrick, Christie (Ameobi 30), Defoe, Dunn.

13 Nov

England (0) 1 *(Carrick 72)*

Holland (0) 0   32,418

England: Kirkland; Wright, Bridge, Davis, Terry, King, Pennant (Greening 68), Carrick, Ameobi, Defoe, Dunn.

12 Feb

Slovenia (0) 0

England (0) 1 *(Ameobi 65)*   350

England: Robinson (Weaver 60); Wright (Knight 60), Konchesky, Dunn (Etherington 46), Riggott, Barry, Pennant, Parker (Prutton 46), Christie, Defoe (Ameobi 61), Jenas.

26 Mar

England (0) 1 *(Barry 59)*

Italy (1) 1 *(Maccarone 15)*   21,642

England: Robinson (Bywater 79); Wright, Samuel, Prutton, Knight (Gardner 79), Barry, Wright-Phillips (Pennant 46), Jenas (Parker 46), Smith, Defoe, Etherington (Crouch 59).

16 Apr

England (0) 0

Portugal (1) 1 *(Tonel 39)*   28,000

England: Robinson (Kirkland 46); Wright (Young 70), Konchesky, Davis (Jenas 55), Riggott, Barry, Dunn (Pennant 46), Carrick, Smith (Zamora 70), Christie (Crouch 46), Johnson S (Defoe 77).

17 May

Switzerland (0) 1 *(Frei 58)*

England (1) 2 *(Defoe 3, Crouch 53)*   16,000

England: Robinson; Young, Konchesky, Davis (Prutton 34), Riggott, Barry, Pennant, Dunn, Crouch (Ameobi 78), Smith, Defoe (Parker 64).

20 May

Italy (0) 2 *(Maccarone 58, 84)*

England (0) 1 *(Barry 64)*   12,980

England: Robinson; Young, Konchesky, Davis, Knight, Riggott, Smith, Dunn, Crouch (Defoe 46), Prutton (Pennant 84), Barry (Zamora 88).

22 May

Portugal (2) 3 *(Teixeira 7, Makukula 20 (pen), Viana 69)*

England (1) 1 *(Smith 43)*   10,000

England: Robinson; Young, Konchesky, Dunn, Knight, Barry, Pennant (Parker 76), Prutton, Smith, Defoe (Zamora 66), Greening (Ameobi 31).

SCOTLAND UNDER-21 INTERNATIONALS

31 Aug

Scotland 1 *(Miller 90 (pen))*
Croatia 1

Scotland: Langfield; McCunnie (Maloney), Cummings, Caldwell S, Caldwell G, Murray, Young (Fowler), Easton, Miller, Severin, McManus (Paterson).

4 Sept

Belgium 0
Scotland 0

Scotland: Esson; Fowler, Cummings, McGuire, Caldwell G, Murray, Mason, Easton (Williams), Miller, Severin, McManus (Maloney).

5 Oct

Scotland 1 *(McNaughton 81)*
Latvia 0

Scotland: Stewart C; Fowler (Canero), Hammell (McNaughton), McGuire, Caldwell G, McCracken, Stewart M, Murray, McManus, Maloney (McPhee), Hughes.

NORTHERN IRELAND UNDER-21 INTERNATIONALS

31 Aug

Denmark 2
Northern Ireland 0

Northern Ireland: Miskelly; Kelly, McCartney (Capaldi), McAreavey (McFlynn), Simms, Holmes, Carlisle (Carson), Toner, Feeney, Kirk, McCann G.

4 Sept

Northern Ireland 1 *(McCann 45)*
Iceland 3

Northern Ireland: Miskelly; Kelly, Capaldi, Close (McAreavey), Simms, Holmes, Carlisle (McFlynn), Toner, Kirk (Feeney), Hamilton, McCann G.

5 Oct

Malta 2
Northern Ireland 2 *(Boyle 14, McCann 51)*

Northern Ireland: Miskelly; Dickson, Holmes, Kelly, Simms, McCann G (McAreavey), Carlisle, Toner (Close), Boyle (Morrison), Hamilton, Capaldi.

12 Feb

Northern Ireland 0
Germany 1

Northern Ireland: Morris (Blayney); Baird, Capaldi, Clyde, Simms (Buchanan), Melaugh, Close, McFlynn (Hunter), Braniff (McVeigh), Black, McCourt (McCann R).

WALES UNDER-21 INTERNATIONALS

31 Aug

Wales 1 *(Day 40)*
Armenia 1

Wales: Walsh; Hillier, Price (De-Vulgt), Gabbidon, Day, Valentine, Roberts, Gibson, Thomas J, Thomas S (Phillips), Maxwell (Lowe).

4 Sept

Norway 2
Wales 0

Wales: Walsh (Jones J); Hillier, Price, Gabbidon, Day, Valentine (Lowe), Roberts, Gibson, Thomas J (Gall), Thomas S, Maxwell.

5 Oct

Wales 1 *(Williams 90)*
Belarus 2

Wales: Walsh; De-Vulgt (Maxwell), Price, Valentine, Day, Phillips, Lowe, Gibson, Thomas J, Thomas S (Gall), Roberts (Williams).

REPUBLIC OF IRELAND UNDER-21 INTERNATIONALS

31 Aug

Republic of Ireland 1 *(Barrett 9)*
Holland 1

Republic of Ireland: Murphy; Quinn B, O'Shea, Gavin, Foy, Byrne S (Quinn A), McPhail, Butler, Healy, Sadlier, Barrett.

5 Oct

Republic of Ireland 3 *(Doyle 55, 60, Reid 64)*
Cyprus 0

Republic of Ireland: Roche; Thompson (Shelley), Goodwin, O'Shea, Foy, Butler, Byrne S, Miller, Doyle (Keane), Reid, Barrett (Burgess).

26 Mar

Republic of Ireland 3 *(Goodwin 21, Burgess 52, Gamble 88)*
Denmark 2

Republic of Ireland: Murphy; Shelley, Goodwin, O'Shea (O'Callaghan), Foy, Miller, Mattis (Gamble), Doyle, Butler, Burgess (Daly), Reid (Byrne S).

16 Apr

Republic of Ireland 3 *(Byrne S 12, Heffernan 16, Reid 58)*
Austria 3

Republic of Ireland: Stack; Shelley (O'Callaghan), O'Shea, Goodwin, Foy, Byrne S, Miller, Doyle (Keane), Butler, Heffernan (Cash), Reid.

BRITISH UNDER-21 APPEARANCES 1976–2002

ENGLAND

Ablett, G. (Liverpool), 1988 v F (1)

Adams, A. (Arsenal). 1985 v Ei, Fi; 1986 v D; 1987 v Se, Y (5)

Adams, N. (Everton), 1987 v Se (1)

Allen, B. (QPR), 1992 v H, M, Cz, F; 1993 v N (sub), T, P, Cz (sub) (8)

Allen, C. A. (Oxford U), 1995 v Br (sub), F (sub) (2)

Allen, C. (QPR), 1980 v EG (sub); (with C Palace), 1981 v N, R (3)

Allen, M. (QPR), 1987 v Se (sub); 1988 v Y (sub) (2)

Allen, P. (West Ham U), 1985 v Ei, R; (with Tottenham H, 1986 v R (3)

Allen, R. W. (Tottenham H), 1998 v F (sub), S.Af, Arg (sub) (3)

Ameobi, F. (Newcastle U), 2001 v Sp (sub), Fi (sub), Alb (sub), M, Gr (sub); 2002 v Ho (sub+1), Slv (sub), Sw (sub), I (sub), P (sub) (11)

Anderson, V. A. (Nottingham F), 1978 v I (1)

Anderton, D. R. (Tottenham H), 1993 v Sp, Sm, Ho, Pol, N, P, Cz, Br, S, F; 1994 v Pol, Sm (12)

Andrews, I. (Leicester C), 1987 v Se (1)

Ardley, N. C. (Wimbledon), 1993 v Pol, N, P, Cz, Br, S, F, 1994 v Pol (sub), Ho, Sm (10)

Ashcroft, L. (Preston NE), 1992 v H (sub) (1)

Atherton, P. (Coventry C), 1992 v T (1)

Atkinson, B. (Sunderland), 1991 v W (sub), Sen, M, USSR (sub), F; 1992 v Pol (sub) (6)

Awford, A. T. (Portsmouth), 1993 v Sp, N, T, P, Cz, Br, S, F; 1994 v Ho (9)

Bailey, G. R. (Manchester U), 1979 v W, Bul; 1980 v D, S (2), EG; 1982 v N; 1983 v D, Gr; 1984 v H, F (2), I, Sp (14)

Baker, G. E. (Southampton), 1981 v N, R (2)

Ball, M. J. (Everton), 1999 v Se, Bul, L, CzR, Pol; 2000 v L, D (sub) (7)

Barker, S. (Blackburn R), 1985 v Is (sub), Ei, R; 1986 v I (4)

Barmby, N. J. (Tottenham H), 1994 v D; 1995 v P, A (sub); (with Everton), 1998 v Sw (4)

Bannister, G. (Sheffield W), 1982 v Pol (1)

Barnes, J. (Watford), 1983 v D, Gr (2)

Barnes, P. S. (Manchester C), 1977 v W (sub), S, Fi, N; 1978 v N, Fi, I (2), Y (9)

Barrett, E. D. (Oldham Ath), 1990 v P, F, USSR, Cz (4)

Barry, G. (Aston Villa), 1999 v CzR, F, H; 2000 v Y; 2001 v Sp, Fi, Alb; 2002 v Ho, G, Alb, Gr, Ho (sub), Slv, I, P, Sw, I, P (18)

Bart-Williams, C. G. (Sheffield W), 1993 v Sp, N, T; 1994 v D, Ru, F, Bel, P; 1995 v P, A, Ei (2), La (2); (with Nottingham F) 1996 v P (sub), A (16)

Batty, D. (Leeds U), 1988 v Sw (sub); 1989 v Gr (sub), Bul, Sen, Ei, US; 1990 v Pol (7)

Bazeley, D. S. (Watford), 1992 v H (sub) (1)

Beagrie, P. (Sheffield U), 1988 v WG, T (2)

Beardsmore, R. (Manchester U), 1989 v Gr, Alb (sub), Pol, Bul, USA (5)

Beattie, J. S. (Southampton), 1999 v CzR (sub), F (sub), Pol, H; 2000 v Pol (5)

Beckham, D. R. J. (Manchester U), 1995 v Br, Mal, An, F; 1996 v P, A (sub), Bel, An, P (9)

Bent, M. N. (Crystal Palace), 1998 v S.Af (sub), Arg (2)

Beeston, C. (Stoke C), 1988 v USSR (1)

Benjamin, T. J. (Leicester C), 2001 v M (sub) (1)

Bertschin, K. E. (Birmingham C), 1977 v S; 1978 v Y (2) (3)

Birtles, G. (Nottingham F), 1980 v Bul, EG (sub) (2)

Blackwell, D. R. (Wimbledon), 1991 v W, T, Sen (sub), M, USSR, F (6)

Blake, M. A. (Aston Villa), 1990 v F (sub), Cz (sub); 1991 v H, Pol, Ei (2), W; 1992 v Pol (8)

Blissett, L. L. (Watford), 1979 v W, Bul, Se; 1980 v D (4)

Booth, A. D. (Huddersfield T), 1995 v La (2 subs); 1996 v N (3)

Bothroyd, J. (Coventry C), 2001 v M (sub) (1)

Bowyer, L. D. (Charlton Ath), 1996 v N (sub), Bel, P, Br; (with Leeds U), 1997 v Mol, I, Sw, Ge; 1998 v Mol; 1999 v F, Pol; 2000 v D, Arg (13)

Bracewell, P. (Stoke C), 1983 v D, Gr (1 + 1 sub), H; 1984 v D, H, F (2), I (2), Sp (2); 1985 v T (13)

Bradbury, L. M. (Portsmouth), 1997 v Pol; (with Manchester C), 1998 v Mol (sub), I (sub) (3)

Bramble, T. M. (Ipswich T), 2001 v Ge, G, Fi, Alb (sub), M; 2002 v Ho (sub) (6)

Branch, P. M. (Everton), 1997 v Pol (sub) (1)

Bradshaw, P. W. (Wolverhampton W), 1977 v W, S; 1978 v Fi, Y (4)

Breacker, T. (Luton T), 1986 v I (2) (2)

Brennan, M. (Ipswich T), 1987 v Y, Sp, T, Mor, F (5)

Bridge, W. M. (Southampton), 1999 v H (sub); 2001 v Sp; 2002 v Ho, G, Alb, Gr, Ho (2) (8)

Bridges, M. (Sunderland), 1997 v Sw (sub); 1999 v F; (with Leeds U), 2000 v D (3)

Brightwell, I. (Manchester C), 1989 v D, Alb; 1990 v Se (sub), Pol (4)

Briscoe, L. S. (Sheffield W), 1996 v Cro, Bel (sub), An, Br; 1997 v Sw (sub) (5)

Brock, K. (Oxford U), 1984 v I, Sp (2); 1986 v I (4)

Broomes, M. C. (Blackburn R), 1997 v Sw, Ge (2)

Brown, M. R. (Manchester C), 1996 v Cro, Bel, An, P (4)

Brown, W. M. (Manchester U), 1999 v Se, Bul, L, CzR, Pol, Se, Bul; 2001 v G (8)

Bull, S. G. (Wolverhampton W), 1989 v Alb (2) Pol; 1990 v Se, Pol (5)

Bullock, M. J. (Barnsley), 1998 v Gr (sub) (1)

Burrows, D. (WBA), 1989 v Se (sub); (with Liverpool), Gr, Alb (2), Pol; 1990 v Se, Pol (7)

Butcher, T. I. (Ipswich T), 1979 v Se; 1980 v D, Bul, S (2), EG (7)

Butt, N. (Manchester U), 1995 v Ei (2), La; 1996 v P, A; 1997 v Ge, Pol (7)

Butters, G. (Tottenham H), 1989 v Bul, Sen (sub), Ei (sub) (3)

Butterworth, I. (Coventry C), 1985 v T, R; (with Nottingham F), 1986 v R, T, D (2), I (2) (8)

Bywater, S. (West Ham U), 2001 v M (sub), Gr; 2002 v Ho (sub), I (sub) (4)

Cadamarteri, D. L. (Everton), 1999 v CzR (sub); 2000 v Y (sub); 2001 v M (sub) (3)

Caesar, G. (Arsenal), 1987 v Mor, USSR (sub), F (3)

Callaghan, N. (Watford), 1983 v D, Gr (sub), H (sub); 1984 v D, H, F (2), I, Sp (9)

Campbell, A. P. (Middlesbrough), 2000 v Y, T (sub), Slo (sub); 2001 v Ge (sub) (4)

Campbell, K. J. (Arsenal), 1991 v H, T (sub); 1992 v G, T (4)

Campbell, S. (Tottenham), 1994 v D, Ru, F, US, Bel, P; 1995 v P, A, Ei; 1996 v N, A (11)

Carbon, M. P. (Derby Co), 1996 v Cro (sub); 1997 v Ge, I, Sw (4)

Carr, C. (Fulham), 1985 v Ei (sub) (1)

Carr, F. (Nottingham F), 1987 v Se, Y, Sp (sub), Mor, USSR; 1988 v WG (sub), T, Y, F (9)

Carragher, J. L. (Liverpool), 1997 v I (sub), Sw, Ge, Pol; 1998 v Mol (sub), I, Gr, Sw (sub), F, S.Af, Arg; 1999 v Se, Bul, L, CzR, F, Pol, Se, Bul; 2000 v L, Pol, D, Arg, Y, I, T, Slo (27)

Carlisle, C. J. (QPR), 2001 v Ge (sub), G (sub), Fi (sub) (3)

Carrick, M. (West Ham U), 2001 v Ge, G, Fi, I, Gr; 2002 v Gr, Ho (2), P (9)

Casper, C. M. (Manchester U), 1995 v Mal (1)

Caton, T. (Manchester C), 1982 v N, H (sub), Pol (2), S; 1983 v WG (2), Gr; 1984 v D, H, F (2), I (2) (14)

Chadwick, L. H. (Manchester U), 2000 v L, D, Arg, I (sub), Slo (sub); 2001 v Ge (sub), I, Sp, Fi, Alb; 2002 v Ho, G, Alb (13)

Challis, T. M. (QPR), 1996 v An, P (2)

Chamberlain, M. (Stoke C), 1983 v Gr; 1984 v F (sub), I, Sp (4)

Chapman, L. (Stoke C), 1981 v Ei (1)

Charles, G. A. (Nottingham F), 1991 v H, W (sub), Ei; 1992 v T (4)

Chettle, S. (Nottingham F), 1988 v M, USSR, Mor, F; 1989 v D, Se, Gr, Alb (2), Bul; 1990 v Se, Pol (12)

Clark, L. R. (Newcastle U), 1992 v Cz, F; 1993 v Sp, N, T, Ho (sub), Pol (sub), Cz, Br, S; 1994 v Ho (11)

Christie, M. N. (Derby Co), 2001 v Fi (sub), Sp, Fi, Alb, M, Gr; 2002 v Ho (sub), Ho, Slv, P (11)

Clegg, M. J. (Manchester U), 1998 v Fr (sub), S.Af (sub) (2)

Clemence, S. N. (Tottenham H), 1999 v Se (sub) (1)

Clough, N. (Nottingham F), 1986 v D (sub); 1987 v Se, Y, T, USSR, F (sub), P; 1988 v WG, T, Y, S (2), M, Mor, F (15)

Cole, A. A. (Arsenal), 1992 v H, Cz (sub), F (sub); (with Bristol C), 1993 v Sm; (with Newcastle U), Pol, N; 1994 v Pol, Ho (8)

Cole, A. (Arsenal), 2001 v Ge, G, Fi, I (4)

Cole, J. J. (West Ham U), 2000 v Arg (sub); 2001 v Ge, Gr; 2002 v G (4)

Coney, D. (Fulham), 1985 v T (sub); 1986 v R; 1988 v T, WG (4)

Connor, T. (Brighton & HA), 1987 v Y (1)

Cooke, R. (Tottenham H), 1986 v D (sub) (1)

Cooke, T. J. (Manchester U), 1996 v Cro, Bel, An (sub), P (4)

Cooper, C. (Middlesbrough), 1988 v F (2), M, USSR, Mor; 1989 v D, Se, Gr (8)

Corrigan, J. T. (Manchester C), 1978 v I (2), Y (3)

Cort, C. E. R. (Wimbledon), 1999 v L (sub), CzR, H (sub), Se, Bul; 2000 v L (sub), Pol, D (sub), Arg, I, T, Slo (12)

Cottee, A. (West Ham U), 1985 v Fi (sub), Is (sub), Ei, R, Fi; 1987 v Sp, P; 1988 v WG (8)

Couzens, A. J. (Leeds U), 1995 v Mal (sub), An, F (sub) (3)

Cowans, G. S. (Aston Villa), 1979 v W, Se; 1980 v Bul, EG; 1981 v R (5)

Cox, N. J. (Aston Villa), 1993 v T, Ho, Pol, N; 1994 v Pol, Sm (6)

Cranson, I. (Ipswich T), 1985 v Fi, Is, R; 1986 v R, I (5)

Cresswell, R. P. W. (York C), 1999 v F (sub); (with Sheffield W) H (sub), Se, Bul (4)

Croft, G. (Grimsby T), 1995 v Br, Mal, An, F (4)

Crooks, G. (Stoke C), 1980 v Bul, S (2), EG (sub) (4)

Crossley, M. G. (Nottingham F), 1990 v P, USSR, Cz (3)

Crouch, P. J. (Portsmouth), 2002 v I (sub), P (sub), Sw (3)

Cundy, J. V. (Chelsea), 1991 v Ei (2); 1992 v Pol (3)

Cunningham, L. (WBA), 1977 v S, Fi, N (sub); 1978 v N, Fi, I (6)

Curbishley, L. C. (Birmingham C), 1981 v Sw (1)

Curtis, J. C. K. (Manchester U), 1998 v I (sub), Gr, Sw, F, S.Af, Arg; 1999 v Se (sub), Bul, I, CzR, F, Pol (sub), H, Se (sub), Bul; 2000 v Pol (16)

Daniel, P. W. (Hull C), 1977 v S, Fi, N; 1978 v Fi, I, Y (2) (7)

Davies, K. C. (Southampton), 1998 v Gr (sub); (with Blackburn R), 1999 v CzR; (with Southampton), 2000 v Y (sub) (3)

Davis, K. G. (Luton T), 1995 v An; 1996 v Cro (sub), P (3)

Davis, P. (Arsenal), 1982 v Pol; 1983 v D, Gr (1 + 1 sub), H; 1987 v T; 1988 v WG, T, Y, Fr (11)

Davis, S. (Fulham), 2001 v Fi, Alb, M, Gr; 2002 v Ho, G, Alb, Ho (2), P, Sw (11)

Day, C. N. (Tottenham H), 1996 v Cro, Bel, Br; (with Crystal Palace), 1997 v Mol, Ge, Sw (6)

D'Avray, M. (Ipswich T), 1984 v I, Sp (sub) (2)

Deehan, J. M. (Aston Villa), 1977 v N; 1978 v N, Fi, I; 1979 v Bul, Se; 1980 v D (7)

Defoe, J. C. (West Ham U), 2001 v M, Gr; 2002 v Ho (sub), G (sub), Alb, Gr, Ho (2), Slv, I, P (sub), Sw, I, P (14)

Dennis, M. E. (Birmingham C), 1980 v Bul; 1981 v N, R (3)

Dichio, D. S. E. (QPR), 1996 v N (sub) (1)

Dickens, A. (West Ham U), 1985 v Fi (sub) (1)

Dicks, J. (West Ham U), 1988 v Sw (sub), M, Mor, F (4)

Digby, F. (Swindon T), 1987 v Sp (sub), USSR, P; 1988 v T; 1990 v Pol (5)

Dillon, K. P. (Birmingham C), 1981 v R (1)

Dixon, K. (Chelsea), 1985 v Fi (1)

Dobson, A. (Coventry C), 1989 v Bul, Sen, Ei, US (4)

Dodd, J. R. (Southampton), 1991 v Pol, Ei, T, Sen, M, F; 1992 v G, Pol (8)

Donowa, L. (Norwich C), 1985 v Is, R (sub), Fi (sub) (3)

Dorigo, A. (Aston Villa), 1987 v Se, Sp, T, Mor, USSR, F, P; 1988 v WG, Y, S (2) (11)

Dozzell, J. (Ipswich T), 1987 v Se, Y (sub), Sp, USSR, F, P; 1989 v Se, Gr (sub); 1990 v Se (sub) (9)

Draper, M. A. (Notts Co), 1991 v Ei (sub); 1992 v G, Pol (3)

Duberry, M. W. (Chelsea), 1997 v Mol, Pol, Ge; 1998 v Mol, Gr (5)

Dunn, D. J. I. (Blackburn R), 1999 v CzR (sub); 2000 v I (sub), T, Slo; 2001 v Ge, G, Fi, I, Sp, M, Gr; 2002 v Ho, Gr, Ho (2), Slv, P, Sw, I, P (20)

Duxbury, M. (Manchester U), 1981 v Sw (sub), Ei (sub), R (sub), Sw; 1982 v N; 1983 v WG (2) (7)

Dyer, B. A. (Crystal Palace), 1994 v Ru, F, US, Bel, P; 1995 v P (sub); 1996 v Cro; 1997 v Mol, Ge; 1998 v Mol, Gr (10)

Dyer, K. C. (Ipswich T), 1998 v Mol, I, Gr, Sw, S.Af, Arg; 1999 v Se, Bul, CzR, Se; (with Newcastle U), 2000 v Y (11)

Dyson, P. I. (Coventry C), 1981 v N, R, Sw, Ei (4)

Eadie, D. M. (Norwich C), 1994 v F (sub), US; 1997 v Mol, Ge (2), I; 1998 v I (7)

Ebbrell, J. (Everton), 1989 v Sen, Ei, US (sub); 1990 v P, F, USSR, Cz; 1991 v H, Pol, Ei, W, T; 1992 v G, T (14)

Edghill, R. A. (Manchester C), 1994 v D, Ru; 1995 v A (3)

Ehiogu, U. (Aston Villa), 1992 v H, M, Cz, F; 1993 v Sp, N, T, Sm, T, Ho, Pol, N; 1994 v Pol, Ho, Sm (15)

Elliott, P. (Luton T), 1985 v Fi; 1986 v T, D (3)

Elliott, R. J. (Newcastle U), 1996 v P, A (2)

Elliott, S. W. (Derby Co), 1998 v F, Arg (sub) (2)

Etherington, N, (Tottenham H), 2002 v Slv (sub), I (2)

Euell, J. J. (Wimbledon), 1998 v F, Arg (sub); 1999 v Se (sub), Bul (se), Pol (sub), H (6)

Fairclough, C. (Nottingham F), 1985 v T, Is, Ei; 1987 v·Sp, T; (with Tottenham H), 1988 v Y, F (7)

Fairclough, D. (Liverpool), 1977 v W (1)

Fashanu, J. (Norwich C), 1980 v EG; 1981 v N (sub), R, Sw, Ei (sub), H; (with Nottingham F), 1982 v N, H, Pol, S; 1983 v WG (sub) (11)

Fear, P. (Wimbledon), 1994 v Ru, F, US (sub) (3)

Fenton, G. A. (Aston Villa), 1995 v Ei (1)

Fenwick, T. W. (C Palace), 1981 v N, R, Sw, Ei; (with QPR); R; 1982 v N, H, S (2); 1983 v WG (2) (11)

Ferdinand, R. G. (West Ham U), 1997 v Sw, Ge; 1998 v I, Gr; 2000 v Y (5)

Fereday, W. (QPR), 1985 v T, Ei (sub). Fi; 1986 v T (sub), I (5)

Flitcroft, G. W. (Manchester C), 1993 v Sm, Hol, N, P, Cz, Br, S, F; 1994 v Pol, Ho (10)

Flowers, T. (Southampton), 1987 v Mor, F; 1988 v WG (sub) (3)

Ford, M. (Leeds U), 1996 v Cro; 1997 v Mol (2)

Forster, N. M. (Brentford), 1995 v Br, Mal, An, F (4)

Forsyth, M. (Derby Co), 1988 v Sw (1)

Foster, S. (Brighton & HA), 1980 v EG (sub) (1)

Fowler, R. B. (Liverpool), 1994 v Sm, Ru, F, US; 1995 v P, A; 1996 v P, A (8)

Froggatt, S. J. (Aston Villa), 1993 v Sp, Sm (sub) (2)

Futcher, P. (Luton T), 1977 v W, S, Fi, N; (with Manchester C), 1978 v N, Fi, I (2), Y (2); 1979 v D (11)

Gabbiadini, M. (Sunderland), 1989 v Bul, USA (2)

Gale, A. (Fulham), 1982 v Pol (1)

Gallen, K. A. (QPR), 1995 v Ei, La (2); 1996 v Cro (4)

Gardner, A. (Tottenham H), 2002 v I (sub) (1)

Gascoigne, P. (Newcastle U), 1987 v Mo, USSR, P; 1988 v WG, Y, S (2), F (2), Sw, M, USSR (sub), Mor (13)

Gayle, H. (Birmingham C), 1984 v I, Sp (2) (3)

Gernon, T. (Ipswich T), 1983 v Gr (1)

Gerrard, P. W. (Oldham Ath), 1993 v T, Ho, Pol, N, P, Cz, Br, S, F; 1994 v D, Ru; 1995 v P, A, Ei (2), La (2); 1996 v P (18)

Gerrard, S. G. (Liverpool), 2000 v L, Pol, D, Y (4)

Gibbs, N. (Watford), 1989 v Mor, USSR, F, P; 1988 v T (5)

Gibson, C. (Aston Villa), 1982 v N (1)

Gilbert, W. A. (C Palace), 1979 v W, Bul; 1980 v Bul; 1981 v N, R, Sw, R, Sw, H; 1982 v N (sub), H (11)

Goddard, P. (West Ham U), 1981 v N, Sw, Ei (sub); 1982 v N (sub), Pol, S; 1983 v WG (2) (8)

Gordon, D. (Norwich C), 1987 v T (sub), Mor (sub), F, P (4)

Gordon, D. D. (Crystal Palace), 1994 v Ru, F, US, Bel, P; 1995 v P, A, Ei (2), La (2); 1996 v P, N (13)

Grant, A. J. (Everton), 1996 v An (sub) (1)

Granville, D. P. (Chelsea), 1997 v Ge (sub), Pol; 1998 v Mol (3)

Gray, A. (Aston Villa), 1988 v S, F (2)

Greening, J. (Manchester U), 1999 v H, Se (sub), Bul; 2000 v Pol; 2001 v Ge, G, Fi, I, Sp (sub), Fi, Alb; (with Middlesbrough), 2002 v Ho, G, Alb, Gr, Ho (sub), I, P (18)

Griffin, A. (Newcastle U), 1999 v H; 2001 v I, Sp (3)

Guppy, S. A. (Leicester C), 1998 v Sw (1)

Haigh, P. (Hull C), 1977 v N (sub) (1)

Hall, M. T. J. (Coventry C), 1997 v Pol (2), I, Sw, Ge; 1998 v Mol, Gr (2) (8)

Hall, R. A. (Southampton), 1992 v H (sub), F; 1993 v Sm, T, Ho, Pol, P, Cz, Br, S, F (11)

Hamilton, D. V. (Newcastle U), 1997 v Pol (1)

Hardyman, P. (Portsmouth), 1985 v Ei; 1986 v D (2)

Hargreaves, O. (Bayern Munich), 2001 v Ge (sub), I, Sp (3)

Harley, J. (Chelsea), 2000 v Arg (sub), T (sub), Slo (3)

Hateley, M. (Coventry C), 1982 v Pol, S; 1983 v Gr (2), H; (with Portsmouth), 1984 v F (2), I, Sp (2) (10)

Hayes, M. (Arsenal), 1987 v Sp, T; 1988 v F (sub) (3)

Hazell, R. J. (Wolverhampton W), 1979 v D (1)

Heaney, N. A. (Arsenal), 1992 v H, M, Cz, F; 1993 v N, T (6)

Heath, A. (Stoke C), 1981 v R, Sw, H; 1982 v N, H; (with Everton), Pol, S; 1983 v WG (8)

Hendon, I. M. (Tottenham H), 1992 v H, M, Cz, F; 1993 v Sp, N, T (7)

Hendrie, L. A.'(Aston Villa), 1996 v Cro (sub); 1998 v Sw (sub); 1999 v Se, Bul, L, F, Pol; 2000 v L, D, Arg, Y, I, Slo (sub) (13)

Hesford, I. (Blackpool), 1981 v Ei (sub), Pol (2), S (2); 1983 v WG (2) (7)

Heskey, E. W. I. (Leicester C), 1997 v I, Ge, Pol (2); 1998 v I, Gr (2), Sw, F, S.Af, Arg; 1999 v Se, Bul, L; 2000 v L; (with Liverpool), Y (16)

Hilaire, V. (C Palace), 1980 v Bul, S (1+1 sub), EG (2); 1981 v N, R, Sw (sub); 1982 v Pol (sub) (9)

Hill, D. R. L. (Tottenham H), 1995 v Br, Mal, An, F (4)

Hillier, D. (Arsenal), 1991 v T (1)

Hinchcliffe, A. (Manchester C), 1989 v D (1)

Hinshelwood, P. A. (C Palace), 1978 v N; 1980 v EG (2)

Hirst, D. (Sheffield W), 1988 v USSR, F; 1989 v D, Bul (sub), Sen, Ei, US (7)

Hislop, N. S. (Newcastle U), 1998 v Sw (1)

Hoddle, G. (Tottenham H), 1977 v W (sub); 1978 v Fi (sub), I (2), Y; 1979 v D, W, Bul; 1980 v S (2), EG (2) (12)

Hodge, S. (Nottingham F), 1983 v Gr (sub); 1984 v D, F, I, Sp (2); (with Aston Villa), 1986 v R, T (8)

Hodgson, D. J. (Middlesbrough), 1981 v N, R (sub), Sw, Ei; 1982 v Pol; 1983 v WG (6)

Holdsworth, D. (Watford), 1989 v Gr (sub) (1)

Holland, C. J. (Newcastle U), 1995 v La; 1996 v N (sub), A (sub), Cro, Bel, An, Br; 1997 v Mol, Pol, Sw (10)

Holland, P. (Mansfield T), 1995 v Br, Mal, An, F (4)

Holloway, D. (Sunderland), 1998 v Sw (sub) (1)

Horne, B. (Millwall), 1989 v Gr (sub), Pol, Bul, Ei, US (5)

Howe, E. J. F. (Bournemouth), 1998 v S.Af (sub), Arg (2)

Hucker, P. (QPR), 1984 v I, Sp (2)

Huckerby, D. (Coventry C), 1997 v I (sub), Sw, Ge (sub), Pol (sub) (4)

Hughes, J. (Arsenal), 1997 v I, Sw, Ge, Pol; 1998 v Mol, I, Gr, Sw (sub) (8)

Humphreys, R. J. (Sheffield W), 1997 v Pol, Ge (sub), Sw (3)

Impey, A. R. (QPR), 1993 v T (1)

Ince, P. (West Ham U), 1989 v Alb; 1990 v Se (2)

Jackson, M. A. (Everton), 1992 v H, M, Cz, F; 1993 v Sm (sub), T, Ho, Pol, N; 1994 v Pol (10)

James, D. (Watford), 1991 v Ei (2), T, Sen, M, USSR, F; 1992 v G, T, Pol (10)

James, J. C. (Luton T), 1990 v F, USSR (2)

Jansen, M. B (Crystal Palace), 1999 v Se, Bul, L; (with Blackburn R) F (sub), Pol; 2000 v I (sub) (6)

Jeffers, F. (Everton), 2000 v L, Arg, I, T, Slo; 2001 v Ge; (with Arsenal), 2002 v Ho, G (sub), Alb (9)

Jemson, N. B. (Nottingham F), 1991 v W (1)

Jenas, J. A. (Newcastle U), 2002 v Slv, I, P (sub) (3)

Joachim, J. K. (Leicester C), 1994 v D (sub); 1995 v P, A, Ei, Br, Mal, An, F; 1996 v N (9)

Johnson, S. A. M. (Crewe Alex), 1999 v L (sub), CzR (sub), F (sub), Pol; (with Derby Co), Se, Bul; 2000 v D, Arg (sub), Y, I, T; 2001 v Fi; 2002 v Ho (sub), Alb (sub); (with Leeds U), P (15)

Johnson, T. (Notts Co), 1991 v H (sub), Ei (sub); 1992 v G, T, Pol; (with Derby Co), M, Cz (sub) (7)

Johnston, C. P. (Middlesbrough), 1981 v N, Ei (2)

Jones, D. R. (Everton), 1977 v W (1)

Jones, C. H. (Tottenham H), 1978 v Y (sub) (1)

Jones, R. (Liverpool), 1993 v Sm, Ho (2)

Keegan, G. A. (Manchester C), 1977 v W (1)

Kenny, W. (Everton), 1993 v T (1)

Keown, M. (Aston Villa), 1987 v Sp, Mor, USSR, P; 1988 v T, S, F (2) (8)

Kerslake, D. (QPR), 1986 v T (1)

Kilcline, B. (Notts C), 1983 v D, Gr (2)

King, A. E. (Everton), 1977 v W; 1978 v Y (2)

King, L. B. (Tottenham H), 2000 v L (sub), I, T, Slo; 2001 v I, Sp (sub), Fi; 2002 v G, Alb, Gr, Ho (2) (12)

Kirkland, C. E. (Coventry C), 2001 v M; (with Liverpool), 2002 v Gr, Ho (2), P (sub) (5)

Kitson, P. (Leicester C), 1991 v Sen (sub), M, F; 1992 v Pol; (with Derby Co), M, Cz, F (7)

Knight, A. (Portsmouth), 1983 v Gr, H (2)

Knight, I. (Sheffield W), 1987 v Se (sub), Y (2)

Knight, Z. (Fulham), 2002 v Slv (sub), I (2), P (4)

Konchesky, P. M. (Charlton Ath), 2002 v Slv, P, Sw, I, P (5)

Kozluk, R. (Derby Co), 1998 v F, Arg (sub) (2)

Lake, P. (Manchester C), 1989 v D, Alb (2), Pol; 1990 v Pol (5)

Lampard, F. J. (West Ham U), 1998 v Gr (2), Sw, F, S.Af, Arg; 1999 v Se, Bul, L, CzR, F, Pol, Se; 2000 v L, Arg, Y, I, T, Slo (19)

Langley, T. W. (Chelsea), 1978 v I (sub) (1)

Lee, D. J. (Chelsea), 1990 v F; 1991 v H, Pol, Ei (2), T, Sen, USSR, F; 1992 v Pol (10)

Lee, R. (Charlton Ath), 1986 v I (sub); 1987 v Se (sub) (2)

Lee, S. (Liverpool), 1981 v R, Sw, H; 1982 v S; 1983 v WG (2) (6)

Le Saux, G. (Chelsea), 1990 v P, F, USSR, Cz (4)

Lowe, D. (Ipswich T), 1988 v F, Sw (sub) (2)

Lukic, J. (Leeds U), 1981 v N, R, Ei, R, Sw, H; 1982 v H (7)

Lund, G. (Grimsby T), 1985 v T; 1986 v R, T (3)

McCall, S. H. (Ipswich T), 1981 v Sw, H; 1982 v H, S; 1983 v WG (2) (6)

McDonald, N. (Newcastle U), 1987 v Se (sub), Sp, T; 1988 v WG, Y (sub) (5)

McGrath, L. (Coventry C), 1986 v D (1)

MacKenzie, S. (WBA), 1982 v N, S (2) (3)

McLeary, A. (Millwall), 1988 v Sw (1)

McMahon, S. (Everton), 1981 v Ei; 1982 v Pol; 1983 v D, Gr (2); (with Aston Villa), 1984 v H (6)

McManaman, S. (Liverpool), 1991 v W, M (sub); 1993 v N, T, Sm, T; 1994 v Pol (7)

Mabbutt, G. (Bristol R), 1982 v Pol (2), S; (with Tottenham H), 1983 v D; 1984 v F; 1986 v D, I (7)

Makin, C. (Oldham Ath), 1994 v Ru (sub), F, US, Bel, P (5)

Marriott, A. (Nottingham F), 1992 v M (1)

Marsh, S. T. (Oxford U), 1998 v F (1)

Marshall, A. J. (Norwich C), 1995 v Mal, An; 1997 v Pol, I (4)

Marshall, I. K. (Norwich C), 1999 v F (sub) (1)

Martin, L. (Manchester U), 1989 v Gr (sub), Alb (sub) (2)

Martyn, N. (Bristol R), 1988 v S (sub), M, USSR, Mor, F; 1989 v D, Se, Gr, Alb (2); 1990 v Se (11)

Matteo, D. (Liverpool), 1994 v F (sub), Bel, P; 1998 v Sw (4)

Matthew, D. (Chelsea), 1990 v P, USSR (sub), Cz; 1991 v Ei, M, USSR, F; 1992 v G (sub), T (9)

May, A. (Manchester C), 1986 v I (sub) (1)

Merson, P. (Arsenal), 1989 v D, Gr, Pol (sub); 1990 v Pol (4)

Middleton, J. (Nottingham F), 1977 v Fi, N; (with Derby Co), 1978 v N (3)

Miller, A. (Arsenal), 1988 v Mor (sub); 1989 v Sen; 1991 v H, Pol (4)

Mills, D. J. (Charlton Ath), 1999 v Se, Bul (sub), L, Pol, H, Se; (with Leeds U), 2000 v L, Pol, D, Arg, Y (sub), I, T, Slo (14)

Mills, G. R. (Nottingham F), 1981 v R; 1982 v N (2)

Mimms, R. (Rotherham U), 1985 v Is (sub), Ei (sub); (with Everton), 1986 v I (3)

Minto, S. C. (Charlton Ath), 1991 v W; 1992 v H, M, Cz; 1993 v T; 1994 v Ho (6)

Moore, I. (Tranmere R), 1996 v Cro (sub), Bel (sub), An, P, Br; 1997 v Mol (sub); (with Nottingham F), Sw (sub) (7)

Moran, S. (Southampton), 1982 v N (sub); 1984 v F (2)

Morgan, S. (Leicester C), 1987 v Se, Y (2)

Morris, J. (Chelsea), 1997 v Pol (sub), Sw (sub), Ge (sub); 1999 v Bul (sub), L (sub), CzR; 2000 v Pol (7)

Mortimer, P. (Charlton Ath), 1989 v Sen, Ei (2)

Moses, A. P. (Barnsley), 1997 v Pol; 1998 v Gr (sub) (2)

Moses, R. M. (WBA), 1981 v N (sub), Sw, Ei, R, Sw, H; 1982 v N (sub); (with Manchester U), H (8)

Mountfield, D. (Everton), 1984 v Sp (1)

Muggleton, C. D. (Leicester C), 1990 v F (1)

Mullins, H. I. (Crystal Palace), 1999 v Pol (sub), H, Bul (3)

Murphy, D. B. (Liverpool), 1998 v Mol, Gr (sub); 2000 v T, Slo (4)

Murray, P. (QPR), 1997 v I, Pol; 1998 v I, Gr (4)

Mutch, A. (Wolverhampton W), 1989 v Pol (1)

Myers, A. (Chelsea), 1995 v Br, Mal, An (sub), F (4)

Naylor, L. M. (Wolverhampton W), 2000 v Arg; 2001 v M, Gr (3)

Nethercott, S. (Tottenham), 1994 v D, Ru, F, US, Bel, P; 1995 v La (2) (8)

Neville, P. J. (Manchester U), 1995 v Br, Mal, An, F; 1996 v P, N (sub); 1997 v Ge (7)

Newell, M. (Luton T), 1986 v D (1 + 1 sub), I (1 + 1 sub) (4)

Newton, A. L. (West Ham U), 2001 v Ge (1)

Newton, E. J. I. (Chelsea), 1993 v T (sub); 1994 v Sm (2)

Newton, S. O. (Charlton Ath), 1997 v Mol, Pol, Ge (3)

Nicholls, A. (Plymouth Arg), 1994 v F (1)

Oakes, M. C. (Aston Villa), 1994 v D (sub), F (sub), US, Bel, P; 1996 v A (6)

Oakes, S. J. (Luton T), 1993 v Br (sub) (1)

Oakley, M. (Southampton), 1997 v Ge; 1998 v F, S.Af, Arg (4)

O'Brien, A. J. (Bradford C), 1999 v F (1)

O'Connor, J. (Everton), 1996 v Cro, An, Br (3)

Oldfield, D. (Luton T), 1989 v Se (1)

Olney, I. A. (Aston Villa), 1990 v P, F, USSR, Cz; 1991 v H, Pol, Ei (2), T; 1992 v Pol (sub) (10)

Ord, R. J. (Sunderland), 1991 v W, M, USSR (3)

Osman, R. C. (Ipswich T), 1979 v W (sub), Se; 1980 v D, S (2), EG (2) (7)

Owen, G. A. (Manchester C), 1977 v S, Fi, N; 1978 v N, Fi, I (2), Y; 1979 v D, W; (with WBA), Bul, Se (sub); 1980 v D, S (2), EG; 1981 v Sw, R; 1982 v N (sub), H; 1983 v WG (2) (22)

Owen, M. J. (Liverpool), 1998 v Gr (1)

Painter, I. (Stoke C), 1986 v I (1)

Palmer, C. (Sheffield W), 1989 v Bul, Sen, Ei, US (4)

Parker, G. (Hull C), 1986 v I (2); (with Nottingham F), F; 1987 v Se, Y, Sp (6)

Parker, P. (Fulham), 1985 v Fi, T, Is (sub), Ei, R, Fi; 1986 v T, D (8)

Parker, S. M. (Charlton Ath), 2001 v Ge (sub), G, Fi (sub), Alb (sub); 2002 v Ho (sub), G (sub), Alb, Slv, I (sub), Sw (sub), I (sub), P (sub) (12)

Parkes, P. B. F. (QPR), 1979 v D (1)

Parkin, S. (Stoke C), 1987 v Sp (sub); 1988 v WG (sub), T, S (sub), F (5)

Parlour, R. (Arsenal), 1992 v H, M, Cz, F; 1993 v Sp, N, T; 1994 v D, Ru, Bel, P; 1995 v A (12)

Peach, D. S. (Southampton), 1977 v S, Fi, N; 1978 v N, I (2) (6)

Peake, A. (Leicester C), 1982 v Pol (1)

Pearce, I. A. (Blackburn R), 1995 v Ei, La; 1996 v N (3)

Pearce, S. (Nottingham F), 1987 v Y (1)

Pennant, J. (Arsenal), 2001 v M (sub); 2002 v Ho (sub), Alb (sub), Gr, Ho (2), Slv, I (sub), P (sub), Sw, I, P (13)

Pickering N. (Sunderland), 1983 v D (sub), Gr, H; 1984 v F (sub + 1), I (2), Sp; 1985 v Is, R, Fi; 1986 v R, T; (with Coventry C), D, I (15)

Platt, D. (Aston Villa), 1988 v M, Mor, F (3)

Plummer, C. S. (QPR), 1996 v Cro (sub), Bel, An, P (sub), Br (5)

Pollock, J. (Middlesbrough), 1995 v Ei (sub); 1996 v N, A (3)

Porter, G. (Watford), 1987 v Sp (sub), T, Mor, USSR, F, P (sub); 1988 v T (sub), Y, S (2), F, Sw (12)

Potter, G. S. (Southampton), 1997 v Mol (1)

Pressman, K. (Sheffield W), 1989 v D (sub) (1)

Proctor, M. (Middlesbrough), 1981 v Ei (sub), Sw; (with Nottingham F) 1982 v N, Pol (4)

Prutton, D. T. (Nottingham F), 2001 v Ge (sub), G (sub), Fi, Sp (sub), M, Gr (sub); 2002 v Ho (sub), G, Gr (sub), Slv (sub), I, Sw (sub), I, P (14)

Purse, D. J. (Birmingham C), 1998 v F. S.Af (2)

Quashie, N. F. (QPR), 1997 v Pol; 1998 v Mol, Gr, Sw (4)

Quinn, W. R. (Sheffield U), 1998 v Mol (sub), I (2)

Ramage, C. D. (Derby Co), 1991 v Pol (sub), W; 1992 v Fr (sub) (3)

Ranson, R. (Manchester C), 1980 v Bul, EG; 1981 v R (sub), R, Sw (1 + 1 sub), H, Pol (2), S (10)

Redknapp, J. F. (Liverpool), 1993 v Sm, Pol, N, P, Cz, Br, S, F; 1994 v Pol, Ho (sub), D, Ru, F, US, Bel, P; 1995 v P, A; 1998 v Sw (19)

Redmond, S. (Manchester C), 1988 v F (2), M, USSR, Mor, F; 1989 v D, Se, Gr, Alb (2), Pol; 1990 v Se, Pol (14)

Reeves, K. P. (Norwich C), 1978 v I, Y (2); 1979 v N, W, Bul, Sw; 1980 v D, S; (with Manchester C) EG (10)

Regis, C. (WBA), 1979 v D, Bul, Se; 1980 v S, EG; 1983 v D (6)

Reid, N. S. (Manchester C), 1981 v H (sub); 1982 v H, Pol (2), S (2) (6)

Reid, P. (Bolton W), 1977 v S, Fi, N; 1978 v Fi, I, Y (6)

Richards, D. I. (Wolverhampton W), 1995 v Br, Mal, An, F (4)

Richards, J. P. (Wolverhampton W), 1977 v Fi, N (2)

Rideout, P. (Aston Villa), 1985 v Fi, Is, Ei (sub), R; (with Bari), 1986 v D (5)

Riggott, C. M. (Derby Co), 2001 v Sp (sub), Fi (sub), Alb, M (sub); 2002 v Ho (sub), Slv, P, Sw (8)

Ripley, S. (Middlesbrough), 1988 v USSR, F (sub); 1989 v D (sub), Se, Gr, Alb (2); 1990 v Se (8)

Ritchie, A. (Brighton & HA), 1982 v Pol (1)

Rix, G. (Arsenal), 1978 v Fi (sub), Y; 1979 v D, Se; 1980 v D (sub), Bul, S (7)

Roberts, A. J. (Millwall), 1995 v Ei, La (2); (with C Palace), 1996 v N, A (5)

Roberts, B. J. (Middlesbrough), 1997 v Sw (sub) (1)

Robins, M. G. (Manchester U), 1990 v P, F, USSR, Cz; 1991 v H (sub), Pol (6)

Robinson, P. P. (Watford), 1999 v Se, Bul; 2000 v Pol (3)

Robinson, P. W. (Leeds U), 2000 v D; 2001 v Ge, G, Fi, Sp; 2002 v Slv, I, P, Sw, I, P (11)

Robson, B. (WBA), 1979 v W, Bul (sub), Se; 1980 v D, Bul, S (2) (7)

Robson, S. (Arsenal), 1984 v I; 1985 v Fi, Is, Fi; 1986 v R, I (with West Ham U); 1988 v S, Sw (8)

Rocastle, D. (Arsenal), 1987 v Se, Y, Sp, T; 1988 v WG, T, Y, S (2), F (2 subs), M, USSR, Mor (14)

Roche, L. P. (Manchester U), 2001 v Fi (1)

Rodger, G. (Coventry C), 1987 v USSR, F, P; 1988 v WG (4)

Rogers, A. (Nottingham F), 1998 v F, S.Af, Arg (3)

Rosario, R. (Norwich C), 1987 v T (sub), Mor, F, P (sub) (4)

Rose, M. (Arsenal), 1997 v Ge (sub), I (2)

Rowell, G. (Sunderland), 1977 v Fi (1)

Ruddock, N. (Southampton), 1989 v Bul (sub), Sen, Ei, US (4)

Rufus, R. R. (Charlton Ath), 1996 v Cro, Bel, An, P, Br; 1997 v I (6)

Ryan, J. (Oldham Ath), 1983 v H (1)

Ryder, S.H. (Walsall), 1995 v Br, An, F (3)

Samuel, J. (Aston Villa), 2002 v I (1)

Samways, V. (Tottenham H), 1988 v Sw (sub), USSR, F; 1989 v D, Se (5)

Sansom, K. G. (C Palace), 1979 v D, W, Bul, Se; 1980 v S (2), EG (2) (8)

Scimeca, R. (Aston Villa), 1996 v P; 1997 v Mol, Pol, Ge, I; 1998 v Mol, I, Gr (2) (9)

Scowcroft, J. B. (Ipswich T), 1997 v Pol, Ge (2), I (sub); 1998 v Gr (sub) (5)

Seaman, D. (Birmingham C), 1985 v Fi, T, Is, Ei, R, Fi; 1986 v R, F, D, I (10)

Sedgley, S. (Coventry C), 1987 v USSR, F (sub), P; 1988 v F; 1989 v D (sub), Se, Gr, Alb (2), Pol; (with Tottenham H), 1990 v Se (11)

Sellars, S. (Blackburn R), 1988 v S (sub), F, Sw (3)

Selley, I. (Arsenal), 1994 v Ru (sub), F (sub), US (3)

Serrant, C. (Oldham Ath), 1998 v Gr (2) (2)

Sharpe, L. (Manchester U), 1989 v Gr; 1990 v P (sub), F, USSR, Cz; 1991 v H, Pol (sub), Ei (8)

Shaw, G. R. (Aston Villa), 1981 v Ei, Sw, H; 1982 v H, S; 1983 v WG (2) (7)

Shearer, A. (Southampton), 1991 v Ei (2), W, T, Sen, M, USSR, F; 1992 v G, T, Pol (11)

Shelton, G. (Sheffield W), 1985 v Fi (1)

Sheringham, T. (Millwall), 1988 v Sw (1)

Sheron, M. N. (Manchester C), 1992 v H, F; 1993 v N (sub), T (sub), Sm, Ho, Pol, N, P, Cz, Br, S, F; 1994 v Pol (sub), Ho, Sm (16)

Sherwood, T. A. (Norwich C), 1990 v P, F, USSR, Cz (4)

Shipperley, N. J. (Chelsea), 1994 v Sm (sub); (with Southampton) 1995 v Ei, La (2); 1996 v P, N, A (7)

Simonsen, S. P. A. (Tranmere R), 1998 v F; (with Everton), 1999 v CzR, F, Bul (4)

Simpson, P. (Manchester C), 1986 v D (sub); 1987 v Y, Mor, F, P (5)

Sims, S. (Leicester C), 1977 v W, S, Fi, N; 1978 v N, Fi, I (2), Y (2) (10)

Sinclair, T. (QPR), 1994 v Ho, Sm, D, Ru, F, US, Bel, P; 1995 v P, Ei (2), La; 1996 v P; (with West Ham U), 1998 v Sw (5)

Sinnott, L. (Watford), 1985 v Is (sub) (1)

Slade, S. A. (Tottenham H), 1996 v Bel, An, P, Br (4)

Slater, S. I. (West Ham U), 1990 v P, USSR (sub), Cz (sub) (3)

Small, B. (Aston Villa), 1993 v Sm, T, Ho, Pol, N, P, Cz, Br, S, F; 1994 v Pol, Sm (12)

Smith, A. (Leeds U), 2000 v D, Arg (sub); 2001 v G, Fi, Sp; 2002 v I, P, Sw, I, P (10)

Smith, D. (Coventry C), 1988 v M, USSR (sub), Mor; 1989 v D, Se, Alb (2), Pol; 1990 v Se, Pol (10)

Smith, M. (Sheffield W), 1981 v Ei, R, Sw, H; 1982 v Pol (sub) (5)

Smith, M. (Sunderland), 1995 v Ei (sub) (1)

Smith, T. W. (Watford), 2001 v Ge (sub) (1)

Snodin, I. (Doncaster R), 1985 v T, Is, R, Fi (4)

Statham, B. (Tottenham H), 1988 v Sw; 1989 v D (sub), Se (3)

Statham, D. J. (WBA), 1978 v Fi, 1979 v W, Bul, Se; 1980 v D; 1983 v D (6)

Stein, B. (Luton T), 1984 v D, H, I (3)

Sterland, M. (Sheffield W), 1984 v D, H, F (2), I, Sp (2) (7)

Steven, T. (Everton), 1985 v Fi, T (2)

Stevens, G. (Brighton & HA), 1983 v H; (with Tottenham H), 1984 v H, F (1+1 sub), I (sub), Sp (1+1 sub); 1986 v I (8)

Stewart, P. (Manchester C), 1988 v F (1)

Stockdale, R. K. (Middlesbrough), 2001 v Ge (sub) (1)

Stuart, G. C. (Chelsea), 1990 v P (sub), F, USSR, Cz; 1991 v T (sub) (5)

Stuart, J. C. (Charlton Ath), 1996 v Bel, An, P, Br (4)

Suckling, P. (Coventry C), 1986 v D; (with Manchester C), 1987 v Se (sub), Y, Sp, T; (with C Palace), 1988 v S (2), F (2), Sw (10)

Summerbee, N.J. (Swindon T), 1993 v P (sub), S (sub), F (3)

Sunderland, A. (Wolverhampton W), 1977 v W (1)

Sutton, C. R. (Norwich), 1993 v Sp (sub), T (sub + 1),Ho, P (sub), Cz, Br, S, F; 1994 v Pol, Ho, Sm, D (13)

Swindlehurst, D. (C Palace), 1977 v W (1)

Sutch, D. (Norwich C), 1992 v H, M, Cz; 1993 v T (4)

Talbot, B. (Ipswich T), 1977 v W (1)

Taylor, M. (Blackburn R), 2001 v M (sub) (1)

Taylor, S. J. (Arsenal), 2002 v Ho, G, Alb (3)

Terry, J. G. (Chelsea), 2001 v Fi, Sp, Fi, Alb, M, Gr; 2002 v Ho (3) (9)

Thatcher, B. D. (Millwall), 1996 v Cro; (with Wimbledon), 1997 v Mol, Pol; 1998 v I (4)

Thelwell, A. A. (Tottenham H), 2001 v Sp (sub) (1)

Thirlwell, P. (Sunderland), 2001 v Ge (sub) (1)

Thomas, D. (Coventry C), 1981 v Ei; 1983 v WG (2), Gr, H; (with Tottenham H), I, Sp (7)

Thomas, M. (Luton T), 1986 v T, D, I (3)

Thomas, M. (Arsenal), 1988 v Y, S, F (2), M, USSR, Mor; 1989 v Gr, Alb (2), Pol; 1990 v Se (12)

Thomas, R. E. (Watford), 1990 v P (1)

Thompson, A. (Bolton W), 1995 v La; 1996 v P (2)

Thompson, D. A. (Liverpool), 1997 v Pol (sub), Ge; 2000 v L (sub), Pol (sub), D (sub), I, T (sub) (7)

Thompson, G. L. (Coventry C), 1981 v R, Sw, H; 1982 v N, H, S (6)

Thorn, A. (Wimbledon), 1988 v WG (sub), Y, S, F, Sw (5)

Thornley, B. L. (Manchester U), 1996 v Bel, P, Br (3)

Tiler, C. (Barnsley), 1990 v P, USSR, Cz; 1991 v H, Pol, Ei (2), T, Sen, USSR, F; (with Nottingham F), 1992 v G, T (13)

Unsworth, D. G. (Everton), 1995 v A, Ei (2), La; 1996 v N, A (6)

Upson, M. J. (Arsenal), 1999 v Se, Bul, L, F; 2000 v L, Pol, D; 2001 v I, Sp (sub), M (sub), Gr (11)

Vassell, D. (Aston Villa), 1999 v H (sub); 2000 v Pol (sub); 2001 v Ge, G, Fi, I, Fi, Alb; 2002 v Ho, G, Gr (11)

Venison, B. (Sunderland), 1983 v D, Gr; 1985 v Fi, T, Is, Fi; 1986 v R, T, D (2) (10)

Vernazza, P. A. P. (Arsenal), 2001 v G (sub); (with Watford), M (sub) (2)

Vinnicombe, C. (Rangers), 1991 v H (sub), Pol, Ei (2), T, Sen, M, USSR (sub), F; 1992 v G, T, Pol (12)

Waddle, C. (Newcastle U), 1985 v Fi (1)

Wallace, D. (Southampton), 1983 v Gr, H; 1984 v D, H, F (2), I, Sp (sub); 1985 v Fi, T, Is; 1986 v R, D, I (14)

Wallace, Ray (Southampton), 1989 v Bul, Sen (sub), Ei; 1990 v Se (4)

Wallace, Rod (Southampton), 1989 v Bul, Ei (sub), US; 1991 v H, Pol, Ei, T, Sen, M, USSR, F (11)

Walker, D. (Nottingham F), 1985 v Fi; 1987 v Se, T; 1988 v WG, T, S (2) (7)

Walker, I. M. (Tottenham H), 1991 v W; 1992 v H, Cz, F; 1993 v Sp, N, T, Sm; 1994 v Pol (9)

Walsh, G. (Manchester U), 1988 v WG, Y (2)

Walsh, P. M. (Luton T), 1983 v D (sub), Gr (2), H (4)

Walters, K. (Aston Villa), 1984 v D (sub), H (sub); 1985 v Is, Ei, R; 1986 v R, T, D, I (sub) (9)

Ward, P. D. (Brighton & HA), 1978 v N; 1980 v EG (2)

Warhurst, P. (Oldham Ath), 1991 v H, Pol, W, Sen, M (sub), USSR, F (sub); (with Sheffield W), 1992 v G (8)

Watson, D. (Norwich C), 1984 v D, F (2), I (2), Sp (2) (7)

Watson, D. N. (Barnsley), 1994 v Ho, Sm; 1995 v Br, F; 1996 v N (5)

Watson, G. (Sheffield W), 1991 v Sen, USSR (2)

Watson, S. C. (Newcastle U), 1993 v Sp (sub), N; 1994 v Sm (sub), D; 1995 v P, A, Ei (2), La (2); 1996 v N, A (12)

Weaver, N. J. (Manchester C), 2000 v L, Pol, Arg, I, T, Slo; 2001 v I, Fi, Alb; 2002 v Slv (sub) (10)

Webb, N. (Portsmouth), 1985 v Ei; (with Nottingham F), 1986 v D (2) (3)

Whelan, P. J. (Ipswich T), 1993 v Sp, T (sub), P (3)

Whelan, N. (Leeds U), 1995 v A (sub), Ei (2)

Wilson, M. A. (Manchester U), 2001 v Sp, Fi (sub), Alb, M (sub); (with Middlesbrough), 2002 v Ho (sub), Alb (sub) (6)

White, D. (Manchester C), 1988 v S (2), F, USSR; 1989 v Se; 1990 v Pol (6)

Whyte, C. (Arsenal), 1982 v S (1+1 sub); 1983 v D, Gr (4)

Wicks, S. (QPR), 1982 v S (1)

Wilkins, R. C. (Chelsea), 1977 v W (1)

Wilkinson, P. (Grimsby T), 1985 v Ei, R (sub); (with Everton), 1986 v R (sub), I (4)

Williams, D. (Sunderland), 1998 v Sw (sub); 1999 v F (2)

Williams, P. (Charlton Ath), 1989 v Bul, Sen, Ei, US (sub) (4)

Williams, P. D. (Derby Co), 1991 v Sen, M, USSR; 1992 v G, T, Pol (6)

Williams, S. C. (Southampton), 1977 v S, Fi, N; 1978 v N, I (1 + 1 sub), Y (2); 1979 v D, Bul, Se (sub); 1980 v D, EG (2) (14)

Winterburn, N. (Wimbledon), 1986 v I (1)

Wise, D. (Wimbledon), 1988 v Sw (1)

Woodcook, A. S. (Nottingham F), 1978 v Fi, I (2)

Woodgate, J. S. (Leeds U), 2000 v Arg (1)

Woodhouse, C. (Sheffield U), 1999 v H, Se, Bul; 2000 v Pol (sub) (4)

Woods, C. C. E. (Nottingham F), 1979 v W (sub), Se; (with QPR), 1980 v Bul, EG; 1981 v Sw; (with Norwich C), 1984 v D (6)

Wright, A. G. (Blackburn), 1993 v Sp, N (2)

Wright, M. (Southampton), 1983 v Gr, H; 1984 v D, H (4)

Wright, R. I. (Ipswich T), 1997 v Ge, Pol; 1998 v Mol, I, Gr (2), SAf, Arg; 1999 v Se, Bul, L, Pol, H, Se; 2000 v Y (15)

Wright, S. J. (Liverpool), 2001 v Ge (sub), G, M (sub); 2002 v Ho (sub), G, Alb, Ho, Slv, I, P (10)

Wright, W. (Everton), 1979 v D, W, Bul; 1980 v D, S (2) (6)

Wright-Phillips, S. C. (Manchester C), 2002 v I (1)

Yates, D. (Notts Co), 1989 v D (sub), Bul, Sen, Ei, US (5)

Young, L. P. (Tottenham H), 1999 v H; 2000 v D (sub), Arg (sub), T, Slo; (with Charlton Ath), 2002 v Ho, Gr, Ho, P (sub), Sw, I, P (12)

Zamora, R. L. (Brighton & HA), 2002 v P (sub), I (sub), P (sub) (3)

SCOTLAND

Aitken, R. (Celtic), 1977 v Cz, Sw; 1978 v Cz, W; 1979 v P, N (2); 1980 v Bel, E; 1984 v EG, Y (2); 1985 v WG, Ic, Sp (16)

Albiston, A. (Manchester U), 1977 v Cz, W, Sw; 1978 v Sw, Cz (5)

Alexander, N. (Stenhousemuir), 1997 v P; 1998 v Bl, Ei, I; (with Livingston), 1999 v Li, Es, Bel (2), CzR, G (10)

Anderson, I. (Dundee), 1997 v Co (sub), US, CzR, P; 1998 v Bl, La, Fi, D (sub), Ei (sub), Ni; 1999 v G (sub), Ei, Ni, CzR; (with Toulouse), 2000 v Bos (15)

Anderson, R. (Aberdeen), 1997 v Es, A, Se; 1998 v La (sub), Fi, Ei, I; 1999 v Es, Bel, G, Ei, Ni, CzR; 2000 v Bos, Es (15)

Anthony, M. (Celtic), 1997 v La (sub), Es (sub), Col (3)

Archdeacon, O. (Celtic), 1987 v WG (sub) (1)

Archibald, A. (Partick T), 1998 v Fi, Ei, Ni, I; 1999 v Li (5)

Archibald, S. (Aberdeen), 1980 v B, E (2), WG; (with Tottenham H), 1981 v D (5)

Bagen, D. (Kilmarnock), 1997 v Es, A (sub), Se (sub), Bl (4)

Bain, K. (Dundee), 1993 v P, I, Ma, P (4)

Baker, M. (St. Mirren), 1993 v F, M, E; 1994 v Ma, A; 1995 v Gr, M, F (sub), Sk (sub); 1996 v H (sub) (10)

Baltacha, S. S. (St Mirren), 2000 v Bos, Li (sub), F (sub) (3)

Bannon, E. J. P. (Hearts), 1979 v US; (with Chelsea), P, N (2); (with Dundee U), 1980 v Bel, WG, E (7)

Beattie, J. (St Mirren), 1992 v D, US, P, Y (4)

Beaumont, D. (Dundee U), 1985 v Ic (1)

Bell, D. (Aberdeen), 1981 v D; 1984 v Y (2)

Bernard, P. R. J. (Oldham Ath), 1992 v R (sub), D, Se (sub), US; 1993 v Sw, P, I, Ma, P, F, Bul, M, E; 1994 v I, Ma (15)

Bett, J. (Rangers), 1981 v Se, D; 1982 v Se, D, I, E (2) (7)

Black, E. (Aberdeen), 1983 v EG, Sw (2), Bel; 1985 v Ic, Sp (2), Ic (8)

Blair, A. (Coventry U), 1980 v E; 1981 v Se; (with Aston Villa), 1982 v Se, D, I (5)

Bollan, G. (Dundee U), 1992 v D, G (sub), US, P, Y; 1993 v Sw, P, I, P, F, Bul, M, E; 1994 v Sw; 1995 v Gr; (with Rangers) v Ru, Sm (17)

Bonar, P. (Raith R), 1997 v A, La, Es (sub), Se (4)

Booth, S. (Aberdeen), 1991 v R (sub), Bul (sub + 1), Pol, F (sub); 1992 v Sw, R, D, Se, US, P, Y; 1993 v Ma, P (14)

Bowes, M. J. (Dunfermline Ath), 1992 v D (sub) (1)

Bowman, D. (Hearts), 1985 v WG (sub) (1)

Boyack, S. (Rangers), 1997 v Se (1)

Boyd, T. (Motherwell), 1987 v WG, Ei (2), Bel; 1988 v Bel (5)

Brazil, A. (Hibernian), 1978 v W (1)

Brazil, A. (Ipswich T), 1979 v N; 1980 v Bel (2), E (2), WG; 1981 v Se; 1982 v Se (8)

Brebner, G. I. (Manchester U), 1997 v Col, CzR (sub), US (sub), P; 1998 v Bl, La, Fi, D; (with Reading), 1999 v Li, Es, Bel (2), CzR, G, Ei, Ni, CzR; (with Hibernian), 2000 v Bos (18)

Brough, J. (Hearts), 1981 v D (1)

Browne, P. (Raith R), 1997 v A (1)

Buchan, J. (Aberdeen), 1997 v Se, Col, CzR, P; 1998 v Bl, La, Fi; 1999 v Li, Es, Bel, CzR, G, Ei (13)

Burchill, M. (Celtic), 1998 v Fi, D (sub); 1999 v Li, Es (sub), Bel (2), CzR, Ei, Ni, CzR; 2000 v Bos, Es; 2001 v La, Bel, Pol (15)

Burke, A. (Kilmarnock), 1997 v Es, A, Bl (sub); 1998 v Ei (sub) (4)

Burley, G. E. (Ipswich T), 1977 v Cz, W, Sw; 1978 v Sw, Cz (5)

Burley, C. (Chelsea), 1992 v D; 1993 v Sw, P, I, P; 1994 v Sw, I (sub) (7)

Burns, H. (Rangers), 1985 v Sp, Ic (sub) (2)

Burns, T. (Celtic), 1977 v Cz, W, E; 1978 v Sw; 1982 v E (5)

Caldwell, G. (Newcastle U), 2000 v F, Ni, W; 2002 v Cro, Bel, La (6)

Caldwell, S. (Newcastle U), 2001 v La, Cro, Bel; 2002 v Cro (4)

Campbell, S. (Dundee), 1989 v N (sub), Y, F (3)

Campbell, S. P. (Leicester C), 1998 v Fi (sub), D, Ei, Ni (sub), I; 1999 v Li, Es, Bel (2), CzR, G, Ei, Ni, CzR (sub); 2000 v Bos (sub) (15)

Canero, P. (Kilmarnock), 2000 v F; 2001 v La (sub), Cro (sub), Bel, Pol; 2002 v La (sub) (6)

Carey, L. A. (Bristol C), 1998 v D (1)

Casey, J. (Celtic), 1978 v W (1)

Christie, M. (Dundee), 1992 v D, P (sub), Y (3)

Clark, R. (Aberdeen), 1977 v Cz, W, Sw (3)

Clarke, S. (St Mirren), 1984 v Bel, EG, Y; 1985 v WG, Ic, Sp (2), Ic (8)

Cleland, A. (Dundee U), 1990 v F, N (2); 1991 v R, Sw, Bul; 1992 v Sw, R, G, Se (2) (11)

Collins, J. (Hibernian), 1988 v Bel, I; 1989 v N, Y, F; 1990 v Y, F, N (8)

Connolly, P. (Dundee U), 1991 v R (sub), Sw, Bul (3)

Connor, R. (Ayr U), 1981 v Se; 1982 v Se (2)

Cooper, D. (Clydebank), 1977 v Cz, W, Sw, E; (with Rangers), 1978 v Sw, Cz (6)

Cooper, N. (Aberdeen), 1982 v D, E (2); 1983 v Bel, EG, Sw (2); 1984 v Bel, EG, Y; 1985 v Ic, Sp, Ic (13)

Crabbe, S. (Hearts), 1990 v Y (sub), F (2)

Craig, M. (Aberdeen), 1998 v Bl, La (2)

Craig, T. (Newcastle U), 1977 v E (1)

Crainey, S. D. (Celtic), 2000 v F (sub) (1)

Crainie, D. (Celtic), 1983 v Sw (sub) (1)

Crawford, S. (Raith R), 1994 v A, Eg, P, Bel; 1995 v Fi, Ru,Gr, Ru, Sm, M, F (sub), Sk (sub), Br (sub); 1996 v Gr, Fi (sub), H (1 + sub), Sp (sub), F (sub) (19)

Creaney, G. (Celtic), 1991 v Sw, Bul (2), Pol, F; 1992 v Sw, R, G (2), Se (2) (11)

Cummings, W. (Chelsea), 2000 v F, Ni; 2001 v La, Cro, Bel, Pol; 2002 v Cro, Bel (8)

Dailly, C. (Dundee U), 1991 v R; 1992 v US, R; 1993 v Sw, P, I, Ic, P, F, Bul, M, E; 1994 v Sw, I, Ma, A, Eg, P, Bel; 1995 v Fi, Ru, Gr, Ru, Sm, M, F, Sk, Br; 1996 v Fi, Sm, H (2), Sp, F (34)

Dalglish, P. (Newcastle U), 1999 v Es, Bel, CzR; (with Norwich C), 2000 v Es (sub), Bos, Li (sub) (6)

Dargo, C. (Raith R), 1998 v Fi, Ei, Ni (sub), I; 1999 v Es, Bel (1+sub), CzR (sub), G, Ni (sub) (10)

Davidson, C. (St Johnstone), 1997 v Se, Bl (2)

Davidson, H. N. (Dundee U), 2000 v Es (sub), Li, F (3)

Dawson, A. (Rangers), 1979 v P, N (2); 1980 v B (2), E (2), WG (8)

Deas, P. A. (St Johnstone), 1992 v D (sub); 1993 v Ma (2)

Dennis, S. (Raith R), 1992 v Sw (1)

Dickov, P. (Arsenal), 1992 v Y; 1993 v F, M, E (4)

Dodds, D. (Dundee U), 1978 v W (1)

Dods, D. (Hibernian), 1997 v La, Es, Se (2), Bl (5)

Doig, C. R. (Nottingham F), 2000 v Ni, W; 2001 v La, Cro, Pol (5)

Donald, G. S. (Hibernian), 1992 v US (sub), P, Y (sub) (3)

Donnelly, S. (Celtic), 1994 v Eg, P, Bel; 1995 v Fi, Gr (sub); 1996 v Gr (sub), Sm, H (2), Sp, F (11)

Dow, A. (Dundee), 1993 v Ma (sub), Ic; (with Chelsea) 1994 v I (3)

Duffy, J. (Dundee), 1987 v Ei (1)

Durie, G. S. (Chelsea), 1987 v WG, Ei, Bel; 1988 v Bel (4)

Durrant, I. (Rangers), 1987 v WG, Ei, Bel; 1988 v E (4)

Doyle, J. (Partick Th), 1981 v D, I (sub) (2)

Easton, C. (Dundee U), 1997 v Col, US, CzR, P; 1998 v Bl, Fi, D, Ei, Ni, I; 1999 v Li, Es, Bel (1+sub); 2000 v Li, F; 2001 v La (sub), Cro, Bel; 2002 v Cro, Bel (21)

Elliot, B. (Celtic), 1998 v Ni; 1999 v Li (sub) (2)

Esson, R. (Aberdeen), 2000 v Li, Ni; 2001 v La, Cro, Bel, Pol; 2002 v Bel (7)

Ferguson, B. (Rangers), 1997 v Col (sub), US, CzR, P; 1998 v Bl, La, Fi, D (sub), Ei, Ni, I; 1999 v Bel (12)

Ferguson, D. (Rangers), 1987 v WG, Ei, Bel; 1988 v E; 1990 v Y (5)

Ferguson, D. (Dundee U), 1992 v D, G, Se (2); 1993 v Sw, I, Ma (7)

Ferguson, D. (Manchester U), 1992 v US, P (sub), Y; 1993 v Sw, Ma (5)

Ferguson, I. (Dundee), 1983 v EG (sub), Sw (sub); 1984 v Bel (sub), EG (4)

Ferguson, I. (Clyde), 1987 v WG (sub), Ei; (with St Mirren), Ei, Bel; 1988 v Bel; (with Rangers), E (sub) (8)

Ferguson, R. (Hamilton A), 1977 v E (1)

Findlay, W. (Hibernian), 1991 v R, Pol, Bul (2), Pol (5)

Fitzpatrick, A. (St Mirren), 1977 v W (sub), Sw (sub), E; 1978 v Sw, Cz (5)

Flannigan, C. (Clydebank), 1993 v Ic (sub) (1)

Fleck, R. (Rangers), 1987 v WG (sub), Ei, Bel; (with Norwich C), 1988 v E (2); 1989 v Y (6)

Fowler, J. (Kilmarnock), 2002 v Cro (sub), Bel, La (3)

Fraser, S. T. (Luton T), 2000 v Ni (sub), W; 2001 v La, Cro (4)

Freedman, D. A. (Barnet), 1995 v Ru (sub + 1), Sm, M, F, Sk, Br; (with C Palace) 1996 v Sm (sub) (8)

Fridge, L. (St Mirren), 1989 v F; 1990 v Y (2)

Fullarton, J. (St. Mirren), 1993 v F, Bul; 1994 v Ma, A, Eg, P, Bel; 1995 v M, F, Sk, Br; 1996 v Gr, Fi, H (sub + 1), Sp (sub), F (17)

Fulton, M. (St Mirren), 1980 v Bel, WG, E; 1981 v Se, D (sub) (5)

Fulton, S. (Celtic), 1991 v R, Sw, Bul, Pol, F; 1992 v G (2) (7)

Gallacher, K. (Dundee U), 1987 v WG, Ei (2), Bel (sub); 1988 v E (2); 1990 v Y (7)

Gallacher, P. (Dundee U), 1999 v Ei, Ni, CzR; 2000 v Bos, Es, Bos, F (7)

Galloway, M. (Hearts), 1989 v F; (with Celtic), 1990 v N (2)

Gardiner, J. (Hibernian), 1993 v F (1)

Geddes, R. (Dundee), 1982 v Se, D, E (2); 1988 v E (5)

Gemmill, S. (Nottingham F), 1992 v Sw, R (sub), G (sub), Se (sub) (4)

Germaine, G. (WBA), 1997 v Se (1)

Gilles, R. (St Mirren), 1997 v A (1 + sub), La, Es (2), Se, Bl (7)

Gillespie, G. (Coventry C), 1979 v US; 1980 v E; 1981 v D; 1982 v Se, D, I (2), E (8)

Glass, S. (Aberdeen), 1995 v M, F, Sk, Br; 1996 v Gr, Fi, H, Sp; 1997 v A (2), Es (11)

Glover, L. (Nottingham F), 1988 v Bel (sub); 1989 v N; 1990 v Y (3)

Goram, A. (Oldham Ath), 1987 v Ei (1)

Gough, C. R. (Dundee U), 1983 v EG, Sw, Bel; 1984 v Y (2) (5)

Graham, D. (Rangers), 1998 v Bl (sub), La (sub), Fi (sub), D, Ei (sub), Ni, I; 1999 v Li (8)

Grant, P. (Celtic), 1985 v WG, Ic, Sp; 1987 v WG, Ei (2), Bel; 1988 v Bel, E (2) (10)

Gray S. (Celtic), 1995 v F, Sk, Br; 1996 v Gr, H, Sp, F (7)

Gray, S. (Aberdeen), 1987 v WG (1)

Gunn, B. (Aberdeen), 1984 v EG, Y (2); 1985 v WG, Ic, Sp (2), Ic; 1990 v F (9)

Hagen, D. (Rangers), 1992 v D (sub), US (sub), P, Y; 1993 v Sw (sub), P, Ic, P (8)

Hammell, S. (Motherwell), 2001 v Pol (sub); 2002 v La (2)

Hamilton, B. (St Mirren), 1989 v Y, F (sub); 1990 v F, N (4)

Hamilton, J. (Dundee), 1995 v Sm (sub), Br; 1996 v Fi (sub), Sm, H (sub), Sp (sub), F; 1997 v A, La, Es, Se; (with Hearts), Es, A, Se (14)

Handyside, P. (Grimsby T), 1993 v Ic (sub), Bul, M, E; 1995 v Ru; 1996 v Fi, Sm (7)

Hannah, D. (Dundee U), 1993 v F (sub), Bul, M; 1994 v A, Eg, P, Bel; 1995 v Fi, Ru (sub), Gr, Ru, M, F, Sk, Br; 1996 v Gr (16)

Harper, K. (Hibernian), 1995 v Ru (sub); 1996 v Fi; 1997 v A (2), La, Es, Se (7)

Hartford, R. A. (Manchester C), 1977 v Sw (1)

Hartley, P. (Millwall), 1997 v A (sub) (1)

Hegarty, P. (Dundee U), 1987 v WG, Bel; 1988 v E (2); 1990 v F, N (6)

Hendry, J. (Tottenham H), 1992 v D (sub) (1)

Hetherston, B. (St Mirren), 1997 v Es (sub) (1)

Hewitt, J. (Aberdeen), 1982 v I; 1983 v EG, Sw (2); 1984 v Bel, Y (sub) (6)

Hogg, G. (Manchester U), 1984 v Y; 1985 v WG, Ic, Sp (4)

Hood, G. (Ayr U), 1993 v F, E (sub); 1994 v A (3)

Horn, R. (Hearts), 1997 v US, CzR, P; 1998 v Bl, La, D (sub) (6)

Howie, S. (Cowdenbeath), 1993 v Ma, Ic, P; 1994 v Sw, I (5)

Hughes, R. D. (Bournemouth), 1999 v CzR, Ei, Ni, CzR; 2000 v Bos, Es; 2001 v La, Cro, Bel (9)

Hughes, S. (Rangers), 2002 v La (1)

Hunter, G. (Hibernian), 1987 v Ei (sub); 1988 v Bel, E (3)

Hunter, P. (East Fife), 1989 v N (sub), F (sub); 1990 v F (sub) (3)

James, K. F. (Falkirk), 1997 v Bl (1)

Jardine, I. (Kilmarnock), 1979 v US (1)

Jess, E. (Aberdeen), 1990 v F (sub), N (sub); 1991 v R, Sw, Bul (2), Pol, F; 1992 v Sw, R, G (2), Se (1 + 1 sub) (14)

Johnson, G. I. (Dundee U), 1992 v US, P, Y; 1993 v Sw, P, Ma (6)

Johnston, A. (Hearts), 1994 v Bel; 1995 v Ru, 1996 v Sp (3)

Johnston, F. (Falkirk), 1993 v Ic (1)

Johnston, M. (Partick Th), 1984 v EG (sub); (with Watford), Y (2) (3)

Jordan, A. J. (Bristol C), 2000 v Bos (sub), Li, F (3)

Jupp, D. A. (Fulham), 1995 v Fi, Ru (2), Sm, M, F, Sk, Br; 1997 v Se (9)

Kirkwood, D. (Hearts), 1990 v Y (1)

Kerr, M. (Kilmarnock), 2001 v Pol (sub) (1)

Kerr, S. (Celtic), 1993 v Bul, M, E; 1994 v Ma, A, Eg, P, Bel; 1995 v Fi, Gr (10)

Kyle, K. (Sunderland), 2001 v La (sub), Cro (sub), Pol (sub) (3)

Lambert, P. (St Mirren), 1991 v R, Sw, Bul (2), Pol, F; 1992 v Sw, R, G (2), Se (11)

Langfield, J. (Dundee), 2000 v W; 2002 v Cro (2)

Lauchlan, J. (Kilmarnock), 1998 v Ei, Ni, I; 1999 v CzR, G, Ni, CzR; 2000 v Bos, Es, Bos, Li (11)

Lavety, B. (St. Mirren), 1993 v Ic, Bul (sub), M (sub), E; 1994 v Ma, A (sub), Eg (sub), Bel (sub); 1995 v Fi (sub) (9)

Lavin, G. (Watford), 1993 v F, Bul, M; 1994 v Ma, Eg, P, Bel (7)

Leighton, J. (Aberdeen), 1982 v I (1)

Levein, C. (Hearts), 1985 v Sp, Ic (2)

Liddell, A. M. (Barnsley), 1994 v Ma (sub); 1995 v Sm (sub), M (sub), F, Sk; 1996 v Gr, Fi, Sm, H (2), Sp, F (sub) (12)

Lindsey, J. (Motherwell), 1979 v US (1)

Locke, G. (Hearts), 1994 v Ma, A, Eg, P; 1995 v Fi; 1996 v Fi, H; 1997 v Es, A, Bl (10)

Love, G. (Hibernian), 1995 v Ru (1)

McAllister, G. (Leicester C), 1990 v N (1)

McAlpine, H. (Dundee U), 1983 v EG, Sw (2), Bel; 1984 v Bel (5)

McAnespie, K. (St Johnstone), 1998 v Fi (sub); 1999 v G (sub); 2000 v Ni, W (4)

McAuley, S. (St. Johnstone), 1993 v P (sub) (1)

McAvennie, F. (St Mirren), 1982 v I, E; 1985 v Is, Ei, R (5)

McBride, J. (Everton), 1981 v D (1)

McBride, J. P. (Celtic), 1998 v Ni (sub), I (sub) (2)

McCall, S. (Bradford C), 1988 v E; (with Everton), 1990 v F (2)

McCann, N. (Dundee), 1994 v A, Eg, P, Bel; 1995 v Fi, Gr (sub), Sm; 1996 v Fi, Sm (9)

McClair, B. (Celtic), 1984 v Bel (sub), EG, Y (1 + 1 sub); 1985 v WG, Ic (8)

McCluskey, G. (Celtic), 1979 v US, P; 1980 v Bel (2); 1982 v D, I (6)

McCluskey, S. (St Johnstone), 1997 v Es (2), A, Se, Col, US, CzR; 1998 v Bl, La, D, Ei (sub), Ni, I; 1999 v Li (14)

McCoist, A. (Rangers), 1984 v Bel (1)

McConnell, I. (Clyde), 1997 v A (sub) (1)

McCracken, D. (Dundee U), 2002 v La (1)

McCulloch, A. (Kilmarnock), 1981 v Se (1)

McCulloch, I. (Notts Co), 1982 v E (2)

McCulloch, L. (Motherwell), 1997 v La (sub), Es (1 + sub), Se (sub + 1), A (sub), Col (sub); 1998 v Bl (sub), Fi (sub), D, Ei, Ni; 1999 v CzR, G (14)

McCunnie, J. (Dundee U), 2001 v Pol; 2002 v Cro (2)

MacDonald, J. (Rangers), 1980 v WG (sub); 1981 v Se; 1982 v Se (sub), L, I (2), E (2 sub) (8)

McDonald, C. (Falkirk), 1995 v Fi (sub), Ru, M (sub), F (sub), Br (sub) (5)

McEwan, C. (Clyde), 1997 v Col, US (sub), CzR (sub), P; (with Raith R), 1998 v Bl, La, Fi, D, Ei, Ni, I; 1999 v Li, Es (sub), Bel (2), CzR, G (sub) (17)

McFarlane, D. (Hamilton A), 1997 v Col, US (sub), P (sub) (3)

McGarry, S. (St Mirren), 1997 v US, CzR, P (sub) (3)

McGarvey, F. (St Mirren), 1977 v E; 1978 v Cz; (with Celtic), 1982 v D (3)

McGarvey, S. (Manchester U), 1982 v E (sub); 1983 v Bel, Sw; 1984 v Bel (4)

McGhee, M. (Aberdeen), 1981 v D (1)

McGinnis, G. (Dundee U), 1985 v Sp (1)

McGrillen, P. (Motherwell), 1994 v Sw (sub), I (2)

McGuire, D. (Aberdeen), 2002 v Bel, La (2)

McInally, J. (Dundee U), 1989 v F (1)

McKenzie, R. (Hearts), 1997 v Es, Bl (2)

McKimmie, S. (Aberdeen), 1985 v WG, Ic (2) (3)

McKinlay, T. (Dundee), 1984 v EG (sub); 1985 v WG, Ic, Sp (2), Ic (6)

McKinlay, W. (Dundee U), 1989 v N, Y (sub), F; 1990 v Y, F, N (6)

McKinnon, R. (Dundee U), 1991 v R, Pol (sub); 1992 v G (2), Se (2) (6)

McLaren, A. (Hearts), 1989 v F; 1990 v Y, N; 1991 v Sw, Bul, Pol, F; 1992 v R, G, Se (2) (11)

McLaren, A. (Dundee U), 1993 v I, Ma (sub); 1994 v Sw, I (sub) (4)

McLaughlin, B. (Celtic), 1995 v Ru, Sm, M, Sk (sub), Br (sub); 1996 v Gr (sub), Sm (sub), H (8)

McLaughlin, J. (Morton), 1981 v D; 1982 v Se, D, I, E (2); 1983 v EG, Sw (2), Bel (10)

McLeish, A. (Aberdeen), 1978 v W; 1979 v US; 1980 v Bel, E (2); 1987 v Ei (6)

MacLeod, A. (Hibernian), 1979 v P, N (2) (3)

McLeod, J. (Dundee U), 1989 v N; 1990 v F (2)

MacLeod, M. (Dumbarton), 1979 v US; (with Celtic), P (sub), N (2); 1980 v Bel (5)

McManus, P. (Hibernian), 2001 v Bel, Pol (sub); 2002 v Cro, Bel, La (5)

McMillan, S. (Motherwell), 1997 v A (sub + sub), Se, Bl (4)

McNab, N. (Tottenham H), 1978 v W (1)

McNally, M. (Celtic), 1991 v Bul; 1993 v Ic (2)

McNamara, J. (Dunfermline Ath), 1994 v A, Bel; 1995 v Gr, Ru, Sm; 1996 v Gr, Fi; (with Celtic), Sm, H (2), Sp, F (12)

McNaughton, K. (Aberdeen), 2002 v La (sub) (1)

McNichol, J. (Brentford), 1979 v P, N (2); 1980 v Bel (2), WG, E (7)

McNiven, D. (Leeds U), 1977 v Cz, W (sub), Sw (sub) (3)

McNiven, S. A. (Oldham Ath), 1996 v Sm (sub) (1)

McPhee, S. (Port Vale), 2002 v La (sub) (1)

McPherson, D. (Rangers), 1984 v Bel; 1985 v Sp; (with Hearts), 1989 v N, Y (4)

McQuilken, J. (Celtic), 1993 v Bul, E (2)

McStay, P. (Celtic), 1983 v EG, Sw (2); 1984 v Y (2) (5)

McWhirter, N. (St Mirren), 1991 v Bul (sub) (1)

Main, A. (Dundee U), 1988 v E; 1989 v Y; 1990 v N (3)

Malcolm, R. (Rangers), 2001 v Pol (1)

Maloney, S. (Celtic), 2002 v Cro (sub), Bel (sub), La (3)

Malpas, M. (Dundee U), 1983 v Bel, Sw (1+1 sub); 1984 v Bel, EG, Y (2); 1985 v Sp (8)

Marshall, S. R. (Arsenal), 1995 v Ru, Gr; 1996 v H, Sp, F (5)

Mason, G. R. (Manchester C), 1999 v Li (sub); (with Dunfermline Ath), 2002 v Bel (2)

Mathieson, D. (Queen of the South), 1997 v Col; 1998 v La; 1999 v G (sub) (3)

May, E. (Hibernian), 1989 v Y (sub), F (2)

Meldrum, C. (Kilmarnock), 1996 v F (sub); 1997 v A (2), La, Es, Se (6)

Melrose, J. (Partick Th), 1977 v Sw; 1979 v US, P, N (2); 1980 v Bel (sub), WG, E (8)

Miller, C. (Rangers), 1995 v Gr, Ru; 1996 v Gr, Sp, F; 1997 v A, La, Es (8)

Miller, J. (Aberdeen), 1987 v Ei (sub); 1988 v Bel; (with Celtic), E; 1989 v N, Y; 1990 v F, N (7)

Miller, K. (Hibernian), 2000 v F, Ni, W; (with Rangers), 2001 v Cro, Bel; 2002 v Cro, Bel (7)

Miller, W. (Aberdeen), 1978 v Sw, Cz (2)

Miller, W. (Hibernian), 1991 v R, Sw, Bul, Pol, F; 1992 v R, G (sub) (7)

Milne, R. (Hearts), 2000 v F (1)

Milne, R. (Dundee U), 1982 v Se (sub); 1984 v Bel, EG (3)

Money, I. C. (St Mirren), 1987 v Ei; 1988 v Bel; 1989 v N (3)

Muir, L. (Hibernian), 1977 v Cz (sub) (1)

Murray, H. (St Mirren), 2000 v F (sub), Ni (sub), W (sub) (3)

Murray, I. (Hibernian), 2001 v Bel (sub), Pol; 2002 v Cro, Bel, La (5)

Murray, N. (Rangers), 1993 v P (sub), Ma, Ic, P; 1994 v Sw, I; 1995 v Fi, Ru, Gr, Sm; 1996 v Gr (sub), Fi, Sm, H (2), F (16)

Murray, R. (Bournemouth), 1993 v Ic (sub) (1)

Narey, D. (Dundee U), 1977 v Cz, Sw; 1978 v Sw, Cz (4)

Naysmith, G. (Hearts), 1997 v La, Es (1 + sub), Se, A, Col, US, CzR, P; 1998 v La, D; 1999 v Es, Bel (2), CzR, G, Ei, CzR; 2000 v Bos, Es, Bos, Li (22)

Neilson, R. (Hearts), 2000 v Ni (1)

Nevin, P. (Chelsea), 1985 v WG, Ic, Sp (2), Ic (5)

Nicholas, C. (Celtic), 1981 v Se; 1983 v EG, Sw, Bel; (with Arsenal), 1984 v Y (6)

Nicholson, B. (Rangers), 1999 v G, Ni, CzR (sub); 2000 v Bos (sub), Es, Bos, Li (7)

Nicol, S. (Ayr U), 1981 v Se; 1982 v Se, D; (with Liverpool), I (2), E (2); 1983 v EG, Sw (2), Bel; 1984 v Bel, EG, Y (14)

Nisbet, S. (Rangers), 1989 v N, Y, F; 1990 v Y, F (5)

Notman, A. M. (Manchester U), 1999 v Li (sub), Es, Bel (sub+sub); 2000 v Li, F (sub), Ni, W; 2001 v La, Cro (10)

O'Brien, B. (Blackburn R), 1999 v Ei (sub), Ni (sub), CzR (sub); 2000 v Bos (sub) (4)

O'Donnell, P. (Motherwell), 1992 v Sw (sub), R, D, G (2), Se (1 + 1 sub); 1993 v P (7)

O'Neil, B. (Celtic), 1992 v D, G, Se (2); 1993 v Sw, P, I (7)

O'Neil, J. (Dundee U), 1991 v Bul (sub) (1)

O'Neill, M. (Clyde), 1995 v Ru (sub), F, Sk, Br; 1997 v Se (sub), Bl (sub) (6)

Orr, N. (Morton), 1978 v W (sub); 1979 v US, P, N (2); 1980 v Bel, E (7)

Parker, K. (St Johnstone), 2001 v Pol (sub) (1)

Parlane, D. (Rangers), 1977 v W (1)

Paterson, C. (Hibernian), 1981 v Se; 1982 v I (2)

Paterson, J. (Dundee U), 1997 v Col, US, CzR; 1999 v Bel (sub+sub); 2000 v Es, Bos, Li; 2002 v Cro (sub) (9)

Payne, G. (Dundee U), 1978 v Sw, Cz, W (3)

Peacock, L. A. (Carlisle U), 1997 v Bl (1)

Pressley, S. (Rangers), 1993 v Ic, F, Bul, M, E; 1994 v Sw, I, M, A, Eg, P, Bel; 1995 v Fi; (with Coventry C), Ru (2), Sm, M, F, Sk, Br; (with Dundee U), 1996 v Gr, Sm, H (2), Sp, F (26)

Provan, D. (Kilmarnock), 1977 v Cz (sub) (1)

Rae, A. (Millwall), 1991 v Bul (sub + 1), F (sub); 1992 v Sw, R, G (sub), Se (2) (8)

Rae, G. (Dundee), 1999 v Ei (sub), Ni, CzR; 2000 v Bos, Es, Bos (6)

Redford, I. (Rangers), 1981 v Se (sub); 1982 v Se, D, I (2), E (6)

Reid, B. (Rangers), 1991 v F; 1992 v D, US, P (4)

Reid, C. (Hibernian), 1993 v Sw, P, I (3)

Reid, M. (Celtic), 1982 v E; 1984 v Y (2)

Reid, R. (St Mirren), 1977 v W, Sw, E (3)

Renicks, S. (Hamilton A), 1997 v Bl (1)

Rice, B. (Hibernian), 1985 v WG (1)

Richardson, L. (St Mirren), 1980 v WG, E (sub) (2)

Ritchie, A. (Morton), 1980 v Bel (1)

Ritchie, P. R. (Hearts), 1996 v H; 1997 v A (2), La, Es (2), Se (7)

Robertson, A. (Rangers) 1991 v F (1)

Robertson, C. (Rangers), 1977 v E (sub) (1)

Robertson, D. (Aberdeen), 1987 v Ei (sub); 1988 v E (2); 1989 v N, Y; 1990 v Y, N (7)

Robertson, H. (Aberdeen), 1994 v Eg; 1995 v Fi (2)

Robertson, J. (Hearts), 1985 v WG, Ic (sub) (2)

Robertson, L. (Rangers), 1993 v F, M (sub), E (sub) (3)

Robertson, S. (St Johnstone), 1998 v Fi, Ni (2)

Roddie, A. (Aberdeen), 1992 v US, P; 1993 v Sw (sub), P, Ic (5)

Ross, T. W. (Arsenal), 1977 v W (1)

Rowson, D. (Aberdeen), 1997 v La, Es, Se (2), Bl (5)

Russell, R. (Rangers), 1978 v W; 1980 v Bel; 1984 v Y (3)

Salton, D. B. (Luton T), 1992 v D, US, P, Y; 1993 v Sw, I (6)

Scott, P. (St Johnstone), 1994 v A (sub), Eg (sub), P, Bel (4)

Scrimgour, D. (St Mirren), 1997 v US, CzR; 1998 v D (3)

Seaton, A. (Falkirk), 1998 v Bl (sub) (1)

Severin, S. D. (Hearts), 2000 v Es, Bos, Li (sub), F, Ni, W; 2001 v La, Bel; 2002 v Cro, Bel (10)

Shannon, R. (Dundee), 1987 v WG, Ei (2), Bel; 1988 v Bel, E (2) (7)

Sharp, G. (Everton), 1982 v E (1)

Sharp, R. (Dunfermline Ath), 1990 v N (sub); 1991 v R, Sw, Bul (4)

Sheerin, P. (Southampton), 1996 v Sm (1)

Shields, G. (Rangers), 1997 v A, La (2)

Simpson, N. (Aberdeen), 1982 v I (2), E; 1983 v EG, Sw (2), Bel; 1984 v Bel, EG, Y; 1985 v Sp (11)

Sinclair, G. (Dumbarton), 1977 v E (1)

Skilling, M. (Kilmarnock), 1993 v Ic (sub); 1994 v I (2)

Smith, B. M. (Celtic), 1992 v G (2), US, P, Y (5)

Smith, G. (Rangers), 1978 v W (1)

Smith, H. G. (Hearts), 1987 v WG, Bel (2)

Sneddon, A. (Celtic), 1979 v US (1)

Speedie, D. (Chelsea), 1985 v Sp (1)

Spencer, J. (Rangers), 1991 v Sw (sub), F; 1992 v Sw (3)

Stanton, P. (Hibernian), 1977 v Cz (1)

Stark, W. (Aberdeen), 1985 v Ic (1)

Stephen, R. (Dundee), 1983 v Bel (sub) (1)

Stevens, G. (Motherwell), 1977 v E (1)

Stewart, C. (Kilmarnock), 2002 v La (1)

Stewart, J. (Kilmarnock), 1978 v Sw, Cz; (with Middlesbrough), 1979 v P (3)

Stewart, M. J. (Manchester U), 2000 v Ni; 2001 v La, Cro, Bel, Pol; 2002 v La (6)

Stewart, R. (Dundee U), 1979 v P, N (2); (with West Ham U), 1980 v Bel (2), E (2), WG; 1981 v D; 1982 v I (2), E (12)

Stillie, D. (Aberdeen), 1995 v Ru (2), Sm, M, F, Sk, Br; 1996 v Gr, Fi, Sm, H (2), Sp, F (14)

Strachan, G. D. (Aberdeen), 1980 v Bel (1)

Strachan, G. D. (Coventry C), 1998 v D, Ei; 1999 v Li, Es, Bel (2); 2000 v Li (7)

Sturrock, P. (Dundee U), 1977 v Cz, W, Sw, E; 1978 v Sw, Cz; 1982 v Se, I, E (9)

Sweeney, S. (Clydebank), 1991 v R, Sw (sub), Bul (2), Pol; 1992 v Sw, R (7)

Tarrant, N. K. (Aston Villa), 1999 v Ni (sub); 2000 v Es (sub), Bos (sub), Li, Ni (sub) (5)

Teale, C. (Clydebank), 1997 v La (sub), Es, Bl; (with Ayr U), 1999 v CzR (sub), G (sub), Ei (sub) (6)

Telfer, P. (Luton T), 1993 v Ma, P; 1994 v Sw (3)

Thomas, K. (Hearts), 1993 v F (sub), Bul, M, E; 1994 v Sw, Ma; 1995 v Gr; 1997 v A (8)

Thompson, S. (Dundee U), 1997 v US, CzR, P; 1998 v Bl, La; 1999 v G (sub), Ei, Ni, CzR; 2000 v Bos, Es, Bos (12)

Thomson, W. (Partick Th), 1977 v E (sub); 1978 v W; (with St Mirren), 1979 v US, N (2); 1980 v Bel (2), E (2), WG (10)

Tolmie, J. (Morton), 1980 v Bel (sub) (1)

Tortolano, J. (Hibernian), 1987 v WG, Ei (2)

Tweed, S. (Hibernian), 1993 v Ic; 1994 v Sw, I (3)

Wales, G. (Hearts), 2000 v F (1)

Walker, A. (Celtic), 1988 v Bel (1)

Wallace, I. (Coventry C), 1978 v Sw (1)

Walsh, C. (Nottingham F), 1984 v EG, Sw (2), Bel; 1984 v EG (5)

Wark, J. (Ipswich T), 1977 v Cz, W, Sw; 1978 v W; 1979 v P; 1980 v E (2), WG (8)

Watson, A. (Aberdeen), 1981 v Se, D; 1982 v D, I (sub) (4)

Watson, K. (Rangers), 1977 v E; 1978 v Sw (sub) (2)

Watt, M. (Aberdeen), 1991 v R, Sw, Bul (2), Pol, F; 1992 v Sw, R, G (2), Se (2) (12)

Whiteford, A. (St Johnstone), 1997 v US (1)

Whyte, D. (Celtic), 1987 v Ei (2), Bel; 1988 v E (2); 1989 v N, Y; 1990 v Y, N (9)

Wilkie, L. (Dundee), 2000 v Bos, F, Ni, W; 2001 v La, Cro (6)

Will, J. A. (Arsenal), 1992 v D (sub), Y; 1993 v Ic (sub) (3)

Williams, G. (Nottingham F), 2002 v Bel (sub) (1)

Wilson, S. (Rangers), 1999 v Es, Bel (2), G, Ei, CzR; 2000 v Bos (7)

Wilson, T. (St Mirren), 1983 v Sw (sub) (1)

Wilson, T. (Nottingham F), 1988 v E; 1989 v N, Y; 1990 v F (4)

Winnie, D. (St Mirren), 1988 v Bel (1)

Wright, P. (Aberdeen), 1989 v Y, F; (with QPR), 1990 v Y (sub) (3)

Wright, S. (Aberdeen), 1991 v Bul, Pol, F; 1992 v Sw, G (2), Se (2); 1993 v Sw, P, I, Ma; 1994 v I, Ma (14)

Wright, T. (Oldham Ath), 1987 v Bel (sub) (1)

Young, Darren. (Aberdeen), 1997 v Es (sub), Se, Col, CzR (sub), P; 1998 v La (sub); 1999 v CzR (sub), G (sub) (8)

Young, Derek. (Aberdeen), 2000 v W; 2001 v Cro (sub), Bel (sub), Pol; 2002 v Cro (5)

WALES

Aizlewood, M. (Luton T), 1979 v E; 1981 v Ho (2)

Baddeley, L. M. (Cardiff C), 1996 v Mol (sub), G (sub) (2)

Balcombe, S. (Leeds U), 1982 v F (sub) (1)

Barnhouse, D. J. (Swansea), 1995 v Mol; 1996 v Mol, Sm (3)

Bater, P. T. (Bristol R), 1977 v E, S (2)

Bellamy, C. D. (Norwich C), 1996 v Sm; 1997 v Sm, T, Bel; 1998 v T, Bel, I; 1999 v I (8)

Bird, A. (Cardiff C), 1993 v Cy (sub); 1994 v Cy (sub); 1995 v Mol, Ge (sub), Bul; 1996 v G (sub) (6)

Blackmore, C. (Manchester U), 1984 v N, Bul, Y (3)

Blake, N. (Cardiff C), 1991 v Pol (sub); 1993 v Cy, Bel, RCS; 1994 v RCS (5)

Blaney, S. D. (West Ham U), 1997 v Sm, Ho, T (3)

Bodin, P. (Cardiff C), 1983 v Y (1)

Bowen, J. P. (Swansea C), 1993 v Cy, Bel (2); 1994 v RCS, R (sub) (5)

Bowen, M. (Tottenham H), 1983 v N; 1984 v Bul, Y (3)

Boyle, T. (C Palace), 1982 v F (1)

Brace, D. P. (Wrexham), 1995 v Ge, Bul (2); 1997 v Sm Ho; 1998 v T (6)

Cegielski, W. (Wrexham), 1977 v E (sub), S (2)

Chapple, S. R. (Swansea C), 1992 v R; 1993 v Cy, Bel (2), RCS; 1994 v RCS; Bul (2) (8)

Charles, J. M. (Swansea C), 1979 v E; 1981 v Ho (2)

Clark, J. (Manchester U), 1978 v S; (with Derby Co), 1979 v E (2)

Coates, J. S. (Swansea C), 1996 v Mol, G; 1997 v Ho, T (sub); 1998 v T (sub) (5)

Coleman, C. (Swansea C), 1990 v Pol; 1991 v E, Pol (3)

Coyne, D. (Tranmere R), 1992 v R; 1994 v Cy (sub), R; 1995 v Mol, Ge, Bul (2) (7)

Curtis, A. T. (Swansea C), 1977 v E (1)

Davies, A. (Manchester U), 1982 v F (2), Ho; 1983 v N, Y, Bul (6)

Davies, D. (Barry T), 1999 v D (sub) (1)

Davies, G. M. (Hereford U), 1993 v Bel, RCS; 1995 v Mol (sub), Ge, Bul (2); (with C Palace) 1996 v Mol (7)

Davies, I. C. (Norwich C), 1978 v S (sub) (1)

Davies, S. (Peterborough U), 1999 v D, Bl, Sw, I, D; (with Tottenham H), 2000 v S; 2001 v Bl, N, Pol, Arm (10)

Day, R. (Manchester U), 2000 v S (sub), Ni; 2001 v Uk, Pol, Uk; 2002 v Arm, N, Bl (6)

Deacy, N. (PSV Eindhoven), 1977 v S (1)

De-Vulgt, L. S. (Swansea C), 2002 v Arm (sub), Bl (2)

Dibble, A. (Cardiff C), 1983 v Bul; 1984 v N, Bul (3)

Doyle, S. C. (Preston NE), 1979 v E (sub); (with Huddersfield T), 1984 v N (2)

Dwyer, P. J. (Cardiff C), 1979 v E (1)

Earnshaw, R. (Cardiff C), 1999 v P (sub), I, D; 2000 v S, Ni; 2001 v Bl (sub), N, Pol (2), Uk (10)

Ebdon, M. (Everton), 1990 v Pol; 1991 v E (2)

Edwards, C. N. H. (Swansea C), 1996 v G; 1997 v Sm, Ho (2), T, Bel; 1998 v T (7)

Edwards, R. I. (Chester), 1977 v S; 1978 v W (2)

Edwards, R. W. (Bristol C), 1991 v Pol; 1992 v R; 1993 v Cy, Bel (2), RCS; 1994 v RCS, Cy, R; 1995 v Ge, Bul; 1996 v Mol G (13)

Evans, A. (Bristol R), 1977 v E (1)

Evans, K. (Leeds U), 1999 v I (sub), D; (with Cardiff C), 2001 v N (sub), Pol (sub) (4)

Evans, P. S. (Shrewsbury T), 1996 v G (1)

Evans, S. J. (Crystal Palace), 2001 v Bl, Arm (2)

Evans, T. (Cardiff C), 1995 v Bul (sub); 1996 v Mol, G (3)

Folland, R. W. (Oxford U), 2000 v Ni (sub) (1)

Foster, M. G. (Tranmere R), 1993 v RCS (1)

Freestone, R. (Chelsea), 1990 v Pol (1)

Gabbidon, D. L. (WBA), 1999 v D, P, Sw, I (sub), D; 2000 v Bl, Sw, S, Ni; (with Cardiff C), 2001 v N, Pol, Arm, Uk, Pol, Uk; 2002 v Arm, N (17)

Gale, D. (Swansea C), 1983 v Bul; 1984 v N (sub) (2)

Gall, K. A. (Bristol R), 2002 v N (sub), Bl (sub) (2)

Gibson, N. D. (Tranmere R), 1999 v D (sub), Bl (sub), P; 2000 v S (sub), Ni; (with Sheffield W), 2001 v Uk, Pol, Uk; 2002 v Arm, N, Bl (11)

Giggs, R. (Manchester U), 1991 v Pol (1)

Giles, D. C. (Cardiff C), 1977 v S; 1978 v S; (with Swansea C), 1981 v Ho; (with C Palace), 1983 v Y (4)

Giles, P. (Cardiff C), 1982 v F (2), Ho (3)

Graham, D. (Manchester U), 1991 v E (1)

Green, R. M. (Wolverhampton W), 1998 v I; 1999 v I, D, Bl, Sw, I, D; 2000 v Bl, S, Ni; 2001 v Bl, N, Pol, Arm, Uk, Pol (16)

Griffith, C. (Cardiff C), 1990 v Pol (1)

Griffiths, C. (Shrewsbury T), 1991 v Pol (sub) (1)

Hall, G. D. (Chelsea), 1990 v Pol (1)

Hartson, J. (Luton T), 1994 v Cy, R; 1995 v Mol, Ge, Bul; (with Arsenal), 1996 v G, Sm; 1997 v Sm, Ho (9)

Haworth, S. O. (Cardiff C), 1997 v Ho, T, Bel; (with Coventry C), 1998 v T, Bel; I; 1999 v I, D; (with Wigan Ath) Bl, Sw; 2000 v Bl, Sw (12)

Hillier, I. M. (Tottenham H), 2001 v Uk (sub), Pol (sub), Uk; (with Luton T), 2002 v Arm, N (5)

Hodges, G. (Wimbledon), 1983 v Y (sub), Bul (sub); 1984 v N, Bul, Y (5)

Holden, A. (Chester C), 1984 v Y (sub) (1)

Holloway, C. D. (Exeter C), 1999 v P, D (2)

Hopkins, J. (Fulham), 1982 v F (sub), Ho; 1983 v N, Y, Bul (5)

Hopkins, S. A. (Wrexham), 1999 v P (sub) (1)

Huggins, D. S. (Bristol C), 1996 v Sm (1)

Hughes, D. R. (Southampton), 1994 v R (1)

Hughes, R. D. (Aston Villa), 1996 v Sm; 1997 v Sm (sub), Ho (2), T, Bel; 1998 v T, Bel, I; 1999 v I, Sw, I; (with Shrewsbury T), 2000 v Sw (13)

Hughes, I. (Bury), 1992 v R; 1993 v Cy, Bel (sub), RCS; 1994 v Cy, R; 1995 v Mol, Ge, Bul; 1996 v Mol (sub), G (11)

Hughes, L. M. (Manchester U), 1983 v N, Y; 1984 v N, Bul, Y (5)

Hughes, W. (WBA), 1977 v E, S; 1978 v S (3)

Jackett, K. (Watford), 1981 v Ho; 1982 v F (2)

James, R. M. (Swansea C), 1977 v E, S; 1978 v S (3)

Jarman, L. (Cardiff C), 1996 v Sm; 1997 v Sm, Ho (2), Bel; 1998 v T, Bel; 1999 v I, P; 2000 v Bl (10)

Jeanne, L. C. (QPR), 1999 v P (sub), Sw, I; 2000 v Bl, Sw, S, Ni; 2001 v Bl (8)

Jelleyman, G. A. (Peterborough U), 1999 v D (sub) (1)

Jenkins, L. D. (Swansea C), 1998 v T (sub); 2000 v Bl, Sw, S, Ni; 2001 v N, Pol, Arm, Uk (9)

Jenkins, S. R. (Swansea C), 1993 v Cy (sub), Bel (2)

Jones, E. P. (Blackpool), 2000 v Ni (sub) (1)

Jones, F. (Wrexham), 1981 v Ho (1)

Jones, J. A. (Swansea C); 2001 v Pol, Uk; 2002 v N (sub) (3)

Jones, L. (Cardiff C), 1982 v F (2), Ho (3)

Jones, M. G. (Leeds U), 1998 v Bel; 1999 v I, D, Bl, Sw, I; 2000 v Sw (7)

Jones, P. L. (Liverpool), 1992 v R; 1993 v Cy, Bel (2), RCS; 1994 v RCS (sub), Cy, R; 1995 v Mol, Ge; 1996 v Mol, G (12)

Jones, R. (Sheffield W), 1994 v R; 1995 v Bul (2) (3)

Jones, V. (Bristol R), 1979 v E; 1981 v Ho (2)

Kendall, L. M. (Crystal Palace), 2001 v N, Pol (2)

Kendall, M. (Tottenham H), 1978 v S (1)

Kenworthy, J. R. (Tranmere R), 1994 v Cy; 1995 v Mol, Bul (3)

Knott, G. R. (Tottenham H), 1996 v Sm (1)

Law, B. J. (QPR), 1990 v Pol; 1991 v E (2)

Letheran, G. (Leeds U), 1977 v E, S (2)

Lewis, D. (Swansea C), 1982 v F (2), Ho; 1983 v N, Y, Bul; 1984 v N, Bul, Y (9)

Lewis, J. (Cardiff C), 1983 v N (1)

Llewellyn, C. M. (Norwich C), 1998 v T (sub), Bel (sub), I; 1999 v I, D, Bl, I; 2000 v Bl, Sw, S; 2001 v N, Pol, Arm, Uk (14)

Loveridge, J. (Swansea C), 1982 v Ho; 1983 v N, Bul (3)

Low, J. D. (Bristol R), 1999 v P; (with Cardiff C), 2002 v Arm (sub), N (sub), Bl (1)

Lowndes, S. R. (Newport Co), 1979 v E; 1981 v Ho; (with Millwall), 1984 v Bul, Y (4)

McCarthy, A. J. (QPR), 1994 v RCS, Cy, R (3)

Maddy, P. (Cardiff C), 1982 v Ho; 1983 v N (sub) (2)

Margetson, M. W. (Manchester C), 1992 v R; 1993 v Cy, Bel (2), RCS; 1994 v RCS, Cy (7)

Martin, A. P. (Crystal Palace), 1999 v D (1)

Marustik, C. (Swansea C), 1982 v F (2); 1983 v Y, Bul; 1984 v N, Bul, Y (7)

Maxwell, L. J. (Liverpool), 1999 v Sw (sub), I; 2000 v Sw (sub), S, Ni; 2001 v Bl, Pol, Arm, Uk, Pol, Uk; (with Cardiff C), 2002 v Arm, N, Bl (sub) (14)

Meaker, M. J. (QPR), 1994 v RCS (sub), R (sub) (2)

Melville, A. K. (Swansea C), 1990 v Pol; (with Oxford U), 1991 v E (2)

Micallef, C. (Cardiff C), 1982 v F, Ho; 1983 v N (3)

Morgan, A. M. (Tranmere R), 1995 v Mol, Bul; 1996 v Mol, G (4)

Mountain, P. D. (Cardiff C), 1997 v Ho, T (2)

Nardiello, D. (Coventry C), 1978 v S (1)

Neilson, A. B. (Newcastle U), 1993 v Cy, Bel (2), RCS; 1994 v RCS, Cy, R (7)

Nicholas, P. (C Palace), 1978 v S; 1979 v E; (with Arsenal), 1982 v F (3)

Nogan, K. (Luton T), 1990 v Pol; 1991 v E (2)

Nogan, L. (Oxford U) 1991 v E (1)

Oster, J. M. (Grimsby T), 1997 v Sm (sub), Ho (sub), T, Bel; (with Everton), 1998 v T, Bel, I; 1999 v I, Sw (9)
Owen, G. (Wrexham), 1991 v E (sub), Pol; 1992 v R; 1993 v Cy, Bel (2); 1994 v Cy, R (8)

Page, R. J. (Watford), 1995 v Mol, Ge, Bul; 1996 v Mol (4)
Partridge, D. W. (West Ham U), 1997 v T (1)
Pascoe, C. (Swansea C), 1983 v Bul (sub); 1984 v N (sub), Bul, Y (4)
Pembridge, M. (Luton T), 1991 v Pol (1)
Perry, J. (Cardiff C), 1990 v Pol; 1991 v E, Pol (3)
Peters, M. (Manchester C), 1992 v R; (with Norwich C), 1993 v Cy, RCS (3)
Phillips, D. (Plymouth Arg), 1984 v N, Bul, Y (3)
Phillips, G. R. (Swansea C), 2001 v Uk (sub); 2002 v Arm (sub), Bl (3)
Phillips, L. (Swansea C), 1979 v E; (with Charlton Ath), 1983 v N (2)
Pontin, K. (Cardiff C), 1978 v S (1)
Powell, L. (Southampton), 1991 v Pol (sub); 1992 v R (sub); 1993 v Bel (sub); 1994 v RCS (4)
Price, J. J. (Swansea C), 1998 v I (sub); 1999 v I (sub), D, Bl, P; 2000 v Bl, Sw (7)
Price, M. D. (Everton), 2001 v Uk. Pol (sub), Uk; (with Hull C), 2002 v Arm, N, Bl (6)
Price, P. (Luton T), 1981 v Ho (1)
Pugh, D. (Doncaster R), 1982 v F (2) (2)
Pugh, S. (Wrexham), 1993 v Bel (2 subs) (2)

Ramasut, M. W. T. (Bristol R), 1997 v Ho, Bel; 1998 v T, I (4)
Ratcliffe, K. (Everton), 1981 v Ho; 1982 v F (2)
Ready, K. (QPR), 1992 v R; 1993 v Bel (2); 1994 v RCS, Cy (5)
Rees, A. (Birmingham C), 1984 v N (1)
Rees, J. (Luton T), 1990 v Pol; 1991 v E, Pol (3)
Roberts, A. (QPR), 1991 v E, Pol (2)
Roberts, C. J. (Cardiff C), 1999 v D (sub) (1)
Roberts, G. (Hull C), 1983 v Bul (1)
Roberts, G. W. (Liverpool), 1997 v Ho, T, Bel; 1998 v T, I; 1999 v I, D, Bl, P; (with Panionios) D; (with Tranmere R), 2000 v Sw (11)
Roberts, J. G. (Wrexham), 1977 v E (1)
Roberts, N. W. (Wrexham), 1999 v I (sub), P; 2000 v Sw (sub) (3)
Roberts, P. (Porthmadog), 1997 v Ho (sub) (1)
Roberts, S. I. (Swansea C), 1999 v Sw, I (sub), D; 2000 v Bl (sub), Ni; 2001 v Bl (sub), N, Pol, Arm, Uk; 2002 v Arm, N, Bl (13)
Roberts, S. W. (Wrexham), 2000 v S; 2001 v Bl, N (sub) (3)
Robinson, C. P. (Wolverhampton W), 1996 v Sm; 1997 v Sm, Ho (2), T, Bel (6)
Robinson, J. (Brighton & HA), 1992 v R; (with Charlton Ath), 1993 v Bel; 1994 v RCS, Cy, R (5)
Rowlands, M. A. J. R. (Manchester C), 1996 v Sm; 1997 v Sm, Ho (1 + sub), T (sub) (5)
Rush, I. (Liverpool), 1981 v Ho; 1982 v F (2)

Savage, R. W. (Crewe Alex), 1995 v Bul; 1996 v Mol, G (3)
Sayer, P. A. (Cardiff C), 1977 v E, S (2)
Searle, D. (Cardiff C), 1991 v Pol (sub); 1992 v R; 1993 v Cy, Bel (2), RCS; 1994 v RCS (6)
Slatter, D. (Chelsea), 2000 v Sw (sub), S; 2001 v Bl, N (sub), Pol (sub), Uk (sub) (6)
Slatter, N. (Bristol R), 1983 v N, Y, Bul; 1984 v N, Bul, Y (6)
Speed, G. A. (Leeds U), 1990 v Pol; 1991 v E, Pol (3)
Stevenson, N. (Swansea C), 1982 v F, Ho (2)
Stevenson, W. B. (Leeds U), 1977 v E, S; 1978 v S (3)
Symons, K. (Portsmouth), 1991 v E, Pol (2)

Taylor, G. K. (Bristol R), 1995 v Ge, Bul (2); 1996 v Mol (4)
Thomas, D. J. (Watford), 1998 v T, Bel (2)
Thomas, J. A. (Blackburn R), 1996 v Sm; 1997 v Sm, Ho (2), T, Bel; 1998 v Bel; 1999 v D, Bl, P; 2000 v Bl (sub); 2001 v Bl, N, Pol, Arm, Uk, Pol, Uk; 2002 v Arm, N, Bl (21)
Thomas, Martin R. (Bristol R), 1979 v E; 1981 v Ho (2)
Thomas, Mickey R. (Wrexham), 1977 v E; 1978 v S (2)

Thomas, S. (Wrexham), 2001 v Pol, Uk; 2002 v Arm, N, Bl (5)
Thomas, D. G. (Leeds U), 1977 v E; 1979 v E; 1984 v N (3)
Tibbott, L. (Ipswich T), 1977 v E, S (2)
Tipton, M. J. (Oldham Ath), 1998 v I (sub); 1999 v P, Sw (sub); 2000 v Ni; 2001 v Arm (sub), Uk (sub) (6)
Tolley, J. C. (Shrewsbury T), 2001 v Pol, Uk (sub) (2)
Twiddy, C. (Plymouth Arg), 1995 v Mol, Ge; 1996 v G (sub) (3)

Vaughan, N. (Newport Co), 1982 v F, Ho (2)
Valentine, R. D. (Everton), 2001 v Pol, Uk; 2002 v Arm, N, Bl (5)

Walsh, D. (Wrexham), 2000 v S, Ni; 2001 v Bl, Arm, Uk; 2002 v Arm, N, Bl (8)
Walsh, I. P. (C Palace), 1979 v E; (with Swansea C), 1983 v Bul (2)
Walton, M. (Norwich C.), 1991 v Pol (sub) (1)
Ward, D. (Notts Co), 1996 v Mol, G (2)
Weston, R. D. (Arsenal), 2001 v Bl, N, Pol; (with Cardiff C), Arm (4)
Williams, A. P. (Southampton), 1998 v Bel, I; 1999 v I, D (sub), Bl, Sw, I; 2000 v Bl, Sw (9)
Williams, A. S. (Blackburn R), 1996 v Sm; 1997 v Sm, Ho, Bel; 1998 v T, Bel, I; 1999 v I, D, Bl, P, Sw, I, D; 2000 v Bl, Sw (16)
Williams, D. (Bristol R), 1983 v Y (1)
Williams, D. I. L. (Liverpool), 1998 v I; 1999 v D, Bl; (with Wrexham) I; 2000 v Bl, S, Ni; 2001 v Bl (9)
Williams, E. (Caernarfon T), 1997 v Ho (sub), T (sub) (2)
Williams, G. (Bristol R), 1983 v Y, Bul (2)
Williams, M. (Manchester U), 2001 v Pol (sub), Uk (sub); 2002 v Bl (sub) (3)
Williams, S. J. (Wrexham), 1995 v Mol, Ge, Bul (2) (4)
Wilmot, R. (Arsenal), 1982 v F (2), Ho; 1983 v N, Y; 1984 v Y (6)
Wright, A. A. (Oxford U), 1998 v Bel, I (sub); 1999 v D (sub) (3)

Young, S. (Cardiff C), 1996 v Sm; 1997 v Sm, Ho (2), Bel (sub) (5)

NORTHERN IRELAND

Bailie, N. (Linfield), 1990 v Is; 1994 v R (sub) (2)
Baird, C. P. (Southampton), 2002 v G (1)
Beatty, S. (Chelsea), 1990 v Is; (with Linfield), 1994 v R (2)
Black, K. T. (Luton T), 1990 v Is (1)
Black, R. Z. (Morecambe), 2002 v G (1)
Blackledge, G. (Portadown), 1978 v Ei (1)
Boyle, W. S. (Leeds U), 1998 v Sw (sub), S (sub); 2001 v CzR (sub), Bul (1+sub), CzR; 2002 v Ma (7)
Braniff, K. R. (Millwall), 2002 v G (1)
Brotherston, N. (Blackburn R), 1978 v Ei (sub) (1)
Buchanan, W. B. (Bolton W), 2002 v G (sub) (1)
Burns, L. (Port Vale), 1998 v Sw, S, Ei; 1999 v T, Fi, Mol, G, Mol, Ei; 2000 v F, T, G, Fi (13)

Capaldi, A. C. (Birmingham C), 2002 v D (sub), Ic, Ma, G (4)
Carlisle, W. T. (Crystal Palace), 2000 v Fi (sub); 2001 v Ma, Ic, Bul (1+sub), CzR; 2002 v D, Ic, Ma (9)
Carroll, R. E. (Wigan Ath), 1998 v S, Ei; 1999 v T, Fi, Mol, G, Mol, Ei; 2000 v T, G, Fi (11)
Carson, S. (Rangers), 2000 v Ma; (wirh Dundee U), 2002 v D (sub) (2)
Clarke, R. D. J. (Portadown), 1999 v Ei (sub), S; 2000 v F (sub), S, W (sub) (5)
Close, B. (Middlesbrough), 2002 v Ic, Ma (sub), G (3)
Clyde, M. G. (Wolverhampton W), 2002 v G (1)
Connell, T. E. (Coleraine), 1978 v Ei (sub) (1)
Coote, A. (Norwich C), 1998 v Sw (sub), S, Ei; 1999 v T, Fi,Mol, G, Mol, Ei; 2000 v F, T, G (12)
Convery, J. (Celtic), 2000 v S, W; 2001 v D, Ic (4)

Devine, D. (Omagh T), 1994 v R (1)
Devine, J. (Glentoran), 1990 v Is (1)
Dickson, H. (Wigan Ath). 2002 v Ma (1)
Dolan, J. (Millwall), 2000 v Fi, Ma, S; 2001 v Ma, D, Ic (6)
Donaghy, M. M. (Larne), 1978 v Ei (1)
Dowie, I. (Luton T), 1990 v Is (1)

Elliott, S. (Glentoran), 1999 v Fi (sub), Ei, S (sub) (3)

Feeney, L. (Linfield), 1998 v Ei (sub); 1999 v T, Fi, Mol; (with Rangers), G (sub), Ei, S; 2000 v Fi (8)
Feeney, W. (Bournemouth), 2002 v D, Ic (sub) (2)
Ferguson, M. (Glentoran), 2000 v T (sub), Ma (sub) (2)
Fitzgerald, D. (Rangers), 1998 v Sw, S; 1999 v T (sub), Fi (4)
Friars, S. M. (Liverpool), 1998 v Sw, S, Ei; (with Ipswich T), 1999 v T, Fi, Mol, G, Mol; 2000 v F, T, G, Ma, S, W; 2001 v Ma, D, Ic, CzR, Bul (2), CzR (21)

Gillespie, K. R. (Manchester U), 1994 v R (1)
Glendinning, M. (Bangor), 1994 v R (1)
Graham, G. L. (Crystal Palace), 1999 v S; 2000 v F, T, G, Fi (5)
Graham, R. S. (QPR), 1999 v Fi (sub), Mol, Ei (sub); 2000 v F (sub), T (sub), G (sub), Fi (sub), Ma, S, W; 2001 v Ma, D, CzR (sub), Bul (sub), CzR (sub) (15)
Gray, P. (Luton T), 1990 v Is (sub) (1)
Griffin, D. J. (St Johnstone), 1998 v S (sub), Ei; 1999 v T, Fi, G, Mol, Ei, S; 2000 v F, T (10)

Hamilton, G. (Blackburn R), 2000 v Ma (sub), S, W (sub); 2001 v Ma, D, Ic, CzR, Bul (2), CzR; (wirh Portadown), 2002 v Ic, Ma (12)
Hamilton, W. R. (Linfield), 1978 v Ei (1)
Harkin, M. P. (Wycombe W), Ma (sub), S (sub), W; 2001 v Ma (sub), D (sub), Ic, CzR, Bul (sub+1) (9)
Harvey, J. (Arsenal), 1978 v Ei (1)
Hawe, S. (Blackburn R), 2001 v Cz (1+sub) (2)
Hayes, T. (Luton T), 1978 v Ei (1)
Healy, D. J. (Manchester U), 1999 v Mol (sub), G (sub), Ei (sub), S; 2000 v F (sub), T, G, Fi (8)
Holmes, S. (Manchester C), Ma, S, W; 2001 v Ma, D, Ic, CzR, Bul (2), CzR; (with Wrexham), 2002 v D, Ic, Ma (13)
Hughes, M. E. (Manchester C), 1990 v Is (sub)
Hunter, M. (Glentoran), 2002 v G (sub) (1)

Ingham, M. (Sunderland), 2001 v CzR, Bul (2), CzR (4)

Johnson, D. M. (Blackburn R), 1998 v Sw, S, Ei; 1999 v T, Fi, G, Mol, Ei; 2000 v F, T, G (11)
Johnston, B. (Cliftonville), 1978 v Ei (1)

Kee, P. V. (Oxford U), 1990 v Is (1)
Kelly, D. (Derry C), 2000 v Ma, W; 2001 v Ma, Ic (sub), CzR, Bul (2), CzR; 2002 v D, Ic, Ma (11)
Kelly, N. (Oldham Ath), 1990 v Is (sub) (1)
Kirk, A. (Hearts), 1999 v S; 2000 v Ma, S, W; 2001 v Ma, D, Ic (sub); 2002 v D, Ic (9)

Lennon, N. F. (Manchester C), 1990 v Is; (with Crewe Alex), 1994 v R (2)
Lyttle, G. (Celtic), 1998 v Sw, S; (with Peterborough U), 1999 v T (sub), Mol (2), S; 2000 v G, Fi (8)

Magee, J. (Bangor), 1994 v R (sub) (1)
Magilton, J. (Liverpool), 1990 v Is (1)
Matthews, N. P. (Blackpool), 1990 v Is (1)
McAreavey, P. (Swindon T), 2000 v Ma, S; 2001 v Ma, D; 2002 v D, Ic (sub), Ma (sub) (7)
McBride, J. (Glentoran), 1994 v R (sub) (1)
McCallion, E. (Coleraine), 1998 v Sw (sub) (1)
McCann, G. S. (West Ham U), 2000 v S (sub), W; 2001 v D (sub), Ic, CzR, Bul (2), CzR; 2002 v D, Ic, Ma (11)

McCann, R. (Rangers), 2002 v G (sub) (1)
McCartney, G. (Sunderland), 2001 v D, CzR, Bul (2); 2002 v D (5)
McCourt, P. (Rochdale), 2002 v G (1)
McCoy, R. K. (Coleraine), 1990 v Is (1)
McCreery, D. (Manchester U), 1978 v Ei (1)
McFlynn, T. M. (QPR), 2000 v Ma (sub), W (sub); 2001 v Ma (sub), CzR (sub), Bul (sub+sub), CzR; (with Woking), 2002 v D (sub), Ic (sub); (with Margate), G (10)
McGibbon, P. C. G. (Manchester U), 1994 v R (1)
McGlinchey, B. (Manchester C), 1998 v Sw, S, Ei; (with Port Vale), 1999 v T, Fi, Mol, G, Mol, Ei, S; (with Gillingham), 2000 v F, G, T, Fi (14)
McIlroy, T. (Linfield), 1994 v R (sub) (1)
McKnight, P. (Rangers), 1998 v Sw; 1999 v T (sub), Mol (sub) (3)
McMahon, G. J. (Tottenham H),1994 v R (sub) (1)
McVeigh, A. (Ayr U), 2002 v G (sub) (1)
McVeigh, P. F. (Tottenham H), 1998 v S (sub), Ei; 1999 v T, Mol, G, Mol, Ei; 2000 v F, T (sub), G (sub), Fi (11)
Melaugh, G. M. (Aston Villa), 2002 v G (1)
Millar, W. P. (Port Vale), 1990 v Is (1)
Miskelly, D. T. (Oldham Ath), 2000 v F, Ma, S, W; 2001 v Ma, D, Ic; 2002 v D, Ic, Ma (10)
Moreland, V. (Glentoran), 1978 v Ei (sub) (1)
Morgan, M. P. T. (Preston NE), 1999 v S (1)
Morris, E. J. (WBA), 2002 v G (1)
Morrison, O. (Sheffield W), 2001 v Bul (sub); 2002 v Ma (sub) (2)
Morrow, A. (Northampton T), 2001 v D (sub) (1)
Mulryne, P. P. (Manchester U), Sw, S, Ei; (with Norwich C), 1999 v G, Mol (5)
Murray, W. (Linfield), 1978 v Ei (sub) (1)

Nicholl, J. M. (Manchester U), 1978 v Ei (1)
Nixon, C. (Glentoran), 2000 v Fi (sub) (1)

O'Hara, G. (Leeds U), 1994 v R (1)
O'Neill, M. A. M. (Hibernian), 1994 v R (1)
O'Neill, J. P. (Leicester C), 1978 v Ei (1)

Patterson, D. J. (Crystal Palace), 1994 v R (1)

Quinn, S. J. (Blackpool), 1994 v R (1)

Robinson, S. (Tottenham H), 1994 v R (1)

Simms, G. (Hartlepool U), 2001 v Bul (2), CzR; 2002 v D, Ic, Ma, G (7)
Skates, G. (Blackburn R), 2000 v Ma; 2001 v Ic (sub), CzR (2) (4)
Sloan, T. (Ballymena U), 1978 v Ei (1)

Taylor, M. S. (Fulham), 1998 v Sw (1)
Toner, C. (Tottenham H), 2000 v Ma (sub), S (sub), W; 2001 v D, Ic, CzR, Bul (2), CzR; 2002 v D, Ic, Ma (12)

Waterman, D. G. (Portsmouth), 1998 v Sw, S, Ei; 1999 v T, Fi, Mol, G, Mol, Ei, S (sub); 2000 v F, T, G, Fi (14)
Wells, D. P. (Barry T), 1999 v S (1)
Whitley, Jeff (Manchester C), 1998 v Sw, S, Ei; 1999 v T, Fi, Mol, G, Ei, S; 2000 v F, G, T, Ma, S, W; 2001 v Ma, Ic (17)

FA SCHOOLS & YOUTH GAMES 2001–02

ENGLAND UNDER-20

Howarth (York C), Halls (Arsenal), Samuel (Aston Villa), Noble (Watford), Reid (Preston NE), Clarke (Everton), Davis (Manchester U), Ricketts (Arsenal), Crouch (Aston Villa), Keenan (Chelsea), Bothroyd (Coventry C), Myhill (Aston Villa), Richardson (Leeds U), Sidwell (Brentford), Konchesky (Charlton Ath), Johnson A (Birmingham C), Murray (Derby Co), Richards (Blackburn R), McSheffrey (Coventry C), Evans (QPR), Jackson (Tottenham H), Lescott (Wolverhampton W), Nolan (Bolton W), Webber (Manchester U), Jenkins (Wimbledon), Henry (Stoke C), Hamshaw (Sheffield W), Parnaby (Middlesbrough), Jagielka (Sheffield U), Armstrong (Oldham Ath), Knight (Huddersfield T loan), Bywater (West Ham U), Pead (Coventry C), McMaster (Leeds U), Bewers (Aston Villa).

22 Nov

England 1 *(Keenan 76)*   **Portugal 0**

England: Howarth (Myhill 46); Halls (Richardson 77), Samuel, Noble (Sidwell 64), Reid (Konchesky 46), Clarke, Davis (Johnson A 46), Ricketts (Murray 46), Crouch (Richards 64), Keenan, Bothroyd (McSheffrey 46).

13 Mar

England 3 *(Davis 25, 50, Richards 80)*   **Finland 0**

England: Evans (Howarth 46); Halls (Richardson 60), Jackson (Jenkins 46), Noble (Henry 67), Clarke (Reid 83), Lescott, Davis (Hamshaw 83), Nolan, Webber (Richards 70), Ricketts, Bothroyd.

10 Apr

Portugal 2   England 0

England: Myhill (Howarth 46); Halls, Jackson, Noble (Sidwell 70), Clarke, Parnaby (Richardson 46), Davis, Ricketts (Jagielka 46), Webber, Keenan (Henry 46), McSheffrey (Hamshaw 46).

6 May

China 0   England 0

England: Evans; Halls (Richardson 55), Armstrong, Jackson, Clarke, Lescott, Knight, Noble, Webber, Davis (Murray 70), McSheffrey (Hamshaw 68).

10 May

Poland 0   England 1 *(Parnaby 46)*

England: Bywater; Jackson (Noble 58), Clarke, Lescott, Knight (McMaster 68), Davis, Murray, Pead, Hamshaw, Parnaby, Richardson.

12 May

Portugal 0   England 1 *(Davis 77)*

England: Howarth; Halls (Richardson 55), Armstrong, Clarke, Knight, Noble, Davis, McSheffrey (Hamshaw 70), McMaster (Pead 65), Parnaby, Bewers.

14 May

Brazil 0   England 0

England: Evans; Jackson, Clarke, Lescott, Knight, Webber, Davis (McSheffrey 66), Pead (Murray 74), Hamshaw, Parnaby, Richardson.

17 May

Japan 0   England 0

Japan won 5-4 on penalties.
England: Evans; Halls, Armstrong, Jackson, Clarke, Lescott, Knight, Webber (McSheffrey 55), Murray, Hamshaw, Bewers (Pead 50).

ENGLAND UNDER-19

Grant (Derby Co), Duncan (QPR), McKie (Tottenham H), Bowditch (Tottenham H), Clark (Sunderland), Davenport (Coventry C), Pennant (Arsenal), O'Neil (Portsmouth), Chopra (Newcastle U), Cooke (Aston Villa), Howard (Southampton), Lonergan (Preston NE),

Hoyte (Arsenal), Hylton (Aston Villa), Fox (Manchester U), Mooniaruck (Manchester U), Moore S (Aston Villa), Prince (Liverpool), O'Hanlon (Everton), Muirhead (Manchester U), Dove (Middlesbrough), Johnson (West Ham U), Jenas (Nottingham F), Morgan (Wimbledon), Thomas (Arsenal), Ashton (Crewe Alex), Welsh (Liverpool), Bent D (Ipswich T), Carter (Birmingham C), Otsemobor (Liverpool), Offiong (Newcastle U), Townson (Rochdale), Bloomfield (Ipswich T), Garry (Arsenal), Cole (Chelsea).

1 Oct

England 2 *(Pennant, Moore S)*   **Iceland 0**

England: Grant (Lonergan); Duncan (Hoyte), McKie (Hylton), Bowditch (Fox), Clark, Davenport, Pennant, O'Neil (Mooniaruck), Chopra (Moore S), Cooke, Howard (Prince).

4 Oct

England 0   Russia 1

England: Grant; Hoyte (Duncan), Hylton (McKie), Bowditch (Fox), O'Hanlon, Clark, Muirhead (Dove), O'Neil, Moore S (Prince), Cooke, Chopra.

7 Nov+

England 4 *(Jenas, Chopra, Ashton 2 (2 pens))*   **Georgia 1**

England: Grant; Hoyte, Hylton, Johnson, Clark, O'Neil, Cooke, Jenas, Chopra, Morgan (Thomas), Ashton (Moore S).

11 Nov+

England 3 *(Jenas, Hoyte, Clark)*   **Hungary 1**

England: Grant; Hoyte, Hylton, Jenas, Johnson, Clark, Chopra, O'Neil, Ashton (Moore S), Cooke, Morgan (Bowditch).

14 Feb

England 3 *(Morgan 8, Bent D 43, 72)*   **Germany 1**

England: Lonergan; Hoyte (Otsemobor 72), Hylton, Welsh (Offiong 84), Johnson, Clark, Bent D, Fox (Townson 64), Ashton (Chopra 46), Carter (Cooke 46), Morgan (Bloomfield 64).

17 Apr+

Lithuania 1   England 1 *(Bent D 33)*

England: Grant; Hoyte, Garry (Hylton 80), Welsh, Johnson, Clark, Chopra, O'Neil, Bent D (Cole 87), Cooke (Fox 70), Townson.

21 Apr+

England 2 *(Chopra 82, Pennant 84)*   **Lithuania 1**

England: Grant; Hoyte, Garry, Bowditch (Fox 85), Johnson, Clark, Pennant, Welsh, Cole (Moore S 53), O'Neil, Bent D (Chopra 68).

ENGLAND UNDER-18

Camp (Derby Co), Taylor R (Tranmere R), Moogan A (Everton), Bentley (Arsenal), Leacock (Fulham), Taylor K (Manchester U), Watt (Blackburn R), Donnelly (Blackburn R), Brown (Sunderland), Richardson (Manchester U), Downing (Middlesbrough), Steele (Peterborough U), Sims (Manchester U), Butler (Liverpool), Kilgallon (Leeds U), Byrne (Manchester U), Cade (Middlesbrough), Birchall (Arsenal), Wettner (Tottenham H), Jones (Manchester U), Mills (Derby Co), Slabber (Tottenham H), Westcarr (Nottingham F), Pidgeley (Chelsea), Schumacher (Everton), Kitamirike (Chelsea), Scothern (Barnsley), Foster (Tottenham H).

4 Mar

Italy 3   England 0

England: Camp (Steele); Taylor R (Sims), Moogan A (Butler), Bentley, Leacock, Taylor K (Kilgallon), Watt (Byrne), Donnelly (Cade), Brown (Birchall), Richardson (Wettner), Downing (Jones).

6 June

Slovakia 0   England 1

England: Steele; Taylor R, Moogan A, Schumacher, Leacock, Bentley, Donnelly (Mills), Downing, Brown (Slabber), Watt (Westcarr), Kilgallon.

7 June

Norway 3   England 2

England: Pidgeley; Schumacher (Taylor R), Kitamirike, Westcarr (Moogan A), Scothern, Donnelly (Bentley), Watt (Downing), Kilgallon, Foster, Slabber (Brown), Mills.

9 June

Portugal 3   England 0

England: Steele (Pidgeley); Moogan A, Schumacher, Leacock, Kitamirike (Taylor R), Bentley, Donnelly, Downing, Brown (Scothern), Watt (Westcarr), Kilgallon (Mills).

ENGLAND UNDER 17

Turnbull (Middlesbrough), Bridges (Aston Villa), Tillen (Chelsea), McDermott (Newcastle U), Hogg (Ipswich T), Small (Arsenal), Croft (Manchester C), Gardner (Newcastle U), Proffitt (Manchester C), Brown (Everton), Doherty (Fulham), Rooney (Everton), Guy (Newcastle U), Eyre (Tottenham H), Sankofa (Charlton Ath), Long (Charlton Ath), Watson L (Watford), Harban (Barnsley), Dodds (Sunderland), Tolley (Peterborough U), Jeffreys (Chelsea), Smyth (Liverpool), Watson J (Tottenham H), Eckersley (Manchester U), Price (Tottenham H), Nowacki (Fulham), Borrowdale (Crystal Palace), Gobern (Wolverhampton W), Benson (Northampton T), Routledge (Crystal Palace), Drench (Blackburn R), Oldham (Barnsley), Biggins (Nottingham F), Sadler (Birmingham C), Groves (Nottingham F), Mannix (Liverpool), Raven (Liverpool), Collins (Sunderland), Samba (Millwall).

12 July 2001

England 1 *(Proffitt 29)*   **Italy 2**

England: Turnbull; Bridges, Tillen, McDermott, Hogg, Small, Croft, Gardner (Rooney 64), Proffitt (Guy 48), Brown, Doherty.

15 July 2001

England 0   Brazil 2

England: Eyre; Small, Tillen, McDermott, Hogg, Sankofa, Croft, Gardner (Proffitt 26), Guy (Rooney 56), Brown, Doherty (Long 63).

1 Aug 2001

Faeroes 1   England 4 *(Jeffreys 22, Smyth 24, Long 40, 79)*

England: Watson L; Harban (Nowacki 41), Dodds, Small, Tolley (Borrowdale 41), Jeffreys (Gobern 58), Smyth (Benson 54), Watson J, Eckersley (Routledge 41), Long, Price.

2 Aug 2001

Finland 1   England 3 *(Oldham 26, 76, Routledge 47)*

England: Drench; Harban, Borrowdale, Dodds (Benson 78), Nowacki, Small (Watson J 71), Oldham, Jeffreys (Tolley 59), Smyth (Price 59), Long (Gobern 75), Routledge.

4 Aug 2001

Norway 1   England 3 *(Routledge 2, Smyth 55, Jeffreys 65)*

England: Watson L; Harban, Dodds (Borrowdale 64), Nowacki, Small, Oldham (Tolley 70), Eckersley, Gobern (Jeffreys 41), Long (Benson 62), Price (Smyth 41), Routledge.

5 Aug 2001

Slovakia 1   England 1 *(Small 65)*
England won 3-1 on penalties.

England: Drench; Harban, Borrowdale, Dodds, Small, Oldham (Price 76), Jeffreys, Smyth, Eckersley, Long, Routledge.

3 Oct 2001

England 3 *(Guy, McDermott, Doherty)*   **Spain 2**

England: Eyre; Biggins (Borrowdale), Sadler, McDermott, Hogg, Sankofa, Rooney, Croft, Guy (Groves), Brown (Gardner), Doherty (Smyth).

22 Nov 2001

England 6 *(Sadler, Smyth, Long, Routledge, Mannix, Rooney)*   **Poland 0**

England: Turnbull (Drench); Bridges (Sankofa), Eckersley, Mannix, Raven, Sadler, Routledge, Croft (McDermott), Smyth (Rooney), Long (Brown), Doherty (Guy).

11 Dec 2001

Portugal 1   England 1 *(Collins 26)*

England: Drench; Biggins (Small 76), Borrowdale, Mannix (Dodds 71), Raven, Collins, Routledge, Croft (Brown 50), Proffitt, Long (Gardner 50), Doherty (Smyth 68).

13 Dec 2001

Portugal 1   England 1 *(Long 69)*

England: Turnbull; Borrowdale, Raven, Collins (Biggins 40), Croft, Proffitt, Small, Brown (Routledge 58), Dodds (Long 34), Smyth (Mannix 40), Gardner (Doherty 68).

13 Feb 2002

England 2 *(Hogg, Doherty)*   **Slovakia 2**

England: Turnbull; Bridges (Biggins), Sadler (Borrowdale), Gardner, Raven, Hogg, Routledge, Croft (Brown), Samba (Groves), Long (Rooney), Doherty (Smyth).

6 Mar 2002+

England 3 *(Gardner 12, Routledge 19, 70)*   **Scotland 1**

England: Turnbull; Biggins, Sadler, Gardner, Raven, Hogg, Routledge (Proffitt 75), Croft (Brown 78), Rooney (Smyth 59), Long, Doherty.

10 Mar 2002+

England 4 *(Long 11, Routledge 53, Rooney 65, Raven 73)*   **Lithuania 0**

England: Drench; Biggins, Sadler (Borrowdale 41), Gardner, Raven, Hogg (Collins 62), Routledge, Croft (Groves 73), Rooney, Long, Smyth.

27 Apr 2002+

Finland 2   England 3 *(Hogg 12, Smyth 41, Doherty 68)*

England: Drench; Biggins, Borrowdale, Gardner, Raven, Hogg, Routledge, Croft, Rooney (Proffitt 58), Long (Mannix 58), Smyth (Doherty 67).

29 Apr 2002+

Holland 0   England 2 *(Rooney 32, Long 54)*

England: Drench; Biggins, Borrowdale, Gardner, Raven, Routledge, Croft (Mannix 74), Rooney (Proffitt 71), Long, Smyth, Sadler.

1 May 2002+

Denmark 0   England 0

England: Eyre; Biggins, Raven, Hogg, Long (Croft 41), Sadler, Mannix, Groves, Brown, Proffitt, Doherty.

4 May 2002+

Yugoslavia 0   England 1 *(Rooney 7)*

England: Drench; Biggins, Borrowdale, Gardner, Raven (Sadler 56), Hogg, Routledge, Croft (Groves 76), Rooney, Long, Smyth.

7 May 2002+

Switzerland 3   England 0

England: Drench; Biggins, Borrowdale, Gardner, Hogg, Routledge, Croft (Mannix 61), Rooney, Long (Proffitt 56), Smyth (Doherty 70), Sadler.

10 May 2002+

Spain 1   England 4 *(Routledge 37, Rooney 40, 52, 72)*

England: Drench; Biggins, Borrowdale, Gardner, Hogg, Routledge, Rooney (Proffitt 76), Sadler, Groves, Brown (Croft 63), Doherty (Smyth 60).

ENGLAND UNDER 16

Heaton (Manchester U), Smith D (Chelsea), Gillan (Bolton W), Doyle (Derby Co), Pettigrew (Chelsea), Taylor S (Newcastle U), Bowditch (Ipswich T), Leadbitter (Sunderland), Moore L (Aston Villa), Nix (Manchester U), Forte (Sheffield U), Martin D (Derby Co), Ifil (Tottenham H), O'Hara (Arsenal), Milner (Leeds U), Nevins (Manchester U), Anyon (Blackburn R), Smith D (Sunderland), Huddlestone (Derby Co), Cartwright (Manchester C), Lennon (Leeds U), Webster (Newcastle U), Jarvis (Norwich C), Giddings (Coventry C), Smith R (Arsenal), Sylvester (Chelsea), Jones (Manchester U), Barcham (Tottenham H), Fontaine (Fulham), Martin D (Wimbledon), McMahon (Middlesbrough), Fisher (Watford), Poulter (Sheffield W), Parrington (West Ham U), Mawer (Watford), Taylor A (Middlesbrough), Knight (Middlesbrough), Roberts (Liverpool), Ashikodi (Millwall), Henry (West Ham U), Jones B (Crewe Alex), Noble (West Ham U), Alnwick (Sunderland), Berry (Crystal Palace), Chapman (Watford).

12 Oct*

England 3 *(Moore L 38, 49, 77)*   **Northern Ireland 0**

England: Heaton; Dean Smith [Chelsea], Gillan (Daniel Martin [Derby Co] 79), Doyle (Ifil 76), Pettigrew, Taylor S, Bowditch, Leadbitter, Moore L, Nix (O'Hara 46), Forte (Milner 63).

25 Oct

England 4 *(Bowditch 16, 58, Leadbitter 15, 24)*   **Spain 3**

England: Heaton; Nevins (Dean Smith 46), Gillan (Daniel Martin 67), Doyle, Pettigrew, Taylor S, Bowditch, Leadbitter, Moore L, O'Hara, Forte.

2 Nov*

England 3 *(Cartwright 7, Jarvis 41, Giddings 69)*

Wales 1

England: Anyon; Ifil, Daniel Smith [Sunderland], Huddlestone, Cartwright, Daniel Martin, Lennon (Sylvester 80), Webster (Jones R 73), Jarvis, Giddings, Smith R (Barcham 73).

12 Nov

England 2 *(Doyle 10, Smith R 79)*   **Holland 1**

England: Heaton; Dean Smith (Nevins 56), Daniel Smith, Doyle, Taylor S, Fontaine, Bowditch (Lennon 73), Leadbitter (Giddings 69), Moore L, O'Hara, Forte (Smith R 60).

15 Nov

England 0   Germany 2

England: Heaton (Anyon 25); Nevins (Dean Smith 40), Daniel Smith, Doyle, Taylor S, Fontaine, Bowditch (Lennon 61), Leadbitter, Moore L, O'Hara (Giddings 40), Forte (Smith R 80).

30 Nov*

Scotland 2   England 4 *(Daniel Martin 7, Jarvis 5, 83, own goal)*

England: David Martin [Wimbledon] (Poulter 40); Ifil, Gillan, Huddlestone, McMahon (Parrington 78), Daniel Martin, Lennon (Sylvester 78), Webster (Milner 40), Jarvis, Nix, Fisher (Mawer 59).

26 Mar

Japan 1   England 3 *(Milner 9, Forte 67, 72)*

England: Poulter; Ifil (Nevins 78), Gillan, Huddlestone (Nix 61), McMahon, Fontaine, Milner (Lennon 74), Leadbitter, Jarvis (Bowditch 67), Giddings, Forte (Webster 74).

28 Mar

Argentina 0   England 0

England: Anyon; Ifil, McMahon, Milner (Forte 46), Giddings, Lennon, Bowditch (Jarvis 46), Nevins (Leadbitter 57), Nix, Webster (Huddlestone 67), Taylor A.

30 Mar

Italy 1   England 2 *(Leadbitter 28, Bowditch 41)*

England: Anyon; Ifil, Gillan (Taylor A 75), Huddlestone, McMahon, Fontaine, Leadbitter, Jarvis (Lennon 68), Forte (Milner 78), Bowditch, Nix (Giddings 40).

1 Apr

Portugal 0   England 2 *(Bowditch 58, Lennon 60)*

England: Anyon; Ifil, Gillan (Fontaine 75), Huddlestone, Milner, Leadbitter, Giddings, Forte (Jarvis 70), Lennon, Bowditch, Taylor A.

2 May

Belgium 1   England 3 *(Smith R 14, Ashikodi 29, Noble 70)*

England: Knight; Roberts, Daniel Smith (Henry 75), Doyle, Pettigrew (Jones B 75), Daniel Martin, Barcham (Sylvester 64), Jones R (Noble 64), Ashikodi, O'Hara, Smith R.

3 May

Israel 1   England 0

England: Alnwick; Daniel Smith, Pettigrew, Barcham (Smith R 61), Jones R (O'Hara 53), Noble (Doyle 39), Jones B, Henry, Berry, Chapman, Sylvester (Ashikodi 40).

4 May

Northern Ireland 1   England 1 *(own goal 60)*

England: Knight; Roberts (Henry 36), Doyle, Pettigrew (Daniel Smith 58), Daniel Martin (Sylvester 78), Ashikodi, O'Hara, Smith R, Jones B, Berry (Barcham 50), Chapman (Jones R 58).

6 May

Scotland 1   England 2 *(Barcham 16, Sylvester 72)*

England: Alnwick; Daniel Smith, Doyle, Daniel Martin (Chapman 61), Barcham, Ashikodi (Sylvester 40), O'Hara, Smith R, Jones B, Henry (Pettigrew 53), Berry.

*Victory Shield; + UEFA Championship.

WOMEN'S FOOTBALL 2001–02

Women's football continues to expand at a rapid rate as evidenced by the increased number of senior competitions, which have recently been implemented. Indeed there were 63 more teams involving over 1,000 women taking part in League and Cup competitions last season.

The most prestigious of the competitions was the National Division Championship, which was again won by Arsenal and for the second year in succession. It was their fifth League title in 10 seasons and their playing record was 49 points from 18 games with an 8-point margin over Doncaster Belles. Their achievements almost matched their men's counterparts who annexed the Premier League and FA Cup double. Not only that but the Highbury club won the Women's FA Umbro Charity Shield by 5-2 over Doncaster Belles and reached the quarter-finals of the inaugural UEFA Women's Cup. Their reserves won the Premier League Southern Division 1 title and the Premier Reserve League Cup with a 7-0 victory over Doncaster Belles.

Surprisingly though the Gunners were not the most successful team. That honour went to the first professional outfit, Fulham Ladies. They completed the double by securing the FA Women's Cup with a 2-1 victory, over clearly the most unlucky team of the season, the Doncaster Belles and easily won the Women's Premier League Cup with a 7-0 victory over Birmingham City. In addition they gained promotion to the Premier National Division itself by winning the Southern Division Championship with 66 points from 22 games with a winning margin of 22 points over Bristol Rovers. The Northern Division title went to Birmingham City with 51 points from 20 matches, a margin of 14 points over Wolverhampton Wanderers. Sunderland in the Midlands/North Division and Ipswich Town in the Southern Division 2 won the other two reserve sections.

Individual domestic achievements went to Marieanne Spacey of Arsenal, who has become arguably the first women's icon in the English game, won the titles of AXA National Division top scorer, AXA Players' Player of the Year and the Sport Relief Special Achievement Award.

Other Honours were achieved by the following:

The Nationwide International Player of the Year	Katie Chapman – Fulham
The Umbro Young Player of the Year	Fara Williams
Umbro "Top Scorer" Awards	Katy Ward – Birmingham City (Northern Division) Marianne Pettersen – Fulham (Southern Division)
The AXA Manager of the Year	Mark Hodgson – Leeds United
The "Club of the Year" Award	Birmingham City
The "She Kicks" Media Award	Lincoln City
The AXA Northern Division Player of the Year	Anne Blackham – Wolves
The AXA FA Cup Final Player of the Match	Mandy Lowe – Doncaster Belles

Perhaps the greatest recognition of women's football has come in the Queen's Birthday Honours List where England Women's National Coach Hope Powell has received an OBE for her work for the sport.

Turning to the International scene Powell has led her side to qualification for the play-offs for the Women's World Cup, the Finals of which take place in China in September 2003. Highlight of the campaign was the 8-0 defeat of rivals Portugal. The England Under 17s and Under 19s have again shown great promise with the Under 19s going out in the semi-finals of the Women's European Cup 1-0 to Germany whilst the Under 17s won the Scotland tournament on goals scored from a very strong USA team.

KEN GOLDMAN

The FA Women's Premier League

National Division

	P	W	D	L	F	A	GD	Pts
Arsenal LFC	18	16	1	1	60	15	45	49
Doncaster Belles LFC	18	13	2	3	57	21	36	41
Charlton Athletic WFC	18	10	1	7	40	24	16	31
Leeds United	18	7	5	6	36	37	-1	26
Everton LFC	18	8	2	8	30	31	-1	26
Tranmere Rovers LFC	18	7	3	8	31	36	-5	24
Brighton & Hove Albion	18	7	3	8	19	33	-14	24
Southampton Saints WFC	18	5	3	10	19	34	-15	18
Barry Town LFC	18	2	3	13	19	49	-30	9
Sunderland AFC Women	18	1	5	12	15	46	-31	8

Northern Division

	P	W	D	L	F	A	GD	Pts
Birmingham City LFC	20	16	3	1	68	21	47	51
Wolverhampton Wanderers	20	11	4	5	39	27	12	37
Oldham Curzon LFC	20	10	6	4	39	22	17	36
Ilkeston Town LFC	20	9	6	5	43	27	16	33
Liverpool LFC	20	8	6	6	41	27	14	30
Bangor City LFC	20	7	8	5	40	36	4	29
Sheffield Wednesday LFC	20	6	7	7	33	38	-5	25
Aston Villa LFC	20	6	6	8	42	39	3	24
Garswood Saints WFC	20	4	6	10	21	47	-26	18
Manchester City LFC	20	4	4	12	19	45	-26	16
Coventry City LFC	20	0	2	18	8	64	-56	2

Southern Division

	P	W	D	L	F	A	GD	Pts
Fulham LFC	22	22	0	0	234	6	228	66
Bristol Rovers WFC	22	14	2	6	72	35	37	44
Millwall Lionesses LFC	22	14	1	7	55	55	0	43
Chelsea LFC	22	13	2	7	59	51	8	41
Langford LFC	22	12	1	9	53	46	7	37
Wimbledon LFC	22	11	3	8	41	55	-14	36
Ipswich Town LFC	22	8	4	10	43	52	-9	28
Barking LFC	22	7	2	13	40	79	-39	23
Newport County LFC	22	6	3	13	37	60	-23	21
*Barnet LFC	22	5	6	11	27	75	-48	18
Queens Park Rangers LFC	22	3	5	14	19	60	-41	14
Berkhamstead Town LFC	22	-1	3	18	10	116	-106	6

* indicates three points deducted.

Midlands/North Reserve Division

	P	W	D	L	F	A	GD	Pts
Sunderland AFC Women	14	11	1	2	53	15	38	34
Doncaster Belles LFC	14	8	1	4	27	21	6	28
Everton LFC	14	8	2	3	45	17	28	26
*Leeds United	14	8	2	4	49	22	27	25
Wolverhampton Wanderers	14	6	0	8	29	37	-8	18
Manchester City LFC	14	4	1	9	33	55	-22	13
Sheffield Wednesday LFC	14	4	1	9	23	64	-41	13
Ilkeston Town LFC	14	1	2	11	12	40	-28	5

* indicates one point deducted.
** indicates three points awarded.

Southern Reserve Division 1

	P	W	D	L	F	A	GD	Pts
Arsenal LFC	6	6	0	0	44	2	42	18
Charlton Athletic WFC	6	5	0	1	28	12	16	15
Fulham LFC	6	4	0	2	27	12	15	12
Brighton & Hove Albion	6	2	0	4	14	12	2	6
Millwall Lionesses LFC	6	2	0	4	7	41	–34	6
Southampton Saints WFC	6	1	0	5	10	27	–17	3
Chelsea LFC	6	1	0	5	3	27	–24	3

Southern Reserve Division 2

	P	W	D	L	F	A	GD	Pts
Ipswich Town LFC	6	5	0	1	24	7	17	15
Newport County LFC	6	5	0	1	16	6	10	15
Langford LFC	6	3	1	2	12	4	8	10
Wimbledon LFC	6	3	1	2	12	11	1	10
Bristol Rovers WFC	6	2	1	3	22	11	+11	7
Barking LFC	6	0	2	4	9	25	–16	2

ENGLAND WOMEN'S RECORD 2001–02

Tournament	Date	Opponents	Venue	Attendance	Score	Goalscorers
5th UEFA Finals, Group Stage	24.06.01	Russia	Jena	1253	1-1	Banks
5th UEFA Finals, Group Stage	27.06.01	Sweden	Jena	1127	0-4	–
5th UEFA Finals, Group Stage	30.06.01	Germany	Jena	11,312	0-3	–
Friendly	23.08.01	Denmark	Northampton	2902	0-3	–
World Cup qualifier	27.09.01	Germany	Kassel	c.10,000	1-3	Yankey
World Cup qualifier	04.11.01	Holland	Grimsby Town	4130	0-0	–
World Cup qualifier	24.11.01	Portugal	Aveiro	c.1500	1-1	Karen Walker
Friendly	25.01.02	Sweden	La Manga	Training game	0-5	–
World Cup qualifier	24.02.02	Portugal	Portsmouth FC	8821	3-0	Fara Williams, Kelly Smith 2
Friendly – Algarve Cup	01.03.02	Norway	Municipal Stadium, Albufeira	c.50	1-3	Angie Banks
Friendly – Algarve Cup	03.03.02	USA	Municipal Stadium, Ferreiras	c.250	0-2	–
Friendly – Algarve Cup	05.03.02	Sweden	Municipal Stadium, Lagos	c.150	3-6	Walker 2, Amanda Barr
Friendly – Algarve Cup	07.03.02	Scotland	Municipal Stadium, Quarteira	c.50	4-1	Walker, Williams, Exley, Burke
World Cup Qualifier	23.03.02	Holland	Zuiderpark Stadion	c.2000	4-1	Chapman, Burke, Smith, Walker
World Cup Qualifer	19.05.02	Germany	Crystal Palace FC	14,107	0-1	–

ENGLAND UNDER-19s

15.11.01	Denmark v England	EC qualifier	3-4	Ellen Maggs, Laura Bassett, Katy Ward
17.11.01	England v Iceland	EC qualifier	2-1	Michelle Hickmott, Katy Ward
19.11.01	England v Czech Republic	EC qualifier	3-0	Kelly McDougall, Katy Ward, Fara Williams
06.03.02	France v England	Friendly	0-1	–
08.03.02	France v England	Friendly	1-2	Katy Ward
03.05.02	England v Norway	EC Finals – Group A	3-1	Michelle Hickmott, Shelley Cox, Kelly McDougall
05.05.02	England v Denmark	EC Finals – Group A	1-2	Faye Dunn
07.05.02	England v Switzerland	EC Finals – Group A	3-4	Faye Dunn, Katy Ward 2
10.05.02	England v Germany	EC Finals – semi final	0-1	–

ENGLAND UNDER-17s

19.07.01	England v Rep. Ireland	Friendly	4-0	Shelly Cox, Kim Holden, Alex Scott 2
21.07.01	England v Rep. Ireland	Friendly	3-1	Jo Potter, Alex Scott, Sarah Smith
31.03.02	England v Rep. Ireland	Scotland Tournament	3-1	Anita Asante 2, Natasha Caswell
03.04.02	England v N. Ireland	Scotland Tournament	7-0	Percival, Griffin, Ta 2, Holden, Emmanuel, Bailey
05.04.02	England v USA	Scotland Tournament	4-2	Kemp, Bailey, Holden, Shakes
07.04.02	England v Scotland	Scotland Tournament	3-5	Asante 2, Caswell

Scotland Tournament Final Table

	P	W	D	L	F	A	GD	Pts
England	4	3	0	1	17	8	9	9
USA	4	3	0	1	14	5	9	9
Rep of Ireland	4	1	1	2	3	6	–3	4
Northern Ireland	4	1	1	2	3	14	–11	4
Scotland	4	1	0	3	6	10	–4	3

AXA FA WOMEN'S CUP 2001–02

FIRST QUALIFYING ROUND

Bury Girls & Ladies v Corwen	14-0	Preston North End v Warrington Grange	3-3
Billingham v Bolton Wanderers (Supporters)	8-2	*Warrington Grange won 3-0 on penalties.*	
Barnsley v Wigan	3-0	Greyhound Gunners v Ossett Albion	2-3
		Gretna w.o. v Morley Spurs withdrew	

Stockport Celtic v Tameside Girls ... 3-2
Newsham PH v Killingworth YPC ... 0-1
Bolton Wanderers v Darlington RA ... 4-0
Windscale v Wakefield ... 4-0
Loughborough Students v Kidderminster Harriers ... 6-4
King's Lynn withdrew v University of Birmingham w.o.
Chaffoteaux v Great Wyrley ... 6-0
Leicester City v Kettering Amazons ... 4-0
Rushden & Diamonds v Kesteven Grantham ... 8-1
Gresley Rovers v Tamworth ... 3-7
Pearl v ES Barwell ... 5-2
Nettleham v Belper Town ... 0-7
Gravesend & Northfleet v Wycombe Wanderers ... 4-1
West Ham United v Brunel University ... 3-2
Woking v Thame United ... 6-2
Slough v Royston Town ... 6-0
Woodham Radars v Abbey Rangers ... 3-7
Haverhill U's v Colney Heath ... 1-3
Barnet Copthall v Leighton United ... 5-0
Brentford v Redbridge Wanderers ... 4-2
Launton v Viking ... 7-1
Crowborough Athletic v Haywards Heath ... 5-3
Denham United v Mansfield Road ... 4-0
Crystal Palace v Woodbridge Town ... 1-0
Sawbridgeworth Town v Tring Town ... 1-5
Malling v London Ladies ... 4-2
Okeford United v Keynsham Town ... 1-4
Newquay v Penzance ... 4-2
Wadebridge Town v Corfe Hills United ... 0-10
Bristol United v Exeter City ... 0-7
Cogan Coronation v Rover Oxford ... 2-4
Dorchester v Wendron ... 17-0
Bournemouth Town v Swindon Spitfires ... 7-0
North Malton Sports v Marjons ... 2-5

SECOND QUALIFYING ROUND
Bolton Wanderers v South Durham Royals ... 9-1
Killingworth YPC v Stockport Celtic ... 4-2
Gretna v Bolton Ambassadors ... 11-0
Thorpe United v Steel City Wanderers ... 5-1
Warrington Grange v Bury Girls & Ladies ... 2-5
Liverpool Feds v Penrith Sapphires ... 3-0
Barnsley v Ossett Albion ... 7-0
Billingham v Windscale ... 5-1
Rushden & Diamonds v Cambridge United ... 4-1
Blaby & Whetstone v Loughborough ... 0-8
Wisbech Town v Tamworth ... 0-13
University of Birmingham v Oadby Town ... 2-3
Leicester City v Pearl ... 5-0
North Staffs v Belper Town ... 0-4
Chaffoteaux v Loughborough Students ... 1-4
Colney Heath v Harringey Borough ... 1-0
Brentford v Chiswick United ... 2-1
Gravesend & Northfleet v Slough ... 2-2
   Gravesend & Northfleet won 5-4 on penalties.
Crystal Palace v West Ham United ... 0-3
Launton v Malling ... 0-7
Tring Town v Barnet Copthall ... 0-5
Luton Town Belles v Stocklake ... 5-2
Woking v Redbridge Raiders ... 1-4
Thatcham Town v Caversham ... 1-12
Denham United v Harlow Town ... 3-1
Newport Pagnall Town v Redhill ... 0-10
Hastings Town v Crowborough Athletic ... 2-3
Croydon Postal withdrew v Abbey Rangers w.o.
Rover Oxford v Launceston ... 8-0
Exeter City v Marjons ... 6-1
Dorchester v Newquay ... 3-2
Wimborne Town v Bournemouth Town ... 2-4
Corfe Hills United v Keynsham Town ... 0-3

FIRST ROUND
Chester City v Blackburn Rovers ... 3-1
Bury Girls & Ladies v Parkgate ... 3-5
Billingham v Liverpool Feds ... 3-3
   Liverpool Feds won 7-6 on penalties.
Newcastle v Bolton Wanderers ... 4-0
Manchester United v Barnsley ... 2-1
Stockport County v Gretna ... 5-2
MFC Ladies v Bradford City ... 2-0
Killingworth YPC v Leeds City Vixens ... 4-2
Chester-Le-Street v Blackpool Wren Rovers ... 0-1
Huddersfield Town v Thorpe United ... 1-0
Rushden & Diamonds v Tamworth ... 1-0
Ilkeston v Leicester City ... 0-1
Highfield Rangers v Oadby Town ... 7-0

Shrewsbury Town v Chesterfield ... 1-4
Lincoln City v Telford United ... 7-1
Cambridge University v Belper Town ... 3-1
Port Vale v Loughborough ... 4-0
Peterborough United v Norwich City Racers ... 2-2
   Peterborough United won 6-5 on penalties.
Derby County v Stafford Rangers ... 1-4
Stowmarket v Lichfield Diamonds ... 5-1
Crowborough Athletic v Brentford ... 5-2
Caversham v Hampton ... 0-1
Chelmsford City v Charlton ... 3-2
Bedford Town Belles v Gravesend & Northfleet ... 6-1
Chesham United v Enfield ... 1-3
Redbridge Raiders v Luton Town Belles ... 4-0
Denham United v Redhill ... 2-4
Gillingham v Colney Heath ... 2-1
Watford v Barnet Copthall ... 4-0
West Ham United v Abbey Rangers ... 4-1
Whitehawk v Malling ... 3-1
Southampton v Yeovil Town ... 1-4
Exeter City v Keynsham Town ... 3-0
Rover Oxford v Portsmouth ... 0-3
Reading Royals v Reading ... 1-3
Swindon Town v Cardiff City ... 3-4
Dorchester v Clevedon Town ... 1-2
Bournemouth Town v Bristol City ... 1-9
Plymouth Argyle v Newton Abbott ... 0-6
Bye: Loughborough Students.

SECOND ROUND
Huddersfield Town v Blackpool Wren Rovers ... 3-1
Manchester United v Liverpool Feds ... 0-1
Stockport County v Killingworth YPC ... 4-1
MFC Ladies v Chester City ... 2-3
Newcastle v Parkgate ... 5-2
Loughborough Students v Peterborough United ... 7-1
Lincoln City v Highfield Rangers ... 3-1
Cambridge University v Stafford Rangers ... 4-0
Port Vale v Rushden & Diamonds ... 0-2
Chesterfield v Leicester City ... 1-3
Redhill v Gillingham ... 4-1
Hampton v Chelmsford City ... 3-2
Stowmarket v Bedford Town Belles ... 2-1
Crowborough Athletic v Redbridge Raiders ... 3-5
Whitehawk v West Ham United ... 0-2
Watford v Enfield ... 1-2
Newton Abbott v Yeovil Town ... 0-3
Portsmouth v Clevedon Town ... 4-1
Bristol City v Reading ... 5-1
Exeter City v Cardiff City ... 2-1

THIRD ROUND
Ilkeston Town v Oldham Curzon ... 1-3
Chester City v Newcastle ... 1-2
Manchester City v Bangor City ... 2-3
Loughborough Students v Aston Villa ... 4-3
Liverpool Feds v Lincoln City ... 0-1
Wolverhampton Wanderers v Leicester City ... 1-0
Liverpool v Garswood Saints ... 0-1
Sheffield Wednesday v Cambridge University ... 3-0
North Notts v Stockport County ... 1-4
Huddersfield Town v Birmingham City ... 1-2
Rushden & Diamonds v Coventry City ... 3-6
Fulham v Newport County ... 12-0
Redbridge Raiders v West Ham United ... 1-0
Langford v Barnet ... 4-1
Enfield v Barking ... 6-4
Hampton v Yeovil Town ... 2-2
   Hampton won 3-2 on penalties.
Wimbledon v Exeter City ... 1-3
Ipswich Town v Chelsea ... 0-2
QPR Ladies v Portsmouth ... 0-3
   Millwall Lionesses w.o. v Stowmarket failed to fulfil fixture.
Redhill v Berkhamsted Town ... 4-0
Bristol City v Bristol Rovers ... 2-6

FOURTH ROUND
Bristol Rovers v Everton ... 2-4
Newcastle v Leeds United ... 2-4
Loughborough Students v Arsenal ... 0-7
Birmingham City v Fulham ... 0-5
Millwall Lionesses v Barry Town ... 2-3
Sheffield Wednesday v Langford ... 2-2
   Langford won 4-2 on penalties.
Hampton v Lincoln City ... 0-1

Tranmere Rovers v Sunderland	4-2
Garswood Saints v Redhill	5-0
Southampton Saints v Portsmouth	3-1
Redbridge Raiders v Wolverhampton Wanderers	1-3
Chelsea v Enfield	0-1
Oldham Curzon v Stockport County	4-0
Exeter City v Coventry City	0-1
Brighton & Hove Albion v Doncaster Belles	2-5
Charlton Athletic v Bangor City	3-0

FIFTH ROUND

Barry Town v Doncaster Belles	0-1
Coventry City v Fulham	0-11
Garswood Saints v Enfield	3-2
Southampton Saints v Oldham Curzon	1-2
Arsenal v Leeds United	3-0
Langford v Charlton Athletic	0-7
Lincoln City v Everton	2-7
Tranmere Rovers v Wolverhampton Wanderers	4-1

SIXTH ROUND

Everton v Fulham	0-4
Tranmere Rovers v Oldham Curzon	6-1

Garswood Saints v Charlton Athletic	0-4
Doncaster Belles v Arsenal	2-1

SEMI-FINALS

Fulham v Charlton Athletic	4-1
Tranmere Rovers v Doncaster Belles	1-3

FINAL (at Selhurst Park)

6 MAY

Doncaster Belles (0) 1 *(Handley 58)*

Fulham (0) 2 *(Yankey 55, Chapman 56)*　　　　10,124

Doncaster Belles: Hall; Hunt C, Utley, Easton, Barr, Lowe, Burke, Exley, Walker, Handley, Hunt G.
Fulham: Johannessen; Jerray-Silver, Unitt, Haugenes (Mork 90), Terp, Phillip, McArthur, Chapman, Moore (Duncan 61), Pettersen, Yankey.
Referee: E. Evans.

AXA FA WOMEN'S PREMIER LEAGUE CUP 2001–02

PRELIMINARY ROUND

Fulham v Millwall Lionesses	12-0
Wimbledon v Coventry	2-0

FIRST ROUND

Arsenal v Ipswich Town	8-0
Aston Villa v Doncaster Belles	2-5
Barking v North Notts	6-1
Berkhamsted Town v Barry Town	0-6
Birmingham City v Barnet	4-0
Everton v Bristol Rovers	3-1
Fulham v Leeds United	8-0
Garswood Saints v Liverpool	1-4
Ilkeston Town v Brighton & Hove Albion	2-0
Langford v Chelsea	2-3
Manchester City v Southampton Saints	0-2
Oldham Curzon v Sheffield Wednesday	3-6
Queens Park Rangers v Charlton Athletic	0-7
Tranmere Rovers v Newport County	5-1
Wimbledon v Bangor City	1-2
Wolverhampton Wanderers v Sunderland	1-3

SECOND ROUND

Arsenal v Sunderland	8-1
Bangor City v Birmingham City	0-1
Charlton Athletic v Fulham	1-5
Doncaster Belles v Barking	5-0
Sheffield Wednesday v Ilkeston Town	1-2
Southampton Saints v Chelsea	4-2
Barry Town v Tranmere Rovers	1-0
Everton v Liverpool	2-0

THIRD ROUND

Barry Town v Arsenal	2-4
Fulham v Southampton Saints	9-1
Ilkeston Town v Birmingham City	0-4
Doncaster Belles v Everton	3-1

SEMI-FINALS

Fulham v Arsenal	3-2
Doncaster Belles v Birmingham City	3-4

FINAL

Fulham v Birmingham City	7-1

Fulham winners of the AXA F.A. Women's Cup in celebratory mood after beating Doncaster Belles 2-1 in the final at Selhurst Park. (Colorsport)

NATIONWIDE CONFERENCE 2001–02

NATIONWIDE CONFERENCE 2001–02 FINAL LEAGUE TABLE

		Home			Goals		Away			Goals			
	P	W	D	L	F	A	W	D	L	F	A	GD	Pts
Boston United	42	12	5	4	53	24	13	4	4	31	18	42	84
Dagenham & Redbridge	42	13	6	2	35	20	11	6	4	35	27	23	84
Yeovil Town	42	6	7	8	27	30	13	6	2	39	23	13	70
Doncaster Rovers	42	11	6	4	41	23	7	7	7	27	23	22	67
Barnet	42	10	4	7	30	19	9	6	6	34	29	16	67
Morecambe	42	12	5	4	30	27	5	6	10	33	40	−4	62
Farnborough Town	42	11	3	7	38	23	7	4	10	28	31	12	61
Margate	42	7	9	5	33	22	7	7	7	26	31	6	58
Telford United	42	8	6	7	34	31	6	9	6	29	27	5	57
Nuneaton Borough	42	9	3	9	33	27	7	6	8	24	30	0	57
Stevenage Borough	42	10	4	7	36	30	5	6	10	21	30	−3	55
Scarborough*	42	9	6	6	27	22	5	8	8	28	41	−8	55
Northwich Victoria	42	9	4	8	32	34	7	3	11	25	36	−13	55
Chester City	42	7	7	7	26	23	8	2	11	28	28	3	54
Southport	42	9	6	6	40	26	4	8	9	13	23	4	53
Leigh Railway Mechanics Institute	42	6	4	11	29	29	9	5	8	27	29	−2	53
Hereford United	42	9	6	6	28	15	5	4	12	22	38	−3	52
Forest Green Rovers	42	7	7	7	28	32	5	8	8	26	44	−22	51
Woking	42	7	5	9	28	29	6	4	11	31	41	−11	48
Hayes	42	6	2	13	27	45	7	3	11	26	35	−27	44
Stalybridge Celtic	42	7	6	8	26	32	4	4	13	14	37	−29	43
Dover Athletic	42	6	5	10	20	25	5	1	15	21	40	−24	39

* 1 point deducted for breach of rule.

NATIONWIDE CONFERENCE LEADING GOALSCORERS 2001–02

	League	LDV	Total
Daryl Clare (Boston United)	24	0	24
Mark Stein (Dagenham & Redbridge)	24	0	24
Ken Charlery (Dagenham & Redbridge)	17	1	18
Mark Cooper (Forest Green Rovers)	17	0	17
Mark Beesley (Chester City)	16	0	16
(Including 8 League goals for Boston United)			
Gregg Blundell (Northwich Victoria)	16	0	16
Leon Braithwaite (Margate)	16	0	16
Simon Parke (Southport)	16	0	16
Lenny Piper (Farnborough Town)	15	0	15
Robbie Talbot (Morecambe)	15	0	15
Michael Twiss (Leigh RMI)	15	0	15
Jamie Paterson (Doncaster Rovers)	14	0	14
Dean Clark (Hayes)	13	0	13
Mark Quayle (Telford United)	13	0	13
Dino Maamria (Leigh RMI)	12	1	13
Ian Hodges (Hayes)	12	0	12
Darren Stamp (Scarborough)	12	0	12
Jeff Vansittart (Farnborough Town)	12	0	12
Simon Weatherstone (Boston United)	12	0	12
Warren Patmore (Woking)	11	0	11

ATTENDANCES BY CLUB 2001–02

	Aggregate 2001–02	Average 2001–02	Highest Attendance 2001–02
Yeovil Town	60,309	2,872	5,061 v Boston United
Boston United	51,128	2,435	4,200 v Nuneaton Borough
Doncaster Rovers	50,579	2,409	4,027 v Boston United
Dagenham & Redbridge	40,225	1,915	3,939 v Chester City
Woking	39,531	1,882	2,817 v Dagenham & Redbridge
Stevenage Borough	36,032	1,716	2,405 v Barnet
Hereford United	32,591	1,552	2,210 v Barnet
Barnet	30,578	1,456	2,456 v Stevenage Borough
Morecambe	27,064	1,289	1,780 v Doncaster Rovers
Nuneaton Borough	26,837	1,278	2,203 v Boston United
Chester City	26,762	1,274	2,148 v Doncaster Rovers
Margate	25,594	1,219	3,676 v Dover Athletic
Scarborough	25,072	1,194	2,349 v Dagenham & Redbridge
Southport	22,008	1,048	1,732 v Morecambe
Dover Athletic	21,545	1,026	2,325 v Margate
Telford United	21,060	1,003	2,168 v Hereford United
Northwich Victoria	18,609	886	1,940 v Chester City
Forest Green Rovers	17,653	841	1,609 v Yeovil Town
Farnborough Town	17,582	837	1,404 v Yeovil Town
Stalybridge Celtic	16,059	765	1,226 v Doncaster Rovers
Hayes	15,457	736	3,249 v Boston United
Leigh RMI	10,462	498	788 v Boston United

NATIONWIDE CONFERENCE 2001–02

Home \ Away	Barnet	Boston United	Chester City	Dagenham & Redbridge	Doncaster Rovers	Dover Athletic	Farnborough Town	Forest Green Rovers	Hayes	Hereford United	Leigh RMI	Margate	Morecambe	Northwich Victoria	Nuneaton Borough	Scarborough	Southport	Stalybridge Celtic	Stevenage Borough	Telford United	Woking	Yeovil Town
Barnet	—	0-1	3-1	4-0	2-0	2-0	0-3	0-1	3-1	2-0	1-1	4-1	1-0	1-0	0-1	1-1	0-0	1-2	0-3	0-0	3-0	2-3
Boston United	1-1	—	0-1	1-2	2-2	4-2	4-0	6-1	4-1	3-4	2-1	0-1	2-1	3-2	4-1	2-2	0-0	4-1	0-0	3-1	4-0	4-0
Chester City	1-0	1-2	—	0-1	1-1	3-0	1-0	2-3	3-1	2-0	1-1	0-3	1-1	1-2	1-0	0-0	0-2	0-0	5-1	2-2	0-2	1-1
Dagenham & Redbridge	1-1	1-0	3-0	—	1-0	1-0	2-1	1-1	1-1	1-0	0-1	4-1	3-2	1-1	2-0	4-2	1-1	2-1	1-0	1-5	3-1	1-1
Doncaster Rovers	2-3	0-1	2-0	0-0	—	2-1	1-1	5-1	5-2	4-0	2-0	1-0	3-3	2-2	2-2	4-3	1-0	0-1	2-0	1-0	1-1	1-2
Dover Athletic	2-2	3-2	1-0	0-1	0-1	—	2-1	1-2	3-2	0-1	0-0	1-0	1-1	4-1	1-2	0-2	0-1	1-0	2-0	1-0	2-2	1-2
Farnborough Town	2-1	0-2	1-1	1-2	0-1	1-0	—	3-0	1-2	4-2	3-0	0-0	2-1	4-1	2-1	4-2	0-1	2-0	6-1	1-1	0-1	1-3
Forest Green Rovers	2-2	0-3	0-2	2-4	0-2	2-1	1-0	—	2-1	1-1	1-2	3-3	3-1	2-0	1-2	1-2	2-1	0-0	0-0	1-1	0-1	1-1
Hayes	0-2	0-2	1-3	2-4	1-5	0-3	0-3	1-1	—	4-1	2-1	2-4	3-1	2-0	1-2	1-2	1-0	0-0	0-2	1-4	4-1	0-4
Hereford United	2-1	0-1	1-0	1-0	3-0	3-0	0-1	0-0	0-1	—	0-1	3-0	0-2	1-0	1-1	6-0	0-0	3-0	1-1	0-1	2-2	0-2
Leigh RMI	3-3	1-2	3-0	2-0	1-4	1-2	3-0	1-1	1-1	2-2	—	2-2	0-1	1-2	0-1	1-1	1-2	1-0	1-2	3-1	3-1	0-1
Margate	0-1	1-1	0-0	1-1	1-1	0-1	2-1	1-1	1-0	0-1	1-2	—	1-1	2-1	1-0	1-1	2-0	8-0	2-1	3-1	4-3	0-1
Morecambe	1-0	0-0	0-3	1-1	1-0	2-1	1-1	2-0	2-1	2-2	1-3	2-1	—	2-1	1-0	2-0	2-2	1-0	0-3	2-1	3-1	1-5
Northwich Victoria	0-3	1-2	3-1	1-2	2-3	2-1	1-2	2-2	1-0	1-0	0-3	1-1	4-3	—	3-0	1-1	3-1	1-0	2-1	2-2	0-3	1-3
Nuneaton Borough	2-3	1-1	1-3	2-0	2-3	3-0	1-1	2-1	0-2	2-0	2-1	0-0	2-3	0-1	—	1-2	3-0	3-1	2-1	1-2	2-0	1-2
Scarborough	3-0	2-0	2-1	0-0	1-0	1-1	1-0	1-1	1-2	3-2	2-5	0-1	0-2	1-2	1-2	—	2-0	1-1	3-1	3-1	1-0	0-0
Southport	0-1	2-3	3-2	2-2	1-0	0-2	2-5	5-1	2-3	1-1	5-0	1-2	1-1	5-1	1-1	1-0	—	3-1	0-0	0-0	2-0	3-0
Stalybridge Celtic	1-1	2-1	0-4	2-3	1-0	0-2	1-1	2-1	1-0	0-2	0-1	2-2	4-3	1-1	4-2	2-3	0-0	—	2-0	0-2	0-2	1-1
Stevenage Borough	3-2	1-2	2-1	1-3	2-3	1-3	1-2	4-1	1-1	3-1	2-1	3-1	3-1	1-0	2-2	2-0	2-1	2-0	—	1-1	1-4	2-3
Telford United	1-2	2-2	0-3	1-4	4-3	0-1	0-1	0-0	0-2	0-1	3-1	2-0	4-1	1-0	0-2	3-0	1-1	3-1	2-1	—	3-3	2-2
Woking	1-3	0-2	2-1	0-2	3-1	4-0	3-2	3-4	0-1	1-0	1-1	1-3	1-3	3-1	0-0	1-2	2-0	3-1	0-0	1-1	—	0-2
Yeovil Town	1-2	0-1	0-1	0-1	3-1	2-0	0-1	1-1	2-1	1-2	2-1	1-2	1-1	3-1	2-1	2-1	0-0	0-2	2-1	1-1	1-3	—

NATIONWIDE CONFERENCE 2001–02
APPEARANCES AND GOALSCORERS

Barnet

Appearances: Arber, 37+1; Bell, 23+6; Berkley, 10+3; Brown, 20+5; D'Arcy, 1+1; Doolan, 16+3; Essandoh, 3+3; Flynn, 34+4; Gledhill, 36+1; Goodhind, 7; Gower, 34+1; Harrison, 36; Heald, 38; Midgley, 30+9; Naisbitt, 6+1; Niven, 25+9; Olayinka, 1; Olshitola, 0+9; Pluck, 5+3; Pope, 0+1; Purches, 0+1; Purser, 26+3; Sawyers, 23+6; Searle, 2+3; Strevens, 24; Taylor, 0+5; Toms, 17+10; Akabu, 3+1.

Goals (64): Midgley 9, Strevens 9, Purser 8 (1 pen), Arber 7 (2 pens), Gower 5, Toms 5, Brown 3, Flynn 3, Bell 2, Berkley 2, Doolan 2 (1 pen), Heald 2, Olshitola 2, Sawyers 2, Essandoh 1, Niven 1, own goal 1.

Boston United

Appearances: Angel, 26+8; Bastock, 41; Beesley, 3+3; Brabin, 1; Brown, 21+5; Charlery, 12; Clare, 39+1; Clifford, 40; Cook, 11+21; Costello, 17+9; Elding, 12+7; Ellender, 36; Evans, 1; Gould, 26+6; Gray, 3; Lodge, 9+3; Marsh, 7; McGarry, 2+4; Monington, 25; Murphy, 6+14; Rodwell, 16; Rusk, 23+4; Scott, 7; Tarrant, 4+6; Thompson, 4; Town, 5+18; Warburton, 5+1; Weatherstone, R. 19+5; Weatherstone, S. 33+1.

Goals (84): Clare 24 (7 pens), Weatherstone S 12, Charlery 8, Elding 6, Angel 4, Town 4, Brown 3, Cook 3, Gould 3, Ellender 2, Murphy 2, Rodwell 2, Rusk 2, Costello 1, Marsh 1, Scott 1, Tarrant 1, Warburton 1, Weatherstone R 1, own goals 3.

Chester City

Appearances: Baxter, 1+1; Beesley, 34+1; Blackburn, 2+8; Bolland, 14; Brabin, 16; Brown, D. 11+2; Brown, W. 2; Carden, 13+2; Carey, 11; Collins, 3+5; Haarhoff, 7+17; Halford, 10; Hill, 13; Hopwood, 0+3; Jenkins, 5+1; Kerr, 4+2; Kilgannon, 8+5; Lancaster, 35; Linighan, 3; Lopez, 4+2; Malkin, 5+4; McElhatton, 8; McGarry, 14; McNiven, 1; O'Brien, C. 9; O'Brien, M. 8+2; Peacock, 6; Porter, 5+2; Roberts, 1+5; Rose, M. 33+1; Rose, S. 8+4; Ruffer, 5+2; Ruscoe, 17+5; Spink, 19+2; Tate, 4; Whittaker, 6+1; Williams, 6+5; Woodyatt, 14+5; Wright, 3+7.

Goals (54): Beesley 16, Blackburn 4, Rose M 4, Ruscoe 4, Whittaker 4, Brabin 3, Brown D 2, McElhatton 2, O'Brien M 2, Porter 2 (1 pen), Ruffer 2, Spink 2, Woodyatt 2, Haarhoff 1, Hill 1, Lancaster 1, Tate 1, Wright 1.

Dagenham & Redbridge

Appearances: Brennan, 8+8; Broom, 11+9; Charlery, 9+4; Cole, 2+2; Forbes, 0+3; Goodwin, 28+1; Gothard, 6+1; Hayzelden, 12+14; Heffer, 34+2; Hill, 12+7; Hooper, 4; Janney, 30+5; Jones, 25+4; Lock, 5+8; McDougald, 4+12; McGavin, 9+17; Roberts, 36; Rodwell, 1; Rooney, 7+4; Shipp, 32+5; Smith, 40+1; Stein, 33+1; Terry, 36+3; Vaughan, 0+2; Vickers, 26+1; West, 12+1.

Goals (70): Stein 24, Charlery 9 (1 pen), McGavin 6 (3 pens), Shipp 5, Hill 3, McDougald 3 (1 pen), Terry 3, Goodwin 2, Vickers 2, Brennan 1, Cole 1, Hayzelden 1, Heffer 1, Janney 1, Jones 1, Lock 1, Smith 1, West 1, own goals 4.

Doncaster Rovers

Appearances: Barnes, 19+4; Barrick, 20+3; Butler, 8+1; Campbell, 23+8; Carden, 10+6; Caudwell, 16+6; Futcher, 4; Gill, 13+10; Green, 5+3; Hawkins, 10+1; Jackson, 14+2; Kelly, 35; Marples, 23+2; Miller, 38+1; Owen, 33; Paterson, 30+6; Penney, 1; Price, 13+4; Ravenhill, 6+4; Richardson, 21; Ryan, 28+1; Sale, 6+9; Sandwith, 5+5; Squires, 29+1; Tierney, 17+4; Warrington, 13; Watson, 0+7; Whitman, 14+10.

Goals (68): Paterson 14 (2 pens), Campbell 8, Whitman 8, Barnes 6 (1 pen), Owen 6 (1 pen), Watson 4, Gill 3, Jackson 3, Sale 3, Caudwell 2, Green 2, Kelly 2 (1 pen), Miller 2, Squires 2, Carden 1, Tierney 1, own goal 1.

Dover Athletic

Appearances: Aggrey, 8; Allen, 12+6; Bathgate, 0+2; Browne, 11+1; Carr, 1+1; Carruthers, 21+4; Cloke, 0+1; Codner, 1; Davies, 15+3; Day, 18+8; Dorrian, 14; Elliott, 0+4; Frost, 0+1; Glover, 0+1; Hickman, 0+3; Hockton, 1; Hyde, 30; Inman, 5+1; James, 9+4; Kelly, 13; Le Bihan, 25+2; Leberl, 42; McRobert, 1+4; Norman, 39; Ovard, 0+5; Parsons, 1; Ramsay, 11+2; Risbridger, 3; Scott, 40; Seabury, 15; Shearer, 28+3; Smith, 12+1; Stant, 1+3; Strouts, 30+2; Tyne, 18+6; Ullathorne, 0+1; Vowden, 23+1; White, 5.

Goals (41): Scott 14 (2 pens), Strouts 5, Kelly 3, Tyne 3, Allen 2, Carruthers 2, Elliott 2, Le Bihan 2, Leberl 2, Seabury 2 (1 pen), Aggrey 1, Bathgate 1, Day 1, Ramsay 1.

Farnborough Town

Appearances: Annon, 30+5; Baptiste, 9+6; Bennetts, 0+1; Benstead, 4+1; Bonfield, 9+2; Bunce, 15+2; Charles, 4; Crawshaw, 6+14; Darlington, 0+1; De Souza, 8+4; Dublin, 4+4; Farrelly, 17; Green, 14+8; Gregory, 16+4; Harper, 15+1; Hicks, 0+3; Hodges, 0+1; Holloway, 12+3; Jones, 3+6; Laker, 36; Lee, 14+3; O'Shea, 22+1; Osborn, 2; Patterson, 24; Pennock, 10; Piper, C. 36+4; Piper, L. 31+11; Rose, 0+1; Taggart, 16+9; Vansittart, 29+5; Warner, 40; Watson, 36.

Goals (66): Piper L 15 (1 pen), Vansittart 12, Lee 7, Piper C 5, Taggart 5, Baptiste 4, Bunce 3, Green 3, Holloway 3, Crawshaw 2, Charles 1, De Souza 1, Laker 1, O'Shea 1, Patterson 1, own goals 2.

Forest Green Rovers

Appearances: Adams, 2+7; Allen, 9+6; Cooper, 37; Coupe, 8+2; Cousins, 31+2; Daley, 6+6; Foster, 38; Freestone, 0+1; Futcher, 18+9; Heggs, 28+2; Hopkins, 6+2; Howey, 15; Impey, 31+1; Jenkins, 36; Jones, 0+1; Langan, 24+1; Lee, 3+2; Lightbody, 3+8; Meechan, 40+2; Middleton, 0+7; Odejayi, 5+1; Pearcey, 3; Perrin, 39+1; Shaw, 21+4; Small, 5; Sykes, 11+1; Tearney, 7+6; Travis, 31+4; Ward, 5.

Goals (54): Cooper 17 (7 pens), Heggs 10 (2 pens), Meechan 8 (2 pens), Lightbody 3, Travis 3, Howey 2, Jenkins 2, Allen 1, Cousins 1, Langan 1, Lee 1, Odejayi 1, Shaw 1, Sykes 1, Ward 1, own goal 1.

Hayes

Appearances: Ashton, 16+5; Austin, 1; Bossu, 31; Brown, 2; Bull, 7; Case, 5+9; Charles, 14; Clark, 38+3; Coppard, 8+5; Currie, 12+5; Daly, 7; Diallo, 3+1; Dick, 3+2; Dyer, 38; Ellverson, 9+2; Everitt, 8+9; Gallen, 13+4; Granville, 1; Grey, 9+4; Hale, 8+4; Harris, 4+1; Highton, 2+2; Hodges, 31+5; Holsgrove, L. 1; Paul Holsgrove, 25+6; Peter Holsgrove, 8+13; Jolly, 2+8; Kodra, 4; Molesley, 32+2; Shipperley, 0+4; Slade, 1; Sladen, 3; Sodje, 6; Spencer, 24+3; Stant, 1+2; Sterling, 39; Stevens, 2+2; Taylor, 3; Warner, D. 1+4; Warner, K. 38; Watts, 2+1.

Goals (53): Clark 13 (1 pen), Hodges 12, Molesley 5, Peter Holsgrove 4, Sterling 4, Charles 3, Dyer 2, Sodje 2, Warner K 2, Everitt 1, Grey 1, Hale 1, Paul Holsgrove 1, Spencer 1, Watts 1.

Hereford United

Appearances: Baker, 37+1; Barnes, 1; Barrick, 7; Capaldi, 12; Clarke, 36; Davidson, 3+9; Diamond, 1+2; Elmes, 26+10; Evans, 0+2; Gardiner, 1+2; Goodwin, 29+3; Hill, 1+2; Holmes, 8; James, C. 5+2; James, T. 41; Jones, 4; Kevan, 2+1; Parry, 39; Piearce, 4+10; Quiggin, 13+8; Robinson, 20+2; Rodgerson, 16; Sedgemore, 1+1; Shirley, 10+5; Snape, 37+1; Voice, 7+4; Webb, 12+1; Williams, G. 40; Williams, M. 12+1; Wright, 37.

Goals (50): Elmes 9, Williams G 9, Parry 5, Snape 5, Robinson 4, Wright 4, Goodwin 3, Piearce 2, Quiggin 2, Voice 2, Clarke 1, James T 1, Rodgerson 1, Shirley 1, Williams M 1 (pen).

Leigh RMI

Appearances: Archer, 0+2; Black, 24+2; Derbyshire, 0+1; Dootson, 2; Durkin, 42; Farrell, 19+4; Felgate, 7+1; Fisher, 2+5; Fitzgerald, 1+1; Fitzpatrick, 2+1; German, 31+5; Hallows, 22+16; Harris, 5; Harrison, 0+4; Hayder, 1+5; Heald, 10+12; Kielty, 22+6; Maamria, 24+5; Monk, 42; Reynolds, 0+3; Ridings, 23; Salt, 15; Scott, 8+6; Skinner, 5; Spencer, 0+4; Spooner, 20+3; Swan, 24+3; Thompson, 5+2; Twiss, 29+4; Udall, 1+2; Westhead, 33.

Goals (56): Twiss 15, Maamria 12 (1 pen), Hallows 8, Black 6 (1 pen), Monk 5, Fisher 3, Heald 2, Ridings 2, Hayder 1, Kielty 1, own goal 1.

Margate

Appearances: Azzopardi, 1+5; Beard, 25+3; Blackford, 12+1; Boardman, 3; Braithwaite, 40+1; Collins, 15+6; Edwards, 41; Graham, 22+4; Hafner, 3+8; Hilaire, 0+3; Keister, 10+1; Lamb, 41; Lincoln, 1; McFlynn, 21; Mitten, 18; Munday, 33+5; O'Connell, 16+1; Porter, 38; Roddis, 11+1; Saunders, 36+2; Sodje, 10+6; Takalobighashi, 0+2; Turner, 24+1; Williams, 35+2; Yorath, 6+2.
Goals (59): Braithwaite 16 (5 pens), Munday 7, Beard 6, Keister 6, Saunders 5, McFlynn 3, Sodje 3, Collins 2, Porter 2, Roddis 2, Boardman 1, Graham 1, Lamb 1, Williams 1, own goals 3.

Morecambe

Appearances: Arnold, 23+4; Black, 13+15; Carlton, 4+7; Colkin, 28+1; Crumblehulme, 5+3; Curtis, 10+13; Drummond, 36; Eastwood, 2+10; Fensome, 24+5; Gouck, 24+4; Hardiker, 18; Hay, 2; Lightfoot, 15; Mawson, 41; McGuire, 32+2; McKearney, 39; Murphy, 16+4; Norman, 23+15; Perkins, 19+2; Porter, 1+5; Quayle, 1+1; Rigoglioso, 19+18; Robinson, 3+1; Stanford, 0+3; Stringfellow, 3+5; Talbot, 25; Thompson, 27+1; Thomson, 2+2; Ubershar, 6+3; Willcock, 1.
Goals (63): Talbot 15 (1 pen), Curtis 8, Arnold 7 (4 pens), Thompson 7, Norman 6, Black 4, Drummond 4, Gouck 3 (1 pen), Lightfoot 3, Rigoglioso 3, Carlton 1, Thomson 1, own goal 1.

Northwich Victoria

Appearances: Bailey, 12+1; Bardsley, 2; Barnard, 39; Blundell, 41; Brownrigg, 5+2; Burke, 26+7; Collins, 9+8; Davis, 1; Dawson, 0+3; Devlin, 33; Garvey, 33+9; Gibson, 42; Grant, 11; Griggs, 1; Illman, 4+6; Ingram, 22; Jones, 11; Knowles, 13+4; Meaker, 5+3; Mike, 17+3; Mitchell, 1+5; Morris, 0+1; Norris, 22+7; Owen, 17+2; Porter, 9; Quinn, 13+17; Royle, 9; Sedgemore, 18+5; Skinner, 4+1; Talbot, 38; Walsh, 4+3.
Goals (58): Blundell 16, Quinn 6, Garvey 5, Grant 4, Mike 4, Devlin 3 (1 pen), Norris 3, Talbot 3, Barnard 2 (1 pen), Burke 2, Illman 2, Brownrigg 1, Jones 1, Meaker 1, Mitchell 1, Owen 1, own goals 2.

Nuneaton Borough

Appearances: Angus, 37; Birch, 5; Burgess, 3+3; Charles, 28+4; Cooper, 7+4; Crowley, 26+2; Dunkley, 2+6; Harkin, 13+1; Harris, 11+2; Howey, 10; Kelly, 3; Kennerdale, 0+2; Lavery, 29+6; Leadbeater, 3+8; Love, 40+1; Mackenzie, 42; McGregor, 17+1; Peake, 22+2; Peyton, 31+2; Sykes, 19+4; Thackeray, 35+2; Tullin, 1; Turner, 10+2; Weaver, 24+5; Whitehall, 10+6; Williams, B. 18+7; Williams, J. 13+1; Wright, 3+3.
Goals (57): Charles 10, Peyton 9 (5 pens), McGregor 8 (2 pens), Whitehall 6, Harris 5, Thackeray 5, Birch 3, Sykes 3, Dunkley 1, Harkin 1, Leadbeater 1, Love 1, Turner 1, Williams J 1, Wright 1, own goal 1.

Scarborough

Appearances: Atkinson, 13+2; Baker, 14+4; Barnwell-Edinbor, 2+2; Bennett, 1; Blunt, 40; Brodie, 17+1; Burley, 3; Burt, 3+4; Connell, 1+6; Crawford, 0+1; Dryden, 4; Elliott, 6+2; Faure, 16+3; Fickling, 7; Fitzsimmons, 16+1; Henderson, 0+1; Hogg, 0+1; Hotte, 17+1; Ingram, 13; Jewell, 0+5; Jones, 6+1; Jordan, 20+1; Keegan, 5; Mann, 2; Newton, 1; O'Riordan, 0+1; Patterson, 17+2; Pounder, 29+7; Rennison, 38+1; Rose, 12+4; Salt, 11; Shepherd, 10; Sherwood, 1+5; Shields, 9; Short, 5; Smith, 4; Stamp, 28+3; Stoker, 24+4; Sugden, 9+4; Swales, 3+4; Tracey, 0+1; Turley, 0+5; Wilford, 9+1; Windross, 5+6; Woods, 37; Wright, 4.
Goals (55): Stamp 12 (1 pen), Blunt 6, Rose 6, Brodie 4, Pounder 4, Rennison 3, Windross 3, Connell 2, Shepherd 2 (1 pen), Shields 2, Sugden 2, Baker 1 (pen), Burt 1, Dryden 1, Elliott 1, Jordan 1, Stoker 1, Wilford 1, own goals 2.

Southport

Appearances: Bauress, 9+3; Clark, 41; Connolly, 0+1; Dickenson, 42; Eastwood, 5+8; Elam, 37+2; Grayston, 36; Howell, 20+1; Jones, B. 36+1; Jones, S. 36+2; Lane, 45+1; Leadbeater, 0+4; MacAuley, 23+5; McGorry, 7+5; Morgan, 0+1; Mulvaney, 0+3; Obong, 2+1; Owen, 3;

Parke, 40+1; Robertson, 21+2; Scott, 3+3; Sullivan, 9+1; Teale, 35+1; Ward, 3; Whitehall, 16+2; Whittaker, 0+; Williams, 3+1.
Goals (53): Parke 16, Jones S 8, Whitehall 6, Teale Elam 4, Lane 4 (1 pen), Jones B 3, Eastwood 2, Sulliv 2, Grayston 1, Howell 1, Leadbeater 1.

Stalybridge Celtic

Appearances: Ayorinde, 19; Barker, 0+2; Batty, 4+ Beesley, 26; Bushell, 16+2; Clements, 2; Courtney, 33+ Crookes, 5+1; Evans, 0+3; Fish, 22+3; Futcher, 2 Ingham, 6; Kelly, 7; Marivat, 0+4; McNeil, 5+8; Mil 2+5; Murphy, 32+7; Parr, 32; Peacock, 29+1; Perki 22+6; Pickford, 32; Scott, 17+3; Shandran, 6+1; Stee 1+3; Trainer, 3+1; Turley, 4+6; Walker, 10+1; Walsh, 1+ Ward, 7; Wharton, 1+7; Williamson, 10+6; Wood, 3 Woodhead, 8; Woods, 36+1.
Goals (40): Courtney 9, Ayorinde 6, Peacock 5, Parr Pickford 4 (1 pen), Kelly 3, Steele 2, Bushell 1, Evans Futcher 1, Murphy 1, Shandran 1, Turley 1, Woods 1.

Stevenage Borough

Appearances: Abbey, 0+1; Armstrong, 4+12; Arnott, Campbell, D. 18+3; Campbell, J. 8+1; Carey, 3; Cast 5+2; Clarke, 27+5; Dean, 0+1; Dreyer, 24; Evers, 6+ Fisher, 13+3; Fitzpatrick, 1+1; Fraser, 5; George, 3+ Goodliffe, 32; Greygoose, 18; Hamsher, 28+1; Ha 12+10; Houghton, 5+2; Howell, 2; Illman, 5+11; Jackso 11+6; Lincoln, 1; Luckett, 1; McMahon, 35+3; Midso 1+3; Morgan, 2+4; Riddle, 5; Shields, 1+1; Sigere, 18+ Smith, 0+5; Sodje, 17+3; Stirling, 8+3; Sturgess, 24+ Tagro, 0+1; Tate, 6; Trott, 22+4; Walters, 10; Watts, Wilkerson, 24; Williams, 26+7; Wormull, 2+1.
Goals (57): Sigere 10, Jackson 7, Clarke 6 (1 pen), Hay McMahon 4, Campbell D 3, Goodliffe 3, Hamsher 3 pens), Williams 3, Wormull 3 (1 pen), Fisher 2, Sodje Tate 2, Armstrong 1, Shields 1, Stirling 1.

Telford United

Appearances: Albrighton, 30+1; Bentley, 28; Crowe, 0+ Davies, 21+6; Edwards, J. 23+5; Edwards, P. 2 Fitzpatrick, 31+7; Fowler, 23; Hanmer, 42; Hateley, Jobling, 32+1; King, 6+7; Martindale, 11+10; Moore, 40; Moore, P. 4+23; Palmer, 28+1; Preece, 5+4; Price, Quayle, 22+2; Scott, 21+5; Smith, 25+8; Wooliscro 28+2.
Goals (63): Quayle 13 (1 pen), Bentley 8, Edwards J Albrighton 5, Fitzpatrick 5, Smith 5, Hanmer Martindale 4 (1 pen), Moore N 2, Moore P 2, Davies Jobling 1, King 1, Palmer 1, Scott 1, own goals 2.

Woking

Appearances: Allman, 0+2; Bevan, 7; Boardman, 12+ Chandler, 14; Dsane, 11+6; Fowler, 8; Graham, 3+ Griffin, 21+9; Haughton, 8+21; Hollingdale, 1 Huckerby, 5+6; Kadi, 5+5; McFlynn, 5+5; McGorry, Moore, 36+1; Patmore, 20+6; Perkins, 24+5; Piper, 4 Pitcher, 13; Pitman, 21+3; Randall, 0+3; Reece, 1 Reeks, 11+6; Roddis, 10+1; Saunders, 17+3; Sharplin 26+4; Smith, 28+1; Steele, P. 9+1; Steele, S. 16+5; Tuck 35; Webber, 3+1; West, 22+2.
Goals (59): Patmore 11 (3 pens), Griffin 10 (1 per Moore 6, Sharpling 5, West 4, Dsane 3, Haughton Huckerby 3, Perkins 3, Steele S 3, Pitcher 2, Boardman Kadi 1, McFlynn 1, Roddis 1, Smith 1 (pen), own goal 1.

Yeovil Town

Appearances: Alford, 27+11; Belgrave, 4+4; Bent, 0+ Brassart, 12+2; Broad, 4; Collis, 1+1; Cooper, 0+ Crittenden, 39+1; Giles, 8+26; Grant, 14+6; Haverc 2+2; Johnson, 36; Kumbar, 5; Lindegaard, 3+ Lockwood, 26+4; McIndoe, 34+1; O'Brien, 7+4; Pluc 24+2; Poole, 1+1; Ramsay, 14+3; Schram, 3+1; Sheffie 14; Skiverton, 23+1; Stansfield, 22+1; Thompson, 11+ Tonkin, 39+1; Turner, 14+7; Way, 22+5; Weale, 2 White, 26+9.
Goals (66): Alford 8, Stansfield 8, Giles 7, McIndoe Grant 5, Johnson 5, Crittenden 4, Ramsay 4, Kumbar Way 3 (1 pen), Belgrave 2, Pluck 2, Brassart 1, Broad Lindegaard 1, Skiverton 1, Thompson 1, Turner 1, ov goals 2.

UNIBOND LEAGUE 2001–02

Premier Division	P	W	Home D	L	Goals F	A	W	Away D	L	Goals F	A	Pts
Burton Albion	44	17	5	0	59	12	14	6	2	47	18	104
Vauxhall Motors	44	16	3	3	50	26	11	5	6	36	29	89
Lancaster City	44	14	4	4	44	26	9	5	8	36	31	78
Worksop Town	44	13	4	5	40	22	10	5	7	34	29	78
Emley	44	15	4	3	43	24	7	5	10	26	30	75
Accrington Stanley	44	10	7	5	47	27	11	2	9	42	37	72
Runcorn FC Halton	44	11	2	9	36	26	10	6	6	40	27	71
Barrow	44	10	7	5	40	25	9	3	10	35	34	67
Altrincham	44	11	3	8	33	28	8	6	8	33	30	66
Bradford Park Avenue	44	11	2	9	45	37	7	3	12	32	39	59
Droylsden	44	11	3	8	32	34	6	5	11	33	44	59
Blyth Spartans	44	9	8	5	30	24	5	8	9	29	38	58
Frickley Athletic*	44	10	4	8	37	37	6	7	9	26	32	58
Gateshead	44	7	8	7	24	30	7	6	9	34	41	56
Whitby Town	44	7	5	10	33	39	8	3	11	28	37	53
Hucknall Town	44	6	5	11	25	35	8	4	10	24	33	51
Marine	44	7	7	8	36	38	4	10	8	26	33	50
Burscough	44	9	4	9	40	38	6	1	15	29	48	50
Gainsborough Trinity	44	9	5	8	36	30	4	5	13	25	46	49
Colwyn Bay	44	7	6	9	27	39	5	5	12	22	43	47
Bishop Auckland	44	5	5	12	22	34	7	3	12	24	34	44
Hyde United	44	5	7	10	29	37	5	3	14	32	50	40
Bamber Bridge*	44	5	4	13	23	40	2	6	14	15	48	30

1 point deducted for breach of rule

First Division	P	W	Home D	L	Goals F	A	W	Away D	L	Goals F	A	Pts
Harrogate Town	42	14	5	2	42	13	11	6	4	38	22	86
Ossett Town	42	12	5	4	37	21	9	8	4	36	23	76
Ashton United	42	14	2	5	50	31	7	10	4	40	32	75
Spennymoor United	42	13	4	4	44	34	9	2	10	31	39	72
Radcliffe Borough	42	11	3	7	46	28	9	5	7	27	23	68
Leek Town	42	12	3	6	35	19	8	5	8	32	32	68
Gretna*	42	10	4	7	30	26	9	3	9	36	40	63
Eastwood Town	42	8	7	6	32	30	9	4	8	29	29	62
Rossendale United	42	5	7	9	31	32	12	3	6	38	26	61
Witton Albion	42	8	6	7	33	23	9	4	8	39	45	61
Guiseley	42	10	4	7	35	28	8	3	10	25	39	61
North Ferriby United	42	8	6	7	36	31	6	10	5	35	29	58
Chorley	42	8	8	6	32	30	8	3	10	27	27	57
Matlock Town**	42	7	6	8	28	22	8	3	10	21	26	51
Trafford	42	7	4	10	31	34	7	5	9	33	46	51
Workington	42	5	4	12	24	32	7	8	6	27	25	48
Farsley Celtic	42	10	3	8	36	32	2	8	11	28	46	47
Belper Town	42	6	6	9	25	30	6	5	10	24	36	47
Lincoln United	42	6	10	5	36	34	5	4	12	26	46	47
Stocksbridge Park Steels	42	8	5	8	33	29	4	4	13	22	47	45
Kendal Town	42	6	5	10	36	42	3	4	14	16	34	36
Ossett Albion	42	6	5	10	29	43	2	3	16	14	49	32

1 point deducted for breach of rule
**3 points deducted for breach of rule*

LEADING GOALSCORERS
(In order of League Goals)

Premier Division

Lge	Cup	Tot	
27	9	36	Terry Fearns (Vauxhall Motors)
26	6	32	Andy Whittaker (Lancaster City)
22	12	34	Paul Mullin (Accrington Stanley)
21	2	23	Lutel James (Accrington Stanley)
20	11	31	Andy Hayward (Bradford Park Avenue)
20	7	27	Glen Robson (Blyth Spartans)
17	16	33	Rod Thornley (Altrincham)
17	6	23	Darren Day (Emley)
16	8	24	Jason Maxwell (Bradford Park Avenue)
16	7	23	Steve Preen (Gateshead)
16	5	21	Paul McNally (Runcorn FC Halton)
16	4	20	Steve Housham (Barrow)
16	2	18	Richie Townsend (Marine)

First Division

Lge	Cup	Tot	
24	8	32	Mark Dobie (Gretna)
24	3	27	Jodie Banin (Radcliffe Borough)
22	7	29	Andy Mason (Chorley)
21	7	28	Robbie Whellans (Farsley Celtic)
21	6	27	Carl Cunningham (Belper Town)
21	5	26	Carl Rendell (Witton Albion)
19	11	30	Phil Denney (Ashton United)
19	7	26	Chris Newton (Farsley Celtic)
18	9	27	Gavin Knight (North Ferriby United)
18	2	20	Dave Whittaker (Leek Town)

ATTENDANCES
Premier Division
Highest Attendances: 2170 Burton Albion v Droylsden
2141 Burton Albion v Bradford Park Avenue
2032 Barrow v Lancaster City

ATTENDANCES
Division One
Highest Attendances: 1109 Harrogate Town v Workington
756 Harrogate Town v Ossett Town
663 Ossett Town v Ossett Albion

Average Cup Attendance: 207 (2000–01 – 186)

UNIBOND LEAGUE – PREMIER DIVISION RESULTS 2001-02

	Accrington Stanley	Altrincham	Bamber Bridge	Barrow	Bishop Auckland	Blyth Spartans	Bradford Park Avenue	Burscough	Burton Albion	Colwyn Bay	Droylsden	Emley	Frickley Athletic	Gainsborough Trinity	Gateshead	Hucknall Town	Hyde United	Lancaster City	Marine	Runcorn FC Halton	Vauxhall Motors	Whitby Town	Worksop Town
Accrington Stanley	—	0-0	2-0	0-3	1-1	0-0	5-1	3-0	3-3	3-0	5-2	0-1	1-1	1-1	2-1	1-2	4-1	3-2	3-1	1-1	2-3	2-3	5-0
Altrincham	3-1	—	4-3	2-1	1-1	2-1	1-0	0-3	0-2	4-0	2-2	1-2	0-2	1-1	3-1	2-0	1-2	1-1	1-0	0-2	0-1	1-0	2-0
Bamber Bridge	0-1	1-1	—	1-0	1-2	0-1	2-1	2-3	0-1	1-2	3-3	2-1	0-2	1-0	1-4	1-4	1-3	1-1	0-1	1-6	1-3	3-0	0-0
Barrow	0-4	2-2	1-1	—	3-1	4-1	2-3	1-0	1-2	1-1	1-2	1-1	3-1	3-0	4-1	6-1	0-0	0-0	1-1	2-1	1-2	2-0	1-0
Bishop Auckland	1-2	2-1	2-0	1-2	—	1-1	0-4	2-1	1-1	1-2	1-2	1-0	1-1	0-1	1-2	0-2	0-2	1-1	0-0	1-3	3-4	1-0	1-2
Blyth Spartans	1-1	0-3	3-1	1-1	2-1	—	4-1	2-1	0-1	2-0	0-0	1-3	3-1	2-2	2-1	1-2	2-0	1-0	0-0	2-2	0-1	2-1	2-2
Bradford Park Avenue	1-2	4-1	5-2	2-0	0-2	2-2	—	0-2	1-4	5-0	3-1	2-1	3-0	2-0	3-5	0-1	3-1	1-0	2-3	3-1	1-3	1-1	1-5
Burscough	3-2	0-2	5-0	3-2	1-0	1-2	0-2	—	0-0	4-0	6-2	1-1	1-0	2-0	2-2	1-3	0-2	0-6	1-1	1-3	2-3	3-1	2-3
Burton Albion	3-1	1-1	1-1	4-0	3-0	4-0	3-0	4-0	—	1-0	1-1	2-1	4-0	3-1	5-1	2-0	5-1	0-3	0-0	1-0	2-1	5-1	1-0
Colwyn Bay	3-0	2-5	0-0	0-5	1-2	1-1	1-2	2-1	1-3	—	1-0	1-0	1-5	4-2	1-2	1-1	4-4	1-2	0-0	1-0	1-0	1-1	0-3
Droylsden	1-5	2-0	0-0	2-0	1-0	0-0	2-2	3-1	0-7	3-2	—	3-2	1-0	1-2	3-0	3-0	3-2	2-0	0-2	0-1	3-2	2-3	0-2
Emley	0-3	2-1	5-0	2-3	0-1	2-1	1-0	3-0	3-2	2-0	4-2	—	2-1	1-2	2-2	3-0	2-1	2-1	3-3	1-0	1-1	0-2	1-1
Frickley Athletic	1-3	3-1	2-0	2-3	2-1	1-5	0-0	3-0	0-5	2-1	3-1	1-1	—	3-1	0-0	0-1	2-2	1-4	3-0	2-4	1-0	1-4	4-0
Gainsborough Trinity	5-2	1-3	5-0	0-1	1-1	2-1	4-1	3-1	2-0	1-2	1-3	1-1	2-2	—	0-0	0-0	1-0	3-2	0-0	1-4	2-1	2-0	0-2
Gateshead	0-0	0-2	1-1	0-0	1-0	1-1	0-7	2-0	1-1	3-3	2-0	2-0	0-0	1-0	—	1-1	4-1	1-2	2-4	0-2	0-2	2-0	0-3
Hucknall Town	1-3	0-0	1-1	2-1	2-3	2-1	1-0	1-2	1-2	1-1	1-0	0-4	3-4	1-4	0-0	—	3-1	0-1	3-2	1-2	1-1	0-1	0-1
Hyde United	2-4	3-2	0-1	1-2	1-3	3-1	2-0	3-2	1-1	1-2	0-3	2-3	0-0	1-1	2-1	0-2	—	1-1	2-2	0-1	0-0	0-1	3-3
Lancaster City	1-0	1-1	4-1	3-3	1-0	4-2	4-0	0-3	1-0	2-1	2-2	0-1	0-2	5-2	2-0	1-0	4-2	—	2-1	1-1	2-0	2-3	2-1
Marine	2-5	1-0	0-1	3-2	2-3	0-2	1-2	3-3	1-1	1-1	2-4	2-0	4-0	1-1	1-3	2-0	2-1	4-4	—	2-0	1-1	0-3	1-1
Runcorn FC Halton	1-0	0-1	3-2	1-3	3-1	1-2	0-2	4-0	1-3	1-0	2-0	1-0	1-0	4-0	1-1	3-1	3-1	4-1	1-1	—	1-2	4-1	0-1
Vauxhall Motors	1-2	2-1	1-0	2-0	3-0	2-2	2-1	3-2	3-2	3-2	1-0	1-1	3-1	4-0	4-1	2-1	2-1	2-0	4-1	3-2	—	0-2	3-2
Whitby Town	2-1	2-3	1-0	2-4	2-1	1-1	2-1	1-3	1-1	2-1	3-0	4-1	1-3	0-4	2-3	2-2	1-2	0-2	2-1	3-2	1-2	—	0-2
Worksop Town	5-0	1-2	1-0	0-1	2-1	2-0	3-2	3-1	0-3	1-0	0-3	0-0	1-1	4-0	1-0	3-2	3-2	0-2	2-1	1-1	3-3	2-0	—

UNIBOND LEAGUE – FIRST DIVISION RESULTS 2001-02

	Ashton United	Belper Town	Chorley	Eastwood Town	Farsley Celtic	Gretna	Guiseley	Harrogate Town	Kendal Town	Leek Town	Lincoln United	Matlock Town	North Ferriby United	Ossett Albion	Ossett Town	Radcliffe Borough	Rossendale United	Spennymoor United	Stocksbridge Park Steels	Trafford	Witton Albion	Workington
Ashton United	—	3-1	0-2	3-2	5-2	6-2	2-1	1-1	3-2	4-1	3-0	0-1	1-3	2-1	1-1	2-1	3-2	2-3	3-0	1-3	4-2	1-0
Belper Town	1-1	—	3-1	1-0	2-2	0-2	0-1	3-4	2-1	3-2	0-0	1-1	2-2	1-0	0-1	0-1	2-3	1-2	1-0	0-3	2-3	0-0
Chorley	1-1	1-1	—	2-2	3-2	5-4	0-1	0-2	4-2	0-0	2-0	0-0	0-2	3-0	2-2	1-2	0-2	2-1	1-0	3-2	1-2	1-2
Eastwood Town	1-1	1-0	0-2	—	1-1	1-2	2-2	2-2	2-0	2-1	1-2	2-1	1-1	2-1	1-2	0-0	1-0	2-1	3-3	3-1	4-5	0-2
Farsley Celtic	1-1	3-0	2-0	1-0	—	3-1	1-2	0-3	3-2	3-3	3-4	3-0	2-0	2-4	2-5	1-3	0-1	0-0	2-1	3-0	0-2	1-0
Gretna	2-0	0-0	1-0	4-1	1-0	—	3-1	0-3	0-0	0-2	2-2	1-2	2-1	2-0	2-1	1-2	0-1	0-1	2-1	4-0	0-2	2-2
Guiseley	2-0	5-4	4-1	0-1	1-0	1-2	—	2-1	1-0	1-2	3-2	0-2	1-1	4-1	0-2	2-1	0-1	3-0	0-2	1-1	1-1	3-3
Harrogate Town	3-0	6-0	0-1	0-0	5-3	2-1	2-0	—	1-0	1-0	5-1	3-2	1-1	4-1	1-1	1-0	6-1	2-0	2-0	1-0	0-0	0-2
Kendal Town	2-2	2-1	1-1	2-3	3-2	1-2	2-0	1-3	—	1-2	1-2	1-3	1-1	0-0	1-1	0-3	0-3	3-1	1-1	0-2	4-2	1-1
Leek Town	2-3	0-1	0-2	2-1	2-0	1-0	1-1	0-0	2-0	—	2-0	2-0	1-3	5-1	1-5	4-1	0-3	1-3	5-0	5-0	3-2	0-0
Lincoln United	2-1	1-3	2-1	0-3	2-2	1-2	2-2	2-1	1-1	4-2	—	1-0	1-1	5-0	1-1	0-3	1-1	2-4	3-3	2-2	1-1	0-1
Matlock Town	0-3	2-0	0-1	1-1	2-1	1-1	0-1	1-1	1-2	1-1	5-0	—	4-2	0-0	0-1	1-1	0-1	0-2	2-0	1-1	5-1	1-2
North Ferriby United	1-1	3-2	2-2	1-3	2-2	6-1	3-0	1-3	2-1	0-0	1-4	0-2	—	3-1	0-1	0-1	2-0	3-2	2-3	1-1	5-1	2-0
Ossett Albion	1-5	1-0	1-3	1-4	2-2	1-1	1-2	2-4	1-0	1-1	3-1	0-2	3-5	—	2-0	1-1	0-4	3-1	0-1	3-5	3-1	0-3
Ossett Town	2-2	0-2	1-3	3-1	1-2	3-1	2-4	0-0	1-0	0-1	5-1	2-0	0-0	2-0	—	1-1	0-4	2-0	3-2	0-0	3-1	2-1
Radcliffe Borough	2-3	0-1	2-1	2-1	1-1	3-2	4-1	4-3	0-1	3-1	0-2	2-0	0-0	4-1	0-3	—	1-3	1-2	5-0	6-1	5-0	1-1
Rossendale United	1-2	0-0	0-3	1-1	5-2	1-0	5-1	1-2	1-1	3-0	2-2	0-3	1-3	2-0	1-1	0-1	—	3-3	0-0	3-4	1-2	1-2
Spennymoor United	2-6	2-2	2-1	1-2	2-1	0-2	3-0	1-0	1-1	0-2	2-0	2-0	2-1	3-2	3-3	2-1	1-1	—	2-1	4-1	4-2	5-4
Stocksbridge Park Steels	3-3	2-1	2-0	0-1	0-1	2-2	2-1	0-1	5-1	2-1	0-0	1-4	1-4	3-0	2-2	3-2	0-1	1-2	—	3-2	1-3	0-0
Trafford	1-3	1-2	3-1	0-1	2-2	1-4	2-1	1-2	0-1	2-1	3-1	3-0	3-2	1-1	1-0	0-1	3-3	1-2	3-1	—	0-1	1-1
Witton Albion	1-1	2-0	1-1	4-0	0-0	1-2	3-1	0-0	0-1	0-4	2-1	1-1	0-0	0-1	1-3	0-2	0-3	5-0	7-2	0-1	—	3-0
Workington	1-1	2-3	0-3	0-1	4-0	0-2	2-1	0-2	2-1	2-4	1-0	0-1	1-1	4-0	1-1	1-1	0-2	2-1	0-1	2-3	1-3	—

UNIBOND LEAGUE CUP 2001–02

GROUP 1	P	W	D	L	F	A	Pts
Blyth Spartans	4	3	0	1	10	6	9
Gateshead	4	2	0	2	8	7	6
Spennymoor United	4	1	2	1	9	7	5
Bishop Auckland	4	1	2	1	5	7	5
Gretna	4	0	2	2	6	11	2

GROUP 2	P	W	D	L	F	A	Pts
Kendal Town	4	4	0	0	14	7	12
Barrow	4	2	0	2	9	10	6
Bamber Bridge	4	2	0	2	5	6	6
Lancaster City	4	1	0	3	10	11	3
Workington	4	1	0	3	4	8	3

GROUP 3	P	W	D	L	F	A	Pts
Bradford Park Avenue	4	4	0	0	11	1	12
Guiseley	4	3	0	1	7	3	9
Harrogate Town	4	1	1	2	5	6	4
Farsley Celtic	4	1	0	3	2	7	3
Whitby Town	4	0	1	3	2	10	1

GROUP 4	P	W	D	L	F	A	Pts
Accrington Stanley	5	4	0	1	11	7	12
Burscough	5	3	0	2	9	4	9
Chorley	5	2	1	2	8	9	7
Rossendale United	5	2	0	3	6	8	6
Marine	5	1	2	2	6	8	5
Radcliffe Borough	5	1	1	3	6	10	4

GROUP 5	P	W	D	L	F	A	Pts
Trafford	5	4	0	1	7	3	12
Altrincham	5	3	0	2	6	5	9
Vauxhall Motors	5	2	2	1	9	8	8
Witton Albion	5	2	1	2	7	5	7
Runcorn FC Halton	5	0	3	2	7	11	3
Colwyn Bay	5	0	2	3	6	10	2

GROUP 6	P	W	D	L	F	A	Pts
Emley	5	4	0	1	11	7	12
Ashton United	5	3	1	1	22	13	10
Droylsden	5	3	1	1	16	9	10
Ossett Town	5	2	1	2	8	10	7
Hyde United	5	1	1	3	9	13	4
Ossett Albion	5	0	0	5	4	18	0

GROUP 7	P	W	D	L	F	A	Pts
Matlock Town	5	2	2	1	7	7	8
Leek Town	5	1	4	0	8	6	7
Hucknall Town	5	2	1	2	8	8	7
Belper Town	5	2	1	2	7	6	7
Eastwood Town	5	1	2	2	7	8	5
Burton Albion	5	1	2	2	5	7	5

GROUP 8	P	W	D	L	F	A	Pts
North Ferriby United	5	3	1	1	7	7	10
Gainsborough Trinity	5	3	0	2	9	7	9
Worksop Town	5	2	1	2	8	6	7
Frickley Athletic	5	2	0	3	11	11	6
Stocksbridge Park Steels	5	1	3	1	5	6	6
Lincoln United	5	1	1	3	8	11	4

Group winners qualified for League Challenge Cup, runners-up for President's Cup and third place for Chairman's Cup.

LEAGUE CHALLENGE CUP

QUARTER-FINALS
Accrington Stanley 1, Emley 0
Bradford Park Avenue 7, Blyth Spartans 1
Kendal Town 2, Trafford 3
Matlock Town 2, North Ferriby United 1

SEMI-FINALS
Accrington Stanley 2, Trafford 1
Matlock Town 1, Bradford Park Avenue 2

FINAL
Bradford Park Avenue 1, 0, Accrington Stanley 0, 1
Accrington Stanley won 5-4 on penalties.

PRESIDENT'S CUP

QUARTER-FINALS
Altrincham 1, Gainsborough Trinity 2
Barrow 2, Gateshead 1
Burscough 1, Ashton United 3
Leek Town 0, Guiseley 1

SEMI-FINALS
Ashton United 4, Barrow 5
Gainsborough Trinity 5, Guiseley 1

FINAL
Barrow 1, Gainsborough Trinity 0

CHAIRMAN'S CUP

QUARTER-FINALS
Droylsden 3, Chorley 3
Droylsden won 3-2 on penalties.
Harrogate Town 2, Bamber Bridge 0
Spennymoor United 4, Hucknall Town 2
Vauxhall Motors 0, Worksop Town 3

SEMI-FINALS
Harrogate Town 0, Droylsden 1
Spennymoor United 0, Worksop Town 1

FINAL
Droylsden 1, Worksop Town 2

DR MARTENS LEAGUE 2001–02

Premier Division

	P	Home			Away			Total			Goals		GD	Pts
		W	D	L	W	D	L	W	D	L	F	A		
Kettering Town	42	12	4	5	15	2	4	27	6	9	80	41	39	87
Tamworth	42	16	5	0	8	8	5	24	13	5	81	41	40	85
Havant & Waterlooville	42	14	4	3	8	5	8	22	9	11	74	50	24	75
Crawley Town	42	12	3	6	9	7	5	21	10	11	67	48	19	73
Newport County	42	10	6	5	9	3	9	19	9	14	61	48	13	66
Tiverton Town	42	10	4	7	7	6	8	17	10	15	70	63	7	61
Moor Green	42	10	6	5	8	1	12	18	7	17	64	62	2	61
Worcester City	42	9	7	5	7	5	9	16	12	14	65	54	11	60
Stafford Rangers	42	13	2	6	4	7	10	17	9	16	70	62	8	60
Ilkeston Town	42	8	8	5	6	8	7	14	16	12	58	61	–3	58
Weymouth	42	9	4	8	6	7	8	15	11	16	59	67	–8	56
Hinckley United	42	10	5	6	4	8	9	14	13	15	64	62	2	55
Folkestone Invicta	42	10	5	6	4	7	10	14	12	16	51	61	–10	54
Cambridge City	42	7	7	7	5	9	7	12	16	14	60	70	–10	52
Welling United	42	8	7	6	5	5	11	13	12	17	69	66	3	51
Hednesford Town	42	9	4	8	6	2	13	15	6	21	59	70	–11	51
Bath City	42	9	3	9	4	8	9	13	11	18	56	65	–9	50
Chelmsford City	42	8	6	7	5	5	11	13	11	18	63	75	–12	50
Newport (IW)	42	6	7	8	6	5	10	12	12	18	38	61	–23	48
King's Lynn	42	6	8	7	5	5	11	11	13	18	44	57	–13	46
Merthyr Tydfil	42	8	7	6	4	1	16	12	8	22	53	71	–18	44
Salisbury City	42	4	5	12	2	3	16	6	8	28	36	87	–51	26

Southern & Eastern Division

	P	Home			Away			Total			Goals		GD	Pts
		W	D	L	W	D	L	W	D	L	F	A		
Hastings Town	42	15	3	3	14	5	2	29	8	5	85	38	47	95
Grantham Town	42	15	5	1	14	1	6	29	6	7	99	43	56	93
Dorchester Town	42	16	4	1	10	6	5	26	10	6	81	36	45	88
Histon	42	15	2	4	8	6	7	23	8	11	83	49	34	77
Stamford	42	15	2	4	9	2	10	24	4	14	76	61	15	76
Fisher Athletic	42	13	4	4	7	6	8	20	10	12	83	56	27	70
Eastbourne Borough	42	11	5	5	10	1	10	21	6	15	63	46	17	69
Dartford	42	11	2	8	7	3	11	18	5	19	62	66	–4	59
Erith & Belvedere	42	8	1	12	10	2	9	18	3	21	75	79	–4	57
Bashley	42	10	7	4	5	4	12	15	11	16	71	64	7	56
Burnham	42	8	3	10	7	7	7	15	10	17	52	54	–2	55
Rugby United	42	10	4	7	6	2	13	16	6	20	56	67	–11	54
Rothwell Town	42	9	3	9	5	5	11	14	8	20	45	66	–21	50
Ashford Town	42	7	3	11	7	3	11	14	6	22	58	78	–20	48
Banbury United*	42	12	2	7	1	7	13	13	9	20	53	66	–13	47
Chatham Town	42	7	6	8	6	2	13	13	8	21	56	87	–31	47
Sittingbourne	42	9	0	12	5	4	12	14	4	24	46	69	–23	46
Spalding United	42	8	4	9	5	2	14	13	6	23	72	84	–12	45
Tonbridge Angels	42	10	3	8	3	3	15	13	6	23	65	80	–15	45
St Leonards	42	7	2	12	7	1	13	14	3	25	52	88	–36	45
Corby Town	42	4	9	8	6	4	11	10	13	19	54	82	–28	43
Wishbech Town	42	6	5	10	5	3	13	11	8	23	56	84	–28	41

1 point deducted for breach of League Rule.

Midland & Western Division

	P	Home			Away			Total			Goals		GD	Pts
		W	D	L	W	D	L	W	D	L	F	A		
Halesowen Town	40	14	3	3	13	6	1	27	9	4	85	24	61	90
Chippenham Town	40	12	6	2	14	3	3	26	9	5	81	28	53	87
Weston-Super-Mare	40	13	3	4	9	7	4	22	10	8	70	38	32	76
Solihull Borough	40	7	9	4	13	2	5	20	11	9	75	42	33	71
Gresley Rovers	40	10	5	5	9	4	7	19	9	12	59	50	9	66
Sutton Coldfield Town	40	12	3	5	5	7	8	17	10	13	74	54	20	61
Mangotsfield United	40	8	5	7	9	4	7	17	9	14	59	59	0	60
Stourport Swifts	40	12	3	5	5	2	13	17	5	18	61	59	2	56
Atherstone United	40	9	5	6	7	3	10	16	8	16	57	58	–1	56
Clevedon Town	40	8	4	8	7	6	7	15	10	15	59	63	–4	55
Bedworth United	40	8	3	9	8	4	8	16	7	17	54	70	–16	55
Evesham United	40	8	2	10	8	4	8	16	6	18	64	69	–5	54
Cirencester Town	40	9	2	9	6	5	9	15	7	18	48	63	–15	52
Gloucester City	40	8	5	7	6	4	10	14	9	17	54	67	–13	51
Cinderford Town	40	10	2	8	1	5	14	11	7	22	54	67	–13	40
Shepshed Dynamo	40	4	6	10	6	4	10	10	10	20	64	84	–20	40
Bilston Town	40	8	2	10	3	5	12	11	7	22	50	72	–22	40
Redditch United	40	7	5	8	4	1	15	11	6	23	47	77	–30	39
Swindon Supermarine	40	6	3	11	5	1	14	11	4	25	52	76	–24	37
Racing Club Warwick	40	7	6	7	1	5	14	8	11	21	38	63	–25	35
Rocester	40	2	8	10	3	4	13	5	12	23	33	75	–42	27

Records for Bloxwich United Football Club have been deleted.

DR MARTENS LEAGUE ATTENDANCES
Premier Average 682
Eastern Division Average 237
Western Division Average 236

LEADING GOALSCORERS
(League and Cup)

Premier Division

Paul Kiely (Stafford Rangers)	29
James Taylor (Havant & Waterlooville)	28
David Laws (Weymouth)	25
Nathan Lamey (Moor Green)	22
Ryan King (Salisbury City)	20
Lee Phillips (Weymouth)	20
Dale Watkins (Kettering Town)	20
Adrian Foster (Bath City)	19
Darren Roberts (Tamworth)	19
Gary Abbott (Welling United)	18
Glen Kirkwood (Ilkeston Town)	18
Adam Webster (Worcester City)	18
Jamie O'Rourke (Havant & Waterlooville)	17
Daniel Carroll (Crawley Town)	15
Timothy Hambley (Havant & Waterlooville)	15
Anthony Hemmings (Tamworth)	15
Daniel Hockton (Chelmsford City)	14
Jamie Lenton (Hinckley United)	14
Mark Owen (Worcester City)	14
Robert Collins (Crawley Town)	13
Neil Davis (Hednesford Town)	13
Darren Collins (Kettering Town)	12

Eastern Division

Darren Adams (Erith & Belvedere)	29
Lee Stephenson (Spalding United)	26
Justin Keeler (Dorchester Town)	25
Daniel O'Hagan (Dorchester Town)	25
Matthew Allen (Eastbourne Borough)	23
Gary Bull (Grantham Town)	22
Simon Austin (Chatham Town)	21
Leroy Huggins (Fisher Athletic)	21
Neil Kennedy (Histon)	21
David Hassett (Ashford Town)	19
Carl Holmes (Stamford)	19

Peter Munns (Histon)	17
Mathew Groves (Dorchester Town)	16
Malcolm Ndekwe (Stamford)	16
Richard Ranshaw (Grantham Town)	16
David Adams (Eastbourne Borough)	15
Mathew Gooderick (Banbury)	15
Wayne Spencer (Corby Town)	15
Ashley Warner (Rugby United)	15
Michael Durkin (Burnham)	14
Christopher Freestone (Rugby United)	14
Benjamin Milner (Banbury United)	14

Western Division

Derek Hall (Solihull Borough)	32
Christopher Partridge (Bedworth United)	22
Jody Bevan (Weston-Super-Mare)	21
Christopher Smith (Solihull Borough)	21
Darren Edwards (Mangotsfield United)	18
Kirk Master (Shepshed Dynamo)	18
Leroy May (Halesowen Town)	18
Karl Bayliss (Gloucester City)	17
James Bent (Chippenham Town)	16
James Cox (Weston-Super-Mare)	16
Mathew Rawlins (Chippenham Town)	16
Paul Danks (Redditch United)	15
David Seal (Mangotsfield United)	15
Lee Booth (Redditch United)	14
Stephen Brown (Chippenham Town)	14
Kevin Charley (Atherstone United)	14
Emeka Ejiofor (Atherstone United)	14
Steven Tweddle (Chippenham Town)	14
Lee Ross (Halesowen Town)	13
Lee McGlinchey (Shepshed Dynamo)	11
Leon Mitchell (Sutton Coldfield Town)	11
Christopher Parkins (Gresley Rovers)	11

DR MARTENS LEAGUE CUP

PRELIMINARY ROUND
Sittingbourne 0, Chatham Town 0
Chatham Town won 3-2 on penalties.
Wisbech Town 1, Spalding United 2

FIRST ROUND
Hednesford Town 1, Evesham United 3
Newport County 1, Bath City 3
Worcester City 2, Rocester 0
Ashford Town 1, Chelmsford City 0
Bilston Town 1, Halesowen Town 0
Burnham 4, St Leonards 2
Cinderford Town 3, Gloucester City 0
Cirencester Town 2, Weston-Super-Mare 1
Clevedon Town 5, Tiverton Town 2
Crawley Town 3, Chatham Town 1
Dorchester Town 4, Bashley 3
Eastbourne Borough 3, Fisher Athletic 1
Erith & Belvedere 1, Folkestone Invicta 2
Grantham Town 1, King's Lynn 2
Hastings Town 3, Dartford 1
Havant & Waterlooville 2, Newport (IW) 0
Hinckley United 1, Atherstone United 4
Kettering Town 3, Corby Town 1
Mangotsfield United 3, Chippenham Town 2
Merthyr Tydfil 5, Swindon Supermarine 0
Moor Green 5, Shepshed Dynamo 4
Rothwell Town 1, Racing Club Warwick 0
Rugby United 1, Banbury United 2
Solihull Borough 1, Sutton Coldfield 0
Spalding United 1, Histon 0
Stafford Rangers 1, Bloxwich United 1
Bloxwich United won 4-1 on penalties.
Stamford 1, Cambridge City 0
Stourport Swifts 4, Redditch United 5
Tamworth 1, Bedworth United 4
Tonbridge Angels 2, Welling United 1
Weymouth 4, Salisbury City 0
Gresley Rovers 1, Ilkeston Town 0

SECOND ROUND
Dorchester Town 3, Weymouth 2
Merthyr Tydfil 2, Clevedon Town 0

Ashford Town 2, Havant & Waterlooville 1
Bath City 3, Cinderford Town 1
Bedworth United 4, Worcester City 0
Bilston Town 2, Banbury United 1
Evesham United 1, Solihull Borough 2
Hastings Town 5, Folkestone Invicta 0
King's Lynn 6, Kettering Town 1
Mangotsfield United 3, Cirencester Town 1
Redditch United 1, Moor Green 4
Stamford 0, Gresley Rovers 1
Tonbridge Angels 1, Eastbourne Borough 2
Crawley Town 6, Burnham 0
Histon 1, Rothwell Town 3
Bloxwich United withdrew v Atherstone United w.o.

THIRD ROUND
Bedworth United 4, Moor Green 3
Bath City 0, Dorchester Town 2
Crawley Town 2, Ashford Town 2
Ashford Town won 4-1 on penalties.
Hastings Town 2, Eastbourne Borough 3
Solihull Borough 4, Bilston Town 0
Atherstone United 2, Gresley Rovers 1
Merthyr Tydfil 3, Mangotsfield United 0
King's Lynn 2, Rothwell Town 1

FOURTH ROUND
Dorchester Town 3, Merthyr Tydfil 0
Solihull Borough 3, Bedworth United 2
Atherstone United 0, King's Lynn 2
Eastbourne Borough 1, Ashford Town 0

SEMI-FINALS
King's Lynn 2, Solihull Borough 1
Dorchester Town 2, Eastbourne Borough 1

FINAL FIRST LEG   535
King's Lynn (0) 0, Dorchester Town (1) 1 *(Andrews 44)*

FINAL SECOND LEG   592
Dorchester Town (2) 3 *(Andrews 13, O'Hagan 25,
Keeler 76)*, King's Lynn (0) 0

DR MARTENS LEAGUE – PREMIER DIVISION RESULTS 2001-02

	Bath City	Cambridge City	Chelmsford City	Crawley Town	Folkestone Invicta	Havant & Waterlooville	Hednesford Town	Hinckley United	Ilkeston Town	Kettering Town	King's Lynn	Merthyr Tydfil	Moor Green	Newport County	Newport (IW)	Salisbury City	Stafford Rangers	Tamworth	Tiverton Town	Welling United	Weymouth	Worcester City
Bath City	—	1-1	1-2	2-0	1-1	2-5	3-4	1-2	1-1	0-1	0-1	4-2	0-2	2-1	0-1	1-0	4-3	1-2	4-2	2-1	2-1	4-0
Cambridge City	1-3	—	0-1	0-0	0-0	0-3	2-1	3-2	2-1	2-1	2-2	2-2	0-1	1-2	2-0	1-3	1-1	1-1	1-3	2-0	2-2	0-2
Chelmsford City	1-3	0-3	—	2-2	1-1	0-3	1-1	0-2	6-1	0-2	2-2	2-1	0-2	3-1	3-0	3-2	0-0	1-1	2-2	1-2	2-1	2-1
Crawley Town	3-0	4-3	2-2	—	1-1	3-0	4-1	1-0	3-0	2-3	1-0	2-1	1-2	0-1	2-0	4-0	1-2	1-2	3-0	2-4	3-0	1-0
Folkestone Invicta	1-1	1-0	2-1	1-1	—	3-0	1-0	1-3	0-2	2-3	1-2	1-0	1-0	3-1	2-2	2-0	2-1	3-3	0-3	0-0	1-3	2-1
Havant & Waterlooville	3-0	4-1	3-1	2-2	2-2	—	2-1	5-0	2-2	1-3	0-0	4-0	3-1	1-3	2-1	6-0	3-3	0-2	3-3	1-0	3-2	1-0
Hednesford Town	1-0	1-1	1-2	4-0	3-1	2-1	—	2-1	2-1	1-2	0-2	3-0	2-1	3-2	1-2	6-0	3-0	1-0	2-1	1-1	2-4	0-3
Hinckley United	2-2	1-2	0-2	0-1	1-2	2-4	4-0	—	2-2	2-1	0-2	1-0	2-1	0-1	1-2	2-1	3-0	1-0	3-4	3-2	2-4	0-0
Ilkeston Town	3-3	2-2	2-0	0-0	2-1	2-0	2-0	2-1	—	0-2	3-1	1-0	2-1	0-1	0-0	2-1	2-2	2-1	0-2	3-1	3-2	1-2
Kettering Town	0-0	1-2	1-1	1-3	3-1	3-1	1-0	1-1	1-2	—	3-0	3-0	1-0	1-2	1-2	4-0	1-0	1-1	0-1	3-1	4-1	4-1
King's Lynn	1-1	1-3	3-0	2-2	2-2	1-1	3-1	2-2	0-1	0-3	—	0-1	1-2	4-2	3-1	2-1	2-0	1-1	1-2	1-2	0-0	1-2
Merthyr Tydfil	3-1	1-3	3-1	2-2	1-0	1-1	3-1	1-1	2-3	0-2	3-1	—	1-2	1-1	3-1	3-2	2-0	1-1	1-2	2-1	7-1	0-0
Moor Green	0-0	1-2	3-1	2-0	4-1	2-1	1-4	1-1	3-0	0-2	4-0	1-0	—	1-2	0-0	0-0	5-0	2-0	1-1	1-1	1-2	3-1
Newport County	1-0	2-2	3-0	4-1	2-0	2-0	0-1	0-2	2-1	0-2	0-0	3-0	2-1	—	0-0	0-0	1-0	0-4	3-0	2-1	1-2	0-2
Newport (IW)	2-1	1-0	2-0	1-1	0-1	0-1	2-0	1-1	2-1	0-2	0-0	0-4	2-1	0-4	—	0-0	1-1	0-4	3-0	1-1	0-0	1-1
Salisbury City	0-1	1-1	2-1	0-3	0-1	2-0	2-0	1-1	1-1	1-2	0-3	0-2	5-0	0-4	1-1	—	1-4	1-2	0-3	0-1	2-3	1-1
Stafford Rangers	2-1	3-0	2-1	2-0	2-1	0-2	3-0	4-2	1-2	2-3	3-2	1-0	3-4	2-1	5-1	3-0	—	0-1	6-2	2-1	2-1	1-1
Tamworth	1-1	2-2	1-0	1-1	1-1	1-1	3-0	2-1	1-1	1-0	4-1	2-0	2-0	2-0	5-1	5-1	1-0	—	3-2	1-0	3-0	3-2
Tiverton Town	3-1	5-0	0-1	2-0	2-0	0-1	2-0	2-1	3-2	1-2	1-1	1-3	2-0	2-0	1-0	1-0	3-3	2-2	—	0-2	0-1	2-0
Welling United	4-0	4-4	2-4	2-3	2-4	1-2	4-1	3-2	1-0	1-1	0-1	3-0	1-1	1-0	3-0	5-1	3-2	3-3	1-1	—	1-1	1-3
Weymouth	0-0	4-2	2-1	1-2	1-1	0-1	0-4	1-1	3-1	4-1	1-0	4-1	0-1	2-1	4-0	6-0	0-1	0-2	2-1	1-1	—	1-2
Worcester City	0-1	1-2	1-1	3-0	1-1	0-0	0-1	4-3	2-2	1-1	3-1	1-0	3-2	0-0	4-0	6-0	1-2	0-2	4-2	2-1	3-3	—

DR MARTENS LEAGUE – MIDLAND & WESTERN DIVISION RESULTS 2001–02

	Atherstone United	Bedworth United	Bilston Town	Chippenham Town	Cinderford Town	Cirencester Town	Clevedon Town	Evesham United	Gloucester City	Gresley Rovers	Halesowen Town	Mangotsfield United	Racing Club Warwick	Redditch United	Rocester	Shepshed Dynamo	Solihull Borough	Stourport Swifts	Sutton Coldfield Town	Swindon Supermarine	Weston-Super-Mare
Atherstone United	—	3-1	4-0	1-3	5-1	4-1	2-2	0-1	1-0	0-0	2-5	1-1	1-0	1-2	2-0	1-1	1-2	2-1	0-0	5-0	0-2
Bedworth United	2-1	—	0-3	1-2	2-4	2-1	1-1	3-0	4-1	0-2	0-3	1-4	1-1	3-1	1-0	0-4	0-2	1-1	2-0	4-2	2-3
Bilston Town	1-3	0-1	—	1-2	4-0	3-1	0-1	3-1	5-1	0-2	1-2	2-6	3-1	3-2	0-1	3-0	0-6	1-0	0-0	1-2	1-1
Chippenham Town	2-0	2-1	2-0	—	0-0	3-0	4-0	1-2	1-0	0-1	2-2	3-0	1-1	4-0	4-0	4-0	3-1	1-0	1-1	1-2	1-1
Cinderford Town	4-1	2-4	2-0	0-1	—	1-1	2-1	4-0	2-1	3-5	0-0	1-4	5-1	4-1	2-1	0-2	3-1	4-0	1-0	0-1	0-1
Cirencester Town	1-0	3-0	1-2	1-3	1-1	—	1-2	2-1	1-1	2-1	0-1	0-4	0-1	1-2	1-2	3-2	4-1	4-0	2-2	0-1	3-4
Clevedon Town	0-3	0-1	3-2	3-2	2-1	2-3	—	0-0	1-3	1-2	2-0	1-2	0-2	2-0	1-0	1-2	1-3	1-0	3-2	2-1	1-0
Evesham United	1-1	3-2	3-1	0-6	0-2	0-3	0-0	—	0-2	1-4	0-3	0-0	2-0	6-0	2-2	1-2	2-4	1-2	1-0	2-1	1-2
Gloucester City	4-1	1-7	5-1	1-1	4-2	0-1	2-3	0-2	—	3-0	0-3	2-1	1-0	2-0	2-2	1-5	1-1	2-0	2-2	1-0	1-2
Gresley Rovers	0-1	1-2	2-0	2-2	0-0	4-2	1-1	1-0	2-0	—	1-2	2-0	0-0	2-1	4-0	2-2	2-0	6-2	2-0	2-0	0-0
Halesowen Town	1-0	0-1	3-0	0-1	1-2	2-0	2-0	3-0	0-0	1-2	—	1-1	6-0	2-1	4-0	6-0	4-1	3-0	2-0	5-1	2-2
Mangotsfield United	3-1	1-1	0-0	1-0	2-0	4-1	0-0	1-3	1-1	2-0	1-1	—	3-3	2-0	4-0	6-2	0-3	3-0	0-1	5-1	1-3
Racing Club Warwick	5-1	0-0	0-1	0-4	0-0	1-3	0-2	1-0	0-1	0-0	6-0	3-3	—	2-0	1-0	2-0	2-1	1-1	1-4	3-1	1-1
Redditch United	1-3	2-1	2-1	1-3	1-0	4-0	2-0	2-2	0-0	0-0	1-3	2-0	2-0	—	5-1	1-1	0-2	1-2	1-0	1-2	1-2
Rocester	0-4	1-0	2-1	0-2	1-1	0-1	1-0	0-1	0-1	1-0	1-1	1-0	1-0	5-1	—	1-1	0-2	1-2	1-3	0-3	2-2
Shepshed Dynamo	1-2	1-3	1-1	1-2	5-2	0-1	1-3	1-1	0-2	2-2	1-2	1-2	0-3	3-2	2-2	—	0-3	1-1	0-0	0-3	3-1
Solihull Borough	1-1	2-0	1-1	0-1	2-2	4-0	0-0	2-3	4-0	0-1	1-1	2-1	2-1	1-1	1-2	0-3	—	1-1	0-0	4-1	1-0
Stourport Swifts	1-1	1-1	5-2	0-0	4-2	2-0	2-1	2-3	2-1	2-0	2-0	1-0	1-0	3-4	4-0	2-0	2-0	—	0-1	3-1	1-0
Sutton Coldfield Town	6-0	1-1	2-1	1-2	1-1	5-1	1-0	1-1	0-1	3-1	2-0	2-1	2-1	2-1	4-0	3-2	0-4	2-0	—	1-0	0-3
Swindon Supermarine	0-1	2-0	1-1	0-3	1-3	1-3	1-2	2-3	1-2	0-2	0-1	2-2	4-0	1-2	1-0	6-2	2-3	3-1	3-1	—	1-1
Weston-Super-Mare	2-0	2-1	1-0	3-1	4-1	0-2	4-1	2-2	0-1	0-0	0-0	1-0	1-0	3-1	3-1	5-0	1-2	4-1	1-2	2-0	—

N.B. Bloxwich United's record expunged from the table.

DR MARTENS LEAGUE – SOUTHERN & EASTERN DIVISION RESULTS 2001-02

	Ashford Town	Banbury United	Bashley	Burnham	Chatham Town	Corby Town	Dartford	Dorchester Town	Eastbourne Borough	Erith & Belvedere	Fisher Athletic	Grantham Town	Hastings Town	Histon	Rothwell Town	Rugby United	Sittingbourne	Spalding	St Leonards	Stamford	Tonbridge Angels	Wisbech Town
Ashford Town	—	3-0	0-0	1-1	0-1	1-4	0-1	0-2	0-1	3-2	2-0	0-3	0-2	1-1	1-2	2-1	6-1	0-3	0-1	2-3	3-2	1-0
Banbury United	2-1	—	4-1	2-2	2-1	1-1	4-1	0-1	3-1	0-3	2-0	4-1	2-3	1-0	1-0	0-1	2-0	3-0	2-1	1-0	0-2	3-0
Bashley	2-3	3-1	—	2-1	4-1	4-2	2-0	1-1	0-2	1-2	2-1	2-1	0-0	2-2	1-1	0-1	1-2	1-1	3-1	0-0	3-3	8-0
Burnham	0-0	0-1	1-0	—	1-1	3-0	0-1	1-3	0-1	1-5	0-0	0-2	1-2	0-6	0-1	2-0	1-2	2-1	2-0	0-1	3-1	3-2
Chatham Town	2-5	3-3	2-4	1-1	—	1-1	1-2	2-2	0-3	2-3	1-1	5-3	1-2	0-4	1-1	1-0	1-2	3-1	1-0	2-1	2-1	4-2
Corby Town	1-1	1-1	1-1	0-0	2-3	—	3-2	2-4	1-0	0-5	3-0	0-1	0-5	2-1	2-1	2-2	0-3	1-5	2-2	1-3	0-0	1-3
Dartford	3-1	1-1	1-0	5-4	2-0	2-0	—	0-1	1-2	4-0	0-1	0-1	3-1	3-1	3-1	3-1	0-2	1-3	2-6	2-0	3-2	2-1
Dorchester Town	6-1	2-0	1-1	2-0	3-1	3-0	2-0	—	2-1	1-0	3-3	1-0	0-0	2-0	1-1	2-2	0-1	2-1	1-0	1-3	0-0	3-1
Eastbourne Borough	1-2	2-1	3-2	0-2	0-2	2-2	1-0	2-1	—	2-2	3-4	2-1	1-2	2-1	2-1	2-3	0-2	2-0	2-0	5-4	3-1	1-1
Erith & Belvedere	2-1	1-1	1-0	0-1	2-0	3-2	2-5	1-1	2-2	—	2-1	4-2	3-2	5-2	0-3	2-3	1-3	2-1	5-2	1-2	2-1	0-1
Fisher Athletic	5-2	2-2	1-1	0-3	5-0	3-0	0-0	2-2	2-0	2-1	—	0-1	0-1	1-1	1-0	2-1	3-2	6-1	4-1	5-3	1-0	2-0
Grantham Town	4-1	4-1	3-1	3-2	6-1	3-0	0-1	1-0	2-0	4-2	0-1	—	1-3	2-0	3-0	6-0	0-0	1-1	3-1	1-1	3-0	2-0
Hastings Town	2-2	4-0	2-0	1-0	2-0	1-2	1-0	0-0	1-0	3-2	2-1	1-3	—	2-0	3-0	4-1	0-0	3-2	0-1	1-0	4-2	2-1
Histon	1-0	2-1	3-1	1-2	2-0	3-1	3-1	2-0	2-1	5-2	1-0	2-0	2-0	—	1-1	4-2	1-2	3-0	1-2	1-0	3-2	0-0
Rothwell Town	0-2	2-2	1-2	1-0	1-1	0-1	1-0	1-0	1-0	0-1	1-4	3-0	3-0	1-1	—	0-1	3-1	2-1	1-0	4-2	0-2	3-2
Rugby United	4-0	1-1	3-1	0-1	1-2	0-1	0-0	2-1	2-1	0-2	3-0	6-0	4-1	4-2	0-0	—	2-0	3-2	2-0	0-1	1-2	0-0
Sittingbourne	0-1	4-1	2-1	1-2	3-0	0-3	0-2	0-2	0-2	1-3	0-4	0-0	0-3	1-0	3-1	2-0	—	2-3	4-3	0-2	3-0	1-2
Spalding	3-2	1-0	2-3	1-1	1-2	2-1	1-1	1-3	2-2	2-3	0-1	2-5	1-5	1-1	5-0	1-3	2-0	—	1-5	1-3	1-0	3-1
St Leonards	2-1	2-1	2-5	0-3	1-2	1-3	2-4	0-3	3-1	2-1	4-1	1-2	1-3	2-2	0-0	3-1	2-1	1-5	—	1-3	2-0	0-3
Stamford	1-3	1-0	2-1	2-0	3-2	3-4	2-0	1-2	1-2	2-2	5-3	1-2	2-5	1-0	7-0	3-1	3-2	2-1	1-3	—	0-1	1-1
Tonbridge Angels	4-0	2-1	4-0	2-2	2-1	2-2	2-0	1-4	0-3	1-2	2-1	1-0	2-0	2-0	2-0	3-1	1-2	3-1	2-0	4-0	—	0-1
Wisbech Town	0-2	2-0	0-3	1-1	3-0	2-1	2-1	1-1	0-1	1-2	1-1	0-6	2-4	1-1	1-4	3-2	1-2	6-1	1-2	1-3	3-1	—

RYMAN FOOTBALL LEAGUE 2001–02

Premier Division

	P	Home					Away					Total						
		W	D	L	F	A	W	D	L	F	A	W	D	L	F	A	GD	Pts
Gravesend & Northfleet	42	14	4	3	43	18	17	2	2	47	15	31	6	5	90	33	57	99
Canvey Island	42	15	3	3	55	25	15	2	4	53	16	30	5	7	108	41	67	95
Aldershot Town	42	12	4	5	44	23	10	3	8	32	28	22	7	13	76	51	25	73
Braintree Town	42	15	2	4	37	20	8	2	11	29	41	23	4	15	66	61	5	73
Purfleet	42	11	8	2	39	20	8	7	6	28	24	19	15	8	67	44	23	72
Grays Athletic	42	12	5	4	33	21	8	5	8	32	34	20	10	12	65	55	10	70
Chesham United	42	11	7	3	40	27	8	3	10	29	26	19	10	13	69	53	16	67
Hendon	42	10	3	8	26	22	9	2	10	40	33	19	5	18	66	55	11	62
Billericay Town	42	8	6	7	32	34	8	7	6	27	26	16	13	13	59	60	-1	61
St Albans City	42	9	5	7	29	25	7	4	10	42	35	16	9	17	71	60	11	57
Hitchin Town	42	7	4	10	31	39	8	6	7	42	42	15	10	17	73	81	-8	55
Sutton United	42	8	9	4	33	26	5	6	10	29	37	13	15	14	62	63	-1	54
Heybridge Swifts	42	7	6	8	34	40	8	3	10	34	45	15	9	18	68	85	-17	54
Kingstonian	42	10	4	7	34	27	3	9	9	16	29	13	13	16	50	56	-6	52
Boreham Wood	42	6	4	11	24	36	9	2	10	26	26	15	6	21	50	62	-12	51
Maidenhead United	42	9	3	9	27	30	6	2	13	24	33	15	5	22	51	63	-12	50
Bedford Town	42	10	1	10	39	32	2	11	8	25	37	12	12	18	64	69	-5	48
Basingstoke Town	42	8	5	8	28	31	3	10	8	22	37	11	15	16	50	68	-18	48
Enfield	42	4	4	13	20	44	7	5	9	28	33	11	9	22	48	77	-29	42
Hampton & Richmond Borough	42	5	8	8	26	32	4	5	12	25	39	9	13	20	51	71	-20	40
Harrow Borough	42	2	5	14	26	54	6	5	10	24	35	8	10	24	50	89	-39	34
Croydon	42	5	3	13	24	40	2	2	17	12	53	7	5	30	36	93	-57	26

Division One

	P	Home					Away					Total						
		W	D	L	F	A	W	D	L	F	A	W	D	L	F	A	GD	Pts
Ford United	42	12	5	4	44	30	15	2	4	48	26	27	7	8	92	56	36	88
Bishop's Stortford	42	15	3	3	60	25	11	6	4	44	26	26	9	7	104	51	53	87
Aylesbury United	42	13	6	2	57	33	10	4	7	39	31	23	10	9	96	64	32	79
Bognor Regis Town	42	10	8	3	36	20	10	5	6	38	35	20	13	9	74	55	19	73
Northwood	42	11	5	5	53	34	8	6	7	39	30	19	11	12	92	64	28	68
Carshalton Athletic	42	11	5	5	38	28	6	11	4	26	25	17	16	9	64	53	11	67
Harlow Town	42	9	4	8	36	30	10	5	6	41	35	19	9	14	77	65	12	66
Slough Town	42	10	4	7	41	24	7	7	7	27	27	17	11	14	68	51	17	62
Uxbridge	42	11	1	9	44	35	7	5	9	24	30	18	6	18	68	65	3	60
Oxford City	42	10	6	5	32	23	7	3	11	27	43	17	9	16	59	66	-7	60
Thame United	42	10	4	7	44	27	5	10	6	31	34	15	14	13	75	61	14	59
Tooting & Mitcham United	42	7	7	7	40	36	9	4	8	30	34	16	11	15	70	70	0	59
Walton & Hersham	42	6	6	9	27	25	10	4	7	48	45	16	10	16	75	70	5	58
Yeading	42	9	6	6	40	31	7	4	10	44	59	16	10	16	84	90	-6	58
Worthing	42	7	2	12	43	41	8	6	7	26	24	15	8	19	69	65	4	53
Staines Town	42	5	9	7	22	26	7	2	12	23	34	12	11	19	45	60	-15	47
Dulwich Hamlet	42	6	5	10	33	42	5	8	8	31	34	11	13	18	64	76	-12	46
Wealdstone	42	6	9	6	32	31	5	3	13	28	51	11	12	19	60	82	-22	45
Bromley	42	7	5	9	20	27	3	6	12	24	47	10	11	21	44	74	-30	41
Whyteleafe	42	6	6	9	30	39	4	5	12	16	47	10	11	21	46	86	-40	41
Barking & East Ham United	42	6	3	12	31	50	2	4	15	30	73	8	7	27	61	123	-62	31
Windsor & Eton	42	5	3	13	34	46	2	2	17	19	47	7	5	30	53	93	-40	26

Division Two

	P	Home					Away					Total						
		W	D	L	F	A	W	D	L	F	A	W	D	L	F	A	GD	Pts
Lewes	42	17	3	1	65	15	12	6	3	43	16	29	9	4	108	31	77	96
Horsham	42	17	3	1	59	14	10	6	5	45	30	27	9	6	104	44	60	90
Berkhamsted Town	42	12	5	4	47	26	11	5	5	35	25	23	10	9	82	51	31	79
Arlesey Town	42	12	4	5	52	28	11	1	9	37	27	23	6	13	89	55	34	75
Banstead Athletic	42	12	3	6	44	25	10	5	6	39	29	22	8	12	83	54	29	74
Leyton Pennant	42	15	2	4	47	27	7	6	8	37	33	22	8	12	84	60	24	74
Great Wakering Rovers	42	12	4	5	43	19	9	4	8	21	20	21	8	13	64	37	27	71
East Thurrock United	42	11	5	5	37	25	10	3	8	30	34	21	8	13	67	59	8	71
Marlow	42	10	5	6	33	26	8	8	5	40	37	18	13	11	73	63	10	67.
Hemel Hempstead Town	42	10	6	5	46	28	8	4	9	36	38	18	10	14	82	66	16	64
Leatherhead	42	11	3	7	42	24	6	3	12	30	38	17	6	19	72	62	10	57
Ashford Town (Mx)	42	8	7	6	33	29	7	4	10	25	42	15	11	16	58	71	-13	56
Metropolitan Police	42	10	4	7	49	35	6	3	12	35	49	16	7	19	84	84	0	55
Barton Rovers	42	9	2	10	28	24	6	7	8	26	36	15	9	18	54	60	-6	54
Hungerford Town	42	7	7	7	27	32	7	2	12	29	43	14	9	19	56	75	-19	51
Tilbury	42	7	4	10	24	28	8	2	11	31	46	15	6	21	55	74	-19	51
Chertsey Town	42	7	6	8	45	52	3	8	10	34	60	10	14	18	79	112	-33	44
Wembley	42	7	4	10	31	35	2	6	13	20	47	9	10	23	51	82	-31	37
Molesey	42	6	6	9	21	32	4	0	17	19	61	10	6	26	40	93	-53	36
Cheshunt	42	2	8	11	28	39	5	5	11	23	45	7	13	22	51	84	-33	34
Wivenhoe Town	42	6	2	13	33	52	2	7	12	22	59	8	9	25	55	111	-56	33
Romford	42	2	4	15	27	59	2	3	16	15	46	4	7	31	42	105	-63	19

Division Three

	P	Home					Away					Total						
		W	D	L	F	A	W	D	L	F	A	W	D	L	F	A	GD	Pts
Croydon Athletic	42	21	0	0	83	14	9	5	7	55	27	30	5	7	138	41	97	95
Hornchurch	42	13	7	1	54	20	12	4	5	42	26	25	11	6	96	46	50	86
Aveley	42	14	4	3	74	28	12	2	7	35	27	26	6	10	109	55	54	84
Bracknell Town	42	17	2	2	59	17	8	6	7	37	37	25	8	9	96	54	42	83
Epsom & Ewell	42	9	9	3	41	24	11	6	4	40	27	20	15	7	81	51	30	75
Egham Town	42	12	6	3	37	23	9	5	7	35	36	21	11	10	72	59	13	74
Wingate & Finchley	42	10	5	6	39	26	10	4	7	41	34	20	9	13	80	60	20	69
Dorking	42	12	5	4	42	27	6	9	6	35	39	18	14	10	77	66	11	68
Tring Town	42	12	4	5	42	25	7	7	7	22	37	19	11	12	64	62	2	68
Corinthian Casuals	42	12	5	4	40	16	6	8	7	29	28	18	13	11	69	44	25	67
Hertford Town	42	12	5	4	45	25	8	2	11	43	49	20	7	15	88	74	14	67
Witham Town	42	11	2	8	38	29	4	8	9	28	43	15	10	17	66	72	–6	55
Ware	42	8	6	7	43	36	6	4	11	31	40	14	10	18	74	76	–2	52
Chalfont St Peter	42	9	2	10	35	39	6	2	13	34	53	15	4	23	69	92	–23	49
Wokingham Town	42	9	3	9	46	47	5	3	13	33	60	14	6	22	79	107	–28	48
Abingdon Town	42	7	5	9	27	27	6	2	13	34	48	13	7	22	61	75	–14	46
Leighton Town	42	6	6	9	35	47	2	6	13	21	48	8	12	22	56	95	–39	36
Kingsbury Town	42	4	6	11	28	42	4	5	12	30	49	8	11	23	58	91	–33	35
Edgware Town	42	4	5	12	38	50	5	2	14	27	51	9	7	26	65	101	–36	34
Flackwell Heath*	42	4	3	14	32	62	5	5	11	21	37	9	8	25	53	99	–46	32
Clapton	42	6	2	13	23	46	3	2	16	22	72	9	4	29	45	118	–73	31
Camberley Town	42	6	7	8	26	36	1	2	18	11	59	7	9	26	37	95	–58	30

* 3 points deducted for fielding an ineligible player.

LEADING GOALSCORERS

Premier Division   *Lge*   *ILC*
		Lge	ILC
31	Lee Boylan (Canvey Island)	27	4
25	Nicky Simpson (Braintree Town)	18	7
24	Simon Martin (St Albans City)	24	
24	Craig Maskell (Hampton & Richmond B)	17	7
24	Kevin Slinn (Bedford Town)	24	
22	Stafford Browne (Aldershot Town)	19	3

Division One
		Lge	ILC
33	Vinnie John (Bishop's Stortford)	33	
31	Nigel Webb (Tooting & Mitcham United)	23	8
30	Matt Miller (Yeading)	27	3
28	Trevor Paul (Bishop's Stortford)	25	3
26	Matt Russell (Bognor Regis Town)	26	
26	Lawrence Yaku (Northwood)	22	4

Divison Two
		Lge	ILC
26	Alex Inglethorpe (Leatherhead)	25	1
24	Darren Greives (Hemel Hempstead Town)	23	1
24	Lee Newman (Lewes)	24	
24	Jamie Taylor (Horsham)	24	
23	Eric Tomlinson (Metropolitan Police)	23	

Division Three
		Lge	ILC
50	John Fowler (Croydon Athletic)	47	3
36	Kevin Cooper (Hertford Town)	36	
26	Chris Woolf (Hornchurch)	23	3
25	Clayton Whittle (Egham Town)	23	2

Lge: Ryman League; ILC: Isthmian League Cup.

LEADING ATTENDANCES

Premier Division
4098 Gravesend & Northfleet v Canvey Island 26.03.2002
2630 Aldershot Town v Canvey Island 29.12.2001
2111 Canvey Island v Gravesend & Northfleet 08.01.2002

Division One
1412 Aylesbury United v Oxford City 20.04.2002
968 Tooting & Mitcham United v Wealdstone 20.04.2002
717 Bishop's Stortford v Harlow Town 26.12.2001

Division Two
962 Horsham v Lewes 01.04.2002
315 Lewes v Horsham 26.12.2001
314 Berkhamsted Town v Hemel Hempstead Town 01.04.2002

Division Three
248 Ware v Hertford Town 01.04.2002
233 Hornchurch v Aveley 12.03.2002
228 Hertford Town v Ware 16.04.2002

RYMAN FOOTBALL LEAGUE – PREMIER DIVISION RESULTS 2001–02

	Aldershot Town	Basingstoke Town	Bedford Town	Billericay Town	Boreham Wood	Braintree Town	Canvey Island	Chesham United	Croydon	Enfield	Gravesend & Northfleet	Grays Athletic	Hampton & Richmond	Harrow Borough	Hendon	Heybridge Swifts	Hitchin Town	Kingstonian	Maidenhead United	Purfleet	St Albans City	Sutton United
Aldershot Town	—	2-2	4-0	1-1	0-2	4-0	1-3	1-0	2-0	3-1	1-2	0-1	4-1	2-1	2-1	3-3	1-2	3-0	4-1	4-1	1-1	1-0
Basingstoke Town	1-1	—	1-1	0-1	1-0	1-2	0-4	1-1	1-0	2-0	1-4	0-2	1-1	2-1	2-1	1-3	2-3	2-1	1-2	2-2	3-1	3-0
Bedford Town	1-2	3-0	—	3-4	2-0	2-0	1-3	2-0	3-2	2-2	0-1	4-0	4-1	3-4	0-5	5-2	0-1	2-1	1-2	1-0	0-1	0-1
Billericay Town	2-0	2-0	0-0	—	0-1	2-4	0-3	0-0	2-0	3-2	1-3	3-2	2-0	1-1	4-6	1-2	1-1	1-1	2-2	2-0	1-5	2-1
Boreham Wood	1-3	0-0	1-0	0-1	—	1-2	0-3	2-1	1-1	1-3	0-2	2-2	3-2	1-2	1-2	2-4	2-1	1-3	2-1	1-0	0-1	1-2
Braintree Town	2-0	3-2	2-1	1-0	1-2	—	2-1	2-0	2-1	2-3	0-2	2-3	3-2	0-0	2-0	2-0	0-1	1-0	2-1	2-2	2-1	3-0
Canvey Island	1-3	5-1	3-3	3-0	0-3	3-2	—	2-1	3-0	3-1	0-2	1-2	1-1	3-0	3-1	6-1	5-3	2-0	2-0	3-0	3-2	1-1
Chesham United	2-1	1-1	1-1	2-0	2-1	4-1	1-5	—	2-1	0-0	0-2	1-2	2-1	2-1	0-2	3-0	5-5	2-0	2-0	0-0	2-0	2-0
Croydon	1-2	1-3	3-3	0-0	0-5	0-4	2-1	2-1	—	0-2	2-2	3-5	1-1	5-0	0-2	3-0	1-2	4-0	1-0	0-1	3-2	1-2
Enfield	1-1	3-0	1-0	0-2	0-1	1-2	0-3	0-1	0-2	—	3-4	1-0	0-0	2-1	1-3	2-3	0-5	2-2	0-2	0-1	2-1	2-2
Gravesend & Northfleet	2-1	0-0	4-1	1-0	3-2	3-0	0-1	0-3	3-4	3-0	—	2-0	2-1	1-2	0-6	4-2	0-5	2-0	0-1	0-3	0-0	3-1
Grays Athletic	3-1	0-0	2-1	0-0	3-0	3-0	0-1	1-4	1-0	3-0	1-2	—	1-1	2-2	1-0	1-1	2-0	2-0	3-2	0-0	3-2	3-3
Hampton & Richmond	1-1	1-1	1-1	1-2	0-2	0-2	1-5	2-1	6-1	0-0	0-2	0-0	—	0-1	0-0	1-3	6-3	0-0	0-1	1-3	0-5	2-1
Harrow Borough	2-3	3-3	2-4	0-2	2-3	1-2	1-1	2-1	1-0	2-4	1-2	1-1	0-1	—	0-1	0-1	1-1	1-3	2-1	1-1	2-6	1-6
Hendon	0-1	1-3	1-2	1-3	2-1	3-0	0-1	0-6	6-0	2-0	0-3	1-0	0-0	0-1	—	1-0	2-2	2-0	0-3	1-2	1-0	4-3
Heybridge Swifts	1-2	5-1	1-1	2-3	0-2	1-1	0-7	1-2	2-0	4-2	1-5	1-3	1-0	1-6	1-0	—	3-1	1-1	1-1	3-3	1-0	2-0
Hitchin Town	0-3	0-1	2-2	3-2	4-1	1-1	2-1	2-1	0-1	1-2	0-0	1-2	1-0	0-1	2-2	2-2	—	1-1	2-0	2-2	0-2	1-1
Kingstonian	2-1	1-1	3-0	4-1	1-1	0-2	2-1	2-3	2-0	0-2	0-4	2-4	1-3	1-1	2-0	0-1	2-2	—	1-0	1-5	2-4	1-1
Maidenhead United	1-2	2-2	2-1	0-2	2-0	2-0	0-1	1-0	2-2	0-1	0-1	3-2	3-0	0-3	3-1	1-2	1-1	0-1	—	1-3	4-2	2-2
Purfleet	2-1	0-0	1-1	1-1	0-1	3-2	0-0	0-4	3-0	0-1	0-3	0-0	2-1	4-2	3-1	3-3	3-1	1-1	1-0	—	2-1	1-1
St Albans City	0-3	2-0	0-0	0-0	1-0	3-1	2-4	2-2	5-1	1-0	0-0	0-5	3-0	0-3	1-0	1-2	1-2	2-2	5-2	0-1	—	2-0
Sutton United	2-0	2-1	2-2	2-2	2-2	3-1	1-4	5-1	5-0	2-0	3-1	3-3	2-0	1-1	2-1	4-1	2-4	0-0	2-1	0-0	1-1	—

RYMAN FOOTBALL LEAGUE – DIVISION ONE RESULTS 2001–02

	Aylesbury United	Barking & East Ham Utd	Bishop's Stortford	Bognor Regis Town	Bromley	Carshalton Athletic	Dulwich Hamlet	Ford United	Harlow Town	Northwood	Oxford City	Slough Town	Staines Town	Thame United	Tooting & Mitcham United	Uxbridge	Walton & Hersham	Wealdstone	Whyteleafe	Windsor & Eton	Worthing	Yeading
Aylesbury United	—	3-2	3-3	2-2	3-1	2-1	3-3	3-4	1-0	3-2	1-4	4-0	2-1	2-3	3-2	0-0	4-2	2-2	8-0	3-2	1-1	4-1
Barking & East Ham Utd	2-1	—	0-4	1-2	2-2	1-2	1-0	1-4	0-6	0-5	1-1	0-1	2-0	2-3	2-1	2-3	3-3	2-1	3-0	2-4	1-3	3-4
Bishop's Stortford	2-2	3-1	—	1-3	3-0	2-1	2-2	4-1	4-1	1-2	2-0	3-2	5-0	3-0	5-0	2-4	2-0	7-1	3-0	2-0	1-1	6-4
Bognor Regis Town	1-1	8-3	0-0	—	2-0	1-1	1-0	1-1	0-0	3-1	3-1	0-0	0-2	2-1	3-1	0-1	3-3	0-1	2-0	2-1	1-1	3-1
Bromley	0-2	3-2	1-1	1-1	—	0-1	1-0	1-2	1-3	2-0	3-2	0-3	1-0	2-2	2-3	1-0	3-2	3-0	2-0	2-2	0-2	2-5
Carshalton Athletic	2-1	1-1	2-0	0-2	3-0	—	0-0	0-5	1-2	1-1	1-2	2-1	1-0	2-2	2-3	4-1	0-3	3-0	2-0	3-1	0-2	2-0
Dulwich Hamlet	3-3	7-1	1-2	2-1	5-3	0-3	—	0-5	1-1	1-4	5-0	0-0	0-1	4-2	0-2	1-1	0-3	3-2	0-3	4-2	1-2	2-0
Ford United	0-3	3-1	2-1	1-3	0-1	1-1	2-2	—	0-2	2-0	1-2	0-2	2-1	4-2	1-1	2-1	6-1	2-1	2-2	1-0	2-1	3-2
Harlow Town	1-3	3-1	1-2	4-0	0-1	2-2	1-2	4-1	—	3-2	4-1	1-4	2-1	2-2	0-1	2-1	0-1	2-0	5-0	0-1	2-0	2-1
Northwood	3-2	2-2	2-2	5-1	2-2	1-1	1-2	1-2	3-2	—	4-1	1-1	4-3	3-1	3-4	2-0	3-5	3-1	3-2	2-0	1-0	4-1
Oxford City	0-2	0-1	1-0	2-2	2-0	1-1	0-0	1-2	1-2	2-2	—	3-0	2-0	1-1	1-0	1-1	0-3	6-0	0-0	3-0	0-1	3-3
Slough Town	3-4	2-1	0-1	0-1	3-0	1-1	3-2	1-2	4-0	2-1	1-2	—	2-0	1-1	3-1	3-0	0-3	1-1	0-0	3-0	4-3	0-2
Staines Town	2-1	2-1	0-0	1-1	0-0	0-0	0-0	2-4	1-3	2-1	0-0	0-1	—	0-0	1-3	1-0	3-1	1-1	3-0	1-0	4-3	3-4
Thame United	0-1	10-2	0-2	1-1	4-1	1-1	1-1	1-2	1-4	2-1	3-0	3-0	4-1	—	0-0	1-0	3-3	4-2	3-0	1-0	0-0	3-4
Tooting & Mitcham United	2-4	5-0	2-3	2-0	4-1	1-1	1-1	0-4	2-4	1-1	3-0	1-1	4-1	2-2	—	0-1	1-0	3-2	2-3	2-1	0-0	4-4
Uxbridge	3-1	3-1	1-3	2-0	1-0	2-0	0-3	1-2	2-3	0-2	3-1	3-1	2-3	1-3	1-1	—	3-4	1-0	2-0	5-3	2-3	6-1
Walton & Hersham	1-1	4-0	0-1	1-0	2-4	2-2	1-1	0-2	1-1	2-2	1-2	1-1	1-0	2-1	1-2	2-1	—	3-3	1-1	4-0	2-0	0-1
Wealdstone	1-0	2-2	2-2	2-3	4-1	1-2	1-3	1-0	1-1	2-2	3-0	2-1	1-0	2-2	3-0	0-0	2-5	—	1-1	1-0	1-1	0-2
Whyteleafe	1-2	2-4	2-4	1-5	1-1	0-0	2-1	1-0	4-2	1-3	4-2	0-2	1-2	0-1	3-0	0-0	2-5	1-2	—	1-0	2-1	1-2
Windsor & Eton	1-3	4-0	1-7	3-4	2-1	1-2	3-0	1-5	6-1	0-3	1-4	3-3	4-2	0-1	0-0	3-2	1-2	3-3	4-0	—	0-1	7-1
Worthing	2-0	2-2	2-4	0-2	2-3	2-3	6-2	1-2	6-1	0-1	2-2	0-3	4-2	0-2	1-2	3-2	1-2	0-2	0-3	2-0	—	1-1
Yeading	1-2	5-2	3-2	3-1	3-3	4-1	1-4	0-1	1-3	3-3	0-1	0-0	1-0	1-1	3-2	1-1	2-1	2-1	4-0	3-1	1-1	—

RYMAN FOOTBALL LEAGUE – DIVISION TWO RESULTS 2001–02

	Arlesey Town	Ashford Town (Mx)	Banstead Athletic	Barton Rovers	Berkhamsted Town	Chertsey Town	Cheshunt	East Thurrock United	Great Wakering Rovers	Hemel Hempstead Town	Horsham	Hungerford Town	Leatherhead	Lewes	Leyton Pennant	Marlow	Metropolitan Police	Molesey	Romford	Tilbury	Wembley	Wivenhoe Town
Arlesey Town	—	0-2	2-2	3-3	0-2	2-1	2-3	2-0	3-2	2-0	4-5	2-1	1-0	1-0	1-1	1-1	5-2	6-0	1-1	5-1	4-1	5-0
Ashford Town (Mx)	2-2	—	2-2	1-2	1-0	2-2	1-1	1-0	1-3	0-1	2-1	2-0	1-3	1-0	2-2	3-3	2-1	1-2	3-1	1-2	4-1	0-0
Banstead Athletic	1-0	0-2	—	3-1	2-1	4-1	6-0	2-0	0-1	0-1	1-0	1-1	1-1	0-1	1-3	3-3	0-3	2-1	6-1	1-0	5-0	1-2
Barton Rovers	0-1	0-1	1-2	—	0-1	3-3	2-0	0-1	1-3	4-3	0-1	2-1	3-1	0-0	1-2	1-3	0-1	2-0	2-0	2-0	1-0	3-1
Berkhamsted Town	3-1	8-1	2-3	3-1	—	2-1	2-2	1-1	0-1	4-2	1-0	0-2	3-0	1-5	3-1	2-2	2-0	7-2	2-0	2-1	1-0	1-1
Chertsey Town	2-6	2-0	1-1	2-2	0-5	—	2-3	1-2	2-0	1-1	1-0	4-1	3-0	1-4	3-1	3-3	1-5	3-0	1-1	3-4	1-0	5-1
Cheshunt	0-3	0-0	1-2	1-2	1-2	1-2	—	1-2	0-0	6-3	0-6	1-2	3-1	1-2	2-3	2-3	2-2	0-1	3-3	2-2	0-0	1-1
East Thurrock United	0-2	2-2	0-4	1-2	1-1	1-2	3-0	—	0-0	2-4	3-3	1-2	3-1	0-3	0-0	2-3	3-0	0-1	1-0	2-1	0-0	1-1
Great Wakering Rovers	1-0	3-0	3-0	3-1	3-1	5-1	3-0	0-0	—	0-1	0-0	3-0	3-0	1-3	0-0	2-1	1-1	4-1	3-0	1-1	4-0	1-3
Hemel Hempstead Town	1-2	1-2	1-0	1-1	2-2	2-2	1-2	6-0	3-2	—	3-1	4-1	3-0	0-1	1-2	1-2	3-1	2-0	3-0	1-1	4-0	6-2
Horsham	3-0	3-1	2-1	3-0	3-0	4-0	6-1	3-1	3-0	3-1	—	2-2	3-0	2-2	1-5	4-0	1-0	3-1	1-4	4-2	2-0	3-3
Hungerford Town	0-3	2-2	2-1	3-0	2-2	2-0	1-1	1-2	3-0	1-0	2-0	—	1-3	2-2	2-0	3-2	1-0	3-1	1-0	3-4	2-2	1-1
Leatherhead	0-3	2-0	0-1	1-3	1-3	1-0	1-3	1-2	1-0	2-2	0-0	7-0	—	4-1	2-0	1-2	8-0	2-1	3-1	3-1	1-1	4-0
Lewes	4-0	2-0	3-0	3-0	2-0	1-4	3-1	1-2	1-3	0-1	2-2	2-2	0-0	—	2-0	1-1	6-2	4-0	0-3	1-2	0-4	5-0
Leyton Pennant	2-1	2-1	1-1	4-1	1-1	6-4	3-0	3-1	2-1	0-1	3-2	2-0	4-1	1-1	—	3-2	6-2	2-0	3-0	1-3	2-1	5-1
Marlow	1-0	1-2	3-0	1-1	1-1	2-2	3-0	2-6	2-1	2-0	3-4	1-0	3-0	1-1	3-2	—	1-4	2-0	2-0	1-2	0-2	1-1
Metropolitan Police	4-1	4-4	0-3	0-1	2-3	1-5	2-2	3-0	1-1	3-1	1-0	3-0	1-0	6-2	1-0	1-4	—	5-1	1-6	4-0	2-0	4-3
Molesey	0-1	0-1	1-4	1-0	0-3	1-1	1-0	0-1	0-2	1-1	1-1	2-4	0-0	0-5	1-1	2-3	1-6	—	4-1	1-3	0-0	2-1
Romford	0-6	4-0	0-3	0-2	0-2	1-1	0-1	2-0	0-1	1-2	0-1	1-0	0-0	0-3	3-0	2-3	1-6	4-1	—	1-0	3-3	1-1
Tilbury	0-1	0-2	2-2	1-2	1-2	0-2	0-0	1-2	1-1	2-1	3-4	3-4	0-3	1-2	0-4	0-1	2-0	3-1	2-3	—	2-2	1-0
Wembley	1-3	4-1	0-4	1-1	1-2	0-2	0-0	2-2	3-4	1-3	2-2	3-4	1-2	0-4	2-3	2-0	0-0	1-3	2-3	6-1	—	2-0
Wivenhoe Town	2-1	2-1	3-2	1-3	3-1	6-3	1-1	3-1	0-1	1-3	0-2	2-1	0-3	2-3	2-1	1-3	2-3	2-3	0-2	0-1	1-3	—

RYMAN FOOTBALL LEAGUE – DIVISION THREE RESULTS 2001-02

	Abingdon Town	Aveley	Bracknell Town	Camberley Town	Chalfont St Peter	Clapton	Corinthian Casuals	Croydon Athletic	Dorking	Edgware Town	Egham Town	Epsom & Ewell	Flackwell Heath	Hertford Town	Hornchurch	Kingsbury Town	Leighton Town	Tring Town	Ware	Wingate & Finchley	Witham Town	Wokingham Town
Abingdon Town	–	1-2	3-1	2-0	1-2	4-0	1-1	1-2	2-2	0-3	0-1	0-2	1-0	0-3	0-2	3-1	0-0	1-1	1-3	1-0	1-1	4-0
Aveley	5-1	–	3-1	3-0	2-1	6-1	2-2	0-3	1-1	5-0	3-1	2-2	4-0	7-0	1-2	4-4	4-3	3-1	4-1	1-3	7-0	7-1
Bracknell Town	3-0	2-0	–	5-0	6-0	5-1	2-0	3-2	3-0	3-1	1-3	1-2	2-0	3-2	0-2	4-0	3-0	2-2	2-1	2-2	2-0	3-1
Camberley Town	2-0	1-3	1-1	–	2-2	0-0	1-1	3-2	1-1	3-2	1-3	1-4	1-1	3-2	0-2	3-1	1-0	1-2	0-4	0-3	2-1	1-2
Chalfont St Peter	3-4	2-0	3-2	1-0	–	3-1	0-1	0-7	6-2	2-0	0-1	0-4	2-3	3-6	1-3	0-2	1-0	0-2	1-4	0-0	1-1	4-1
Clapton	1-0	0-2	3-4	1-0	0-2	–	0-2	0-7	1-2	4-2	0-1	0-1	0-2	1-4	1-2	1-1	2-1	1-2	1-0	1-4	1-1	2-3
Corinthian Casuals	1-0	5-2	4-1	2-0	1-0	5-0	–	4-2	4-0	3-0	3-3	0-0	0-0	6-0	3-0	4-0	2-0	8-0	3-0	2-0	1-0	5-2
Croydon Athletic	4-0	5-2	4-1	2-0	4-0	8-1	4-2	–	4-0	3-0	1-1	4-2	6-1	2-0	2-6	3-0	2-0	3-0	2-1	4-0	1-0	5-2
Dorking	2-1	1-1	1-1	4-1	4-1	4-1	0-3	2-1	–	4-2	3-0	2-2	1-2	1-2	3-1	5-2	0-2	3-0	0-0	4-0	0-0	1-0
Edgware Town	0-5	2-2	2-0	2-2	1-3	0-1	1-1	0-3	1-4	–	1-4	1-1	1-2	3-2	2-1	5-2	7-1	6-3	2-3	3-4	2-5	1-1
Egham Town	0-0	1-2	0-1	3-1	2-1	1-0	1-1	1-1	2-2	3-0	–	1-1	1-0	1-1	2-0	2-2	3-0	2-1	1-1	4-2	3-1	1-4
Epsom & Ewell	3-1	0-3	3-3	2-1	5-1	3-0	1-0	2-2	2-2	3-1	0-0	–	1-0	0-8	1-3	2-1	1-1	1-2	2-0	0-1	1-1	5-1
Flackwell Heath	4-1	0-2	3-5	1-2	5-3	0-5	1-1	3-7	0-3	0-3	1-2	1-2	–	2-0	2-0	4-2	2-2	1-1	0-2	1-3	6-2	2-0
Hertford Town	3-1	0-2	0-2	3-0	1-2	5-1	0-0	0-0	1-1	0-2	5-2	3-2	1-1	–	1-1	2-2	3-1	3-0	2-1	1-1	1-1	3-2
Hornchurch	2-2	2-1	0-0	5-1	6-3	6-0	4-0	3-2	3-0	2-3	2-0	0-0	1-3	1-1	–	1-0	1-1	4-1	1-0	4-2	2-4	5-1
Kingsbury Town	4-2	0-3	1-2	3-1	0-3	0-2	0-0	0-6	1-2	3-2	2-2	2-3	1-3	1-2	1-1	–	1-1	0-1	4-4	1-4	1-1	2-6
Leighton Town	0-3	1-2	2-2	3-0	1-0	5-2	0-3	1-0	3-3	1-1	0-2	1-2	3-1	1-0	3-2	1-2	–	0-0	4-2	1-4	2-0	2-2
Tring Town	4-0	3-0	1-1	3-0	2-4	6-1	1-0	1-0	0-3	3-3	0-3	2-0	0-0	1-0	1-2	2-1	3-1	–	0-1	1-2	1-1	0-5
Ware	3-0	0-4	4-2	6-0	1-1	4-2	5-2	0-4	0-0	6-1	5-1	1-3	3-2	1-2	2-2	2-1	0-0	0-1	–	1-1	2-3	5-0
Wingate & Finchley	1-4	0-0	0-1	2-0	2-0	5-2	2-1	3-1	1-3	2-0	2-2	0-2	0-0	0-1	1-1	3-2	4-1	0-0	2-1	–	3-2	1-1
Witham Town	0-3	1-2	0-1	5-0	2-3	0-0	0-2	3-1	3-1	2-0	4-2	0-3	4-1	1-0	1-1	1-0	4-3	0-0	0-2	3-2	–	3-0
Wokingham Town	3-6	0-2	2-6	1-1	4-2	2-1	2-6	0-5	2-2	2-0	0-2	5-2	3-1	5-2	1-2	2-4	1-2	0-0	7-0	2-1	2-0	–

ISTHMIAN LEAGUE CUP 2001–02

PRELIMINARY ROUND
Abingdon Town 3, Ashford Town (Middlesex) 1
Arlesey Town 4, Wingate & Finchley 0
Aveley 2, Corinthian Casuals 3
Banstead Athletic 3, Barton Rovers 3
Barton Rovers 1, Banstead Athletic 0
Berkhamsted Town 2, Leighton Town 3
Camberley Town 1, Chertsey Town 0
Clapton 0, Epsom & Ewell 2
Croydon Athletic 4, Ware 3
Dorking 2, Hertford Town 4
Egham Town 2, Wivenhoe Town 0
Flackwell Heath 2, Marlow 5
Hemel Hempstead Town 5, East Thurrock United 1
Hornchurch 0, Wokingham Town 0
Wokingham Town 0, Hornchurch 4
Hungerford Town 2, Cheshunt 1
Kingsbury Town 1, Barking 2
Leatherhead 2, Leyton Pennant 3
Lewes 4, Witham Town 0
Metropolitan Police 2, Great Wakering Rovers 1
Romford 1, Molesey 2
Tilbury 3, Tring Town 2
Tooting & Mitcham United 3, Bracknell Town 2
Wealdstone 5, Edgware Town 2
Wembley 2, Horsham 0
Windsor & Eton 1, Chalfont St Peter 0

FIRST ROUND
Aldershot Town 5, Croydon 1
Aylesbury United 1, Metropolitan Police 3
Barking & East Ham United 3, Hampton & Richmond
  Borough 8
Basingstoke Town 2, Kingstonian 0
Boreham Wood 1, Leyton Pennant 2
Braintree Town 2, Abingdon Town 2
Abingdon Town 0, Braintree Town 4
Bromley 2, Billericay Town 0
Canvey Island 3, Lewes 2
Carshalton Athletic 0, Worthing 2
Chesham United 2, St Albans City 0
Corinthian Casuals 2, Whyteleafe 1
Enfield 4, Egham Town 1
Ford United 1, Epsom & Ewell 0
Gravesend & Northfleet 2, Arlesey Town 1
Grays Athletic 5, Bedford Town 1
Harlow Town 1, Northwood 2
Harrow Borough 3, Camberley Town 0
Hemel Hempstead Town 1, Croydon Athletic 3
Hertford Town 0, Hendon 3
Hitchin Town 8, Walton & Hersham 2
Hornchurch 5, Bognor Regis Town 2
Hungerford Town 0, Maidenhead United 3
Marlow 1, Barton Rovers 2
Molesey 4, Leighton Town 1
Oxford City 0, Bishop's Stortford 4

Purfleet 0, Yeading 1
Staines Town 2, Heybridge Swifts 0
Sutton United 5, Dulwich Hamlet 3
Thame United 1, Windsor & Eton 0
Uxbridge 1, Tooting & Mitcham United 1
Tooting & Mitcham United 3, Uxbridge 1
Wealdstone 6, Tilbury 1
Wembley 4, Slough Town 6

SECOND ROUND
Bishop's Stortford 2, Canvey Island 4
Braintree Town 4, Molesey 1
Bromley 0, Corinthian Casuals 1
Chesham United 0, Enfield 2
Ford United 4, Barton Rovers 1
Gravesend & Northfleet 4, Basingstoke Town 1
Hampton & Richmond Borough 5, Maidenhead United 3
Harrow Borough 1, Northwood 4
Hendon 0, Aldershot Town 2
Hornchurch 0, Leyton Pennant 2
Metropolitan Police 1, Wealdstone 2
Slough Town 0, Hitchin Town 1
Staines Town 0, Grays Athletic 2
Thame United 1, Sutton United 3
Tooting & Mitcham United 2, Croydon Athletic 0
Yeading 3, Worthing 2

THIRD ROUND
Aldershot Town 3, Corinthian Casuals 0
Braintree Town 3, Canvey Island 5
Enfield 4, Hitchin Town 0
Gravesend & Northfleet 1, Tooting & Mitcham United 2
Leyton Pennant 0, Northwood 1
Sutton United 1, Grays Athletic 7
Wealdstone 3, Ford United 2
Yeading 1, Hampton & Richmond Borough 3

FOURTH ROUND
Grays Athletic 2, Aldershot Town 3
Hampton & Richmond Borough 1, Enfield 0
Northwood 3, Canvey Island 1
Wealdstone 0, Tooting & Mitcham United 1

SEMI-FINALS, FIRST LEG
Aldershot Town 2, Hampton & Richmond Borough 2
Northwood 4, Tooting & Mitcham United 2

SEMI-FINALS, SECOND LEG
Hampton & Richmond Borough 1, Aldershot Town 0
Tooting & Mitcham United 1, Northwood 1

FINAL
Hampton & Richmond Borough (1) 2 *(Gough 45,*
  O'Connor 77)
Northwood (1) 3 *(Cook 43, 74, Yaku 92)*   *aet* 262

FA UMBRO TROPHY 2001–02

FIRST ROUND

Bilston Town v Gresley Rovers	1-1, 0-0
Gresley Rovers won 5-4 on penalties.	
Hednesford Town v Racing Club Warwick	5-0
Trafford v Ossett Albion	1-1, 3-0
Blyth Spartans v Burscough	2-0
Workington v Lincoln United	0-2
Gateshead v Redditch United	4-0
Ashton United v Rocester	4-1
Moor Green v Bamber Bridge	3-0
Matlock Town v Marine	1-1, 2-3
Ossett Town v Hyde United	1-1, 1-3
Grantham v Stamford	1-0
Gretna v Witton Albion	3-1
Guiseley v Stafford Rangers	0-0, 2-4
Droylsden v Frickley Athletic	1-1, 1-1
Frickley Athletic won 4-3 on penalties.	
Corby Town v Vauxhall Motors	0-3
Harrogate Town v Colwyn Bay	2-0
Radcliffe Borough v Accrington Stanley	0-0, 0-2
Ilkeston Town v Gainsborough Trinity	1-0
Chorley v Farsley Celtic	0-1
Rossendale United v Bedworth United	3-3, 0-2
Atherstone United v Spennymoor United	1-2
Barrow v Halesowen Town	2-1
Kendal Town v Bradford (Park Avenue)	3-2
Sutton Coldfield Town v Hucknall Town	1-0
North Ferriby United v Shepshed Dynamo	4-1
Hinckley United v Eastwood Town	2-1
Bloxwich United v Solihull Borough	2-3
Belper Town v Runcorn	0-4
Leek Town v Tamworth	0-1
Spalding United v Altrincham	0-0, 2-3
Stocksbridge Park Steels v Whitby Town	1-1, 0-2
Slough Town v Aylesbury United	0-2
Dulwich Hamlet v Evesham United	3-1
Chippenham Town v Walton & Hersham	1-4
Ashford Town v Bromley	1-2
Barking & East Ham United v Cinderford Town	1-3
Dartford v Braintree Town	0-3
Northwood v Maidenhead United	0-1
Hitchin Town v Kingstonian	1-2
Uxbridge v Cirencester Town	3-3, 1-4
Worcester City v Mangotsfield United	1-1, 1-2
Sittingbourne v Fisher Athletic	1-3
Whyteleafe v Hampton & Richmond Borough	0-5
Tonbridge Angels v Merthyr Tydfil	3-3, 2-3
Croydon v Ford United	4-0
Bedford Town v Worthing	0-1
Crawley Town v Newport (IW)	2-0
Gravesend & Northfleet v Chelmsford City	2-3
Heybridge Swifts v Erith & Belvedere	3-1
Histon v Weston-Super-Mare	3-0
Tooting & Mitcham United v Salisbury City	2-4
Oxford City v Bashley	1-0
Banbury United v Windsor & Eton	1-1, 2-3
Wealdstone v Bishop's Stortford	5-1
Carshalton Athletic v St Leonards	2-3
Havant & Waterlooville v Grays Athletic	2-3
Harrow Borough v Dorchester Town	0-0, 1-0
Eastbourne Borough v Chatham Town	2-3
Bath City v Newport County	4-1
Cambridge City v Gloucester City	1-1, 3-5
Rothwell Town v Billericay Town	0-1
Folkestone Invicta v Tiverton Town	2-1
Enfield v Hastings Town	3-1
Kettering Town v Swindon Super Marine	4-2
Purfleet v Boreham Wood	3-3, 0-5
Staines Town v Thame United	1-1, 2-1
Clevedon Town v Harlow Town	2-1
Burnham v Yeading	1-4
Hendon v Sutton United	2-1
Rugby United v Bognor Regis Town	1-1, 0-3
Wisbech Town v St Albans City	
Bye: Stourport Swifts	

SECOND ROUND

Accrington Stanley v Altrincham	1-1, 1-1
Altrincham won 3-1 on penalties.	
Moor Green v Trafford	2-1

Worksop Town v Marine	3-2
Runcorn FC Halton v Farsley Celtic	4-2
North Ferriby United v Spennymoor United	4-2
Gretna v Emley	0-1
Stafford Rangers v Vauxhall Motors	0-3
Lincoln United v Solihull Borough	0-1
Whitby Town v Blyth Spartans	1-2
Bedworth United v Gresley Rovers	1-4
Kendal Town v Harrogate Town	1-2
Lancaster City v Hinckley United	2-1
Hyde United v Ilkeston Town	0-4
Barrow v Burton Albion	1-1, 0-5
Stourport Swifts v Bishop Auckland	5-4
Grantham Town v Frickley Athletic	5-1
Hednesford Town v Gateshead	2-1
Sutton Coldfield Town v Tamworth	0-3
King's Lynn v Ashton United	4-1
Kingstonian v Cirencester Town	6-2
Dulwich Hamlet v Billericay Town	2-1
Mangotsfield United v Dorchester Town	3-1
Fisher Athletic v Merthyr Tydfil	5-1
Purfleet v Kettering Town	2-1
Tiverton Town v Croydon	6-0
Bashley v Burnham	1-1, 4-1
Bishop's Stortford v Grays Athletic	1-1, 2-3
Eastbourne Borough v Bedford Town	0-0, 2-1
Hampton & Richmond Borough v Harlow Town	2-2, 2-1
Banbury United v Cambridge City	0-2
Walton & Hersham v Newport County	2-3
Bromley v Tooting & Mitcham United	1-1, 1-3
Welling United v Erith & Belvedere	8-1
Braintree Town v Basingstoke Town	1-1, 2-0
Carshalton Athletic v Newport (IW)	1-0
Thame United v Bognor Regis Town	1-5
Chesham United v Weymouth	4-0
Cinderford Town v Gravesend & Northfleet	0-2
Enfield v Histon	2-2, 1-3
Maidenhead United v Hendon	1-2
Aylesbury United v Aldershot Town	0-2
Canvey Island v St Albans City	5-1

THIRD ROUND

Scarborough v Hednesford Town	2-0
Leigh RMI v Emley	2-2, 4-1
Worksop Town v Tamworth	4-3
Chester City v Stourport Swifts	1-1, 3-0
Southport v Gresley Rovers	1-1, 0-1
Northwich Victoria v Boston United	3-1
Solihull Borough v Runcorn FC Halton	3-0
Stalybridge Celtic v Nuneaton Borough	1-1, 2-1
Burton Albion v Blyth Spartans	3-0
Ilkeston Town v Telford United	0-2
Vauxhall Motors v Lancaster City	4-0
North Ferriby United v Altrincham	3-2
Morecambe v King's Lynn	2-0
Doncaster Rovers v Harrogate Town	2-0
Grantham Town v Moor Green	2-1
Grays Athletic v Welling United	2-3
Chesham United v Hereford United	3-4
Dulwich Hamlet v Braintree Town	3-1
Margate v Hayes	5-1
Stevenage Borough v Dover Athletic	0-5
Fisher Athletic v Barnet	1-1, 1-3
Histon v Gravesend & Northfleet	1-1, 1-3
Hampton & Richmond Borough v Newport County	2-0
Bashley v Bognor Regis Town	2-1
Tiverton Town v Yeovil Town	1-3
Dagenham & Redbridge v Eastbourne Borough	1-0
Forest Green Rovers v Aldershot Town	1-1, 3-2
Canvey Island v Purfleet	2-2, 1-0
Mangotsfield United v Tooting & Mitcham United	3-2
Cambridge City v Hendon	1-1, 0-2
Farnborough Town v Carshalton Athletic	1-1, 5-0
Woking v Kingstonian	2-1

FOURTH ROUND

Morecambe v Gresley Rovers	5-0
Farnborough Town v Burton Albion	1-1, 2-3
Gravesend & Northfleet v Hendon	2-1

Chester City v Solihull Borough	0-0, 4-2
Woking v Welling United	4-2
North Ferriby United v Braintree Town	4-4, 2-2
Braintree Town won 5-4 on penalties.	
Yeovil Town v Doncaster Rovers	1-1, 5-4
Margate v Leigh RMI	2-0
Vauxhall Motors v Northwich Victoria	0-4
Dagenham & Redbridge v Telford United	0-2
Mangotsfield United v Stalybridge Celtic	0-1
Forest Green Rovers v Worksop Town	1-0
Grantham Town v Canvey Island	1-4
Hereford United v Hampton & Richmond Borough	4-1
Barnet v Scarborough	0-0, 2-2
Scarborough won 5-4 on penalties.	
Stevenage Borough v Bashley	1-0

FIFTH ROUND

Scarborough v Morecambe	1-1, 0-3
Gravesend & Northfleet v Stalybridge Celtic	0-2
Margate v Braintree Town	1-1, 2-1
Stevenage Borough v Forest Green Rovers	3-2
Yeovil Town v Canvey Island	2-1
Burton Albion v Woking	3-0
Chester City v Hereford United	2-1
Northwich Victoria v Telford United	3-2

SIXTH ROUND

Margate v Morecambe	1-2
Northwich Victoria v Yeovil Town	0-2
Stevenage Borough v Stalybridge Celtic	1-0
Burton Albion v Chester City	2-0

SEMI-FINAL (two legs)

Yeovil Town v Burton Albion	4-0, 1-2
Morecambe v Stevenage Borough	1-2, 0-2

FINAL (at Villa Park)

12 MAY

Yeovil Town (1) 2 *(Alford 12, Stansfield 66)*
Stevenage Borough (0) 0   18,809

Yeovil Town: Weale; Lockwood, Tonkin, Skiverton, Pluck (White), Johnson, Crittenden (Lindegaard), Way, Alford (Giles), Stansfield, McIndoe.
Stevenage Borough: Wilkerson; Hamsher, Fraser, Goodliffe, Trott, Fisher, Evers (Williams), Sigere (Campbell D), Jackson, Clarke, Wormull (Sterling).
Referee: N. Barry (N. Lincolnshire).

Yeovil Town's Carl Alford scores the opening goal in the F.A. Umbro Trophy final. Yeovil ran out 2-0 winners over Stevenage Borough. (Actionimages)

FA CARLSBERG VASE 2001–02

FIRST QUALIFYING ROUND

Cheadle Town v Washington Nissan	1-2
West Auckland Town v Ashington	5-2
Winterton Rangers v North Shields	3-2
Willington v Parkgate	2-3
Sheffield v Rossington Main	3-3, 1-1
Rossington Main won 5-4 on penalties.	
Poulton Victoria v Pickering Town	0-2
Glasshoughton Welfare v Whickham	2-0
Warsborough Bridge MW v Armthorpe Welfare	4-0
Chester-Le-Street Town v Ramsbottom United	4-1
Norton & Stockton Ancients v Nelson	2-2, 0-3
Oldham Town v Chadderton	1-4
Maine Road v Billingham Synthonia	2-3
Selby Town v Easington Colliery	2-1
Maltby Main v Peterlee Newtown	1-1, 0-5
Warrington Town v Bottesford Town	9-1
Hebburn v Esh Winning	1-5
Walsall Wood v North Notts	0-1
Gedling Town v Deeping Rangers	3-2
Rainworth MW v Highfield Rangers	3-2
Halesowen Harriers v Stourbridge	2-1
St Andrews v Birstall United	1-1, 2-0
Dunkirk v Friar Lane OB	1-4
Westfields v Stratford Town	2-3
Kimberley Town v Kidsgrove Athletic	0-3
Stapenhill v Tividale	0-2
Ibstock Welfare v Oldbury United	1-1, 2-1
Quorn v Stafford Town	1-0
Marconi v Heath Hayes	3-2
Gornal Athletic v Chasetown	1-2
Anstey Nomads v Cheslyn Haw	1-4
Beaconsfield SYCOB v Brache Sparta	5-1
Fakenham Town v Needham Market	2-0
Chalfont St Peter v Thetford Town	2-0
Tring Town v Southall	2-0
Norwich United v Biggleswade Town	3-1
Newmarket Town v Wroxham	0-3
Bowers United v Harringey Borough	4-2
Ford Sports Daventry v Biggleswade United	3-2
Dunstable Town v Ware	2-1
Whitney Academy v Letchworth	1-2
Somersham Town v Wembley	0-5
Witham Town v Edgware Town	3-1
Saffron Walden Town v Maldon Town	1-11
Leyton v Hoddesdon Town	1-0
Kingsbury Town v Soham Town Rangers	0-4
Eynesbury Rovers v Brook House	0-1
Ilford v Welwyn Garden City	3-0
AFC Wallingford v Cornard United	0-4
Henley Town v Harwich & Parkeston	2-0
Mildenhall Town v Bugbrooke St Michaels	2-1
Burnham Ramblers v Hertford Town	2-1
Haverhill Rovers v Woodbridge Town	2-1
Ringmer v Horsham YMCA	2-0
VCD Athletic v Cray Wanderers	1-2
Merstham v Southwick	6-2
Moneyfields v Whitchurch United	0-1
AFC Newbury v Hillingdon Borough	2-0
Lymington Town v Walton Casuals	3-0
Wick v Camberley Town	1-2
Didcot Town v Gosport Borough	0-5
Erith Town v Ash United	0-1
Whitstable Town v Redhill	1-0
Molesey v Viking Greenford	5-1
Lewes v Alton Town	4-2
Corinthian Casuals v Blackfield & Langley	2-3
Three Bridges v Banstead Athletic	4-1
Maidstone United v Carterton Town	4-3
Elmore v Bristol Manor Farm	1-2
Willand Rovers v Welton Rovers	3-0
Team Bath v Corsham Town	1-1, 1-5
Torrington v Pershore Town	2-0
St Blazey v Backwell United	1-0
Barnstaple Town v Chard Town	5-0
Bitton v Warminster Town	3-2
Melksham Town v Street	0-2
Highworth Town v Bridgwater Town	2-1
Calne Town v Shortwood United	

SECOND QUALIFYING ROUND

Parkgate v Cammell Laird	3-3, 2-4
Newcastle Benfield Saints v Peterlee Newtown	2-4
Curzon Ashton v Atherton Collieries	5-2
Denaby United v Shotton Comrades	3-2
Warrington Town v Yorkshire Amateur	5-1
Darwen v Bacup Borough	0-5
Billingham Synthonia v Horden CW	4-0
Winterton Rangers v Atherton LR	0-1
Alnwick Town v Squires Gate	3-4
Newcastle Blue Star v Glasshoughton Welfare	1-0
Guisborough Town v West Allotment Celtic	2-0
Nelson v Garforth Town	8-0
Blackpool Mechanics v Brandon United	3-1
Woodleigh Sports v Warsborough Bridge MW	2-0
Harrogate Railway v Brodsworth	3-1
Great Harwood Town v Shildon	0-4
Northallerton Town v West Auckland Town	2-3
Prescot Cables v Morpeth Town	2-0
Colne v Whitley Bay	0-1
Louth United v Fleetwood Freeport	4-3
Rossington Main v Bridlington Town	2-0
Flixton v Salford City	3-2
Hall Road Rangers v Stand Athletic	4-0
Durham City v South Shields	2-0
Pickering Town v Selby Town	0-4
Holker Old Boys v Chester-Le-Street Town	2-3
Liversedge v Thackley	
Washington Ikeda Hoover v	
Jarrow Roofing Boldon CA	1-1, 2-6
Thornaby v Abbey Hey	4-2
Pontefract Collieries v Castleton Gabriels	1-3
Goole v Hallam	1-3
Chadderton v Evenwood Town	0-3
Esh Winning v Crook Town	3-1
Washington Nissan v Penrith	4-1
Seaham Red Star v Skelmersdale United	1-0
Tadcaster Albion v Hatfield Main	2-3
Knypersley Victoria v Rainworth MW	1-3
Clapwell v Pegasus Juniors	1-2
Cheslyn Hay v Kidsgrove Athletic	2-5
Long Eaton United v Boldmere St Michaels	3-2
Brierley & Hagley Alliance v Holwell Sports	2-1
Alvechurch v Shirebrook Town	0-5
Kirby Muxloe v Glossop North End	0-2
Ibstock Welfare v Holbech United	1-0
Lincoln Moorlands v Willenhall Town	1-2
Causeway United v West Midlands Police	2-0
Barrow Town v Shawbury United	3-0
Quorn v Grosvenor Park	2-3
Star v Halesowen Harriers	3-1
Marconi v Bolehill Swifts	2-2, 3-3
Friar Lane OB v Studley BKL	3-4
South Normanton Athletic v Bridgnorth Town	2-3
Nuneaton Griff v Downes Sports	0-4
Malvern Town v Blackstone	1-3
Ludlow Town v Stratford Town	1-6
Dudley Town v Cradleigh Town	1-2
Collingham v Meir KA	2-1
Handrahan Timbers v Buxton	0-4
Pelsall Villa v Tividale	1-2
Gedling Town v Chasetown	4-1
Bourne Town v North Notts	0-1
Kings Heath v St Andrews	1-2
Wolverhampton Casuals v Staveley MW	1-1
Wolverhampton Casuals withdrew; Staveley MW w.o.	
Shifnal Town v Leek CSOB	0-4
Ford Sports Daventry v Hullbridge Sports	3-2
Wotton Blue Cross v Buckingham Town	1-2
Stewarts & Lloyds v Wellingborough Town	9-2
Witton United v Rothwell Corinthians	1-2
Bowers United v Leighton Town	2-4
Stowmarket Town v St Neots Town	2-3
Felixstowe & Walton United v	
Great Wakering Rovers	1-3
Mildenhall Town v Haverhill Rovers	1-1, 1-0
Leyton Pennant v Sawbridgeworth Town	2-0
Fakenham Town v Norwich United	1-3
Long Buckby v Clapton	2-0
Concord Rangers v St Ives Town	2-1
Halstead Town v Tring Town	1-2
Colney Heath v March Town United	11-0

Cockfosters v Warboys Town	5-2
Southend Manor v Hoddesdon Town	1-2
Wivenhoe Town v Ruislip Manor	1-0
Royston Town v Brimsdown Rovers	3-2
Langford v Maldon Town	1-4
Brook House v Stanway Rovers	5-0
Kempston Rovers v Wroxham	0-3
Beaconsfield SYCOB v Tilbury	1-2
AFC Wallingford v North Leigh	5-1
Ipswich Wanderers v Yaxley	2-0
Ely City v Letchworth	1-2
Tiptree United v Potters Bar Town	7-0
Milton Keynes City v St Margaretsbury	1-1, 5-1
Potton United v Southall Town	1-5
Wingate & Finchley v Stansted	2-2, 4-2
Northampton Spencer v Welwyn Garden City	4-1
Downham Town v Clacton Town	0-8
Harwich & Parkeston v Dunstable Town	0-2
Flackwell Heath v Bedford United	2-1
Chalfont St Peter v Aveley	0-4
Bury Town v Somersett Ambury V&E	4-5
Witham Town v Dereham Town	1-2
Harefield United v Harpenden Town	5-4
Kingsbury Town v Great Yarmouth Town	2-1
Holmer Green v East Thurrock United	1-3
Leverstock Green v Desborough Town	0-2
Brentwood v Hanwell Town	2-1
Hadleigh United v Burnham Ramblers	3-2
Wembley v Cheshunt	3-1
Bicester Town v Brightlingsea United	2-0
Hythe Town v Bedfont	1-1, 0-3
Reading Town v Abingdon Town	1-3
Tunbridge Wells v Lordswood	2-5
Littlehampton Town v Peacehaven & Telscombe	3-3, 2-3
Abingdon United v Epsom & Ewell	2-0
Beckingham Town v Wokingham Town	0-3
VCD Athletic v Godalming & Guildford	5-0
Moneyfields v Molesey	2-1
Arundel v Banstead Athletic	1-5
Wick v Slade Green	1-0
Metropolitan Police v Ash United	2-3
Lancing v Fleet Town	3-2
Greenwich Borough v Chessington United	3-0
Horsham v Chichester City United	1-3
Whitehawk v Lymington Town	1-0
Fareham Town v Selsey	0-1
Hailsham Town v Corinthian Casuals	1-3
East Preston v Oakwood	1-4
Chessington & Hook United v Chertsey Town	4-2
Farnham Town v Redhill	2-1
Maidstone United v Hungerford Town	4-2
Hillingdon Borough v Milton United	4-2
Wantage Town v Lewes	0-1
Dorking v Cobham	3-0
Sandhurst Town v Eastbourne Town	1-0
Pagham v Ringmer	0-5
Eastbourne United v Bracknell Town	0-3
Thatcham Town v East Grinstead Town	4-1
Hassocks v Chipstead	3-0
BAT Sports v Southwick	3-2
Gosport Borough v Andover	2-2, 2-4
Egham Town v Eastleigh	5-1
Brislington v Team Bath	0-1
Bromyard Town v Harrow Hill	4-3
Bournemouth v Bridport	0-2
Pershore Town v Frome Town	0-4
Portland United v Amesbury Town	0-0, 2-0
Bishop Sutton v Keynsham Town	4-2
Wotton Bassett Town v Calne Town	3-2
Downton v Bridgwater Town	0-3
Bideford v Fareford Town	2-1
Barnstaple Town v Shepton Mallet	3-2
Bitton v Almondsbury Town	0-2
Devizes Town v Odd Down	2-0
Melksham Town v Clevedon United	3-1
St Blazey v Gloucester United	1-0
Minehead Town v Christchurch	2-6
Bemerton Heath Harlequins v Cullompton Rangers	6-1
Paulton Rovers v Dawlish Town	2-3
Ilfracombe Town v Welton Rovers	2-0
Elmore v Westbury United	3-0
Tuffley Rovers v Wellington Town	2-1

FIRST ROUND

Nantwich Town v Castleton Gabriels	2-1
Esh Winning v Jarrow Roofing Boldon CA	1-0

Hall Road Rangers v Harrogate Railway	2-5
Hatfield Main v Guisborough Town	3-4
Rossington Main v Curzon Ashton	1-2
Prescot Cables v Blackpool Mechanics	5-0
Seaham Red Star v Thornaby	0-1
Tow Law Town v Cammell Laird	3-1
West Auckland Town v Evenwood Town	4-1
Dunston FB v Whitley Bay	2-3
Warrington Town v Durham City	1-2
Atherton LR v Hallam	1-2
Newcastle Blue Star v Winsford United	0-5
Congleton Town v Shildon	4-2
Mossley v Flixton	3-0
Pickering Town v Denaby United	2-0
Chester-Le-Street Town v Peterlee Newtown	1-4
Squires Gate v Bacup Borough	2-1
Thackley v Woodleigh Sports	1-2
Louth United v Nelson	1-3
Washington Nissan v Billingham Synthonia	7-9
Barrow Town v North Notts	2-1
Blackstone v Staveley MW	1-0
Rainworth MW v Studley BKW	0-5
Grosvenor Park v Tividale	1-2
Glossop North End v Raunds Town	1-2
Leek CSOB v Kidsgrove Athletic	1-7
Marconi v Rothwell Corinthians	2-1
Stewarts & Lloyds v Pegasus Juniors	3-0
Buxton v Downs Sports	2-1
Shirebrook Town v Causeway United	0-1
St Andrews v Bridgnorth Town	2-4
Barwell v Willenhall Town	3-0
Heanor Town v Paget Rangers	3-2
Cradleigh Town v Bromsgrove Rovers	0-4
Gedling Town v Alfreton Town	4-4, 0-2
Brierley & Hagleigh Alliance v Desborough Town	2-4
Star v Long Eaton United	2-1
Boston Town v Collingham	3-2
Ibstock Welfare v Stratford Town	1-1, 0-3
Long Buckby v Bromyard Town	1-3
Great Wakering Rovers v Hoddesdon Town	3-1
Norwich United v Colney Heath	1-2
Tiptree United v Cockfosters	3-1
Wingate & Finchley v Harefield United	1-1, 1-2
Tring Town v Southall Town	0-3
Somersett Ambury V&E v Barton Rovers	2-3
Diss Town v Concord Rangers	1-1, 2-3
Mildenhall Town v Bicester Town	2-0
Letchworth v London Colney	0-4
Dereham Town v Buckingham Town	4-1
Hadleigh United v Maldon Town	2-1
Flackwell Heath v Clacton Town	0-4
Leighton Town v Kingsbury Town	0-2
AFC Sudbury v Hemel Hempstead Town	5-1
Coggenhoe United v Ipswich Wanderers	3-1
Leyton Pennant v Dunstable Town	6-1
Brackley Town v Lowestoft Town	5-3
Gorleston v Ford Sports Daventry	2-4
Wembley v St Neots Town	0-2
Milton Keynes City v Northampton Spencer	3-1
Wivenhoe Town v Brook House	0-1
Royston Town v Wroxham	0-1
Bracknell Town v Hillingdon Borough	2-0
Wokingham Town v Sandhurst Town	1-2
Lordswood v Corinthian Casuals	2-0
Ash United v Leatherhead	7-2
Selsey v Chessington & Hook United	2-0
AFC Wallingford v Herne Bay	4-2
Greenwich Borough v Wick	7-3
East Thurrock United v Ringmer	0-3
Burgess Hill Town v Egham Town	4-0
Banstead Athletic v Deal Town	3-2
Sidley United v Hassocks	3-1
Farnham Town v Aveley	0-1
Maidstone United v Bedfont	1-0
Abingdon Town v Peacehaven & Telscombe	1-0
Dorking v VCD Athletic	2-1
Saltdean United v Abingdon United	0-5
Romford v Brentwood	4-3
Tilbury v Whitehawk	3-0
Lewes v Oakwood	6-1
Lancing v Ramsgate	2-0
Portland United v Frome Town	3-0
Lymington & New Milton v Bridport	4-0
Bideford v Elmore	1-3
Almondsbury Town v Team Bath	0-3
Chichester City United v Barnstaple Town	6-0

Ilfracombe Town v Bishop Sutton 0-2
Bemerton Heath Harlequins v Dawlish Town 4-2
Bridgwater Town v Melksham Town 2-3
Moneyfields v Tuffley Rovers 5-0
Andover v Yate Town 2-1
Wotton Bassett Town v St Blazey 0-2
Devizes Town v Christchurch 2-3
BAT Sports v Thatcham Town 1-7

SECOND ROUND
Marske United v Hallam 1-2
Winsford United v St Helens Town 2-4
Durham City v Mossley 3-2
Harrogate Railway v West Auckland Town 1-3
Guisborough Town v Whitley Bay 2-2, 0-2
Tow Law Town v Congleton Town 5-0
Billingham Town v Curzon Ashton 2-1
Squires Gate v Billingham Synthonia 0-3
Peterlee Newtown v Consett 3-4
Clitheroe v Nelson 1-1, 3-1
Woodleigh Sports v Pickering Town 0-3
Eccleshill United v Bedlington Terriers 1-2
Nantwich Town v Esh Winning 4-3
Thornaby v Prescot Cables 1-4
Barwell v Borrowash Victoria 4-0
Brigg Town v Causeway United 6-0
Arnold Town v Barrow Town 2-1
Stewarts & Lloyds v Star 5-3
Mickelover Sports v Milton Keynes City 1-2
Bridgnorth Town v Desborough Town 3-1
Boston Town v Heanor Town 0-3
Blackstone v Coggenhoe United 0-3
Bromsgrove Rovers v Ford Sports Daventry 2-0
Kidsgrove Athletic v Bromyard Town 7-0
Rushall Olympic v Marconi 2-1
Alfreton Town v Newcastle Town 0-2
Raunds Town v Stratford Town 6-1
Tividale v Oadby Town 1-4
Studley BKW v Buxton 6-1
Banstead Athletic v Ringmer 4-2
Brook House v AFC Sudbury 1-5
Great Wakering Rovers v London Colney 3-1
Selsey v Concord Rangers 2-0
Brackley Town v Berkhamsted Town 2-5
Wroxham v Abingdon United 7-1
Mildenhall Town v Maidstone United 3-0
Aveley v Kingsbury Town 3-4
Tilbury v Barton Rovers 2-2
  Abandoned 81 minutes; referee injured. 2-1
Abingdon Town v Clacton Town 3-2
Harefield United v Croydon Athletic 1-2
Tiptree United v Colney Heath 3-2
Romford v St Neots Town 0-3
Sidley United v Dereham Town 1-2
Lewes v Hornchurch 3-1
Arlesey Town v Hadleigh United 7-1
Lancing v Stotfold 2-4
Dorking v Greenwich Borough 2-0
Corinthian Casuals v Burgess Hill Town 0-3
Ashford Town (Middlesex) v Leyton Pennant 0-2
Westfield v AFC Wallingford 1-0
Thamesmead Town v Southall Town 2-0
Cowes Sports v Christchurch 2-0
Thatcham Town v Bishop Sutton 1-2
Lymington & New Milton v Wimborne Town 1-2
AFC Totton v Melksham Town 0-5
Cove v Bemerton Heath Harlequins 4-2
Moneyfields v Portland United 3-4
Marlow v Porthleven 2-4
Andover v Taunton Town 4-0
Ash United v Falmouth Town 5-2
St Blazey v Elmore 2-0
Team Bath v Bracknell Town 2-4
Chichester City United v Hallen 4-4, 2-1
Brockenhurst v Sandhurst Town

THIRD ROUND
Bedlington Terriers v Bridgnorth Town 3-0
Prescot Cables v Newcastle Town 4-0
West Auckland Town v Nantwich Town 1-0
St Helens Town v Billingham Synthonia 3-1
Tow Law Town v Bromsgrove Rovers 1-0
  Abandoned 76 minutes: fog.
Coggenhoe United v Clitheroe 3-1
                                        1-5

Arnold Town v Consett 2-1
Billingham Town v Whitley Bay 1-2
Raunds Town v Durham City 1-1, 1-3
Oadby Town v Kidsgrove Athletic 1-2
Barwell v Rushall Olympic 0-3
Pickering Town v Stewarts & Lloyds 2-0
Heanor Town v Hallam 2-1
Studley BKL v Brigg Town 2-3
Croydon Athletic v Brockenhurst 5-2
Thamesmead Town v Bemerton Heath Harlequins 0-2
Great Wakering Rovers v Thatcham Town 2-0
Moneyfields v Porthleven 3-4
Lewes v Hallen 3-0
Cowes Sports v Tiptree United 1-3
Leyton Pennant v Mildenhall Town 1-2
Ash United v Stotfold 3-1
Wimborne Town v Taunton Town 1-2
AFC Wallingford v Abingdon Town 0-1
Milton Keynes City v St Blazey 3-1
Team Bath v Arlesey Town 0-1
AFC Sudbury v Berkhamsted Town 4-1
Dorking v Kingsbury Town 3-2
Banstead Athletic v Dereham Town 0-2
Tilbury v Wroxham 1-1, 1-2
Melksham Town v St Neots Town 2-3
Burgess Hill Town v Selsey 4-0

FOURTH ROUND
Abingdon Town v Clitheroe 0-3
Ash United v Tow Law Town 0-3
Burgess Hill Town v Dorking 1-1, 1-1
  Burgess Hill Town won 3-2 on penalties.
AFC Sudbury v Croydon Athletic 5-0
Arlesey Town v St Helens Town 1-0
Bemerton Heath Harlequins v Great Wakering
  Rovers 0-2
Kidsgrove Athletic v Lewes 0-2
Bedlington Terriers v Brigg Town 1-4
Pickering Town v Tiptree United 0-3
Rushall Olympic v St Neots Town 1-2
Whitley Bay v Milton Keynes City 5-1
Porthleven v Mildenhall Town 1-0
Prescot Cables v Wroxham 4-5
Taunton Town v West Auckland Town 3-2
Arnold Town v Heanor Town 2-1
Dereham Town v Durham City 2-2, 0-2

FIFTH ROUND
Whitley Bay v Brigg Town 3-3, 3-0
Durham City v St Neots Town 2-1
Wroxham v Arnold Town 3-1
Arlesey Town v Clitheroe 0-3
Lewes v Tow Law Town 4-1
AFC Sudbury v Great Wakering Rovers 2-1
Burgess Hill Town v Porthleven 4-0
Tiptree United v Taunton Town 1-1, 2-1

SIXTH ROUND
Lewes v AFC Sudbury 1-2
Clitheroe v Whitley Bay 1-2
Durham City v Wroxham 2-1
Burgess Hill Town v Tiptree United 1-2

SEMI-FINALS (two legs)
AFC Sudbury v Tiptree United 0-2, 0-0
Whitley Bay v Durham City 2-1, 0-0

FINAL (at Villa Park)

11 MAY
Tiptree United (0) 0
Whitley Bay (0) 1 *(Chandler 97)* 4742

Tiptree United: Haygreen; Battell, Brady, Houghton, Fish, Wall, Streetly (Gillespie), Wareham (Snow), Aransibia (Parnell), Barefield, Daly.
Whitley Bay: Caffrey; Sunderland, Walmsley, Dixon (Neil), Anderson, Locker, Bowes (Carr), Walton, Chandler, Fenwick (Cuggy), Middleton.
aet.
Referee: A. Kaye (Wakefield).

THE AXA FA YOUTH CUP 2001–02
(in association with *The Times*)

FIRST QUALIFYING ROUND

Witton Albion v Workington	3-2
Crook Town v Gretna	3-5
Guiseley v Chester City	0-3
Altrincham v Leek Town	3-2
Consett v Northwich Victoria	1-5
Emley v Chester-Le-Street Town	3-2
Dunston FB v Marine	5-5
Marine won 7-6 on penalties.	
Farsley Celtic v Pontefract Collieries	5-0
Hallam v Selby Town	2-0
Thackley v Nantwich Town	3-1
Alfreton Town v Warrington Town	1-2
Lancaster City v Kendal Town	5-3
Stocksbridge Park Steels v Bottesford Town	3-0
Ossett Town v Burscough	1-5
Chadderton v Winsford United	2-1
Congleton Town v Morecambe	1-8
Rugby United v Matlock Town	1-2
Marconi v Belper Town	1-0
Burton Albion v Malvern Town	6-1
Redditch United v Oadby Town	0-2
Northampton Spencer v Racing Club Warwick	1-0
Sutton Coldfield Town v Banbury United	6-2
Telford United v Corby Town	4-3
Handrahan Timbers v Lincoln United	2-5
Bedworth United v Boldmere St Michaels	0-1
Worksop Town v Atherton Collieries	2-0
New Mills v Barrow	5-1
Scarborough v Glossop North End	5-0
Dudley Sports v Eynesbury Rovers	4-1
Hinckley United v Atherstone United	4-0
Hednesford Town v Willenhall Town	5-1
Nuneaton Borough v Birstall United	1-0
Gresley Rovers v Mickelover Sports	2-0
Paget Rangers v Long Buckby	19-0
Stamford withdrew v Boston United w.o.	
Hucknall Town w.o. v Bromsgrove Rovers withdrew	
Kettering Town v St Ives Town	3-1
Gornal Athletic v Alvechurch	1-3
Grantham Town v Chasetown	4-0
Holbeach United v Arnold Town	1-2
Bloxwich United w.o. v Holwell Sports withdrew	
Newcastle Town withdrew v St Neots Town w.o.	
Aylesbury United v Romford	3-2
Cambridge City v Chelmsford City	5-1
Wingate & Finchley v Brentwood	3-6
Uxbridge v Leighton Town	3-5
Hitchin Town v Northwood	4-0
Wealdstone v Hemel Hempstead Town	0-3
Ruislip Manor v Boreham Wood	1-0
Braintree Town v Canvey Island	0-1
Ipswich Wanderers v Bugbrooke St Michaels	2-1
Clapton v Barton Rovers	3-0
Potters Bar Town v Wroxham	2-1
Concord Rangers v Bury Town	0-6
Marlow v Milton Keynes City	5-4
Letchworth v Leyton	3-3
Leyton won 5-4 on penalties.	
Kempston Rovers v Southend Manor	3-7
Soham Town Rangers v Bowers United	3-1
AFC Wallingford v Hullbridge Sports	1-3
Bedford Town v Cheshunt	3-0
Heybridge Swifts v Tiptree United	1-3
Great Wakering Rovers v Tilbury	3-0
Newmarket Town v Burnham Ramblers	0-2
Royston Town v Welwyn Garden City	5-1
Chesham United v Arlesey Town	2-1
Erith Town v Whyteleafe	2-0
Whitstable Town v Three Bridges	3-3
Whitstable Town won 3-1 on penalties.	
Dulwich Hamlet v Chichester City United	1-2
Chipstead v Chessington United	3-1
Horsham v Camberley Town	4-3
Molesey v Sittingbourne	5-1
Tooting & Mitcham United v Burgess Hill Town	1-1
Tooting & Mitcham United won 4-3 on penalties.	
Littlehampton Town v Walton & Hersham	1-2
Lordswood v Sutton United	1-2

Leatherhead v Hillingdon Borough	4-2
Eastbourne Town v Bracknell Town	3-3
Eastbourne Town won 4-1 on penalties.	
Reading Town v Merstham	8-2
Woking v Dartford	7-2
Sandhurst Town v Gravesend & Northfleet	1-11
Westfield v Ashford Town (Middx)	2-3
Eastbourne United v Fisher Athletic	0-1
Dover Athletic v Thamesmead Town	1-2
Walton Casuals v Crowborough Athletic	1-4
Wokingham Town v Lewes	4-2
Kingstonian v Croydon Athletic	1-1
Kingstonian won 8-7 on penalties.	
Croydon v Tonbridge Angels	0-2
Yeovil Town v Bournemouth	5-0
Thatcham Town v Frome Town	3-1
Evesham United v Chippenham Town	1-5
Street v Eastleigh	0-1
Salisbury City v Newport County	1-2
Brislington v Bath City	1-2
AFC Newbury v Gloucester City	0-3
Coggenhoe United v Wisbech Town	3-2
Hornchurch v Ware	1-3
Clacton Town v Edgware Town	0-5
Hoddesdon Town v Purfleet	0-2
Ilford v Beaconsfield SYCOB	1-0
Southall withdrew v Witham Town w.o.	
Haringey Borough v Stevenage Borough	1-4
St Albans City v Great Yarmouth Town	3-1
Saltdean United v Bedfont	5-5
Saltdean United won 4-2 on penalties.	
Greenwich Borough v Didcot Town	1-2
North Leigh v Alton Town	2-1
Leyton Pennant v Abingdon United	2-3
Chatham Town v Havant & Waterlooville	0-3
Beckenham Town v Farnborough Town	3-2
Milton United v Banstead Athletic	3-4
Aldershot Town v Thame United	5-3
Carshalton Athletic v Horndean	7-0
Bristol Manor Farm v Worcester City	1-3
Cirencester Town v Cinderford Town	10-0
Forest Green Rovers v Bashley	2-4
Tring Town withdrew v Hayes w.o.	
Woodbridge Town v Ford United	2-0
Godalming & Guildford withdrew v Welling United	w.o.
Fleet Town w.o. v Faversham Town removed	

SECOND QUALIFYING ROUND

Witton Albion v Lancaster City	1-2
Thackley v Chadderton	2-0
Burscough v New Mills	7-0
Stocksbridge Park Steels v Worksop Town	3-1
Doncaster Rovers v Emley	4-3
Warrington Town v Farsley Celtic	1-3
Northwich Victoria v Morecambe	1-5
Marine v Chester City	3-3
Marine won 4-3 on penalties.	
Gresley Rovers v Telford United	0-2
Kettering Town v St Neots Town	6-1
Matlock Town v Lincoln United	0-3
Grantham Town v Burton Albion	5-4
Hinckley United v Hucknall Town	0-1
Dudley Sports v Marconi	0-1
Hednesford Town v Arnold Town	7-2
Alvechurch v Oadby Town	2-1
Tamworth v Northampton Spencer	2-1
Boldmere St Michaels v Boston United	2-4
Bloxwich United v Paget Rangers	2-0
Bedford Town v Canvey Island	1-3
Bishop's Stortford v Chesham United	3-7
Ruislip Manor v Woodbridge Town	4-4
Woodbridge Town won 5-4 on penalties.	
Ware v St Albans City	0-2
Great Wakering Rovers v Leyton	0-2
Burnham Ramblers v Coggenhoe United	0-2
Cambridge City v Hitchin Town	4-2
Lowestoft Town v Royston Town	6-1
Brentwood v Edgware Town	2-5

Potters Bar Town v Witham Town | 7-1
Bury Town v Leighton Town | 3-4
Tiptree United v Hullbridge Sports | 1-3
Ilford v Purfleet | 1-3
Abingdon w.o. v Thamesmead Town withdrew
Ashford Town (Middx) v Crowborough Athletic | 0-2
Wokingham Town v North Leigh | 10-0
Horsham YMCA v Folkestone Invicta | 0-6
Chipstead v Carshalton Athletic | 0-4
Whitstable Town v Tooting & Mitcham United | 0-3
Gravesend & Northfleet v Sutton United | 1-2
Cobham v Tonbridge Angels | 1-3
Horsham v Walton & Hersham | 0-3
Welling United v Didcot Town | 4-1
Fisher Athletic v Molesey | 1-0
Banstead Athletic v Beckenham Town | 1-2
Eastbourne Town v Leatherhead | 1-2
Eastleigh v Thatcham Town | 4-3
Hallam v Scarborough | 1-2
Altrincham v Gretna | 3-1
Nuneaton Borough v Sutton Coldfield Town | 1-0
Ipswich Wanderers v Marlow | 2-1
Stevenage Borough v Soham Town Rangers | 5-0
Aylesbury United v Southend Manor | 2-2
Southend Manor won 3-2 on penalties.
Histon v Hayes | 0-3
Clapton v Hemel Hempstead Town | 4-1
Erith Town v Havant & Waterlooville | 2-3
Saltdean United v Reading Town | 1-1
Saltdean United won 3-2 on penalties.
Moneyfields v Woking | 1-3
Aldershot Town v Fleet Town | 3-0
Kingstonian v Dulwich Hamlet | 1-1
Kingstonian won 5-4 on penalties.
Gloucester City v Chippenham Town | 4-2
Yeovil Town v Bath City | 7-5
Worcester City v Bashley | 2-8
Cirencester Town v Mangotsfield United | 3-2
Newport County v Basingstoke Town | 3-0

THIRD QUALIFYING ROUND

Thackley v Lancaster City | 3-1
Burscough v Marine | 2-0
Doncaster Rovers v Scarborough | 0-2
Morecambe v Altrincham | 1-2
Farsley Celtic v Stocksbridge Park Steels | 1-4
Boston United v Grantham Town | 6-2
Telford United v Alvechurch | 3-1
Marconi v Kettering Town | 2-0
Hucknall Town v Tamworth | 3-0
Hednesford Town v Bloxwich United | 2-4
Nuneaton Borough v Lincoln United | 1-4
Ipswich Wanderers v Hayes | 1-4
Leighton Town v Stevenage Borough | 1-3
Coggenhoe United v Southend Manor | 2-1
Cambridge City v Ware | 0-1
Chesham United v Canvey Island | 9-1
Edgware Town v Woodbridge Town | 5-0
Potters Bar Town v Clapton | 1-2
Leyton v Purfleet | 3-2
Lowestoft Town v Hullbridge Sports | 0-4
Abingdon United v Woking | 1-4
Fisher Athletic v Crowborough Athletic | 3-1
Kingstonian v Havant & Waterlooville | 2-4
Tooting & Mitcham United v Carshalton Athletic | 0-2
Folkestone Invicta v Wokingham Town | 2-2
Walton & Hersham v Saltdean United
Walton & Hersham won 5-4 on penalties.
Welling United v Sutton United | 1-4
Aldershot Town v Leatherhead | 6-1
Tonbridge Angels v Beckenham Town | 2-0
Eastleigh v Cirencester Town | 2-6
Yeovil Town v Bashley | 3-2
Newport County v Gloucester City | 6-2

FIRST ROUND

Rushden & Diamonds v Stoke City | 0-3
Peterborough United v Bury | 5-3
Tranmere Rovers v Wigan Athletic | 4-2
Huddersfield Town v Chesterfield | 4-1
Thackley v Port Vale | 0-2
Scarborough v Burscough | 1-2
York City v Hartlepool United | 0-3
Halifax Town v Shrewsbury Town | 2-0
Macclesfield Town v Kidderminster Harriers | 0-1
Wrexham v Altrincham | 2-1

Grantham Town v Telford United | 1-0
Oldham Athletic v Hednesford Town | 4-3
Notts County v Lincoln United | 3-1
Blackpool v Mansfield Town | 3-2
Farsley Celtic v Darlington | 2-0
Carlisle United v Hucknall Town | 4-0
Hull City v Lincoln City | 5-0
Rochdale v Marconi | 8-0
Scunthorpe United v Northampton Town | 1-0
Reading v Woking | 6-0
Leyton Orient v Carshalton Athletic | 3-0
Cardiff City v Aldershot Town | 0-0
Cardiff City won 3-0 on penalties.
Plymouth Argyle v Sutton United | 0-1
AFC Bournemouth v Queens Park Rangers | 1-3
Yeovil Town v Tonbridge Angels | 2-1
Torquay United v Cambridge United | 1-1
Torquay United won 4-3 on penalties.
Potters Bar Town v Edgware Town | 4-3
Bristol Rovers v Cambridge City | 4-2
Crowborough Athletic v Newport County | 1-2
Swindon Town v Southend Manor | 3-0
Brentford v Exeter City | 4-1
Swansea City v Cirencester Town | 1-2
Wokingham Town v Brighton & Hove Albion | 1-4
Cheltenham Town v Luton Town | 3-4
Southend United v Walton & Hersham | 3-1
Bristol City v Lowestoft Town | 2-1
Hayes v Colchester United | 0-5
Purfleet v Stevenage Borough | 3-3
Purfleet won 3-2 on penalties.
Canvey Island v Wycombe Wanderers | 2-5
Kingstonian v Oxford United | 2-0

SECOND ROUND

Port Vale v Burscough | 2-1
Kidderminster Harriers v Scunthorpe United | 2-0
Stoke City v Hartlepool United | 0-2
Tranmere Rovers v Rochdale | 5-0
Notts County v Huddersfield Town | 3-2
Farsley Celtic v Wrexham | 0-5
Peterborough United v Oldham Athletic | 4-3
Halifax Town v Blackpool | 3-2
Carlisle United v Hull City | 0-2
Swindon Town v Grantham Town | 5-0
Torquay United v Purfleet | 2-2
Torquay United won 3-2 on penalties.
Cardiff City v Sutton United | 1-2
Newport County v Brighton & Hove Albion | 1-3
Queens Park Rangers v Leyton Orient | 3-2
Yeovil Town v Kingstonian | 3-2
Luton Town v Brentford | 0-2
Bristol Rovers v Colchester United | 2-3
Wycombe Wanderers v Cirencester Town | 3-0
Southend United v Reading | 0-2
Potters Bar Town v Bristol City | 0-3

THIRD ROUND

Crystal Palace v Wolverhampton Wanderers | 1-1
Crystal Palace won 4-2 on penalties.
Leeds United v Liverpool | 1-0
Coventry City v Southampton | 3-0
Manchester City v Burnley | 3-0
Derby County v Barnsley | 1-3
Ipswich Town v Bristol City | 5-0
West Ham United v Everton | 1-2
Middlesbrough v Notts County | 5-0
Tranmere Rovers v Sheffield Wednesday | 4-1
Blackburn Rovers v Chelsea | 4-0
Crewe Alexandra v Portsmouth | 1-0
Brighton & Hove Albion v Hull City | 4-0
Norwich City v Newcastle United | 2-1
Rotherham United v Gillingham | 1-2
Halifax Town v Reading | 1-2
Aston Villa v Wimbledon | 2-1
Arsenal v Colchester United | 5-0
Sunderland v Nottingham Forest | 2-4
Grimsby Town v Peterborough United | 3-2
Watford v Stockport County | 1-0
Hartlepool United v Brentford | 2-2
Hartlepool United won 5-4 on penalties.
West Bromwich Albion v Millwall | 1-0
Kidderminster Harriers v Sutton United | 3-1
Bolton Wanderers v Bradford City | 2-1
Birmingham City v Torquay United | 3-1
Preston North End v Fulham | 0-1

Charlton Athletic v Leicester City — 0-1
Walsall v Tottenham Hotspur — 1-5
Sheffield United v Wycombe Wanderers — 1-3
Yeovil Town v Swindon Town — 0-2
Port Vale v Wrexham — 1-0
Queens Park Rangers v Manchester United — 1-3

FOURTH ROUND
Everton v West Bromwich Albion — 2-0
Port Vale v Fulham — 0-3
Bolton Wanderers v Tottenham Hotspur — 1-2
Reading v Barnsley — 0-3
Middlesbrough v Leeds United — 1-1
  Leeds United won 4-3 on penalties.
Kidderminster Harriers v Grimsby Town — 2-1
Manchester City v Gillingham — 7-1
Aston Villa v Tranmere Rovers — 4-3
Crewe Alexandra v Arsenal — 0-1
Brighton & Hove Albion v Leicester City — 3-2
Wycombe Wanderers v Norwich City — 1-1
  Wycombe Wanderers won 7-6 on penalties.
Nottingham Forest v Watford — 5-1
Ipswich Town v Coventry City — 3-1
Blackburn Rovers v Swindon Town — 2-1
Birmingham City v Manchester United — 2-3
Crystal Palace v Hartlepool United — 1-2

FIFTH ROUND
Barnsley v Wycombe Wanderers — 0-0
  Barnsley won 5-4 on penalties.
Manchester United v Hartlepool United — 3-2
Leeds United v Tottenham Hotspur — 0-1
Aston Villa v Brighton & Hove Albion — 2-0
Nottingham Forest v Kidderminster Harriers — 3-0
Arsenal v Blackburn Rovers — 0-2
Fulham v Ipswich Town — 3-2
Everton v Manchester City — 4-2

SIXTH ROUND
Tottenham Hotspur v Blackburn Rovers — 2-0
Everton v Nottingham Forest — 2-1
Fulham v Aston Villa — 0-3
Manchester United v Barnsley — 3-3
  Barnsley won 3-1 on penalties.

SEMI-FINALS (TWO LEGS)
Aston Villa v Barnsley — 3-1, 3-1
Everton v Tottenham Hotspur — 2-1, 2-1

FINAL FIRST LEG

14 MAY

Everton (1) 1 *(Rooney 25)* — 15,280
Aston Villa (1) 4 *(Moore S 37, 53, Hynes 68, Moore L 80)*

Everton: Pettinger; Moogan B, Crowder, Moogan A (Colbeck 74), Schumacher, Garside, Brown, Beck, Symes, Rooney, Carney.
Aston Villa: Henderson; Wells, Whittingham, Marshall, O'Connor (Amoo 83), Ridgewell, Davis, Hynes (Husbands 89), Moore L (Atkinson 90), Foley, Moore S.
Referee: B. Knight (Kent).

FINAL SECOND LEG

18 MAY

Aston Villa (0) 0

Everton (0) 1 *(Brown 75)* — 18,651

Aston Villa: Henderson; Wells, Whittingham, Marshall, Amoo, Ridgewell, Hynes (Scullion 87), Davis, Moore L (Husbands 90), Foley, Moore S.
Everton: Pettinger; Moogan B, Crowder, Moogan A, Schumacher, Garside, Brown, Beck (Hopkins 64), Symes, Rooney, Carney.
Referee: B. Knight (Kent).

SEMI-PROFESSIONAL INTERNATIONALS

UNIBOND FOUR NATIONS TOURNAMENT

England 1 (Weatherstone S), Wales 1 — (425)
Republic of Ireland 2, Scotland 0 — (210)
England 1 (Moore), Republic of Ireland 2 — (515)
Scotland 1, Wales 2 — (150)
England 2 (Weatherstone S, Drummond), Scotland 0 — (827)
Republic of Ireland 2, Wales 5 — (420)

	P	W	D	L	F	A	Pts
Wales	3	2	1	0	8	4	7
Republic of Ireland	3	2	0	1	6	6	6
England	3	1	1	1	4	3	4
Scotland	3	0	0	3	1	6	0

England XI 2, USA 1 — (548)
England XI 1, Holland 0 — (824)

FA UMBRO SUNDAY CUP 2001–02

FIRST ROUND
Fantail Manfast v Ford Motors	4-0
Sandon Dock v Orchard Park	1-3
Bolton Woods v Allerton	2-3
Britannia w.o. v Frames withdrew.	
Prestige Brighams v Queens Park	3-2
Canon v A3 (Canada)	1-6
East Bowling Unity v Cramlington Benedictine	5-0
Ship Inn v Smith & Nephew	1-2
Nicosia w.o. v Northwood withdrew.	
Grosvenor Park v Rolls Royce Celtic	1-2
Standens Barn v Slade Celtic	2-0
Capel Plough w.o. v Bretforton Sports Vic failed to appear.	
Lodge Cottrell v Duke of York	0-1
Wyrley Club v Readflex Rangers	2-0
Holly Lane Delta v Greyhound Dog	0-1
Pilot withdrew v Jolly Farmers w.o.	
Stile v Mackadown Lane	1-2
Trooper v Toll Inn	1-5
Lebeq Tavern Courage v Percival	1-0
St Joseph's (Luton) v Rainham Sports	1-0
Moat v Old Oak	3-0
Wishing Well v Ouzavich	4-0
Gossoms End v Hammer	1-2
Pioneer v Heybridge Social	3-2
St Joseph's (South Oxhey) v Theale	1-2
Grasshoppers v Kempston Fox	1-1
Grasshoppers won 4-3 on penalties.	
Mayfair United v Lewsey Social	5-0
Poole Wanderers v Palmeston WMC	1-2
Reading Irish v Queensmen	3-2

SECOND ROUND
Fantail Manfast v Orchard Park	1-0
Britannia v East Bowling Unity	3-2
Allerton v Prestige Brighams	1-0
Mainstay v Oakenshaw	2-2
Oakenshaw won 3-2 on penalties.	
A3 (Canada) v Smith & Nephew	4-3
Flathouse unable to provide venue v Rolls Royce Celtic awarded tie.	
Nicosia v Brossley Town	3-0
Lobster v Cheadle United	2-0
Hartlepool Lion Hillcarter v Town Green	1-0
Burnley Boys withdrew v Hessle Rangers w.o.	
Seymour v Wedgwood	4-4
Seymour won 5-3 on penalties.	
Clubmoor Nalgo v Western Approaches	5-1
Salerno v Albion Sports	0-1
Mackadown Lane v St Joseph's (Luton)	0-4
Jolly Farmers v Wyrley Club	1-3
Schofields v Standens Barn	5-2
Moat v Hammer	2-0
St Gerards v Duke of York	2-6
FC Houghton Centre v Axe & Compass	5-1
Mayfair United v Palmeston WMC	3-0
Pioneer v Belstone	1-3
Celtic SC v Biggleswade	5-1
Melton Youth OB v Concord Rangers	3-2
Hexton v Watford Labour	2-0
Azaad Sports v Wishing Well	1-2

Greyhound Dog v Lebeq Tavern Courage	1-3
Theale v Toll Inn	3-2
Capel Plough v Peacock	1-1
Peacock won 5-4 on penalties.	
Little Paxton v Grasshoppers	4-2
Longfleet St Marys v Reading Irish	2-1
Bournemouth Electric v Finch Hampstead Athletic	3-1
Bye: General Panel Sports.	

THIRD ROUND
Britannia v Allerton	4-4
Britannia won 4-3 on penalties.	
Fantail Manfast v Hartlepool Lion Hillcarter	0-1
Hessle Rangers v Lobster	1-2
Seymour v Nicosia	6-3
Seymour removed from competition for fielding a suspended player.	
Rolls Royce Celtic v Oakenshaw	3-1
Clubmoor Nalgo v Wyrley Club	1-1
Clubmoor Nalgo won 4-3 on penalties.	
A3 (Canada) v Albion Sports	4-5
Mayfair United v St Joseph's (Luton)	0-4
Melton Youth OB v Hexton	2-5
Moat v Lebeq Tavern Courage	1-2
Celtic SC v Wishing Well	2-1
Schofields v General Panel Sports	2-0
Peacock v Theale	3-4
Little Paxton v Longfleet St Marys	5-0
Duke of York v Belstone	4-0
FC Houghton Centre v Bournemouth Electric	3-1

FOURTH ROUND
Britannia v Schofields	6-0
Lobster v Hartlepool Lion Hillcarter	1-4
Nicosia v Albion Sports	3-3
Albion Sports won 4-2 on penalties.	
Clubmoor Nalgo v Rolls Royce Celtic	2-2
Rolls Royce Celtic won 5-4 on penalties.	
St Joseph's (Luton) v FC Houghton Centre	1-2
Lebeq Tavern Courage v Hexton	3-1
Celtic SC v Duke of York	3-4
Little Paxton v Theale	1-0

FIFTH ROUND
Duke of York v Rolls Royce Celtic	1-3
FC Houghton Centre v Little Paxton	2-3
Hartlepool Lion Hillcarter v Albion Sports	0-0
Albion Sports won 4-3 on penalties.	
Britannia v Lebeq Tavern Courage	7-0

SEMI-FINALS
Rolls Royce Celtic v Britannia	1-2
Little Paxton v Albion Sports	0-0
Little Paxton won 4-3 on penalties.	

FINAL
Britannia v Little Paxton	2-0

FA COUNTY YOUTH CHALLENGE CUP 2001–02

FIRST ROUND

Leicestershire & Rutland v Staffordshire	4-2
Durham v Cumberland	5-0
Isle of Man v Cheshire	0-1
East Riding v Lincolnshire	4-1
Manchester v Lancashire	1-3
Essex v Surrey	7-1
Suffolk v Berks & Bucks	2-1
Hampshire v Norfolk	6-2
Hertfordshire v Sussex	1-5
Herefordshire v Somerset	0-4
Kent v Guernsey	3-2
Worcestershire v Bedfordshire	2-1
Devon v Jersey	0-1
Dorset v Wiltshire	2-3

SECOND ROUND

Liverpool v Northumberland	1-2
Leicestershire & Rutland v East Riding	0-1
West Riding v Lancashire	1-3
Sheffield & Hallamshire v Birmingham	0-3
Westmorland v Durham	0-7
Shropshire v Nottinghamshire	0-3
North Riding v Cheshire	1-3
Sussex v Oxfordshire	4-4
Oxfordshire won 4-2 on penalties.	
Suffolk v Gloucestershire	3-2
Jersey v Kent	2-0
Worcestershire v Somerset	2-1
Wiltshire v Army	5-0

London v Hampshire	1-3
Middlesex v Huntingdonshire	5-1
Essex v Northamptonshire	5-0
Cornwall v Cambridgeshire	3-0

THIRD ROUND

East Riding v Middlesex	1-3
Cheshire v Northumberland	3-0
Suffolk v Hampshire	6-2
Oxfordshire v Nottinghamshire	1-6
Worcestershire v Lancashire	2-3
Cornwall v Jersey	0-1
Durham v Essex	3-0
Wiltshire v Birmingham	2-3

FOURTH ROUND

Middlesex v Birmingham	1-2
Jersey v Lancashire	1-2
Durham v Suffolk	2-1
Cheshire v Nottinghamshire	1-3

SEMI-FINALS

Nottinghamshire v Birmingham	0-3
Durham v Lancashire	2-1

FINAL

Birmingham v Durham	2-1

FA XI REPRESENTATIVE MATCHES

19 Nov

FA XI 3 *(Peyton, Marples, Pickford)*
Northern Premier League 4

FA XI: Woods (Scarborough), Dickinson (Southport), Lane (Southport), Marples (Doncaster R), Durkin (Leigh RMI), Clarke (Southport), Beesley (Stalybridge C), Twiss (Leigh RMI), Scott (Stalybridge C), Drummond (Morecambe), Elliott (Scarborough), Pickford (Stalybridge C), Peyton (Nuneaton B), Kilbane (Lancaster C), Whittaker (Lancaster C), Talbot (Morecambe).
Attendance: 602 at Altrincham.

20 Nov

FA XI 3 *(Sharpling 3)*
Southern League 3

Southern League won 4-1 on penalties.
FA XI: Farrelly (Farnborough T), Hyde (Dover Ath), Warner (Farnborough T), Bunce (Farnborough T), West (Woking), Porter (Margate), Edwards (Margate), Tonkin (Yeovil T), Roddis (Woking), Turner (Margate), Moore (Woking), Patterson (Farnborough T), Sharpling (Woking), Braithwaite (Margate), Perkins (Woking).
Attendance: 632 at Crawley.

21 Nov

FA XI 0
Isthmian League 2

FA XI: Wilkerson (Stevenage B), Perrin (Forest Green R), Travis (Forest Green R), Brennan (Dagenham & R), Smith (Dagenham & R), Heald (Barnet), Arber (Barnet), Sturgess (Stevenage B), Bell (Barnet), McMahon (Stevenage B), Charles (Nuneaton B), Clark (Hayes), Charlery (Dagenham & R), Scott (Dover Ath), Strevens (Barnet).
Attendance: 403 at Bishop's Stortford.

15 Jan

FA XI 1 *(Blundell)*
British Universities 1

FA XI: Anderson (Burton A), Bailey (Burton A), Wall (Burton A), Brunskill (Droylsden), Jenkins (Hednesford T), Shakespeare (Hednesford T), Barnard, Blundell, Garvey, Ingram, Norris (all Northwich Vic), Edwards, Hanmer, Moore, Palmer, Smith (all Telford U).
Attendance: 301 at Hednesford.

25 Mar

FA XI 3 (Hambley, Taylor, Cooper)
Combined Services 1

FA XI: Key (Kingstonian), McLeod (Grays Ath), Southon (Purfleet), Laker (Farnborough T), Wilkinson (Basingstoke T), McFarlane (Purfleet), Carrol (Crawley T), Hambley (Havant & W), Vansittart (Farnborough T), Taylor (Havant & W), Holloway (Farnborough T), Bristow (Basingstoke T), Tarr (Basingstoke T), Judge (Crawley T), Cooper (Grays Ath), Bowes (Purfleet).
at RAF Uxbridge.

UNIVERSITY FOOTBALL 2001–02

118th UNIVERSITY MATCH

(at QPR, 30th March 2002)

Oxford 0, Cambridge 0

Oxford: Casarella; Addley, Woodcock, Redmayne, Oehmke, Adamson, Rishworth (Paterson 46), Ratcliffe (Ross 90), Okkaya (Johnson 90), Lowe, Durnford.
Cambridge: Heath; Pett, Smith, Dimmock, Brett (Butler 46), Owles, Hall (Lewis 90), Harding, Walsh (Farbairn 74), Glamocak, Garwood-Gowers.
Referee: D'Urso.

UNIVERSITY OF LONDON UNION MEN'S COMPETITIONS

(*Limited to one game against each member*)

Premier Division	P	W	D	L	F	A	Pts
London School of Economics	11	9	1	1	35	8	28
University College	11	9	1	1	34	14	28
Royal Holloway College	11	7	0	4	16	15	21
R Free, UC & Middx Hospitals M S	11	6	1	4	35	20	19
Imperial College School of Medicine	11	5	1	5	17	20	16
Imperial College*	11	5	1	5	19	18	15
Goldsmiths' College*	11	4	2	5	15	11	13
Queen Mary Westfield College	11	3	4	4	16	27	13
King's College*	11	2	6	3	28	26	11
Guy's, King's & St Thomas's M S*	11	3	1	7	10	30	9
St George's Hospital M S*	11	1	3	7	14	23	5
St Barts & R. London Hospitals M C	11	0	3	8	11	38	3

Division 1	P	W	D	L	F	A	Pts
Royal Holloway College Res	11	10	0	1	61	15	30
University College Res	11	8	1	2	35	11	25
King's College 3rd	10	6	2	2	43	22	20
Imperial College Res	11	6	0	5	32	18	18
London School of Economics 3rd	10	5	3	2	21	19	18
London School of Economics Res**	11	6	1	4	29	16	17
Queen Mary Westfeld College Res	11	5	2	4	23	26	17
University College 3rd	11	3	3	5	21	22	12
Imperial College Sch Med Res	11	3	2	6	21	36	11
Goldsmiths' College Res*	10	2	2	6	13	27	7
King's College 4th	10	1	0	9	10	55	3
King's College Res*	9	0	0	9	6	48	0

Division 2	P	W	D	L	F	A	Pts
Royal Holloway College 4th	10	9	0	1	29	10	27
Imperial College 3rd	10	5	4	1	19	9	19
Royal Holloway College 3rd	10	6	1	3	32	25	19
Guy's, King's & St Thomas's M S Res	10	5	2	3	34	19	17
R Free, UC & Middx Hosp M S Res	10	5	2	3	22	17	17
London School of Economics 4th	10	4	2	4	26	30	14
University College 4th	10	3	3	4	15	15	12
Imperial College 4th	10	3	1	6	19	28	10
Imperial College Sch Med Res 3rd	10	2	2	6	16	29	7
Queen Mary Westfield College 3rd	8	1	1	6	20	32	4
Wye College*	9	1	0	8	7	25	2

*Point deducted for breach of rule
**2 points deducted for breach of rule

Division 3—11 teams
Won by School of Oriental & African Studies
(*Played as conventional Leagues*)
Division 4—13 teams
Won by London School of Economics 5th
Division 5—12 teams
Won by R College of Science (Imperial College)

Challenge Cup
LSE 1:2* Royal Holloway 1:1*
Reserves' Challenge Cup
LSE Res 1:2* Imperial College 1:1*
Reserves' Plate
LSE 4th 1:2* R Free M x & UC MS 3rd 1:1*
Vase
U C 6th 0 Imperial 6th 2

BRITISH UNIVERSITIES SPORTS ASSOCIATION CHAMPIONSHIP

Men's Championship
Semi-Final
Loughborough 1, Exeter 0
Bath 2, Brunel West London 1
Final
Loughborough 2, Bath 0
Men's Shield
Southampton 3, Glasgow 2
Men's Trophy (2nd teams and below)
Brunel West London 1, Bath 0

Women's Championship
Final
Crewe & Alsager 3, Loughborough 2
Women's Shield
Leeds 6, Bath 2
Women's Trophy (2nd teams and below)
Loughborough 2, Manchester 1

UNIVERSITY OF LONDON UNION WOMEN'S LEAGUES

Premier Division	P	W	D	L	F	A	Pts
Guy's, King's & St Thomas's M S	10	9	1	0	81	8	28
Queen Mary Westfield College	10	8	1	1	69	11	25
University College	10	4	1	5	35	35	13
London School of Economics	10	4	0	6	29	40	12
Imperial College	10	2	1	7	10	58	7
School of Oriental & African Studies	10	0	2	8	5	77	2

Division 1	P	W	D	L	F	A	Pts
Royal Holloway College	10	8	1	1	64	15	25
King's College	10	6	3	1	41	9	21
Royal Veterinary College	10	2	4	4	10	17	10
R Free, UC & Middx Hosp M S	10	3	1	6	8	19	10
Goldsmiths' College	10	3	1	6	2	65	10
St George's Hospital M S	10	2	2	6	19	19	8

Division 2	P	W	D	L	F	A	Pts
Guy's, King's & St Thomas's MS Res	8	7	0	1	30	7	21
R Free, UC & Middx Hosp M S Res	8	5	0	3	18	15	15
University College Res	8	5	0	3	17	17	15
Wye College	8	3	0	5	10	26	9
Royal Holloway College Res	8	0	0	8	8	18	0

Challenge Cup
GKT 1*:2 Q Mary Westfield 1*:1

LONDON UNIVERSITY REPRESENTATIVE XI

v Southern Olympian League	Won	3-0
v Cambridge University	Drawn	0-0
v Old Boys' League	Drawn	1-1
v Army Crusaders	Won	6-0
v Amateur Football Alliance	Lost	1-2
v Arthurian League	Lost	2-3
v London Legal League	Won	5-1

SCHOOLS FOOTBALL 2001–02

BOODLE & DUNTHORNE INDEPENDENT SCHOOLS FA CUP 2001–02

FIRST ROUND
Aldenham 1, Forest 5
Bolton 1, Shrewsbury 2
Bradfield 0, Victoria College, Jersey 0
(aet; Bradfield won 5-3 on penalties).
Charterhouse 0, Brentwood 4
Haileybury 6, Dover College 0
KES, Witley 0, St Bede's College 4
King's, Chester 3, Ardingly 1
Manchester GS 1, Repton 0
QEGS, Blackburn 5, Kimbolton 0
Wolverhampton GS 2, St Bede's (Hailsham) 1

SECOND ROUND
Alleyn's 4, John Lyon 2
Batley GS 1, Manchester GS 5
Chigwell 4, Malvern 1
City of London 0, Latymer Upper 5
Eton 3, Bradfield 1
Forest 9, Emanuel 1
Grange 2, Brentwood 9
Haileybury 2, QEGS, Blackburn 5
Hampton 0, Wolverhampton GS 0
(aet; Wolverhampton GS won 8-7 on penalties).
Hulme GS 6, Wellingborough 0
Lancing 3, King's, Chester 1
Millfield 0, St Bede's College 2
St Edmund's, Canterbury 0, Highgate 1
St Mary's, Crosby 3, Winchester 4, *(aet)*
Shrewsbury 4, Bury GS 1
Westminster 7, Oswestry 0

THIRD ROUND
Brentwood 5, Westminster 1
Eton 4, Latymer Upper 1
Forest 4, Manchester GS 2
Highgate 0, St Bede's College 6
Hulme GS 1, Shrewsbury 2
Lancing 2, Chigwell 1
QEGS, Blackburn 2, Wolverhampton GS 3 *(aet)*
Winchester 5, Alleyn's 1

FOURTH ROUND
Brentwood 2, Shrewsbury 1
Eton 4, Winchester 0
Lancing 2, Forest 2
(aet; Lancing won 4-3 on penalties).
Wolverhampton GS 0, St Bede's College 1

SEMI-FINALS
Brentwood 3, Eton 0
St Bede's College 2, Lancing 0

FINAL (at Leicester City)
Brentwood 1 *(Harlow)*
St Bede's College 1 *(A. Fetherston)* 1100
(aet; Brentwood won 3-0 on penalties.)
Brentwood: J. Redwood; C. Adams, J. Pryor, P. Harlow,
B. Harris, D. Ward, P. Barker, A. Hodges, J. Harrison, T.
Winothai, A. Worricker (A. Martin).
St Bede's College: P. Walker; C. Turnbull, M. Fetherston,
M. Gandy, S. Lukes (J. Clarke), P. Ireland, M. Rogers, R.
Monteiro, M. Mozley, A. Stapleton (L. Finnigan), A.
Fetherston (F. Mansaray).
Referee: D. Elleray (Harrow).

ESFA WAGONWHEELS 5-A-SIDE COMPETITION
U.12 FINALS
Staged at JJB Soccerdome, Wigan.

BOYS FINAL:
St Ignatius College (Enfield) 4, Bradon Forest School
(Swindon) 3

GIRLS FINAL:
Thomas Telford School (Telford) 1, Newlands School
(Middlesbrough) 0

ESFA PREMIER LEAGUE U.19 INTER-COUNTY TROPHY
FINAL:
Merseyside County 1, Somerset County 4
Played at Goodison Park.

ESFA U.19 INDIVIDUAL SCHOOLS TROPHY
FINAL:
Bluecoat School (Merseyside) 2, Hartridge High School
(Gwent) 3
Played at Anfield.

ESFA U.19 SCHOOLS & COLLEGES TROPHY
FINAL:
West Notts College (Nottingham) 0, Cirencester College
(Gloucestershire) 6
Played at Meadow Lane.

ESFA SCHOOLSNET U.16 INDIVIDUAL SCHOOLS CUP
FINAL:
Arrow Vale High School (Worcestershire) 2, Kingshurst
City Technical College (West Midlands) 1
Played at Redditch United.

ESFA U.16 PREMIER LEAGUE INTER COUNTY TROPHY
FINAL:
Nottingham County 2, Kent County 0
Played at Meadow Lane.

ESFA GIRLS U.16 INTER COUNTY TROPHY
FINAL:
Merseyside County 3, Kent County 1
Played at Goodison Park.

ESFA GIRLS U.16 INDIVIDUAL SCHOOLS CUP
FINAL:
Frome Community College (Somerset) 3, Countesthorpe
College (Leicester) 1
Played at Ashton Gate.

ESFA WIZARDS U.15 INTER ASSOCIATION TROPHY
FINAL (two legs):
Cardiff 2, North Tyneside 1
Plyaed at Ninian Park.
North Tyneside 2, Cardiff 0
Played at Killingworth YPC.

ESFA GERRARD U.14 INDIVIDUAL SCHOOLS CUP
FINAL:
Vermuyden School (Humberside) 2, Edmonton County
School (Middlesex) 1
Played at Villa Park.

ESFA U.13 LONDON SCHOOLS COCA-COLA CUP
BOYS FINAL:
Edenham High School (Croydon) 2, Shenfield High
School (Essex) 0
Played at Stamford Bridge.

GIRLS FINAL:
Sacred Heart High School (Shepherd's Bush) 2, Sanders
Draper School (Hornchurch) 1
Played at Stamford Bridge.

ADIDAS COMMUNITY CUP GIRLS U.13 6-A-SIDE
FINAL:
Trinity School (Carlisle) – Blackburn Rovers F.C. 1, St
Edmund's Girl School (Salisbury) – Southampton F.C. 0

RAILTRACK PLAY SAFE TROPHY U.11 6-A-SIDE
FINAL:
Farnborough Road School (Southport) – Everton F.C. 3,
Cranborne School (Potters Bar) – Barnet F.C. 1

ESFA MANCHESTER UNITED 7-A-SIDE COMPETITIONS
Year 6 Ryelands Middle School (Northampton) 1,
Eastlands Junior School (Mansfield) 2
Year 7 Featherstone Sports College (Middlesex) 0,
Ormesby Comprehensive School (Middlesbrough) 3

ESFA U.11 7-A-SIDE INTER ASSOCIATION COMPETITION
FINAL:
Winners Bexley after 1-0 win over Oldham.

ESFA U.11 SMALLS SCHOOL SOCCER SIXES
Winners Corpus Christi.

ESFA U.11 6-A-SIDE INDIVIDUAL SCHOOLS COMPETITION
Winners Farnborough Road.

AVON INSURANCE COMBINATION 2001–02

With only three points separating the top three teams, this was one of the closest finishes to the Avon Insurance Combination ever. QPR ran out worthy winners, but were hard pressed by both Crystal Palace and Brentford. The Avon Insurance Combination Cup will be concluded on 14 August of this year with Bristol City playing Luton Town but not until Bristol had won a thrilling sudden death penalty shoot out against Portsmouth by 6 goals to 5!

The main purpose of the Avon Insurance Combination is to allow member clubs to bring players through from the youth team and to give potential its chance as well as give trials to youngsters released by other teams.

Many international players have graced the Avon Insurance Combination and used it as a stepping stone to stardom. Without the Avon Insurance Combination there would be little chance for home-grown players to develop in the face of readily available foreign talent, and many promising careers would be over before they had really started.

2001–02 SEASON SUMMARY
Champions – QPR
League Cup Winners – Bristol City v Luton Town
 (14 August 2002, 7pm)
Top Scorer – Gareth Williams, Crystal Palace
Fair Play Award – Colchester
Avon Insurance Enterprise Award – Norwich
Avon Insurance Programme Award – Brentford

Division One	P	W	D	L	F	A	GD	Pts
QPR	24	14	6	4	52	22	30	48
Crystal P	24	14	5	5	50	26	24	47
Brentford	24	13	6	5	48	33	15	45
Portsmouth	24	12	6	6	36	22	14	38
Cardiff C	24	11	5	8	41	31	10	38
Peterborough U	24	12	2	10	41	39	2	38
Millwall	24	10	7	7	43	36	7	37
Luton T	24	10	7	7	39	30	9	37
Reading	24	10	6	8	35	25	10	36
Southend U	24	9	8	7	35	29	–6	35
Leyton Orient	24	11	2	11	37	53	–16	35
Norwich C	24	9	7	8	40	38	2	34
Oxford U	24	9	7	8	30	35	–5	34
Brighton & HA	24	7	11	6	30	27	3	32
Barnet	24	10	2	12	31	34	–3	32
Cheltenham T	24	9	5	10	30	43	–13	32
Gillingham	24	8	6	10	31	34	–3	30
Bristol R	24	9	4	11	31	34	–3	31
Bristol C	24	7	7	10	33	35	–2	28
Colchester U	24	7	5	12	32	38	–6	26
Cambridge U	24	7	4	13	29	43	–14	25
Wycombe W	24	7	3	14	31	44	–13	24
Bournemouth	24	6	5	13	26	47	–21	23
Northampton T	24	4	10	10	25	42	–17	22
Swindon T	24	4	6	14	22	38	–16	18

AVON INSURANCE LEAGUE 2001–02

The Avon Insurance League Premier, First and Second Divisions were very tightly contested this season. Preston North End were crowned the Avon Insurance League Premiership Champions after they beat Burnley at home in the final game of the season, whilst Barnsley, despite losing to Burnley in their final game, secured second spot from Tranmere on goal difference!

Walsall managed to win the Avon Insurance First Division despite a late run of form from Bury. Bury were 6th in the league at the start of April, before they went on to win all of their three games in hand, scoring 14 goals and only conceding one, including smashing five past both Lincoln and Blackpool, and finishing second in the league!

A 3-1 victory against Hartlepool in their final game of the season ensured that Macclesfield won the honour of being crowned Avon Insurance League Division Two Champions.

Doncaster Rovers won the Avon Insurance League Cup Final beating Burnley 2-0 and Lee Trundle of Wrexham, Mark Goodfellow of Stoke City and Notts County's Paul Heffernan won the Divisional Top Scorer Awards.

West Bromwich Albion won the Avon Insurance Enterprise Award and Tranmere Rovers the Avon Insurance Programme Award.

Premier Division	P	W	D	L	F	A	GD	Pts
Preston NE	24	14	2	8	46	40	6	44
Barnsley	24	12	5	7	43	31	12	41
Tranmere R	24	12	5	7	40	32	8	41
Sheffield U	24	10	9	5	38	31	7	39
Burnley	24	11	6	7	43	40	3	39
Rotherham U	24	10	8	6	42	31	11	38
Wolverhampton W	24	11	4	9	25	22	3	37
Birmingham C	24	9	7	8	35	26	9	34
Huddersfield T	24	7	10	7	36	34	2	31
Oldham Ath	24	5	9	10	30	44	–14	24
WBA	24	5	8	11	20	29	–9	23
Wrexham	24	5	6	13	41	49	–8	21
Port Vale	24	3	5	16	19	49	–30	14

Division One	P	W	D	L	F	A	GD	Pts
Walsall	22	14	3	5	52	22	30	45
Bury	22	13	2	7	45	34	11	41
Scunthorpe U	22	12	2	8	39	37	2	38
Grimsby T	22	11	3	8	42	34	8	36
Stoke C	22	10	3	9	52	27	25	33
Doncaster R	22	10	3	9	44	33	11	33
Shrewsbury T	22	9	3	10	35	35	0	30
Lincoln C	22	7	8	7	21	34	–13	29
Darlington	22	8	4	10	27	38	–11	28
Blackpool	22	5	6	11	28	48	–20	21
Stockport Co	22	5	6	11	26	51	–25	21
York C	22	5	3	14	19	37	–18	18

Division Two	P	W	D	L	F	A	GD	Pts
Macclesfield T	20	14	3	3	37	13	24	45
Hull C	20	13	4	3	53	27	26	43
Kidderminster H	20	12	2	6	40	27	13	38
Notts Co	20	9	6	5	36	22	14	33
Mansfield T	20	9	4	7	31	31	0	31
Hartlepool U	20	9	1	10	39	32	7	28
Wigan Ath	20	7	4	9	36	34	2	25
Rochdale	20	6	4	10	29	35	–6	22
Chesterfield	20	5	2	13	22	58	–36	17
Halifax T	20	4	3	13	23	45	–22	15
Carlisle U	20	3	5	12	17	39	–22	14

FA PREMIER RESERVE LEAGUE 2001–02

FA PREMIER RESERVE LEAGUE – NORTH SECTION

	P	W	D	L	F	A	GD	Pts
Manchester U	24	12	7	5	47	28	+19	43
Newcastle U	24	13	3	8	46	28	+18	42
Middlesbrough	24	12	6	6	39	28	+11	42
Sunderland	24	12	4	8	43	28	+15	40
Bolton W	24	12	3	9	45	40	+5	39
Manchester C	24	10	7	7	40	28	+12	37
Blackburn R	24	11	4	9	41	30	+11	37
Leeds U	24	10	4	10	25	33	–8	34
Liverpool	24	9	6	9	56	52	+4	33
Everton	24	8	8	8	30	30	0	32
Aston Villa	24	7	4	13	26	49	–23	25
Bradford C	24	5	6	13	27	56	–29	21
Sheffield W	24	2	4	18	26	61	–35	10

Leading Appearances

Bewers (Aston Villa)	24
Pilkington (Everton)	24
Greer (Blackburn R)	23
McLeod (Everton)	23
Hudson (Middlesbrough)	23
Bellion (Sunderland)	23
Smith (Aston Villa)	22
O'Brien (Blackburn R)	22
Shuker (Manchester C)	22
Kerr (Newcastle U)	22
Byrne (Sunderland)	22
Kyle (Sunderland)	22

Leading Goalscorers

Mellor (Liverpool)	15
Kyle (Sunderland)	11
Windass (Middlesbrough)	10
Holdsworth (Bolton W)	9
Killen (Manchester C)	9
Lua-Lua (Newcastle U)	9
Chadwick (Everton)	8
Webber (Manchester U)	8
Ostenstad (Blackburn R)	7
Shuker (Manchester C)	7

HIGHEST ATTENDANCE 9028
Sunderland v Newcastle U

	Aston Villa	Blackburn R	Bolton W	Bradford C	Everton	Leeds U	Liverpool	Manchester C	Manchester U	Middlesbrough	Newcastle U	Sheffield W	Sunderland
Aston Villa	—	1-0	3-1	2-0	5-1	0-2	2-2	1-1	1-0	0-3	1-0	2-1	0-1
Blackburn R	5-0	—	1-1	3-1	0-0	4-0	4-3	0-1	1-3	1-2	0-1	2-1	1-0
Bolton W	2-1	1-2	—	3-3	2-1	1-1	2-1	0-1	0-3	3-0	1-1	6-2	1-4
Bradford C	4-1	1-0	0-2	—	1-2	0-3	1-3	0-1	2-7	1-1	1-2	3-3	1-1
Everton	1-1	3-0	2-1	2-2	—	2-0	0-1	1-1	1-3	1-0	1-0	1-1	2-0
Leeds U	2-2	0-5	0-2	0-1	1-0	—	1-1	1-2	0-2	0-0	1-0	1-1	1-3
Liverpool	4-2	2-2	4-2	7-1	1-1	1-2	—	2-2	1-1	3-4	3-2	4-2	2-1
Manchester C	2-0	4-1	1-2	4-0	1-3	3-4	6-0	—	1-1	0-0	0-1	2-3	3-2
Manchester U	1-0	1-2	2-4	1-1	2-1	1-2	3-2	1-1	—	1-0	0-0	5-1	3-0
Middlesbrough	1-0	0-3	1-2	3-0	1-0	1-0	4-3	1-1	1-2	—	1-2	4-1	2-1
Newcastle U	6-1	4-0	2-1	5-0	1-1	0-1	4-2	2-0	5-2	1-4	—	1-1	2-4
Sheffield W	2-0	0-4	1-3	0-2	1-1	0-1	1-2	0-1	1-3	1-2	0-2	—	0-2
Sunderland	7-0	0-0	3-1	0-1	4-2	2-0	2-1	1-0	0-0	1-1	0-2	4-2	—

Manchester United League appearances (includes playing substitutes): Blomqvist 1; Brown 3; Butt 3; Carroll 8; Chadwick 7; Clegg M 10; Clegg S 1; Cole 1; Colkin 1; Davis 18; Djordjic 18; Fletcher 1; Fortune 13; Forlan 2; Fox 7; Irwin 4; Johnsen 1; Lynch 4; May 11; McDermott 3; Muirhead 9; Nardiello 19; Neville P 3; O'Shea 10; Pugh 12; Rankin 7; Rachubka 4; Richardson 5; Roche 18; Sampson 2; Sims 1; Solskjaer 2; Steele 1; Stewart 18; Tate 7; Tierney 19; Timm 2; Van der Gouw 7; Wallwork 17; Webber 16; Williams B 3; Williams M 10; Wood 5; Yorke 8.

Goals: Webber 8, Davis 6, Fortune 4, Chadwick 3, Wallwork 3, Yorke 3, Forlan 2, May 2, Muirhead 2, Nardiello 2, Pugh 2, Stewart 2, Djordjic 1, Lynch 1, O'Shea 1, Richardson 1, Solskjaer 1, Timm 1, Wood 1, own goal 1.

FA PREMIER RESERVE LEAGUE – SOUTH SECTION

	P	W	D	L	F	A	GD	Pts
Ipswich T	26	17	5	4	54	26	+28	56
Arsenal	26	15	5	6	49	27	+22	50
Derby Co	26	15	5	6	47	31	+16	50
Fulham	26	14	5	7	54	33	+21	47
Southampton	26	10	6	10	35	30	+5	36
West Ham U	26	9	7	10	39	32	+7	34
Charlton Ath	26	9	7	10	37	41	–4	34
Tottenham H	26	10	4	12	29	38	–9	34
Chelsea	26	9	7	10	28	40	–12	34
Nottingham F	26	9	5	12	28	40	–12	32
Leicester C	26	7	8	11	32	44	–12	29
Wimbledon	26	8	3	15	34	52	–18	27
Coventry C	26	6	7	13	29	42	–13	25
Watford	26	4	5	15	30	51	–21	17

Leading Appearances

Collis (Charlton Ath)	26
Juan (Arsenal)	25
Bolder (Derby Co)	24
Godfrey (Watford)	24
Riza (West Ham U)	24
Heath (Leicester C)	23
MacDonald (Southampton)	23
Neill (Wimbledon)	23
Pead (Coventry C)	23
Swonnell (Watford)	23
Willock (Fulham)	23

Leading Goalscorers

Bent D (Ipswich T)	21
Cole (Chelsea)	10
Nowland (Wimbledon)	9
Aliadiere (Arsenal)	8
Bolder (Derby Co)	8
Willock (Fulham)	8
Ambrose (Ipswich T)	7
Foley (Watford)	7
Morris (Derby Co)	7
Riza (West Ham U)	7
Robinson (Wimbledon)	7

HIGHEST ATTENDANCE 10,025
Southampton v Arsenal

	Arsenal	Charlton Ath	Chelsea	Coventry C	Derby Co	Fulham	Ipswich T	Leicester C	Nottingham F	Southampton	Tottenham H	Watford	West Ham U	Wimbledon
Arsenal	—	0-0	5-0	0-0	0-1	1-0	2-3	3-1	0-1	4-0	2-2	2-1	2-1	
Charlton Ath	1-4	—	0-1	1-0	0-1	3-3	2-3	3-2	0-3	3-1	3-0	0-2	2-1	2-1
Chelsea	0-4	3-1	—	1-0	1-1	1-1	1-2	0-1	0-1	0-3	0-2	1-1	2-1	1-1
Coventry C	3-2	1-2	0-0	—	2-2	1-3	0-1	1-0	2-3	0-2	0-1	0-3	2-2	2-1
Derby Co	5-0	3-1	5-1	3-2	—	2-0	0-3	2-0	0-1	2-1	2-0	4-1	3-2	2-1
Fulham	0-2	1-1	1-0	1-2	4-2	—	2-0	4-0	3-0	1-2	3-1	2-0	3-1	3-0
Ipswich T	2-1	0-1	4-0	4-1	2-1	3-3	—	2-0	0-1	2-0	2-0	3-1	3-2	6-1
Leicester C	1-1	2-2	0-0	1-1	1-0	2-5	0-1	—	5-1	1-1	2-1	0-0	0-3	3-2
Nottingham F	1-2	1-0	1-0	1-1	2-2	0-4	2-1	2-1	—	0-0	1-0	4-2	2-1	1-2
Southampton	1-0	1-0	3-3	4-1	0-1	1-1	2-4	2-2	1-0	—	1-0	0-3	0-0	0-2
Tottenham H	1-4	2-1	2-2	3-2	1-2	2-1	0-0	2-1	1-0	0-0	—	2-1	2-2	0-0
Watford	1-1	0-1	1-1	2-1	5-2	0-1	0-1	2-2	2-0	1-0		—	1-3	4-1
West Ham U	1-2	0-1	1-0	1-1	2-1	1-2	1-2	0-1	2-2	0-0	2-1	0-1	—	2-0
Wimbledon	0-2	3-4	1-2	0-1	2-1	1-2	4-2	1-0	0-4					—

Ipswich Town League appearances (includes playing substitutes): Abidallah 14; Ambrose 22; Armstrong 2; Ardun 11; Beevers 14; Bent D 22; Bloomfield 15; Bramble 6; Branagan 4; Brown 8; Burton 4; Clapham 2; Counago 12; Croft 13; Dickinson 7; Gaardso 16; Graaven 2; Hogg 3; Karic 3; Le Pen 13; Logan 12; Magilton 3; Marshall 7; McGreal 2; Miller J 19; Miller T 13; Naylor 4; Nicholls 21; Peralta 4; Price 5; Reuser 7; Richards 12; Robinson 4; Salmon 10; Snowdon 10; Stewart 1; Venus 2; Westlake 11; Wilnis 14.

Goals: Bent D 21, Ambrose 7, Counago 4, Reuser 4, Logan 3, Peralta 3, Le Pen 2, Miller T 2, Robinson 2, Armstrong 1, Dickinson 1, Gaardso 1, McGreal 1, Miller J 1, Nicholls 1.

FA ACADEMY UNDER-17 LEAGUE 2001–02

Group A	P	W	D	L	F	A	GD	Pts
Tottenham H	24	13	7	4	38	20	+18	46
Arsenal	24	13	4	7	48	25	+23	43
Crystal Palace	24	11	4	9	43	44	−1	37
Charlton Ath	24	7	7	10	36	39	−3	28
Wimbledon	24	7	5	12	31	41	−10	26
Southampton	24	7	4	13	30	39	−9	25
Millwall	24	7	4	13	33	49	−16	25
Bristol C	24	6	5	13	32	51	−19	23
Reading	24	7	2	15	25	51	−26	23

Group B	P	W	D	L	F	A	GD	Pts
Aston Villa	22	15	4	3	53	18	+35	49
Birmingham C	22	12	3	7	45	23	+22	39
Leicester C	22	11	4	7	37	31	+6	37
West Ham U	22	10	5	7	28	25	+3	35
Ipswich T	22	10	3	9	43	38	+5	33
Watford	22	8	4	10	24	33	−9	28
Wolverhampton W	22	5	6	11	21	40	−19	21
Fulham	22	5	5	12	29	61	−32	20

Group C	P	W	D	L	F	A	GD	Pts
Liverpool	24	19	5	0	75	16	+59	62
Blackburn R	24	13	8	3	53	21	+32	47
Manchester U	24	13	6	5	68	27	+41	45
Coventry C	24	10	6	8	37	38	−1	36
Crewe Alex	24	10	5	9	28	36	−8	35
Manchester C	24	7	9	8	37	40	−3	30
Bolton W	24	5	2	17	33	60	−27	17
Everton	24	4	4	16	18	47	−29	16
Wrexham	24	2	5	17	19	71	−52	11

Group D	P	W	D	L	F	A	GD	Pts
Newcastle U	24	15	4	5	61	25	+36	49
Sunderland	24	12	10	2	49	24	+25	46
Leeds U	24	11	7	6	39	24	+15	40
Derby Co	24	10	5	9	52	38	+14	35
Sheffield U	24	10	5	9	36	39	−3	35
Nottingham F	24	11	2	11	33	44	−11	35
Barnsley	24	10	2	12	34	50	−16	32
Middlesbrough	24	9	2	13	24	32	−8	29
Sheffield W	24	3	5	16	29	61	−32	14

UNDER-17 PLAY-OFFS

Group 1	P	W	D	L	F	A	GD	Pts
Tottenham H	2	1	1	0	3	2	+1	4
Coventry C	2	1	0	1	3	2	+1	3
Barnsley	2	0	1	1	2	4	−2	1

Group 2	P	W	D	L	F	A	GD	Pts
Arsenal	3	3	0	0	7	2	+5	9
Nottingham F	3	1	1	1	5	3	+2	4
West Ham U	3	1	1	1	4	4	0	4
Everton	3	0	0	3	1	8	−7	0

Group 3	P	W	D	L	F	A	GD	Pts
Aston Villa	3	2	1	0	8	4	+4	7
Middlesbrough	3	1	2	0	6	3	+3	5
Manchester C	3	1	1	1	5	5	0	4
Charlton Ath	3	0	0	3	3	10	−7	0

Group 4	P	W	D	L	F	A	GD	Pts
Manchester U	3	2	1	0	9	1	+8	7
Birmingham C	3	1	1	1	3	3	0	4
Southampton	3	1	0	2	1	3	−2	3
Sheffield W	3	1	0	2	2	8	−6	3

Group 5	P	W	D	L	F	A	GD	Pts
Sheffield U	3	2	0	1	4	2	+2	6
Liverpool	3	1	2	0	2	0	+2	5

Group 5 cont	P	W	D	L	F	A	GD	Pts
Reading	3	1	1	1	2	4	−2	4
Leicester C	3	0	1	2	1	3	−2	1

Group 6	P	W	D	L	F	A	GD	Pts
Blackburn R	3	2	1	0	6	2	+4	7
Wolverhampton W	3	2	0	1	4	2	+2	6
Derby Co	3	1	1	1	4	2	+2	4
Millwall	3	0	0	3	1	9	−8	0

Group 7	P	W	D	L	F	A	GD	Pts
Newcastle U	3	3	0	0	12	1	+11	9
Crewe Alex	3	1	1	1	8	4	+4	4
Wimbledon	3	1	0	2	5	7	−2	3
Fulham	3	0	1	2	4	9	−5	1

Group 8	P	W	D	L	F	A	GD	Pts
Ipswich T	3	2	1	0	6	2	+4	7
Bolton W	3	2	0	1	6	4	+2	6
Sunderland	3	1	0	2	2	5	−3	3
Bristol C	3	0	1	2	1	4	−3	1

Group 9	P	W	D	L	F	A	GD	Pts
Leeds U	3	2	1	0	8	1	+7	7
Crystal Palace	3	1	2	0	9	5	+4	5
Watford	3	1	1	1	7	5	+2	4
Wrexham	3	0	0	3	0	13	−13	0

QUARTER-FINALS
Arsenal 1, Newcastle U 2
Tottenham H 1, Sheffield U 2
Aston Villa 1, Leeds U 2
Manchester U 2, Ipswich T 1

SEMI-FINALS
Sheffield U 2, Newcastle U 3
Leeds U 0, Manchester U 2

FINAL (two legs)
Manchester U 2, Newcastle U 3
Newcastle U 2, Manchester U 0

FA ACADEMY UNDER-19 LEAGUE 2001–02

Group A	P	W	D	L	F	A	GD	Pts
Arsenal	27	17	7	3	63	22	+41	58
Chelsea	27	12	10	5	54	37	+17	46
Crystal Palace	27	11	7	9	45	35	+10	40
Tottenham H	27	10	9	8	43	28	+15	39
Charlton Ath	27	10	4	13	45	48	−3	34
Millwall	27	9	7	11	37	45	−8	34
Southampton	27	10	2	15	42	51	−9	32
Bristol C	27	9	5	13	39	59	−20	32
Wimbledon	27	6	9	12	28	39	−11	27
Reading	27	5	5	17	31	61	−30	20

Group B	P	W	D	L	F	A	GD	Pts
Ipswich T	26	17	7	2	69	38	+31	58
West Ham U	26	12	8	6	45	37	+8	44
Birmingham C	26	12	5	9	48	44	+4	41
Fulham	26	9	6	11	44	47	−3	33
Wolverhampton W	26	8	8	10	24	29	−5	32
Leicester C	26	8	7	11	33	37	−4	31
Norwich C	26	8	5	13	41	64	−23	29
Aston Villa	26	6	10	10	42	50	−8	28
Watford	26	7	7	12	28	44	−16	28

Group C	P	W	D	L	F	A	GD	Pts
Liverpool	28	18	7	3	74	37	+37	61
Manchester U	28	19	4	5	62	36	+26	61
Manchester C	28	15	5	8	53	38	+15	50
Crewe Alex	28	14	7	7	55	47	+8	49
Coventry C	28	12	6	10	49	37	+12	42
Everton	28	11	9	8	43	31	+12	42
Blackburn R	28	8	9	11	45	43	+2	33
Stoke C	28	7	6	15	40	46	−6	27
Bolton W	28	5	6	17	39	59	−20	21
Wrexham	28	1	2	25	25	103	−78	5

Group D	P	W	D	L	F	A	GD	Pts
Nottingham F	28	20	6	2	61	21	+40	66
Derby Co	28	16	2	10	58	33	+25	50
Newcastle U	28	14	5	9	72	42	+30	47
Middlesbrough	28	13	8	7	37	27	+10	47
Leeds U	28	13	6	9	52	45	+7	45
Sunderland	28	7	13	8	25	28	−3	34
Barnsley	28	10	3	15	36	56	−20	33
Sheffield U	28	6	8	14	36	55	−19	26
Huddersfield T	28	7	4	17	35	70	−35	25
Sheffield W	28	5	6	17	32	61	−29	21

UNDER-19 PLAY-OFFS

SEMI-FINALS
Ipswich T 1, Arsenal 2
Nottingham F 1, Liverpool 2

FINAL (two legs)
Liverpool 1, Arsenal 5
Arsenal 2, Liverpool 3

NON-LEAGUE TABLES 2001–02

DORSET COMBINATION

	P	W	D	L	F	A	Pts
Hamworthy Recreation	34	25	5	4	79	27	80
Sherborne Town	34	23	6	5	66	34	75
Holt United	34	22	5	7	83	41	71
Shaftesbury	34	21	8	5	74	37	71
Hamworthy United (–3)	34	21	6	7	85	42	66
Dorchester Town Reserves	34	21	2	11	88	50	65
Gillingham Town	34	19	6	9	59	31	63
Westland Sports	34	19	4	11	82	55	61
Bournemouth Sports (–6)	34	12	7	15	57	61	37
Weymouth Sports	34	8	9	17	46	77	33
Bridport Reserves	34	9	5	20	35	68	32
Blandford United	34	9	5	20	29	73	32
Cobham Sports	34	7	10	17	38	71	31
Sturminster Newton United	34	7	7	20	48	70	28
Wareham Rangers (–3)	34	7	9	18	44	73	27
Witchampton United	34	6	9	19	38	79	27
Allendale	34	6	8	20	46	73	26
Stourpaine	34	7	3	24	42	77	24

HAMPSHIRE LEAGUE

	P	W	D	L	F	A	Pts
Alton Town	40	31	4	5	95	35	97
East Cowes Victoria (–3)	40	30	5	5	125	52	92
Winchester City	40	28	6	6	132	35	90
Vosper Thorneycroft	40	25	7	8	86	35	82
Poole Town	40	24	8	8	86	49	80
Locksheath	40	23	3	14	90	61	72
Liss Athletic	40	21	5	14	81	84	68
Brading Town	40	18	10	12	83	61	64
Horndean (+3)	40	17	7	16	78	66	61
Ringwood Town	40	16	11	13	67	63	59
Portsmouth RN	40	15	10	15	69	59	55
Stockbridge	40	15	6	19	65	80	51
Pirelli General	40	13	7	20	71	100	46
Lymington Town	40	12	9	19	55	80	45
Petersfield Town	40	11	6	23	56	78	39
Hythe & Dibden	40	10	8	22	49	77	38
Bishops Waltham Town	40	10	7	23	40	79	37
Andover New Street	40	10	6	24	55	86	36
Esso Fawley	40	9	4	27	53	111	31
Amesbury Town	40	8	6	26	46	114	30
AFC Aldermaston	40	5	3	32	44	121	18

EXPRESS & STAR WEST MIDLANDS LEAGUE

Premier	P	W	D	L	F	A	Pts
Causeway United	46	29	12	5	107	55	99
Tividale (–3)	46	27	10	9	94	57	88
Wolverhampton Casuals	46	26	8	12	89	69	86
Little Drayton Rangers	46	23	13	10	95	57	82
Westfields	46	24	9	13	89	53	81
Ledbury Town	46	26	3	17	104	85	81
Star	46	24	8	14	91	65	80
Kington Town	46	21	14	11	77	41	77
Malvern Town	46	21	11	14	88	55	74
Heath Hayes	46	19	13	14	60	53	70
Brierley & Hagley	46	18	15	13	75	60	69
Tipton Town	46	19	11	16	74	50	68
Wellington	46	18	11	17	63	69	65
Lye Town	46	16	15	15	59	47	63
Ettingshall Holy Trinity	46	17	12	17	68	73	63
Wolverhampton United	46	15	11	20	79	81	56
Bustleholme	46	15	10	21	79	93	55
Shawbury United	46	13	14	19	69	83	53
Darlaston Town	46	14	10	22	69	100	52
Bromyard Town	46	11	10	25	73	97	43
Gornal Athletic	46	7	15	24	54	112	36
Smethwick Rangers	46	11	3	32	70	147	36
Walsall Wood	46	7	12	27	52	96	33
Dudley Town	46	3	6	37	42	122	15

MIDLAND COMBINATION

	P	W	D	L	F	A	Pts
Grosvenor Park	42	31	4	7	111	39	97
Coventry Sphinx	42	27	13	2	91	41	94
Nuneaton Griff	42	26	6	10	98	54	84
Romulus	42	22	7	13	88	59	73
Feckenham	42	20	11	11	78	64	71
Pershore Town	42	20	7	15	86	68	67
West Midlands Police	42	18	7	17	69	75	61
Coventry Marconi	42	16	12	14	74	66	60
Massey Ferguson	42	17	9	16	82	81	60
Coleshill Town	42	18	5	19	76	68	59
Shirley Town	42	18	5	19	97	102	59
Handsworth Continental Star	42	16	9	17	76	75	57
Highgate United	42	13	12	17	70	75	51
Kings Heath	42	14	9	19	62	71	51
Meir KA	42	13	11	18	64	71	50
Handrahan Timbers	42	12	13	17	49	66	49
Cheslyn Hay	42	14	6	22	51	83	48
County Sports	42	11	13	18	64	108	46
Bolehall Swifts	42	11	11	20	68	84	44
Alvechurch	42	10	10	22	58	79	40
Alveston	42	11	5	26	56	89	38
Southam United	42	8	7	27	52	102	31

MIDLAND ALLIANCE

	P	W	D	L	F	A	Pts
Stourbridge	42	27	7	8	82	39	88
Bromsgrove Rovers	42	26	9	7	94	41	87
Wednesfield	42	24	9	9	73	39	81
Stratford Town	42	24	7	11	81	49	79
Rushall Olympic	42	22	11	9	81	50	77
Oadby Town	42	21	12	9	78	62	75
Quorn	42	20	10	12	76	55	70
Barwell	42	15	17	10	67	44	62
Studley BKL	42	16	12	14	76	57	60
Ludlow Town	42	15	14	13	58	53	59
Bridgnorth Town	42	18	5	19	74	73	59
Willenhall Town	42	16	9	17	65	62	57
Boldmere St Michaels	42	15	11	16	43	51	56
Halesowen Harriers	42	16	8	18	56	69	56
Paget Rangers	42	10	19	13	58	55	49
Stafford Town	42	13	6	23	59	88	45
Pelsall Villa	42	10	12	20	39	70	42
Chasetown	42	9	13	20	43	74	40
Shifnal Town	42	9	10	23	36	77	37
Knypersley Victoria	42	10	5	27	51	82	35
Oldbury United	42	7	11	24	39	77	32
Cradley Town	42	5	11	26	36	98	26

COMBINED COUNTIES LEAGUE

	P	W	D	L	F	A	Pts
AFC Wallingford	42	33	5	4	134	39	104
Ash United	42	31	7	4	137	44	100
Chipstead	42	24	8	10	90	55	80
Bedfont	42	23	8	11	80	58	77
Withdean 2000	42	21	13	8	84	52	76
Hartley Wintney	42	21	9	12	109	77	72
Raynes Park Vale (+2)	42	18	13	11	79	56	69
Southall	41	20	8	13	97	77	68
Walton Casuals	42	20	7	15	88	63	67
Feltham	42	18	10	14	77	64	64
Chessington & Hook	42	16	9	17	81	73	57
Westfield	42	15	12	15	69	61	57
Sandhurst Town	42	16	6	20	73	74	54
Farnham Town (+3)	41	14	6	21	54	75	51
Cove (–2)	42	15	6	21	72	86	49
Chessington United	42	13	8	21	60	79	47
Godalming & Guildford	42	12	9	21	57	88	45
Cobham	42	12	7	23	62	76	43
Viking Greenford (+2)	42	11	7	24	55	106	42
Merstham	42	9	8	25	59	106	35
Reading Town	42	8	5	29	47	115	29
Cranleigh	42	4	3	35	26	166	15

SUSSEX LEAGUE

Division One

	P	W	D	L	F	A	Pts
urgess Hill Town	38	28	6	4	100	33	90
ingmer	38	23	5	10	86	46	74
hichester City United	38	21	4	13	72	66	67
elsey	38	19	9	10	69	54	66
dley United	38	18	11	9	70	36	65
ailsham Town	38	20	2	16	62	55	62
hree Bridges	38	18	7	13	82	61	61
agham	38	17	8	13	80	67	59
rundel	38	17	6	15	52	63	57
orsham YMCA	38	16	6	16	74	58	54
assocks	38	15	8	15	57	65	53
eacehaven & Telscombe	38	15	7	16	58	63	52
hitehawk	38	14	9	15	69	55	51
ick	38	15	3	20	56	64	48
edhill	38	12	5	21	65	83	41
ttlehampton Town	38	11	7	20	64	84	40
dlesham	38	11	7	20	55	78	40
outhwick	38	10	9	19	44	76	39
astbourne United	38	9	10	19	48	67	37
altdean United	38	3	7	28	40	129	16

Division Two

	P	W	D	L	F	A	Pts
ye & Iden United	34	26	3	5	102	33	81
horeham	34	22	7	5	74	32	73
ast Preston	34	20	9	5	89	48	69
astbourne Town	34	20	5	9	84	39	65
ast Grinstead Town	34	18	10	6	70	40	64
ancing	34	13	10	11	58	48	49
roadbridge Heath	34	14	7	13	63	54	49
orthing United	34	13	9	12	65	63	48
eaford	34	13	8	13	65	63	47
rawley Down	34	12	9	13	58	50	45
estfield	34	13	6	15	65	59	45
akwood	34	12	8	14	45	55	44
ealden	34	13	4	17	55	68	43
ile Oak	34	11	4	19	42	70	37
inewater Association	34	10	6	18	53	91	36
ving SC	34	10	5	19	40	78	35
orrington	34	4	6	24	31	74	18
osham	34	2	4	28	31	125	10

DEVON LEAGUE

	P	W	D	L	F	A	Pts
artmouth	38	28	7	3	125	45	91
ewton Abbot	38	25	8	5	107	45	83
ospers Oak Villa	38	24	4	10	82	38	76
ewton Abbot Spurs	38	24	1	13	76	61	73
ybridge Town	38	22	6	10	107	61	72
uckland Athletic	38	19	9	10	91	59	66
udleigh Salterton	38	20	2	16	70	87	62
opsham Town (–3)	38	18	7	13	95	72	58
ttery St Mary	38	16	7	15	77	52	55
lphington	38	15	8	15	65	86	53
eavitree United	38	16	4	18	71	76	52
ullompton Rangers	38	14	7	17	64	67	49
xeter Civil Service	38	13	9	16	60	72	48
lburton Villa	38	14	6	18	64	82	48
ymstock United	38	13	7	18	61	71	46
artington SC	38	11	9	18	63	76	42
oke Gabriel	38	10	4	24	63	104	34
rediton United	38	9	5	24	52	74	32
ppledore	38	8	7	23	57	84	31
uckfastleigh Rangers (–3)	38	2	1	35	32	170	4

MINERVA SPARTAN SOUTH MIDLANDS LEAGUE

Premier Division

	P	W	D	L	F	A	Pts
ondon Colney	38	28	8	2	119	32	92
etchworth	38	25	7	6	105	45	82
anwell Town	38	25	6	7	114	64	81
ilton Keynes City	38	22	9	7	76	39	75
t Margaretsbury	38	20	8	10	74	55	68
rook House	38	19	7	12	89	63	64
unstable Town	38	18	8	12	74	54	62
oyston Town	38	15	13	10	82	58	58
iggleswade Town	38	16	9	13	73	64	57
eaconsfield SYCOB	38	15	10	13	84	52	55
omersett Ambury V&E	38	16	5	17	75	60	53
aringey Borough	38	13	9	16	53	74	48
otters Bar Town	38	14	5	19	71	77	47
oddesdon Town	38	12	8	18	50	56	44
Holmer Green	38	12	6	20	59	98	42
Hillingdon Borough	38	11	6	21	63	76	39
Ruislip Manor	38	9	6	23	47	82	33
Bedford United	38	8	7	23	38	114	31
Brache Sparta	38	7	4	27	45	109	25
New Bradwell St Peter	38	3	3	32	25	144	12

NORTH WEST COUNTIES LEAGUE

Division One

	P	W	D	L	F	A	Pts
Kidsgrove Athletic	44	31	9	4	125	47	102
Prescot Cables	44	29	10	5	110	42	97
Salford City	44	29	10	5	91	40	97
St Helens Town	44	28	6	10	101	44	90
Newcastle Town	44	22	11	11	97	66	77
Clitheroe	44	22	10	12	73	53	76
Winsford United	44	19	12	13	72	71	69
Mossley	44	18	14	12	82	63	68
Skelmersdale United	44	19	5	20	87	89	62
Woodley Sports	44	16	12	16	58	65	60
Warrington Town	44	16	11	17	78	72	59
Ramsbottom United	44	15	10	19	75	73	55
Curzon Ashton	44	16	7	21	74	72	55
Fleetwood Freeport	44	13	13	18	70	86	52
Nantwich Town	44	12	15	17	63	90	51
Congleton Town	44	13	11	20	71	79	50
Atherton Collieries	44	13	8	23	66	91	47
Abbey Hey	44	12	11	21	62	101	47
Glossop North End	44	13	7	24	78	105	46
Atherton LR	44	11	11	22	62	88	44
Flixton	44	11	9	24	61	112	42
Maine Road	44	8	7	29	68	115	31
Great Harwood Town	44	5	11	28	39	99	26

Division Two

	P	W	D	L	F	A	Pts
Stand Athletic	40	30	5	5	110	47	95
Alsager	40	24	9	7	77	31	81
Squires Gate	40	24	9	7	103	60	81
Stone Dominoes	40	25	3	12	71	40	78
Formby	40	21	14	5	76	39	77
Bootle	40	19	7	14	82	64	64
Norton United	40	19	7	14	56	51	64
Blackpool Mechanics	40	18	9	13	69	48	63
Nelson	40	18	9	13	63	63	63
Leek CSOB	40	17	8	15	62	65	59
Darwen	40	15	10	15	77	74	55
Bacup Borough	40	13	13	14	52	66	52
Padiham	40	14	8	18	69	66	50
Colne	40	14	8	18	61	72	50
Chadderton	40	15	5	20	65	81	50
Ashton Town	40	13	6	21	65	85	45
Cheadle Town	40	10	8	22	67	85	38
Castleton Gabriels	40	10	3	27	61	95	33
Holker Old Boys	40	7	9	24	43	79	30
Daisy Hill	40	8	4	28	49	114	28
Oldham Town	40	7	4	29	50	113	25

JEWSON EASTERN COUNTIES LEAGUE

Premier Division

	P	W	D	L	F	A	Pts
AFC Sudbury	42	32	4	6	139	54	100
Wroxham	42	29	6	7	113	47	93
Lowestoft Town	42	24	8	10	106	55	80
Clacton Town	42	20	16	6	83	41	76
Gorleston	42	21	8	13	78	69	71
Stowmarket Town	42	20	10	12	75	64	70
Bury Town	42	19	7	16	70	53	64
Woodbridge Town	42	16	14	12	62	61	62
Ely City	42	19	5	18	71	72	62
Maldon Town	42	17	10	15	78	78	61
Mildenhall Town	42	18	7	17	68	68	61
Dereham Town	42	16	7	19	59	64	55
Soham Town Rangers (–1)	42	16	8	18	68	80	55
Fakenham Town	42	13	13	16	59	66	52
Tiptree United	42	13	10	19	53	69	49
Diss Town	42	14	7	21	66	84	49
Great Yarmouth Town	42	13	9	20	41	65	48
Harwich & Parkeston	42	13	5	24	46	81	44
Newmarket Town	42	10	13	19	65	89	43
Ipswich Wanderers	42	11	8	23	53	69	41
Felixstowe & Walton	42	7	9	26	38	88	30
Swaffham Town	42	7	4	31	39	113	25

Division One

	P	W	D	L	F	A	Pts
Norwich United	36	25	7	4	83	22	82
Histon Reserves	36	25	4	7	99	34	79
Haverhill Rovers	36	23	7	6	85	31	76
Leiston	36	24	4	8	74	36	76
Needham Market	36	22	5	9	79	42	71
King's Lynn Reserves	36	19	8	9	84	44	65
Stanway Rovers	36	18	5	13	72	52	59
Somersham Town	36	15	8	13	51	60	53
Wisbech Town Reserves	36	15	5	16	58	64	50
Cambridge City Reserves	36	13	7	16	79	67	46
Cornard United	36	14	3	19	60	73	45
Whitton United	36	12	6	18	49	58	42
Halstead Town	36	11	8	17	53	68	41
Hadleigh United	36	11	8	17	51	72	41
Downham Town	36	11	5	20	60	82	38
Warboys Town	36	9	7	20	38	75	34
Brightlingsea United	36	9	4	23	49	105	31
Thetford Town	36	7	6	23	37	97	27
March Town United	36	3	5	28	45	124	14

REDFERN REMOVERS
CENTRAL MIDLANDS LEAGUE

Supreme Division

	P	W	D	L	F	A	Pts
Shirebrook Town	38	29	3	6	105	25	90
Hucknall Rolls Royce	38	26	8	4	94	39	86
Long Eaton United	38	26	6	6	84	39	84
South Normanton Athletic	38	22	6	10	82	51	72
Sneinton	38	20	5	13	73	42	65
Greenwood Meadows	38	19	7	12	79	55	64
Heanor Town	38	18	8	12	69	53	62
North Notts	38	17	9	12	62	53	60
Dunkirk	38	17	6	15	62	70	57
Teversal	38	15	11	12	75	61	56
Sandiacre Town	38	15	7	16	71	68	52
Holbrook	38	15	6	17	70	63	51
Graham Street Prims	38	15	3	20	55	76	48
Askern Welfare	38	12	11	15	59	54	47
Clipstone Welfare	38	11	8	19	45	76	41
Collingham	38	10	9	19	59	63	39
Bottesford Town (–1)	38	10	7	21	41	79	36
Nettleham	38	9	4	25	43	85	31
Kimberley Town	38	3	9	26	27	98	18
Selston	38	3	3	32	37	142	12

NORTHERN COUNTIES EAST LEAGUE

Premier Division

	P	W	D	L	F	A	Pts
Alfreton Town	38	27	5	6	94	36	86
Brigg Town	38	25	5	8	90	46	80
Hallam	38	21	6	11	72	62	69
Pickering Town	38	20	8	10	70	38	68
Harrogate Railway	38	17	10	11	83	61	61
Armthorpe Welfare	38	17	7	14	56	58	58
Selby Town	38	14	12	12	47	47	54
Thackley	38	14	11	13	48	47	53
Sheffield	38	14	10	14	54	62	52
Arnold Town	38	13	10	15	53	55	49
Liversedge	38	14	6	18	59	66	48
Goole AFC	38	13	9	16	43	51	48
Eccleshill United	38	13	9	16	60	72	48
Glapwell	38	12	10	16	66	71	46
Brodsworth MW (–3)	38	13	9	16	68	74	45
Borrowash Victoria	38	10	13	15	49	67	43
Glasshoughton Welfare	38	10	10	18	49	62	40
Denaby United	38	11	5	22	47	78	38
Buxton	38	8	13	17	43	61	37
Garforth Town	38	8	4	26	46	83	28

Division One

	P	W	D	L	F	A	Pts
Gedling Town	30	21	5	4	75	42	68
Bridlington Town	30	20	4	6	73	26	64
Worsborough Bridge	30	18	8	4	70	37	62
Lincoln Moorlands	30	15	6	9	52	41	51
Mickleover Sports	30	16	2	12	51	42	50
Maltby Main	30	15	3	12	54	44	48
Winterton Rangers	30	14	6	10	44	36	48
Rossington Main	30	12	7	11	44	46	43
Hall Road Rangers	30	12	7	11	54	57	43
Hatfield Main	30	10	7	13	50	47	37
Louth United	30	10	5	15	36	46	35
Yorkshire Amateur	30	8	6	16	33	47	30
Tadcaster Albion	30	9	3	18	40	62	30
Parkgate	30	8	3	19	53	80	27
Staveley MW	30	4	12	14	32	60	24
Pontefract Collieries	30	4	4	22	23	71	16

JEWSON WESSEX LEAGUE

	P	W	D	L	F	A
Andover	44	30	6	8	138	53
Fleet Town (–1)	44	29	9	6	107	59
AFC Totton	44	29	7	8	104	50
Gosport Borough	44	26	11	7	101	41
Brockenhurst	44	27	2	15	99	57
Lymington & New Milton (–6)	44	26	6	12	94	47
AFC Newbury	44	22	12	10	87	51
Wimborne Town	44	21	14	9	82	53
Moneyfields	44	23	7	14	98	64
Fareham Town	44	21	13	10	72	54
Bemerton Heath H	44	18	11	15	103	84
Thatcham Town	44	19	8	17	94	77
Eastleigh	44	18	9	17	91	71
Portland United	44	17	8	19	81	66
Christchurch	44	16	7	21	61	80
Cowes Sports	44	15	9	20	66	73
Blackfield & Langley	44	16	5	23	82	121
Bournemouth	44	14	7	23	61	84
BAT Sports	44	13	8	23	46	67
Whitchurch United	44	5	5	34	27	116
Downton	44	5	4	35	42	139
Hamble ASSC	44	4	4	36	33	119
Swanage & Herston	44	3	6	35	31	174

KENT LEAGUE

	P	W	D	L	F	A
Maidstone United	30	20	6	4	72	32
VCD Athletic	30	20	6	4	67	31
Deal Town	30	19	5	6	79	38
Thamesmead Town	30	17	6	7	59	39
Cray Wanderers	30	15	6	9	56	44
Ramsgate	30	13	5	12	57	50
Herne Bay (–3)	30	13	5	12	53	49
Tunbridge Wells	30	10	10	10	45	46
Beckenham Town	30	11	7	12	43	45
Whitstable Town	30	9	9	12	43	51
Lordswood (+3)	30	8	9	13	44	55
Slade Green	30	11	2	17	35	47
Erith Town	30	10	3	17	42	60
Hythe Town	30	8	7	15	31	49
Greenwich Borough	30	5	4	21	31	70
Faversham Town	30	3	6	21	30	81

BRITISH ENERGY
KENT COUNTY LEAGUE

	P	W	D	L	F	A
Bearsted	26	21	4	1	75	16
Sevenoaks Town	26	16	5	5	83	33
Milton Athletic	26	15	8	3	65	27
Stansfield O&BC	26	14	5	7	43	39
New Romney	26	12	3	11	52	50
Beauwater	26	11	4	11	48	48
Wickham Park	26	11	3	12	60	60
Sheerness East	26	10	5	11	38	38
Crockenhill	26	10	5	11	44	45
Snodland	26	8	5	13	38	72
Lydd Town	26	9	1	16	40	60
Greenways	26	7	4	15	36	52
Phoenix Sports	26	7	3	16	38	65
Thames Polytechnic	26	2	3	21	23	78

FORESTERS ESSEX SENIOR LEAGUE

	P	W	D	L	F	A
Leyton	30	24	3	3	75	23
Enfield Town	30	22	3	5	83	28
Burnham Ramblers	30	17	2	11	57	42
Concord Rangers	30	16	2	12	65	51
Southend Manor	30	14	7	9	58	42
Bowers United (–2)	30	13	9	8	70	51
Sawbridgeworth Town	30	13	7	10	59	54
Stansted	30	12	6	12	55	54
Ilford	30	11	5	14	51	49
Basildon United	30	10	7	13	58	64
Saffron Waldon Town	30	10	6	14	40	62
Hullbridge Sports	30	9	6	15	44	76
Barkingside	30	8	8	14	44	50
Brentwood	30	8	6	16	45	53
Eton Manor	30	4	7	19	40	73
Woodford Town	30	5	4	21	29	101

HELLENIC LEAGUE

Premier Division

	P	W	D	L	F	A	Pts
orth Leigh	42	30	8	4	97	36	98
oucester United	42	29	6	7	106	48	93
ate Town	42	24	13	5	105	39	85
bingdon United	42	24	8	10	86	51	80
dcot Town	42	24	6	12	93	56	78
irford Town	42	21	10	11	72	42	73
ackley Town	42	20	9	13	70	55	69
affley Rovers	42	19	11	12	53	61	68
ortwood United	42	20	7	15	67	66	67
shops Cleeve	42	19	8	15	79	51	65
arterton Town	42	18	10	14	71	48	64
antage Town	42	15	10	17	67	65	55
gasus Juniors	42	16	5	21	65	92	53
uthall Town	42	14	9	19	55	66	51
ighworth Town	42	14	7	21	66	77	49
enley Town	42	12	10	20	51	65	46
rencester Academy	42	11	11	20	61	71	44
dmondsbury Town	42	12	6	24	53	84	42
ootton Bassett Town	42	11	9	22	39	75	42
cester Town	42	9	6	27	58	97	33
arrow Hill	42	7	2	33	31	104	23
heltenham Saracens	42	3	9	30	30	126	18

Division One West

	P	W	D	L	F	A	Pts
ook Norton	32	22	8	2	69	21	74
wsey Vale	32	20	5	7	80	39	65
rdley United	32	18	8	6	83	51	62
arton	32	18	4	10	63	52	58
oss Town	32	15	10	7	56	41	55
interbourne United	32	15	9	8	73	41	54
iddle Barton	32	13	8	11	62	64	47
d Woodstock Town	32	11	10	11	47	38	43
rivenham	32	12	6	14	57	63	42
dlington	32	11	8	13	36	38	41
ipping Norton	32	10	7	15	49	68	37
almesbury Victoria	32	8	11	13	49	53	35
asington Sports	32	9	8	15	37	54	35
anfield	32	7	9	16	40	61	30
rencester United	32	8	4	20	36	69	28
eadington Amateurs	32	6	7	19	40	79	25
etcombe	32	3	10	19	42	87	19

Division One East

	P	W	D	L	F	A	Pts
nchampstead	32	20	6	6	73	40	66
ston Clinton	32	19	7	6	76	37	64
S Basingstoke	32	16	7	9	64	53	55
artin Baker Sports	32	15	8	9	68	43	53
nglefield Green	32	16	4	12	64	51	52
ilton United	32	12	13	7	50	37	49
sley Sports	32	14	5	13	53	53	47
restwood	32	13	6	13	58	58	45
enn & Tylers Green	32	12	8	12	56	50	44
ton Wick	32	12	6	14	53	59	42
uarry Nomads	32	12	6	14	54	74	42
rayton Wanderers	32	11	4	17	56	86	37
eppard	32	8	11	13	39	46	35
ayners Lane	32	9	7	16	44	55	34
ounslow Borough	32	8	10	14	55	66	34
nalfont Wasps (-3)	32	6	9	17	44	72	24

EVERARDS BREWERY LEICESTERSHIRE SENIOR LEAGUE

	P	W	D	L	F	A	Pts
oalville Town	34	23	6	5	90	42	75
riar Lane OB	34	21	9	4	88	39	72
hurnby Rangers	34	20	6	8	77	39	66
Andrews SC	34	19	3	12	73	50	60
rby Muxloe SC	34	17	9	8	63	44	60
aby & Whetstone Athletic	34	16	6	12	37	48	54
eicester YMCA	34	15	8	11	51	43	53
olwell Sports	34	15	6	13	63	43	51
stock Welfare	34	14	8	12	52	46	50
ighfield Rangers	34	13	10	11	51	49	49
ownes Sports	34	13	8	13	55	47	47
hurmaston Town	34	12	9	13	59	63	45
listown	34	11	7	16	42	61	40
arrow Town	34	10	9	15	44	50	39
nstey Nomads	34	7	7	20	34	64	28
irstall United	34	6	9	19	28	69	27
ylestone Park OB	34	7	3	24	32	68	24
hringstone United	34	3	5	26	22	94	14

ALBANY NORTHERN LEAGUE

Division One

	P	W	D	L	F	A	Pts
Bedlington Terriers	40	28	8	4	104	35	92
Tow Law Town	40	26	7	7	90	44	85
Dunston Federation	40	22	9	9	86	53	75
Marske United	40	21	8	11	56	48	71
Whitley Bay	40	20	8	12	78	49	68
Durham City	40	19	11	10	87	62	68
West Auckland Town	40	19	11	10	80	57	68
Brandon United	40	17	8	15	68	53	59
Billingham Town	40	16	9	15	67	66	57
Billingham Synthonia	40	15	10	15	79	75	55
Guisborough Town (-3)	40	16	9	15	68	63	54
Jarrow Roofing	40	15	8	17	62	74	53
Peterlee Newtown	40	14	10	16	54	60	52
Chester Le Street	40	14	7	19	63	68	49
Washington Ikeda Hoover	40	13	5	22	54	74	44
Consett	40	11	10	19	60	65	43
Newcastle Blue Star (-3)	40	13	6	21	56	80	42
Morpeth Town	40	10	10	20	48	70	40
Ashington (-3)	40	11	8	21	62	98	38
Thornaby	40	8	5	27	48	96	29
Seaham Red Star (-3)	40	6	5	29	38	118	20

Division Two

	P	W	D	L	F	A	Pts
Shildon	38	28	4	6	135	51	88
Prudhoe Town	38	26	7	5	104	32	85
Esh Winning	38	27	4	7	93	39	85
Penrith	38	26	4	8	101	42	82
Easington Colliery	38	24	5	9	87	47	77
Horden CW	38	21	9	8	87	55	72
Washington Nissan	38	23	3	12	95	68	72
South Shields	38	18	8	12	62	41	62
Northallerton Town	38	17	10	11	59	52	61
Kennek Ryhope CA	38	17	8	13	65	47	59
Crook Town	38	16	6	16	53	60	54
Norton&Stockton Ancients	38	14	7	17	66	71	49
Alnwick Town	38	12	12	14	63	74	48
Hebburn Town	38	12	6	20	52	97	42
Evenwood Town	38	8	5	25	46	96	29
Whickham	38	7	5	26	50	90	26
Willington	38	6	6	26	52	114	24
Murton	38	5	7	26	34	108	22
Eppleton CW (-6)	38	6	6	26	42	91	18
Shotton Comrades	38	4	4	30	45	116	16

EAGLE BITTER UNITED COUNTIES

Premier Division

	P	W	D	L	F	A	Pts
Ford Sports Daventry	40	31	6	3	95	30	99
Holbeach United	40	25	5	10	110	52	80
Cogenhoe United	40	24	8	8	83	57	80
Raunds Town	40	21	11	8	95	54	74
Desborough Town	40	22	8	10	85	48	74
St Neots Town	40	23	4	13	80	47	73
Wootton Blue Cross	40	21	9	10	74	50	72
Boston Town	40	20	8	12	93	50	68
Stotfold	40	20	8	12	75	48	68
Deeping Rangers	40	20	6	14	79	56	66
Yaxley	40	16	11	13	73	57	59
Blackstone	40	16	5	19	57	68	53
Bourne Town	40	15	8	17	57	75	53
S & L Corby	40	14	7	19	61	72	49
Daventry Town	40	13	7	20	59	71	46
Buckingham Town	40	13	7	20	78	91	46
Northampton Spencer	40	12	4	24	52	63	40
Long Buckby	40	8	6	26	43	93	30
Kempston Rovers	40	8	3	29	45	101	27
Bugbrooke St Michael	40	6	6	28	27	110	24
Wellingborough Town	40	1	3	36	29	157	10

Division One

	P	W	D	L	F	A	Pts
Newport Pagnell Town	32	25	3	4	115	36	78
Sileby Rangers	32	20	8	4	90	26	68
Woodford United	32	18	5	9	61	39	59
Wellingborough Whitworths	32	16	10	6	57	46	58
Thrapston Town	32	16	8	8	77	52	56
Higham Town	32	16	8	8	66	44	56
Blisworth	32	15	8	9	50	31	53
Harrowby United	32	16	5	11	65	59	53
Irchester United	32	14	8	10	58	61	50
Olney Town	32	14	7	11	52	44	49
Cottingham	32	10	9	13	57	77	39
Northampton ON Cheneks	32	9	8	15	60	76	35
Eynesbury Rovers	32	9	6	17	43	59	33
Rothwell Corinthians	32	6	11	15	46	54	29
Potton United	32	5	3	24	38	107	18
St Ives Town	32	2	6	24	35	99	12
Burton Park Wanderers	32	2	5	25	33	93	11

SCREWFIX DIRECT WESTERN LEAGUE

Premier Division	P	W	D	L	F	A	Pts
Bideford	38	28	7	3	105	37	91
Taunton Town	38	26	5	7	104	43	83
Brislington	38	24	11	3	72	32	83
Team Bath	38	22	7	9	74	36	73
Devizes Town	38	22	4	12	72	51	70
Dawlish Town	38	21	6	11	86	56	69
Paulton Rovers	38	18	11	9	77	54	65
Bridgwater Town	38	17	9	12	53	45	60
Backwell United	38	16	9	13	56	41	57
Melksham Town	38	15	9	14	47	46	54
Odd Down	38	13	11	14	49	45	50
Barnstaple Town	38	12	8	18	57	66	44
Keynsham Town	38	11	9	18	47	71	42
Elmore	38	10	7	21	47	96	37
Bishop Sutton	38	9	8	21	53	89	35
Yeovil Town Reserves	38	10	4	24	57	86	34
Bridport	38	9	6	23	51	86	33
Welton Rovers	38	7	9	22	46	67	30
Bristol Manor Farm	38	7	8	23	30	80	29
Westbury United	38	7	4	27	35	91	25

Division One	P	W	D	L	F	A	Pts
Frome Town	38	29	5	4	104	22	92
Bath City Res (–3)	38	24	12	2	79	22	81
Exmouth Town	38	23	11	4	84	39	80
Torrington	38	23	5	10	87	49	74
Clyst Rovers	38	18	11	9	73	53	65
Bitton	38	18	9	11	66	55	63
Shepton Mallet Town	38	18	8	12	59	47	62
Street	38	17	10	11	76	58	61
Corsham Town	38	14	13	11	55	48	55
Hallen	38	16	6	16	69	60	54
Chard Town	38	14	8	16	66	59	50
Larkhall Athletic	38	13	8	17	55	71	47
Weston St Johns	38	13	7	18	71	78	46
Ilfracombe	38	14	4	20	59	84	46
Willand Rovers	38	9	15	14	59	58	42
Cadbury Heath	38	10	7	21	55	84	37
Wellington	38	9	8	21	48	89	35
Minehead Town	38	9	5	24	52	90	32
Calne Town	38	6	7	25	40	86	25
Warminster Town	38	2	3	33	35	140	9

CARLSBERG SOUTH WESTERN LEAGUE

	P	W	D	L	F	A	
St Blazey	36	33	3	0	120	25	1
Porthleven	36	27	4	5	105	32	
Holsworthy	36	24	5	7	94	47	
Liskeard Athletic	36	24	4	8	121	54	
Plymouth Parkway	36	21	6	9	88	50	
Penzance	36	16	8	12	79	62	
Tavistock	36	16	7	13	62	52	
Falmouth Town	36	16	6	14	82	86	
Saltash United	36	15	5	16	62	76	
Newquay	36	14	7	15	76	68	
Bodmin Town	36	13	9	14	66	81	
Torpoint Athletic	36	13	6	17	67	74	
Wadebridge Town	36	13	6	17	58	70	
Launceston	36	12	2	22	65	91	
Millbrook	36	8	7	21	44	94	
Callington Town	36	8	5	23	57	112	
Truro City	36	6	10	20	57	82	
Penryn Athletic	36	8	3	25	42	84	
St Austell	36	2	3	31	20	125	

HIGHLAND LEAGUE

	P	W	D	L	F	A	GD
Fraserburgh	28	20	4	4	71	36	35
Deveronvale	28	19	4	5	68	27	41
Buckie Thistle	28	15	8	5	51	27	24
Clachnacuddin	28	13	10	5	60	39	21
Keith	28	14	5	9	57	37	20
Cove Rangers	28	12	7	9	72	60	12
Inverurie	28	12	4	12	48	43	5
Brora Rangers	28	12	4	12	47	55	–8
Huntly	28	11	6	11	46	36	10
Forres Mechanics	28	9	10	9	49	46	3
Lossiemouth	28	9	6	13	23	40	–17
Nairn County	28	6	8	14	44	61	–17
Fort William	28	7	2	19	30	61	–31
Wick Academy	28	5	4	19	20	59	–39
Rothes	28	2	6	20	24	83	–59

AMATEUR FOOTBALL ALLIANCE 2001–02

AFA SENIOR CUP

1st Round Proper
vil Service 4 Glyn Old Boys 5
d Parkonians 5 Mill Hill Village 6
is 3 Old Salvatorians 4
ld Cholmeleians 1 Old Salesians 3
ld Elizabethans 0 Old Isleworthians 1
d Wilsonians 2 Old Bromleians 1
orsemen 1 Albanian 4
ld Grammarians w/o Mill Hill County Old Boys w/d
ale End Athletic 1 Parkfield 0
d Actonians Assn 3 Old Wokingians 0
ast Barnet Old Grammarians 4 William Fitt 0
hertsey Old Salesians 2 Carshalton 0
d Westminster Citz 4 Old Brentwoods 1
roomfield 7 Old Danes 4
Alexandra Park 1 Latymer Old Boys 2
est Wickham 5 Old Westminsters 4
outh Bank Cuaco 4 Old Esthameians 6
ueen Mary College O B 1 HSBC 5
lleyn Old Boys 0 Old Vaughanians 1
ancing Old Boys 0 Old Owens 1
ardinal Manning O B 3 Old Meadonians 4
ld Bealonians 2 Crouch End Vampires 3
B Eagles 1 Bank of England 0
CL Academicals 3 Old Lyonian 0
ld Suttonians 1 Old Reptonians 4
ld Parmiterians 4 Ulysses 1
ensbury 1 Southgate County 4
ld Tiffinians 1 Old Foresters 4
niversity of Herts 2 Old Aloysians 6
erton 1 Polytechnic 4
on Artillery Coy w/o Wood Green O B w/d
ottsborough 12 Wandsworth Borough 1

2nd Round Proper
lyn Old Boys 1 Mill Hill Village 5
ld Salvatorians 3 Old Salesians 2
aet; p – penalties.

Old Isleworthians 0 Old Wilsonians 5
Albanian 1*:3p Old Grammarians 1*:4p
Hale End Athletic 0 Old Actonians Assn 1
E Barnet O Gramm'ns 5 Chertsey Old Salesians 2
Old Westminster Citz 3 Broomfield 0
Latymer Old Boys 2 West Wickham 5
Old Esthameians 3 H S B C 1
Old Vaughanians 1 Old Owens 4
Old Meadonians 2 Crouch End Vampires 1
BB Eagles 1 UCL Academicals 4
Old Reptonians 3 Old Parmiterians 2
Southgate County 1 Old Foresters 0
Old Aloysians 1 Polytechnic 5
Hon Artillery Company 1 Nottsborough 3

3rd Round Proper
Mill Hill Village 5 Old Salvatorians 2
Old Wilsonians 5 Old Grammarians 1*:4p
Old Actonians Assn 4 E Barnet O Gramm'ns 2
Old Westminster Citz 1 West Wickham 4
Old Esthameians 3 Old Owens 1
Old Meadonians 2*:3p UCL Academicals 2*:0p
Old Reptonians 2*:4 Southgate County 2*:2
Polytechnic 2 Nottsborough 0

4th Round Proper
Mill Hill Village 2 Old Wilsonians 3
Old Actonians Assn 2 West Wickham 0
Old Esthameians 1*:6p Old Meadonians 1*:7p
Old Reptonians 2 Polytechnic 4

Semi-finals
Old Wilsonians 0 Old Actonians Assn 1
Old Meadonians 3 Polytechnic 1

Final
Old Actonians Assn 1*:2p Old Meadonians 1*:4p

OTHER AFA CUP FINALS

ssex Senior
ale End Athletic 5 Old Parmiterians 3
iddlesex Senior
olytechnic 3 Old Actonians Assn 1
urrey Senior
SBC 2 Carshalton 0
ntermediate
ld Aloysians Res 1* Old Owens Res 0*
anior
ld Aloysians 3rd 0 Old Challoners Res 1
inor
at'l Westmin'r Bank 4th 0 Old Tenisonians 4th 3
eterans
inchmore Hill 2 Old Parmiterians 1
pen Veterans
enford Senior 4 Old Parmiterians 2
reenland
ld Ignatians 4 Old Wokingians 0
ssex Intermediate
ld Buckwellians Res 0 Hale End Athletic Res 5
ent Intermediate
P Morgan 1st 2 Dresdner Kleinwort Wasserstein 1st 3
iddlesex Intermediate
ld Hamptonians 3rd 1 BB Eagles Res 2
urrey Intermediate
ottsborough Res 3 Carshalton Res 2
enior Novets
. Finchleians 5th 1 Civil Service 5th 3
ntermediate Novets
orsemen 6th 2 Old Actonians Assn 6th 6
anior Novets
utcasts 1st 3* Old Actonians 8th 2*

YOUTH Saturday
U-18
Battersea Park Rangers 4 Young Parmiterians 1
U-16
Thornton United 2 Young Parmiterians 1
U-15
Sheen Tigers 2 Providence 1
U-14
Parmiterians "A" 3 Prohawks 1
U-13
St Johns' Walworth 1 London Lions 7
U-12
Bethwin Boys 1 Providence 5
U-11
Bec United 5 Bethwin Boys 0

YOUTH Sunday
U-18
Alexandra Park 0 Old Latymerians 2
U-16
Aloysians 3* Carshalton 2*
U-13
Palace North 4 Palace South 0
U-12
Palace South 1 Palace North 3
U-11
Parmiterians 2* Palace Raiders 3*

*aet.

ARTHUR DUNN CUP

ld Chigwellians 2 Old Reptonians 1

ARTHURIAN LEAGUE

PREMIER DIVISION	P	W	D	L	F	A	Pts
Old Reptonians	16	11	3	2	43	23	25
Old Brentwoods	16	9	5	2	39	21	23
Old Carthusians	16	8	3	5	39	30	19
Old Etonians	16	6	2	8	42	35	14
Lancing Old Boys	16	7	0	9	37	38	14
Old Harrovians	16	6	2	8	33	39	14
Old Salopians	16	6	1	9	24	40	13
Old Chigwellians	16	5	3	8	33	41	13
Old Cholmeleians*	16	3	3	10	24	49	7

DIVISION 1	P	W	D	L	F	A	Pts
Old Westminsters	14	13	1	0	50	9	27
Old Foresters	14	11	0	3	59	18	22
Old Bradfieldians	14	8	1	5	46	21	17
Old Wykehamists	14	6	2	6	26	38	14
Old Witleians	14	6	0	8	26	40	12
Old Malvernians	14	4	1	9	21	41	9
Old Aldenhamians	14	4	1	9	23	45	9
Old Wellingburians*	14	1	0	13	18	57	0

DIVISION 2	P	W	D	L	F	A	Pts
Old Salopians Res	12	7	2	3	40	26	16
Old Etonians Res	12	7	2	3	33	21	16
Old Carthusians Res	12	6	2	4	22	23	14
Old Chigwellians Res	12	6	1	5	22	24	13
Old Etonians 3rd	12	4	2	6	23	24	10
Old Brentwoods Res	12	4	2	6	26	38	10
Lancing Old Boys Res	12	1	3	8	16	26	5

DIVISION 3	P	W	D	L	F	A	Pts
Old Cholmeleians Res*	12	9	1	2	35	9	17
Old Carthusians 3rd	12	6	3	3	26	17	15
Old Foresters 3rd	12	4	4	4	19	24	12
Old Bradfieldians Res	12	4	3	5	25	22	11
Old Aldenhamians Res	12	3	4	5	30	49	10
Old Foresters Res	12	4	1	7	34	29	9
Old Harrovians Res	12	3	2	7	18	37	8

* 2 points deducted for breach of rule

DIVISION 4–8 teams
Won by Old Haileyburians
DIVISION 5–6 teams
Won by Old Westminster Res
JUNIOR LEAGUE CUP
Old Haileyburians 5 Old Etonians 3rd 1
DERRIK MOORE MEMORIAL CUP
Old Cholmeleians Vets 3 Old Brentwoods Vets 0
JIM DIXSON SIX-A-SIDE CUP
Won by Old Chigwellians

LONDON FINANCIAL FOOTBALL ASSOCIATION

DIVISION ONE	P	W	D	L	F	A	Pts
Dresdner Kleinwort Wasserstein	16	12	3	1	60	23	39
Coutts & Co	16	11	2	3	38	21	35
Mount Pleasant Post Office	16	8	4	4	47	27	28
J P Morgan	16	6	4	6	36	28	22
Granby	16	5	6	5	32	31	21
Bank of America	16	5	5	6	35	41	20
Royal Sun Alliance	16	3	4	9	30	48	13
Chelsea Exiles*	16	3	3	10	25	65	11
Citibank	16	1	5	10	25	44	8

DIVISION TWO	P	W	D	L	F	A	Pts
Churchill Insurance	21	16	2	3	94	46	50
Zurich Eagle Star	21	16	1	4	107	38	49
Marsh	21	11	4	6	62	50	37
Royal Sun Alliance Res	21	7	7	7	63	49	28
Granby Res	21	4	7	10	39	66	19
C Hoare & Co	21	5	4	12	50	88	19
Coutts & Co Res	21	4	5	12	37	71	17
Foreign & Commonwealth Office	21	3	6	12	34	78	15

DIVISION THREE	P	W	D	L	F	A	Pts
Citibank Res	16	10	4	2	49	24	34
Marsh Res	16	10	3	3	63	26	33
Salomon Smith Barney	16	10	2	4	47	30	32
Royal Bank of Scotland	16	9	3	4	59	37	30
Royal Sun Alliance 3rd	16	8	1	7	50	32	25
Credit Suisse First Boston	16	6	1	9	42	57	19
Temple Bar	16	3	5	8	33	45	14
Zurich Eagle Star Res	16	4	2	10	28	61	14
Customs & Excise	16	1	1	14	19	78	4

DIVISION FOUR

DIVISION FOUR	P	W	D	L	F	A	Pts
Marsh 3rd	16	11	2	3	58	39	—
Granby 4th	16	10	2	4	45	35	—
Temple Bar Res	16	9	1	6	56	36	—
Standard Chartered Bank	16	7	3	6	40	28	—
GEFC	16	7	2	7	45	47	—
Granby 3rd	16	6	3	7	30	37	—
Bank of Ireland	16	5	4	7	42	39	—
Royal Bank of Scotland Res	16	5	1	10	30	52	—
South Bank Cuaco 5th	16	2	2	12	32	65	—

*1 point deducted for breach of rule

CHALLENGE CUP
Bank of England 3 Coutts & Co 1

LONDON LEGAL LEAGUE

DIVISION I	P	W	D	L	F	A	Pts
Denton Wilde Sapte (A)	18	12	3	3	52	18	—
Eversheds	18	11	1	6	40	25	—
Slaughter & May	18	10	2	6	47	34	—
Gray's Inn*	18	9	3	6	36	19	—
KPMG ICE	18	9	1	8	31	33	—
Linklaters & Alliance	18	9	0	9	35	40	—
Lovells	18	7	5	6	31	39	—
Fleet FRK*	18	5	3	10	25	30	—
Clifford Chance	18	4	3	11	30	46	—
Nabarro Nathanson	18	3	1	14	19	62	—

DIVISION II	P	W	D	L	F	A	Pts
Watson Farley & Williams	18	15	2	1	53	17	—
CMS Cameron McKenna	18	12	1	5	49	27	—
Allen & Overy	18	8	3	7	48	34	—
Baker & McKenzie	18	8	3	7	28	40	—
Norton Rose	18	8	1	9	49	45	—
Herbert Smith	18	7	4	7	26	43	—
Simmons & Simmons	18	8	0	10	41	33	—
Nicholson Graham & Jones**	18	7	2	9	34	38	—
Barlow Lyde & Gilbert	18	6	2	10	30	43	—
Taylor Joynson Garrett**	18	1	2	15	16	54	—

DIVISION III	P	W	D	L	F	A	Pts
Freshfields	18	14	2	2	60	20	—
Richards Butler	18	13	1	4	78	33	—
Titmuss Sainer Dechert	18	11	1	6	49	31	—
Macfarlanes**	18	8	2	8	51	50	—
Financial Services A	18	5	7	6	43	49	—
S J Berwin & Co	18	6	3	9	31	23	—
Hammonds Suddards Edge*	18	7	1	10	16	29	—
Denton Wilde Sapte (B)	18	6	0	12	21	63	—
Pegasus (Inner Temple)	18	4	4	10	36	55	—
Stephenson Harwood	18	5	1	12	30	62	—

* 1 point deducted for breach of rule
** 2 points deducted for breach of rule

LEAGUE CHALLENGE CUP
Denton Wilde Sapte 'A' 4 KPMG ICE 2
WEAVERS ARMS CHALLENGE CUP
Herbert Smith 6 Allen & Overy 4

LONDON OLD BOYS' CUPS
Senior
Old Wilsonians 1 Latymer Old Boys 0
Intermediate
Albanian Res 2 Old Bradfieldians 0
Junior
Old Challoners Res 1 Old Suttonians 3rd 0
Minor
Holland Park O B Res 2 Old Edmontonians 3rd 1
Novets
Old Uffingtonians 3rd 2 Old Edmontonians 4th 3
Drummond
Old Actonians Assn 6th 3 Albanian 6th 0
Nemean
Old Actonians Assn 8th 1 Old Edmontonians 6th 0
Veterans'
Phoenix Old Boys 1 Old Meadonians 0

OLD BOYS' INVITATION CUPS
Senior
Old Wilsonians 3* Old Salesians 2*
Junior
Old Finchleians Res 3* Old Owens Res 2*
Minor
Old Minchendenians 3 Old Tenisonians 3rd 1

th XIs
Old Finchleians 4th 4 Old Stationers 4th 2
th XIs
Old Minchendenians 5th 4* Old Westmin'r Citz 5th 2*
th XIs
Old Minchendenian 6th 5* Old Finchleians 6th 2*
th XIs
Glyn Old Boys 7th 4 Old Parkonians 7th 0
'eterans'
Old Esthameians 0*:3p Old Westminster Citizens 0*:0p
aet; p – penalties.

MIDLAND AMATEUR ALLIANCE

Premier Division

	P	W	D	L	F	A	Pts
Caribbean Cavaliers	24	19	3	2	87	38	60
Nottingham Trent University	24	15	4	5	84	40	49
Nottinghamshire	24	15	4	5	64	28	49
Old Elizabethans	24	12	3	9	66	56	39
Ashland Rovers	24	11	4	9	64	54	37
Squareform Stealers	24	10	5	9	69	65	35
Bassingfield	24	11	1	12	58	59	34
Magdala Amateurs Res	24	10	3	11	48	50	33
Lady Bay	24	9	3	12	54	67	30
Woodborough United	24	9	3	12	45	62	30
ASC Dayncourt Res	24	9	2	13	45	75	29
Racing Athletic	24	5	3	16	38	68	18
(ex Horse & Jockey)							
Wollaton 3rd	24	2	0	22	34	94	6

Division 1

	P	W	D	L	F	A	Pts
Bracken Park	26	20	6	0	75	22	66
Pakistan Centre	26	18	4	4	92	28	58
Nottinghamshire Res	26	17	3	6	78	45	54
Beeston Old Boys Assn	26	15	4	7	68	45	49
Wollaton 4th	26	15	4	7	61	43	49
Sherwood Forest	26	12	2	12	57	66	38
Old Elizabethans Res	26	11	3	12	65	61	36
County NALGO	26	9	5	12	55	75	32
Southwell Arms	26	8	7	11	70	67	31
Bassingfield Res	26	8	6	12	52	69	30
Old Bemrosians	26	8	4	16	30	60	22
Derbyshire Amateurs Res	26	5	0	21	35	83	15
Brunts Old Boys	26	3	4	19	37	89	13

Division 2

	P	W	D	L	F	A	Pts
ASC Dayncourt 3rd	28	20	2	6	80	36	62
Edwinstowe FC	28	17	5	6	91	42	56
Magdala Arms 3rd	28	18	1	9	92	66	55
Nottinghamshire 3rd	28	16	3	9	65	45	51
Caribbean Cavaliers Res	28	15	4	9	87	64	49
Old Elizabethans 3rd	28	15	4	9	65	49	49
West Bridgford United	28	14	2	12	70	54	44
Beeston O B Assn Res	28	12	6	10	55	47	42
F L L Aerospace Res	28	11	5	12	73	67	38
Tibshelf Old Boys	28	11	4	13	64	67	37
Derbyshire Amateurs 3rd	28	11	2	15	65	91	35
Wollaton 5th	28	10	2	16	76	71	32
Dynamo	28	8	3	17	74	99	27
EMTEC	28	5	2	21	47	146	17
Old Bemrosians Res	28	3	3	22	33	93	12

LEAGUE SENIOR CUP
Nottingham Trent University 3 Lady Bay 1
LEAGUE INTERMEDIATE CUP
Southwell Amateurs 0 Pakistan Centre 2
LEAGUE MINOR CUP
ASC Dayncourt 3rd 2 Wollaton 5th 1

OLD BOYS' LEAGUE

PREMIER DIVISION

	P	W	D	L	F	A	Pts
Old Meadonians	20	13	3	4	52	22	42
Old Danes	20	12	5	3	50	28	41
Old Aloysians	20	10	6	4	53	30	36
Old Ignatians	20	10	5	5	44	35	35
Old Hamptonians	20	10	4	6	44	38	34
Old Wilsonians	20	7	6	7	43	32	27
Old Salvatorians	20	7	5	8	26	37	26
Old Vaughanians	20	6	4	10	44	41	22
Cardinal Manning Old Boys	20	5	4	11	39	67	19
Phoenix Old Boys	20	4	2	14	33	66	14
Shene Old Grammarians	20	3	2	15	35	67	11

SENIOR DIVISION 1

	P	W	D	L	F	A	Pts
Latymer Old Boys	18	16	1	1	77	14	49
Old Tiffinians	18	12	2	4	55	22	38
Old Isleworthians	18	11	2	5	53	28	35
Old Manorians	18	9	3	6	36	33	30
Old Dorkinians	18	6	7	5	30	32	25
Glyn Old Boys	18	8	1	9	27	48	25
Old Suttonians	18	4	4	10	24	46	16
Old Tenisonians	18	4	3	11	18	48	15
Enfield Old Grammarians	18	3	3	12	20	47	12
Old Minchendenians	18	3	2	13	32	54	11

SENIOR DIVISION 2

	P	W	D	L	F	A	Pts
Old Wokingians	20	18	2	0	54	17	56
Queen Mary College Old Boys	20	13	3	4	46	26	42
Old Buckwellians	20	11	4	5	62	38	37
Wood Green Old Boys	20	11	2	7	64	47	35
Old Reigatians	20	10	2	8	46	29	32
John Fisher Old Boys	20	8	2	10	32	31	26
Old Sedcopians	20	6	3	11	44	64	21
Latymer Old Boys Res	20	6	3	11	34	56	21
Old Kingsburians*	20	5	3	12	40	59	15
Phoenix Old Boys Res	20	4	2	14	31	56	14
Old Vaughanians Res	20	4	2	14	38	68	14

SENIOR DIVISION 3

	P	W	D	L	F	A	Pts
Old Aloysians Res	22	14	2	6	62	33	44
Old Tenisonians Res	22	13	5	4	44	23	44
Old Egbertians	22	12	4	6	42	24	40
Old Salvatorians Res	22	10	7	5	56	47	37
Clapham Old Xavierians	22	10	4	8	51	39	34
Old Wilsonians Res	22	10	3	9	52	34	33
Old Hamptonians Res	22	10	2	10	33	36	32
Mickleham Old Boxhillians	22	7	7	8	43	50	28
Old Meadonians Res	22	7	5	10	53	67	26
Old Manorians Res	22	6	3	13	33	54	21
Old St Marys	22	5	3	14	30	67	18
Fitzwilliam Old Boys	22	4	3	15	37	62	15

* 3 points deducted for breach of rule

Intermediate Division South–12 teams
Won by Chertsey Old Salesians
Intermediate Division North–12 teams
Won by Old Challoners

NORTHERN
Division 1–11 teams
Won by Old Edmontonians Res
Division 2–10 teams
Won by Old Minchendenians 3rd
Division 3–9 teams
Won by Old Edmontonians 4th
Division 4–9 teams
Won by Old Edmontonians 5th
Division 5–8 teams
Won by Holland Park Old Boys 5th
Division 6–9 teams
Won by Old Egbertians 6th

SOUTHERN
Division 1–10 teams
Won by Old Tenisonians 4th
Division 2–11 teams
Won by Old Guildfordians
Division 3–9 teams
Won by Sinjuns Res
Division 4–10 teams
Won by Clapham Old Xavierians 4th
Division 5–9 teams
Won by Glyn Old Boys 6th
Division 6–11 teams
Won by Old Strandians
Division 7–9 teams
Won by Mickleham Old Boxhillians Res
Division 8–8 teams
Won by Old Tiffinians 5th

WESTERN
Division 1–10 teams
Won by Old Challoners Res
Division 2–10 teams
Won by Old Salvatorians 4th
Division 3–11 teams
Won by Old Uxonians Res
Division 4–11 teams
Won by Old Uffingtonians Res
Division 5–10 teams
Won by Old Uffingtonians 3rd

SOUTHERN AMATEUR LEAGUE

SENIOR SECTION

DIVISION 1	P	W	D	L	F	A	Pts
Old Owens	22	16	1	5	50	18	49
BB Eagles	22	12	6	4	53	33	42
(formerly Barclays Bank)							
Civil Service	22	13	1	8	46	34	40
Broomfield	22	11	3	8	49	34	36
Old Esthameians	22	10	5	7	45	34	35
Polytechnic	22	11	2	9	40	42	35
Old Actonians Association	22	9	6	7	36	26	33
Alleyn Old Boys	22	8	5	9	36	42	29
Norsemen	22	8	1	13	39	47	25
East Barnet Old Grammarians	22	6	4	12	28	56	22
Carshalton	22	5	2	15	29	59	17
Crouch End Vampires	22	4	2	16	30	56	14

DIVISION 2	P	W	D	L	F	A	Pts
Old Salesians	22	16	5	1	69	21	53
HSBC	22	16	3	3	62	30	51
West Wickham	22	15	5	2	46	15	50
Old Bromleians	22	12	4	6	48	26	40
Old Parkonians	22	10	5	7	42	39	35
Old Lyonians	22	8	5	9	42	53	29
Old Finchleians	22	6	7	9	37	53	25
Lensbury	22	6	5	11	34	36	23
Winchmore Hill	22	7	2	13	24	37	23
Lloyds TSB Bank	22	5	3	14	36	52	18
Old Stationers	22	4	1	17	24	51	13
National Westminster Bank	22	3	3	16	27	78	10

* 2 points deducted for breach of rule

DIVISION 3	P	W	D	L	F	A	Pts
Nottsborough	22	18	3	1	92	16	57
South Bank Cuaco	22	14	6	2	44	21	48
(Merged Clubs)							
Bank of England	22	15	1	6	56	22	46
Alexandra Park	22	13	3	6	50	33	42
Kew Association	22	11	4	7	55	54	37
Old Parmiterians	22	10	3	9	60	48	33
Southgate Olympic	22	7	2	13	31	62	23
Merton	22	6	4	12	36	51	22
Ibis	22	5	6	11	30	48	21
Old Latymerians	22	6	2	14	37	52	20
Old Westminster Citizens	22	5	3	14	32	72	18
Brentham	22	3	1	18	43	87	10

RESERVE TEAM SECTION
Division 1–12 teams
Won by East Barnet Old Grammarians Res
Division 2–12 teams
Won by Polytechnic Res
Division 3–12 teams
Won by Nottsborough Res
Third Team Section
Division 1–12 teams
Won by Old Finchleians 3rd
Division 2–12 teams
Won by Old Latymerians 3rd
Division 3–12 teams
Won by Carshalton 3rd
Fourth Team Section
Division 1–12 teams
Won by Old Finchleians 4th
Division 2–11 teams
Won by West Wickham 4th
Division 3–11 teams
Won by Nottsborough 4th
Fifth Team Section
Division 1–11 teams
Won by Old Finchleians 5th
Division 2–10 teams
Won by HSBC 5th
Division 3–9 teams
Won by Old Esthameians 5th
Sixth Team Section
Division 1–12 teams
Won by Old Parmiterians 6th
Division 2–10 teams
Won by Kew Association 6th
Minor Section
Division 1–10 teams
Won by Old Finchleians 7th
Division 2–10 teams
Won by Kew Association 7th
Division 3–11 teams
Won by Old Parmiterians 9th

SOUTHERN OLYMPIAN LEAGUE

SENIOR SECTION

PREMIER DIVISION	P	W	D	L	F	A	Pts
Hale End Athletic	18	12	4	2	44	17	40
UCL Academicals	18	10	2	6	47	27	32
Parkfield	18	8	6	4	29	23	30
Albanian	18	8	5	5	25	24	29
Honorable Artillery Company	18	7	5	6	36	30	26
Mill Hill Village	18	7	3	8	40	41	24
Southgate County	18	6	4	8	31	42	22
Ulysses	18	5	5	8	30	40	20
Old Grammarians	18	5	4	9	33	43	19
Old Woodhouseians	18	1	4	13	27	55	7

DIVISION TWO	P	W	D	L	F	A	Pts
Old Bealonians	18	14	1	3	66	29	43
St Marys College	18	11	2	5	36	21	35
Kings Old Boys	18	10	3	5	44	27	33
University of Hertford	18	9	2	7	46	33	29
Economicals	18	9	2	7	38	32	29
Pegasus	18	7	5	6	38	26	26
Wandsworth Borough	18	6	3	9	28	52	21
Brent	18	6	2	10	25	53	20
Centymca	18	3	4	11	28	50	13
City of London	18	1	4	13	30	56	7

DIVISION THREE	P	W	D	L	F	A	Pts
BBC	20	18	1	1	96	28	55
The Rugby Clubs	20	13	2	5	88	42	41
London Welsh	20	11	5	4	65	40	38
Witan	20	9	6	5	43	43	33
Hampstead Heathens	20	9	5	6	52	43	32
London Airways	20	8	1	11	42	71	25
Bluepoint	20	6	4	10	38	46	22
Ealing Association	20	6	2	12	39	81	20
The Comets	20	4	4	12	35	51	16
Fulham Compton	20	4	4	12	32	57	16
Inland Revenue	20	3	4	13	24	52	13

INTERMEDIATE SECTION
Division 1–10 teams
Won by Old Woodhouseians Res
Division 2–9 teams
Won by Honourable Artillery Company Res
Division 3–8 teams
Won by Mill Hill Village 3rd

JUNIOR SECTION
DIVISION ONE NORTH–9 teams
Won by Mill Hill Village 4th
DIVISION TWO NORTH–9 teams
Won by Old Bealonians 5th
DIVISION THREE NORTH–7 teams
Won by UCL Academicals 6th
DIVISION ONE SOUTH WEST–9 teams
Won by Witan Res
DIVISION TWO SOUTH WEST–9 teams
Won by Witan 3rd

LEAGUE CUPS
SENIOR
Southgate County 2* UCL Academicals 1*
INTERMEDIATE
Albanian Res 1* UCL Academicals Res 0*
JUNIOR
Mill Hill Village 3rd 3* Albanian 3rds 2*
MANDER
Mill Hill Village 4th 5 Old Woodhouseians 4th 0
BURNTWOOD TROPHY
Mill Hill Village 5th 4 Old Bealonians 5th 1
VETERANS'
Albanian 2* UCL Academicals 1*
*aet.

IMPORTANT ADDRESSES

The Football Association: A. Crozier, 25 Soho Square, London W1D 4FA. *020 7745 4545*

Scotland: David Taylor, Hampden Park, Glasgow G42 9AY. *0141 616 6000*

Northern Ireland (Irish FA): D. I. Bowen, 20 Windsor Avenue, Belfast BT9 6EG. *028 9066 9458*

Wales: A. Evans, 3 Westgate Street, Cardiff, South Glamorgan CF1 1DD. *029 2037 2325*

Republic of Ireland (FA of Ireland): 80 Merrion Square South, Dublin 2. *00353 16766864*

International Federation (FIFA): P. O. Box 85 8030 Zurich, Switzerland. *00 411 384 9595. Fax: 00 411 384 9696*

Union of European Football Associations: G. Aigner, Route de Geneve 46, Case Postale CH-1260 Nyon, Switzerland. *0041 22 994 44 44. Fax: 0041 22 994 44 88*

THE LEAGUES

The Premier League: R. Scudamore, 11 Connaught Place, London W2 2ET. *020 7298 1600*

The Football League: D. Burns, The Football League, Unit 5, Edward VII Quay, Navigation Way, Preston, Lancashire PR2 2YF. *01772 325800. Fax 01772 325801*

Scottish Premier League: R. Mitchell, Hampden Park, Somerville Drive, Glasgow G42 9BA. *0141 646 6962*

The Scottish League: P. Donald, Hampden Park, Glasgow G42 9AY. *0141 616 6000*

The Irish League: H. Wallace, 96 University Street, Belfast BT7 1HE. *028 9024 2888*

Football League of Ireland: D. Crowther, 80 Merrion Square, Dublin 2. *00353 16765120*

Nationwide Conference: J. A. Moules, Chief Executive, Riverside House, 14b High Street, Crayford, DA1 4HG. *01322 411021*

Central League: A. Williamson, The Football League, Unit 5, Edward VII Quay, Navigation Way, Preston, Lancashire PR2 2YF. *01772 325801. Fax 01772 325801*

Eastern Counties League: B. A. Badcock, 41 The Copse, Southwood, Farnborough, Hampshire GU14 0QD. *01252 387588*

Football Combination: D. A. Daughtery, 3 Eastergate, Little Common, Bexhill-on-Sea, East Sussex TN31 4NU. *01424 848061*

Hellenic League: B. King, 83 Queens Road, Carterton, Oxon OX18 3YF. *01993 212738*

Kent League: R. Vinter, Bakery House, The Street, Chilham, Canterbury, Kent CT4 8BX. *01227 730457*

Leicestershire Senior League: R. J. Holmes, 8 Huntsmans Close, Markfield, Leics LE67 9XE. *01530 243093*

Manchester League: P. Platt, 26A Stalybridge Road, Mottram Hyde, Cheshire SK14 6NE. *01457 763821*

Midland Combination: N. Harvey, 115 Millfield Road, Handsworth Wood, Birmingham B20 1ED. *0121 357 4172*

Northern Premier: R. D. Bayley, 22 Woburn Drive, Hale, Altrincham, Cheshire WA15 8LZ. *0161 980 7007*

Northern League: T. Golightly, 85 Park Road North, Chester-le-Street, Co Durham DH3 3SA. *0191 3882056*

Isthmian League: N. Robinson, 226 Rye Lane, Peckham SE15 4NL. *020 8409 1978. Fax: 020 7639 5726*

Southern League: D. J. Strudwick, P.O. Box 90, Worcester, WR3 8RX. *01905 757509*

Spartan South Midlands League: M. Mitchell, 26 Leighton Court, Dunstable, Beds LU6 1EW. *01582 667291*

United Counties League: R. Gamble, 8 Bostock Avenue, Northampton NN1 4LW. *01604 637766*

Western League: K. A. Clarke, 32 Westmead Lane, Chippenham, Wilts SN15 3HZ. *01249 464467*

West Midlands Regional League: N. R. Juggins, 14 Badger Way, Blackwell, Bromsgrove, Worcs B60 1EX. *0121 445 2953*

Northern Counties (East): B. Wood, 6 Restmore Avenue, Guiseley, Leeds LS20 9DG. *01943 874558*

Central Midlands Football League: Frank Harwood, 103 Vestry Road, Oakwood, Derby, Derbyshire DE21 2BN. *01332 832372*

Combined Counties League: Clive R. Tidey, 22 Silo Road, Farncombe, Godalming, Surrey GU7 3PA. *01483 428453*

Essex Senior League: David Walls, Bramley Cottage, 2 Birch Street, Colchester CO2 0NW. *0207 587 4139*

Lancashire Football League: Barbara Howarth, 86 Windsor Road, Great Harwood, Blackburn, Lancs BB6 7RR. *01254 886267*

Midland Football Alliance: Peter Dagger, 32 Drysdale Close, Wickhamford, Worcs WR11 6RZ. *01386 831763*

North West Counties Football League: G. J. Wilkinson, 46 Oaklands Drive, Penwortham, Preston, Lancs PR1 0XY. *01772 746312*

Wessex League: Tom Lindon, 63 Downs Road, South Wonston, Winchester, Hants SO21 3EW. *01962 884760*

South Western League: R. Rowe, 5 Alverton Gardens, Truro, Cornwall TR1 1JA. *01872 242190*

COUNTY FOOTBALL ASSOCIATIONS

Bedfordshire: P. D. Brown, Century House, Skimpot Road, Dunstable, Beds LU5 4JU. *01582 565111*

Berks and Bucks: B. G. Moore, 15a London Street, Faringdon, Oxon SN7 7HD. *01367 242099*

Birmingham County: D. Shelton, County FA Offices, Rayhall Lane, Great Barr, Birmingham B43 6JF. *0121 357 4278*

Cambridgeshire: R. K. Pawley, City Ground, Milton Road, Cambridge CB4 1FA. *01223 576770*

Cheshire: Mrs M. Dunford, The Cottage, Hartford Moss Rec Centre, Winnington, Northwich CW8 4BG. *01606 871166*

Cornwall: B. Cudmore, 1 High Cross Street, St. Austell, Cornwall PL25 4AB. *01726 74080*

Cumberland: G. Turrell, 17 Oxford Street, Workington, Cumbria CA14 2AL. *01900 872310*

Derbyshire: K. Compton, No 8–9 Stadium, Business Court, Millenium Way, Pride Park, Derby DE24 8HZ. *01332 361422*

Devon County: C. Davidson, County HQ, Coach Road, Newton Abbot, Devon TQ12 1EJ. *01626 332077*

Dorset County: P. Hough, County Ground, Blandford Close, Hamworthy, Poole, Dorset BH15 4BF. *01202 682375*

Durham: J. Topping, 'Codeslaw', Ferens Park, Durham DH1 1JZ. *0191 3848653*

East Riding County: D. R. Johnson, 50 Boulevard, Hull HU3 2TB. *01482 221158*

Essex County: P. Sammons, 31 Mildmay Road, Chelmsford, Essex CM2 0DN. *01245 357727*

Gloucestershire: P. Britton, Oaklands Park, Almondsbury, Bristol BS32 4AG. *01454 615888*

Guernsey: D. Dorey, Haut Regard, St. Clair Hill, St. Sampson's, Guernsey, GY2 4DT, CI. *01481 246231*

Hampshire: L. Jones, William Pickford House, 8 Ashwood Gardens, off Winchester Road, Southampton SO16 7PW. *023 8079 1110*

Herefordshire: J. S. Lambert, County Ground Offices, Widemarsh Common, Hereford HR4 9NA. *01432 342179*

Hertfordshire: E. King, County Ground, Baldock Road, Letchworth, Herts SG6 2EN. *01462 677622*

Huntingdonshire: M. M. Armstrong, Cromwell Chambers, 8 St Johns Street, Huntingdon, Cambs PE29 6DD. *01480 414422*

Isle of Man: Mrs A. Garrett, P.O. Box 53, The Bowl, Douglas IOM IM99 1GY. *01624 615576*

Jersey: S. Monks, Rocqueberg View, Rue De Samares, St. Clement, Jersey JE2 6LS. *01534 852642*

Kent County: K. T. Masters, 69 Maidstone Road, Chatham, Kent ME4 6DT. *01634 843824*

Lancashire: J. Kenyon, The County Ground, Thurston Road, Leyland, Preston, Lancs PR5 1LF. *01772 624000*

Leicestershire and Rutland: P. Morrison, Holmes Park, Dog and Gun Lane, Whetstone, Leicester LE8 6FA. *0116 2867828*

Lincolnshire: J. Griffin, PO Box 26, 12 Dean Road, Lincoln LN2 4DP. *01522 524917*

Liverpool County: F. L. J. Hunter, Liverpool Soccer Centre, Walton Hall Park, Walton Hall Avenue, Liverpool L4 9XP. *0151 523 4488*

London: D. Fowkes, 6 Aldworth Grove, London SE13 6HY. *020 8690 9626*

Manchester County: John Dutton, Brantingham Road, Chorlton, Manchester M21 0TT. *0161 881 0299*

Middlesex County: P. J. Clayton, 39 Roxborough Road, Harrow, Middx HA1 1NS. *020 8424 8524*

Norfolk County: R. J. Howlett, Plantation Park, Blofield, Norwich, Norfolk, NR13 4PL. *01603 717177*

Northamptonshire: B. Walden, 2 Duncan Close, Moulton Park, Northampton NN3 6WL. *01604 670741*

North Riding County: M. Jarvis, Southlands Centre, Ormesby Road, Middlesbrough TS3 0HB. *01642 318603*

Northumberland: R. E. Maughan, Churchill Pavilion, Hartley Avenue, Whitley Bay NE26 3FA. *0191 2530656*

Nottinghamshire: M. Kilbee, 7 Clarendon Stree Nottingham NG1 5HS. *0115 9418954*

Oxfordshire: I. Mason, P.O. Box 62, Witney, Oxo OX28 1HA. *01993 778586*

Sheffield and Hallamshire: J. Hope-Gill, Clegg Hous 69 Cornish Place, Cornish Street, Shalesmoo Sheffield S6 3AF. *0114 241 4999*

Shropshire: D. Rowe, Gay Meadow, Abbey Foregat Shrewsbury SY2 6AB. *01743 362769*

Somerset & Avon (South): Mrs H. Marchment, 30 Nort Road, Midsomer Norton, Radstock BA3 2QD. *0176 410280*

Staffordshire: B. J. Adshead, County Showgroun Weston Road, Stafford ST18 0BD. *01785 256994*

Suffolk County: Felaw Maltings, 44 Felaw Street, Ipswic IP2 8SJ. *01473 407290*

Surrey County: R. Ward, 321 Kingston Road, Leather head, Surrey KT22 7TU. *01372 373543*

Sussex County: Ken Benham, County Office, Culve Road, Lancing, West Sussex BN15 9AX. *01903 753547*

Westmorland: P. G. Ducksbury, Unit 1, Angel Court, 2 Highgate, Kendal, Cumbria LA9 4DA. *01539 730946*

West Riding County: R. Carter, Fleet Lane, Woodles ford, Leeds LS26 8NX. *0113 2821222*

Wiltshire: M. G. Benson, Covingham Square, Covinghan Swindon SN3 5AA. *01793 525245*

Worcestershire: M. R. Leggett, Craftsman House, D Salis Drive, Hampton Lovett Industrial Estate Droitwich WR9 0QE. *01905 827137*

OTHER USEFUL ADDRESSES

Amateur Football Alliance: M. L. Brown, 55 Islington Park Street, London N1 1QB. *020 7359 3493*

English Schools FA: Ms A. Pritchard, 1/2 Eastgate Street, Stafford ST16 2NN. *01785 51142*

Oxford University: M. Matthews, University College, Oxford OX1 4BH. *01865 276648*

Cambridge University: Dr J. A. Little, St Catherine's College, Cambridge CB2 1RL. *01223 334376*

Army: Major W. T. E. Thomson ASCB (MOD), Clayton Barracks, Thornhill Road, Aldershot, Hants GU11 2BG. *01252 348571/4*

Royal Air Force: Sqn Ldr R. Moorehouse, OC PACS, RAF Coltishall, Norwich. *01603 737361 ext 7306*

Royal Navy: Lt-Cdr S. Vasey, RN Sports Office, HMS Temeraire, Portsmouth, Hants PO1 2HB. *023 9272 2671*

British Universities Sports Association: G. Gregory-Jones, Chief Executive: BUSA, 8 Union Street, London SE1 1SZ. *020 7357 8555*

British Olympic Association: 6 John Prince's Street, London W1M 0DH. *020 7408 2029*

The Football Supporters Federation: Chairman: Ian D. Todd MBE, 8 Wyke Close, Wyke Gardens, Isleworth, Middlesex TW7 5PE. *020 8847 2905 (and fax). Mobile: 0961 558908.* National Secretary: Mark Agate, "The Stadium", 14 Coombe Close, Lordswood, Chatham, Kent ME5 8NU. *01634 319461 (and fax)*

National Playing Fields Association: Col. R. Satterthwaite, O.B.E., 578b Catherine Place, London, SW1.

Professional Footballers' Association: G. Taylor, 2 Oxford Court, Bishopsgate, Off Lower Mosley Street, Manchester M2 3WQ. *0161 236 0575*

Referees' Association: A. Smith, 1 Westhill Road, Coundon, Coventry CV6 2AD. *024 7660 1701*

Women's Football Alliance: Miss K. Doyle, The Football Association, 25 Soho Square, London W1D 4FA. *020 7745 4545*

Institute of Football Management and Administration: Camkin House, 8 Charles Court, Budbrooke Road, Warwick CV34 5LZ. *01926 411384. Fax: 01926 411041*

Football Administrators Association: as above.

Commercial and Marketing Managers Association: a above.

Management Stats Association: as above.

League Managers Association: as above.

The Association of Football Statisticians: R. J. Spiller PO Box 5828, Basildon, Essex SS15 5GQ. *0126 416020 (and fax 01268-543559)*

The Football Programme Directory: David Stacey, 'Th Beeches', 66 Southend Road, Wickford, Esse SS11 8EN. *01268 732041 (and fax)*

England Football Supporters Association: Publicit Officer, David Stacey, 'The Beeches', 66 Southend Road Wickford, Essex SS11 8EN. *01268 732041 (and fax)*

World Cup (1966) Association: as above.

The Ninety-Two Club: 104 Gilda Crescent, Whitchurch Bristol BS14 9LD.

Scottish 38 Club: Mark Byatt, 6 Greenfields Close Loughton, Essex IG10 3HG. *0181 508 6088*

The Football Trust: Second Floor, Walkden House, 10 Melton Street, London NW1 2EJ. *020 7388 4504*

Association of Provincial Football Supporters Clubs ii London: Stephen Moon, 32 Westminster Gardens Barking, Essex IG11 0BJ. *020 8594 2367*

World Association of Friends of English Football Carlisle Hill, Gluck, Habichthof 2, D24939 Flensburg Germany. *0049 461 4700222*

Football Postcard Collectors Club: PRO: Bryan Horsnell 275 Overdown Road, Tilehurst, Reading RG31 6NX *0118 9424448 (and fax)*

UK Programme Collectors Club: Secretary, John Litster 46 Milton Road, Kirkcaldy, Fife KY1 1TL. *0159 268718. Fax: 01592 595069*

Programme Monthly: as above.

Scottish Football Historians Association: as above.

Phil Gould (Licensed Football Agent), c/o Whoppi Management Ltd, P. O. Box 27204, London N11 2WS *07071 732 468. Fax: 07070 732 469*

The Scandinavian Union of Supporters of British Football: Postboks, 15 Stovner, N-0913 Oslo, Norway.

Football Writers' Association: Executive Secretary, Ken Montgomery, 6 Chase Lane, Barkingside, Essex IG6 1BH. *0208 554 2455 (and fax)*

FOOTBALL CLUB CHAPLAINCY

ootball clubs, in common for example with churches, businesses and Christian ministers, all xperience periods when progress appears to be slow to the point of being non-existent, and yet the iscerning eye can see features which do indicate headway. That's where the Football Chaplains are at he time this little article is being prepared.

Thus, without any earth-shattering movements over the last year or so, it is now our evaluation that omewhere approaching three quarters of the Premier and Football League clubs now benefit to some egree from the ministry of a chaplain, and those who are happy to acknowledge an appointed official chaplain are listed below. Equally, the effectiveness in and value to a club of such a person is learly increasingly understood and welcomed not simply within our own sport, for chaplaincy, based pon the Association Football model, has now expanded and overlapped into both Rugby codes. This particularly emphasised by the close involvement of chaplains (including several of 'our' men, on emporary transfers only!) with the officials and each of the participating teams in the 2000 Rugby eague World Cup, and also, to the expressed pleasure of Sir Alex Ferguson, no less, over the last ouple of years, within the world of horseracing.

Again, slightly more than forty of the football chaplains gathered at their national conference at illeshall last autumn, where the speakers included a triumvirate comprising a First Division chairman, former, famous top flight player and a key off-field employee of a major Premiership outfit, all of whom encouraged the chaplains as to their relevance and value within our game.

However, perhaps the most useful cameo from the chaplains' conference, for those football club fficials and readers from clubs that are exploring the possibility of making such an appointment, came rom one of the longest serving chaplains in the country during an observation that one of our number is now in his fortieth season at his club and another handful are nearing their thirtieth: 'Chaplains', he aid, 'are there for the long haul, not for the quick fix. Where the right man (or, occasionally, lady) is nvited to serve a club in such a supportive role, he (she) usually matures in it like a fine vintage!'

Surely, a case (pun intended!) of 'More port, Vicar?'!!

THE REV

OFFICIAL CHAPLAINS TO FA PREMIERSHIP AND FOOTBALL LEAGUE CLUBS

Rev Steven Hawkins—Bristol R; Rev Catherine Bell—Luton T; Rev Richard Chewter—Exeter C; Rev Peter Bye—Carlisle U; Rev Ken Howles—Blackburn R; Rev David Langdon—QPR; Rev Andrew Taggart—Torquay U; Rev Gary Piper—Fulham; Rev David Jeans—Sheffield W; Rev Peter Amos—Barnsley; Rev Nigel Sands—Crystal Palace; Rev Barry Kirk—Reading; Rev Graham pencer—Leicester C; Rev Martin Short and Very Rev John Richardson—Bradford C; Rev Kevan McCormack—Ipswich T; Rev John Boyers—Manchester U; Rev Allen Bagshawe—Hull C; Rev Martin Butt—Walsall; Rev David Tully—Newcastle U; Rev Derek Cleave—Bristol C; Rev Fr Alan Poulter and Fr Gerald Courell—Tranmere R; Rev Brian Rice—Hartlepool U; Rev Matt Baker and Rev effrey Heskins—Charlton Ath; Revs Andy Cowley and John Graham—Watford; Rev Owen Beament—Millwall; Rev Michael Chantry—Oxford U; Rev Elwin Cockett—West Ham U; Rev Michael Futens—Derby Co; Rev Mick Woodhead—Sheffield U; Rev Ken Hawkins—Birmingham C; Rev Alan Comfort—Leyton Orient; Rev Simon Stevenette—Swindon T; Rev John Hall-Matthews— Wolverhampton W; Rev Canon Michael Hunter—Grimsby T; Rev Steve Collis—Port Vale; Rev Chris Cullwick—York C; Rev Ken Baker—Northampton T; Rev Mark Hirst—Burnley; Rev Tony Porter— Manchester C; Rev Richard Hayton—Gillingham; Rev Clive Andrews—Notts Co; Fr Andrew McMahon—Southampton; Rev Chris Nelson—Preston North End; Rev Henry Corbett and Rev Harry Ross—Everton; Rev Paul Brown—Wrexham; Rev Jeff Howden—Plymouth Argyle; Rev Andy Rimmer—Portsmouth; Rev Alan Hayday—Scunthorpe U; Rev Tim Welch—Shrewsbury T; Rev ames Booth—Southend U; Rev Philip Hearn—Kidderminster H; Rev David Ottley—Bury; Capt Nigel Tansley—Crewe Alex; Rev Billy Montgomery—Stockport Co; Rev Ken Hipkiss—WBA; Canon Roger Knight—Rushden & Diamonds; Rev Kevin Johns—Swansea C; Rev Anthony Wareham— Peterborough U.

The chaplains hope that those who read this page will see the value and benefit of chaplaincy work in football and will take appropriate steps to spread the word where this is possible. They would also like to thank the editors of the Rothmans Yearbook *for their continued support for this specialist and growing area of work.*

The following addresses may be helpful: SCORE (Sports Chaplaincy Offering Resources and Encouragement), PO Box 123, Sale, Manchester M33 4ZA and Christians in Sport, PO Box 93, Oxford OX2 7YP

OBITUARIES

Sune Andersson (Born Soedertaejle, Sweden, 22 February 1921. Died Solna, Stockholm, Sweden, 29 April 2002.) Sun Andersson played at left half for Sweden when they defeated Yugoslavia 3-1 to take the Olympic Games gold medal a Wembley Stadium in 1948. He won a total of 28 caps for his country and was also a member of the team that finishe third in the 1950 World Cup. At club level he played for AIK before spending two years as a professional in Italy wit Roma.

Gerald Ashby (Born circa 1949. Died December 2001.) Gerald Ashby was a well-known referee who took charge of th 1995 FA Cup final between Everton and Manchester United. After retiring he became a referee's assessor and a UEFA match delegate.

Jeff Astle (Born Eastwood, Notts, 13 May 1942. Died Burton-upon-Trent, Staffs, 19 January 2002.) Jeff Astle was prolific centre forward for West Bromwich Albion in the 1960s and 1970s. He began his career at Notts County when he partnered the young Tony Hateley for a while, and was sold to the Baggies for a bargain fee in September 1964. H scored 171 goals in all competitions while at the Hawthorns, including a dramatic winner in extra time in the 1968 F Cup final against Everton. He won five full caps for England, one B cap and appeared twice for the Football League.

Ken Aston, MBE (Born Colchester, 1 September 1915. Died 23 October 2001.) Ken Aston qualified as a referee in 193 and went on to take charge of the European Championships final (1961) and FA Cup final (1963). He refereed at th 1962 World Cup finals before joining the FIFA Referees' Committee and was in charge of the referees for the 196 1970 and 1974 World Cup finals. He achieved fame as the man to introduce the red and yellow card system and also th number board for substitutes, so that it was clear which player was to be replaced.

Billy Ayre (Born Crookhill, Co Durham, 7 May 1952. Died Southport, 16 April 2002.) Billy Ayre made his name as solid central defender in non-league football with Scarborough, appearing in the team that won the FA Trophy in bot 1976 and 1977. He subsequently joined the full-time ranks and went on to make over 300 Football League appearance with Hartlepool, Halifax (two spells) and Mansfield. He then entered a career in management, taking charge of Halifa Blackpool, Scarborough and Cardiff. He was working as a coach with Bury at the time of his death, which was as result of lymph node cancer.

Stanley Barnes (Born Devon, circa 1914. Died Chingford, Essex, July 2001.) Stanley Barnes never managed to appea in senior football in peacetime, but played over 50 games for Clapton Orient during World War Two.

Youssef Belkhouja (Born Morocco, circa 1977. Died Casablanca, Morocco, 29 September 2001.) Youssef Belkhouj was a Moroccan international player who collapsed and died from a massive heart attack while playing for his clu WAC against local rivals Raja Casablanca in their semi-final tie of the Coupe du Trône last September.

Said Belqola (Born Tiflet, Morocco, 1956. Died Rabat, Morocco, 15 June 2002.) Said Belqola graduated to refereeing a international level in 1993 and reached the peak of his career four years later when he took charge of the Africa Nations' Cup final and the World Cup final between France and Brazil. He was the first African to referee a World Cup final.

Graham Bent (Born Ruabon, 6 October 1945. Died 2002.) Capped by Wales at schoolboy and amateur level, Graham spent two years as an apprentice before joining Wrexham in July 1963. He made 12 first-team appearances for th Robins over the next couple of seasons before returning to the Midlands where he played for a number of prominen non-league clubs.

Josef Bican (Born Vienna, Austria, 25 September 1913. Died Prague, Czech Republic, 12 December 2001.) Josef Bica was one of the legendary goal-scorers in Central European football, netting a total of more than 500 senior goals fo Rapid Vienna, SK Admira, Slavia Prague and VK Vitkovice. He represented Austria in the 1934 World Cup finals an was also capped by Czechoslavakia.

George Bray (Born Oswaldtwistle, Lancs, 11 November 1918. Died Hapton, Burnley, Lancs, 13 February 2002.) George Bray served Burnley for over 50 years firstly as a player and then as a member of the backroom staff. He made his first team debut in the last pre-war season, and by the time peace returned he was a regular at left half. He was an importan member of the Clarets' team that won promotion from Division Two and lost to Charlton in the FA Cup final in the 1946–47 season. George continued to play at first-team level until the start of the 1951–52 campaign. He made over 25 senior appearances at Turf Moor before joining the training staff and it was not until 1992 that he finally retired.

Bobby Brennan (Born Belfast, 14 March 1925. Died Norwich, 1 January 2002.) A talented inside forward, Bobby Brennan played over 400 Football League games for Luton, Birmingham City, Fulham and Norwich City. He was a member of the Canaries' team that reached the FA Cup semi-finals in 1958–59 whilst still a Third Division club. He wor five caps for Northern Ireland and also made one appearance for the Irish league representative team early in his caree when he was with Distillery.

Dick Bright (Born circa 1922. Died 2002.) Although Dick Bright failed to make a senior appearance in League footbal he played almost 100 games in the emergency competitions during World War Two principally for Burnley, although he also guested for Preston North End and Birmingham City.

James 'Buster' Brown (Born Cumnock, Ayrshire, 16 February 1924. Died January 2002.) Buster Brown was a centre forward with Motherwell, Chesterfield, Bradford City, Queen of the South and Carlisle in the immediate post-wa period. He had the distinction of scoring 'Well's first goal when peacetime activities resumed when he netted in a 4-2 defeat by Rangers.

Tommy Burden (Born Andover, Hants, 21 February 1924. Died Street, Somerset, October 2001.) Tommy Burden began his career at Wolves, but made no senior appearances and moved on to Chester in November 1945. He went on to make his name as a talented wing half throughout the 1940s and '50s, principally with Leeds United and Bristol City He was a member of the City team that won the Division Three South title in 1954–55.

Jack Callender

Tommy Callender

ommy Burdett (Born Hetton-le-Hole, Co Durham, 29 October 1915. Died 25 November 2001.) Tommy Burdett was a inside right or centre forward who played a total of 30 Football League games for Hull and Lincoln City in the years ading up to the Second World War. He was also on the books of Fulham and Bury without making an appearance, ad played for a number of clubs as a guest during the war.

rnie Butler (Born Box, Wilts, 13 May 1919. Died Portsmouth, January 2002.) Ernie Butler was the goalkeeper for ortsmouth when they won successive Football League titles in 1948–49 and 1949–50. In total he played in 240 League ad cup games for Pompey, before retiring after breaking a bone in his hand.

ack Callender (Born West Wylam, Northumberland, 2 April 1923. Died Gateshead, 22 May 2001.) Jack Callender was right half for Gateshead in the immediate post-war period and held the club record of 470 Football League appearaces. He played alongside his brother Tommy, whose death is reported below, in the team that reached the FA Cup uarter-finals in 1952–53, defeating Liverpool on the way.

ommy Callender (Born Wylam, nr Newcastle on Tyne, 20 September 1920. Died Lobley Hill, Gateshead, February 002.) Tommy Callender was a stalwart centre half who won three caps for England at schoolboy level in 1935. He egan his professional career with Lincoln City, but was best known for his time at Gateshead. He made over 400 ppearances for the North-East club between 1946 and 1957 and was a member of the team that reached the FA Cup uarter-finals in 1952–53 before falling to Bolton Wanderers in front of a crowd of over 17,000 at Redheugh Park.

ke Clarke (Born Tipton, Staffs, 9 January 1915. Died Canterbury, Kent, 2 April 2002.) Ike Clarke was a brave centre rward who made his name at West Bromwich Albion where his career spanned ten years, although interrupted by the econd World War. At the age of 32 he joined Portsmouth, then a power in the land, and went on to play in their outanding team of the immediate post-war period, featuring in the title-winning sides of 1948–49 and 1949–50. He scored goals in 224 Football League appearances, before enjoying a spell as player-manager of Yeovil Town.

lebson (Born Itiuba, Bahia, Brazil, 4 September 1978. Died Bahia State, 22 June 2001.) Clebson was a prominent right ack in Brazilian domestic football who was a member of the Vasco da Gama team that won a double of the Copa ercosur and Brazilian national championship in 2000–01. He died in a car accident.

orman Coe (Born Swansea, 6 December 1940. Died Northampton, 24 October 2001.) Norman Coe was a goalkeeper ith Northampton Town during their rise from the Fourth Division to the First during the early 1960s. Although a serve for much of his time at the County Ground he enjoyed a lengthy spell in the line-up during the 1965–66 season, e only occasion the Cobblers have appeared in the top flight.

llan Collins (Born Kilmarnock, 24 January 1919. Died Kilmarnock, 10 April 2002.) Allan Collins was an inside or cene forward who scored over 50 goals for Kilmarnock between 1936 and 1948, and was a member of the team that lost to ast Fife in the replayed Scottish Cup final of 1938. He later played for Raith Rovers and Stenhousemuir.

ugh Colvan (Born Port Glasgow, 24 September 1925. Died Port Glasgow, 26 February 2002.) Hugh Colvan was an side forward who played for Hibs in the period after the war before having a brief spell at Rochdale where he made a ngle Football League appearance. He subsequently joined Derry City, and was a member of the team that defeated lentoran in 1949 to win the Irish Cup for the first time in the club's history.

Arthur Crowe (Born Dundee. Died Ayrshire, June 2002.) Arthur Crowe was a wing half who joined St Johnstone fro Dundee juniors Stobswell. He went on to make 21 first-team appearances for the Perth club between 1945 and 1948.

Bob Curry (Born Gateshead, 2 November 1918. Died Halstead, Essex, 30 June 2001.) Bob Curry captained t Colchester United team that reached the FA Cup fifth round as a Southern League club in 1947–48, causing a sensatic by knocking First Division Huddersfield Town out of the competition in the third round. He went on to lead the tea back to the Football League in 1950 but after a season moved on to Clacton Town. Earlier in his career he had mac one appearance for Sheffield Wednesday before the war.

Mitchell Downie (Born Irvine, Ayrshire, 9 February 1923. Died West Yorkshire, 12 July 2001.) Mitchell Down enjoyed a successful career north of the border with Hibernian, Kilmarnock and Airdrie before moving south to jo Bradford Park Avenue in August 1950. He went on to make over 450 Football League appearances, playing for bo Bradford clubs, Lincoln City and Doncaster Rovers.

Roy Dwight (Born Dartford, 9 January 1933. Died Woolwich, London, 9 April 2002.) Roy Dwight is always remer bered for his role for Nottingham Forest in the 1959 FA Cup final when he scored after nine minutes and was th stretchered off with a broken leg. A goal-scoring outside right or centre forward, his career had begun at Fulham whe he spent eight years on the club's books. He took some time to recover from his injury and drifted into non-league foc ball with Gravesend before his former colleague Jimmy Hill brought him to Coventry and he later also played f Millwall. Roy was the uncle of pop star Elton John.

Olivier Eggiman (Born circa 1919. Died April 2002.) Olivier won 44 caps for Switzerland for whom he appeared in bo the 1950 and 1954 World Cup finals. A centre half, he was a member of domestic title-winning sides with three clubs Lausanne, Servette and La Chaux-de-Fonds.

Bobby Evans (Born Glasgow, 16 July 1927. Died Airdrie, 1 September 2001.) Bobby Evans was a legendary half bac who made more than 500 senior appearances for Celtic in the 1940s and '50s. He was a member of the team that won domestic double in 1953–54 and led the club to their first ever victory in the Scottish League Cup final in 1956–57. H won 48 caps for Scotland, captaining the team in the 1958 World Cup finals, and appeared on 25 occasions for th Scottish League. He later played for Chelsea, Newport County (as player-manager), Morton, Third Lanark and Raith.

Aaron Flahavan (Born Southampton, 12 December 1975. Died Bournemouth, 4 August 2001.) Aaron was a talente young goalkeeper who had just established himself as first choice at Portsmouth in the 2000–01 campaign when he trag cally died in a car accident shortly before the start of last season. An accomplished 'keeper who showed good commar of his area, he made just over 100 senior appearances for Pompey.

Jim Fraser (Born circa 1946. Died 20 March 2002.) Jim captained Dunfermline Athletic in the mid-1960s and had th misfortune to miss out on a place in the 1968 Scottish Cup final victory over Hearts after breaking a leg. Although began his career as a winger, he soon converted to become a cultured centre half or sweeper. He made around 2(senior appearances for the Pars before concluding with a spell at Airdrie.

Tommy Gallacher (Born Renfrew, 13 July 1922. Died Dundee, 24 November 2001.) Tommy Gallacher was a talente right half who made over 250 appearances for Dundee between 1947 and 1956. He was a member of the team th defeated Rangers 3-2 in the 1951–52 Scottish League Cup final and also won a cap for the Scottish League against th Football League. He began his career with Queen's Park and also guested for Aberdeen during the war. He was later well-known football writer for the *Dundee Courier*.

Ray Gill (Born Manchester, 8 December 1924. Died Rochdale, 17 September 2001.) Ray Gill held the record of 4(Football League appearances for Chester. A wholehearted full back, he began his career at Manchester City before movir to Sealand Road in August 1951. He spent 11 years with the club and occasionally featured as an emergency centre forwar

Jovan Gojkovic (Born Cacak, Yugoslavia, 7 January 1975. Died Belgrade, Yugoslavia, 22 December 2001.) Jova Gojkovic was a midfielder who made his name with Red Star Belgrade before joining Greek club Iraklis. He won or cap for his country, appearing against Israel in December 1998. He died as a result of a car crash in central Belgrade.

Ken Green (Born Plaistow, London, 27 April 1924. Died Sutton Coldfield, West Midlands, June 2001.) Ken Gree made over 400 first-team appearances for Birmingham City, his only senior club. A hard-tackling full back known the nickname 'Slasher', he played for the Blues when they lost to Manchester City in the 1956 FA Cup final, and was member of two Second Division championship-winning sides. He won representative honours for the Football Leagu against the Scottish and Irish Leagues in 1953 and for England B against Yugoslavia B and Switzerland B the followir year.

Charlie Gronbach (Born circa 1910. Died 2002.) Charlie Gronbach played at full back for Cowdenbeath and East Fi before the Second World War and later served Cowdenbeath as chairman from 1964 to 1981.

Les Hall (Born St Albans, 1 October 1921. Died 2001.) Les Hall joined Luton from St Albans City during World Wa Two and went on to make 91 first-team appearances at centre half for the Hatters before moving on to Hem Hempstead in 1955.

Stan Harland (Born Liverpool, 19 June 1940. Died Yeovil, Somerset, 30 August 2001.) Stan Harland was captain of th Swindon Town team that provided a major upset when they defeated Arsenal in the 1969 Football League Cup fina He made almost 500 Football League appearances as a wing half in a lengthy career that also saw him play for Bradfo City, Carlisle and Birmingham City. He later had a spell as manager of Yeovil Town.

Ian Harnett (Born circa 1927. Died Scotland, 23 June 2001.) Ian Harnett played for 15 years with Queen's Park, princ pally at full back, and also represented Scotland at amateur level on many occasions. He later became president of th famous Scottish amateur club.

Eric Harper, MBE (Born Aberdeen, circa 1928. Died Stonehaven, 18 December 2001.) Eric Harper was right back fc the Aberdeen Sunnybank team that defeated Lochee Harp to win the Scottish Junior Cup in 1954 and later played pr fessionally for Forfar Athletic and Elgin City. He worked for many years as a secretary and agent for the Conservativ Party in Scotland.

Nandor Hidegkuti heading home for Hungary in the 1954 World Cup semi-final against Uruguay. The Hungarians won 4-2 after extra time in arguably the finest World Cup match in history.

Bill Harvey (Born Grimsby, 1920. Died February 2002.) Bill Harvey played a handful of first-team games at outside right for Grimsby Town during World War Two and later appeared in the Midland League with Boston United and Scarborough. He went on to coach Bristol City and Swindon and had spells as manager of Luton and Grimsby Town.

Mike Haughney (Born Paisley, 10 December 1925. Died Peoria, Illinois, USA, 23 February 2002.) Mike Haughney was a versatile player who was equally at home at right back or centre forward, but it was in the former role that he won his only cap for Scotland against England in April 1954. His career with Celtic, his only senior club, spanned the period 1949 to 1957 during which he made over 200 first-team appearances. He was also a member of the team that lifted the Scottish League and Cup double in 1953–54. Soon after leaving the club he moved to the USA.

Bert Head (Born Midsomer Norton, Somerset, 8 June 1916. Died 4 February 2002.) Bert Head made over 250 senior appearances, principally at centre half, for Torquay and Bury between 1936 and 1953, but was much better known for his time as a manager with Crystal Palace. He led the Eagles to a place in the top flight for the first time in their history in 1968–69 and kept them there for the next four seasons. He also had a spell as manager of Swindon Town where he discovered Mike Summerbee and Don Rogers.

Brian Henderson (Born Allendale, Northumberland, 12 June 1930. Died 7 November 2001.) Brian Henderson was a wholehearted full back for Darlington for 12 seasons, making a total of 422 Football League appearances between 1952 and 1964. A member of the team that reached the fifth round of the FA Cup in 1957–58, his career was ended after he suffered a broken leg against Stockport County in January 1964.

Doug Henderson (Born Southampton, 6 March 1913. Died Southampton, 29 May 2002.) Doug Henderson was one of the oldest surviving Southampton players at the time of his death. A reliable full back, he made 24 senior appearances for Saints before joining Bristol City in the 1939 close season. When war broke out he joined the Southampton Police force and he remained with them until his retirement in 1978.

Ron Hewitt (Born Flint, 21 June 1928. Died September 2001.) Ron Hewitt won five caps for Wales, all in 1958, and played in the World Cup quarter-final tie against Brazil. His best years were spent at Wrexham, for whom he played over 200 times but also appeared for Walsall, Darlington, Cardiff City, Coventry City and Chester. A goal-scoring inside forward, he netted a total of 155 senior goals and won representative honours for Division Three North against Division Three South in October 1956.

Nandor Hidegkuti (Born Budapest, Hungary, 3 March 1922. Died Budapest, Hungary, 14 February 2002.) Nandor Hidegkuti was one of the stars of Hungary's all-conquering team of the 1950s. He created a sensation playing as a deep-lying centre forward against England at Wembley in 1953, the tactic confusing the home defenders to such an extent that he netted a hat-trick in the Magyars' 6-3 win. He won 68 caps in all and played in the 1954 World Cup final against West Germany. He played all his senior club football with MTK Budapest and later coached Fiorentina to victory against Rangers in the 1960–61 European Cup Winners' Cup final.

Tommy Hough (Born Preston, 17 January 1922. Died Preston, 2 July 2001.) Tommy Hough was a promising inside forward who lost the best years of his career to the Second World War. He signed for Preston North End in May 1939 and made a handful of wartime appearances, also guesting for Blackburn Rovers, and later played three times for Barrow in the 1946–47 season.

Stewart Imlach (Born Lossiemouth, 6 January 1932. Died October 2001.) Stewart Imlach was one of the heroes of Nottingham Forest's victory over Luton in the 1959 FA Cup final, creating both of his side's goals on a day when they won 2-1 despite losing Roy Dwight early on with a broken leg. A talented outside left, he made over 400 Football League appearances, and also played for Bury, Derby County, Luton Town, Coventry City and Crystal Palace. He was capped four times by Scotland for whom he featured in the 1958 World Cup finals in Sweden.

Barry Jepson (Born Alfreton, Derbys, 29 December 1929. Died December 2001.) Barry Jepson was a prolific centre forward in the lower divisions in the 1950s. He netted 85 League goals in 168 appearances for Mansfield, Chester and Southport between 1954 and 1960. He scored five times for Chester against York City in February 1958.

Leslie Johnston (Born Glasgow, 16 August 1920. Died Clayton, Staffs, October 2001.) Leslie Johnston developed as a centre forward with Clyde during the Second World War and won a wartime cap for Scotland when he came on as substitute in the 6-1 defeat by England at Hampden in April 1945. He later had a brief spell at Hibernian before returning to Clyde where he won two full caps in the summer of 1948, appearing against Belgium and Switzerland. He then had a season at Celtic before joining Stoke City, where he scored a creditable 22 goals from 88 games, before concluding his career at Shrewsbury Town.

Steve Kenworthy (Born Wrexham, 6 November 1959. Died Wrexham, 26 June 2001.) Steve Kenworthy was a left back who began his career with Wrexham, for whom he made 20 appearances in a four-year spell as a professional, before finishing his senior career at Bury in the 1981–82 season.

David Kipiani (Born Tbilisi, USSR, 18 November 1951. Died Tbilisi, Georgia, 17 September 2001.) David Kipiani was one of the legendary figures of Georgian football. Capped 19 times by the USSR, he was 'Player of the Year' in 1977 and was a member of the Dynamo Tbilisi team that won the European Cup Winners' Cup in 1981. He later became a respected coach and led the Georgian national team until shortly before his death, which came as a result of a car accident.

Ladislao Kubala (Born Budapest, Hungary, 10 June 1927. Died Barcelona, Spain, 17 May 2002.) One of the great stars of the Barcelona team of the 1950s, Ladislao Kubala was a brilliant forward with great skills on the ball and a powerful shot. He was a member of the Barça team that won the Spanish League title on four occasions, and scored over 250 goals for them in just over 300 appearances. He played international football for three countries – Hungary, Czechoslovakia and Spain – and later enjoyed a successful career in coaching, including an 11-year spell in charge of Spain's national team.

Arthur Lightening (Born Durban, South Africa, 1 April 1936. Died Durban, South Africa, October 2001.) Arthur Lightening was one of the many South Africans who came to play in the Football League in the 1950s. A goalkeeper, he made 171 appearances for Nottingham Forest, Coventry City and Middlesbrough before returning to Durban.

Harry Liley (Born Trowbridge, Wilts, 19 August 1918. Died Weston-Super-Mare, Somerset, 17 September 2001.) Harry Liley was a goalkeeper for Bristol Rovers, making 27 Football League appearances between 1946 and 1951. He later spent several seasons with Bath in the Southern League.

Valery Lobanovsky (Born Kiev, USSR, 6 January 1939. Died Ukraine, 13 May 2002.) Valery Lobanovsky was one of the key figures in modern Ukrainian football. He coached Dynamo Kiev to victory in the European Cup Winners' Cup final in 1975 and 1986, and led the national team until ill health forced his retirement in November 2001. Such was his importance that he was given a state funeral when 80,000 fans, including the country's president, came to pay their respects.

Maurice Lockier (Born Bristol, 27 November 1924. Died 23 December 2001.) Maurice Lockier was an outside left on Bristol Rovers' books between 1947 and 1952, but only made two senior appearances, playing in the final two games of the 1949–50 season. He was later with Bath City and Trowbridge Town.

Stan Lynn (Born Bolton, 18 June 1928. Died 28 April 2002.) Stan Lynn was a tough-tackling right back who was known as 'Stan the Wham' on account of his powerful kicking. He began his career with Accrington Stanley before he was sold to Aston Villa for a £10,000 fee in 1950. He went on to play nearly 300 games for Villa and appeared in the 1957 FA Cup final when they defeated Manchester United. He was later a member of the team that won the Second Division title in 1959–60 and also played in two League Cup finals, the second of which was for Birmingham City who he had joined in October 1961. In January 1958 he became the first full back to score a hat-trick in a First Division game playing for Villa against Sunderland.

John McAlindon (Born Carlisle, 25 December 1930. Died February 2002.) John McAlindon was a lively centre forward who played 18 games for Celtic in the 1950s. He also played for Albion Rovers on loan in 1948–49 and made a dozen appearances for Shrewsbury Town in the 1957–58 season.

Alan McAvoy (Born Wigton, Cumberland, 4 October 1963. Died Maryport, Cumbria, 6 December 2001.) Alan McAvoy enjoyed a brief career as an inside forward with Blackpool in the early 1980s making six Football League appearances in the 1981–82 season.

Jimmy McPhie (Born Bonnybridge, 25 August 1920. Died Falkirk, 24 February 2002.) Jimmy McPhie was a talented full back who made almost 300 appearances for Falkirk and appeared in the 1947 Scottish League Cup final when the Bairns were defeated 4-1 by East Fife. Capped three times for Scotland at schoolboy level, he guested for Preston North End during World War Two and won a wartime cap against Wales in November 1945.

Reg Matthews (Born Coventry, 20 December 1932. Died Coventry, 7 October 2001.) Reg Matthews won five full caps for England and appeared twice for the Football League representative team in the mid-1950s while still a Third Division player. An agile 'keeper, he established himself as first choice for Coventry City during the 1954–55 season and was sold to Chelsea for £22,500 (a record fee for a goalkeeper) in November 1956. He later played over 200 games for Derby County, but failed to add to his international honours after leaving Highfield Road.

Harry Mattinson (Born Ireby, Cumberland, 20 July 1925. Died South Shields, 8 June 2001.) After spending his early career with Sunderland and Middlesbrough, Harry joined Preston in March 1949 and was centre half in the team that won the Second Division title in 1950–51, although he suffered a badly broken leg playing against Huddersfield in an FA Cup game in January of 1951 that kept him out of action for some time. Altogether he made 124 Football League appearances for North End and stayed with the club until 1960 when he joined Queen of the South.

Jason Mayele (Born Kinshasa, DR Congo, 4 January 1976. Died Verona, Italy, 2 March 2002.) Jason Mayele had recently joined Serie A club Chievo when he was killed in a car accident. A striker, he began his professional career in France with Chateauroux, moving on to Cagliari and then Chievo soon after the start of the 2001–02 season. He was a member of the DR Congo squad that reached the quarter-final of the 2002 African Nations' Cup.

Bertie Mee, OBE (Born Bulwell, Notts, 25 December 1920. Died 22 October 2001.) Bertie Mee was the manager of the Arsenal team that achieved a League and FA Cup double in 1970–71. He had played as a winger for Derby County and Mansfield Town before the war and guested for Southampton during the hostilities before injury forced his retirement. He later qualified as a physiotherapist, joining Arsenal in that capacity in 1960 and after gaining coaching qualifications he was appointed manager in June 1966. After two Football League Cup final defeats the Gunners won the Inter Cities Fairs Cup in 1970 and the double the following season. He stayed at Highbury until 1976 and was later a director of Watford.

Vittorio Mero (Born Vercelli, Italy, 21 May 1974. Died 23 January 2002.) A defender with Serie A club Brescia, Vittorio died in a car accident early in 2002. He had previously been on the books of Parma and Ravenna.

Neil Midgley (Born circa 1943. Died 8 July 2001.) Neil Midgley was a leading referee and took charge of the 1987 FA Cup final between Coventry City and Tottenham Hotspur. He later became a referee's assessor for both the Premiership and UEFA.

Tommy Millar (Born Edinburgh, 3 December 1928. Died August 2001.) Tommy was a tough full back who joined Colchester United from Bo'ness United in June 1959. He spent two years at Layer Road before moving to Dundee United where he went on to make over 250 senior appearances before suffering a broken leg which effectively brought his career to an end.

Charlie Mitten (Born Rangoon, Burma, 17 January 1921. Died Stockport, 2 January 2002.) Charlie Mitten was a very skilful left winger with exceptional ball control and the ability to deliver the perfect cross. He developed with Manchester United, making his debut on the resumption of peacetime football and playing in the team that defeated Blackpool in the 1948 FA Cup final. In 1950 he attracted controversy when he moved to the rebel Colombian Dimayor league, returning 12 months later and after a completing a period of suspension imposed by the FA he joined Fulham. He later had a spell as player-manager of Mansfield Town and also managed Newcastle from 1958 to 1961. He made one appearance for England in an unofficial international against Scotland in August 1946 in aid of the Bolton Disaster Fund.

Charlie Mitten

Brian Moore (Born Benenden, Kent, 28 February 1932. Died Kent, 1 September 2001.) Brian Moore was a well-respected football commentator, firstly with BBC Radio, for whom he commentated on the 1966 World Cup final, and then for ITV television from 1968. He presented *On the Ball* and *The Big Match*, retiring after the 1998 World Cup final between France and Brazil.

Bob Morton (Born Aston Clinton, Beds, 25 September 1927. Died Eaton Bray, Beds, April 2002.) Bob Morton made a record 495 Football League appearances for Luton Town between 1948 and 1964, mostly at right half. A one-club man, the high point of his career was playing for the Hatters in the 1959 FA Cup final when they lost to Nottingham Forest. He also won a cap for England B against Switzerland in March 1956 and toured South Africa with an FA XI later the same year.

Sizwe Motaung (Born Newcastle, Natal, South Africa, 7 October 1970. Died Newcastle, Natal, South Africa, August 2001.) Sizwe Motaung was a defender who won 49 caps for South Africa in the 1990s and was a member of the team that defeated Tunisia to win the African Nations' Cup in 1996.

Ambrose Mulraney (Born Wishaw, Lanarks, 18 May 1916. Died 2001.) Ambrose Mulraney joined Ipswich Town in November 1936 and had the distinction of scoring the club's first ever hat-trick in the Football League. He guested as a winger for a number of clubs during World War Two, eventually signing for Birmingham City. However he played just one season of peacetime football for the Blues, later drifting into non-league football with Shrewsbury Town and Kidderminster, before making a surprise come back with First Division Aston Villa, making 12 appearances in the 1948–49 season.

Danny Murphy (Born Warrington, Cheshire, 10 May 1922. Died June 2001.) Danny Murphy made almost 300 Football League appearances for Bolton Wanderers, Crewe Alexandra and Rochdale between 1946 and 1957. A sound left half, he signed for Wanderers in February 1943 and played almost 100 games for them in the emergency wartime competitions.

Marc North (Born Ware, Herts, 29 May 1966. Died Southend, 25 September 2001.) Marc North originally joined Luton Town as a goalkeeper, but soon switched to playing as a striker and it was in the latter role that he enjoyed a successful career in the 1980s. He made over 150 appearances for Luton, Grimsby Town and Leicester City and also played on loan for Lincoln City, Scunthorpe United and Birmingham City. He was a member of the Mariners team that reached the fifth round of the FA Cup in 1988–89 after which he was sold to Leicester.

Billy O'Rourke (Born Nottingham, 2 April 1960. Died Preston, 24 January 2002.) Billy O'Rourke was a goalkeeper with Burnley, Blackpool, Chester and Tranmere in the late 1970s and 1980s. He was an ever present for Blackpool when they won promotion from the Fourth Division in 1984–85, when he was the club's 'Player of the Year', and helped to preserve Tranmere Rovers' Football League status in the nail-biting finish to the 1986–87 campaign.

Liam O'Sullivan (Born 28 October 1981. Died Haddington, East Lothian, 29 April 2002.) Liam was a young defender on the books at Hibernian. He had played for the club's U21 team and had experienced senior football in loan spells at Clydebank and Brechin City. His tragic death occurred at a time when he was recovering from a long-term injury.

David Paris (Born Dundee, circa 1921. Died Dundee, 14 August 2001.) David Paris was a prolific goal-scorer in Scottish football in the late 1940s and early 1950s. He joined East Fife shortly before war broke out and returned to the club after Army service. He spent much of the 1946–47 season on loan at Stirling Albion scoring 22 goals in 12 games and shooting them to a double of the Division C League and League Cup trophies. He later played for Montrose and Brechin City where he continued to find the net with regularity.

Roy Paul (Born Ton Pentre, 18 April 1920. Died Treorchy, 21 May 2002.) Roy Paul was one of the stars of Welsh football in the 1950s. He won 33 caps between 1949 and 1956, captaining his country with distinction. A classy wing half, he made his name with Swansea Town, and came close to joining the exodus of top British players to Colombia in 1950 before changing his mind and returning to sign for Manchester City. He captained City to victory over Birmingham City in the 1956 FA Cup final and made a total of 430 senior appearances for his two clubs before retiring in 1957.

Joe Payne (Born Swansea, 29 June 1921. Died Daventry, 12 September 2001.) Joe Payne was an inside forward who served Swansea Town, Newport County, Scunthorpe United and Northampton Town in the immediate post-war period. He appeared in Scunthorpe's first-ever Football League match against Shrewsbury in August 1950. On retiring from the game he spent many years on the backroom staff at Northampton and later had a spell as manager of Rushden Town.

Serhiy Perkhun (Born Dnipropetrovsk, Ukraine, 4 September 1977. Died Moscow, 28 August 2001.) Serhiy was a young goalkeeper starting out on a promising career when he died after falling into a coma after an accidental collision while playing for CSKA Moscow against Anzhi Makhachkala in a Russian Premier League match. Capped by Ukraine at U21 level, he made his full international debut against Latvia shortly before his death.

Ron Phillips (Born Worsley, Lancs, 30 March 1947. Died Walkden, Lancs, April 2002.) Ron Phillips was a talented left winger who made over 300 senior appearances for Bolton Wanderers, Chesterfield, Bury and Chester between 1966 and 1981. He was a member of the Bolton team that won the Third Division championship in 1972–73.

David Pyle (Born Trowbridge, Wilts, 12 December 1936. Died Trowbridge, Wilts, February 2002.) David Pyle was a reliable centre half who played over 150 games for Bristol Rovers between 1957 and 1962, and was a member of the team that reached the FA Cup quarter-final in 1957–58. He later had a season with Bristol City before retiring from the game.

Jimmy Quinn (Born Croy, 23 November 1947. Died 24 April 2002.) Jimmy was the grandson of the legendary Celtic player Jimmy Quinn, but never managed to establish himself at Parkhead. A versatile player who featured as a forward and at full back, he also had spells with Clyde (on loan), Sheffield Wednesday and Hamilton Academicals.

Duggie Reid (Born West Kilbride, 3 October 1917. Died 8 February 2002.) Duggie Reid was inside forward for the Portsmouth team that won consecutive Football League titles in 1948–49 and 1949–50. He began his career with Stockport County before joining Pompey in March 1946 and he went on to play over 300 games for the Fratton Park club, latterly featuring at centre half. Afterwards he worked for many years as the club groundsman.

Pedro Richards (Born Edmonton, Middlesex, 11 November 1956. Died Nottingham, 23 December 2001.) Pedro Richards was a defender who made over 450 senior appearances for Notts County between 1974 and 1986. He was a member of the team that won promotion to the old First Division in 1980–81 and helped them stay in the top flight for three seasons before they were relegated.

Norman Rigby (Born Warsop, Notts, 23 May 1923. Died Newark, Notts, 21 August 2001.) Norman Rigby was one of Peterborough United's greatest ever servants. In a 20-year association with Posh he led the team to five consecutive Midland League titles and then the Fourth Division championship at the first attempt in 1960–61. He subsequently had a spell as manager of the team in the late 1960s. A tough-tackling centre half, his career had begun with Notts County, for whom he made almost 50 appearances in the seasons after the war.

Frank Rist (Born Leyton, Essex, 30 March 1914. Died Highams Park, Essex, 9 September 2001.) Frank Rist was a centre half who played 47 games for Charlton Athletic, whom he joined in June 1933. He guested for Clapton Orient during World War Two and after leaving the Valley he signed for Colchester United, then a top Southern League club. He also played county cricket for Essex.

Jackie Roberts (Born Swansea, 30 June 1918. Died June 2001.) Jackie began his career for Bolton Wanderers in 1936 as an inside right before switching to play at full back after the war. In all he made over 150 appearances for Wanderers and later spent a season at Swansea Town before leaving the full-time game. Earlier he had played as a guest for Norwich City during wartime Army service. He won his only cap for Wales against Belgium in May 1949.

Tommy Robertson (Born Kincardine, 1935. Died Melbourne, Australia, 4 September 2001.) Tommy Robertson made his only appearance for Rangers against Brechin City in the semi-final of the Scottish League Cup in 1957–58. He also played for Dundee, Queen of the South and Cowdenbeath before moving to Australia.

Tom Saunders (Born Liverpool, circa 1921. Died 4 July 2001.) Tom Saunders was a member of the famous Liverpool bootroom, and an important behind the scenes influence at Anfield. A former schoolteacher, he coached the England Schools team and later became youth development officer for the Reds under Bill Shankly. He was on the club's staff until retiring in 1986 and later served as a director.

Alex Scott (Born Falkirk, 22 November 1936. Died September 2001.) Alex Scott made his name as a goal-scoring winger with Rangers in the 1950s and 1960s. A member of four Scottish League championship-winning sides, he also played in the final of the European Cup Winners' Cup in 1961. He moved south to join Everton in February 1963, helping the Blues to the Football League title in 1962–63 and the FA Cup in 1966. He later wound down his career with spells at Hibernian and Falkirk. He won representative honours for the Scottish League and was capped 16 times by Scotland between 1956 and 1966.

Frank Scrine (Born Swansea, 9 January 1925. Died 5 October 2001.) Frank Scrine played over 200 games for Swansea Town and Oldham Athletic in a career that spanned the years 1944 to 1956. He was a key member of the Swans team that won the Division Three South title in 1948–49 and was capped twice by Wales, playing at inside left against England and Northern Ireland during the 1949–50 season.

Les Sealey (Born Bethnal Green, London, 29 September 1957. Died 19 August 2001.) Les Sealey spent much of his career as a journeyman goalkeeper for Coventry City and Luton Town, seeing little success. He received a surprise boost when Manchester United manager Alex Ferguson signed him on loan in March 1990 and he went on to replace Jim Leighton for the FA Cup final replay following a 3-3 draw in the first match. United won the match and he stayed at Old Trafford the following season when he was a member of the team that defeated Barcelona to take the European Cup Winners' Cup. In total he made over 550 senior appearances for ten clubs.

Ray Seary (Born Slough, Berks, 18 September 1952. Died Histon, Cambs, 5 December 2001.) Ray Seary served Queen's Park Rangers as an apprentice but only received the briefest experience of senior football at Loftus Road before moving on to Cambridge United early in 1974. He was a regular at left back for the U's for most of the next two-and-a-half seasons before leaving the game to join the Cambridgeshire Police Force.

Ronnie Sharp (Born 30 January 1948. Died Mexico. 2002.) Ronnie Sharp was a midfield player who was a member of the Cowdenbeath team that finished runners-up to Falkirk in the Scottish Second Division in 1969–70. He later moved to the United States and had a successful career with Miami Toros and Fort Lauderdale Strikers.

John Sharples (Born Wolverhampton, 8 August 1934. Died 1 September 2001.) John Sharples was a well built full back who had his introduction to senior football with Aston Villa in the 1958–59 season when deputising for the injured Peter Aldis. He joined Walsall in the summer of 1959 and after spending some time establishing himself in the team, he went on to make 131 League and cup appearances over the next five seasons.

Frank Sims (Born Lincoln, 12 September 1931. Died Nottingham, 28 November 2001.) Frank Sims was a stalwart centre half who spent eight seasons with Lincoln City between 1950 and 1958. Principally a back up to Tony Emery, he made just three first-team appearances but otherwise played regularly for the Imps' reserves in the Midland League.

Jimmy Smith (Born Arbroath, 16 October 1937. Died April 2002.) Jimmy Smith was a full back who won schoolboy honours for Scotland and joined Preston North End as a teenager. He spent 11 seasons at Deepdale, making over 300 first-team appearances and playing in the team that were defeated by West Ham in the 1964 FA Cup final. He later spent three seasons with Stockport County before leaving the full-time game.

George Smith (Born Portsmouth, 24 March 1919. Died Albury, NSW, Australia, 21 December 2001.) George Smith was a wing half who made his debut for Southampton in the final season before World War Two broke out. After wartime service in the RAF he went on to play just over 100 games for the Saints and then had a brief spell at Crystal Palace before emigrating to Australia.

Jim Smith (Born Angus, circa 1921. Died Forfar, 15 December 2001.) Jim Smith was a long-serving centre half for Brechin City throughout the 1940s and 1950s.

Fritz Walter carried off in triumph after Germany's 1954 victory over Hungary.

Tom Staniforth (Born Carlisle, 15 December 1980. Died York, 19 August 2001.) Tom Staniforth was a promising young central defender who was a young professional yet to make his senior debut for Sheffield Wednesday. He died tragically after suffering a fit while on a night out with friends.

Colin Syme (Born Rosyth, 23 June 1924. Died Leicester, 2 October 2001.) Colin Syme joined Torquay United from Dunfermline Athletic in December 1946, and played his only senior game shortly afterwards on Christmas Day that year, when he lined up at outside right for the Gulls in their 6-1 defeat at Crystal Palace.

Ernst Stojaspal (Born Austria, 14 January 1925. Died France, April 2002.) Ernst Stojaspal was a forward who scored 15 goals in 32 appearances for Austria. He was a member of the Austrian team that finished third in the 1954 World Cup finals. He made his name as a goal-scorer with FK Austria before joining Strasbourg in 1954 and he remained in France for the rest of his career.

Bill Thomas (Born Derby, 18 November 1918. Died Bristol, November 2001.) Bill Thomas was an inside forward who joined Bristol City in October 1944 and played regularly in wartime football. He remained at Ashton Gate for four seasons after the resumption of the game and made 77 appearances for the Robins scoring 18 goals.

Arthur Thomson (Born Edinburgh, 2 September 1948. Died Edinburgh, 7 March 2002.) Arthur Thomson was a tall wing half who never managed to make the first team at Chelsea, but went on to enjoy a successful spell with Hearts. He later moved south to join Oldham, but never really established himself at Boundary Park and in December 1970 he signed for Raith Rovers where he concluded his senior career.

Kurtis Townsend (Born Waltham Forest, London, 28 August 1983. Died 15 December 2001.) Kurtis Townsend was a young full back who spent the 2000–01 season as a professional at Wimbledon. He later joined Cheshunt and tragically died in a car accident while on his way to play for the club shortly before Christmas.

Mickey Trotman (Born Arima, Trinidad, 21 October 1974. Died Arima, Trinidad, 3 October 2001.) Mickey Trotman was a midfield player who was a current international with Trinidad & Tobago at the time of his death, which came as a result of a car accident. A member of the team that won the Copa Caribe in 1999 and 2001, he played for the US-A League club Rochester Rhinos.

Paul Vaessen (Born Gillingham, 16 October 1961. Died Bristol, 8 August 2001.) Paul Vaessen was a young star at Arsenal in the early 1980s. The pinnacle of his career was scoring the winner against Juventus to take the Gunners into the final of the European Cup Winners' Cup in 1980. Injuries eventually forced him into an early retirement and he died in Bristol in tragic circumstances during the summer of 2001.

Velibor Vasovic (Born Yugoslavia, 3 October 1939. Died Yugoslavia, 4 March 2002.) Velibor Vasovic was a central defender and captain of the great Ajax team of the early 1970s. He began his career with Partizan Belgrade, for whom he appeared in the 1966 European Cup final defeat by Real Madrid. In December of that year he signed for Ajax and went on to lead the team to victory over Panathinaikos in the 1971 European Cup final before retiring and returning to Yugoslavia. He won 32 caps for his country and gained a runners-up medal in the 1968 European Championships when they lost a replayed final to Italy.

Vava (Born Recife, Brazil, 12 November 1934. Died Rio de Janeiro, Brazil, 19 January 2002.) Vava was a centre forward who played for Brazil's World Cup-winning teams in 1958 and 1962. He scored twice against Sweden in '58 and added another against Czechoslovakia four years later to become the first player to score in consecutive World Cup finals. He played most of his football in Brazil for Vasco da Gama, but also had a spell in Europe with Atletico Madrid.

William Walmsley (Born Kilmarnock. Died 3 September 2001.) William Walmsley was an outside left who made one appearance for Rangers against Clyde in the 1946–47 season.

Fritz Walter (Born Kaiserslautern, Germany, 31 October 1920. Died Enkenbach-Alsenborn, Germany, 17 June 2002.) Fritz Walter captained the West German team that surprisingly defeated Hungary to win the World Cup in 1954, a success that enabled his country to fully integrate into the football world once more following several years of isolation after the Second World War. An attacking midfield player, he won 61 caps for his country and scored 33 goals. A one-club man he played for Kaiserslautern for over 20 years, scoring at almost a goal-a-game. He also led his country at the 1958 World Cup finals, when they finished in fourth place, announcing his retirement soon afterwards.

Craig Watson (Born circa 1942. Died Glasgow, 7 November 2001.) Craig Watson was a member of the Rangers team that defeated Morton to win the Scottish League Cup in 1963–64. An outside left, he made 20 appearances for the Ibrox club between 1962 and 1966 and later played for Morton before emigrating to South Africa.

Derek Whiteford (Born circa 1947. Died Shotts, North Lanarkshire, 12 January 2002.) Derek Whiteford played over 400 games for Airdrie, captaining them in the 1975 Scottish Cup final, when they lost 3-1 to Celtic, and also when they won the Spring Cup in 1975–76. He began his career as a defender with Hibernian, later switching to a more attacking role. He also played for Dumbarton and Falkirk and had spells as manager of Albion Rovers and Airdrie.

Jimmy Whittle, MBE (Born Hamilton, 5 September 1929. Died 2001.) Jimmy Whittle was an inside or centre forward with Hearts from 1947 until 1956; primarily a reserve, he scored 18 goals in 49 first-team appearances. He played two games on loan for Southampton in the 1953–54 season while on National Service and later played for Ayr United. An accountant by profession he was awarded the MBE in 1983 for his work with the Red Cross.

Darwell Williams (Born Llanelli, 4 November 1926. Died 13 October 2001.) Darwell Williams was a wing half who joined Swansea Town from Loughor Rovers in 1946 and went on to make 130 League appearances for the Swans before being released in May 1954.

Willie Wilson (Born East Lothian, circa 1943. Died November 2001.) Willie Wilson was a goalkeeper for Hibernian in the 1960s, and featured in many of their famous European clashes during the decade.

Sir Walter Winterbottom, CBE, OBE (Born Oldham, Lancs, 31 January 1913. Died Guildford, Surrey, 16 February 2002.) Walter Winterbottom was England's longest serving manager and guided the team through four World Cup final tournaments. He had been a promising centre half with Manchester United before the war, but a spine condition led him to pursue a career in teaching and then coaching. He was appointed as national director of coaching by the FA in 1946 and became England manager the following May, although team selection was still in the hands of an FA committee. Although a reforming influence, his early years in the job saw English football at a low ebb following defeats by the USA in the 1950 World Cup and then the disasters against Hungary in 1953–54. Nevertheless he was relatively successful (78 wins from 139 games) and laid the foundations for victory in 1966.

Kenneth Wolstenholme (Born Worsley, Lancs, 1920. Died Torquay, 25 March 2002.) Kenneth Wolstenholme is best known as the television commentator who remarked during the closing stages of the 1966 World Cup final, 'Some people are on the pitch. They think it's all over ... it is now,' as Geoff Hurst scored England's fourth goal to complete their victory. He commentated for BBC Television from 1948, covering five World Cups and 22 FA Cup finals and was widely regarded as the 'voice of football', setting new standards for the quality of his work.

Alf Wood (Born Walsall, 14 May 1915. Died Aberdare, 17 December 2001.) Alf Wood served Coventry City as a player and then as a coach for over 20 years. He joined the Sky Blues in December 1935, but played only a couple of games before war broke out. He went to establish himself as the club's regular goalkeeper in 1946–47 and made 209 consecutive Football League appearances before moving on to Northampton Town in December 1951. He played almost 150 games for the Cobblers before joining the coaching staff at Highfield Road, although he continued to play in an emergency and made his last appearances at the age of 43. He later had a spell as manager of Walsall.

Ray Wood (Born Hebburn, Co Durham, 11 June 1931. Died Bexhill, East Sussex, 7 July 2002.) Ray Wood will always be remembered as the goalkeeper who suffered a fractured cheekbone playing in the 1957 FA Cup final for Manchester United against Aston Villa, an injury that arguably cost United the match. He made his bow in senior football with Darlington in the 1949–50 season before moving to Old Trafford where he played over 200 first-team games and was a survivor of the 1958 Munich Air Crash. His career tally of appearances topped 400 after further spells with Huddersfield, Bradford City and Barnsley, while he also won three full caps for England in the mid-1950s.

Willie Woodburn (Born Edinburgh, 8 August 1919. Died Edinburgh, 2 December 2001.) One of the all-time greats for Rangers, Willie Woodburn was the centre half in the team that won a domestic treble in 1948–49. He won four Scottish League championships and four Scottish Cups during his time at Ibrox, making more than 300 appearances for the club. He also gained 24 caps for Scotland, but was later banned for life by the SFA after being sent off in the 1954–55 season.

Derek Woodley (Born Isleworth, Middlesex, 2 March 1942. Died Essex, January 2002.) Derek Woodley was a talented schoolboy footballer, winning five caps for England at U15 level in 1957 and creating a record for scoring the fastest ever goal at Wembley Stadium when he netted after just 13 seconds against Wales. An outside right, he never really made the grade with West Ham United, despite gaining England youth honours, but is best remembered for a lengthy spell at Southend United. He later played for Charlton Athletic and Gillingham before retiring from the game in 1971.

Zizinho (Born Sao Gonzalo, Brazil, 14 September 1922. Died Niteroi, Rio de Janeiro, Brazil, 7 February 2002.) Zizinho was an attacking midfield player who won over 50 caps for Brazil, for whom he was a member of the teams that won the Copa America in 1949 and finished runners-up to Uruguay in the 1950 World Cup finals. He played his club football with Flamengo, Bangu and FC Sao Paulo.

IAN NANNESTAD
(Soccer History Magazine)

THE FA BARCLAYCARD PREMIERSHIP and NATIONWIDE FOOTBALL LEAGUE FIXTURES 2002–03

Reproduced under Copyright/Database Licence No. PRINT/ALL/3014. Copyright © The FA Premier League/The Football League Limited 2002.

*Sky Sports; †Premiership Plus pay per view

Saturday, 10 August 2002
Nationwide Football League Division 1
Bradford C v Wolverhampton W
Burnley v Brighton & HA
Coventry C v Sheffield U
Derby Co v Reading
Leicester C v Watford
Millwall v Rotherham U
Norwich C v Grimsby T
Portsmouth v Nottingham F
Preston NE v Crystal P
Sheffield W v Stoke C
*Walsall v Ipswich T (5:35)
Wimbledon v Gillingham

Nationwide Football League Division 2
Bristol C v Blackpool
Cheltenham T v Wigan Ath
Colchester U v Stockport Co
Huddersfield T v Brentford
Luton T v Peterborough U
Mansfield T v Plymouth Arg
Northampton T v Crewe Alex
Notts Co v Wycombe W
Oldham Ath v Cardiff C
Port Vale v Tranmere R
QPR v Chesterfield
Swindon T v Barnsley

Nationwide Football League Division 3
Boston U v Bournemouth
Cambridge U v Darlington
Carlisle U v Hartlepool U
Hull C v Southend U
Kidderminster H v Lincoln C
Macclesfield T v York C
Oxford U v Bury
Rochdale v Leyton Orient
Scunthorpe U v Wrexham
Shrewsbury T v Exeter C
Swansea C v Rushden & D'monds
Torquay U v Bristol R

Sunday, 11 August 2002
FA Community Shield
*Arsenal v Liverpool (2:00)

Nationwide Football League Division 1
*Bradford C v Wolverhampton W (4:30)

Tuesday, 13 August 2002
Nationwide Football League Division 1
Brighton & HA v Coventry C
Crystal P v Bradford C (8:00)
Gillingham v Derby Co
Grimsby T v Wimbledon
*Reading v Sheffield W (7:45)
Rotherham U v Norwich C
Sheffield U v Portsmouth
Watford v Millwall
Wolverhampton W v Walsall

Nationwide Football League Division 2
Barnsley v Cheltenham T
Blackpool v Luton T
Brentford v Bristol C

Cardiff C v Port Vale
Chesterfield v Swindon T
Crewe Alex v Notts Co
Peterborough U v Oldham Ath
Plymouth Arg v Huddersfield T
Stockport Co v QPR
Tranmere R v Colchester U
Wigan Ath v Mansfield T
Wycombe W v Northampton T

Nationwide Football League Division 3
Bournemouth v Kidderminster H
Bristol R v Hull C
Bury v Cambridge U
Darlington v Swansea C (7:30)
Exeter C v Scunthorpe U
Hartlepool U v Boston U
Leyton Orient v Macclesfield T
Lincoln C v Rochdale
Rushden & D'monds v Torquay U
Southend U v Carlisle U
Wrexham v Oxford U
York C v Shrewsbury T

Wednesday, 14 August 2002
Nationwide Football League Division 1
Nottingham F v Preston NE
*Stoke C v Leicester C (7:45)

Saturday, 17 August 2002
FA Barclaycard Premiership
Blackburn R v Sunderland
Charlton Ath v Chelsea
Everton v Tottenham H
Fulham v Bolton W
Leeds U v Manchester C
Manchester U v WBA
Southampton v Middlesbrough

Nationwide Football League Division 1
Brighton & HA v Norwich C
Crystal P v Portsmouth
Gillingham v Millwall
*Grimsby T v Derby Co (5:35)
Nottingham F v Sheffield W
Reading v Coventry C
Rotherham U v Preston NE
Sheffield U v Walsall
Stoke C v Bradford C
Watford v Wimbledon
Wolverhampton W v Burnley

Nationwide Football League Division 2
Barnsley v QPR
Blackpool v Swindon T
Brentford v Oldham Ath
Cardiff C v Northampton T
Chesterfield v Port Vale
Crewe Alex v Colchester U
Peterborough U v Huddersfield T
Plymouth Arg v Luton T
Stockport Co v Notts Co
Tranmere R v Cheltenham T
Wigan Ath v Bristol C
Wycombe W v Mansfield T

Nationwide Football League Division 3
Bournemouth v Cambridge U

Bristol R v Rochdale
Bury v Swansea C
Darlington v Oxford U
Exeter C v Hull C
Hartlepool U v Macclesfield T
Leyton Orient v Scunthorpe U
Lincoln C v Carlisle U
Rushden & D'monds v
 Kidderminster H
Southend U v Shrewsbury T
Wrexham v Boston U
York C v Torquay U

Nationwide Conference
Burton A v Scarborough
Chester C v Kettering T
Dag & Red v Leigh RMI
Doncaster R v Barnet
Halifax T v Telford U
Hereford U v Farnborough T
Margate v Morecambe
Southport v Nuneaton B
Stevenage B v Northwich Vic
Woking v Forest Green R
Yeovil T v Gravesend & N

Sunday, 18 August 2002
FA Barclaycard Premiership
*Arsenal v Birmingham C (4:05)
†Aston Villa v Liverpool (2:00)

Nationwide Football League Division 1
Ipswich T v Leicester C

Monday, 19 August 2002
FA Barclaycard Premiership
*Newcastle U v West Ham U (8:00)

Nationwide Conference
Telford U v Chester C

Tuesday, 20 August 2002
Nationwide Conference
Barnet v Yeovil T
Farnborough T v Stevenage B
Forest Green R v Hereford U
Gravesend & N v Dag & Red
Kettering T v Margate
Leigh RMI v Doncaster R
Morecambe v Halifax T
Northwich Vic v Burton A
Nuneaton B v Woking
Scarborough v Southport

Friday, 23 August 2002
FA Barclaycard Premiership
*Chelsea v Manchester U (8:00)

Nationwide Football League Division 2
Northampton T v Blackpool

Saturday, 24 August 2002
FA Barclaycard Premiership
Birmingham C v Blackburn R
Bolton W v Charlton Ath
Liverpool v Southampton
*Manchester C v Newcastle U (12:15)
Middlesbrough v Fulham
Sunderland v Everton

Tottenham H v Aston Villa
†WBA v Leeds U (5:30)
West Ham U v Arsenal

Nationwide Football League Division 1
Bradford C v Grimsby T
Burnley v Sheffield U
Coventry C v Crystal P
Derby Co v Wolverhampton W
Leicester C v Reading
Millwall v Ipswich T
Norwich C v Gillingham
Portsmouth v Watford
Preston NE v Stoke C
Sheffield W v Rotherham U
Walsall v Nottingham F
Wimbledon v Brighton & HA

Nationwide Football League Division 2
Bristol C v Wycombe W
Cheltenham T v Plymouth Arg
Colchester U v Brentford
Huddersfield T v Crewe Alex
Luton T v Barnsley
Mansfield T v Chesterfield
Notts Co v Wigan Ath
Oldham Ath v Tranmere R
Port Vale v Stockport Co
QPR v Peterborough U
Swindon T v Cardiff C

Nationwide Football League Division 3
Boston U v Lincoln C
Cambridge U v Leyton Orient
Carlisle U v Bristol R
Hull C v Bury
Kidderminster H v Exeter C
Macclesfield T v Wrexham
Oxford U v Southend U
Rochdale v Darlington
Scunthorpe U v York C
Shrewsbury T v Rushden & D'monds
Swansea C v Bournemouth
Torquay U v Hartlepool U

Nationwide Conference
Barnet v Chester C
Farnborough T v Halifax T
Forest Green R v Southport
Gravesend & N v Hereford U
Kettering T v Woking
Leigh RMI v Burton A
Morecambe v Yeovil T
Northwich Vic v Margate
Nuneaton B v Stevenage B
Scarborough v Dag & Red
Telford U v Doncaster R

Monday, 26 August 2002

Nationwide Football League Division 1
Brighton & HA v Walsall (3:00)
Gillingham v Preston NE (3:00)
Grimsby T v Portsmouth (3:00)
Ipswich T v Bradford C
Rotherham U v Derby Co (3:00)
Sheffield U v Millwall (3:00)
Stoke C v Norwich C (3:00)
*Watford v Coventry C (1:00)

Nationwide Football League Division 2
Barnsley v Notts Co (3:00)
Blackpool v Oldham Ath (3:00)
Brentford v Swindon T (3:00)
Cardiff C v Luton T (3:00)
Peterborough U v Colchester U (3:00)
Plymouth Arg v Bristol C (3:00)
Stockport Co v Mansfield T (3:00)
Tranmere R v Huddersfield T (3:00)
Wigan Ath v Port Vale (3:00)
Wycombe W v QPR (3:00)

Nationwide Football League Division 3
Bury v Shrewsbury T (3:00)
Exeter C v Torquay U (3:00)
Hartlepool U v Hull C (3:00)
Leyton Orient v Kidderminster H (3:00)
Lincoln C v Macclesfield T (3:00)
Rushden & D'monds v Scunthorpe U (3:00)
Southend U v Cambridge U (3:00)
Wrexham v Rochdale (3:00)
York C v Boston U (3:00)

Nationwide Conference
*Burton A v Barnet (7.45)
Chester C v Scarborough
Dag & Red v Telford U
Doncaster R v Farnborough T
Halifax T v Northwich Vic
Hereford U v Morecambe
Margate v Forest Green R
Southport v Kettering T
Stevenage B v Gravesend & N
Woking v Leigh RMI
Yeovil T v Nuneaton B

Tuesday, 27 August 2002

FA Barclaycard Premiership
†Arsenal v WBA (8:00)
Charlton Ath v Tottenham H

Nationwide Football League Division 1
Crystal P v Leicester C (8:00)
Reading v Burnley (8:00)
Wolverhampton W v Sheffield W

Nationwide Football League Division 2
Chesterfield v Northampton T
Crewe Alex v Cheltenham T

Nationwide Football League Division 3
Bournemouth v Oxford U
Bristol R v Swansea C
Darlington v Carlisle U (7:30)

Wednesday, 28 August 2002

FA Barclaycard Premiership
Aston Villa v Manchester C
Blackburn R v Liverpool (8:00)
Everton v Birmingham C (8:00)
*Fulham v West Ham U (8:00)
Leeds U v Sunderland
Newcastle U v Bolton W – postponed
*Alternative date required due to
European Cup Qualifier*
Southampton v Chelsea

Nationwide Football League Division 1
Nottingham F v Wimbledon

Saturday, 31 August 2002

FA Barclaycard Premiership
Birmingham C v Leeds U
Manchester C v Everton
Middlesbrough v Blackburn R
Sunderland v Manchester U
Tottenham H v Southampton
WBA v Fulham
West Ham U v Charlton Ath

Nationwide Football League Division 1
Bradford C v Rotherham U
Burnley v Crystal P
*Coventry C v Nottingham F (5:35)
Derby Co v Stoke C
Leicester C v Gillingham
Millwall v Grimsby T
Norwich C v Watford
Portsmouth v Brighton & HA
Walsall v Reading
Wimbledon v Wolverhampton W

Nationwide Football League Division 2
Bristol C v Tranmere R
Cheltenham T v Cardiff C
Colchester U v Wigan Ath
Huddersfield T v Blackpool
Luton T v Chesterfield
Mansfield T v Crewe Alex
Northampton T v Barnsley
Notts Co v Brentford
Oldham Ath v Wycombe W
Port Vale v Peterborough U
QPR v Plymouth Arg
Swindon T v Stockport Co

Nationwide Football League Division 3
Boston U v Bury
Cambridge U v Rushden & D'monds
Carlisle U v Exeter C
Hull C v Leyton Orient
Kidderminster H v Darlington
Macclesfield T v Bournemouth
Oxford U v Hartlepool U
Rochdale v Southend U
Scunthorpe U v Bristol R
Shrewsbury T v Lincoln C
Swansea C v York C
Torquay U v Wrexham

Nationwide Conference
Barnet v Halifax T
Farnborough T v Dag & Red
Forest Green R v Chester C
Gravesend & N v Southport
Kettering T v Yeovil T
Leigh RMI v Margate
Morecambe v Stevenage B
Northwich Vic v Doncaster R
Nuneaton B v Hereford U
Scarborough v Woking
Telford U v Burton A

Sunday, 1 September 2002

FA Barclaycard Premiership
†Bolton W v Aston Villa (2:00)
*Chelsea v Arsenal (4:05)

Nationwide Football League Division 1
Preston NE v Ipswich T (2:00)
*Sheffield W v Sheffield U (12:00)

Monday, 2 September 2002

FA Barclaycard Premiership
*Liverpool v Newcastle U (8:00)

Nationwide Conference
Stevenage B v Telford U

Tuesday, 3 September 2002

FA Barclaycard Premiership
†Manchester U v Middlesbrough (8:00)

Nationwide Conference
Burton A v Forest Green R
Chester C v Morecambe
Dag & Red v Nuneaton B
Doncaster R v Kettering T
Halifax T v Scarborough
Hereford U v Northwich Vic
Margate v Barnet
Southport v Leigh RMI
Woking v Gravesend & N
Yeovil T v Farnborough T

Saturday, 7 September 2002

Nationwide Football League Division 1
Bradford C v Coventry C
Derby Co v Burnley

Gillingham v Portsmouth
Grimsby T v Ipswich T
Millwall v Brighton & HA
Norwich C v Sheffield U
Rotherham U v Reading
Sheffield W v Crystal P
Stoke C v Nottingham F
Watford v Walsall
Wimbledon v Leicester C
Wolverhampton W v Preston NE

Nationwide Football League Division 2
Blackpool v Tranmere R
Brentford v Luton T
Bristol C v Northampton T
Colchester U v Cheltenham T
Crewe Alex v Chesterfield
Huddersfield T v Barnsley
Mansfield T v QPR
Notts Co v Oldham Ath
Plymouth Arg v Cardiff C
Stockport Co v Peterborough U
Swindon T v Port Vale
Wigan Ath v Wycombe W

Nationwide Football League Division 3
Bury v York C
Cambridge U v Hull C
Carlisle U v Rochdale
Darlington v Wrexham
Exeter C v Bournemouth
Kidderminster H v Boston U
Lincoln C v Scunthorpe U
Macclesfield T v Bristol R
Oxford U v Torquay U
Rushden & D'monds v Southend U
Shrewsbury T v Leyton Orient
Swansea C v Hartlepool U

Nationwide Conference
Barnet v Telford U
Burton A v Halifax T
Chester C v Leigh RMI
*Doncaster R v Dag & Red (12:15)
Gravesend & N v Nuneaton B
Margate v Stevenage B
Morecambe v Forest Green R
Scarborough v Kettering T
Southport v Farnborough T
Woking v Hereford U
Yeovil T v Northwich Vic

Tuesday, 10 September 2002
FA Barclaycard Premiership
*Arsenal v Manchester C (8:00)
Middlesbrough v Sunderland

Wednesday, 11 September 2002
FA Barclaycard Premiership
Aston Villa v Charlton Ath
Blackburn R v Chelsea (8:00)
Fulham v Tottenham H
Liverpool v Birmingham C (8:00)
Manchester U v Bolton W (8:00)
†Newcastle U v Leeds U (8:00)
Southampton v Everton
West Ham U v WBA

Saturday, 14 September 2002
FA Barclaycard Premiership
Bolton W v Liverpool
Charlton Ath v Arsenal
Chelsea v Newcastle U
Everton v Middlesbrough
*Leeds U v Manchester U (12:00)
Sunderland v Fulham
WBA v Southampton

Nationwide Football League Division 1
Brighton & HA v Gillingham
Burnley v Stoke C
Coventry C v Grimsby T
Crystal P v Wolverhampton W
Leicester C v Derby Co
Nottingham F v Watford
Portsmouth v Millwall
Preston NE v Sheffield W
Reading v Wimbledon
Sheffield U v Rotherham U
Walsall v Bradford C

Nationwide Football League Division 2
Barnsley v Plymouth Arg
Cardiff C v Stockport Co
Cheltenham T v Bristol C
Chesterfield v Wigan Ath
Luton T v Notts Co
Northampton T v Huddersfield T
Oldham Ath v Mansfield T
Peterborough U v Crewe Alex
Port Vale v Colchester U
QPR v Swindon T
Tranmere R v Brentford
Wycombe W v Blackpool

Nationwide Football League Division 3
Boston U v Oxford U
Bournemouth v Bury
Bristol R v Exeter C
Hartlepool U v Darlington
Hull C v Carlisle U
Leyton Orient v Lincoln C
Rochdale v Shrewsbury T
Scunthorpe U v Kidderminster H
Southend U v Macclesfield T
Torquay U v Cambridge U
Wrexham v Swansea C
York C v Rushden & D'monds

Nationwide Conference
Dag & Red v Burton A
Farnborough T v Scarborough
Forest Green R v Gravesend & N
Halifax T v Doncaster R
Hereford U v Chester C
Kettering T v Morecambe
Leigh RMI v Barnet
Northwich Vic v Woking
Nuneaton B v Margate
Stevenage B v Yeovil T
Telford U v Southport

Sunday, 15 September 2002
FA Barclaycard Premiership
*Birmingham C v Aston Villa (4:05)
†Manchester C v Blackburn R (2:00)

Nationwide Football League Division 1
Ipswich T v Norwich C (1:00)

Monday, 16 September 2002
FA Barclaycard Premiership
*Tottenham H v West Ham U (8:00)

Nationwide Conference
Telford U v Scarborough

Tuesday, 17 September 2002
Nationwide Football League Division 1
Brighton & HA v Stoke C
Burnley v Millwall
Crystal P v Derby Co (8:00)
Leicester C v Bradford C
Portsmouth v Wimbledon
Preston NE v Watford
Sheffield U v Grimsby T
Walsall v Rotherham U

Nationwide Football League Division 2
Barnsley v Blackpool
Cardiff C v Brentford
Cheltenham T v Swindon T
Chesterfield v Stockport Co
Luton T v Mansfield T
Northampton T v Colchester U
Oldham Ath v Bristol C
Peterborough U v Plymouth Arg
Port Vale v Notts Co
QPR v Huddersfield T
Tranmere R v Wigan Ath
Wycombe W v Crewe Alex

Nationwide Football League Division 3
Bournemouth v Rushden & D'monds
Bristol R v Bury
Hartlepool U v Lincoln C
Hull C v Macclesfield T
Leyton Orient v Oxford U
Rochdale v Cambridge U
Scunthorpe U v Carlisle U (7:30)
Southend U v Kidderminster H
Torquay U v Shrewsbury T
Wrexham v Exeter C
York C v Darlington

Nationwide Conference
Barnet v Farnborough T
Burton A v Gravesend & N
Dag & Red v Kettering T
Doncaster R v Southport
Forest Green R v Stevenage B
Halifax T v Chester C
Hereford U v Yeovil T
Leigh RMI v Nuneaton B
Northwich Vic v Morecambe
Woking v Margate

Wednesday, 18 September 2002
Nationwide Football League Division 1
Coventry C v Sheffield W
Ipswich T v Wolverhampton W
Nottingham F v Gillingham
Reading v Norwich C (8:00)

Nationwide Football League Division 3
Boston U v Swansea C

Saturday, 21 September 2002
FA Barclaycard Premiership
Arsenal v Bolton W
Liverpool v WBA
Manchester U v Tottenham H
Middlesbrough v Birmingham C
Southampton v Charlton Ath
West Ham U v Manchester C

Nationwide Football League Division 1
Bradford C v Burnley
Derby Co v Preston NE
Gillingham v Sheffield U
Grimsby T v Nottingham F
Millwall v Walsall
Norwich C v Portsmouth
Rotherham U v Brighton & HA
Sheffield W v Leicester C
Stoke C v Ipswich T
Watford v Crystal P
Wimbledon v Coventry C
Wolverhampton W v Reading

Nationwide Football League Division 2
Blackpool v Port Vale
Brentford v Wycombe W
Bristol C v QPR
Colchester U v Oldham Ath
Crewe Alex v Tranmere R

Huddersfield T v Luton T
Mansfield T v Cheltenham T
Notts Co v Cardiff C
Plymouth Arg v Chesterfield
Stockport Co v Barnsley
Swindon T v Northampton T
Wigan Ath v Peterborough U

Nationwide Football League Division 3
Bury v Hartlepool U
Cambridge U v York C
Carlisle U v Boston U
Darlington v Bournemouth
Exeter C v Leyton Orient
Kidderminster H v Rochdale
Lincoln C v Southend U
Macclesfield T v Scunthorpe U
Oxford U v Hull C
Rushden & D'monds v Wrexham
Shrewsbury T v Bristol R
Swansea C v Torquay U

Nationwide Conference
Chester C v Dag & Red
Farnborough T v Leigh RMI
Gravesend & N v Telford U
Kettering T v Northwich Vic
Margate v Doncaster R
Morecambe v Woking
Nuneaton B v Forest Green R
Scarborough v Barnet
Southport v Burton A
Stevenage B v Hereford U
Yeovil T v Halifax T

Sunday, 22 September 2002

FA Barclaycard Premiership
†Aston Villa v Everton (2:00)
Blackburn R v Leeds U
*Newcastle U v Sunderland (4:05)

Monday, 23 September 2002

FA Barclaycard Premiership
*Fulham v Chelsea (8:00)

Nationwide Conference
Stevenage B v Barnet

Tuesday, 24 September 2002

Nationwide Football League Division 1
Ipswich T v Burnley

Nationwide Conference
Chester C v Burton A
Farnborough T v Forest Green R
Gravesend & N v Doncaster R
Kettering T v Hereford U
Margate v Dag & Red
Morecambe v Telford U
Nuneaton B v Northwich Vic
Scarborough v Leigh RMI
Southport v Halifax T
*Yeovil T v Woking (7:45)

Saturday, 28 September 2002

FA Barclaycard Premiership
†Birmingham C v Newcastle U (5:30)
Bolton W v Southampton
Charlton Ath v Manchester U
Chelsea v West Ham U
Everton v Fulham
*Leeds U v Arsenal (12:00)
Manchester C v Liverpool
Sunderland v Aston Villa
Tottenham H v Middlesbrough

Nationwide Football League Division 1
Brighton & HA v Grimsby T
Burnley v Wimbledon
Coventry C v Millwall
Crystal P v Gillingham
Ipswich T v Derby Co
Leicester C v Wolverhampton W
Nottingham F v Rotherham U
Portsmouth v Bradford C
Preston NE v Norwich C
Reading v Stoke C
Sheffield U v Watford
Walsall v Sheffield W

Nationwide Football League Division 2
Barnsley v Wigan Ath
Cardiff C v Crewe Alex
Cheltenham T v Notts Co
Chesterfield v Blackpool
Luton T v Swindon T
Northampton T v Mansfield T
Oldham Ath v Huddersfield T
Peterborough U v Brentford
Port Vale v Bristol C
QPR v Colchester U
Tranmere R v Stockport Co
Wycombe W v Plymouth Arg

Nationwide Football League Division 3
Boston U v Cambridge U
Bournemouth v Carlisle U
Bristol R v Kidderminster H
Hartlepool U v Rushden & D'monds
Hull C v Swansea C
Leyton Orient v Darlington
Rochdale v Macclesfield T
Scunthorpe U v Shrewsbury T
Southend U v Exeter C
Torquay U v Lincoln C
Wrexham v Bury
York C v Oxford U

Nationwide Conference
Barnet v Morecambe
Burton A v Margate
Dag & Red v Southport
Doncaster R v Chester C
Forest Green R v Kettering T
Halifax T v Nuneaton B
Hereford U v Scarborough
Leigh RMI v Yeovil T
Northwich Vic v Gravesend & N
Telford U v Farnborough T
Woking v Stevenage B

Monday, 30 September 2002

FA Barclaycard Premiership
*WBA v Blackburn R (8:00)

Saturday, 5 October 2002

FA Barclaycard Premiership
Fulham v Charlton Ath
Middlesbrough v Bolton W
Newcastle U v WBA
Southampton v Manchester C
West Ham U v Birmingham C

Nationwide Football League Division 1
Bradford C v Preston NE
Derby Co v Walsall
Gillingham v Coventry C
Grimsby T v Reading
Millwall v Nottingham F
Norwich C v Leicester C
Rotherham U v Portsmouth
Sheffield W v Burnley
Stoke C v Crystal P
Watford v Brighton & HA

Wimbledon v Ipswich T
Wolverhampton W v Sheffield U

Nationwide Football League Division 2
Blackpool v Cheltenham T
Brentford v Barnsley
Bristol C v Chesterfield
Colchester U v Wycombe W
Crewe Alex v QPR
Huddersfield T v Port Vale
Mansfield T v Tranmere R
Notts Co v Peterborough U
Plymouth Arg v Northampton T
Stockport Co v Luton T
Swindon T v Oldham Ath
Wigan Ath v Cardiff C

Nationwide Football League Division 3
Bury v Southend U
Cambridge U v Wrexham
Carlisle U v Torquay U
Darlington v Bristol R
Exeter C v York C
Kidderminster H v Hull C
Lincoln C v Bournemouth
Macclesfield T v Boston U
Oxford U v Scunthorpe U
Rushden & D'monds v Leyton Orient
Shrewsbury T v Hartlepool U
Swansea C v Rochdale

Nationwide Conference
Forest Green R v Barnet
Gravesend & N v Scarborough
Hereford U v Dag & Red
Kettering T v Telford U
Margate v Chester C
Morecambe v Leigh RMI
Northwich Vic v Farnborough T
Nuneaton B v Doncaster R
Stevenage B v Halifax T
Woking v Burton A
Yeovil T v Southport

Sunday, 6 October 2002

FA Barclaycard Premiership
†Arsenal v Sunderland (2:00)
Aston Villa v Leeds U
Blackburn R v Tottenham H
*Liverpool v Chelsea (4:05)

Monday, 7 October 2002

FA Barclaycard Premiership
*Manchester U v Everton (8:00)

Nationwide Conference
Telford U v Forest Green R

Tuesday, 8 October 2002

Nationwide Conference
Barnet v Gravesend & N
Burton A v Yeovil T
Chester C v Nuneaton B
Dag & Red v Woking
Doncaster R v Stevenage B
Farnborough T v Margate
Halifax T v Kettering T
Leigh RMI v Hereford U
Scarborough v Morecambe
Southport v Northwich Vic

Saturday, 12 October 2002

Nationwide Football League Division 1
Bradford C v Derby Co
Burnley v Walsall
Coventry C v Norwich C
Crystal P v Reading

Ipswich T v Sheffield W
Millwall v Wimbledon
Nottingham F v Brighton & HA
Preston NE v Leicester C
Rotherham U v Gillingham
Sheffield U v Stoke C
Watford v Grimsby T
Wolverhampton W v Portsmouth

Nationwide Football League Division 2
Barnsley v Bristol C
Cardiff C v Wycombe W
Chesterfield v Tranmere R
Huddersfield T v Notts Co
Luton T v Cheltenham T
Northampton T v Brentford
Peterborough U v Mansfield T
Plymouth Arg v Wigan Ath
Port Vale v Oldham Ath
QPR v Blackpool
Stockport Co v Crewe Alex
Swindon T v Colchester U

Nationwide Football League Division 3
Boston U v Torquay U
Bournemouth v Hartlepool U
Bristol R v Lincoln C
Bury v Darlington
Carlisle U v Shrewsbury T
Exeter C v Rushden & D'monds
Hull C v Rochdale
Kidderminster H v Macclesfield T
Oxford U v Swansea C
Scunthorpe U v Cambridge U
Southend U v York C
Wrexham v Leyton Orient

Nationwide Conference
Barnet v Nuneaton B
Burton A v Hereford U
Chester C v Gravesend & N
Dag & Red v Morecambe
Doncaster R v Forest Green R
Farnborough T v Kettering T
Halifax T v Margate
Leigh RMI v Stevenage B
Scarborough v Northwich Vic
Southport v Woking
Telford U v Yeovil T

Friday, 18 October 2002
Nationwide Football League Division 2
Colchester U v Chesterfield

Saturday, 19 October 2002
FA Barclaycard Premiership
Blackburn R v Newcastle U
Everton v Arsenal
Fulham v Manchester U
†Leeds U v Liverpool (12:00)
Manchester C v Chelsea
Sunderland v West Ham U
WBA v Birmingham C

Nationwide Football League Division 1
Derby Co v Nottingham F
Gillingham v Watford
Grimsby T v Rotherham U
Leicester C v Burnley
Norwich C v Millwall
Portsmouth v Coventry C
Reading v Ipswich T
Sheffield W v Bradford C
Stoke C v Wolverhampton W
Walsall v Preston NE
Wimbledon v Crystal P

Nationwide Football League Division 2
Blackpool v Cardiff C
Brentford v Port Vale
Bristol C v Swindon T
Cheltenham T v QPR
Crewe Alex v Plymouth Arg
Mansfield T v Huddersfield T
Notts Co v Northampton T
Oldham Ath v Luton T
Tranmere R v Barnsley
Wigan Ath v Stockport Co
Wycombe W v Peterborough U

Nationwide Football League Division 3
Cambridge U v Oxford U
Darlington v Boston U
Hartlepool U v Wrexham
Leyton Orient v Bournemouth
Lincoln C v Exeter C
Macclesfield T v Carlisle U
Rochdale v Scunthorpe U
Rushden & D'monds v Bury
Shrewsbury T v Kidderminster H
Swansea C v Southend U
Torquay U v Hull C
York C v Bristol R

Nationwide Conference
Forest Green R v Scarborough
Gravesend & N v Leigh RMI
Hereford U v Halifax T
Kettering T v Barnet
Margate v Southport
Morecambe v Farnborough T
Northwich Vic v Dag & Red
Nuneaton B v Telford U
Stevenage B v Burton A
Woking v Chester C
Yeovil T v Doncaster R

Sunday, 20 October 2002
FA Barclaycard Premiership
*Charlton Ath v Middlesbrough (4:05)
Tottenham H v Bolton W (4:05)

Nationwide Football League Division 1
Brighton & HA v Sheffield U

Monday, 21 October 2002
FA Barclaycard Premiership
*Aston Villa v Southampton (8:00)

Friday, 25 October 2002
Nationwide Football League Division 3
Southend U v Hartlepool U

Saturday, 26 October 2002
FA Barclaycard Premiership
Arsenal v Blackburn R
Birmingham C v Manchester C
Chelsea v WBA
Liverpool v Tottenham H
Manchester U v Aston Villa
Middlesbrough v Leeds U
Newcastle U v Charlton Ath

Nationwide Football League Division 1
Bradford C v Norwich C
Burnley v Portsmouth
Coventry C v Walsall
Crystal P v Brighton & HA
Ipswich T v Gillingham
Millwall v Derby Co
Nottingham F v Leicester C
Preston NE v Reading
Rotherham U v Stoke C
Sheffield U v Wimbledon

Watford v Sheffield W
Wolverhampton W v Grimsby T

Nationwide Football League Division 2
Barnsley v Wycombe W
Cardiff C v Tranmere R
Chesterfield v Notts Co
Huddersfield T v Colchester U
Luton T v Wigan Ath
Northampton T v Cheltenham T
Peterborough U v Bristol C
Plymouth Arg v Blackpool
Port Vale v Crewe Alex
QPR v Oldham Ath
Stockport Co v Brentford
Swindon T v Mansfield T

Nationwide Football League Division 3
Boston U v Rochdale
Bournemouth v York C
Bristol R v Leyton Orient
Bury v Macclesfield T
Carlisle U v Swansea C
Exeter C v Darlington
Hull C v Rushden & D'monds
Kidderminster H v Cambridge U
Oxford U v Shrewsbury T
Scunthorpe U v Torquay U
Wrexham v Lincoln C

Sunday, 27 October 2002
FA Barclaycard Premiership
†Southampton v Fulham (2:00)
*West Ham U v Everton (4:05)

Monday, 28 October 2002
FA Barclaycard Premiership
*Bolton W v Sunderland (8:00)

Tuesday, 29 October 2002
Nationwide Football League Division 1
Brighton & HA v Ipswich T
Gillingham v Wolverhampton W
Grimsby T v Burnley
Leicester C v Coventry C
Norwich C v Nottingham F
Portsmouth v Preston NE
Reading v Bradford C
Walsall v Crystal P
Wimbledon v Rotherham U

Nationwide Football League Division 2
Blackpool v Stockport Co
Brentford v Plymouth Arg
Bristol C v Huddersfield T
Cheltenham T v Port Vale
Colchester U v Barnsley
Crewe Alex v Luton T
Mansfield T v Cardiff C
Notts Co v Swindon T
Oldham Ath v Northampton T
Tranmere R v Peterborough U
Wigan Ath v QPR
Wycombe W v Chesterfield

Nationwide Football League Division 3
Cambridge U v Carlisle U
Darlington v Scunthorpe U
Hartlepool U v Bristol R
Leyton Orient v Southend U
Lincoln C v Bury
Macclesfield T v Oxford U
Rochdale v Exeter C
Rushden & D'monds v Boston U
Shrewsbury T v Hull C
Swansea C v Kidderminster H
Torquay U v Bournemouth
York C v Wrexham

Wednesday, 30 October 2002
Nationwide Football League Division 1
Derby Co v Sheffield U
Sheffield W v Millwall
Stoke C v Watford

Friday, 1 November 2002
Nationwide Football League Division 2
Mansfield T v Colchester U

Nationwide Football League Division 3
Hartlepool U v York C

Saturday, 2 November 2002
FA Barclaycard Premiership
Birmingham C v Bolton W
Blackburn R v Aston Villa
Fulham v Arsenal
Leeds U v Everton
Liverpool v West Ham U
Manchester U v Southampton
WBA v Manchester C

Nationwide Football League Division 1
Brighton & HA v Bradford C
Coventry C v Rotherham U
Grimsby T v Gillingham
Ipswich T v Crystal P
Nottingham F v Sheffield U
Portsmouth v Leicester C
Preston NE v Burnley
Reading v Millwall (12:00)
Sheffield W v Derby Co
Walsall v Stoke C
Watford v Wolverhampton W
Wimbledon v Norwich C

Nationwide Football League Division 2
Brentford v Blackpool
Bristol C v Notts Co
Cardiff C v Peterborough U
Cheltenham T v Huddersfield T
Chesterfield v Barnsley
Northampton T v Luton T
Oldham Ath v Stockport Co
Port Vale v QPR
Tranmere R v Plymouth Arg
Wigan Ath v Crewe Alex
Wycombe W v Swindon T

Nationwide Football League Division 3
Boston U v Exeter C
Bournemouth v Bristol R
Cambridge U v Swansea C
Carlisle U v Oxford U
Darlington v Lincoln C
Hull C v Scunthorpe U
Leyton Orient v Bury
Macclesfield T v Shrewsbury T
Rochdale v Rushden & D'monds
Southend U v Wrexham
Torquay U v Kidderminster H

Nationwide Conference
Barnet v Northwich Vic
Burton A v Morecambe
Chester C v Yeovil T
Dag & Red v Forest Green R
Doncaster R v Hereford U
Farnborough T v Nuneaton B
Halifax T v Gravesend & N
Leigh RMI v Kettering T
Scarborough v Margate
Southport v Stevenage B
Telford U v Woking

Sunday, 3 November 2002
FA Barclaycard Premiership
*Charlton Ath v Sunderland (4:05)
†Tottenham H v Chelsea (2:00)

Monday, 4 November 2002
FA Barclaycard Premiership
*Newcastle U v Middlesbrough (8:00)

Saturday, 9 November 2002
FA Barclaycard Premiership
Arsenal v Newcastle U
Aston Villa v Fulham
Bolton W v WBA
Chelsea v Birmingham C
Everton v Charlton Ath
*Manchester C v Manchester U (12:15)
Middlesbrough v Liverpool
Southampton v Blackburn R
West Ham U v Leeds U

Nationwide Football League Division 1
Bradford C v Wimbledon
Burnley v Coventry C
Crystal P v Nottingham F
Derby Co v Portsmouth
Gillingham v Reading
Leicester C v Walsall
Millwall v Preston NE
Norwich C v Sheffield W
Rotherham U v Watford
Sheffield U v Ipswich T
Stoke C v Grimsby T
Wolverhampton W v Brighton & HA

Nationwide Football League Division 2
Barnsley v Cardiff C
Blackpool v Wigan Ath
Colchester U v Bristol C
Crewe Alex v Brentford
Huddersfield T v Wycombe W
Luton T v Port Vale
Notts Co v Mansfield T
Peterborough U v Chesterfield
Plymouth Arg v Oldham Ath
QPR v Northampton T
Stockport Co v Cheltenham T
Swindon T v Tranmere R

Nationwide Football League Division 3
Bristol R v Southend U
Bury v Torquay U
Exeter C v Hartlepool U
Kidderminster H v Carlisle U
Lincoln C v Hull C
Oxford U v Rochdale
Rushden & D'monds v Darlington
Scunthorpe U v Boston U
Shrewsbury T v Cambridge U
Swansea C v Macclesfield T
Wrexham v Bournemouth
York C v Leyton Orient

Nationwide Conference
Forest Green R v Halifax T
Gravesend & N v Farnborough T
Hereford U v Southport
Kettering T v Burton A
Margate v Telford U
Morecambe v Doncaster R
Northwich Vic v Leigh RMI
Nuneaton B v Scarborough
Stevenage B v Chester C
Woking v Barnet
Yeovil T v Dag & Red

Sunday, 10 November 2002
FA Barclaycard Premiership
*Sunderland v Tottenham H (4:05)

Saturday, 16 November 2002
FA Barclaycard Premiership
Arsenal v Tottenham H
Birmingham C v Fulham
Blackburn R v Everton
Chelsea v Middlesbrough
Leeds U v Bolton W
Liverpool v Sunderland
Manchester C v Charlton Ath
Newcastle U v Southampton
WBA v Aston Villa

Nationwide Football League Division 1
Brighton & HA v Derby Co
Coventry C v Wolverhampton W
Gillingham v Sheffield W
Grimsby T v Preston NE
Millwall v Leicester C
Norwich C v Crystal P
Nottingham F v Bradford C
Portsmouth v Stoke C
Rotherham U v Burnley
Sheffield U v Reading
Watford v Ipswich T
Wimbledon v Walsall

Sunday, 17 November 2002
FA Barclaycard Premiership
*West Ham U v Manchester U (4:05)

Friday, 22 November 2002
Nationwide Football League Division 2
Cardiff C v Chesterfield

Saturday, 23 November 2002
FA Barclaycard Premiership
Aston Villa v West Ham U
Bolton W v Chelsea
Everton v WBA
Fulham v Liverpool
*Manchester U v Newcastle U (12:15)
Middlesbrough v Manchester C
Southampton v Arsenal
Sunderland v Birmingham C

Nationwide Football League Division 1
Bradford C v Sheffield U
Burnley v Norwich C
Crystal P v Grimsby T
Derby Co v Wimbledon
Ipswich T v Coventry C
Leicester C v Rotherham U
Preston NE v Brighton & HA
Reading v Watford
Sheffield W v Portsmouth
Stoke C v Millwall
Walsall v Gillingham
Wolverhampton W v Nottingham F

Nationwide Football League Division 2
Brentford v Wigan Ath
Crewe Alex v Blackpool
Huddersfield T v Swindon T
Luton T v QPR
Mansfield T v Bristol C
Northampton T v Port Vale
Notts Co v Colchester U
Oldham Ath v Cheltenham T
Peterborough U v Barnsley
Plymouth Arg v Stockport Co
Wycombe W v Tranmere R

Nationwide Football League Division 3
Bristol R v Wrexham
Carlisle U v Bury
Exeter C v Cambridge U
Hull C v Boston U
Kidderminster H v Oxford U
Leyton Orient v Hartlepool U
Lincoln C v Rushden & D'monds
Macclesfield T v Torquay U
Rochdale v York C
Scunthorpe U v Swansea C
Shrewsbury T v Darlington
Southend U v Bournemouth

Nationwide Conference
Barnet v Forest Green R
Burton A v Woking
Chester C v Margate
Dag & Red v Hereford U
Doncaster R v Nuneaton B
Farnborough T v Northwich Vic
Halifax T v Stevenage B
Leigh RMI v Morecambe
Scarborough v Gravesend & N
Southport v Yeovil T
Telford U v Kettering T

Sunday, 24 November 2002

FA Barclaycard Premiership
*Charlton Ath v Blackburn R (4:05)
Tottenham H v Leeds U

Saturday, 30 November 2002

FA Barclaycard Premiership
Arsenal v Aston Villa
Birmingham C v Tottenham H
Blackburn R v Fulham
Chelsea v Sunderland
Leeds U v Charlton Ath
Manchester C v Bolton W
Newcastle U v Everton
WBA v Middlesbrough

Nationwide Football League Division 1
Brighton & HA v Reading
Coventry C v Preston NE
Gillingham v Stoke C
Grimsby T v Leicester C
Millwall v Bradford C
Norwich C v Derby Co
Nottingham F v Ipswich T
Portsmouth v Walsall
Rotherham U v Wolverhampton W
Sheffield U v Crystal P
Watford v Burnley
Wimbledon v Sheffield W

Nationwide Football League Division 2
Barnsley v Oldham Ath
Blackpool v Notts Co
Bristol C v Crewe Alex
Cheltenham T v Brentford
Chesterfield v Huddersfield T
Colchester U v Plymouth Arg
Port Vale v Mansfield T
QPR v Cardiff C
Stockport Co v Wycombe W
Swindon T v Peterborough U
Tranmere R v Luton T
Wigan Ath v Northampton T

Nationwide Football League Division 3
Boston U v Leyton Orient
Bournemouth v Scunthorpe U
Bury v Exeter C
Cambridge U v Macclesfield T
Darlington v Southend U
Hartlepool U v Kidderminster H

Oxford U v Lincoln C
Rushden & D'monds v Bristol R
Swansea C v Shrewsbury T
Torquay U v Rochdale
Wrexham v Hull C
York C v Carlisle U

Nationwide Conference
Doncaster R v Woking
Farnborough T v Burton A
Halifax T v Dag & Red
Hereford U v Barnet
Kettering T v Nuneaton B
Leigh RMI v Telford U
Morecambe v Gravesend & N
Northwich Vic v Forest Green R
Southport v Chester C
Stevenage B v Scarborough
Yeovil T v Margate

Sunday, 1 December 2002

FA Barclaycard Premiership
*Liverpool v Manchester U (12:15)

Monday, 2 December 2002

FA Barclaycard Premiership
*West Ham U v Southampton (8:00)

Saturday, 7 December 2002

FA Barclaycard Premiership
Aston Villa v Newcastle U
Bolton W v Blackburn R
Charlton Ath v Liverpool
Everton v Chelsea
Fulham v Leeds U
*Manchester U v Arsenal (12:15)
Middlesbrough v West Ham U
Southampton v Birmingham C
Sunderland v Manchester C

Nationwide Football League Division 1
Bradford C v Gillingham
Burnley v Nottingham F
Crystal P v Millwall
Derby Co v Watford
Ipswich T v Rotherham U
Leicester C v Sheffield U
Preston NE v Wimbledon
Reading v Portsmouth
Sheffield W v Brighton & HA
Stoke C v Coventry C
Walsall v Grimsby T
Wolverhampton W v Norwich C

Nationwide Conference
Barnet v Southport
Burton A v Doncaster R
Chester C v Farnborough T
Dag & Red v Stevenage B
Forest Green R v Leigh RMI
Gravesend & N v Kettering T
Margate v Hereford U
Nuneaton B v Morecambe
Scarborough v Yeovil T
Telford U v Northwich Vic
Woking v Halifax T

Sunday, 8 December 2002

FA Barclaycard Premiership
*Tottenham H v WBA (4:05)

Saturday, 14 December 2002

FA Barclaycard Premiership
Aston Villa v WBA
Charlton Ath v Manchester C
Everton v Blackburn R
Fulham v Birmingham C

Manchester U v West Ham U
Middlesbrough v Chelsea
Southampton v Newcastle U
Tottenham H v Arsenal

Nationwide Football League Division 1
Bradford C v Nottingham F
Burnley v Rotherham U
Crystal P v Norwich C
Derby Co v Brighton & HA
Ipswich T v Watford
Leicester C v Millwall
Preston NE v Grimsby T
Reading v Sheffield U
Sheffield W v Gillingham
Stoke C v Portsmouth
Walsall v Wimbledon
Wolverhampton W v Coventry C

Nationwide Football League Division 2
Brentford v Chesterfield
Cardiff C v Bristol C
Crewe Alex v Barnsley
Huddersfield T v Stockport Co
Luton T v Colchester U
Mansfield T v Blackpool
Northampton T v Tranmere R
Notts Co v QPR
Oldham Ath v Wigan Ath
Peterborough U v Cheltenham T
Plymouth Arg v Swindon T
Wycombe W v Port Vale

Nationwide Football League Division 3
Bristol R v Oxford U
Carlisle U v Wrexham
Exeter C v Swansea C
Hull C v Darlington
Kidderminster H v York C
Leyton Orient v Torquay U
Lincoln C v Cambridge U
Macclesfield T v Rushden & D'monds
Rochdale v Hartlepool U
Scunthorpe U v Bury
Shrewsbury T v Bournemouth
Southend U v Boston U

Nationwide Conference
Dag & Red v Doncaster R
Farnborough T v Southport
Forest Green R v Morecambe
Halifax T v Burton A
Hereford U v Woking
Kettering T v Scarborough
Leigh RMI v Chester C
Northwich Vic v Yeovil T
Nuneaton B v Gravesend & N
Stevenage B v Margate
Telford U v Barnet

Sunday, 15 December 2002

FA Barclaycard Premiership
*Sunderland v Liverpool (4:05)

Monday, 16 December 2002

FA Barclaycard Premiership
*Bolton W v Leeds U (8:00)

Friday, 20 December 2002

Nationwide Football League Division 1
Brighton & HA v Leicester C

Nationwide Football League Division 2
Stockport Co v Northampton T

Nationwide Football League Division 3
Hartlepool U v Scunthorpe U
York C v Lincoln C

Saturday, 21 December 2002

FA Barclaycard Premiership
Arsenal v Middlesbrough
Birmingham C v Charlton Ath
Blackburn R v Manchester U
Chelsea v Aston Villa
Leeds U v Southampton
Newcastle U v Fulham
WBA v Sunderland
West Ham U v Bolton W

Nationwide Football League Division 1
Coventry C v Derby Co
Gillingham v Burnley
Grimsby T v Sheffield W
Millwall v Wolverhampton W
Norwich C v Walsall
Nottingham F v Reading
Portsmouth v Ipswich T
Rotherham U v Crystal P
Sheffield U v Preston NE
Watford v Bradford C
Wimbledon v Stoke C

Nationwide Football League Division 2
Barnsley v Mansfield T
Blackpool v Peterborough U
Bristol C v Luton T
Cheltenham T v Wycombe W
Chesterfield v Oldham Ath
Colchester U v Cardiff C
Port Vale v Plymouth Arg
QPR v Brentford
Swindon T v Crewe Alex
Tranmere R v Notts Co
Wigan Ath v Huddersfield T

Nationwide Football League Division 3
Boston U v Shrewsbury T
Bournemouth v Hull C
Bury v Rochdale
Cambridge U v Bristol R
Darlington v Macclesfield T
Oxford U v Exeter C
Rushden & D'monds v Carlisle U
Swansea C v Leyton Orient
Torquay U v Southend U
Wrexham v Kidderminster H

Nationwide Conference
Barnet v Leigh RMI
Burton A v Dag & Red
Chester C v Hereford U
Doncaster R v Halifax T
Gravesend & N v Forest Green R
Margate v Nuneaton B
Morecambe v Kettering T
Scarborough v Farnborough T
Southport v Telford U
Woking v Northwich Vic
Yeovil T v Stevenage B

Sunday, 22 December 2002

FA Barclaycard Premiership
*Liverpool v Everton (4:05)

Monday, 23 December 2002

FA Barclaycard Premiership
*Manchester C v Tottenham H (8:00)

Thursday, 26 December 2002

FA Barclaycard Premiership
Birmingham C v Everton (3:00)
Bolton W v Newcastle U (3:00)
Chelsea v Southampton (12:00)
Liverpool v Blackburn R (3:00)
Manchester C v Aston Villa (3:00)

*Middlesbrough v Manchester U (4:00)
Sunderland v Leeds U (3:00)
Tottenham H v Charlton Ath (12:00)
WBA v Arsenal (3:00)
West Ham U v Fulham (12:00)

Nationwide Football League Division 1
Bradford C v Stoke C (3:00)
Burnley v Wolverhampton W (3:00)
Coventry C v Reading (3:00)
Derby Co v Grimsby T (3:00)
Leicester C v Ipswich T (3:00)
Millwall v Gillingham (12:00)
Norwich C v Brighton & HA (3:00)
Portsmouth v Crystal P (3:00)
Preston NE v Rotherham U (3:00)
Sheffield W v Nottingham F (3:00)
Walsall v Sheffield U (3:00)
Wimbledon v Watford (12:00)

Nationwide Football League Division 2
Bristol C v Plymouth Arg (12:00)
Cheltenham T v Crewe Alex (3:00)
Colchester U v Peterborough U (3:00)
Huddersfield T v Tranmere R (3:00)
Luton T v Cardiff C (12:00)
Mansfield T v Stockport Co (3:00)
Northampton T v Chesterfield (3:00)
Notts Co v Barnsley (3:00)
Oldham Ath v Blackpool (3:00)
Port Vale v Wigan Ath (3:00)
QPR v Wycombe W (12:00)
Swindon T v Brentford (3:00)

Nationwide Football League Division 3
Boston U v York C (3:00)
Cambridge U v Southend U (3:00)
Carlisle U v Darlington (3:00)
Hull C v Hartlepool U (3:00)
Kidderminster H v Leyton Orient (3:00)
Macclesfield T v Lincoln C (3:00)
Oxford U v Bournemouth (3:00)
Rochdale v Wrexham
Scunthorpe U v Rushden & D'monds (3:00)
Shrewsbury T v Bury (3:00)
Swansea C v Bristol R (1:00)
Torquay U v Exeter C (11:00)

Nationwide Conference
Barnet v Dag & Red
Farnborough T v Woking
Forest Green R v Yeovil T
Gravesend & N v Margate
Kettering T v Stevenage B
Leigh RMI v Halifax T
Morecambe v Southport
Northwich Vic v Chester C
Nuneaton B v Burton A
Scarborough v Doncaster R
Telford U v Hereford U

Saturday, 28 December 2002

FA Barclaycard Premiership
Aston Villa v Middlesbrough
Blackburn R v West Ham U
Charlton Ath v WBA
Everton v Bolton W
Fulham v Manchester C
Leeds U v Chelsea
Manchester U v Birmingham C
Southampton v Sunderland

Nationwide Football League Division 1
Brighton & HA v Burnley
Crystal P v Preston NE
Gillingham v Wimbledon
Grimsby T v Norwich C

Ipswich T v Walsall
Nottingham F v Portsmouth
Reading v Derby Co
Rotherham U v Millwall
Sheffield U v Coventry C
Stoke C v Sheffield W
Watford v Leicester C
Wolverhampton W v Bradford C

Nationwide Football League Division 2
Barnsley v Port Vale
Blackpool v Colchester U
Brentford v Mansfield T
Chesterfield v Cheltenham T
Crewe Alex v Oldham Ath
Peterborough U v Northampton T (12:00)
Plymouth Arg v Notts Co
Stockport Co v Bristol C
Tranmere R v QPR
Wigan Ath v Swindon T
Wycombe W v Luton T

Nationwide Football League Division 3
Bournemouth v Rochdale
Bristol R v Boston U
Bury v Kidderminster H
Darlington v Torquay U
Exeter C v Macclesfield T
Hartlepool U v Cambridge U
Leyton Orient v Carlisle U
Lincoln C v Swansea C
Rushden & D'monds v Oxford U
Southend U v Scunthorpe U
Wrexham v Shrewsbury T (12:00)
York C v Hull C

Nationwide Conference
Burton A v Northwich Vic
Chester C v Telford U
Dag & Red v Gravesend & N
Doncaster R v Leigh RMI
Halifax T v Morecambe
Hereford U v Forest Green R
Margate v Kettering T
Southport v Scarborough
Stevenage B v Farnborough T
Woking v Nuneaton B
Yeovil T v Barnet

Sunday, 29 December 2002

FA Barclaycard Premiership
*Arsenal v Liverpool (4:05)
Newcastle U v Tottenham H

Nationwide Football League Division 2
Cardiff C v Huddersfield T

Wednesday, 1 January 2003

FA Barclaycard Premiership
Arsenal v Chelsea (3:00)
Aston Villa v Bolton W (3:00)
Blackburn R v Middlesbrough (3:00)
Charlton Ath v West Ham U (3:00)
Everton v Manchester C (3:00)
Fulham v WBA (3:00)
Leeds U v Birmingham C (3:00)
Manchester U v Sunderland (3:00)
*Newcastle U v Liverpool (7.45)
Southampton v Tottenham H (3:00)

Nationwide Football League Division 1
Brighton & HA v Wimbledon (3:00)
Crystal P v Coventry C (3:00)
Gillingham v Norwich C (3:00)
Grimsby T v Bradford C (3:00)
Ipswich T v Millwall (3:00)
Nottingham F v Walsall (3:00)
Reading v Leicester C (3:00)

Rotherham U v Sheffield W (3:00)
Sheffield U v Burnley (3:00)
Stoke C v Preston NE (3:00)
Watford v Portsmouth (3:00)
Wolverhampton W v Derby Co (3:00)

Nationwide Football League Division 2
Barnsley v Northampton T (3:00)
Blackpool v Huddersfield T (3:00)
Brentford v Colchester U (3:00)
Cardiff C v Swindon T (3:00)
Chesterfield v Luton T (3:00)
Crewe Alex v Mansfield T (3:00)
Peterborough U v QPR (3:00)
Plymouth Arg v Cheltenham T (3:00)
Stockport Co v Port Vale (3:00)
Tranmere R v Oldham Ath (3:00)
Wigan Ath v Notts Co (3:00)
Wycombe W v Bristol C (3:00)

Nationwide Football League Division 3
Bournemouth v Swansea C (3:00)
Bristol R v Torquay U (3:00)
Bury v Hull C (3:00)
Darlington v Rochdale
Exeter C v Kidderminster H (3:00)
Hartlepool U v Carlisle U (3:00)
Leyton Orient v Cambridge U (3:00)
Lincoln C v Boston U (3:00)
Rushden & D'monds v Shrewsbury T (3:00)
Southend U v Oxford U (3:00)
Wrexham v Macclesfield T (3:00)
York C v Scunthorpe U (3:00)

Nationwide Conference
Burton A v Nuneaton B
Chester C v Northwich Vic
Dag & Red v Barnet
Doncaster R v Scarborough
Halifax T v Leigh RMI
Hereford U v Telford U
Margate v Gravesend & N
Southport v Morecambe
Stevenage B v Kettering T
Woking v Farnborough T
Yeovil T v Forest Green R

Saturday, 4 January 2003
Nationwide Football League Division 2
Bristol C v Brentford
Cheltenham T v Barnsley
Colchester U v Tranmere R
Huddersfield T v Plymouth Arg
Luton T v Blackpool
Mansfield T v Wigan Ath
Northampton T v Wycombe W
Notts Co v Crewe Alex
Oldham Ath v Peterborough U
Port Vale v Cardiff C
QPR v Stockport Co
Swindon T v Chesterfield

Nationwide Football League Division 3
Boston U v Hartlepool U
Cambridge U v Bury
Carlisle U v Southend U
Hull C v Bristol R
Kidderminster H v Bournemouth
Macclesfield T v Leyton Orient
Oxford U v Wrexham
Rochdale v Lincoln C
Scunthorpe U v Exeter C
Shrewsbury T v York C
Swansea C v Darlington
Torquay U v Rushden & D'monds

Nationwide Conference
Barnet v Doncaster R
Farnborough T v Hereford U
Forest Green R v Woking
Gravesend & N v Yeovil T
Kettering T v Chester C
Leigh RMI v Dag & Red
Morecambe v Margate
Northwich Vic v Stevenage B
Nuneaton B v Southport
Scarborough v Burton A
Telford U v Halifax T

Saturday, 11 January 2003
FA Barclaycard Premiership
Birmingham C v Arsenal
Bolton W v Fulham
Chelsea v Charlton Ath
Liverpool v Aston Villa
Manchester C v Leeds U
Middlesbrough v Southampton
Sunderland v Blackburn R
Tottenham H v Everton
WBA v Manchester U
West Ham U v Newcastle U

Nationwide Football League Division 1
Bradford C v Crystal P
Burnley v Ipswich T
Coventry C v Brighton & HA
Derby Co v Gillingham
Leicester C v Stoke C
Millwall v Watford
Norwich C v Rotherham U
Portsmouth v Sheffield U
Preston NE v Nottingham F
Sheffield W v Reading
Walsall v Wolverhampton W
Wimbledon v Grimsby T

Nationwide Football League Division 2
Bristol C v Wigan Ath
Cheltenham T v Tranmere R
Colchester U v Crewe Alex
Huddersfield T v Peterborough U
Luton T v Plymouth Arg
Mansfield T v Wycombe W
Northampton T v Cardiff C (12:00)
Notts Co v Stockport Co
Oldham Ath v Brentford
Port Vale v Chesterfield
QPR v Barnsley
Swindon T v Blackpool

Nationwide Football League Division 3
Boston U v Wrexham
Cambridge U v Bournemouth
Carlisle U v Lincoln C
Hull C v Exeter C
Kidderminster H v Rushden & D'monds
Macclesfield T v Hartlepool U
Oxford U v Darlington
Rochdale v Bristol R
Scunthorpe U v Leyton Orient
Shrewsbury T v Southend U
Swansea C v Bury
Torquay U v York C

Friday, 17 January 2003
Nationwide Football League Division 3
Bournemouth v Macclesfield T

Saturday, 18 January 2003
FA Barclaycard Premiership
Arsenal v West Ham U
Aston Villa v Tottenham H

Blackburn R v Birmingham C
Charlton Ath v Bolton W
Everton v Sunderland
Fulham v Middlesbrough
Leeds U v WBA
Manchester C v Chelsea
Newcastle U v Manchester C
Southampton v Liverpool

Nationwide Football League Division 1
Brighton & HA v Portsmouth
Crystal P v Burnley
Gillingham v Leicester C
Grimsby T v Millwall
Ipswich T v Preston NE
Nottingham F v Coventry C
Reading v Walsall
Rotherham U v Bradford C
Sheffield U v Sheffield W
Stoke C v Derby Co
Watford v Norwich C
Wolverhampton W v Wimbledon

Nationwide Football League Division 2
Barnsley v Luton T
Blackpool v Northampton T
Brentford v Notts Co
Cardiff C v Cheltenham T
Chesterfield v Mansfield T
Crewe Alex v Huddersfield T
Peterborough U v Port Vale
Plymouth Arg v QPR
Stockport Co v Swindon T
Tranmere R v Bristol C
Wigan Ath v Colchester U
Wycombe W v Oldham Ath

Nationwide Football League Division 3
Bristol R v Scunthorpe U
Bury v Boston U
Darlington v Kidderminster H
Exeter C v Carlisle U
Hartlepool U v Oxford U
Leyton Orient v Hull C
Lincoln C v Shrewsbury T
Rushden & D'monds v Cambridge U
Southend U v Rochdale
Wrexham v Torquay U
York C v Swansea C

Nationwide Conference
Burton A v Leigh RMI
Chester C v Barnet
Dag & Red v Scarborough
Doncaster R v Telford U
Halifax T v Farnborough T
Hereford U v Gravesend & N
Margate v Northwich Vic
Southport v Forest Green R
Stevenage B v Nuneaton B
Woking v Kettering T
Yeovil T v Morecambe

Saturday, 25 January 2003
Nationwide Football League Division 2
Bristol C v Stockport Co
Cheltenham T v Chesterfield
Colchester U v Blackpool
Huddersfield T v Cardiff C
Luton T v Wycombe W
Mansfield T v Brentford
Northampton T v Peterborough U (12:00)
Notts Co v Plymouth Arg
Oldham Ath v Crewe Alex
Port Vale v Barnsley
QPR v Tranmere R
Swindon T v Wigan Ath

Nationwide Football League Division 3
Boston U v Bristol R
Cambridge U v Hartlepool U
Carlisle U v Leyton Orient
Hull C v York C
Kidderminster H v Bury
Macclesfield T v Exeter C
Oxford U v Rushden & D'monds
Rochdale v Bournemouth
Scunthorpe U v Southend U
Swansea C v Lincoln C
Torquay U v Darlington

Nationwide Conference
Barnet v Burton A
Farnborough T v Doncaster R
Forest Green R v Margate
Gravesend & N v Stevenage B
Kettering T v Southport
Leigh RMI v Woking
Morecambe v Hereford U
Northwich Vic v Halifax T
Nuneaton B v Yeovil T
Scarborough v Chester C
Telford U v Dag & Red

Sunday, 26 January 2003
Nationwide Football League Division 3
Shrewsbury T v Wrexham (12:00)

Tuesday, 28 January 2003
FA Barclaycard Premiership
Birmingham C v Manchester U
Bolton W v Everton (8:00)
Middlesbrough v Aston Villa
Sunderland v Southampton (8:00)
WBA v Charlton Ath

Wednesday, 29 January 2003
FA Barclaycard Premiership
Chelsea v Leeds U
Liverpool v Arsenal (8:00)
Manchester C v Fulham
Tottenham H v Newcastle U
West Ham U v Blackburn R

Friday, 31 January 2003
Nationwide Football League Division 3
Bournemouth v Boston U

Saturday, 1 February 2003
FA Barclaycard Premiership
Arsenal v Fulham
Aston Villa v Blackburn R
Bolton W v Birmingham C
Chelsea v Tottenham H
Everton v Leeds U
Manchester C v WBA
Middlesbrough v Newcastle U
Southampton v Manchester U
Sunderland v Charlton Ath
West Ham U v Liverpool

Nationwide Football League Division 1
Bradford C v Ipswich T
Burnley v Reading
Coventry C v Watford
Derby Co v Rotherham U
Leicester C v Crystal P
Millwall v Sheffield U
Norwich C v Stoke C
Portsmouth v Grimsby T
Preston NE v Gillingham
Sheffield W v Wolverhampton W
Walsall v Brighton & HA
Wimbledon v Nottingham F

Nationwide Football League Division 2
Barnsley v Swindon T
Blackpool v Bristol C
Brentford v Huddersfield T
Cardiff C v Oldham Ath
Chesterfield v QPR
Crewe Alex v Northampton T
Peterborough U v Luton T (12:00)
Plymouth Arg v Mansfield T
Stockport Co v Colchester U
Tranmere R v Port Vale
Wigan Ath v Cheltenham T
Wycombe W v Notts Co

Nationwide Football League Division 3
Bristol R v Carlisle U
Bury v Oxford U
Darlington v Cambridge U
Exeter C v Shrewsbury T
Hartlepool U v Torquay U
Leyton Orient v Rochdale
Lincoln C v Kidderminster H
Rushden & D'monds v Swansea C
Southend U v Hull C
Wrexham v Scunthorpe U

Sunday, 2 February 2003
Nationwide Football League Division 3
York C v Macclesfield T

Saturday, 8 February 2003
FA Barclaycard Premiership
Birmingham C v Chelsea
Blackburn R v Southampton
Charlton Ath v Everton
Fulham v Aston Villa
Leeds U v West Ham U
Liverpool v Middlesbrough
Manchester U v Manchester C
Newcastle U v Arsenal
Tottenham H v Sunderland
WBA v Bolton W

Nationwide Football League Division 1
Brighton & HA v Wolverhampton W
Coventry C v Burnley
Grimsby T v Stoke C
Ipswich T v Sheffield U
Nottingham F v Crystal P
Portsmouth v Derby Co
Preston NE v Millwall
Reading v Gillingham
Sheffield W v Norwich C
Walsall v Leicester C
Watford v Rotherham U
Wimbledon v Bradford C

Nationwide Football League Division 2
Brentford v Crewe Alex
Bristol C v Colchester U
Cardiff C v Barnsley
Cheltenham T v Stockport Co
Chesterfield v Peterborough U
Mansfield T v Notts Co
Northampton T v QPR
Oldham Ath v Plymouth Arg
Port Vale v Luton T
Tranmere R v Swindon T
Wigan Ath v Blackpool
Wycombe W v Huddersfield T

Nationwide Football League Division 3
Boston U v Scunthorpe U
Bournemouth v Wrexham
Cambridge U v Shrewsbury T
Carlisle U v Kidderminster H
Darlington v Rushden & D'monds
Hartlepool U v Exeter C
Hull C v Lincoln C

Leyton Orient v York C
Macclesfield T v Swansea C
Rochdale v Oxford U
Southend U v Bristol R
Torquay U v Bury

Nationwide Conference
Burton A v Telford U
Chester C v Forest Green R
Dag & Red v Farnborough T
Doncaster R v Northwich Vic
Halifax T v Barnet
Hereford U v Nuneaton B
Margate v Leigh RMI
Southport v Gravesend & N
Stevenage B v Morecambe
Woking v Scarborough
Yeovil T v Kettering T

Friday, 14 February 2003
Nationwide Football League Division 2
Colchester U v Mansfield T

Saturday, 15 February 2003
Nationwide Football League Division 1
Bradford C v Brighton & HA
Burnley v Preston NE
Crystal P v Ipswich T
Derby Co v Sheffield W
Gillingham v Grimsby T
Leicester C v Portsmouth
Millwall v Reading (1:00)
Norwich C v Wimbledon
Rotherham U v Coventry C
Sheffield U v Nottingham F
Stoke C v Walsall
Wolverhampton W v Watford

Nationwide Football League Division 2
Barnsley v Chesterfield
Blackpool v Brentford
Crewe Alex v Wigan Ath
Huddersfield T v Cheltenham T
Luton T v Northampton T
Notts Co v Bristol C
Peterborough U v Cardiff C
Plymouth Arg v Tranmere R
QPR v Port Vale
Stockport Co v Oldham Ath
Swindon T v Wycombe W

Nationwide Football League Division 3
Bristol R v Bournemouth
Bury v Leyton Orient
Exeter C v Boston U
Kidderminster H v Torquay U
Lincoln C v Darlington
Oxford U v Carlisle U
Rushden & D'monds v Rochdale
Scunthorpe U v Hull C
Shrewsbury T v Macclesfield T
Swansea C v Cambridge U
Wrexham v Southend U
York C v Hartlepool U

Nationwide Conference
Barnet v Margate
Farnborough T v Yeovil T
Forest Green R v Burton A
Gravesend & N v Woking
Kettering T v Doncaster R
Leigh RMI v Southport
Morecambe v Chester C
Northwich Vic v Hereford U
Nuneaton B v Dag & Red
Scarborough v Halifax T
Telford U v Stevenage B

Friday, 21 February 2003
Nationwide Football League Division 2
Cardiff C v Plymouth Arg

Saturday, 22 February 2003
FA Barclaycard Premiership
Birmingham C v Liverpool
Bolton W v Manchester U
Charlton Ath v Aston Villa
Chelsea v Blackburn R
Everton v Southampton
Leeds U v Newcastle U
Manchester C v Arsenal
Sunderland v Middlesbrough
Tottenham H v Fulham
WBA v West Ham U

Nationwide Football League Division 1
Brighton & HA v Millwall
Burnley v Derby Co
Coventry C v Bradford C
Crystal P v Sheffield W
Ipswich T v Grimsby T
Leicester C v Wimbledon
Nottingham F v Stoke C
Portsmouth v Gillingham
Preston NE v Wolverhampton W
Reading v Rotherham U
Sheffield U v Norwich C
Walsall v Watford

Nationwide Football League Division 2
Barnsley v Huddersfield T
Cheltenham T v Colchester U
Chesterfield v Crewe Alex
Luton T v Brentford
Northampton T v Bristol C
Oldham Ath v Notts Co
Peterborough U v Stockport Co
Port Vale v Swindon T
QPR v Mansfield T
Tranmere R v Blackpool
Wycombe W v Wigan Ath

Nationwide Football League Division 3
Boston U v Kidderminster H
Bournemouth v Exeter C
Bristol R v Macclesfield T
Hartlepool U v Swansea C
Hull C v Cambridge U
Leyton Orient v Shrewsbury T
Rochdale v Carlisle U
Scunthorpe U v Lincoln C
Southend U v Rushden & D'monds
Torquay U v Oxford U
Wrexham v Darlington
York C v Bury

Nationwide Conference
Barnet v Scarborough
Burton A v Southport
Dag & Red v Chester C
Doncaster R v Margate
Forest Green R v Nuneaton B
Halifax T v Yeovil T
Hereford U v Stevenage B
Leigh RMI v Farnborough T
Northwich Vic v Kettering T
Telford U v Gravesend & N
Woking v Morecambe

Saturday, 1 March 2003
FA Barclaycard Premiership
Arsenal v Charlton Ath
Aston Villa v Birmingham C
Blackburn R v Manchester C
Fulham v Sunderland
Liverpool v Bolton W

Manchester U v Leeds U
Middlesbrough v Everton
Newcastle U v Chelsea
Southampton v WBA
West Ham U v Tottenham H

Nationwide Football League Division 1
Bradford C v Walsall
Derby Co v Leicester C
Gillingham v Brighton & HA
Grimsby T v Coventry C
Millwall v Portsmouth
Rotherham U v Sheffield U
Sheffield W v Preston NE
Stoke C v Burnley
Watford v Nottingham F
Wimbledon v Reading
Wolverhampton W v Crystal P

Nationwide Football League Division 2
Blackpool v Wycombe W
Brentford v Tranmere R
Bristol C v Cheltenham T
Colchester U v Port Vale
Crewe Alex v Peterborough U
Huddersfield T v Northampton T
Mansfield T v Oldham Ath
Notts Co v Luton T
Plymouth Arg v Barnsley
Stockport Co v Cardiff C
Swindon T v QPR
Wigan Ath v Chesterfield

Nationwide Football League Division 3
Bury v Bournemouth
Cambridge U v Torquay U
Carlisle U v Hull C
Darlington v Hartlepool U
Exeter C v Bristol R
Kidderminster H v Scunthorpe U
Lincoln C v Leyton Orient
Macclesfield T v Southend U
Oxford U v Boston U
Rushden & D'monds v York C
Shrewsbury T v Rochdale
Swansea C v Wrexham

Nationwide Conference
Chester C v Halifax T
Farnborough T v Barnet
Gravesend & N v Burton A
Kettering T v Dag & Red
Margate v Woking
Morecambe v Northwich Vic
Nuneaton B v Leigh RMI
Scarborough v Telford U
Southport v Doncaster R
Stevenage B v Forest Green R
Yeovil T v Hereford U

Sunday, 2 March 2003
Nationwide Football League Division 1
Norwich C v Ipswich T (1:00)

Tuesday, 4 March 2003
Nationwide Football League Division 1
Bradford C v Leicester C
Gillingham v Nottingham F
Grimsby T v Sheffield U
Millwall v Burnley
Rotherham U v Walsall
Watford v Preston NE
Wimbledon v Portsmouth
Wolverhampton W v Ipswich T

Nationwide Football League Division 2
Blackpool v Barnsley
Brentford v Cardiff C

Bristol C v Oldham Ath
Colchester U v Northampton T
Crewe Alex v Wycombe W
Huddersfield T v QPR
Mansfield T v Luton T
Notts Co v Port Vale
Plymouth Arg v Peterborough U
Stockport Co v Chesterfield
Wigan Ath v Tranmere R

Nationwide Football League Division 3
Bury v Bristol R
Cambridge U v Rochdale
Carlisle U v Scunthorpe U
Darlington v York C (7:30)
Exeter C v Wrexham
Kidderminster H v Southend U
Lincoln C v Hartlepool U
Macclesfield T v Hull C
Oxford U v Leyton Orient
Rushden & D'monds v Bournemouth
Shrewsbury T v Torquay U
Swansea C v Boston U

Wednesday, 5 March 2003
Nationwide Football League Division 1
Derby Co v Crystal P
Norwich C v Reading
Sheffield W v Coventry C
Stoke C v Brighton & HA

Nationwide Football League Division 2
Swindon T v Cheltenham T

Friday, 7 March 2003
Nationwide Football League Division 3
Hartlepool U v Bury

Saturday, 8 March 2003
Nationwide Football League Division 1
Brighton & HA v Rotherham U
Burnley v Bradford C
Coventry C v Wimbledon
Crystal P v Watford
Ipswich T v Stoke C
Leicester C v Sheffield W
Nottingham F v Grimsby T
Portsmouth v Norwich C
Preston NE v Derby Co
Reading v Wolverhampton W
Sheffield U v Gillingham
Walsall v Millwall

Nationwide Football League Division 2
Barnsley v Stockport Co
Cardiff C v Notts Co
Cheltenham T v Mansfield T
Chesterfield v Plymouth Arg
Luton T v Huddersfield T
Northampton T v Swindon T
Oldham Ath v Colchester U
Peterborough U v Wigan Ath
Port Vale v Blackpool
QPR v Bristol C
Tranmere R v Crewe Alex
Wycombe W v Brentford

Nationwide Football League Division 3
Boston U v Carlisle U
Bournemouth v Darlington
Bristol R v Shrewsbury T
Hull C v Oxford U
Leyton Orient v Exeter C
Rochdale v Kidderminster H
Scunthorpe U v Macclesfield T
Southend U v Lincoln C
Torquay U v Swansea C
Wrexham v Rushden & D'monds
York C v Cambridge U

Nationwide Conference
Barnet v Stevenage B
Burton A v Chester C
Dag & Red v Margate
Doncaster R v Gravesend & N
Forest Green R v Farnborough T
Halifax T v Southport
Hereford U v Kettering T
Leigh RMI v Scarborough
Northwich Vic v Nuneaton B
Telford U v Morecambe
Woking v Yeovil T

Friday, 14 March 2003
Nationwide Football League Division 2
Tranmere R v Cardiff C

Saturday, 15 March 2003
FA Barclaycard Premiership
Aston Villa v Manchester U
Blackburn R v Arsenal
Charlton Ath v Newcastle U
Everton v West Ham U
Fulham v Southampton
Leeds U v Middlesbrough
Manchester C v Birmingham C
Sunderland v Bolton W
Tottenham H v Liverpool
WBA v Chelsea

Nationwide Football League Division 1
Brighton & HA v Nottingham F
Derby Co v Bradford C
Gillingham v Rotherham U
Grimsby T v Watford
Leicester C v Preston NE
Norwich C v Coventry C
Portsmouth v Wolverhampton W
Reading v Crystal P
Sheffield W v Ipswich T
Stoke C v Sheffield U
Walsall v Burnley
Wimbledon v Millwall (12:00)

Nationwide Football League Division 2
Blackpool v Plymouth Arg
Brentford v Stockport Co
Bristol C v Peterborough U
Cheltenham T v Northampton T
Colchester U v Huddersfield T
Crewe Alex v Port Vale
Mansfield T v Swindon T
Notts Co v Chesterfield
Oldham Ath v QPR
Wigan Ath v Luton T
Wycombe W v Barnsley

Nationwide Football League Division 3
Cambridge U v Kidderminster H
Darlington v Exeter C
Hartlepool U v Southend U
Leyton Orient v Bristol R
Lincoln C v Wrexham
Macclesfield T v Bury
Rochdale v Boston U
Rushden & D'monds v Hull C
Shrewsbury T v Oxford U
Swansea C v Carlisle U
Torquay U v Scunthorpe U
York C v Bournemouth

Nationwide Conference
Chester C v Doncaster R
Farnborough T v Telford U
Gravesend & N v Northwich Vic
Kettering T v Forest Green R
Margate v Burton A
Morecambe v Barnet
Nuneaton B v Halifax T

Scarborough v Hereford U
Southport v Dag & Red
Stevenage B v Woking
Yeovil T v Leigh RMI

Tuesday, 18 March 2003
Nationwide Football League Division 1
Bradford C v Sheffield W
Burnley v Leicester C
Crystal P v Wimbledon (8:00)
Ipswich T v Reading
Millwall v Norwich C
Preston NE v Walsall
Rotherham U v Grimsby T
Sheffield U v Brighton & HA
Watford v Gillingham
Wolverhampton W v Stoke C

Nationwide Football League Division 2
Barnsley v Tranmere R
Cardiff C v Blackpool
Chesterfield v Colchester U
Huddersfield T v Mansfield T
Luton T v Oldham Ath
Northampton T v Notts Co
Peterborough U v Wycombe W
Plymouth Arg v Crewe Alex
Port Vale v Brentford
QPR v Cheltenham T
Stockport Co v Wigan Ath

Nationwide Football League Division 3
Bournemouth v Leyton Orient
Bristol R v York C
Bury v Rushden & D'monds
Carlisle U v Macclesfield T
Exeter C v Lincoln C
Hull C v Torquay U
Kidderminster H v Shrewsbury T
Oxford U v Cambridge U
Scunthorpe U v Rochdale (7:30)
Southend U v Swansea C
Wrexham v Hartlepool U

Wednesday, 19 March 2003
Nationwide Football League Division 1
Coventry C v Portsmouth
Nottingham F v Derby Co

Nationwide Football League Division 2
Swindon T v Bristol C

Nationwide Football League Division 3
Boston U v Darlington

Friday, 21 March 2003
Nationwide Football League Division 2
Cardiff C v Mansfield T

Saturday, 22 March 2003
FA Barclaycard Premiership
Arsenal v Everton
Birmingham C v WBA
Bolton W v Tottenham H
Chelsea v Manchester C
Liverpool v Leeds U
Manchester U v Fulham
Middlesbrough v Charlton Ath
Newcastle U v Blackburn R
Southampton v Aston Villa
West Ham U v Sunderland

Nationwide Football League Division 1
Bradford C v Reading
Burnley v Grimsby T
Coventry C v Leicester C
Crystal P v Walsall

Ipswich T v Brighton & HA
Millwall v Sheffield W
Nottingham F v Norwich C
Preston NE v Portsmouth
Rotherham U v Wimbledon
Sheffield U v Derby Co
Watford v Stoke C
Wolverhampton W v Gillingham

Nationwide Football League Division 2
Barnsley v Colchester U
Chesterfield v Wycombe W
Huddersfield T v Bristol C
Luton T v Crewe Alex
Northampton T v Oldham Ath
Peterborough U v Tranmere R
Plymouth Arg v Brentford
Port Vale v Cheltenham T
QPR v Wigan Ath
Stockport Co v Blackpool
Swindon T v Notts Co

Nationwide Football League Division 3
Boston U v Rushden & D'monds
Bournemouth v Torquay U
Bristol R v Hartlepool U
Bury v Lincoln C
Carlisle U v Cambridge U
Exeter C v Rochdale
Hull C v Shrewsbury T
Kidderminster H v Swansea C
Oxford U v Macclesfield T
Scunthorpe U v Darlington
Southend U v Leyton Orient
Wrexham v York C

Nationwide Conference
Barnet v Hereford U
Burton A v Farnborough T
Chester C v Southport
Dag & Red v Halifax T
Forest Green R v Northwich Vic
Gravesend & N v Morecambe
Margate v Yeovil T
Nuneaton B v Kettering T
Scarborough v Stevenage B
Telford U v Leigh RMI
Woking v Doncaster R

Friday, 28 March 2003
Nationwide Football League Division 3
Swansea C v Oxford U

Saturday, 29 March 2003
Nationwide Football League Division 1
Brighton & HA v Crystal P
Derby Co v Millwall
Gillingham v Ipswich T
Grimsby T v Wolverhampton W
Leicester C v Nottingham F
Norwich C v Bradford C
Portsmouth v Burnley
Reading v Preston NE
Sheffield W v Watford
Stoke C v Rotherham U
Walsall v Coventry C
Wimbledon v Sheffield U

Nationwide Football League Division 2
Blackpool v QPR
Brentford v Northampton T
Bristol C v Barnsley
Cheltenham T v Luton T
Colchester U v Swindon T
Crewe Alex v Stockport Co
Mansfield T v Peterborough U
Notts Co v Huddersfield T
Oldham Ath v Port Vale

Tranmere R v Chesterfield
Wigan Ath v Plymouth Arg
Wycombe W v Cardiff C

Nationwide Football League Division 3
Cambridge U v Scunthorpe U
Darlington v Bury
Hartlepool U v Bournemouth
Leyton Orient v Wrexham
Lincoln C v Bristol R
Macclesfield T v Kidderminster H
Rochdale v Hull C
Rushden & D'monds v Exeter C
Shrewsbury T v Carlisle U
Torquay U v Boston U
York C v Southend U

Nationwide Conference
Doncaster R v Burton A
Farnborough T v Chester C
Halifax T v Woking
Hereford U v Margate
Kettering T v Gravesend & N
Leigh RMI v Forest Green R
Morecambe v Nuneaton B
Northwich Vic v Telford U
Southport v Barnet
Stevenage B v Dag & Red
Yeovil T v Scarborough

Friday, 4 April 2003
Nationwide Football League Division 2
Northampton T v Wigan Ath

Saturday, 5 April 2003
FA Barclaycard Premiership
Aston Villa v Arsenal
Bolton W v Manchester C
Charlton Ath v Leeds U
Fulham v Blackburn R
Manchester U v Liverpool
Middlesbrough v WBA
Southampton v West Ham U
Sunderland v Chelsea
Tottenham H v Birmingham C

Nationwide Football League Division 1
Bradford C v Millwall
Burnley v Watford
Crystal P v Sheffield U
Derby Co v Norwich C
Ipswich T v Nottingham F
Leicester C v Grimsby T
Preston NE v Coventry C
Reading v Brighton & HA
Sheffield W v Wimbledon
Stoke C v Gillingham
Walsall v Portsmouth
Wolverhampton W v Rotherham U

Nationwide Football League Division 2
Brentford v Cheltenham T
Cardiff C v QPR
Crewe Alex v Bristol C
Huddersfield T v Chesterfield
Luton T v Tranmere R
Mansfield T v Port Vale
Notts Co v Blackpool
Oldham Ath v Barnsley
Peterborough U v Swindon T
Plymouth Arg v Colchester U
Wycombe W v Stockport Co

Nationwide Football League Division 3
Bristol R v Rushden & D'monds
Carlisle U v York C
Exeter C v Bury
Hull C v Wrexham

Kidderminster H v Hartlepool U
Leyton Orient v Boston U
Lincoln C v Oxford U
Macclesfield T v Cambridge U
Rochdale v Torquay U
Scunthorpe U v Bournemouth
Shrewsbury T v Swansea C
Southend U v Darlington

Nationwide Conference
Forest Green R v Doncaster R
Gravesend & N v Chester C
Hereford U v Burton A
Kettering T v Farnborough T
Margate v Halifax T
Morecambe v Dag & Red
Northwich Vic v Scarborough
Nuneaton B v Barnet
Stevenage B v Leigh RMI
Woking v Southport
Yeovil T v Telford U

Sunday, 6 April 2003
FA Barclaycard Premiership
Everton v Newcastle U

Saturday, 12 April 2003
FA Barclaycard Premiership
Arsenal v Southampton
Birmingham C v Sunderland
Blackburn R v Charlton Ath
Chelsea v Bolton W
Leeds U v Tottenham H
Liverpool v Fulham
Manchester C v Middlesbrough
Newcastle U v Manchester U
WBA v Everton
West Ham U v Aston Villa

Nationwide Football League Division 1
Brighton & HA v Preston NE
Coventry C v Ipswich T
Gillingham v Walsall
Grimsby T v Crystal P
Millwall v Stoke C
Norwich C v Burnley
Nottingham F v Wolverhampton W
Portsmouth v Sheffield W
Rotherham U v Leicester C
Sheffield U v Bradford C
Watford v Reading
Wimbledon v Derby Co

Nationwide Football League Division 2
Barnsley v Peterborough U
Blackpool v Crewe Alex
Bristol C v Mansfield T
Cheltenham T v Oldham Ath
Chesterfield v Cardiff C
Colchester U v Notts Co
Port Vale v Northampton T
QPR v Luton T
Stockport Co v Plymouth Arg
Swindon T v Huddersfield T
Tranmere R v Wycombe W
Wigan Ath v Brentford

Nationwide Football League Division 3
Boston U v Hull C
Bournemouth v Southend U
Bury v Carlisle U
Cambridge U v Exeter C
Darlington v Shrewsbury T
Hartlepool U v Leyton Orient
Oxford U v Kidderminster H
Rushden & D'monds v Lincoln C
Swansea C v Scunthorpe U
Torquay U v Macclesfield T

Wrexham v Bristol R
York C v Rochdale

Nationwide Conference
Barnet v Kettering T
Burton A v Stevenage B
Chester C v Woking
Dag & Red v Northwich Vic
Doncaster R v Yeovil T
Farnborough T v Morecambe
Halifax T v Hereford U
Leigh RMI v Gravesend & N
Scarborough v Forest Green R
Southport v Margate
Telford U v Nuneaton B

Friday, 18 April 2003
FA Barclaycard Premiership
Tottenham H v Manchester C (3:00)

Nationwide Football League Division 2
Northampton T v Stockport Co

Saturday, 19 April 2003
FA Barclaycard Premiership
Aston Villa v Chelsea
Bolton W v West Ham U
Charlton Ath v Birmingham C
Everton v Liverpool
Fulham v Newcastle U
Manchester U v Blackburn R
Middlesbrough v Arsenal
Southampton v Leeds U
Sunderland v WBA

Nationwide Football League Division 1
Bradford C v Watford
Burnley v Gillingham
Crystal P v Rotherham U
Derby Co v Coventry C
Ipswich T v Portsmouth
Leicester C v Brighton & HA
Preston NE v Sheffield U
Reading v Nottingham F
Sheffield W v Grimsby T
Stoke C v Wimbledon
Walsall v Norwich C
Wolverhampton W v Millwall

Nationwide Football League Division 2
Brentford v QPR
Cardiff C v Colchester U
Crewe Alex v Swindon T
Huddersfield T v Wigan Ath
Luton T v Bristol C
Mansfield T v Barnsley
Notts Co v Tranmere R
Oldham Ath v Chesterfield
Peterborough U v Blackpool
Plymouth Arg v Port Vale
Wycombe W v Cheltenham T

Nationwide Football League Division 3
Bristol R v Cambridge U
Carlisle U v Rushden & D'monds
Exeter C v Oxford U
Hull C v Bournemouth
Kidderminster H v Wrexham
Leyton Orient v Swansea C
Lincoln C v York C
Macclesfield T v Darlington
Rochdale v Bury
Scunthorpe U v Hartlepool U
Shrewsbury T v Boston U
Southend U v Torquay U

Nationwide Conference
Forest Green R v Telford U

Gravesend & N v Barnet
Hereford U v Leigh RMI
Kettering T v Halifax T
Margate v Farnborough T
Morecambe v Scarborough
Northwich Vic v Southport
Nuneaton B v Chester C
Stevenage B v Doncaster R
Woking v Dag & Red
Yeovil T v Burton A

Monday, 21 April 2003

FA Barclaycard Premiership
Arsenal v Manchester U (3:00)
Birmingham C v Southampton (3:00)
Blackburn R v Bolton W (3:00)
Chelsea v Everton (3:00)
Liverpool v Charlton Ath (3:00)
Manchester C v Sunderland (3:00)
Newcastle U v Aston Villa (3:00)
WBA v Tottenham H (3:00)
West Ham U v Middlesbrough (3:00)

Nationwide Football League Division 1
Brighton & HA v Sheffield W (3:00)
Coventry C v Stoke C (3:00)
Gillingham v Bradford C (3:00)
Grimsby T v Walsall (3:00)
Millwall v Crystal P (3:00)
Norwich C v Wolverhampton W (3:00)
Nottingham F v Burnley (3:00)
Portsmouth v Reading (3:00)
Rotherham U v Ipswich T (3:00)
Sheffield U v Leicester C (3:00)
Watford v Derby Co (3:00)

Nationwide Football League Division 2
Barnsley v Crewe Alex (3:00)
Blackpool v Mansfield T (3:00)
Cheltenham T v Peterborough U (3:00)
Chesterfield v Brentford (3:00)
Colchester U v Luton T (3:00)
Port Vale v Wycombe W (3:00)
QPR v Notts Co (3:00)
Stockport Co v Huddersfield T (3:00)
Swindon T v Plymouth Arg (3:00)
Tranmere R v Northampton T (3:00)
Wigan Ath v Oldham Ath (3:00)

Nationwide Football League Division 3
Boston U v Southend U (3:00)
Bury v Scunthorpe U (3:00)
Cambridge U v Lincoln C (3:00)
Darlington v Hull C (3:00)
Hartlepool U v Rochdale (3:00)
Oxford U v Bristol R (3:00)
Rushden & D'monds v Macclesfield T (3:00)
Swansea C v Exeter C (3:00)
Torquay U v Leyton Orient (3:00)
Wrexham v Carlisle U (3:00)
York C v Kidderminster H (3:00)

Nationwide Conference
Barnet v Woking
Burton A v Kettering T
Chester C v Stevenage B
Dag & Red v Yeovil T
Doncaster R v Morecambe
Farnborough T v Gravesend & N
Halifax T v Forest Green R
Leigh RMI v Northwich Vic
Scarborough v Nuneaton B
Southport v Hereford U
Telford U v Margate

Tuesday, 22 April 2003

FA Barclaycard Premiership
Leeds U v Fulham

Nationwide Football League Division 1
Wimbledon v Preston NE

Nationwide Football League Division 2
Bristol C v Cardiff C

Nationwide Football League Division 3
Bournemouth v Shrewsbury T

Saturday, 26 April 2003

FA Barclaycard Premiership
Birmingham C v Middlesbrough
Bolton W v Arsenal
Charlton Ath v Southampton
Chelsea v Fulham
Everton v Aston Villa
Leeds U v Blackburn R
Manchester C v West Ham U
Sunderland v Newcastle U
Tottenham H v Manchester U
WBA v Liverpool

Nationwide Football League Division 1
Brighton & HA v Watford
Burnley v Sheffield W
Coventry C v Gillingham
Crystal P v Stoke C
Ipswich T v Wimbledon
Leicester C v Norwich C
Nottingham F v Millwall
Portsmouth v Rotherham U
Preston NE v Bradford C
Reading v Grimsby T
Sheffield U v Wolverhampton W
Walsall v Derby Co

Nationwide Football League Division 2
Barnsley v Brentford
Cardiff C v Wigan Ath
Cheltenham T v Blackpool
Chesterfield v Bristol C
Luton T v Stockport Co
Northampton T v Plymouth Arg
Oldham Ath v Swindon T
Peterborough U v Notts Co
Port Vale v Huddersfield T
QPR v Crewe Alex
Tranmere R v Mansfield T
Wycombe W v Colchester U

Nationwide Football League Division 3
Boston U v Macclesfield T
Bournemouth v Lincoln C
Bristol R v Darlington
Hartlepool U v Shrewsbury T
Hull C v Kidderminster H
Leyton Orient v Rushden & D'monds
Rochdale v Swansea C
Scunthorpe U v Oxford U
Southend U v Bury
Torquay U v Carlisle U
Wrexham v Cambridge U
York C v Exeter C

Nationwide Conference
Forest Green R v Dag & Red
Gravesend & N v Halifax T
Hereford U v Doncaster R
Kettering T v Leigh RMI
Margate v Scarborough
Morecambe v Burton A
Northwich Vic v Barnet

Nuneaton B v Farnborough T
Stevenage B v Southport
Woking v Telford U
Yeovil T v Chester C

Saturday, 3 May 2003

FA Barclaycard Premiership
Arsenal v Leeds U
Aston Villa v Sunderland
Blackburn R v WBA
Fulham v Everton
Liverpool v Manchester C
Manchester U v Charlton Ath
Middlesbrough v Tottenham H
Newcastle U v Birmingham C
Southampton v Bolton W
West Ham U v Chelsea

Nationwide Football League Division 2
Blackpool v Chesterfield
Brentford v Peterborough U
Bristol C v Port Vale
Colchester U v QPR
Crewe Alex v Cardiff C
Huddersfield T v Oldham Ath
Mansfield T v Northampton T
Notts Co v Cheltenham T
Plymouth Arg v Wycombe W
Stockport Co v Tranmere R
Swindon T v Luton T
Wigan Ath v Barnsley

Nationwide Football League Division 3
Bury v Wrexham
Cambridge U v Boston U
Carlisle U v Bournemouth
Darlington v Leyton Orient
Exeter C v Southend U
Kidderminster H v Bristol R
Lincoln C v Torquay U
Macclesfield T v Rochdale
Oxford U v York C
Rushden & D'monds v Hartlepool U
Shrewsbury T v Scunthorpe U
Swansea C v Hull C

Sunday, 4 May 2003

Nationwide Football League Division 1
Bradford C v Portsmouth
Derby Co v Ipswich T
Gillingham v Crystal P
Grimsby T v Brighton & HA
Millwall v Coventry C
Norwich C v Preston NE
Rotherham U v Nottingham F
Sheffield W v Walsall
Stoke C v Reading
Watford v Sheffield U
Wimbledon v Burnley
Wolverhampton W v Leicester C

Sunday, 11 May 2003

FA Barclaycard Premiership
Birmingham C v West Ham U (4:00)
Bolton W v Middlesbrough (4:00)
Charlton Ath v Fulham (4:00)
Chelsea v Liverpool (4:00)
Everton v Manchester U (4:00)
Leeds U v Aston Villa (4:00)
Manchester C v Southampton (4:00)
Sunderland v Arsenal (4:00)
Tottenham H v Blackburn R (4:00)
WBA v Newcastle U (4:00)

FA BARCLAYCARD PREMIERSHIP FIXTURES 2002–03

Reproduced under Copyright/Database Licence No. PRINT/ALL3014. Copyright © The FA Premier League Limited 2002.

	Arsenal	Aston Villa	Birmingham C	Blackburn R	Bolton W	Charlton Ath	Chelsea	Everton	Fulham	Leeds U	Liverpool	Manchester C	Manchester U	Middlesbrough	Newcastle U	Southampton	Sunderland	Tottenham H	WBA	West Ham U
Arsenal	—	30.11	18.8	26.10	21.9	1.3	1.1	22.3	1.2	3.5	29.12	10.9	21.4	21.12	9.11	12.4	6.10	16.11	27.8	18.1
Aston Villa	5.4	—	1.3	1.2	1.1	11.9	19.4	22.9	9.11	6.10	18.8	28.8	15.3	28.12	7.12	21.10	3.5	18.1	14.12	23.11
Birmingham C	11.1	15.9	—	24.8	2.11	21.12	8.2	26.12	9.11	31.8	22.2	26.10	28.1	26.4	28.9	21.4	12.4	30.11	22.3	11.5
Blackburn R	15.3	2.11	18.1	—	21.4	12.4	11.9	16.11	30.11	22.9	28.8	1.3	21.12	1.1	19.10	8.2	17.8	6.10	3.5	26.12
Bolton W	26.4	1.9	1.2	7.12	—	24.8	23.11	28.1	11.1	16.12	14.9	5.4	22.2	11.5	26.12	8.2	17.8	22.3	9.11	19.4
Charlton Ath	14.9	22.2	19.4	24.11	18.1	—	17.8	8.2	11.5	5.4	7.12	14.12	28.9	20.10	15.3	28.9	3.11	27.8	26.12	1.1
Chelsea	1.9	21.12	9.11	22.2	12.4	11.1	—	21.4	26.4	29.1	11.5	22.3	23.8	16.11	14.9	26.12	30.11	1.2	26.10	28.9
Everton	19.10	26.4	28.8	14.12	26.12	9.11	7.12	—	28.9	1.2	19.4	1.1	11.5	16.11	6.4	22.2	18.1	17.8	23.11	15.3
Fulham	2.11	8.2	14.12	5.4	17.8	5.10	23.9	3.5	—	1.2	23.11	26.12	19.10	14.9	19.4	15.3	1.3	11.9	1.1	28.8
Leeds U	28.9	11.5	1.1	26.4	16.11	30.11	26.12	2.11	22.4	—	19.10	26.12	14.9	15.3	22.2	21.12	28.8	12.4	18.1	8.2
Liverpool	29.1	11.1	11.9	26.12	1.3	21.4	6.10	22.12	12.4	22.3	—	3.5	1.12	8.2	2.9	24.8	16.11	26.10	21.9	2.11
Manchester C	22.2	26.12	15.3	15.9	30.11	16.11	19.10	31.8	29.1	11.1	28.9	—	9.11	12.4	24.8	11.5	21.4	23.12	1.2	26.4
Manchester U	7.12	26.10	26.12	19.4	11.9	3.5	18.1	7.10	22.3	1.3	5.4	8.2	—	3.9	23.11	12.11	1.1	21.9	17.8	14.12
Middlesbrough	19.4	28.1	21.9	31.8	5.10	14.12	14.12	1.3	24.8	26.10	9.11	23.11	26.12	—	1.2	11.1	10.9	3.5	5.4	7.12
Newcastle U	8.2	21.4	3.5	22.3	28.8	26.10	1.3	30.11	1.3	26.10	1.1	26.12	12.4	4.11	—	16.11	22.9	29.12	5.10	17.8
Southampton	23.11	22.3	7.12	9.11	3.5	21.9	28.8	11.9	27.10	19.4	18.1	5.10	12.4	17.8	14.12	—	26.12	16.11	1.3	1.1
Sunderland	11.5	28.9	23.11	11.1	15.3	1.2	5.4	24.8	14.9	26.12	14.12	7.12	31.8	22.2	29.1	28.1	—	10.11	19.4	19.10
Tottenham H	14.12	24.8	5.4	11.5	20.10	26.12	3.11	11.1	22.2	24.11	15.3	18.4	26.4	28.9	29.1	31.8	8.2	—	8.12	16.9
WBA	26.12	16.11	19.10	30.9	8.2	28.1	15.3	12.4	31.8	24.8	26.4	2.11	11.1	30.11	11.5	14.9	21.12	21.4	—	22.2
West Ham U	24.8	12.4	5.10	29.1	21.12	31.8	3.5	27.10	26.12	9.11	1.2	21.9	17.11	21.4	11.1	2.12	22.3	1.3	11.9	—

NATIONWIDE FOOTBALL LEAGUE FIXTURES 2002–03

Reproduced under Copyright/Database Licence No. PRINT/ALL/3014. Copyright © The Football League Limited 2002.

DIVISION ONE

	Bradford C	Brighton & HA	Burnley	Coventry C	Crystal Palace	Derby Co	Gillingham	Grimsby T	Ipswich T	Leicester C	Millwall	Norwich C	Nottingham F	Portsmouth	Preston NE	Reading	Rotherham U	Sheffield U	Sheffield W	Stoke C	Walsall	Watford	Wimbledon	Wolverhampton W
Bradford C	—	15.2	21.9	7.9	11.1	12.10	7.12	24.8	1.2	4.3	5.4	26.10	14.12	4.5	5.10	22.3	31.8	23.11	18.3	26.12	1.3	19.4	9.11	11.8
Brighton & HA	2.11	—	28.12	13.8	29.3	16.11	14.9	28.9	29.10	20.12	22.2	17.8	15.3	18.1	12.4	30.11	8.3	20.10	21.4	17.9	26.8	26.4	1.1	8.2
Burnley	8.3	10.8	—	9.11	31.8	22.2	19.4	22.3	11.1	18.3	17.9	23.11	7.12	26.10	15.2	1.2	14.12	24.8	26.4	14.9	12.10	5.4	28.9	26.12
Coventry C	22.2	11.1	8.2	—	24.8	21.12	26.4	14.9	12.4	22.3	28.9	12.10	31.8	19.3	30.11	26.12	2.11	10.8	18.9	21.4	26.4	1.2	8.3	16.11
Crystal Palace	13.8	26.10	18.1	1.1	—	17.9	28.9	23.11	15.2	27.8	16.11	14.12	9.11	17.8	28.12	12.10	19.4	5.4	22.2	31.8	26.10	8.3	18.3	14.9
Derby Co	15.3	14.12	7.9	19.4	5.3	—	11.1	26.12	4.5	1.3	29.3	5.4	19.10	9.11	26.8	10.8	1.2	30.10	15.2	31.8	29.10	7.12	23.11	24.8
Gillingham	21.4	1.3	21.12	5.10	4.5	13.8	—	15.2	29.3	18.1	17.8	1.1	4.3	7.9	26.8	9.11	15.3	19.10	16.11	30.11	12.4	23.11	28.12	29.10
Grimsby T	1.1	4.5	29.10	1.3	12.4	17.8	15.2	—	7.9	30.11	31.8	28.12	21.9	26.8	16.11	5.10	19.10	4.3	16.11	30.11	21.4	9.11	13.8	29.3
Ipswich T	26.8	22.3	24.9	23.11	1.2	28.9	2.11	7.9	—	18.8	24.8	15.9	29.10	21.12	1.9	19.10	21.4	9.11	15.3	12.10	10.8	16.11	5.10	18.9
Leicester C	17.9	19.4	19.10	29.10	21.4	14.9	26.10	5.4	18.8	—	16.11	18.3	5.10	2.11	12.10	1.1	12.4	1.9	28.12	12.10	28.12	8.2	7.9	28.9
Millwall	30.11	7.9	4.3	4.5	16.11	26.10	31.8	31.8	24.8	16.11	—	26.4	29.10	14.9	8.2	2.11	13.8	26.8	30.10	23.11	8.3	19.4	12.10	21.12
Norwich City	29.3	26.12	12.4	15.3	8.2	30.11	26.12	10.8	2.3	5.10	19.10	—	29.10	13.8	22.2	8.2	26.8	19.4	18.9	28.9	26.8	18.1	15.2	7.12
Nottingham F	16.11	12.10	21.4	18.1	30.11	19.3	24.8	8.3	30.11	26.10	26.4	22.3	—	28.12	10.8	21.12	4.5	15.2	7.9	24.8	1.3	1.2	28.8	5.4
Portsmouth	28.9	31.8	29.3	19.10	26.12	8.2	18.9	1.2	21.12	2.11	14.9	13.8	28.12	—	29.10	12.10	5.10	23.11	24.8	21.9	5.4	1.1	5.4	12.10
Preston NE	26.4	23.11	2.11	5.4	10.8	8.3	22.2	14.12	1.9	12.10	8.2	22.2	10.8	29.10	—	26.10	29.3	21.12	14.9	14.9	19.10	4.3	19.4	7.9
Reading	29.10	5.4	27.8	17.8	15.3	28.12	1.2	26.4	19.10	1.1	2.11	8.2	21.12	12.10	26.10	—	22.2	9.11	14.12	26.10	31.8	12.4	7.12	21.9
Rotherham U	18.1	21.9	16.11	15.2	21.12	26.8	8.2	18.3	21.4	12.4	13.8	26.8	4.5	5.10	29.3	22.2	—	14.12	13.8	26.10	4.3	9.11	14.9	30.11
Sheffield U	12.4	18.3	1.1	28.12	30.11	22.3	12.10	17.9	9.11	1.9	26.8	19.4	15.2	23.11	21.12	9.11	14.12	—	1.1	12.10	17.8	28.9	22.3	26.4
Sheffield W	19.10	7.12	5.10	5.3	7.9	2.11	8.3	7.12	15.3	28.12	30.10	18.9	7.9	24.8	14.9	14.12	13.8	1.1	—	28.9	28.9	30.11	14.9	1.2
Stoke C	17.8	5.3	1.3	29.10	7.9	18.1	14.12	12.10	21.9	12.10	23.11	28.9	24.8	21.9	14.9	26.10	26.10	12.10	28.9	—	10.8	4.5	10.8	2.11
Walsall	14.9	1.2	15.3	29.3	29.10	26.4	5.4	19.4	10.8	14.8	8.3	26.8	1.3	5.4	19.10	31.8	4.3	17.8	28.9	15.2	—	15.2	14.12	19.10
Watford	21.12	24.8	30.11	26.8	21.9	21.4	18.3	12.10	16.11	8.2	19.4	18.1	1.2	1.1	4.3	12.4	9.11	28.9	30.11	4.5	15.2	—	17.8	2.11
Wimbledon	8.2	5.10	5.4	21.9	19.10	12.4	10.8	11.1	5.10	7.9	12.10	15.2	28.8	5.4	19.4	7.12	14.9	22.3	14.9	10.8	14.12	17.8	—	31.8
Wolverhampton W	28.12	9.11	17.8	14.12	1.3	1.1	22.3	26.10	4.3	5.4	19.4	7.12	5.4	12.10	7.9	21.9	30.11	26.4	1.2	2.11	19.10	2.11	31.8	—

NATIONWIDE FOOTBALL LEAGUE FIXTURES 2002–03

Reproduced under Copyright/Database Licence No. PRINT/ALL/3014. Copyright © The Football League Limited 2002.

DIVISION TWO

	Barnsley	Blackpool	Brentford	Bristol C	Cardiff C	Cheltenham T	Chesterfield	Colchester U	Crewe Alex	Huddersfield T	Luton T	Mansfield T	Northampton T	Notts Co	Oldham Ath	Peterborough U	Plymouth Arg	Port Vale	QPR	Stockport Co	Swindon T	Tranmere R	Wigan Ath	Wycombe W
Barnsley	—	17.9	26.4	12.10	9.11	13.8	15.2	22.3	21.4	22.2	18.1	21.12	1.1	26.8	30.11	12.4	14.9	28.12	17.8	8.3	1.2	18.3	28.9	26.10
Blackpool	4.3	—	15.2	1.2	19.10	5.10	3.5	28.12	12.4	1.1	13.8	21.4	18.1	30.11	26.8	21.12	15.3	21.9	29.3	29.10	17.8	7.9	9.11	1.3
Brentford	5.10	2.11	—	13.8	4.3	5.4	14.12	1.1	8.2	1.2	7.9	28.12	29.3	18.1	17.8	3.5	29.10	19.10	19.4	15.3	26.8	31.8	23.11	21.9
Bristol C	29.3	10.8	4.1	—	22.4	1.3	5.10	8.2	30.11	29.10	21.12	12.4	7.9	2.11	4.3	15.3	26.12	3.5	21.9	25.1	19.10	31.8	11.1	24.8
Cardiff C	8.2	18.3	17.9	14.12	—	18.1	22.11	19.4	28.9	29.12	26.8	21.3	17.8	8.3	1.2	21.4	24.8	13.8	5.4	14.9	1.1	26.10	26.4	12.10
Cheltenham T	4.1	26.4	30.11	14.9	31.8	—	25.1	22.2	26.12	2.11	29.3	8.3	27.8	28.9	12.4	21.4	24.8	29.10	19.10	8.2	17.9	11.1	10.8	21.12
Chesterfield	2.11	28.9	21.4	26.4	12.4	28.12	—	18.3	22.2	30.11	1.1	18.1	27.8	26.10	21.12	8.2	8.3	17.8	1.2	17.9	13.8	12.10	14.9	22.3
Colchester U	29.10	25.1	24.8	8.2	19.4	22.2	18.3	—	11.1	17.8	12.10	22.2	26.12	17.9	23.11	26.8	5.4	14.9	18.1	23.11	13.8	12.10	24.8	5.10
Crewe Alex	14.12	9.11	9.11	5.4	3.5	26.12	22.2	11.1	—	18.1	21.9	11.1	10.8	4.1	12.4	14.9	10.8	26.4	26.10	23.11	21.12	15.2	1.1	17.9
Huddersfield T	7.9	31.8	10.8	22.3	25.1	2.11	30.11	17.8	18.1	—	21.9	18.3	2.11	1.3	3.5	17.8	4.1	5.10	4.3	24.8	23.11	26.8	17.8	9.11
Luton T	24.8	4.1	22.2	9.11	26.12	8.3	1.1	21.4	21.9	21.9	—	17.9	4.3	14.9	19.10	1.2	11.1	29.3	17.9	26.8	29.3	30.11	26.8	3.5
Mansfield T	19.4	14.12	25.1	29.10	29.10	17.9	18.1	22.2	11.1	17.9	17.9	—	3.5	8.2	1.3	10.8	10.8	1.3	23.11	8.2	26.8	26.4	4.1	7.8
Northampton T	31.8	23.8	12.10	22.2	11.1	27.8	27.8	26.12	10.8	2.11	4.3	28.9	—	18.3	22.3	25.1	5.10	19.4	8.2	18.3	20.12	21.4	4.4	4.1
Notts Co	26.12	5.4	31.8	15.2	21.9	28.9	26.10	17.9	4.1	1.3	1.3	9.11	19.10	—	7.9	5.10	25.1	4.3	14.12	2.11	29.10	21.12	24.8	10.8
Oldham Ath	5.4	26.12	11.1	17.9	10.8	12.4	21.12	13.8	25.1	18.3	18.3	1.3	19.10	14.9	—	4.1	8.2	29.3	15.3	2.11	26.4	24.8	14.12	31.8
Peterborough U	23.11	19.4	28.9	26.10	15.2	14.12	9.11	26.8	14.9	17.8	1.2	12.10	28.12	26.4	13.8	—	4.1	18.1	15.3	2.11	26.4	24.8	14.12	31.8
Plymouth Arg	1.3	26.10	22.3	26.8	7.9	24.8	8.3	5.4	10.8	10.8	11.1	10.8	5.10	17.9	9.11	4.3	—	19.4	17.9	22.2	14.12	22.3	12.10	3.5
Port Vale	25.1	8.3	18.3	28.9	4.1	29.10	17.8	26.10	26.4	22.3	17.8	30.11	12.4	17.9	12.10	31.8	21.12	—	19.4	24.8	22.2	10.8	26.12	21.4
QPR	11.1	12.10	21.12	8.3	30.11	19.10	1.2	14.9	26.10	26.4	17.9	21.4	9.11	21.4	12.10	24.8	31.8	2.11	—	4.1	14.9	25.1	22.3	26.12
Stockport Co	21.9	22.3	26.10	28.12	14.9	8.2	17.9	22.2	23.11	24.8	5.10	26.8	17.8	21.4	26.10	4.1	31.8	7.9	1.1	—	18.1	3.5	18.3	15.2
Swindon T	10.8	11.1	26.12	19.3	1.1	17.9	13.8	12.4	21.12	12.4	26.8	26.10	20.12	22.3	5.10	30.11	12.4	7.9	1.3	31.8	—	9.11	25.1	15.2
Tranmere R	19.10	22.2	14.9	14.3	26.8	11.1	12.10	12.4	15.2	26.8	26.10	26.4	21.4	21.12	30.11	30.11	12.4	1.2	1.3	31.8	8.2	—	17.9	12.4
Wigan Ath	3.5	8.2	12.4	17.8	13.8	15.3	14.3	5.10	1.1	17.8	1.1	21.4	1.1	1.1	21.4	29.10	2.11	29.3	29.10	19.10	28.12	4.3	—	7.9
Wycombe W	15.3	14.9	8.3	1.1	29.3	19.4	17.8	26.4	17.9	9.11	29.12	13.8	4.1	10.8	28.0	14.12	29.3	26.8	14.12	26.8	5.4	21.11	22.3	—

NATIONWIDE FOOTBALL FIXTURES 2002–03

Reproduced under Copyright/Database Licence No. PRINT/ALL/3014. Copyright © The Football League Limited 2002.

DIVISION THREE

	Boston U	AFC Bournemouth	Bristol R	Bury	Cambridge U	Carlisle U	Darlington	Exeter C	Hartlepool U	Hull C	Kidderminster H	Leyton O	Lincoln C	Macclesfield T	Oxford U	Rochdale	Rushden & D	Scunthorpe U	Shrewsbury T	Southend U	Swansea C	Torquay U	Wrexham	York C
Boston U	—	10.8	25.1	31.8	28.9	8.3	19.3	2.11	4.1	12.4	22.2	30.11	24.8	26.4	14.9	26.10	22.3	8.2	21.12	21.4	18.9	12.10	11.1	26.12
AFC Bournemouth	31.1	—	2.11	14.9	17.8	28.9	8.3	22.2	12.10	21.12	13.8	18.3	26.4	17.1	27.8	28.12	17.9	30.11	22.4	12.4	1.1	22.3	8.2	26.10
Bristol R	28.12	15.2	—	17.9	19.4	1.2	26.4	14.9	22.3	13.8	28.9	26.10	12.10	22.2	14.12	17.8	5.4	18.1	8.3	9.11	27.8	1.1	23.11	18.3
Bury	18.1	1.3	4.3	—	13.8	12.4	12.10	30.11	21.9	1.1	28.12	15.2	22.3	26.10	1.2	21.12	18.3	21.4	26.8	5.10	17.8	9.11	3.5	7.9
Cambridge U	3.5	11.1	21.12	4.1	—	29.10	10.8	12.4	25.1	7.9	15.3	24.8	21.4	30.11	19.10	4.3	31.8	29.3	8.2	26.12	2.11	1.3	5.10	21.9
Carlisle U	21.9	3.5	24.8	23.11	22.3	—	26.12	31.8	25.1	1.3	8.2	25.1	11.1	18.3	2.11	7.9	19.4	4.3	12.10	4.1	26.10	5.10	14.12	5.4
Darlington	19.10	21.9	5.10	29.3	1.2	27.8	—	15.3	10.8	21.4	18.1	3.5	2.11	21.12	17.8	1.1	8.2	29.10	12.4	30.11	13.8	28.12	7.9	4.3
Exeter C	15.2	7.9	1.3	5.4	23.11	27.8	15.3	—	9.11	26.8	1.1	21.9	17.9	2.11	26.4	15.3	8.2	13.8	18.3	3.5	14.12	26.8	4.3	5.10
Hartlepool U	13.8	29.3	7.3	5.4	28.12	1.3	19.4	26.12	—	26.10	21.4	24.8	17.8	18.1	7.9	21.4	1.1	8.2	26.4	15.3	28.9	13.8	18.3	5.10
Hull C	23.11	19.4	4.1	14.12	1.1	1.3	21.4	26.8	26.10	—	30.11	12.4	8.2	17.8	18.1	21.4	28.9	20.12	2.11	10.8	28.9	18.3	5.4	25.1
Kidderminster H	7.9	4.1	3.5	25.1	15.3	8.2	18.1	1.1	21.4	30.11	—	26.8	14.9	10.8	23.11	1.2	11.1	1.3	18.3	4.3	22.3	2.11	29.3	14.12
Leyton O	5.4	19.10	15.3	2.11	24.8	25.1	3.5	21.9	24.8	12.4	26.8	—	14.9	13.8	17.9	1.2	26.4	17.8	22.2	29.10	19.4	14.12	29.3	8.2
Lincoln C	1.1	5.10	29.3	29.10	21.4	11.1	2.11	17.9	11.1	8.2	14.9	14.9	—	26.8	29.10	26.12	23.11	7.9	18.1	21.9	28.12	3.5	15.3	19.4
Macclesfield T	5.10	31.8	7.9	15.3	30.11	18.3	21.12	2.11	18.1	17.8	10.8	13.8	26.8	—	22.3	29.10	14.12	21.9	2.11	5.10	8.2	23.11	24.8	10.8
Oxford U	1.3	26.12	21.4	10.8	19.10	2.11	17.8	26.4	7.9	18.1	23.11	29.10	30.11	22.3	—	9.11	25.1	5.10	26.10	24.8	12.10	7.9	4.1	3.5
Rochdale	15.3	25.1	11.1	19.4	4.3	7.9	1.1	15.3	21.4	21.4	1.2	26.4	21.9	28.9	9.11	—	2.11	15.2	18.3	4.1	26.4	5.4	26.12	23.11
Rushden & D	29.10	4.3	30.11	19.10	31.8	19.4	8.2	8.2	1.1	28.9	11.1	26.4	23.11	14.12	25.1	2.11	—	26.8	25.1	24.8	26.4	13.8	26.12	23.11
Scunthorpe U	9.11	5.4	31.8	14.12	21.9	26.12	12.10	13.8	5.10	29.10	19.10	7.9	22.2	8.3	31.8	18.3	26.12	—	3.5	28.12	23.11	26.10	10.8	24.8
Shrewsbury T	19.4	14.12	21.9	26.12	31.8	21.9	22.3	23.11	10.8	5.10	19.10	7.9	31.8	15.2	1.1	1.3	24.8	3.5	—	11.1	5.4	4.3	26.1	4.1
Southend U	14.12	23.11	8.2	26.8	26.8	13.8	5.4	21.4	25.1	29.10	17.9	22.3	8.3	14.9	1.1	18.1	10.8	28.12	17.8	—	18.3	19.4	2.11	12.10
Swansea C	4.3	24.8	26.12	11.1	15.2	26.4	25.1	21.4	7.9	3.5	29.10	21.2	25.1	14.9	28.3	5.10	30.11	12.4	30.11	19.10	—	21.9	1.3	31.8
Torquay U	29.3	29.10	10.8	8.2	14.9	26.4	28.9	17.9	25.1	26.12	2.11	21.4	28.9	12.4	22.2	30.11	4.1	15.3	17.9	21.12	8.3	—	31.8	11.1
Wrexham	17.8	9.11	12.4	28.9	26.4	21.4	22.2	17.9	18.3	30.11	21.12	12.10	26.10	1.1	13.8	26.8	8.3	1.2	28.12	15.2	14.9	18.1	—	22.3
York C	26.8	15.3	19.10	22.2	8.3	30.11	17.9	26.4	15.2	28.12	21.4	9.11	20.12	2.2	28.9	12.4	14.9	1.1	13.8	29.3	18.1	17.8	29.10	—

THE SCOTTISH PREMIERSHIP and FOOTBALL LEAGUE FIXTURES 2002–03

Reproduced under Copyright/Database Licence No. PRINT/ALL/3014.
Copyright © The Scottish Premier League Limited/The Scottish Football League 2002.

Saturday, 3 August 2002

Scottish Premier League
Celtic v Dunfermline Ath
Dundee v Hearts
Hibernian v Aberdeen
Kilmarnock v Rangers
Livingston v Motherwell
Partick T v Dundee U

Scottish League Division 1
Arbroath v Ross Co
Ayr U v Falkirk
Inverness CT v Alloa Ath
Queen of the S v Clyde
St Mirren v St Johnstone

Scottish League Division 2
Airdrie U v Forfar Ath
Brechin C v Berwick R
Cowdenbeath v Hamilton A
Raith R v Stranraer
Stenhousemuir v Dumbarton

Scottish League Division 3
East Stirlingshire v Montrose
Gretna v Morton
Peterhead v East Fife
Queen's Park v Elgin C
Stirling Albion v Albion R

Saturday, 10 August 2002

Scottish Premier League
Aberdeen v Celtic
Dundee U v Kilmarnock
Dunfermline Ath v Livingston
Hearts v Hibernian
Motherwell v Partick T
Rangers v Dundee

Scottish League Division 1
Alloa Ath v Arbroath
Clyde v Ayr U
Falkirk v St Mirren
Ross Co v Queen of the S
St Johnstone v Inverness CT

Scottish League Division 2
Berwick R v Raith R
Dumbarton v Brechin C
Forfar Ath v Stenhousemuir
Hamilton A v Airdrie U
Stranraer v Cowdenbeath

Scottish League Division 3
Albion R v Peterhead
East Fife v East Stirlingshire
Elgin C v Gretna
Montrose v Queen's Park
Morton v Stirling Albion

Saturday, 17 August 2002

Scottish Premier League
Celtic v Dundee U
Dunfermline Ath v Dundee

Hibernian v Rangers
Kilmarnock v Motherwell

Scottish League Division 1
Arbroath v Clyde
Ayr U v Ross Co
Inverness CT v Falkirk
Queen of the S v St Johnstone
St Mirren v Alloa Ath

Scottish League Division 2
Airdrie U v Stranraer
Brechin C v Hamilton A
Cowdenbeath v Forfar Ath
Raith R v Dumbarton
Stenhousemuir v Berwick R

Scottish League Division 3
East Stirlingshire v Albion R
Gretna v Montrose
Peterhead v Morton
Queen's Park v East Fife
Stirling Albion v Elgin C

Sunday, 18 August 2002

Scottish Premier League
Aberdeen v Hearts
Partick T v Livingston

Saturday, 24 August 2002

Scottish Premier League
Dundee v Hibernian
Hearts v Dunfermline Ath
Livingston v Kilmarnock
Partick T v Celtic

Scottish League Division 1
Alloa Ath v Falkirk
Arbroath v St Johnstone
Clyde v St Mirren
Inverness CT v Ross Co
Queen of the S v Ayr U

Scottish League Division 2
Brechin C v Forfar Ath
Cowdenbeath v Raith R
Dumbarton v Airdrie U
Hamilton A v Berwick R
Stenhousemuir v Stranraer

Scottish League Division 3
East Fife v Montrose
Elgin C v Peterhead
Gretna v Albion R
Morton v Queen's Park
Stirling Albion v East Stirlingshire

Sunday, 25 August 2002

Scottish Premier League
Dundee U v Motherwell
Rangers v Aberdeen

Saturday, 31 August 2002

Scottish Premier League
Dundee U v Dundee
Dunfermline Ath v Rangers
Hearts v Kilmarnock
Motherwell v Hibernian

Scottish League Division 1
Ayr U v Arbroath
Falkirk v Queen of the S
Ross Co v Clyde
St Johnstone v Alloa Ath
St Mirren v Inverness CT

Scottish League Division 2
Airdrie U v Cowdenbeath
Berwick R v Dumbarton
Forfar Ath v Hamilton A
Raith R v Stenhousemuir
Stranraer v Brechin C

Scottish League Division 3
Albion R v East Fife
East Stirlingshire v Morton
Montrose v Elgin C
Peterhead v Stirling Albion
Queen's Park v Gretna

Sunday, 1 September 2002

Scottish Premier League
Aberdeen v Partick T
Celtic v Livingston

Wednesday, 11 September 2002

Scottish Premier League
Aberdeen v Dundee U
Dundee v Livingston
Hibernian v Dunfermline Ath
Kilmarnock v Partick T
Motherwell v Celtic
Rangers v Hearts

Saturday, 14 September 2002

Scottish Premier League
Celtic v Hibernian
Dundee U v Dunfermline Ath
Hearts v Motherwell
Kilmarnock v Aberdeen
Livingston v Rangers
Partick T v Dundee

Scottish League Division 1
Arbroath v St Mirren
Ayr U v St Johnstone
Clyde v Alloa Ath
Queen of the S v Inverness CT
Ross Co v Falkirk

Scottish League Division 2
Berwick R v Stranraer
Brechin C v Cowdenbeath
Dumbarton v Forfar Ath
Raith R v Airdrie U
Stenhousemuir v Hamilton A

...ottish League Division 3
gin C v East Fife
retna v Peterhead
orton v Albion R
ueen's Park v East Stirlingshire
rling Albion v Montrose

...turday, 21 September 2002

...ottish Premier League
undee v Celtic
unfermline Ath v Motherwell
earts v Dundee U
bernian v Kilmarnock
vingston v Aberdeen

...ottish League Division 1
loa Ath v Ayr U
lkirk v Clyde
verness CT v Arbroath
Johnstone v Ross Co
Mirren v Queen of the S

...ottish League Division 2
rdrie U v Brechin C
owdenbeath v Stenhousemuir
rfar Ath v Berwick R
amilton A v Raith R
anraer v Dumbarton

...ottish League Division 3
bion R v Elgin C
st Fife v Stirling Albion
st Stirlingshire v Gretna
ontrose v Morton
terhead v Queen's Park

...nday, 22 September 2002

...ottish Premier League
angers v Partick T

...turday, 28 September 2002

...ottish Premier League
berdeen v Dunfermline Ath
eltic v Kilmarnock
undee U v Rangers
bernian v Livingston
otherwell v Dundee
rtick T v Hearts

...ottish League Division 1
yr U v St Mirren
yde v Inverness CT
lkirk v St Johnstone
ueen of the S v Arbroath
oss Co v Alloa Ath

...ottish League Division 2
rwick R v Cowdenbeath
umbarton v Hamilton A
aith R v Brechin C
enhousemuir v Airdrie U
anraer v Forfar Ath

...ottish League Division 3
st Stirlingshire v Elgin C
retna v Stirling Albion
ontrose v Peterhead
orton v East Fife
ueen's Park v Albion R

...turday, 5 October 2002

...ottish Premier League
undee v Kilmarnock
unfermline Ath v Partick T
bernian v Dundee U

Livingston v Hearts
Motherwell v Aberdeen

Scottish League Division 1
Alloa Ath v Queen of the S
Arbroath v Falkirk
Inverness CT v Ayr U
St Johnstone v Clyde
St Mirren v Ross Co

Scottish League Division 2
Airdrie U v Berwick R
Brechin C v Stenhousemuir
Cowdenbeath v Dumbarton
Forfar Ath v Raith R
Hamilton A v Stranraer

Scottish League Division 3
Albion R v Montrose
East Fife v Gretna
Elgin C v Morton
Peterhead v East Stirlingshire
Stirling Albion v Queen's Park

Sunday, 6 October 2002

Scottish Premier League
Celtic v Rangers

Saturday, 19 October 2002

Scottish Premier League
Aberdeen v Dundee
Dundee U v Livingston
Hearts v Celtic
Kilmarnock v Dunfermline Ath
Partick T v Hibernian
Rangers v Motherwell

Scottish League Division 1
Alloa Ath v Inverness CT
Clyde v Queen of the S
Falkirk v Ayr U
Ross Co v Arbroath
St Johnstone v St Mirren

Scottish League Division 2
Airdrie U v Hamilton A
Brechin C v Dumbarton
Cowdenbeath v Stranraer
Raith R v Berwick R
Stenhousemuir v Forfar Ath

Scottish League Division 3
East Stirlingshire v East Fife
Gretna v Elgin C
Peterhead v Albion R
Queen's Park v Montrose
Stirling Albion v Morton

Saturday, 26 October 2002

Scottish Premier League
Aberdeen v Hibernian
Dundee U v Partick T
Dunfermline Ath v Celtic
Hearts v Dundee
Motherwell v Livingston
Rangers v Kilmarnock

Scottish League Division 1
Arbroath v Alloa Ath
Ayr U v Clyde
Inverness CT v St Johnstone
Queen of the S v Ross Co
St Mirren v Falkirk

Scottish League Division 2
Berwick R v Brechin C

Dumbarton v Stenhousemuir
Forfar Ath v Airdrie U
Hamilton A v Cowdenbeath
Stranraer v Raith R

Scottish League Division 3
Albion R v Stirling Albion
East Fife v Peterhead
Elgin C v Queen's Park
Montrose v East Stirlingshire
Morton v Gretna

Saturday, 2 November 2002

Scottish Premier League
Celtic v Aberdeen
Dundee v Rangers
Hibernian v Hearts
Kilmarnock v Dundee U
Livingston v Dunfermline Ath
Partick T v Motherwell

Scottish League Division 1
Alloa Ath v St Johnstone
Arbroath v Ayr U
Clyde v Ross Co
Inverness CT v St Mirren
Queen of the S v Falkirk

Scottish League Division 2
Brechin C v Stranraer
Cowdenbeath v Airdrie U
Dumbarton v Berwick R
Hamilton A v Forfar Ath
Stenhousemuir v Raith R

Scottish League Division 3
East Fife v Albion R
Elgin C v Montrose
Gretna v Queen's Park
Morton v East Stirlingshire
Stirling Albion v Peterhead

Saturday, 9 November 2002

Scottish Premier League
Dundee U v Celtic
Hearts v Aberdeen
Livingston v Partick T
Motherwell v Kilmarnock
Rangers v Hibernian

Scottish League Division 1
Ayr U v Queen of the S
Falkirk v Alloa Ath
Ross Co v Inverness CT
St Johnstone v Arbroath
St Mirren v Clyde

Scottish League Division 2
Airdrie U v Dumbarton
Berwick R v Hamilton A
Forfar Ath v Brechin C
Raith R v Cowdenbeath
Stranraer v Stenhousemuir

Scottish League Division 3
Albion R v Gretna
East Stirlingshire v Stirling Albion
Montrose v East Fife
Peterhead v Elgin C
Queen's Park v Morton

Sunday, 10 November 2002

Scottish Premier League
Dundee v Dunfermline Ath

Saturday, 16 November 2002

Scottish Premier League
Aberdeen v Rangers
Celtic v Partick T
Dunfermline Ath v Hearts
Hibernian v Dundee
Kilmarnock v Livingston
Motherwell v Dundee U

Scottish League Division 1
Alloa Ath v Clyde
Falkirk v Ross Co
Inverness CT v Queen of the S
St Johnstone v Ayr U
St Mirren v Arbroath

Scottish League Division 2
Airdrie U v Raith R
Cowdenbeath v Brechin C
Forfar Ath v Dumbarton
Hamilton A v Stenhousemuir
Stranraer v Berwick R

Scottish League Division 3
Albion R v Morton
East Fife v Elgin C
East Stirlingshire v Queen's Park
Montrose v Stirling Albion
Peterhead v Gretna

Saturday, 23 November 2002

Scottish Premier League
Dundee v Dundee U
Hibernian v Motherwell
Kilmarnock v Hearts
Livingston v Celtic
Partick T v Aberdeen
Rangers v Dunfermline Ath

Scottish League Division 1
Arbroath v Inverness CT
Ayr U v Alloa Ath
Clyde v Falkirk
Queen of the S v St Mirren
Ross Co v St Johnstone

Scottish League Division 2
Berwick R v Forfar Ath
Brechin C v Airdrie U
Dumbarton v Stranraer
Raith R v Hamilton A
Stenhousemuir v Cowdenbeath

Scottish League Division 3
Elgin C v Albion R
Gretna v East Stirlingshire
Morton v Montrose
Queen's Park v Peterhead
Stirling Albion v East Fife

Saturday, 30 November 2002

Scottish Premier League
Celtic v Motherwell
Dundee U v Aberdeen
Dunfermline Ath v Hibernian
Hearts v Rangers
Livingston v Dundee
Partick T v Kilmarnock

Scottish League Division 1
Alloa Ath v Ross Co
Arbroath v Queen of the S
Inverness CT v Clyde
St Johnstone v Falkirk
St Mirren v Ayr U

Scottish League Division 2
Berwick R v Airdrie U
Dumbarton v Cowdenbeath
Raith R v Forfar Ath
Stenhousemuir v Brechin C
Stranraer v Hamilton A

Scottish League Division 3
East Stirlingshire v Peterhead
Gretna v East Fife
Montrose v Albion R
Morton v Elgin C
Queen's Park v Stirling Albion

Wednesday, 4 December 2002

Scottish Premier League
Aberdeen v Kilmarnock
Dundee v Partick T
Dunfermline Ath v Dundee U
Hibernian v Celtic
Motherwell v Hearts
Rangers v Livingston

Saturday, 7 December 2002

Scottish Premier League
Aberdeen v Motherwell
Dundee U v Hibernian
Hearts v Livingston
Kilmarnock v Dundee
Partick T v Dunfermline Ath
Rangers v Celtic

Scottish League Division 1
Ayr U v Inverness CT
Clyde v St Johnstone
Falkirk v Arbroath
Queen of the S v Alloa Ath
Ross Co v St Mirren

Saturday, 14 December 2002

Scottish Premier League
Dundee v Motherwell
Dunfermline Ath v Aberdeen
Hearts v Partick T
Kilmarnock v Celtic
Livingston v Hibernian
Rangers v Dundee U

Scottish League Division 1
Alloa Ath v St Mirren
Clyde v Arbroath
Falkirk v Inverness CT
Ross Co v Ayr U
St Johnstone v Queen of the S

Scottish League Division 2
Airdrie U v Stenhousemuir
Brechin C v Raith R
Cowdenbeath v Berwick R
Forfar Ath v Stranraer
Hamilton A v Dumbarton

Scottish League Division 3
Albion R v Queen's Park
East Fife v Morton
Elgin C v East Stirlingshire
Peterhead v Montrose
Stirling Albion v Gretna

Saturday, 21 December 2002

Scottish Premier League
Aberdeen v Livingston
Celtic v Dundee
Dundee U v Hearts
Kilmarnock v Hibernian

Motherwell v Dunfermline Ath
Partick T v Rangers

Scottish League Division 1
Arbroath v Ross Co
Ayr U v Falkirk
Inverness CT v Alloa Ath
Queen of the S v Clyde
St Mirren v St Johnstone

Scottish League Division 2
Airdrie U v Forfar Ath
Brechin C v Berwick R
Cowdenbeath v Hamilton A
Raith R v Stranraer
Stenhousemuir v Dumbarton

Scottish League Division 3
East Stirlingshire v Montrose
Gretna v Morton
Peterhead v East Fife
Queen's Park v Elgin C
Stirling Albion v Albion R

Thursday, 26 December 2002

Scottish Premier League
Celtic v Hearts
Dundee v Aberdeen
Dunfermline Ath v Kilmarnock
Hibernian v Partick T
Livingston v Dundee U
Motherwell v Rangers

Saturday, 28 December 2002

Scottish League Division 1
Ayr U v Arbroath
Falkirk v Queen of the S
Ross Co v Clyde
St Johnstone v Alloa Ath
St Mirren v Inverness CT

Scottish League Division 2
Berwick R v Stenhousemuir
Dumbarton v Raith R
Forfar Ath v Cowdenbeath
Hamilton A v Brechin C
Stranraer v Airdrie U

Scottish League Division 3
Albion R v East Stirlingshire
East Fife v Queen's Park
Elgin C v Stirling Albion
Montrose v Gretna
Morton v Peterhead

Sunday, 29 December 2002

Scottish Premier League
Celtic v Dunfermline Ath
Dundee v Hearts
Hibernian v Aberdeen
Kilmarnock v Rangers
Livingston v Motherwell
Partick T v Dundee U

Wednesday, 1 January 2003

Scottish League Division 1
Alloa Ath v Falkirk
Arbroath v St Johnstone
Clyde v St Mirren
Inverness CT v Ross Co
Queen of the S v Ayr U

Scottish League Division 2
Brechin C v Forfar Ath
Cowdenbeath v Raith R

umbarton v Airdrie U
amilton A v Berwick R
enhousemuir v Stranraer

ottish League Division 3
ast Fife v Montrose
gin C v Peterhead
retna v Albion R
orton v Queen's Park
irling Albion v East Stirlingshire

hursday, 2 January 2003
ottish Premier League
berdeen v Celtic
undee U v Kilmarnock
unfermline Ath v Livingston
earts v Hibernian
otherwell v Partick T
angers v Dundee

aturday, 4 January 2003
ottish League Division 1
rbroath v St Mirren
yr U v St Johnstone
yde v Alloa Ath
ueen of the S v Inverness CT
oss Co v Falkirk

aturday, 11 January 2003
ottish League Division 1
lloa Ath v Ayr U
alkirk v Clyde
verness CT v Arbroath
Johnstone v Ross Co
Mirren v Queen of the S

ottish League Division 2
irdrie U v Cowdenbeath
erwick R v Dumbarton
orfar Ath v Hamilton A
aith R v Stenhousemuir
ranraer v Brechin C

ottish League Division 3
lbion R v East Fife
ast Stirlingshire v Morton
ontrose v Elgin C
eterhead v Stirling Albion
ueen's Park v Gretna

aturday, 18 January 2003
ottish League Division 1
lloa Ath v Queen of the S
rbroath v Falkirk
verness CT v Ayr U
Johnstone v Clyde
Mirren v Ross Co

ottish League Division 2
erwick R v Stranraer
rechin C v Cowdenbeath
umbarton v Forfar Ath
aith R v Airdrie U
enhousemuir v Hamilton A

ottish League Division 3
gin C v East Fife
retna v Peterhead
orton v Albion R
ueen's Park v East Stirlingshire
irling Albion v Montrose

uesday, 28 January 2003
ottish Premier League
artick T v Livingston

Wednesday, 29 January 2003
Scottish Premier League
Aberdeen v Hearts
Celtic v Dundee U
Dunfermline Ath v Dundee
Hibernian v Rangers
Kilmarnock v Motherwell

Saturday, 1 February 2003
Scottish Premier League
Dundee v Hibernian
Hearts v Dunfermline Ath
Livingston v Kilmarnock
Partick T v Celtic

Scottish League Division 1
Ayr U v St Mirren
Clyde v Inverness CT
Falkirk v St Johnstone
Queen of the S v Arbroath
Ross Co v Alloa Ath

Scottish League Division 2
Airdrie U v Brechin C
Cowdenbeath v Stenhousemuir
Forfar Ath v Berwick R
Hamilton A v Raith R
Stranraer v Dumbarton

Scottish League Division 3
Albion R v Elgin C
East Fife v Stirling Albion
East Stirlingshire v Gretna
Montrose v Morton
Peterhead v Queen's Park

Sunday, 2 February 2003
Scottish Premier League
Dundee U v Motherwell
Rangers v Aberdeen

Saturday, 8 February 2003
Scottish Premier League
Aberdeen v Partick T
Celtic v Livingston
Dundee U v Dundee
Dunfermline Ath v Rangers
Hearts v Kilmarnock
Motherwell v Hibernian

Scottish League Division 1
Arbroath v Clyde
Ayr U v Ross Co
Inverness CT v Falkirk
Queen of the S v St Johnstone
St Mirren v Alloa Ath

Scottish League Division 2
Berwick R v Cowdenbeath
Dumbarton v Hamilton A
Raith R v Brechin C
Stenhousemuir v Airdrie U
Stranraer v Forfar Ath

Scottish League Division 3
East Stirlingshire v Elgin C
Gretna v Stirling Albion
Montrose v Peterhead
Morton v East Fife
Queen's Park v Albion R

Saturday, 15 February 2003
Scottish Premier League
Aberdeen v Dundee U
Dundee v Livingston

Hibernian v Dunfermline Ath
Kilmarnock v Partick T
Motherwell v Celtic
Rangers v Hearts

Scottish League Division 1
Alloa Ath v Arbroath
Clyde v Ayr U
Falkirk v St Mirren
Ross Co v Queen of the S
St Johnstone v Inverness CT

Scottish League Division 2
Airdrie U v Berwick R
Brechin C v Stenhousemuir
Cowdenbeath v Dumbarton
Forfar Ath v Raith R
Hamilton A v Stranraer

Scottish League Division 3
Albion R v Montrose
East Fife v Gretna
Elgin C v Morton
Peterhead v East Stirlingshire
Stirling Albion v Queen's Park

Saturday, 22 February 2003
Scottish League Division 2
Berwick R v Raith R
Dumbarton v Brechin C
Forfar Ath v Stenhousemuir
Hamilton A v Airdrie U
Stranraer v Cowdenbeath

Scottish League Division 3
Albion R v Peterhead
East Fife v East Stirlingshire
Elgin C v Gretna
Montrose v Queen's Park
Morton v Stirling Albion

Saturday, 1 March 2003
Scottish Premier League
Celtic v Hibernian
Dundee U v Dunfermline Ath
Hearts v Motherwell
Kilmarnock v Aberdeen
Livingston v Rangers
Partick T v Dundee

Scottish League Division 1
Alloa Ath v St Johnstone
Arbroath v Ayr U
Clyde v Ross Co
Inverness CT v St Mirren
Queen of the S v Falkirk

Scottish League Division 2
Airdrie U v Stranraer
Brechin C v Hamilton A
Cowdenbeath v Forfar Ath
Raith R v Dumbarton
Stenhousemuir v Berwick R

Scottish League Division 3
East Stirlingshire v Albion R
Gretna v Montrose
Peterhead v Morton
Queen's Park v East Fife
Stirling Albion v Elgin C

Saturday, 8 March 2003
Scottish Premier League
Celtic v Rangers
Dundee v Kilmarnock
Dunfermline Ath v Partick T

Hibernian v Dundee U
Livingston v Hearts
Motherwell v Aberdeen

Scottish League Division 1
Ayr U v Queen of the S
Falkirk v Alloa Ath
Ross Co v Inverness CT
St Johnstone v Arbroath
St Mirren v Clyde

Scottish League Division 2
Airdrie U v Dumbarton
Berwick R v Hamilton A
Forfar Ath v Brechin C
Raith R v Cowdenbeath
Stranraer v Stenhousemuir

Scottish League Division 3
Albion R v Gretna
East Stirlingshire v Stirling Albion
Montrose v East Fife
Peterhead v Elgin C
Queen's Park v Morton

Saturday, 15 March 2003
Scottish Premier League
Aberdeen v Dundee
Dundee U v Livingston
Hearts v Celtic
Kilmarnock v Dunfermline Ath
Partick T v Hibernian
Rangers v Motherwell

Scottish League Division 1
Arbroath v Inverness CT
Ayr U v Alloa Ath
Clyde v Falkirk
Queen of the S v St Mirren
Ross Co v St Johnstone

Scottish League Division 2
Brechin C v Stranraer
Cowdenbeath v Airdrie U
Dumbarton v Berwick R
Hamilton A v Forfar Ath
Stenhousemuir v Raith R

Scottish League Division 3
East Fife v Albion R
Elgin C v Montrose
Gretna v Queen's Park
Morton v East Stirlingshire
Stirling Albion v Peterhead

Saturday, 22 March 2003
Scottish League Division 2
Berwick R v Forfar Ath
Brechin C v Airdrie U
Dumbarton v Stranraer
Raith R v Hamilton A
Stenhousemuir v Cowdenbeath

Scottish League Division 3
Elgin C v Albion R
Gretna v East Stirlingshire
Morton v Montrose
Queen's Park v Peterhead
Stirling Albion v East Fife

Saturday, 5 April 2003
Scottish Premier League
Dundee v Celtic
Dunfermline Ath v Motherwell

Hearts v Dundee U
Kilmarnock v Hibernian
Livingston v Aberdeen
Rangers v Partick T

Scottish League Division 1
Alloa Ath v Clyde
Falkirk v Ross Co
Inverness CT v Queen of the S
St Johnstone v Ayr U
St Mirren v Arbroath

Scottish League Division 2
Airdrie U v Raith R
Cowdenbeath v Brechin C
Forfar Ath v Dumbarton
Hamilton A v Stenhousemuir
Stranraer v Berwick R

Scottish League Division 3
Albion R v Morton
East Fife v Elgin C
East Stirlingshire v Queen's Park
Montrose v Stirling Albion
Peterhead v Gretna

Saturday, 12 April 2003
Scottish Premier League
Aberdeen v Dunfermline Ath
Celtic v Kilmarnock
Dundee U v Rangers
Hibernian v Livingston
Motherwell v Dundee
Partick T v Hearts

Scottish League Division 1
Alloa Ath v Ross Co
Arbroath v Queen of the S
Inverness CT v Clyde
St Johnstone v Falkirk
St Mirren v Ayr U

Scottish League Division 2
Berwick R v Airdrie U
Dumbarton v Cowdenbeath
Raith R v Forfar Ath
Stenhousemuir v Brechin C
Stranraer v Hamilton A

Scottish League Division 3
East Stirlingshire v Peterhead
Gretna v East Fife
Montrose v Albion R
Morton v Elgin C
Queen's Park v Stirling Albion

Saturday, 19 April 2003
Scottish League Division 1
Ayr U v Inverness CT
Clyde v St Johnstone
Falkirk v Arbroath
Queen of the S v Alloa Ath
Ross Co v St Mirren

Scottish League Division 2
Airdrie U v Stenhousemuir
Brechin C v Raith R
Cowdenbeath v Berwick R
Forfar Ath v Stranraer
Hamilton A v Dumbarton

Scottish League Division 3
Albion R v Queen's Park
East Fife v Morton

Elgin C v East Stirlingshire
Peterhead v Montrose
Stirling Albion v Gretna

Saturday, 26 April 2003
Scottish League Division 1
Alloa Ath v Inverness CT
Clyde v Queen of the S
Falkirk v Ayr U
Ross Co v Arbroath
St Johnstone v St Mirren

Scottish League Division 2
Berwick R v Brechin C
Dumbarton v Stenhousemuir
Forfar Ath v Airdrie U
Hamilton A v Cowdenbeath
Stranraer v Raith R

Scottish League Division 3
Albion R v Stirling Albion
East Fife v Peterhead
Elgin C v Queen's Park
Montrose v East Stirlingshire
Morton v Gretna

Saturday, 3 May 2003
Scottish League Division 1
Arbroath v Alloa Ath
Ayr U v Clyde
Inverness CT v St Johnstone
Queen of the S v Ross Co
St Mirren v Falkirk

Scottish League Division 2
Airdrie U v Hamilton A
Brechin C v Dumbarton
Cowdenbeath v Stranraer
Raith R v Berwick R
Stenhousemuir v Forfar Ath

Scottish League Division 3
East Stirlingshire v East Fife
Gretna v Elgin C
Peterhead v Albion R
Queen's Park v Montrose
Stirling Albion v Morton

Saturday, 10 May 2003
Scottish League Division 1
Alloa Ath v St Mirren
Clyde v Arbroath
Falkirk v Inverness CT
Ross Co v Ayr U
St Johnstone v Queen of the S

Scottish League Division 2
Berwick R v Stenhousemuir
Dumbarton v Raith R
Forfar Ath v Cowdenbeath
Hamilton A v Brechin C
Stranraer v Airdrie U

Scottish League Division 3
Albion R v East Stirlingshire
East Fife v Queen's Park
Elgin C v Stirling Albion
Montrose v Gretna
Morton v Peterhead

OTHER FIXTURES 2002–03

ly 2002

/7 Sat/Sun	UEFA Intertoto Cup 2 (1)
/14 Sat/Sun	UEFA Intertoto Cup 2 (2)
Wed	UEFA Champions League 1Q (1)
/21 Sat/Sun	UEFA Intertoto Cup 3 (1)
Wed	UEFA Champions League 1Q (2)
Sat	UEFA Intertoto Cup 3 (2)
Wed	UEFA Champions League 2Q (1)
	UEFA Intertoto Cup Semi-Final (1)

ugust 2002

Sat	
Wed	UEFA Champions League 2Q (2)
	UEFA Intertoto Cup Semi-Final (2)
Sat	Football League Commences
Sun	F.A. Community Shield
	Arsenal v Liverpool at The Millennium Stadium, Cardiff – 2.00
/14 Tues/Wed	UEFA Champions League 3Q (1)
	UEFA Intertoto Cup Final (1)
Thu	UEFA Cup Q (1)
Sat	F.A. Premier League Commences
Sun	Start of F.A. Women's Premier League
Wed	Friendly Internationals
Fri	UEFA Super Cup
Sat	F.A. Cup EP
Mon	Bank Holiday
Tue	UEFA Intertoto Cup Final (2)
/28 Tue/Wed	UEFA Champions League 3Q (2)
Thu	UEFA Cup Q (2)
Sat	F.A. Cup P

eptember 2002

Sat	UEFA 2004 Qualifying Internationals
	F.A. Vase 1Q
	F.A. Youth Cup 1Q*
Sun	F.A. Women's Cup 1Q
	F.A. Women's Premier League Cup P
Wed	F.L. Worthington Cup 1
Sat	F.A. Cup 1Q
/18 Tue/Wed	UEFA Champions League Match Day (1)
Thu	UEFA Cup 1 (1)
Sat	F.A. Vase 2Q
	F.A. Youth Cup 2Q*
Sun	F.A. Women's Premier League Cup 1
4/25 Tue/Wed	UEFA Champions League Match Day (2)
Sat	F.A. Cup 2Q
Sun	F.A. Women's Cup 2Q

ctober 2002

1/2 Tue/Wed	UEFA Champions League Match Day (3)
Wed	F.L. Worthington Cup 2
Thu	UEFA Cup 1 (2)
Sat	F.A. Trophy P
	F.A. Youth Cup 3Q*
	F.A. County Youth Cup 1*
Sun	F.A. Sunday Cup 1
Sat	Slovakia v England – UEFA 2004 Qualifying
	F.A. Cup 3Q
Wed	England v FYR Macedonia – UEFA 2004 Qualifying
Sat	F.A. Vase 1P
2/23 Tue/Wed	UEFA Champions League Match Day (4)

23 Wed	F.L. LDV Vans Trophy 1
26 Sat	F.A. Cup 4Q
27 Sun	F.A. Women's Cup 1P
	F.A. Youth Cup 1P*
	F.A. Women's Premier League Cup 2
29/30 Tue/Wed	UEFA Champions League Match Day (5)
31 Wed	UEFA Cup 2 (1)

November 2002

2 Sat	F.A. Trophy 1
3 Sun	F.A. Sunday Cup 2
6 Wed	F.L. Worthington Cup 3
9 Sat	F.A. Vase 2P
	F.A. Youth Cup 2P*
	F.A. County Youth Cup 2*
10 Sun	F.A. Women's Cup 2P
12/13 Tue/Wed	UEFA Champions League Match Day (6)
13 Wed	F.L. LDV Vans Trophy 2
14 Thu	UEFA Cup 2 (2)
16 Sat	F.A. Cup 1P
20 Wed	Friendly Internationals
24 Sun	F.A. Women's Premier League Cup 3
26/27 Tue/Wed	UEFA Champions League Match Day (7)
27 Wed	F.A. Cup 1R
28 Thu	UEFA Cup 3 (1)
30 Sat	F.A. Trophy 2

December 2002

1 Sun	F.A. Sunday Cup 3
3 Tue	Inter-Continental Cup
4 Wed	F.L. Worthington Cup 4
7 Sat	F.A. Cup 2P
	F.A. Vase 3P
	F.A. Youth Cup 3P*
8 Sun	F.A. Women's Cup 3P
10/11 Tue/Wed	UEFA Champions League Match Day (8)
11 Wed	F.L. LDV Vans Trophy QF
12 Thu	UEFA Cup 3 (2)
14 Sat	F.A. County Youth Cup 3*
18 Wed	F.A. Cup 2R
	F.L. Worthington Cup 5
24 Tue	Christmas Eve
25 Wed	Christmas Day
26 Thu	Boxing Day

January 2003

1 Wed	New Year's Day
4 Sat	F.A. Cup 3P
5 Sun	F.A. Women's Cup 4P
8 Wed	F.L. Worthington Cup SF1
11 Sat	F.A. Trophy 3
12 Sun	F.A. Sunday Cup 4
15 Wed	F.A. Cup 3R
18 Sat	F.A. Vase 4P
19 Sun	F.A. Women's Premier League Cup SF
22 Wed	F.L. Worthington Cup SF2
	F.L. LDV Vans Trophy SF
25 Sat	F.A. Cup 4P
	F.A. Youth Cup 4P*
26 Sun	F.A. Women's Cup 5P

February 2003

1 Sat	F.A. Trophy 4
	F.A. County Youth Cup 4*

2 Sun	F.A. Sunday Cup 5
5 Wed	F.A. Cup 4R
8 Sat	F.A. Vase 5P
9 Sun	F.A. Women's Cup 6P
12 Wed	International (Friendly)
15 Sat	F.A. Cup 5P
	F.A. Youth Cup 5P*
18/19 Tue/Wed	UEFA Champions League
	Match Day (9)
19 Wed	F.L. LDV Vans Trophy Area Final 1
20 Thu	UEFA Cup 4 (1)
22 Sat	F.A. Trophy 5
25/26 Tue/Wed	UEFA Champions League
	Match Day (10)
26 Wed	F.A. Cup 5R
	F.L. LDV Vans Trophy Area Final 2
27 Thu	UEFA Cup 4 (2)

March 2003

1 Sat	F.A. Vase 6P
2 Sun	F.L. Worthington Cup Final
8 Sat	F.A. Cup 6P
	F.A. Youth Cup 6P*
	F.A. County Youth Cup Semi Final*
11/12 Tue/Wed	UEFA Champions League
	Match Day (11)
13 Thu	UEFA Cup Quarter Final
15 Sat	F.A. Trophy 6
16 Sun	F.A. Sunday Cup Semi Final
	F.A. Women's Premier League Cup Final
18/19 Tue/Wed	UEFA Champions League
	Match Day (12)
19 Wed	F.A. Cup 6R
20 Thu	UEFA Cup Quarter Final (2)
22 Sat	F.A. Vase Semi Final (1)
29 Sat	Liechtenstein v England – UEFA 2004
	Qualifying
	F.A. Vase Semi Final (2)
	F.A. Youth Cup Semi Final 1st Leg*
30 Sun	F.A. Women's Cup Semi Final

April 2003

2 Wed	England v Turkey – UEFA 2004 Qualifying
5 Sat	F.A. Trophy Semi Final (1)
6 Sun	F.L. LDV Vans Trophy Final
8/9 Tue/Wed	UEFA Champions League
	Quarter Final (1)
10 Thu	UEFA Cup Semi Final (1)
12 Sat	F.A. Trophy Semi Final (2)
	F.A. Youth Cup Semi Final 2nd Leg*
13 Sun	F.A. Cup Semi Finals
18 Fri	Good Friday
21 Mon	Easter Monday

22/23 Tue/Wed	UEFA Champions League
	Quarter Final (2)
24 Thu	UEFA Cup Semi Final (2)
26 Sat	F.A. County Youth Cup Final
27 Sun	F.A. Sunday Cup Final
30 Wed	International (Friendly)

May 2003

3 Sat	End of Football League
5 Mon	Bank Holiday
6/7 Tue/Wed	UEFA Champions League Semi Final (
10 Sat	End of Premier League
	F.A. Vase Final
11 Sun	F.A. Trophy Final (prov)
	F.L. Play-off Semi Final (1)
13/14 Tue/Wed	UEFA Champions League Semi Final
14 Wed	F.L. Play-off Semi Final (2)
15 Thu	F.A. Youth Cup Cup Final 1 (prov)
17 Sat	F.A. Cup Final
18 Sun	F.A. Trophy Final (prov)
21 Wed	UEFA Cup Final
22 Thu	F.A. Youth Cup Final 2 (prov)
24 Sat	F.L. 3rd Division Play-off Final
25 Sun	F.L. 2nd Division Play-off Final
26 Mon	F.L. 1st Division Play-off Final
28 Wed	UEFA Champions League Final

June 2003

11 Wed	England v Slovakia – UEFA 2004
	Qualifying

*Closing date of round

Other UEFA 2004 Qualifying Ties

Sat 6 Sept 2003
FYR Macedonia v England

Wed 10 Sept 2003
England v Liechtenstein

Sat 11 Oct 2003
Turkey v England

Final Competition

Draw – 30 November 2003
Opening match, Porto – 12 June 2004
End of group stage – 23 June 2004
Quarter-Final 1 – 26 June 2004
Quarter-Final 2 – 27 June 2004
Semi-Final 1 – 30 June 2004
Semi-Final 2 – 1 July 2004
Final – 4 July 2004

STOP PRESS

nables lands Leeds job ... Man U sign a 50-50 £303m 13-year merchandising deal with Nike ... AFC Wimbledon act 4657 to a friendly ... Portuguese striker Joao Pinto banned for four months, fined £22,500 for punching World referee ... Football League clubs picket Granada/Carlton offices ... Ray Lewington named as Watford manager, rtin Hinshelwood at Brighton ... Referees to crack down on verbal abuse ... Frank Taylor OBE only reporter to vive 1958 Munich air crash dies at 81 ... Man U pay British record £30m for Leeds' Rio Ferdinand ...

mmer transfers completed and pending: **Arsenal:** Pascal Cygan (Lille) £2.5m; **Aston Villa:** Marcus Allback erenveen) £2m; Stefan Postma (De Graafschap) £1.5m; Michael Boulding (Grimsby T) Free; Lee Grant (York C) lisclosed; **Birmingham C:** Robbie Savage (Leicester C) £2.5m; Aliou Cisse (Paris St Germain) £1.5m; Kenny nningham (Wimbledon) undisclosed. **Blackburn R:** Marc Sebastian Pelzer (Kaiserslautern) undisclosed; Andy Todd arlton Ath) £750,000. **Bolton W:** Bulent Akin (Galatasaray) undisclosed; Delroy Facey (Huddersfield T) Tribunal; -Jay Okocha (Paris St Germain) Free; Youri Djorkaeff (Kaiserslautern) Free; Bernard Mendy (Paris St Germain) n. **Chelsea:** Enrique De Lucas (Espanyol) Free. **Everton:** Joseph Yobo (Marseille) £5m; Richard Wright (Arsenal) m; Li Weifeng (Shenzhen) Loan; Lee Tie (Liaoning) Loan. **Fulham:** Martin Herrera (Alaves) Free; Facundo Sava mnasia) undisclosed; Martin Djetou (Parma) Loan; Junichi Inamoto (Gamba Osaka) Loan. **Liverpool:** El-Hadji uf (Lens) £10m; Bruno Cheyrou (Lille) £3.7m; Salif Diao (Sedan) undisclosed; Alou Diarra (Bayern Munich) Free. nchester C: Sylvain Distin (Paris St Germain) £4m; Mikkel Bischoff (AB Copenhagen) £750,000; Marc Vivien Foe on) £550,000; Nicolas Anelka (Paris St Germain) £13m (club record); Vicente Matias Vuoso (Independiente) £3.5m; one Loran (Volendam) undisclosed; Peter Schmeichel (Aston Villa) Free. **Manchester U:** Rio Ferdinand (Leeds U) n; **Middlesbrough:** Massimo Maccarone (Empoli) £8.15m; Franck Queudrue (Lens) £2.5m; Geremi (Real Madrid) n. **Newcastle U:** Hugo Viana (Sporting Lisbon) £8.5m; Titus Bramble (Ipswich T) £5m. **Southampton:** Michael mas Myhre (Besiktas) Free. **Sunderland:** Phil Babb (Sporting Lisbon) Free; Sean Thornton (Tranmere R) Tribunal; nsson (Troyes) £2m. **Tottenham H:** Jonathan Blondel (Mouscron) Free; Rohan Ricketts (Arsenal) Free. A: Ronnie Wallwork (Manchester U) Free; Joe Murphy (Tranmere R) undisclosed. **West Ham U:** Youssef Soufiane xerre) Free; Raimond Van der Gouw (Manchester U) Free.

er moves: Alex Manninger, Arsenal to Espanyol £1m; Sam Dalla Bona, Chelsea to Milan £1m; Chris Barker, nsley to Cardiff £600,000; Ricardo Fuller, Tivoli Gardens to Preston NE £500,000; Hayden Foxe, West Ham U to tsmouth £400,000; Ben Burgess, Blackburn R to Stockport Co £400,000; Clint Hill, Tranmere R to Oldham Ath 5,000; Tyrone Mears, Manchester C to Preston NE £200,000; Richard Hughes, Bournemouth to Portsmouth 0,000; Steve Robinson, Preston NE to Luton T £50,000; Paul Edwards, Swindon T to Wrexham Free; Ian Breckin, esterfield to Wigan Ath Free; Lee Hardy, Oldham Ath to Macclesfield T Free; Rod Wallace, Bolton W to ingham Free; David Zdrillic, Unterhaching to Walsall Free; Ian Stevens, Carlisle U to Shrewsbury T Free; Rigobert g, West Ham U to Lens; Matthew Robinson, Reading to Oxford U Free; Daniel Maye, Port Vale to Southend U; tt McNiven, Oldham Ath to Oxford U Free; John Anderson, Livingston to Hull U Free; Ritchie Appleby, derminster H to Hull C Free; Gunnar Halle, Bradford C to Lillestrom Free; Paul Harsley, Halifax T to rthampton T; Greg Lincoln, Margate to Northampton T Free; Matt Murphy, Bury to Swansea C Free; Paul Reid, y to Swansea C; Greg Shields, Charlton Ath to Kilmarnock Free; Allan Smart, Oldham Ath to Dundee U; David th, Grimsby T to Swansea C; Tony Thorpe Bristol C to Luton T Free; David Robertson, Leeds U to Montrose; rick Suffo, Sheffield U to Numancia; Matthew Taylor, Luton T to Portsmouth; Jon Beswetherick, Plymouth Arg to ffield W; Mark Boyd, Newcastle U to Port Vale Free; Tom Cowan, Cambridge U to York C Free; Dean Cropper, ffield W to Lincoln C Free; Andy Dibble, Stockport Co to Wrexham; Craig Faulconbridge, Wrexham to Wycombe Free; James Goodwin, Celtic to Stockport Co Free; Bradley Hughes, Watford to Grimsby T Free; Damien Lynch, tingham F to Bohemians, Free; Kesiena Metitiri, West Ham U to Bristol C Free; Neil Moore, Telford U to nsfield T Free; Carl Muggleton, Cheltenham T to Chesterfield Free; Kevin Muscat, Wolverhampton W to Rangers e; George O'Callaghan, Port Vale to Cork C; Dion Scott, Walsall to Mansfield T Free; Gareth Sheldon, Scunthorpe o Exeter C; Greg Strong, Motherwell to Hull C; James Thomas, Blackburn R to Swansea C Free; Martin Thomas, ord U to Exeter C Free; Simon Weaver, Nuneaton B to Lincoln C Free; Dean Gordon, Middlesbrough to Coventry Danny Butterfield, Grimsby T to Crystal Palace Free; Paul Heckingbottom, Darlington to Norwich C Free; Shaka op, West Ham U to Portsmouth Free; Steve Yates, Tranmere R to Sheffield U Free; Stuart McCall, Bradford C to ffield U; Iffy Onuora, Gillingham to Sheffield U; Karl Colley, Newcastle U to Sheffield U Free; Lloyd Owusu, nsfield W Free; Chris Greenacre, Mansfield T to Stoke C Free; Dani Rodrigues, Southampton to Walsall e; Ivar Ingimarsson, Brentford to Wolverhampton W Free; Chris Brandon, Torquay U to Chesterfield Free; Paul kers, Oldham Ath to Northampton T; Marc Bircham, Millwall to QPR; Kevin Gray, Huddersfield T to Tranmere R e; Alan Connell, Ipswich T to Bournemouth Free; Adam Barrett, Mansfield T to Bristol R; Anwar U'ddin, Sheffield o Bristol R; Kevin Austin, Cambridge U to Bristol R; Guiliano Grazioli, Swindon T to Bristol R; Danny Boxall, ntford to Bristol R; Paul Tait, Crewe Alex to Bristol R; Matt Clarke, Halifax T to Darlington; James Coppinger, wcastle U to Exeter C; Ian Ashbee, Cambridge U to Hull C; Sean Parrish, Chesterfield to Kidderminster H Free; Steele, Brighton & HA to Oxford U Free; James Hunt, Northampton T to Oxford U Free; Chris Beech, dersfield T to Rochdale Free; David Moss, Falkirk to Swansea C Free; Sam Collins, Bury to Port Vale; Omer Riza, st Ham U to Cambridge U; Frode Kippe, Liverpool to Lillestrom Free; Brian Shelley, Bohemians to Carlisle U; hael Jackson, Cheltenham T to Swansea C Free; Jonathan Keavney, Carmarthen T to Swansea C Free; Scott Donald, Southampton to Huddersfield; Gino Padula, Wigan Ath to QPR Free; Des Walker, unattached to tingham F; David Beresford, Hull C to Plymouth Arg; Nathan Lowndes, Livingston to Plymouth Arg; Cedric ssel, Wolverhampton W to Mons; Tommy Johnson, Kilmarnock to Gillingham; Paul Wheatcroft, Bolton W to nthorpe U; Jason Jones, Swansea C to Llanelli; Gareth Whalley, Bradford C to Cardiff C; Nick Culkin, Manchester o QPR; Eddie Youds, Charlton Ath to Huddersfield T; Stuart Elliott, Motherwell to Hull C; Rikhardur Dadason, ke C to Lillestrom; Paul Evans, Jong Cosmos to Sheffield W; Shaun Smith, Crewe Alex to Hull C; Sean Dyche, wall to Watford; Laurent D'Jaffo, Sheffield U to Aberdeen; Lee Harper, Walsall to Northampton T; Robert Quinn, ord U to Bristol R; Shane Nicholson, Sheffield U to Tranmere R; Lee Hodges, Scunthorpe U to Rochdale; Gary ft, Ipswich T to Cardiff C; Danny Sonner, Birmingham C to Walsall; Simon Grayson, Blackburn R to Blackpool; l Robinson, Wolverhampton W to Portsmouth; Paul Trollope, Coventry C to Northampton T.

ns: Gary Caldwell, Newcastle U to Coventry C; Leon Knight, Chelsea to Sheffield W; Vincent Pericard, Juventus to tsmouth; Matteo Sereni, Ipswich T to Brescia; Scott Bevan, Southampton to Huddersfield T; Jacinto Ela Eyene, hampton to Hercules; John Halls, Liam Chilvers and Steve Sidwell (all Arsenal) to Beveren; Paddy Kenny, Bury to ffield U; Alex Nyarko, Everton to Paris St Germain; Matt Gadsby, Walsall to Mansfield T.

ally: Mali fax number 00223 230322.

Now you can buy any of these other bestselling sports titles from your bookshop or *direct from the publisher.*

FREE P&P AND UK DELIVERY
(Overseas and Ireland £3.50 per book)

Playfair Football Annual 2002–2003	Glenda Rollin and Jack Rollin	£6.99
1966 and All That	Geoff Hurst	£6.99
Psycho	Stuart Pearce	£6.99
The Autobiography	David Batty	£6.99
Priceless	Rodney Marsh	£7.99
The Autobiography	Gareth Edwards	£7.99
The Autobiography	John Barnes	£6.99
Ultra Nippon	Jonathan Birchall	£7.99
Barmy Army	Dougie Brimson	£6.99
Vinnie	Vinnie Jones	£6.99
Manchester United Ruined My Life	Colin Shindler	£6.99
God Save the Team	Eddy Brimson	£6.99
A Lot of Hard Yakka	Simon Hughes	£6.99
Left Foot Forward	Garry Nelson	£6.99

TO ORDER SIMPLY CALL THIS NUMBER

01235 400 414

or visit our website:
www.madaboutbooks.com

Prices and availability subject to change without notice.